Official 2010 National Football League Record & Fact Book

National Football League
280 Park Avenue, New York, N.Y. 10017 (212) 450-2000. NFL Internet Address: http://www.NFL.com

Printed in the United States of America.

A National Football League Book.

Compiled by the NFL Communications Department and Seymour Siwoff, Elias Sports Bureau.
Statistics by Elias Sports Bureau.

Edited by Jon Zimmer, NFL Communications Department, and Matt Marini. Layout by William Tham. Cover design by NFL Creative.
Produced by NFL Communications Department.

Cover photograph of Drew Brees of the Super Bowl XLIV champion New Orleans Saints by David Stluka, AP Photo.

Time Inc. Home Entertainment
1271 Avenue of the Americas, New York, N.Y. 10020
Manufactured in the United States of America.
First printing, July 2010.
10 9 8 7 6 5 4 3 2 1

TABLE OF CONTENTS

Additional sections available online at www.NFLmedia.com.

2010 SCHEDULE AND NOTE CALENDAR

All times local. Dates and times subject to change.
Nationally televised games indicated by network in parentheses.

	Sunday, August 8	Hall of Fame Game at Canton, Ohio	
		Cincinnati _____ vs. Dallas _____	(NBC) 8:00
PRESEASON/WEEK 1	**Thursday, August 12**	New Orleans _____ at New England _____	7:30
		Carolina _____ at Baltimore _____	(ESPN) 8:00
		Oakland _____ at Dallas _____	8:00
	Friday, August 13	Jacksonville _____ at Philadelphia _____	7:30
		Buffalo _____ at Washington _____	7:30
		Kansas City _____ at Atlanta _____	8:00
	Saturday, August 14	Tampa Bay _____ at Miami _____	7:00
		Detroit _____ at Pittsburgh _____	7:30
		Houston _____ at Arizona _____	5:00
		Cleveland _____ at Green Bay _____	7:00
		Minnesota _____ at St. Louis _____	7:00
		Chicago _____ at San Diego _____	6:00
		Tennessee _____ at Seattle _____	7:00
	Sunday, August 15	San Francisco _____ at Indianapolis _____	1:00
		Denver _____ at Cincinnati _____	7:00
	Monday, August 16	New York Giants _____ at New York Jets _____	(ESPN) 8:00
PRESEASON/WEEK 2	**Thursday, August 19**	Indianapolis _____ at Buffalo (Toronto)_____	7:30
		New England _____ at Atlanta _____	(FOX) 8:00
	Friday, August 20	Philadelphia _____ at Cincinnati _____	(FOX) 8:00
	Saturday, August 21	Pittsburgh _____ at New York Giants _____	7:00
		Baltimore _____ at Washington _____	7:00
		St. Louis _____ at Cleveland _____	7:30
		Miami _____ at Jacksonville _____	7:30
		Kansas City _____ at Tampa Bay _____	7:30
		New York Jets _____ at Carolina _____	8:00
		Houston _____ at New Orleans _____	7:00
		Oakland _____ at Chicago _____	7:30
		Detroit _____ at Denver _____	7:00
		Dallas _____ at San Diego _____	6:00
		Green Bay _____ at Seattle _____	7:00
	Sunday, August 22	Minnesota _____ at San Francisco _____	(NBC) 5:00
	Monday, August 23	Arizona _____ at Tennessee _____	(ESPN) 7:00
PRESEASON/WEEK 3	**Thursday, August 26**	St. Louis _____ at New England _____	7:30
		Indianapolis _____ at Green Bay _____	(ESPN) 7:00
	Friday, August 27	Atlanta _____ at Miami _____	7:00
		Washington _____ at New York Jets _____	7:00
		Philadelphia _____ at Kansas City _____	7:00
		San Diego _____ at New Orleans _____	(CBS) 7:00
	Saturday, August 28	Cleveland _____ at Detroit _____	5:30
		Cincinnati _____ at Buffalo _____	6:30
		New York Giants _____ at Baltimore _____	7:30
		Jacksonville _____ at Tampa Bay _____	7:30
		Tennessee _____ at Carolina _____	8:00
		Dallas _____ at Houston _____	(CBS) 7:00
		Seattle _____ at Minnesota _____	7:00
		Arizona _____ at Chicago _____	7:30
		San Francisco _____ at Oakland _____	6:00
	Sunday, August 29	Pittsburgh _____ at Denver _____	(FOX) 6:00

PRESEASON/WEEK 4

Thursday, September 2

Buffalo _____ at Detroit _____	7:00
Cincinnati _____ at Indianapolis _____	7:00
New England _____ at New York Giants _____	7:00
Atlanta _____ at Jacksonville _____	7:30
New York Jets _____ at Philadelphia _____	7:30
Carolina _____ at Pittsburgh _____	7:30
Chicago _____ at Cleveland _____	8:00
Miami _____ at Dallas _____	7:00
Tampa Bay _____ at Houston _____	7:00
Green Bay _____ at Kansas City _____	7:00
Denver _____ at Minnesota _____	7:00
Baltimore _____ at St. Louis _____	7:00
New Orleans _____ at Tennessee _____	7:00
Washington _____ at Arizona _____	7:00
Seattle _____ at Oakland _____	7:00
San Diego _____ at San Francisco _____	7:00

NFL KICKOFF 2010

KICKOFF WEEKEND

Thursday, September 9

Minnesota _____ at New Orleans _____	(NBC) 7:30

Sunday, September 12
FOX-TV National Weekend

Miami _____ at Buffalo _____	1:00
Detroit _____ at Chicago _____	12:00
Indianapolis _____ at Houston _____	12:00
Denver _____ at Jacksonville _____	1:00
Cincinnati _____ at New England _____	1:00
Carolina _____ at New York Giants _____	1:00
Atlanta _____ at Pittsburgh _____	1:00
Cleveland _____ at Tampa Bay _____	1:00
Oakland _____ at Tennessee _____	12:00
Green Bay _____ at Philadelphia _____	4:15
Arizona _____ at St. Louis _____	3:15
San Francisco _____ at Seattle _____	1:15
Dallas _____ at Washington _____	(NBC) 8:20

Monday, September 13

Baltimore _____ at New York Jets _____	(ESPN) 7:00
San Diego _____ at Kansas City _____	(ESPN) 9:15

SECOND WEEK

Sunday, September 19
CBS-TV National Weekend

Arizona _____ at Atlanta _____	1:00
Tampa Bay _____ at Carolina _____	1:00
Baltimore _____ at Cincinnati _____	1:00
Kansas City _____ at Cleveland _____	1:00
Chicago _____ at Dallas _____	12:00
Philadelphia _____ at Detroit _____	1:00
Buffalo _____ at Green Bay _____	12:00
Miami _____ at Minnesota _____	12:00
Pittsburgh _____ at Tennessee _____	12:00
Seattle _____ at Denver _____	2:05
St. Louis _____ at Oakland _____	1:05
New England _____ at New York Jets _____	4:15
Jacksonville _____ at San Diego _____	1:15
Houston _____ at Washington _____	4:15
New York Giants _____ at Indianapolis _____	(NBC) 8:20

Monday, September 20

New Orleans _____ at San Francisco	(ESPN) 5:30

THIRD WEEK

Sunday, September 26
CBS-TV National Weekend

Cleveland _____ at Baltimore _____	1:00
Cincinnati _____ at Carolina _____	1:00
Dallas _____ at Houston _____	12:00
San Francisco _____ at Kansas City _____	12:00
Detroit _____ at Minnesota _____	12:00
Buffalo _____ at New England _____	1:00
Atlanta _____ at New Orleans _____	12:00
Tennessee _____ at New York Giants _____	1:00
Pittsburgh _____ at Tampa Bay _____	1:00
Philadelphia _____ at Jacksonville _____	4:05
Washington _____ at St. Louis _____	3:05
Oakland _____ at Arizona _____	1:15
Indianapolis _____ at Denver _____	2:15
San Diego _____ at Seattle _____	1:15
New York Jets _____ at Miami _____	(NBC) 8:20

Monday, September 27

Green Bay _____ at Chicago _____	(ESPN) 7:30

2010 SCHEDULE AND NOTE CALENDAR

FOURTH WEEK
Open Date: Dallas, Kansas City, Minnesota, Tampa Bay

Sunday, October 3	San Francisco _____ at Atlanta _____	1:00
FOX-TV National Weekend	New York Jets _____ at Buffalo _____	1:00
	Cincinnati _____ at Cleveland _____	1:00
	Detroit _____ at Green Bay _____	12:00
	Carolina _____ at New Orleans _____	12:00
	Baltimore _____ at Pittsburgh _____	1:00
	Seattle _____ at St. Louis _____	12:00
	Denver _____ at Tennessee _____	12:00
	Indianapolis _____ at Jacksonville _____	4:05
	Houston _____ at Oakland _____	1:05
	Washington _____ at Philadelphia _____	4:15
	Arizona _____ at San Diego _____	1:15
	Chicago _____ at New York Giants _____	(NBC) 8:20
Monday, October 4	New England _____ at Miami _____	(ESPN) 8:30

FIFTH WEEK
Open Date: Miami, New England, Pittsburgh, Seattle

Sunday, October 10	Denver _____ at Baltimore _____	1:00
CBS-TV National Weekend	Jacksonville _____ at Buffalo _____	1:00
	Chicago _____ at Carolina _____	1:00
	Tampa Bay _____ at Cincinnati _____	1:00
	Atlanta _____ at Cleveland _____	1:00
	St. Louis _____ at Detroit _____	1:00
	Kansas City _____ at Indianapolis _____	1:00
	New York Giants _____ at Houston _____	12:00
	Green Bay _____ at Washington _____	1:00
	New Orleans _____ at Arizona _____	1:05
	Tennessee _____ at Dallas _____	3:15
	San Diego _____ at Oakland _____	1:15
	Philadelphia _____ at San Francisco	(NBC) 5:20
Monday, October 11	Minnesota _____ at New York Jets _____	(ESPN) 8:30

SIXTH WEEK
Open Date: Arizona, Buffalo, Carolina, Cincinnati

Sunday, October 17	Seattle _____ at Chicago _____	12:00
FOX-TV National Weekend	Miami _____ at Green Bay _____	12:00
	Kansas City _____ at Houston _____	12:00
	Baltimore _____ at New England _____	1:00
	Detroit _____ at New York Giants _____	1:00
	Atlanta _____ at Philadelphia _____	1:00
	Cleveland _____ at Pittsburgh _____	1:00
	San Diego _____ at St. Louis _____	12:00
	New Orleans _____ at Tampa Bay _____	1:00
	New York Jets _____ at Denver _____	2:05
	Oakland _____ at San Francisco _____	1:05
	Dallas _____ at Minnesota _____	3:15
	Indianapolis _____ at Washington _____	(NBC) 8:20
Monday, October 18	Tennessee _____ at Jacksonville _____	(ESPN) 8:30

SEVENTH WEEK
Open Date: Detroit, Houston, Indianapolis, New York Jets

Sunday, October 24	Cincinnati _____ at Atlanta _____	1:00
CBS-TV National Weekend	Buffalo _____ at Baltimore _____	1:00
	San Francisco _____ at Carolina _____	1:00
	Washington _____ at Chicago _____	12:00
	Jacksonville _____ at Kansas City _____	12:00
	Pittsburgh _____ at Miami _____	1:00
	Cleveland _____ at New Orleans _____	12:00
	St. Louis _____ at Tampa Bay _____	1:00
	Philadelphia _____ at Tennessee _____	12:00
	Arizona _____ at Seattle _____	1:05
	New England _____ at San Diego _____	1:15
	Oakland _____ at Denver _____	2:15
	Minnesota _____ at Green Bay _____	(NBC) 7:20
Monday, October 25	New York Giants _____ at Dallas _____	(ESPN) 7:30

EIGHTH WEEK
Open Date: Atlanta, Baltimore, Chicago, Cleveland, New York Giants, Philadelphia

INTERNATIONAL SERIES 2010

Sunday, October 31	Miami _____ at Cincinnati _____	1:00
FOX-TV National Weekend	Jacksonville _____ at Dallas _____	12:00
	Washington _____ at Detroit _____	1:00
	Buffalo _____ at Kansas City _____	12:00
	Green Bay _____ at New York Jets _____	1:00
	Carolina _____ at St. Louis _____	12:00
	Denver _____ at San Francisco (London) _____	5:00
	Tennessee _____ at San Diego _____	1:05
	Minnesota _____ at New England _____	4:15
	Seattle _____ at Oakland _____	1:15
	Tampa Bay _____ at Arizona _____	1:15
	Pittsburgh _____ at New Orleans _____	(NBC) 7:20
Monday, November 1	Houston _____ at Indianapolis _____	(ESPN) 8:30

NINTH WEEK
Open Date: Denver, Jacksonville, St. Louis, San Francisco, Tennessee, Washington

Sunday, November 7	Tampa Bay _____ at Atlanta _____	1:00
CBS-TV National Weekend	Miami _____ at Baltimore _____	1:00
	Chicago _____ at Buffalo (Toronto) _____	1:00
	New Orleans _____ at Carolina _____	1:00
	New England _____ at Cleveland _____	1:00
	New York Jets _____ at Detroit _____	1:00
	San Diego _____ at Houston _____	12:00
	Arizona _____ at Minnesota _____	12:00
	New York Giants _____ at Seattle _____	1:05
	Indianapolis _____ at Philadelphia _____	4:15
	Kansas City _____ at Oakland _____	1:15
	Dallas _____ at Green Bay _____	(NBC) 7:20
Monday, November 8	Pittsburgh _____ at Cincinnati _____	(ESPN) 8:30

TENTH WEEK
Open Date: Green Bay, New Orleans, Oakland, San Diego

Thursday, November 11	Baltimore _____ at Atlanta _____	(NFLN) 8:20
Sunday, November 14	Detroit _____ at Buffalo _____	1:00
FOX-TV National Weekend	Minnesota _____ at Chicago _____	12:00
	New York Jets _____ at Cleveland _____	1:00
	Cincinnati _____ at Indianapolis _____	1:00
	Houston _____ at Jacksonville _____	1:00
	Tennessee _____ at Miami _____	1:00
	Carolina _____ at Tampa Bay _____	1:00
	Kansas City _____ at Denver _____	2:05
	Dallas _____ at New York Giants _____	4:15
	Seattle _____ at Arizona _____	2:15
	St. Louis _____ at San Francisco _____	1:15
	New England _____ at Pittsburgh _____	(NBC) 8:20
Monday, November 15	Philadelphia _____ at Washington _____	(ESPN) 8:30

ELEVENTH WEEK

Thursday, November 18	Chicago _____ at Miami _____	8:20
Sunday, November 21	Baltimore _____ at Carolina _____	1:00
CBS-TV National Weekend	Buffalo _____ at Cincinnati _____	1:00
	Detroit _____ at Dallas _____	12:00
	Cleveland _____ at Jacksonville _____	1:00
	Arizona _____ at Kansas City _____	12:00
	Green Bay _____ at Minnesota _____	12:00
	Houston _____ at New York Jets _____	1:00
	Oakland _____ at Pittsburgh _____	1:00
	Washington _____ at Tennessee _____	12:00
	Seattle _____ at New Orleans _____	3:05
	Atlanta _____ at St. Louis _____	3:05
	Tampa Bay _____ at San Francisco _____	1:05
	Indianapolis _____ at New England _____	4:15
	New York Giants _____ at Philadelphia * _____	(NBC) 8:20
Monday, November 22	Denver _____ at San Diego _____	(ESPN) 5:30

**Sunday Night Games In Weeks 11-16 Subject to Change*

TWELFTH WEEK

THANKSGIVING 2010

Thursday, November 25	New England _____ at Detroit _____		(CBS) 12:30
	New Orleans _____ at Dallas _____		(FOX) 3:15
	Cincinnati _____ at New York Jets _____		(NFLN) 8:20
Sunday, November 28	Green Bay _____ at Atlanta _____		1:00
FOX-TV National Weekend	Tampa Bay _____ at Baltimore _____		1:00
	Pittsburgh _____ at Buffalo _____		1:00
	Philadelphia _____ at Chicago _____		12:00
	Carolina _____ at Cleveland _____		1:00
	Tennessee _____ at Houston _____		12:00
	Jacksonville _____ at New York Giants _____		1:00
	Minnesota _____ at Washington _____		1:00
	Kansas City _____ at Seattle _____		1:05
	Miami _____ at Oakland _____		1:05
	St. Louis _____ at Denver _____		2:15
	San Diego _____ at Indianapolis * _____		(NBC) 8:20
Monday, November 29	San Francisco _____ at Arizona _____		(ESPN) 6:30

**Sunday Night Games In Weeks 11-16 Subject to Change*

THIRTEENTH WEEK

Thursday, December 2	Houston _____ at Philadelphia _____	(NFLN) 8:20
Sunday, December 5	New Orleans _____ at Cincinnati _____	1:00
FOX-TV National Weekend	Chicago _____ at Detroit _____	1:00
	San Francisco _____ at Green Bay _____	12:00
	Denver _____ at Kansas City _____	12:00
	Cleveland _____ at Miami _____	1:00
	Buffalo _____ at Minnesota _____	12:00
	Washington _____ at New York Giants _____	1:00
	Atlanta _____ at Tampa Bay _____	1:00
	Jacksonville _____ at Tennessee _____	12:00
	Oakland _____ at San Diego _____	1:05
	St. Louis _____ at Arizona _____	2:15
	Dallas _____ at Indianapolis _____	4:15
	Carolina _____ at Seattle _____	1:15
	Pittsburgh _____ at Baltimore * _____	(NBC) 8:20
Monday, December 6	New York Jets _____ at New England _____	(ESPN) 8:30

**Sunday Night Games In Weeks 11-16 Subject to Change*

FOURTEENTH WEEK

Thursday, December 9	Indianapolis _____ at Tennessee _____	(NFLN) 7:20
Sunday, December 12	Cleveland _____ at Buffalo _____	1:00
CBS-TV National Weekend	Atlanta _____ at Carolina _____	1:00
	New England _____ at Chicago _____	12:00
	Green Bay _____ at Detroit _____	1:00
	Oakland _____ at Jacksonville _____	1:00
	New York Giants _____ at Minnesota _____	12:00
	Cincinnati _____ at Pittsburgh _____	1:00
	Tampa Bay _____ at Washington _____	1:00
	St. Louis _____ at New Orleans _____	3:05
	Seattle _____ at San Francisco _____	1:05
	Denver _____ at Arizona _____	2:15
	Miami _____ at New York Jets _____	4:15
	Kansas City _____ at San Diego _____	1:15
	Philadelphia _____ at Dallas * _____	(NBC) 7:20
Monday, December 13	Baltimore _____ at Houston _____	(ESPN) 7:30

**Sunday Night Games In Weeks 11-16 Subject to Change*

FIFTEENTH WEEK

Thursday, December 16	San Francisco _____ at San Diego _____	(NFLN) 5:20
Sunday, December 19	New Orleans _____ at Baltimore _____	1:00
CBS-TV National Weekend	Arizona _____ at Carolina _____	1:00
	Cleveland _____ at Cincinnati _____	1:00
	Washington _____ at Dallas _____	12:00
	Jacksonville _____ at Indianapolis _____	1:00
	Buffalo _____ at Miami _____	1:00
	Philadelphia _____ at New York Giants _____	1:00
	Kansas City _____ at St. Louis _____	12:00
	Detroit _____ at Tampa Bay _____	1:00
	Houston _____ at Tennessee _____	12:00
	Atlanta _____ at Seattle _____	1:05
	Denver _____ at Oakland _____	1:15
	New York Jets _____ at Pittsburgh _____	4:15
	Green Bay _____ at New England * _____	(NBC) 8:20
Monday, December 20	Chicago _____ at Minnesota _____	(ESPN) 7:30

**Sunday Night Games In Weeks 11-16 Subject to Change*

SIXTEENTH WEEK

Thursday, December 23	Carolina _____ at Pittsburgh _____	(NFLN) 8:20
Saturday, December 25	Dallas _____ at Arizona _____	(NFLN) 5:30
Sunday, December 26	New England _____ at Buffalo _____	1:00
FOX-TV National Weekend	New York Jets _____ at Chicago _____	12:00
	Baltimore _____ at Cleveland _____	1:00
	Washington _____ at Jacksonville _____	1:00
	Tennessee _____ at Kansas City _____	12:00
	Detroit _____ at Miami _____	1:00
	Minnesota _____ at Philadelphia _____	1:00
	San Francisco _____ at St. Louis _____	12:00
	Seattle _____ at Tampa Bay _____	1:00
	Houston _____ at Denver _____	2:05
	Indianapolis _____ at Oakland _____	1:05
	New York Giants _____ at Green Bay _____	3:15
	San Diego _____ at Cincinnati * _____	(NBC) 8:20
Monday, December 27	New Orleans _____ at Atlanta _____	(ESPN) 8:30

**Sunday Night Games In Weeks 11-16 Subject to Change*

SEVENTEENTH WEEK

Sunday, January 2	Carolina _____ at Atlanta _____	1:00
CBS-TV and FOX-TV National Weekend	Cincinnati _____ at Baltimore _____	1:00
	Pittsburgh _____ at Cleveland _____	1:00
	Minnesota _____ at Detroit _____	1:00
	Chicago _____ at Green Bay _____	12:00
	Jacksonville _____ at Houston _____	12:00
	Tennessee _____ at Indianapolis _____	1:00
	Oakland _____ at Kansas City _____	12:00
	Miami _____ at New England _____	1:00
	Tampa Bay _____ at New Orleans _____	12:00
	Buffalo _____ at New York Jets _____	1:00
	Dallas _____ at Philadelphia _____	1:00
	New York Giants _____ at Washington _____	1:00
	San Diego _____ at Denver _____	2:15
	Arizona _____ at San Francisco _____	1:15
	St. Louis _____ at Seattle _____	1:15

**Sunday Night Game In Week 17 TBD*

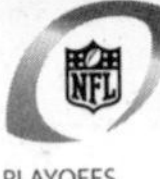

Wild Card Playoff Games
Site Priorities
Two Wild Card teams (division non-champions with best two records) from each conference and the division champions with the third and fourth-best record in each conference will enter the first round of the playoffs. The division champion with the third-best record will play host to the Wild Card team with the second-best record. The division champion with the fourth-best record will play host to the Wild Card team with the best record. There are no restrictions on intra-division games.

Saturday, January 8, 2011

American Football Conference

__________ at __________ (NBC)

National Football Conference

__________ at __________ (NBC)

Sunday, January 9, 2011

American Football Conference

__________ at __________ (CBS)

National Football Conference

__________ at __________ (FOX)

Divisional Playoff Games
Site Priorities
In each conference, the two division champions with the highest won-lost-tied percentage during the regular season will play host to the Wild Card winners. The division champion with the best record in each conference is assured of playing the lowest seeded Wild Card survivor. There are no restrictions on intra-division games.

Saturday, January 15, 2011

American Football Conference

__________ at __________ (CBS)

National Football Conference

__________ at __________ (FOX)

Sunday, January 16, 2011

American Football Conference

__________ at __________ (CBS)

National Football Conference

__________ at __________ (FOX)

Championship Games
Site Priorities for Championship Games
The home teams will be the surviving playoff winners with the highest seeds. A Wild Card team cannot play host unless two Wild Card teams are in the game, in which case the Wild Card team that was seeded highest in the first round of the playoffs will be the home team.

Sunday, January 23, 2011

American Football Conference

__________ at __________ (CBS)

National Football Conference

__________ at __________ (FOX)

AFC-NFC Pro Bowl

PRO BOWL

Sunday, January 30, 2011

AFC-NFC Pro Bowl at Aloha Stadium, Hawaii

AFC__________ vs. NFC __________ (FOX)

Super Bowl XLV

SUPER BOWL XLV

Sunday, February 6, 2011

Super Bowl XLV at Cowboys Stadium, North Texas

__________ vs. __________ (FOX)

2010 NATIONALLY TELEVISED PRIMETIME GAMES

All times E.T.

Thursday, Sept. 9	Minnesota at New Orleans (NBC)	8:30
Sunday, Sept. 12	Dallas at Washington (NBC)	8:20
Monday, Sept. 13	Baltimore at New York Jets (ESPN)	7:00
	San Diego at Kansas City (ESPN)	10:15
Sunday, Sept. 19	New York Giants at Indianapolis (NBC)	8:20
Monday, Sept. 20	New Orleans at San Francisco (ESPN)	8:30
Sunday, Sept. 26	New York Jets at Miami (NBC)	8:20
Monday, Sept. 27	Green Bay at Chicago (ESPN)	8:30
Sunday, Oct. 3	Chicago at New York Giants (NBC)	8:20
Monday, Oct. 4	New England at Miami (ESPN)	8:30
Sunday, Oct. 10	Philadelphia at San Francisco (NBC)	8:20
Monday, Oct. 11	Minnesota at New York Jets (ESPN)	8:30
Sunday, Oct. 17	Indianapolis at Washington (NBC)	8:20
Monday, Oct. 18	Tennessee at Jacksonville (ESPN)	8:30
Sunday, Oct. 24	Minnesota at Green Bay (NBC)	8:20
Monday, Oct. 25	New York Giants at Dallas (ESPN)	8:30
Sunday, Oct. 31	Pittsburgh at New Orleans (NBC)	8:20
Monday, Nov. 1	Houston at Indianapolis (ESPN)	8:30
Sunday, Nov. 7	Dallas at Green Bay (NBC)	8:20
Monday, Nov. 8	Pittsburgh at Cincinnati (ESPN)	8:30
Thursday, Nov. 11	Baltimore at Atlanta (NFL Network)	8:20
Sunday, Nov. 14	New England at Pittsburgh (NBC)	8:20
Monday, Nov. 15	Philadelphia at Washington (ESPN)	8:30
Thursday, Nov. 18	Chicago at Miami (NFL Network)	8:20
Sunday, Nov. 21	New York Giants at Philadelphia (NBC)*	8:20
Monday, Nov. 22	Denver at San Diego (ESPN)	8:30
Thursday, Nov. 25	New England at Detroit (CBS)	12:30
	New Orleans at Dallas (FOX)	4:15
	Cincinnati at New York Jets (NFL Network)	8:20
Sunday, Nov. 28	San Diego at Indianapolis (NBC)*	8:20
Monday, Nov. 29	San Francisco at Arizona (ESPN)	8:30
Thursday, Dec. 2	Houston at Philadelphia (CBS)	8:20
Sunday, Dec. 5	Pittsburgh at Baltimore (NBC)*	8:20
Monday, Dec. 6	New York Jets at New England (ESPN)	8:30
Thursday, Dec. 9	Indianapolis at Tennessee (NFL Network)	8:20
Sunday, Dec. 12	Philadelphia at Dallas (NBC)*	8:20
Monday, Dec. 13	Baltimore at Houston (ESPN)	8:30
Thursday, Dec. 16	San Francisco at San Diego (NFL Network)	8:20
Sunday, Dec. 19	Green Bay at New England (NBC)*	8:20
Monday, Dec. 20	Chicago at Minnesota (ESPN)	8:30
Thursday, Dec. 23	Carolina at Pittsburgh (NFL Network)	8:20
Saturday, Dec. 25	Dallas at Arizona (NFL Network)	7:30
Sunday, Dec. 26	San Diego at Cincinnati (NBC)*	8:20
Monday, Dec. 27	New Orleans at Atlanta (ESPN)	8:30
Sunday, Jan. 2	To be determined (NBC)*	8:20

**The NFL again will utilize "flexible scheduling" in 2010.*

Flexible scheduling moves will be announced at least 12 days before games in Weeks 11-16. In Week 17, the flexible scheduling move will be announced at least six days before the game. Flexible scheduling will ensure quality matchups on Sunday night in those weeks and give "surprise" teams a chance to play their way on to primetime.

POSTSEASON GAMES

Saturday, January 8	AFC and NFC Wild Card Playoffs (NBC)
Sunday, January 9	AFC and NFC Wild Card Playoffs (CBS and FOX)
Saturday, January 15	AFC and NFC Divisional Playoffs (CBS and FOX)
Sunday, January 16	AFC and NFC Divisional Playoffs (CBS and FOX)
Sunday, January 23	AFC and NFC Championship Games (CBS and FOX)
Sunday, January 30	AFC-NFC Pro Bowl in Hawaii (FOX)
Sunday, February 6	Super Bowl XLV in North Texas (FOX)

IMPORTANT DATES

2010

Mid-July — Preseason training camps open. Clubs not permitted to open official preseason camp earlier than July 5. Veteran players cannot be required to report earlier than 15 days prior to club's first preseason game.

July 15 — Deadline at 4 P.M., New York time, for any club that designated a Franchise Player to sign such player to a multi-year contract or extension. After this date, the player may sign only a one-year contract with the designating club for the 2010 season, and such contract cannot be extended until after the Club's last regular season game.

July 22 — Signing period ends at 4 P.M., New York time, for Transition Players with outstanding tenders. After this date and through 4 P.M., New York time, on the Tuesday after the 10th regular season weekend, Old Club has exclusive negotiating rights to these players.

July 22# — Signing period ends at 4 P.M., New York time, for Unrestricted Free Agents to whom a June 1 tender was made by Old Club. After this date and through 4 P.M., New York time, on the Tuesday after the 10th regular season weekend, Old Club has exclusive negotiating rights to these players.
#or the first scheduled day of the first NFL training camp, whichever is later.

August 10 — Deadline for players under contract to report to earn a season of free-agency credit.

August 6-8 — Hall of Fame Weekend.

August 8 — Pro Football Hall of Fame Game, Canton, Ohio: Cincinnati vs. Dallas

August 12-16 — First Preseason Weekend.

August 13 — If a Drafted Rookie has not signed with his club by this date, he may not be traded to any other club in 2010.

August 14-18 — Deadline for club to provide written notice to certain unsigned players and the NFLPA of its intent to place them on the Exempt List if they fail to report no later than one day prior to the club's second preseason game. Any player who fails to report prior to the deadline will be ineligible to play or receive compensation for at least three games (preseason or regular season) from the time that he reports.

August 31 — Roster cut-down to maximum of 75 players on Active List by 4 P.M., New York time.

September 1 — All tryouts on this date and for the remainder of the season must be reported to the League office.

September 4 — Roster cut-down to maximum of 53 players on Active/Inactive List by 6 P.M., New York time. Clubs may dress minimum of 42 and maximum of 45 players and Third Quarterback for each regular-season and postseason game.

September 4 — Simultaneously with the cut-down to 53, clubs that have players in the categories of Active/Physically Unable to Perform or Active/Non-Football Injury or Illness must take one of the following options: place player on Reserve/Physically Unable to Perform or Reserve/Non-Football Injury or Illness, whichever is applicable; ask waivers; terminate; trade; or continue to count him on Active List.

September 5 — After 12 noon, New York time, clubs may establish a Practice Squad of eight players by signing free agents who do not have an accrued season of free-agency credit or who were on the 45-player Active List for less than nine regular-season games during their only Accrued Season(s). A player cannot participate on the Practice Squad for more than three seasons.

September 8 — All clubs are required to file a personnel (injury) report with their conference information manager by 4:00 p.m., New York time. Reports are to be filed every Wednesday, Thursday and Friday before a regular-season game by 4:00 p.m., New York time (or as soon as possible after the completion of practice). An update must also be reported if there is any change in a player's condition after Friday.

September 9-13 — Regular Season opens.

September 9-13 — Beginning on these dates vested veterans terminated from the Active List or Inactive List (and from Reserve/Injured if the player is placed on Reserve/Injured after the beginning of the regular season) are entitled to receive, after the end of the regular-season schedule, Termination Pay pursuant to the terms of the CBA.

September 28 — Priority on multiple waiver claims is now based on the current season's standing.

October 19 — Beginning the day after the conclusion of the sixth regular-season weekend and continuing through the day after the conclusion of the ninth regular-season weekend, clubs are permitted to begin practicing players on Reserve/Physically Unable to Perform and Reserve/Non-Football Injury or Illness for a period not to exceed 21 days. Players may be activated during the 21-day practice period or until 4 P.M., New York time, on the day after the conclusion of the 21-day period.

October 19 — All trading ends at 4 P.M., New York time.

October 20 — Players with at least four previous pension-credited seasons are subject to the waiver system for the remainder of the regular season and postseason.

November 16 Signing period ends at 4 P.M., New York time, for Franchise Players who are eligible to receive Offer Sheets.

November 16 Deadline for clubs to sign by 4 P.M., New York time, their unsigned Franchise and Transition Players, including Franchise Players who were eligible to receive Offer Sheets until this date. If still unsigned after this date, such players are prohibited from playing in NFL in 2010.

November 16 Deadline for clubs to sign by 4 P.M., New York time, their Unrestricted Free Agents to whom June 1 tender was made. If still unsigned after this date, such players are prohibited from playing in NFL in 2010.

November 16 Deadline for clubs to sign by 4 P.M., New York time, their Restricted Free Agents to whom June 1 tender was made. If such players remain unsigned, they are prohibited from playing in NFL in 2010.

November 16 Deadline for clubs to sign Drafted players by 4 P.M., New York time. If such players remain unsigned, they are prohibited from playing in NFL in 2010.

December 3 Deadline for reinstatement of players in Reserve List categories of Retired, Did Not Report, and Exclusive Rights, and of players who were placed on Reserve/Left Squad in a previous season.

December 31 Deadline for waiver requests in 2010, except for "special waiver requests," which have a 10-day claiming period, with termination or assignment delayed until after the Super Bowl.

2011

January 3 Clubs may begin signing free-agent players for the 2011 season.

January 8-9 Wild Card Playoff Games.

January 15-16 Divisional Playoff Games.

January 23 AFC and NFC Championship Games.

January 30 AFC-NFC Pro Bowl, Aloha Stadium, Honolulu, Hawaii.

February 6 Super Bowl XLV, Cowboys Stadium, North Texas.

2012

February 5* Super Bowl XLVI, Lucas Oil Stadium, Indianapolis, Indiana.

2013

February 3* Super Bowl XLVII, Louisiana Superdome, New Orleans, Louisiana.

2014

February 2* Super Bowl XLVIII, New Meadowlands Stadium, New York - New Jersey.

**Tentative date.*

NFL ON THE INTERNET

The NFL is online to provide fans and media quick and easy access to all the latest professional football information.

NFL.COM—(http://NFL.com)

NFL.com, the league's year-round home page on the Internet, enters its 14th season in cyberspace. The site provides NFL information during the regular season, postseason, and offseason, including:

NEWS/STATS: Up-to-the-minute NFL news, plus game previews, injury reports, and player and team stats.

GAMEDAY COVERAGE: Live game coverage with play-by-play, scores, and statistics, including graphical drive charts and comprehensive scoreboard that reloads automatically with the latest information.

VIDEO HIGHLIGHTS: The site showcases NFL Films video highlights of the previous week's games as well as upcoming matchups. Video also supports feature stories and team highlight clips from every game last season. In addition, exclusive NFL Network programming is featured.

TEAM AREAS: Customized areas for all 32 clubs, featuring updated rosters, depth charts, and all the latest team news.

SUPERBOWL.COM—(http://SuperBowl.com)

Look for SuperBowl.com in late December for complete coverage of the playoffs and Super Bowl XLV. The multimedia site follows all postseason action and features audio and video clips of past Super Bowls.

During the week leading up to Super Bowl XLV, the site will go "live" from North Texas, providing coverage of events, press conferences, and chats with Super Bowl players and coaches. On Super Bowl Sunday, SuperBowl.com will showcase a live Internet cybercast, complete with online commentators calling the action. The site also features digital photos from the game, live public address audio and press box announcements, and live audio from foreign broadcasts.

NFL.COM/ESPANOL POWERED BY UNIVISION.COM—(http://NFL.COM/ESPANOL)

The official Spanish-language site of the NFL provides in depth information on teams and players, and offers highlights of every NFL game in Spanish. The site includes Hispanic player diaries, live radio broadcasts, up-to-date stats, fantasy football, and Tu Pasión, the NFL's interactive community for Hispanic fans.

NFLPPK.COM (http://nflppk.com)

NFLPPK.com is the NFL's website focused on the NFL Punt, Pass and Kick Program. Established in 1961, NFL PPK is one of the largest & most recognized grassroots programs and part of NFL PLAY 60, which encourages kids to be active for at least 60 minutes a day. Boys and girls ages 8-15 nationwide have the opportunity to test their punting, passing and kicking skills against their peers in a competitive environment. Our website is a resource for coaches, parents, and youth organizations who want to learn how to host their own NFL PPK local competition or find and register their children in an event in their community.

NFLFLAG.COM (http://nflflag.com)

NFLFLAG.com focuses on the NFL FLAG Program, which is also part of NFL PLAY 60. Boys and girls ages 5-17 nationwide have the opportunity to display their skills in a non-contact environment by playing against their peers in five-on-five flag football games. Our website is a resource for league organizers, coaches, parents and youth organizations who want to start or find a local NFL FLAG league in their area as well as promote a positive experience for their youth participants.

NFLRUSH.COM—(http://www.NFLRUSH.com)

NFLRUSH.com, which is targeted to kids 6-15, is the official kids' website of the National Football League, offering unique customizable content, games, fantasy football for kids, contests, videos, fun daily features on NFL players and information on the NFL's Youth Football programs. NFLRUSH.com also features fun and interactive fitness information as part of the NFL PLAY 60 campaign, which encourages kids to be active for 60 minutes a day. The NFLRUSH ZONE, a role playing game on NFLRUSH.com, is an immersive virtual world where kids are able to create avatars, join their favorite team, play games, chat, watch cartoons and compete with friends in safe and fun environment.

USAFOOTBALL.COM—(http://usafootball.com)

USA Football is an independent, non-profit organization which is leading the growth and development of youth, high school and international amateur football. USA Football helps youth and amateur football organizations keep the sport fun, safe, and accessible by offering resources focused on coaching education, league enhancement, officiating development and health and safety awareness. The organization also serves as the designated United States representatives to the International Federation of American Football. Based Indianapolis, USA Football was endowed by the NFL and NFLPA in 2002.

JOINTHETEAM.COM—(http://JoinTheTeam.com)

JoinTheTeam.com is the official website dedicated to the off-the-field community work of the NFL and the member clubs. The site provides news and information regarding how the NFL gives back and serves as a useful tool for individuals who are looking for a way to make a difference in their communities. The site also serves as the online home for NFL Charities, and provides opportunities to learn about and apply for funding. JoinTheTeam.com highlights the ways the league, our teams and our fans come together to make a difference through community involvement.

PROFOOTBALLHOF.COM—(http://profootballhof.com)

Profootballhof.com is the official site of the Pro Football Hall of Fame in Canton, Ohio. In addition to a complete visitor's guide to the Hall, the site features bios, stories and Q & A's with Hall of Fame inductees, a detailed archive of football history, and information on appearances by members of the Hall.

OFFICIAL NFL TEAM SITES

In addition to a dedicated area on NFL.com, all 32 teams have their own Websites, which have separate URLs, and are linked from NFL.com.

Arizona Cardinals (www.azcardinals.com)
Atlanta Falcons (www.atlantafalcons.com)
Baltimore Ravens (www.baltimoreravens.com)
Buffalo Bills (www.buffalobills.com)
Carolina Panthers (www.panthers.com)
Chicago Bears (www.chicagobears.com)
Cincinnati Bengals (www.bengals.com)
Cleveland Browns (www.clevelandbrowns.com)
Dallas Cowboys (www.dallascowboys.com)
Denver Broncos (www.denverbroncos.com)
Detroit Lions (www.detroitlions.com)
Green Bay Packers (www.packers.com)
Houston Texans (www.houstontexans.com)
Indianapolis Colts (www.colts.com)
Jacksonville Jaguars (www.jaguars.com)
Kansas City Chiefs (www.kcchiefs.com)
Miami Dolphins (www.miamidolphins.com)
Minnesota Vikings (www.vikings.com)
New England Patriots (www.patriots.com)
New Orleans Saints (www.neworleanssaints.com)
New York Giants (www.giants.com)
New York Jets (www.newyorkjets.com)
Oakland Raiders (www.raiders.com)
Philadelphia Eagles (www.philadelphiaeagles.com)
Pittsburgh Steelers (www.steelers.com)
St. Louis Rams (www.stlouisrams.com)
San Diego Chargers (www.chargers.com)
San Francisco 49ers (www.sf49ers.com)
Seattle Seahawks (www.seahawks.com)
Tampa Bay Buccaneers (www.buccaneers.com)
Tennessee Titans (www.titansonline.com)
Washington Redskins (www.redskins.com)

NFL Network provides fans with a network to call their own. Seven days a week, 24 hours a day, 365 days a year, fans turn to NFL Network to receive information and insight straight from the field, team headquarters, league offices and everywhere the NFL is making news.

NFL Network gives fans unprecedented year-round access to all NFL events, including the Super Bowl, Playoffs, regular season, preseason, Pro Bowl, Pro Football Hall of Fame induction weekend, NFL Draft, Scouting Combine, Senior Bowl, league meetings, minicamps and training camps.

In addition, NFL Network is the only place on television for fans to view NFL games outside their initial live airings. From original broadcast versions of past Super Bowls, in-week replays of current games, original network telecasts of classic NFL regular season and postseason games, to every preseason game, and regular season *Thursday Night Football* games—NFL Network is truly the year-round destination for football fans. NFL Network is available on cable, telcos and satellite television through your local service provider. If your provider doesn't currently offer NFL Network, please call (866) NFL-NETWORK or log on to IWantNFLNetwork.com for more information.

KEY PROGRAMMING

EXCLUSIVE LIVE PRIMETIME GAMES

NFL Network's eight-game, regular-season Thursday Night primetime schedule kicks off in high definition on November 11. Each game, at 8:00 PM ET, will be preceded by a two-hour pregame show and followed by a live post-game show.

NFL TOTAL ACCESS

NFL Network's signature show is the football show of record. *NFL Total Access* is uniquely structured to see the game through the participants' eyes, airing at 7:00 PM ET Monday through Saturday.

Covering all 32 teams, *NFL Total Access* features interviews with players, coaches and other key league personnel. Using "Team Cams" at every facility, *NFL Total Access* has the ability to go live to any NFL team headquarters at any time.

NFL GAMEDAY MORNING

The information packed *NFL GameDay Morning* is the first NFL pregame show on the air Sundays at 9:00 AM ET during the regular season and playoffs, providing fans with the earliest news and notes as well as live reports from around the league.

NFL GAMEDAY SCOREBOARD

After Sunday's early games conclude, *NFL GameDay Scoreboard* takes viewers around the league for post-game press conferences and game highlights. *NFL GameDay Scoreboard* airs at 4:00 PM ET on Sundays and continues through the Sunday afternoon games.

NFL GAMEDAY HIGHLIGHTS

Following the late afternoon games, *NFL GameDay Highlights* analysts Deion Sanders and Michael Irvin join host Rich Eisen to analyze the events of the day. Includes highlights from all completed games, insider commentary, on-field interviews and post-game press conferences.

NFL GAMEDAY FINAL

After each Sunday's final game, the 90-minute *NFL GameDay Final* delivers comprehensive coverage of the day's action. Host Rich Eisen is joined by Steve Mariucci and Deion Sanders. *NFL GameDay Final* kicks off at 11:30 PM ET and features highlights, post-game press conferences, on-field interviews, analysis and more in wrapping up each NFL Sunday.

NFL REPLAY

NFL games will be re-aired with the original television announcers and cameras. This offering features the most exciting games each week in an abbreviated format (eliminating halftime and other non-critical elements). Enhancements to each broadcast include additional camera angles, sideline sound and post-game interviews.

In addition, *NFL Replay Real-Time* gives fans a unique minute-by-minute look at what happened in the previous afternoon's games as they unfolded in real time.

PLAYBOOK

NFL Network uses the "all 22" game film watched each week by coaches and players to present football's ultimate chalkboard show. Four times each week, *Playbook* offers 60-minute strategy sessions with NFL Network analysts, who focus on each week's key matchups and discuss technique and game planning with coaches and players.

AMERICA'S GAME

The Sports Emmy-winning original series continues its profiles of Super Bowl champions with the 2009 New Orleans Saints.

NFL's TOP 10

Putting a fresh twist on the countdown genre, *NFL's Top 10* is a fast-paced series that provides an irreverent look at some of the most intriguing subjects in the NFL, creating and debating a top ten list for each category. Each 60-minute episode counts down from No. 10 to the top ranking in each category.

SOUND FX

The sounds of the game that only NFL Films can capture – with exclusive on-field and sideline microphone access – will be featured on *Sound FX*.

NFL CLASSIC GAMES

The only place on television to catch the complete network broadcasts of classic NFL regular season and playoff games is on NFL Network. Each *NFL Classic Games* telecast features the original network announcers and graphics.

PRESEASON GAMES

NFL Network is the only place on television where fans can view all 65 NFL preseason games in high-definition, including encores of the 11 live national preseason telecasts.

SCHEDULING FORMULA

The NFL expanded to 32 teams in 2002 with the addition of the Houston Texans. In addition, the NFL realigned for the first time since 1970—into eight divisions of four teams each—and the scheduling formula that was introduced guarantees for the first time that all teams play each other on a regular, rotating basis. Although the number of teams has increased to 32, the number of playoff teams remains the same at 12.

Under the NFL scheduling formula, every team within a division plays 16 games as follows:

- Home and away against its three division opponents (6 games).
- The four teams from another division within its conference on a rotating three-year cycle (4 games).
- The four teams from a division in the other conference on a rotating four-year cycle (4 games).
- Two intraconference games based on the prior year's standings (2 games). These games will match a first-place team against the first-place teams in the two same-conference divisions the team is not scheduled to play that season. The second-place, third-place, and fourth-place teams in a conference will be matched in the same way each year.

The schedule format takes each team through a cycle of games—home and away—against every other team in the league. From 2002-2009, every team played every other team at least twice—once home and once away. After the 2008 season, a decision was made to continue with the same rotation in 2010 and beyond.

In determining how to begin the divisional rotation in 2002, the displacement of teams from their old divisions in the new alignment was taken into account. Preference was given to scheduling games with former division rivals and other regional opponents for clubs realigned from otherwise intact divisions.

FUTURE SCHEDULING ROTATION

		2010	2011
AFC EAST	Intraconference	AFCN	AFCW
	Interconference	NFCN	NFCE
AFC NORTH	Intraconference	AFCE	AFCS
	Interconference	NFCS	NFCN
AFC SOUTH	Intraconference	AFCW	AFCN
	Interconference	NFCE	NFCS
AFC WEST	Intraconference	AFCS	AFCE
	Interconference	NFCW	NFCN
NFC EAST	Intraconference	NFCN	NFCW
	Interconference	AFCS	AFCE
NFC NORTH	Intraconference	NFCE	NFCS
	Interconference	AFCE	AFCW
NFC SOUTH	Intraconference	NFCW	NFCN
	Interconference	AFCN	AFCS
NFC WEST	Intraconference	NFCS	NFCE
	Interconference	AFCW	AFCN

AFC EAST NON-DIVISIONAL OPPONENTS 2010-11

BUFFALO BILLS

	2010 Home	2010 Away	2011 Home	2011 Away
Intraconference by Division	CLE	BALT	DEN	KC
	PITT	CIN	OAK	SD
Interconference by Division	CHI	GB	PHIL	DALL
	DET	MINN	WASH	NYG
Intraconference by Position	AFCS	AFCW	AFCS	AFCN

MIAMI DOLPHINS

	2010 Home	2010 Away	2011 Home	2011 Away
Intraconference by Division	CLE	BALT	DEN	KC
	PITT	CIN	OAK	SD
Interconference by Division	CHI	GB	PHIL	DALL
	DET	MINN	WASH	NYG
Intraconference by Position	AFCS	AFCW	AFCS	AFCN

NEW ENGLAND PATRIOTS

	2010 Home	2010 Away	2011 Home	2011 Away
Intraconference by Division	BALT	CLE	KC	DEN
	CIN	PITT	SD	OAK
Interconference by Division	GB	CHI	DALL	PHIL
	MINN	DET	NYG	WASH
Intraconference by Position	AFCS	AFCW	AFCS	AFCN

NEW YORK JETS

	2010 Home	2010 Away	2011 Home	2011 Away
Intraconference by Division	BALT	CLE	KC	DEN
	CIN	PITT	SD	OAK
Interconference by Division	GB	CHI	DALL	PHIL
	MINN	DET	NYG	WASH
Intraconference by Position	AFCS	AFCW	AFCS	AFCN

AFC NORTH NON-DIVISIONAL OPPONENTS 2010-11

BALTIMORE RAVENS

	2010 Home	2010 Away	2011 Home	2011 Away
Intraconference by Division	BUFF	NE	HOU	JAX
	MIA	NYJ	IND	TENN
Interconference by Division	NO	ATL	ARIZ	STL
	TB	CAR	SF	SEA
Intraconference by Position	AFCW	AFCS	AFCE	AFCW

CINCINNATI BENGALS

	2010 Home	2010 Away	2011 Home	2011 Away
Intraconference by Division	BUFF	NE	HOU	JAX
	MIA	NYJ	IND	TENN
Interconference by Division	NO	ATL	ARIZ	STL
	TB	CAR	SF	SEA
Intraconference by Position	AFCW	AFCS	AFCE	AFCW

CLEVELAND BROWNS

	2010 Home	2010 Away	2011 Home	2011 Away
Intraconference by Division	NE	BUFF	JAX	HOU
	NYJ	MIA	TENN	IND
Interconference by Division	ATL	NO	STL	ARIZ
	CAR	TB	SEA	SF
Intraconference by Position	AFCW	AFCS	AFCE	AFCW

PITTSBURGH STEELERS

	2010 Home	2010 Away	2011 Home	2011 Away
Intraconference by Division	NE	BUFF	JAX	HOU
	NYJ	MIA	TENN	IND
Interconference by Division	ATL	NO	STL	ARIZ
	CAR	TB	SEA	SF
Intraconference by Position	AFCW	AFCS	AFCE	AFCW

AFC SOUTH NON-DIVISIONAL OPPONENTS 2010-11

HOUSTON TEXANS

	2010 Home	2010 Away	2011 Home	2011 Away
Intraconference by Division	KC	DEN	CLE	BALT
	SD	OAK	PITT	CIN
Interconference by Division	DALL	PHIL	ATL	NO
	NYG	WASH	CAR	TB
Intraconference by Position	AFCN	AFCE	AFCW	AFCE

INDIANAPOLIS COLTS

	2010 Home	2010 Away	2011 Home	2011 Away
Intraconference by Division	KC	DEN	CLE	BALT
	SD	OAK	PITT	CIN
Interconference by Division	DALL	PHIL	ATL	NO
	NYG	WASH	CAR	TB
Intraconference by Position	AFCN	AFCE	AFCW	AFCE

JACKSONVILLE JAGUARS

	2010 Home	2010 Away	2011 Home	2011 Away
Intraconference by Division	DEN	KC	BALT	CLE
	OAK	SD	CIN	PITT
Interconference by Division	PHIL	DALL	NO	ATL
	WASH	NYG	TB	CAR
Intraconference by Position	AFCN	AFCE	AFCW	AFCE

TENNESSEE TITANS

	2010 Home	2010 Away	2011 Home	2011 Away
Intraconference by Division	DEN	KC	BALT	CLE
	OAK	SD	CIN	PITT
Interconference by Division	PHIL	DALL	NO	ATL
	WASH	NYG	TB	CAR
Intraconference by Position	AFCN	AFCE	AFCW	AFCE

AFC WEST NON-DIVISIONAL OPPONENTS 2010-11

DENVER BRONCOS

	2010 Home	2010 Away	2011 Home	2011 Away
Intraconference by Division	HOU	JAX	NE	BUFF
	IND	TENN	NYJ	MIA
Interconference by Division	STL	ARIZ	CHI	GB
	SEA	SF	DET	MINN
Intraconference by Position	AFCE	AFCN	AFCN	AFCS

KANSAS CITY CHIEFS

	2010 Home	2010 Away	2011 Home	2011 Away
Intraconference by Division	JAX	HOU	BUFF	NE
	TENN	IND	MIA	NYJ
Interconference by Division	ARIZ	STL	GB	CHI
	SF	SEA	MINN	DET
Intraconference by Position	AFCE	AFCN	AFCN	AFCS

OAKLAND RAIDERS

	2010 Home	2010 Away	2011 Home	2011 Away
Intraconference by Division	HOU	JAX	NE	BUFF
	IND	TENN	NYJ	MIA
Interconference by Division	STL	ARIZ	CHI	GB
	SEA	SF	DET	MINN
Intraconference by Position	AFCE	AFCN	AFCN	AFCS

SAN DIEGO CHARGERS

	2010 Home	2010 Away	2011 Home	2011 Away
Intraconference by Division	JAX	HOU	BUFF	NE
	TENN	IND	MIA	NYJ
Interconference by Division	ARIZ	STL	GB	CHI
	SF	SEA	MINN	DET
Intraconference by Position	AFCE	AFCN	AFCN	AFCS

NFC EAST NON-DIVISIONAL OPPONENTS 2010-11

DALLAS COWBOYS

	2010 Home	2010 Away	2011 Home	2011 Away
Intraconference by Division	CHI	GB	STL	ARIZ
	DET	MINN	SEA	SF
Interconference by Division	JAX	HOU	BUFF	NE
	TENN	IND	MIA	NYJ
Intraconference by Position	NFCS	NFCW	NFCN	NFCS

NEW YORK GIANTS

	2010 Home	2010 Away	2011 Home	2011 Away
Intraconference by Division	CHI	GB	STL	ARIZ
	DET	MINN	SEA	SF
Interconference by Division	JAX	HOU	BUFF	NE
	TENN	IND	MIA	NYJ
Intraconference by Position	NFCS	NFCW	NFCN	NFCS

PHILADELPHIA EAGLES

	2010 Home	2010 Away	2011 Home	2011 Away
Intraconference by Division	GB	CHI	ARIZ	STL
	MINN	DET	SF	SEA
Interconference by Division	HOU	JAX	NE	BUFF
	IND	TENN	NYJ	MIA
Intraconference by Position	NFCS	NFCW	NFCN	NFCS

WASHINGTON REDSKINS

	2010 Home	2010 Away	2011 Home	2011 Away
Intraconference by Division	GB	CHI	ARIZ	STL
	MINN	DET	SF	SEA
Interconference by Division	HOU	JAX	NE	BUFF
	IND	TENN	NYJ	MIA
Intraconference by Position	NFCS	NFCW	NFCN	NFCS

NFC NORTH NON-DIVISIONAL OPPONENTS 2010-11

CHICAGO BEARS

	2010 Home	2010 Away	2011 Home	2011 Away
Intraconference by Division	PHIL	DALL	ATL	NO
	WASH	NYG	CAR	TB
Interconference by Division	NE	BUFF	KC	DEN
	NYJ	MIA	SD	OAK
Intraconference by Position	NFCW	NFCS	NFCW	NFCE

DETROIT LIONS

	2010 Home	2010 Away	2011 Home	2011 Away
Intraconference by Division	PHIL	DALL	ATL	NO
	WASH	NYG	CAR	TB
Interconference by Division	NE	BUFF	KC	DEN
	NYJ	MIA	SD	OAK
Intraconference by Position	NFCW	NFCS	NFCW	NFCE

GREEN BAY PACKERS

	2010 Home	2010 Away	2011 Home	2011 Away
Intraconference by Division	DALL	PHIL	NO	ATL
	NYG	WASH	TB	CAR
Interconference by Division	BUFF	NE	DEN	KC
	MIA	NYJ	OAK	SD
Intraconference by Position	NFCW	NFCS	NFCW	NFCE

MINNESOTA VIKINGS

	2010 Home	2010 Away	2011 Home	2011 Away
Intraconference by Division	DALL	PHIL	NO	ATL
	NYG	WASH	TB	CAR
Interconference by Division	BUFF	NE	DEN	KC
	MIA	NYJ	OAK	SD
Intraconference by Position	NFCW	NFCS	NFCW	NFCE

NFC SOUTH NON-DIVISIONAL OPPONENTS 2010-11

ATLANTA FALCONS

	2010 Home	2010 Away	2011 Home	2011 Away
Intraconference by Division	ARIZ	STL	GB	CHI
	SF	SEA	MINN	DET
Interconference by Division	BALT	CLE	JAX	HOU
	CIN	PITT	TENN	IND
Intraconference by Position	NFCN	NFCE	NFCE	NFCW

CAROLINA PANTHERS

	2010 Home	2010 Away	2011 Home	2011 Away
Intraconference by Division	ARIZ	STL	GB	CHI
	SF	SEA	MINN	DET
Interconference by Division	BALT	CLE	JAX	HOU
	CIN	PITT	TENN	IND
Intraconference by Position	NFCN	NFCE	NFCE	NFCW

NEW ORLEANS SAINTS

	2010 Home	2010 Away	2011 Home	2011 Away
Intraconference by Division	STL	ARIZ	CHI	GB
	SEA	SF	DET	MINN
Interconference by Division	CLE	BALT	HOU	JAX
	PITT	CIN	IND	TENN
Intraconference by Position	NFCN	NFCE	NFCE	NFCW

TAMPA BAY BUCCANEERS

	2010 Home	2010 Away	2011 Home	2011 Away
Intraconference by Division	STL	ARIZ	CHI	GB
	SEA	SF	DET	MINN
Interconference by Division	CLE	BALT	HOU	JAX
	PITT	CIN	IND	TENN
Intraconference by Position	NFCN	NFCE	NFCE	NFCW

NFC WEST NON-DIVISIONAL OPPONENTS 2010-11

ARIZONA CARDINALS

	2010 Home	2010 Away	2011 Home	2011 Away
Intraconference by Division	NO	ATL	DALL	PHIL
	TB	CAR	NYG	WASH
Interconference by Division	DEN	KC	CLE	BALT
	OAK	SD	PITT	CIN
Intraconference by Position	NFCE	NFCN	NFCS	NFCN

ST. LOUIS RAMS

	2010 Home	2010 Away	2011 Home	2011 Away
Intraconference by Division	ATL	NO	PHIL	DALL
	CAR	TB	WASH	NYG
Interconference by Division	KC	DEN	BALT	CLE
	SD	OAK	CIN	PITT
Intraconference by Position	NFCE	NFCN	NFCS	NFCN

SAN FRANCISCO 49ERS

	2010 Home	2010 Away	2011 Home	2011 Away
Intraconference by Division	NO	ATL	DALL	PHIL
	TB	CAR	NYG	WASH
Interconference by Division	DEN	KC	CLE	BALT
	OAK	SD	PITT	CIN
Intraconference by Position	NFCE	NFCN	NFCS	NFCN

SEATTLE SEAHAWKS

	2010 Home	2010 Away	2011 Home	2011 Away
Intraconference by Division	ATL	NO	PHIL	DALL
	CAR	TB	WASH	NYG
Interconference by Division	KC	DEN	BALT	CLE
	SD	OAK	CIN	PITT
Intraconference by Position	NFCE	NFCN	NFCS	NFCN

TOP ACTIVE PASSERS

1,000 or more attempts

		Yrs.	Att.	Comp.	Pct. Comp.	Yards	TD	Pct. TD	Had Int.	Pct. Int.	Ratings Pts.
1.	Aaron Rodgers, G.B.	5	1,136	726	63.9	8,801	59	5.2	21	1.8	97.2
2.	Philip Rivers, S.D.	6	1,914	1,207	63.1	14,951	106	5.5	45	2.4	95.8
3.	Tony Romo, Dal.	6	1,857	1,178	63.4	15,045	107	5.8	55	3.0	95.6
4.	Peyton Manning, Ind.	12	6,531	4,232	64.8	50,128	366	5.6	181	2.8	95.2
5.	Tom Brady, N.E.	10	4,218	2,672	63.3	30,844	225	5.3	99	2.3	93.3
6.	Drew Brees, N.O.	9	4,164	2,697	64.8	30,646	202	4.9	110	2.6	91.9
7.	Ben Roethlisberger, Pit.	6	2,411	1,526	63.3	19,302	127	5.3	81	3.4	91.7
8.	Matt Schaub, Hou.	6	1,413	923	65.3	11,087	59	4.2	40	2.8	91.3
9.	Chad Pennington, Mia.	10	2,469	1,631	66.1	17,804	102	4.1	64	2.6	90.1
10.	Carson Palmer, Cin.	6	2,631	1,662	63.2	18,724	128	4.9	80	3.0	87.9
11.	Daunte Culpepper, *	11	3,199	2,016	63.0	24,153	149	4.7	106	3.3	87.8
12.	Brett Favre, Min.	19	9,811	6,083	62.0	69,329	497	5.1	317	3.2	86.6
13.	Donovan McNabb, Was.	11	4,746	2,801	59.0	32,873	216	4.6	100	2.1	86.5
14.	David Garrard, Jac.	8	1,915	1,170	61.1	13,269	66	3.4	39	2.0	84.9
15.	Marc Bulger, *	8	3,171	1,969	62.1	22,814	122	3.8	93	2.9	84.4
16.	Mark Brunell, *	16	4,624	2,753	59.5	31,928	182	3.9	107	2.3	83.9
17.	Jay Cutler, Chi.	4	1,775	1,098	61.9	12,690	81	4.6	63	3.5	83.8
18.	Matt Hasselbeck, Sea.	11	3,835	2,306	60.1	26,578	164	4.3	111	2.9	83.3
19.	Jason Campbell, Oak.	4	1,637	1,002	61.2	10,860	55	3.4	38	2.3	82.3
20.	Jake Delhomme, Cle.	9	2,755	1,630	59.2	19,892	123	4.5	94	3.4	82.1
21.	Byron Leftwich, Pit.	7	1,545	900	58.3	10,218	58	3.8	41	2.7	79.6
22.	Matt Cassel, K.C.	5	1,048	620	59.2	6,870	39	3.7	29	2.8	79.6
23.	Eli Manning, NYG	6	2,793	1,593	57.0	18,644	125	4.5	88	3.2	79.2
24.	Charlie Batch, Pit.	12	1,461	819	56.1	10,050	57	3.9	44	3.0	77.9
25.	Kyle Orton, Den.	4	1,454	841	57.8	9,121	51	3.5	39	2.7	76.9

TOP ACTIVE SCORERS

(number in parentheses represents 2-point conversions scored)

		Yrs.	TD	FG	PAT	TP
1.	Matt Stover, *	19	0	471	591	2,004
2.	Jason Hanson, Det.	18	0	427	554	1,835
3.	John Kasay, Car.	19	0	408	507	1,731
4.	Adam Vinatieri, Ind.	14	0	338	514(1)	1,530
5.	Ryan Longwell, Min.	13	0	322	536	1,502
6.	Olindo Mare, Sea.	13	0	303	405	1,314
7.	David Akers, Phi.	12	0	262	396	1,182
8.	Kris Brown, Hou.	11	0	252	347	1,103
9.	Joe Nedney, S.F.	14	0	245	328	1,063
10.	Jay Feely, Ari.	9	0	231	320	1,013
11.	Rian Lindell, Buf.	10	0	233	306	1,005
12.	Sebastian Janikowski, Oak.	10	0	229	313	1,000
13.	Phil Dawson, Cle.	11	1	229	273	966
14.	LaDainian Tomlinson, NYJ	9	153	0	0	918
15.	Neil Rackers, Hou.	10	0	205	290	905
16.	Randy Moss, N.E.	12	149	0	0(4)	902
17.	Terrell Owens, *	14	147	0	0(3)	888
18.	Shayne Graham, *	9	0	196	276	864
19.	Jeff Reed, Pit.	8	0	189	288	855
20.	Josh Brown, St.L.	7	0	166	258	756
21.	Nate Kaeding, S.D.	6	0	150	303	753
22.	Matt Bryant, Atl.	8	0	145	191	626
23.	Lawrence Tynes, NYG	6	0	119	225	582
24.	Rob Bironas, Ten.	5	0	136	167	575
	Robbie Gould, Chi.	5	0	134	173	575

**Free agent; subject to developments.*

TOP ACTIVE SCORERS (TOUCHDOWNS)

		Yrs.	Rush	Rec.	Ret.	Tot.
1.	LaDainian Tomlinson, NYJ	9	138	15	0	153
2.	Randy Moss, N.E.	12	0	148	1	149
3.	Terrell Owens, *	14	3	144	0	147
4.	Isaac Bruce, S.F.	16	0	91	0	91
5.	Joey Galloway, Was.	15	1	77	5	83
6.	Tony Gonzalez, Atl.	13	0	82	0	82
7.	Hines Ward, Pit.	12	1	78	0	79
8.	Clinton Portis, Was.	8	73	5	0	78
9.	Ahman Green, *	12	60	14	0	74
	Torry Holt, N.E.	11	0	74	0	74
	Fred Taylor, N.E.	12	66	8	0	74
12.	Ricky Williams, Mia.	9	62	7	0	69
13.	Brian Westbrook, *	8	37	29	2	68
14.	Thomas Jones, K.C.	10	62	3	0	65
15.	Reggie Wayne, Ind.	9	0	63	0	63
16.	Jamal Lewis, *	9	58	4	0	62
	Derrick Mason, Bal.	13	0	59	3	62
	Muhsin Muhammad, *	14	0	62	0	62
	Chad Ochocinco, Cin.	9	0	62	0	62
20.	Larry Johnson, Was.	7	55	6	0	61
21.	Larry Fitzgerald, Ari.	6	0	59	0	59
	Antonio Gates, S.D.	7	0	59	0	59
23.	Steve Smith, Car.	9	2	50	6	58
24.	Chris Chambers, K.C.	9	0	57	0	57
25.	Maurice Jones-Drew, Jac.	4	49	5	2	56

NFL ACTIVE STATISTICAL LEADERS

TOP ACTIVE RUSHERS

	Yrs.	Att.	Yards	TD
1. LaDainian Tomlinson, NYJ	9	2,880	12,490	138
2. Fred Taylor, N.E.	12	2,491	11,540	66
3. Jamal Lewis, *	9	2,542	10,607	58
4. Clinton Portis, Was.	8	2,176	9,696	73
5. Thomas Jones, K.C.	10	2,280	9,217	62
6. Ahman Green, *	12	2,056	9,205	60
7. Ricky Williams, Mia.	9	2,164	8,892	62
8. Steven Jackson, St.L.	6	1,548	6,707	41
9. Larry Johnson, Was.	7	1,421	6,219	55
10. Brian Westbrook, *	8	1,308	5,995	37
11. Willis McGahee, Bal.	6	1,441	5,787	50
12. Frank Gore, S.F.	5	1,168	5,561	32
13. Willie Parker, Was.	6	1,253	5,378	24
14. Julius Jones, Sea.	6	1,220	4,845	22
15. Adrian Peterson, Min.	3	915	4,484	40
16. Chester Taylor, Chi.	8	1,028	4,396	22
17. Ronnie Brown, Mia.	5	928	4,081	31
18. Marion Barber, Dal.	5	929	3,984	43
19. Michael Vick, Phi.	7	553	3,954	23
20. Maurice Jones-Drew, Jac.	4	842	3,924	49
21. DeAngelo Williams, Car.	4	754	3,850	30
22. Michael Turner, Atl.	6	782	3,827	33
23. LaMont Jordan, *	9	897	3,734	28
24. Michael Bennett, Oak.	9	840	3,692	13
25. Cedric Benson, Cin.	5	935	3,591	18

TOP ACTIVE SCRIMMAGE YARDS LEADERS

	Yrs.	Rush	Rec	Total	TD
1. LaDainian Tomlinson, NYJ	9	12,490	3,955	16,445	153
2. Isaac Bruce, S.F.	16	139	15,208	15,347	91
3. Terrell Owens, *	14	251	14,951	15,202	147
4. Randy Moss, N.E.	12	159	14,465	14,624	148
5. Fred Taylor, N.E.	12	11,540	2,378	13,918	74
6. Torry Holt, N.E.	11	57	13,382	13,439	74
7. Jamal Lewis, *	9	10,607	1,879	12,486	62
8. Ahman Green, *	12	9,205	2,883	12,088	74
9. Tony Gonzalez, Atl.	13	14	11,807	11,821	82
10. Clinton Portis, Was.	8	9,696	1,963	11,659	78
11. Muhsin Muhammad, *	14	64	11,438	11,502	62
12. Hines Ward, Pit.	12	430	10,947	11,377	79
13. Ricky Williams, Mia.	9	8,892	2,382	11,274	69
14. Joey Galloway, Was.	15	496	10,777	11,273	78
15. Derrick Mason, Bal.	13	3	11,089	11,092	59
16. Thomas Jones, K.C.	10	9,217	1,858	11,075	65
17. Chad Ochocinco, Cin.	9	175	9,952	10,127	62
18. Brian Westbrook, *	8	5,995	3,790	9,785	66
19. Reggie Wayne, Ind.	9	0	9,393	9,393	63
20. Donald Driver, G.B.	11	217	9,050	9,267	50
21. Steven Jackson, St.L.	10	6,707	2,287	8,994	48
22. Laveranues Coles, *	10	231	8,609	8,840	49
23. Steve Smith, Car.	9	295	8,330	8,625	52
24. Andre Johnson, Hou.	7	36	7,948	7,984	42
25. Chris Chambers, K.C.	9	373	7,435	7,808	57

TOP ACTIVE PASS RECEIVERS

	Yrs.	No.	Yards	TD
1. Isaac Bruce, S.F.	16	1,024	15,208	91
2. Terrell Owens, *	14	1,006	14,951	144
3. Tony Gonzalez, Atl.	13	999	11,807	82
4. Randy Moss, N.E.	12	926	14,465	148
5. Torry Holt, N.E.	11	920	13,382	74
6. Hines Ward, Pit.	12	895	10,947	78
7. Derrick Mason, Bal.	13	863	11,089	59
8. Muhsin Muhammad, *	14	860	11,438	62
9. Joey Galloway, Was.	15	689	10,777	77
10. Chad Ochocinco, Cin.	9	684	9,952	62
11. Reggie Wayne, Ind.	9	676	9,393	63
12. Laveranues Coles, *	10	674	8,609	49
13. Donald Driver, G.B.	11	647	9,050	49
14. Andre Johnson, Hou.	7	587	7,948	42
15. Anquan Boldin, Bal.	7	586	7,520	44
T.J. Houshmandzadeh, Sea.	9	586	6,693	40
17. Steve Smith, Car.	9	574	8,330	50
18. Marty Booker, *	11	539	6,703	37
19. LaDainian Tomlinson, NYJ	9	530	3,955	15
20. Larry Fitzgerald, Ari.	6	523	7,067	59
Jason Witten, Dal.	7	523	5,965	27
22. Chris Chambers, K.C.	9	518	7,435	57
23. Santana Moss, Was.	9	500	7,443	46
24. Antonio Gates, S.D.	7	479	6,223	59
25. Jeremy Shockey, N.O.	8	469	5,280	30

TOP ACTIVE INTERCEPTORS

	Yrs.	No.	Yards	TD
1. Darren Sharper, N.O.	13	63	1,412	11
2. Ty Law, *	15	53	828	7
3. Champ Bailey, Den.	11	46	446	4
Ed Reed, Bal.	8	46	1,255	6
5. Charles Woodson, G.B.	12	45	785	9
6. Dre' Bly, *	11	43	652	5
7. Ronde Barber, T.B.	13	37	653	7
8. Brian Dawkins, Den.	14	36	515	2
9. Walt Harris, *	14	35	332	4
Asante Samuel, Phi.	7	35	494	4
11. Shawn Springs, N.E.	13	33	429	2
12. Anthony Henry, *	9	31	533	3
13. Nate Clements, S.F.	9	30	436	5
14. Ray Lewis, Bal.	14	28	473	2
Rashean Mathis, Jac.	7	28	487	3
16. Deon Grant, NYG	9	26	267	0
DeAngelo Hall, Was.	6	26	589	2
18. Ken Lucas, *	9	25	298	1
Lawyer Milloy, Sea.	14	25	205	1
20. Chris Gamble, Car.	6	24	283	2
21. Terence Newman, Dal.	7	23	249	2
Adrian Wilson, Ari.	9	23	489	2
23. Charles Tillman, Chi.	7	22	342	3
24. Nick Harper, *	9	21	286	1
Al Harris, G.B.	12	21	407	3
Fred Smoot, *	9	21	194	1
Deshea Townsend, *	12	21	190	3
Antoine Winfield, Min.	11	21	178	2

TOP ACTIVE PUNT RETURNERS

40 or more punt returns

	Yrs.	No.	Yards	Avg.	TD
1. Roscoe Parrish, Buf.	5	118	1,445	12.2	3
2. Clifton Smith, T.B.	2	46	556	12.1	1
3. Quan Cosby, Cin.	1	40	474	11.9	0
4. Santana Moss, Was.	9	112	1,268	11.3	3
5. Devin Hester, Chi.	4	145	1,636	11.3	7
6. DeSean Jackson, Phi.	2	79	881	11.2	3
7. Josh Cribbs, Cle.	5	103	1,141	11.1	2
8. Domenik Hixon, NYG	3	48	530	11.0	1
9. Will Blackmon, G.B.	4	47	515	11.0	3
10. Jacoby Jones, Hou.	3	101	1,098	10.9	2
11. Eddie Royal, Den.	2	44	475	10.8	1
12. Hank Poteat, *	9	77	788	10.2	1
13. Dennis Northcutt, Det.	10	255	2,592	10.2	3
14. Wes Welker, N.E.	6	203	2,056	10.1	0
15. Nate Clements, S.F.	9	82	816	10.0	2
16. Nate Burleson, Det.	7	156	1,523	9.8	3
17. Patrick Crayton, Dal.	6	111	1,066	9.6	2
18. Jim Leonhard, NYJ	5	52	499	9.6	0
19. Joey Galloway, Was.	15	141	1,349	9.6	5
20. Mewelde Moore, Pit.	6	83	792	9.5	2
21. Kevin Faulk, N.E.	11	99	932	9.4	0
22. Leon Washington, Sea.	4	64	599	9.4	0
23. Steve Smith, Car.	9	172	1,606	9.3	4
24. Mark Jones, Ten.	6	159	1,483	9.3	0
25. Phillip Buchanon, Was.	8	118	1,075	9.1	3

TOP ACTIVE KICKOFF RETURNERS

40 or more kickoff returns

	Yrs.	No.	Yards	Avg.	TD
1. Clifton Smith, T.B.	2	67	1,894	28.3	1
2. Leodis McKelvin, Buf.	2	57	1,589	27.9	1
3. Danieal Manning, Chi.	4	68	1,895	27.9	1
4. Percy Harvin, Min.	1	42	1,156	27.5	2
5. Ellis Hobbs, Phi.	5	125	3,394	27.2	3
6. Stefan Logan, Pit.	1	55	1,466	26.7	0
7. Josh Cribbs, Cle.	5	265	7,049	26.6	8
8. Terrence McGee, Buf.	7	207	5,450	26.3	5
9. Maurice Jones-Drew, Jac.	4	79	2,054	26.0	2
10. Laurence Maroney, N.E.	4	41	1,062	25.9	0
11. Jerious Norwood, Atl.	4	117	2,987	25.5	0
12. Leon Washington, Sea.	4	117	2,986	25.5	4
13. Quintin Demps, Phi.	2	58	1,469	25.3	1
14. Courtney Roby, N.O.	4	88	2,222	25.3	1
15. Michael Turner, Atl.	6	44	1,111	25.3	0
16. Darren Sproles, S.D.	5	207	5,212	25.2	2
17. Eric Weems, Atl.	3	49	1,233	25.2	0
18. Josh Wilson, Sea.	3	94	2,350	25.0	1
19. Eddie Royal, Den.	2	49	1,221	24.9	1
20. Pierre Thomas, N.O.	3	68	1,677	24.7	0
21. Chris Carr, Bal.	5	249	6,140	24.7	0
22. Domenik Hixon, NYG	3	80	1,966	24.6	1
23. Danny Amendola, St.L.	1	66	1,618	24.5	0
24. Jamaal Charles, K.C.	2	51	1,246	24.4	1
25. Jacoby Jones, Hou.	3	41	996	24.3	1

TOP ACTIVE PUNTERS

50 or more punts

	Yrs.	No.	Avg.	LG
1. Shane Lechler, Oak.	10	778	47.3	73
2. Brett Kern, Ten.	2	110	46.0	67
3. Donnie Jones, St.L.	6	449	45.5	80
4. Jon Ryan, Sea.	4	310	45.3	72
5. Mat McBriar, Dal.	6	371	45.0	75
6. Andy Lee, S.F.	6	554	44.9	82
7. Brandon Fields, Mia.	3	226	44.5	71
8. Ben Graham, Ari.	5	335	44.4	69
9. Chris Kluwe, Min.	5	391	44.4	70
10. Pat McAfee, Ind.	1	64	44.3	60
11. Mike Scifres, S.D.	7	393	44.2	71
12. Dustin Colquitt, K.C.	5	397	44.1	81
13. Sam Koch, Bal.	4	321	43.8	74
14. Brian Moorman, Buf.	9	700	43.6	84
15. Thomas Morstead, N.O.	1	58	43.6	60
16. Hunter Smith, *	11	634	43.2	69
17. Kevin Huber, Cin.	1	86	43.2	61
18. Steve Weatherford, NYJ	4	279	43.0	66
19. Mitch Berger, *	15	847	42.9	75
20. Craig Hentrich, *	16	1,150	42.9	78
21. Jeremy Kapinos, G.B.	3	88	42.8	58
22. Josh Bidwell, Was.	10	727	42.8	68
23. Dave Zastudil, Cle.	8	581	42.7	67
24. Jason Baker, Car.	9	637	42.7	70
25. Sav Rocca, Phi.	3	226	42.6	65

TOP ACTIVE QUARTERBACK SACKERS

	Yrs.	No.
1. Jason Taylor, NYJ	13	127.5
2. Joey Porter, Ari.	11	92.0
3. Trevor Pryce, Bal.	13	90.0
4. John Abraham, Atl.	10	89.5
5. Leonard Little, *	12	87.5
6. Greg Ellis, *	12	84.0
Dwight Freeney, Ind.	8	84.0
8. Julius Peppers, Chi.	8	81.0
9. Aaron Schobel, Buf.	9	78.0
10. Jevon Kearse, *	11	74.0
11. Jared Allen, Min.	6	72.0
12. Shaun Ellis, NYJ	10	68.0
13. Darren Howard, *	10	67.0
Adewale Ogunleye, *	9	67.0
15. DeMarcus Ware, Dal.	5	64.5
16. Andre Carter, Was.	9	63.5
17. Robert Mathis, Ind.	7	63.0
18. Phillip Daniels, Was.	14	60.0
Vonnie Holliday, Den.	12	60.0
20. Terrell Suggs, Bal.	7	57.5
21. Mike Vrabel, K.C.	13	57.0
22. Justin Smith, S.F.	9	56.5
23. Aaron Kampman, Jac.	8	54.0
24. Chike Okeafor, *	10	53.0
Adalius Thomas, *	10	53.0

COACHES RECORDS

ACTIVE COACHES' CAREER RECORDS (Order Based on Career Victories)
Start of 2010 Season

			Regular Season				Postseason			Career			
Coach	**Team(s)**	**Yrs.**	**Won**	**Lost**	**Tied**	**Pct.**	**Won**	**Lost**	**Pct.**	**Won**	**Lost**	**Tied**	**Pct.**
Bill Belichick	Cleveland Browns, New England Patriots	15	148	92	0	.617	15	5	.750	163	97	0	.627
Mike Shanahan	Los Angeles Raiders, Denver Broncos, Washington Redskins	16	146	98	0	.598	8	5	.615	154	103	0	.599
Jeff Fisher	Houston/Tennessee Oilers, Tennessee Titans	15	136	110	0	.553	5	6	.455	141	116	0	.549
Tom Coughlin	Jacksonville Jaguars, New York Giants	14	123	101	0	.549	8	7	.533	131	108	0	.548
Andy Reid	Philadelphia Eagles	11	108	67	1	.616	10	8	.556	118	75	1	.611
Norv Turner	Washington Redskins, Oakland Raiders, San Diego Chargers	12	90	98	1	.479	4	4	.500	94	102	1	.480
Wade Phillips	New Orleans Saints, Denver Broncos, Buffalo Bills, Atlanta Falcons, Dallas Cowboys	10	81	54	0	.600	1	5	.167	82	59	0	.582
John Fox	Carolina Panthers	8	71	57	0	.555	5	3	.625	76	60	0	.559
Jack Del Rio	Jacksonville Jaguars	7	57	55	0	.509	1	2	.333	58	57	0	.504
Marvin Lewis	Cincinnati Bengals	7	56	55	1	.504	0	2	.000	56	57	1	.496
Lovie Smith	Chicago Bears	6	52	44	0	.542	2	2	.500	54	46	0	.540
Sean Payton	New Orleans Saints	4	38	26	0	.594	4	1	.800	42	27	0	.609
Mike McCarthy	Green Bay Packers	4	38	26	0	.594	1	2	.333	39	28	0	.582
Brad Childress	Minnesota Vikings	4	36	28	0	.563	1	2	.333	37	30	0	.552
Pete Carroll	New York Jets, New England Patriots, Seattle Seahawks	4	33	31	0	.516	1	2	.333	34	33	0	.507
Mike Tomlin	Pittsburgh Steelers	3	31	17	0	.646	3	1	.750	34	18	0	.654
Gary Kubiak	Houston Texans	4	31	33	0	.484	0	0	—	31	33	0	.484
Ken Whisenhunt	Arizona Cardinals	3	27	21	0	.563	4	2	.667	31	23	0	.574
Eric Mangini	New York Jets, Cleveland Browns	4	28	36	0	.438	0	1	.000	28	37	0	.431
John Harbaugh	Baltimore Ravens	2	20	12	0	.625	3	2	.600	23	14	0	.622
Mike Smith	Atlanta Falcons	2	20	12	0	.625	0	1	.000	20	13	0	.606
Chan Gailey	Dallas Cowboys, Buffalo Bills	2	18	14	0	.563	0	2	.000	18	16	0	.529
Tony Sparano	Miami Dolphins	2	18	14	0	.563	0	1	.000	18	15	0	.545
Jim Caldwell	Indianapolis Colts	1	14	2	0	.875	2	1	.667	16	3	0	.842
Mike Singletary	San Francisco 49ers	2	13	12	0	.520	0	0	—	13	12	0	.520
Rex Ryan	New York Jets	1	9	7	0	.563	2	1	.667	11	8	0	.579
Tom Cable	Oakland Raiders	2	9	19	0	.321	0	0	—	9	19	0	.321
Josh McDaniels	Denver Broncos	1	8	8	0	.500	0	0	—	8	8	0	.500
Todd Haley	Kansas City Chiefs	1	4	12	0	.250	0	0	—	4	12	0	.250
Raheem Morris	Tampa Bay Buccaneers	1	3	13	0	.188	0	0	—	3	13	0	.188
Jim Schwartz	Detroit Lions	1	2	14	0	.125	0	0	—	2	14	0	.125
Steve Spagnuolo	St. Louis Rams	1	1	15	0	.063	0	0	—	1	15	0	.063

COACHES WITH 100 CAREER VICTORIES (Order Based on Career Victories)
Start of 2010 Season

		Regular Season					Postseason			Career			
Coach	**Team(s)**	**Yrs.**	**Won**	**Lost**	**Tied**	**Pct.**	**Won**	**Lost**	**Pct.**	**Won**	**Lost**	**Tied**	**Pct.**
Don Shula	Baltimore Colts, Miami Dolphins	33	328	156	6	.677	19	17	.528	347	173	6	.666
George Halas	Chicago Bears	40	318	148	31	.682	6	3	.667	324	151	31	.682
Tom Landry	Dallas Cowboys	29	250	162	6	.607	20	16	.556	270	178	6	.603
Earl (Curly) Lambeau	Green Bay Packers, Chicago Cardinals, Washington Redskins	33	226	132	22	.631	3	2	.600	229	134	22	.631
Chuck Noll	Pittsburgh Steelers	23	193	148	1	.566	16	8	.667	209	156	1	.572
Marty Schottenheimer	Cleveland Browns, Kansas City Chiefs, Washington Redskins, San Diego Chargers	21	200	126	1	.613	5	13	.278	205	139	1	.596
Dan Reeves	Denver Broncos, New York Giants, Atlanta Falcons	23	190	165	2	.535	11	9	.550	201	174	2	.536
Chuck Knox	Los Angeles Rams, Buffalo Bills, Seattle Seahawks	22	186	147	1	.558	7	11	.389	193	158	1	.550
Bill Parcells	New York Giants, New England Patriots, New York Jets, Dallas Cowboys	19	172	130	1	.569	11	8	.579	183	138	1	.570
Mike Holmgren	Green Bay Packers, Seattle Seahawks	17	161	111	0	.592	13	11	.542	174	122	0	.588
Joe Gibbs	Washington Redskins	16	154	94	0	.621	17	7	.708	171	101	0	.629
Paul Brown	Cleveland Browns, Cincinnati Bengals	21	166	100	6	.624	4	8	.333	170	108	6	.612
Bud Grant	Minnesota Vikings	18	158	96	5	.621	10	12	.455	168	108	5	.608
Bill Belichick	Cleveland Browns, New England Patriots	15	148	92	0	.617	15	5	.750	163	97	0	.627
Bill Cowher	Pittsburgh Steelers	15	149	90	1	.623	12	9	.571	161	99	1	.619
Mike Shanahan	Los Angeles Raiders, Denver Broncos, Washington Redskins	16	146	98	0	.598	8	5	.615	154	103	0	.599
Marv Levy	Kansas City Chiefs, Buffalo Bills	17	143	112	0	.561	11	8	.579	154	120	0	.562
Steve Owen	New York Giants	23	151	100	17	.602	2	8	.200	153	108	17	.586
Tony Dungy	Tampa Bay Buccaneers, Indianapolis Colts	13	139	69	0	.668	9	10	.474	148	79	0	.652
Jeff Fisher	Houston/Tennessee Oilers, Tennessee Titans	15	136	110	0	.553	5	6	.455	141	116	0	.549
Hank Stram	Kansas City Chiefs, New Orleans Saints	17	131	97	10	.574	5	3	.625	136	100	10	.576
Weeb Ewbank	Baltimore Colts, New York Jets	20	130	129	7	.502	4	1	.800	134	130	7	.508
Tom Coughlin	Jacksonville Jaguars, New York Giants	14	123	101	0	.549	8	7	.533	131	108	0	.548
Mike Ditka	Chicago Bears, New Orleans Saints	14	121	95	0	.560	6	6	.500	127	101	0	.557
Dick Vermeil	Philadelphia Eagles, St. Louis Rams, Kansas City Chiefs	15	120	109	0	.524	6	5	.545	126	114	0	.525
Jim Mora	New Orleans Saints, Indianapolis Colts	15	125	106	0	.541	0	6	.000	125	112	0	.527
George Seifert	San Francisco 49ers, Carolina Panthers	11	114	62	0	.648	10	5	.667	124	67	0	.649
Sid Gillman	Los Angeles Rams, Los Angeles-San Diego Chargers, Houston Oilers	18	122	99	7	.552	1	5	.167	123	104	7	.542
George Allen	Los Angeles Rams, Washington Redskins	12	116	47	5	.712	2	7	.222	118	54	5	.686
Andy Reid	Philadelphia Eagles	11	108	67	1	.616	10	8	.556	118	75	1	.611
Dennis Green	Minnesota Vikings, Arizona Cardinals	13	113	94	0	.546	4	8	.333	117	102	0	.534
Don Coryell	St. Louis Cardinals, San Diego Chargers	14	111	83	1	.572	3	6	.333	114	89	1	.561
John Madden	Oakland Raiders	10	103	32	7	.759	9	7	.563	112	39	7	.739
Ray (Buddy) Parker	Chicago Cardinals, Detroit Lions, Pittsburgh Steelers	15	104	75	9	.581	3	1	.750	107	76	9	.585
Vince Lombardi	Green Bay Packers, Washington Redskins	10	96	34	6	.739	9	1	.900	105	35	6	.750
Tom Flores	Oakland-Los Angeles Raiders, Seattle Seahawks	12	97	87	0	.527	8	3	.727	105	90	0	.538
Bill Walsh	San Francisco 49ers	10	92	59	1	.609	10	4	.714	102	63	1	.617
Jon Gruden	Oakland Raiders, Tampa Bay Buccaneers	11	95	81	0	.540	5	4	.556	100	85	0	.541

Active coaches in bold.
From 1920-71, tie games were not included in winning percentage.

WHAT TO LOOK FOR IN 2010

The **Chicago Bears** need seven regular-season victories to become the first team in NFL history with 700 regular-season victories. Chicago's all-time regular-season record is 693-507-42.

The **Detroit Lions** need three victories to reach 500 total victories. Detroit's all-time record is 497-593-32.

The **Arizona Cardinals** need 11 victories to reach 500 total victories. Arizona's all-time record is 489-687-39.

The **Cleveland Browns** need six victories to reach 450 total victories. Cleveland's all-time record is 444-403-10.

The **Kansas City Chiefs** need seven victories to reach 400 total victories. Kansas City's all-time record is 393-372-12.

The **Houston Texans** need one victory to reach 50 total victories. Houston's all-time record is 49-79-0.

The **Indianapolis Colts** have advanced to the playoffs in each of the past eight seasons and can tie the NFL record for most consecutive playoff appearances if they qualify for the 2010 postseason. Indianapolis would join Dallas (1975-1983) as the only teams with nine consecutive playoff appearances.

Indianapolis needs 12 regular-season wins to become the first team in NFL history with eight consecutive 12-win seasons. Indianapolis is the only team to accomplish the feat in seven consecutive seasons.

Bill Belichick, New England, needs 12 victories to pass Bud Grant (168), Paul Brown (170), Joe Gibbs (171) and Mike Holmgren (174) for 10th place all-time in career victories. In 15 seasons, Belichick has 163 career victories (see Shanahan note).

Mike Shanahan, Washington, needs 10 victories to pass Bill Cowher (161) and Bill Belichick (163) for 14th place all-time in career victories. In 16 seasons, Shanahan has 154 career victories (see Belichick note).

Jeff Fisher, Tennessee, needs nine victories to become the 19th coach in NFL history to win 150 games. In 15 seasons, Fisher has 141 career victories.

Norv Turner, San Diego, needs six victories to reach 100 for his career. In 12 seasons, Turner has 94 career victories.

Brett Favre, Minnesota, needs three touchdown passes to become the first player in NFL history with 500 career touchdown passes. In 19 seasons, Favre is the all-time leader with 497 touchdown passes.

Favre needs 671 passing yards to become the first player in NFL history with 70,000 passing yards. In 19 seasons, Favre is the all-time leader with 69,329 career passing yards.

Favre needs 189 pass attempts to become the first player in NFL history with 10,000 attempts. In 19 seasons, Favre is the all-time leader with 9,811 career pass attempts.

Favre needs to play in the first 13 games of the season to become the second player in NFL history to play in 300 consecutive games. Favre, whose streak began on September 13, 1992 and stands at 287 games, would join Jeff Feagles (336) as the only players to accomplish the feat.

Favre has passed for 3,000 yards in a season 18 times in his 19-year career and can extend his NFL record with another 3,000-yard season. Favre also holds the record for the most consecutive seasons with 3,000 passing yards with 18 (active).

In his 19-year career, Favre has passed for four touchdowns in a game 23 times – an NFL record. Favre needs two more four-touchdown games to become the first player with 25 four-touchdown pass games in NFL history (see Manning note).

Favre has led the league in touchdown passes four times in his career and can surpass Johnny Unitas, Len Dawson and Steve Young (4) for the most seasons leading the league in touchdown passes.

Peyton Manning, Indianapolis, needs 4,000 passing yards to become the first player in NFL history with 11 4,000-yard seasons. Manning is the only quarterback to accomplish the feat in 10 seasons.

Manning needs 25 touchdown passes to become the first player in NFL history to throw 25 touchdown passes in 13 consecutive seasons. Manning is the only player to have 12 consecutive seasons with 25 touchdown passes.

Manning has passed for 3,000 yards in each of the past 12 seasons and owns the second-longest streak of consecutive 3,000-yard seasons (Brett Favre, 18). Manning is the only player in NFL history to start a career with 12 consecutive 3,000-yard seasons.

Manning has led the league in touchdown passes three times in his career and can tie Brett Favre, Johnny Unitas, Len Dawson and Steve Young (4) for the most seasons leading the league in touchdown passes (see Favre note).

Manning has passed for 400 yards in a game seven times in his career. Manning needs one 400-yard passing game to surpass Joe Montana and Warren Moon (7) for the second-most games with 400 yards passing in NFL history (Dan Marino, 13).

Manning needs 34 touchdown passes to become the third player in NFL history with 400 touchdown passes. Manning would join Dan Marino (420) and Brett Favre (497) as the only players to accomplish the feat. In 12 seasons, Manning has thrown 366 touchdown passes.

Manning needs 1,348 passing yards to surpass John Elway (51,475) to move into third place all-time. In 12 seasons, Manning has passed for 50,128 yards.

Manning has 21 games with four or more touchdown passes and needs three such games to surpass Brett Favre (23) for the most games with four touchdown passes in NFL history (see Favre note).

LaDainian Tomlinson, New York Jets, needs 10 rushing touchdowns to extend his NFL-record streak of consecutive 10-touchdown seasons to begin a career to 10.

Tomlinson needs seven touchdowns to become the third player with 160 touchdowns. Tomlinson would join Jerry Rice (208) and Emmitt Smith (175) as the only players to accomplish the feat. In nine seasons, Tomlinson has scored 153 touchdowns (see Moss and Owens notes).

Tomlinson needs 12 rushing touchdowns to become the second player with 150 rushing touchdowns. Tomlinson has scored 138 rushing touchdowns and would join Emmitt Smith (164) as the only players to accomplish the feat.

Tomlinson has four 200-yard rushing games in his career. Tomlinson needs two 200-yard games to surpass Tiki Barber (5) and tie O.J. Simpson (6) for the most all-time.

Tomlinson needs 1,000 rushing yards to become the fifth player in NFL history with nine 1,000-yard rushing seasons. Only Walter Payton (10), Barry Sanders (10), Curtis Martin (10) and Emmitt Smith (11) have accomplished the feat.

Tomlinson needs 555 scrimmage yards to become the eighth player in NFL history with 17,000 scrimmage yards. In nine seasons, Tomlinson has 16,445 scrimmage yards.

Chris Johnson, Tennessee, needs 100 rushing yards in each of his next four games to surpass Marcus Allen (11) and Barry Sanders (14) for the most consecutive 100-yard games in NFL history. Johnson has rushed for 100 yards in each of his past 11 games.

Randy Moss, New England, needs five touchdowns to surpass LaDainian Tomlinson (153) for third place all-time (see Owens and Tomlinson notes). In 12 seasons, Moss has scored 149 touchdowns.

Moss needs two receiving touchdowns to become the second player in NFL history with 150 receiving TDs. Moss can join Jerry Rice (197) as the only other player in NFL history with 150 receiving touchdowns (see Owens note). In 12 seasons, Moss has 148 touchdown receptions.

Moss has recorded 1,000 receiving yards in a season 10

times in his 12-year NFL career. Moss can join Jerry Rice (14) as the only players in NFL history with 11 seasons with 1,000 receiving yards.

Moss has led the league in touchdown receptions five times in his career and can tie Jerry Rice (6) for the second-most seasons leading the league in touchdown receptions (Don Hutson, 9).

Moss needs 535 receiving yards to become the third player in NFL history with 15,000 receiving yards. Moss would join Isaac Bruce (15,208) and Jerry Rice (22,895) as the only players to accomplish the feat (see Owens note). In 12 seasons, Moss has 14,465 receiving yards.

Moss needs 74 receptions to become the seventh player in NFL history with 1,000 receptions (see Gonzalez note). In 11 seasons, Moss has 926 receptions.

Terrell Owens needs six receiving touchdowns to become the second player in NFL history with 150 receiving TDs. Owens can join Jerry Rice (197) as the only other player in NFL history with 150 receiving touchdowns (see Moss note). In 14 seasons, Owens has 144 receiving touchdowns.

Owens needs seven touchdowns to surpass Randy Moss (149) and LaDainian Tomlinson (153) to move into third place all-time (see Moss and Tomlinson notes). In 14 seasons, Owens has scored 147 touchdowns.

Owens has recorded 1,000 receiving yards in a season nine times in his 14-year NFL career. Owens can join Jerry Rice (14) and Randy Moss (10) as the only players in NFL history with 10 seasons with 1,000 receiving yards (see Moss note).

Owens needs 49 receiving yards to become the third player in NFL history with 15,000 receiving yards. Owens would join Isaac Bruce (15,208) and Jerry Rice (22,895) as the only players to accomplish the feat (see Moss note). In 14 seasons, Owens has 14,951 receiving yards.

Owens needs 89 receptions to surpass Isaac Bruce (1,024) and Tim Brown (1,094) for fourth place all-time (see Bruce note). In 14 seasons, Owens has 1,006 receptions.

Isaac Bruce, San Francisco, needs 71 receptions to surpass Tim Brown (1,094) for fourth place all-time (see Owens note). In 16 seasons, Bruce has 1,024 receptions.

Andre Johnson, Houston, needs 100 receptions to become the third player in NFL history with four 100-catch seasons. Johnson can join Marvin Harrison and Jerry Rice (4) as the only players with four 100-reception seasons (see Marshall and Welker notes).

Johnson needs 1,500 receiving yards to become the first player in NFL history with three consecutive 1,500-yard seasons. Johnson can also join Marvin Harrison (3) and Jerry Rice (4) as the only players with three 1,500-yard seasons.

Johnson needs three games with 10 receptions and 100 receiving yards to become the NFL's all-time career leader. Johnson has 13 games with at least 10 catches and 100 receiving yards in his career and can surpass Marvin Harrison (14) and Jerry Rice (15) for the most such games in NFL history.

Brandon Marshall, Miami, has caught at least 100 passes in each of the past three seasons. Marshall can join Marvin Harrison (4) as the only players to catch 100 passes in four consecutive seasons (see Johnson and Welker notes).

Wes Welker, New England, has caught at least 100 passes in each of the past three seasons. Welker can join Marvin Harrison (4) as the only players to catch 100 passes in four consecutive seasons (see Johnson and Marshall notes).

Chad Ochocinco, Cincinnati, needs 48 receiving yards to reach 10,000. In his nine-year career, Ochocinco has 9,952 receiving yards.

Reggie Wayne, Indianapolis, needs 607 receiving yards to reach 10,000. In his nine-year career, Wayne has 9,393 receiving yards.

Tony Gonzalez, Atlanta, needs one reception to become the first tight end in NFL history with 1,000 receptions. In 13 seasons, Gonzalez has 999 receptions – the most ever by a tight end.

Gonzalez needs 50 receptions to become the first tight end in NFL history with 13 consecutive 50-reception seasons. Gonzalez is the only tight end in NFL history with 12 consecutive 50-reception seasons.

Jason Taylor, New York Jets, needs 10.5 sacks to surpass Rickey Jackson (128.0), Leslie O'Neal (132.5), Lawrence Taylor (132.5), John Randle (137.5), and Richard Dent (137.5) to move into sixth place all-time. In 13 seasons, Taylor has 127.5 sacks.

Darren Sharper, New Orleans, needs two interception return touchdowns to surpass Rod Woodson (12) for the most all-time (see C. Woodson note). In 13 seasons, Sharper has 11 interception return touchdowns.

Sharper needs 72 interception return yards to surpass Rod Woodson (1,483) for the most all-time. In 13 seasons, Sharper has 1,412 interception return yards.

Sharper needs six interceptions to surpass Ronnie Lott (63), Ken Riley (65), and Dick "Night Train" Lane (68) to move into fourth place all-time. In 13 seasons, Sharper has 63 interceptions.

Charles Woodson, Green Bay, needs one interception return touchdown to become the third player in NFL history with 10 interception return touchdowns. Woodson would join Darren Sharper (11) and Rod Woodson (12) as the only players to accomplish the feat. In 12 seasons, Charles Woodson has nine interception return touchdowns.

DRAFT LIST FOR 2010

75th Annual NFL Draft, April 22-24, 2010
+Denotes Compensatory Selection
#Denotes Underclassman Selection

ARIZONA CARDINALS
1. Dan Williams—26, DT, Tennessee
2. Daryl Washington—47, LB, Texas Christian
   from TENNESSEE through NEW ENGLAND
3. Andre Roberts—88, WR, Citadel, from BALTIMORE
4. O'Brien Schofield—130, LB, Wisconsin
   from NEW ORLEANS
5. John Skelton—155, QB, Fordham
   from PHILADELPHIA through
   NEW YORK JETS and PITTSBURGH
6. Jorrick Calvin—201, DB, Troy, from NEW ORLEANS
7. Jim Dray—233, TE, Stanford

ATLANTA FALCONS
1. Sean Weatherspoon—19, LB, Missouri
3. Corey Peters—83, DT, Kentucky
   + Mike Johnson—98, G, Alabama
4. Joe Hawley—117, C, Nevada-Las Vegas
5.+Dominique Franks—135, DB, Oklahoma
   from WASHINGTON through ST. LOUIS
   + Kerry Meier—165, WR, Kansas
6. Shann Schillinger—171, DB, Montana

BALTIMORE RAVENS
2. Sergio Kindle—43, LB, Texas, from MIAMI through DENVER
   Terrence Cody—57, DT, Alabama
3. Ed Dickson—70, TE, Oregon
   from SEATTLE through PHILADELPHIA
   and DENVER
4. Dennis Pitta—114, TE, Brigham Young, from DENVER
5. David Reed—156, WR, Utah
   Arthur Jones—157, DT, Syracuse, from ARIZONA
6. Ramon Harewood—194, T, Morehouse

BUFFALO BILLS
1. C.J. Spiller—9, RB, Clemson
2. Torell Troup—41, DT, Central Florida
3. Alex Carrington—72, DE, Arkansas State
4. Marcus Easley—107, WR, Connecticut
5. Ed Wang—140, T, Virginia Tech
6. Arthur Moats—178, LB, James Madison
   Danny Batten—192, LB, South Dakota State
   from PHILADELPHIA
7. Levi Brown—209, QB, Troy, from DETROIT
   Kyle Calloway—216, G, Iowa

CAROLINA PANTHERS
2.#Jimmy Clausen—48, QB, Notre Dame
3. Brandon LaFell—78, WR, Louisiana State
   Armanti Edwards—89, WR, Appalachian State
   from ARIZONA through NEW ENGLAND
4. Eric Norwood—124, DE, South Carolina
   from ARIZONA through NEW YORK JETS
6. Greg Hardy—175, DE, Mississippi, from OAKLAND
   David Gettis—198, WR, Baylor, from NEW YORK JETS
   + Jordan Pugh—202, DB, Texas A&M
   + Tony Pike—204, QB, Cincinnati
7. R.J. Stanford—223, DB, Utah
   + Robert McClain—249, DB, Connecticut

CHICAGO BEARS
3.#Major Wright—75, DB, Florida
4. Corey Wootton—109, DE, Northwestern
5.#Joshua Moore—141, DB, Kansas State
6. Dan LeFevour—181, QB, Central Michigan
7. J'Marcus Webb—218, T, West Texas A&M

CINCINNATI BENGALS
1.#Jermaine Gresham—21, TE, Oklahoma
2.#Carlos Dunlap—54, DE, Florida
3. Jordan Shipley—84, WR, Texas
   + Brandon Ghee—96, DB, Wake Forest
4. Geno Atkins—120, DT, Georgia
   + Roddrick Muckelroy—131, LB, Texas
5. Otis Hudson—152, G, Eastern Illinois
6.#Dezmon Briscoe—191, WR, Kansas
7. Reggie Stephens—228, C, Iowa State

CLEVELAND BROWNS
1.#Joe Haden—7, DB, Florida
2. T.J. Ward—38, DB, Oregon
   Montario Hardesty—59, RB, Tennessee
   from DALLAS through PHILADELPHIA
3. Colt McCoy—85, QB, Texas
   from NEW ENGLAND through OAKLAND
   Shawn Lauvao—92, G, Arizona State
   from NEW YORK JETS
5. Larry Asante—160, DB, Nebraska
   from NEW YORK JETS
6.#Carlton Mitchell—177, WR, South Florida
   # Clifton Geathers—186, DE, South Carolina

DALLAS COWBOYS
1.#Dez Bryant—24, WR, Oklahoma State
   from PHILADELPHIA through DENVER
   and NEW ENGLAND
2. Sean Lee—55, LB, Penn State
   from PHILADELPHIA
4. Akwasi Owusu-Ansah—126, DB, Indiana (Pa.)
   from SAN DIEGO through MIAMI
6. Sam Young—179, T, Notre Dame
   from MIAMI
   Jamar Wall—196, DB, Texas Tech
7. Sean Lissemore—234, DT, William & Mary

DENVER BRONCOS
1.#Demaryius Thomas—22, WR, Georgia Tech
   from NEW ENGLAND
   Tim Tebow—25, QB, Florida
   from BALTIMORE
2. Zane Beadles—45, T, Utah
3. J.D. Walton—80, C, Baylor
   Eric Decker—87, WR, Minnesota
   from PHILADELPHIA
5. Perrish Cox—137, DB, Oklahoma State
   from CLEVELAND through PHILADELPHIA
6. Eric Olsen—183, G, Notre Dame
7. Syd'Quan Thompson—225, DB, California
   from PITTSBURGH through TAMPA BAY
   Jammie Kirlew—232, LB, Indiana
   from BALTIMORE through TAMPA BAY

DETROIT LIONS
1. Ndamukong Suh—2, DT, Nebraska
   # Jahvid Best—30, RB, California, from MINNESOTA
3.#Amari Spievey—66, DB, Iowa
4. Jason Fox—128, T, Miami, from MINNESOTA
7. Willie Young—213, DE, North Carolina State
   from SEATTLE
   + Tim Toone—255, WR, Weber State

GREEN BAY PACKERS
1.#Bryan Bulaga—23, T, Iowa
2. Mike Neal—56, DE, Purdue
3.#Morgan Burnett—71, DB, Georgia Tech
from CLEVELAND through PHILADELPHIA
5. Andrew Quarless—154, TE, Penn State
+ Marshall Newhouse—169, T, Texas Christian
6. James Starks—193, RB, Buffalo
7. C.J. Wilson—230, DE, East Carolina

HOUSTON TEXANS
1.#Kareem Jackson—20, DB, Alabama
2. Ben Tate—58, RB, Auburn
from ARIZONA through NEW ENGLAND
3. Earl Mitchell—81, DT, Arizona
4. Darryl Sharpton—102, LB, Miami, from KANSAS CITY
Garrett Graham—118, TE, Wisconsin
5. Sherrick McManis—144, DB, Northwestern,
from CAROLINA through KANSAS CITY
6. Shelley Smith—187, G, Colorado State
Trindon Holliday—197, KR, Louisiana State
from SAN DIEGO
7. Dorin Dickerson—227, WR, Pittsburgh

INDIANAPOLIS COLTS
1. Jerry Hughes—31, DE, Texas Christian
2. Pat Angerer—63, LB, Iowa
3. Kevin Thomas—94, DB, Southern California
4. Jacques McClendon—129, G, Tennessee
5. Brody Eldridge—162, TE, Oklahoma
7. Ricardo Mathews—238, DE, Cincinnati
+ Kavell Conner—240, LB, Clemson
+ Ray Fisher—246, DB, Indiana

JACKSONVILLE JAGUARS
1. Tyson Alualu—10, DT, California
3. D'Anthony Smith—74, DT, Louisiana Tech
5. Larry Hart—143, DE, Central Arkansas
Austen Lane—153, DE, Murray State
from NEW ENGLAND through TAMPA BAY
and OAKLAND
6. Deji Karim—180, RB, Southern Illinois
+ Scotty McGee—203, KR, James Madison

KANSAS CITY CHIEFS
1.#Eric Berry—5, DB, Tennessee
2. Dexter McCluster—36, RB, Mississippi
Javier Arenas—50, DB, Alabama, from ATLANTA
3. Jon Asamoah—68, G, Illinois
Tony Moeaki—93, TE, Iowa
from MINNESOTA through HOUSTON
5. Kendrick Lewis—136, DB, Mississippi
Cameron Sheffield—142, LB, Troy, from MIAMI

MIAMI DOLPHINS
1. Jared Odrick—28, DT, Penn State, from SAN DIEGO
2. Koa Misi—40, LB, Utah
from SEATTLE through SAN DIEGO
3. John Jerry—73, G, Mississippi
4. A.J. Edds—119, LB, Iowa
from NEW ENGLAND through DALLAS
5. Nolan Carroll—145, DB, Maryland, from SAN FRANCISCO
Reshad Jones—163, DB, Georgia
from NEW ORLEANS through PHILADELPHIA,
ST. LOUIS and WASHINGTON
7. Chris McCoy—212, LB, Middle Tennessee
from KANSAS CITY
+ Austin Spitler—252, LB, Ohio State

MINNESOTA VIKINGS
2. Chris Cook—34, DB, Virginia, from DETROIT
Toby Gerhart—51, RB, Stanford, from HOUSTON
4.#Everson Griffen—100, DE, Southern California
from DETROIT
5. Chris DeGeare—161, G, Wake Forest
+ NateTriplett—167, LB, Minnesota
6. Joe Webb—199, WR, Alabama-Birmingham
7. Mickey Shuler—214, TE, Penn State
from CLEVELAND through DETROIT
Ryan D'Imperio—237, RB, Rutgers

NEW ENGLAND PATRIOTS
1. Devin McCourty—27, DB, Rutgers, from DALLAS
2.#Rob Gronkowski—42, TE, Arizona
from CHICAGO through TAMPA BAY
and OAKLAND
Jermaine Cunningham—53, DE, Florida
Brandon Spikes—62, LB, Florida
from MINNESOTA through HOUSTON
3. Taylor Price—90, WR, Ohio, from DALLAS
4.#Aaron Hernandez—113, TE, Florida
from SAN FRANCISCO through DENVER
5. Zoltan Mesko—150, P, Michigan, from HOUSTON
6.+Ted Larsen—205, C, North Carolina State
7. Thomas Welch—208, T, Vanderbilt
from ST. LOUIS through WASHINGTON
+ Brandon Deaderick—247, DE, Alabama
+ Kade Weston—248, DT, Georgia
+ Zac Robinson—250, QB, Oklahoma State

NEW ORLEANS SAINTS
1. Patrick Robinson—32, DB, Florida State
2. Charles Brown—64, T, Southern California
3. Jimmy Graham—95, TE, Miami
4. Al Woods—123, DT, Louisiana State
from BALTIMORE through ARIZONA
5. Matt Tennant—158, C, Boston College
from DALLAS through DENVER, NEW ENGLAND,
OAKLAND and JACKSONVILLE
7. Sean Canfield—239, QB, Oregon State

NEW YORK GIANTS
1.#Jason Pierre-Paul—15, DE, South Florida
2.#Linval Joseph—46, DT, East Carolina
3.#Chad Jones—76, DB, Louisiana State
4. Phillip Dillard—115, LB, Nebraska
5. Mitch Petrus—147, G, Arkansas
6. Adrian Tracy—184, LB, William & Mary
7. Matt Dodge—221, P, East Carolina

NEW YORK JETS
1. Kyle Wilson—29, DB, Boise State
2. Vladimir Ducasse—61, T, Massachusetts
4.#Joe McKnight—112, RB, Southern California
from CAROLINA
5. John Conner—139, RB, Kentucky, from SEATTLE

DRAFT LIST FOR 2010

OAKLAND RAIDERS
1.#Rolando McClain—8, LB, Alabama
2. Lamarr Houston—44, DE, Texas
from JACKSONVILLE through NEW ENGLAND
3. Jared Veldheer—69, T, Hillsdale
4.#Bruce Campbell—106, T, Maryland
Jacoby Ford—108, WR, Clemson, from JACKSONVILLE
5. Walter McFadden—138, DB, Auburn
6. Travis Goethel—190, LB, Arizona State
from NEW ENGLAND
7. Jeremy Ware—215, DB, Michigan State
+ Stevie Brown—251, DB, Michigan

PHILADELPHIA EAGLES
1. Brandon Graham—13, DE, Michigan
from SAN FRANCISCO through DENVER
2. Nate Allen—37, DB, South Florida, from WASHINGTON
3. Daniel Te'o-Nesheim—86, DE, Washington
from GREEN BAY
4. Trevard Lindley—105, DB, Kentucky, from CLEVELAND
Keenan Clayton—121, LB, Oklahoma
Mike Kafka—122, QB, Northwestern, from GREEN BAY
Clay Harbor—125, TE, Missouri State, from DALLAS
5. Ricky Sapp—134, DE, Clemson
from TAMPA BAY through CLEVELAND
Riley Cooper—159, WR, Florida, from SAN DIEGO
6. Charles Scott—200, RB, Louisiana State
from INDIANAPOLIS
7. Jamar Chaney—220, LB, Mississippi State
from DENVER through DETROIT
+ Jeff Owens—243, DT, Georgia
+ Kurt Coleman—244, DB, Ohio State

PITTSBURGH STEELERS
1.#Maurkice Pouncey—18, C, Florida
2.#Jason Worilds—52, LB, Virginia Tech
3. Emmanuel Sanders—82, WR, Southern Methodist
4.#Thaddeus Gibson—116, LB, Ohio State
5. Chris Scott—151, T, Tennessee
+ Crezdon Butler—164, DB, Clemson
+ Stevenson Sylvester—166, LB, Utah
6.#Jonathan Dwyer—188, RB, Georgia Tech
Antonio Brown—195, WR, Central Michigan
from ARIZONA
7.+Doug Worthington—242, DE, Ohio State

ST. LOUIS RAMS
1.#Sam Bradford—1, QB, Oklahoma
2. Rodger Saffold—33, T, Indiana
3. Jerome Murphy—65, DB, South Florida
4. Mardy Gilyard—99, WR, Cincinnati
5. Michael Hoomanawanui—132, TE, Illinois
Hall Davis—149, DE, Louisiana-Lafayette, from ATLANTA
6. Fendi Onobun—170, TE, Houston
Eugene Sims—189, DE, West Texas A&M, from ATLANTA
7. Marquis Johnson—211, DB, Alabama
from WASHINGTON
George Selvie—226, DE, South Florida, from ATLANTA
+ Josh Hull—254, LB, Penn State

SAN DIEGO CHARGERS
1.#Ryan Mathews—12, RB, Fresno State, from MIAMI
3. Donald Butler—79, LB, Washington
from SAN FRANCISCO
4. Darrell Stuckey—110, DB, Kansas, from MIAMI
5. Cam Thomas—146, DT, North Carolina
from DENVER through DETROIT, CLEVELAND and PHILADELPHIA
+ Jonathan Crompton—168, QB, Tennessee
7. Dedrick Epps—235, TE, Miami

SAN FRANCISCO 49ERS
1.#Anthony Davis—11, T, Rutgers
from CHICAGO through DENVER
Mike Iupati—17, G, Idaho, from CAROLINA
2. Taylor Mays—49, DB, Southern California
3.#Navorro Bowman—91, LB, Penn State, from SAN DIEGO
6. Anthony Dixon—173, RB, Mississippi State
from KANSAS CITY through MIAMI
and SAN DIEGO
Nate Byham—182, TE, Pittsburgh
+ Kyle Williams—206, WR, Arizona State
7. Phillip Adams—224, DB, South Carolina State

SEATTLE SEAHAWKS
1. Russell Okung—6, T, Oklahoma State
Earl Thomas—14, DB, Texas, from DENVER
2.#Golden Tate—60, WR, Notre Dame, from SAN DIEGO
4. Walter Thurmond—111, DB, Oregon
from TENNESSEE
E.J. Wilson—127, DE, North Carolina
from NEW YORK JETS through PHILADELPHIA
5. Kam Chancellor—133, DB, Virginia Tech, from DETROIT
6. Anthony McCoy—185, TE, Southern California
from TENNESSEE
7. Dexter Davis—236, LB, Arizona State,
from NEW YORK JETS
+ Jameson Konz—245, WR, Kent State

TAMPA BAY BUCCANEERS
1.#Gerald McCoy—3, DT, Oklahoma
2.#Brian Price—35, DT, UCLA
Arrelious Benn—39, WR, Illinois, from OAKLAND
3. Myron Lewis—67, DB, Vanderbilt
4.#Mike Williams—101, WR, Syracuse
6. Brent Bowden—172, P, Virginia Tech
7. Cody Grimm—210, DB, Virginia Tech
Dekoda Watson—217, LB, Florida State
from JACKSONVILLE
+ Erik Lorig—253, DE, Stanford

TENNESSEE TITANS
1.#Derrick Morgan—16, DE, Georgia Tech
3.#Damian Williams—77, WR, Southern California
#+Rennie Curran—97, LB, Georgia
4. Alterraun Verner—104, DB, UCLA, from SEATTLE
5. Robert Johnson—148, DB, Utah
6. Rusty Smith—176, QB, Florida Atlantic, from SEATTLE
+ Myron Rolle—207, DB, Florida State
7. Marc Mariani—222, WR, Montana
+ David Howard—241, DT, Brown

WASHINGTON REDSKINS
1. Trent Williams—4, T, Oklahoma
3. Choice Exercised in 2009 Supplemental Draft
for Jeremy Jarmon, DE, Kentucky
4. Perry Riley—103, LB, Louisiana State
6. Dennis Morris—174, TE, Louisiana Tech
reacquired through MIAMI
7. Terrence Austin—219, WR, UCLA, from MIAMI
Erik Cook—229, C, New Mexico, from NEW ENGLAND
Selvish Capers—231, T, West Virginia
from PHILADELPHIA through NEW ENGLAND, DENVER and NEW ENGLAND

NUMBER OF PLAYERS DRAFTED—2010

BY POSITION:

Defensive Backs	52
Linebackers	35
Wide Receivers	30
Defensive Ends	28
Defensive Tackles	20
Tight Ends	19
Tackles	19
Running Backs	15
Quarterbacks	13
Guards	12
Centers	7
Punters	3
Kick Returners	2

BY COLLEGE:

Florida	9
Alabama	7
Oklahoma	7
Southern California	7
Iowa	6
Louisiana State	6
Penn State	6
Tennessee	6
Texas	6
Utah	6
Clemson	5
Georgia	5
South Florida	5
Virginia Tech	5
Arizona State	4
Georgia Tech	4
Miami	4
Mississippi	4
Notre Dame	4
Ohio State	4
Oklahoma State	4
California	3
Cincinnati	3
East Carolina	3
Florida State	3
Illinois	3
Indiana	3
Kansas	3
Kentucky	3
Michigan	3
Nebraska	3
Northwestern	3
Oregon	3
Rutgers	3
Stanford	3
Texas Christian	3
Troy	3
UCLA	3
Arizona	2
Auburn	2
Baylor	2
Central Michigan	2
Connecticut	2
James Madison	2
Louisiana Tech	2
Maryland	2
Minnesota	2
Mississippi State	2
Montana	2
North Carolina	2
North Carolina State	2
Pittsburgh	2
South Carolina	2
Syracuse	2
Vanderbilt	2
Wake Forest	2
Washington	2
West Texas A&M	2
William & Mary	2
Wisconsin	2
Alabama-Birmingham	1
Appalachian State	1
Arkansas	1
Arkansas State	1
Boise State	1
Boston College	1
Brigham Young	1
Brown	1
Buffalo	1
Central Arkansas	1
Central Florida	1
Citadel	1
Colorado State	1
Eastern Illinois	1
Florida Atlantic	1
Fordham	1
Fresno State	1
Hillsdale	1
Houston	1
Idaho	1
Indiana (Pa.)	1
Iowa State	1
Kansas State	1
Kent State	1
Louisiana-Lafayette	1
Massachusetts	1
Michigan State	1
Middle Tennessee State	1
Missouri	1
Missouri State	1
Morehouse	1
Murray State	1
Nevada-Las Vegas	1
New Mexico	1
Ohio	1
Oregon State	1
Purdue	1
South Carolina State	1
South Dakota State	1
Southern Illinois	1
Southern Methodist	1
Texas A&M	1
Texas Tech	1
Virginia	1
Weber State	1
West Virginia	1

BY CONFERENCE:

Southeastern	49
Big Ten	34
Atlantic Coast	31
Big 12	30
Pacific 10	28
Big East	18
Mountain West	13
Conference USA	7
Sun Belt	7
Colonial Athletic	5
Mid-American	5
Western Athletic	5
Independent	4
Big Sky	3
Missouri Valley Football	3
Lone Star	2
Ohio Valley	2
Southern	2
Great Lakes Intercollegiate Athletic	1
Ivy	1
Mid-Eastern Athletic	1
Patriot	1
Pennsylvania State Athletic	1
Southern Intercollegiate Athletic	1
Southland	1

UNDERCLASSMEN IN THE DRAFT

Year	DIA	Drafted	In Top 10
1990	28	18	5
1991	23	19	1
1992	30	21	5
1993	34	24	5
1994	31	25	6
1995	33	22	2
1996	24	16	4
1997	34	25	6
1998	32	19	3
1999	31	22	5
2000	26	20	4
2001	35	27	5
2002	38	26	2
2003	47	32	5
2004	43	35	5
2005	51	37	4
2006	52	33	6
2007	40	29	5
2008	53	39	4
2009	46	41	5
2010	53	46	5

WAIVERS

The waiver system is a procedure by which player contracts or NFL rights to players are made available by a club to other clubs in the League. During the procedure, the 31 other clubs either file claims to obtain the players or waive the opportunity to do so—thus the term "waiver." Claiming clubs are assigned players on a priority based on the inverse of won-and-lost standing. The claiming period is 24 hours from the first business day after the Super Bowl through the conclusion of the regular season. If a player passes through waivers unclaimed, he becomes a free agent. All waivers are no recall and no withdrawal. Under the Collective Bargaining Agreement, from the beginning of the waiver system each year through the trading deadline (October 19, 2010), any veteran who has acquired four years of pension credit is not subject to the waiver system if the club desires to release him. After the trading deadline, such players are subject to the waiver system.

ACTIVE/INACTIVE LIST

The Active/Inactive List is the principal status for players participating for a club. It consists of all players under contract who are eligible for preseason, regular-season, and postseason games. Teams are permitted to open training camp with no more than 80 players under contract and thereafter must meet two mandatory roster reductions prior to the season opener. Teams will be permitted an Active List of 45 players and an Inactive List of eight players for each regular-season and postseason game. Provided that a club has two quarterbacks on its 45-player Active List, a third quarterback from its Inactive List is permitted to dress for the game, but if he enters the game during the first three quarters, the other two quarterbacks are thereafter prohibited from playing. Teams also are permitted to establish Practice Squads of up to eight players who are eligible to participate in practice, but these players remain free agents and are eligible to sign with any other team in the league.

August 31....................Roster reduction to 75 players
September 4.................Roster reduction to 53 players
September 5.................Teams establish a Practice Squad of up to eight players

In addition to the squad limits described above, the overall roster limit of 80 players remains in effect throughout the regular season and postseason. The overall limit is applicable to players on a team's Active, Inactive, and certain Exempt Lists, players on the Practice Squad, and players on the Reserve List as Injured, Physically Unable to Perform, Non-Football Illness/Injury, and Suspended by Club.

RESERVE LIST

The Reserve List is a status for players who, for reasons of injury, retirement, military service, or other circumstances, are not immediately available for participation with a club. Players on Reserve/Injured are not eligible to practice or return to the Active/Inactive List in the same season that they are placed on Reserve. Players in the category of Reserve/Retired, Reserve/Did Not Report, Reserve/Exclusive Rights, and players who were placed in the category of Reserve/Left Squad in a previous season may not be reinstated during the period from 30 days before the end of the regular season through the postseason.

TRADES

Unrestricted trading between the AFC and NFC is allowed in 2010 through October 19, after which trading will end until 2011.

ANNUAL ACTIVE PLAYER LIMITS

NFL

Year(s)	Limit
1991-2010	45**
1985-90	45
1983-84	49
1982	45†-49
1978-81	45
1975-77	43
1974	47
1964-73	40
1963	37
1961-62	36
1960	38
1959	36
1957-58	35
1951-56	33
1949-50	32
1948	35
1947	35*-34
1945-46	33
1943-44	28
1940-42	33
1938-39	30
1936-37	25
1935	24
1930-34	20
1926-29	18
1925	16

** 45 plus a third quarterback
† 45 for first two games
* 35 for first three games

AFL

Year(s)	Limit
1966-69	40
1965	38
1964	34
1962-63	33
1960-61	35

NFL FREE AGENCY MOVEMENT

The following chart details veteran free agents who signed with new teams:

	Unrestricted	Restricted	Transition	Franchise	TOTALS
1993	108	8	4	1	121
1994	121	7	4	0	132
1995	171	6	2	0	179
1996	100	4	2	0	106
1997	86	2	2	0	90
1998	112	4	1	2	119
1999	115	2	1	0	118
2000	107	4	0	0	111
2001	93	4	0	0	97
2002	130	1	0	0	131
2003	111	5	1	0	117
2004	124	1	1	0	126
2005	104	3	0	0	107
2006	149	4	1	0	154
2007	126	4	0	0	130
2008	132	3	0	0	135
2009	128	0	0	0	128

The following procedures will be used to break standings ties for postseason playoffs and to determine regular-season schedules.

Note: Tie games count as one-half win and one-half loss for both clubs.

TO BREAK A TIE WITHIN A DIVISION

If, at the end of the regular season, two or more clubs in the same division finish with the best won-lost-tied percentage, the following steps will be taken until a champion is determined:

TWO CLUBS

1. Head-to-head (best won-lost-tied percentage in games between the clubs.)
2. Best won-lost-tied percentage in games played within the division.
3. Best won-lost-tied percentage in common games.
4. Best won-lost-tied percentage in games played within the conference.
5. Strength of victory.
6. Strength of schedule.
7. Best combined ranking among conference teams in points scored and points allowed.
8. Best combined ranking among all teams in points scored and points allowed.
9. Best net points in common games.
10. Best net points in all games.
11. Best net touchdowns in all games
12. Coin toss.

THREE OR MORE CLUBS

(Note: If two clubs remain tied after a third club is eliminated during any step, tie-breaker reverts to Step 1 of the two-club format.)

1. Head-to-head (best won-lost-tied percentage in games among the clubs.)
2. Best won-lost-tied percentage in games played within the division.
3. Best won-lost-tied percentage in common games.
4. Best won-lost-tied percentage in games played within the conference.
5. Strength of victory.
6. Strength of schedule.
7. Best combined ranking among conference teams in points scored and points allowed.
8. Best combined ranking among all teams in points scored and points allowed.
9. Best net points in common games.
10. Best net points in all games.
11. Best net touchdowns in all games.
12. Coin toss.

TO BREAK A TIE FOR THE WILD-CARD TEAM

If it is necessary to break ties to determine the two Wild Card clubs from each conference, the following steps will be taken:

A. If all the tied clubs are from the same division, apply division tie-breaker.

B. If the tied clubs are from different divisions, apply the following steps:

TWO CLUBS

1. Head-to-head, if applicable.
2. Best won-lost-tied percentage in the games played within the conference.
3. Best won-lost-tied percentage in common games, minimum of four.
4. Strength of victory.
5. Strength of schedule.
6. Best combined ranking among conference teams in points scored and points allowed.
7. Best combined ranking among all teams in points scored and points allowed.
8. Best net points in conference games.
9. Best net points in all games.
10. Best net touchdowns in all games.
11. Coin toss.

THREE OR MORE CLUBS

1. Apply division tie-breaker to eliminate all but highest ranked club in each division prior to proceeding to Step 2. The original seeding within a division upon application of the division tie-breaker remains the same for all subsequent applications of the procedure that are necessary to identify the Wild Card participants.
2. Head-to-head sweep (apply only if one club has defeated each of the others or one club has lost to each of the others).
3. Best won-lost-tied percentage in games played within the conference.
4. Best won-lost-tied percentage in common games, minimum of four.
5. Strength of victory.
6. Strength of schedule.
7. Best combined ranking among conference teams in points scored and points allowed.
8. Best combined ranking among all teams in points scored and points allowed.
9. Best net points in conference games.
10. Best net points in all games.
11. Best net touchdowns in all games.
12. Coin toss.

When the first Wild Card team has been identified, the procedure is repeated to name the second Wild Card (i.e., eliminate all but the highest ranked club in each division prior to proceeding to Step 2.) In situations where three teams from the same division are involved in the procedure, the original seeding of the teams remains the same for subsequent applications of the tie-breaker if the top-ranked team in that division qualifies for a Wild Card berth.

OTHER TIE-BREAKING PROCEDURES

1. Only one club advances to the playoffs in any tie-breaking step. Remaining tied clubs revert to the first step of the applicable division or Wild Card tie-breakers. As an example, if two clubs remain tied in any tie-breaker step after all other clubs have been eliminated, the procedure reverts to Step 1 of the two-club format to determine the winner. When one club wins the tie-breaker, all other clubs revert to Step 1 of the applicable two-club or three-club format.
2. In comparing records against common opponents among tied teams, the best won-lost-tied percentage is the deciding factor since teams may have played an unequal number of games.
3. To determine home-field priority among division-titlists, apply Wild Card tie-breakers.
4. To determine home-field priority for Wild Card qualifiers, apply division tie-breakers (if teams are from the same division) or Wild Card tie-breakers (if teams are from different divisions).
5. To determine the best combined ranking among conference teams in points scored and points allowed, add a team's position in the two categories, and the lowest score wins. For example, if Team A is first in points scored and second in points allowed, its combined ranking is "3." If Team B is third in points scored and first in points allowed, its combined ranking is "4." Team A then wins the tiebreaker. If two teams are tied for a position, both teams are awarded the ranking as if they held it solely. For example, if Team A and Team B are tied for first in points scored, each team is assigned a ranking of "1" in that category, and if Team C is third, its ranking will still be "3."

TIE-BREAKING PROCEDURE FOR SELECTION MEETING

1. Clubs not participating in the playoffs shall select in the first through 20th positions in reverse standings order.
2. The Super Bowl winner is last and Super Bowl loser is next-to-last.
3. The losers of the Conference Championship games shall select 29th and 30th based on won-lost-tied percentage.
4. The losers of the Divisional playoff games shall select 25th through 28th based on won-lost-tied percentage.
5. The losers of the Wild Card games shall select 21st through 24th based on won-lost-tied percentage.

If ties exist in any grouping except (2) above, such ties shall be broken by strength-of-schedule. If any ties cannot be broken by strength-of-schedule, the divisional or conference tie-breakers, if applicable, shall be applied. Any ties that still exist shall be broken by a coin flip.

INSTANT REPLAY

The NFL uses a system of Referee Replay Review to aid officiating.

Prior to the two-minute warning of each half, a Coaches' Challenge System will be in effect. After the two-minute warning, and throughout any overtime period, a Referee Review will be initiated by a Replay Assistant from a Replay Booth.

The following procedures will be used:

Reviews by Referee: All Replay Reviews will be conducted by the Referee on a field-level monitor after consultation with the other covering official(s), prior to review. A decision will be reversed only when the Referee has *indisputable visual evidence* available to him that warrants the change.

Coaches' Challenge: In each game, a team will be permitted two challenges that will initiate Referee Replay reviews. Each challenge will require the use of a team time out. If a challenge is upheld, the time out will be restored to the challenging team. If both challenges are upheld, a third challenge will be awarded to the challenging team. No challenges will be recognized from a team that has exhausted its time outs.

Replay Assistant's Request for Review: After the two-minute warning of each half, and throughout any overtime period, any review will be initiated by a Replay Assistant. There is no limit to the number of reviews that may be initiated by the Replay Assistant. His ability to initiate a review will be unrelated to the number of time outs that either team has remaining, and no time out will be charged for any review initiated by the Replay Assistant.

Time Limit: Each review will be a maximum of 60 seconds in length, timed from when the Referee begins his review of the replay at the field-level monitor.

Reviewable Plays: The Replay System will cover the following play situations only:

A) Plays Governed by Sideline, Goal Line, End Zone, End Line, and Goal Posts:

1. Scoring plays, including a runner breaking the plane of the goal line.
2. Pass complete/incomplete/intercepted at sideline, goal line, end zone, and end line.
3. Runner/receiver in or out of bounds.
4. Recovery of loose ball in or out of bounds.

B) Passing Plays:

1. Pass ruled complete/incomplete/intercepted in the field of play.
2. Touching of a forward pass by an ineligible receiver.
3. Touching of a forward pass by a defensive player.
4. Quarterback (Passer) forward pass or fumble.
5. Illegal forward pass beyond line of scrimmage.
6. Illegal forward pass after change of possession.
7. Forward or backward pass thrown from behind line of scrimmage.

C) Other Reviewable Plays:

1. Runner ruled not down by defensive contact.
2. Runner ruled down by defensive contact and there is a recovery by defense.
3. Forward progress with respect to first down.
4. Touching of a kick.
5. Number of players on the field.
6. Recovery of loose ball in the field of play, including those ruled to have hit sideline.
7. A field goal or try attempt when it is lower than the top of the uprights.
8. Illegal forward handoff.

INSTANT REPLAY HISTORY

From 1986-1991, a limited system of Instant Replay was used on a year-by-year basis. Replay also was experimented with during the 1996 and 1998 preseasons. For the 1999 season, the NFL introduced a system of Referee Replay Review to aid officiating. That system was extended on a one-year basis for the 2000 season and then approved for the next three years through 2003. The system was extended on a five-year basis in March 2004 and was later installed permanently in March 2007.

Following are the results of the different systems:

REGULAR SEASON, 1986-1991

Year	Games	Plays Closely Reviewed	Reversals
1986	224	374	38
1987	210	490	57
1988	224	537	53
1989	224	492	65
1990	224	504	73
1991	224	570	90
TOTAL	1,330	2,967	376

PRESEASON, 1996, 1998

Year	Games	Challenges	Reversals
1996	10	13	3
1998	10	10	3
TOTAL	20	23	6

REGULAR SEASON, 1999-2009

Year	Games	Total Replay Reviews	Challenges	Reversals
1999	248	195	133	57
2000	248	247	179	84
2001	248	258	191	89
2002	256	294	208	94
2003	256	255	184	66
2004	256	283	233	88
2005	256	295	223	92
2006	256	311	237	107
2007	256	327	250	122
2008	256	315	229	117
2009	256	328	228	126
TOTAL	2,792	3,108	2,295	1,042

The AFC

American Football Conference
North Division
Team Colors: Black, Purple, and Metallic Gold
1 Winning Drive
Owings Mills, Maryland 21117
Telephone: (410) 701-4000

2010 SCHEDULE
PRESEASON

Aug. 12	**Carolina**	8:00
Aug. 21	at Washington	7:00
Aug. 28	**N.Y. Giants**	7:30
Sep. 2	at St. Louis	7:00

REGULAR SEASON

Sep. 13	at New York Jets (Mon)	7:00
Sep. 19	at Cincinnati	1:00
Sep. 26	**Cleveland**	1:00
Oct. 3	at Pittsburgh	1:00
Oct. 10	**Denver**	1:00
Oct. 17	at New England	1:00
Oct. 24	**Buffalo**	1:00
Oct. 31	BYE	
Nov. 7	**Miami**	1:00
Nov. 11	at Atlanta (Thu)	8:20
Nov. 21	at Carolina	1:00
Nov. 28	**Tampa Bay**	1:00
Dec. 5	**Pittsburgh**	* 8:20
Dec. 13	at Houston (Mon)	7:30
Dec. 19	**New Orleans**	1:00
Dec. 26	at Cleveland	1:00
Jan. 2	**Cincinnati**	1:00

** Sunday night games in Weeks 11-17 subject to change*

Stadium: M&T Bank Stadium (opened in 1998) • **Capacity:** 71,008
1101 Russell Street
Baltimore, Maryland 21230
Playing Surface: Sportexe Momentum
Training Camp: McDaniel College
2 College Hill
Westminster, MD 21157

M&T BANK STADIUM

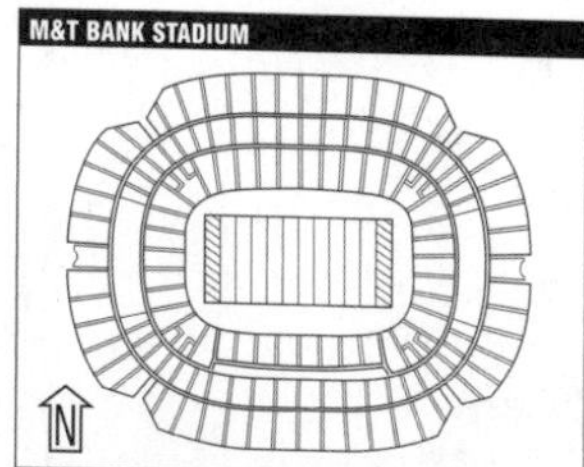

CLUB OFFICIALS
Owner: Steve Bisciotti
President: Dick Cass
Executive Vice President/General Manager: Ozzie Newsome
Senior Vice President/Public and Community Relations: Kevin Byrne
Vice President of Football Administration: Pat Moriarty
Vice President of Medical Services/Head Certified Athletic Trainer: Bill Tessendorf
Vice President, Corporate Sales and Development: Mark Burdett
Vice President and Chief Financial Officer: Jeff Goering
Vice President, Regional Partnerships and Sales: Ed Burchell
Vice President, Marketing: Gabrielle Dow
Vice President, Operations: Bob Eller
Vice President, Information Technology: Bill Jankowski
Vice President, Ticket Sales and Operations: Baker Koppelman
Vice President, National Partnerships and Sales: Kevin Rochlitz
Vice President, Broadcasting: Larry Rosen
Vice President, Stadium Operations: Roy Sommerhof
Vice President of Digital Media: Michelle Andres
Director of Player Personnel: Eric DeCosta
Director of College Scouting: Joe Hortiz
Director of Pro Personnel: Vincent Newsome
Assistant Director of Pro Personnel: Chad Alexander
Director of Player Development: O.J. Brigance
Director of Media Relations: Chad Steele
Assistant Director of Player Development: Harry Swayne
Pro Scout: Mark Azevedo
Scouts: Joe Douglas, Jack Glowik, Milt Hendrickson, Andrew Weidl, Lonnie Young
Equipment Manager: Ed Carroll
Director of Football Video Operations: Jon Dubé
Assistant Director of Football Video Operations: Mark Bienvenu
Senior Director, Fields & Grounds/Head Groundskeeper: Don Follett
Director of Premium Services/Suites: Theresa Abato
Controller: Jim Coller
Director, Broadcasting Administration: Don DiRaddo
Director, Information Technology: Nick Fusee
Director, Human Resources: Elizabeth Jackson
Director of Community Relations: Melanie LeGrande
Director, Security: Darren Sanders

COACHING HISTORY
(124-112-1)
Records include postseason games

1996-98	Ted Marchibroda	16-31-1
1999-2007	Brian Billick	85-67-0
2008-09	John Harbaugh	23-14-0

PAID ATTENDANCE
Home 555,907 Away 496,088
Total 1,051,995
Single-game home record, 71,382 (12/03/07)
Single-season home record, 557,792 (2008)

2010 DRAFT CHOICES

Round	Name	Pos.	College
2	Sergio Kindle	LB	Texas
	Terrence Cody	DT	Alabama
3	Ed Dickson	TE	Oregon
4	Dennis Pitta	TE	Brigham Young
5	David Reed	WR	Utah
	Arthur Jones	DT	Syracuse
6	Ramon Harewood	T	Morehouse

BALTIMORE RAVENS

2009 TEAM RECORD

PRESEASON (4-0)

Date	Result	Opponent
8/13	W 23-0	Washington
8/24	W 24-23	New York Jets
8/29	W 17-13	at Carolina
9/3	W 20-3	at Atlanta

REGULAR SEASON (9-7)

Date	Result	Opponent
9/13	W 38-24	Kansas City
9/20	W 31-26	at San Diego
9/27	W 34-3	Cleveland
10/4	L 21-27	at New England
10/11	L 14-17	Cincinnati
10/18	L 31-33	at Minnesota
11/1	W 30-7	Denver
11/8	L 7-17	at Cincinnati
11/16	W 16-0	at Cleveland
11/22	L 15-17	Indianapolis
11/29	W 20-17	Pittsburgh (OT)
12/7	L 14-27	at Green Bay
12/13	W 48-3	Detroit
12/20	W 31-7	Chicago
12/27	L 20-23	at Pittsburgh
1/3	W 21-13	at Oakland

(OT) Overtime

POSTSEASON (1-1)

Date	Result	Opponent
1/10	W 33-14	at New England
1/16	L 3-20	at Indianapolis

SCORE BY PERIODS

Ravens	77	81	123	107	3	— 391
Opponents	57	95	47	62	0	— 261

2009 TEAM STATISTICS

	Ravens	Opp.
Total First Downs	320	280
Rushing	115	82
Passing	187	164
Penalty	18	34
3rd Down: Made/Att	89/214	80/218
3rd Down Pct.	41.6	36.7
4th Down: Made/Att	6/13	7/17
4th Down Pct.	46.2	41.2
Possession Avg.	29:18	30:42
Total Net Yards	5619	4808
Avg. Per Game	351.2	300.5
Total Plays	1014	991
Avg. Per Play	5.5	4.9
Net Yards Rushing	2200	1492
Avg. Per Game	137.5	93.3
Total Rushes	468	435
Net Yards Passing	3419	3316
Avg. Per Game	213.7	207.3
Sacked/Yards Lost	36/218	32/190
Gross Yards	3637	3506
Att./Completions	510/321	524/306
Completion Pct.	62.9	58.4
Had Intercepted	13	22
Punts/Average	74/43.1	79/43.4
Net Punting Avg.	74/37.9	79/37.2
Penalties/Yards	115/1094	88/741
Fumbles/Ball Lost	19/9	20/10
Touchdowns	47	27
Rushing	22	8
Passing	21	17
Returns	4	2

2009 INDIVIDUAL STATISTICS

PASSING	Att.	Comp.	Yds.	Pct.	TD	Int.	Tkld.	Rate
Flacco	499	315	3613	63.1	21	12	36/218	88.9
T. Smith	9	5	24	55.6	0	1	0/0	21.3
Clayton	1	1	0	100.0	0	0	0/0	79.2
Rice	1	0	0	0.0	0	0	0/0	39.6
Ravens	510	321	3637	62.9	21	13	36/218	87.4
Opponents	524	306	3506	58.4	17	22	32/190	71.9

SCORING	TD R	TD P	TD Rt	PAT	FG	Saf	PTS
McGahee	12	2	0	0/0	0/0	0	84
Cundiff TM	0	0	0	19/19	12/17	0	55
Hauschka TM	0	0	0	27/28	9/13	0	54
Rice	7	1	0	0/0	0/0	0	48
Mason	0	7	0	0/0	0/0	0	42
Heap	0	6	0	0/0	0/0	0	36
Clayton	0	2	0	0/0	0/0	0	12
L. McClain	2	0	0	0/0	0/0	0	12
K. Washington	0	2	0	0/0	0/0	0	12
Edwards	0	0	1	0/0	0/0	0	6
Landry	0	0	1	0/0	0/0	0	6
Reed	0	0	1	0/0	0/0	0	6
T. Smith	1	0	0	0/0	0/0	0	6
Webb	0	0	1	0/0	0/0	0	6
D. Williams	0	1	0	0/0	0/0	0	6
Ravens	22	21	4	46/47	21/30	0	391
Opponents	8	17	2	27/27	24/27	0	261

2-Pt. Conversions: Ravens 0-0, Opponents 0-0

RUSHING	No.	Yds	Avg	LG	TD
Rice	254	1339	5.3	59t	7
McGahee	109	544	5.0	77t	12
L. McClain	46	180	3.9	20	2
Flacco	35	56	1.6	10	0
T. Smith	8	31	3.9	15t	1
Clayton	4	28	7.0	12	0
Parmele	5	17	3.4	7	0
Heap	1	2	2.0	2	0
Mason	1	2	2.0	2	0
K. Washington	1	1	1.0	1	0
Lawrence	4	0	0.0	4	0
Ravens	468	2200	4.7	77t	22
Opponents	435	1492	3.4	58	8

RECEIVING	No.	Yds	Avg	LG	TD
Rice	78	702	9.0	63	1
Mason	73	1028	14.1	72t	7
Heap	53	593	11.2	31	6
Clayton	34	480	14.1	54	2
K. Washington	34	431	12.7	28	2
L. McClain	21	141	6.7	19	0
McGahee	15	85	5.7	14	2
D. Williams	8	142	17.8	34	1
L. Smith	2	31	15.5	26	0
Jones	1	8	8.0	8	0
Lawrence	1	4	4.0	4	0
Oher	1	-8	-8.0	-8	0
Ravens	321	3637	11.3	72t	21
Opponents	306	3506	11.5	81t	17

INTERCEPTIONS	No.	Yds	Avg	LG	TD
Landry	4	89	22.3	48t	1
Foxworth	4	34	8.5	19	0
Reed	3	111	37.0	52t	1
Carr	2	24	12.0	13	0
Zbikowski	2	13	6.5	21	0
J. Johnson	2	8	4.0	8	0
Ellerbe	1	28	28.0	28	0
Kruger	1	26	26.0	26	0
Barnes	1	4	4.0	4	0
Ayanbadejo	1	0	0.0	0	0
Walker	1	0	0.0	0	0
Lewis	0	9	—	9	0
Ravens	22	346	15.7	52t	2
Opponents	13	195	15.0	70	0

PUNTING	No.	Yds.	Avg.	In 20	LG
Koch	73	3188	43.7	26	60
Ravens	74	3188	43.1	26	60
Opponents	79	3426	43.4	24	61

PUNT RETURNS	Ret	FC	Yds	Avg	LG	TD
Carr	32	17	262	8.2	34	0
Reed	7	1	29	4.1	9	0
Webb	0	0	-1	—	-1	0
Ravens	39	18	290	7.4	34	0
Opponents	38	12	287	7.6	49t	1

KICKOFF RETURNS	No.	Yds	Avg	LG	TD
Webb	35	918	26.2	95t	1
Carr	13	315	24.2	41	0
Parmele	9	283	31.4	53	0
L. McClain	1	17	17.0	17	0
Edwards	1	14	14.0	14	0
Ravens	59	1547	26.2	95t	1
Opponents	77	1565	20.3	53	0

FIELD GOALS	1-19	20-29	30-39	40-49	50+
Cundiff TM	0/0	5/5	4/7	3/3	0/2
Hauschka TM	0/0	1/1	5/7	3/5	0/0
Ravens	0/0	6/6	9/14	6/8	0/2
Opponents	0/0	12/12	9/11	2/3	1/1

SACKS	No.
Pryce	6.5
J. Johnson	6.0
Suggs	4.5
Barnes	3.0
Gregg	3.0
Lewis	3.0
Carr	1.5
Ngata	1.5
Ayanbadejo	1.0
Edwards	1.0
Webb	1.0
Ravens	32.0
Opponents	36.0

RECORD HOLDERS

INDIVIDUAL RECORDS—CAREER

Category	Name	Performance
Rushing (Yds.)	Jamal Lewis, 2000-06	7,801
Passing (Yds.)	Kyle Boller, 2003-08	7,846
Passing (TDs)	Vinny Testaverde, 1996-97	51
Receiving (No.)	Todd Heap, 2001-09	427
Receiving (Yds.)	Derrick Mason, 2005-09	4,975
Interceptions	Ed Reed, 2002-09	46
Punting (Avg.)	Sam Koch, 2006-09	43.8
Punt Return (Avg.)	Jermaine Lewis, 1996-2001	11.8
Kickoff Return (Avg.)	Corey Harris, 1998-2001	24.0
Field Goals	Matt Stover, 1996-2008	354
Touchdowns (Tot.)	Jamal Lewis, 2000-06	47
Points	Matt Stover, 1996-2008	1,464
*Sacks	Peter Boulware, 1997-2005	70.0

INDIVIDUAL RECORDS—SINGLE SEASON

Category	Name	Performance
Rushing (Yds.)	Jamal Lewis, 2003	2,066
Passing (Yds.)	Vinny Testaverde, 1996	4,177
Passing (TDs)	Vinny Testaverde, 1996	33
Receiving (No.)	Derrick Mason, 2007	103
Receiving (Yds.)	Michael Jackson, 1996	1,201
Interceptions	Ed Reed, 2004, 2008	9
Punting (Avg.)	Sam Koch, 2008	45.0
Punt Return (Avg.)	Jermaine Lewis, 2000	16.1
Kickoff Return (Avg.)	Corey Harris, 1998	27.6
Field Goals	Matt Stover, 2000	35
Touchdowns (Tot.)	Michael Jackson, 1996	14
	Jamal Lewis, 2003	14
	Willis McGahee, 2009	14
Points	Matt Stover, 2000	135
*Sacks	Peter Boulware, 2001	15.0

INDIVIDUAL RECORDS—SINGLE GAME

Category	Name	Performance
Rushing (Yds.)	Jamal Lewis, 9-14-03	295
Passing (Yds.)	Vinny Testaverde, 10-27-96	429
Passing (TDs)	Tony Banks, 9-10-00	5
Receiving (No.)	Priest Holmes, 10-11-98	13
Receiving (Yds.)	Qadry Ismail, 12-12-99	268
Interceptions	Many times	2
	Last time by Domonique Foxworth, 12-20-09	
Field Goals	Matt Stover, 9-21-97, 12-26-99, 10-28-00, 10-14-07	5
	Billy Cundiff, 11-22-09	5
Touchdowns (Tot.)	Marcus Robinson, 11-23-03	4
Points	Marcus Robinson, 11-23-03	24
*Sacks	Michael McCrary, 11-8-98	4.0
	Peter Boulware, 1-7-02	4.0

**Sacks became an official statistic in 1982.*

BALTIMORE RAVENS

2010 VETERAN ROSTER

No.	Name	Pos.	Ht.	Wt.	Birthdate	NFL Exp.	College	Hometown	How Acq.	'09 Games/ Starts
96	Ayanbadejo, Brendon	LB	6-1	225	9/6/76	8	UCLA	Santa Cruz, Calif.	UFA(Chi)-'08	4/1
50	Barnes, Antwan	LB	6-1	240	10/19/84	4	Florida International	Miami, Fla.	D4a-'07	11/0
12	Beck, John	QB	6-2	215	8/21/81	4	Brigham Young	Mesa, Ariz.	FA-'09	0*
77	Birk, Matt	C	6-4	309	7/23/76	13	Harvard	St. Paul, Minn.	UFA(Minn)-'09	16/16
81	t- Boldin, Anquan	WR	6-1	217	10/3/80	8	Florida State	Pahokee, Fla.	T(Ariz)-'10	15/15*
54	Burgess, Prescott	LB	6-3	247	3/6/84	4	Michigan	Warren, Ohio	D6-'07	13/0
25	Carr, Chris	CB/RS	5-10	180	4/30/83	6	Boise State	Reno, Nev.	UFA(Tenn)-'09	16/4
65	Chester, Chris	G/C	6-3	315	1/12/83	5	Oklahoma	Tustin, Calif.	D2-'06	16/13
89	+Clayton, Mark	WR	5-10	190	7/2/82	6	Oklahoma	Arlington, Texas	D1-'05	14/12
64	Cousins, Oniel	T	6-4	314	6/29/84	3	Texas-El Paso	Fullerton, Calif.	D3c-'08	4/3
7	Cundiff, Billy	K	6-1	207	3/30/80	6	Drake	Harlan, Iowa	FA-'09	7/0
96	Divens, Lamar	DT	6-3	338	11/12/85	3	Tennessee State	Fayetteville, Tenn.	FA-'08	0*
59	Ellerbe, Dannell	LB	6-1	243	11/29/85	2	Georgia	Hamlet, N.C.	FA-'09	13/3
5	Flacco, Joe	QB	6-6	235	1/16/85	3	Delaware	Audubon, N.J.	D1-'08	16/16
24	Foxworth, Domonique	CB	5-11	180	3/27/83	6	Maryland	Randallstown, Md.	UFA(Atl)-'09	16/16
71	+Gaither, Jared	T	6-9	340	3/18/86	4	Maryland	White Plains, Md.	SD5-'07	11/11
40	Gerard, K.J.	S	6-1	192	4/22/86	2	Northern Arizona	Fountain Valley, Calif.	FA-'09	3/0
56	Gooden, Tavares	LB	6-1	242	10/7/84	3	Miami	Fort Lauderdale, Fla.	D3a-'08	12/12
97	Gregg, Kelly	DT	6-0	315	11/1/76	11	Oklahoma	Edmond, Okla.	FA-'00	16/13
66	Grubbs, Ben	G	6-3	315	3/10/84	4	Auburn	Eclectic, Ala.	D1-'07	16/16
62	Hale, David	G/T	6-6	310	3/3/83	3	Weber State	Plain City, Utah	D4b-'08	12/0
14	Harper, Justin	WR	6-3	215	2/24/85	3	Virginia Tech	Catawba, N.C.	D7a-'08	2/0
86	Heap, Todd	TE	6-5	245	3/16/80	10	Arizona State	Mesa, Ariz.	D1-'01	16/16
95	Johnson, Jarret	DE	6-3	265	8/14/81	8	Alabama	Cedar Key, Fla.	D4a-'03	16/16
48	Jones, Edgar	LB/DE	6-3	258	12/1/84	4	Southeast Missouri	Rayville, La.	FA-'07	16/0
70	Katula, Matt	LS	6-6	262	8/22/82	6	Wisconsin	Brookfield, Wisc.	FA-'05	16/0
4	+Koch, Sam	P	6-1	220	8/13/82	5	Nebraska	Seward, Neb.	D6a-'06	16/0
99	Kruger, Paul	LB/DE	6-4	270	2/15/86	2	Utah	Orem, Utah	D2-'09	9/1
26	+Landry, Dawan	S	6-0	210	12/30/82	5	Georgia Tech	Ama, La.	D5a-'06	16/16
32	Lawrence, Matt	RB	6-1	209	5/5/85	2	Massachusetts	Bloomfield, Conn.	FA-'08	8/0
52	Lewis, Ray	LB	6-1	250	5/15/75	15	Miami	Lakeland, Fla.	D1b-'96	16/16
85	Mason, Derrick	WR	5-10	192	1/17/74	14	Michigan State	Detroit, Mich.	FA-'05	16/16
53	McClain, Jameel	LB	6-1	250	7/25/85	3	Syracuse	Philadelphia, Pa.	FA-'08	16/1
33	+McClain, Le'Ron	FB	6-0	260	12/27/84	4	Alabama	Northport, Ala.	D4b-'07	16/14
23	McGahee, Willis	RB	6-0	235	10/21/81	8	Miami	Miami, Fla.	T(Buff)-'07	16/1
91	McKinney, Brandon	NT	6-2	360	8/24/83	5	Michigan State	Dayton, Ohio	FA-'08	7/0
79	Moll, Tony	G/T	6-5	311	8/23/83	5	Nevada	Sonoma, Calif.	T(GB)-'09	5/0
43	Nakamura, Haruki	S	5-10	200	4/18/86	3	Cincinnati	Cleveland, Ohio	D6-'08	9/0
92	Ngata, Haloti	DT	6-4	345	1/21/84	5	Oregon	Salt Lake City, Utah	D1-'06	14/13
74	Oher, Michael	T	6-4	310	5/28/86	2	Mississippi	Memphis, Tenn.	D1-'09	16/16
34	Parmele, Jalen	RB	5-11	220	12/30/85	3	Toledo	Midland, Mich.	FA-'08	7/0
30	Paschal, Marcus	S	6-0	201	8/31/84	3	Iowa	Largo, Fla.	FA-'09	2/0
58	Phillips, Jason	LB	6-1	244	2/14/86	2	Texas Christian	Waller, Texas	D5a-'09	0*
17	Price, Maurice	WR	6-1	200	9/11/85	2	Charleston Southern	Orlando, Fla.	FA-'09	0*
90	Pryce, Trevor	DE	6-5	290	8/3/75	14	Clemson	Winter Park, Fla.	FA-'06	16/8
93	Redding, Cory	DE	6-4	292	11/15/80	8	Texas	Houston, Texas	UFA(Sea)-'10	15/3*
20	Reed, Ed	S	5-11	200	9/11/78	9	Miami	St. Rose, La.	D1-'02	12/12
76	Reitz, Joe	T	6-7	305	8/24/85	2	Western Michigan	Fishers, Ind.	FA-'08	0*
27	Rice, Ray	RB	5-8	210	1/22/87	3	Rutgers	New Rochelle, N.Y.	D2-'08	16/15
69	Rodgers, Stefan	T	6-5	317	11/3/81	3	Lambuth	Little Rock, Ark.	FA-'09	0*
11	Smith, Marcus	WR	6-1	215	1/11/85	3	New Mexico	San Diego, Calif.	D4a-'08	0*
10	Smith, Troy	QB	6-0	225	7/20/84	4	Ohio State	Cleveland, Ohio	D5-'07	4/0
18	Stallworth, Donte'	WR	6-0	200	11/10/80	8	Tennessee	Del Paso Heights, Calif.	FA-'10	0*
55	Suggs, Terrell	LB	6-3	260	10/11/82	8	Arizona State	Chandler, Ariz.	D1a-'03	13/13
98	Talavou, Kelly	NT	6-2	350	10/4/84	3	Utah	Fountain Valley, Calif.	FA-'08	3/0
41	#Walker, Frank	CB	5-11	200	8/6/81	8	Tuskegee	Tuskegee, Ala.	UFA(GB)-'08	14/1
31	+Washington, Fabian	CB	5-11	180	6/9/83	6	Nebraska	Bradenton, Fla.	T(Oak)-'08	10/10
21	Webb, Lardarius	CB/RS	5-10	175	10/12/85	2	Nicholls State	Opelika, Ala.	D3-'09	14/4
29	Williams, Cary	CB	6-1	185	12/23/84	2	Washburn	Hollywood, Fla.	FA-'09	5/1
87	Williams, Demetrius	WR	6-2	202	3/28/83	5	Oregon	Concord, Calif.	D4a-'06	13/0
73	Yanda, Marshal	G/T	6-3	313	9/15/84	4	Iowa	Anamosa, Iowa	D3b-'07	16/9
28	Zbikowski, Tom	S	5-11	210	5/22/85	3	Notre Dame	Arlington Heights, Ill.	D3b-'08	15/4

* Beck inactive third quarterback all 16 games; Boldin played 15 games for Arizona in '09; Divens missed '09 season because of injury; Phillips missed '09 season because of injury; Price was inactive with Baltimore in '08; Redding played 15 games for Seattle; Reitz missed '08 season because of injury; Rodgers last active with Jacksonville and Philadelphia in '08; M. Smith missed '09 season because of injury; Stallworth played 11 games for Cleveland in '08.

t- Ravens traded for Boldin (Ariz).

\# Unrestricted free agent; subject to developments.

\+ Restricted free agent; subject to developments.

Players lost through free agency (2): DT Justin Bannan (Den; 16 games in '09); DE Dwan Edwards (Buff; 16).

Also played with Ravens in '09—K Steven Hauschka (9 games), CB Corey Ivy (2), TE L.J. Smith (12), WR David Tyree (10), WR Kelley Washington (15).

2010 FIRST-YEAR ROSTER

Name	Pos.	Ht.	Wt.	Birthdate	College	Hometown	How Acq.
Anthony, Rodelin	WR	6-5	230	5/17/87	Nevada-Las Vegas	Immokalee, Fla.	FA
Bujnoch, Digger (1)	C	6-5	280	6/19/85	Cincinnati	Cincinnati, Ohio	FA
Cody, Terrence	DT	6-4	360	6/28/88	Alabama	Fort Myers, Fla.	D2b
Cox, Morgan	LS	6-4	226	4/26/86	Tennessee	Collierville, Tenn.	FA
Dickson, Ed	TE	6-4	250	7/25/87	Oregon	Bellflower, Calif.	D3
Drew, Davon (1)	TE	6-4	255	12/9/85	East Carolina	New Bern, N.C.	D5b-'09
Fletcher, John	DL	6-6	265	12/6/85	Wyoming	Arvada, Colo.	FA
Hall, Ashton	DB	5-10	196	8/18/88	Marshall	Kingsland, Ga.	FA
Hannon, Chris (1)	WR	6-3	205	2/18/84	Tennessee	Sarasota, Fla.	FA
Harewood, Ramon	T	6-6	340	2/3/87	Morehouse	St. Michael, Barbados	D6
Jones, Arthur	DT	6-3	305	6/3/86	Syracuse	Endicott, N.Y.	D5b
Kindle, Sergio	LB	6-3	250	9/20/87	Texas	Dallas, Texas	D2a
Mattison, Bryan (1)	OL/DL	6-3	295	5/15/84	Iowa	Mishawaka, Ind.	FA-'08
McClellan, Albert	LB/DE	6-2	254	6/4/86	Marshall	Lakeland, Fla.	FA
McLaughlin, Mike	FB	6-0	245	5/11/87	Boston College	Woburn, Mass.	FA
Miller, Prince	CB	5-8	198	1/14/88	Georgia	Duncan, S.C.	FA
Pitta, Dennis	TE	6-4	245	6/29/85	Brigham Young	Moorpark, Calif.	D4
Reed, David	WR	6-0	190	3/22/87	Utah	New Britain, Conn.	D5a
Riley, Eron (1)	WR	6-3	205	8/5/87	Duke	Savannah, Ga.	FA-'09
Sanders, Daniel (1)	G/C	6-2	316	2/3/86	Colorado	Vista, Calif.	FA
Smith, Courtney	CB	5-11	195	10/17/84	Central Washington	Stockton, Calif.	FA
Steele, Curtis	RB	6-0	190	3/24/87	Memphis	Franklin, Tenn.	FA
VanDeSteeg, William (1)	LB	6-4	256	9/22/85	Minnesota	Silver Lake, Minn.	FA-'09

The term NFL Rookie is defined as a player who is in his first season of professional football and has not been on the roster of another professional football team for any regular-season or postseason games. A Rookie is designated by an "R" on NFL rosters. Players who have been active in another professional football league or players who have NFL experience, including either preseason training camp or being on an Active List or Inactive List, or on Reserve/Injured or Reserve/Physically Unable to Perform for fewer than six regular-season games, are termed NFL First-Year Players. An NFL First-Year Player is designated by a "1" on NFL rosters. Thereafter, a player is credited with an additional year of experience for each season in which he accumulates six games on the Active List or Inactive List, or on Reserve/Injured or Reserve/Physically Unable to Perform.

Log on to www.baltimoreravens.com for an up-to-date roster.

COACHING STAFF

Head Coach,
John Harbaugh

Pro Career: John Harbaugh was hired as the third head coach in Baltimore Ravens history on January 19, 2008. In 2009, Harbaugh became the 10th NFL head coach since 1990 to reach the playoffs in his first two seasons. In 2008, his initial campaign with Baltimore, Harbaugh led the Ravens to an 11-5 record and a berth in the AFC Championship game. Baltimore set an NFL record for most wins (13) by a team with both a rookie head coach and a quarterback (Joe Flacco). Harbaugh spent his first 10 NFL seasons (1998-2007) with the Philadelphia Eagles, nine seasons as its special teams coordinator and one season (2007) as the secondary coach. Harbaugh was the 2001 NFL Special Teams Coach of the Year, as selected by his coaching peers. Career record: 23-14.

Background: Harbaugh played defensive back at Miami (Ohio) from 1980-83 and earned a degree in political science. He coached collegiately at Western Michigan (1984-86), Pittsburgh (1987), Morehead State (1988), Cincinnati (1989-1996), and Indiana (1997).

Personal: Born in Perrysburg, Ohio on September 23, 1962, Harbaugh and his wife, Ingrid, have a daughter, Alison. He is the son of longtime college coach Jack Harbaugh, and his brother, Jim, the current Stanford head coach, was an NFL quarterback for 14 years, including 1998 with Baltimore. John's brother-in-law, Tom Crean, Indiana University's basketball coach, is married to his sister, Joani.

ASSISTANT COACHES

Roy Anderson, defensive assistant; born October 5, 1979, Tallahassee, Fla. Quarterback Howard 1997-2001. No pro playing experience. Pro coach: Joined Ravens in 2009.

Clarence Brooks, defensive line; born May 20, 1951, New York, N.Y. Guard Massachusetts 1970-73. No pro playing experience. College coach: Massachusetts 1976-1980, Syracuse 1981-89, Arizona 1990-92. Pro coach: Chicago Bears 1993-98, Cleveland Browns 1999, Miami Dolphins 2000-04, joined Ravens in 2005.

Cam Cameron, offensive coordinator; born February 6, 1961, Chapel Hill, N.C. Quarterback Indiana 1980-83. No pro playing experience. College coach: Michigan 1984-1993, Indiana 1997-2001 (head coach). Pro coach: Washington Redskins 1994-96, San Diego Chargers 2002-06, Miami Dolphins 2007 (head coach), joined Ravens in 2008.

John Dunn, asst. strength and conditioning; born July 22, 1965, Great Barrington, Mass. Guard Penn State 1974-77. No pro playing experience. College coach: Penn State 1978. Pro coach: Washington Redskins 1984-86, Los Angeles Raiders 1987-89, San Diego Chargers 1990-96, New York Giants 1997-2003, Washington Redskins 2004-05, joined Ravens in 2008.

Wade Harman, tight ends; born October 1, 1963, Corydon, Iowa. Linebacker Drake 1985, Utah State 1986. No pro playing experience. College coach: Utah State 1987-1991, Pacific 1992-95, Morningside 1996. Pro coach: Minnesota Vikings 1997-98, joined Ravens in 1999.

Jim Hostler, wide receivers; born November 11, 1966, Pittsburgh. Defensive back Indiana (Pa.) 1986-89. No pro playing experience. College coach: Indiana (Pa.) 1990-92, 1994-99, Juniata (Pa.) 1993. Pro coach: Kansas City Chiefs 2000, New Orleans Saints 2001-02, New York Jets 2003-04, San Francisco 49ers 2005-07, joined Ravens in 2008.

Marwan Maalouf, asst. special teams; born November 26, 1976, Beirut, Lebanon. Guard Baldwin-Wallace 1997-99. No pro playing experience. College coach: Baldwin-Wallace 2000, Fordham 2001, Rutgers 2002-03. Pro coach: Cleveland Browns 2004-06, joined Ravens in 2008.

John Matsko, offensive line; born February 2, 1951, Cleveland. Fullback Kent State 1970-73. No pro playing experience. College coach: Kent State 1973, Miami (Ohio) 1974-75, 1977, North Carolina 1978-1984, Navy 1985, Arizona 1986, Southern California 1987-1991. Pro coach: Phoenix Cardinals 1992-93, New Orleans Saints 1994-96, N.Y. Giants 1997-98, St. Louis Rams 1999-2005, Kansas City Chiefs 2006-07, joined Ravens in 2008.

Greg Mattison, defensive coordinator; born November 15, 1949, Madison, Wisc. Guard Wisconsin-LaCrosse 1967-1970. No pro playing experience. College coach: Illinois 1976, Cornell 1977, Northwestern 1978-1980, Western Michigan 1981-86, Navy 1987-88, Texas A&M 1989-1991, Michigan 1992-96, Notre Dame 1997-2004, Florida 2005-07. Pro coach: Joined Ravens in 2008.

Andy Moeller, asst. offensive line; June 15, 1964, Grand Rapids, Mich. Linebacker Michigan 1983-86. No pro playing experience. College coach: Indiana 1987, Army 1988-1993, Missouri 1994-99, Michigan 2000-07. Pro coach: Joined Ravens in 2008.

Ted Monachino, outside linebackers; born October 15, 1966, Council Bluffs, Iowa. Defensive lineman Missouri 1988-1990. No pro playing experience. College coach: Texas Christian 1996-97, James Madison 1998, Southwest Missouri State 1999, Boise State 2000, Arizona State 2001-05. Pro coach: Jacksonville Jaguars 2006-09, joined Ravens in 2010.

Wilbert Montgomery, running backs; born September 16, 1954, Greenville, Miss. Running back Abilene Christian 1973-76. Pro running back Philadelphia Eagles 1977-1984, Detroit Lions 1985. Pro Coach: St. Louis Rams 1997-2005, Detroit Lions 2006-07, joined Ravens in 2008.

Chuck Pagano, secondary; born October 2, 1960, Boulder, Colo. Safety Wyoming 1980-83. No pro playing experience. College coach: Southern California 1984-85, Miami 1986, Boise State 1987-88, East Carolina 1989, Nevada-Las Vegas 1990-91, East Carolina 1992-94, Miami 1995-2000, North Carolina 2007. Pro coach: Cleveland Browns 2001-04, Oakland Raiders 2005-06, joined Ravens in 2008.

Dean Pees, linebackers; born September 4, 1949, Dunkirk, Ohio. Attended Bowling Green State. No college or pro playing experience. College coach: Findlay 1979-1982, Miami (Ohio) 1983-86, Naval Academy 1987-89, Toledo 1990-93, Notre Dame 1994, Michigan State 1995-97, Kent State 1998-2003. Pro coach: New England Patriots 2004-09, joined Ravens in 2010.

Bob Rogucki, strength and conditioning; born September 27, 1953, Clarksburg, W.Va. No college or pro playing experience. College coach: Penn State 1981, Weber State 1982, Army 1983-89. Pro coach: Arizona Cardinals 1990-2003, Jacksonville Jaguars 2004, Philadelphia Eagles 2006-07, joined Ravens in 2008.

Jerry Rosburg, special teams coordinator/ asst. head coach; born November 24, 1955, Fairmont, Minn. Linebacker North Dakota State 1974-77. No pro playing experience. College coach: Northern Michigan 1981-86, Western Michigan 1987-1991, Cincinnati 1992-95, Minnesota 1996, Boston College 1997-98, Notre Dame 1999-2000. Pro coach: Cleveland Browns 2001-06, Atlanta Falcons 2007, joined Ravens in 2008.

Al Saunders, senior offensive assistant; born February 1, 1947, London, England. Defensive back San Jose State 1966-68. No pro playing experience. College coach: Southern California 1970-71, Missouri 1972, Utah State 1973-75, California 1976-1981, Tennessee 1982. Pro coach: San Diego Chargers 1983-88 (head coach 1986-88), Kansas City Chiefs 1989-1998, St. Louis Rams 1999-2000, Kansas City Chiefs 2001-05, Washington Redskins 2006-07, St. Louis Rams 2008, joined Ravens in 2009.

Craig Ver Steeg, offensive assistant; born September 11, 1960, Inglewood, Calif. No college or pro playing experience. College coach: Southern California 1984-85, Utah 1986-89, Cincinnati 1990-93, Harvard 1994-95, Illinois 1998-2000, Utah 2001-02, Rutgers 2003-07. Pro coach: Chicago Bears 1996-97, joined Ravens in 2008.

Matt Weiss, head coach's assistant; born March 1, 1983, New Haven, Conn. Punter Vanderbilt 2001-02. No pro playing experience. College coach: Stanford 2008. Pro coach: Joined Ravens in 2009.

Jim Zorn, quarterbacks; born May 10, 1953, Whittier, Calif. Quarterback Cal Poly Pomona 1973-74. Pro quarterback Seattle Seahawks 1976-1984, Green Bay Packers 1985, Winnipeg Blue Bombers (CFL) 1986, Tampa Bay Buccaneers 1987. College coach: Boise State 1989-1991, Utah State 1992-94, Minnesota 1995-96. Pro coach: Seattle Seahawks 1997, 2001-07, Detroit Lions 1998-2000, Washington Redskins 2008-09 (head coach), joined Ravens in 2010.

American Football Conference
East Division
Team Colors: Dark Navy, Red, Royal, and Nickel
One Bills Drive
Orchard Park, New York 14127-2296
Telephone: (716) 648-1800

2010 SCHEDULE

PRESEASON

Aug. 13	at Washington	7:30
Aug. 19	**Indianapolis** (Toronto)	7:30
Aug. 28	**Cincinnati**	6:30
Sep. 2	at Detroit	7:00

REGULAR SEASON

Sep. 12	**Miami**	1:00
Sep. 19	at Green Bay	12:00
Sep. 26	at New England	1:00
Oct. 3	**New York Jets**	1:00
Oct. 10	**Jacksonville**	1:00
Oct. 17	BYE	
Oct. 24	at Baltimore	1:00
Oct. 31	at Kansas City	12:00
Nov. 7	**Chicago** (Toronto)	1:00
Nov. 14	**Detroit**	1:00
Nov. 21	at Cincinnati	1:00
Nov. 28	**Pittsburgh**	1:00
Dec. 5	at Minnesota	12:00
Dec. 12	**Cleveland**	1:00
Dec. 19	at Miami	1:00
Dec. 26	**New England**	1:00
Jan. 2	at New York Jets	1:00

Stadium: Ralph Wilson Stadium (opened in 1973) • **Capacity:** 73,967
One Bills Drive
Orchard Park, New York
14127-2296
Playing Surface: AstroPlay
Training Camp: St. John Fisher College
Rochester, N.Y. 14618

RALPH WILSON STADIUM

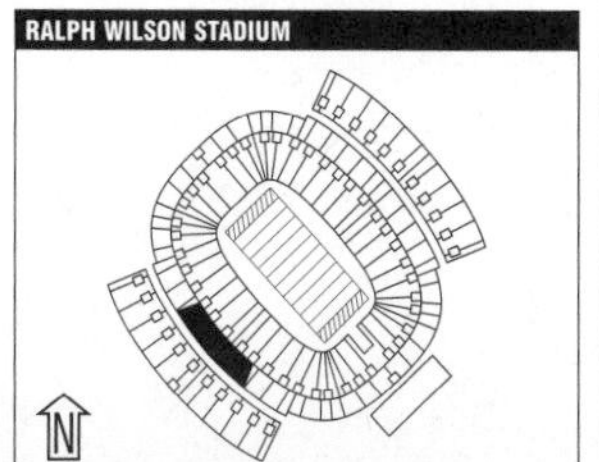

CLUB OFFICIALS

Owner and President: Ralph C. Wilson, Jr.
Chief Executive Officer: Russ Brandon
Treasurer: Jeffrey C. Littmann
General Manager: Buddy Nix
Senior Vice President of Marketing and Broadcasting: Marc Honan
Senior Vice President of Football Administration: Jim Overdorf
Senior Vice President of Business Development: Bruce Popko
Senior Vice President of Business Operations: Dave Wheat
Vice President of Communications: Scott Berchtold
Vice President of Stadium Operations: Joe Frandina
Vice President of Community Relations: Gretchen Geitter
Vice President of College Scouting: Tom Modrak
Vice President of Government Relations and External Affairs: Bill Munson
Vice President of Strategic Planning: Mary Owen
Consultant: Christy Wilson Hofmann
Assistant General Manager/Director of Pro Personnel: Doug Whaley
Executive Director of Information Technology: Dan Evans
Director of Security: Chris Clark
Director of Stadium Operations: Perry Dix
Director of Merchandise: Tim Kehoe
Director of Player Programs: Paul Lancaster
Controller: Frank Wojnicki
Equipment Manager: Dave Hojnowski, Jeff Mazurek
Assistant Equipment Managers: Randy Ribbeck, Spencer Haws
Head Athletic Trainer: Bud Carpenter
Athletic Trainers: Chris Fischetti, Shone Gipson, Greg McMillen
Video Director: Henry Kunttu
Assistant Video Director: Greg Estes
Video System Analyst: Wes Burnard
Coordinator of College Scouting: Doug Majeski
Scouts: Rashaan Curry, Brian Fisher, Brad Forsyth, Matt Hand (BLESTO), Shawn Heilen, Tom Roth, (emeritus) David G. Smith, (emeritus) David W. Smith

COACHING HISTORY
(368-409-8)

Records include postseason games

1960-61	Buster Ramsey	11-16-1
1962-65	Lou Saban	38-18-3
1966-68	Joe Collier*	13-17-1
1968	Harvey Johnson	1-10-1
1969-1970	John Rauch	7-20-1
1971	Harvey Johnson	1-13-0
1972-76	Lou Saban**	32-29-1
1976-77	Jim Ringo	3-20-0
1978-1982	Chuck Knox	38-38-0
1983-85	Kay Stephenson***	10-26-0
1985-86	Hank Bullough****	4-17-0
1986-1997	Marv Levy	123-78-0
1998-2000	Wade Phillips	29-21-0
2001-03	Gregg Williams	17-31-0
2004-05	Mike Mularkey	14-18-0
2006-09	Dick Jauron#	24-33-0
2009	Perry Fewell	3-4-0

*Released after two games in 1968
**Resigned after five games in 1976
***Released after four games in 1985
****Released after nine games in 1986
#Released after nine games in 2009

PAID ATTENDANCE

Home 528,327 Away 515,222
Total 1,043,549
Single-game home record, 80,368 (10/4/92)
Single-season home record, 635,889 (1991)

2010 DRAFT CHOICES

Round	Name	Pos.	College
1	C.J. Spiller	RB	Clemson
2	Torell Troup	DT	Central Florida
3	Alex Carrington	DE	Arkansas St.
4	Marcus Easley	WR	Connecticut
5	Ed Wang	T	Virginia Tech
6	Arthur Moats	LB	James Madison
	Danny Batten	LB	South Dakota St.
7	Levi Brown	QB	Troy
	Kyle Calloway	G	Iowa

BUFFALO BILLS

2009 TEAM RECORD

PRESEASON (1-4)

Date	Result	Opponent
8/9	L 18-21	vs. Tennessee, at Canton, OH
8/15	W 27-20	Chicago
8/22	L 17-31	at Green Bay
8/29	L 0-17	at Pittsburgh
9/3	L 6-17	Detroit

REGULAR SEASON (6-10)

Date	Result	Opponent
9/14	L 24-25	at New England
9/20	W 33-20	Tampa Bay
9/27	L 7-27	New Orleans
10/4	L 10-38	at Miami
10/11	L 3-6	Cleveland
10/18	W 16-13	at New York Jets (OT)
10/25	W 20-9	at Carolina
11/1	L 10-31	Houston
11/15	L 17-41	at Tennessee
11/22	L 15-18	at Jacksonville
11/29	W 31-14	Miami
12/3	L 13-19	New York Jets
12/13	W 16-10	at Kansas City
12/20	L 10-17	New England
12/27	L 3-31	at Atlanta
1/3	W 30-7	Indianapolis

(OT) Overtime

SCORE BY PERIODS

	1	2	3	4	OT		Total
Bills	74	67	37	77	3	—	258
Opponents	44	115	48	119	0	—	326

2009 TEAM STATISTICS

	Bills	Opp.
Total First Downs	233	310
Rushing	81	134
Passing	126	157
Penalty	26	19
3rd Down: Made/Att	51/198	97/240
3rd Down Pct.	25.8	40.4
4th Down: Made/Att	7/15	14/26
4th Down Pct.	46.7	53.8
Possession Avg.	27:50	32:10
Total Net Yards	4382	5449
Avg. Per Game	273.9	340.6
Total Plays	911	1086
Avg. Per Play	4.8	5.0
Net Yards Rushing	1867	2501
Avg. Per Game	116.7	156.3
Total Rushes	424	535
Net Yards Passing	2515	2948
Avg. Per Game	157.2	184.3
Sacked/Yards Lost	46/274	32/189
Gross Yards	2789	3137
Att./Completions	441/256	519/295
Completion Pct.	58.0	56.8
Had Intercepted	19	28
Punts/Average	90/46.6	78/41.2
Net Punting Avg.	90/40.2	78/37.4
Penalties/Yards	107/855	107/919
Fumbles/Ball Lost	24/11	21/5
Touchdowns	25	37
Rushing	6	19
Passing	17	14
Returns	2	4

2009 INDIVIDUAL STATISTICS

PASSING	Att.	Comp.	Yds.	Pct.	TD	Int.	Tkld.	Rate
Fitzpatrick	227	127	1422	55.9	9	10	21/127	69.7
Edwards	183	110	1169	60.1	6	7	23/139	73.8
Brohm TM	29	17	146	58.6	0	2	2/8	43.2
Jackson	1	1	27	100.0	1	0	0/0	158.3
Moorman	1	1	25	100.0	1	0	0/0	158.3
Bills	441	256	2789	58.0	17	19	46/274	71.7
Opponents	519	295	3137	56.8	14	28	32/189	61.1

SCORING	TD R	TD P	TD Rt	PAT	FG	Saf	PTS
Lindell	0	0	0	24/24	28/33	0	108
Evans	0	7	0	0/0	0/0	0	42
Owens	1	5	0	0/0	0/0	0	36
Jackson	2	2	0	0/0	0/0	0	24
Lynch	2	0	0	0/0	0/0	0	12
Denney	0	1	0	0/0	0/0	0	6
Fitzpatrick	1	0	0	0/0	0/0	0	6
Nelson	0	1	0	0/0	0/0	0	6
Reed	0	1	0	0/0	0/0	0	6
Schobel	0	0	1	0/0	0/0	0	6
Whitner	0	0	1	0/0	0/0	0	6
Bills	6	17	2	24/24	28/33	0	258
Opponents	19	14	4	32/32	22/28	1	326

2-Pt. Conversions: Bills 0-1, Opponents 2-5.

RUSHING	No.	Yds	Avg	LG	TD
Jackson	237	1062	4.5	43	2
Lynch	120	450	3.8	47	2
Fitzpatrick	31	141	4.5	31t	1
Edwards	14	106	7.6	20	0
Owens	6	54	9.0	29t	1
McIntyre	5	34	6.8	25	0
Omon TM	5	22	4.4	7	0
Parrish	2	4	2.0	9	0
Brohm TM	3	-3	-1.0	-1	0
Jenkins	1	-3	-3.0	-3	0
Bills	424	1867	4.4	47	6
Opponents	535	2501	4.7	76t	19

RECEIVING	No.	Yds	Avg	LG	TD
Owens	55	829	15.1	98t	5
Jackson	46	371	8.1	21	2
Evans	44	612	13.9	50	7
Lynch	28	179	6.4	35	0
Reed	27	291	10.8	29	1
Nelson	17	156	9.2	25	1
Schouman	9	103	11.4	27	0
Fine	9	64	7.1	11	0
McIntyre	7	55	7.9	18	0
Stupar	6	40	6.7	17	0
Parrish	3	34	11.3	16	0
St. Johnson	2	10	5.0	5	0
Denney	1	25	25.0	25t	1
Klopfenstein	1	11	11.0	11	0
Hardy	1	9	9.0	9	0
Bills	256	2789	10.9	98t	17
Opponents	295	3137	10.6	52	14

INTERCEPTIONS	No.	Yds	Avg	LG	TD
Byrd	9	118	13.1	37	0
Wilson	4	23	5.8	27	0
Posluszny	3	20	6.7	17	0
Whitner	2	104	52.0	76t	1
C. Harris	2	7	3.5	7	0
B. Scott	1	27	27.0	27	0
Schobel	1	26	26.0	26t	1
Florence	1	7	7.0	7	0
McGee	1	3	3.0	3	0
Corner	1	0	0.0	0	0
Draft	1	0	0.0	0	0
Mace	1	0	0.0	0	0
Wendling	1	0	0.0	0	0
Bills	28	335	12.0	76t	2
Opponents	19	194	10.2	31t	3

PUNTING	No.	Yds.	Avg.	In 20	LG
Moorman	90	4192	46.6	25	73
Bills	90	4192	46.6	25	73
Opponents	78	3216	41.2	30	63

PUNT RETURNS	Ret	FC	Yds	Avg	LG	TD
Parrish	24	13	133	5.5	31	0
Jackson	6	5	69	11.5	27	0
Reed	3	0	0	0.0	0	0
Youboty	0	0	16	—	16	0
Bills	33	18	218	6.6	31	0
Opponents	49	12	377	7.7	52	0

KICKOFF RETURNS	No.	Yds	Avg	LG	TD
Jackson	41	1014	24.7	71	0
Parrish	11	258	23.5	31	0
McKelvin	5	121	24.2	33	0
Jenkins	3	45	15.0	19	0
McGee	1	30	30.0	30	0
Omon TM	1	26	26.0	26	0
Sp. Johnson	1	12	12.0	12	0
Stupar	1	11	11.0	11	0
Bills	64	1517	23.7	71	0
Opponents	59	1271	21.5	52	0

FIELD GOALS	1-19	20-29	30-39	40-49	50+
Lindell	0/0	12/12	9/9	6/9	1/3
Bills	0/0	12/12	9/9	6/9	1/3
Opponents	1/1	9/9	7/8	3/6	2/4

SACKS	No.
Schobel	10.0
Kelsay	5.0
Williams	4.0
Denney	2.0
Sp. Johnson	2.0
B. Scott	2.0
Stroud	2.0
Wilson	2.0
Draft	1.0
Posluszny	1.0
(group)	1.0
Bills	32.0
Opponents	46.0

RECORD HOLDERS

INDIVIDUAL RECORDS—CAREER

Category	Name	Performance
Rushing (Yds.)	Thurman Thomas, 1988-1999	11,938
Passing (Yds.)	Jim Kelly, 1986-1996	35,467
Passing (TDs)	Jim Kelly, 1986-1996	237
Receiving (No.)	Andre Reed, 1985-1999	941
Receiving (Yds.)	Andre Reed, 1985-1999	13,095
Interceptions	George (Butch) Byrd, 1964-1970	40
Punting (Avg.)	Brian Moorman, 2001-09	43.6
Punt Return (Avg.)	Roscoe Parrish, 2005-09	12.3
Kickoff Return (Avg.)	O.J. Simpson, 1969-1977	30.0
Field Goals	Steve Christie, 1992-2000	234
Touchdowns (Tot.)	Andre Reed, 1985-1999	87
	Thurman Thomas, 1988-1999	87
Points	Steve Christie, 1992-2000	1,011
*Sacks	Bruce Smith, 1985-1999	**171.0

INDIVIDUAL RECORDS—SINGLE SEASON

Category	Name	Performance
Rushing (Yds.)	O.J. Simpson, 1973	2,003
Passing (Yds.)	Drew Bledsoe, 2002	4,359
Passing (TDs)	Jim Kelly, 1991	33
Receiving (No.)	Eric Moulds, 2002	100
Receiving (Yds.)	Eric Moulds, 1998	1,368
Interceptions	Billy Atkins, 1961	10
	Tom Janik, 1967	10
Punting (Avg.)	Brian Moorman, 2009	46.6
Punt Return (Avg.)	Roscoe Parrish, 2007	16.3
Kickoff Return (Avg.)	Terrence McGee, 2005	30.24
Field Goals	Steve Christie, 1998	33
Touchdowns (Tot.)	O.J. Simpson, 1975	23
Points	Steve Christie, 1998	140
*Sacks	Bruce Smith, 1990	19.0

INDIVIDUAL RECORDS—SINGLE GAME

Category	Name	Performance
Rushing (Yds.)	O.J. Simpson, 11-25-76	273
Passing (Yds.)	Drew Bledsoe, 9-15-02	463
Passing (TDs)	Jim Kelly, 9-8-91	6
Receiving (No.)	Andre Reed, 11-20-94	15
Receiving (Yds.)	Lee Evans, 11-19-06	265
Interceptions	Many times	3
	Last time by Nate Clements, 10-20-02	
Field Goals	Steve Christie, 10-20-96	6
Touchdowns (Tot.)	Cookie Gilchrist, 12-8-63	5
Points	Cookie Gilchrist, 12-8-63	30
*Sacks	Cornelius Bennett, 12-27-87	4.0
	Bruce Smith, 12-9-90, 9-18-94	4.0

**Sacks became an official statistic in 1982.*
***NFL Record*

BUFFALO BILLS

2010 VETERAN ROSTER

No.	Name	Pos.	Ht.	Wt.	Birthdate	NFL Exp.	College	Hometown	How Acq.	'09 Games/ Starts
77	Bell, Demetrius	T	6-5	307	5/3/1984	2	Northwestern State	Summerfield, La.	D7a-'08	8/8
4	Brohm, Brian	QB	6-3	223	9/23/85	3	Louisville	Louisville, Ky.	FA-'09	1/1
31	Byrd, Jairus	DB	5-10	200	10/7/86	2	Oregon	Clayton, Mo.	D2a-'09	14/11
73	Chambers, Kirk	T	6-7	315	3/19/79	6	Stanford	Provo, Utah	UFA-'09	14/9
27	Corner, Reggie	CB	5-9	175	11/17/83	3	Akron	Canton, Ohio	D4a-'08	16/8
33	Corto, Jon	LB	6-1	220	9/3/84	3	Sacred Heart	Orchard Park, N.Y.	FA-'08	16/1
54	Davis, Andra	LB	6-1	251	12/23/78	9	Florida	Live Oak, Fla.	FA-'10	16/13*
98	Edwards, Dwan	DL	6-3	290	5/16/81	6	Oregon State	Columbus, Mont.	UFA(Balt)-'10	16/9*
5	Edwards, Trent	QB	6-4	231	10/30/83	4	Stanford	Los Gatos, Calif.	D3-'07	8/7
93	Ellis, Chris	LB	6-4	261	2/11/85	4	Virginia Tech	Hampton, Va.	D3-'08	3/0
56	Ellison, Keith	LB	6-0	229	2/6/84	5	Oregon State	Redondo Beach, Calif.	D6-'06	8/8
83	Evans, Lee	WR	5-10	197	3/11/81	7	Wisconsin	Bedford, Ohio	D1a-'04	16/16
14	Fitzpatrick, Ryan	QB	6-2	225	11/24/82	5	Harvard	Gilbert, Ariz.	UFA(Cin)-'09	9/7
29	Florence, Drayton	CB	6-0	195	12/19/80	8	Tuskegee	Ocala, Fla.	FA-'09	14/13
61	Gaddis, Christian	C	6-1	300	10/5/84	2	Villanova	North Miami Beach, Fla.	FA-'09	1/0
74	Green, Cornell	OL	6-6	315	8/25/76	9	Central Florida	St. Petersburg, Fla.	UFA(Oak)-'10	12/12*
63	Hangartner, Geoff	C	6-5	301	4/22/82	6	Texas A&M	New Braunfels, Texas	UFA(Car)-'09	16/16
84	Hardy, James	WR	6-5	220	12/24/85	3	Indiana	Fort Wayne, Ind.	D2-'08	2/0
47	Harris, Cary	DB	5-11	187	3/22/87	2	Southern California	Pacoima, Calif.	D6-'09	4/1
54	Harris, Nic	LB	6-2	232	10/6/86	2	Oklahoma	Alexandria, La.	D5-'09	15/2
17	Jackson, Chad	WR	6-1	223	3/6/85	3	Florida	Hoover, Ala.	FA-'10	0*
22	Jackson, Fred	RB	6-1	215	2/20/81	4	Coe College	Fort Worth, Texas	FA-'06	16/11
91	Johnson, Spencer	DT	6-3	286	12/12/81	7	Auburn	Silas, Ala.	UFA(Minn)-'08	16/3
13	Johnson, Steve	WR	6-2	202	7/22/86	3	Kentucky	San Francisco, Calif.	D7b-'08	5/0
90	Kelsay, Chris	LB	6-4	261	10/31/79	8	Nebraska	Auburn, Neb.	D2-'03	16/16
87	Klopfenstein, Joe	TE	6-5	262	11/9/83	4	Colorado	Aurora, Colo.	FA-'09	1/1
25	Lankster, Ellis	DB	5-9	190	6/3/87	2	West Virginia	Whistler, Ala.	D7-'09	10/0
67	Levitre, Andy	LG	6-2	305	5/15/86	2	Oregon State	Los Gatos, Calif.	D2b-'09	16/16
9	Lindell, Rian	K	6-3	233	1/20/77	11	Washington State	Vancouver, Wash.	FA-'03	16/0
23	Lynch, Marshawn	RB	5-11	215	4/22/86	4	California	Oakland, Calif.	D1-'07	13/6
82	Matthews, Michael	TE	6-4	270	10/9/83	4	Georgia Tech	Altadena, Calif.	FA-'10	7/0*
58	Maybin, Aaron	LB	6-4	250	4/6/88	2	Penn State	Ellicott City, Md.	D1a-'09	16/0
97	McCargo, John	DT	6-2	307	8/19/83	5	North Carolina State	Drakes Branch, Va.	D1b-'06	11/1
24	McGee, Terrence	CB	5-9	198	10/14/80	8	Northwestern State	Athens, Texas	D4a-'03	11/10
38	McIntyre, Corey	FB	6-0	258	1/25/79	6	West Virginia	Indiantown, Fla.	FA-'08	15/4
28	McKelvin, Leodis	CB	5-10	184	9/1/85	3	Troy	Waycross, Ga.	D1-'08	3/3
69	Meredith, Jamon	T	6-5	304	5/11/86	2	South Carolina	Simpsonville, S.C.	FA-'09	8/4
55	Mitchell, Kawika	LB	6-1	253	10/10/79	8	South Florida	Winter Springs, Fla.	UFA(NYG)-'08	5/5
8	Moorman, Brian	P	6-0	172	2/5/76	10	Pittsburg State	Sedgwick, Kan.	FA-'01	16/0
89	Nelson, Shawn	TE	6-5	240	10/5/85	2	Southern Mississippi	Gonzales, La.	D4-'09	13/12
11	Parrish, Roscoe	WR	5-9	178	7/16/82	6	Miami	Miami, Fla.	D2-'05	11/0
51	Posluszny, Paul	LB	6-1	238	10/10/84	4	Penn State	Aliquippa, Pa.	D2-'07	12/12
76	Ramsey, Andre	G	6-5	322	7/24/87	2	Ball State	Cordele, Ga.	FA-'09	2/0
65	Sanborn, Garrison	LS	6-0	240	7/31/85	2	Florida State	Tampa, Fla.	FA-'09	16/0
94	Schobel, Aaron	LB	6-4	243	9/1/77	10	Texas Christian	Columbus, Texas	D2a-'01	16/16
80	Schouman, Derek	TE	6-2	223	3/11/85	4	Boise State	Eagle, Idaho	D7a-'07	2/2
43	Scott, Bryan	S	6-1	219	4/13/81	8	Penn State	Doylestown, Pa.	FA-'07	9/9
	Simpson, Chad	RB	5-9	216	8/22/85	3	Morgan State	Miami, Fla.	FA-'09	14/0*
99	Stroud, Marcus	DT	6-6	310	6/25/78	10	Georgia	Thomasville, Ga.	T(Jax)-'08	15/15
88	Stupar, Jonathan	TE	6-3	254	7/24/84	2	Virginia	State College, Pa.	UA-'09	14/2
20	Whitner, Donte	S	5-10	208	7/24/85	5	Ohio State	Cleveland, Ohio	D1a-'06	10/8
95	Williams, Kyle	DT	6-1	306	6/10/83	5	Louisiana State	Ruston, La.	D5a-'06	14/14
37	Wilson, George	S	6-0	212	3/14/81	5	Arkansas	Paducah, Ky.	FA-'04	16/12
70	Wood, Eric	RG	6-4	315	3/18/86	2	Louisville	Cincinnati, Ohio	D1b-'09	10/10
26	Youboty, Ashton	CB	5-11	189	7/7/84	5	Ohio State	Klein, Texas	D3-'06	11/1

* Davis played 16 games with Denver in '09; D. Edwards played 16 games with Baltimore; Green played in 12 games with Oakland; C. Jackson last active with Denver in '08; Matthews played 3 games with Detroit and 4 games with New England; Simpson played 14 games with Indianapolis.

Players lost through free agency (2): OL Richie Incognito (Mia; 3 games in '09), OL Jonathan Scott (Det; 10).

Also played with Bills in '09—LB Marcus Buggs (5 games), OL Brad Butler (2), DE Ryan Denney (16), LB Chris Draft (11), TE Derek Fine (8), OL Nick Hennessey (1), WR Justin Jenkins (12), DB Todd Johnson (8), DL Corey Mace (2), LB Ryan Manalac (1), OL Seth McKinney (8), RB Xavier Omon (4), WR Terrell Owens (16), LB Ashlee Palmer (14), WR Josh Reed (14), OL Kendall Simmons (3), LB Josh Stamer (2), DB John Wendling (16).

2010 FIRST-YEAR ROSTER

Name	Pos.	Ht.	Wt.	Birthdate	College	Hometown	How Acq.
Allen, Sean	C	6-3	305	3/4/88	East Carolina	Wilson, N.C.	FA
Batten, Danny	LB	6-4	250	12/8/87	South Dakota State	Gilbert, Ariz.	D6b
Bell, Joique	RB	5-11	220	8/4/86	Wayne State	Benton Harbor, Mich.	FA
Brown, Levi	QB	6-4	225	3/11/87	Troy	Mt. Juliet, Tenn.	D7a
Calloway, Kyle	G	6-7	315	6/21/87	Iowa	Belleville, Ill.	D7b
Carrington, Alex	DE	6-5	284	6/19/87	Arkansas State	Tupelo, Miss.	D3
Coleman, Antonio	LB	6-1	248	9/1/86	Auburn	Mobile, Ala.	FA
Croner, Will	DE	6-2	279	11/14/86	Howard	Wilmington, Del.	FA
Destin, John	DB	5-11	191	8/17/86	Tulsa	Belle Glade, Fla.	FA
Duncan, Rashaad (1)	DT	6-2	315	12/10/86	Pittsburgh	Belle Glade, Fla.	FA-'09
Easley, Marcus	WR	6-2	207	11/2/87	Connecticut	Stratford, Conn.	D4
Favorite, Marlon (1)	DT	6-1	317	6/22/86	Louisiana State	Harvey, La.	FA
Ferguson, Rodney (1)	FB	6-0	234	8/25/86	New Mexico	Flint, Mich.	FA
Guerra, Jorge	G	6-3	300	10/15/87	Texas A&M-Kingsville	Roma, Texas	FA
Harris, Dominique	DB	6-2	213	4/14/87	Temple	Washington, D.C.	FA
Harvey, Lonnie (1)	DT	6-3	342	1/20/87	Morgan State	Baltimore, Md.	FA-'09
Hennessey, Nick (1)	OL	6-5	291	7/2/86	Colgate	Danvers, Mass.	FA-'09
Howard, Cordaro	T	6-4	314	7/2/87	Georgia Tech	Phoenix City, Ala.	FA
Huggins, Felton (1)	WR	6-2	186	2/15/83	Southeastern Louisiana	Zachary, La.	FA
Johnson, Brett	FS	6-1	194	2/27/87	California	Las Vegas, Nev.	FA
Jones, Donald	WR	6-0	214	12/17/87	Youngstown State	Plainfield, N.J.	FA
Manalac, Ryan (1)	LB	6-0	235	10/20/85	Cincinnati	Pickerington, Ohio	FA-'09
Moats, Arthur	LB	6-2	250	3/14/88	James Madison	Portsmouth, Va.	D6a
Nelson, David	WR	6-5	217	11/7/86	Florida	Wichita Falls, Texas	FA
Roosevelt, Naaman	WR	6-0	189	12/24/87	Buffalo	Buffalo, N.Y.	FA
Sargeant, Lydell (1)	DB	6-1	187	1/31/87	Penn State	Lompoc, Calif.	FA-'09
Spiller, C.J.	RB	5-11	196	8/5/87	Clemson	Lake Butler, Fla.	D1
Troup, Torell	NT	6-3	315	6/23/88	Central Florida	Conyers, Ga.	D2
Virgil, Stephan	DB	5-11	189	4/3/87	Virginia Tech	Rocky Mount, N.C.	FA
Wang, Ed	T	6-5	301	3/12/87	Virginia Tech	Ashburn, Va.	D5
Watkins, Jason (1)	OL	6-6	325	6/10/85	Florida	New Orleans, La.	FA-'09
Wright, Mike	LB	6-1	241	6/6/86	Utah	Bountiful, Utah	FA

The term NFL Rookie is defined as a player who is in his first season of professional football and has not been on the roster of another professional football team for any regular-season or postseason games. A Rookie is designated by an "R" on NFL rosters. Players who have been active in another professional football league or players who have NFL experience, including either preseason training camp or being on an Active List or Inactive List, or on Reserve/Injured or Reserve/Physically Unable to Perform for fewer than six regular-season games, are termed NFL First-Year Players. An NFL First-Year Player is designated by a "1" on NFL rosters. Thereafter, a player is credited with an additional year of experience for each season in which he accumulates six games on the Active List or Inactive List, or on Reserve/Injured or Reserve/Physically Unable to Perform.

Log on to www.buffalobills.com for an up-to-date roster.

COACHING STAFF

Head Coach,
Chan Gailey

Pro Career: Gailey was named Buffalo's fifteenth head coach on January 19, 2010. Gailey has over three decades of coaching experience, including head coaching experience in college, World League and the NFL. Gailey served as head coach of the Dallas Cowboys from 1998-99, leading the Cowboys to playoff berths in each season. With the Cowboys, in 1998, Gailey became the first coach in NFC Eastern Division history to lead his team to a perfect 8-0 record in division play and a 10-6 overall record. In 1999, Gailey followed that with an 8-8 campaign and his second consecutive playoff appearance. Gailey also has four stints as offensive coordinator in the NFL with Denver (1989-1990), Pittsburgh (1996-97), Miami (2000-01) and Kansas City (2008). Gailey has spent nine of his previous 15 NFL season as either a head coach or offensive coordinator. During those nine seasons, his teams have made the playoffs seven times and boasted a 1,000-yard rusher on seven different occasions. In total, he has made playoff appearances in 11 of his 15 seasons in NFL coaching. His résumé also boasts four Super Bowl berths, including one with Pittsburgh (XXX) and three with Denver (XXI, XXII and XXIV). Gailey served as the head coach at Georgia Tech (2002-07), becoming the first coach in school history to lead the Yellow Jackets to bowl appearance in his first six seasons. Compiled a 44-33 overall record. He began his NFL career as an assistant with Denver (1985-1990). Career record: 18-16.

Background: A former collegiate quarterback at Florida, Gailey was a three-year letterwinner for the Gators. He coached collegiately at Florida (1974-75), Troy State (1976-78), Air Force (1979-1982). Gailey was an all-state quarterback at Americus High School in Americus, Ga.

Personal: Born January 5, 1952, Gainesville, Ga. Chan and his wife, Laurie, have two sons, Tate and Andrew. The Gaileys also have two grandsons.

ASSISTANT COACHES

Bob Bicknell, tight ends; born November, 13, 1969, Holliston, Mass. Tight end Boston College 1988-1991. No pro playing experience. College coach: Boston University 1993-97, Temple 2006. Pro coach: Frankfurt Galaxy (NFLE) 1998-99, Berlin Thunder 2000-03 (NFLE), Cologne Centurions (NFLE) 2004-05, Kansas City Chiefs 2007-09, joined Bills in 2010.

George Catavolos, defensive backs; born May 8, 1945, Chicago. Defensive back Purdue 1964-67. No pro playing experience. College coach: Purdue 1967-68, 1971-76, Middle Tennessee State 1969, Louisville 1970, Kentucky 1977-1981, Tennessee 1982-83. Pro coach: Indianapolis Colts 1984-1994, 1998-2001, Carolina Panthers 1995-97, Washington Redskins 2002-03, Detroit Lions 2004-05, joined Bills in 2006.

Eric Ciano, co-head strength and conditioning; born August 8, 1973, Waltham, Mass. Offensive line Springfield (Mass.) College 1993-97. No pro playing experience. College coach: Tennessee 1997-99, Louisiana Tech 2000-02, Tennessee 2002-04, Georgia Tech 2005-09. Pro coach: Joined Bills in 2010.

George Cortez, quarterbacks; born February 11, 1951, Port Arthur, Texas. No college or pro playing experience. College coach: Rice 1979-1982, Lamar 1987-89, Southern Methodist 1995-96, California 2002-05. Pro coach: Montreal Alouettes (CFL) 1984-86, Ottawa Roughriders (CFL) 1990-91, Calgary Stampeders (CFL) 1992-94, 1997-2001, 2007-09, joined Bills in 2010.

DeMontie Cross, inside linebackers; born February 26, 1974, St. Louis, Mo. Free safety Missouri 1994-96. No pro playing experience. College coach: Missouri 1998-99, Sam Houston State 2000, Iowa State 2001-05. Pro coach: Joined Bills in 2006.

Joe D'Alessandris, offensive line; born April, 29, 1954, Aliquippa, Pa. Guard Western Carolina 1972-76. No pro playing experience. College coach: Western Carolina 1977-78, Livingston 1979-1983, Memphis 1984-85, Tennessee-Chattanooga 1986-89, Samford 1993, Texas A&M 1994, Pittsburgh 1996, Duke 1997-2001, Georgia Tech 2002-07. Pro coach: Ottawa Rough Riders (CFL) 1990, Birmingham Fire (WLAF) 1991-92, Memphis (AFL) 1995, Kansas City Chiefs 2008-09, joined Bills in 2010.

Daryl Daye, asst. to the head coach; born February 1, 1963, Las Cruces, N.M. Linebacker Louisiana State 1981-85. No pro playing experience. College coach: Louisiana State 1986-88, Southern Mississippi 1989-1990, Liberty University 1991-98, Nicholls State 1999-2003, Louisiana State 2004, Southern University 2005, Missouri Southern State 2006-09. Pro coach: Joined Bills in 2010.

Bruce DeHaven, special teams coordinator; born September 6, 1948, Trousdale, Kan. Attended Southwestern (Kan.) College. No college or pro playing experience. College coach: Kansas 1979-1981, New Mexico State 1982. Pro coach: New Jersey Generals (USFL) 1983, Pittsburgh Maulers (USFL) 1984, Orlando Renegades (USFL) 1985, Buffalo Bills 1987-1999, San Francisco 49ers 2000-02, Dallas Cowboys 2003-06, Seattle Seahawks 2007-09, re-joined Bills in 2010.

George Edwards, defensive coordinator; born January 16, 1967, Siler City, N.C. Linebacker Duke 1985-89. No pro playing experience. College coach: Florida 1990-91, Appalachian State 1992-95, Duke 1996, Georgia 1997. Pro coach: Dallas Cowboys 1998-2001, Washington Redskins 2002-03, Cleveland Browns 2004, Miami Dolphins 2005-09, joined Bills in 2010.

John Gamble, co-head strength and conditioning; born June 26, 1957, Richmond, Va. Linebacker Hampton 1975-78. No pro playing experience. College coach: Virginia 1982-1993. Pro coach: Miami Dolphins 1994-2005, joined Bills in 2010.

Stan Hixon, wide receivers; born July 24, 1957, Lakeland, Fla. Wide receiver Iowa State 1975-78. No pro playing experience. College coach: Morehead State 1980-82, Appalachian State 1983-88, South Carolina 1989-1992, Wake Forest 1993-94, Georgia Tech 1995-99, Louisiana State 2000-03. Pro coach: Washington Redskins 2004-09, joined Bills in 2010.

Bobby Johnson, asst. offensive line; born February 28, 1963, Akron, Ohio. Offensive line Miami (Ohio) 1992-94. No pro playing experience. College coach: Akron 1995-98, Miami (Ohio) 1999-2004, Indiana 2005-09. Pro coach: Joined Bills in 2010.

Stan Kwan, asst. special teams; born November 2, 1967, Phoenix. Attended South Mountain (Ariz.) C.C., San Diego State. No college or pro playing experience. Pro coach: San Diego Chargers 1991-96, Detroit Lions 1997-2000, Arizona Cardinals 2001-03, Detroit Lions 2004-09, joined Bills in 2010.

Curtis Modkins, offensive coordinator/ running backs; born November 15, 1970, Marlin, Texas. Running back Texas Christian 1989-1992. No pro playing experience. College coach: Texas Christian 1995-97, New Mexico 1998-2001, Georgia Tech 2002-07. Pro coach: Kansas City Chiefs 2008, Arizona Cardinals 2009, joined Bills in 2010.

Kevin Patullo, offensive quality control; born July 14, 1981, Hillsborough, N.J. Quarterback/wide receiver South Florida 1999-2001. College coach: South Florida 2002-03, Arizona 2004-06. Pro coach: Kansas City Chiefs 2007-2008, joined Bills in 2010.

Bob Sanders, outside linebackers; born December 5, 1953, Jacksonville, N.C. Linebacker Davidson College 1973-75. No pro playing experience. College coach: Georgia Tech 1978, East Carolina 1980-82, Richmond 1983-84, Duke 1985-89, Florida 1990-2000. Pro coach: Miami Dolphins 2001-04, Green Bay Packers 2005-08, joined Bills in 2009.

Giff Smith, defensive line; born October 23, 1968, Atlanta. Defensive end Georgia Southern 1986-1990. No pro playing experience. Attended College coach: Arkansas 1991-93, Georgia 1994-1995, Georgia Southern 1996-98, Tulane 1999-2003, Georgia Tech 2004-09. Pro coach: Joined Bills in 2010.

Adrian White, defensive quality control; born April 6, 1964, Orange Park, Fla. Defensive back Southern Illinois 1983, Florida 1985-86. Pro defensive back: New York Giants 1987-1991, Green Bay Packers 1992, New England Patriots 1993. Pro coach: Rhein Fire (NFLE) 2001-07, joined Bills in 2008.

American Football Conference
North Division
Team Colors: Black, Orange, and White
One Paul Brown Stadium
Cincinnati, Ohio 45202-3492
Telephone: (513) 621-3550
Ticket Office (513) 621-TDTD (8383)

2010 SCHEDULE

PRESEASON

Aug. 8	vs. Dallas, at Canton, OH	8:00
Aug. 15	**Denver**	7:00
Aug. 20	**Philadelphia**	8:00
Aug. 28	at Buffalo	6:30
Sep. 2	at Indianapolis	7:00

REGULAR SEASON

Sep. 12	at New England	1:00
Sep. 19	**Baltimore**	1:00
Sep. 26	at Carolina	1:00
Oct. 3	at Cleveland	1:00
Oct. 10	**Tampa Bay**	1:00
Oct. 17	BYE	
Oct. 24	at Atlanta	1:00
Oct. 31	**Miami**	1:00
Nov. 8	**Pittsburgh** (Mon)	8:30
Nov. 14	at Indianapolis	1:00
Nov. 21	**Buffalo**	1:00
Nov. 25	at New York Jets (Thu)	8:20
Dec. 5	**New Orleans**	1:00
Dec. 12	at Pittsburgh	1:00
Dec. 19	**Cleveland**	1:00
Dec. 26	**San Diego**	* 8:20
Jan. 2	at Baltimore	1:00

** Sunday night games in Weeks 11-17 subject to change*

Stadium: Paul Brown Stadium
(opened in 2000)
• **Capacity:** 65,515
One Paul Brown Stadium
Cincinnati, Ohio 45202-3492
Playing Surface: Synthetic
Training Camp: Georgetown College
Georgetown, KY 40324

PAUL BROWN STADIUM

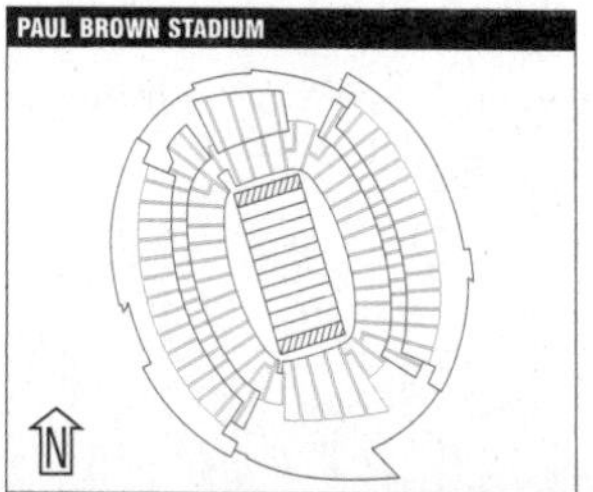

CLUB OFFICIALS

President: Mike Brown
Senior Vice President: Pete Brown
Executive Vice President: Katie Blackburn
Vice President: Paul Brown
Vice President: John Sawyer
Vice President: Troy Blackburn
Business Manager: Bill Connelly
Chief Financial Officer: Bill Scanlon
Director of Business Development: Bob Bedinghaus
Managing Director of Paul Brown Stadium: Eric Brown
Directors of Technology: Michael Kayes, Jo Ann Ralstin
Bengals.com Editor: Geoff Hobson
Director of Security: Rusty Guy
Director of Sales and Public Affairs: Jeff Berding
Director of Corporate Sales and Marketing: Vince Cicero
Ticket Manager: Tim Kelly
Director of Player Relations: Eric Ball
Director of Football Operations: Jim Lippincott
Director of Player Personnel: Duke Tobin
Public Relations Director: Jack Brennan
Athletic Trainer: Paul Sparling
Equipment Manager: Jeff Brickner
Video Director: Travis Brammer

COACHING HISTORY
(287-369-2)

Records include postseason games

1968-1975	Paul Brown	55-59-1
1976-78	Bill Johnson*	18-15-0
1978-79	Homer Rice	8-19-0
1980-83	Forrest Gregg	34-27-0
1984-1991	Sam Wyche	64-68-0
1992-96	Dave Shula**	19-52-0
1996-2000	Bruce Coslet***	21-39-0
2000-02	Dick LeBeau	12-33-0
2003-09	Marvin Lewis	56-57-1

* Resigned after five games in 1978
** Released after seven games in 1996
*** Resigned after three games in 2000

PAID ATTENDANCE

Home 495,803 Away 512,394
Total 1,008,197
Single-game home record, 66,188 (10/28/07)
Single-season home record, 516,154 (2006)

2010 DRAFT CHOICES

Round	Name	Pos.	College
1	Jermaine Gresham	TE	Oklahoma
2	Carlos Dunlap	DE	Florida
3	Jordan Shipley	WR	Texas
	Brandon Ghee	CB	Wake Forest
4	Geno Atkins	DT	Georgia
	Roddrick Muckelroy	LB	Texas
5	Otis Hudson	G	Eastern Illinois
6	Dezmon Briscoe	WR	Kansas
7	Reggie Stephens	C	Iowa State

CINCINNATI BENGALS

2009 TEAM RECORD

PRESEASON (2-2)

Date	Result		Opponent
8/14	L	7-17	at New Orleans
8/20	W	7-6	at New England
8/27	L	21-24	St. Louis
9/3	W	38-7	Indianapolis

REGULAR SEASON (10-6)

Date	Result		Opponent
9/13	L	7-12	Denver
9/20	W	31-24	at Green Bay
9/27	W	23-20	Pittsburgh
10/4	W	23-20	at Cleveland (OT)
10/11	W	17-14	at Baltimore
10/18	L	17-28	Houston
10/25	W	45-10	Chicago
11/8	W	17-7	Baltimore
11/15	W	18-12	at Pittsburgh
11/22	L	17-20	at Oakland
11/29	W	16-7	Cleveland
12/6	W	23-13	Detroit
12/13	L	10-30	at Minnesota
12/20	L	24-27	at San Diego
12/27	W	17-10	Kansas City
1/3	L	0-37	at New York Jets

(OT) Overtime

REGULAR SEASON (0-1)

1/9	L	14-24	N.Y. Jets

SCORE BY PERIODS

Bengals	61	118	49	74	3	— 305
Opponents	55	96	61	79	0	— 291

2009 TEAM STATISTICS

	Bengals	Opp.
Total First Downs	295	276
Rushing	109	95
Passing	159	165
Penalty	27	16
3rd Down: Made/Att	93/229	81/210
3rd Down Pct.	40.6	38.6
4th Down: Made/Att	10/14	7/15
4th Down Pct.	71.4	46.7
Possession Avg.	31:59	28:01
Total Net Yards	4946	4822
Avg. Per Game	309.1	301.4
Total Plays	1011	980
Avg. Per Play	4.9	4.9
Net Yards Rushing	2056	1573
Avg. Per Game	128.5	98.3
Total Rushes	505	399
Net Yards Passing	2890	3249
Avg. Per Game	180.6	203.1
Sacked/Yards Lost	29/244	34/237
Gross Yards	3134	3486
Att./Completions	477/286	547/318
Completion Pct.	60.0	58.1
Had Intercepted	13	19
Punts/Average	86/43.2	83/43.9
Net Punting Avg.	86/36.3	83/35.3
Penalties/Yards	114/863	99/767
Fumbles/Ball Lost	24/12	17/6
Touchdowns	34	32
Rushing	9	12
Passing	21	18
Returns	4	2

2009 INDIVIDUAL STATISTICS

PASSING	Att.	Comp.	Yds.	Pct.	TD	Int.	Tkld.	Rate
C. Palmer	466	282	3094	60.5	21	13	26/213	83.6
O'Sullivan	11	4	40	36.4	0	0	3/31	47.5
Bengals	477	286	3134	60.0	21	13	29/244	82.7
Opponents	547	318	3486	58.1	18	19	34/237	73.6

SCORING	TD R	TD P	TD Rt	PAT	FG	Saf	PTS
Graham	0	0	0	28/29	23/28	0	97
Ochocinco	0	9	0	0/0	0/0	0	54
Benson	6	0	0	0/0	0/0	0	36
Coles	0	5	0	0/0	0/0	0	30
C. Palmer	3	0	0	0/0	0/0	0	20
Caldwell	0	3	0	0/0	0/0	0	18
Foschi	0	2	0	0/0	0/0	0	12
Henry	0	2	0	0/0	0/0	0	12
Fanene	0	0	1	0/0	0/0	0	6
Geathers	0	0	1	0/0	0/0	0	6
Joseph	0	0	1	0/0	0/0	0	6
Scott	0	0	1	0/0	0/0	0	6
Leonard	0	0	0	0/0	0/0	0	2
Bengals	9	21	4	28/29	23/28	0	305
Opponents	12	18	2	30/30	23/29	0	291

2-Pt. Conversions: Leonard, C. Palmer. Bengals 2-5, Opponents 0-2.

RUSHING	No.	Yds	Avg	LG	TD
Benson	301	1251	4.2	42	6
Scott	74	321	4.3	61	0
L. Johnson TM	46	204	4.4	27	0
C. Palmer	39	93	2.4	15	3
Leonard	27	84	3.1	11	0
Ochocinco	3	32	10.7	26	0
Caldwell	3	22	7.3	15	0
Crocker	1	21	21.0	21	0
O'Sullivan	3	12	4.0	6	0
Coles	2	10	5.0	8	0
Je. Johnson	4	8	2.0	4	0
Huber	1	0	0.0	0	0
Cosby	1	-2	-2.0	-2	0
Bengals	505	2056	4.1	61	9
Opponents	399	1573	3.9	57	12

RECEIVING	No.	Yds	Avg	LG	TD
Ochocinco	72	1047	14.5	50	9
Caldwell	51	432	8.5	24	3
Coles	43	514	12.0	40	5
Leonard	30	217	7.2	18	0
Foschi	27	260	9.6	27	2
Benson	17	111	6.5	19	0
Coats	16	150	9.4	23	0
Henry	12	236	19.7	73	2
Je. Johnson	6	41	6.8	9	0
Scott	5	67	13.4	23	0
Cosby	4	55	13.8	23	0
L. Johnson TM	3	4	1.3	6	0
Bengals	286	3134	11.0	73	21
Opponents	318	3486	11.0	87t	18

INTERCEPTIONS	No.	Yds	Avg	LG	TD
Joseph	6	92	15.3	32	1
Hall	6	47	7.8	26	0
Crocker	2	38	19.0	20	0
Fanene	1	45	45.0	45t	1
Rucker	1	26	26.0	26	0
Ndukwe	1	9	9.0	9	0
Nelson	1	2	2.0	2	0
Rivers	1	0	0.0	0	0
Bengals	19	259	13.6	45t	2
Opponents	13	184	14.2	52t	2

PUNTING	No.	Yds.	Avg.	In 20	LG
Huber	86	3713	43.2	24	61
Bengals	86	3713	43.2	24	61
Opponents	83	3641	43.9	25	66

PUNT RETURNS	Ret	FC	Yds	Avg	LG	TD
Cosby	40	19	474	11.9	60	0
Bengals	40	19	474	11.9	60	0
Opponents	39	15	393	10.1	50	0

KICKOFF RETURNS	No.	Yds	Avg	LG	TD
Caldwell	29	539	18.6	39	0
Scott	16	504	31.5	96t	1
Cosby	13	239	18.4	31	0
Leonard	2	38	19.0	24	0
Hall	1	22	22.0	22	0
Coles	1	14	14.0	14	0
Bengals	62	1356	21.9	96t	1
Opponents	58	1289	22.2	58	0

FIELD GOALS	1-19	20-29	30-39	40-49	50+
Graham	0/0	10/11	8/10	3/3	2/4
Bengals	0/0	10/11	8/10	3/3	2/4
Opponents	1/1	6/7	8/9	5/5	3/7

SACKS	No.
Odom	8.0
Fanene	6.0
Geathers	3.5
Dh. Jones	3.5
M Johnson	3.0
T. Johnson	2.0
Ndukwe	2.0
B. Johnson	1.5
Maualuga	1.0
Rivers	1.0
Rucker	1.0
Trent	1.0
Sims	0.5
Bengals	34.0
Opponents	29.0

RECORD HOLDERS

INDIVIDUAL RECORDS—CAREER

Category	Name	Performance
Rushing (Yds.)	Corey Dillon, 1997-2003	8,061
Passing (Yds.)	Ken Anderson, 1971-1986	32,838
Passing (TDs)	Ken Anderson, 1971-1986	197
Receiving (No.)	Chad Ochocinco, 2001-09	684
Receiving (Yds.)	Chad Ochocinco, 2001-09	9,952
Interceptions	Ken Riley, 1969-1983	65
Punting (Avg.)	Dave Lewis, 1970-73	43.8
Punt Return (Avg.)	Mike Martin, 1983-89	9.9
Kickoff Return (Avg.)	Lemar Parrish, 1970-77	24.7
Field Goals	Jim Breech, 1980-1992	225
Touchdowns (Tot.)	Pete Johnson, 1977-1983	70
Points	Jim Breech, 1980-1992	1,151
*Sacks	Eddie Edwards, 1977-1988	47.5

INDIVIDUAL RECORDS—SINGLE SEASON

Category	Name	Performance
Rushing (Yds.)	Rudi Johnson, 2005	1,458
Passing (Yds.)	Carson Palmer, 2007	4,131
Passing (TDs)	Carson Palmer, 2005	32
Receiving (No.)	T.J. Houshmandzadeh, 2007	112
Receiving (Yds.)	Chad Ochocinco, 2007	1,440
Interceptions	Deltha O'Neal, 2005	10
Punting (Avg.)	Dave Lewis, 1970	46.2
Punt Return (Avg.)	Lemar Parrish, 1974	18.8
Kickoff Return (Avg.)	Tremain Mack, 1999	27.1
Field Goals	Shayne Graham, 2007	31
Touchdowns (Tot.)	Carl Pickens, 1995	17
Points	Shayne Graham, 2005	131
*Sacks	Eddie Edwards, 1983	13.0

INDIVIDUAL RECORDS—SINGLE GAME

Category	Name	Performance
Rushing (Yds.)	Corey Dillon, 10-22-00	278
Passing (Yds.)	Boomer Esiason, 10-7-90	490
Passing (TDs)	Carson Palmer, 9-16-07	6
Receiving (No.)	Carl Pickens, 10-11-98	13
Receiving (Yds.)	Chad Ochocinco, 11-12-06	260
Interceptions	Many times	3
	Last time by Leon Hall, 12-21-08	
Field Goals	Shayne Graham, 11-11-07	7
Touchdowns (Tot.)	Larry Kinnebrew, 10-28-84	4
	Corey Dillon, 12-4-97	4
Points	Larry Kinnebrew, 10-28-84	24
	Corey Dillon, 12-4-97	24
*Sacks	Antwan Odom, 9-20-09	5.0

**Sacks became an official statistic in 1982.*

CINCINNATI BENGALS

2010 VETERAN ROSTER

No.	Name	Pos.	Ht.	Wt.	Birthdate	NFL Exp.	College	Hometown	How Acq.	'09 Games/ Starts
32	Benson, Cedric	HB	5-11	225	12/28/82	6	Texas	Midland, Texas	FA-'08	13/13
81	Bryant, Antonio	WR	6-1	205	3/9/81	8	Pittsburgh	Miami, Fla.	UFA(TB)-'10	13/11*
87	Caldwell, Andre	WR	6-0	200	4/15/85	3	Florida	Tampa, Fla.	D3b-'08	16/3
86	Coats, Daniel	TE	6-3	264	4/16/84	4	Brigham Young	Layton, Utah	FA-'07	16/11
80	Coffman, Chase	TE	6-6	257	11/10/86	2	Missouri	Peculiar, Mo.	D3b-'09	0*
73	Collins, Anthony	T	6-5	315	11/2/85	3	Kansas	Beaumont, Texas	D4-'08	14/7
64	Cook, Kyle	C	6-3	312	7/25/83	3	Michigan State	Macomb, Mich.	FA-'07	16/16
12	Cosby, Quan	WR	5-9	196	12/23/82	2	Texas	Mart, Texas	FA-'09	16/0
42	Crocker, Chris	S	5-11	200	3/9/80	8	Marshall	Chesapeake, Va.	FA-'08	13/13
16	Davis, Chris	WR	5-10	181	1/23/84	3	Florida State	St. Petersburg, Fla.	FA-'10	0*
68	Fanene, Jonathan	DE/DT	6-4	292	3/19/82	6	Utah	Pago Pago, American Samoa	D7-'05	16/10
91	Geathers, Robert	DE	6-3	280	8/11/83	7	Georgia	Georgetown, S.C.	D4b-'04	15/15
17	#Graham, Shayne	K	6-0	205	12/9/77	10	Virginia Tech	Dublin, Va.	W(Car)-'03	16/0
29	Hall, Leon	CB	5-11	199	12/9/84	4	Michigan	Vista, Calif.	D1-'07	16/16
46	Harris, Clark	LS/TE	6-5	257	7/10/84	2	Rutgers	Manahawkin, N.J.	FA-'09	11/0
95	Harris, Orien	DT	6-3	300	6/3/83	3	Miami	Newark, Del.	FA-'09	4/0
34	Hebert, Kyries	S	6-3	220	10/9/80	3	Louisiana-Lafayette	Lafayette, La.	FA-'08	15/0
52	Hodge, Abdul	LB	6-0	240	9/9/82	5	Iowa	Lauderdale Lakes, Fla.	FA-'08	16/0
10	Huber, Kevin	P	6-1	210	7/16/85	2	Cincinnati	Cincinnati, Ohio	D5-'09	16/0
53	Jeanty, Rashad	LB	6-2	247	4/17/83	5	Central Florida	Miami, Fla.	FA-'06	15/1
59	Johnson, Brandon	LB	6-5	243	4/5/83	5	Louisville	Birmingham, Ala.	FA-'08	16/3
23	#Johnson, Jeremi	FB	5-11	275	9/4/80	8	Western Kentucky	Louisville, Ky.	FA-'09	16/8
93	Johnson, Michael	DE	6-7	260	2/7/87	2	Georgia Tech	Selma, Ala.	D3a-'09	16/0
99	Johnson, Tank	DT	6-3	305	12/7/81	7	Washington	Tempe, Ariz.	UFA(Dall)-'09	14/13
24	Jones, Adam	CB	5-10	186	9/30/83	4	West Virginia	Atlanta, Ga.	FA-'10	0*
20	Jones, David	CB	6-0	196	9/19/85	4	Wingate	Greenville, S.C.	W(NO)-'07	12/0
57	Jones, Dhani	LB	6-1	240	2/22/78	11	Michigan	Potomac, Md.	FA-'07	16/16
18	Jones, Matt	WR	6-6	218	4/22/83	5	Arkansas	Fort Smith, Ark.	FA-'10	0*
22	Joseph, Johnathan	CB	5-11	193	4/16/84	5	South Carolina	Rock Hill, S.C.	D1-'06	16/16
82	#Kelly, Reggie	TE	6-4	256	2/22/77	12	Mississippi State	Aberdeen, Miss.	UFA(Atl)-'03	0*
40	Leonard, Brian	HB	6-1	230	2/3/84	4	Rutgers	Gouverneur, N.Y.	T(StL)-'09	14/1
62	Livings, Nate	G	6-5	330	3/16/82	3	Louisiana State	Lake Charles, La.	FA-'06	14/9
50	Luigs, Jonathan	C	6-4	315	8/11/86	2	Arkansas	Little Rock, Ark.	D4-'09	8/0
66	Mathis, Evan	G	6-5	295	11/1/81	6	Alabama	Homewood, Ala.	FA-'08	13/7
58	Maualuga, Rey	LB	6-2	255	1/20/87	2	Southern California	Eureka, Calif.	D2-'09	15/15
41	Ndukwe, Chinedum	S	6-2	224	3/4/85	4	Notre Dame	Powell, Ohio	D7b-'07	16/12
43	Nelson, Tom	S	5-11	203	12/4/86	2	Illinois State	Arlington Heights, Ill.	CFA-'09	12/3
2	Nugent, Mike	K	5-10	190	3/2/82	6	Ohio State	Centerville, Ohio	FA-'10	6/0*
85	Ochocinco, Chad	WR	6-1	192	1/9/78	10	Oregon State	Miami, Fla.	D2-'01	16/15
98	Odom, Antwan	DE	6-5	280	9/24/81	7	Alabama	Bayou La Batre, Ala.	UFA(Tenn)-'08	6/6
4	O'Sullivan, J.T.	QB	6-2	230	8/25/79	8	California, Davis	Burbank, Calif.	UFA(SF)-'09	3/0
9	Palmer, Carson	QB	6-5	235	12/27/79	8	Southern California	Mission Viejo, Calif.	D1-'03	16/16
5	Palmer, Jordan	QB	6-5	235	5/30/84	3	Texas-El Paso	Mission Viejo, Calif.	FA-'08	0*
94	Peko, Domata	DT	6-3	318	11/27/84	5	Michigan State	Pago Pago, American Samoa	D4-'06	11/11
26	Ratliff, Keiwan	CB	5-11	188	4/19/81	7	Florida	Columbus, Ohio	FA-'09	8/0*
3	Rayner, Dave	K	6-2	210	10/26/82	4	Michigan State	Oxford, Mich.	FA-'10	0*
55	Rivers, Keith	LB	6-2	240	5/5/86	3	Southern California	Lake Mary, Fla.	D1-'08	13/13
74	Roland, Dennis	T	6-9	325	3/10/83	3	Georgia	Bolivar, Mo.	FA-'08	16/12
92	Rucker, Frostee	DE	6-3	285	9/14/83	5	Southern California	Tustin, Calif.	D3-'06	12/1
65	Santucci, Dan	C	6-4	304	9/6/83	4	Notre Dame	Harwood Heights, Ill.	PS(Ind)-'07	0*
28	Scott, Bernard	HB	5-10	200	2/10/84	2	Abilene Christian	Vernon, Texas	D6b-'09	13/2
70	Shirley, Jason	G	6-5	338	9/30/85	2	Fresno State	Fontana, Calif.	D5-'08	0*
89	Simpson, Jerome	WR	6-2	195	2/4/86	3	Coastal Carolina	Reidsville, N.C.	D2--'08	2/0
90	Sims, Pat	DT	6-2	325	11/29/85	3	Auburn	Fort Lauderdale, Fla.	D3a-'08	16/8
51	Skuta, Dan	LB	6-2	251	4/21/86	2	Grand Valley State	Flint, Mich.	FA-'09	8/0
71	Smith, Andre	T	6-4	335	1/25/87	2	Alabama	Birmingham, Ala.	D1-'09	6/1
25	Trent, Morgan	CB	6-1	195	12/14/85	2	Michigan	San Diego, Calif.	D6a-'09	16/0
37	Vakapuna, Fui	FB	6-0	260	3/9/84	2	Brigham Young	Glendale, Utah	PS(Ariz)-'09	0*
77	Whitworth, Andrew	T	6-7	335	12/12/81	5	Louisiana State	West Monroe, La.	D2-'06	16/16
63	Williams, Bobbie	G	6-4	345	9/25/76	11	Arkansas	Jefferson, Texas	UFA(Phil)-'04	16/16
31	Williams, Roy	S	6-0	222	8/14/80	9	Oklahoma	Union City, Calif.	FA-'09	4/4
27	Wilson, Gibril	S	6-0	205	11/12/81	7	Tennessee	San Jose, Calif.	FA-'10	16/14*

* Bryant played 13 games with Tampa Bay in '09; Coffman inactive for 12 games and on Reserve/Injured for 4 games; Davis last active with Tennessee in '08; A. Jones last active with Dallas in '08; M. Jones last active with Jacksonville in '08; Kelly missed '09 season because of injury; Nugent played 4 games with Tampa Bay and 2 games with Arizona; J. Palmer inactive third quarterback for 16 games; Ratliff played 8 games with Pittsburgh; Rayner last active with Cincinnati in '08; Santucci missed '09 season because of injury; Shirley missed '08 season because of injury; Vakapuna inactive for 9 games; Wilson played 16 games with Miami.

\# Unrestricted free agent; subject to developments.

Players lost through free agency (1): HB Larry Johnson (Wash; 7 games in '09).

Also played with Bengals in '09—WR Laveranues Coles (16 games), TE J.P. Foschi (15), WR Chris Henry (8), TE Darius Hill (1), G Scott Kooistra (4), S Rico Murray (4), CB Geoffrey Pope (4), WR Maurice Purify (5), LS/TE Brad St. Louis (5), DT Shaun Smith (3).

2010 FIRST-YEAR ROSTER

Name	Pos.	Ht.	Wt.	Birthdate	College	Hometown	How Acq.
Alem, Rahim	DE	6-3	251	2/25/87	Louisiana State	New Orleans, La.	FA
Atkins, Geno	DT	6-1	293	3/28/88	Georgia	Pembroke Pines, Fla.	D4a
Briscoe, Dezmon	WR	6-2	207	8/31/89	Kansas	Dallas, Texas	D6
Brown, Freddie (1)	WR	6-4	198	6/24/86	Utah	La Verne, Calif.	FA-'09
Dunlap, Carlos	DE	6-6	277	2/28/89	Florida	North Charleston, S.C.	D2
Eason, Cordera	HB	6-0	226	9/7/87	Mississippi	Meridian, Miss.	FA
Evans, Bryan	S	5-11	193	12/12/86	Georgia	Jacksonville, Fla.	FA
Ghee, Brandon	CB	6-0	192	6/6/87	Wake Forest	Fayetteville, N.C.	D3b
Gresham, Jermaine	TE	6-5	261	6/16/88	Oklahoma	Ardmore, Okla.	D1
Hill, Darius (1)	TE	6-7	245	8/26/85	Ball State	Blue Springs, Mo.	FA-'09
Hudson, Otis	G	6-5	320	7/19/86	Eastern Illinois	Barrington, Ill.	D5
Manns, Gabriel	T	6-6	323	12/9/86	North Carolina Central	Winston-Salem, N.C.	FA
McDonald, Clinton (1)	DT	6-2	290	1/6/87	Memphis	Jacksonville, Ark.	D7b-'09
Miles, Jeromy	S	6-2	210	7/20/87	Massachusetts	Sicklerville, N.J.	FA
Mitchell, Andrew	T	6-5	308	6/12/85	Oklahoma State	Choctaw, Oklahoma	FA
Muckelroy, Roddrick	LB	6-2	246	10/27/86	Texas	Hallsville, Texas	D4b
Murray, Rico (1)	S	5-11	202	8/21/87	Kent State	Cincinnati, Ohio	FA'09
Peerman, Cedric (1)	HB	5-9	210	10/10/86	Virginia	Gladys, Va.	W(Det)
Purify, Maurice (1)	WR	6-3	226	1/17/86	Nebraska	Eureka, Calif.	FA-'08
Rey, Vincent	LB	6-2	240	9/6/87	Duke	Far Rockaway, N.Y.	FA
Richardson, Jake	P	6-1	198	10/5/85	Miami (Ohio)	Oxford, Ohio	FA
Shipley, Jordan	WR	6-0	193	12/23/85	Texas	Burnet, Texas	D3a
Stephens, Reggie	C	6-3	314	8/28/87	Iowa State	Rowlett, Texas	D7
Tronzo, Joe	FB	5-11	242	6/10/87	Louisville	Louisville, Ky.	FA
Willingham, DeAngelo (1)	S	6-0	200	1/15/87	Tennessee	Calhoun, S.C.	W(Sea)
Windt, Mike	LS	6-1	251	5/29/86	Cincinnati	Cincinnati, Ohio	FA

The term NFL Rookie is defined as a player who is in his first season of professional football and has not been on the roster of another professional football team for any regular-season or postseason games. A Rookie is designated by an "R" on NFL rosters. Players who have been active in another professional football league or players who have NFL experience, including either preseason training camp or being on an Active List or Inactive List, or on Reserve/Injured or Reserve/Physically Unable to Perform for fewer than six regular-season games, are termed NFL First-Year Players. An NFL First-Year Player is designated by a "1" on NFL rosters. Thereafter, a player is credited with an additional year of experience for each season in which he accumulates six games on the Active List or Inactive List, or on Reserve/Injured or Reserve/Physically Unable to Perform.

Log on to www.bengals.com for an up-to-date roster.

CINCINNATI BENGALS

COACHING STAFF

Head Coach,
Marvin Lewis

Pro Career: After establishing himself as a record-setting NFL defensive coordinator, Lewis was named the ninth head coach in Bengals history on January 14, 2003. Last season, he directed his second AFC North Division championship for Cincinnati, as the team posted a 10-6 record that included the franchise's first-ever unbeaten record (6-0) in division play. He was named NFL Coach of the Year by the Associated Press and by *Pro Football Weekly*/Pro Football Writers of America. Now in his eighth season, Lewis ties Bengals founder Paul Brown (1968-1975) and Sam Wyche (1984-1991) for most seasons as Bengals head coach. He is tied for ninth place among active NFL head coaches for most career seasons as an NFL head coach. He has posted 56 wins in his first seven seasons, second in Bengals history, and he could pass Wyche (64) into first place with nine wins in 2010. Lewis' other division championship season for Cincinnati was in 2005. Prior to joining the Bengals, Lewis was Washington Redskins defensive coordinator (2002), serving as assistant head coach in addition to his coordinator's role. He spent six seasons (1996-2001) as defensive coordinator with the Baltimore Ravens, a tenure that included a Super Bowl victory in the 2000 season. In 2000, Lewis' defense set the NFL record for fewest points allowed in a 16-game campaign (165), and the unit has been widely considered as one of the best NFL defenses of all time. Baltimore's 970 rushing yards allowed in 2000 was the fewest in NFL history for a 16-game season. The Ravens' four shutouts were the most in the NFL since 1976. Prior to joining Baltimore, Lewis spent four seasons (1992-95) with the Pittsburgh Steelers as linebackers coach, guiding the careers of Pro Bowl selections Chad Brown, Kevin Greene, Levon Kirkland and Gregg Lloyd. Career record: 56-57-1.

Background: Earned All-Big Sky Conference honors as a linebacker at Idaho State (1978-1980), and saw action at quarterback and free safety. Received his bachelor's degree in physical education from Idaho State in 1981, and earned his Master's degree in athletic administration in 1982. Inducted into Idaho State's Hall of Fame in 2001. Began his coaching career at Idaho State (1981-84). The team finished 12-1 during his first season and won the NCAA Division I-AA championship. Was also the linebackers coach at Long Beach State (1985-86), New Mexico (1987-89), and Pittsburgh (1990-91).

Personal: Born September 23, 1958, McDonald, Pa. Lewis and his wife, Peggy, have two children—Whitney and Marcus.

ASSISTANT COACHES

Paul Alexander, asst. head coach/offensive line; born February 12, 1960, Rochester, N.Y. Tackle Cortland State 1979-1981. No pro playing experience. College coach: Penn State 1982-84, Michigan 1985-86, Central Michigan 1987-1991. Pro coach: New York Jets 1992-93, joined Bengals in 1994.

Jim Anderson, running backs; born March 27, 1948, Harrisburg, Pa. Linebacker/defensive end California Western 1967-69. No pro playing experience. College coach: California Western 1970-71, Scottsdale (Ariz.) C.C. 1973, Nevada-Las Vegas 1974-75, Southern Methodist 1976-1980, Stanford 1981-83. Pro coach: Joined Bengals in 1984.

Bob Bratkowski, offensive coordinator; born December 2, 1955, San Angelo, Texas. Wide receiver Washington State 1975-77. No pro playing experience. College coach: Missouri 1978-1980, Weber State 1981-85, Wyoming 1986, Washington State 1987-88, Miami 1989-1991. Pro coach: Seattle Seahawks 1992-98, Pittsburgh Steelers 1999-2000, joined Bengals in 2001.

Kyle Caskey, offensive quality control; born Dec. 7, 1978, Daingerfield, Texas. Tight end Texas A&M 1997-98. No pro playing experience. College coach: Louisiana-Monroe 2004-05, Indiana State 2006-08, Mississippi 2009. Pro coach: Joined Bengals in 2010.

Louie Cioffi, asst. defensive backs; born September 21, 1973, Greenlawn, N.Y. Attended SUNY-Stony Brook. No college or pro playing experience. College coach: C.W. Post 1995-96. Pro coach: New York Jets 1993-94, joined Bengals in 1997.

Kevin Coyle, defensive backs; born January 14, 1956, Staten Island, N.Y. Defensive back Massachusetts 1975-77. No pro playing experience. College coach: Cincinnati 1978-79, Arkansas 1980, U.S. Merchant Marine Academy 1981, Holy Cross 1982-1990, Syracuse 1991-93, Maryland 1994-96, Fresno State 1997-2000. Pro coach: Joined Bengals in 2001.

Jeff FitzGerald, linebackers; born April 18, 1960, Burbank, Calif. Linebacker Oregon State 1980. No pro playing experience. College coach: Cincinnati 1985, Alabama 1986-89, San Diego State 1994-97. Pro coach: Tampa Bay Buccaneers 1990-93, Washington Redskins 1998-99, Arizona Cardinals 2000-03, Baltimore Ravens 2004-07, joined Bengals in 2008.

Jeff Friday, asst. strength and conditioning; born Oct. 11, 1966, Milwaukee, Wis. Attended Wisconsin-Milwaukee. No college or pro playing experience. College coach: Illinois State 1990-91, Northwestern 1992-95. Pro coach: Minnesota Vikings 1996-98, Baltimore Ravens 1999-2007, joined Bengals in 2010.

Paul Guenther, staff assistant; born Nov. 22, 1971, Richboro, Pa. Linebacker Ursinus College 1990-93. No pro playing experience. College coach: Western Maryland 1994-95, Ursinus College 1996, 1997-2001 (head coach 1997-2001), Jacksonville 1997. Pro coach: Washington Redskins 2002-03, joined Bengals in 2005.

Jay Hayes, defensive line; born March 3, 1960, South Fayette, Pa. Defensive end Idaho 1978-1981. Pro defensive end/linebacker Michigan Panthers (USFL) 1984, Memphis Showboats (USFL) 1985. College coach: Notre Dame 1988-1991, California 1992-94, Wisconsin 1995-98. Pro coach: Pittsburgh Steelers 1999-2001, Minnesota Vikings 2002, joined Bengals in 2003.

Jonathan Hayes, tight ends; born Aug. 11, 1962, South Fayette, Pa. Linebacker/tight end Iowa 1981-84. Pro tight end Kansas City Chiefs 1985-1993, Pittsburgh Steelers 1994-96. College coach: Oklahoma 1999-2002. Pro coach: Joined Bengals in 2003.

Chip Morton, strength and conditioning; born November 27, 1962, Hamden, Conn. Attended North Carolina. No college or pro playing experience. College coach: Ohio State 1985-86, Penn State 1987-1991. Pro coach: San Diego Chargers 1992-94, Carolina Panthers 1995-98, Baltimore Ravens 1999-2001, Washington Redskins 2002, joined Bengals in 2003.

Mike Sheppard, wide receivers; born October 29, 1951, Tulsa, Okla. Wide receiver Cal Lutheran 1969-1972. No pro playing experience. College coach: Cal Lutheran 1974-76, Brigham Young 1977-78, U.S. International 1979, Idaho State 1980-81, Long Beach State 1982, 1984-86, Kansas 1983, New Mexico 1987-1991, California 1992. Pro coach: Cleveland Browns 1993-95, Baltimore Ravens 1996, San Diego Chargers 1997-98, Seattle Seahawks 1999-2000, Buffalo Bills 2001, New Orleans Saints 2002-05, joined Bengals in 2007.

Darrin Simmons, special teams; born April 9, 1973, Elkhart, Kan. Punter Kansas 1993-95. No pro playing experience. College coach: Kansas 1996, Minnesota 1997. Pro coach: Baltimore Ravens 1998, Carolina Panthers 1999-2002, joined Bengals in 2003.

Ken Zampese, quarterbacks; born July 19, 1967, Santa Maria, Calif. Wide receiver San Diego 1985-88. No pro playing experience. College coach: San Diego 1989, Southern California 1990-91, Northern Arizona 1992-95, Miami (Ohio) 1996-97. Pro coach: Philadelphia Eagles 1998, Green Bay Packers 1999, St. Louis Rams 2000-02, joined Bengals in 2003.

Mike Zimmer, defensive coordinator; born June 5, 1956, Peoria, Ill. Quarterback/linebacker Illinois State 1974-76. No pro playing experience. College coach: Missouri 1979-1980, Weber State 1981-88, Washington State 1989-1993. Pro coach: Dallas Cowboys 1994-2006, Atlanta Falcons 2007, joined Bengals in 2008.

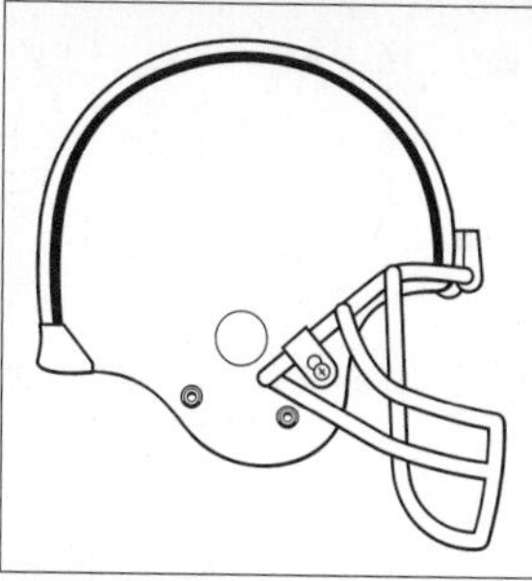

American Football Conference
North Division
Team Colors: Brown, Orange, and White
76 Lou Groza Blvd.
Berea, Ohio 44017
Telephone: (440) 891-5000

2010 SCHEDULE
PRESEASON

Aug. 14	at Green Bay	7:00
Aug. 21	**St. Louis**	7:30
Aug. 28	at Detroit	5:30
Sep. 2	**Chicago**	8:00

REGULAR SEASON

Sep. 12	at Tampa Bay	1:00
Sep. 19	**Kansas City**	1:00
Sep. 26	at Baltimore	1:00
Oct. 3	**Cincinnati**	1:00
Oct. 10	**Atlanta**	1:00
Oct. 17	at Pittsburgh	1:00
Oct. 24	at New Orleans	12:00
Oct. 31	BYE	
Nov. 7	**New England**	1:00
Nov. 14	**New York Jets**	1:00
Nov. 21	at Jacksonville	1:00
Nov. 28	**Carolina**	1:00
Dec. 5	at Miami	1:00
Dec. 12	at Buffalo	1:00
Dec. 19	at Cincinnati	1:00
Dec. 26	**Baltimore**	1:00
Jan. 2	**Pittsburgh**	1:00

Stadium: Cleveland Browns Stadium
(opened in 1999)
• **Capacity:** 73,300
100 Alfred Lerner Way
Cleveland, Ohio 44114
Playing Surface: Grass
Headquarters/Training Camp:
76 Lou Groza Boulevard
Berea, Ohio 44017

CLEVELAND BROWNS STADIUM

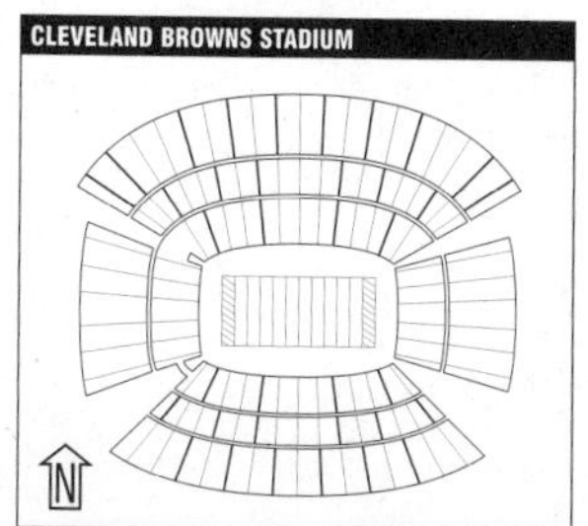

CLUB OFFICIALS
Owner: Randolph D. Lerner
President: Mike Holmgren
General Manager: Tom Heckert
Head Coach: Eric Mangini
Executive Vice President, Business Operations: Bryan Wiedmeier
Senior Advisor to the President: Gil Haskell
General Counsel & Special Counsel to the President: Fred Nance
Executive Advisor: Jim Brown
Senior Vice President: Lew Merletti
Senior Vice President, Finance & Administration: David A. Jenkins
Senior Vice President, Business Development: Jim Ross
Vice President, Integrated Sales & Marketing: Jim Frevola
Vice President, Tickets Sales & Service: Chris Gallagher
Vice President, Media Relations: Neal Gulkis
Vice President, Security: Carl Meyer
Vice President, Sales & Marketing: Brett Reynolds
Vice President, Football Operations: Mark Schiefelbein
Vice President, Football Administration: Matt Thomas
Director, Stadium Operations: Todd Argust
Director, Marketing Communications: Reagan Berube
Director, Video: Chad Bogard
Director, Player Development: Jerry Butler
Director, Information Technology: Brandon Covert
Director, Operations: Phil Dangerfield
Director, Pro Personnel: Keith Gilbertson
Director, Community Relations: Renee Harvey
Director, Corporate Sales & Client Services: Scott Klein
Director, Alumni Relations: Dino Lucarelli
Director, Marketing Services: George Muller
Director, Media Sales: Dana Nagel
Director, Administration: Mike Nikolaus
Director, Client Services: Nicole Peters
Director, Retail and Concessions: Julie Ann Reeder
Director, Suite Operations: Joe Ricciuti
Controller: Laurie Rice
Director, College Scouting: Pat Roberts
Director, Finance: Gregory Rush
Director, Player Personnel: Jon Sandusky
Director, Marketing and Customer Service: John Schulze
Head Athletic Trainer: Joe Sheehan
Head Equipment Manager: Brad Melland
Head Groundskeeper: Chris Powell

COACHING HISTORY
(444-403-10)
Records include postseason games

1950-1962	Paul Brown	115-49-5
1963-1970	Blanton Collier	79-38-2
1971-74	Nick Skorich	30-26-2
1975-77	Forrest Gregg*	18-23-0
1977	Dick Modzelewski	0-1-0
1978-1984	Sam Rutigliano**	47-52-0
1984-88	Marty Schottenheimer	46-31-0
1989-1990	Bud Carson***	12-14-1
1990	Jim Shofner	1-6-0
1991-95	Bill Belichick	37-45-0
1999-2000	Chris Palmer	5-27-0
2001-04	Butch Davis****	24-36-0
2004	Terry Robiskie	1-4-0
2005-08	Romeo Crennel	24-40-0
2009	Eric Mangini	5-11-0

*Resigned after 13 games in 1977
**Released after eight games in 1984
***Released after nine games in 1990
****Resigned after 11 games in 2004

PAID ATTENDANCE
Home 516,748 Away 494,089
Total 1,010,837
Single-game home record, 85,073 (9/21/70)
Single-season home record, 620,496 (1980)

2010 DRAFT CHOICES

Round	Name	Pos.	College
1	Joe Haden	DB	Florida
2	T.J. Ward	DB	Oregon
	Montario Hardesty	RB	Tennessee
3	Colt McCoy	QB	Texas
	Shawn Lauvao	G	Arizona St.
5	Larry Asante	DB	Nebraska
6	Carlton Mitchell	WR	South Florida
	Clifton Geathers	DE	South Carolina

CLEVELAND BROWNS

2009 TEAM RECORD

PRESEASON (2-2)

Date	Result	Opponent
8/15	L 0-17	at Green Bay
8/22	W 27-10	Detroit
8/29	W 23-17	Tennessee
9/3	L 23-26	at Chicago

REGULAR SEASON (5-11)

Date	Result	Opponent
9/13	L 20-34	Minnesota
9/20	L 6-27	at Denver
9/27	L 3-34	at Baltimore
10/4	L 20-23	Cincinnati (OT)
10/11	W 6-3	at Buffalo
10/18	L 14-27	at Pittsburgh
10/25	L 3-31	Green Bay
11/1	L 6-30	at Chicago
11/16	L 0-16	Baltimore
11/22	L 37-38	at Detroit
11/29	L 7-16	at Cincinnati
12/6	L 23-30	San Diego
12/10	W 13-6	Pittsburgh
12/20	W 41-34	at Kansas City
12/27	W 23-9	Oakland
1/3	W 23-17	Jacksonville

(OT) Overtime

SCORE BY PERIODS

Browns	66	70	46	63	0	— 245
Opponents	65	132	87	88	3	— 375

2009 TEAM STATISTICS

	Browns	Opp.
Total First Downs	237	336
Rushing	102	120
Passing	118	189
Penalty	17	27
3rd Down: Made/Att	76/233	86/221
3rd Down Pct.	32.6	38.9
4th Down: Made/Att	10/15	10/20
4th Down Pct.	66.7	50.0
Possession Avg.	28:28	31:32
Total Net Yards	4163	6229
Avg. Per Game	260.2	389.3
Total Plays	971	1072
Avg. Per Play	4.3	5.8
Net Yards Rushing	2087	2314
Avg. Per Game	130.4	144.6
Total Rushes	498	506
Net Yards Passing	2076	3915
Avg. Per Game	129.8	244.7
Sacked/Yards Lost	30/179	40/234
Gross Yards	2255	4149
Att./Completions	443/219	526/313
Completion Pct.	49.4	59.5
Had Intercepted	18	10
Punts/Average	94/42.3	77/43.1
Net Punting Avg.	94/37.8	77/35.4
Penalties/Yards	77/678	101/812
Fumbles/Ball Lost	21/13	17/9
Touchdowns	25	41
Rushing	10	15
Passing	11	22
Returns	4	4

2009 INDIVIDUAL STATISTICS

PASSING	Att.	Comp.	Yds.	Pct.	TD	Int.	Tkld.	Rate
Quinn	256	136	1339	53.1	8	7	19/104	67.2
D. Anderson	182	81	888	44.5	3	10	11/75	42.1
Cribbs	4	1	18	25.0	0	1	0/0	6.3
Dawson	1	1	10	100.0	0	0	0/0	108.3
Browns	443	219	2255	49.4	11	18	30/179	55.8
Opponents	526	313	4149	59.5	22	10	40/234	90.6

SCORING	TD R	TD P	TD Rt	PAT	FG	Saf	PTS
Dawson	0	0	0	18/19	17/19	0	69
J. Harrison	5	2	0	0/0	0/0	0	42
Cribbs	1	1	4	0/0	0/0	0	36
Cundiff TM	0	0	0	4/4	6/6	0	22
Massaquoi	0	3	0	0/0	0/0	0	18
D. Anderson	2	0	0	0/0	0/0	0	12
Gaines TM	0	1	0	0/0	0/0	0	6
Heiden	0	1	0	0/0	0/0	0	6
Jennings	1	0	0	0/0	0/0	0	6
Quinn	1	0	0	0/0	0/0	0	6
Royal	0	1	0	0/0	0/0	0	6
Stuckey TM	0	1	0	0/0	0/0	0	6
Vickers	0	1	0	0/0	0/0	0	6
Ja. Lewis	0	0	0	0/0	0/0	0	2
Browns	10	11	4	22/23	23/25	1	245
Opponents	15	22	4	39/41	30/36	0	375

2-Pt. Conversions: Ja. Lewis.
Browns 1-2, Opponents 0-0.

RUSHING	No.	Yds	Avg	LG	TD
J. Harrison	194	862	4.4	71t	5
Ja. Lewis	143	500	3.5	18	0
Cribbs	55	381	6.9	37	1
Jennings	63	220	3.5	16	1
Quinn	20	98	4.9	24	1
Davis	9	15	1.7	5	0
D. Anderson	10	8	0.8	3	2
Stuckey TM	2	6	3.0	6	0
Hodges TM	1	0	0.0	0	0
Massaquoi	1	-3	-3.0	-3	0
Browns	498	2087	4.2	71t	10
Opponents	506	2314	4.6	64t	15

RECEIVING	No.	Yds	Avg	LG	TD
Massaquoi	34	624	18.4	59t	3
J. Harrison	34	220	6.5	18	2
Furrey	23	170	7.4	22	0
Cribbs	20	135	6.8	35	1
Stuckey TM	19	198	10.4	40t	1
Moore	12	158	13.2	24	0
Royal	11	134	12.2	29	1
Edwards TM	10	139	13.9	24	0
Heiden	10	73	7.3	14	1
Jennings	9	56	6.2	19	0
Ja. Lewis	8	88	11.0	19	0
Vickers	8	27	3.4	12	1
Robiskie	7	106	15.1	43	0
Gaines TM	5	59	11.8	24	1
Estandia TM	4	45	11.3	18	0
Davis	4	5	1.3	2	0
Quinn	1	18	18.0	18	0
Browns	219	2255	10.3	59t	11
Opponents	313	4149	13.3	75t	22

INTERCEPTIONS	No.	Yds	Avg	LG	TD
E. Wright	4	74	18.5	47	0
Pool	4	33	8.3	32	0
McDonald	1	39	39.0	39	0
Bowens	1	15	15.0	15	0
Browns	10	161	16.1	47	0
Opponents	18	281	15.6	48t	2

PUNTING	No.	Yds.	Avg.	In 20	LG
Zastudil	49	2188	44.7	25	60
Hodges TM	45	1789	39.8	15	54
Browns	94	3977	42.3	40	60
Opponents	77	3322	43.1	26	66

PUNT RETURNS	Ret	FC	Yds	Avg	LG	TD
Cribbs	38	3	452	11.9	67t	1
Lawson	1	0	4	4.0	4	0
Browns	39	3	456	11.7	67t	1
Opponents	40	21	262	6.6	36	0

KICKOFF RETURNS	No.	Yds	Avg	LG	TD
Cribbs	56	1542	27.5	103t	3
Lawson	5	43	8.6	13	0
J. Harrison	3	55	18.3	39	0
Furrey	1	12	12.0	12	0
Estandia TM	1	9	9.0	9	0
Trusnik TM	1	9	9.0	9	0
Elam	1	0	0.0	0	0
Vickers	1	0	0.0	0	0
Browns	69	1670	24.2	103t	3
Opponents	52	984	18.9	46	0

FIELD GOALS	1-19	20-29	30-39	40-49	50+
Dawson	0/0	7/7	5/5	5/6	0/1
Cundiff TM	1/1	4/4	1/1	0/0	0/0
Browns	1/1	11/11	6/6	5/6	0/1
Opponents	1/1	7/8	15/18	5/6	2/3

SACKS	No.
Wimbley	6.5
Bowens	5.5
Roth	4.0
Co. Williams	4.0
Benard	3.5
Maiava	2.5
Trusnik	2.5
Rogers	2.0
Coleman	1.5
Schaefering	1.5
R. Smith	1.5
M Adams	1.0
Elam	1.0
McDonald	1.0
Pool	1.0
Poteat	1.0
Browns	40.0
Opponents	30.0

RECORD HOLDERS

INDIVIDUAL RECORDS—CAREER

Category	Name	Performance
Rushing (Yds.)	Jim Brown, 1957-1965	12,312
Passing (Yds.)	Brian Sipe, 1974-1983	23,713
Passing (TDs)	Brian Sipe, 1974-1983	154
Receiving (No.)	Ozzie Newsome, 1978-1990	662
Receiving (Yds.)	Ozzie Newsome, 1978-1990	7,980
Interceptions	Thom Darden, 1972-74, 1976-1981	45
Punting (Avg.)	Dave Zastudil, 2006-09	44.1
Punt Return (Avg.)	Greg Pruitt, 1973-1981	11.8
Kickoff Return (Avg.)	Joshua Cribbs, 2005-09	26.6
Field Goals	Lou Groza, 1950-59, 1961-67	234
Touchdowns (Tot.)	Jim Brown, 1957-1965	126
Points	Lou Groza, 1950-59, 1961-67	1,349
*Sacks	Clay Matthews, 1978-1993	62.0

INDIVIDUAL RECORDS—SINGLE SEASON

Category	Name	Performance
Rushing (Yds.)	Jim Brown, 1963	1,863
Passing (Yds.)	Brian Sipe, 1980	4,132
Passing (TDs)	Brian Sipe, 1980	30
Receiving (No.)	Ozzie Newsome, 1983	89
	Ozzie Newsome, 1984	89
	Kellen Winslow, 2006	89
Receiving (Yds.)	Braylon Edwards, 2007	1,289
Interceptions	Thom Darden, 1978	10
	Anthony Henry, 2001	10
Punting (Avg.)	Gary Collins, 1965	46.7
Punt Return (Avg.)	Leroy Kelly, 1965	15.6
Kickoff Return (Avg.)	Billy Lefear, 1975	31.7
Field Goals	Phil Dawson, 2008	30
Touchdowns (Tot.)	Jim Brown, 1965	21
Points	Jim Brown, 1965	126
*Sacks	Reggie Camp, 1984	14.0

INDIVIDUAL RECORDS—SINGLE GAME

Category	Name	Performance
Rushing (Yds.)	Jerome Harrison, 12-20-09	286
Passing (TDs)	Frank Ryan, 12-12-64	5
	Bill Nelsen, 11-2-69	5
	Brian Sipe, 10-7-79	5
	Kelly Holcomb, 11-28-04	5
	Derek Anderson, 9-16-07	5
Receiving (No.)	Ozzie Newsome, 10-14-84	14
Receiving (Yds.)	Ozzie Newsome, 10-14-84	191
Interceptions	Many times	3
	Last time by Anthony Henry, 11-18-01	
Field Goals	Phil Dawson, 11-5-06	6
Touchdowns (Tot.)	Dub Jones, 11-25-51	**6
Points	Dub Jones, 11-25-51	36
*Sacks	Andra Davis, 11-9-03	4.0

**Sacks became an official statistic in 1982.*
***NFL Record*

CLEVELAND BROWNS

2010 VETERAN ROSTER

No.	Name	Pos.	Ht.	Wt.	Birthdate	NFL Exp.	College	Hometown	How Acq.	'09 Games/ Starts
20	Adams, Mike	DB	5-11	200	3/24/81	7	Delaware	Paterson, N.J.	UFA(SF)-'07	16/9
85	Allen, Jake	WR	6-4	196	1/18/85	2	Mississippi College	Laurel, Miss.	W(GB)-'09	2/0
50	Barton, Eric	LB	6-3	245	9/29/77	12	Maryland	Alexandria, Va.	UFA(NYJ)-'09	8/8
58	Benard, Marcus	LB	6-2	256	7/26/85	2	Jackson State	Adrian, Mich.	FA-'09	6/0
96	Bowens, David	LB	6-3	265	7/3/77	12	Western Illinois	Detroit, Mich.	UFA(NYJ)-'09	16/15
36	Bowie, John	DB	5-11	190	5/11/84	3	Cincinnati	Columbus, Ohio	FA-'10	3/0*
23	t- Brown, Sheldon	DB	5-10	200	3/19/79	9	South Carolina	Fort Lawn, S.C.	T(Phil)-'10	16/16*
29	Brown, Thomas	RB	5-8	203	5/15/86	2	Georgia	Tucker, Ga.	FA-'08	0*
90	Coleman, Kenyon	DL	6-5	295	4/10/79	9	UCLA	Alta Loma, Calif.	T(NYJ)-'09	13/13
54	Costanzo, Blake	LB	6-1	235	4/14/84	4	Lafayette	Franklin Lakes, N.J.	W(Buff)-'09	16/0
16	Cribbs, Joshua	WR	6-1	215	6/9/83	6	Kent State	Washington, D.C.	FA-'05	16/12
21	Davis, James	RB	5-11	218	1/1/86	2	Clemson	Atlanta, Ga.	D6c-'09	2/0
4	Dawson, Phil	K	5-11	200	1/23/75	12	Texas	Dallas, Texas	FA-'99	11/0
17	Delhomme, Jake	QB	6-2	215	1/10/75	12	Louisiana-Lafayette	Breaux Bridge, La.	FA-'10	11/11*
26	+Elam, Abram	DB	6-0	207	10/15/81	5	Kent State	Riviera Beach, Fla.	T(NYJ)-'09	16/16
88	Estandia, Greg	TE	6-8	266	11/18/82	4	Nevada-Las Vegas	Moorpark, Calif.	W(Jax)-'09	6/0*
25	Francies, Coye	DB	6-0	185	11/15/86	2	San Jose State	Sacramento, Calif.	D6b-'09	6/0
99	Fujita, Scott	LB	6-5	250	4/28/79	9	California	Ventura, Calif.	UFA(NO)-'10	11/10*
	#Furrey, Mike	WR	6-0	195	3/12/77	7	Northern Iowa	Grove City, Ohio	FA-'09	16/4
63	Ghiaciuc, Eric	OL	6-4	303	5/28/81	6	Central Michigan	Oxford, Mich.	FA-'10	16/16*
51	t- Gocong, Chris	LB	6-2	263	11/16/83	5	Cal Poly San Luis Obispo	Santa Barbara, Calif.	T(Phil)-'10	15/11*
35	+Harrison, Jerome	RB	5-9	205	2/26/83	5	Washington State	Kalamazoo, Mich.	D5a-'06	14/7
28	t- Hillis, Peyton	RB	6-2	250	1/21/86	3	Arkansas	Conway, Ark.	T(Den)-'10	14/2*
2	Hodges, Reggie	P	6-0	220	1/26/82	4	Ball State	Champaign, Ill	FA-'09	12/0*
52	+Jackson, D'Qwell	LB	6-0	240	9/26/83	5	Maryland	Largo, Fla.	D2-'06	6/6
34	Jennings, Chris	RB	5-10	218	12/12/85	2	Arizona	Yuma, Ariz.	FA-'09	9/1
74	Kooistra, Scott	OL	6-6	335	10/14/80	8	North Carolina State	Gouverneur, N.Y.	FA-'10	4/0*
30	Lawson, Gerard	DB	5-10	195	1/12/85	3	Oregon State	Las Vegas, Nev.	FA-'08	5/0
61	Lewis, Jonathan	DL	6-0	305	7/12/84	3	Virginia Tech	Richmond, Va.	FA-'09	0*
55	Mack, Alex	OL	6-4	311	11/19/85	2	California	Santa Barbara, Calif.	D1-'09	16/16
56	Maiava, Kaluka	LB	6-0	229	12/27/86	2	Southern California	Wailuku, Hawaii	D4-'09	16/3
11	Massaquoi, Mohamed	WR	6-2	207	11/24/86	2	Georgia	Charlotte, N.C.	D2b-'09	16/11
22	McDonald, Brandon	DB	5-10	185	8/26/85	4	Memphis	Collins, Miss.	D5-'07	16/10
89	Moore, Evan	TE	6-6	247	1/3/85	2	Stanford	Brea, Calif.	FA-'09	5/0
69	Mosley, C.J.	DL	6-3	305	8/6/83	6	Missouri	Fort Leonard Wood, Mo.	UFA(NYJ)-'09	12/1
79	Pashos, Tony	OL	6-6	325	8/3/80	8	Illinois	Palos Heights, Ill.	UFA(SF)-'10	5/1*
64	Pontbriand, Ryan	LS	6-2	255	10/1/79	8	Rice	Houston, Texas	D5a-'03	16/0
	#Poteat, Hank	DB	5-10	195	8/31/77	9	Pittsburgh	Harrisburg, Pa.	UFA(NYJ)-'09	16/2
5	Ratliff, Brett	QB	6-4	224	8/8/85	3	Utah	Chico, Calif.	T(NYJ)-'09	0*
37	Roberson, Chris	DB	5-11	190	6/3/83	4	Eastern Michigan	Detroit, Mich.	FA-'10	0*
67	Robinson, Derreck	DL	6-4	295	3/3/82	4	Iowa	Minneapolis, Minn.	FA-'09	3/0
38	Robinson, Ramzee	DB	5-10	190	2/20/84	4	Alabama	Huntsville, Ala.	W(Phil)-'09	7/0*
80	Robiskie, Brian	WR	6-3	209	12/3/87	2	Ohio State	Cleveland, Ohio	D2a-'09	11/1
92	Rogers, Shaun	DL	6-4	350	3/12/79	10	Texas	LaPorte, Texas	T(Det)-'08	11/11
53	+Roth, Matt	LB	6-4	275	10/14/82	6	Iowa	Villa Park, Ill.	W(Mia)-'09	10/6*
84	Royal, Robert	TE	6-4	257	5/15/79	9	Louisiana State	New Orleans, La.	FA-'09	13/11
71	Rubin, Ahtyba	DL	6-2	330	7/25/86	3	Iowa State	Fort Belvoir, Va.	D6a-'08	16/5
81	Smith, Alex	TE	6-4	258	5/22/82	6	Stanford	Denver, Colo.	FA-'10	16/5*
39	Smith, DeAngelo	DB	5-11	200	7/17/86	2	Cincinnati	Columbus, Ohio	W(Det)-'10	7/0*
98	Smith, Robaire	DL	6-5	310	11/15/77	11	Michigan State	Flint, Mich.	UFA(Tenn)-'07	15/15
27	Sorensen, Nick	DB	6-3	210	7/31/78	10	Virginia Tech	Winter Haven, Fla.	FA-'07	16/0
78	St. Clair, John	OL	6-6	320	7/15/77	11	Virginia	Roanoke, Va.	UFA(Chi)-'09	14/14
65	Steinbach, Eric	OL	6-6	295	4/4/80	8	Iowa	Lockport, Ill.	UFA(Cin)-'07	16/16
10	Steptoe, Syndric	WR	5-9	200	12/6/84	3	Arizona	Bryan, Texas	D7b-'07	0*
83	t- Stuckey, Chansi	WR	6-0	196	10/4/83	4	Clemson	Warner Robins, Ga.	T(NYJ)-'09	15/1*
73	Thomas, Joe	OL	6-6	312	12/4/84	4	Wisconsin	Brookfield, Wisc.	D1a-'07	16/16
93	t- Trusnik, Jason	LB	6-4	250	6/6/84	4	Ohio Northern	Macedonia, Ohio	T(NYJ)-'09	16/10*
	#Tucker, Ryan	OL	6-6	315	6/12/75	13	Texas Christian	Midland, Texas	UFA(StL)-'02	0*
57	Veikune, David	LB	6-2	257	12/12/85	2	Hawaii	Wahiawa, Hawaii	D2c-'09	10/0
41	Ventrone, Ray	DB	5-10	200	10/21/82	5	Villanova	Pittsburgh, Pa.	FA-'09	14/0
47	+Vickers, Lawrence	FB	6-0	250	5/8/83	5	Colorado	Houston, Texas	D6a-'06	16/9
6	t- Wallace, Seneca	QB	5-11	205	8/6/80	8	Iowa State	Sacramento, Calif.	T(Sea)-'10	13/2*
82	Watson, Benjamin	TE	6-3	255	12/18/80	7	Georgia	Rock Hill, S.C.	UFA(NE)-'10	16/7*
77	Womack, Floyd	OL	6-4	328	11/15/78	10	Mississippi State	Cleveland, Miss.	UFA(Sea)-'09	15/15
24	Wright, Eric	DB	5-10	190	7/24/85	4	Nevada-Las Vegas	San Francisco, Calif.	D2-'07	16/16
68	Yates, Billy	OL	6-2	305	4/15/80	7	Texas A&M	Fort Worth, Texas	FA-'09	6/0
15	Zastudil, Dave	P	6-3	220	10/26/78	9	Ohio University	Bay Village, Ohio	UFA(Balt)-'06	8/0

* Bowie played 3 games with Oakland in '09; S. Brown played 16 games with Philadelphia; T. Brown last active with Atlanta in '08; Delhomme played 11 games with Carolina; Estandia played 2 games with Jacksonville and 4 with Cleveland; Fujita played 11 games with New Orleans; Ghiaciuc played 16 games with Cincinnati; Gocong played 15 games with Philadelphia; Hillis played 14 games with Denver; Hodges played 4 games with Tennessee and 8 games with Cleveland; Kooistra played 4 games with Cincinnati; Lewis last active with Arizona in '06; Pashos played 5 games with San Francisco; Ratliff inactive for 14 games; Roberson missed '09 season with Detroit because of injury; D. Robinson last active with Miami in '07; R. Robinson played 3 games with Philadelphia and 4 games with Cleveland; Roth played 4 games with Miami and 6 games with Cleveland; A. Smith played 16 games with Philadelphia; D. Smith played 7 games with Detroit; Steptoe missed '09 season because of injury; Stuckey played 4 games with N.Y. Jets and 11 games with Cleveland; Trusnik played 4 games with N.Y. Jets and 12 with Cleveland; Tucker missed '09 season because of injury; Wallace played 13 games with Seattle; Watson played 16 games with New England.

\# Unrestricted free agent, subject to developments.

t- Browns traded for S. Brown (Phil), Gocong (Phil), Hillis (Den), Stuckey (NYJ), Trusnik (NYJ), and Wallace (Sea).

Traded—WR Braylon Edwards (4 games in '09) to N.Y. Jets, LB Alex Hall (14) to Philadelphia, QB Brady Quinn (10) to Denver, DL Corey Williams (16) to Detroit, LB Kamerion Wimbley (15) to Oakland.

Players lost through free agency (2): TE Michael Gaines (Hou; 9 games in '09); OL Rex Hadnot (Ariz; 9).

Also played with Browns in '09—QB Derek Anderson (8 games), LB Titus Brown (1), K Billy Cundiff (5), OL Hank Fraley (15), LB Arnold Harrison (4), TE Steve Heiden (7), RB Jamal Lewis (9), DB Anthony Madison (4), DB Brodney Pool (11), DL Brian Schaefering (5), LB Josh Stamer (2).

2010 FIRST-YEAR ROSTER

Name	Pos.	Ht.	Wt.	Birthdate	College	Hometown	How Acq.
Adams, Titus (1)	DL	6-4	305	1/28/83	Nebraska	Omaha, Neb.	W(NE)-'09
Asante, Larry	DB	6-0	210	3/7/88	Nebraska	Alexandria, Va.	D5
Bender, Casey	OL	6-5	295	12/22/86	South Dakota State	Lindsay, Neb.	FA
Brown, Titus (1)	LB	6-3	250	3/27/86	Mississippi State	Tuscaloosa, Ala.	FA-'08
Burney, Benjamin	DB	5-11	205	3/29/87	Colorado	Lone Tree, Colo.	FA
Capizzi, Jason (1)	OL	6-9	330	6/19/83	Indiana (Pa.)	Gibsonia, Pa.	FA-'09
Chancellor, Chris	DB	5-9	180	12/22/86	Clemson	Miami, Fla.	FA
Collins, Jed (1)	RB	6-1	249	3/3/86	Washington State	San Juan Capistrano, Calif.	FA-'09
English, Auston	LB	6-3	250	3/10/87	Oklahoma	Canadian, Texas	FA
Geathers, Cliff	DL	6-7	300	12/11/87	South Carolina	Georgetown, S.C.	D6b
Grennan, Keith (1)	DL	6-4	298	5/20/84	Eastern Washington	Edmonds, Wa.	FA-'09
Haden, Joe	DB	5-11	190	4/14/89	Florida	Fort Washington, Md.	D1
Haggerty, Johnathan	WR	6-1	195	2/5/88	Southwestern Oklahoma State	Dallas, Texas	FA
Hardesty, Montario	RB	6-0	225	2/1/87	Tennessee	New Bern, N.C.	D2b
Lauvao, Shawn	OL	6-3	315	10/26/87	Arizona State	Honolulu, Hawaii	D3b
McCoy, Colt	QB	6-1	215	9/5/86	Texas	Tuscola, Texas	D3a
Miller, Swanson	DL	6-4	310	3/24/86	Oklahoma State	Alachua, Fla.	FA
Mitchell, Carlton	WR	6-3	215	4/6/88	South Florida	Gainesville, Fla.	D6a
Morton, Dion	WR	5-8	160	2/5/86	Colorado State	Riverside, Calif.	FA
Murray, Pat (1)	OL	6-3	316	10/31/84	Truman State	Fort Dodge, Iowa	FA-'09
Reinders, Joel	OL	6-7	320	10/2/87	Waterloo	Oakville, Ontario, Canada	FA
Schaefering, Brian (1)	DL	6-4	295	8/20/83	Lindenwood	St. Louis, Mo.	FA-'09
Ward, T.J.	DB	5-10	200	12/12/86	Oregon	San Francisco, Calif.	D2a

The term NFL Rookie is defined as a player who is in his first season of professional football and has not been on the roster of another professional football team for any regular-season or postseason games. A Rookie is designated by an "R" on NFL rosters. Players who have been active in another professional football league or players who have NFL experience, including either preseason training camp or being on an Active List or Inactive List, or on Reserve/Injured or Reserve/Physically Unable to Perform for fewer than six regular-season games, are termed NFL First-Year Players. An NFL First-Year Player is designated by a "1" on NFL rosters. Thereafter, a player is credited with an additional year of experience for each season in which he accumulates six games on the Active List or Inactive List, or on Reserve/Injured or Reserve/Physically Unable to Perform.

Log on to www.clevelandbrowns.com for an up-to-date roster.

COACHING STAFF

Head Coach, Eric Mangini

Pro Career: Eric Mangini was named the twelfth full-time head coach in Browns history on January 8, 2009. This is Mangini's fifth season as an NFL head coach, having led the Jets (2006-08) to a three-year record of 23-25, before joining the Browns in 2009. In his first season at the helm, Mangini led the Browns to a 5-11 mark, including closing the season with four consecutive victories. The Jets put together winning marks in two of Mangini's three seasons at the helm, including a record of 10-6 in 2006, when the Jets earned the 12th postseason berth in franchise history. Overall, Mangini is entering his 16th season in the NFL. Prior to joining the Jets, he spent six seasons (2000-05) on the staff of the New England Patriots, the first five as defensive backs coach and the final one as defensive coordinator. During Mangini's tenure there, the Patriots captured three Super Bowl titles. Mangini's first NFL coaching position came as an assistant on the Browns' staff in 1995. He moved with the team to Baltimore in 1996, serving as a quality control/offensive assistant for the Ravens that year. He joined Bill Parcells' staff with the Jets in 1997, serving as a defensive assistant/quality control coach for three seasons. While completing his Wesleyan degree in Melbourne, Australia, Mangini served as the head coach and defensive coordinator for the Kewe Colts, a semi-professional football team, and led them to back-to-back titles. Career record: 28-37.

Background: Mangini set a school record with 36.5 sacks as a nose tackle in college for Wesleyan (Conn.) from 1989-1990, 1992-93. He was voted a first-team all-star by NESCAC and ECAC New England Division III.

Personal: Born January 19, 1971, Hartford, Conn. Mangini and his wife, Julie, have three sons, Jake, Luke and Zack.

ASSISTANT COACHES

Gary Brown, running backs; born July 1, 1969, Williamsport, Pa. Running back Penn State 1987-1990. Pro running back Houston Oilers 1991-95, San Diego Chargers 1995, New York Giants 1998-99. College coach: Lycoming 2003-04, Susquehanna 2006-07, Rutgers 2008. Pro coach: New York Giants 2005, joined Browns in 2009.

Bryan Cox, defensive line; born February 17, 1968, East St. Louis, Mo. Linebacker Western Illinois 1987-1990. Pro linebacker Miami Dolphins 1991-95, Chicago Bears 1996-97, New York Jets 1998-2000, New England Patriots 2001, New Orleans Saints 2002. Pro coach: New York Jets 2006-08, joined Browns in 2009.

Brian Daboll, offensive coordinator; born April 14, 1975, Welland, Ontario, Canada. Safety Rochester 1995-97. No pro playing experience. College coach: William & Mary 1997, Michigan State 1998-99. Pro coach: New England Patriots 2000-06, New York Jets 2007-08, joined Browns in 2009.

Andy Dickerson, defensive quality control; born January 29, 1982, Wilmington, Del. Offensive lineman Tufts 1999-2002. No pro playing experience. College coach: Tufts 2003. Pro coach: New York Jets 2006-08, joined Browns in 2009.

Matt Eberflus, linebackers; born May 17, 1970, Toledo, Ohio. Linebacker Toledo 1988-1991. No pro playing experience. College coach: Toledo 1992-2000, Missouri 2001-08. Pro coach: Joined Browns in 2009.

Steve Hagen, tight ends; born September 15, 1961, Forest City, Iowa. Wide receiver Cal Lutheran 1979-1982. No pro playing experience. College coach: Illinois 1983, Kansas 1984-85, Northern Arizona 1986-88, Notre Dame 1989-1990, Kent State 1991, Nevada 1992-93, Nevada-Las Vegas 1994-95, Wartburg 1996, San Jose State 1997-98, California 1999-2000, Fresno State 2006, North Carolina 2007-08. Pro coach: Cleveland Browns 2001-04, re-joined Browns in 2009.

Jerome Henderson, defensive backs; born August 8, 1969, Portsmouth, Va. Defensive back Clemson 1987-1990. Pro cornerback New England Patriots 1991-93, 1996, Buffalo Bills 1993-94, Philadelphia Eagles 1995, New York Jets 1997-98. Pro coach: New York Jets 2006-08, joined Browns in 2009.

Kent Johnson, strength and conditioning; born February 21, 1966, Mexia, Texas. Defensive back Stephen F. Austin 1974-77. No pro playing experience. College coach: Northwestern Louisiana 1979-1980, Northeast Louisiana 1980-81, Alabama 1985-86, 2004-05. Pro coach: Tampa Bay Buccaneers 1987-1991, Green Bay Packers 1992-98, Seattle Seahawks 1999-2003, joined Browns in 2010.

Rick Lyle, asst. strength and conditioning; born February 26, 1971, Monroe, La. Defensive lineman Missouri 1989-1993. Pro defensive lineman Cleveland Browns 1994-95, Baltimore Ravens 1996, New York Jets 1997-2001, New England Patriots 2002-03. Pro coach: New York Jets 2006-08, joined Browns in 2009.

George McDonald, wide receivers; born May 10, 1976, Buena Park, Calif. Wide receiver Illinois 1995-98. No pro playing experience. College coach: Ball State 2000, Northern Illinois 2001-03, Stanford 2004, Western Michigan 2005-06, Minnesota 2007-08. Pro coach: Joined Browns in 2009.

Rob Ryan, defensive coordinator; born December 13, 1962, Ardmore, Okla. Linebacker Oklahoma State 1984, Southwestern Oklahoma State 1985-86. No pro playing experience. College coach: Western Kentucky 1987, Ohio State 1988, Tennessee State 1989-1993, Hutchinson (Kan.) C.C. 1996, Oklahoma State 1997-99. Pro coach: Arizona Cardinals 1994-95, New England Patriots 2000-03, Oakland Raiders 2004-08, joined Browns in 2009.

Brad Seely, asst. head coach/special teams coordinator; born September 6, 1956, Vinton, Iowa. Tackle/guard South Dakota State 1974-77. No pro playing experience. College coach: Colorado State 1979-1980, Southern Methodist 1981, North Carolina State 1982, Pacific 1983, Oklahoma State 1984-88. Pro coach: Indianapolis Colts 1989-1993, New York Jets 1994, Carolina Panthers 1995-98, New England Patriots 1999-2008, joined Browns in 2009.

Carl Smith, quarterbacks; born April 26, 1948, Wasco, Calif. Quarterback Bakersfield 1966-67, defensive back Cal Poly-San Luis Obispo 1969-1970. No pro playing experience. College coach: Cal Poly-San Luis Obispo 1971, Colorado 1972-73, Southwestern Louisiana 1974-78, Lamar 1979-1981, North Carolina State 1982, Southern California 2004. Pro coach: Philadelphia/Baltimore Stars 1983-85, New Orleans Saints 1986-1996, New England Patriots 1997-99, Cleveland Browns 2001-03, Jacksonville Jaguars 2005-06, re-joined Browns in 2009.

George Warhop, offensive line; born September 19, 1961, Riverside, Calif. Guard/center Mt. San Jacinto (Calif.) J.C. 1979-1980, Cincinnati 1981-82. No pro playing experience. College coach: Cincinnati 1983, Kansas 1984-86, Vanderbilt 1987-89, New Mexico 1990, Southern Methodist 1993, Boston College 1994-95. Pro coach: London Monarchs (World League) 1991-92, St. Louis Rams 1996-97, Arizona Cardinals 1998-2002, Dallas Cowboys 2003-04, San Francisco 49ers 2005-08, joined Browns in 2009.

American Football Conference
West Division
Team Colors: Orange, Broncos Navy Blue, and White
13655 Broncos Parkway
Englewood, Colorado 80112
Telephone: (303) 649-9000

2010 SCHEDULE

PRESEASON

Aug. 15	at Cincinnati	7:00
Aug. 21	**Detroit**	7:00
Aug. 29	**Pittsburgh**	6:00
Sep. 2	at Minnesota	7:00

REGULAR SEASON

Sep. 12	at Jacksonville	1:00
Sep. 19	**Seattle**	2:05
Sep. 26	**Indianapolis**	2:15
Oct. 3	at Tennessee	12:00
Oct. 10	at Baltimore	1:00
Oct. 17	**New York Jets**	2:05
Oct. 24	**Oakland**	2:15
Oct. 31	at San Francisco (London)	5:00
Nov. 7	BYE	
Nov. 14	**Kansas City**	2:05
Nov. 22	at San Diego (Mon)	5:30
Nov. 28	**St. Louis**	2:15
Dec. 5	at Kansas City	12:00
Dec. 12	at Arizona	2:15
Dec. 19	at Oakland	1:15
Dec. 26	**Houston**	2:05
Jan. 2	**San Diego**	2:15

Stadium: INVESCO Field at Mile High (opened in 2001) •**Capacity:** 76,125
1701 Bryant Street
Denver, Colorado 80204
Playing Surface: DD Grassmaster
Training Camp: 13655 Broncos Parkway
Englewood, Colorado 80112

INVESCO FIELD AT MILE HIGH

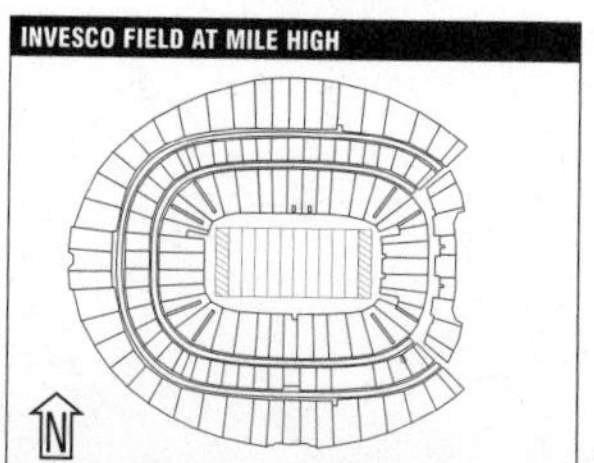

CLUB OFFICIALS
President-Chief Executive Officer: Pat Bowlen
Head Coach: Josh McDaniels
Chief Operating Officer: Joe Ellis

FOOTBALL STAFF
General Manager: Brian Xanders
Vice President, Team Administration/ Assistant to Head Coach: Mark Thewes
Director of Football Administration: Mike Bluem
Head Athletic Trainer: Steve Antonopulos
Director of Video Operations: Steve Scarnecchia

BUSINESS STAFF
General Counsel/Senior Vice President of Administration: Rich Slivka
Vice President of Corporate Communications: Jim Saccomano
Vice President of Marketing and Sales: Dennis Moore
Vice President of Community Development: Cindy Kellogg
Executive Director of Media Relations: Patrick Smyth
Executive Director of Ticket Operations and Administration: Kirk Dyer

STADIUM MANAGEMENT COMPANY
Senior Vice President of Business Development: Mac Freeman

COACHING HISTORY
(411-367-10)
Records include postseason games

1960-61	Frank Filchock	7-20-1
1962-64	Jack Faulkner*	9-22-1
1964-66	Mac Speedie**	6-19-1
1966	Ray Malavasi	4-8-0
1967-1971	Lou Saban***	20-42-3
1971	Jerry Smith	2-3-0
1972-76	John Ralston	34-33-3
1977-1980	Robert (Red) Miller	42-25-0
1981-1992	Dan Reeves	117-79-1
1993-94	Wade Phillips	16-17-0
1995-2008	Mike Shanahan	146-91-0
2009	Josh McDaniels	8-8-0

*Released after four games in 1964
**Resigned after two games in 1966
***Resigned after nine games in 1971

PAID ATTENDANCE
Home 590,433 Away 520,424
Total 1,110,857
Single-game home record, 76,716 (11/9/09)
Single-season home record, 597,984 (2007)

2010 DRAFT CHOICES

Round	Name	Pos.	College
1	Demaryius Thomas	WR	Georgia Tech
	Tim Tebow	QB	Florida
2	Zane Beadles	T	Utah
3	J.D. Walton	C	Baylor
	Eric Decker	WR	Minnesota
5	Perrish Cox	DB	Oklahoma St.
6	Eric Olsen	G	Notre Dame
7	Syd'Quan Thompson	DB	California
	Jammie Kirlew	LB	Indiana

DENVER BRONCOS

2009 TEAM RECORD

PRESEASON (1-3)

Date	Result		Opponent
8/14	L	16-17	at San Francisco
8/22	L	13-27	at Seattle
8/30	L	17-27	Chicago
9/3	W	19-0	Arizona

REGULAR SEASON (8-8)

Date	Result		Opponent
9/13	W	12-7	at Cincinnati
9/20	W	27-6	Cleveland
9/27	W	23-3	at Oakland
10/4	W	17-10	Dallas
10/11	W	20-17	New England (OT)
10/19	W	34-23	at San Diego
11/1	L	7-30	at Baltimore
11/9	L	10-28	Pittsburgh
11/15	L	17-27	at Washington
11/22	L	3-32	San Diego
11/26	W	26-6	New York Giants
12/6	W	44-13	at Kansas City
12/13	L	16-28	at Indianapolis
12/20	L	19-20	Oakland
12/27	L	27-30	at Philadelphia
1/3	L	24-44	Kansas City

(OT) Overtime

SCORE BY PERIODS

Broncos	57	80	101	85	3	—	326
Opponents	84	82	57	101	0	—	324

2009 TEAM STATISTICS

	Broncos	Opp.
Total First Downs	306	290
Rushing	95	99
Passing	186	167
Penalty	25	24
3rd Down: Made/Att	78/215	81/218
3rd Down Pct.	36.3	37.2
4th Down: Made/Att	7/18	8/16
4th Down Pct.	38.9	50.0
Possession Avg.	30:03	29:57
Total Net Yards	5463	5040
Avg. Per Game	341.4	315.0
Total Plays	1032	1007
Avg. Per Play	5.3	5.0
Net Yards Rushing	1836	2059
Avg. Per Game	114.8	128.7
Total Rushes	440	458
Net Yards Passing	3627	2981
Avg. Per Game	226.7	186.3
Sacked/Yards Lost	34/198	39/241
Gross Yards	3825	3222
Att./Completions	558/341	510/298
Completion Pct.	61.1	58.4
Had Intercepted	13	17
Punts/Average	78/43.4	76/46.3
Net Punting Avg.	78/36.7	76/40.0
Penalties/Yards	93/800	78/726
Fumbles/Ball Lost	15/10	30/13
Touchdowns	34	34
Rushing	9	11
Passing	21	18
Returns	4	5

2009 INDIVIDUAL STATISTICS

PASSING	Att.	Comp.	Yds.	Pct.	TD	Int.	Tkld.	Rate
Orton	541	336	3802	62.1	21	12	29/159	86.8
Simms	17	5	23	29.4	0	1	5/39	15.1
Broncos	558	341	3825	61.1	21	13	34/198	84.4
Opponents	510	298	3222	58.4	18	17	39/241	75.0

SCORING	TD R	TD P	TD Rt	PAT	FG	Saf	PTS
Prater	0	0	0	32/32	30/35	0	122
Marshall	0	10	0	0/0	0/0	0	60
Moreno	7	2	0	0/0	0/0	0	54
Stokley	0	4	0	0/0	0/0	0	24
Gaffney	0	2	0	0/0	0/0	0	12
Royal	0	0	2	0/0	0/0	0	12
Scheffler	0	2	0	0/0	0/0	0	12
Ayers	0	0	1	0/0	0/0	0	6
Buckhalter	1	0	0	0/0	0/0	0	6
Goodman	0	0	1	0/0	0/0	0	6
Graham	0	1	0	0/0	0/0	0	6
Hillis	1	0	0	0/0	0/0	0	6
Broncos	9	21	4	32/32	30/35	0	326
Opponents	11	18	5	33/34	29/31	0	324

2-Pt. Conversions: Broncos 0-2, Opponents 0-0.

RUSHING	No.	Yds	Avg	LG	TD
Moreno	247	947	3.8	36	7
Buckhalter	120	642	5.4	45t	1
Jordan	25	86	3.4	13	0
Orton	24	71	3.0	13	0
Hillis	13	54	4.2	13	1
Marshall	7	39	5.6	14	0
Royal	1	1	1.0	1	0
Simms	3	-4	-1.3	-1	0
Broncos	440	1836	4.2	45t	9
Opponents	458	2059	4.5	56t	11

RECEIVING	No.	Yds	Avg	LG	TD
Marshall	101	1120	11.1	75t	10
Gaffney	54	732	13.6	49	2
Royal	37	345	9.3	20	0
Scheffler	31	416	13.4	52	2
Buckhalter	31	240	7.7	30	0
Graham	28	289	10.3	24	1
Moreno	28	213	7.6	27	2
Stokley	19	327	17.2	87t	4
Lloyd	8	117	14.6	44	0
Hillis	4	19	4.8	6	0
Kuper	0	7	—	7	0
Broncos	341	3825	11.2	87t	21
Opponents	298	3222	10.8	53	18

INTERCEPTIONS	No.	Yds	Avg	LG	TD
Goodman	5	65	13.0	30	0
Bailey	3	18	6.0	11	0
McBath	2	28	14.0	25	0
Hill	2	18	9.0	18	0
Dawkins	2	0	0.0	0	0
Law	1	37	37.0	37	0
Scheffler	1	5	5.0	5	0
Woodyard	1	0	0.0	0	0
Broncos	17	171	10.1	37	0
Opponents	13	237	18.2	60t	3

PUNTING	No.	Yds.	Avg.	In 20	LG
Berger	51	2142	42.0	13	65
Kern TM	27	1245	46.1	9	64
Broncos	78	3387	43.4	22	65
Opponents	76	3520	46.3	27	65

PUNT RETURNS	Ret	FC	Yds	Avg	LG	TD
Royal	30	13	335	11.2	71t	1
A. Smith	10	3	47	4.7	21	0
McKinley	3	0	32	10.7	14	0
Hill	1	0	0	0.0	0	0
Barrett	0	0	5	—	5	0
Broncos	44	16	419	9.5	71t	1
Opponents	36	16	363	10.1	77t	1

KICKOFF RETURNS	No.	Yds	Avg	LG	TD
Royal	26	621	23.9	93t	1
Buckhalter	8	184	23.0	41	0
McKinley	7	158	22.6	30	0
Hillis	6	134	22.3	24	0
A. Smith	4	75	18.8	23	0
Quinn	1	19	19.0	19	0
Larsen	1	13	13.0	13	0
Hochstein	1	6	6.0	6	0
Jordan	1	6	6.0	6	0
Thomas	1	1	1.0	1	0
Polumbus	1	0	0.0	0	0
Broncos	57	1217	21.4	93t	1
Opponents	49	1115	22.8	95t	1

FIELD GOALS	1-19	20-29	30-39	40-49	50+
Prater	0/0	14/14	6/8	8/10	2/3
Broncos	0/0	14/14	6/8	8/10	2/3
Opponents	1/1	8/8	7/7	9/10	4/5

SACKS	No.
Dumervil	17.0
Holliday	5.0
Reid	4.0
Davis	3.5
D. Williams	3.5
Hill	2.0
Goodman	1.0
Haggan	1.0
Peterson	1.0
L. Smith	1.0
Broncos	39.0
Opponents	34.0

RECORD HOLDERS

INDIVIDUAL RECORDS—CAREER

Category	Name	Performance
Rushing (Yds.)	Terrell Davis, 1995-2002	7,607
Passing (Yds.)	John Elway, 1983-1998	51,475
Passing (TDs)	John Elway, 1983-1998	300
Receiving (No.)	Rod Smith, 1995-2007	849
Receiving (Yds.)	Rod Smith, 1995-2007	11,389
Interceptions	Steve Foley, 1976-1986	44
Punting (Avg.)	Jim Fraser, 1962-64	45.2
Punt Return (Avg.)	Darrien Gordon, 1997-98	12.5
Kickoff Return (Avg.)	Abner Haynes, 1965-66	26.3
Field Goals	Jason Elam, 1993-2007	395
Touchdowns (Tot.)	Rod Smith, 1995-2007	71
Points	Jason Elam, 1993-2007	1,786
*Sacks	Simon Fletcher, 1985-1995	97.5

INDIVIDUAL RECORDS—SINGLE SEASON

Category	Name	Performance
Rushing (Yds.)	Terrell Davis, 1998	2,008
Passing (Yds.)	Jay Cutler, 2008	4,526
Passing (TDs)	John Elway, 1997	27
	Jake Plummer, 2004	27
Receiving (No.)	Rod Smith, 2001	113
Receiving (Yds.)	Rod Smith, 2000	1,602
Interceptions	Goose Gonsoulin, 1960	11
Punting (Avg.)	Tom Rouen, 1998	46.9
Punt Return (Avg.)	Floyd Little, 1967	16.9
Kickoff Return (Avg.)	Bill Thompson, 1969	28.5
Field Goals	Jason Elam, 1995, 2001	31
Touchdowns (Tot.)	Terrell Davis, 1998	23
Points	Terrell Davis, 1998	138
*Sacks	Elvis Dumervil, 2009	17.0

INDIVIDUAL RECORDS—SINGLE GAME

Category	Name	Performance
Rushing (Yds.)	Mike Anderson, 12-3-00	251
Passing (Yds.)	Jake Plummer, 10-31-04	499
Passing (TDs)	Frank Tripucka, 10-28-62	5
	John Elway, 11-18-84	5
	Gus Frerotte, 11-19-00	5
Receiving (No.)	Brandon Marshall, 12-13-09	**21
Receiving (Yds.)	Shannon Sharpe, 10-20-02	214
Interceptions	Goose Gonsoulin, 9-18-60	**4
	Willie Brown, 11-15-64	**4
	Deltha O'Neal, 10-7-01	**4
Field Goals	Gene Mingo, 10-6-63	5
	Rich Karlis, 11-20-83	5
	Jason Elam, 9-3-95, 10-13-02	5
Touchdowns (Tot.)	Clinton Portis, 12-7-03	5
Points	Clinton Portis, 12-7-03	30
*Sacks	Karl Mecklenburg, 9-15-85, 12-1-85	4.0
	Simon Fletcher, 11-4-90	4.0
	Elvis Dumervil, 9-20-09	4.0

**Sacks became an official statistic in 1982.*
***NFL Record*

DENVER BRONCOS

2010 VETERAN ROSTER

No.	Name	Pos.	Ht.	Wt.	Birthdate	NFL Exp.	College	Hometown	How Acq.	'09 Games/ Starts
26	Arrington, J.J.	RB	5-9	212	1/23/83	5	California	Rocky Mount, N.C.	FA-'10	0*
58	Atkins, Baraka	LB/DE	6-4	268	9/28/84	4	Miami	Sarasota, Fla.	FA-'10	0*
56	Ayers, Robert	LB/DE	6-3	274	9/6/85	2	Tennessee	Bennettsville, S.C.	D1b-'09	15/1
51	Ayodele, Akin	LB	6-2	245	9/17/79	9	Purdue	Irving, Texas	FA-'10	16/15*
24	Bailey, Champ	CB	6-0	192	6/22/78	12	Georgia	Folkston, Ga.	T(Was)-'04	16/16
75	Baker, Chris	DL	6-2	329	10/8/87	2	Hampton	Windsor, Conn.	FA-'09	1/0
35	Ball, Lance	RB	5-9	220	6/19/85	2	Maryland	Teaneck, N.J.	FA-'09	0*
99	Bannan, Justin	DL	6-3	310	4/18/79	9	Colorado	Fair Oaks, Calif.	UFA(Balt)-'10	16/2*
36	Barrett, Josh	S	6-2	225	1/22/84	3	Arizona State	Reno, Nev.	D7-'08	14/0
67	Batiste, D'Anthony	T	6-4	314	3/29/82	5	Louisiana-Lafayette	Marksville, La.	FA-'09	8/0*
3	Brandstater, Tom	QB	6-5	223	10/21/84	2	Fresno State	Turlock, Calif.	D6-'09	0*
30	Bruton, David	S	6-2	211	7/23/87	2	Notre Dame	Miamisburg, Ohio	D4a-'09	14/1
28	Buckhalter, Correll	RB	6-0	223	10/6/78	10	Nebraska	Collins, Miss.	UFA(Phil)-'09	14/7
78	Clady, Ryan	T	6-6	325	9/6/86	3	Boise State	Rialto, Calif.	D1-'08	16/16
20	Dawkins, Brian	S	6-0	210	10/13/73	15	Clemson	Jacksonville, Fla.	UFA(Phil)-'09	16/1
92	Dumervil, Elvis	OLB/DE	5-11	248	1/19/84	5	Louisville	Miami, Fla.	D4b-'06	16/14
91	Fields, Ronald	DL	6-2	314	9/13/81	6	Mississippi State	Bogalusa, La.	UFA(SF)-'09	16/16
10	Gaffney, Jabar	WR	6-2	200	12/1/80	9	Florida	Jacksonville, Fla.	UFA(NE)-'09	16/7
21	Goodman, André	CB	5-10	184	8/11/78	9	South Carolina	Greenville, S.C.	UFA(Mia)-'09	16/16
89	Graham, Daniel	TE	6-3	257	1/16/78	9	Colorado	Denver, Colo.	UFA(NE)-'07	16/14
93	Green, Jarvis	DL	6-3	285	1/12/79	9	Louisiana State	Donaldson, La.	UFA(NE)-'10	13/12*
	Greisen, Nick	LB	6-1	242	8/10/79	9	Wisconsin	Sturgeon Bay, Wisc.	FA-'10	0*
57	Haggan, Mario	LB/DE	6-3	267	3/3/80	8	Mississippi State	Clarksdale, Miss.	FA-'08	16/16
74	Harris, Ryan	T	6-5	300	3/11/85	4	Notre Dame	St. Paul, Minn.	D3-'07	8/8
23	Hill, Renaldo	S	5-11	205	1/12/78	10	Michigan State	Detroit, Mich.	UFA(Mia)-'09	15/15
71	Hochstein, Russ	OL	6-4	305	10/7/77	10	Nebraska	Hartington, Neb.	T(NE)-'09	15/10
33	Jones, Nate	CB	5-10	185	6/15/82	7	Rutgers	Scotch Plains, N.J.	UFA(Mia)-'10	16/5
73	Kuper, Chris	G	6-4	303	12/19/82	5	North Dakota	Anchorage, Alaska	D5-'06	15/15
46	Larsen, Spencer	LB/FB	6-2	243	3/4/84	3	Arizona	Gilbert, Ariz.	D6-'08	9/1
84	Lloyd, Brandon	WR	6-0	194	7/5/81	8	Illinois	Blue Springs, Mo.	FA-'09	2/1
31	McBath, Darcel	S	6-1	198	10/28/85	2	Texas Tech	Gainesville, Texas	D2b-'09	13/0
98	McBean, Ryan	DL	6-5	297	4/23/84	3	Oklahoma State	Euless, Texas	FA-'08	14/14
60	McChesney, Matt	G	6-3	333	1/6/81	3	Colorado	Longmont, Colo.	FA-'10	0*
11	McKinley, Kenny	WR	6-0	183	1/31/87	2	South Carolina	Austell, Ga.	D5-'09	8/0
27	Moreno, Knowshon	RB	5-11	210	7/16/87	2	Georgia	Middletown, N.J.	D1a-'09	16/9
94	Moss, Jarvis	LB/DE	6-7	257	8/3/84	4	Florida	Denton, Texas	D1-'07	7/0
70	Olsen, Seth	G	6-5	308	12/17/85	2	Iowa	Omaha, Neb.	D4b-'09	3/0
8	Orton, Kyle	QB	6-4	225	1/14/82	6	Purdue	Runnels, Iowa	T(Chi)-'09	16/15
66	Paxton, Lonie	LS	6-2	281	3/13/78	11	Sacramento State	Corona, Calif.	UFA(NE)-'09	16/0
76	Polumbus, Tyler	T	6-8	300	4/10/85	3	Colorado	Greenwood Village, Colo.	FA-'08	15/8
5	Prater, Matt	K	5-10	187	8/10/84	4	Central Florida	Estero, Fla.	PS(Mia)-'07	16/0
9	t- Quinn, Brady	QB	6-3	235	10/27/84	4	Notre Dame	Dublin, Ohio	T(Cle)-'10	10/9*
81	Quinn, Richard	TE	6-4	255	9/6/86	2	North Carolina	Maple Heights, Ohio	D2c-'09	15/0
95	Reid, Darrell	LB/DE	6-2	270	6/20/82	6	Minnesota	Freehold, N.J.	UFA(Ind)-'09	16/0
19	Royal, Eddie	WR	5-10	180	5/21/86	3	Virginia Tech	Chantilly, Va.	D2-'08	14/12
22	Smith, Alphonso	CB	5-9	190	10/20/85	2	Wake Forest	Pahokee, Fla.	D2a-'09	15/0
97	Smith, Le Kevin	DL	6-3	308	7/21/82	5	Nebraska	Macon, Ga.	T(NE)-'09	13/2
14	Stokley, Brandon	WR	6-0	192	6/23/76	12	Southwestern Louisiana	Lafayette, La.	FA-'07	16/2
79	Thomas, Marcus	DL	6-3	316	9/23/85	4	Florida	Jacksonville, Fla.	D4-'07	16/0
55	Williams, D.J.	LB	6-1	242	7/20/82	7	Miami	Concord, Calif.	D1-'04	16/16
76	Williams, Jamal	DL	6-3	348	4/28/76	13	Oklahoma State	Washington, D.C.	FA-'10	1/1*
12	Willis, Matthew	WR	6-0	190	4/13/84	3	UCLA	Anaheim, Calif.	FA-'08	1/1
59	Woodyard, Wesley	LB	6-0	222	7/21/86	3	Kentucky	LaGrange, Ga.	FA-'08	16/0

* Arrington missed the '09 season because of injury; Atkins inactive for 2 games with San Francisco in '09; Ayodele played 16 games for Miami in '09; Ball last active with Indianapolis in '08; Bannan played 16 games with Baltimore; Batiste played 8 games with Washington; Brandstater inactive third quarterback all 16 games; Green played 13 games with New England; Greisen missed '09 season because of injury; McChesney last active with Miami in '08; Quinn played 10 games with Cleveland; J. Williams played 1 game with San Diego.

t- Broncos traded for Quinn (Cle).

Traded—FB Peyton Hillis (14 games in '09) to Cleveland, WR Brandon Marshall (15) to Miami, TE Tony Scheffler (15) to Detroit.

Players lost through free agency (1): G/C Ben Hamilton (Sea; 15 games in '09).

Also played with Broncos in '09—P Mitch Berger (10 games), CB Tony Carter (2), LB Andra Davis (16), S Vernon Fox (2), T Brandon Gorin (6), DL Vonnie Holliday (16), RB LaMont Jordan (9), P Brett Kern (6), CB Ty Law (7), DL Kenny Peterson (16), QB Chris Simms (3), C Casey Wiegmann (16), CB Jack Williams (7).

2010 FIRST-YEAR ROSTER

Name	Pos.	Ht.	Wt.	Birthdate	College	Hometown	How Acq.
Alexander, Kevin	LB/DE	6-4	265	7/1/87	Clemson	Lake Butler, Fla.	FA
Arnett, Alric	WR	6-2	189	6/26/87	West Virginia	Belle Glade, Fla.	FA
Baker, Toney	RB	5-10	225	6/16/86	North Carolina State	Jamestown, N.C.	FA
Baston, Jaron	DL	6-1	305	4/10/87	Missouri	Blue Spring, Mo.	FA
Beadles, Zane	T	6-4	305	11/19/86	Utah	Sandy, Utah	D2
Bishop, Devin	LB	6-1	239	7/17/86	California	Vacaville, Calif.	FA
Bosworth, Korey	LB/DE	6-1	242	11/21/86	UCLA	Plano, Texas	FA
Branson, Marquez (1)	TE	6-2	241	2/14/87	Central Arkansas	Starkville, Miss.	FA-'09
Carter, Tony (1)	CB	5-9	175	5/24/86	Florida State	Jacksonville, Fla.	FA-'09
Colquitt, Britton (1)	P	6-3	204	3/20/85	Tennessee	Knoxville, Tenn.	FA-'09
Cox, Perrish	CB	6-0	195	1/10/87	Oklahoma State	Waco, Texas	D5
Decker, Eric	WR	6-2	215	3/15/87	Minnesota	Cold Spring, Min.	D3b
Duncun, Paul	T	6-7	315	6/18/87	Notre Dame	Dallas, Ga.	FA
Fry, Dustin (1)	C	6-3	326	10/3/83	Clemson	Summerville, S.C.	FA
Garland, Ben	DL	6-5	275	4/6/81	Air Force	Grand Junction, Colo.	FA
Geer, Riar	TE	6-4	250	12/19/86	Colorado	Fruita, Colo.	FA
Hall, Bruce (1)	RB	5-11	205	3/18/85	Mississippi	Orlando, Fla.	FA
Honeycutt, Patrick	WR	5-9	172	12/30/86	Middle Tennessee State	Hoover, Ala.	FA
Kelley, Braxton (1)	LB	6-0	242	10/24/86	Kentucky	LaGrange, Ga.	FA-'09
Kirlew, Jammie	LB/DE	6-3	264	5/12/87	Indiana	Orlando, Fla.	D7b
Lyons, Dicky (1)	WR	5-11	190	11/19/85	Kentucky	New Orleans, La.	FA
Marinelli, Chris	T	6-7	300	3/3/87	Stanford	Boston, Mass.	FA
McCarthy, Kyle	S	6-1	210	9/30/86	Notre Dame	Youngstown, Ohio	FA
Olsen, Eric	G	6-4	305	6/16/88	Notre Dame	Brooklyn, N.Y.	D6
Overbay, Nathan	TE	6-5	270	1/4/87	Eastern Washington	Chehalis, Wash.	FA
Stehle, Jeff	DL	6-6	310	4/4/87	Wisconsin	Staten Island, N.Y.	FA
Tebow, Tim	QB	6-3	245	8/14/87	Florida	Jacksonville, Fla.	D1b
Thomas, Demaryius	WR	6-3	229	12/25/87	Georgia Tech	Montrose, Ga.	D1a
Thompson, Syd'Quan	CB	5-9	187	2/7/87	California	Sacramento, Calif.	D7a
Trapasso, A.J. (1)	P	5-11	225	2/6/86	Ohio State	Pickerington, Ohio	FA
Vaughn, Cassius	CB	5-11	195	11/3/87	Mississippi	Memphis, Tenn.	FA
Walton, J.D.	C	6-3	305	3/24/87	Baylor	Allen, Texas	D3a
Williams, Landis	WR	5-10	174	10/23/88	Maine	Pemberton, N.J.	FA

The term NFL Rookie is defined as a player who is in his first season of professional football and has not been on the roster of another professional football team for any regular-season or postseason games. A Rookie is designated by an "R" on NFL rosters. Players who have been active in another professional football league or players who have NFL experience, including either preseason training camp or being on an Active List or Inactive List, or on Reserve/Injured or Reserve/Physically Unable to Perform for fewer than six regular-season games, are termed NFL First-Year Players. An NFL First-Year Player is designated by a "1" on NFL rosters. Thereafter, a player is credited with an additional year of experience for each season in which he accumulates six games on the Active List or Inactive List, or on Reserve/Injured or Reserve/Physically Unable to Perform.

Log on to www.denverbroncos.com for an up-to-date roster.

COACHING STAFF

Head Coach,
Josh McDaniels

Pro Career: Became the twelfth head coach in Broncos history on January 12, 2009. McDaniels joins the Broncos after spending the previous eight seasons (2001-2008) with the New England Patriots, including the last three years (2006-08) as the club's offensive coordinator/quarterbacks coach. McDaniels helped the Patriots win three Super Bowls, four AFC championships and six division titles while posting the NFL's best overall record (111-34) during his eight years in New England. The Patriots had seven 10-win seasons with McDaniels on staff, including the 2007 campaign when New England became the first team in NFL history to post a 16-0 regular-season record. McDaniels joined the Patriots in 2001 as a personnel/coaching assistant. In 2003 he acquired additional responsibility working with the defensive backs. In 2004 he acted as the club's quarterbacks coach and on January 20, 2006 the Patriots promoted McDaniels to offensive coordinator/quarterbacks coach. McDaniels is the fifth-youngest coach in NFL history (32 years, 8 months) at the time of his hire. He is the youngest active coach in the league and the youngest in the history of the Denver Broncos. Career record: 8-8.

Background: McDaniels was a quarterback and kicker at Canton McKinley High School (Canton, Ohio). Was a quarterback/wide receiver at John Carroll from 1995-98. No pro playing experience. He was a college coach at Michigan State in 1999.

Personal: Born in Barberton, Ohio on April 22, 1976. He and his wife, Laura, have one son Jack Thomas, and one daughter, Maddie.

ASSISTANT COACHES

Craig Auckerman, defensive assistant; born November 22, 1976. Defensive back/wide receiver Findlay 1995-98. No pro playing experience. College coach: Findlay 2000, Miami (Ohio) 2001-02, Western Kentucky 2003-04, Kent State 2009. Pro coach: Joined Broncos in 2010.

Clancy Barone, offensive line; born July 26, 1963, San Andreas, Calif. Offensive lineman Cal State-Sacramento 1981-82, Nevada 1985-86. No pro playing experience. College coach: American River (Calif.) J.C. 1987-89, Cal State-Sacramento 1990-92, Texas A&M 1993, Eastern Illinois 1994-96, Wyoming 1997-99, Houston 2000-02, Texas State 2003. Pro coach: Atlanta Falcons 2004-06, San Diego Chargers 2007-08, joined Broncos in 2009.

Keith Burns, asst. special teams; born May 16, 1972, Greeleyville, S.C. Linebacker Oklahoma State 1991-94. Pro linebacker Denver Broncos 1994-98, 2000-03, 2005-06, Chicago Bears 1999, Tampa Bay Buccaneers 2004. Pro coach: Joined Broncos in 2007.

Brian Callahan, coaching assistant; born June 10, 1984, Champaign, Ill. Quarterback UCLA 2002-06. No pro playing experience. College coach: UCLA 2006-07. Pro coach: Joined Broncos in 2010.

Ed Donatell, secondary; born February 4, 1957, Akron, Ohio. Defensive back Glenville (W. Va.) State 1975-78. College coach: Kent State 1979-1980, Washington 1981-82, 2008, Pacific 1983-85, Idaho 1986-88, Cal State-Fullerton 1989. Pro coach: New York Jets 1990-94, Denver Broncos 1995-99, Green Bay Packers 2000-03, Atlanta Falcons 2004-06, re-joined Broncos in 2009.

Adam Gase, wide receivers; born March 29, 1978, Ypsilanti, Mich. Attended Michigan State. No college or pro playing experience. College coach: Louisiana State 2000-02. Pro coach: Detroit Lions 2003-07, San Francisco 49ers 2008, joined Broncos in 2009.

Bob Ligashesky, tight ends; born June 2, 1962, Pittsburgh. Linebacker Indiana (Pa.) 1983-84. No pro playing experience. College coach: Wake Forest 1985, Arizona State 1986-89, Kent State 1990, Bowling Green 1991-99, Pittsburgh 2000-03. Pro coach: Jacksonville Jaguars 2004, St. Louis Rams 2005-06, Pittsburgh Steelers 2007-09, joined Broncos in 2010.

Justin Lovett, strength and conditioning assistant; born January 8, 1977, Dayton, Ohio. Wide receiver Findlay 1995-96. No pro playing experience. College coach: Texas-El Paso 2008. Pro coach: Joined Broncos in 2010.

Don Martindale, defensive coordinator; born May 19, 1963, Dayton, Ohio. Linebacker Defiance College 1984-86. No pro playing experience. College coach: Defiance 1987, Notre Dame 1994-95, Cincinnati 1996-98, Western Illinois 1999, Western Kentucky 2000-02. Pro coach: Oakland Raiders 2004-08, joined Broncos in 2009.

Mike McCoy, offensive coordinator; born April 1, 1972, San Francisco. Quarterback Long Beach State 1990-91, Utah 1992-94. Pro quarterback Amsterdam Admirals (NFLE) 1997, Calgary Stampeders (CFL) 1999. Pro coach: Carolina Panthers 1999-2008, joined Broncos in 2009.

Ben McDaniels, quarterbacks; born June 6, 1980, Barberton, Ohio. Quarterback Kent State 1999-2002. No pro playing experience. College coach: Minnesota 2004-05. Pro coach: Joined Broncos in 2009.

Wayne Nunnely, defensive line, born March 29, 1952, Los Angeles. Fullback Nevada-Las Vegas 1972-75. No pro playing experience. College coach: Nevada-Las Vegas 1976, 1982-89 (head coach 1986-89), Cal Poly-Pomona 1977-78, Cal State-Fullerton 1979, Pacific 1980-81, Southern California 1991-92, UCLA 1993-94. Pro coach: New Orleans Saints 1995-96, San Diego Chargers 1997-2008, joined Broncos in 2009.

Roman Phifer, asst. linebackers; born March 5, 1968, Charlotte, N.C. Linebacker UCLA 1987-1990. Linebacker Los Angeles/St. Louis Rams 1991-98, New York Jets 1999-2000, New England Patriots 2001-04, New York Giants 2005. Pro coach: Joined Broncos in 2009.

Mike Priefer, special teams coordinator; born August 21, 1966, Cleveland. Attended U.S. Naval Academy. No college or pro playing experience. College coach: Navy 1994-96, Youngstown State 1997-98, Virginia Military Institute 1999, Northern Illinois 2000-01. Pro coach: Jacksonville Jaguars 2002, New York Giants 2003-05, Kansas City Chiefs 2007-08, joined Broncos in 2009.

Jay Rodgers, defensive assistant; born August 29, 1976, St. Paul, Minn. Quarterback Indiana 1996-98, Missouri State 1999. No pro playing experience. College coach: Missouri State 2004, Stephen F. Austin 2005-06, Iowa State 2007-08. Pro coach: Joined Broncos in 2009.

Greg Saporta, asst. strength and conditioning; born February 2, 1957, New York, N.Y. Wide receiver Buffalo State 1977-79. No pro playing experience. College coach: Florida 1981-88, 1993-94, North Carolina 1989-1992. Pro coach: Joined Broncos in 1995.

Eric Studesville, running backs; born May 29, 1967, Madison, Wisc. Defensive back Wisconsin-Whitewater 1985-88. No pro playing experience. College coach: Wingate 1994, Kent State 1995-96. Pro coach: Chicago Bears 1997-2000, New York Giants 2001-03, Buffalo Bills 2004-2009, joined Broncos in 2010

Mark Thewes, vice president of team administration/asst. to the head coach; born September 13, 1976, Canton, Ohio. Attended Miami (Ohio). No college or pro playing experience. Pro coach: Joined Broncos in 2009.

Rich Tuten, strength and conditioning; born December 30, 1953, Columbia, S.C. Nose guard Clemson 1976-78. No pro playing experience. College coach: Florida 1979-1988, 1993-94, North Carolina 1989-1992. Pro coach: Joined Broncos in 1995.

Bob Wylie, asst. offensive line; born February 16, 1951, West Warwick, R.I. Linebacker Colorado 1969-1971. No pro playing experience. College coach: Brown 1980-82, Holy Cross 1983-84, Ohio 1985-87, Colorado State 1988-89, Cincinnati 1996, Syracuse 2005-06. Pro coach: New York Jets 1990-91, Tampa Bay Buccaneers 1992-95, Cincinnati Bengals 1997-98, Chicago Bears 1999-2003, Arizona Cardinals 2004, Winnipeg Blue Bombers (CFL) 2007-08, Saskatchewan Roughriders (CFL) 2009, joined Broncos in 2010.

American Football Conference
South Division
Team Colors: Deep Steel Blue, Battle Red, and Liberty White
Two Reliant Park
Houston, Texas 77054
Telephone: (832) 667-2000

2010 SCHEDULE

PRESEASON

Aug. 14 at Arizona..........................5:00
Aug. 21 at New Orleans...................7:00
Aug. 28 **Dallas**...............................7:05
Sep. 2 **Tampa Bay**.........................7:00

REGULAR SEASON

Sep. 12 **Indianapolis** 12:00
Sep. 19 at Washington 4:15
Sep. 26 **Dallas** 12:00
Oct. 3 at Oakland 1:05
Oct. 10 **New York Giants**.............12:00
Oct. 17 **Kansas City** 12:00
Oct. 24 BYE
Nov. 1 at Indianapolis (Mon) 8:30
Nov. 7 **San Diego** 12:00
Nov. 14 at Jacksonville 1:00
Nov. 21 at New York Jets 1:00
Nov. 28 **Tennessee** 12:00
Dec. 2 at Philadelphia (Thu) 8:20
Dec. 13 **Baltimore** (Mon) 7:30
Dec. 19 at Tennessee 12:00
Dec. 26 at Denver 2:05
Jan. 2 **Jacksonville** 12:00

Stadium: Reliant Stadium (opened in 2002) • **Capacity:** 71,054 Houston, Texas 77054
Playing Surface: Grass
Training Camp: Methodist Training Center

RELIANT STADIUM

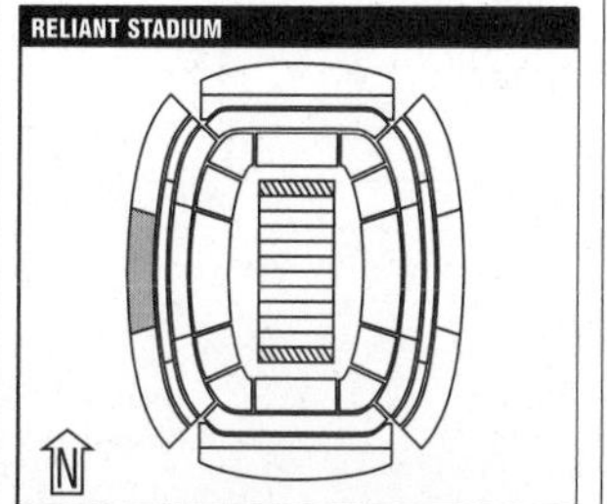

CLUB OFFICIALS

Chairman and CEO: Robert C. McNair
Vice Chairman: Philip J. Burguiéres
Vice Chairman: D. Cal McNair
General Manager: Rick Smith
President: Jamey Rootes
Senior Vice President, Treasurer and CFO: Scott Schwinger
Senior Vice President, General Counsel and CAO: Suzie Thomas
Vice President and Controller: Marilan Logan
Vice President of Security: Ryan Reichert
Vice President, Ticketing and Event Management: John Schriever
Vice President, Finance: Greg Watson
Director of Football Administration: Chris Olsen
Director of Football Operations: Lloyd Richards
Director of Player Development: Sean Washington
Director of College Scouting: Dale Strahm
Director of Pro Personnel: Brian Gardner
Associate Director of Pro Scouting: Bobby Grier
Pro Scout: Kevin Murphy
Coordinator of College Scouting: Mike Maccagnan
National College Scout: Ed Lambert
College Scouts: Jon Carr, Ryan Cavanaugh, Mike Martin, Bob Merritt, Nathan Trott
Head Athletic Trainer: Geoff Kaplan
Coordinator of Rehabilitation: Roland Ramirez
Assistant Athletic Trainer: Jon Ishop
Director of Equipment Services: Jay Brunetti
Equipment Services Assistants: Mike Parson, Christian Snell
Director of Video Operations: Joe Malota
Assistant Director of Video Operations: Bob Ford
Video Operations Assistant: Tim Borg
Director of Public Relations: Kevin Cooper
Director of Corporate Development: Greg Grissom
Risk Manager: Jan Kelly
Corporate Counsel: Greg Kondritz
Director of Human Resources: Glenda Morrison
Director of Event Services: Diane Crossey
Director of Marketing: Melissa Rentz
Director, Digital Media & Publications: Nick Schenck
Director of Information Technology: Jeff Schmitz
Assistant Treasurer: Jon Southern
Director of Premium Seating: Brian Varnadoe
Director of Ticket Sales: Derek Beeman
Director of Accounting: Tamala Theeck

COACHING HISTORY
(49-79-0)

2002-05 Dom Capers................18-46-0
2006-09 Gary Kubiak................31-33-0

PAID ATTENDANCE

Home 549,713 Away 470,549
Total 1,020,262
Single-game home record, 71,153 (11/23/09)
Single-season home record, 555,421 (2004)

2010 DRAFT CHOICES

Round	Name	Pos.	College
1	Kareem Jackson	DB	Alabama
2	Ben Tate	RB	Auburn
3	Earl Mitchell	DT	Arizona
4	Darryl Sharpton	LB	Miami
	Garrett Graham	TE	Wisconsin
5	Sherrick McManis	DB	Northwestern
6	Shelley Smith	G	Colorado St.
	Trindon Holliday	KR	Louisiana St.
7	Dorin Dickerson	WR	Pittsburgh

HOUSTON TEXANS

2009 TEAM RECORD

PRESEASON (2-2)

Date	Result	Opponent
8/15	W 16-10	at Kansas City
8/22	L 14-38	New Orleans
8/31	L 10-17	Minnesota
9/4	W 27-20	at Tampa Bay

REGULAR SEASON (9-7)

Date	Result	Opponent
9/13	L 7-24	New York Jets
9/20	W 34-31	at Tennessee
9/27	L 24-31	Jacksonville
10/4	W 29-6	Oakland
10/11	L 21-28	at Arizona
10/18	W 28-17	at Cincinnati
10/25	W 24-21	San Francisco
11/1	W 31-10	at Buffalo
11/8	L 17-20	at Indianapolis
11/23	L 17-20	Tennessee
11/29	L 27-35	Indianapolis
12/6	L 18-23	at Jacksonville
12/13	W 34-7	Seattle
12/20	W 16-13	at St. Louis
12/27	W 27-20	at Miami
1/3	W 34-27	New England

SCORE BY PERIODS

Texans	89	131	75	93	0 —	388
Opponents	57	135	58	83	0 —	333

2009 TEAM STATISTICS

	Texans	Opp.
Total First Downs	340	300
Rushing	93	91
Passing	231	175
Penalty	16	34
3rd Down: Made/Att	82/204	79/201
3rd Down Pct.	40.2	39.3
4th Down: Made/Att	8/12	9/21
4th Down Pct.	66.7	42.9
Possession Avg.	31:54	28:06
Total Net Yards	6129	5198
Avg. Per Game	383.1	324.9
Total Plays	1043	974
Avg. Per Play	5.9	5.3
Net Yards Rushing	1475	1711
Avg. Per Game	92.2	106.9
Total Rushes	425	396
Net Yards Passing	4654	3487
Avg. Per Game	290.9	217.9
Sacked/Yards Lost	25/149	30/187
Gross Yards	4803	3674
Att./Completions	593/399	548/344
Completion Pct.	67.3	62.8
Had Intercepted	17	14
Punts/Average	67/42.8	76/46.8
Net Punting Avg.	67/39.4	76/40.4
Penalties/Yards	95/833	92/728
Fumbles/Ball Lost	21/11	27/13
Touchdowns	46	39
Rushing	13	17
Passing	29	19
Returns	4	3

2009 INDIVIDUAL STATISTICS

PASSING	Att.	Comp.	Yds.	Pct.	TD	Int.	Tkld.	Rate
Schaub	583	396	4770	67.9	29	15	25/149	98.6
Grossman	9	3	33	33.3	0	1	0/0	5.6
C. Brown	1	0	0	0.0	0	1	0/0	0.0
Texans	593	399	4803	67.3	29	17	25/149	96.3
Opponents	548	344	3674	62.8	19	14	30/187	83.2

SCORING	TD R	TD P	TD Rt	PAT	FG	Saf	PTS
K. Brown	0	0	0	43/44	21/32	0	106
A. Johnson	0	9	0	0/0	0/0	0	56
J. Jones	0	6	1	0/0	0/0	0	42
Slaton	3	4	0	0/0	0/0	0	42
Daniels	0	5	0	0/0	0/0	0	30
Moats	4	1	0	0/0	0/0	0	30
C. Brown	3	0	0	0/0	0/0	0	18
Foster	3	0	0	0/0	0/0	0	18
Pollard	0	0	2	0/0	0/0	0	12
Walter	0	2	0	0/0	0/0	0	12
Barber	0	0	1	0/0	0/0	0	6
Dreessen	0	1	0	0/0	0/0	0	6
Leach	0	1	0	0/0	0/0	0	6
Cushing	0	0	0	0/0	0/0	1	2
Diles	0	0	0	0/0	0/0	1	2
Texans	13	29	4	43/44	21/32	2	388
Opponents	17	19	3	39/39	20/23	0	333

2-Pt. Conversions: A. Johnson.
Texans 1-2, Opponents 0-0.

RUSHING	No.	Yds	Avg	LG	TD
Slaton	131	437	3.3	32t	3
Moats	101	390	3.9	17	4
C. Brown	79	267	3.4	13	3
Foster	54	257	4.8	24	3
Schaub	48	57	1.2	19	0
Walter	4	26	6.5	13	0
J. Jones	3	22	7.3	17	0
A. Johnson	2	10	5.0	7	0
Grossman	3	9	3.0	8	0
Texans	425	1475	3.5	32t	13
Opponents	396	1711	4.3	91t	17

RECEIVING	No.	Yds	Avg	LG	TD
A. Johnson	101	1569	15.5	72t	9
Walter	53	611	11.5	41	2
Slaton	44	417	9.5	38t	4
Daniels	40	519	13.0	44	5
D. Anderson	38	370	9.7	27	0
J. Jones	27	437	16.2	45	6
Dreessen	26	320	12.3	25t	1
Leach	20	155	7.8	26	1
C. Brown	16	74	4.6	12	0
Moats	13	106	8.2	20	1
Foster	8	93	11.6	20	0
Casey	6	64	10.7	32	0
A. Davis	6	59	9.8	21	0
Hill	1	9	9.0	9	0
Texans	399	4803	12.0	72t	29
Opponents	344	3674	10.7	69t	19

INTERCEPTIONS	No.	Yds	Avg	LG	TD
Pollard	4	121	30.3	70t	1
Cushing	4	26	6.5	20	0
Wilson	2	29	14.5	16	0
Reeves	1	19	19.0	19	0
Busing	1	14	14.0	14	0
Barber	1	3	3.0	3	0
McCain	1	0	0.0	0	0
Texans	14	212	15.1	70t	1
Opponents	17	294	17.3	91t	3

PUNTING	No.	Yds.	Avg.	In 20	LG
Turk	67	2866	42.8	24	62
Texans	67	2866	42.8	24	62
Opponents	76	3557	46.8	27	67

PUNT RETURNS	Ret	FC	Yds	Avg	LG	TD
J. Jones	39	14	426	10.9	62	0
Martinez	6	1	23	3.8	11	0
Texans	45	15	449	10.0	62	0
Opponents	24	24	104	4.3	18	0

KICKOFF RETURNS	No.	Yds	Avg	LG	TD
A. Davis	33	782	23.7	63	0
J. Jones	24	638	26.6	95t	1
Leach	2	23	11.5	15	0
Martinez	1	6	6.0	6	0
Busing	1	0	0.0	0	0
Casey	1	0	0.0	0	0
De. Robinson	1	0	0.0	0	0
Walter	1	0	0.0	0	0
Texans	64	1449	22.6	95t	1
Opponents	71	1597	22.5	71	0

FIELD GOALS	1-19	20-29	30-39	40-49	50+
K. Brown	0/0	11/13	6/9	2/6	2/4
Texans	0/0	11/13	6/9	2/6	2/4
Opponents	0/0	5/5	4/5	4/5	7/8

SACKS	No.
Williams	9.0
Barwin	4.5
Antonio Smith	4.5
Cushing	4.0
Zgonina	2.5
Okoye	1.5
Pollard	1.5
Ryans	1.0
(group)	1.0
Cody	0.5
Texans	30.0
Opponents	25.0

RECORD HOLDERS

INDIVIDUAL RECORDS—CAREER

Category	Name	Performance
Rushing (Yds.)	Domanick Williams, 2003-06	3,195
Passing (Yds.)	David Carr, 2002-06	13,391
Passing (TDs)	David Carr, 2002-06	59
Receiving (No.)	Andre Johnson, 2003-09	587
Receiving (Yds.)	Andre Johnson, 2003-09	7,948
Interceptions	Dunta Robinson, 2004-09	13
Punting (Avg.)	Chad Stanley, 2002-06	41.0
Punt Return (Avg.)	Jacoby Jones, 2007-09	10.9
Kickoff Return (Avg.)	André Davis, 2007-09	25.4
Field Goals	Kris Brown, 2002-09	172
Touchdowns (Tot.)	Andre Johnson, 2003-09	42
Points	Kris Brown, 2002-09	767
*Sacks	Mario Williams, 2006-08	30.5

INDIVIDUAL RECORDS—SINGLE SEASON

Category	Name	Performance
Rushing (Yds.)	Steve Slaton, 2008	1,282
Passing (Yds.)	Matt Schaub, 2009	4,770
Passing (TDs)	David Carr, 2004	16
Receiving (No.)	Andre Johnson, 2008	115
Receiving (Yds.)	Andre Johnson, 2008	1,575
Interceptions	Marcus Coleman, 2003	7
Punting (Avg.)	Matt Turk, 2009	42.7
Punt Return (Avg.)	Jacoby Jones, 2008	12.1
Kickoff Return (Avg.)	André Davis, 2007	30.3
Field Goals	Kris Brown, 2008	29
Touchdowns (Tot.)	Domanick Williams, 2004	14
Points	Kris Brown, 2008	124
*Sacks	Mario Williams, 2007	14.0

INDIVIDUAL RECORDS—SINGLE GAME

Category	Name	Performance
Rushing (Yds.)	Domanick Williams, 12-26-04	158
Passing (Yds.)	Matt Schaub, 12-7-08	414
Passing (TDs)	Sage Rosenfels, 10-21-07	4
	Matt Schaub, 9-20-09, 10-18-09	4
Receiving (No.)	Andre Johnson, 10-10-04, 11-27-05	12
	Kevin Walter, 10-14-07	12
Receiving (Yds.)	Andre Johnson, 12-14-08	207
Interceptions	Aaron Glenn, 12-8-02	2
	Marcus Coleman, 9-7-03	2
	Kenny Wright, 9-28-03	2
	Dunta Robinson, 10-3-04	2
	Bernard Pollard, 11-8-09	2
Field Goals	Kris Brown, 9-7-03, 12-4-05, 10-7-07	5
Touchdowns (Tot.)	Ryan Moats, 11-1-09	3
Points	Ryan Moats, 11-1-09	18
*Sacks	Mario Williams, 12-13-07	3.5

**Sacks became an official statistic in 1982.*

HOUSTON TEXANS

2010 VETERAN ROSTER

No.	Name	Pos.	Ht.	Wt.	Birthdate	NFL Exp.	College	Hometown	How Acq.	'09 Games/ Starts
52	Adibi, Xavier	LB	6-2	242	10/18/84	3	Virginia Tech	Hampton, Va.	D4-'08	16/0
89	Anderson, David	WR	5-10	196	7/28/83	5	Colorado State	Thousand Oaks, Calif.	D7-'06	16/8
34	Barber, Dominique	S	6-0	215	8/2/86	3	Minnesota	Wayzata, Minn.	D6-'08	13/6
98	Barwin, Connor	DE	6-4	254	10/15/86	2	Cincinnati	Detroit, Mich.	D2-'09	16/0
32	Bennett, Fred	CB	6-1	201	12/31/83	4	South Carolina	Manning, S.C.	D4-'07	10/3
57	Bentley, Kevin	LB	6-0	248	12/29/79	9	Northwestern	North Hills, Calif.	UFA(Sea)-'08	16/0
50	Bing, Darnell	LB	6-2	220	9/10/84	2	Southern California	Long Beach, Calif.	FA-'09	4/0*
65	Brisiel, Mike	G	6-5	300	3/14/83	3	Colorado State	Fayetteville, Ark.	FA-'06	5/5
22	#Brown, Chris	RB	6-3	235	4/17/81	8	Colorado	Naperville, Ill.	UFA(Tenn)-'08	14/4
76	Brown, Duane	T	6-4	315	8/30/85	3	Virginia Tech	Richmond, Va.	D1-'08	16/16
3	Brown, Kris	K	5-11	215	12/23/76	12	Nebraska	Southlake, Texas	RFA(Pitt)-'02	16/0
93	Bulman, Tim	DE	6-4	275	10/31/82	4	Boston College	Dorchester, Mass.	FA-'06	15/1
40	#Busing, John	S	6-2	218	9/1/83	5	Miami (Ohio)	Alpharetta, Ga.	FA-'09	16/4
78	Butler, Rashad	T	6-4	308	2/10/83	5	Miami	West Palm Beach, Fla.	W(Car)-07	15/0
62	Caldwell, Antoine	C	6-3	305	4/19/86	2	Alabama	Montgomery, Ala.	D3-'09	11/3
53	#Campbell, Khary	LB	6-2	224	4/4/79	9	Bowling Green	Toledo, Ohio	FA-'09	1/0
86	Casey, James	TE	6-3	240	9/22/84	2	Rice	Azle, Texas	D5-'09	15/0
95	Cody, Shaun	DT	6-4	310	1/22/83	6	Southern California	Hacienda Heights, Calif.	UFA(Det)-'09	14/13
56	Cushing, Brian	LB	6-3	260	1/24/87	2	Southern California	Park Ridge, N.J.	D1-'09	16/16
81	Daniels, Owen	TE	6-3	250	11/9/82	5	Wisconsin	Naperville, Ill.	D4-'06	8/8
11	Davis, André	WR	6-1	200	6/12/79	9	Virginia Tech	Niskayuna, N.Y.	UFA(Buff)-'07	14/1
54	Diles, Zac	LB	6-2	245	6/11/85	4	Kansas State	Tulare, Calif.	D7-'07	16/13
85	Dreessen, Joel	TE	6-4	250	7/26/82	5	Colorado State	Fort Morgan, Colo.	FA-'07	16/11
25	#Ferguson, Nick	S	5-11	204	11/27/74	11	Georgia Tech	Miami, Fla.	UFA(Den)-'08	10/1
23	Foster, Arian	RB	6-1	224	8/24/86	2	Tennessee	San Diego, Calif.	FA-'09	6/1
82	Gaines, Michael	TE	6-4	277	3/30/80	7	Central Florida	Tallahassee, Fla.	UFA(Cle)-'10	10/7*
27	Henry, Chris	RB	5-11	230	6/6/85	4	Arizona	Stockton, Calif.	FA-'09	2/0*
87	Hill, Anthony	TE	6-6	265	1/2/85	2	North Carolina State	Houston, Texas	D4b-'09	5/0
96	Jamison, Tim	DE	6-3	270	2/26/86	2	Michigan	Riverdale, Ill.	FA-'09	7/0
80	Johnson, Andre	WR	6-3	225	7/11/81	8	Miami	Miami, Fla.	D1-'03	16/16
12	Jones, Jacoby	WR	6-2	210	7/11/84	4	Lane College	New Orleans, La.	D3-'07	15/1
44	Leach, Vonta	FB	6-0	255	11/6/81	7	East Carolina	Rowland, N.C.	FA-'06	16/4
17	Martinez, Glenn	WR	6-1	190	11/30/81	5	Saginaw Valley	Tampa, Fla.	FA-'09	7/0
41	McCain, Brice	CB	5-9	185	12/10/86	2	Utah	Terrell, Texas	D6-'09	16/1
21	Moats, Ryan	RB	5-8	210	12/17/82	6	Louisiana Tech	Dallas, Texas	FA-'08	14/2
28	Molden, Antwaun	CB	6-1	202	1/23/85	3	Eastern Kentucky	Cleveland, Ohio	D3a-'08	4/0
55	Myers, Chris	C	6-4	295	9/15/81	6	Miami	Miami, Fla.	T(Den)-'08	16/16
72	Nading, Jesse	DE	6-5	268	7/3/1985	2	Colorado State	Highlands Ranch, Colo.	FA-'08	1/0
97	Okam, Frank	DT	6-5	340	10/16/85	3	Texas	Dallas, Texas	D5-'08	3/0
91	Okoye, Amobi	DT	6-2	315	6/10/87	4	Louisville	Huntsville, Ala.	D1-'07	16/16
7	Orlovsky, Dan	QB	6-5	230	8/18/83	6	Connecticut	Shelton, Conn.	UFA(Det)-'09	0*
38	Parson, Mark	CB	5-10	188	5/9/86	2	Ohio	Richmond, Va.	FA-'09	0*
48	#Pittman, Bryan	LS	6-3	265	1/20/77	8	Washington	Auburn, Wash.	FA-'09	7/0*
69	#Pitts, Chester	G	6-4	308	6/2679	9	San Diego State	Inglewood, Calif.	D2-'02	2/2
31	Pollard, Bernard	S	6-1	224	12/23/84	5	Purdue	Fort Wayne, Ind.	FA-'09	13/13
29	Quin, Glover	CB	6-0	205	1/15/86	2	New Mexico	Summitt, Miss.	D4a-'09	15/12
4	Rackers, Neil	K	6-1	206	8/16/76	11	Illinois	St. Louis, Mo.	UFA(Ariz)-'10	14/0*
35	Reeves, Jacques	CB	5-11	195	10/8/82	7	Purdue	Lancaster, Texas	UFA(Dall)-'08	12/4
70	#Reyes, Tutan	G	6-3	310	10/28/77	11	Mississippi	Queens, N.Y.	FA-'09	0*
66	Robinson, DelJuan	DT	6-3	320	7/1/84	3	Mississippi State	Hernando, Miss.	FA-'07	10/0
42	#Russell, Brian	S	6-2	210	2/5/78	9	San Diego State	West Covina, Calif.	FA-'09	12/1*
59	Ryans, DeMeco	LB	6-1	250	7/28/84	5	Alabama	Bessemer, Ala.	D2-'06	16/16
74	#Salaam, Ephraim	T	6-7	310	6/19/76	13	San Diego State	Sacramento, Calif.	FA-'09	5/0*
8	Schaub, Matt	QB	6-5	240	6/25/81	7	Virginia	West Chester, Pa.	T(Atl)-'07	16/16
20	Slaton, Steve	RB	5-9	215	1/4/86	3	West Virginia	Levittown, Pa.	D3b-'08	11/10
94	Smith, Antonio	DE	6-4	295	10/21/81	7	Oklahoma State	Oklahoma City, Okla.	UFA(Ariz)-'09	16/15
74	Smith, Wade	G	6-4	296	4/26/81	7	Memphis	Dallas, Texas	UFA(KC)-'10	16/9*
64	Studdard, Kasey	G	6-3	302	7/1/84	4	Texas	Lone Tree, Colo.	D6-'07	16/14
51	#Thompson, Chaun	LB	6-2	250	5/22/80	8	West Texas A&M	Mount Pleasant, Texas	UFA(Cle)-'08	3/0
1	Turk, Matt	P	6-5	251	6/16/68	15	Wisconsin-Whitewater	Greenfield, Wisc.	FA-'07	16/0
83	Walter, Kevin	WR	6-3	218	8/4/81	8	Eastern Michigan	Vernon Hills, Ill.	RFA(Cin)-'06	14/14
63	White, Chris	C	6-2	290	2/28/83	6	Southern Mississippi	Winona, Miss.	FA-'06	12/8
90	Williams, Mario	DE	6-6	295	1/31/85	5	North Carolina State	Richlands, N.C.	D1-'06	16/16
26	Wilson, Eugene	S	5-10	202	8/17/80	8	Illinois	Merrillville, Ind.	FA-'08	8/8
73	Winston, Eric	T	6-7	314	11/17/83	5	Miami	Midland, Texas	D3b-'06	16/16
92	#Zgonina, Jeff	DT	6-2	285	5/24/70	18	Purdue	Chicago, Ill.	UFA(Mia)-'07	16/2

* Bing played 4 games for Detroit in '09; Gaines played 1 game for Chicago and 9 games for Cleveland; Henry played 2 games with Tennessee; Orlovsky inactive third quarterback all 16 games; Parson inactive for 6 games; Pittman played 4 games for Atlanta and 3 games with Houston; Rackers played 14 games for Arizona; Reyes inactive for 1 game with N.Y. Giants and 11 games with Houston; Russell played 9 games with Jacksonville and 3 games with Houston; Salaam played 5 games for Detroit; W. Smith played 16 games for Kansas City.

\# Unrestricted free agent; subject to developments.

Players lost through free agency (2): QB Rex Grossman (Wash; 1 game in '09); CB Dunta Robinson (Atl; 16).

Also played with Texans in '09—None.

2010 FIRST-YEAR ROSTER

Name	Pos.	Ht.	Wt.	Birthdate	College	Hometown	How Acq.
Booty, John David (1)	QB	6-3	213	1/3/85	Southern California	Shreveport, La.	FA
Corcoran, Jack	FB	6-1	230	6/26/87	Rutgers	Atlantic City, N.J.	FA
Crawford, London	WR	6-2	205	10/19/86	Arkansas	Mobile, Ala.	FA
Dickerson, Dorin	WR	6-2	222	3/31/88	Pittsburgh	Imperial, Pa.	D7
Egboh, Pannel (1)	DE	6-6	276	3/23/86	Stanford	Mesquite, Texas	FA-'09
Graham, Garrett	TE	6-3	243	8/4/86	Wisconsin	Brick, N.J.	D4b
Greenhouse, Isaiah	LB	6-2	232	7/15/87	Northwestern State	Marksville, La.	FA
Helms, Brett (1)	C	6-2	295	4/16/86	Louisiana State	Stuttgart, Ark.	FA-'09
Holliday, Trindon	WR	5-5	159	4/27/86	Louisiana State	Zachary, La.	D6b
Jackson, Kareem	CB	5-10	196	4/10/88	Alabama	Macon, Ga.	D1
Johnson, Jeremiah (1)	RB	5-9	210	2/15/87	Oregon	Los Angeles, Calif.	FA-'09
Maneri, Steve	T	6-6	275	3/20/88	Temple	Saddle Brook, N.J.	FA
Matte, Kristian	G	6-2	291	9/3/85	Concordia	St. Hubert, Quebec, Canada	FA
McManis, Sherrick	CB	6-1	195	12/19/87	Northwestern	Peoria, Ill.	D5
Mitchell, Earl	DT	6-3	296	9/25/87	Arizona	Galena Park, Texas	D3
Nolan, Troy (1)	S	6-2	207	9/7/86	Arizona State	Woodland Hills, Calif.	D7-'09
Patterson, Will	LB	6-1	237	7/20/87	Indiana	Indianapolis, Ind.	FA
Pemberton, Cole	T	6-7	318	7/1/87	Colorado State	Highlands Ranch, Colo.	FA
Polk, Nicholas	S	6-0	219	10/6/86	Indiana	Milwaukee, Wisc.	FA
Sharpton, Darryl	LB	5-11	236	1/1/88	Miami	Coral Gables, Fla.	D4a
Sheehan, Tyler	QB	6-4	227	11/17/87	Bowling Green	Cincinnati, Ohio	FA
Sheppard, Malcolm	DT	6-2	291	2/13/88	Arkansas	Bainbridge, Ga.	FA
Singfield, Pierre	CB	5-11	196	9/25/87	Arizona State	Arvada, Colo.	FA
Smith, Shelley	G	6-4	300	5/21/87	Colorado State	Phoenix, Ariz.	D6a
Stenavich, Adam (1)	T	6-4	305	3/11/83	Michigan	Marshfield, Wisc.	FA-'08
Stross, Trey	WR	6-4	200	6/29/87	Iowa	Avon Lake, Ohio	FA
Tate, Ben	RB	5-11	220	8/21/88	Auburn	Salisbury, Md.	D2
Ulatoski, Adam	T	6-6	310	12/17/85	Texas	Southlake, Texas	FA
Unrein, Will	DE	6-4	270	3/25/87	Wyoming	Eaton, Colo.	FA
Webster, Aaron	S	6-2	211	7/20/88	Cincinnati	Detroit, Mich.	FA
Williams, Torri	S	6-2	208	8/29/86	Purdue	Leander, Texas	FA

The term NFL Rookie is defined as a player who is in his first season of professional football and has not been on the roster of another professional football team for any regular-season or postseason games. A Rookie is designated by an "R" on NFL rosters. Players who have been active in another professional football league or players who have NFL experience, including either preseason training camp or being on an Active List or Inactive List, or on Reserve/Injured or Reserve/Physically Unable to Perform for fewer than six regular-season games, are termed NFL First-Year Players. An NFL First-Year Player is designated by a "1" on NFL rosters. Thereafter, a player is credited with an additional year of experience for each season in which he accumulates six games on the Active List or Inactive List, or on Reserve/Injured or Reserve/Physically Unable to Perform.

Log on to www.houstontexans.com for an up-to-date roster.

COACHING STAFF

Head Coach,
Gary Kubiak

Pro Career: Gary Kubiak was introduced as the second head coach in Houston Texans history on January 26, 2006. Kubiak returned to Houston after spending 20 of the previous 23 years in the Denver area. Kubiak's record as Texans head coach is 31-33, making him the franchise's winningest head coach. He guided the Texans to a 9-7 record in 2009, highlighted by a season-ending four-game win streak to capture the franchise's first winning season. Houston narrowly missed its first-ever playoff berth, losing a tie-breaker for the final spot. The 2009 Texans set franchise records for total offense, scoring offense, total defense and scoring defense. A franchise-record five players earned trips to the Pro Bowl, led by Pro Bowl MVP Matt Schaub. In 2008, he Texans overcame an 0-4 start that was due in part to the damage inflicted by Hurricane Ike and finished 8-8. Houston became just the ninth squad in NFL history to finish .500 or better after an 0-4 start. In 2007, the Texans broke even for the first time, finishing at 8-8. Houston went 7-3 outside of the AFC West and set a franchise record with a 6-2 mark at home. It was the first time the Texans posted a winning mark at Reliant Stadium. In his first year as a head coach, Kubiak guided the Texans to a 6-10 record, tripling the team's win total of the year before. Prior to joining the Texans, Kubiak spent the previous 11 years (1995-2005) as Denver's offensive coordinator, helping guide the Broncos to back-to-back World Championships in Super Bowls XXXII and XXXIII and three AFC West Division titles. Kubiak tutored Hall of Fame QB John Elway from 1995-98 and RB Terrell Davis was named NFL Most Valuable Player in 1998. In Kubiak's 11 years in Denver, the Broncos had 28 Pro Bowl players on the offensive side of the ball. Kubiak began his coaching career as the running backs coach at Texas A&M (1992-93). Kubiak started his NFL coaching career with the San Francisco 49ers as the quarterbacks coach, winning Super Bowl XXIX in his only season (1994). Kubiak is a veteran of six Super Bowls—three as a player and three as a coach. Career record: 31-33.

Background: Kubiak starred at quarterback for Texas A&M from 1979-1982, earning all-Southwest Conference honors as a senior. He played for the Broncos from 1983-1991 as John Elway's backup. Kubiak played in 119 career games, tossed 14 touchdowns, and was a part of three teams that reached the Super Bowl.

Personal: Born August 15, 1961 in Houston. He and his wife, Rhonda, have three sons—Klint, Klay, and Klein.

ASSISTANT COACHES

John Benton, offensive line; born December 13, 1963, Los Angeles. Offensive lineman Colorado State 1986-1990. No pro playing experience. College coach: California University (Pa.) 1990-94, Colorado State 1996-2003. Pro coach: St. Louis Rams 2004-05, joined Texans in 2006.

Frank Bush, defensive coordinator; born January 10, 1963, Athens, Ga. Linebacker North Carolina State 1981-84. Pro linebacker Houston Oilers 1985-86. Pro coach: Houston Oilers 1987-1991 (scout), 1992-94, Denver Broncos 1995-2003, Arizona Cardinals 2004-06, joined Texans in 2007.

Perry Carter, defensive assistant; born August 15, 1971, McComb, Miss. Defensive back Southern Mississippi 1989-1993. Pro defensive back Arizona Cardinals 1994, Kansas City Chiefs 1995, Oakland Raiders 1996-98, Edmonton Eskimos (CFL) 2000-01, Montreal Alouettes (CFL) 2002, British Columbia Lions (CFL) 2003-04. College coach: Texas A&M-Commerce 2004. Pro coach: Hamburg Sea Devils (NFLEL) 2006, joined Texans in 2006.

Rick Dennison, offensive coordinator; born June 22, 1958, Kalispell, Mont. Tight end Colorado State 1976-79. Pro linebacker Denver Broncos 1982-1990. Pro coach: Denver Broncos 1995-2009, joined Texans in 2010.

David Gibbs, defensive backs; born January 10, 1968, Mount Airy, N.C. Defensive back Colorado 1987-1990. No pro playing experience. College coach: Oklahoma 1991-92, Colorado 1993-94, Kansas 1995-96, Minnesota 1997-2000, Auburn 2005. Pro coach: Denver Broncos 2001-04, Kansas City Chiefs 2006-08, joined Texans in 2009.

Chick Harris, running backs; born September 21, 1945, Durham, N.C. Running back Northern Arizona 1966-69. No pro playing experience. College coach: Colorado State 1970-71, Long Beach State 1972-73, Washington 1975-1980. Pro coach: Detroit Wheels (WFL) 1974, Buffalo Bills 1981-82, Seattle Seahawks 1983-1991, Los Angeles Rams 1992-94, Carolina Panthers 1995-2001, joined Texans in 2002.

Johnny Holland, linebackers; born March 11, 1965, Belleville, Texas. Linebacker Texas A&M 1983-86. Pro linebacker Green Bay Packers 1987-1993. Pro coach: Green Bay Packers 1995-99, Seattle Seahawks 2000-02, Detroit Lions 2003-05, joined Texans in 2006.

Larry Kirksey, wide receivers; born January 6, 1951, Harlan, Ky. Wide receiver Eastern Kentucky 1970-73. No pro playing experience. College coach: Miami (Ohio) 1974-76, Kentucky 1977-1981, Kansas 1982, Kentucky State 1983 (head coach), Florida 1984-88, Pittsburgh 1989, Alabama 1990-93, Texas A&M 2000, Middle Tennessee State 2006. Pro coach: San Francisco 49ers 1994-99, Detroit Lions 2001-02, Jacksonville Jaguars 2003, Denver Broncos 2004, joined Texans in 2007.

Greg Knapp, quarterbacks; born March 5, 1963, Long Beach, Calif. Quarterback San Diego State 1982-85. No pro playing experience. College coach: Sacramento State 1986-1994. Pro coach: San Francisco 49ers 1995-2003, Atlanta Falcons 2004-06, Oakland Raiders 2007-08, Seattle Seahawks 2009, joined Texans in 2010.

Bill Kollar, asst. head coach/defensive line; born November 27, 1952, Warren, Ohio. Defensive end Montana State 1971-73. Pro defensive end Cincinnati Bengals 1974-76, Tampa Bay Buccaneers 1977-1981. College coach: Illinois 1985-87, Purdue 1988-89. Pro coach: Tampa Bay Buccaneers 1984, Atlanta Falcons 1990-2000, St. Louis Rams 2001-05, Buffalo Bills 2006-08, joined Texans in 2009.

Marc Lubick, offensive assistant; born November 13, 1977, Bozeman, Mont. Defensive back Montana State 1996-99. No pro playing experience. College coach: Colorado State 2000-02, 2005-09. Pro coach: St. Louis Rams 2003-04 (scout), joined Texans in 2010.

Joe Marciano, special teams coordinator; born February 10, 1954, Dunmore, Pa. Quarterback Temple 1972-75. No pro playing experience. College coach: East Stroudsburg State 1977, Rhode Island 1978-79, Villanova 1980, Penn State 1981, Temple 1982. Pro coach: Philadelphia/Baltimore Stars (USFL) 1983-85, New Orleans Saints 1986-1995, Tampa Bay Buccaneers 1996-2001, joined Texans in 2002.

Bruce Matthews, offensive assistant; born August 8, 1961, Raleigh, N.C. Offensive lineman Southern California, 1979-1982. Pro offensive lineman Houston Oilers/Tennessee Titans 1983-2001. Inducted into Pro Football Hall of Fame in 2007. Pro coach: Joined Texans in 2009.

Brian Pariani, tight ends; born July 2, 1965, San Francisco. No college or pro playing experience. College coach: UCLA 1989, Syracuse 2005. Pro coach: San Francisco 49ers 1991-94, Denver Broncos 1994-2004, joined Texans in 2006.

Frank Pollack, asst. offensive line; born November 5, 1967, Camp Springs, Md. Offensive lineman Northern Arizona 1985-89. Pro offensive lineman San Francisco 49ers 1990-97. College coach: Northern Arizona 2005-06. Pro coach: Joined Texans in 2007.

Ray Rhodes, senior defensive assistant; born October 20, 1950, Mexia, Texas. Running back Texas Christian 1969-1970, wide receiver/defensive back/kick returner Tulsa 1972-73. Pro wide receiver/defensive back New York Giants 1974-79, San Francisco 49ers 1980. Pro coach: San Francisco 49ers 1981-1991, 1994, Green Bay Packers 1992-93, 1999 (head coach 1999), Philadelphia Eagles 1995-98 (head coach), Washington Redskins 2000, Denver Broncos 2001-02, Seattle Seahawks 2003-07, joined Texans in 2008.

Robert Saleh, asst. linebackers; born January 31, 1979, Dearborn, Mich. Tight end Northern Michigan 1997-2000. No pro playing experience. College coach: Michigan State 2002-03, Central Michigan 2004. Pro coach: Joined Texans in 2005.

American Football Conference
South Division
Team Colors: Royal Blue and White
P.O. Box 535000
Indianapolis, Indiana 46253
Telephone: (317) 297-2658

2010 SCHEDULE

PRESEASON

Aug. 15	**San Francisco**	1:00
Aug. 19	at Buffalo	7:30
Aug. 26	at Green Bay	7:00
Sep. 2	**Cincinnati**	7:00

REGULAR SEASON

Sep. 12	at Houston	12:00
Sep. 19	**New York Giants**	8:20
Sep. 26	at Denver	2:15
Oct. 3	at Jacksonville	4:05
Oct. 10	**Kansas City**	1:00
Oct. 17	at Washington	8:20
Oct. 24	BYE	
Nov. 1	**Houston** (Mon)	8:30
Nov. 7	at Philadelphia	4:15
Nov. 14	**Cincinnati**	1:00
Nov. 21	at New England	4:15
Nov. 28	**San Diego**	* 8:20
Dec. 5	**Dallas**	4:15
Dec. 9	at Tennessee (Thu)	7:20
Dec. 19	**Jacksonville**	1:00
Dec. 26	at Oakland	1:05
Jan. 2	**Tennessee**	1:00

** Sunday night games in Weeks 11-17 subject to change*

Stadium: Lucas Oil Stadium (opened in 2008) • **Capacity:** 63,000
500 South Capitol Avenue
Indianapolis, Indiana 46225
Playing Surface: FieldTurf
Training Camp: Rose-Hulman Institute
5500 Wabash Avenue
Terre Haute, IN 47803

LUCAS OIL STADIUM

CLUB OFFICIALS

Owner and CEO: James Irsay
President: Bill Polian
Head Coach: Jim Caldwell
Vice President: Carlie Irsay-Gordon
Vice President: Casey Irsay Foyt
Senior Executive Vice President: Pete Ward
Senior Vice President of Sales and Marketing: Tom Zupancic
Vice President and General Manager: Chris Polian
Vice President-Finance: Kurt Humphrey
Vice President-Ticket Operations/Guest Services: Larry Hall
Vice President-Public Relations: Craig Kelley
Vice President of Sponsorship Sales: Jay Souers
Vice President of Premium Seating and Ticket Sales: Greg Hylton
Director of Football Administration: Steve Champlin
Director of Player Personnel: Tom Telesco
Director of Pro Player Personnel: Clyde Powers
Associate Director of Pro Personnel: Kevin Rogers
Equipment Manager: Jon Scott
Video Director: Marty Heckscher
Head Athletic Trainer: Dave Hammer
Director of Rehabilitation: Erin Barill
Assistant Director of Public Relations: Vernon Cheek
Manager of Publicity: Justin Dickens
Assistant Equipment Managers: Mike Mays, Sean Sullivan, Brian Seabrooks
Assistant Trainers: Dave Walston, Bryant Baugh
Assistant Video Director: John Starliper

COACHING HISTORY

Baltimore 1953-1983
(460-409-7)
Records include postseason games

1953	Keith Molesworth	3-9-0
1954-1962	Weeb Ewbank	61-52-1
1963-69	Don Shula	73-26-4
1970-72	Don McCafferty*	26-11-1
1972	John Sandusky	4-5-0
1973-74	Howard Schnellenberger**	4-13-0
1974	Joe Thomas	2-9-0
1975-79	Ted Marchibroda	41-36-0
1980-81	Mike McCormack	9-23-0
1982-84	Frank Kush***	11-28-1
1984	Hal Hunter	0-1-0
1985-86	Rod Dowhower****	5-24-0
1986-1991	Ron Meyer#	36-36-0
1991	Rick Venturi	1-10-0
1992-95	Ted Marchibroda	32-35-0
1996-97	Lindy Infante	12-21-0
1998-2001	Jim Mora	32-34-0
2002-08	Tony Dungy	92-33-0
2009	Jim Caldwell	16-3-0

*Released after five games in 1972
**Released after three games in 1974
***Resigned after 15 games in 1984
****Released after 13 games in 1986
#Released after five games in 1991

PAID ATTENDANCE

Home 518,109 Away 519,157
Total 1,037,266
Single-game home record, 67,650 (1/24/10)
Single-season home record, 518,109 (2009)

2010 DRAFT CHOICES

Round	Name	Pos.	College
1	Jerry Hughes	DE	Texas Christian
2	Pat Angerer	LB	Iowa
3	Kevin Thomas	DB	Southern California
4	Jacques McClendon	G	Tennessee
5	Brody Eldridge	TE	Oklahoma
7	Ricardo Mathews	DE	Cincinnati
	Kavell Conner	LB	Clemson
	Ray Fisher	DB	Indiana

INDIANAPOLIS COLTS

2009 TEAM RECORD

PRESEASON (1-3)

Date	Result	Opponent
8/14	L 3-13	Minnesota
8/20	W 23-15	Philadelphia
8/29	L 17-18	at Detroit
9/3	L 7-38	at Cincinnati

REGULAR SEASON (14-2)

Date	Result	Opponent
9/13	W 14-12	Jacksonville
9/21	W 27-23	at Miami
9/27	W 31-10	at Arizona
10/4	W 34-17	Seattle
10/11	W 31-9	at Tennessee
10/25	W 42-6	at St. Louis
11/1	W 18-14	San Francisco
11/8	W 20-17	Houston
11/15	W 35-34	New England
11/22	W 17-15	at Baltimore
11/29	W 35-27	at Houston
12/6	W 27-17	Tennessee
12/13	W 28-16	Denver
12/17	W 35-31	at Jacksonville
12/27	L 15-29	New York Jets
1/3	L 7-30	at Buffalo

POSTSEASON (2-1)

Date	Result	Opponent
1/16	W 20-3	Baltimore
1/24	W 30-17	New York Jets
2/7	L 17-31	vs. New Orleans, at South Florida

SCORE BY PERIODS

Colts	96	147	58	115	0	— 416
Opponents	66	105	52	84	0	— 307

2009 TEAM STATISTICS

	Colts	Opp.
Total First Downs	339	320
Rushing	69	106
Passing	241	203
Penalty	29	11
3rd Down: Made/Att	95/193	104/231
3rd Down Pct.	49.2	45.0
4th Down: Made/Att	5/11	6/19
4th Down Pct.	45.5	31.6
Possession Avg.	27:40	32:20
Total Net Yards	5809	5427
Avg. Per Game	363.1	339.2
Total Plays	980	1084
Avg. Per Play	5.9	5.0
Net Yards Rushing	1294	2024
Avg. Per Game	80.9	126.5
Total Rushes	366	467
Net Yards Passing	4515	3403
Avg. Per Game	282.2	212.7
Sacked/Yards Lost	13/90	34/228
Gross Yards	4605	3631
Att./Completions	601/402	583/372
Completion Pct.	66.9	63.8
Had Intercepted	19	16
Punts/Average	64/44.3	65/44.4
Net Punting Avg.	64/37.8	65/40.5
Penalties/Yards	74/546	92/889
Fumbles/Ball Lost	11/5	20/10
Touchdowns	53	31
Rushing	16	10
Passing	34	19
Returns	3	2

2009 INDIVIDUAL STATISTICS

PASSING	Att.	Comp.	Yds.	Pct.	TD	Int.	Tkld.	Rate
Manning	571	393	4500	68.8	33	16	10/74	99.9
Painter	28	8	83	28.6	0	2	3/16	9.8
Addai	1	1	22	100.0	1	0	0/0	158.3
Wayne	1	0	0	0.0	0	1	0/0	0.0
Colts	601	402	4605	66.9	34	19	13/90	95.4
Opponents	583	372	3631	63.8	19	16	34/228	80.6

SCORING	TD R	TD P	TD Rt	PAT	FG	Saf	PTS
Addai	10	3	0	0/0	0/0	0	78
Clark	0	10	0	0/0	0/0	0	60
Stover	0	0	0	33/33	9/11	0	60
Wayne	0	10	0	0/0	0/0	0	60
Collie	0	7	0	0/0	0/0	0	42
Vinatieri	0	0	0	17/18	7/9	0	38
Garcon	0	4	0	0/0	0/0	0	24
Brown	3	0	0	0/0	0/0	0	18
Simpson	2	0	1	0/0	0/0	0	18
Hart	1	0	0	0/0	0/0	0	6
Lacey	0	0	1	0/0	0/0	0	6
Session	0	0	1	0/0	0/0	0	6
Colts	16	34	3	50/51	16/20	0	416
Opponents	10	19	2	27/27	30/36	0	307

2-Pt. Conversions: Colts 0-2, Opponents 2-4.

RUSHING	No.	Yds	Avg	LG	TD
Addai	219	828	3.8	21t	10
Brown	78	281	3.6	45	3
Simpson	15	102	6.8	31t	2
Hart	26	70	2.7	15	1
Clark	2	11	5.5	7	0
Garcon	2	10	5.0	17	0
Painter	3	4	1.3	10	0
Collie	2	1	0.5	2	0
Manning	19	-13	-0.7	3	0
Colts	366	1294	3.5	45	16
Opponents	467	2024	4.3	64t	10

RECEIVING	No.	Yds	Avg	LG	TD
Wayne	100	1264	12.6	65t	10
Clark	100	1106	11.1	80t	10
Collie	60	676	11.3	39t	7
Addai	51	336	6.6	25	3
Garcon	47	765	16.3	66	4
Brown	11	169	15.4	72	0
Robinson	9	62	6.9	19	0
Santi	8	107	13.4	31	0
Hart	5	54	10.8	14	0
Baskett TM	4	28	7.0	9	0
Tamme	3	35	11.7	21	0
Simpson	3	1	0.3	5	0
Cloherty	1	2	2.0	2	0
Colts	402	4605	11.5	80t	34
Opponents	372	3631	9.8	63t	19

INTERCEPTIONS	No.	Yds	Avg	LG	TD
Bethea	4	19	4.8	19	0
Lacey	3	53	17.7	35t	1
Session	2	35	17.5	27t	1
Jennings	2	13	6.5	13	0
Sanders	1	29	29.0	29	0
Brackett	1	8	8.0	8	0
Hayden	1	6	6.0	6	0
Jackson	1	3	3.0	3	0
Powers	1	1	1.0	1	0
Colts	16	167	10.4	35t	2
Opponents	19	229	12.1	42	0

PUNTING	No.	Yds.	Avg.	In 20	LG
McAfee	64	2837	44.3	21	60
Colts	64	2837	44.3	21	60
Opponents	65	2883	44.4	25	59

PUNT RETURNS	Ret	FC	Yds	Avg	LG	TD
Rushing	21	22	119	5.7	22	0
Silva	7	1	32	4.6	7	0
Jennings	1	0	0	0.0	0	0
Colts	29	23	151	5.2	22	0
Opponents	36	15	301	8.4	69	0

KICKOFF RETURNS	No.	Yds	Avg	LG	TD
Simpson	38	898	23.6	93t	1
Rushing	7	127	18.1	22	0
Giguere	5	122	24.4	36	0
Do. Brown	1	21	21.0	21	0
Silva	1	19	19.0	19	0
Dawson	1	14	14.0	14	0
Robinson	1	10	10.0	10	0
Collie	1	8	8.0	8	0
Colts	55	1219	22.2	93t	1
Opponents	60	1519	25.3	106t	1

FIELD GOALS	1-19	20-29	30-39	40-49	50+
Stover	0/0	2/2	5/6	2/2	0/1
Vinatieri	1/1	3/3	1/2	2/2	0/1
Colts	1/1	5/5	6/8	4/4	0/2
Opponents	0/0	4/4	13/14	11/14	2/4

SACKS	No.
Freeney	13.5
Mathis	9.5
Brock	3.5
Foster	2.5
Brackett	1.0
A. Johnson	1.0
Keiaho	1.0
Wheeler	1.0
Muir	0.5
Session	0.5
Colts	34.0
Opponents	13.0

RECORD HOLDERS

INDIVIDUAL RECORDS—CAREER

Category	Name	Performance
Rushing (Yds.)	Edgerrin James, 1999-2005	9,226
Passing (Yds.)	Peyton Manning, 1998-2009	50,128
Passing (TDs)	Peyton Manning, 1998-2009	366
Receiving (No.)	Marvin Harrison, 1996-2008	1,102
Receiving (Yds.)	Marvin Harrison, 1996-2008	14,580
Interceptions	Bob Boyd, 1960-68	57
Punting (Avg.)	Chris Gardocki, 1995-98	44.8
Punt Return (Avg.)	Ron Gardin, 1970-71	13.5
Kickoff Return (Avg.)	Jim Duncan, 1969-1971	32.6
Field Goals	Mike Vanderjagt, 1998-2005	217
Touchdowns (Tot.)	Marvin Harrison, 1996-2008	128
Points	Mike Vanderjagt, 1998-2005	995
*Sacks	Dwight Freeney, 2002-09	84.0

INDIVIDUAL RECORDS—SINGLE SEASON

Category	Name	Performance
Rushing (Yds.)	Edgerrin James, 2000	1,709
Passing (Yds.)	Peyton Manning, 2004	4,557
Passing (TDs)	Peyton Manning, 2004	49
Receiving (No.)	Marvin Harrison, 2002	**143
Receiving (Yds.)	Marvin Harrison, 2002	1,722
Interceptions	Tom Keane, 1953	11
Punting (Avg.)	Rohn Stark, 1985	45.9
Punt Return (Avg.)	T.J. Rushing, 2007	13.1
Kickoff Return (Avg.)	Jim Duncan, 1970	35.4
Field Goals	Mike Vanderjagt, 2003	37
Touchdowns (Tot.)	Lenny Moore, 1964	20
Points	Mike Vanderjagt, 2003	157
*Sacks	Dwight Freeney, 2004	16.0

INDIVIDUAL RECORDS—SINGLE GAME

Category	Name	Performance
Rushing (Yds.)	Edgerrin James, 10-15-00	219
Passing (Yds.)	Peyton Manning, 10-31-04	472
Passing (TDs)	Peyton Manning, 9-28-03, 11-25-04	6
Receiving (No.)	Marvin Harrison, 12-26-99, 11-17-02	14
	Dallas Clark, 11-8-09	14
Receiving (Yds.)	Raymond Berry, 11-10-57	224
Interceptions	Many times	3
	Last time by Mike Prior, 12-20-92	
Field Goals	Many times	5
	Last time by Mike Vanderjagt, 12-7-03	
Touchdowns (Tot.)	Many times	4
	Last time by Joseph Addai, 11-26-06	
Points	Many times	24
	Last time by Joseph Addai, 11-26-06	
*Sacks	Johnie Cooks, 11-25-84	4.5

**Sacks became an official statistic in 1982.*
***NFL Record*

INDIANAPOLIS COLTS

2010 VETERAN ROSTER

No.	Name	Pos.	Ht.	Wt.	Birthdate	NFL Exp.	College	Hometown	How Acq.	'09 Games/ Starts
29	Addai, Joseph	RB	5-11	214	5/3/83	5	Louisiana State	Houston, Texas	D1-'06	15/15
62	Alleman, Andy	G	6-4	310	11/20/83	4	Akron	Massillon, Ohio	FA-'10	9/3*
94	Baldwin, Ervin	DE	6-2	260	8/25/86	2	Michigan State	Oglethorpe, Ga.	FA-'09	3/0
41	#Bethea, Antoine	DB	5-11	203	7/7/84	5	Howard	Newport News, Va.	D6b-'06	16/16
58	Brackett, Gary	LB	5-11	235	5/23/80	8	Rutgers	Glassboro, N.J.	FA-'03	14/14
31	Brown, Donald	RB	5-10	210	4/11/87	2	Connecticut	Atlantic Highland, N.J.	D1-'09	11/1
33	Bullitt, Melvin	DB	6-1	201	11/13/84	4	Texas A&M	Bryan, Texas	FA-'07	14/12
44	Clark, Dallas	TE/FB	6-3	252	6/12/79	8	Iowa	Livermore, Iowa	D1-'03	16/16
17	Collie, Austin	WR	6-0	200	11/11/85	2	Brigham Young	El Dorado Hills, Calif.	D4-'09	16/5
96	Dawson, Keyunta	DE	6-3	254	9/13/85	4	Texas Tech	Shreveport, La.	D7-'07	12/2
66	DeVan, Kyle	OL	6-2	306	2/10/85	2	Oregon State	Vacaville, Calif.	FA-'09	15/9
71	Diem, Ryan	T	6-6	331	7/1/79	10	Northern Illinois	Carol Stream, Ill.	D4-'01	15/15
68	Foster, Eric	DT	6-2	265	4/5/85	3	Rutgers	Homestead, Fla.	FA-'08	16/5
93	Freeney, Dwight	DE	6-1	268	2/19/80	9	Syracuse	Hartford, Conn.	D1-'02	14/9
85	Garcon, Pierre	WR	6-0	210	8/8/86	3	Mount Union	West Palm Beach, Fla.	D6d-'08	14/13
14	Giguere, Sam	WR	5-11	215	7/11/85	2	Sherbrooke	Sherbrooke, Quebec	FA-'09	1/0
52	Glenn, Cody	LB	6-0	240	10/6/86	2	Nebraska	Rusk, Texas	FA-'09	9/0
11	Gonzalez, Anthony	WR	6-0	193	9/18/84	4	Ohio State	Cleveland, Ohio	D1-'07	1/1
32	Hart, Mike	RB	5-9	206	4/9/86	3	Michigan	Syracuse, N.Y.	D6c-'08	9/0
26	Hayden, Kelvin	DB	6-0	195	7/23/83	6	Illinois	Chicago, Ill.	D2-'05	9/8
59	Humber, Ramon	LB	5-11	232	8/10/87	2	North Dakota State	Brooklyn Park, Minn.	FA-'09	16/2
99	Johnson, Antonio	DT	6-3	310	12/8/84	4	Mississippi State	Leland, Miss.	FA-'08	15/15
74	Johnson, Charlie	T	6-4	305	5/2/84	5	Oklahoma State	Sherman, Texas	D6a-'06	12/12
27	Lacey, Jacob	CB	5-10	177	5/28/87	2	Oklahoma State	Garland, Texas	FA-'09	16/9
18	Manning, Peyton	QB	6-5	230	3/24/76	13	Tennessee	New Orleans, La.	D1-'98	16/16
98	Mathis, Robert	DE	6-2	235	2/26/81	8	Alabama A&M	Atlanta, Ga.	D5a-'03	14/9
1	McAfee, Pat	P	6-1	220	5/2/87	2	West Virginia	Plum, Pa.	D7a-'09	16/0
95	Moala, Fili	DT	6-4	303	6/23/85	2	Southern Cal	Buena Park, Calif..	D2a-'09	10/1
90	Muir, Daniel	DT	6-2	312	9/12/83	4	Kent State	Riverdale, Md.	W(GB)-'08	16/10
7	Painter, Curtis	QB	6-4	230	6/24/85	2	Purdue	Yorktown, Ind.	D6-'09	2/0
78	Pollak, Mike	G	6-3	301	2/16/85	3	Arizona State	Scottsdale, Ariz.	D2-'08	14/7
25	Powers, Jerraud	DB	5-10	192	7/19/87	2	Auburn	Decatur, Ala.	D3-'09	12/12
61	Richard, Jamey	G	6-5	295	10/9/84	3	Buffalo	Weston, Conn.	D7-'08	9/0
47	Robinson, Gijon	TE	6-1	255	10/12/84	3	Missouri Western State	Waynesville, Mo.	FA-'08	13/10
21	Sanders, Bob	DB	5-8	206	2/24/81	7	Iowa	Erie, Pa.	D2b-'04	2/2
86	Santi, Tom	TE	6-3	250	11/22/85	3	Virginia	Nashville, Tenn.	D6a-'08	3/2
63	Saturday, Jeff	C	6-2	295	6/8/75	12	North Carolina	Tucker, Ga.	FA-'99	16/16
55	Session, Clint	LB	6-0	235	9/9/84	4	Pittsburgh	Pompano Beach, Fla.	D4c-'07	14/14
40	Silva, Jamie	DB	5-11	204	12/14/84	3	Boston College	East Providence, R.I.	FA-'08	14/0
48	Snow, Justin	TE	6-3	240	12/21/76	11	Baylor	Abilene, Texas	FA-'00	16/0
84	Tamme, Jacob	TE	6-3	236	3/15/85	3	Kentucky	Danville, Ky.	D4-'08	16/1
79	Terry, Adam	T	6-8	335	9/1/82	5	Syracuse	Queensbury, N.Y.	FA-'10	0*
67	Ugoh, Tony	T	6-5	301	11/17/83	4	Arkansas	Houston, Texas	D2a-'07	15/12
4	Vinatieri, Adam	K	6-0	202	12/28/72	15	South Dakota State	Rapid City, S.D.	UFA(NE)-'06	6/0
87	Wayne, Reggie	WR	6-0	198	11/17/78	10	Miami	New Orleans, La.	D1b-'01	16/16
50	Wheeler, Philip	LB	6-2	240	12/12/84	3	Georgia Tech	Columbus, Ga.	D3-'08	16/7

* Alleman played 9 games with Kansas City in '09; Terry last active with Baltimore in '08.

Also played with Colts in '09—K Shane Andrus (1 game), WR Hank Baskett (11), DE Raheem Brock (16), TE Colin Cloherty (1), T Dan Federkeil (6), DB Aaron Francisco (10), DT John Gill (2), LB Tyjuan Hagler (7), DB De'von Hall (4), DB Marlin Jackson (4), DB Tim Jennings (15), DT Ed Johnson (4), LB Freddy Keiaho (16), G Ryan Lilja (16), DB Anthony Madison (3), DB T.J. Rushing (15), LB Jordan Senn (2), RB Chad Simpson (14), QB Jim Sorgi (1), K Matt Stover (10), DE Josh Thomas (2), T Michael Toudouze (2).

2010 FIRST-YEAR ROSTER

Name	Pos.	Ht.	Wt.	Birthdate	College	Hometown	How Acq.
Anderson, Trevor	DE	6-0	241	1/13/87	Michigan State	Detroit, Mich.	FA
Angerer, Pat	LB	6-0	235	1/31/87	Iowa	Bettendorf, Iowa	D2
Cadogan, Gerald (1)	T	6-5	310	1/16/86	Penn State	Portsmouth, Ohio	FA
Caldwell, David	DB	5-11	212	5/19/87	William & Mary	Montclair, N.J.	FA
Chick, John (1)	DE	6-4	250	11/20/82	Utah State	Gillette, Wyo.	FA
Cloherty, Colin (1)	TE	6-2	245	9/16/87	Brown	Bethesda, Md.	FA-'09
Conner, Kavell	LB	6-0	242	2/23/87	Clemson	Richmond, Va.	D7b
Eldridge, Brody	TE	6-5	265	3/31/87	Oklahoma	La Cygne, Kan.	D5
Fisher, Ray	DB	5-9	185	9/12/87	Indiana	Cleveland, Ohio	D7c
Gill, John (1)	DT	6-3	302	10/28/86	Northwestern	Los Altos, Calif.	FA-'09
Guice, Dudley (1)	WR	6-3	209	5/28/86	Northwestern State	Fayette, Miss.	FA
Hemby, Jordan	DB	5-11	190	7/21/87	North Carolina	Morgantown, N.C.	FA
Hiller, Tim	QB	6-4	229	12/13/86	Western Michigan	Parma, Ohio	FA
Hughes, Jerry	DE	6-2	255	8/13/88	Texas Christian	Sugar Land, Texas	D1
James, Brandon	KR	5-7	176	12/21/87	Florida	St. Augustine, Fla.	FA
James, Javarris	RB	6-0	215	9/18/87	Miami	Immokalee, Fla.	FA
King, Brandon	DB	5-10	194	1/28/87	Purdue	Warner Robins, Ga.	FA
King, Mitch (1)	DT	6-2	282	5/5/86	Iowa	Burlington, Iowa	FA
Lambert, Terrail (1)	DB	5-10	190	12/1/85	Notre Dame	Oxnard, Calif.	FA
Linkenbach, Jeff	T	6-4	311	6/9/87	Cincinnati	Sandusky, Ohio	FA
Mathews, Ricardo	DT	6-3	294	7/30/87	Cincinnati	Jacksonville, Fla.	D7a
Matthews, John (1)	WR	6-0	197	7/19/86	San Diego	Aurora, Colo.	FA
McClendon, Jacques	G	6-3	324	12/10/87	Tennessee	Cleveland, Tenn.	D4
Moore, Devin (1)	RB	5-9	190	11/6/85	Wyoming	Indianapolis, Ind.	FA
Newton, Mike	DB	5-10	197	11/11/87	Buffalo	Pasadena, Md.	FA
Peat, Gregg	G	6-3	299	9/16/87	Oregon State	Mission Viejo, Calif.	FA
Renkart, Brandon (1)	LB	6-2	236	12/29/84	Rutgers	Piscataway, N.J.	FA
Ricks, Jake	NT	6-3	288	6/6/87	Auburn	Muscle Shoals, Ala.	FA
Skolnitsjy, J.D. (1)	DT	6-5	255	11/6/86	James Madison	Fairfax, Va.	W(Wash)
Smith, Taj (1)	WR	6-0	192	9/30/83	Syracuse	Newark, N.J.	FA
Swenson, Brett	K	5-8	173	2/10/88	Michigan State	Pompano Beach, Fla.	FA
Thomas, Jaimie (1)	G	6-4	330	8/24/86	Maryland	Harrisburg, Pa.	FA
Thomas, Kevin	DB	6-0	192	9/20/86	Southern California	Oxnard, Calif.	D3
Tuihalamaka, Vuna	LB	6-0	230	2/28/87	Arizona	Inglewood, Calif.	FA
Turner, Thad	DB	5-11	188	4/30/87	Ohio	Marietta, Ga.	FA
Tyshovnytsky, Andrew	T	6-4	317	1/25/88	Fordham	Wayne, Pa.	FA
White, Blair	WR	6-2	205	2/20/87	Michigan State	Saginaw, Mich.	FA
Willy, Drew (1)	QB	6-3	217	11/13/86	Buffalo	Randolph, N.J.	FA

The term NFL Rookie is defined as a player who is in his first season of professional football and has not been on the roster of another professional football team for any regular-season or postseason games. A Rookie is designated by an "R" on NFL rosters. Players who have been active in another professional football league or players who have NFL experience, including either preseason training camp or being on an Active List or Inactive List, or on Reserve/Injured or Reserve/Physically Unable to Perform for fewer than six regular-season games, are termed NFL First-Year Players. An NFL First-Year Player is designated by a "1" on NFL rosters. Thereafter, a player is credited with an additional year of experience for each season in which he accumulates six games on the Active List or Inactive List, or on Reserve/Injured or Reserve/Physically Unable to Perform.

Log on to www.colts.com for an up-to-date roster.

INDIANAPOLIS COLTS

COACHING STAFF

Head Coach,
Jim Caldwell

Pro Career: Jim Caldwell was named head coach of the club on January 13, 2009 and enters his second season as head coach of the Colts. In first season, Caldwell guided the Colts to 14 consecutive victories to start the season, the longest winning streak for a coach beginning his career in NFL history. The season culminated with the Colts making their fourth-ever Super Bowl appearance. Prior to his head-coaching promotion, Caldwell had served with Indianapolis from 2002-08. He was elevated to associate head coach with the club on January 21, 2008. Caldwell spent his first three seasons as quarterbacks coach before earning the expanded title of assistant head coach prior to the 2005 season. Indianapolis (2003-09) extended its NFL mark to seven consecutive seasons with at least 12 victories. The club also led the NFL with an eighth consecutive playoff appearance, a span that includes Caldwell's tenure in Indianapolis. The Colts extended their streak of double-digit victory seasons to eight, tying the second-longest streak in NFL history. The Colts are the only franchise in NFL history to win seven or more consecutive regular-season games in six consecutive seasons. Caldwell joined Indianapolis from Tampa Bay, where he served as quarterbacks coach during the 2001 season. He spent 1993-2000 as head coach at Wake Forest and served as an assistant coach at Southern Illinois (1978-1980), Northwestern (1981), Colorado (1982-84), Louisville (1985) and Penn State (1986-1992). Career record: 16-3.

Background: Caldwell was a four-year starter (1973-76) as a defensive back at Iowa and worked as a graduate assistant for the Hawkeyes in 1977. He holds a bachelor's degree from Iowa.

Personal: Born January 16, 1955 in Beloit, Wis. Jim and his wife, Cheryl, have four children: Jimmy, Jermaine, Jared, and Natalie.

ASSISTANT COACHES

Clyde Christensen, offensive coordinator; born January 28, 1956, Covina, Calif. Quarterback Fresno City College 1975, North Carolina 1976-78. No pro playing experience. College coach: Mississippi 1979, East Tennessee State 1980-82, Temple 1983-85, East Carolina 1986-88, Holy Cross 1989-1990, South Carolina 1991, Maryland 1992-93, Clemson 1994-95. Pro coach: Tampa Bay Buccaneers 1996-2001, joined Colts in 2002.

Jim Bob Cooter, offensive assistant; born July 3, 1984, Fayetteville, Tenn. Quarterback Tennessee 2002-06. No pro playing experience. College coach: Tennessee 2007-08. Pro coach: Joined Colts in 2009.

Larry Coyer, defensive coordinator; born April 19, 1943, Huntington, W.Va. Quarterback Marshall 1961-64. No pro playing experience. College coach: Marshall 1965-67, Bowling Green 1968-1973, Iowa 1974-77, Oklahoma State 1978, Iowa State 1979-1982, 1995-96, UCLA 1987-89, Houston 1990, Ohio State 1991-92, East Carolina 1993, Pittsburgh 1997-99. Pro coach: Michigan Panthers (USFL) 1983-84, Memphis Showboats (USFL) 1985, New York Jets 1994, Denver Broncos 2000-06, Tampa Bay Buccaneers 2007-08, joined Colts in 2009.

Richard Howell, asst. strength and conditioning; born February 19, 1972, Bladenboro, N.C. Quarterback Davidson 1990-93. No pro playing experience. College coach: Davidson 1994-98, North Carolina 1998-99. Pro coach: Barcelona Dragons (NFLE) 1999, joined Colts in 2000.

Gene Huey, running backs; born July 20, 1947, Uniontown, Pa. Defensive back-wide receiver Wyoming 1965-68. Pro running back San Diego Chargers 1969. College coach: Wyoming 1970-73, New Mexico 1974-76, Nebraska 1977-1986, Arizona State 1987, Ohio State 1988-1991. Pro coach: Joined Colts in 1992.

Pete Metzelaars, offensive line; born May 24, 1960, Three Rivers, Mich. Tight end Wabash College 1978-1981. Pro tight end Seattle Seahawks 1982-84, Buffalo Bills 1985-1994, Carolina Panthers 1995, Detroit Lions 1996-97. College coach: Wingate 2003. Pro coach: Barcelona Dragons (NFLE) 2003, joined Colts in 2004.

Tom Moore, senior offensive assistant; born November 7, 1938, Owatonna, Minn. Quarterback Iowa 1957-1960. No pro playing experience. College coach: Iowa 1961-62, Dayton 1965-68, Wake Forest 1969, Georgia Tech 1970-71, Minnesota 1972-73, 1975-76. Pro coach: New York Stars (WFL) 1974, Pittsburgh Steelers 1977-1989, Minnesota Vikings 1990-93, Detroit Lions 1994-96, New Orleans Saints 1997, joined Colts in 1998.

Mike Murphy, linebackers; born September 25, 1944, New York, N.Y. Guard/linebacker Huron (S.D.) 1963-66. No pro playing experience. College coach: Vermont 1970-73, Idaho State 1974-76, Western Illinois 1977-78. Pro coach: Saskatchewan Roughriders (CFL) 1979-1983, Chicago Blitz (USFL) 1984, Detroit Lions 1985-89, Arizona Cardinals 1990-93, Seattle Seahawks 1995-97, joined Colts in 1998.

Rod Perry, special assistant to the defense; born September 11, 1953, Fresno, Calif. Defensive back Colorado 1972-74. Pro cornerback Los Angeles Rams 1975-1982, Cleveland Browns 1983-84. College coach: Columbia 1985, Fresno City College 1986, Fresno State 1987-88. Pro coach: Seattle Seahawks 1989-1991, Los Angeles Rams 1992-94, Houston Oilers 1995-96, San Diego Chargers 1997-2001, Carolina Panthers 2002-06, joined Colts in 2007.

Ron Prince, asst. offensive line; born September 18, 1969, Omaha, Neb. Offensive lineman Dodge City (Kan.) C.C. 1988-89, Appalachian State 1990-91. No pro playing experience. College coach: Dodge City C.C. 1992, Alabama A&M 1993, South Carolina State 1994, James Madison 1995-97, Cornell 1998-2000, Virginia 2001-05, 2009, Kansas State 2006-08 (head coach). Pro coach: Joined Colts in 2010.

Frank Reich, quarterbacks; born December 4, 1961, Freeport, N.Y. Quarterback Maryland 1981-84. Pro quarterback Buffalo Bills 1985-1994, Carolina Panthers 1995, New York Jets 1996, Detroit Lions 1997-98. Pro coach: Joined Colts in 2008.

Ray Rychleski, special teams; born September 27, 1957, Old Forge, Pa. Attended Millersville (Pa.) State College. No college or pro playing experience. College coach: Temple 1981-88, Northeastern 1989-1990, Penn State 1991, East Stroudsburg 1992, Wake Forest 1993-2000, Maryland 2001-07, South Carolina 2008. Pro coach: Joined Colts in 2009.

Bill Teerlinck, defensive assistant; born July 23, 1978, Champaign, Ill. Defensive end Chadron State 2000-02. No pro playing experience. College coach: Indiana 2003-04, Illinois State 2005-06. Pro coach: Joined Colts in 2007.

John Teerlinck, defensive line; born April 9, 1951, Rochester, N.Y. Defensive lineman Western Illinois 1970-73. Pro defensive tackle San Diego Chargers 1974-77. College coach: Iowa Lakes J.C. 1977, Eastern Illinois 1978-79, Illinois 1980-82. Pro coach: Chicago Blitz (USFL) 1983-84, Arizona Wranglers/Outlaws (USFL) 1985-86, Cleveland Browns 1989-1990, Los Angeles Rams 1991, Minnesota Vikings 1992-94, Detroit Lions 1995-96, Denver Broncos 1997-2001, joined Colts in 2002.

Ricky Thomas, tight ends; born March 29, 1965, London, England. Safety Alabama 1983-86. No pro playing experience. College coach: Kentucky 1996, Gardner-Webb 1997. Pro coach: Tampa Bay Buccaneers 1997-2001, joined Colts in 2002.

Jon Torine, strength and conditioning; born November 16, 1973, Livingston, N.J. Linebacker Springfield (Mass.) College 1991. No pro playing experience. Pro coach: Buffalo Bills 1995-97, joined Colts in 1998.

Ron Turner, wide receivers; born December 5, 1953, Martinez, Calif. Wide receiver Diablo Valley (Calif.) C.C. 1973-74, Pacific 1975-76. No pro playing experience. College coach: Pacific 1977, Arizona 1978-1980, Northwestern 1981-82, Pittsburgh 1983-84, Southern California 1985-87, Texas A&M 1988, Stanford 1989-1991, San Jose State 1992 (head coach), Illinois 1997-2004 (head coach). Pro coach: Chicago Bears 1993-96, 2005-09, joined Colts in 2010.

Alan Williams, defensive backs; born November 4, 1969, Norfolk, Va. Running back William & Mary 1988-1991. No pro playing experience. College coach: William & Mary 1996-2000. Pro coach: Tampa Bay Buccaneers 2001, joined Colts in 2002.

American Football Conference
South Division
Team Colors: Teal, Black, and Gold
Jacksonville Municipal Stadium
One Stadium Place
Jacksonville, Florida 32202
Telephone: (904) 633-6000

2010 SCHEDULE

PRESEASON

Aug. 13	at Philadelphia	7:30
Aug. 21	**Miami**	7:30
Aug. 28	at Tampa Bay	7:30
Sep. 2	**Atlanta**	7:30

REGULAR SEASON

Sep. 12	**Denver**	1:00
Sep. 19	at San Diego	1:15
Sep. 26	**Philadelphia**	4:05
Oct. 3	**Indianapolis**	4:05
Oct. 10	at Buffalo	1:00
Oct. 18	**Tennessee** (Mon)	8:30
Oct. 24	at Kansas City	12:00
Oct. 31	at Dallas	12:00
Nov. 7	BYE	
Nov. 14	**Houston**	1:00
Nov. 21	**Cleveland**	1:00
Nov. 28	at New York Giants	1:00
Dec. 5	at Tennessee	12:00
Dec. 12	**Oakland**	1:00
Dec. 19	at Indianapolis	1:00
Dec. 26	**Washington**	1:00
Jan. 2	at Houston	12:00

Stadium: Jacksonville Municipal Stadium (opened in 1995)
•**Capacity:** 67,246
One Stadium Place
Jacksonville, Florida 32202
Playing Surface: Grass
Training Camp: Jacksonville Municipal Stadium
One Stadium Place
Jacksonville, Florida 32202

JACKSONVILLE MUNICIPAL STADIUM

CLUB OFFICIALS

Chairman and Chief Executive Officer: Wayne Weaver
Senior Vice President/Football Operations: Paul Vance
Senior Vice President/Chief Financial Officer: Bill Prescott
Senior Vice President/Communications and Media: Dan Edwards
Senior Vice President/Sales and Marketing: Macky Weaver

General Manager/Senior Vice President, Player Personnel: Gene Smith
Director, Player Personnel: Terry McDonough
Assistant Director, College Personnel: Tim Mingey
Assistant Director, Pro Personnel: Louis Clark
National Scout: Andy Dengler
Regional Scouts: Jason DesJarlais, Marty Miller, Chris Prescott, Brian Simmons
Pro Scout: Chris Driggers
BLESTO Scout: Jake Peetz
Scouting Assistant, College and Pro Personnel: Patrick Mularkey

Executive Director of Football Operations: Skip Richardson
Executive Director of Information Technology: Bruce Swindell
Director of Ticket Operations: Tim Bishko
Associate General Counsel: Sashi Brown
Director of Football Administration: Tim Walsh
Head Athletic Trainer: Michael Ryan
Video Director: Mike Perkins
Equipment Manager: Drew Hampton
Manager, Communications: Ryan Robinson
Executive Assistant to Senior VP, Communications and Media: Alisa Abbott

Chair & Chief Executive Officer, Jaguars Foundation: Delores Barr Weaver
Executive Director: Peter Racine

COACHING HISTORY
(130-121-0)

Records include postseason games

1995-2002	Tom Coughlin	72-64-0
2003-09	Jack Del Rio	58-57-0

PAID ATTENDANCE

Home 367,063 Away 524,749
Total 891,812
Single-game home record, 74,143 (12/28/98)
Single-season home record, 561,472 (1998)

2010 DRAFT CHOICES

Round	Name	Pos.	College
1	Tyson Alualu	DT	California
3	D'Anthony Smith	DT	Louisiana Tech
5	Larry Hart	DE	Central Arkansas
	Austen Lane	DE	Murray State
6	Deji Karim	RB	Southern Illinois
	Scotty McGee	RS	James Madison

JACKSONVILLE JAGUARS

2009 TEAM RECORD

PRESEASON (3-1)

Date	Result	Opponent
8/17	L 9-12	at Miami
8/22	L 23-24	Tampa Bay
8/27	L 32-33	at Philadelphia
9/3	W 24-17	Washington

REGULAR SEASON (7-9)

Date	Result	Opponent
9/13	L 12-14	at Indianapolis
9/20	L 17-31	Arizona
9/27	W 31-24	at Houston
10/4	W 37-17	Tennessee
10/11	L 0-41	at Seattle
10/18	W 23-20	St. Louis (OT)
11/1	L 13-30	at Tennessee
11/8	W 24-21	Kansas City
11/15	W 24-22	at New York Jets
11/22	W 18-15	Buffalo
11/29	L 3-20	at San Francisco
12/6	W 23-18	Houston
12/13	L 10-14	Miami
12/17	L 31-35	Indianapolis
12/27	L 7-35	at New England
1/3	L 17-23	at Cleveland

(OT) Overtime

SCORE BY PERIODS

Jaguars	48	113	46	80	3	— 290
Opponents	69	157	75	79	0	— 380

2009 TEAM STATISTICS

	Jaguars	Opp.
Total First Downs	300	307
Rushing	114	100
Passing	170	191
Penalty	16	16
3rd Down: Made/Att	102/226	94/209
3rd Down Pct.	45.1	45.0
4th Down: Made/Att	12/21	12/17
4th Down Pct.	57.1	70.6
Possession Avg.	30:08	29:52
Total Net Yards	5385	5637
Avg. Per Game	336.6	352.3
Total Plays	1010	982
Avg. Per Play	5.3	5.7
Net Yards Rushing	2029	1863
Avg. Per Game	126.8	116.4
Total Rushes	447	458
Net Yards Passing	3356	3774
Avg. Per Game	209.8	235.9
Sacked/Yards Lost	44/243	14/79
Gross Yards	3599	3853
Att./Completions	519/315	510/345
Completion Pct.	60.7	67.6
Had Intercepted	10	15
Punts/Average	72/41.9	62/44.9
Net Punting Avg.	72/38.3	62/39.5
Penalties/Yards	70/542	64/498
Fumbles/Ball Lost	26/13	22/10
Touchdowns	34	44
Rushing	19	12
Passing	15	28
Returns	0	4

2009 INDIVIDUAL STATISTICS

PASSING	Att.	Comp.	Yds.	Pct.	TD	Int.	Tkld.	Rate
Garrard	516	314	3597	60.9	15	10	42/236	83.5
McCown	3	1	2	33.3	0	0	2/7	42.4
Jaguars	519	315	3599	60.7	15	10	44/243	83.2
Opponents	510	345	3853	67.6	28	15	14/79	96.0

SCORING	TD R	TD P	TD Rt	PAT	FG	Saf	PTS
Jones-Drew	15	1	0	0/0	0/0	0	96
Scobee	0	0	0	30/31	18/28	0	84
Sims-Walker	0	7	0	0/0	0/0	0	42
Garrard	3	0	0	0/0	0/0	0	20
M. Lewis	0	2	0	0/0	0/0	0	12
Miller	0	2	0	0/0	0/0	0	12
Hughes	0	1	0	0/0	0/0	0	6
Jennings	1	0	0	0/0	0/0	0	6
M. Thomas	0	1	0	0/0	0/0	0	6
Wilford	0	1	0	0/0	0/0	0	6
Jaguars	19	15	0	30/31	18/28	0	290
Opponents	12	28	4	38/38	24/28	1	380

2-Pt. Conversions: Garrard.
Jaguars 1-3, Opponents 2-6.

RUSHING	No.	Yds	Avg	LG	TD
Jones-Drew	312	1391	4.5	80t	15
Garrard	77	323	4.2	30	3
Jennings	39	202	5.2	28t	1
M. Thomas	12	86	7.2	22	0
Jones	4	23	5.8	11	0
Miller	1	3	3.0	3	0
Owens	2	1	0.5	3	0
Jaguars	447	2029	4.5	80t	19
Opponents	458	1863	4.1	89t	12

RECEIVING	No.	Yds	Avg	LG	TD
Sims-Walker	63	869	13.8	61t	7
Jones-Drew	53	374	7.1	19	1
Holt	51	722	14.2	63	0
M. Thomas	48	453	9.4	28	1
M. Lewis	32	518	16.2	47	2
Miller	21	212	10.1	62	2
Jennings	16	101	6.3	14	0
Wilford	11	123	11.2	30	1
Dillard	6	106	17.7	33	0
Hughes	5	70	14.0	35t	1
Jones	5	14	2.8	9	0
Williamson	3	34	11.3	13	0
Potter	1	3	3.0	3	0
Jaguars	315	3599	11.4	63	15
Opponents	345	3853	11.2	98t	28

INTERCEPTIONS	No.	Yds	Avg	LG	TD
D. Cox	4	6	1.5	6	0
Mathis	3	46	15.3	29	0
A. Smith TM	2	34	17.0	30	0
Alexander	2	23	11.5	22	0
Groves	1	37	37.0	37	0
Durant	1	27	27.0	27	0
Considine	1	25	25.0	25	0
D. Smith	1	10	10.0	10	0
Jaguars	15	208	13.9	37	0
Opponents	10	234	23.4	56	1

PUNTING	No.	Yds.	Avg.	In 20	LG
Podlesh	72	3017	41.9	23	64
Jaguars	72	3017	41.9	23	64
Opponents	62	2784	44.9	21	70

PUNT RETURNS	Ret	FC	Yds	Avg	LG	TD
M. Thomas	14	4	118	8.4	44	0
Witherspoon TM	7	3	78	11.1	42	0
Jones-Drew	2	0	19	9.5	12	0
Hughes	2	0	18	9.0	11	0
Middleton TM	1	0	0	0.0	0	0
Starks	1	0	0	0.0	0	0
Jaguars	27	7	233	8.6	44	0
Opponents	38	15	159	4.2	13	0

KICKOFF RETURNS	No.	Yds	Avg	LG	TD
M. Thomas	26	644	24.8	43	0
Witherspoon TM	24	568	23.7	42	0
Jones-Drew	4	102	25.5	30	0
Jennings	3	56	18.7	24	0
Owens	3	49	16.3	29	0
Underwood	2	38	19.0	24	0
Miller	2	19	9.5	16	0
Ellison	1	16	16.0	16	0
Wilford	1	0	0.0	0	0
Jaguars	66	1492	22.6	43	0
Opponents	47	1069	22.7	93t	1

FIELD GOALS	1-19	20-29	30-39	40-49	50+
Scobee	0/0	7/8	4/4	3/7	4/9
Jaguars	0/0	7/8	4/4	3/7	4/9
Opponents	0/0	12/12	4/5	7/8	1/3

SACKS	No.
J. Henderson	3.0
Harvey	2.0
Knighton	1.5
D. Smith	1.5
Durant	1.0
Ellison	1.0
Hayward	1.0
Ingram	1.0
Landri	1.0
Stanley	1.0
Jaguars	14.0
Opponents	44.0

RECORD HOLDERS

INDIVIDUAL RECORDS—CAREER

Category	Name	Performance
Rushing (Yds.)	Fred Taylor, 1998-2008	11,271
Passing (Yds.)	Mark Brunell, 1995-2003	25,698
Passing (TDs)	Mark Brunell, 1995-2003	144
Receiving (No.)	Jimmy Smith, 1995-2005	862
Receiving (Yds.)	Jimmy Smith, 1995-2005	12,287
Interceptions	Rashean Mathis, 2003-09	28
Punting (Avg.)	Bryan Barker, 1995-2000	43.5
Punt Return (Avg.)	Bobby Shaw, 2002	12.4
Kickoff Return (Avg.)	Maurice Jones-Drew, 2006-09	26.0
Field Goals	Mike Hollis, 1995-2001	175
Touchdowns (Tot.)	Fred Taylor, 1998-2008	70
Points	Mike Hollis, 1995-2001	764
*Sacks	Tony Brackens, 1996-2003	55.0

INDIVIDUAL RECORDS—SINGLE SEASON

Category	Name	Performance
Rushing (Yds.)	Fred Taylor, 2003	1,572
Passing (Yds.)	Mark Brunell, 1996	4,367
Passing (TDs)	Mark Brunell, 1998, 2000	20
Receiving (No.)	Jimmy Smith, 1999	116
Receiving (Yds.)	Jimmy Smith, 1999	1,636
Interceptions	Rashean Mathis, 2006	8
Punting (Avg.)	Bryan Barker, 1998	45.0
Punt Return (Avg.)	Reggie Barlow, 1998	12.9
Kickoff Return (Avg.)	Maurice Jones-Drew, 2006	27.7
Field Goals	Mike Hollis, 1997, 1999	31
Touchdowns (Tot.)	Fred Taylor, 1998	17
Points	Mike Hollis, 1997	134
*Sacks	Tony Brackens, 1999	12.0

INDIVIDUAL RECORDS—SINGLE GAME

Category	Name	Performance
Rushing (Yds.)	Fred Taylor, 11-19-00	234
Passing (Yds.)	Mark Brunell, 9-22-96	432
Passing (TDs)	Mark Brunell, 11-29-98	4
	Quinn Gray, 12-30-07	4
Receiving (No.)	Keenan McCardell, 10-20-96	16
Receiving (Yds.)	Jimmy Smith, 9-10-00	291
Interceptions	Many times	2
	Last time by Rashean Mathis, 11-5-06	
Field Goals	Mike Hollis, 12-1-96, 11-30-97, 9-10-00	5
	Josh Scobee, 11-25-07	5
Touchdowns (Tot.)	James Stewart, 10-12-97	5
Points	James Stewart, 10-12-97	30
*Sacks	Kelvin Pritchett, 10-5-97	3.0
	John Henderson, 10-6-02	3.0
	Paul Spicer, 9-25-05	3.0

**Sacks became an official statistic in 1982.*

JACKSONVILLE JAGUARS

2010 VETERAN ROSTER

No.	Name	Pos.	Ht.	Wt.	Birthdate	NFL Exp.	College	Hometown	How Acq.	'09 Games/ Starts
42	Alexander, Gerald	S	6-2	204	6/28/84	4	Boise State	Rancho Cucamonga, Calif.	T(Det)-'09	15/10
50	Allen, Russell	LB	6-3	234	5/5/86	2	San Diego State	Oceanside, Calif.	FA-'09	16/5
78	Black, Jordan	T	6-5	305	1/28/80	6	Notre Dame	Garland, Texas	FA-'08	9/2
41	Brackenridge, Tyron	DB	5-11	189	6/30/84	3	Washington State	Pasadena, Calif.	W(NYJ)-'09	16/5
73	Britton, Eben	T	6-6	310	10/14/87	2	Arizona	Burbank, Calif.	D2-'09	15/15
48	Cain, Jeremy	LS	6-1	245	3/24/80	5	Massachusetts	Boynton Beach, Fla.	W(Wash)-'09	16/0
26	Coe, Michael	DB	6-0	190	12/17/83	3	Alabama State	Memphis, Tenn.	PS(NYG)-'09	5/0
37	Considine, Sean	S	6-0	212	12/17/82	6	Iowa	Byron, Ill.	UFA(Phil)-'09	11/6
21	Cox, Derek	CB	6-1	190	9/22/86	2	William & Mary	Greenville, N.C.	D3b-'09	16/16
60	Crummey, Andrew	OL	6-5	301	10/22/84	2	Maryland	Van Wert, Ohio	FA-'10	0*
87	Dillard, Jarett	WR	5-10	187	12/21/85	2	Rice	San Antonio, Texas	D5-'09	7/0
56	Durant, Justin	LB	6-1	240	9/20/85	4	Hampton	Florence, S.C.	D2-'07	13/13
99	Ellison, Atiyyah	DL	6-3	322	9/29/81	3	Missouri	St. Louis, Mo.	PS(SF)-'08	15/6
65	Forney, Kynan	G	6-3	302	9/8/78	10	Hawaii	Nacogdoches, Texas	FA-'09	3/0
9	Garrard, David	QB	6-1	236	2/14/78	9	East Carolina	Durham, N.C.	D4-'02	16/16
36	Greene, Courtney	S	6-0	212	11/23/86	2	Rutgers	New Rochelle, N.Y.	FA-'09	9/0
91	Harvey, Derrick	DE	6-5	281	11/9/86	3	Florida	Greenbelt, Md.	D1-'08	16/16
97	Hayward, Reggie	DE	6-5	275	3/14/79	10	Iowa State	Dolton, Ill.	UFA(Den)-'05	1/1
16	Hughes, Nate	WR	6-2	195	1/18/85	2	Alcorn State	Starkville, Miss.	FA-'08	8/0
23	Jennings, Rashad	RB	6-1	235	3/26/85	2	Liberty	Forest, Va.	D7a-'09	15/0
33	Jones, Greg	FB/RB	6-1	254	5/9/81	7	Florida State	Beaufort, S.C.	D2b-'04	13/7
32	Jones-Drew, Maurice	RB	5-7	208	3/23/85	5	UCLA	Antioch, Calif.	D2-'06	16/16
74	Kampman, Aaron	DE	6-4	260	11/30/79	9	Iowa	Kesley, Iowa	UFA(GB)-'10	9/9*
54	Keiaho, Freddy	LB	5-11	228	12/18/82	5	San Diego State	Ventura, Calif.	FA-'10	16/2*
96	Knighton, Terrance	DT	6-3	325	7/4/86	2	Temple	Windsor, Conn.	D3a-'09	16/16
57	Lehman, Teddy	LB	6-1	249	11/18/81	6	Oklahoma	Tulsa, Okla.	FA-'10	0*
89	Lewis, Marcedes	TE	6-6	275	5/19/84	5	UCLA	Long Beach, Calif.	D1-'06	15/15
67	Manuwai, Vince	G	6-2	333	7/12/80	8	Hawaii	Honolulu, Hawaii	D3-'03	16/16
27	Mathis, Rashean	CB	6-1	193	8/27/80	8	Bethune-Cookman	Jacksonville, Fla.	D2-'03	10/10
12	McCown, Luke	QB	6-4	217	7/12/81	6	Louisiana Tech	Jacksonville, Texas	T(TB)-'09	3/0
79	McQuistan, Paul	OL	6-6	315	4/30/83	4	Weber State	San Diego, Calif.	FA-'09	0*
63	Meester, Brad	C	6-3	311	3/23/77	11	Northern Iowa	Parkersburg, Iowa	D2-'00	16/16
29	Middleton, William	CB	5-11	194	7/28/86	2	Furman	Marist, Ga.	PS(Atl)-'09	12/0
86	Miller, Zach	TE	6-4	245	10/4/84	2	Nebraska-Omaha	Wahoo, Neb.	D6-'09	14/0
94	Mincey, Jeremy	DL	6-3	270	12/14/83	3	Florida	Statesboro, Ga.	FA-'10	0*
75	Monroe, Eugene	T	6-5	320	4/18/87	2	Virginia	Plainfield, N.J.	D1-'09	15/13
55	t-Morrison, Kirk	LB	6-2	240	2/19/82	5	San Diego State	Oakland, Calif.	T(Oak)-'10	16/16*
46	Navarre, Jeremy	DE	6-3	279	3/16/87	2	Maryland	Joppatowne, Md.	FA-'09	6/0
25	Nelson, Reggie	S	5-11	202	9/21/83	4	Florida	Melbourne, Fla.	D1-'07	16/14
77	Nwaneri, Uche	G/C	6-3	329	3/20/84	4	Purdue	Garland, Texas	D5a-'07	16/13
81	Osgood, Kassim	WR	6-5	220	5/20/80	8	San Diego State	Salinas, Calif.	UFA(SD)-'10	16/1*
24	Owens, Montell	FB	5-10	225	5/4/84	5	Maine	Wilmington, Del.	FA-'06	16/0
3	Podlesh, Adam	P	5-11	200	8/11/83	4	Maryland	Pittsford, N.Y.	D4a-'07	16/0
10	Scobee, Josh	K	6-1	210	6/23/82	7	Louisiana Tech	Longview, Texas	D5a-'04	16/0
11	Sims-Walker, Mike	WR	6-2	214	11/21/84	4	Central Florida	Orlando, Fla.	D3-'07	15/14
20	Smith, Anthony	S	6-0	200	9/20/83	5	Syracuse	Hubbard, Ohio	W(StL)-'09	8/2
52	Smith, Daryl	LB	6-2	249	3/14/82	7	Georgia Tech	Albany, Ga.	D2a-'04	16/16
31	Starks, Scott	CB	5-9	178	6/27/83	6	Wisconsin	St. Louis, Mo.	D3-'05	5/0
80	Thomas, Mike	WR	5-8	198	6/4/87	2	Arizona	DeSoto, Texas	D4-'09	14/4
19	Underwood, Tiquan	WR	6-1	178	2/17/87	2	Rutgers	New Brunswick, N.J.	D7b-'09	3/0
85	Wilford, Ernest	TE	6-4	235	1/14/79	7	Virginia Tech	Richmond, Va.	FA-'09	15/7
90	Williams, Julius	DE	6-2	260	7/19/86	2	Connecticut	Decatur, Ga.	FA-'09	11/1
84	Williamson, Troy	WR	6-1	203	4/30/83	6	South Carolina	Jackson, S.C.	T(Minn)-'08	2/1

* Crummey last active with Cincinnati in '08; Kampman played 9 games with Green Bay in '09; Keiaho played 16 games with Indianapolis; Lehman last activ with Buffalo in '08; McQuistan inactive for 7 games; Mincey last active with Jacksonville in '08; Morrison played 16 games with Oakland; Osgood played 16 games with San Diego.

t- Jaguars traded for Morrison (Oak).

Traded—DE Quentin Groves (16 games in '09) to Oakland.

Also played with Jaguars in '09—FB Brock Bolen (3 games), DB Kennard Cox (4), LB Torrance Daniels (1), TE Greg Estandia (2), DE Chris Harrington (3), DT John Henderson (15), WR Torry Holt (15), LB Clint Ingram (13), LB Brian Iwuh (13), DT Derek Landri (7), DT Greg Peterson (2), TE Zach Potter (1), S Brian Russell (9), LB Adam Seward (3), LB Bryan Smith (6), DT Montavious Stanley (15), T Tra Thomas (8), OL Maurice Williams (5), CB Brian Witherspoon (7), DE James Wyche (2).

2010 FIRST-YEAR ROSTER

Name	Pos.	Ht.	Wt.	Birthdate	College	Hometown	How Acq.
Alualu, Tyson	DT	6-3	294	5/12/87	California	Honolulu, Hawaii	D1
Baldridge, Daniel	T	6-8	311	10/21/85	Marshall	Opelousas, La.	FA
Bolen, Brock (1)	FB	6-0	233	3/24/85	Louisville	Germantown, Ohio	FA-'09
Bosworth, Kyle	LB	6-1	236	11/21/86	UCLA	Plano, Texas	FA
Carey, Don (1)	DB	5-11	192	2/14/87	Norfolk State	Norfolk, Va.	W(Cle)-'09
Caussin, Mike	TE	6-5	252	2/26/87	James Madison	Springfield, Va.	FA
Curry, Walter (1)	DL	6-4	309	6/18/81	Albany State	Crescent City, Fla.	FA
Cutrera, Jacob	LB	6-3	238	5/18/88	Louisiana State	Lafayette, La.	FA
Denmark, Clarence (1)	WR	5-11	185	9/29/85	Arkansas-Monticello	Jacksonville, Fla.	FA-'09
Estes, John	C	6-2	302	3/25/87	Hawaii	Stockton, Calif.	FA
Gordy, Josh	CB	5-11	195	2/9/87	Central Michigan	Warthen, Ga.	FA
Harmon, Jason	WR	6-2	214	1/27/87	Florida Atlantic	Tampa, Fla.	FA
Harrington, Chris (1)	DE	6-5	260	1/19/85	Texas A&M	Houston, Texas	PS(Ariz)-'09
Harris, Trevor	QB	6-2	223	5/31/86	Edinboro	Waldo, Ohio	FA
Hart, Larry	DE	6-0	248	7/16/87	Central Arkansas	Madison, Miss.	D5a
Haslam, Kevin	T	6-5	304	11/8/86	Rutgers	Mahwah, N.J.	FA
Hawkins, Chris	CB	6-0	186	4/12/86	Louisiana State	Walker, La.	FA
Kackert, Chad	RB	5-9	199	9/15/86	New Hampshire	Simi Valley, Calif.	FA
Karim, Deji	RB/KR	5-8	209	11/18/86	Southern Illinois	Oklahoma City, Okla.	D6a
Lane, Austen	DE	6-5	274	11/9/87	Murray State	Iola, Wisc.	D5b
Malone, Robert	P	6-2	234	2/4/88	Fresno State	Riverside, Calif.	FA
McGaha, Chris	WR	6-1	199	10/21/86	Arizona State	Phoenix, Ariz.	FA
McGee, Scotty	RS/CB	5-8	182	12/4/86	James Madison	Virginia Beach, Va.	D6b
Morgan, Aaron	LB	6-4	238	12/30/88	Louisiana-Monroe	Amite, La.	FA
Newton, Cecil (1)	C	6-2	310	3/20/86	Tennessee State	Atlanta, Ga.	FA-'09
Patrick, Allen (1)	RB	6-1	200	2/15/84	Oklahoma	Conway, S.C.	FA-'09
Potter, Zach (1)	TE	6-7	280	5/4/86	Nebraska	Omaha, Neb.	FA-'09
Quaye, Kommonyan	DT	6-1	307	5/11/87	South Dakota	Brookland Park, Minn.	FA
Smith, D'Anthony	DT	6-2	298	6/9/88	Louisiana Tech	Pickering, La.	D3
Stallings, Ben	FB	5-10	248	8/27/87	Lambuth	Indianola, Miss.	FA
Stephenson, Cameron (1)	G	6-3	326	6/18/83	Rutgers	Inglewood, Calif.	PS(NO)-'08
Thomas, Roren	WR	5-10	172	9/21/87	Lindenwood	St. Louis, Mo.	FA
Whitehead, Terrell	S	6-1	194	9/18/88	Norfolk State	Virginia Beach, Va.	FA

The term NFL Rookie is defined as a player who is in his first season of professional football and has not been on the roster of another professional football team for any regular-season or postseason games. A Rookie is designated by an "R" on NFL rosters. Players who have been active in another professional football league or players who have NFL experience, including either preseason training camp or being on an Active List or Inactive List, or on Reserve/Injured or Reserve/Physically Unable to Perform for fewer than six regular-season games, are termed NFL First-Year Players. An NFL First-Year Player is designated by a "1" on NFL rosters. Thereafter, a player is credited with an additional year of experience for each season in which he accumulates six games on the Active List or Inactive List, or on Reserve/Injured or Reserve/Physically Unable to Perform.

Log on to www.jaguars.com for an up-to-date roster.

JACKSONVILLE JAGUARS

COACHING STAFF

Head Coach,
Jack Del Rio

Pro Career: Jack Del Rio was named head coach of the Jaguars on January 17, 2003, becoming the second head coach in franchise history. He is one of 11 current coaches with 50 career wins. In 2007, the Jaguars posted an 11-5 record and won the franchise's first playoff game since 1999. In 2006, the Jaguars finished second in the NFL in total defense and third in rushing offense but fell just shy of the playoffs with an 8-8 record. Jacksonville finished with a 12-4 record in 2005 and Del Rio guided the franchise to its first postseason appearance since 1999. In 2004, the Jaguars registered a 9-7 record for the franchise's first winning season since 1999. Del Rio was the defensive coordinator for Carolina in 2002. Was linebackers coach for Baltimore (1999-2001), helping the team win Super Bowl XXXV. Del Rio previously coached in New Orleans (1997-98). Spent 11 years as an NFL linebacker. In 1985, he was a third-round choice of New Orleans and was named to the NFL's All-Rookie team. Del Rio also played for Kansas City (1987-88), Dallas (1989-1991), and Minnesota (1992-95). He played in the Pro Bowl following the 1994 season. Career record: 58-57.

Background: Four-year starter (1981-84) at linebacker at Southern California, and earned consensus All-America honors as a senior. He was co-MVP of the 1985 Rose Bowl. Drafted by baseball's Toronto Blue Jays in 1981, he batted .340 while playing catcher on USC's baseball team. Has a political science degree from Kansas.

Personal: Born April 4, 1963 in Castro Valley, Calif. Jack and his wife, Linda, live in Jacksonville, and have three daughters, Lauren, Hope, and Aubrey, and a son, Luke.

ASSISTANT COACHES

Ben Albert, asst. defensive line; born March 19, 1972, Paterson, N.J. Defensive lineman Massachusetts 1990-94. No pro playing experience. College coach: Massachusetts 1995-96, 2002-03, Richmond 1997-2000, 2004, Rutgers 2001, Delaware 2006-09. Pro coach: Joined Jaguars in 2010.

Rob Boras, tight ends; born September 30, 1970, Glen Ellyn, Ill. Center DePauw 1988-1991. No pro playing experience. College coach: DePauw 1992-93, Texas 1994-97, Benedictine 1998 (head coach), Nevada-Las Vegas 1999-2003. Pro coach: Chicago Bears 2004-09, joined Jaguars in 2010.

Earnest Byner, running backs; born September 15, 1962, Milledgeville, Ga. Running back East Carolina 1980-83. Pro running back Cleveland Browns 1984-88, 1994-95, Washington Redskins 1989-1993, Baltimore Ravens 1996-97. Pro coach: Washington Redskins 2004-07, Tennessee Titans 2008-09, joined Jaguars in 2010.

Johnny Cox, quality control/ offense; born February 5, 1972, Denver. Wide receiver Fort Lewis College 1990-93. No pro playing experience. College coach: Fort Lewis College 1994, North Dakota State 1996, Texas 1997-98, Fort Lewis College 1999, North Dakota State 2000-02, Holy Cross 2007. Pro coach: Tampa Bay Buccaneers 2008, joined Jaguars in 2009.

Joe Cullen, defensive line; born December 15, 1967, Quincy, Mass. Nose guard Massachusetts 1986-89. No pro playing experience. College coach: Massachusetts 1990-91, Richmond 1992-98, 2000, Louisiana State 1999, Memphis 2001, Indiana 2002-04, Illinois 2005, Idaho State 2009. Pro coach: Detroit Lions 2006-08, joined Jaguars in 2010.

Mark Duffner, linebackers; born July 19, 1953, Annandale, Va. Defensive lineman William & Mary 1972-74. No pro playing experience. College coach: Ohio State 1975-76, Cincinnati 1977-1980, Holy Cross 1981-1991 (head coach 1986-1991), Maryland 1992-1996 (head coach). Pro coach: Cincinnati Bengals 1997-2002, Green Bay Packers 2003-2005, joined Jaguars in 2006.

Jason George, asst. strength and conditioning; born October 3, 1968, Winnipeg, Manitoba, Canada. Safety Manitoba 1991-1992. No pro playing experience. College coach: Kansas 1997-98, Fordham 1998-2008. Pro coach: Joined Jaguars in 2009.

Matt Griffin, offensive staff assistant; born May 9, 1968, Gardner, Mass. Quarterback New Hampshire 1987-1991. No pro playing experience. College coach: Plymouth State 1992-93, Richmond 1994, Northeastern 1995-96, Tennessee-Martin 1997-98, 2003-05 (head coach 2003-05), Maine 1999-2002, Murray State 2006-09 (head coach). Pro coach: Joined Jaguars in 2010.

Andy Heck, offensive line; born January 1, 1967, Fargo, N.D. Tackle Notre Dame 1985-88. Pro tackle Seattle 1989-1993, Chicago 1994-98, Washington 1999-2000. College coach: Virginia 2001-03. Pro coach: Joined Jaguars in 2003.

Ron Heller, offensive staff assistant; born August 25, 1962, East Meadow, N.Y. Offensive tackle Penn State 1980-83. Pro offensive tackle Tampa Bay Buccaneers 1984-87, Philadelphia Eagles 1988-1992, Miami Dolphins 1993-95. Pro coach: Amsterdam Admirals (NFLE) 2004, 2006-07, Toronto Argonauts (CFL) 2009, joined Jaguars in 2010.

Nate Kaczor, asst. special teams; born April 8, 1967, Scott City, Kan. Center Utah State 1986-89. No pro playing experience. College coach: Utah State 1991-99, Nebraska-Kerney 2000-03, Idaho 2004-05, Louisiana-Monroe 2006-07. Pro coach: Joined Jaguars in 2008.

Thom Kaumeyer, asst. defensive backs; born March 17, 1967, LaJolla, Calif. Safety Palomar (JC) College 1985-86, Oregon 1987-88. Pro safety Seattle Seahawks 1989-1990, New York Giants 1991-92. College coach: Palomar College 1991-94, 1998-2000 (head coach 1994), Onward Kashiyama Ltd. (head coach, Japan) 1995-96, San Diego State 2002-06, Tulane 2007, Kentucky 2008. Pro coach: Atlanta Falcons 2001-02, joined Jaguars in 2008.

Dirk Koetter, offensive coordinator; born February 5, 1959, Pocatello, Idaho. Quarterback Idaho State 1978-1981. No pro playing experience. College coach: San Francisco State 1985, Texas El-Paso 1986-88, Missouri 1989-1993, Boston College 1994-95, Oregon 1996-97, Boise State 1998-2000 (head coach), Arizona State 2001-06 (head coach). Pro coach: Joined Jaguars in 2007.

Todd Monken, wide receivers; born February 2, 1966, Wheaton, Ill. Quarterback Knox College 1987-1989. No pro playing experience. College coach: Grand Valley State 1989-1990, Notre Dame 1991-92, Eastern Michigan 1993-99, Louisiana Tech 2000-01, Oklahoma State 2002-04, Louisiana State 2005-06. Pro coach: Joined Jaguars in 2007.

Russ Purnell, special teams coordinator; born June 12, 1948, Chicago. Center Orange Coast (Calif.) J.C. 1966-67, Whittier College 1968-69. No pro playing experience. College coach: Whittier College 1970-71, Southern California 1982-85. Pro coach: Seattle Seahawks 1986-1994, Houston Oilers/Tennessee Titans 1995-98, Baltimore Ravens 1999-2001, Indianapolis Colts 2002-2008, joined Jaguars in 2009.

Luke Richesson, strength and conditioning; born April 29, 1974, Kansas City, Missouri. Defensive back Kansas 1992-96. No pro playing experience. College coach: Wyoming 1998, Arizona State 1999-2000. Pro coach: Joined Jaguars in 2009.

Mike Shula, quarterbacks; born June 3, 1965, Baltimore. Quarterback Alabama 1984-86. No pro playing experience. College coach: Alabama 2003-06 (head coach). Pro coach: Miami Dolphins 1991-92, Chicago Bears 1993-95, Tampa Bay Buccaneers 1996-99, Miami Dolphins 2000-02, joined Jaguars in 2007.

Mel Tucker, defensive coordinator; born January 4, 1972, Cleveland. Defensive back Wisconsin 1992-95. No pro playing experience. College coach: Michigan State 1997-98, Miami (Ohio) 1999, Louisiana State 2000, Ohio State 2001-04. Pro coach: Cleveland Browns 2005-08, joined Jaguars in 2009.

Cory Undlin, defensive backs; born June 29, 1971, St. Cloud, Minn. Defensive back California Lutheran 1990-94. No pro playing experience. College coach: California Lutheran 1998-2001, Fresno State 2002-03. Pro coach: New England Patriots 2004, Cleveland Browns 2005-08, joined Jaguars in 2009.

American Football Conference
West Division
Team Colors: Red, Gold, and White
One Arrowhead Drive
Kansas City, Missouri 64129
Telephone: (816) 920-9300

2010 SCHEDULE

PRESEASON

Aug. 13	at Atlanta	8:00
Aug. 21	at Tampa Bay	7:30
Aug. 27	**Philadelphia**	7:00
Sep. 2	**Green Bay**	7:00

REGULAR SEASON

Sep. 13	**San Diego** (Mon)	9:15
Sep. 19	at Cleveland	1:00
Sep. 26	**San Francisco**	12:00
Oct. 3	BYE	
Oct. 10	at Indianapolis	1:00
Oct. 17	at Houston	12:00
Oct. 24	**Jacksonville**	12:00
Oct. 31	**Buffalo**	12:00
Nov. 7	at Oakland	1:15
Nov. 14	at Denver	2:05
Nov. 21	**Arizona**	12:00
Nov. 28	at Seattle	1:05
Dec. 5	**Denver**	12:00
Dec. 12	at San Diego	1:15
Dec. 19	at St. Louis	12:00
Dec. 26	**Tennessee**	12:00
Jan. 2	**Oakland**	12:00

Stadium: Arrowhead Stadium (opened in 1972, fully renovated in 2010) • **Capacity:** 76,416
One Arrowhead Drive
Kansas City, Missouri 64129
Playing Surface: Grass
Training Camp:
Missouri Western State Univ.
St. Joseph, MO 64507

ARROWHEAD STADIUM

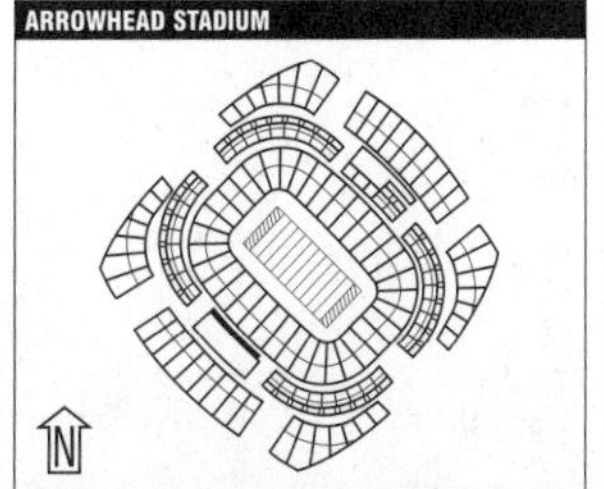

CLUB OFFICIALS

Chairman of the Board: Clark Hunt
General Manager: Scott Pioli
Assistant General Manager: Joel Collier
Director of College Scouting: Phil Emery
Director of Pro Personnel: Ray Farmer
Director of Football Administration: Trip MacCracken
Director of Player Development: Katie Douglass
President: Denny Thum
Executive Vice President/COO: Mark Donovan
Vice President of Sales and Marketing: Tammy Fruits
Vice President of Media and Marketing: Rob Alberino
Director of Finance/Treasurer: Dale Young
Director of Logistics: Ken Blume
Director of Special Events: Gary Spani
Director of Community Relations: Brenda Sniezek
Director of Ticket Operations: Doug Hopkins
Director of Sales and Service: David Steffano
Associate Director of Public Relations: Pete Moris
Equipment Manager: Mike Davidson
Asst. Equipment Mangers: Allen Wright, Chris Shropshire, Kyle Crumbaugh
Head Athletic Trainer: David Price
Assistant Athletic Trainers: David Glover, Jimmy Ntelekos, Nick Potter
Director of Video Operations: Pat Brazil
Assistant Director Video Operations: Ken Radino
Video Assistant: Josh Schmidt

COACHING HISTORY

Dallas Texans 1960-62
(393-372-12)
Records include postseason games

1960-1974	Hank Stram	129-79-10
1975-77	Paul Wiggin*	11-24-0
1977	Tom Bettis	1-6-0
1978-1982	Marv Levy	31-42-0
1983-86	John Mackovic	30-35-0
1987-88	Frank Gansz	8-22-1
1989-1998	Marty Schottenheimer	104-65-1
1999-2000	Gunther Cunningham	16-16-0
2001-05	Dick Vermeil	44-37-0
2006-08	Herm Edwards	15-34-0
2009	Todd Haley	4-12-0

*Released after seven games in 1977

PAID ATTENDANCE

Home 482,837 Away 499,533
Total 982,370
Single-game home record, *82,893 (10/2/00)
Single-season home record, 629,569 (1999)
*Arrowhead Stadium attendance: 78,502
Kauffman Stadium attendance: 4,391

2010 DRAFT CHOICES

Round	Name	Pos.	College
1	Eric Berry	DB	Tennessee
2	Dexter McCluster	WR	Mississippi
	Javier Arenas	DB	Alabama
3	Jon Asamoah	OL	Illinois
	Tony Moeaki	TE	Iowa
5	Kendrick Lewis	DB	Mississippi
	Cameron Sheffield	LB	Troy

KANSAS CITY CHIEFS

2009 TEAM RECORD

PRESEASON (0-4)

Date	Result	Opponent
8/15	L 10-16	Houston
8/21	L 13-17	at Minnesota
8/29	L 10-14	Seattle
9/3	L 9-17	at St. Louis

REGULAR SEASON (4-12)

Date	Result	Opponent
9/13	L 24-38	at Baltimore
9/20	L 10-13	Oakland
9/27	L 14-34	at Philadelphia
10/4	L 16-27	New York Giants
10/11	L 20-26	Dallas (OT)
10/18	W 14-6	at Washington
10/25	L 7-37	San Diego
11/8	L 21-24	at Jacksonville
11/15	W 16-10	at Oakland
11/22	W 27-24	Pittsburgh (OT)
11/29	L 14-43	at San Diego
12/6	L 13-44	Denver
12/13	L 10-16	Buffalo
12/20	L 34-41	Cleveland
12/27	L 10-17	at Cincinnati
1/3	W 44-24	at Denver

(OT) Overtime

SCORE BY PERIODS

Chiefs	29	83	61	118	3 —	294
Opponents	93	110	100	115	6 —	424

2009 TEAM STATISTICS

	Chiefs	Opp.
Total First Downs	256	318
Rushing	91	122
Passing	139	178
Penalty	26	18
3rd Down: Made/Att	62/227	85/223
3rd Down Pct.	27.3	38.1
4th Down: Made/Att	14/29	6/11
4th Down Pct.	48.3	54.5
Possession Avg.	27:37	32:23
Total Net Yards	4851	6211
Avg. Per Game	303.2	388.2
Total Plays	1019	1062
Avg. Per Play	4.8	5.8
Net Yards Rushing	1929	2504
Avg. Per Game	120.6	156.5
Total Rushes	438	531
Net Yards Passing	2922	3707
Avg. Per Game	182.6	231.7
Sacked/Yards Lost	45/261	22/137
Gross Yards	3183	3844
Att./Completions	536/296	509/302
Completion Pct.	55.2	59.3
Had Intercepted	17	15
Punts/Average	97/45.0	79/44.1
Net Punting Avg.	97/40.8	79/39.4
Penalties/Yards	84/667	106/821
Fumbles/Ball Lost	31/10	23/13
Touchdowns	31	48
Rushing	8	18
Passing	18	25
Returns	5	5

2009 INDIVIDUAL STATISTICS

PASSING	Att.	Comp.	Yds.	Pct.	TD	Int.	Tkld.	Rate
Cassel	493	271	2924	55.0	16	16	42/243	69.9
Croyle	40	23	230	57.5	2	0	3/18	90.6
Bradley TM	1	1	26	100.0	0	0	0/0	118.8
Gutierrez	1	1	3	100.0	0	0	0/0	79.2
Castille	1	0	0	0.0	0	1	0/0	0.0
Chiefs	536	296	3183	55.2	18	17	45/261	70.8
Opponents	509	302	3844	59.3	25	15	22/137	87.1

SCORING	TD R	TD P	TD Rt	PAT	FG	Saf	PTS
Succop	0	0	0	29/29	25/29	0	104
Charles	7	1	1	0/0	0/0	0	56
Bowe	0	4	0	0/0	0/0	0	24
Chambers TM	0	4	0	0/0	0/0	0	24
Bradley TM	0	2	0	0/0	0/0	0	12
D. Johnson	0	0	2	0/0	0/0	0	12
Ryan	0	2	0	0/0	0/0	0	12
Wade	0	2	0	0/0	0/0	0	12
Castille	0	1	0	0/0	0/0	0	6
Cox	1	0	0	0/0	0/0	0	6
McGraw	0	0	1	0/0	0/0	0	6
Pope	0	1	0	0/0	0/0	0	6
Studebaker	0	0	1	0/0	0/0	0	6
Vrabel	0	1	0	0/0	0/0	0	6
Hali	0	0	0	0/0	0/0	1	2
Chiefs	8	18	5	29/29	25/29	1	294
Opponents	18	25	5	47/47	29/37	1	424

2-Pt. Conversions: Charles.
Chiefs 1-2, Opponents 0-0.

RUSHING	No.	Yds	Avg	LG	TD
Charles	190	1120	5.9	76t	7
L. Johnson TM	132	377	2.9	19	0
Cassel	50	189	3.8	13	0
Castille	14	55	3.9	16	0
Savage	10	45	4.5	11	0
Lawrence	2	42	21.0	26	0
Ko. Smith	15	33	2.2	12	0
Battle	7	21	3.0	12	0
Bradley TM	2	20	10.0	22	0
Wade	3	11	3.7	8	0
J. Williams	6	6	1.0	5	0
Cox	3	5	1.7	2	1
McGraw	1	4	4.0	4	0
Thigpen TM	1	2	2.0	2	0
Colquitt	1	0	0.0	0	0
Long TM	1	-1	-1.0	-1	0
Chiefs	438	1929	4.4	76t	8
Opponents	531	2504	4.7	78	18

RECEIVING	No.	Yds	Avg	LG	TD
Bowe	47	589	12.5	41	4
Charles	40	297	7.4	49	1
Chambers TM	36	608	16.9	61	4
Wade	36	367	10.2	25	2
Bradley TM	24	320	13.3	50	2
Long TM	20	178	8.9	30	0
Pope	20	174	8.7	29	1
Ryan	14	135	9.6	43	2
L. Johnson TM	12	76	6.3	22	0
Cox	10	79	7.9	19	0
Cottam	9	120	13.3	26	0
Savage	7	51	7.3	12	0
Engram	5	61	12.2	18	0
Copper	4	68	17.0	50	0
Castille	4	37	9.3	20t	1
Ko. Smith	2	9	4.5	5	0
O'Connell	2	7	3.5	4	0
Battle	2	-3	-1.5	3	0
Lawrence	1	9	9.0	9	0
Vrabel	1	1	1.0	1t	1
Chiefs	296	3183	10.8	61	18
Opponents	302	3844	12.7	64t	25

INTERCEPTIONS	No.	Yds	Avg	LG	TD
Flowers	5	38	7.6	33	0
D. Johnson	3	175	58.3	70	2
M. Brown	3	13	4.3	10	0
Studebaker	2	96	48.0	94	0
Carr	1	31	31.0	31	0
McGraw	1	27	27.0	27	0
Chiefs	15	380	25.3	94	2
Opponents	17	160	9.4	37	0

PUNTING	No.	Yds.	Avg.	In 20	LG
Colquitt	96	4361	45.4	41	70
Chiefs	97	4361	45.0	41	70
Opponents	79	3482	44.1	31	73

PUNT RETURNS	Ret	FC	Yds	Avg	LG	TD
Wade	21	19	160	7.6	18	0
Savage	6	1	36	6.0	19	0
Leggett	5	1	13	2.6	10	0
Bradley TM	0	2	0	—	—	0
Engram	0	1	0	—	—	0
Chiefs	32	24	209	6.5	19	0
Opponents	40	24	285	7.1	44	0

KICKOFF RETURNS	No.	Yds	Avg	LG	TD
Charles	36	925	25.7	97t	1
Lawrence	16	317	19.8	29	0
Savage	8	160	20.0	29	0
Bradley TM	7	123	17.6	24	0
Long TM	6	106	17.7	22	0
Cox	2	9	4.5	9	0
Copper	1	18	18.0	18	0
Studebaker	1	8	8.0	8	0
Chiefs	77	1666	21.6	97t	1
Opponents	60	1446	24.1	103t	2

FIELD GOALS	1-19	20-29	30-39	40-49	50+
Succop	0/0	10/10	7/7	6/7	2/5
Chiefs	0/0	10/10	7/7	6/7	2/5
Opponents	1/1	11/11	7/8	7/11	3/6

SACKS	No.
Hali	8.5
Gilberry	4.5
M. Brown	2.0
Magee	2.0
Vrabel	2.0
Dorsey	1.0
D. Johnson	1.0
McGraw	1.0
Chiefs	22.0
Opponents	45.0

RECORD HOLDERS

INDIVIDUAL RECORDS—CAREER

Category	Name	Performance
Rushing (Yds.)	Priest Holmes, 2001-07	6,070
Passing (Yds.)	Len Dawson, 1962-1975	28,507
Passing (TDs)	Len Dawson, 1962-1975	237
Receiving (No.)	Tony Gonzalez, 1997-2008	916
Receiving (Yds.)	Tony Gonzalez, 1997-2008	10,940
Interceptions	Emmitt Thomas, 1966-1978	58
Punting (Avg.)	Dustin Colquitt, 2005-09	44.1
Punt Return (Avg.)	Noland Smith, 1967-69	11.1
Kickoff Return (Avg.)	Noland Smith, 1967-69	26.8
Field Goals	Nick Lowery, 1980-1993	329
Touchdowns (Tot.)	Priest Holmes, 2001-07	83
Points	Nick Lowery, 1980-1993	1,466
*Sacks	Derrick Thomas, 1989-1999	126.5

INDIVIDUAL RECORDS—SINGLE SEASON

Category	Name	Performance
Rushing (Yds.)	Larry Johnson, 2006	1,789
Passing (Yds.)	Trent Green, 2004	4,591
Passing (TDs)	Len Dawson, 1964	30
Receiving (No.)	Tony Gonzalez, 2004	102
Receiving (Yds.)	Derrick Alexander, 2000	1,391
Interceptions	Emmitt Thomas, 1974	12
Punting (Avg.)	Jerrel Wilson, 1973	45.5
Punt Return (Avg.)	Dante Hall, 2003	16.3
Kickoff Return (Avg.)	Dave Grayson, 1962	29.7
Field Goals	Nick Lowery, 1990	34
Touchdowns (Tot.)	Priest Holmes, 2003	27
Points	Priest Holmes, 2003	162
*Sacks	Derrick Thomas, 1990	20.0

INDIVIDUAL RECORDS—SINGLE GAME

Category	Name	Performance
Rushing (Yds.)	Jamaal Charles, 1-3-10	259
Passing (Yds.)	Elvis Grbac, 11-5-00	504
Passing (TDs)	Len Dawson, 11-1-64	6
Receiving (No.)	Tony Gonzalez, 1-2-05	14
Receiving (Yds.)	Stephone Paige, 12-22-85	309
Interceptions	Bobby Ply, 12-16-62	**4
	Bobby Hunt, 10-4-64	**4
	Deron Cherry, 9-29-85	**4
Field Goals	Many times	5
	Last time by Nick Lowery, 9-20-93	
Touchdowns (Tot.)	Abner Haynes, 11-26-61	5
Points	Abner Haynes, 11-26-61	30
*Sacks	Derrick Thomas, 11-11-90	**7.0

**Sacks became an official statistic in 1982.*
***NFL Record*

KANSAS CITY CHIEFS

2010 VETERAN ROSTER

No.	Name	Pos.	Ht.	Wt.	Birthdate	NFL Exp.	College	Hometown	How Acq.	'09 Games/ Starts
76	Albert, Branden	T	6-5	316	11/4/84	3	Glen Burnie, Md.	Virginia	D1b-'08	14/14
26	Battle, Jackie	RB	6-2	238	10/1/83	3	Humble, Texas	Houston	FA-'08	5/0
59	Belcher, Jovan	LB	6-2	228	7/24/87	2	West Babylon, N.Y.	Maine	FA-'09	16/3
82	Bowe, Dwayne	WR	6-2	221	9/21/84	4	Miami, Fla.	Louisiana State	D1-'07	11/9
61	Brown, Colin	G	6-7	335	8/29/85	2	Braymer, Mo.	Missouri	D5-'09	0*
39	Carr, Brandon	CB	6-0	207	5/19/86	3	Flint, Mich.	Grand Valley State	D5-'08	16/16
7	Cassel, Matt	QB	6-4	230	5/17/82	6	Chatsworth, Calif.	Southern California	T(NE)-'09	15/15
46	Castille, Tim	RB	5-11	238	5/29/84	4	Birmingham, Ala.	Alabama	FA-'09	7/0
84	Chambers, Chris	WR	5-11	210	8/12/78	10	Bedford, Ohio	Wisconsin	FA-'09	16/14*
25	Charles, Jamaal	RB	5-11	199	12/27/86	3	Port Arthur, Texas	Texas	D3a-'08	15/10
2	Colquitt, Dustin	P	6-3	210	5/6/82	6	Knoxville, Tenn.	Tennessee	D3-05	16/0
10	Copper, Terrance	WR	6-0	207	3/12/82	7	Washington, N.C.	East Carolina	UFA(Balt)-'09	15/2
87	Cottam, Brad	TE	6-7	269	11/28/84	3	Germantown, Tenn.	Tennessee	D3b-'08	8/1
42	Cox, Mike	FB	6-0	252	7/11/85	3	Lewisberry, Pa.	Georgia Tech	FA-'08	16/10
12	Croyle, Brodie	QB	6-2	206	2/6/83	5	Rainbow City, Ala.	Alabama	D3-'06	3/1
34	Daniels, Travis	CB	6-1	195	9/8/82	6	Hollywood, Fla.	Louisiana State	FA-'09	9/1
72	Dorsey, Glenn	DE	6-1	297	8/1/85	3	Gonzales, La.	Louisiana State	D1a-'08	15/14
95	Edwards, Ron	DT	6-3	315	7/12/79	10	Houston, Texas	Texas A&M	UFA(Buff)-'06	16/14
24	Flowers, Brandon	CB	5-9	187	2/18/86	3	Delray Beach, Fla.	Virginia Tech	D2-'08	15/15
43	Gafford, Thomas	LS	6-2	250	1/29/83	3	Friendswood, Texas	Houston	FA-'09	16/0
92	Gilberry, Wallace	DE	6-2	268	12/5/84	3	Bay Minette, Ala.	Alabama	FA-'08	16/0
9	Gutierrez, Matt	QB	6-4	230	6/9/84	4	Concord, Calif.	Idaho State	W(NE)-'09	1/0
91	Hali, Tamba	LB	6-3	275	11/3/83	5	Teaneck, N.J.	Penn State	D1-'06	16/16
52	Herron, David	LB	6-1	239	6/17/84	3	Warren, Ohio	Michigan State	FA-'09	10/0
94	Jackson, Tyson	DE	6-4	296	6/6/86	2	Edgard, La.	Louisiana State	D1-'09	16/14
56	Johnson, Derrick	LB	6-3	242	11/22/82	6	Waco, Texas	Texas	D1-05	15/3
20	Jones, Thomas	RB	5-10	212	8/19/78	11	Big Stone Gap, Va.	Virginia	FA-'10	16/16*
14	Lawrence, Quinten	WR	6-0	184	9/21/84	2	Carencro, La.	McNeese State	D6-'09	6/1
31	Leggett, Maurice	CB/S	5-11	188	10/2/86	3	Pittsburgh, Pa.	Valdosta State	FA-'08	10/1
65	Lilja, Ryan	G	6-2	290	10/15/81	7	Shawnee Mission, Kan.	Kansas State	FA-'10	16/16*
17	Long, Lance	WR	5-11	186	5/4/85	2	Macomb, Miss.	Mississippi State	FA-'09	8/1*
71	Magee, Alex	DE	6-3	298	4/28/87	2	Oswego, Ill.	Purdue	D3-'09	15/1
51	Mays, Corey	LB	6-1	245	11/27/83	5	Chicago, Ill.	Notre Dame	FA-'09	16/13
47	McGraw, Jon	S	6-3	208	4/2/79	9	Manhattan, Kan.	Kansas State	UFA(Det)-'07	14/9
38	Morgan, DaJuan	S	6-0	203	10/21/85	3	Riviera Beach, Fla.	North Carolina State	D3c-'08	13/2
60	Ndukwe, Ikechuku	G/T	6-4	325	7/17/82	4	Dublin, Ohio	Northwestern	T(Mia)-'09	12/3
64	Niswanger, Rudy	C	6-5	301	11/9/82	5	Monroe, La.	Louisiana State	FA-'06	16/16
75	O'Callaghan, Ryan	T	6-7	330	7/19/83	5	Redding, Calif.	California	W(NE)-'09	14/12
85	O'Connell, Jake	TE	6-3	250	11/6/85	2	Naples, Fla.	Miami (Ohio)	D7b-'09	4/2
44	Page, Jarrad	S	6-0	225	10/19/84	5	San Leandro, Calif.	UCLA	D7-'06	5/5
45	Pope, Leonard	TE	6-8	264	9/10/83	5	Americus, Ga.	Georgia	FA-'09	13/8
67	Richardson, Barry	T	6-6	319	5/15/86	3	Mt. Pleasant, S.C.	Clemson	D6a-'08	10/1
23	Richardson, Mike	CB	5-11	190	2/18/84	4	Warner Robins, Ga.	Notre Dame	FA-'09	11/1
21	Smith, Kolby	RB	5-11	219	12/15/84	4	Tallahassee, Fla.	Louisville	D5a-'07	4/0
90	Smith, Shaun	DT	6-2	325	8/19/81	6	Wichita, Kan.	South Carolina	FA-'10	3/0*
96	Studebaker, Andy	LB	6-3	248	9/16/85	3	Eureka, Ill.	Wheaton	FA-'08	16/2
6	Succop, Ryan	K	6-2	218	9/19/86	2	Hickory, N.C.	South Carolina	D7c-'09	16/0
83	Urban, Jerheme	WR	6-3	207	11/26/80	6	Victoria, Texas	Trinity (Texas)	FA-'10	10/0*
50	Vrabel, Mike	LB	6-4	261	8/14/75	14	Akron, Ohio	Ohio State	T(NE)-'09	14/14
97	Walters, Pierre	LB	6-5	269	3/25/86	2	Westchester, Ill.	Eastern Illinois	CA-'09	3/0
27	Washington, Donald	CB	6-1	197	7/28/86	2	Indianapolis, Ind.	Ohio State	D4-'09	8/0
54	Waters, Brian	G	6-3	320	2/18/77	11	Waxahachie, Texas	North Texas	FA-00	15/15
62	Wiegmann, Casey	C	6-2	285	7/20/73	15	Parkersburg, Iowa	Iowa	FA-'10	16/16*
53	Williams, Demorrio	LB	6-1	232	7/6/80	7	Beckville, Texas	Nebraska	UFA(Atl)-'08	16/13

* Brown missed '09 season because of injury; Chambers played 7 games with San Diego and 9 games with Kansas City in '09; Jones played 16 games with N.Y. Jets; Lilja played 16 games with Indianapolis; Long played 1 game with Arizona and 7 games with Kansas City; S. Smith played three games with Cincinnati; Urban played 10 games with Arizona; Wiegmann played 16 games with Denver.

Traded—QB Tyler Thigpen (1 game in '09) to Miami, DT Tank Tyler (6) to Carolina.

Players lost through free agency (3): TE Sean Ryan (Wash; 10), G/T Wade Smith (Hou; 16), WR Bobby Wade (Wash; 12).

Also played with Chiefs in '09—C/G Andy Alleman (9 games), LB Monty Beisel (3), WR Mark Bradley (13), S Mike Brown (16), CB Ricardo Colclough (1), WR Bobby Engram (5), DE/DT Dion Gales (3), G Mike Goff (8), RB Larry Johnson (7), DT Derek Lokey (2), S Ricky Price (2), LB Justin Rogers (1), RB Dantrell Savage (5), DT Kenny Smith (6), RB Javarris Williams (4).

2010 FIRST-YEAR ROSTER

Name	Pos.	Ht.	Wt.	Birthdate	College	Hometown	How Acq.
Arenas, Javier	DB	5-9	197	10/28/87	Alabama	Tampa, Fla.	D2b
Asamoah, Jon	OL	6-4	305	7/21/88	Illinois	Park Forest, Ill.	D3a
Bates, Jackie (1)	CB	5-10	180	10/12/86	Hampton	Concord, Calif.	FA
Berry, Eric	DB	6-0	211	12/29/88	Tennessee	Fairburn, Ga.	D1
Brown, Garrett	DL	6-1	309	9/20/88	Minnesota	Fairfield, Conn.	FA
Cole, Justin	LB	6-3	242	11/22/87	San Jose State	Chino Hills, Calif.	FA
Eastman, Tyler	OL	6-5	310	6/9/87	Maine	Old Town, Maine	FA
Gales, Dion (1)	DE/DT	6-5	259	8/17/85	Troy	New Orleans, La.	FA-'09
Greenwood, Bobby (1)	DE	6-5	278	3/2/87	Alabama	Prattville, Ala.	FA
Grimes, David (1)	WR	5-9	183	12/31/86	Notre Dame	Los Angeles, Calif.	FA
Gunnell, Rich	WR	5-11	197	1/12/87	Boston College	Lawrenceville, N.J.	FA
Harris, Darryl (1)	G	6-4	300	1/14/85	Mississippi	Clarksdale, Miss.	FA-'09
Horne, Jeremy	WR	6-2	193	10/25/86	Massachusetts	New Berlin, N.Y.	FA
Jeanpierre, Lemuel	OL	6-3	301	5/19/87	South Carolina	Orlando, Fla.	FA
Johnson, Michael	LB	6-0	254	9/8/86	North Alabama	Panama City, Fla.	FA
Johnson, Tervaris	RB	6-2	248	6/14/88	Miami	Opa-locka, Fla.	FA
Landry, Nick	OL	6-5	291	10/16/87	Tulane	Beaumont, Texas	FA
Langford, Reshard (1)	S	6-1	213	2/6/86	Vanderbilt	Tanner, Ala.	FA-'09
Lewis, Andrew	OL	6-4	298	2/20/87	Oklahoma State	Joplin, Mo.	FA
Lewis, Kendrick	DB	6-0	198	6/16/88	Mississippi	Gainesville, Ga.	D5a
Lokey, Derek (1)	DT	6-1	300	11/25/85	Texas	Denton, Texas	FA-'09
McCluster, Dexter	WR	5-8	170	8/25/88	Mississippi	Largo, Fla.	D2a
Moeaki, Tony	TE	6-3	252	6/8/87	Iowa	Wheaton, Ill.	D3b
Moore, Kestahn (1)	RB	5-10	214	4/13/87	Florida	Arlington, Texas	FA
Palko, Tyler (1)	QB	6-1	215	8/9/83	Pittsburgh	Imperial, Pa.	FA
Porter, Jermail (1)	OL	6-5	310	5/24/86	Kent State	Akron, Ohio	FA
Price, Ricky (1)	S	6-1	195	9/16/87	Oklahoma State	Houston, Texas	FA-'09
Sheffield, Cameron	DB	6-2	257	2/12/88	Troy	Portal, Ga.	D5b
Williams, Javarris (1)	RB	5-10	223	4/8/86	Tennessee State	Richmond, Texas	D7a-'09

The term NFL Rookie is defined as a player who is in his first season of professional football and has not been on the roster of another professional football team for any regular-season or postseason games. A Rookie is designated by an "R" on NFL rosters. Players who have been active in another professional football league or players who have NFL experience, including either preseason training camp or being on an Active List or Inactive List, or on Reserve/Injured or Reserve/Physically Unable to Perform for fewer than six regular-season games, are termed NFL First-Year Players. An NFL First-Year Player is designated by a "1" on NFL rosters. Thereafter, a player is credited with an additional year of experience for each season in which he accumulates six games on the Active List or Inactive List, or on Reserve/Injured or Reserve/Physically Unable to Perform.

Log on to www.kcchiefs.com for an up-to-date roster.

KANSAS CITY CHIEFS

COACHING STAFF

Head Coach,
Todd Haley

Pro Career: Todd Haley was named head coach of the Kansas City Chiefs on February 6, 2009. He is entering his 16th season in the National Football League and his 14th campaign in a coaching capacity in 2010. The Chiefs improved in 30 different statistical categories in Haley's inaugural campaign compared to the 2008 season. Most notably, Kansas City led the NFL in Red Zone scoring percentage (89.5%) and ranked eighth in defensive three-and-out percentage (24.4%). The Chiefs also improved from 29th to 12th in the comprehensive NFL special teams rankings compiled by Rick Gosselin of the *Dallas Morning News*. Only three teams showed more dramatic improvement in that area than the Chiefs. Haley has been on the coaching staff of four different franchises that have reached the playoffs—Arizona, Dallas, Chicago and the N.Y. Jets—serving under head coach Bill Parcells in both Dallas and with the N.Y. Jets. He joined the Chiefs after a two-year stint as the offensive coordinator of the Arizona Cardinals (2007-08). In 2008, Haley helped the Cardinals claim their first division crown since 1975 as Arizona earned a berth in Super Bowl XLIII. The Cardinals offense tied for third in the league in scoring, registering a franchise-record 427 points (26.7 ppg), while ranking fourth in total offense (365.8 ypg). Under Haley in 2007, the Cardinals were fifth in the league in passing (254.1 ypg) and set a single-season franchise record with 32 TD passes. Served three seasons as passing game coordinator/wide receivers coach for Dallas (2004-06). Joined the Cowboys after a three-year tour of duty as wide receivers coach for Chicago (2001-03). In 2001, the Bears went 13-3 and won the NFC Central for the first time since 1990. Served as the N.Y. Jets wide receivers coach from 1999-2000 after serving as an offensive assistant/quality control coach from 1997-98. Haley began his NFL career with the Jets as a scouting department assistant in 1995. Career record: 4-12.

Background: Haley earned a degree in communications from the University of North Florida in 1991 and received that school's 2009 Distinguished Alumni Achievement Award. Haley attended Upper St. Clair High School in Pittsburgh, and is the son of longtime NFL personnel man Dick Haley, who was one of the architects of the great Steelers teams of the 1970s.

Personal: Born on February 28, 1967 in Atlanta, Georgia. He and his wife, Chrissy, have four daughters: Taylor, Peyton, Kady, and Ella and one son, Richard Todd, Jr.

ASSISTANT COACHES

Richie Anderson, wide receivers; born September 13, 1971, Sandy Springs, Md. Running back Penn State 1989-1992. Pro running back New York Jets 1993-2002, Dallas Cowboys 2003-04. Pro coach: New York Jets 2006, joined Chiefs in 2010.

Maurice Carthon, asst. head coach; born April 24, 1961, Chicago. Running back Arkansas State 1979-1982. Pro running back New Jersey Generals (USFL) 1983-85, New York Giants 1985-1991, Indianapolis Colts 1992. Pro coach: New England Patriots 1994-96, New York Jets 1997-2000, Detroit Lions 2001-02, Dallas Cowboys 2003-04, Cleveland Browns 2005-06, Arizona Cardinals 2007-08, joined Chiefs in 2009.

Mike Clark, strength and conditioning; born August 22, 1954, Wichita, Kan. Center Ottawa 1973-76. No pro playing experience. College coach: Kansas 1977-78, 1982, Wyoming 1981, Oregon 1983-87, Southern California 1988-89, Texas A&M 1990-2003. Pro coach: Seattle Seahawks 2004-09, joined Chiefs in 2010.

Romeo Crennel, defensive coordinator; born June 18, 1947, Lynchburg, Va. Defensive lineman Western Kentucky 1966-69. No pro playing experience. College coach: Western Kentucky 1970-74, Texas Tech 1975-77, Mississippi 1978-79, Georgia 1980. Pro coach: New York Giants 1981-1992, New England Patriots 1993-96, 2001-04, New York Jets 1997-99, Cleveland Browns 2000, 2005-08 (head coach), joined Chiefs in 2010.

Gary Gibbs, linebackers; born August 13, 1952, Beaumont, Texas. Linebacker Oklahoma 1972-74. No pro playing experience. College coach: Oklahoma 1975-1994 (head coach 1989-1994), Georgia 2000, Louisiana State 2001. Pro coach: Dallas Cowboys 2002-04, New Orleans Saints 2006-08, joined Chiefs in 2009.

Steve Hoffman, special teams; born September 8, 1958, Camden, N.J. Quarterback/running back/wide receiver Dickinson College 1977-1980. Pro punter Washington Federals (USFL) 1983. College coach: Miami 1985-87. Pro coach: Dallas Cowboys 1989-2004, Atlanta Falcons 2006, Miami Dolphins 2007-08, joined Chiefs in 2009.

Bill Muir, offensive line; born October 26, 1942, Pittsburgh. Tackle Susquehanna 1962-64. No pro playing experience. College coach: Susquehanna 1965, Delaware Valley 1966-67, Rhode Island 1970-71, Idaho State 1972-73, Southern Methodist 1976-77. Pro coach: Orlando (Continental Football League) 1968-69, Houston/Shreveport Steamer (WFL) 1974-75, New England Patriots 1982-84, Detroit Lions 1985-88, Indianapolis Colts 1989-1991, Philadelphia Eagles 1992-94, New York Jets 1995-2001, Tampa Bay Buccaneers 2002-08, joined Chiefs in 2009.

Bernie Parmalee, tight ends; born September 16, 1967, Jersey City, N.J. Running back Ball State 1988-1991. Pro running back Miami Dolphins 1992-98, New York Jets 1999-2000. College coach: Notre Dame 2005-09. Pro coach: Miami Dolphins 2002-04, joined Chiefs in 2010.

Pat Perles, asst. offensive line; born October 2, 1963, Detroit. Defensive tackle Michigan State 1982-85. No pro playing experience. College coach: Toledo 1989-1991, Michigan State 2000-02, North Dakota State 2003-08. Pro coach: L.A. Rams 1992-93, Saskatchewan Roughriders (CFL) 1994-96, Winnipeg Blue Bombers (CFL) 1997, Hamilton Tigercats (CFL) 1998-99, joined Chiefs in 2009.

Anthony Pleasant, defensive line; born January 27, 1968, Century, Fla. Defensive end Tennessee State 1987-89. Pro defensive end Cleveland Browns 1990-95, Baltimore Ravens 1996, Atlanta Falcons 1997, New York Jets 1998-99, San Francisco 49ers 2000, New England Patriots 2001-03. Pro coach: Joined Chiefs in 2010.

Brent Salazar, asst. strength and conditioning; born May 22, 1980, Denver. Attended New Mexico. No college or pro playing experience. College coach: New Mexico 2002-03, Nevada-Las Vegas 2004, Pacific 2006. Pro coach: Joined Chiefs in 2007.

Nick Sirianni, offensive quality control; born June 15, 1981, Jamestown, N.Y. Wide receiver Mount Union 2000-03. No pro playing experience. College coach: Mount Union 2004-05, Indiana (Pa.) 2006-08. Pro coach: Joined Chiefs in 2009.

Otis Smith, defensive quality control; born October 22, 1965, New Orleans. Defensive back Taft (CA) Junior College 1986-87, Missouri 1988-89. Pro defensive back Philadelphia Eagles 1991-94, New York Jets 1995-96, 1997-99, New England Patriots 1996, 2000-02, Detroit Lions 2003. Pro coach: Philadelphia Eagles 2008, joined Chiefs in 2010.

Emmitt Thomas, defensive backs; born June 3, 1943, Angleton, Tex. Quarterback/wide receiver Bishop (TX) College 1963-65. Pro defensive back Kansas City Chiefs 1966-1978. Inducted into Pro Football Hall of Fame 2008. College coach: Central Missouri State 1979-1980. Pro coach: St. Louis Cardinals 1981-85, Washington Redskins 1986-1994, Philadelphia Eagles 1995-98, Green Bay Packers 1999, Minnesota Vikings 2000-01, Atlanta Falcons 2002-09 (interim head coach 2007), re-joined Chiefs in 2010.

Charlie Weis, offensive coordinator; born March 30, 1956, Trenton N.J. Attended Notre Dame. No college or pro playing experience. College coach: South Carolina 1985-88, Notre Dame 2005-09 (head coach). Pro coach: New York Giants 1990-92, New England Patriots 1993-96, 2000-04, New York Jets 1997-99, joined Chiefs in 2010.

Adam Zimmer, defensive assistant/asst. linebackers; born January 13, 1984, Ogden, Utah. Defensive back Trinity (Texas) 2002-05. No pro playing experience. Pro coach: New Orleans Saints 2006-09, joined Chiefs in 2010.

American Football Conference
East Division
Team Colors: Aqua, Coral, Blue, and White
7500 S.W. 30th Street
Davie, Florida 33314
Telephone: (954) 452-7000

2010 SCHEDULE

PRESEASON

Aug. 14	**Tampa Bay**	7:00
Aug. 21	at Jacksonville	7:30
Aug. 27	**Atlanta**	7:00
Sep. 2	at Dallas	7:00

REGULAR SEASON

Sep. 12	at Buffalo	1:00
Sep. 19	at Minnesota	12:00
Sep. 26	**New York Jets**	8:20
Oct. 4	**New England** (Mon)	8:30
Oct. 10	BYE	
Oct. 17	at Green Bay	12:00
Oct. 24	**Pittsburgh**	1:00
Oct. 31	at Cincinnati	1:00
Nov. 7	at Baltimore	1:00
Nov. 14	**Tennessee**	1:00
Nov. 18	**Chicago** (Thu)	8:20
Nov. 28	at Oakland	1:05
Dec. 5	**Cleveland**	1:00
Dec. 12	at New York Jets	4:15
Dec. 19	**Buffalo**	1:00
Dec. 26	**Detroit**	1:00
Jan. 2	at New England	1:00

Stadium: Sun Life Stadium (opened in 1987)
•**Capacity:** 75,192
2269 Dan Marino Blvd.
Miami Gardens, Florida 33056
Playing Surface: Grass (PAT)
Training Camp: Nova Southeastern Univ.
7500 S.W. 30th Street
Davie, Florida 33314

SUN LIFE STADIUM

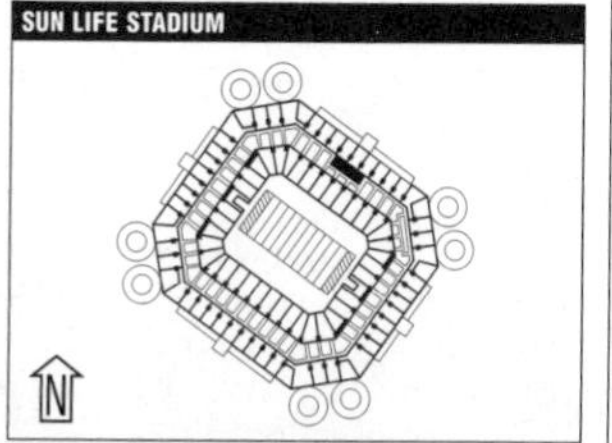

CLUB OFFICIALS

Chairman of the Board/Managing General Partner: Stephen M. Ross
Chief Executive Officer: Mike Dee
Executive Vice President-Football Operations: Bill Parcells
General Manager: Jeff Ireland
Chief Administrative Officer: Harold Talisman
Senior Vice President of Football Operations: Dawn Aponte
Senior Vice President-Operations: Bill Galante
Senior Vice President-Media Relations: Harvey Greene
Senior Vice President-Public Affairs: Adam Grossman
Senior Vice President-Chief Technology Officer: Tery Howard
Senior Vice President-Corporate Partnerships and Integrated Media: Jim Rushton
Senior Vice President-Finance and Administration: Jill R. Strafaci
Senior Vice President-Sales and Ticket Operations: Mark Tilson
Assistant Director of Player Personnel: Brian Gaine
Director of College Scouting: Chris Grier
Player Personnel Coordinator: Chris Shea
Head Athletic Trainer: Kevin O'Neill
Equipment Manager: Joe Cimino
Video Director: Bob Hack
Senior Director of Internet and Publications: Scott Stone
Director of Media Relations: Jason Jenkins
Director of Communications: Fitz Ollison
Senior Director of Programming and Production: Jeff Griffith
Senior Director of Cheerleaders and Entertainment: Dorie Grogan
Cheerleader Coordinator: Emily Snow
Director of Records and Archives: Kristin Hingston
Alumni, Youth and Special Projects: Nat Moore
Senior Director of Community Relations: Ilona Wolpin
Director of Youth Programs: Twan Russell
Director of Security: Stuart Weinstein

COACHING HISTORY
(407-301-4)

Records include postseason games

1966-69	George Wilson	15-39-2
1970-1995	Don Shula	274-147-2
1996-99	Jimmy Johnson	38-31-0
2000-04	Dave Wannstedt*	43-33-0
2004	Jim Bates	3-4-0
2005-06	Nick Saban	15-17-0
2007	Cam Cameron	1-15-0
2008-09	Tony Sparano	18-15-0

*Resigned after nine games in 2004

PAID ATTENDANCE

Home 540,342 Away 544,472
Total 1,084,814
Single-game home record, 75,283 (10/27/96)
Single-season home record, 592,161 (1999)

2010 DRAFT CHOICES

Round	Name	Pos.	College
1	Jared Odrick	DT	Penn State
2	Koa Misi	LB	Utah
3	John Jerry	G	Mississippi
4	A.J. Edds	LB	Iowa
5	Nolan Carroll	DB	Maryland
	Reshad Jones	DB	Georgia
7	Chris McCoy	LB	Middle Tennessee
	Austin Spitler	LB	Ohio State

MIAMI DOLPHINS

2009 TEAM RECORD

PRESEASON (4-0)

Date	Result	Opponent
8/17	W 12-9	Jacksonville
8/22	W 27-17	Carolina
8/27	W 10-6	at Tampa Bay
9/3	W 10-7	at New Orleans

REGULAR SEASON (7-9)

Date	Result	Opponent
9/13	L 7-19	at Atlanta
9/21	L 23-27	Indianapolis
9/27	L 13-23	at San Diego
10/4	W 38-10	Buffalo
10/12	W 31-27	New York Jets
10/25	L 34-46	New Orleans
11/1	W 30-25	at New York Jets
118	L 17-27	at New England
11/15	W 25-23	Tampa Bay
11/19	W 24-17	at Carolina
11/29	L 14-31	at Buffalo
12/6	W 22-21	New England
12/13	W 14-10	at Jacksonville
12/20	L 24-27	at Tennessee (OT)
12/27	L 20-27	Houston
1/3	L 24-30	Pittsburgh

(OT) Overtime

SCORE BY PERIODS

Dolphins	57	106	81	116	0 —	360
Opponents	68	101	78	140	3 —	390

2009 TEAM STATISTICS

	Dolphins	Opp.
Total First Downs	333	297
Rushing	129	88
Passing	188	184
Penalty	16	25
3rd Down: Made/Att	120/245	69/198
3rd Down Pct.	49.0	34.8
4th Down: Made/Att	13/18	8/15
4th Down Pct.	72.2	53.3
Possession Avg.	31:54	28:06
Total Net Yards	5401	5589
Avg. Per Game	337.6	349.3
Total Plays	1088	968
Avg. Per Play	5.0	5.8
Net Yards Rushing	2231	1835
Avg. Per Game	139.4	114.7
Total Rushes	509	435
Net Yards Passing	3170	3754
Avg. Per Game	198.1	234.6
Sacked/Yards Lost	34/226	44/242
Gross Yards	3396	3996
Att./Completions	545/331	489/281
Completion Pct.	60.7	57.5
Had Intercepted	19	15
Punts/Average	75/46.3	67/44.1
Net Punting Avg.	75/39.8	67/38.4
Penalties/Yards	78/640	73/589
Fumbles/Ball Lost	27/10	17/6
Touchdowns	41	42
Rushing	22	16
Passing	15	23
Returns	4	3

2009 INDIVIDUAL STATISTICS

PASSING	Att.	Comp.	Yds.	Pct.	TD	Int.	Tkld.	Rate
Henne	451	274	2878	60.8	12	14	26/176	75.2
Pennington	74	51	413	68.9	1	2	6/32	76.0
Thigpen TM	8	4	83	50.0	1	2	0/0	87.0
Brown	6	2	22	33.3	1	0	1/9	84.7
White	5	0	0	0.0	0	0	1/9	39.6
R. Williams	1	0	0	0.0	0	1	0/0	0.0
Dolphins	545	331	3396	60.7	15	19	34/226	73.3
Opponents	489	281	3996	57.5	23	15	44/242	86.9

SCORING	TD R	TD P	TD Rt	PAT	FG	Saf	PTS
Carpenter	0	0	0	37/38	25/28	0	112
R. Williams	11	2	0	0/0	0/0	0	80
Brown	8	0	0	0/0	0/0	0	48
B. Hartline	1	3	0	0/0	0/0	0	24
Ginn	0	1	2	0/0	0/0	0	18
Hilliard	1	2	0	0/0	0/0	0	18
Bess	0	2	0	0/0	0/0	0	12
Fasano	0	2	0	0/0	0/0	0	12
Haynos	0	2	0	0/0	0/0	0	12
V. Davis	0	0	1	0/0	0/0	0	6
Henne	1	0	0	0/0	0/0	0	6
Sperry	0	1	0	0/0	0/0	0	6
Taylor	0	0	1	0/0	0/0	0	6
Dolphins	22	15	4	37/38	25/28	0	360
Opponents	16	23	3	35/37	33/39	0	390

2-Pt. Conversions: R. Williams.
Dolphins 1-3, Opponents 2-5.

RUSHING	No.	Yds	Avg	LG	TD
R. Williams	241	1121	4.7	68t	11
Brown	147	648	4.4	45	8
Polite	37	123	3.3	13	0
Hilliard	23	89	3.9	18	1
White	21	81	3.9	33	0
Ginn	7	48	6.9	22	0
Cobbs	6	36	6.0	19	0
Henne	16	32	2.0	12	1
B. Hartline	4	29	7.3	16t	1
Bess	2	11	5.5	11	0
Pennington	3	7	2.3	4	0
Sheets TM	1	5	5.0	5	0
Thigpen TM	1	1	1.0	1	0
Dolphins	509	2231	4.4	68t	22
Opponents	435	1835	4.2	50	16

RECEIVING	No.	Yds	Avg	LG	TD
Bess	76	758	10.0	34t	2
Camarillo	50	552	11.0	29	0
Ginn	38	454	11.9	53t	1
R. Williams	35	264	7.5	59	2
B. Hartline	31	506	16.3	67	3
Fasano	31	339	10.9	27	2
Hilliard	20	158	7.9	18	2
Haynos	19	162	8.5	21	2
Brown	14	98	7.0	27	0
Polite	11	51	4.6	10	0
Sperry	3	31	10.3	13	1
Cobbs	3	23	7.7	10	0
Dolphins	331	3396	10.3	67	15
Opponents	281	3996	14.2	81t	23

INTERCEPTIONS	No.	Yds	Avg	LG	TD
V. Davis	4	64	16.0	26	1
Bell	3	48	16.0	29	0
W. Allen	2	27	13.5	21	0
N. Jones	2	0	0.0	0	0
Culver	1	23	23.0	23	0
Crowder	1	2	2.0	2	0
Taylor	1	0	0.0	0	0
Torbor	1	0	0.0	0	0
Dolphins	15	164	10.9	29	1
Opponents	19	261	13.7	54t	3

PUNTING	No.	Yds.	Avg.	In 20	LG
Fields	75	3472	46.3	25	66
Dolphins	75	3472	46.3	25	66
Opponents	67	2953	44.1	22	66

PUNT RETURNS	Ret	FC	Yds	Avg	LG	TD
Bess	28	13	209	7.5	22	0
Ginn	5	0	28	5.6	12	0
Dolphins	33	13	237	7.2	22	0
Opponents	43	13	369	8.6	31	0

KICKOFF RETURNS	No.	Yds	Avg	LG	TD
Ginn	52	1296	24.9	101t	2
Cobbs	16	361	22.6	39	0
B. Hartline	3	36	12.0	18	0
Polite	2	24	12.0	12	0
Berger	1	13	13.0	13	0
Torbor	1	9	9.0	9	0
Dolphins	75	1739	23.2	101t	2
Opponents	71	1557	21.9	87	0

FIELD GOALS	1-19	20-29	30-39	40-49	50+
Carpenter	0/0	9/9	7/8	8/9	1/2
Dolphins	0/0	9/9	7/8	8/9	1/2
Opponents	0/0	11/11	7/8	9/14	6/6

SACKS	No.
Porter	9.0
Starks	7.0
Taylor	7.0
Wake	5.5
Langford	2.5
Merling	2.5
Anderson	2.0
Bell	1.5
McDaniel	1.5
Crowder	1.0
N. Jones	1.0
Moses	1.0
Torbor	1.0
Wilson	1.0
Baker	0.5
Dolphins	44.0
Opponents	34.0

RECORD HOLDERS

INDIVIDUAL RECORDS—CAREER

Category	Name	Performance
Rushing (Yds.)	Larry Csonka, 1968-1974, 1979	6,737
Passing (Yds.)	Dan Marino, 1983-1999	61,361
Passing (TDs)	Dan Marino, 1983-1999	420
Receiving (No.)	Mark Clayton, 1983-1992	550
Receiving (Yds.)	Mark Duper, 1982-1992	8,869
Interceptions	Jake Scott, 1970-75	35
Punting (Avg.)	Brandon Fields, 2007-09	44.2
Punt Return (Avg.)	Jeff Ogden, 2000-01	13.7
Kickoff Return (Avg.)	Mercury Morris, 1969-1975	26.5
Field Goals	Olindo Mare, 1997-2006	245
Touchdowns (Tot.)	Mark Clayton, 1983-1992	82
Points	Olindo Mare, 1997-2006	1,048
*Sacks	Jason Taylor, 1997-2007, 2009	124.0

INDIVIDUAL RECORDS—SINGLE SEASON

Category	Name	Performance
Rushing (Yds.)	Ricky Williams, 2002	1,853
Passing (Yds.)	Dan Marino, 1984	**5,084
Passing (TDs)	Dan Marino, 1984	48
Receiving (No.)	O.J. McDuffie, 1998	90
Receiving (Yds.)	Mark Clayton, 1984	1,389
Interceptions	Dick Westmoreland, 1967	10
Punting (Avg.)	John Kidd, 1996	46.3
Punt Return (Avg.)	Jeff Ogden, 2000	17.0
Kickoff Return (Avg.)	Duriel Harris, 1976	32.9
Field Goals	Olindo Mare, 1999	39
Touchdowns (Tot.)	Mark Clayton, 1984	18
Points	Olindo Mare, 1999	144
*Sacks	Jason Taylor, 2002	18.5

INDIVIDUAL RECORDS—SINGLE GAME

Category	Name	Performance
Rushing (Yds.)	Ricky Williams, 12-1-02	228
Passing (Yds.)	Dan Marino, 10-23-88	521
Passing (TDs)	Bob Griese, 11-24-77	6
	Dan Marino, 9-21-86	6
Receiving (No.)	Chris Chambers, 12-4-05	15
Receiving (Yds.)	Chris Chambers, 12-4-05	238
Interceptions	Dick Anderson, 12-3-73	**4
Field Goals	Olindo Mare, 10-17-99	6
Touchdowns (Tot.)	Paul Warfield, 12-15-73	4
	Mark Ingram, 11-27-94	4
	Ronnie Brown, 9-21-08	4
Points	Paul Warfield, 12-15-73	24
	Mark Ingram, 11-27-94	24
	Ronnie Brown, 9-21-08	24
*Sacks	Doug Betters, 9-4-83	4.0
	E.J. Junior, 10-6-91	4.0
	Joey Porter, 9-21-08	4.0

**Sacks became an official statistic in 1982.*
***NFL Record*

MIAMI DOLPHINS

2010 VETERAN ROSTER

No.	Name	Pos.	Ht.	Wt.	Birthdate	NFL Exp.	College	Hometown	How Acq.	'09 Games/ Starts
79	Alama-Francis, Ikaika	DE	6-5	290	12/4/84	4	Hawaii	Kailua, Hawaii	FA-'09	0*
32	Allen, Jason	CB	6-1	200	7/5/83	5	Tennessee	Muscle Shoals, Ala.	D1-'06	16/1
25	Allen, Will	CB	5-10	195	8/5/78	10	Syracuse	Syracuse, N.Y.	UFA(NYG)-'06	6/6
56	Anderson, Charlie	LB	6-4	250	12/8/81	7	Mississippi	Jackson, Miss.	UFA(Hou)-'08	16/2
90	Baker, Ryan	DE	6-5	295	11/25/84	2	Purdue	Indianapolis, Ind	FA-'09	5/0
37	Bell, Yeremiah	S	6-0	205	3/3/78	7	Eastern Kentucky	Winchester, Ky.	D6c-'03	16/15
67	Berger, Joe	G	6-5	315	5/25/82	6	Michigan Tech	Newaygo, Mich.	UFA(Dall)-'09	16/6
15	Bess, Davone	WR	5-10	190	9/13/85	3	Hawaii	Oakland, Calif.	FA-'08	16/2
23	Brown, Ronnie	RB	6-0	230	12/12/81	6	Auburn	Cartersville, Ga.	D1-'05	9/9
83	Camarillo, Greg	WR	6-1	190	4/18/82	5	Stanford	Menlo Park, Calif.	W(SD)-'07	16/16
72	Carey, Vernon	T	6-5	340	7/31/81	7	Miami	Miami, Fla.	D1-'04	16/16
5	Carpenter, Dan	K	6-2	225	11/25/85	3	Montana	Helena, Mont.	FA-'08	16/0
30	Clemons, Chris	S	6-1	210	9/15/85	2	Clemson	Arcadia, Fla.	D5b-'09	11/2
38	Cobbs, Patrick	RB	5-8	205	1/31/83	5	North Texas	Tecumseh, Okla.	FA-'06	5/0
52	Crowder, Channing	LB	6-2	250	12/2/83	6	Florida	Atlanta, Ga.	D3-'05	13/13
29	Culver, Tyrone	S	6-1	210	7/6/83	5	Fresno State	Palmdale, Calif.	FA-'08	16/2
58	Dansby, Karlos	LB	6-4	250	11/3/81	7	Auburn	Birmingham, Ala.	UFA(Ariz)-'10	16/16*
21	Davis, Vontae	CB	5-11	203	5/27/88	2	Illinois	Washington, D.C.	D1-'09	16/9
92	Denney, John	LS	6-5	255	12/13/78	6	Brigham Young	Thornton, Colo.	FA-'05	16/0
51	t- Dobbins, Tim	LB	6-1	246	12/10/82	5	Iowa State	Nashville, Tenn.	T(SD)-'10	14/2*
71	Dotson, Lionel	DE	6-4	290	2/11/85	3	Arizona	Houston, Texas	D7-'08	2/0
80	Fasano, Anthony	TE	6-4	255	4/20/84	5	Notre Dame	Verona, N.J.	T(Dall)-'08	14/14
95	Ferguson, Jason	DT	6-3	310	11/28/74	14	Georgia	Tupelo, Miss.	T(Dall)-'08	10/10
2	Fields, Brandon	P	6-5	245	5/21/84	4	Michigan State	Toledo, Ohio	D7b-'07	16/0
63	Gardner, Andrew	T	6-6	305	4/4/86	2	Georgia Tech	Tyrone, Ga.	D6-'09	1/0
75	Garner, Nate	T	6-7	325	1/18/85	3	Arkansas	Roland, Ark	W(NYJ)-'08	16/8
64	Grove, Jake	C	6-4	300	1/22/80	7	Virginia Tech	Forest, Va.	UFA(Oak)-'09	12/10
60	Hartline, Andrew	OL	6-5	300	9/1/85	2	Central Michigan	Baroda, Mich.	FA-'09	0*
82	Hartline, Brian	WR	6-2	195	11/22/86	2	Ohio State	North Canton, Ohio	D4-'09	16/2
81	Haynos, Joey	TE	6-8	270	8/28/84	3	Maryland	Rockville, Md.	FA-'08	16/8
7	Henne, Chad	QB	6-3	230	7/2/85	3	Michigan	Wyomissing, Pa.	D2b-'08	14/13
26	Hilliard, Lex	RB	5-11	240	7/30/84	2	Montana	Kalispell, Mont.	D6c-'08	16/0
68	Incognito, Richie	G	6-3	324	7/5/83	6	Nebraska	Englewood, N.J.	FA-'10	12/12*
57	Johnston, Brian	DE	6-5	269	5/2/86	2	Gardner-Webb	San Diego, Calif.	FA-'10	0*
70	Langford, Kendall	DE	6-6	295	1/27/86	3	Hampton	Petersburg, Va.	D3-'08	16/13
77	Long, Jake	T	6-7	317	5/9/85	3	Michigan	Lapeer, Mich.	D1-'08	16/16
	t- Marshall, Brandon	WR	6-4	230	3/23/84	5	Central Florida	Winter Park, Fla.	T(Den)-'10	15/13*
78	McDaniel, Tony	DT	6-7	305	1/20/85	5	Tennessee	Columbia, S.C.	T(Jax)-'09	16/0
97	Merling, Phillip	DE	6-4	295	4/19/85	3	Clemson	St. Matthews, S.C.	D2a-'08	16/2
93	Moses, Quentin	LB	6-5	260	11/18/83	4	Georgia	Athens, Ga.	FA-'07	10/0
76	Murtha, Lydon	T	6-7	315	11/13/85	2	Nebraska	Hutchinson, Minn.	FA-'09	1/0
27	Oglesby, Evan	CB	5-11	182	12/18/81	5	North Alabama	Toccoa, Ga.	FA-'09	1/0
10	Pennington, Chad	QB	6-3	230	6/26/76	11	Marshall	Knoxville, Tenn.	FA-'08	3/3
36	Polite, Lousaka	FB	6-0	245	9/14/81	6	Pittsburgh	Pittsburgh, Pa.	FA-'08	16/9
22	Sheets, Kory	RB	5-11	206	3/31/85	2	Purdue	Bloomfield, Conn.	FA-'09	2/0
65	Smiley, Justin	G	6-3	310	11/11/81	7	Alabama	Ellabell, Ga.	UFA(SF)-'08	15/12
24	Smith, Sean	CB	6-3	214	7/14/87	2	Utah	Pasadena, Calif.	D2b-'09	16/16
96	Soliai, Paul	DT	6-4	355	12/30/83	4	Utah	Pago Pago, American Samoa	D4-'07	14/9
85	Sperry, Kory	TE	6-4	238	4/10/85	2	Colorado State	Pueblo, Colo.	FA-'09	8/1
94	Starks, Randy	DE	6-3	305	12/14/83	7	Maryland	Waldorf, Md.	UFA(Tenn)-'08	16/16
16	t- Thigpen, Tyler	QB	6-1	224	4/14/84	4	Coastal Carolina	Winnsboro, S.C.	T(KC)-'09	2/0*
66	Thomas, Donald	G	6-4	310	9/25/85	3	Connecticut	New Haven, Conn.	D6b-'08	16/12
53	Torbor, Reggie	LB	6-2	250	1/25/81	7	Auburn	Baton Rouge, La.	UFA(NYG)-'08	16/2
84	Turner, Patrick	WR	6-5	220	5/19/87	2	Southern California	West Madison, Tenn	D3-'09	2/0
91	Wake, Cameron	LB	6-3	250	1/30/82	2	Penn State	Hyattsville, Md.	FA-'09	14/1
50	Walden, Erik	LB	6-2	250	8/21/85	3	Middle Tennessee	Dublin, Ga.	W(KC)-'08	11/0
6	White, Pat	QB	6-0	190	2/25/86	2	West Virginia	Daphne, Ala	D2a-'09	13/0
34	Williams, Ricky	RB	5-10	230	5/21/77	10	Texas	San Diego, Calif.	T(NO)-'02	16/7

* Alama-Francis inactive for 6 games; Dansby played 16 games with Arizona in '09; Dobbins played 14 games with San Diego; A. Hartline did not play in 3 games; Incognito played 9 games with St. Louis and 3 games with Buffalo; Johnston missed '09 season because of injury; Marshall 15 games with Denver; Thigpen played in 1 game with Kansas City and 1 game with Miami.

t- Dolphins traded for Dobbins (SD), Marshall (Den), Thigpen (KC).

Traded—WR Ted Ginn Jr. (16 games in '09) to San Francisco.

Players lost through free agency (2): CB Nathan Jones (Den; 16 games in '09), LB Jason Taylor (NYJ; 16).

Also played with Dolphins in '09—LB Akin Ayodele (16 games), LB J.D. Folsom (2), LB William Kershaw (1), LB Joey Porter (14), S Gibril Wilson (16).

2010 FIRST-YEAR ROSTER

Name	Pos.	Ht.	Wt.	Birthdate	College	Hometown	How Acq.
Amaya, Jonathan	DB	6-2	190	11/25/88	Nevada	Diamond Bar, Calif.	FA
Carroll, Nolan	CB	6-1	202	1/16/87	Maryland	Green Grove Spring, Fla.	D5a
Davis, Tristan (1)	RB	5-10	212	5/5/86	Auburn	East Point, Ga.	FA
Edds, A.J.	LB	6-4	246	9/18/87	Iowa	Greenwood, Ind.	D4
Feinga, Ray (1)	G	6-4	337	5/8/86	Brigham Young	West Valley City, Utah	FA
Folsom, J.D. (1)	LB	6-3	230	8/19/84	Weber State	Salmon, Idaho	FA
Grice-Mullen, Ryan (1)	WR	5-11	180	9/12/86	Hawaii	Rialto, Calif.	FA
Ivey, Travis	DT	6-4	325	12/22/86	Maryland	Riverdale, Md.	FA
Jerry, John	G	6-5	328	6/14/86	Mississippi	Batesville, Miss.	D3
Johnson, Taurus (1)	WR	6-1	205	4/13/86	South Florida	Cape Coral, Fla.	FA
Jones, Reshad	S	6-1	214	2/25/88	Georgia	Atlanta, Ga.	D5b
Lumbala, Rolly (1)	FB	6-2	238	1/30/86	Idaho	Libreville, Gabon	FA
McCoy, Chris	LB	6-3	261	11/25/86	Middle Tennessee State	Villa Rica, Ga.	D7a
Misi, Koa	LB	6-3	251	1/17/87	Utah	Santa Rosa, Calif.	D2
Moore, Marlon	WR	6-0	190	9/3/87	Fresno State	Sacramento, Calif.	FA
Ness, Nate (1)	S	6-1	190	9/5/86	Arizona	Gardena, Calif.	FA
Odrick, Jared	DE	6-5	304	12/31/87	Penn State	Lebanon County, Pa.	D1
Pruitt, Julius (1)	WR	6-2	206	12/30/85	Ouachita Baptist	Newport, Ark.	FA
Spitler, Austin	LB	6-2	243	10/26/86	Ohio State	Bellbrook, Ohio	D7b
Tsoumpas, Dimitri (1)	G	6-4	315	9/26/85	Weber State	Edmonton, Alberta, Calif.	FA
Wallace, A.J.	CB	6-1	195	5/23/88	Penn State	Pomfret, Md.	FA
Wallace, Roberto	WR	6-4	225	5/10/86	San Diego State	Oceanside, Calif.	FA
Weaver, Ross	DB	6-1	203	1/9/87	Michigan State	Southfield, Mich.	FA

The term NFL Rookie is defined as a player who is in his first season of professional football and has not been on the roster of another professional football team for any regular-season or postseason games. A Rookie is designated by an "R" on NFL rosters. Players who have been active in another professional football league or players who have NFL experience, including either preseason training camp or being on an Active List or Inactive List, or on Reserve/Injured or Reserve/Physically Unable to Perform for fewer than six regular-season games, are termed NFL First-Year Players. An NFL First-Year Player is designated by a "1" on NFL rosters. Thereafter, a player is credited with an additional year of experience for each season in which he accumulates six games on the Active List or Inactive List, or on Reserve/Injured or Reserve/Physically Unable to Perform.

Log on to www.miamidolphins.com for an up-to-date roster.

MIAMI DOLPHINS

COACHING STAFF

Head Coach,

Tony Sparano

Pro Career: Became the eighth head coach in Dolphins history on January 16, 2008. In his first season led the Dolphins to the greatest turnaround in NFL history as Miami posted an 11-5 regular season record while capturing the teams first AFC East Division title since 2000. Sparano had spent the previous five seasons (2003-07) on the staff of the Dallas Cowboys, during which time the team made three playoff appearances. He tutored the Cowboys' offensive line the last three years while also holding the title of assistant head coach the past two seasons. He coached the team's tight ends his first two seasons in Dallas. Prior to joining the Cowboys, Sparano had NFL stops in Cleveland (1999-2000), Washington (2001) and Jacksonville (2002). Career record: 18-15.

Background: Sparano was a four-year letterman as a center at the University of New Haven, where he earned his degree in criminal law. He began his coaching career at his alma mater in 1984 before moving on to Boston University as offensive coordinator in 1989. He returned to New Haven as the school's head coach in 1994, and manned that spot for the next five years.

Personal: Born October 7, 1961 in West Haven, Conn. He and his wife, Jeanette, have two sons, Tony and Andrew, and one daughter, Ryan Leigh.

ASSISTANT COACHES

John Bonamego, special teams coordinator; born August 14, 1963, Waynesboro, Pa. Wide receiver/quarterback Central Michigan 1985-86. No pro playing experience. College coach: Maine 1988-91, Lehigh 1992, Army 1993-98. Pro coach: Jacksonville Jaguars 1999-2002, Green Bay Packers 2003-05, New Orleans Saints 2006-07, joined Dolphins in 2008.

Todd Bowles, asst. head coach/secondary; born November 18, 1963, Elizabeth, N.J. Defensive back Temple 1982-85. Pro defensive back Washington Redskins 1986-1990, 1992-93, San Francisco 49ers 1991. College coach: Morehouse College 1997, Grambling State 1998-99. Pro coach: New York Jets 2000, Cleveland Browns 2001-04, Dallas Cowboys 2005-07, joined Dolphins in 2008.

Steve Bush, offensive quality control; born December 21, 1959, Denville, N.J. Defensive back Southern Connecticut State 1978-1981. No pro playing experience. College coach: Southern Connecticut State 1982-83, Springfield College 1984-85, New Haven 1986-87, Boston University 1988-89, Syracuse 2000-04. Pro coach: Joined Dolphins in 2008.

David Corrao, defensive quality control; born June 11, 1974. Running back University of San Diego 1992. No pro playing experience. College coach: Syracuse 2000-03, Northeastern 2004, Mississippi 2005-07. Pro coach: Joined Dolphins in 2008.

Joe Danna, defensive assistant; born April 3, 1977, Midland, Mich. Wide receiver Central Michigan 1995-98. No pro playing experience. College coach: Central Michigan 1999-2000, 2002-05, Georgia 2001, Georgia Southern 2006, James Madison 2007. Pro coach: Atlanta Falcons 2008-09, joined Dolphins in 2010.

Dave DeGuglielmo, offensive line; born July 15, 1968, Cambridge, Mass. Attended Boston University. No college or pro playing experience. College coach: Boston College 1991-92, Boston University 1993-96, Connecticut 1997-98, South Carolina 1999-2003. Pro coach: New York Giants 2004–08, joined Dolphins in 2009.

George DeLeone, tight ends; born May 9, 1948, New Haven, Conn. Offensive lineman Connecticut 1966-67. No pro playing experience. College coach: Southern Connecticut State 1970-79, Rutgers 1980-83, Holy Cross 1984, Syracuse 1985-1996, 1998-2004, Mississippi 2005, Temple 2006-07. Pro coach: San Diego Chargers 1997, joined Dolphins in 2008.

Karl Dorrell, wide receivers; born December 18, 1968, Alameda, Calif. Wide receiver UCLA 1982-86. No pro playing experience. College coach: UCLA 1988, 2003-07 (head coach 2003-07), Central Florida 1989, Northern Arizona 1990-91, Colorado 1992-93, 1995-98, Arizona State 1994, Washington 1999. Pro coach: Denver Broncos 2000-02, joined Dolphins in 2008.

Dan Henning, offensive coordinator; born June 21, 1942, Bronx, N.Y. Quarterback William & Mary 1962-64. Pro quarterback San Diego Chargers 1964, 1966-67. College coach: Florida State 1968-1970, 1974, Virginia Tech 1971, 1973, Boston College 1994-96 (head coach). Pro coach: Houston Oilers 1972, New York Jets 1976-78, 1998-2000, Miami Dolphins 1979-1980, Washington Redskins 1981-82, 1987-88, Atlanta Falcons 1983-86 (head coach), San Diego Chargers 1989-1991 (head coach), Detroit Lions 1992-93, Buffalo Bills 1997, Carolina Panthers 2002-06, re-joined Dolphins in 2008.

David Lee, quarterbacks; born July 2, 1953, Cape Girardeau, Mo. Quarterback Vanderbilt 1971-74. No pro playing experience. College coach: Tennessee-Martin 1975-76, Vanderbilt 1977, Mississippi 1978-1982, New Mexico 1983, Arkansas 1984-88, 2001-02, 2007, Texas-El Paso 1989-1993 (head coach), Rice 1994-2000. Pro coach: Dallas Cowboys 2003-06, joined Dolphins in 2008.

Evan Marcus, head strength and conditioning; born January 2, 1968, Cranford, N.J. Tackle Ithaca College 1986-1990. No pro playing experience. College coach: Arizona State 1991-92, Rutgers 1993, Maryland 1994, Texas 1995-97, Louisville 1998-99, Virginia 2003-06. Pro coach: New Orleans Saints 2000-02, Atlanta Falcons 2007, joined Dolphins in 2008.

Mike Nolan, defensive coordinator; born March 7, 1965, Haverhill, Mass. Safety Oregon 1978-1980. No pro playing experience. College coach: Oregon 1981, Stanford 1982-83, Rice 1984-85, Louisiana State 1986. Pro coach: Denver Broncos 1987-1992, 2009, New York Giants 1993-96, Washington Redskins 1997-99, New York Jets 2000, Baltimore Ravens 2001-04, San Francisco 49ers 2005-08 (head coach), joined Dolphins in 2010.

Dave Puloka, asst. strength and conditioning; born January 12, 1979, Arlington, Mass. Linebacker Holy Cross 1997-2000. No pro playing experience College coach: Stevens Institute of Technology 2005, Virginia 2006. Pro coach: Atlanta Falcons 2007, joined Dolphins in 2008.

Darren Rizzi, asst. special teams; born July 21, 1970, Hillsdale, N.J. Tight end Rhode Island 1988-1991. College coach: Rhode Island 1992, Colgate 1993, New Haven 1993-97, Northeastern 1998, New Haven 1999-2001 (head coach), Rutgers 2002-07, Rhode Island 2008 (head coach). Pro coach: Joined Dolphins in 2009.

Kacy Rodgers, defensive line; born June 24, 1969, Humboldt, Tennessee. Linebacker/defensive end Tennessee 1988-1991. Pro linebacker Shreveport Pirates (CFL) 1994. College coach: Tennessee-Martin 1994-97, Louisiana-Monroe 1998, Middle Tennessee State 1999-2001, Arkansas 2002. Pro coach: Dallas Cowboys 2003-07, joined Dolphins in 2008.

James Saxon, running backs; born March 23, 1966, Beaufort, S.C. Running back American River (Calif.) J.C. 1984-85, San Jose State 1986-87. Pro running back Kansas City Chiefs 1988-1991, Miami Dolphins 1992-94, Philadelphia Eagles 1995. College coach: Rutgers 1997-98, Menlo College 1999. Pro coach: Buffalo Bills 2000, Kansas City Chiefs 2001-07, joined Dolphins in 2008.

Bill Sheridan, linebackers; born January 27, 1959, Detroit. Linebacker Grand Valley State 1979-1982. No pro playing experience. College coach: Michigan 1985-86, Maine 1987-88, Cincinnati 1989-1991, Army 1992-97, Michigan State 1998-2000, Notre Dame 2001, Michigan 2002-04. Pro coach: New York Giants 2005-09, joined Dolphins in 2010.

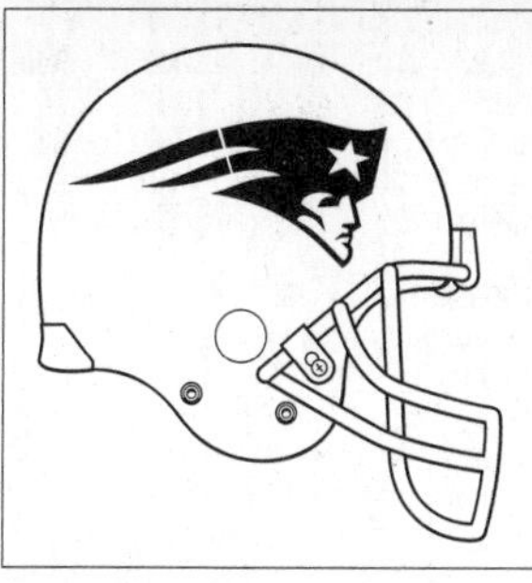

American Football Conference
East Division
Team Colors: Blue, Red, Silver, and White
Gillette Stadium
One Patriot Place
Foxborough, Massachusetts 02035
Telephone: (508) 543-8200

2010 SCHEDULE

PRESEASON

Aug. 12	**New Orleans**	7:30
Aug. 19	at Atlanta	8:00
Aug. 26	**St. Louis**	7:30
Sep. 2	at New York Giants	7:00

REGULAR SEASON

Sep. 12	**Cincinnati**	1:00
Sep. 19	at New York Jets	4:15
Sep. 26	**Buffalo**	1:00
Oct. 4	at Miami (Mon)	8:30
Oct. 10	BYE	
Oct. 17	**Baltimore**	1:00
Oct. 24	at San Diego	1:15
Oct. 31	**Minnesota**	4:15
Nov. 7	at Cleveland	1:00
Nov. 14	at Pittsburgh	8:20
Nov. 21	**Indianapolis**	4:15
Nov. 25	at Detroit (Thu)	12:30
Dec. 6	**New York Jets** (Mon)	8:30
Dec. 12	at Chicago	12:00
Dec. 19	**Green Bay**	* 8:20
Dec. 26	at Buffalo	1:00
Jan. 2	**Miami**	1:00

** Sunday night games in Weeks 11-17 subject to change*

Stadium: Gillette Stadium
(opened in 2002)
• **Capacity:** 68,756
One Patriot Place
Foxborough, Massachusetts 02035
Playing Surface: FieldTurf
Training Camp: Gillette Stadium
Foxborough, MA 02035

GILLETTE STADIUM

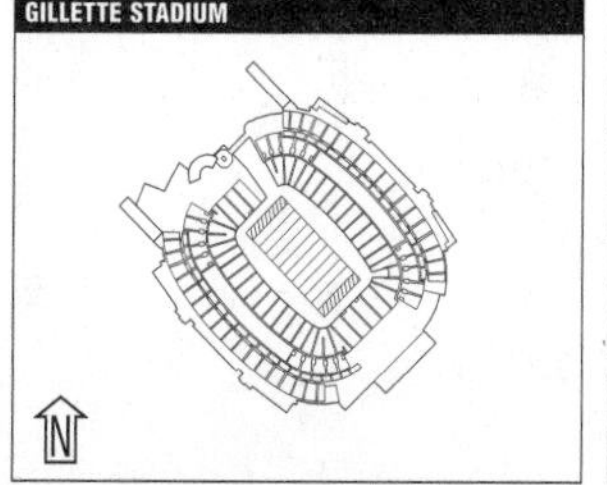

CLUB OFFICIALS

Chairman & CEO: Robert K. Kraft
President: Jonathan A. Kraft
Chief Administrative Officer: Jim Hausmann
Director of Strategic Initiatives and Retail Operations: Brian Bilello
Vice President of Human Resources: Robin Boudreau
Chief Operating Officer of TeamOps Security: Mark Briggs
Equipment Manager: Don Brocher
Director of Player Personnel: Nick Caserio
Vice President of Information Technology: Pat Curley
Video Director: Jimmy Dee
Vice President of Marketing Operations: Jennifer Ferron
Director of New Business Development & Operational Initiatives: Jessica Gelman
Senior Advisor: Robyn Glaser
Director of Ticket Operations: Maryruth Hughey
Vice President of Media Relations: Stacey James
Publisher / Editor-in-Chief and Director of Interactive Media: Fred Kirsch
Vice President of Sales: Murray Kohl
President of New England Patriots Charitable Foundation: Josh Kraft
Director of Research: Richard Miller
Vice President of Stadium Business Development and External Affairs: Dan Murphy
Director of Football / Head Coach Administration: Berj Najarian
Vice President of Stadium Operations: Jim Nolan
Vice President of Marketing Integration and Events: David Pearlstein
Senior Football Advisor: Floyd Reese
Executive Producer of Broadcast Production: Matt Smith
Director of Cheerleaders: Tracy Sormanti
Executive Director of Community Affairs: Andre Tippett
Head Athletic Trainer: Jim Whalen
Vice President of Finance: Jim Wilson

COACHING HISTORY

Boston 1960-1970
(408-374-9)
Records include postseason games

1960-61	Lou Saban*	7-12-0
1961-68	Mike Holovak	53-47-9
1969-1970	Clive Rush**	5-16-0
1970-72	John Mazur***	9-21-0
1972	Phil Bengtson	1-4-0
1973-78	Chuck Fairbanks****	46-41-0
1978	Hank Bullough-Ron Erhardt#	0-1-0
1979-1981	Ron Erhardt	21-27-0
1982-84	Ron Meyer##	18-16-0
1984-89	Raymond Berry	51-41-0
1990	Rod Rust	1-15-0
1991-92	Dick MacPherson	8-24-0
1993-96	Bill Parcells	34-34-0
1997-99	Pete Carroll	28-23-0
2000-09	Bill Belichick	126-52-0

*Released after five games in 1961
**Released after seven games in 1970
***Resigned after nine games in 1972
****Suspended for final regular-season game in 1978
#Co-coaches
##Released after eight games in 1984

PAID ATTENDANCE

Home 561,481 Away 573,643
Total 1,135,124
Single-game home record, 71,768 (11/30/08)
Single-season home record, 579,182 (2007)

2010 DRAFT CHOICES

Round	Name	Pos.	College
1	Devin McCourty	DB	Rutgers
2	Rob Gronkowski	TE	Arizona
	Jermaine Cunningham	DE	Florida
	Brandon Spikes	LB	Florida
3	Taylor Price	WR	Ohio
4	Aaron Hernandez	TE	Florida
5	Zoltan Mesko	P	Michigan
6	Ted Larsen	OL	North Carolina St.
7	Thomas Welch	OL	Vanderbilt
	Brandon Deaderick	DL	Alabama
	Kade Weston	DL	Georgia
	Zac Robinson	QB	Oklahoma St.

NEW ENGLAND PATRIOTS

2009 TEAM RECORD

PRESEASON (3-1)

Date	Result	Opponent
8/13	W 27-25	at Philadelphia
8/20	L 6-7	Cincinnati
8/28	W 27-24	at Washington
9/3	W 38-27	New York Giants

REGULAR SEASON (10-6)

Date	Result	Opponent
9/14	W 25-24	Buffalo
9/20	L 9-16	at New York Jets
9/27	W 26-10	Atlanta
10/4	W 27-21	Baltimore
10/11	L 17-20	at Denver (OT)
10/18	W 59-0	Tennessee
10/25	W 35-7	at Tampa Bay
11/8	W 27-17	Miami
11/15	L 34-35	at Indianapolis
11/22	W 31-14	New York Jets
11/30	L 17-38	at New Orleans
12/6	L 21-22	at Miami
12/13	W 20-10	Carolina
12/20	W 17-10	at Buffalo
12/27	W 35-7	Jacksonville
1/3	L 27-34	at Houston

(OT) Overtime

POSTSEASON (0-1)

Date	Result	Opponent
1/10	L 14-33	Baltimore

SCORE BY PERIODS

Patriots	99	183	70	75	0 —	427
Opponents	47	89	53	93	3 —	285

2009 TEAM STATISTICS

	Patriots	Opp.
Total First Downs	373	289
Rushing	114	80
Passing	222	193
Penalty	37	16
3rd Down: Made/Att	90/206	72/194
3rd Down Pct.	43.7	37.1
4th Down: Made/Att	11/22	10/21
4th Down Pct.	50.0	47.6
Possession Avg.	32:55	27:05
Total Net Yards	6357	5123
Avg. Per Game	397.3	320.2
Total Plays	1076	941
Avg. Per Play	5.9	5.4
Net Yards Rushing	1921	1768
Avg. Per Game	120.1	110.5
Total Rushes	466	398
Net Yards Passing	4436	3355
Avg. Per Game	277.3	209.7
Sacked/Yards Lost	18/104	31/229
Gross Yards	4540	3584
Att./Completions	592/390	512/300
Completion Pct.	65.9	58.6
Had Intercepted	13	18
Punts/Average	57/39.0	79/41.4
Net Punting Avg.	57/34.1	79/35.4
Penalties/Yards	81/743	91/780
Fumbles/Ball Lost	17/9	28/10
Touchdowns	50	35
Rushing	19	6
Passing	28	25
Returns	3	4

2009 INDIVIDUAL STATISTICS

PASSING	Att.	Comp.	Yds.	Pct.	TD	Int.	Tkld.	Rate
Brady	565	371	4398	65.7	28	13	16/86	96.2
Hoyer	27	19	142	70.4	0	0	2/18	82.6
Patriots	592	390	4540	65.9	28	13	18/104	95.6
Opponents	512	300	3584	58.6	25	18	31/229	81.7

SCORING	TD R	TD P	TD Rt	PAT	FG	Saf	PTS
Gostkowski	0	0	0	47/47	26/31	0	125
Moss	0	13	0	0/0	0/0	0	80
Maroney	9	0	0	0/0	0/0	0	54
Watson	0	5	0	0/0	0/0	0	30
F. Taylor	4	0	0	0/0	0/0	0	24
Welker	0	4	0	0/0	0/0	0	24
Faulk	2	1	0	0/0	0/0	0	18
Aiken	0	2	0	0/0	0/0	0	12
Baker	0	2	0	0/0	0/0	0	12
Morris	2	0	0	0/0	0/0	0	12
Bodden	0	0	1	0/0	0/0	0	6
Brady	1	0	0	0/0	0/0	0	6
Butler	0	0	1	0/0	0/0	0	6
Edelman	0	1	0	0/0	0/0	0	6
Hoyer	1	0	0	0/0	0/0	0	6
Meriweather	0	0	1	0/0	0/0	0	6
Patriots	19	28	3	47/47	26/31	0	427
Opponents	6	25	4	33/34	14/20	0	285

2-Pt. Conversions: Moss.
Patriots 1-3, Opponents 0-1.

RUSHING	No.	Yds	Avg	LG	TD
Maroney	194	757	3.9	45t	9
Faulk	62	335	5.4	29	2
Morris	73	319	4.4	55	2
F. Taylor	63	269	4.3	19	4
Green-Ellis	26	114	4.4	29	0
Brady	29	44	1.5	9	1
Welker	5	36	7.2	11	0
Hoyer	10	25	2.5	20	1
Tate	1	11	11.0	11	0
Slater	1	6	6.0	6	0
Edelman	2	5	2.5	5	0
Patriots	466	1921	4.1	55	19
Opponents	398	1768	4.4	50	6

RECEIVING	No.	Yds	Avg	LG	TD
Welker	123	1348	11.0	58	4
Moss	83	1264	15.2	71t	13
Edelman	37	359	9.7	29	1
Faulk	37	301	8.1	38t	1
Watson	29	404	13.9	36	5
Aiken	20	326	16.3	81t	2
Morris	19	180	9.5	35	0
Baker	14	142	10.1	36t	2
Maroney	14	99	7.1	17	0
Galloway TM	7	67	9.6	19	0
Stanback	3	22	7.3	9	0
F. Taylor	2	17	8.5	13	0
Green-Ellis	2	11	5.5	6	0
Patriots	390	4540	11.6	81t	28
Opponents	300	3584	11.9	75t	25

INTERCEPTIONS	No.	Yds	Avg	LG	TD
Meriweather	5	149	29.8	56	1
Bodden	5	60	12.0	53t	1
Butler	3	91	30.3	91t	1
Wilhite	2	17	8.5	17	0
Springs	1	8	8.0	8	0
Chung	1	2	2.0	2	0
Moss	1	0	0.0	0	0
Patriots	18	327	18.2	91t	3
Opponents	13	146	11.2	38	1

PUNTING	No.	Yds.	Avg.	In 20	LG
Hanson	56	2221	39.7	18	56
Patriots	57	2221	39.0	18	56
Opponents	79	3267	41.4	22	64

PUNT RETURNS	Ret	FC	Yds	Avg	LG	TD
Welker	27	16	338	12.5	69	0
Edelman	6	1	63	10.5	35	0
Faulk	5	2	31	6.2	15	0
Patriots	38	19	432	11.4	69	0
Opponents	20	16	180	9.0	31	0

KICKOFF RETURNS	No.	Yds	Avg	LG	TD
Maroney	13	279	21.5	52	0
Slater	11	269	24.5	35	0
Edelman	11	241	21.9	32	0
Faulk	6	144	24.0	32	0
Butler	5	104	20.8	26	0
Tate	4	106	26.5	34	0
Welker	2	45	22.5	27	0
Stanback	1	22	22.0	22	0
Connolly	1	16	16.0	16	0
Patriots	54	1226	22.7	52	0
Opponents	70	1705	24.4	51	0

FIELD GOALS	1-19	20-29	30-39	40-49	50+
Gostkowski	0/0	7/7	12/13	5/8	2/3
Patriots	0/0	7/7	12/13	5/8	2/3
Opponents	0/0	6/6	4/6	3/4	1/4

SACKS	No.
Banta-Cain	10.0
D. Burgess	5.0
Wright	5.0
A. Thomas	3.0
Chung	2.0
Guyton	1.5
Mayo	1.5
Green	1.0
Ninkovich	1.0
Warren	1.0
Patriots	31.0
Opponents	18.0

RECORD HOLDERS

INDIVIDUAL RECORDS—CAREER

Category	Name	Performance
Rushing (Yds.)	Sam Cunningham, 1973-79, 1981-82	5,453
Passing (Yds.)	Tom Brady, 2000-09	30,844
Passing (TDs)	Tom Brady, 2000-09	225
Receiving (No.)	Troy Brown, 1993-2007	557
Receiving (Yds.)	Stanley Morgan, 1977-1989	10,352
Interceptions	Raymond Clayborn, 1977-1989	36
	Ty Law, 1995-2004	36
Punting (Avg.)	Tom Tupa, 1996-98	44.7
Punt Return (Avg.)	Mack Herron, 1973-75	12.0
Kickoff Return (Avg.)	Ellis Hobbs, 2005-08	27.7
Field Goals	Adam Vinatieri, 1996-2005	263
Touchdowns (Tot.)	Stanley Morgan, 1977-1989	68
Points	Adam Vinatieri, 1996-2005	1,158
*Sacks	Andre Tippett, 1982-1993	100.0

INDIVIDUAL RECORDS—SINGLE SEASON

Category	Name	Performance
Rushing (Yds.)	Corey Dillon, 2004	1,635
Passing (Yds.)	Tom Brady, 2007	4,806
Passing (TDs)	Tom Brady, 2007	**50
Receiving (No.)	Wes Welker, 2009	123
Receiving (Yds.)	Randy Moss, 2007	1,493
Interceptions	Ron Hall, 1964	11
Punting (Avg.)	Tom Tupa, 1997	45.8
Punt Return (Avg.)	Mack Herron, 1974	14.8
Kickoff Return (Avg.)	Raymond Clayborn, 1977	31.0
Field Goals	Stephen Gostkowski, 2008	36
Touchdowns (Tot.)	Randy Moss, 2007	23
Points	Gino Cappelletti, 1964	155
*Sacks	Andre Tippett, 1984	18.5

INDIVIDUAL RECORDS—SINGLE GAME

Category	Name	Performance
Rushing (Yds.)	Tony Collins, 9-18-83	212
Passing (Yds.)	Drew Bledsoe, 11-13-94	426
Passing (TDs)	Tom Brady, 10-21-07, 10-18-09	6
Receiving (No.)	Troy Brown, 9-22-02	16
Receiving (Yds.)	Terry Glenn, 10-3-99	214
Interceptions	Many times	3
	Last time by Leigh Bodden 11-22-09	
Field Goals	Gino Cappelletti, 10-4-64	6
Touchdowns (Tot.)	Randy Moss, 11-18-07	4
Points	Gino Cappelletti, 12-18-65	24
*Sacks	Andre Tippett, 10-26-86	3.5
	Chris Slade, 11-20-94	3.5

**Sacks became an official statistic in 1982.*
***NFL Record*

NEW ENGLAND PATRIOTS

2010 VETERAN ROSTER

No.	Name	Pos.	Ht.	Wt.	Birthdate	NFL Exp.	College	Hometown	How Acq.	'09 Games/ Starts
88	Aiken, Sam	WR	6-2	215	12/14/80	8	North Carolina	Kenansville, N.C.	UFA(Buff)-'08	14/7
52	Alexander, Eric	LB	6-2	240	2/8/82	6	Louisiana State	Port Arthur, Texas	FA-'04	14/0
27	Arrington, Kyle	CB	5-10	196	8/12/86	2	Hofstra	Accokeek, Md.	FA-'09	8/0
95	Banta-Cain, Tully	LB	6-2	250	8/28/80	8	California	Sunnyvale, Calif.	FA-'09	16/10
23	Bodden, Leigh	CB	6-1	193	9/24/81	8	Duquesne	Hyattsville, Md.	FA-'09	15/14
97	Brace, Ron	DL	6-3	330	12/18/86	2	Boston College	Worcester, Mass.	D2b-'09	9/2
12	Brady, Tom	QB	6-4	225	8/3/77	11	Michigan	San Mateo, Calif.	D6b-'00	16/16
	#Burgess, Derrick	LB	6-2	260	8/12/78	10	Mississippi	Greenbelt, Md.	T(Oak)-'09	16/6
66	Bussey, George	OL	6-3	305	10/24/84	2	Louisville	Louisville	D5-'09	0*
28	Butler, Darius	CB	5-10	185	3/18/86	2	Connecticut	Ft. Lauderdale, Fla.	D2c-'09	14/5
25	Chung, Patrick	S	5-11	212	8/19/87	2	Oregon	Rancho Cucamonga, Calif.	D2a-'09	16/1
63	Connolly, Dan	G/C	6-4	313	9/2/82	5	Southeast Missouri St.	St. Louis, Mo.	FA-'08	14/4
98	Crable, Shawn	LB	6-5	243	12/26/84	3	Michigan	Massillon, Ohio	D3a-'08	0*
82	Crumpler, Alge	TE	6-2	262	12/23/77	9	North Carolina	Wilmington, N.C.	UFA(Tenn)-'10	16/14*
49	Davis, Bruce	LB	6-3	252	9/2/85	2	UCLA	Houston, Texas	FA-'09	0*
11	Edelman, Julian	WR	6-0	198	5/22/86	2	Kent State	Redwood City, Calif.	D7a-'09	11/7
33	Faulk, Kevin	RB	5-8	202	6/5/76	12	Louisiana State	Carencro, La.	D2-'99	15/7
62	Gordon, Amon	DL	6-2	305	10/13/81	5	Stanford	San Diego, Calif.	FA-'10	0*
3	Gostkowski, Stephen	K	6-1	215	1/28/84	5	Memphis	Madison, Miss.	D4b-'06	16/0
42	Green-Ellis, BenJarvus	RB	5-11	215	7/2/85	3	Mississippi	New Orleans, La.	FA-'08	12/0
59	Guyton, Gary	LB	6-3	245	11/14/85	3	Georgia Tech	Hinesville, Ga.	FA-'08	16/16
	#Hanson, Chris	P	6-2	202	10/25/76	12	Marshall	Sharpsburg, Ga.	FA-'07	16/0
84	Holt, Torry	WR	6-0	200	6/5/76	12	North Carolina State	Gibsonville, N.C.	FA-'10	15/12*
8	Hoyer, Brian	QB	6-2	215	10/13/85	2	Michigan State	North Olmsted, Ohio	FA-'09	5/0
47	Ingram, Jake	LS	6-3	235	10/23/85	2	Hawaii	Mililani, Hawaii	D6a-'09	16/0
77	Kaczur, Nick	T	6-4	315	7/28/79	6	Toledo	Brantford, Ontario	D3b-'05	14/13
67	Koppen, Dan	C	6-2	296	9/12/79	8	Boston College	Whitehall, Pa.	D5-'03	16/16
64	LeVoir, Mark	T	6-7	310	7/29/82	4	Notre Dame	Eden Prairie, Minn.	W(StL)-'08	10/0
92	Lewis, Damione	DL	6-2	301	3/1/78	10	Miami	Sulphur Springs, Texas	FA-'10	16/16*
72	Light, Matt	T	6-4	305	6/23/78	10	Purdue	Greenville, Ohio	D2-'01	11/11
38	Lockett, Bret	DB	6-1	224	10/7/86	2	UCLA	Diamond Bar, Calif.	W(Cle)-'09	10/0
70	Mankins, Logan	G	6-4	310	3/10/82	6	Fresno State	Catheys Valley, Calif.	D1-'05	16/16
39	Maroney, Laurence	RB	5-11	220	2/5/85	5	Minnesota	St. Louis, Mo.	D1-'06	15/5
51	Mayo, Jerod	LB	6-1	245	2/23/86	3	Tennessee	Hampton, Va.	D1-'08	13/12
30	McGowan, Brandon	S	5-11	210	9/26/83	6	Maine	Jersey City, N.J.	UFA(Chi)-'09	16/11
44	McKenzie, Tyrone	LB	6-2	240	12/11/85	2	South Florida	Riverview, Fla.	D3b-'09	0*
31	Meriweather, Brandon	S	5-11	200	1/14/84	4	Miami	Apopka, Fla.	D1-'07	16/11
34	Morris, Sammy	RB	6-0	220	3/23/77	11	Texas Tech	San Antonio, Texas	UFA (Mia)-'07	12/5
81	Moss, Randy	WR	6-4	210	2/13/77	13	Marshall	Rand, W. Va.	T(Oak)-'07	16/16
93	Murrell, Marques	LB	6-2	250	3/20/85	4	Appalachian State	Fayetteville, N.C.	FA(NYJ)-'09	10/0*
61	Neal, Stephen	G	6-4	305	10/9/76	9	Cal State-Bakersfield	San Diego, Calif.	FA-'01	12/12
50	Ninkovich, Rob	LB	6-2	255	2/1/84	5	Purdue	Blue Island, Ill.	FA-'09	15/0
60	Ohrnberger, Rich	OL	6-2	300	2/14/86	2	Penn State	East Meadow, N.Y.	D4-'09	3/0
86	Patten, David	WR	5-10	190	8/19/74	13	Western Carolina	Columbia, S.C.	FA-'09	0*
91	Pryor, Myron	DL	6-1	310	6/13/86	2	Kentucky	Louisville, Ky.	D6b-'09	13/0
9	Rowe, Jeff	QB	6-5	221	3/21/84	3	Nevada	Reno, Nev.	FA-'09	0*
36	Sanders, James	S	5-10	210	11/11/83	6	Fresno State	Porterville, Calif.	D4-'05	14/5
18	Slater, Matthew	WR	6-0	200	9/9/85	3	UCLA	Anaheim, Calif.	D5-'08	14/0
29	Springs, Shawn	CB	6-0	204	3/11/75	14	Ohio State	Silver Spring, Md.	FA-'09	12/8
15	Stanback, Isaiah	QB/WR	6-2	208	8/16/84	4	Washington	Seattle, Was.	FA-'09	6/2
19	Tate, Brandon	WR	6-1	195	10/5/87	2	North Carolina	Burlington, N.C.	D3a-'09	2/1
	Taylor, Chris	RB	6-0	224	11/7/83	4	Indiana	Memphis, Tenn.	FA-'09	0*
21	Taylor, Fred	RB	6-1	228	1/27/76	13	Florida	Pahokee, Fla.	FA-'09	6/1
76	Vollmer, Sebastian	OL	6-8	315	7/10/84	2	Houston	Kaarst, Germany	D2d-'09	14/8
68	Warren, Gerard	DL	6-4	325	7/25/78	10	Florida	Lake Butler, Fla.	FA-'10	16/16*
94	Warren, Ty	DL	6-5	300	2/6/81	7	Texas A&M	Bryan, Texas	D1-'03	13/12
83	Welker, Wes	WR	5-9	185	5/1/81	7	Texas Tech	Oklahoma City, Okla.	T(Mia)-'07	14/13
69	Wendell, Ryan	C	6-2	285	3/4/86	2	Fresno State	Diamond Bar, Calif.	FA-'08	2/0
22	Wheatley, Terrence	CB	5-9	185	5/5/85	3	Colorado	Plano, Texas	D2-'08	5/0
75	Wilfork, Vince	NT	6-2	325	11/4/81	7	Miami	Boynton Beach, Fla.	D1a-'04	13/13
24	Wilhite, Jonathan	CB	5-11	185	2/23/84	3	Auburn	Monroe, La.	D4-'08	14/8
48	Williams, Thomas	LB	6-1	237	12/25/84	2	Southern California	Vacaville, Calif.	FA-'09	0*
58	Woods, Pierre	LB	6-5	255	1/6/82	5	Michigan	Cleveland, Ohio	FA-'06	16/5
99	Wright, Mike	DL	6-4	295	3/1/82	6	Cincinnati	Cincinnati, Ohio	FA-'05	16/9

* Bussey missed '09 season because of injury; Crable missed '08 season because of injury: Crumpler played 16 games with Tennessee in '09; Davis last active in '08 with Pittsburgh; Gordon played 2 games with Tennessee in '08; Holt played 15 games with Jacksonville; Lewis played 16 games with Carolina; McKenzie missed '09 season because of injury; Murrell played 10 games with N.Y. Jets; Patten played 5 games with New Orleans in '08; Rowe last active with Cincinnati in '08; C. Taylor missed '09 season because of injury; T. Williams last active with Jacksonville in '08; Warren played 16 games with Oakland.

Unrestricted free agent; subject to developments.

Players lost through free agency (2): DL Jarvis Green (Den; 13 games in '09); TE Benjamin Watson (Cle; 16).

Also played with Patriots in '09—DL Titus Adams (2 games), TE Chris Baker (16), WR Joey Galloway (3), TE Michael Matthews (4), DL Terdell Sands (1), LB Junior Seau (7), G Kendall Simmons (1), LB Adalius Thomas (14).

2010 FIRST-YEAR ROSTER

Name	Pos.	Ht.	Wt.	Birthdate	College	Hometown	How Acq.
Agnone, Robbie (1)	TE	6-6	260	10/2/85	Delaware	Etters, Pa.	FA
Anderson, Bryan	WR	6-5	215	12/19/86	Central Michigan	Rockford, Michigan	FA
Barnes, Tyree (1)	WR	6-0	196	4/15/86	Navy	Hampton, Va.	FA
Brown, Sergio	S	6-2	205	5/22/88	Notre Dame	Maywood, Ill.	FA
Cunningham, Jermaine	LB	6-3	266	4/24/88	Florida	Stone Mountain, Ga.	D2b
Deaderick, Brandon	DL	6-4	287	8/19/87	Alabama	Elizabethtown Ky.	D7b
Farnham, Buddy	WR	6-0	185	5/22/87	Brown	Andover, Mass.	FA
Fletcher, Dane	DE	6-2	244	9/14/86	Montana State	Bozeman, Mont.	FA
Grady, Adrian (1)	DL	6-1	290	11/21/85	Louisville	Nicholls, Ga.	FA
Gronkowski, Rob	TE	6-6	265	5/14/89	Arizona	Pittsburgh, Pa.	D2a
Hernandez, Aaron	TE	6-2	250	11/6/89	Florida	Bristol, Conn.	D4
Jenkins, Darnell (1)	WR	5-10	191	12/31/82	Miami	Miami, Fla.	FA
Johnson, Terrence	DB	5-9	190	7/5/86	California (Pa.)	Pittsburgh, Pa.	FA
Kettani, Eric (1)	RB	5-11	235	3/26/87	Navy	Kirtland, Ohio	FA
King, David	P	6-0	200	8/24/81	No College	Melbourne, Australia	FA
Larsen, Ted	OL	6-2	304	6/13/87	North Carolina State	Palm Harbor, Fla.	D6
Love, Kyle	DL	6-1	301	9/14/86	Mississippi State	Fairburn, Ga.	FA
McCourty, Devin	CB	5-10	193	8/13/87	Rutgers	Montvale, N.J.	D1
Mesko, Zoltan	P	6-5	231	3/16/86	Michigan	Twinsburg, Ohio	D5
Myers, Rob (1)	TE	6-4	240	4/9/86	Utah State	Houston, Texas	FA
Paschal, Pat	RB	5-11	206	3/21/87	North Dakota State	Johns Creek, Ga.	FA
Price, Taylor	WR	6-0	212	10/8/87	Ohio	Hilliard, Ohio	D3
Richard, Darryl (1)	DL	6-4	290	6/17/86	Georgia Tech	Destrehan, La.	D7b-'09
Robinson, Zac	QB	6-3	218	9/29/86	Oklahoma State	Littleton, Colo.	D7d
Spikes, Brandon	LB	6-2	249	9/3/87	Florida	Shelby, N.C.	D2c
Ventrone, Ross	DB	5-8	190	9/27/86	Villanova	Pittsburgh, Pa.	FA
Welch, Thomas	OL	6-7	310	6/19/87	Vanderbilt	Brentwood, Tenn.	D7a
Weston, Kade	DL	6-5	315	11/29/86	Georgia	Red Banks, N.J.	D7c
White, Shun (1)	WR	5-8	195	12/9/85	Navy	Memphis, Tenn.	FA
Wise, John	OL	6-5	298	9/13/85	Illinois	Pittsfield, Ill.	FA

The term NFL Rookie is defined as a player who is in his first season of professional football and has not been on the roster of another professional football team for any regular-season or postseason games. A Rookie is designated by an "R" on NFL rosters. Players who have been active in another professional football league or players who have NFL experience, including either preseason training camp or being on an Active List or Inactive List, or on Reserve/Injured or Reserve/Physically Unable to Perform for fewer than six regular-season games, are termed NFL First-Year Players. An NFL First-Year Player is designated by a "1" on NFL rosters. Thereafter, a player is credited with an additional year of experience for each season in which he accumulates six games on the Active List or Inactive List, or on Reserve/Injured or Reserve/Physically Unable to Perform.

Log on to www.patriots.com for an up-to-date roster.

COACHING STAFF

Head Coach,
Bill Belichick

Pro Career: Bill Belichick is in his 36th season as an NFL coach and is the only head coach in NFL history to win three Super Bowl titles in a four-year span. In his first 10 seasons as Patriots head coach, he has won 126 games – more than any other head coach in NFL history through his first 10 years with a team. Hired by Chairman and CEO Robert Kraft on Jan. 27, 2000, Belichick is in his 11th season as New England's head coach in 2010. Through 10 seasons, Belichick has delivered three Super Bowl championships, four conference titles, seven division crowns and 14 playoff victories, while posting an overall record of 126-52. Belichick directed the Patriots to victories in Super Bowls XXXVI (2001), XXXVIII (2003) and XXXIX (2004), and in 2007 he became the first NFL head coach to guide his team to a 16-0 regular season. Only one coach (Pittsburgh's Chuck Noll, 4) has won more Super Bowls than Belichick, and his three Super Bowl titles tie Washington's Joe Gibbs and San Francisco's Bill Walsh for second place on the NFL's all-time list. Belichick's Patriots teams own the all-time NFL records for consecutive total victories, including the postseason (21 from 2003-04) and consecutive playoff victories (10 from 2001-05). Under Belichick, the Patriots also established the NFL mark for consecutive regular-season victories (21 from 2006-08) before the record was topped by Indianapolis (23 from 2008-09). Belichick owns the second best postseason record in NFL history (15-5) and is the winningest NFL head coach since 2001 (121-41). Over a 100-game span from 2003-08, he directed the Patriots to an 82-18 record – the best record for any 100-game span in NFL history. Belichick (.627) has the fifth highest winning percentage among coaches with at least 150 wins, trailing only four Hall of Famers: George Halas, Don Shula, Curly Lambeau and Joe Gibbs. Belichick's recent accomplishments are the latest triumphs in a career during which he has helped produce five Super Bowl titles, seven conference championships and 14 division titles since entering the NFL in 1975. He won his first two Super Bowls as the defensive coordinator for the New York Giants in 1986 and 1990 before claiming three Super Bowl championships with the Patriots. George Seifert is the only other man to have won multiple Super Bowls both as a head coach and as an assistant coach. Belichick launched his career in 1975 as a special assistant with the Baltimore Colts, then became an assistant special teams coach with Detroit (1976-77) and Denver (1978). In 1979, he joined the New York Giants to begin a 12-season stint in which he contributed to two Super Bowl championships as New York's defensive coordinator. Belichick was named head coach of the Cleveland Browns in 1991, becoming the youngest head coach in the NFL at age 38. By 1994, Belichick brought the Browns back to the playoffs, finishing 11-5 and advancing to the second round of the playoffs, while allowing a league-low 204 total points. In 1996, Belichick joined New England and was a key contributor to the team's rebound from a 6-10 season in 1995 to an 11-5 season and the team's first division title in 10 years en route to the Patriots' appearance in Super Bowl XXXI. Belichick then spent three seasons with the New York Jets from 1997 to 1999, helping New York improve from a 1-15 season in 1996 to an appearance in the AFC Championship Game in 1998. Career record: 163-97.

Background: Belichick was a center/tight end at Wesleyan 1971-74.

Personal: Born April 16, 1952, Nashville.

ASSISTANT COACHES

Josh Boyer, defensive backs; born January 21, 1977, Heath, Ohio. Wide receiver/defensive back Muskingum College 1996-99. No pro playing experience. College coach: King's College (Pa.) 2000, Dayton 2001, Kent State 2002-03, Bryant University 2004, South Dakota School of Mines and Technology 2005. Pro coach: Joined Patriots in 2006.

Corwin Brown, defensive assistant; born April 25, 1970, Chicago. Cornerback Michigan 1988-1992. Pro cornerback New England Patriots 1993-96, New York Jets 1997-98, Detroit Lions 1999-2000. College coach: Virginia 2001-03, Notre Dame 2007-09. Pro coach: New York Jets 2004-06, joined Patriots in 2010.

Ivan Fears, running backs; born November 15, 1954, Portsmouth, Va. Running back William & Mary 1973-75. No pro playing experience. College coach: William & Mary 1977-79, Syracuse 1980-1990. Pro coach: New England Patriots 1991-92, Chicago Bears 1993-98, re-joined Patriots in 1999.

Brian Ferentz, offensive assistant; born March 28, 1983, Iowa City, Iowa. Offensive lineman Iowa 2001-05. No pro playing experience. Pro coach: Joined Patriots in 2009.

Brian Flores, asst. coach offense/special teams; born February 24, 1981, Brooklyn, N.Y. Linebacker Boston College 1999-2003. No pro playing experience. Pro coach: Joined Patriots in 2008.

Patrick Graham, defensive assistant; born January 24, 1979, Des Plaines, Ill. Defensive line Yale 1997-2001. College coach: Wagner College 2002-03, Richmond 2004-06, Notre Dame 2007-08. Pro coach: Joined Patriots in 2009.

Pepper Johnson, defensive line; born July 29, 1964, Detroit. Linebacker Ohio State 1982-85. Pro linebacker New York Giants 1986-1992, Cleveland Browns 1993-95, Detroit Lions 1996, New York Jets 1997-98. Pro coach: Joined Patriots in 2001.

Harold Nash, asst. strength and conditioning; born May 5, 1970, New Orleans. Defensive back Louisiana-Lafayette 1988-1993. Pro defensive back Shreveport Pirates (CFL) 1994-95, Montreal Alouettes (CFL) 1996-99, Winnipeg Blue Bombers (CFL) 1999-2003, Edmonton Eskimos (CFL) 2004. Pro coach: Joined Patriots in 2005.

Bill O'Brien, quarterbacks; born October 23, 1969, Andover, Mass. Linebacker/defensive end Brown 1990-92. No pro playing experience. College coach: Brown 1993-94, Georgia Tech 1995-2002, Maryland 2003-04, Duke 2005-06. Pro Coach: Joined Patriots in 2007.

Scott O'Brien, special teams; born June 25, 1957, Superior, Wisc. Linebacker Wisconsin-Superior 1975-78. No pro playing experience. College coach: Wisconsin-Superior 1980-82, Nevada-Las Vegas 1983-85, Rice 1986, Pittsburgh 1987-1990. Pro coach: Cleveland Browns 1991-95, Baltimore Ravens 1996-98, Carolina Panthers 1999-2004, Miami Dolphins 2005-06, Denver Broncos 2007-08, joined Patriots in 2009.

Chad O'Shea, receivers; born December 18, 1972, Houston. Quarterback Marshall 1991-93, Houston 1994-95. No pro playing experience. College coach: Houston 1996-99, Southern Mississippi 2000-02. Pro coach: Kansas City Chiefs 2003-05, Minnesota Vikings 2006-08, joined Patriots in 2009.

Matt Patricia, linebackers; born Sept. 13, 1974. Center-guard Rensselaer 1992-96. No pro playing experience. College coach: Rensselaer 1996, Amherst 1999-2000, Syracuse 2001-03. Pro coach: Joined Patriots in 2004.

Dante Scarnecchia, asst. head coach/offensive line; born February 15, 1948, Los Angeles. Center/guard California Western 1968-1970. No pro playing experience. College coach: California Western 1970-72, Iowa State 1973-74, Southern Methodist 1975-76, Pacific 1977-78, Northern Arizona 1979, Southern Methodist 1980-81. Pro coach: New England Patriots 1982-88, Indianapolis Colts 1989-1990, re-joined Patriots in 1991.

Mike Woicik, strength and conditioning; born September 26, 1956, Baltimore. Attended Boston College. No college or pro playing experience. College coach: Springfield College 1978-1980, Syracuse 1980-89. Pro coach: Dallas Cowboys 1990-96, New Orleans Saints 1997-99, joined Patriots in 2000.

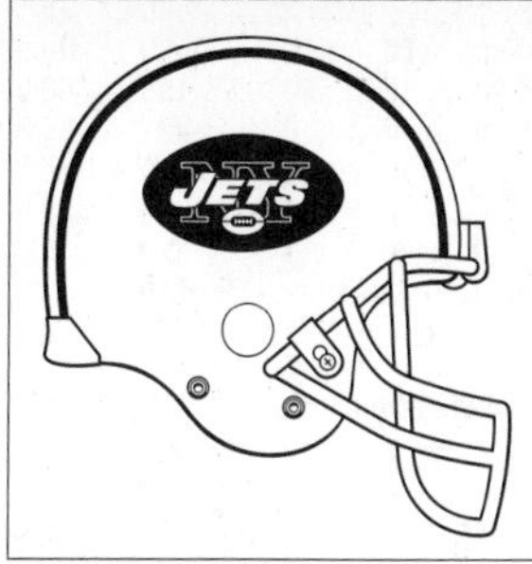

American Football Conference
East Division
Team Colors: Green and White
1 Jets Drive
Florham Park, New Jersey 07932
Telephone (973) 549-4800

2010 SCHEDULE

PRESEASON

Aug. 16	**N.Y. Giants**	8:00
Aug. 21	at Carolina	8:00
Aug. 27	**Washington**	7:00
Sep. 2	at Philadelphia	7:30

REGULAR SEASON

Sep. 13	**Baltimore** (Mon)	7:00
Sep. 19	**New England**	4:15
Sep. 26	at Miami	8:20
Oct. 3	at Buffalo	1:00
Oct. 11	**Minnesota** (Mon)	8:30
Oct. 17	at Denver	2:05
Oct. 24	BYE	
Oct. 31	**Green Bay**	1:00
Nov. 7	at Detroit	1:00
Nov. 14	at Cleveland	1:00
Nov. 21	**Houston**	1:00
Nov. 25	**Cincinnati** (Thu)	8:20
Dec. 6	at New England (Mon)	8:30
Dec. 12	**Miami**	4:15
Dec. 19	at Pittsburgh	4:15
Dec. 26	at Chicago	12:00
Jan. 2	**Buffalo**	1:00

Stadium: New Meadowlands Stadium (opens in 2010)
•**Capacity:** 82,500
East Rutherford, New Jersey 07073
Playing Surface: FieldTurf
Training Camp: SUNY Cortland
Cortland, New York 13045

NEW MEADOWLANDS STADIUM

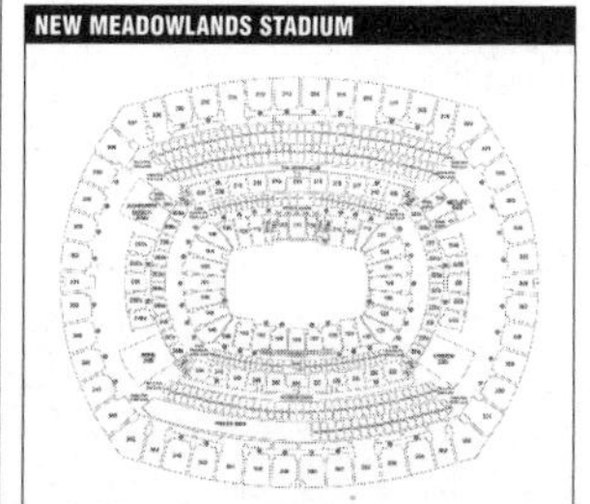

CLUB OFFICIALS

Chairman and CEO: Robert Wood Johnson IV
Executive V.P., Business Operations: Matt Higgins
Executive V.P., Finance & Stadium Development: Thad Sheely
Executive V.P., General Manager: Mike Tannenbaum
Assistant General Manager: Scott Cohen
Chief Financial Officer: Brian Friedman
Associate General Counsel/ Director, Legal Affairs: Hymie Elhai
V.P., College Scouting: Joey Clinkscales
V.P., Finance: Mike Gerstle
V.P., Broadcasting & Production: Bob Parente
V.P., Corporate Sales: Marc Riccio
V.P., Consumer Sales & Service: Robert Sullivan
V.P., Security: Steve Yarnell
Senior Personnel Executive: Terry Bradway
Assistant Director, Player Personnel: JoJo Wooden
Director, Pro Personnel: Brendan Phophett
Pro Scout: Brock Sunderland
Assistant, Pro Personnel: Cole Hufnagel
Assistant Director, College Scouting: Michael Davis
Coordinator, College Scouting: Dan Zbojovsky
National Scout: Jim Cochran
Personnel Scouts: Jeff Bauer, Matt Bazirgan, Joe Bommarito, Jesse Kaye, Jay Mandolesi, Gary Smith
Assistant, Player Personnel: Kathryn Smith
Director, Football Administration: Ari Nissim
Manager, Football Administration: Jacqueline Davidson
Senior Director, Athletic Training: John Mellody
Assistant Athletic Trainers: Josh Koch, Dave Zuffelato
Senior Director, Sales: Bob Brennfleck
Senior Director, Multimedia & Production: Rich Gentile
Senior Director, Ticket Operations: Jeff Hecker
Senior Director, Corporate Partnerships: Jennifer Linn
Senior Director, IT: Tom Murphy
Senior Director, Merchandising: Chris Pierce
Senior Director, Media Relations: Bruce Speight
Senior Director, Marketing: Victoria Vitarelli
Director, Equipment: Gus Granneman
Manager, Equipment: Vito Contento
Assistant Manager, Equipment: Jim Gallione
Assistant, Equipment: Brendan Burger
Director, Community Relations: Jesse Linder
Director, Events & Game Operations: Brian Mulligan
Director, Player Development: David Szott
Director, Video: Tim Tubito

COACHING HISTORY

New York Titans 1960-62
(350-420-8)
Records include postseason games

1960-61	Sammy Baugh	14-14-0
1962	Clyde (Bulldog) Turner	5-9-0
1963-1973	Weeb Ewbank	73-78-6
1974-75	Charley Winner*	9-14-0
1975	Ken Shipp	1-4-0
1976	Lou Holtz**	3-10-0
1976	Mike Holovak	0-1-0
1977-1982	Walt Michaels	41-49-1
1983-89	Joe Walton	54-59-1
1990-93	Bruce Coslet	26-39-0
1994	Pete Carroll	6-10-0
1995-96	Rich Kotite	4-28-0
1997-99	Bill Parcells	30-20-0
2000	Al Groh	9-7-0
2001-05	Herman Edwards	41-44-0
2006-08	Eric Mangini	23-26-0
2009	Rex Ryan	11-8-0

*Released after nine games in 1975
**Resigned after 13 games in 1976

PAID ATTENDANCE

Home 590,652 Away 476,369
Total 1,067,021
Single-game home record, 79,572 (11/19/06)
Single-season home record, 628,773 (2002)

2010 DRAFT CHOICES

Round	Name	Pos.	College
1	Kyle Wilson	DB	Boise State
2	Vladimir Ducasse	T	Massachusetts
4	Joe McKnight	RB	Southern California
5	John Conner	RB	Kentucky

NEW YORK JETS

2009 TEAM RECORD

PRESEASON (2-2)

Date	Result	Opponent
8/14	L 20-23	St. Louis
8/24	L 23-24	at Baltimore
8/29	W 27-25	at New York Giants
9/3	W 38-27	Philadelphia

REGULAR SEASON (9-7)

Date	Result	Opponent
9/13	W 24-7	at Houston
9/20	W 16-9	New England
9/27	W 24-17	Tennessee
10/4	L 10-24	at New Orleans
10/12	L 27-31	at Miami
10/18	L 13-16	Buffalo (OT)
10/25	W 38-0	at Oakland
11/1	L 25-30	Miami
11/15	L 22-24	Jacksonville
11/22	L 14-31	at New England
11/29	W 17-6	Carolina
12/3	W 19-13	at Buffalo
12/13	W 26-3	at Tampa Bay
12/20	L 7-10	Atlanta
12/27	W 29-15	at Indianapolis
1/3	W 37-0	Cincinnati

(OT) Overtime

POSTSEASON (2-1)

Date	Result	Opponent
1/9	W 24-14	at Cincinnati
1/17	W 17-14	at San Diego
1/24	L 17-30	at Indianapolis

SCORE BY PERIODS

	1	2	3	4	OT		Total
Jets	81	108	79	80	0	—	348
Opponents	52	70	47	64	3	—	236

2009 TEAM STATISTICS

	Jets	Opp.
Total First Downs	280	237
Rushing	132	87
Passing	131	128
Penalty	17	22
3rd Down: Made/Att	86/232	69/219
3rd Down Pct.	37.1	31.5
4th Down: Made/Att	15/20	7/19
4th Down Pct.	75.0	36.8
Possession Avg.	31:43	28:17
Total Net Yards	5136	4037
Avg. Per Game	321.0	252.3
Total Plays	1030	953
Avg. Per Play	5.0	4.2
Net Yards Rushing	2756	1578
Avg. Per Game	172.3	98.6
Total Rushes	607	420
Net Yards Passing	2380	2459
Avg. Per Game	148.8	153.7
Sacked/Yards Lost	30/216	32/245
Gross Yards	2596	2704
Att./Completions	393/210	501/259
Completion Pct.	53.4	51.7
Had Intercepted	21	17
Punts/Average	80/42.0	99/43.2
Net Punting Avg.	80/36.7	99/37.2
Penalties/Yards	88/677	87/680
Fumbles/Ball Lost	24/9	22/14
Touchdowns	37	26
Rushing	21	11
Passing	12	8
Returns	4	7

2009 INDIVIDUAL STATISTICS

PASSING	Att.	Comp.	Yds.	Pct.	TD	Int.	Tkld.	Rate
Sanchez	364	196	2444	53.8	12	20	26/195	63.0
Clemens	26	13	125	50.0	0	0	4/21	63.8
B. Smith	1	1	27	100.0	0	0	0/0	118.8
Edwards TM	1	0	0	0.0	0	0	0/0	39.6
Weatherford	1	0	0	0.0	0	1	0/0	0.0
Jets	393	210	2596	53.4	12	21	30/216	62.0
Opponents	501	259	2704	51.7	8	17	32/245	58.8

SCORING	TD R	TD P	TD Rt	PAT	FG	Saf	PTS
Feely	0	0	0	32/32	30/36	0	122
Jones	14	0	0	0/0	0/0	0	84
Edwards TM	0	4	0	0/0	0/0	0	26
Cotchery	1	3	0	0/0	0/0	0	24
Sanchez	3	0	0	0/0	0/0	0	18
B. Smith	1	0	2	0/0	0/0	0	18
Keller	0	2	0	0/0	0/0	0	14
Greene	2	0	0	0/0	0/0	0	12
Clowney	0	1	0	0/0	0/0	0	6
Douglas	0	0	1	0/0	0/0	0	6
Hartsock	0	1	0	0/0	0/0	0	6
Revis	0	0	1	0/0	0/0	0	6
Stuckey TM	0	1	0	0/0	0/0	0	6
Jets	21	12	4	32/32	30/36	0	348
Opponents	11	8	7	23/24	19/23	0	236

2-Pt. Conversions: Edwards, Keller.
Jets 2-5, Opponents 0-2.

RUSHING	No.	Yds	Avg	LG	TD
Jones	331	1402	4.2	71t	14
Greene	108	540	5.0	33t	2
L. Washington	72	331	4.6	33	0
B. Smith	18	207	11.5	57	1
Sanchez	36	106	2.9	14t	3
Woodhead	15	64	4.3	16	0
Richardson	7	48	6.9	19	0
Weatherford	2	42	21.0	26	0
Cotchery	2	7	3.5	6t	1
Keller	1	7	7.0	7	0
Clemens	12	1	0.1	6	0
Clowney	3	1	0.3	13	0
Jets	607	2756	4.5	71t	21
Opponents	420	1578	3.8	35	11

RECEIVING	No.	Yds	Avg	LG	TD
Cotchery	57	821	14.4	53	3
Keller	45	522	11.6	40	2
Edwards TM	35	541	15.5	65t	4
L. Washington	15	131	8.7	33	0
Clowney	14	191	13.6	53	1
Stuckey TM	11	120	10.9	30t	1
Jones	10	58	5.8	28	0
Woodhead	8	87	10.9	24	0
B. Smith	7	63	9.0	19	0
Richardson	3	10	3.3	5	0
Wright	2	21	10.5	14	0
E. Smith	1	27	27.0	27	0
Hartsock	1	2	2.0	2t	1
Mulligan	1	2	2.0	2	0
Jets	210	2596	12.4	65t	12
Opponents	259	2704	10.4	59	8

PUNTING	No.	Yds.	Avg.	In 20	LG
Weatherford	80	3357	42.0	25	66
Jets	80	3357	42.0	25	66
Opponents	99	4277	43.2	25	66

INTERCEPTIONS	No.	Yds	Avg	LG	TD
Revis	6	121	20.2	67t	1
Lowery	3	41	13.7	34	0
Rhodes	3	17	5.7	11	0
Harris	2	24	12.0	14	0
Leonhard	1	44	44.0	44	0
Sheppard	1	0	0.0	0	0
E. Smith	1	0	0.0	0	0
Jets	17	247	14.5	67t	1
Opponents	21	309	14.7	99t	2

PUNT RETURNS	Ret	FC	Yds	Avg	LG	TD
Cotchery	23	12	236	10.3	31	0
Leonhard	21	13	173	8.2	37	0
B. Smith	2	0	27	13.5	21	0
L. Washington	2	1	16	8.0	12	0
Revis	2	0	5	2.5	3	0
Jets	50	26	457	9.1	37	0
Opponents	27	26	238	8.8	40	0

KICKOFF RETURNS	No.	Yds	Avg	LG	TD
L. Washington	16	385	24.1	43	0
B. Smith	10	310	31.0	106t	1
Lowery	5	128	25.6	44	0
Miller TM	5	115	23.0	27	0
Clowney	3	81	27.0	37	0
Cotchery	1	17	17.0	17	0
Woodhead	1	16	16.0	16	0
E. Smith	1	9	9.0	9	0
Leonhard	1	7	7.0	7	0
Turner	1	6	6.0	6	0
Jets	44	1074	24.4	106t	1
Opponents	70	1685	24.1	101t	2

FIELD GOALS	1-19	20-29	30-39	40-49	50+
Feely	0/0	6/6	12/15	11/14	1/1
Jets	0/0	6/6	12/15	11/14	1/1
Opponents	0/0	8/8	5/5	6/10	0/0

SACKS	No.
Pace	8.0
Ellis	6.5
Harris	5.5
Leonhard	2.5
Ihedigbo	2.0
Strickland	2.0
Thomas	2.0
Douglas	1.5
Scott	1.0
Westerman	1.0
Jets	32.0
Opponents	30.0

RECORD HOLDERS

INDIVIDUAL RECORDS—CAREER

Category	Name	Performance
Rushing (Yds.)	Curtis Martin, 1998-2005	10,302
Passing (Yds.)	Joe Namath, 1965-1976	27,057
Passing (TDs)	Joe Namath, 1965-1976	170
Receiving (No.)	Don Maynard, 1960-1972	627
Receiving (Yds.)	Don Maynard, 1960-1972	11,732
Interceptions	Bill Baird, 1963-69	34
Punting (Avg.)	Ben Graham, 2005-08	43.6
Punt Return (Avg.)	Dick Christy, 1961-63	16.2
Kickoff Return (Avg.)	Justin Miller, 2005-07, 2009	26.9
Field Goals	Pat Leahy, 1974-1991	304
Touchdowns (Tot.)	Don Maynard, 1960-1972	88
Points	Pat Leahy, 1974-1991	1,470
*Sacks	Mark Gastineau, 1979-1988	74.0

INDIVIDUAL RECORDS—SINGLE SEASON

Category	Name	Performance
Rushing (Yds.)	Curtis Martin, 2004	1,697
Passing (Yds.)	Joe Namath, 1967	4,007
Passing (TDs)	Vinny Testaverde, 1998	29
Receiving (No.)	Al Toon, 1988	93
Receiving (Yds.)	Don Maynard, 1967	1,434
Interceptions	Dainard Paulson, 1964	12
Punting (Avg.)	Curley Johnson, 1965	45.3
Punt Return (Avg.)	Dick Christy, 1961	21.3
Kickoff Return (Avg.)	Bobby Humphery, 1984	30.7
Field Goals	Jim Turner, 1968	34
Touchdowns (Tot.)	Thomas Jones, 2008	15
Points	Jim Turner, 1968	145
*Sacks	Mark Gastineau, 1984	22.0

INDIVIDUAL RECORDS—SINGLE GAME

Category	Name	Performance
Rushing (Yds.)	Thomas Jones, 10-18-09	210
Passing (Yds.)	Joe Namath, 9-24-72	496
Passing (TDs)	Joe Namath, 9-24-72	6
	Brett Favre, 9-28-08	6
Receiving (No.)	Clark Gaines, 9-21-80	17
Receiving (Yds.)	Don Maynard, 11-17-68	228
Interceptions	Many times	3
	Last time by Ty Law, 1-1-06	
Field Goals	Jim Turner, 11-3-68	6
	Bobby Howfield, 12-3-72	6
Touchdowns (Tot.)	Wesley Walker, 9-21-86	4
Points	Wesley Walker, 9-21-86	24
*Sacks	Mark Gastineau, 11-6-83, 9-2-84	4.0
	John Abraham, 11-4-01	4.0

**Sacks became an official statistic in 1982.*

NEW YORK JETS

2010 VETERAN ROSTER

No.	Name	Pos.	Ht.	Wt.	Birthdate	NFL Exp.	College	Hometown	How Acq.	'09 Games/ Starts
3	Ainge, Erik	QB	6-5	221	6/12/86	3	Tennessee	Hillsboro, Ore.	D5-'08	0*
88	Allison, Aundrae	WR	6-0	198	6/25/84	4	East Carolina	Kannapolis, N.C.	W(Minn)-'09	0*
11	Clemens, Kellen	QB	6-2	221	6/7/83	5	Oregon	Burns, Ore.	D2-'06	10/1
87	Clowney, David	WR	6-0	188	7/7/85	3	Virginia Tech	Delray Beach, Fla.	FA-'07	13/3
34	Cole, Marquice	CB	5-10	190	11/13/83	2	Northwestern	Hazel Crest, Ill.	FA-'09	11/0
30	Coleman, Drew	CB	5-9	180	4/22/83	5	Texas Christian	Henderson, Texas	D6-'06	15/1
42	Condren, Brannon	S	6-1	205	8/19/86	3	Troy	Fort Walton Beach, Fla.	FA-'10	0*
89	Cotchery, Jerricho	WR	6-0	203	6/16/82	7	North Carolina State	Birmingham, Ala.	D4a-'04	14/12
31	t-Cromartie, Antonio	CB	6-2	203	4/15/84	5	Florida State	Tallahassee, Fla.	T(SD)-'10	16/16*
54	Cummings, Kenwin	LB	6-3	250	7/23/86	2	Wingate	Maxton, N.C.	FA-'08	0*
43	Davis, Jason	FB	5-10	242	11/2/83	2	Illinois	St. Louis, Mo.	FA-'10	0*
85	#Dearth, James	LS	6-4	265	1/22/76	10	Tarleton State	Scurry, Texas	FA-'01	16/0
70	DeVito, Mike	DE	6-3	305	6/10/84	4	Maine	Wellfleet, Mass.	FA-'07	15/1
93	#Douglas, Marques	DE	6-2	290	5/5/77	10	Howard	Greensboro, N.C.	FA-'09	16/12
17	t-Edwards, Braylon	WR	6-3	215	2/21/83	6	Michigan	Detroit, Mich.	T(Cle)-'09	16/15*
92	Ellis, Shaun	DE	6-5	285	6/24/77	11	Tennessee	Anderson, S.C.	D1a-'00	15/15
60	Ferguson, D'Brickashaw	T	6-6	310	12/10/83	5	Virginia	Freeport, N.Y.	D1a-'06	16/16
2	Folk, Nick	K	6-1	222	11/5/84	4	Arizona	Hollywood, Calif.	FA-'10	14/0*
51	#Fowler, Ryan	LB	6-3	250	5/20/82	7	Duke	Redington Shores, Fla.	FA-'09	8/0
50	Gholston, Vernon	LB	6-3	264	6/5/86	3	Ohio State	Detroit, Mich.	D1a-'08	14/3
23	Greene, Shonn	RB	5-11	226	8/21/85	2	Iowa	Sicklerville, N.J.	D3-'09	14/0
52	Harris, David	LB	6-2	245	1/21/84	4	Michigan	Grand Rapids, Mich.	D2-'07	16/16
84	Hartsock, Ben	TE	6-4	270	7/5/80	7	Ohio State	Chillicothe, Ohio	FA-'09	16/7
10	t-Holmes, Santonio	WR	5-11	192	3/3/84	5	Ohio State	Belle Glade, Fla.	T(Pitt)-'10	16/16*
78	Hunter, Wayne	T	6-5	320	7/2/81	7	Hawaii	Honolulu, Hawaii	FA-'07	16/1
44	Ihedigbo, James	S	6-1	210	12/3/83	4	Massachusetts	Amherst, Mass.	FA-'08	15/0
53	#Izzo, Larry	LB	5-10	225	9/26/74	15	Rice	Fort Belvoir, Va.	UFA(NE)-'09	12/0
77	Jenkins, Kris	DT	6-4	360	8/3/79	10	Maryland	Ypsilanti, Mich.	T(Car)-'08	6/6
81	Keller, Dustin	TE	6-2	248	9/25/84	3	Purdue	Lafayette, Ind.	D1b-'08	16/12
56	Laury, Lance	LB	6-2	237	1/17/82	5	South Carolina	Hopkins, S.C.	FA-'10	16/0*
36	Leonhard, Jim	S	5-8	186	10/27/82	6	Wisconsin	Ladysmith, Wisc.	UFA(Balt)-'09	16/16
26	Lowery, Dwight	CB	5-11	198	1/23/86	3	San Jose State	Santa Cruz, Calif.	D4-'08	13/5
74	Mangold, Nick	C	6-4	305	1/13/84	5	Ohio State	Centerville, Ohio	D1b-'06	16/16
65	Moore, Brandon	G	6-3	305	6/3/80	8	Illinois	Gary, Ind.	FA-'03	16/16
82	Mulligan, Matthew	TE	6-4	270	1/18/85	2	Maine	West Enfield, Maine	W(Tenn)-'09	5/1
7	O'Connell, Kevin	QB	6-5	225	5/25/85	3	San Diego State	Carlsbad, Calif.	T(Det)-'09	0*
97	Pace, Calvin	LB	6-4	265	10/28/80	8	Wake Forest	Douglasville, Ga.	UFA(Ariz)-'08	12/12
79	Pitoitua, Ropati	DE	6-8	310	4/6/85	2	Washington State	Spanaway, Wash.	FA-'08	8/0
22	Pool, Brodney	S	6-2	210	5/24/84	6	Oklahoma	Corpus Christi, Texas	FA-'10	11/10*
91	Pouha, Sione	DT	6-3	325	2/3/79	6	Utah	Salt Lake City, Utah	D3-'05	16/14
24	Revis, Darrelle	CB	5-11	198	7/14/85	4	Pittsburgh	Aliquippa, Pa.	D1-'07	16/16
49	Richardson, Tony	FB	6-1	238	12/17/71	16	Auburn	Daleville, Ala.	UFA(Minn)-'08	16/10
6	Sanchez, Mark	QB	6-2	225	11/11/86	2	Southern California	Mission Viejo, Calif.	D1-'09	15/15
57	Scott, Bart	LB	6-2	240	8/18/80	9	Southern Illinois	Detroit, Mich.	UFA(Balt)-'09	16/16
68	Slauson, Matt	G	6-5	315	2/18/86	2	Nebraska	Colorado Springs, Colo.	D6-'09	3/0
16	Smith, Brad	WR	6-2	210	12/12/83	5	Missouri	Youngstown, Ohio	D4a-'06	13/2
33	Smith, Eric	S	6-1	205	3/17/83	5	Michigan State	Groveport, Ohio	D3b-'06	16/4
	Taylor, Jason	LB	6-6	255	9/1/74	14	Akron	Pittsburgh, Pa.	UFA(Mia)-'10	16/15*
99	Thomas, Bryan	LB	6-4	266	6/7/79	9	Alabama-Birmingham	Birmingham, Ala.	D1-'02	16/14
21	Tomlinson, LaDainian	RB	5-10	221	6/23/79	10	Texas Christian	Rosebud, Texas	FA-'10	14/14*
75	Turner, Robert	OL	6-4	308	8/20/84	3	New Mexico	Austin, Texas	FA-'07	13/3
32	Washington, Chauncey	RB	5-11	222	4/29/85	2	Southern California	Torrance, Calif.	FA-'09	2/0*
9	Weatherford, Steve	P	6-3	210	12/17/82	5	Illinois	Terre Haute, Ind.	FA-'09	16/0
55	Westerman, Jamaal	LB	6-3	255	2/21/85	2	Rutgers	Brampton, Ontario, Canada	FA-'09	14/0
83	Woodhead, Danny	WR	5-9	195	12/3/83	3	Chadron State	North Platte, Neb.	FA-'08	10/0
67	Woody, Damien	OL	6-3	330	11/3/77	12	Boston College	Beaverdam, Va.	UFA(Det)-'08	16/16
98	Wright, Rodrique	DE	6-5	300	7/31/84	3	Texas	Houston, Texas	FA-'10	0*

* Ainge inactive for 15 games; Allison missed '09 season because of injury; Condren last active with Miami in '08; Cromartie played 16 games with San Diego in '09; Cummings inactive for 7 games; Davis last active with Chicago in '08; Edwards played 4 games with Cleveland and 12 games with N.Y. Jets; Folk played 14 games with Dallas; Holmes played 16 games with Pittsburgh; Laury played 16 with Seattle; O'Connell inactive for 16 games; Pool played 11 games with Cleveland; Taylor played 16 games with Miami; Tomlinson played 14 games with San Diego; Washington played 2 games with Dallas; Wright last active with Miami during '08 postseason.

t- Jets traded for Cromartie (SD), Edwards (Cle), Holmes (Pitt).

Traded—S Kerry Rhodes (16 games in '09) to Arizona, WR Chansi Stuckey (4) to Cleveland, LB Jason Trusnik (4) to Cleveland, RB Leon Washington (7) to Seattle.

Players lost through free agency (1): K Jay Feely (Ariz; 16 games in '09).

Also played with Jets in '09—DB Ahmad Carroll (6 games), G Alan Faneca (16), DT Howard Greeen (12), RB Thomas Jones (16), DB Justin Miller (1), LB Marques Murrell (10), CB Lito Sheppard (11), CB Donald Strickland (9), WR Wallace Wright (16).

2010 FIRST-YEAR ROSTER

Name	Pos.	Ht.	Wt.	Birthdate	College	Hometown	How Acq.
Basped, Kevin	LB	6-4	254	5/19/88	Nevada	Sacramento, Calif.	FA
Buckman, Keith	G	6-5	321	2/5/87	North Dakota State	Belfield, N.D.	FA
Butler, Ezra (1)	LB	6-2	248	11/20/84	Nevada	Calabasas, Calif.	FA
Conley, TJ (1)	P	6-3	220	8/29/85	Idaho	Walla Walla, Wash.	FA
Conner, John	FB	5-11	246	6/8/87	Kentucky	West Chester, Ohio	D5
Cumberland, Jeff	TE	6-4	249	5/2/87	Illinois	Columbus, Ohio	FA
Davis, Britt (1)	WR	6-3	205	4/23/86	Northern Illinois	Melrose Park, Ill.	FA
Ducasse, Vladimir	OL	6-5	330	10/15/87	Massachusetts	Stamford, Conn.	D2
Gay, Dan (1)	T	6-4	303	8/29/86	Baylor	Lafayette, La.	FA
Green, S.J. (1)	WR	6-3	220	6/20/85	South Florida	Brandon, Fla.	FA
Henry, Marcus (1)	WR	6-4	212	2/21/86	Kansas	Lawton, Okla.	D6
Jackson, Brian	CB	6-0	198	5/4/87	Oklahoma	De Soto, Texas	FA
Kroul, Matt (1)	DL	6-3	280	2/25/86	Iowa	Mount Vernon, Iowa	FA
Lamb, Jason	DE	6-4	284	3/3/87	Baylor	Richardson, Texas	FA
Mauga, Joshua (1)	LB	6-1	243	6/20/87	Nevada	Fallon, Nev.	FA
McKnight, Joe	RB	5-11	194	4/16/88	Southern California	River Ridge, La.	D4
Parenton, Michael (1)	C	6-2	287	11/2/85	Tulane	Thibodaux, La.	FA
Purdum, Tanner (1)	LS	6-3	270	8/15/84	Baker	Enid, Okla.	FA
Reamer, Cory	LB	6-3	231	5/6/87	Alabama	Hoover, Ala.	FA
Satele, Brashton	LB	6-0	241	11/8/87	Hawaii	Mililani, Hawaii	FA
Smith, Bo (1)	DB	6-0	190	6/8/83	Weber State	Owensboro, Ky.	FA
Steinkuhler, Ty (1)	DL	6-3	280	9/11/85	Nebraska	Lincoln, Neb.	FA
Stitser, Clint	K	6-1	200	5/19/85	Fresno State	Reno, Nev.	FA
Stommes, Matt	T	6-6	311	10/17/86	Minnesota	Richmond, Minn.	FA
Tanner, Charlie	G	6-3	305	6/3/86	Texas	Austin, Texas	FA
Taylor, Larry (1)	WR	5-6	177	5/30/85	Connecticut	Fort Lauderdale, Fla.	FA
Turkovich, Michael (1)	T	6-6	301	11/27/86	Notre Dame	Johnstown, Pa.	FA
Warren, Donovan	S	5-11	195	1/31/89	Michigan	Long Beach, Calif.	FA
Williams, Ernest	DT	6-0	281	7/3/86	Pittsburgh	Monessen, Pa.	FA
Wilson, Kyle	CB	5-10	194	5/30/87	Boise State	Piscataway, N.J.	D1

The term NFL Rookie is defined as a player who is in his first season of professional football and has not been on the roster of another professional football team for any regular-season or postseason games. A Rookie is designated by an "R" on NFL rosters. Players who have been active in another professional football league or players who have NFL experience, including either preseason training camp or being on an Active List or Inactive List, or on Reserve/Injured or Reserve/Physically Unable to Perform for fewer than six regular-season games, are termed NFL First-Year Players. An NFL First-Year Player is designated by a "1" on NFL rosters. Thereafter, a player is credited with an additional year of experience for each season in which he accumulates six games on the Active List or Inactive List, or on Reserve/Injured or Reserve/Physically Unable to Perform.

Log on to www.newyorkjets.com for an up-to-date roster.

COACHING STAFF

Head Coach,
Rex Ryan

Pro Career: Named the 15th full-time head coach of the New York Jets on January 19, 2009. In his first season, Ryan guided his team to a 9-7 record en route to the AFC Championship Game. Under Ryan, the Jets' rushing attack ranked first in the NFL and the defense finished first in total defense, points allowed and passing defense. Ryan spent 10 seasons with the Baltimore Ravens, including 2008 as the assistant head coach/defensive coordinator. Since becoming defensive coordinator in 2005, the Ravens never finished lower than sixth in total defense. From 1999-2008, the Ravens ranked first in the NFL for fewest points allowed, fewest rushing yards allowed, most takeaways, most interceptions and most interceptions returned for touchdowns. Ravens allowed fewest points in NFL history for 16-game season (165) in 2000 en route to winning Super Bowl XXXV. Began NFL career with Arizona under his father, Buddy Ryan, as coach for defensive line (1994) and linebackers (1995). Career record: 11-8.

Background: Coached at Eastern Kentucky (1987-88), New Mexico Highlands (1989), Morehead State (1990-93), Cincinnati (1996-97) and Oklahoma (1998). Played defensive end at Southwestern Oklahoma State with his twin brother, Rob, who is currently the Cleveland defensive coordinator. Earned his Bachelor's and Master's Degree in Physical Education at Eastern Kentucky.

Personal: Born December 13, 1963, Ardmore, Okla. Ryan and his wife Michelle have two sons, Payton and Seth.

ASSISTANT COACHES

Sal Alosi, head strength and conditioning; born May 11, 1977, Massapequa, N.Y. Linebacker Hofstra 1996-2000. No pro playing experience. College coach: Hofstra 2001. Pro coach: New York Jets 2002-05, Atlanta Falcons 2006, re-joined Jets in 2007.

Mike Bloomgren, offensive assistant; born January 25, 1977, Tallahassee, Fla. Culver-Stockton tight end 1996. No pro playing experience. College coach: Florida State 1997-98 Alabama 1999-2001, Catawba College 2002-04, Delta State 2005-06. Pro coach: Joined Jets in 2007.

Bill Callahan, asst. head coach/offense; born July, 31 1956, Chicago. Quarterback Benedictine 1975-77. No pro playing experience. College coach: Illinois 1980-86, Northern Arizona 1987-88, Southern Illinois 1989, Wisconsin 1990-94, Nebraska 2004-2007 (head coach). Pro coach: Philadelphia Eagles 1995-97, Oakland Raiders 1998-2003 (head coach 2002-03), joined Jets in 2008.

Mark Carrier, defensive line; born April 28, 1968, Lake Charles, La. Defensive back Southern California 1987-89. Pro defensive back Chicago Bears 1990-96, Detroit Lions 1997-99, Washington Redskins 2000. College coach: Arizona State 2004-05. Pro coach: Baltimore Ravens 2006-09, joined Jets in 2010.

Matt Cavanaugh, quarterbacks; born October 27, 1956, Youngstown, Ohio. Quarterback Pittsburgh 1974-77. Pro quarterback New England Patriots 1978-1982, San Francisco 49ers 1983-85, Philadelphia Eagles 1986-89, New York Giants 1990-91. College coach: Pittsburgh 1991-93, 2005-08. Pro coach: Arizona Cardinals 1994-95, San Francisco 49ers 1996, Chicago Bears 1997-98, Baltimore Ravens 1999-2004, joined Jets in 2009.

Mike Devlin, tight ends/asst. offensive line; born November 16, 1969, Blacksburg, Va. Offensive line Iowa 1989-1992. Pro offensive lineman Buffalo Bills 1993-95, Arizona Cardinals 1996-99. College coach: Toledo 2004-05. Pro coach: Arizona Cardinals 2000-03, joined Jets in 2006.

Henry Ellard, wide receivers; born July 21, 1961, Fresno, Calif. Wide receiver Fresno State 1979-1982. Pro wide receiver/punt returner Los Angeles Rams 1983-1993, Washington Redskins 1994-98, New England Patriots 1998. College coach: Fresno State 2000. Pro coach: St. Louis Rams 2001-08, joined Jets in 2009.

Ben Kotwica, asst. special teams; born December 8, 1974, Tinley Park, Ill. Linebacker Army 1995-97. No pro playing experience. Pro coach: Joined Jets in 2007.

Anthony Lynn, running backs; born December 21, 1968, McKinney, Texas. Running back Texas Tech 1987-1991. Pro running back Denver Broncos 1993, 1997-99, San Francisco 49ers 1995-96. Pro coach: Denver Broncos 2000-02, Jacksonville Jaguars 2003-04, Dallas Cowboys 2005-06, Cleveland Browns 2007-08, joined Jets in 2009.

Jim O'Neil, quality control/defense; born Oct. 26, 1978, Philadelphia. Defensive end Towson University 1997-2000. No pro playing experience. College coach: SUNY-Albany 2001, Pennsylvania 2002, Northwestern 2003-04, Towson University 2005, Eastern Michigan 2006-08. Pro coach: Joined Jets in 2009.

Mike Pettine, defensive coordinator; born September 25, 1966, Doylestown, Pa. Safety Virginia 1984-87. No pro playing experience. College coach: Pittsburgh 1993-94. Pro coach: Baltimore Ravens 2003-08, joined Jets in 2009.

Brian Schottenheimer, offensive coordinator; born October 16, 1973, Denver. Quarterback Kansas 1992, Florida 1993-96. No pro playing experience. College coach: Syracuse 1999, Southern California 2000. Pro coach: St. Louis Rams 1997, Kansas City Chiefs 1998, Washington Redskins 2001, San Diego Chargers 2002-05, joined Jets in 2006.

Bob Sutton, defensive assistant/linebackers; born January 28, 1951, Ypsilanti, Mich. Attended Eastern Michigan. No college or pro playing experience. College coach: Michigan 1972-73, Syracuse 1974, Western Michigan 1975-76, 1980-81, Illinois 1977-79, North Carolina State 1982, Army 1983-1999 (head coach 1991-99). Pro coach: Joined Jets in 2000.

Kyle Thorne, asst. strength and conditioning; born August 4, 1980, Tucson, Ariz. Linebacker Hofstra 2000-01. Pro linebacker/wide receiver Hawaiian Islanders (AF2) 2004. Pro coach: Billings Outlaws (IFL) 2005, Everton Football Club (EPL) 2007-09, joined Jets in 2009.

Dennis Thurman, defensive backs; born April 13, 1956, Los Angeles, Calif. Defensive back Southern California 1974-77. Pro defensive back Dallas Cowboys 1978-1985, St. Louis Cardinals 1986, Phoenix Cardinals 1988-89. College coach: Southern California 1993-2000. Pro coach: Ohio Glory (WLAF) 1992, Baltimore Ravens 2002-07, joined Jets in 2009.

Jeff Weeks, defensive assistant; born May 30, 1962, Denver. Wide receiver Southwest Oklahoma State 1982-84, Northwest Oklahoma State 1985. College coach: Western Kentucky 1987-88, Morehead State 1990-91, Phoenix CC 1996, Oklahoma 1999, Fort Scott (Kan.) C.C. 2001-04, Southeast Oklahoma State 2005, Texas A&M- Kingsville 2006. Pro coach: Oakland Raiders 2008, joined Jets in 2009.

Mike Westhoff, special teams coordinator; born January 10, 1948, Pittsburgh. Linebacker Wyoming 1965, center/linebacker Wichita State 1967-69. College coach: Indiana 1974-75, Dayton 1976, Indiana State 1977, Northwestern 1978-1980, Texas Christian 1981. Pro coach: Baltimore Colts 1982-83, Indianapolis Colts 1984, Arizona Outlaws (USFL) 1985, Miami Dolphins 1986-2000, joined Jets in 2001.

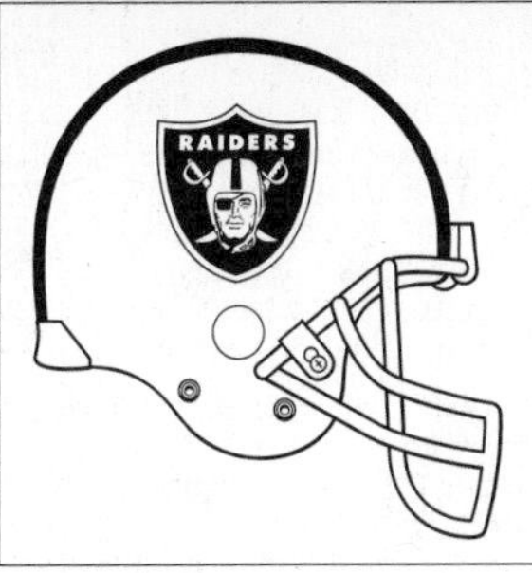

American Football Conference
West Division
Team Colors: Silver and Black
1220 Harbor Bay Parkway
Alameda, California 94502
Telephone: (510) 864-5000

2010 SCHEDULE

PRESEASON

Aug. 12	at Dallas	8:00
Aug. 21	at Chicago	7:30
Aug. 28	**San Francisco**	6:00
Sep. 2	**Seattle**	7:00

REGULAR SEASON

Sep. 12	at Tennessee	12:00
Sep. 19	**St. Louis**	1:05
Sep. 26	at Arizona	1:15
Oct. 3	**Houston**	1:05
Oct. 10	**San Diego**	1:15
Oct. 17	at San Francisco	1:05
Oct. 24	at Denver	2:15
Oct. 31	**Seattle**	1:15
Nov. 7	**Kansas City**	1:15
Nov. 14	BYE	
Nov. 21	at Pittsburgh	1:00
Nov. 28	**Miami**	1:05
Dec. 5	at San Diego	1:05
Dec. 12	at Jacksonville	1:00
Dec. 19	**Denver**	1:15
Dec. 26	**Indianapolis**	1:05
Jan. 2	at Kansas City	12:00

Stadium: Oakland Coliseum
(opened in 1966)
• **Capacity:** 63,132
7000 Coliseum Way
Oakland, CA 94621-1917
Playing Surface: Grass
Training Camp: Napa Valley Marriott
Napa, California 94558

OAKLAND COLISEUM

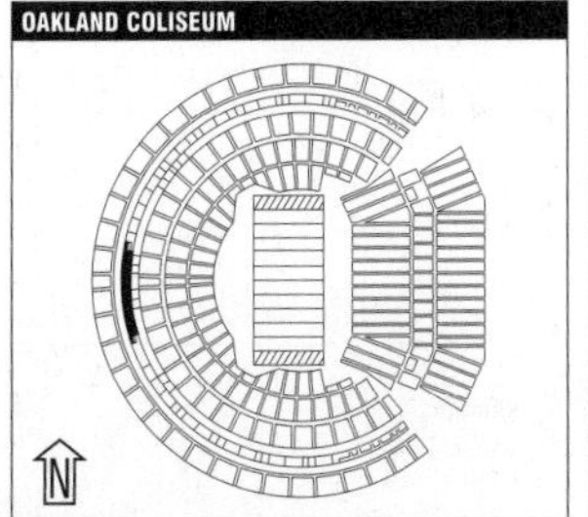

CLUB OFFICIALS

Owner: Al Davis
Chief Executive: Amy Trask
Legal: Jeff Birren, Dan Ventrelle
Finance: Marc Badain, Tom Blanda, Derek Person, Ed Villanueva
Special Projects: Willie Brown, Jim Otto,
Public Relations: John Herrera, Will Kiss, Mike Taylor
Tickets, Suites & Premium Seats: Ethel Brual, Jay Chess, Adam Feldman, Qiava Harper, Courtney Jeffries, Ryan Robbins, Mark Shearer
Multi-Cultural Initiatives: Elena Valenzuela
Internet: Jerry Knaak
Marketing/Sponsorships: Farnoush Ansari, Morris Bradshaw, Paul Engl, Robert Kinnard, Meka White
Community Relations: Scott Fink
Youth Initiatives: Rosie Bone
Raiderettes: Karen Kovac
Trainers: Chris Cortez, H. Rod Martin, Scott Touchet
Equipment: Wale Adefela, Danny Molina, Bob Romanski, Richard Romanski
Video Operations: Dave Nash, Jim Otten, John Otten
Broadcasting: Vittorio DeBartolo, Brad Phinney, Jeanette Thompson
Computer Operations: Benny Hong, Matthew Pasco, Shawn Testa

COACHING HISTORY

Oakland 1960-1981
Los Angeles 1982-1994
(435-353-11)
Records include postseason games

1960-61	Eddie Erdelatz*	6-10-0
1961-62	Marty Feldman**	2-15-0
1962	Red Conkright	1-8-0
1963-65	Al Davis	23-16-3
1966-68	John Rauch	35-10-1
1969-1978	John Madden	112-39-7
1979-1987	Tom Flores	91-56-0
1988-89	Mike Shanahan***	8-12-0
1989-1994	Art Shell	56-41-0
1995-96	Mike White	15-17-0
1997	Joe Bugel	4-12-0
1998-2001	Jon Gruden	40-28-0
2002-03	Bill Callahan	17-18-0
2004-05	Norv Turner	9-23-0
2006	Art Shell	2-14-0
2007-08	Lane Kiffin****	5-15-0
2008-09	Tom Cable	9-19-0

* Released after two games in 1961
** Released after five games in 1962
*** Released after four games in 1989
**** Released after four games in 2008

PAID ATTENDANCE

Home 338,157 Away 552,237
Total 890,394
Single-game home record, 62,660 (11/3/02)
Single-season home record, 471,151 (2002)

2010 DRAFT CHOICES

Round	Name	Pos.	College
1	Rolando McClain	LB	Alabama
2	Lamarr Houston	DE	Texas
3	Jared Veldheer	T	Hillsdale
4	Bruce Campbell	T	Maryland
	Jacoby Ford	WR	Clemson
5	Walter McFadden	DB	Auburn
6	Travis Goethel	LB	Arizona St.
7	Jeremy Ware	DB	Michigan St.
	Stevie Brown	DB	Michigan

OAKLAND RAIDERS

2009 TEAM RECORD

PRESEASON (1-3)

Date	Result	Opponent
8/13	W 31-10	Dallas
8/22	L 20-21	at San Francisco
8/29	L 7-45	New Orleans
9/3	L 21-31	at Seattle

REGULAR SEASON (5-11)

Date	Result	Opponent
9/14	L 20-24	San Diego
9/20	W 13-10	at Kansas City
9/27	L 3-23	Denver
10/4	L 6-29	at Houston
10/11	L 7-44	at New York Giants
10/18	W 13-9	Philadelphia
10/25	L 0-38	New York Jets
11/1	L 16-24	at San Diego
11/15	L 10-16	Kansas City
11/22	W 20-17	Cincinnati
11/26	L 7-24	at Dallas
12/6	W 27-24	at Pittsburgh
12/13	L 13-34	Washington
12/20	W 20-19	at Denver
12/27	L 9-23	at Cleveland
1/3	L 13-21	Baltimore

SCORE BY PERIODS

Raiders	36	78	22	61	0 —	197
Opponents	100	136	49	94	0 —	379

2009 TEAM STATISTICS

	Raiders	Opp.
Total First Downs	234	314
Rushing	81	126
Passing	131	158
Penalty	22	30
3rd Down: Made/Att	63/213	77/216
3rd Down Pct.	29.6	35.6
4th Down: Made/Att	10/21	9/14
4th Down Pct.	47.6	64.3
Possession Avg.	28:18	31:42
Total Net Yards	4258	5791
Avg. Per Game	266.1	361.9
Total Plays	944	1023
Avg. Per Play	4.5	5.7
Net Yards Rushing	1701	2488
Avg. Per Game	106.3	155.5
Total Rushes	410	548
Net Yards Passing	2557	3303
Avg. Per Game	159.8	206.4
Sacked/Yards Lost	49/318	37/228
Gross Yards	2875	3531
Att./Completions	485/255	438/259
Completion Pct.	52.6	59.1
Had Intercepted	18	8
Punts/Average	96/51.1	77/42.8
Net Punting Avg.	96/43.9	77/39.5
Penalties/Yards	117/920	86/684
Fumbles/Ball Lost	30/15	29/12
Touchdowns	17	41
Rushing	7	24
Passing	10	16
Returns	0	1

2009 INDIVIDUAL STATISTICS

PASSING	Att.	Comp.	Yds.	Pct.	TD	Int.	Tkld.	Rate
J. Russell	246	120	1287	48.8	3	11	33/207	50.0
Gradkowski	150	82	1007	54.7	6	3	11/71	80.6
Frye	87	53	581	60.9	1	4	5/40	65.3
Bush	1	0	0	0.0	0	0	0/0	39.6
Losman	1	0	0	0.0	0	0	0/0	39.6
Raiders	485	255	2875	52.6	10	18	49/318	62.0
Opponents	438	259	3531	59.1	16	8	37/228	89.5

SCORING	TD R	TD P	TD Rt	PAT	FG	Saf	PTS
Janikowski	0	0	0	17/17	26/29	0	95
Murphy	0	4	0	0/0	0/0	0	24
Bush	3	0	0	0/0	0/0	0	18
Fargas	3	0	0	0/0	0/0	0	18
Z. Miller	0	3	0	0/0	0/0	0	18
Schilens	0	2	0	0/0	0/0	0	12
Heyward-Bey	0	1	0	0/0	0/0	0	6
McFadden	1	0	0	0/0	0/0	0	6
Raiders	7	10	0	17/17	26/29	0	197
Opponents	24	16	1	41/41	30/40	1	379

2-Pt. Conversions: Raiders 0-0, Opponents 0-0.

RUSHING	No.	Yds	Avg	LG	TD
Bush	123	589	4.8	60	3
Fargas	129	491	3.8	35	3
McFadden	104	357	3.4	28	1
Gradkowski	18	108	6.0	21	0
J. Russell	18	44	2.4	15	0
Frye	4	41	10.3	26	0
Murphy	6	31	5.2	13	0
Higgins	2	21	10.5	19	0
Heyward-Bey	2	19	9.5	20	0
O'Neal	1	0	0.0	0	0
G. Russell	3	0	0.0	2	0
Raiders	410	1701	4.1	60	7
Opponents	548	2488	4.5	77t	24

RECEIVING	No.	Yds	Avg	LG	TD
Z. Miller	66	805	12.2	86t	3
Murphy	34	521	15.3	75t	4
Schilens	29	365	12.6	25	2
McFadden	21	245	11.7	48	0
Higgins	19	263	13.8	33	0
Fargas	17	113	6.6	14	0
Bush	17	105	6.2	17	0
G. Russell	12	96	8.0	20	0
Stewart	10	78	7.8	19	0
Heyward-Bey	9	124	13.8	24	1
Watkins	8	90	11.3	28	0
Lawton	7	31	4.4	14	0
Myers	4	19	4.8	6	0
Reece	2	20	10.0	11	0
Raiders	255	2875	11.3	86t	10
Opponents	259	3531	13.6	63	16

INTERCEPTIONS	No.	Yds	Avg	LG	TD
C. Johnson	3	20	6.7	20	0
Huff	3	15	5.0	10	0
Asomugha	1	0	0.0	0	0
Eugene	1	0	0.0	0	0
Raiders	8	35	4.4	20	0
Opponents	18	259	14.4	44	0

PUNTING	No.	Yds.	Avg.	In 20	LG
Lechler	96	4909	51.1	30	70
Raiders	96	4909	51.1	30	70
Opponents	77	3299	42.8	28	65

PUNT RETURNS	Ret	FC	Yds	Avg	LG	TD
Higgins	34	21	177	5.2	19	0
J. Walker	1	0	0	0.0	0	0
Williams	1	0	0	0.0	0	0
Eugene	0	2	0	—	—	0
Raiders	36	23	177	4.9	19	0
Opponents	63	13	459	7.3	27	0

KICKOFF RETURNS	No.	Yds	Avg	LG	TD
Holland	28	550	19.6	60	0
G. Russell	18	330	18.3	41	0
Rankin TM	6	108	18.0	23	0
J. Miller TM	6	106	17.7	27	0
Reece	3	58	19.3	23	0
Stewart	2	19	9.5	11	0
Williams	2	11	5.5	7	0
Lawton	1	17	17.0	17	0
Raiders	66	1199	18.2	60	0
Opponents	42	1078	25.7	95t	1

FIELD GOALS	1-19	20-29	30-39	40-49	50+
Janikowski	0/0	3/3	8/8	9/10	6/8
Raiders	0/0	3/3	8/8	9/10	6/8
Opponents	0/0	10/10	9/13	9/12	2/5

SACKS	No.
Ellis	7.0
Scott	7.0
Seymour	4.0
Shaughnessy	4.0
Richardson	3.0
Howard	2.0
Morrison	2.0
Warren	2.0
Mitchell	1.5
Branch	1.0
Kelly	1.0
Routt	1.0
(group)	1.0
Huff	0.5
Raiders	37.0
Opponents	49.0

RECORD HOLDERS

INDIVIDUAL RECORDS—CAREER

Category	Name	Performance
Rushing (Yds.)	Marcus Allen, 1982-1992	8,545
Passing (Yds.)	Ken Stabler, 1970-79	19,078
Passing (TDs)	Ken Stabler, 1970-79	150
Receiving (No.)	Tim Brown, 1988-2003	1,070
Receiving (Yds.)	Tim Brown, 1988-2003	14,734
Interceptions	Willie Brown, 1967-1978	39
	Lester Hayes, 1977-1986	39
Punting (Avg.)	Shane Lechler, 2000-09	**47.3
Punt Return (Avg.)	Claude Gibson, 1963-65	12.6
Kickoff Return (Avg.)	Jack Larscheid, 1960-61	28.4
Field Goals	Sebastian Janikowski, 2000-09	229
Touchdowns (Tot.)	Tim Brown, 1988-2003	104
Points	Sebastian Janikowski, 2000-09	1,000
*Sacks	Greg Townsend, 1983-1993, 1997	107.5

INDIVIDUAL RECORDS—SINGLE SEASON

Category	Name	Performance
Rushing (Yds.)	Marcus Allen, 1985	1,759
Passing (Yds.)	Rich Gannon, 2002	4,689
Passing (TDs)	Daryle Lamonica, 1969	34
Receiving (No.)	Tim Brown 1997	104
Receiving (Yds.)	Tim Brown, 1997	1,408
Interceptions	Lester Hayes, 1980	13
Punting (Avg.)	Shane Lechler, 2009	51.1
Punt Return (Avg.)	Claude Gibson, 1964	14.4
Kickoff Return (Avg.)	Harold Hart, 1975	30.5
Field Goals	Jeff Jaeger, 1993	35
Touchdowns (Tot.)	Marcus Allen, 1984	18
Points	Jeff Jaeger, 1993	132
*Sacks	Derrick Burgess, 2005	16.0

INDIVIDUAL RECORDS—SINGLE GAME

Category	Name	Performance
Rushing (Yds.)	Napoleon Kaufman, 10-19-97	227
Passing (Yds.)	Cotton Davidson, 10-25-64	427
Passing (TDs)	Tom Flores, 12-22-63	6
	Daryle Lamonica, 10-19-69	6
Receiving (No.)	Tim Brown, 12-21-97	14
Receiving (Yds.)	Art Powell, 12-22-63	247
Interceptions	Many times	3
	Last time by Rod Woodson, 9-29-02	
Field Goals	Jeff Jaeger, 12-11-94	5
	Sebastian Janikowski, 10-29-00, 10-5-03, 11-18-07	5
Touchdowns (Tot.)	Art Powell, 12-22-63	4
	Marcus Allen, 9-24-84	4
	Harvey Williams, 11-16-97	4
Points	Art Powell, 12-22-63	24
	Marcus Allen, 9-24-84	24
	Harvey Williams, 11-16-97	24
*Sacks	Howie Long, 10-2-83	5.0

**Sacks became an official statistic in 1982.*
***NFL Record*

OAKLAND RAIDERS

2010 VETERAN ROSTER

No.	Name	Pos.	Ht.	Wt.	Birthdate	NFL Exp.	College	Hometown	How Acq.	'09 Games/ Starts
21	Asomugha, Nnamdi	CB	6-2	210	7/6/81	8	California	Los Angeles, Calif.	D1-'03	16/16
69	Barnes, Khalif	T	6-5	325	4/21/82	6	Washington	Spring Valley, Calif.	UFA(Jax)-'09	6/2
32	Bennett, Michael	RB	5-9	205	8/13/78	10	Wisconsin	Milwaukee, Wisc.	FA-'10	6/0*
10	Bodiford, Shaun	WR	5-11	185	5/4/82	4	Portland State	Federal Way, Wash.	FA-'10	0*
7	Boller, Kyle	QB	6-3	220	6/17/81	7	California	Newhall, Calif.	UFA(StL)-'09	7/4*
30	Boyd, Jerome	S	6-2	225	5/26/86	2	Oregon	Los Angeles, Calif.	FA-'09	1/0
33	Branch, Tyvon	S	6-0	205	12/11/86	3	Connecticut	Cicero, N.Y.	D4-'08	16/16
57	Brown, Ricky	LB	6-2	235	12/27/83	5	Boston College	Cincinnati, Ohio	FA-'06	5/5
90	Bryant, Desmond	DT	6-5	290	12/15/85	2	Harvard	Elizabethtown, N.C.	FA-'09	16/0
29	Bush, Michael	RB	6-1	245	6/16/84	3	Louisville	Louisville, Ky.	D4-'07	16/7
8	t- Campbell, Jason	QB	6-5	230	12/31/81	6	Auburn	Taylorsville, Miss.	T(Wash)-'10	16/16*
66	Carlisle, Cooper	G	6-5	295	8/11/77	11	Florida	McComb, Miss.	UFA(Den)-'07	16/16
25	Cartwright, Rock	RB	5-8	215	12/3/79	9	Kansas State	Conroe, Texas	FA-'10	16/2*
59	Condo, Jon	LS/LB	6-3	250	8/26/81	5	Maryland	Philipsburg, Pa.	FA-'06	16/0
78	Cooper, Chris	DT	6-5	285	2/27/77	8	Nebraska-Omaha	Lincoln, Neb.	FA-'10	0*
50	Ekejiuba, Isaiah	LB	6-4	240	10/5/81	6	Virginia	Somerset, N.J.	FA-'05	16/0
31	Eugene, Hiram	S	6-2	200	11/24/80	5	Louisiana Tech	Jeanerette, La.	FA-'06	14/4
13	Figurs, Yamon	WR	5-11	185	1/10/82	4	Kansas State	Fort Pierce, Fla.	FA-'10	6/0*
3	Frye, Charlie	QB	6-4	220	8/28/81	6	Akron	Willard, Ohio	UFA(Sea)-'09	3/3
76	Gallery, Robert	G	6-7	325	7/26/80	7	Iowa	Masonville, Iowa	D1-'04	6/6
5	Gradkowski, Bruce	QB	6-1	220	1/27/83	5	Toledo	Pittsburgh, Pa.	W(Cle)-'09	7/4
52	t- Groves, Quentin	LB	6-3	265	7/5/84	3	Auburn	Greenville, Miss.	T(Jax)-'10	16/7*
97	Gunheim, Greyson	DE	6-5	265	4/4/86	3	Washington	Sebastopol. Calif.	D4-'09	0*
75	Henderson, Mario	T	6-7	300	10/29/84	4	Florida State	Lehigh Acres, Fla.	D3-'07	16/16
85	Heyward-Bey, Darrius	WR	6-2	210	2/26/87	2	Maryland	Owings Mills, Md.	D1-'09	11/11
15	Higgins, Johnnie Lee	WR	5-11	185	9/8/83	4	Texas-El Paso	Sweeny, Texas	D3-'07	15/5
17	Holland , Jonathan	WR	6-1	195	6/18/85	3	Louisiana Tech	Archibald, La.	D7-'07	14/0
53	Howard, Thomas	LB	6-3	240	7/14/83	5	Texas-El Paso	Lubbock, Texas	D2-'06	16/15
24	Huff, Michael	S	6-1	205	3/6/83	5	Texas	Irving, Texas	D1-'06	16/12
11	Janikowski, Sebastian	K	6-2	250	3/2/78	11	Florida State	Daytona Beach, Fla.	D1-'00	16/0
37	Johnson, Chris	CB	6-1	200	9/25/79	7	Louisville	Longview, Texas	UFA(KC)-'07	15/15
94	Joseph, William	DT	6-5	310	9/3/79	7	Miami	Miami, Fla.	FA-'09	6/0
93	Kelly, Tommy	DT	6-6	300	12/27/80	7	Mississippi State	Jackson, Miss.	FA-'04	16/16
44	Lawton, Luke	FB	6-0	240	8/26/80	5	McNeese State	New Iberia, La.	FA-'08	13/3
9	Lechler, Shane	P	6-2	225	8/7/76	11	Texas A&M	Sealy, Texas	D5-'00	16/0
	+Losman, J.P.	QB	6-2	210	3/12/81	7	Tulane	Venice, Calif.	FA-'09	1/0
20	McFadden, Darren	RB	6-2	210	8/27/87	3	Arkansas	North Little Rock, Ark.	D1-'08	12/7
89	Miller, Nick	WR	5-9	180	3/29/87	2	Southern Utah	Mesa, Ariz.	FA-'09	0*
80	Miller, Zach	TE	6-5	255	12/11/85	4	Arizona State	Phoenix, Ariz.	D2-'07	15/15
34	Mitchell, Mike	S	6-1	220	6/10/87	2	Ohio	Florence, Ky.	D2-'09	16/0
51	Morris, Chris	C/G	6-4	305	2/2/83	5	Michigan State	Temperance, Mich.	D7-'06	16/10
18	Murphy, Louis	WR	6-2	200	5/11/87	2	Florida	St. Petersburg, Fla.	D4-'09	16/9
83	Myers, Brandon	TE	6-4	250	9/4/85	2	Iowa	Iowa City, Iowa	D6-'09	11/2
56	Nixon, David	LB	6-3	235	3/16/85	2	Brigham Young	College Station, Texas	FA-'09	3/0
58	Norris, Slade	LB	6-2	245	10/25/85	2	Oregon State	Portland, Ore.	D4-'09	4/0
82	Owens, John	TE	6-3	255	1/10/80	9	Notre Dame	Hyattsville, Md.	FA-'10	16/3*
72	Pears, Erik	T	6-8	305	4/21/82	5	Colorado State	Denver, Colo.	UFA(Den)-'09	12/4
45	Reece, Marcel	FB	6-2	240	6/23/85	2	Washington	Hesperia, Calif.	FA-'08	2/0
98	Richardson, Jay	DE	6-6	280	1/27/84	4	Ohio State	Washington, D.C.	D5-'07	16/0
26	Routt, Stanford	CB	6-1	195	7/26/83	6	Houston	Austin, Texas	D2-'05	16/1
22	+Russell, Gary	RB	5-11	215	9/8/86	4	Minnesota	Columbus, Ohio	FA-'09	12/4
64	Satele, Samson	C	6-3	300	11/29/84	4	Hawaii	Kailua, Hawaii	T(Mia)-'09	16/12
81	Schilens, Chaz	WR	6-4	225	11/7/85	3	San Diego State	Mesa, Ariz.	D7-'08	8/8
91	Scott, Trevor	DE	6-5	255	8/30/84	3	Buffalo	Potsdam, N.Y.	D6-'08	16/6
92	Seymour, Richard	DE	6-6	310	10/6/79	10	Georgia	Gadsden, S.C.	T(NE)-'09	16/16
77	Shaughnessy, Matt	DE	6-5	270	9/23/86	2	Wisconsin	Norwich, Conn.	D3-'09	16/2
86	Stewart, Tony	TE	6-5	260	8/9/79	10	Penn State	Allentown, Pa.	UFA(Cin)-'07	15/4
36	Thomas, Joey	CB	6-1	190	8/29/80	5	Montana State	Seattle, Wash.	FA-'10	0*
70	Walker, Langston	T	6-8	360	9/3/79	9	California	Oakland, Calif.	FA-'09	7/2
19	Watkins, Todd	WR	6-3	195	6/22/83	3	Brigham Young	La Mesa, Calif.	FA-'08	13/1
54	Williams, Sam	LB	6-5	260	7/28/80	8	Fresno State	Clayton, Calif.	D3-'03	16/2
96	t- Wimbley, Kamerion	LB	6-4	255	10/13/83	5	Florida State	Wichita, Kan.	T(Cle)-10	15/15*

* Bennett played 6 games for San Diego in '09; Bodiford missed '08 season with Green Bay because of injury; Boller played 7 games for St. Louis; Campbell played 16 games for Washington; Cartwright played 16 games for Washington; Cooper missed '08 season with Seattle because of injury; Figurs played 3 games for Detroit and 3 games for Tampa Bay; Groves played 16 games for Jacksonville; Gunheim inactive for 1 game; N. Miller inactive for 15 games; Owens played 16 games for Seattle; Thomas last active with Miami in '08; Wimbley played 15 games for Cleveland.

\+ Restricted free agent; subject to developments.

t- Raiders traded for Campbell (Wash), Groves (Jax), Wimbley (Cle).

Traded—LB Kirk Morrison (16 games in '09) to Jacksonville.

Players lost through free agency (1): T Cornell Green (Buff; 12 games in '09).

Also played with Raiders in '09—LB Jon Alston (9 games), CB John Bowie (3), DE Greg Ellis (14), RB Justin Fargas (12), G Paul McQuistan (3), CB Justin Miller (1), RB Oren O'Neal (4), RB Louis Rankin (2), QB JaMarcus Russell (12), WR Javon Walker (3), DT Gerard Warren (16).

2010 FIRST-YEAR ROSTER

Name	Pos.	Ht.	Wt.	Birthdate	College	Hometown	How Acq.
Brown, Stevie	S	5-11	215	7/17/87	Michigan	Columbus, Ind.	D7
Campbell, Bruce	G	6-6	315	5/25/88	Maryland	Hamden, Conn.	D4
Daniels, Alex	DE	6-4	260	11/27/86	Cincinnati	Columbus, Ohio	FA
Ford, Jacoby	WR	5-9	185	7/27/87	Clemson	Royal Palm Beach, Fla.	D4
Goethel, Travis	LB	6-2	240	7/27/87	Arizona State	Vista, Calif.	D6
Heard, Kellen	DT	6-6	355	10/17/85	Memphis	Wharton, Texas	FA
Houston, Lamarr	DE	6-3	305	6/24/87	Texas	Colorado Springs, Colo.	D2
Hubbard, Paul	WR	6-2	225	6/12/85	Wisconsin	Colorado Springs, Colo.	FA
McClain, Rolando	LB	6-3	255	7/14/89	Alabama	Decatur, Ala.	D1
McFadden, Walter	CB	5-10	180	1/21/87	Auburn	Pompano Beach, Fla.	D5
Moline, Chane	FB	6-0	250	7/23/87	UCLA	Mission Viejo, Calif.	FA
Parsons, Alex	OL	6-4	300	9/14/87	Southern California	Irvine, Calif.	FA
Rodd, Brandon	G	6-4	305	11/1/85	Arizona State	Aiea, Hawaii	FA
Tonga, Manase	FB	5-11	245	2/28/84	Brigham Young	San Mateo, Calif.	FA
Veldheer, Jared	T	6-8	315	6/14/87	Hillsdale	Grand Rapids, Mich.	D3
Ware, Jeremy	CB	5-10	185	9/18/86	Michigan State	Fort Myers, Fla.	D7
Waters, Swayze	K	5-11	180	5/18/87	Alabama-Birmingham	Jackson, Miss.	FA

The term NFL Rookie is defined as a player who is in his first season of professional football and has not been on the roster of another professional football team for any regular-season or postseason games. A Rookie is designated by an "R" on NFL rosters. Players who have been active in another professional football league or players who have NFL experience, including either preseason training camp or being on an Active List or Inactive List, or on Reserve/Injured or Reserve/Physically Unable to Perform for fewer than six regular-season games, are termed NFL First-Year Players. An NFL First-Year Player is designated by a "1" on NFL rosters. Thereafter, a player is credited with an additional year of experience for each season in which he accumulates six games on the Active List or Inactive List, or on Reserve/Injured or Reserve/Physically Unable to Perform.

Log on to www.raiders.com for an up-to-date roster.

OAKLAND RAIDERS

COACHING STAFF

Head Coach,
Tom Cable

Pro Career: Named interim head coach following four regular season games in 2008 season, then became 17th head coach in Raiders history in February 2009. Cable was offensive line coach of the Oakland Raiders from 2007-08, where in 2007 he coached a unit that contributed to the Silver and Black finishing sixth in the NFL in both rushing and Inside-the-20 touchdown percentage. He was offensive line coach for the Atlanta Falcons in 2006, where he tutored a unit that helped the Falcons lead the NFL in rushing. Career record: 9-19.

Background: Offensive lineman Idaho 1982-86. College coach: Idaho 1987-88, San Diego State 1989, Cal State-Fullerton 1990, Nevada-Las Vegas 1991, California 1992-97, Colorado 1998-99, Idaho 2000-03 (head coach 2001-03), UCLA 2004-05. He was offensive coordinator and offensive line coach at UCLA from 2004-05, where he helped develop one of the most productive offensive units in the nation. In 2005, coordinated a UCLA offense that averaged 431 yards in total offense per game while earning 10 wins and a bowl berth. In 2004, the Bruins on offense under Cable improved by over 1,000 yards from the previous season while averaging 410 yards per game. Cable was head coach of the University of Idaho from 2001-03. During his tenure at Idaho, his teams averaged 424.1 yards of total offense per game. He spent two years at the University of Colorado. In 1998, he served as the offensive line coach and the following year was promoted to offensive coordinator. Under his direction, the Buffaloes' offense was ranked 14th in the nation in 1999, averaging 424.9 yards per game. Spent six seasons (1992-97) as offensive line coach at the University of California, where he tutored four first team All-Pac-10 selections.

Personal: Born November 26, 1964, in Merced, Calif. Cable and his wife Carol have four children—Ryan, Amanda, Alexander, and Zachery.

ASSISTANT COACHES

John Fassel, special teams coordinator; born January 10, 1974, Anaheim, Calif. Wide receiver/quarterback Pacific 1994-95, Weber State 1996-98. No pro playing experience. College coach: Bucknell 1999, 2001, Idaho State 2000, New Mexico Highlands 2002-03. Pro coach: Amsterdam Admirals (NFLE) 2000, Baltimore Ravens 2005-07; joined Raiders in 2008.

Paul Hackett, quarterbacks; born July 5, 1947, Burlington, Vt. Quarterback Cal-Davis 1965-68. No pro playing experience. College coach: Cal-Davis 1969-1971, California 1972-75, Southern California 1976-1980, 1998-2000 (head coach 1998-2000), Pittsburgh 1989-1992 (head coach 1990-92). Pro coach: Cleveland Browns 1981-82, San Francisco 49ers 1983-85, Dallas Cowboys 1986-88, Kansas City Chiefs 1993-97, New York Jets 2001-04, Tampa Bay Buccaneers 2005-07, joined Raiders in 2008.

Mike Haluchak, linebackers; born Nov. 28, 1949, Concord, Calif. Linebacker Southern California 1967-1970. No pro playing experience. College coach: Southern California 1976-77, Cal State-Fullerton 1978, Pacific 1979-1980, California 1981, North Carolina State 1982. Pro coach: Oakland Invaders (USFL) 1983-85, San Diego Chargers 1986-1991, Cincinnati Bengals 1992-93, Washington Redskins 1994-96, New York Giants 1997-99, St. Louis Rams 2000-02, Jacksonville Jaguars 2003-04, Cleveland Browns 2005-08, joined Raiders in 2009.

Adam Henry, tight ends; born April 27, 1972, Beaumont, Texas. Wide receiver McNeese State 1992-93. Pro receiver New Orleans Saints 1995. College coach: McNeese State 1996-2006. Pro coach: Joined Raiders in 2007.

Hue Jackson, offensive coordinator; born October 22, 1965, Los Angeles. Quarterback Pacific 1985-86. No pro playing experience. College coach: Pacific 1987-89, Cal State-Fullerton 1990, Arizona State 1992-95, California 1996, Southern California 1997-2000. Pro coach: London Monarchs (WFL) 1991, Washington Redskins 2001-03, Cincinnati Bengals 2004-06, Atlanta Falcons 2007, Baltimore Ravens 2008, joined Raiders in 2010.

Sanjay Lal, wide receivers; born July 23, 1969, London, England. Wide receiver UCLA 1989, Washington 1990-92. Pro wide receiver St. Louis Rams 1998, Scottish Claymores (World League) 1999. College coach: Los Medanos (Calif.) College 2003, Saint Mary's College 2004, California 2005-06, joined Raiders in 2007.

John Marshall, defensive coordinator; born October 2, 1945, Arroyo Grande, Calif. Linebacker Washington State 1964. No pro playing experience. College coach: Oregon 1970-76, Southern California 1977-79. Pro coach: Green Bay Packers 1980-82, Indianapolis Colts 1986-88, San Francisco 49ers 1989-1998, Carolina Panthers 1999-2001, Detroit Lions 2002, Seattle Seahawks 2003-08, joined Raiders in 2009.

Jim Michalczik, offensive line; born June 7, 1966, Port Angeles, Wash. Offensive lineman Washington State 1995-1998. Pro offensive lineman Arizona Cardinals 1989. College coach: Miami 1990-91, Montana State 1992-98, Oregon State 1999-2001, California 2002-08, Washington 2009. Pro coach: Joined Raiders in 2009.

Chris Morgan, asst. offensive line; born September 24 1976, Killeen, Texas. Offensive lineman Colorado 1996-99. No pro playing experience. College coach: Idaho 2003. Pro coach: Joined Raiders in 2009.

Brad Roll, strength & conditioning; July 4, 1958, Houston. Center Blinn (Tex.) J.C. 1976-77, Stephen F. Austin 1978-79. No pro playing experience. College coach: Stephen F. Austin 1980, Southwestern Louisiana 1981-86, Kansas 1987-88, Miami 1989-1992. Pro coach: Tampa Bay Buccaneers 1993-95, Miami Dolphins 1996-2003, Buffalo Bills 2004-05, St. Louis Rams 2006-07, joined Raiders in 2008.

Kevin Ross, defensive assistant; born January 16, 1962, Camden, N.J. Defensive back Temple 1980-83. Pro defensive back Kansas City Chiefs 1984-1993, 1997, Atlanta Falcons 1994-95, San Diego Chargers 1996. Pro coach: Minnesota Vikings 2003-05, San Diego Chargers 2007-08, joined Raiders in 2010.

Kelly Skipper, tight ends; born July 25, 1967, Brawley, Calif. Running back Fresno State 1985-88. No pro playing experience. College coach: Fresno State 1989-1997, UCLA 1998-2002, Washington State 2003-06. Pro coach: Joined Raiders in 2007.

Ted Tollner, passing game coordinator; born May 29, 1940, San Francisco, Calif. Quarterback Cal Poly-San Luis Obispo 1959-61. No pro playing experience. College coach: College of San Mateo 1971-72 (head coach), San Diego State 1973-1980, 1994-2001 (head coach 1994-2001), Brigham Young 1981, Southern California 1982-86 (head coach 1983-86). Pro coach: Buffalo Bills 1987-88, San Diego Chargers 1989-1991, San Francisco 2002-04, Detroit Lions 2005, San Francisco 49ers 2007-08, joined Raiders in 2009.

Lionel Washington, defensive backs; born October 21, 1960, New Orleans. Defensive back Tulane 1979-1982. Pro defensive back St. Louis Cardinals 1983-86, Los Angeles/Oakland Raiders 1987-1994, 1997, Denver Broncos 1995-96. Pro coach: Green Bay Packers 1999-2008, joined Raiders in 2009.

Mike Waufle, defensive line; born June 27, 1954, Hornell, N.Y. U.S. Marines 1972-75. Defensive lineman Bakersfield (Calif.) J.C. 1975-76, Utah State 1977-78. No pro playing experience. College coach: Alfred 1979, Utah State 1980-84, Fresno State 1985-88, UCLA 1989, Oregon State 1990-91, California 1992-97. Pro coach: Oakland Raiders 1998-2003, New York Giants 2004-09, re-joined Raiders in 2010.

American Football Conference
North Division
Team Colors: Black and Gold
3400 South Water Street
Pittsburgh, Pennsylvania 15203
Telephone: (412) 432-7800

2010 SCHEDULE

PRESEASON

Aug. 14	**Detroit**	7:30
Aug. 21	at New York Giants	7:00
Aug. 29	at Denver	6:00
Sep. 2	**Carolina**	7:30

REGULAR SEASON

Sep. 12	**Atlanta**	1:00
Sep. 19	at Tennessee	12:00
Sep. 26	at Tampa Bay	1:00
Oct. 3	**Baltimore**	1:00
Oct. 10	BYE	
Oct. 17	**Cleveland**	1:00
Oct. 24	at Miami	1:00
Oct. 31	at New Orleans	7:20
Nov. 8	at Cincinnati (Mon)	8:30
Nov. 14	**New England**	8:20
Nov. 21	**Oakland**	1:00
Nov. 28	at Buffalo	1:00
Dec. 5	at Baltimore	* 8:20
Dec. 12	**Cincinnati**	1:00
Dec. 19	**New York Jets**	4:15
Dec. 23	**Carolina** (Thu)	8:20
Jan. 2	at Cleveland	1:00

** Sunday night games in Weeks 11-17 subject to change*

Stadium: Heinz Field (opened in 2001)
• **Capacity:** 65,050
100 Art Rooney Avenue
Pittsburgh, Pennsylvania 15212
Playing Surface: DD GrassMaster
Training Camp: St. Vincent College
Latrobe, PA 15650

HEINZ FIELD

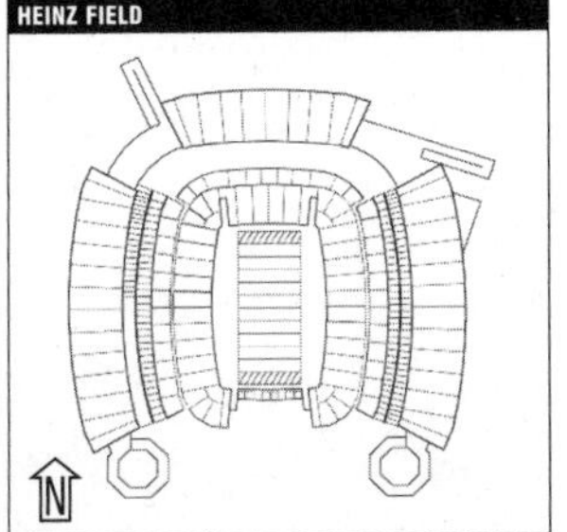

CLUB OFFICIALS

Chairman: Daniel M. Rooney
President: Arthur J. Rooney II
Vice President: John R. McGinley
Vice President: Arthur J. Rooney Jr.
Administration Advisor: Charles H. Noll
Director of Planning & Development: Mark Hart
Director of Finance: Bob Tyler
Director of Business & Administration: Omar Khan
Director of Football Operations: Kevin Colbert
College Scouting Coordinator: Ron Hughes
Pro Scouting Coordinator: Brandon Hunt
Head Athletic Trainer: John Norwig
Director of Marketing: Tony Quatrini
Communications Coordinator: Dave Lockett
Public Relations/Media Manager: Burt Lauten
Director of Stadium Management: Jim Sacco
Video Coordinator: Bob McCartney
Human Relations/Office Coordinator: Geraldine Glenn
Ticket Manager: Ben Lentz

COACHING HISTORY

Pittsburgh Pirates 1933-39
(565-528-21)
Records include postseason games

1933	Forrest (Jap) Douds	3-6-2
1934	Luby DiMelio	2-10-0
1935-36	Joe Bach	10-14-0
1937-39	Johnny (Blood) McNally*	6-19-0
1939-1940	Walt Kiesling	3-13-3
1941	Bert Bell**	0-2-0
	Aldo (Buff) Donelli***	0-5-0
1941-44	Walt Kiesling****	13-20-2
1945	Jim Leonard	2-8-0
1946-47	Jock Sutherland	13-10-1
1948-1951	Johnny Michelosen	20-26-2
1952-53	Joe Bach	11-13-0
1954-56	Walt Kiesling	14-22-0
1957-1964	Raymond (Buddy) Parker	51-47-6
1965	Mike Nixon	2-12-0
1966-68	Bill Austin	11-28-3
1969-1991	Chuck Noll	209-156-1
1992-2006	Bill Cowher	161-99-1
2007-09	Mike Tomlin	34-17-0

*Released after three games in 1939
**Resigned after two games in 1941
***Released after five games in 1941
****Co-coach with Earle (Greasy) Neale in Philadelphia-Pittsburgh merger in 1943 and with Phil Handler in Chicago Cardinals-Pittsburgh merger in 1944

PAID ATTENDANCE

Home 517,599 Away 526,483
Total 1,044,082
Single-game home record, 64,965 (10/26/08)
Single-season home record, 517,599 (2009)

2010 DRAFT CHOICES

Round	Name	Pos.	College
1	Maurkice Pouncey	C	Florida
2	Jason Worilds	LB	Virginia Tech
3	Emmanuel Sanders	WR	Southern Methodist
4	Thaddeus Gibson	LB	Ohio State
5	Chris Scott	T	Tennessee
	Crezdon Butler	DB	Clemson
	Stevenson Sylvester	LB	Utah
6	Jonathan Dwyer	RB	Georgia Tech
	Antonio Brown	WR	Central Michigan
7	Doug Worthington	DT	Ohio State

PITTSBURGH STEELERS

2009 TEAM RECORD

PRESEASON (3-1)

Date	Result	Opponent
8/13	W 20-10	Arizona
8/22	L 13-17	at Washington
8/29	W 17-0	Buffalo
9/3	W 21-10	at Carolina

REGULAR SEASON (9-7)

Date	Result	Opponent
9/10	W 13-10	Tennessee (OT)
9/20	L 14-17	at Chicago
9/27	L 20-23	at Cincinnati
10/4	W 38-28	San Diego
10/11	W 28-20	at Detroit
10/18	W 27-14	Cleveland
10/25	W 27-17	Minnesota
11/9	W 28-10	at Denver
11/15	L 12-18	Cincinnati
11/22	L 24-27	at Kansas City (OT)
11/29	L 17-20	at Baltimore (OT)
12/6	L 24-27	Oakland
12/10	L 6-13	at Cleveland
12/20	W 37-36	Green Bay
12/27	W 23-20	Baltimore
1/3	W 30-24	at Miami

(OT) Overtime

SCORE BY PERIODS

Steelers	81	126	61	97	3 —	368
Opponents	52	75	56	135	6 —	324

2009 TEAM STATISTICS

	Steelers	Opp.
Total First Downs	331	274
Rushing	96	70
Passing	210	186
Penalty	25	18
3rd Down: Made/Att	80/203	96/227
3rd Down Pct.	39.4	42.3
4th Down: Made/Att	8/12	7/10
4th Down Pct.	66.7	70.0
Possession Avg.	32:13	27:47
Total Net Yards	5941	4885
Avg. Per Game	371.3	305.3
Total Plays	1014	967
Avg. Per Play	5.9	5.1
Net Yards Rushing	1793	1438
Avg. Per Game	112.1	89.9
Total Rushes	428	372
Net Yards Passing	4148	3447
Avg. Per Game	259.3	215.4
Sacked/Yards Lost	50/348	47/314
Gross Yards	4496	3761
Att./Completions	536/351	548/319
Completion Pct.	65.5	58.2
Had Intercepted	14	12
Punts/Average	72/42.7	86/42.8
Net Punting Avg.	72/37.1	86/37.8
Penalties/Yards	85/769	102/903
Fumbles/Ball Lost	21/11	21/10
Touchdowns	41	37
Rushing	10	7
Passing	28	22
Returns	3	8

2009 INDIVIDUAL STATISTICS

PASSING	Att.	Comp.	Yds.	Pct.	TD	Int.	Tkld.	Rate
Roethlisberger	506	337	4328	66.6	26	12	50/348	100.5
Dixon	26	12	145	46.2	1	1	0/0	60.6
Batch	2	1	17	50.0	0	0	0/0	79.2
Moore	1	1	6	100.0	1	0	0/0	131.3
Holmes	1	0	0	0.0	0	1	0/0	0.0
Steelers	536	351	4496	65.5	28	14	50/348	98.1
Opponents	548	319	3761	58.2	22	12	47/314	83.4

SCORING	TD R	TD P	TD Rt	PAT	FG	Saf	PTS
Reed	0	0	0	41/41	27/31	0	122
Mendenhall	7	1	0	0/0	0/0	0	48
Miller	0	6	0	0/0	0/0	0	36
Wallace	0	6	0	0/0	0/0	0	36
Ward	0	6	0	0/0	0/0	0	36
Holmes	0	5	0	0/0	0/0	0	30
Moore	0	2	0	0/0	0/0	0	12
Roethlisberger	2	0	0	0/0	0/0	0	12
Carter	0	0	1	0/0	0/0	0	6
Dixon	1	0	0	0/0	0/0	0	6
Fox	0	0	1	0/0	0/0	0	6
Parker	0	1	0	0/0	0/0	0	6
Spaeth	0	1	0	0/0	0/0	0	6
Woodley	0	0	1	0/0	0/0	0	6
Steelers	10	28	3	41/41	27/31	0	368
Opponents	7	22	8	32/32	22/29	0	324

2-Pt. Conversions: Steelers 0-0, Opponents 2-5.

RUSHING	No.	Yds	Avg	LG	TD
Mendenhall	242	1108	4.6	60	7
Parker	98	389	4.0	34	0
Moore	35	118	3.4	15	0
Roethlisberger	40	82	2.1	15	2
Wallace	5	48	9.6	21	0
Dixon	3	27	9.0	24t	1
Davis	2	15	7.5	14	0
Holmes	3	6	2.0	7	0
Steelers	428	1793	4.2	60	10
Opponents	372	1438	3.9	37	7

RECEIVING	No.	Yds	Avg	LG	TD
Ward	95	1167	12.3	54	6
Holmes	79	1248	15.8	57	5
Miller	76	789	10.4	41	6
Wallace	39	756	19.4	60t	6
Mendenhall	25	261	10.4	26	1
Moore	21	153	7.3	19t	2
Parker	6	64	10.7	27t	1
Spaeth	5	25	5.0	9	1
Da. Johnson	2	9	4.5	5	0
Grisham	1	14	14.0	14	0
Logan	1	5	5.0	5	0
Sweed	1	5	5.0	5	0
Steelers	351	4496	12.8	60t	28
Opponents	319	3761	11.8	83t	22

INTERCEPTIONS	No.	Yds	Avg	LG	TD
Polamalu	3	17	5.7	16	0
Clark	3	0	0.0	0	0
Carter	2	53	26.5	48t	1
Fox	1	82	82.0	82t	1
Taylor	1	20	20.0	20	0
Farrior	1	18	18.0	18	0
Townsend	1	-1	-1.0	-1	0
Steelers	12	189	15.8	82t	2
Opponents	14	398	28.4	94	2

PUNTING	No.	Yds.	Avg.	In 20	LG
Sepulveda	72	3074	42.7	29	60
Steelers	72	3074	42.7	29	60
Opponents	86	3684	42.8	28	63

PUNT RETURNS	Ret	FC	Yds	Avg	LG	TD
Logan	30	15	280	9.3	25	0
Moore	3	9	3	1.0	2	0
Holmes	2	1	6	3.0	3	0
J. Harrison	1	0	1	1.0	1	0
Steelers	36	25	290	8.1	25	0
Opponents	33	18	325	9.8	55	0

KICKOFF RETURNS	No.	Yds	Avg	LG	TD
Logan	55	1466	26.7	83	0
Moore	4	44	11.0	13	0
Burnett	3	23	7.7	13	0
Wallace	1	26	26.0	26	0
Davis	1	13	13.0	13	0
Mendenhall	1	8	8.0	8	0
Spaeth	1	1	1.0	1	0
Steelers	66	1581	24.0	83	0
Opponents	74	1795	24.3	98t	4

FIELD GOALS	1-19	20-29	30-39	40-49	50+
Reed	1/1	7/7	15/16	4/5	0/2
Steelers	1/1	7/7	15/16	4/5	0/2
Opponents	1/1	9/9	4/7	8/9	0/3

SACKS	No.
Woodley	13.5
J. Harrison	10.0
Timmons	7.0
Farrior	3.0
Keisel	3.0
Hampton	2.5
Smith	2.0
Carter	1.0
Gay	1.0
Hood	1.0
Kirschke	1.0
Taylor	1.0
(group)	1.0
Steelers	47.0
Opponents	50.0

RECORD HOLDERS

INDIVIDUAL RECORDS—CAREER

Category	Name	Performance
Rushing (Yds.)	Franco Harris, 1972-1983	11,950
Passing (Yds.)	Terry Bradshaw, 1970-1983	27,989
Passing (TDs)	Terry Bradshaw, 1970-1983	212
Receiving (No.)	Hines Ward, 1998-2009	895
Receiving (Yds.)	Hines Ward, 1998-2009	10,947
Interceptions	Mel Blount, 1970-1983	57
Punting (Avg.)	Bobby Joe Green, 1960-61	45.7
Punt Return (Avg.)	Bobby Gage, 1949-1950	14.9
Kickoff Return (Avg.)	Lynn Chandnois, 1950-56	29.6
Field Goals	Gary Anderson, 1982-1994	309
Touchdowns (Tot.)	Franco Harris, 1972-1983	100
Points	Gary Anderson, 1982-1994	1,343
*Sacks	Jason Gildon, 1994-2003	77.0

INDIVIDUAL RECORDS—SINGLE SEASON

Category	Name	Performance
Rushing (Yds.)	Barry Foster, 1992	1,690
Passing (Yds.)	Ben Roethlisberger, 2009	4,328
Passing (TDs)	Ben Roethlisberger, 2007	32
Receiving (No.)	Hines Ward, 2002	112
Receiving (Yds.)	Yancey Thigpen, 1997	1,398
Interceptions	Mel Blount, 1975	11
Punting (Avg.)	Bobby Joe Green, 1961	47.0
Punt Return (Avg.)	Bobby Gage, 1949	16.0
Kickoff Return (Avg.)	Lynn Chandnois, 1952	35.2
Field Goals	Norm Johnson, 1995	34
Touchdowns (Tot.)	Willie Parker, 2006	16
Points	Norm Johnson, 1995	141
*Sacks	James Harrison, 2008	16.0

INDIVIDUAL RECORDS—SINGLE GAME

Category	Name	Performance
Rushing (Yds.)	Willie Parker, 12-7-06	223
Passing (Yds.)	Ben Roethlisberger, 12-20-09	503
Passing (TDs)	Terry Bradshaw, 11-15-81	5
	Mark Malone, 9-8-85	5
	Ben Roethlisberger, 11-5-07	5
Receiving (No.)	Courtney Hawkins, 11-1-98	14
Receiving (Yds.)	Plaxico Burress, 11-10-02	253
Interceptions	Jack Butler, 12-13-53	**4
Field Goals	Gary Anderson, 10-23-88	6
	Jeff Reed, 12-1-02	6
Touchdowns (Tot.)	Ray Mathews, 10-17-54	4
	Roy Jefferson, 11-3-68	4
Points	Ray Mathews, 10-17-54	24
	Roy Jefferson, 11-3-68	24
*Sacks	Chad Brown, 10-13-96	4.5

**Sacks became an official statistic in 1982.*
***NFL Record*

PITTSBURGH STEELERS

2010 VETERAN ROSTER

No.	Name	Pos.	Ht.	Wt.	Birthdate	NFL Exp.	College	Hometown	How Acq.	'09 Games/ Starts
26	Allen, Will	S	6-1	200	6/16/78	7	Ohio State	Dayton, Ohio	UFA(TB)-'10	8/2*
55	Bailey, Patrick	LB	6-4	235	11/18/81	3	Duke	Elmendorf, Texas	FA-'08	16/0
16	Batch, Charlie	QB	6-2	216	12/4/70	13	Eastern Michigan	Homestead, Pa.	FA-'02	1/0
81	Battle, Arnaz	WR	6-1	208	2/21/76	8	Notre Dame	Dallas, Texas	UFA(SF)-'10	15/0*
27	Burnett, Joe	CB	5-10	192	11/27/82	2	Central Florida	Eustis, Fla.	D5a-'09	15/0
25	Clark, Ryan	S	5-11	205	10/11/75	9	Louisiana State	Marrero, La.	UFA(Wash)-'06	15/15
74	Colon, Willie	T	6-3	315	4/8/79	5	Hofstra	Bronx, N.Y.	D4a-'06	16/16
10	Dixon, Dennis	QB	6-3	209	1/10/81	3	Oregon	San Leandro, Calif.	D5-'08	1/1
93	Eason, Nick	DE	6-3	305	5/28/76	8	Clemson	Lyons, Ga.	FA-'07	8/5
79	Essex, Trai	G/T	6-5	324	12/4/78	6	Northwestern	Fort Wayne, Ind.	D3-'05	16/16
51	Farrior, James	LB	6-2	243	1/5/71	14	Virginia	Ettrick, Va.	UFA(NYJ)-'02	16/16
50	Foote, Larry	LB	6-1	239	6/11/76	9	Michigan	Detroit, Mich.	UFA(Det)-'10	14/14*
73	Foster, Ramon	T	6-6	325	1/6/82	2	Tennessee	Henning, Tenn.	FA-'09	14/4
57	Fox, Keyaron	LB	6-3	235	1/23/78	7	Georgia Tech	Atlanta, Ga.	UFA(KC)-'08	16/3
54	Frazier, Andre	LB	6-5	245	6/28/78	6	Cincinnati	Cincinnati, Ohio	FA-'07	14/0
22	Gay, William	CB	5-10	190	12/31/80	4	Louisville	Tallahassee, Fla.	D5b-'07	16/14
98	Hampton, Casey	NT	6-1	325	9/2/73	10	Texas	Galveston, Texas	D1-'01	16/16
77	Harris, Ra'Shon	DE	6-5	300	8/25/82	2	Oregon	Pensacola, Fla.	D6-'09	0*
31	Harris, Tuff	S	6-0	198	1/22/79	4	Montana	Colstrip, Mont.	FA-'09	0*
92	Harrison, James	LB	6-0	242	5/3/74	7	Kent State	Akron, Ohio	FA-'04	16/16
62	Hartwig, Justin	C	6-5	312	11/20/74	9	Kansas	Mankato, Minn.	UFA(Car)-'08	16/16
66	Hills, Tony	T	6-5	304	11/3/80	3	Texas	Houston, Texas	D4-'08	1/0
76	Hoke, Chris	NT	6-2	305	4/5/72	9	Brigham Young	Long Beach, Calif.	FA-'01	16/0
96	Hood, Ziggy	DE	6-3	300	2/15/83	2	Missouri	Amarillo, Texas	D1-'09	16/0
85	Johnson, David	TE	6-2	260	8/25/83	2	Arkansas State	Pine Bluff, Ala.	D7b-'09	15/3
99	Keisel, Brett	DE	6-5	285	9/18/74	9	Brigham Young	Greybull, Wyo.	D7b-'02	15/15
68	Kemoeatu, Chris	G	6-3	344	1/3/79	6	Utah	Kahuka, Hawaii	D6-'05	12/12
4	t- Leftwich, Byron	QB	6-5	250	1/13/76	8	Marshall	Washington, D.C.	T(TB)-'10	3/3*
64	Legursky, Doug	C	6-1	315	6/8/82	2	Marshall	Beckley, W.Va.	FA-'08	9/0
20	Lewis, Keenan	CB	6-0	208	5/16/82	2	Oregon State	New Orleans, La.	D3c-'09	4/0
11	Logan, Stefan	WR	5-6	180	6/1/77	2	South Dakota	Miami, Fla.	FA-'09	16/1
15	London, Brandon	WR	6-4	210	10/15/80	2	Massachusetts	Richmond, Va.	FA-'10	0*
37	Madison, Anthony	CB	5-9	180	10/7/77	5	Alabama	Thomasville, Ala.	FA-'09	9/0*
	t- McFadden, Bryant	CB	6-0	190	11/20/77	6	Florida State	Hollywood, Fla.	T(Ariz)-'10	16/16*
49	McHugh, Sean	TE	6-5	265	5/26/78	7	Penn State	University Heights, Ohio	FA-'08	0*
34	Mendenhall, Rashard	RB	5-10	225	6/18/83	3	Illinois	Skokie, Ill.	D1-'08	16/12
83	Miller, Heath	TE	6-5	256	10/21/78	6	Virginia	Swords Creek, Va.	D1-'05	16/16
21	Moore, Mewelde	RB	5-11	209	7/23/78	7	Tulane	Hammond, La.	UFA(Minn)-'08	16/0
29	Mundy, Ryan	S	6-1	209	2/10/81	2	West Virginia	Pittsburgh, Pa.	D6b-'08	16/0
71	Paxson, Scott	DT	6-4	292	2/2/79	2	Penn State	Philadelphia, Pa.	FA-'10	0*
30	Pittman, David	DB	5-11	185	10/13/79	4	Northwestern State (La.)	Gramercy, La.	FA-'10	0*
43	Polamalu, Troy	S	5-10	207	4/18/77	8	Southern California	Tenmile, Ore.	D1-'03	5/5
82	Randle El, Antwaan	WR	5-10	185	8/16/75	9	Indiana	Riverdale, Ill.	FA-'10	16/3*
3	Reed, Jeff	K	5-11	225	4/8/75	9	North Carolina	Charlotte, N.C.	FA-'02	16/0
61	Retkofsky, Jared	LS	6-5	260	3/15/79	3	Texas Christian	Austin, Texas	FA-'09	2/0
7	Roethlisberger, Ben	QB	6-5	241	3/1/78	7	Miami (Ohio)	Findlay, Ohio	D1-'04	15/15
72	Scott, Jonathan	T	6-6	318	1/9/79	4	Texas	Dallas, Texas	FA-'10	10/8*
9	Sepulveda, Daniel	P	6-3	230	1/11/80	4	Baylor	Austin, Texas	D4a-'07	16/0
91	Smith, Aaron	DE	6-5	298	4/18/72	12	Northern Colorado	Colorado Springs, Colo.	D4-'99	5/5*
89	Spaeth, Matt	TE	6-7	270	11/23/79	4	Minnesota	St. Michael, Minn.	D3-'07	16/7
78	Starks, Max	T	6-8	345	1/9/78	7	Florida	Orlando, Fla.	D3-'04	16/16
80	Sweed, Limas	WR	6-4	220	12/24/80	3	Texas	Brenham, Texas	D2-'08	9/0
24	Taylor, Ike	CB	6-2	195	5/4/76	8	Louisiana-Lafayette	Gretna, La.	D4-'03	16/16
94	Timmons, Lawrence	LB	6-1	234	5/13/82	4	Florida State	Florence, S.C.	D1-'07	14/13
65	Urbik, Kraig	G	6-5	323	9/22/81	2	Wisconsin	Hudson, Wisc.	D3a-'09	0*
17	Wallace, Mike	WR	6-0	199	7/31/82	2	Mississippi	New Orleans, La.	D3b-'09	16/5
86	Ward, Hines	WR	6-0	205	3/7/72	13	Georgia	Forest Park, Ga.	D3b-'98	16/16
60	Warren, Greg	LS	6-3	252	10/17/77	6	North Carolina	Goldsboro, N.C.	FA-'05	14/0
48	Williams, Renauld	LB	6-0	228	2/22/77	3	Hofstra	Westbury, N.Y.	FA-'10	0*
56	Woodley, LaMarr	LB	6-2	265	11/2/80	4	Michigan	Saginaw, Mich.	D2-'07	16/16

* Allen played 8 games with Tampa Bay in '09; Battle played 15 games with San Francisco; Foote played 14 games with Detroit; L. Harris inactive for 11 games; T. Harris last active with Tennessee in '08; Leftwich played 3 games with Tampa Bay; London last active with Miami in '08; Madison played 4 games with Cleveland and 5 games with Pittsburgh; McFadden played 16 games with Arizona; McHugh missed '09 season because of injury; Paxson last active with Pittsburgh in '08; Pittman last active with New Orleans and Houston in '08; Randle El played 16 games with Washington; Scott played 10 games with Buffalo; Urbik inactive for 16 games; Williams last active with San Francisco in '06.

t- Steelers traded for Leftwich (TB) and McFadden (Ariz).

Traded—WR Santonio Holmes (16 games in '09) to N.Y. Jets.

Players lost through free agency (1): RB Willie Parker (Wash; 14 games in '09).

Also played with Steelers in '09—LB Rocky Boiman (6 games), S Tyrone Carter (16), FB Carey Davis (6), WR Tyler Grisham (4), LB Arnold Harrison (6), DB Corey Ivy (1), DE Travis Kirschke (12), WR Shaun McDonald (4), CB Keiwan Ratliff (8), RB Isaac Redman (1), RB Frank Summers (2), CB Deshea Townsend (16), LB Donovan Woods (1).

2010 FIRST-YEAR ROSTER

Name	Pos.	Ht.	Wt.	Birthdate	College	Hometown	How Acq.
Bright, Eugene (1)	TE	6-4	268	4/17/81	Purdue	Bryn Mawr, Pa.	FA-'09
Brooks, Dorian	G	6-2	306	4/15/83	James Madison	Richmond, Va.	FA
Brown, Antonio	WR	5-10	186	7/9/84	Central Michigan	Miami, Fla.	D6b
Butler, Crezdon	CB	6-0	191	5/25/83	Clemson	Asheville, N.C.	D5b
Chery, Jason (1)	WR	5-10	192	5/30/81	Louisiana-Lafayette	Delray Beach, Fla.	FA-'09
Cromartie-Smith, Da'Mon	S	6-2	210	2/18/83	Texas-El Paso	Riverside, Calif.	FA
Czech, Piotr (1)	K	6-5	210	8/16/82	Wagner	Olesnica, Poland	FA
Doggett, Derrick (1)	LB	6-3	210	12/30/80	Oregon State	San Diego, Calif.	FA
Dwyer, Jonathan	RB	5-11	229	7/25/85	Georgia Tech	Marietta, Ga.	D6a
Gibson, Thaddeus	LB	6-2	243	10/20/83	Ohio State	Euclid, Ohio	D4
Graessle, Adam (1)	P	6-4	215	11/24/80	Pittsburgh	Dublin, Ohio	FA
Grisham, Tyler (1)	WR	5-11	180	6/10/83	Clemson	Birmingham, Ala.	FA-'09
Jolly, Kyle	T	6-6	300	7/21/83	North Carolina	Powhatan, Va.	FA
McLendon, Steve (1)	DT	6-4	280	1/2/82	Troy	Ozark, Ala.	FA-'09
Pouncey, Maurkice	C	6-4	304	7/23/85	Florida	Lakeland, Fla.	D1
Redman, Isaac (1)	RB	6-0	230	11/9/80	Bowie State	Paulsboro, N.J.	FA-'09
Sanders, Emmanuel	WR	5-11	180	3/16/83	Southern Methodist	Bellville, Texas	D3
Scott, Chris	T	6-4	319	8/3/83	Tennessee	Riverdale, Ga.	D5a
Summers, Frank (1)	RB	5-10	240	9/5/81	Nevada-Las Vegas	Oakland, Calif.	D5b-'09
Sylvester, Stevenson	LB	6-2	231	7/17/84	Utah	Las Vegas, Nev.	D5c
Taylor, Demetrius	FB	6-0	273	11/25/82	Virginia Tech	Jacksonville, Fla.	FA
Thompson, Cordarrow	DT	6-2	301	10/1/83	Virginia Tech	Stafford, Va.	FA
Thornton, Justin	S	6-1	213	7/12/83	Kansas	Saint Joseph, Mo.	FA
Vierling, Bradley	C	6-3	290	5/17/82	Vanderbilt	Warminster, Pa.	FA
Vincent, Justin (1)	RB	5-10	219	1/24/79	Louisiana State	Lake Charles, La.	FA-'09
Williams, Johnny (1)	LB	6-2	246	2/19/82	Kentucky	Jacksonville, Fla.	FA-'09
Williams, Trae (1)	CB	5-10	195	1/29/81	South Florida	Plant City, Fla.	FA-'09
Witten, Lindsey	LB	6-4	250	4/27/84	Connecticut	Cleveland, Ohio	FA
Worilds, Jason	LB	6-2	262	3/2/84	Virginia Tech	Carteret, N.J.	D2
Worthington, Doug	DT	6-5	292	8/9/83	Ohio State	Athol Springs, N.Y.	D7

The term NFL Rookie is defined as a player who is in his first season of professional football and has not been on the roster of another professional football team for any regular-season or postseason games. A Rookie is designated by an "R" on NFL rosters. Players who have been active in another professional football league or players who have NFL experience, including either preseason training camp or being on an Active List or Inactive List, or on Reserve/Injured or Reserve/Physically Unable to Perform for fewer than six regular-season games, are termed NFL First-Year Players. An NFL First-Year Player is designated by a "1" on NFL rosters. Thereafter, a player is credited with an additional year of experience for each season in which he accumulates six games on the Active List or Inactive List, or on Reserve/Injured or Reserve/Physically Unable to Perform.

Log on to www.steelers.com for an up-to-date roster.

PITTSBURGH STEELERS

COACHING STAFF

Head Coach,
Mike Tomlin

Pro Career: Named the sixteenth head coach in Steelers history when he replaced Bill Cowher on January 22, 2007. Became the youngest coach (36 years, 323 days) in NFL history to win a Super Bowl when the Steelers defeated the Arizona Cardinals, 27-23, in Super Bowl XLIII on February 1, 2009. The only coach in Steelers' history to win division titles each of his first two seasons, Tomlin's club posted a 9-7 record last season. In 2008, Tomlin directed the Steelers to a 12-4 record, winning his second-consecutive AFC North title. In his first season, Tomlin guided the Steelers to a 10-6 record and their first AFC North title since 2004. Tomlin was the Minnesota Vikings defensive coordinator in 2006 after spending the previous five seasons (2001-05) as defensive backs coach for the Tampa Bay Buccaneers. Tomlin coached one of the top defensive backfields in the NFL for the Buccaneers, culminating with its performance in Super Bowl XXXVII. The secondary recorded four interceptions, returning two for touchdowns to help Tampa Bay capture the franchise's first Super Bowl title. Tomlin served two seasons as the defensive backs coach at the University of Cincinnati (1999-2000) before going to Tampa Bay. Prior to joining the Cincinnati staff, Tomlin had a short stint on the coaching staff at Tennessee-Martin and then spent two seasons at Arkansas State. He spent the 1996 season as a graduate assistant at Memphis. Tomlin began his coaching career in 1995 as wide receivers coach at Virginia Military Institute. Career record: 34-18.

Background: Was a three-year starter at wide receiver at William & Mary (1990-94) and finished his career with 101 receptions for 2,046 yards and a school-record 20 touchdown receptions. A first-team All-Yankee Conference selection in 1994, he established a school record with a 20.2 yards per catch average. Tomlin was a teammate of current Viking Pro Bowl safety Darren Sharper at William and Mary. Graduated in 1994 with a degree in sociology.

Personal: Born in Hampton, Va., on March 15, 1972. He and his wife, Kiya, have two sons, Dino and Mason, and a daughter Harlyn Quinn.

ASSISTANT COACHES

Bruce Arians, offensive coordinator; born October 3, 1952, Paterson, N.J. Quarterback Virginia Tech 1970-74. No pro playing experience. College coach: Virginia Tech 1975-77, Mississippi State 1978-1980, Alabama 1981-82, Temple 1983-88 (head coach), Mississippi State 1993-95, Alabama 1997. Pro coach: Kansas City Chiefs 1989-1992, New Orleans Saints 1996, Indianapolis Colts 1998-2000, Cleveland Browns 2001-03, joined Steelers in 2004.

Keith Butler, linebackers; born May 16, 1956, Anniston, Ala. Linebacker Memphis 1974-77. Pro linebacker Seattle Seahawks 1978-1987. College coach: Memphis 1990-97, Arkansas State 1998. Pro coach: Cleveland Browns 1999-2002, joined Steelers in 2003.

James Daniel, tight ends; born January 17, 1953, Wetumpka, Ala. Guard Alabama State 1970-73. No pro playing experience. College coach: Auburn 1981-1992. Pro coach: New York Giants 1993-96, Atlanta Falcons 1997-2003, joined Steelers in 2004.

Al Everest, special teams; born August 22, 1950, Santa Barbara, Calif. Safety Southern Methodist 1970-71. No pro playing experience. College coach: Southern Methodist 1972, North Texas 1973-74, Cameron University 1974-75. Pro coach: Arizona Cardinals 1996-99, New Orleans Saints 2000-05, San Francisco 49ers 2007-09, joined Steelers in 2010.

Randy Fichtner, quarterbacks; born November 7, 1963, Cleveland. Defensive back Purdue 1982-85. No pro playing experience. College coach: Michigan 1986-87, Southern California 1988, Nevada-Las Vegas 1989, Memphis 1990-93, Purdue 1994-96, Arkansas State 1997-2000, Memphis 2001-06. Pro coach: Joined Steelers in 2007.

Ray Horton, defensive backs; born April 12, 1960, Tacoma, Wash. Defensive back Washington 1979-1982. Pro defensive back Cincinnati Bengals 1983-88, Dallas Cowboys 1989-1992. Pro coach: Washington Redskins 1994-96, Cincinnati Bengals 1997-2001, Detroit Lions 2002-03, joined Steelers in 2004.

Amos Jones, asst. special teams; born December 31, 1959, Tallahassee, Fla.. Safety/running back Alabama 1978-1980. No pro playing experience. College coach: Alabama 1981-82, Temple 1983-88, Alabama 1990-91, Pittsburgh 1992, Tulane 1995-96, Cincinnati 1999-2002, James Madison 2003, Mississippi State 2004-06. Pro coach: British Columbia (CFL) 1997, joined Steelers in 2007.

Sean Kugler, offensive line; born August 9, 1966, Lockport, N.Y. Offensive line Texas-El Paso 1985-89. No pro playing experience. College coach: Texas-El Paso 1993-2000, Boise State 2006. Pro coach: Detroit Lions 2001-05, Buffalo Bills 2007-09, joined Steelers in 2010.

Dick LeBeau, defensive coordinator; born September 9, 1937, London, Ohio. Defensive back Ohio State 1955-58. Pro cornerback Detroit Lions 1959-1972. Pro coach: Philadelphia Eagles 1973-75, Green Bay Packers 1976-79, Cincinnati Bengals 1980-1991, 1997-2002 (head coach 2000-02), Pittsburgh Steelers 1992-96, Buffalo Bills 2003, re-joined Steelers in 2004.

John Mitchell, defensive line; born October 14, 1951, Mobile, Ala. Defensive end Eastern Arizona J.C. 1969-1970, Alabama 1971-72. No pro playing experience. College coach: Alabama 1973-76, Arkansas 1977-1982, Temple 1986, Louisiana State 1987-1990. Pro coach: Birmingham Stallions (USFL) 1983-85, Cleveland Browns 1991-93, joined Steelers in 1994.

Scottie Montgomery, wide receivers; born May 26, 1978, Shelby, N.C. Wide receiver Duke 1996-99. Pro wide receiver Carolina Panthers 2000, Denver Broncos 2000-02, Oakland Raiders 2003, Georgia Force (AFL) 2005. College coach: Duke 2006-09. Pro coach: Joined Steelers in 2010.

Kirby Wilson, running backs; born August 24, 1961, Los Angeles. Running back/wide receiver Pasadena (Calif.) C.C. 1979-1980, Illinois 1981-82. Pro cornerback Winnipeg Blue Bombers (CFL) 1983, Toronto Argonauts (CFL) 1984. College coach: Pasadena (Calif.) C.C. 1989-1990, Southern Illinois 1991-92, Wyoming 1993-94, Iowa State 1995-96, Southern California 2001. Pro coach: New England Patriots 1997-99, Washington Redskins 2000, Tampa Bay Buccaneers 2002-03, Arizona Cardinals 2004-06, joined Steelers in 2007.

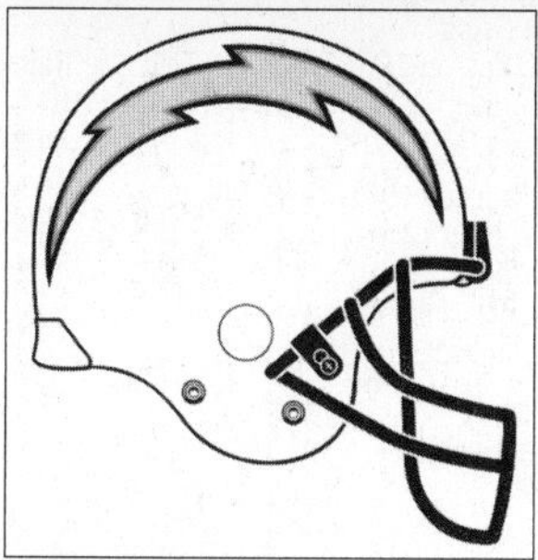

American Football Conference
West Division
Team Colors: Navy Blue, Powder Blue, White, and Gold
P.O. Box 609609
San Diego, California 92160-9609
Telephone: (858) 874-4500

2010 SCHEDULE
PRESEASON

Aug. 14	**Chicago**	6:00
Aug. 21	**Dallas**	6:00
Aug. 27	at New Orleans	7:00
Sep. 2	at San Francisco	7:00

REGULAR SEASON

Sep. 13	at Kansas City (Mon)	9:15
Sep. 19	**Jacksonville**	1:15
Sep. 26	at Seattle	1:15
Oct. 3	**Arizona**	1:15
Oct. 10	at Oakland	1:15
Oct. 17	at St. Louis	12:00
Oct. 24	**New England**	1:15
Oct. 31	**Tennessee**	1:05
Nov. 7	at Houston	12:00
Nov. 14	BYE	
Nov. 22	**Denver** (Mon)	5:30
Nov. 28	at Indianapolis	* 8:20
Dec. 5	**Oakland**	1:05
Dec. 12	**Kansas City**	1:15
Dec. 16	**San Francisco** (Thu)	5:20
Dec. 26	at Cincinnati	* 8:20
Jan. 2	at Denver	2:15

** Sunday night games in Weeks 11-17 subject to change*

Stadium: Qualcomm Stadium (opened in 1967)
•**Capacity:** 70,000 (app.)
9449 Friars Road
San Diego, California 92108
Playing Surface: Grass
Training Camp: Chargers Park
4020 Murphy Canyon Rd.
San Diego, CA 92123

QUALCOMM STADIUM

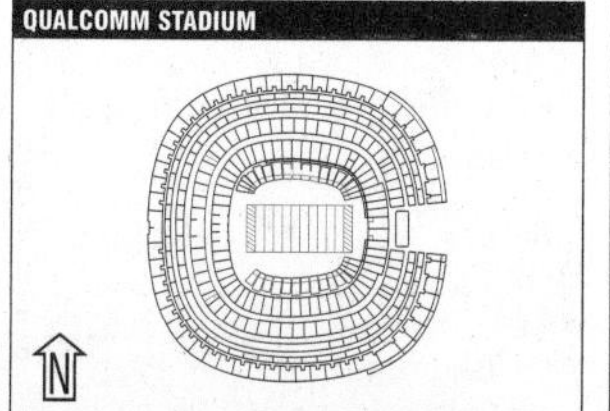

CLUB OFFICIALS
Owner: Alex G. Spanos
President/CEO: Dean A. Spanos
Executive Vice President: Michael A. Spanos
Executive Vice President-Executive Officer: A.G. Spanos
Executive Vice President-General Manager: A.J. Smith
Executive Vice President: Jeremiah T. Murphy
Executive Vice President of Football Operations-Assistant General Manager: Ed McGuire
Executive Vice President-Chief Financial Officer: Jeanne M. Bonk
Senior Vice President-Chief Marketing Officer: Ken Derrett
Director of Player Personnel: Jimmy Raye
Director of College Scouting: John Spanos
Director of Pro Scouting: Dennis Abraham
Senior Executive: Randy Mueller
Head Athletic Trainer: James Collins
Director of Video Operations: Brian Duddy
Equipment Manager: Bob Wick
Director of Player Development: Arthur Hightower
Vice President of Marketing Partnerships: Dennis O'Leary
Senior Director of Ticket Sales and Service: Todd Poulsen
Director of Business Operations: John Hinek
Director of Public Relations: Bill Johnston
Director of Public Affairs & Corporate/Community Relations: Kimberley Layton
Director of Security: Dick Lewis
Director of Stadium/Game Operations & Events: Sean O'Connor
Controller: Marsha Wells
Director of Ticket Operations: Michael L. Dougherty

COACHING HISTORY
Los Angeles 1960
(385-386-11)
Records include postseason games

1960-69	Sid Gillman*	83-51-6
1969-1970	Charlie Waller	9-7-3
1971	Sid Gillman**	4-6-0
1971-73	Harland Svare***	7-17-2
1973	Ron Waller	1-5-0
1974-78	Tommy Prothro****	21-39-0
1978-1986	Don Coryell#	72-60-0
1986-88	Al Saunders	17-22-0
1989-1991	Dan Henning	16-32-0
1992-96	Bobby Ross	50-36-0
1997-98	Kevin Gilbride	6-16-0
1998	June Jones	3-7-0
1999-2001	Mike Riley	14-34-0
2002-06	Marty Schottenheimer	47-35-0
2007-09	Norv Turner	35-19-0

*Retired after nine games in 1969
**Resigned after 10 games in 1971
***Resigned after eight games in 1973
****Resigned after four games in 1978
#Resigned after eight games in 1986
##Released after six games in 1998

PAID ATTENDANCE
Home 539,948 Away 544,239
Total 1,084,187
Single-game home record, 69,288 (11/7/99)
Single-season home record, 547,937 (2005)

2010 DRAFT CHOICES

Round	Name	Pos.	College
1	Ryan Mathews	RB	Fresno St.
3	Donald Butler	LB	Washington
4	Darrell Stuckey	DB	Kansas
5	Cam Thomas	DT	North Carolina
	Jonathan Crompton	QB	Tennessee
7	Dedrick Epps	TE	Miami

SAN DIEGO CHARGERS

2009 TEAM RECORD

PRESEASON (2-2)

Date	Result	Opponent
8/15	L 14-20	Seattle
8/22	W 17-6	at Arizona
8/29	L 24-27	at Atlanta
9/4	W 26-7	San Francisco

REGULAR SEASON (13-3)

Date	Result	Opponent
9/14	W 24-20	at Oakland
9/20	L 26-31	Baltimore
9/27	W 23-13	Miami
10/4	L 28-38	at Pittsburgh
10/19	L 23-34	Denver
10/25	W 37-7	at Kansas City
11/1	W 24-16	Oakland
11/8	W 21-20	at New York Giants
11/15	W 31-23	Philadelphia
11/22	W 32-3	at Denver
11/29	W 43-14	Kansas City
12/6	W 30-23	at Cleveland
12/13	W 20-17	at Dallas
12/20	W 27-24	Cincinnati
12/25	W 42-17	at Tennessee
1/3	W 23-20	Washington

POSTSEASON (0-1)

Date	Result	Opponent
1/17	L 14-17	New York Jets

SCORE BY PERIODS

Chargers	103	120	107	124	0 —	454
Opponents	51	98	57	114	0 —	320

2009 TEAM STATISTICS

	Chargers	Opp.
Total First Downs	330	309
Rushing	80	112
Passing	222	177
Penalty	28	20
3rd Down: Made/Att	83/187	82/203
3rd Down Pct.	44.4	40.4
4th Down: Made/Att	5/10	10/20
4th Down Pct.	50.0	50.0
Possession Avg.	29:58	30:02
Total Net Yards	5761	5232
Avg. Per Game	360.1	327.0
Total Plays	972	991
Avg. Per Play	5.9	5.3
Net Yards Rushing	1423	1884
Avg. Per Game	88.9	117.8
Total Rushes	427	422
Net Yards Passing	4338	3348
Avg. Per Game	271.1	209.3
Sacked/Yards Lost	26/168	35/221
Gross Yards	4506	3569
Att./Completions	519/338	534/326
Completion Pct.	65.1	61.0
Had Intercepted	10	14
Punts/Average	52/45.0	63/43.0
Net Punting Avg.	52/39.2	63/37.6
Penalties/Yards	78/570	103/795
Fumbles/Ball Lost	14/7	24/11
Touchdowns	51	35
Rushing	17	10
Passing	29	23
Returns	5	2

2009 INDIVIDUAL STATISTICS

PASSING	Att.	Comp.	Yds.	Pct.	TD	Int.	Tkld.	Rate
Rivers	486	317	4254	65.2	28	9	25/167	104.4
Volek	31	20	231	64.5	1	1	1/1	84.2
Naanee	1	1	21	100.0	0	0	0/0	118.8
Tomlinson	1	0	0	0.0	0	0	0/0	39.6
Chargers	519	338	4506	65.1	29	10	26/168	103.1
Opponents	534	326	3569	61.0	23	14	35/221	84.2

SCORING	TD R	TD P	TD Rt	PAT	FG	Saf	PTS
Kaeding	0	0	0	50/51	32/35	0	146
Tomlinson	12	0	0	0/0	0/0	0	72
V. Jackson	0	9	0	0/0	0/0	0	54
Gates	0	8	0	0/0	0/0	0	48
Sproles	3	4	1	0/0	0/0	0	48
Tolbert	1	3	0	0/0	0/0	0	24
Hester	0	0	2	0/0	0/0	0	12
Naanee	0	2	0	0/0	0/0	0	12
Chambers TM	0	1	0	0/0	0/0	0	6
Floyd	0	1	0	0/0	0/0	0	6
Oliver	0	0	1	0/0	0/0	0	6
Rivers	1	0	0	0/0	0/0	0	6
Weddle	0	0	1	0/0	0/0	0	6
Wilson	0	1	0	0/0	0/0	0	6
Chargers	17	29	5	50/51	32/35	1	454
Opponents	10	23	2	33/33	25/29	0	320

2-Pt. Conversions: Chargers 0-0, Opponents 1-2.

RUSHING	No.	Yds	Avg	LG	TD
Tomlinson	223	730	3.3	36	12
Sproles	93	343	3.7	21	3
Tolbert	25	148	5.9	32	1
Hester	21	74	3.5	15	0
Bennett	23	65	2.8	14	0
Rivers	26	50	1.9	15	1
V. Jackson	3	11	3.7	12	0
Naanee	3	7	2.3	10	0
Cr. Davis	1	4	4.0	4	0
Volek	9	-9	-1.0	-1	0
Chargers	427	1423	3.3	36	17
Opponents	422	1884	4.5	36	10

RECEIVING	No.	Yds	Avg	LG	TD
Gates	79	1157	14.6	56	8
V. Jackson	68	1167	17.2	55	9
Floyd	45	776	17.2	53	1
Sproles	45	497	11.0	81t	4
Naanee	24	242	10.1	23	2
Tomlinson	20	154	7.7	36	0
Tolbert	17	192	11.3	66t	3
Chambers TM	9	122	13.6	20	1
Hester	9	24	2.7	5	0
Bennett	6	65	10.8	33	0
Cr. Davis	6	52	8.7	11	0
Manumaleuna	5	13	2.6	11	0
Wilson	4	28	7.0	21	1
Osgood	1	17	17.0	17	0
Chargers	338	4506	13.3	81t	29
Opponents	326	3569	10.9	84	23

INTERCEPTIONS	No.	Yds	Avg	LG	TD
Jammer	3	25	8.3	21	0
Cromartie	3	17	5.7	16	0
Weddle	2	44	22.0	31t	1
Cason	2	22	11.0	22	0
Oliver	1	34	34.0	34	0
Dobbins	1	13	13.0	13	0
Gregory	1	13	13.0	13	0
Siler	1	5	5.0	5	0
Chargers	14	173	12.4	34	1
Opponents	10	88	8.8	33	0

PUNTING	No.	Yds.	Avg.	In 20	LG
Scifres	52	2342	45.0	23	65
Chargers	52	2342	45.0	23	65
Opponents	63	2711	43.0	21	69

PUNT RETURNS	Ret	FC	Yds	Avg	LG	TD
Sproles	26	12	183	7.0	77t	1
Cr. Davis	0	1	0	—	—	0
Chargers	26	13	183	7.0	77t	1
Opponents	23	16	265	11.5	71t	1

KICKOFF RETURNS	No.	Yds	Avg	LG	TD
Sproles	54	1300	24.1	66	0
Cr. Davis	4	79	19.8	23	0
Cromartie	3	41	13.7	22	0
Wilson	1	13	13.0	13	0
Hester	1	9	9.0	9	0
Chargers	63	1442	22.9	66	0
Opponents	87	1909	21.9	93t	1

FIELD GOALS	1-19	20-29	30-39	40-49	50+
Kaeding	2/2	17/17	4/4	6/8	3/4
Chargers	2/2	17/17	4/4	6/8	3/4
Opponents	1/1	12/12	7/7	5/8	0/1

SACKS	No.
Phillips	7.0
Merriman	4.0
Boone	3.0
Burnett	2.5
Castillo	2.0
English	2.0
Gregory	2.0
Harris	2.0
Siler	2.0
Weddle	1.5
Cesaire	1.0
Dobbins	1.0
Ellison	1.0
Nwagbuo	1.0
Oliver	1.0
Scott	1.0
(group)	1.0
Chargers	35.0
Opponents	26.0

RECORD HOLDERS

INDIVIDUAL RECORDS—CAREER

Category	Name	Performance
Rushing (Yds.)	LaDainian Tomlinson, 2001-09	12,490
Passing (Yds.)	Dan Fouts, 1973-1987	43,040
Passing (TDs)	Dan Fouts, 1973-1987	254
Receiving (No.)	Charlie Joiner, 1976-1986	586
Receiving (Yds.)	Lance Alworth, 1962-1970	9,585
Interceptions	Gill Byrd, 1983-1992	42
Punting (Avg.)	Mike Scifres, 2003-09	44.2
Punt Return (Avg.)	Darrien Gordon, 1993-96	13.6
Kickoff Return (Avg.)	Leslie (Speedy) Duncan, 1964-1970	25.3
Field Goals	John Carney, 1990-2000	261
Touchdowns (Tot.)	LaDainian Tomlinson, 2001-09	153
Points	John Carney, 1990-2000	1,076
*Sacks	Leslie O'Neal, 1986-1995	105.5

INDIVIDUAL RECORDS—SINGLE SEASON

Category	Name	Performance
Rushing (Yds.)	LaDainian Tomlinson, 2006	1,815
Passing (Yds.)	Dan Fouts, 1981	4,802
Passing (TDs)	Philip Rivers, 2008	34
Receiving (No.)	LaDainian Tomlinson, 2003	100
Receiving (Yds.)	Lance Alworth, 1965	1,602
Interceptions	Antonio Cromartie, 2007	10
Punting (Avg.)	Darren Bennett, 2000	46.2
Punt Return (Avg.)	Leslie (Speedy) Duncan, 1965	15.5
Kickoff Return (Avg.)	Keith Lincoln, 1962	28.4
Field Goals	John Carney, 1994	34
Touchdowns (Tot.)	LaDainian Tomlinson, 2006	**31
Points	LaDainian Tomlinson, 2006	**186
*Sacks	Leslie O'Neal, 1992	17.0
	Shawne Merriman, 2006	17.0

INDIVIDUAL RECORDS—SINGLE GAME

Category	Name	Performance
Rushing (Yds.)	LaDainian Tomlinson, 12-28-03	243
Passing (Yds.)	Dan Fouts, 10-19-80, 12-11-82	444
Passing (TDs)	Dan Fouts, 11-22-81	6
Receiving (No.)	Kellen Winslow, 10-7-84	15
Receiving (Yds.)	Wes Chandler, 12-20-82	260
Interceptions	Many times	3
	Last time by Antonio Cromartie, 11-11-07	
Field Goals	John Carney, 9-5-93, 9-18-93	6
	Greg Davis, 10-5-97	6
Touchdowns (Tot.)	Kellen Winslow, 11-22-81	5
Points	Kellen Winslow, 11-22-81	30
*Sacks	Leslie O'Neal, 11-16-86	5.0

**Sacks became an official statistic in 1982.*
***NFL Record*

SAN DIEGO CHARGERS

2010 VETERAN ROSTER

No.	Name	Pos.	Ht.	Wt.	Birthdate	NFL Exp.	College	Hometown	How Acq.	'09 Games/ Starts
90	Applewhite, Antwan	LB	6-3	246	12/31/85	3	San Diego State	Los Angeles, Calif.	FA-'07	1/0
97	Bingham, Ryon	DE/DT	6-3	303	6/6/81	6	Nebraska	Sandy, Utah	D7a-'04	0*
50	Binn, David	LS	6-3	228	2/6/72	17	California	San Mateo, Calif.	FA-'94	16/0
70	Boone, Alfonso	DE	6-3	305	1/11/76	10	Mt. San Antonio JC (Calif.)	Saginaw, Mich.	FA-'09	13/4
99	Burnett, Kevin	LB	6-3	240	12/24/82	6	Tennessee	Compton, Calif.	FA-'09	11/8
20	Cason, Antoine	CB	6-0	190	7/9/86	3	Arizona	Long Beach, Calif.	D1-'08	16/1
93	Castillo, Luis	DE	6-3	290	8/4/83	6	Northwestern	Garfield, N.J.	D1b-'05	14/14
74	Cesaire, Jacques	DE	6-2	295	8/30/80	8	So. Connecticut State	Gardner, Mass.	FA-'03	13/13
75	Clark, Corey	T	6-5	325	6/21/84	2	Texas A&M	Spring Branch, Texas	D7-'08	1/0
66	Clary, Jeromey	T	6-6	320	11/5/83	4	Kansas State	Mansfield, Texas	D6a-'06	10/10
54	Cooper, Stephen	LB	6-1	235	6/19/79	8	Maine	Wareham, Mass.	FA-'03	16/16
84	Davis, Buster	WR	6-1	210	10/2/85	4	Louisiana State	New Orleans, La.	D1-'07	1/0
68	Dielman, Kris	G	6-4	320	2/3/81	8	Indiana	Troy, Ohio	FA-'03	16/16
62	Dombrowski, Brandyn	G/T	6-5	323	4/3/85	2	San Diego State	Henderson, Nev.	FA-'08	16/8
25	Ellison, Kevin	S	6-1	221	1/8/87	2	Southern California	Redondo Beach, Calif.	D6-'09	13/9
52	English, Larry	LB	6-2	255	1/22/86	2	Northern Illinois	Aurora, Ill.	D1-'09	16/2
80	+Floyd, Malcom	WR	6-5	225	9/8/81	5	Wyoming	Sacramento, Calif.	FA-'04	16/9
71	Garay, Antonio	DT	6-4	320	11/30/79	4	Boston College	Rahway, N.J.	FA-'09	2/0
85	Gates, Antonio	TE	6-4	260	6/18/80	8	Kent State	Detroit, Mich.	FA-'03	16/16
69	Green, Tyronne	G	6-2	308	4/6/86	2	Auburn	Pensacola, Fla.	D4b-'09	4/0
28	Gregory, Steve	S	5-11	195	1/8/83	5	Syracuse	Staten Island, N.Y.	FA-'06	16/6
61	Hardwick, Nick	C	6-4	295	9/2/81	7	Purdue	Indianapolis, Ind.	D3b-'04	3/3
22	Hester, Jacob	FB	5-11	235	5/8/85	3	Louisiana State	Shreveport, La.	D3-'08	15/10
53	Holt, James	LB	6-2	223	11/24/86	2	Kansas	Altus, Okla.	FA-'09	9/0
26	Hughes, Brandon	CB	5-11	181	5/23/86	2	Oregon State	Bloomington, Ill.	D5-'09	0*
33	Hughes, Dante	CB	5-10	190	8/21/85	4	California	Los Angeles, Calif.	FA-'09	1/0
83	+Jackson, Vincent	WR	6-5	230	1/14/83	6	Northern Colorado	Colorado Springs, Colo.	D2-'05	15/15
23	Jammer, Quentin	CB	6-0	204	6/19/79	9	Texas	Angleton, Texas	D1-'02	16/16
96	+Johnson, Travis	DE/DT	6-3	311	4/26/82	6	Florida State	Sherman Oaks, Calif.	T(Hou)-'09	13/0
10	Kaeding, Nate	K	6-0	187	3/26/82	7	Iowa	Coralville, Iowa	D3a-'04	16/0
92	Martin, Vaughn	DE/DT	6-4	320	4/18/86	2	Western Ontario	London, Ontario, Canada	D4a-'09	10/0
29	Mason, Marcus	RB	5-9	215	6/23/84	3	Youngstown State	Rockville, Md.	FA-'10	9/0*
73	+McNeill, Marcus	T	6-7	336	11/16/83	5	Auburn	Ellenwood, Ga.	D2-'06	16/16
56	+Merriman, Shawne	LB	6-4	265	5/25/84	6	Maryland	Upper Marlboro, Md.	D1a-'05	14/14
63	Mruczkowski, Scott	C	6-5	325	4/5/82	6	Bowling Green	Garfield Heights, Ohio	D7-'05	14/13
11	Naanee, Legedu	WR	6-2	220	9/16/83	4	Boise State	Portland, Ore.	D5-'07	15/1
9	Novak, Nick	K	6-0	198	8/21/81	4	Maryland	Charlottesville, Va.	FA-'10	0*
91	Nwagbuo, Ogemdi	DE/DT	6-4	303	12/24/85	2	Michigan State	Spring Valley, Calif.	FA-'08	12/5
27	Oliver, Paul	CB	5-11	210	3/30/84	4	Georgia	Kennesaw, Ga.	D4(Supp)-'07	16/3
95	Phillips, Shaun	LB	6-3	262	5/13/81	7	Purdue	Willingboro, N.J.	D4-'04	16/16
17	Rivers, Philip	QB	6-5	228	12/8/81	7	North Carolina State	Athens, Ala.	T(NYG)-'04	16/16
5	Scifres, Mike	P	6-2	221	10/8/80	8	Western Illinois	Destrehan, La.	D5-'03	16/0
98	Scott, Ian	DT	6-3	315	11/8/81	8	Florida	Gainesville, Fla.	FA-'08	12/7
59	Siler, Brandon	LB	6-2	239	12/5/85	4	Florida	Orlando, Fla.	D7-'07	16/6
41	Spillman, C.J.	S	6-0	196	5/6/86	2	Marshall	Louisville, Ky.	FA-'09	5/1
43	Sproles, Darren	RB/KR	5-6	185	6/20/83	6	Kansas State	Olathe, Kan.	D4-'05	16/2
30	Strickland, Donald	CB	5-10	185	11/27/80	7	Colorado	San Francisco, Calif.	FA-'10	9/2*
35	Tolbert, Mike	FB	5-9	243	11/23/85	3	Coastal Carolina	Douglasville, Ga.	FA-'08	16/2
94	Tucker, Jyles	LB	6-3	258	9/18/83	4	Wake Forest	Dover, N.J.	FA-'07	7/0
31	Vasher, Nathan	CB	5-11	185	11/17/81	7	Texas	Texarkana, Texas	FA-'10	15/2*
65	Vasquez, Louis	G	6-5	325	4/11/87	2	Texas Tech	Corsicana, Texas	D3-'09	14/14
7	Volek, Billy	QB	6-2	214	4/28/76	11	Fresno State	Fresno, Calif.	T(Tenn)-'06	4/0
32	Weddle, Eric	S	5-11	200	1/4/85	4	Utah	Alta Loma, Calif.	D2-'07	13/13
88	Wilson, Kris	TE	6-2	245	8/22/81	7	Pittsburgh	Lancaster, Pa.	FA-'08	16/0

* Bingham missed '09 season because of injury; B. Hughes missed '09 season because of injury; Mason played 9 games with Washington in '09; Novak last played with Kansas City in '08; Strickland played 9 games with N.Y. Jets; Vasher played 15 games with Chicago.

\+ Restricted free agent; subject to developments.

Traded—CB Antonio Cromartie (16 games in '09) to N.Y. Jets, LB Tim Dobbins (14) to Miami, QB Charlie Whitehurst (0) to Seattle.

Players lost through free agency (2): TE Brandon Manumaleuna (Chi; 16 games in '09), WR Kassim Osgood (Jax; 16).

Also played with Chargers in '09—RB Michael Bennett (6 games), DB Simeon Castille (1), WR Chris Chambers (7), DE Andre Coleman (2), LB Marques Harris (4), OL Dennis Norman (10), T Jon Runyan (5), RB LaDainian Tomlinson (14), DT Jamal Williams (1).

2010 FIRST-YEAR ROSTER

Name	Pos.	Ht.	Wt.	Birthdate	College	Hometown	How Acq.
Ajirotutu, Seyi	WR	6-3	206	6/12/87	Fresno State	El Dorado Hills, Calif.	FA
Banks, Gary (1)	WR	6-0	193	11/4/81	Troy	Melvin, Ala.	FA-'08
Beckwith, Darry (1)	LB	6-0	234	5/15/87	Louisiana State	Baton Rouge, La.	FA-'09
Bond, Brady	T	6-6	300	6/4/86	Oklahoma State	Garber, Okla.	FA
Brinkley, Curtis (1)	RB	5-9	208	9/20/85	Syracuse	Philadelphia, Pa.	FA-'09
Brockel, Richie	TE	6-1	251	7/24/86	Boise State	Phoenix, Ariz.	FA
Butler, Donald	LB	6-1	235	10/17/88	Washington	Fair Oaks, Calif.	D3
Crompton, Jonathan	QB	6-3	222	7/25/87	Tennessee	Waynesville, N.C.	D5b
Epps, Dedrick	TE	6-4	246	6/19/88	Miami	Richmond, Va.	D7
Farr, DajLeon	TE	6-5	256	10/5/86	Memphis	Houston, Texas	FA
Goodman, Richard	WR	6-0	192	4/23/87	Florida State	Ft. Lauderdale, Fla.	FA
Hansen, Jeff	C/G	6-4	301	9/24/86	Montana State	Great Falls, Mont.	FA
Jackson, Cory	FB	6-0	250	3/12/88	Maryland	Morgantown, W. Va.	FA
Jackson, Jordyn	WR	5-9	187	6/8/86	Eastern Oregon	Camas, Wash.	FA
Jeffries, Justin	T	6-5	320	9/17/88	Kentucky	Louisville, Ky.	FA
Johnson, Cort	P	5-10	195	5/1/86	West Texas A&M	Amarillo, Texas	FA
Jones, Derrick (1)	DE	6-4	315	11/14/84	Grand Valley State	Yermo, Calif.	FA-'09
Lang, Brandon	LB	6-3	266	6/18/86	Troy	Tucker, Ga.	FA
Latsko, Billy (1)	FB	5-10	233	2/16/84	Florida	Gainesville, Fla.	FA-'08
Mathews, Ryan	RB	6-0	218	10/10/87	Fresno State	Bakersfield, Calif.	D1
McDonald, Ryan (1)	C	6-4	293	8/21/85	Illinois	Holland, Mich.	FA-'09
McNeal, Shawnbrey	RB	5-9	190	10/17/88	Southern Methodist	Dallas, Texas	FA
Otterson, Ryan	T	6-5	291	11/29/86	Wyoming	Brighton, Colo.	FA
Richmond, Nick	T	6-8	309	5/1/87	Texas Christian	Garland, Texas	FA
Simmons, Traye	CB	5-9	180	1/18/87	Minnesota	Marietta, Ga.	FA
Smith, Ernest	WR	6-3	200	3/18/88	Baylor	New Orleans, La.	FA
Stuckey, Darrell	S	5-11	204	6/16/87	Kansas	Kansas City, Kan.	FA
Thomas, Cam	DT	6-4	335	12/12/86	North Carolina	Eagle Springs, N.C.	D5a
Thompson, Marcel	WR	6-2	204	10/26/87	Lindenwood	San Francisco, Calif.	FA
Walters, Bryan	WR	6-0	190	11/4/87	Cornell	Bothell, Wash.	FA
Williams, Jeremy	WR	6-0	203	1/23/87	Tulane	Baytown, Texas	FA
Wilson, Kion	LB	6-0	235	10/24/86	South Florida	Jacksonville, Fla.	FA

The term NFL Rookie is defined as a player who is in his first season of professional football and has not been on the roster of another professional football team for any regular-season or postseason games. A Rookie is designated by an "R" on NFL rosters. Players who have been active in another professional football league or players who have NFL experience, including either preseason training camp or being on an Active List or Inactive List, or on Reserve/Injured or Reserve/Physically Unable to Perform for fewer than six regular-season games, are termed NFL First-Year Players. An NFL First-Year Player is designated by a "1" on NFL rosters. Thereafter, a player is credited with an additional year of experience for each season in which he accumulates six games on the Active List or Inactive List, or on Reserve/Injured or Reserve/Physically Unable to Perform.

Log on to www.chargers.com for an up-to-date roster.

SAN DIEGO CHARGERS

COACHING STAFF

Head Coach,
Norv Turner

Pro Career: A veteran coach of 25 NFL seasons, Turner became the 14th head coach in team history on February 19, 2007. In his first three seasons, Turner has led the Chargers to three-straight AFC West titles. In the postseason, he led the Chargers to the 2007 AFC Championship Game and the 2008 and 2009 Divisional Playoffs. A two-time Super Bowl champion as an offensive coordinator with the Dallas Cowboys, Turner was the offensive coordinator for the San Francisco 49ers in 2006. A Bay Area native from Martinez, California, this is Turner's second stint with the Chargers. He spent the 2001 season as the Bolts' offensive coordinator. Turner's 25 years of coaching experience include 12 as a head coach—seven for the Washington Redskins (1994-2000), two with the Oakland Raiders (2004-05), and three with the Chargers (2007-09). In 1999, he led the Redskins to a division title. He spent 13 seasons as an NFL assistant coach, including seven as an offensive coordinator with the Cowboys (1991-93), Chargers (2001), Dolphins (2002-03), and 49ers (2006). Turner began his NFL coaching career as an assistant with the Rams in 1985. He coached wide receivers from 1985-86 before adding the responsibility of the team's tight ends from 1987-1990. Turner made his coaching mark during his three seasons in Dallas as the Cowboys won back-to-back Super Bowls (XXVII and XXVIII) following the 1992 and 1993 seasons. Career record: 94-102-1.

Background: Turner played quarterback at Oregon, spending two seasons behind former Charger and NFL Hall of Fame quarterback Dan Fouts. Turner coached at Oregon (1975) and Southern California (1976-1984). During his nine-year tenure at USC, the Trojans played in four Rose Bowls, winning all four. One of those was a win over Michigan after the 1978 season that capped a 12-1 season and gave USC the National Championship.

Personal: Born in LeJeune, N.C., May 17, 1952. Turner and his wife, Nancy, have three children—Scott, Stephanie, and Drew.

ASSISTANT COACHES

Rob Chudzinski, tight ends/asst. head coach; born May 12, 1968, Toledo, Ohio. Tight end Miami 1986-90. No pro playing experience. College coach: Miami 1994-2003. Pro coach: Cleveland Browns 2004, 2007-08, San Diego Chargers 2005-06, rejoined Chargers in 2009.

Steve Crosby, special teams; born July 3, 1950, Great Bend, Kan. Running back Fort Hayes State 1970-73. Pro running back New York Giants 1974-76. College coach: Vanderbilt 1998-2001. Pro coach: Miami Dolphins 1979-1982, Atlanta Falcons 1983-84, 1986-89, Cleveland Browns 1985, 1991-95, New England Patriots 1990, joined Chargers in 2002.

Cris Dishman, asst. secondary; born August 13, 1965, Louisville, Kentucky. Cornerback Purdue 1984-87. Pro cornerback Houston Oilers 1988-1996, Washington Redskins 1997-98, Kansas City Chiefs 1999, Minnesota Vikings 2000. College coach: Menlo College 2006-08. Pro coach: Joined Chargers in 2009.

Hal Hunter, offensive line; born July 8, 1959, Canonsburg, Pa. Linebacker Northwestern 1978. College coach: William & Mary 1982, Pittsburgh 1983-84, Columbia 1985, Indiana (Pa.) 1986, Akron 1987-1990, Vanderbilt 1991-94, Louisiana State 1995-99, Indiana 2000-01, North Carolina 2002-05. Pro coach: Joined Chargers in 2006.

Jeff Hurd, strength and conditioning; born April 24, 1958, Pomona, Calif. No college or pro playing experience. College coach: Fort Hays State 1984, Delta State 1985-86, Clemson 1986-87, Western Michigan 1987-1992, Tulsa 1994. Pro coach: Jacksonville Jaguars 1995-97, Kansas City Chiefs 1998-2006, joined Chargers in 2007.

Don Johnson, defensive line; born November 3, 1954, Newark, N.J. Linebacker Jersey City State 1973-76. College coach: Jersey City State 1984-85. Riverside (Calif.) C.C. 1987-1990, Cal State-Fullerton 1991-92, Nevada 1995-98, UCLA 1999-2004. Pro coach: Chicago Bears 2005-06, Oakland Raiders 2007-08, joined Chargers in 2009.

Charlie Joiner, receivers; born October 14, 1947, Many, La. Wide receiver Grambling State 1965-68. Pro defensive back/wide receiver Houston Oilers 1969-1972, Cincinnati Bengals 1972-75, San Diego Chargers 1976-1986. Inducted into Pro Football Hall of Fame 1996. Pro coach: San Diego Chargers 1987-1991, Buffalo Bills 1992-2000, Kansas City Chiefs 2001-07, re-joined Chargers in 2008.

John Pagano, outside linebackers; born March 30, 1967, Boulder, Colo. Linebacker Mesa State College 1985-88. No pro playing experience. College coach: Mesa State College 1989, Nevada-Las Vegas 1990-91, Louisiana Tech 1994, Mississippi 1995. Pro coach: New Orleans Saints 1996-97, Indianapolis Colts 1998-2001, joined Chargers in 2002.

John Ramsdell, quarterbacks; born August 16, 1954, Lafayette, Ind. Running back Springfield (Mass.) College 1972-75. No pro playing experience. College coach: San Francisco State 1976-77, Long Beach State 1978, Pacific 1979-1982, Oregon 1983-1994. Pro coach: St. Louis Rams 1995-2005, joined Chargers in 2006.

Ron Rivera, defensive coordinator; born January 7, 1962, Fort Ord, Calif. Linebacker California 1980-83. Pro linebacker Chicago Bears 1984-1992. Pro coach: Chicago Bears 1997-98, 2004-06, Philadelphia Eagles 1999-2003, joined Chargers in 2007.

Clarence Shelmon, offensive coordinator; born September 17, 1952, Bossier City, La. Running back Houston 1971-75. No pro playing experience. College coach: Army 1978-1980, Indiana 1981-83, Arizona 1984-86, Southern California 1987-1990. Pro coach: Los Angeles Rams 1991, Seattle Seahawks 1992-97, Dallas Cowboys 1998-2001, joined Chargers in 2002.

Vernon Stephens, asst. strength and conditioning; born November 30, 1974, Jacksonville. No college or pro playing experience. College coach: North Florida 1999-2002, Colorado 2003-06. Pro coach: Jacksonville Jaguars 2002-03, joined Chargers in 2007.

Mike Sullivan, offensive line; born December 22, 1967, Chicago. Offensive lineman Miami 1986-90. Pro offensive lineman Dallas Cowboys 1991, Tampa Bay Buccaneers 1992-95. College coach: Miami 2000, Western Michigan 2005-06. Pro coach: Cleveland Browns 2001-04, 2007-08, joined Chargers in 2009.

Steven Wilks, secondary; born August 8, 1969, Charlotte. Defensive back Appalachian State 1987-1991. Pro defensive back/wide receiver Charlotte Rage (AFL) 1993. College coach: Johnson C. Smith 1995-96, Savannah State 1997-99, Illinois State 2000, Appalachian State 2001, East Tennessee State 2002, Bowling Green State 2003, Notre Dame 2004, Washington 2005. Pro coach: Chicago Bears 2006-08, joined Chargers in 2009.

Greg Williams, asst. linebackers; born March 12, 1976, Chicago. Wide receiver/defensive back North Carolina 1994-97. Pro defensive back Amsterdam Admirals (NFL Europe) 1999-2000, San Francisco Demons (XFL) 2001, Indiana Firebirds (AFL) 2001-03, Chicago Rush (AFL) 2004. College coach: Arizona State 2003, College of DuPage 2004-05, Arkansas Tech 2006-07, Pittsburgh 2008. Pro coach: Joined Chargers in 2009.

Ollie Wilson, running backs; born March 3, 1951, Worcester, Mass. Wide receiver Springfield 1971-73. No pro playing experience. College coach: Springfield 1975, Northeastern 1976-1982, California 1983-1990. Pro coach: Atlanta Falcons 1991-96, 2002-07, San Diego Chargers 1997-2001, re-joined Chargers in 2008.

American Football Conference
South Division
Team Colors: Navy, Titans Blue, Red, Silver
460 Great Circle Road
Nashville, Tennessee 37228
Telephone: (615) 565-4000

2010 SCHEDULE
PRESEASON

Aug. 14	at Seattle	7:00
Aug. 23	**Arizona**	7:00
Aug. 28	at Carolina	8:00
Sep. 2	**New Orleans**	7:00

REGULAR SEASON

Sep. 12	**Oakland**	12:00
Sep. 19	**Pittsburgh**	12:00
Sep. 26	at New York Giants	1:00
Oct. 3	**Denver**	12:00
Oct. 10	at Dallas	3:15
Oct. 18	at Jacksonville (Mon)	8:30
Oct. 24	**Philadelphia**	12:00
Oct. 31	at San Diego	1:05
Nov. 7	BYE	
Nov. 14	at Miami	1:00
Nov. 21	**Washington**	12:00
Nov. 28	at Houston	12:00
Dec. 5	**Jacksonville**	12:00
Dec. 9	**Indianapolis** (Thu)	7:20
Dec. 19	**Houston**	12:00
Dec. 26	at Kansas City	12:00
Jan. 2	at Indianapolis	1:00

Stadium: LP Field
(opened in 1999)
•**Capacity:** 69,143
One Titans Way
Nashville, Tennessee 37213
Playing Surface: Natural Grass
Training Camp: Baptist Sports Park
460 Great Circle Road
Nashville, TN 37228

LP FIELD

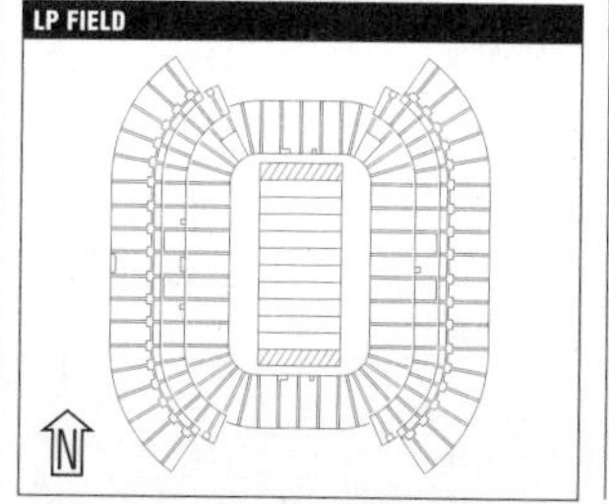

CLUB OFFICIALS
Owner/Chairman of the Board/CEO/ President: K.S. (Bud) Adams, Jr.
Senior Executive V.P./General Counsel: Steve Underwood
Executive V.P./Head Coach: Jeff Fisher
Executive V.P./General Manager: Mike Reinfeldt
Executive V.P. of Administration/Facilities: Don MacLachlan
Vice President/Asst. General Counsel: Elza Bullock
Vice President/Community Affairs: Bob Hyde
Vice President/CFO: Jenneen Kaufman
Senior Director of Football Administration: Vincent Marino
National Supervisor of College Scouting: C.O. Brocato
Director of College Scouting—Eastern Region: Mike Ackerley
Scouting Coordinator: Blake Beddingfield
Senior Director of Sales and Operations: Stuart Spears
Operations Manager: Brent Akers
Director of Broadcasting: Mike Keith
Vice President/Marketing: Ralph Ockenfels
Director of Information Systems: Russ Hudson
Director of Internet Operations/Publications: Gary Glenn
Director of Media Relations: Robbie Bohren
Asst. Director of Media Relations: Dwight Spradlin
Director of Security: Steve Berk
Senior Director of Ticketing: Marty Collins
Director of Pro Personnel: Lake Dawson
Director of Player Development: Tina Tuggle
Director of Cheerleading: Stacie Kinder
Director of Suite and Club Services: Bill Wainwright
Marketing Manager: Brad McClanahan
Head Athletic Trainer: Brad Brown
Assistant Athletic Trainers: Don Moseley, Casey Carter
Equipment Manager: Paul Noska
Video Director: Anthony Pastrana
General Manager of LP Field: Walter Overton
Manager of Community Relations: Tresa Halbrooks
Club Member Manager: Anthony Hall
Head Groundskeeper: Terry Porch

COACHING HISTORY
Houston 1960-1996
(385-398-6)
Records include postseason games

1960-61	Lou Rymkus*	12-7-1
1961	Wally Lemm	10-0-0
1962-63	Frank (Pop) Ivy	17-12-0
1964	Sammy Baugh	4-10-0
1965	Hugh Taylor	4-10-0
1966-1970	Wally Lemm	28-40-4
1971	Ed Hughes	4-9-1
1972-73	Bill Peterson**	1-18-0
1973-74	Sid Gillman	8-15-0
1975-1980	O.A. (Bum) Phillips	59-38-0
1981-83	Ed Biles***	8-23-0
1983	Chuck Studley	2-8-0
1984-85	Hugh Campbell****	8-22-0
1985-89	Jerry Glanville	35-35-0
1990-94	Jack Pardee#	44-35-0
1994-2009	Jeff Fisher	141-116-0

* Released after five games in 1961
** Released after five games in 1973
*** Resigned after six games in 1983
**** Released after 14 games in 1985
# Released after 10 games in 1994

PAID ATTENDANCE
Home 534,449 Away 512,744
Total 1,047,193
Single-game home record, 69,149, many times (last: 12/18/05)
Single-season home record, 553,192 (2005)

2010 DRAFT CHOICES

Round	Name	Pos.	College
1	Derrick Morgan	DE	Georgia Tech
3	Damian Williams	WR	Southern California
	Rennie Curran	LB	Georgia
4	Alterraun Verner	DB	UCLA
5	Robert Johnson	DB	Utah
6	Rusty Smith	QB	Florida Atlantic
	Myron Rolle	DB	Florida St.
7	Marc Mariani	WR	Montana
	David Howard	DT	Brown

TENNESSEE TITANS

2009 TEAM RECORD

PRESEASON (3-2)

Date	Result	Opponent
8/9	W 21-18	vs. Buffalo, at Canton, OH
8/15	W 27-20	Tampa Bay
8/21	L 10-30	at Dallas
8/29	L 17-23	at Cleveland
9/3	W 27-13	Green Bay

REGULAR SEASON (8-8)

Date	Result	Opponent
9/10	L 10-13	at Pittsburgh (OT)
9/20	L 31-34	Houston
9/27	L 17-24	at New York Jets
10/4	L 17-37	at Jacksonville
10/11	L 9-31	Indianapolis
10/18	L 0-59	at New England
11/1	W 30-13	Jacksonville
11/8	W 34-27	at San Francisco
11/15	W 41-17	Buffalo
11/23	W 20-17	at Houston
11/29	W 20-17	Arizona
12/6	L 17-27	at Indianapolis
12/13	W 47-7	St. Louis
12/20	W 27-24	Miami (OT)
12/25	L 17-42	San Diego
1/3	W 17-13	at Seattle

(OT) Overtime

SCORE BY PERIODS

Titans	77	103	67	104	3	—	354
Opponents	82	169	77	71	3	—	402

2009 TEAM STATISTICS

	Titans	Opp.
Total First Downs	288	323
Rushing	115	89
Passing	154	210
Penalty	19	24
3rd Down: Made/Att	89/214	89/218
3rd Down Pct.	41.6	40.8
4th Down: Made/Att	12/22	12/17
4th Down Pct.	54.5	70.6
Possession Avg.	28:27	31:33
Total Net Yards	5623	5850
Avg. Per Game	351.4	365.6
Total Plays	990	1038
Avg. Per Play	5.7	5.6
Net Yards Rushing	2592	1711
Avg. Per Game	162.0	106.9
Total Rushes	499	402
Net Yards Passing	3031	4139
Avg. Per Game	189.4	258.7
Sacked/Yards Lost	15/73	32/224
Gross Yards	3104	4363
Att./Completions	476/271	604/404
Completion Pct.	56.9	66.9
Had Intercepted	15	20
Punts/Average	69/43.4	76/44.3
Net Punting Avg.	69/38.7	76/39.5
Penalties/Yards	98/821	94/724
Fumbles/Ball Lost	27/16	20/7
Touchdowns	39	48
Rushing	19	16
Passing	16	31
Returns	4	1

2009 INDIVIDUAL STATISTICS

PASSING	Att.	Comp.	Yds.	Pct.	TD	Int.	Tkld.	Rate
Young	259	152	1879	58.7	10	7	9/36	82.8
Collins	216	119	1225	55.1	6	8	6/37	65.5
Johnson	1	0	0	0.0	0	0	0/0	39.6
Titans	476	271	3104	56.9	16	15	15/73	74.8
Opponents	604	404	4363	66.9	31	20	32/224	91.2

SCORING	TD R	TD P	TD Rt	PAT	FG	Saf	PTS
Bironas	0	0	0	37/37	27/32	0	118
Johnson	14	2	0	0/0	0/0	0	98
Washington	0	6	0	0/0	0/0	0	36
Britt	0	3	0	0/0	0/0	0	18
Gage	0	3	0	0/0	0/0	0	18
Fuller	0	0	2	0/0	0/0	0	12
White	2	0	0	0/0	0/0	0	12
Young	2	0	0	0/0	0/0	0	12
Collins	1	0	0	0/0	0/0	0	6
Crumpler	0	1	0	0/0	0/0	0	6
Finnegan	0	0	1	0/0	0/0	0	6
Hood	0	0	1	0/0	0/0	0	6
Scaife	0	1	0	0/0	0/0	0	6
Titans	19	16	4	37/37	27/32	0	354
Opponents	16	31	1	46/47	22/27	0	402

2-Pt. Conversions: Johnson.
Titans 1-2, Opponents 1-1.

RUSHING	No.	Yds	Avg	LG	TD
Johnson	358	2006	5.6	91t	14
Young	55	281	5.1	44	2
White	64	222	3.5	11	2
Ringer	8	48	6.0	32	0
Collins	11	15	1.4	10t	1
Washington	2	15	7.5	14	0
Hall	1	5	5.0	5	0
Titans	499	2592	5.2	91t	19
Opponents	402	1711	4.3	80t	16

RECEIVING	No.	Yds	Avg	LG	TD
Johnson	50	503	10.1	69t	2
Washington	47	569	12.1	35	6
Scaife	45	440	9.8	27	1
Britt	42	701	16.7	57	3
Gage	28	383	13.7	49	3
Crumpler	27	222	8.2	27	1
Hall	12	79	6.6	15	0
Cook	9	74	8.2	17	0
Hawkins	7	110	15.7	32	0
White	3	14	4.7	7	0
M. Jones	1	9	9.0	9	0
Titans	271	3104	11.5	69t	16
Opponents	404	4363	10.8	72t	31

INTERCEPTIONS	No.	Yds	Avg	LG	TD
Finnegan	5	194	38.8	80	1
Hood	3	91	30.3	43	1
Fuller	3	71	23.7	45t	2
Bulluck	3	45	15.0	23	0
Hope	3	24	8.0	24	0
Harper	1	4	4.0	4	0
Griffin	1	3	3.0	3	0
McRath	1	1	1.0	1	0
Titans	20	433	21.7	80	4
Opponents	15	121	8.1	26	0

PUNTING	No.	Yds.	Avg.	In 20	LG
Kern TM	37	1665	45	18	67
Hodges TM	22	868	39.5	1	50
Hentrich	9	422	46.9	3	60
Bironas	1	40	40	0	40
Titans	69	2995	43.4	22	67
Opponents	76	3364	44.3	32	64

PUNT RETURNS	Ret	FC	Yds	Avg	LG	TD
Pearman	11	8	112	10.2	18	0
Kaesviharn	9	8	34	3.8	10	0
Mouton	6	3	37	6.2	15	0
Finnegan	4	1	14	3.5	11	0
M. Jones	3	2	23	7.7	15	0
Titans	33	22	220	6.7	18	0
Opponents	29	17	208	7.2	37	0

KICKOFF RETURNS	No.	Yds	Avg	LG	TD
Britt	24	523	21.8	56	0
M. Jones	13	264	20.3	27	0
Ringer	9	181	20.1	25	0
Pearman	8	174	21.8	27	0
Griffin	6	143	23.8	31	0
McCourty	3	72	24.0	27	0
Crumpler	3	20	6.7	15	0
Mouton	1	14	14.0	14	0
Stevens	1	14	14.0	14	0
Hall	1	12	12.0	12	0
Titans	69	1417	20.5	56	0
Opponents	71	1714	24.1	99t	1

FIELD GOALS	1-19	20-29	30-39	40-49	50+
Bironas	0/0	8/8	4/6	10/12	5/6
Titans	0/0	8/8	4/6	10/12	5/6
Opponents	0/0	9/9	8/9	4/6	1/3

SACKS	No.
Ford	5.5
T. Brown	5.0
Hayes	4.0
J. Jones	4.0
Vanden Bosch	3.0
Hope	2.0
Tulloch	2.0
Fuller	1.0
Griffin	1.0
Kearse	1.0
Marks	1.0
Thornton	1.0
(group)	1.0
Haye	0.5
Titans	32.0
Opponents	15.0

RECORD HOLDERS

INDIVIDUAL RECORDS—CAREER

Category	Name	Performance
Rushing (Yds.)	Eddie George, 1996-2003	10,009
Passing (Yds.)	Warren Moon, 1984-1993	33,685
Passing (TDs)	Warren Moon, 1984-1993	196
Receiving (No.)	Ernest Givins, 1986-1994	542
Receiving (Yds.)	Ernest Givins, 1986-1994	7,935
Interceptions	Jim Norton, 1960-68	45
Punting (Avg.)	Greg Montgomery, 1988-1993	43.6
Punt Return (Avg.)	Billy Johnson, 1974-1980	13.2
Kickoff Return (Avg.)	Bobby Jancik, 1962-67	26.5
Field Goals	Al Del Greco, 1991-2000	246
Touchdowns (Tot.)	Eddie George, 1996-2003	74
Points	Al Del Greco, 1991-2000	1,060
*Sacks	Ray Childress, 1985-1995	75.5

INDIVIDUAL RECORDS—SINGLE SEASON

Category	Name	Performance
Rushing (Yds.)	Chris Johnson, 2009	2,006
Passing (Yds.)	Warren Moon, 1991	4,690
Passing (TDs)	George Blanda, 1961	36
Receiving (No.)	Charley Hennigan, 1964	101
Receiving (Yds.)	Charley Hennigan, 1961	1,746
Interceptions	Fred Glick, 1963	12
	Mike Reinfeldt, 1979	12
Punting (Avg.)	Craig Hentrich, 1998	47.2
Punt Return (Avg.)	Billy Johnson, 1977	15.4
Kickoff Return (Avg.)	Ken Hall, 1960	31.3
Field Goals	Al Del Greco, 1998	36
Touchdowns (Tot.)	Earl Campbell, 1979	19
Points	Al Del Greco, 1998	136
*Sacks	William Fuller, 1991	15.0

INDIVIDUAL RECORDS—SINGLE GAME

Category	Name	Performance
Rushing (Yds.)	Chris Johnson, 11-1-09	228
Passing (Yds.)	Warren Moon, 12-16-90	527
Passing (TDs)	George Blanda, 11-19-61	**7
Receiving (No.)	Charley Hennigan, 10-13-61	13
	Haywood Jeffires, 10-13-91	13
	Drew Bennett, 12-19-04	13
Receiving (Yds.)	Charley Hennigan, 10-13-61	272
Interceptions	Many times	3
	Last time by Keith Bulluck, 9-24-07	
Field Goals	Rob Bironas, 10-21-07	**8
Touchdowns (Tot.)	Billy Cannon, 12-10-61	5
Points	Billy Cannon, 12-10-61	30
*Sacks	William Fuller, 11-28-93	4.0

**Sacks became an official statistic in 1982.*
***NFL Record*

TENNESSEE TITANS

2010 VETERAN ROSTER

No.	Name	Pos.	Ht.	Wt.	Birthdate	NFL Exp.	College	Hometown	How Acq.	'09 Games/ Starts
56	Allred, Colin	LB	6-1	238	4/15/83	3	Baylor	Dallas, Texas	FA-'07	12/2
54	Amano, Eugene	G/C	6-3	310	3/1/82	7	Southeast Missouri State	San Diego, Calif.	D7-'04	16/15
58	Amato, Ken	LB/LS	6-2	245	5/18/77	8	Montana State	Miami, Fla.	FA-'03	16/0
93	Babin, Jason	DE	6-3	267	5/24/80	7	Western Michigan	Kalamazoo, Mich.	UFA(Phil)-'10	12/0*
98	Ball, Dave	DE	6-5	277	1/4/81	6	UCLA	Dixon, Calif.	FA-'08	11/1
2	Bironas, Rob	K	6-0	215	1/29/78	6	Georgia Southern	Louisville, Ky.	FA-'05	16/0
18	Britt, Kenny	WR	6-3	218	9/19/88	2	Rutgers	Bayonne, N.J.	D1-'09	16/6
79	Brown, Kareem	DL	6-4	260	1/30/84	2	Miami	Miami, Fla.	FA-'09	0*
97	Brown, Tony	DT	6-3	290	9/29/80	6	Memphis	Chattanooga, Tenn.	FA-'06	15/15
53	#Bulluck, Keith	LB	6-3	235	4/4/77	11	Syracuse	New City, N.Y.	D1-'00	14/14
5	Collins, Kerry	QB	6-5	245	12/30/72	16	Penn State	Lebanon, Pa.	UFA(Oak)-'06	7/6
89	Cook, Jared	TE	6-5	246	4/7/87	2	South Carolina	Suwanee, Ga.	D3-'09	14/0
19	Edison, Dominique	WR	6-2	204	7/16/86	2	Stephen F. Austin	San Augustine, Texas	D6-'09	5/0
31	Finnegan, Cortland	CB	5-10	188	2/2/84	5	Samford	Milton, Fla.	D7-'06	13/13
78	Ford, Jacob	DE	6-4	256	7/20/83	4	Central Arkansas	Memphis, Tenn.	D6-'07	15/0
22	Fuller, Vincent	S	6-1	190	8/3/82	6	Virginia Tech	Baltimore, Md.	D4-'05	13/1
12	Gage, Justin	WR	6-4	212	1/24/81	8	Missouri	Jefferson City, Mo.	UFA(Chi)-'07	12/10
33	Griffin, Michael	S	6-0	202	1/4/85	4	Texas	Austin, Texas	D1-'07	16/15
45	Hall, Ahmard	FB	5-11	242	11/13/79	5	Texas	Angleton, Texas	FA-'06	16/7
20	#Harper, Nick	CB	5-10	182	9/10/74	10	Fort Valley State	Baldwin, Ga.	UFA(Ind)-'07	11/11
64	Harris, Leroy	G/C	6-3	302	6/6/84	4	North Carolina State	Raleigh, N.C.	D4-'07	15/2
87	Hawkins, Lavelle	WR	5-11	190	7/12/86	3	California	Stockton, Calif.	D4-'08	10/0
75	Haye, Jovan	DT	6-2	285	6/21/82	6	Vanderbilt	Fort Lauderdale, Fla.	UFA(TB)-'09	15/15
95	Hayes, William	DE	6-3	272	5/2/85	3	Winston-Salem State	High Point, N.C.	D4-'08	16/11
26	Hill, Tye	CB	5-10	185	6/3/82	5	Clemson	St. George, S.C.	FA-'10	8/3*
37	Hood, Rod	CB	5-11	198	10/3/81	8	Auburn	Columbus, Ga.	FA-'09	5/4
24	Hope, Chris	S	6-0	208	9/29/80	9	Florida State	Rock Hill, S.C.	UFA(Pitt)-'06	16/16
90	Howard, Marcus	DE	6-0	237	10/12/85	2	Georgia	Huger, S.C.	FA-'10	0*
28	Johnson, Chris	RB	5-11	200	9/23/85	3	East Carolina	Orlando, Fla.	D1-'08	16/16
91	Jones, Jason	DT	6-5	280	5/23/86	3	Eastern Michigan	Detroit, Mich.	D2-'08	7/0
84	Jones, Mark	WR	5-9	185	11/3/80	7	Tennessee	Wallingford, Pa.	UFA(Car)-'09	3/0
26	#Kaesviharn, Kevin	S	6-1	200	8/29/76	10	Augustana (S.D.)	Paramount, Calif.	FA-'09	13/0
90	#Kearse, Jevon	DE	6-4	265	9/3/76	12	Florida	Ft. Myers, Fla.	FA-'08	6/4
59	Keglar, Stanford	LB	6-2	240	7/4/85	3	Purdue	Indianapolis, Ind.	D4-'08	12/0
6	Kern, Brett	P	6-2	215	2/17/86	3	Toledo	Grand Island, N.Y.	W(Den)-'09	16/0*
70	Kropog, Troy	T/G	6-6	309	7/31/86	2	Tulane	Metairie, La.	D4-'09	1/0
94	Marks, Sen'Derrick	DT	6-2	306	2/23/87	2	Auburn	Mobile, Ala.	D2-'09	9/0
68	#Mawae, Kevin	C	6-4	289	1/23/71	17	Louisiana State	Leesville, La.	UFA(NYJ)-'06	16/16
30	McCourty, Jason	CB	6-0	193	8/13/87	2	Rutgers	Nyack, N.Y.	D6-'09	15/3
51	McRath, Gerald	LB	6-3	231	6/16/86	2	Southern Mississippi	Powder Springs, Ga.	D4-'09	16/5
29	Mouton, Ryan	CB	5-9	187	9/23/86	2	Hawaii	Houston, Texas	D3-'09	14/2
23	Nickey, Donnie	S	6-3	210	4/25/80	8	Ohio State	Plain City, Ohio	D5-'03	16/1
66	Otto, Mike	T	6-5	308	7/24/83	3	Purdue	Kokomo, Ind.	D7-'07	14/0
35	Pearman, Alvin	RB	5-10	204	8/10/82	5	Virginia	Charlotte, N.C.	FA-'09	5/0
21	Ringer, Javon	RB	5-9	205	2/2/87	2	Michigan State	Dayton, Ohio	D5-'09	6/0
71	Roos, Michael	T	6-7	315	10/5/82	6	Eastern Washington	Vancouver, Wash.	D2-'05	16/16
80	Scaife, Bo	TE	6-3	249	1/6/81	6	Texas	Denver, Colo.	D6-'05	14/10
73	Scott, Jake	G	6-5	295	4/16/81	7	Idaho	Lewiston, Idaho	UFA(Ind)-'08	16/16
8	Simms, Chris	QB	6-4	220	8/29/80	8	Texas	Ramapo, N.J.	FA-'08	3/1*
88	Stevens, Craig	TE	6-3	255	9/1/84	3	California	Rancho Palos Verdes, Calif.	D3-'08	12/2
76	Stewart, David	T	6-7	318	8/28/82	6	Mississippi State	Moulton, Ala.	D4-'05	15/15
50	Thornton, David	LB	6-2	225	11/1/78	9	North Carolina	Goldsboro, N.C.	UFA(Ind)-'06	11/11
44	Togafau, Pago	LB	5-11	240	1/10/84	3	Idaho State	Long Beach, Calif.	W(Ariz)-'10	2/0*
55	Tulloch, Stephen	LB	5-11	235	1/1/85	5	North Carolina State	Miami, Fla.	D4-'06	16/13
85	Washington, Nate	WR	6-1	185	8/28/83	6	Tiffin	Toledo, Ohio	UFA(Pitt)-'09	16/15
81	Williams, Paul	WR	6-1	205	12/2/83	3	Fresno State	Avenal, Calif.	D3-'07	0*
52	Winborn, Jamie	LB	5-11	230	5/14/79	9	Vanderbilt	Wetumpka, Ala.	FA-'09	2/0
4	Witherspoon, Will	LB	6-1	240	8/19/80	9	Georgia	Panama City, Fla.	FA-'10	17/16*
10	Young, Vince	QB	6-5	233	5/18/83	5	Texas	Houston, Texas	D1-'06	12/10

* Babin played 12 games with Philadelphia in '09; K. Brown last active with N.Y. Jets in '08; Hill played 8 games with Atlanta; Howard last active with Indianapolis in '08; Kern played 6 games with Denver and 10 games with Tennessee; Simms played 3 games with Denver; Togafau played 2 games with Arizona; Williams last active with Tennessee in '08; Witherspoon played 6 games with St. Louis and 11 with Philadelphia.

\# Unrestricted free agent; subject to developments.

Traded—DT Kevin Vickerson (13 games in '09) to Seattle, RB LenDale White (13) to Seattle.

Retired—Craig Hentrich, 16-year punter, 2 games.

Players lost through free agency (2): TE Alge Crumpler (NE; 16 games in '09), DE Kyle Vanden Bosch (Det; 16).

Also played with Titans in '09—DE Eric Bakhtiarai (3 games), RB Chris Henry (2), P Reggie Hodges (4), G Fernando Velasco (1), DB Cary Williams (4).

2010 FIRST-YEAR ROSTER

Name	Pos.	Ht.	Wt.	Birthdate	College	Hometown	How Acq.
Alfred, Kenny	C	6-2	290	7/29/86	Washington State	Gig Harbor, Wash.	FA
Bakhtiari, Eric (1)	DE	6-3	285	12/2/84	San Diego	Burlingame, Calif.	FA-'09
Blount, LeGarrette	RB	6-0	241	12/5/86	Oregon	Madison, Fla.	FA
Curran, Rennie	LB	5-11	235	11/10/88	Georgia	Snellville, Ga.	D3
Durand, Ryan (1)	G	6-5	305	11/17/85	Syracuse	Leominster, Mass.	D7-'09
Harris, Gerald	TE	6-1	259	4/16/88	Mississippi	Terrell, Texas	FA
Howard, David	DT	6-3	293	8/31/87	Brown	Columbia, Md.	D7
Howell, Nick	T	6-5	300	10/10/86	Southern California	Fresno, Calif.	FA
Johnson, Robert	S	6-2	203	2/13/87	Utah	Los Angeles, Calif.	D5
Johnson, Stafon	RB	5-11	214	2/6/88	Southern California	Bellflower, Calif.	FA
Joseph, Joe	DT	6-2	300	10/20/85	Miami	Orlando, Fla.	FA
Lewko, Jake	LB	6-1	237	10/7/87	Pennsylvania	Camden, N.J.	FA
Lindsay, Dominique	RB	5-10	201	12/8/86	East Carolina	Charlotte, N.C.	FA
Love, Jamar (1)	CB	6-0	191	11/8/86	Arkansas	North Little Rock, Ark.	FA-'09
Malecki, John	G	6-2	298	5/26/88	Pittsburgh	Murrysville, Pa.	FA
Mariani, Marc	WR	6-1	190	5/2/87	Montana	Havre, Mont.	D7
Matthews, Kevin	C	6-3	298	2/4/87	Texas A&M	Houston, Texas	FA
McCaskill, Nevin (1)	T	6-4	300	12/29/83	Hampton	Tallahassee, Fla.	FA
McSwain, Mico	WR	6-0	208	3/7/84	North Alabama	Richton, Miss.	FA
Moore, Jay (1)	DE	6-4	280	8/16/83	Nebraska	Elkhorn, Neb.	FA
Morgan, Derrick	DE	6-3	266	1/6/89	Georgia Tech	Coatesville, Pa.	D1
Morris, Phillip (1)	WR	6-3	175	7/2/86	South Carolina State	Timmonsville, S.C.	FA-'09
Pfahler, Steve	TE	6-4	250	8/21/87	Montana	Frenchtown, Mont.	FA
Rivera, Mike (1)	LB	6-2	245	1/10/86	Kansas	Shawnee Mission, Kan.	FA-'09
Rolle, Myron	S	6-2	215	10/30/86	Florida State	Galloway, N.J.	D6
Rose, Willie	FB	6-1	236	3/23/87	Florida Atlantic	Lutz, Fla.	FA
Schmitt, Ricky (1)	P/K	6-3	210	8/17/85	Shepherd (W. Va.)	Virginia Beach, Va.	FA
Schommer, Nick (1)	S	6-0	201	1/3/86	North Dakota State	Prescott, Wis.	D7-'09
Sewall, Bobby	WR	6-0	197	2/29/88	Brown	Portsmouth, R.I.	FA
Smith, Rusty	QB	6-5	230	1/28/87	Florida Atlantic	Jacksonville, Fla.	D6
Trahan, Patrick	LB	6-2	234	11/7/86	Mississippi	New Orleans, La.	FA
Velasco, Fernando (1)	C/G	6-4	304	2/22/85	Georgia	Wrens, Ga.	FA-'08
Verner, Alterraun	CB	5-10	189	12/13/88	UCLA	Carson, Calif.	D4
Williams, Damian	WR	6-1	197	5/26/88	Southern California	Springdale, Ark.	D3

The term NFL Rookie is defined as a player who is in his first season of professional football and has not been on the roster of another professional football team for any regular-season or postseason games. A Rookie is designated by an "R" on NFL rosters. Players who have been active in another professional football league or players who have NFL experience, including either preseason training camp or being on an Active List or Inactive List, or on Reserve/Injured or Reserve/Physically Unable to Perform for fewer than six regular-season games, are termed NFL First-Year Players. An NFL First-Year Player is designated by a "1" on NFL rosters. Thereafter, a player is credited with an additional year of experience for each season in which he accumulates six games on the Active List or Inactive List, or on Reserve/Injured or Reserve/Physically Unable to Perform.

Log on to www.titansonline.com for an up-to-date roster.

TENNESSEE TITANS

COACHING STAFF

Head Coach,
Jeff Fisher

Pro Career: Officially became the franchise's fifteenth head coach on January 5, 1995, after closing his first campaign with the Oilers as head coach/defensive coordinator. He replaced Jack Pardee on November 14, 1994, coaching the remaining six games as head coach. Fisher holds the franchise mark for wins with 141 over his 15-year coaching career. Fisher, the NFL's current leader in head coaching tenure, has led the Titans to six playoff appearance in the past 11 years. In 2008, Tennessee's 13-3 record, which included a franchise-best 10 consecutive wins to start the season, matched the best record in franchise history and led to an AFC South title. In 2009, he moved into 20th place in NFL history in career wins among head coaches, and he ranks 10th in league history in games coached with one team (257). Fisher has led the Titans to two AFC Championship Games and a berth in Super Bowl XXXIV. In 2000, Fisher became only the fifth coach in NFL history to lead his team to consecutive 13-win seasons, joining Mike Holmgren, George Seifert, Marv Levy, and Mike Ditka. Fisher originally joined the Oilers in 1994 as the defensive coordinator, after serving as defensive backs coach for the San Francisco 49ers (1992-93). In 1991, Fisher served as the defensive coordinator for the Rams. He began his coaching career with the Philadelphia Eagles in 1986, where he handled defensive backs until becoming the NFL's youngest defensive coordinator in 1988. Spent five seasons as a cornerback and kick returner for the Bears (1981-85). Assisted defensive coordinator Buddy Ryan in Bears' 1985 Super Bowl season after being placed on injured reserve with ankle injury. Career record: 141-116.

Background: Played at Southern California (1977-1980) for John Robinson in a star-studded defensive backfield that included Ronnie Lott, Dennis Smith, and Joey Browner. Member of the USC team that won the national championship in 1978. Also served as the Trojans' backup placekicker and was a Pac-10 All-Academic selection in 1980.

Personal: Born February 25, 1958, in Culver City, Calif. Fisher has three children, sons Brandon and Trenton, and daughter Tara.

ASSISTANT COACHES

Chuck Cecil, defensive coordinator; born November 8, 1964, Red Bluff, Calif. Defensive back Arizona 1983-87. Pro safety Green Bay Packers 1988-1992, Phoenix Cardinals 1993, Houston Oilers 1995. Pro coach: Joined Titans in 2001.

Marty Galbraith, asst. special teams; born February 3, 1950, Joplin, Mo. Defensive back Missouri Southern 1971-73. No pro playing experience. College coach: Purdue 1977, Wake Forest 1978-1982, Louisiana State 1987-88, Wake Forest 1989-1990, Pittsburgh 1991, Georgia Tech 1992-93, Marshall 1998-99, North Carolina State 2000-02, Duke 2004. Pro coach: Tampa Bay Bandits (USFL) 1983-84, Kansas City Chiefs 1985, Arizona Outlaws (USFL) 1986, Arizona Cardinals 2003, joined Titans in 2005.

Fred Graves, wide receivers; born March 2, 1950, Los Angeles, Calif. Halfback/split end Utah 1968-1971. Pro halfback California Suns 1973 (World Football League). College coach: Northeast Missouri State 1975-76, Western Illinois 1977-78, New Mexico State 1979-1981, Utah 1982-2000. Pro coach: Buffalo Bills 2001-03, Cleveland Browns 2004, Detroit Lions 2005, joined Titans in 2007.

Tim Hauck, asst. secondary; born December 20, 1966, Butte, Mont. Defensive back Pacific 1985, Montana 1986-89. Pro safety New England Patriots 1990, Green Bay Packers 1991-94, Denver Broncos 1995-96, Seattle Seahawks 1997, Indianapolis Colts 1998, Philadelphia Eagles 1999-2002, San Francisco 49ers 2002. College coach: Montana 2004-07, UCLA 2008. Pro coach: Joined Titans in 2009.

Mike Heimerdinger, offensive coordinator; born October 13, 1952, DeKalb, Ill. Wide receiver Eastern Illinois 1970-74. No pro playing experience. College coach: Florida 1980, Air Force 1981, North Texas State 1982, Florida 1983-87, Cal State-Fullerton 1988, Rice 1989-1993, Duke 1994. Pro coach: Denver Broncos 1995-99, Tennessee Titans 2000-04, N.Y. Jets 2005, Denver Broncos 2006-07, re-joined Titans in 2008.

Craig Johnson, quarterbacks; born March 3, 1960, Rome, N.Y. Quarterback Wyoming 1978-1982. No pro playing experience. College coach: Wyoming 1983, Arkansas 1984, Army 1985, Rutgers 1986-88, Virginia Military Institute 1989-1991, Northwestern 1992-96, Maryland 1997-99. Pro coach: Joined Titans in 2000.

Dowell Loggains, offensive quality control; born October 1, 1980, Newport, Ark. Quarterback Arkansas 2000-04. No pro playing experience. Pro coach: Dallas Cowboys 2005, joined Titans in 2006.

Alan Lowry, special teams; born November 21, 1950, Miami, Okla. Defensive back/quarterback Texas 1970-72. No pro playing experience. College coach: Virginia Tech 1974, Wyoming 1975, Texas 1977-1981. Pro coach: Dallas Cowboys 1982-1990, Tampa Bay Buccaneers 1991, San Francisco 49ers 1992-95, joined Titans/Oilers in 1996.

Dave McGinnis, linebackers; born August 7, 1951, Independence, Kan. Defensive back Texas Christian 1970-72. No pro playing experience. College coach: Texas Christian 1973-74, 1982, Missouri 1975-77, Indiana State 1978, 1980-81, Kansas State 1983-85. Pro coach: Chicago Bears 1986-1995, Arizona Cardinals 1996-2003 (head coach 2000-2003), joined Titans in 2004.

Mike Munchak, offensive line; born March 5, 1960, Scranton, Pa. Guard-tackle Penn State 1979-1981. Pro guard Houston Oilers 1982-1993. Inducted into Pro Football Hall of Fame 2001. Pro coach: Joined Titans/Oilers in 1994.

Kennedy Pola, running backs; born November 22, 1963, Pago, Pago, American Samoa. Fullback Southern California 1982-85. No pro playing experience. College coach: UCLA 1992-93, San Diego State 1994-96, Colorado 1997-98, San Diego State 1999, Southern California 2000-03. Pro coach: Cleveland Browns 2004, Jacksonville Jaguars 2005-09, joined Titans in 2010.

Marcus Robertson, defensive backs; born October 2, 1969, Pasadena, Calif. Defensive back Iowa State 1987-1990. Pro safety Houston Oilers/Tennessee Titans 1991-2000, Seattle Seahawks 2001-02. Pro coach: Joined Titans in 2007.

Rayna Stewart, defensive quality control; born June 18, 1973, Oklahoma City, Okla. Defensive back/linebacker Northern Arizona 1992-95. Pro defensive back Houston/Tennessee Oilers 1996-97, Miami Dolphins 1998, Jacksonville Jaguars 1999-2000. College coach: Northwestern 2007-08. Pro coach: Joined Titans in 2009.

Jim Washburn, defensive line; born December 2, 1949, Shelby, N.C. Offensive lineman Gardner-Webb 1969-1973. No pro playing experience. College coach: Southern Methodist 1976, Lees McRae (N.C.) J.C. 1977-78, Livingston 1979, New Mexico 1980-82, South Carolina 1983-88, Purdue 1989, Arkansas 1994-97, Houston 1998. Pro coach: London Monarchs (WLAF) 1991, Charlotte Rage (AFL) 1993, joined Titans in 1999.

Steve Watterson, strength and rehabilitation; born November 27, 1956, Newport, R.I. Attended Rhode Island. No college or pro playing experience. Pro coach: Philadelphia Eagles 1984-85, joined Titans/Oilers in 1986.

Richie Wessman, offensive asst.: born December 10, 1980, San Clemente, Calif. Quarterback Orange Coast College 1999, Southern California 2000-01. No pro playing experience. College coach: Southern California 2003-04. Pro coach: Joined Titans in 2009.

John Zernhelt, tight ends, born January 4, 1954, Pottsville, Pa. Offensive lineman Maryland 1974-77. No pro playing experience. College coach: Ferrum 1977-1980, Marshall 1981, East Carolina 1982-86, Maryland 1987-1991, Rice 1992-93, Duke 1994-95, South Carolina 1996-98, James Madison 1999-2002, The Citadel 2003-04. Pro coach: New York Jets 2005, joined Titans in 2006.

The NFC

National Football Conference
West Division
Team Colors: Cardinal Red, Black, and White
8701 S. Hardy Drive
Tempe, Arizona 85284
Telephone: (602) 379-0101

2010 SCHEDULE

PRESEASON

Aug. 14	**Houston**	5:00
Aug. 23	at Tennessee	7:00
Aug. 28	at Chicago	7:30
Sep. 2	**Washington**	7:00

REGULAR SEASON

Sep. 12	at St. Louis	3:15
Sep. 19	at Atlanta	1:00
Sep. 26	**Oakland**	1:15
Oct. 3	at San Diego	1:15
Oct. 10	**New Orleans**	1:05
Oct. 17	BYE	
Oct. 24	at Seattle	1:05
Oct. 31	**Tampa Bay**	1:15
Nov. 7	at Minnesota	12:00
Nov. 14	**Seattle**	2:15
Nov. 21	at Kansas City	12:00
Nov. 29	**San Francisco** (Mon)	6:30
Dec. 5	**St. Louis**	2:15
Dec. 12	**Denver**	2:15
Dec. 19	at Carolina	1:00
Dec. 25	**Dallas** (Sat)	5:30
Jan. 2	at San Francisco	1:15

Stadium: University of Phoenix Stadium (opened in 2006)
•**Capacity:** 65,000
1 Cardinals Drive
Glendale, Arizona 85305
Playing Surface: Grass
Training Camp: Northern Arizona University
Flagstaff, Arizona 86011

UNIVERSITY OF PHOENIX STADIUM

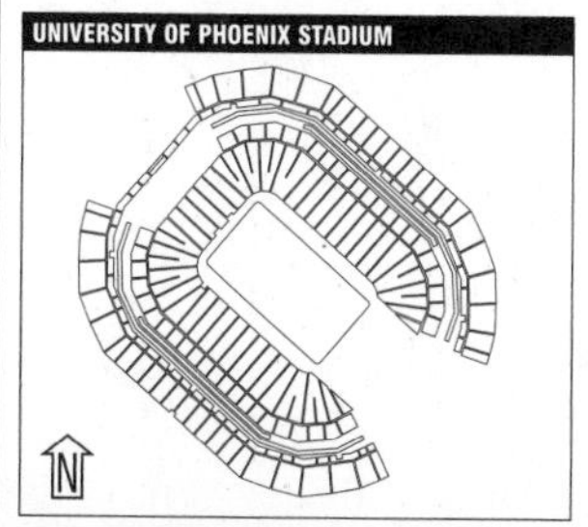

CLUB OFFICIALS

Owner: William V. Bidwill
President: Michael Bidwill
General Manager: Rod Graves
Executive Vice President/Chief Operating Officer: Ron Minegar
Chief Financial Officer: Greg Lee
General Counsel: David Koeninger
Vice President, Media Relations: Mark Dalton
Vice President, Marketing: Lisa Manning
Vice President, Business Development: Steve Ryan
Vice President, Information Technology: Mark Feller
Vice President, Security: Rick Knight
Vice President, Stadium Operations: John Drum
Senior Director, Player Programs: Anthony Edwards
Senior Director, Community Relations: Luis Zendejas
Senior Director, Ticketing: Steve Bomar
Senior Director, Ticket Sales: Ron Campbell
Director, Player Personnel: Steve Keim
Director, Pro Personnel: T.J. McCreight
Director, Football Administration: Reggie Terry
Director, Broadcasting/Executive Producer: Tim DeLaney
Director, Cheerleading: Heather Karberg
Website Manager: Darren Urban
Video Director: Rob Brakel
Head Athletic Trainer: Tom Reed
Assistant Athletic Trainers: Jim Shearer, Jeff Herndon, Chad Cook
Equipment Manager: Mark Ahlemeier
Assistant Equipment Manager: Steve Christensen

COACHING HISTORY

Chicago 1920-1959, St. Louis 1960-1987 (489-687-39)

Records include postseason games

1920-22	John (Paddy) Driscoll	17-8-4
1923-24	Arnold Horween	13-8-1
1925-26	Norman Barry	16-8-2
1927	Guy Chamberlin	3-7-1
1928	Fred Gillies	1-5-0
1929	Dewey Scanlon	6-6-1
1930	Ernie Nevers	5-6-2
1931	LeRoy Andrews*	0-1-0
1931	Ernie Nevers	5-3-0
1932	Jack Chevigny	2-6-2
1933-34	Paul Schissler	6-15-1
1935-38	Milan Creighton	16-26-4
1939	Ernie Nevers	1-10-0
1940-42	Jimmy Conzelman	8-22-3
1943-45	Phil Handler**	1-29-0
1946-48	Jimmy Conzelman	27-10-0
1949	Phil Handler-Buddy Parker***	2-4-0
1949	Raymond (Buddy) Parker	4-1-1
1950-51	Earl (Curly) Lambeau****	7-15-0
1951	Phil Handler-Cecil Isbell#	1-1-0
1952	Joe Kuharich	4-8-0
1953-54	Joe Stydahar	3-20-1
1955-57	Ray Richards	14-21-1
1958-1961	Frank (Pop) Ivy##	15-31-2
1961	Chuck Drulis-Ray Prochaska-Ray Willsey###	2-0-0
1962-65	Wally Lemm	27-26-3
1966-1970	Charley Winner	35-30-5
1971-72	Bob Hollway	8-18-2
1973-77	Don Coryell	42-29-1
1978-79	Bud Wilkinson####	9-20-0
1979	Larry Wilson	2-1-0
1980-85	Jim Hanifan	39-50-1
1986-89	Gene Stallings@	23-34-1
1989	Hank Kuhlmann	0-5-0
1990-93	Joe Bugel	20-44-0
1994-95	Buddy Ryan	12-20-0
1996-2000	Vince Tobin@@	29-44-0
2000-03	Dave McGinnis	17-40-0
2004-06	Dennis Green	16-32-0
2007-09	Ken Whisenhunt	31-23-0

* Resigned after one game in 1931
** Co-coach with Walt Kiesling in Chicago Cardinals-Pittsburgh merger in 1944
*** Co-coaches for first six games in 1949
**** Resigned after 10 games in 1951
\# Co-coaches
\## Resigned after 12 games in 1961
\### Co-coaches
\#### Released after 13 games in 1979
@ Released after 11 games in 1989
@@ Released after seven games in 2000

PAID ATTENDANCE

Home 495,595 Away 469,823
Total 965,418
Single-game home record, 73,025* (9/19/93)
Single-season home record, 516,646 (2007)
*Team also had attendance of 103,467 for regular-season home game at Azteca Stadium, Mexico City, Mexico

2010 DRAFT CHOICES

Round	Name	Pos.	College
1	Dan Williams	DT	Tennessee
2	Daryl Washington	LB	Texas Christian
3	Andre Roberts	WR	The Citadel
4	O'Brien Schofield	LB	Wisconsin
5	John Skelton	QB	Fordham
6	Jorrick Calvin	DB	Troy
7	Jim Dray	TE	Stanford

ARIZONA CARDINALS

2009 TEAM RECORD

PRESEASON (0-4)

Date	Result	Opponent
8/13	L 10-20	at Pittsburgh
8/22	L 6-17	San Diego
8/28	L 37-44	Green Bay
9/3	L 0-19	at Denver

REGULAR SEASON (10-6)

Date	Result	Opponent
9/13	L 16-20	San Francisco
9/20	W 31-17	at Jacksonville
9/27	L 10-31	Indianapolis
10/11	W 28-21	Houston
10/18	W 27-3	at Seattle
10/25	W 24-17	at New York Giants
11/1	L 21-34	Carolina
11/8	W 41-21	at Chicago
11/15	W 31-20	Seattle
11/22	W 21-13	at St. Louis
11/29	L 17-20	at Tennessee
12/6	W 30-17	Minnesota
12/14	L 9-24	at San Francisco
12/20	W 31-24	at Detroit
12/27	W 31-10	St. Louis
1/3	L 7-33	Green Bay

POSTSEASON (1-1)

Date	Result	Opponent
1/10	W 51-45	Green Bay (OT)
1/16	L 14-45	at New Orleans

(OT) Overtime

SCORE BY PERIODS

Cardinals	76	132	82	85	0	— 375
Opponents	67	101	62	95	0	— 325

2009 TEAM STATISTICS

	Cardinals	Opp.
Total First Downs	317	289
Rushing	77	81
Passing	215	188
Penalty	25	20
3rd Down: Made/Att	69/190	82/232
3rd Down Pct.	36.3	35.3
4th Down: Made/Att	5/9	12/24
4th Down Pct.	55.6	50.0
Possession Avg.	29:52	30:08
Total Net Yards	5510	5543
Avg. Per Game	344.4	346.4
Total Plays	985	1038
Avg. Per Play	5.6	5.3
Net Yards Rushing	1494	1804
Avg. Per Game	93.4	112.8
Total Rushes	365	402
Net Yards Passing	4016	3739
Avg. Per Game	251.0	233.7
Sacked/Yards Lost	26/184	43/259
Gross Yards	4200	3998
Att./Completions	594/392	593/346
Completion Pct.	66.0	58.3
Had Intercepted	18	21
Punts/Average	86/47.0	84/44.9
Net Punting Avg.	86/40.6	84/39.4
Penalties/Yards	108/886	104/840
Fumbles/Ball Lost	32/18	20/8
Touchdowns	46	38
Rushing	16	13
Passing	27	22
Returns	3	3

2009 INDIVIDUAL STATISTICS

PASSING	Att.	Comp.	Yds.	Pct.	TD	Int.	Tkld.	Rate
Warner	513	339	3753	66.1	26	14	24/172	93.2
Leinart	77	51	435	66.2	0	3	2/12	64.6
St. Pierre	4	2	12	50.0	1	1	0/0	56.3
Cardinals	594	392	4200	66.0	27	18	26/184	89.1
Opponents	593	346	3998	58.3	22	21	43/259	76.4

SCORING	TD R	TD P	TD Rt	PAT	FG	Saf	PTS
Rackers	0	0	0	37/38	16/17	0	85
Fitzgerald	0	13	0	0/0	0/0	0	78
Hightower	8	0	0	0/0	0/0	0	48
B. Wells	7	0	0	0/0	0/0	0	42
Boldin	1	4	0	0/0	0/0	0	30
Breaston	0	3	0	0/0	0/0	0	18
Nugent TM	0	0	0	8/8	2/2	0	14
Patrick	0	2	0	0/0	0/0	0	12
Stephens-Howling	0	1	1	0/0	0/0	0	12
Wright	0	2	0	0/0	0/0	0	12
Becht	0	1	0	0/0	0/0	0	6
Doucet	0	1	0	0/0	0/0	0	6
Rodgers-Cromartie	0	0	1	0/0	0/0	0	6
Rolle	0	0	1	0/0	0/0	0	6
Cardinals	16	27	3	45/46	18/19	0	375
Opponents	13	22	3	38/38	19/25	1	325

2-Pt. Conversions: Cardinals 0-0, Opponents 0-0

RUSHING	No.	Yds	Avg	LG	TD
B. Wells	176	793	4.5	33	7
Hightower	143	598	4.2	50	8
Breaston	2	44	22.0	25	0
Wright	3	17	5.7	8	0
Stephens-Howling	6	15	2.5	5	0
Boldin	3	12	4.0	5t	1
Warner	21	10	0.5	10	0
Rolle	1	9	9.0	9	0
St. Pierre	1	2	2.0	2	0
Leinart	9	-6	-0.7	1	0
Cardinals	365	1494	4.1	50	16
Opponents	402	1804	4.5	85t	13

RECEIVING	No.	Yds	Avg	LG	TD
Fitzgerald	97	1092	11.3	34t	13
Boldin	84	1024	12.2	44	4
Hightower	63	428	6.8	23	0
Breaston	55	712	12.9	45	3
Urban	18	186	10.3	40	0
Doucet	17	214	12.6	29	1
Patrick	12	146	12.2	28	2
B. Wells	12	143	11.9	25	0
Stephens-Howling	10	83	8.3	15	1
Wright	9	53	5.9	10	2
Becht	7	61	8.7	16	1
Spach	4	38	9.5	22	0
Kreider	4	20	5.0	8	0
Cardinals	392	4200	10.7	45	27
Opponents	346	3998	11.6	72	22

INTERCEPTIONS	No.	Yds	Avg	LG	TD
Rodgers-Cromartie	6	77	12.8	49t	1
Wilson	5	56	11.2	41	0
Rolle	4	71	17.8	29	0
R. Brown	1	85	85.0	80	0
Ware	1	18	18.0	18	0
Adams	1	17	17.0	17	0
Dansby	1	11	11.0	11	0
Dockett	1	3	3.0	3	0
Toler	1	0	0.0	0	0
Cardinals	21	338	16.1	80	1
Opponents	18	312	17.3	101t	3

PUNTING	No.	Yds.	Avg.	In 20	LG
Graham	86	4045	47.0	42	64
Cardinals	86	4045	47.0	42	64
Opponents	84	3774	44.9	30	64

PUNT RETURNS	Ret	FC	Yds	Avg	LG	TD
Breaston	38	11	253	6.7	64	0
Rolle	6	2	55	9.2	27	0
Toler	1	0	0	0.0	0	0
Cardinals	45	13	308	6.8	64	0
Opponents	47	14	493	10.5	62	0

KICKOFF RETURNS	No.	Yds	Avg	LG	TD
Stephens-Howling	52	1257	24.2	99t	1
Wright	2	27	13.5	18	0
Cardinals	54	1284	23.8	99t	1
Opponents	61	1248	20.5	63	0

FIELD GOALS	1-19	20-29	30-39	40-49	50+
Rackers	0/0	4/4	6/6	6/7	0/0
Nugent TM	1/1	0/0	0/0	1/1	0/0
Cardinals	1/1	4/4	6/6	7/8	0/0
Opponents	0/0	8/8	8/10	1/3	2/4

SACKS	No.
Campbell	7.0
Dockett	7.0
Berry	6.0
Haggans	5.0
Okeafor	4.5
Branch	2.0
Davis	2.0
Iwebema	2.0
Wilson	2.0
Rolle	1.5
Banks	1.0
Dansby	1.0
B. Robinson	1.0
(group)	1.0
Cardinals	43.0
Opponents	26.0

RECORD HOLDERS

INDIVIDUAL RECORDS—CAREER

Category	Name	Performance
Rushing (Yds.)	Ottis Anderson, 1979-1986	7,999
Passing (Yds.)	Jim Hart, 1966-1983	34,639
Passing (TDs)	Jim Hart, 1966-1983	209
Receiving (No.)	Anquan Boldin, 2003-09	586
Receiving (Yds.)	Roy Green, 1979-1990	8,497
Interceptions	Larry Wilson, 1960-1972	52
Punting (Avg.)	Ben Graham, 2008-09	46.1
Punt Return (Avg.)	Charley Trippi, 1947-1955	13.7
Kickoff Return (Avg.)	Ollie Matson, 1952, 1954-58	28.5
Field Goals	Jim Bakken, 1962-1978	282
Touchdowns (Tot.)	Roy Green, 1979-1990	70
Points	Jim Bakken, 1962-1978	1,380
*Sacks	Freddie Joe Nunn, 1985-1993	66.5

INDIVIDUAL RECORDS—SINGLE SEASON

Category	Name	Performance
Rushing (Yds.)	Ottis Anderson, 1979	1,605
Passing (Yds.)	Neil Lomax, 1984	4,614
Passing (TDs)	Kurt Warner, 2008	30
Receiving (No.)	Larry Fitzgerald, 2005	103
Receiving (Yds.)	David Boston, 2001	1,598
Interceptions	Bob Nussbaumer, 1949	12
Punting (Avg.)	Ben Graham, 2009	47.0
Punt Return (Avg.)	John (Red) Cochran, 1949	20.9
Kickoff Return (Avg.)	Ollie Matson, 1958	35.5
Field Goals	Neil Rackers, 2005	**40
Touchdowns (Tot.)	John David Crow, 1962	17
Points	Neil Rackers, 2005	140
*Sacks	Simeon Rice, 1999	16.5

INDIVIDUAL RECORDS—SINGLE GAME

Category	Name	Performance
Rushing (Yds.)	LeShon Johnson, 9-22-96	214
Passing (Yds.)	Boomer Esiason, 11-10-96 (OT)	522
Passing (TDs)	Jim Hardy, 10-2-50	6
	Charley Johnson, 9-26-65, 11-2-69	6
Receiving (No.)	Sonny Randle, 11-4-62	16
Receiving (Yds.)	Sonny Randle, 11-4-62	256
Interceptions	Bob Nussbaumer, 11-13-49	**4
	Jerry Norton, 11-20-60	**4
	Kwamie Lassiter, 12-27-98	**4
Field Goals	Jim Bakken, 9-24-67	7
Touchdowns (Tot.)	Ernie Nevers, 11-28-29	**6
Points	Ernie Nevers, 11-28-29	**40
*Sacks	Curtis Greer, 12-18-83	4.5

**Sacks became an official statistic in 1982.*
***NFL Record*

ARIZONA CARDINALS

2010 VETERAN ROSTER

No.	Name	Pos.	Ht.	Wt.	Birthdate	NFL Exp.	College	Hometown	How Acq.	'09 Games/ Starts
41	Abdullah, Hamza	S	6-2	216	8/20/83	6	Washington State	Los Angeles, Calif.	FA-'09	1/0
27	Adams, Michael	CB	5-8	181	6/17/85	4	Louisiana-Lafayette	Dallas, Texas	FA-'07	16/1
42	Ali, Charles	FB	6-2	255	8/23/84	3	Arkansas-Pine Bluff	St. Louis, Mo.	FA-'10	0*
3	Anderson, Derek	QB	6-6	230	6/15/83	6	Oregon State	Scappoose, Ore.	FA-'10	8/7*
23	Barksdale, Rashad	CB	6-0	208	5/11/84	2	Albany	Hudson, N.Y.	FA-'09	0*
84	Becht, Anthony	TE	6-6	270	8/8/77	11	West Virginia	Drexel Hill, Pa.	FA-'09	16/10
52	Beisel, Monty	LB	6-3	244	11/9/86	10	Kansas State	Coral Springs, Fla.	FA-'09	6/0
78	Branch, Alan	DT	6-5	338	12/29/84	4	Michigan	Rio Rancho, N.M.	D2-'07	16/0
15	Breaston, Steve	WR	6-0	189	8/20/83	4	Michigan	North Braddock, Pa.	D5-'07	15/6
73	Bridges, Jeremy	G/T	6-4	326	4/19/80	8	Southern Mississippi	South Pike, Miss.	FA-'09	16/4
32	Broughton, Nehemiah	FB	5-11	255	11/4/82	4	The Citadel	Charleston, S.C.	FA-'09	0*
50	Brown, Cody	LB	6-3	244	8/20/78	2	Connecticut	Douglass, Kan.	D2-'09	0*
75	Brown, Levi	T	6-5	324	3/16/84	4	Penn State	Norfolk, Va.	D1-'07	16/16
86	Byrd, Dominique	TE	6-3	255	2/7/84	4	Southern California	Minneapolis, Minn.	FA-'10	0*
93	Campbell, Calais	DE	6-8	290	9/1/86	3	Miami	Aurora, Colo.	D2-'08	16/15
71	Clark, Jeremy	DE	6-3	309	9/6/83	2	Alabama	Daphne, Ala.	FA-'09	0*
62	Claxton, Ben	C	6-2	301	7/30/80	4	Mississippi	Dublin, Ga.	FA-'09	1/0
59	Davis, Will	LB	6-2	261	6/2/86	2	Illinois	Greenbelt, Md.	D6-'09	11/0
90	Dockett, Darnell	DT	6-4	285	5/27/81	7	Florida State	Burtonsville, Md.	D3-'04	16/16
80	Doucet, Early	WR	6-0	212	10/28/85	3	Louisiana State	St. Martinville, La.	D3-'08	9/0
94	Dykes, Keilen	DT	6-3	305	9/6/84	2	West Virginia	Youngstown, Ohio	FA-'08	2/0
4	Feely, Jay	K	5-10	205	5/26/76	10	Michigan	Tampa, Fla.	UFA(NYJ)-'10	16/0*
11	Fitzgerald, Larry	WR	6-3	217	8/31/83	7	Pittsburgh	Minneapolis, Minn.	D1-'04	16/16
5	Graham, Ben	P	6-5	235	11/2/73	6	Deakin (Australia)	Geelong, Australia	FA-'08	16/0
70	Hadnot, Rex	G/C	6-2	320	1/28/82	7	Houston	Lufkin, Texas	UFA(Cle)-'10	9/6*
53	Haggans, Clark	LB	6-4	243	1/10/77	11	Colorado State	Torrance, Calif.	UFA(Pitt)-'08	16/14
54	Hayes, Gerald	LB	6-1	246	10/10/80	8	Pittsburgh	Paterson, N.J.	D3-'03	14/13
95	Highsmith, Ali	LB	6-1	230	1/20/85	3	Louisiana State	Miami, Fla.	FA-'08	14/2
34	Hightower, Tim	RB	6-0	222	5/23/86	3	Richmond	Alexandria, Va.	D5-'08	16/16
91	Iwebema, Kenny	DE	6-4	280	2/6/85	3	Iowa	Arlington, Texas	D4-'08	11/0
67	Johnson, Herman	G/T	6-7	382	1/29/85	2	Louisiana State	Denton, Texas	D5-'09	0*
49	Johnson, Rashad	S	5-11	203	1/2/86	2	Alabama	Sulligent, Ala.	D3-'09	10/1
44	Jones, Herana-Daze	S	5-11	206	4/15/82	5	Indiana	Louisville, Kent.	FA-'10	1/0*
72	Keith, Brandon	G/T	6-5	338	11/21/84	3	Northern Iowa	McAlester, Okla.	D7-'08	3/0
82	Leach, Mike	LS	6-2	238	10/18/76	11	William & Mary	Jefferson Township, N.J.	FA-'09	16/0
7	Leinart, Matt	QB	6-5	232	5/11/83	5	Southern California	Santa Ana, Calif.	D1-'06	8/1
51	Lenon, Paris	LB	6-2	235	11/26/77	9	Richmond	Lynchburg, Va.	UFA(StL)-'10	15/10*
76	+Lutui, Deuce	G	6-4	338	5/5/83	5	Southern California	Mesa, Ariz.	D2-'06	16/16
45	Maui'a, Reagan	FB	6-0	260	7/6/84	3	Hawaii	Lodi, Calif.	FA-'10	0*
37	McBride, Trumaine	CB	5-9	181	9/24/85	4	Mississippi	Clarksdale, Miss.	FA-'10	1/0*
47	Miller, Justin	CB	5-11	190	2/14/84	6	Clemson	Owensboro, Ky.	FA-'10	2/0*
89	Patrick, Ben	TE	6-3	264	8/23/84	4	Delaware	Savannah, Ga.	D7-'07	9/7
55	Porter, Joey	LB	6-3	255	3/22/77	12	Colorado State	Bakersfield, Calif.	FA-'10	14/14*
25	t-Rhodes, Kerry	S	6-3	214	8/2/82	6	Louisville	Bessemer, Ala.	T(NYJ)-'10	16/14*
97	Robinson, Bryan	DT	6-4	304	6/22/74	14	Fresno State	Toledo, Ohio	UFA(Cin)-'08	16/15
29	Rodgers-Cromartie, Dominique	CB	6-2	182	4/7/86	3	Tennessee State	Bradenton, Fla.	D1-'08	16/16
63	Sendlein, Lyle	C	6-3	305	3/16/84	4	Texas	Scottsdale, Ariz.	FA-'07	16/16
83	Spach, Stephen	TE	6-4	260	7/18/82	5	Fresno State	Clovis, Calif.	FA-'08	7/5
36	Stephens-Howling, LaRod	RB	5-7	180	4/26/87	2	Pittsburgh	Johnstown, Pa.	D7a-'09	16/2
28	Toler, Greg	CB	6-0	191	1/2/85	2	Saint Paul's (Va.)	Washington, D.C.	D4-'09	13/0
56	Walker, Reggie	LB	6-0	238	12/15/86	2	Kansas State	Sacramento, Calif.	FA-'09	7/0
22	Ware, Matt	S	6-2	215	12/2/82	7	UCLA	Santa Monica, Calif.	W(Phil)-'06	11/1
96	Washington, Mark	LB	6-3	245	8/20/85	2	Texas State-San Marcos	Long Beach, Calif.	FA-'09	0*
98	Watson, Gabe	DT	6-4	329	9/24/83	5	Michigan	Southfield, Mich.	D4-'06	16/0
26	Wells, Beanie	RB	6-1	228	8/7/88	2	Ohio State	Akron, Ohio	D1-'09	16/0
74	Wells, Reggie	G	6-4	312	11/3/80	8	Clarion (Pa.)	Library, Pa.	D6a-'03	16/16
24	Wilson, Adrian	S	6-3	226	10/12/79	10	North Carolina State	High Point, N.C.	D3-'01	16/16
31	Wright, Jason	RB	5-10	212	7/12/82	7	Northwestern	Diamond Bar, Calif.	UFA(Cle)-'09	16/0

* Ali inactive for 2 games with Baltimore; Anderson played 8 games with Cleveland in '09; Barksdale last active with Kansas City in '07; Broughton last active with Washington in '06; C. Brown missed '09 season because of injury; Byrd inactive for 10 games; Clark last active with N.Y. Giants in '08; Feely played 16 games with N.Y. Jets; Hadnot played 9 games with Cleveland; H. Johnson inactive for 16 games; Jones played 1 game with New Orleans; Lenon played 15 games with St. Louis; Maui'a last active with Cincinnati in '08; McBride played 1 game with Chicago; Miller played 2 games with Oakland and 1 game with N.Y. Jets; Porter played 14 games with Miami; Rhodes played 16 games with N.Y. Jets; Washington last active with Miami in '07.

t- Cardinals traded for Rhodes (NYJ).

Traded—WR Anquan Boldin (15 games in '09) to Baltimore.

Retired—Kurt Warner, 12-year quarterback, 15 games in '09.

Players lost through free agency (3): LB Karlos Dansby (Mia; 16 games in '09), WR Sean Morey (Sea; 13), K Neil Rackers (Hou; 14).

Also played with Cardinals in '09—DE Bertrand Berry (15 games), CB Ralph Brown (16), T Mike Gandy (12), FB Dan Kreider (14), WR Lance Long (1), CB Bryant McFadden (16), K Mike Nugent (2), LB Chike Okeafor (13), S Antrel Rolle (15), QB Brian St. Pierre (1), LB Pago Togafau (2), WR Jerheme Urban (10).

2010 FIRST-YEAR ROSTER

Name	Pos.	Ht.	Wt.	Birthdate	College	Hometown	How Acq.
Baggs, Stevie (1)	LB	6-1	241	12/30/81	Bethune-Cookman	Orlando, Fla	FA
Bowser, Deryn	WR	6-1	210	4/3/87	Akron	Los Angeles, Calif.	FA
Calvin, Jorrick	CB	5-10	184	7/17/87	Troy	Baton Rouge, La.	D6
Dray, Jim	TE	6-5	255	12/31/86	Stanford	Paramus, N.J.	D7
Gant, Ed (1)	WR	6-3	190	1/24/87	North Alabama	Fort Myers, Fla	FA-'09
Green, Marshay	CB	5-9	175	1/14/86	Mississippi	Bastrop, La.	FA
Hall, Max	QB	6-1	201	10/1/85	Brigham Young	Mesa, Ariz.	FA
Jefferson, A.J.	CB	6-0	190	4/4/88	Fresno State	Bakersfield, Calif.	FA
Jones, Onrea (1)	WR	6-0	202	12/22/83	Hampton	Williamsburg, Va.	FA-'08
Kees, Ryan (1)	DE	6-6	275	4/2/86	St. Cloud State	Eagan, Minn.	FA-'09
Knips, Casey	T	6-8	300	3/2/87	South Dakota State	Adrian, Minn	FA
Komar, Max	WR	5-11	202	11/30/87	Idaho	Auburn, Wash.	FA
Moosman, David	C	6-5	293	9/2/86	Michigan	Libertyville, Ill.	FA
Mougey, Darren (1)	WR	6-5	215	4/7/85	San Diego State	Scottsdale, Ariz.	FA
Muhtadi, Dean (1)	DE/DT	6-3	296	7/17/86	Maryland	Alexandria, Va.	FA
Palmer, Jonathan (1)	G	6-4	336	12/3/83	Auburn	Ellenwood, Ga.	FA-'09
Pestock, Tom (1)	G/T	6-6	317	9/13/84	Northwest Missouri State	Lenexa, Kan.	FA-'09
Roberts, Andre	WR	5-11	195	1/9/88	The Citadel	Columbia, S.C.	D3
Schofield, O'Brien	LB	6-2	231	4/3/87	Wisconsin	Chicago, Ill.	D4
Skelton, John	QB	6-5	244	3/17/88	Fordham	El Paso, Texas	D5
Smith, Alfonso	RB	6-1	208	1/23/87	Kentucky	Louisville, Ky.	FA
Stewart, Juamorris	WR	6-3	205	12/6/86	Southern	Baton Rouge, La.	FA
Tyler, Devin	T	6-7	308	7/2/86	Temple	Suitland, Md.	FA
Washington, Daryl	LB	6-2	230	10/9/86	Texas Christian	Irving, Texas	D2
Williams, Dan	DT	6-2	327	6/1/87	Tennessee	Memphis, Tenn.	D1
Williams, Stephen	WR	6-5	199	6/29/86	Toledo	Houston, Texas	FA

The term NFL Rookie is defined as a player who is in his first season of professional football and has not been on the roster of another professional football team for any regular-season or postseason games. A Rookie is designated by an "R" on NFL rosters. Players who have been active in another professional football league or players who have NFL experience, including either preseason training camp or being on an Active List or Inactive List, or on Reserve/Injured or Reserve/Physically Unable to Perform for fewer than six regular-season games, are termed NFL First-Year Players. An NFL First-Year Player is designated by a "1" on NFL rosters. Thereafter, a player is credited with an additional year of experience for each season in which he accumulates six games on the Active List or Inactive List, or on Reserve/Injured or Reserve/Physically Unable to Perform.

Log on to www.azcardinals.com for an up-to-date roster.

COACHING STAFF

Head Coach, Ken Whisenhunt

Pro Career: Became an NFL head coach for the first time when hired by Arizona on January 14, 2007. After establishing himself as one of the NFL's top coaches in his first three seasons, was rewarded with an extension on February 25, 2010 that keeps him under contract with the Cardinals through 2013 with a team option for 2014. Is the first coach in franchise history with a .500 record or better in each of his first three seasons. His 31-23 overall record in that span places him fourth on the franchise career wins list and his 4-2 postseason record is among the league leaders in winning percentage. Led the Cardinals to NFC West titles in 2008 and '09, the team's first back-to-back division crowns since 1974-75. Arizona's 8-8 mark in his first season was the team's best record since going 9-7 in 1998. The 2008 season brought the franchise's first postseason appearance since 1998, first division crown since 1975, and first home playoff game since 1947. It ended with the team's first-ever conference title and Super Bowl appearance. Arizona's 12 total wins in 2008 were the most in team history and the Cardinals won more postseason contests in January (3) than they had in their entire history (2). In the 54 total games played in Whisenhunt's two seasons as head coach, the Cardinals have scored 20-or-more points in 41 of them (76%) and 30-plus points in 22 (41%). Prior to joining the Cardinals, Whisenhunt spent the previous six seasons as an assistant on Bill Cowher's staff with the Pittsburgh Steelers, the first three as tight ends coach and the last three as offensive coordinator. Whisenhunt took over as Pittsburgh's offensive coordinator in 2004, the same year the team drafted quarterback Ben Roethlisberger, who went on to set an NFL record with wins in his first 13 career starts en route to Offensive Rookie of the Year honors. The next season he became the youngest quarterback in NFL history to win a Super Bowl and finished third in the league in passer rating (98.6). Whisenhunt previously coached at the pro level with the New York Jets (tight ends, 2000), Cleveland Browns (special teams, 1999) and Baltimore Ravens (tight ends, 1997-98). He began his coaching career in the collegiate ranks with Vanderbilt for two seasons (1995-96). Whisenhunt was selected in the 12th round of the 1985 NFL Draft by the Atlanta Falcons out of Georgia Tech. He went on to play nine NFL seasons with the Falcons (1985-88), Washington Redskins (1989-90), and New York Jets (1991-93). In 74 career games (37 starts), he caught 62 passes for 601 yards and 6 touchdowns. Career record: 31-23.

Background: After going to Georgia Tech as a walk-on, he played four seasons as a tight end/H-back. He finished his Yellow Jackets' career ranked second on the receiving yardage list (1,264 yards) and fourth in receptions (82). As a senior in 1984, He was a consensus All-ACC and honorable mention All-America selection when he averaged 19.1 yards-per-catch.

Personal: Born February 28, 1962 in Atlanta. Whisenhunt earned a degree in civil engineering from Georgia Tech. Ken and his wife, Alice, have two children—Kenneth, Jr. and Mary Ashley.

ASSISTANT COACHES

Ron Aiken, defensive line; born August 18, 1955, Moncks Corner, S.C. Guard/center North Carolina A&T 1973-76. No pro playing experience. College coach: Bethany College 1979-1981, Tarkio College 1982-84, Rensselaer Polytechnic Institute 1985, Langston 1986-89, New Mexico 1990-94, Vanderbilt 1995-96, Texas 1997, San Diego State 1998, Iowa 1999-2006. Pro coach: Joined Cardinals in 2007.

Rick Courtright, asst. defensive backs; born January 4, 1961, Miami. Linebacker Wheaton College 1980-83. No pro playing experience. College coach: Washington 1991-92, Minnesota-Morris 1993, Ohio 1994, Idaho State 1995, Idaho 1996-99, Murray State 2000, Western Illinois 2001-03. Pro coach: Joined Cardinals in 2004.

Bill Davis, defensive coordinator; born November 5, 1965, Youngstown, Ohio. Quarterback Cincinnati 1984-88. College coach: Michigan State 1990-91. Pro coach: Pittsburgh Steelers 1992-94, Carolina Panthers 1995-98, Cleveland Browns 1999, Green Bay Packers 2000, Atlanta Falcons 2001-03, New York Giants 2004, San Francisco 49ers 2005-06, joined Cardinals in 2007.

Chad Grimm, offensive quality control; born May 18, 1985, Fairfax, Va. Linebacker Virginia Tech 2003-06. No pro playing experience. Pro coach: Joined Cardinals in 2009.

Russ Grimm, asst. head coach/run game coordinator/offensive line; born May 2, 1959, Scottdale, Pa. Center Pittsburgh 1977-1980. Pro guard Washington Redskins 1981-1991. Inducted into Pro Football Hall of Fame in 2010. Pro coach: Washington Redskins 1992-2000, Pittsburgh Steelers 2001-06, joined Cardinals in 2007.

Donnie Henderson, defensive backs; born May 17, 1957, Baltimore. Defensive back Utah State 1978-79. No pro playing experience. College coach: Utah State 1983-88, Idaho 1989, California 1990-91, Arizona State 1992-97, Houston 1998. Pro coach: Baltimore Ravens 1999-2003, N.Y. Jets 2004-05, Detroit Lions 2006, Jacksonville Jaguars 2008, joined Cardinals in 2010.

Freddie Kitchens, tight ends; born November 29, 1974, Gadsden, Ala. Quarterback Alabama 1994-97. No pro playing experience. College coach: Glenville State College 1999, Louisiana State 2000, North Texas 2001-03, Mississippi State 2004-05. Pro coach: Dallas Cowboys 2006, joined Cardinals in 2007.

John Lott, strength and conditioning; born May 9, 1964, Denton, Texas. Offensive lineman North Texas 1983-86. Pro offensive lineman Pittsburgh Steelers 1987. College coach: North Texas 1989-1990, Houston 1991-96. Pro coach: New York Jets 1997-2004, Cleveland Browns 2005-06, joined Cardinals in 2007.

John McNulty, wide receivers; born May 29, 1968, Scranton, Pa. Safety Penn State 1988-1990. No pro playing experience. College coach: Michigan 1991-94, Connecticut 1995-97, Rutgers 2004-08. Pro coach: Jacksonville Jaguars 1998-2002, Dallas Cowboys 2003, joined Cardinals in 2009.

Chris Miller, quarterbacks; born August 9, 1965, Pomona, Calif. Quarterback Oregon 1983-86. Pro quarterback Atlanta Falcons 1987-1993, St. Louis Rams 1994-95, Denver Broncos 1999. Pro coach: Joined Cardinals in 2009.

Mike Miller, passing game coordinator; born April 9, 1970, Plum Borough, Pa. Attended Clarion. No college or pro playing experience. College coach: Robert Morris 1997-98, 2006. Pro coach: Pittsburgh Steelers 1999-2003, Buffalo Bills 2004-05, Berlin Thunder (NFLE) 2006, joined Cardinals in 2007.

Matt Raich, linebackers; born August 16, 1970, Monaca, Pa. Middle linebacker Westminster College 1989-1992. No pro playing experience. College coach: Westminster 1993-94, Robert Morris 1996-98, 2000-02, Glenville State 1999. Pro coach: Pittsburgh Steelers 2004-06, joined Cardinals in 2007.

Tommie Robinson, running backs; born April 4, 1963, Columbus, Ga. Safety Troy State 1982-85. No pro playing experience. College coach: Arkansas 1991, Utah State 1992-93, TCU 1994-97, Nevada-Las Vegas 1998, Oklahoma State 2001, Georgia Tech 2002-05, Memphis 2006, Miami 2007-09. Pro coach: Dallas Cowboys 1998-2000, joined Cardinals in 2010.

Ryan Slowik, defensive quality control; born Dec. 27, 1980, Chicago. Safety Wisconsin-Oshkosh 2002-03. No pro playing experience. College coach: Wisconsin-Oshkosh 2004. Pro coach: Denver Broncos 2005-08, joined Cardinals in 2009.

Kevin Spencer, special teams; born November 2, 1953, Queens, N.Y. Outside linebacker Springfield College 1971. No pro playing experience. College coach: SUNY-Cortland 1975-76, Cornell 1979-1980, Ithaca 1981-86, Wesleyan 1987-1991. Pro coach: Cleveland Browns 1991-94, Oakland Raiders 1995-97, Indianapolis Colts 1998-2001, Pittsburgh Steelers 2002-06, joined Cardinals in 2007.

National Football Conference
South Division
Team Colors: Black, Red, Silver, and White
4400 Falcon Parkway
Flowery Branch, Georgia 30542
Telephone: (770) 965-3115

2010 SCHEDULE

PRESEASON

Aug. 13	**Kansas City**	8:00
Aug. 19	**New England**	8:00
Aug. 27	at Miami	7:00
Sep. 2	at Jacksonville	7:30

REGULAR SEASON

Sep. 12	at Pittsburgh	1:00
Sep. 19	**Arizona**	1:00
Sep. 26	at New Orleans	12:00
Oct. 3	**San Francisco**	1:00
Oct. 10	at Cleveland	1:00
Oct. 17	at Philadelphia	1:00
Oct. 24	**Cincinnati**	1:00
Oct. 31	BYE	
Nov. 7	**Tampa Bay**	1:00
Nov. 11	**Baltimore** (Thu)	8:20
Nov. 21	at St. Louis	3:05
Nov. 28	**Green Bay**	1:00
Dec. 5	at Tampa Bay	1:00
Dec. 12	at Carolina	1:00
Dec. 19	at Seattle	1:05
Dec. 27	**New Orleans** (Mon)	8:30
Jan. 2	**Carolina**	1:00

Stadium: Georgia Dome
(opened in 1992)
• **Capacity:** 71,228
One Georgia Dome Drive
Atlanta, Georgia 30313
Playing Surface: FieldTurf
Training Camp: Atlanta Falcons
4400 Falcon Parkway
Flowery Branch, GA 30542

GEORGIA DOME

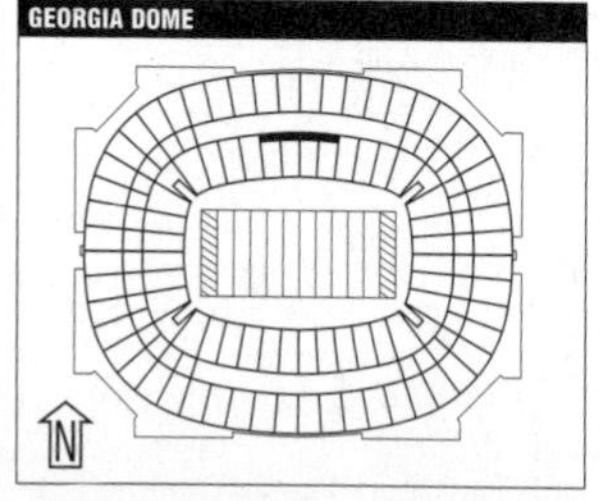

CLUB OFFICIALS

Owner & CEO: Arthur M. Blank
President: Rich McKay
General Manager: Thomas Dimitroff
Head Coach: Mike Smith
Director of Human Resources: Karen Walters
Vice President & CFO: Greg Beadles
Controller: Rob Geoffroy
Vice President of Football Communications: Reggie Roberts
Vice President of Information Technology: Danny Branch
Vice President of Marketing: Jim Smith
Vice President of Sales: Dave Cohen
Senior Director of Media Relations: Frank Kleha
Senior Director of Player Development: Kevin Winston
Director of Logistics and Facilities: Spencer Treadwell
Director of Ticket Operations: Mike Gilsenan
Director of Community Relations: Kendyl Baugh Moss
Director of Event Marketing: Roddy White
Director of Football Operations: Nick Polk
Director of Player Personnel: Les Snead
Director of College Scouting: David Caldwell
Assistant Director of Player Personnel: Lionel Vital
Eastern Regional Scout: Marvin Allen
Western Regional Scout: Mark Olson
Area Scouts: Bob Harrison, Shepley Heard, Bob Kronenberg, Taylor Morton, Robinson Payne
Pro Scouts: Ran Carthon, DeJuan Polk
Scouting Assistant: Anthony Robinson
Head Athletic Trainer: Marty Lauzon
Assistant Athletic Trainer: James Williams
Assistant Athletic Trainer: Danny Long
Video Director: Mike Crews
Video Assistants: Phil Tieman, Daniel Wayne
Equipment Manager: Brian Boigner
Director of Sponsorship Sales: Tim Zulawski
Director of Retail: Chris DiPierri
Director of New Media: Dan Levak
Football Communications Manager: Matt Conti
Football Communications Coordinator: Brian Cearns

COACHING HISTORY
(282-399-6)

Records include postseason games

1966-68	Norb Hecker*	4-26-1
1968-1974	Norm Van Brocklin**	37-49-3
1974-76	Marion Campbell***	6-19-0
1976	Pat Peppler	3-6-0
1977-1982	Leeman Bennett	47-44-0
1983-86	Dan Henning	22-41-1
1987-89	Marion Campbell****	11-32-0
1989	Jim Hanifan	0-4-0
1990-93	Jerry Glanville	28-38-0
1994-96	June Jones	19-30-0
1997-2003	Dan Reeves#	52-61-1
2003	Wade Phillips	2-1-0
2004-06	Jim Mora	27-23-0
2007	Bobby Petrino##	3-10-0
2007	Emmitt Thomas	1-2-0
2008-09	Mike Smith	20-13-0

*Released after three games in 1968
**Released after eight games in 1974
***Released after five games in 1976
****Retired after 12 games in 1989
#Released after 13 games in 2003
##Resigned after 13 games in 2007

PAID ATTENDANCE

Home 530,999 Away 538,144
Total 1,069,143
Single-game home record, 71,151 (10/22/06)
Single-season home record, 553,979 (1992)

2010 DRAFT CHOICES

Round	Name	Pos.	College
1	Sean Weatherspoon	LB	Missouri
3	Corey Peters	DT	Kentucky
	Mike Johnson	G	Alabama
4	Joe Hawley	C	Nevada-Las Vegas
5	Dominique Franks	DB	Oklahoma
	Kerry Meier	WR	Kansas
6	Shann Schillinger	DB	Montana

ATLANTA FALCONS

2009 TEAM RECORD

PRESEASON (2-2)

Date	Result	Opponent
8/15	L 26-27	at Detroit
8/21	W 20-13	at St. Louis
8/29	W 27-24	San Diego
9/3	L 3-20	Baltimore

REGULAR SEASON (9-7)

Date	Result	Opponent
9/13	W 19-7	Miami
9/20	W 28-20	Carolina
9/27	L 10-26	at New England
10/11	W 45-10	at San Francisco
10/18	W 21-14	Chicago
10/25	L 21-37	at Dallas
11/2	L 27-35	at New Orleans
11/08	W 31-17	Washington
11/15	L 19-28	at Carolina
11/22	L 31-34	at New York Giants (OT)
11/29	W 20-17	Tampa Bay
12/6	L 7-34	Philadelphia
12/13	L 23-26	New Orleans
12/20	W 10-7	at New York Jets
12/27	W 31-3	Buffalo
1/3	W 20-10	at Tampa Bay

(OT) Overtime

SCORE BY PERIODS

Falcons	78	116	60	109	0 —	363
Opponents	53	125	55	89	3 —	325

2009 TEAM STATISTICS

	Falcons	Opp.
Total First Downs	330	303
Rushing	105	89
Passing	192	197
Penalty	33	17
3rd Down: Made/Att	91/216	97/214
3rd Down Pct.	42.1	45.3
4th Down: Made/Att	16/23	8/17
4th Down Pct.	69.6	47.1
Possession Avg.	29:47	30:13
Total Net Yards	5447	5582
Avg. Per Game	340.4	348.9
Total Plays	1048	997
Avg. Per Play	5.2	5.6
Net Yards Rushing	1876	1711
Avg. Per Game	117.3	106.9
Total Rushes	451	433
Net Yards Passing	3571	3871
Avg. Per Game	223.2	241.9
Sacked/Yards Lost	27/126	28/170
Gross Yards	3697	4041
Att./Completions	570/332	536/335
Completion Pct.	58.2	62.5
Had Intercepted	17	15
Punts/Average	63/41.8	62/42.5
Net Punting Avg.	63/36.3	62/36.5
Penalties/Yards	78/664	110/892
Fumbles/Ball Lost	19/8	23/13
Touchdowns	44	38
Rushing	15	10
Passing	26	25
Returns	3	3

2009 INDIVIDUAL STATISTICS

PASSING	Att.	Comp.	Yds.	Pct.	TD	Int.	Tkld.	Rate
Ryan	451	263	2916	58.3	22	14	19/92	80.9
Redman	119	69	781	58.0	4	3	8/34	78.4
Falcons	570	332	3697	58.2	26	17	27/126	80.4
Opponents	536	335	4041	62.5	25	15	28/170	89.5

SCORING	TD R	TD P	TD Rt	PAT	FG	Saf	PTS
Elam	0	0	0	32/33	12/19	0	68
White	0	11	0	0/0	0/0	0	66
Turner	10	0	0	0/0	0/0	0	60
Gonzalez	0	6	0	0/0	0/0	0	36
Bryant	0	0	0	10/10	7/10	0	31
Snelling	4	1	0	0/0	0/0	0	30
Peelle	0	2	0	0/0	0/0	0	12
Weems	0	2	0	0/0	0/0	0	12
Biermann	0	0	1	0/0	0/0	0	6
Booker	0	1	0	0/0	0/0	0	6
Hill	0	0	1	0/0	0/0	0	6
Jenkins	0	1	0	0/0	0/0	0	6
Mughelli	0	1	0	0/0	0/0	0	6
Norwood	0	1	0	0/0	0/0	0	6
Ryan	1	0	0	0/0	0/0	0	6
Sidbury	0	0	1	0/0	0/0	0	6
Falcons	15	26	3	42/43	19/29	0	363
Opponents	10	25	3	37/38	20/28	0	325

2-Pt. Conversions: Falcons 0-1, Opponents 0-0

RUSHING	No.	Yds	Avg	LG	TD
Turner	178	871	4.9	58t	10
Snelling	142	613	4.3	31	4
Norwood	76	252	3.3	21	0
Weems	8	53	6.6	31	0
Ryan	30	49	1.6	7	1
Stecker	5	15	3.0	6	0
Mughelli	4	10	2.5	4	0
Booker	1	7	7.0	7	0
Redman	6	4	0.7	5	0
White	1	2	2.0	2	0
Falcons	451	1876	4.2	58t	15
Opponents	433	1711	4.0	45t	10

RECEIVING	No.	Yds	Avg	LG	TD
White	85	1153	13.6	90t	11
Gonzalez	83	867	10.4	27	6
Jenkins	50	635	12.7	50t	1
Snelling	30	259	8.6	38	1
Norwood	19	186	9.8	38	1
Booker	16	181	11.3	27	1
Peelle	12	115	9.6	32	2
Finneran	11	111	10.1	19	0
Mughelli	7	51	7.3	21	1
Weems	6	50	8.3	30t	2
Turner	5	35	7.0	10	0
Stecker	5	34	6.8	14	0
Haynes	3	20	6.7	10	0
Falcons	332	3697	11.1	90t	26
Opponents	335	4041	12.1	65t	25

INTERCEPTIONS	No.	Yds	Avg	LG	TD
Grimes	6	17	2.8	11	0
DeCoud	3	25	8.3	15	0
Owens	2	13	6.5	13	0
Hill	1	62	62.0	62t	1
Peterson	1	39	39.0	39	0
Houston	1	4	4.0	4	0
Williams	1	-2	-2.0	-2	0
Falcons	15	158	10.5	62t	1
Opponents	17	306	18.0	83t	2

PUNTING	No.	Yds.	Avg.	In 20	LG
Koenen	61	2598	42.6	18	70
Bryant	1	36	36.0	1	36
Falcons	63	2634	41.8	19	70
Opponents	62	2632	42.5	16	60

PUNT RETURNS	Ret	FC	Yds	Avg	LG	TD
Weems	27	14	270	10.0	28	0
Falcons	27	14	270	10.0	28	0
Opponents	27	18	289	10.7	73t	1

KICKOFF RETURNS	No.	Yds	Avg	LG	TD
Weems	48	1214	25.3	62	0
Stecker	3	54	18.0	21	0
Finneran	2	22	11.0	16	0
Norwood	1	39	39.0	39	0
Zinger	1	7	7.0	7	0
Falcons	55	1336	24.3	62	0
Opponents	46	945	20.5	39	0

FIELD GOALS	1-19	20-29	30-39	40-49	50+
Elam	0/0	4/4	4/8	3/5	1/2
Bryant	0/0	2/2	4/4	0/2	1/2
Falcons	0/0	6/6	8/12	3/7	2/4
Opponents	0/0	2/2	13/18	4/5	1/3

SACKS	No.
Babineaux	6.0
Abraham	5.5
Biermann	5.0
Nicholas	3.0
DeCoud	2.0
Johnson	2.0
Davis	1.0
Jackson	1.0
Peterson	1.0
Sidbury	1.0
Anderson	0.5
Falcons	28.0
Opponents	27.0

RECORD HOLDERS

INDIVIDUAL RECORDS—CAREER

Category	Name	Performance
Rushing (Yds.)	Gerald Riggs, 1982-88	6,631
Passing (Yds.)	Steve Bartkowski, 1975-1985	23,470
Passing (TDs)	Steve Bartkowski, 1975-1985	154
Receiving (No.)	Terance Mathis, 1994-2001	573
Receiving (Yds.)	Terance Mathis, 1994-2001	7,349
Interceptions	Rolland Lawrence, 1973-1980	39
Punting (Avg.)	Rick Donnelly, 1985-89	42.6
Punt Return (Avg.)	Darrien Gordon, 2001	14.1
Kickoff Return (Avg.)	Darrick Vaughn, 2000-01	25.7
Field Goals	Morten Andersen, 1995-2000, 2006-07	184
Touchdowns (Tot.)	Terance Mathis, 1994-2001	57
Points	Morten Andersen, 1995-2000, 2006-07	806
Sacks*	Chuck Smith, 1992-99	58.5

INDIVIDUAL RECORDS—SINGLE SEASON

Category	Name	Performance
Rushing (Yds.)	Jamal Anderson, 1998	1,846
Passing (Yds.)	Jeff George, 1995	4,143
Passing (TDs)	Steve Bartkowski, 1980	31
Receiving (No.)	Terance Mathis, 1994	111
Receiving (Yds.)	Roddy White, 2008	1,382
Interceptions	Scott Case, 1988	10
Punting (Avg.)	Billy Lothridge, 1968	44.3
Punt Return (Avg.)	Darrien Gordon, 2001	14.1
Kickoff Return (Avg.)	Darrick Vaughn, 2000	27.7
Field Goals	Jay Feely, 2002	32
Touchdowns (Tot.)	Michael Turner, 2008	17
Points	Jay Feely, 2002	138
Sacks*	John Abraham, 2008	16.5

INDIVIDUAL RECORDS—SINGLE GAME

Category	Name	Performance
Rushing (Yds.)	Michael Turner, 9-7-08	220
Passing (Yds.)	Chris Chandler, 12-23-01	431
Passing (TDs)	Wade Wilson, 12-13-92	5
Receiving (No.)	William Andrews, 11-15-81	15
Receiving (Yds.)	Roddy White, 10-11-09	210
Interceptions	Many times	2
	Last time by Brent Grimes, 12-20-09	
Field Goals	Norm Johnson, 11-13-94	6
Touchdowns (Tot.)	T.J. Duckett, 12-12-04	4
	Michael Turner, 11-23-08	4
Points	T.J. Duckett, 12-12-04	24
	Michael Turner, 11-23-08	24
Sacks*	Chuck Smith, 10-12-97	5.0

**Sacks became an official statistic in 1982.*

ATLANTA FALCONS

2010 VETERAN ROSTER

No.	Name	Pos.	Ht.	Wt.	Birthdate	NFL Exp.	College	Hometown	How Acq.	'09 Games/ Starts
55	Abraham, John	DE	6-4	263	5/6/78	11	South Carolina	Timmonsville, S.C.	T(NYJ)-'06	16/15
59	Adkins, Spencer	LB	5-11	242	5/16/87	2	Miami	Naples, Fla.	D6-'09	5/0
98	Anderson, Jamaal	DE	6-6	289	2/6/86	4	Arkansas	Little Rock, Ark.	D1-'07	13/13
95	Babineaux, Jonathan	DT	6-2	296	10/12/81	6	Iowa	Port Arthur, Texas	D2-'05	16/16
72	Baker, Sam	T	6-5	307	5/30/85	3	Southern California	Tustin, Calif.	D1b-'08	14/14
71	Biermann, Kroy	DE	6-3	260	9/12/85	3	Montana	Hardin, Mont.	D5b-'08	16/2
63	Blalock, Justin	OG	6-4	329	12/20/83	4	Texas	Dallas, Texas	D2a-'07	16/16
3	Bryant, Matt	K	5-9	200	5/29/75	9	Baylor	Orange, Texas	FA-'09	5/0
77	Clabo, Tyson	T	6-6	331	10/17/81	6	Wake Forest	Knoxville, Tenn.	FA-'06	16/16
26	Coleman, Erik	S	5-10	207	5/6/82	7	Washington State	Sacramento, Calif.	FA-'08	16/16
73	Dahl, Harvey	G	6-5	305	6/24/81	4	Nevada-Reno	Fallon, Nev.	FA-'07	11/11
92	Davis, Chauncey	DE	6-2	262	1/27/83	6	Florida State	Bartow, Fla.	D4-'05	16/4
28	DeCoud, Thomas	S	6-2	205	3/19/85	3	California	Vallejo, Calif.	D3c-'08	16/16
83	Douglas, Harry	WR	6-0	182	9/16/84	2	Louisville	Jonesboro, Ga.	D3b-'08	0*
86	Finneran, Brian	WR	6-5	210	1/31/76	10	Villanova	Mission Viejo, Calif.	FA-'00	10/2
27	Giordano, Matt	S	5-11	200	10/16/82	6	California	Clovis, Calif.	FA-'10	5/0*
88	Gonzalez, Tony	TE	6-5	243	2/27/76	14	California	Torrance, Calif.	T(KC)-'09	16/16
20	Grimes, Brent	CB	5-10	181	7/19/83	3	Shippensburg	Philadelphia, Pa.	FA-'07	16/9
6	Hauschka, Steve	K	6-4	210	6/29/85	3	North Carolina State	Needham, Mass.	FA-'09	9/0*
22	Jackson, Chevis	CB	5-11	193	12/11/85	3	Louisiana State	Mobile, Ala.	D3a-'08	15/2
12	Jenkins, Michael	WR	6-4	217	6/18/82	7	Ohio State	Tampa, Fla.	D1b-'04	15/9
	Jerry, Peria	DT	6-2	294	8/23/84	2	Mississippi	Batesville, Miss.	D1-'09	2/2
93	Johnson, Thomas	DT	6-2	304	6/24/81	3	Middle Tennessee State	Memphis, Tenn.	FA-'09	13/10
49	Klecko, Dan	FB	5-11	275	1/12/81	7	Temple	Chester, Pa.	FA-'10	0*
9	Koenen, Michael	P	5-11	198	7/13/82	6	Western Washington	Ferndale, Wash.	FA-'05	16/0
97	Lewis, Trey	DT	6-3	316	5/23/85	3	Washburn	Topeka, Kan.	D6a-'07	9/1
50	Lofton, Curtis	LB	6-0	242	6/2/86	3	Oklahoma	Kingfisher, Okla.	D2-'08	16/16
62	McClure, Todd	C	6-1	296	2/16/77	12	Louisiana State	Baton Rouge, La.	D7a-'99	16/16
	Moore, William	S	6-0	218	5/18/85	2	Missouri	Hayti, Mo.	D2-'09	2/0
34	Mughelli, Ovie	FB	6-1	252	6/10/80	8	Wake Forest	Boston, Mass.	UFA(Balt)-'07	14/7
54	Nicholas, Stephen	LB	6-3	230	5/1/83	4	South Florida	Jacksonville, Fla.	D4a-'07	16/14
32	Norwood, Jerious	RB	5-11	209	7/29/83	5	Mississippi State	Jackson, Miss.	D3-'06	10/4
76	Ojinnaka, Quinn	G	6-5	299	4/23/84	5	Syracuse	Seabrook, Md.	D5-'06	9/5
21	Owens, Christopher	CB	5-9	179	12/1/86	2	San Jose State	Los Angeles, Calif.	D3-'09	16/6
87	Peelle, Justin	TE	6-4	251	3/15/79	9	Oregon	Fresno, Calif.	FA-'08	15/9
53	Peterson, Mike	LB	6-1	233	6/17/76	12	Florida	Gainesville, Fla.	UFA(Jax)-'09	16/16
8	Redman, Chris	QB	6-3	229	7/7/77	8	Louisville	Louisville, Ky.	FA-'07	5/2
75	Reynolds, Garrett	T	6-7	317	7/1/87	2	North Carolina	Knoxville, Tenn.	D5b-'09	5/0
23	Robinson, Dunta	CB	5-10	182	4/11/82	7	South Carolina	Athens, Ga.	UFA(Hous)-'10	16/16*
66	Romberg, Brett	C	6-2	293	10/10/79	7	Miami	Windsor, Ontario, Canada	FA-'09	9/0
2	Ryan, Matt	QB	6-4	213	5/17/85	3	Boston College	Exton, Pa.	D1a-'08	14/14
1	Shockley, D.J.	QB	6-0	218	3/23/83	3	Georgia	College Park, Ga.	FA-'09	0*
90	Sidbury, Lawrence	DE	6-3	265	2/6/86	2	Richmond	Cheltenham, Md.	D4-'09	16/0
44	Snelling, Jason	RB	5-11	223	12/29/83	4	Virginia	Chester, Va.	D7-'07	14/3
74	Svitek, Will	T	6-6	309	1/8/82	5	Stanford	Prague, Czech Republic	FA-'09	13/2
33	Turner, Michael	RB	5-10	244	2/13/82	7	Northern Illinois	Waukegan, Ill.	UFA(SD)-'08	11/11
99	Walker, Vance	DT	6-2	307	4/26/87	2	Georgia Tech	Fort Mill, S.C.	D7-'09	10/1
14	Weems, Eric	WR	5-9	194	7/4/85	3	Bethune-Cookman	Ormond Beach, Fla.	FA-'07	16/0
84	White, Roddy	WR	6-0	212	11/2/81	6	Alabama-Birmingham	James Island, S.C.	D1-'05	16/16
29	Williams, Brian	DB	5-11	202	7/2/79	9	North Carolina State	High Point, N.C.	FA-'09	5/5
52	Wire, Coy	LB	6-0	225	11/7/78	9	Stanford	Camp Hill, Pa.	FA' 08	16/1
82	Zelenka, Joe	LS	6-3	260	3/9/76	12	Wake Forest	Cleveland, Ohio	FA-'09	5/0
89	Zinger, Keith	TE	6-4	258	10/9/84	2	Louisiana State	Leesville, La.	D7b-'08	15/2

* Douglas missed '09 season because of injury; Giordano played 5 games with Green Bay in '09; Hauschka played 9 games with Baltimore; Klecko last active with Philadelphia in '08; Robinson played 16 games with Houston; Shockley inactive third quarterback for 16 games.

Traded—CB Chris Houston (12 games in '09) to Detroit.

Also played with Falcons in '09—WR Marty Booker (16 games), S Eric Brock (2), S Jamaal Fudge (2), LB Tony Gilbert (12), FB Verron Haynes (7), CB Tye Hill (9), LB Robert James (1), S Charlie Peprah (2), G Bryan Pittman (4), LS Mike Schneck (7), RB Aaron Stecker (9).

2010 FIRST-YEAR ROSTER

Name	Pos.	Ht.	Wt.	Birthdate	College	Hometown	How Acq.
Banks, Leroy	TE	6-3	243	12/12/87	Southern Mississippi	Memphis, Tenn.	FA
Bergeron, Troy (1)	WR	6-2	195	12/3/83	No College	New Orleans, La.	FA-'09
Bruggeman, Rob (1)	C	6-4	293	3/21/86	Iowa	Cedar Rapids, Iowa	FA-'09
Bryant, Trey	DT	6-2	315	6/2/87	Baylor	Dallas, Texas	FA
Buckley, Tim	WR	6-1	185	8/19/88	Alcorn State	Madison, Miss.	FA
Bush, Rafael	S	5-11	180	5/12/87	South Carolina State	Williston, S.C.	FA
Daniels, Dominique	CB	6-2	190	6/20/88	Nicholls State	Gibsonton, Fla.	FA
Derricks, Gabe	CB	6-3	202	1/8/88	San Diego	Oak Park, Calif.	FA
Drescher, Justin	LS	6-1	230	1/1/88	Colorado	Southlake, Texas	FA
Franks, Dominique	CB	6-0	192	10/8/87	Oklahoma	Tulsa, Okla.	D5a
Harvey, Brandyn	WR	6-4	205	11/6/87	Villanova	Spring Valley, Calif.	FA
Hawley, Joe	C	6-3	310	10/22/88	Nevada-Las Vegas	Yorba Linda, Calif.	D4
Henley, Rajon	DE	6-3	244	3/22/88	Texas Tech	Galveston, Texas	FA
James, Robert (1)	LB	5-11	220	12/26/83	Arizona State	Glendale, Ariz.	D5a-'08
Johnson, Mike	G	6-6	305	4/2/87	Alabama	Pensacola, Fla.	D3b
Johnson, Weston	LB	6-3	233	1/15/87	Wyoming	Wray, Colo.	FA
Lindholm, Garrett	K	5-9	190	8/10/88	Tarleton State	Pflugerville, Texas	FA
Meier, Kerry	WR	6-3	220	11/12/86	Kansas	Pittsburg, Kan.	D5b
Nance, Dimitri	RB	5-10	218	2/18/88	Arizona State	Euless, Texas	FA
Palmer, Michael	TE	6-5	260	1/18/88	Clemson	Stone Mountain, Ga.	FA
Peek, Colin	TE	6-6	255	6/4/86	Alabama	Ponte Vedra, Fla.	FA
Peters, Corey	DT	6-3	295	6/8/88	Kentucky	Louisville, Ky.	D3a
Schillinger, Shann	S	6-0	202	5/22/86	Montana	Baker, Mont.	D6
Schlueter, Blake (1)	C	6-2	279	4/22/86	Texas Christian	Ganado, Texas	FA-'09
Smith, Antone (1)	RB	5-9	190	9/17/85	Florida State	Pahokee, Fla.	FA-'09
Stephens, Emmanuel	DE	6-3	255	2/17/87	Mississippi	Houston, Texas	FA
Strickland, Andy (1)	WR	6-0	197	9/2/87	Wofford	Gaffney, S.C.	FA-'09
Valdez, Jose (1)	G	6-6	324	12/13/86	Arkansas	St. Francis, Wisc.	FA-'09
Walker, Daylan	DB	5-9	177	9/22/86	Arkansas State	Milan, Tenn.	FA
Ward, Eric	QB	6-2	210	4/12/87	Richmond	Atlanta, Ga.	FA
Weatherspoon, Sean	LB	6-2	245	12/29/87	Missouri	Jasper, Texas	D1
Wilson, John Parker (1)	QB	6-2	218	10/17/85	Alabama	Hoover, Ala.	FA-'09
Wolfe, Ryan	WR	6-2	210	11/23/86	Nevada-Las Vegas	Santa Clarita, Calif.	FA
Woods, Bear	LB	6-0	245	1/22/87	Troy	MacClenny, Fla.	FA

The term NFL Rookie is defined as a player who is in his first season of professional football and has not been on the roster of another professional football team for any regular-season or postseason games. A Rookie is designated by an "R" on NFL rosters. Players who have been active in another professional football league or players who have NFL experience, including either preseason training camp or being on an Active List or Inactive List, or on Reserve/Injured or Reserve/Physically Unable to Perform for fewer than six regular-season games, are termed NFL First-Year Players. An NFL First-Year Player is designated by a "1" on NFL rosters. Thereafter, a player is credited with an additional year of experience for each season in which he accumulates six games on the Active List or Inactive List, or on Reserve/Injured or Reserve/Physically Unable to Perform.

Log on to www.atlantafalcons.com for an up-to-date roster.

COACHING STAFF

Head Coach,

Mike Smith

Pro Career: Mike Smith was named the 14th head coach in Atlanta Falcons franchise history on January 23, 2008. In two seasons with the team he has compiled a 20-12 record, a playoff appearance in 2008 and back-to-back winning seasons for the first time in franchise history. Smith's two-year regular-season winning percentage of .625 is the second-best mark for an Atlanta head coach in their first two years with the team. His home record since his rookie campaign is 13-3, which ranks second in the NFL over that time span. In 2008, Smith guided the Falcons to an 11-5 record, marking a seven-win turnaround from the previous season. For his efforts, he was named the Associated Press and *Sporting News* NFL Coach of the Year. From 2003-07, Smith served as the defensive coordinator for the Jacksonville Jaguars following a four-year stint with the Baltimore Ravens from 1999-2002, which included the team's 2000 Super Bowl season. Before joining the NFL ranks, Smith coached at San Diego State (1982-85), Morehead State (1986), and Tennessee Tech (1987-1998). Career record: 20-13.

Background: Smith played linebacker for the Winnipeg Blue Bombers of the CFL in 1982. He played at East Tennessee (1977-1981) and was named defensive MVP twice at his position. Smith led the team with 186 tackles as a senior.

Personal: A native of Daytona Beach, Florida, Smith was born on November 30, 1959 in Chicago, Illinois. He and his wife Julie have one daughter, Logan, who is eight years old.

ASSISTANT COACHES

Keith Armstrong, special teams coordinator; born December 15, 1963, Levittown, Pa. Running back Temple 1983-86. No pro playing experience. College coach: Temple 1987, Miami 1988, Akron 1989, Oklahoma State 1990-92, Notre Dame 1993. Pro coach: Atlanta Falcons 1994-96, Chicago Bears 1997-2000, Miami Dolphins 2001-2007, re-joined Falcons 2008.

Jonas Beauchemin, strength and conditioning assistant; born October 11, 1984, Burlington, Vt. Attended Keene State. No college or pro playing experience. Pro coach: Joined Falcons in 2009.

Paul Boudreau, offensive line; born December 30, 1949, Arlington, Mass. Guard Boston College 1970-73. No pro playing experience. Pro coach: New Orleans Saints 1987-1993, Detroit Lions 1994-96, New England Patriots 1997-98, Miami Dolphins 1999-2000, Carolina Panthers 2001-02, Jacksonville Jaguars 2003-05, St. Louis Rams 2006-07, joined Falcons in 2008.

Gerald Brown, running backs; born September 4, 1959, Sweetwater, Tenn. Attended Memphis State. No college or pro playing experience. College coach: Tennessee Tech 1991-2000, Indiana 2002-07. Pro coach: Joined Falcons in 2008.

Mark Collins, defensive assistant; born August 30, 1975, Sault Ste. Marie, Mich. Defensive end/outside linebacker East Tennessee State 1995-98. No pro playing experience. College coach: East Tennessee State 1999-2002, Michigan 2003-04, Elon, 2005, Georgia Southern, 2006, Georgia 2007, Louisiana-Monroe 2009. Pro coach: Joined Falcons in 2010.

Paul Dunn, asst. offensive line; born July 7, 1960, Philadelphia. Offensive lineman Pittsburgh 1978-1982. No pro playing experience. College coach: Pittsburgh 1983, 2005-07, Penn State 1984-85, Edinboro 1986-88, Rutgers 1989, Maine 1990-93, Cincinnati 1994-95, Vanderbilt 1996-97, Kansas State 1998-2002, Kentucky 2003-04. Pro coach: Joined Falcons in 2008.

Jeff Fish, director of athletic performance; born June 6, 1966, Ithaca, N.Y. Wide receiver Western Carolina 1985-88. No pro playing experience. College coach: Western Michigan 1989, Clemson 1991-92, Kent State 1993-94, Tulsa 1995-97, Missouri 2001-03. Pro coach: Tampa Bay Buccaneers 1997, Kansas City Chiefs 1998-2000, Oakland Raiders 2004-07, joined Falcons in 2008.

Ray Hamilton, defensive line; born January 20, 1951, Omaha, Neb. Nose tackle Oklahoma 1969-1972. Pro defensive lineman New England Patriots 1973-1981. College coach: Tennessee 1992. Pro coach: New England Patriots 1985-89, Tampa Bay Buccaneers 1991, Los Angeles Raiders 1993-94, New York Jets 1994-96, 2000, New England Patriots 1997-99, Cleveland Browns 2001-02, Jacksonville Jaguars 2003-07, joined Falcons in 2008.

Bill Hughan, asst. strength and conditioning; born February 8, 1975, Oxford, Conn. Attended Springfield College. No college or pro playing experience. College coach: Yale 1997-98, Columbia 1999-2000, Missouri 2001-03. Pro coach: Oakland Raiders 2004-07, joined Falcons in 2008.

Tim Lewis, secondary; born December 18, 1961, Quakertown, Pa. Cornerback Pittsburgh 1979-1982. Pro cornerback Green Bay Packers 1983-86. Pro coach: Pittsburgh Steelers 1995-2003, New York Giants 2004-06, Carolina Panthers 2007-08, Seattle Seahawks 2009, joined Falcons in 2010.

Mike Mularkey, offensive coordinator; born November 19, 1961, Ft. Lauderdale, Fla. Tight end Florida 1979-1982. Pro tight end Minnesota Vikings 1983-88, Pittsburgh Steelers 1989-1991. College coach: Concordia 1993. Pro coach: Tampa Bay Buccaneers 1994-1995, Pittsburgh Steelers 1996-2003, Buffalo Bills 2004-05 (head coach), Miami Dolphins 2006-07, joined Falcons in 2008.

Bill Musgrave, asst. head coach/quarterbacks; born November 11, 1967, Grand Junction, Colo. Quarterback Oregon 1987-1990. Pro quarterback San Francisco 49ers 1991-94, Denver Broncos 1995-96. College coach: Virginia 2001-02. Pro coach: Oakland Raiders 1997, Philadelphia Eagles 1998, Carolina Panthers 1999-2000, Jacksonville Jaguars 2003-04, Washington Redskins 2005, joined Falcons in 2006.

Glenn Pires, linebackers; born September 13, 1958, New Bedford, Mass. Offensive lineman Springfield College 1976-79. No pro playing experience. College coach: Dartmouth 1985-88, Syracuse 1989-1994, Michigan State 1995. Pro coach: Arizona Cardinals 1996-2000, Detroit Lions 2001-02, Miami Dolphins 2003-07, joined Falcons in 2008.

Alvin Reynolds, defensive backs; born June 24, 1959, Pineville, La. Safety Indiana State 1978-1981. No pro playing experience. College coach: Indiana State 1982-1992. Pro coach: Denver Broncos 1993-95, Baltimore Ravens 1996-98, Carolina Panthers 1999-2002, Jacksonville Jaguars 2003-07, joined Falcons in 2008.

Terry Robiskie, wide receivers; born November 12, 1954, New Orleans. Running back Louisiana State 1973-76. Pro running back Oakland Raiders 1977-79, Miami Dolphins 1980-81. Pro coach: Los Angeles Raiders 1982-1993, Washington Redskins 1994-2000 (interim head coach 2000), Cleveland Browns 2001-06 (interim head coach 2004), Miami Dolphins 2007, joined Falcons in 2008.

Chris Scelfo, tight ends; born September 30, 1963, New Iberia, La. Center Northeast Louisiana 1981-84. No pro playing experience. College coach: Northeast Louisiana 1986-87, Oklahoma 1988-89, Marshall 1990-95, Georgia 1996-98, Tulane 1998-2006. Pro coach: Joined Falcons in 2008.

Eric Sutulovich, asst. special teams; born February 28, 1974, Kansas City, Kan. Tight end Louisiana Tech 1993-95. No pro playing experience. College coach: Louisiana Tech 1997-99, Pittsburgh 2000, Kansas 2006. Pro coach: Houston Texans 2002-05, Detroit Lions 2008, joined Falcons in 2009.

Glenn Thomas, offensive assistant; born September 22, 1977, Eastland, Texas. Attended Texas Tech. No college or pro playing experience. College coach: Texas Tech 1998-2001, Midwestern State 2001-07. Pro coach: Joined Falcons in 2008.

Brian VanGorder, defensive coordinator; born April 17, 1959, Jackson, Mich. Linebacker Wayne State 1979-1980. No pro playing experience. College coach: Grand Valley State 1989-1991, Wayne State 1992-94 (head coach), Central Florida 1995-97, Central Michigan 1998-99, Western Illinois 2000, Georgia 2001-04, Georgia Southern 2006 (head coach). Pro coach: Jacksonville Jaguars 2005, joined Falcons in 2007.

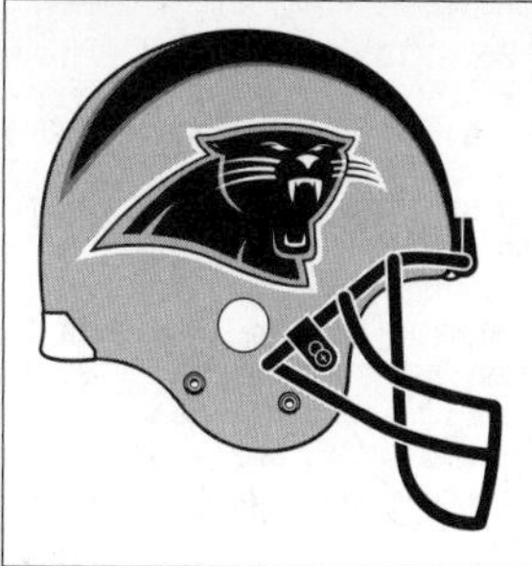

National Football Conference
South Division
Team Colors: Black, Panther Blue, and Silver
800 South Mint Street
Charlotte, North Carolina 28202-1502
Telephone: (704) 358-7000

2010 SCHEDULE

PRESEASON

Aug. 12	at Baltimore	8:00
Aug. 21	**New York Jets**	8:00
Aug. 28	**Tennessee**	8:00
Sep. 2	at Pittsburgh	7:30

REGULAR SEASON

Sep. 12	at New York Giants	1:00
Sep. 19	**Tampa Bay**	1:00
Sep. 26	**Cincinnati**	1:00
Oct. 3	at New Orleans	12:00
Oct. 10	**Chicago**	1:00
Oct. 17	BYE	
Oct. 24	**San Francisco**	1:00
Oct. 31	at St. Louis	12:00
Nov. 7	**New Orleans**	1:00
Nov. 14	at Tampa Bay	1:00
Nov. 21	**Baltimore**	1:00
Nov. 28	at Cleveland	1:00
Dec. 5	at Seattle	1:15
Dec. 12	**Atlanta**	1:00
Dec. 19	**Arizona**	1:00
Dec. 23	at Pittsburgh (Thu)	8:20
Jan. 2	at Atlanta	1:00

Stadium: Bank of America Stadium (opened in 1996) • **Capacity:** 73,504 Charlotte, North Carolina 28202-1502
Playing Surface: Grass
Training Camp: Wofford College Spartanburg, South Carolina 29303

BANK OF AMERICA STADIUM

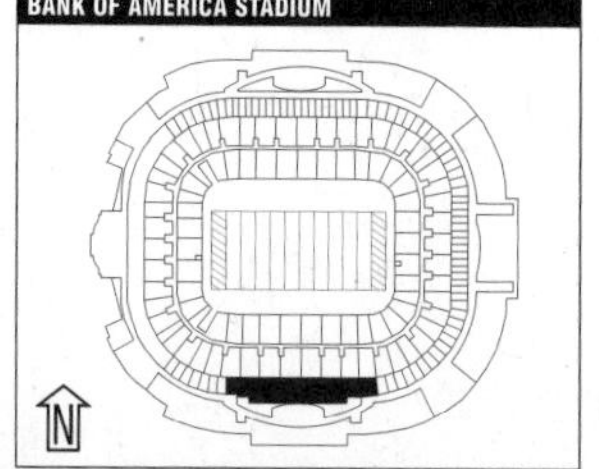

CLUB OFFICIALS

Owner/Founder: Jerry Richardson
President, Panthers Football LLC: Danny Morrison
General Manager: Marty Hurney
General Counsel: Richard Thigpen
Chief Financial Officer: Dave Olsen
Controller: Mike Dudan
Director of Pro Scouting: Mark Koncz
Director of College Scouting: Don Gregory
College Scouts: Jeff Beathard, Ryan Cowden, Khary Darlington, Robert Haines, Jeff Morrow, John Peterson, Pete Russell, Mike Szabo
Director of Communications: Charlie Dayton
Media Relations Manager: Steven Drummond
Public Relations Assistant: Deedee Mills
Director of Ticket Operations: Phil Youtsey
Director of Community Relations and Cheerleader/Mascot Programs: Riley Fields
Director of Sponsor Sales and Services: John Berger
Director of Broadcast Administration: Henry Thomas
Executive Producer-Television: Greg Brannon
Executive Producer-Radio: David Langton
Director of Team Administration: Rob Rogers
Director of Team Operations: Brandon Beane
Video Director: Mark Hobbs
Assistant Video Director: Jeff Mueller
Head Trainer: Ryan Vermillion
Assistant Trainer: Mark Shermansky
Equipment Manager: Jackie Miles
Assistant Equipment Manager: Don Toner
Director of Security: Gene Brown
Stadium Operations Manager: Scott Paul
Director of Entertainment and Panthervision: Kyle Ritchie
Facility Manager: Matthew Getz
Head Groundskeeper: Tom Vaughan
Director of Human Resources: Jackie Jeffries

COACHING HISTORY
(123-127-0)

Records include postseason games

1995-98	Dom Capers	31-35-0
1999-2001	George Seifert	16-32-0
2002-09	John Fox	76-60-0

PAID ATTENDANCE

Home 577,168 Away 528,913
Total 1,106,081
Single-game home record, 76,136 (12/10/95)
Single-season home record, 579,192 (2006)

2010 DRAFT CHOICES

Round	Name	Pos.	College
2	Jimmy Clausen	QB	Notre Dame
3	Brandon LaFell	WR	Louisiana St.
	Armanti Edwards	WR	Appalachian St.
4	Eric Norwood	DE	South Carolina
6	Greg Hardy	DE	Mississippi
	David Gettis	WR	Baylor
	Jordan Pugh	DB	Texas A&M
	Tony Pike	QB	Cincinnati
7	R.J. Stanford	DB	Utah
	Robert McClain	DB	Connecticut

CAROLINA PANTHERS

2009 TEAM RECORD

PRESEASON (0-4)

Date	Result	Opponent
8/17	L 17-24	at New York Giants
8/22	L 17-27	at Miami
8/29	L 13-17	Baltimore
9/3	L 10-21	Pittsburgh

REGULAR SEASON (8-8)

Date	Result	Opponent
9/13	L 10-38	Philadelphia
9/20	L 20-28	at Atlanta
9/28	L 7-21	at Dallas
10/11	W 20-17	Washington
10/18	W 28-21	at Tampa Bay
10/25	L 9-20	Buffalo
11/1	W 34-21	at Arizona
11/8	L 20-30	at New Orleans
11/15	W 28-19	Atlanta
11/19	L 17-24	Miami
11/29	L 6-17	at New York Jets
12/6	W 16-6	Tampa Bay
12/13	L 10-20	at New England
12/20	W 26-7	Minnesota
12/27	W 41-9	at New York Giants
1/3	W 23-10	New Orleans

SCORE BY PERIODS

Panthers	68	109	43	95	0	— 315
Opponents	48	102	72	86	0	— 308

2009 TEAM STATISTICS

	Panthers	Opp.
Total First Downs	289	290
Rushing	123	109
Passing	152	155
Penalty	14	26
3rd Down: Made/Att	82/220	70/197
3rd Down Pct.	37.3	35.5
4th Down: Made/Att	9/20	9/17
4th Down Pct.	45.0	52.9
Possession Avg.	30:13	29:47
Total Net Yards	5297	5053
Avg. Per Game	331.1	315.8
Total Plays	1023	976
Avg. Per Play	5.2	5.2
Net Yards Rushing	2498	1997
Avg. Per Game	156.1	124.8
Total Rushes	525	450
Net Yards Passing	2799	3056
Avg. Per Game	174.9	191.0
Sacked/Yards Lost	33/271	31/193
Gross Yards	3070	3249
Att./Completions	465/264	495/305
Completion Pct.	56.8	61.6
Had Intercepted	20	22
Punts/Average	77/43.5	74/44.8
Net Punting Avg.	77/36.6	74/38.2
Penalties/Yards	88/698	82/632
Fumbles/Ball Lost	23/11	28/15
Touchdowns	35	36
Rushing	18	15
Passing	16	14
Returns	1	7

2009 INDIVIDUAL STATISTICS

PASSING	Att.	Comp.	Yds.	Pct.	TD	Int.	Tkld.	Rate
Delhomme	321	178	2015	55.5	8	18	23/187	59.4
M. Moore	138	85	1053	61.6	8	2	9/78	98.5
McCown	6	1	2	16.7	0	0	1/6	39.6
Panthers	465	264	3070	56.8	16	20	33/271	70.5
Opponents	495	305	3249	61.6	14	22	31/193	71.7

SCORING	TD R	TD P	TD Rt	PAT	FG	Saf	PTS
Kasay	0	0	0	31/32	22/27	0	97
Stewart	10	1	0	0/0	0/0	0	66
S. Smith	0	7	0	0/0	0/0	0	44
D. Williams	7	0	0	0/0	0/0	0	44
King	0	3	0	0/0	0/0	0	18
Hoover	1	1	0	0/0	0/0	0	12
Rosario	0	2	0	0/0	0/0	0	12
Jarrett	0	1	0	0/0	0/0	0	6
Muhammad	0	1	0	0/0	0/0	0	6
Peppers	0	0	1	0/0	0/0	0	6
Thomas TM	0	0	0	0/0	0/0	1	2
Panthers	18	16	1	31/32	22/27	2	315
Opponents	15	14	7	33/33	19/27	0	308

2-Pt. Conversions: S. Smith, D. Williams.
Panthers 2-3, Opponents 1-3.

RUSHING	No.	Yds	Avg	LG	TD
Stewart	221	1133	5.1	67t	10
D. Williams	216	1117	5.2	77	7
Sutton	12	68	5.7	20	0
Delhomme	17	60	3.5	11	0
Hoover	20	52	2.6	18	1
Goodson	22	49	2.2	11	0
S. Smith	5	22	4.4	17	0
M. Moore	12	-3	-0.3	5	0
Panthers	525	2498	4.8	77	18
Opponents	450	1997	4.4	46t	15

RECEIVING	No.	Yds	Avg	LG	TD
S. Smith	65	982	15.1	66	7
Muhammad	53	581	11.0	27	1
D. Williams	29	252	8.7	30	0
Rosario	26	313	12.0	26	2
King	25	200	8.0	32	3
Stewart	18	139	7.7	19	1
Jarrett	17	196	11.5	30t	1
Barnidge	12	242	20.2	55	0
Sutton	6	62	10.3	13	0
K. Moore	6	59	9.8	22	0
Hoover	4	23	5.8	12	1
Goodson	2	15	7.5	13	0
C. Martin	1	6	6.0	6	0
Panthers	264	3070	11.6	66	16
Opponents	305	3249	10.7	63	14

INTERCEPTIONS	No.	Yds	Avg	LG	TD
Gamble	4	55	13.8	41	0
Marshall	4	47	11.8	28	0
Beason	3	46	15.3	18	0
S. Martin	3	35	11.7	23	0
C. Harris	3	3	1.0	3	0
T. Davis	2	24	12.0	24	0
Peppers	2	13	6.5	13t	1
Godfrey	1	12	12.0	12	0
Panthers	22	235	10.7	41	1
Opponents	20	339	17.0	67t	3

PUNTING	No.	Yds.	Avg.	In 20	LG
Baker	76	3352	44.1	22	61
Panthers	77	3352	43.5	22	61
Opponents	74	3312	44.8	30	70

PUNT RETURNS	Ret	FC	Yds	Avg	LG	TD
Munnerlyn	31	10	278	9.0	37	0
K. Moore	2	1	4	2.0	4	0
Gamble	1	0	0	0.0	0	0
Panthers	34	11	282	8.3	37	0
Opponents	41	18	452	11.0	85t	1

KICKOFF RETURNS	No.	Yds	Avg	LG	TD
Goodson	17	352	20.7	33	0
Sutton	14	302	21.6	32	0
K. Moore	10	219	21.9	55	0
King	3	37	12.3	14	0
Rosario	2	41	20.5	22	0
Stewart	2	17	8.5	17	0
Barnidge	1	16	16.0	16	0
Schwartz	1	16	16.0	16	0
Munnerlyn	1	15	15.0	15	0
Panthers	51	1015	19.9	55	0
Opponents	51	1267	24.8	97t	1

FIELD GOALS	1-19	20-29	30-39	40-49	50+
Kasay	0/0	7/7	9/10	5/6	1/4
Panthers	0/0	7/7	9/10	5/6	1/4
Opponents	1/1	7/7	4/7	7/11	0/1

SACKS	No.
Peppers	10.5
Brayton	5.0
C. Johnson	4.0
Beason	3.0
Brown	2.5
T. Davis	1.5
Anderson	1.0
Hayden	1.0
Leonard	1.0
Wesley	1.0
D. Lewis	0.5
Panthers	31.0
Opponents	33.0

RECORD HOLDERS

INDIVIDUAL RECORDS—CAREER

Category	Name	Performance
Rushing (Yds.)	DeAngelo Williams, 2006-09	3,850
Passing (Yds.)	Jake Delhomme, 2003-09	19,258
Passing (TDs)	Jake Delhomme, 2003-09	120
Receiving (No.)	Muhsin Muhammad, 1996-2004, 2008-09	696
Receiving (Yds.)	Muhsin Muhammad, 1996-2004, 2008-09	9,255
Interceptions	Eric Davis, 1996-2000	25
Punting (Avg.)	Todd Sauerbrun, 2001-04	45.5
Punt Return (Avg.)	Winslow Oliver, 1996-98	10.7
Kickoff Return (Avg.)	Michael Bates, 1996-2000	25.7
Field Goals	John Kasay, 1995-2009	326
Touchdowns (Tot.)	Steve Smith, 2001-09	58
Points	John Kasay, 1995-2009	1,390
*Sacks	Julius Peppers, 2002-09	81.0

INDIVIDUAL RECORDS—SINGLE SEASON

Category	Name	Performance
Rushing (Yds.)	DeAngelo Williams, 2008	1,515
Passing (Yds.)	Steve Beuerlein, 1999	4,436
Passing (TDs)	Steve Beuerlein, 1999	36
Receiving (No.)	Steve Smith, 2005	103
Receiving (Yds.)	Steve Smith, 2005	1,563
Interceptions	Doug Evans, 2001	8
Punting (Avg.)	Todd Sauerbrun, 2001	47.5
Punt Return (Avg.)	Winslow Oliver, 1996	11.5
Kickoff Return (Avg.)	Michael Bates, 1996	30.2
Field Goals	John Kasay, 1996	37
Touchdowns (Tot.)	DeAngelo Williams, 2008	20
Points	John Kasay, 1996	145
*Sacks	Kevin Greene, 1998	15.0

INDIVIDUAL RECORDS—SINGLE GAME

Category	Name	Performance
Rushing (Yds.)	DeAngelo Williams, 12-8-08	186
Passing (Yds.)	Chris Weinke, 12-10-06	423
Passing (TDs)	Steve Beuerlein, 1-2-00	5
Receiving (No.)	Steve Smith, 11-20-05	14
Receiving (Yds.)	Steve Smith, 10-30-05	201
Interceptions	Deon Grant, 9-22-02	3
Field Goals	John Kasay, 12-5-04	6
Touchdowns (Tot.)	DeAngelo Williams, 11-30-08, 12-21-08	4
Points	DeAngelo Williams, 11-30-08, 12-21-08	24
*Sacks	Many times	3.0
	Julius Peppers, 11-9-08	

**Sacks became an official statistic in 1982.*

CAROLINA PANTHERS

2010 VETERAN ROSTER

No.	Name	Pos.	Ht.	Wt.	Birthdate	NFL Exp.	College	Hometown	How Acq.	'09 Games/ Starts
50	Anderson, James	LB	6-2	235	9/26/83	5	Virginia Tech	Chesapeake, Va.	D3a-'06	16/7
7	Baker, Jason	P	6-2	205	5/17/78	10	Iowa	Fort Wayne, Ind.	T(Den)-'05	16/0
82	Barnidge, Gary	TE	6-5	247	9/22/85	3	Louisville	Middleburg, Fla.	D5-'08	16/3
52	Beason, Jon	LB	6-0	237	1/14/85	4	Miami	Miramar, Fla.	D1-'07	16/16
73	Bernadeau, Mackenzy	G	6-4	308	1/3/86	3	Bentley	Waltham, Mass.	D7c-'08	16/7
96	Brayton, Tyler	DE	6-6	280	11/20/79	8	Colorado	Pasco, Wash.	UFA(Oak)-'08	15/15
91	Brown, Everette	DE	6-1	256	8/7/87	2	Florida State	Stantonsburg, N.C.	D2a-'09	15/1
55	Connor, Dan	LB	6-2	231	11/2/85	3	Penn State	Wallingford, Pa.	D3b-'08	16/0
56	Culberson, Quinton	LB	6-1	236	10/21/85	4	Mississippi State	Jackson, Miss.	FA-'09	5/0
71	Davis, C.J.	G	6-2	308	2/2/87	2	Pittsburgh	Imperial, Pa.	FA-'09	0*
58	Davis, Thomas	LB	6-0	240	3/22/83	6	Georgia	Shellman, Ga.	D1-'05	7/7
42	Fiammetta, Tony	FB	6-0	242	8/22/86	2	Syracuse	Walkersville, Md.	D4a-'09	10/2
21	Francisco, Aaron	S	6-2	207	7/3/83	6	Brigham Young	Kahuku, Hawaii	FA-'10	10/2*
20	Gamble, Chris	CB	6-1	200	3/11/83	7	Ohio State	Sunrise, Fla.	D1-'04	16/16
30	Godfrey, Charles	S	5-11	205	11/15/85	3	Iowa	Baytown, Texas	D3a-'08	12/11
33	Goodson, Mike	RB	6-0	212	5/23/87	2	Texas A&M	Klein, Texas	D4b-'09	8/0
69	Gross, Jordan	T	6-4	305	7/20/80	8	Utah	Fruitland, Idaho	D1-'03	9/9
98	Hayden, Nick	DT	6-4	292	2/4/86	2	Wisconsin	Hartland, Wisc.	D6-'08	10/3
25	Hudson, Marcus	S	6-2	200	11/15/82	5	North Carolina State	Homestead, Fla.	FA-'10	12/0*
60	Irvin, Corvey	DT	6-3	302	5/3/85	2	Georgia	Augusta, Ga.	D3-'09	0*
44	Jackson, Dexter	WR	5-9	182	8/5/86	2	Appalachian State	Dunwoody, Ga.	FA-'10	0*
44	Jansen, J.J.	LS	6-2	256	1/20/86	3	Notre Dame	Phoenix, Ariz.	T(GB)-'09	16/0
80	Jarrett, Dwayne	WR	6-4	219	9/11/86	4	Southern California	New Brunswick, N.J.	D2a-'07	13/2
95	Johnson, Charles	DE	6-2	275	7/10/86	4	Georgia	Hawkinsville, Ga.	D3-'07	13/2
99	Johnson, Ed	DT	6-2	296	12/18/83	2	Penn State	Detroit, Mich.	FA-'10	4/4*
95	Justice, Steve	C	6-3	293	5/26/84	2	Wake Forest	New Smyrna Beach, Fla.	FA-'09	0*
67	Kalil, Ryan	C	6-2	295	3/29/85	4	Southern California	Corona, Calif.	D2b-'07	16/16
4	Kasay, John	K	5-10	210	10/27/69	20	Georgia	Athens, Ga.	UFA(Sea)-'95	16/0
47	King, Jeff	TE	6-3	260	2/19/83	5	Virginia Tech	Pulaski, Va.	D5-'06	16/15
61	Landri, Derek	DT	6-2	290	9/21/83	4	Notre Dame	Concord, Calif.	W(Jax)-'09	7/0*
94	Leonard, Louis	DT	6-4	325	7/16/84	4	Fresno State	Los Angeles, Calif.	T(Cle)-'09	2/1
31	Marshall, Richard	CB	5-11	189	12/12/84	5	Fresno State	Los Angeles, Calif.	D2-'06	16/16
83	Martin, Charly	WR	6-1	212	3/20/84	2	West Texas A&M	Farmington, N.M.	FA-'09	7/0
23	Martin, Sherrod	CB	6-1	198	10/12/84	2	Troy	Griffin, Ga.	D2b-'09	16/5
66	Moore, Eric	DE	6-4	268	2/28/81	5	Florida State	Pahokee, Fla.	FA-'10	0*
81	Moore, Kenneth	WR	5-11	195	2/19/85	3	Wake Forest	Charlotte, N.C.	FA-'08	12/1
3	Moore, Matt	QB	6-3	202	8/9/84	4	Oregon State	Valencia, Calif.	W(Dall)-'07	7/5
41	Munnerlyn, Captain	CB	5-8	186	4/10/88	2	South Carolina	Mobile, Ala.	D7-'09	15/4
79	Otah, Jeff	T	6-6	330	6/17/86	3	Pittsburgh	New Castle, Del.	D1b-'08	13/13
64	Petitti, Rob	T	6-6	327	5/21/82	5	Pittsburgh	Rumson, N.J.	FA-'09	0*
72	Robinson, Duke	G	6-5	330	10/10/86	2	Oklahoma	Atlanta, Ga.	D5-'09	1/0
88	Rosario, Dante	TE	6-4	250	10/25/84	4	Oregon	Dayton, Ore.	D5a-'07	14/8
74	Schwartz, Geoff	T	6-6	331	7/11/86	2	Oregon	Los Angeles, Calif.	D7b-'08	15/3
57	Senn, Jordan	LB	5-11	224	6/11/84	3	Portland State	Beaverton, Ore.	FA-'09	6/0
89	Smith, Steve	WR	5-9	185	5/12/79	10	Utah	Los Angeles, Calif.	D3-'01	15/15
28	Stewart, Jonathan	RB	5-10	235	3/21/87	3	Oregon	Fort Lewis, Wash.	D1a-'08	16/3
22	Sutton, Tyrell	RB	5-8	213	12/19/86	2	Northwestern	Akron, Ohio	FA-'09	7/1
97	Taylor, Hilee	DE	6-2	250	7/18/86	3	North Carolina	Laurinburg, N.C.	D7a-'08	5/0
93 t-	Tyler, Tank	DE	6-2	306	2/14/85	4	North Carolina State	Fayetteville, N.C.	T(KC)-'09	12/2*
70	Wharton, Travelle	G	6-4	312	5/19/81	7	South Carolina	Simpsonville, S.C.	D3-'04	16/16
34	Williams, DeAngelo	RB	5-9	217	4/25/83	5	Memphis	Wynne, Ark.	D1-'06	13/13
53 t-	Williams, Jamar	LB	6-0	237	6/14/84	5	Arizona State	Houston, Texas	T(Chi)-'09	16/2*
65	Williams, Garry	T	6-3	296	8/20/86	2	Kentucky	Louisville, Ky.	FA-'09	7/0
27	Wilson, C.J.	CB	6-1	195	4/2/85	4	Baylor	Terrell, Texas	FA-'07	7/0
15	Wright, Wallace	WR	6-1	197	2/1/84	4	North Carolina	Fayetteville, N.C.	FA-'10	16/0*

* Francisco played 10 games with Indianapolis in '09; Hudson played 12 games with San Francisco; Irvin missed '09 season because of injury; Jackson last active with Tampa Bay in '08; E. Johnson played 4 games with Indianapolis; Justice last active with Indianapolis in '08, Landri played 7 games with Jacksonville; E. Moore last active with St. Louis in '07; Petitti inactive for 3 games; Tyler played 6 games with Kansas City and 6 games with Carolina; J. Williams played 16 games with Chicago; Wright played 16 games with N.Y. Jets.

t- Panthers traded for Tyler (KC) and J. Williams (Chi).

Traded—S Chris Harris (13 games in '09) to Chicago.

Players lost through free agency (3): QB A.J. Feeley (StL; 0 games in '09), DE Julius Peppers (Chi; 16), CB Dante Wesley (Det; 15).

Also played with Panthers in '09—DT Antwon Burton (2 games), QB Jake Delhomme (11), LB Na'il Diggs (15), T Ra'Shon Harris (2), FB Brad Hoover (11), LB Landon Johnson (10), DT Damione Lewis (16), K Rhys Lloyd (16), QB Josh McCown (1), WR Muhsin Muhammad (14), LB Kelvin Smith (3), S Quinton Teal (16), DT Hollis Thomas (13), G Keydrick Vincent (16).

2010 FIRST-YEAR ROSTER

Name	Pos.	Ht.	Wt.	Birthdate	College	Hometown	How Acq.
Cantwell, Hunter (1)	QB	6-4	236	12/30/85	Louisville	Paducah, Ky.	FA-'09
Carter, Todd (1)	K	6-1	190	6/7/86	Grand Valley State	Flint, Mich.	FA
Clausen, Jimmy	QB	6-2	222	9/21/87	Notre Dame	Thousand Oaks, Calif.	D2
Edwards, Armanti	WR	5-11	182	3/8/88	Appalachian State	Greenwood, S.C.	D3b
Franklin, Noah	G	6-5	313	7/1/86	Oklahoma State	Vinita, Okla.	FA
George, Andrew	TE	6-4	247	7/23/84	Brigham Young	Englewood, Colo.	FA
Gettis, David	WR	6-3	216	8/27/87	Baylor	Los Angeles, Calif.	D6b
Gregory, Kurtis	G	6-4	308	8/7/86	Missouri	Alma, Mo.	FA
Guy, Trent	WR	5-8	171	8/22/87	Louisville	Charlotte, N.C.	FA
Hardy, Greg	DE	6-4	277	7/28/88	Mississippi	Memphis, Tenn.	D6a
Haudan, Blake	P	6-0	220	9/2/86	Minnesota	Toledo, Ohio	FA
Hisatake, Ray	G	6-3	305	9/18/86	Hawaii	Daly City, Calif.	FA
Ivy, Mortty (1)	LB	6-1	239	4/26/86	West Virginia	Monroeville, Pa.	FA-'09
Jackson, Rashawn	FB	6-1	239	1/15/87	Virginia	Jersey City, N.J.	FA
LaFell, Brandon	WR	6-2	211	11/4/86	Louisiana State	Houston, Texas	D3a
McClain, Robert	CB	5-9	195	7/22/88	Connecticut	Lusby, Md.	D7b
Neblett, Andre	DT	6-0	295	6/7/88	Temple	Rahway, N.J.	FA
Norwood, Eric	DE/LB	6-1	241	5/24/88	South Carolina	Kennesaw, Ga.	D4
O'Hanlon, Matt	S	5-11	207	10/5/85	Nebraska	Bellevue, Neb.	FA
Ortmann, Mark	T	6-6	295	6/24/86	Michigan	Klein, Texas	FA
Pettrey, Aaron	K	6-1	201	6/17/86	Ohio State	Raceland, Ky.	FA
Pike, Tony	QB	6-6	222	3/10/86	Cincinnati	Cincinnati, Ohio	D6d
Porter, Dan	RB	5-9	196	7/31/87	Louisiana Tech	Baton Rouge, La.	FA
Pugh, Jordan	S	5-11	196	1/29/88	Texas A&M	Plano, Texas	D6c
Stanford, R.J.	CB	5-10	183	5/6/88	Utah	Chino, Calif.	D7a
Vaughan, Josh (1)	RB	6-0	232	12/3/86	Richmond	Richmond, Va.	FA
Walker, Marcus (1)	CB	5-11	191	5/23/86	Oklahoma	Waco, Texas	FA-'09
Ware, Sean	LB	6-2	237	1/31/87	New Hampshire	Bristol, Conn.	FA
Warren, Brett (1)	LB	6-0	232	3/7/85	Virginia Tech	Clifton, Va.	FA
Young, Oliver	WR	6-2	197	10/25/85	South Carolina State	Charleston, S.C.	FA

The term NFL Rookie is defined as a player who is in his first season of professional football and has not been on the roster of another professional football team for any regular-season or postseason games. A Rookie is designated by an "R" on NFL rosters. Players who have been active in another professional football league or players who have NFL experience, including either preseason training camp or being on an Active List or Inactive List, or on Reserve/Injured or Reserve/Physically Unable to Perform for fewer than six regular-season games, are termed NFL First-Year Players. An NFL First-Year Player is designated by a "1" on NFL rosters. Thereafter, a player is credited with an additional year of experience for each season in which he accumulates six games on the Active List or Inactive List, or on Reserve/Injured or Reserve/Physically Unable to Perform.

Log on to www.panthers.com for an up-to-date roster.

CAROLINA PANTHERS

COACHING STAFF

Head Coach,
John Fox

Pro Career: Became third coach in Carolina Panthers history on January 25, 2002. In 2008, guided the Panthers to the third division title in franchise history. During tenure from 2002-08, 68 overall victories stand as the second-highest total in the NFC. Since arrival in 2002, the Panthers have ranked among the NFL's top 10 in total defense in five of eight seven seasons. In 2005, directed team to second NFC championship appearance in three seasons. Became the fifth head coach in NFL history to record four career postseason road wins. Equaled an NFL record with four consecutive postseason road wins. In 2004, directed Carolina team that overcame a 1-7 record to end the regular season with mark of 7-9. Of the 28 NFL teams that began season with 1-7 record since 1990, Panthers became only third team to finish season with seven victories. In 2003, guided Panthers to Super Bowl XXXVIII two years after inheriting team that won one game in 2001. Joined Vince Lombardi and Bill Parcells as the only coaches in NFL history to inherit a one-win team and guide it to the playoffs in their second season. In 2002, engineered a six-game turn-around that ranks second for rookie head coaches since 1978. In 2002, the Panthers became the only team since 1970 to improve from thirty-first to second in total defense in one season. Prior to joining Carolina he served as the defensive coordinator for the N.Y. Giants (1997-2001). In 2000, Fox helped the Giants reach Super Bowl XXXV, including posting the first shutout in a conference title game since 1986. Before joining the Giants, Fox was a consultant for the Rams (1996), defensive coordinator for the Raiders (1994-95), defensive backs coach for the Chargers (1992-93) and Steelers (1989-1991), and secondary coach for the USFL's Los Angeles Express (1985). Career record: 76-60.

Background: Defensive back at San Diego State (1976-77). Coached at San Diego State (1978), U.S. International (1979) Boise State (1980), Long Beach State (1981), Utah (1982), Kansas (1983), Iowa State (1984), and Pittsburgh (1986-88). Received bachelor's degree in physical education and earned a teaching credential from San Diego State.

Personal: Born February 8, 1955, in Virginia Beach, Va. He and his wife, Robin, have four children—Mathew, Mark, Cody, and Halle.

ASSISTANT COACHES

Brian Baker, defensive line; born June 20, 1962, Baltimore. Linebacker Maryland 1981-83. College coach: Maryland 1984-85, Army 1986, Georgia Tech 1987-1995. Pro coach: San Diego Chargers 1996, Detroit Lions 1997-2000, Minnesota Vikings 2001-05, St. Louis Rams 2006-08, joined Panthers in 2009.

Geep Chryst, tight ends/quality control-offense; born June 25, 1962, Madison, Wis. Linebacker Princeton 1981-84. Pro linebacker Orlando Thunder (WFL) 1992. College coach: Wisconsin-Platteville 1987, Wisconsin 1988, Wyoming 1989-1990. Pro coach: Orlando Thunder (WL) 1991, Chicago Bears 1991-95, Arizona Cardinals 1996-98, 2001-03, San Diego Chargers 1999-2000, joined Panthers in 2006.

Jeff Davidson, offensive coordinator; born Oct. 3, 1967, Akron, Ohio. Offensive lineman Ohio State 1986-89. Pro offensive lineman Denver Broncos 1990-92, New Orleans Saints 1994. Pro coach: New Orleans Saints 1995-96, New England Patriots 1997-2004, Cleveland Browns 2005-06, joined Panthers in 2007.

Sam Garnes, asst. special teams/strength and conditioning; born July 12, 1974, Bronx, N.Y. Safety Cincinnati 1992-96. Pro safety N.Y. Giants 1997-2001, N.Y. Jets 2002-03. Pro coach: Cologne Centurions (NFL Europe) 2006, Las Vegas Locomotives (UFL) 2009, joined Panthers in 2010.

Mike Gillhamer, secondary; born February 20, 1956, Oakland. Defensive back Carroll College 1972, Wenatchee (Wash.) J.C. 1973, Humboldt State 1974-75. No pro playing experience. College coach: College of the Sequoias 1979-1983, Weber State 1984, Utah 1985-89, San Jose State 1990-93, Nevada 1994-95, Oregon 2001-02, Louisville 2003. Pro coach: New York Giants 1997-2000, joined Panthers in 2004.

David Magazu, offensive line; born June 10, 1957, Taunton Mass. Defensive tackle Springfield College 1976-79. No pro playing experience. College coach: Ithaca 1980, Western Michigan 1981, Eastern Michigan 1982, Michigan 1983, Northern Illinois 1984, Ball State 1985-86, Navy 1987-89, Indiana State 1990-91, Colorado State 1992-94, Kentucky 1995-96, Memphis 1997-98, Boston College 1999-2002. Pro coach: Joined Panthers in 2003.

Ron Meeks, defensive coordinator; born August 27, 1954, Jacksonville. Defensive back Arkansas State 1972-76. Pro defensive back Hamilton Tiger-Cats (CFL) 1977-79, Ottawa Rough Riders (CFL) 1979, Toronto Argonauts (CFL) 1980-81. College coach: Arkansas State 1984-85, Miami 1986-87, New Mexico State 1988, Fresno State 1989-1990. Pro coach: Dallas Cowboys 1991, Cincinnati Bengals 1992-96, Atlanta Falcons 1997-99, Washington Redskins 2000, St. Louis Rams 2001, Indianapolis Colts 2002-08, joined Panthers in 2009.

Sam Mills III, quality control/defense; born May 20, 1978, Long Branch, N.J. Cornerback Montclair State 1997-98. No pro playing experience. Pro coach: Joined Panthers in 2006.

Ron Milus, secondary; born November 25, 1963, Tacoma, Wash. Cornerback Washington 1982-85. College coach: Washington 1991-98, Texas A&M 1999. Pro coach: Denver Broncos 2000-02, Arizona Cardinals 2003, New York Giants 2004-05, St. Louis Rams 2006-08, joined Panthers in 2009.

Jeff Rodgers, special teams; January 12, 1978, St. Paul, Minn. Linebacker North Texas 1996-99. College coach: Arizona 2001-02, Kansas State 2008. Pro coach: San Francisco 49ers 2003-07, joined Panthers in 2009.

Rip Scherer, quarterbacks, passing game coordinator; born August 3, 1952, Quarterback: William & Mary 1970-73. College coach: Penn State 1974-75, North Carolina State 1976, Hawaii 1977-78, Virginia 1979, Georgia Tech 1980-86, Alabama 1987, Arizona 1988-1990, James Madison 1991-94 (head coach), Memphis 1995-2000 (head coach), Kansas 2001, Southern Mississippi 2003-04. Pro coach: Cleveland Browns 2005-2008, joined Panthers in 2009.

Jerry Simmons, strength and conditioning; born June 15, 1954, Elkhart, Kan. Linebacker Fort Hays State 1976-77. No pro playing experience. College coach: Fort Hays State 1978, Clemson 1980, Rice 1981-82, Southern California 1983-87. Pro coach: New England Patriots 1988-1990, Cleveland Browns/Baltimore Ravens 1991-98, joined Panthers in 1999.

Jim Skipper, asst. head coach/running backs; born January 23, 1949, Breaux Bridge, La. Defensive back Whittier College 1971-72. No pro playing experience. College coach: Cal Poly-Pomona 1974-76, San Jose State 1977-78, Pacific 1979, Oregon 1980-82. Pro coach: Philadelphia/Baltimore Stars (USFL) 1983-85, New Orleans Saints 1986-1995, Arizona Cardinals 1996, New York Giants 1997-2000, San Francisco Demons (XFL) 2001 (head coach), joined Panthers in 2002.

Richard Smith, linebackers; born October 17, 1955, Los Angeles. Offensive lineman Rio Hondo (Calif.) J.C. 1975-76, Fresno State 1977-78. College coach: Rio Hondo (Calif.) J.C. 1979-1980, Cal State-Fullerton 1981-83, California 1984-86, Arizona 1987. Pro coach: Houston Oilers 1988-1992, Denver Broncos 1993-96, San Francisco 49ers 1997-2002, Detroit Lions 2003-04, Miami Dolphins 2005, Houston Texans 2006-08, joined Panthers in 2009.

Tyke Tolbert, wide receivers; born September 15, 1967, Conroe, Texas. Wide receiver Louisiana State 1988-1990. No pro playing experience. College coach: Louisiana State 1994, Ohio 1995, Northeast Louisiana 1995-97, Auburn 1998, Louisiana-Lafayette 1999-2001, Florida 2002. Pro coach: Arizona Cardinals 2003, Buffalo Bills 2004-09, joined Panthers in 2010.

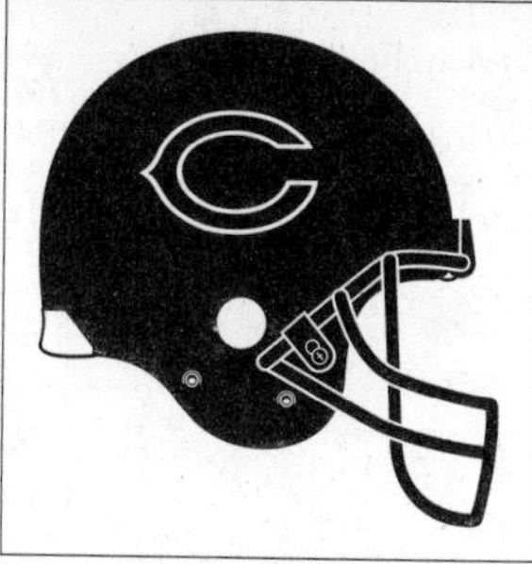

National Football Conference
North Division
Team Colors: Navy Blue, Orange, and White
Halas Hall at Conway Park
1000 Football Drive
Lake Forest, Illinois 60045
Telephone: (847) 295-6600

2010 SCHEDULE

PRESEASON

Aug. 14	at San Diego	6:00
Aug. 21	**Oakland**	7:30
Aug. 28	**Arizona**	7:30
Sep. 2	at Cleveland	8:00

REGULAR SEASON

Sep. 12	**Detroit**	12:00
Sep. 19	at Dallas	12:00
Sep. 27	**Green Bay** (Mon)	7:30
Oct. 3	at New York Giants	8:20
Oct. 10	at Carolina	1:00
Oct. 17	**Seattle**	12:00
Oct. 24	**Washington**	12:00
Oct. 31	BYE	
Nov. 7	at Buffalo (Toronto)	1:00
Nov. 14	**Minnesota**	12:00
Nov. 18	at Miami (Thu)	8:20
Nov. 28	**Philadelphia**	12:00
Dec. 5	at Detroit	1:00
Dec. 12	**New England**	12:00
Dec. 20	at Minnesota (Mon)	7:30
Dec. 26	**New York Jets**	12:00
Jan. 2	at Green Bay	12:00

Stadium: Soldier Field (opened in 1924)
•**Capacity:** 61,500
1410 S. Museum Campus Dr.
Chicago, Illinois 60605
Playing Surface: Natural Grass
Training Camp: Olivet-Nazarene Univ.
Bourbonnais, Illinois
60901

SOLDIER FIELD

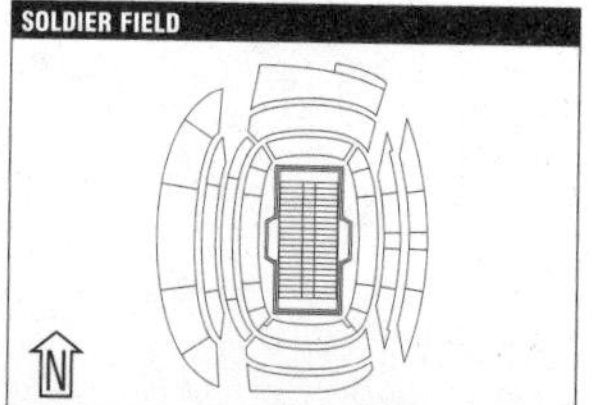

CLUB OFFICIALS

Chairman of the Board: Michael B. McCaskey
Secretary: Virginia H. McCaskey
President and CEO: Ted Phillips
General Manager: Jerry Angelo
Vice President: Tim McCaskey
Senior Director of Special Projects: Pat McCaskey
Senior Director of Ticket Operations: George McCaskey
Senior Director of Business Development & Alumni Relations: Brian McCaskey
Senior Director of Administration: John Bostrom
Senior Director of Finance & Treasurer: Karen Murphy
Senior Director of Corporate Sales & Marketing: Chris Hibbs
Senior Director of Corporate Communications: Scott Hagel
Senior Director of Football Administration and General Counsel: Cliff Stein
Director of Pro Personnel: Tim Ruskell
Assistant Director of Pro Personnel: Kevin Turks
Pro Scout: Dennard Wilson
Director of Player Development: Isaiah Harris
Director of Video Services: Dave Hendrickson
Assistant Video Director: Dean Pope
College Video Coordinator: Dan Tuohy
Video Assistant: Jack Dowling
Head Athletic Trainer: Tim Bream
Assistant Trainers: Chris Hanks, Jeremy Smith
Director of Rehabilitation: Bobby Slater
Head Equipment Manager: Tony Medlin
Assistant Equipment Managers: Carl Piekarski, John Perkins, Joseph Shaw
Scouts: Chris Ballard, Marty Barrett, Rex Hogan, Ted Monago, Mark Sadowski, Jeff Shiver
Director of Community Relations: Caroline Guip Schrenker
Director of Broadcasting & Scoreboard Operations: Greg Miller
Media Services Manager: Jim Christman
Media Relations Coordinator: Mike Corbo
Media Relations Assistant: Cary Dohman

COACHING HISTORY

Decatur Staleys 1920, Chicago Staleys 1921
(709-524-42)
Records include postseason games

1920-29	George Halas	84-31-19
1930-32	Ralph Jones	24-10-7
1933-1942	George Halas*	88-24-4
1942-45	Hunk Anderson-Luke Johnsos**	24-12-2
1946-1955	George Halas	76-43-2
1956-57	John (Paddy) Driscoll	14-10-1
1958-1967	George Halas	76-53-6
1968-1971	Jim Dooley	20-36-0
1972-74	Abe Gibron	11-30-1
1975-77	Jack Pardee	20-23-0
1978-1981	Neill Armstrong	30-35-0
1982-1992	Mike Ditka	112-68-0
1993-98	Dave Wannstedt	41-57-0
1999-2003	Dick Jauron	35-46-0
2004-09	Lovie Smith	54-46-0

*Retired after five games to enter U.S. Navy
**Co-coaches

PAID ATTENDANCE

Home 484,090 Away 513,666
Total 997,756
Single-game home record, 66,900 (9/5/93)
Single-season home record, 527,769 (1999)

2010 DRAFT CHOICES

Round	Name	Pos.	College
3	Major Wright	DB	Florida
4	Corey Wootton	DE	Northwestern
5	Joshua Moore	DB	Kansas State
6	Dan LeFevour	QB	Central Michigan
7	J'Marcus Webb	T	West Texas A&M

CHICAGO BEARS

2009 TEAM RECORD

PRESEASON (3-1)

Date	Result	Opponent
8/15	L 20-27	at Buffalo
8/22	W 17-3	N.Y. Giants
8/30	W 27-17	at Denver
9/3	W 26-23	Cleveland

REGULAR SEASON (7-9)

Date	Result	Opponent
9/13	L 15-21	at Green Bay
9/20	W 17-14	Pittsburgh
9/27	W 25-19	at Seattle
10/4	W 48-24	Detroit
10/18	L 14-21	at Atlanta
10/25	L 10-45	at Cincinnati
11/1	W 30-6	Cleveland
11/8	L 21-41	Arizona
11/12	L 6-10	at San Francisco
11/22	L 20-24	Philadelphia
11/29	L 10-36	at Minnesota
12/6	W 17-9	St. Louis
12/13	L 14-21	Green Bay
12/20	L 7-31	at Baltimore
12/28	W 36-30	Minnesota (OT)
1/3	W 37-23	at Detroit

(OT) Overtime

SCORE BY PERIODS

Bears	36	106	85	94	6 —	327
Opponents	96	112	69	98	0 —	375

2009 TEAM STATISTICS

	Bears	Opp.
Total First Downs	262	312
Rushing	71	105
Passing	170	186
Penalty	21	21
3rd Down: Made/Att	81/217	93/226
3rd Down Pct.	37.3	41.2
4th Down: Made/Att	7/18	6/13
4th Down Pct.	38.9	46.2
Possession Avg.	28:27	31:33
Total Net Yards	4965	5404
Avg. Per Game	310.3	337.8
Total Plays	971	1033
Avg. Per Play	5.1	5.2
Net Yards Rushing	1492	2022
Avg. Per Game	93.3	126.4
Total Rushes	373	467
Net Yards Passing	3473	3382
Avg. Per Game	217.1	211.4
Sacked/Yards Lost	35/204	35/272
Gross Yards	3677	3654
Att./Completions	563/340	531/341
Completion Pct.	60.4	64.2
Had Intercepted	27	13
Punts/Average	77/41.4	71/42.6
Net Punting Avg.	77/37.4	71/36.3
Penalties/Yards	100/836	88/744
Fumbles/Ball Lost	26/7	27/15
Touchdowns	36	43
Rushing	6	14
Passing	27	29
Returns	3	0

2009 INDIVIDUAL STATISTICS

PASSING	Att.	Comp.	Yds.	Pct.	TD	Int.	Tkld.	Rate
Cutler	555	336	3666	60.5	27	26	35/204	76.8
Hanie	7	3	11	42.9	0	1	0/0	10.7
Maynard	1	1	0	100.0	0	0	0/0	79.2
Bears	563	340	3677	60.4	27	27	35/204	75.6
Opponents	531	341	3654	64.2	29	13	35/272	92.3

SCORING	TD R	TD P	TD Rt	PAT	FG	Saf	PTS
Gould	0	0	0	33/33	24/28	0	105
Olsen	0	8	0	0/0	0/0	0	48
Knox	0	5	1	0/0	0/0	0	36
Forté	4	0	0	0/0	0/0	0	26
Aromashodu	0	4	0	0/0	0/0	0	24
Bennett	0	2	1	0/0	0/0	0	20
K. Davis	0	3	0	0/0	0/0	0	18
Hester	0	3	0	0/0	0/0	0	18
Clark	0	2	0	0/0	0/0	0	12
Cutler	1	0	0	0/0	0/0	0	6
Tillman	0	0	1	0/0	0/0	0	6
Wolfe	1	0	0	0/0	0/0	0	6
Manning	0	0	0	0/0	0/0	1	2
Bears	6	27	3	33/33	24/28	1	327
Opponents	14	29	0	38/40	25/33	0	375

2-Pt. Conversions: Bennett, Forté.
Bears 2-2, Opponents 2-3.

RUSHING	No.	Yds	Avg	LG	TD
Forté	258	929	3.6	61	4
Bell	40	220	5.5	72	0
Cutler	40	173	4.3	30	1
Wolfe	22	120	5.5	36	1
Peterson	7	51	7.3	15	0
Hester	6	-1	-0.2	7	0
Bears	373	1492	4.0	72	6
Opponents	467	2022	4.3	62t	14

RECEIVING	No.	Yds	Avg	LG	TD
Olsen	60	612	10.2	41	8
Hester	57	757	13.3	48	3
Forté	57	471	8.3	37	0
Bennett	54	717	13.3	71	2
Knox	45	527	11.7	68	5
Aromashodu	24	298	12.4	39t	4
Clark	19	145	7.6	26	2
K. Davis	9	75	8.3	18	3
R. Davis	5	35	7.0	10	0
McKie	5	13	2.6	8	0
Wolfe	2	12	6.0	12	0
Peterson	2	11	5.5	7	0
Bell	1	4	4.0	4	0
Bears	340	3677	10.8	71	27
Opponents	341	3654	10.7	50t	29

INTERCEPTIONS	No.	Yds	Avg	LG	TD
Bowman	6	67	11.2	39	0
Tillman	2	35	17.5	21t	1
Manning	1	35	35.0	35	0
Harris	1	6	6.0	6	0
Vasher	1	1	1.0	1	0
Briggs	1	0	0.0	0	0
Hillenmeyer	1	0	0.0	0	0
Bears	13	144	11.1	39	1
Opponents	27	365	13.5	67	0

PUNTING	No.	Yds.	Avg.	In 20	LG
Maynard	77	3191	41.4	26	66
Bears	77	3191	41.4	26	66
Opponents	71	3026	42.6	21	61

PUNT RETURNS	Ret	FC	Yds	Avg	LG	TD
Hester	24	5	187	7.8	33	0
Bennett	14	2	143	10.2	49t	1
Knox	1	0	0	0.0	0	0
Bears	39	7	330	8.5	49t	1
Opponents	34	14	272	8.0	53	0

KICKOFF RETURNS	No.	Yds	Avg	LG	TD
Knox	32	927	29.0	102t	1
Manning	28	744	26.6	59	0
R. Davis	9	114	12.7	22	0
Hester	7	156	22.3	44	0
Bennett	2	40	20.0	22	0
Aromashodu	1	18	18.0	18	0
Idonije	1	0	0.0	0	0
Bears	80	1999	25.0	102t	1
Opponents	64	1552	24.3	62	0

FIELD GOALS	1-19	20-29	30-39	40-49	50+
Gould	0/0	9/9	6/6	7/10	2/3
Bears	0/0	9/9	6/6	7/10	2/3
Opponents	0/0	6/6	8/12	8/12	3/3

SACKS	No.
Ogunleye	6.5
A. Brown	6.0
Anderson	3.5
Briggs	2.5
Harris	2.5
Hillenmeyer	2.5
Idonije	2.5
A. Adams	2.0
Afalava	2.0
Roach	2.0
Harrison	1.0
Manning	1.0
(group)	1.0
Bears	35.0
Opponents	35.0

RECORD HOLDERS

INDIVIDUAL RECORDS—CAREER

Category	Name	Performance
Rushing (Yds.)	Walter Payton, 1975-1987	16,726
Passing (Yds.)	Sid Luckman, 1939-1950	14,686
Passing (TDs)	Sid Luckman, 1939-1950	137
Receiving (No.)	Walter Payton, 1975-1987	492
Receiving (Yds.)	Johnny Morris, 1958-1967	5,059
Interceptions	Gary Fencik, 1976-1987	38
Punting (Avg.)	George Gulyanics, 1947-1952	44.5
Punt Return (Avg.)	George McAfee, 1940-41, 1945-1950	**12.8
Kickoff Return (Avg.)	Gale Sayers, 1965-1971	**30.6
Field Goals	Kevin Butler, 1985-1995	243
Touchdowns (Tot.)	Walter Payton, 1975-1987	125
Points	Kevin Butler, 1985-1995	1,116
*Sacks	Richard Dent, 1983-1993, 1995	124.5

INDIVIDUAL RECORDS—SINGLE SEASON

Category	Name	Performance
Rushing (Yds.)	Walter Payton, 1977	1,852
Passing (Yds.)	Erik Kramer, 1995	3,838
Passing (TDs)	Erik Kramer, 1995	29
Receiving (No.)	Marty Booker, 2001	100
Receiving (Yds.)	Marcus Robinson, 1999	1,400
Interceptions	Mark Carrier, 1990	10
Punting (Avg.)	Bobby Joe Green, 1963	46.5
Punt Return (Avg.)	Harry Clark, 1943	15.8
Kickoff Return (Avg.)	Gale Sayers, 1967	37.7
Field Goals	Robbie Gould, 2006	32
Touchdowns (Tot.)	Gale Sayers, 1965	22
Points	Kevin Butler, 1985	144
*Sacks	Richard Dent, 1984	17.5

INDIVIDUAL RECORDS—SINGLE GAME

Category	Name	Performance
Rushing (Yds.)	Walter Payton, 11-20-77	275
Passing (Yds.)	Johnny Lujack, 12-11-49	468
Passing (TDs)	Sid Luckman, 11-14-43	**7
Receiving (No.)	Jim Keane, 10-23-49	14
Receiving (Yds.)	Harlon Hill, 10-31-54	214
Interceptions	Many times	3
	Last time by Mark Carrier, 12-9-90	
Field Goals	Roger LeClerc, 12-3-61	5
	Mac Percival, 10-20-68	5
Touchdowns (Tot.)	Gale Sayers, 12-12-65	**6
Points	Gale Sayers, 12-12-65	36
*Sacks	Richard Dent, 11-4-84, 12-27-87	4.5

**Sacks became an official statistic in 1982.*
***NFL Record*

CHICAGO BEARS

2010 VETERAN ROSTER

No.	Name	Pos.	Ht.	Wt.	Birthdate	NFL Exp.	College	Hometown	How Acq.	'09 Games/ Starts
95	Adams, Anthony	DT	6-0	310	6/18/80	8	Penn State	Detroit, Mich.	UFA(SF)-'07	16/8
24	Afalava, Al	S	5-11	212	1/20/87	2	Oregon State	Laie, Hawai'i	D6-'09	13/13
97	+Anderson, Mark	DE	6-4	255	5/26/83	5	Alabama	Tulsa, Okla.	D5-'06	16/2
89	Angulo, Richard	TE	6-8	260	8/13/80	5	Western New Mexico	Albuquerque, N.M.	FA-'10	0*
19	Aromashodu, Devin	WR	6-2	201	5/23/84	4	Auburn	Miami, Fla.	FA-'08	10/2
14	Basanez, Brett	QB	6-1	208	5/11/83	2	Northwestern	Arlington Heights, Ill.	UFA(Car)-'09	0*
67	Beekman, Josh	G/C	6-2	310	6/30/83	4	Boston College	Amsterdam, N.Y.	D4-'07	11/4
32	Bell, Kahlil	RB	5-11	212	12/10/86	2	UCLA	Ft. Collins, Colo.	FA-'09	7/0
80	Bennett, Earl	WR	6-0	204	3/23/87	3	Vanderbilt	Birmingham, Ala.	D3a-'08	16/15
35	Bowman, Zackary	CB	6-1	193	11/18/84	3	Nebraska	Anchorage, Alaska	D5a-'08	16/12
55	Briggs, Lance	LB	6-1	242	11/12/80	8	Arizona	Sacramento, Calif.	D3-'03	15/15
36	Bullocks, Josh	S	6-0	207	2/28/83	6	Nebraska	Chattanooga, Tenn.	UFA(NO)-'09	12/4
88	Clark, Desmond	TE	6-3	249	4/20/77	12	Wake Forest	Lakeland, Fla.	UFA(Mia)-'03	11/7
6	Cutler, Jay	QB	6-3	233	4/29/83	5	Vanderbilt	Santa Claus, Ind.	T(Den)-'09	16/16
87	Davis, Kellen	TE	6-7	262	10/11/85	3	Michigan State	Adrian, Mich.	D5b-'08	16/2
81	Davis, Rashied	WR	5-9	187	7/24/79	6	San Jose State	Granada Hills, Calif.	FA-'05	16/0
22	Forté, Matt	RB	6-2	218	12/10/85	3	Tulane	Slidell, La.	D2-'08	16/16
63	Garza, Roberto	G/C	6-2	310	3/26/79	10	Texas A&M-Kingsville	Rio Hondo, Texas	UFA(Atl)-'05	16/16
70	Gilbert, Jarron	DT	6-5	285	9/30/86	2	San Jose State	Chino, Calif.	D3a-'09	4/0
9	Gould, Robbie	K	6-0	185	12/30/81	6	Penn State	Lock Haven, Pa.	FA-'05	16/0
21	Graham, Corey	CB	6-0	198	7/25/85	4	New Hampshire	Buffalo, N.Y.	D5b-'07	16/1
12	Hanie, Caleb	QB	6-2	225	9/11/85	3	Colorado State	Forney, Texas	FA-'08	3/0
t-	Harris, Chris	S	6-0	207	8/6/82	6	Louisiana-Monroe	Little Rock, Ark.	T(Car)-'10	13/13*
91	Harris, Tommie	DT	6-3	295	4/29/83	7	Oklahoma	Killeen, Texas	D1-'04	15/15
94	Harrison, Marcus	DT	6-3	312	7/10/84	3	Arkansas	Little Rock, Ark.	D3b-'08	16/9
23	Hester, Devin	WR/PR	5-11	190	11/4/82	5	Miami	Riviera Beach, Fla.	D2b-'06	13/12
92	Hillenmeyer, Hunter	LB	6-4	238	10/28/80	8	Vanderbilt	Nashville, Tenn.	FA-'03	14/13
71	Idonije, Israel	DL	6-6	270	11/17/80	7	Manitoba	Lagos, Nigeria	FA-'03	15/0
17	Iglesias, Juaquin	WR	6-1	205	8/22/87	2	Oklahoma	Killeen, Texas	D3b-'09	1/0
26	Jennings, Tim	CB	5-8	185	12/24/83	5	Georgia	Orangeburg, S.C.	FA-'10	15/5*
13	Knox, Johnny	WR	6-0	185	11/3/86	2	Abilene Christian	Houston, Texas	D5a-'09	15/0
57	Kreutz, Olin	C	6-2	292	6/9/77	13	Washington	Honolulu, Hawaii	D3-'98	16/16
60	Louis, Lance	G	6-3	305	4/24/85	2	San Diego State	New Orleans, La.	D7a-'09	0*
65	Mannelly, Patrick	LS	6-5	265	4/18/75	13	Duke	Atlanta, Ga.	D6b-'98	16/0
38	+Manning, Danieal	S/KR	5-11	202	8/9/82	5	Abilene Christian	Corsicana, Texas	D2a-'06	15/10
86	Manumaleuna, Brandon	TE	6-2	295	1/4/80	10	Arizona	Torrance, Calif.	UFA(SD)-'10	16/5*
72	Marten, James	T	6-8	310	4/18/84	3	Boston College	Indianapolis, Ind.	FA-'09	0*
4	Maynard, Brad	P	6-1	188	2/9/74	14	Ball State	Sheridan, Ind.	UFA(NYG)-'01	16/0
98	#McClover, Darrell	LB	6-1	226	8/25/81	7	Miami	Coconut Creek, Fla.	FA-'06	13/0
69	Melton, Henry	DE	6-3	260	10/11/86	2	Texas	Grapevine, Texas	D4a-'09	0*
30	Moore, D.J.	CB	5-9	183	3/22/87	2	Vanderbilt	Spartanburg, S.C.	D4b-'09	3/0
93	#Ogunleye, Adewale	DE	6-4	260	8/9/77	10	Indiana	Staten Island, N.Y.	T(Mia)-'04	14/14
82	Olsen, Greg	TE	6-5	255	3/11/85	4	Miami	Wayne, N.J.	D1-'07	16/15
68	Omiyale, Frank	G	6-4	315	11/23/82	6	Tennessee Tech	Whites Creek, Tenn.	UFA(Car)-'09	16/12
44	Payne, Kevin	S	6-0	212	12/5/83	4	Louisiana-Monroe	Junction City, Ark.	D5a-'07	13/5
90	Peppers, Julius	DE	6-7	283	1/18/80	9	North Carolina	Bailey, N.C.	UFA(Car)-'10	16/14*
29	#Peterson, Adrian	RB	5-10	212	7/1/79	9	Georgia Southern	Alachua, Fla.	D6a-'02	14/0
53	Roach, Nick	LB	6-1	234	6/16/85	4	Northwestern	Milwaukee, Wisc.	FA-'07	16/15
78	Shaffer, Kevin	T	6-5	318	3/2/80	9	Tulsa	Lancaster, Pa.	FA-'09	16/5
58	Shaw, Tim	LB	6-1	236	3/27/84	3	Penn State	Livonia, Mich.	FA-'09	15/0
20	Steltz, Craig	S	6-1	210	5/7/86	3	Louisiana State	Metairie, La.	D4-'08	12/2
29	Taylor, Chester	RB	5-11	213	9/22/79	9	Toledo	River Rouge, Mich.	UFA(Minn)-'10	16/0*
33	Tillman, Charles	CB	6-1	198	2/23/81	8	Louisiana-Lafayette	Copperas Cove, Texas	D2-'03	15/15
59	Tinoisamoa, Pisa	LB	6-1	230	7/15/81	8	Hawaii	Vista, Calif.	FA-'09	2/2
75	Toeaina, Matt	DT	6-2	308	10/9/84	3	Oregon	Utulei, American Samoa	FA-'07	1/0
54	Urlacher, Brian	LB	6-4	258	5/25/78	11	New Mexico	Lovington, N.M.	D1-'00	1/1
74	Williams, Chris	T	6-6	315	8/26/85	3	Vanderbilt	Glynn, La.	D1-'08	16/16
43	Williams, Eddie	FB	6-1	249	8/22/87	2	Idaho	San Mateo, Calif.	FA-'10	0*
25	Wolfe, Garrett	RB	5-7	185	8/17/84	4	Northern Illinois	Chicago, Ill.	D3a-'07	8/0

* Angulo last active with Jacksonville in '08; Basanez inactive 1 game; Jennings played 15 games with Indianapolis in '09; Louis inactive 13 games; Manumaleuna played 16 games with San Diego; Marten inactive 3 games; Melton missed '09 season because of injury; Peppers played 16 games with Carolina; Taylor played 16 games with Minnesota; E. Williams inactive 3 games with Washington.

t- Bears traded for C. Harris (Car).

Traded—S Kevin Payne (13 games in '09) to St. Louis, LB Jamar Williams (16) to Carolina.

Also played with Bears in '09—DE Gaines Adams (10 games), DE Alex Brown (16), TE Michael Gaines (1), LB Cato June (1), CB Trumaine McBride (1), FB Jason McKie (16), T Orlando Pace (12), CB Woodny Turenne (1), CB Nathan Vasher (15).

2010 FIRST-YEAR ROSTER

Name	Pos.	Ht.	Wt.	Birthdate	College	Hometown	How Acq.
Asiata, Johan (1)	G	6-4	300	12/19/85	Nevada-Las Vegas	Kalihi, Hawaii	FA-'09
Barnes, Freddie	WR	5-11	210	12/6/86	Bowling Green	Chicago Heights, Ill.	FA
Brock, Kevin (1)	TE	6-5	255	4/9/1986	Rutgers	Hackensack, N.J.	FA-'09
Brown, Cornelius	CB	5-11	198	2/26/88	Texas-El Paso	Houston, Texas	FA
Hall, Vic	WR	5-9	185	9/24/86	Virginia	Lynchburg, Va.	FA
Horn, Levi	T	6-6	320	10/2/86	Montana	Spokane, Wash.	FA
LeFevour, Dan	QB	6-3	230	3/19/87	Central Michigan	Downers Grove, Ill.	D6
Malast, Kevin (1)	LB	6-1	233	6/6/86	Rutgers	Manchester, N.J.	FA-'09
Mathews, Greg	WR	6-2	209	1/28/88	Michigan	Orlando, Fla.	FA
Mayberry, Matt	LB	6-1	230	8/6/87	Indiana	Darien, Ill.	FA
McGee, Richmond (1)	P	6-4	203	4/25/83	Texas	Garland, Texas	FA-'09
Minor, Brandon	RB	6-0	214	7/24/88	Michigan	Richmond, Va.	FA
Moore, Joshua	CB	5-11	188	8/20/88	Kansas State	Ft. Lauderdale, Fla.	D5
Peterman, Eric (1)	WR	6-1	202	11/18/86	Northwestern	Sherman, Ill.	FA-'09
Robinson, Antonio	WR	6-3	195	11/30/85	Nicholls State	Miami, Fla.	FA
Saddler-McQueen, Jimmy	DT	6-2	297	8/4/87	Texas A&M-Kingsville	Houston, Texas	FA
Scott, Quentin	S	6-3	220	5/31/88	Northern Iowa	Little Rock, Ark.	FA
Spicer, Averell	DT	6-1	305	4/26/87	Southern California	Rancho Cucamonga, Calif.	FA
Ta'ufo'ou, Will (1)	FB	5-11	247	6/19/86	California	San Carlos, Calif.	FA-'09
Turenne, Woodny (1)	CB	6-0	184	1/25/87	Louisville	Ft. Lauderdale, Fla.	FA-'09
Turner, Barry	DE	6-3	259	1/7/87	Nebraska	Antioch, Tenn.	FA
Walter, Tim	C	6-4	294	12/9/86	Colorado State	Manhattan Beach, Calif.	FA
Webb, J'Marcus	T	6-7	328	8/8/88	West Texas A&M	Mesquite, Texas	D7
Wilson, Lawrence	DE	6-4	274	7/21/87	Ohio State	Akron, Ohio	FA
Wootton, Corey	DE	6-6	270	6/22/87	Northwestern	Rutherford, N.J.	D4
Wright, Major	S	5-11	206	7/1/88	Florida	Miramar, Fla.	D3

The term NFL Rookie is defined as a player who is in his first season of professional football and has not been on the roster of another professional football team for any regular-season or postseason games. A Rookie is designated by an "R" on NFL rosters. Players who have been active in another professional football league or players who have NFL experience, including either preseason training camp or being on an Active List or Inactive List, or on Reserve/Injured or Reserve/Physically Unable to Perform for fewer than six regular-season games, are termed NFL First-Year Players. An NFL First-Year Player is designated by a "1" on NFL rosters. Thereafter, a player is credited with an additional year of experience for each season in which he accumulates six games on the Active List or Inactive List, or on Reserve/Injured or Reserve/Physically Unable to Perform.

Log on to www.chicagobears.com for an up-to-date roster.

CHICAGO BEARS

COACHING STAFF

Head Coach,
Lovie Smith

Pro Career: Named the thirteenth head coach in Chicago Bears history on January 15, 2004. Smith enters his seventh season as the head coach of the Chicago Bears with a regular season coaching record of 52-44 (.542). Those 52 wins are third most in franchise history, trailing only Hall of Famers George Halas and Mike Ditka. Smith also has a 2-2 postseason record, including an NFC Championship and the Bears first Super Bowl appearance in 21 years (2006), to give him the third-most playoff victories in team history behind the six of Halas and Ditka. Registering a career-high 13 wins in 2006 to tie predecessor Dick Jauron for the most victories by a Bears head coach in his third season, Smith led Chicago to home-field advantage in the NFC Playoffs and the team's first NFC Championship since its Super Bowl season of 1985. A year earlier, Smith earned the 2005 AP NFL Coach of the Year Award after turning a 1-3 start to the season into 11 victories, the most by a second-year coach in club annals, and the second seed in the NFC Playoffs. Fueled by an eight-game win streak, Smith led a worst-to-first revival in the NFC North division as the Bears six-win improvement from the previous season was tied for the biggest in the NFL in 2005. In Smith's first season, Chicago posted a 5-11 record. The Bears rank second in the NFL from 2004-07 with 140 takeaways and 14 touchdowns scored via defensive return. Smith came to Chicago from St. Louis (2001-03), where he served as defensive coordinator. In 2001 he helped the Rams return to the Super Bowl after missing the playoffs the previous season. Smith previously coached the linebackers for the Tampa Bay Buccaneers (1996-2000). Career record: 54-46.

Background: Played at Tulsa (1976-79), where he was a linebacker before moving to strong safety and earning two-time All-America and three-time All-Missouri Conference defensive back honors. Began his coaching career at his hometown high school (Big Sandy, Texas) in 1980 before moving to Cascia Hall Prep in Tulsa the following year. Two years later Smith began coaching collegiately at Tulsa (1983-86), Wisconsin (1987), Arizona State (1988-1991), Kentucky (1992), Tennessee (1993-94), and Ohio State (1995).

Personal: Born May 8, 1958, Gladewater, Texas. Lovie and his wife MaryAnne have three sons—Mikal, Matthew and Miles and twin grandsons—Malachi and Noah.

ASSISTANT COACHES

Jim Arthur, strength and conditioning assistant; born July 12, 1978. Attended Springfield (Mass.) College. No college or pro playing experience. College coach: Springfield (Mass.) College 2000, Louisiana Tech 2001, Boston College 2002. Pro coach: Joined Bears in 2005.

Bob Babich, linebackers; born February 20, 1961, Aliquippa, Pa. Linebacker Mesa (Colo.) C.C. 1979-1980, Tulsa 1981-82. No pro playing experience. College coach: Tulsa 1984-87, 1990, Wisconsin 1988-89, Bowling Green 1991, East Carolina 1992-93, Pittsburgh 1994-96, North Dakota State 1997-2002 (head coach). Pro coach: St. Louis Rams 2003, joined Bears in 2004.

Gill Byrd, asst. defensive backs/safeties; born February 20, 1961, San Francisco. Cornerback San Jose State 1979-1982. Pro cornerback San Diego Chargers 1983-1992. Pro coach: St. Louis Rams 2003-05, joined Bears in 2006.

Shane Day, quarterbacks; born September 27, 1974, Manhattan, Kan. Attended Kansas State. Wide receiver Rhodes College 1995-96. No pro playing experience. College coach: Michigan 2005-06. Pro coach: San Francisco 49ers 2007-09, joined Bears in 2010.

Mike DeBord, tight ends; born February 7, 1956, Muncie, Ind. Offensive line Manchester College 1974-77. No pro playing experience. College coach: Franklin 1982-83, Fort Hays State 1984-86, Eastern Illinois 1987-88, Ball State 1989, Colorado State 1990-91, Northwestern 1992, Michigan 1992-99, 2004-07, Central Michigan 2000-03 (head coach). Pro coach: Seattle Seahawks 2008-09, joined Bears in 2010.

Darryl Drake, wide receivers; born December 11, 1956, Louisville, Ky. Wide receiver Western Kentucky 1975-78. Pro wide receiver Washington Redskins 1979, Ottawa Rough Riders (CFL) 1981, Cincinnati Bengals 1983. College coach: Western Kentucky 1983-1991, Georgia 1992-96, Baylor 1997, Texas 1998-2003. Pro coach: Joined Bears in 2004.

Andrew Hayes-Stoker, offensive quality control; born January 9, 1979, Arlington, Texas. Running back Texas Christian 1999-2001. No pro playing experience. Pro coach: Joined Bears in 2010.

Jon Hoke, defensive backs; born January 24, 1957, Kettering, Ohio. Defensive back Ball State 1976-79. Pro defensive back Chicago Bears 1980. College coach: Bowling Green 1983-86, San Diego State 1987-88, Kent State 1989-1993, Missouri 1994-98, Florida 1999-2001. Pro coach: Houston Texans 2002-08, joined Bears in 2009.

Rusty Jones, director of physical development; born August 14, 1953. Attended Springfield (Mass.) College. No college or pro playing experience. College coach: Springfield (Mass.) College 1979-1982. Pro coach: Buffalo Bills 1985-2004, joined Bears in 2005.

Rod Marinelli, defensive coordinator/asst. head coach; born July 13, 1949, Rosemead, Calif. Offensive/defensive tackle Utah 1968, offensive tackle California Lutheran 1970-72. No pro playing experience. College coach: Utah State 1976, California 1983-1991, Arizona State 1992-94, Southern California 1995. Pro coach: Tampa Bay Buccaneers 1996-2005, Detroit Lions 2006-08 (head coach), joined Bears in 2009.

Mike Martz, offensive coordinator; born May 13, 1951, Sioux Falls, S.D. Tight end Fresno State 1972. No pro playing experience. College coach: San Diego Mesa C.C. 1974, 1976-77, San Jose State 1975, Santa Ana College 1978, Fresno State 1979, Pacific 1980-81, Minnesota 1982, Arizona State 1983-1991. Pro coach: L.A./St. Louis Rams 1992-96, 1999-2005 (head coach 2000-05), Washington Redskins 1997-98, Detroit Lions 2006-07, San Francisco 49ers 2008, joined Bears in 2010.

Mikal Smith, defensive quality control; born November 16, 1976, Dallas. Safety Arizona 1995-97. No pro playing experience. College coach: Trinity International 2006-07. Pro coach: Joined Bears in 2010.

Tim Spencer, running backs; born December 10, 1960, Martin Ferry, Ohio. Running back Ohio State 1979-1982. Pro running back Chicago Blitz (USFL) 1983, Arizona Wranglers (USFL) 1984, Memphis Showboats (USFL) 1985, San Diego Chargers 1985-1990. College coach: Ohio State 1994-2003. Pro coach: Joined Bears in 2004.

Chris Tabor, asst. special teams; born March 4, 1971, St. Joseph, Mo. Quarterback Benedictine College 1989-1992. No pro playing experience. College coach: Hutchinson (Kan.) C.C. 1994, Central Methodist College 1995-96, Missouri 1997-2000, Culver-Stockton College 2001 (head coach), Utah State 2002-04, Western Michigan 2005-07. Pro coach: Joined Bears in 2008.

Mike Tice, offensive line; born February 2, 1959, Bay Shore, N.Y. Quarterback Maryland 1977-1980. Pro tight end Seattle Seahawks 1981-88, 1990-91, Washington Redskins 1989, Minnesota Vikings 1992-93, 1995. Pro coach: Minnesota Vikings 1996-2005 (head coach 2001-05), Jacksonville Jaguars 2006-09, joined Bears in 2010.

Dave Toub, special teams coordinator; born June 1, 1962, Ossining, N.Y. Offensive lineman Springfield College 1980-81, Texas-El Paso 1983-84. No pro playing experience. College coach: Texas El-Paso 1987-89, Missouri 1989-2000. Pro coach: Philadelphia Eagles 2001-03, joined Bears in 2004.

Eric Washington, defensive line; born October 29, 1969, Shreveport, La. Grambling State 1989-1991. No pro playing experience. College coach: Texas A&M 1997-98, Ohio 2001-03, Northwestern 2004-07. Pro coach: Joined Bears in 2008.

National Football Conference
East Division
Team Colors: Royal Blue, Metallic Silver Blue, and White
Cowboys Center, One Cowboys Parkway
Irving, Texas 75063
Telephone: (972) 556-9900

2010 SCHEDULE

PRESEASON

Aug. 8	vs. Cincinnati, at Canton, OH	8:00
Aug. 12	**Oakland**	8:00
Aug. 21	at San Diego	6:00
Aug. 28	at Houston	7:00
Sep. 2	**Miami**	7:00

REGULAR SEASON

Sep. 12	at Washington	8:20
Sep. 19	**Chicago**	12:00
Sep. 26	at Houston	12:00
Oct. 3	BYE	
Oct. 10	**Tennessee**	3:15
Oct. 17	at Minnesota	3:15
Oct. 25	**New York Giants** (Mon)	7:30
Oct. 31	**Jacksonville**	12:00
Nov. 7	at Green Bay	7:20
Nov. 14	at New York Giants	4:15
Nov. 21	**Detroit**	12:00
Nov. 25	**New Orleans** (Thu)	3:15
Dec. 5	at Indianapolis	4:15
Dec. 12	**Philadelphia**	* 7:20
Dec. 19	**Washington**	12:00
Dec. 25	at Arizona (Sat)	5:30
Jan. 2	at Philadelphia	1:00

** Sunday night games in Weeks 11-17 subject to change*

Stadium: Cowboys Stadium (opened in 2009)
•**Capacity:** 80,000 (expandable to 100,000 for special events)
One Legends Way
Arlington, Texas 76011
Playing Surface: Sportfield Softtop
Training Camp: Alamodome
San Antonio, TX 78203
River Ridge Field
Oxnard, CA 93030

COWBOYS STADIUM

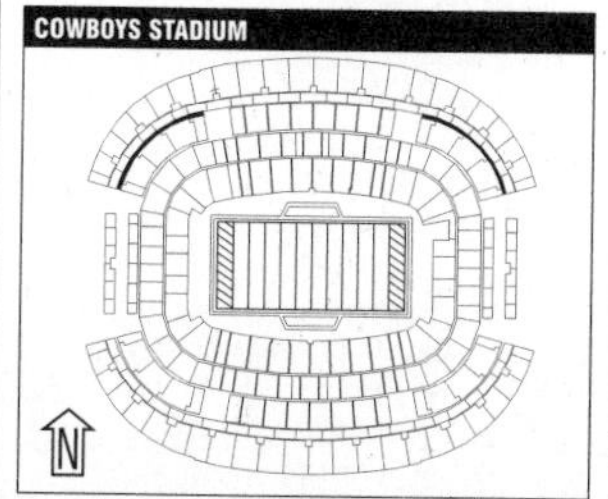

CLUB OFFICIALS

Owner/President/General Manager: Jerry Jones
Chief Operating Officer/Executive Vice President/Director of Player Personnel: Stephen Jones
Executive Vice President/VP of Brand Management/President Charity Foundation: Charlotte Anderson
Executive Vice President/Chief Sales and Marketing Officer: Jerry Jones Jr.
CFO: George Mitchell
Senior Vice President, Sales and Marketing: Greg McElroy
Senior Vice President and General Counsel: Alec Scheiner
Vice President Public Relations/Communications: Rich Dalrymple
Director of Corporate Communications: Brett Daniels
Director of Community Relations and Alumni Affairs: Emily Robbins
Director of College and Pro Scouting: Tom Ciskowski
Director of Operations: Bruce Mays
Director of Player Development: Bryan Wansley
Director of Information Technology: Peter Walsh
Director of Broadcasting: Scott Purcel
Internet Director: Derek Eagleton
Director of Ticket Operations: Ann Bihari
Head Athletic Trainer: Jim Maurer
Equipment Manager: Mike McCord
Video Director: Robert Blackwell
Cheerleader Director: Kelli Finglass

COACHING HISTORY

(467-339-6)
Records include postseason games

1960-1988	Tom Landry	270-178-6
1989-1993	Jimmy Johnson	51-37-0
1994-97	Barry Switzer	45-26-0
1998-99	Chan Gailey	18-16-0
2000-02	Dave Campo	15-33-0
2003-06	Bill Parcells	34-32-0
2007-09	Wade Phillips	34-17-0

PAID ATTENDANCE

Home 629,749 Away 574,899
Total 1,204,648
Single-game home record, 105,121 (9/20/09)
Single-season home record, 629,749 (2009)

2010 DRAFT CHOICES

Round	Name	Pos.	College
1	Dez Bryant	WR	Oklahoma St.
2	Sean Lee	LB	Penn State
4	Akwasi Owusu-Ansah	DB	Indiana (PA)
6	Sam Young	T	Notre Dame
	Jamar Wall	DB	Texas Tech
7	Sean Lissemore	DT	William & Mary

DALLAS COWBOYS

2009 TEAM RECORD

PRESEASON (2-2)

Date	Result	Opponent
8/13	L 10-31	at Oakland
8/21	W 30-10	Tennessee
8/29	L 13-20	San Francisco
9/4	W 35-31	at Minnesota

REGULAR SEASON (11-5)

Date	Result	Opponent
9/13	W 34-21	at Tampa Bay
9/20	L 31-33	New York Giants
9/28	W 21-7	Carolina
10/4	L 10-17	at Denver
10/11	W 26-20	at Kansas City (OT)
10/25	W 37-21	Atlanta
11/1	W 38-17	Seattle
11/8	W 20-16	at Philadelphia
11/15	L 7-17	at Green Bay
11/22	W 7-6	Washington
11/26	W 24-7	Oakland
12/6	L 24-31	at New York Giants
12/13	L 17-20	San Diego
12/19	W 24-17	at New Orleans
12/27	W 17-0	at Washington
1/3	W 24-0	Philadelphia

(OT) Overtime

POSTSEASON (1-1)

Date	Result	Opponent
1/9	W 34-14	Philadelphia
1/17	L 3-34	at Minnesota

SCORE BY PERIODS

	1	2	3	4	OT	Total
Cowboys	71	98	80	106	6	— 361
Opponents	27	80	34	109	0	— 250

2009 TEAM STATISTICS

	Cowboys	Opp.
Total First Downs	335	286
Rushing	110	74
Passing	203	186
Penalty	22	26
3rd Down: Made/Att	82/202	70/200
3rd Down Pct.	40.6	35.0
4th Down: Made/Att	4/11	6/12
4th Down Pct.	36.4	50.0
Possession Avg.	32:04	27:56
Total Net Yards	6390	5054
Avg. Per Game	399.4	315.9
Total Plays	1020	979
Avg. Per Play	6.3	5.2
Net Yards Rushing	2103	1448
Avg. Per Game	131.4	90.5
Total Rushes	436	365
Net Yards Passing	4287	3606
Avg. Per Game	267.9	225.4
Sacked/Yards Lost	34/196	42/268
Gross Yards	4483	3874
Att./Completions	550/347	572/344
Completion Pct.	63.1	60.1
Had Intercepted	9	11
Punts/Average	72/45.1	92/44.4
Net Punting Avg.	72/39.9	92/37.8
Penalties/Yards	115/892	93/768
Fumbles/Ball Lost	20/10	23/10
Touchdowns	43	28
Rushing	14	7
Passing	26	19
Returns	3	2

2009 INDIVIDUAL STATISTICS

PASSING	Att.	Comp.	Yds.	Pct.	TD	Int.	Tkld.	Rate
Romo	550	347	4483	63.1	26	9	34/196	97.6
Cowboys	550	347	4483	63.1	26	9	34/196	97.6
Opponents	572	344	3874	60.1	19	11	42/268	83.5

SCORING	TD R	TD P	TD Rt	PAT	FG	Saf	PTS
Folk	0	0	0	36/36	18/28	0	90
Austin	0	11	0	0/0	0/0	0	66
Barber	7	0	0	0/0	0/0	0	42
Crayton	0	5	2	0/0	0/0	0	42
R. Williams	0	7	0	0/0	0/0	0	42
Choice	3	0	0	0/0	0/0	0	20
Jones	3	0	0	0/0	0/0	0	18
Witten	0	2	0	0/0	0/0	0	12
Suisham TM	0	0	0	5/5	2/3	0	11
Hurd	0	1	0	0/0	0/0	0	6
Newman	0	0	1	0/0	0/0	0	6
Romo	1	0	0	0/0	0/0	0	6
Cowboys	14	26	3	41/41	20/31	0	361
Opponents	7	19	2	28/28	18/26	0	250

2-Pt. Conversions: Choice.
Cowboys 1-1, Opponents 0-0.

RUSHING	No.	Yds	Avg	LG	TD
Barber	214	932	4.4	35	7
Jones	116	685	5.9	56	3
Choice	64	349	5.5	66	3
Romo	35	105	3.0	17	1
Crayton	4	28	7.0	20	0
Ogletree	1	6	6.0	6	0
Austin	2	-2	-1.0	11	0
Cowboys	436	2103	4.8	66	14
Opponents	365	1448	4.0	35	7

RECEIVING	No.	Yds	Avg	LG	TD
Witten	94	1030	11.0	69	2
Austin	81	1320	16.3	60t	11
R. Williams	38	596	15.7	66t	7
Crayton	37	622	16.8	80t	5
Barber	26	221	8.5	42	0
Jones	19	119	6.3	30	0
Bennett	15	159	10.6	21	0
Choice	15	132	8.8	28	0
Hurd	7	121	17.3	53	1
Ogletree	7	96	13.7	21	0
Phillips	7	62	8.9	23	0
Anderson	1	5	5.0	5	0
Cowboys	347	4483	12.9	80t	26
Opponents	344	3874	11.3	74t	19

INTERCEPTIONS	No.	Yds	Avg	LG	TD
Jenkins	5	0	0.0	0	0
Newman	3	36	12.0	27t	1
Scandrick	1	0	0.0	0	0
Sensabaugh	1	0	0.0	0	0
Spencer	1	-3	-3.0	-3	0
Cowboys	11	33	3.0	27t	1
Opponents	9	96	10.7	34t	1

PUNTING	No.	Yds.	Avg.	In 20	LG
McBriar	72	3249	45.1	38	63
Cowboys	72	3249	45.1	38	63
Opponents	92	4084	44.4	36	69

PUNT RETURNS	Ret	FC	Yds	Avg	LG	TD
Crayton	36	23	437	12.1	82t	2
Newman	2	0	-11	-5.5	0	0
Ogletree	1	0	0	0.0	0	0
Cowboys	39	23	426	10.9	82t	2
Opponents	38	23	314	8.3	79t	1

KICKOFF RETURNS	No.	Yds	Avg	LG	TD
Jones	30	678	22.6	41	0
Ogletree	8	166	20.8	32	0
Austin	7	157	22.4	29	0
Rossum TM	1	16	16.0	16	0
Anderson	1	15	15.0	15	0
Cowboys	47	1032	22.0	41	0
Opponents	47	967	20.6	67	0

FIELD GOALS	1-19	20-29	30-39	40-49	50+
Folk	1/1	5/6	6/7	5/12	1/2
Suisham TM	0/0	1/1	0/1	1/1	0/0
Cowboys	1/1	6/7	6/8	6/13	1/2
Opponents	0/0	4/5	7/9	6/7	1/5

SACKS	No.
Ware	11.0
Ratliff	6.0
Spencer	6.0
Bowen	3.0
Brooking	3.0
Butler	3.0
Spears	2.5
B. Carpenter	2.0
James	2.0
Olshansky	1.5
Hatcher	1.0
Scandrick	1.0
Cowboys	42.0
Opponents	34.0

RECORD HOLDERS

INDIVIDUAL RECORDS—CAREER

Category	Name	Performance
Rushing (Yds.)	Emmitt Smith, 1990-2002	**17,162
Passing (Yds.)	Troy Aikman, 1989-2000	32,942
Passing (TDs)	Troy Aikman, 1989-2000	165
Receiving (No.)	Michael Irvin, 1988-1999	750
Receiving (Yds.)	Michael Irvin, 1988-1999	11,904
Interceptions	Mel Renfro, 1964-1977	52
Punting (Avg.)	Mat McBriar, 2004-09	45.0
Punt Return (Avg.)	Deion Sanders, 1995-99	13.3
Kickoff Return (Avg.)	Mel Renfro, 1964-1977	26.4
Field Goals	Rafael Septien, 1978-1986	162
Touchdowns (Tot.)	Emmitt Smith, 1990-2002	164
Points	Emmitt Smith, 1990-2002	986
*Sacks	Jim Jeffcoat, 1983-1994	94.5

INDIVIDUAL RECORDS—SINGLE SEASON

Category	Name	Performance
Rushing (Yds.)	Emmitt Smith, 1995	1,773
Passing (Yds.)	Tony Romo, 2009	4,483
Passing (TDs)	Tony Romo, 2007	36
Receiving (No.)	Michael Irvin, 1995	111
Receiving (Yds.)	Michael Irvin, 1995	1,603
Interceptions	Everson Walls, 1981	11
Punting (Avg.)	Mat McBriar, 2006	48.2
Punt Return (Avg.)	Bob Hayes, 1968	20.8
Kickoff Return (Avg.)	Mel Renfro, 1965	30.0
Field Goals	Richie Cunningham, 1997	34
Touchdowns (Tot.)	Emmitt Smith, 1995	25
Points	Emmitt Smith, 1995	150
*Sacks	DeMarcus Ware, 2008	20.0

INDIVIDUAL RECORDS—SINGLE GAME

Category	Name	Performance
Rushing (Yds.)	Emmitt Smith, 10-31-93	237
Passing (Yds.)	Don Meredith, 11-10-63	460
Passing (TDs)	Many times Last time by Tony Romo, 11-23-06	5
Receiving (No.)	Jason Witten, 12-9-07	15
Receiving (Yds.)	Miles Austin, 10-11-09	250
Interceptions	Many times Last time by Terence Newman, 12-14-03	3
Field Goals	Chris Boniol, 11-18-96	7
	Billy Cundiff, 9-15-03	7
Touchdowns (Tot.)	Many times Last time by Terrell Owens, 11-18-07	4
Points	Many times Last time by Terrell Owens, 11-18-07	24
*Sacks	Jim Jeffcoat, 11-10-85	5.0

**Sacks became an official statistic in 1982.*
***NFL Record*

DALLAS COWBOYS

2010 VETERAN ROSTER

No.	Name	Pos.	Ht.	Wt.	Birthdate	NFL Exp.	College	Hometown	How Acq.	'09 Games/ Starts
34	Anderson, Deon	FB	5-10	246	1/27/83	4	Connecticut	Providence, R.I.	D6b-'07	16/9
19	+Austin, Miles	WR	6-3	214	6/30/84	5	Monmouth	Garfield, N.J.	FA-'06	16/9
20	Ball, Alan	CB	6-1	188	3/29/85	3	Illinois	Detroit, Mich.	D7b-'07	16/3
24	Barber, Marion	RB	6-0	222	6/10/83	6	Minnesota	Wayzata, Minn.	D4a-'05	15/15
78	t- Barron, Alex	T	6-7	315	9/28/82	6	Florida State	Orangeburg, S.C.	T(StL)-'10	16/16*
80	Bennett, Martellus	TE	6-6	266	3/10/87	3	Texas A&M	Alief, Texas	D2-'08	14/6
72	Bowen, Stephen	DE	6-5	306	3/28/84	5	Hofstra	Wheatley Heights, N.Y.	FA-'06	16/2
79	Brewster, Robert	T	6-4	320	7/30/86	2	Ball State	Cincinnati, Ohio	D3-'09	0*
51	Brooking, Keith	LB	6-2	242	10/30/75	13	Georgia Tech	Senoia, Ga.	UFA(Atl)-'09	16/14
18	Buehler, David	K	6-2	228	2/5/87	2	Southern California	Anaheim, Calif.	D5c-'09	16/0
57	Butler, Victor	LB	6-2	246	7/29/87	2	Oregon State	Rialto, Calif.	D4b-'09	16/1
23	Choice, Tashard	RB	5-10	212	11/20/84	3	Georgia Tech	Riverdale, Ga.	D4-'08	16/0
75	Colombo, Marc	T	6-8	318	10/8/78	9	Boston College	Bridgewater, Mass.	FA-'05	9/9
84	Crayton, Patrick	WR	6-0	204	4/7/79	7	Northwestern Okla. St.	DeSoto, Texas	D7b-'04	16/6
70	Davis, Leonard	G	6-6	353	9/5/78	10	Texas	Wortham, Texas	UFA(Ariz)-'07	16/16
29	Floyd, Marquis	CB	6-0	190	3/17/80	2	West Georgia	Monroe, Ga.	FA-'09	0*
68	Free, Doug	T	6-6	313	1/6/84	4	Northern Illinois	Manitowoc, Wis.	D4b-'07	16/7
26	Gordon, Cletis	CB	6-1	205	4/23/83	5	Jackson State	Amite City, La.	FA-'09	1/0
65	Gurode, Andre	C	6-4	318	3/6/79	9	Colorado	Houston, Texas	D2a-'02	16/16
36	Hamlin, Michael	S	6-2	213	11/21/85	2	Clemson	Lamar, S.C.	D5b-'09	6/0
97	Hatcher, Jason	DE	6-6	305	7/13/82	5	Grambling State	Jena, La.	D3b-'06	16/0
55	Hodge, Stephen	LB	6-0	238	7/17/87	2	Texas Christian	Tatum, Texas	D6a-'09	0*
64	Holland, Montrae	G	6-2	326	5/21/80	8	Florida State	Ore, Texas	FA-'10	0*
17	Hurd, Sam	WR	6-2	208	4/24/85	5	Northern Illinois	San Antonio, Texas	FA-'06	16/1
56	James, Bradie	LB	6-2	247	1/17/81	8	Louisiana State	Monroe, La.	D4-'03	16/16
21	Jenkins, Mike	CB	5-10	198	3/22/85	3	South Florida	Bradenton, Fla.	D1b-'08	16/15
98	Johnson, Curtis	LB	6-3	237	2/16/85	3	Clark Atlanta	Syracuse, N.Y.	W(Ind)-'09	3/0
28	Jones, Felix	RB	6-0	218	5/8/87	3	Arkansas	Tulsa, Okla.	D1a-'08	14/1
3	Kitna, Jon	QB	6-2	230	9/21/72	14	Central Washington	Tacoma, Wash.	T(Det)-'09	0*
63	Kosier, Kyle	G	6-5	307	11/27/78	9	Arizona State	Peoria, Ariz.	UFA(Det)-'06	16/16
91	Ladouceur, Louis-Philippe	LS	6-4	256	3/13/81	6	California	Pointe-Claire, Quebec	FA-'05	16/0
1	McBriar, Mat	P	6-1	220	7/8/79	7	Hawaii	East Brighton, Australia	FA-'04	16/0
7	McGee, Stephen	QB	6-3	218	9/27/85	2	Texas A&M	Burnet, Texas	D4a-'09	0*
77	McQuistan, Pat	T	6-6	317	4/30/83	5	Weber State	Lebanon, Ore.	D7a-'06	7/0
41	Newman, Terence	CB	5-11	191	9/4/78	8	Kansas State	Salina, Kan.	D1-'03	16/16
53	Octavien, Steve	LB	6-0	246	11/25/84	2	Nebraska	Belle Glade, Fla.	FA-'08	14/0
85	Ogletree, Kevin	WR	6-0	192	8/5/87	2	Virginia	Queens, N.Y.	FA-'09	11/0
99	Olshansky, Igor	DE	6-6	315	5/3/82	7	Oregon	San Francisco, Calif.	UFA(SD)-'09	16/14
89	Phillips, John	TE	6-5	255	6/11/87	2	Virginia	Warm Springs, Va.	D6b-'09	16/4
69	+Preston, Duke	C	6-5	311	6/12/82	6	Illinois	San Diego, Calif.	FA-'09	0*
71	Procter, Cory	C	6-4	311	10/18/82	6	Montana	Gig Harbor, Wash.	FA-'05	12/0
90	Ratliff, Jay	NT	6-4	303	8/29/81	6	Auburn	Valdosta, Ga.	D7-'05	16/16
9	Romo, Tony	QB	6-2	226	4/21/80	8	Eastern Illinois	Burlington, Wisc.	FA-'03	16/16
32	Scandrick, Orlando	CB	5-10	193	2/10/87	3	Boise State	Los Alamitos, Calif.	D5-'08	16/4
43	+Sensabaugh, Gerald	S	6-0	210	6/13/83	6	North Carolina	Kingsport, Tenn.	UFA(Jax)-'09	15/15
95	Siavii, Junior	NT	6-5	318	11/14/78	5	Oregon	Pago Pago, American Samoa	FA-'09	16/0
96	Spears, Marcus	DE	6-4	309	3/8/83	6	Louisiana State	Baton Rouge, La.	D1b-'05	16/14
93	Spencer, Anthony	LB	6-3	256	1/23/84	4	Purdue	Fort Wayne, Ind.	D1-'07	16/16
94	Ware, DeMarcus	LB	6-4	262	7/31/82	6	Troy	Auburn, Ala.	D1a-'05	16/15
25	Watkins, Patrick	S	6-5	218	12/18/82	5	Florida State	Tallahassee, Fla.	D5-'06	13/1
59	Williams, Brandon	LB	6-3	248	6/21/88	2	Texas Tech	Fort Worth, Texas	D4c-'09	0*
58	Williams, Jason	LB	6-1	246	2/21/86	2	Western Illinois	Chicago, Ill.	D3a-'09	5/0
52	Williams, Leon	LB	6-2	250	7/30/83	4	Miami	Brooklyn, N.Y.	FA-'10	0*
11	Williams, Roy	WR	6-3	215	12/20/81	7	Texas	Odessa, Texas	T(Det)-'08	15/13
82	Witten, Jason	TE	6-5	263	5/6/82	8	Tennessee	Elizabethton, Tenn.	D3-'03	16/16
50	Woods, Donovan	LB	6-2	230	7/27/85	2	Oklahoma State	Oklahoma City, Okla.	FA-'09	1/0*

* Barron played 16 games with St. Louis in '09; Brewster missed '09 season because of injury; Floyd inactive for 2 games with Cleveland; Hodge missed '09 season because of injury; Holland inactive for 16 games; Kitna did not play in 16 games; McGee inactive third quarterback all 16 games; Preston inactive for 15 games; B. Wiliams missed '09 season because of injury; L. Williams last active with Cleveland in '08; Woods played 1 game with Pittsburgh.

\+ Restricted free agent; subject to developments.

t- Cowboys traded for Barron (StL).

Traded—LB Bobby Carpenter (16 games in '09) to St. Louis.

Also played with Cowboys in '09—T Flozell Adams (16 games), K Nick Folk (14), S Ken Hamlin (12), CB Allen Rossum (1), K Shaun Suisham (2), RB Chauncey Washington (2), CB Marvin White (3).

2010 FIRST-YEAR ROSTER

Name	Pos.	Ht.	Wt.	Birthdate	College	Hometown	How Acq.
Alvarado, Delbert	P/K	6-0	200	1/3/89	South Florida	Tampa, Fla.	FA
Aumavae, Junior	NT	6-2	315	4/29/86	Minnesota State	Palmer, Alaska	FA
Barker, Will	T	6-7	315	7/3/87	Virginia	Bryan Mawr, Pa.	FA
Bright, Travis (1)	G	6-4	320	1/5/83	Brigham Young	Queen Creek, Ariz.	FA-'09
Bryant, Dez	WR	6-1	217	11/4/88	Oklahoma State	Lufkin, Texas	D1
Church, Barry	S	6-1	222	2/11/88	Toledo	Pittsburgh, Pa.	FA
Costa, Phil	G/C	6-3	307	7/11/87	Maryland	Moorestown, N.J.	FA
Dixon, Marcus (1)	DE	6-4	285	9/16/84	Hampton	Rome, Ga.	FA-'08
Donaldson, Herb (1)	RB	5-11	225	12/13/85	Western Illinois	St. Louis, Mo.	FA-'09
Greer, Rashaun	WR	6-0	206	2/10/87	Colorado State	North Las Vegas, Nev.	FA
Gronkowski, Chris	FB	6-2	239	12/26/86	Arizona	Amherst, N.Y.	FA
Holley, Jesse (1)	WR	6-2	213	1/8/84	North Carolina	Roselle, N.J.	FA-'09
Hudgins, Terrell	WR	6-2	229	2/24/87	Elon	Rocky Mount, N.C.	FA
Hughes, Connor (1)	K	5-10	172	10/4/83	Virginia	Newport News, Va.	FA
Johnson, Manuel (1)	WR	5-11	195	10/14/86	Oklahoma	Gilmer, Texas	D7b-'09
Lee, Sean	LB	6-2	236	7/22/86	Penn State	Pittsburgh, Pa.	D2
Lissemore, Sean	DL	6-3	298	9/11/87	William & Mary	Durmont, N.J.	D7
McCann, Bryan	CB	5-10	182	9/29/87	Southern Methodist	Oklahoma City, Okla.	FA
McCray, Danny	S	6-0	214	3/10/88	Louisiana State	Houston, Texas	FA
Miller, Lonyae	RB	5-11	221	4/29/88	Fresno State	Fontana, Calif.	FA
Nichols, Matt	QB	6-2	220	3/19/87	Eastern Washington	Cottonwood, Calif.	FA
Owusu-Ansah, Akwasi	S	6-0	207	4/10/88	Indiana (Pa.)	Columbus, Ohio	D4
Ryan, Titus (1)	WR	6-0	190	5/19/84	Concordia College	Tuscaloosa, Ala.	FA
Sicko, Scott	TE	6-4	251	1/30/88	New Hampshire	Stillwater, N.Y.	FA
Teofilo, Chet	G/C	6-4	309	5/8/86	California	Chula Vista, Calif.	FA
Tepper, Mike	T	6-5	320	12/11/85	California	Cypress, Calif.	FA
Tow-Arnett, Nick	TE	6-3	241	9/7/84	Minnesota	Redwood Falls, Minn.	FA
Tucker, Verran	WR	6-2	202	6/26/88	California	Torrance, Calif.	FA
Wall, Jamar	CB	5-10	203	1/10/88	Texas Tech	Plainview, Texas	D6b
Washington, Lorenzo	DE	6-4	291	12/2/86	Alabama	Loganville, Ga.	FA
Young, Sam	T	6-8	316	6/24/87	Notre Dame	Coral Springs, Fla.	D6a

The term NFL Rookie is defined as a player who is in his first season of professional football and has not been on the roster of another professional football team for any regular-season or postseason games. A Rookie is designated by an "R" on NFL rosters. Players who have been active in another professional football league or players who have NFL experience, including either preseason training camp or being on an Active List or Inactive List, or on Reserve/Injured or Reserve/Physically Unable to Perform for fewer than six regular-season games, are termed NFL First-Year Players. An NFL First-Year Player is designated by a "1" on NFL rosters. Thereafter, a player is credited with an additional year of experience for each season in which he accumulates six games on the Active List or Inactive List, or on Reserve/Injured or Reserve/Physically Unable to Perform.

Log on to www.dallascowboys.com for an up-to-date roster.

DALLAS COWBOYS

COACHING STAFF

Head Coach,
Wade Phillips

Pro Career: Was named the seventh coach in club history on February 8, 2007. He led the Cowboys to a 13-3 record in 2007 becoming the third head coach since the NFL merger to reach 13 wins in his first season with a club. In guiding the Cowboys to the playoffs, he has now reached the playoffs in the first season in each of the last seven times he has taken over as a head coach or defensive coordinator. In 2009, he led the team to an 11-5 record, its second NFC East title under Phillips and the club's first playoff win since 1996. Following the season, he was awarded a two-year contract extension. Phillips brought 30 years of NFL coaching experience, including five as a head coach and 20 as a defensive coordinator, to the Cowboys. In his eight full seasons as a head coach, Phillips has produced a 79-51 record and guided his teams to five playoff appearances. He has had only one non-winning season as a head coach. His .600 career winning percentage in the regular season is fourth among active NFL head coaches with 40 or more games. Over the last 20 years as a head coach or coordinator, he has been a part of only four teams that have had non-winning records. During that time he has worked with a defense that ranked in the NFL's top 10 eleven times. Phillips served as the defensive coordinator for the San Diego Chargers (2004-06) and Atlanta Falcons (2002-03), finishing the 2003 season as interim head coach for the Falcons (posting a 2-1 record). Phillips also served as interim head coach in New Orleans for four games in 1985 (1-3 record). During the 1998-2000 seasons as head coach in Buffalo, the Bills compiled a record of 29-19. Phillips took the reins after a 6-10 finish in 1997 and reversed the team's fortunes by leading it to a 10-6 record and the playoffs in 1998. His 1999 team led the NFL in total defense, went 11-5 and earned another trip to the postseason. Before becoming the Bills head coach in 1998, he was the team's defensive coordinator (1995-97). Phillips had a two-year stint as Denver's head coach (1993-94), after serving as defensive coordinator the previous four seasons. He led the Broncos to a playoff berth in his first season (1993). He was the Philadelphia Eagles defensive coordinator and linebackers coach (1986-88). His first coordinator's position came with the New Orleans Saints (1981-85). He began his NFL coaching career with the Houston Oilers (1976-1980) under his father, longtime NFL coach Bum Phillips. Career record: 82-59.

Background: Played linebacker at Houston (1966-68). Served as a college coach at Houston (1969), Oklahoma State (1973-74), and Kansas (1975).

Personal: Born June 21, 1947, in Orange, Texas. He and his wife Laurie, have one son, Wesley, and one daughter, Tracy.

ASSISTANT COACHES

Dave Campo, secondary; born July 18, 1947, Groton, Conn. Defensive back Central Connecticut State 1967-1970. No pro playing experience. College coach: Central Connecticut State 1971-72, Albany 1973, Bridgeport 1974, Pittsburgh 1975, Washington State 1976, Boise State 1977-79, Oregon State 1980, Weber State 1981-82, Iowa State 1983, Syracuse 1984-86, Miami 1987-88. Pro coach: Dallas Cowboys 1989-2002 (head coach 2000-02), Cleveland Browns 2003-04, Jacksonville Jaguars 2005-07, re-joined Cowboys in 2008.

Joe DeCamillis, special teams coordinator; born June 29, 1965, Arvada, Colo. Attended Wyoming. No college or pro playing experience. Pro coach: Denver Broncos 1988-1992, New York Giants 1993-96, Atlanta Falcons 1997-2006, Jacksonville Jaguars 2007-08, joined Cowboys in 2009.

Jason Garrett, asst. head coach/offensive coordinator; born March 28, 1966, Abington, Pa. Quarterback Princeton 1987-88. Pro quarterback San Antonio Riders (World League) 1991, Ottawa RoughRiders (CFL) 1991, Dallas Cowboys 1993-99, New York Giants 2000-03, Tampa Bay Buccaneers 2004, Miami Dolphins 2004. College coach: Princeton 1990. Pro coach: Miami Dolphins 2005-06, joined Cowboys in 2007.

John Garrett, tight ends; born March 2, 1965, Danville, Pa. Wide receiver Columbia 1983-85, Princeton 1986-87. Pro wide receiver Cincinnati Bengals 1989, Buffalo Bills 1991, San Antonio Riders (World League) 1991. College coach: Virginia 2004-06. Pro coach: Cincinnati Bengals 1995-98, 2001-02, Arizona Cardinals 1999-2000, joined Cowboys in 2007.

Reggie Herring, linebackers; born July 3, 1959, Myrtle Beach, S.C. Linebacker Florida State 1978-1980. No pro playing experience. College coach: Oklahoma State 1981-85, Auburn 1986-1991, Texas Christian 1992-93, Clemson 1994-2001, North Carolina State 2004, Arkansas 2005-07 (interim head coach 2007). Pro coach: Houston Texans 2002-03, joined Cowboys in 2008.

Hudson Houck, offensive line; born January 7, 1943, Los Angeles. Center Southern California 1962-64. No pro playing experience. College coach: Southern California 1970-72, 1976-1982, Stanford 1973-75. Pro coach: Los Angeles Rams 1983-1991, Seattle Seahawks 1992, Dallas Cowboys 1993-2001, San Diego Chargers 2002-04, Miami Dolphins 2005-07, re-joined Cowboys in 2008.

Joe Juraszek, strength and conditioning; born June 8, 1958, Chicago. Linebacker/defensive end New Mexico 1976-1980. No pro playing experience. College coach: Oklahoma 1981-86, 1993-96, Texas Tech 1987-1992. Pro coach: Joined Cowboys in 1997.

Bobby King, defensive quality control/asst. linebackers; born June 29, 1978, Louisville, Kentucky. Defensive line Texas El-Paso 1998-2000. No pro playing experience. College coach: Texas El-Paso 2002-03, West Texas A&M 2005, 2008-09, Baylor 2006-07. Pro coach: Joined Cowboys in 2010.

Brett Maxie, secondary/safeties; born January 13, 1962, Dallas. Safety Texas Southern 1982-84. Pro safety New Orleans Saints 1985-1993, Atlanta Falcons 1994, Carolina Panthers 1995-96, San Francisco 49ers 1997. Pro coach: Carolina Panthers 1998, San Francisco 49ers 1999-2003, Miami Dolphins 2007, joined Cowboys in 2008.

Paul Pasqualoni, defensive line; born August 16, 1949, Cheshire, Conn. Linebacker Penn State 1968-1971. College coach: Southern Connecticut State 1976-1981, Western Connecticut State 1982-86 (head coach), Syracuse 1987-2004 (head coach 1991-2004). Pro coach: Dallas Cowboys 2005-07, Miami Dolphins 2008-09, re-joined Cowboys in 2010.

Skip Peete, running backs; born January 30, 1963, Mesa, Ariz. Wide receiver Arizona 1981-82, Kansas 1984-85. Pro wide receiver New York Jets 1987. College coach: Pittsburgh 1988-1992, Michigan State 1993-94, Rutgers 1995, UCLA 1996-97. Pro coach: Oakland Raiders 1998-2006, joined Cowboys in 2007.

Wes Phillips, offensive assistant/offensive quality control; born February 17, 1979, Houston. Quarterback Texas-El Paso 1997-2001. Pro quarterback San Diego Riptide (AFL2) 2002-03. College coach: Texas-El Paso 2003, West Texas A&M 2004-05, Baylor 2006. Pro coach: Joined Cowboys in 2007.

Ray Sherman, wide receivers; born November 27, 1951, Berkeley, Calif. Wide receiver/defensive back Fresno State 1971-72. No pro playing experience. College coach: San Jose State 1974, California 1975, 1981, Michigan State 1976-77, Wake Forest 1978-1980, Purdue 1982-85, Georgia 1986-87. Pro coach: Houston Oilers 1988-89, Atlanta Falcons 1990, San Francisco 49ers 1991-93, New York Jets 1994, Minnesota Vikings 1995-97, 1999, Pittsburgh Steelers 1998, Green Bay Packers 2000-04, Tennessee Titans 2005-06, joined Cowboys in 2007.

Wade Wilson, quarterbacks; born February 1, 1959, Commerce, Texas. Quarterback East Texas State 1977-1980. Pro quarterback Minnesota Vikings 1981-1991, Atlanta Falcons 1992, New Orleans Saints 1993-94, Dallas Cowboys 1995-97, Oakland Raiders 1998-99. Pro coach: Dallas Cowboys 2000-02, Chicago Bears 2004-06, re-joined Cowboys in 2007.

National Football Conference
North Division
Team Colors: Honolulu Blue and Silver
222 Republic Drive
Allen Park, Michigan 48101
Telephone: (313) 216-4000

2010 SCHEDULE

PRESEASON

Aug. 14	at Pittsburgh	7:30
Aug. 21	at Denver	7:00
Aug. 28	**Cleveland**	5:30
Sep. 2	**Buffalo**	7:00

REGULAR SEASON

Sep. 12	at Chicago	12:00
Sep. 19	**Philadelphia**	1:00
Sep. 26	at Minnesota	12:00
Oct. 3	at Green Bay	12:00
Oct. 10	**St. Louis**	1:00
Oct. 17	at New York Giants	1:00
Oct. 24	BYE	
Oct. 31	**Washington**	1:00
Nov. 7	**New York Jets**	1:00
Nov. 14	at Buffalo	1:00
Nov. 21	at Dallas	12:00
Nov. 25	**New England** (Thu)	12:30
Dec. 5	**Chicago**	1:00
Dec. 12	**Green Bay**	1:00
Dec. 19	at Tampa Bay	1:00
Dec. 26	at Miami	1:00
Jan. 2	**Minnesota**	1:00

Stadium: Ford Field (opened in 2002)
•**Capacity:** 64,500
2000 Brush Street
Detroit, Michigan 48226
Playing Surface: FieldTurf
Training Camp: 222 Republic Drive
Allen Park, Michigan
48101

FORD FIELD

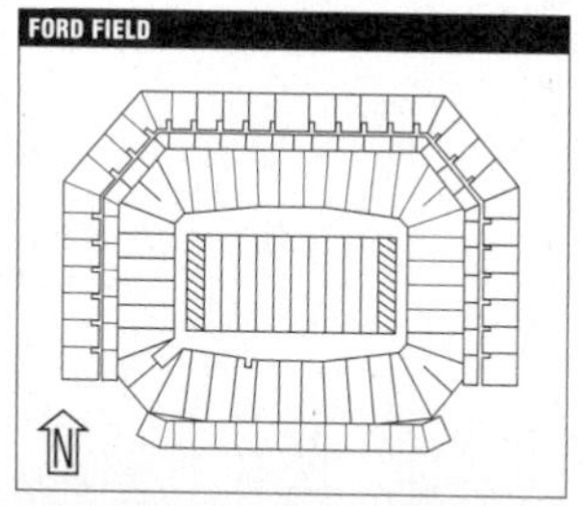

CLUB OFFICIALS

Chairman and Owner: William Clay Ford
Vice Chairman: William Clay Ford, Jr.
President: Tom Lewand
Senior Vice President & General Manager: Martin Mayhew
Senior Vice President of Communications: Bill Keenist
Senior Vice President & CFO: Tom Lesnau
Corporate Secretary: David Hempstead
Senior Personnel Executive: James Harris
Vice President of Pro Personnel: Sheldon White
Vice President of Football Operations: Cedric Saunders
Director of College Scouting: Scott McEwen
Player Personnel: Cary Conklin, Dennis Gentry, Chad Henry, Rob Lohman, Miller McCalmon, Silas McKinnie, Lance Newmark, Charlie Sanders, Dave Sears, Dave Uyrus
Senior Director of Community Affairs: Tim Pendell
Director of Media Relations: Matt Barnhart
Director of Broadcasting and Production: Bryan Bender
Director of Ticket Operations: Mark Graham
Coordinator of Athletic Medicine/Athletic Trainer: Dean Kleinschmidt
Athletic Trainer: Al Bellamy
Equipment Manager: Tim O'Neill
Video Director: Robert Yanagi

COACHING HISTORY

Portsmouth Spartans 1930-33
(497-593-32)
Records include postseason games

1930	Hal (Tubby) Griffen	5-6-3
1931-36	George (Potsy) Clark	49-20-6
1937-38	Earl (Dutch) Clark	14-8-0
1939	Elmer (Gus) Henderson	6-5-0
1940	George (Potsy) Clark	5-5-1
1941-42	Bill Edwards*	4-9-1
1942	John Karcis	0-8-0
1943-47	Charles (Gus) Dorais	20-31-2
1948-1950	Alvin (Bo) McMillin	12-24-0
1951-56	Raymond (Buddy) Parker	50-24-2
1957-1964	George Wilson	55-45-6
1965-66	Harry Gilmer	10-16-2
1967-1972	Joe Schmidt	43-35-7
1973	Don McCafferty	6-7-1
1974-76	Rick Forzano**	15-17-0
1976-77	Tommy Hudspeth	11-13-0
1978-1984	Monte Clark	43-63-1
1985-88	Darryl Rogers***	18-40-0
1988-1996	Wayne Fontes	67-71-0
1997-2000	Bobby Ross****	27-32-0
2000	Gary Moeller	4-3-0
2001-02	Marty Mornhinweg	5-27-0
2003-05	Steve Mariucci#	15-28-0
2005	Dick Jauron	1-4-0
2006-08	Rod Marinelli	10-38-0
2009	Jim Schwartz	2-14-0

*Released after three games in 1942
**Resigned after four games in 1976
***Released after 11 games in 1988
****Resigned after nine games in 2000
#Released after 11 games in 2005

PAID ATTENDANCE

Home 382,188 Away 513,319
Total 895,507
Single-game home record, 80,444 (12/20/81)
Single-season home record, 644,904 (1980)

2010 DRAFT CHOICES

Round	Name	Pos.	College
1	Ndamukong Suh	DT	Nebraska
	Jahvid Best	RB	California
3	Amari Spievey	DB	Iowa
4	Jason Fox	T	Miami
7	Willie Young	DE	North Carolina St.
	Tim Toone	WR	Weber St.

DETROIT LIONS

2009 TEAM RECORD

PRESEASON (3-1)

Date	Result	Opponent
8/15	W 27-26	Atlanta
8/22	L 10-27	at Cleveland
8/29	W 18-17	Indianapolis
9/3	W 17-6	at Buffalo

REGULAR SEASON (2-14)

Date	Result	Opponent
9/13	L 27-45	at New Orleans
9/20	L 13-27	Minnesota
9/27	W 19-14	Washington
10/4	L 24-48	at Chicago
10/11	L 20-28	Pittsburgh
10/18	L 0-26	at Green Bay
11/1	L 10-17	St. Louis
11/8	L 20-32	at Seattle
11/15	L 10-27	at Minnesota
11/22	W 38-37	Cleveland
11/26	L 12-34	Green Bay
12/6	L 13-23	at Cincinnati
12/13	L 3-48	at Baltimore
12/20	L 24-31	Arizona
12/27	L 6-20	at San Francisco
1/3	L 23-37	Chicago

SCORE BY PERIODS

Lions	80	63	51	68	0 —	262
Opponents	88	158	127	121	0 —	494

2009 TEAM STATISTICS

	Lions	Opp.
Total First Downs	281	332
Rushing	82	95
Passing	168	213
Penalty	31	24
3rd Down: Made/Att	84/234	85/210
3rd Down Pct.	35.9	40.5
4th Down: Made/Att	7/26	10/15
4th Down Pct.	26.9	66.7
Possession Avg.	28:57	31:03
Total Net Yards	4784	6274
Avg. Per Game	299.0	392.1
Total Plays	1037	1029
Avg. Per Play	4.6	6.1
Net Yards Rushing	1616	2025
Avg. Per Game	101.0	126.6
Total Rushes	409	458
Net Yards Passing	3168	4249
Avg. Per Game	198.0	265.6
Sacked/Yards Lost	43/303	26/150
Gross Yards	3471	4399
Att./Completions	585/316	545/371
Completion Pct.	54.0	68.1
Had Intercepted	32	9
Punts/Average	74/42.9	66/43.6
Net Punting Avg.	74/36.8	66/38.9
Penalties/Yards	98/768	113/944
Fumbles/Ball Lost	25/9	26/14
Touchdowns	28	57
Rushing	9	18
Passing	16	35
Returns	3	4

2009 INDIVIDUAL STATISTICS

PASSING	Att.	Comp.	Yds.	Pct.	TD	Int.	Tkld.	Rate
Stafford	377	201	2267	53.3	13	20	24/169	61.0
Culpepper	157	89	945	56.7	3	6	14/107	64.8
Stanton	51	26	259	51.0	0	6	5/27	26.1
Lions	585	316	3471	54.0	16	32	43/303	58.1
Opponents	545	371	4399	68.1	35	9	26/150	107.0

SCORING	TD R	TD P	TD Rt	PAT	FG	Saf	PTS
Hanson	0	0	0	25/25	21/28	0	88
K. Smith	4	1	0	0/0	0/0	1	32
C. Johnson	0	5	0	0/0	0/0	0	30
Heller	0	3	0	0/0	0/0	0	18
B. Johnson	0	3	0	0/0	0/0	0	18
Delmas	0	0	2	0/0	0/0	1	14
Morris	2	0	0	0/0	0/0	0	14
Pettigrew	0	2	0	0/0	0/0	0	12
Stafford	2	0	0	0/0	0/0	0	12
A. Brown	0	1	0	0/0	0/0	0	6
James	0	0	1	0/0	0/0	0	6
Northcutt	0	1	0	0/0	0/0	0	6
Stanton	1	0	0	0/0	0/0	0	6
Lions	9	16	3	25/25	21/28	2	262
Opponents	18	35	4	55/55	31/34	1	494

2-Pt. Conversions: Morris.
Lions 1-3, Opponents 1-2.

RUSHING	No.	Yds	Avg	LG	TD
K. Smith	217	747	3.4	31	4
Morris	93	384	4.1	64t	2
A. Brown	27	131	4.9	19	0
Stafford	20	108	5.4	21	2
Culpepper	18	91	5.1	32	0
C. Johnson	7	73	10.4	19	0
Felton	15	46	3.1	10	0
Stanton	9	33	3.7	11	1
D. Williams	1	4	4.0	4	0
Pearson	1	1	1.0	1	0
Figurs TM	1	-2	-2.0	-2	0
Lions	409	1616	4.0	64t	9
Opponents	458	2025	4.4	61	18

RECEIVING	No.	Yds	Avg	LG	TD
C. Johnson	67	984	14.7	75t	5
K. Smith	41	415	10.1	63	1
B. Johnson	35	417	11.9	36	3
Northcutt	35	357	10.2	47	1
Pettigrew	30	346	11.5	30	2
Heller	29	296	10.2	24	3
Morris	26	210	8.1	19	0
Fitzsimmons	18	128	7.1	12	0
Felton	13	133	10.2	27	0
A. Brown	9	84	9.3	26t	1
D. Williams	6	52	8.7	19	0
Nordin	2	26	13.0	14	0
T. Smith	2	7	3.5	4	0
Figurs TM	1	7	7.0	7	0
Standeford	1	5	5.0	5	0
Gronkowski	1	4	4.0	4	0
Lions	316	3471	11.0	75t	16
Opponents	371	4399	11.9	68	35

INTERCEPTIONS	No.	Yds	Avg	LG	TD
Delmas	2	130	65.0	101t	1
James	2	41	20.5	38t	1
Henry	2	26	13.0	26	0
Simpson	1	8	8.0	8	0
Levy	1	5	5.0	5	0
D. White	1	0	0.0	0	0
Lions	9	210	23.3	101t	2
Opponents	32	508	15.9	61t	3

PUNTING	No.	Yds.	Avg.	In 20	LG
N. Harris	74	3174	42.9	20	56
Lions	74	3174	42.9	20	56
Opponents	66	2878	43.6	34	64

PUNT RETURNS	Ret	FC	Yds	Avg	LG	TD
Northcutt	22	15	189	8.6	43	0
Buchanon	4	0	34	8.5	18	0
Witherspoon TM	2	0	10	5.0	9	0
Lions	28	15	233	8.3	43	0
Opponents	41	14	354	8.6	45	0

KICKOFF RETURNS	No.	Yds	Avg	LG	TD
A. Brown	42	951	22.6	87	0
D. Williams	42	931	22.2	34	0
Witherspoon TM	4	72	18.0	31	0
Northcutt	3	66	22.0	34	0
Follett	2	12	6.0	10	0
Fitzsimmons	1	10	10.0	10	0
Jennings	1	8	8.0	8	0
Felton	1	0	0.0	0	0
Lions	96	2050	21.4	87	0
Opponents	58	1353	23.3	102t	1

FIELD GOALS	1-19	20-29	30-39	40-49	50+
Hanson	0/0	5/5	8/9	7/10	1/4
Lions	0/0	5/5	8/9	7/10	1/4
Opponents	0/0	13/14	10/11	7/8	1/1

SACKS	No.
Avril	5.5
Hunter	5.0
Peterson	4.5
Foote	2.0
Fluellen	1.5
McBride	1.5
Bryan	1.0
Buchanon	1.0
J. Cohen	1.0
Delmas	1.0
Dizon	1.0
(group)	1.0
Lions	26.0
Opponents	43.0

RECORD HOLDERS

INDIVIDUAL RECORDS—CAREER

Category	Name	Performance
Rushing (Yds.)	Barry Sanders, 1989-1998	15,269
Passing (Yds.)	Bobby Layne, 1950-58	15,710
Passing (TDs)	Bobby Layne, 1950-58	118
Receiving (No.)	Herman Moore, 1991-2001	670
Receiving (Yds.)	Herman Moore, 1991-2001	9,174
Interceptions	Dick LeBeau, 1959-1972	62
Punting (Avg.)	Yale Lary, 1952-53, 1956-1964	44.3
Punt Return (Avg.)	Jack Christiansen, 1951-58	12.8
Kickoff Return (Avg.)	Pat Studstill, 1961-67	25.7
Field Goals	Jason Hanson, 1992-2009	427
Touchdowns (Tot.)	Barry Sanders, 1989-1998	109
Points	Jason Hanson, 1992-2009	1,835
*Sacks	Robert Porcher, 1992-2003	95.5

INDIVIDUAL RECORDS—SINGLE SEASON

Category	Name	Performance
Rushing (Yds.)	Barry Sanders, 1997	2,053
Passing (Yds.)	Scott Mitchell, 1995	4,338
Passing (TDs)	Scott Mitchell, 1995	32
Receiving (No.)	Herman Moore, 1995	123
Receiving (Yds.)	Herman Moore, 1995	1,686
Interceptions	Don Doll, 1950	12
	Jack Christiansen, 1953	12
Punting (Avg.)	Yale Lary, 1963	48.9
Punt Return (Avg.)	Pat Studstill, 1962	15.8
Kickoff Return (Avg.)	Mel Gray, 1994	28.4
Field Goals	Jason Hanson, 1993	34
Touchdowns (Tot.)	Barry Sanders, 1991	17
Points	Jason Hanson, 1995	132
*Sacks	Robert Porcher, 1999	15.0

INDIVIDUAL RECORDS—SINGLE GAME

Category	Name	Performance
Rushing (Yds.)	Barry Sanders, 11-13-94	237
Passing (Yds.)	Charlie Batch, 11-18-01	436
Passing (TDs)	Gary Danielson, 12-9-78	5
Receiving (No.)	Herman Moore, 12-4-95	14
Receiving (Yds.)	Cloyce Box, 12-3-50	302
Interceptions	Don Doll, 10-23-49	**4
Field Goals	Garo Yepremian, 11-13-66	6
	Jason Hanson, 10-17-99	6
Touchdowns (Tot.)	Dutch Clark, 10-22-34	4
	Cloyce Box, 12-3-50	4
	Barry Sanders, 11-24-91	4
Points	Dutch Clark, 10-22-34	24
	Cloyce Box, 12-3-50	24
	Barry Sanders, 11-24-91	24
*Sacks	Bill Gay, 9-4-83	5.5

**Sacks became an official statistic in 1982.*
***NFL Record*

DETROIT LIONS

2010 VETERAN ROSTER

No.	Name	Pos.	Ht.	Wt.	Birthdate	NFL Exp.	College	Hometown	How Acq.	'09 Games/ Starts
92	Avril, Cliff	DE	6-3	260	4/8/86	3	Purdue	Green Cove Springs, Fla.	D3c-'08	13/11
76	Backus, Jeff	T	6-5	305	9/21/77	10	Michigan	Norcross, Ga.	D1-'01	16/16
21	Brown, Aaron	RB	6-1	205	10/10/85	2	Texas Christian	Katy, Texas	D6-'09	15/1
94	Bryan, Copeland	DE	6-4	253	7/14/83	3	Arizona	San Jose, Calif.	W(Buff)-'09	5/1
27	Bullocks, Daniel	S	6-0	212	2/28/83	5	Nebraska	Chattanooga, Tenn.	D2-'06	0*
13	Burleson, Nate	WR	6-0	198	8/19/81	8	Nevada	Seattle, Wash.	UFA(Sea)-'10	13/12*
77	Cherilus, Gosder	T	6-7	325	6/28/84	3	Boston College	Somerville, Mass.	D1-'08	15/15
46	Ciurciu, Vinny	LB	6-0	240	5/2/80	8	Boston College	Hackensack, N.J.	FA-'09	9/0
87	Clark, Brian	WR	6-2	204	12/26/83	5	North Carolina State	Tampa, Fla.	FA-'10	14/0*
60	Cohen, Joe	DT	6-2	310	6/6/84	3	Florida	Melbourne, Fla.	FA-'09	7/0
98	Cohen, Landon	DT	6-3	300	8/3/86	3	Ohio	Spartanburg, S.C.	D7-'08	14/3
26	Delmas, Louis	S	5-11	202	4/12/87	2	Western Michigan	North Miami Beach, Fla.	D2-'09	15/15
95	DeVries, Jared	DE	6-4	275	6/11/76	12	Iowa	Aplington, Iowa	D3-'99	0*
57	Dizon, Jordon	LB	6-0	232	1/16/86	3	Colorado	Kauai, Hawaii	D2-'08	16/0
38	Dorsey, DeDe	RB	5-11	210	8/1/84	5	Lindenwood	Broken Arrow, Okla.	FA-'10	0*
45	Felton, Jerome	FB	6-0	246	7/3/86	3	Furman	Madisonville, Tenn.	D5b-'08	13/8
96	Fluellen, Andre	DT	6-2	302	3/7/85	3	Florida State	Cartersville, Ga.	D3b-'08	14/3
49	Follett, Zack	LB	6-1	236	7/3/87	2	California	Clovis, Calif.	D7-'09	12/0
18	Fowler, Eric	WR	6-3	210	10/17/84	2	Grand Valley	New Haven, Mich.	FA-'09	3/0
65	Gandy, Dylan	C	6-3	295	3/8/82	5	Texas Tech	Harlingen, Texas	FA-'09	15/5
4	Hanson, Jason	K	6-0	190	6/17/70	19	Washington State	Spokane, Wash.	D2b-'92	16/0
2	Harris, Nick	P	6-2	218	7/23/78	10	California	Avondale, Ariz.	W(Cin)-'03	16/0
89	Heller, Will	TE	6-6	275	2/28/81	9	Georgia Tech	Dunwoody, Ga.	UFA(Sea)-'09	16/9
79	Hill, Sammie	DT	6-4	329	11/8/86	2	Stillman	West Blocton, Ala.	D4-'09	13/12
14	t-Hill, Shaun	QB	6-3	220	1/9/80	9	Maryland	Parsons, Kan	T(SF)-'10	6/6*
78	Hillard, Cory	T	6-6	300	4/26/85	4	Oklahoma State	New Orleans, La.	FA-'09	0*
23	t-Houston, Chris	CB	5-11	178	10/18/84	4	Arkansas	Austin, Texas	T(Atl)-'10	12/10*
97	Hunter, Jason	DE	6-4	271	8/28/83	5	Appalachian State	Charlotte, N.C.	W(GB)-'09	14/10
68	Jansen, Jon	T	6-6	305	1/28/76	12	Michigan	Clawson, Mich.	FA-'09	11/2
80	Johnson, Bryant	WR	6-3	215	3/7/81	8	Penn State	Baltimore City, Md.	UFA(SF)-'09	16/16
81	Johnson, Calvin	WR	6-5	236	9/29/85	4	Georgia Tech	Tyrone, Ga.	D1-'07	14/14
55	Johnson, Landon	LB	6-2	232	3/13/81	7	Purdue	Lubbock, Texas	FA-'10	10/3*
29	King, Eric	CB	5-10	190	5/10/82	6	Wake Forest	Owings Mills, Md.	UFA(Tenn)-'09	4/1
54	Levy, DeAndre	LB	6-2	238	3/26/87	2	Wisconsin	Milwaukee, Wisc.	D3a-'09	16/10
40	Manuel, Marquand	S	6-0	213	7/11/79	9	Florida	Miami, Fla.	FA-'09	9/6
75	McBride, Turk	DE	6-2	278	5/30/85	4	Tennessee	Camden, N.J.	W(KC)-'09	11/3
28	Morris, Maurice	RB	5-11	216	12/1/79	9	Oregon	Chester, S.C.	UFA(Sea)-'09	14/3
48	Muhlbach, Don	LS	6-4	265	8/17/81	7	Texas A&M	Lufkin, Texas	FA-'04	15/0
85	Nordin, Jake	TE	6-3	255	7/8/84	3	Northern Illinois	Lake Lillian, Minn.	FA-'09	4/1
86	Northcutt, Dennis	WR	5-11	172	12/22/77	11	Arizona	Los Angeles, Calif.	T(Jax)-'09	16/2
58	Palmer, Ashlee	LB	6-1	236	4/7/86	2	Mississippi	Compton, Calif.	W(Buff)-'10	14/2*
66	Peterman, Stephen	G	6-4	323	1/11/82	6	Louisiana State	Waveland, Miss.	FA-'06	9/9
59	Peterson, Julian	LB	6-3	245	7/28/78	11	Michigan State	Washington, D.C.	T(Sea)-'09	16/14
84	Pettigrew, Brandon	TE	6-5	265	2/23/85	2	Oklahoma State	Tyler, Texas	D1b-'09	11/11
51	Raiola, Dominic	C	6-1	295	12/30/78	10	Nebraska	Honolulu, Hawaii	D2a-'01	16/16
63	Ramirez, Manny	G	6-3	326	2/13/83	4	Texas Tech	Houston, Texas	D4b-'07	13/12
74	Schuening, Roy	G	6-3	315	4/18/85	2	Oregon State	Pendleton, Ore.	W(Oak)-'09	0*
30	Simpson, Ko	S	6-1	202	11/9/83	5	South Carolina	Rock Hill, S.C.	T(Buff)-'09	8/5
67	t-Sims, Rob	G	6-3	312	12/6/83	5	Ohio State	Macedonia, Ohio	T(Sea)-'10	14/14*
34	Smith, Kevin	RB	6-1	217	12/17/86	3	Central Florida	Miami, Fla.	D3-'08	13/13
9	Stafford, Matthew	QB	6-3	232	2/7/88	2	Georgia	Highland Park, Texas	D1a-'09	10/10
5	Stanton, Drew	QB	6-3	230	5/7/84	4	Michigan State	Farmington Hills, Mich.	D2a-'07	3/1
93	Vanden Bosch, Kyle	DE	6-4	278	11/17/78	10	Nebraska	Larchwood, Iowa	UFA(Tenn)-'10	16/16*
41	Wade, Jonathan	CB	5-10	198	3/27/84	4	Tennessee	Shreveport, La.	FA-'10	15/4*
	Wesley, Dante	CB	6-1	215	4/5/79	8	Arkansas-Pine Bluff	Pine Bluff, Ark.	UFA(Car)-'10	15/0*
25	White, Marvin	CB	6-1	199	12/5/83	4	Texas Christian	Port Barre, La.	W(Dall)-'09	10/6
99	t-Williams, Corey	DT	6-4	320	8/17/80	7	Arkansas State	Camden, Ark.	T(Clev)-'10	16/2*
12	Williams, Derrick	WR	5-11	197	7/6/86	2	Penn State	Greenbelt, Md.	D3b-'09	11/0
31	Williams, Jack	CB	5-9	183	3/27/85	3	Kent State	Norfolk, Va.	W(Den)-'09	1/0

* Bullocks missed '09 season because of injury; Burleson played 13 games with Seattle; Clark played 14 games with Tampa Bay; DeVries missed '09 season because of injury; Dorsey inactive 1 game for Cincinnati; Hill played 6 games with San Francisco; Hilliard inactive for 4 games; Houston played 12 games with Atlanta; L. Johnson played 10 games with Carolina; Palmer played 14 games with Buffalo; Schuening inactive for 1 game with Oakland and 3 games with Detroit; Sims played 14 games with Seattle; Vanden Bosch played 16 games with Tennessee; Wade played 15 games with St. Louis; Wesley played 15 games with Carolina; C. Williams played 16 games with Cleveland.

t- Lions traded for Sh. Hill (SF), Houston (Atl), Sims (Sea), C. Williams (Cle).

Traded—DE Robert Henderson (0 games in '09) to Seattle, LB Ernie Sims (11) to Philadelphia.

Players lost through free agency (1): LB Larry Foote (Pitt; 14 games in '09).

Also played with Lions in '09—LB Darnell Bing (4 games), CB Phillip Buchanon (13), QB Daunte Culpepper (13), DT Chartric Darby (2), CB Demarcus Faggins (2), WR Yamon Figurs (3), TE Casey FitzSimmons (12), TE Dan Gronkowski (2), CB Anthony Henry (14), DB Kevin Hobbs (14), TE Nathan Hodel (1), DT Grady Jackson (15), CB William James (16), WR Adam Jennings (1), G Daniel Loper (8), TE Michael Matthews (3), CB Marcus McCauley (1), S Kalvin Pearson (12), RB Cedric Peerman (2), T Ephraim Salaam (5), CB DeAngelo Smith (7), FB Terrelle Smith (8), WR John Standeford (2), DE Dewayne White (10), CB Brian Witherspoon (1), CB Jahi Word-Daniels (2).

2010 FIRST-YEAR ROSTER

Name	Pos.	Ht.	Wt.	Birthdate	College	Hometown	How Acq.
Berry, Aaron	CB	5-11	180	6/25/88	Pittsburgh	Harrisburg, Pa.	FA
Best, Jahvid	RB	5-10	199	1/30/89	California	Richmond, Calif.	D1b
Callaway, Robert	DT	6-5	312	2/14/88	Saginaw Valley State	Mt. Morris, Mich.	FA
Campbell, Caleb (1)	LB	6-2	237	6/19/86	Army	Perryton, Texas	FA
Canfield, Trevor (1)	G	6-5	307	1/10/86	Cincinnati	Cincinnati, Ohio	W(Sea)
Clapp, Matt	FB	6-2	246	12/6/86	Oklahoma	Phoenix, Ariz.	FA
Dickson, Richard	TE	6-2	245	11/17/87	Louisiana State	Ocean Springs, Miss.	FA
Fox, Jason	T	6-6	314	5/2/88	Miami	Fort Worth, Texas	D4
Gerberry, Dan (1)	C	6-3	302	11/10/85	Ball State	Austintown, Ohio	FA-'09
Gronkowski, Dan (1)	TE	6-5	260	1/21/85	Maryland	Amherst, N.Y.	D7c-'09
Hefney, Jonathan (1)	CB	5-9	185	2/27/85	Tennessee	Rock Hill, S.C.	FA
Ihekwoaba, Chima	DE	6-4	260	11/3/88	Wilfrid Laurier	Burlington, Ontario, Canada	FA-
Mitchell, Marko (1)	WR	6-4	218	3/11/85	Nevada-Reno	York, Ala.	W(Wash)
Moore, Mike	WR	6-2	210	4/6/86	Georgia	Coconut Creek, Fla.	FA
Parks, Contrevious	WR	5-10	190	2/21/88	Stephen F. Austin	Killeen, Texas	FA
Pratt, Paul (1)	CB	5-10	185	5/1/85	Nevada-Reno	Woodland Hills, Calif.	FA-'09
Quarterman, Kurt (1)	G	6-5	348	10/5/83	Louisville	Albany, Ga.	FA-'09
Scroggins, Sam	LS	6-5	240	2/17/86	West Virginia State	Florissant, Mo.	FA
Spievey, Amari	CB	5-11	195	4/15/88	Iowa	Middleton, Conn.	D3
Suh, Ndamukong	DT	6-4	307	1/6/87	Nebraska	Portland, Ore.	D1a
Toone, Tim	WR	5-10	185	2/14/85	Weber State	Peoria, Ariz.	D7b
Word-Daniels, Jahi (1)	CB	6-0	194	11/19/86	Georgia Tech	Hoover, Ala.	FA-'09
Young, Willie	DE	6-4	251	9/19/85	North Carolina State	Palm Beach Gardens, Fla.	D7a

The term NFL Rookie is defined as a player who is in his first season of professional football and has not been on the roster of another professional football team for any regular-season or postseason games. A Rookie is designated by an "R" on NFL rosters. Players who have been active in another professional football league or players who have NFL experience, including either preseason training camp or being on an Active List or Inactive List, or on Reserve/Injured or Reserve/Physically Unable to Perform for fewer than six regular-season games, are termed NFL First-Year Players. An NFL First-Year Player is designated by a "1" on NFL rosters. Thereafter, a player is credited with an additional year of experience for each season in which he accumulates six games on the Active List or Inactive List, or on Reserve/Injured or Reserve/Physically Unable to Perform.

Log on to www.detroitlions.com for an up-to-date roster.

DETROIT LIONS

COACHING STAFF

Head Coach,
Jim Schwartz

Pro Career: Named Lions' twenty-fifth head coach on January 16, 2009. Schwartz enters his second season in Detroit and the next phase of a rebuilding plan that overturned the roster by more than 50-percent heading into his first season. He came to Detroit following 10 seasons with the Tennessee Titans, including the past eight as defensive coordinator. As the Titans' defensive coordinator since 2001, Schwartz's defensive unit held firm in two major defensive categories that factored significantly in the team's overall success; rushing defense and third-down conversion. From 2001-08, Tennessee ranked fifth in rushing yards allowed per game (103.5) and sixth in third-down conversion percentage (36.1). Before joining the Titans in 1999, he spent three years (1996-98) as a defensive assistant/quality control coach with the Baltimore Ravens. During his tenure in Baltimore, he also coached the team's outside linebackers. After the Cleveland Browns moved to Baltimore following the 1995 season, Schwartz made the transition from player personnel to coaching. From 1993-95, he worked in the Browns' player personnel department, serving as both a college and pro scout. Career record: 2-14.

Background: Schwartz worked on the college level for four years before moving onto the NFL. He began his coaching career as a graduate assistant coach at the University of Maryland, tutoring the Terrapins' linebackers in 1989 and then served as graduate assistant at the University of Minnesota (1990). He became a position coach in the secondary at North Carolina Central (1991) before moving to Colgate (1992) as linebackers coach. Played collegiately at Georgetown University where he lettered four years at linebacker. In 1988 he earned numerous honors that include Division III CoSIDA/GTE Academic All-America, All-America and team captain.

Personal: Born June 2, 1966, in Baltimore, Md. He and his wife, Kathy, have twins Christian and Allison along with a younger daughter Maria. He earned a degree in economics at Georgetown as well as Distinguished Economics Graduate honors.

ASSISTANT COACHES

Jason Arapoff, director of physical development; born July 8, 1965, Weymouth, Mass. Defensive back Springfield College 1985-88. No college or pro playing experience. Pro coach: Washington Redskins 1992-2000, joined Lions in 2001.

Bradford Banta, asst. special teams; born December 14, 1979, Baton Rouge, La. Tight end Southern California 1990-93, Pro tight end/long snapper Indianapolis Colts 1993-99, New York Jets 2000, Detroit Lions 2001-03, Buffalo Bills 2004. College coach: Tennessee-Chattanooga 2007. Pro coach: Joined Lions in 2008.

Matt Burke, linebackers; born March 25, 1976, Hudson, Mass. Safety Dartmouth 1994-97. No pro playing experience. College coach: Boston College 2000-02, Harvard 2003. Pro coach: Tennessee Titans 2006-08, joined Lions in 2009.

Don Clemons, defensive quality control; born February 15, 1954, Newark, N.J. Defensive end Muhlenberg (Pa.) 1973-76. No pro playing experience. College coach: Kutztown State 1977-78, New Mexico 1979, Arizona State 1980-84. Pro coach: Joined Lions in 1985.

Danny Crossman, special teams: born January 17, 1967, El Paso, Texas. Defensive back Kansas 1985, Pittsburgh 1987-89. Pro defensive back Washington Redskins 1990, Detroit Lions 1991-92. College coach: U.S. Coast Guard Academy 1993, Western Kentucky 1994-96, Central Florida 1997-98, Georgia Tech 1999-2001, Michigan State 2002. Pro coach: Carolina Panthers 2003-09, joined Lions in 2010.

Gunther Cunningham, defensive coordinator; born June 19, 1946, Munich, Germany. Linebacker/placekicker Oregon 1966-68. No pro playing experience. College coach: Oregon 1969-1971, Arkansas 1972, Stanford 1973-76, California 1977-1980. Pro coach: Hamilton Tiger-Cats (CFL) 1981, Baltimore/Indianapolis Colts 1982-84, San Diego Chargers 1985-1990, L.A. Raiders 1991-94, Kansas City Chiefs 1995-2000, 2004-08 (head coach 1999-2000), Tennessee Titans 2001-03, joined Lions in 2009.

Todd Downing, offensive quality control: born July 22, 1980, Eden Prairie, Minn. Attended Minnesota. No college or pro playing experience. Pro coach: Minnesota Vikings 2003-05, St. Louis Rams 2006-08, joined Lions in 2009.

Sam Gash, running backs; born March 7, 1969, Henderson, N.C. Fullback Penn State 1987-1991. Pro fullback New England Patriots 1992-97, Buffalo Bills 1998-99, 2003, Baltimore Ravens 2000-02. Pro coach: New York Jets 2005-06, joined Lions in 2007.

Shawn Jefferson, wide receivers; born February 22, 1969, Jacksonville. Wide receiver Central Florida 1988-1990. Pro wide receiver San Diego Chargers 1991-95, New England Patriots 1996-99, Atlanta Falcons 2000-02, Detroit Lions 2003. Pro coach: Joined Lions in 2005.

Kris Kocurek, defensive line; born November 15, 1978. Defensive tackle Texas Tech 1997-2000. Pro defensive tackle Seattle Seahawks 2001, Tennessee Titans 2002. College coach: Texas Tech 2003, Texas A&M-Kingsville 2004-05, Texas A&M-Commerce 2006, West Texas A&M 2007, Stephen F. Austin State 2008. Pro coach: Joined Lions in 2009.

Tim Lappano, tight ends: born October 14, 1956, Spokane, Wash. Running back Idaho 1978-1981. No pro playing experience. College coach: Idaho 1982-85, Wyoming 1986, Washington State 1987-1991, California 1992-95, Wyoming 1996, Purdue 1997, Oregon State 2000-02, Washington 2005-08. Pro coach: Seattle Seahawks 1998, San Francisco 49ers 2003-04, joined Lions in 2009.

Scott Linehan, offensive coordinator; born September 17, 1963, Sunnyside, Wash. Quarterback Idaho 1982-86. No pro playing experience. College coach: Idaho 1989-1990, 1992-93, Nevada-Las Vegas 1991, Washington 1994-98, Louisville 1999-2001. Pro coach: Minnesota Vikings 2002-04, Miami Dolphins 2005, St Louis Rams 2006-08 (head coach), joined Lions in 2009.

Ted Rath, strength and conditioning assistant: born November 22, 1983. Linebacker Toledo 2003-06. No pro playing experience. College coach: Toledo 2007-09. Pro coach: Joined Lions in 2009.

Daron Roberts, asst. secondary; born November 29, 1978, Mt. Pleasant, Texas. Attended Texas. No college or pro playing experience. Pro coach: Kansas City Chiefs 2007-08, joined Lions in 2009.

Tim Walton, secondary; born March 11, 1971. Defensive back Ohio State 1990-94. No pro playing experience. College coach: Bowling Green 1995-99, Memphis 2000-01, 2008, Syracuse 2002, Louisiana State 2003, Miami 2004-07. Pro coach: Joined Lions in 2009.

George Yarno, offensive line; born August 12, 1957, Spokane, Wash. Offensive line Washington State 1975-78. Pro offensive line Tampa Bay Buccaneers 1979-1983, 1985-87, Denver Gold (USFL) 1984-85, Atlanta Falcons 1988, Houston Oilers 1989, Green Bay Packers 1990. College coach: Louisiana State 2001-02, Washington State 2003-07. Pro coach: Tampa Bay Buccaneers 2008, joined Lions in 2009.

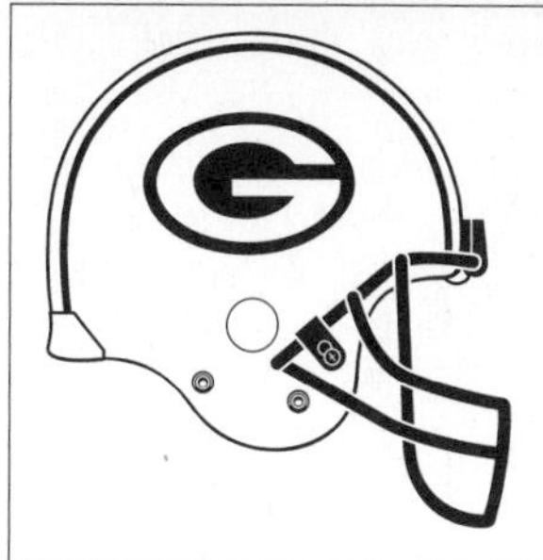

National Football Conference
North Division
Team Colors: Dark Green, Gold, and White
Lambeau Field Atrium
1265 Lombardi Avenue
Green Bay, Wisconsin 54304
Telephone: (920) 569-7500

2010 SCHEDULE

PRESEASON

Aug. 14	**Cleveland**	7:00
Aug. 21	at Seattle	7:00
Aug. 26	**Indianapolis**	7:00
Sep. 2	at Kansas City	7:00

REGULAR SEASON

Sep. 12	at Philadelphia	4:15
Sep. 19	**Buffalo**	12:00
Sep. 27	at Chicago (Mon)	7:30
Oct. 3	**Detroit**	12:00
Oct. 10	at Washington	1:00
Oct. 17	**Miami**	12:00
Oct. 24	**Minnesota**	7:20
Oct. 31	at New York Jets	1:00
Nov. 7	**Dallas**	7:20
Nov. 14	BYE	
Nov. 21	at Minnesota	12:00
Nov. 28	at Atlanta	1:00
Dec. 5	**San Francisco**	12:00
Dec. 12	at Detroit	1:00
Dec. 19	at New England	*8:20
Dec. 26	**New York Giants**	3:15
Jan. 2	**Chicago**	12:00

** Sunday night games in Weeks 11-17 subject to change*

Stadium: Lambeau Field (opened in 1957)
•**Capacity:** 72,928
1265 Lombardi Avenue
Green Bay, Wisconsin 54304
Playing Surface: DD GrassMaster
Training Camp: St. Norbert College
De Pere, Wisconsin 54115

LAMBEAU FIELD

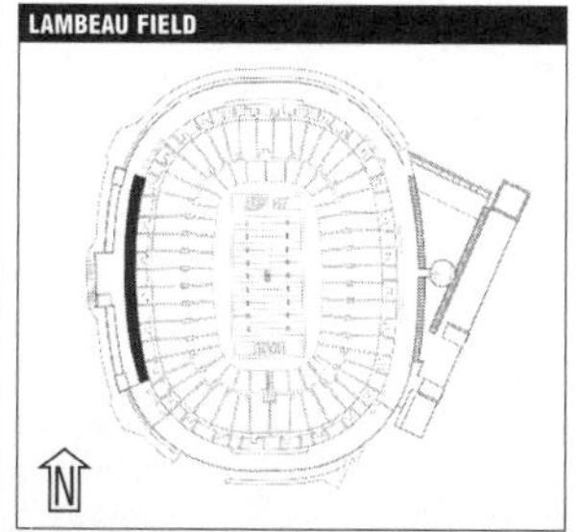

CLUB OFFICIALS

President and Chief Executive Officer: Mark Murphy
Executive Vice President/General Manager/Director of Football Operations: Ted Thompson
Vice President of Football Administration/Player Finance: Russ Ball
Vice President of Finance: Paul Baniel
Vice President of Sales and Marketing: Tim Connolly
Vice President of Organizational/Staff Development: Betsy Mitchell
Vice President of Administration/General Counsel: Jason Wied
Director of College Scouting: John Dorsey
Director-Football Operations: Reggie McKenzie
Director of Player Development: Rob Davis
Director of Public Relations: Jeff Blumb
Assistant Directors of Public Relations: Sarah Quick, Adam Woullard
Public Relations Coordinator: Rob Crane
Manager of Corporate Communications: Aaron Popkey
Director of Ticket Operations: Mark Wagner
Director of Marketing and Corporate Sales: Craig Benzel
Director of Premium Sales and Guest Services: Jennifer Ark
Director of Retail Operations: Kate Hogan
Director of Information Technology: Wayne Wichlacz
Director of Facility Operations: Ted Eisenreich
Director of Corporate Security/Risk Management: Doug Collins
Manager of Community Outreach: Cathy Dworak
Internet Coordinator: Duke Bobber
Assistant Director of College Scouting: Shaun Herock
College Scouts: Lee Gissendaner, Brian Gutekunst, Alonzo Highsmith, Sam Seale, Jon-Eric Sullivan, Richmond Williams
Scouting Coordinator: Danny Mock
Scouting Assistant: Chad Brinker
Assistant Directors of Pro Personnel: Tim Terry, Eliot Wolf
Director of Research and Development: Mike Eayrs
Coaching Administrator: Curtis Fuller
Strength and Conditioning Assistant: Thadeus Jackson
Football Administration Coordinator: Matt Klein
Video Director: Bob Eckberg
Head Athletic Trainer: Pepper Burruss
Equipment Manager: Gordon (Red) Batty

COACHING HISTORY
(679-534-36)

Records include postseason games

1921-1949	Earl (Curly) Lambeau	212-106-21
1950-53	Gene Ronzani*	14-31-1
1953	Hugh Devore-Ray (Scooter) McLean**	0-2-0
1954-57	Lisle Blackbourn	17-31-0
1958	Ray (Scooter) McLean	1-10-1
1959-1967	Vince Lombardi	98-30-4
1968-1970	Phil Bengtson	20-21-1
1971-74	Dan Devine	25-28-4
1975-1983	Bart Starr	53-77-3
1984-87	Forrest Gregg	25-37-1
1988-1991	Lindy Infante	24-40-0
1992-98	Mike Holmgren	84-42-0
1999	Ray Rhodes	8-8-0
2000-05	Mike Sherman	59-43-0
2006-09	Mike McCarthy	39-28-0

*Resigned after 10 games in 1953
**Co-coaches

PAID ATTENDANCE

Home 565,666 Away 489,745
Total 1,055,411
Single-game home record, 71,213 (11/1/09)
Single-season home record, 566,418 (2007)

2010 DRAFT CHOICES

Round	Name	Pos.	College
1	Bryan Bulaga	T	Iowa
2	Mike Neal	DE	Purdue
3	Morgan Burnett	DB	Georgia Tech
5	Andrew Quarless	TE	Penn State
	Marshall Newhouse	T	Texas Christian
6	James Starks	RB	Buffalo
7	C.J. Wilson	DE	East Carolina

GREEN BAY PACKERS

2009 TEAM RECORD

PRESEASON (3-1)

Date	Result	Opponent
8/15	W 17-0	Cleveland
8/22	W 31-21	Buffalo
8/28	W 44-37	at Arizona
9/3	L 13-27	at Tennessee

REGULAR SEASON (11-5)

Date	Result	Opponent
9/13	W 21-15	Chicago
9/20	L 24-31	Cincinnati
9/27	W 36-17	at St. Louis
10/5	L 23-30	at Minnesota
10/18	W 26-0	Detroit
10/25	W 31-3	at Cleveland
11/1	L 26-38	Minnesota
11/8	L 28-38	at Tampa Bay
11/15	W 17-7	Dallas
11/22	W 30-24	San Francisco
11/26	W 34-12	at Detroit
12/7	W 27-14	Baltimore
12/13	W 21-14	at Chicago
12/20	L 36-37	at Pittsburgh
12/27	W 48-10	Seattle
1/3	W 33-7	at Arizona

POSTSEASON (0-1)

Date	Result	Opponent
1/10	L 45-51	at Arizona (OT)

(OT) Overtime

SCORE BY PERIODS

Packers	115	154	58	134	0	— 461
Opponents	52	84	65	96	0	— 297

2009 TEAM STATISTICS

	Packers	Opp.
Total First Downs	335	272
Rushing	102	68
Passing	201	168
Penalty	32	36
3rd Down: Made/Att	103/219	76/211
3rd Down Pct.	47.0	36.0
4th Down: Made/Att	3/9	10/25
4th Down Pct.	33.3	40.0
Possession Avg.	33:03	26:57
Total Net Yards	6065	4551
Avg. Per Game	379.1	284.4
Total Plays	1042	948
Avg. Per Play	5.8	4.8
Net Yards Rushing	1885	1333
Avg. Per Game	117.8	83.3
Total Rushes	438	371
Net Yards Passing	4180	3218
Avg. Per Game	261.3	201.1
Sacked/Yards Lost	51/312	37/232
Gross Yards	4492	3450
Att./Completions	553/357	540/294
Completion Pct.	64.6	54.4
Had Intercepted	8	30
Punts/Average	67/43.1	74/45.0
Net Punting Avg.	67/34.1	74/40.2
Penalties/Yards	118/1057	107/914
Fumbles/Ball Lost	20/8	24/10
Touchdowns	54	36
Rushing	20	5
Passing	30	29
Returns	4	2

2009 INDIVIDUAL STATISTICS

PASSING	Att.	Comp.	Yds.	Pct.	TD	Int.	Tkld.	Rate
Rodgers	541	350	4434	64.7	30	7	50/306	103.2
Flynn	12	7	58	58.3	0	1	1/6	36.1
Packers	553	357	4492	64.6	30	8	51/312	101.8
Opponents	540	294	3450	54.4	29	30	37/232	68.8

SCORING	TD R	TD P	TD Rt	PAT	FG	Saf	PTS
Crosby	0	0	0	48/49	27/36	0	129
Grant	11	0	0	0/0	0/0	0	66
Driver	0	6	0	0/0	0/0	0	36
Finley	0	5	0	0/0	0/0	0	30
J. Jones	0	5	0	0/0	0/0	0	30
Rodgers	5	0	0	0/0	0/0	0	30
Jennings	0	4	0	0/0	0/0	0	28
Havner	0	4	0	0/0	0/0	0	24
Jackson	2	1	0	0/0	0/0	0	20
Kuhn	1	2	0	0/0	0/0	0	18
Woodson	0	0	3	0/0	0/0	0	18
Nelson	0	2	0	0/0	0/0	0	12
Green	1	0	0	0/0	0/0	0	6
D. Lee	0	1	0	0/0	0/0	0	6
Matthews	0	0	1	0/0	0/0	0	6
Packers	20	30	4	48/49	27/36	1	461
Opponents	5	29	2	34/34	13/17	3	297

2-Pt. Conversions: Jennings 2, Jackson. Packers 3-5, Opponents 1-2.

RUSHING	No.	Yds	Avg	LG	TD
Grant	282	1253	4.4	62t	11
Rodgers	58	316	5.4	35	5
Green	41	160	3.9	26	1
Jackson	37	111	3.0	9	2
D. Wynn	6	19	3.2	6	0
Kuhn	8	18	2.3	5	1
Driver	1	13	13.0	13	0
Flynn	5	-5	-1.0	-1	0
Packers	438	1885	4.3	62t	20
Opponents	371	1333	3.6	42	5

RECEIVING	No.	Yds	Avg	LG	TD
Driver	70	1061	15.2	71t	6
Jennings	68	1113	16.4	83t	4
Finley	55	676	12.3	62t	5
D. Lee	37	260	7.0	19	1
J. Jones	32	440	13.8	74t	5
Grant	25	197	7.9	27	0
Nelson	22	320	14.5	51	2
Jackson	21	187	8.9	17	1
Havner	7	112	16.0	45t	4
Kuhn	7	47	6.7	14	2
Hall	5	41	8.2	13	0
Green	3	18	6.0	12	0
D. Wynn	2	19	9.5	11	0
Johnson	2	4	2.0	4	0
Tauscher	1	-3	-3.0	-3	0
Packers	357	4492	12.6	83t	30
Opponents	294	3450	11.7	68	29

INTERCEPTIONS	No.	Yds	Avg	LG	TD
Woodson	9	179	19.9	45t	3
Collins	6	110	18.3	31	0
T. Williams	4	94	23.5	67	0
Bigby	4	14	3.5	14	0
Hawk	2	42	21.0	29	0
Harris	2	29	14.5	29	0
Jenkins	1	4	4.0	4	0
Bush	1	3	3.0	3	0
Jolly	1	2	2.0	2	0
Packers	30	477	15.9	67	3
Opponents	8	171	21.4	80	1

PUNTING	No.	Yds.	Avg.	In 20	LG
Kapinos	66	2891	43.8	15	58
Packers	67	2891	43.1	15	58
Opponents	74	3329	45.0	31	64

PUNT RETURNS	Ret	FC	Yds	Avg	LG	TD
Nelson	17	6	90	5.3	14	0
T. Williams	13	5	135	10.4	45	0
Blackmon	3	1	11	3.7	6	0
Woodson	1	0	0	0.0	0	0
Packers	34	12	236	6.9	45	0
Opponents	40	7	403	10.1	60	0

KICKOFF RETURNS	No.	Yds	Avg	LG	TD
Nelson	25	635	25.4	54	0
Blackmon	10	233	23.3	28	0
Green	9	196	21.8	37	0
Jackson	2	36	18.0	23	0
Woodson	2	30	15.0	18	0
Havner	2	26	13.0	16	0
T. Williams	2	26	13.0	24	0
Bishop	1	6	6.0	6	0
Dietrich-Smith	1	5	5.0	5	0
Packers	54	1193	22.1	54	0
Opponents	80	1824	22.8	83	0

FIELD GOALS	1-19	20-29	30-39	40-49	50+
Crosby	1/1	13/13	7/9	4/7	2/6
Packers	1/1	13/13	7/9	4/7	2/6
Opponents	0/0	4/4	3/4	5/7	1/2

SACKS	No.
Matthews	10.0
Jenkins	4.5
Barnett	4.0
B. Jones	4.0
Kampman	3.5
Chillar	2.0
Woodson	2.0
Collins	1.0
Harris	1.0
Hawk	1.0
Jolly	1.0
Poppinga	1.0
Raji	1.0
T. Williams	1.0
Packers	37.0
Opponents	51.0

RECORD HOLDERS

INDIVIDUAL RECORDS—CAREER

Category	Name	Performance
Rushing (Yds.)	Ahman Green, 2000-06, 2009	8,322
Passing (Yds.)	Brett Favre, 1992-2007	**61,655
Passing (TDs)	Brett Favre, 1992-2007	**442
Receiving (No.)	Donald Driver, 1999-2009	647
Receiving (Yds.)	James Lofton, 1978-1986	9,656
Interceptions	Bobby Dillon, 1952-59	52
Punting (Avg.)	Craig Hentrich, 1994-97	42.8
Punt Return (Avg.)	Desmond Howard, 1996, 1999	13.8
Kickoff Return (Avg.)	Travis Williams, 1967-1970	26.7
Field Goals	Ryan Longwell, 1997-2005	226
Touchdowns (Tot.)	Don Hutson, 1935-1945	105
Points	Ryan Longwell, 1997-2005	1,054
*Sacks	Kabeer Gbaja-Biamila, 2000-08	74.5

INDIVIDUAL RECORDS—SINGLE SEASON

Category	Name	Performance
Rushing (Yds.)	Ahman Green, 2003	1,883
Passing (Yds.)	Lynn Dickey, 1983	4,458
Passing (TDs)	Brett Favre, 1996	39
Receiving (No.)	Sterling Sharpe, 1993	112
Receiving (Yds.)	Robert Brooks, 1995	1,497
Interceptions	Irv Comp, 1943	10
Punting (Avg.)	Craig Hentrich, 1997	45.0
Punt Return (Avg.)	Billy Grimes, 1950	19.1
Kickoff Return (Avg.)	Travis Williams, 1967	**41.1
Field Goals	Chester Marcol, 1972	33
	Ryan Longwell, 2000	33
Touchdowns (Tot.)	Ahman Green, 2003	20
Points	Paul Hornung, 1960	176
*Sacks	Tim Harris, 1989	19.5

INDIVIDUAL RECORDS—SINGLE GAME

Category	Name	Performance
Rushing (Yds.)	Ahman Green, 12-28-03	218
Passing (Yds.)	Lynn Dickey, 10-12-80	418
Passing (TDs)	Many times	5
	Last time by Brett Favre, 9-27-98	
Receiving (No.)	Don Hutson, 11-22-42	14
Receiving (Yds.)	Billy Howton, 10-21-56	257
Interceptions	Bobby Dillon, 11-26-53	**4
	Willie Buchanon, 9-24-78	**4
Field Goals	Chris Jacke, 11-11-90, 10-14-96	5
	Ryan Longwell, 9-24-00	5
Touchdowns (Tot.)	Paul Hornung, 12-12-65	5
Points	Paul Hornung, 10-8-61	33
*Sacks	Vonnie Holliday, 12-22-02	5.0

**Sacks became an official statistic in 1982.*
***NFL Record*

GREEN BAY PACKERS

2010 VETERAN ROSTER

No.	Name	Pos.	Ht.	Wt.	Birthdate	NFL Exp.	College	Hometown	How Acq.	'09 Games/ Starts
78	Barbre, Allen	T	6-4	305	6/22/84	4	Missouri Southern St.	Granby, Mo.	D4-'07	10/7
56	Barnett, Nick	LB	6-2	236	5/27/81	8	Oregon State	Fontana, Calif.	D1-'03	16/16
26	Bell, Josh	CB	5-11	177	1/8/85	3	Baylor	Dallas, Texas	FA-'09	4/0
20	Bigby, Atari	S	5-11	213	9/19/81	5	Central Florida	Miami, Fla.	FA-'05	13/11
55	Bishop, Desmond	LB	6-2	238	7/24/84	4	California	Fairfield, Calif.	D6b-'07	16/0
27	Blackmon, Will	CB	6-0	206	10/27/84	5	Boston College	Warwick, R.I.	D4b-'06	3/0
24	Bush, Jarrett	CB/S	6-0	200	5/21/84	5	Utah State	Vacaville, Calif.	W(Car)-'06	16/3
54	Chillar, Brandon	LB	6-3	237	10/21/82	7	UCLA	Carlsbad, Calif.	UFA(StL)-'08	12/4
76	Clifton, Chad	T	6-5	320	6/26/76	11	Tennessee	Martin, Tenn.	D2-'00	12/12
73	Colledge, Daryn	G	6-4	308	2/11/82	5	Boise State	North Pole, Alaska	D2a-'06	16/16
36	Collins, Nick	S	5-11	207	8/16/83	6	Bethune-Cookman	Cross City, Fla.	D2a-'05	16/16
2	Crosby, Mason	K	6-1	207	9/3/84	4	Colorado	Georgetown, Texas	D6c-'07	16/0
62	Dietrich-Smith, Evan	G/C	6-2	305	7/19/86	2	Idaho State	Salinas, Calif.	FA-'09	13/0
80	Driver, Donald	WR	6-0	194	2/2/75	12	Alcorn State	Houston, Texas	D7b-'99	16/16
88	Finley, Jermichael	TE	6-5	247	3/26/87	3	Texas	Diboll, Texas	D3-'08	13/10
10	Flynn, Matt	QB	6-2	225	6/20/85	3	Louisiana State	Tyler, Texas	D7a-'08	15/0
39	Ford, Trevor	CB	6-0	188	2/19/86	2	Troy	Miami, Fla.	FA-'09	3/0
68	Giacomini, Breno	T	6-7	311	9/27/85	3	Louisville	Malden, Mass.	D5-'08	0*
61	Goode, Brett	LS	6-1	261	11/2/84	3	Arkansas	Fort Smith, Ark.	FA-'08	16/0
25	Grant, Ryan	RB	6-1	222	12/9/82	4	Notre Dame	Ramsey, N.J.	T(NYG)-'07	16/16
35	Hall, Korey	FB	6-0	236	8/5/83	4	Boise State	Glenns Ferry, Idaho	D6a-'07	11/5
91	Harrell, Justin	DE	6-4	320	2/14/84	4	Tennessee	Martin, Tenn.	D1-'07	0*
31	Harris, Al	CB	6-1	190	12/7/74	13	Texas A&M-Kingsville	Pompano Beach, Fla.	T(Phil)-'03	10/10
41	Havner, Spencer	TE	6-3	250	2/2/83	2	UCLA	Grass Valley, Calif.	FA-'08	16/1
50	Hawk, A.J.	LB	6-1	250	1/6/84	5	Ohio State	Centerville, Ohio	D1-'06	16/14
32	Jackson, Brandon	RB	5-10	216	10/2/85	4	Nebraska	Horn Lake, Miss.	D2-'07	12/0
77	Jenkins, Cullen	DE	6-2	305	1/20/81	7	Central Michigan	Belleville, Mich.	FA-'04	16/16
85	Jennings, Greg	WR	5-11	198	9/21/83	5	Western Michigan	Kalamazoo, Mich.	D2b-'06	16/13
45	Johnson, Quinn	FB	6-1	255	9/30/86	2	Louisiana State	Edgard, La.	D5a-'09	9/0
97	Jolly, Johnny	DE	6-3	325	2/21/83	5	Texas A&M	Houston, Texas	D6a-'06	16/16
59	Jones, Brad	LB	6-3	239	4/1/86	2	Colorado	East Lansing, Mich.	D7-'09	14/7
89	Jones, James	WR	6-1	208	3/31/84	4	San Jose State	San Jose, Calif.	D3a-'07	16/3
30	Kuhn, John	FB	6-0	250	9/9/82	5	Shippensburg	York, Pa.	W(Pitt)-'07	14/6
70	Lang, T.J.	T/G	6-4	316	9/20/87	2	Eastern Michigan	Birmingham, Mich.	D4-'09	16/3
86	Lee, Donald	TE	6-4	248	8/31/80	8	Mississippi State	Maben, Miss.	FA-'05	16/10
22	Lee, Pat	CB	6-0	194	2/20/84	3	Auburn	Miami, Fla.	D2c-'08	0*
28	Lumpkin, Kregg	RB	5-11	228	5/15/84	2	Georgia	Stone Mountain, Ga.	FA-'08	0*
29	Martin, Derrick	S	5-10	198	5/16/85	5	Wyoming	Denver, Colo.	T(Balt)-'09	14/1
52	Matthews, Clay	LB	6-3	250	5/14/86	2	Southern California	Agoura Hills, Calif.	D1b-'09	16/13
87	Nelson, Jordy	WR	6-3	217	5/31/85	3	Kansas State	Riley, Kan.	D2a-'08	13/0
46	Peprah, Charlie	S	5-11	203	2/24/83	5	Alabama	Plano, Texas	FA-'10	2/0*
79	Pickett, Ryan	NT	6-2	340	10/8/79	10	Ohio State	Zephyrhills, Fla.	UFA(StL)-'06	13/9
51	Poppinga, Brady	LB	6-3	250	9/21/79	6	Brigham Young	Evanston, Wyo.	D4b-'05	15/3
90	Raji, B.J.	NT	6-2	337	7/11/86	2	Boston College	Washington Township, N.J.	D1a-'09	14/1
12	Rodgers, Aaron	QB	6-2	220	12/2/83	6	California	Chico, Calif.	D1-'05	16/16
71	Sitton, Josh	G	6-3	322	6/6/86	3	Central Florida	Pensacola, Fla.	D4b-'08	16/16
72	Spitz, Jason	C/G	6-3	307	12/19/82	5	Louisville	Jacksonville, Fla.	D3b-'06	5/4
16	Swain, Brett	WR	6-0	203	6/21/85	2	San Diego State	Carlsbad, Calif.	D7b-'08	6/0
65	Tauscher, Mark	T	6-3	316	6/17/77	11	Wisconsin	Auburndale, Wis.	D7a-'00	8/8
33	Underwood, Brandon	CB	6-1	191	6/24/86	2	Cincinnati	Hamilton, Ohio	D6b-'09	11/0
63	Wells, Scott	C	6-2	300	1/7/81	7	Tennessee	Brentwood, Tenn.	FA-'04	15/14
38	Williams, Tramon	CB	5-11	191	3/16/83	4	Louisiana Tech	Napoleonville, La.	FA-'06	16/10
21	Woodson, Charles	CB	6-1	202	10/7/76	13	Michigan	Fremont, Ohio	UFA(Oak)-'06	16/16
94	Wynn, Jarius	DE	6-3	285	8/29/86	2	Georgia	Lincolnton, Ga.	D6a-'09	11/0

* Giacomini inactive for 16 games: Harrell missed '09 season because of injury; Lee missed '09 season because of injury; Lumpkin last active with Green Bay in '08; Peprah played 2 games with Atlanta in '09.

Players lost through free agency (1): Aaron Kampman (Jax; 9 games in '09).

Also played with Packers in '09—WR Jake Allen (1 game), WR Biren Ealy (1), S Matt Giordano (5), RB Ahman Green (8), P Jeremy Kapinos (16), DE Michael Montgomery (10), LB Cyril Obiozor (5), S Aaron Rouse (2), LB Jeremy Thompson (6), NT Anthony Toribio (1), RB DeShawn Wynn (4).

2010 FIRST-YEAR ROSTER

Name	Pos.	Ht.	Wt.	Birthdate	College	Hometown	How Acq.
Bryan, Chris	P	6-5	210	3/6/82	No College	Melbourne, Australia	FA
Bulaga, Bryan	T	6-5	314	3/21/89	Iowa	Woodstock, Ill.	D1
Burnett, Morgan	S	6-1	209	1/13/89	Georgia Tech	College Park, Ga.	D3
Campbell, Chris	T	6-5	328	9/22/86	Eastern Illinois	Chicago, Ill.	FA
Clark, D.J. (1)	CB	6-1	200	11/30/86	Idaho State	Oceanside, Calif.	FA-'09
Crabtree, Tom (1)	TE	6-4	245	11/4/85	Miami (Ohio)	Carroll, Ohio	FA-'09
Daniels, Stanley (1)	G	6-4	328	11/30/84	Washington	San Diego, Calif.	FA-'09
Dillon, Charles (1)	WR	6-0	202	1/30/86	Washington State	Oxnard, Calif.	FA
Francois, Robert (1)	LB	6-3	255	5/14/85	Boston College	Byfield, Mass.	FA-'09
Gore, Shawn	WR	6-0	200	4/12/87	Bishop's (Canada)	Toronto, Ontario, Canada	FA
Jones, Khalil (1)	S	6-1	212	12/10/85	Miami	Miami, Fla.	FA-09
Joseph, Alex	LB	6-2	238	7/6/88	Temple	Stamford, Conn.	FA
Knicky, Tim	LB	6-4	251	1/1/88	Stephen F. Austin	Cedar Park, Texas	FA
Levine, Anthony	S	5-11	195	3/27/87	Tennessee State	Winston-Salem, N.C.	FA
Masthay, Tim (1)	P	6-1	197	3/16/87	Kentucky	Murray, Ky.	FA
McDonald, Nick	G	6-4	316	6/27/87	Grand Valley State	Sterling Heights, Mich.	FA
Moturi, Jeff	WR	5-11	186	4/4/86	Texas-El Paso	Irving, Texas	FA
Mullins, Aleric	NT	6-1	319	4/4/86	North Carolina	Wendell, N.C.	FA
Neal, Mike	DE	6-3	294	6/26/87	Purdue	Merrillville, Ind.	D2
Newhouse, Marshall	T/G	6-4	319	9/29/88	Texas Christian	Dallas, Texas	D5b
Obiozor, Cyril (1)	LB	6-4	249	9/26/86	Texas A&M	Pearland, Texas	FA-'09
Pizzotti, Chris (1)	QB	6-5	226	6/29/86	Harvard	Reading, Mass.	FA-'09
Porter, Quinn	RB	6-0	205	2/2/86	Stillman College	Quartz Hill, Calif.	FA
Quarless, Andrew	TE	6-4	252	10/6/88	Penn State	Uniondale, N.Y.	D5a
Russell, John	LB	6-3	260	7/11/87	Wake Forest	Jacksonville, Fla.	FA
Shepard, Noah	QB	6-2	223	12/31/86	South Dakota	Broomfield, Colo.	FA
Shields, Sam	CB	5-11	184	12/8/87	Miami	Sarasota, Fla.	FA
Starks, James	RB	6-2	218	2/25/86	Buffalo	Niagara Falls, N.Y.	D6
Talley, Ronald (1)	DE	6-3	286	2/21/86	Delaware	Detroit, Mich.	FA-'09
Toribio, Anthony (1)	NT	6-1	315	3/1/85	Carson-Newman	Miami, Fla.	FA-'08
West, Chastin	WR	6-0	212	5/1/87	Fresno State	Moorpark, Calif.	FA
Williams, Patrick (1)	WR	6-1	204	1/13/86	Colorado	DeSoto, Texas	FA-'09
Wilson, C.J.	DE	6-3	290	3/30/87	East Carolina	Pinetown, N.C.	D7
Zombo, Frank	LB	6-3	254	3/5/87	Central Michigan	Sterling Heights, Mich.	FA

The term NFL Rookie is defined as a player who is in his first season of professional football and has not been on the roster of another professional football team for any regular-season or postseason games. A Rookie is designated by an "R" on NFL rosters. Players who have been active in another professional football league or players who have NFL experience, including either preseason training camp or being on an Active List or Inactive List, or on Reserve/Injured or Reserve/Physically Unable to Perform for fewer than six regular-season games, are termed NFL First-Year Players. An NFL First-Year Player is designated by a "1" on NFL rosters. Thereafter, a player is credited with an additional year of experience for each season in which he accumulates six games on the Active List or Inactive List, or on Reserve/Injured or Reserve/Physically Unable to Perform.

Log on to www.packers.com for an up-to-date roster.

GREEN BAY PACKERS

COACHING STAFF

Head Coach,
Mike McCarthy

Pro Career: Named the fourteenth head coach in team history January 12, 2006. Offense has ranked in Top 10 in total yards each of his four years as head coach, accumulating most points (461), fewest turnovers (16) and third-most yards (6,065) in team history in 2009. Named Motorola Coach of the Year, matched a franchise record with 13 wins, and won NFC North Division title in 2007. Became the first coach since Vince Lombardi to lead team to a championship game in his second season. Had returned to Green Bay after serving as the team's quarterbacks coach in 1999. Subsequently was a highly successful offensive coordinator for the New Orleans Saints (2000-04). With McCarthy calling plays, the Saints racked up 10 offensive team records and 26 individual marks. He was named NFC Assistant Coach of the Year by *USA Today* in 2000, and New Orleans led the league with 432 points and 49 touchdowns in 2002. The list of quarterbacks he has coached includes Joe Montana, Elvis Grbac, Rich Gannon, Brett Favre, Aaron Rodgers, Matt Hasselbeck, Aaron Brooks, Jake Delhomme, Marc Bulger, Steve Bono, and Jeff Blake—a collection that combines for 36 career Pro Bowl selections and nine Super Bowl starts. Career record: 39-28.

Background: Graduated with business administration degree from Baker University. Was an all-conference tight end (1985-86), helping the school to a NAIA Division II runner-up finish as a senior captain. Coached collegiately at Fort Hays State (1987-88) and Pittsburgh (1989-1992), before moving to the NFL with the Chiefs (1993-98), Packers (1999), Saints (2000-04) and 49ers (2005).

Personal: Born November 10, 1963, in Pittsburgh. Family includes daughters Alexandra and Gabrielle, wife Jessica and boys Jack and George.

ASSISTANT COACHES

Edgar Bennett, running backs; born February 15, 1969, Jacksonville. Running back Florida State 1987, 1989-1991. Pro running back Green Bay Packers 1992-96, Chicago Bears 1998-99. Pro coach: Joined Packers in 2001.

James Campen, offensive line; born June 11, 1964, Sacramento, Calif. Center Sacramento City (Calif.) J.C. 1982-83, Tulane 1984-85. Pro center New Orleans Saints 1987-88, Green Bay Packers 1989-1993. Pro coach: Joined Packers in 2004.

Dom Capers, defensive coordinator; born August 7, 1950, Cambridge, Ohio. Defensive back Mount Union 1968-1971. No pro playing experience. College coach: Kent State 1972-74, Hawaii 1975-76, San Jose State 1977, California 1978-79, Tennessee 1980-81, Ohio State 1982-83. Pro coach: Philadelphia/Baltimore Stars (USFL) 1984-85, New Orleans Saints 1986-1991, Pittsburgh Steelers 1992-94, Carolina Panthers 1995-98 (head coach), Jacksonville Jaguars 1999-2000, Houston Texans 2001-05 (head coach), Miami Dolphins 2006-07, New England Patriots 2008, joined Packers in 2009.

Tom Clements, quarterbacks; born June 18, 1953, McKees Rocks, Pa. Quarterback Notre Dame 1972-74. Pro quarterback Ottawa Rough Riders (CFL) 1975-78, Hamilton Tiger-Cats (CFL) 1979, 1981-82, Kansas City Chiefs 1980, Winnipeg Blue Bombers (CFL) 1983-87. College coach: Notre Dame 1992-95. Pro coach: New Orleans Saints 1997-99, Kansas City Chiefs 2000, Pittsburgh Steelers 2001-03, Buffalo Bills 2004-05, joined Packers in 2006.

Jerry Fontenot, asst. offensive line; born November 21, 1966, Lafayette, La. Guard Texas A&M 1985-88. Pro center Chicago Bears 1989-1996, New Orleans Saints 1997-2003, Cincinnati Bengals 2004. Pro coach: Joined Packers in 2006.

Kevin Greene, outside linebackers; born July 31, 1962, Schenectady, N.Y. Linebacker Auburn 1980-85. Pro linebacker Los Angeles Rams 1985-1992, Pittsburgh Steelers 1993-95, Carolina Panthers 1996, San Francisco 49ers 1997, Carolina Panthers 1998-99. Pro coach: Joined Packers in 2009.

Mark Lovat, strength & conditioning coordinator; born Oct. 9, 1969, Pocatello, Idaho. Attended Butler. No college or pro playing experience. Pro coach: Joined Packers in 1999.

Ben McAdoo, tight ends; born July 7, 1977, Homer City, Pa. Attended Indiana University (Pa.). No college or pro playing experience. College coach: Michigan State 2001, Fairfield 2002, Pittsburgh 2003, Akron 2004, Stanford 2005. Pro coach: New Orleans Saints 2004, San Francisco 49ers 2005, joined Packers in 2006.

Scott McCurley, defensive quality control; born August 1, 1980, New Castle, Pa. Linebacker Pittsburgh 1998-2002. No pro playing experience. College coach: Pittsburgh 2003-05. Pro coach: Joined Packers in 2006.

Chad Morton, special teams assistant; born April 4, 1977, Torrance, Calif. Running back Southern California 1995-99. Pro running back New Orleans Saints 2000, New York Jets 2001-02, Washington Redskins 2003-04, New York Giants 2005-06. Pro coach: Joined Packers in 2009.

Winston Moss, asst. head coach/inside linebackers; born December 24, 1965, Miami. Linebacker Miami 1983-86. Pro linebacker Tampa Bay Buccaneers 1987-1990, Los Angeles Raiders 1991-94, Seattle Seahawks 1995-97. Pro coach: Seattle Seahawks 1998, New Orleans Saints 2000-05, joined Packers in 2006.

Darren Perry, secondary-safeties; born December 29, 1968, Norfolk, Va. Safety Penn State 1989-1991. Pro safety Pittsburgh Steelers 1992-98, San Diego Chargers 1999, New Orleans Saints 2000. Pro coach: Cincinnati Bengals 2002, Pittsburgh Steelers 2003-06, Oakland Raiders 2007-08, joined Packers in 2009.

Joe Philbin, offensive coordinator; born July 2, 1961, Springfield, Mass. Tight end Washington & Jefferson 1980. No pro playing experience. College coach: Tulane 1984-85, Worcester Tech 1986-87, U.S. Merchant Marine Academy 1988-89, Allegheny 1990-93, Ohio University 1994, Northeastern 1995-96, Harvard 1997-98, Iowa 1999-2002. Pro coach: Joined Packers in 2003.

Dave Redding, asst. strength & conditioning; born June 14, 1952, Holdenville, Okla. Defensive end Nebraska 1971-75. No pro playing experience. College coach: Nebraska 1976, Washington State 1977, Missouri 1978-1981. Pro coach: Cleveland Browns 1982-88, Kansas City Chiefs 1989-1997, Washington Redskins 2001, San Diego Chargers 2002-06, joined Packers in 2009.

Jimmy Robinson, wide receivers; born January 3, 1953, Atlanta. Wide receiver Georgia Tech 1972-74. Pro wide receiver New York Giants 1976-79, San Francisco 49ers 1980, Denver Broncos 1981. College coach: Georgia Tech 1987-89. Pro coach: Memphis Showboats (USFL) 1984-85, Atlanta Falcons 1990-93, Indianapolis Colts 1994-97, New York Giants 1998-2003, New Orleans Saints 2004-05, joined Packers in 2006.

John Rushing, offensive quality control; born February 26, 1972, Merced, Calif. Defensive back Washington State 1991-94. No pro playing experience. College coach: Willamette (Ore.) 1996-97, Boise State 1998-99, Montana State 2000-02, Utah State 2003-08. Pro coach: Joined Packers in 2009.

Shawn Slocum, special teams coordinator; born February 21, 1965, Bryan, Texas. Linebacker Texas A&M 1983-84. No pro playing experience. College coach: Texas A&M 1989, 1991-97, 2000-02, Pittsburgh 1990, Southern California 1998-99, Mississippi 2005. Pro coach: Joined Packers in 2006.

Mike Trgovac, defensive line; born February 27, 1959, Youngstown, Ohio. Defensive lineman Michigan 1977-1980. No pro playing experience. College coach: Michigan 1984-85, Ball State 1986-88, Navy 1989, Colorado State 1990-91, Notre Dame 1992-94. Pro coach: Philadelphia Eagles 1995-98, Green Bay Packers 1999, Washington Redskins 2000-01, Carolina Panthers 2002-08, re-joined Packers in 2009.

Joe Whitt, Jr., secondary-cornerbacks; born July 19, 1978, Auburn, Ala. Wide receiver Auburn 1997-99. No pro playing experience. College coach: Auburn 2000-01, The Citadel 2002, Louisville 2003-06. Pro coach: Atlanta Falcons 2007, joined Packers in 2008.

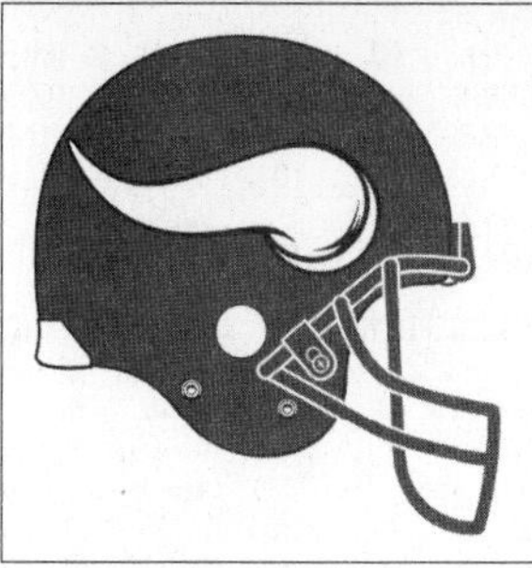

National Football Conference
North Division
Team Colors: Purple, Gold, and White
9520 Viking Drive
Eden Prairie, Minnesota 55344
Telephone: (952) 828-6500

2010 SCHEDULE

PRESEASON

Aug. 14	at St. Louis	7:00
Aug. 22	at San Francisco	7:00
Aug. 28	**Seattle**	7:00
Sep. 2	**Denver**	7:00

REGULAR SEASON

Sep. 9	at New Orleans (Thu)	7:30
Sep. 19	**Miami**	12:00
Sep. 26	**Detroit**	12:00
Oct. 3	BYE	
Oct. 11	at New York Jets (Mon)	8:30
Oct. 17	**Dallas**	3:15
Oct. 24	at Green Bay	7:20
Oct. 31	at New England	4:15
Nov. 7	**Arizona**	12:00
Nov. 14	at Chicago	12:00
Nov. 21	**Green Bay**	12:00
Nov. 28	at Washington	1:00
Dec. 5	**Buffalo**	12:00
Dec. 12	**New York Giants**	12:00
Dec. 20	**Chicago** (Mon)	7:30
Dec. 26	at Philadelphia	1:00
Jan. 2	at Detroit	1:00

Stadium: Mall of America Field at Hubert H. Humphrey Metrodome (opened in 1982)
•**Capacity:** 64,121
500 11th Avenue South
Minneapolis, Minnesota 55415
Playing Surface: FieldTurf
Training Camp: Minnesota State-Mankato
Mankato, Minnesota
56001

HUBERT H. HUMPHREY METRODOME

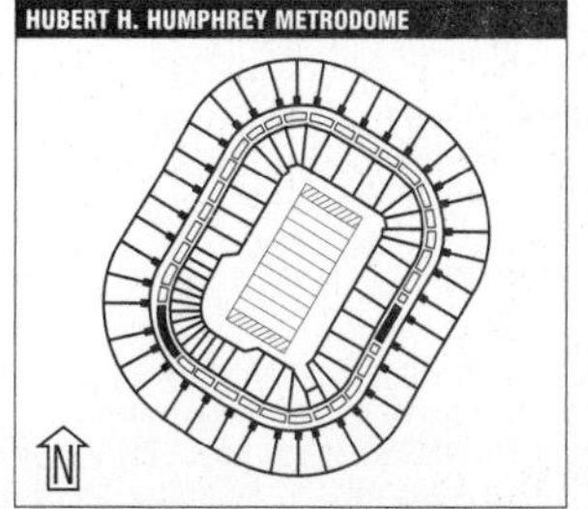

CLUB OFFICIALS

Owner/Chairman: Zygi Wilf
Owner/President: Mark Wilf
Owner/Vice Chairman: Leonard Wilf
Ownership Partners: Reggie Fowler, Alan Landis, David Mandelbaum
Vice President of Public Affairs/Stadium Development: Lester Bagley
Vice President of Football Operations: Rob Brzezinski
Vice President of Sales and Marketing: Steve LaCroix
Vice President of Finance: Steve Poppen
Vice President of Player Personnel: Rick Spielman
Vice President of Operations and Legal Counsel: Kevin Warren
Director of College Scouting: Scott Studwell
Director of Public Relations: Bob Hagan
Director of Community Relations: Brad Madson
Director of Operations/Team Travel: Luther Hippe
Director of Operations/Stadium and Logistics: Chad Lundeen
Director of Ticketing and Hospitality: Phil Huebner
Director of Video: Bob Marcus
Executive Director of Player Development/Legal: Les Pico
Director of Security: Kim Klawiter
Head Athletic Trainer: Eric Sugarman
Equipment Manager: Dennis Ryan
Director of Marketing & Business Development: Dannon Hulskotter
Director of Corporate Sales: Mike Slates
Director of Civic and Business Affairs: Kimberly Fields
Facilities Director: Nick Tigue

COACHING HISTORY
(426-352-9)

Records include postseason games

1961-66	Norm Van Brocklin	29-51-4
1967-1983	Bud Grant	161-99-5
1984	Les Steckel	3-13-0
1985	Bud Grant	7-9-0
1986-1991	Jerry Burns	55-46-0
1992-2001	Dennis Green*	101-70-0
2001-05	Mike Tice	33-34-0
2006-09	Brad Childress	37-30-0

*Resigned after 15 games in 2001

PAID ATTENDANCE

Home 499,567 Away 514,756
Total 1,014,323
Single-game home record, 64,482 (11/2/03)
Single-season home record, 510,741 (1998)

2010 DRAFT CHOICES

Round	Name	Pos.	College
2	Chris Cook	DB	Virginia
	Toby Gerhart	RB	Stanford
4	Everson Griffen	DE	Southern California
5	Chris DeGeare	G	Wake Forest
	Nate Triplett	LB	Minnesota
6	Joe Webb	WR	Ala.-Birmingham
7	Mickey Shuler	TE	Penn State
	Ryan D'Imperio	RB	Rutgers

MINNESOTA VIKINGS

2009 TEAM RECORD

PRESEASON (3-1)

Date	Result	Opponent
8/14	W 13-3	at Indianapolis
8/21	W 17-13	Kansas City
8/31	W 17-10	at Houston
9/4	L 31-35	Dallas

REGULAR SEASON (12-4)

Date	Result	Opponent
9/13	W 34-20	at Cleveland
9/20	W 27-13	at Detroit
9/27	W 27-24	San Francisco
10/5	W 30-23	Green Bay
10/11	W 38-10	at St. Louis
10/18	W 33-31	Baltimore
10/25	L 17-27	at Pittsburgh
11/1	W 38-26	at Green Bay
11/15	W 27-10	Detroit
11/22	W 35-9	Seattle
11/29	W 36-10	Chicago
12/6	L 17-30	at Arizona
12/13	W 30-10	Cincinnati
12/20	L 7-26	at Carolina
12/28	L 30-36	at Chicago (OT)
1/3	W 44-7	New York Giants

POSTSEASON (1-1)

Date	Result	Opponent
1/17	W 34-3	Dallas
1/24	L 28-31	at New Orleans (OT)

(OT) Overtime

SCORE BY PERIODS

Vikings	69	156	111	134	0 —	470
Opponents	29	101	56	120	6 —	312

2009 TEAM STATISTICS

	Vikings	Opp.
Total First Downs	343	271
Rushing	99	63
Passing	220	183
Penalty	24	25
3rd Down: Made/Att	100/223	69/200
3rd Down Pct.	44.8	34.5
4th Down: Made/Att	8/12	5/12
4th Down Pct.	66.7	41.7
Possession Avg.	32:40	27:20
Total Net Yards	6074	4888
Avg. Per Game	379.6	305.5
Total Plays	1054	940
Avg. Per Play	5.8	5.2
Net Yards Rushing	1918	1394
Avg. Per Game	119.9	87.1
Total Rushes	467	357
Net Yards Passing	4156	3494
Avg. Per Game	259.8	218.4
Sacked/Yards Lost	34/247	48/318
Gross Yards	4403	3812
Att./Completions	553/377	535/341
Completion Pct.	68.2	63.7
Had Intercepted	7	11
Punts/Average	73/43.9	89/44.7
Net Punting Avg.	73/37.8	89/38.2
Penalties/Yards	101/757	109/902
Fumbles/Ball Lost	19/11	35/13
Touchdowns	56	36
Rushing	19	5
Passing	34	26
Returns	3	5

2009 INDIVIDUAL STATISTICS

Passing	Att.	Comp.	Yds.	Pct.	TD	Int.	Tkld.	Rate
Favre	531	363	4202	68.4	33	7	34/247	107.2
Jackson	21	14	201	66.7	1	0	0/0	113.4
Rice	1	0	0	0.0	0	0	0/0	39.6
Vikings	553	377	4403	68.2	34	7	34/247	107.3
Opponents	535	341	3812	63.7	26	11	48/318	92.5

SCORING	TD R	TD P	TD Rt	PAT	FG	Saf	PTS
Longwell	0	0	0	54/55	26/28	0	132
Peterson	18	0	0	0/0	0/0	0	108
Shiancoe	0	11	0	0/0	0/0	0	66
Harvin	0	6	2	0/0	0/0	0	48
Rice	0	8	0	0/0	0/0	0	48
Berrian	0	4	0	0/0	0/0	0	24
Dugan	0	2	0	0/0	0/0	0	12
Taylor	1	1	0	0/0	0/0	0	12
J. Allen	0	0	1	0/0	0/0	1	8
Lewis	0	1	0	0/0	0/0	0	6
Tahi	0	1	0	0/0	0/0	0	6
Vikings	19	34	3	54/55	26/28	1	470
Opponents	5	26	5	30/31	22/26	0	312

2-Pt. Conversions: Vikings 0-1, Opponents 0-4

RUSHING	No.	Yds	Avg	LG	TD
Peterson	314	1383	4.4	64t	18
Taylor	94	338	3.6	25	1
Harvin	15	135	9.0	35	0
Young	12	53	4.4	10	0
Dugan	3	7	2.3	5	0
Favre	9	7	0.8	4	0
Tahi	3	5	1.7	2	0
Jackson	17	-10	-0.6	6	0
Vikings	467	1918	4.1	64t	19
Opponents	357	1394	3.9	42	5

RECEIVING	No.	Yds	Avg	LG	TD
Rice	83	1312	15.8	63	8
Harvin	60	790	13.2	51t	6
Shiancoe	56	566	10.1	27	11
Berrian	55	618	11.2	40	4
Taylor	44	389	8.8	33	1
Peterson	43	436	10.1	63	0
Kleinsasser	10	70	7.0	21	0
Tahi	10	67	6.7	32	1
Lewis	8	96	12.0	32t	1
Dugan	6	52	8.7	25	2
J. Johnson	1	9	9.0	9	0
Favre	1	-2	-2.0	-2	0
Vikings	377	4403	11.7	63	34
Opponents	341	3812	11.2	63	26

INTERCEPTIONS	No.	Yds	Avg	LG	TD
Griffin	4	-2	-0.5	0	0
Greenway	3	49	16.3	36	0
A. Allen	1	0	0.0	0	0
Ty. Johnson	1	0	0.0	0	0
Winfield	1	0	0.0	0	0
J. Allen	1	-4	-4.0	-4	0
Vikings	11	43	3.9	36	0
Opponents	7	120	17.1	82t	1

PUNTING	No.	Yds.	Avg.	In 20	LG
Kluwe	73	3202	43.9	24	60
Vikings	73	3202	43.9	24	60
Opponents	89	3979	44.7	21	67

PUNT RETURNS	Ret	FC	Yds	Avg	LG	TD
Reynaud	30	13	308	10.3	36	0
J. Johnson	16	3	134	8.4	24	0
Berrian	2	0	13	6.5	8	0
A. Allen	0	1	0	—	—	0
Vikings	48	18	455	9.5	36	0
Opponents	33	13	260	7.9	67t	1

KICKOFF RETURNS	No.	Yds	Avg	LG	TD
Harvin	42	1156	27.5	101t	2
Dugan	5	38	7.6	13	0
Reynaud	4	90	22.5	30	0
Robison	2	7	3.5	7	0
Kennedy	1	6	6.0	6	0
Rice	1	0	0.0	0	0
Tahi	1	0	0.0	0	0
Vikings	56	1297	23.2	101t	2
Opponents	91	2060	22.6	77	0

FIELD GOALS	1-19	20-29	30-39	40-49	50+
Longwell	1/1	10/10	5/6	8/9	2/2
Vikings	1/1	10/10	5/6	8/9	2/2
Opponents	0/0	8/8	10/10	4/7	0/1

SACKS	No.
J. Allen	14.5
Edwards	8.5
K Williams	6.0
Robison	4.5
Kennedy	3.0
Leber	2.5
E.J. Henderson	2.0
P. Williams	2.0
(group)	2.0
Abdullah	1.0
A. Allen	1.0
Winfield	1.0
Vikings	48.0
Opponents	34.0

RECORD HOLDERS

INDIVIDUAL RECORDS—CAREER

Category	Name	Performance
Rushing (Yds.)	Robert Smith, 1993-2000	6,818
Passing (Yds.)	Fran Tarkenton, 1961-66, 1972-78	33,098
Passing (TDs)	Fran Tarkenton, 1961-66, 1972-78	239
Receiving (No.)	Cris Carter, 1990-2001	1,004
Receiving (Yds.)	Cris Carter, 1990-2001	12,383
Interceptions	Paul Krause, 1968-1979	53
Punting (Avg.)	Chris Kluwe, 2005-09	44.4
Punt Return (Avg.)	Mewelde Moore, 2004-07	10.4
Kickoff Return (Avg.)	Charlie West, 1968-1973	25.5
Field Goals	Fred Cox, 1963-1977	282
Touchdowns (Tot.)	Cris Carter, 1990-2001	110
Points	Fred Cox, 1963-1977	1,365
*Sacks	John Randle, 1990-2000	114.0

INDIVIDUAL RECORDS—SINGLE SEASON

Category	Name	Performance
Rushing (Yds.)	Adrian Peterson, 2008	1,760
Passing (Yds.)	Daunte Culpepper, 2004	4,717
Passing (TDs)	Daunte Culpepper, 2004	39
Receiving (No.)	Cris Carter, 1994, 1995	122
Receiving (Yds.)	Randy Moss, 2003	1,632
Interceptions	Paul Krause, 1975	10
Punting (Avg.)	Chris Kluwe, 2008	47.6
Punt Return (Avg.)	David Palmer, 1995	13.2
Kickoff Return (Avg.)	Aundrae Allison, 2007	28.7
Field Goals	Gary Anderson, 1998	35
Touchdowns (Tot.)	Chuck Foreman, 1975	22
Points	Gary Anderson, 1998	164
*Sacks	Chris Doleman, 1989	21.0

INDIVIDUAL RECORDS—SINGLE GAME

Category	Name	Performance
Rushing (Yds.)	Adrian Peterson, 11-4-07	**296
Passing (Yds.)	Tommy Kramer, 11-2-86	490
Passing (TDs)	Joe Kapp, 9-28-69	**7
Receiving (No.)	Rickey Young, 12-16-79	15
Receiving (Yds.)	Sammy White, 11-7-76	210
Interceptions	Many Times	3
	Last time by Darren Sharper, 11-13-05	
Field Goals	Rich Karlis, 11-5-89	7
Touchdowns (Tot.)	Chuck Foreman, 12-20-75	4
	Ahmad Rashad, 9-2-79	4
Points	Chuck Foreman, 12-20-75	24
	Ahmad Rashad, 9-2-79	24
*Sacks	Randy Holloway, 9-16-84	5.0

**Sacks became an official statistic in 1982.*
***NFL Record*

MINNESOTA VIKINGS

2010 VETERAN ROSTER

No.	Name	Pos.	Ht.	Wt.	Birthdate	NFL Exp.	College	Hometown	How Acq.	'09 Games/ Starts
39	Abdullah, Husain	S	6-0	204	7/27/85	3	Washington State	Pomona, Calif.	FA-'08	14/0
21	Allen, Asher	CB	5-9	194	1/22/88	2	Georgia	Tucker, Ga.	D3-'09	10/1
69	Allen, Jared	DE	6-6	270	4/3/82	7	Idaho State	Los Gatos, Calif.	T(KC)-'08	16/16
87	Berrian, Bernard	WR	6-1	185	12/27/80	7	Fresno State	Winton, Calif.	UFA(Chi)-'08	16/15
15	Biddle, Taye	WR	6-1	185	2/27/83	2	Mississippi	Decatur, Ala.	FA-'10	0*
54	Brinkley, Jasper	LB	6-1	252	7/12/85	2	South Carolina	Thomson, Ga.	D5-'09	16/4
62	Cook, Ryan	T	6-6	328	5/8/83	5	New Mexico	Albuquerque, N.M.	D2b-'06	16/0
68	Cooper, Jon	C	6-2	291	10/1/86	2	Oklahoma	Fort Collins, Colo.	FA-'09	1/0
83	Dugan, Jeff	TE	6-4	258	4/8/81	7	Maryland	Pittsburgh, Pa.	D7-'04	16/3
93	+Edwards, Ray	DE	6-5	268	1/1/85	5	Purdue	Cincinnati, Ohio	D4-'06	16/16
90	Evans, Fred	DT	6-4	305	11/6/83	5	Texas St.-San Marcos	Morgan Park, Ill.	FA-'07	13/0
59	Farwell, Heath	LB	6-0	235	12/31/81	6	San Diego State	Corona, Calif.	FA-'05	16/0
4	Favre, Brett	QB	6-2	222	10/10/69	20	Southern Mississippi	Kiln, Miss.	FA-'09	16/16
37	Frampton, Eric	S	5-11	205	2/6/84	4	Washington State	San Jose, Calif.	W(Det)-'07	16/0
52	Greenway, Chad	LB	6-2	242	1/12/83	5	Iowa	Mt. Vernon, S.D.	D1-'06	16/16
23	Griffin, Cedric	CB	6-0	203	11/11/82	5	Texas	San Antonio, Texas	D2a-'06	16/16
98	Guion, Letroy	DT	6-4	303	6/21/87	3	Florida State	Starke, Fla.	D5b-'08	7/0
12	Harvin, Percy	WR	5-11	184	5/28/88	2	Florida	Virginia Beach, Va.	D1-'09	15/7
56	Henderson, E.J.	LB	6-1	245	8/3/80	8	Maryland	Aberdeen, Md.	D2-'03	12/12
50	Henderson, Erin	LB	6-3	244	7/1/86	3	Maryland	Aberdeen, Md.	FA-'08	2/0
64	Herrera, Anthony	G	6-2	315	6/14/80	7	Tennessee	Naples, Fla.	FA-'04	14/14
76	Hutchinson, Steve	G	6-5	313	11/1/77	10	Michigan	Ft. Lauderdale, Fla.	RFA(Sea)-'06	16/16
7	Jackson, Tarvaris	QB	6-2	225	4/21/83	5	Alabama State	Montgomery, Ala.	D2c-'06	8/0
11	Johnson, Jaymar	WR	6-0	176	7/10/84	2	Jackson State	Gary, Ind.	D6b-'08	6/0
25	Johnson, Tyrell	S	6-0	207	5/19/85	3	Arkansas State	Rison, Ark.	D2-'08	15/15
73	Kennedy, Jimmy	DT	6-5	320	11/15/79	8	Penn State	Yonkers, N.Y.	FA(Jax)-'08	13/1
40	Kleinsasser, Jim	TE	6-3	272	1/31/77	12	North Dakota	Carrington, N.D.	D2-'99	16/8
5	Kluwe, Chris	P	6-4	215	12/24/81	6	UCLA	Los Alamitos, Calif.	W(Sea)-'05	16/0
51	Leber, Ben	LB	6-3	244	12/7/78	9	Kansas State	Vermillion, S.D.	UFA(SD)-'06	16/13
57	Leman, J	LB	6-2	240	3/1/85	2	Illinois	Champaign, Ill.	FA-'09	0/0
17	Lewis, Greg	WR	6-0	185	2/12/80	8	Illinois	Matteson, Ill.	FA-'09	13/1
9	Lloyd, Rhys	K	6-0	238	6/5/82	4	Minnesota	Apple Valley, Minn.	FA-'10	16/0*
71	Loadholt, Phil	T	6-8	343	1/21/86	2	Oklahoma	Fountain, Colo.	D2-'09	15/15
46	Loeffler, Cullen	LS	6-5	241	1/27/81	7	Texas	Ingram, Texas	FA-'04	16/0
8	Longwell, Ryan	K	6-0	200	8/16/74	14	California	Bend, Ore.	UFA(GB)-'06	16/0
74	McKinnie, Bryant	T	6-8	335	9/23/79	9	Miami	Woodbury, N.J.	D1-'02	16/16
45	Mills, Garrett	TE	6-1	235	10/12/83	4	Tulsa	Jenks, Okla.	W(NE)-'07	0*
92	Mitchell, Jayme	DE	6-6	285	3/15/84	5	Mississippi	Jackson, Miss.	FA-'06	4/0
99	Montgomery, Mike	DE	6-5	282	8/18/83	6	Texas A&M	Carthage, Texas	FA-'10	10/0*
55	Onatolu, Kenny	LB	6-2	225	10/8/82	2	Nebraska-Omaha	Papillion, Neb.	FA-'09	16/0
28	Peterson, Adrian	RB	6-1	217	3/21/85	4	Oklahoma	Palestine, Texas	D1-'07	16/15
60	Radovich, Drew	T	6-5	305	6/20/85	2	Southern California	Mission Viejo, Calif.	FA-'09	0*
27	Reynaud, Darius	RB	5-9	201	12/29/84	3	West Virginia	Boutte, La.	FA-'08	11/0
18	Rice, Sidney	WR	6-4	202	9/1/86	4	South Carolina	Gaffney, S.C.	D2-'07	16/15
96	Robison, Brian	DE	6-3	259	4/27/83	4	Texas	Splendora, Texas	D4-'07	16/0
2	Rosenfels, Sage	QB	6-4	225	3/6/78	10	Iowa State	Maquoketa, Iowa	T(Hou)-'09	0*
33	Sanford, Jamarca	S	5-10	200	8/27/85	2	Mississippi	Batesville, Miss.	D7-'09	14/1
22	Sapp, Benny	CB	5-9	190	1/20/81	7	Northern Iowa	Ft. Lauderdale, Fla.	UFA(KC)-'08	16/7
29	Sheppard, Lito	CB	5-10	194	4/8/81	9	Florida	Jacksonville, Fla.	FA-'10	11/9*
81	Shiancoe, Visanthe	TE	6-4	250	6/18/80	8	Morgan State	Laurel, Md.	UFA(NYG)-'07	16/14
65	Sullivan, John	C	6-4	301	8/8/85	3	Notre Dame	Old Greenwich, Conn.	D6a-'08	16/16
38	Tahi, Naufahu	FB	6-0	254	10/30/81	5	Brigham Young	West Valley City, Utah	PS(Cin)-'06	15/2
93	Williams, Kevin	DT	6-5	311	8/16/80	8	Oklahoma State	Fordyce, Ark.	D1-'03	16/16
20	Williams, Madieu	S	6-1	203	10/18/81	7	Maryland	Lanham, Md.	UFA(Cin)-'08	16/16
94	Williams, Pat	DT	6-3	317	10/24/72	14	Texas A&M	Monroe, La.	UFA(Buff)-'05	15/15
26	Winfield, Antoine	CB	5-9	180	6/24/77	12	Ohio State	Akron, Ohio	UFA(Buff)-'04	10/9
34	Young, Albert	RB	5-10	209	2/25/85	2	Iowa	Moorestown, N.J.	FA-'08	7/0

* Biddle inactive with N.Y. Giants in '08; Lloyd played 16 games with Carolina in '09; Mills inactive for 4 games; Montgomery played 10 games for Green Bay; Radovich inactive with Minnesota in '08; Rosenfels inactive third quarterback for 16 games; Sheppard played 11 games with N.Y. Jets.

Players lost through free agency (2): T Artis Hicks (Wash; 16 games in '09), RB Chester Taylor (Chi; 16).

Also played with Vikings in '09—CB Karl Paymah (12 games).

2010 FIRST-YEAR ROSTER

Name	Pos.	Ht.	Wt.	Birthdate	College	Hometown	How Acq.
Adamski, Eddie	C	6-3	284	10/4/86	Northern Illinois	Kildeer, Ill.	FA
Anderson, Colt (1)	S	5-10	194	10/25/85	Montana	Butte, Mont.	FA-'09
Archer, R.J.	QB	6-2	220	8/5/87	William & Mary	Earlysville, Va.	FA
Austin, Thomas	G	6-4	310	11/14/86	Clemson	Camden, S.C.	FA
Battles, Adrian	G	6-3	311	10/30/86	Minnesota State	Milwaukee, Wisc.	FA
Brown, Patrick (1)	T	6-5	310	12/25/86	Central Florida	St. Charles, Ill.	FA-'09
Clark, Chris (1)	T	6-5	315	10/1/85	Southern Mississippi	New Orleans, La.	FA-'08
Cook, Chris	CB	6-2	212	2/15/87	Virginia	Lynchburg, Va.	D2a
DeGeare, Chris	T	6-4	335	2/17/87	Wake Forest	Kernersville, N.C.	D5a
D'Imperio, Ryan	FB	6-3	240	8/15/87	Rutgers	Sewell, N.J.	D7b
Gerhart, Toby	RB	6-0	231	3/28/87	Stanford	Norco, Calif.	D2b
Griffen, Everson	DE	6-3	273	12/22/87	Southern California	Avondale, Ariz.	D4
Hamilton, Marquis	WR	6-3	222	6/18/87	Iowa State	Edmond, Okla.	FA
Hanson, Matt	T	6-7	315	3/29/86	Midwestern State	Linden, Calif.	FA
Hernandez, Tommy	C	6-2	290	4/26/87	California-Davis	Chino Hills, Calif.	FA
Johnson, Ian (1)	RB	5-11	212	10/10/86	Boise State	San Dimas, Calif.	FA-'09
Johnson, James (1)	RB	5-11	205	9/6/84	Kansas State	Port Arthur, Texas	FA
Johnson, Tremaine (1)	DT	6-2	285	9/26/85	Louisiana State	Galena Park, Texas	FA-'09
McKinley, Cedric	DE	6-6	281	3/26/87	Minnesota	Bratt, Fla.	FA
Noethlich, Bill	T	6-7	308	11/10/86	Southwest Minnesota State	Doland, S.D.	FA
Rhea, Aaron	WR	6-1	202	4/29/87	Stephen F. Austin	Houston, Texas	FA
Sherels, Marcus	CB	5-10	175	9/30/87	Minnesota	Rochester, Minn.	FA
Shuler, Mickey	TE	6-4	251	10/9/86	Penn State	Enola, Pa.	D7a
Skinner, Terrell	S	6-2	214	2/24/87	Maryland	St. Petersburg, Fla.	FA
Small, Ray	WR	5-11	180	3/25/87	Ohio State	Cleveland, Ohio	FA
Tindal, Kelton	WR	6-3	195	10/27/87	Newberry	Sumter, S.C.	FA
Triplett, Nate	LB	6-3	247	3/15/87	Minnesota	Delano, Minn.	D5b
Webb, Joe	WR	6-4	220	11/14/86	Alabama-Birmingham	Birmingham, Ala.	D6
Williams II, Angelo	CB	5-11	185	6/16/87	Ferris State	Jackson, Mich.	FA
Winn, Marlon	T	6-6	287	7/3/86	Texas Tech	Waxahachie, Texas	FA
Wright, DeAndre (1)	CB	5-11	190	4/13/86	New Mexico	Brandywine, Md.	FA-'09

The term NFL Rookie is defined as a player who is in his first season of professional football and has not been on the roster of another professional football team for any regular-season or postseason games. A Rookie is designated by an "R" on NFL rosters. Players who have been active in another professional football league or players who have NFL experience, including either preseason training camp or being on an Active List or Inactive List, or on Reserve/Injured or Reserve/Physically Unable to Perform for fewer than six regular-season games, are termed NFL First-Year Players. An NFL First-Year Player is designated by a "1" on NFL rosters. Thereafter, a player is credited with an additional year of experience for each season in which he accumulates six games on the Active List or Inactive List, or on Reserve/Injured or Reserve/Physically Unable to Perform.

Log on to www.vikings.com for an up-to-date roster.

COACHING STAFF

Head Coach,
Brad Childress

Pro Career: Named the seventh head coach in Vikings' history on January 6, 2006. This marks Childress' 33rd season coaching, including his thirteenth on an NFL sideline. Childress led Minnesota to successive division titles for the first time in 32 years in 2008 and 2009, posting records of 10-6 and 12-4, respectively, to claim the franchise's first two NFC North crowns. The Vikings hosted a playoff game in each of the last two seasons after not doing so since 2000, and in 2009 made the franchise's eighth NFC Championship appearance. Ten Vikings were recognized with Pro Bowl berths in 2009, including Brett Favre, and NFL touchdown-leader Adrian Peterson. Minnesota's 2009 offense (5th) and defense (6th) were both ranked in the NFL's top 10 in the same season for the first time since 1994. The Vikings led the NFL in rush defense for three consecutive years under Childress from 2006-08, a league first since the 1970 AFL-NFL merger. The 2007 Vikings became the first team in franchise history to rank No. 1 in the NFL in rushing offense and rushing defense. Was an assistant coach with the Eagles (1999-2005, the last four as offensive coordinator), when the Eagles reached Super Bowl XXXIX and played in four straight NFC Championship Games. He began his NFL coaching career as the Colts' quarterbacks coach (1985). Career record: 37-30.

Background: Coached at Illinois (1978-1984), Northern Arizona (1986-89), Utah (1990), and Wisconsin (1991-98). Childress played quarterback and wide receiver at Illinois before transferring to Eastern Illinois, where he graduated with a bachelor's degree in psychology.

Personal: Born June 27, 1956 in Aurora, Ill. He and his wife Dru-Ann have four children: Cara, Kyle, Andrew, and Christopher.

ASSISTANT COACHES

Juney Barnett, asst. strength and conditioning; born January 11, 1979, Philadelphia. Defensive back Bloomsburg 1997-2000. College coach: Bloomsburg 2001, Army 2005. Pro coach: Rhein Fire (NFLE) 2004-05, joined Vikings in 2006.

Darrell Bevell, offensive coordinator; born January 6, 1970, Yuma, Ariz. Quarterback Northern Arizona 1989, Wisconsin 1992-95. No pro playing experience. College coach: Westmar 1996, Iowa State 1997, Connecticut 1998-99. Pro coach: Green Bay Packers 2000-05, joined Vikings in 2006.

Eric Bieniemy, running backs; born August 15, 1969, New Orleans. Running back Colorado 1987-1990. Pro running back San Diego Chargers 1991-94, Cincinnati Bengals 1995-98, Philadelphia Eagles 1999. College coach: Colorado 2001-02, UCLA 2003-05. Pro coach: Joined Vikings in 2006.

Karl Dunbar, defensive line; born May 18, 1967, Plaisance, La. Defensive lineman Louisiana State 1986-89. Pro defensive lineman Pittsburgh Steelers 1990, New Orleans Saints 1992-93, Arizona Cardinals 1994-95. College coach: Nicholls State 1998-99, Louisiana State 2000-01, 2005, Oklahoma State 2002-03. Pro coach: Chicago Bears 2004, joined Vikings in 2006.

Ryan Ficken, offensive assistant/wide receivers; born February 20, 1980, Aurora, Colo. Wide receiver Arizona State 1998-99. No pro playing experience. College coach: UCLA 2004-06. Pro coach: Joined Vikings in 2007.

Leslie Frazier, defensive coordinator/asst. head coach; born April 3, 1959, Columbus, Miss. Defensive back Alcorn State 1977-1980. Pro defensive back Chicago Bears 1981-86. College coach: Trinity (Ill.) College 1988-1996 (head coach), Illinois 1997-98. Pro coach Philadelphia Eagles 1999-2002, Cincinnati Bengals 2003-04, Indianapolis Colts 2005-06, joined Vikings in 2007.

Jim Hueber, asst. offensive line; born August 14, 1948, Philadelphia. Center South Dakota 1966-67. No pro playing experience. College coach: Cincinnati 1974, Dodge City (Kan.) C.C. 1975-78, Wichita State 1979-1980, Temple 1981-82, Memphis State 1983, Minnesota 1984-1991, Wisconsin 1992-2005. Pro coach: Joined Vikings in 2006.

Jeff Imamura, defensive assistant/linebackers; born May 22, 1974, Lubbock, Texas. Attended Texas Christian. No college or pro playing experience. College coach: Texas Christian 1997-99, Northern Arizona 2000-02, Saginaw Valley State 2003. Pro coach: Joined Vikings in 2006.

Jimmie Johnson, tight ends; born October 6, 1966, Augusta, Ga. Tight end Howard 1985-88. Pro tight end Washington Redskins 1989-1991, Detroit Lions 1992-93, Kansas City Chiefs 1994, Philadelphia Eagles 1995-98. College coach: South Carolina State 2001, Shaw 2002-03, Texas Southern 2004-05. Pro coach: Joined Vikings in 2006.

Tom Kanavy, strength and conditioning; born April 8, 1970, Archibald, Pa. Attended Penn State. No college or pro playing experience. College coach: Miami 1993, Penn State 1993-95. Pro coach: Philadelphia Eagles 1995-2005, joined Vikings in 2006.

Pat Morris, offensive line; born April 7, 1954, Cleveland. Offensive lineman Southern California 1972-75. College coach: Southern California 1976-77, 1983-86, Northern Arizona 1978, Minnesota 1979-1982, Michigan State 1987-1994, Stanford 1995-96. Pro coach: San Francisco 49ers 1997-2003, Detroit Lions 2004-05, joined Vikings in 2006.

Brian Murphy, special teams coordinator; born July 17, 1969, Elmwood Park, Ill. Defensive lineman Lehigh 1988-1991. No pro playing experience. College coach: Benedictine 1992, Wisconsin 1994-96, 2002-05, Baylor 1997, San Diego 1998, Lehigh 1999. Pro coach: Joined Vikings in 2006.

Fred Pagac, linebackers; born April 26, 1952, Richeyville, Pa. Tight end Ohio State 1971-73. Pro tight end Chicago Bears 1974, Tampa Bay Buccaneers 1976. College coach: Ohio State 1978-2000. Pro coach: Oakland Raiders 2001-03, Kansas City Chiefs 2004-05, joined Vikings in 2006.

Dennis Polian, asst. to head coach; born November 10, 1976, Bronx, N.Y. Attended Villanova and Boston College. No college or pro playing experience. Pro coach: Hamilton Tiger-Cats (CFL) 2008, joined Vikings in 2009.

Diron Reynolds, asst. defensive line; born February 23, 1971, Aiken, S.C. Linebacker Wake Forest 1990-93. No pro playing experience. College coach: Wake Forest 1997-2000, Indiana 2001. Pro coach: Indianapolis Colts 2002-06, Miami Dolphins 2007, joined Vikings in 2009.

Kevin Rogers, quarterbacks; born September 7, 1951, Brooklyn, N.Y. Linebacker Massanutten Academy 1969-1970, William & Mary 1971-73. College coach: Ohio State 1977-78, William & Mary 1980-82, Navy 1983-1990, Syracuse 1991-98, Notre Dame 1999-2001, Virginia Tech 2002-05. Pro coach: Joined Vikings in 2006.

Matt Sheldon, asst. defensive backs; born February 26, 1969, Berwyn, Ill. Cornerback Minnesota 1987-1991. No pro playing experience. College coach: Wisconsin 1997-99. Pro coach: St. Louis Rams 2001-2005, Buffalo Bills 2006-09, joined Vikings in 2010.

Ryan Silverfield, defensive assistant/defensive line; born August 4, 1980, Jacksonville, Fla. Attended Hampden-Sydney. No college or pro playing experience. College coach: Hampden-Sydney 2000-03, Jacksonville 2005, Central Florida 2006-07. Pro coach: Joined Vikings in 2008.

Kevin Stefanski, quality control-offense/quarterbacks; born May 8, 1982, Philadelphia. Safety Pennsylvania 2000-04. College coach: Pennsylvania 2005. Pro coach: Joined Vikings in 2006.

George Stewart, wide receivers; born December 29, 1958, Little Rock, Ark. Guard Arkansas 1977-1980. No pro playing experience. College coach: Minnesota 1984-85, Notre Dame 1986-88. Pro coach: Pittsburgh Steelers 1989-1991, Tampa Bay Buccaneers 1992-95, San Francisco 49ers 1996-2002, Atlanta Falcons 2003-06, joined Vikings in 2007.

Martin Streight, asst. strength and conditioning; born June 20, 1969, Trenton, N.J. Attended Indiana (Penn.). No college or pro playing experience. College coach: Penn State 1994, Princeton 1995-96. Pro coach: Philadelphia Eagles 1995-96, Arizona Cardinals 1997-2003, Scottish Claymores (NFLE) 2003, Berlin Thunder (NFLE) 2004-05, joined Vikings in 2006.

Chris White, asst. special teams; born June 29, 1967, Haverhill, Mass. Quarterback Colby College 1986-89. No pro playing experience. College coach: Syracuse 1990-92, 2000-08, Arkansas State 1992-93, Holy Cross 1993-94, UNLV 1996-98, Cal Poly-San Luis Obispo 1999. Pro coach: Joined Vikings in 2009.

Joe Woods, defensive backs; born June 25, 1970, Natrona Heights, Pa. Safety Illinois State 1988-1991. College coach: Muskingum 1992, Eastern Michigan 1993, Northwestern (La.) State 1994, Grand Valley State 1994-96, Kent State 1997, Hofstra 1998-2000, Western Michigan 2001-03. Pro coach: Tampa Bay Buccaneers 2004-05, joined Vikings in 2006.

National Football Conference
South Division
Team Colors: Old Gold, Black, and White
5800 Airline Drive
Metairie, Louisiana 70003
Telephone: (504) 733-0255

2010 SCHEDULE

PRESEASON

Aug. 12	at New England	7:30
Aug. 21	**Houston**	7:00
Aug. 27	**San Diego**	7:00
Sep. 2	at Tennessee	7:00

REGULAR SEASON

Sep. 9	**Minnesota** (Thu)	7:30
Sep. 20	at San Francisco (Mon)	5:30
Sep. 26	**Atlanta**	12:00
Oct. 3	**Carolina**	12:00
Oct. 10	at Arizona	1:05
Oct. 17	at Tampa Bay	1:00
Oct. 24	**Cleveland**	12:00
Oct. 31	**Pittsburgh**	7:20
Nov. 7	at Carolina	1:00
Nov. 14	BYE	
Nov. 21	**Seattle**	3:05
Nov. 25	at Dallas (Thu)	3:15
Dec. 5	at Cincinnati	1:00
Dec. 12	**St. Louis**	3:05
Dec. 19	at Baltimore	1:00
Dec. 27	at Atlanta (Mon)	8:30
Jan. 2	**Tampa Bay**	12:00

Stadium: Louisiana Superdome (opened in 1975) • **Capacity:** 68,000
1500 Poydras Street
New Orleans, Louisiana 70112
Playing Surface: Sportexe Momentum
Training Camp: New Orleans Saints
Metairie, Louisiana 70003

LOUISIANA SUPERDOME

CLUB OFFICIALS

Owner/President: Tom Benson
Owner/Executive Vice President: Rita Benson LeBlanc
Executive Vice President/General Manager: Mickey Loomis
Executive Vice President/Chief Financial Officer: Dennis Lauscha
Vice President of Communications: Greg Bensel
Vice President of Marketing and Business Development: Ben Hales
Vice President/General Counsel: Vicky Neumeyer
Vice President of Ticket and Suite Sales: Mike Stanfield
Director of Football Administration: Khai Harley
Director of Operations: James Nagaoka
Pro Scouting Director: Ryan Pace
Pro Scouts: Terry Fontenot, Ryan Powell
Director of College Scouting: Rick Reiprish
Assistant Director of College Scouting: Brian Adams
College Scouting Coordinator: Jason Mitchell
Area Scouts: Mike Baugh, Dwaune Jones, Josh Lucas, Jim Monos, Mike Neu, Terry Wooden
Combine Scout: Ryan Hollern
Player Personnel Assistant: Joseph Laine
Equipment Manager: Dan Simmons
Assistant Equipment Manager: Glennon (Silky) Powell
Equipment Assistant: John Baumgartner
Head Athletic Trainer: Scottie B. Patton
Assistant Athletic Trainers: Duane Brooks, Kevin Mangum
Video Director: Dave Desposito
Director of Player Development: Fred McAfee
Senior Director of Communications: Doug Miller
Communications Managers: Dave Lawrence, Justin Macione
Director of Photography: Michael C. Hebert
Director of Community Affairs: Nick Karl
Information Technology/Network Manager: Jeff Huffman
Facilities Manager: Terry Ashburn
Administrative Director: Jay Romig

COACHING HISTORY
(280-384-5)

Records include postseason games

1967-70	Tom Fears*	13-34-2
1970-72	J.D. Roberts	7-25-3
1973-75	John North**	11-23-0
1975	Ernie Hefferle	1-7-0
1976-77	Hank Stram	7-21-0
1978-80	Dick Nolan***	15-29-0
1980	Dick Stanfel	1-3-0
1981-85	O.A. (Bum) Phillips****	27-42-0
1985	Wade Phillips	1-3-0
1986-96	Jim Mora#	93-78-0
1996	Rick Venturi	1-7-0
1997-99	Mike Ditka	15-33-0
2000-05	Jim Haslett	46-52-0
2006-09	Sean Payton	42-27-0

*Released after seven games in 1970
**Released after six games in 1975
***Released after 12 games in 1980
****Resigned after 12 games in 1985
#Resigned after eight games in 1996

PAID ATTENDANCE

Home 531,897 Away 532,327
Total 1,064,224
Single-game home record, 70,940 (9/2/79)
Single-season home record, 548,728 (1992)

2010 DRAFT CHOICES

Round	Name	Pos.	College
1	Patrick Robinson	DB	Florida State
2	Charles Brown	T	Southern California
3	Jimmy Graham	TE	Miami
4	Al Woods	DT	Louisiana State
5	Matt Tennant	C	Boston College
7	Sean Canfield	QB	Oregon State

NEW ORLEANS SAINTS

2009 TEAM RECORD

PRESEASON (3-1)

Date	Result	Opponent
8/14	W 17-7	Cincinnati
8/22	W 38-14	at Houston
8/29	W 45-7	at Oakland
9/3	L 7-10	Miami

REGULAR SEASON (13-3)

Date	Result	Opponent
9/13	W 45-27	Detroit
9/20	W 48-22	at Philadelphia
9/27	W 27-7	at Buffalo
10/4	W 24-10	New York Jets
10/18	W 48-27	New York Giants
10/25	W 46-34	at Miami
11/2	W 35-27	Atlanta
11/8	W 30-20	Carolina
11/15	W 28-23	at St. Louis
11/22	W 38-7	at Tampa Bay
11/30	W 38-17	New England
12/6	W 33-30	at Washington (OT)
12/13	W 26-23	at Atlanta
12/19	L 17-24	Dallas
12/27	L 17-20	Tampa Bay (OT)
1/3	L 10-23	at Carolina

POSTSEASON (3-0)

Date	Result	Opponent
1/16	W 45-14	Arizona
1/24	W 31-28	Minnesota (OT)
2/7	W 31-17	vs. Indianapolis, at South Florida

(OT) Overtime

SCORE BY PERIODS

Saints	85	176	107	139	3	— 510
Opponents	106	93	91	48	3	— 341

2009 TEAM STATISTICS

	Saints	Opp.
Total First Downs	348	310
Rushing	115	111
Passing	215	175
Penalty	18	24
3rd Down: Made/Att	88/197	82/216
3rd Down Pct.	44.7	38.0
4th Down: Made/Att	6/15	11/24
4th Down Pct.	40.0	45.8
Possession Avg.	31:10	28:50
Total Net Yards	6461	5724
Avg. Per Game	403.8	357.8
Total Plays	1032	1044
Avg. Per Play	6.3	5.5
Net Yards Rushing	2106	1955
Avg. Per Game	131.6	122.2
Total Rushes	468	435
Net Yards Passing	4355	3769
Avg. Per Game	272.2	235.6
Sacked/Yards Lost	20/135	35/192
Gross Yards	4490	3961
Att./Completions	544/378	574/330
Completion Pct.	69.5	57.5
Had Intercepted	12	26
Punts/Average	58/43.6	71/43.0
Net Punting Avg.	58/36.0	71/38.9
Penalties/Yards	89/787	86/717
Fumbles/Ball Lost	25/16	18/13
Touchdowns	64	37
Rushing	21	19
Passing	34	15
Returns	9	3

2009 INDIVIDUAL STATISTICS

PASSING	Att.	Comp.	Yds.	Pct.	TD	Int.	Tkld.	Rate
Brees	514	363	4388	70.6	34	11	20/135	109.6
Brunell	30	15	102	50.0	0	1	0/0	44.0
Saints	544	378	4490	69.5	34	12	20/135	106.0
Opponents	574	330	3961	57.5	15	26	35/192	68.6

SCORING	TD R	TD P	TD Rt	PAT	FG	Saf	PTS
Carney	0	0	0	50/52	13/17	0	89
Meachem	0	9	1	0/0	0/0	0	60
Colston	0	9	0	0/0	0/0	0	54
Bush	5	3	0	0/0	0/0	0	48
P. Thomas	6	2	0	0/0	0/0	0	48
Hartley	0	0	0	10/11	9/11	0	37
Bell	5	0	0	0/0	0/0	0	30
H. Evans	1	2	0	0/0	0/0	0	18
Sharper	0	0	3	0/0	0/0	0	18
Shockey	0	3	0	0/0	0/0	0	18
Brees	2	0	0	0/0	0/0	0	12
Hamilton	2	0	0	0/0	0/0	0	12
Henderson	0	2	0	0/0	0/0	0	12
Moore	0	2	0	0/0	0/0	0	12
Ayodele	0	0	1	0/0	0/0	0	6
Dinkins	0	1	0	0/0	0/0	0	6
Greer	0	0	1	0/0	0/0	0	6
Hargrove	0	0	1	0/0	0/0	0	6
Porter	0	0	1	0/0	0/0	0	6
Roby	0	0	1	0/0	0/0	0	6
D. Thomas	0	1	0	0/0	0/0	0	6
Saints	21	34	9	60/63	22/28	0	510
Opponents	19	15	3	36/36	27/32	1	341

2-Pt. Conversions: Saints 0-1, Opponents 0-1.

RUSHING	No.	Yds	Avg	LG	TD
P. Thomas	147	793	5.4	34t	6
Bell	172	654	3.8	35	5
Bush	70	390	5.6	55	5
Hamilton	35	125	3.6	19	2
Meachem	6	82	13.7	41	0
Brees	22	33	1.5	10	2
H. Evans	5	16	3.2	6	1
Henderson	4	13	3.3	13	0
Colston	1	6	6.0	6	0
Eckel	2	6	3.0	7	0
Brunell	4	-12	-3.0	-1	0
Saints	468	2106	4.5	55	21
Opponents	435	1955	4.5	68t	19

RECEIVING	No.	Yds	Avg	LG	TD
Colston	70	1074	15.3	68	9
Henderson	51	804	15.8	75t	2
Shockey	48	569	11.9	66	3
Bush	47	335	7.1	29	3
Meachem	45	722	16.0	54t	9
P. Thomas	39	302	7.7	36	2
D. Thomas	35	356	10.2	37	1
Moore	14	153	10.9	22	2
H. Evans	10	70	7.0	13t	2
Hamilton	5	48	9.6	16	0
Dinkins	5	22	4.4	8	1
Bell	4	12	3.0	9	0
Eckel	2	14	7.0	8	0
Humphrey	1	7	7.0	7	0
Roby	1	6	6.0	6	0
Brees	1	-4	-4.0	-4	0
Saints	378	4490	11.9	75t	34
Opponents	330	3961	12.0	71t	15

INTERCEPTIONS	No.	Yds	Avg	LG	TD
Sharper	9	376	41.8	99t	3
Porter	4	72	18.0	54t	1
Vilma	3	25	8.3	11	0
Greer	2	59	29.5	48t	1
Shanle	2	16	8.0	13	0
Reis	1	33	33.0	33	0
Gay	1	25	25.0	25	0
Young	1	24	24.0	24	0
Jenkins	1	14	14.0	14	0
McKenzie	1	8	8.0	8	0
Smith	1	0	0.0	0	0
Saints	26	652	25.1	99t	5
Opponents	12	133	11.1	41	0

PUNTING	No.	Yds.	Avg.	In 20	LG
Morstead	58	2528	43.6	18	60
Saints	58	2528	43.6	18	60
Opponents	71	3055	43.0	19	61

PUNT RETURNS	Ret	FC	Yds	Avg	LG	TD
Bush	27	9	130	4.8	23	0
Henderson	4	5	16	4.0	11	0
Sharper	1	1	6	6.0	6	0
Moore	1	2	0	0.0	0	0
Saints	33	17	152	4.6	23	0
Opponents	25	13	358	14.3	77t	1

KICKOFF RETURNS	No.	Yds	Avg	LG	TD
Roby	42	1154	27.5	97t	1
Meachem	6	148	24.7	42	0
Hamilton	3	15	5.0	15	0
Bell	2	45	22.5	28	0
Charleston	2	11	5.5	11	0
P. Thomas	1	19	19.0	19	0
Dinkins	1	1	1.0	1	0
Saints	57	1393	24.4	97t	1
Opponents	74	1813	24.5	87	0

FIELD GOALS	1-19	20-29	30-39	40-49	50+
Carney	0/0	6/6	5/8	2/3	0/0
Hartley	1/1	3/3	5/6	0/0	0/1
Saints	1/1	9/9	10/14	2/3	0/1
Opponents	0/0	7/9	14/15	6/6	0/2

SACKS	No.
Smith	13.0
Grant	5.5
Hargrove	5.0
Ellis	2.0
Vilma	2.0
Ayodele	1.5
Rom Harper	1.5
McCray	1.5
Fujita	1.0
Gay	1.0
Sharper	0.5
Torrence	0.5
Saints	35.0
Opponents	20.0

RECORD HOLDERS

INDIVIDUAL RECORDS—CAREER

Category	Name	Performance
Rushing (Yds.)	Deuce McAllister, 2001-08	6,096
Passing (Yds.)	Archie Manning, 1971-1982	21,734
Passing (TDs)	Drew Brees, 2006-09	122
Receiving (No.)	Eric Martin, 1985-1993	532
Receiving (Yds.)	Eric Martin, 1985-1993	7,854
Interceptions	Dave Waymer, 1980-89	37
Punting (Avg.)	Mark Royals, 1997-98	45.8
Punt Return (Avg.)	Mel Gray, 1986-88	13.4
Kickoff Return (Avg.)	Courtney Roby, 2008-09	26.7
Field Goals	Morten Andersen, 1982-1994	302
Touchdowns (Tot.)	Deuce McAllister, 2001-08	55
Points	Morten Andersen, 1982-1994	1,318
*Sacks	Rickey Jackson, 1981-1993	115.0

INDIVIDUAL RECORDS—SINGLE SEASON

Category	Name	Performance
Rushing (Yds.)	George Rogers, 1981	1,674
Passing (Yds.)	Drew Brees, 2008	5,069
Passing (TDs)	Drew Brees, 2008, 2009	34
Receiving (No.)	Marques Colston, 2007	98
Receiving (Yds.)	Joe Horn, 2004	1,399
Interceptions	Dave Whitsell, 1967	10
Punting (Avg.)	Mark Royals, 1997	45.9
Punt Return (Avg.)	Mel Gray, 1987	14.7
Kickoff Return (Avg.)	John Gilliam, 1967	30.1
Field Goals	Morten Andersen, 1985	31
	John Carney, 2002	31
Touchdowns (Tot.)	Dalton Hilliard, 1989	18
Points	John Carney, 2002	130
*Sacks	Pat Swilling, 1991	17.0
	La'Roi Glover, 2000	17.0

INDIVIDUAL RECORDS—SINGLE GAME

Category	Name	Performance
Rushing (Yds.)	George Rogers, 9-4-83	206
Passing (Yds.)	Drew Brees, 11-19-06	510
Passing (TDs)	Billy Kilmer, 11-2-69	6
	Drew Brees, 9-13-09	6
Receiving (No.)	Tony Galbreath, 9-10-78	14
Receiving (Yds.)	Wes Chandler, 9-2-79	205
Interceptions	Tommy Myers, 9-3-78	3
	Dave Waymer, 10-6-85	3
	Reggie Sutton, 10-18-87	3
	Gene Atkins, 12-22-91	3
	Sammy Knight, 9-9-01	3
Field Goals	Many times	5
	Last time by John Carney, 9-26-04	
Touchdowns (Tot.)	Joe Horn, 12-14-03	4
	Reggie Bush, 12-3-06	4
Points	Joe Horn, 12-14-03	24
	Reggie Bush, 12-3-06	24
*Sacks	Many times	4.0
	Last time by Wayne Martin, 9-21-97	

**Sacks became an official statistic in 1982.*

NEW ORLEANS SAINTS

2010 VETERAN ROSTER

No.	Name	Pos.	Ht.	Wt.	Birthdate	NFL Exp.	College	Hometown	How Acq.	'09 Games/ Starts
53	Arnoux, Stanley	LB	6-0	233	9/9/86	2	Wake Forest	Sunrise, Fla.	D4b-'09	0*
87	Arrington, Adrian	WR	6-3	192	11/7/85	2	Michigan	Cedar Rapids, Iowa	D7-'08	0*
92	Ayodele, Remi	DT	6-2	318	4/22/83	4	Oklahoma	Grand Prairie, Texas	FA-'08	15/13
9	Brees, Drew	QB	6-0	209	1/15/79	10	Purdue	Austin, Texas	UFA(SD)-'06	15/15
96	Brown, Alex	DE	6-3	260	6/4/79	9	Florida	White Springs, Fla.	FA-'10	16/16*
70	+Brown, Jammal	T	6-6	313	3/30/81	6	Oklahoma	Lawton, Okla.	D1-'05	0*
11	#Brunell, Mark	QB	6-1	217	9/17/70	18	Washington	Santa Maria, Calif.	FA-'08	16/1
25	Bush, Reggie	RB	6-0	203	3/2/85	5	Southern California	Spring Valley, Calif.	D1-'06	14/8
74	Bushrod, Jermon	T	6-5	315	8/19/84	4	Towson	King George, Va.	D4b-'07	15/14
52	Casillas, Jonathan	LB	6-1	227	6/3/87	2	Wisconsin	New Brunswick, N.J.	FA-'09	11/2
97	Charleston, Jeff	DE	6-4	265	1/19/83	4	Idaho State	Oregon City, Ore.	FA-'09	16/0
12	Colston, Marques	WR	6-4	225	6/5/83	5	Hofstra	Harrisburg, Pa.	D7b-'06	16/14
10	Daniel, Chase	QB	6-0	225	10/7/86	2	Missouri	Southlake, Texas	FA-'09	0*
56	Dunbar, Jo-Lonn	LB	6-0	226	3/13/85	3	Boston College	Syracuse, N.Y.	FA-'08	9/3
98	Ellis, Sedrick	DT	6-1	307	7/9/85	3	Southern California	Chino, Calif.	D1-'08	10/10
44	Evans, Heath	FB	6-0	250	12/30/78	10	Auburn	West Palm Beach, Fla.	UFA(NE)-'09	6/5
73	Evans, Jahri	G	6-4	318	8/22/83	5	Bloomsburg	Philadelphia, Pa.	D4-'06	16/16
54	Evans, Troy	LB	6-3	238	12/3/77	9	Cincinnati	Cincinnati, Ohio	UFA(Hou)-'07	16/2
20	Gay, Randall	CB	5-11	190	5/5/82	7	Louisiana State	Brusly, La.	UFA(NE)-'08	14/7
75	Goddard, Na'Shan	G/T	6-5	315	4/23/83	2	South Carolina	Dayton, Ohio	FA-'10	0*
76	Goodwin, Jonathan	C	6-3	318	12/2/78	9	Michigan	Richland, S.C.	UFA(NYJ)-'06	16/16
33	Greer, Jabari	CB	5-11	180	2/11/82	7	Tennessee	Jackson, Tenn.	UFA(Buff)-'09	9/8
30	Hamilton, Lynell	RB	6-0	235	8/5/85	2	San Diego State	Stockton, Calif.	FA-'08	9/1
69	Hargrove, Anthony	DT/DE	6-3	272	7/20/83	6	Georgia Tech	Punta Gorda, Fla.	UFA(Buff)-'09	16/6
13	Harper, Rod	WR	6-0	209	3/26/85	2	Murray State	Bradenton, Fla.	FA-'09	0*
41	+Harper, Roman	S	6-1	200	12/11/82	5	Alabama	Prattville, Ala.	D2-'06	15/15
5	Hartley, Garrett	K	5-8	196	5/16/86	3	Oklahoma	Southlake, Texas	FA-'08	5/0
19	Henderson, Devery	WR	5-11	200	3/26/82	7	Louisiana State	Opelousas, La.	D2a-'04	16/11
43	Hill, P.J.	RB	5-10	218	1/3/87	2	Wisconsin	East Elmhurst, N.Y.	W(Wash)-'10	0*
84	Humphrey, Tory	TE	6-2	255	1/20/83	4	Central Michigan	Saginaw, Mich.	FA-'09	1/0
27	Jenkins, Malcolm	CB	6-0	204	12/20/87	2	Ohio State	Piscataway, N.J.	D1-'09	14/6
35	Jones, Reggie	CB	6-0	193	3/15/86	2	Portland State	Federal Way, Wash.	FA-'09	0*
45	Keasey, Zak	FB	6-0	235	3/19/82	3	Princeton	Lake Orion, Mich.	FA-'10	0*
57	Kyle, Jason	LS	6-3	242	5/12/72	16	Arizona State	Tempe, Ariz.	FA-'09	16/0
60	Leckey, Nick	C	6-3	291	3/12/82	7	Kansas State	Grapevine, Texas	UFA(StL)-'09	8/0
95	Leisle, Rodney	DT	6-3	315	2/5/81	4	UCLA	Bakersfield, Calif.	FA-'09	1/0
46	Mailei, Marcus	FB	6-0	255	10/30/86	2	Weber State	Salt Lake City, Utah	FA-'09	2/0
93	McCray, Bobby	DE	6-6	260	8/8/81	7	Florida	Homestead, Fla.	UFA(Jax)-'08	16/0
17	Meachem, Robert	WR	6-2	210	9/28/84	4	Tennessee	Tulsa, Okla.	D1-'07	16/7
50	Mitchell, Marvin	LB	6-3	249	10/21/84	4	Tennessee	Norfolk, Va.	D7-'07	14/2
16	+Moore, Lance	WR	5-9	190	8/31/83	5	Toledo	Westerville, Ohio	FA-'07	7/0
6	Morstead, Thomas	P	6-4	225	3/7/86	2	Southern Methodist	Pearland, Texas	D5-'09	16/0
77	Nicks, Carl	G	6-5	343	5/14/85	3	Nebraska	Salinas, Calif.	D5b-'08	16/16
22	Porter, Tracy	CB	5-11	186	8/11/86	3	Indiana	Port Allen, La.	D2-'08	12/11
90	Pressley, DeMario	DT	6-3	301	11/3/85	3	North Carolina State	Greensboro, N.C.	D5a-'08	7/0
31	Prioleau, Pierson	S	5-11	188	8/6/77	12	Virginia Tech	Alvin, S.C.	UFA(Jax)-'09	16/1
39	Reis, Chris	S	6-1	215	9/19/83	4	Georgia Tech	Roswell, Ga.	FA-'07	15/1
15	Roby, Courtney	WR	6-0	189	1/10/83	5	Indiana	Indianapolis, Ind.	FA-'09	15/0
58	Shanle, Scott	LB	6-2	245	11/23/79	8	Nebraska	St. Edward, Neb.	T(Dall)-'06	14/14
42	Sharper, Darren	S	6-2	210	11/3/75	14	William & Mary	Richmond, Va.	UFA(Min)-'09	14/14
88	Shockey, Jeremy	TE	6-5	251	8/18/80	9	Miami	Ada, Okla.	T(NYG)-'08	13/12
91	Smith, Will	DE	6-3	282	7/4/81	7	Ohio State	Utica, N.Y.	D1-'04	16/16
78	Stinchcomb, Jon	T	6-5	315	8/27/79	8	Georgia	Lilburn, Ga.	D2-'03	16/16
64	Strief, Zach	T	6-7	320	9/22/83	5	Northwestern	Milford, Ohio	D7a-'06	16/2
85	Thomas, David	TE	6-3	248	7/5/83	5	Texas	Plainview, Texas	T(NE)-'09	15/8
23	+Thomas, Pierre	RB	5-11	215	12/18/84	4	Illinois	Lynwood, Ill.	FA-'07	14/6
24	Torrence, Leigh	CB	5-11	179	1/4/82	5	Stanford	Atlanta, Ga.	W(Wash)-'08	5/0
21	Vaughn, Chip	S	6-2	221	10/26/85	2	Wake Forest	Fairfax, Va.	D4a-'09	0*
51	Vilma, Jonathan	LB	6-1	230	4/16/82	7	Miami	Coral Gables, Fla.	T(NYJ)-'08	15/15
59	Waters, Anthony	LB	6-3	238	7/25/84	4	Clemson	Lake View, S.C.	FA-'09	3/0
99	Wilkerson, Jimmy	DE/DT	6-2	270	1/4/81	8	Oklahoma	Naples, Texas	UFA(TB)-'10	15/15*
28	Young, Usama	S	6-0	200	5/8/85	4	Kent State	Largo, Md.	D3a-'07	12/1

* Arnoux missed '09 season because of injury; Arrington missed '09 season because of injury; A. Brown played 16 games with Chicago in '09; J. Brown missed '09 season because of injury; Daniel inactive for 7 games and active but did not play in 1 game; Goddard last active with Seattle in '08; Rod Harper missed '09 season because of injury; Hill did not play in 1 game with Philadelphia; Jones missed '09 season because of injury; Keasey last active with San Francisco in '08; Vaughn missed '09 season because of injury; Wilkerson played in 15 games with Tampa Bay.

\# Unrestricted free agent; subject to developments.

\+ Restricted free agent; subject to developments.

Players lost through free agency (2): RB Mike Bell (Phil; 13 games in '09), LB Scott Fujita (Cle; 11).

Also played with Saints in '09—K John Carney (11 games), DT Kendrick Clancy (2), TE Darnell Dinkins (11), FB Kyle Eckel (7), CB Greg Fassitt (1), DE Charles Grant (16), S Herana-Daze Jones (1), CB Chris McAlister (2), CB Mike McKenzie (5), G Jamar Nesbit (13), TE Buck Ortega (1).

2010 FIRST-YEAR ROSTER

Name	Pos.	Ht.	Wt.	Birthdate	College	Hometown	How Acq.
Billings, Montez	WR	6-1	181	6/15/86	Auburn	Pelham, Ala.	FA
Brown, Carlos	RB	6-0	212	4/28/88	Michigan	Franklin, Ga.	FA
Brown, Charles	T	6-5	297	4/10/87	Southern California	Chino Hills, Calif.	D2
Canfield, Sean	QB	6-4	223	11/12/86	Oregon State	Carlsbad, Calif.	D7
Carter, Brandon	G	6-6	319	9/10/86	Texas Tech	Longview, Texas	FA
Coleman, Harry	LB	6-2	212	11/10/85	Louisiana State	Baldwin, La.	FA
Duckworth, Tim (1)	G	6-4	318	9/14/82	Auburn	Taylorsville, Miss.	FA-'09
Ducré, Christian	RB	5-11	225	4/8/87	Mississippi State	LaCombe, La.	FA
Fassitt, Greg (1)	CB	5-11	186	4/4/85	Grambling State	New Orleans, La.	FA-'09
Galette, Junior	DE	6-2	258	3/27/88	Stillman	Spring Valley, N.Y.	FA
Graham, Jimmy	TE	6-6	260	11/24/86	Miami	Goldsboro, N.C.	D3
Gresham, Clint	LS	6-3	238	8/24/86	Texas Christian	Corpus Christi, Texas	FA
Hamilton, Ryan	S	6-1	206	2/16/87	Vanderbilt	Wycombe, Pa.	FA
Heyman, Earl (1)	DT	6-1	289	9/5/87	Louisville	Louisville, Ky.	FA-'09
Ivory, Chris	RB	6-0	222	3/22/88	Tiffin	Longview, Texas	FA
Lorenzen, Tyler (1)	TE	6-5	229	12/24/85	Connecticut	Fremont, Iowa	FA-'09
Maxwell, Sam	LB	6-2	244	5/13/87	Kentucky	Hartwell, Ga.	FA
Parnell, Jermey (1)	T	6-6	278	7/20/86	Mississippi	Gosnell, Ark.	FA-'09
Robinson, Patrick	CB	5-11	191	9/7/87	Florida State	Miami, Fla.	D1
Ross, Jay	DT	6-3	302	10/3/87	East Carolina	Wilmington, N.C.	FA
Sharpe, Brandon	DE	6-2	254	12/22/86	Texas Tech	Lyons, Ga.	FA
Sharpe, Glenn (1)	CB	6-0	184	2/27/84	Miami	Miami, Fla.	FA
Simon, Matt (1)	WR	6-1	199	12/4/85	Northern Illinois	Farmington, Minn.	FA
Tennant, Matt	C	6-4	300	3/19/87	Boston College	Cincinnati, Ohio	D5
Tonga, Joe	G	6-4	313	12/8/84	Indiana (Pa.)	Taylorsville, Utah	FA
Woods, Al	DT	6-4	307	3/25/87	Louisiana State	Elton, La.	D4
Young, Marcell	CB	6-0	183	9/2/87	Jackson State	Jackson, Miss.	FA

The term NFL Rookie is defined as a player who is in his first season of professional football and has not been on the roster of another professional football team for any regular-season or postseason games. A Rookie is designated by an "R" on NFL rosters. Players who have been active in another professional football league or players who have NFL experience, including either preseason training camp or being on an Active List or Inactive List, or on Reserve/Injured or Reserve/Physically Unable to Perform for fewer than six regular-season games, are termed NFL First-Year Players. An NFL First-Year Player is designated by a "1" on NFL rosters. Thereafter, a player is credited with an additional year of experience for each season in which he accumulates six games on the Active List or Inactive List, or on Reserve/Injured or Reserve/Physically Unable to Perform.

Log on to www.neworleanssaints.com for an up-to-date roster.

NEW ORLEANS SAINTS

COACHING STAFF

Head Coach,
Sean Payton

Pro Career: Named the fourteenth head coach in Saints history on Jan. 18, 2006 and twice in his first four seasons led the Saints to NFC South division titles, NFC Championship Game appearances and their first Super Bowl appearance and victory in Super Bowl XLIV. Earned unanimous NFL coach of the year honors in his first season in 2006 and received the same honors from some outlets in 2009. Considered one of the NFL's brightest offensive minds, the Saints have ranked among the league's most productive offenses each season since his arrival, including finishing first in the NFL in 2009, 2008 and 2006 and ranking fourth in 2007. He arrived in New Orleans following a three-year stint with Dallas Cowboys, serving as the assistant head coach/passing game coordinator in 2005 after spending his first two seasons as assistant head coach/quarterbacks. Additional experience includes four years with the New York Giants (1999-2002), the last three seasons as offensive coordinator. Also previously worked for the Philadelphia Eagles (1997-98) as quarterbacks coach. Career record: 42-27.

Background: Earned a degree in communications at Eastern Illinois, where he departed with a school-record 10,665 passing yards, then the third-highest total in NCAA Division I-AA history. A three-time All-American, Payton had brief playing stops with Chicago of the Arena Football League, the Ottawa Rough Riders of the Canadian Football League and the Chicago Bears in 1987. Inducted into the Eastern Illinois Hall of Fame in 2000, Payton coached collegiately at San Diego State (1988-89, 1992-93), Indiana State (1990-91), and Miami (Ohio) in 1994-95.

Personal: Born Dec. 29, 1963 in San Mateo, Calif. and raised in Naperville, Ill, Payton and his wife, Beth, have a daughter, Meghan, and a son, Connor.

ASSISTANT COACHES

Dennis Allen, secondary; born Sept. 22, 1972, Atlanta. Safety Texas A&M 1992-95. No pro playing experience. College coach: Texas A&M 1996-99, Tulsa 2000-01. Pro coach: Atlanta Falcons 2002-05, joined Saints in 2006.

Charles Byrd, asst. strength and conditioning; born June 24, 1981, Oxford, Ohio. Defensive back Morehead State 2001-04. Pro defensive back Las Vegas Gladiators (AFL) 2006. College coach: Miami (Ohio) 2006-07. Pro coach: Joined Saints in 2008.

Pete Carmichael Jr., offensive coordinator; born October 6, 1971, Framingham, Mass. Attended Boston College. No college or pro playing experience. College coach: New Hampshire 1994, Louisiana Tech 1995-99. Pro coach: Cleveland Browns 2000, Washington Redskins 2001, San Diego Chargers 2002-05, joined Saints in 2006.

Dan Dalrymple, head strength and conditioning; born Aug. 26, 1965, Cleveland. Offensive lineman Miami (Ohio) 1983-86. No pro playing experience. College coach: Miami (Ohio) 1987-2005. Pro coach: Joined Saints in 2006.

Bret Ingalls, running backs; born Aug. 19, 1960, San Jose, Calif. Running back Wichita State 1979-1981. No pro playing experience. College coach: Idaho 1982-88, San Diego State 1989-1993, Eastern Michigan 1994, Louisville 1995-96, Northern Iowa 1997-99, Idaho 2000-03, Indiana State 2004, Miami (Ohio) 2005, Northwestern 2006-08. Pro coach: Joined Saints in 2009.

Bill Johnson, defensive line; born June 23, 1955, Monroe, La. Defensive lineman Northwestern (La.) State 1976-79. No pro playing experience. College coach: Northwestern (La.) 1980-84, McNeese State 1985-86, Miami 1987, Louisiana Tech 1988-89, Arkansas 1990-91, 2000, Texas A&M 1992-99. Pro coach: Atlanta Falcons 2001-06, Denver Broncos 2007-08, joined Saints in 2009.

Curtis Johnson, wide receivers; born November 5, 1961, New Orleans. Wide receiver Idaho 1979-1983. No pro playing experience. College coach: Idaho 1987-88, San Diego State 1989-1993, Southern Methodist 1994, California 1995, Miami 1996-2005. Pro coach: Joined Saints in 2006.

Travis Jones, asst. defensive line; born June 6, 1972, Milledgeville, Ga. Linebacker Georgia 1991-94. Pro linebacker Baltimore Stallions (CFL) 1995. College coach: Georgia: 1997, Appalachian State 1998-2000, Kansas 2001-02, Louisiana State 2003-04. Pro coach: Miami Dolphins 2005-07, joined Saints in 2008.

Aaron Kromer, offensive line/running game; born April 30, 1967, Sandusky, Ohio. Offensive tackle Miami (Ohio) 1986-89. No pro playing experience. College coach: Miami (Ohio) 1990-98, Northwestern 1999-2000. Pro coach: Oakland Raiders 2001-04, Tampa Bay Buccaneers 2005-07, joined Saints in 2008.

Joe Lombardi, quarterbacks; born June 6, 1981, Seattle. Tight end Air Force 1992-94. No pro playing experience. College coach: Dayton 1996-98, Virginia Military Institute 1999, Bucknell 2000, Mercyhurst 2002-05. Pro coach: New York/New Jersey Hitmen (XFL) 2001, Atlanta Falcons 2006, joined Saints in 2007.

Mike Mallory, asst. special teams; born Nov. 16, 1962, Bowling Green, Ohio. Linebacker Michigan 1982-85. No pro playing experience. College coach: Indiana 1986-87, Kent State 1989-1990, Eastern Illinois 1991-92, Rhode Island 1993-95, Northern Illinois 1996-99, Maryland 2000, Illinois 2001-05, Kansas 2006, Louisville 2007. Pro coach: Joined Saints in 2008.

Terry Malone, tight ends; born February 26, 1960, Buffalo. Tight end Holy Cross 1978-1982. No pro playing experience. College coach: Arizona 1983-84, Holy Cross 1985, Bowling Green 1986-1995, Boston College 1996, Michigan 1997-2005. Pro coach: Joined Saints in 2006.

Greg McMahon, special teams coordinator; born Jan. 2, 1960, Rantoul, Ill. Defensive back Eastern Illinois 1978-1981. No pro playing experience. College coach: Eastern Illinois 1982, Minnesota 1983-84, North Alabama 1985-87, Southern Illinois 1988, Valdosta State 1989, Nevada Las-Vegas 1990-91, Illinois 1992-2004, East Carolina 2005. Pro coach: Joined Saints in 2006.

Tony Oden, asst. secondary; born June 30, 1973, Cleveland. Linebacker Baldwin-Wallace College 1991-95. No pro playing experience. College coach: Millersville (Penn.) 1996, Boston College 1997, Army 1998-99, East Carolina 2000-02, Eastern Michigan 2003. Pro coach: Houston Texans 2004-05, joined Saints in 2006.

Carter Sheridan, offensive assistant/asst. player programs; born Nov. 20, 1977, New Orleans. Defensive back Florida A&M 1996-98. No pro playing experience. Pro coach: Joined Saints in 2006.

Frank Smith, coaching assistant; born February 21, 1981, Milwaukee. Offensive lineman Miami (Ohio) 1999-2003. No pro playing experience. College coach: Miami (Ohio) 2004-05, Butler 2006-09. Pro coach: Joined Saints in 2010.

Marcus Ungaro, coaching assistant; born October 9, 1984, Seattle. Defensive back Southwestern College 2004-05. No pro playing experience. Pro coach: Joined Saints in 2010.

Joe Vitt, asst. head coach/linebackers, born August 23, 1954, Syracuse, N.Y. Linebacker Towson State 1974-78. No pro playing experience. Pro coach: Baltimore Colts 1979-1981, Seattle Seahawks 1982-1991, Los Angeles Rams 1992-94, Philadelphia Eagles 1995-98, Green Bay Packers 1999, Kansas City Chiefs 2000-03, St. Louis Rams 2004-05 (head coach, final 11 games of 2005), joined Saints in 2006.

Blake Williams, coaching assistant; born Dec. 30, 1984, Independence, Mo. Defensive back Princeton 2003-07. No pro playing experience. Pro coach: Washington Redskins 2006-07, Jacksonville Jaguars 2008, joined Saints in 2009.

Gregg Williams, defensive coordinator; born July 15, 1958, Excelsior Springs, Mo. Quarterback Northeastern Missouri State 1976-79. No pro playing experience. College coach: Houston 1988-89. Pro coach: Houston Oilers/Tennessee Titans 1990-2000, Buffalo Bills 2001-03 (head coach), Washington Redskins 2004-07, Jacksonville Jaguars 2008, joined Saints in 2009.

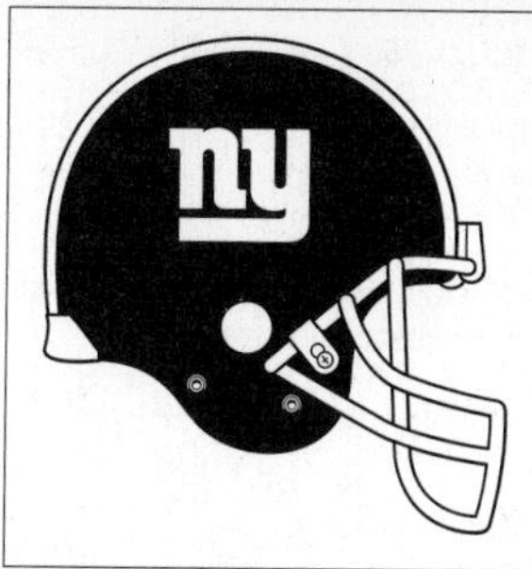

National Football Conference
East Division
Team Colors: Blue, Red, and White
Timex Performance Center
1925 Giants Drive
East Rutherford, New Jersey 07073
Telephone: (201) 935-8111

2010 SCHEDULE

PRESEASON

Aug. 16	at New York Jets	8:00
Aug. 21	**Pittsburgh**	7:00
Aug. 28	at Baltimore	7:30
Sep. 2	**New England**	7:00

REGULAR SEASON

Sep. 12	**Carolina**	1:00
Sep. 19	at Indianapolis	8:20
Sep. 26	**Tennessee**	1:00
Oct. 3	**Chicago**	8:20
Oct. 10	at Houston	12:00
Oct. 17	**Detroit**	1:00
Oct. 25	at Dallas (Mon)	7:30
Oct. 31	BYE	
Nov. 7	at Seattle	1:05
Nov. 14	**Dallas**	4:15
Nov. 21	at Philadelphia	* 8:20
Nov. 28	**Jacksonville**	1:00
Dec. 5	**Washington**	1:00
Dec. 12	at Minnesota	12:00
Dec. 19	**Philadelphia**	1:00
Dec. 26	at Green Bay	3:15
Jan. 2	at Washington	1:00

** Sunday night games in Weeks 11-17 subject to change*

Stadium: New Meadowlands Stadium
(opens in 2010)
• **Capacity:** 82,500
East Rutherford, New Jersey 07073
Playing Surface: FieldTurf
Training Camp: University at Albany
1400 Washington Avenue
Albany, New York 12222

NEW MEADOWLANDS STADIUM

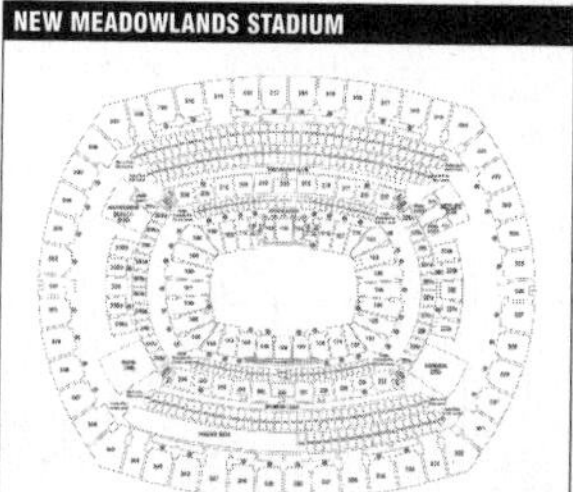

CLUB OFFICIALS

President/CEO: John K. Mara
Chairman/EVP: Steve Tisch
Treasurer: Jonathan Tisch
Senior Vice President-General Manager: Jerry Reese
Senior Vice President and Chief Marketing Officer: Michael Stevens
Vice President-Player Evaluations: Chris Mara
Vice President and Chief Financial Officer: Christine Procops
Senior Vice President-Marketing: John Maguire
Vice President-Marketing: Rusty Hawley
VP/Medical Services: Ronnie Barnes
Vice President-Communications: Pat Hanlon
Vice President, Media and Partnerships: Dan Lynch
Vice President and Executive Producer, Giants Entertainment: Don Sperling
Vice President Business Development: Doug Smoyer
Assistant General Manager: Kevin Abrams
Director of Pro Player Personnel: David Gettleman
Assistant Director of Pro Player Personnel: Ken Sternfeld
Director of College Scouting: Marc Ross
Director of Research and Development: Raymond J. Walsh, Jr.
Director of Player Development: Charles Way
Pro Personnel Assistants: Jeremy Breit, Matthew Shauger
Director of Promotions: Frank Mara
Ticket Manager: John Gorman
Director of Administration: Jim Phelan
Controller: Steven Hamrahi
Director of Community Relations: Allison Stangeby
Director of Creative Services: Doug Murphy
Director of Public/Media Relations: Peter John-Baptiste
Assistant Director of Communications: Avis Roper
Head Athletic Trainer: Ronnie Barnes
Assistant Athletic Trainers: Steve Kennelly, Byron Hansen, Leigh Weiss
Equipment/Locker Room Manager: Ed Wagner, Jr.
Equipment Director: Joseph Skiba
Assistant Equipment Managers: Ed Skiba, Tim Slaman
Video Director: Dave Maltese
Assistant Video Directors: Carmen Pizzano, Ed Triggs, Steve Venditti
Assistant Director of Community Relations: Ethan Medley
Directors of Information Technology: Julie Glisky, Justin Warren
Director of Marketing Services & Youth Programs: Beth Roche

COACHING HISTORY
(646-542-33)
Records include postseason games

1925	Bob Folwell	8-4-0
1926	Joe Alexander	8-4-1
1927-28	Earl Potteiger	15-8-3
1929-1930	LeRoy Andrews*	24-5-1
1930	Benny Friedman-Steve Owen	2-0-0
1931-1953	Steve Owen	153-108-17
1954-1960	Jim Lee Howell	55-29-4
1961-68	Allie Sherman	57-54-4
1969-1973	Alex Webster	29-40-1
1974-76	Bill Arnsparger**	7-28-0
1976-78	John McVay	14-23-0
1979-1982	Ray Perkins	24-35-0
1983-1990	Bill Parcells	85-52-1
1991-92	Ray Handley	14-18-0
1993-96	Dan Reeves	32-34-0
1997-2003	Jim Fassel	60-56-1
2004-09	Tom Coughlin	59-44-0

*Released after 15 games in 1930
**Released after seven games in 1976

PAID ATTENDANCE

Home 629,417 Away 575,959
Total 1,205,376
Single-game home record, 79,378 (1/8/06)
Single-season home record, 629,874 (2004)

2010 DRAFT CHOICES

Round	Name	Pos.	College
1	Jason Pierre-Paul	DE	South Florida
2	Linval Joseph	DT	East Carolina
3	Chad Jones	DB	Louisiana State
4	Phillip Dillard	LB	Nebraska
5	Mitch Petrus	G	Arkansas
6	Adrian Tracy	LB	William & Mary
7	Matt Dodge	P	East Carolina

NEW YORK GIANTS

2009 TEAM RECORD

PRESEASON (1-3)

Date	Result	Opponent
8/17	W 24-17	Carolina
8/22	L 3-17	at Chicago
8/29	L 25-27	New York Jets
9/3	L 27-38	at New England

REGULAR SEASON (8-8)

Date	Result	Opponent
9/13	W 23-17	Washington
9/20	W 33-31	at Dallas
9/27	W 24-0	at Tampa Bay
10/4	W 27-16	at Kansas City
10/11	W 44-7	Oakland
10/18	L 27-48	at New Orleans
10/25	L 17-24	Arizona
11/1	L 17-40	at Philadelphia
11/8	L 20-21	San Diego
11/22	W 34-31	Atlanta (OT)
11/26	L 6-26	at Denver
12/6	W 31-24	Dallas
12/13	L 38-45	Philadelphia
12/21	W 45-12	at Washington
12/27	L 9-41	Carolina
1/3	L 7-44	at Minnesota

(OT) Overtime

SCORE BY PERIODS

Giants	57	159	77	106	3	— 402
Opponents	64	169	100	94	0	— 427

2009 TEAM STATISTICS

	Giants	Opp.
Total First Downs	323	308
Rushing	103	103
Passing	194	182
Penalty	26	23
3rd Down: Made/Att	90/210	77/199
3rd Down Pct.	42.9	38.7
4th Down: Made/Att	9/15	12/19
4th Down Pct.	60.0	63.2
Possession Avg.	31:34	28:26
Total Net Yards	5856	5198
Avg. Per Game	366.0	324.9
Total Plays	1017	953
Avg. Per Play	5.8	5.5
Net Yards Rushing	1837	1773
Avg. Per Game	114.8	110.8
Total Rushes	443	423
Net Yards Passing	4019	3425
Avg. Per Game	251.2	214.1
Sacked/Yards Lost	32/227	32/237
Gross Yards	4246	3662
Att./Completions	542/338	498/314
Completion Pct.	62.4	63.1
Had Intercepted	14	13
Punts/Average	64/40.7	72/44.0
Net Punting Avg.	64/36.0	72/38.0
Penalties/Yards	95/802	88/678
Fumbles/Ball Lost	30/17	28/11
Touchdowns	46	54
Rushing	14	21
Passing	28	31
Returns	4	2

2009 INDIVIDUAL STATISTICS

PASSING	Att.	Comp.	Yds.	Pct.	TD	Int.	Tkld.	Rate
Manning	509	317	4021	62.3	27	14	30/216	93.1
Carr	33	21	225	63.6	1	0	2/11	93.6
Giants	542	338	4246	62.4	28	14	32/227	93.2
Opponents	498	314	3662	63.1	31	13	32/237	95.1

SCORING	TD R	TD P	TD Rt	PAT	FG	Saf	PTS
Tynes	0	0	0	45/45	27/32	0	126
Bradshaw	7	0	0	0/0	0/0	0	42
Smith	0	7	0	0/0	0/0	0	42
Jacobs	5	1	0	0/0	0/0	0	36
Nicks	0	6	0	0/0	0/0	0	36
Boss	0	5	0	0/0	0/0	0	30
Manningham	0	5	0	0/0	0/0	0	30
Hixon	0	1	1	0/0	0/0	0	12
Carr	1	0	0	0/0	0/0	0	6
Hagan	0	1	0	0/0	0/0	0	6
Hedgecock	0	1	0	0/0	0/0	0	6
B. Johnson	0	0	1	0/0	0/0	0	6
Moss	0	1	0	0/0	0/0	0	6
Thomas	0	0	1	0/0	0/0	0	6
Umenyiora	0	0	1	0/0	0/0	0	6
Ware	1	0	0	0/0	0/0	0	6
Giants	14	28	4	45/45	27/32	0	402
Opponents	21	31	2	47/51	18/21	0	427

2-Pt. Conversions: Giants 0-1, Opponents 1-3.

RUSHING	No.	Yds	Avg	LG	TD
Jacobs	224	835	3.7	31	5
Bradshaw	163	778	4.8	38	7
Ware	13	73	5.6	14	1
Manning	17	65	3.8	14	0
G. Johnson	13	43	3.3	11	0
Carr	9	27	3.0	12t	1
Boss	1	16	16.0	16	0
Nicks	2	8	4.0	9	0
Feagles	1	-8	-8.0	-8	0
Giants	443	1837	4.1	38	14
Opponents	423	1773	4.2	66t	21

RECEIVING	No.	Yds	Avg	LG	TD
Smith	107	1220	11.4	51	7
Manningham	57	822	14.4	49	5
Nicks	47	790	16.8	68t	6
Boss	42	567	13.5	35	5
Bradshaw	21	207	9.9	55	0
Jacobs	18	184	10.2	74t	1
Hixon	15	187	12.5	61t	1
Hagan	8	101	12.6	23t	1
Beckum	8	55	6.9	15	0
Da. Johnson	5	32	6.4	14	0
Hedgecock	4	23	5.8	9	1
Ware	3	15	5.0	14	0
Moss	1	18	18.0	18t	1
Barden	1	16	16.0	16	0
Pascoe	1	9	9.0	9	0
Giants	338	4246	12.6	74t	28
Opponents	314	3662	11.7	60t	31

INTERCEPTIONS	No.	Yds	Avg	LG	TD
Thomas	5	87	17.4	33	1
B. Johnson	2	83	41.5	49	1
Phillips	2	22	11.0	22	0
Blackburn	1	24	24.0	24	0
Goff	1	5	5.0	5	0
M. Johnson	1	0	0.0	0	0
Webster	1	0	0.0	0	0
Rouse TM	0	0	—	—	0
Giants	13	221	17.0	49	2
Opponents	14	106	7.6	37	0

PUNTING	No.	Yds.	Avg.	In 20	LG
Feagles	64	2604	40.7	23	59
Giants	64	2604	40.7	23	59
Opponents	72	3169	44.0	26	59

PUNT RETURNS	Ret	FC	Yds	Avg	LG	TD
Hixon	17	17	256	15.1	79t	1
Moss	11	0	74	6.7	16	0
Bradshaw	6	1	55	9.2	20	0
Webster	1	0	8	8.0	8	0
Dockery	1	0	0	0.0	0	0
Giants	36	18	393	10.9	79t	1
Opponents	28	14	258	9.2	72t	1

KICKOFF RETURNS	No.	Yds	Avg	LG	TD
Hixon	57	1291	22.6	68	0
Moss	6	109	18.2	29	0
Ware	2	37	18.5	20	0
Nicks	1	16	16.0	16	0
G. Johnson	1	15	15.0	15	0
Hedgecock	1	8	8.0	8	0
Beckum	1	3	3.0	3	0
Blackburn	1	3	3.0	3	0
Beatty	1	0	0.0	0	0
Giants	71	1482	20.9	68	0
Opponents	77	1619	21.0	53	0

FIELD GOALS	1-19	20-29	30-39	40-49	50+
Tynes	0/0	10/12	11/13	5/6	1/1
Giants	0/0	10/12	11/13	5/6	1/1
Opponents	0/0	8/8	8/9	2/3	0/1

SACKS	No.
Umenyiora	7.0
Tuck	6.0
Kiwanuka	3.0
D. Clark	2.0
Robbins	2.0
Bernard	1.0
Boley	1.0
Cofield	1.0
Goff	1.0
B. Johnson	1.0
M. Johnson	1.0
Pierce	1.0
Rouse	1.0
Sintim	1.0
Thomas	1.0
Tollefson	1.0
Blackburn	0.5
Canty	0.5
Giants	32.0
Opponents	32.0

RECORD HOLDERS

INDIVIDUAL RECORDS—CAREER

Category	Name	Performance
Rushing (Yds.)	Tiki Barber, 1997-2006	10,449
Passing (Yds.)	Phil Simms, 1979-1993	33,462
Passing (TDs)	Phil Simms, 1979-1993	199
Receiving (No.)	Amani Toomer, 1996-2008	668
Receiving (Yds.)	Amani Toomer, 1996-2008	9,497
Interceptions	Emlen Tunnell, 1948-1958	74
Punting (Avg.)	Don Chandler, 1956-1964	43.8
Punt Return (Avg.)	Ward Cuff, 1941-45	12.1
Kickoff Return (Avg.)	Rocky Thompson, 1971-73	27.2
Field Goals	Pete Gogolak, 1966-1974	126
Touchdowns (Tot.)	Frank Gifford, 1952-1964	78
Points	Pete Gogolak, 1966-1974	646
*Sacks	Michael Strahan, 1993-2007	141.5

INDIVIDUAL RECORDS—SINGLE SEASON

Category	Name	Performance
Rushing (Yds.)	Tiki Barber, 2005	1,860
Passing (Yds.)	Kerry Collins, 2002	4,073
Passing (TDs)	Y.A. Tittle, 1963	36
Receiving (No.)	Steve Smith, 2009	107
Receiving (Yds.)	Amani Toomer, 2002	1,343
Interceptions	Otto Schnellbacher, 1951	11
	Jim Patton, 1958	11
Punting (Avg.)	Don Chandler, 1959	46.6
Punt Return (Avg.)	Merle Hapes, 1942	15.5
Kickoff Return (Avg.)	John Salscheider, 1949	31.6
Field Goals	Ali Haji-Sheikh, 1983	35
	Jay Feely, 2005	35
	John Carney, 2008	35
Touchdowns (Tot.)	Joe Morris, 1985	21
Points	Jay Feely, 2005	148
*Sacks	Michael Strahan, 2001	**22.5

INDIVIDUAL RECORDS—SINGLE GAME

Category	Name	Performance
Rushing (Yds.)	Tiki Barber, 12-30-06	234
Passing (Yds.)	Phil Simms, 10-13-85	513
Passing (TDs)	Y.A. Tittle, 10-28-62	**7
Receiving (No.)	Tiki Barber, 1-2-00	13
Receiving (Yds.)	Del Shofner, 10-28-62	269
Interceptions	Many times	3
	Last time by Terry Kinard, 9-20-87	
Field Goals	Joe Danelo, 10-18-81	6
Touchdowns (Tot.)	Ron Johnson, 10-2-72	4
	Earnest Gray, 9-7-80	4
	Rodney Hampton, 9-24-95	4
Points	Ron Johnson, 10-2-72	24
	Earnest Gray, 9-7-80	24
	Rodney Hampton, 9-24-95	24
*Sacks	Osi Umenyiora, 9-30-07	6.0

**Sacks became an official statistic in 1982.*
***NFL Record*

NEW YORK GIANTS

2010 VETERAN ROSTER

No.	Name	Pos.	Ht.	Wt.	Birthdate	NFL Exp.	College	Hometown	How Acq.	'09 Games/ Starts
93	Alford, Jay	DT	6-3	304	5/28/83	4	Penn State	Orange, N.J.	D3-'07	0*
13	Barden, Ramses	WR	6-6	227	1/1/86	2	Cal Poly	La Canada Flintridge, Calif.	D3-'09	3/0
65	Beatty, Will	T	6-6	307	3/2/85	2	Connecticut	York, Pa.	D2-'09	16/4
47	Beckum, Travis	TE	6-3	239	1/24/87	2	Wisconsin	Milwaukee, Wisc.	D3-'09	15/2
78	Bender, Jacob	OL	6-6	316	4/25/85	3	Nicholls State	Mayo, Md.	FA-'09	0*
95	Bernard, Rocky	DT	6-3	308	4/19/79	9	Texas A&M	Baytown, Texas	UFA(Sea)-'09	15/0
57	Blackburn, Chase	LB	6-3	247	6/10/83	6	Akron	Marysville, Ohio	FA-'05	16/7
59	Boley, Michael	LB	6-3	223	8/24/82	6	Southern Miss	Elkmont, Ala.	UFA(Atl)-'09	11/11
77	Boothe, Kevin	G	6-5	315	7/5/83	5	Cornell	Fort Lauderdale, Fla.	W(Oak)-'07	16/2
89	Boss, Kevin	TE	6-6	253	1/11/84	4	Western Oregon	Philomath, Ore.	D5-'07	15/15
44	Bradshaw, Ahmad	RB	5-9	198	3/19/86	4	Marshall	Bluefield, Va.	D7b-'07	15/1
37	Brown, Courtney	DB	6-1	204	2/10/84	3	Cal Poly	Berkeley, Calif.	FA-'10	0*
99	Canty, Chris	DL	6-7	304	11/10/82	6	Virginia	Charlotte, N.C.	UFA(Dall)-'09	8/4
85	Chandler, Scott	TE	6-7	272	7/23/85	2	Iowa	Bedford, Texas	FA-'09	0*
96	Cofield, Barry	DT	6-4	306	3/19/84	5	Northwestern	Cleveland Heights, Ohio	D4a-'06	16/16
51	DeOssie, Zak	LB	6-4	249	5/24/84	4	Brown	No. Andover, Mass.	D4-'07	16/0
66	Diehl, David	T	6-5	319	9/15/80	8	Illinois	Oak Lawn, Ill.	D5-'03	16/16
54	Goff, Jonathan	LB	6-2	236	12/12/85	3	Vanderbilt	Lynn, Mass.	D5-'08	16/4
34	Grant, Deon	S	6-2	215	3/14/79	11	Tennessee	Augusta, Ga.	FA-'10	16/16*
80	Hagan, Derek	WR	6-2	215	9/21/84	5	Arizona State	Palmdale, Calif.	FA-'08	16/0
39	Hedgecock, Madison	FB	6-3	266	8/27/81	6	North Carolina	Wallburg, N.C.	W(StL)-'07	16/9
87	Hixon, Domenik	WR	6-2	182	10/8/84	5	Akron	Columbus, Ohio	W(Den)-'07	14/2
27	Jacobs, Brandon	RB	6-4	264	7/6/82	6	Southern Illinois	Napoleonville, La.	D4-'05	15/15
25	Johnson, Bruce	CB	5-11	182	12/18/87	2	Miami	Live Oak, Fla.	FA-'09	16/5
29	Johnson, D.J.	DB	6-1	191	11/7/85	2	Jackson Stats	Texas City, Texas	FA-'09	3/0
33	Johnson, Gartrell	RB	5-10	219	6/21/86	2	Colorado State	Miami Springs, Fla.	W(SD)-'09	10/0
20	Johnson, Michael	S	6-2	207	5/9/84	4	Arizona	Round Rock, Texas	D7a-'07	15/14
53	Kehl, Bryan	LB	6-2	237	6/16/84	3	Brigham Young	Salt Lake City, Utah	D4-'08	14/1
94	Kiwanuka, Mathias	DE	6-5	265	3/8/83	5	Boston College	Indianapolis, Ind.	D1-'06	16/6
61	Koets, Adam	T	6-5	300	1/7/84	4	Oregon State	Santa Ana, Calif.	D6-'07	2/0
10	Manning, Eli	QB	6-4	225	1/3/81	7	Mississippi	New Orleans, La.	T(SD)-'04	16/16
82	Manningham, Mario	WR	5-11	183	5/25/86	3	Michigan	Warren, Ohio	D3-'08	14/10
67	McKenzie, Kareem	T	6-6	327	5/24/79	10	Penn State	Willingboro, N.J.	UFA(NYJ)-'05	12/12
83	Moss, Sinorice	WR	5-8	185	12/28/83	5	Miami	Miami, Fla.	D2-'06	8/0
88	Nicks, Hakeem	WR	6-0	215	1/14/88	2	North Carolina	Charlotte, N.C.	D1-'09	14/6
60	O'Hara, Shaun	C	6-3	303	6/23/77	11	Rutgers	Hillsborough, N.J.	UFA(Cle)-'04	16/16
86	Pascoe, Bear	TE	6-5	251	2/23/86	2	Fresno State	Porterville, Calif.	FA-'09	4/1
21	Phillips, Kenny	S	6-2	210	11/24/86	3	Miami	Miami, Fla.	D1-'08	2/2
30	Rashad, Sha'reff	S	6-0	198	10/6/86	2	Central Florida	Jacksonville, Fla.	FA-'09	0*
26	Rolle, Antrel	S	6-0	208	12/16/82	5	Miami	Homestead, Fla.	FA-'10	15/15*
31	Ross, Aaron	CB	6-0	197	9/15/82	4	Texas	Tyler, Texas	D1-'07	4/1
69	Seubert, Rich	G	6-3	310	3/30/79	10	Western Illinois	Marshfield, Wisc.	FA-'01	14/14
52	Sintim, Clint	LB	6-2	256	2/21/86	2	Virginia	Woodbridge, Va.	D2-'09	11/0
12	Smith, Steve	WR	5-11	195	5/6/85	4	Southern California	Woodland Hills, Calif.	D2-'07	16/15
76	Snee, Chris	G	6-3	317	1/18/82	7	Boston College	Montrose, Pa.	D2-'04	16/16
19	Sorgi, Jim	QB	6-5	196	12/3/80	7	Wisconsin	Fraser, Mich.	FA-'10	1/0*
24	Thomas, Terrell	CB	6-0	199	1/8/85	3	Southern California	Alto Loma, Calif.	D2-'08	16/16
71	Tollefson, Dave	DE	6-4	255	7/10/82	4	N.W. Missouri State	Concord, Calif.	FA-'07	15/0
91	Tuck, Justin	DE	6-5	274	3/29/83	6	Notre Dame	Kellyton, Ala.	D3-'05	16/15
9	Tynes, Lawrence	K	6-1	202	6/3/78	7	Troy	Milton, Fla.	T(KC)-'07	16/0
72	Umenyiora, Osi	DE	6-3	261	11/16/81	8	Troy	Auburn, Ala.	D2-'03	16/11
28	Ware, D.J.	RB	6-0	234	2/18/85	4	Georgia	Rockmart, Ga.	FA-'07	8/0
23	Webster, Corey	CB	6-0	202	3/2/82	6	Louisiana State	Vacherie, La.	D2-'05	13/13
79	Whimper, Guy	T	6-5	302	5/21/83	5	East Carolina	Havelock, N.C.	D4-'06	6/0
58	Wilkinson, Gerris	LB	6-3	231	4/5/83	5	Georgia Tech	Oakland, Calif.	D3-'06	9/0

* Alford missed '09 season because of injury; Bender last active with San Francisco in '08; C. Brown last active with Dallas in '08; Chandler inactive for 2 games; Grant played 16 games with Seattle in '09; Rashad inactive for 1 game; Rolle played 15 games with Arizona; Sorgi played 1 game with Indianapolis.

Retired—Jeff Feagles, 22-year punter, 16 games in '09.

Players lost through free agency (2): QB David Carr (SF; 6 games in '09); DT Fred Robbins (StL; 16).

Also played with Giants in '09—S CC Brown (16 games), CB Kevin Dockery (11), TE Darcy Johnson (13), LB Antonio Pierce (9).

2010 FIRST-YEAR ROSTER

Name	Pos.	Ht.	Wt.	Birthdate	College	Hometown	How Acq.
Anderson, Vince (1)	DB	6-2	205	12/8/84	Webber International	Lake City, Fla.	FA-'09
Ballard, Jake	TE	6-6	256	12/2/87	Ohio State	Springboro, Ohio	FA
Bond, Jy (1)	P	6-2	215	4/22/79	No College	Melbourne, Australia	FA
Brown, Tim	WR	5-8	165	11/9/87	Rutgers	Miami, Fla.	FA
Butler, Carson (1)	TE	6-0	255	8/21/87	Michigan	Detroit, Mich.	FA
Calhoun, Duke	WR	6-4	205	9/1/87	Memphis	Memphis, Tenn.	FA
Campbell, Lee	LB	6-3	246	8/11/88	Minnesota	Naples, Fla.	FA
Collins, Nate	DT	6-2	290	12/14/87	Virginia	Port Chester, N.Y.	FA
Cordle, Jim	C	6-4	297	8/22/87	Ohio State	Lancaster, Ohio	FA
Cruz, Victor	WR	6-1	200	11/11/86	Massachusetts	Paterson, N.J.	FA
Dillard, Phillip	LB	6-0	245	12/10/86	Nebraska	Tulsa, Okla.	D4
Dodge, Matt	P/K	6-1	224	5/30/87	East Carolina	Morehead City, N.C.	D7
Greco, Michael	S	6-3	217	2/26/87	Central Florida	Fort Lauderdale, Fla.	FA
Hendricks, Dwayne	DT	6-4	300	3/17/86	Miami	Millville, N.J.	FA-'09
Hill, Tommie (1)	DE	6-6	245	11/28/85	Colorado State	Englewood, Colo.	FA
Ingram, Kenny	LB	6-5	239	2/27/86	Florida State	Orlando, Fla.	FA-'09
Johnson, Jerome (1)	FB	6-1	265	1/19/85	Nevada-Reno	Los Angeles, Calif.	FA
Jones, Chad	S	6-2	221	10/5/88	Louisiana State	Baton Rouge, La.	D3
Joseph, Linval	DT	6-4	319	10/10/88	East Carolina	Gainesville, Fla.	D2
Landolt, Dennis	G	6-4	306	10/15/86	Penn State	Burlington, N.J.	FA
Okpokowuruk, Ayanga	DE	6-3	250	6/19/87	Duke	Charlotte, N.C.	FA
Petrus, Mitch	G	6-3	307	5/11/87	Arkansas	Carlisle, Ark.	D5
Pierre-Paul, Jason	DE	6-5	270	1/1/89	South Florida	Deerfield Beach, Fla.	D1
Randolph, Dominic	QB	6-3	223	11/11/86	Holy Cross	Cincinnati, Ohio	FA
Swank, Sam (1)	K	6-0	193	10/5/85	Wake Forest	Jacksonville Beach, Fla.	FA
Tracy, Adrian	LB	6-2	248	4/6/87	William & Mary	Sterling, Va.	D6
Williams, Seth	CB	5-11	185	10/24/86	Richmond	Fayetteville, N.C.	FA

The term NFL Rookie is defined as a player who is in his first season of professional football and has not been on the roster of another professional football team for any regular-season or postseason games. A Rookie is designated by an "R" on NFL rosters. Players who have been active in another professional football league or players who have NFL experience, including either preseason training camp or being on an Active List or Inactive List, or on Reserve/Injured or Reserve/Physically Unable to Perform for fewer than six regular-season games, are termed NFL First-Year Players. An NFL First-Year Player is designated by a "1" on NFL rosters. Thereafter, a player is credited with an additional year of experience for each season in which he accumulates six games on the Active List or Inactive List, or on Reserve/Injured or Reserve/Physically Unable to Perform.

Log on to www.giants.com for an up-to-date roster.

NEW YORK GIANTS

COACHING STAFF

Head Coach,
Tom Coughlin

Pro Career: Was named the sixteenth head coach in Giants history on January 6, 2004. This season marks Coughlin's seventh with the Giants and fifteenth as an NFL head coach. The Giants finished the 2009 season with an 8-8 record. In the 2008 season the Giants finished with a 12-4 record, which won the NFC East division. Coughlin directed the Giants 17-14 win over the New England Patriots in Super Bowl XLII on February 3, 2008, the third championship in the teams history. Coached the Giants to an 11-5 record, the NFC East title and the playoffs in 2005-06, his second and third seasons with the team. Coughlin previously spent eight years (1995-2002) with the Jacksonville Jaguars. Under Coughlin, the Jaguars had the most victories of any NFL expansion team in its first seven seasons. They were also the only expansion team in NFL history to advance to the playoffs four times in their first five seasons. Coughlin's team went 9-7 in 1996 and an NFL-best 14-2 in 1999, both times reaching the AFC Championship Game. Coughlin previously coached the Philadelphia Eagles (1984-85), Green Bay Packers (1986-87), and Giants (1988-1990). He was a member of the Giants' Super Bowl XXV champion coaching staff. Career record: 131-108.

Background: Served as head coach at Boston College (1991-93), and coached at Syracuse (1969, 1974-1980), Rochester Institute of Technology 1970-73 (head coach), and Boston College (1981-83). Played wingback for Syracuse (1965-67).

Personal: Born August 31, 1946, Waterloo, N.Y. Tom and his wife Judy have two daughters, Keli and Katie; two son-in-laws named Chris; two sons, Brian and Tim; two daughters-in-law, Andrea (Tim's wife) and Susie (Brian's wife); and five grandchildren, Emma Rose, Dylan, Shea, Cooper, and Caroline.

ASSISTANT COACHES

Jack Bicknell, Jr., asst. offensive line; born Feb 7, 1963, North Plainfield, N.J. Center Boston College 1981-85. No pro playing experience. College coach: Boston College 1985-87, 2007-08, New Hampshire 1987-1996, Louisiana Tech 1997-2006 (head coach 1999-2006). Pro coach: Joined Giants in 2009.

Perry Fewell, defensive coordinator; born September 7, 1962, Gastonia, N.C. Defensive back Lenoir-Rhyne 1981-84. No pro playing experience. College coach: North Carolina 1985-86, Army 1987, 1992-94, Kent State 1988-1991, Vanderbilt 1995-97. Pro coach: Jacksonville Jaguars 1998-2002, St. Louis Rams 2003-04, Chicago Bears 2005, Buffalo Bills 2006-09, joined Giants in 2010.

Pat Flaherty, offensive line; born April 27, 1956, Hanover, Pa. Center East Stroudsburg 1974-77. No pro playing experience. College coach: East Stroudsburg 1980-81, Penn State 1982-83, Rutgers 1984-1991, East Carolina 1992, Wake Forest 1993-98, Iowa 1999. Pro coach: Washington Redskins 2000, Chicago Bears 2001-03, joined Giants in 2004.

Kevin Gilbride, offensive coordinator; born August 27, 1951, New Haven, Conn. Quarterback/tight end Southern Connecticut State 1971-73. No pro playing experience. College coach: Idaho State 1974-75, Tufts 1976-77, American International 1978-79. Southern Connecticut State 1980-84, East Carolina 1987-88. Pro coach: Ottawa Rough Riders (CFL) 1985-86, Houston Oilers 1989-1994, Jacksonville Jaguars 1995-96, San Diego Chargers 1997-98 (head coach), Pittsburgh Steelers 1999-2000, Buffalo Bills 2002-2003, joined Giants in 2004.

Kevin Gilbride, Jr., offensive quality control; born December 14, 1979, Jacksonville. Quarterback, Hawaii 2000. No pro playing experience. College coach: Syracuse 2004-05, Georgetown 2006, Temple 2007-09. Pro coach: Joined Giants in 2010.

Peter Giunta, secondary/corners; born August 11, 1956, Salem, Mass. Running back/defensive back Northeastern 1974-77. No pro playing experience. College coach: Penn State 1981-83, Brown 1984-87, Lehigh 1988-1990. Pro coach: Philadelphia Eagles 1991-94, N.Y. Jets 1995-96, St. Louis Rams 1997-2000, Kansas City Chiefs 2001-2005, joined Giants in 2006.

Jim Hermann, linebackers; born December 8, 1960, Hollywood, Calif. Linebacker Michigan 1979-1982. No pro playing experience. College coach: Michigan 1983, 1986-2005. Pro coach: New York Jets 2006-2008, joined Giants in 2009.

Al Holcomb, defensive quality control; born October 22, 1970, Queens, N.Y. Attended West Virginia. No college or pro playing experience. College coach: Temple 1995-96, Colby College 1997, Bloomsburg 1998-2003, Kutztown 2004-05, Lafayette 2006-08. Pro coach: Joined Giants in 2009.

Jerald Ingram, running backs; born December 24, 1960, Dayton, Ohio. Fullback Michigan 1979-1983. College coach: Michigan 1984, Ball State 1985-1990, Boston College 1991-93. Pro coach: Jacksonville Jaguars 1994-2002, joined Giants in 2004.

Thomas McGaughey, asst. special teams coordinator; born May 8, 1973, Chicago. Safety Houston 1991-95. Pro safety Philadelphia Eagles 1996, Barcelona Dragons (NFLE) 1997. College coach Houston 1997, 2003-04. Pro coach: Scottish Claymores (NFLE) 2002, Kansas City Chiefs 2002, Denver Broncos 2005-06, joined Giants in 2007.

David Merritt Sr., secondary/safeties; born September 8, 1971, Raleigh, N.C. Linebacker North Carolina State 1989-1992. Pro linebacker Miami Dolphins 1993, Arizona Cardinals 1993-96, Rhein Fire (NFLE) 1997. College coach: Chattanooga 1997, Virginia Military Institute 1998-2000. Pro coach: New York Jets 2001-2003, joined Giants in 2004.

Robert Nunn, defensive line; born June 10, 1965, Apache, Okla. Linebacker Oklahoma State 1984-87. No pro playing experience. College coach: Northeastern Oklahoma 1988, Tennessee 1989-1990, Georgia Military 1991-99. Pro coach: Miami Dolphins 2000-02, 2004, Washington Redskins 2003, Green Bay Packers 2005-08, Tampa Bay Buccaneers 2009, joined Giants in 2010.

Jerry Palmieri, strength and conditioning; born October 30, 1958, Englewood, N.J. Attended Montclair State. No college or pro playing experience. College coach: North Carolina 1982-83, Oklahoma State 1984-86, Kansas State 1987-1992, Boston College 1993-94. Pro coach: Jacksonville Jaguars 1995-2002, New Orleans Saints 2003, joined Giants in 2004.

Marcus Paul, asst. strength and conditioning; born April 1, 1966, Orlando, Fla. Safety Syracuse 1984-88. Pro safety Chicago Bears 1989-1993, Tampa Buccaneers 1993. Pro coach: New Orleans Saints 1998-99, New England Patriots 2000-04, New York Jets 2005-2006, joined Giants in 2007.

Michael Pope, tight ends; born March 15, 1942, Monroe, N.C. Quarterback Lenoir-Rhyne 1962-64. No pro playing experience. College coach: Florida State 1970-74, Texas Tech 1975-77, Mississippi 1978-1982. Pro coach: New York Giants 1983-1991, Cincinnati Bengals 1992-93, New England Patriots 1994-96, Washington Redskins 1997-99, re-joined Giants in 2000.

Tom Quinn, special teams coordinator; born January 27, 1968, Pasadena, Calif. Linebacker Arizona 1986-1990. No pro playing experience. College coach; Davidson College 1991, James Madison 1992-94, Boston 1995, Holy Cross 1996-98, San Jose State 1999-2001, Stanford 2002-05. Pro coach: Joined Giants in 2006.

Sean Ryan, wide receivers; born May 1, 1972, Glenn Falls, N.Y. Defensive back Hamilton College 1994. No pro playing experience. College coach: Albany 1998-99, Colgate 2000, Boston College 2001-02, Columbia 2003-04, Harvard 2006. Pro coach: Joined Giants in 2007.

Mike Sullivan, quarterbacks; born January 28, 1967, Santa Maria, Calif. Defensive back Army 1987-88. No pro playing experience. College coach: Mt. San Jacinto (Calif.) J.C. 1993, Humboldt State 1993-94, Army 1995-96, 1999-2000, Youngstown State 1997-98, Ohio 2001. Pro coach: Jacksonville Jaguars 2002-03, joined Giants in 2004.

National Football Conference
East Division
Team Colors: Midnight Green, Silver, Black, and White
NovaCare Complex
One NovaCare Way
Philadelphia, Pennsylvania 19145
Telephone: (215) 463-2500

2010 SCHEDULE

PRESEASON

Aug. 13	**Jacksonville**	7:30
Aug. 20	at Cincinnati	8:00
Aug. 27	at Kansas City	7:00
Sep. 2	**N.Y. Jets**	7:30

REGULAR SEASON

Sep. 12	**Green Bay**	4:15
Sep. 19	at Detroit	1:00
Sep. 26	at Jacksonville	4:05
Oct. 3	**Washington**	4:15
Oct. 10	at San Francisco	5:20
Oct. 17	**Atlanta**	1:00
Oct. 24	at Tennessee	12:00
Oct. 31	BYE	
Nov. 7	**Indianapolis**	4:15
Nov. 15	at Washington (Mon)	8:30
Nov. 21	**New York Giants**	* 8:20
Nov. 28	at Chicago	12:00
Dec. 2	**Houston** (Thu)	8:20
Dec. 12	at Dallas	* 7:20
Dec. 19	at New York Giants	1:00
Dec. 26	**Minnesota**	1:00
Jan. 2	**Dallas**	1:00

** Sunday night games in Weeks 11-17 subject to change*

Stadium: Lincoln Financial Field (opened in 2003)
•**Capacity:** 69,144
One Lincoln Financial Field Way
Philadelphia, Pennsylvania 19148
Playing Surface: Natural Grass
Training Camp: Lehigh University
Bethlehem, PA 18015

LINCOLN FINANCIAL FIELD

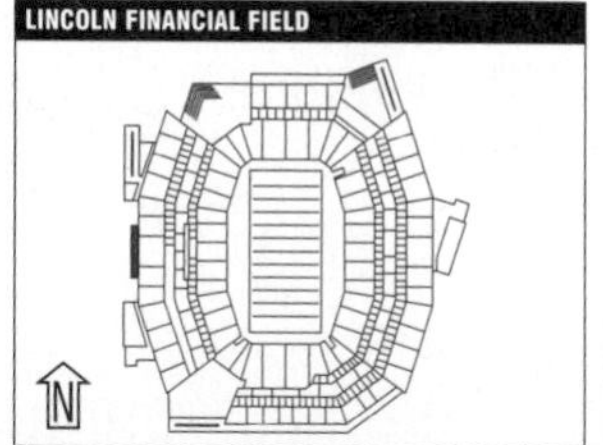

CLUB OFFICIALS

Chairman/Chief Executive Officer: Jeffrey Lurie
President: Joe Banner
Head Coach/Executive Vice President of Football Operations: Andy Reid
General Manager: Howie Roseman
Director of Player Personnel: Ryan Grigson
Senior Vice President/Public Affairs and Government Relations: Pamela Browner White
Chief Operating Officer: Don Smolenski
Vice President of Sales and Service: Marlyse Fant
Executive Director of Eagles Youth Partnership: Sarah Martinez-Helfman
Director of Pro Personnel: Louis Riddick
Director of Football Media Relations: Derek Boyko
Senior Vice President/Chief Marketing Officer: Tim McDermott
Director of Human Resources: Kristie Pappal
Manager of Community Relations: Julie Hirshey
Director of Events: Leonard Bonacci
Director of Ticket Operations: Laini Delawter
Director of Ticket Client Relations: Leo Carlin
Director of Merchandise: Brendan McQuillen
Travel Manager: Tracey Leinen
Director of Team Security: David Young
Head Athletic Trainer: Rick Burkholder
Asst. Athletic Trainers: Steve Condon, Chris Peduzzi
Video Director: Mike Dougherty
Head Equipment Manager: John Hatfield

COACHING HISTORY
(518-554-26)

Records include postseason games

1933-35	Lud Wray	9-21-1
1936-1940	Bert Bell	10-44-2
1941-1950	Earle (Greasy) Neale*	66-44-5
1951	Alvin (Bo) McMillin**	2-0-0
1951	Wayne Millner	2-8-0
1952-55	Jim Trimble	25-20-3
1956-57	Hugh Devore	7-16-1
1958-1960	Lawrence (Buck) Shaw	20-16-1
1961-63	Nick Skorich	15-24-3
1964-68	Joe Kuharich	28-41-1
1969-1971	Jerry Williams***	7-22-2
1971-72	Ed Khayat	8-15-2
1973-75	Mike McCormack	16-25-1
1976-1982	Dick Vermeil	57-51-0
1983-85	Marion Campbell****	17-29-1
1985	Fred Bruney	1-0-0
1986-1990	Buddy Ryan	43-38-1
1991-94	Rich Kotite	37-29-0
1995-98	Ray Rhodes	30-36-1
1999-2009	Andy Reid	118-75-1

*Co-coach with Walt Kiesling in Philadelphia-Pittsburgh merger in 1943
**Retired after two games in 1951
***Released after three games in 1971
****Released after 15 games in 1985

PAID ATTENDANCE

Home 539,984 Away 566,921
Total 1,106,905
Single-game home record, 72,111 (11/1/81)
Single-season home record, 557,325 (1980)

2010 DRAFT CHOICES

Round	Name	Pos.	College
1	Brandon Graham	DE	Michigan
2	Nate Allen	DB	South Florida
3	Daniel Te'o-Nesheim	DE	Washington
4	Trevard Lindley	DB	Kentucky
	Keenan Clayton	LB	Oklahoma
	Mike Kafka	QB	Northwestern
	Clay Harbor	TE	Missouri St.
5	Ricky Sapp	DE	Clemson
	Riley Cooper	WR	Florida
6	Charles Scott	RB	Louisiana St.
7	Jamar Chaney	LB	Mississippi St.
	Jeff Owens	DT	Georgia
	Kurt Coleman	DB	Ohio St.

PHILADELPHIA EAGLES

2009 TEAM RECORD

PRESEASON (1-3)

Date	Result	Opponent
8/13	L 25-27	New England
8/20	L 15-23	at Indianapolis
8/27	W 33-32	Jacksonville
9/3	L 27-38	at New York Jets

REGULAR SEASON (11-5)

Date	Result	Opponent
9/13	W 38-10	at Carolina
9/20	L 22-48	New Orleans
9/27	W 34-14	Kansas City
10/11	W 33-14	Tampa Bay
10/18	L 9-13	at Oakland
10/26	W 27-17	at Washington
11/1	W 40-17	New York Giants
11/8	L 16-20	Dallas
11/15	L 23-31	at San Diego
11/22	W 24-20	at Chicago
11/29	W 27-24	Washington
12/6	W 34-7	at Atlanta
12/13	W 45-38	at New York Giants
12/20	W 27-13	San Francisco
12/27	W 30-27	Denver
1/3	L 0-24	at Dallas

POSTSEASON (0-1)

Date	Result	Opponent
1/9	L 14-34	at Dallas

SCORE BY PERIODS

Eagles	122	151	72	84	0 —	429
Opponents	58	101	107	71	0 —	337

2009 TEAM STATISTICS

	Eagles	Opp.
Total First Downs	290	295
Rushing	87	81
Passing	182	179
Penalty	21	35
3rd Down: Made/Att	75/207	73/221
3rd Down Pct.	36.2	33.0
4th Down: Made/Att	6/14	17/30
4th Down Pct.	42.9	56.7
Possession Avg.	28:15	31:46
Total Net Yards	5726	5137
Avg. Per Game	357.9	321.1
Total Plays	975	1037
Avg. Per Play	5.9	5.0
Net Yards Rushing	1637	1675
Avg. Per Game	102.3	104.7
Total Rushes	384	413
Net Yards Passing	4089	3462
Avg. Per Game	255.6	216.4
Sacked/Yards Lost	38/291	44/316
Gross Yards	4380	3778
Att./Completions	553/335	580/354
Completion Pct.	60.6	61.0
Had Intercepted	13	25
Punts/Average	76/42.4	80/45.1
Net Punting Avg.	76/38.3	80/37.2
Penalties/Yards	115/951	104/789
Fumbles/Ball Lost	23/10	25/13
Touchdowns	47	39
Rushing	14	11
Passing	27	27
Returns	6	1

2009 INDIVIDUAL STATISTICS

PASSING	Att.	Comp.	Yds.	Pct.	TD	Int.	Tkld.	Rate
McNabb	443	267	3553	60.3	22	10	35/264	92.9
Kolb	96	62	741	64.6	4	3	3/27	88.9
Vick	13	6	86	46.2	1	0	0/0	93.8
Westbrook	1	0	0	0.0	0	0	0/0	39.6
Eagles	553	335	4380	60.6	27	13	38/291	92.0
Opponents	580	354	3778	61.0	27	25	44/316	77.6

SCORING	TD R	TD P	TD Rt	PAT	FG	Saf	PTS
Akers	0	0	0	43/45	32/37	0	139
D. Jackson	1	9	2	0/0	0/0	0	72
Celek	0	8	0	0/0	0/0	0	48
McCoy	4	0	0	0/0	0/0	0	26
Maclin	0	4	0	0/0	0/0	0	24
Weaver	2	2	0	0/0	0/0	0	24
Avant	0	3	0	0/0	0/0	0	20
S. Brown	0	0	2	0/0	0/0	0	12
McNabb	2	0	0	0/0	0/0	0	12
Vick	2	0	0	0/0	0/0	0	12
Westbrook	1	1	0	0/0	0/0	0	12
Abiamiri	0	0	1	0/0	0/0	0	6
Buckley	1	0	0	0/0	0/0	0	6
Kolb	1	0	0	0/0	0/0	0	6
Witherspoon TM	0	0	1	0/0	0/0	0	6
Howard	0	0	0	0/0	0/0	1	2
Eagles	14	27	6	43/45	32/37	2	429
Opponents	11	27	1	38/38	21/24	0	337

2-Pt. Conversions: Avant, McCoy.
Eagles 2-2, Opponents 1-1.

RUSHING	No.	Yds	Avg	LG	TD
McCoy	155	637	4.1	66t	4
Weaver	70	323	4.6	41t	2
Westbrook	61	274	4.5	25	1
McNabb	37	140	3.8	27	2
D. Jackson	11	137	12.5	67t	1
Vick	24	95	4.0	34	2
Buckley	15	44	2.9	9	1
Kolb	5	-1	-0.2	5	1
Garcia	3	-2	-0.7	0	0
R. Brown	1	-3	-3.0	-3	0
Maclin	2	-7	-3.5	-1	0
Eagles	384	1637	4.3	67t	14
Opponents	413	1675	4.1	72	11

RECEIVING	No.	Yds	Avg	LG	TD
Celek	76	971	12.8	47t	8
D. Jackson	62	1156	18.6	71t	9
Maclin	56	773	13.8	56	4
Avant	41	587	14.3	58	3
McCoy	40	308	7.7	45	0
Westbrook	25	181	7.2	34	1
Weaver	15	140	9.3	59	2
R. Brown	9	155	17.2	43	0
K. Curtis	6	77	12.8	19	0
Smith	3	25	8.3	11	0
Baskett TM	1	6	6.0	6	0
McNabb	1	1	1.0	1	0
Eagles	335	4380	13.1	71t	27
Opponents	354	3778	10.7	86t	27

INTERCEPTIONS	No.	Yds	Avg	LG	TD
Samuel	9	117	13.0	37	0
S. Brown	5	152	30.4	83t	1
Jones	2	37	18.5	37	0
Mikell	2	16	8.0	16	0
Jordan	2	14	7.0	11	0
Hanson	2	8	4.0	6	0
Demps	1	12	12.0	12	0
Witherspoon TM	1	9	9.0	9t	1
White	1	5	5.0	5	0
Eagles	25	370	14.8	83t	2
Opponents	13	131	10.1	97t	1

PUNTING	No.	Yds.	Avg.	In 20	LG
Rocca	76	3222	42.4	26	61
Eagles	76	3222	42.4	26	61
Opponents	80	3604	45.1	29	64

PUNT RETURNS	Ret	FC	Yds	Avg	LG	TD
D. Jackson	29	15	441	15.2	85t	2
Maclin	6	4	30	5.0	27	0
Eagles	35	19	471	13.5	85t	2
Opponents	39	15	229	5.9	26	0

KICKOFF RETURNS	No.	Yds	Avg	LG	TD
Hobbs	20	481	24.1	63	0
Harris	19	394	20.7	32	0
Maclin	7	124	17.7	28	0
Demps	6	155	25.8	48	0
Weaver	2	33	16.5	18	0
Babin	2	0	0.0	0	0
Smith	1	4	4.0	4	0
D. Jackson	1	0	0.0	0	0
Eagles	58	1191	20.5	63	0
Opponents	81	1907	23.5	52	0

FIELD GOALS	1-19	20-29	30-39	40-49	50+
Akers	1/1	11/11	8/9	11/13	1/3
Eagles	1/1	11/11	8/9	11/13	1/3
Opponents	0/0	11/11	2/3	7/9	1/1

SACKS	No.
T. Cole	12.5
J. Parker	8.0
Howard	6.5
Clemons	3.0
Babin	2.5
Abiamiri	2.0
Gaither	1.5
M. Patterson	1.5
Bunkley	1.0
Dixon	1.0
Gocong	1.0
Jones	1.0
Jordan	1.0
Witherspoon	1.0
Hanson	0.5
Eagles	44.0
Opponents	38.0

RECORD HOLDERS

INDIVIDUAL RECORDS—CAREER

Category	Name	Performance
Rushing (Yds.)	Wilbert Montgomery, 1977-1984	6,538
Passing (Yds.)	Donovan McNabb, 1999-2009	32,873
Passing (TDs)	Donovan McNabb, 1999-2009	216
Receiving (No.)	Harold Carmichael, 1971-1983	589
Receiving (Yds.)	Harold Carmichael, 1971-1983	8,978
Interceptions	Bill Bradley, 1969-1976	34
	Eric Allen, 1988-1994	34
	Brian Dawkins, 1996-2008	34
Punting (Avg.)	Joe Muha, 1946-1950	42.9
Punt Return (Avg.)	Ernie Steele, 1942-48	16.8
Kickoff Return (Avg.)	Steve Van Buren, 1944-1951	26.7
Field Goals	David Akers, 1999-2009	262
Touchdowns (Tot.)	Harold Carmichael, 1971-1983	79
Points	David Akers, 1999-2009	1,180
*Sacks	Reggie White, 1985-1992	124.0

INDIVIDUAL RECORDS—SINGLE SEASON

Category	Name	Performance
Rushing (Yds.)	Wilbert Montgomery, 1979	1,512
Passing (Yds.)	Donovan McNabb, 2008	3,916
Passing (TDs)	Sonny Jurgensen, 1961	32
Receiving (No.)	Brian Westbrook, 2007	90
Receiving (Yds.)	Mike Quick, 1983	1,409
Interceptions	Bill Bradley, 1971	11
Punting (Avg.)	Joe Muha, 1948	47.2
Punt Return (Avg.)	Steve Van Buren, 1944	15.3
Kickoff Return (Avg.)	Al Nelson, 1972	29.1
Field Goals	David Akers, 2008	33
Touchdowns (Tot.)	Steve Van Buren, 1945	18
Points	David Akers, 2008	144
*Sacks	Reggie White, 1987	21.0

INDIVIDUAL RECORDS—SINGLE GAME

Category	Name	Performance
Rushing (Yds.)	Steve Van Buren, 11-27-49	205
Passing (Yds.)	Donovan McNabb, 12-5-04	464
Passing (TDs)	Adrian Burk, 10-17-54	**7
Receiving (No.)	Don Looney, 12-1-40	14
	Brian Westbrook, 11-4-07	14
Receiving (Yds.)	Tommy McDonald, 12-10-60	237
Interceptions	Russ Craft, 9-24-50	**4
Field Goals	Tom Dempsey, 11-12-72	6
Touchdowns (Tot.)	Many times	4
	Last time by Brian Westbrook, 11-27-08	
Points	Bobby Walston, 10-17-54	25
*Sacks	Clyde Simmons, 9-15-91	4.5
	Hugh Douglas, 10-18-98	4.5

**Sacks became an official statistic in 1982.*
***NFL Record*

PHILADELPHIA EAGLES

2010 VETERAN ROSTER

No.	Name	Pos.	Ht.	Wt.	Birthdate	NFL Exp.	College	Hometown	How Acq.	'09 Games/ Starts
95	Abiamiri, Victor	DE	6-4	267	1/14/86	4	Notre Dame	Baltimore, Md.	D2b-'07	13/5
2	Akers, David	K	5-10	200	12/9/74	12	Louisville	Lexington, Ky.	FA-'99	16/0
76	Andrews, Stacy	G/T	6-7	340	6/2/81	7	Mississippi	Camden, Ark.	UFA(Cin)-'09	10/2
81	Avant, Jason	WR	6-0	212	4/20/83	5	Michigan	Chicago, Ill.	D4b-'06	16/9
84	Baskett, Hank	WR	6-4	220	9/4/82	5	New Mexico	Clovis, N.M.	FA-'10	12/0*
26	Bell, Mike	RB	6-0	225	4/23/83	5	Arizona	Tolleson, Ariz.	RFA(NO)-'10	13/3*
55	Bradley, Stewart	LB	6-4	255	11/2/83	4	Nebraska	Salt Lake City, Utah	D3a-'07	0*
34	Buckley, Eldra	RB	5-9	207	6/23/85	2	Tennessee-Chattanooga	Charleston, Miss.	W(SD)-'09	16/0
97	Bunkley, Brodrick	DT	6-2	306	11/23/83	5	Florida State	Tampa, Fla.	D1-'06	16/16
87	Celek, Brent	TE	6-4	255	1/25/85	4	Cincinnati	Cincinnati, Ohio	D5b-'07	16/15
59	Cole, Nick	G/C	6-0	350	7/28/84	5	New Mexico State	Lawton, Okla.	FA-'06	16/16
58	Cole, Trent	LB/DE	6-3	270	10/5/82	6	Cincinnati	Xenia, Ohio	D5a-'05	16/16
39	Demps, Quintin	S	5-11	206	6/29/85	3	Texas-El Paso	San Antonio, Texas	D4b-'08	9/0
64	Dixon, Antonio	DT	6-3	322	7/17/85	2	Miami	Miami, Fla.	W(Wash)-'09	16/0
46	Dorenbos, Jon	LS	6-0	250	7/21/80	8	Texas-El Paso	Garden Grove, Calif.	FA-'06	16/0
65	Dunlap, King	T	6-8	310	9/9/85	3	Auburn	Brentwood, Tenn.	D7-'08	12/0
53	Fokou, Moise	LB	6-1	236	8/28/85	2	Maryland	Potomac, Md.	D7b-'09	16/4
96	Gaither, Omar	LB	6-2	235	3/18/84	5	Tennessee	Charlotte, N.C.	D5b-'06	5/3
57	t-Hall, Alex	LB	6-5	250	8/17/85	3	St. Augustine's	Glenarden, Md.	T(Cle)-'10	14/0*
21	Hanson, Joselio	CB	5-9	185	8/13/81	6	Texas Tech	Playa Del Rey, Calif.	FA-'06	12/1
24	Harris, Macho	S	5-11	198	2/16/86	2	Virginia Tech	Highland Springs, Va.	D5b-'09	15/8
79	Herremans, Todd	G/T	6-6	321	10/13/82	6	Saginaw Valley State	Ravenna, Mich.	D4b-'05	11/11
31	Hobbs, Ellis	CB	5-9	195	5/16/83	6	Iowa State	DeSoto, Texas	T(NE)-'09	8/0
88	Ingram, Cornelius	TE	6-4	245	6/10/85	2	Florida	Hawthorne, Fla.	D5a-'09	0*
10	Jackson, DeSean	WR	5-10	175	12/1/86	3	California	Long Beach, Calif.	D2b-'08	15/15
67	Jackson, Jamaal	C	6-4	325	5/8/80	7	Delaware State	Miami, Fla.	FA-'03	15/15
28	Jackson, Marlin	DB	6-0	196	6/30/83	6	Michigan	Sharon, Pa	FA-'10	4/0*
62	Jean-Gilles, Max	G	6-3	358	11/19/83	5	Georgia	Miami, Fla.	D4a-'06	13/5
56	Jordan, Akeem	LB	6-1	230	8/17/85	4	James Madison	Harrisonburg, Va.	FA-'07	12/10
74	Justice, Winston	T	6-6	320	9/14/84	5	Southern California	Long Beach, Calif.	D2-'06	16/16
4	Kolb, Kevin	QB	6-3	218	8/24/84	4	Houston	Stephenville, Texas	D2a-'07	5/2
93	Laws, Trevor	DT	6-1	304	6/14/85	3	Notre Dame	Apple Valley, Minn.	D2a-'08	11/0
18	Maclin, Jeremy	WR	6-0	198	5/11/88	2	Missouri	Kirkwood, Mo.	D1-'09	15/13
51	Mays, Joe	LB	5-11	246	7/6/85	3	North Dakota State	Chicago, Ill.	D6b-'08	11/1
25	McCoy, LeSean	RB	5-11	208	7/12/88	2	Pittsburgh	Harrisburg, Pa.	D2-'09	16/4
77	McGlynn, Mike	G	6-4	315	3/8/85	3	Pittsburgh	Austintown, Ohio	D4a-'08	0*
27	Mikell, Quintin	S	5-10	206	9/16/80	8	Boise State	Eugene, Ore.	FA-'03	16/16
75	Parker, Juqua	DE	6-2	250	5/15/78	10	Oklahoma State	Houston, Texas	FA-'05	16/11
23	Patterson, Dimitri	CB	5-10	190	6/18/83	5	Tuskegee	Orlando, Fla.	FA-'09	11/0
98	Patterson, Mike	DT	6-1	300	9/1/83	6	Southern California	Los Alamitos, Calif.	D1-'05	16/16
71	Peters, Jason	T	6-4	340	1/22/82	7	Arkansas	Queen City, Texas	T(Buff)-'09	15/15
30	Pope, Geoff	CB	6-0	190	6/21/84	3	Howard	Detroit, Mich.	FA-'09	5/0*
6	Rocca, Sav	P	6-5	265	11/20/73	4	None	Lakeside, Australia	FA-'07	16/0
89	Rucker, Martin	TE	6-5	255	5/4/85	2	Missouri	St. Joseph, Mo.	FA-'09	0*
22	Samuel, Asante	CB	5-10	185	1/6/81	8	Central Florida	Lauderdale Lakes, Fla.	UFA(NE)-'08	16/16
50	t-Sims, Ernie	LB	6-0	230	12/23/84	5	Florida State	Tallahassee, Fla.	T(Det)-'10	11/8*
91	t-Tapp, Darryl	DE	6-1	270	9/13/84	5	Virginia Tech	Chesapeake, Va.	T(Sea)-'10	16/5*
78	Tupou, Fenuki	T	6-5	323	5/2/85	2	Oregon	Antelope, Calif.	D5c-'09	0*
7	Vick, Michael	QB	6-0	215	6/26/80	9	Virginia Tech	Newport News, Va.	FA-'09	12/1
43	Weaver, Leonard	FB	6-0	250	9/23/82	6	Carson-Newman	Satellite, Fla.	UFA(Sea)-'09	16/8
32	Wright, Dwayne	FB	5-11	228	6/2/83	2	Fresno State	San Diego, Calif.	FA-'10	0*

* Baskett played 1 game with Philadelphia and 11 games with Indianapolis in '09; Bell played 13 games with New Orleans; Bradley missed '09 season because of injury; Hall played 14 games with Cleveland; Ingram missed '09 season because of injury; M. Jackson played 4 games with Indianapolis; McGlynn did not play in 1 game; Pope played 4 games with Cincinnati and 1 game with Philadelphia; Rucker inactive for 3 games; Sims played 11 games with Detroit; Tapp played 16 games with Seattle; Tupou missed '09 season because of injury; Wright last active with Buffalo in '07.

t- Eagles traded for Hall (Cle), Sims (Det), Tapp (Sea).

Traded—CB Sheldon Brown (16 games in '09) to Cleveland, WR Reggie Brown (14) to Tampa Bay, DE Chris Clemons (16) to Seattle, WR Brandon Gibson (1) to St. Louis, LB Chris Gocong (15) to Cleveland, QB Donovan McNabb (14) to Washington.

Players lost through free agency (2): DE Jason Babin (Tenn; 12 games in '09), S Sean Jones (TB; 15).

Also played with Eagles in '09—WR Kevin Curtis (3 games), QB Jeff Garcia (1), DE Darren Howard (16), CB Jack Ikegwuonu (1), WR Jordan Norwood (1), DB Ramzee Robinson (3), TE Alex Smith (16), LB Jeremiah Trotter (13), RB Brian Westbrook (8), LB Tracy White (16), LB Will Witherspoon (11).

2010 FIRST-YEAR ROSTER

Name	Pos.	Ht.	Wt.	Birthdate	College	Hometown	How Acq.
Allen, Nate	S	6-0	207	11/30/87	South Florida	Cape Coral, Fla.	D2
Chaney, Jamar	LB	6-0	242	10/11/86	Mississippi State	St. Lucie, Fla.	D6b
Clayton, Keenan	LB	6-1	229	6/3/87	Oklahoma	Sulphur Springs, Texas	D4b
Coleman, Kurt	S	5-10	192	7/1/88	Ohio State	Clayton, Ohio	D7b
Collins, Dobson (1)	WR	6-2	167	7/12/87	Gardner-Webb	Stone Mountain, Ga.	FA-'09
Cooper, Blue	WR	6-2	185	3/27/86	Tennessee-Chattanooga	Rome, Ga.	FA
Cooper, Riley	WR	6-3	222	9/9/87	Florida	Clearwater, Fla.	D5b
Duncan, Zipp	G	6-5	297	7/15/87	Kentucky	Magnolia, Ky.	FA
Elliott, Joey	QB	6-3	215	8/2/86	Purdue	Evansville, Ind.	FA
Flemming, Keithon	RB	5-10	208	8/26/86	West Texas A&M	Mesquite, Texas	FA
Graham, Brandon	DE	6-2	268	4/3/88	Michigan	Detroit, Mich.	D1
Hall, Chad	WR	5-8	180	5/23/86	Air Force	Atlanta, Ga.	FA
Harbor, Clay	TE	6-2	252	7/2/87	Missouri State	Dwight, Ill.	D4d
Howard, Austin	T	6-7	333	3/22/87	Northern Iowa	Davenport, Iowa	FA
Isdaner, Greg (1)	G	6-4	325	2/25/87	West Virginia	Gladwyne, Pa.	FA
Jurovich, Kevin	WR	6-0	188	6/30/86	San Jose State	San Jose, Calif.	FA
Kafka, Mike	QB	6-3	225	7/25/87	Northwestern	Chicago, Ill.	D4c
Lindley, Trevard	CB	5-11	183	2/2/86	Kentucky	Hiram, Ga.	D4a
Mallett, Martell (1)	RB	5-11	200	5/13/86	Arkansas-Pine Bluff	Pine Bluff, Ark.	FA
McCuller, Jeraill	T	6-6	328	9/8/87	North Carolina State	Jamesville, N.C.	FA
Moncur, Eric	DE	6-1	237	11/28/84	Miami	Miami, Fla.	FA
Morris, Josh (1)	CB	5-11	186	7/3/86	Weber State	Ada, Okla.	FA
Norwood, Jordan (1)	WR	5-11	180	9/28/86	Penn State	Honolulu, Hawaii	FA-'09
Owens, Jeff	DT	6-1	304	10/14/86	Georgia	Sunrise, Fla.	D7a
Parrish, Ken (1)	P	6-1	210	6/22/84	East Stroudsburg	East Stroudsburg, Pa.	FA-'09
Pender, David	CB	6-0	180	12/4/87	Purdue	Folkston, Ga.	FA
Reynolds, Dallas (1)	G	6-4	314	4/23/84	Brigham Young	Provo, Utah	FA-'09
Ross, Devin	CB	5-10	183	5/25/88	Arizona	Cucamonga, Calif.	FA
Sapp, Ricky	DE	6-4	252	11/14/86	Clemson	Bamberg, S.C.	D5a
Scott, Charles	RB	5-11	238	8/8/88	Louisiana State	Saline, La.	D6a
Shipley, A.Q. (1)	CB	6-1	315	5/22/86	Penn State	Coraopolis, Pa.	FA
Simonds, Pat	WR	6-5	229	8/5/88	Colgate	Sidney, N.Y.	FA
Te'o-Nesheim, Daniel	DE	6-3	263	6/12/87	Washington	Waikoloa, Hawaii	D3
Zardas, Chris	FB	6-0	238	12/23/86	Massachusetts	Wakefield, Mass.	FA

The term NFL Rookie is defined as a player who is in his first season of professional football and has not been on the roster of another professional football team for any regular-season or postseason games. A Rookie is designated by an "R" on NFL rosters. Players who have been active in another professional football league or players who have NFL experience, including either preseason training camp or being on an Active List or Inactive List, or on Reserve/Injured or Reserve/Physically Unable to Perform for fewer than six regular-season games, are termed NFL First-Year Players. An NFL First-Year Player is designated by a "1" on NFL rosters. Thereafter, a player is credited with an additional year of experience for each season in which he accumulates six games on the Active List or Inactive List, or on Reserve/Injured or Reserve/Physically Unable to Perform.

Log on to www.philadelphiaeagles.com for an up-to-date roster.

COACHING STAFF

Head Coach/Executive Vice President of Football Operations, Andy Reid

Pro Career: Reid has earned NFL coach of the year honors twice, compiled the best win total (118), winning percentage (.611), and playoff victory total (10) in team history. He has captured five division titles and five trips to the NFC Championship game. Since he was hired in 1999, no other franchise has earned more divisional playoff round appearances (7) or conference championships (5) than Philadelphia. Among coaches with 100 games under their belt entering 2010, Reid's .611 overall winning percentage is 14th in NFL history and second among active coaches, behind New England's Bill Belichick (.632). In his 18-year NFL coaching career, Reid's teams have made the playoffs 14 times (19-13 record). He has coached in the Super Bowl three times, the NFC Championship game nine times, and the Pro Bowl five times. Reid became the 20th head coach in franchise history on January 11, 1999, and was promoted to head coach/executive vice president of football operations in 2001. He was named NFL coach of the year in 2000 and 2002. He joined the Eagles after a seven-year stint as an assistant coach with Green Bay (1992-98) under Mike Holmgren. With Green Bay, Reid helped the Packers earn a Super Bowl XXXI victory over New England. Career record: 118-75-1.

Background: Coached at Brigham Young (1982), San Francisco State (1983-85), Northern Arizona (1986), Texas-El Paso (1987-88), and Missouri (1989-1991). Reid first met Holmgren, who was a member of BYU's coaching staff, when Reid was an offensive tackle and guard on three Cougar Holiday Bowl teams. Reid graduated with a bachelor's degree in physical education. He also received a master's degree in professional leadership in physical education and athletics.

Personal: Born in Los Angeles on March 19, 1958, Reid and his wife Tammy have five children—Garrett, Britt, Crosby, Drew Ann, and Spencer.

ASSISTANT COACHES

Bobby April, special teams coordinator; born April 15, 1963. Linebacker/defensive end Nicholls State 1972-75. No pro playing experience. College coach: Southern Mississippi 1978, Tulane 1979, Arizona 1980-86, Southern California 1987-1990. Pro coach: Atlanta Falcons 1991-93, Pittsburgh Steelers 1994-95, New Orleans Saints 1996-99, St. Louis Rams 2001-02, Buffalo Bills 2004-09, joined Eagles in 2010.

Mike Caldwell, asst. linebackers; born August 31, 1971. Linebacker Middle Tennessee State 1989-1992. Pro linebacker Cleveland Browns 1993-95, Baltimore Ravens 1996, Arizona Cardinals 1997, Philadelphia Eagles 1998-2001, Chicago Bears 2002, Carolina Panthers 2003. Pro coach: Joined Eagles in 2008.

Juan Castillo, offensive line; born October 8, 1959, Port Isabel, Texas. Linebacker Texas A&I (now Texas A&M-Kingsville) 1978-1980. Pro linebacker San Antonio Gunslingers (USFL) 1984-85. College coach: Texas A&I/Texas A&M-Kingsville 1982-85, 1990-94. Pro coach: Joined Eagles in 1995.

David Culley, wide receivers; born September 17, 1955, Sparta, Tenn. Quarterback Vanderbilt 1973-77. No pro playing experience. College coach: Austin Peay 1978, Vanderbilt 1979-1981, Middle Tennessee State 1982, Tennessee-Chattanooga 1983, Western Kentucky 1984, Southwestern Louisiana 1985-88, Texas-El Paso 1989-1990, Texas A&M 1991-93. Pro coach: Tampa Bay Buccaneers 1994-95, Pittsburgh Steelers 1996-1998, joined Eagles in 1999.

Dick Jauron, senior asst./defensive backs; born October 7, 1950. Running back Yale, 1970-72. Pro safety Detroit Lions 1973-77, Cincinnati Bengals 1978-1980. Pro coach: Buffalo Bills 1985, Green Bay Packers 1986-1994, Jacksonville Jaguars 1995-98, Chicago Bears 1999-2003 (head coach), Detroit Lions 2004-05 (head coach 2005), Buffalo Bills 2006-09 (head coach), joined Eagles in 2010.

Sean McDermott, defensive coordinator; born March 21, 1974, Omaha, Neb. Safety William & Mary 1994-97. No pro playing experience. College coach: William & Mary 1998. Pro coach: Joined Eagles in 1998.

Tom Melvin, tight ends; born October 1, 1961, Redwood City, Calif. Offensive lineman San Francisco State 1982-83. No pro playing experience. College coach: San Francisco State 1984-85, Northern Arizona 1986-87, California-Santa Barbara 1988-1990, Occidental College 1991-98. Pro coach: Joined Eagles in 1999.

Marty Mornhinweg, asst. head coach/ \offensive coordinator; born March 29, 1962, Edmond, Okla. Quarterback Montana 1981-84. Pro quarterback Denver Dynamite (AFL) 1987. College coach: Montana 1985, Texas-El Paso 1986-87, Northern Arizona 1988, 1994, Southeast Missouri State 1989-1990, Missouri 1991-93. Pro coach: Green Bay Packers 1995-96, San Francisco 49ers 1997-2000, Detroit Lions 2001-02 (head coach), joined Eagles in 2003.

Jeff Nixon, special teams quality control; born October 16, 1974, Rochester, Pa. Running back West Virginia 1993-94, Penn State 1996. No pro playing experience. College coach: Penn State 1997, Princeton 1998, Shippensburg 1999-2002, Tennessee-Chattanooga 2003-05, Temple 2006. Pro coach: Joined Eagles in 2007.

Doug Pederson, offensive quality control; born January 31, 1968, Bellingham, Wash. Quarterback Louisiana-Monroe 1987-1990. Pro experience: Miami Dolphins 1993-95, Green Bay Packers 1995-98, 2001-04, Philadelphia Eagles 1999, Cleveland Browns 2000. Pro coach: Joined Eagles in 2009.

Barry Rubin, strength and conditioning; born June 25, 1957. Running back/punter Louisiana State 1976-77, tight end/punter Northwestern (La.) State 1978-1980. No pro playing experience. College coach: Northeast Louisiana 1981-83, 1987-1990, 1994, Louisiana State 1984-85. Pro coach: Green Bay Packers 1995-2005, joined Eagles in 2008.

Rory Segrest, defensive line; born May 20, 1973, Waycross, Ga. Tackle Alabama 1991-93. No pro playing experience. College coach: Alabama 1994-97, Auburn 1997-98, Southeast Missouri State 1999-2001, Samford 2002-05. Pro coach: Joined Eagles in 2006.

Bill Shuey, linebackers; born October 5, 1974, Bethlehem, Pa. Attended Slippery Rock. No college or pro playing experience. Pro coach: Joined Eagles in 2003.

James Urban, quarterbacks; born December 1, 1973, Mechanicsburg, Pa. Wide receiver Washington and Lee 1993-96. No pro playing experience. College coach: Clarion 1997-98, Pennsylvania 1999-2004. Pro coach: Joined Eagles in 2007.

Ted Williams, running backs; born November 17, 1943, Lyons, Texas. Attended Cal Poly-Pomona. No college or pro playing experience. College coach: UCLA 1980-89, Washington State 1991-93, Arizona 1994. Pro coach: Joined Eagles in 1995.

Michael Zordich, defensive quality control; born October 12, 1963;. Safety Penn State 1982-85. Pro safety New York Jets 1987-88, Phoenix Cardinals 1989-1993, Philadelphia Eagles 1994-98. Pro coach: Joined Eagles in 2009.

National Football Conference
West Division
Team Colors: New Century Gold, Millennium Blue, and White
One Rams Way
St. Louis, Missouri 63045
Telephone: (314) 982-7267

2010 SCHEDULE

PRESEASON

Aug. 14	**Minnesota**	7:00
Aug. 21	at Cleveland	7:30
Aug. 26	at New England	7:30
Sep. 2	**Baltimore**	7:00

REGULAR SEASON

Sep. 12	**Arizona**	3:15
Sep. 19	at Oakland	1:05
Sep. 26	**Washington**	3:05
Oct. 3	**Seattle**	12:00
Oct. 10	at Detroit	1:00
Oct. 17	**San Diego**	12:00
Oct. 24	at Tampa Bay	1:00
Oct. 31	**Carolina**	12:00
Nov. 7	BYE	
Nov. 14	at San Francisco	1:15
Nov. 21	**Atlanta**	3:05
Nov. 28	at Denver	2:15
Dec. 5	at Arizona	2:15
Dec. 12	at New Orleans	3:05
Dec. 19	**Kansas City**	12:00
Dec. 26	**San Francisco**	12:00
Jan. 2	at Seattle	1:15

Stadium: Edward Jones Dome
(opened in 1995)
• **Capacity:** 66,000
901 N. Broadway
St. Louis, Missouri 63101
Playing Surface: FieldTurf
Training Camp: Russell Training Center
1 Rams Way
St. Louis, Missouri 63045

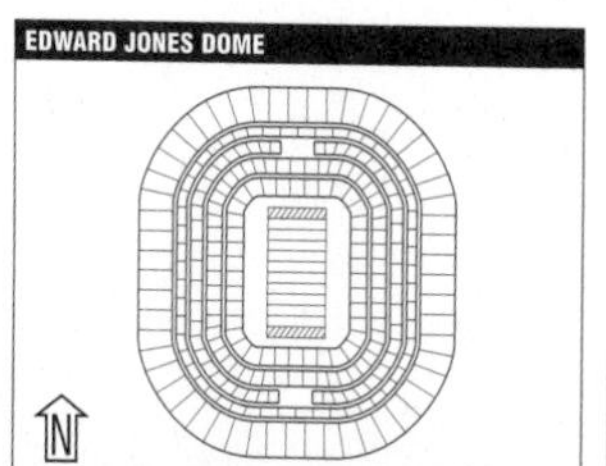

EDWARD JONES DOME

CLUB OFFICIALS

Owner/Chairman: Dale "Chip" Rosenbloom
Owner/Partner: Lucia Rodriguez
Owner/Vice Chairman: Stan Kroenke
General Manager: Billy Devaney
Executive Vice President Of Football Operations/Chief Operating Officer: Kevin Demoff
Director of Player Personnel: Lawrence McCutcheon
Treasurer: Jeff Brewer
Executive Vice President of Marketing and Sales: Bob Reif
Vice President of Finance: Michael T. Naughton
Vice President of Operations: John Oswald
Vice President of Ticketing: Mike O'Keefe
Senior Director of Communications: Ted Crews
Director of Media Relations: Artis Twyman
Director of Corporate Sales: Chad Watson
Vice President of Marketing: Adam Jacobs
Vice President of Corporate Communications and Civic Affairs: Molly Higgins
Director of Community Relations: Michael Yarbrough
Vice President of Player Personnel: Mike Williams
Director of College Scouting: John Mancini
Head Trainer: Reggie Scott
Assistant Trainers: James Lomax, Tyler Williams, Byron Cunningham
Equipment Manager: Todd Hewitt
Assistant Equipment Manager: Jim Lake
Scouts: Ray Agnew, Drew Casani, Luke Driscoll, Brad Holmes, Steve Kazor

COACHING HISTORY

Cleveland 1937-1945, Los Angeles 1946-1994
(523-507-20)
Records include postseason games

1937-38	Hugo Bezdek*	1-13-0
1938	Art Lewis	4-4-0
1939-1942	Earl (Dutch) Clark	16-26-2
1944	Aldo (Buff) Donelli	4-6-0
1945-46	Adam Walsh	16-5-1
1947	Bob Snyder	6-6-0
1948-49	Clark Shaughnessy	14-8-3
1950-52	Joe Stydahar**	19-9-0
1952-54	Hamp Pool	23-11-2
1955-59	Sid Gillman	28-32-1
1960-62	Bob Waterfield***	9-24-1
1962-65	Harland Svare	14-31-3
1966-1970	George Allen	49-19-4
1971-72	Tommy Prothro	14-12-2
1973-77	Chuck Knox	57-20-1
1978-1982	Ray Malavasi	43-36-0
1983-1991	John Robinson	79-74-0
1992-94	Chuck Knox	15-33-0
1995-96	Rich Brooks	13-19-0
1997-99	Dick Vermeil	25-26-0
2000-05	Mike Martz****	56-36-0
2005	Joe Vitt	4-7-0
2006-08	Scott Linehan#	11-25-0
2008	Jim Haslett	2-10-0
2009	Steve Spagnuolo	1-15-0

* Released after three games in 1938
** Resigned after one game in 1952
*** Resigned after eight games in 1962
**** Took medical leave after five games in 2005
\# Released after four games in 2008

PAID ATTENDANCE

Home 427,115 Away 476,157
Total 903,272
Single-game home record, 66,273 (12/10/00)
Single-season home record, 520,926 (1999)

2010 DRAFT CHOICES

Round	Name	Pos.	College
1	Sam Bradford	QB	Oklahoma
2	Rodger Saffold	T	Indiana
3	Jerome Murphy	DB	South Florida
4	Mardy Gilyard	WR	Cincinnati
5	Michael Hoomanawanui	TE	Illinois
	Hall Davis	DE	Louisiana-Lafayette
6	Fendi Onobun	TE	Houston
	Eugene Sims	DE	West Texas A&M
7	Marquis Johnson	DB	Alabama
	George Selvie	DE	South Florida
	Josh Hall	LB	Penn State

ST. LOUIS RAMS

2009 TEAM RECORD

PRESEASON (3-1)

Date	Result	Opponent
8/14	W 23-20	at N.Y. Jets
8/21	L 13-20	Atlanta
8/27	W 24-21	at Cincinnati
9/3	W 17-9	Kansas City

REGULAR SEASON (1-15)

Date	Result	Opponent
9/13	L 0-28	at Seattle
9/20	L 7-9	at Washington
9/27	L 17-36	Green Bay
10/4	L 0-35	at San Francisco
10/11	L 10-38	Minnesota
10/18	L 20-23	at Jacksonville (OT)
10/25	L 6-42	Indianapolis
11/1	W 17-10	at Detroit
11/15	L 23-28	New Orleans
11/22	L 13-21	Arizona
11/29	L 17-27	Seattle
12/6	L 9-17	at Chicago
12/13	L 7-47	at Tennessee
12/20	L 13-16	Houston
12/27	L 10-31	at Arizona
1/3	L 6-28	San Francisco

(OT) Overtime

SCORE BY PERIODS

Rams	16	74	25	60	0	— 175
Opponents	87	114	93	139	3	— 436

2009 TEAM STATISTICS

	Rams	Opp.
Total First Downs	259	333
Rushing	79	127
Passing	159	182
Penalty	21	24
3rd Down: Made/Att	73/226	91/209
3rd Down Pct.	32.3	43.5
4th Down: Made/Att	10/28	6/12
4th Down Pct.	35.7	50.0
Possession Avg.	28:58	31:02
Total Net Yards	4470	5965
Avg. Per Game	279.4	372.8
Total Plays	998	1016
Avg. Per Play	4.5	5.9
Net Yards Rushing	1784	2201
Avg. Per Game	111.5	137.6
Total Rushes	411	500
Net Yards Passing	2686	3764
Avg. Per Game	167.9	235.3
Sacked/Yards Lost	44/284	25/149
Gross Yards	2970	3913
Att./Completions	543/312	491/315
Completion Pct.	57.5	64.2
Had Intercepted	21	8
Punts/Average	90/46.8	75/44.3
Net Punting Avg.	90/41.7	75/36.9
Penalties/Yards	100/834	80/613
Fumbles/Ball Lost	24/12	26/12
Touchdowns	17	54
Rushing	4	24
Passing	12	22
Returns	1	8

2009 INDIVIDUAL STATISTICS

PASSING	Att.	Comp.	Yds.	Pct.	TD	Int.	Tkld.	Rate
Bulger	247	140	1469	56.7	5	6	14/85	70.7
Boller	176	98	899	55.7	3	6	17/117	61.2
Null	119	73	566	61.3	3	9	13/82	49.9
Jo. Brown	1	1	36	100.0	1	0	0/0	158.3
Rams	543	312	2970	57.5	12	21	44/284	64.0
Opponents	491	315	3913	64.2	22	8	25/149	96.9

SCORING	TD R	TD P	TD Rt	PAT	FG	Saf	PTS
Jo. Brown	0	0	0	16/16	19/24	0	73
Avery	0	5	0	0/0	0/0	0	30
Jackson	4	0	0	0/0	0/0	0	24
Fells	0	3	0	0/0	0/0	0	18
Amendola	0	1	0	0/0	0/0	0	6
B. Gibson TM	0	1	0	0/0	0/0	0	6
Little	0	0	1	0/0	0/0	0	6
McMichael	0	1	0	0/0	0/0	0	6
Robinson	0	1	0	0/0	0/0	0	6
Rams	4	12	1	16/16	19/24	0	175
Opponents	24	22	8	51/52	19/22	1	436

2-Pt. Conversions: Rams 0-1, Opponents 1-2.

RUSHING	No.	Yds	Avg	LG	TD
Jackson	324	1416	4.4	58	4
Darby	27	152	5.6	51	0
Boller	13	76	5.8	16	0
Ogbonnaya	11	50	4.5	18	0
Avery	4	30	7.5	15	0
Gado	14	26	1.9	11	0
Bulger	8	22	2.8	7	0
Karney	2	8	4.0	8	0
Null	5	6	1.2	3	0
Amendola	3	-2	-0.7	8	0
Rams	411	1784	4.3	58	4
Opponents	500	2201	4.4	62t	24

RECEIVING	No.	Yds	Avg	LG	TD
Jackson	51	322	6.3	38	0
Avery	47	589	12.5	50	5
Amendola	43	326	7.6	25	1
B. Gibson TM	34	348	10.2	23	1
McMichael	34	332	9.8	35	1
Burton	25	253	10.1	25	0
Fells	21	273	13.0	36t	3
Darby	18	96	5.3	13	0
Robinson	13	167	12.8	45	1
Bajema	8	94	11.8	27	0
Martin	6	99	16.5	33	0
Karney	6	16	2.7	9	0
Gado	3	25	8.3	13	0
Ogbonnaya	1	19	19.0	19	0
Carter	1	6	6.0	6	0
Kent	1	5	5.0	5	0
Rams	312	2970	9.5	50	12
Opponents	315	3913	12.4	73t	22

INTERCEPTIONS	No.	Yds	Avg	LG	TD
J. Butler	3	17	5.7	17	0
Laurinaitis	2	28	14.0	21	0
Atogwe	2	21	10.5	12	0
Little	1	36	36.0	36t	1
Rams	8	102	12.8	36t	1
Opponents	21	321	15.3	65t	4

PUNTING	No.	Yds.	Avg.	In 20	LG
D. Jones	90	4212	46.8	34	63
Rams	90	4212	46.8	34	63
Opponents	75	3326	44.3	25	70

PUNT RETURNS	Ret	FC	Yds	Avg	LG	TD
Amendola	31	11	360	11.6	56	0
Stanley	3	1	37	12.3	24	0
Q. Butler	2	2	-2	-1.0	0	0
Roach	1	0	0	0.0	0	0
Rams	37	14	395	10.7	56	0
Opponents	41	12	260	6.3	29	0

KICKOFF RETURNS	No.	Yds	Avg	LG	TD
Amendola	66	1618	24.5	58	0
Darby	4	54	13.5	23	0
Bajema	2	26	13.0	14	0
Gado	1	23	23.0	23	0
Avery	1	19	19.0	19	0
Grant	1	14	14.0	14	0
Karney	1	10	10.0	10	0
Rams	76	1764	23.2	58	0
Opponents	43	1032	24.0	97t	1

FIELD GOALS	1-19	20-29	30-39	40-49	50+
Jo. Brown	0/0	5/5	4/5	4/7	6/7
Rams	0/0	5/5	4/5	4/7	6/7
Opponents	1/1	10/10	5/5	2/3	1/3

SACKS	No.
Little	6.5
Long	5.0
Hall	4.5
Dahl	2.0
Laurinaitis	2.0
Ah You	1.0
Atogwe	1.0
Grant	1.0
Ramsey	1.0
Ryan	1.0
Rams	25.0
Opponents	44.0

RECORD HOLDERS

INDIVIDUAL RECORDS—CAREER

Category	Name	Performance
Rushing (Yds.)	Eric Dickerson, 1983-87	7,245
Passing (Yds.)	Jim Everett, 1986-1993	23,758
Passing (TDs)	Roman Gabriel, 1962-1972	154
Receiving (No.)	Isaac Bruce, 1994-2007	942
Receiving (Yds.)	Isaac Bruce, 1994-2007	14,109
Interceptions	Ed Meador, 1959-1970	46
Punting (Avg.)	Danny Villanueva, 1960-64	44.3
Punt Return (Avg.)	Az-Zahir Hakim, 1998-2001	11.4
Kickoff Return (Avg.)	Ron Brown, 1984-89, 1991	26.3
Field Goals	Jeff Wilkins, 1997-2007	265
Touchdowns (Tot.)	Marshall Faulk, 1999-2005	85
Points	Jeff Wilkins, 1997-2007	1,223
*Sacks	Leonard Little, 1998-2008	81.0

INDIVIDUAL RECORDS—SINGLE SEASON

Category	Name	Performance
Rushing (Yds.)	Eric Dickerson, 1984	**2,105
Passing (Yds.)	Kurt Warner, 2001	4,830
Passing (TDs)	Kurt Warner, 1999	41
Receiving (No.)	Isaac Bruce, 1995	119
Receiving (Yds.)	Isaac Bruce, 1995	1,781
Interceptions	Dick (Night Train) Lane, 1952	**14
Punting (Avg.)	Donnie Jones, 2008	50.0
Punt Return (Avg.)	Woodley Lewis, 1952	18.5
Kickoff Return (Avg.)	Verda (Vitamin T) Smith, 1950	33.7
Field Goals	Jeff Wilkins, 2003	39
Touchdowns (Tot.)	Marshall Faulk, 2000	26
Points	Jeff Wilkins, 2003	163
*Sacks	Kevin Carter, 1999	17.0

INDIVIDUAL RECORDS—SINGLE GAME

Category	Name	Performance
Rushing (Yds.)	Willie Ellison, 12-5-71	247
Passing (Yds.)	Norm Van Brocklin, 9-28-51	**554
Passing (TDs)	Many times Last time by Kurt Warner, 10-10-99	5
Receiving (No.)	Tom Fears, 12-3-50	18
Receiving (Yds.)	Willie Anderson, 11-26-89	**336
Interceptions	Many times Last time by Keith Lyle, 12-15-96	3
Field Goals	Bob Waterfield, 12-9-51	5
	Jeff Wilkins, 10-1-00	5
Touchdowns (Tot.)	Many times Last time by Marshall Faulk, 10-20-02	4
Points	Many times Last time by Marshall Faulk, 10-20-02	24
*Sacks	Gary Jeter, 9-18-88	5.0

**Sacks became an official statistic in 1982.*
***NFL Record*

ST. LOUIS RAMS

2010 VETERAN ROSTER

No.	Name	Pos.	Ht.	Wt.	Birthdate	NFL Exp.	College	Hometown	How Acq.	'09 Games/ Starts
94	Adeyanju, Victor	DE	6-4	284	2/11/83	5	Indiana	Chicago, Ill.	D4-'06	10/1
99	Ah You, C.J.	DE	6-4	270	7/7/82	2	Oklahoma	Highland, Utah	FA-'07	8/1
62	Allen III, Roger	G	6-3	323	2/10/86	2	Missouri Western State	Raytown, Mo.	FA-'09	2/1
16	Amendola, Danny	WR	5-11	186	11/2/85	2	Texas Tech	The Woodlands, Texas	FA-'09	14/2
50	Asiodu, K.C.	LB	6-2	242	11/24/86	2	Central Oklahoma	Chino Hills, Calif.	FA-'09	10/0
21	Atogwe, Oshiomogho	S	5-11	205	6/23/81	6	Stanford	Windsor, Ontario (Canada)	D3a-'05	12/12
17	Avery, Donnie	WR	5-11	183	6/12/84	3	Houston	Alief, Texas	D2-'08	16/16
47	Bajema, Billy	TE	6-4	259	10/31/82	6	Oklahoma State	Oklahoma City, Okla.	UFA(SF)-'09	16/5
24	Bartell, Ron	CB	6-1	206	2/22/82	6	Howard	Detroit, Mich.	D2-'05	15/15
41	Bassey, Eric	S	6-1	215	1/3/83	3	Oklahoma	Garland, Texas	FA-'07	0*
63	Bell, Jacob	G	6-5	300	3/2/81	7	Miami (Ohio)	Cleveland, Ohio	UFA(Tenn)-'08	13/13
60	Brown, Jason	C	6-3	328	5/5/83	6	North Carolina	Henderson, N.C.	UFA(Balt)-'09	16/16
3	Brown, Josh	K	6-0	205	4/29/79	8	Nebraska	Foyil, Okla.	UFA(Sea)-'08	16/0
14	Burton, Keenan	WR	6-0	206	10/29/84	3	Kentucky	Louisville, Ky.	D4b-'08	9/6
37	Butler, James	S	6-3	209	9/7/82	6	Georgia Tech	Bainbridge, Ga.	UFA(NYG)-'09	13/13
36	Butler, Quincy	CB	6-1	188	11/25/83	3	Texas Christian	San Antonio, Texas	W(Dall)-'08	14/7
52	t- Carpenter, Bobby	LB	6-2	250	8/1/83	5	Ohio State	Lancaster, Ohio	T(Dall)-'10	16/2*
57	Chamberlain, Chris	LB	6-1	230	9/30/85	3	Tulsa	Bethany, Okla.	D7a-'08	16/0
70	Conover, Sean	DE	6-5	275	7/31/84	3	Bucknell	Whitman, Mass.	FA-'09	0*
43	Dahl, Craig	S	6-1	209	6/17/85	4	North Dakota State	Mankato, Minn.	FA-'09	14/8
34	Darby, Kenneth	RB	5-10	219	12/26/82	3	Alabama	Huntsville, Ala.	FA-'08	16/1
53	Diggs, Na'il	LB	6-4	240	7/8/78	11	Ohio State	Los Angeles, Calif.	FA-'10	15/11*
35	Dockery, Kevin	CB	5-8	188	1/8/84	5	Mississippi State	Hernando, Miss.	FA-'10	15/15*
54	Douglas, Dominic	LB	6-1	240	1/13/87	2	Mississippi State	Clinton, Miss.	FA-'09	4/0
69	Douzable, Leger	DT	6-4	305	5/31/86	2	Central Florida	Tampa, Fla.	FA-'09	12/1
4	Feeley, A.J.	QB	6-3	220	5/16/77	10	Oregon	Caldwell, Idaho	UFA(Car)-'10	0*
46	Fells, Daniel	TE	6-4	272	9/23/83	4	California-Davis	Fullerton, Calif.	FA-'08	14/4
32	Fletcher, Bradley	CB	6-0	198	6/25/86	2	Iowa	Youngstown, Ohio	D3-'09	7/3
	Fraley, Hank	C/G	6-3	310	9/21/77	11	Robert Morris	Gaithersburg, MD	FA-'10	15/4*
35	Gado, Samkon	RB	5-10	227	11/13/82	4	Liberty	Columbia, S.C.	FA-'09	15/0
11	t- Gibson, Brandon	WR	6-0	210	8/13/87	2	Washington State	Puyallup, Wash.	T(Phil)-'09	10/4*
71	Gibson, Gary	DT	6-3	300	5/5/82	5	Rutgers	Lafayette, N.Y.	FA-'09	5/5
73	Goldberg, Adam	T	6-7	309	8/12/80	7	Wyoming	Edina, Minn.	T(Minn)-'06	16/14
25	Gorrer, Danny	CB	6-0	185	6/1/86	2	Texas A&M	Port Arthur, Texas	FA-'09	3/1
59	Grant, Larry	LB	6-1	251	2/16/85	2	Ohio State	Sacramento, Calif.	FA-'08	16/0
79	Greco, John	G	6-4	329	3/24/85	3	Toledo	Youngstown, Ohio	D3-'08	11/3
96	Hall, James	DE	6-2	281	2/4/77	11	Michigan	New Orleans, La.	T(Det)-'07	14/14
42	Hart, Clinton	S	6-0	208	7/20/77	7	Central Florida C.C.	Bushnell, Fla.	FA-'09	3/0
39	Jackson, Steven	RB	6-2	236	7/22/83	6	Oregon State	Las Vegas, Nev.	D1-'04	15/15
87	Johnson, Darcy	TE	6-5	252	2/11/83	5	Central Florida	St. Augustine, Fla.	FA-'10	13/4*
5	Jones, Donnie	P	6-2	225	7/5/80	7	Louisiana State	Baton Rouge, La.	RFA(Mia)-'07	16/0
44	Karney, Mike	FB	5-11	260	7/6/81	7	Arizona State	Kent, Wash.	FA-'09	14/8
82	Kent, Jordan	WR	6-4	219	7/24/84	3	Oregon	Eugene, Ore.	FA-'09	5/0
31	King, Justin	CB	5-11	188	5/11/87	3	Penn State	Pittsburgh, Pa.	D4a-'08	15/7
55	Laurinaitis, James	LB	6-2	247	12/3/86	2	Ohio State	Plymouth, Minn.	D2-'09	16/16
91	Little, Leonard	DE	6-3	267	10/19/74	12	Tennessee	Asheville, N.C.	D3-'98	13/13
72	Long, Chris	DE	6-3	276	3/28/85	3	Virginia	Charlottesville, Va.	D1-'08	16/4
45	Massey, Chris	LS	6-0	237	8/21/79	9	Marshall	Chesapeake, W. Va.	D7-'02	7/0
84	McMichael, Randy	TE	6-3	246	6/28/79	8	Georgia	Fort Valley, Ga.	FA-'07	16/16
67	Miller, Drew	C	6-5	303	7/6/85	2	Florida	Paducah, Ky.	FA-'09	0*
9	Null, Keith	QB	6-4	219	9/24/85	2	West Texas A&M	Lampasas, Texas	D6-'09	4/4
22	Ogbonnaya, Chris	RB	6-0	225	5/20/86	2	Texas	Houston, Texas	D7-'09	2/0
30	t- Payne, Kevin	S	6-0	212	12/5/83	4	Louisiana-Monroe	Junction City, Ark.	T(Chi)-'10	13/5*
99	Ramsey, LaJuan	DT	6-3	300	3/19/84	3	Southern California	Compton, Calif.	W(Tenn)-'09	15/5
27	Roach, David	S	6-2	216	8/9/85	2	Texas Christian	Abilene, Texas	FA-'08	15/0
98	Robbins, Fred	DT	6-4	325	3/26/77	11	Wake Forest	Pensacola, Fla.	UFA(NYG)-'10	16/12*
19	Robinson, Laurent	WR	6-2	197	5/20/85	4	Illinois State	Rockledge, Fla.	T(Atl)-'09	3/3
95	Ryan, Clifton	DT	6-3	324	2/18/84	4	Michigan State	Saginaw, Mich.	D5b-'07	16/15
97	Scott, Darell	DT	6-3	315	3/15/86	2	Clemson	Columbia, S.C.	D4-'09	12/5
66	Setterstrom, Mark	G	6-4	318	3/3/84	5	Minnesota	Northfield, Minn.	D7b-'06	10/3
77	Smith, Jason	T	6-5	307	4/30/86	2	Baylor	Dallas, Texas	D1-'09	8/5
64	Trautwein, Phil	T	6-6	308	4/15/86	2	Florida	Voorhees, N.J.	FA-'09	4/0
58	Vobora, David	LB	6-1	239	4/8/86	3	Idaho	Eugene, Ore.	D7b-'08	12/10
76	Wyche, James	DE	6-5	279	4/19/82	5	Syracuse	Roosevelt, N.Y.	W(Jax)-'09	3/0*

* Bassey missed '09 season because of injury: Carpenter played 16 games with Dallas in '09; Conover last active with Tennessee in '07; Diggs played 15 games with Carolina; Dockery played 11 games with N.Y. Giants; Feeley did not play in 5 games with Carolina; Fraley played 15 games with Cleveland; B. Gibson played 1 game with Philadelphia and 9 games with St. Louis; Johnson played 13 games with N.Y. Giants; Miller last active with Jacksonville in '08; Payne played 13 games with Chicago; Robbins played 16 games with N.Y. Giants; Wyche played 2 games with Jacksonville and 1 with St. Louis.

t- Rams traded for Carpenter (Dall), B. Gibson (Phil) and Payne (Chi).

Traded—T Alex Barron (16 games in '09) to Dallas, DT Adam Carriker (0) to Washington, LB Will Witherspoon (6) to Philadelphia.

Players lost through free agency (2): QB Kyle Boller (Oak; 7 games in '09), LB Paris Lenon (Ariz; 14).

Also played with Rams in '09—QB Marc Bulger (9 games), WR Tim Carter (2), LB Quinton Culberson (1), S Clinton Hart (3), G Richie Incognito (9), WR Nate Jones (1), WR Ruvell Martin (8), LS Ryan Neill (9), WR/CB Cord Parks (2), DT LaJuan Ramsey (15), CB Anthony Smith (2), WR Derek Stanley (2), DT Hollis Thomas (3), CB Jonathan Wade (15).

2010 FIRST-YEAR ROSTER

Name	Pos.	Ht.	Wt.	Birthdate	College	Hometown	How Acq.
Bradford, Sam	QB	6-4	223	11/8/87	Oklahoma	Oklahoma City, Okla.	D1
Bradwell, Chris (1)	DT	6-5	280	12/17/83	Troy	Johns Creek, Ga.	FA-'09
Butler, Eric (1)	TE	6-2	265	9/13/84	Mississippi State	Moss Point, Miss.	FA-'09
Cudjo, Jermelle	DT	6-2	293	9/28/86	Central Oklahoma	Lawton, Okla.	FA
Curry, Dominique	WR	6-2	227	8/16/87	California (Pa.)	Philadelphia, Pa.	FA
Davis, Hall	DE	6-4	240	3/2/87	Louisiana-Lafayette	Baton Rouge, La.	D5b
Foster, Brooks (1)	WR	6-1	205	4/9/86	North Carolina	Boling Springs, S.C.	D5-'09
Gilyard, Mardy	WR	5-11	179	12/2/86	Cincinnati	Bunnell, Fla.	D4
Harris, Freddie	LB	6-2	227	6/21/86	Central Oklahoma	Coppell, Texas	FA
Harris, Martin	S	5-11	201	7/29/87	Fresno State	Stockton, Calif.	FA
Hoomanawanui, Michael	TE	6-4	264	7/4/88	Illinois	Bloomington, Ill.	D5a
Hull, Josh	LB	6-3	237	5/21/87	Penn State	Millheim, Pa.	D7c
Jackson, Cardia	LB	6-0	237	4/13/88	Louisiana-Monroe	Monroe, La.	FA
Johnson, Marquis	DB	5-11	192	5/18/88	Alabama	Sarasota, Fla.	D7a
Jones, Jeromy	S	5-11	202	11/20/86	Idaho	Las Vegas, Nev.	FA
Lawrence, Simoni	LB	6-0	232	2/1/88	Minnesota	Upper Darby, Pa	FA
Lewis, Mark (1)	G	6-3	305	7/17/85	Oregon	Arroyo Grande, Calif.	FA-'09
Lewis, Thaddeus	QB	6-0	215	2/1/88	Duke	Opa-locka, Fla.	FA
McCoy, Jamie	FB	6-2	240	7/21/87	Texas A&M	Midland, Texas	FA
McKee, Ryan (1)	T	6-6	291	11/4/86	Southern Mississippi	Daphne, Ala.	W(NYJ)-'09
McRae, Brandon	WR	6-3	208	3/5/86	Mississippi State	Chester, Va.	FA
Moore, Nick (1)	WR	6-2	186	6/25/86	Toledo	Columbus, Ohio	FA
Murphy, Jerome	CB	6-0	196	1/13/87	South Florida	Elizabeth, N.J.	D3
Onobun, Fendi	TE	6-6	249	11/17/86	Houston	Houston, Texas	D6a
Owens, Roderick	WR	6-0	183	1/28/87	Florida State	Jacksonville, Fla.	FA
Parks, Cord (1)	WR/CB	5-10	185	11/12/86	Northeastern	Stone Mountain, Ga.	FA-'09
Reid, Ernest	DT	6-2	320	9/14/1986	Univ. of Mary	Laie, Hawaii	FA
Saffold, Rodger	T	6-5	318	6/6/88	Indiana	Bedford, Ohio	D2
Selvie, George	DE	6-4	250	3/6/87	South Florida	Pensacola, Fla.	D7b
Sims, Eugene	DE	6-6	235	3/18/86	West Texas A&M	Mize, Miss.	D6b
Stewart, Darian	S	5-11	216	8/4/88	South Carolina	Huntsville, Ala.	FA
Thompson, Antoine	CB	5-11	189	10/3/87	Reno	Norfolk, Va.	FA
Tinsley, Kennedy	FB	6-0	225	12/4/86	North Carolina	Greensboro, N.C.	FA
Toston, Keith	RB	6-0	214	5/6/87	Oklahoma State	Angleton, Texas	FA
Woolridge, DeMaundray	RB	5-9	241	4/4/87	Idaho	Keller, Texas	FA
Young, Eric (1)	T	6-3	304	11/22/83	Tennessee	Union, S.C.	FA-'09

The term NFL Rookie is defined as a player who is in his first season of professional football and has not been on the roster of another professional football team for any regular-season or postseason games. A Rookie is designated by an "R" on NFL rosters. Players who have been active in another professional football league or players who have NFL experience, including either preseason training camp or being on an Active List or Inactive List, or on Reserve/Injured or Reserve/Physically Unable to Perform for fewer than six regular-season games, are termed NFL First-Year Players. An NFL First-Year Player is designated by a "1" on NFL rosters. Thereafter, a player is credited with an additional year of experience for each season in which he accumulates six games on the Active List or Inactive List, or on Reserve/Injured or Reserve/Physically Unable to Perform.

Log on to www.stlouisrams.com for an up-to-date roster.

COACHING STAFF

Head Coach,

Steve Spagnuolo

Pro Career: Named the twenty-fifth head coach in franchise history on January 19, 2009. Spagnuolo was defensive coordinator of the New York Giants from 2007-08. In 2007, the Giants' defense ranked seventh in the NFL in yards allowed after ranking 25th in 2006. The Giants were in the NFL's top 10 in eight statistical categories and led the league with 53 quarterback sacks. The Giants beat the undefeated New England Patriots 17-14 in Super Bowl XLII. The Giants' defense held the Patriots to nearly 130 yards less than their season average. New England scored 14 points in the Super Bowl after averaging more than 36 points per game in the regular season. In 2008, Spagnuolo's defense improved from seventh to fifth in the NFL in total defense as the Giants won the NFC East. Spagnuolo spent eight seasons (1999-2006) with the Philadelphia Eagles, serving as defensive assistant/safeties from 1999-2000, defensive backs coach from 2001-03 and linebackers coach from 2004-06. From 1999-2005, the Eagles played in four NFC Championship games and one Super Bowl. Spagnuolo served as defensive line/special teams coach with the Barcelona Dragons of the WLAF in 1992 and was defensive coordinator/linebackers coach for NFL Europe's Frankfurt Galaxy in 1998. Spagnuolo worked as pro personnel intern with the Washington Redskins in 1983 and as a scout with the San Diego Chargers in 1993. Career record: 1-15.

Background: Wide receiver at Springfield (Mass.) College (1978-1981). Coached collegiately at Massachusetts (1982-83), Lafayette (1984-86), Connecticut (1987-1991), Maine (1993-94), Rutgers (1994-95), and Bowling Green (1996-97).

Personal: Born December 21, 1959 in Whitinsville, Mass. He is married to wife, Maria.

ASSISTANT COACHES

Nolan Cromwell, wide receivers; born January 30, 1955, Smith Center, Kan. Defensive back/quarterback Kansas 1973-76. Pro safety Los Angeles Rams 1977-1987. College coach: Texas A&M 2008-09. Pro coach: Los Angeles Rams 1991, Green Bay Packers 1992-98, Seattle Seahawks 1999-2007, re-joined Rams in 2010.

Sylvester Croom, running backs; born September 25, 1954, Tuscaloosa, Ala. Linebacker/tight end/center Alabama 1971-74. Pro center New Orleans Saints 1975. College coach: Alabama 1976-1986, Mississippi State 2004-08 (head coach). Pro coach: Tampa Bay Buccaneers 1987-1990, Indianapolis Colts 1991, San Diego Chargers 1992-96, Detroit Lions 1997-2000, Green Bay Packers 2001-03, joined Rams in 2009.

Richard Curl, asst. head coach/quarterbacks; born May 4, 1940, Chester, Pa. Quarterback Richmond 1958-1962. No pro playing experience. College coach: Trenton State 1973-74, Rutgers 1975-1980, 1983-89, Virginia 1981-82, Boston College 1990. Pro coach: Barcelona Dragons (NFLE) 1991-97, Frankfurt Galaxy (NFLE) 1998-2000, New York Jets 2003-05, Kansas City Chiefs 2006-08, joined Rams in 2009.

Andre Curtis, secondary/safeties; born December 8, 1976, Beaverdam, Va. Linebacker Virginia Military Institute 1996-99. No pro playing experience. College coach: Virginia Military Institute 2000-03, Georgia Southern 2004-05. Pro coach: New York Giants 2006-08, joined Rams in 2009.

Brendan Daly, defensive line; born September 10, 1975, Springfield, Ill. Tight End Drake 1993-96. No pro playing experience. College coach: Drake 1998, Villanova 1999, 2005, Maryland 2000, Oklahoma State 2001-2003, Illinois State 2004. Pro coach: Minnesota Vikings 2006-08, joined Rams in 2009.

Chuck Faucette, asst. strength; born October 7, 1963, Willingboro, N.J. Linebacker Maryland 1983-86. Pro linebacker San Diego Chargers 1987-89. College coach: Texas 1999-2001, 2007, Southern Methodist 2002-06. Pro coach: Hamilton TigerCats (CFL) 1990-92, joined Rams in 2008.

Paul Ferraro, linebackers; born April 30, 1959, Ridgewood, N.J. Safety Springfield College 1978-1981. No pro playing experience. College coach: Massachusetts 1982, Syracuse 1983, Villanova 1984-86, Dartmouth 1987, Catholic University 1988, Maine 1989, Ohio University 1990, Bowling Green 1991-98, Georgia Tech 1999-2000, Rutgers 2001-04. Pro coach: Carolina Panthers 2005, Minnesota Vikings 2006-08, joined Rams in 2009.

Ken Flajole, defensive coordinator; born October 4, 1954, Seattle. Linebacker Carroll College 1972, Wenatchee Valley Community College 1973, Pacific Lutheran 1974-75. No pro playing experience. College coach: Pacific Lutheran 1977-78, Washington 1979, Montana 1980-85, Texas-El Paso 1986-88, Missouri 1989-1993, Richmond 1994, Hawaii 1995, Nevada 1996-97. Pro coach: Green Bay Packers 1998, Seattle Seahawks 1999-2002, Carolina Panthers 2003-08, joined Rams in 2009.

Rock Gullickson, strength; born April 11, 1955, Moorhead, Minn. Guard Moorhead State 1973-76. No pro playing experience. College coach: Moorhead State 1978, Maryville State (N.D.) 1979-1980, South Dakota State 1981, Montana State 1982-89, Rutgers 1990-92, Texas 1993-97, Louisville 1998-99. Pro coach: New Orleans Saints 2000-05, Green Bay Packers 2006-08, joined Rams in 2009.

Matt House, defensive quality control; born May 17, 1978, Harrison, Mich. No pro playing experience. College coach: Michigan State 2001-02, North Carolina 2003-04, Gardner-Webb 2005, Buffalo 2006-07. Pro coach: Carolina Panthers 2008, joined Rams in 2009.

Frank Leonard, tight ends; born April 5, 1958, Wethersfield, Conn. Cornerback Central Connecticut State 1976, 1978-1980. No pro playing experience. College coach: Western Connecticut 1982-84, Central Connecticut State 1985-86, Western Connecticut 1987-89, Connecticut 1990-93, Richmond 1994-2003, Kansas State 2007-08. Pro coach: Joined Rams in 2009.

Steve Loney, offensive line; born April 26, 1952, Marshalltown, Iowa. Guard Iowa State 1971-72. No pro playing experience. College coach: Iowa State 1974, 1995-97, Missouri Western 1975-76, Morehead State 1979-1983, Citadel 1984-86, Colorado State 1989-1992, Connecticut 1994, Minnesota 1998-99, Iowa State 2000-01, Drake 2007. Pro coach: Arizona Cardinals 1993, Minnesota Vikings 2002-05, Arizona Cardinals 2006, joined Rams in 2008.

Clayton Lopez, secondary/cornerbacks; born May 26, 1970, Los Angeles. Defensive back Nevada 1991-94. No pro playing experience. College coach: Nevada 1995-98. Pro coach: Seattle Seahawks 1999-2003, Oakland Raiders 2004-05, Detroit Lions 2006-08, joined Rams in 2009.

Tom McMahon, special teams coordinator; born July 12, 1969, Helena, Mont. Corner Carroll College 1988-1992. No pro playing experience. College coach: Carroll College 1992, 1994, Utah State 1995-2005, Louisville 2006. Pro coach: Atlanta Falcons 2007-08, joined Rams in 2009.

Pat Shurmur, offensive coordinator; born April 14, 1965, Ann Arbor, Mich. Center/linebacker Michigan State 1983-87. No pro playing experience. College coach: Michigan State 1988-1997, Stanford 1998. Pro coach: Philadelphia Eagles 1999-2008, joined Rams in 2009.

Andy Sugarman, quality control/offense; born May 23, 1972, Lafayette, Calif. No college or pro playing experience. College coach: California-Berkeley 1991-97. Pro coach: San Francisco 49ers 1998-2002, Detroit Lions 2003-05, Atlanta Falcons 2007, joined Rams in 2009.

Derius Swinton, quality control special teams; born April 26, 1985, Newport News, Va. Safety Hampton 2003-06. No pro playing experience. College coach: Tennessee 2007-08. Pro coach: Joined Rams in 2009.

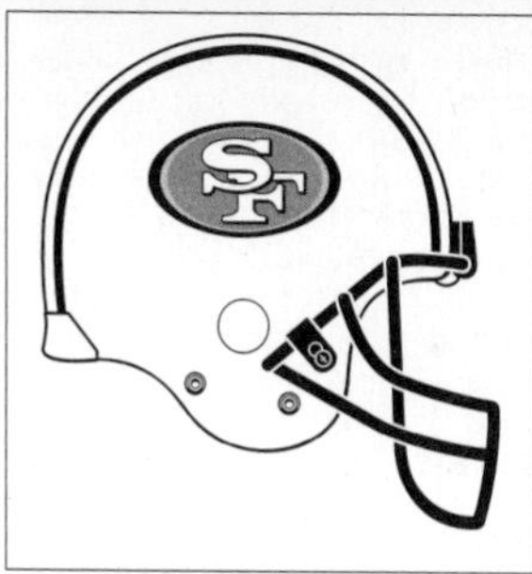

National Football Conference
West Division
Team Colors: 49ers Gold, 49ers Red, and Beige
4949 Centennial Boulevard
Santa Clara, California 95054
Telephone: (408) 562-4949

2010 SCHEDULE

PRESEASON

Aug. 15	at Indianapolis	1:00
Aug. 22	**Minnesota**	5:00
Aug. 28	at Oakland	6:00
Sep. 2	**San Diego**	7:00

REGULAR SEASON

Sep. 12	at Seattle	1:15
Sep. 20	**New Orleans** (Mon)	5:30
Sep. 26	at Kansas City	12:00
Oct. 3	at Atlanta	1:00
Oct. 10	**Philadelphia**	5:20
Oct. 17	**Oakland**	1:05
Oct. 24	at Carolina	1:00
Oct. 31	**Denver** (London)	5:00
Nov. 7	BYE	
Nov. 14	**St. Louis**	1:15
Nov. 21	**Tampa Bay**	1:05
Nov. 29	at Arizona (Mon)	6:30
Dec. 5	at Green Bay	12:00
Dec. 12	**Seattle**	1:05
Dec. 16	at San Diego (Thu)	5:20
Dec. 26	at St. Louis	12:00
Jan. 2	**Arizona**	1:15

Stadium: Candlestick Park (opened in 1960)
•**Capacity:** 69,732
San Francisco, California 94124
Playing Surface: Natural Grass
Training Camp: Marie P. DeBartolo Sports Center
4949 Centennial Boulevard
Santa Clara, CA 95054

CANDLESTICK PARK

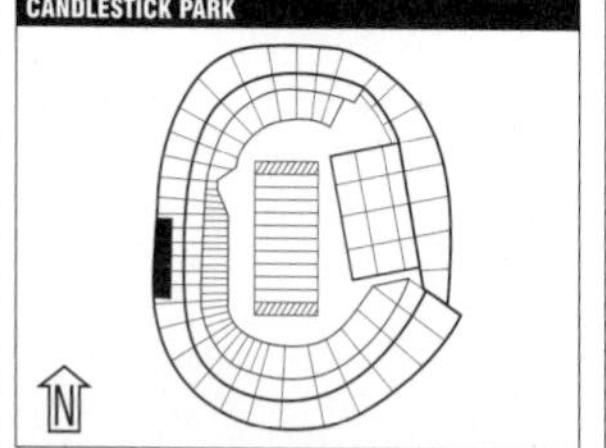

CLUB OFFICIALS

OWNERSHIP

Co-Chairman/Owner: Denise DeBartolo York
Co-Chairman/Owner: John York
Team President/CEO: Jed York
Limited Partner: Rick and Carla Morabito

MANAGEMENT

Executive Vice President of Football Administration: Lal Heneghan
Executive Vice President of Football & Business Operations: Paraag Marathe
Director of Player Personnel: Trent Baalke
Director of Pro Personnel: Tom Gamble
Vice President of Football Affairs: Keena Turner
Vice President/CFO: Larry MacNeil
Vice President of Marketing: Michael P. Williams
Vice President of Stadium Operations & Security: Jim Mercurio
Chief Sales Officer: John Vidalin
Vice President Communications and Government Relations: Lisa Lang
Vice President of Business Development: Mike Redlick
Vice President of Ticketing & Suites: Jamie Brandt
Director of Public Relations: Bob Lange
Head Athletic Trainer: Jeff Ferguson
Equipment Manager: Steve Urbaniak
Director of Video Operations: Keith Yanagi
Controller: Debye Whelchel
Director of Finance: Scott Sabatino
Director of Security: Fred Formosa

Director of Information Technology: Alexander Ignacio
Director of Alumni Relations: Guy McIntrye
Director of Player Development: Ty Knott
Senior Manager of Ticket Office: Lynn Carrozzi
Business Operations Consultant: Dwight Clark
Senior Human Resources Manager: Tina De Vora Rojas
Director of Community Relations/49ers Foundation: Joanne Pasternack

COACHING HISTORY
(483-404-13)

Records include postseason games

1950-54	Lawrence (Buck) Shaw	33-25-2
1955	Norman (Red) Strader	4-8-0
1956-58	Frankie Albert	19-17-1
1959-1963	Howard (Red) Hickey*	27-27-1
1963-67	Jack Christiansen	26-38-3
1968-1975	Dick Nolan	56-56-5
1976	Monte Clark	8-6-0
1977	Ken Meyer	5-9-0
1978	Pete McCulley**	1-8-0
1978	Fred O'Connor	1-6-0
1979-1988	Bill Walsh	102-63-1
1989-1996	George Seifert	108-35-0
1997-2002	Steve Mariucci	60-43-0
2003-04	Dennis Erickson	9-23-0
2005-08	Mike Nolan***	18-37-0
2008-09	Mike Singletary	13-12-0

* Resigned after three games in 1963
** Released after nine games in 1978
*** Released after seven games in 2008

PAID ATTENDANCE

Home 485,667 Away 505,584
Total 991,251
Single-game home record, 69,014 (11/13/94)
Single-season home record, 544,228 (1999)

2010 DRAFT CHOICES

Round	Name	Pos.	College
1	Anthony Davis	T	Rutgers
	Mike Iupati	G	Idaho
2	Taylor Mays	DB	Southern California
3	Navorro Bowman	LB	Penn State
6	Anthony Dixon	RB	Mississippi St.
	Nate Byham	TE	Pittsburgh
	Kyle Williams	WR	Arizona St.
7	Phillip Adams	DB	South Carolina St.

SAN FRANCISCO 49ERS

2009 TEAM RECORD

PRESEASON (3-1)

Date	Result	Opponent
8/14	W 17-16	Denver
8/22	W 21-20	Oakland
8/29	W 20-13	at Dallas
9/4	L 7-26	at San Diego

REGULAR SEASON (8-8)

Date	Result	Opponent
9/13	W 20-16	at Arizona
9/20	W 23-10	Seattle
9/27	L 24-27	at Minnesota
10/4	W 35-0	St. Louis
10/11	L 10-45	Atlanta
10/25	L 21-24	at Houston
11/1	L 14-18	at Indianapolis
11/8	L 27-34	Tennessee
11/12	W 10-6	Chicago
11/22	L 24-30	at Green Bay
11/29	W 20-3	Jacksonville
12/6	L 17-20	at Seattle
12/14	W 24-9	Arizona
12/20	L 13-27	at Philadelphia
12/27	W 20-6	Detroit
1/3	W 28-6	at St. Louis

SCORE BY PERIODS

49ers	62	93	72	103	0	—	330
Opponents	57	116	33	75	0	—	281

2009 TEAM STATISTICS

	49ers	Opp.
Total First Downs	238	278
Rushing	77	77
Passing	137	176
Penalty	24	25
3rd Down: Made/Att	65/218	88/240
3rd Down Pct.	29.8	36.7
4th Down: Made/Att	12/21	6/15
4th Down Pct.	57.1	40.0
Possession Avg.	29:47	30:14
Total Net Yards	4652	5222
Avg. Per Game	290.8	326.4
Total Plays	939	1050
Avg. Per Play	5.0	5.0
Net Yards Rushing	1600	1552
Avg. Per Game	100.0	97.0
Total Rushes	371	426
Net Yards Passing	3052	3670
Avg. Per Game	190.8	229.4
Sacked/Yards Lost	40/241	44/293
Gross Yards	3293	3963
Att./Completions	528/312	580/352
Completion Pct.	59.1	60.7
Had Intercepted	14	18
Punts/Average	99/47.6	95/45.2
Net Punting Avg.	99/41.0	95/41.5
Penalties/Yards	98/758	114/969
Fumbles/Ball Lost	24/10	29/15
Touchdowns	39	28
Rushing	12	12
Passing	23	14
Returns	4	2

2009 INDIVIDUAL STATISTICS

PASSING	Att.	Comp.	Yds.	Pct.	TD	Int.	Tkld.	Rate
A. Smith	372	225	2350	60.5	18	12	22/134	81.5
S. Hill	155	87	943	56.1	5	2	18/107	79.6
Spurlock TM	1	0	0	0.0	0	0	0/0	39.6
49ers	528	312	3293	59.1	23	14	40/241	80.8
Opponents	580	352	3963	60.7	14	18	44/293	76.2

SCORING	TD R	TD P	TD Rt	PAT	FG	Saf	PTS
Nedney	0	0	0	33/33	17/21	0	84
V. Davis	0	13	0	0/0	0/0	0	78
Gore	10	3	0	0/0	0/0	0	78
Morgan	0	3	0	0/0	0/0	0	18
Crabtree	0	2	0	0/0	0/0	0	12
J. Hill	0	2	0	0/0	0/0	0	12
Schmitt	0	0	0	2/2	2/3	0	8
Clements	0	0	1	0/0	0/0	0	6
Coffee	1	0	0	0/0	0/0	0	6
McDonald	0	0	1	0/0	0/0	0	6
McKillop	0	0	1	0/0	0/0	0	6
Norris	1	0	0	0/0	0/0	0	6
Willis	0	0	1	0/0	0/0	0	6
Andrus TM	0	0	0	4/4	0/0	0	4
49ers	12	23	4	39/39	19/24	0	330
Opponents	12	14	2	26/27	29/34	0	281

2-Pt. Conversions: 49ers 0-0, Opponents 0-1.

RUSHING	No.	Yds	Avg	LG	TD
Gore	229	1120	4.9	80t	10
Coffee	83	226	2.7	17	1
S. Hill	8	70	8.8	22	0
Morgan	5	61	12.2	20	0
A. Smith	24	51	2.1	11	0
Norris	14	41	2.9	15	1
Del. Walker	3	34	11.3	16	0
Spurlock TM	1	3	3.0	3	0
Robinson	3	2	0.7	4	0
Bruce	1	-8	-8.0	-8	0
49ers	371	1600	4.3	80t	12
Opponents	426	1552	3.6	41	12

RECEIVING	No.	Yds	Avg	LG	TD
V. Davis	78	965	12.4	73t	13
Morgan	52	527	10.1	61	3
Gore	52	406	7.8	48	3
Crabtree	48	625	13.0	50	2
Bruce	21	264	12.6	50	0
Del. Walker	21	233	11.1	39	0
Coffee	11	76	6.9	12	0
J. Hill	9	90	10.0	30	2
Norris	7	31	4.4	11	0
Robinson	6	24	4.0	8	0
Battle	5	40	8.0	12	0
Jones	1	18	18.0	18	0
A. Smith	1	-6	-6.0	-6	0
49ers	312	3293	10.6	73t	23
Opponents	352	3963	11.3	90t	14

INTERCEPTIONS	No.	Yds	Avg	LG	TD
Goldson	4	39	9.8	34	0
Bly	3	66	22.0	31	0
Willis	3	33	11.0	23t	1
Brown	2	52	26.0	51	0
Spencer	2	2	1.0	2	0
Roman	1	27	27.0	27	0
Franklin	1	10	10.0	10	0
Clements	1	8	8.0	8	0
M. Lewis	1	0	0.0	0	0
49ers	18	237	13.2	51	1
Opponents	14	168	12.0	43	1

PUNTING	No.	Yds.	Avg.	In 20	LG
Lee	99	4711	47.6	30	64
49ers	99	4711	47.6	30	64
Opponents	95	4295	45.2	31	67

PUNT RETURNS	Ret	FC	Yds	Avg	LG	TD
Battle	21	10	61	2.9	18	0
Rossum TM	12	1	84	7.0	14	0
Jones	9	1	26	2.9	13	0
Clements	4	1	38	9.5	12	0
R. Smith	3	0	7	2.3	9	0
49ers	49	13	216	4.4	18	0
Opponents	57	14	495	8.7	56	0

KICKOFF RETURNS	No.	Yds	Avg	LG	TD
Robinson	18	414	23.0	40	0
Morgan	13	367	28.2	76	0
Rossum TM	7	152	21.7	40	0
Del. Walker	5	85	17.0	25	0
Battle	3	68	22.7	26	0
Coffee	3	42	14.0	16	0
Balmer	2	7	3.5	4	0
Norris	1	0	0.0	0	0
49ers	52	1135	21.8	76	0
Opponents	65	1415	21.8	101t	1

FIELD GOALS	1-19	20-29	30-39	40-49	50+
Nedney	0/0	4/4	7/8	4/6	2/3
Schmitt	0/0	0/1	2/2	0/0	0/0
49ers	0/0	4/5	9/10	4/6	2/3
Opponents	0/0	11/12	8/8	6/9	4/5

SACKS	No.
Lawson	6.5
Brooks	6.0
J. Smith	6.0
Haralson	5.0
Spikes	4.0
Willis	4.0
McDonald	3.0
Franklin	2.0
Goldson	2.0
Evans	1.5
Bly	1.0
M. Lewis	1.0
Roman	1.0
Sopoaga	1.0
49ers	44.0
Opponents	40.0

RECORD HOLDERS

INDIVIDUAL RECORDS—CAREER

Category	Name	Performance
Rushing (Yds.)	Joe Perry, 1950-1960, 1963	7,344
Passing (Yds.)	Joe Montana, 1979-1992	35,124
Passing (TDs)	Joe Montana, 1979-1992	244
Receiving (No.)	Jerry Rice, 1985-2000	1,281
Receiving (Yds.)	Jerry Rice, 1985-2000	19,247
Interceptions	Ronnie Lott, 1981-1990	51
Punting (Avg.)	Andy Lee, 2004-09	44.9
Punt Return (Avg.)	Dana McLemore, 1982-87	10.8
Kickoff Return (Avg.)	Abe Woodson, 1958-1964	29.4
Field Goals	Ray Wersching, 1977-1987	190
Touchdowns (Tot.)	Jerry Rice, 1985-2000	187
Points	Jerry Rice, 1985-2000	1,130
*Sacks	Bryant Young, 1994-2007	89.5

INDIVIDUAL RECORDS—SINGLE SEASON

Category	Name	Performance
Rushing (Yds.)	Frank Gore, 2006	1,695
Passing (Yds.)	Jeff Garcia, 2000	4,278
Passing (TDs)	Steve Young, 1998	36
Receiving (No.)	Jerry Rice, 1995	122
Receiving (Yds.)	Jerry Rice, 1995	**1,848
Interceptions	Dave Baker, 1960	10
	Ronnie Lott, 1986	10
Punting (Avg.)	Andy Lee, 2008	47.8
Punt Return (Avg.)	Dana McLemore, 1982	22.3
Kickoff Return (Avg.)	Joe Arenas, 1953	34.4
Field Goals	Jeff Wilkins, 1996	30
Touchdowns (Tot.)	Jerry Rice, 1987	23
Points	Jerry Rice, 1987	138
*Sacks	Fred Dean, 1983	17.5

INDIVIDUAL RECORDS—SINGLE GAME

Category	Name	Performance
Rushing (Yds.)	Frank Gore, 11-19-06	212
Passing (Yds.)	Joe Montana, 10-14-90	476
Passing (TDs)	Joe Montana, 10-14-90	6
Receiving (No.)	Terrell Owens, 12-17-00	20
Receiving (Yds.)	Jerry Rice, 12-18-95	289
Interceptions	Dave Baker, 12-4-60	**4
Field Goals	Ray Wersching, 10-16-83	6
	Jeff Wilkins, 9-29-96	6
Touchdowns (Tot.)	Jerry Rice, 10-14-90	5
Points	Jerry Rice, 10-14-90	30
*Sacks	Fred Dean, 11-13-83	6.0

**Sacks became an official statistic in 1982.*
***NFL Record*

SAN FRANCISCO 49ERS

2010 VETERAN ROSTER

No.	Name	Pos.	Ht.	Wt.	Birthdate	NFL Exp.	College	Hometown	How Acq.	'09 Games/ Starts
64	Baas, David	G	6-4	330	9/28/81	6	Michigan	Sarasota, Fla.	D2-'05	16/16
96	Balmer, Kentwan	DT	6-5	315	10/15/86	3	North Carolina	Weldon, N.C.	D1-'08	11/0
50	Briggs, Diyral	LB	6-4	230	10/31/85	2	Bowling Green	Mt. Healthy, Ohio	FA-'09	4/0
55	Brooks, Ahmad	LB	6-3	259	3/14/84	5	Virginia	Fairfax, Va.	W(Cin)-'08	14/0
25	Brown, Tarell	CB	5-10	193	1/6/85	4	Texas	Mesquite, Texas	D5-'07	16/4
88	Bruce, Isaac	WR	6-0	188	11/10/72	17	Memphis	Fort Lauderdale, Fla.	FA-'08	10/7
5	Carr, David	QB	6-3	216	7/21/79	9	Fresno State	Bakersfield, Calif.	UFA(NYG)-'10	6/0*
22	Clements, Nate	CB	6-0	205	12/12/79	10	Ohio State	Shaker Heights, Ohio	UFA(Buff)-'07	7/6
29	Coffee, Glen	RB	6-0	209	5/1/87	2	Alabama	Fort Walton Beach, Fla.	D3-'09	14/2
15	Crabtree, Michael	WR	6-1	214	9/14/87	2	Texas Tech	Dallas, Texas	D1-'09	11/11
88	Curtis, Tony	TE	6-5	251	2/11/83	4	Portland State	Seaside, Calif.	FA-'10	0*
7	Davis, Nate	QB	6-1	226	5/5/87	2	Ball State	Bellaire, Ohio	D5b-'09	0*
85	Davis, Vernon	TE	6-3	250	1/31/84	5	Maryland	Washington, D.C.	D1a-'06	16/16
93	Evans, Demetric	DT	6-4	275	9/3/79	9	Georgia	Haynesville, La.	UFA(Wash)-'09	14/0
92	Franklin, Aubrayo	NT	6-1	317	8/27/80	8	Tennessee	Johnson City, Tenn.	UFA(Balt)-'07	16/16
19 t-	Ginn, Ted	WR	5-11	180	4/12/85	4	Ohio State	Cleveland, Ohio	T(Mia)-'10	16/12*
38	Goldson, Dashon	S	6-2	200	9/18/84	4	Washington	Carson, Calif.	D4b-'07	16/16
21	Gore, Frank	RB	5-9	217	5/14/83	6	Miami	Coral Gables, Fla.	D3a-'05	14/14
98	Haralson, Parys	LB	6-0	255	1/24/84	5	Tennessee	Flora, Miss.	D5a-'06	16/16
66	Heitmann, Eric	C	6-3	312	2/24/80	9	Stanford	Katy, Texas	D7a-'02	16/16
89	Hill, Jason	WR	6-0	202	2/20/85	4	Washington State	San Francisco, Calif.	D3a-'07	11/0
31	James, William	CB	6-0	200	6/15/79	10	Western Illinois	Uniontown, Pa.	UFA(Det)-'10	16/14*
95	Jean Francois, Ricky	DT	6-3	295	11/23/86	2	Louisiana State	Miami, Fla.	D7b-'09	3/0
86	Jennings, Brian	TE/LS	6-5	242	10/14/76	11	Arizona State	Mesa, Ariz.	D7b-'00	16/0
81	Jones, Brandon	WR	6-1	212	10/6/82	6	Oklahoma	Texarkana, Texas	UFA(Tenn)-'09	8/0
54	LaBoy, Travis	LB	6-3	250	8/20/81	6	Hawaii	Honolulu, Hawaii	FA-'10	0*
99	Lawson, Manny	LB	6-5	240	7/3/84	5	North Carolina State	Goldsboro, N.C.	D1b-'06	16/16
4	Lee, Andy	P	6-2	180	8/11/82	7	Pittsburgh	Westminster, S.C.	D6a-'04	16/0
32	Lewis, Michael	S	6-1	222	4/29/80	9	Colorado	Houston, Texas	UFA(Phil)-'07	15/15
91	McDonald, Ray	DT	6-3	290	9/2/84	4	Florida	Belle Glade, Fla.	D3b-'07	16/0
56	McKillop, Scott	LB	6-1	244	3/4/86	2	Pittsburgh	Export, Pa.	D5a-'09	16/0
84	Morgan, Josh	WR	6-0	219	6/20/85	3	Virginia Tech	Washington, D.C.	D6-'08	16/15
6	Nedney, Joe	K	6-5	234	3/22/73	15	San Jose State	San Jose, Calif.	FA-'05	14/0
44	Norris, Moran	FB	6-1	250	6/16/78	10	Kansas	Houston, Texas	UFA(Det)-'09	16/7
61	Patrick, Chris	T	6-5	305	8/22/84	2	Nebraska	Ithaca, Mich.	FA-'09	3/0
41	Paymah, Karl	CB	6-0	195	11/29/82	6	Washington State	Culver City, Calif.	FA-'10	12/2*
62	Rachal, Chilo	T/G	6-4	315	3/15/86	3	Southern California	Compton, Calif.	D2-'08	16/15
24	Robinson, Michael	RB	6-1	223	2/6/83	5	Penn State	Richmond, Va.	D4-'06	15/0
65	Sims, Barry	T	6-5	300	12/1/74	12	Utah	Park City, Utah	FA-'08	16/7
11	Smith, Alex	QB	6-4	217	5/7/84	6	Utah	San Diego, Calif.	D1-'05	11/10
94	Smith, Justin	DT	6-4	285	9/30/79	10	Missouri	Jefferson City, Mo.	UFA(Cin)-'08	16/16
20	Smith, Keith	CB	5-11	191	3/20/80	6	McNeese State	Leesville, La.	FA-'09	3/0
30	Smith, Reggie	S	6-1	200	9/3/86	3	Oklahoma	Edmond, Okla.	D3-'08	10/0
68	Snyder, Adam	T/G	6-6	325	1/30/82	6	Oregon	Fullerton, Calif.	D3b-'05	16/16
90	Sopoaga, Isaac	DT	6-2	330	9/4/81	7	Hawaii	Pago Pago, American Samoa	D4a-'04	16/16
36	Spencer, Shawntae	CB	6-1	190	2/22/82	7	Pittsburgh	Rankin, Pa.	D2b-'04	16/16
51	Spikes, Takeo	LB	6-2	242	12/17/76	13	Auburn	Sandersville, Ga.	FA-'08	15/15
74	Staley, Joe	T	6-5	315	8/30/84	4	Central Michigan	Rockford, Mich.	D1b-'07	9/9
28	Taylor, Curtis	S	6-2	209	7/13/85	2	Louisiana State	Bogalusa, La.	D7a-'09	7/0
46	Walker, Delanie	TE	6-0	242	8/12/84	5	Central Missouri	Texarkana, Texas	D6a-'06	16/8
78	Walker, Derek	DT	6-4	271	9/16/86	2	Illinois	Glendale Heights, Ill.	W(Sea)-'09	0*
59	Wallace, Cody	C	6-4	300	11/26/84	3	Texas A&M	Cuero, Texas	D4-'08	1/0
57	Wilhelm, Matt	LB	6-2	245	2/2/81	8	Ohio State	Oberlin, Ohio	FA-'09	11/1
52	Willis, Patrick	LB	6-1	240	1/25/85	4	Mississippi	Bruceton, Tenn.	D1a-'07	16/16
69	Wragge, Tony	G	6-4	310	8/14/79	6	New Mexico State	Bloomfield, Neb.	FA-'05	15/0
17	Zeigler, Dominique	WR	6-3	185	10/11/84	2	Baylor	Kalamazoo, Mich.	FA-'07	0*

* Carr played 6 games with N.Y. Giants in '09; Curtis inactive for 3 games with Baltimore; N. Davis inactive third quarterback for all 16 games; Ginn played 16 games with Miami; James played 16 games with Detroit; LaBoy last active with Arizona '08; Paymah played 12 games with Minnesota; Der. Walker inactive for 1 game; Zeigler last active with San Francisco in '08.

t- 49ers traded for Ginn (Mia).

Retired—Jeff Ulbrich, 10-year linebacker, 4 games in '09.

Players lost through free agency (2): WR Arnaz Battle (Pitt; 15 games in '09), T Tony Pashos (Cle: 5).

Also played with 49ers in '09—CB Dre' Bly (16 games), LB Marques Harris (4), QB Shaun Hill (6), CB Marcus Hudson (12), FB Brit Miller (5), S Mark Roman (16), CB Allen Rossum (3), P Ricky Schmitt (1), WR Micheal Spurlock (4).

2010 FIRST-YEAR ROSTER

Name	Pos.	Ht.	Wt.	Birthdate	College	Hometown	How Acq.
Adams, Phillip	CB	5-11	192	7/20/88	South Carolina State	Rock Hill, S.C.	D7
Andrus, Shane (1)	K	5-10	190	10/2/80	Murray State	Murray, Tenn.	FA
Balogun, Mike	LB	6-0	240	9/28/83	Oklahoma	Upper Marlboro, Md.	FA
Boone, Alex (1)	T	6-7	328	5/4/87	Ohio State	Lakewood, Ohio	FA-'09
Bowman, Navorro	LB	6-0	242	5/28/88	Penn State	Suitland, Md.	D3
Brock, Tramaine	CB	5-10	197	8/20/88	Belhaven	Gulfport, Miss.	FA
Brown, Jarrett	QB	6-3	224	9/21/87	West Virginia	West Palm Beach, Fla.	FA
Burnett, Martail (1)	LB	6-3	262	1/10/85	Utah	Los Angeles, Calif.	FA-'09
Byham, Nate	TE	6-4	264	6/27/88	Pittsburgh	Franklin, Pa.	D6b
Caulcrick, Jehuu (1)	FB	6-0	250	8/6/83	Michigan State	Findley Lake, N.Y.	FA
Davis, Anthony	T	6-5	323	10/11/89	Rutgers	Piscataway, N.J.	D1a
de la Puente, Brian (1)	G	6-3	306	5/13/85	California	Los Angeles, Calif.	FA
Dixon, Anthony	RB	6-1	233	9/24/87	Mississippi State	Jackson, Mich.	D6a
Finley, Joe Jon (1)	TE	6-6	251	1/30/85	Oklahoma	Arlington, Texas	FA-'08
Grant, Bakari	WR	6-3	195	6/24/87	California-Davis	Oakland, Calif.	FA
Iupati, Mike	G	6-5	331	5/12/87	Idaho	American Samoa	D1b
Kristick, Keaton	LB	6-3	234	4/25/88	Oregon State	Naperville, Ill.	FA
Long, Brandon (1)	LB	6-3	254	9/6/86	Michigan State	Canton, Ohio	FA
Long, Scott	WR	6-2	216	10/22/86	Louisville	Southport, N.C.	FA
Maragos, Chris	S	5-10	200	1/6/87	Wisconsin	Racine, Wisc.	FA
Mays, Taylor	S	6-3	230	2/7/88	Southern California	Seattle, Wash.	D2
Miller, Brit (1)	FB	6-0	243	9/15/86	Illinois	Decatur, Ill.	W(Car)-'09
Mitchell, Khalif (1)	DT	6-5	318	4/7/85	East Carolina	Virginia Beach, Va.	FA-'09
Perry, Jared	WR	6-1	177	3/29/88	Missouri	La Marque, Texas	FA
Stoudamire, Patrick	CB	5-10	206	2/21/88	Western Illinois	Portland, Ore.	FA
Vann, LeRoy	CB/RS	5-8	177	11/18/86	Florida A&M	Tampa, Fla.	FA
Williams, Kyle	WR	5-10	186	7/19/88	Arizona State	San Jose, Calif.	D6c

The term NFL Rookie is defined as a player who is in his first season of professional football and has not been on the roster of another professional football team for any regular-season or postseason games. A Rookie is designated by an "R" on NFL rosters. Players who have been active in another professional football league or players who have NFL experience, including either preseason training camp or being on an Active List or Inactive List, or on Reserve/Injured or Reserve/Physically Unable to Perform for fewer than six regular-season games, are termed NFL First-Year Players. An NFL First-Year Player is designated by a "1" on NFL rosters. Thereafter, a player is credited with an additional year of experience for each season in which he accumulates six games on the Active List or Inactive List, or on Reserve/Injured or Reserve/Physically Unable to Perform.

Log on to www.sf49ers.com for an up-to-date roster.

SAN FRANCISCO 49ERS

COACHING STAFF

Head Coach,

Mike Singletary

Pro Career: Named the sixteenth head coach in 49ers history on October 20, 2008, Mike Singletary enters his third season at the helm of the San Francisco 49ers. Singletary is in his eighth season as an NFL coach after a 12-year Pro Football Hall of Fame playing career with the Chicago Bears. Prior to being named head coach of the 49ers, Singletary served as the assistant head coach/defense for San Francisco from 2006 to 2008 after spending one year as the assistant head coach/linebackers in 2005. He was the inside linebackers coach for the Baltimore Ravens from 2003 to 2004. Inducted into the Hall of Fame in 1998, Singletary played linebacker for the Chicago Bears (1981-1992) after being drafted in the second round of the 1981 NFL Draft out of Baylor. The former Bears captain played in a team-record 10 consecutive Pro Bowls and was also named All-Pro eight times. Career record: 13-12.

Background: Singletary earned All-America honors as both a junior and senior at Baylor. He was the only junior selected to the All-Southwest Conference Team of the 1970s. Singletary is a graduate of Evan E. Worthing (Tex.) High School in Houston.

Personal: Born October 9, 1958, Houston. He and wife Kim have seven children.

ASSISTANT COACHES

Ray Brown, asst. offensive line; born December 12, 1962, Marion, Ark. Offensive lineman Arkansas State 1982-85. Pro offensive lineman St. Louis/Phoenix Cardinals 1986-88, Washington Redskins 1989-1995, 2004-05, San Francisco 49ers 1996-2001, Detroit Lions 2002-03. Pro coach: Washington Redskins 2006, Buffalo Bills 2008-09, joined 49ers in 2010.

Duane Carlisle, strength and conditioning; born Nov. 13, 1965, Haverhill, Mass. Attended Maryland. No college or pro playing experience. Pro coach: Speed development consultant for Philadelphia Eagles 2000-04, joined 49ers in 2005.

Wendell Davis, asst. wide receivers; born January 3, 1966, Shreveport, La. Wide receiver Louisiana State 1984-87. Pro wide receiver Chicago Bears 1988-1993, Indianapolis Colts 1995. Pro coach: Joined 49ers in 2009.

Dave Fipp, asst. special teams; born August 8, 1974, Albuquerque, N.M. Safety Arizona 1994-97. No pro playing experience. College coach: Holy Cross 1998-99, Arizona 2000, Cal Poly 2001-03, Nevada 2004, San Jose State 2005-07. Pro coach: Joined 49ers in 2008.

Al Harris, pass rush specialist; born December 31, 1956, Bangor, Me. Defensive end Arizona State 1975-78. Pro defensive end Chicago Bears 1979-1988, Philadelphia Eagles 1989-1990. Pro coach: Joined 49ers in 2009.

Pete Hoener, tight ends; born June 14, 1954, Peoria, Ill. Tight end/defensive end Bradley 1969-1970. College coach: Missouri 1975-76, Illinois State 1977, Indiana State 1978-1984, Illinois 1986-88, Purdue 1989-1990, Texas Christian 1991-97, Iowa State 1998-99, Texas A&M 2000. Pro coach: St. Louis Cardinals 1985-86, Arizona Cardinals 2003, Chicago Bears 2004, joined 49ers in 2005.

Mike Johnson, quarterbacks; born May 2, 1967, Los Angeles. Quarterback Arizona State 1985-86, Akron 1988-89. Pro quarterback Arizona Cardinals 1990, San Antonio Riders (WLAF) 1991-92, British Columbia Lions (CFL) 1992-93, Shreveport Pirates (CFL) 1994-95. College coach: Oregon State 1997-99. Pro coach: San Diego Chargers 2000-01, Atlanta Falcons 2002-05, Baltimore Ravens 2006-07, joined 49ers in 2009.

Vance Joseph, secondary assistant; born September 20, 1972, Marrero, La. Defensive back Colorado 1990-94. Pro defensive back New York Jets 1995, Indianapolis Colts 1996. College coach: Colorado 1999-2001, 2002-03, Wyoming 2002, Bowling Green State 2004. Pro coach: Joined 49ers in 2005.

Johnnie Lynn, special assistant to head coach/secondary; born December 19, 1956, Los Angeles. Defensive back UCLA 1975-78. Pro defensive back New York Jets 1979-1986. College coach: Arizona 1988-1993. Pro coach: Tampa Bay Buccaneers 1994-95, San Francisco 49ers 1996, New York Giants 1997-2003, Baltimore Ravens 2004-05, joined 49ers in 2006.

Greg Manusky, defensive coordinator; born August 12, 1966, Wilkes-Barre, Pa. Linebacker Colgate 1983-87. Pro linebacker Washington Redskins 1988-1990, Minnesota Vikings 1991-93, Kansas City Chiefs 1994-99. Pro coach: Washington Redskins 2001, San Diego Chargers 2002-06, joined 49ers in 2007.

Jason Michael, offensive assistant; born October 15, 1978, Portsmouth, Ohio. Quarterback Western Kentucky 1999-2002. No pro playing experience. College coach: Tennessee 2003-04, 2008. Pro coach: Oakland Raiders 2005, New York Jets 2006-07, joined 49ers in 2009.

Tom Rathman, running backs; born October 7, 1962, Grand Island, Neb. Running back Nebraska 1983-85. Pro running back San Francisco 49ers 1986-1993, Los Angeles Raiders 1994. College coach: Menlo College (Calif.) 1996. Pro coach: San Francisco 1997-2002, Detroit Lions 2003-05, Oakland Raiders 2007-08, re-joined 49ers in 2009.

Jimmy Raye, offensive coordinator; born March 26, 1946, Fayetteville, N.C. Quarterback Michigan State 1964-68. Pro defensive back Philadelphia Eagles 1969. College coach: Michigan State 1971-75, Wyoming 1976. Pro coach: San Francisco 49ers 1977, Detroit Lions 1978-79, Atlanta Falcons 1980-82, 1987-89, Los Angeles Rams 1983-84, 1991, Tampa Bay Buccaneers 1985-86, New England Patriots 1990, Kansas City Chiefs 1992-2000, Washington Redskins 2001, New York Jets 2002-03, Oakland Raiders 2004-05, New York Jets 2006-08, re-joined 49ers in 2009.

Kurt Schottenheimer, special teams coordinator; born October 1, 1949, McDonald, Pa. Quarterback Coffeyville (Kan.) J.C. 1967-68, defensive back Miami 1969-1970. No pro playing experience. College coach: William Paterson 1974, Michigan State 1978-1982, Tulane 1983, Louisiana State 1984-85, Notre Dame 1986. Pro coach: Cleveland Browns 1987-88, Kansas City Chiefs 1989-2000, Washington Redskins 2001, Detroit Lions 2002-03, Green Bay Packers 2004, St. Louis Rams 2005, Green Bay Packers 2006, joined 49ers in 2010.

Vantz Singletary, inside linebackers; born November 23, 1965, Houston, Texas. Linebacker Blinn College 1985-86, Kansas State 1987-88. No pro playing experience. College coach: Trinity International 1992-96, Southern 1997-98, Hawaii 1999-2005, Tennessee-Chattanooga 2006-07, Buffalo 2008. Pro coach: Joined 49ers in 2009.

Mike Solari, offensive line, born January 16, 1955, Daly City, Calif. Offensive lineman San Diego State 1972-75. No pro playing experience. College coach: Mira Costa (Calif.) J.C. 1978, U.S. International 1979, Boise State 1980, Cincinnati 1981-82, Kansas 1983-85, Pittsburgh 1986, Alabama 1990-91. Pro coach: Dallas Cowboys 1987-88, Phoenix Cardinals 1989, San Francisco 49ers 1992-1996, Kansas City Chiefs 1997-2007, Seattle Seahawks 2008-09, rejoined 49ers in 2010.

Jerry Sullivan, wide receivers/senior assistant; born July 13, 1944, Miami, Fla. Quarterback Florida State 1963-64. No pro playing experience. College coach: Kansas State 1971-72, Texas Tech 1973-75, South Carolina 1976-1982, Indiana 1983, Louisiana State 1984-1990, Ohio State 1991. Pro coach: San Diego Chargers 1992-96, Detroit Lions 1997-2000, Arizona Cardinals 2001-03, Miami Dolphins 2004, joined 49ers in 2005.

Jason Tarver, outside linebackers/defensive assistant; born August 28, 1974, Stanford, Calif. Defensive back West Valley College 1994-95. No pro playing experience. College coach: West Valley College 1996-97, UCLA 1998-2000. Pro coach: Joined 49ers in 2001.

Jim Tomsula, defensive line; born April 14, 1967, Homestead, Pa. Middle Tennessee State 1985-86, Catawba College 1987-1990. No pro playing experience. College coach: Charleston Southern 1997. Pro coach: England Monarchs (NFL Europe) 1998, Scottish Claymores (NFL Europe) 1999-2003, Berlin Thunder (NFL Europe) 2004-05, Rhein Fire (NFL Europa) 2006 (head coach), joined 49ers in 2007.

Mark Uyeyama, asst. strength and conditioning; born December 2, 1975, Vancouver, B.C. Nose Guard Butte C.C. 1994-95, Northern State 1996-97. No pro playing experience. College coach: Arizona State 2001-03, Utah State 2004-07. Pro coach: joined 49ers in 2008.

National Football Conference
West Division
Team Colors: Seahawks Blue, Seahawks Navy, Seahawks Bright Green
Virginia Mason Athletic Center
12 Seahawks Way
Renton, Washington 98056
Telephone: (425) 203-8000

2010 SCHEDULE
PRESEASON

Aug. 14	**Tennessee**	7:00
Aug. 21	**Green Bay**	7:00
Aug. 28	at Minnesota	7:00
Sep. 2	at Oakland	7:00

REGULAR SEASON

Sep. 12	**San Francisco**	1:15
Sep. 19	at Denver	2:05
Sep. 26	**San Diego**	1:15
Oct. 3	at St. Louis	12:00
Oct. 10	BYE	
Oct. 17	at Chicago	12:00
Oct. 24	**Arizona**	1:05
Oct. 31	at Oakland	1:15
Nov. 7	**New York Giants**	1:05
Nov. 14	at Arizona	2:15
Nov. 21	at New Orleans	3:05
Nov. 28	**Kansas City**	1:05
Dec. 5	**Carolina**	1:15
Dec. 12	at San Francisco	1:05
Dec. 19	**Atlanta**	1:05
Dec. 26	at Tampa Bay	1:00
Jan. 2	**St. Louis**	1:15

Stadium: Qwest Field
(opened in 2002)
• **Capacity:** 67,000
Playing Surface: FieldTurf
Training Camp: VMAC
Renton, WA 98056

QWEST FIELD

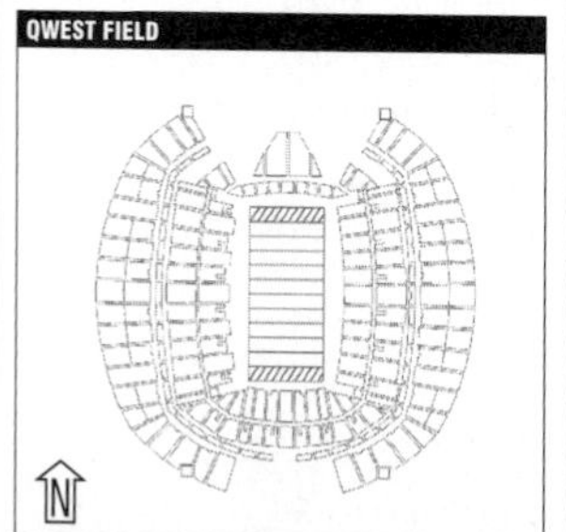

CLUB OFFICIALS
Chairman: Paul Allen
CEO: Tod Leiweke
Executive Vice President of Football Operations & Head Coach: Pete Carroll
General Manager: John Schneider
COO: John Rizzardini
CFO & VP/Finance: Karen Harrison
VP/Football Operations: Will Lewis
VP/Football Administration: John Izdik
VP/Player Personnel: Ruston Webster
VP/Community Outreach: Mike Flood
VP/General Counsel: Lance Lopes
VP/Corporate Partnerships: Ron Jenkins
Director of Marketing: Bill Chapin
Director of Corp. Hospitality, Suite Sales & Service: Amy Sprangers
Director of Pro Personnel: Tag Ribary
VP/Communications & Broadcasting: Dave Pearson
Director of Communications: Lane Gammel
Director of Community Outreach: Sandy Gregory
Director of Ticket Sales/Operations: Chuck Arnold
Gameday Presentation: Rick Crawford
Video Director Football: Thom Fermstad
Head Athletic Trainer: Sam Ramsden
Equipment Manager: Erik Kennedy
Team Travel: Jeremy Young

COACHING HISTORY
(262-287-0)
Records include postseason games

1976-1982	Jack Patera*	35-59-0
1982	Mike McCormack	4-3-0
1983-1991	Chuck Knox	83-67-0
1992-94	Tom Flores	14-34-0
1995-98	Dennis Erickson	31-33-0
1999-2008	Mike Holmgren	90-80-0
2009	Jim Mora	5-11-0

*Released after two games in 1982

PAID ATTENDANCE
Home 525,691 Away 501,286
Total 1,026,977
Single-game home record, 68,681 (12/16/00)
Single-season home record, 533,657 (2007)

2010 DRAFT CHOICES

Round	Name	Pos.	College
1	Russell Okung	T	Oklahoma St.
	Earl Thomas	DB	Texas
2	Golden Tate	WR	Notre Dame
4	Walter Thurmond	DB	Oregon
	E.J. Wilson	DE	North Carolina
5	Kam Chancellor	DB	Virginia Tech
6	Anthony McCoy	TE	Southern California
7	Dexter Davis	LB	Arizona St.
	Jameson Konz	WR	Kent St.

SEATTLE SEAHAWKS

2009 TEAM RECORD

PRESEASON (4-0)

Date	Result	Opponent
8/15	W 20-14	at San Diego
8/22	W 27-13	Denver
8/29	W 14-10	at Kansas City
9/3	W 31-21	Oakland

REGULAR SEASON (5-11)

Date	Result	Opponent
9/13	W 28-0	St. Louis
9/20	L 10-23	at San Francisco
9/27	L 19-25	Chicago
10/04	L 17-34	at Indianapolis
10/11	W 41-0	Jacksonville
10/18	L 3-27	Arizona
11/01	L 17-38	at Dallas
18	W 32-20	Detroit
11/15	L 20-31	at Arizona
11/22	L 9-35	at Minnesota
11/29	W 27-17	at St. Louis
12/6	W 20-17	San Francisco
12/13	L 7-34	at Houston
12/20	L 7-24	Tampa Bay
12/27	L 10-48	at Green Bay
1/3	L 13-17	Tennessee

SCORE BY PERIODS

Seahawks	37	118	46	79	0 —	280
Opponents	100	109	104	77	0 —	390

2009 TEAM STATISTICS

	Seahawks	Opp.
Total First Downs	297	305
Rushing	80	80
Passing	184	204
Penalty	33	21
3rd Down: Made/Att	75/225	87/223
3rd Down Pct.	33.3	39.0
4th Down: Made/Att	8/19	6/12
4th Down Pct.	42.1	50.0
Possession Avg.	27:31	32:29
Total Net Yards	5069	5703
Avg. Per Game	316.8	356.4
Total Plays	1045	1024
Avg. Per Play	4.9	5.6
Net Yards Rushing	1566	1776
Avg. Per Game	97.9	111.0
Total Rushes	395	428
Net Yards Passing	3503	3927
Avg. Per Game	218.9	245.4
Sacked/Yards Lost	41/268	28/185
Gross Yards	3771	4112
Att./Completions	609/372	568/374
Completion Pct.	61.1	65.8
Had Intercepted	19	13
Punts/Average	89/46.1	82/47.2
Net Punting Avg.	89/38.7	82/41.5
Penalties/Yards	95/840	111/971
Fumbles/Ball Lost	33/12	21/10
Touchdowns	30	46
Rushing	7	17
Passing	20	27
Returns	3	2

2009 INDIVIDUAL STATISTICS

PASSING	Att.	Comp.	Yds.	Pct.	TD	Int.	Tkld.	Rate
Hasselbeck	488	293	3029	60.0	17	17	32/209	75.1
S. Wallace	120	78	700	65.0	3	2	9/59	81.9
Ryan	1	1	42	100.0	0	0	0/0	118.8
Seahawks	609	372	3771	61.1	20	19	41/268	76.7
Opponents	568	374	4112	65.8	27	13	28/185	93.4

SCORING	TD R	TD P	TD Rt	PAT	FG	Saf	PTS
Mare	0	0	0	28/28	24/26	0	100
Carlson	0	7	0	0/0	0/0	0	42
Forsett	4	1	0	0/0	0/0	0	30
J. Jones	2	2	0	0/0	0/0	0	24
Burleson	0	3	0	0/0	0/0	0	18
Houshmandzadeh	0	3	0	0/0	0/0	0	18
Branch	0	2	0	0/0	0/0	0	12
Wilson	0	0	2	0/0	0/0	0	12
Griffith	0	1	0	0/0	0/0	0	6
Reed	0	0	1	0/0	0/0	0	6
Schmitt	0	1	0	0/0	0/0	0	6
S. Wallace	1	0	0	0/0	0/0	0	6
Seahawks	7	20	3	28/28	24/26	0	280
Opponents	17	27	2	44/44	22/31	0	390

2-Pt. Conversions: Seahawks 0-2, Opponents 2-2.

RUSHING	No.	Yds	Avg	LG	TD
J. Jones	177	663	3.7	62t	2
Forsett	114	619	5.4	35	4
James	46	125	2.7	10	0
Hasselbeck	26	119	4.6	23	0
Rankin TM	8	36	4.5	12	0
Griffith	4	6	1.5	3	0
Burleson	2	4	2.0	2	0
S. Wallace	16	2	0.1	10	1
Ryan	1	0	0.0	0	0
Branch	1	-8	-8.0	-8	0
Seahawks	395	1566	4.0	62t	7
Opponents	428	1776	4.1	80t	17

RECEIVING	No.	Yds	Avg	LG	TD
Houshmandzadeh	79	911	11.5	53	3
Burleson	63	812	12.9	44t	3
Carlson	51	574	11.3	42	7
Branch	45	437	9.7	35	2
Forsett	41	350	8.5	47	1
J. Jones	35	232	6.6	49	2
Griffith	19	118	6.2	25	1
Butler	15	175	11.7	32	0
Schmitt	6	21	3.5	10	1
Rankin TM	5	33	6.6	14	0
Obomanu	4	41	10.3	12	0
James	3	19	6.3	7	0
Owens	3	16	5.3	8	0
S. Wallace	2	29	14.5	24	0
Morrah	1	3	3.0	3	0
Seahawks	372	3771	10.1	53	20
Opponents	374	4112	11.0	64t	27

INTERCEPTIONS	No.	Yds	Avg	LG	TD
Hawthorne	3	9	3.0	5	0
Grant	3	7	2.3	7	0
Wilson	2	126	63.0	65t	2
Babineaux	2	18	9.0	18	0
Trufant	2	4	2.0	4	0
Lucas	1	0	0.0	0	0
Seahawks	13	164	12.6	65t	2
Opponents	19	202	10.6	70t	1

PUNTING	No.	Yds.	Avg.	In 20	LG
Ryan	88	4068	46.2	28	70
Mare	1	32	32.0	1	32
Seahawks	89	4100	46.1	29	70
Opponents	82	3872	47.2	21	67

PUNT RETURNS	Ret	FC	Yds	Avg	LG	TD
Burleson	30	3	254	8.5	29	0
Forsett	16	9	92	5.8	20	0
Seahawks	46	12	346	7.5	29	0
Opponents	43	17	479	11.1	82t	1

KICKOFF RETURNS	No.	Yds	Avg	LG	TD
Forsett	18	432	24.0	46	0
Rankin TM	16	358	22.4	41	0
Obomanu	11	293	26.6	45	0
Wilson	11	212	19.3	29	0
Butler	1	16	16.0	16	0
Reed	1	3	3.0	3	0
Burleson	1	2	2.0	2	0
Vallos	1	0	0.0	0	0
Seahawks	60	1316	21.9	46	0
Opponents	46	1059	23.0	53	0

FIELD GOALS	1-19	20-29	30-39	40-49	50+
Mare	0/0	9/9	10/11	5/6	0/0
Seahawks	0/0	9/9	10/11	5/6	0/0
Opponents	1/1	5/6	8/11	5/9	3/4

SACKS	No.
Kerney	5.0
Jackson	4.5
Hawthorne	4.0
Tapp	2.5
Curry	2.0
Redding	2.0
Babineaux	1.5
Mebane	1.5
Hill	1.0
Reed	1.0
Tatupu	1.0
Terrill	1.0
Wilson	1.0
Seahawks	28.0
Opponents	41.0

RECORD HOLDERS

INDIVIDUAL RECORDS—CAREER

Category	Name	Performance
Rushing (Yds.)	Shaun Alexander, 2000-07	9,429
Passing (Yds.)	Matt Hasselbeck, 2001-09	26,433
Passing (TDs)	Dave Krieg, 1980-1991	195
Receiving (No.)	Steve Largent, 1976-1989	819
Receiving (Yds.)	Steve Largent, 1976-1989	13,089
Interceptions	Dave Brown, 1976-1986	50
Punting (Avg.)	Jon Ryan, 2008-09	45.9
Punt Return (Avg.)	Charlie Rogers, 1999-2001	12.7
Kickoff Return (Avg.)	Steve Broussard, 1995-98	23.2
Field Goals	Norm Johnson, 1982-1990	159
Touchdowns (Tot.)	Shaun Alexander, 2000-07	112
Points	Norm Johnson, 1982-1990	810
*Sacks	Jacob Green, 1980-1991	97.5

INDIVIDUAL RECORDS—SINGLE SEASON

Category	Name	Performance
Rushing (Yds.)	Shaun Alexander, 2005	1,880
Passing (Yds.)	Matt Hasselbeck, 2007	3,966
Passing (TDs)	Dave Krieg, 1984	32
Receiving (No.)	Bobby Engram, 2007	94
Receiving (Yds.)	Steve Largent, 1985	1,287
Interceptions	John Harris, 1981	10
	Kenny Easley, 1984	10
Punting (Avg.)	Jon Ryan, 2009	46.2
Punt Return (Avg.)	Charlie Rogers, 1999	14.5
Kickoff Return (Avg.)	Charlie Rogers, 2000	24.9
Field Goals	Todd Peterson, 1999	34
Touchdowns (Tot.)	Shaun Alexander, 2005	28
Points	Shaun Alexander, 2005	168
*Sacks	Michael Sinclair, 1998	16.5

INDIVIDUAL RECORDS—SINGLE GAME

Category	Name	Performance
Rushing (Yds.)	Shaun Alexander, 11-11-01	266
Passing (Yds.)	Matt Hasselbeck, 12-29-02	449
Passing (TDs)	Dave Krieg, 12-2-84, 9-15-85, 11-28-88	5
	Warren Moon, 10-26-97	5
	Matt Hasselbeck, 11-23-03, 9-24-06	5
Receiving (No.)	Steve Largent, 10-18-87	15
Receiving (Yds.)	Steve Largent, 10-18-87	261
Interceptions	Kenny Easley, 9-3-84	3
	Eugene Robinson, 12-6-92	3
	Darryl Williams, 9-21-97	3
	Lofa Tatupu, 12-2-07	3
	Marcus Trufant, 12-9-07	3
Field Goals	Norm Johnson, 9-20-87, 12-18-88	5
Touchdowns (Tot.)	Shaun Alexander, 9-29-02	5
Points	Shaun Alexander, 9-29-02	30
*Sacks	Many times	4.0
	Last time by Darryl Tapp, 10-21-07	

**Sacks became an official statistic in 1982.*

SEATTLE SEAHAWKS

2010 VETERAN ROSTER

No.	Name	Pos.	Ht.	Wt.	Birthdate	NFL Exp.	College	Hometown	How Acq.	'09 Games/ Starts
25	Adams, Jamar	S	6-2	212	11/29/85	3	Michigan	Charlotte, N.C.	FA-'08	6/0
27	Babineaux, Jordan	S	6-0	206	8/31/82	7	Southern Arkansas	Port Arthur, Texas	FA-'04	16/16
86	Baker, Chris	TE	6-3	258	11/18/79	9	Michigan State	Queens, N.Y.	FA-'10	16/7*
83	Branch, Deion	WR	5-9	192	7/18/79	9	Louisville	Albany, Ga.	T(NE)-'06	14/5
79	Bryant, Red	DT	6-4	318	4/18/84	3	Texas A&M	Jasper, Texas	D4-'08	6/1
11	Butler, Deon	WR	5-10	182	1/4/86	2	Penn State	Woodbridge, Va.	D3-'09	16/0
89	Carlson, John	TE	6-5	251	5/12/84	3	Notre Dame	Litchfield, Minn.	D2-'08	16/16
91	t-Clemons, Chris	DE	6-2	240	10/30/81	7	Georgia	Griffin, Ga.	T(Phi)-'10	16/0*
90	Cole, Colin	DT	6-1	330	6/24/80	8	Iowa	Ft. Lauderdale, Fla.	UFA(GB)-'09	16/15
59	Curry, Aaron	LB	6-2	254	4/6/86	2	Wake Forest	Fayetteville, N.C.	D1-'09	14/12
20	Forsett, Justin	RB	5-8	194	10/14/85	3	California	Arlington, Texas	D7a-'08	16/3
32	Ganther, Quinton	RB	5-9	214	7/15/84	5	Utah	Oakland, Calif.	FA-'10	8/4*
64	Gibson, Mike	G	6-3	305	11/18/85	3	California	Napa, Calif.	PS(Phil)-'09	3/0
50	Hamilton, Ben	G	6-4	290	8/18/77	10	Minnesota	Plymouth, Minn.	UFA(Den)-'10	15/8*
18	Hass, Mike	WR	6-1	206	1/2/83	4	Oregon State	Portland, Ore.	FA-'09	1/0
8	Hasselbeck, Matt	QB	6-4	225	9/25/75	12	Boston College	Westwood, Mass.	T(GB)-'01	14/14
57	Hawthorne, David	LB	6-0	240	5/14/85	3	Texas Christian	Corsicana, Texas	FA-'08	16/11
99	t-Henderson, Robert	DE	6-3	283	11/9/83	2	Southern Mississippi	Ponchatoula, La.	T(Det)-'10	0*
54	Herring, Will	LB	6-3	243	8/28/83	4	Auburn	Opelika, Ala.	D5-'07	16/7
56	Hill, Leroy	LB	6-1	238	9/14/82	6	Clemson	Haddock, Ga.	D3b-'05	11/11
84	Houshmandzadeh, T.J.	WR	6-2	203	9/26/77	10	Oregon State	Barstow, Calif.	UFA(Cin)-'09	16/16
95	Jackson, Lawrence	DE	6-4	271	8/30/85	3	Southern California	Inglewood, Calif.	D1-'08	15/10
21	Jennings, Kelly	CB	5-11	180	11/30/82	5	Miami	Live Oak, Fla.	D1-'06	16/6
22	Jones, Julius	RB	5-10	208	8/14/81	7	Notre Dame	Big Stone Gap, Va.	UFA(Dall)-'08	14/14
34	Lewis, Roy	CB	5-10	190	5/19/85	3	Washington	Los Angeles, Calif.	FA-'09	9/0
75	Locklear, Sean	T	6-4	308	5/29/81	7	North Carolina State	Lumberton, N.C.	D3-'04	10/10
10	Mare, Olindo	K	5-11	190	6/6/73	15	Syracuse	Cooper City, Fla.	FA-'08	16/0
82	Martin, Ruvell	WR	6-4	220	8/10/82	5	Saginaw Valley State	Muskegon, Mich.	FA-'10	8/0*
52	McCoy, Matt	LB	6-0	235	10/14/82	6	San Diego State	Tustin, Calif.	FA-'10	12/2*
92	Mebane, Brandon	DT	6-1	301	1/15/85	4	California	Los Angeles, Calif.	D3-'07	15/15
17	Morey, Sean	WR	5-11	193	2/6/76	10	Brown	Marshfield, Mass.	UFA(Ariz)-'10	13/0*
88	Morrah, Cameron	TE	6-3	244	3/18/87	2	California	Claremont, Calif.	D7c-'09	3/0
87	Obomanu, Ben	WR	6-0	206	10/30/83	5	Auburn	Selma, Ala.	D7b-'06	14/0
47	Pociask, Jason	TE	6-3	259	2/9/83	4	Wisconsin	Indianapolis, Ind.	FA-'09	0*
40	Rankin, Louis	RB	6-1	205	5/4/85	3	Washington	Stockton, Calif.	FA-'09	9/0
98	Reed, Nick	DE	6-1	247	9/1/87	2	Oregon	Trabuco Canyon, Calif.	D7b-'09	16/0
9	Ryan, Jon	P	6-0	222	11/26/81	5	Regina	Regina, Saskatchewan	FA-'08	16/0
35	Schmitt, Owen	FB	6-2	247	2/13/85	3	West Virginia	Fairfax, Va.	D5-'08	15/1
65	Spencer, Chris	C	6-3	312	3/28/82	6	Mississippi	Madison, Miss.	D1-'05	14/14
51	Tatupu, Lofa	LB	6-0	242	11/15/82	6	Southern California	Wrentham, Mass.	D2-'05	5/5
14	Teel, Mike	QB	6-3	230	1/6/86	2	Rutgers	Ramsey, N.J.	D6-'09	0*
93	Terrill, Craig	DT	6-2	295	6/27/80	7	Purdue	Lebanon, Ind.	D6-'04	13/1
23	Trufant, Marcus	CB	5-11	197	12/25/80	8	Washington State	Tacoma, Wash.	D1-'03	10/9
60	Unger, Max	C/G	6-5	309	4/14/86	2	Oregon	Kailua-Kona, Hawaii	D2-'09	16/16
69	Vallos, Steve	C	6-3	312	12/28/83	4	Wake Forest	Boardman, Ohio	D7-'07	16/3
94	t-Vickerson, Kevin	DT	6-5	305	1/8/83	5	Michigan State	Detroit, Mich.	T(Tenn)-'10	13/2*
30	t-Washington, Leon	RB	5-8	195	8/29/82	5	Florida State	Jacksonville, Fla.	T(NYJ)-'10	7/0*
24	t-White, LenDale	RB	6-1	235	12/20/84	5	Southern California	Park Hill, Colo.	T(Tenn)-'10	13/0*
6	t-Whitehurst, Charlie	QB	6-4	220	8/6/82	5	Clemson	Alpharetta, Ga.	T(SD)-'10	0*
1	Williams, Mike	WR	6-5	235	1/4/84	4	Southern California	Tampa, Fla.	FA-'10	0*
15	Williams, Reggie	WR	6-4	212	5/17/83	6	Washington	Tacoma, Wash.	FA-'10	0*
74	Willis, Ray	T	6-6	315	8/13/82	6	Florida State	Angleton, Texas	D4-'05	16/16
26	Wilson, Josh	CB	5-9	192	3/11/85	4	Maryland	Upper Marlboro, Md.	D2-'07	12/11
66	Wrotto, Mansfield	G	6-3	320	10/12/84	4	Georgia Tech	Snellville, Ga.	D4b-'07	6/1

* Baker played 16 games with New England in '09; Clemons played 16 games with Philadelphia; Ganther played 8 games with Washington; Hamilton played 15 games with Denver; Henderson missed '08 season with N.Y. Giants with injury; Martin played 8 games with St. Louis; McCoy played 12 games with Tampa Bay; Morey played 13 games with Arizona; Pociask last active with N.Y. Jets in '07; Teel inactive third quarterback for 16 games; Vickerson played 13 games with Tennessee; Washington played 7 games with N.Y. Jets; White played 13 games with Tennessee; Whitehurst inactive third quarterback for San Diego for 16 games; M. Williams last played with Tennessee in '07; R. Williams last played with Jacksonville in '08.

t- Seahawks traded for Clemons (Phil), Henderson (Det), Vickerson (Tenn), Washington (NYJ), White (Tenn) and Whitehurst (SD).

Traded—G Rob Sims (Det; 14 games in '09), DE Darryl Tapp (Phil; 16), QB Seneca Wallace (Cle; 13).

Retired—Walter Jones, 13-year tackle, missed '09 due to injury; Patrick Kerney, 11-year defensive end, 14 games in '09.

Players lost through free agency (2): WR Nate Burleson (Det; 13 games in '09), DE Cory Redding (Balt; 15).

Also played with Seahawks in '09—CB Travis Fisher (4 games), T Brandon Frye (4), S Deon Grant (16), FB Justin Griffith (13), LS Kevin Houser (14), RB Edgerrin James (7), LB Lance Laury (16), LB D.D. Lewis (12), CB Ken Lucas (16), T Damion McIntosh (10), S Lawyer Milloy (16), TE John Owens (16), LS Jeff Robinson (2), S C.J. Wallace (5), T Kyle Williams (2).

2010 FIRST-YEAR ROSTER

Name	Pos.	Ht.	Wt.	Birthdate	College	Hometown	How Acq.
Brindley, James	S	5-11	196	2/1/88	Utah State	Grass Valley, Calif.	FA
Brown, Marcus	CB	6-0	195	1/27/87	Arkansas State	Marianna, Ark.	FA
Burkhart, Kyle	T	6-4	293	9/18/86	Southern Mississippi	Kinsley, Kan.	FA
Byers, Jeff	C/G	6-3	301	9/7/85	Southern California	Fort Collins, Colo.	FA
Carter, Patrick (1)	WR	6-3	215	2/6/85	Louisville	St. Petersburg, Fla.	FA-'09
Carter, Reggie	LB	5-11	238	6/16/87	UCLA	Los Angeles, Calif.	FA
Chancellor, Kam	S	6-3	232	4/3/88	Virginia Tech	Norfolk, Va.	D5
Cox, Kennard (1)	CB	6-0	197	8/17/85	Pittsburgh	Miami, Fla.	FA
Davis, Dexter	DE	6-1	244	11/10/86	Arizona State	Phoenix, Ariz.	D7a
Devenny, Patrick	TE	6-3	239	3/19/87	Colorado	Roseville, Calif.	FA
Dixon, Kevin	LB	6-2	257	5/7/87	Troy	Sebring, Fla.	FA
Erickson, Mitch (1)	G	6-6	290	5/14/85	South Dakota State	Hutchinson, Minn.	FA
Foley, Ricky (1)	DE	6-2	258	4/2/81	York	Toronto, Ontario	FA
Granger, DeMarcus	DT	6-2	332	9/4/86	Oklahoma	Dallas, Texas	FA
Hancock, Quintin	WR	6-2	211	9/13/87	Tennessee	St. Augustine, Fla.	FA
Harris, Will	S	6-0	204	12/29/86	Southern California	Covina, Calif.	FA
Heygood, Anthony (1)	LB	6-1	232	4/3/86	Purdue	Chester, Pa.	FA-'09
Jones, Mike (1)	WR	6-4	212	9/9/86	Arizona State	Humsle, Texas	FA-'09
Konz, Jameson	WR	6-3	234	7/2/86	Kent State	Uniontown, Ohio	D7b
MacDonald, Patrick (1)	LS	6-2	265	2/20/82	Alberta	Toronto, Ontario	FA
Malone, Tom (1)	P	6-0	205	3/29/84	Southern California	Lake Elsinore, Calif.	FA
McCoy, Anthony	TE	6-4	259	12/28/87	Southern California	Fresno, Calif.	D6
Martinez, Adrian	C	6-3	317	11/4/87	Colorado State	San Clemente, Calif.	FA
Okung, Russell	T	6-5	310	10/7/87	Oklahoma State	Houston, Texas	D1a
Pawelek, Joe	LB	6-2	237	12/8/86	Baylor	San Antonio, Texas	FA
Phillips, Jacob	T	6-6	299	1/19/88	Belhaven	Baton Rouge, La.	FA
Pinkard, Josh	CB	6-1	214	4/2/86	Southern California	Oxnard, Calif.	FA
Powdrell, Ryan (1)	FB	5-11	254	12/20/83	Southern California	Rancho Santa Margarita, Calf.	FA
Rose, Rob	DE	6-4	294	12/24/87	Ohio State	Cleveland, Ohio	FA
Tate, Golden	WR	5-10	202	8/2/88	Notre Dame	Hendersonville, Tenn.	D2
Thomas, Earl	S	5-10	202	5/7/89	Texas	Orange, Texas	D1b
Thurmond, Walter	CB	5-11	190	8/12/87	Oregon	West Covina, Calif.	D4a
Willingham, DeAngelo (1)	CB	6-0	200	1/15/87	Tennessee	Calhoun, S.C.	FA-'09
Wilson, E.J.	DE	6-2	289	10/28/87	North Carolina	Lawrenceville, Va.	D4b

The term NFL Rookie is defined as a player who is in his first season of professional football and has not been on the roster of another professional football team for any regular-season or postseason games. A Rookie is designated by an "R" on NFL rosters. Players who have been active in another professional football league or players who have NFL experience, including either preseason training camp or being on an Active List or Inactive List, or on Reserve/Injured or Reserve/Physically Unable to Perform for fewer than six regular-season games, are termed NFL First-Year Players. An NFL First-Year Player is designated by a "1" on NFL rosters. Thereafter, a player is credited with an additional year of experience for each season in which he accumulates six games on the Active List or Inactive List, or on Reserve/Injured or Reserve/Physically Unable to Perform.

Log on to www.seahawks.com for an up-to-date roster.

SEATTLE SEAHAWKS

COACHING STAFF

Head Coach,
Pete Carroll

Pro Career: Named as Seattle's eighth head coach on January 11, 2010. Began his NFL career as defensive backs coach for the Buffalo Bills (1984) and Minnesota Vikings (1985-89), before becoming the N.Y. Jets defensive coordinator (1990-93) and head coach (1994). He spent two years as the San Francisco 49ers defensive coordinator (1995-96) before leading the New England Patriots to a 27-21 record and two playoff appearances as head coach (1997-99). Carroll's overall head coaching record is 33-31 in the regular season and 1-2 in the postseason. He returns to the NFL after spending the previous nine years (2001-09) as head coach at USC, where he won seven consecutive Pac-10 titles (2002-08), two national championships and led the Trojans to a 97-19 record. Career record: 34-33.

Background: Two-time All-Pacific Coast Conference safety at Pacific (1971-72). Earned degree in business administration (1973) and secondary teaching credential and master's degree in physical education (1976) from Pacific. College coach: Pacific 1974-76, 1983, Arkansas 1977, Iowa State 1978, Ohio State 1979, North Carolina State 1980-82, USC 2001-09.

Personal: Born September 15, 1951 in San Francisco. He and his wife, Glena, have three children: Brennan, Nate, Jaime, and one grandson: Dillon.

ASSISTANT COACHES

Jeremy Bates, offensive coordinator; August 27, 1976, Manhattan, Kan. Quarterback Tennessee 1995, Rice 1997-99. No pro playing experience. College coach: Southern California 2009. Pro coach: Tampa Bay Buccaneers 2002-04, New York Jets 2005, Denver Broncos 2006-08, joined Seahawks in 2010.

Casey (Gus) Bradley, defensive coordinator; born July 5, 1966, Zumbrota, Minn. Safety/punter North Dakota State 1984-88. No pro playing experience. College coach: North Dakota State 1990-91, 1996-2005, Fort Lewis College 1992-96. Pro coach: Tampa Bay Buccaneers 2006-2008, joined Seahawks in 2009.

Kippy Brown, wide receivers; born March 6, 1955, Sweetwater, Tenn. Quarterback Memphis State 1974-77. No pro playing experience. College coach: Memphis State 1978-1980, Louisville 1982, Tennessee 1983-89, 1993-94, 2009. Pro coach: New York Jets 1990-92, Tampa Bay Buccaneers 1995, Miami Dolphins 1996-99, Green Bay Packers 2000, Houston Texans 2002-05, Detroit Lions 2006-08, joined Seahawks in 2010.

Luke Butkus, quality control/offensive line; born June 26, 1979, Steger, Ill. Center Illinois 1998-2001. Pro center Rhein Fire (NFL Europe) 2003, Cologne Centurions (NFL Europe) 2004. College coach: Oregon 2005-06. Pro coach: Chicago Bears 2007-09, joined Seahawks in 2010.

Dave Canales, quality control/offense; born May 7, 1981, Carson, Calif. Wide receiver Azusa Pacific 2000-03. No pro playing experience. College coach: El Camino (Calif). J.C. 2006-08, Southern California 2009. Pro coach: Joined Seahawks in 2010.

Chris Carlisle, head strength & conditioning; born August 7, 1962, Mason City, Iowa. Offensive lineman North Iowa Area Community College 1980-81, Chadron (Neb.) State College 1982-83. No pro playing experience. College coach: Arkansas 1992-93, Trinity Valley (Texas) C.C. 1997, Tennessee 1998-2000, Southern California 2001-09. Pro coach: Joined Seahawks in 2010.

Jedd Fisch, quarterbacks; born May 5, 1976, Livingston, N.J. Attended Florida. No college or pro playing experience. College coach: Florida 1999-2000, Minnesota 2009. Pro coach: Houston Texans 2001-03, Baltimore Ravens 2004-07, Denver Broncos 2008, joined Seahawks in 2010.

Mondray Gee, asst. strength & conditioning; born June 15, 1976, Detroit. Attended Michigan State. No college or pro playing experience. College coach: Michigan State 2000-01. Pro coach: Detroit Lions 2001-07, Green Bay Packers 2008-09, joined Seahawks in 2010.

Alex Gibbs, offensive line; born February 22, 1941, Morganton, N.C. Running back/defensive back Davidson 1959-1963. No pro playing experience. College coach: Duke 1969-1970, Kentucky 1971-72, West Virginia 1973-74, Ohio State 1975-78, Auburn 1979-1981, Georgia 1982-83. Pro coach: Denver Broncos 1984-87, 1995-2003, Oakland Raiders 1988-89, San Diego Chargers 1990-91, Indianapolis Colts 1992, Kansas City Chiefs 1993-94, Atlanta Falcons 2004-06, Houston Texans 2008-09, joined Seahawks in 2010.

Jerry Gray, defensive backs; born December 16, 1962, Lubbock, Texas. Safety Texas 1981-84. Pro defensive back Los Angeles Rams 1985-1991, Houston Oilers 1992, Tampa Bay Buccaneers 1993. College coach: Southern Methodist 1995-96. Pro coach: Tennessee Titans 1997-2000, Buffalo Bills 2001-05, Washington Redskins 2006-09, joined Seahawks in 2010.

Pat McPherson, tight ends; born April 15, 1969, Santa Clara, Calif. Linebacker Santa Clara 1991-92. No pro playing experience. Pro coach: San Francisco 49ers 1996, Denver Broncos 1998-2008, joined Seahawks in 2010.

Ken Norton, Jr., linebackers; born September 29, 1966, Lincoln, Ill. Linebacker UCLA 1984-87. Pro linebacker Dallas Cowboys 1988-1993, San Francisco 49ers 1994-2000. College coach: Southern California 2004-09. Pro coach: Joined Seahawks in 2010.

Mike Phair, defensive assistant; born November 8, 1969, Mesa, Ariz. Linebacker Mesa (Ariz.) C.C. 1988-89, Arizona State 1990-91. No pro playing experience. College coach: Arizona State 1999-2000, Tiffin University 2001. Pro coach: Joined Seahawks in 2008.

Dan Quinn, defensive line; born September 11, 1970, Orange, N.J. Defensive lineman Salisbury State 1990-93. No pro playing experience. College coach: William & Mary 1994, Virginia Military Institute 1995, Hofstra 1997-2000. Pro coach: San Francisco 49ers 2001-04, Miami Dolphins 2005-06, New York Jets 2007-08, joined Seahawks in 2009.

Kris Richard, asst. defensive backs; born October 28, 2978, Carson, Calif. Defensive back Southern California 1998-2001. Pro defensive back Seattle Seahawks 2002-04, San Francisco 49ers 2005. College coach: Southern California 2008-09. Pro coach: Joined Seahawks in 2010.

Brian Schneider, special teams coordinator; born May 16, 1971, San Diego. Linebacker Colorado State 1989-1993. No pro playing experience. College coach: Colorado State 1994-2002, UCLA 2003-05, Iowa State 2006, Air Force 2007, Southern California 2009. Pro coach: Oakland Raiders 2007-08, joined Seahawks in 2010.

Rocky Seto, quality control/defense; born March 12, 1976, Arcadia, Calif. Linebacker Southern California 1997-98. No pro playing experience. College coach: Southern California 1999-2009. Pro coach: Joined Seahawks in 2010.

Sherman Smith, running backs; born November 1, 1954, Youngstown, Ohio. Quarterback Miami (Ohio) 1972-75. Pro running back Seattle Seahawks 1976-1982, San Diego Chargers 1983-84. College coach: Miami (Ohio) 1990-91, Illinois 1992-94. Pro coach: Houston Oilers/Tennessee Titans 1995-2007, Washington Redskins 2008-09, joined Seahawks in 2010.

Jeff Ulbrich, special teams assistant; born February 17, 1977, San Jose, Calif. Linebacker Hawaii 1996-99. Pro linebacker San Francisco 49ers 2000-09. Pro coach: Joined Seahawks in 2010.

Art Valero, asst. offensive line; born May 12, 1958, La Mirada, Calif. Guard Boise State 1979-1980. No pro playing experience. College coach: Boise State 1981-82, Iowa State 1983, Long Beach State 1984-86, New Mexico 1987-89, Idaho 1990-94, Utah State 1995-97, Louisville 1998-2001. Pro coach: Tampa Bay Buccaneers 2002-07, St. Louis Rams 2008-09, joined Seahawks in 2010.

Jamie Yanchar, asst. strength & conditioning, born December 29, 1963, Cleveland. Attended Louisville. No college or pro playing experience. College coach: Southern California 1990-2009. Pro coach: Joined Seahawks in 2010.

National Football Conference
South Division
Team Colors: Buccaneer Red, Pewter, Black, and Orange
One Buccaneer Place
Tampa, Florida 33607
Telephone: (813) 870-2700

2010 SCHEDULE

PRESEASON

Aug. 14	at Miami	7:00
Aug. 21	**Kansas City**	7:30
Aug. 28	**Jacksonville**	7:30
Sep. 2	at Houston	8:00

REGULAR SEASON

Sep. 12	**Cleveland**	1:00
Sep. 19	at Carolina	1:00
Sep. 26	**Pittsburgh**	1:00
Oct. 3	BYE	
Oct. 10	at Cincinnati	1:00
Oct. 17	**New Orleans**	1:00
Oct. 24	**St. Louis**	1:00
Oct. 31	at Arizona	1:15
Nov. 7	at Atlanta	1:00
Nov. 14	**Carolina**	1:00
Nov. 21	at San Francisco	1:05
Nov. 28	at Baltimore	1:00
Dec. 5	**Atlanta**	1:00
Dec. 12	at Washington	1:00
Dec. 19	**Detroit**	1:00
Dec. 26	**Seattle**	1:00
Jan. 2	at New Orleans	12:00

Stadium: Raymond James Stadium (opened in 1998)
• **Capacity:** 65,908
Tampa, Florida 33607
Playing Surface: Grass
Training Camp: One Buccaneer Place
Tampa, Florida 33607

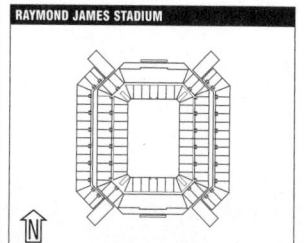

RAYMOND JAMES STADIUM

N

CLUB OFFICIALS

Owner/President: Malcolm Glazer
Co-Chairman: Bryan Glazer
Co-Chairman: Joel Glazer
Co-Chairman: Edward Glazer
General Manager: Mark Dominik
Vice President of Business Administration: Brian Ford
Director of Football Administration: Digger Daley
Director of College Scouting: Dennis Hickey
Director of Player Development: Eric Vance
Director of Football Technology: Chris Wells
National Scout: Jim Abrams
College Scouts: Brian Hudspeth, Byron Kiefer, Tom Throckmorton, Seth Turner
Combine Scout: Tony Kinkela
Pro Scouts: Shelton Quarles, Justin Sheridan
Assistant to the Head Coach: Jay Kaiser
College Personnel Assistant: Andre Ford
Senior Director of Sales and Advertising: Jason Layton
General Counsel: Manny Alvare
Chief Financial Officer: Joe Fada
Director of Communications: Jonathan Grella
Public Relations Manager: Jason Wahlers
Public Relations Coordinator: Dan Berglund
Director of Community Relations: Miray Holmes
Director of Creative Services: Darren Morgan
Director of Marketing and Business Development: Jeff Ajluni
Director of Security and Facilities: Andres Trescastro
Director of Special Events and Team Operations: Killeen Mullen
Director of Sports Medicine and Performance: Todd Toriscelli
Director of Rehabilitation: Shannon Merrick
Team Nutritionist : Kevin Luhrs
Head Equipment Manager: James Sorenson
Assistant Equipment Manager: Mike Myrick
Video Director: Dave Levy
Assistant Video Director: Chris Bryan
Broadcasting Operations Manager: Jeff Ryan
Cheerleading Manager: Catherine Boyd
Human Resources Generalist: Raeni Ware
Player Benefits and Alumni Program Manager: Jill Hobbs
IT Manager: Ed Johnston
Purchasing Manager: Brian Mathiews
Special Events and Team Operations Manager: Jim Mackes
Ticket Operations Manager: Alex Bohne
Video Production Manager: Ed Bottger
Website Manager: Scott Smith

COACHING HISTORY
(214-332-1)

Records include postseason games

1976-1984	John McKay	45-91-1
1985-86	Leeman Bennett	4-28-0
1987-1990	Ray Perkins*	19-41-0
1990-91	Richard Williamson	4-15-0
1992-95	Sam Wyche	23-41-0
1996-2001	Tony Dungy	56-46-0
2002-08	Jon Gruden	60-57-0
2009	Raheem Morris	3-13-0

*Released after 13 games in 1990

PAID ATTENDANCE

Home 437,062 Away 555,859
Total 992,921
Single-game home record, 73,523 (12/7/97)
Single-season home record, 545,980 (1979)

2010 DRAFT CHOICES

Round	Name	Pos.	College
1	Gerald McCoy	DT	Oklahoma
2	Brian Price	DT	UCLA
	Arrelious Benn	WR	Illinois
3	Myron Lewis	DB	Vanderbilt
4	Mike Williams	WR	Syracuse
6	Brent Bowden	P	Virginia Tech
7	Cody Grimm	DB	Virginia Tech
	Dekoda Watson	LB	Florida St.
	Erik Lorig	DE	Stanford

TAMPA BAY BUCCANEERS

2009 TEAM RECORD

PRESEASON (1-3)

Date	Result	Opponent
8/15	L 20-27	at Tennessee
8/22	W 24-23	at Jacksonville
8/27	L 6-10	Miami
9/4	L 20-27	Houston

REGULAR SEASON (3-13)

Date	Result	Opponent
9/13	L 21-34	Dallas
9/20	L 20-33	at Buffalo
9/27	L 0-24	New York Giants
10/4	L 13-16	at Washington
10/11	L 14-33	at Philadelphia
10/18	L 21-28	Carolina
10/25	L 7-35	New England
11/8	W 38-28	Green Bay
11/15	L 23-25	at Miami
11/22	L 7-38	New Orleans
11/29	L 17-20	at Atlanta
12/6	L 6-16	at Carolina
12/13	L 3-26	New York Jets
12/20	W 24-7	at Seattle
12/27	W 20-17	at New Orleans (OT)
1/3	L 10-20	Atlanta

(OT) Overtime

SCORE BY PERIODS

Buccaneers	34	73	38	96	3 —	244
Opponents	108	118	74	100	0 —	400

2009 TEAM STATISTICS

	Buccaneers	Opp.
Total First Downs	246	324
Rushing	80	129
Passing	148	171
Penalty	18	24
3rd Down: Made/Att	71/218	86/214
3rd Down Pct.	32.6	40.2
4th Down: Made/Att	9/22	9/15
4th Down Pct.	40.9	60.0
Possession Avg.	28:31	31:29
Total Net Yards	4600	5849
Avg. Per Game	287.5	365.6
Total Plays	961	1039
Avg. Per Play	4.8	5.6
Net Yards Rushing	1627	2531
Avg. Per Game	101.7	158.2
Total Rushes	404	529
Net Yards Passing	2973	3318
Avg. Per Game	185.8	207.4
Sacked/Yards Lost	33/161	28/166
Gross Yards	3134	3484
Att./Completions	524/279	482/301
Completion Pct.	53.2	62.4
Had Intercepted	29	19
Punts/Average	87/41.7	72/42.8
Net Punting Avg.	87/36.3	72/35.3
Penalties/Yards	93/696	80/731
Fumbles/Ball Lost	25/5	18/10
Touchdowns	28	46
Rushing	5	16
Passing	18	28
Returns	5	2

2009 INDIVIDUAL STATISTICS

PASSING	Att.	Comp.	Yds.	Pct.	TD	Int.	Tkld.	Rate
Freeman	290	158	1855	54.5	10	18	20/102	59.8
J. Johnson	125	63	685	50.4	4	8	11/59	50.9
Leftwich	107	58	594	54.2	4	3	2/0	71.2
Clayton	1	0	0	0.0	0	0	0/0	39.6
D. Johnson	1	0	0	0.0	0	0	0/0	39.6
Buccaneers	524	279	3134	53.2	18	29	33/161	59.8
Opponents	482	301	3484	62.4	28	19	28/166	87.2

SCORING	TD R	TD P	TD Rt	PAT	FG	Saf	PTS
Barth	0	0	0	12/12	14/19	0	54
Williams	4	3	0	0/0	0/0	0	42
Winslow	0	5	0	0/0	0/0	0	30
A. Bryant	0	4	0	0/0	0/0	0	24
Ward	1	2	0	0/0	0/0	0	18
Jackson	0	0	2	0/0	0/0	0	12
Nugent TM	0	0	0	6/6	2/6	0	12
Stroughter	0	1	1	0/0	0/0	0	12
Clayton	0	1	0	0/0	0/0	0	8
Andrus TM	0	0	0	6/6	0/1	0	6
Barber	0	0	1	0/0	0/0	0	6
Spurlock TM	0	0	1	0/0	0/0	0	6
Stevens	0	1	0	0/0	0/0	0	6
Stovall	0	1	0	0/0	0/0	0	6
Freeman	0	0	0	0/0	0/0	0	2
Buccaneers	5	18	5	24/24	16/26	0	244
Opponents	16	28	2	44/46	26/32	1	400

2-Pt. Conversions: Clayton, Freeman. Buccaneers 2-4, Opponents 0-0.

RUSHING	No.	Yds	Avg	LG	TD
Williams	211	823	3.9	35	4
Ward	114	409	3.6	28	1
Freeman	30	161	5.4	20	0
J. Johnson	22	148	6.7	29	0
Graham	14	66	4.7	17	0
Smith	4	7	1.8	4	0
Winslow	1	7	7.0	7	0
Leftwich	6	6	1.0	4	0
Askew	1	0	0.0	0	0
Pressley TM	1	0	0.0	0	0
Buccaneers	404	1627	4.0	35	5
Opponents	529	2531	4.8	45	16

RECEIVING	No.	Yds	Avg	LG	TD
Winslow	77	884	11.5	42t	5
A. Bryant	39	600	15.4	42t	4
Stroughter	31	334	10.8	35	1
Williams	28	217	7.8	22t	3
Stovall	24	366	15.3	38	1
Ward	20	150	7.5	38	2
Clayton	16	230	14.4	47	1
Stevens	15	130	8.7	17	1
Graham	14	109	7.8	16	0
Clark	6	65	10.8	17	0
Gilmore	3	23	7.7	9	0
Smith	2	4	2.0	3	0
Askew	2	3	1.5	4	0
Penn	1	15	15.0	15	0
Pressley TM	1	2	2.0	2	0
Freeman	0	1	—	1	0
Zuttah	0	1	—	1	0
Buccaneers	279	3134	11.2	47	18
Opponents	301	3484	11.6	80t	28

INTERCEPTIONS	No.	Yds	Avg	LG	TD
Talib	5	99	19.8	32	0
Jackson	5	86	17.2	35t	2
Mack	3	36	12.0	36	0
Hayes	2	21	10.5	20	0
Piscitelli	2	7	3.5	4	0
Ba. Ruud	1	23	23.0	21	0
Black	1	3	3.0	3	0
Buccaneers	19	275	14.5	36	2
Opponents	29	492	17.0	76t	2

PUNTING	No.	Yds.	Avg.	In 20	LG
D. Johnson	62	2558	41.3	16	63
Paulescu TM	24	1022	42.6	8	61
Barth	1	46	46.0	0	46
Buccaneers	87	3626	41.7	24	63
Opponents	72	3083	42.8	22	63

PUNT RETURNS	Ret	FC	Yds	Avg	LG	TD
Smith	23	8	232	10.1	21	0
Stroughter	12	0	119	9.9	33	0
Spurlock TM	3	0	90	30.0	77t	1
Figurs TM	2	2	21	10.5	12	0
Buccaneers	40	10	462	11.6	77t	1
Opponents	38	17	311	8.2	34	0

KICKOFF RETURNS	No.	Yds	Avg	LG	TD
Smith	31	902	29.1	83	0
Stroughter	11	324	29.5	97t	1
Spurlock TM	8	170	21.3	32	0
Figurs TM	5	105	21.0	27	0
Huggins	2	52	26.0	30	0
Graham	2	38	19.0	21	0
Stovall	1	20	20.0	20	0
Crowder	1	11	11.0	11	0
Hayward	1	8	8.0	8	0
Buccaneers	62	1630	26.3	97t	1
Opponents	46	878	19.1	37	0

FIELD GOALS	1-19	20-29	30-39	40-49	50+
Barth	0/0	2/2	4/6	5/7	3/4
Nugent TM	0/0	1/1	1/2	0/3	0/0
Andrus TM	0/0	0/0	0/0	0/1	0/0
Buccaneers	0/0	3/3	5/8	5/11	3/4
Opponents	0/0	9/10	6/7	10/13	1/2

SACKS	No.
S. White	6.5
Wilkerson	6.0
Crowder	3.5
Hayes	3.0
Barber	2.0
R. Miller	2.0
Black	1.5
Adams	1.0
Bennett	1.0
Sims	1.0
Hovan	0.5
Buccaneers	28.0
Opponents	33.0

RECORD HOLDERS

INDIVIDUAL RECORDS—CAREER

Category	Name	Performance
Rushing (Yds.)	James Wilder, 1981-89	5,957
Passing (Yds.)	Vinny Testaverde, 1987-1992	14,820
Passing (TDs)	Vinny Testaverde, 1987-1992	77
Receiving (No.)	James Wilder, 1981-89	430
Receiving (Yds.)	Mark Carrier, 1987-1992	5,018
Interceptions	Ronde Barber, 1997-2008	37
Punting (Avg.)	Josh Bidwell, 2004-08	44.0
Punt Return (Avg.)	Clifton Smith, 2008	14.1
Kickoff Return (Avg.)	Aaron Stecker, 2000-03	23.8
Field Goals	Martín Gramatica, 1999-2004	137
Touchdowns (Tot.)	Mike Alstott, 1996-2006	71
Points	Martín Gramatica, 1999-2004	592
*Sacks	Warren Sapp, 1995-2003	77.0

INDIVIDUAL RECORDS—SINGLE SEASON

Category	Name	Performance
Rushing (Yds.)	James Wilder, 1984	1,544
Passing (Yds.)	Brad Johnson, 2003	3,811
Passing (TDs)	Brad Johnson, 2003	26
Receiving (No.)	Keyshawn Johnson, 2001	106
Receiving (Yds.)	Mark Carrier, 1989	1,422
Interceptions	Ronde Barber, 2001	10
Punting (Avg.)	Josh Bidwell, 2005	45.6
Punt Return (Avg.)	Karl Williams, 1996	21.1
Kickoff Return (Avg.)	Sammie Stroughter, 2009	29.5
Field Goals	Martín Gramatica, 2002	32
	Matt Bryant, 2008	32
Touchdowns (Tot.)	James Wilder, 1984	13
Points	Matt Bryant, 2008	131
*Sacks	Warren Sapp, 2000	16.5

INDIVIDUAL RECORDS—SINGLE GAME

Category	Name	Performance
Rushing (Yds.)	James Wilder, 11-6-83	219
Passing (Yds.)	Doug Williams, 11-16-80	486
Passing (TDs)	Steve DeBerg, 9-13-87	5
	Brad Johnson, 11-3-02	5
Receiving (No.)	James Wilder, 9-15-85	13
	Earnest Graham, 10-21-07	13
Receiving (Yds.)	Mark Carrier, 12-6-87	212
Interceptions	Ronde Barber, 12-23-01, 12-4-05	3
	Aqib Talib, 9-21-08	3
Field Goals	Martín Gramatica, 12-29-02	5
Touchdowns (Tot.)	Jimmie Giles, 10-20-85	4
Points	Jimmie Giles, 10-20-85	24
*Sacks	Marcus Jones, 10-19-00	4.0
	Simeon Rice, 10-12-03	4.0

**Sacks became an official statistic in 1982.*

TAMPA BAY BUCCANEERS

2010 VETERAN ROSTER

No.	Name	Pos.	Ht.	Wt.	Birthdate	NFL Exp.	College	Hometown	How Acq.	'09 Games/ Starts
50	Alston, Jon	LB	6-0	235	6/4/83	5	Stanford	Shreveport, La.	FA-'10	9/4*
20	Barber, Ronde	CB	5-10	184	4/7/75	14	Virginia	Roanoke, Va.	D3b-'97	16/16
10	Barth, Connor	K	5-11	193	4/11/86	3	North Carolina	Wilmington, N.C.	FA-'09	9/0
71	Bennett, Michael	DL	6-4	274	11/13/85	2	Texas A&M	Alief, Texas	W(Sea)-'09	7/0
31	Biggers, E.J.	CB	6-0	180	6/13/87	2	Western Michigan	North Miami Beach, Fla.	D7a-'09	0*
58	Black, Quincy	LB	6-2	240	2/28/84	4	New Mexico	Chicago, Ill.	D3-'07	16/13
16	Bradley, Mark	WR	6-1	201	1/29/82	6	Oklahoma	Pine Bluff, Ark.	FA-'09	13/6*
15	t-Brown, Reggie	WR	6-1	197	1/13/81	6	Georgia	Carrollton, Ga.	T(Phil)-'10	14/2*
12	Carpenter, Rudy	QB	6-2	212	4/15/86	2	Arizona State	Westlake Village, Calif.	FA-'09	0*
80	Clayton, Michael	WR	6-4	215	10/13/82	7	Louisiana State	Baton Rouge, La.	D1-'04	13/11
61	Compas, Jonathan	C	6-3	300	1/9/86	2	California-Davis	Carlsbad, Calif.	W(Oak)-'09	2/0
96	Crowder, Tim	DE	6-4	260	6/30/85	4	Texas	Tyler, Texas	FA-'09	15/4
59	Crowell, Angelo	LB	6-1	246	8/16/81	8	Virginia	North Forsythe, N.C.	UFA(Buff)-'09	0*
69	Dotson, Demar	T	6-9	315	10/11/85	2	Southern Miss	Alexandria, La.	FA-'09	9/0
48	Economos, Andrew	LS	6-1	250	6/24/82	5	Georgia Tech	Atlanta, Ga.	FA-'06	16/0
52	Faine, Jeff	C	6-3	291	4/6/81	8	Notre Dame	Sanford, Fla.	UFA(NO)-'08	12/12
5	Freeman, Josh	QB	6-6	248	1/13/88	2	Kansas State	Kansas City, Mo.	D1-'09	10/9
68	Fulton, Xavier	T	6-5	301	4/18/86	2	Illinois	Flossmoor, Ill.	D5-'09	0*
88	Gilmore, John	TE	6-5	257	9/21/79	9	Penn State	West Lawn, Pa.	UFA(Chi)-'08	13/2
34	Graham, Earnest	RB	5-9	225	1/15/80	7	Florida	Ft. Myers, Fla.	FA-'03	13/6
54	Hayes, Geno	LB	6-1	226	8/10/87	3	Florida State	Greenville, Fla.	D6-'08	15/13
57	Hayward, Adam	LB	6-1	240	6/23/84	4	Portland State	Westminster, Calif.	D6-'07	15/1
36	Jackson, Tanard	S	6-0	200	7/21/85	4	Syracuse	Potomac, Md.	D4-'07	12/12
11	Johnson, Josh	QB	6-3	205	5/15/86	3	San Diego	Oakland, Calif.	D5-'08	6/4
26	Jones, Sean	S	6-1	220	3/2/82	7	Georgia	Atlanta, Ga.	UFA(Phil)-'10	15/9*
75	Joseph, Davin	G	6-3	313	11/22/83	5	Oklahoma	Hallandale, Fla.	D1-'06	16/16
53	Koutouvides, Niko	LB	6-2	238	3/25/81	7	Purdue	Plainville, Conn.	FA-'09	16/0
77	Lee, James	T	6-4	305	8/17/85	3	South Carolina State	Belle Glade, Fla.	W(Cle)-'08	0*
41	Lynch, Corey	S	6-0	206	5/7/85	3	Appalachian State	Ft. Myers, Fla.	FA-'09	13/0
33	Mack, Elbert	CB	5-10	175	7/14/86	3	Troy	Wichita, Kan.	FA-'08	15/3
90	Miller, Roy	DT	6-2	310	7/9/87	2	Texas	Killeen, Texas	D3-'09	15/1
92	Moore, Dre	DT	6-4	305	6/9/85	2	Maryland	Charlotte, N.C.	D4-'08	7/0
94	Moore, Kyle	DE/DT	6-5	272	10/25/86	2	Southern California	Warner Robins, Ga.	D4-'09	8/0
83	Nunn, Terrence	WR	6-0	195	7/25/86	2	Nebraska	Houston, Texas	FA-'09	0*
70	Penn, Donald	T	6-5	305	4/27/83	5	Utah State	Playa Del Rey, Calif.	FA-'06	16/16
21	Piscitelli, Sabby	S	6-3	224	8/24/83	4	Oregon State	Boca Raton, Fla.	D2b-'07	16/15
45	Pressley, Chris	FB	5-11	260	8/8/86	2	Wisconsin	Woodbury, N.J.	FA-'09	7/3
29	Roberson, Derrick	CB	5-10	182	3/12/85	2	Rutgers	Ft. Lauderdale, Fla.	FA-'09	6/0
51	Ruud, Barrett	LB	6-2	241	5/20/83	6	Nebraska	Lincoln, Neb.	D2-'05	16/16
98	Sims, Ryan	DT	6-4	315	5/4/80	9	North Carolina	Spartanburg, S.C.	T(KC)-'07	16/16
22	Smith, Clifton	RB	5-9	190	7/4/85	3	Fresno State	Fresno, Calif.	FA-'08	11/0
81	Spurlock, Micheal	WR	5-11	200	1/31/83	3	Mississippi	Indianola, Miss.	FA-'09	6/0*
86	Stevens, Jerramy	TE	6-7	260	11/13/79	9	Washington	Olympia, Wash.	UFA(Sea)-'07	16/8
85	Stovall, Maurice	WR	6-5	220	2/21/85	5	Notre Dame	Philadelphia, Pa.	D3-'06	15/7
18	Stroughter, Sammie	WR	5-10	189	1/3/86	2	Oregon State	Sacramento, Calif.	D7b-'09	13/0
25	Talib, Aqib	CB	6-1	205	2/13/86	3	Kansas	Richardson, Texas	D1-'08	15/15
65	Trueblood, Jeremy	T	6-8	320	5/10/83	5	Boston College	Indianapolis, Ind.	D2-'06	16/16
28	Ward, Derrick	RB	5-11	228	8/30/80	7	Ottawa (Kan.)	Moreno Valley, Calif.	UFA(NYG)-'09	14/1
91	White, Stylez G.	DE	6-3	270	7/25/79	4	Minnesota	Newark, N.J.	FA-'07	15/8
24	Williams, Carnell	RB	5-11	217	4/21/82	6	Auburn	Attalla, Ala.	D1-'05	16/15
82	Winslow, Kellen	TE	6-4	240	7/21/83	7	Miami	San Diego, Calif.	T(Cle)-'09	16/14
76	Zuttah, Jeremy	G	6-4	308	6/1/86	3	Rutgers	Edison, N.J.	D3-'08	16/16

* Alston played 9 games with Oakland in '09; Biggers missed '09 season because of injury; Bradley played 13 games with Kansas City; Brown played 14 games with Philadelphia; Carpenter inactive for 6 games; Crowell missed '09 season because of injury; Fulton missed '09 season because of injury; Jones played 15 games with Philadelphia; Lee inactive for 9 games; Nunn did not play 1 game; Spurlock played 4 games with San Francisco.

t- Buccaneers traded for Brown (Phil).

Traded—DE Gaines Adams (5 games in '09) to Chicago, QB Byron Leftwich (3) to Pittsburgh.

Players lost through free agency (3): S Will Allen (Pitt; 8 games in '09), WR Antonio Bryant (Cin; 13), DE Jimmy Wilkerson (NO; 15).

Also played with Buccaneers in '09—CB Brandon Anderson (3 games), K Shane Andrus (3), CB Kyle Arrington (1), FB B.J. Askew (5), S Steve Cargile (1), WR Brian Clark (14), CB Torrie Cox (11), WR Yamon Figurs (3), CB Marcus Hamilton (1), DT Chris Hovan (16), RB Kareem Huggins (3), P Dirk Johnson (11), G Marcus Johnson (6), C/G Sean Mahan (6), LB Matt McCoy (12), G Shawn Murphy (1), K Mike Nugent (4), P Sam Paulescu (5), S Jermaine Phillips (2), LB Rod Wilson (8).

2010 FIRST-YEAR ROSTER

Name	Pos.	Ht.	Wt.	Birthdate	College	Hometown	How Acq.
Adeniji, Damola	WR	6-3	213	6/16/87	Oregon State	Eugene, Ore.	FA
Anderson, Brandon (1)	CB	5-10	179	12/10/85	Akron	Dublin, Va.	FA-'09
Benn, Arrelious	WR	6-2	220	9/8/88	Illinois	Washington, D.C.	D2b
Bowden, Brent	P	6-3	202	5/21/87	Virginia Tech	Chantilly, Va.	D6
Brooks, Chris	WR	6-2	215	2/5/87	Nebraska	St. Louis, Mo.	FA
Cook, Emanuel (1)	S	5-10	185	1/20/88	South Carolina	Riviera Beach, Fla.	FA-'09
Dile, Marc (1)	OL	6-4	300	5/5/86	South Florida	Miami, Fla.	FA-'09
Evans, Maurice (1)	DE	6-2	264	8/14/88	Penn State	Brooklyn, N.Y.	FA-'09
Gilbeaux, Brandon	DE	6-3	270	6/9/87	Delaware	Washington, D.C.	FA
Grimes, Lee	G	6-6	309	1/28/87	Texas A&M	Brownwood, Texas	FA
Grimm, Cody	S	5-11	210	2/26/87	Virginia Tech	Fairfax, Va.	D7a
Hall, De'von (1)	S	6-3	215	9/8/87	Utah State	Reseda, Calif.	W(Ind)-'09
Hardman, Derek	T	6-6	300	9/13/86	Eastern Kentucky	Spencer, W. Va.	FA
Huggins, Kareem (1)	RB	5-9	198	5/24/86	Hofstra	Irvington, N.J.	FA-'09
Johnson, George	DE	6-4	265	12/11/87	Rutgers	Glassboro, N.J.	FA
Lawrence, Hunter	K	6-0	187	6/28/88	Texas	Boerne, Texas	FA
Lewis, Myron	CB	6-2	203	11/24/87	Vanderbilt	Pompano Beach, Fla.	D3
Lorig, Erik	DE	6-4	275	11/17/86	Stanford	Palos Verdes, Calif.	D7c
Mastrud, Jeron	TE	6-6	253	12/17/87	Kansas State	Beaverton, Ore.	FA
McCoy, Gerald	DT	6-4	295	2/25/88	Oklahoma	Oklahoma City, Okla.	D1
McCoy, Rico	LB	6-0	224	11/6/87	Tennessee	Washington, D.C.	FA
Okeafor, Rob	G	6-3	320	1/7/88	Florida A&M	Jacksonville, Fla.	FA
Parker, Preston	WR	6-0	200	2/13/87	North Alabama	Delray Beach, Fla.	FA
Pasco, Darrell	CB	6-0	170	1/28/87	Georgia Southern	Clearwater, Fla.	FA
Price, Brian	DT	6-1	303	4/10/89	UCLA	Los Angeles, Calif.	D2a
Purvis, Ryan (1)	TE	6-4	260	5/8/86	Boston College	Reinholds, Pa.	FA-'09
Render, Sergio	G	6-3	313	9/13/86	Virginia Tech	Newnan, Ga.	FA
Robinson, Lee (1)	LB	6-2	256	4/23/87	Alcorn State	Liberty, Miss.	FA-'09
Rogan, Dennis	S	5-10	178	12/27/88	Tennessee	Knoxville, Tenn.	FA
Ruffin, James	DE	6-4	263	2/6/87	Northern Iowa	Burnsville, Minn.	FA
Snead, Jevan	QB	6-3	220	9/2/87	Mississippi	Stephenville, Texas	FA
Taylor, Rendrick	FB	6-2	265	4/3/87	Clemson	Clio, S.C.	FA
Urrutia, Mario (1)	WR	6-6	232	1/18/86	Louisville	Louisville, Ky.	FA-'09
Watson, Dekoda	LB	6-2	240	3/3/88	Florida State	Aiken, S.C.	D7b
Williams, James	T	6-5	295	7/3/88	Harvard	Chesnut Hill, Mass.	FA
Williams, Mike	WR	6-2	212	5/18/87	Syracuse	Buffalo, N.Y.	D4

The term NFL Rookie is defined as a player who is in his first season of professional football and has not been on the roster of another professional football team for any regular-season or postseason games. A Rookie is designated by an "R" on NFL rosters. Players who have been active in another professional football league or players who have NFL experience, including either preseason training camp or being on an Active List or Inactive List, or on Reserve/Injured or Reserve/Physically Unable to Perform for fewer than six regular-season games, are termed NFL First-Year Players. An NFL First-Year Player is designated by a "1" on NFL rosters. Thereafter, a player is credited with an additional year of experience for each season in which he accumulates six games on the Active List or Inactive List, or on Reserve/Injured or Reserve/Physically Unable to Perform.

Log on to www.buccaneers.com for an up-to-date roster.

TAMPA BAY BUCCANEERS

COACHING STAFF

Head Coach, Raheem Morris

Pro Career: Morris was named the eighth head coach in Buccaneers history on January 17, 2009. Prior to being named the head coach, he worked as the Buccaneers defensive backs coach from 2007-08, as assistant defensive back coach from 2004-05, as defensive assistant in 2003 and as a defensive quality control coach in 2002. After Tampa Bay fell to 19th in the NFL in pass defense in 2006, Morris led a resurgence in his return as he guided the Buccaneers pass defense to the league's top ranking en route to the NFC South division title in 2007. In five of his seasons with Tampa Bay, the Bucs ranked in the top five in the NFL in total defense, including No. 1 rankings in 2005 and 2002, when the club captured its first world title in Super Bowl XXXVII. He spent time with the New York Jets serving a defensive minority internship in 2001. Career record: 3-13.

Background: Safety at Hofstra (1994-97), graduating with a degree in physical education. Coached collegiately at Hofstra (1998, 2000-01), Cornell (1999) and Kansas State (2006).

Personal: Born September 3, 1976 in Irvington, New Jersey.

ASSISTANT COACHES

Joe Baker, linebackers; born June 29, 1969, Glen Ridge, N.J. Wide receiver Princeton 1987-1990. No pro playing experience. College coach: East Stroudsburg 1991, Samford 1993, Wisconsin 1999. Pro coach: Birmingham Fire (WFL) 1992, Jacksonville Jaguars 1995-98, New Orleans Saints 2000-04, Green Bay Packers 2005, St. Louis Rams 2006, Denver Broncos 2007-08, joined Buccaneers in 2009.

Tim Berbenich, asst. wide receivers; born December 19, 1979, Huntington, N.Y. Wide receiver Hamilton College 1998-2001. No pro playing experience. Pro coach: New York Jets 2003-05, joined Buccaneers in 2006.

Richard Bisaccia, associate head coach/special teams coordinator; born June 3, 1960, Yonkers, N.Y. Defensive back Yankton College 1979-1982. Pro defensive back Philadelphia Stars (USFL) 1983. College coach: Wayne State College 1983-87, South Carolina 1988-1993, Clemson 1994-98, Mississippi 1999-2001. Pro coach: Joined Buccaneers in 2002.

Tim Holt, offensive assistant; born November 29, 1973, Dighton, Mass. Offensive line Southern Connecticut State 1991-94. No pro playing experience. College coach: Southern Connecticut State 1995-96, 2004-07, Lehigh 1997-98, Cornell 1999-2000, American International 2001-03, Stonehill 2008. Pro coach: Joined Buccaneers in 2009.

Chris Keenan, asst. strength and conditioning; born November 3, 1980, Creston, Iowa. Fullback Drake 1999-2001. No pro playing experience. College coach: Iowa State 2003, Tulane 2006-2008. Pro coach: Minnesota Vikings 2004-05, Tampa Bay Buccaneers 2006, re-joined Buccaneers in 2009.

Jimmy Lake, defensive backs; born December 17, 1976, San Francisco. Safety Eastern Washington 1995-98. No pro playing experience. College coach: Eastern Washington 1999-2003, Washington 2004, Montana State 2005. Pro coach: Tampa Bay Buccaneers 2006-07, Detroit Lions 2008, re-joined Buccaneers in 2010.

Steve Logan, running backs; born February 3, 1953, Lawton, Okla. No college or pro playing experience. College coach: Oklahoma State 1980, Hutchinson J.C. 1981-82, Tulsa 1983-84, Colorado 1985-86, Mississippi State 1987-88, East Carolina 1989-2002, Boston College 2007-08. Pro coach: Berlin Thunder (NFL Europe) 2004-05, Rhein Fire (NFL Europe) 2006, joined Buccaneers in 2009.

Pete Mangurian, offensive line; born June 17, 1955, Los Angeles. Defensive tackle Louisiana State 1975-78. No pro playing experience. College coach: Southern Methodist 1979-1980, New Mexico State 1981, Stanford 1982-83, Louisiana State 1984-87, Cornell 1998-2000. Pro coach: Denver Broncos 1988-1992, New York Giants 1993-96, Atlanta Falcons 1997, 2001-03, New England Patriots 2005-08, joined Buccaneers in 2009.

Chris Mosley, defensive assistant; born December 5, 1977, Jacksonville. Running back Southeast Missouri State 1997-98, Washington & Jefferson 1999-2001. No pro playing experience. College coach: Boston College 2007, Princeton 2008. Pro coach: Joined Buccaneers in 2009.

Greg Olson, offensive coordinator; born March 1, 1963, Richland, Wash. Quarterback, Spokane Falls (Wash.) J.C. 1981-82. No pro playing experience. College coach: Washington State 1987-1989, Central Washington 1990-1993, Idaho 1994-1996, Purdue 1997-2000, 2002. Pro coach: San Francisco 49ers 2001, Chicago Bears 2003, Detroit Lions 2004-2005, St. Louis Rams 2006-2007, joined Buccaneers in 2008.

Alfredo Roberts, tight ends; born March 17, 1965, Fort Lauderdale, Fla. Tight end Miami 1983-87. Pro tight end Kansas City Chiefs 1988-1990, Dallas Cowboys 1991-93. College coach: Florida Atlantic 1999-2002. Pro coach: Jacksonville Jaguars 2003-06, Cleveland Browns 2007-08, joined Buccaneers in 2009.

Kurtis Shultz, head strength and conditioning; born March 10, 1972, Baltimore. Attended Maryland. No college or pro playing experience. College coach: Loyola (Md.) 1995-98, Maryland and Johns Hopkins 1999-2002. Pro coach: Cincinnati Bengals 2003, Minnesota Vikings 2004-05, joined Buccaneers in 2006.

Byron Storer, asst. special teams; born May 1, 1984, Modesto, Calif. Fullback California 2002-06. Pro fullback Tampa Bay Buccaneers 2007-09. Pro coach: Joined Buccaneers in 2009.

Dwayne Stukes, asst. defensive backs; born January 24, 1977, Portsmith, Va. Cornerback/safety Virginia 1996-1999. Pro safety Berlin Thunder (NFL Europe) 2001-2002, Colorado Crush (AFL) 2004. Pro coach: Joined Buccaneers in 2006.

Alex Van Pelt, quarterbacks; born May 1, 1970, Pittsburgh. Quarterback Pittsburgh 1989-1992. Pro quarterback Buffalo Bills 1995-2003. College coach: Buffalo 2005. Pro coach: Frankfurt Galaxy (NFLE) 2005, Buffalo Bills 2006-09, joined Buccaneers in 2010.

Todd Wash, defensive line; born July 19, 1968, Miles City, Mont. Linebacker North Dakota State 1988-1991. No pro playing experience. College coach: Fort Lewis College 1996-99, Nebraska-Kearney 2000-01, North Dakota State 2002-03, 2005-06, Missouri Southern State 2004. Pro coach: Joined Buccaneers in 2006.

Eric Yarber, wide receivers; born September 22, 1963, Chicago. Wide receiver Idaho 1984-85. Pro wide receiver Washington Redskins 1986-88. College coach: Idaho 1996, Nevada-Las Vegas 1997, Oregon State 1999-2002, Washington 2005-06, Arizona State 2007-09. Pro coach: Seattle Seahawks 1998, San Francisco 49ers 2003-04, joined Buccaneers in 2010.

National Football Conference
East Division
Team Colors: Burgundy and Gold
Redskins Park
21300 Redskins Park Drive
Ashburn, Virginia 20147
Telephone: (703) 726-7000

2010 SCHEDULE

PRESEASON

Aug. 13	**Buffalo**	7:30
Aug. 21	**Baltimore**	7:00
Aug. 27	at New York Jets	7:00
Sep. 2	at Arizona	7:00

REGULAR SEASON

Sep. 12	**Dallas**	8:20
Sep. 19	**Houston**	4:15
Sep. 26	at St. Louis	3:05
Oct. 3	at Philadelphia	4:15
Oct. 10	**Green Bay**	1:00
Oct. 17	**Indianapolis**	8:20
Oct. 24	at Chicago	12:00
Oct. 31	at Detroit	1:00
Nov. 7	BY	
Nov. 15	**Philadelphia** (Mon)	8:30
Nov. 21	at Tennessee	12:00
Nov. 28	**Minnesota**	1:00
Dec. 5	at New York Giants	1:00
Dec. 12	**Tampa Bay**	1:00
Dec. 19	at Dallas	1:00
Dec. 26	at Jacksonville	1:00
Jan. 2	**New York Giants**	1:00

Stadium: FedExField (opened in 1997)
•**Capacity:** 91,704
1600 FedEx Way
Landover, Maryland 20785
Playing Surface: Natural Grass
Training Camp: Redskins Park
Ashburn, Virginia 20147

FEDEXFIELD

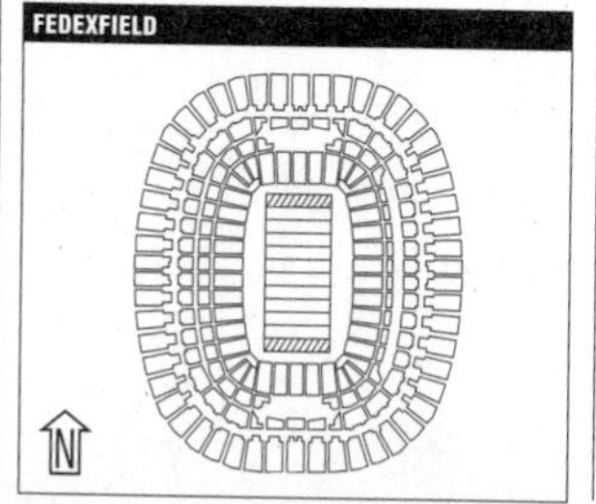

CLUB OFFICIALS

Owner: Daniel M. Snyder
Chief Operating Officer: Dave Donovan
Chief Financial Officer: Nico Foris
Executive Vice President/General Manager: Bruce Allen
Executive Vice President/Head Coach: Mike Shanahan
Senior Vice President: Tony Wyllie
Chief Marketing Officer: Mitch Gershman
Senior Vice President, Stadium Operations: Lon Rosenberg
Director of Player Personnel: Scott Campbell
Director of Pro Personnel: Morocco Brown
Pro Scouts: Richard Mann II, Alex Santos
College Scouts: Bill Baker, Chip Flanagan, Tim Gribble, Shemy Schembechler, Jim Zeches
Vice President, Football Administration: Eric Schaffer
Executive Director of Communications: Zack Bolno
Leadership Council/Community Affairs: BJ Corriveau
Director of Football Administration: Paul Kelly
Video Director: Mike Bracken
Video Department: Bobby Slowik
Head Athletic Trainer: Larry Hess
Assistant Athletic Trainers: Eric Steward, Elliott Jermyn, Eli Bisnett-Cobb
Equipment Manager: Brad Berlin
Assistant Equipment Manager: Anders Beutel, Chris Collins

COACHING HISTORY

Boston 1932-36
(564-523-27)
Records include postseason games

1932	Lud Wray	4-4-2
1933-34	William (Lone Star) Dietz	11-11-2
1935	Eddie Casey	2-8-1
1936-1942	Ray Flaherty	56-23-3
1943	Arthur (Dutch) Bergman	7-4-1
1944-45	Dudley DeGroot	14-6-1
1946-48	Glen (Turk) Edwards	16-18-1
1949	John Whelchel*	3-3-1
1949-1951	Herman Ball**	4-16-0
1951	Dick Todd	5-4-0
1952-53	Earl (Curly) Lambeau	10-13-1
1954-58	Joe Kuharich	26-32-2
1959-1960	Mike Nixon	4-18-2
1961-65	Bill McPeak	21-46-3
1966-68	Otto Graham	17-22-3
1969	Vince Lombardi	7-5-2
1970	Bill Austin	6-8-0
1971-77	George Allen	69-35-1
1978-1980	Jack Pardee	24-24-0
1981-1992	Joe Gibbs	140-65-0
1993	Richie Petitbon	4-12-0
1994-2000	Norv Turner***	50-60-1
2000	Terry Robiskie	1-2-0
2001	Marty Schottenheimer	8-8-0
2002-03	Steve Spurrier	12-20-0
2004-07	Joe Gibbs	31-36-0
2008-09	Jim Zorn	12-20-0

*Released after seven games in 1949
**Released after three games in 1951
***Released after 13 games in 2000

PAID ATTENDANCE

Home 681,703 Away 511,376
Total 1,193,079
Single-game home record, 90,910 (12/30/07)
Single-season home record, * 711,471 (2007)
NFL Record

2010 DRAFT CHOICES

Round	Name	Pos.	College
1	Trent Williams	T	Oklahoma
4	Perry Riley	LB	Louisiana St.
6	Dennis Morris	TE	Louisiana Tech
7	Terrence Austin	WR	UCLA
	Erik Cook	C	New Mexico
	Selvish Capers	T	West Virginia

WASHINGTON REDSKINS

2009 TEAM RECORD

PRESEASON (1-3)

Date	Result		Opponent
8/13	L	0-23	at Baltimore
8/22	W	17-13	Pittsburgh
8/28	L	24-27	New England
9/3	L	17-24	at Jacksonville

REGULAR SEASON (4-12)

Date	Result		Opponent
9/13	L	17-23	at New York Giants
9/20	W	9-7	St. Louis
9/27	L	14-19	at Detroit
10/4	W	16-13	Tampa Bay
10/11	L	17-20	at Carolina
10/18	L	6-14	Kansas City
10/26	L	17-27	Philadelphia
11/8	L	17-31	at Atlanta
11/15	W	27-17	Denver
11/22	L	6-7	at Dallas
11/29	L	24-27	at Philadelphia
12/6	L	30-33	New Orleans (OT)
12/13	W	34-13	at Oakland
12/21	L	12-45	New York Giants
12/27	L	0-17	Dallas
1/3	L	20-23	at San Diego

(OT) Overtime

SCORE BY PERIODS

Redskins	41	74	84	67	0	—	266
Opponents	96	118	30	89	3	—	336

2009 TEAM STATISTICS

	Redskins	Opp.
Total First Downs	280	280
Rushing	72	85
Passing	191	176
Penalty	17	19
3rd Down: Made/Att	86/216	87/219
3rd Down Pct.	39.8	39.7
4th Down: Made/Att	7/22	4/17
4th Down Pct.	31.8	23.5
Possession Avg.	28:49	31:11
Total Net Yards	5000	5115
Avg. Per Game	312.5	319.7
Total Plays	970	1000
Avg. Per Play	5.2	5.1
Net Yards Rushing	1510	1799
Avg. Per Game	94.4	112.4
Total Rushes	391	449
Net Yards Passing	3490	3316
Avg. Per Game	218.1	207.3
Sacked/Yards Lost	46/307	40/241
Gross Yards	3797	3557
Att./Completions	533/340	511/314
Completion Pct.	63.8	61.4
Had Intercepted	16	11
Punts/Average	76/40.6	70/41.8
Net Punting Avg.	76/36.1	70/38.5
Penalties/Yards	85/679	98/763
Fumbles/Ball Lost	30/12	21/6
Touchdowns	29	34
Rushing	8	10
Passing	21	19
Returns	0	5

2009 INDIVIDUAL STATISTICS

PASSING	Att.	Comp.	Yds.	Pct.	TD	Int.	Tkld.	Rate
Campbell	507	327	3618	64.5	20	15	43/285	86.4
Collins	23	12	144	52.2	0	0	2/11	71.6
H. Smith	2	1	35	50.0	1	1	0/0	95.8
Portis	1	0	0	0.0	0	0	0/0	39.6
Randle El	0	0	0	—	0	0	1/11	—
Redskins	533	340	3797	63.8	21	16	46/307	85.5
Opponents	511	314	3557	61.4	19	11	40/241	85.7

SCORING	TD R	TD P	TD Rt	PAT	FG	Saf	PTS
Suisham TM	0	0	0	20/21	18/21	0	74
Davis	0	6	0	0/0	0/0	0	36
Gano	0	0	0	6/7	4/4	0	18
Ganther TM	3	0	0	0/0	0/0	0	18
Moss	0	3	0	0/0	0/0	0	18
D. Thomas	0	3	0	0/0	0/0	0	18
Yoder	0	3	0	0/0	0/0	0	18
Betts	2	0	0	0/0	0/0	0	12
Cooley	0	2	0	0/0	0/0	0	12
Portis	1	1	0	0/0	0/0	0	12
Sellers	0	2	0	0/0	0/0	0	12
Campbell	1	0	0	0/0	0/0	0	6
Cartwright	0	1	0	0/0	0/0	0	6
H. Smith	1	0	0	0/0	0/0	0	6
Redskins	8	21	0	26/28	22/25	0	266
Opponents	10	19	5	31/31	31/36	2	336

2-Pt. Conversions: Redskins 0-1, Opponents 2-3.

RUSHING	No.	Yds	Avg	LG	TD
Portis	124	494	4.0	78	1
Campbell	46	236	5.1	21	1
Cartwright	64	228	3.6	34	0
Betts	56	210	3.8	18	2
Ganther TM	62	201	3.2	13	3
Mason	32	127	4.0	20	0
Moss	2	8	4.0	6	0
H. Smith	1	8	8.0	8t	1
Collins	1	0	0.0	0	0
D. Thomas	3	-2	-.7	2	0
Redskins	391	1510	3.9	78	8
Opponents	449	1799	4.0	67t	10

RECEIVING	No.	Yds	Avg	LG	TD
Moss	70	902	12.9	59t	3
Randle El	50	530	10.6	44	0
Davis	48	509	10.6	29	6
Cooley	29	332	11.4	25	2
Cartwright	27	242	9.0	51	1
Kelly	25	347	13.9	84	0
D. Thomas	25	325	13.0	40	3
Betts	17	179	10.5	25	0
Sellers	17	176	10.4	47	2
Ganther TM	9	99	11.0	42	0
Portis	9	57	6.3	10t	1
Mason	6	58	9.7	17	0
Mitchell	4	32	8.0	11	0
Yoder	4	9	2.3	3t	3
Redskins	340	3797	11.2	84	21
Opponents	314	3557	11.3	75t	19

PUNTING	No.	Yds.	Avg.	In 20	LG
H. Smith	57	2356	41.3	23	59
Pakulak	13	498	38.3	4	57
Paulescu TM	3	150	50.0	0	53
Suisham TM	3	80	26.7	1	32
Redskins	76	3084	40.6	28	59
Opponents	70	2929	41.8	30	68

INTERCEPTIONS	No.	Yds	Avg	LG	TD
Hall	4	114	28.5	44	0
McIntosh	2	27	13.5	18	0
Moore	1	14	14.0	14	0
Doughty	1	13	13.0	13	0
Landry	1	12	12.0	13	0
Tryon	1	3	3.0	3	0
Fletcher	1	2	2.0	2	0
Redskins	11	185	16.8	44	0
Opponents	16	291	18.2	62t	3

PUNT RETURNS	Ret	FC	Yds	Avg	LG	TD
Randle El	17	19	102	6.0	43	0
Moss	11	1	52	4.7	11	0
Hall	2	2	-2	-1.0	0	0
Barnes	1	0	0	0.0	0	0
Westbrook	1	0	0	0.0	0	0
Redskins	32	22	152	4.8	43	0
Opponents	32	26	220	6.9	29	0

KICKOFF RETURNS	No.	Yds	Avg	LG	TD
Cartwright	39	868	22.3	42	0
D. Thomas	20	439	22.0	39	0
Mason	2	31	15.5	18	0
Betts	1	29	29.0	29	0
Ganther TM	1	25	25.0	25	0
Sellers	1	13	13.0	13	0
Wilson	1	8	8.0	8	0
Redskins	65	1413	21.7	42	0
Opponents	56	1104	19.7	55	0

FIELD GOALS	1-19	20-29	30-39	40-49	50+
Suisham TM	0/0	8/9	5/6	5/5	0/1
Gano	0/0	2/2	0/0	2/2	0/0
Redskins	0/0	10/11	5/6	7/7	0/1
Opponents	1/1	12/12	8/8	9/12	1/3

SACKS	No.
Carter	11.0
Orakpo	11.0
Haynesworth	4.0
Alexander	2.0
Doughty	2.0
Fletcher	2.0
Golston	2.0
Griffin	2.0
Daniels	1.0
Landry	1.0
Tryon	1.0
Wilson	1.0
Redskins	40.0
Opponents	46.0

RECORD HOLDERS

INDIVIDUAL RECORDS—CAREER

Category	Name	Performance
Rushing (Yds.)	John Riggins, 1976-79, 1981-85	7,472
Passing (Yds.)	Joe Theismann, 1974-1985	25,206
Passing (TDs)	Sammy Baugh, 1937-1952	187
Receiving (No.)	Art Monk, 1980-1993	888
Receiving (Yds.)	Art Monk, 1980-1993	12,028
Interceptions	Darrell Green, 1983-2001	54
Punting (Avg.)	Sammy Baugh, 1937-1952	45.1
Punt Return (Avg.)	Johnny Williams, 1952-53	12.8
Kickoff Return (Avg.)	Bobby Mitchell, 1962-68	28.5
Field Goals	Mark Moseley, 1974-1986	263
Touchdowns (Tot.)	Charley Taylor, 1964-1977	90
Points	Mark Moseley, 1974-1986	1,206
*Sacks	Dexter Manley, 1981-89	91.0

INDIVIDUAL RECORDS—SINGLE SEASON

Category	Name	Performance
Rushing (Yds.)	Clinton Portis, 2005	1,516
Passing (Yds.)	Jay Schroeder, 1986	4,109
Passing (TDs)	Sonny Jurgensen, 1967	31
Receiving (No.)	Art Monk, 1984	106
Receiving (Yds.)	Santana Moss, 2005	1,483
Interceptions	Dan Sandifer, 1948	13
Punting (Avg.)	Sammy Baugh, 1940	**51.4
Punt Return (Avg.)	Johnny Williams, 1952	15.3
Kickoff Return (Avg.)	Mike Nelms, 1981	29.7
Field Goals	Mark Moseley, 1983	33
Touchdowns (Tot.)	John Riggins, 1983	24
Points	Mark Moseley, 1983	161
*Sacks	Dexter Manley, 1986	18.5

INDIVIDUAL RECORDS—SINGLE GAME

Category	Name	Performance
Rushing (Yds.)	Gerald Riggs, 9-17-89	221
Passing (Yds.)	Sammy Baugh, 10-31-43	446
Passing (TDs)	Sammy Baugh, 10-31-43, 11-23-47	6
	Mark Rypien, 11-10-91	6
Receiving (No.)	Art Monk, 12-15-85, 11-4-90	13
	Kelvin Bryant, 12-7-86	13
Receiving (Yds.)	Anthony Allen, 10-4-87	255
Interceptions	Sammy Baugh, 11-14-43	**4
	Dan Sandifer, 10-31-48	**4
Field Goals	Many times	5
	Last time by Shaun Suisham, 11-4-07	
Touchdowns (Tot.)	Dick James, 12-17-61	4
	Larry Brown, 12-16-73	4
Points	Dick James, 12-17-61	24
	Larry Brown, 12-16-73	24
*Sacks	Dexter Manley, 10-2-88	4.0
	Ken Harvey, 11-23-97	4.0
	Phillip Daniels, 12-18-05	4.0

**Sacks became an official statistic in 1982.*
***NFL Record*

WASHINGTON REDSKINS

2010 VETERAN ROSTER

No.	Name	Pos.	Ht.	Wt.	Birthdate	NFL Exp.	College	Hometown	How Acq.	'09 Games/ Starts
	#Albright, Ethan	LS	6-5	248	5/1/71	16	North Carolina	Greensboro, N.C.	UFA(Buff)-'01	16/0
97	Alexander, Lorenzo	LB/DE	6-1	297	5/31/83	4	California	Berkeley, Calif.	FA-'07	16/0
25	Barnes, Kevin	CB	6-1	188	9/15/86	2	Maryland	Glen Burnie, Md.	D3-'09	4/0
10	Bartel, Richard	QB	6-3	230	2/3/83	2	Tarleton State	Grapevine, Texas	FA-'09	0*
3	Bidwell, Josh	P	6-3	220	3/13/73	11	Oregon	Winston, Ore.	FA-'10	0*
54	Blades, H.B.	LB	5-10	242	9/30/84	4	Pittsburgh	Plantation, Fla.	D6-'07	16/1
55	Bowen, Alvin	LB	6-1	222	12/24/83	3	Iowa State	East Orange, N.J.	FA-'09	0*
15	Brennan, Colt	QB	6-3	206	8/16/83	3	Hawaii	Irvine, Calif.	D6-'08	0*
76	Bryant, Anthony	DL	6-3	335	11/6/81	4	Alabama	Greensboro, Ala	FA-'10	0*
31	Buchanon, Phillip	CB	5-11	186	9/19/80	9	Miami	Ft. Myers, Fla.	FA-'10	13/11*
	t- Carriker, Adam	DL	6-6	296	5/6/84	4	Nebraska	Kennewick, Wash.	T(StL)-'10	0*
99	Carter, Andre	LB	6-4	253	5/12/79	10	California	San Jose, Calif.	UFA(SF)-'06	16/16
47	Cooley, Chris	TE	6-3	250	7/11/82	6	Utah State	Logan, Utah	D3-'04	7/7
93	Daniels, Phillip	DL	6-6	311	3/4/73	15	Georgia	Donalsonville, Ga.	UFA(Chi)-'04	16/16
86	Davis, Fred	TE	6-4	257	1/15/86	3	Southern California	Toledo, Ohio	D2-'08	16/11
66	Dockery, Derrick	G	6-6	326	9/7/80	8	Texas	Lakeview, Texas	FA-'09	16/16
37	Doughty, Reed	S	6-1	205	11/4/82	5	Northern Colorado	Johnstown, Colo.	D6-'06	15/7
57	Draft, Chris	LB	5-11	232	2/26/76	13	Stanford	Anaheim, Calif.	UFA(Buff)-'10	11/3*
69	Fanaika, Paul	G	6-5	327	4/9/86	2	Arizona State	Milbrae, Calif.	FA-'09	0*
59	Fletcher, London	LB	5-10	245	5/19/75	13	John Carroll	Cleveland, Ohio	FA(Buff)-'07	16/16
84	Galloway, Joey	WR	5-11	197	11/20/71	15	Ohio State	Bellair, Ohio	UFA(NE)-'10	3/2*
56	Gatewood, Curtis	LB	6-3	240	5/18/85	2	Vanderbilt	Memphis, Tenn.	FA-'09	0*
64	Golston, Kedric	DL	6-4	290	5/30/83	5	Georgia	Tyrone, Ga.	D6-'06	16/6
72	Green, Howard	DL	6-2	320	1/12/79	7	Louisiana State	Donaldsville, La.	FA-'10	12/0*
8	Grossman, Rex	QB	6-1	217	8/23/80	8	Florida	Bloomington, Ind.	UFA(Hou)-'10	1/0*
83	Hagans, Marques	WR	5-10	205	12/29/82	2	Virginia	Hampton, Va.	FA-'10	0*
23	Hall, DeAngelo	CB	5-10	195	11/19/83	7	Virginia Tech	Chesapeake, Va.	FA-'08	13/12
92	Haynesworth, Albert	DL	6-6	350	6/17/81	9	Tennessee	Hartsville, S.C.	UFA(Tenn)-'09	12/12
51	Henson, Robert	LB	6-0	242	1/27/86	2	Texas Christian	Longview, Texas	D6-'09	6/0
74	Heyer, Stephon	T	6-6	330	1/16/84	4	Maryland	Lawrenceville, Ga.	FA-'07	16/16
75	Hicks, Artis	T/G	6-4	335	11/28/78	9	Memphis	Jackson, Tenn.	UFA(Minn)-'10	16/3*
29	Holmes, Lendy	S	6-1	201	10/26/85	2	Oklahoma	Dallas, Texas	FA-'09	8/0
48	Horton, Chris	S	6-1	211	12/29/84	3	UCLA	New Orleans. La.	D7-'08	8/5
91	Jackson, Rob	LB	6-4	269	11/3/85	2	Kansas State	West Haven, Conn.	D7-'08	5/0
90	Jarmon, Jeremy	LB	6-3	277	11/20/87	2	Kentucky	Collierville, Tenn.	SD3-'09	11/0
27	Johnson, Larry	RB	6-1	230	11/19/79	8	Penn State	State College, Pa.	UFA(Cin)-'10	14/7*
	#Jones, Levi	T	6-5	307	8/24/79	9	Arizona State	Eloy, Ariz.	FA-'09	9/8
12	Kelly, Malcolm	WR	6-4	227	12/30/86	3	Oklahoma	Longview, Texas	D2-'08	16/9
96	Kemoeatu, Maake	DL	6-5	345	1/10/79	9	Utah	Kahuku, Hawaii	FA-'10	0*
30	Landry, LaRon	S	6-0	210	10/14/84	4	Louisiana State	Ama, La.	D1-'07	15/15
78	Lichtensteiger, Kory	C	6-2	289	3/22/85	2	Bowling Green	Van Wert, Ohio	FA-'10	0*
38	McCauley, Marcus	CB	6-0	203	9/3/83	4	Fresno State	Rancho Cordova, Calif.	FA-'09	1/0*
52	McIntosh, Rocky	LB	6-2	238	11/15/82	5	Miami	Gaffney, S.C.	D2-'06	16/15
5	t- McNabb, Donovan	QB	6-2	240	11/25/76	12	Syracuse	Chicago, Ill.	T(Phil)-'10	14/14*
63	Montgomery, Will	G	6-3	305	2/13/83	4	Virginia Tech	Clifton, Va.	FA-'08	16/3
41	Moore, Kareem	S	5-11	218	8/13/84	3	Nicholls State	Okolona, Miss.	D6-'08	16/1
89	Moss, Santana	WR	5-10	200	6/1/79	10	Miami	Miami, Fla.	T(NYJ)-'05	16/16
98	Orakpo, Brian	LB	6-4	260	7/31/86	2	Texas	Houston, Texas	D1-'09	16/16
39	Parker, Willie	RB	5-10	209	11/11/80	7	North Carolina	Clinton, N.C.	UFA(Pitt)-'10	14/3*
79	Peterson, Greg	DL	6-5	315	1/21/84	4	North Carolina Central	Kenansville, N.C.	FA-'10	2/0*
26	Portis, Clinton	RB	5-11	221	9/1/81	9	Miami	Gainesville, Fla.	T(Den)-'04	8/8
61	Rabach, Casey	CB	6-4	295	9/24/77	10	Wisconsin	Sturgeon Bay, Wisc.	UFA(Balt)-'05	16/16
75	Rinehart, Chad	G/T	6-5	310	5/4/85	3	Northern Iowa	Boone, Iowa	D3-'08	5/4
73	Robinson, William	T	6-5	297	12/20/84	2	San Diego State	Pomona, Calif.	FA-'09	1/0
22	Rogers, Carlos	CB	6-0	190	7/2/81	6	Auburn	Augusta, Ga.	D1-'05	16/15
85	Ryan, Sean	TE	6-5	260	3/27/80	7	Boston College	Buffalo, N.Y.	UFA(KC)-'10	10/8
75	Scott, Darrion	DL	6-3	289	10/25/81	28	Ohio State	Charleston, W. Va.	FA-'10	0*
45	Sellers, Mike	FB	6-3	280	7/21/75	11	Walla Walla (Wash.) C.C.	North Thurston, Wash.	FA-'04	15/8
	#Smith, Hunter	P	6-2	209	8/9/77	12	Notre Dame	Sherman, Texas	UFA(Ind)-'09	13/0
	#Smoot, Fred	CB	5-11	185	4/17/79	10	Mississippi State	Jackson, Miss.	FA-'07	15/7
11	Thomas, Devin	WR	6-2	215	11/15/86	3	Michigan State	Ann Arbor, Mich.	D2-'08	14/10
46	Torain, Ryan	RB	6-1	225	8/10/86	24	Arizona State	Topeka, Kan.	FA-'10	0*
20	Tryon, Justin	CB	5-9	183	5/29/84	3	Arizona State	Palmdale, Calif.	D4-'08	15/1
88	Vickers, Lee	TE	6-6	275	3/13/81	2	North Alabama	Athens, Ala.	FA-'10	0*
19	Wade, Bobby	WR	5-10	186	2/25/81	8	Arizona	Orange County, Calif.	UFA(KC)-'10	12/6*
34	Westbrook, Byron	CB	5-10	198	12/26/84	2	Salisbury	Washington, D.C.	FA-'07	15/1
50	Williams, Edwin	C/G	6-3	315	12/10/86	2	Maryland	Washington, D.C.	FA-'09	4/2

71	Williams, Mike	G	6-7	337	1/11/80	6	Texas	Dallas, Texas	FA-'09	9/8
87	Williams, Roydell	WR	6-0	187	3/14/81	4	Tulane	New Orleans. La.	FA-'10	0*
95	Wilson, Chris	LB	6-4	247	7/10/82	4	Northwood	Flint, Mich.	FA-'07	16/0
97	#Wynn, Renaldo	DE	6-3	296	9/3/74	14	Notre Dame	Chicago, Ill.	UFA(NYG)-'09	2/0
87	#Yoder, Todd	TE	6-4	251	3/18/78	11	Vanderbilt	New Palestine, Ind.	FA-'06	16/1

* Bartel inactive for 6 games; Bidwell missed '09 season because of injury; Bowen inactive for 5 games; Brennan missed '09 season because of injury; Bryant last active with Miami in '07; Buchanon played 13 games with Detroit in '09; Carriker missed '09 season because of injury; Draft played 11 games with Buffalo; Fanaika inactive for 5 games; Galloway played 3 games with New England; Gatewood inactive for 3 games; Green played 12 games with N.Y. Jets; Grossman played 1 game with Houston; Hagans last active with Kansas City in '08; Hicks played 16 games with Minnesota; Johnson played 7 games with Kansas City and 7 games with Cincinnati; Kemoeatu missed '09 season because of injury; Lichtensteiger last active with Denver in '08; McCauley inactive for 1 game; McNabb played 14 games with Philadelphia; Parker played 14 games with Pittsburgh; Peterson played 2 games with Jacksonville; Ryan played 10 games with Kansas City; Scott last active with Minnesota in '07; Torain last active with Denver in '08; Vickers last active with Baltimore in '07; Wade played 12 games with Kansas City; R. Williams last active with Tennessee in '07.

t- Redskins traded for Carriker (StL) and McNabb (Phil).

Traded—QB Jason Campbell (16 games in '09) to Oakland.

Retired—Chris Samuels, 10-year tackle, 5 games in '09.

Also played with Redskins in '09—OL D'Anthony Batiste (8 games), RB Ladell Betts (8), RB Rock Cartwright (16), QB Todd Collins (3), K Graham Gano (4), RB Quinton Ganther (8), DT Cornelius Griffin (15), RB Marcus Mason (9), WR Marko Mitchell (10), DT Anthony Montgomery (7), P Glenn Pakulak (2), P Sam Paulescu (1), WR Antwaan Randle El (16), K Shaun Suisham (12), G Randy Thomas (2),

2010 FIRST-YEAR ROSTER

Name	Pos.	Ht.	Wt.	Birthdate	College	Hometown	How Acq.
Armstrong, Anthony (1)	WR	5-11	183	3/23/83	West Texas A&M	Indianapolis, Ind.	FA-'09
Austin, Terrence	WR	5-11	172	8/24/88	UCLA	Long Beach, Calif.	D7
Capers, Selvish	T	6-5	308	11/13/85	West Virginia	Kenner, La.	D7
Cook, Erik	C	6-6	318	7/5/87	New Mexico	Albuquerque, N.M.	D7
Dutch, Doug (1)	CB	5-11	199	2/15/86	Michigan	Washington, D.C.	FA-'09
Gano, Graham (1)	K	6-2	200	4/9/87	Florida State	Pensacola, Fla.	FA-'09
Holmes, Antoine (1)	DL	6-2	289	3/25/86	North Carolina State	Williamsburg, Va.	FA-'09
Jacobs, Trey	DL	6-4	295	6/1/88	Liberty	Eau Claire, S.C.	FA
Medlock, Justin (1)	K	5-11	201	10/23/83	UCLA	Fremont, Calif.	FA
Morris, Dennis	FB/TE	6-2	265	2/15/87	Louisiana Tech	Shreveport, La.	D6
Oldenburg, Clint (1)	T	6-5	302	9/9/83	Colorado State	Campbell County, Wy.	FA-'09
Paulsen, Logan	TE	6-5	264	2/26/87	UCLA	Northridge, Calif.	FA
Riley, Perry	LB	6-0	240	5/3/88	Louisiana State	Ellenwood, Ga.	D4
Russell, Anderson	S	6-0	205	5/30/87	Ohio State	Atlanta, Ga.	FA
Sundberg, Nick (1)	LS	6-0	245	7/29/87	California	Phoenix, Ariz.	FA
Williams, Keiland	RB	5-11	223	8/14/86	Louisiana State	Lafayette, La.	FA
Williams, Trent	T	6-5	314	8/19/88	Oklahoma	Longview, Texas	D1
Young, Darrel (1)	FB	5-11	245	4/8/87	Villanova	Amityville, N.Y.	FA-'09

The term NFL Rookie is defined as a player who is in his first season of professional football and has not been on the roster of another professional football team for any regular-season or postseason games. A Rookie is designated by an "R" on NFL rosters. Players who have been active in another professional football league or players who have NFL experience, including either preseason training camp or being on an Active List or Inactive List, or on Reserve/Injured or Reserve/Physically Unable to Perform for fewer than six regular-season games, are termed NFL First-Year Players. An NFL First-Year Player is designated by a "1" on NFL rosters. Thereafter, a player is credited with an additional year of experience for each season in which he accumulates six games on the Active List or Inactive List, or on Reserve/Injured or Reserve/Physically Unable to Perform.

Log on to www.washingtonredskins.com for an up-to-date roster.

COACHING STAFF

Head Coach,
Mike Shanahan

Pro Career: Became the 28th coach in franchise history when he replaced Jim Zorn on January 6, 2010. Mike Shanahan joins the Redskins after spending 14 seasons as head coach of the Denver Broncos (1995-2008). Shanahan led the Broncos to back-to-back Super Bowl championships in 1997 and 1998, becoming just the fifth head coach to accomplish that feat, and is the only coach to win seven consecutive postseason games in a two-year period. During his NFL career, Shanahan has been a part of teams that have played in nine conference championship games and six Super Bowls. In 30 seasons as a pro and college coach, Shanahan's teams have participated in postseason or bowl games 22 times. Under Shanahan's guidance, Denver set then-NFL records by posting the most victories in both a two-year (33, 1997-98) and three-year (46, 1996-98) span. In 17 years (14 with Denver and three as offensive coordinator with the San Francisco 49ers), Shanahan's offenses have finished number one in the NFL four times, second three times and third twice. Shanahan was an assistant with Denver (1984-87, 1989-1991) and San Francisco (1992-94). Returned to Denver as quarterbacks coach on October 6, 1989, after posting 8-12 record as the Los Angeles Raiders' head coach. Career record: 154-103.

Background: Shanahan coached at Oklahoma (1975-76), Northern Arizona (1977), Eastern Illinois (1978), Minnesota (1979), and Florida (1980-83).

Personal: Born in Oak Park, Illinois, on August 24, 1952. He was a wishbone quarterback/defensive back at Eastern Illinois. Mike and his wife, Peggy, have two children—Kyle and Krystal.

ASSISTANT COACHES

Malcolm Blacken, asst. strength and conditioning; born October 12, 1965, Richmond, Va. Running back Virginia Tech 1984-88. No pro playing experience. College coach: South Carolina 1990-91, George Mason 1992-94, Virginia 1995. Pro coach: Washington Redskins 1996-2000, Detroit Lions 2001-09, joined Redskins in 2010.

Jacob Burney, defensive line; born January 24, 1959, Chattanooga, Tenn. Defensive tackle Tennessee-Chattanooga 1977-1980. No pro playing experience. College coach: New Mexico 1983-86, Tulsa 1987, Mississippi State 1988, Wisconsin 1989, UCLA 1990-92, Tennessee 1993. Pro coach: Cleveland Browns/Baltimore Ravens 1994-98, Carolina Panthers 1999-2001, Denver Broncos 2002-08, joined Redskins in 2010.

Jon Embree, tight ends; born October 15, 1965, Los Angeles. Tight end Colorado 1983-86. Pro tight end Los Angeles Rams 1987-88. College coach: Colorado 1991, 1993-2002, UCLA 2003-05. Pro coach: Kansas City Chiefs 2006-08, joined Redskins in 2010.

Chad Englehart, asst. strength and conditioning; born June 5, 1981, New Orleans, La. Attended Southeastern Louisiana. No college or pro playing experience. College coach: New Orleans 2006. Pro coach: Florida Tuskers (UFL) 2009, joined Redskins in 2010.

Richmond Flowers, coaching assistant; born May 4, 1978, Birmingham, Ala. Wide receiver Duke 1996, 1998-99, Tennessee-Chattanooga 2000. Pro wide receiver Dallas Cowboys 2001, Washington Redskins 2002. Pro coach: joined Redskins in 2010.

Chris Foerster, offensive line; born October 12, 1961, Milwaukee, Wis. Center Colorado State 1979-1982. No pro playing experience. College coach: Colorado State 1983-87, Stanford 1988-1991, Minnesota 1992. Pro coach: Minnesota Vikings 1993-95, Tampa Bay Buccaneers 1996-2001, Indianapolis Colts 2002-03, Miami Dolphins 2004, Baltimore Ravens 2005-07, San Francisco 49ers 2008-09, joined Redskins in 2010.

Jim Haslett, defensive coordinator; born December 9, 1955, Pittsburgh. Defensive end Indiana (Pa.) 1975-78. Pro linebacker Buffalo Bills 1979-1986, N.Y. Jets 1987. College coach: Buffalo 1988-1990. Pro coach: Sacramento Surge (NFLE) 1991-92, Los Angeles Raiders 1993-94, New Orleans Saints 1995-96, Pittsburgh Steelers 1997-99, New Orleans Saints 2000-05 (head coach), St. Louis Rams 2006-08 (head coach 2008), Florida Tuskers (UFL head coach 2009), joined Redskins in 2010.

Richard Hightower, special teams assistant; born September 15, 1980, Houston. Wide receiver/defensive back Texas 1998-2002. No pro playing experience. College coach: Minnesota 2009. Pro coach: Houston Texans 2006-08, joined Redskins 2010.

Steve Jackson, safeties; born April 8, 1969, Houston. Defensive back Purdue 1987-1990. Pro defensive back Houston Oilers/Tennessee Titans 1991-99. Pro coach: Buffalo Bills 2001-03, joined Redskins in 2004.

Matt LeFleur, quarterbacks; born November 3, 1979, Mt. Pleasant, Mich. Quarterback/wide receiver Western Michigan 1998-99, Saginaw Valley State 2000-02. Pro quarterback Omaha Beef (NIFL) 2002, Billings Outlaws (NIFL) 2002. College coach: Saginaw Valley State 2003, Central Michigan 2004-05, Northern Michigan 2006, Ashland 2007. Pro coach: Houston Texans 2006-08, joined Redskins in 2010.

Keenan McCardell, wide receivers; born January 6, 1970, Houston. Wide receiver Nevada-Las Vegas 1987-1990. Pro wide receiver Washington Redskins 1991, 2007, Cleveland Browns 1992-95, Jacksonville Jaguars 1996-2001, Tampa Bay Buccaneers 2002-03, San Diego Chargers 2004-06. Pro coach: Joined Redskins in 2010.

Sean McVay, offensive assistant; born January 24, 1986, Marietta, Ga. Wide receiver Miami (Ohio) 2004-07. No pro playing experience. Pro coach: Tampa Bay Buccaneers 2008, Florida Tuskers (UFL) 2009, joined Redskins in 2010.

Kirk Olivadotti, defensive assistant; born January 1, 1974, Wilmington, Del. Wide receiver Purdue 1992-96. No pro playing experience. College coach: Marine Maritime Academy 1997, Indiana State 1998-99. Pro coach: Joined Redskins in 2000.

Kyle Shanahan, offensive coordinator; born December 14, 1979, Minneapolis. Wide receiver Duke 1998-99, Texas 2000-02. No pro playing experience. College coach: UCLA 2003. Pro coach: Tampa Bay Buccaneers 2004-05, Houston Texans 2006-09, joined Redskins in 2010.

Bob Slowik, defensive backs; born May 16, 1954, Pittsburgh. Defensive back Delaware 1973-76. No pro playing experience. College coach: Delaware 1977-78, Florida 1979-1982, Drake 1983, Rutgers 1984-89, East Carolina 1990-91. Pro coach: Dallas Cowboys 1992, Chicago Bears 1993-98, Cleveland Browns 1999, Green Bay Packers 2000-04, Denver Broncos 2005-2008, joined Redskins 2010.

Danny Smith, special teams; born September 7, 1953, Pittsburgh. Defensive back Edinboro State 1972-75. No pro playing experience. College coach: Edinboro State 1976, Clemson 1979, William & Mary 1980-83, Citadel 1984-86, Georgia Tech 1987-1994. Pro coach: Philadelphia Eagles 1995-98, Detroit Lions 1999-2000, Buffalo Bills 2001-03, joined Redskins in 2004.

Lou Spanos, linebackers; born March 27, 1971, Pittsburgh. Center Tulsa 1989-1992. No pro playing experience. College coach: Tulsa 1993. Pro coach: Pittsburgh Steelers 1994-2009, joined Redskins in 2010.

Bobby Turner, asst. head coach/running backs; born May 6, 1949, East Chicago, Ind. Defensive back Indiana State 1968-1971. No pro playing experience. College coach: Indiana State 1975-1982, Fresno State 1983-88, Ohio State 1989-1990, Purdue 1991-94. Pro coach: Denver Broncos 1995-2009, joined Redskins in 2010.

Ray Wright, strength and conditioning; born December 30, 1971, Fort Worth, Texas. Running back/wide receiver Duke 1990-95. No pro playing experience. College coach: Cornell 2000, Maryland 2001. Pro coach: Houston Texans 2002-09, joined Washington in 2010.

2009 Season in Review

TRADES

2009 TRADES (since May 1)

Defensive tackle **Orien Harris** from Cincinnati to St. Louis for running back **Brian Leonard**. (5/7)

Wide receiver **Dennis Northcutt** from Jacksonville to Detroit for defensive back **Gerald Alexander**. (7/1)

Wide receiver **Ron Curry** from Detroit to St. Louis for defensive tackle **Orien Harris**. (7/22)

Defensive end **Derrick Burgess** from Oakland to New England for Patriots' unannounced selections. (8/7)

Defensive tackle **LeKevin Smith** and an unannounced selection from New England to Denver for an unannounced selection. (8/17)

Center **Andy Alleman** and Guard **Ikechuku Ndukwe** from Miami to Kansas City for a Chiefs' unannounced selection. (8/24)

Guard **Russ Hochstein** from New England to Denver for an unannounced selection. (8/25)

Defensive tackle **Travis Johnson** from Houston to San Diego for Chargers' unannounced selection. (8/31)

Defensive tackle **Louis Leonard** from Cleveland to Carolina for Panthers' unannounced selection. (9/1)

Defensive back **Tye Hill** from St. Louis to Atlanta for Falcons' unannounced selection. (9/1)

Defensive back **Ko Simpson** from Buffalo to Detroit for Lions' unannounced selection. (9/4)

Defensive back **Derrick Martin** from Baltimore to Green Bay for tackle **Tony Moll**. (9/5)

Tight end **David Thomas** from New England to New Orleans for Saints' unannounced selection. (9/5)

Tight end **Michael Matthews** from the New York Giants to New England for Patriots' unannounced selection. (9/5)

Quarterback **Kevin O'Connell** from Detroit to the New York Jets for Jets' unannounced selection. (9/6)

Defensive end **Richard Seymour** from New England to Oakland for Raiders' unannounced selection. (9/6)

Quarterback **Luke McCown** from Tampa Bay to Jacksonville for Jaguars' unannounced selection. (9/6)

Linebacker **Prescott Burgess** from Baltimore to New England for Patriots' unannounced selection. (9/22)

Quarterback **Tyler Thigpen** from Kansas City to Miami for Dolphins' unannounced selection. (9/29)

Wide receiver **Braylon Edwards** from Cleveland to the New York Jets for wide receiver **Chansi Stuckey**, linebacker **Jason Trusnik**, and Jets' unannounced selections. (10/7)

Defensive end **Gaines Adams** from Tampa Bay to Chicago for the Bears' unannounced selection. (10/17)

Defensive tackle **Tank Tyler** from Kansas City to Carolina for Panthers' unannounced selection. (10/20)

Linebacker **Will Witherspoon** from St. Louis to Philadelphia for wide receiver **Brandon Gibson** and Eagles' unannounced selection. (10/20)

** Draft choice number is listed if club later traded the pick.*

2010 TRADES

Defensive end **Corey Williams** and Browns' seventh-round selection from Cleveland to Detroit for the Broncos' fifth-round selection in 2010 (#146) and sixth-round selection in 2010 (#214). (3/5)

Cornerback **Antonio Cromartie** from San Diego to N.Y. Jets for Jets' unannounced selection. (3/5)

Wide receiver **Anquan Boldin** and Cardinals' fifth-round selection (DT **Arthur Jones**) from Arizona to Baltimore for the Ravens' third-round selection (WR **Andre Roberts**) and fourth-round selection in 2010 (#123). (3/6)

Defensive back **Kerry Rhodes** from N.Y. Jets to Arizona for the Cardinals' fourth-round selection in 2010 (#124) and an unannounced selection. (3/8)

Defensive back **Chris Houston** from Atlanta to Detroit for the Lions' sixth-round selection in 2010 (DB **Shann Schillinger**) and an unannounced selection. (3/8)

Quarterback **Seneca Wallace** from Seattle to Cleveland for an unannounced selection. (3/9)

Wide receiver **Reggie Brown** from Philadelphia to Tampa Bay for an unannounced selection. (3/9)

Quarterback **Brady Quinn** from Cleveland to Denver for running back **Peyton Hillis** and two unannounced selections. (3/15)

Linebacker **Kamerion Wimbley** from Cleveland to Oakland for the Patriots' third-round selection in 2010 (#85). (3/15)

Quarterback **Shaun Hill** from San Francisco to Detroit for an unannounced selection. (3/15)

Defensive end **Chris Clemons** and the Jets' fourth-round selection in 2010 (DE **E.J. Wilson**) from Philadelphia to Seattle for defensive end **Darryl Tapp**. (3/17)

Quarterback **Charlie Whitehurst** and second-round selection (WR **Golden Tate**) from San Diego to Seattle for the Seahawks' second-round selection (#40) and an unannounced selection. (3/18)

Defensive back **Sheldon Brown** and linebacker **Chris Gocong** from Philadelphia to Cleveland for linebacker **Alex Hall**, the Browns' fourth-round selection in 2010 (DB **Trevard Lindley**) and fifth-round selection in 2010 (#137). (4/2)

Quarterback **Donovan McNabb** from Philadelphia to Washington for the Redskins' second-round selection (DB **Nate Allen**) for an unannounced selection. (4/5)

Defensive end **Robert Henderson** and the Lions' fifth-round selection in 2010 (DE **Kam Chancellor**) from Detroit to Seattle for guard **Rob Sims** and the Seahawks' seventh-round selection in 2010 (DE **Willie Young**). (4/5)

Wide receiver **Santonio Holmes** from Pittsburgh to N.Y. Jets for the Eagles' fifth-round selection in 2010 (#155). (4/12)

Wide receiver **Brandon Marshall** from Denver to Miami for the Dolphins' second-round selection in 2010 (#43) and an unannounced selection. (4/14)

Wide receiver **Ted Ginn** from Miami to San Francisco for the 49ers' fifth-round selection in 2010 (DB **Nolan Carroll**). (4/16)

Three-way trade: Denver receives the Browns' fifth-round selection in 2010 from Philadelphia (DB **Perrish Cox**); Philadelphia receives linebacker **Ernie Sims**; Detroit receives tight end **Tony Scheffler** and the Broncos' seventh-round selection in 2010 (LB **Jamar Chaney**). (4/19)

Quarterback **Byron Leftwich** from Tampa Bay to Pittsburgh for the Steelers' seventh-round selection in 2010 (#225). (4/21)

Defensive tackle **Adam Carriker**, the Saints' fifth-round selection (#163) and the Rams' seventh-round selection (#208) from St. Louis to Washington for the Redskins' fifth-round selection in 2010 (#135) and seventh-round selection in 2010 (DB **Marquis Johnson**). (4/21)

Linebacker **Quentin Groves** from Jacksonville to Oakland for the Cowboys' fifth-round selection in 2010 (#158). (4/22)

Denver trades Bears' first-round selection in 2010 (T **Anthony Davis**) from Denver to San Francisco for the 49ers' first-round selection in 2010 (#13) and fourth-round selection in 2010 (#113). (4/22)

Linebacker **Tim Dobbins** and the Chargers' first-round selection in 2010 (DT **Jared Odrick**), the Seahawks' second-round selection in 2010 (LB **Koa Misi**), and the Chargers' fourth-round selection in 2010 (#126) from San Diego to Miami for the Dolphins' first-round selection in 2010 (RB **Ryan Mathews**), fourth-round selection in 2010 (DB **Darrell Stuckey**), and the Chiefs' sixth-round selection in 2010 (#173). (4/22)

Denver trades 49ers' first-round selection in 2010 (DE **Brandon Graham**) from Denver to Philadelphia for the Eagles' first-round selection in 2010 (#24), the Seahawks' third-round selection in 2010 (#70) and the Eagles' third-round selection in 2010 (WR **Eric Decker**). (4/22)

Denver trades Eagles' first-round selection in 2010 (#24) and 49ers' fourth-round selection in 2010 (#113) from Denver to New England for the Patriots' first-round selection in 2010 (WR **Demaryius Thomas**). (4/22)

Denver trades Dolphins' second-round selection in 2010 (LB **Sergio Kindle**), Seahawks' third-round selection in 2010 (TE **Ed Dickson**), and the Broncos' fourth-round selection (TE **Dennis Pitta**) from Denver to Baltimore for the Ravens' first-round selection in 2010 (QB **Tim Tebow**). (4/22)

Detroit trades Lions' second-round selection in 2010 (DB **Chris Cook**), fourth-round selection in 2010 (DE **Everson Griffen**), and the Browns' seventh-round selection in 2010 (TE **Mickey Shuler**) from Detroit to Minnesota for the Vikings' first-round selection in 2010 (RB **Jahvid Best**) and fourth-round selection in 2010 (T **Jason Fox**). (4/22)

Oakland trades Raiders' third-round selection in 2009 (WR **Arrelious Benn**) from Oakland to Tampa Bay for the Bears' second-round selection in 2010 (#42) and the Patriots' fifth-round selection in 2010 (#153). (4/22)

New England trades Jaguars' second-round selection in 2010 (DE **Lamarr Houston**) and Patriots' sixth-round selection in 2010 (LB **Travis Goethel**) from New England to Oakland for the Bears' second-round selection in 2010 (TE **Rob Gronkowski**). (4/23)

Arizona trades Cardinals' second-round selection in 2010 (#58) and third-round selection in 2010 (#89) from Arizona to New England for the Titans' second-round selection in 2010 (LB **Daryl Washington**). (4/23)

Houston trades Texans' second-round selection in 2010 (RB **Toby Gerhart**) from Houston to Minnesota for the Vikings' second-round selection in 2010 (#62) and third-round selection in 2010 (#93). (4/23)

Dallas trades Cowboys' second-round selection in 2010 (#59) and fourth-round selection in 2010 (TE **Clay Harbor**) from Dallas to Philadelphia for the Eagles' second-round selection in 2010 (LB **Sean Lee**). (4/23)

Houston trades Vikings' second-round selection in 2010 (LB **Brandon Spikes**) and the Texans' fifth-round selection in 2010 (P **Zoltan Mesko**) from Houston to New England for the Cardinals' second-round selection in 2010 (RB **Ben Tate**). (4/23)

Cleveland trades Browns' third-round selection in 2010 (#71), Buccaneers' fifth-round selection in 2010 (DE **Ricky Sapp**), and the Broncos' fifth-round selection in 2010 (#146) from Cleveland to Philadelphia for the Cowboys' second-round selection in 2010 (RB **Montario Hardesty**). (4/23)

Green Bay trades Packers' third-round selection in 2010 (DE **Daniel Te'o-Nesheim**) and fourth-round choice in 2010 (QB **Mike Kafka**) from Green Bay to Philadelphia for the Browns' third-round selection in 2010 (DB **Morgan Burnett**). (4/23)

San Diego trades Chargers' third-round selection in 2010 (LB **Navorro Bowman**), the Chiefs' sixth-round selection in 2010 (RB **Anthony Dixon**), and the Chargers' fourth-round selection in 2011 from San Diego to San Francisco for the 49ers' third-round selection in 2010 (LB **Donald Butler**). (4/23)

Carolina trades Panthers' second-round selection in 2011 from Carolina to New England for the Cardinals' third-round selection in 2010 (WR **Armanti Edwards**). (4/23)

Houston trades Vikings' third-round selection in 2010 (TE **Tony Moeaki**) from Houston to Kansas City for the Chiefs' fourth-round selection in 2010 (LB **Darryl Sharpton**) and Panthers' fifth-round selection in 2010 (DB **Sherrick McManis**). (4/23)

Seattle trades Seahawks' fourth-round selection in 2010 (DB **Alterraun Verner**) and sixth-round selection in 2010 (QB **Rusty Smith**) from Seattle to Tennessee for defensive tackle **Kevin Vickerson**, running back **LenDale White**, the Titans' fourth-round selection in 2010 (DB **Walter Thurmond**) and sixth-round selection in 2010 (TE **Anthony McCoy**). (4/24)

Jacksonville trades Jaguars' fourth-round selection in 2010 (WR **Jacoby Ford**) from Jacksonville to Oakland for linebacker **Kirk Morrison** and the Patriots' fifth-round selection in 2010 (DE **Austen Lane**). (4/24)

Carolina trades Panthers' fourth-round selection in 2010 (RB **Joe McKnight**) from Carolina to N.Y. Jets for the Cardinals' fourth-round selection in 2010 (DE **Eric Norwood**) and the Jets' sixth-round selection in 2010 (WR **David Gettis**). (4/24)

Dallas trades Patriots' fourth-round selection in 2010 (LB **A.J. Edds**) from Dallas to Miami for the Chargers' fourth-round selection in 2010 (DB **Akwasi Owusu-Ansah**) and the Dolphins' sixth-round selection in 2010 (T **Sam Young**). (4/24)

Arizona trades Ravens' fourth-round selection in 2010 (DT **Al Woods**) from Arizona to New Orleans for the Saints' fourth-round selection in 2010 (LB **O'Brien Schofield**) and sixth-round selection in 2010 (DB **Jorrick Calvin**). (4/24)

Atlanta trades Falcons' fifth-round selection in 2010 (DE **Hall Davis**) and sixth-round selection in 2010 (DE **Eugene Sims**) from Atlanta to St. Louis for the Redskins' fifth-round selection in 2010 (DB **Dominique Franks**). (4/24)

Running back **Leon Washington** and the Jets' seventh-round selection in 2010 (LB **Dexter Davis**) from N.Y. Jets to Seattle for the Seahawks' fifth-round selection in 2010 (RB **John Conner**). (4/24)

Philadelphia trades Broncos' fifth-round selection in 2010 (DT **Cam Thomas**) from Philadelphia to San Diego for the Chargers' fifth-round selection in 2010 (WR **Riley Cooper**) and fifth-round selection in 2011. (4/24)

Cornerback **Bryant McFadden** and the Cardinals' sixth-round selection in 2010 (WR **Antonio Brown**) from Arizona to Pittsburgh for the Eagles' fifth-round selection in 2010 (QB **John Skelton**). (4/24)

Quarterback **Jason Campbell** from Washington to Oakland for an unannounced selection. (4/24)

Jacksonville trades Cowboys' fifth-round selection in 2010 (C **Matt Tennant**) from Jacksonville to New Orleans for the Saints' fourth-round selection in 2011. (4/24)

Miami trades Redskins' sixth-round selection in 2010 (TE **Dennis Morris**) and the Dolphins' seventh-round selection in 2010 (WR **Terrence Austin**) from Miami to Washington for the Saints' fifth-round selection in 2010 (DB **Reshad Jones**). (4/24)

New England trades Patriots' seventh-round selection in 2010 (C **Erik Cook**) and the Eagles' seventh-round selection in 2010 (T **Selvish Capers**) from New England to Washington for the Rams' seventh-round selection in 2010 (T **Thomas Welch**). (4/24)

Detroit trades Broncos' seventh-round selection in 2010 (LB **Jamar Chaney**) from Detroit to Philadelphia for the Eagles' sixth-round selection in 2011. (4/24)

Denver trades Broncos' fifth-round selection in 2011 from Denver to Tampa Bay for the Steelers' seventh-round selection in 2010 (DB **Syd'Quan Thompson**) and the Ravens' seventh-round selection in 2010 (LB **Jammie Kirlew**). (4/24)

Defensive back **Chris Harris** from Carolina to Chicago for linebacker **Jamar Williams**. (4/27)

Defensive back **Kevin Payne** from Chicago to St. Louis for an unannounced selection. (4/29)

Linebacker **Bobby Carpenter** from Dallas to St. Louis for tackle **Alex Barron**. (5/10)

** Draft choice number is listed if club later traded the pick.*

2009 PRESEASON STANDINGS/RESULTS

PRESEASON STANDINGS

AMERICAN FOOTBALL CONFERENCE

East Division

	W	L	T	Pct.	Pts.	OP
Miami	4	0	0	1.000	59	39
New England	3	1	0	.750	98	83
New York Jets	2	2	0	.500	108	99
Buffalo	1	4	0	.200	72	106

North Division

	W	L	T	Pct.	Pts.	OP
Baltimore	4	0	0	1.000	84	39
Pittsburgh	3	1	0	.750	71	37
Cincinnati	2	2	0	.500	73	54
Cleveland	2	2	0	.500	73	70

South Division

	W	L	T	Pct.	Pts.	OP
Tennessee	3	2	0	.600	102	104
Houston	2	2	0	.500	67	85
Indianapolis	1	3	0	.250	50	84
Jacksonville	1	3	0	.250	88	86

West Division

	W	L	T	Pct.	Pts.	OP
San Diego	2	2	0	.500	81	60
Denver	1	3	0	.250	65	71
Oakland	1	3	0	.250	79	107
Kansas City	0	4	0	.000	42	64

AFC PRESEASON RECORDS—TEAM BY TEAM

East Division

BUFFALO (1-4)

18	Tennessee (a)	21
27	Chicago	20
21	at Green Bay	31
0	at Pittsburgh	17
6	Detroit	17
72		106

MIAMI (4-0)

12	Jacksonville	9
27	Carolina	17
10	at Tampa Bay	6
10	at New Orleans	7
59		39

NEW ENGLAND (3-1)

27	at Philadelphia	25
6	Cincinnati	7
27	at Washington	24
38	New York Giants	27
98		83

N.Y. JETS (2-2)

20	St. Louis	23
23	at Baltimore	24
27	at New York Giants	25
38	Philadelphia	27
108		99

North Division

BALTIMORE (4-0)

23	Washington	0
24	New York Jets	23
17	at Carolina	13
20	at Atlanta	3
84		39

CINCINNATI (2-2)

7	at New Orleans	17
7	at New England	6
21	St. Louis	24
38	Indianapolis	7
73		54

CLEVELAND (2-2)

0	at Green Bay	17
27	Detroit	10
23	Tennessee	17
23	at Chicago	26
73		70

PITTSBURGH (3-1)

20	Arizona	10
13	at Washington	17
17	Buffalo	0
21	at Carolina	10
71		37

South Division

HOUSTON (2-2)

16	at Kansas City	10
14	New Orleans	38
10	Minnesota	17
27	at Tampa Bay	20
67		85

INDIANAPOLIS (1-3)

3	Minnesota	13
23	Philadelphia	15
17	at Detroit	18
7	at Cincinnati	38
50		84

JACKSONVILLE (1-3)

9	at Miami	12
23	Tampa Bay	24
32	at Philadelphia	33
24	Washington	17
88		86

TENNESSEE (3-2)

21	Buffalo (a)	18
27	Tampa Bay	20
10	at Dallas	30
17	at Cleveland	23
27	Green Bay	13
102		104

West Division

DENVER (1-3)

16	at San Francisco	17
13	at Seattle	27
17	Chicago	27
19	Arizona	0
65		71

KANSAS CITY (0-4)

10	Houston	16
13	at Minnesota	17
10	Seattle	14
9	at St. Louis	17
42		64

OAKLAND (1-3)

31	Dallas	10
20	at San Francisco	21
7	New Orleans	45
21	at Seattle	31
79		107

SAN DIEGO (2-2)

14	Seattle	20
17	at Arizona	6
24	at Atlanta	27
26	San Francisco	7
81		60

(a) Pro Football Hall of Fame Game at Canton, Ohio

NFC PRESEASON RECORDS—TEAM BY TEAM

East Division

DALLAS (2-2)

10	at Oakland	31
30	Tennessee	10
13	San Francisco	20
35	at Minnesota	31
88		92

N.Y. GIANTS (1-3)

24	Carolina	17
3	at Chicago	17
25	New York Jets	27
27	at New England	38
79		99

PHILADELPHIA (1-3)

25	New England	27
15	at Indianapolis	23
33	Jacksonville	32
27	at New York Jets	38
100		120

WASHINGTON (1-3)

0	at Baltimore	23
17	Pittsburgh	13
24	New England	27
17	Jacksonville	24
58		87

North Division

CHICAGO (3-1)

20	at Buffalo	27
17	New York Giants	3
27	at Denver	17
26	Cleveland	23
90		70

DETROIT (3-1)

27	Atlanta	26
10	at Cleveland	27
18	Indianapolis	17
17	at Buffalo	6
72		76

GREEN BAY (3-1)

17	Cleveland	0
31	Buffalo	21
44	at Arizona	37
13	at Tennessee	27
105		85

MINNESOTA (3-1)

13	Seattle	3
17	at Baltimore	13
17	Pittsburgh	10
31	at Dallas	35
78		61

South Division

ATLANTA (2-2)

26	at Detroit	27
20	at St. Louis	13
27	San Diego	24
3	Baltimore	20
76		84

CAROLINA (0-4)

17	at New York Giants	24
17	at Miami	27
13	Baltimore	17
10	Pittsburgh	21
57		89

NEW ORLEANS (3-1)

17	Cincinnati	7
38	at Houston	14
45	at Oakland	7
7	Miami	10
107		38

TAMPA BAY (1-3)

20	at Tennessee	27
24	at Jacksonville	23
6	Miami	10
20	Houston	27
70		87

West Division

ARIZONA (0-4)

10	at Pittsburgh	20
6	San Diego	17
37	Green Bay	44
0	at Denver	19
53		100

ST. LOUIS (3-1)

23	at New York Jets	20
13	Atlanta	20
24	at Cincinnati	21
17	Kansas City	9
77		70

SAN FRANCISCO (3-1)

17	Denver	16
21	Oakland	20
20	at Dallas	13
7	at San Diego	26
65		75

SEATTLE (4-0)

20	at San Diego	14
27	Denver	13
14	at Kansas City	10
31	Oakland	21
92		58

PRESEASON STANDINGS

NATIONAL FOOTBALL CONFERENCE

East Division

	W	L	T	Pct.	Pts.	OP
Dallas	2	2	0	.500	88	92
New York Giants	1	3	0	.250	79	99
Philadelphia	1	3	0	.250	100	120
Washington	1	3	0	.250	58	87

North Division

	W	L	T	Pct.	Pts.	OP
Chicago	3	1	0	.750	90	70
Detroit	3	1	0	.750	72	76
Green Bay	3	1	0	.750	105	85
Minnesota	3	1	0	.750	78	61

South Division

	W	L	T	Pct.	Pts.	OP
New Orleans	3	1	0	.750	107	38
Atlanta	2	2	0	.500	76	84
Tampa Bay	1	3	0	.250	70	87
Carolina	0	4	0	.000	57	89

West Division

	W	L	T	Pct.	Pts.	OP
Seattle	4	0	0	1.000	92	58
St. Louis	3	1	0	.750	77	70
San Francisco	3	1	0	.750	65	75
Arizona	0	4	0	.000	53	100

2009 AFC RESULTS

AMERICAN FOOTBALL CONFERENCE

BALTIMORE RAVENS (9-7)

38	Kansas City	24
31	at San Diego	26
34	Cleveland	3
21	at New England	27
14	Cincinnati	17
31	at Minnesota	33
30	Denver	7
7	at Cincinnati	17
16	at Cleveland	0
15	Indianapolis	17
20	Pittsburgh (OT)	17
14	at Green Bay	27
48	Detroit	3
31	Chicago	7
20	at Pittsburgh	23
21	at Oakland	13
391		261

BUFFALO BILLS (6-10)

24	at New England	25
33	Tampa Bay	20
7	New Orleans	27
10	at Miami	38
3	Cleveland	6
16	at New York Jets (OT)	13
20	at Carolina	9
10	Houston	31
17	at Tennessee	41
15	at Jacksonville	18
31	Miami	14
13	New York Jets	19
16	at Kansas City	10
10	New England	17
3	at Atlanta	31
30	Indianapolis	7
258		326

CINCINNATI BENGALS (10-6)

7	Denver	12
31	at Green Bay	24
23	Pittsburgh	20
23	at Cleveland (OT)	20
17	at Baltimore	14
17	Houston	28
45	Chicago	10
17	Baltimore	7
18	at Pittsburgh	12
17	at Oakland	20
16	Cleveland	7
23	Detroit	13
10	at Minnesota	30
24	at San Diego	27
17	Kansas City	10
0	at New York Jets	37
305		291

CLEVELAND BROWNS (5-11)

20	Minnesota	34
6	at Denver	27
3	at Baltimore	34
20	Cincinnati (OT)	23
6	at Buffalo	3
14	at Pittsburgh	27
3	Green Bay	31
6	at Chicago	30
0	Baltimore	16
37	at Detroit	38
7	at Cincinnati	16
23	San Diego	30
13	Pittsburgh	6
41	at Kansas City	34
23	Oakland	9
23	Jacksonville	17
245		375

DENVER BRONCOS (8-8)

12	at Cincinnati	7
27	CLEVELAND	6
23	at Oakland	3
17	Dallas	10
20	New England (OT)	17
34	at San Diego	23
7	at Baltimore	30
10	Pittsburgh	28
17	at Washington	27
3	San Diego	32
26	New York Giants	6
44	at Kansas City	13
16	at Indianapolis	28
19	Oakland	20
27	at Philadelphia	30
24	Kansas City	44
326		324

HOUSTON TEXANS (9-7)

7	New York Jets	24
34	at Tennessee	31
24	Jacksonville	31
29	Oakland	6
21	at Arizona	28
28	at Cincinnati	17
24	San Francisco	21
31	at Buffalo	10
17	at Indianapolis	20
17	Tennessee	20
27	Indianapolis	35
18	at Jacksonville	23
34	Seattle	7
16	at St. Louis	13
27	at Miami	20
34	New England	27
388		333

INDIANAPOLIS COLTS (14-2)

14	Jacksonville	12
27	at Miami	23
31	at Arizona	10
34	Seattle	17
31	at Tennessee	9
42	at St. Louis	6
18	San Francisco	14
20	Houston	17
35	New England	34
17	at Baltimore	15
35	at Houston	27
27	Tennessee	17
28	Denver	16
35	at Jacksonville	31
15	New York Jets	29
7	at Buffalo	30
416		307

JACKSONVILLE JAGUARS (7-9)

12	at Indianapolis	14
17	Arizona	31
31	at Houston	24
37	Tennessee	17
0	at Seattle	41
23	St. Louis (OT)	20
13	at Tennessee	30
24	Kansas City	21
24	at New York Jets	22
18	Buffalo	15
3	at San Francisco	20
23	Houston	18
10	Miami	14
31	Indianapolis	35
7	at New England	35
17	at Cleveland	23
290		380

KANSAS CITY CHIEFS (4-12)

24	at Baltimore	38
10	Oakland	13
14	at Philadelphia	34
16	New York Giants	27
20	Dallas (OT)	26
14	at Washington	6
7	San Diego	37
21	at Jacksonville	24
16	at Oakland	10
27	Pittsburgh (OT)	24
14	at San Diego	43
13	Denver	44
10	Buffalo	16
34	Cleveland	41
10	at Cincinnati	17
44	at Denver	24
294		424

MIAMI DOLPHINS (7-9)

7	at Atlanta	19
23	Indianapolis	27
13	at San Diego	23
38	Buffalo	10
31	New York Jets	27
34	New Orleans	46
30	at New York Jets	25
17	at New England	27
25	Tampa Bay	23
24	at Carolina	17
14	at Buffalo	31
22	New England	21
14	at Jacksonville	10
24	at Tennessee (OT)	27
20	Houston	27
24	Pittsburgh	30
360		390

NEW ENGLAND PATRIOTS (10-6)

25	Buffalo	24
9	at New York Jets	16
26	Atlanta	10
27	Baltimore	21
17	at Denver (OT)	20
59	Tennessee	0
35	at Tampa Bay	7
27	Miami	17
34	at Indianapolis	35
31	New York Jets	14
17	at New Orleans	38
21	at Miami	22
20	Carolina	10
17	at Buffalo	10
35	Jacksonville	7
27	at Houston	34
427		285

NEW YORK JETS (9-7)

24	at Houston	7
16	New England	9
24	Tennessee	17
10	at New Orleans	24
27	at Miami	31
13	Buffalo (OT)	16
38	at Oakland	0
25	Miami	30
22	Jacksonville	24
14	at New England	31
17	Carolina	6
19	at Buffalo	13
26	at Tampa Bay	3
7	Atlanta	10
29	at Indianapolis	15
37	Cincinnati	0
348		236

OAKLAND RAIDERS (5-11)

20	San Diego	24
13	at Kansas City	10
3	Denver	23
6	at Houston	29
7	at New York Giants	44
13	Philadelphia	9
0	New York Jets	38
16	at San Diego	24
10	Kansas City	16
20	Cincinnati	17
7	at Dallas	24
27	at Pittsburgh	24
13	Washington	34
20	at Denver	19
9	at Cleveland	23
13	Baltimore	21
197		379

PITTSBURGH STEELERS (9-7)

13	Tennessee (OT)	10
14	at Chicago	17
20	at Cincinnati	23
38	San Diego	28
28	at Detroit	20
27	Cleveland	14
27	Minnesota	17
28	at Denver	10
12	Cincinnati	18
24	at Kansas City (OT)	27
17	at Baltimore (OT)	20
24	Oakland	27
6	at Cleveland	13
37	Green Bay	36
23	Baltimore	20
30	at Miami	24
368		324

SAN DIEGO CHARGERS (13-3)

24	at Oakland	20
26	Baltimore	31
23	Miami	13
28	at Pittsburgh	38
23	Denver	34
37	at Kansas City	7
24	Oakland	16
21	at New York Giants	20
31	Philadelphia	23
32	at Denver	3
43	Kansas City	14
30	at Cleveland	23
20	at Dallas	17
27	Cincinnati	24
42	at Tennessee	17
23	Washington	20
454		320

TENNESSEE TITANS (8-8)

10	at Pittsburgh (OT)	13
31	Houston	34
17	at New York Jets	24
17	at Jacksonville	37
9	Indianapolis	31
0	at New England	59
30	Jacksonville	13
34	at San Francisco	27
41	Buffalo	17
20	at Houston	17
20	Arizona	17
17	at Indianapolis	27
47	St. Louis	7
27	Miami (OT)	24
17	San Diego	42
17	at Seattle	13
354		402

NATIONAL FOOTBALL CONFERENCE

ARIZONA CARDINALS (10-6)

16	San Francisco	20
31	at Jacksonville	17
10	Indianapolis	31
28	Houston	21
27	at Seattle	3
24	at New York Giants	17
21	Carolina	34
41	at Chicago	21
31	Seattle	20
21	at St. Louis	13
17	at Tennessee	20
30	Minnesota	17
9	at San Francisco	24
31	at Detroit	24
31	ST. LOUIS	10
7	Green Bay	33
375		325

ATLANTA FALCONS (9-7)

19	Miami	7
28	Carolina	20
10	at New England	26
45	at San Francisco	10
21	Chicago	14
21	at Dallas	37
27	at New Orleans	35
31	Washington	17
19	at Carolina	28
31	at New York Giants (OT)	34
20	Tampa Bay	17
7	Philadelphia	34
23	New Orleans	26
10	at New York Jets	7
31	Buffalo	3
20	at Tampa Bay	10
363		325

CAROLINA PANTHERS (8-8)

10	Philadelphia	38
20	at Atlanta	28
7	at Dallas	21
20	Washington	17
28	at Tampa Bay	21
9	Buffalo	20
34	at Arizona	21
20	at New Orleans	30
28	Atlanta	19
17	Miami	24
6	at New York Jets	17
16	Tampa Bay	6
10	at New England	20
26	Minnesota	7
41	at New York Giants	9
23	New Orleans	10
315		308

CHICAGO BEARS (7-9)

15	at Green Bay	21
17	Pittsburgh	14
25	at Seattle	19
48	Detroit	24
14	at Atlanta	21
10	at Cincinnati	45
30	Cleveland	6
21	Arizona	41
6	at San Francisco	10
20	Philadelphia	24
10	at Minnesota	36
17	St. Louis	9
14	Green Bay	21
7	at Baltimore	31
36	Minnesota (OT)	30
37	at Detroit	23
327		375

DALLAS COWBOYS (11-5)

34	at Tampa Bay	21
31	New York Giants	33
21	Carolina	7
10	at Denver	17
26	at Kansas City (OT)	20
37	Atlanta	21
38	Seattle	17
20	at Philadelphia	16
7	at Green Bay	17
7	Washington	6
24	Oakland	7
24	at New York Giants	31
17	San Diego	20
24	at New Orleans	17
17	at Washington	0
24	Philadelphia	0
361		250

DETROIT LIONS (2-14)

27	at New Orleans	45
13	Minnesota	27
19	Washington	14
24	at Chicago	48
20	Pittsburgh	28
0	at Green Bay	26
10	St. Louis	17
20	at Seattle	32
10	at Minnesota	27
38	Cleveland	37
12	Green Bay	34
13	at Cincinnati	23
3	at Baltimore	48
24	Arizona	31
6	at San Francisco	20
23	Chicago	37
262		494

GREEN BAY PACKERS (11-5)

21	Chicago	15
24	Cincinnati	31
36	at St. Louis	17
23	at Minnesota	30
26	Detroit	0
31	at Cleveland	3
26	Minnesota	38
28	at Tampa Bay	38
17	Dallas	7
30	San Francisco	24
34	at Detroit	12
27	Baltimore	14
21	at Chicago	14
36	at Pittsburgh	37
48	Seattle	10
33	at Arizona	7
461		297

MINNESOTA VIKINGS (12-4)

34	at Cleveland	20
27	at Detroit	13
27	San Francisco	24
30	Green Bay	23
38	at St. Louis	10
33	Baltimore	31
17	at Pittsburgh	27
38	at Green Bay	26
27	Detroit	10
35	Seattle	9
36	Chicago	10
17	at Arizona	30
30	Cincinnati	10
7	at Carolina	26
30	at Chicago (OT)	36
44	New York Giants	7
470		312

NEW ORLEANS SAINTS (13-3)

45	Detroit	27
48	at Philadelphia	22
27	at Buffalo	7
24	New York Jets	10
48	New York Giants	27
46	at Miami	34
35	Atlanta	27
30	Carolina	20
28	at St. Louis	23
38	at Tampa Bay	7
38	New England	17
33	at Washington (OT)	30
26	at Atlanta	23
17	Dallas	24
17	Tampa Bay (OT)	20
10	at Carolina	23
510		341

NEW YORK GIANTS (8-8)

23	Washington	17
33	at Dallas	31
24	at Tampa Bay	0
27	at Kansas City	16
44	Oakland	7
27	at New Orleans	48
17	Arizona	24
17	at Philadelphia	40
20	San Diego	21
34	Atlanta (OT)	31
6	at Denver	26
31	Dallas	24
38	Philadelphia	45
45	at Washington	12
9	Carolina	41
7	at Minnesota	44
402		427

PHILADELPHIA EAGLES (11-5)

38	at Carolina	10
22	New Orleans	48
34	Kansas City	14
33	Tampa Bay	14
9	at Oakland	13
27	at Washington	17
40	New York Giants	17
16	Dallas	20
23	at San Diego	31
24	at Chicago	20
27	Washington	24
34	at Atlanta	7
45	at New York Giants	38
27	San Francisco	13
30	Denver	27
0	at Dallas	24
429		337

ST. LOUIS RAMS (1-15)

0	at Seattle	28
7	at Washington	9
17	Green Bay	36
0	at San Francisco	35
10	Minnesota	38
20	at Jacksonville (OT)	23
6	Indianapolis	42
17	at Detroit	10
23	New Orleans	28
13	Arizona	21
17	Seattle	27
9	at Chicago	17
7	at Tennessee	47
13	Houston	16
10	at Arizona	31
6	San Francisco	28
175		436

SAN FRANCISCO 49ERS (8-8)

20	at Arizona	16
23	Seattle	10
24	at Minnesota	27
35	St. Louis	0
10	Atlanta	45
21	at Houston	24
14	at Indianapolis	18
27	Tennessee	34
10	Chicago	6
24	at Green Bay	30
20	Jacksonville	3
17	at Seattle	20
24	Arizona	9
13	at Philadelphia	27
20	Detroit	6
28	at St. Louis	6
330		281

SEATTLE SEAHAWKS (5-11)

28	St. Louis	0
10	at San Francisco	23
19	Chicago	25
17	at Indianapolis	34
41	Jacksonville	0
3	Arizona	27
17	at Dallas	38
32	Detroit	20
20	at Arizona	31
9	at Minnesota	35
27	at St. Louis	17
20	San Francisco	17
7	at Houston	34
7	Tampa Bay	24
10	at Green Bay	48
13	Tennessee	17
280		390

TAMPA BAY BUCCANEERS (3-13)

21	Dallas	34
20	at Buffalo	33
0	New York Giants	24
13	at Washington	16
14	at Philadelphia	33
21	Carolina	28
7	New England	35
38	Green Bay	28
23	at Miami	25
7	New Orleans	38
17	at Atlanta	20
6	at Carolina	16
3	New York Jets	26
24	at Seattle	7
20	at New Orleans (OT)	17
10	Atlanta	20
244		400

WASHINGTON REDSKINS (4-12)

17	at New York Giants	23
9	St. Louis	7
14	at Detroit	19
16	Tampa Bay	13
17	at Carolina	20
6	Kansas City	14
17	Philadelphia	27
17	at Atlanta	31
27	Denver	17
6	at Dallas	7
24	at Philadelphia	27
30	New Orleans (OT)	33
34	at Oakland	13
12	New York Giants	45
0	Dallas	17
20	at San Diego	23
266		336

FINAL STANDINGS

AMERICAN FOOTBALL CONFERENCE

East Division	W	L	T	Pct.	Pts.	OP
* New England	10	6	0	.625	427	285
# New York Jets	9	7	0	.563	348	236
Miami	7	9	0	.438	360	390
Buffalo	6	10	0	.375	258	326
North Division	**W**	**L**	**T**	**Pct.**	**Pts.**	**OP**
* Cincinnati	10	6	0	.625	305	291
# Baltimore	9	7	0	.563	391	261
Pittsburgh	9	7	0	.563	368	324
Cleveland	5	11	0	.313	245	375
South Division	**W**	**L**	**T**	**Pct.**	**Pts.**	**OP**
* Indianapolis	14	2	0	.875	416	307
Houston	9	7	0	.563	388	333
Tennessee	8	8	0	.500	354	402
Jacksonville	7	9	0	.438	290	380
West Division	**W**	**L**	**T**	**Pct.**	**Pts.**	**OP**
* San Diego	13	3	0	.813	454	320
Denver	8	8	0	.500	326	324
Oakland	5	11	0	.313	197	379
Kansas City	4	12	0	.250	294	424

NATIONAL FOOTBALL CONFERENCE

East Division	W	L	T	Pct.	Pts.	OP
* Dallas	11	5	0	.688	361	250
# Philadelphia	11	5	0	.688	429	337
New York Giants	8	8	0	.500	402	427
Washington	4	12	0	.250	266	336
North Division	**W**	**L**	**T**	**Pct.**	**Pts.**	**OP**
* Minnesota	12	4	0	.750	470	312
# Green Bay	11	5	0	.688	461	297
Chicago	7	9	0	.438	327	375
Detroit	2	14	0	.125	262	494
South Division	**W**	**L**	**T**	**Pct.**	**Pts.**	**OP**
* New Orleans	13	3	0	.813	510	341
Atlanta	9	7	0	.563	363	325
Carolina	8	8	0	.500	315	308
Tampa Bay	3	13	0	.188	244	400
West Division	**W**	**L**	**T**	**Pct.**	**Pts.**	**OP**
* Arizona	10	6	0	.625	375	325
San Francisco	8	8	0	.500	330	281
Seattle	5	11	0	.313	280	390
St. Louis	1	15	0	.063	175	436

** Division champion*
 # Wild Card team

New England finished ahead of Cincinnati based on better strength of victory (.450 to Bengals' .438). Baltimore finished ahead of Pittsburgh based on better division record (3-3 to Steelers' 2-4). New York Jets finished ahead of Baltimore for first Wild Card based on better record vs. common opponents (4-1 to Ravens' 1-4) and ahead of Houston based on better conference record (7-5 to Texans' 6-6). Baltimore was second Wild Card based on better conference record than Houston (7-5 to Texans' 6-6). Dallas finished ahead of Philadelphia based on head-to-head sweep (2-0). Green Bay was first Wild Card ahead of Philadelphia based on better record vs. common opponents (4-1 to Eagles' 3-2).

WILD-CARD PLAYOFFS

AFC
New York Jets 24, CINCINNATI 14
Baltimore 33, NEW ENGLAND 14
NFC
DALLAS 34, Philadelphia 14
ARIZONA 51, Green Bay 45 (OT)

DIVISIONAL PLAYOFFS

AFC
INDIANAPOLIS 20, Baltimore 3
New York Jets 17, SAN DIEGO 14
NFC
NEW ORLEANS 45, Arizona 14
MINNESOTA 34, Dallas 3

CHAMPIONSHIP GAMES

AFC
INDIANAPOLIS 30, New York Jets 17
NFC
NEW ORLEANS 31, Minnesota 28 (OT)

AFC-NFC PRO BOWL

AFC 41, NFC 34
at Sun Life Stadium, Miami, Florida

SUPER BOWL XLIV

New Orleans 31, Indianapolis 17
at Sun Life Stadium, Miami, Florida

Home teams in playoff games are indicated in CAPS.

FIRST WEEK STANDINGS

American Football Conference

East Division	W	L	T	Pct.	Pts.	OP
New England	1	0	0	1.000	25	24
New York Jets	1	0	0	1.000	24	7
Buffalo	0	1	0	.000	24	25
Miami	0	1	0	.000	7	19
North Division	**W**	**L**	**T**	**Pct.**	**Pts.**	**OP**
Baltimore	1	0	0	1.000	38	24
Pittsburgh	1	0	0	1.000	13	10
Cincinnati	0	1	0	.000	7	12
Cleveland	0	1	0	.000	20	34
South Division	**W**	**L**	**T**	**Pct.**	**Pts.**	**OP**
Indianapolis	1	0	0	1.000	14	12
Houston	0	1	0	.000	7	24
Jacksonville	0	1	0	.000	12	14
Tennessee	0	1	0	.000	10	13
West Division	**W**	**L**	**T**	**Pct.**	**Pts.**	**OP**
Denver	1	0	0	1.000	12	7
San Diego	1	0	0	1.000	24	20
Kansas City	0	1	0	.000	24	38
Oakland	0	1	0	.000	20	24

National Football Conference

East Division	W	L	T	Pct.	Pts.	OP
Dallas	1	0	0	1.000	34	21
New York Giants	1	0	0	1.000	23	17
Philadelphia	1	0	0	1.000	38	10
Washington	0	1	0	.000	17	23
North Division	**W**	**L**	**T**	**Pct.**	**Pts.**	**OP**
Green Bay	1	0	0	1.000	21	15
Minnesota	1	0	0	1.000	34	20
Chicago	0	1	0	.000	15	21
Detroit	0	1	0	.000	27	45
South Division	**W**	**L**	**T**	**Pct.**	**Pts.**	**OP**
Atlanta	1	0	0	1.000	19	7
New Orleans	1	0	0	1.000	45	27
Carolina	0	1	0	.000	10	38
Tampa Bay	0	1	0	.000	21	34
West Division	**W**	**L**	**T**	**Pct.**	**Pts.**	**OP**
San Francisco	1	0	0	1.000	20	16
Seattle	1	0	0	1.000	28	0
Arizona	0	1	0	.000	16	20
St. Louis	0	1	0	.000	0	28

WEEK 1 RESULTS

Thursday, September 10
PITTSBURGH 13, Tennessee 10 (OT)

Sunday, September 13
ATLANTA 19, Miami 7
BALTIMORE 38, Kansas City 24
Philadelphia 38, CAROLINA 10
Denver 12, CINCINNATI 7
Minnesota 34, CLEVELAND 20
New York Jets 24, HOUSTON 7
INDIANAPOLIS 14, Jacksonville 12
NEW ORLEANS 45, Detroit 27
Dallas 34, TAMPA BAY 21
San Francisco 20, ARIZONA 16
NEW YORK GIANTS 23, Washington 17
SEATTLE 28, St. Louis 0
GREEN BAY 34, Chicago 15

Monday, September 14
NEW ENGLAND 25, Buffalo 24
San Diego 24, OAKLAND 20

In the 2009 Week By Week section, home teams are indicated by ALL CAPS.

**For game recaps, box scores, and video highlights, please visit www.NFL.com/scores.*

SECOND WEEK STANDINGS

American Football Conference

East Division	W	L	T	Pct.	Pts.	OP
New York Jets	2	0	0	1.000	40	16
Buffalo	1	1	0	.500	57	45
New England	1	1	0	.500	34	40
Miami	0	2	0	.000	30	46
North Division	**W**	**L**	**T**	**Pct.**	**Pts.**	**OP**
Baltimore	2	0	0	1.000	69	50
Cincinnati	1	1	0	.500	38	36
Pittsburgh	1	1	0	.500	27	27
Cleveland	0	2	0	.000	26	61
South Division	**W**	**L**	**T**	**Pct.**	**Pts.**	**OP**
Indianapolis	2	0	0	1.000	41	35
Houston	1	1	0	.500	41	55
Jacksonville	0	2	0	.000	29	45
Tennessee	0	2	0	.000	41	47
West Division	**W**	**L**	**T**	**Pct.**	**Pts.**	**OP**
Denver	2	0	0	1.000	39	13
Oakland	1	1	0	.500	33	34
San Diego	1	1	0	.500	50	51
Kansas City	0	2	0	.000	34	51

National Football Conference

East Division	W	L	T	Pct.	Pts.	OP
New York Giants	2	0	0	1.000	56	48
Dallas	1	1	0	.500	65	54
Philadelphia	1	1	0	.500	60	58
Washington	1	1	0	.500	26	30
North Division	**W**	**L**	**T**	**Pct.**	**Pts.**	**OP**
Minnesota	2	0	0	1.000	61	33
Chicago	1	1	0	.500	32	35
Green Bay	1	1	0	.500	45	46
Detroit	0	2	0	.000	40	72
South Division	**W**	**L**	**T**	**Pct.**	**Pts.**	**OP**
Atlanta	2	0	0	1.000	47	27
New Orleans	2	0	0	1.000	93	49
Carolina	0	2	0	.000	30	66
Tampa Bay	0	2	0	.000	41	67
West Division	**W**	**L**	**T**	**Pct.**	**Pts.**	**OP**
San Francisco	2	0	0	1.000	43	26
Arizona	1	1	0	.500	47	37
Seattle	1	1	0	.500	38	23
St. Louis	0	2	0	.000	7	37

WEEK 2 RESULTS

Sunday, September 20
ATLANTA 28, Carolina 20
Minnesota 27, DETROIT 13
Cincinnati 31, GREEN BAY 24
Arizona 31, JACKSONVILLE 17
Oakland 13, KANSAS CITY 10
NEW YORK JETS 16, New England 9
New Orleans 48, PHILADELPHIA 22
Houston 34, TENNESSEE 31
WASHINGTON 9, St. Louis 7
BUFFALO 33, Tampa Bay 20
SAN FRANCISCO 23, Seattle 10
CHICAGO 17, Pittsburgh 14
DENVER 27, Cleveland 6
Baltimore 31, SAN DIEGO 26
New York Giants 33, DALLAS 31

Monday, September 21
Indianapolis 27, MIAMI 23

THIRD WEEK STANDINGS

American Football Conference

East Division	W	L	T	Pct.	Pts.	OP
New York Jets	3	0	0	1.000	64	33
New England	2	1	0	.667	60	50
Buffalo	1	2	0	.333	64	72
Miami	0	3	0	.000	43	69
North Division	**W**	**L**	**T**	**Pct.**	**Pts.**	**OP**
Baltimore	3	0	0	1.000	103	53
Cincinnati	2	1	0	.667	61	56
Pittsburgh	1	2	0	.333	47	50
Cleveland	0	3	0	.000	29	95
South Division	**W**	**L**	**T**	**Pct.**	**Pts.**	**OP**
Indianapolis	3	0	0	1.000	72	45
Houston	1	2	0	.333	65	86
Jacksonville	1	2	0	.333	60	69
Tennessee	0	3	0	.000	58	71
West Division	**W**	**L**	**T**	**Pct.**	**Pts.**	**OP**
Denver	3	0	0	1.000	62	16
San Diego	2	1	0	.667	73	64
Oakland	1	2	0	.333	36	57
Kansas City	0	3	0	.000	48	85

National Football Conference

East Division	W	L	T	Pct.	Pts.	OP
New York Giants	3	0	0	1.000	80	48
Dallas	2	1	0	.667	86	61
Philadelphia	2	1	0	.667	94	72
Washington	1	2	0	.333	40	49
North Division	**W**	**L**	**T**	**Pct.**	**Pts.**	**OP**
Minnesota	3	0	0	1.000	88	57
Chicago	2	1	0	.667	57	54
Green Bay	2	1	0	.667	81	63
Detroit	1	2	0	.333	59	86
South Division	**W**	**L**	**T**	**Pct.**	**Pts.**	**OP**
New Orleans	3	0	0	1.000	120	56
Atlanta	2	1	0	.667	57	53
Carolina	0	3	0	.000	37	87
Tampa Bay	0	3	0	.000	41	91
West Division	**W**	**L**	**T**	**Pct.**	**Pts.**	**OP**
San Francisco	2	1	0	.667	67	53
Arizona	1	2	0	.333	57	68
Seattle	1	2	0	.333	57	48
St. Louis	0	3	0	.000	24	73

WEEK 3 RESULTS

Sunday, September 27
BALTIMORE 34, Cleveland 3
DETROIT 19, Washington 14
Jacksonville 31, HOUSTON 24
MINNESOTA 27, San Francisco 24
NEW ENGLAND 26, Atlanta 10
NEW YORK JETS 24, Tennessee 17
PHILADELPHIA 34, Kansas City 14
Green Bay 36, ST. LOUIS 17
New York Giants 24, TAMPA BAY 0
New Orleans 27, BUFFALO 7
Chicago 25, SEATTLE 19
CINCINNATI 23, Pittsburgh 20
Denver 23, OAKLAND 3
SAN DIEGO 23, Miami 13
Indianapolis 31, ARIZONA 10

Monday, September 28
DALLAS 21, Carolina 7

FOURTH WEEK STANDINGS

American Football Conference

East Division	W	L	T	Pct.	Pts.	OP
New England	3	1	0	.750	87	71
New York Jets	3	1	0	.750	74	57
Buffalo	1	3	0	.250	74	110
Miami	1	3	0	.250	81	79
North Division	**W**	**L**	**T**	**Pct.**	**Pts.**	**OP**
Baltimore	3	1	0	.750	124	80
Cincinnati	3	1	0	.750	84	76
Pittsburgh	2	2	0	.500	85	78
Cleveland	0	4	0	.000	49	118
South Division	**W**	**L**	**T**	**Pct.**	**Pts.**	**OP**
Indianapolis	4	0	0	1.000	106	62
Houston	2	2	0	.500	94	92
Jacksonville	2	2	0	.500	97	86
Tennessee	0	4	0	.000	75	108
West Division	**W**	**L**	**T**	**Pct.**	**Pts.**	**OP**
Denver	4	0	0	1.000	79	26
San Diego	2	2	0	.500	101	102
Oakland	1	3	0	.250	42	86
Kansas City	0	4	0	.000	64	112

National Football Conference

East Division	W	L	T	Pct.	Pts.	OP
New York Giants	4	0	0	1.000	107	64
Philadelphia	2	1	0	.667	94	72
Dallas	2	2	0	.500	96	78
Washington	2	2	0	.500	56	62
North Division	**W**	**L**	**T**	**Pct.**	**Pts.**	**OP**
Minnesota	4	0	0	1.000	118	80
Chicago	3	1	0	.750	105	78
Green Bay	2	2	0	.500	104	93
Detroit	1	3	0	.250	83	134
South Division	**W**	**L**	**T**	**Pct.**	**Pts.**	**OP**
New Orleans	4	0	0	1.000	144	66
Atlanta	2	1	0	.667	57	53
Carolina	0	3	0	.000	37	87
Tampa Bay	0	4	0	.000	54	107
West Division	**W**	**L**	**T**	**Pct.**	**Pts.**	**OP**
San Francisco	3	1	0	.750	102	53
Arizona	1	2	0	.333	57	68
Seattle	1	3	0	.250	74	82
St. Louis	0	4	0	.000	24	108

WEEK 4 RESULTS

Sunday, October 4

CHICAGO 48, Detroit 24
Cincinnati 23, CLEVELAND 20 (OT)
HOUSTON 29, Oakland 6
INDIANAPOLIS 34, Seattle 17
JACKSONVILLE 37, Tennessee 17
New York Giants 27, KANSAS CITY 16
NEW ENGLAND 27, Baltimore 21
WASHINGTON 16, Tampa Bay 13
MIAMI 38, Buffalo 10
NEW ORLEANS 24, New York Jets 10
DENVER 17, Dallas 10
SAN FRANCISCO 35, St. Louis 0
PITTSBURGH 38, San Diego 28

Monday, October 5

MINNESOTA 30, Green Bay 23

Byes: Arizona, Atlanta, Carolina, Philadelphia

FIFTH WEEK STANDINGS

American Football Conference

East Division	W	L	T	Pct.	Pts.	OP
New England	3	2	0	.600	104	91
New York Jets	3	2	0	.600	101	88
Miami	2	3	0	.400	112	106
Buffalo	1	4	0	.200	77	116
North Division	**W**	**L**	**T**	**Pct.**	**Pts.**	**OP**
Cincinnati	4	1	0	.800	101	90
Baltimore	3	2	0	.600	138	97
Pittsburgh	3	2	0	.600	113	98
Cleveland	1	4	0	.200	55	121
South Division	**W**	**L**	**T**	**Pct.**	**Pts.**	**OP**
Indianapolis	5	0	0	1.000	137	71
Houston	2	3	0	.400	115	120
Jacksonville	2	3	0	.400	97	127
Tennessee	0	5	0	.000	84	139
West Division	**W**	**L**	**T**	**Pct.**	**Pts.**	**OP**
Denver	5	0	0	1.000	99	43
San Diego	2	2	0	.500	101	102
Oakland	1	4	0	.200	49	130
Kansas City	0	5	0	.000	84	138

National Football Conference

East Division	W	L	T	Pct.	Pts.	OP
New York Giants	5	0	0	1.000	151	71
Philadelphia	3	1	0	.750	127	86
Dallas	3	2	0	.600	122	98
Washington	2	3	0	.400	73	82
North Division	**W**	**L**	**T**	**Pct.**	**Pts.**	**OP**
Minnesota	5	0	0	1.000	156	90
Chicago	3	1	0	.750	105	78
Green Bay	2	2	0	.500	104	93
Detroit	1	4	0	.200	103	162
South Division	**W**	**L**	**T**	**Pct.**	**Pts.**	**OP**
New Orleans	4	0	0	1.000	144	66
Atlanta	3	1	0	.750	102	63
Carolina	1	3	0	.250	57	104
Tampa Bay	0	5	0	.000	68	140
West Division	**W**	**L**	**T**	**Pct.**	**Pts.**	**OP**
San Francisco	3	2	0	.600	112	98
Arizona	2	2	0	.500	85	89
Seattle	2	3	0	.400	115	82
St. Louis	0	5	0	.000	34	146

WEEK 5 RESULTS

Sunday, October 11

Cincinnati 17, BALTIMORE 14
Cleveland 6, BUFFALO 3
CAROLINA 20, Washington 17
Pittsburgh 28, DETROIT 20
Dallas 26, KANSAS CITY 20 (OT)
NEW YORK GIANTS 44, Oakland 7
PHILADELPHIA 33, Tampa Bay 14
Minnesota 38, ST. LOUIS 10
Atlanta 45, SAN FRANCISCO 10
ARIZONA 28, Houston 21
DENVER 20, New England 17 (OT)
SEATTLE 41, Jacksonville 0
Indianapolis 31, TENNESSEE 9

Monday, October 12

MIAMI 31, New York Jets 27

Byes: Chicago, Green Bay, New Orleans, San Diego

SIXTH WEEK STANDINGS

American Football Conference

East Division	W	L	T	Pct.	Pts.	OP
New England	4	2	0	.667	163	91
New York Jets	3	3	0	.500	114	104
Miami	2	3	0	.400	112	106
Buffalo	2	4	0	.333	93	129
North Division	**W**	**L**	**T**	**Pct.**	**Pts.**	**OP**
Cincinnati	4	2	0	.667	118	118
Pittsburgh	4	2	0	.667	140	112
Baltimore	3	3	0	.500	169	130
Cleveland	1	5	0	.167	69	148
South Division	**W**	**L**	**T**	**Pct.**	**Pts.**	**OP**
Indianapolis	5	0	0	1.000	137	71
Houston	3	3	0	.500	143	137
Jacksonville	3	3	0	.500	120	147
Tennessee	0	6	0	.000	84	198
West Division	**W**	**L**	**T**	**Pct.**	**Pts.**	**OP**
Denver	6	0	0	1.000	133	66
San Diego	2	3	0	.400	124	136
Oakland	2	4	0	.333	62	139
Kansas City	1	5	0	.167	98	144

National Football Conference

East Division	W	L	T	Pct.	Pts.	OP
New York Giants	5	1	0	.833	178	119
Dallas	3	2	0	.600	122	98
Philadelphia	3	2	0	.600	136	99
Washington	2	4	0	.333	79	96
North Division	**W**	**L**	**T**	**Pct.**	**Pts.**	**OP**
Minnesota	6	0	0	1.000	189	121
Chicago	3	2	0	.600	119	99
Green Bay	3	2	0	.600	130	93
Detroit	1	5	0	.167	103	188
South Division	**W**	**L**	**T**	**Pct.**	**Pts.**	**OP**
New Orleans	5	0	0	1.000	192	93
Atlanta	4	1	0	.800	123	77
Carolina	2	3	0	.400	85	125
Tampa Bay	0	6	0	.000	89	168
West Division	**W**	**L**	**T**	**Pct.**	**Pts.**	**OP**
Arizona	3	2	0	.600	112	92
San Francisco	3	2	0	.600	112	98
Seattle	2	4	0	.333	118	109
St. Louis	0	6	0	.000	54	169

WEEK 6 RESULTS

Sunday, October 18

Houston 28, CINCINNATI 17
GREEN BAY 26, Detroit 0
JACKSONVILLE 23, St. Louis 20 (OT)
MINNESOTA 33, Baltimore 31
NEW ORLEANS 48, New York Giants 27
PITTSBURGH 27, Cleveland 14
Carolina 28, TAMPA BAY 21
Kansas City 14, WASHINGTON 6
OAKLAND 13, Philadelphia 9
Arizona 27, SEATTLE 3
NEW ENGLAND 59, Tennessee 0
Buffalo 16, NEW YORK JETS 13 (OT)
ATLANTA 21, Chicago 14

Monday, October 19

Denver 34, SAN DIEGO 23

Byes: Dallas, Indianapolis, Miami, San Francisco

SEVENTH WEEK STANDINGS

American Football Conference

East Division	W	L	T	Pct.	Pts.	OP
New England	5	2	0	.714	198	98
New York Jets	4	3	0	.571	152	104
Buffalo	3	4	0	.429	113	138
Miami	2	4	0	.333	146	152
North Division	**W**	**L**	**T**	**Pct.**	**Pts.**	**OP**
Cincinnati	5	2	0	.714	163	128
Pittsburgh	5	2	0	.714	167	129
Baltimore	3	3	0	.500	169	130
Cleveland	1	6	0	.143	72	179
South Division	**W**	**L**	**T**	**Pct.**	**Pts.**	**OP**
Indianapolis	6	0	0	1.000	179	77
Houston	4	3	0	.571	167	158
Jacksonville	3	3	0	.500	120	147
Tennessee	0	6	0	.000	84	198
West Division	**W**	**L**	**T**	**Pct.**	**Pts.**	**OP**
Denver	6	0	0	1.000	133	66
San Diego	3	3	0	.500	161	143
Oakland	2	5	0	.286	62	177
Kansas City	1	6	0	.143	105	181

National Football Conference

East Division	W	L	T	Pct.	Pts.	OP
New York Giants	5	2	0	.714	195	143
Dallas	4	2	0	.667	159	119
Philadelphia	4	2	0	.667	163	116
Washington	2	5	0	.286	96	123
North Division	**W**	**L**	**T**	**Pct.**	**Pts.**	**OP**
Minnesota	6	1	0	.857	206	148
Green Bay	4	2	0	.667	161	96
Chicago	3	3	0	.500	129	144
Detroit	1	5	0	.167	103	188
South Division	**W**	**L**	**T**	**Pct.**	**Pts.**	**OP**
New Orleans	6	0	0	1.000	238	127
Atlanta	4	2	0	.667	144	114
Carolina	2	4	0	.333	94	145
Tampa Bay	0	7	0	.000	96	203
West Division	**W**	**L**	**T**	**Pct.**	**Pts.**	**OP**
Arizona	4	2	0	.667	136	109
San Francisco	3	3	0	.500	133	122
Seattle	2	4	0	.333	118	109
St. Louis	0	7	0	.000	60	211

WEEK 7 RESULTS

Sunday, October 25

CINCINNATI 45, Chicago 10
Green Bay 31, CLEVELAND 3
HOUSTON 24, San Francisco 21
San Diego 37, KANSAS CITY 7
PITTSBURGH 27, Minnesota 17
Indianapolis 42, ST. LOUIS 6
New England 35, TAMPA BAY 7 (London)
Buffalo 20, CAROLINA 9
New York Jets 38, OAKLAND 0
DALLAS 37, Atlanta 21
New Orleans 46, MIAMI 34
Arizona 24, NEW YORK GIANTS 17

Monday, October 26

Philadelphia 27, WASHINGTON 17

Byes: Baltimore, Denver, Detroit, Jacksonville, Seattle, Tennessee

EIGHTH WEEK STANDINGS

American Football Conference

East Division	W	L	T	Pct.	Pts.	OP
New England	5	2	0	.714	198	98
New York Jets	4	4	0	.500	177	134
Miami	3	4	0	.429	176	177
Buffalo	3	5	0	.375	123	169
North Division	**W**	**L**	**T**	**Pct.**	**Pts.**	**OP**
Cincinnati	5	2	0	.714	163	128
Pittsburgh	5	2	0	.714	167	129
Baltimore	4	3	0	.571	199	137
Cleveland	1	7	0	.125	78	209
South Division	**W**	**L**	**T**	**Pct.**	**Pts.**	**OP**
Indianapolis	7	0	0	1.000	197	91
Houston	5	3	0	.625	198	168
Jacksonville	3	4	0	.429	133	177
Tennessee	1	6	0	.143	114	211
West Division	**W**	**L**	**T**	**Pct.**	**Pts.**	**OP**
Denver	6	1	0	.857	140	96
San Diego	4	3	0	.571	185	159
Oakland	2	6	0	.250	78	201
Kansas City	1	6	0	.143	105	181

National Football Conference

East Division	W	L	T	Pct.	Pts.	OP
Dallas	5	2	0	.714	197	136
Philadelphia	5	2	0	.714	203	133
New York Giants	5	3	0	.625	212	183
Washington	2	5	0	.286	96	123
North Division	**W**	**L**	**T**	**Pct.**	**Pts.**	**OP**
Minnesota	7	1	0	.875	244	174
Chicago	4	3	0	.571	159	150
Green Bay	4	3	0	.571	187	134
Detroit	1	6	0	.143	113	205
South Division	**W**	**L**	**T**	**Pct.**	**Pts.**	**OP**
New Orleans	7	0	0	1.000	273	154
Atlanta	4	3	0	.571	171	149
Carolina	3	4	0	.429	128	166
Tampa Bay	0	7	0	.000	96	203
West Division	**W**	**L**	**T**	**Pct.**	**Pts.**	**OP**
Arizona	4	3	0	.571	157	143
San Francisco	3	4	0	.429	147	140
Seattle	2	5	0	.286	135	147
St. Louis	1	7	0	.125	77	221

WEEK 8 RESULTS

Sunday, November 1

BALTIMORE 30, Denver 7
Houston 31, BUFFALO 10
CHICAGO 30, Cleveland 6
DALLAS 38, Seattle 17
St. Louis 17, DETROIT 10
Minnesota 38, GREEN BAY 26
INDIANAPOLIS 18, San Francisco 14
Miami 30, NEW YORK JETS 25
SAN DIEGO 24, Oakland 16
TENNESSEE 30, Jacksonville 13
Carolina 34, ARIZONA 21
PHILADELPHIA 40, New York Giants 17

Monday, November 2

NEW ORLEANS 35, Atlanta 27

Byes: Cincinnati, Kansas City, New England, Pittsburgh, Tampa Bay, Washington

NINTH WEEK STANDINGS

American Football Conference

East Division	W	L	T	Pct.	Pts.	OP
New England	6	2	0	.750	225	115
New York Jets	4	4	0	.500	177	134
Buffalo	3	5	0	.375	123	169
Miami	3	5	0	.375	193	204
North Division	**W**	**L**	**T**	**Pct.**	**Pts.**	**OP**
Cincinnati	6	2	0	.750	180	135
Pittsburgh	6	2	0	.750	195	139
Baltimore	4	4	0	.500	206	154
Cleveland	1	7	0	.125	78	209
South Division	**W**	**L**	**T**	**Pct.**	**Pts.**	**OP**
Indianapolis	8	0	0	1.000	217	108
Houston	5	4	0	.556	215	188
Jacksonville	4	4	0	.500	157	198
Tennessee	2	6	0	.250	148	238
West Division	**W**	**L**	**T**	**Pct.**	**Pts.**	**OP**
Denver	6	2	0	.750	150	124
San Diego	5	3	0	.625	206	179
Oakland	2	6	0	.250	78	201
Kansas City	1	7	0	.125	126	205

National Football Conference

East Division	W	L	T	Pct.	Pts.	OP
Dallas	6	2	0	.750	217	152
Philadelphia	5	3	0	.625	219	153
New York Giants	5	4	0	.556	232	204
Washington	2	6	0	.250	113	154
North Division	**W**	**L**	**T**	**Pct.**	**Pts.**	**OP**
Minnesota	7	1	0	.875	244	174
Chicago	4	4	0	.500	180	191
Green Bay	4	4	0	.500	215	172
Detroit	1	7	0	.125	133	237
South Division	**W**	**L**	**T**	**Pct.**	**Pts.**	**OP**
New Orleans	8	0	0	1.000	303	174
Atlanta	5	3	0	.625	202	166
Carolina	3	5	0	.375	148	196
Tampa Bay	1	7	0	.125	134	231
West Division	**W**	**L**	**T**	**Pct.**	**Pts.**	**OP**
Arizona	5	3	0	.625	198	164
San Francisco	3	5	0	.375	174	174
Seattle	3	5	0	.375	167	167
St. Louis	1	7	0	.125	77	221

WEEK 9 RESULTS

Sunday, November 8

ATLANTA 31, Washington 17
Arizona 41, CHICAGO 21
CINCINNATI 17, Baltimore 7
INDIANAPOLIS 20, Houston 17
JACKSONVILLE 24, Kansas City 21
NEW ENGLAND 27, Miami 17
TAMPA BAY 38, Green Bay 28
NEW ORLEANS 30, Carolina 20
SEATTLE 32, Detroit 20
San Diego 21, NEW YORK GIANTS 20
Tennessee 34, SAN FRANCISCO 27
Dallas 20, PHILADELPHIA 16

Monday, November 9

Pittsburgh 28, DENVER 10

Byes: Buffalo, Cleveland, Minnesota, New York Jets, Oakland, St. Louis

TENTH WEEK STANDINGS

American Football Conference

East Division	W	L	T	Pct.	Pts.	OP
New England	6	3	0	.667	259	150
Miami	4	5	0	.444	218	227
New York Jets	4	5	0	.444	199	158
Buffalo	3	6	0	.333	140	210
North Division	**W**	**L**	**T**	**Pct.**	**Pts.**	**OP**
Cincinnati	7	2	0	.778	198	147
Pittsburgh	6	3	0	.667	207	157
Baltimore	5	4	0	.556	222	154
Cleveland	1	8	0	.111	78	225
South Division	**W**	**L**	**T**	**Pct.**	**Pts.**	**OP**
Indianapolis	9	0	0	1.000	252	142
Houston	5	4	0	.556	215	188
Jacksonville	5	4	0	.556	181	220
Tennessee	3	6	0	.333	189	255
West Division	**W**	**L**	**T**	**Pct.**	**Pts.**	**OP**
Denver	6	3	0	.667	167	151
San Diego	6	3	0	.667	237	202
Kansas City	2	7	0	.222	142	215
Oakland	2	7	0	.222	88	217

National Football Conference

East Division	W	L	T	Pct.	Pts.	OP
Dallas	6	3	0	.667	224	169
New York Giants	5	4	0	.556	232	204
Philadelphia	5	4	0	.556	242	184
Washington	3	6	0	.333	140	171
North Division	**W**	**L**	**T**	**Pct.**	**Pts.**	**OP**
Minnesota	8	1	0	.889	271	184
Green Bay	5	4	0	.556	232	179
Chicago	4	5	0	.444	186	201
Detroit	1	8	0	.111	143	264
South Division	**W**	**L**	**T**	**Pct.**	**Pts.**	**OP**
New Orleans	9	0	0	1.000	331	197
Atlanta	5	4	0	.556	221	194
Carolina	4	5	0	.444	176	215
Tampa Bay	1	8	0	.111	157	256
West Division	**W**	**L**	**T**	**Pct.**	**Pts.**	**OP**
Arizona	6	3	0	.667	229	184
San Francisco	4	5	0	.444	184	180
Seattle	3	6	0	.333	187	198
St. Louis	1	8	0	.111	100	249

WEEK 10 RESULTS

Thursday, November 12
SAN FRANCISCO 10, Chicago 6

Sunday, November 15
CAROLINA 28, Atlanta 19
MIAMI 25, Tampa Bay 23
MINNESOTA 27, Detroit 10
Jacksonville 24, NEW YORK JETS 22
Cincinnati 18, PITTSBURGH 12
New Orleans 28, ST. LOUIS 23
TENNESSEE 41, Buffalo 17
WASHINGTON 27, Denver 17
Kansas City 16, OAKLAND 10
ARIZONA 31, Seattle 20
GREEN BAY 17, Dallas 7
SAN DIEGO 31, Philadelphia 23
INDIANAPOLIS 35, New England 34

Monday, November 16
Baltimore 16, CLEVELAND 0

Byes: Houston, New York Giants

ELEVENTH WEEK STANDINGS

American Football Conference

East Division	W	L	T	Pct.	Pts.	OP
New England	7	3	0	.700	290	164
Miami	5	5	0	.500	242	244
New York Jets	4	6	0	.400	213	189
Buffalo	3	7	0	.300	155	228
North Division	**W**	**L**	**T**	**Pct.**	**Pts.**	**OP**
Cincinnati	7	3	0	.700	215	167
Pittsburgh	6	4	0	.600	231	184
Baltimore	5	5	0	.500	237	171
Cleveland	1	9	0	.100	115	263
South Division	**W**	**L**	**T**	**Pct.**	**Pts.**	**OP**
Indianapolis	10	0	0	1.000	269	157
Jacksonville	6	4	0	.600	199	235
Houston	5	5	0	.500	232	208
Tennessee	4	6	0	.400	209	272
West Division	**W**	**L**	**T**	**Pct.**	**Pts.**	**OP**
San Diego	7	3	0	.700	269	205
Denver	6	4	0	.600	170	183
Kansas City	3	7	0	.300	169	239
Oakland	3	7	0	.300	108	234

National Football Conference

East Division	W	L	T	Pct.	Pts.	OP
Dallas	7	3	0	.700	231	175
New York Giants	6	4	0	.600	266	235
Philadelphia	6	4	0	.600	266	204
Washington	3	7	0	.300	146	178
North Division	**W**	**L**	**T**	**Pct.**	**Pts.**	**OP**
Minnesota	9	1	0	.900	306	193
Green Bay	6	4	0	.600	262	203
Chicago	4	6	0	.400	206	225
Detroit	2	8	0	.200	181	301
South Division	**W**	**L**	**T**	**Pct.**	**Pts.**	**OP**
New Orleans	10	0	0	1.000	369	204
Atlanta	5	5	0	.500	252	228
Carolina	4	6	0	.400	193	239
Tampa Bay	1	9	0	.100	164	294
West Division	**W**	**L**	**T**	**Pct.**	**Pts.**	**OP**
Arizona	7	3	0	.700	250	197
San Francisco	4	6	0	.400	208	210
Seattle	3	7	0	.300	196	233
St. Louis	1	9	0	.100	113	270

WEEK 11 RESULTS

Thursday, November 19
Miami 24, CAROLINA 17

Sunday, November 22
Indianapolis 17, BALTIMORE 15
DALLAS 7, Washington 6
DETROIT 38, Cleveland 37
GREEN BAY 30, San Francisco 24
JACKSONVILLE 18, Buffalo 15
KANSAS CITY 27, Pittsburgh 24 (OT)
MINNESOTA 35, Seattle 9
NEW YORK GIANTS 34, Atlanta 31 (OT)
New Orleans 38, TAMPA BAY 7
Arizona 21, ST. LOUIS 13
San Diego 32, DENVER 3
NEW ENGLAND 31, New York Jets 14
OAKLAND 20, Cincinnati 17
Philadelphia 24, CHICAGO 20

Monday, November 23
Tennessee 20, HOUSTON 17

TWELFTH WEEK STANDINGS

American Football Conference

East Division	W	L	T	Pct.	Pts.	OP
New England	7	4	0	.636	307	202
Miami	5	6	0	.455	256	275
New York Jets	5	6	0	.455	230	195
Buffalo	4	7	0	.364	186	242
North Division	**W**	**L**	**T**	**Pct.**	**Pts.**	**OP**
Cincinnati	8	3	0	.727	231	174
Baltimore	6	5	0	.545	257	188
Pittsburgh	6	5	0	.545	248	204
Cleveland	1	10	0	.091	122	279
South Division	**W**	**L**	**T**	**Pct.**	**Pts.**	**OP**
Indianapolis*	11	0	0	1.000	304	184
Jacksonville	6	5	0	.545	202	255
Houston	5	6	0	.455	259	243
Tennessee	5	6	0	.455	229	289
West Division	**W**	**L**	**T**	**Pct.**	**Pts.**	**OP**
San Diego	8	3	0	.727	312	219
Denver	7	4	0	.636	196	189
Kansas City	3	8	0	.273	183	282
Oakland	3	8	0	.273	115	258

National Football Conference

East Division	W	L	T	Pct.	Pts.	OP
Dallas	8	3	0	.727	255	182
Philadelphia	7	4	0	.636	293	228
New York Giants	6	5	0	.545	272	261
Washington	3	8	0	.273	170	205
North Division	**W**	**L**	**T**	**Pct.**	**Pts.**	**OP**
Minnesota	10	1	0	.909	342	203
Green Bay	7	4	0	.636	296	215
Chicago	4	7	0	.364	216	261
Detroit	2	9	0	.182	193	335
South Division	**W**	**L**	**T**	**Pct.**	**Pts.**	**OP**
New Orleans	11	0	0	1.000	407	221
Atlanta	6	5	0	.545	272	245
Carolina	4	7	0	.364	199	256
Tampa Bay	1	10	0	.091	181	314
West Division	**W**	**L**	**T**	**Pct.**	**Pts.**	**OP**
Arizona	7	4	0	.636	267	217
San Francisco	5	6	0	.455	228	213
Seattle	4	7	0	.364	223	250
St. Louis	1	10	0	.091	130	297

**Clinched division title*

WEEK 12 RESULTS

Thursday, November 26
Green Bay 34, DETROIT 12
DALLAS 24, Oakland 7
DENVER 26, New York Giants 6

Sunday, November 29
ATLANTA 20, Tampa Bay 17
BUFFALO 31, Miami 14
CINCINNATI 16, Cleveland 7
Indianapolis 35, HOUSTON 27
NEW YORK JETS 17, Carolina 6
PHILADELPHIA 27, Washington 24
Seattle 27, ST. LOUIS 17
SAN DIEGO 43, Kansas City 14
SAN FRANCISCO 20, Jacksonville 3
MINNESOTA 36, Chicago 10
TENNESSEE 20, Arizona 17
BALTIMORE 20, Pittsburgh 17 (OT)

Monday, November 30
NEW ORLEANS 38, New England 17

THIRTEENTH WEEK STANDINGS

American Football Conference

East Division	W	L	T	Pct.	Pts.	OP
New England	7	5	0	.583	328	224
Miami	6	6	0	.500	278	296
New York Jets	6	6	0	.500	249	208
Buffalo	4	8	0	.333	199	261
North Division	**W**	**L**	**T**	**Pct.**	**Pts.**	**OP**
Cincinnati	9	3	0	.750	254	187
Baltimore	6	6	0	.500	271	215
Pittsburgh	6	6	0	.500	272	231
Cleveland	1	11	0	.083	145	309
South Division	**W**	**L**	**T**	**Pct.**	**Pts.**	**OP**
Indianapolis*	12	0	0	1.000	331	201
Jacksonville	7	5	0	.583	225	273
Houston	5	7	0	.417	277	266
Tennessee	5	7	0	.417	246	316
West Division	**W**	**L**	**T**	**Pct.**	**Pts.**	**OP**
San Diego	9	3	0	.750	342	242
Denver	8	4	0	.667	240	202
Oakland	4	8	0	.333	142	282
Kansas City	3	9	0	.250	196	326

National Football Conference

East Division	W	L	T	Pct.	Pts.	OP
Dallas	8	4	0	.667	279	213
Philadelphia	8	4	0	.667	327	235
New York Giants	7	5	0	.583	303	285
Washington	3	9	0	.250	200	238
North Division	**W**	**L**	**T**	**Pct.**	**Pts.**	**OP**
Minnesota	10	2	0	.833	359	233
Green Bay	8	4	0	.667	323	229
Chicago	5	7	0	.417	233	270
Detroit	2	10	0	.167	206	358
South Division	**W**	**L**	**T**	**Pct.**	**Pts.**	**OP**
New Orleans*	12	0	0	1.000	440	251
Atlanta	6	6	0	.500	279	279
Carolina	5	7	0	.417	215	262
Tampa Bay	1	11	0	.083	187	330
West Division	**W**	**L**	**T**	**Pct.**	**Pts.**	**OP**
Arizona	8	4	0	.667	297	234
San Francisco	5	7	0	.417	245	233
Seattle	5	7	0	.417	243	267
St. Louis	1	11	0	.083	139	314

**Clinched division title*

WEEK 13 RESULTS

Thursday, December 3
New York Jets 19, BUFFALO 13 (Toronto)

Sunday, December 6
Philadelphia 34, ATLANTA 7
CAROLINA 16, Tampa Bay 6
CHICAGO 17, St. Louis 9
CINCINNATI 23, Detroit 13
INDIANAPOLIS 27, Tennessee 17
JACKSONVILLE 23, Houston 18
Denver 44, KANSAS CITY 13
MIAMI 22, New England 21
Oakland 27, PITTSBURGH 24
New Orleans 33, WASHINGTON 30 (OT)
San Diego 30, CLEVELAND 23
NEW YORK GIANTS 31, Dallas 24
SEATTLE 20, San Francisco 17
ARIZONA 30, Minnesota 17

Monday, December 7
GREEN BAY 27, Baltimore 14

FOURTEENTH WEEK STANDINGS

American Football Conference

East Division	W	L	T	Pct.	Pts.	OP
New England	8	5	0	.615	348	234
Miami	7	6	0	.538	292	306
New York Jets	7	6	0	.538	275	211
Buffalo	5	8	0	.385	215	271
North Division	**W**	**L**	**T**	**Pct.**	**Pts.**	**OP**
Cincinnati	9	4	0	.692	264	217
Baltimore	7	6	0	.538	319	218
Pittsburgh	6	7	0	.462	278	244
Cleveland	2	11	0	.154	158	315
South Division	**W**	**L**	**T**	**Pct.**	**Pts.**	**OP**
Indianapolis*	13	0	0	1.000	359	217
Jacksonville	7	6	0	.538	235	287
Houston	6	7	0	.462	311	273
Tennessee	6	7	0	.462	293	323
West Division	**W**	**L**	**T**	**Pct.**	**Pts.**	**OP**
San Diego	10	3	0	.769	362	259
Denver	8	5	0	.615	256	230
Oakland	4	9	0	.308	155	316
Kansas City	3	10	0	.231	206	342

National Football Conference

East Division	W	L	T	Pct.	Pts.	OP
Philadelphia	9	4	0	.692	372	273
Dallas	8	5	0	.615	296	233
New York Giants	7	6	0	.538	341	330
Washington	4	9	0	.308	234	251
North Division	**W**	**L**	**T**	**Pct.**	**Pts.**	**OP**
Minnesota#	11	2	0	.846	389	243
Green Bay	9	4	0	.692	344	243
Chicago	5	8	0	.385	247	291
Detroit	2	11	0	.154	209	406
South Division	**W**	**L**	**T**	**Pct.**	**Pts.**	**OP**
New Orleans*	13	0	0	1.000	466	274
Atlanta	6	7	0	.462	302	305
Carolina	5	8	0	.385	225	282
Tampa Bay	1	12	0	.077	190	356
West Division	**W**	**L**	**T**	**Pct.**	**Pts.**	**OP**
Arizona	8	5	0	.615	306	258
San Francisco	6	7	0	.462	269	242
Seattle	5	8	0	.385	250	301
St. Louis	1	12	0	.077	146	361

**Clinched division title*
#Clinched playoff berth

WEEK 14 RESULTS

Thursday, December 10
CLEVELAND 13, Pittsburgh 6

Sunday, December 13
New Orleans 26, ATLANTA 23
BALTIMORE 48, Detroit 3
Green Bay 21, CHICAGO 14
HOUSTON 34, Seattle 7
INDIANAPOLIS 28, Denver 16
Miami 14, JACKSONVILLE 10
Buffalo 16, KANSAS CITY 10
MINNESOTA 30, Cincinnati 10
NEW ENGLAND 20, Carolina 10
New York Jets 26, TAMPA BAY 3
Washington 34, OAKLAND 13
TENNESSEE 47, St. Louis 7
San Diego 20, DALLAS 17
Philadelphia 45, NEW YORK GIANTS 38

Monday, December 14
SAN FRANCISCO 24, Arizona 9

FIFTEENTH WEEK STANDINGS

American Football Conference

East Division	W	L	T	Pct.	Pts.	OP
New England	9	5	0	.643	365	244
Miami	7	7	0	.500	316	333
New York Jets	7	7	0	.500	282	221
Buffalo	5	9	0	.357	225	288
North Division	**W**	**L**	**T**	**Pct.**	**Pts.**	**OP**
Cincinnati	9	5	0	.643	288	244
Baltimore	8	6	0	.571	350	225
Pittsburgh	7	7	0	.500	315	280
Cleveland	3	11	0	.214	199	349
South Division	**W**	**L**	**T**	**Pct.**	**Pts.**	**OP**
Indianapolis*	14	0	0	1.000	394	248
Houston	7	7	0	.500	327	286
Jacksonville	7	7	0	.500	266	322
Tennessee	7	7	0	.500	320	347
West Division	**W**	**L**	**T**	**Pct.**	**Pts.**	**OP**
San Diego*	11	3	0	.786	389	283
Denver	8	6	0	.571	275	250
Oakland	5	9	0	.357	175	335
Kansas City	3	11	0	.214	240	383

National Football Conference

East Division	W	L	T	Pct.	Pts.	OP
Philadelphia#	10	4	0	.714	399	286
Dallas	9	5	0	.643	320	250
New York Giants	8	6	0	.571	386	342
Washington	4	10	0	.286	246	296
North Division	**W**	**L**	**T**	**Pct.**	**Pts.**	**OP**
Minnesota*	11	3	0	.786	396	269
Green Bay	9	5	0	.643	380	280
Chicago	5	9	0	.357	254	322
Detroit	2	12	0	.143	233	437
South Division	**W**	**L**	**T**	**Pct.**	**Pts.**	**OP**
New Orleans*	13	1	0	.929	483	298
Atlanta	7	7	0	.500	312	312
Carolina	6	8	0	.429	251	289
Tampa Bay	2	12	0	.143	214	363
West Division	**W**	**L**	**T**	**Pct.**	**Pts.**	**OP**
Arizona*	9	5	0	.643	337	282
San Francisco	6	8	0	.429	282	269
Seattle	5	9	0	.357	257	325
St. Louis	1	13	0	.071	159	377

**Clinched division title*
#Clinched playoff berth

WEEK 15 RESULTS

Thursday, December 17
Indianapolis 35, JACKSONVILLE 31

Saturday, December 19
Dallas 24, NEW ORLEANS 17

Sunday, December 20
BALTIMORE 31, Chicago 7
New England 17, BUFFALO 10
Arizona 31, DETROIT 24
Cleveland 41, KANSAS CITY 34
Atlanta 10, NEW YORK JETS 7
PHILADELPHIA 27, San Francisco 13
Houston 16, ST. LOUIS 13
TENNESSEE 27, Miami 24 (OT)
Oakland 20, DENVER 19
SAN DIEGO 27, Cincinnati 24
PITTSBURGH 37, Green Bay 36
Tampa Bay 24, SEATTLE 7
CAROLINA 26, Minnesota 7

Monday, December 21
New York Giants 45, WASHINGTON 12

SIXTEENTH WEEK STANDINGS

American Football Conference

East Division	W	L	T	Pct.	Pts.	OP
New England*	10	5	0	.667	400	251
New York Jets	8	7	0	.533	311	236
Miami	7	8	0	.467	336	360
Buffalo	5	10	0	.333	228	319
North Division	**W**	**L**	**T**	**Pct.**	**Pts.**	**OP**
Cincinnati*	10	5	0	.667	305	254
Baltimore	8	7	0	.533	370	248
Pittsburgh	8	7	0	.533	338	300
Cleveland	4	11	0	.267	222	358
South Division	**W**	**L**	**T**	**Pct.**	**Pts.**	**OP**
Indianapolis*	14	1	0	.933	409	277
Houston	8	7	0	.533	354	306
Jacksonville	7	8	0	.467	273	357
Tennessee	7	8	0	.467	337	389
West Division	**W**	**L**	**T**	**Pct.**	**Pts.**	**OP**
San Diego*	12	3	0	.800	431	300
Denver	8	7	0	.533	302	280
Oakland	5	10	0	.333	184	358
Kansas City	3	12	0	.200	250	400

National Football Conference

East Division	W	L	T	Pct.	Pts.	OP
Philadelphia#	11	4	0	.733	429	313
Dallas#	10	5	0	.667	337	250
New York Giants	8	7	0	.533	395	383
Washington	4	11	0	.267	246	313
North Division	**W**	**L**	**T**	**Pct.**	**Pts.**	**OP**
Minnesota*	11	4	0	.733	426	305
Green Bay#	10	5	0	.667	428	290
Chicago	6	9	0	.400	290	352
Detroit	2	13	0	.133	239	457
South Division	**W**	**L**	**T**	**Pct.**	**Pts.**	**OP**
New Orleans*	13	2	0	.867	500	318
Atlanta	8	7	0	.533	343	315
Carolina	7	8	0	.467	292	298
Tampa Bay	3	12	0	.200	234	380
West Division	**W**	**L**	**T**	**Pct.**	**Pts.**	**OP**
Arizona*	10	5	0	.667	368	292
San Francisco	7	8	0	.467	302	275
Seattle	5	10	0	.333	267	373
St. Louis	1	14	0	.067	169	408

**Clinched division title*
#Clinched playoff berth

WEEK 16 RESULTS

Friday, December 25
San Diego 42, TENNESSEE 17

Sunday, December 27
ATLANTA 31, Buffalo 3
CINCINNATI 17, Kansas City 10
CLEVELAND 23, Oakland 9
GREEN BAY 48, Seattle 10
Houston 27, MIAMI 20
NEW ENGLAND 35, Jacksonville 7
Tampa Bay 20, NEW ORLEANS 17 (OT)
Carolina 41, NEW YORK GIANTS 9
PITTSBURGH 23, Baltimore 20
ARIZONA 31, St. Louis 10
SAN FRANCISCO 20, Detroit 6
New York Jets 29, INDIANAPOLIS 15
PHILADELPHIA 30, Denver 27
Dallas 17, WASHINGTON 0

Monday, December 28
CHICAGO 36, Minnesota 30 (OT)

SEVENTEENTH WEEK STANDINGS

American Football Conference

East Division	W	L	T	Pct.	Pts.	OP
New England*	10	6	0	.625	427	285
New York Jets#	9	7	0	.563	348	236
Miami	7	9	0	.438	360	390
Buffalo	6	10	0	.375	258	326
North Division	**W**	**L**	**T**	**Pct.**	**Pts.**	**OP**
Cincinnati*	10	6	0	.625	305	291
Baltimore#	9	7	0	.563	391	261
Pittsburgh	9	7	0	.563	368	324
Cleveland	5	11	0	.313	245	375
South Division	**W**	**L**	**T**	**Pct.**	**Pts.**	**OP**
Indianapolis*	14	2	0	.875	416	307
Houston	9	7	0	.563	388	333
Tennessee	8	8	0	.500	354	402
Jacksonville	7	9	0	.438	290	380
West Division	**W**	**L**	**T**	**Pct.**	**Pts.**	**OP**
San Diego*	13	3	0	.813	454	320
Denver	8	8	0	.500	326	324
Oakland	5	11	0	.313	197	379
Kansas City	4	12	0	.250	294	424

National Football Conference

East Division	W	L	T	Pct.	Pts.	OP
Dallas*	11	5	0	.688	361	250
Philadelphia#	11	5	0	.688	429	337
New York Giants	8	8	0	.500	402	427
Washington	4	12	0	.250	266	336
North Division	**W**	**L**	**T**	**Pct.**	**Pts.**	**OP**
Minnesota*	12	4	0	.750	470	312
Green Bay#	11	5	0	.688	461	297
Chicago	7	9	0	.438	327	375
Detroit	2	14	0	.125	262	494
South Division	**W**	**L**	**T**	**Pct.**	**Pts.**	**OP**
New Orleans*	13	3	0	.813	510	341
Atlanta	9	7	0	.563	363	325
Carolina	8	8	0	.500	315	308
Tampa Bay	3	13	0	.188	244	400
West Division	**W**	**L**	**T**	**Pct.**	**Pts.**	**OP**
Arizona*	10	6	0	.625	375	325
San Francisco	8	8	0	.500	330	281
Seattle	5	11	0	.313	280	390
St. Louis	1	15	0	.063	175	436

**Clinched division title*
#Clinched wild-card berth

WEEK 17 RESULTS

Sunday, January 3, 2010
BUFFALO 30, Indianapolis 7
CAROLINA 23, New Orleans 10
CLEVELAND 23, Jacksonville 17
Chicago 37, DETROIT 23
HOUSTON 34, New England 27
Pittsburgh 30, MIAMI 24
MINNESOTA 44, New York Giants 7
San Francisco 28, ST. LOUIS 6
Atlanta 20, TAMPA BAY 10
Green Bay 33, ARIZONA 7
DALLAS 24, Philadelphia 0
Kansas City 44, DENVER 24
Baltimore 21, OAKLAND 13
SAN DIEGO 23, Washington 20
Tennessee 17, SEATTLE 13
NEW YORK JETS 37, Cincinnati 0

2009 NFL PAID ATTENDANCE BREAKDOWN

Games	Attendance	Average
NFL Preseason Total		
65	3,810,074	58,617
NFL Regular-Season Total		
256	16,651,126	65,043
NFL Postseason Total		
12	823,882	68,657
NFL All Games		
333	21,285,082	63,919

1.1-MILLION CLUB

During the 2009 season, seven teams drew more than 1.1 million paid attendance home and away during the regular season. The New York Giants led the league in regular-season paid attendance (1,205,376). For the tenth consecutive year, the Washington Redskins led the league in home paid attendance (681,703).

Team	Total Paid Home Attendance	Total Paid Visiting Attendance	Total Paid Attendance
New York Giants	629,417	575,959	1,205,376
Dallas	629,749	574,899	1,204,648
Washington	681,703	511,376	1,193,079
New England	561,481	573,643	1,135,124
Denver	590,433	520,424	1,110,857
Philadelphia	539,984	566,921	1,106,905
Carolina	577,168	528,913	1,106,081

For complete year-by-year attendance records, see pages 527-528.

2009 AFC PLAYERS OF THE WEEK

	Offense		Defense		Special Teams	
Week 1	QB	Tom Brady, New England	LB	David Harris, N.Y. Jets	K	Jeff Reed, Pittsburgh
Week 2	QB	Matt Schaub, Houston	DE	Antwan Odom, Cincinnati	K	Rian Lindell, Buffalo
Week 3	RB	Maurice Jones-Drew, Jacksonville	LB	Brendon Ayanbadejo, Baltimore	LB	Jason Trusnik, N.Y. Jets
Week 4	RB	Rashard Mendenhall, Pittsburgh	CB	Champ Bailey, Denver	KR/WR	Jacoby Jones, Houston
Week 5	QB	Kyle Orton, Denver	LB	James Harrison, Pittsburgh	P	Dave Zastudil, Cleveland
Week 6	QB	Tom Brady, New England	LB	Brian Cushing, Houston	KR/WR	Eddie Royal, Denver
Week 7	QB	Carson Palmer, Cincinnati	S	Brandon Meriweather, New England	P	Brian Moorman, Buffalo
Week 8	RB	Chris Johnson, Tennessee	LB	Brian Cushing, Houston	WR/KR	Ted Ginn Jr., Miami
Week 9	TE	Dallas Clark, Indianapolis	S	Tyrone Carter, Pittsburgh	K	Stephen Gostkowski, New England
Week 10	QB	Peyton Manning, Indianapolis	S	Mike Brown, Kansas City	KR/RB	Bernard Scott, Cincinnati
Week 11	RB	Ricky Williams, Miami	CB	Leigh Bodden, New England	KR/RB	Jamaal Charles, Kansas City
Week 12	QB	Vince Young, Tennessee	CB	Darrelle Revis, N.Y. Jets	K	Matt Prater, Denver
Week 13	QB	Bruce Gradkowski, Oakland	LB	Justin Durant, Jacksonville	K	Dan Carpenter, Miami
Week 14	WR	Brandon Marshall, Denver	LB	Keith Bulluck, Tennessee	KR/WR	Joshua Cribbs, Cleveland
Week 15	QB	Ben Roethlisberger, Pittsburgh	CB	Domonique Foxworth, Baltimore	KR/WR	Joshua Cribbs, Cleveland
Week 16	QB	Tom Brady, New England	LB	LaMarr Woodley, Pittsburgh	KR/WR	Brad Smith, N.Y. Jets
Week 17	RB	Willis McGahee, Baltimore	LB	Derrick Johnson, Kansas City	K	Nate Kaeding, San Diego

2009 AFC PLAYERS OF THE MONTH

	Offense		Defense		Special Teams	
September	QB	Peyton Manning, Indianapolis	DE	Antwan Odom, Cincinnati	K	Matt Prater, Denver
October	QB	Tom Brady, New England	LB	James Harrison, Pittsburgh	KR/WR	Eddie Royal, Denver
November	RB	Chris Johnson, Tennessee	DE	Robert Mathis, Indianapolis	KR/WR	Ted Ginn Jr., Miami
December	QB	Philip Rivers, San Diego	CB	Darrelle Revis, N.Y. Jets	KR/WR	Joshua Cribbs, Cleveland

2009 NFC PLAYERS OF THE WEEK

	Offense		Defense		Special Teams	
Week 1	QB	Drew Brees, New Orleans	DE	Justin Tuck. N.Y. Giants	PR/WR	DeSean Jackson, Philadelphia
Week 2	RB	Frank Gore, San Francisco	LB	Chad Greenway, Minnesota	DE	Calais Campbell, Arizona
Week 3	QB	Kevin Kolb, Philadelphia	LB	Lance Briggs, Chicago	KR/WR	Percy Harvin, Minnesota
Week 4	QB	Brett Favre, Minnesota	S	Darren Sharper, New Orleans	KR/WR	Johnny Knox, Chicago
Week 5	WR	Miles Austin, Dallas	CB	Dominique Rodgers-Cromartie, Arizona	P	Jason Baker, Carolina
Week 6	QB	Drew Brees, New Orleans	S	Thomas DeCoud, Atlanta	KR/WR	Sammie Stroughter, Tampa Bay
Week 7	WR	DeSean Jackson, Philadelphia	S	Adrian Wilson, Arizona	PR/WR	Patrick Crayton, Dallas
Week 8	QB	Brett Favre, Minnesota	DE	Julius Peppers, Carolina	K	Josh Brown, St. Louis
Week 9	QB	Kurt Warner, Arizona	DT	Anthony Hargrove, New Orleans	KR/PR	Clifton Smith, Tampa Bay
Week 10	WR	Sidney Rice, Minnesota	CB	Charles Woodson, Green Bay	P	Hunter Smith, Washington
Week 11	QB	Matthew Stafford, Detroit	LB	Michael Boley, N.Y. Giants	P	Thomas Morstead, New Orleans
Week 12	QB	Drew Brees, New Orleans	CB	Charles Woodson, Green Bay	KR	LaRod Stephens-Howling, Arizona
Week 13	QB	Kurt Warner, Arizona	LB	Clay Matthews, Green Bay	PR	Domenik Hixon, N.Y. Giants
Week 14	RB	Frank Gore, San Francisco	LB	Brian Orakpo, Washington	PR/WR	DeSean Jackson, Philadelphia
Week 15	RB	Jonathan Stewart, Carolina	LB	DeMarcus Ware, Dallas	P	Ben Graham, Arizona
Week 16	QB	Jay Cutler, Chicago	LB	Jon Beason, Carolina	PR/KR	Micheal Spurlock, Tampa Bay
Week 17	QB	Brett Favre, Minnesota	LB	Anthony Spencer, Dallas	P	Thomas Morstead, New Orleans

2009 NFC PLAYERS OF THE MONTH

	Offense		Defense		Special Teams	
September	QB	Drew Brees, New Orleans	CB	Charles Woodson, Green Bay	PR/WR	DeSean Jackson, Philadelphia
October	QB	Aaron Rodgers, Green Bay	S	Darren Sharper, New Orleans	KR/WR	Johnny Knox, Chicago
November	QB	Brett Favre, Minnesota	CB	Charles Woodson, Green Bay	K	David Akers, Philadelphia
December	QB	Tony Romo, Dallas	CB	Charles Woodson, Green Bay	PR/WR	DeSean Jackson, Philadelphia

2009 NFL ROOKIES OF THE MONTH

	Offense (College)		Defense (College)	
September	QB	Mark Sanchez, N.Y. Jets (Southern California)	S	Louis Delmas, Detroit (Western Michigan)
October	WR	Hakeem Nicks, N.Y. Giants (North Carolina)	S	Jairus Byrd, Buffalo (Oregon)
November	WR	Percy Harvin, Minnesota (Florida)	LB	Brian Cushing, Houston (Southern California)
December	T	Michael Oher, Baltimore (Mississippi)	LB	Brian Cushing, Houston (Southern California)

2009 PRO FOOTBALL AWARDS/ALL-PRO TEAMS

2009 PRO FOOTBALL AWARDS

ASSOCIATED PRESS

Most Valuable Player	Peyton Manning
Offensive Player of the Year	Chris Johnson
Defensive Player of the Year	Charles Woodson
Offensive Rookie of the Year	Percy Harvin
Defensive Rookie of the Year	Brian Cushing
Coach of the Year	Marvin Lewis
Comeback Player of the Year	Tom Brady

THE SPORTING NEWS

Offensive Player of the Year	Drew Brees
Defensive Player of the Year	Charles Woodson
Rookie of the Year	Percy Harvin
Coach of the Year	Sean Payton

PRO FOOTBALL WEEKLY/PFWA

Executive of the Year	Bill Polian
Most Valuable Player	Peyton Manning
Defensive Most Valuable Player	Charles Woodson
Offensive Rookie of the Year	Percy Harvin
Defensive Rookie of the Year	Brian Cushing
Coach of the Year	Marvin Lewis
Assistant Coach of the Year	Mike Zimmer
Golden Toe	Shane Lechler
Comeback Player of the Year	Tom Brady
Most Improved Player of the Year	Miles Austin

SPORTS ILLUSTRATED

Most Valuable Player	Peyton Manning
Offensive Rookie of the Year	Percy Harvin
Defensive Rookie of the Year	Brian Cushing
Coach of the Year	Marvin Lewis

MAXWELL CLUB PLAYER OF THE YEAR

(Bert Bell Trophy)	Drew Brees

MAXWELL CLUB COACH OF THE YEAR

(Earle "Greasy" Neale Trophy)	Sean Payton

DIET PEPSI ROOKIE OF THE YEAR

Rookie of the Year	Percy Harvin

FEDEX AIR & GROUND NFL PLAYERS OF THE YEAR

FedEx Express NFL Player of the Year	Drew Brees
FedEx Ground NFL Player of the Year	Chris Johnson

WALTER PAYTON/ NFL MAN OF THE YEAR

Man of the Year	Brian Waters
Man of the Year Finalist	London Fletcher
Man of the Year Finalist	Mike Furrey

SUPER BOWL XLIV MOST VALUABLE PLAYER

Pete Rozelle Trophy	Drew Brees

AFC-NFC 2010 PRO BOWL MOST VALUABLE PLAYER

Pro Bowl MVP	Matt Schaub

2009 ALL-PRO TEAMS

2009 PFW/PFWA ALL-PRO TEAM

Selected by *Pro Football Weekly* and the Professional Football Writers of America

Offense:

Peyton Manning, Indianapolis	Quarterback
Adrian Peterson, Minnesota	Running Back
Chris Johnson, Tennessee	Running Back
Dallas Clark, Indianapolis	Tight End
Andre Johnson, Houston	Wide Receiver
Wes Welker, New England	Wide Receiver
Ryan Clady, Denver	Tackle
Joe Thomas, Cleveland	Tackle
Jahri Evans, New Orleans	Guard
Steve Hutchinson, Minnesota	Guard
Nick Mangold, N.Y. Jets	Center

Defense:

Jared Allen, Minnesota	End
Dwight Freeney, Indianapolis	End
Haloti Ngata, Baltimore	Tackle
Kevin Williams, Minnesota	Tackle
DeMarcus Ware, Dallas	Outside Linebacker
Elvis Dumervil, Denver	Outside Linebacker
Patrick Willis, San Francisco	Middle Linebacker
Charles Woodson, Green Bay	Cornerback
Darrelle Revis, N.Y. Jets	Cornerback
Darren Sharper, New Orleans	Safety
Adrian Wilson, Arizona	Safety

Special Teams:

Nate Kaeding, San Diego	Kicker
Shane Lechler, Oakland	Punter
Joshua Cribbs, Cleveland	Kick Returner
DeSean Jackson, Philadelphia	Punt Returner
Kassim Osgood, San Diego	Special Teams Player

2009 ASSOCIATED PRESS ALL-PRO TEAM

Selected by the Associated Press

Offense:

Peyton Manning, Indianapolis	Quarterback
Adrian Peterson, Minnesota	Running Back
Chris Johnson, Tennessee	Running Back
Leonard Weaver, Philadelphia	Fullback
Dallas Clark, Indianapolis	Tight End
Andre Johnson, Houston	Wide Receiver
Wes Welker, New England	Wide Receiver
Ryan Clady, Denver	Tackle
Joe Thomas, Cleveland	Tackle
Jahri Evans, New Orleans	Guard
Steve Hutchinson, Minnesota	Guard
Nick Mangold, N.Y. Jets	Center

Defense:

Jared Allen, Minnesota	End
Dwight Freeney, Indianapolis	End
Jay Ratliff, Dallas	Tackle
Kevin Williams, Minnesota	Tackle
DeMarcus Ware, Dallas	Outside Linebacker
Elvis Dumervil, Denver	Outside Linebacker
Ray Lewis, Baltimore	Inside Linebacker
Patrick Willis, San Francisco	Inside Linebacker
Charles Woodson, Green Bay	Cornerback
Darrelle Revis, N.Y. Jets	Cornerback
Darren Sharper, New Orleans	Safety
Adrian Wilson, Arizona	Safety

Special Teams:

Nate Kaeding, San Diego	Kicker
Shane Lechler, Oakland	Punter
Joshua Cribbs, Cleveland	Kick Returner

2009 ALL-NFL TEAM

Selected by the Associated Press, *Pro Football Weekly,* and the Professional Football Writers of America

Offense:

Peyton Manning, Indianapolis (PFW, AP)	Quarterback
Adrian Peterson, Minnesota (PFW, AP)	Running Back
Chris Johnson, Tennessee (PFW, AP)	Running Back
Leonard Weaver, Philadelphia (AP)	Fullback
Dallas Clark, Indianapolis (PFW, AP)	Tight End
Andre Johnson, Houston (PFW, AP)	Wide Receiver
Wes Welker, New England (PFW, AP)	Wide Receiver
Ryan Clady, Denver (PFW, AP)	Tackle
Joe Thomas, Cleveland (PFW, AP)	Tackle
Jahri Evans, New Orleans (PFW, AP)	Guard
Steve Hutchinson, Minnesota (PFW, AP)	Guard
Nick Mangold, N.Y. Jets (PFW, AP)	Center

Defense:

Jared Allen, Minnesota (PFW, AP)	End
Dwight Freeney, Indianapolis (PFW, AP)	End
Haloti Ngata, Baltimore (PFW)	Tackle
Jay Ratliff, Dallas (AP)	Tackle
Kevin Williams, Minnesota (PFW, AP)	Tackle
DeMarcus Ware, Dallas (PFW, AP)	Outside Linebacker
Elvis Dumervil, Denver (PFW, AP)	Outside Linebacker
Ray Lewis, Baltimore (AP)	Inside Linebacker
Patrick Willis, San Francisco (PFW, AP)	Inside Linebacker
Charles Woodson, Green Bay (PFW, AP)	Cornerback
Darrelle Revis, N.Y. Jets (PFW, AP)	Cornerback
Darren Sharper, New Orleans (PFW, AP)	Safety
Adrian Wilson, Arizona (PFW, AP)	Safety

Special Teams:

Nate Kaeding, San Diego (PFW, AP)	Kicker
Shane Lechler, Oakland (PFW, AP)	Punter
Joshua Cribbs, Cleveland (PFW, AP)	Kick Returner
DeSean Jackson, Philadelphia (PFW)	Punt Returner
Kassim Osgood, San Diego (PFW)	Special Teams Player

2009 PFW/PFWA ALL-ROOKIE TEAM

Selected by *Pro Football Weekly* and the Professional Football Writers of America

Offense:

Mark Sanchez, N.Y. Jets	Quarterback
Knowshon Moreno, Denver	Running Back
Beanie Wells, Arizona	Running Back
Brandon Pettigrew, Detroit	Tight End
Percy Harvin, Minnesota	Wide Receiver
Austin Collie, Indianapolis	Wide Receiver
Michael Oher, Baltimore	Tackle
Phil Loadholt, Minnesota	Tackle
Andy Levitre, Buffalo	Guard
Louis Vasquez, San Diego	Guard
Alex Mack, Cleveland	Center

Defense:

Tyson Jackson, Kansas City	Defensive Lineman
Terrance Knighton, Jacksonville	Defensive Lineman
B.J. Raji, Green Bay	Defensive Lineman
Matt Shaughnessy, Oakland	Defensive Lineman
Clay Matthews, Green Bay	Outside Linebacker
Brian Orakpo, Washington	Outside Linebacker
Brian Cushing, Houston	Middle Linebacker
Vontae Davis, Miami	Cornerback
Jacob Lacey, Indianapolis	Cornerback
Jairus Byrd, Buffalo	Safety
Louis Delmas, Detroit	Safety

Special Teams:

Ryan Succop, Kansas City	Kicker
Pat McAfee, Indianapolis	Punter
Quan Cosby, Cincinnati	Punt Returner
Percy Harvin, Minnesota	Kickoff Returner
LaRod Stephens-Howling, Arizona	Special Teams Player

2009 BEST PERFORMANCES

TEN BEST RUSHING PERFORMANCES, 2009

	Att.	Yards	TD
1. Jerome Harrison Cleveland vs. Kansas City, Dec. 20	34	286	3
2. Jamaal Charles Kansas City vs. Denver, Jan. 3	25	259	2
3. Chris Johnson Tennessee vs. Jacksonville, Nov. 1	24	228	2
4. Fred Jackson Buffalo vs. Indianapolis, Jan 3	33	212	0
5. Thomas Jones N.Y. Jets vs. Buffalo, Oct. 18	22	210	1
6. Frank Gore San Francisco vs. Seattle, Sept. 20	16	207	2
7. Jonathan Stewart Carolina vs. N.Y. Giants, Dec. 27	28	206	1
8. Chris Johnson Tennessee vs. Houston, Sept. 20	16	197	2
9. Cedric Benson Cincinnati vs. Chicago, Oct. 25	37	189	1
10. Adrian Peterson Minnesota vs. Cleveland, Sept. 13	25	180	3

There were 116 100-yard rushing performances in 2009.

MOST 100-YARD RUSHING PERFORMANCES, 2009

Player, Team	100-Yd. Games
Chris Johnson, Tennessee	12
Steven Jackson, St. Louis	7
Thomas Jones, New York Jets	7
Cedric Benson, Cincinnati	6
Jamaal Charles, Kansas City	5
Frank Gore, San Francisco	5
Maurice Jones-Drew, Jacksonville	5
Jonathan Stewart, Carolina	5
Jerome Harrison, Cleveland	4
Ray Rice, Baltimore	4
Michael Turner, Atlanta	4
DeAngelo Williams, Carolina	4
Ricky Williams, Miami	4
Ryan Grant, Green Bay	3
Rashard Mendenhall, Pittsburgh	3
Adrian Peterson, Minnesota	3
Ahmad Bradshaw, New York Giants	2
Ronnie Brown, Miami	2
Correll Buckhalter, Denver	2
Michael Bush, Oakland	2
Justin Forsett, Seattle	2
Matt Forté, Chicago	2
Fred Jackson, Buffalo	2
21 players tied with	1

100-YARD RUSHING, 2009 POSTSEASON

Wild Card

Cedric Benson, Cincinnati	169 yards vs. New York Jets
Ray Rice, Baltimore	159 yards vs. New England
Felix Jones, Dallas	148 yards vs. Philadelphia
Shonn Greene, New York Jets	135 yards vs. Cincinnati

Divisional

Shonn Greene, New York Jets	128 yards vs. San Diego

Championship

Adrian Peterson, Minnesota	122 yards vs. New Orleans

Super Bowl XLIV

None

TEN BEST PASSING PERFORMANCES, 2009

	Att.	Comp.	Yds.	TD
1. Ben Roethlisberger Pittsburgh vs. Green Bay, Dec. 20	46	29	503	3
2. Donovan McNabb Philadelphia vs. San Diego, Nov. 15	55	35	450	2
3. Philip Rivers San Diego vs. Baltimore, Sept. 20	45	25	436	2
4. Kyle Orton Denver vs. Kansas City, Jan. 3	56	32	431	1
5. Matthew Stafford Detroit vs. Cleveland, Nov. 22	43	26	422	5
6. Drew Brees New Orleans vs. Washington, Dec. 6	49	35	419	2
7. Ben Roethlisberger Pittsburgh vs. Cleveland, Oct. 18	35	23	417	2
8. Ben Roethlisberger Pittsburgh vs. Kansas City, Nov. 22	42	32	398	3
9. Matt Schaub Houston vs. Cincinnati, Oct. 18	40	28	392	4
Brett Favre Minnesota vs. Chicago, Nov. 29	48	32	392	3
Tony Romo Dallas vs. N.Y. Giants, Dec. 6	55	41	392	3

There were 104 300-yard passing performances in 2009.

MOST 300-YARD PASSING PERFORMANCES, 2009

Player, Team	300-Yd. Games
Peyton Manning, Indianapolis	9
Matt Schaub, Houston	9
Tony Romo, Dallas	8
Tom Brady, New England	7
Drew Brees, New Orleans	7
Brett Favre, Minnesota	6
Philip Rivers, San Diego	5
Aaron Rodgers, Green Bay	5
Ben Roethlisberger, Pittsburgh	5
Kurt Warner, Arizona	4
Jay Cutler, Chicago	3
Joe Flacco, Baltimore	3
David Garrard, Jacksonville	3
Chad Henne, Miami	3
Eli Manning, New York Giants	3
Donovan McNabb, Philadelphia	3
Jason Campbell, Washington	2
Jake Delhomme, Carolina	2
Matt Hasselbeck, Seattle	2
Kevin Kolb, Philadelphia	2
Kyle Orton, Denver	2
11 players tied with	1

300-YARD PASSING, 2009 POSTSEASON

Wild Card

Aaron Rodgers, Green Bay	423 yards vs. Arizona
Kurt Warner, Arizona	379 yards vs. Green Bay

Divisional

None

Championship

Peyton Manning, Indianapolis	377 yards vs. New York Jets
Brett Favre, Minnesota	310 yards vs. New Orleans

Super Bowl XLIV

Peyton Manning, Indianapolis	333 yards vs. New Orleans

TEN BEST RECEIVING PERFORMANCES, 2009

	No.	Yards	TD
1. Miles Austin Dallas vs. Kansas City, Oct. 11	10	250	2
2. Jabar Gaffney Denver vs. Kansas City, Jan. 3	14	213	0
3. Roddy White Atlanta vs. San Francisco, Oct. 11	8	210	2
4. Sidney Rice Minnesota vs. Detroit, Dec. 13	7	201	0
5. Brandon Marshall Denver vs. Indianapolis, Dec. 13	21	200	2
6. Terrell Owens Buffalo vs. Jacksonville, Nov. 22	9	197	1
7. Andre Johnson Houston vs. St. Louis, Dec. 20	9	196	0
8. Andre Johnson Houston vs. Seattle, Dec. 13	11	193	2
9. Wes Welker New England vs. New York Jets, Nov. 22	15	192	0
10. Dallas Clark Indianapolis vs. Miami, Sept. 21	7	183	1

There were 163 100-yard receiving performances in 2009.

MOST 100-YARD RECEIVING PERFORMANCES, 2009

Player, Team	100-Yd. Games
Vincent Jackson, San Diego	6
Andre Johnson, Houston	6
Wes Welker, New England	6
Miles Austin, Dallas	5
DeSean Jackson, Philadelphia	5
Greg Jennings, Green Bay	5
Randy Moss, New England	5
Hines Ward, Pittsburgh	5
Reggie Wayne, Indianapolis	5
Sidney Rice, Minnesota	4
Roddy White, Atlanta	4
Anquan Boldin, Arizona	3
Brent Celek, Philadelphia	3
Vernon Davis, San Francisco	3
Larry Fitzgerald, Arizona	3
Antonio Gates, San Diego	3
Santonio Holmes, Pittsburgh	3
Calvin Johnson, Detroit	3
Brandon Marshall, Denver	3
Chad Ochocinco, Cincinnati	3
Mike Sims-Walker, Jacksonville	3
Steve Smith, New York Giants	3
Jason Witten, Dallas	3
Kenny Britt, Tennessee	2
Nate Burleson, Seattle	2
Chris Chambers, Kansas City	2
Dallas Clark, Indianapolis	2
Marques Colston, New Orleans	2
Donald Driver, Green Bay	2
Pierre Garcon, Indianapolis	2
Devery Henderson, New Orleans	2
T.J. Houshmandzadeh, Seattle	2
Mario Manningham, New York Giants	2
Derrick Mason, Baltimore	2
Mohamed Massaquoi, Cleveland	2
Zach Miller, Oakland	2
Hakeem Nicks, New York Giants	2
Steve Smith, Carolina	2
Kellen Winslow, Tampa Bay	2
39 players tied with	1

100-YARD RECEIVING, 2009 POSTSEASON

Wild Card

Jermichael Finley, Green Bay	159 yards vs. Arizona
Jeremy Maclin, Philadelphia	146 yards vs. Dallas
Greg Jennings, Green Bay	130 yards vs. Arizona
Steve Breaston, Arizona	125 yards vs. Green Bay

Divisional

Sidney Rice, Minnesota	141 yards. vs. Dallas
Vincent Jackson, San Diego	111 yards vs. New York Jets

Championship

Pierre Garcon, Indianapolis	151 yards vs. New York Jets
Austin Collie, Indianapolis	123 yards vs. New York Jets
Bernard Berrian, Minnesota	102 yards vs. New Orleans
Jerricho Cotchery, New York Jets	102 yards vs. Indianapolis
Braylon Edwards, New York Jets	100 yards vs. Indianapolis

Super Bowl XLIV

None

TOP QUARTERBACK SACK PERFORMANCES, 2009

	No.
1. Antwan Odom Cincinnati vs. Green Bay, Sept. 20	5.0
2. Jared Allen Minnesota vs. Green Bay, Oct. 5	4.5
3. Elvis Dumervil Denver vs. Cleveland, Sept. 20	4.0
Brian Orakpo Washington vs. Oakland, Dec. 13	4.0
5. Justin Smith San Francisco vs. St. Louis, Jan. 3	3.5
6. James Harrison Pittsburgh vs. Detroit, Oct. 11	3.0
Jimmy Wilkerson, Tampa Bay vs. Philadelphia, Oct. 11	3.0
Calvin Pace New York Jets vs. Oakland, Oct. 25	3.0
Jared Allen Minnesota vs. Green Bay, Nov. 1	3.0
Darnell Dockett Arizona vs. Tennessee, Nov. 29	3.0
Tamba Hali Kansas City vs. Denver, Dec. 6	3.0
Ahmad Brooks San Francisco vs. Arizona, Dec. 14	3.0
Tully Banta-Cain New England vs. Buffalo, Dec. 20	3.0
Aaron Schobel Buffalo vs. Atlanta, Dec. 27	3.0

There were 14 3.0-plus sack performances in 2009.

MOST 3.0-PLUS SACK PERFORMANCES, 2009

Player, Team	3.0-Sack Games
Jared Allen, Minnesota	2
12 players tied with	1

3.0 SACK PERFORMANCES, 2009 POSTSEASON

Wild Card

None

Divisional

Ray Edwards, Minnesota — 3.0 vs. Dallas

Championship

None

Super Bowl XLIV

None

For week-by-week listings of top performances from 1970 to the present, please visit www.NFL.com/stats/topperformers.

2009 TEAM STATISTICS

AMERICAN FOOTBALL CONFERENCE OFFENSE

	Balt.	Buff.	Cin.	Cle.	Den.	Hou.	Ind.	Jax.	KC	Mia.	NE	NYJ	Oak.	Pitt.	SD	Tenn.
First Downs	320	233	295	237	306	340	339	300	256	333	373	280	234	331	330	288
Rushing	115	81	109	102	95	93	69	114	91	129	114	132	81	96	80	115
Passing	187	126	159	118	186	231	241	170	139	188	222	131	131	210	222	154
Penalty	18	26	27	17	25	16	29	16	26	16	37	17	22	25	28	19
Rushes	468	424	505	498	440	425	366	447	438	509	466	607	410	428	427	499
Net Yds. Gained	2200	1867	2056	2087	1836	1475	1294	2029	1929	2231	1921	2756	1701	1793	1423	2592
Avg. Gain	4.7	4.4	4.1	4.2	4.2	3.5	3.5	4.5	4.4	4.4	4.1	4.5	4.1	4.2	3.3	5.2
Avg. Yds. per Game	137.5	116.7	128.5	130.4	114.8	92.2	80.9	126.8	120.6	139.4	120.1	172.3	106.3	112.1	88.9	162.0
Passes Attempted	510	441	477	443	558	593	601	519	536	545	592	393	485	536	519	476
Completed	321	256	286	219	341	399	402	315	296	331	390	210	255	351	338	271
% Completed	62.9	58.0	60.0	49.4	61.1	67.3	66.9	60.7	55.2	60.7	65.9	53.4	52.6	65.5	65.1	56.9
Total Yds. Gained	3637	2789	3134	2255	3825	4803	4605	3599	3183	3396	4540	2596	2875	4496	4506	3104
Times Sacked	36	46	29	30	34	25	13	44	45	34	18	30	49	50	26	15
Yds. Lost	218	274	244	179	198	149	90	243	261	226	104	216	318	348	168	73
Net Yds. Gained	3419	2515	2890	2076	3627	4654	4515	3356	2922	3170	4436	2380	2557	4148	4338	3031
Avg. Yds. per Game	213.7	157.2	180.6	129.8	226.7	290.9	282.2	209.8	182.6	198.1	277.3	148.8	159.8	259.3	271.1	189.4
Net Yds. per Pass Play	6.26	5.16	5.71	4.39	6.13	7.53	7.35	5.96	5.03	5.47	7.27	5.63	4.79	7.08	7.96	6.17
Yds. Gained per Comp.	11.33	10.89	10.96	10.30	11.22	12.04	11.46	11.43	10.75	10.26	11.64	12.36	11.27	12.81	13.33	11.45
Combined Net Yds. Gained	5619	4382	4946	4163	5463	6129	5809	5385	4851	5401	6357	5136	4258	5941	5761	5623
% Total Yds. Rushing	39.2	42.6	41.6	50.1	33.6	24.1	22.3	37.7	39.8	41.3	30.2	53.7	39.9	30.2	24.7	46.1
% Total Yds. Passing	60.8	57.4	58.4	49.9	66.4	75.9	77.7	62.3	60.2	58.7	69.8	46.3	60.1	69.8	75.3	53.9
Avg. Yds. per Game	351.2	273.9	309.1	260.2	341.4	383.1	363.1	336.6	303.2	337.6	397.3	321.0	266.1	371.3	360.1	351.4
Ball Control Plays	1014	911	1011	971	1032	1043	980	1010	1019	1088	1076	1030	944	1014	972	990
Avg. Yds. per Play	5.5	4.8	4.9	4.3	5.3	5.9	5.9	5.3	4.8	5.0	5.9	5.0	4.5	5.9	5.9	5.7
Avg. Time of Poss.	29:18	27:50	31:59	28:28	30:03	31:54	27:40	30:08	27:37	31:54	32:55	31:43	28:18	32:13	29:58	28:27
Third Down Efficiency	41.6	25.8	40.6	32.6	36.3	40.2	49.2	45.1	27.3	49.0	43.7	37.1	29.6	39.4	44.4	41.6
Had Intercepted	13	19	13	18	13	17	19	10	17	19	13	21	18	14	10	15
Yds. Opp Returned	195	194	184	281	237	294	229	234	160	261	146	309	259	398	88	121
Ret. by Opp. for TD	0	3	2	2	3	3	0	1	0	3	1	2	0	2	0	0
Punts	74	90	86	94	78	67	64	72	97	75	57	80	96	72	52	69
Yds. Punted	3188	4192	3713	3977	3387	2866	2837	3017	4361	3472	2221	3357	4909	3074	2342	2995
Avg. Yds. per Punt	43.1	46.6	43.2	42.3	43.4	42.8	44.3	41.9	45.0	46.3	39.0	42.0	51.1	42.7	45.0	43.4
Punt Returns	39	33	40	39	44	45	29	27	32	33	38	50	36	36	26	33
Yds. Returned	290	218	474	456	419	449	151	233	209	237	432	457	177	290	183	220
Avg. Yds. per Return	7.4	6.6	11.9	11.7	9.5	10.0	5.2	8.6	6.5	7.2	11.4	9.1	4.9	8.1	7.0	6.7
Returned for TD	0	0	0	1	1	0	0	0	0	0	0	0	0	0	1	0
Kickoff Returns	59	64	62	69	57	64	55	66	77	75	54	44	66	66	63	69
Yds. Returned	1547	1517	1356	1670	1217	1449	1219	1492	1666	1739	1226	1074	1199	1581	1442	1417
Avg. Yds. per Return	26.2	23.7	21.9	24.2	21.4	22.6	22.2	22.6	21.6	23.2	22.7	24.4	18.2	24.0	22.9	20.5
Returned for TD	1	0	1	3	1	1	1	0	1	2	0	1	0	0	0	0
Fumbles	19	24	24	21	15	21	11	26	31	27	17	24	30	21	14	27
Lost	9	11	12	13	10	11	5	13	10	10	9	9	15	11	7	16
Out of Bounds	2	2	2	1	0	3	2	2	2	4	0	4	4	3	2	0
Own Rec. for TD	0	0	0	0	0	1	0	0	0	0	0	0	0	0	0	0
Opp. Rec. by	10	5	6	9	13	13	9	10	13	6	10	14	12	10	10	7
Opp. Rec. for TD	1	0	1	0	2	1	0	0	1	1	0	1	0	1	2	0
Penalties	115	107	114	77	93	95	74	70	84	78	81	88	117	85	78	98
Yds. Penalized	1094	855	863	678	800	833	546	542	667	640	743	677	920	769	570	821
Total Points Scored	391	258	305	245	326	388	416	290	294	360	427	348	197	368	454	354
Total TDs	47	25	34	25	34	46	53	34	31	41	50	37	17	41	51	39
TDs Rushing	22	6	9	10	9	13	16	19	8	22	19	21	7	10	17	19
TDs Passing	21	17	21	11	21	29	34	15	18	15	28	12	10	28	29	16
TDs on Ret. and Rec.	4	2	4	4	4	4	3	0	5	4	3	4	0	3	5	4
Extra Point Kicks	46	24	28	22	32	43	50	30	29	37	47	32	17	41	50	37
Extra Point Kicks Att.	47	24	29	23	32	44	51	31	29	38	47	32	17	41	51	37
2Pt Conversions	0	0	2	1	0	1	0	1	1	1	1	2	0	0	0	1
2Pt Conversions Att.	0	1	5	2	2	2	2	3	2	3	3	5	0	0	0	2
Safeties	0	0	0	1	0	2	0	0	1	0	0	0	0	0	1	0
Field Goals Made	21	28	23	23	30	21	16	18	25	25	26	30	26	27	32	27
Field Goals Attempted	30	33	28	25	35	32	20	28	29	28	31	36	29	31	35	32
% Successful	70.0	84.8	82.1	92.0	85.7	65.6	80.0	64.3	86.2	89.3	83.9	83.3	89.7	87.1	91.4	84.4

AMERICAN FOOTBALL CONFERENCE DEFENSE

	Balt.	Buff.	Cin.	Cle.	Den.	Hou.	Ind.	Jax.	KC	Mia.	NE	NYJ	Oak.	Pitt.	SD	Tenn.
First Downs	280	310	276	336	290	300	320	307	318	297	289	237	314	274	309	323
Rushing	82	134	95	120	99	91	106	100	122	88	80	87	126	70	112	89
Passing	164	157	165	189	167	175	203	191	178	184	193	128	158	186	177	210
Penalty	34	19	16	27	24	34	11	16	18	25	16	22	30	18	20	24
Rushes	435	535	399	506	458	396	467	458	531	435	398	420	548	372	422	402
Net Yds. Gained	1492	2501	1573	2314	2059	1711	2024	1863	2504	1835	1768	1578	2488	1438	1884	1711
Avg. Gain	3.4	4.7	3.9	4.6	4.5	4.3	4.3	4.1	4.7	4.2	4.4	3.8	4.5	3.9	4.5	4.3
Avg. Yds. per Game	93.3	156.3	98.3	144.6	128.7	106.9	126.5	116.4	156.5	114.7	110.5	98.6	155.5	89.9	117.8	106.9
Passes Attempted	524	519	547	526	510	548	583	510	509	489	512	501	438	548	534	604
Completed	306	295	318	313	298	344	372	345	302	281	300	259	259	319	326	404
% Completed	58.4	56.8	58.1	59.5	58.4	62.8	63.8	67.6	59.3	57.5	58.6	51.7	59.1	58.2	61.0	66.9
Total Yds. Gained	3506	3137	3486	4149	3222	3674	3631	3853	3844	3996	3584	2704	3531	3761	3569	4363
Times Sacked	32	32	34	40	39	30	34	14	22	44	31	32	37	47	35	32
Yds. Lost	190	189	237	234	241	187	228	79	137	242	229	245	228	314	221	224
Net Yds. Gained	3316	2948	3249	3915	2981	3487	3403	3774	3707	3754	3355	2459	3303	3447	3348	4139
Avg. Yds. per Game	207.3	184.3	203.1	244.7	186.3	217.9	212.7	235.9	231.7	234.6	209.7	153.7	206.4	215.4	209.3	258.7
Net Yds. per Pass Play	5.96	5.35	5.59	6.92	5.43	6.03	5.52	7.20	6.98	7.04	6.18	4.61	6.95	5.79	5.88	6.51
Yds. Gained per Comp.	11.46	10.63	10.96	13.26	10.81	10.68	9.76	11.17	12.73	14.22	11.95	10.44	13.63	11.79	10.95	10.80
Combined Net Yds. Gained	4808	5449	4822	6229	5040	5198	5427	5637	6211	5589	5123	4037	5791	4885	5232	5850
% Total Yds. Rushing	31.0	45.9	32.6	37.1	40.9	32.9	37.3	33.0	40.3	32.8	34.5	39.1	43.0	29.4	36.0	29.2
% Total Yds. Passing	69.0	54.1	67.4	62.9	59.1	67.1	62.7	67.0	59.7	67.2	65.5	60.9	57.0	70.6	64.0	70.8
Avg. Yds. per Game	300.5	340.6	301.4	389.3	315.0	324.9	339.2	352.3	388.2	349.3	320.2	252.3	361.9	305.3	327.0	365.6
Ball Control Plays	991	1086	980	1072	1007	974	1084	982	1062	968	941	953	1023	967	991	1038
Avg. Yds. per Play	4.9	5.0	4.9	5.8	5.0	5.3	5.0	5.7	5.8	5.8	5.4	4.2	5.7	5.1	5.3	5.6
Avg. Time of Poss.	30:42	32:10	28:01	31:32	29:57	28:06	32:20	29:52	32:23	28:06	27:05	28:17	31:42	27:47	30:02	31:33
Third Down Efficiency	36.7	40.4	38.6	38.9	37.2	39.3	45.0	45.0	38.1	34.8	37.1	31.5	35.6	42.3	40.4	40.8
Intercepted By	22	28	19	10	17	14	16	15	15	15	18	17	8	12	14	20
Yds. Returned By	346	335	259	161	171	212	167	208	380	164	327	247	35	189	173	433
Returned for TD	2	2	2	0	0	1	2	0	2	1	3	1	0	2	1	4
Punts	79	78	83	77	76	76	65	62	79	67	79	99	77	86	63	76
Yds. Punted	3426	3216	3641	3322	3520	3557	2883	2784	3482	2953	3267	4277	3299	3684	2711	3364
Avg. Yds. per Punt	43.4	41.2	43.9	43.1	46.3	46.8	44.4	44.9	44.1	44.1	41.4	43.2	42.8	42.8	43.0	44.3
Punt Returns	38	49	39	40	36	24	36	38	40	43	20	27	63	33	23	29
Yds. Returned	287	377	393	262	363	104	301	159	285	369	180	238	459	325	265	208
Avg. Yds. per Return	7.6	7.7	10.1	6.6	10.1	4.3	8.4	4.2	7.1	8.6	9.0	8.8	7.3	9.8	11.5	7.2
Returned for TD	1	0	0	0	1	0	0	0	0	0	0	0	0	0	1	0
Kickoff Returns	77	59	58	52	49	71	60	47	60	71	70	70	42	74	87	71
Yds. Returned	1565	1271	1289	984	1115	1597	1519	1069	1446	1557	1705	1685	1078	1795	1909	1714
Avg. Yds. per Return	20.3	21.5	22.2	18.9	22.8	22.5	25.3	22.7	24.1	21.9	24.4	24.1	25.7	24.3	21.9	24.1
Returned for TD	0	0	0	0	1	0	1	1	2	0	0	2	1	4	1	1
Fumbles	20	21	17	17	30	27	20	22	23	17	28	22	29	21	24	20
Lost	10	5	6	9	13	13	10	10	13	6	10	14	12	10	11	7
Out of Bounds	0	1	3	4	3	1	2	3	5	2	2	0	3	0	2	0
Own Rec. for TD	0	0	0	0	0	0	0	0	0	0	0	1	0	0	0	0
Opp. Rec. by	8	11	12	13	10	10	5	13	10	9	9	9	15	11	7	16
Opp. Rec. for TD	0	1	0	2	0	0	1	1	2	0	2	2	0	2	0	0
Penalties	88	107	99	101	78	92	92	64	106	73	91	87	86	102	103	94
Yds. Penalized	741	919	767	812	726	728	889	498	821	589	780	680	684	903	795	724
Total Points Scored	261	326	291	375	324	333	307	380	424	390	285	236	379	324	320	402
Total TDs	27	37	32	41	34	39	31	44	48	42	35	26	41	37	35	48
TDs Rushing	8	19	12	15	11	17	10	12	18	16	6	11	24	7	10	16
TDs Passing	17	14	18	22	18	19	19	28	25	23	25	8	16	22	23	31
TDs on Ret. and Rec.	2	4	2	4	5	3	2	4	5	3	4	7	1	8	2	1
Extra Point Kicks	27	32	30	39	33	39	27	38	47	35	33	23	41	32	33	46
Extra Point Kicks Att.	27	32	30	41	34	39	27	38	47	37	34	24	41	32	33	47
2Pt Conversions	0	2	0	0	0	0	2	2	0	2	0	0	0	2	1	1
2Pt Conversions Att.	0	5	2	0	0	0	4	6	0	5	1	2	0	5	2	1
Safeties	0	1	0	0	0	0	0	1	1	0	0	0	1	0	0	1
Field Goals Made	24	22	23	30	29	20	30	24	29	33	14	19	30	22	25	22
Field Goals Attempted	27	28	29	36	31	23	36	28	37	39	20	23	40	29	29	27
% Successful	88.9	78.6	79.3	83.3	93.5	87.0	83.3	85.7	78.4	84.6	70.0	82.6	75.0	75.9	86.2	81.5

2009 TEAM STATISTICS

NATIONAL FOOTBALL CONFERENCE OFFENSE

	Ariz.	Atl.	Car.	Chi.	Dall.	Det.	GB	Minn.	NO	NYG	Phil.	StL	SF	Sea.	TB	Wash.
First Downs	317	330	289	262	335	281	335	343	348	323	290	259	238	297	246	280
Rushing	77	105	123	71	110	82	102	99	115	103	87	79	77	80	80	72
Passing	215	192	152	170	203	168	201	220	215	194	182	159	137	184	148	191
Penalty	25	33	14	21	22	31	32	24	18	26	21	21	24	33	18	17
Rushes	365	451	525	373	436	409	438	467	468	443	384	411	371	395	404	391
Net Yds. Gained	1494	1876	2498	1492	2103	1616	1885	1918	2106	1837	1637	1784	1600	1566	1627	1510
Avg. Gain	4.1	4.2	4.8	4.0	4.8	4.0	4.3	4.1	4.5	4.1	4.3	4.3	4.3	4.0	4.0	3.9
Avg. Yds. per Game	93.4	117.3	156.1	93.3	131.4	101.0	117.8	119.9	131.6	114.8	102.3	111.5	100.0	97.9	101.7	94.4
Passes Attempted	594	570	465	563	550	585	553	553	544	542	553	543	528	609	524	533
Completed	392	332	264	340	347	316	357	377	378	338	335	312	312	372	279	340
% Completed	66.0	58.2	56.8	60.4	63.1	54.0	64.6	68.2	69.5	62.4	60.6	57.5	59.1	61.1	53.2	63.8
Total Yds. Gained	4200	3697	3070	3677	4483	3471	4492	4403	4490	4246	4380	2970	3293	3771	3134	3797
Times Sacked	26	27	33	35	34	43	51	34	20	32	38	44	40	41	33	46
Yds. Lost	184	126	271	204	196	303	312	247	135	227	291	284	241	268	161	307
Net Yds. Gained	4016	3571	2799	3473	4287	3168	4180	4156	4355	4019	4089	2686	3052	3503	2973	3490
Avg. Yds. per Game	251.0	223.2	174.9	217.1	267.9	198.0	261.3	259.8	272.2	251.2	255.6	167.9	190.8	218.9	185.8	218.1
Net Yds. per Pass Play	6.48	5.98	5.62	5.81	7.34	5.04	6.92	7.08	7.72	7.00	6.92	4.58	5.37	5.39	5.34	6.03
Yds. Gained per Comp.	10.71	11.14	11.63	10.81	12.92	10.98	12.58	11.68	11.88	12.56	13.07	9.52	10.55	10.14	11.23	11.17
Combined Net Yds. Gained	5510	5447	5297	4965	6390	4784	6065	6074	6461	5856	5726	4470	4652	5069	4600	5000
% Total Yds. Rushing	27.1	34.4	47.2	30.1	32.9	33.8	31.1	31.6	32.6	31.4	28.6	39.9	34.4	30.9	35.4	30.2
% Total Yds. Passing	72.9	65.6	52.8	69.9	67.1	66.2	68.9	68.4	67.4	68.6	71.4	60.1	65.6	69.1	64.6	69.8
Avg. Yds. per Game	344.4	340.4	331.1	310.3	399.4	299.0	379.1	379.6	403.8	366.0	357.9	279.4	290.8	316.8	287.5	312.5
Ball Control Plays	985	1048	1023	971	1020	1037	1042	1054	1032	1017	975	998	939	1045	961	970
Avg. Yds. per Play	5.6	5.2	5.2	5.1	6.3	4.6	5.8	5.8	6.3	5.8	5.9	4.5	5.0	4.9	4.8	5.2
Avg. Time of Poss.	29:52	29:47	30:13	28:27	32:04	28:57	33:03	32:40	31:10	31:34	28:15	28:58	29:47	27:31	28:31	28:49
Third Down Efficiency	36.3	42.1	37.3	37.3	40.6	35.9	47.0	44.8	44.7	42.9	36.2	32.3	29.8	33.3	32.6	39.8
Had Intercepted	18	17	20	27	9	32	8	7	12	14	13	21	14	19	29	16
Yds. Opp Returned	312	306	339	365	96	508	171	120	133	106	131	321	168	202	492	291
Ret. by Opp. for TD	3	2	3	0	1	3	1	1	0	0	1	4	1	1	2	3
Punts	86	63	77	77	72	74	67	73	58	64	76	90	99	89	87	76
Yds. Punted	4045	2634	3352	3191	3249	3174	2891	3202	2528	2604	3222	4212	4711	4100	3626	3084
Avg. Yds. per Punt	47.0	41.8	43.5	41.4	45.1	42.9	43.1	43.9	43.6	40.7	42.4	46.8	47.6	46.1	41.7	40.6
Punt Returns	45	27	34	39	39	28	34	48	33	36	35	37	49	46	40	32
Yds. Returned	308	270	282	330	426	233	236	455	152	393	471	395	216	346	462	152
Avg. Yds. per Return	6.8	10.0	8.3	8.5	10.9	8.3	6.9	9.5	4.6	10.9	13.5	10.7	4.4	7.5	11.6	4.8
Returned for TD	0	0	0	1	2	0	0	0	0	1	2	0	0	0	1	0
Kickoff Returns	54	55	51	80	47	96	54	56	57	71	58	76	52	60	62	65
Yds. Returned	1284	1336	1015	1999	1032	2050	1193	1297	1393	1482	1191	1764	1135	1316	1630	1413
Avg. Yds. per Return	23.8	24.3	19.9	25.0	22.0	21.4	22.1	23.2	24.4	20.9	20.5	23.2	21.8	21.9	26.3	21.7
Returned for TD	1	0	0	1	0	0	0	2	1	0	0	0	0	0	1	0
Fumbles	32	19	23	26	20	25	20	19	25	30	23	24	24	33	25	30
Lost	18	8	11	7	10	9	8	11	16	17	10	12	10	12	5	12
Out of Bounds	3	2	3	1	4	2	0	2	4	2	4	1	2	2	1	6
Own Rec. for TD	0	0	0	0	0	0	0	0	0	0	0	0	0	0	0	0
Opp. Rec. by	8	13	15	15	10	13	10	13	13	11	13	11	15	10	10	6
Opp. Rec. for TD	0	2	0	0	0	1	1	1	3	1	2	0	2	1	0	0
Penalties	108	78	88	100	115	98	118	101	89	95	115	100	98	95	93	85
Yds. Penalized	886	664	698	836	892	768	1057	757	787	802	951	834	758	840	696	679
Total Points Scored	375	363	315	327	361	262	461	470	510	402	429	175	330	280	244	266
Total TDs	46	44	35	36	43	28	54	56	64	46	47	17	39	30	28	29
TDs Rushing	16	15	18	6	14	9	20	19	21	14	14	4	12	7	5	8
TDs Passing	27	26	16	27	26	16	30	34	34	28	27	12	23	20	18	21
TDs on Ret. and Rec.	3	3	1	3	3	3	4	3	9	4	6	1	4	3	5	0
Extra Point Kicks	45	42	31	33	41	25	48	54	60	45	43	16	39	28	24	26
Extra Point Kicks Att.	46	43	32	33	41	25	49	55	63	45	45	16	39	28	24	28
2Pt Conversions	0	0	2	2	1	1	3	0	0	0	2	0	0	0	2	0
2Pt Conversions Att.	0	1	3	2	1	3	5	1	1	1	2	1	0	2	4	1
Safeties	0	0	2	1	0	2	1	1	0	0	2	0	0	0	0	0
Field Goals Made	18	19	22	24	20	21	27	26	22	27	32	19	19	24	16	22
Field Goals Attempted	19	29	27	28	31	28	36	28	28	32	37	24	24	26	26	25
% Successful	94.7	65.5	81.5	85.7	64.5	75.0	75.0	92.9	78.6	84.4	86.5	79.2	79.2	92.3	61.5	88.0

NATIONAL FOOTBALL CONFERENCE DEFENSE

	Ariz.	Atl.	Car.	Chi.	Dall.	Det.	GB	Minn.	NO	NYG	Phil.	StL	SF	Sea.	TB	Wash.
First Downs	289	303	290	312	286	332	272	271	310	308	295	333	278	305	324	280
Rushing	81	89	109	105	74	95	68	63	111	103	81	127	77	80	129	85
Passing	188	197	155	186	186	213	168	183	175	182	179	182	176	204	171	176
Penalty	20	17	26	21	26	24	36	25	24	23	35	24	25	21	24	19
Rushes	402	433	450	467	365	458	371	357	435	423	413	500	426	428	529	449
Net Yds. Gained	1804	1711	1997	2022	1448	2025	1333	1394	1955	1773	1675	2201	1552	1776	2531	1799
Avg. Gain	4.5	4.0	4.4	4.3	4.0	4.4	3.6	3.9	4.5	4.2	4.1	4.4	3.6	4.1	4.8	4.0
Avg. Yds. per Game	112.8	106.9	124.8	126.4	90.5	126.6	83.3	87.1	122.2	110.8	104.7	137.6	97.0	111.0	158.2	112.4
Passes Attempted	593	536	495	531	572	545	540	535	574	498	580	491	580	568	482	511
Completed	346	335	305	341	344	371	294	341	330	314	354	315	352	374	301	314
% Completed	58.3	62.5	61.6	64.2	60.1	68.1	54.4	63.7	57.5	63.1	61.0	64.2	60.7	65.8	62.4	61.4
Total Yds. Gained	3998	4041	3249	3654	3874	4399	3450	3812	3961	3662	3778	3913	3963	4112	3484	3557
Times Sacked	43	28	31	35	42	26	37	48	35	32	44	25	44	28	28	40
Yds. Lost	259	170	193	272	268	150	232	318	192	237	316	149	293	185	166	241
Net Yds. Gained	3739	3871	3056	3382	3606	4249	3218	3494	3769	3425	3462	3764	3670	3927	3318	3316
Avg. Yds. per Game	233.7	241.9	191.0	211.4	225.4	265.6	201.1	218.4	235.6	214.1	216.4	235.3	229.4	245.4	207.4	207.3
Net Yds. per Pass Play	5.88	6.86	5.81	5.98	5.87	7.44	5.58	5.99	6.19	6.46	5.55	7.29	5.88	6.59	6.51	6.02
Yds. Gained per Comp.	11.55	12.06	10.65	10.72	11.26	11.86	11.73	11.18	12.00	11.66	10.67	12.42	11.26	10.99	11.57	11.33
Combined Net Yds. Gained	5543	5582	5053	5404	5054	6274	4551	4888	5724	5198	5137	5965	5222	5703	5849	5115
% Total Yds. Rushing	32.5	30.7	39.5	37.4	28.7	32.3	29.3	28.5	34.2	34.1	32.6	36.9	29.7	31.1	43.3	35.2
% Total Yds. Passing	67.5	69.3	60.5	62.6	71.3	67.7	70.7	71.5	65.8	65.9	67.4	63.1	70.3	68.9	56.7	64.8
Avg. Yds. per Game	346.4	348.9	315.8	337.8	315.9	392.1	284.4	305.5	357.8	324.9	321.1	372.8	326.4	356.4	365.6	319.7
Ball Control Plays	1038	997	976	1033	979	1029	948	940	1044	953	1037	1016	1050	1024	1039	1000
Avg. Yds. per Play	5.3	5.6	5.2	5.2	5.2	6.1	4.8	5.2	5.5	5.5	5.0	5.9	5.0	5.6	5.6	5.1
Avg. Time of Poss.	30:08	30:13	29:47	31:33	27:56	31:03	26:57	27:20	28:50	28:26	31:46	31:02	30:14	32:29	31:29	31:11
Third Down Efficiency	35.3	45.3	35.5	41.2	35.0	40.5	36.0	34.5	38.0	38.7	33.0	43.5	36.7	39.0	40.2	39.7
Intercepted By	21	15	22	13	11	9	30	11	26	13	25	8	18	13	19	11
Yds. Returned By	338	158	235	144	33	210	477	43	652	221	370	102	237	164	275	185
Returned for TD	1	1	1	1	1	2	3	0	5	2	2	1	1	2	2	0
Punts	84	62	74	71	92	66	74	89	71	72	80	75	95	82	72	70
Yds. Punted	3774	2632	3312	3026	4084	2878	3329	3979	3055	3169	3604	3326	4295	3872	3083	2929
Avg. Yds. per Punt	44.9	42.5	44.8	42.6	44.4	43.6	45.0	44.7	43.0	44.0	45.1	44.3	45.2	47.2	42.8	41.8
Punt Returns	47	27	41	34	38	41	40	33	25	28	39	41	57	43	38	32
Yds. Returned	493	289	452	272	314	354	403	260	358	258	229	260	495	479	311	220
Avg. Yds. per Return	10.5	10.7	11.0	8.0	8.3	8.6	10.1	7.9	14.3	9.2	5.9	6.3	8.7	11.1	8.2	6.9
Returned for TD	0	1	1	0	1	0	0	1	1	1	0	0	0	1	0	0
Kickoff Returns	61	46	51	64	47	58	80	91	74	77	81	43	65	46	46	56
Yds. Returned	1248	945	1267	1552	967	1353	1824	2060	1813	1619	1907	1032	1415	1059	878	1104
Avg. Yds. per Return	20.5	20.5	24.8	24.3	20.6	23.3	22.8	22.6	24.5	21.0	23.5	24.0	21.8	23.0	19.1	19.7
Returned for TD	0	0	1	0	0	1	0	0	0	0	0	1	1	0	0	0
Fumbles	20	23	28	27	23	26	24	35	18	28	25	26	29	21	18	21
Lost	8	13	15	15	10	14	10	13	13	11	13	12	15	10	10	6
Out of Bounds	5	1	1	3	4	1	1	6	1	4	2	2	3	1	2	4
Own Rec. for TD	0	0	0	0	0	0	0	0	0	0	0	0	0	0	0	0
Opp. Rec. by	18	8	11	7	10	9	8	11	15	17	10	12	10	12	5	12
Opp. Rec. for TD	0	0	2	0	0	0	0	2	2	1	0	3	0	0	0	2
Penalties	104	110	82	88	93	113	107	109	86	88	104	80	114	111	80	98
Yds. Penalized	840	892	632	744	768	944	914	902	717	678	789	613	969	971	731	763
Total Points Scored	325	325	308	375	250	494	297	312	341	427	337	436	281	390	400	336
Total TDs	38	38	36	43	28	57	36	36	37	54	39	54	28	46	46	34
TDs Rushing	13	10	15	14	7	18	5	5	19	21	11	24	12	17	16	10
TDs Passing	22	25	14	29	19	35	29	26	15	31	27	22	14	27	28	19
TDs on Ret. and Rec.	3	3	7	0	2	4	2	5	3	2	1	8	2	2	2	5
Extra Point Kicks	38	37	33	38	28	55	34	30	36	47	38	51	26	44	44	31
Extra Point Kicks Att.	38	38	33	40	28	55	34	31	36	51	38	52	27	44	46	31
2Pt Conversions	0	0	1	2	0	1	1	0	0	1	1	1	0	2	0	2
2Pt Conversions Att.	0	0	3	3	0	2	2	4	1	3	1	2	1	2	0	3
Safeties	1	0	0	0	0	1	3	0	1	0	0	1	0	0	1	2
Field Goals Made	19	20	19	25	18	31	13	22	27	18	21	19	29	22	26	31
Field Goals Attempted	25	28	27	33	26	34	17	26	32	21	24	22	34	31	32	36
% Successful	76.0	71.4	70.4	75.8	69.2	91.2	76.5	84.6	84.4	85.7	87.5	86.4	85.3	71.0	81.3	86.1

2009 TEAM STATISTICS

AFC, NFC, AND NFL SUMMARY

	AFC Offense Total	AFC Offense Average	AFC Defense Total	AFC Defense Average	NFC Offense Total	NFC Offense Average	NFC Defense Total	NFC Defense Average	NFL Total	NFL Average
First Downs	4795	299.7	4780	298.8	4773	298.3	4788	299.3	9568	299.0
Rushing	1616	101.0	1601	100.1	1462	91.4	1477	92.3	3078	96.2
Passing	2815	175.9	2825	176.6	2931	183.2	2921	182.6	5746	179.6
Penalty	364	22.8	354	22.1	380	23.8	390	24.4	744	23.3
Rushes	7357	459.8	7182	448.9	6731	420.7	6906	431.6	14088	440.3
Net Yds. Gained	31190	1949.4	30743	1921.4	28549	1784.3	28996	1812.3	59739	1866.8
Avg. Gain	—	4.2	—	4.3	—	4.2	—	4.2	—	4.2
Avg. Yds. per Game	—	121.8	—	120.1	—	111.5	—	113.3	—	116.7
Passes Attempted	8224	514.0	8402	525.1	8809	550.6	8631	539.4	17033	532.3
Completed	4981	311.3	5041	315.1	5391	336.9	5331	333.2	10372	324.1
% Completed	—	60.6	—	60.0	—	61.2	—	61.8	—	60.9
Total Yds. Gained	57343	3583.9	58010	3625.6	61574	3848.4	60907	3806.7	118917	3716.2
Times Sacked	524	32.8	535	33.4	577	36.1	566	35.4	1101	34.4
Yds. Lost	3309	206.8	3425	214.1	3757	234.8	3641	227.6	7066	220.8
Net Yds. Gained	54034	3377.1	54585	3411.6	57817	3613.6	57266	3579.1	111851	3495.3
Avg. Yds. per Game	—	211.1	—	213.2	—	225.8	—	223.7	—	218.5
Net Yds. per Pass Play	—	6.18	—	6.11	—	6.16	—	6.23	—	6.17
Yds. Gained per Comp.	—	11.51	—	11.51	—	11.42	—	11.43	—	11.47
Combined Net Yds. Gained	85224	5326.5	85328	5333.0	86366	5397.9	86262	5391.4	171590	5362.2
% Total Yds. Rushing	—	36.6	—	36.0	—	33.1	—	33.6	—	34.8
% Total Yds. Passing	—	63.4	—	64.0	—	66.9	—	66.4	—	65.2
Avg. Yds. per Game	—	332.9	—	333.3	—	337.4	—	337.0	—	335.1
Ball Control Plays	16105	1006.6	16119	1007.4	16117	1007.3	16103	1006.4	32222	1006.9
Avg. Yds. per Play	—	5.3	—	5.3	—	5.4	—	5.4	—	5.3
Third Down Efficiency	—	38.9	—	38.9	—	38.2	—	38.3	—	38.6
Interceptions	249	15.6	260	16.3	276	17.3	265	16.6	525	16.4
Yds. Returned	3590	224.4	3807	237.9	4061	253.8	3844	240.3	7651	239.1
Returned for TD	22	1.4	23	1.4	26	1.6	25	1.6	48	1.5
Punts	1223	76.4	1222	76.4	1228	76.8	1229	76.8	2451	76.6
Yds. Punted	53908	3369.3	53386	3336.6	53825	3364.1	54347	3396.7	107733	3366.7
Avg. Yds. per Punt	—	44.1	—	43.7	—	43.8	—	44.2	—	44.0
Punt Returns	580	36.3	578	36.1	602	37.6	604	37.8	1182	36.9
Yds. Returned	4895	305.9	4575	285.9	5127	320.4	5447	340.4	10022	313.2
Avg. Yds. per Return	—	8.4	—	7.9	—	8.5	—	9.0	—	8.5
Returned for TD	3	0.2	3	0.2	7	0.4	7	0.4	10	0.3
Kickoff Returns	1010	63.1	1018	63.6	994	62.1	986	61.6	2004	62.6
Yds. Returned	22811	1425.7	23298	1456.1	22530	1408.1	22043	1377.7	45341	1416.9
Avg. Yds. per Return	—	22.6	—	22.9	—	22.7	—	22.4	—	22.6
Returned for TD	12	0.8	14	0.9	6	0.4	4	0.3	18	0.6
Fumbles	352	22.0	358	22.4	398	24.9	392	24.5	750	23.4
Lost	171	10.7	159	9.9	176	11.0	188	11.8	347	10.8
Out of Bounds	33	2.1	31	1.9	39	2.4	41	2.6	72	2.3
Own Rec. for TD	1	0.1	1	0.1	0	0.0	0	0.0	1	0.0
Opp. Rec.	157	9.8	168	10.5	186	11.6	175	10.9	343	10.7
Opp. Rec. for TD	11	0.7	13	0.8	14	0.9	12	0.8	25	0.8
Penalties	1454	90.9	1463	91.4	1576	98.5	1567	97.9	3030	94.7
Yds. Penalized	12018	751.1	12056	753.5	12905	806.6	12867	804.2	24923	778.8
Total Points Scored	5421	338.8	5357	334.8	5570	348.1	5634	352.1	10991	343.5
Total TDs	605	37.8	597	37.3	642	40.1	650	40.6	1247	39.0
TDs Rushing	227	14.2	212	13.3	202	12.6	217	13.6	429	13.4
TDs Passing	325	20.3	328	20.5	385	24.1	382	23.9	710	22.2
TDs on Ret. and Rec.	53	3.3	57	3.6	55	3.4	51	3.2	108	3.4
Extra Point Kicks	565	35.3	555	34.7	600	37.5	610	38.1	1165	36.4
Extra Point Kicks Att.	573	35.8	563	35.2	612	38.3	622	38.9	1185	37.0
2Pt Conversions	11	0.7	12	0.8	13	0.8	12	0.8	24	0.8
2Pt Conversions Att.	32	2.0	33	2.1	28	1.8	27	1.7	60	1.9
Safeties	5	0.3	4	0.3	9	0.6	10	0.6	14	0.4
Field Goals Made	398	24.9	396	24.8	358	22.4	360	22.5	756	23.6
Field Goals Attempted	482	30.1	482	30.1	448	28.0	448	28.0	930	29.1
% Successful	—	82.6	—	82.2	—	79.9	—	80.4	—	81.3

CLUB LEADERS

	Offense	Defense
First Downs	New England 373	N.Y. Jets 237
Rushing	N.Y. Jets 132	Minnesota 63
Passing	Indianapolis 241	N.Y. Jets 128
Penalty	New England 37	Indianapolis 11
Rushes	N.Y. Jets 607	Minnesota 357
Net Yds. Gained	N.Y. Jets 2756	Green Bay 1333
Avg. Gain	Tennessee 5.2	Baltimore 3.4
Passes Attempted	Seattle 609	Oakland 438
Completed	Indianapolis 402	N.Y. Jets & Oak. 259
% Completed	New Orleans 69.5	N.Y. Jets 51.7
Total Yds. Gained	Houston 4803	N.Y. Jets 2704
Times Sacked	Indianapolis 13	Minnesota 48
Yds. Lost	Tennessee 73	Minnesota 318
Net Yds. Gained	Houston 4654	N.Y. Jets 2459
Net Yds. per Pass Play	San Diego 8.0	N.Y. Jets 4.6
Yds. Gained per Comp.	San Diego 13.3	Indianapolis 9.8
Combined Net Yds. Gained	New Orleans 6461	N.Y. Jets 4037
% Total Yds. Rushing	N.Y. Jets 53.7	Minnesota 28.5
% Total Yds. Passing	Indianapolis 77.7	Buffalo 54.1
Ball Control Plays	Miami 1088	Minnesota 940
Avg. Yds. per Play	Dallas 6.3	N.Y. Jets 4.2
Avg. Time of Poss.	Green Bay 33:03	—
Third Down Efficiency	Indianapolis 49.2	N.Y. Jets 31.5
Interceptions	—	Green Bay 30
Yds. Returned	—	New Orleans 652
Returned for TD	—	New Orleans 5
Punts	San Francisco 99	—
Yds. Punted	Oakland 4909	—
Avg. Yds. per Punt	Oakland 51.1	—
Punt Returns	N.Y. Jets 50	New England 20
Yds. Returned	Cincinnati 474	Houston 104
Avg. Yds. per Return	Philadelphia 13.5	Jacksonville 4.2
Returned for TD	Dallas & Philadelphia 2	—
Kickoff Returns	Detroit 96	Oakland 42
Yds. Returned	Detroit 2050	Tampa Bay 878
Avg. Yds. per Return	Tampa Bay 26.3	Cleveland 18.9
Returned for TD	Cleveland 3	—
Total Points Scored	New Orleans 510	N.Y. Jets 236
Total TDs	New Orleans 64	N.Y. Jets 26
TDs Rushing	Baltimore & Miami 22	Green Bay & Minnesota 5
TDs Passing	Indianapolis & Minnesota & New Orleans 34	N.Y. Jets 8
TDs on Ret. and Rec.	New Orleans 9	Chicago 0
Extra Point Kicks	New Orleans 60	N.Y. Jets 23
2-Point Conversions	Green Bay 3	—
Safeties	Carolina & Detroit & Houston & Philadelphia 2	—
Field Goals Made	Philadelphia & San Diego 32	Green Bay 13
Field Goals Attempted	Philadelphia 37	Green Bay 17
% Successful	Arizona 94.7	Dallas 69.2

NFL CLUB RANKINGS BY YARDS

	Offense			Defense		
	Total	Rush	Pass	Total	Rush	Pass
Arizona	14	28	12	20	17	23
Atlanta	16	15	14	21	10T	28
Baltimore	13	5	18	3	5	8T
Buffalo	30	16	30	19	30	2
Carolina	19	3	27	8	22	4
Chicago	23	29	17	17	23	13
Cincinnati	24	9	26	4	7	6
Cleveland	32	8	32	31	28	29
Dallas	2	7	6	9	4	20
Denver	15	18	13	7	26	3
Detroit	26	24	21	32	25	32
Green Bay	6	14	7	2	*1	5
Houston	4	30	*1	13T	10T	18
Indianapolis	9	32	2	18	24	14
Jacksonville	18	10	19	23	19	27
Kansas City	25	11	25	30	31	22
Miami	17	4	20	22	18	24
Minnesota	5	13	8	6	2	19
New England	3	12	3	11	13	12
New Orleans	*1	6	4	25	21	26
New York Giants	8	17	11	13T	14	15
New York Jets	20	*1	31	*1	8	*1
Oakland	31	21	29	26	29	7
Philadelphia	11	22	10	12	9	17
Pittsburgh	7	19	9	5	3	16
St. Louis	29	20	28	29	27	25
San Diego	10	31	5	16	20	11
San Francisco	27	25	22	15	6	21
Seattle	21	26	15	24	15	30
Tampa Bay	28	23	24	27	32	10
Tennessee	12	2	23	28	10T	31
Washington	22	27	16	10	16	8T

T = Tied for position * = League Leader

AFC TAKEAWAYS/GIVEAWAYS

	Takeaways			Giveaways			Net
	Int	Fum	Total	Int	Fum	Total	Diff.
Baltimore	22	10	32	13	9	22	+10
San Diego	14	11	25	10	7	17	+8
Denver	17	13	30	13	10	23	+7
New England	18	10	28	13	9	22	+6
Buffalo	28	5	33	19	11	30	+3
Indianapolis	16	10	26	19	5	24	+2
Jacksonville	15	10	25	10	13	23	+2
Kansas City	15	13	28	17	10	27	+1
N.Y. Jets	17	14	31	21	9	30	+1
Cincinnati	19	6	25	13	12	25	0
Houston	14	13	27	17	11	28	-1
Pittsburgh	12	10	22	14	11	25	-3
Tennessee	20	7	27	15	16	31	-4
Miami	15	6	21	19	10	29	-8
Cleveland	10	9	19	18	13	31	-12
Oakland	8	12	20	18	15	33	-13
Totals	260	159	419	249	171	420	-1

NFC TAKEAWAYS/GIVEAWAYS

	Takeaways			Giveaways			Net
	Int	Fum	Total	Int	Fum	Total	Diff.
Green Bay	30	10	40	8	8	16	+24
Philadelphia	25	13	38	13	10	23	+15
New Orleans	26	13	39	12	16	28	+11
San Francisco	18	15	33	14	10	24	+9
Carolina	22	15	37	20	11	31	+6
Minnesota	11	13	24	7	11	18	+6
Atlanta	15	13	28	17	8	25	+3
Dallas	11	10	21	9	10	19	+2
Tampa Bay	19	10	29	29	5	34	-5
Chicago	13	15	28	27	7	34	-6
Arizona	21	8	29	18	18	36	-7
N.Y. Giants	13	11	24	14	17	31	-7
Seattle	13	10	23	19	12	31	-8
Washington	11	6	17	16	12	28	-11
St. Louis	8	12	20	21	12	33	-13
Detroit	9	14	23	32	9	41	-18
Totals	265	188	453	276	176	452	+1

2009 INDIVIDUAL STATISTICS—SCORING

SCORING

POINTS

AFC: 146 Nate Kaeding, San Diego
NFC: 139 David Akers, Philadelphia

TOUCHDOWNS

NFC: 18 Adrian Peterson, Minnesota
AFC: 16 Chris Johnson, Tennessee
16 Maurice Jones-Drew, Jacksonville

EXTRA POINT KICKS

NFC: 54 Ryan Longwell, Minnesota
AFC: 50 Nate Kaeding, San Diego

TWO-POINT EXTRA POINT PLAYS

NFC: 2 Greg Jennings, Green Bay
AFC: 1 Jamaal Charles, Kansas City
1 Braylon Edwards, Cleveland-N.Y. Jets
1 David Garrard, Jacksonville
1 Andre Johnson, Houston
1 Chris Johnson, Tennessee
1 Dustin Keller, N.Y. Jets
1 Brian Leonard, Cincinnati
1 Jamal Lewis, Cleveland
1 Randy Moss, New England
1 Carson Palmer, Cincinnati
1 Ricky Williams, Miami

FIELD GOALS

AFC: 32 Nate Kaeding, San Diego
NFC: 32 David Akers, Philadelphia

FIELD GOAL ATTEMPTS

NFC: 37 David Akers, Philadelphia
AFC: 36 Jay Feely, N.Y. Jets

LONGEST FIELD GOAL

AFC: 61 Sebastian Janikowski, Oakland at Cleveland, December 27
NFC: 55 Josh Brown, St. Louis vs. Seattle, November 29

MOST POINTS, GAME

AFC: 18 Chris Johnson, Tennessee vs. Houston, September 20 (3 TD)
18 Maurice Jones-Drew, Jacksonville at Houston, September 27 (3 TD)
18 Maurice Jones-Drew, Jacksonville vs. St. Louis, October 18 (3 TD) - (OT)
18 Randy Moss, New England vs. Tennessee, October 18 (3 TD)
18 Ricky Williams, Miami vs. New Orleans, October 25 (3 TD)
18 Ryan Moats, Houston at Buffalo, November 1 (3 TD)
18 Ricky Williams, Miami at Carolina, November 19 (3 TD)
18 Dallas Clark, Indianapolis vs. Denver, December 13 (3 TD)
18 Chris Johnson, Tennessee vs. St. Louis, December 13 (3 TD)
18 Jerome Harrison, Cleveland at Kansas City, December 20 (3 TD)
18 Darren Sproles, San Diego at Tennessee, December 25 (3 TD)
18 Randy Moss, New England vs. Jacksonville, December 27 (3 TD)
18 Willis McGahee, Baltimore at Oakland, January 3 (3 TD)

NFC: 18 Adrian Peterson, Minnesota at Cleveland, September 13 (3 TD)
18 Michael Turner, Atlanta at San Francisco, October 11 (3 TD)
18 Vernon Davis, San Francisco at Houston, October 25 (3 TD)
18 Greg Olsen, Chicago vs. Arizona, November 8 (3 TD)
18 Brandon Jackson, Green Bay vs. Seattle, December 27 (3 TD)

TEAM LEADERS, POINTS

AFC: BALTIMORE, 84, Willis McGahee; BUFFALO, 108, Rian Lindell; CINCINNATI, 97, Shayne Graham; CLEVELAND, 69, Phil Dawson; DENVER, 122, Matt Prater; HOUSTON, 106, Kris Brown; INDIANAPOLIS, 78, Joseph Addai; JACKSONVILLE, 96, Maurice Jones-Drew; KANSAS CITY, 104, *Ryan Succop; MIAMI, 112, Dan Carpenter; NEW ENGLAND, 125, Stephen Gostkowski; N.Y. JETS, 122, Jay Feely; OAKLAND, 95, Sebastian Janikowski; PITTSBURGH, 122, Jeff Reed; SAN DIEGO, 146, Nate Kaeding; TENNESSEE, 118, Rob Bironas

NFC: ARIZONA, 85, Neil Rackers; ATLANTA, 68, Jason Elam; CAROLINA, 97, John Kasay; CHICAGO, 105, Robbie Gould; DALLAS, 90, Nick Folk; DETROIT, 88, Jason Hanson; GREEN BAY, 129, Mason Crosby; MINNESOTA, 132, Ryan Longwell; NEW ORLEANS, 89, John Carney; N.Y. GIANTS, 126, Lawrence Tynes; PHILADELPHIA, 139, David Akers; ST. LOUIS, 73, Josh Brown; SAN FRANCISCO, 84, Joe Nedney; SEATTLE, 100, Olindo Mare; TAMPA BAY, 54, Connor Barth; WASHINGTON, 74, Shaun Suisham

TEAM CHAMPION

NFC: 510 New Orleans
AFC: 454 San Diego

NFL TOP TEN SCORERS—KICKERS

	XP	XPA	FG	FGA	PTS
Kaeding, Nate, S.D.	50	51	32	35	146
Akers, David, Phi.	43	45	32	37	139
Longwell, Ryan, Min.	54	55	26	28	132
Crosby, Mason, G.B.	48	49	27	36	129
Tynes, Lawrence, NY-G	45	45	27	32	126
Gostkowski, Stephen, N.E.	47	47	26	31	125
Feely, Jay, NYJ	32	32	30	36	122
Prater, Matt, Den.	32	32	30	35	122
Reed, Jeff, Pit.	41	41	27	31	122
Bironas, Rob, Ten.	37	37	27	32	118

NFL TOP TEN SCORERS—NONKICKERS

	TD	TDR	TDP	TDM	2-PT.	PTS
Peterson, Adrian, Min.	18	18	0	0	0	108
Johnson, Chris, Ten.	16	14	2	0	1	98
Jones-Drew, Maurice, Jac.	16	15	1	0	0	96
Jones, Thomas, NYJ	14	14	0	0	0	84
McGahee, Willis, Bal.	14	12	2	0	0	84
Moss, Randy, N.E.	13	0	13	0	1	80
Williams, Ricky, Mia.	13	11	2	0	1	80
Addai, Joseph, Ind.	13	10	3	0	0	78
Davis, Vernon, S.F.	13	0	13	0	0	78
Fitzgerald, Larry, Ariz	13	0	13	0	0	78
Gore, Frank, S.F.	13	10	3	0	0	78

AFC—INDIVIDUAL SCORERS

KICKERS

	XP	XPA	FG	FGA	PTS
Kaeding, Nate, S.D.	50	51	32	35	146
Gostkowski, Stephen, N.E.	47	47	26	31	125
Feely, Jay, NYJ	32	32	30	36	122
Prater, Matt, Den.	32	32	30	35	122
Reed, Jeff, Pit.	41	41	27	31	122
Bironas, Rob, Ten.	37	37	27	32	118
Carpenter, Dan, Mia.	37	38	25	28	112
Lindell, Rian, Buf.	24	24	28	33	108
Brown, Kris, Hou.	43	44	21	32	106
* Succop, Ryan, K.C.	29	29	25	29	104
Graham, Shayne, Cin.	28	29	23	28	97
Janikowski, Sebastian, Oak.	17	17	26	29	95
Scobee, Josh, Jac.	30	31	18	28	84
Cundiff, Billy, Cle.-Bal.	23	23	18	23	77
Dawson, Phil, Cle.	18	19	17	19	69
Stover, Matt, Ind.	33	33	9	11	60
Hauschka, Steven, Bal.	27	28	9	13	54
Vinatieri, Adam, Ind.	17	18	7	9	38

NONKICKERS

	TD	TDR	TDP	TDM	2-PT.	PTS
Johnson, Chris, Ten.	16	14	2	0	1	98
Jones-Drew, Maurice, Jac.	16	15	1	0	0	96
Jones, Thomas, NYJ	14	14	0	0	0	84
McGahee, Willis, Bal.	14	12	2	0	0	84
Moss, Randy, N.E.	13	0	13	0	1	80
Williams, Ricky, Mia.	13	11	2	0	1	80
Addai, Joseph, Ind.	13	10	3	0	0	78
Tomlinson, LaDainian, S.D.	12	12	0	0	0	72
Clark, Dallas, Ind.	10	0	10	0	0	60
Marshall, Brandon, Den.	10	0	10	0	0	60
Wayne, Reggie, Ind.	10	0	10	0	0	60
Charles, Jamaal, K.C.	9	7	1	1	1	56
Johnson, Andre, Hou.	9	0	9	0	1	56
Jackson, Vincent, S.D.	9	0	9	0	0	54
Maroney, Laurence, N.E.	9	9	0	0	0	54
* Moreno, Knowshon, Den.	9	7	2	0	0	54
Ochocinco, Chad, Cin.	9	0	9	0	0	54
Brown, Ronnie, Mia.	8	8	0	0	0	48
Gates, Antonio, S.D.	8	0	8	0	0	48
Mendenhall, Rashard, Pit.	8	7	1	0	0	48
Rice, Ray, Bal.	8	7	1	0	0	48
Sproles, Darren, S.D.	8	3	4	1	0	48
* Collie, Austin, Ind.	7	0	7	0	0	42
Evans, Lee, Buf.	7	0	7	0	0	42
Harrison, Jerome, Cle.	7	5	2	0	0	42
Jones, Jacoby, Hou.	7	0	6	1	0	42
Mason, Derrick, Bal.	7	0	7	0	0	42
Sims-Walker, Mike, Jac.	7	0	7	0	0	42
Slaton, Steve, Hou.	7	3	4	0	0	42
Benson, Cedric, Cin.	6	6	0	0	0	36
Cribbs, Josh, Cle.	6	1	1	4	0	36
Heap, Todd, Bal.	6	0	6	0	0	36
Miller, Heath, Pit.	6	0	6	0	0	36
Owens, Terrell, Buf.	6	1	5	0	0	36
* Wallace, Mike, Pit.	6	0	6	0	0	36
Ward, Hines, Pit.	6	0	6	0	0	36
Washington, Nate, Ten.	6	0	6	0	0	36
Chambers, Chris, S.D.-K.C.	5	0	5	0	0	30
Coles, Laveranues, Cin.	5	0	5	0	0	30
Daniels, Owen, Hou.	5	0	5	0	0	30
Holmes, Santonio, Pit.	5	0	5	0	0	30
Moats, Ryan, Hou.	5	4	1	0	0	30
Watson, Benjamin, N.E.	5	0	5	0	0	30
Edwards, Braylon, NYJ	4	0	4	0	1	26
Bowe, Dwayne, K.C.	4	0	4	0	0	24
Cotchery, Jerricho, NYJ	4	1	3	0	0	24
Garcon, Pierre, Ind.	4	0	4	0	0	24
* Hartline, Brian, Mia.	4	1	3	0	0	24
Jackson, Fred, Buf.	4	2	2	0	0	24
* Murphy, Louis, Oak.	4	0	4	0	0	24
Stokley, Brandon, Den.	4	0	4	0	0	24
Taylor, Fred, N.E.	4	4	0	0	0	24
Tolbert, Mike, S.D.	4	1	3	0	0	24
Welker, Wes, N.E.	4	0	4	0	0	24
Garrard, David, Jac.	3	3	0	0	1	20
Palmer, Carson, Cin.	3	3	0	0	1	20
* Britt, Kenny, Ten.	3	0	3	0	0	18
Brown, Chris, Hou.	3	3	0	0	0	18
* Brown, Donald, Ind.	3	3	0	0	0	18
Bush, Michael, Oak.	3	3	0	0	0	18
Caldwell, Andre, Cin.	3	0	3	0	0	18
Fargas, Justin, Oak.	3	3	0	0	0	18
Faulk, Kevin, N.E.	3	2	1	0	0	18
* Foster, Arian, Hou.	3	3	0	0	0	18
Gage, Justin, Ten.	3	0	3	0	0	18
Ginn, Ted Jr., Mia.	3	0	1	2	0	18
Hilliard, Lex, Mia.	3	1	2	0	0	18
* Massaquoi, Mohamed, Cle.	3	0	3	0	0	18
Miller, Zach, Oak.	3	0	3	0	0	18
* Sanchez, Mark, NYJ	3	3	0	0	0	18
Simpson, Chad, Ind.	3	2	0	1	0	18
Smith, Brad, NYJ	3	1	0	2	0	18
Keller, Dustin, NYJ	2	0	2	0	1	14
Aiken, Sam, N.E.	2	0	2	0	0	12
Anderson, Derek, Cle.	2	2	0	0	0	12
Baker, Chris, N.E.	2	0	2	0	0	12
Bess, Davone, Mia.	2	0	2	0	0	12
Bradley, Mark, K.C.	2	0	2	0	0	12
Clayton, Mark, Bal.	2	0	2	0	0	12
Fasano, Anthony, Mia.	2	0	2	0	0	12
Foschi, J.P., Cin.	2	0	2	0	0	12
Fuller, Vincent, Ten.	2	0	0	2	0	12
Gaffney, Jabar, Den.	2	0	2	0	0	12
* Greene, Shonn, NYJ	2	2	0	0	0	12
Haynos, Joey, Mia.	2	0	2	0	0	12
Henry, Chris, Cin.	2	0	2	0	0	12
Hester, Jacob, S.D.	2	0	0	2	0	12
Johnson, Derrick, K.C.	2	0	0	2	0	12
Lewis, Marcedes, Jac.	2	0	2	0	0	12
Lynch, Marshawn, Buf.	2	2	0	0	0	12
McClain, Le'Ron, Bal.	2	2	0	0	0	12
* Miller, Zach, Jac.	2	0	2	0	0	12
Moore, Mewelde, Pit.	2	0	2	0	0	12
Morris, Sammy, N.E.	2	2	0	0	0	12
Naanee, Legedu, S.D.	2	0	2	0	0	12
Pollard, Bernard, Hou.	2	0	0	2	0	12
Roethlisberger, Ben, Pit.	2	2	0	0	0	12
Royal, Eddie, Den.	2	0	0	2	0	12
Ryan, Sean, K.C.	2	0	2	0	0	12
Scheffler, Tony, Den.	2	0	2	0	0	12
Schilens, Chaz, Oak.	2	0	2	0	0	12
Stuckey, Chansi, NYJ-Cle.	2	0	2	0	0	12
Wade, Bobby, K.C.	2	0	2	0	0	12
Walter, Kevin, Hou.	2	0	2	0	0	12
Washington, Kelley, Bal.	2	0	2	0	0	12
White, LenDale, Ten.	2	2	0	0	0	12
Young, Vince, Ten.	2	2	0	0	0	12
* Ayers, Robert, Den.	1	0	0	1	0	6
Barber, Dominique, Hou.	1	0	0	1	0	6
Bodden, Leigh, N.E.	1	0	0	1	0	6
Brady, Tom, N.E.	1	1	0	0	0	6
Buckhalter, Correll, Den.	1	1	0	0	0	6
* Butler, Darius, N.E.	1	0	0	1	0	6
Carter, Tyrone, Pit.	1	0	0	1	0	6
Castille, Tim, K.C.	1	0	1	0	0	6

2009 INDIVIDUAL STATISTICS—SCORING

	TD	TDR	TDP	TDM	2-PT.	PTS
Clowney, David, NYJ	1	0	1	0	0	6
Collins, Kerry, Ten.	1	1	0	0	0	6
Cox, Mike, K.C.	1	1	0	0	0	6
Crumpler, Alge, Ten.	1	0	1	0	0	6
* Davis, Vontae, Mia.	1	0	0	1	0	6
Denney, Ryan, Buf.	1	0	1	0	0	6
Dixon, Dennis, Pit.	1	1	0	0	0	6
Douglas, Marques, NYJ	1	0	0	1	0	6
Dreessen, Joel, Hou.	1	0	1	0	0	6
* Edelman, Julian, N.E.	1	0	1	0	0	6
Edwards, Dwan, Bal.	1	0	0	1	0	6
Fanene, Jonathan, Cin.	1	0	0	1	0	6
Finnegan, Cortland, Ten.	1	0	0	1	0	6
Fitzpatrick, Ryan, Buf.	1	1	0	0	0	6
Floyd, Malcom, S.D.	1	0	1	0	0	6
Fox, Keyaron, Pit.	1	0	0	1	0	6
Gaines, Michael, Cle.	1	0	1	0	0	6
Geathers, Robert, Cin.	1	0	0	1	0	6
Goodman, Andre', Den.	1	0	0	1	0	6
Graham, Daniel, Den.	1	0	1	0	0	6
Hart, Mike, Ind.	1	1	0	0	0	6
Hartsock, Ben, NYJ	1	0	1	0	0	6
Heiden, Steve, Cle.	1	0	1	0	0	6
Henne, Chad, Mia.	1	1	0	0	0	6
* Heyward-Bey, Darrius, Oak.	1	0	1	0	0	6
Hillis, Peyton, Den.	1	1	0	0	0	6
Hood, Roderick, Ten.	1	0	0	1	0	6
* Hoyer, Brian, N.E.	1	1	0	0	0	6
Hughes, Nate, Jac.	1	0	1	0	0	6
* Jennings, Chris, Cle.	1	1	0	0	0	6
* Jennings, Rashad, Jac.	1	1	0	0	0	6
Joseph, Johnathan, Cin.	1	0	0	1	0	6
* Lacey, Jacob, Ind.	1	0	0	1	0	6
Landry, Dawan, Bal.	1	0	0	1	0	6
Leach, Vonta, Hou.	1	0	1	0	0	6
McFadden, Darren, Oak.	1	1	0	0	0	6
McGraw, Jon, K.C.	1	0	0	1	0	6
Meriweather, Brandon, N.E.	1	0	0	1	0	6
* Nelson, Shawn, Buf.	1	0	1	0	0	6
Oliver, Paul, S.D.	1	0	0	1	0	6
Parker, Willie, Pit.	1	0	1	0	0	6
Pope, Leonard, K.C.	1	0	1	0	0	6
Quinn, Brady, Cle.	1	1	0	0	0	6
Reed, Ed, Bal.	1	0	0	1	0	6
Reed, Josh, Buf.	1	0	1	0	0	6
Revis, Darrelle, NYJ	1	0	0	1	0	6
Rivers, Philip, S.D.	1	1	0	0	0	6
Royal, Robert, Cle.	1	0	1	0	0	6
Scaife, Bo, Ten.	1	0	1	0	0	6
Schobel, Aaron, Buf.	1	0	0	1	0	6
* Scott, Bernard, Cin.	1	0	0	1	0	6
Session, Clint, Ind.	1	0	0	1	0	6
Smith, Troy, Bal.	1	1	0	0	0	6
Spaeth, Matt, Pit.	1	0	1	0	0	6
* Sperry, Kory, Mia.	1	0	1	0	0	6
Studebaker, Andy, K.C.	1	0	0	1	0	6
Taylor, Jason, Mia.	1	0	0	1	0	6
* Thomas, Mike, Jac.	1	0	1	0	0	6
Vickers, Lawrence, Cle.	1	0	1	0	0	6
Vrabel, Mike, K.C.	1	0	1	0	0	6
* Webb, Lardarius, Bal.	1	0	0	1	0	6
Weddle, Eric, S.D.	1	0	0	1	0	6
Whitner, Donte, Buf.	1	0	0	1	0	6
Wilford, Ernest, Jac.	1	0	1	0	0	6
Williams, Demetrius, Bal.	1	0	1	0	0	6
Wilson, Kris, S.D.	1	0	1	0	0	6
Woodley, LaMarr, Pit.	1	0	0	1	0	6
* Cushing, Brian, Hou.	0	0	0	0	0	^2
Diles, Zac, Hou.	0	0	0	0	0	^2
Hali, Tamba, K.C.	0	0	0	0	0	^2
Leonard, Brian, Cin.	0	0	0	0	1	2
Lewis, Jamal, Cle.	0	0	0	0	1	2

*^ Safety; *Player that was a rookie in 2009*
Team safety credited to Baltimore, Jacksonville, and San Diego

NFC—INDIVIDUAL SCORERS

KICKERS

	XP	XPA	FG	FGA	PTS
Akers, David, Phi.	43	45	32	37	139
Longwell, Ryan, Min.	54	55	26	28	132
Crosby, Mason, G.B.	48	49	27	36	129
Tynes, Lawrence, NY-G	45	45	27	32	126
Gould, Robbie, Chi.	33	33	24	28	105
Mare, Olindo, Sea.	28	28	24	26	100
Kasay, John, Car.	31	32	22	27	97
Folk, Nick, Dal.	36	36	18	28	90
Carney, John, N.O.	50	52	13	17	89
Hanson, Jason, Det.	25	25	21	28	88
Rackers, Neil, Ariz	37	38	16	17	85
Suisham, Shaun, Was.-Dal.	25	26	20	24	85
Nedney, Joe, S.F.	33	33	17	21	84
Brown, Josh, St.L	16	16	19	24	73
Elam, Jason, Atl.	32	33	12	19	68
Barth, Connor, T.B.	12	12	14	19	54
Hartley, Garrett, N.O.	10	11	9	11	37
Bryant, Matt, Atl.	10	10	7	10	31
Nugent, Mike, T.B.-Ariz	14	14	4	8	26
* Gano, Graham, Was.	6	7	4	4	18
Andrus, Shane, T.B.-S.F.	10	10	0	1	10
Schmitt, Ricky, S.F.	2	2	2	3	8

NONKICKERS

	TD	TDR	TDP	TDM	X2G	PTS
Peterson, Adrian, Min.	18	18	0	0	0	108
Davis, Vernon, S.F.	13	0	13	0	0	78
Fitzgerald, Larry, Ariz	13	0	13	0	0	78
Gore, Frank, S.F.	13	10	3	0	0	78
Jackson, DeSean, Phi.	12	1	9	2	0	72
Austin, Miles, Dal.	11	0	11	0	0	66
Grant, Ryan, G.B.	11	11	0	0	0	66
Shiancoe, Visanthe, Min.	11	0	11	0	0	66
Stewart, Jonathan, Car.	11	10	1	0	0	66
White, Roddy, Atl.	11	0	11	0	0	66
Meachem, Robert, N.O.	10	0	9	1	0	60
Turner, Michael, Atl.	10	10	0	0	0	60
Colston, Marques, N.O.	9	0	9	0	0	54
Bush, Reggie, N.O.	8	5	3	0	0	48
Celek, Brent, Phi.	8	0	8	0	0	48
* Harvin, Percy, Min.	8	0	6	2	0	48
Hightower, Tim, Ariz	8	8	0	0	0	48
Olsen, Greg, Chi.	8	0	8	0	0	48
Rice, Sidney, Min.	8	0	8	0	0	48
Thomas, Pierre, N.O.	8	6	2	0	0	48
Smith, Steve, Car.	7	0	7	0	1	44
Williams, DeAngelo, Car.	7	7	0	0	1	44
Barber, Marion, Dal.	7	7	0	0	0	42
Bradshaw, Ahmad, NY-G	7	7	0	0	0	42
Carlson, John, Sea.	7	0	7	0	0	42
Crayton, Patrick, Dal.	7	0	5	2	0	42
Smith, Steve, NY-G	7	0	7	0	0	42
* Wells, Beanie, Ariz	7	7	0	0	0	42
Williams, Cadillac, T.B.	7	4	3	0	0	42
Williams, Roy E., Dal.	7	0	7	0	0	42
Davis, Fred, Was.	6	0	6	0	0	36
Driver, Donald, G.B.	6	0	6	0	0	36
Gonzalez, Tony, Atl.	6	0	6	0	0	36

2009 INDIVIDUAL STATISTICS—SCORING

	TD	TDR	TDP	TDM	2-PT.	PTS
Jacobs, Brandon, NY-G	6	5	1	0	0	36
* Knox, Johnny, Chi.	6	0	5	1	0	36
* Nicks, Hakeem, NY-G	6	0	6	0	0	36
Smith, Kevin, Det.	5	4	1	0	0	^32
Avery, Donnie, St.L	5	0	5	0	0	30
Bell, Mike, N.O.	5	5	0	0	0	30
Boldin, Anquan, Ariz	5	1	4	0	0	30
Boss, Kevin, NY-G	5	0	5	0	0	30
Finley, Jermichael, G.B.	5	0	5	0	0	30
Forsett, Justin, Sea.	5	4	1	0	0	30
Johnson, Calvin, Det.	5	0	5	0	0	30
Jones, James, G.B.	5	0	5	0	0	30
Manningham, Mario, NY-G	5	0	5	0	0	30
Rodgers, Aaron, G.B.	5	5	0	0	0	30
Snelling, Jason, Atl.	5	4	1	0	0	30
Winslow, Kellen, T.B.	5	0	5	0	0	30
Jennings, Greg, G.B.	4	0	4	0	2	28
Forté, Matt, Chi.	4	4	0	0	1	26
* McCoy, LeSean, Phi.	4	4	0	0	1	26
Aromashodu, Devin, Chi.	4	0	4	0	0	24
Berrian, Bernard, Min.	4	0	4	0	0	24
Bryant, Antonio, T.B.	4	0	4	0	0	24
Havner, Spencer, G.B.	4	0	4	0	0	24
Jackson, Steven, St.L	4	4	0	0	0	24
Jones, Julius, Sea.	4	2	2	0	0	24
* Maclin, Jeremy, Phi.	4	0	4	0	0	24
Weaver, Leonard, Phi.	4	2	2	0	0	24
Avant, Jason, Phi.	3	0	3	0	1	20
Bennett, Earl, Chi.	3	0	2	1	1	20
Choice, Tashard, Dal.	3	3	0	0	1	20
Jackson, Brandon, G.B.	3	2	1	0	1	20
Breaston, Steve, Ariz	3	0	3	0	0	18
Burleson, Nate, Sea.	3	0	3	0	0	18
Davis, Kellen, Chi.	3	0	3	0	0	18
Evans, Heath, N.O.	3	1	2	0	0	18
Fells, Daniel, St.L	3	0	3	0	0	18
Ganther, Quinton, Was.	3	3	0	0	0	18
Heller, Will, Det.	3	0	3	0	0	18
Hester, Devin, Chi.	3	0	3	0	0	18
Houshmandzadeh, T.J., Sea.	3	0	3	0	0	18
Johnson, Bryant, Det.	3	0	3	0	0	18
Jones, Felix, Dal.	3	3	0	0	0	18
King, Jeff, Car.	3	0	3	0	0	18
Kuhn, John, G.B.	3	1	2	0	0	18
Morgan, Josh, S.F.	3	0	3	0	0	18
Moss, Santana, Was.	3	0	3	0	0	18
Sharper, Darren, N.O.	3	0	0	3	0	18
Shockey, Jeremy, N.O.	3	0	3	0	0	18
Thomas, Devin, Was.	3	0	3	0	0	18
Ward, Derrick, T.B.	3	1	2	0	0	18
Woodson, Charles, G.B.	3	0	0	3	0	18
Yoder, Todd, Was.	3	0	3	0	0	18
* Delmas, Louis, Det.	2	0	0	2	0	^14
Morris, Maurice, Det.	2	2	0	0	1	14
Betts, Ladell, Was.	2	2	0	0	0	12
Branch, Deion, Sea.	2	0	2	0	0	12
Brees, Drew, N.O.	2	2	0	0	0	12
Brown, Sheldon, Phi.	2	0	0	2	0	12
Clark, Desmond, Chi.	2	0	2	0	0	12
Cooley, Chris, Was.	2	0	2	0	0	12
* Crabtree, Michael, S.F.	2	0	2	0	0	12
Dugan, Jeff, Min.	2	0	2	0	0	12
Hamilton, Lynell, N.O.	2	2	0	0	0	12
Henderson, Devery, N.O.	2	0	2	0	0	12
Hill, Jason, S.F.	2	0	2	0	0	12
Hixon, Domenik, NY-G	2	0	1	1	0	12
Hoover, Brad, Car.	2	1	1	0	0	12
Jackson, Tanard, T.B.	2	0	0	2	0	12
McNabb, Donovan, Phi.	2	2	0	0	0	12
Moore, Lance, N.O.	2	0	2	0	0	12
Nelson, Jordy, G.B.	2	0	2	0	0	12
Patrick, Ben, Ariz	2	0	2	0	0	12
Peelle, Justin, Atl.	2	0	2	0	0	12
* Pettigrew, Brandon, Det.	2	0	2	0	0	12
Portis, Clinton, Was.	2	1	1	0	0	12
Rosario, Dante, Car.	2	0	2	0	0	12
Sellers, Mike, Was.	2	0	2	0	0	12
* Stafford, Matthew, Det.	2	2	0	0	0	12
* Stephens-Howling, LaRod, Ariz	2	0	1	1	0	12
* Stroughter, Sammie, T.B.	2	0	1	1	0	12
Taylor, Chester, Min.	2	1	1	0	0	12
Vick, Michael, Phi.	2	2	0	0	0	12
Weems, Eric, Atl.	2	0	2	0	0	12
Westbrook, Brian, Phi.	2	1	1	0	0	12
Wilson, Josh, Sea.	2	0	0	2	0	12
Witten, Jason, Dal.	2	0	2	0	0	12
Wright, Jason, Ariz	2	0	2	0	0	12
Allen, Jared, Min.	1	0	0	1	0	^8
Clayton, Michael, T.B.	1	0	1	0	1	8
Abiamiri, Victor, Phi.	1	0	0	1	0	6
Amendola, Danny, St.L	1	0	1	0	0	6
Ayodele, Remi, N.O.	1	0	0	1	0	6
Barber, Ronde, T.B.	1	0	0	1	0	6
Becht, Anthony, Ariz	1	0	1	0	0	6
Biermann, Kroy, Atl.	1	0	0	1	0	6
Booker, Marty, Atl.	1	0	1	0	0	6
* Brown, Aaron, Det.	1	0	1	0	0	6
Buckley, Eldra, Phi.	1	1	0	0	0	6
Campbell, Jason, Was.	1	1	0	0	0	6
Carr, David, NY-G	1	1	0	0	0	6
Cartwright, Rock, Was.	1	0	1	0	0	6
Clements, Nate, S.F.	1	0	0	1	0	6
* Coffee, Glen, S.F.	1	1	0	0	0	6
Cutler, Jay, Chi.	1	1	0	0	0	6
Dinkins, Darnell, N.O.	1	0	1	0	0	6
Doucet, Early, Ariz	1	0	1	0	0	6
* Gibson, Brandon, St.L	1	0	1	0	0	6
Green, Ahman, G.B.	1	1	0	0	0	6
Greer, Jabari, N.O.	1	0	0	1	0	6
Griffith, Justin, Sea.	1	0	1	0	0	6
Hagan, Derek, NY-G	1	0	1	0	0	6
Hargrove, Anthony, N.O.	1	0	0	1	0	6
Hedgecock, Madison, NY-G	1	0	1	0	0	6
Hill, Tye, Atl.	1	0	0	1	0	6
Hurd, Sam, Dal.	1	0	1	0	0	6
James, William, Det.	1	0	0	1	0	6
Jarrett, Dwayne, Car.	1	0	1	0	0	6
Jenkins, Michael, Atl.	1	0	1	0	0	6
* Johnson, Bruce, NY-G	1	0	0	1	0	6
Kolb, Kevin, Phi.	1	1	0	0	0	6
Lee, Donald, G.B.	1	0	1	0	0	6
Lewis, Greg, Min.	1	0	1	0	0	6
Little, Leonard, St.L	1	0	0	1	0	6
* Matthews, Clay, G.B.	1	0	0	1	0	6
McDonald, Ray, S.F.	1	0	0	1	0	6
* McKillop, Scott, S.F.	1	0	0	1	0	6
McMichael, Randy, St.L	1	0	1	0	0	6
Moss, Sinorice, NY-G	1	0	1	0	0	6
Mughelli, Ovie, Atl.	1	0	1	0	0	6
Muhammad, Muhsin, Car.	1	0	1	0	0	6
Newman, Terence, Dal.	1	0	0	1	0	6
Norris, Moran, S.F.	1	1	0	0	0	6
Northcutt, Dennis, Det.	1	0	1	0	0	6
Norwood, Jerious, Atl.	1	0	1	0	0	6
Peppers, Julius, Car.	1	0	0	1	0	6
Porter, Tracy, N.O.	1	0	0	1	0	6
* Reed, Nick, Sea.	1	0	0	1	0	6
Robinson, Laurent, St.L	1	0	1	0	0	6

2009 INDIVIDUAL STATISTICS—SCORING

	TD	TDR	TDP	TDM	2-PT.	PTS
Roby, Courtney, N.O.	1	0	0	1	0	6
Rodgers-Cromartie, Dominique, Ariz	1	0	0	1	0	6
Rolle, Antrel, Ariz	1	0	0	1	0	6
Romo, Tony, Dal.	1	1	0	0	0	6
Ryan, Matt, Atl.	1	1	0	0	0	6
Schmitt, Owen, Sea.	1	0	1	0	0	6
* Sidbury, Lawrence, Atl.	1	0	0	1	0	6
Smith, Hunter, Was.	1	1	0	0	0	6
Spurlock, Micheal, T.B.	1	0	0	1	0	6
Stanton, Drew, Det.	1	1	0	0	0	6
Stevens, Jerramy, T.B.	1	0	1	0	0	6
Stovall, Maurice, T.B.	1	0	1	0	0	6
Tahi, Naufahu, Min.	1	0	1	0	0	6
Thomas, David, N.O.	1	0	1	0	0	6
Thomas, Terrell, NY-G	1	0	0	1	0	6
Tillman, Charles, Chi.	1	0	0	1	0	6
Umenyiora, Osi, NY-G	1	0	0	1	0	6
Wallace, Seneca, Sea.	1	1	0	0	0	6
Ware, Danny, NY-G	1	1	0	0	0	6
Willis, Patrick, S.F.	1	0	0	1	0	6
Witherspoon, Will, Phi.	1	0	0	1	0	6
Wolfe, Garrett, Chi.	1	1	0	0	0	6
* Freeman, Josh, T.B.	0	0	0	0	1	2
Howard, Darren, Phi.	0	0	0	0	0	^2
Manning, Danieal, Chi.	0	0	0	0	0	^2
Thomas, Hollis, Car.	0	0	0	0	0	^2

^ Safety
** Player that was a rookie in 2009*

AMERICAN FOOTBALL CONFERENCE—SCORING

	TD	TDR	TDP	TDM	XKG	XKAtt	X2G	X2Att	FG	FGA	SAF	POINTS
San Diego	51	17	29	5	50	51	0	0	32	35	1	454
New England	50	19	28	3	47	47	1	3	26	31	0	427
Indianapolis	53	16	34	3	50	51	0	2	16	20	0	416
Baltimore	47	22	21	4	46	47	0	0	21	30	0	391
Houston	46	13	29	4	43	44	1	2	21	32	2	388
Pittsburgh	41	10	28	3	41	41	0	0	27	31	0	368
Miami	41	22	15	4	37	38	1	3	25	28	0	360
Tennessee	39	19	16	4	37	37	1	2	27	32	0	354
N.Y. Jets	37	21	12	4	32	32	2	5	30	36	0	348
Denver	34	9	21	4	32	32	0	2	30	35	0	326
Cincinnati	34	9	21	4	28	29	2	5	23	28	0	305
Kansas City	31	8	18	5	29	29	1	2	25	29	1	294
Jacksonville	34	19	15	0	30	31	1	3	18	28	0	290
Buffalo	25	6	17	2	24	24	0	1	28	33	0	258
Cleveland	25	10	11	4	22	23	1	2	23	25	1	245
Oakland	17	7	10	0	17	17	0	0	26	29	0	197
AFC Total	605	227	325	53	565	573	11	32	398	482	5	5421
AFC Average	37.8	14.2	20.3	3.3	35.3	35.8	0.7	2.0	24.9	30.1	0.3	338.8

NATIONAL FOOTBALL CONFERENCE—SCORING

	TD	TDR	TDP	TDM	XKG	XKAtt	X2G	X2Att	FG	FGA	SAF	POINTS
New Orleans	64	21	34	9	60	63	0	1	22	28	0	510
Minnesota	56	19	34	3	54	55	0	1	26	28	1	470
Green Bay	54	20	30	4	48	49	3	5	27	36	1	461
Philadelphia	47	14	27	6	43	45	2	2	32	37	2	429
N.Y. Giants	46	14	28	4	45	45	0	1	27	32	0	402
Arizona	46	16	27	3	45	46	0	0	18	19	0	375
Atlanta	44	15	26	3	42	43	0	1	19	29	0	363
Dallas	43	14	26	3	41	41	1	1	20	31	0	361
San Francisco	39	12	23	4	39	39	0	0	19	24	0	330
Chicago	36	6	27	3	33	33	2	2	24	28	1	327
Carolina	35	18	16	1	31	32	2	3	22	27	2	315
Seattle	30	7	20	3	28	28	0	2	24	26	0	280
Washington	29	8	21	0	26	28	0	1	22	25	0	266
Detroit	28	9	16	3	25	25	1	3	21	28	2	262
Tampa Bay	28	5	18	5	24	24	2	4	16	26	0	244
St. Louis	17	4	12	1	16	16	0	1	19	24	0	175
NFC Total	642	202	385	55	600	612	13	28	358	448	9	5570
NFC Average	40.1	12.6	24.1	3.4	37.5	38.3	0.8	1.8	22.4	28.0	0.6	348.1
NFL Total	1247	429	710	108	1165	1185	24	60	756	930	14	10991
NFL Average	39.0	13.4	22.2	3.4	36.4	37.0	0.8	1.9	23.6	29.1	0.4	343.5

FIELD GOALS

FIELD GOAL PERCENTAGE

NFC: .941 Neil Rackers, Arizona
AFC: .914 Nate Kaeding, San Diego

FIELD GOALS

AFC: 32 Nate Kaeding, San Diego
NFC: 32 David Akers, Philadelphia

FIELD GOAL ATTEMPTS

NFC: 37 David Akers, Philadelphia
AFC: 36 Jay Feely, N.Y. Jets

FIELD GOALS, GAME

AFC: 5 Billy Cundiff, Baltimore vs. Indianapolis, November 22 (6 attempts)
NFC: 4 Lawrence Tynes, N.Y. Giants at Dallas, September 20 (5 attempts)
4 Olindo Mare, Seattle vs. Chicago, September 27 (6 attempts)
4 Mason Crosby, Green Bay vs. Detroit, October 18 (4 attempts)
4 Ryan Longwell, Minnesota vs. Baltimore, October 18 (4 attempts)
4 Olindo Mare, Seattle vs. Detroit, November 8 (4 attempts)
4 Robbie Gould, Chicago vs. Philadelphia, November 22 (5 attempts)
4 David Akers, Philadelphia vs. Washington, November 29 (4 attempts)
4 Garrett Hartley, New Orleans at Washington, December 6 (5 attempts) - (OT)

LONGEST FIELD GOAL

AFC: 61 Sebastian Janikowski, Oakland at Cleveland, December 27
NFC: 55 Josh Brown, St. Louis vs. Seattle, November 29

AVERAGE YARDS MADE

AFC: 42.5 Sebastian Janikowski, Oakland
NFC: 41.6 Connor Barth, Tampa Bay

AMERICAN FOOTBALL CONFERENCE—FIELD GOALS

	FG	FGA	Pct	Long
Cleveland	23	25	.920	49
San Diego	32	35	.914	55
Oakland	26	29	.897	61
Miami	25	28	.893	52
Pittsburgh	27	31	.871	46
Kansas City	25	29	.862	53
Denver	30	35	.857	51
Buffalo	28	33	.848	56
Tennessee	27	32	.844	53
New England	26	31	.839	53
N.Y. Jets	30	36	.833	55
Cincinnati	23	28	.821	53
Indianapolis	16	20	.800	48
Baltimore	21	30	.700	46
Houston	21	32	.656	56
Jacksonville	18	28	.643	52
AFC Total	398	482	—	61
AFC Average	24.9	30.1	.826	—

NATIONAL FOOTBALL CONFERENCE—FIELD GOALS

	FG	FGA	Pct	Long
Arizona	18	19	.947	48
Minnesota	26	28	.929	52
Seattle	24	26	.923	47
Washington	22	25	.880	48
Philadelphia	32	37	.865	52
Chicago	24	28	.857	52
N.Y. Giants	27	32	.844	52
Carolina	22	27	.815	50
St. Louis	19	24	.792	55
San Francisco	19	24	.792	51
New Orleans	22	28	.786	46
Detroit	21	28	.750	50
Green Bay	27	36	.750	52
Atlanta	19	29	.655	51
Dallas	20	31	.645	51
Tampa Bay	16	26	.615	54
NFC Total	358	448	—	55
NFC Average	22.4	28.0	.799	—
League Total	756	930	—	61
League Average	23.6	29.1	.813	—

2009 INDIVIDUAL STATISTICS—FIELD GOALS

AFC—INDIVIDUAL FIELD GOALS

	1-19 Yards	20-29 Yards	30-39 Yards	40-49 Yards	50 or Longer	Totals	Avg Yds Att	Avg Yds Made	Avg Yds Miss	Long
Kaeding, Nate, S.D.	2-2 1.000	17-17 1.000	4-4 1.000	6-8 .750	3-4 .750	32-35 .914	33.4	32.2	46.3	55
Janikowski, Sebastian, Oak.	0-0 —	3-3 1.000	8-8 1.000	9-10 .900	6-8 .750	26-29 .897	43.9	42.5	56.0	61
Dawson, Phil, Cle.	0-0 —	7-7 1.000	5-5 1.000	5-6 .833	0-1 .000	17-19 .895	35.2	33.7	47.5	49
Carpenter, Dan, Mia.	0-0 —	9-9 1.000	7-8 .875	8-9 .889	1-2 .500	25-28 .893	36.5	35.2	47.0	52
Reed, Jeff, Pit.	1-1 1.000	7-7 1.000	15-16 .938	4-5 .800	0-2 .000	27-31 .871	34.9	33.2	46.5	46
* Succop, Ryan, K.C.	0-0 —	10-10 1.000	7-7 1.000	6-7 .857	2-5 .400	25-29 .862	36.4	34.0	51.0	53
Prater, Matt, Den.	0-0 —	14-14 1.000	6-8 .750	8-10 .800	2-3 .667	30-35 .857	35.2	33.8	44.0	51
Lindell, Rian, Buf.	0-0 —	12-12 1.000	9-9 1.000	6-9 .667	1-3 .333	28-33 .848	35.2	32.7	49.2	56
Bironas, Rob, Ten.	0-0 —	8-8 1.000	4-6 .667	10-12 .833	5-6 .833	27-32 .844	40.0	39.1	44.8	53
Gostkowski, Stephen, N.E.	0-0 —	7-7 1.000	12-13 .923	5-8 .625	2-3 .667	26-31 .839	35.7	34.5	42.0	53
Feely, Jay, NYJ	0-0 —	6-6 1.000	12-15 .800	11-14 .786	1-1 1.000	30-36 .833	37.7	36.7	42.3	55
Graham, Shayne, Cin.	0-0 —	10-11 .909	8-10 .800	3-3 1.000	2-4 .500	23-28 .821	33.9	32.8	39.0	53
Cundiff, Billy, Cle.-Bal.	1-1 1.000	9-9 1.000	5-8 .625	3-3 1.000	0-2 .000	18-23 .783	32.9	30.7	40.8	46
Brown, Kris, Hou.	0-0 —	11-13 .846	6-9 .667	2-6 .333	2-4 .500	21-32 .656	35.5	32.4	41.5	56
Scobee, Josh, Jac.	0-0 —	7-8 .875	4-4 1.000	3-7 .429	4-9 .444	18-28 .643	40.4	35.8	48.5	52
(Nonqualifiers)										
Hauschka, Steven, Bal.	0-0 —	1-1 1.000	5-7 .714	3-5 .600	0-0 —	9-13 .692	37.5	36.4	39.8	44
Stover, Matt, Ind.	0-0 —	2-2 1.000	5-6 .833	2-2 1.000	0-1 .000	9-11 .818	35.4	33.9	42.0	43
Vinatieri, Adam, Ind.	1-1 1.000	3-3 1.000	1-2 .500	2-2 1.000	0-1 .000	7-9 .778	33.6	31.1	42.0	48
AFC Totals	5-5 1.000	143-147 .973	123-145 .848	96-126 .762	31-59 .525	398-482 .826	36.4	34.7	44.7	61
NFL Totals	11-11 1.000	264-273 .967	240-287 .836	186-255 .729	55-104 .529	756-930 .813	36.5	34.7	44.1	61

Leader based on overall percentage, minimum 16 field goals

NFC—INDIVIDUAL FIELD GOALS

	1-19 Yards	20-29 Yards	30-39 Yards	40-49 Yards	50 or Longer	Totals	Avg Yds Att	Avg Yds Made	Avg Yds Miss	Long
Rackers, Neil, Ariz	0-0	4-4	6-6	6-7	0-0	16-17	36.2	35.5	48.0	48
	—	1.000	1.000	.857	—	.941				
Longwell, Ryan, Min.	1-1	10-10	5-6	8-9	2-2	26-28	34.3	33.7	41.5	52
	1.000	1.000	.833	.889	1.000	.929				
Mare, Olindo, Sea.	0-0	9-9	10-11	5-6	0-0	24-26	33.8	33.4	38.5	47
	—	1.000	.909	.833	—	.923				
Akers, David, Phi.	1-1	11-11	8-9	11-13	1-3	32-37	36.4	34.8	46.6	52
	1.000	1.000	.889	.846	.333	.865				
Gould, Robbie, Chi.	0-0	9-9	6-6	7-10	2-3	24-28	37.5	35.7	48.5	52
	—	1.000	1.000	.700	.667	.857				
Tynes, Lawrence, NY-G	0-0	10-12	11-13	5-6	1-1	27-32	33.9	34.1	33.2	52
	—	.833	.846	.833	1.000	.844				
Suisham, Shaun, Was.-Dal.	0-0	9-10	5-7	6-6	0-1	20-24	33.3	32.8	35.5	48
	—	.900	.714	1.000	.000	.833				
Kasay, John, Car.	0-0	7-7	9-10	5-6	1-4	22-27	36.9	34.5	47.6	50
	—	1.000	.900	.833	.250	.815				
Nedney, Joe, S.F.	0-0	4-4	7-8	4-6	2-3	17-21	38.9	37.2	45.8	51
	—	1.000	.875	.667	.667	.810				
Brown, Josh, St.L	0-0	5-5	4-5	4-7	6-7	19-24	40.4	39.1	45.4	55
	—	1.000	.800	.571	.857	.792				
Carney, John, N.O.	0-0	6-6	5-8	2-3	0-0	13-17	33.1	31.2	39.3	46
	—	1.000	.625	.667	—	.765				
Crosby, Mason, G.B.	1-1	13-13	7-9	4-7	2-6	27-36	36.3	32.8	46.6	52
	1.000	1.000	.778	.571	.333	.750				
Hanson, Jason, Det.	0-0	5-5	8-9	7-10	1-4	21-28	39.6	36.6	48.4	50
	—	1.000	.889	.700	.250	.750				
Barth, Connor, T.B.	0-0	2-2	4-6	5-7	3-4	14-19	41.8	41.6	42.4	54
	—	1.000	.667	.714	.750	.737				
Folk, Nick, Dal.	1-1	5-6	6-7	5-12	1-2	18-28	37.4	34.4	42.6	51
	1.000	.833	.857	.417	.500	.643				
Elam, Jason, Atl.	0-0	4-4	4-8	3-5	1-2	12-19	36.5	34.7	39.6	50
	—	1.000	.500	.600	.500	.632				
(Nonqualifiers)										
Hartley, Garrett, N.O.	1-1	3-3	5-6	0-0	0-1	9-11	33.6	30.6	47.5	38
	1.000	1.000	.833	—	.000	.818				
Bryant, Matt, Atl.	0-0	2-2	4-4	0-2	1-2	7-10	38.3	34.3	47.7	51
	—	1.000	1.000	.000	.500	.700				
Nugent, Mike, T.B.-Ariz	1-1	1-1	1-2	1-4	0-0	4-8	38.4	31.5	45.3	48
	1.000	1.000	.500	.250	—	.500				
* Gano, Graham, Was.	0-0	2-2	0-0	2-2	0-0	4-4	33.5	33.5	—	46
	—	1.000	—	1.000	—	1.000				
Schmitt, Ricky, S.F.	0-0	0-1	2-2	0-0	0-0	2-3	33.3	36.0	28.0	39
	—	.000	1.000	—	—	.667				
Andrus, Shane, T.B.	0-0	0-0	0-0	0-1	0-0	0-1	43.0	—	43.0	0
	—	—	—	.000	—	.000				
NFC Totals	6-6	121-126	117-142	90-129	24-45	358-448	36.5	34.8	43.5	55
	1.000	.960	.824	.698	.533	.799				
NFL Totals	11-11	264-273	240-287	186-255	55-104	756-930	36.5	34.7	44.1	61
	1.000	.967	.836	.729	.529	.813				

Leader based on overall percentage, minimum 16 field goals
** Player that was a rookie in 2009*

2009 INDIVIDUAL STATISTICS—RUSHING

RUSHING

YARDS

AFC: 2006 Chris Johnson, Tennessee
NFC: 1416 Steven Jackson, St. Louis

YARDS, GAME

AFC: 286 Jerome Harrison, Cleveland at Kansas City, December 20 (34 attempts, 3 TD)
NFC: 207 Frank Gore, San Francisco vs. Seattle, September 20 (16 attempts, 2 TD)

LONGEST

AFC: 91 Chris Johnson, Tennessee vs. Houston, September 20 - TD
NFC: 80 Frank Gore, San Francisco vs. Seattle, September 20 - TD

ATTEMPTS

AFC: 358 Chris Johnson, Tennessee
NFC: 324 Steven Jackson, St. Louis

ATTEMPTS, GAME

AFC: 39 Jerome Harrison, Cleveland vs. Oakland, December 27 (148 yards, 1 TD)
NFC: 30 DeAngelo Williams, Carolina at Tampa Bay, October 18 (152 yards, 2 TD)

YARDS PER ATTEMPT

NFC: 5.9 Felix Jones, Dallas
AFC: 5.9 Jamaal Charles, Kansas City

TOUCHDOWNS

NFC: 18 Adrian Peterson, Minnesota
AFC: 15 Maurice Jones-Drew, Jacksonville

TEAM LEADERS, YARDS

AFC: BALTIMORE, 1339, Ray Rice; BUFFALO, 1062, Fred Jackson; CINCINNATI, 1251, Cedric Benson; CLEVELAND, 862, Jerome Harrison; DENVER, 947, *Knowshon Moreno; HOUSTON, 437, Steve Slaton; INDIANAPOLIS, 828, Joseph Addai; JACKSONVILLE, 1391, Maurice Jones-Drew; KANSAS CITY, 1120, Jamaal Charles; MIAMI, 1121, Ricky Williams; NEW ENGLAND, 757, Laurence Maroney; N.Y. JETS, 1402, Thomas Jones; OAKLAND, 589, Michael Bush; PITTSBURGH, 1108, Rashard Mendenhall; SAN DIEGO, 730, LaDainian Tomlinson; TENNESSEE, 2006, Chris Johnson

NFC: ARIZONA, 793, *Beanie Wells; ATLANTA, 871, Michael Turner; CAROLINA, 1133, Jonathan Stewart; CHICAGO, 929, Matt Forté; DALLAS, 932, Marion Barber; DETROIT, 747, Kevin Smith; GREEN BAY, 1253, Ryan Grant; MINNESOTA, 1383, Adrian Peterson; NEW ORLEANS, 793, Pierre Thomas; N.Y. GIANTS, 835, Brandon Jacobs; PHILADELPHIA, 637, *LeSean McCoy; ST. LOUIS, 1416, Steven Jackson; SAN FRANCISCO, 1120, Frank Gore; SEATTLE, 663, Julius Jones; TAMPA BAY, 823, Cadillac Williams; WASHINGTON, 494, Clinton Portis

TEAM CHAMPION

AFC: 2756 N.Y. Jets
NFC: 2498 Carolina

**Player that was a rookie in 2009*

NFL TOP TEN RUSHERS

	Att	Yards	Avg	Long	TD
Johnson, Chris, Ten.	358	2006	5.6	91t	14
Jackson, Steven, St.L	324	1416	4.4	58	4
Jones, Thomas, NYJ	331	1402	4.2	71t	14
Jones-Drew, Maurice, Jac.	312	1391	4.5	80t	15
Peterson, Adrian, Min.	314	1383	4.4	64t	18
Rice, Ray, Bal.	254	1339	5.3	59t	7
Grant, Ryan, G.B.	282	1253	4.4	62t	11
Benson, Cedric, Cin.	301	1251	4.2	42	6
Stewart, Jonathan, Car.	221	1133	5.1	67t	10
Williams, Ricky, Mia.	241	1121	4.7	68t	11

AFC—INDIVIDUAL RUSHERS

	Att	Yards	Avg	Long	TD
Johnson, Chris, Ten.	358	2006	5.6	91t	14
Jones, Thomas, NYJ	331	1402	4.2	71t	14
Jones-Drew, Maurice, Jac.	312	1391	4.5	80t	15
Rice, Ray, Bal.	254	1339	5.3	59t	7
Benson, Cedric, Cin.	301	1251	4.2	42	6
Williams, Ricky, Mia.	241	1121	4.7	68t	11
Charles, Jamaal, K.C.	190	1120	5.9	76t	7
Mendenhall, Rashard, Pit.	242	1108	4.6	60	7
Jackson, Fred, Buf.	237	1062	4.5	43	2
* Moreno, Knowshon, Den.	247	947	3.8	36	7
Harrison, Jerome, Cle.	194	862	4.4	71t	5
Addai, Joseph, Ind.	219	828	3.8	21t	10
Maroney, Laurence, N.E.	194	757	3.9	45t	9
Tomlinson, LaDainian, S.D.	223	730	3.3	36	12
Brown, Ronnie, Mia.	147	648	4.4	45	8
Buckhalter, Correll, Den.	120	642	5.4	45t	1
Bush, Michael, Oak.	123	589	4.8	60	3
Johnson, Larry, K.C.-Cin.	178	581	3.3	27	0
McGahee, Willis, Bal.	109	544	5.0	77t	12
* Greene, Shonn, NYJ	108	540	5.0	33t	2
Lewis, Jamal, Cle.	143	500	3.5	18	0
Fargas, Justin, Oak.	129	491	3.8	35	3
Lynch, Marshawn, Buf.	120	450	3.8	47	2
Slaton, Steve, Hou.	131	437	3.3	32t	3
Moats, Ryan, Hou.	101	390	3.9	17	4
Parker, Willie, Pit.	98	389	4.0	34	0
Cribbs, Josh, Cle.	55	381	6.9	37	1
McFadden, Darren, Oak.	104	357	3.4	28	1
Sproles, Darren, S.D.	93	343	3.7	21	3
Faulk, Kevin, N.E.	62	335	5.4	29	2
Washington, Leon, NYJ	72	331	4.6	33	0
Garrard, David, Jac.	77	323	4.2	30	3
* Scott, Bernard, Cin.	74	321	4.3	61	0
Morris, Sammy, N.E.	73	319	4.4	55	2
* Brown, Donald, Ind.	78	281	3.6	45	3
Young, Vince, Ten.	55	281	5.1	44	2
Taylor, Fred, N.E.	63	269	4.3	19	4
Brown, Chris, Hou.	79	267	3.4	13	3
* Foster, Arian, Hou.	54	257	4.8	24	3
White, LenDale, Ten.	64	222	3.5	11	2
* Jennings, Chris, Cle.	63	220	3.5	16	1
Smith, Brad, NYJ	18	207	11.5	57	1
* Jennings, Rashad, Jac.	39	202	5.2	28t	1
Cassel, Matt, K.C.	50	189	3.8	13	0
McClain, Le'Ron, Bal.	46	180	3.9	20	2
Tolbert, Mike, S.D.	25	148	5.9	32	1
Fitzpatrick, Ryan, Buf.	31	141	4.5	31t	1
Polite, Lousaka, Mia.	37	123	3.3	13	0
Moore, Mewelde, Pit.	35	118	3.4	15	0
Green-Ellis, BenJarvus, N.E.	26	114	4.4	29	0
Gradkowski, Bruce, Oak.	18	108	6.0	21	0
Edwards, Trent, Buf.	14	106	7.6	20	0
* Sanchez, Mark, NYJ	36	106	2.9	14t	3
Simpson, Chad, Ind.	15	102	6.8	31t	2
Quinn, Brady, Cle.	20	98	4.9	24	1

	Att	Yards	Avg	Long	TD
Palmer, Carson, Cin.	39	93	2.4	15	3
Hilliard, Lex, Mia.	23	89	3.9	18	1
Jordan, LaMont, Den.	25	86	3.4	13	0
* Thomas, Mike, Jac.	12	86	7.2	22	0
Leonard, Brian, Cin.	27	84	3.1	11	0
Roethlisberger, Ben, Pit.	40	82	2.1	15	2
* White, Pat, Mia.	21	81	3.9	33	0
Hester, Jacob, S.D.	21	74	3.5	15	0
Orton, Kyle, Den.	24	71	3.0	13	0
Hart, Mike, Ind.	26	70	2.7	15	1
Bennett, Michael, S.D.	23	65	2.8	14	0
Woodhead, Danny, NYJ	15	64	4.3	16	0
Schaub, Matt, Hou.	48	57	1.2	19	0
Flacco, Joe, Bal.	35	56	1.6	10	0
Castille, Tim, K.C.	14	55	3.9	16	0
Hillis, Peyton, Den.	13	54	4.2	13	1
Owens, Terrell, Buf.	6	54	9.0	29t	1
Rivers, Philip, S.D.	26	50	1.9	15	1
Ginn, Ted Jr., Mia.	7	48	6.9	22	0
Richardson, Tony, NYJ	7	48	6.9	19	0
* Ringer, Javon, Ten.	8	48	6.0	32	0
* Wallace, Mike, Pit.	5	48	9.6	21	0
Savage, Dantrell, K.C.	10	45	4.5	11	0
Brady, Tom, N.E.	29	44	1.5	9	1
Russell, JaMarcus, Oak.	18	44	2.4	15	0
* Lawrence, Quinten, K.C.	2	42	21.0	26	0
Weatherford, Steve, NYJ	2	42	21.0	26	0
Frye, Charlie, Oak.	4	41	10.3	26	0
Marshall, Brandon, Den.	7	39	5.6	14	0
Cobbs, Patrick, Mia.	6	36	6.0	19	0
Welker, Wes, N.E.	5	36	7.2	11	0
McIntyre, Corey, Buf.	5	34	6.8	25	0
Smith, Kolby, K.C.	15	33	2.2	12	0
Henne, Chad, Mia.	16	32	2.0	12	1
Ochocinco, Chad, Cin.	3	32	10.7	26	0
* Murphy, Louis, Oak.	6	31	5.2	13	0
Smith, Troy, Bal.	8	31	3.9	15t	1
* Hartline, Brian, Mia.	4	29	7.3	16t	1
Clayton, Mark, Bal.	4	28	7.0	12	0
Dixon, Dennis, Pit.	3	27	9.0	24t	1
Walter, Kevin, Hou.	4	26	6.5	13	0
* Hoyer, Brian, N.E.	10	25	2.5	20	1
Jones, Greg, Jac.	4	23	5.8	11	0
Caldwell, Andre, Cin.	3	22	7.3	15	0
Jones, Jacoby, Hou.	3	22	7.3	17	0
Omon, Xavier, Buf.	5	22	4.4	7	0
Battle, Jackie, K.C.	7	21	3.0	12	0
Crocker, Chris, Cin.	1	21	21.0	21	0
Higgins, Johnnie Lee, Oak.	2	21	10.5	19	0
Bradley, Mark, K.C.	2	20	10.0	22	0
* Heyward-Bey, Darrius, Oak.	2	19	9.5	20	0
Parmele, Jalen, Bal.	5	17	3.4	7	0
Collins, Kerry, Ten.	11	15	1.4	10t	1
Davis, Carey, Pit.	2	15	7.5	14	0
* Davis, James, Cle.	9	15	1.7	5	0
Washington, Nate, Ten.	2	15	7.5	14	0
O'Sullivan, J.T., Cin.	3	12	4.0	6	0
Bess, Davone, Mia.	2	11	5.5	11	0
Clark, Dallas, Ind.	2	11	5.5	7	0
Jackson, Vincent, S.D.	3	11	3.7	12	0
* Tate, Brandon, N.E.	1	11	11.0	11	0
Wade, Bobby, K.C.	3	11	3.7	8	0
Coles, Laveranues, Cin.	2	10	5.0	8	0
Garcon, Pierre, Ind.	2	10	5.0	17	0
Johnson, Andre, Hou.	2	10	5.0	7	0
Grossman, Rex, Hou.	3	9	3.0	8	0
Anderson, Derek, Cle.	10	8	0.8	3	2
Johnson, Jeremi, Cin.	4	8	2.0	4	0

	Att	Yards	Avg	Long	TD
Cotchery, Jerricho, NYJ	2	7	3.5	6t	1
Keller, Dustin, NYJ	1	7	7.0	7	0
Naanee, Legedu, S.D.	3	7	2.3	10	0
Pennington, Chad, Mia.	3	7	2.3	4	0
Holmes, Santonio, Pit.	3	6	2.0	7	0
Slater, Matt, N.E.	1	6	6.0	6	0
Stuckey, Chansi, Cle.	2	6	3.0	6	0
* Williams, Javarris, K.C.	6	6	1.0	5	0
Cox, Mike, K.C.	3	5	1.7	2	1
* Edelman, Julian, N.E.	2	5	2.5	5	0
Hall, Ahmard, Ten.	1	5	5.0	5	0
* Sheets, Kory, Mia.	1	5	5.0	5	0
Davis, Craig, S.D.	1	4	4.0	4	0
McGraw, Jon, K.C.	1	4	4.0	4	0
* Painter, Curtis, Ind.	3	4	1.3	10	0
Parrish, Roscoe, Buf.	2	4	2.0	9	0
* Miller, Zach, Jac.	1	3	3.0	3	0
Thigpen, Tyler, K.C.-Mia.	2	3	1.5	2	0
Heap, Todd, Bal.	1	2	2.0	2	0
Mason, Derrick, Bal.	1	2	2.0	2	0
Clemens, Kellen, NYJ	12	1	0.1	6	0
Clowney, David, NYJ	3	1	0.3	13	0
* Collie, Austin, Ind.	2	1	0.5	2	0
Owens, Montell, Jac.	2	1	0.5	3	0
Royal, Eddie, Den.	1	1	1.0	1	0
Washington, Kelley, Bal.	1	1	1.0	1	0
Colquitt, Dustin, K.C.	1	0	0.0	0	0
Hodges, Reggie, Cle.	1	0	0.0	0	0
* Huber, Kevin, Cin.	1	0	0.0	0	0
Lawrence, Matt, Bal.	4	0	0.0	4	0
O'Neal, Oren, Oak.	1	0	0.0	0	0
Russell, Gary, Oak.	3	0	0.0	2	0
Long, Lance, K.C.	1	-1	-1.0	-1	0
* Cosby, Quan, Cin.	1	-2	-2.0	-2	0
Brohm, Brian, Buf.	3	-3	-1.0	-1	0
Jenkins, Justin, Buf.	1	-3	-3.0	-3	0
* Massaquoi, Mohamed, Cle.	1	-3	-3.0	-3	0
Simms, Chris, Den.	3	-4	-1.3	-1	0
Volek, Billy, S.D.	9	-9	-1.0	-1	0
Manning, Peyton, Ind.	19	-13	-0.7	3	0

t = Touchdown
Leader based on most yards gained
** Player that was a rookie in 2009*

NFC—INDIVIDUAL RUSHERS

	Att	Yards	Avg	Long	TD
Jackson, Steven, St.L	324	1416	4.4	58	4
Peterson, Adrian, Min.	314	1383	4.4	64t	18
Grant, Ryan, G.B.	282	1253	4.4	62t	11
Stewart, Jonathan, Car.	221	1133	5.1	67t	10
Gore, Frank, S.F.	229	1120	4.9	80t	10
Williams, DeAngelo, Car.	216	1117	5.2	77	7
Barber, Marion, Dal.	214	932	4.4	35	7
Forté, Matt, Chi.	258	929	3.6	61	4
Turner, Michael, Atl.	178	871	4.9	58t	10
Jacobs, Brandon, NY-G	224	835	3.7	31	5
Williams, Cadillac, T.B.	211	823	3.9	35	4
Thomas, Pierre, N.O.	147	793	5.4	34t	6
* Wells, Beanie, Ariz	176	793	4.5	33	7
Bradshaw, Ahmad, NY-G	163	778	4.8	38	7
Smith, Kevin, Det.	217	747	3.4	31	4
Jones, Felix, Dal.	116	685	5.9	56	3
Jones, Julius, Sea.	177	663	3.7	62t	2
Bell, Mike, N.O.	172	654	3.8	35	5
* McCoy, LeSean, Phi.	155	637	4.1	66t	4
Forsett, Justin, Sea.	114	619	5.4	35	4

2009 INDIVIDUAL STATISTICS—RUSHING

	Att	Yards	Avg	Long	TD
Snelling, Jason, Atl.	142	613	4.3	31	4
Hightower, Tim, Ariz	143	598	4.2	50	8
Portis, Clinton, Was.	124	494	4.0	78	1
Ward, Derrick, T.B.	114	409	3.6	28	1
Bush, Reggie, N.O.	70	390	5.6	55	5
Morris, Maurice, Det.	93	384	4.1	64t	2
Choice, Tashard, Dal.	64	349	5.5	66	3
Taylor, Chester, Min.	94	338	3.6	25	1
Weaver, Leonard, Phi.	70	323	4.6	41t	2
Rodgers, Aaron, G.B.	58	316	5.4	35	5
Westbrook, Brian, Phi.	61	274	4.5	25	1
Norwood, Jerious, Atl.	76	252	3.3	21	0
Campbell, Jason, Was.	46	236	5.1	21	1
Cartwright, Rock, Was.	64	228	3.6	34	0
* Coffee, Glen, S.F.	83	226	2.7	17	1
* Bell, Kahlil, Chi.	40	220	5.5	72	0
Betts, Ladell, Was.	56	210	3.8	18	2
Ganther, Quinton, Was.	62	201	3.2	13	3
Cutler, Jay, Chi.	40	173	4.3	30	1
* Freeman, Josh, T.B.	30	161	5.4	20	0
Green, Ahman, G.B.	41	160	3.9	26	1
Darby, Kenneth, St.L	27	152	5.6	51	0
Johnson, Josh, T.B.	22	148	6.7	29	0
McNabb, Donovan, Phi.	37	140	3.8	27	2
Jackson, DeSean, Phi.	11	137	12.5	67t	1
* Harvin, Percy, Min.	15	135	9.0	35	0
* Brown, Aaron, Det.	27	131	4.9	19	0
Mason, Marcus, Was.	32	127	4.0	20	0
Hamilton, Lynell, N.O.	35	125	3.6	19	2
James, Edgerrin, Sea.	46	125	2.7	10	0
Wolfe, Garrett, Chi.	22	120	5.5	36	1
Hasselbeck, Matt, Sea.	26	119	4.6	23	0
Jackson, Brandon, G.B.	37	111	3.0	9	2
* Stafford, Matthew, Det.	20	108	5.4	21	2
Romo, Tony, Dal.	35	105	3.0	17	1
Vick, Michael, Phi.	24	95	4.0	34	2
Culpepper, Daunte, Det.	18	91	5.1	32	0
Meachem, Robert, N.O.	6	82	13.7	41	0
Boller, Kyle, St.L	13	76	5.8	16	0
Johnson, Calvin, Det.	7	73	10.4	19	0
Ware, Danny, NY-G	13	73	5.6	14	1
Hill, Shaun, S.F.	8	70	8.8	22	0
* Sutton, Tyrell, Car.	12	68	5.7	20	0
Graham, Earnest, T.B.	14	66	4.7	17	0
Manning, Eli, NY-G	17	65	3.8	14	0
Morgan, Josh, S.F.	5	61	12.2	20	0
Delhomme, Jake, Car.	17	60	3.5	11	0
Weems, Eric, Atl.	8	53	6.6	31	0
Young, Albert, Min.	12	53	4.4	10	0
Hoover, Brad, Car.	20	52	2.6	18	1
Peterson, Adrian, Chi.	7	51	7.3	15	0
Smith, Alex, S.F.	24	51	2.1	11	0
* Ogbonnaya, Chris, St.L	11	50	4.5	18	0
* Goodson, Mike, Car.	22	49	2.2	11	0
Ryan, Matt, Atl.	30	49	1.6	7	1
Felton, Jerome, Det.	15	46	3.1	10	0
Breaston, Steve, Ariz	2	44	22.0	25	0
Buckley, Eldra, Phi.	15	44	2.9	9	1
* Johnson, Gartrell, NY-G	13	43	3.3	11	0
Norris, Moran, S.F.	14	41	2.9	15	1
Rankin, Louis, Sea.	8	36	4.5	12	0
Walker, Delanie, S.F.	3	34	11.3	16	0
Brees, Drew, N.O.	22	33	1.5	10	2
Stanton, Drew, Det.	9	33	3.7	11	1
Avery, Donnie, St.L	4	30	7.5	15	0
Crayton, Patrick, Dal.	4	28	7.0	20	0
Carr, David, NY-G	9	27	3.0	12t	1
Gado, Samkon, St.L	14	26	1.9	11	0
Bulger, Marc, St.L	8	22	2.8	7	0
Smith, Steve, Car.	5	22	4.4	17	0
Wynn, DeShawn, G.B.	6	19	3.2	6	0
Kuhn, John, G.B.	8	18	2.3	5	1
Wright, Jason, Ariz	3	17	5.7	8	0
Boss, Kevin, NY-G	1	16	16.0	16	0
Evans, Heath, N.O.	5	16	3.2	6	1
Stecker, Aaron, Atl.	5	15	3.0	6	0
* Stephens-Howling, LaRod, Ariz	6	15	2.5	5	0
Driver, Donald, G.B.	1	13	13.0	13	0
Henderson, Devery, N.O.	4	13	3.3	13	0
Boldin, Anquan, Ariz	3	12	4.0	5t	1
Mughelli, Ovie, Atl.	4	10	2.5	4	0
Warner, Kurt, Ariz	21	10	0.5	10	0
Rolle, Antrel, Ariz	1	9	9.0	9	0
Karney, Mike, St.L	2	8	4.0	8	0
Moss, Santana, Was.	2	8	4.0	6	0
* Nicks, Hakeem, NY-G	2	8	4.0	9	0
Smith, Hunter, Was.	1	8	8.0	8t	1
Booker, Marty, Atl.	1	7	7.0	7	0
Dugan, Jeff, Min.	3	7	2.3	5	0
Favre, Brett, Min.	9	7	0.8	4	0
Smith, Clifton, T.B.	4	7	1.8	4	0
Winslow, Kellen, T.B.	1	7	7.0	7	0
Colston, Marques, N.O.	1	6	6.0	6	0
Eckel, Kyle, N.O.	2	6	3.0	7	0
Griffith, Justin, Sea.	4	6	1.5	3	0
Leftwich, Byron, T.B.	6	6	1.0	4	0
* Null, Keith, St.L	5	6	1.2	3	0
* Ogletree, Kevin, Dal.	1	6	6.0	6	0
Tahi, Naufahu, Min.	3	5	1.7	2	0
Burleson, Nate, Sea.	2	4	2.0	2	0
Redman, Chris, Atl.	6	4	0.7	5	0
* Williams, Derrick, Det.	1	4	4.0	4	0
Spurlock, Micheal, S.F.	1	3	3.0	3	0
Robinson, Michael, S.F.	3	2	0.7	4	0
St. Pierre, Brian, Ariz	1	2	2.0	2	0
Wallace, Seneca, Sea.	16	2	0.1	10	1
White, Roddy, Atl.	1	2	2.0	2	0
Pearson, Kalvin, Det.	1	1	1.0	1	0
Askew, B.J., T.B.	1	0	0.0	0	0
Collins, Todd, Was.	1	0	0.0	0	0
* Pressley, Chris, T.B.	1	0	0.0	0	0
Ryan, Jon, Sea.	1	0	0.0	0	0
Hester, Devin, Chi.	6	-1	-0.2	7	0
Kolb, Kevin, Phi.	5	-1	-0.2	5	1
Amendola, Danny, St.L	3	-2	-0.7	8	0
Austin, Miles, Dal.	2	-2	-1.0	11	0
Figurs, Yamon, Det.	1	-2	-2.0	-2	0
Garcia, Jeff, Phi.	3	-2	-0.7	0	0
Thomas, Devin, Was.	3	-2	-0.7	2	0
Brown, Reggie, Phi.	1	-3	-3.0	-3	0
Moore, Matt, Car.	12	-3	-0.3	5	0
Flynn, Matt, G.B.	5	-5	-1.0	-1	0
Leinart, Matt, Ariz	9	-6	-0.7	1	0
* Maclin, Jeremy, Phi.	2	-7	-3.5	-1	0
Branch, Deion, Sea.	1	-8	-8.0	-8	0
Bruce, Isaac, S.F.	1	-8	-8.0	-8	0
Feagles, Jeff, NY-G	1	-8	-8.0	-8	0
Jackson, Tarvaris, Min.	17	-10	-0.6	6	0
Brunell, Mark, N.O.	4	-12	-3.0	-1	0

t = Touchdown
Leader based on most yards gained
** Player that was a rookie in 2009*

AMERICAN FOOTBALL CONFERENCE—RUSHING

	Att	Yards	Avg	Long	TD
N.Y. Jets	607	2756	4.5	71t	21
Tennessee	499	2592	5.2	91t	19
Miami	509	2231	4.4	68t	22
Baltimore	468	2200	4.7	77t	22
Cleveland	498	2087	4.2	71t	10
Cincinnati	505	2056	4.1	61	9
Jacksonville	447	2029	4.5	80t	19
Kansas City	438	1929	4.4	76t	8
New England	466	1921	4.1	55	19
Buffalo	424	1867	4.4	47	6
Denver	440	1836	4.2	45t	9
Pittsburgh	428	1793	4.2	60	10
Oakland	410	1701	4.1	60	7
Houston	425	1475	3.5	32t	13
San Diego	427	1423	3.3	36	17
Indianapolis	366	1294	3.5	45	16
AFC Total	7357	31190	4.2	91t	227
AFC Average	459.8	1949.4	4.2	—	14.2

NATIONAL FOOTBALL CONFERENCE—RUSHING

	Att	Yards	Avg	Long	TD
Carolina	525	2498	4.8	77	18
New Orleans	468	2106	4.5	55	21
Dallas	436	2103	4.8	66	14
Minnesota	467	1918	4.1	64t	19
Green Bay	438	1885	4.3	62t	20
Atlanta	451	1876	4.2	58t	15
N.Y. Giants	443	1837	4.1	38	14
St. Louis	411	1784	4.3	58	4
Philadelphia	384	1637	4.3	67t	14
Tampa Bay	404	1627	4.0	35	5
Detroit	409	1616	4.0	64t	9
San Francisco	371	1600	4.3	80t	12
Seattle	395	1566	4.0	62t	7
Washington	391	1510	3.9	78	8
Arizona	365	1494	4.1	50	16
Chicago	373	1492	4.0	72	6
NFC Total	6731	28549	4.2	80t	202
NFC Average	420.7	1784.3	4.2	—	12.6
League Total	14088	59739	—	91t	429
League Average	440.3	1866.8	4.2	—	13.4

2009 INDIVIDUAL STATISTICS—PASSING

PASSING

HIGHEST RATING
NFC: 109.6 Drew Brees, New Orleans
AFC: 104.4 Philip Rivers, San Diego

COMPLETION PERCENTAGE
NFC: 70.6 Drew Brees, New Orleans
AFC: 68.8 Peyton Manning, Indianapolis

ATTEMPTS
AFC: 583 Matt Schaub, Houston
NFC: 555 Jay Cutler, Chicago

COMPLETIONS
AFC: 396 Matt Schaub, Houston
NFC: 363 Drew Brees, New Orleans
363 Brett Favre, Minnesota

YARDS
AFC: 4770 Matt Schaub, Houston
NFC: 4483 Tony Romo, Dallas

YARDS, GAME
AFC: 503 Ben Roethlisberger, Pittsburgh vs. Green Bay, December 20 (29-46, 3 TD)
NFC: 450 Donovan McNabb, Philadelphia at San Diego, November 15 (35-55, 2 TD)

LONGEST
AFC: 98 Ryan Fitzpatrick (to Terrell Owens) Buffalo at Jacksonville, November 22 - TD
NFC: 90 Matt Ryan (to Roddy White) Atlanta at San Francisco, October 11 - TD

YARDS PER ATTEMPT
AFC: 8.75 Philip Rivers, San Diego
NFC: 8.54 Drew Brees, New Orleans

TOUCHDOWN PASSES
NFC: 34 Drew Brees, New Orleans
AFC: 33 Peyton Manning, Indianapolis

TOUCHDOWN PASSES, GAME
AFC: 6 Tom Brady, New England vs. Tennessee, October 18 (29-34, 380 yards)
NFC: 6 Drew Brees, New Orleans vs. Detroit, September 13 (26-34, 358 yards)

LOWEST INTERCEPTION PERCENTAGE
AFC: 1.9 Philip Rivers, San Diego
NFC: 1.3 Aaron Rodgers, Green Bay

TEAM CHAMPION (MOST NET YARDS)
AFC: 4654 Houston
NFC: 4355 New Orleans

NFL TOP TEN PASSERS

	Att	Comp	Pct Comp	Yds	Avg Gain	TD	Pct TD	Long	Int	Pct Int	Sack	Yds Lost	Rating Points
Brees, Drew, N.O.	514	363	70.6	4388	8.54	34	6.6	75t	11	2.1	20	135	109.6
Favre, Brett, Min.	531	363	68.4	4202	7.91	33	6.2	63	7	1.3	34	247	107.2
Rivers, Philip, S.D.	486	317	65.2	4254	8.75	28	5.8	81t	9	1.9	25	167	104.4
Rodgers, Aaron, G.B.	541	350	64.7	4434	8.20	30	5.5	83t	7	1.3	50	306	103.2
Roethlisberger, Ben, Pit.	506	337	66.6	4328	8.55	26	5.1	60t	12	2.4	50	348	100.5
Manning, Peyton, Ind.	571	393	68.8	4500	7.88	33	5.8	80t	16	2.8	10	74	99.9
Schaub, Matt, Hou.	583	396	67.9	4770	8.18	29	5.0	72t	15	2.6	25	149	98.6
Romo, Tony, Dal.	550	347	63.1	4483	8.15	26	4.7	80t	9	1.6	34	196	97.6
Brady, Tom, N.E.	565	371	65.7	4398	7.78	28	5.0	81t	13	2.3	16	86	96.2
Warner, Kurt, Ariz	513	339	66.1	3753	7.32	26	5.1	45	14	2.7	24	172	93.2

AMERICAN FOOTBALL CONFERENCE—PASSING

	Att	Comp	Pct Comp	Gross Yards	Sacked	Yds Lost	Net Yards	Yds/ Att	Yards/ Comp	TD	Pct TD	Long	Int	Pct Int
Houston	593	399	67.3	4803	25	149	4654	8.10	12.04	29	4.89	72t	17	2.9
Indianapolis	601	402	66.9	4605	13	90	4515	7.66	11.46	34	5.66	80t	19	3.2
New England	592	390	65.9	4540	18	104	4436	7.67	11.64	28	4.73	81t	13	2.2
San Diego	519	338	65.1	4506	26	168	4338	8.68	13.33	29	5.59	81t	10	1.9
Pittsburgh	536	351	65.5	4496	50	348	4148	8.39	12.81	28	5.22	60t	14	2.6
Denver	558	341	61.1	3825	34	198	3627	6.85	11.22	21	3.76	87t	13	2.3
Baltimore	510	321	62.9	3637	36	218	3419	7.13	11.33	21	4.12	72t	13	2.5
Jacksonville	519	315	60.7	3599	44	243	3356	6.93	11.43	15	2.89	63	10	1.9
Miami	545	331	60.7	3396	34	226	3170	6.23	10.26	15	2.75	67	19	3.5
Kansas City	536	296	55.2	3183	45	261	2922	5.94	10.75	18	3.36	61	17	3.2
Cincinnati	477	286	60.0	3134	29	244	2890	6.57	10.96	21	4.40	73	13	2.7
Tennessee	476	271	56.9	3104	15	73	3031	6.52	11.45	16	3.36	69t	15	3.2
Oakland	485	255	52.6	2875	49	318	2557	5.93	11.27	10	2.06	86t	18	3.7
Buffalo	441	256	58.0	2789	46	274	2515	6.32	10.89	17	3.85	98t	19	4.3
N.Y. Jets	393	210	53.4	2596	30	216	2380	6.61	12.36	12	3.05	65t	21	5.3
Cleveland	443	219	49.4	2255	30	179	2076	5.09	10.30	11	2.48	59t	18	4.1
AFC Total	8224	4981	—	57343	524	3309	54034	—	—	325	—	98t	249	—
AFC Average	514.0	311.3	60.6	3583.9	32.8	206.8	3377.1	6.97	11.51	20.3	4.0	—	15.6	3.0

NATIONAL FOOTBALL CONFERENCE—PASSING

	Att	Comp	Pct Comp	Gross Yards	Sacked	Yds Lost	Net Yards	Yds/ Att	Yards/ Comp	TD	Pct TD	Long	Int	Pct Int
Green Bay	553	357	64.6	4492	51	312	4180	8.12	12.58	30	5.42	83t	8	1.4
New Orleans	544	378	69.5	4490	20	135	4355	8.25	11.88	34	6.25	75t	12	2.2
Dallas	550	347	63.1	4483	34	196	4287	8.15	12.92	26	4.73	80t	9	1.6
Minnesota	553	377	68.2	4403	34	247	4156	7.96	11.68	34	6.15	63	7	1.3
Philadelphia	553	335	60.6	4380	38	291	4089	7.92	13.07	27	4.88	71t	13	2.4
N.Y. Giants	542	338	62.4	4246	32	227	4019	7.83	12.56	28	5.17	74t	14	2.6
Arizona	594	392	66.0	4200	26	184	4016	7.07	10.71	27	4.55	45	18	3.0
Washington	533	340	63.8	3797	46	307	3490	7.12	11.17	21	3.94	84	16	3.0
Seattle	609	372	61.1	3771	41	268	3503	6.19	10.14	20	3.28	53	19	3.1
Atlanta	570	332	58.2	3697	27	126	3571	6.49	11.14	26	4.56	90t	17	3.0
Chicago	563	340	60.4	3677	35	204	3473	6.53	10.81	27	4.80	71	27	4.8
Detroit	585	316	54.0	3471	43	303	3168	5.93	10.98	16	2.74	75t	32	5.5
San Francisco	528	312	59.1	3293	40	241	3052	6.24	10.55	23	4.36	73t	14	2.7
Tampa Bay	524	279	53.2	3134	33	161	2973	5.98	11.23	18	3.44	47	29	5.5
Carolina	465	264	56.8	3070	33	271	2799	6.60	11.63	16	3.44	66	20	4.3
St. Louis	543	312	57.5	2970	44	284	2686	5.47	9.52	12	2.21	50	21	3.9
NFC Total	8809	5391	—	61574	577	3757	57817	—	—	385	—	90t	276	—
NFC Average	550.6	336.9	61.2	3848.4	36.1	234.8	3613.6	6.99	11.42	24.1	4.4	—	17.3	3.1
League Total	17033	10372	—	118917	1101	7066	111851	—	—	710	—	98t	525	—
League Average	532.3	324.1	60.9	3716.2	34.4	220.8	3495.3	6.98	11.47	22.2	4.2	—	16.4	3.1

2009 INDIVIDUAL STATISTICS—PASSING

AFC—INDIVIDUAL PASSERS

	Att	Comp	Pct Comp	Yds	Avg Gain	TD	Pct TD	Long	Int	Pct Int	Sack	Yds Lost	Rating Points
Rivers, Philip, S.D.	486	317	65.2	4254	8.75	28	5.8	81t	9	1.9	25	167	104.4
Roethlisberger, Ben, Pit.	506	337	66.6	4328	8.55	26	5.1	60t	12	2.4	50	348	100.5
Manning, Peyton, Ind.	571	393	68.8	4500	7.88	33	5.8	80t	16	2.8	10	74	99.9
Schaub, Matt, Hou.	583	396	67.9	4770	8.18	29	5.0	72t	15	2.6	25	149	98.6
Brady, Tom, N.E.	565	371	65.7	4398	7.78	28	5.0	81t	13	2.3	16	86	96.2
Flacco, Joe, Bal.	499	315	63.1	3613	7.24	21	4.2	72t	12	2.4	36	218	88.9
Orton, Kyle, Den.	541	336	62.1	3802	7.03	21	3.9	87t	12	2.2	29	159	86.8
Palmer, Carson, Cin.	466	282	60.5	3094	6.64	21	4.5	73	13	2.8	26	213	83.6
Garrard, David, Jac.	516	314	60.9	3597	6.97	15	2.9	63	10	1.9	42	236	83.5
Young, Vince, Ten.	259	152	58.7	1879	7.25	10	3.9	66t	7	2.7	9	36	82.8
Henne, Chad, Mia.	451	274	60.8	2878	6.38	12	2.7	67	14	3.1	26	176	75.2
Cassel, Matt, K.C.	493	271	55.0	2924	5.93	16	3.2	61	16	3.2	42	243	69.9
Fitzpatrick, Ryan, Buf.	227	127	55.9	1422	6.26	9	4.0	98t	10	4.4	21	127	69.7
Quinn, Brady, Cle.	256	136	53.1	1339	5.23	8	3.1	59t	7	2.7	19	104	67.2
* Sanchez, Mark, NYJ	364	196	53.8	2444	6.71	12	3.3	65t	20	5.5	26	195	63.0
Russell, JaMarcus, Oak.	246	120	48.8	1287	5.23	3	1.2	86t	11	4.5	33	207	50.0
(Nonqualifiers)													
Croyle, Brodie, K.C.	40	23	57.5	230	5.75	2	5.0	50	0	0.0	3	18	90.6
Volek, Billy, S.D.	31	20	64.5	231	7.45	1	3.2	50	1	3.2	1	1	84.2
* Hoyer, Brian, N.E.	27	19	70.4	142	5.26	0	0.0	17	0	0.0	2	18	82.6
Gradkowski, Bruce, Oak.	150	82	54.7	1007	6.71	6	4.0	75t	3	2.0	11	71	80.6
Pennington, Chad, Mia.	74	51	68.9	413	5.58	1	1.4	21	2	2.7	6	32	76.0
Edwards, Trent, Buf.	183	110	60.1	1169	6.39	6	3.3	46	7	3.8	23	139	73.8
Collins, Kerry, Ten.	216	119	55.1	1225	5.67	6	2.8	69t	8	3.7	6	37	65.5
Frye, Charlie, Oak.	87	53	60.9	581	6.68	1	1.1	33	4	4.6	5	40	65.3
Clemens, Kellen, NYJ	26	13	50.0	125	4.81	0	0.0	26	0	0.0	4	21	63.8
Dixon, Dennis, Pit.	26	12	46.2	145	5.58	1	3.8	33t	1	3.8	0	0	60.6
O'Sullivan, J.T., Cin.	11	4	36.4	40	3.64	0	0.0	16	0	0.0	3	31	47.5
Brohm, Brian, Buf.	29	17	58.6	146	5.03	0	0.0	15	2	6.9	2	8	43.2
Anderson, Derek, Cle.	182	81	44.5	888	4.88	3	1.6	43	10	5.5	11	75	42.1
Simms, Chris, Den.	17	5	29.4	23	1.35	0	0.0	7	1	5.9	5	39	15.1
* Painter, Curtis, Ind.	28	8	28.6	83	2.96	0	0.0	22	2	7.1	3	16	9.8
(Fewer than 10 attempts)													
Addai, Joseph, Ind.	1	1	100.0	22	22.00	1	100.0	22t	0	0.0	0	0	158.3
Batch, Charlie, Pit.	2	1	50.0	17	8.50	0	0.0	17	0	0.0	0	0	79.2
Bradley, Mark, K.C.	1	1	100.0	26	26.00	0	0.0	26	0	0.0	0	0	118.8
Brown, Chris, Hou.	1	0	0.0	0	0.00	0	0.0	—	1	100.0	0	0	0.0
Brown, Ronnie, Mia.	6	2	33.3	22	3.67	1	16.7	21	0	0.0	1	9	84.7
Bush, Michael, Oak.	1	0	0.0	0	0.00	0	0.0	—	0	0.0	0	0	39.6
Castille, Tim, K.C.	1	0	0.0	0	0.00	0	0.0	—	1	100.0	0	0	0.0
Clayton, Mark, Bal.	1	1	100.0	0	0.00	0	0.0	0	0	0.0	0	0	79.2
Cribbs, Josh, Cle.	4	1	25.0	18	4.50	0	0.0	18	1	25.0	0	0	6.3
Dawson, Phil, Cle.	1	1	100.0	10	10.00	0	0.0	10	0	0.0	0	0	108.3
Edwards, Braylon, NYJ	1	0	0.0	0	0.00	0	0.0	—	0	0.0	0	0	39.6
Grossman, Rex, Hou.	9	3	33.3	33	3.67	0	0.0	21	1	11.1	0	0	5.6
Gutierrez, Matt, K.C.	1	1	100.0	3	3.00	0	0.0	3	0	0.0	0	0	79.2
Holmes, Santonio, Pit.	1	0	0.0	0	0.00	0	0.0	—	1	100.0	0	0	0.0
Jackson, Fred, Buf.	1	1	100.0	27	27.00	1	100.0	27t	0	0.0	0	0	158.3
Johnson, Chris, Ten.	1	0	0.0	0	0.00	0	0.0	—	0	0.0	0	0	39.6
Losman, J.P., Oak.	1	0	0.0	0	0.00	0	0.0	—	0	0.0	0	0	39.6
McCown, Luke, Jac.	3	1	33.3	2	0.67	0	0.0	2	0	0.0	2	7	42.4
Moore, Mewelde, Pit.	1	1	100.0	6	6.00	1	100.0	6t	0	0.0	0	0	131.3
Moorman, Brian, Buf.	1	1	100.0	25	25.00	1	100.0	25t	0	0.0	0	0	158.3
Naanee, Legedu, S.D.	1	1	100.0	21	21.00	0	0.0	21	0	0.0	0	0	118.8
Rice, Ray, Bal.	1	0	0.0	0	0.00	0	0.0	—	0	0.0	0	0	39.6
Smith, Brad, NYJ	1	1	100.0	27	27.00	0	0.0	27	0	0.0	0	0	118.8
Smith, Troy, Bal.	9	5	55.6	24	2.67	0	0.0	9	1	11.1	0	0	21.3
Thigpen, Tyler, Mia.	8	4	50.0	83	10.38	1	12.5	34t	2	25.0	0	0	87.0
Tomlinson, LaDainian, S.D.	1	0	0.0	0	0.00	0	0.0	—	0	0.0	0	0	39.6
Wayne, Reggie, Ind.	1	0	0.0	0	0.00	0	0.0	—	1	100.0	0	0	0.0
Weatherford, Steve, NYJ	1	0	0.0	0	0.00	0	0.0	—	1	100.0	0	0	0.0
* White, Pat, Mia.	5	0	0.0	0	0.00	0	0.0	—	0	0.0	1	9	39.6
Williams, Ricky, Mia.	1	0	0.0	0	0.00	0	0.0	—	1	100.0	0	0	0.0

t = Touchdown
Leader based on rating points, minimum 224 attempts
* *Player that was a rookie in 2009*

NFC—INDIVIDUAL PASSERS

	Att	Comp	Pct Comp	Yds	Avg Gain	TD	Pct TD	Long	Int	Pct Int	Sack	Yds Lost	Rating Points
Brees, Drew, N.O.	514	363	70.6	4388	8.54	34	6.6	75t	11	2.1	20	135	109.6
Favre, Brett, Min.	531	363	68.4	4202	7.91	33	6.2	63	7	1.3	34	247	107.2
Rodgers, Aaron, G.B.	541	350	64.7	4434	8.20	30	5.5	83t	7	1.3	50	306	103.2
Romo, Tony, Dal.	550	347	63.1	4483	8.15	26	4.7	80t	9	1.6	34	196	97.6
Warner, Kurt, Ariz	513	339	66.1	3753	7.32	26	5.1	45	14	2.7	24	172	93.2
Manning, Eli, NY-G	509	317	62.3	4021	7.90	27	5.3	74t	14	2.8	30	216	93.1
McNabb, Donovan, Phi.	443	267	60.3	3553	8.02	22	5.0	60t	10	2.3	35	264	92.9
Campbell, Jason, Was.	507	327	64.5	3618	7.14	20	3.9	84	15	3.0	43	285	86.4
Smith, Alex, S.F.	372	225	60.5	2350	6.32	18	4.8	73t	12	3.2	22	134	81.5
Ryan, Matt, Atl.	451	263	58.3	2916	6.47	22	4.9	90t	14	3.1	19	92	80.9
Cutler, Jay, Chi.	555	336	60.5	3666	6.61	27	4.9	71	26	4.7	35	204	76.8
Hasselbeck, Matt, Sea.	488	293	60.0	3029	6.21	17	3.5	53	17	3.5	32	209	75.1
Bulger, Marc, St.L	247	140	56.7	1469	5.95	5	2.0	50	6	2.4	14	85	70.7
* Stafford, Matthew, Det.	377	201	53.3	2267	6.01	13	3.4	75t	20	5.3	24	169	61.0
* Freeman, Josh, T.B.	290	158	54.5	1855	6.40	10	3.4	42t	18	6.2	20	102	59.8
Delhomme, Jake, Car.	321	178	55.5	2015	6.28	8	2.5	52	18	5.6	23	187	59.4
(Nonqualifiers)													
Jackson, Tarvaris, Min.	21	14	66.7	201	9.57	1	4.8	34t	0	0.0	0	0	113.4
Moore, Matt, Car.	138	85	61.6	1053	7.63	8	5.8	66	2	1.4	9	78	98.5
Vick, Michael, Phi.	13	6	46.2	86	6.62	1	7.7	43	0	0.0	0	0	93.8
Carr, David, NY-G	33	21	63.6	225	6.82	1	3.0	37t	0	0.0	2	11	93.6
Kolb, Kevin, Phi.	96	62	64.6	741	7.72	4	4.2	71t	3	3.1	3	27	88.9
Wallace, Seneca, Sea.	120	78	65.0	700	5.83	3	2.5	39t	2	1.7	9	59	81.9
Hill, Shaun, S.F.	155	87	56.1	943	6.08	5	3.2	61	2	1.3	18	107	79.6
Redman, Chris, Atl.	119	69	58.0	781	6.56	4	3.4	50t	3	2.5	8	34	78.4
Collins, Todd, Was.	23	12	52.2	144	6.26	0	0.0	46	0	0.0	2	11	71.6
Leftwich, Byron, T.B.	107	58	54.2	594	5.55	4	3.7	47	3	2.8	2	0	71.2
Culpepper, Daunte, Det.	157	89	56.7	945	6.02	3	1.9	38	6	3.8	14	107	64.8
Leinart, Matt, Ariz	77	51	66.2	435	5.65	0	0.0	28	3	3.9	2	12	64.6
Boller, Kyle, St.L	176	98	55.7	899	5.11	3	1.7	35	6	3.4	17	117	61.2
Johnson, Josh, T.B.	125	63	50.4	685	5.48	4	3.2	35	8	6.4	11	59	50.9
* Null, Keith, St.L	119	73	61.3	566	4.76	3	2.5	25	9	7.6	13	82	49.9
Brunell, Mark, N.O.	30	15	50.0	102	3.40	0	0.0	18	1	3.3	0	0	44.0
Flynn, Matt, G.B.	12	7	58.3	58	4.83	0	0.0	17	1	8.3	1	6	36.1
Stanton, Drew, Det.	51	26	51.0	259	5.08	0	0.0	30	6	11.8	5	27	26.1
(Fewer than 10 attempts)													
Brown, Josh, St.L	1	1	100.0	36	36.00	1	100.0	36t	0	0.0	0	0	158.3
Clayton, Michael, T.B.	1	0	0.0	0	0.00	0	0.0	—	0	0.0	0	0	39.6
Hanie, Caleb, Chi.	7	3	42.9	11	1.57	0	0.0	5	1	14.3	0	0	10.7
Johnson, Dirk, T.B.	1	0	0.0	0	0.00	0	0.0	—	0	0.0	0	0	39.6
Maynard, Brad, Chi.	1	1	100.0	0	0.00	0	0.0	0	0	0.0	0	0	79.2
McCown, Josh, Car.	6	1	16.7	2	0.33	0	0.0	2	0	0.0	1	6	39.6
Portis, Clinton, Was.	1	0	0.0	0	0.00	0	0.0	—	0	0.0	0	0	39.6
Randle El, Antwaan, Was.	0	0	—	0	—	0	—	—	0	—	1	11	—
Rice, Sidney, Min.	1	0	0.0	0	0.00	0	0.0	—	0	0.0	0	0	39.6
Ryan, Jon, Sea.	1	1	100.0	42	42.00	0	0.0	42	0	0.0	0	0	118.8
Smith, Hunter, Was.	2	1	50.0	35	17.50	1	50.0	35t	1	50.0	0	0	95.8
Spurlock, Micheal, S.F.	1	0	0.0	0	0.00	0	0.0	—	0	0.0	0	0	39.6
St. Pierre, Brian, Ariz	4	2	50.0	12	3.00	1	25.0	9	1	25.0	0	0	56.3
Westbrook, Brian, Phi.	1	0	0.0	0	0.00	0	0.0	—	0	0.0	0	0	39.6

t = Touchdown
Leader based on rating points, minimum 224 attempts
* *Player that was a rookie in 2009*

2009 INDIVIDUAL STATISTICS—PASS RECEIVING

PASS RECEIVING

RECEPTIONS

AFC: 123 Wes Welker, New England

NFC: 107 Steve Smith, N.Y. Giants

RECEPTIONS, GAME

AFC: 21 Brandon Marshall, Denver at Indianapolis, December 13 (200 yards, 2 TD)

NFC: 14 Jason Witten, Dallas at N.Y. Giants, December 6 (156 yards, 0 TD)

YARDS

AFC: 1569 Andre Johnson, Houston

NFC: 1320 Miles Austin, Dallas

YARDS, GAME

NFC: 250 Miles Austin, Dallas at Kansas City, October 11 (10 receptions, 2 TD) - (OT)

AFC: 213 Jabar Gaffney, Denver vs. Kansas City, January 3 (14 receptions, 0 TD)

LONGEST

AFC: 98 Terrell Owens (from Ryan Fitzpatrick) Buffalo at Jacksonville, November 22 - TD

NFC: 90 Roddy White (from Matt Ryan) Atlanta at San Francisco, October 11 - TD

YARDS PER RECEPTION

AFC: 19.4* Mike Wallace, Pittsburgh

NFC: 18.6 DeSean Jackson, Philadelphia

TOUCHDOWNS

AFC: 13 Randy Moss, New England

NFC: 13 Vernon Davis, San Francisco

13 Larry Fitzgerald, Arizona

TEAM LEADERS, RECEPTIONS

AFC: BALTIMORE, 78, Ray Rice; BUFFALO, 55, Terrell Owens; CINCINNATI, 72, Chad Ochocinco; CLEVELAND, 34, *Jerome Harrison, Mohamed Massaquoi; DENVER, 101, Brandon Marshall; HOUSTON, 101, Andre Johnson; INDIANAPOLIS, 100, Dallas Clark, Reggie Wayne; JACKSONVILLE, 63, Mike Sims-Walker; KANSAS CITY, 47, Dwayne Bowe; MIAMI, 76, Davone Bess; NEW ENGLAND, 123, Wes Welker; N.Y. JETS, 57, Jerricho Cotchery; OAKLAND, 66, Zach Miller; PITTSBURGH, 95, Hines Ward; SAN DIEGO, 79, Antonio Gates; TENNESSEE, 50, Chris Johnson

NFC: ARIZONA, 97, Larry Fitzgerald; ATLANTA, 85, Roddy White; CAROLINA, 65, Steve Smith; CHICAGO, 60, Greg Olsen; DALLAS, 94, Jason Witten; DETROIT, 67, Calvin Johnson; GREEN BAY, 70, Donald Driver; MINNESOTA, 83, Sidney Rice; NEW ORLEANS, 70, Marques Colston; N.Y. GIANTS, 107, Steve Smith; PHILADELPHIA, 76, Brent Celek; ST. LOUIS, 51, Steven Jackson; SAN FRANCISCO, 78, Vernon Davis; SEATTLE, 79, T.J. Houshmandzadeh; TAMPA BAY, 77, Kellen Winslow; WASHINGTON, 70, Santana Moss

** Player that was a rookie in 2009*

NFL TOP TEN PASS RECEIVERS

	No	Yards	Avg	Long	TD
Welker, Wes, N.E.	123	1348	11.0	58	4
Smith, Steve, NY-G	107	1220	11.4	51	7
Johnson, Andre, Hou.	101	1569	15.5	72t	9
Marshall, Brandon, Den.	101	1120	11.1	75t	10
Clark, Dallas, Ind.	100	1106	11.1	80t	10
Wayne, Reggie, Ind.	100	1264	12.6	65t	10
Fitzgerald, Larry, Ariz	97	1092	11.3	34t	13
Ward, Hines, Pit.	95	1167	12.3	54	6
Witten, Jason, Dal.	94	1030	11.0	69	2
White, Roddy, Atl.	85	1153	13.6	90t	11

NFL TOP TEN RECEIVERS BY YARDS

	Yards	No	Avg	Long	TD
Johnson, Andre, Hou.	1569	101	15.5	72t	9
Welker, Wes, N.E.	1348	123	11.0	58	4
Austin, Miles, Dal.	1320	81	16.3	60t	11
Rice, Sidney, Min.	1312	83	15.8	63	8
Moss, Randy, N.E.	1264	83	15.2	71t	13
Wayne, Reggie, Ind.	1264	100	12.6	65t	10
Holmes, Santonio, Pit.	1248	79	15.8	57	5
Smith, Steve, NY-G	1220	107	11.4	51	7
Jackson, Vincent, S.D.	1167	68	17.2	55	9
Ward, Hines, Pit.	1167	95	12.3	54	6

AFC—INDIVIDUAL RECEIVERS

	No	Yards	Avg	Long	TD
Welker, Wes, N.E.	123	1348	11.0	58	4
Johnson, Andre, Hou.	101	1569	15.5	72t	9
Marshall, Brandon, Den.	101	1120	11.1	75t	10
Wayne, Reggie, Ind.	100	1264	12.6	65t	10
Clark, Dallas, Ind.	100	1106	11.1	80t	10
Ward, Hines, Pit.	95	1167	12.3	54	6
Moss, Randy, N.E.	83	1264	15.2	71t	13
Holmes, Santonio, Pit.	79	1248	15.8	57	5
Gates, Antonio, S.D.	79	1157	14.6	56	8
Rice, Ray, Bal.	78	702	9.0	63	1
Miller, Heath, Pit.	76	789	10.4	41	6
Bess, Davone, Mia.	76	758	10.0	34t	2
Mason, Derrick, Bal.	73	1028	14.1	72t	7
Ochocinco, Chad, Cin.	72	1047	14.5	50	9
Jackson, Vincent, S.D.	68	1167	17.2	55	9
Miller, Zach, Oak.	66	805	12.2	86t	3
Sims-Walker, Mike, Jac.	63	869	13.8	61t	7
* Collie, Austin, Ind.	60	676	11.3	39t	7
Cotchery, Jerricho, NYJ	57	821	14.4	53	3
Owens, Terrell, Buf.	55	829	15.1	98t	5
Gaffney, Jabar, Den.	54	732	13.6	49	2
Walter, Kevin, Hou.	53	611	11.5	41	2
Heap, Todd, Bal.	53	593	11.2	31	6
Jones-Drew, Maurice, Jac.	53	374	7.1	19	1
Holt, Torry, Jac.	51	722	14.2	63	0
Caldwell, Andre, Cin.	51	432	8.5	24	3
Addai, Joseph, Ind.	51	336	6.6	25	3
Camarillo, Greg, Mia.	50	552	11.0	29	0
Johnson, Chris, Ten.	50	503	10.1	69t	2
* Thomas, Mike, Jac.	48	453	9.4	28	1
Garcon, Pierre, Ind.	47	765	16.3	66	4
Bowe, Dwayne, K.C.	47	589	12.5	41	4
Washington, Nate, Ten.	47	569	12.1	35	6
Jackson, Fred, Buf.	46	371	8.1	21	2
Floyd, Malcom, S.D.	45	776	17.2	53	1
Chambers, Chris, S.D.-K.C.	45	730	16.2	61	5
Edwards, Braylon, Cle.-NYJ	45	680	15.1	65t	4
Keller, Dustin, NYJ	45	522	11.6	40	2
Sproles, Darren, S.D.	45	497	11.0	81t	4
Scaife, Bo, Ten.	45	440	9.8	27	1
Evans, Lee, Buf.	44	612	13.9	50	7
Slaton, Steve, Hou.	44	417	9.5	38t	4

	No	Yards	Avg	Long	TD
Coles, Laveranues, Cin.	43	514	12.0	40	5
* Britt, Kenny, Ten.	42	701	16.7	57	3
Daniels, Owen, Hou.	40	519	13.0	44	5
Charles, Jamaal, K.C.	40	297	7.4	49	1
* Wallace, Mike, Pit.	39	756	19.4	60t	6
Ginn, Ted Jr., Mia.	38	454	11.9	53t	1
Anderson, David, Hou.	38	370	9.7	27	0
* Edelman, Julian, N.E.	37	359	9.7	29	1
Royal, Eddie, Den.	37	345	9.3	20	0
Faulk, Kevin, N.E.	37	301	8.1	38t	1
Wade, Bobby, K.C.	36	367	10.2	25	2
Williams, Ricky, Mia.	35	264	7.5	59	2
* Massaquoi, Mohamed, Cle.	34	624	18.4	59t	3
* Murphy, Louis, Oak.	34	521	15.3	75t	4
Clayton, Mark, Bal.	34	480	14.1	54	2
Washington, Kelley, Bal.	34	431	12.7	28	2
Harrison, Jerome, Cle.	34	220	6.5	18	2
Lewis, Marcedes, Jac.	32	518	16.2	47	2
* Hartline, Brian, Mia.	31	506	16.3	67	3
Scheffler, Tony, Den.	31	416	13.4	52	2
Fasano, Anthony, Mia.	31	339	10.9	27	2
Buckhalter, Correll, Den.	31	240	7.7	30	0
Stuckey, Chansi, NYJ-Cle.	30	318	10.6	40t	2
Leonard, Brian, Cin.	30	217	7.2	18	0
Watson, Benjamin, N.E.	29	404	13.9	36	5
Schilens, Chaz, Oak.	29	365	12.6	25	2
Gage, Justin, Ten.	28	383	13.7	49	3
Graham, Daniel, Den.	28	289	10.3	24	1
* Moreno, Knowshon, Den.	28	213	7.6	27	2
Lynch, Marshawn, Buf.	28	179	6.4	35	0
Jones, Jacoby, Hou.	27	437	16.2	45	6
Reed, Josh, Buf.	27	291	10.8	29	1
Foschi, J.P., Cin.	27	260	9.6	27	2
Crumpler, Alge, Ten.	27	222	8.2	27	1
Dreessen, Joel, Hou.	26	320	12.3	25t	1
Mendenhall, Rashard, Pit.	25	261	10.4	26	1
Bradley, Mark, K.C.	24	320	13.3	50	2
Naanee, Legedu, S.D.	24	242	10.1	23	2
Furrey, Mike, Cle.	23	170	7.4	22	0
McFadden, Darren, Oak.	21	245	11.7	48	0
* Miller, Zach, Jac.	21	212	10.1	62	2
Moore, Mewelde, Pit.	21	153	7.3	19t	2
McClain, Le'Ron, Bal.	21	141	6.7	19	0
Aiken, Sam, N.E.	20	326	16.3	81t	2
Long, Lance, K.C.	20	178	8.9	30	0
Pope, Leonard, K.C.	20	174	8.7	29	1
Hilliard, Lex, Mia.	20	158	7.9	18	2
Leach, Vonta, Hou.	20	155	7.8	26	1
Tomlinson, LaDainian, S.D.	20	154	7.7	36	0
Cribbs, Josh, Cle.	20	135	6.8	35	1
Stokley, Brandon, Den.	19	327	17.2	87t	4
Higgins, Johnnie Lee, Oak.	19	263	13.8	33	0
Morris, Sammy, N.E.	19	180	9.5	35	0
Haynos, Joey, Mia.	19	162	8.5	21	2
Tolbert, Mike, S.D.	17	192	11.3	66t	3
* Nelson, Shawn, Buf.	17	156	9.2	25	1
Fargas, Justin, Oak.	17	113	6.6	14	0
Benson, Cedric, Cin.	17	111	6.5	19	0
Bush, Michael, Oak.	17	105	6.2	17	0
Coats, Daniel, Cin.	16	150	9.4	23	0
* Jennings, Rashad, Jac.	16	101	6.3	14	0
Brown, Chris, Hou.	16	74	4.6	12	0
Washington, Leon, NYJ	15	131	8.7	33	0
McGahee, Willis, Bal.	15	85	5.7	14	2
Johnson, Larry, K.C.-Cin.	15	80	5.3	22	0
Clowney, David, NYJ	14	191	13.6	53	1
Baker, Chris, N.E.	14	142	10.1	36t	2
Ryan, Sean, K.C.	14	135	9.6	43	2
Maroney, Laurence, N.E.	14	99	7.1	17	0
Brown, Ronnie, Mia.	14	98	7.0	27	0
Moats, Ryan, Hou.	13	106	8.2	20	1
Henry, Chris, Cin.	12	236	19.7	73	2
Moore, Evan, Cle.	12	158	13.2	24	0
Russell, Gary, Oak.	12	96	8.0	20	0
Hall, Ahmard, Ten.	12	79	6.6	15	0
* Brown, Donald, Ind.	11	169	15.4	72	0
Royal, Robert, Cle.	11	134	12.2	29	1
Wilford, Ernest, Jac.	11	123	11.2	30	1
Polite, Lousaka, Mia.	11	51	4.6	10	0
Cox, Mike, K.C.	10	79	7.9	19	0
Stewart, Tony, Oak.	10	78	7.8	19	0
Heiden, Steve, Cle.	10	73	7.3	14	1
Jones, Thomas, NYJ	10	58	5.8	28	0
* Heyward-Bey, Darrius, Oak.	9	124	13.8	24	1
Cottam, Brad, K.C.	9	120	13.3	26	0
Schouman, Derek, Buf.	9	103	11.4	27	0
* Cook, Jared, Ten.	9	74	8.2	17	0
Fine, Derek, Buf.	9	64	7.1	11	0
Robinson, Gijon, Ind.	9	62	6.9	19	0
* Jennings, Chris, Cle.	9	56	6.2	19	0
Hester, Jacob, S.D.	9	24	2.7	5	0
Williams, Demetrius, Bal.	8	142	17.8	34	1
Lloyd, Brandon, Den.	8	117	14.6	44	0
Santi, Tom, Ind.	8	107	13.4	31	0
* Foster, Arian, Hou.	8	93	11.6	20	0
Watkins, Todd, Oak.	8	90	11.3	28	0
Lewis, Jamal, Cle.	8	88	11.0	19	0
Woodhead, Danny, NYJ	8	87	10.9	24	0
Vickers, Lawrence, Cle.	8	27	3.4	12	1
Hawkins, Lavelle, Ten.	7	110	15.7	32	0
* Robiskie, Brian, Cle.	7	106	15.1	43	0
Galloway, Joey, N.E.	7	67	9.6	19	0
Smith, Brad, NYJ	7	63	9.0	19	0
McIntyre, Corey, Buf.	7	55	7.9	18	0
Savage, Dantrell, K.C.	7	51	7.3	12	0
Lawton, Luke, Oak.	7	31	4.4	14	0
* Dillard, Jarett, Jac.	6	106	17.7	33	0
Bennett, Michael, S.D.	6	65	10.8	33	0
* Casey, James, Hou.	6	64	10.7	32	0
Parker, Willie, Pit.	6	64	10.7	27t	1
Davis, Andre, Hou.	6	59	9.8	21	0
Davis, Craig, S.D.	6	52	8.7	11	0
Johnson, Jeremi, Cin.	6	41	6.8	9	0
Stupar, Jonathan, Buf.	6	40	6.7	17	0
Hughes, Nate, Jac.	5	70	14.0	35t	1
* Scott, Bernard, Cin.	5	67	13.4	23	0
Engram, Bobby, K.C.	5	61	12.2	18	0
Gaines, Michael, Cle.	5	59	11.8	24	1
Hart, Mike, Ind.	5	54	10.8	14	0
Baskett, Hank, Phi.-Ind.	5	34	6.8	9	0
Spaeth, Matt, Pit.	5	25	5.0	9	1
Jones, Greg, Jac.	5	14	2.8	9	0
Manumaleuna, Brandon, S.D.	5	13	2.6	11	0
Copper, Terrance, K.C.	4	68	17.0	50	0
* Cosby, Quan, Cin.	4	55	13.8	23	0
Estandia, Greg, Cle.	4	45	11.3	18	0
Castille, Tim, K.C.	4	37	9.3	20t	1
Wilson, Kris, S.D.	4	28	7.0	21	1
Hillis, Peyton, Den.	4	19	4.8	6	0
* Myers, Brandon, Oak.	4	19	4.8	6	0
* Davis, James, Cle.	4	5	1.3	2	0
Tamme, Jacob, Ind.	3	35	11.7	21	0
Parrish, Roscoe, Buf.	3	34	11.3	16	0
Williamson, Troy, Jac.	3	34	11.3	13	0
* Sperry, Kory, Mia.	3	31	10.3	13	1
Cobbs, Patrick, Mia.	3	23	7.7	10	0

2009 INDIVIDUAL STATISTICS—PASS RECEIVING

	No	Yards	Avg	Long	TD
Stanback, Isaiah, N.E.	3	22	7.3	9	0
White, LenDale, Ten.	3	14	4.7	7	0
Richardson, Tony, NYJ	3	10	3.3	5	0
Simpson, Chad, Ind.	3	1	0.3	5	0
Smith, L.J., Bal.	2	31	15.5	26	0
Wright, Wallace, NYJ	2	21	10.5	14	0
Reece, Marcel, Oak.	2	20	10.0	11	0
Taylor, Fred, N.E.	2	17	8.5	13	0
Green-Ellis, BenJarvus, N.E.	2	11	5.5	6	0
Johnson, Steve, Buf.	2	10	5.0	5	0
* Johnson, David, Pit.	2	9	4.5	5	0
Smith, Kolby, K.C.	2	9	4.5	5	0
* O'Connell, Jake, K.C.	2	7	3.5	4	0
Battle, Jackie, K.C.	2	-3	-1.5	3	0
Smith, Eric, NYJ	1	27	27.0	27	0
Denney, Ryan, Buf.	1	25	25.0	25t	1
Quinn, Brady, Cle.	1	18	18.0	18	0
Osgood, Kassim, S.D.	1	17	17.0	17	0
* Grisham, Tyler, Pit.	1	14	14.0	14	0
Klopfenstein, Joe, Buf.	1	11	11.0	11	0
Hardy, James, Buf.	1	9	9.0	9	0
* Hill, Anthony, Hou.	1	9	9.0	9	0
Jones, Mark, Ten.	1	9	9.0	9	0
* Lawrence, Quinten, K.C.	1	9	9.0	9	0
Jones, Edgar, Bal.	1	8	8.0	8	0
Logan, Stefan, Pit.	1	5	5.0	5	0
Sweed, Limas, Pit.	1	5	5.0	5	0
Lawrence, Matt, Bal.	1	4	4.0	4	0
* Potter, Zach, Jac.	1	3	3.0	3	0
* Cloherty, Colin, Ind.-	1	2	2.0	2	0
Hartsock, Ben, NYJ	1	2	2.0	2t	1
Mulligan, Matthew, NYJ	1	2	2.0	2	0
Vrabel, Mike, K.C.	1	1	1.0	1t	1
* Oher, Michael, Bal.	1	-8	-8.0	-8	0
Kuper, Chris, Den.	0	7	—	7	0

*t = Touchdown; * Player that was a rookie in 2009*
Leader based on receptions

NFC—INDIVIDUAL RECEIVERS

	No	Yards	Avg	Long	TD
Smith, Steve, NY-G	107	1220	11.4	51	7
Fitzgerald, Larry, Ariz	97	1092	11.3	34t	13
Witten, Jason, Dal.	94	1030	11.0	69	2
White, Roddy, Atl.	85	1153	13.6	90t	11
Boldin, Anquan, Ariz	84	1024	12.2	44	4
Rice, Sidney, Min.	83	1312	15.8	63	8
Gonzalez, Tony, Atl.	83	867	10.4	27	6
Austin, Miles, Dal.	81	1320	16.3	60t	11
Houshmandzadeh, T.J., Sea.	79	911	11.5	53	3
Davis, Vernon, S.F.	78	965	12.4	73t	13
Winslow, Kellen, T.B.	77	884	11.5	42t	5
Celek, Brent, Phi.	76	971	12.8	47t	8
Colston, Marques, N.O.	70	1074	15.3	68	9
Driver, Donald, G.B.	70	1061	15.2	71t	6
Moss, Santana, Was.	70	902	12.9	59t	3
Jennings, Greg, G.B.	68	1113	16.4	83t	4
Johnson, Calvin, Det.	67	984	14.7	75t	5
Smith, Steve, Car.	65	982	15.1	66	7
Burleson, Nate, Sea.	63	812	12.9	44t	3
Hightower, Tim, Ariz	63	428	6.8	23	0
Jackson, DeSean, Phi.	62	1156	18.6	71t	9
* Harvin, Percy, Min.	60	790	13.2	51t	6
Olsen, Greg, Chi.	60	612	10.2	41	8
Manningham, Mario, NY-G	57	822	14.4	49	5
Hester, Devin, Chi.	57	757	13.3	48	3
Forté, Matt, Chi.	57	471	8.3	37	0
* Maclin, Jeremy, Phi.	56	773	13.8	56	4
Shiancoe, Visanthe, Min.	56	566	10.1	27	11
Breaston, Steve, Ariz	55	712	12.9	45	3
Finley, Jermichael, G.B.	55	676	12.3	62t	5
Berrian, Bernard, Min.	55	618	11.2	40	4
Bennett, Earl, Chi.	54	717	13.3	71	2
Muhammad, Muhsin, Car.	53	581	11.0	27	1
Morgan, Josh, S.F.	52	527	10.1	61	3
Gore, Frank, S.F.	52	406	7.8	48	3
Henderson, Devery, N.O.	51	804	15.8	75t	2
Carlson, John, Sea.	51	574	11.3	42	7
Jackson, Steven, St.L	51	322	6.3	38	0
Jenkins, Michael, Atl.	50	635	12.7	50t	1
Randle El, Antwaan, Was.	50	530	10.6	44	0
* Crabtree, Michael, S.F.	48	625	13.0	50	2
Shockey, Jeremy, N.O.	48	569	11.9	66	3
Davis, Fred, Was.	48	509	10.6	29	6
* Nicks, Hakeem, NY-G	47	790	16.8	68t	6
Avery, Donnie, St.L	47	589	12.5	50	5
Bush, Reggie, N.O.	47	335	7.1	29	3
Meachem, Robert, N.O.	45	722	16.0	54t	9
* Knox, Johnny, Chi.	45	527	11.7	68	5
Branch, Deion, Sea.	45	437	9.7	35	2
Taylor, Chester, Min.	44	389	8.8	33	1
Peterson, Adrian, Min.	43	436	10.1	63	0
Amendola, Danny, St.L	43	326	7.6	25	1
Boss, Kevin, NY-G	42	567	13.5	35	5
Avant, Jason, Phi.	41	587	14.3	58	3
Smith, Kevin, Det.	41	415	10.1	63	1
Forsett, Justin, Sea.	41	350	8.5	47	1
* McCoy, LeSean, Phi.	40	308	7.7	45	0
Bryant, Antonio, T.B.	39	600	15.4	42t	4
Thomas, Pierre, N.O.	39	302	7.7	36	2
Williams, Roy E., Dal.	38	596	15.7	66t	7
Crayton, Patrick, Dal.	37	622	16.8	80t	5
Lee, Donald, G.B.	37	260	7.0	19	1
Johnson, Bryant, Det.	35	417	11.9	36	3
Northcutt, Dennis, Det.	35	357	10.2	47	1
Thomas, David, N.O.	35	356	10.2	37	1
Jones, Julius, Sea.	35	232	6.6	49	2
* Gibson, Brandon, St.L	34	348	10.2	23	1
McMichael, Randy, St.L	34	332	9.8	35	1
Jones, James, G.B.	32	440	13.8	74t	5
* Stroughter, Sammie, T.B.	31	334	10.8	35	1
* Pettigrew, Brandon, Det.	30	346	11.5	30	2
Snelling, Jason, Atl.	30	259	8.6	38	1
Cooley, Chris, Was.	29	332	11.4	25	2
Heller, Will, Det.	29	296	10.2	24	3
Williams, DeAngelo, Car.	29	252	8.7	30	0
Williams, Cadillac, T.B.	28	217	7.8	22t	3
Cartwright, Rock, Was.	27	242	9.0	51	1
Rosario, Dante, Car.	26	313	12.0	26	2
Barber, Marion, Dal.	26	221	8.5	42	0
Morris, Maurice, Det.	26	210	8.1	19	0
Kelly, Malcolm, Was.	25	347	13.9	84	0
Thomas, Devin, Was.	25	325	13.0	40	3
Burton, Keenan, St.L	25	253	10.1	25	0
King, Jeff, Car.	25	200	8.0	32	3
Grant, Ryan, G.B.	25	197	7.9	27	0
Westbrook, Brian, Phi.	25	181	7.2	34	1
Stovall, Maurice, T.B.	24	366	15.3	38	1
Aromashodu, Devin, Chi.	24	298	12.4	39t	4
Nelson, Jordy, G.B.	22	320	14.5	51	2
Fells, Daniel, St.L	21	273	13.0	36t	3
Bruce, Isaac, S.F.	21	264	12.6	50	0
Walker, Delanie, S.F.	21	233	11.1	39	0
Bradshaw, Ahmad, NY-G	21	207	9.9	55	0
Jackson, Brandon, G.B.	21	187	8.9	17	1
Ward, Derrick, T.B.	20	150	7.5	38	2

	No	Yards	Avg	Long	TD
Norwood, Jerious, Atl.	19	186	9.8	38	1
Clark, Desmond, Chi.	19	145	7.6	26	2
Jones, Felix, Dal.	19	119	6.3	30	0
Griffith, Justin, Sea.	19	118	6.2	25	1
Urban, Jerheme, Ariz	18	186	10.3	40	0
Jacobs, Brandon, NY-G	18	184	10.2	74t	1
Stewart, Jonathan, Car.	18	139	7.7	19	1
Fitzsimmons, Casey, Det.	18	128	7.1	12	0
Darby, Kenneth, St.L	18	96	5.3	13	0
Doucet, Early, Ariz	17	214	12.6	29	1
Jarrett, Dwayne, Car.	17	196	11.5	30t	1
Betts, Ladell, Was.	17	179	10.5	25	0
Sellers, Mike, Was.	17	176	10.4	47	2
Clayton, Michael, T.B.	16	230	14.4	47	1
Booker, Marty, Atl.	16	181	11.3	27	1
Hixon, Domenik, NY-G	15	187	12.5	61t	1
* Butler, Deon, Sea.	15	175	11.7	32	0
Bennett, Martellus, Dal.	15	159	10.6	21	0
Weaver, Leonard, Phi.	15	140	9.3	59	2
Choice, Tashard, Dal.	15	132	8.8	28	0
Stevens, Jerramy, T.B.	15	130	8.7	17	1
Moore, Lance, N.O.	14	153	10.9	22	2
Graham, Earnest, T.B.	14	109	7.8	16	0
Robinson, Laurent, St.L	13	167	12.8	45	1
Felton, Jerome, Det.	13	133	10.2	27	0
Barnidge, Gary, Car.	12	242	20.2	55	0
Patrick, Ben, Ariz	12	146	12.2	28	2
* Wells, Beanie, Ariz	12	143	11.9	25	0
Peelle, Justin, Atl.	12	115	9.6	32	2
Finneran, Brian, Atl.	11	111	10.1	19	0
* Coffee, Glen, S.F.	11	76	6.9	12	0
* Stephens-Howling, LaRod, Ariz	10	83	8.3	15	1
Evans, Heath, N.O.	10	70	7.0	13t	2
Kleinsasser, Jimmy, Min.	10	70	7.0	21	0
Tahi, Naufahu, Min.	10	67	6.7	32	1
Brown, Reggie, Phi.	9	155	17.2	43	0
Ganther, Quinton, Was.	9	99	11.0	42	0
Hill, Jason, S.F.	9	90	10.0	30	2
* Brown, Aaron, Det.	9	84	9.3	26t	1
Davis, Kellen, Chi.	9	75	8.3	18	3
Portis, Clinton, Was.	9	57	6.3	10t	1
Wright, Jason, Ariz	9	53	5.9	10	2
Hagan, Derek, NY-G	8	101	12.6	23t	1
Lewis, Greg, Min.	8	96	12.0	32t	1
Bajema, Billy, St.L	8	94	11.8	27	0
* Beckum, Travis, NY-G	8	55	6.9	15	0
Hurd, Sam, Dal.	7	121	17.3	53	1
Havner, Spencer, G.B.	7	112	16.0	45t	4
* Ogletree, Kevin, Dal.	7	96	13.7	21	0
* Phillips, John, Dal.	7	62	8.9	23	0
Becht, Anthony, Ariz	7	61	8.7	16	1
Mughelli, Ovie, Atl.	7	51	7.3	21	1
Kuhn, John, G.B.	7	47	6.7	14	2
Norris, Moran, S.F.	7	31	4.4	11	0
Martin, Ruvell, St.L	6	99	16.5	33	0
Curtis, Kevin, Phi.	6	77	12.8	19	0
Clark, Brian, T.B.	6	65	10.8	17	0
* Sutton, Tyrell, Car.	6	62	10.3	13	0
Moore, Kenny, Car.	6	59	9.8	22	0
Mason, Marcus, Was.	6	58	9.7	17	0
Dugan, Jeff, Min.	6	52	8.7	25	2
* Williams, Derrick, Det.	6	52	8.7	19	0
Weems, Eric, Atl.	6	50	8.3	30t	2
Robinson, Michael, S.F.	6	24	4.0	8	0
Schmitt, Owen, Sea.	6	21	3.5	10	1
Karney, Mike, St.L	6	16	2.7	9	0
Hamilton, Lynell, N.O.	5	48	9.6	16	0
Hall, Korey, G.B.	5	41	8.2	13	0

	No	Yards	Avg	Long	TD
Battle, Arnaz, S.F.	5	40	8.0	12	0
Davis, Rashied, Chi.	5	35	7.0	10	0
Turner, Michael, Atl.	5	35	7.0	10	0
Stecker, Aaron, Atl.	5	34	6.8	14	0
Rankin, Louis, Sea.	5	33	6.6	14	0
Johnson, Darcy, NY-G	5	32	6.4	14	0
Dinkins, Darnell, N.O.	5	22	4.4	8	1
McKie, Jason, Chi.	5	13	2.6	8	0
Obomanu, Ben, Sea.	4	41	10.3	12	0
Spach, Stephen, Ariz	4	38	9.5	22	0
* Mitchell, Marko, Was.	4	32	8.0	11	0
Hedgecock, Madison, NY-G	4	23	5.8	9	1
Hoover, Brad, Car.	4	23	5.8	12	1
Kreider, Dan, Ariz	4	20	5.0	8	0
Bell, Mike, N.O.	4	12	3.0	9	0
Yoder, Todd, Was.	4	9	2.3	3t	3
Gado, Samkon, St.L	3	25	8.3	13	0
Smith, Alex, Phi.	3	25	8.3	11	0
Gilmore, John, T.B.	3	23	7.7	9	0
Haynes, Verron, Atl.	3	20	6.7	10	0
James, Edgerrin, Sea.	3	19	6.3	7	0
Green, Ahman, G.B.	3	18	6.0	12	0
Owens, John, Sea.	3	16	5.3	8	0
Ware, Danny, NY-G	3	15	5.0	14	0
Wallace, Seneca, Sea.	2	29	14.5	24	0
Nordin, Jake, Det.	2	26	13.0	14	0
Wynn, DeShawn, G.B.	2	19	9.5	11	0
* Goodson, Mike, Car.	2	15	7.5	13	0
Eckel, Kyle, N.O.	2	14	7.0	8	0
Wolfe, Garrett, Chi.	2	12	6.0	12	0
Peterson, Adrian, Chi.	2	11	5.5	7	0
Smith, Terrelle, Det.	2	7	3.5	4	0
* Johnson, Quinn, G.B.	2	4	2.0	4	0
Smith, Clifton, T.B.	2	4	2.0	3	0
Askew, B.J., T.B.	2	3	1.5	4	0
* Ogbonnaya, Chris, St.L	1	19	19.0	19	0
Jones, Brandon, S.F.	1	18	18.0	18	0
Moss, Sinorice, NY-G	1	18	18.0	18t	1
* Barden, Ramses, NY-G	1	16	16.0	16	0
Penn, Donald, T.B.	1	15	15.0	15	0
Johnson, Jaymar, Min.	1	9	9.0	9	0
* Pascoe, Bear, NY-G	1	9	9.0	9	0
Figurs, Yamon, Det.	1	7	7.0	7	0
Humphrey, Tory, N.O.	1	7	7.0	7	0
Carter, Tim, St.L	1	6	6.0	6	0
* Martin, Charly, Car.	1	6	6.0	6	0
Roby, Courtney, N.O.	1	6	6.0	6	0
Anderson, Deon, Dal.	1	5	5.0	5	0
Kent, Jordan, St.L	1	5	5.0	5	0
Standeford, John, Det.	1	5	5.0	5	0
* Bell, Kahlil, Chi.	1	4	4.0	4	0
* Gronkowski, Dan, Det.	1	4	4.0	4	0
* Morrah, Cameron, Sea.	1	3	3.0	3	0
* Pressley, Chris, T.B.	1	2	2.0	2	0
McNabb, Donovan, Phi.	1	1	1.0	1	0
Favre, Brett, Min.	1	-2	-2.0	-2	0
Tauscher, Mark, G.B.	1	-3	-3.0	-3	0
Brees, Drew, N.O.	1	-4	-4.0	-4	0
Smith, Alex, S.F.	1	-6	-6.0	-6	0
* Freeman, Josh, T.B.	0	1	—	1	0
Zuttah, Jeremy, T.B.	0	1	—	1	0

*t = Touchdown; * Player that was a rookie in 2009*
Leader based on receptions

2009 INDIVIDUAL STATISTICS—INTERCEPTIONS

INTERCEPTIONS

INTERCEPTIONS

AFC: 9 * Jairus Byrd, Buffalo
NFC: 9 Asante Samuel, Philadelphia
9 Darren Sharper, New Orleans
9 Charles Woodson, Green Bay

INTERCEPTIONS, GAME

AFC: 3 Leigh Bodden, New England vs. N.Y. Jets, November 22 (60 yards, 1 TD)
NFC: 3 Aqib Talib, Tampa Bay at Washington, October 4 (61 yards, 0 TD)

YARDS

NFC: 376 Darren Sharper, New Orleans
AFC: 194 Cortland Finnegan, Tennessee

LONGEST

NFC: 101 * Louis Delmas, Detroit vs. Arizona, December 20 - TD
AFC: 94 Andy Studebaker, Kansas City vs. Pittsburgh, November 22 - (OT)

TOUCHDOWNS

NFC: 3 Darren Sharper, New Orleans
3 Charles Woodson, Green Bay
AFC: 2 Vincent Fuller, Tennessee
2 Derrick Johnson, Kansas City

TEAM LEADERS, INTERCEPTIONS

AFC: BALTIMORE, 4, Domonique Foxworth, Dawan Landry; BUFFALO, 9, *Jairus Byrd; CINCINNATI, 6, Leon Hall, Johnathan Joseph; CLEVELAND, 4, Brodney Pool, Eric Wright; DENVER, 5, Andre' Goodman; HOUSTON, 4, *Brian Cushing, Bernard Pollard; INDIANAPOLIS, 4, Antoine Bethea; JACKSONVILLE, 4, *Derek Cox; KANSAS CITY, 5, Brandon Flowers; MIAMI, 4, *Vontae Davis; NEW ENGLAND, 5, Leigh Bodden, Brandon Meriweather; N.Y. JETS, 6, Darrelle Revis; OAKLAND, 3, Michael Huff, Chris Johnson; PITTSBURGH, 3, Ryan Clark, Troy Polamalu; SAN DIEGO, 3, Antonio Cromartie, Quentin Jammer; TENNESSEE, 5, Cortland Finnegan

NFC: ARIZONA, 6, Dominique Rodgers-Cromartie; ATLANTA, 6, Brent Grimes; CAROLINA, 4, Chris Gamble, Richard Marshall; CHICAGO, 6, Zack Bowman; DALLAS, 5, Mike Jenkins; DETROIT, 2, *Louis Delmas, Anthony Henry, William James; GREEN BAY, 9, Charles Woodson; MINNESOTA, 4, Cedric Griffin; NEW ORLEANS, 9, Darren Sharper; N.Y. GIANTS, 5, Terrell Thomas; PHILADELPHIA, 9, Asante Samuel; ST. LOUIS, 3, James Butler; SAN FRANCISCO, 4, Dashon Goldson; SEATTLE, 3, Deon Grant, David Hawthorne; TAMPA BAY, 5, Tanard Jackson, Aqib Talib; WASHINGTON, 4, DeAngelo Hall

TEAM CHAMPION

NFC: 30 Green Bay
AFC: 28 Buffalo

NFL TOP TEN INTERCEPTORS

	No	Yards	Avg	Long	TD
* Byrd, Jairus, Buf.	9	118	13.1	37	0
Samuel, Asante, Phi.	9	117	13.0	37	0
Sharper, Darren, N.O.	9	376	41.8	99t	3
Woodson, Charles, G.B.	9	179	19.9	45t	3
Bowman, Zack, Chi.	6	67	11.2	39	0
Collins, Nick, G.B.	6	110	18.3	31	0
Grimes, Brent, Atl.	6	17	2.8	11	0
Hall, Leon, Cin.	6	47	7.8	26	0
Joseph, Johnathan, Cin.	6	92	15.3	32	1
Revis, Darrelle, NYJ	6	121	20.2	67t	1
Rodgers-Cromartie, Dominique, Ariz	6	77	12.8	49t	1

AFC—INDIVIDUAL INTERCEPTORS

	No	Yards	Avg	Long	TD
* Byrd, Jairus, Buf.	9	118	13.1	37	0
Revis, Darrelle, NYJ	6	121	20.2	67t	1
Joseph, Johnathan, Cin.	6	92	15.3	32	1
Hall, Leon, Cin.	6	47	7.8	26	0
Finnegan, Cortland, Ten.	5	194	38.8	80	1
Meriweather, Brandon, N.E.	5	149	29.8	56	1
Goodman, Andre', Den.	5	65	13.0	30	0
Bodden, Leigh, N.E.	5	60	12.0	53t	1
Flowers, Brandon, K.C.	5	38	7.6	33	0
Pollard, Bernard, Hou.	4	121	30.3	70t	1
Landry, Dawan, Bal.	4	89	22.3	48t	1
Wright, Eric, Cle.	4	74	18.5	47	0
* Davis, Vontae, Mia.	4	64	16.0	26	1
Foxworth, Domonique, Bal.	4	34	8.5	19	0
Pool, Brodney, Cle.	4	33	8.3	32	0
* Cushing, Brian, Hou.	4	26	6.5	20	0
Wilson, George, Buf.	4	23	5.8	27	0
Bethea, Antoine, Ind.	4	19	4.8	19	0
* Cox, Derek, Jac.	4	6	1.5	6	0
Johnson, Derrick, K.C.	3	175	58.3	70	2
Reed, Ed, Bal.	3	111	37.0	52t	1
* Butler, Darius, N.E.	3	91	30.3	91t	1
Hood, Roderick, Ten.	3	91	30.3	43	1
Fuller, Vincent, Ten.	3	71	23.7	45t	2
* Lacey, Jacob, Ind.	3	53	17.7	35t	1
Bell, Yeremiah, Mia.	3	48	16.0	29	0
Mathis, Rashean, Jac.	3	46	15.3	29	0
Bulluck, Keith, Ten.	3	45	15.0	23	0
Lowery, Dwight, NYJ	3	41	13.7	34	0
Jammer, Quentin, S.D.	3	25	8.3	21	0
Hope, Chris, Ten.	3	24	8.0	24	0
Johnson, Chris, Oak.	3	20	6.7	20	0
Posluszny, Paul, Buf.	3	20	6.7	17	0
Bailey, Champ, Den.	3	18	6.0	11	0
Cromartie, Antonio, S.D.	3	17	5.7	16	0
Polamalu, Troy, Pit.	3	17	5.7	16	0
Rhodes, Kerry, NYJ	3	17	5.7	11	0
Huff, Michael, Oak.	3	15	5.0	10	0
Brown, Mike, K.C.	3	13	4.3	10	0
Clark, Ryan, Pit.	3	0	0.0	0	0
Whitner, Donte, Buf.	2	104	52.0	76t	1
Studebaker, Andy, K.C.	2	96	48.0	94	0
Carter, Tyrone, Pit.	2	53	26.5	48t	1
Weddle, Eric, S.D.	2	44	22.0	31t	1
Crocker, Chris, Cin.	2	38	19.0	20	0
Session, Clint, Ind.	2	35	17.5	27t	1
Smith, Anthony, Jac.	2	34	17.0	30	0
Wilson, Eugene, Hou.	2	29	14.5	16	0
* McBath, Darcel, Den.	2	28	14.0	25	0
Allen, Will, Mia.	2	27	13.5	21	0
Carr, Chris, Bal.	2	24	12.0	13	0
Harris, David, NYJ	2	24	12.0	14	0
Alexander, Gerald, Jac.	2	23	11.5	22	0
Cason, Antoine, S.D.	2	22	11.0	22	0
Hill, Renaldo, Den.	2	18	9.0	18	0
Wilhite, Jonathan, N.E.	2	17	8.5	17	0
Jennings, Tim, Ind.	2	13	6.5	13	0
Zbikowski, Tom, Bal.	2	13	6.5	21	0
Johnson, Jarret, Bal.	2	8	4.0	8	0
* Harris, Cary, Buf.	2	7	3.5	7	0

	No	Yards	Avg	Long	TD
Dawkins, Brian, Den.	2	0	0.0	0	0
Jones, Nate, Mia.	2	0	0.0	0	0
Fox, Keyaron, Pit.	1	82	82.0	82t	1
Fanene, Jonathan, Cin.	1	45	45.0	45t	1
Leonhard, Jim, NYJ	1	44	44.0	44	0
McDonald, Brandon, Cle.	1	39	39.0	39	0
Groves, Quentin, Jac.	1	37	37.0	37	0
Law, Ty, Den.	1	37	37.0	37	0
Oliver, Paul, S.D.	1	34	34.0	34	0
Carr, Brandon, K.C.	1	31	31.0	31	0
Sanders, Bob, Ind.	1	29	29.0	29	0
* Ellerbe, Dannell, Bal.	1	28	28.0	28	0
Durant, Justin, Jac.	1	27	27.0	27	0
McGraw, Jon, K.C.	1	27	27.0	27	0
Scott, Bryan, Buf.	1	27	27.0	27	0
* Kruger, Paul, Bal.	1	26	26.0	26	0
Rucker, Frostee, Cin.	1	26	26.0	26	0
Schobel, Aaron, Buf.	1	26	26.0	26t	1
Considine, Sean, Jac.	1	25	25.0	25	0
Culver, Tyrone, Mia.	1	23	23.0	23	0
Taylor, Ike, Pit.	1	20	20.0	20	0
Reeves, Jacques, Hou.	1	19	19.0	19	0
Farrior, James, Pit.	1	18	18.0	18	0
Bowens, David, Cle.	1	15	15.0	15	0
Busing, John, Hou.	1	14	14.0	14	0
Dobbins, Tim, S.D.	1	13	13.0	13	0
Gregory, Steve, S.D.	1	13	13.0	13	0
Smith, Daryl, Jac.	1	10	10.0	10	0
Ndukwe, Chinedum, Cin.	1	9	9.0	9	0
Brackett, Gary, Ind.	1	8	8.0	8	0
Springs, Shawn, N.E.	1	8	8.0	8	0
Florence, Drayton, Buf.	1	7	7.0	7	0
Hayden, Kelvin, Ind.	1	6	6.0	6	0
Scheffler, Tony, Den.	1	5	5.0	5	0
Siler, Brandon, S.D.	1	5	5.0	5	0
Barnes, Antwan, Bal.	1	4	4.0	4	0
Harper, Nick, Ten.	1	4	4.0	4	0
Barber, Dominique, Hou.	1	3	3.0	3	0
Griffin, Michael, Ten.	1	3	3.0	3	0
Jackson, Marlin, Ind.	1	3	3.0	3	0
McGee, Terrence, Buf.	1	3	3.0	3	0
* Chung, Pat, N.E.	1	2	2.0	2	0
Crowder, Channing, Mia.	1	2	2.0	2	0
* Nelson, Tom, Cin.	1	2	2.0	2	0
* McRath, Gerald, Ten.	1	1	1.0	1	0
* Powers, Jerraud, Ind.	1	1	1.0	1	0
Asomugha, Nnamdi, Oak.	1	0	0.0	0	0
Ayanbadejo, Brendon, Bal.	1	0	0.0	0	0
Corner, Reggie, Buf.	1	0	0.0	0	0
Draft, Chris, Buf.	1	0	0.0	0	0
Eugene, Hiram, Oak.	1	0	0.0	0	0
Mace, Corey, Buf.	1	0	0.0	0	0
* McCain, Brice, Hou.	1	0	0.0	0	0
Moss, Randy, N.E.	1	0	0.0	0	0
Rivers, Keith, Cin.	1	0	0.0	0	0
Sheppard, Lito, NYJ	1	0	0.0	0	0
Smith, Eric, NYJ	1	0	0.0	0	0
Taylor, Jason, Mia.	1	0	0.0	0	0
Torbor, Reggie, Mia.	1	0	0.0	0	0
Walker, Frank, Bal.	1	0	0.0	0	0
Wendling, John, Buf.	1	0	0.0	0	0
Woodyard, Wesley, Den.	1	0	0.0	0	0
Townsend, Deshea, Pit.	1	-1	-1.0	-1	0
Lewis, Ray, Bal.	0	9	—	9	0

*t = Touchdown; *Player that was a rookie in 2009*
Leader based on interceptions

NFC—INDIVIDUAL INTERCEPTORS

	No	Yards	Avg	Long	TD
Sharper, Darren, N.O.	9	376	41.8	99t	3
Woodson, Charles, G.B.	9	179	19.9	45t	3
Samuel, Asante, Phi.	9	117	13.0	37	0
Collins, Nick, G.B.	6	110	18.3	31	0
Rodgers-Cromartie, Domin, Ariz	6	77	12.8	49t	1
Bowman, Zack, Chi.	6	67	11.2	39	0
Grimes, Brent, Atl.	6	17	2.8	11	0
Brown, Sheldon, Phi.	5	152	30.4	83t	1
Talib, Aqib, T.B.	5	99	19.8	32	0
Thomas, Terrell, NY-G	5	87	17.4	33	1
Jackson, Tanard, T.B.	5	86	17.2	35t	2
Wilson, Adrian, Ariz	5	56	11.2	41	0
Jenkins, Mike, Dal.	5	0	0.0	0	0
Hall, DeAngelo, Was.	4	114	28.5	44	0
Williams, Tramon, G.B.	4	94	23.5	67	0
Porter, Tracy, N.O.	4	72	18.0	54t	1
Rolle, Antrel, Ariz	4	71	17.8	29	0
Gamble, Chris, Car.	4	55	13.8	41	0
Marshall, Richard, Car.	4	47	11.8	28	0
Goldson, Dashon, S.F.	4	39	9.8	34	0
Bigby, Atari, G.B.	4	14	3.5	14	0
Griffin, Cedric, Min.	4	-2	-0.5	0	0
Bly, Dre', S.F.	3	66	22.0	31	0
Greenway, Chad, Min.	3	49	16.3	36	0
Beason, Jon, Car.	3	46	15.3	18	0
Mack, Elbert, T.B.	3	36	12.0	36	0
Newman, Terence, Dal.	3	36	12.0	27t	1
* Martin, Sherrod, Car.	3	35	11.7	23	0
Willis, Patrick, S.F.	3	33	11.0	23t	1
DeCoud, Thomas, Atl.	3	25	8.3	15	0
Vilma, Jonathan, N.O.	3	25	8.3	11	0
Butler, James, St.L	3	17	5.7	17	0
Hawthorne, David, Sea.	3	9	3.0	5	0
Grant, Deon, Sea.	3	7	2.3	7	0
Harris, Chris, Car.	3	3	1.0	3	0
* Delmas, Louis, Det.	2	130	65.0	101t	1
Wilson, Josh, Sea.	2	126	63.0	65t	2
* Johnson, Bruce, NY-G	2	83	41.5	49	1
Greer, Jabari, N.O.	2	59	29.5	48t	1
Brown, Tarell, S.F.	2	52	26.0	51	0
Hawk, A.J., G.B.	2	42	21.0	29	0
James, William, Det.	2	41	20.5	38t	1
Jones, Sean, Phi.	2	37	18.5	37	0
Tillman, Charles, Chi.	2	35	17.5	21t	1
Harris, Al, G.B.	2	29	14.5	29	0
* Laurinaitis, James, St.L	2	28	14.0	21	0
McIntosh, Rocky, Was.	2	27	13.5	18	0
Henry, Anthony, Det.	2	26	13.0	26	0
Davis, Thomas, Car.	2	24	12.0	24	0
Phillips, Kenny, NY-G	2	22	11.0	22	0
Atogwe, Oshiomogho, St.L	2	21	10.5	12	0
Hayes, Geno, T.B.	2	21	10.5	20	0
Babineaux, Jordan, Sea.	2	18	9.0	18	0
Mikell, Quintin, Phi.	2	16	8.0	16	0
Shanle, Scott, N.O.	2	16	8.0	13	0
Jordan, Akeem, Phi.	2	14	7.0	11	0
* Owens, Chris, Atl.	2	13	6.5	13	0
Peppers, Julius, Car.	2	13	6.5	13t	1
Hanson, Joselio, Phi.	2	8	4.0	6	0
Piscitelli, Sabby, T.B.	2	7	3.5	4	0
Trufant, Marcus, Sea.	2	4	2.0	4	0
Spencer, Shawntae, S.F.	2	2	1.0	2	0
Brown, Ralph, Ariz	1	85	85.0	80	0
Hill, Tye, Atl.	1	62	62.0	62t	1
Peterson, Mike, Atl.	1	39	39.0	39	0
Little, Leonard, St.L	1	36	36.0	36t	1
Manning, Danieal, Chi.	1	35	35.0	35	0
Reis, Chris, N.O.	1	33	33.0	33	0

2009 INDIVIDUAL STATISTICS—INTERCEPTIONS

	No	Yards	Avg	Long	TD
Roman, Mark, S.F.	1	27	27.0	27	0
Gay, Randall, N.O.	1	25	25.0	25	0
Blackburn, Chase, NY-G	1	24	24.0	24	0
Young, Usama, N.O.	1	24	24.0	24	0
Ruud, Barrett, T.B.	1	23	23.0	21	0
Ware, Matt, Ariz	1	18	18.0	18	0
Adams, Michael, Ariz	1	17	17.0	17	0
* Jenkins, Malcolm, N.O.	1	14	14.0	14	0
Moore, Kareem, Was.	1	14	14.0	14	0
Doughty, Reed, Was.	1	13	13.0	13	0
Demps, Quintin, Phi.	1	12	12.0	12	0
Godfrey, Charles, Car.	1	12	12.0	12	0
Landry, LaRon, Was.	1	12	12.0	13	0
Dansby, Karlos, Ariz	1	11	11.0	11	0
Franklin, Aubrayo, S.F.	1	10	10.0	10	0
Witherspoon, Will, Phi.	1	9	9.0	9t	1
Clements, Nate, S.F.	1	8	8.0	8	0
McKenzie, Mike, N.O.	1	8	8.0	8	0
Simpson, Ko, Det.	1	8	8.0	8	0
Harris, Tommie, Chi.	1	6	6.0	6	0
Goff, Jonathan, NY-G	1	5	5.0	5	0
* Levy, DeAndre, Det.	1	5	5.0	5	0
White, Tracy, Phi.	1	5	5.0	5	0
Houston, Chris, Atl.	1	4	4.0	4	0
Jenkins, Cullen, G.B.	1	4	4.0	4	0
Black, Quincy, T.B.	1	3	3.0	3	0
Bush, Jarrett, G.B.	1	3	3.0	3	0
Dockett, Darnell, Ariz	1	3	3.0	3	0
Tryon, Justin, Was.	1	3	3.0	3	0
Fletcher, London, Was.	1	2	2.0	2	0
Jolly, Johnny, G.B.	1	2	2.0	2	0
Vasher, Nathan, Chi.	1	1	1.0	1	0
* Allen, Asher, Min.	1	0	0.0	0	0
Briggs, Lance, Chi.	1	0	0.0	0	0
Hillenmeyer, Hunter, Chi.	1	0	0.0	0	0
Johnson, Tyrell, Min.	1	0	0.0	0	0
Johnson, Michael, NY-G	1	0	0.0	0	0
Lewis, Michael, S.F.	1	0	0.0	0	0
Lucas, Ken, Sea.	1	0	0.0	0	0
Scandrick, Orlando, Dal.	1	0	0.0	0	0
Sensabaugh, Gerald, Dal.	1	0	0.0	0	0
Smith, Will, N.O.	1	0	0.0	0	0
* Toler, Greg, Ariz.	1	0	0.0	0	0
Webster, Corey, NY-G	1	0	0.0	0	0
White, Dewayne, Det.	1	0	0.0	0	0
Winfield, Antoine, Min.	1	0	0.0	0	0
Williams, Brian, Atl.	1	-2	-2.0	-2	0
Spencer, Anthony, Dal.	1	-3	-3.0	-3	0
Allen, Jared, Min.	1	-4	-4.0	-4	0

t = Touchdown; Leader based on interceptions
** Player that was a rookie in 2009*

AMERICAN FOOTBALL CONFERENCE—INTERCEPTIONS

	No	Yards	Avg	Long	TD
Buffalo	28	335	12.0	76t	2
Baltimore	22	346	15.7	52t	2
Tennessee	20	433	21.7	80	4
Cincinnati	19	259	13.6	45t	2
New England	18	327	18.2	91t	3
Denver	17	171	10.1	37	0
N.Y. Jets	17	247	14.5	67t	1
Indianapolis	16	167	10.4	35t	2
Jacksonville	15	208	13.9	37	0
Kansas City	15	380	25.3	94	2
Miami	15	164	10.9	29	1
Houston	14	212	15.1	70t	1
San Diego	14	173	12.4	34	1
Pittsburgh	12	189	15.8	82t	2
Cleveland	10	161	16.1	47	0
Oakland	8	35	4.4	20	0
AFC Total	260	3807	14.6	94	23
AFC Average	16.3	237.9	14.6	—	1.4

NATIONAL FOOTBALL CONFERENCE—INTERCEPTIONS

	No	Yards	Avg	Long	TD
Green Bay	30	477	15.9	67	3
New Orleans	26	652	25.1	99t	5
Philadelphia	25	370	14.8	83t	2
Carolina	22	235	10.7	41	1
Arizona	21	338	16.1	80	1
Tampa Bay	19	275	14.5	36	2
San Francisco	18	237	13.2	51	1
Atlanta	15	158	10.5	62t	1
Chicago	13	144	11.1	39	1
N.Y. Giants	13	221	17.0	49	2
Seattle	13	164	12.6	65t	2
Dallas	11	33	3.0	27t	1
Minnesota	11	43	3.9	36	0
Washington	11	185	16.8	44	0
Detroit	9	210	23.3	101t	2
St. Louis	8	102	12.8	36t	1
NFC Total	265	3844	14.5	101t	25
NFC Average	16.6	240.3	14.5	—	1.6
League Total	525	7651	—	101t	48
League Average	16.4	239.1	14.6	—	1.5

KICKOFF RETURNS

YARDS PER RETURN
NFC: 29.1 Clifton Smith, Tampa Bay
AFC: 27.5 Josh Cribbs, Cleveland

YARDS
NFC: 1618 Danny Amendola, St. Louis
AFC: 1542 Josh Cribbs, Cleveland

YARDS, GAME
AFC: 299 Ted Ginn Jr., Miami at N.Y. Jets, November 1 (6 returns, 2 TD)
NFC: 230 Domenik Hixon, N.Y. Giants at New Orleans, October 18 (7 returns, 0 TD)

LONGEST
AFC: 106 Brad Smith, N.Y. Jets at Indianapolis, December 27 - TD
NFC: 102 * Johnny Knox, Chicago vs. Detroit, October 4 - TD

RETURNS
NFC: 66 Danny Amendola, St. Louis
AFC: 56 Josh Cribbs, Cleveland

RETURNS, GAME
NFC: 9 Danny Amendola, St. Louis at Tennessee, December 13 (217 yards, 0 TD)
AFC: 7 * Lardarius Webb, Baltimore at Minnesota, October 18 (165 yards, 0 TD)
7 Darren Sproles, San Diego vs. Denver, October 19 (149 yards, 0 TD)
7 Fred Jackson, Buffalo at Tennessee, November 15 (167 yards, 0 TD)
7 Mark Bradley, Kansas City vs. Cleveland, December 20 (123 yards, 0 TD)
7 * Kenny Britt, Tennessee vs. San Diego, December 25 (96 yards, 0 TD)

TOUCHDOWNS
AFC: 3 Josh Cribbs, Cleveland
NFC: 2 * Percy Harvin, Minnesota

TEAM CHAMPION
NFC: 26.3 Tampa Bay
AFC: 26.2 Baltimore

NFL TOP TEN KICKOFF RETURNERS

	No	Yards	Avg	Long	TD
Smith, Clifton, T.B.	31	902	29.1	83	0
* Knox, Johnny, Chi.	32	927	29.0	102t	1
Cribbs, Josh, Cle.	56	1542	27.5	103t	3
* Harvin, Percy, Min.	42	1156	27.5	101t	2
Roby, Courtney, N.O.	42	1154	27.5	97t	1
Logan, Stefan, Pit.	55	1466	26.7	83	0
Jones, Jacoby, Hou.	24	638	26.6	95t	1
Manning, Danieal, Chi.	28	744	26.6	59	0
* Webb, Lardarius, Bal.	35	918	26.2	95t	1
Charles, Jamaal, K.C.	36	925	25.7	97t	1

AFC—INDIVIDUAL KICKOFF RETURNERS

	No	Yards	Avg	Long	TD
Cribbs, Josh, Cle.	56	1542	27.5	103t	3
Logan, Stefan, Pit.	55	1466	26.7	83	0
Jones, Jacoby, Hou.	24	638	26.6	95t	1
* Webb, Lardarius, Bal.	35	918	26.2	95t	1
Charles, Jamaal, K.C.	36	925	25.7	97t	1
Ginn, Ted Jr., Mia.	52	1296	24.9	101t	2
* Thomas, Mike, Jac.	26	644	24.8	43	0
Jackson, Fred, Buf.	41	1014	24.7	71	0
Sproles, Darren, S.D.	54	1300	24.1	66	0
Royal, Eddie, Den.	26	621	23.9	93t	1
Davis, Andre, Hou.	33	782	23.7	63	0
Simpson, Chad, Ind.	38	898	23.6	93t	1
* Britt, Kenny, Ten.	24	523	21.8	56	0
Holland, Jonathan, Oak.	28	550	19.6	60	0
Caldwell, Andre, Cin.	29	539	18.6	39	0
(Nonqualifiers)					
Russell, Gary, Oak.	18	330	18.3	41	0
* Scott, Bernard, Cin.	16	504	31.5	96t	1
Washington, Leon, NYJ	16	385	24.1	43	0
Cobbs, Patrick, Mia.	16	361	22.6	39	0
Lawrence, Quinten, K.C.	16	317	19.8	29	0
Carr, Chris, Bal.	13	315	24.2	41	0
Maroney, Laurence, N.E.	13	279	21.5	52	0
Jones, Mark, Ten.	13	264	20.3	27	0
* Cosby, Quan, Cin.	13	239	18.4	31	0
Slater, Matt, N.E.	11	269	24.5	35	0
Parrish, Roscoe, Buf.	11	258	23.5	31	0
* Edelman, Julian, N.E.	11	241	21.9	32	0
Miller, Justin, Oak.-NYJ	11	221	20.1	27	0
Smith, Brad, NYJ	10	310	31.0	106t	1
Parmele, Jalen, Bal.	9	283	31.4	53	0
* Ringer, Javon, Ten.	9	181	20.1	25	0
Buckhalter, Correll, Den.	8	184	23.0	41	0
Pearman, Alvin, Ten.	8	174	21.8	27	0
Savage, Dantrell, K.C.	8	160	20.0	29	0
* McKinley, Kenny, Den.	7	158	22.6	30	0
Rushing, T.J., Ind.	7	127	18.1	22	0
Bradley, Mark, K.C.	7	123	17.6	24	0
Faulk, Kevin, N.E.	6	144	24.0	32	0
Griffin, Michael, Ten.	6	143	23.8	31	0
Hillis, Peyton, Den.	6	134	22.3	24	0
Long, Lance, K.C.	6	106	17.7	22	0
Lowery, Dwight, NYJ	5	128	25.6	44	0
Giguere, Samuel, Ind.	5	122	24.4	36	0
McKelvin, Leodis, Buf.	5	121	24.2	33	0
* Butler, Darius, N.E.	5	104	20.8	26	0
Lawson, Gerard, Cle.	5	43	8.6	13	0
* Tate, Brandon, N.E.	4	106	26.5	34	0
Jones-Drew, Maurice, Jac.	4	102	25.5	30	0
Davis, Craig, S.D.	4	79	19.8	23	0
* Smith, Alphonso, Den.	4	75	18.8	23	0
Moore, Mewelde, Pit.	4	44	11.0	13	0
Clowney, David, NYJ	3	81	27.0	37	0
* McCourty, Jason, Ten.	3	72	24.0	27	0
Reece, Marcel, Oak.	3	58	19.3	23	0
* Jennings, Rashad, Jac.	3	56	18.7	24	0
Harrison, Jerome, Cle.	3	55	18.3	39	0
Owens, Montell, Jac.	3	49	16.3	29	0
Jenkins, Justin, Buf.	3	45	15.0	19	0
Cromartie, Antonio, S.D.	3	41	13.7	22	0
* Hartline, Brian, Mia.	3	36	12.0	18	0
* Burnett, Joe, Pit.	3	23	7.7	13	0
Crumpler, Alge, Ten.	3	20	6.7	15	0
Welker, Wes, N.E.	2	45	22.5	27	0
Leonard, Brian, Cin.	2	38	19.0	24	0
* Underwood, Tiquan, Jac.	2	38	19.0	24	0
Polite, Lousaka, Mia.	2	24	12.0	12	0
Leach, Vonta, Hou.	2	23	11.5	15	0
* Miller, Zach, Jac.	2	19	9.5	16	0
Stewart, Tony, Oak.	2	19	9.5	11	0
Williams, Sam, Oak.	2	11	5.5	7	0
Cox, Mike, K.C.	2	9	4.5	9	0
McGee, Terrence, Buf.	1	30	30.0	30	0
Omon, Xavier, Buf.	1	26	26.0	26	0
* Wallace, Mike, Pit.	1	26	26.0	26	0
Hall, Leon, Cin.	1	22	22.0	22	0
Stanback, Isaiah, N.E.	1	22	22.0	22	0

2009 INDIVIDUAL STATISTICS—KICKOFF RETURNS

	No	Yards	Avg	Long	TD
* Brown, Donald, Ind.	1	21	21.0	21	0
* Quinn, Richard, Den.	1	19	19.0	19	0
Silva, Jamie, Ind.	1	19	19.0	19	0
Copper, Terrance, K.C.	1	18	18.0	18	0
Cotchery, Jerricho, NYJ	1	17	17.0	17	0
Lawton, Luke, Oak.	1	17	17.0	17	0
McClain, Le'Ron, Bal.	1	17	17.0	17	0
Connolly, Dan, N.E.	1	16	16.0	16	0
Ellison, Atiyyah, Jac.	1	16	16.0	16	0
Woodhead, Danny, NYJ	1	16	16.0	16	0
Coles, Laveranues, Cin.	1	14	14.0	14	0
Dawson, Keyunta, Ind.	1	14	14.0	14	0
Edwards, Dwan, Bal.	1	14	14.0	14	0
* Mouton, Ryan, Ten.	1	14	14.0	14	0
Stevens, Craig, Ten.	1	14	14.0	14	0
Berger, Joe, Mia.	1	13	13.0	13	0
Davis, Carey, Pit.	1	13	13.0	13	0
Larsen, Spencer, Den.	1	13	13.0	13	0
Wilson, Kris, S.D.	1	13	13.0	13	0
Furrey, Mike, Cle.	1	12	12.0	12	0
Hall, Ahmard, Ten.	1	12	12.0	12	0
Johnson, Spencer, Buf.	1	12	12.0	12	0
Stupar, Jonathan, Buf.	1	11	11.0	11	0
Robinson, Gijon, Ind.	1	10	10.0	10	0
Estandia, Greg, Cle.	f1	9	9.0	9	0
Hester, Jacob, S.D.	1	9	9.0	9	0
Smith, Eric, NYJ	1	9	9.0	9	0
Torbor, Reggie, Mia.	1	9	9.0	9	0
Trusnik, Jason, Cle.	1	9	9.0	9	0
* Collie, Austin, Ind.	1	8	8.0	8	0
Mendenhall, Rashard, Pit.	1	8	8.0	8	0
Studebaker, Andy, K.C.	1	8	8.0	8	0
Leonhard, Jim, NYJ	1	7	7.0	7	0
Hochstein, Russ, Den.	1	6	6.0	6	0
Jordan, LaMont, Den.	1	6	6.0	6	0
Martinez, Glenn, Hou.	1	6	6.0	6	0
Turner, Robert, NYJ	1	6	6.0	6	0
Spaeth, Matt, Pit.	f1	1	1.0	1	0
Thomas, Marcus, Den.	1	1	1.0	1	0
Busing, John, Hou.	1	0	0.0	0	0
* Casey, James, Hou.	1	0	0.0	0	0
Elam, Abram, Cle.	1	0	0.0	0	0
Polumbus, Tyler, Den.	1	0	0.0	0	0
Robinson, DelJuan, Hou.	1	0	0.0	0	0
Vickers, Lawrence, Cle.	1	0	0.0	0	0
Walter, Kevin, Hou.	1	0	0.0	0	0
Wilford, Ernest, Jac.	1	0	0.0	0	0
Coats, Daniel, Cin.	f0	0	—	—	0
Corto, Jon, Buf.	f0	0	—	—	0
Eason, Nick, Pit.	f0	0	—	—	0
Haynos, Joey, Mia.	f0	0	—	—	0

t = Touchdown; f = Fair Catch
Leader based on average return, minimum 20 returns
* *Player that was a rookie in 2009*

NFC—INDIVIDUAL KICKOFF RETURNERS

	No	Yards	Avg	Long	TD
Smith, Clifton, T.B.	31	902	29.1	83	0
* Knox, Johnny, Chi.	32	927	29.0	102t	1
* Harvin, Percy, Min.	42	1156	27.5	101t	2
Roby, Courtney, N.O.	42	1154	27.5	97t	1
Manning, Danieal, Chi.	28	744	26.6	59	0
Nelson, Jordy, G.B.	25	635	25.4	54	0
Weems, Eric, Atl.	48	1214	25.3	62	0
Amendola, Danny, St.L	66	1618	24.5	58	0
* Stephens-Howling, LaRod, Ariz	52	1257	24.2	99t	1
Hobbs, Ellis, Phi.	20	481	24.1	63	0
Witherspoon, Brian, Jac.-Det.	28	640	22.9	42	0
Hixon, Domenik, NY-G	57	1291	22.6	68	0
* Brown, Aaron, Det.	42	951	22.6	87	0
Jones, Felix, Dal.	30	678	22.6	41	0
Cartwright, Rock, Was.	39	868	22.3	42	0
* Williams, Derrick, Det.	42	931	22.2	34	0
Thomas, Devin, Was.	20	439	22.0	39	0
Rankin, Louis, Oak.-Sea.	22	466	21.2	41	0
(Nonqualifiers)					
* Harris, Macho, Phi.	19	394	20.7	32	0
Forsett, Justin, Sea.	18	432	24.0	46	0
Robinson, Michael, S.F.	f18	414	23.0	40	0
* Goodson, Mike, Car.	17	352	20.7	33	0
* Sutton, Tyrell, Car.	14	302	21.6	32	0
Morgan, Josh, S.F.	13	367	28.2	76	0
* Stroughter, Sammie, T.B.	11	324	29.5	97t	1
Obomanu, Ben, Sea.	11	293	26.6	45	0
Wilson, Josh, Sea.	11	212	19.3	29	0
Blackmon, Will, G.B.	10	233	23.3	28	0
Moore, Kenny, Car.	10	219	21.9	55	0
Green, Ahman, G.B.	9	196	21.8	37	0
Davis, Rashied, Chi.	9	114	12.7	22	0
Spurlock, Micheal, T.B.	8	170	21.3	32	0
Rossum, Allen, S.F.-Dal.	8	168	21.0	40	0
* Ogletree, Kevin, Dal.	8	166	20.8	32	0
Austin, Miles, Dal.	7	157	22.4	29	0
Hester, Devin, Chi.	7	156	22.3	44	0
* Maclin, Jeremy, Phi.	7	124	17.7	28	0
Demps, Quintin, Phi.	6	155	25.8	48	0
Meachem, Robert, N.O.	6	148	24.7	42	0
Moss, Sinorice, NY-G	6	109	18.2	29	0
Figurs, Yamon, T.B.	5	105	21.0	27	0
Walker, Delanie, S.F.	5	85	17.0	25	0
Dugan, Jeff, Min.	5	38	7.6	13	0
Reynaud, Darius, Min.	4	90	22.5	30	0
Darby, Kenneth, St.L	4	54	13.5	23	0
Battle, Arnaz, S.F.	3	68	22.7	26	0
Northcutt, Dennis, Det.	3	66	22.0	34	0
Stecker, Aaron, Atl.	3	54	18.0	21	0
* Coffee, Glen, S.F.	3	42	14.0	16	0
King, Jeff, Car.	3	37	12.3	14	0
Hamilton, Lynell, N.O.	3	15	5.0	15	0
Huggins, Kareem, T.B.	2	52	26.0	30	0
Bell, Mike, N.O.	2	45	22.5	28	0
Rosario, Dante, Car.	2	41	20.5	22	0
Bennett, Earl, Chi.	2	40	20.0	22	0
Graham, Earnest, T.B.	2	38	19.0	21	0
Ware, Danny, NY-G	2	37	18.5	20	0
Jackson, Brandon, G.B.	f2	36	18.0	23	0
Weaver, Leonard, Phi.	2	33	16.5	18	0
Mason, Marcus, Was.	2	31	15.5	18	0
Woodson, Charles, G.B.	2	30	15.0	18	0
Wright, Jason, Ariz	2	27	13.5	18	0
Bajema, Billy, St.L	2	26	13.0	14	0
Havner, Spencer, G.B.	2	26	13.0	16	0
Williams, Tramon, G.B.	2	26	13.0	24	0
Finneran, Brian, Atl.	2	22	11.0	16	0
Stewart, Jonathan, Car.	2	17	8.5	17	0
* Follett, Zack, Det.	2	12	6.0	10	0
Charleston, Jeff, N.O.	2	11	5.5	11	0
Balmer, Kentwan, S.F.	2	7	3.5	4	0
Robison, Brian, Min.	f2	7	3.5	7	0
Babin, Jason, Phi.	2	0	0.0	0	0
Norwood, Jerious, Atl.	1	39	39.0	39	0
Betts, Ladell, Was.	1	29	29.0	29	0
Ganther, Quinton, Was.	1	25	25.0	25	0
Gado, Samkon, St.L	1	23	23.0	23	0
Stovall, Maurice, T.B.	1	20	20.0	20	0
Avery, Donnie, St.L	1	19	19.0	19	0
Thomas, Pierre, N.O.	1	19	19.0	19	0

	No	Yards	Avg	Long	TD
Aromashodu, Devin, Chi.	1	18	18.0	18	0
Barnidge, Gary, Car.	1	16	16.0	16	0
* Butler, Deon, Sea.	1	16	16.0	16	0
* Nicks, Hakeem, NY-G	1	16	16.0	16	0
Schwartz, Geoff, Car.	1	16	16.0	16	0
Anderson, Deon, Dal.	1	15	15.0	15	0
* Johnson, Gartrell, NY-G	1	15	15.0	15	0
* Munnerlyn, Captain, Car.	1	15	15.0	15	0
Grant, Larry, St.L	1	14	14.0	14	0
Sellers, Mike, Was.	1	13	13.0	13	0
Crowder, Tim, T.B.	f1	11	11.0	11	0
Fitzsimmons, Casey, Det.	1	10	10.0	10	0
Karney, Mike, St.L	1	10	10.0	10	0
Hayward, Adam, T.B.	1	8	8.0	8	0
Hedgecock, Madison, NY-G	1	8	8.0	8	0
Jennings, Adam, Det.	1	8	8.0	8	0
Wilson, Chris, Was.	1	8	8.0	8	0
Zinger, Keith, Atl.	1	7	7.0	7	0
Bishop, Desmond, G.B.	f1	6	6.0	6	0
Kennedy, Jimmy, Min.	1	6	6.0	6	0
* Dietrich-Smith, Evan, G.B.	1	5	5.0	5	0
Smith, Alex, Phi.	1	4	4.0	4	0
* Beckum, Travis, NY-G	1	3	3.0	3	0
Blackburn, Chase, NY-G	1	3	3.0	3	0
* Reed, Nick, Sea.	1	3	3.0	3	0
Burleson, Nate, Sea.	1	2	2.0	2	0
Dinkins, Darnell, N.O.	1	1	1.0	1	0
* Beatty, William, NY-G	1	0	0.0	0	0
Felton, Jerome, Det.	1	0	0.0	0	0
Idonije, Israel, Chi.	1	0	0.0	0	0
Jackson, DeSean, Phi.	1	0	0.0	0	0
Norris, Moran, S.F.	1	0	0.0	0	0
Rice, Sidney, Min.	1	0	0.0	0	0
Tahi, Naufahu, Min.	1	0	0.0	0	0
Vallos, Steve, Sea.	1	0	0.0	0	0
McCoy, Matt, T.B.	f0	0	—	—	0

t = Touchdown; f = Fair Catch
Leader based on average return, minimum 20 returns
** Player that was a rookie in 2009*

AMERICAN FOOTBALL CONFERENCE—KICKOFF RETURNS

	No	Yards	Avg	Long	TD
Baltimore	59	1547	26.2	95t	1
N.Y. Jets	44	1074	24.4	106t	1
Cleveland	69	1670	24.2	103t	3
Pittsburgh	66	1581	24.0	83	0
Buffalo	64	1517	23.7	71	0
Miami	75	1739	23.2	101t	2
San Diego	63	1442	22.9	66	0
New England	54	1226	22.7	52	0
Houston	64	1449	22.6	95t	1
Jacksonville	66	1492	22.6	43	0
Indianapolis	55	1219	22.2	93t	1
Cincinnati	62	1356	21.9	96t	1
Kansas City	77	1666	21.6	97t	1
Denver	57	1217	21.4	93t	1
Tennessee	69	1417	20.5	56	0
Oakland	66	1199	18.2	60	0
AFC Total	1010	22811	22.6	106t	12
AFC Average	63.1	1425.7	22.6	—	0.8

NATIONAL FOOTBALL CONFERENCE—KICKOFF RETURNS

	No	Yards	Avg	Long	TD
Tampa Bay	62	1630	26.3	97t	1
Chicago	80	1999	25.0	102t	1
New Orleans	57	1393	24.4	97t	1
Atlanta	55	1336	24.3	62	0
Arizona	54	1284	23.8	99t	1
St. Louis	76	1764	23.2	58	0
Minnesota	56	1297	23.2	101t	2
Green Bay	54	1193	22.1	54	0
Dallas	47	1032	22.0	41	0
Seattle	60	1316	21.9	46	0
San Francisco	52	1135	21.8	76	0
Washington	65	1413	21.7	42	0
Detroit	96	2050	21.4	87	0
N.Y. Giants	71	1482	20.9	68	0
Philadelphia	58	1191	20.5	63	0
Carolina	51	1015	19.9	55	0
NFC Total	994	22530	22.7	102t	6
NFC Average	62.1	1408.1	22.7	—	0.4
League Total	2004	45341	—	106t	18
League Average	62.6	1416.9	22.6	—	0.6

2009 INDIVIDUAL STATISTICS—PUNTING

PUNTING

AVERAGE YARDS PER PUNT

AFC: 51.1 Shane Lechler, Oakland
NFC: 47.6 Andy Lee, San Francisco

NET AVERAGE YARDS PER PUNT

AFC: 43.9 Shane Lechler, Oakland
NFC: 41.7 Donnie Jones, St. Louis

LONGEST

AFC: 73 Brian Moorman, Buffalo at Kansas City, December 13
NFC: 70 Jon Ryan, Seattle vs. St. Louis, September 13
70 Michael Koenen, Atlanta at Carolina, November 15

PUNTS

NFC: 99 Andy Lee, San Francisco
AFC: 96 Dustin Colquitt, Kansas City
96 Shane Lechler, Oakland

PUNTS, GAME

AFC: 11 Shane Lechler, Oakland vs. Kansas City, November 15 (531 yards)
NFC: 11 Donnie Jones, St. Louis vs. San Francisco, January 3 (551 yards)

TEAM CHAMPION

AFC: 51.1 Oakland
NFC: 47.6 San Francisco

AMERICAN FOOTBALL CONFERENCE—PUNTING

	Total Punts	Yards	Long	Avg	TB	Blk	Opp Ret	Return Yards	In 20	Net Avg
Oakland	96	4909	70	51.1	12	0	63	459	30	43.9
Buffalo	90	4192	73	46.6	10	0	49	377	25	40.2
Miami	75	3472	66	46.3	6	0	43	369	25	39.8
San Diego	52	2342	65	45.0	2	0	23	265	23	39.2
Kansas City	97	4361	70	45.0	6	1	40	285	41	40.8
Indianapolis	64	2837	60	44.3	6	0	36	301	21	37.8
Denver	78	3387	65	43.4	8	0	36	363	22	36.7
Tennessee	69	2995	67	43.4	6	0	29	208	22	38.7
Cincinnati	86	3713	61	43.2	10	0	39	393	24	36.3
Baltimore	74	3188	60	43.1	5	1	38	287	26	37.9
Houston	67	2866	62	42.8	6	0	24	104	24	39.4
Pittsburgh	72	3074	60	42.7	4	0	33	325	29	37.1
Cleveland	94	3977	60	42.3	8	0	40	262	40	37.8
N.Y. Jets	80	3357	66	42.0	9	0	27	238	25	36.7
Jacksonville	72	3017	64	41.9	5	0	38	159	23	38.3
New England	57	2221	56	39.0	5	1	20	180	18	34.1
AFC Total	1223	53908	73	—	108	3	578	4575	418	—
AFC Average	76.4	3369.3	—	44.1	6.8	0.2	36.1	285.9	26.1	38.6

NATIONAL FOOTBALL CONFERENCE—PUNTING

	Total Punts	Yards	Long	Avg	TB	Blk	Opp Ret	Return Yards	In 20	Net Avg
San Francisco	99	4711	64	47.6	8	0	57	495	30	41.0
Arizona	86	4045	64	47.0	3	0	47	493	42	40.6
St. Louis	90	4212	63	46.8	10	0	41	260	34	41.7
Seattle	89	4100	70	46.1	9	0	43	479	29	38.7
Dallas	72	3249	63	45.1	3	0	38	314	38	39.9
Minnesota	73	3202	60	43.9	9	0	33	260	24	37.8
New Orleans	58	2528	60	43.6	4	0	25	358	18	36.0
Carolina	77	3352	61	43.5	4	1	41	452	22	36.6
Green Bay	67	2891	58	43.1	10	1	40	403	15	34.1
Detroit	74	3174	56	42.9	5	0	41	354	20	36.8
Philadelphia	76	3222	61	42.4	4	0	39	229	26	38.3
Atlanta	63	2634	70	41.8	3	1	27	289	19	36.3
Tampa Bay	87	3626	63	41.7	8	0	38	311	24	36.3
Chicago	77	3191	66	41.4	2	0	34	272	26	37.4
N.Y. Giants	64	2604	59	40.7	2	0	28	258	23	36.0
Washington	76	3084	59	40.6	6	0	32	220	28	36.1
NFC Total	1228	53825	70	—	90	3	604	5447	418	—
NFC Average	76.8	3364.1	—	43.8	5.6	0.2	37.8	340.4	26.1	37.9
NFL Total	2451	107733	73	—	198	6	1182	10022	836	—
NFL Average	76.6	3366.7	—	44.0	6.2	0.2	36.9	313.2	26.1	38.3

NFL TOP TEN PUNTERS

	No	Yards	Long	Avg	Total Punts	TB	Blk	Opp Ret	Return Yards	In 20	Net Avg
Lechler, Shane, Oak.	96	4909	70	51.1	96	12	0	63	459	30	43.9
Lee, Andy, S.F.	99	4711	64	47.6	99	8	0	57	495	30	41.0
Graham, Ben, Ariz	86	4045	64	47.0	86	3	0	47	493	42	40.6
Jones, Donnie, St.L	90	4212	63	46.8	90	10	0	41	260	34	41.7
Moorman, Brian, Buf.	90	4192	73	46.6	90	10	0	49	377	25	40.2
Fields, Brandon, Mia.	75	3472	66	46.3	75	6	0	43	369	25	39.8
Ryan, Jon, Sea.	88	4068	70	46.2	88	9	0	43	479	28	38.7
Kern, Brett, Den.-Ten.	64	2910	67	45.5	64	10	0	27	249	27	38.5
Colquitt, Dustin, K.C.	96	4361	70	45.4	97	6	1	40	285	41	40.8
McBriar, Mat, Dal.	72	3249	63	45.1	72	3	0	38	314	38	39.9

AFC—INDIVIDUAL PUNTERS

	No	Yards	Long	Avg	Total Punts	TB	Blk	Opp Ret	Return Yards	In 20	Net Avg
Lechler, Shane, Oak.	96	4909	70	51.1	96	12	0	63	459	30	43.9
Moorman, Brian, Buf.	90	4192	73	46.6	90	10	0	49	377	25	40.2
Fields, Brandon, Mia.	75	3472	66	46.3	75	6	0	43	369	25	39.8
Kern, Brett, Den.-Ten.	64	2910	67	45.5	64	10	0	27	249	27	38.5
Colquitt, Dustin, K.C.	96	4361	70	45.4	97	6	1	40	285	41	40.8
Scifres, Mike, S.D.	52	2342	65	45.0	52	2	0	23	265	23	39.2
Zastudil, Dave, Cle.	49	2188	60	44.7	49	5	0	22	170	25	39.1
* McAfee, Pat, Ind.	64	2837	60	44.3	64	6	0	36	301	21	37.8
Koch, Sam, Bal.	73	3188	60	43.7	74	5	1	38	287	26	37.9
* Huber, Kevin, Cin.	86	3713	61	43.2	86	10	0	39	393	24	36.3
Turk, Matt, Hou.	67	2866	62	42.8	67	6	0	24	104	24	39.4
Sepulveda, Daniel, Pit.	72	3074	60	42.7	72	4	0	33	325	29	37.1
Berger, Mitch, Den.	51	2142	65	42.0	51	2	0	23	169	13	37.9
Weatherford, Steve, NYJ	80	3357	66	42.0	80	9	0	27	238	25	36.7
Podlesh, Adam, Jac.	72	3017	64	41.9	72	5	0	38	159	23	38.3
Hanson, Chris, N.E.	56	2221	56	39.7	57	5	1	20	180	18	34.1
Hodges, Reggie, Ten.-Cle.	67	2657	54	39.7	67	5	0	30	220	16	34.9
(Nonqualifiers)											
Hentrich, Craig, Ten.	9	422	60	46.9	9	0	0	3	25	3	44.1
Bironas, Rob, Ten.	1	40	40	40.0	1	0	0	0	0	0	40.0

Leader based on average, minimum 40 punts

NFC—INDIVIDUAL PUNTERS

	No	Yards	Long	Avg	Total Punts	TB	Blk	Opp Ret	Return Yards	In 20	Net Avg
Lee, Andy, S.F.	99	4711	64	47.6	99	8	0	57	495	30	41.0
Graham, Ben, Ariz	86	4045	64	47.0	86	3	0	47	493	42	40.6
Jones, Donnie, St.L	90	4212	63	46.8	90	10	0	41	260	34	41.7
Ryan, Jon, Sea.	88	4068	70	46.2	88	9	0	43	479	28	38.7
McBriar, Mat, Dal.	72	3249	63	45.1	72	3	0	38	314	38	39.9
Baker, Jason, Car.	76	3352	61	44.1	77	4	1	41	452	22	36.6
Kluwe, Chris, Min.	73	3202	60	43.9	73	9	0	33	260	24	37.8
Kapinos, Jeremy, G.B.	66	2891	58	43.8	67	10	1	40	403	15	34.1
* Morstead, Thomas, N.O.	58	2528	60	43.6	58	4	0	25	358	18	36.0
Harris, Nick, Det.	74	3174	56	42.9	74	5	0	41	354	20	36.8
Koenen, Michael, Atl.	61	2598	70	42.6	62	3	1	27	289	18	36.3
Rocca, Sav, Phi.	76	3222	61	42.4	76	4	0	39	229	26	38.3
Maynard, Brad, Chi.	77	3191	66	41.4	77	2	0	34	272	26	37.4
Smith, Hunter, Was.	57	2356	59	41.3	57	5	0	22	158	23	36.8
Johnson, Dirk, T.B.	62	2558	63	41.3	62	3	0	29	222	16	36.7
Feagles, Jeff, NY-G	64	2604	59	40.7	64	2	0	28	258	23	36.0
(Nonqualifiers)											
Paulescu, Sam, Was.-T.B.	27	1172	61	43.4	27	5	0	10	83	8	36.6
Pakulak, Glenn, Was.	13	498	57	38.3	13	1	0	7	46	4	33.2
Suisham, Shaun, Was.	3	80	32	26.7	3	0	0	1	4	1	25.3
Barth, Connor, T.B.	1	46	46	46.0	1	0	0	1	18	0	28.0
Bryant, Matt, Atl.	1	36	36	36.0	1	0	0	0	0	1	36.0
Mare, Olindo, Sea.	1	32	32	32.0	1	0	0	0	0	1	32.0

Leader based on average, minimum 40 punts
* Player that was a rookie in 2009

PUNT RETURNS

YARDS PER RETURN
NFC: 15.2 DeSean Jackson, Philadelphia
AFC: 12.5 Wes Welker, New England

YARDS
AFC: 474 * Quan Cosby, Cincinnati
NFC: 441 DeSean Jackson, Philadelphia

YARDS, GAME
AFC: 120 Josh Cribbs, Cleveland vs. Cincinnati, October 4 (6 returns, 0 TD) - (OT)
NFC: 116 Patrick Crayton, Dallas vs. Seattle, November 1 (4 returns, 1 TD)

LONGEST
NFC: 85 DeSean Jackson, Philadelphia at Carolina, September 13 - TD
AFC: 77 Darren Sproles, San Diego vs. Denver, October 19 - TD

RETURNS
AFC: 40 * Quan Cosby, Cincinnati
NFC: 38 Steve Breaston, Arizona

RETURNS, GAME
AFC: 7 Jacoby Jones, Houston vs. Oakland, October 4 (60 yards, 0 TD)
NFC: 7 Sinorice Moss, N.Y. Giants vs. Oakland, October 11 (48 yards, 0 TD)
7 Nate Burleson, Seattle vs. San Francisco, December 6 (61 yards, 0 TD)

FAIR CATCHES
NFC: 23 Patrick Crayton, Dallas
AFC: 22 T.J. Rushing, Indianapolis

TOUCHDOWNS
NFC: 2 Patrick Crayton, Dallas
2 DeSean Jackson, Philadelphia
AFC: 1 Josh Cribbs, Cleveland
1 Eddie Royal, Denver
1 Darren Sproles, San Diego

TEAM CHAMPION
NFC: 13.5 Philadelphia
AFC: 11.9 Cincinnati

NFL TOP TEN PUNT RETURNERS

	No	FC	Yards	Avg	Long	TD
Jackson, DeSean, Phi.	29	15	441	15.2	85t	2
Welker, Wes, N.E.	27	16	338	12.5	69	0
Crayton, Patrick, Dal.	36	23	437	12.1	82t	2
Cribbs, Josh, Cle.	38	3	452	11.9	67t	1
* Cosby, Quan, Cin.	40	19	474	11.9	60	0
Amendola, Danny, St.L	31	11	360	11.6	56	0
Royal, Eddie, Den.	30	13	335	11.2	71t	1
Jones, Jacoby, Hou.	39	14	426	10.9	62	0
Reynaud, Darius, Min.	30	13	308	10.3	36	0
Cotchery, Jerricho, NYJ	23	12	236	10.3	31	0

AFC—INDIVIDUAL PUNT RETURNERS

	No	FC	Yards	Avg	Long	TD
Welker, Wes, N.E.	27	16	338	12.5	69	0
Cribbs, Josh, Cle.	38	3	452	11.9	67t	1
* Cosby, Quan, Cin.	40	19	474	11.9	60	0
Royal, Eddie, Den.	30	13	335	11.2	71t	1
Jones, Jacoby, Hou.	39	14	426	10.9	62	0
Cotchery, Jerricho, NYJ	23	12	236	10.3	31	0
Logan, Stefan, Pit.	30	15	280	9.3	25	0
Leonhard, Jim, NYJ	21	13	173	8.2	37	0
Carr, Chris, Bal.	32	17	262	8.2	34	0
Wade, Bobby, K.C.	21	19	160	7.6	18	0
Bess, Davone, Mia.	28	13	209	7.5	22	0
Sproles, Darren, S.D.	26	12	183	7.0	77t	1
Rushing, T.J., Ind.	21	22	119	5.7	22	0
Parrish, Roscoe, Buf.	24	13	133	5.5	31	0
Higgins, Johnnie Lee, Oak.	34	21	177	5.2	19	0
(Nonqualifiers)						
* Thomas, Mike, Jac.	14	4	118	8.4	44	0
Pearman, Alvin, Ten.	11	8	112	10.2	18	0
* Smith, Alphonso, Den.	10	3	47	4.7	21	0
Kaesviharn, Kevin, Ten.	9	8	34	3.8	10	0
Silva, Jamie, Ind.	7	1	32	4.6	7	0
Reed, Ed, Bal.	7	1	29	4.1	9	0
Jackson, Fred, Buf.	6	5	69	11.5	27	0
* Edelman, Julian, N.E.	6	1	63	10.5	35	0
* Mouton, Ryan, Ten.	6	3	37	6.2	15	0
Savage, Dantrell, K.C.	6	1	36	6.0	19	0
Martinez, Glenn, Hou.	6	1	23	3.8	11	0
Faulk, Kevin, N.E.	5	2	31	6.2	15	0
Ginn, Ted Jr., Mia.	5	0	28	5.6	12	0
Leggett, Maurice, K.C.	5	1	13	2.6	10	0
Finnegan, Cortland, Ten.	4	1	14	3.5	11	0
* McKinley, Kenny, Den.	3	0	32	10.7	14	0
Jones, Mark, Ten.	3	2	23	7.7	15	0
Moore, Mewelde, Pit.	3	9	3	1.0	2	0
Reed, Josh, Buf.	3	0	0	0.0	0	0
Smith, Brad, NYJ	2	0	27	13.5	21	0
Jones-Drew, Maurice, Jac.	2	0	19	9.5	12	0
Hughes, Nate, Jac.	2	0	18	9.0	11	0
Washington, Leon, NYJ	2	1	16	8.0	12	0
Holmes, Santonio, Pit.	2	1	6	3.0	3	0
Revis, Darrelle, NYJ	2	0	5	2.5	3	0
Lawson, Gerard, Cle.	1	0	4	4.0	4	0
Harrison, James, Pit.	1	0	1	1.0	1	0
Hill, Renaldo, Den.	1	0	0	0.0	0	0
Jennings, Tim, Ind.	1	0	0	0.0	0	0
* Middleton, William, Jac.	1	0	0	0.0	0	0
Starks, Scott, Jac.	1	0	0	0.0	0	0
Walker, Javon, Oak.	1	0	0	0.0	0	0
Williams, Sam, Oak.	1	0	0	0.0	0	0
Youboty, Ashton, Buf.	0	0	16	—	16	0
Barrett, Josh, Den.	0	0	5	—	5	0
Davis, Craig, S.D.	0	1	0	—	—	0
Engram, Bobby, K.C.	0	1	0	—	—	0
Eugene, Hiram, Oak.	0	2	0	—	—	0
* Webb, Lardarius, Bal.	0	0	-1	—	-1	0

t = Touchdown
Leader based on average return, minimum 20 returns
** Player that was a rookie in 2009*

NFC—INDIVIDUAL PUNT RETURNERS

	No	FC	Yards	Avg	Long	TD
Jackson, DeSean, Phi.	29	15	441	15.2	85t	2
Crayton, Patrick, Dal.	36	23	437	12.1	82t	2
Amendola, Danny, St.L	31	11	360	11.6	56	0
Reynaud, Darius, Min.	30	13	308	10.3	36	0
Smith, Clifton, T.B.	23	8	232	10.1	21	0
Weems, Eric, Atl.	27	14	270	10.0	28	0
* Munnerlyn, Captain, Car.	31	10	278	9.0	37	0
Northcutt, Dennis, Det.	22	15	189	8.6	43	0
Burleson, Nate, Sea.	30	3	254	8.5	29	0
Hester, Devin, Chi.	24	5	187	7.8	33	0
Breaston, Steve, Ariz	38	11	253	6.7	64	0
Bush, Reggie, N.O.	27	9	130	4.8	23	0
Battle, Arnaz, S.F.	21	10	61	2.9	18	0
(Nonqualifiers)						
Hixon, Domenik, NY-G	17	17	256	15.1	79t	1
Randle El, Antwaan, Was.	17	19	102	6.0	43	0
Nelson, Jordy, G.B.	17	6	90	5.3	14	0
Johnson, Jaymar, Min.	16	3	134	8.4	24	0
Forsett, Justin, Sea.	16	9	92	5.8	20	0
Bennett, Earl, Chi.	14	2	143	10.2	49t	1
Williams, Tramon, G.B.	13	5	135	10.4	45	0
* Stroughter, Sammie, T.B.	12	0	119	9.9	33	0
Rossum, Allen, S.F.	12	1	84	7.0	14	0
Moss, Sinorice, NY-G	11	0	74	6.7	16	0
Moss, Santana, Was.	11	1	52	4.7	11	0
Witherspoon, Brian, Jac.-Det.	9	3	88	9.8	42	0
Jones, Brandon, S.F.	9	1	26	2.9	13	0
Bradshaw, Ahmad, NY-G	6	1	55	9.2	20	0
Rolle, Antrel, Ariz	6	2	55	9.2	27	0
* Maclin, Jeremy, Phi.	6	4	30	5.0	27	0
Clements, Nate, S.F.	4	1	38	9.5	12	0
Buchanon, Phillip, Det.	4	0	34	8.5	18	0
Henderson, Devery, N.O.	4	5	16	4.0	11	0
Spurlock, Micheal, T.B.	3	0	90	30.0	77t	1
Stanley, Derek, St.L	3	1	37	12.3	24	0
Blackmon, Will, G.B.	3	1	11	3.7	6	0
Smith, Reggie, S.F.	3	0	7	2.3	9	0
Figurs, Yamon, T.B.	2	2	21	10.5	12	0
Berrian, Bernard, Min.	2	0	13	6.5	8	0
Moore, Kenny, Car.	2	1	4	2.0	4	0
Butler, Quincy, St.L	2	2	-2	-1.0	0	0
Hall, DeAngelo, Was.	2	2	-2	-1.0	0	0
Newman, Terence, Dal.	2	0	-11	-5.5	0	0
Webster, Corey, NY-G	1	0	8	8.0	8	0
Sharper, Darren, N.O.	1	1	6	6.0	6	0
* Barnes, Kevin, Was.	1	0	0	0.0	0	0
Dockery, Kevin, NY-G	1	0	0	0.0	0	0
Gamble, Chris, Car.	1	0	0	0.0	0	0
* Knox, Johnny, Chi.	1	0	0	0.0	0	0
Moore, Lance, N.O.	1	2	0	0.0	0	0
* Ogletree, Kevin, Dal.	1	0	0	0.0	0	0
Roach, David, St.L	1	0	0	0.0	0	0
* Toler, Greg, Ariz.	1	0	0	0.0	0	0
Westbrook, Byron, Was.	1	0	0	0.0	0	0
Woodson, Charles, G.B.	1	0	0	0.0	0	0
* Allen, Asher, Min.	0	1	0	—	—	0
Bradley, Mark, K.C.-T.B.	0	2	0	—	—	0

t = Touchdown
Leader based on average return, minimum 20 returns
** Player that was a rookie in 2009*

AMERICAN FOOTBALL CONFERENCE—PUNT RETURNS

	No	FC	Yards	Avg	Long	TD
Cincinnati	40	19	474	11.9	60	0
Cleveland	39	3	456	11.7	67t	1
New England	38	19	432	11.4	69	0
Houston	45	15	449	10.0	62	0
Denver	44	16	419	9.5	71t	1
N.Y. Jets	50	26	457	9.1	37	0
Jacksonville	27	7	233	8.6	44	0
Pittsburgh	36	25	290	8.1	25	0
Baltimore	39	18	290	7.4	34	0
Miami	33	13	237	7.2	22	0
San Diego	26	13	183	7.0	77t	1
Tennessee	33	22	220	6.7	18	0
Buffalo	33	18	218	6.6	31	0
Kansas City	32	24	209	6.5	19	0
Indianapolis	29	23	151	5.2	22	0
Oakland	36	23	177	4.9	19	0
AFC Total	580	284	4895	8.4	77t	3
AFC Average	36.3	17.8	305.9	8.4	—	0.2

NATIONAL FOOTBALL CONFERENCE—PUNT RETURNS

	No	FC	Yards	Avg	Long	TD
Philadelphia	35	19	471	13.5	85t	2
Tampa Bay	40	10	462	11.6	77t	1
Dallas	39	23	426	10.9	82t	2
N.Y. Giants	36	18	393	10.9	79t	1
St. Louis	37	14	395	10.7	56	0
Atlanta	27	14	270	10.0	28	0
Minnesota	48	18	455	9.5	36	0
Chicago	39	7	330	8.5	49t	1
Detroit	28	15	233	8.3	43	0
Carolina	34	11	282	8.3	37	0
Seattle	46	12	346	7.5	29	0
Green Bay	34	12	236	6.9	45	0
Arizona	45	13	308	6.8	64	0
Washington	32	22	152	4.8	43	0
New Orleans	33	17	152	4.6	23	0
San Francisco	49	13	216	4.4	18	0
NFC Total	602	238	5127	8.5	85t	7
NFC Average	37.6	14.9	320.4	8.5	—	0.4
League Total	1182	522	10022	—	85t	10
League Average	36.9	16.3	313.2	8.5	—	0.3

2009 INDIVIDUAL STATISTICS—SACKS

SACKS

MOST SACKS

AFC: 17.0 Elvis Dumervil, Denver
NFC: 14.5 Jared Allen, Minnesota

MOST SACKS, GAME

AFC: 5.0 Antwan Odom, Cincinnati at Green Bay, September 20
NFC: 4.5 Jared Allen, Minnesota vs. Green Bay, October 5

TEAM LEADERS, SACKS

AFC: BALTIMORE, 6.5, Trevor Pryce; BUFFALO, 10, Aaron Schobel; CINCINNATI, 8, Antwan Odom; CLEVELAND, 6.5, Kamerion Wimbley; DENVER, 17, Elvis Dumervil; HOUSTON, 9, Mario Williams; INDIANAPOLIS, 13.5, Dwight Freeney; JACKSONVILLE, 3, John Henderson; KANSAS CITY, 8.5, Tamba Hali; MIAMI, 9, Joey Porter; NEW ENGLAND, 10, Tully Banta-Cain; N.Y. JETS, 8, Calvin Pace; OAKLAND, 7, Greg Ellis, Trevor Scott; PITTSBURGH, 13.5, LaMarr Woodley; SAN DIEGO, 7, Shaun Phillips; TENNESSEE, 5.5, Jacob Ford

NFC: ARIZONA, 7, Calais Campbell, Darnell Dockett; ATLANTA, 6, Jonathan Babineaux; CAROLINA, 10.5, Julius Peppers; CHICAGO, 6.5, Adewale Ogunleye; DALLAS, 11, DeMarcus Ware; DETROIT, 5.5, Cliff Avril; GREEN BAY, 10, *Clay Matthews; MINNESOTA, 14.5, Jared Allen; NEW ORLEANS, 13, Will Smith; N.Y. GIANTS, 7, Osi Umenyiora; PHILADELPHIA, 12.5, Trent Cole; ST. LOUIS, 6.5, Leonard Little; SAN FRANCISCO, 6.5, Manny Lawson; SEATTLE, 5, Patrick Kerney; TAMPA BAY, 6.5, Stylez White; WASHINGTON, 11, *Brian Orakpo, Andre Carter

TEAM CHAMPION

NFC: 48 Minnesota
AFC: 47 Pittsburgh

NFL TOP TEN LEADERS—SACKS

	Sacks
Dumervil, Elvis, Den.	17.0
Allen, Jared, Min.	14.5
Freeney, Dwight, Ind.	13.5
Woodley, LaMarr, Pit.	13.5
Smith, Will, N.O.	13.0
Cole, Trent, Phi.	12.5
Carter, Andre, Was.	11.0
* Orakpo, Brian, Was.	11.0
Ware, DeMarcus, Dal.	11.0
Peppers, Julius, Car.	10.5

AMERICAN FOOTBALL CONFERENCE—SACKS

	Sacks	Yards
Pittsburgh	47	314
Miami	44	242
Cleveland	40	234
Denver	39	241
Oakland	37	228
San Diego	35	221
Cincinnati	34	237
Indianapolis	34	228
Baltimore	32	190
Buffalo	32	189
N.Y. Jets	32	245
Tennessee	32	224
New England	31	229
Houston	30	187
Kansas City	22	137
Jacksonville	14	79
AFC Total	535	3425
AFC Average	33.4	214.1

NATIONAL FOOTBALL CONFERENCE—SACKS

	Sacks	Yards
Minnesota	48	318
Philadelphia	44	316
San Francisco	44	293
Arizona	43	259
Dallas	42	268
Washington	40	241
Green Bay	37	232
Chicago	35	272
New Orleans	35	192
N.Y. Giants	32	237
Carolina	31	193
Atlanta	28	170
Seattle	28	185
Tampa Bay	28	166
Detroit	26	150
St. Louis	25	149
NFC Total	566	3641
NFC Average	35.4	227.6
League Total	1101	7066
League Average	34.4	220.8

AFC—INDIVIDUAL SACKS

	Sacks
Dumervil, Elvis, Den.	17.0
Freeney, Dwight, Ind.	13.5
Woodley, LaMarr, Pit.	13.5
Banta-Cain, Tully, N.E.	10.0
Harrison, James, Pit.	10.0
Schobel, Aaron, Buf.	10.0
Mathis, Robert, Ind.	9.5
Porter, Joey, Mia.	9.0
Williams, Mario, Hou.	9.0
Hali, Tamba, K.C.	8.5
Odom, Antwan, Cin.	8.0
Pace, Calvin, NYJ	8.0
Ellis, Greg, Oak.	7.0
Phillips, Shaun, S.D.	7.0
Scott, Trevor, Oak.	7.0
Starks, Randy, Mia.	7.0
Taylor, Jason, Mia.	7.0
Timmons, Lawrence, Pit.	7.0
Ellis, Shaun, NYJ	6.5
Pryce, Trevor, Bal.	6.5
Wimbley, Kamerion, Cle.	6.5
Fanene, Jonathan, Cin.	6.0
Johnson, Jarret, Bal.	6.0
Bowens, David, Cle.	5.5
Ford, Jacob, Ten.	5.5
Harris, David, NYJ	5.5
Wake, Cameron, Mia.	5.5
Brown, Tony, Ten.	5.0
Burgess, Derrick, N.E.	5.0
Holliday, Vonnie, Den.	5.0
Kelsay, Chris, Buf.	5.0
Wright, Mike, N.E.	5.0
* Barwin, Connor, Hou.	4.5
Gilberry, Wallace, K.C.	4.5
Smith, Antonio, Hou.	4.5
Suggs, Terrell, Bal.	4.5
* Cushing, Brian, Hou.	4.0
Hayes, William, Ten.	4.0
Jones, Jason, Ten.	4.0
Merriman, Shawne, S.D.	4.0
Reid, Darrell, Den.	4.0
Roth, Matt, Cle.	4.0
Seymour, Richard, Oak.	4.0
* Shaughnessy, Matt, Oak.	4.0
Williams, Corey, Cle.	4.0
Williams, Kyle, Buf.	4.0
* Benard, Marcus, Cle.	3.5
Brock, Raheem, Ind.	3.5
Davis, Andra, Den.	3.5
Geathers, Robert, Cin.	3.5
Jones, Dhani, Cin.	3.5
Williams, D.J., Den.	3.5
Barnes, Antwan, Bal.	3.0
Boone, Alfonso, S.D.	3.0
Farrior, James, Pit.	3.0
Gregg, Kelly, Bal.	3.0
Henderson, John, Jac.	3.0
* Johnson, Michael, Cin.	3.0
Keisel, Brett, Pit.	3.0
Lewis, Ray, Bal.	3.0
Richardson, Jay, Oak.	3.0
Thomas, Adalius, N.E.	3.0
Vanden Bosch, Kyle, Ten.	3.0
Burnett, Kevin, S.D.	2.5
Foster, Eric, Ind.	2.5
Hampton, Casey, Pit.	2.5
Langford, Kendall, Mia.	2.5
Leonhard, Jim, NYJ	2.5

	Sacks
* Maiava, Kaluka, Cle.	2.5
Merling, Phillip, Mia.	2.5
Trusnik, Jason, Cle.	2.5
Zgonina, Jeff, Hou.	2.5
Anderson, Charlie, Mia.	2.0
Brown, Mike, K.C.	2.0
Castillo, Luis, S.D.	2.0
* Chung, Pat, N.E.	2.0
Denney, Ryan, Buf.	2.0
* English, Larry, S.D.	2.0
Gregory, Steve, S.D.	2.0
Harris, Marques, S.D.	2.0
Harvey, Derrick, Jac.	2.0
Hill, Renaldo, Den.	2.0
Hope, Chris, Ten.	2.0
Howard, Thomas, Oak.	2.0
Ihedigbo, James, NYJ	2.0
Johnson, Spencer, Buf.	2.0
Johnson, Tank, Cin.	2.0
* Magee, Alex, K.C.	2.0
Morrison, Kirk, Oak.	2.0
Ndukwe, Chinedum, Cin.	2.0
Rogers, Shaun, Cle.	2.0
Scott, Bryan, Buf.	2.0
Siler, Brandon, S.D.	2.0
Smith, Aaron, Pit.	2.0
Strickland, Donald, NYJ	2.0
Stroud, Marcus, Buf.	2.0
Thomas, Bryan, NYJ	2.0
Tulloch, Stephen, Ten.	2.0
Vrabel, Mike, K.C.	2.0
Warren, Gerard, Oak.	2.0
Wilson, George, Buf.	2.0
Bell, Yeremiah, Mia.	1.5
Carr, Chris, Bal.	1.5
Coleman, Kenyon, Cle.	1.5
Douglas, Marques, NYJ	1.5
Guyton, Gary, N.E.	1.5
Johnson, Brandon, Cin.	1.5
* Knighton, Terrance, Jac.	1.5
Mayo, Jerod, N.E.	1.5
McDaniel, Tony, Mia.	1.5
* Mitchell, Mike, Oak.	1.5
Ngata, Haloti, Bal.	1.5
Okoye, Amobi, Hou.	1.5
Pollard, Bernard, Hou.	1.5
Schaefering, Brian, Cle.	1.5
Smith, Daryl, Jac.	1.5
Smith, Robaire, Cle.	1.5
Weddle, Eric, S.D.	1.5
Adams, Mike, Cle.	1.0
Ayanbadejo, Brendon, Bal.	1.0
Brackett, Gary, Ind.	1.0
Branch, Tyvon, Oak.	1.0
Carter, Tyrone, Pit.	1.0
Cesaire, Jacques, S.D.	1.0
Crowder, Channing, Mia.	1.0
Dobbins, Tim, S.D.	1.0
Dorsey, Glenn, K.C.	1.0
Draft, Chris, Buf.	1.0
Durant, Justin, Jac.	1.0
Edwards, Dwan, Bal.	1.0
Elam, Abram, Cle.	1.0
Ellison, Atiyyah, Jac.	1.0
* Ellison, Kevin, S.D.	1.0
Fuller, Vincent, Ten.	1.0
Gay, William, Pit.	1.0
Goodman, Andre', Den.	1.0
Green, Jarvis, N.E.	1.0

	Sacks
Griffin, Michael, Ten.	1.0
Haggan, Mario, Den.	1.0
Hayward, Reggie, Jac.	1.0
* Hood, Ziggy, Pit.	1.0
Ingram, Clint, Jac.	1.0
Johnson, Antonio, Ind.	1.0
Johnson, Derrick, K.C.	1.0
Jones, Nate, Mia.	1.0
Kearse, Jevon, Ten.	1.0
Keiaho, Freddy, Ind.	1.0
Kelly, Tommy, Oak.	1.0
Kirschke, Travis, Pit.	1.0
Landri, Derek, Jac.	1.0
* Marks, Sen'Derrick, Ten.	1.0
* Maualuga, Rey, Cin.	1.0
McDonald, Brandon, Cle.	1.0
McGraw, Jon, K.C.	1.0
Moses, Quentin, Mia.	1.0
Ninkovich, Rob, N.E.	1.0
Nwagbuo, Ogemdi, S.D.	1.0
Oliver, Paul, S.D.	1.0
Peterson, Kenny, Den.	1.0
Pool, Brodney, Cle.	1.0
Posluszny, Paul, Buf.	1.0
Poteat, Hank, Cle.	1.0
Rivers, Keith, Cin.	1.0
Routt, Stanford, Oak.	1.0
Rucker, Frostee, Cin.	1.0
Ryans, DeMeco, Hou.	1.0
Scott, Bart, NYJ	1.0
Scott, Ian, S.D.	1.0
Smith, Le Kevin, Den.	1.0
Stanley, Montavious, Jac.	1.0
Taylor, Ike, Pit.	1.0
Thornton, David, Ten.	1.0
Torbor, Reggie, Mia.	1.0
* Trent, Morgan, Cin.	1.0
Warren, Ty, N.E.	1.0
* Webb, Lardarius, Bal.	1.0
* Westerman, Jamaal, NYJ	1.0
Wheeler, Philip, Ind.	1.0
Wilson, Gibril, Mia.	1.0
* Baker, Ryan, Mia.	0.5
Cody, Shaun, Hou.	0.5
Haye, Jovan, Ten.	0.5
Huff, Michael, Oak.	0.5
Muir, Daniel, Ind.	0.5
Session, Clint, Ind.	0.5
Sims, Pat, Cin.	0.5

** Player that was a rookie in 2009*

NFC—INDIVIDUAL SACKS

	Sacks
Allen, Jared, Min.	14.5
Smith, Will, N.O.	13.0
Cole, Trent, Phi.	12.5
Carter, Andre, Was.	11.0
* Orakpo, Brian, Was.	11.0
Ware, DeMarcus, Dal.	11.0
Peppers, Julius, Car.	10.5
* Matthews, Clay, G.B.	10.0
Edwards, Ray, Min.	8.5
Parker, Juqua, Phi.	8.0
Campbell, Calais, Ariz	7.0
Dockett, Darnell, Ariz	7.0
Umenyiora, Osi, NY-G	7.0
Howard, Darren, Phi.	6.5
Lawson, Manny, S.F.	6.5
Little, Leonard, St.L	6.5
Ogunleye, Adewale, Chi.	6.5
White, Stylez, T.B.	6.5
Babineaux, Jonathan, Atl.	6.0
Berry, Bertrand, Ariz	6.0
Brooks, Ahmad, S.F.	6.0
Brown, Alex, Chi.	6.0
Ratliff, Jay, Dal.	6.0
Smith, Justin, S.F.	6.0
Spencer, Anthony, Dal.	6.0
Tuck, Justin, NY-G	6.0
Wilkerson, Jimmy, T.B.	6.0
Williams, Kevin, Min.	6.0
Abraham, John, Atl.	5.5
Avril, Cliff, Det.	5.5
Grant, Charles, N.O.	5.5
Biermann, Kroy, Atl.	5.0
Brayton, Tyler, Car.	5.0
Haggans, Clark, Ariz	5.0
Haralson, Parys, S.F.	5.0
Hargrove, Anthony, N.O.	5.0
Hunter, Jason, Det.	5.0
Kerney, Patrick, Sea.	5.0
Long, Chris, St.L	5.0
Hall, James, St.L	4.5
Jackson, Lawrence, Sea.	4.5
Jenkins, Cullen, G.B.	4.5
Okeafor, Chike, Ariz	4.5
Peterson, Julian, Det.	4.5
Robison, Brian, Min.	4.5
Barnett, Nick, G.B.	4.0
Hawthorne, David, Sea.	4.0
Haynesworth, Albert, Was.	4.0
Johnson, Charles, Car.	4.0
* Jones, Brad, G.B.	4.0
Spikes, Takeo, S.F.	4.0
Willis, Patrick, S.F.	4.0
Anderson, Mark, Chi.	3.5
Crowder, Tim, T.B.	3.5
Kampman, Aaron, G.B.	3.5
Beason, Jon, Car.	3.0
Bowen, Stephen, Dal.	3.0
Brooking, Keith, Dal.	3.0
* Butler, Victor, Dal.	3.0
Clemons, Chris, Phi.	3.0
Hayes, Geno, T.B.	3.0
Kennedy, Jimmy, Min.	3.0
Kiwanuka, Mathias, NY-G	3.0
McDonald, Ray, S.F.	3.0
Nicholas, Stephen, Atl.	3.0
Babin, Jason, Phi.	2.5
Briggs, Lance, Chi.	2.5
* Brown, Everette, Car.	2.5

2009 INDIVIDUAL STATISTICS—SACKS

	Sacks
Harris, Tommie, Chi.	2.5
Hillenmeyer, Hunter, Chi.	2.5
Idonije, Israel, Chi.	2.5
Leber, Ben, Min.	2.5
Spears, Marcus, Dal.	2.5
Tapp, Darryl, Sea.	2.5
Abiamiri, Victor, Phi.	2.0
Adams, Anthony, Chi.	2.0
* Afalava, Al, Chi.	2.0
Alexander, Lorenzo, Was.	2.0
Barber, Ronde, T.B.	2.0
Branch, Alan, Ariz	2.0
Carpenter, Bobby, Dal.	2.0
Chillar, Brandon, G.B.	2.0
Clark, Danny, NY-G	2.0
* Curry, Aaron, Sea.	2.0
Dahl, Craig, St.L	2.0
* Davis, Will, Ariz	2.0
DeCoud, Thomas, Atl.	2.0
Doughty, Reed, Was.	2.0
Ellis, Sedrick, N.O.	2.0
Fletcher, London, Was.	2.0
Foote, Larry, Det.	2.0
Franklin, Aubrayo, S.F.	2.0
Goldson, Dashon, S.F.	2.0
Golston, Kedric, Was.	2.0
Griffin, Cornelius, Was.	2.0
Henderson, E.J., Min.	2.0
Iwebema, Kenny, Ariz	2.0
James, Bradie, Dal.	2.0
Johnson, Thomas, Atl.	2.0
* Laurinaitis, James, St.L	2.0
* Miller, Roy, T.B.	2.0
Redding, Cory, Sea.	2.0
Roach, Nick, Chi.	2.0
Robbins, Fred, NY-G	2.0
Vilma, Jonathan, N.O.	2.0
Williams, Pat, Min.	2.0
Wilson, Adrian, Ariz	2.0
Woodson, Charles, G.B.	2.0
Ayodele, Remi, N.O.	1.5
Babineaux, Jordan, Sea.	1.5
Black, Quincy, T.B.	1.5
Davis, Thomas, Car.	1.5
Evans, Demetric, S.F.	1.5
Fluellen, Andre, Det.	1.5
Gaither, Omar, Phi.	1.5
Harper, Roman, N.O.	1.5
McBride, Turk, Det.	1.5
McCray, Bobby, N.O.	1.5
Mebane, Brandon, Sea.	1.5
Olshansky, Igor, Dal.	1.5
Patterson, Mike, Phi.	1.5
Rolle, Antrel, Ariz	1.5
Abdullah, Husain, Min.	1.0
Adams, Gaines, T.B.	1.0
Ah You, C.J., St.L	1.0
* Allen, Asher, Min.	1.0
Anderson, James, Car.	1.0
Atogwe, Oshiomogho, St.L	1.0
Banks, Jason, Ariz	1.0
* Bennett, Michael, T.B.	1.0
Bernard, Rocky, NY-G	1.0
Bly, Dre', S.F.	1.0
Boley, Michael, NY-G	1.0
Bryan, Copeland, Det.	1.0
Buchanon, Phillip, Det.	1.0
Bunkley, Brodrick, Phi.	1.0
Cofield, Barry, NY-G	1.0
Cohen, Joe, Det.	1.0
Collins, Nick, G.B.	1.0
Daniels, Phillip, Was.	1.0
Dansby, Karlos, Ariz	1.0
Davis, Chauncey, Atl.	1.0
* Delmas, Louis, Det.	1.0
* Dixon, Antonio, Phi.	1.0
Dizon, Jordon, Det.	1.0
Fujita, Scott, N.O.	1.0
Gay, Randall, N.O.	1.0
Gocong, Chris, Phi.	1.0
Goff, Jonathan, NY-G	1.0
Grant, Larry, St.L	1.0
Harris, Al, G.B.	1.0
Harrison, Marcus, Chi.	1.0
Hatcher, Jason, Dal.	1.0
Hawk, A.J., G.B.	1.0
Hayden, Nick, Car.	1.0
Hill, Leroy, Sea.	1.0
Jackson, Chevis, Atl.	1.0
* Johnson, Bruce, NY-G	1.0
Johnson, Michael, NY-G	1.0
Jolly, Johnny, G.B.	1.0
Jones, Sean, Phi.	1.0
Jordan, Akeem, Phi.	1.0
Landry, LaRon, Was.	1.0
Leonard, Louis, Car.	1.0
Lewis, Michael, S.F.	1.0
Manning, Danieal, Chi.	1.0
Peterson, Mike, Atl.	1.0
Pierce, Antonio, NY-G	1.0
Poppinga, Brady, G.B.	1.0
* Raji, B.J., G.B.	1.0
Ramsey, LaJuan, St.L	1.0
* Reed, Nick, Sea.	1.0
Robinson, Bryan, Ariz	1.0
Roman, Mark, S.F.	1.0
Rouse, Aaron, NY-G	1.0
Ryan, Clifton, St.L	1.0
Scandrick, Orlando, Dal.	1.0
* Sidbury, Lawrence, Atl.	1.0
Sims, Ryan, T.B.	1.0
* Sintim, Clint, NY-G	1.0
Sopoaga, Isaac, S.F.	1.0
Tatupu, Lofa, Sea.	1.0
Terrill, Craig, Sea.	1.0
Thomas, Terrell, NY-G	1.0
Tollefson, Dave, NY-G	1.0
Tryon, Justin, Was.	1.0
Wesley, Dante, Car.	1.0
Williams, Tramon, G.B.	1.0
Wilson, Chris, Was.	1.0
Wilson, Josh, Sea.	1.0
Winfield, Antoine, Min.	1.0
Witherspoon, Will, Phi.	1.0
Anderson, Jamaal, Atl.	0.5
Blackburn, Chase, NY-G	0.5
Canty, Chris, NY-G	0.5
Hanson, Joselio, Phi.	0.5
Hovan, Chris, T.B.	0.5
Lewis, Damione, Car.	0.5
Sharper, Darren, N.O.	0.5
Torrence, Leigh, N.O.	0.5

** Player that was a rookie in 2009*

2010 PLAYER RANKINGS AND PROJECTIONS

The *NFL.com 2010 Fantasy Football Preview*, available at newsstands now, contains 160 pages of fantasy football facts, tips, and projections for the upcoming season. The following eight pages display the projections for the running backs, wide receivers, quarterbacks, tight ends, and kickers for the 2010 season, as devised by the magazine's experts. Pick up a copy of the *NFL.com 2010 Fantasy Football Preview* today.

RUNNING BACKS	Rushing Yards	Rushing Touchdowns	Receptions	Receiving Yards	Receiving Touchdowns	Total Touchdowns
1. Chris Johnson, Tennessee	1252	13	47	465	3	16
2. Adrian Peterson, Minnesota	1550	16	38	395	1	17
3. Maurice Jones-Drew, Jacksonville	1295	13	58	440	2	15
4. Ray Rice, Baltimore	1240	9	67	650	2	11
5. Michael Turner, Atlanta	1505	16	7	25	0	16
6. Frank Gore, San Francisco	1285	9	47	395	2	11
7. Rashard Mendenhall, Pittsburgh	1320	9	31	320	1	10
8. Steven Jackson, St. Louis	1365	7	45	385	1	8
9. Cedric Benson, Cincinnati	1480	9	21	145	0	9
10. Shonn Greene, N.Y. Jets	1370	12	8	30	0	12
11. Jamaal Charles, Kansas City	1155	8	51	380	1	9
12. DeAngelo Williams, Carolina	1210	8	36	300	1	9
13. Ryan Grant, Green Bay	1215	9	20	175	0	9
14. Ryan Mathews, San Diego	1230	8	17	185	0	8
15. Knowshon Moreno, Denver	1105	8	35	245	1	9
16. LeSean McCoy, Philadelphia	870	6	55	430	3	9
17. Joseph Addai, Indianapolis	870	8	44	300	3	11
18. Beanie Wells, Arizona	1065	9	20	165	0	9
19. Ronnie Brown, Miami	1005	8	14	210	1	9
20. Jonathan Stewart, Carolina	1030	10	15	125	0	10
21. Pierre Thomas, New Orleans	820	7	35	310	2	9
22. Matt Forté, Chicago	790	5	53	420	2	7
23. Brandon Jacobs, N.Y. Giants	990	8	12	125	0	2
24. Jerome Harrison, Cleveland	850	6	42	265	2	8
25. Jahvid Best, Detroit	975	6	27	180	1	7
26. Marion Barber, Dallas	805	7	31	245	1	8
27. LenDale White, Seattle	955	8	16	95	0	8
28. Fred Jackson, Buffalo	905	4	30	280	1	5
29. Felix Jones, Dallas	965	6	23	145	0	6
30. C.J. Spiller, Buffalo	780	5	18	265	2	7
31. Clinton Portis, Washington	910	7	18	135	0	7
32. Ben Tate, Houston	945	7	12	95	0	7
33. Carnell Williams, Tampa Bay	860	5	23	180	2	7
34. Darren McFadden, Oakland	825	5	36	315	0	5
35. Ahmad Bradshaw, N.Y. Giants	785	6	27	220	1	7
36. LaDainian Tomlinson, N.Y. Jets	670	6	34	285	1	7
37. Thomas Jones, Kansas City	735	7	15	90	1	8
38. Chester Taylor, Chicago	550	4	41	340	2	6
39. Laurence Maroney, New England	725	7	11	80	1	8
40. Reggie Bush, New Orleans	435	4	55	415	3	7
41. Donald Brown, Indianapolis	635	5	20	265	1	6
42. Ricky Williams, Miami	635	5	28	205	1	6
43. Montario Hardesty, Cleveland	825	5	8	65	0	5
44. Tim Hightower, Arizona	435	6	49	335	1	7
45. Steve Slaton, Houston	530	4	38	360	1	5
46. Kevin Smith, Detroit	665	4	29	285	0	4
47. Michael Bush, Oakland	815	4	21	140	0	4
48. Darren Sproles, San Diego	365	2	40	445	4	6
49. Willis McGahee, Baltimore	570	8	18	100	0	8
50. Leon Washington, Seattle	455	3	38	360	2	5
51. Marshawn Lynch, Buffalo	510	4	28	255	1	5
52. Larry Johnson, Washington	565	5	15	90	1	6
53. Derrick Ward, Tampa Bay	540	2	20	175	2	4
54. Sammy Morris, New England	505	4	22	210	0	4
55. Correll Buckhalter, Denver	550	2	28	225	1	3
56. Mike Bell, Philadelphia	505	5	10	75	0	5
57. Arian Foster, Houston	505	4	11	95	0	4
58. Brian Westbrook, Free Agent	360	2	31	215	2	4

	Rushing Yards	Rushing Touchdowns	Receptions	Receiving Yards	Receiving Touchdowns	Total Touchdowns
59. Toby Gerhart, Minnesota	420	5	4	20	0	5
60. Bernard Scott, Cincinnati	505	2	9	85	0	2
61. Tashard Choice, Dallas	395	3	18	155	0	3
62. Willie Parker, Washington	420	4	8	70	0	4
63. Fred Taylor, New England	490	3	8	55	0	3
64. Lynell Hamilton, New Orleans	445	4	6	40	0	4
65. Jerious Norwood, Atlanta	245	1	25	285	2	3
66. Mewelde Moore, Pittsburgh	220	1	31	310	2	3
67. Jason Snelling, Atlanta	365	4	0	90	0	4
68. Javon Ringer, Tennessee	385	2	11	80	1	3
69. Jonathan Dwyer, Pittsburgh	340	2	6	10	0	2
70. Justin Forsett, Seattle	135	1	21	205	1	2
71. Maurice Morris, Detroit	290	1	18	110	0	1
72. Joe McKnight, N.Y. Jets	265	1	20	130	0	1
73. Kevin Faulk, New England	140	1	29	250	0	1
74. Brandon Jackson, Green Bay	130	1	26	195	1	2
75. Glen Coffee, San Francisco	305	1	14	75	0	1
76. Rashad Jennings, Jacksonville	245	1	20	130	0	1
77. Julius Jones, Seattle	270	1	18	120	0	1
78. Leonard Weaver, Philadelphia	245	1	20	130	0	1
79. James Davis, Cleveland	285	1	16	70	0	1
80. Le'Ron McClain, Baltimore	160	2	16	130	0	2
81. Peyton Hillis, Cleveland	240	2	8	45	0	2
82. Albert Young, Minnesota	205	2	8	55	0	2
83. Ryan Moats, Houston	165	2	8	55	0	2
84. Aaron Brown, Indianapolis	195	1	10	65	0	1
85. Kenneth Darby, St. Louis	140	1	10	105	0	1

For more in-depth analysis, pick up a copy of the NFL.com 2010 Fantasy Football Preview, *available at newsstands today.*

WIDE RECEIVERS

		Receptions	Yards	Touchdowns
1.	Andre Johnson, Houston	107	1545	10
2.	Larry Fitzgerald, Arizona	91	1230	11
3.	Randy Moss, New England	77	1205	12
4.	Reggie Wayne, Indianapolis	93	1325	9
5.	DeSean Jackson, Philadelphia	67	1205	10
6.	Miles Austin, Dallas	76	1215	9
7.	Calvin Johnson, Detroit	75	1235	8
8.	Roddy White, Atlanta	82	1205	9
9.	Vincent Jackson, San Diego	76	1190	9
10.	Brandon Marshall, Miami	92	1180	9
11.	Sidney Rice, Minnesota	78	1235	8
12.	Marques Colston, New Orleans	74	1135	9
13.	Steve Smith, N.Y. Giants	93	1150	8
14.	Greg Jennings, Green Bay	73	1210	7
15.	Anquan Boldin, Baltimore	87	1160	7
16.	Steve Smith, Carolina	77	1085	7
17.	Chad Ochocinco, Cincinnati	71	1060	8
18.	Dwayne Bowe, Kansas City	74	1055	7
19.	Hines Ward, Pittsburgh	79	1045	7
20.	Percy Harvin, Minnesota	67	830	7
21.	Wes Welker, New England	83	1085	5
22.	Mike Sims-Walker, Jacksonville	70	980	7
23.	Robert Meachem, New Orleans	55	895	8
24.	Michael Crabtree, San Francisco	74	1000	7
25.	Mike Wallace, Pittsburgh	61	915	8
26.	Hakeem Nicks, N.Y. Giants	64	970	7
27.	Santana Moss, Washington	77	1015	6
28.	Pierre Garcon, Indianapolis	54	890	7
29.	Jeremy Maclin, Philadelphia	67	920	6
30.	Steve Breaston, Arizona	69	965	5
31.	Donald Driver, Green Bay	63	970	5
32.	Terrell Owens, Free Agent	58	820	6
33.	Derrick Mason, Baltimore	62	910	5
34.	Santonio Holmes, N.Y. Jets	56	875	5
35.	Lee Evans, Buffalo	58	875	5
36.	Eddie Royal, Denver	72	810	5
37.	Kenny Britt, Tennessee	60	870	5
38.	Devin Aromashodu, Chicago	61	810	6
39.	T.J. Houshmandzadeh, Seattle	73	925	4
40.	Antonio Bryant, Cincinnati	61	850	5
41.	Jerricho Cotchery, N.Y. Jets	63	835	5
42.	Chris Chambers, Kansas City	54	830	5
43.	Roy Williams, Dallas	51	770	6
44.	Braylon Edwards, N.Y. Jets	53	805	5
45.	Mario Manningham, N.Y. Giants	57	825	5
46.	Austin Collie, Indianapolis	65	720	6
47.	Nate Burleson, Detroit	58	840	4
48.	Kevin Walter, Houston	53	755	5
49.	Johnny Knox, Chicago	56	725	6
50.	Julian Edelman, New England	55	715	5
51.	Chaz Schilens, Oakland	60	755	5
52.	Malcom Floyd, San Diego	52	870	3
53.	Demaryius Thomas, Denver	51	775	4
54.	Bernard Berrian, Minnesota	58	735	5
55.	Nate Washington, Tennessee	52	655	6
56.	Devin Hester, Chicago	49	680	4
57.	Davone Bess, Miami	68	805	3
58.	Devin Thomas, Washington	54	735	4
59.	Laurent Robinson, St. Louis	63	735	4
60.	Donnie Avery, St. Louis	52	690	4
61.	Anthony Gonzalez, Indianapolis	51	705	5
62.	Dez Bryant, Dallas	42	670	4
63.	Mohamed Massaquoi, Cleveland	50	705	4
64.	Devery Henderson, New Orleans	51	730	3
65.	Arrelious Benn, Tampa Bay	49	700	4
66.	Joshua Cribbs, Cleveland	37	450	2
67.	Deion Branch, Seattle	48	690	4
68.	Earl Bennett, Chicago	47	690	3
69.	Josh Morgan, San Francisco	56	615	3

WIDE RECEIVERS	Receptions	Yards	Touchdowns
70. Jabar Gaffney, Denver	41	615	4
71. Early Doucet, Arizona	55	615	3
72. Louis Murphy, Oakland	50	620	2
73. Michael Jenkins, Atlanta	40	550	3
74. James Jones, Green Bay	40	480	4
75. Andre Caldwell, Cincinnati	45	525	3

For more in-depth analysis, pick up a copy of the NFL.com 2010 Fantasy Football Preview, *available at newsstands today.*

QUARTERBACKS

	Player	Passing Yards	Passing Touchdowns	Rushing Yards	Rushing Touchdowns
1.	Aaron Rodgers, Green Bay	4575	32	255	4
2.	Drew Brees, New Orleans	4725	32	25	1
3.	Peyton Manning, Indianapolis	4400	31	15	1
4.	Tom Brady, New England	4450	29	55	1
5.	Philip Rivers, San Diego	4300	30	65	1
6.	Matt Schaub, Houston	4575	27	45	0
7.	Tony Romo, Dallas	4300	25	70	2
8.	Brett Favre, Minnesota	4125	29	15	1
9.	Jay Cutler, Chicago	4250	26	140	1
10.	Eli Manning, N.Y. Giants	4125	25	40	1
11.	Kevin Kolb, Philadelphia	3950	25	25	0
12.	Donovan McNabb, Washington	3625	22	155	1
13.	Joe Flacco, Baltimore	3925	24	65	0
14.	Matt Ryan, Atlanta	3750	24	55	1
15.	Vince Young, Tennessee	3075	17	425	2
16.	Ben Roethlisberger, Pittsburgh	2975	18	105	1
17.	Carson Palmer, Cincinnati	3450	22	30	1
18.	Alex Smith, San Francisco	3525	21	120	1
19.	Matthew Stafford, Detroit	3650	19	140	1
20.	Mark Sanchez, N.Y. Jets	3375	18	125	2
21.	Chad Henne, Miami	3750	19	30	0
22.	David Garrard, Jacksonville	3325	16	240	1
23.	Matt Cassel, Kansas City	3325	18	205	1
24.	Matt Leinart, Arizona	3525	18	70	2
25.	Kyle Orton, Denver	3425	17	50	0
26.	Matt Hasselbeck, Seattle	3325	16	85	0
27.	Matt Moore, Carolina	3325	17	35	0
28.	Josh Freeman, Tampa Bay	3050	15	245	1
29.	Jake Delhomme, Cleveland	2850	14	45	0
30.	Trent Edwards, Buffalo	2375	13	160	1
31.	Sam Bradford, St. Louis	2625	15	65	1
32.	Dennis Dixon, Pittsburgh	875	8	135	1
33.	JaMarcus Russell, Oakland	1725	11	85	0
34.	Michael Vick, Philadelphia	850	3	110	2
35.	Bruce Gradkowski, Oakland	1050	6	80	0
36.	Jimmy Clausen, Carolina	950	6	25	0
37.	Charlie Whitehurst, Seattle	800	6	35	0
38.	Jason Campbell, Oakland	750	4	55	0
39.	Derek Anderson, Arizona	925	6	20	0
40.	Brady Quinn, Denver	750	4	45	0
41.	Seneca Wallace, Cleveland	750	5	40	1
42.	Ryan Fitzpatrick, Buffalo	775	5	80	1
43.	Chad Pennington, Miami	620	3	10	0
44.	Brian Brohm, Buffalo	620	3	5	0
45.	Josh Johnson, Tampa Bay	420	2	65	0

FANTASY SECTION

TIGHT ENDS	Receptions	Yards	Touchdowns
1. Dallas Clark, Indianapolis	91	1025	10
2. Antonio Gates, San Diego	72	1050	8
3. Vernon Davis, San Francisco	69	910	9
4. Brent Celek, Philadelphia	71	925	8
5. Jason Witten, Dallas	91	1000	5
6. Tony Gonzalez, Atlanta	75	890	6
7. Jermichael Finley, Green Bay	63	775	7
8. Owen Daniels, Houston	74	885	5
9. Kellen Winslow, Tampa Bay	83	840	5
10. Visanthe Shiancoe, Minnesota	51	585	9
11. Chris Cooley, Washington	68	770	5
12. Heath Miller, Pittsburgh	65	700	6
13. John Carlson, Seattle	58	665	6
14. Greg Olsen, Chicago	42	585	6
15. Zach Miller, Oakland	62	760	3
16. Dustin Keller, N.Y. Jets	54	625	5
17. Kevin Boss, N.Y. Giants	47	590	5
18. Jeremy Shockey, New Orleans	55	630	4
19. Todd Heap, Baltimore	48	520	5
20. Brandon Pettigrew, Detroit	46	515	4
21. Benjamin Watson, Cleveland	36	480	4
22. Fred Davis, Washington	33	380	4
23. Bo Scaife, Tennessee	52	520	2
24. Tony Scheffler, Detroit	35	440	2
25. Marcedes Lewis, Jacksonville	33	415	2
26. Spencer Havner, Green Bay	34	435	2
27. Martellus Bennett, Dallas	30	340	2
28. David Thomas, New Orleans	27	315	2
29. Dante Rosario, Carolina	30	275	2
30. Desmond Clark, Chicago	27	310	1

For more in-depth analysis, pick up a copy of the NFL.com 2010 Fantasy Football Preview, *available at newsstands today.*

KICKERS	PTS	XP/XPA	FG/FGA
1. Stephen Gostkowski, New England	143	53/53	30/34
2. Garrett Hartley, New Orleans	141	48/48	31/35
3. Nate Kaeding, San Diego	136	46/46	30/34
4. David Akers, Philadelphia	134	41/41	31/37
5. Mason Crosby, Green Bay	129	45/45	28/36
6. Ryan Longwell, Minnesota	128	47/47	27/32
7. Rob Bironas, Tennessee	125	38/38	29/36
8. Matt Prater, Denver	123	36/36	29/36
9. Lawrence Tynes, N.Y. Giants	123	42/43	27/33
10. Robbie Gould, Chicago	121	40/40	27/32
11. Jay Feely, Arizona	122	35/35	29/32
12. Ryan Succop, Kansas City	119	32/32	29/34
13. Billy Cundiff, Baltimore	119	41/41	26/35
14. Dan Carpenter, Miami	114	39/39	25/27
15. Sebastian Janikowski, Oakland	107	20/20	29/33
16. Adam Vinatieri, Indianapolis	113	38/39	25/29
17. Neil Rackers, Houston	110	35/35	25/33
18. Jeff Reed, Pittsburgh	113	38/38	25/29
19. Shayne Graham, Cincinnati	111	33/33	26/31
20. John Kasay, Carolina	110	35/35	25/30
21. Nick Folk, N.Y. Jets	110	38/39	24/31
22. Rian Lindell, Buffalo	108	27/27	27/32
23. Matt Bryant, Atlanta	109	34/34	25/30
24. Olindo Mare, Seattle	105	30/30	25/29
25. Joe Nedney, San Francisco	104	29/29	25/31
26. Jason Hanson, Detroit	102	33/33	23/25
27. Phil Dawson, Cleveland	99	30/30	23/28
28. Josh Brown, St. Louis	98	29/29	23/26
29. David Buehler, Dallas	96	39/39	19/24
30. Graham Gano, Washington	90	27/27	21/26

FANTASY SECTION

DEFENSE/ SPECIAL TEAMS	Yards Per Game	Points Per Game	Takeaways	Sacks	Touchdowns DEF & RET
1. Jets	260.5	15.1	34	35	4
2. Vikings	297.3	18.8	24	49	4
3. Eagles	297.5	19.3	32	46	6
4. Packers	299.1	19.7	33	33	5
5. Ravens	295.9	16.9	35	37	5
6. Steelers	279.6	17.8	25	44	3
7. Saints	344.2	23.5	31	34	6
8. 49ers	324.9	18.3	29	41	4
9. Cowboys	303.7	17.1	22	45	4
10. Bears	318.4	18.7	29	41	5
11. Chargers	320.9	20.8	27	31	4
12. Giants	309.8	21.5	24	38	4
13. Dolphins	319.1	20.1	27	41	3
14. Patriots	311.6	18.3	27	34	3
15. Broncos	322.3	21.8	26	35	3
16. Cardinals	337.9	22.6	24	38	3
17. Bengals	311.7	20.1	26	31	4
18. Panthers	320.1	21	33	28	2
19. Texans	318.5	20.2	23	30	4
20. Bills	336.8	21.2	27	31	3
21. Colts	328.5	18.8	26	32	3
22. Titans	341.6	22.3	27	28	4
23. Falcons	331.4	19.5	23	33	3
24. Redskins	297.6	19.5	19	30	1
25. Browns	366.2	22.6	23	37	3
26. Raiders	370.3	22.5	22	42	3
27. Seahawks	381.7	23.6	20	31	3
28. Chiefs	386.2	25.3	28	18	4
29. Buccaneers	401.1	24.6	24	25	3
30. Jaguars	345.6	22.9	19	22	2
31. Lions	386.9	28.4	21	33	3
32. Rams	410.7	26.5	22	28	2

For more in-depth analysis, pick up a copy of the NFL.com 2010 Fantasy Football Preview, *available at newsstands today.*

Inside the Numbers

GREATEST COMEBACKS IN NFL HISTORY
(Most Points Overcome To Win Game)

REGULAR SEASON GAMES

FROM 28 POINTS BEHIND TO WIN:
December 7, 1980, at San Francisco

New Orleans	14	21	0	0	0	— 35
San Francisco	0	7	14	14	3	— 38

NO — Harris 33 pass from Manning (Ricardo kick)
NO — Childs 21 pass from Manning (Ricardo kick)
NO — Holmes 1 run (Ricardo kick)
SF — Solomon 57 punt return (Wersching kick)
NO — Holmes 1 run (Ricardo kick)
NO — Harris 41 pass from Manning (Ricardo kick)
SF — Montana 1 run (Wersching kick)
SF — Clark 71 pass from Montana (Wersching kick)
SF — Solomon 14 pass from Montana (Wersching kick)
SF — Elliott 7 run (Wersching kick)
SF — FG Wersching 36

FROM 26 POINTS BEHIND TO WIN:
September 21, 1997, at Buffalo

Indianapolis	14	12	0	9	— 35
Buffalo	0	10	6	21	— 37

Ind — Bailey 10 pass from Harbaugh (Blanchard kick)
Ind — Faulk 10 run (Blanchard kick)
Ind — FG Blanchard 39
Ind — FG Blanchard 36
Ind — FG Blanchard 49
Ind — FG Blanchard 22
Buff — Johnson 16 pass from Collins (Christie kick)
Buff — FG Christie 27
Buff — A. Smith 15 run (2-pt attempt failed)
Ind — FG Blanchard 25
Buff — Early 4 pass from Collins (Christie kick)
Buff — A. Smith 1 run (Christie kick)
Buff — A. Smith 54 run (Christie kick)
Ind — Harrison 2 pass from Justin (2-pt attempt failed)

FROM 25 POINTS BEHIND TO WIN:
November 8, 1987, at St. Louis

Tampa Bay	7	7	14	0	— 28
St. Louis	0	3	0	28	— 31

TB — Carrier 5 pass from DeBerg (Igwebuike kick)
TB — Carter 3 pass from DeBerg (Igwebuike kick)
StL — FG Gallery 31
TB — Smith 34 pass from DeBerg (Igwebuike kick)
TB — Smith 3 run (Igwebuike kick)
StL — Awalt 4 pass from Lomax (Gallery kick)
StL — Noga 23 fumble recovery (Gallery kick)
StL — J. Smith 11 pass from Lomax (Gallery kick)
StL — J. Smith 17 pass from Lomax (Gallery kick)

FROM 24 POINTS BEHIND TO WIN:
October 27, 1946, at Washington

Philadelphia	0	0	14	14	— 28
Washington	10	14	0	0	— 24

Wash — Rosato 2 run (Poillon kick)
Wash — FG Poillon 28
Wash — Rosato 4 run (Poillon kick)
Wash — Lapka recovered fumble in end zone (Poillon kick)
Phil — Steele 1 run (Lio kick)
Phil — Pritchard 45 pass from Thompson (Lio kick)
Phil — Steinke 7 pass from Thompson (Lio kick)
Phil — Ferrante 30 pass from Thompson (Lio kick)

FROM 24 POINTS BEHIND TO WIN:
October 20, 1957, at Detroit

Baltimore	7	14	6	0	— 27
Detroit	0	3	7	21	— 31

Balt — Mutscheller 15 pass from Unitas (Rechichar kick)
Det — FG Martin 47
Balt — Moore 72 pass from Unitas (Rechichar kick)
Balt — Mutscheller 52 pass from Unitas (Rechichar kick)
Balt — Moore 4 pass from Unitas (kick failed)
Det — Junker 14 pass from Rote (Layne kick)
Det — Cassady 26 pass from Layne (Layne kick)
Det — Johnson 1 run (Layne kick)
Det — Cassady 29 pass from Layne (Layne kick)

FROM 24 POINTS BEHIND TO WIN:
October 25, 1959, at Minneapolis

Philadelphia	0	0	21	7	— 28
Chicago Cardinals	7	10	7	0	— 24

Cardinals — Crow 10 pass from Roach (Conrad kick)
Cardinals — J. Hill 77 blocked field goal return (Conrad kick)
Cardinals — FG Conrad 15
Cardinals — Lane 37 interception return (Conrad kick)
Phil — Barnes 1 run (Walston kick)
Phil — McDonald 29 pass from Van Brocklin (Walston kick)
Phil — Barnes 2 run (Walston kick)
Phil — McDonald 22 pass from Van Brocklin (Walston kick)

FROM 24 POINTS BEHIND TO WIN:
October 23, 1960, at Denver

Boston	10	7	7	0	— 24
Denver	0	0	14	17	— 31

Bos — FG Cappelletti 12
Bos — Colclough 10 pass from Songin (Cappelletti kick)
Bos — Wells 6 pass from Songin (Cappelletti kick)
Bos — Miller 47 pass from Songin (Cappelletti kick)
Den — Carmichael 21 pass from Tripucka (Mingo kick)
Den — Jessup 19 pass from Tripucka (Mingo kick)
Den — Carmichael 35 lateral from Taylor, pass from Tripucka (Mingo kick)
Den — Taylor 8 pass from Tripucka (Mingo kick)
Den — FG Mingo 9

FROM 24 POINTS BEHIND TO WIN:
December 15, 1974, at Miami

New England	21	3	0	3	— 27
Miami	0	17	7	10	— 34

NE — Hannah recovered fumble in end zone (J. Smith kick)
NE — Sanders 23 interception return (J. Smith kick)
NE — Herron 4 pass from Plunkett (J. Smith kick)
NE — FG J. Smith 46
Mia — Nottingham 1 run (Yepremian kick)
Mia — Baker 37 pass from Morrall (Yepremian kick)
Mia — FG Yepremian 28
Mia — Baker 46 pass from Morrall (Yepremian kick)
NE — FG J. Smith 34
Mia — Nottingham 2 run (Yepremian kick)
Mia — FG Yepremian 40

FROM 24 POINTS BEHIND TO WIN:
December 4, 1977, at Minnesota

San Francisco	0	10	14	3	— 27
Minnesota	0	0	7	21	— 28

SF — Delvin Williams 2 run (Wersching kick)
SF — FG Wersching 31
SF — Dave Williams 80 kickoff return (Wersching kick)
SF — Delvin Williams 5 run (Wersching kick)
Minn — McClanahan 15 pass from Lee (Cox kick)
Minn — Rashad 8 pass from Kramer (Cox kick)
Minn — Tucker 9 pass from Kramer (Cox kick)
SF — FG Wersching 31
Minn — S. White 69 pass from Kramer (Cox kick)

FROM 24 POINTS BEHIND TO WIN:
September 23, 1979, at Denver

Seattle	10	10	14	0	— 34
Denver	0	10	21	6	— 37

Sea — FG Herrera 28
Sea — Doornink 5 run (Herrera kick)
Den — FG Turner 27
Sea — Doornink 5 run (Herrera kick)
Den — Armstrong 2 run (Turner kick)
Sea — FG Herrera 22
Sea — McCullum 13 pass from Zorn (Herrera kick)
Sea — Smith 1 run (Herrera kick)
Den — Studdard 2 pass from Morton (Turner kick)
Den — Moses 11 pass from Morton (Turner kick)
Den — Upchurch 35 pass from Morton (Turner kick)

Den — Lytle 1 run (kick failed)

FROM 24 POINTS BEHIND TO WIN:
September 23, 1979, at Cincinnati

Houston	0	10	17	0	3	—	30
Cincinnati	14	10	0	3	0	—	27

Cin — Johnson 1 run (Bahr kick)
Cin — Alexander 2 run (Bahr kick)
Cin — Johnson 1 run (Bahr kick)
Cin — FG Bahr 52
Hou — Burrough 35 pass from Pastorini (Fritsch kick)
Hou — FG Fritsch 33
Hou — Campbell 8 run (Fritsch kick)
Hou — Caster 22 pass from Pastorini (Fritsch kick)
Hou — FG Fritsch 47
Cin — FG Bahr 55
Hou — FG Fritsch 29

FROM 24 POINTS BEHIND TO WIN:
November 22, 1982, at Los Angeles

San Diego	10	14	0	0	—	24
L.A. Raiders	0	7	14	7	—	28

SD — FG Benirschke 19
SD — Scales 29 pass from Fouts (Benirschke kick)
SD — Muncie 2 run (Benirschke kick)
SD — Muncie 1 run (Benirschke kick)
Raiders — Christensen 1 pass from Plunkett (Bahr kick)
Raiders — Allen 3 run (Bahr kick)
Raiders — Allen 6 run (Bahr kick)
Raiders — Hawkins 1 run (Bahr kick)

FROM 24 POINTS BEHIND TO WIN:
September 26, 1988, at Denver

L.A. Raiders	0	0	14	13	3	—	30
Denver	7	17	0	3	0	—	27

Den — Dorsett 1 run (Karlis kick)
Den — Dorsett 1 run (Karlis kick)
Den — Sewell 7 pass from Elway (Karlis kick)
Den — FG Karlis 39
Raiders — Smith 40 pass from Schroeder (Bahr kick)
Raiders — Smith 42 pass from Schroeder (Bahr kick)
Raiders — FG Bahr 28
Raiders — Allen 4 run (Bahr kick)
Den — FG Karlis 25
Raiders — FG Bahr 44
Raiders — FG Bahr 35

FROM 24 POINTS BEHIND TO WIN:
December 6, 1992, at Tampa

L.A. Rams	0	3	21	7	—	31
Tampa Bay	6	21	0	0	—	27

TB — FG Murray 34
TB — FG Murray 47
TB — Armstrong 81 pass from Testaverde (Murray kick)
TB — Jones 26 fumble recovery (Murray kick)
Rams — FG Zendejas 18
TB — Carrier 10 pass from Testaverde (Murray kick)
Rams — Anderson 40 pass from Everett (Zendejas kick)
Rams — Chadwick 27 pass from Everett (Zendejas kick)
Rams — Lang 1 run (Zendejas kick)
Rams — Carter 8 pass from Everett (Zendejas kick)

POSTSEASON GAMES

FROM 32 POINTS BEHIND TO WIN:
AFC First-Round Playoff Game
January 3, 1993, at Buffalo

Houston	7	21	7	3	0	—	38
Buffalo	3	0	28	7	3	—	41

Hou — Jeffires 3 pass from Moon (Del Greco kick)
Buff — FG Christie 36
Hou — Slaughter 7 pass from Moon (Del Greco kick)
Hou — Duncan 26 pass from Moon (Del Greco kick)
Hou — Jeffires 27 pass from Moon (Del Greco kick)
Hou — McDowell 58 interception return (Del Greco kick)
Buff — Davis 1 run (Christie kick)
Buff — Beebe 38 pass from Reich (Christie kick)
Buff — Reed 26 pass from Reich (Christie kick)
Buff — Reed 18 pass from Reich (Christie kick)
Buff — Reed 17 pass from Reich (Christie kick)
Hou — FG Del Greco 26
Buff — FG Christie 32

FROM 24 POINTS BEHIND TO WIN:
NFC First-Round Playoff Game
January 5, 2003, at San Francisco

N.Y. Giants	7	21	10	0	—	38
San Francisco	7	7	8	17	—	39

SF — Owens 76 pass from Garcia (Chandler kick)
NYG — Toomer 12 pass from Collins (Bryant kick)
NYG — Shockey 2 pass from Collins (Bryant kick)
SF — Barlow 1 run (Chandler kick)
NYG — Toomer 8 pass from Collins (Bryant kick)
NYG — Toomer 24 pass from Collins (Bryant kick)
NYG — Barber 6 run (Bryant kick)
NYG — FG Bryant 21
SF — Owens 26 pass from Garcia (Owens from Garcia)
SF — Garcia 14 run (Owens from Garcia)
SF — Garcia 14 run (Owens from Garcia)
SF — FG Chandler 25
SF — Streets 13 pass from Garcia (2-pt attempt failed)

FROM 20 POINTS BEHIND TO WIN:
Western Conference Playoff Game
December 22, 1957, at San Francisco

Detroit	0	7	14	10	—	31
San Francisco	14	10	3	0	—	27

SF — Owens 34 pass from Tittle (Soltau kick)
SF — McElhenny 47 pass from Tittle (Soltau kick)
Det — Junker 4 pass from Rote (Martin kick)
SF — Wilson 12 pass from Tittle (Soltau kick)
SF — FG Soltau 25
SF — FG Soltau 10
Det — Tracy 2 run (Martin kick)
Det — Tracy 58 run (Martin kick)
Det — Gedman 3 run (Martin kick)
Det — FG Martin 14

FROM 18 POINTS BEHIND TO WIN:
NFC Divisional Playoff Game
December 23, 1972, at San Francisco

Dallas	3	10	0	17	—	30
San Francisco	7	14	7	0	—	28

SF — Washington 97 kickoff return (Gossett kick)
Dall — FG Fritsch 37
SF — Schreiber 1 run (Gossett kick)
SF — Schreiber 1 run (Gossett kick)
Dall — FG Fritsch 45
Dall — Alworth 28 pass from Morton (Fritsch kick)
SF — Schreiber 1 run (Gossett kick)
Dall — FG Fritsch 27
Dall — Parks 20 pass from Staubach (Fritsch kick)
Dall — Sellers 10 pass from Staubach (Fritsch kick)

FROM 18 POINTS BEHIND TO WIN:
AFC Divisional Playoff Game
January 4, 1986, at Miami

Cleveland	7	7	7	0	—	21
Miami	3	0	14	7	—	24

Mia — FG Reveiz 51
Cle — Newsome 16 pass from Kosar (Bahr kick)
Cle — Byner 21 run (Bahr kick)
Cle — Byner 66 run (Bahr kick)
Mia — Moore 6 pass from Marino (Reveiz kick)
Mia — Davenport 31 run (Reveiz kick)
Mia — Davenport 1 run (Reveiz kick)

FROM 18 POINTS BEHIND TO WIN:
AFC Divisional Playoff Game
January 21, 2007, at Indianapolis

New England	7	14	7	6	—	34
Indianapolis	3	3	15	17	—	38

NE — Mankins 0 fumble recovery (Gostkowski kick)
Ind — FG Vinatieri 42
NE — Dillon 7 run (Gostkowski kick)
NE — Samuel 39 interception return (Gostkowski kick)
Ind — FG Vinatieri 26
Ind — Manning 1 run (Vinatieri kick)
Ind — Klecko 1 pass from Manning (Harrison from Manning)
NE — Gaffney 6 pass from Brady (Gostkowski kick)
Ind — Saturday 0 fumble recovery (Vinatieri kick)
NE — FG Gostkowski 28
Ind — FG Vinatieri 36
NE — FG Gostkowski 43
Ind — Addai 3 run (Vinatieri kick)

RECORDS FOR NFL TEAMS FOR MOST POINTS IN A GAME (REGULAR SEASON ONLY)

Note: *When the record has been achieved more than once, only the most recent game is shown; summaries are listed in alphabetical order by conference. Bold face indicates team holding record.*

BALTIMORE RAVENS

December 13, 2009, at Baltimore

Detroit	0	3	0	0	— 3
Baltimore	3	17	21	7	— 48

TD: Balt—Willis McGahee 2, Derrick Mason, Le'Ron McClain, Ray Rice, Troy Smith. TD Passes: Balt—Joe Flacco. FG: Balt—Billy Cundiff 2; Det—Jason Hanson.

BUFFALO BILLS

September 18, 1966, at Buffalo

Miami	3	7	0	14	— 24
Buffalo	21	27	3	7	— 58

TD: Buff—Bobby Burnett 2, Butch Byrd 2, Jack Spikes 2, Bobby Crockett, Jack Kemp; Mia—Dave Kocourek, Bo Roberson, John Roderick. TD Passes: Buff—Jack Kemp, Daryle Lamonica; Mia—George Wilson 3. FG: Buff—Booth Lusteg; Mia—Gene Mingo.

CINCINNATI BENGALS

December 17, 1989, at Cincinnati

Houston	0	0	0	7	— 7
Cincinnati	21	10	21	9	— 61

TD: Cin—Eddie Brown 2, Eric Ball, James Brooks, Ira Hillary, Rodney Holman, Tim McGee, Craig Taylor; Hou—Lorenzo White. TD Passes: Cin—Boomer Esiason 4, Erik Wilhelm. FG: Cin—Jim Breech 2.

CLEVELAND BROWNS

November 7, 1954, at Cleveland

Washington	0	3	0	0	— 3
Cleveland	13	14	21	14	— 62

TD: Cle—Darrell Brewster 2, Mo Bassett, Ken Gorgal, Otto Graham, Dub Jones, Dante Lavelli, Curley Morrison. TD Passes: Cle—George Ratterman 3, Otto Graham. FG: Cle—Lou Groza 2; Wash—Vic Janowicz.

DENVER BRONCOS

October 6, 1963, at Denver

San Diego	13	7	0	14	— 34
Denver	3	14	9	24	— 50

TD: Den—Lionel Taylor 2, Goose Gonsoulin, Gene Prebola, Donnie Stone; SD—Keith Lincoln 2, Lance Alworth, Paul Lowe, Jacque MacKinnon. TD Passes: Den—John McCormick 3; SD—Tobin Rote 3, John Hadl 2. FG: Den—Gene Mingo 5.

HOUSTON TEXANS

December 30, 2007 at Houston

Jacksonville	7	7	7	7	— 28
Houston	0	21	14	7	— 42

TD: Jax—Earnest Wilford 2, Matt Jones, Reggie Williams; Hou—Andre Davis 2, Ron Dayne 2, Owen Daniels, Darius Walker. TD Passes: Jax—Quinn Gray 4; Hou—Sage Rosenfels.

INDIANAPOLIS COLTS

December 12, 1976, at Baltimore

Buffalo	3	3	7	7	— 20
Baltimore Colts	7	13	28	10	— 58

TD: Balt—Roger Carr, Raymond Chester, Glenn Doughty, Roosevelt Leaks, Derrel Luce, Lydell Mitchell, Howard Stevens; Buff—Bob Chandler, O.J. Simpson. TD Passes: Balt—Bert Jones 3; Buff—Gary Marangi. FG: Balt—Toni Linhart 3; Buff—George Jakowenko 2.

JACKSONVILLE JAGUARS

December 23, 2007, at Jacksonville

Oakland	0	3	0	8	— 11
Jacksonville	14	14	7	14	— 49

TD: Oak—Zach Miller; Jac—Richard Angulo, David Garrard, Greg Jones, Matt Jones, Maurice Jones-Drew, Fred Taylor, Reggie Williams. TD Passes: Oak—JaMarcus Russell; Jac—David Garrard 2, Quinn Gray 2. FG: Oak—Sebastian Janikowski.

KANSAS CITY CHIEFS

September 7, 1963, at Denver

Kansas City	14	14	21	10	— 59
Denver	0	7	0	0	— 7

TD: KC—Chris Burford 2, Frank Jackson 2, Dave Grayson, Abner Haynes, Sherrill Headrick, Curtis McClinton; Den—Lionel Taylor. TD Passes: KC—Len Dawson 4, Curtis McClinton; Den—Mickey Slaughter. FG: KC—Tommy Brooker.

MIAMI DOLPHINS

November 24, 1977, at St. Louis

Miami	14	14	20	7	— 55
St. Louis Cardinals	7	0	0	7	— 14

TD: Mia—Nat Moore 3, Gary Davis, Duriel Harris, Leroy Harris, Benny Malone, Andre Tillman; StL—Ike Harris, Terry Metcalf. TD Passes: Mia—Bob Griese 6; StL—Jim Hart.

NEW ENGLAND PATRIOTS

October 18, 2009, at New England

Tennessee	0	0	0	0	— 0
New England	10	35	14	0	— 59

TD: NE—Randy Moss 3, Wes Welker 2, Kevin Faulk, Brian Hoyer, Laurence Maroney. TD Passes: NE—Tom Brady 6. FG: NE—Stephen Gostkowski.

NEW YORK JETS

November 17, 1985, at New York

Tampa Bay	14	7	7	0	— 28
New York Jets	17	24	14	7	— 62

TD: NYJ—Mickey Shuler 3, Johnny Hector 2, Tony Paige, Al Toon, Wesley Walker; TB—James Wilder 2, Kevin House, Calvin Magee. TD Passes: NYJ—Ken O'Brien 5; TB—Steve DeBerg 2. FG: NYJ—Pat Leahy 2.

OAKLAND RAIDERS

September 29, 2002 at Oakland

Tennessee	7	0	12	6	— 25
Oakland	21	10	7	14	— 52

TD: Oak—Tim Brown, Phillip Buchanon, Charlie Garner, Terry Kirby, Jerry Porter, Jim Rice, Rod Woodson; Tenn—Drew Bennett, Eddie George, Justin McCareins, John Simon. TD Passes: Oak—Rich Gannon 4; Tenn—Steve McNair 2. FG: Oak—Sebastian Janikowski.

PITTSBURGH STEELERS

November 30, 1952, at Pittsburgh

New York Giants	0	0	7	0	— 7
Pittsburgh	14	14	7	28	— 63

TD: Pitt—Lynn Chandnois 2, Dick Hensley 2, Jack Butler, George Hays, Ray Mathews, Ed Modzelewski, Elbie Nickel; NYG—Bill Stribling. TD Passes: Pitt—Jim Finks 4, Gary Kerkorian; NYG—Tom Landry.

SAN DIEGO CHARGERS

December 22, 1963, at San Diego

Denver	7	10	3	0	— 20
San Diego	10	16	10	22	— 58

TD: SD—Paul Lowe 2, Chuck Allen, Bobby Jackson, Dave Kocourek, Keith Lincoln, Jacque MacKinnon; Den—Billy Joe, Donnie Stone. TD Passes: SD—John Hadl, Tobin Rote; Den—Don Breaux. FG: SD—George Blair 3; Den—Gene Mingo 2.

TENNESSEE TITANS

December 9, 1990, at Houston

Cleveland	0	7	7	0	— 14
Houston Oilers	14	31	7	6	— 58

TD: Hou—Lorenzo White 4, Ernest Givins, Leonard Harris, Tony Jones, Terry Kinard; Cle—Eric Metcalf 2. TD Passes: Hou—Warren Moon 2, Cody Carlson; Cle—Bernie Kosar. FG: Hou—Teddy Garcia.

ARIZONA CARDINALS

November 13, 1949, at New York

Chicago Cardinals	7	31	14	13	— 65
New York Bulldogs	7	0	6	7	— 20

TD: Chi—Red Cochran 2, Pat Harder 2, Bill Dewell, Mel Kutner, Bob Ravensburg, Vic Schwall, Charlie Trippi; NY—Joe Golding, Frank Muehlheuser, Johnny Rauch. TD Passes: Chi—Paul Christman 3, Jim Hardy 3; NY—Bobby Layne. FG: Chi—Pat Harder.

ATLANTA FALCONS

September 16, 1973, at New Orleans

Atlanta	0	24	21	17	— 62
New Orleans	0	0	7	0	— 7

TD: Atl—Ken Burrow 2, Eddie Ray 2, Wes Chesson, Tom Hayes, Art Malone, Joe Profit; NO—Bill Butler. TD Passes: Atl—Dick Shiner 3, Bob Lee; NO—Archie Manning. FG: Atl—Nick Mike-Mayer 2.

CAROLINA PANTHERS

December 8, 2002, at Carolina

Cincinnati	7	10	14	0	— 31
Carolina	9	7	21	15	— 52

TD: Car—Steve Smith 3, Dee Brown, Muhsin Muhammad, Al Wallace, Wesley Walls; Cin—Peter Warrick 2, Jon Kitna, Takeo Spikes. TD Passes: Car—Rodney Peete 3; Cin—Jon Kitna 2. FG: Cin—Neil Rackers.

CHICAGO BEARS

December 7, 1980, at Chicago

Green Bay	0	7	0	0	— 7
Chicago	0	28	13	20	— 61

TD: Chi—Walter Payton 3, Brian Baschnagel, Robin Earl, Roland Harper, Willie McClendon, Len Walterscheid, Rickey Watts; GB—James Lofton. TD Passes: Chi—Vince Evans 3; GB—Lynn Dickey.

DALLAS COWBOYS

October 12, 1980, at Dallas

San Francisco	0	7	0	7	— 14
Dallas	14	24	14	7	— 59

TD: Dall—Drew Pearson 3, Ron Springs 2, Tony Dorsett, Billy Joe DuPree, Robert Newhouse; SF—Dwight Clark 2. TD Passes: Dall—Danny White 4; SF—Steve DeBerg 2. FG: Dall—Rafael Septien.

DETROIT LIONS

November 27, 1997, at Detroit

Chicago	14	6	0	0	— 20
Detroit	3	14	17	21	— 55

TD: Det—Herman Moore, Johnnie Morton, Ron Rivers, Barry Sanders 3, Tracy Scroggins; Chi—Raymont Harris, Ricky Proehl. TD Passes: Det—Scott Mitchell 2; Chi—Erik Kramer. FG: Det—Jason Hanson 2; Chi—Jeff Jaeger 2.

GREEN BAY PACKERS

October 7, 1945, at Milwaukee

Detroit	0	7	7	7	— 21
Green Bay	0	41	9	7	— 57

TD: GB—Don Hutson 4, Charley Brock, Irv Comp, Ted Fritsch, Clyde Goodnight; Det—Chuck Fenenbock, John Greene, Bob Westfall. TD Passes: GB—Tex McKay 4, Lou Brock, Irv Comp; Det—Dave Ryan.

MINNESOTA VIKINGS

October 18, 1970, at Minnesota

Dallas	3	3	0	7	— 13
Minnesota	14	20	17	3	— 54

TD: Minn—Clint Jones 2, Ed Sharockman 2, John Beasley, Dave Osborn; Dall—Calvin Hill. TD Pass: Minn—Gary Cuozzo. FG: Minn—Fred Cox 4; Dall—Mike Clark 2.

NEW ORLEANS SAINTS

November 24, 2008, at New Orleans

Green Bay	7	14	0	8	— 29
New Orleans	14	10	21	6	— 51

TD: NO—Lance Moore 2, Pierre Thomas 2, Billy Miller, Deuce McAllister, Marques Colston; GB—John Kuhn, Greg Jennings, Ruvell Martin, Aaron Rodgers. TD Pass: NO—Drew Brees 4; GB—Aaron Rodgers 2. FG: NO—Garrett Hartley.

NEW YORK GIANTS

November 26, 1972, at New York

Philadelphia	3	7	0	0	— 10
New York Giants	14	24	10	14	— 62

TD: NYG—Don Herrmann 2, Ron Johnson 2, Bob Tucker 2, Randy Johnson; Phil—Harold Jackson. TD Passes: NYG—Norm Snead 3, Randy Johnson 2; Phil—John Reaves. FG: NYG—Pete Gogolak 2; Phil—Tom Dempsey.

PHILADELPHIA EAGLES

November 6, 1934, at Philadelphia

Cincinnati Reds	0	0	0	0	— 0
Philadelphia	26	6	12	20	— 64

TD: Phil—Joe Carter 3, Swede Hanson 3, Marvin Ellstrom, Roger Kirkman, Ed Matesic, Ed Storm. TD Passes: Phil—Ed Matesic 2, Albert Weiner 2, Marvin Elstrom.

ST. LOUIS RAMS

October 22, 1950, at Los Angeles

Baltimore	13	0	7	7	— 27
Los Angeles Rams	21	14	14	21	— 70

TD: LA—Bob Boyd 2, Vitamin T. Smith 2, Tom Fears, Elroy (Crazylegs) Hirsch, Dick Hoerner, Ralph Pasquariello, Dan Towler, Bob Waterfield; Balt—Chet Mutryn 2, Adrian Burk, Billy Stone. TD Passes: LA—Norm Van Brocklin 2, Bob Waterfield 2, Glenn Davis; Balt—Adrian Burk 3.

SAN FRANCISCO 49ERS

October 18, 1992, at San Francisco

Atlanta	7	3	0	7	— 17
San Francisco	21	21	14	0	— 56

TD: SF—Jerry Rice 3, Ricky Watters 3, Brent Jones, Tom Rathman; Atl—Michael Haynes, Jason Phillips. TD Passes: SF—Steve Young 3; Atl—Chris Miller, Wade Wilson. FG: Atl—Norm Johnson.

SEATTLE SEAHAWKS

October 30, 1977, at Seattle

Buffalo	3	0	7	7	— 17
Seattle	14	28	7	7	— 56

TD: Sea—Steve Largent 2, Duke Fergerson, Al Hunter, David Sims, Sherman Smith, Don Testerman, Jim Zorn; Buff—Joe Ferguson, John Kimbrough. TD Passes: Sea—Jim Zorn 4; Buff—Joe Ferguson. FG: Buff—Carson Long.

TAMPA BAY BUCCANEERS

December 23, 2001, at Tampa Bay

New Orleans	0	0	7	14	— 21
Tampa Bay	17	13	3	15	— 48

TD: TB—Mike Alstott, Ronde Barber, Warrick Dunn, Dave Moore, Karl Williams; NO—Joe Horn 2, Eddie Williams. TD Passes: TB—Brad Johnson 3; NO—Aaron Brooks 3. FG: TB—Martin Gramatica 4.

WASHINGTON REDSKINS

November 27, 1966, at Washington

New York Giants	0	14	14	13	— 41
Washington	13	21	14	24	— 72

TD: Wash—A.D. Whitfield 3, Brig Owens 2, Charley Taylor 2, Rickie Harris, Joe Don Looney, Bobby Mitchell; NYG—Allen Jacobs, Homer Jones, Dan Lewis, Joe Morrison, Aaron Thomas, Gary Wood. TD Passes: Wash—Sonny Jurgensen 3; NYG—Gary Wood 2, Tom Kennedy. FG: Wash—Charlie Gogolak.

RECORDS OF NFL TEAMS SINCE 1970 AFL-NFL MERGER

AFC	W	L	T	Pct.	Division Titles	Playoff Berths	Postseason Record	Super Bowl Record
Miami	372	242	2	.606	13	22	20-20	2-3
Pittsburgh	372	242	2	.606	19	24	31-18	6-1
Denver	355	255	6	.581	10	17	17-15	2-4
Oakland	333	277	6	.546	12	18	22-15	3-1
New England	324	292	0	.526	11	16	20-13	3-3
Jacksonville**	125	115	0	.521	2	6	5-6	0-0
Baltimore***	116	107	1	.520	2	6	8-5	1-0
Indianapolis	308	306	2	.502	12	18	15-16	2-1
Tennessee	301	313	2	.490	5	16	12-16	0-1
Kansas City	298	311	7	.489	5	11	3-11	0-0
San Diego	289	322	5	.473	10	12	9-12	0-1
Buffalo	289	325	2	.471	7	13	12-13	0-4
Cleveland+	253	312	3	.448	6	11	4-11	0-0
Cincinnati	275	340	1	.447	7	9	5-9	0-2
N.Y. Jets	271	343	2	.442	2	11	8-11	0-0
Houston****	49	79	0	.383	0	0	0-0	0-0

NFC	W	L	T	Pct.	Division Titles	Playoff Berths	Postseason Record	Super Bowl Record
Dallas	367	249	0	.596	17	26	32-21	5-3
Minnesota	355	259	2	.578	16	24	17-24	0-3
San Francisco	345	268	3	.563	17	21	25-16	5-0
Washington	337	277	2	.549	6	16	20-13	3-2
Philadelphia	315	293	8	.518	7	18	15-18	0-2
St. Louis	313	299	4	.511	11	19	16-18	1-2
Green Bay	310	298	8	.510	8	14	13-13	1-1
Chicago	306	309	1	.498	9	13	9-12	1-1
N.Y. Giants	302	311	3	.493	7	14	16-11	3-1
Carolina**	117	123	0	.488	3	4	6-4	0-1
Seattle*	255	277	0	.479	6	10	7-10	0-1
Atlanta	264	347	5	.432	3	9	6-9	0-1
New Orleans	263	349	4	.430	4	7	5-6	1-0
Arizona	251	359	6	.412	4	6	5-6	0-1
Detroit	248	364	4	.406	3	9	1-9	0-0
Tampa Bay*	208	323	1	.392	6	10	6-9	1-0

**Entered NFL in 1976.*
***Entered NFL in 1995.*
****Entered NFL in 1996.*
*****Entered NFL in 2002.*
+Did not play, 1996-98.
Oakland totals include L.A. Raiders, 1982-1994.
Tennessee totals include Houston, 1970-1996.
Indianapolis totals include Baltimore, 1970-1983.
St. Louis totals include L.A. Rams, 1970-1994.
Arizona totals include St. Louis, 1970-1987, and Phoenix, 1988-1993.
Tie games before 1972 are not calculated in won-lost percentage.

HOME RECORDS OF NFL TEAMS SINCE 1970 AFL-NFL MERGER

AFC	W	L	T	Pct.
Pittsburgh	222	85	1	.722
Denver	215	90	4	.704
Miami	213	93	1	.695
Baltimore***	73	38	1	.656
Jacksonville**	74	46	0	.617
New England	186	122	0	.604
Oakland	184	122	2	.601
Kansas City	180	124	3	.592
Tennessee	172	135	1	.560
Cincinnati	169	138	1	.550
Buffalo	169	139	1	.549
San Diego	165	140	2	.541
Indianapolis	163	143	2	.533
Cleveland+	140	141	2	.498
N.Y. Jets	145	161	1	.474
Houston****	30	34	0	.469

NFC	W	L	T	Pct.
Dallas	210	98	0	.682
Minnesota	210	98	1	.681
Washington	192	113	2	.629
San Francisco	188	118	2	.614
Green Bay	185	118	5	.609
Chicago	182	125	1	.593
Philadelphia	176	130	3	.575
Seattle*	153	114	0	.573
St. Louis	172	134	2	.562
N.Y. Giants	165	143	1	.536
Carolina**	64	56	0	.533
Detroit	162	145	1	.528
Atlanta	159	149	1	.516
Arizona	149	155	3	.490
Tampa Bay*	129	136	1	.487
New Orleans	140	167	1	.456

**Entered NFL in 1976.*
***Entered NFL in 1995.*
****Entered NFL in 1996.*
*****Entered NFL in 2002.*
+Did not play, 1996-98.
Oakland totals include L.A. Raiders, 1982-1994.
Tennessee totals include Houston, 1970-1996.
Indianapolis totals include Baltimore, 1970-1983.
St. Louis totals include L.A. Rams, 1970-1994.
Arizona totals include St. Louis, 1970-1987, and Phoenix, 1988-1993.
Tie games before 1972 are not calculated in won-lost percentage.

ROAD RECORDS OF NFL TEAMS SINCE 1970 AFL-NFL MERGER

AFC	W	L	T	Pct.
Miami	159	149	1	.516
Oakland	149	155	4	.490
Pittsburgh	150	157	1	.489
Indianapolis	145	163	0	.471
Denver	140	165	2	.459
New England	138	170	0	.448
Jacksonville**	51	69	0	.425
Tennessee	129	178	1	.420
N.Y. Jets	126	182	1	.409
San Diego	124	182	3	.406
Cleveland+	113	171	1	.398
Buffalo	120	186	1	.392
Kansas City	118	187	4	.388
Baltimore***	43	69	0	.384
Cincinnati	106	202	0	.344
Houston****	19	45	0	.297

NFC	W	L	T	Pct.
San Francisco	157	150	1	.511
Dallas	157	151	0	.510
Minnesota	145	161	1	.474
Washington	145	164	0	.469
St. Louis	141	165	2	.461
Philadelphia	139	163	5	.461
N.Y. Giants	137	168	2	.450
Carolina**	53	67	0	.442
Green Bay	125	180	3	.410
New Orleans	123	182	3	.404
Chicago	124	184	0	.403
Seattle*	102	163	0	.385
Atlanta	105	198	4	.347
Arizona	102	204	3	.334
Tampa Bay**	79	187	0	.297
Detroit	86	219	3	.283

**Entered NFL in 1976.*
***Entered NFL in 1995.*
****Entered NFL in 1996.*
*****Entered NFL in 2002.*
+Did not play, 1996-98.
Oakland totals include L.A. Raiders, 1982-1994.
Tennessee totals include Houston, 1970-1996.
Indianapolis totals include Baltimore, 1970-1983.
St. Louis totals include L.A. Rams, 1970-1994.
Arizona totals include St. Louis, 1970-1987, and Phoenix, 1988-1993.
Tie games before 1972 are not calculated in won-lost percentage.

RECORDS OF TEAMS ON KICKOFF WEEKEND

AFC	W	L	T	Pct.	Longest W Strk.	Longest L Strk.	Current Streak
Denver	32	17	1	.653	4	4	W-3
Jacksonville	9	6	0	.600	6	3	L-3
San Diego	29	21	0	.580	6	6	W-1
Pittsburgh	39	32	4	.549	7	3	W-7
Miami	23	20	1	.535	11	5	L-4
Indianapolis	34	31	1	.523	8	8	W-1
Kansas City	26	24	0	.520	7	4	L-4
New England	26	24	0	.520	6	3	W-6
Tennessee	26	24	0	.520	4	3	L-1
Oakland	24	26	0	.480	5	7	L-7
Cleveland	27	30	0	.474	5	6	L-5
Cincinnati	19	23	0	.452	4	4	L-2
N.Y. Jets	22	28	0	.440	3	5	W-2
Baltimore	6	8	0	.429	2	4	W-2
Buffalo	20	30	0	.400	6	5	L-1
Houston	3	5	0	.375	2	3	L-2

NFC	W	L	T	Pct.	Longest W Strk.	Longest L Strk.	Current Streak
Dallas	34	15	1	.694	17	5	W-3
N.Y. Giants	48	32	5	.600	4	3	W-2
Chicago	50	35	5	.588	9	6	L-1
Minnesota	28	20	1	.583	5	3	W-1
Green Bay	50	36	3	.581	5	6	W-3
Atlanta	24	20	0	.545	5	3	W-2
Detroit	42	36	2	.538	10	4	L-2
St. Louis	38	34	0	.528	5	6	L-3
San Francisco	31	28	1	.525	5	3	W-1
Washington	37	37	4	.500	6	5	L-2
Philadelphia	31	44	1	.413	5	9	W-2
Arizona	35	52	2	.402	6	7	L-1
Carolina	6	9	0	.400	3	4	L-1
Tampa Bay	13	21	0	.382	3	5	L-4
Seattle	12	22	0	.353	3	8	W-1
New Orleans	15	28	0	.349	2	6	W-2

Kansas City totals include Dallas Texans, 1960-62.
Oakland totals include L.A. Raiders, 1982-1994.
San Diego totals include L.A. Chargers, 1960.
Indianapolis totals include Baltimore, 1953-1983.
Tennessee total include Houston, 1960-1996.
New England totals include Boston, 1960-1970.
St. Louis totals include Cleveland, 1937-1942 and 1944-45, and L.A. Rams, 1946-1994.
Detroit totals include Portsmouth, 1930-33.
Arizona totals include Chi. Cardinals, 1920-1959, St. Louis, 1960-1987, and Phoenix, 1988-1993.
Chicago totals include Decatur, 1920.
Washington totals include Boston Braves, 1932 and Boston Redskins, 1933-36.
NOTE: All tied games occurred prior to 1972, when calculation of ties in percentage as half-win.

RECORDS OF NFL TEAMS, 2000-09

AFC	W	L	T	Pct.	Division Titles	Playoff Berths	Postseason Record	Super Bowl Record
Indianapolis	115	45	0	.719	6	9	9-8	1-1
New England	112	48	0	.700	7	7	14-4	3-1
Pittsburgh	103	56	1	.647	5	6	10-4	2-0
Denver	93	67	0	.581	1	4	1-4	0-0
Baltimore	92	68	0	.575	2	6	8-5	1-0
Tennessee	91	69	0	.569	3	5	2-5	0-0
San Diego	85	75	0	.531	5	5	3-5	0-0
N.Y. Jets	80	80	0	.500	1	5	4-5	0-0
Miami	79	81	0	.494	2	3	1-3	0-0
Jacksonville	76	84	0	.475	0	2	1-2	0-0
Kansas City	70	90	0	.438	1	2	0-2	0-0
Cincinnati	68	91	1	.428	2	2	0-2	0-0
Buffalo	66	94	0	.413	0	0	0-0	0-0
Oakland	62	98	0	.388	3	3	4-3	0-1
Houston	49	79	0	.383	0	0	0-0	0-0
Cleveland	57	103	0	.356	0	1	0-1	0-0

Houston entered NFL in 2002.

NFC	W	L	T	Pct.	Division Titles	Playoff Berths	Postseason Record	Super Bowl Record
Philadelphia	103	56	1	.647	5	8	10-8	0-1
Green Bay	95	65	0	.594	4	6	3-6	0-0
N.Y. Giants	88	72	0	.550	3	6	6-5	1-1
Minnesota	84	76	0	.525	3	4	3-4	0-0
New Orleans	83	77	0	.519	3	3	5-2	1-0
Dallas	82	78	0	.513	2	4	1-4	0-0
Seattle	82	78	0	.513	4	5	4-5	0-1
Chicago	81	79	0	.506	3	3	2-3	0-1
Carolina	79	81	0	.494	2	3	5-3	0-1
Tampa Bay	79	81	0	.494	3	5	3-4	1-0
Atlanta	75	84	1	.472	1	3	2-3	0-0
St. Louis	71	89	0	.444	2	4	3-4	0-1
Washington	70	90	0	.438	0	2	1-2	0-0
San Francisco	68	92	0	.425	1	2	1-2	0-0
Arizona	62	98	0	.388	2	2	4-2	0-1
Detroit	42	118	0	.263	0	0	0-0	0-0

Seattle was in AFC from 2000-01.

HOME RECORDS, 2000-09

AFC	W-L-T	Pct.
New England	61-19-0	.763
Indianapolis	60-20-0	.750
Baltimore	58-22-0	.725
Pittsburgh	57-22-1	.719
Denver	54-26-0	.675
San Diego	49-31-0	.613
Tennessee	49-31-0	.613
Miami	45-35-0	.563
Jacksonville	44-36-0	.550
Kansas City	43-37-0	.538
N.Y. Jets	43-37-0	.538
Cincinnati	41-38-1	.519
Buffalo	38-42-0	.475
Houston	30-34-0	.469
Oakland	35-45-0	.438
Cleveland	31-49-0	.388

Houston entered NFL in 2002.

NFC	W-L-T	Pct.
Minnesota	55-25-0	.688
Green Bay	53-27-0	.663
Philadelphia	52-28-0	.650
Seattle	51-29-0	.638
Chicago	49-31-0	.613
Dallas	48-32-0	.600
Tampa Bay	46-34-0	.575
Atlanta	43-37-0	.538
N.Y. Giants	43-37-0	.538
San Francisco	43-37-0	.538
Carolina	42-38-0	.525
Arizona	40-40-0	.500
St. Louis	40-40-0	.500
Washington	40-40-0	.500
New Orleans	38-42-0	.475
Detroit	29-51-0	.363

Seattle was in AFC from 2000-01.

ROAD RECORDS, 2000-09

AFC	W-L-T	Pct.
Indianapolis	55-25-0	.688
New England	51-29-0	.638
Pittsburgh	46-34-0	.575
Tennessee	42-38-0	.525
Denver	39-41-0	.488
N.Y. Jets	37-43-0	.463
San Diego	36-44-0	.450
Baltimore	34-46-0	.425
Miami	34-46-0	.425
Jacksonville	32-48-0	.400
Buffalo	28-52-0	.350
Cincinnati	27-53-0	.338
Kansas City	27-53-0	.338
Oakland	27-53-0	.338
Cleveland	26-54-0	.325
Houston	19-45-0	.297

Houston entered NFL in 2002.

NFC	W-L-T	Pct.
Philadelphia	51-28-1	.644
New Orleans	45-35-0	.563
N.Y. Giants	45-35-0	.563
Green Bay	42-38-0	.525
Carolina	37-43-0	.463
Dallas	34-46-0	.425
Tampa Bay	33-47-0	.413
Atlanta	32-47-1	.406
Chicago	32-48-0	.400
St. Louis	31-49-0	.388
Seattle	31-49-0	.388
Washington	30-50-0	.375
Minnesota	29-51-0	.363
San Francisco	25-55-0	.313
Arizona	22-58-0	.275
Detroit	13-67-0	.163

Seattle was in AFC from 2000-01.

RECORDS BY MONTHS, 2000-09

	Sept.	Oct.	Nov.	Dec.	Total	
AFC	W-L-T	W-L-T	W-L-T	W-L-T	W-L-T	Pct.
Indianapolis	26- 6-0	27-10-0	31-12-0	31-17-0	115- 45-0	.719
New England	19-13-0	29-12-0	27-14-0	37- 9-0	112- 48-0	.700
Pittsburgh	16-16-0	28-10-0	24-17-1	35-13-0	103- 56-1	.647
Denver	25-10-0	23-16-0	22-17-0	23-24-0	93- 67-0	.581
Baltimore	20-12-0	18-21-0	27-17-0	27-18-0	92- 68-0	.575
Tennessee	14-18-0	23-17-0	24-15-0	30-19-0	91- 69-0	.569
San Diego	16-18-0	20-19-0	21-19-0	28-19-0	85- 75-0	.531
N.Y. Jets	17-16-0	17-22-0	22-17-0	24-25-0	80- 80-0	.500
Miami	14-19-0	16-21-0	24-18-0	25-23-0	79- 81-0	.494
Jacksonville	18-15-0	15-23-0	21-19-0	22-27-0	76- 84-0	.475
Kansas City	14-20-0	21-18-0	15-25-0	20-27-0	70- 90-0	.438
Cincinnati	13-20-0	15-25-0	19-20-1	21-26-0	68- 91-1	.428
Buffalo	14-19-0	18-22-0	15-24-0	19-29-0	66- 94-0	.413
Oakland	16-17-0	15-23-0	16-25-0	15-33-0	62- 98-0	.388
Houston	7-19-0	14-17-0	10-22-0	18-21-0	49- 79-0	.383
Cleveland	12-23-0	16-22-0	13-27-0	16-31-0	57-103-0	.356

Houston entered the NFL in 2002.
September totals include August; December totals include January.

	Sept.	Oct.	Nov.	Dec.	Total	
NFC	W-L-T	W-L-T	W-L-T	W-L-T	W-L-T	Pct.
Philadelphia	20-14-0	23-14-0	28-14-1	32-14-0	103- 56-1	.647
Green Bay	20-15-0	18-17-0	23-20-0	34-13-0	95- 65-0	.594
N.Y. Giants	22-11-0	25-14-0	18-23-0	23-24-0	88- 72-0	.550
Minnesota	18-16-0	22-15-0	25-17-0	19-28-0	84- 76-0	.525
New Orleans	17-16-0	24-16-0	21-18-0	21-27-0	83- 77-0	.519
Dallas	19-14-0	21-18-0	24-18-0	18-28-0	82- 78-0	.513
Seattle	20-13-0	13-24-0	23-19-0	26-22-0	82- 78-0	.513
Chicago	13-20-0	20-17-0	22-20-0	26-22-0	81- 79-0	.506
Carolina	16-16-0	19-22-0	17-23-0	27-20-0	79- 81-0	.494
Tampa Bay	18-15-0	17-23-0	22-17-0	22-26-0	79- 81-0	.494
Atlanta	18-16-0	18-19-0	20-21-1	19-28-0	75- 84-1	.472
St. Louis	14-21-0	20-18-0	16-23-0	21-27-0	71- 89-0	.444
Washington	16-16-0	18-23-0	14-26-0	22-25-0	70- 90-0	.438
San Francisco	13-20-0	13-26-0	18-22-0	24-24-0	68- 92-0	.425
Arizona	10-23-0	16-21-0	16-26-0	20-28-0	62- 98-0	.388
Detroit	12-20-0	10-27-0	11-34-0	9-37-0	42-118-0	.263

Seattle was in the AFC from 2000-01.
September totals include August; December totals include January.

INSIDE THE NUMBERS

TAKEAWAYS/GIVEAWAYS, 2000-09

AFC	Takeaways Int.	Fum.	Total	Giveaways Int.	Fum.	Total	Net.Diff.
New England	182	116	298	131	106	237	+61
Indianapolis	159	127	286	142	92	234	+52
Baltimore	213	125	338	157	140	297	+41
Kansas City	157	127	284	156	96	252	+32
Pittsburgh	163	128	291	154	105	259	+32
Jacksonville	156	104	260	117	115	232	+28
N.Y. Jets	169	116	285	172	89	261	+24
Denver	153	129	282	160	100	260	+22
San Diego	173	105	278	153	103	256	+22
Tennessee	175	112	287	150	119	269	+18
Cincinnati	165	123	288	174	112	286	+2
Miami	172	119	291	173	123	296	-5
Buffalo	157	106	263	157	129	286	-23
Oakland	147	100	247	153	134	287	-40
Houston	101	84	185	131	97	228	-43
Cleveland	175	98	273	201	122	323	-50

Houston entered NFL in 2002.

NFC	Takeaways Int.	Fum.	Total	Giveaways Int.	Fum.	Total	Net.Diff.
Tampa Bay	205	117	322	157	112	269	+53
Philadelphia	165	133	298	135	120	255	+43
Carolina	185	142	327	176	123	299	+28
Green Bay	198	111	309	171	117	288	+21
Atlanta	160	126	286	157	112	269	+17
Seattle	159	120	279	162	114	276	+3
N.Y. Giants	149	121	270	155	118	273	-3
Chicago	171	134	305	185	128	313	-8
New Orleans	157	128	285	161	134	295	-10
San Francisco	160	106	266	155	125	280	-14
Minnesota	154	113	267	163	131	294	-27
Washington	149	99	248	141	134	275	-27
Detroit	141	138	279	218	105	323	-44
Dallas	141	115	256	187	123	310	-54
Arizona	155	114	269	195	145	340	-71
St. Louis	150	128	278	217	141	358	-80

Seattle was in the AFC from 2000-01.

BEST TAKEAWAY/GIVEAWAY DIFFERENTIAL, SEASON

+43 Washington, 1983
+26 Kansas City, 1990
+25 N.Y. Giants, 1997

HIGH AND LOW SINGLE-GAME YARDAGE TOTALS, 2000-09

Most Total Yards, Game

645 Pittsburgh vs. Atlanta, Nov. 10, 2002 (OT)
619 New England vs. Tennessee, Oct. 18, 2009
614 St. Louis vs. San Diego, Oct. 1, 2000
605 Minnesota at New Orleans, Oct. 17, 2004
595 New Orleans vs. Cincinnati, Nov. 19, 2006

Fewest Total Yards, Game

26 Cleveland at Buffalo, Dec. 12, 2004
47 Houston at Pittsburgh, Dec. 8, 2002
53 Cleveland at Jacksonville, Dec. 3, 2000
72 Cincinnati at N.Y. Jets, Jan. 3, 2010
77 Oakland vs. Atlanta, Nov. 2, 2008

Most Yards Rushing, Game

407 Cincinnati vs. Denver, Oct. 22, 2000
378 Minnesota vs. San Diego, Nov. 4, 2007
375 Jacksonville vs. Indianapolis, Dec. 10, 2006
351 Cleveland at Kansas City, Dec. 20, 2009
343 Baltimore vs. Cleveland, Sept. 14, 2003

Fewest Yards Rushing, Game

-18 Detroit at Arizona, Nov. 11, 2007
-3 Detroit vs. Minnesota, Dec. 10, 2006
1 Dallas at Washington, Dec. 30, 2007
4 Cincinnati at Baltimore, Sept. 24, 2000
4 Seattle at Minnesota, Nov. 22, 2009

Most Yards Passing, Game

504 New Orleans vs. Cincinnati, Nov. 19, 2006
499 Denver vs. Atlanta, Oct. 31, 2004
474 Kansas City at Oakland, Nov. 5, 2000
473 N.Y. Jets at Baltimore, Dec. 24, 2000
472 Indianapolis at Kansas City, Oct. 31, 2004
472 Pittsburgh vs. Green Bay, Dec. 20, 2009

Fewest Yards Passing, Game

-9 Cleveland at Jacksonville, Dec. 3, 2000
-7 Tennessee at New England, Oct. 18, 2009
-5 Houston at Oakland, Dec. 3, 2006
-3 Cleveland at Buffalo, Dec. 12, 2004
0 Oakland at San Diego, Dec. 28, 2003
Cincinnati at N.Y. Jets, Jan. 3, 2010

NFL INDIVIDUAL LEADERS, 2000-09

Points

David Akers	1,169
Ryan Longwell	1,141
Jason Elam	1,137
Matt Stover	1,120
Adam Vinatieri	1,061

Touchdowns

LaDainian Tomlinson	153
Randy Moss	120
Terrell Owens	116
Shaun Alexander	112
Marvin Harrison	95

Field Goals

Matt Stover	269
David Akers	259
Jason Elam	250
Ryan Longwell	244
Two tied	233

Rushes

LaDainian Tomlinson	2,880
Edgerrin James	2,659
Jamal Lewis	2,542
Thomas Jones	2,280
Shaun Alexander	2,187

Rushing Yards

LaDainian Tomlinson	12,490
Edgerrin James	10,693
Jamal Lewis	10,607
Clinton Portis	9,696
Fred Taylor	9,585

Rushing TDs

LaDainian Tomlinson	138
Shaun Alexander	100
Priest Holmes	78
Clinton Portis	73
Edgerrin James	67

Pass Attempts

Brett Favre	5,460
Peyton Manning	5,423
Donovan McNabb	4,530
Tom Brady	4,218
Drew Brees	4,164

Completions

Peyton Manning	3,575
Brett Favre	3,424
Drew Brees	2,697
Donovan McNabb	2,695
Tom Brady	2,672

Passing Yards

Peyton Manning	42,254
Brett Favre	38,435
Donovan McNabb	31,925
Tom Brady	30,844
Drew Brees	30,646

TD Passes

Peyton Manning	314
Brett Favre	262
Tom Brady	225
Donovan McNabb	208
Drew Brees	202

Receptions

Torry Holt	868
Tony Gonzalez	831
Hines Ward	819
Derrick Mason	816
Marvin Harrison	791

Reception Yards

Torry Holt	12,594
Randy Moss	11,739
Terrell Owens	11,644
Derrick Mason	10,481
Marvin Harrison	10,439

Receiving TDs

Randy Moss	120
Terrell Owens	114
Marvin Harrison	95
Hines Ward	71
Torry Holt	68

Interceptions

Darren Sharper	58
Ed Reed	46
Champ Bailey	41
Dre' Bly	40
Charles Woodson	39

Sacks

Jason Taylor	111.0
Joey Porter	90.0
John Abraham	89.5
Michael Strahan	89.0
Leonard Little	87.0

NFL GAMES IN WHICH A TEAM HAS SCORED 60 OR MORE POINTS

(Home team in capitals)

Regular Season

WASHINGTON 72, New York Giants 41	November 27, 1966
LOS ANGELES RAMS 70, Baltimore 27	October 22, 1950
Chicago Cardinals 65, NEW YORK BULLDOGS 20	November 13, 1949
LOS ANGELES RAMS 65, Detroit 24	October 29, 1950
PHILADELPHIA 64, Cincinnati 0	November 6, 1934
CHICAGO CARDINALS 63, New York Giants 35	October 17, 1948
AKRON 62, Oorang 0	October 29, 1922
PITTSBURGH 62, New York Giants 7	November 30, 1952
CLEVELAND 62, New York Giants 14	December 6, 1953
CLEVELAND 62, Washington 3	November 7, 1954
NEW YORK GIANTS 62, Philadelphia 10	November 26, 1972
Atlanta 62, NEW ORLEANS 7	September 16, 1973
NEW YORK JETS 62, Tampa Bay 28	November 17, 1985
CHICAGO 61, San Francisco 20	December 12, 1965
Cincinnati 61, HOUSTON 17	December 17, 1972
CHICAGO 61, Green Bay 7	December 7, 1980
CINCINNATI 61, Houston 7	December 17, 1989
ROCK ISLAND 60, Evansville 0	October 15, 1922
CHICAGO CARDINALS 60, Rochester 0	October 7, 1923

Postseason

Chicago Bears 73, WASHINGTON 0	December 8, 1940
JACKSONVILLE 62, Miami 7	January 15, 2000

YOUNGEST AND OLDEST PLAYERS IN NFL IN 2009

10 Youngest Players	Birthdate	Games	Starts	Position
Kenny Britt, Tennessee	9/19/88	16	6	WR
Beanie Wells, Arizona	8/7/88	16	0	RB
LeSean McCoy, Philadelphia	7/12/88	16	4	RB
Percy Harvin, Minnesota	5/28/88	15	8	WR
Vontae Davis, Miami	5/27/88	16	9	CB
Jeremy Maclin, Philadelphia	5/11/88	15	13	WR
Captain Munnerlyn, Carolina	4/10/88	15	4	CB
Aaron Maybin, Buffalo	4/6/88	16	0	DE
Matthew Stafford, Detroit	2/7/88	10	10	QB
Asher Allen, Minnesota	1/22/88	10	1	CB

10 Oldest Players	Birthdate	Games	Starts	Position
John Carney, New Orleans	4/20/64	11	0	K
Jeff Feagles, N.Y. Giants	3/7/66	16	0	P
Matt Stover, Indianapolis	1/27/68	10	0	K
Matt Turk, Houston	6/16/68	16	0	P
Junior Seau, New England	1/19/69	7	0	LB
Brett Favre, Minnesota	10/10/69	16	16	QB
John Kasay, Carolina	10/27/69	16	0	K
Jeff Robinson, Seattle	2/20/70	2	0	LS
Jeff Garcia, Philadelphia	2/24/70	1	0	QB
Jason Elam, Atlanta	3/8/70	11	0	K

YOUNGEST AND OLDEST REGULAR STARTERS BY POSITION IN 2009

Minimum: 8 Games Started

	Youngest		Oldest	
QB	2/7/88	Matthew Stafford, Det.	10/10/69	Brett Favre, Min.
RB	7/16/87	Knowshon Moreno, Den.	12/17/71	Tony Richardson, N.Y. Jets
WR	5/28/88	Percy Harvin, Min.	5/5/73	Muhsin Muhammad, Car.
TE	3/26/87	Jermichael Finley, G.B.	2/27/76	Tony Gonzalez, Atl.
T	10/14/87	Eben Britton, Jac.	5/18/75	Flozell Adams, Dal.
G	4/11/87	Louis Vasquez, S.D.	9/25/76	Bobbie Williams, Cin.
C	11/19/85	Alex Mack, Cle.	1/23/71	Kevin Mawae, Ten.
DE	11/9/86	Derrick Harvey, Jac.	3/4/73	Phillip Daniels, Was.
DT	6/10/87	Amobi Okoye, Hou.	10/24/72	Pat Williams, Min.
LB	8/10/87	Geno Hayes, T.B.	9/1/74	Jason Taylor, Mia.
CB	5/27/88	Vontae Davis, Mia.	9/10/74	Nick Harper, Ten.
S	4/12/87	Louis Delmas, Det.	10/13/73	Brian Dawkins, Den.

OLDEST INDIVIDUAL SINGLE-SEASON OR SINGLE-GAME RECORDS IN NFL RECORD & FACT BOOK

Most Points, Game—40, Ernie Nevers, Chi. Cardinals vs. Chi. Bears, Nov. 28, 1929 (6-td, 4-pat)

Most Touchdowns Rushing, Game—6, Ernie Nevers, Chi. Cardinals vs. Chi. Bears, Nov. 28, 1929

Highest Rushing Average Gain, Season (Qualifiers)—8.44, Beattie Feathers, Chi. Bears, 1934 (119-1,004)

Highest Punting Average, Season (Qualifiers)—51.40, Sammy Baugh, Washington, 1940 (35-1,799)

Highest Punting Average, Rookie, Season (Qualifiers)—45.92, Frank Sinkwich, Detroit, 1943 (12-551)

Highest Punting Average, Game (minimum: 4 punts)—61.75, Bob Cifers, Detroit vs. Chi. Bears, Nov. 24, 1946 (4-247)

Highest Average Gain, Pass Receptions, Season (minimum: 24 receptions)—32.58, Don Currivan, Boston, 1947 (24-782)

Highest Average Gain, Passing, Game (minimum: 20 passes)—18.58, Sammy Baugh, Washington vs. Boston, Oct. 31, 1948 (24-446)

Most Touchdowns, Fumble Recoveries, Game—2, Fred (Dippy) Evans, Chi. Bears vs. Washington, Nov. 28, 1948

Most Yards Gained, Intercepted Passes, Rookie, Season—301, Don Doll, Detroit, 1949

Most Passes Had Intercepted, Game—8, Jim Hardy, Chi. Cardinals vs. Philadelphia, Sept. 24, 1950

Highest Kickoff Return Average, Game (minimum: 3 returns)—73.50, Wally Triplett, Detroit vs. Los Angeles, Oct. 29, 1950 (4-294)

Highest Punt Return Average, Season (Qualifiers)—23.00, Herb Rich, Baltimore, 1950 (12-276)

Highest Punt Return Average, Rookie, Season (Qualifiers)—23.00, Herb Rich, Baltimore, 1950 (12-276)

Most Yards Passing, Game—554, Norm Van Brocklin, Los Angeles vs. N.Y. Yanks, Sept. 28, 1951

Most Touchdowns, Punt Returns, Rookie, Season—4, Jack Christiansen, Detroit, 1951

Most Interceptions By, Season—14, Dick (Night Train) Lane, Los Angeles, 1952

Most Interceptions By, Rookie, Season—14, Dick (Night Train) Lane, Los Angeles, 1952

Highest Average Gain, Passing, Season (Qualifiers)—11.17, Tommy O'Connell, Cleveland, 1957 (110-1,229)

Most Yards Gained, Pass Receptions, Rookie, Season—1,473, Bill Groman, Houston, 1960

NFL INDIVIDUAL LEADERS OVER RECENT SEASONS

Points

Last 2 Seasons		Last 3 Seasons		Last 4 Seasons	
283	David Akers	410	Stephen Gostkowski	527	Nate Kaeding
273	Stephen Gostkowski	397	Mason Crosby	513	Stephen Gostkowski
273	Nate Kaeding	391	David Akers	493	David Akers
259	Ryan Longwell	391	Nate Kaeding	493	Robbie Gould
256	Mason Crosby	378	Rob Bironas	476	Rob Bironas

Touchdowns

Last 2 Seasons		Last 3 Seasons		Last 4 Seasons	
30	Maurice Jones-Drew	47	Randy Moss	73	LaDainian Tomlinson
29	Thomas Jones	42	LaDainian Tomlinson	56	Maurice Jones-Drew
28	Adrian Peterson	41	Adrian Peterson	50	Randy Moss
27	Michael Turner	40	Maurice Jones-Drew	44	Marion Barber
27	DeAngelo Williams	35	Two tied	44	Terrell Owens

Field Goals

Last 2 Seasons		Last 3 Seasons		Last 4 Seasons	
65	David Akers	91	Rob Bironas	113	Rob Bironas
62	Stephen Gostkowski	89	David Akers	113	Robbie Gould
59	Nate Kaeding	85	Mason Crosby	109	Nate Kaeding
58	Rian Lindell	83	Stephen Gostkowski	107	David Akers
56	Rob Bironas	83	Nate Kaeding	105	Rian Lindell

Rushes

Last 2 Seasons		Last 3 Seasons		Last 4 Seasons	
677	Adrian Peterson	931	Thomas Jones	1,227	Thomas Jones
621	Thomas Jones	915	Adrian Peterson	1,178	LaDainian Tomlinson
609	Chris Johnson	830	LaDainian Tomlinson	1,160	Steven Jackson
594	Ryan Grant	814	Steven Jackson	1,041	Frank Gore
577	Steven Jackson	791	Clinton Portis	1,034	Jamal Lewis

Rushing Yards

Last 2 Seasons		Last 3 Seasons		Last 4 Seasons	
3,234	Chris Johnson	4,484	Adrian Peterson	5,129	LaDainian Tomlinson
3,143	Adrian Peterson	3,833	Thomas Jones	5,043	Thomas Jones
2,714	Thomas Jones	3,460	Steven Jackson	4,988	Steven Jackson
2,632	DeAngelo Williams	3,412	Ryan Grant	4,953	Frank Gore
2,570	Michael Turner	3,349	DeAngelo Williams	4,484	Adrian Peterson

Rushing Touchdowns

Last 2 Seasons		Last 3 Seasons		Last 4 Seasons	
28	Adrian Peterson	40	Adrian Peterson	66	LaDainian Tomlinson
27	Thomas Jones	38	LaDainian Tomlinson	49	Maurice Jones-Drew
27	Maurice Jones-Drew	36	Maurice Jones-Drew	40	Adrian Peterson
27	Michael Turner	29	DeAngelo Williams	38	Marion Barber
25	DeAngelo Williams	28	Two tied	34	Two tied

Passes

Last 2 Seasons		Last 3 Seasons		Last 4 Seasons	
1,171	Jay Cutler	1,801	Drew Brees	2,355	Drew Brees
1,149	Drew Brees	1,641	Peyton Manning	2,201	Brett Favre
1,126	Peyton Manning	1,638	Jay Cutler	2,198	Peyton Manning
1,111	Kurt Warner	1,588	Brett Favre	2,039	Eli Manning
1,077	Aaron Rodgers	1,562	Kurt Warner	1,884	Philip Rivers

Completions

Last 2 Seasons		Last 3 Seasons		Last 4 Seasons	
776	Drew Brees	1,216	Drew Brees	1,572	Drew Brees
764	Peyton Manning	1,101	Peyton Manning	1,463	Peyton Manning
740	Kurt Warner	1,062	Brett Favre	1,405	Brett Favre
720	Jay Cutler	1,021	Kurt Warner	1,204	Eli Manning
706	Brett Favre	1,017	Jay Cutler	1,190	Philip Rivers

Passing Yards

Last 2 Seasons		Last 3 Seasons		Last 4 Seasons	
9,457	Drew Brees	13,880	Drew Brees	18,298	Drew Brees
8,502	Peyton Manning	12,542	Peyton Manning	16,939	Peyton Manning
8,472	Aaron Rodgers	12,142	Tony Romo	15,714	Brett Favre
8,336	Kurt Warner	11,829	Brett Favre	15,045	Tony Romo
8,263	Philip Rivers	11,753	Kurt Warner	14,803	Philip Rivers

Last 2 Seasons		Last 3 Seasons		Last 4 Seasons	
Touchdown Passes					
68	Drew Brees	96	Drew Brees	122	Drew Brees
62	Philip Rivers	91	Peyton Manning	122	Peyton Manning
60	Peyton Manning	88	Tony Romo	107	Tony Romo
58	Aaron Rodgers	83	Three tied	105	Philip Rivers
56	Kurt Warner			102	Tom Brady
Receptions					
234	Wes Welker	346	Wes Welker	413	Wes Welker
216	Andre Johnson	307	Brandon Marshall	379	Andre Johnson
205	Brandon Marshall	293	Larry Fitzgerald	373	T.J. Houshmandzadeh
193	Larry Fitzgerald	286	Reggie Wayne	372	Reggie Wayne
182	Reggie Wayne	283	T.J. Houshmandzadeh	362	Larry Fitzgerald
Receiving Yards					
3,144	Andre Johnson	3,995	Andre Johnson	5,229	Reggie Wayne
2,535	Roddy White	3,932	Larry Fitzgerald	5,142	Andre Johnson
2,523	Larry Fitzgerald	3,919	Reggie Wayne	4,878	Larry Fitzgerald
2,513	Wes Welker	3,765	Randy Moss	4,571	Steve Smith
2,409	Reggie Wayne	3,737	Roddy White	4,416	Two tied
Receiving Touchdowns					
25	Larry Fitzgerald	47	Randy Moss	50	Randy Moss
24	Randy Moss	35	Larry Fitzgerald	43	Terrell Owens
18	Visanthe Shiancoe	30	Terrell Owens	41	Larry Fitzgerald
18	Roddy White	27	Dallas Clark	35	Reggie Wayne
17	Two tied	26	Reggie Wayne	34	Antonio Gates
Interceptions					
16	Charles Woodson	20	Charles Woodson	29	Asante Samuel
13	Nick Collins	19	Ed Reed	28	Charles Woodson
13	Asante Samuel	19	Asante Samuel	24	Ed Reed
12	Ed Reed	15	Oshiomogho Atogwe	18	Three tied
11	Darrelle Revis	15	Antonio Cromartie		
Sacks					
31.0	DeMarcus Ware	45.0	DeMarcus Ware	56.5	DeMarcus Ware
29.0	Jared Allen	44.5	Jared Allen	52.0	Jared Allen
26.5	Joey Porter	35.0	Mario Williams	43.0	Elvis Dumervil
26.0	James Harrison	34.5	Elvis Dumervil	42.0	Trent Cole
25.0	Two tied	34.5	James Harrison	40.5	Two tied

NFL TEAM LEADERS OVER RECENT SEASONS

Last 2 Seasons		Last 3 Seasons		Last 4 Seasons	
Highest Won-Lost Percentage					
.813	Indianapolis	.813	Indianapolis	.797	Indianapolis
.688	Minnesota	.771	New England	.766	New England
.656	Five tied	.688	Dallas	.719	San Diego
		.667	San Diego	.656	Dallas
		.646	Two tied	.609	Two tied
Most Points					
973	New Orleans	1,426	New England	1,811	New England
893	San Diego	1,352	New Orleans	1,797	San Diego
880	Green Bay	1,315	Green Bay	1,765	New Orleans
849	Minnesota	1,305	San Diego	1,670	Indianapolis
845	Philadelphia	1,243	Indianapolis	1,616	Green Bay
Most Total Yards					
13,032	New Orleans	18,812	New Orleans	25,076	New Orleans
12,242	Houston	18,784	New England	24,153	New England
12,204	New England	17,753	Dallas	23,525	Dallas
11,902	Dallas	17,614	Green Bay	23,166	Philadelphia
11,796	Denver	17,579	Houston	23,072	Green Bay

Most Rushing Yards

Last 2 Seasons		Last 3 Seasons		Last 4 Seasons	
4,935	Carolina	6,900	Tennessee	9,114	Tennessee
4,791	Tennessee	6,890	Minnesota	8,778	Atlanta
4,760	N.Y. Jets	6,759	Carolina	8,735	Jacksonville
4,576	Baltimore	6,503	N.Y. Giants	8,710	Minnesota
4,355	N.Y. Giants	6,461	N.Y. Jets	8,659	N.Y. Giants

Most Passing Yards

Last 2 Seasons		Last 3 Seasons		Last 4 Seasons	
9,332	New Orleans	13,646	New Orleans	18,149	New Orleans
8,921	Houston	12,755	Arizona	16,950	Indianapolis
8,690	Arizona	12,736	New England	16,417	Arizona
8,609	Indianapolis	12,672	Houston	16,136	New England
8,196	San Diego	12,642	Indianapolis	16,122	Green Bay

Fewest Turnovers

Last 2 Seasons		Last 3 Seasons		Last 4 Seasons	
37	Green Bay	58	New England	76	San Diego
37	San Diego	60	Indianapolis	79	Indianapolis
41	Indianapolis	61	Green Bay	85	New England
42	Miami	61	San Diego	90	Atlanta
43	Two tied	68	Jacksonville	91	Jacksonville

Fewest Points Allowed

Last 2 Seasons		Last 3 Seasons		Last 4 Seasons	
505	Baltimore	816	Pittsburgh	1,090	Baltimore
547	Pittsburgh	867	Indianapolis	1,105	New England
592	N.Y. Jets	868	New England	1,131	Pittsburgh
594	New England	889	Baltimore	1,227	Indianapolis
605	Indianapolis	926	Philadelphia	1,242	N.Y. Jets

Fewest Total Yards Allowed

Last 2 Seasons		Last 3 Seasons		Last 4 Seasons	
8,680	Pittsburgh	12,942	Pittsburgh	17,747	Pittsburgh
8,985	Baltimore	13,810	Baltimore	18,035	Baltimore
9,307	N.Y. Jets	14,508	Philadelphia	19,390	New England
9,526	Philadelphia	14,617	N.Y. Jets	19,757	Philadelphia
9,567	Minnesota	14,620	Washington	19,780	Minnesota

Fewest Rushing Yards Allowed

Last 2 Seasons		Last 3 Seasons		Last 4 Seasons	
2,624	Minnesota	3,809	Minnesota	4,794	Minnesota
2,722	Pittsburgh	4,062	Baltimore	5,276	Baltimore
2,794	Baltimore	4,160	Pittsburgh	5,572	Pittsburgh
3,096	N.Y. Jets	4,667	Dallas	6,326	Dallas
3,151	Philadelphia	4,684	Philadelphia	6,569	New England

Fewest Passing Yards Allowed

Last 2 Seasons		Last 3 Seasons		Last 4 Seasons	
5,958	Pittsburgh	8,782	Pittsburgh	11,724	Indianapolis
6,191	Baltimore	9,043	Tampa Bay	12,068	Oakland
6,211	N.Y. Jets	9,176	Indianapolis	12,175	Pittsburgh
6,219	Buffalo	9,365	N.Y. Jets	12,397	Tampa Bay
6,315	Tampa Bay	9,618	New England	12,587	N.Y. Jets

Most Opponents' Turnovers

Last 2 Seasons		Last 3 Seasons		Last 4 Seasons	
68	Green Bay	97	San Diego	137	Chicago
67	Philadelphia	96	Green Bay	129	Baltimore
66	Baltimore	94	Tampa Bay	129	Green Bay
62	Carolina	93	Chicago	125	San Diego
61	Two tied	92	Two tied	121	Arizona

RETIRED UNIFORM NUMBERS IN NFL

AFC

Baltimore	None	
Buffalo	Jim Kelly	12
Cincinnati	Bob Johnson	54
Cleveland	Otto Graham	14
	Jim Brown	32
	Ernie Davis	45
	Don Fleming	46
	Lou Groza	76
Denver	John Elway	7
	Frank Tripucka	18
	Floyd Little	44
Houston	None	
Indianapolis	Johnny Unitas	19
	Buddy Young	22
	Lenny Moore	24
	Art Donovan	70
	Jim Parker	77
	Raymond Berry	82
	Gino Marchetti	89
Jacksonville	None	
Kansas City	Jan Stenerud	3
	Len Dawson	16
	Emmitt Thomas	18
	Abner Haynes	28
	Stone Johnson	33
	Mack Lee Hill	36
	Derrick Thomas	58
	Willie Lanier	63
	Bobby Bell	78
	Buck Buchanan	86
Miami	Bob Griese	12
	Dan Marino	13
	Larry Csonka	39
New England	Gino Cappelletti	20
	Mike Haynes	40
	Steve Nelson	57
	John Hannah	73
	Bruce Armstrong	78
	Jim Lee Hunt	79
	Bob Dee	89
New York Jets	Joe Namath	12
	Don Maynard	13
	Joe Klecko	73
Oakland	None	
Pittsburgh	Ernie Stautner	70
San Diego	Dan Fouts	14
	Lance Alworth	19
Tennessee	Warren Moon	1
	Earl Campbell	34
	Jim Norton	43
	Mike Munchak	63
	Elvin Bethea	65
	Bruce Matthews	74

NFC

Arizona	Larry Wilson	8
	Pat Tillman	40
	Stan Mauldin	77
	J.V. Cain	88
	Marshall Goldberg	99
Atlanta	Steve Bartkowski	10
	William Andrews	31
	Jeff Van Note	57
	Tommy Nobis	60
Carolina	Sam Mills	51
Chicago	Bronko Nagurski	3
	George McAfee	5
	George Halas	7
	Willie Galimore	28
	Walter Payton	34
	Gale Sayers	40
	Brian Piccolo	41
	Sid Luckman	42
	Dick Butkus	51
	Bill Hewitt	56
	Bill George	61
	Bulldog Turner	66
	Red Grange	77
Dallas	None	
Detroit	Dutch Clark	7
	Bobby Layne	22
	Doak Walker	37
	Joe Schmidt	56
	Chuck Hughes	85
Green Bay	Tony Canadeo	3
	Don Hutson	14
	Bart Starr	15
	Ray Nitschke	66
	Reggie White	92
Minnesota	Fran Tarkenton	10
	Mick Tingelhoff	53
	Jim Marshall	70
	Korey Stringer	77
	Cris Carter	80
	Alan Page	88
New Orleans	Jim Taylor	31
	Doug Atkins	81
New York Giants	Ray Flaherty	1
	Tuffy Leemans	4
	Mel Hein	7
	Phil Simms	11
	Y.A. Tittle	14
	Frank Gifford	16
	Al Blozis	32
	Joe Morrison	40
	Charlie Conerly	42
	Ken Strong	50
	Lawrence Taylor	56
Philadelphia	Steve Van Buren	15
	Tom Brookshier	40
	Pete Retzlaff	44
	Chuck Bednarik	60
	Al Wistert	70
	Reggie White	92
	Jerome Brown	99
St. Louis	Bob Waterfield	7
	Eric Dickerson	29
	Merlin Olsen	74
	Deacon Jones	75
	Jackie Slater	78
	Jack Youngblood	85
San Francisco	Steve Young	8
	John Brodie	12
	Joe Montana	16
	Joe Perry	34
	Jimmy Johnson	37
	Hugh McElhenny	39
	Ronnie Lott	42
	Charlie Krueger	70
	Leo Nomellini	73
	Bob St. Clair	79
	Dwight Clark	87
Seattle	"Fans/the twelfth man"	12
	Steve Largent	80
Tampa Bay	Lee Roy Selmon	63
Washington	Sammy Baugh	33

INSIDE THE NUMBERS

The NFL rates its passers for statistical purposes against a fixed performance standard based on statistical achievements of all qualified pro passers since 1960. The current system replaced one that rated passers in relation to their position in a total group based on various criteria. The current system, which was adopted in 1973, removes inequities that existed in the former method and, at the same time, provides a means of comparing passing performances from one season to the next.

It is important to remember that the system is used to rate passers, not quarterbacks. Statistics do not reflect leadership, play-calling, and other intangible factors that go into making a successful professional quarterback. Four categories are used as a basis for compiling a rating:

—Percentage of completions per attempt
—Average yards gained per attempt
—Percentage of touchdown passes per attempt
—Percentage of interceptions per attempt

The average standard is 1.000. The bottom is .000. To earn a 2.000 rating, a passer must perform at exceptional levels, i.e., 70 percent in completions, 10 percent in touchdowns, 1.5 percent in interceptions, and 11 yards average gain per pass attempt. The maximum a passer can receive in any category is 2.375.

For example, to gain a 2.375 in completion percentage, a passer would have to complete 77.5 percent of his passes. The NFL record is 70.55 by Ken Anderson (Cincinnati, 1982). To earn a 2.375 in percentage of touchdowns, a passer would have to achieve a percentage of 11.9. The record is 13.9 by Sid Luckman (Chicago, 1943). To gain 2.375 in percentage of interceptions, a passer would have to go the entire season without an interception. The 2.375 figure in average yards is 12.50, compared with the NFL record of 11.17 by Tommy O'Connell (Cleveland, 1957).

In order to make the rating more understandable, the point rating is then converted into a scale of 100, with 158.3 being the highest rating a passer can achieve. In cases where statistical performance has been superior, it is possible for a passer to surpass a 100 rating. For example, take Peyton Manning's record-setting season in 2004 when he completed 336 of 497 passes for 4,557 yards, 49 touchdowns, and 10 interceptions. The four calculations would be:

—Percentage of Completions—336 of 497 is 67.60 percent. Subtract 30 from the completion percentage (37.60) and multiply the result by 0.05. The result is a point rating of 1.880.
Note: If the result is less than zero (Comp. Pct. less than 30.0), award zero points. If the results are greater than 2.375 (Comp. Pct. greater than 77.5), award 2.375.

—Average Yards Gained Per Attempt—4,557 yards divided by 497 attempts is 9.17. Subtract three yards from yards-per-attempt (6.17) and multiply the result by 0.25. The result is 1.543.
Note: If the result is less than zero (yards per attempt less than 3.0), award zero points. If the result is greater than 2.375 (yards per attempt greater than 12.5), award 2.375 points.

—Percentage of Touchdown Passes—49 touchdowns in 497 attempts is 9.86 percent. Multiply the touchdown percentage by 0.2. The result is 1.972.
Note: If the result is greater than 2.375 (touchdown percentage greater than 11.875), award 2.375.

—Percentage of Interceptions—10 interceptions in 497 attempts is 2.01 percent. Multiply the interception percentage by 0.25 (0.503) and subtract the number from 2.375. The result is 1.872.
Note: If the result is less than zero (interception percentage greater than 9.5), award zero points.

The sum of the four steps is (1.880 + 1.543 + 1.972 + 1.872) 7.267. The sum is then divided by six (1.211) and multiplied by 100. In this case, the result is 121.1. This same formula can be used to determine a passer rating for any player who attempts at least one pass.

Forty-eight qualifying passers have had a single-season passer rating of 100 or higher. The following is a list of the Top 25 single-season passer ratings among qualifying players:

TOP 25 NFL SINGLE-SEASON PASSER RATINGS (QUALIFYING PLAYERS)

Player, Team	Season	Rating	Att.	Comp.	Pct.	Yds.	Yds. Avg.	TD	TD Pct.	Int.	Int. Pct.
Peyton Manning, Indianapolis	2004	*121.1	497	336	67.6	4,557	9.17	49	9.9	10	2.0
Tom Brady, New England	2007	117.2	578	398	68.9	4,806	8.31	*50	8.7	8	1.4
Steve Young, San Francisco	1994	112.8	461	324	70.2	3,969	8.61	35	7.6	10	2.2
Joe Montana, San Francisco	1989	112.4	386	271	70.2	3,521	9.12	26	6.7	8	2.1
Daunte Culpepper, Minnesota	2004	110.9	548	379	69.2	4,717	8.61	39	7.1	11	2.0
Milt Plum, Cleveland	1960	110.4	250	151	60.4	2,297	9.19	21	8.4	5	2.0
Sammy Baugh, Washington	1945	109.9	182	128	70.3	1,669	9.17	11	6.0	4	2.2
Drew Brees, New Orleans	2009	109.6	514	363	*70.6	4,388	8.54	34	6.6	11	2.1
Kurt Warner, St. Louis	1999	109.2	499	325	65.1	4,353	8.72	41	8.2	13	2.6
Dan Marino, Miami	1984	108.9	564	362	64.2	*5,084	9.01	48	8.5	17	3.0
Sid Luckman, Chicago Bears	1943	107.5	202	110	54.5	2,194	10.86	28	13.9	12	5.9
Brett Favre, Minnesota	2009	107.2	531	363	68.4	4,202	7.91	30	5.6	7	1.3
Steve Young, San Francisco	1992	107.0	402	268	66.7	3,465	8.62	25	6.2	7	1.7
Randall Cunningham, Minnesota	1998	106.0	425	259	60.9	3,704	8.72	34	8.0	10	2.4
Philip Rivers, San Diego	2008	105.5	478	312	65.3	4,009	8.39	34	7.1	11	2.3
Bart Starr, Green Bay	1966	105.0	251	156	62.2	2,257	8.99	14	5.6	3	1.2
Drew Brees, San Diego	2004	104.8	400	262	65.5	3,159	7.90	27	6.8	7	1.8
Roger Staubach, Dallas	1971	104.8	211	126	59.7	1,882	8.92	15	7.1	4	1.9
Y.A. Tittle, N.Y. Giants	1963	104.8	367	221	60.2	3,145	8.57	36	9.8	14	3.8
Donovan McNabb, Philadelphia	2004	104.7	469	300	64.0	3,875	8.06	31	6.6	8	1.7
Steve Young, San Francisco	1997	104.7	356	241	67.7	3,029	8.51	19	5.3	6	1.7
Philip Rivers, San Diego	2009	104.4	486	317	65.2	4,254	8.75	28	5.7	9	1.9
Bart Starr, Green Bay	1968	104.3	171	109	63.7	1,617	9.46	15	8.8	8	4.7
Chad Pennington, N.Y. Jets	2002	104.2	399	275	68.9	3,120	7.82	22	5.5	6	1.5
Ben Roethlisberger, Pittsburgh	2007	104.1	404	264	65.3	3,154	7.81	32	7.9	11	2.7

**NFL Record*

HIGHEST NFL POSTSEASON PASSER RATINGS (MINIMUM: 150 ATTEMPTS)

Player	Games	Att.	Cmp.	Pct.	Yards	Avg. Gain	TD	Int.	Rating
Bart Starr	10	213	130	61.0	1,753	8.23	15	3	104.8
Drew Brees	6	225	150	66.7	1,648	7.32	13	2	103.7
Kurt Warner	13	462	307	66.5	3,952	8.55	31	14	102.8
Joe Montana	23	734	460	62.7	5,772	7.86	45	21	95.6
Ken Anderson	6	166	110	66.3	1,321	7.96	9	6	93.5
Joe Theismann	10	211	128	60.7	1,782	8.45	11	7	91.4
Troy Aikman	16	502	320	63.7	3,849	7.67	23	17	88.3
Peyton Manning	18	692	435	62.9	5,164	7.46	28	19	87.6
Ben Roethlisberger	10	278	172	61.9	2,239	8.05	15	12	87.2
Brett Favre	24	791	481	60.8	5,855	7.40	44	30	86.3

HIGHEST NFL POSTSEASON PASSER RATINGS, ACTIVE PLAYERS (MINIMUM: 150 ATTEMPTS)

Player	Games	Att.	Cmp.	Pct.	Yards	Avg. Gain	TD	Int.	Rating
Drew Brees	6	225	150	66.7	1,648	7.32	13	2	103.7
Peyton Manning	18	692	435	62.9	5,164	7.46	28	19	87.6
Ben Roethlisberger	10	278	172	61.9	2,239	8.05	15	12	87.2
Brett Favre	24	791	481	60.8	5,855	7.40	44	30	86.3
Tom Brady	18	637	395	62.0	4,108	6.45	28	15	85.5
Jake Delhomme	8	226	130	57.5	1,847	8.17	12	10	83.3
Donovan McNabb	16	577	341	59.1	3,752	6.50	24	17	80.0
Matt Hasselbeck	9	325	189	58.2	2,211	6.80	11	8	79.9
Philip Rivers	7	229	134	58.5	1,820	7.95	8	9	79.2
Eli Manning	7	193	113	58.5	1,297	6.72	8	7	77.6

ALL-TIME RANKINGS OF PLAYERS IN FOUR CATEGORIES THAT DETERMINE NFL PASSER RATING

Minimum: 1,500 Attempts

COMPLETION PERCENTAGE	Pct.	Att.	Comp.
Chad Pennington	66.06	2,469	1,631
Kurt Warner	65.50	4,070	2,666
Peyton Manning	64.80	6,531	4,232
Drew Brees	64.77	4,164	2,697
Steve Young	64.28	4,149	2,667
Tony Romo	63.44	1,857	1,178
Tom Brady	63.35	4,218	2,672
Ben Roethlisberger	63.29	2,411	1,526
Joe Montana	63.24	5,391	3,409
Carson Palmer	63.17	2,631	1,662

AVERAGE YARDS PER PASS	Avg.	Att.	Yards
Otto Graham	8.63	1,565	13,499
Sid Luckman	8.42	1,744	14,686
Norm Van Brocklin	8.16	2,895	23,611
Tony Romo	8.10	1,857	15,045
Ben Roethlisberger	8.01	2,411	19,302
Steve Young	7.98	4,149	33,124
Kurt Warner	7.95	4,070	32,344
Ed Brown	7.85	1,987	15,600
Bart Starr	7.85	3,149	24,718
Philip Rivers	7.81	1,914	14,951

TOUCHDOWN PERCENTAGE	Pct.	Att.	TD
Sid Luckman	7.86	1,744	137
Frank Ryan	6.99	2,133	149
Len Dawson	6.39	3,741	239
Daryle Lamonica	6.31	2,601	164
Sammy Baugh	6.24	2,995	187
Charlie Conerly	6.11	2,833	173
Bob Waterfield	6.00	1,617	97
Earl Morrall	5.99	2,689	161
Sonny Jurgensen	5.98	4,262	255
Norm Van Brocklin	5.98	2,895	173

INTERCEPTION PERCENTAGE	Pct.	Att.	Int.
David Garrard	2.04	1,915	39
Neil O'Donnell	2.11	3,229	68
Donovan McNabb	2.11	4,746	100
Jeff Garcia	2.26	3,676	83
Mark Brunell	2.31	4,624	107
Jason Campbell	2.32	1,637	38
Tom Brady	2.35	4,218	99
Philip Rivers	2.35	1,914	45
Steve Bono	2.47	1,701	42
Rich Gannon	2.47	4,206	104

STARTING RECORDS OF ACTIVE NFL QUARTERBACKS

Minimum: 10 starts

	W-L-T	Pct.
Tom Brady	97-30-0	.764
Philip Rivers	46-18-0	.719
Ben Roethlisberger	60-26-0	.698
Tony Romo	38-17-0	.691
Peyton Manning	131-61-0	.682
Matt Ryan	20-10-0	.667
Vince Young	26-13-0	.667
Donovan McNabb	92-49-1	.651
Brett Favre	181-104-0	.635
Joe Flacco	20-12-0	.625
Shaun Hill	10- 6-0	.625
Rex Grossman	19-12-0	.613
Kyle Orton	29-19-0	.604
Jake Delhomme	54-38-0	.587
Eli Manning	50-37-0	.575
Michael Vick	38-28-1	.575
Drew Brees	68-53-0	.562
Matt Hasselbeck	63-54-0	.538
Chad Henne	7- 6-0	.538
Chad Pennington	43-37-0	.538
Mark Sanchez	8- 7-0	.533
Aaron Rodgers	17-15-0	.531
Tarvaris Jackson	10- 9-0	.526
Carson Palmer	42-39-0	.519
Mark Brunell	78-73-0	.517
Todd Collins	10-10-0	.500
David Garrard	31-31-0	.500
Sage Rosenfels	6- 6-0	.500
Byron Leftwich	24-25-0	.490
Matt Schaub	19-21-0	.475
Derek Anderson	16-18-0	.471
Matt Cassel	14-16-0	.467
Trent Edwards	14-16-0	.467
A.J. Feeley	7- 8-0	.467
Kerry Collins	79-91-0	.465
Jay Cutler	24-29-0	.453
Charlie Batch	22-28-0	.440
Chris Simms	7- 9-0	.438
Kyle Boller	20-26-0	.435
Marc Bulger	41-54-0	.432
Patrick Ramsey	10-14-0	.417
Matt Leinart	7-10-0	.412
Daunte Culpepper	41-59-0	.410
Jon Kitna	46-69-0	.400
Alex Smith	16-24-0	.400
Josh McCown	12-19-0	.387
Jason Campbell	20-32-0	.385
Ryan Fitzpatrick	8-14-1	.370
Seneca Wallace	5- 9-0	.357
Chris Redman	4- 8-0	.333
Bruce Gradkowski	5-11-0	.313
Charlie Frye	7-16-0	.304
J.P. Losman	10-23-0	.303
Billy Volek	3- 7-0	.300
David Carr	23-56-0	.291
JaMarcus Russell	7-18-0	.280
Brady Quinn	3- 9-0	.250
Matthew Stafford	2- 8-0	.200
Tyler Thigpen	1-10-0	.091

TEAMS THAT FINISHED IN FIRST PLACE IN THEIR DIVISION THE SEASON AFTER FINISHING IN LAST PLACE

Season	Team	Record	Prior Season
1967	Houston	9-4-1	*3-11-0
1968	Minnesota	8-6-0	3- 8-3
1970	Cincinnati	8-6-0	4- 9-1
1970	San Francisco	10-3-1	4- 8-2
1972	Green Bay	10-4-0	4- 8-2
1975	Baltimore	10-4-0	2-12-0
1979	Tampa Bay	10-6-0	5-11-0
1981	Cincinnati	12-4-0	6-10-0
1987	Indianapolis	9-6-0	3-13-0
1988	Cincinnati	12-4-0	4-11-0
1990	Cincinnati	9-7-0	8- 8-0
1991	Denver	12-4-0	5-11-0
1992	San Diego	11-5-0	4-12-0
1993	Detroit	10-6-0	5-11-0
1997	N.Y. Giants	10-5-1	6-10-0
1999	Indianapolis	13-3-0	3-13-0
1999	St. Louis	13-3-0	4-12-0
2000	New Orleans	10-6-0	3-13-0
2001	Chicago	13-3-0	5-11-0
2001	New England	11-5-0	5-11-0
2003	Carolina	11-5-0	7- 9-0
2003	Kansas City	13-3-0	*8- 8-0
2004	Atlanta	11-5-0	5-11-0
2004	San Diego	12-4-0	*4-12-0
2005	Chicago	11-5-0	5-11-0
2005	Tampa Bay	11-5-0	5-11-0
2006	Baltimore	13-3-0	*6-10-0
2006	New Orleans	10-6-0	3-13-0
2006	Philadelphia	10-6-0	6-10-0
2007	Tampa Bay	9-7-0	4-12-0
2008	Miami	11-5-0	1-15-0
2009	New Orleans	13-3-0	8-8-0

**tied for last place*

LONGEST WINNING STREAKS SINCE 1970

23	Indianapolis, 2008-09	(9 in 2008; 14 in 2009)
21	New England, 2006-08	(3 in 2006, 16 in 2007, 2 in 2008)
18	New England, 2003-04	(12 in 2003, 6 in 2004)
16	Miami, 1971-73	(1 in 1971, 14 in 1972, 1 in 1973)
16	Miami, 1983-84	(5 in 1983, 11 in 1984)
16	Pittsburgh, 2004-05	(14 in 2004, 2 in 2005)
15	San Francisco, 1989-90	(5 in 1989, 10 in 1990)
14	Oakland, 1976-77	(10 in 1976, 4 in 1977)
14	Denver, 1997-98	(1 in 1997, 13 in 1998)
13	Minnesota, 1974-75	(3 in 1974, 10 in 1975)
13	Chicago, 1984-85	(1 in 1984, 12 in 1985)
13	N.Y. Giants, 1989-90	(3 in 1989, 10 in 1990)
13	Indianapolis, 2005	
13	Tennessee, 2007-08	(3 in 2007, 10 in 2008)
13	New Orleans, 2009	
12	Washington, 1990-91	(1 in 1990, 11 in 1991)
11	Pittsburgh, 1975	
11	Baltimore, 1975-76	(9 in 1975, 2 in 1976)
11	Chicago, 1986-87	(7 in 1986, 4 in 1987)
11	Houston, 1993	
11	San Francisco, 1997	
11	Jacksonville, 1999	
11	Indianapolis, 1999	
11	Seattle, 2005	
11	San Diego	(10 in 2006, 1 in 2007)
11	San Diego, 2009 (current)	

NFL PLAYOFF APPEARANCES BY SEASONS

Team	Number of Seasons in Playoffs
Dallas	30
N.Y. Giants	30
St. Louis	27
Minnesota	26
Green Bay	25
Pittsburgh	25
Chicago	24
Cleveland	24
Indianapolis	23
Miami	22
Philadelphia	22
San Francisco	22
Washington	22
Oakland	21

Team	Number of Seasons in Playoffs
Tennessee	21
Buffalo	17
Denver	17
New England	17
San Diego	17
Kansas City	15
Detroit	14
N.Y. Jets	13
Seattle	10
Tampa Bay	10
Atlanta	9
Cincinnati	9
Arizona	8
New Orleans	7
Baltimore	6
Jacksonville	6
Carolina	4

TEAMS IN SUPER BOWL CONTENTION (1978-2009)

	With 3 Weeks to Play	With 2 Weeks to Play	With 1 Week to Play
2009	24	19	17
2008	22	19	18
2007	23	20	15
2006	25	24	20
2005	18	17	14
2004	*27	*26	17
2003	22	17	14
2002	21	21	19
2001	23	16	13
2000	19	17	16
1999	23	20	16
1998	22	19	14
1997	22	18	14
1996	23	21	13
1995	*27	21	18
1994	25	22	15
1993	20	18	16
1992	20	16	14
1991	20	18	13
1990	23	20	15
1989	21	18	17
1988	21	18	15
1987	19	19	15
1986	19	17	14
1985	21	18	13
1984	18	14	13
1983	24	19	15
1982	27	25	*22
1981	21	20	16
1980	20	14	12
1979	19	15	13
1978	20	17	12

RECORD OF TEAMS ON THE ROAD (1970-2009)

Year	W	L	T	Pct
1970	72	101	9	.420
1971	74	100	8	.429
1972	87	90	5	.492
1973	66	109	7	.382
1974	82	99	1	.453
1975	81	101	0	.445
1976	83	112	1	.426
1977	83	113	0	.423
1978	93	130	1	.417
1979	92	132	0	.411
1980	101	122	1	.453
1981	84	139	1	.377
1982	57	68	1	.456
1983	104	119	1	.467
1984	94	129	1	.422
1985	80	144	0	.357
1986	104	118	2	.469
1987	95	114	1	.455
1988	92	131	1	.413
1989	95	128	1	.426
1990	93	131	0	.415
1991	92	132	0	.411
1992	88	136	0	.393
1993	101	123	0	.451
1994	96	128	0	.429
1995	96	144	0	.400
1996	91	149	0	.379
1997	93	145	2	.392
1998	89	151	0	.371
1999	100	148	0	.403
2000	110	138	0	.444
2001	112	136	0	.452
2002	107	148	1	.420
2003	99	157	0	.387
2004	111	145	0	.434
2005	105	151	0	.410
2006	120	136	0	.469
2007	109	147	0	.426
2008	109	146	1	.428
2009	110	146	0	.430

GAMES DECIDED BY 7 POINTS OR FEWER AND 3 POINTS OR FEWER (1970-2009)

	Games Decided by 7 Points or Fewer	Games Decided by 3 Points or Fewer
1970	59 of 182 (32.4%)	34 of 182 (18.7%)
1971	76 of 182 (41.8%)	35 of 182 (19.2%)
1972	71 of 182 (39.0%)	38 of 182 (20.9%)
1973	60 of 182 (32.9%)	28 of 182 (15.4%)
1974	91 of 182 (50.0%)	37 of 182 (20.3%)
1975	62 of 182 (34.1%)	35 of 182 (19.2%)
1976	73 of 196 (37.2%)	38 of 196 (19.4%)
1977	85 of 196 (43.4%)	36 of 196 (18.4%)
1978	108 of 224 (48.2%)	49 of 224 (21.9%)
1979	104 of 224 (46.4%)	51 of 224 (22.8%)
1980	108 of 224 (48.2%)	58 of 224 (25.9%)
1981	91 of 224 (40.6%)	60 of 224 (26.8%)
1982	61 of 126 (48.4%)	33 of 126 (26.2%)
1983	106 of 224 (47.3%)	54 of 224 (24.1%)
1984	95 of 224 (42.4%)	58 of 224 (25.9%)
1985	87 of 224 (38.8%)	38 of 224 (17.0%)
1986	106 of 224 (47.3%)	48 of 224 (21.4%)
1987	99 of 210 (47.1%)	40 of 210 (19.0%)
1988	113 of 224 (50.4%)	62 of 224 (27.7%)
1989	107 of 224 (47.8%)	55 of 224 (24.6%)
1990	97 of 224 (43.3%)	54 of 224 (24.1%)
1991	112 of 224 (50.0%)	57 of 224 (25.4%)
1992	88 of 224 (39.3%)	48 of 224 (21.4%)
1993	*105 of 224 (46.9%)	53 of 224 (23.7%)
1994	115 of 224 (51.3%)	60 of 224 (26.8%)
1995	115 of 240 (47.9%)	61 of 240 (25.4%)
1996	109 of 240 (45.4%)	47 of 240 (19.6%)
1997	111 of 240 (46.3%)	67 of 240 (27.9%)
1998	113 of 240 (47.1%)	50 of 240 (20.8%)
1999	115 of 248 (46.4%)	**64 of 248 (25.8%)
2000	109 of 248 (44.0%)	61 of 248 (24.6%)
2001	121 of 248 (48.8%)	62 of 248 (25.0%)
2002	126 of 256 (49.2%)	63 of 256 (24.6%)
2003	124 of 256 (48.4%)	60 of 256 (23.4%)
2004	116 of 256 (45.3%)	61 of 256 (23.8%)
2005	114 of 256 (44.5%)	60 of 256 (23.4%)
2006	117 of 256 (45.7%)	61 of 256 (23.8%)
2007	110 of 256 (43.0%)	55 of 256 (21.5%)
2008	115 of 256 (44.9%)	50 of 256 (19.5%)
2009	110 of 256 (43.0%)	54 of 256 (21.1%)

*Week record: Dec. 11-13, 1993 (Week 15), 12 of 14 games (86%) decided by 7 points or fewer.

**Week record: Oct. 10-11, 1999 (Week 5), 10 of 14 games (71%) decided by 3 points or fewer.

GAMES DECIDED BY 8 PTS. OR FEWER (1994-2009)

1994	121 of 224 (54.0%)	2004	121 of 256 (47.3%)
1995	123 of 240 (51.3%)	2005	123 of 256 (48.0%)
1996	115 of 240 (47.9%)	2006	126 of 256 (49.2%)
1997	120 of 240 (50.0%)	2007	120 of 256 (46.9%)
1998	120 of 240 (50.0%)	2008	118 of 256 (46.1%)
1999	124 of 248 (50.0%)	2009	120 of 256 (46.9%)
2000	119 of 248 (48.0%)		
2001	*128 of 248 (51.6%)		
2002	137 of 256 (53.5%)		
2003	132 of 256 (51.6%)		

*Week record: Oct. 14-15, 2001 (Week 5), 12 of 14 games (86%) decided by 8 points or fewer

TWO-POINT CONVERSION RESULTS (1994-2009)

1994	59 of 116 (50.9%)	2002	47 of 98 (48.0%)
1995	40 of 104 (38.5%)	2003	29 of 66 (43.9%)
1996	44 of 92 (47.8%)	2004	37 of 76 (48.7%)
1997	47 of 109 (43.1%)	2005	27 of 53 (50.9%)
1998	41 of 105 (39.1%)	2006	21 of 41 (51.2%)
1999	31 of 84 (36.9%)	2007	30 of 61 (49.2%)
2000	35 of 85 (41.2%)	2008	28 of 68 (41.2%)
2001	40 of 90 (44.4%)	2009	24 of 60 (40.0%)

RECORDS AFTER BYE WEEKS (1990-2009)

AFC		NFC	
Baltimore	9- 5	Arizona	10-11
Buffalo	14- 7	Atlanta	11-10
Cincinnati	5-15-1	Carolina	7- 8
Cleveland	6-10	Chicago	13- 8
Denver	15- 6	Dallas	16- 5
Houston	2- 6	Detroit	9-12
Indianapolis	12- 9	Green Bay	12- 9
Jacksonville	7- 8	Minnesota	17- 4
Kansas City	12- 9	New Orleans	9-12
Miami	12- 9	N.Y. Giants	6-15
New England	12- 9	Philadelphia	17- 4
N.Y. Jets	11-10	San Francisco	8-13
Oakland	9-12	Seattle	5-16
Pittsburgh	12- 9	St. Louis	11-10
San Diego	10-10	Tampa Bay	9-12
Tennessee	13- 8	Washington	11-10

2009 RECORDS OF TEAMS IN CLOSE GAMES

AFC	Overall Record	Decided by 8 Pts. or Fewer	Decided By 3 Pts. or Fewer
Baltimore	9- 7	3-5	1-4
Buffalo	6-10	2-5	1-3
Cincinnati	10- 6	6-3	3-2
Cleveland	5-11	4-3	1-2
Denver	8- 8	3-2	1-2
Houston	9- 7	5-6	3-2
Indianapolis	14- 2	8-0	4-0
Jacksonville	7- 9	6-4	4-1
Kansas City	4-12	3-6	1-2
Miami	7- 9	6-4	2-1
New England	10- 6	3-5	1-3
N.Y. Jets	9- 7	3-5	0-3
Oakland	5-11	5-4	4-0
Pittsburgh	9- 7	5-7	3-5
San Diego	13- 3	8-1	4-0
Tennessee	8- 8	5-3	3-2

NFC	Overall Record	Decided by 8 Pts. or Fewer	Decided By 3 Pts. or Fewer
Arizona	10- 6	4-2	0-1
Atlanta	9- 7	4-3	2-2
Carolina	8- 8	2-2	1-0
Chicago	7- 9	4-5	1-0
Dallas	11- 5	4-4	1-2
Detroit	2-14	2-3	1-0
Green Bay	11- 5	3-3	0-1
Minnesota	12- 4	3-1	2-0
New Orleans	13- 3	4-2	2-1
N.Y. Giants	8- 8	4-3	2-1
Philadelphia	11- 5	4-3	2-0
San Francisco	8- 8	2-6	0-3
Seattle	5-11	1-2	1-0
St. Louis	1-15	1-6	0-3
Tampa Bay	3-13	1-4	1-3
Washington	4-12	2-8	2-5

SUPER BOWL CHAMPIONS THAT DID NOT MAKE PLAYOFFS THE FOLLOWING YEAR

Pittsburgh—Super Bowl XLIII champions did not make playoffs in 2009 season.

Pittsburgh—Super Bowl XL champions did not make playoffs in 2006 season.

Tampa Bay—Super Bowl XXXVII champions did not make playoffs in 2003 season.

New England—Super Bowl XXXVI champions did not make playoffs in the 2002 season.

Denver—Super Bowl XXXIII champions did not make playoffs in the 1999 season.

N.Y. Giants—Super Bowl XXV champions did not make playoffs in the 1991 season.

Washington—Super Bowl XXII champions did not make playoffs in the 1988 season.

N.Y. Giants—Super Bowl XXI champions did not make playoffs in the 1987 season.

San Francisco—Super Bowl XVI champions did not make playoffs in the 1982 season.

Oakland—Super Bowl XV champions did not make playoffs in the 1981 season.

Pittsburgh—Super Bowl XIV champions did not make playoffs in the 1980 season.

Kansas City—Super Bowl IV champions did not make playoffs in the 1970 season.

Green Bay—Super Bowl II champions did not make playoffs in the 1968 season.

NON-DIVISION WINNERS THAT PLAYED IN SUPER BOWL

2007 New York Giants ....Super Bowl XLII
(Defeated New England, 17-14)

2005 Pittsburgh Steelers ....Super Bowl XL
(Defeated Seattle, 21-10)

2000 Baltimore Ravens ....Super Bowl XXXV
(Defeated N.Y. Giants, 34-7)

1999 Tennessee Titans..............................Super Bowl XXXIV
(Lost to St. Louis, 23-16)

1997 Denver Broncos.................................Super Bowl XXXII
(Defeated Green Bay, 31-24)

1992 Buffalo Bills ....Super Bowl XXVII
(Lost to Dallas, 52-17)

1985 New England Patriots...............................Super Bowl XX
(Lost to Chicago, 46-10)

1980 Oakland Raiders ....Super Bowl XV
(Defeated Philadelphia, 27-10)

1975 Dallas Cowboys ....Super Bowl X
(Lost to Pittsburgh, 21-17)

1969 Kansas City Chiefs ....Super Bowl IV
(Defeated Minnesota, 23-7)

TEAMS AT OR UNDER .500 IN POSTSEASON PLAY

2008	San Diego Chargers	8-8
2006	New York Giants	8-8
2004	Minnesota Vikings	8-8
2004	St. Louis Rams	8-8
1999	Dallas Cowboys	8-8
1999	Detroit Lions	8-8
1991	New York Jets	8-8
1990	New Orleans Saints	8-8
1985	Cleveland Browns	8-8
1982	Cleveland Browns	4-5
1982	Detroit Lions	4-5
1969	Houston Oilers	6-6-2

TEAMS TO BEAT OPPOSING TEAM THREE TIMES IN A SEASON SINCE 1970

Year	Team	Opponent
2009	Dallas Cowboys	Philadelphia Eagles
2008	Pittsburgh Steelers	Baltimore Ravens
2004	St. Louis Rams	Seattle Seahawks
2002	Pittsburgh Steelers	Cleveland Browns
2000	New York Giants	Philadelphia Eagles
1999	Tennessee Titans	Jacksonville Jaguars
1997	Green Bay Packers	Tampa Bay Buccaneers
1997	New England Patriots	Miami Dolphins
1994	Pittsburgh Steelers	Cleveland Browns
1993	Los Angeles Raiders	Denver Broncos
1991	Kansas City Chiefs	Los Angeles Raiders
1986	New York Giants	Washington Redskins
1982	Miami Dolphins	New York Jets

COLDEST NFL GAMES ON RECORD

-13 degrees (-48 degree wind chill)—December 31, 1967, Lambeau Field, Green Bay, Wisconsin, NFL Championship (Green Bay 21, Dallas 17)

-9 degrees (-59 degree wind chill)—January 10, 1982, Riverfront Stadium, Cincinnati, Ohio, AFC Championship (Cincinnati 27, San Diego 7)

-1 degrees (-23 degree wind chill)—January 20, 2008, Lambeau Field, Green Bay, Wisconsin, NFC Championship (N.Y. Giants 23, Green Bay 20 in OT)

TEAM LEADERS

Offense	Most Scored		Fewest Scored	
1st Quarter	122	Philadelphia	16	St. Louis
2nd Quarter	183	New England	63	Detroit
3rd Quarter	123	Baltimore	22	Oakland
4th Quarter	139	New Orleans	60	St. Louis
Defense	**Most Scored**		**Fewest Scored**	
1st Quarter	108	Tampa Bay	27	Dallas
2nd Quarter	169	NYG and Tenn.	70	N.Y. Jets
3rd Quarter	127	Detroit	30	Washington
4th Quarter	140	Miami	48	New Orleans

2009 NFL SCORE BY QUARTERS

AFC Offense	1	2	3	4	OT	PTS
San Diego	103	120	107	124	0	454
New England	99	183	70	75	0	427
Indianapolis	96	147	58	115	0	416
Baltimore	77	81	123	107	3	391
Houston	89	131	75	93	0	388
Pittsburgh	81	126	61	97	3	368
Miami	57	106	81	116	0	360
Tennessee	77	103	67	104	3	354
N.Y. Jets	81	108	79	80	0	348
Denver	57	80	101	85	3	326
Cincinnati	61	118	49	74	3	305
Kansas City	29	83	61	118	3	294
Jacksonville	48	113	46	80	3	290
Buffalo	74	67	37	77	3	258
Cleveland	66	70	46	63	0	245
Oakland	36	78	22	61	0	197

NFC Offense	1	2	3	4	OT	PTS
New Orleans	85	176	107	139	3	510
Minnesota	69	156	111	134	0	470
Green Bay	115	154	58	134	0	461
Philadelphia	122	151	72	84	0	429
N.Y. Giants	57	159	77	106	3	402
Arizona	76	132	82	85	0	375
Atlanta	78	116	60	109	0	363
Dallas	71	98	80	106	6	361
San Francisco	62	93	72	103	0	330
Chicago	36	106	85	94	6	327
Carolina	68	109	43	95	0	315
Seattle	37	118	46	79	0	280
Washington	41	74	84	67	0	266
Detroit	80	63	51	68	0	262
Tampa Bay	34	73	38	96	3	244
St. Louis	16	74	25	60	0	175

AFC Defense	1	2	3	4	OT	PTS
N.Y. Jets	52	70	47	64	3	236
Baltimore	57	95	47	62	0	261
New England	47	89	53	93	3	285
Cincinnati	55	96	61	79	0	291
Indianapolis	66	105	52	84	0	307
San Diego	51	98	57	114	0	320
Denver	84	82	57	101	0	324
Pittsburgh	52	75	56	135	6	324
Buffalo	44	115	48	119	0	326
Houston	57	135	58	83	0	333
Cleveland	65	132	87	88	3	375
Oakland	100	136	49	94	0	379
Jacksonville	69	157	75	79	0	380
Miami	68	101	78	140	3	390
Tennessee	82	169	77	71	3	402
Kansas City	93	110	100	115	6	424

NFC Defense	1	2	3	4	OT	PTS
Dallas	27	80	34	109	0	250
San Francisco	57	116	33	75	0	281
Green Bay	52	84	65	96	0	297
Carolina	48	102	72	86	0	308
Minnesota	29	101	56	120	6	312
Arizona	67	101	62	95	0	325
Atlanta	53	125	55	89	3	325
Washington	96	118	30	89	3	336
Philadelphia	58	101	107	71	0	337
New Orleans	106	93	91	48	3	341
Chicago	96	112	69	98	0	375
Seattle	100	109	104	77	0	390
Tampa Bay	108	118	74	100	0	400
N.Y. Giants	64	169	100	94	0	427
St. Louis	87	114	93	139	3	436
Detroit	88	158	127	121	0	494
NFL TOTALS	**2,178**	**3,566**	**2,174**	**3,028**	**45**	**10,991**

INSIDE THE NUMBERS

2010 TOP 100 TELEVISION MARKETS
(NFL TEAM MARKETS IN BOLD)

RANK	MARKET	TV HOUSEHOLDS	% of U.S.
1	**New York**	**7,493,530**	**6.524**
2	Los Angeles	5,659,170	4.927
3	**Chicago**	**3,501,010**	**3.048**
4	**Philadelphia**	**2,955,190**	**2.573**
5	**Dallas-Ft. Worth**	**2,544,410**	**2.215**
6	**San Francisco-Oak-San Jose**	**2,503,400**	**2.179**
7	**Boston (Manchester)**	**2,410,180**	**2.098**
8	**Atlanta**	**2,387,520**	**2.079**
9	**Washington, DC (Hagrstwn)**	**2,335,040**	**2.033**
10	**Houston**	**2,123,460**	**1.849**
11	**Detroit**	**1,890,220**	**1.646**
12	**Phoenix (Prescott)**	**1,873,930**	**1.631**
13	**Seattle-Tacoma**	**1,833,990**	**1.597**
14	**Tampa-St. Pete (Sarasota)**	**1,805,810**	**1.572**
15	**Minneapolis-St. Paul**	**1,732,050**	**1.508**
16	**Denver**	**1,539,380**	**1.340**
17	**Miami-Ft. Lauderdale**	**1,538,090**	**1.339**
18	**Cleveland-Akron (Canton)**	**1,520,750**	**1.324**
19	Orlando-Daytona Bch-Melbrn	1,455,620	1.267
20	Sacramnto-Stkton-Modesto	1,404,580	1.223
21	**St. Louis**	**1,249,450**	**1.088**
22	Portland, OR	1,188,770	1.035
23	**Pittsburgh**	**1,154,950**	**1.005**
24	**Charlotte**	**1,147,910**	**0.999**
25	**Indianapolis**	**1,119,760**	**0.975**
26	Raleigh-Durham (Fayetvlle)	1,107,820	0.964
27	**Baltimore**	**1,093,170**	**0.952**
28	**San Diego**	**1,073,390**	**0.934**
29	**Nashville**	**1,019,010**	**0.887**
30	Hartford & New Haven	1,010,630	0.880
31	Salt Lake City	944,060	0.822
32	**Kansas City**	**941,360**	**0.820**
33	**Cincinnati**	**918,670**	**0.800**
34	Columbus, OH	904,030	0.787
35	Milwaukee	901,790	0.785
36	Greenvll-Spart-Ashevll-And	865,810	0.754
37	San Antonio	830,000	0.723
38	West Palm Beach-Ft. Pierce	776,080	0.676
39	Harrisburg-Lncstr-Leb-York	743,420	0.647
40	Birmingham (Ann and Tusc)	742,140	0.646
41	Grand Rapids-Kalmzoo-B.Crk	740,430	0.645
42	Las Vegas	721,780	0.628
43	Norfolk-Portsmth-Newpt Nws	709,880	0.618
44	Albuquerque-Santa Fe	694,040	0.604
45	Oklahoma City	694,030	0.604
46	Greensboro-H.Point-W.Salem	691,380	0.602
47	**Jacksonville**	**679,120**	**0.591**
48	Austin	678,730	0.591
49	Louisville	668,310	0.582
50	Memphis	667,660	0.581

2010 TOP 100 TELEVISION MARKETS
(NFL TEAM MARKETS IN BOLD)

RANK	MARKET	TV HOUSEHOLDS	% of U.S.
51	**New Orleans**	**633,930**	**0.552**
52	**Buffalo**	**633,220**	**0.551**
53	Providence-New Bedford	619,610	0.539
54	Wilkes Barre-Scranton	593,480	0.517
55	Fresno-Visalia	579,180	0.504
56	Little Rock-Pine Bluff	564,490	0.491
57	Albany-Schenectady-Troy	554,070	0.482
58	Richmond-Petersburg	553,950	0.482
59	Knoxville	552,380	0.481
60	Mobile-Pensacola (Ft Walt)	534,730	0.466
61	Tulsa	528,070	0.460
62	Lexington	506,340	0.441
63	Charleston-Huntington	501,530	0.437
64	Ft. Myers-Naples	500,110	0.435
65	Dayton	482,590	0.420
66	Tucson (Sierra Vista)	465,100	0.405
67	Roanoke-Lynchburg	461,220	0.402
68	Flint-Saginaw-Bay City	458,020	0.399
69	Wichita-Hutchinson Plus	452,710	0.394
70	**Green Bay-Appleton**	**443,420**	**0.386**
71	Honolulu	433,240	0.377
72	Des Moines-Ames	432,310	0.376
73	Toledo	423,100	0.368
74	Springfield, MO	422,740	0.368
75	Spokane	419,350	0.365
76	Omaha	410,350	0.357
77	Portland-Auburn	408,120	0.355
78	Paducah-Cape Girard-Harsbg	399,690	0.348
79	Columbia, SC	398,620	0.347
80	Rochester, NY	392,190	0.341
81	Huntsville-Decatur (Flor)	390,900	0.340
82	Shreveport	386,180	0.336
83	Syracuse	385,440	0.336
84	Champaign&Sprngfld-Decatur	384,620	0.335
85	Madison	377,260	0.328
86	Chattanooga	365,400	0.318
87	Harlingen-Wslco-Brnsvl-McA	354,150	0.308
88	Cedar Rapids-Wtrlo-IWC&Dub	346,030	0.301
89	Waco-Temple-Bryan	339,570	0.296
90	Jackson, MS	336,520	0.293
91	South Bend-Elkhart	336,130	0.293
92	Colorado Springs-Pueblo	334,710	0.291
93	Tri-Cities, TN-VA	334,620	0.291
94	Burlington-Plattsburgh	330,650	0.288
95	Baton Rouge	326,890	0.285
96	Savannah	322,030	0.280
97	Charleston, SC	311,190	0.271
98	El Paso (Las Cruces)	310,760	0.271
99	Davenport-R.Island-Moline	308,910	0.269
100	Ft. Smith-Fay-Sprngdl-Rgrs	298,330	0.260
TOTAL NFL MARKETS		**54,095,320**	**47.094**
TOTAL TOP 100 MARKETS		**98,823,060**	**86.033**
TOTAL MARKETS		**114,866,380**	**100.000**

ALL-TIME REGULAR-SEASON RECORDS OF CURRENT NFL TEAMS

AFC

BALTIMORE RAVENS

Season	All Games W	L	T	Home Games W	L	T	Road Games W	L	T
1996	4	12		4	4		0	8	
1997	6	9	1	3	4	1	3	5	
1998	6	10		4	4		2	6	
1999	8	8		4	4		4	4	
2000	12	4		6	2		6	2	
2001	10	6		6	2		4	4	
2002	7	9		4	4		3	5	
2003	10	6		7	1		3	5	
2004	9	7		6	2		3	5	
2005	6	10		6	2		0	8	
2006	13	3		7	1		6	2	
2007	5	11		4	4		1	7	
2008	11	5		6	2		5	3	
2009	9	7		6	2		3	5	
	116	107	1	73	38	1	43	69	

BUFFALO BILLS

Season	All Games W	L	T	Home Games W	L	T	Road Games W	L	T
1960	5	8	1	3	4		2	4	1
1961	6	8		2	5		4	3	
1962	7	6	1	3	3	1	4	3	
1963	7	6	1	4	2	1	3	4	
1964	12	2		6	1		6	1	
1965	10	3	1	5	2		5	1	1
1966	9	4	1	4	2	1	5	2	
1967	4	10		2	5		2	5	
1968	1	12	1	1	6		0	6	1
1969	4	10		4	3		0	7	
1970	3	10	1	1	6		2	4	1
1971	1	13		1	6		0	7	
1972	4	9	1	2	4	1	2	5	
1973	9	5		5	2		4	3	
1974	9	5		5	2		4	3	
1975	8	6		3	4		5	2	
1976	2	12		1	6		1	6	
1977	3	11		1	6		2	5	
1978	5	11		4	4		1	7	
1979	7	9		3	5		4	4	
1980	11	5		6	2		5	3	
1981	10	6		7	1		3	5	
1982	4	5		4	1		0	4	
1983	8	8		3	5		5	3	
1984	2	14		2	6		0	8	
1985	2	14		2	6		0	8	
1986	4	12		3	5		1	7	
1987	7	8		4	4		3	4	
1988	12	4		8	0		4	4	
1989	9	7		6	2		3	5	
1990	13	3		8	0		5	3	
1991	13	3		7	1		6	2	
1992	11	5		6	2		5	3	
1993	12	4		6	2		6	2	
1994	7	9		4	4		3	5	
1995	10	6		6	2		4	4	
1996	10	6		7	1		3	5	
1997	6	10		4	4		2	6	
1998	10	6		6	2		4	4	
1999	11	5		6	2		5	3	
2000	8	8		5	3		3	5	
2001	3	13		1	7		2	6	
2002	8	8		5	3		3	5	
2003	6	10		4	4		2	6	
2004	9	7		5	3		4	4	
2005	5	11		4	4		1	7	
2006	7	9		4	4		3	5	
2007	7	9		4	4		3	5	
2008	7	9		3	5		4	4	
2009	6	10		3	5		3	5	
	354	394	8	203	172	4	151	222	4

CINCINNATI BENGALS

Season	All Games W	L	T	Home Games W	L	T	Road Games W	L	T
1968	3	11		2	5		1	6	
1969	4	9	1	4	3		0	6	1
1970	8	6		5	2		3	4	
1971	4	10		3	4		1	6	
1972	8	6		4	3		4	3	
1973	10	4		7	0		3	4	
1974	7	7		4	3		3	4	
1975	11	3		6	1		5	2	
1976	10	4		6	1		4	3	
1977	8	6		5	2		3	4	
1978	4	12		3	5		1	7	
1979	4	12		4	4		0	8	
1980	6	10		3	5		3	5	
1981	12	4		6	2		6	2	
1982	7	2		4	0		3	2	
1983	7	9		4	4		3	5	
1984	8	8		5	3		3	5	
1985	7	9		5	3		2	6	
1986	10	6		6	2		4	4	
1987	4	11		1	7		3	4	
1988	12	4		8	0		4	4	
1989	8	8		5	3		3	5	
1990	9	7		5	3		4	4	
1991	3	13		3	5		0	8	
1992	5	11		3	5		2	6	
1993	3	13		3	5		0	8	
1994	3	13		2	6		1	7	
1995	7	9		3	5		4	4	
1996	8	8		6	2		2	6	
1997	7	9		6	2		1	7	
1998	3	13		1	7		2	6	
1999	4	12		2	6		2	6	
2000	4	12		3	5		1	7	
2001	6	10		4	4		2	6	
2002	2	14		1	7		1	7	
2003	8	8		5	3		3	5	
2004	8	8		5	3		3	5	
2005	11	5		5	3		6	2	
2006	8	8		4	4		4	4	
2007	7	9		5	3		2	6	
2008	4	11	1	3	4	1	1	7	
2009	10	6		6	2		4	4	
	282	360	2	175	146	1	107	214	1

CLEVELAND BROWNS*

Season	All Games W	L	T	Home Games W	L	T	Road Games W	L	T
1950	10	2		5	1		5	1	
1951	11	1		6	0		5	1	
1952	8	4		4	2		4	2	
1953	11	1		6	0		5	1	
1954	9	3		5	1		4	2	
1955	9	2	1	5	1		4	1	1
1956	5	7		1	5		4	2	
1957	9	2	1	6	0		3	2	1
1958	9	3		4	2		5	1	
1959	7	5		3	3		4	2	
1960	8	3	1	4	2		4	1	1

Season	All Games W	L	T	Home Games W	L	T	Road Games W	L	T
1961	8	5	1	4	3		4	2	1
1962	7	6	1	4	2	1	3	4	
1963	10	4		5	2		5	2	
1964	10	3	1	5	1	1	5	2	
1965	11	3		5	2		6	1	
1966	9	5		5	2		4	3	
1967	9	5		6	1		3	4	
1968	10	4		5	2		5	2	
1969	10	3	1	5	1	1	5	2	
1970	7	7		4	3		3	4	
1971	9	5		4	3		5	2	
1972	10	4		4	3		6	1	
1973	7	5	2	5	1	1	2	4	1
1974	4	10		3	4		1	6	
1975	3	11		3	4		0	7	
1976	9	5		6	1		3	4	
1977	6	8		2	5		4	3	
1978	8	8		5	3		3	5	
1979	9	7		5	3		4	4	
1980	11	5		6	2		5	3	
1981	5	11		3	5		2	6	
1982	4	5		2	2		2	3	
1983	9	7		6	2		3	5	
1984	5	11		2	6		3	5	
1985	8	8		5	3		3	5	
1986	12	4		6	2		6	2	
1987	10	5		5	2		5	3	
1988	10	6		6	2		4	4	
1989	9	6	1	5	2	1	4	4	
1990	3	13		2	6		1	7	
1991	6	10		3	5		3	5	
1992	7	9		4	4		3	5	
1993	7	9		4	4		3	5	
1994	11	5		6	2		5	3	
1995	5	11		3	5		2	6	
1999	2	14		0	8		2	6	
2000	3	13		2	6		1	7	
2001	7	9		4	4		3	5	
2002	9	7		3	5		6	2	
2003	5	11		2	6		3	5	
2004	4	12		3	5		1	7	
2005	6	10		4	4		2	6	
2006	4	12		2	6		2	6	
2007	10	6		7	1		3	5	
2008	4	12		1	7		3	5	
2009	5	11		3	5		2	6	
	433	383	10	233	174	5	200	209	5

*Did not play from 1996-98.

DENVER BRONCOS

Season	All Games W	L	T	Home Games W	L	T	Road Games W	L	T
1960	4	9	1	2	4	1	2	5	
1961	3	11		2	5		1	6	
1962	7	7		3	4		4	3	
1963	2	11	1	2	5		0	6	1
1964	2	11	1	2	4	1	0	7	
1965	4	10		2	5		2	5	
1966	4	10		3	4		1	6	
1967	3	11		1	6		2	5	
1968	5	9		3	4		2	5	
1969	5	8	1	4	2	1	1	6	
1970	5	8	1	3	3	1	2	5	
1971	4	9	1	2	4	1	2	5	
1972	5	9		3	4		2	5	
1973	7	5	2	3	3	1	4	2	1
1974	7	6	1	3	3	1	4	3	
1975	6	8		5	2		1	6	

Season	All Games W	L	T	Home Games W	L	T	Road Games W	L	T
1976	9	5		6	1		3	4	
1977	12	2		6	1		6	1	
1978	10	6		6	2		4	4	
1979	10	6		6	2		4	4	
1980	8	8		4	4		4	4	
1981	10	6		8	0		2	6	
1982	2	7		1	4		1	3	
1983	9	7		6	2		3	5	
1984	13	3		7	1		6	2	
1985	11	5		6	2		5	3	
1986	11	5		7	1		4	4	
1987	10	4	1	7	1		3	3	1
1988	8	8		6	2		2	6	
1989	11	5		6	2		5	3	
1990	5	11		4	4		1	7	
1991	12	4		7	1		5	3	
1992	8	8		7	1		1	7	
1993	9	7		5	3		4	4	
1994	7	9		4	4		3	5	
1995	8	8		6	2		2	6	
1996	13	3		8	0		5	3	
1997	12	4		8	0		4	4	
1998	14	2		8	0		6	2	
1999	6	10		3	5		3	5	
2000	11	5		6	2		5	3	
2001	8	8		6	2		2	6	
2002	9	7		5	3		4	4	
2003	10	6		6	2		4	4	
2004	10	6		6	2		4	4	
2005	13	3		8	0		5	3	
2006	9	7		4	4		5	3	
2007	7	9		5	3		2	6	
2008	8	8		4	4		4	4	
2009	8	8		4	4		4	4	
	394	352	10	239	133	7	155	219	3

HOUSTON TEXANS

Season	All Games W	L	T	Home Games W	L	T	Road Games W	L	T
2002	4	12		2	6		2	6	
2003	5	11		3	5		2	6	
2004	7	9		3	5		4	4	
2005	2	14		2	6		0	8	
2006	6	10		4	4		2	6	
2007	8	8		6	2		2	6	
2008	8	8		6	2		2	6	
2009	9	7		4	4		5	3	
	49	79		30	34		19	45	

INDIANAPOLIS COLTS*

Season	All Games W	L	T	Home Games W	L	T	Road Games W	L	T
1953	3	9		2	4		1	5	
1954	3	9		2	4		1	5	
1955	5	6	1	4	1	1	1	5	
1956	5	7		4	2		1	5	
1957	7	5		4	2		3	3	
1958	9	3		6	0		3	3	
1959	9	3		4	2		5	1	
1960	6	6		4	2		2	4	
1961	8	6		5	2		3	4	
1962	7	7		3	4		4	3	
1963	8	6		4	3		4	3	
1964	12	2		7	1		5	1	
1965	10	3	1	5	2		5	1	1
1966	9	5		5	2		4	3	
1967	11	1	2	6	0	1	5	1	1
1968	13	1		6	1		7	0	

Season	All Games			Home Games			Road Games		
	W	L	T	W	L	T	W	L	T
1969	8	5	1	4	2	1	4	3	
1970	11	2	1	5	1	1	6	1	
1971	10	4		5	2		5	2	
1972	5	9		2	5		3	4	
1973	4	10		3	4		1	6	
1974	2	12		0	7		2	5	
1975	10	4		5	2		5	2	
1976	11	3		6	1		5	2	
1977	10	4		6	1		4	3	
1978	5	11		2	6		3	5	
1979	5	11		3	5		2	6	
1980	7	9		2	6		5	3	
1981	2	14		1	7		1	7	
1982	0	8	1	0	3	1	0	5	
1983	7	9		3	5		4	4	
1984	4	12		2	6		2	6	
1985	5	11		4	4		1	7	
1986	3	13		1	7		2	6	
1987	9	6		4	4		5	2	
1988	9	7		6	2		3	5	
1989	8	8		6	2		2	6	
1990	7	9		3	5		4	4	
1991	1	15		0	8		1	7	
1992	9	7		4	4		5	3	
1993	4	12		2	6		2	6	
1994	8	8		5	3		3	5	
1995	9	7		5	3		4	4	
1996	9	7		6	2		3	5	
1997	3	13		2	6		1	7	
1998	3	13		3	5		0	8	
1999	13	3		7	1		6	2	
2000	10	6		6	2		4	4	
2001	6	10		3	5		3	5	
2002	10	6		5	3		5	3	
2003	12	4		5	3		7	1	
2004	12	4		7	1		5	3	
2005	14	2		7	1		7	1	
2006	12	4		8	0		4	4	
2007	13	3		6	2		7	1	
2008	12	4		6	2		6	2	
2009	14	2		7	1		7	1	
	441	390	7	238	177	5	203	213	2

*includes Baltimore Colts (1953-1983).

JACKSONVILLE JAGUARS

Season	All Games			Home Games			Road Games		
	W	L	T	W	L	T	W	L	T
1995	4	12		2	6		2	6	
1996	9	7		7	1		2	6	
1997	11	5		7	1		4	4	
1998	11	5		7	1		4	4	
1999	14	2		7	1		7	1	
2000	7	9		4	4		3	5	
2001	6	10		3	5		3	5	
2002	6	10		3	5		3	5	
2003	5	11		5	3		0	8	
2004	9	7		4	4		5	3	
2005	12	4		6	2		6	2	
2006	8	8		6	2		2	6	
2007	11	5		6	2		5	3	
2008	5	11		2	6		3	5	
2009	7	9		5	3		2	6	
	125	115		74	46		51	69	

KANSAS CITY CHIEFS*

Season	All Games			Home Games			Road Games		
	W	L	T	W	L	T	W	L	T
1960	8	6		5	2		3	4	
1961	6	8		4	3		2	5	
1962	11	3		6	1		5	2	
1963	5	7	2	4	3		1	4	2
1964	7	7		4	3		3	4	
1965	7	5	2	5	2		2	3	2
1966	11	2	1	4	2	1	7	0	
1967	9	5		4	3		5	2	
1968	12	2		6	1		6	1	
1969	11	3		6	1		5	2	
1970	7	5	2	4	1	2	3	4	
1971	10	3	1	7	0		3	3	1
1972	8	6		3	4		5	2	
1973	7	5	2	5	1	1	2	4	1
1974	5	9		1	6		4	3	
1975	5	9		3	4		2	5	
1976	5	9		1	6		4	3	
1977	2	12		1	6		1	6	
1978	4	12		3	5		1	7	
1979	7	9		3	5		4	4	
1980	8	8		3	5		5	3	
1981	9	7		5	3		4	4	
1982	3	6		2	2		1	4	
1983	6	10		5	3		1	7	
1984	8	8		5	3		3	5	
1985	6	10		5	3		1	7	
1986	10	6		6	2		4	4	
1987	4	11		3	4		1	7	
1988	4	11	1	4	4		0	7	1
1989	8	7	1	5	3		3	4	1
1990	11	5		6	2		5	3	
1991	10	6		6	2		4	4	
1992	10	6		7	1		3	5	
1993	11	5		7	1		4	4	
1994	9	7		5	3		4	4	
1995	13	3		8	0		5	3	
1996	9	7		5	3		4	4	
1997	13	3		8	0		5	3	
1998	7	9		5	3		2	6	
1999	9	7		6	2		3	5	
2000	7	9		5	3		2	6	
2001	6	10		3	5		3	5	
2002	8	8		6	2		2	6	
2003	13	3		8	0		5	3	
2004	7	9		4	4		3	5	
2005	10	6		7	1		3	5	
2006	9	7		6	2		3	5	
2007	4	12		2	6		2	6	
2008	2	14		1	7		1	7	
2009	4	12		1	7		3	5	
	385	359	12	228	145	4	157	214	8

*includes Dallas Texans (1960-62).

MIAMI DOLPHINS

Season	All Games			Home Games			Road Games		
	W	L	T	W	L	T	W	L	T
1966	3	11		2	5		1	6	
1967	4	10		4	3		0	7	
1968	5	8	1	1	5	1	4	3	
1969	3	10	1	2	4	1	1	6	
1970	10	4		6	1		4	3	
1971	10	3	1	6	1		4	2	1
1972	14	0		7	0		7	0	
1973	12	2		7	0		5	2	
1974	11	3		7	0		4	3	
1975	10	4		5	2		5	2	
1976	6	8		3	4		3	4	
1977	10	4		6	1		4	3	
1978	11	5		7	1		4	4	

Season	All Games W	L	T	Home Games W	L	T	Road Games W	L	T
1979	10	6		6	2		4	4	
1980	8	8		5	3		3	5	
1981	11	4	1	6	1	1	5	3	
1982	7	2		4	0		3	2	
1983	12	4		7	1		5	3	
1984	14	2		7	1		7	1	
1985	12	4		8	0		4	4	
1986	8	8		4	4		4	4	
1987	8	7		4	3		4	4	
1988	6	10		4	4		2	6	
1989	8	8		4	4		4	4	
1990	12	4		7	1		5	3	
1991	8	8		5	3		3	5	
1992	11	5		6	2		5	3	
1993	9	7		4	4		5	3	
1994	10	6		6	2		4	4	
1995	9	7		5	3		4	4	
1996	8	8		4	4		4	4	
1997	9	7		6	2		3	5	
1998	10	6		7	1		3	5	
1999	9	7		5	3		4	4	
2000	11	5		5	3		6	2	
2001	11	5		7	1		4	4	
2002	9	7		7	1		2	6	
2003	10	6		4	4		6	2	
2004	4	12		3	5		1	7	
2005	9	7		5	3		4	4	
2006	6	10		4	4		2	6	
2007	1	15		1	7		0	8	
2008	11	5		5	3		6	2	
2009	7	9		4	4		3	5	
	387	281	4	222	110	3	165	171	1

NEW ENGLAND PATRIOTS*

Season	All Games W	L	T	Home Games W	L	T	Road Games W	L	T
1960	5	9		3	4		2	5	
1961	9	4	1	4	2	1	5	2	
1962	9	4	1	6	1		3	3	1
1963	7	6	1	5	1	1	2	5	
1964	10	3	1	4	2	1	6	1	
1965	4	8	2	1	4	2	3	4	
1966	8	4	2	4	2	1	4	2	1
1967	3	10	1	2	4		1	6	1
1968	4	10		2	5		2	5	
1969	4	10		2	5		2	5	
1970	2	12		1	6		1	6	
1971	6	8		5	2		1	6	
1972	3	11		2	5		1	6	
1973	5	9		3	4		2	5	
1974	7	7		3	4		4	3	
1975	3	11		2	5		1	6	
1976	11	3		6	1		5	2	
1977	9	5		6	1		3	4	
1978	11	5		5	3		6	2	
1979	9	7		6	2		3	5	
1980	10	6		6	2		4	4	
1981	2	14		2	6		0	8	
1982	5	4		3	1		2	3	
1983	8	8		5	3		3	5	
1984	9	7		5	3		4	4	
1985	11	5		7	1		4	4	
1986	11	5		4	4		7	1	
1987	8	7		5	3		3	4	
1988	9	7		7	1		2	6	
1989	5	11		3	5		2	6	
1990	1	15		0	8		1	7	
1991	6	10		4	4		2	6	
1992	2	14		1	7		1	7	
1993	5	11		3	5		2	6	
1994	10	6		5	3		5	3	
1995	6	10		3	5		3	5	
1996	11	5		6	2		5	3	
1997	10	6		6	2		4	4	
1998	9	7		6	2		3	5	
1999	8	8		5	3		3	5	
2000	5	11		3	5		2	6	
2001	11	5		6	2		5	3	
2002	9	7		5	3		4	4	
2003	14	2		8	0		6	2	
2004	14	2		8	0		6	2	
2005	10	6		5	3		5	3	
2006	12	4		5	3		7	1	
2007	16	0		8	0		8	0	
2008	11	5		5	3		6	2	
2009	10	6		8	0		2	6	
	387	360	9	219	152	6	168	208	3

includes Boston Patriots (1960-1970).

NEW YORK JETS*

Season	All Games W	L	T	Home Games W	L	T	Road Games W	L	T
1960	7	7		3	4		4	3	
1961	7	7		5	2		2	5	
1962	5	9		2	5		3	4	
1963	5	8	1	4	2	1	1	6	
1964	5	8	1	5	1	1	0	7	
1965	5	8	1	3	3	1	2	5	
1966	6	6	2	4	3		2	3	2
1967	8	5	1	4	2	1	4	3	
1968	11	3		6	1		5	2	
1969	10	4		5	2		5	2	
1970	4	10		2	5		2	5	
1971	6	8		4	3		2	5	
1972	7	7		4	3		3	4	
1973	4	10		2	4		2	6	
1974	7	7		3	4		4	3	
1975	3	11		1	6		2	5	
1976	3	11		2	5		1	6	
1977	3	11		1	6		2	5	
1978	8	8		4	4		4	4	
1979	8	8		6	2		2	6	
1980	4	12		2	6		2	6	
1981	10	5	1	6	2		4	3	1
1982	6	3		3	1		3	2	
1983	7	9		2	6		5	3	
1984	7	9		3	5		4	4	
1985	11	5		7	1		4	4	
1986	10	6		5	3		5	3	
1987	6	9		4	4		2	5	
1988	8	7	1	5	2	1	3	5	
1989	4	12		1	7		3	5	
1990	6	10		3	5		3	5	
1991	8	8		4	4		4	4	
1992	4	12		3	5		1	7	
1993	8	8		3	5		5	3	
1994	6	10		4	4		2	6	
1995	3	13		2	6		1	7	
1996	1	15		0	8		1	7	
1997	9	7		5	3		4	4	
1998	12	4		7	1		5	3	
1999	8	8		4	4		4	4	
2000	9	7		5	3		4	4	
2001	10	6		3	5		7	1	
2002	9	7		5	3		4	4	
2003	6	10		4	4		2	6	

Season	All Games W	L	T	Home Games W	L	T	Road Games W	L	T
2004	10	6		6	2		4	4	
2005	4	12		4	4		0	8	
2006	10	6		4	4		6	2	
2007	4	12		3	5		1	7	
2008	9	7		5	3		4	4	
2009	9	7		4	4		5	3	
	340	408	8	186	186	5	154	222	3

*includes New York Titans (1960-62).

OAKLAND RAIDERS*

Season	All Games W	L	T	Home Games W	L	T	Road Games W	L	T
1960	6	8		3	4		3	4	
1961	2	12		1	6		1	6	
1962	1	13		1	6		0	7	
1963	10	4		6	1		4	3	
1964	5	7	2	5	2		0	5	2
1965	8	5	1	5	2		3	3	1
1966	8	5	1	3	3	1	5	2	
1967	13	1		7	0		6	1	
1968	12	2		6	1		6	1	
1969	12	1	1	7	0		5	1	1
1970	8	4	2	6	1		2	3	2
1971	8	4	2	5	1	1	3	3	1
1972	10	3	1	5	1	1	5	2	
1973	9	4	1	5	2		4	2	1
1974	12	2		6	1		6	1	
1975	11	3		6	1		5	2	
1976	13	1		7	0		6	1	
1977	11	3		6	1		5	2	
1978	9	7		4	4		5	3	
1979	9	7		6	2		3	5	
1980	11	5		6	2		5	3	
1981	7	9		4	4		3	5	
1982	8	1		4	0		4	1	
1983	12	4		6	2		6	2	
1984	11	5		6	2		5	3	
1985	12	4		7	1		5	3	
1986	8	8		3	5		5	3	
1987	5	10		3	5		2	5	
1988	7	9		3	5		4	4	
1989	8	8		7	1		1	7	
1990	12	4		6	2		6	2	
1991	9	7		5	3		4	4	
1992	7	9		5	3		2	6	
1993	10	6		5	3		5	3	
1994	9	7		4	4		5	3	
1995	8	8		4	4		4	4	
1996	7	9		4	4		3	5	
1997	4	12		2	6		2	6	
1998	8	8		4	4		4	4	
1999	8	8		5	3		3	5	
2000	12	4		7	1		5	3	
2001	10	6		5	3		5	3	
2002	11	5		6	2		5	3	
2003	4	12		4	4		0	8	
2004	5	11		3	5		2	6	
2005	4	12		2	6		2	6	
2006	2	14		2	6		0	8	
2007	4	12		2	6		2	6	
2008	5	11		4	4		1	7	
2009	5	11		2	6		3	5	
	410	335	11	230	145	3	180	190	8

*includes Los Angeles Raiders (1982-1994).

PITTSBURGH STEELERS*

Season	All Games W	L	T	Home Games W	L	T	Road Games W	L	T
1933	3	6	2	2	3		1	3	2
1934	2	10		1	5		1	5	
1935	4	8		2	5		2	3	
1936	6	6		4	1		2	5	
1937	4	7		2	4		2	3	
1938	2	9		0	5		2	4	
1939	1	9	1	1	4		0	5	1
1940	2	7	2	1	2	2	1	5	
1941	1	9	1	1	4		0	5	1
1942	7	4		3	2		4	2	
1945	2	8		1	4		1	4	
1946	5	5	1	4	1		1	4	1
1947	8	4		5	1		3	3	
1948	4	8		4	2		0	6	
1949	6	5	1	3	2	1	3	3	
1950	6	6		2	4		4	2	
1951	4	7	1	1	4	1	3	3	
1952	5	7		2	4		3	3	
1953	6	6		3	3		3	3	
1954	5	7		4	2		1	5	
1955	4	8		3	2		1	6	
1956	5	7		3	3		2	4	
1957	6	6		4	2		2	4	
1958	7	4	1	5	1		2	3	1
1959	6	5	1	3	2	1	3	3	
1960	5	6	1	4	2		1	4	1
1961	6	8		4	3		2	5	
1962	9	5		4	3		5	2	
1963	7	4	3	5	0	2	2	4	1
1964	5	9		2	5		3	4	
1965	2	12		1	6		1	6	
1966	5	8	1	3	3	1	2	5	
1967	4	9	1	1	6		3	3	1
1968	2	11	1	1	6		1	5	1
1969	1	13		1	6		0	7	
1970	5	9		4	3		1	6	
1971	6	8		5	2		1	6	
1972	11	3		7	0		4	3	
1973	10	4		7	1		3	3	
1974	10	3	1	5	2		5	1	1
1975	12	2		6	1		6	1	
1976	10	4		6	1		4	3	
1977	9	5		6	1		3	4	
1978	14	2		7	1		7	1	
1979	12	4		8	0		4	4	
1980	9	7		6	2		3	5	
1981	8	8		5	3		3	5	
1982	6	3		4	0		2	3	
1983	10	6		4	4		6	2	
1984	9	7		6	2		3	5	
1985	7	9		5	3		2	6	
1986	6	10		4	4		2	6	
1987	8	7		4	3		4	4	
1988	5	11		4	4		1	7	
1989	9	7		4	4		5	3	
1990	9	7		6	2		3	5	
1991	7	9		5	3		2	6	
1992	11	5		7	1		4	4	
1993	9	7		6	2		3	5	
1994	12	4		7	1		5	3	
1995	11	5		6	2		5	3	
1996	10	6		7	1		3	5	
1997	11	5		7	1		4	4	
1998	7	9		5	3		2	6	
1999	6	10		2	6		4	4	
2000	9	7		4	4		5	3	
2001	13	3		7	1		6	2	

Season	All Games W	L	T	Home Games W	L	T	Road Games W	L	T
2002	10	5	1	5	2	1	5	3	
2003	6	10		4	4		2	6	
2004	15	1		8	0		7	1	
2005	11	5		5	3		6	2	
2006	8	8		5	3		3	5	
2007	10	6		7	1		3	5	
2008	12	4		6	2		6	2	
2009	9	7		6	2		3	5	
	529	495	20	312	197	9	217	298	11

*includes Pittsburgh Pirates (1933-39).

SAN DIEGO CHARGERS*

Season	All Games W	L	T	Home Games W	L	T	Road Games W	L	T
1960	10	4		5	2		5	2	
1961	12	2		6	1		6	1	
1962	4	10		3	4		1	6	
1963	11	3		6	1		5	2	
1964	8	5	1	4	3		4	2	1
1965	9	2	3	4	1	2	5	1	1
1966	7	6	1	5	2		2	4	1
1967	8	5	1	5	2	1	3	3	
1968	9	5		4	3		5	2	
1969	8	6		5	2		3	4	
1970	5	6	3	2	3	2	3	3	1
1971	6	8		6	1		0	7	
1972	4	9	1	2	5		2	4	1
1973	2	11	1	2	5		0	6	1
1974	5	9		3	4		2	5	
1975	2	12		1	6		1	6	
1976	6	8		3	4		3	4	
1977	7	7		3	4		4	3	
1978	9	7		5	3		4	4	
1979	12	4		7	1		5	3	
1980	11	5		6	2		5	3	
1981	10	6		5	3		5	3	
1982	6	3		3	1		3	2	
1983	6	10		4	4		2	6	
1984	7	9		4	4		3	5	
1985	8	8		6	2		2	6	
1986	4	12		2	6		2	6	
1987	8	7		4	3		4	4	
1988	6	10		3	5		3	5	
1989	6	10		4	4		2	6	
1990	6	10		3	5		3	5	
1991	4	12		3	5		1	7	
1992	11	5		6	2		5	3	
1993	8	8		4	4		4	4	
1994	11	5		5	3		6	2	
1995	9	7		5	3		4	4	
1996	8	8		5	3		3	5	
1997	4	12		2	6		2	6	
1998	5	11		4	4		1	7	
1999	8	8		4	4		4	4	
2000	1	15		1	7		0	8	
2001	5	11		4	4		1	7	
2002	8	8		5	3		3	5	
2003	4	12		2	6		2	6	
2004	12	4		7	1		5	3	
2005	9	7		4	4		5	3	
2006	14	2		8	0		6	2	
2007	11	5		7	1		4	4	
2008	8	8		5	3		3	5	
2009	13	3		6	2		7	1	
	375	370	11	212	161	5	163	209	6

*includes Los Angeles Chargers (1960).

TENNESSEE TITANS*

Season	All Games W	L	T	Home Games W	L	T	Road Games W	L	T
1960	10	4		6	1		4	3	
1961	10	3	1	6	1		4	2	1
1962	11	3		6	1		5	2	
1963	6	8		4	3		2	5	
1964	4	10		3	4		1	6	
1965	4	10		3	4		1	6	
1966	3	11		3	4		0	7	
1967	9	4	1	5	2		4	2	1
1968	7	7		3	4		4	3	
1969	6	6	2	4	2	1	2	4	1
1970	3	10	1	1	6		2	4	1
1971	4	9	1	3	3	1	1	6	
1972	1	13		1	6		0	7	
1973	1	13		0	7		1	6	
1974	7	7		3	4		4	3	
1975	10	4		5	2		5	2	
1976	5	9		3	4		2	5	
1977	8	6		5	2		3	4	
1978	10	6		5	3		5	3	
1979	11	5		6	2		5	3	
1980	11	5		6	2		5	3	
1981	7	9		5	3		2	6	
1982	1	8		1	4		0	4	
1983	2	14		2	6		0	8	
1984	3	13		2	6		1	7	
1985	5	11		4	4		1	7	
1986	5	11		4	4		1	7	
1987	9	6		5	2		4	4	
1988	10	6		7	1		3	5	
1989	9	7		6	2		3	5	
1990	9	7		6	2		3	5	
1991	11	5		7	1		4	4	
1992	10	6		5	3		5	3	
1993	12	4		7	1		5	3	
1994	2	14		2	6		0	8	
1995	7	9		3	5		4	4	
1996	8	8		2	6		6	2	
1997	8	8		6	2		2	6	
1998	8	8		3	5		5	3	
1999	13	3		8	0		5	3	
2000	13	3		7	1		6	2	
2001	7	9		3	5		4	4	
2002	11	5		6	2		5	3	
2003	12	4		7	1		5	3	
2004	5	11		2	6		3	5	
2005	4	12		3	5		1	7	
2006	8	8		4	4		4	4	
2007	10	6		5	3		5	3	
2008	13	3		7	1		6	2	
2009	8	8		5	3		3	5	
	371	379	6	215	161	2	156	218	4

*includes Houston (1960-1996) and Tennessee Oilers (1997-98).

NFC

ARIZONA CARDINALS*

Season	All Games W	L	T	Home Games W	L	T	Road Games W	L	T
1920	6	2	2	5	1	1	1	1	1
1921	3	3	2	3	3	1	0	0	1
1922	8	3		8	3		0	0	
1923	8	4		8	3		0	1	
1924	5	4	1	5	3	1	0	1	
1925	11	2	1	11	2		0	0	1
1926	5	6	1	3	3		2	3	1
1927	3	7	1	2	3	1	1	4	
1928	1	5		1	1		0	4	
1929	6	6	1	3	2		3	4	1

Season	All Games W	L	T	Home Games W	L	T	Road Games W	L	T
1930	5	6	2	3	2		2	4	2
1931	5	4		3	0		2	4	
1932	2	6	2	1	2	1	1	4	1
1933	1	9	1	0	4	1	1	5	
1934	5	6		2	2		3	4	
1935	6	4	2	2	2		4	2	2
1936	3	8	1	3	1	1	0	7	
1937	5	5	1	1	3		4	2	1
1938	2	9		1	4		1	5	
1939	1	10		0	4		1	6	
1940	2	7	2	2	1	1	0	6	1
1941	3	7	1	0	3	1	3	4	
1942	3	8		2	2		1	6	
1943	0	10		0	3		0	7	
1945	1	9		0	3		1	6	
1946	6	5		2	2		4	3	
1947	9	3		5	0		4	3	
1948	11	1		5	1		6	0	
1949	6	5	1	2	3	1	4	2	
1950	5	7		3	3		2	4	
1951	3	9		1	5		2	4	
1952	4	8		2	4		2	4	
1953	1	10	1	0	5	1	1	5	
1954	2	10		2	4		0	6	
1955	4	7	1	3	2	1	1	5	
1956	7	5		4	2		3	3	
1957	3	9		0	6		3	3	
1958	2	9	1	1	4	1	1	5	
1959	2	10		2	4		0	6	
1960	6	5	1	3	2	1	3	3	
1961	7	7		3	4		4	3	
1962	4	9	1	2	4	1	2	5	
1963	9	5		3	4		6	1	
1964	9	3	2	4	1	1	5	2	1
1965	5	9		2	5		3	4	
1966	8	5	1	5	1	1	3	4	
1967	6	7	1	3	3	1	3	4	
1968	9	4	1	4	2	1	5	2	
1969	4	9	1	3	4		1	5	1
1970	8	5	1	6	1		2	4	1
1971	4	9	1	1	5	1	3	4	
1972	4	9	1	2	5		2	4	1
1973	4	9	1	2	4	1	2	5	
1974	10	4		5	2		5	2	
1975	11	3		6	1		5	2	
1976	10	4		6	1		4	3	
1977	7	7		4	3		3	4	
1978	6	10		3	5		3	5	
1979	5	11		3	5		2	6	
1980	5	11		2	6		3	5	
1981	7	9		5	3		2	6	
1982	5	4		1	3		4	1	
1983	8	7	1	4	3	1	4	4	
1984	9	7		5	3		4	4	
1985	5	11		4	4		1	7	
1986	4	11	1	3	5		1	6	1
1987	7	8		4	3		3	5	
1988	7	9		4	4		3	5	
1989	5	11		2	6		3	5	
1990	5	11		3	5		2	6	
1991	4	12		2	6		2	6	
1992	4	12		3	5		1	7	
1993	7	9		4	4		3	5	
1994	8	8		5	3		3	5	
1995	4	12		3	5		1	7	
1996	7	9		5	3		2	6	
1997	4	12		3	5		1	7	
1998	9	7		5	3		4	4	
1999	6	10		4	4		2	6	
2000	3	13		3	5		0	8	
2001	7	9		3	5		4	4	
2002	5	11		3	5		2	6	
2003	4	12		4	4		0	8	
2004	6	10		5	3		1	7	
2005	5	11		3	5		2	6	
2006	5	11		3	5		2	6	
2007	8	8		6	2		2	6	
2008	9	7		6	2		3	5	
2009	10	6		4	4		6	2	
	483	670	39	282	290	22	201	380	17

**includes Chicago Cardinals (1920-1959), St. Louis Cardinals (1960-1987), and Phoenix Cardinals (1988-1993).*

ATLANTA FALCONS

Season	All Games W	L	T	Home Games W	L	T	Road Games W	L	T
1966	3	11		1	6		2	5	
1967	1	12	1	1	5	1	0	7	
1968	2	12		1	6		1	6	
1969	6	8		4	3		2	5	
1970	4	8	2	3	4		1	4	2
1971	7	6	1	4	3		3	3	1
1972	7	7		4	3		3	4	
1973	9	5		4	3		5	2	
1974	3	11		2	5		1	6	
1975	4	10		3	4		1	6	
1976	4	10		3	4		1	6	
1977	7	7		4	3		3	4	
1978	9	7		7	1		2	6	
1979	6	10		3	5		3	5	
1980	12	4		6	2		6	2	
1981	7	9		4	4		3	5	
1982	5	4		2	3		3	1	
1983	7	9		4	4		3	5	
1984	4	12		2	6		2	6	
1985	4	12		3	5		1	7	
1986	7	8	1	2	5	1	5	3	
1987	3	12		2	6		1	6	
1988	5	11		2	6		3	5	
1989	3	13		3	5		0	8	
1990	5	11		5	3		0	8	
1991	10	6		6	2		4	4	
1992	6	10		5	3		1	7	
1993	6	10		4	4		2	6	
1994	7	9		5	3		2	6	
1995	9	7		7	1		2	6	
1996	3	13		2	6		1	7	
1997	7	9		3	5		4	4	
1998	14	2		8	0		6	2	
1999	5	11		4	4		1	7	
2000	4	12		3	5		1	7	
2001	7	9		3	5		4	4	
2002	9	6	1	5	3		4	3	1
2003	5	11		2	6		3	5	
2004	11	5		7	1		4	4	
2005	8	8		4	4		4	4	
2006	7	9		3	5		4	4	
2007	4	12		3	5		1	7	
2008	11	5		7	1		4	4	
2009	9	7		6	2		3	5	
	276	390	6	166	169	2	110	221	4

CAROLINA PANTHERS

Season	All Games W	L	T	Home Games W	L	T	Road Games W	L	T
1995	7	9		5	3		2	6	

Season	All Games W	L	T	Home Games W	L	T	Road Games W	L	T
1996	12	4		8	0		4	4	
1997	7	9		2	6		5	3	
1998	4	12		2	6		2	6	
1999	8	8		5	3		3	5	
2000	7	9		5	3		2	6	
2001	1	15		0	8		1	7	
2002	7	9		4	4		3	5	
2003	11	5		6	2		5	3	
2004	7	9		3	5		4	4	
2005	11	5		5	3		6	2	
2006	8	8		4	4		4	4	
2007	7	9		2	6		5	3	
2008	12	4		8	0		4	4	
2009	8	8		5	3		3	5	
	117	123		64	56		53	67	

CHICAGO BEARS*

Season	All Games W	L	T	Home Games W	L	T	Road Games W	L	T
1920	10	1	2	6	0	1	4	1	1
1921	9	1	1	9	1	1	0	0	
1922	9	3		7	1		2	2	
1923	9	2	1	7	1	1	2	1	
1924	6	1	4	5	0	3	1	1	1
1925	9	5	3	7	1	1	2	4	2
1926	12	1	3	10	0	2	2	1	1
1927	9	3	2	7	1	1	2	2	1
1928	7	5	1	6	3		1	2	1
1929	4	9	2	1	5	2	3	4	
1930	9	4	1	5	2	1	4	2	
1931	8	5		6	3		2	2	
1932	7	1	6	6	1	1	1	0	5
1933	10	2	1	6	0		4	2	1
1934	13	0		5	0		8	0	
1935	6	4	2	1	2	2	5	2	
1936	9	3		3	1		6	2	
1937	9	1	1	4	1		5	0	1
1938	6	5		2	3		4	2	
1939	8	3		4	1		4	2	
1940	8	3		5	0		3	3	
1941	10	1		5	1		5	0	
1942	11	0		6	0		5	0	
1943	8	1	1	5	0		3	1	1
1944	6	3	1	4	0	1	2	3	
1945	3	7		2	3		1	4	
1946	8	2	1	4	1	1	4	1	
1947	8	4		4	2		4	2	
1948	10	2		5	1		5	1	
1949	9	3		5	1		4	2	
1950	9	3		6	0		3	3	
1951	7	5		3	3		4	2	
1952	5	7		3	3		2	4	
1953	3	8	1	1	4	1	2	4	
1954	8	4		4	2		4	2	
1955	8	4		5	1		3	3	
1956	9	2	1	6	0		3	2	1
1957	5	7		2	4		3	3	
1958	8	4		5	1		3	3	
1959	8	4		4	2		4	2	
1960	5	6	1	4	2		1	4	1
1961	8	6		5	2		3	4	
1962	9	5		4	3		5	2	
1963	11	1	2	6	0	1	5	1	1
1964	5	9		2	5		3	4	
1965	9	5		5	2		4	3	
1966	5	7	2	4	1	2	1	6	
1967	7	6	1	3	3	1	4	3	
1968	7	7		2	5		5	2	
1969	1	13		1	6		0	7	
1970	6	8		3	4		3	4	
1971	6	8		4	3		2	5	
1972	4	9	1	1	5	1	3	4	
1973	3	11		1	6		2	5	
1974	4	10		4	3		0	7	
1975	4	10		3	4		1	6	
1976	7	7		4	3		3	4	
1977	9	5		5	2		4	3	
1978	7	9		4	4		3	5	
1979	10	6		6	2		4	4	
1980	7	9		5	3		2	6	
1981	6	10		4	4		2	6	
1982	3	6		2	2		1	4	
1983	8	8		5	3		3	5	
1984	10	6		6	2		4	4	
1985	15	1		8	0		7	1	
1986	14	2		7	1		7	1	
1987	11	4		6	2		5	2	
1988	12	4		7	1		5	3	
1989	6	10		4	4		2	6	
1990	11	5		7	1		4	4	
1991	11	5		6	2		5	3	
1992	5	11		4	4		1	7	
1993	7	9		3	5		4	4	
1994	9	7		5	3		4	4	
1995	9	7		5	3		4	4	
1996	7	9		6	2		1	7	
1997	4	12		2	6		2	6	
1998	4	12		3	5		1	7	
1999	6	10		3	5		3	5	
2000	5	11		3	5		2	6	
2001	13	3		7	1		6	2	
2002	4	12		3	5		1	7	
2003	7	9		6	2		1	7	
2004	5	11		2	6		3	5	
2005	11	5		7	1		4	4	
2006	13	3		6	2		7	1	
2007	7	9		4	4		3	5	
2008	9	7		6	2		3	5	
2009	7	9		5	3		2	6	
	693	507	42	409	210	24	284	297	18

includes Decatur Staleys (1920) and Chicago Staleys (1921).

DALLAS COWBOYS

Season	All Games W	L	T	Home Games W	L	T	Road Games W	L	T
1960	0	11	1	0	6		0	5	1
1961	4	9	1	2	4	1	2	5	
1962	5	8	1	2	4	1	3	4	
1963	4	10		3	4		1	6	
1964	5	8	1	2	4	1	3	4	
1965	7	7		5	2		2	5	
1966	10	3	1	6	1		4	2	1
1967	9	5		5	2		4	3	
1968	12	2		5	2		7	0	
1969	11	2	1	6	0	1	5	2	
1970	10	4		6	1		4	3	
1971	11	3		6	1		5	2	
1972	10	4		5	2		5	2	
1973	10	4		6	1		4	3	
1974	8	6		5	2		3	4	
1975	10	4		5	2		5	2	
1976	11	3		6	1		5	2	
1977	12	2		6	1		6	1	
1978	12	4		7	1		5	3	
1979	11	5		6	2		5	3	
1980	12	4		8	0		4	4	

Season	All Games W	L	T	Home Games W	L	T	Road Games W	L	T
1981	12	4		8	0		4	4	
1982	6	3		3	2		3	1	
1983	12	4		6	2		6	2	
1984	9	7		5	3		4	4	
1985	10	6		7	1		3	5	
1986	7	9		3	5		4	4	
1987	7	8		3	4		4	4	
1988	3	13		1	7		2	6	
1989	1	15		0	8		1	7	
1990	7	9		5	3		2	6	
1991	11	5		6	2		5	3	
1992	13	3		7	1		6	2	
1993	12	4		6	2		6	2	
1994	12	4		6	2		6	2	
1995	12	4		6	2		6	2	
1996	10	6		6	2		4	4	
1997	6	10		5	3		1	7	
1998	10	6		6	2		4	4	
1999	8	8		7	1		1	7	
2000	5	11		3	5		2	6	
2001	5	11		4	4		1	7	
2002	5	11		4	4		1	7	
2003	10	6		6	2		4	4	
2004	6	10		4	4		2	6	
2005	9	7		5	3		4	4	
2006	9	7		4	4		5	3	
2007	13	3		6	2		7	1	
2008	9	7		6	2		3	5	
2009	11	5		6	2		5	3	
	434	314	6	246	127	4	188	187	2

DETROIT LIONS*

Season	All Games W	L	T	Home Games W	L	T	Road Games W	L	T
1930	5	6	3	5	1	2	0	5	1
1931	11	3		8	0		3	3	
1932	6	2	4	3	0	2	3	2	2
1933	6	5		4	1		2	4	
1934	10	3		6	2		4	1	
1935	7	3	2	5	0	1	2	3	1
1936	8	4		5	1		3	3	
1937	7	4		4	2		3	2	
1938	7	4		4	3		3	1	
1939	6	5		4	2		2	3	
1940	5	5	1	3	3		2	2	1
1941	4	6	1	3	2		1	4	1
1942	0	11		0	7		0	4	
1943	3	6	1	2	2	1	1	4	
1944	6	3	1	4	2		2	1	1
1945	7	3		4	1		3	2	
1946	1	10		1	5		0	5	
1947	3	9		2	4		1	5	
1948	2	10		2	4		0	6	
1949	4	8		2	4		2	4	
1950	6	6		4	2		2	4	
1951	7	4	1	3	3	1	4	1	
1952	9	3		6	1		3	2	
1953	10	2		5	1		5	1	
1954	9	2	1	5	0	1	4	2	
1955	3	9		3	4		0	5	
1956	9	3		5	1		4	2	
1957	8	4		5	1		3	3	
1958	4	7	1	2	4		2	3	1
1959	3	8	1	2	4		1	4	1
1960	7	5		5	1		2	4	
1961	8	5	1	2	5		6	0	1
1962	11	3		7	0		4	3	
1963	5	8	1	3	3	1	2	5	
1964	7	5	2	3	3	1	4	2	1
1965	6	7	1	2	4	1	4	3	
1966	4	9	1	3	4		1	5	1
1967	5	7	2	3	4		2	3	2
1968	4	8	2	1	4	2	3	4	
1969	9	4	1	5	2		4	2	1
1970	10	4		6	1		4	3	
1971	7	6	1	3	4		4	2	1
1972	8	5	1	5	2		3	3	1
1973	6	7	1	4	3		2	4	1
1974	7	7		5	2		2	5	
1975	7	7		4	3		3	4	
1976	6	8		5	2		1	6	
1977	6	8		5	2		1	6	
1978	7	9		5	3		2	6	
1979	2	14		2	6		0	8	
1980	9	7		6	2		3	5	
1981	8	8		7	1		1	7	
1982	4	5		2	3		2	2	
1983	9	7		6	2		3	5	
1984	4	11	1	2	5	1	2	6	
1985	7	9		6	2		1	7	
1986	5	11		1	7		4	4	
1987	4	11		1	6		3	5	
1988	4	12		2	6		2	6	
1989	7	9		4	4		3	5	
1990	6	10		3	5		3	5	
1991	12	4		8	0		4	4	
1992	5	11		3	5		2	6	
1993	10	6		5	3		5	3	
1994	9	7		6	2		3	5	
1995	10	6		7	1		3	5	
1996	5	11		4	4		1	7	
1997	9	7		6	2		3	5	
1998	5	11		4	4		1	7	
1999	8	8		6	2		2	6	
2000	9	7		4	4		5	3	
2001	2	14		2	6		0	8	
2002	3	13		3	5		0	8	
2003	5	11		5	3		0	8	
2004	6	10		3	5		3	5	
2005	5	11		3	5		2	6	
2006	3	13		2	6		1	7	
2007	7	9		5	3		2	6	
2008	0	16		0	8		0	8	
2009	2	14		2	6		0	8	
	490	583	32	307	242	14	183	341	18

**includes Portsmouth Spartans (1930-33).*

GREEN BAY PACKERS

Season	All Games W	L	T	Home Games W	L	T	Road Games W	L	T
1921	3	2	1	2	1		1	1	1
1922	4	3	3	4	1	1	0	2	2
1923	7	2	1	4	2	1	3	0	
1924	7	4		5	0		2	4	
1925	8	5		6	0		2	5	
1926	7	3	3	4	1	2	3	2	1
1927	7	2	1	6	1		1	1	1
1928	6	4	3	2	2	2	4	2	1
1929	12	0	1	5	0		7	0	1
1930	10	3	1	6	0		4	3	1
1931	12	2		8	0		4	2	
1932	10	3	1	5	0	1	5	3	
1933	5	7	1	3	2	1	2	5	
1934	7	6		4	2		3	4	
1935	8	4		5	2		3	2	
1936	10	1	1	5	1		5	0	1

Season	All Games W	L	T	Home Games W	L	T	Road Games W	L	T
1937	7	4		3	2		4	2	
1938	8	3		4	2		4	1	
1939	9	2		4	1		5	1	
1940	6	4	1	4	2		2	2	1
1941	10	1		4	1		6	0	
1942	8	2	1	4	1		4	1	1
1943	7	2	1	2	1	1	5	1	
1944	8	2		5	0		3	2	
1945	6	4		4	1		2	3	
1946	6	5		2	3		4	2	
1947	6	5	1	4	2		2	3	1
1948	3	9		2	4		1	5	
1949	2	10		1	5		1	5	
1950	3	9		3	3		0	6	
1951	3	9		2	4		1	5	
1952	6	6		3	3		3	3	
1953	2	9	1	1	5		1	4	1
1954	4	8		2	4		2	4	
1955	6	6		5	1		1	5	
1956	4	8		2	4		2	4	
1957	3	9		1	5		2	4	
1958	1	10	1	1	4	1	0	6	
1959	7	5		4	2		3	3	
1960	8	4		4	2		4	2	
1961	11	3		6	1		5	2	
1962	13	1		7	0		6	1	
1963	11	2	1	6	1		5	1	1
1964	8	5	1	4	3		4	2	1
1965	10	3	1	6	1		4	2	1
1966	12	2		6	1		6	1	
1967	9	4	1	4	2	1	5	2	
1968	6	7	1	2	5		4	2	1
1969	8	6		5	2		3	4	
1970	6	8		4	3		2	5	
1971	4	8	2	3	3	1	1	5	1
1972	10	4		4	3		6	1	
1973	5	7	2	3	2	2	2	5	
1974	6	8		4	3		2	5	
1975	4	10		3	4		1	6	
1976	5	9		4	3		1	6	
1977	4	10		2	5		2	5	
1978	8	7	1	5	2	1	3	5	
1979	5	11		4	4		1	7	
1980	5	10	1	4	4		1	6	1
1981	8	8		4	4		4	4	
1982	5	3	1	3	1		2	2	1
1983	8	8		5	3		3	5	
1984	8	8		5	3		3	5	
1985	8	8		5	3		3	5	
1986	4	12		1	7		3	5	
1987	5	9	1	2	5	1	3	4	
1988	4	12		2	6		2	6	
1989	10	6		6	2		4	4	
1990	6	10		3	5		3	5	
1991	4	12		2	6		2	6	
1992	9	7		6	2		3	5	
1993	9	7		6	2		3	5	
1994	9	7		7	1		2	6	
1995	11	5		7	1		4	4	
1996	13	3		8	0		5	3	
1997	13	3		8	0		5	3	
1998	11	5		7	1		4	4	
1999	8	8		5	3		3	5	
2000	9	7		6	2		3	5	
2001	12	4		7	1		5	3	
2002	12	4		8	0		4	4	
2003	10	6		5	3		5	3	
2004	10	6		4	4		6	2	
2005	4	12		3	5		1	7	
2006	8	8		3	5		5	3	
2007	13	3		7	1		6	2	
2008	6	10		4	4		2	6	
2009	11	5		6	2		5	3	
	654	518	36	376	211	16	278	307	20

MINNESOTA VIKINGS

Season	All Games W	L	T	Home Games W	L	T	Road Games W	L	T
1961	3	11		3	4		0	7	
1962	2	11	1	1	5	1	1	6	
1963	5	8	1	3	4		2	4	1
1964	8	5	1	4	3		4	2	1
1965	7	7		2	5		5	2	
1966	4	9	1	2	5		2	4	1
1967	3	8	3	1	4	2	2	4	1
1968	8	6		4	3		4	3	
1969	12	2		7	0		5	2	
1970	12	2		7	0		5	2	
1971	11	3		5	2		6	1	
1972	7	7		3	4		4	3	
1973	12	2		7	0		5	2	
1974	10	4		4	3		6	1	
1975	12	2		7	0		5	2	
1976	11	2	1	6	0	1	5	2	
1977	9	5		5	2		4	3	
1978	8	7	1	5	3		3	4	1
1979	7	9		5	3		2	6	
1980	9	7		5	3		4	4	
1981	7	9		5	3		2	6	
1982	5	4		4	1		1	3	
1983	8	8		3	5		5	3	
1984	3	13		2	6		1	7	
1985	7	9		4	4		3	5	
1986	9	7		5	3		4	4	
1987	8	7		5	3		3	4	
1988	11	5		7	1		4	4	
1989	10	6		8	0		2	6	
1990	6	10		4	4		2	6	
1991	8	8		4	4		4	4	
1992	11	5		5	3		6	2	
1993	9	7		4	4		5	3	
1994	10	6		6	2		4	4	
1995	8	8		6	2		2	6	
1996	9	7		5	3		4	4	
1997	9	7		5	3		4	4	
1998	15	1		8	0		7	1	
1999	10	6		6	2		4	4	
2000	11	5		7	1		4	4	
2001	5	11		5	3		0	8	
2002	6	10		4	4		2	6	
2003	9	7		6	2		3	5	
2004	8	8		5	3		3	5	
2005	9	7		6	2		3	5	
2006	6	10		3	5		3	5	
2007	8	8		5	3		3	5	
2008	10	6		6	2		4	4	
2009	12	4		8	0		4	4	
	407	326	9	237	131	4	170	195	5

NEW ORLEANS SAINTS

Season	All Games W	L	T	Home Games W	L	T	Road Games W	L	T
1967	3	11		2	5		1	6	
1968	4	9	1	3	4		1	5	1
1969	5	9		3	4		2	5	
1970	2	11	1	2	5		0	6	1

Season	All Games W	L	T	Home Games W	L	T	Road Games W	L	T
1971	4	8	2	2	4	1	2	4	1
1972	2	11	1	2	5		0	6	1
1973	5	9		5	2		0	7	
1974	5	9		4	3		1	6	
1975	2	12		2	5		0	7	
1976	4	10		2	5		2	5	
1977	3	11		2	5		1	6	
1978	7	9		3	5		4	4	
1979	8	8		3	5		5	3	
1980	1	15		0	8		1	7	
1981	4	12		2	6		2	6	
1982	4	5		2	3		2	2	
1983	8	8		5	3		3	5	
1984	7	9		3	5		4	4	
1985	5	11		3	5		2	6	
1986	7	9		4	4		3	5	
1987	12	3		6	1		6	2	
1988	10	6		5	3		5	3	
1989	9	7		5	3		4	4	
1990	8	8		5	3		3	5	
1991	11	5		6	2		5	3	
1992	12	4		6	2		6	2	
1993	8	8		4	4		4	4	
1994	7	9		3	5		4	4	
1995	7	9		4	4		3	5	
1996	3	13		2	6		1	7	
1997	6	10		3	5		3	5	
1998	6	10		4	4		2	6	
1999	3	13		3	5		0	8	
2000	10	6		3	5		7	1	
2001	7	9		3	5		4	4	
2002	9	7		4	4		5	3	
2003	8	8		5	3		3	5	
2004	8	8		3	5		5	3	
2005	3	13		1	7		2	6	
2006	10	6		4	4		6	2	
2007	7	9		3	5		4	4	
2008	8	8		6	2		2	6	
2009	13	3		6	2		7	1	
	275	378	5	148	180	1	127	198	4

NEW YORK GIANTS

Season	All Games W	L	T	Home Games W	L	T	Road Games W	L	T
1925	8	4		7	2		1	2	
1926	8	4	1	5	2	1	3	2	
1927	11	1	1	7	1		4	0	1
1928	4	7	2	1	2	2	3	5	
1929	13	1	1	7	1		6	0	1
1930	13	4		6	2		7	2	
1931	7	6	1	4	2	1	3	4	
1932	4	6	2	3	2	1	1	4	1
1933	11	3		7	0		4	3	
1934	8	5		5	1		3	4	
1935	9	3		4	2		5	1	
1936	5	6	1	3	3	1	2	3	
1937	6	3	2	4	2	1	2	1	1
1938	8	2	1	6	1		2	1	1
1939	9	1	1	6	0		3	1	1
1940	6	4	1	4	3		2	1	1
1941	8	3		5	2		3	1	
1942	5	5	1	3	2	1	2	3	
1943	6	3	1	4	2		2	1	1
1944	8	1	1	5	1		3	0	1
1945	3	6	1	2	4		1	2	1
1946	7	3	1	5	1	1	2	2	
1947	2	8	2	2	3	1	0	5	1
1948	4	8		2	4		2	4	
1949	6	6		2	4		4	2	
1950	10	2		5	1		5	1	
1951	9	2	1	5	1		4	1	1
1952	7	5		2	4		5	1	
1953	3	9		2	4		1	5	
1954	7	5		4	2		3	3	
1955	6	5	1	4	1	1	2	4	
1956	8	3	1	4	1	1	4	2	
1957	7	5		3	3		4	2	
1958	9	3		5	1		4	2	
1959	10	2		5	1		5	1	
1960	6	4	2	1	3	2	5	1	
1961	10	3	1	4	2	1	6	1	
1962	12	2		6	1		6	1	
1963	11	3		5	2		6	1	
1964	2	10	2	2	5		0	5	2
1965	7	7		3	4		4	3	
1966	1	12	1	1	6		0	6	1
1967	7	7		5	2		2	5	
1968	7	7		3	4		4	3	
1969	6	8		5	2		1	6	
1970	9	5		5	2		4	3	
1971	4	10		1	6		3	4	
1972	8	6		4	3		4	3	
1973	2	11	1	2	4	1	0	7	
1974	2	12		0	7		2	5	
1975	5	9		2	5		3	4	
1976	3	11		3	4		0	7	
1977	5	9		3	4		2	5	
1978	6	10		5	3		1	7	
1979	6	10		4	4		2	6	
1980	4	12		2	6		2	6	
1981	9	7		4	4		5	3	
1982	4	5		2	3		2	2	
1983	3	12	1	1	7		2	5	1
1984	9	7		6	2		3	5	
1985	10	6		6	2		4	4	
1986	14	2		8	0		6	2	
1987	6	9		5	3		1	6	
1988	10	6		5	3		5	3	
1989	12	4		7	1		5	3	
1990	13	3		7	1		6	2	
1991	8	8		5	3		3	5	
1992	6	10		4	4		2	6	
1993	11	5		6	2		5	3	
1994	9	7		4	4		5	3	
1995	5	11		3	5		2	6	
1996	6	10		3	5		3	5	
1997	10	5	1	6	2		4	3	1
1998	8	8		5	3		3	5	
1999	7	9		4	4		3	5	
2000	12	4		5	3		7	1	
2001	7	9		5	3		2	6	
2002	10	6		5	3		5	3	
2003	4	12		1	7		3	5	
2004	6	10		3	5		3	5	
2005	11	5		7	1		4	4	
2006	8	8		3	5		5	3	
2007	10	6		3	5		7	1	
2008	12	4		7	1		5	3	
2009	8	8		4	4		4	4	
	626	518	33	348	242	16	278	276	17

PHILADELPHIA EAGLES

Season	All Games W	L	T	Home Games W	L	T	Road Games W	L	T
1933	3	5	1	2	3	1	1	2	
1934	4	7		2	4		2	3	

Season	All Games W	L	T	Home Games W	L	T	Road Games W	L	T
1935	2	9		0	5		2	4	
1936	1	11		1	6		0	5	
1937	2	8	1	0	5	1	2	3	
1938	5	6		2	3		3	3	
1939	1	9	1	1	3	1	0	6	
1940	1	10		1	4		0	6	
1941	2	8	1	1	4	1	1	4	
1942	2	9		0	5		2	4	
1944	7	1	2	3	1	2	4	0	
1945	7	3		6	0		1	3	
1946	6	5		3	2		3	3	
1947	8	4		6	1		2	3	
1948	9	2	1	6	0		3	2	1
1949	11	1		6	0		5	1	
1950	6	6		2	4		4	2	
1951	4	8		1	5		3	3	
1952	7	5		4	2		3	3	
1953	7	4	1	5	0	1	2	4	
1954	7	4	1	5	1		2	3	1
1955	4	7	1	4	2		0	5	1
1956	3	8	1	2	3	1	1	5	
1957	4	8		3	3		1	5	
1958	2	9	1	2	4		0	5	1
1959	7	5		5	1		2	4	
1960	10	2		5	1		5	1	
1961	10	4		5	2		5	2	
1962	3	10	1	2	5		1	5	1
1963	2	10	2	1	5	1	1	5	1
1964	6	8		3	4		3	4	
1965	5	9		2	5		3	4	
1966	9	5		5	2		4	3	
1967	6	7	1	5	2		1	5	1
1968	2	12		1	6		1	6	
1969	4	9	1	2	5		2	4	1
1970	3	10	1	3	3	1	0	7	
1971	6	7	1	3	4		3	3	1
1972	2	11	1	0	6	1	2	5	
1973	5	8	1	4	3		1	5	1
1974	7	7		5	2		2	5	
1975	4	10		2	5		2	5	
1976	4	10		2	5		2	5	
1977	5	9		4	3		1	6	
1978	9	7		5	3		4	4	
1979	11	5		5	3		6	2	
1980	12	4		7	1		5	3	
1981	10	6		6	2		4	4	
1982	3	6		1	4		2	2	
1983	5	11		1	7		4	4	
1984	6	9	1	5	3		1	6	1
1985	7	9		4	4		3	5	
1986	5	10	1	2	5	1	3	5	
1987	7	8		4	4		3	4	
1988	10	6		5	3		5	3	
1989	11	5		6	2		5	3	
1990	10	6		6	2		4	4	
1991	10	6		4	4		6	2	
1992	11	5		8	0		3	5	
1993	8	8		3	5		5	3	
1994	7	9		5	3		2	6	
1995	10	6		6	2		4	4	
1996	10	6		5	3		5	3	
1997	6	9	1	6	2		0	7	1
1998	3	13		3	5		0	8	
1999	5	11		4	4		1	7	
2000	11	5		5	3		6	2	
2001	11	5		4	4		7	1	
2002	12	4		7	1		5	3	
2003	12	4		5	3		7	1	
2004	13	3		7	1		6	2	
2005	6	10		4	4		2	6	
2006	10	6		5	3		5	3	
2007	8	8		3	5		5	3	
2008	9	6	1	6	2		3	4	1
2009	11	5		6	2		5	3	
	494	531	25	280	238	12	214	293	13

ST. LOUIS RAMS*

Season	All Games W	L	T	Home Games W	L	T	Road Games W	L	T
1937	1	10		0	5		1	5	
1938	4	7		2	2		2	5	
1939	5	5	1	3	2	1	2	3	
1940	4	6	1	3	1	1	1	5	
1941	2	9		1	4		1	5	
1942	5	6		3	2		2	4	
1944	4	6		1	2		3	4	
1945	9	1		4	0		5	1	
1946	6	4	1	3	2		3	2	1
1947	6	6		3	3		3	3	
1948	6	5	1	3	2	1	3	3	
1949	8	2	2	5	1		3	1	2
1950	9	3		5	1		4	2	
1951	8	4		5	2		3	2	
1952	9	3		5	1		4	2	
1953	8	3	1	5	1		3	2	1
1954	6	5	1	3	2	1	3	3	
1955	8	3	1	5	1		3	2	1
1956	4	8		4	2		0	6	
1957	6	6		5	1		1	5	
1958	8	4		4	2		4	2	
1959	2	10		0	6		2	4	
1960	4	7	1	2	3	1	2	4	
1961	4	10		4	3		0	7	
1962	1	12	1	0	7		1	5	1
1963	5	9		3	4		2	5	
1964	5	7	2	3	2	2	2	5	
1965	4	10		3	4		1	6	
1966	8	6		5	2		3	4	
1967	11	1	2	5	1	1	6	0	1
1968	10	3	1	5	2		5	1	1
1969	11	3		5	2		6	1	
1970	9	4	1	3	3	1	6	1	
1971	8	5	1	4	2	1	4	3	
1972	6	7	1	4	3		2	4	1
1973	12	2		7	0		5	2	
1974	10	4		6	1		4	3	
1975	12	2		6	1		6	1	
1976	10	3	1	5	2		5	1	1
1977	10	4		7	0		3	4	
1978	12	4		6	2		6	2	
1979	9	7		4	4		5	3	
1980	11	5		6	2		5	3	
1981	6	10		4	4		2	6	
1982	2	7		1	4		1	3	
1983	9	7		5	3		4	4	
1984	10	6		5	3		5	3	
1985	11	5		6	2		5	3	
1986	10	6		6	2		4	4	
1987	6	9		3	4		3	5	
1988	10	6		4	4		6	2	
1989	11	5		6	2		5	3	
1990	5	11		2	6		3	5	
1991	3	13		2	6		1	7	
1992	6	10		4	4		2	6	
1993	5	11		3	5		2	6	
1994	4	12		3	5		1	7	

Season	All Games W	L	T	Home Games W	L	T	Road Games W	L	T
1995	7	9		4	4		3	5	
1996	6	10		4	4		2	6	
1997	5	11		2	6		3	5	
1998	4	12		2	6		2	6	
1999	13	3		8	0		5	3	
2000	10	6		5	3		5	3	
2001	14	2		6	2		8	0	
2002	7	9		6	2		1	7	
2003	12	4		8	0		4	4	
2004	8	8		6	2		2	6	
2005	6	10		3	5		3	5	
2006	8	8		4	4		4	4	
2007	3	13		1	7		2	6	
2008	2	14		1	7		1	7	
2009	1	15		0	8		1	7	
	504	483	20	279	209	10	225	274	10

includes Cleveland Rams (1937-1942, 1944-45) and Los Angeles Rams (1946-1994).

SAN FRANCISCO 49ERS

Season	All Games W	L	T	Home Games W	L	T	Road Games W	L	T
1950	3	9		3	3		0	6	
1951	7	4	1	5	1		2	3	1
1952	7	5		3	3		4	2	
1953	9	3		5	1		4	2	
1954	7	4	1	4	2		3	2	1
1955	4	8		2	4		2	4	
1956	5	6	1	3	3		2	3	1
1957	8	4		5	1		3	3	
1958	6	6		4	2		2	4	
1959	7	5		4	2		3	3	
1960	7	5		3	3		4	2	
1961	7	6	1	5	1	1	2	5	
1962	6	8		1	6		5	2	
1963	2	12		2	5		0	7	
1964	4	10		3	4		1	6	
1965	7	6	1	4	2	1	3	4	
1966	6	6	2	4	2	1	2	4	1
1967	7	7		3	4		4	3	
1968	7	6	1	3	3	1	4	3	
1969	4	8	2	3	3	1	1	5	1
1970	10	3	1	5	1	1	5	2	
1971	9	5		4	3		5	2	
1972	8	5	1	4	2	1	4	3	
1973	5	9		3	4		2	5	
1974	6	8		3	4		3	4	
1975	5	9		2	5		3	4	
1976	8	6		4	3		4	3	
1977	5	9		3	4		2	5	
1978	2	14		2	6		0	8	
1979	2	14		2	6		0	8	
1980	6	10		4	4		2	6	
1981	13	3		7	1		6	2	
1982	3	6		0	5		3	1	
1983	10	6		4	4		6	2	
1984	15	1		7	1		8	0	
1985	10	6		5	3		5	3	
1986	10	5	1	6	2		4	3	1
1987	13	2		6	1		7	1	
1988	10	6		4	4		6	2	
1989	14	2		6	2		8	0	
1990	14	2		6	2		8	0	
1991	10	6		7	1		3	5	
1992	14	2		7	1		7	1	
1993	10	6		6	2		4	4	
1994	13	3		7	1		6	2	
1995	11	5		6	2		5	3	
1996	12	4		6	2		6	2	
1997	13	3		8	0		5	3	
1998	12	4		8	0		4	4	
1999	4	12		3	5		1	7	
2000	6	10		4	4		2	6	
2001	12	4		7	1		5	3	
2002	10	6		5	3		5	3	
2003	7	9		6	2		1	7	
2004	2	14		1	7		1	7	
2005	4	12		3	5		1	7	
2006	7	9		4	4		3	5	
2007	5	11		3	5		2	6	
2008	7	9		4	4		3	5	
2009	8	8		6	2		2	6	
	465	396	13	257	173	7	208	223	6

SEATTLE SEAHAWKS

Season	All Games W	L	T	Home Games W	L	T	Road Games W	L	T
1976	2	12		1	6		1	6	
1977	5	9		3	4		2	5	
1978	9	7		5	3		4	4	
1979	9	7		5	3		4	4	
1980	4	12		0	8		4	4	
1981	6	10		5	3		1	7	
1982	4	5		3	2		1	3	
1983	9	7		5	3		4	4	
1984	12	4		7	1		5	3	
1985	8	8		5	3		3	5	
1986	10	6		7	1		3	5	
1987	9	6		6	2		3	4	
1988	9	7		5	3		4	4	
1989	7	9		3	5		4	4	
1990	9	7		5	3		4	4	
1991	7	9		5	3		2	6	
1992	2	14		1	7		1	7	
1993	6	10		4	4		2	6	
1994	6	10		3	5		3	5	
1995	8	8		5	3		3	5	
1996	7	9		4	4		3	5	
1997	8	8		4	4		4	4	
1998	8	8		6	2		2	6	
1999	9	7		5	3		4	4	
2000	6	10		3	5		3	5	
2001	9	7		6	2		3	5	
2002	7	9		3	5		4	4	
2003	10	6		8	0		2	6	
2004	9	7		5	3		4	4	
2005	13	3		8	0		5	3	
2006	9	7		5	3		4	4	
2007	10	6		7	1		3	5	
2008	4	12		2	6		2	6	
2009	5	11		4	4		1	7	
	255	277		153	114		102	163	

TAMPA BAY BUCCANEERS

Season	All Games W	L	T	Home Games W	L	T	Road Games W	L	T
1976	0	14		0	7		0	7	
1977	2	12		1	6		1	6	
1978	5	11		3	5		2	6	
1979	10	6		5	3		5	3	
1980	5	10	1	2	5	1	3	5	
1981	9	7		6	2		3	5	
1982	5	4		4	1		1	3	
1983	2	14		1	7		1	7	
1984	6	10		6	2		0	8	
1985	2	14		2	6		0	8	

Season	All Games W	L	T	Home Games W	L	T	Road Games W	L	T
1986	2	14		1	7		1	7	
1987	4	11		2	5		2	6	
1988	5	11		3	5		2	6	
1989	5	11		2	6		3	5	
1990	6	10		4	4		2	6	
1991	3	13		3	5		0	8	
1992	5	11		3	5		2	6	
1993	5	11		3	5		2	6	
1994	6	10		4	4		2	6	
1995	7	9		5	3		2	6	
1996	6	10		5	3		1	7	
1997	10	6		5	3		5	3	
1998	8	8		6	2		2	6	
1999	11	5		7	1		4	4	
2000	10	6		6	2		4	4	
2001	9	7		5	3		4	4	
2002	12	4		6	2		6	2	
2003	7	9		3	5		4	4	
2004	5	11		4	4		1	7	
2005	11	5		6	2		5	3	
2006	4	12		3	5		1	7	
2007	9	7		6	2		3	5	
2008	9	7		6	2		3	5	
2009	3	13		1	7		2	6	
	208	323	1	129	136	1	79	187	

WASHINGTON REDSKINS*

Season	All Games W	L	T	Home Games W	L	T	Road Games W	L	T
1932	4	4	2	2	3	1	2	1	1
1933	5	5	2	4	2		1	3	2
1934	6	6		4	3		2	3	
1935	2	8	1	2	5		0	3	1
1936	7	5		4	3		3	2	
1937	8	3		4	2		4	1	
1938	6	3	2	3	1	1	3	2	1
1939	8	2	1	5	0	1	3	2	
1940	9	2		6	0		3	2	
1941	6	5		4	2		2	3	
1942	10	1		5	1		5	0	
1943	6	3	1	4	2		2	1	1
1944	6	3	1	4	2		2	1	1
1945	8	2		6	0		2	2	
1946	5	5	1	3	2	1	2	3	
1947	4	8		4	2		0	6	
1948	7	5		4	2		3	3	
1949	4	7	1	3	3		1	4	1
1950	3	9		1	5		2	4	
1951	5	7		2	4		3	3	
1952	4	8		1	5		3	3	
1953	6	5	1	3	3		3	2	1
1954	3	9		3	3		0	6	
1955	8	4		3	3		5	1	
1956	6	6		4	2		2	4	
1957	5	6	1	2	3	1	3	3	
1958	4	7	1	3	2	1	1	5	
1959	3	9		2	4		1	5	
1960	1	9	2	1	4	1	0	5	1
1961	1	12	1	1	6		0	6	1
1962	5	7	2	3	4		2	3	2
1963	3	11		1	6		2	5	
1964	6	8		4	3		2	5	
1965	6	8		3	4		3	4	
1966	7	7		4	3		3	4	
1967	5	6	3	2	4	1	3	2	2
1968	5	9		3	4		2	5	
1969	7	5	2	4	2	1	3	3	1
1970	6	8		4	3		2	5	
1971	9	4	1	4	2	1	5	2	
1972	11	3		6	1		5	2	
1973	10	4		7	0		3	4	
1974	10	4		6	1		4	3	
1975	8	6		5	2		3	4	
1976	10	4		5	2		5	2	
1977	9	5		5	2		4	3	
1978	8	8		5	3		3	5	
1979	10	6		6	2		4	4	
1980	6	10		4	4		2	6	
1981	8	8		5	3		3	5	
1982	8	1		3	1		5	0	
1983	14	2		7	1		7	1	
1984	11	5		7	1		4	4	
1985	10	6		5	3		5	3	
1986	12	4		7	1		5	3	
1987	11	4		6	1		5	3	
1988	7	9		4	4		3	5	
1989	10	6		4	4		6	2	
1990	10	6		7	1		3	5	
1991	14	2		7	1		7	1	
1992	9	7		6	2		3	5	
1993	4	12		3	5		1	7	
1994	3	13		0	8		3	5	
1995	6	10		4	4		2	6	
1996	9	7		5	3		4	4	
1997	8	7	1	5	2	1	3	5	
1998	6	10		4	4		2	6	
1999	10	6		6	2		4	4	
2000	8	8		4	4		4	4	
2001	8	8		4	4		4	4	
2002	7	9		5	3		2	6	
2003	5	11		3	5		2	6	
2004	6	10		3	5		3	5	
2005	10	6		6	2		4	4	
2006	5	11		3	5		2	6	
2007	9	7		5	3		4	4	
2008	8	8		4	4		4	4	
2009	4	12		3	5		1	7	
	541	506	27	313	222	11	228	284	16

**includes Boston Braves (1932) and Boston Redskins (1933-36).*

History

PRO FOOTBALL HALL OF FAME

The Professional Football Hall of Fame is located in Canton, Ohio, site of the organizational meeting on September 17, 1920, from which the National Football League evolved. The NFL recognized Canton as the Hall of Fame site on April 27, 1961. Canton area individuals, foundations, and companies donated almost $400,000 in cash and services to provide funds for the construction of the original two-building complex, which was dedicated on September 7, 1963. Since that time, the Hall added three buildings with major expansion projects in 1971, 1978, and 1995. The Hall's largest-ever expansion, a $9.2 million project, was completed in early fall 1995. With the fifth building, the Hall's size is now 82,307 square feet, more than four times its original size.

The Hall has renovated four of its six major exhibition galleries in recent years. The Lamar Hunt Super Bowl Gallery, featuring the Super Bowl Theater, opened in summer 2009. The Moments, Memories & Mementos Gallery and Pro Football Today Gallery were opened—one in 2008 preceded by a brand new Hall of Fame Gallery, home to enshrinees bronze busts, in 2003. Other highlights of the Hall include an extensive archive and information center and a large museum store. Throughout the years, the Pro Football Hall of Fame has become an extremely popular tourist attraction. Since its opening, the Hall has had more than eight million visitors.

New members of the Pro Football Hall of Fame are elected annually by a 44-member National Board of Selectors, made up of media representatives from every league city, eleven at-large representatives, and a representative of the Pro Football Writers of America. Between four and seven new members are elected each year. An affirmative vote of approximately 80 percent is needed for election.

Any fan may nominate any eligible player or contributor simply by writing to the Pro Football Hall of Fame. Players and coaches must have last played or coached at least five years before he is eligible. Contributors (administrators, owners, *et al.*) may be elected while they are still active.

The charter class of 17 enshrinees was elected in 1963 and the honor roll now stands at 260 (156 living as of May 1, 2010) with the election of a seven-man class in 2010. That class consists of Russ Grimm, Rickey Jackson, Dick LeBeau, Floyd Little, John Randle, Jerry Rice, and Emmitt Smith.

ROSTER OF MEMBERS

HERB ADDERLEY
Cornerback. 6-0, 205. Born in Philadelphia, Pennsylvania, June 8, 1939. Michigan State. Inducted in 1980. 1961-69 Green Bay Packers, 1970-72 Dallas Cowboys. **Highlights:** 48 interceptions, 7 touchdowns. Played in four Super Bowls, five Pro Bowls.

TROY AIKMAN
Quarterback. 6-4, 219. Born in West Covina, California, November 21, 1966. Oklahoma, UCLA. Inducted in 2006. 1989-2000 Dallas Cowboys. **Highlights:** His 90 wins in 1990s make him winningest quarterback of any decade. Led Cowboys to three Super Bowl wins. Passed for 32,942 yards, 165 touchdowns. Named to six Pro Bowls.

GEORGE ALLEN
Coach. Born in Detroit, Michigan, April 29, 1918. Died December 31, 1990. Alma College, Eastern Michigan, Marquette, Michigan. Inducted in 2002. 1966-1970 Los Angeles Rams, 1971-77 Washington Redskins. **Highlights:** 118-54-5 overall record. Never suffered a losing season, and ranked tenth in coaching victories at time of retirement.

MARCUS ALLEN
Running back. 6-2, 210. Born in San Diego, California, March 26, 1960. Southern California. Inducted in 2003. 1982-1992 Los Angeles Raiders, 1993-1997 Kansas City Chiefs. **Highlights:** First player in NFL history to tally 10,000 rushing yards and 5,000 receiving yards. MVP, Super Bowl XVIII.

LANCE ALWORTH
Wide receiver. 6-0, 184. Born in Houston, Texas, August 3, 1940. Arkansas. Inducted in 1978. 1962-1970 San Diego Chargers, 1971-72 Dallas Cowboys. **Highlights:** 542 receptions for 10,266 yards, 85 touchdowns. All-AFL seven times, seven All-Star games.

DOUG ATKINS
Defensive end. 6-8, 275. Born in Humboldt, Tennessee, May 8, 1930. Tennessee. Inducted in 1982. 1953-54 Cleveland Browns, 1955-1966 Chicago Bears, 1967-69 New Orleans Saints. **Highlights:** Eight Pro Bowls, All-NFL four times. Played for 17 years, 205 games.

MORRIS (RED) BADGRO
End. 6-0, 190. Born in Orillia, Washington, December 1, 1902. Died July 13, 1998. Southern California. Inducted in 1981. 1927-28 New York Yankees, 1930-35 New York Giants, 1936 Brooklyn Dodgers. **Highlights:** First- or second-team All-NFL four times. Scored first touchdown in NFL Championship Game series.

LEM BARNEY
Cornerback. 6-0, 190. Born in Gulfport, Mississippi, September 8, 1945. Jackson State. Inducted in 1992. 1967-1977 Detroit Lions. **Highlights:** 56 interceptions for 1,077 yards, 11 touchdowns (7 defensive, 4 special teams). Seven Pro Bowls, All-NFL/NFC four times.

CLIFF BATTLES
Halfback. 6-1, 195. Born in Akron, Ohio, May 1, 1910. Died April 28, 1981. West Virginia Wesleyan. Inducted in 1968. 1932 Boston Braves, 1933-36 Boston Redskins, 1937 Washington Redskins. **Highlights:** NFL rushing champion 1932, 1937. First to gain more than 200 yards in a game, 1933.

SAMMY BAUGH
Quarterback. 6-2, 180. Born in Temple, Texas, March 17, 1914. Died December 17, 2008. Texas Christian. Inducted in 1963. 1937-1952 Washington Redskins. **Highlights:** Charter enshrinee. Six-time NFL passing leader. NFL passing, punting, interception champ, 1943.

CHUCK BEDNARIK
Center-linebacker. 6-3, 230. Born in Bethlehem, Pennsylvania, May 1, 1925. Pennsylvania. Inducted in 1967. 1949-1962 Philadelphia Eagles. **Highlights:** Eight Pro Bowls. Missed three games in 14 years. Named NFL all-time center, 1969.

BERT BELL
Team owner. Commissioner. Born in Philadelphia, Pennsylvania, February 25, 1895. Died October 11, 1959. Pennsylvania. Inducted in 1963. 1933-1940 Philadelphia Eagles, 1941-42 Pittsburgh Steelers, 1943 Phil-Pitt, 1944 Card-Pitt, 1945-46 Pittsburgh Steelers. Commissioner, 1946-1959. **Highlights:** Charter enshrinee. Built NFL image as commissioner, 1946-1959. Set up long-term television policies.

BOBBY BELL
Linebacker. 6-4, 225. Born in Shelby, North Carolina, June 17, 1940. Minnesota. Inducted in 1983. 1963-1974 Kansas City Chiefs. **Highlights:** 26 interceptions. All-AFL/AFC eight times. Nine career touchdowns, 1 on onside kick return.

RAYMOND BERRY
End. 6-2, 187. Born in Corpus Christi, Texas, February 27, 1933. Southern Methodist. Inducted in 1973. 1955-1967 Baltimore Colts. **Highlights:** 631 receptions for 9,275 yards, 68 touchdowns. Set NFL title game mark with 12 catches for 178 yards, 1958.

ELVIN BETHEA
Defensive end. 6-2, 260. Born in Trenton, New Jersey, March 1, 1946. North Carolina A&T. Inducted in 2003. 1968-1983 Houston Oilers. **Highlights:** Led team in sacks six times. Elected to eight Pro Bowls. Played for 16 years, 210 games.

CHARLES W. BIDWILL SR.
Team owner. Born in Chicago, Illinois, September 16, 1895. Died April 19, 1947. Loyola of Chicago. Inducted in 1967. 1933-1943 Chicago Cardinals, 1944 Card-Pitt, 1945-47 Chicago Cardinals. **Highlights:** Guiding light for NFL during depression years. Built famous "Dream Backfield."

FRED BILETNIKOFF
Wide receiver. 6-1, 190. Born in Erie, Pennsylvania, February 23, 1943. Florida State. Inducted in 1988. 1965-1978 Oakland Raiders. **Highlights:** 589 receptions for 8,974 yards, 76 touchdowns. 40 catches 10 straight years. MVP, Super Bowl XI.

GEORGE BLANDA
Quarterback-kicker. 6-2, 215. Born in Youngwood, Pennsylvania, September 17, 1927. Kentucky. Inducted in 1981. 1949-1958 Chicago Bears, 1950 Baltimore Colts, 1960-66 Houston Oilers, 1967-1975 Oakland Raiders. **Highlights:** 2,002 career points. 26-season, 340-game career longest in NFL history at retirement.

MEL BLOUNT
Cornerback. 6-3, 205. Born in Vidalia, Georgia, April 10, 1948. Southern University. Inducted in 1989. 1970-1983 Pittsburgh Steelers. **Highlights:** 57 interceptions for 736 yards. NFL defensive MVP, 1975. Played in five Pro Bowls.

TERRY BRADSHAW
Quarterback. 6-3, 210. Born in Shreveport, Louisiana, September 2, 1948. Louisiana Tech. Inducted in 1989. 1970-1983 Pittsburgh Steelers. **Highlights:** 27,989 yards passing, 212 touchdowns. MVP in Super Bowls XIII, XIV.

BOB (BOOMER) BROWN
Tackle. 6-4, 280. Born in Cleveland, Ohio, December 8, 1941. Nebraska. Inducted in 2004. 1964-68 Philadelphia Eagles, 1969-1970 Los Angeles Rams, 1971-73 Oakland Raiders. **Highlights:** All-NFL seven of 10 seasons, six Pro Bowls. Named to 1960s All-Decade Team.

JIM BROWN
Fullback. 6-2, 228. Born in St. Simons, Georgia, February 17, 1936. Syracuse. Inducted in 1971. 1957-1965 Cleveland Browns. **Highlights:** 12,312 yards rushing, 756 points. Led NFL rushers eight years. Nine consecutive Pro Bowls.

PAUL BROWN
Coach. Born in Norwalk, Ohio, September 7, 1908. Died August 5, 1991. Miami (Ohio). Inducted in 1967. 1946-49 Cleveland Browns (AAFC), 1950-1962 Cleveland Browns. **Highlights:** Built Cleveland dynasty with 167-53-8 record, four AAFC titles, three NFL crowns. Returned to coaching with Cincinnati Bengals after induction, 1968-1975.

ROOSEVELT BROWN
Tackle. 6-3, 255. Born in Charlottesville, Virginia, October 20, 1932. Died June 9, 2004. Morgan State. Inducted in 1975. 1953-1965 New York Giants. **Highlights:** All-NFL eight consecutive years, nine Pro Bowls. NFL's lineman of year, 1956.

WILLIE BROWN
Cornerback. 6-1, 210. Born in Yazoo City, Mississippi, December 2, 1940. Grambling. Inducted in 1984. 1963-66 Denver Broncos, 1967-1978 Oakland Raiders. **Highlights:** 54 interceptions for 472 yards. Scored on 75-yard interception in Super Bowl XI.

BUCK BUCHANAN
Defensive tackle. 6-7, 274. Born in Gainesville, Alabama, September 10, 1940. Died July 16, 1992. Grambling. Inducted in 1990. 1963-1975 Kansas City Chiefs. **Highlights:** Led Chiefs defensive efforts in Super Bowl I, IV. Did not miss a game in 13 years.

NICK BUONICONTI
Linebacker. 5-11, 220. Born in Springfield, Massachusetts, December 15, 1940. Notre Dame. Inducted in 2001. 1962-68 Boston Patriots, 1969-1974, 1976 Miami Dolphins. **Highlights:** All-AFL/AFC eight times. Named to AFL's All-Time Team.

DICK BUTKUS
Linebacker. 6-3, 245. Born in Chicago, Illinois, December 9, 1942. Illinois. Inducted in 1979. 1965-1973 Chicago Bears. **Highlights:** All-NFL six years, eight consecutive Pro Bowls. 27 fumble recoveries.

EARL CAMPBELL
Running back. 5-11, 233. Born in Tyler, Texas, March 29, 1955. Texas. Inducted in 1991. 1978-1984 Houston Oilers, 1984-85 New Orleans Saints. **Highlights:** 9,407 yards rushing, 74 touchdowns. 1,934 yards rushing in 1980, including four games with at least 200 yards.

TONY CANADEO
Halfback. 5-11, 195. Born in Chicago, Illinois, May 5, 1919. Died November 29, 2003. Gonzaga. Inducted in 1974. 1941-44, 1946-1952 Green Bay Packers. **Highlights:** Two-way player. Third player to rush for 1,000 yards in single season, 1949.

JOE CARR
NFL president. Born in Columbus, Ohio, October 23, 1879. Died May 20, 1939. Did not attend college. Inducted in 1963. President, 1921-1939 National Football League. **Highlights:** Charter enshrinee. NFL co-organizer, 1920. Introduced standard player contract.

HARRY CARSON
Linebacker. 6-2, 237. Born in Florence, South Carolina, November 26, 1953. South Carolina State. Inducted in 2006. 1976-1988 New York Giants. **Highlights:** 11 career interceptions. Named to nine Pro Bowls. Named first- or second-team All-NFL six times.

DAVE CASPER
Tight end. 6-4, 240. Born in Bemidji, Minnesota, February 2, 1952. Notre Dame. Inducted in 2002. 1974-1980 Oakland Raiders, 1980-83 Houston Oilers, 1983 Minnesota Vikings, 1984 Los Angeles Raiders. **Highlights:** 378 receptions for 5,216 yards, 52 touchdowns. Five consecutive Pro Bowls.

GUY CHAMBERLIN
End. Coach. 6-2, 196. Born in Blue Springs, Nebraska, January 16, 1894. Died April 4, 1967. Nebraska. Inducted in 1965. 1919 Canton Bulldogs, 1920-21 Decatur Staleys/Chicago Staleys, player-coach 1922-23 Canton Bulldogs, 1924 Cleveland Bulldogs, 1925-26 Frankford Yellowjackets, 1927-28 Chicago Cardinals. **Highlights:** Player-coach of four NFL championship teams. Six-year coaching record of 58-16-7.

JACK CHRISTIANSEN
Safety. 6-1, 185. Born in Sublette, Kansas, December 20, 1928. Died June 29, 1986. Colorado State. Inducted in 1970. 1951-58 Detroit Lions. **Highlights:** 46 interceptions. NFL interception leader, 1953, 1957. Eight punt returns for touchdowns.

EARL (DUTCH) CLARK
Quarterback. 6-0, 185. Born in Fowler, Colorado, October 11, 1906. Died August 5, 1978. Colorado College. Inducted in 1963. 1931-32 Portsmouth Spartans, 1934-38 Detroit Lions. **Highlights:** Charter enshrinee. NFL scoring champion three years. Led Lions to 1935 NFL title.

GEORGE CONNOR
Tackle-linebacker. 6-3, 240. Born in Chicago, Illinois, January 21, 1925. Died March 31, 2003. Holy Cross, Notre Dame. Inducted in 1975. 1948-1955 Chicago Bears. **Highlights:** All-NFL at three positions—T, DT, LB. All-NFL five years. Played in first four Pro Bowls.

JIMMY CONZELMAN
Quarterback. Coach. Team owner. 6-0, 180. Born in St. Louis, Missouri, March 6, 1898. Died July 31, 1970. Washington of St. Louis. Inducted in 1964. 1920 Decatur Staleys, 1921-22 Rock Island Independents, 1922-24 Milwaukee Badgers; owner-coach 1925-26 Detroit Panthers; player-coach 1927-29, coach 1930 Providence Steam Roller; coach 1940-42, 1946-48 Chicago Cardinals. **Highlights:** Player-coach of four NFL teams in 1920's. Coached Cardinals to 1947 NFL crown.

LOU CREEKMUR
Tackle-guard. 6-4, 255. Born in Hopelawn, New Jersey. January 22, 1927. Died July 5, 2009. William & Mary. Inducted in 1996. 1950-59 Detroit Lions. **Highlights:** All-NFL six times, twice at guard and four times at tackle. Selected to eight Pro Bowls and played on three NFL championship teams.

LARRY CSONKA
Running back. 6-3, 235. Born in Stow, Ohio, December 25, 1946. Syracuse. Inducted in 1987. 1968-1974, 1979 Miami Dolphins, 1976-78 New York Giants. **Highlights:** 8,081 yards rushing, 68 touchdowns. MVP Super Bowl VIII. Only 21 fumbles in 1,891 carries and 106 receptions.

AL DAVIS
Team, League Administrator. Born in Brockton, Massachusetts, July 4, 1929. Wittenberg, Syracuse. Inducted in 1992. 1963-1981, 1995-present Oakland Raiders, 1982-1994 Los Angeles Raiders, 1966 American Football League. **Highlights:** Only person to serve in pros as personnel assistant, scout, assistant coach, head coach, general manager, commissioner, team owner/CEO.

WILLIE DAVIS
Defensive end. 6-3, 245. Born in Lisbon, Louisiana, July 24, 1934. Grambling. Inducted in 1981. 1958-59 Cleveland Browns, 1960-69 Green Bay Packers. **Highlights:** All-NFL five seasons, five Pro Bowls. Did not miss game in 12-year career.

LEN DAWSON
Quarterback. 6-0, 190. Born in Alliance, Ohio, June 20, 1935. Purdue. Inducted in 1987. 1957-59 Pittsburgh Steelers, 1960-61 Cleveland Browns, 1962 Dallas Texans, 1963-1975 Kansas City Chiefs. **Highlights:** 28,711 yards passing, 239 touchdowns. Four AFL passing crowns. MVP, Super Bowl IV.

FRED DEAN
Defensive end. 6-3, 230. Born in Arcadia, Louisiana, February 24, 1952. Louisiana Tech. Inducted in 2008. 1975-1981 San Diego Chargers, 1981-85 San Francisco 49ers. **Highlights:** Had career-high 17.5 sacks in 1983. Played on two Super Bowl championship teams with 49ers (Super Bowls XVI, XIX).

JOE DeLAMIELLEURE
Guard. 6-3, 254. Born in Detroit, Michigan, March 16, 1951. Michigan State. Inducted in 2003. 1973-1979, 1985 Buffalo Bills, 1980-1984 Cleveland Browns. **Highlights:** Selected All-Pro and All-AFC six consecutive times, 1975-1980. Named to six Pro Bowls. Played 13 years, 185 games.

ERIC DICKERSON
Running back. 6-3, 220. Born in Sealy, Texas, September 2, 1960. Southern Methodist. Inducted in 1999. 1983-87 Los Angeles Rams, 1987-1991 Indianapolis Colts, 1992 Los Angeles Raiders, 1993 Atlanta Falcons. **Highlights:** Rushed for 13,259 career yards, including an NFL record 2,105 yards in 1984. All-Pro five times, six Pro Bowls.

DAN DIERDORF
Tackle. 6-3, 290. Born in Canton, Ohio, June 29, 1949. Michigan. Inducted in 1996. 1971-1983 St. Louis Cardinals. **Highlights:** All-Pro five times, played in six Pro Bowls, named NFL's best blocker three times.

MIKE DITKA
Tight end. 6-3, 225. Born in Carnegie, Pennsylvania, October 18, 1939. Pittsburgh. Inducted in 1988. 1961-66 Chicago Bears, 1967-68 Philadelphia Eagles, 1969-1972 Dallas Cowboys. **Highlights:** 427 receptions for 5,812 yards, 43 touchdowns. First tight end selected to Hall of Fame. Five consecutive Pro Bowls.

ART DONOVAN
Defensive tackle. 6-3, 265. Born in Bronx, New York, June 5, 1925. Boston College. Inducted in 1968. 1950 Baltimore Colts, 1951 New York Yanks, 1952 Dallas Texans, 1953-1961 Baltimore Colts. **Highlights:** Five Pro Bowls. Vital part of Baltimore's climb to powerhouse status in 1950s.

TONY DORSETT
Running back. 5-11, 184. Born in Rochester, Pennsylvania, April 7, 1954. Pittsburgh. Inducted in 1994. 1977-1987 Dallas Cowboys, 1988 Denver Broncos. **Highlights:** 12,739 yards rushing, 398 receptions, 91 touchdowns. Ran record 99 yards for touchdown vs. Minnesota, January, 1983.

JOHN (PADDY) DRISCOLL
Quarterback. 5-11, 160. Born in Evanston, Illinois, January 11, 1896. Died June 29, 1968. Northwestern. Inducted in 1965. 1919 Hammond Pros, 1920 Decatur Staleys, 1920-25 Chicago Cardinals, 1926-29 Chicago Bears. **Highlights:** All-NFL seven times. Dropkicked record 4 field goals in one game, 1925.

BILL DUDLEY
Halfback. 5-10, 182. Born in Bluefield, Virginia, December 24, 1921. Died February 4, 2010. Virginia. Inducted in 1966. 1942, 1945-46 Pittsburgh Steelers, 1947-49 Detroit Lions, 1950-51, 1953 Washington Redskins. **Highlights:** Won NFL rushing, interception, punt return titles, 1946. All-NFL 1942, 1946, and 1947.

ALBERT GLEN (TURK) EDWARDS
Tackle. 6-2, 260. Born in Mold, Washington, September 28, 1907. Died January 12, 1973. Washington State. Inducted in 1969. 1932 Boston Braves, 1933-36 Boston Redskins, 1937-1940 Washington Redskins. **Highlights:** All-NFL 1932-34, 1936, 1937. Steamrolling blocker, smothering tackler.

CARL ELLER
Defensive end. 6-6, 247. Born in Winston-Salem, North Carolina, January 25, 1942. Minnesota. Inducted in 2004. 1964-1978 Minnesota Vikings, 1979 Seattle Seahawks. **Highlights:** Fixture on Vikings' "Purple People Eaters" defensive line, All-Pro five time, elected to six Pro Bowls.

JOHN ELWAY
Quarterback. 6-3, 215. Born in Port Angeles, Washington, June 28, 1960. Stanford. Inducted in 2004. 1983-1998 Denver Broncos. **Highlights:** Passed for 51,475 yards, 300 touchdowns. Named to nine Pro Bowls. NFL MVP, 1987; MVP, Super Bowl XXXIII.

WEEB EWBANK
Coach. Born in Richmond, Indiana, May 6, 1907. Died November 17, 1998. Miami (Ohio). Inducted in 1978. 1954-1962 Baltimore Colts, 1963-1973 New York Jets. **Highlights:** Only coach to win championships in both NFL, AFL. Led both Colts (1958 and 1959) and Jets (1968) to championships.

TOM FEARS
End. 6-2, 215. Born in Guadalajara, Mexico, December 3, 1922. Died January 4, 2000. Santa Clara, UCLA. Inducted in 1970. 1948-1956 Los Angeles Rams. **Highlights:** 400 receptions for 5,397 yards, 38 touchdowns. Led NFL receivers first three seasons. Had then-record 18 receptions in single game.

JIM FINKS
Administrator. Born in St. Louis, Missouri, August 31, 1927. Died May 8, 1994. Tulsa. Inducted 1995. 1964-1973 Minnesota Vikings, 1974-1982 Chicago Bears, 1986-1993 New Orleans Saints. **Highlights:** Developed Vikings, Bears, Saints—all teams with losing records—into winners.

RAY FLAHERTY
Coach. Born in Spokane, Washington, September 1, 1903. Died July 19, 1994. Gonzaga. Inducted in 1976. 1936-1942 Boston/Washington Redskins, 1946-48 New York Yankees (AAFC), 1949 Chicago Hornets (AAFC). **Highlights:** 82-41-5 coaching record. Introduced screen pass in 1937 title game and platoon system.

LEN FORD
Defensive end. 6-4, 260. Born in Washington, D.C., February 18, 1926. Died March 14, 1972. Morgan State, Michigan. Inducted in 1976. 1948-49 Los Angeles Dons (AAFC), 1950-57 Cleveland Browns, 1958 Green Bay Packers. **Highlights:** All-NFL five times, four Pro Bowls. Recovered 20 opponents' fumbles.

DAN FORTMANN
Guard. 6-0, 210. Born in Pearl River, New York, April 11, 1916. Died May 23, 1995. Colgate. Inducted in 1965. 1936-1943 Chicago Bears. **Highlights:** At 20, became youngest starter in NFL. First- or second-team All-NFL every season of career.

DAN FOUTS
Quarterback. 6-3, 210. Born in San Francisco, California, June 10, 1951. Oregon. Inducted in 1993. 1973-1987 San Diego Chargers. **Highlights:** 43,040 passing yards, 254 touchdowns. Six Pro Bowls, NFL MVP, 1982.

BENNY FRIEDMAN
Quarterback. 5-10, 183. Born in Cleveland, Ohio, March 18, 1905. Died November 23, 1982. Michigan. Inducted in 2005. 1927 Cleveland Bulldogs, 1928 Detroit Wolverines, 1929-1931 New York Giants, 1932-34 Brooklyn Dodgers. **Highlights:** NFL's first great passer. Set league mark for touchdowns with 20 in 1929. Led NFL in touchdown passes each of his first four seasons.

FRANK GATSKI
Center. 6-3, 240. Born in Farmington, West Virginia, March 18, 1919. Marshall, Auburn. Died November 22, 2005. Inducted in 1985. 1946-49 Cleveland Browns (AAFC), 1950-56 Cleveland Browns, 1957 Detroit Lions. **Highlights:** Never missed game in high school, college, or pro football. Played 11 championship games, winning eight.

BILL GEORGE
Linebacker. 6-2, 230. Born in Waynesburg, Pennsylvania, October 27, 1929. Died September 30, 1982. Wake Forest. Inducted in 1974. 1952-1965 Chicago Bears, 1966 Los Angeles Rams. **Highlights:** All-NFL eight years, eight consecutive Pro Bowls. 14 years of service, longest of any Bears player.

JOE GIBBS
Coach. Born in Mocksville, North Carolina, November 25, 1940. Cerritos (Calif.) J.C., San Diego State. Inducted in 1996. 1981-1992 Washington Redskins. **Highlights:** 124-60-0 record in regular season, 16-5 in postseason, including four Super Bowl appearances—winning three. Won 10 or more games eight times.

FRANK GIFFORD
Halfback. 6-1, 195. Born in Santa Monica, California, August 16, 1930. Southern California. Inducted in 1977. 1952-1960, 1962-64 New York Giants. **Highlights:** Starred on both offense and defense. Named to eight Pro Bowls, 1956 NFL player of the year.

SID GILLMAN
Coach. Born in Minneapolis, Minnesota, October 26, 1911. Died January 3, 2003. Ohio State. Inducted in 1983. 1955-59 Los Angeles Rams, 1960-69, 1971 Los Angeles/San Diego Chargers, 1973-74 Houston Oilers. **Highlights:** 123-104-7 coaching record. First to win division titles in both NFL, AFL.

OTTO GRAHAM
Quarterback. 6-1, 195. Born in Waukegan, Illinois, December 6, 1921. Died December 17, 2003. Northwestern. Inducted in 1965. 1946-49 Cleveland Browns (AAFC), 1950-55 Cleveland Browns. **Highlights:** 23,584 passing yards, 174 touchdowns. Guided Browns to 10 division or league crowns in 10 years.

HAROLD (RED) GRANGE
Halfback. 6-0, 185. Born in Forksville, Pennsylvania, June 13, 1903. Died January 28, 1991. Illinois. Inducted in 1963. 1925, 1929-1934 Chicago Bears, 1926 New York Yankees (AFL), 1927 New York Yankees. **Highlights:** Charter enshrinee. Nicknamed "Galloping Ghost." Name produced first huge pro football crowds.

BUD GRANT
Coach. Born in Superior, Wisconsin, May 20, 1927. Minnesota. Inducted in 1994. 1967-1983, 1985 Minnesota Vikings. **Highlights:** 168-108-5 coaching record. Led Vikings to 11 division championships, four Super Bowls.

DARRELL GREEN
Cornerback. 5-8, 176. Born in Houston, Texas, February 15, 1960. Texas A&I. Inducted in 2008. 1983-2002 Washington Redskins. **Highlights:** 54 interceptions, 621 yards, 6 TDs. Played 20 seasons. Recorded interception in NFL record 19 straight seasons. Selected to seven Pro Bowls.

JOE GREENE
Defensive tackle. 6-4, 260. Born in Temple, Texas, September 24, 1946. North Texas State. Inducted in 1987. 1969-1981 Pittsburgh Steelers. **Highlights:** NFL defensive player of the year, 1972, 1974. Four-time Super Bowl champion, 10 Pro Bowls.

FORREST GREGG
Tackle. 6-4, 250. Born in Birthright, Texas, October 18, 1933. Southern Methodist. Inducted in 1977. 1956, 1958-1970 Green Bay Packers, 1971 Dallas Cowboys. **Highlights:** Played 188 consecutive games. Nine Pro Bowls. Played on six NFL championship teams, three Super Bowl winners.

BOB GRIESE
Quarterback. 6-1, 190. Born in Evansville, Indiana, February 3, 1945. Purdue. Inducted in 1990. 1967-1980 Miami Dolphins. **Highlights:** 25,092 passing yards, 192 touchdowns. Led Miami to three AFC titles, Super Bowl VII, VIII wins.

RUSS GRIMM
Guard. 6-3, 273. Born in Scottdale, Pennsylvania, May 2, 1959. Pittsburgh. Inducted in 2010. 1981-1991 Washington Redskins. **Highlights:** Member of famed "Hogs" offensive line, All-NFL four times, four Pro Bowls. Member of All-Decade Team 1980s.

LOU GROZA
Tackle-kicker. 6-3, 250. Born in Martins Ferry, Ohio, January 25, 1924. Died November 29, 2000. Ohio State. Inducted in 1974. 1946-49 Cleveland Browns (AAFC), 1950-59, 1961-67 Cleveland Browns. **Highlights:** 1,608 points in 21 years. Nine Pro Bowls, All-NFL six years. NFL player of the year, 1954.

JOE GUYON
Halfback. 6-1, 180. Born on White Earth Indian Reservation, Minnesota, November 26, 1892. Died November 27, 1971. Carlisle, Georgia Tech. Inducted in 1966. 1919-1920 Canton Bulldogs, 1921 Cleveland Indians, 1922-23 Oorang Indians, 1924 Rock Island Independents, 1924-25 Kansas City Cowboys, 1927 New York Giants. **Highlights:** Touchdown pass gave Giants victory over Bears to win 1927 championship.

GEORGE HALAS
End. Coach. Team owner. Born in Chicago, Illinois, February 2, 1895. Died October 31, 1983. Illinois. Inducted in 1963. Player-coach 1920 Decatur Staleys, 1921 Chicago Staleys, 1922-29 Chicago Bears; coach 1933-1942, 1946-1955, 1958-1967 Chicago Bears. **Highlights:** Charter enshrinee. 324 coaching wins. Only person associated with NFL throughout first 50 years. Coached Bears 40 seasons, won six NFL titles.

JACK HAM
Linebacker. 6-1, 225. Born in Johnstown, Pennsylvania, December 23, 1948. Penn State. Inducted in 1988. 1971-1982 Pittsburgh Steelers. **Highlights:** Won four Super Bowls, 21 opponents' fumbles recovered, 32 interceptions. Eight consecutive Pro Bowls.

DAN HAMPTON
Defensive tackle-defensive end. 6-5, 264. Born in Oklahoma City, Oklahoma, September 19, 1957. Arkansas. Inducted in 2002. 1979-1990 Chicago Bears. **Highlights:** A versatile player, he earned all-pro honors at both defensive tackle and defensive end. Named to four Pro Bowls.

JOHN HANNAH
Guard. 6-3, 265. Born in Canton, Georgia, April 4, 1951. Alabama. Inducted in 1991. 1973-1985 New England Patriots. **Highlights:** Renowned as premier guard of era. All-Pro 10 years, nine Pro Bowls.

FRANCO HARRIS
Running back. 6-2, 225. Born in Fort Dix, New Jersey, March 7, 1950. Penn State. Inducted in 1990. 1972-1983 Pittsburgh Steelers, 1984 Seattle Seahawks. **Highlights:** 12,120 rushing yards, 100 total touchdowns. 1,556 rushing yards in 19 postseason games. MVP in Super Bowl IX.

BOB HAYES
Wide receiver. 5-11, 185. Born in Jacksonville, Florida, December 20, 1942. Died September 18, 2002. Florida A&M. Inducted in 2009. 1965-1974 Dallas Cowboys, 1975 San Francisco 49ers. **Highlights:** Olympic gold medalist with world class speed led Cowboys in receiving three times. 371 receptions for 7,414 yards, 71 TDs. Three Pro Bowls.

MIKE HAYNES
Cornerback. 6-2, 195. Born in Denison, Texas, July 1, 1953. Arizona State. Inducted in 1997. 1976-1982 New England Patriots, 1983-89 Los Angeles Raiders. **Highlights:** Defensive rookie of the year. Selected to nine Pro Bowls and intercepted 46 passes, plus one pick in Super Bowl XVIII.

ED HEALEY
Tackle. 6-3, 220. Born in Indian Orchard, Massachusetts, December 28, 1894. Died December 9, 1978. Dartmouth. Inducted in 1964. 1920-22 Rock Island Independents, 1922-27 Chicago Bears. **Highlights:** Two-way star. Perennial all-pro with Bears.

MEL HEIN
Center. 6-2, 225. Born in Redding, California, August 22, 1909. Died January 31, 1992. Washington State. Inducted in 1963. 1931-1945 New York Giants. **Highlights:** Charter enshrinee. 60-minute regular for 15 years. All-NFL eight consecutive years.

TED HENDRICKS
Linebacker. 6-7, 235. Born in Guatemala City, Guatemala, November 1, 1947. Miami. Inducted in 1990. 1969-1973 Baltimore Colts, 1974 Green Bay Packers, 1975-1981 Oakland Raiders, 1982-83 Los Angeles Raiders. **Highlights:** 25 blocked field goals, extra points, and punts, 26 interceptions. Played in 215 consecutive games.

WILBUR (PETE) HENRY
Tackle. 6-0, 250. Born in Mansfield, Ohio, October 31, 1897. Died February 7, 1952. Washington & Jefferson. Inducted in 1963. 1920-23, 1925-26 Canton Bulldogs, 1927 New York Giants, 1927-28 Pottsville Maroons. **Highlights:** Charter enshrinee. Largest player of his time at 250 pounds. Bulwark of Canton's championship lines.

ARNIE HERBER
Quarterback. 6-0, 200. Born in Green Bay, Wisconsin, April 2, 1910. Died October 14, 1969. Wisconsin, Regis College. Inducted in 1966. 1930-1940 Green Bay Packers, 1944-45 New York Giants. **Highlights:** NFL passing leader 1932, 1934, 1936. Came out of retirement to lead 1944 Giants to NFL Eastern crown.

BILL HEWITT
End. 5-11, 191. Born in Bay City, Michigan, October 8, 1909. Died January 14, 1947. Michigan. Inducted in 1971. 1932-36 Chicago Bears, 1937-39 Philadelphia Eagles, 1943 Phil-Pitt. **Highlights:** First to be named all-NFL with two teams—1933, 1934, 1936 Bears; 1937 Eagles.

GENE HICKERSON
Guard. 6-3, 248. Born in Trenton, Tennessee, February 15, 1935. Died October 20, 2008. Mississippi. Inducted in 2007. 1958-1973 Cleveland Browns. **Highlights:** Blocked for three Hall of Fame running backs. Voted to six straight Pro Bowls. Named to NFL's All-Decade Team of the 1960s.

CLARKE HINKLE
Fullback. 5-11, 201. Born in Toronto, Ohio, April 10, 1909. Died November 9, 1988. Bucknell. Inducted in 1964. 1932-1941 Green Bay Packers. **Highlights:** 3,860 yards rushing, 379 points. Fullback on offense, linebacker on defense.

ELROY (CRAZYLEGS) HIRSCH
Halfback-end. 6-2, 190. Born in Wausau, Wisconsin, June 17, 1923. Died January 28, 2004. Wisconsin, Michigan. Inducted in 1968. 1946-48 Chicago Rockets (AAFC), 1949-1957 Los Angeles Rams. **Highlights:** 387 receptions for 7,029 yards, 60 touchdowns. Key part of Rams' revolutionary "three end" offense, 1949.

PAUL HORNUNG
Halfback. 6-2, 220. Born in Louisville, Kentucky, December 23, 1935. Notre Dame. Inducted in 1986. 1957-1962, 1964-66 Green Bay Packers. **Highlights:** 760 points. Led NFL scorers three years, including record 176 points, 1960. Record 19 points scored in 1961 NFL title game.

KEN HOUSTON
Safety. 6-3, 198. Born in Lufkin, Texas, November 12, 1944. Prairie View A&M. Inducted in 1986. 1967-1972 Houston Oilers, 1973-1980 Washington Redskins. **Highlights:** 49 interceptions, 898 yards, 9 touchdowns. NFL's premier strong safety of 1970s. 12 Pro Bowls.

ROBERT (CAL) HUBBARD
Tackle. 6-5, 250. Born in Keytesville, Missouri, October 31, 1900. Died October 17, 1977. Centenary, Geneva. Inducted in 1963. 1927-28, 1936 New York Giants, 1929-1933, 1935 Green Bay Packers, 1936 Pittsburgh Pirates. **Highlights:** Charter enshrinee. Most feared lineman of his time. All-NFL six years, 1927-29, 1931-33.

SAM HUFF
Linebacker. 6-1, 230. Born in Morgantown, West Virginia, October 4, 1934. West Virginia. Inducted in 1982. 1956-1963 New York Giants, 1964-67, 1969 Washington Redskins. **Highlights:** 30 interceptions. Played in six NFL title games, five Pro Bowls. Redskins player-coach, 1969.

LAMAR HUNT
Team owner. Born in El Dorado, Arkansas, August 2, 1932. Died December 13, 2006. Southern Methodist. Inducted in 1972. 1960-2006 Dallas Texans/Kansas City Chiefs. **Highlights:** Driving force behind organization of AFL. Spearheaded merger negotiations with NFL, 1966.

DON HUTSON
End. 6-1, 180. Born in Pine Bluff, Arkansas, January 31, 1913. Died June 26, 1997. Alabama. Inducted in 1963. 1935-1945 Green Bay Packers. **Highlights:** Charter enshrinee. 488 receptions for 7,991 yards, 99 touchdowns. NFL receiving champion eight years. NFL MVP, 1941, 1942.

MICHAEL IRVIN
Wide receiver. 6-2, 207. Born in Ft. Lauderdale, Florida, March 5, 1966. Miami. Inducted in 2007. 1988-1999 Dallas Cowboys. **Highlights:** 750 career receptions for 11,904 yards, 65 touchdowns. Had NFL record eleven 100-yard receiving games, 1995.

RICKEY JACKSON
Linebacker. 6-2, 243. Born in Pahokee, Florida, March 20, 1958. Pittsburgh. Inducted in 2010. 1981-1993 New Orleans Saints, 1994-95 San Francisco 49ers. **Highlights:** Recorded double-digit sacks in six seasons. Six Pro Bowls, named All-Pro four times. Finished career as defensive end with 49ers.

JIMMY JOHNSON
Cornerback. 6-2, 187. Born in Dallas, Texas, March 31, 1938. UCLA. Inducted in 1994. 1961-1976 San Francisco 49ers. **Highlights:** 47 interceptions for 615 yards. Five Pro Bowls. Opposing passers avoided throwing in his area.

JOHN HENRY JOHNSON
Fullback. 6-2, 225. Born in Waterproof, Louisiana, November 24, 1929. St. Mary's, Arizona State. Inducted in 1987. 1954-56 San Francisco 49ers, 1957-59 Detroit Lions, 1960-65 Pittsburgh Steelers, 1966 Houston Oilers. **Highlights:** 6,803 yards rushing, 55 total touchdowns. Member of San Francisco's "Million-Dollar" backfield.

CHARLIE JOINER
Wide receiver. 5-11, 180. Born in Many, Louisiana, October 14, 1947. Grambling. Inducted in 1996. 1969-1972 Houston Oilers, 1972-75 Cincinnati Bengals, 1976-1986 San Diego Chargers. **Highlights:** 750 receptions for 12,146 yards and 65 touchdowns. Played 18 seasons, 239 games, most ever for wide receiver at time of retirement.

DAVID (DEACON) JONES
Defensive end. 6-5, 260. Born in Eatonville, Florida, December 9, 1938. South Carolina State, Mississippi Vocational. Inducted in 1980. 1961-1971 Los Angeles Rams, 1972-73 San Diego Chargers, 1974 Washington Redskins. **Highlights:** Specialized in quarterback "sacks," a term he invented. Unanimous all-league five consecutive years.

STAN JONES
Guard-defensive tackle. 6-1, 250. Born in Altoona, Pennsylvania, November 24, 1931. Maryland. Inducted in 1991. 1954-1965 Chicago Bears, 1966 Washington Redskins. **Highlights:** Seven consecutive Pro Bowls. First to rely on weightlifting for football preparation.

HENRY JORDAN
Defensive tackle, 6-3, 240. Born in Emporia, Virginia, January 26, 1935. Died February 21, 1977. Virginia. Inducted in 1995. 1957-58 Cleveland Browns, 1959-1969 Green Bay Packers. **Highlights:** Fixture at DT during Packers' dynasty. Played in four Pro Bowls, seven NFL title games, Super Bowls I, II.

SONNY JURGENSEN
Quarterback. 6-0, 203. Born in Wilmington, North Carolina, August 23, 1934. Duke. Inducted in 1983. 1957-1963 Philadelphia Eagles, 1964-1974 Washington Redskins. **Highlights:** 32,224 yards passing, 255 touchdowns, 82.63 passer rating. Surpassed 3,000 yards passing in five seasons.

JIM KELLY
Quarterback. 6-3, 225. Born in Pittsburgh, Pennsylvania, February 14, 1960. Miami. Inducted in 2002. 1986-1996 Buffalo Bills. **Highlights:** Passed for more than 3,000 yards eight times. Mastered the no-huddle offense that propelled Bills to four consecutive Super Bowls.

LEROY KELLY
Running back. 6-0, 205. Born in Philadelphia, Pennsylvania, May 20, 1942. Morgan State. Inducted in 1994. 1964-1973 Cleveland Browns. **Highlights:** 7,274 yards rushing, 90 total touchdowns, 1,000-yard rusher first three years as starter. Punt return champion, 1965.

WALT KIESLING
Guard. Coach. 6-2, 245. Born in St. Paul, Minnesota, March 27, 1903. Died March 2, 1962. St. Thomas (Minnesota). Inducted in 1966. 1926-27 Duluth Eskimos, 1928 Pottsville Maroons, 1929-1933 Chicago Cardinals, 1934 Chicago Bears, 1935-36 Green Bay Packers, 1937-38 Pittsburgh Pirates; coach, 1939 Pittsburgh Pirates, 1940-42 Pittsburgh Steelers; co-coach, 1943 Phil-Pitt, 1944 Card-Pitt; coach, 1954-56 Pittsburgh Steelers. **Highlights:** 34-year career as pro player, assistant coach, head coach. Led Steelers to first winning season, 1942.

FRANK (BRUISER) KINARD
Tackle. 6-1, 210. Born in Pelahatchie, Mississippi, October 23, 1914. Died September 7, 1985. Mississippi. Inducted in 1971. 1938-1943 Brooklyn Dodgers, 1944 Brooklyn Tigers, 1946-47 New York Yankees (AAFC). **Highlights:** First man to earn both All-NFL, All-AAFC honors. Out because of injury only once.

PAUL KRAUSE
Safety. 6-3, 200. Born in Flint, Michigan, February 19, 1942. Iowa. Inducted in 1998. 1964-67 Washington Redskins, 1968-1979 Minnesota Vikings. **Highlights:** NFL all-time leader with 81 interceptions. Played in eight Pro Bowls. Starting safety in four Super Bowls.

EARL (CURLY) LAMBEAU
Coach. Born in Green Bay, Wisconsin, April 9, 1898. Died June 1, 1965. Notre Dame. Inducted in 1963. 1919-1949 Green Bay Packers, 1950-51 Chicago Cardinals, 1952-53 Washington Redskins. **Highlights:** Charter enshrinee. 229-134-22 coaching record with six NFL championships. Founded pre-NFL Packers, 1919.

JACK LAMBERT
Linebacker. 6-4, 220. Born in Mantua, Ohio, July 8, 1952. Kent State. Inducted in 1990. 1974-1984 Pittsburgh Steelers. **Highlights:** Leader of 'Steel Curtain.' NFL defensive player of year in 1976, nine Pro Bowls.

TOM LANDRY
Coach. Born in Mission, Texas, September 11, 1924. Died February 12, 2000. Texas. Inducted in 1990. 1960-1988 Dallas Cowboys. **Highlights:** 270-178-6 coaching record. 20 consecutive winning seasons. Innovator on offense and defense.

DICK (NIGHT TRAIN) LANE
Cornerback. 6-2, 210. Born in Austin, Texas, April 16, 1928. Died January 29, 2002. Scottsbluff Junior College. Inducted in 1974. 1952-53 Los Angeles Rams, 1954-59 Chicago Cardinals, 1960-65 Detroit Lions. **Highlights:** 68 interceptions for 1,207 yards, 5 touchdowns. Record 14 interceptions as rookie. Seven Pro Bowls.

JIM LANGER
Center. 6-2, 255. Born in Little Falls, Minnesota, May 16, 1948. South Dakota State. Inducted in 1987. 1970-79 Miami Dolphins, 1980-81 Minnesota Vikings. **Highlights:** Played every offensive down in Dolphins' perfect 1972 season. Six Pro Bowls.

WILLIE LANIER
Linebacker. 6-1, 245. Born in Clover, Virginia, August 21, 1945. Morgan State. Inducted in 1986. 1967-1977 Kansas City Chiefs. **Highlights:** 27 interceptions. Defensive star in Super Bowl IV upset. Nicknamed 'Contact' for ferocious tackling.

STEVE LARGENT
Wide receiver. 5-11, 191. Born in Tulsa, Oklahoma, September 28, 1954, Tulsa. Inducted in 1995. 1976-1989 Seattle Seahawks. **Highlights:** 819 receptions for 13,089 yards, 100 touchdowns. Receptions in 177 consecutive games.

YALE LARY
Safety. 5-11, 189. Born in Fort Worth, Texas, November 24, 1930. Texas A&M. Inducted in 1979. 1952-53, 1956-1964 Detroit Lions. **Highlights:** 50 interceptions. Three NFL punting crowns, three touchdowns on punt returns. Nine Pro Bowls.

DANTE LAVELLI
End. 6-0, 199. Born in Hudson, Ohio, February 23, 1923. Died January 20, 2009. Ohio State. Inducted in 1975. 1946-49 Cleveland Browns (AAFC), 1950-56 Cleveland Browns. **Highlights:** 386 receptions for 6,488 yards, 62 touchdowns. 24 catches in six NFL title games.

BOBBY LAYNE
Quarterback. 6-2, 190. Born in Santa Anna, Texas, December 19, 1926. Died December 1, 1986. Texas. Inducted in 1967. 1948 Chicago Bears, 1949 New York Bulldogs, 1950-58 Detroit Lions, 1958-1962 Pittsburgh Steelers. **Highlights:** 26,768 yards passing, 196 touchdowns, 2,451 yards rushing. Late touchdown pass won 1953 NFL title game.

DICK LeBEAU
Cornerback. 6-1, 185. Born in London, Ohio, September 9, 1937. Ohio State. Inducted in 2010. 1959-1972 Detroit Lions. **Highlights:** Recorded 62 career interceptions for 762 yards, 3 TDs, ranked third all-time in interceptions at retirement. Voted to three Pro Bowls.

ALPHONSE (TUFFY) LEEMANS
Fullback. 6-0, 200. Born in Superior, Wisconsin, November 12, 1912. Died January 19, 1979. Oregon, George Washington. Inducted in 1978. 1936-1943 New York Giants. **Highlights:** 3,132 yards rushing, 2,318 yards passing, 422 yards receiving. Led NFL rushers as rookie, 1936.

MARV LEVY
Coach. Born in Chicago, Illinois, August 3, 1925. Wyoming, Coe College, Harvard. Inducted in 2001. 1978-1982 Kansas City Chiefs, 1986-1997 Buffalo Bills. **Highlights:** Led Bills to unprecedented four consecutive Super Bowls. Had 154-120 record. Coaching victories ranked 10th when retired.

BOB LILLY
Defensive tackle. 6-5, 260. Born in Olney, Texas, July 26, 1939. Texas Christian. Inducted in 1980. 1961-1974 Dallas Cowboys. **Highlights:** Eleven Pro Bowls. Played 196 consecutive games. Foundation of great Dallas defensive units.

FLOYD LITTLE
Running back. 5-10, 196. Born in New Haven, Connecticut, July 4, 1942. Syracuse. Inducted in 2010. 1967-1975 Denver Broncos. **Highlights:** Broncos' first 1,000-yard rusher, won NFL rushing title in 1971. Amassed more than 12,000 career all-purpose yards, 54 TDs, five AFL All-Star Games/Pro Bowls.

LARRY LITTLE
Guard. 6-1, 265. Born in Groveland, Georgia, November 2, 1945. Bethune-Cookman. Inducted in 1993. 1967-68 San Diego Chargers, 1969-1980 Miami Dolphins. **Highlights:** Five Pro Bowls, started in three Super Bowls. Epitome of powerful Dolphins rushing game of 1970s.

JAMES LOFTON
Wide receiver. 6-3, 192. Born in Fort Ord, California, July 5, 1956. Stanford. Inducted in 2003. 1978-1986 Green Bay Packers, 1987-88 Los Angeles Raiders, 1989-1992 Buffalo Bills, 1993 Los Angeles Rams, 1993 Philadelphia Eagles. **Highlights:** Played 16 seasons, 233 games. Caught 764 passes for 75 touchdowns and a then-record 14,004 yards. All-Pro four times, eight Pro Bowls.

VINCE LOMBARDI
Coach. Born in Brooklyn, New York, June 11, 1913. Died September 3, 1970. Fordham. Inducted in 1971. 1959-1967 Green Bay Packers, 1969 Washington Redskins. **Highlights:** 105-35-6 coaching record in 10 years, including five NFL titles and victories in Super Bowls I and II.

HOWIE LONG
Defensive end. 6-5, 268. Born in Somerville, Massachusetts, January 6, 1960. Villanova. Inducted in 2000. 1981-1993 Oakland/Los Angeles Raiders. **Highlights:** All-Pro 1983, 1984, 1985. Named All-AFC four times, 1983-1986. Eight Pro Bowls.

RONNIE LOTT
Cornerback-safety. 6-0, 203. Born in Albuquerque, New Mexico, May 8, 1959. Southern California. Inducted in 2000. 1981-1990 San Francisco 49ers, 1991-92 Los Angeles Raiders, 1993-94 New York Jets. **Highlights:** Ten Pro Bowls, 63 career interceptions, and was named to the NFL's 75th Anniversary Team.

SID LUCKMAN
Quarterback. 6-0, 195. Born in Brooklyn, New York, November 21, 1916. Died July 5, 1998. Columbia. Inducted in 1965. 1939-1950 Chicago Bears. **Highlights:** 137 touchdown passes. All-NFL five times. League MVP in 1943.

WILLIAM ROY (LINK) LYMAN
Tackle. 6-2, 252. Born in Table Rock, Nebraska, November 30, 1898. Died December 28, 1972. Nebraska. Inducted in 1964. 1922-23, 1925 Canton Bulldogs, 1924 Cleveland Bulldogs, 1925 Frankford Yellowjackets, 1926-28, 1930-31, 1933-34 Chicago Bears. **Highlights:** Played for four NFL champions. In 16 seasons of college and pro football, played on one losing team.

TOM MACK
Guard. 6-3, 250. Born in Cleveland, Ohio, November 1, 1943. Michigan. Inducted in 1999. 1966-1978 Los Angeles Rams. **Highlights:** Never missed a game in entire 184-game career. Elected to 11 Pro Bowls.

JOHN MACKEY
Tight end. 6-2, 224. Born in New York, New York, September 24, 1941. Syracuse. Inducted in 1992. 1963-1971 Baltimore Colts, 1972 San Diego Chargers. **Highlights:** 331 receptions for 5,236 yards, 38 touchdowns. Second tight end to enter Hall of Fame.

JOHN MADDEN
Coach. Born in Austin, Minnesota, April 10, 1936. San Mateo Junior College, California Polytechnic College at San Luis Obispo. Inducted in 2006. 1969-1978 Oakland Raiders. **Highlights:** Became one of youngest coaches in history when hired at age 32. 112-39-7 overall record. Owns best regular season winning percentage among coaches with 100 wins.

TIM MARA
Team owner. Born in New York, New York, July 29, 1887. Died February 16, 1959. Did not attend college. Inducted in 1963. 1925-1959 New York Giants. **Highlights:** Charter enshrinee. Founder of New York Giants. Built team into powerhouse winning four NFL titles, 10 division titles.

WELLINGTON MARA
Team owner. Born in New York, New York, August 14, 1916. Died October 25, 2005. Fordham. Inducted in 1997. 1937-2005 New York Giants. **Highlights:** Lifetime contributor to NFL and New York Giants. Worked as Giants' ballboy, secretary, vice-president, president and co-CEO. NFC president 1984-present.

GINO MARCHETTI
Defensive end. 6-4, 245. Born in Smithers, West Virginia, January 2, 1927. San Francisco. Inducted in 1972. 1952 Dallas Texans, 1953-1964, 1966 Baltimore Colts. **Highlights:** Named top defensive end of NFL's first 50 years. 10 consecutive Pro Bowls. All-NFL seven times.

DAN MARINO
Quarterback. 6-4, 218. Born in Pittsburgh, Pennsylvania, September 15, 1961. Pittsburgh. Inducted in 2005. 1983-1999 Miami Dolphins. **Highlights:** Held NFL records for career passing yardage (61,361), completions (4,967), attempts (8,358), and touchdowns (420). Voted to nine Pro Bowls.

GEORGE PRESTON MARSHALL
Team owner. Born in Grafton, West Virginia, October 11, 1896. Died August 9, 1969. Randolph-Macon. Inducted in 1963. 1932 Boston Braves, 1933-36 Boston Redskins, 1937-1969 Washington Redskins. **Highlights:** Charter enshrinee. Sponsored progressive rules changes. Organized first team band, pioneered halftime shows.

OLLIE MATSON
Halfback. 6-2, 220. Born in Trinity, Texas, May 1, 1930. San Francisco. Inducted in 1972. 1952, 1954-58 Chicago Cardinals, 1959-1962 Los Angeles Rams, 1963 Detroit Lions, 1964-66 Philadelphia Eagles. **Highlights:** Nine touchdowns on kickoff, punt returns. Traded for nine players in 1959.

BRUCE MATTHEWS
Guard-tackle-center. 6-5, 289. Born in Raleigh, North Carolina, August 8, 1961. Southern California. Inducted in 2007. 1983-2001 Houston Oilers/Tennessee Oilers/Tennessee Titans. **Highlights:** Played in 296 games, most ever by positional player at time of his retirement. Named to a record-tying 14 straight Pro Bowls. All-Pro nine times, All-AFC 12 times.

DON MAYNARD
Wide receiver. 6-1, 185. Born in Crosbyton, Texas, January 25, 1935. Texas Western. Inducted in 1987. 1958 New York Giants, 1960-62 New York Titans, 1963-1972 New York Jets, 1973 St. Louis Cardinals. **Highlights:** 633 receptions for 11,834 yards, 88 touchdowns. At least 50 catches and 1,000 yards in five different seasons.

GEORGE McAFEE
Halfback. 6-0, 177. Born in Corbin, Kentucky, March 13, 1918. Died March 4, 2009. Duke. Inducted in 1966. 1940-41, 1945-1950 Chicago Bears. **Highlights:** Two-way star. 25 interceptions, 234 points. Career punt-return average of 12.78 yards per return.

MIKE McCORMACK
Tackle. 6-4, 250. Born in Chicago, Illinois, June 21, 1930. Kansas. Inducted in 1984. 1951 New York Yanks, 1954-1962 Cleveland Browns. **Highlights:** Excelled as offensive right tackle for eight years. Six Pro Bowls.

RANDALL McDANIEL
Guard. 6-3, 276. Born in Phoenix, Arizona, December 19, 1964. Arizona State. Inducted in 2009. 1988-1999 Minnesota Vikings, 2000-01 Tampa Bay Buccaneers. **Highlights:** 12 Pro Bowls, All-Pro nine straight times. Blocked for six different 1,000-yard rushers, five 3,000-yard passers.

TOMMY McDONALD
Wide receiver. 5-9, 175. Born in Roy, New Mexico, July 26, 1934. Oklahoma. Inducted in 1998. 1957-1963 Philadelphia Eagles, 1964 Dallas Cowboys, 1965-66 Los Angeles Rams, 1967 Atlanta Falcons, 1968 Cleveland Browns. **Highlights:** Recorded 495 receptions for 8,410 yards, 84 touchdowns.

HUGH McELHENNY
Halfback. 6-1, 198. Born in Los Angeles, California, December 31, 1928. Washington. Inducted in 1970. 1952-1960 San Francisco 49ers, 1961-62 Minnesota Vikings, 1963 New York Giants, 1964 Detroit Lions. **Highlights:** 5,281 rushing yards, 360 points. Totaled 11,369 yards rushing, receiving, and returning kicks.

JOHNNY (BLOOD) McNALLY
Halfback. 6-0, 185. Born in New Richmond, Wisconsin, November 27, 1903. Died November 28, 1985. Notre Dame, St. John's (Minnesota). Inducted in 1963. 1925-26 Milwaukee Badgers, 1926-27 Duluth Eskimos, 1928 Pottsville Maroons, 1929-1933, 1935-36 Green Bay Packers, 1934 Pittsburgh Pirates; player-coach, 1937-38 Pittsburgh Pirates. **Highlights:** Charter enshrinee. 49 touchdowns, 297 points in 14 seasons with five teams.

MIKE MICHALSKE
Guard. 6-0, 209. Born in Cleveland, Ohio, April 24, 1903. Died October 26, 1983. Penn State. Inducted in 1964. 1926 New York Yankees (AFL), 1927-28 New York Yankees, 1929-1935, 1937 Green Bay Packers. **Highlights:** Anchored Packers' championship lines, 1929-1931. First guard enshrined in Canton.

WAYNE MILLNER
End. 6-0, 191. Born in Roxbury, Massachusetts, January 31, 1913. Died November 19, 1976. Notre Dame. Inducted in 1968. 1936 Boston Redskins, 1937-1941, 1945 Washington Redskins. **Highlights:** Redskins' all-time leader with 124 catches when retired. 55- and 78-yard touchdown receptions in 1937 NFL Championship Game.

BOBBY MITCHELL
Running back-wide receiver. 6-0, 195. Born in Hot Springs, Arkansas, June 6, 1935. Illinois. Inducted in 1983. 1958-1961 Cleveland Browns, 1962-68 Washington Redskins. **Highlights:** 91 touchdowns, including 8 on kickoff and punt returns. 14,078 combined yards.

RON MIX
Tackle. 6-4, 255. Born in Los Angeles, California, March 10, 1938. Southern California. Inducted in 1979. 1960 Los Angeles Chargers, 1961-69 San Diego Chargers, 1971 Oakland Raiders. **Highlights:** All-AFL nine times. Only two holding penalties in 10 years with the Chargers.

ART MONK
Wide receiver. 6-3, 210. Born in White Plains, New York, December 5, 1957. Syracuse. Inducted in 2008. 1980-1993 Washington Redskins, 1994 New York Jets, 1995 Philadelphia Eagles. **Highlights:** 940 receptions, 12,721 yards, 68 TDs. Set then-single season record, 106 catches, 1984. Had 50 or more catches in a season nine times.

JOE MONTANA
Quarterback. 6-2, 200. Born in New Eagle, Pennsylvania, June, 11, 1956. Notre Dame. Inducted in 2000. 1979-1992 San Francisco 49ers, 1993-94 Kansas City Chiefs. **Highlights:** MVP in Super Bowl's XVI, XIX, and XXIV. Eight Pro Bowls and All-NFL three times.

WARREN MOON
Quarterback. 6-3, 212. Born in Los Angeles, California, November 18, 1956. West Los Angeles Junior College, Washington. Inducted in 2006. 1984-1993 Houston Oilers, 1994-1996 Minnesota Vikings, 1997-1998 Seattle Seahawks, 1999-2000 Kansas City Chiefs. **Highlights:** Passed for 49,325 yards and 291 touchdowns in 17 NFL seasons. Elected to nine Pro Bowls including eight straight. Threw for 3,000 yards in nine seasons.

LENNY MOORE
Flanker-running back. 6-1, 198. Born in Reading, Pennsylvania, November 25, 1933. Penn State. Inducted in 1975. 1956-1967 Baltimore Colts. **Highlights:** From 1963-65, scored touchdowns in record 18 consecutive games. 113 career touchdowns, 12,451 combined net yards.

MARION MOTLEY
Fullback. 6-1, 238. Born in Leesburg, Georgia, June 5, 1920. Died June 27, 1999. South Carolina State, Nevada. Inducted in 1968. 1946-49 Cleveland Browns (AAFC), 1950-53 Cleveland Browns, 1955 Pittsburgh Steelers. **Highlights:** AAFC's all-time rushing champion. Led league in rushing in first NFL season.

MIKE MUNCHAK
Guard. 6-3, 281. Born in Scranton, Pennsylvania, March 5, 1960. Penn State. Inducted in 2001. 1982-1993 Houston Oilers. **Highlights:** Devastating blocker, All-AFC seven times, elected to nine Pro Bowls.

ANTHONY MUÑOZ
Tackle. 6-6, 278. Born in Ontario, California, August 19, 1958. Southern California. Inducted in 1998. 1980-1992 Cincinnati Bengals. **Highlights:** All-Pro choice 11 consecutive years, 1981-1991. Selected to 11 straight Pro Bowls.

GEORGE MUSSO
Guard-tackle. 6-2, 270. Born in Collinsville, Illinois. April 8, 1910. Died September 5, 2000. Millikin. Inducted in 1982. 1933-1944 Chicago Bears. **Highlights:** First player to achieve All-NFL status at two positions—tackle in 1935 and guard in 1937.

BRONKO NAGURSKI
Fullback. 6-2, 225. Born in Rainy River, Ontario, Canada, November 3, 1908. Died January 7, 1990. Minnesota. Inducted in 1963. 1930-37, 1943 Chicago Bears. **Highlights:** Charter enshrinee. 2,778 rushing yards in nine seasons. All-NFL five times.

JOE NAMATH
Quarterback. 6-2, 200. Born in Beaver Falls, Pennsylvania, May 31, 1943. Alabama. Inducted in 1985. 1965-1976 New York Jets, 1977 Los Angeles Rams. **Highlights:** First quarterback to pass for more than 4,000 yards in season, 1967. Guaranteed, delivered victory over Colts in Super Bowl III.

EARLE (GREASY) NEALE
Coach. Born in Parkersburg, West Virginia, November 5, 1891. Died November 2, 1973. West Virginia Wesleyan. Inducted in 1969. 1941-42, 1944-1950 Philadelphia Eagles; co-coach, 1943 Phil-Pitt. **Highlights:** Turned Eagles into winners with three consecutive division crowns, NFL championships in 1948 and 1949.

ERNIE NEVERS
Fullback. 6-1, 205. Born in Willow River, Minnesota, June 11, 1903. Died May 3, 1976. Stanford. Inducted in 1963. 1926-27 Duluth Eskimos, 1929-1931 Chicago Cardinals. **Highlights:** Charter enshrinee. Holds NFL's longest-standing record, 40 points in one game in 1929.

OZZIE NEWSOME
Tight end. 6-2, 232. Born in Muscle Shoals, Alabama, March 16, 1956. Alabama. Inducted in 1999. 1978-1990 Cleveland Browns. **Highlights:** Finished career as all-time leader among tight ends with 662 receptions for 7,980 yards.

RAY NITSCHKE
Linebacker. 6-3, 235. Born in Elmwood Park, Illinois, December 29, 1936. Died March 8, 1998. Illinois. Inducted in 1978. 1958-1972 Green Bay Packers. **Highlights:** MVP of 1962 title game. Named NFL's all-time linebacker in 1969.

CHUCK NOLL
Coach. Born in Cleveland, Ohio, January 5, 1932. Dayton. Inducted in 1993. 1969-1991 Pittsburgh Steelers. **Highlights:** Coached for 23 years. Only coach to win four Super Bowl titles (IX, X, XIII, XIV).

LEO NOMELLINI
Defensive tackle. 6-3, 264. Born in Lucca, Italy, June 19, 1924. Died October 17, 2000. Minnesota. Inducted in 1969. 1950-1963 San Francisco 49ers. **Highlights:** Played every 49ers game for 14 seasons. 10 Pro Bowls.

MERLIN OLSEN
Defensive tackle. 6-5, 270. Born in Logan, Utah, September 15, 1940. Died March 11, 2010. Utah State. Inducted in 1982. 1962-1976 Los Angeles Rams. **Highlights:** Member of the Fearsome "Foursome. Named" to 14 consecutive Pro Bowls, Rams' all-time team.

JIM OTTO
Center. 6-2, 255. Born in Wausau, Wisconsin, January 5, 1938. Miami. Inducted in 1980. 1960-1974 Oakland Raiders. **Highlights:** Named AFL's all-time center. Played in 210 games, 12 AFL All-Star Games or Pro Bowls, six AFL/AFC title games.

STEVE OWEN
Tackle. Coach. 6-2, 235. Born in Cleo Springs, Oklahoma, April 21, 1898. Died May 17, 1964. Phillips. Inducted in 1966. 1924-25 Kansas City Cowboys, 1925 Cleveland Bulldogs, 1926-1931, 1933 New York Giants; coach, 1930-1953 New York Giants. **Highlights:** Both player and coach. Coached Giants to record of 155-108-17, eight divisional titles, two NFL championships.

ALAN PAGE
Defensive tackle. 6-4, 225. Born in Canton, Ohio, August 7, 1945. Notre Dame. Inducted in 1988. 1967-1978 Minnesota Vikings, 1978-1981 Chicago Bears. **Highlights:** Dominating defensive tackle played in 218 consecutive games, four Super Bowls. Won league MVP honors in 1971.

CLARENCE (ACE) PARKER
Quarterback. 5-11, 168. Born in Portsmouth, Virginia, May 17, 1912. Duke. Inducted in 1972. 1937-1941 Brooklyn Dodgers, 1945 Boston Yanks, 1946 New York Yankees (AAFC). **Highlights:** Two-way threat. Two-time All-NFL performer, league MVP in 1940.

JIM PARKER
Guard-tackle. 6-3, 273. Born in Macon, Georgia, April 3, 1934. Died July 18, 2005. Ohio State. Inducted in 1973. 1957-1967 Baltimore Colts. **Highlights:** First full-time offensive lineman elected to Hall of Fame. All-NFL eight consecutive years, eight Pro Bowls.

WALTER PAYTON
Running back. 5-10, 202. Born in Columbia, Mississippi, July 25, 1954. Died November 1, 1999. Jackson State. Inducted in 1993. 1975-1987 Chicago Bears. **Highlights:** NFL's all-time leading rusher with 16,726 yards and combined net yardage with 21,803 at time of retirement.

JOE PERRY
Fullback. 6-0, 200. Born in Stevens, Arkansas, January 22, 1927. Compton Junior College. Inducted in 1969. 1948-49 San Francisco 49ers (AAFC), 1950-1960, 1963 San Francisco 49ers, 1961-62 Baltimore Colts. **Highlights:** First player in NFL history to gain 1,000 yards two consecutive seasons. 12,532 combined yards.

PETE PIHOS
End. 6-1, 210. Born in Orlando, Florida, October 22, 1923. Indiana. Inducted in 1970. 1947-1955 Philadelphia Eagles. **Highlights:** Three-time NFL receiving champion. Caught winning touchdown in 1949 NFL Championship Game.

FRITZ POLLARD
Halfback-Coach. 5-9, 165. Born in Chicago, Illinois, January 27, 1894. Died May 11, 1986. Brown. Inducted in 2005. 1919-1921, 1925-26 Akron Pros/Indians, 1922 Milwaukee Badgers, 1923, 1925 Hammond Pros, 1925 Providence Steam Roller. **Highlights:** True pioneer as one of two African American players in the NFL in 1920 and helped lead Akron to league title that season. In 1921, became the league's first black head coach.

JOHN RANDLE
Defensive tackle. 6-1, 278. Born in Hearne, Texas, December 12, 1967. Trinity Valley Community College; Texas A&I. Inducted in 2010. 1990-2000 Minnesota Vikings, 2001-03 Seattle Seahawks. **Highlights:** Undrafted free agent rookie, record eight straight seasons with 10 or more sacks, had 137.5 career sacks. Voted to seven Pro Bowls, named All-Pro/NFC six consecutive years, All-AFC once.

HUGH (SHORTY) RAY
Supervisor of officials 1938-1952. Born in Highland Park, Illinois, September 21, 1884. Died September 16, 1956. Illinois. Inducted in 1966. **Highlights:** Supervisor of Officials, 1938-1952. Streamlined rules to improve game tempo, player safety.

DAN REEVES
Team owner. Born in New York, New York, June 30, 1912. Died April 15, 1971. Georgetown. Inducted in 1967. 1941-45 Cleveland Rams, 1946-1971 Los Angeles Rams. **Highlights:** Moved Rams to Los Angeles in 1946 and opened up West Coast to pro football. First postwar owner to sign African-American player.

MEL RENFRO
Cornerback-safety. 6-0, 192. Born in Houston, Texas, December 30, 1941. Oregon. Inducted in 1996. 1964-1977 Dallas Cowboys. **Highlights:** 52 interceptions for 626 yards and 3 touchdowns. Also added 842 yards on punt returns, 2,246 yards on kickoff returns. Elected to Pro Bowl first 10 seasons.

JERRY RICE
Wide receiver. 6-2, 200. Born in Starksville, Mississippi, October 13, 1962. Mississippi Valley State. Inducted in 2010. 1985-2000 San Francisco 49ers, 2001-04 Oakland Raiders, 2004 Seattle Seahawks. **Highlights:** NFL's all-time reception leader with 1,549 catches for 22,895 yards, 208 total touchdowns. Had 14 seasons with 1,000 yards receiving; 23,546 combined net yards. All-Pro 11 times, Super Bowl XXIII MVP.

JOHN RIGGINS
Running back. 6-2, 240. Born in Seneca, Kansas, August 4, 1949. Kansas. Inducted in 1992. 1971-75 New York Jets, 1976-79, 1981-85 Washington Redskins. **Highlights:** 11,352 rushing yards, 116 total touchdowns. MVP of Super Bowl XVII with 166 rushing yards including game-winning 43-yard touchdown.

JIM RINGO
Center. 6-2, 230. Born in Orange, New Jersey, November 21, 1931. Died November 19, 2007. Syracuse. Inducted in 1981. 1953-1963 Green Bay Packers, 1964-67 Philadelphia Eagles. **Highlights:** Ten-time Pro Bowl selection, seven-time All-NFL selection. Started in then-record 182 consecutive games.

ANDY ROBUSTELLI
Defensive end. 6-0, 230. Born in Stamford, Connecticut, December 6, 1925. Arnold College. Inducted in 1971. 1951-55 Los Angeles Rams, 1956-1964 New York Giants. **Highlights:** Anchored defense in eight championship games. Named NFL's top player in 1962.

ART ROONEY
Team owner. Born in Coulterville, Pennsylvania, January 27, 1901. Died August 25, 1988. Georgetown, Duquesne. Inducted in 1964. 1933-39 Pittsburgh Pirates, 1940-42, 1945-1988 Pittsburgh Steelers, 1943 Phil-Pitt, 1944 Card-Pitt. **Highlights:** Founded Pittsburgh Pirates in 1933 and renamed them Steelers in 1940. Team won four Super Bowls in 1970s.

DAN ROONEY
Team owner. Born in Pittsburgh, Pennsylvania, July, 20, 1932. Duquesne. Inducted in 2000. 1955-present Pittsburgh Steelers. **Highlights:** Has been on the board of directors for the NFL Trust Fund, NFL Films, and Scheduling Committee. Played a key role in the labor agreement reached in 1993 between the NFL owners and players.

PETE ROZELLE
Commissioner. Born in South Gate, California, March 1, 1926. Died December 6, 1996. Compton Junior College, San Francisco. Inducted in 1985. Commissioner, 1960-1989. **Highlights:** Negotiated first league-wide television contract in 1962. Generally recognized as premiere commissioner in all of sports. Credited with making NFL the nation's most popular sport.

BOB ST. CLAIR
Tackle. 6-9, 265. Born in San Francisco, California, February 18, 1931. San Francisco, Tulsa. Inducted in 1990. 1953-1963 San Francisco 49ers. **Highlights:** Exceptional offensive lineman. Also played goal-line defense and had 10 blocked field goals, 1956.

BARRY SANDERS
Running back. 5-8, 203. Born in Wichita, Kansas, July 16, 1968. Oklahoma State. Inducted in 2004. 1989-1998 Detroit Lions. **Highlights:** 15,269 rushing yards, 99 touchdowns. Rushed for 1,000 yards in each of 10 seasons. NFL co-MVP, 1997. Selected to 10 Pro Bowls.

CHARLIE SANDERS
Tight end. 6-4, 230. Born in Richlands, North Carolina, August 25, 1946. Minnesota. Inducted in 2007. 1968-1977 Detroit Lions. **Highlights:** 336 career receptions for 4,817 yards and 31 touchdowns. Selected to seven Pro Bowls. Named to the NFL's All-Decade Team of 1970s.

GALE SAYERS
Running back. 6-0, 200. Born in Wichita, Kansas, May 30, 1943. Kansas. Inducted in 1977. 1965-1971 Chicago Bears. **Highlights:** Broke into league by scoring rookie-record 22 touchdowns. Led league in rushing in 1966, 1969. MVP of three Pro Bowls.

JOE SCHMIDT
Linebacker. 6-0, 222. Born in Pittsburgh, Pennsylvania, January 18, 1932. Pittsburgh. Inducted in 1973. 1953-1965 Detroit Lions. **Highlights:** 24 interceptions. Lions' team captain for nine years. Mastered middle linebacker position that evolved in 1950s.

TEX SCHRAMM
Team president-general manager. Born in San Gabriel, California, June 2, 1920. Died July 15, 2003. Texas. Inducted in 1991. 1947-1956 Los Angeles Rams. 1960-1989 Dallas Cowboys. **Highlights:** Played prominent role in AFL-NFL merger. Chairman of Competition Committee from 1966-1988.

LEE ROY SELMON
Defensive end. 6-3, 250. Born in Eufaula, Oklahoma, October 20, 1954. Oklahoma. Inducted in 1995. 1976-1984 Tampa Bay Buccaneers. **Highlights:** 78½ sacks, 380 quarterback pressures, forced 28 fumbles. Six consecutive Pro Bowl selections.

BILLY SHAW
Guard. 6-2, 258. Born in Natchez, Mississippi, December 15, 1938. Georgia Tech. Inducted in 1999. 1961-69 Buffalo Bills. **Highlights:** First player who played entire career in AFL to be elected to Hall of Fame. Named to AFL's all-time team.

ART SHELL
Tackle. 6-5, 285. Born in Charleston, South Carolina, November 26, 1946. Maryland State-Eastern Shore. Inducted in 1989. 1968-82 Oakland/Los Angeles Raiders. **Highlights:** Cornerstone of Raiders' offensive line in 1970s. 207 regular-season games, 23 postseason games, eight Pro Bowls.

DON SHULA
Coach. Born in Grand River, Ohio, January 4, 1930. John Carroll. Inducted in 1997. 1963-69 Baltimore Colts, 1970-1995 Miami Dolphins. **Highlights:** Won more games (347) than any coach in NFL history. Won two Super Bowl titles, including Super Bowl VII when Dolphins recorded NFL's only perfect season (17-0).

O.J. SIMPSON
Running back. 6-1, 212. Born in San Francisco, California, July 9, 1947. City College (San Francisco), Southern California. Inducted in 1985. 1969-1977 Buffalo Bills, 1978-79 San Francisco 49ers. **Highlights:** In 1973, became first player to rush for 2,000 yards in season. Finished career with four rushing titles, 11,236 yards.

MIKE SINGLETARY
Linebacker. 6-0, 230. Born in Houston, Texas, October 9, 1958. Baylor. Inducted in 1998. 1981-1992 Chicago Bears. **Highlights:** All-Pro choice eight times and All-NFC nine consecutive seasons. Selected to 10 Pro Bowls.

JACKIE SLATER
Tackle. 6-4, 277. Born in Jackson, Mississippi, May 27, 1954. Jackson State. Inducted in 2001. 1976-1995 Los Angeles/St. Louis Rams. **Highlights:** Played 20 seasons, 259 games. Blocked for seven different 1,000-yard rushers. Seven Pro Bowls.

BRUCE SMITH
Defensive end. 6-4, 280. Born in Norfolk, Virginia, June 18, 1963. Virginia Tech. Inducted in 2009. 1985-1999 Buffalo Bills, 2000-03 Washington Redskins. **Highlights:** NFL's all-time leader in sacks with 200. Named All-Pro nine times, 11 Pro Bowls. Selected to NFL's All-Decade Team of 1980s and 1990s.

EMMITT SMITH
Running back. 5-9, 207. Born in Pensacola, Florida, May 15, 1969. Florida. Inducted in 2010. 1990-2002 Dallas Cowboys, 2003-04 Arizona Cardinals. **Highlights:** Won four rushing titles in five years, recorded record 11 straight 1,000-yard seasons. NFL's all-time leading rusher with 18,355 yards, 164 rushing TDs. Won NFL MVP and Super Bowl XXVIII MVP in 1993.

JACKIE SMITH
Tight end. 6-4, 232. Born in Columbia, Mississippi, February 23, 1940. Northwestern State (Louisiana). Inducted in 1994. 1963-1977 St. Louis Cardinals, 1978 Dallas Cowboys. **Highlights:** 480 receptions for 7,918 yards, 40 touchdowns. Third tight end to be elected to Hall of Fame.

JOHN STALLWORTH
Wide receiver. 6-2, 191. Born in Tuscaloosa, Alabama, July 15, 1952. Alabama A&M. Inducted in 2002. 1974-1987 Pittsburgh Steelers. **Highlights:** 537 receptions for 8,723 yards, 63 touchdowns. Scored go-ahead touchdown in Super Bowl XIV on 73-yard reception.

BART STARR
Quarterback. 6-1, 200. Born in Montgomery, Alabama, January 9, 1934. Alabama. Inducted in 1977. 1956-1971 Green Bay Packers. **Highlights:** Quarterbacked Packers to six division titles, five NFL titles, and first two Super Bowls in which he was MVP.

ROGER STAUBACH
Quarterback. 6-3, 202. Born in Cincinnati, Ohio, February 5, 1942. New Mexico Military Institute, Navy. Inducted in 1985. 1969-1979 Dallas Cowboys. **Highlights:** Led Cowboys to four NFC titles and victories in Super Bowls VI, XII. When retired, 83.4 career passer rating was best of all time.

ERNIE STAUTNER
Defensive tackle. 6-2, 235. Born in Prinzing-by-Cham, Bavaria, April 20, 1925. Died February 16, 2006. Boston College. Inducted in 1969. 1950-1963 Pittsburgh Steelers. **Highlights:** Played in nine Pro Bowls and won the best lineman award in 1957. Recorded 3 safeties.

JAN STENERUD
Kicker. 6-2, 190. Born in Fetsund, Norway, November 26, 1942. Montana State. Inducted in 1991. 1967-1979 Kansas City Chiefs, 1980-83 Green Bay Packers, 1984-85 Minnesota Vikings. **Highlights:** 1,699 points on 580 extra points, 373 field goals. First pure placekicker to enter Hall of Fame.

DWIGHT STEPHENSON
Center. 6-2, 255. Born in Murfreesboro, North Carolina, November 20, 1957. Alabama. Inducted in 1998. 1980-87 Miami Dolphins. **Highlights:** Recognized as premier center of his time. All-Pro, All-AFC five straight years. Selected to five Pro Bowls.

HANK STRAM
Coach. Born in Chicago, Illinois, January 3, 1923. Died July 4, 2005. Purdue. Inducted in 2003. 1960-1974 Dallas Texans/Kansas City Chiefs, 1976-1977 New Orleans Saints. **Highlights:** Overall record of 136-100-10. Recorded most wins in AFL history. Guided teams to titles in 1962, 1966, and 1969. Led Chiefs to AFL win in Super Bowl IV.

KEN STRONG
Halfback. 5-11, 210. Born in West Haven, Connecticut, April 21, 1906. Died October 5, 1979. New York University. Inducted in 1967. 1929-1932 Staten Island Stapletons, 1933-35, 1939, 1944-47 New York Giants, 1936-37 New York Yanks (AFL). **Highlights:** Scored 17 points to lead Giants to victory in 1934 'Sneakers' game, led NFL with 64 points, 1933.

JOE STYDAHAR
Tackle. 6-4, 230. Born in Kaylor, Pennsylvania, March 17, 1912. Died March 23, 1977. West Virginia. Inducted in 1967. 1936-1942, 1945-46 Chicago Bears. **Highlights:** One of stalwarts of Bears' 'Monsters of the Midway.' Played on five divisional, three NFL championship teams.

LYNN SWANN
Wide receiver. 5-11, 180. Born in Alcoa, Tennessee, March 7, 1952. Southern California. Inducted in 2001. 1974-1982 Pittsburgh Steelers. **Highlights:** All-AFC three times. Selected to three Pro Bowls. MVP, Super Bowl X.

FRAN TARKENTON
Quarterback. 6-0, 185. Born in Richmond, Virginia, February 3, 1940. Georgia. Inducted in 1986. 1961-66, 1972-78 Minnesota Vikings, 1967-1971 New York Giants. **Highlights:** At retirement, held NFL records for attempts (6,467), completions (3,686), yards (47,003), and touchdowns (342). Four touchdowns passes in first NFL game.

CHARLEY TAYLOR
Running back-wide receiver. 6-3, 210. Born in Grand Prairie, Texas, September 28, 1941. Arizona State. Inducted in 1984. 1964-1975, 1977 Washington Redskins. **Highlights:** Won rookie of year honors as running back. Switched to wide receiver and won receiving titles in 1966, 1967.

JIM TAYLOR
Fullback. 6-0, 216. Born in Baton Rouge, Louisiana, September 20, 1935. Hinds Junior College; Louisiana State. Inducted in 1976. 1958-1966 Green Bay Packers, 1967 New Orleans Saints. **Highlights:** 8,597 rushing yards, 558 points. In 1962, led league in rushing and scoring with 19 touchdowns.

LAWRENCE TAYLOR
Linebacker. 6-3, 237. Born in Williamsburg, Virginia, February 4, 1959. North Carolina. Inducted in 1999. 1981-1993 New York Giants. **Highlights:** Redefined the position of outside linebacker. All-Pro nine times, 10 Pro Bowls. NFL MVP in 1986.

DERRICK THOMAS
Linebacker. 6-3, 243. Born in Miami, Florida, January 1, 1967. Died February 8, 2000. Alabama. Inducted in 2009. 1989-1999 Kansas City Chiefs. **Highlights:** Set NFL record with 7 sacks in one game. Recorded most sacks in NFL during 1990s. Nine Pro Bowls. Named to NFL's All-Decade Team of 1990s.

EMMITT THOMAS
Cornerback. 6-2, 192. Born in Angleton, Texas, June 3, 1943. Bishop. Inducted in 2008. 1966-1978 Kansas City Chiefs. **Highlights:** Undrafted free agent. 58 interceptions, 937 yards, 5 TDs. Ranked fifth all-time in interceptions at retirement. Interception leader —AFL, 1969 and NFL, 1974.

THURMAN THOMAS
Running back. 5-10, 198. Born in Houston, Texas, May 16, 1966. Oklahoma State. Inducted in 2007. 1988-1999 Buffalo Bills, 2000 Miami Dolphins. **Highlights:** Amassed 16,532 total yards including 12,074 yards rushing. Scored 88 touchdowns. Only player in history to lead league in yards from scrimmage four straight seasons.

JIM THORPE
Halfback. 6-1, 190. Born in Prague, Oklahoma, May 28, 1888. Died March 28, 1953. Carlisle. Inducted in 1963. 1915-17, 1919-1920, 1926 Canton Bulldogs, 1921 Cleveland Indians, 1922-23 Oorang Indians, 1924 Rock Island Independents, 1925 New York Giants, 1928 Chicago Cardinals. **Highlights:** Charter enshrinee. First president of American Professional Football Association, 1920. Played for 12 seasons.

ANDRE TIPPETT
Linebacker. 6-3, 240. Born in Birmingham, Alabama, December 27, 1959. Iowa; Ellsworth (IA) Jr. College. Inducted in 2008. 1982-1993 New England Patriots. **Highlights:** Recorded 100 career sacks including personal best 18.5 sacks, 1984. Named to five straight Pro Bowls, 1985-89.

Y.A. TITTLE
Quarterback. 6-0, 200. Born in Marshall, Texas, October 24, 1926. Louisiana State. Inducted in 1971. 1948-49 Baltimore Colts (AAFC), 1950 Baltimore Colts, 1951-1960 San Francisco 49ers, 1961-64 New York Giants. **Highlights:** 33,070 yards, 242 touchdowns. 33 touchdown passes in 1962 and 36 in 1963. Two-time league MVP.

GEORGE TRAFTON
Center. 6-2, 235. Born in Chicago, Illinois, December 6, 1896. Died September 5, 1971. Notre Dame. Inducted in 1964. 1920-1932 Decatur Staleys/Chicago Staleys/ Chicago Bears. **Highlights:** First center to snap with one hand. Named top NFL center of 1920s.

CHARLEY TRIPPI
Halfback-quarterback. 6-0, 185. Born in Pittston, Pennsylvania, December 14, 1922. Georgia. Inducted in 1968. 1947-1955 Chicago Cardinals. **Highlights:** One of football's most versatile performers. Played halfback five years, quarterback for two, defense for two.

EMLEN TUNNELL
Safety. 6-1, 200. Born in Bryn Mawr, Pennsylvania, March 29, 1925. Died July 22, 1975. Toledo, Iowa. Inducted in 1967. 1948-1958 New York Giants, 1959-1961 Green Bay Packers. **Highlights:** 79 interceptions. Gained more yards on kickoff, punt, and interception returns (924) in 1952 than that season's NFL rushing leader.

CLYDE (BULLDOG) TURNER
Center. 6-2, 235. Born in Plains, Texas, March 10, 1919. Died October 30, 1998. Hardin-Simmons. Inducted in 1966. 1940-1952 Chicago Bears. **Highlights:** Anchored defense for four NFL championship teams, including 4 interceptions in five title games.

JOHNNY UNITAS
Quarterback. 6-1, 195. Born in Pittsburgh, Pennsylvania, May 7, 1933. Died September 11, 2002. Louisville. Inducted in 1979. 1956-1972 Baltimore Colts, 1973 San Diego Chargers. **Highlights:** 40,239 passing yards, 290 touchdowns. Led Colts to two NFL championships. Passed for at least one touchdown in 47 consecutive games.

GENE UPSHAW
Guard. 6-5, 255. Born in Robstown, Texas, August 15, 1945. Died August 20, 2008. Texas A & I. Inducted in 1987. 1967-1981 Oakland Raiders. **Highlights:** Premier guard of his era played in 10 AFL/AFC Championship Games, three Super Bowls, seven Pro Bowls.

NORM VAN BROCKLIN
Quarterback. 6-1, 190. Born in Eagle Butte, South Dakota, March 15, 1926. Died May 2, 1983. Oregon. Inducted in 1971. 1949-1957 Los Angeles Rams, 1958-1960 Philadelphia Eagles. **Highlights:** NFL-record 554 yards passing in 1951 season opener. Guided Eagles to NFL crown as league's Most Outstanding Player in 1960.

STEVE VAN BUREN
Halfback. 6-1, 200. Born in La Ceiba, Honduras, December 28, 1920. Louisiana State. Inducted in 1965. 1944-1951 Philadelphia Eagles. **Highlights:** Four-time rushing champion. Won 1944 punt-return title and was 1945 kick-off-return champion.

DOAK WALKER
Halfback. 5-11, 173. Born in Dallas, Texas, January 1, 1927. Died September 27, 1998. Southern Methodist. Inducted in 1986. 1950-55 Detroit Lions. **Highlights:** 534 points. Won two NFL scoring titles. Had winning 67-yard scoring run in 1952 title game.

BILL WALSH
Coach. Born in Los Angeles, California, November 30, 1931. Died July 30, 2007. San Jose State. Inducted in 1993. 1979-1988 San Francisco 49ers. **Highlights:** 102-63-1 coaching record. Guided 49ers to three Super Bowl titles (XVI, XIX, XXIII) in 10 years.

PAUL WARFIELD
Wide receiver. 6-0, 188. Born in Warren, Ohio, November 28, 1942. Ohio State. Inducted in 1983. 1964-69, 1976-77 Cleveland Browns, 1970-74 Miami Dolphins. **Highlights:** 8,565 yards receiving, 85 touchdowns. Eight-time Pro Bowl player. Key to both Cleveland and Miami offenses.

BOB WATERFIELD
Quarterback. 6-2, 200. Born in Elmira, New York, July 26, 1920. Died March 25, 1983. UCLA. Inducted in 1965. 1945 Cleveland Rams, 1946-1952 Los Angeles Rams. **Highlights:** NFL MVP as rookie in 1945 and led Rams to NFL title. Grabbed 20 interceptions in limited defensive duties.

MIKE WEBSTER
Center. 6-2, 260. Born in Tomahawk, Wisconsin, March 18, 1952. Died September 24, 2002. Wisconsin. Inducted in 1997. 1974-1988 Pittsburgh Steelers, 1989-1990 Kansas City Chiefs. **Highlights:** Played in 245 games, nine Pro Bowls, and won four Super Bowls during 17-year career.

ROGER WEHRLI
Cornerback. 6-0, 190. Born in New Point, Missouri, November 26, 1947. Missouri. Inducted in 2007. 1969-1982 St. Louis Cardinals. **Highlights:** 40 career interceptions. Named to the NFL's All-Decade Team of 1970s. All-Pro five times, selected to seven Pro Bowls.

ARNIE WEINMEISTER
Defensive tackle. 6-4, 235. Born in Rhein, Saskatchewan, Canada, March 23, 1923. Died June 29, 2000. Washington. Inducted in 1984. 1948-49 New York Yankees (AAFC), 1950-53 New York Giants. **Highlights:** Dominant defensive tackle of his time. Four-time All-NFL selection, four Pro Bowls.

RANDY WHITE
Defensive tackle. 6-4, 265. Born in Pittsburgh, Pennsylvania, January 15, 1953. Maryland. Inducted in 1994. 1975-1988 Dallas Cowboys. **Highlights:** Missed only one game in 14 seasons. Co-MVP of Super Bowl XII. Nine-time Pro Bowl selection.

REGGIE WHITE
Defensive end. 6-5, 291. Born in Chattanooga, Tennessee, December 19, 1961. Died December 26, 2004. Tennessee. Inducted in 2006. 1985-1992 Philadelphia Eagles, 1993-1998 Green Bay Packers, 2000 Carolina Panthers. **Highlights:** Retired as all-time sack leader with 198. Named All-Pro 13 of 15 seasons including 10 as first-team selection. Named to 13 straight Pro Bowls.

DAVE WILCOX
Linebacker. 6-3, 241. Born in Ontario, Oregon, September, 29, 1942. Boise State, Oregon. Inducted in 2000. 1964-1974 San Francisco 49ers. **Highlights:** Seven Pro Bowls, All-NFL five times. Missed only one game because of injury.

BILL WILLIS
Guard. 6-2, 215. Born in Columbus, Ohio, October 5, 1921. Died November 27, 2007. Ohio State. Inducted in 1977. 1946-1953 Cleveland Browns (AAFC/NFL). **Highlights:** Two-way player who excelled on defense. Four-time All-NFL player, played in three Pro Bowls.

LARRY WILSON
Safety. 6-0, 190. Born in Rigby, Idaho, March 24, 1938. Utah. Inducted in 1978. 1960-1972 St. Louis Cardinals. **Highlights:** 52 interceptions. Had interception in seven consecutive games in 1966. Made "safety blitz" famous.

RALPH WILSON, JR.
Owner-founder. Born in Columbus, Ohio, October 17, 1918. Virginia, Michigan. Inducted in 2009. 1960-present Buffalo Bills. **Highlights:** Founded team. Bills teams captured back-to-back AFL titles in mid-1960s. Unprecedented four straight Super Bowl appearances.

KELLEN WINSLOW
Tight end. 6-5, 250. Born in St. Louis, Missouri, November 5, 1957. Missouri. Inducted in 1995. 1979-1987 San Diego Chargers **Highlights:** 541 receptions for 6,741 yards, 45 touchdowns. 13 catches, blocked field goal in 1981 playoff win over Miami.

ALEX WOJCIECHOWICZ
Center. 6-0, 235. Born in South River, New Jersey, August 12, 1915. Died July 13, 1992. Fordham. Inducted in 1968. 1938-1946 Detroit Lions, 1946-1950 Philadelphia Eagles. **Highlights:** One of league's first iron men. Played both ways for eight years with Lions.

WILLIE WOOD
Safety. 5-10, 190. Born in Washington, D.C., December 23, 1936. Southern California. Inducted in 1989. 1960-1971 Green Bay Packers. **Highlights:** 48 interceptions. Competed in six NFL Championship Games and Super Bowls I and II.

ROD WOODSON
Cornerback-safety. 6-0, 200. Born in Fort Wayne, Indiana, March 10, 1965. Purdue. Inducted in 2009. 1987-1996 Pittsburgh Steelers, 1997 San Francisco 49ers, 1998-2001 Baltimore Ravens, 2002-03 Oakland Raiders. **Highlights:** 71 interceptions returned for 1,483 yards and NFL record 12 TDs. Named NFL Defensive Player of Year, 1993. Member of NFL's 75th Anniversary Team. 11 Pro Bowls.

RAYFIELD WRIGHT
Tackle. 6-6, 255. Born in Griffin, Georgia, August 23, 1945. Fort Valley State. Inducted in 2006. 1967-1979 Dallas Cowboys. **Highlights:** Named first- or second-team All-Pro and voted to Pro Bowl six straight seasons, 1971-76. Played in six NFC championship games and five Super Bowls. Named to NFL's All-Decade Team of 1970s.

RON YARY
Tackle. 6-5, 255. Born in Chicago, Illinois, July 16, 1946. Cerritos (Calif.) J.C., Southern California. Inducted in 2001. 1968-1981 Minnesota Vikings, 1982 Los Angeles Rams. **Highlights:** All-Pro six consecutive seasons, All-NFC eight consecutive years. Named to seven Pro Bowls. Started in four Super Bowls and five NFL/NFC Championship Games.

STEVE YOUNG
Quarterback. 6-2, 205. Born in Salt Lake City, Utah, October 11, 1961. Brigham Young. Inducted in 2005. 1985-86 Tampa Bay Buccaneers, 1987-1999 San Francisco 49ers. **Highlights:** Led the NFL in passing a record-tying six times. Passed for more than 33,000 yards and 232 touchdowns in career. MVP of Super Bowl XXIX. Elected to seven Pro Bowls.

JACK YOUNGBLOOD
Defensive end. 6-4, 247. Born in Jacksonville, Florida, January 26, 1950. Florida. Inducted in 2001. 1971-1984 Los Angeles Rams. **Highlights:** Played in club-record 201 consecutive games. Played in five NFC Championship Games, one Super Bowl. Named All-Pro five times, All-NFC seven times. Elected to seven consecutive Pro Bowls. Lions.

GARY ZIMMERMAN
Tackle. 6-6, 294. Born in Fullerton, California, December 13, 1961. Oregon. Inducted in 2008. 1986-1992 Minnesota Vikings, 1993-97 Denver Broncos. **Highlights:** Named to seven Pro Bowls. One of handful of players to be named to two NFL All-Decade Teams, 1980s and 1990s.

ENSHRINEES BY YEAR OF INDUCTION

**Deceased*
(Date of enshrinement in parentheses)

1963 CHARTER CLASS
(September 7, 1963)
Sammy Baugh*
Bert Bell*
Joe Carr*
Earl (Dutch) Clark*
Harold (Red) Grange*
George Halas*
Mel Hein*
Wilbur (Pete) Henry*
Robert (Cal) Hubbard*
Don Hutson*
Earl (Curly) Lambeau*
Tim Mara*
George Preston Marshall*
John (Blood) McNally*
Bronko Nagurski*
Ernie Nevers*
Jim Thorpe*

CLASS OF 1964
(September 6, 1964)
Jimmy Conzelman*
Ed Healey*
Clarke Hinkle*
William Roy (Link) Lyman*
Mike Michalske*
Art Rooney*
George Trafton*

CLASS OF 1965
(September 12, 1965)
Guy Chamberlin*
John (Paddy) Driscoll*
Dan Fortmann*
Otto Graham*
Sid Luckman*
Steve Van Buren
Bob Waterfield*

CLASS OF 1966
(September 17, 1966)
Bill Dudley*
Joe Guyon*
Arnie Herber*
Walt Kiesling*
George McAfee*
Steve Owen*
Hugh (Shorty) Ray*
Clyde (Bulldog) Turner*

CLASS OF 1967
(August 5, 1967)
Chuck Bednarik
Charles W. Bidwill Sr.*
Paul Brown*
Bobby Layne*
Dan Reeves*
Ken Strong*
Joe Stydahar*
Emlen Tunnell*

CLASS OF 1968
(August 3, 1968)
Cliff Battles*
Art Donovan
Elroy (Crazylegs) Hirsch*
Wayne Millner*
Marion Motley*
Charley Trippi
Alex Wojciechowicz*

CLASS OF 1969
(September 13, 1969)
Albert Glen (Turk) Edwards*
Earle (Greasy) Neale*
Leo Nomellini*
Joe Perry
Ernie Stautner*

CLASS OF 1970
(August 8, 1970)
Jack Christiansen*
Tom Fears*
Hugh McElhenny
Pete Pihos

CLASS OF 1971
(July 31, 1971)
Jim Brown
Bill Hewitt*
Frank (Bruiser) Kinard*
Vince Lombardi*
Andy Robustelli
Y. A. Tittle
Norm Van Brocklin*

CLASS OF 1972
*(July 29, 1972)*Lamar Hunt*
Gino Marchetti
Ollie Matson
Clarence (Ace) Parker

CLASS OF 1973
(July 28, 1973)
Raymond Berry
Jim Parker*
Joe Schmidt

CLASS OF 1974
(July 27, 1974)
Tony Canadeo*
Bill George*
Lou Groza*
Dick (Night Train) Lane*

CLASS OF 1975
(August 2, 1975)
Roosevelt Brown*
George Connor*
Dante Lavelli*
Lenny Moore

CLASS OF 1976
(July 24, 1976)
Ray Flaherty*
Len Ford*
Jim Taylor

CLASS OF 1977
(July 30, 1977)
Frank Gifford
Forrest Gregg
Gale Sayers
Bart Starr
Bill Willis*

CLASS OF 1978
(July 29, 1978)
Lance Alworth
Weeb Ewbank*
Alphonse (Tuffy) Leemans*
Ray Nitschke*
Larry Wilson

CLASS OF 1979
(July 28, 1979)
Dick Butkus
Yale Lary
Ron Mix
Johnny Unitas*

CLASS OF 1980
(August 2, 1980)
Herb Adderley
David (Deacon) Jones
Bob Lilly
Jim Otto

CLASS OF 1981
(August 1, 1981)
Morris (Red) Badgro*
George Blanda
Willie Davis
Jim Ringo*

CLASS OF 1982
(August 7, 1982)
Doug Atkins
Sam Huff
George Musso*
Merlin Olsen*

CLASS OF 1983
(July 30, 1983)
Bobby Bell
Sid Gillman*
Sonny Jurgensen
Bobby Mitchell
Paul Warfield

CLASS OF 1984
(July 28, 1984)
Willie Brown
Mike McCormack
Charley Taylor
Arnie Weinmeister*

CLASS OF 1985
(August 3, 1985)
Frank Gatski*
Joe Namath
Pete Rozelle*
O. J. Simpson
Roger Staubach

PRO FOOTBALL HALL OF FAME

CLASS OF 1986
(August 2, 1986)
Paul Hornung
Ken Houston
Willie Lanier
Fran Tarkenton
Doak Walker*

CLASS OF 1987
(August 8, 1987)
Larry Csonka
Len Dawson
Joe Greene
John Henry Johnson
Jim Langer
Don Maynard
Gene Upshaw*

CLASS OF 1988
(July 30, 1988)
Fred Biletnikoff
Mike Ditka
Jack Ham
Alan Page

CLASS OF 1989
(August 5, 1989)
Mel Blount
Terry Bradshaw
Art Shell
Willie Wood

CLASS OF 1990
(August 4, 1990)
Buck Buchanan*
Bob Griese
Franco Harris
Ted Hendricks
Jack Lambert
Tom Landry*
Bob St. Clair

CLASS OF 1991
(July 27, 1991)
Earl Campbell
John Hannah
Stan Jones
Tex Schramm*
Jan Stenerud

CLASS OF 1992
(August 1, 1992)
Lem Barney
Al Davis
John Mackey
John Riggins

CLASS OF 1993
(July 31, 1993)
Dan Fouts
Larry Little
Chuck Noll
Walter Payton*
Bill Walsh*

CLASS OF 1994
(July 30, 1994)
Tony Dorsett
Bud Grant
Jimmy Johnson
Leroy Kelly
Jackie Smith
Randy White

CLASS OF 1995
(July 29, 1995)
Jim Finks*
Henry Jordan*
Steve Largent
Lee Roy Selmon
Kellen Winslow

CLASS OF 1996
(July 27, 1996)
Lou Creekmur*
Dan Dierdorf
Joe Gibbs
Charlie Joiner
Mel Renfro

CLASS OF 1997
(July 26, 1997)
Mike Haynes
Wellington Mara*
Don Shula
Mike Webster*

CLASS OF 1998
(August 1, 1998)
Paul Krause
Tommy McDonald
Anthony Muñoz
Mike Singletary
Dwight Stephenson

CLASS OF 1999
(August 7, 1999)
Eric Dickerson
Tom Mack
Ozzie Newsome
Billy Shaw
Lawrence Taylor

CLASS OF 2000
(July 29, 2000)
Howie Long
Ronnie Lott
Joe Montana
Dan Rooney
Dave Wilcox

CLASS OF 2001
(August 4, 2001)
Nick Buoniconti
Marv Levy
Mike Munchak
Jackie Slater
Lynn Swann
Ron Yary
Jack Youngblood

CLASS OF 2002
(August 3, 2002)
George Allen*
Dave Casper
Dan Hampton
Jim Kelly
John Stallworth

CLASS OF 2003
(August 3, 2003)
Marcus Allen
Elvin Bethea
Joe DeLamielleure
James Lofton
Hank Stram*

CLASS OF 2004
(August 8, 2004)
Bob (Boomer) Brown
Carl Eller
John Elway
Barry Sanders

CLASS OF 2005
(August 7, 2005)
Benny Friedman*
Dan Marino
Fritz Pollard*
Steve Young

CLASS OF 2006
(*August 6, 2006*)
Troy Aikman
Harry Carson
John Madden
Warren Moon
Reggie White*
Rayfield Wright

CLASS OF 2007
(*August 4, 2007*)
Gene Hickerson*
Michael Irvin
Bruce Matthews
Charlie Sanders
Thurman Thomas
Roger Wehrli

CLASS OF 2008
(*August 2, 2008*)
Fred Dean
Darrell Green
Art Monk
Emmitt Thomas
Andre Tippett
Gary Zimmerman

CLASS OF 2009
(*August 8, 2009*)
Bob Hayes*
Randall McDaniel
Bruce Smith
Derrick Thomas*
Ralph Wilson, Jr.
Rod Woodson

CLASS OF 2010
(*August 7, 2010*)
Russ Grimm
Rickey Jackson
Dick LeBeau
Floyd Little
John Randle
Jerry Rice
Emmitt Smith

PRO FOOTBALL HALL OF FAME GAME (47)

Date	Winner	Loser	Attendance
August 11, 1962	New York Giants 21 (tie)	St. Louis Cardinals 21 (tie)	14,000
September 8, 1963	Pittsburgh Steelers 16	Cleveland Browns 7	18,462
September 6, 1964	Baltimore Colts 48	Pittsburgh Steelers 17	11,479
September 12, 1965	Washington Redskins 20	Detroit Lions 3	14,416
1966	No game was played		
August 5, 1967	Philadelphia Eagles 28	Cleveland Browns 13	17,304
August 3, 1968	Chicago Bears 30	Dallas Cowboys 24	14,578
September 13, 1969	Green Bay Packers 38	Atlanta Falcons 24	17,411
August 8, 1970	New Orleans Saints 14	Minnesota Vikings 13	17,932
July 31, 1971	Los Angeles Rams (NFC) 17	Houston Oilers (AFC) 6	19,384
July 29, 1972	Kansas City Chiefs (AFC) 23	New York Giants (NFC) 17	19,304
July 28, 1973	San Francisco 49ers (NFC) 20	New England Patriots (AFC) 7	19,685
July 27, 1974	St. Louis Cardinals (NFC) 21	Buffalo Bills (AFC) 13	17,286
August 2, 1975	Washington Redskins (NFC) 17	Cincinnati Bengals (AFC) 9	19,360
July 24, 1976	Denver Broncos (AFC) 10	Detroit Lions (NFC) 7	17,639
July 30, 1977	Chicago Bears (NFC) 20	New York Jets (AFC) 6	19,057
July 29, 1978	Philadelphia Eagles (NFC) 17	Miami Dolphins (AFC) 3	19,255
July 28, 1979	Oakland Raiders (AFC) 20	Dallas Cowboys (NFC) 13	20,648
August 2, 1980*	San Diego Chargers (AFC) 0	Green Bay Packers (NFC) 0	19,972
August 1, 1981	Cleveland Browns (AFC) 24	Atlanta Falcons (NFC) 10	23,921
August 7, 1982	Minnesota Vikings (NFC) 30	Baltimore Colts (AFC) 14	23,379
July 30, 1983	Pittsburgh Steelers (AFC) 27	New Orleans Saints (NFC) 14	23,909
July 28, 1984	Seattle Seahawks (AFC) 38	Tampa Bay Buccaneers (NFC) 0	22,250
August 3, 1985	New York Giants (NFC) 21	Houston Oilers (AFC) 20	23,940
August 2, 1986	New England Patriots (AFC) 21	St. Louis Cardinals (NFC) 16	22,739
August 8, 1987	San Francisco 49ers (NFC) 20	Kansas City Chiefs (AFC) 7	23,826
July 30, 1988	Cincinnati Bengals (AFC) 14	Los Angeles Rams (NFC) 7	23,801
August 5, 1989	Washington Redskins (NFC) 31	Buffalo Bills (AFC) 6	23,948
August 4, 1990	Chicago Bears (NFC) 13	Cleveland Browns (AFC) 0	23,952
July 27, 1991	Detroit Lions (NFC) 14	Denver Broncos (AFC) 3	23,815
August 1, 1992	New York Jets (AFC) 41	Philadelphia Eagles (NFC) 14	23,853
July 31, 1993	Los Angeles Raiders (AFC) 19	Green Bay Packers (NFC) 3	23,863
July 30, 1994	Atlanta Falcons (NFC) 21	San Diego Chargers (AFC) 17	23,185
July 29, 1995	Carolina Panthers (NFC) 20	Jacksonville Jaguars (AFC) 14	24,625
July 27, 1996	Indianapolis Colts (AFC) 10	New Orleans Saints (NFC) 3	23,376
July 26, 1997	Minnesota Vikings (NFC) 28	Seattle Seahawks (AFC) 26	23,846
August 1, 1998	Tampa Bay Buccaneers (NFC) 30	Pittsburgh Steelers (AFC) 6	23,875
August 9, 1999	Cleveland Browns (AFC) 20	Dallas Cowboys (NFC) 17 (OT)	25,156
July 31, 2000	New England Patriots (AFC) 20	San Francisco 49ers (NFC) 0	22,840
August 6, 2001	St. Louis Rams (NFC) 17	Miami Dolphins (AFC) 10	22,736
August 5, 2002	New York Giants (NFC) 34	Houston Texans (AFC) 17	22,461
August 4, 2003**	Kansas City Chiefs (AFC) 9	Green Bay Packers (NFC) 0	22,385
August 9, 2004	Washington Redskins (NFC) 20	Denver Broncos (AFC) 17	22,177
August 8, 2005	Chicago Bears (NFC) 27	Miami Dolphins (AFC) 24	22,292
August 6, 2006	Oakland Raiders (AFC) 16	Philadelphia Eagles (NFC) 10	22,200
August 5, 2007	Pittsburgh Steelers (AFC) 20	New Orleans Saints (NFC) 7	22,302
August 3, 2008	Washington Redskins (NFC) 30	Indianapolis Colts (AFC) 16	22,216
August 9, 2009	Tennessee Titans (AFC) 21	Buffalo Bills (AFC) 18	22,153

**Game called with 5:29 remaining in the fourth quarter because of severe thunder and lightning.*

***Game called with 5:49 remaining in the third quarter because of lightning and torrential rain.*

CHRONOLOGY OF PROFESSIONAL FOOTBALL

1869
Rutgers and Princeton played a college soccer football game, the first ever, November 6. The game used modified London Football Association rules. During the next seven years, rugby gained favor with the major eastern schools over soccer, and modern football began to develop from rugby.

1876
At the Massasoit convention, the first rules for American football were written. Walter Camp, who would become known as the father of American football, first became involved with the game.

1892
In an era in which football was a major attraction of local athletic clubs, an intense competition between two Pittsburgh-area clubs, the Allegheny Athletic Association (AAA) and the Pittsburgh Athletic Club (PAC), led to the making of the first professional football player. Former Yale All-America guard William (Pudge) Heffelfinger was paid $500 by the AAA to play in a game against the PAC, becoming the first person to be paid to play football, November 12. The AAA won the game 4-0 when Heffelfinger picked up a PAC fumble and ran 35 yards for a touchdown.

1893
The Pittsburgh Athletic Club signed one of its players, probably halfback Grant Dibert, to the first known pro football contract, which covered all of the PAC's games for the year.

1895
John Brallier became the first football player to openly turn pro, accepting $10 and expenses to play for the Latrobe YMCA against the Jeannette Athletic Club.

1896
The Allegheny Athletic Association team fielded the first completely professional team for its abbreviated two-game season.

1897
The Latrobe Athletic Association football team went entirely professional, becoming the first team to play a full season with only professionals.

1898
A touchdown was changed from four points to five.

Chris O'Brien formed a neighborhood team, which played under the name the Morgan Athletic Club, on the south side of Chicago. The team later became known as the Normals, then the Racine (for a street in Chicago) Cardinals, the Chicago Cardinals, the St. Louis Cardinals, the Phoenix Cardinals, and, in 1994, the Arizona Cardinals. The team remains the oldest continuing operation in pro football.

1900
William C. Temple took over the team payments for the Duquesne Country and Athletic Club, becoming the first known individual club owner.

1902
Baseball's Philadelphia Athletics, managed by Connie Mack, and the Philadelphia Phillies formed professional football teams, joining the Pittsburgh Stars in the first attempt at a pro football league, named the National Football League. The Athletics won the first night football game ever played, 39-0 over Kanaweola AC at Elmira, New York, November 21.

All three teams claimed the pro championship for the year, but the league president, Dave Berry, named the Stars the champions. Pitcher Rube Waddell was with the Athletics, and pitcher Christy Mathewson a fullback for Pittsburgh.

The first World Series of pro football, actually a five-team tournament, was played among a team made up of players from both the Athletics and the Phillies, but simply named New York; the New York Knickerbockers; the Syracuse AC; the Warlow AC; and the Orange (New Jersey) AC at New York's original Madison Square Garden. New York and Syracuse played the first indoor football game before 3,000, December 28. Syracuse, with Glen (Pop) Warner at guard, won 6-0 and went on to win the tournament.

1903
The Franklin (Pa.) Athletic Club won the second and last World Series of pro football over the Oreos AC of Asbury Park, New Jersey; the Watertown Red and Blacks; and the Orange AC.

Pro football was popularized in Ohio when the Massillon Tigers, a strong amateur team, hired four Pittsburgh pros to play in the season-ending game against Akron. At the same time, pro football declined in the Pittsburgh area, and the emphasis on the pro game moved west from Pennsylvania to Ohio.

1904
A field goal was changed from five points to four.

Ohio had at least seven pro teams, with Massillon winning the Ohio Independent Championship, that is, the pro title. Talk surfaced about forming a state-wide league to end spiraling salaries brought about by constant bidding for players and to write universal rules for the game. The feeble attempt to start the league failed.

Halfback Charles Follis signed a contract with the Shelby (Ohio) AC, making him the first known black pro football player.

1905
The Canton AC, later to become known as the Bulldogs, became a professional team. Massillon again won the Ohio League championship.

1906
The forward pass was legalized. The first authenticated pass completion in a pro game came on October 25, when George (Peggy) Parratt of Massillon threw a completion to Dan (Bullet) Riley in a victory over a combined Benwood-Moundsville team.

Arch-rivals Canton and Massillon, the two best pro teams in America, played twice, with Canton winning the first game but Massillon winning the second and the Ohio League championship. A betting scandal and the financial disaster wrought upon the two clubs by paying huge salaries caused a temporary decline in interest in pro football in the two cities and, somewhat, throughout Ohio.

1909
A field goal dropped from four points to three.

1912
A touchdown was increased from five points to six.

Jack Cusack revived a strong pro team in Canton.

1913
Jim Thorpe, a former football and track star at the Carlisle Indian School (Pa.) and a double gold medal winner at the 1912 Olympics in Stockholm, played for the Pine Village Pros in Indiana.

1915
Massillon again fielded a major team, reviving the old rivalry with Canton. Cusack signed Thorpe to play for Canton for $250 a game.

1916
With Thorpe and former Carlisle teammate Pete Calac starring, Canton went 9-0-1, won the Ohio League championship, and was acclaimed the pro football champion.

1917
Despite an upset by Massillon, Canton again won the Ohio League championship.

1919
Canton again won the Ohio League championship, despite the team having been turned over from Cusack to Ralph Hay. Thorpe and Calac were joined in the backfield by Joe Guyon.

Earl (Curly) Lambeau and George Calhoun organized the Green Bay Packers. Lambeau's employer at the Indian Packing Company provided $500 for equipment and allowed the team to use the company field for practices. The Packers went 10-1.

1920
Pro football was in a state of confusion due to three major problems: dramatically rising salaries; players continually jumping from one team to another following the highest offer; and the use of college players still enrolled in school. A league in which all the members would follow the same rules seemed the answer. An

organizational meeting, at which the Akron Pros, Canton Bulldogs, Cleveland Indians, and Dayton Triangles were represented, was held at the Jordan and Hupmobile auto showroom in Canton, Ohio, August 20. This meeting resulted in the formation of the American Professional Football Conference.

A second organizational meeting was held in Canton, September 17. The teams were from four states—Akron, Canton, Cleveland, and Dayton from Ohio; the Hammond Pros and Muncie Flyers from Indiana; the Rochester Jeffersons from New York; and the Rock Island Independents, Decatur Staleys, and Racine Cardinals from Illinois. The name of the league was changed to the American Professional Football Association. Hoping to capitalize on his fame, the members elected Thorpe president; Stanley Cofall of Cleveland was elected vice president. A membership fee of $100 per team was charged to give an appearance of respectability, but no team ever paid it. Scheduling was left up to the teams, and there were wide variations, both in the overall number of games played and in the number played against APFA member teams.

Four other teams—the Buffalo All-Americans, Chicago Tigers, Columbus Panhandles, and Detroit Heralds—joined the league sometime during the year. On September 26, the first game featuring an APFA team was played at Rock Island's Douglas Park. A crowd of 800 watched the Independents defeat the St. Paul Ideals 48-0. A week later, October 3, the first game matching two APFA teams was held. At Triangle Park, Dayton defeated Columbus 14-0, with Lou Partlow of Dayton scoring the first touchdown in a game between Association teams. The same day, Rock Island defeated Muncie 45-0.

By the beginning of December, most of the teams in the APFA had abandoned their hopes for a championship, and some of them, including the Chicago Tigers and the Detroit Heralds, had finished their seasons, disbanded, and had their franchises canceled by the Association. Four teams—Akron, Buffalo, Canton, and Decatur—still had championship as-pirations, but a series of late-season games among them left Akron as the only undefeated team in the Association. At one of these games, Akron sold tackle Bob Nash to Buffalo for $300 and five percent of the gate receipts—the first APFA player deal.

1921

At the league meeting in Akron, April 30, the championship of the 1920 season was awarded to the Akron Pros. The APFA was reorganized, with Joe Carr of the Columbus Panhandles named president and Carl Storck of Dayton secretary-treasurer. Carr moved the Association's headquarters to Columbus, drafted a league constitution and by-laws, gave teams territorial rights, restricted player movements, developed membership criteria for the franchises, and issued standings for the first time, so that the APFA would have a clear champion.

The Association's membership increased to 22 teams, including the Green Bay Packers, who were awarded to John Clair of the Acme Packing Company.

Thorpe moved from Canton to the Cleveland Indians, but he was hurt early in the season and played very little.

A.E. Staley turned the Decatur Staleys over to player-coach George Halas, who moved the team to Cubs Park in Chicago. Staley paid Halas $5,000 to keep the name Staleys for one more year. Halas made halfback Ed (Dutch) Sternaman his partner.

Player-coach Fritz Pollard of the Akron Pros became the first black head coach.

The Staleys claimed the APFA championship with a 9-1-1 record, as did Buffalo at 9-1-2. Carr ruled in favor of the Staleys, giving Halas his first championship.

1922

After admitting the use of players who had college eligibility remaining during the 1921 season, Clair and the Green Bay management withdrew from the APFA, January 28. Curly Lambeau promised to obey league rules and then used $50 of his own money to buy back the franchise. Bad weather and low attendance plagued the Packers, and Lambeau went broke, but local merchants arranged a $2,500 loan for the club. A public nonprofit corporation was set up to operate the team, with Lambeau as head coach and manager.

The American Professional Football Association changed its name to the National Football League, June 24. The Chicago Staleys became the Chicago Bears.

The NFL fielded 18 teams, including the new Oorang Indians of Marion, Ohio, an all-Indian team featuring Thorpe, Joe Guyon, and Pete Calac, and sponsored by the Oorang dog kennels.

Canton, led by player-coach Guy Chamberlin and tackles Link Lyman and Wilbur (Pete) Henry, emerged as the league's first true powerhouse, going 10-0-2.

1923

For the first time, all of the franchises considered to be part of the NFL fielded teams. Thorpe played his second and final season for the Oorang Indians. Against the Bears, Thorpe fumbled, and Halas picked up the ball and returned it 98 yards for a touchdown, a record that would last until 1972.

Canton had its second consecutive undefeated season, going 11-0-1 for the NFL title.

1924

The league had 18 franchises, including new ones in Kansas City, Kenosha, and Frankford, a section of Philadelphia. League champion Canton, successful on the field but not at the box office, was purchased by the owner of the Cleveland franchise, who kept the Canton franchise inactive, while using the best players for his Cleveland team, which he renamed the Bulldogs. Cleveland won the title with a 7-1-1 record.

1925

Five new franchises were admitted to the NFL—the New York Giants, who were awarded to Tim Mara and Billy Gibson for $500; the Detroit Panthers, featuring Jimmy Conzelman as owner, coach, and tailback; the Providence Steam Roller; a new Canton Bulldogs team; and the Pottsville Maroons, who had been perhaps the most successful independent pro team. The NFL established its first player limit, at 16 players.

Late in the season, the NFL made its greatest coup in gaining national recognition. Shortly after the University of Illinois season ended in November, All-America halfback Harold (Red) Grange signed a contract to play with the Chicago Bears. On Thanksgiving Day, a crowd of 36,000—the largest in pro football history—watched Grange and the Bears play the Chicago Cardinals to a scoreless tie at Wrigley Field. At the beginning of December, the Bears left on a barnstorming tour that saw them play eight games in 12 days, in St. Louis, Philadelphia, New York City, Washington, Boston, Pittsburgh, Detroit, and Chicago. A crowd of 73,000 watched the game against the Giants at the Polo Grounds, helping assure the future of the troubled NFL franchise in New York. The Bears then played nine more games in the South and West, including a game in Los Angeles, in which 75,000 fans watched them defeat the Los Angeles Tigers in the Los Angeles Memorial Coliseum.

Pottsville and the Chicago Cardinals were the top contenders for the league title, with Pottsville winning a late-season meeting 21-7. Pottsville scheduled a game against a team of former Notre Dame players for Shibe Park in Philadelphia. Frankford lodged a protest not only because the game was in Frankford's protected territory, but because it was being played the same day as a Yellow Jackets home game. Carr gave three different notices forbidding Pottsville to play the game, but Pottsville played anyway, December 12. That day, Carr fined the club, suspended it from all rights and privileges (including the right to play for the NFL championship), and re-turned its franchise to the league. The Cardinals, who ended the season with the best record in the league, were named the 1925 champions.

1926
Grange's manager, C.C. Pyle, told the Bears that Grange wouldn't play for them unless he was paid a five-figure salary and given one-third ownership of the team. The Bears refused. Pyle leased Yankee Stadium in New York City, then petitioned for an NFL franchise. After he was refused, he started the first American Football League. It lasted one season and included Grange's New York Yankees and eight other teams. The AFL champion Philadelphia Quakers played a December game against the New York Giants, seventh in the NFL, and the Giants won 31-0. At the end of the season, the AFL folded.

Halas pushed through a rule that prohibited any team from signing a player whose college class had not graduated.

The NFL grew to 22 teams, including the Duluth Eskimos, who signed All-America fullback Ernie Nevers of Stanford, giving the league a gate attraction to rival Grange. The 15-member Eskimos, dubbed the Iron Men of the North, played 29 exhibition and league games, 28 on the road, and Nevers played in all but 29 minutes of them.

Frankford edged the Bears for the championship, despite Halas having obtained John (Paddy) Driscoll from the Cardinals. On December 4, the Yellow Jackets scored in the final two minutes to defeat the Bears 7-6 and move ahead of them in the standings.

1927
At a special meeting in Cleveland, April 23, Carr decided to secure the NFL's future by eliminating the financially weaker teams and consolidating the quality players onto a limited number of more successful teams. The new-look NFL dropped to 12 teams, and the center of gravity of the league left the Midwest, where the NFL had started, and began to emerge in the large cities of the East. One of the new teams was Grange's New York Yankees, but Grange suffered a knee injury and the Yankees finished in the middle of the pack. The NFL championship was won by the cross-town rival New York Giants, who posted 10 shutouts in 13 games.

1928
Grange and Nevers both retired from pro football, and Duluth disbanded, as the NFL was reduced to only 10 teams. The Providence Steam Roller of Jimmy Conzelman and Pearce Johnson won the championship, playing in the Cycledrome, a 10,000-seat oval that had been built for bicycle races.

1929
Chris O'Brien sold the Chicago Cardinals to David Jones, July 27.

The NFL added a fourth official, the field judge, July 28.

Grange and Nevers returned to the NFL. Nevers scored six rushing touchdowns and four extra points as the Cardinals beat Grange's Bears 40-6, November 28. The 40 points set a record that remains the NFL's oldest.

Providence became the first NFL team to host a game at night under floodlights, against the Cardinals, November 6.

The Packers added back Johnny Blood (McNally), tackle Cal Hubbard, and guard Mike Michalske, and won their first NFL championship, edging the Giants, who featured quarterback Benny Friedman.

1930
Dayton, the last of the NFL's original franchises, was purchased by William B. Dwyer and John C. Depler, moved to Brooklyn, and renamed the Dodgers. The Portsmouth, Ohio, Spartans entered the league.

The Packers edged the Giants for the title, but the most improved team was the Bears. Halas retired as a player and replaced himself as coach of the Bears with Ralph Jones, who refined the T-formation by introducing wide ends and a halfback in motion. Jones also introduced rookie All-America fullback-tackle Bronko Nagurski.

The Giants defeated a team of former Notre Dame players coached by Knute Rockne 22-0 before 55,000 at the Polo Grounds, December 14. The proceeds went to the New York Unemployment Fund to help those suffering because of the Great Depression, and the easy victory helped give the NFL credibility with the press and the public.

1931
The NFL decreased to 10 teams, and halfway through the season the Frankford franchise folded. Carr fined the Bears, Packers, and Portsmouth $1,000 each for using players whose college classes had not graduated.

The Packers won an unprecedented third consecutive title, beating out the Spartans, who were led by rookie backs Earl (Dutch) Clark and Glenn Presnell.

1932
George Preston Marshall, Vincent Bendix, Jay O'Brien, and M. Dorland Doyle were awarded a franchise for Boston, July 9. Despite the presence of two rookies—halfback Cliff Battles and tackle Glen (Turk) Edwards—the new team, named the Braves, lost money and Marshall was left as the sole owner at the end of the year.

NFL membership dropped to eight teams, the lowest in history. Official statistics were kept for the first time. The Bears and the Spartans finished the season in the first-ever tie for first place. After the season finale, the league office arranged for an additional regular-season game to determine the league champion. The game was moved indoors to Chicago Stadium because of bitter cold and heavy snow. The arena allowed only an 80-yard field that came right to the walls. The goal posts were moved from the end lines to the goal lines and, for safety, inbounds lines or hashmarks where the ball would be put in play were drawn 10 yards from the walls that butted against the sidelines. The Bears won 9-0, December 18, scoring the winning touchdown on a two-yard pass from Nagurski to Grange. The Spartans claimed Nagurski's pass was thrown from less than five yards behind the line of scrimmage, violating the existing passing rule, but the play stood.

1933
The NFL, which long had followed the rules of college football, made a number of significant changes from the college game for the first time and began to develop rules serving its needs and the style of play it preferred. The innovations from the 1932 championship game—inbounds line or hashmarks and goal posts on the goal lines—were adopted. Also the forward pass was legalized from anywhere behind the line of scrimmage, February 25.

Marshall and Halas pushed through a proposal that divided the NFL into two divisions, with the winners to meet in an annual championship game, July 8.

Three new franchises joined the league—the Pittsburgh Pirates of Art Rooney, the Philadelphia Eagles of Bert Bell and Lud Wray, and the Cincinnati Reds. The Staten Island Stapletons suspended operations for a year, but never returned to the league.

Halas bought out Sternaman, became sole owner of the Bears, and reinstated himself as head coach. Marshall changed the name of the Boston Braves to the Redskins. David Jones sold the Chicago Cardinals to Charles W. Bidwill.

In the first NFL Championship Game scheduled before the season, the Western Division champion Bears defeated the Eastern Division champion Giants 23-21 at Wrigley Field, December 17.

1934
G.A. (Dick) Richards purchased the Portsmouth Spartans, moved them to Detroit, and renamed them the Lions.

Professional football gained new prestige when the Bears were matched against the best college football players in the first Chicago College All-Star Game, August 31. The game ended in a scoreless tie before 79,432 at Soldier Field.

The Cincinnati Reds lost their first eight games, then were suspended from the league for defaulting on payments. The St. Louis Gunners, an independent team, joined the NFL by buying the Cincinnati franchise and went 1-2 the last three weeks.

Rookie Beattie Feathers of the Bears became the NFL's first 1,000-yard rusher, gaining 1,004 on 101 carries. The Thanksgiving Day game between the Bears and the Lions became the first NFL game broadcast nationally, with Graham McNamee the announcer for NBC radio.

In the championship game, on an extremely cold and icy day at the Polo Grounds, the Giants trailed the Bears 13-3 in the third quarter before changing to basketball shoes for better footing. The Giants won 30-13 in what has come to be known as the Sneakers Game, December 9.

The player waiver rule was adopted, December 10.

1935
The NFL adopted Bert Bell's proposal to hold an annual draft of college players, to begin in 1936, with teams selecting in an inverse order of finish, May 19. The inbounds line or hashmarks were moved nearer the center of the field, 15 yards from the sidelines.

All-America end Don Hutson of Alabama joined Green Bay. The Lions defeated the Giants 26-7 in the NFL Championship Game, December 15.

1936
There were no franchise transactions for the first year since the formation of the NFL. It also was the first year in which all member teams played the same number of games.

The Eagles made University of Chicago halfback and Heisman Trophy winner Jay Berwanger the first player ever selected in the NFL draft, February 8. The Eagles traded his rights to the Bears, but Berwanger never played pro football. The first player selected to actually sign was the number-two pick, Riley Smith of Alabama, who was selected by Boston.

A rival league was formed, and it became the second to call itself the American Football League. The Boston Shamrocks were its champions.

Because of poor attendance, Marshall, the owner of the host team, moved the Championship Game from Boston to the Polo Grounds in New York. Green Bay defeated the Redskins 21-6, December 13.

1937
Homer Marshman was granted a Cleveland franchise, named the Rams, February 12. Marshall moved the Redskins to Washington, D.C., February 13. The Redskins signed TCU All-America tailback Sammy Baugh, who led them to a 28-21 victory over the Bears in the NFL Championship Game, December 12.

The Los Angeles Bulldogs had an 8-0 record to win the AFL title, but then the 2-year-old league folded.

1938
At the suggestion of Halas, Hugh (Shorty) Ray became a technical advisor on rules and officiating to the NFL. A new rule called for a 15-yard penalty for roughing the passer.

Rookie Byron (Whizzer) White of the Pittsburgh Pirates led the NFL in rushing. The Giants defeated the Packers 23-17 for the NFL title, December 11.

Marshall, *Los Angeles Times* sports editor Bill Henry, and promoter Tom Gallery established the Pro Bowl game between the NFL champion and a team of pro all-stars.

1939
The New York Giants defeated the Pro All-Stars 13-10 in the first Pro Bowl, at Wrigley Field, Los Angeles, January 15.

Carr, NFL president since 1921, died in Columbus, May 20. Carl Storck was named acting president, May 25.

An NFL game was televised for the first time when NBC broadcast the Brooklyn Dodgers-Philadelphia Eagles game from Ebbets Field to the approximately 1,000 sets then in New York, October 22.

Green Bay defeated New York 27-0 in the NFL Championship Game, December 10 at Milwaukee. NFL attendance exceeded 1 million in a season for the first time, reaching 1,071,200.

1940
A six-team rival league, the third to call itself the American Football League, was formed, and the Columbus Bullies won its championship.

Halas' Bears, with additional coaching by Clark Shaughnessy of Stanford, defeated the Redskins 73-0 in the NFL Championship Game, December 8. The game, which was the most decisive victory in NFL history, popularized the Bears' T-formation with a man-in-motion. It was the first championship carried on network radio, broadcast by Red Barber to 120 stations of the Mutual Broadcasting System, which paid $2,500 for the rights.

Art Rooney sold the Pittsburgh franchise to Alexis Thompson, December 9, then bought part interest in the Philadelphia Eagles.

Bell and Rooney traded the Eagles to Thompson for the Pirates, then re-named their new team the Steelers.

1941
Elmer Layden was named the first Commissioner of the NFL, March 1; Storck, the acting president, resigned, April 5. NFL headquarters were moved to Chicago.

Homer Marshman sold the Rams to Daniel F. Reeves and Fred Levy, Jr.

The league by-laws were revised to provide for playoffs in case there were ties in division races, and sudden-death overtimes in case a playoff game was tied after four quarters. An official *NFL Record Manual* was published for the first time.

Columbus again won the championship of the AFL, but the two-year-old league then folded.

The Bears and the Packers finished in a tie for the Western Division championship, setting up the first divisional playoff game in league history. The Bears won 33-14, then defeated the Giants 37-9 for the NFL championship, December 21.

1942
Players departing for service in World War II depleted the rosters of NFL teams. Halas left the Bears in midseason to join the Navy, and Luke Johnsos and Heartley (Hunk) Anderson served as co-coaches as the Bears went 11-0 in the regular season. The Redskins defeated the Bears 14-6 in the NFL Championship Game, December 13.

1943
The Cleveland Rams, with co-owners Reeves and Levy in the service, were granted permission to suspend operations for one season, April 6. Levy transferred his stock in the team to Reeves, April 16.

The NFL adopted free substitution, April 7. The league also made the wearing of helmets mandatory and approved a 10-game schedule for all teams.

Philadelphia and Pittsburgh were granted permission to merge for one season, June 19. The team, known as Phil-Pitt (and called the Steagles by fans), divided home games between the two cities, and Earle (Greasy) Neale of Philadelphia and Walt Kiesling of Pittsburgh served as co-coaches. The merger automatically dissolved the last day of the season, December 5.

Ted Collins was granted a franchise for Boston, to become active in 1944.

Sammy Baugh led the league in passing, punting, and interceptions. He led the Redskins to a tie with the Giants for the Eastern Division title, and then to a 28-0 victory in a divisional playoff game. The Bears beat the Redskins 41-21 in the NFL Championship Game, December 26.

1944
Collins, who had wanted a franchise in Yankee Stadium in New York, named his new team in Boston the Yanks. Cleveland resumed operations. The Brooklyn Dodgers changed their name to the Tigers.

Coaching from the bench was legalized, April 20.

The Cardinals and the Steelers were granted permission to merge for one year under the name Card-Pitt, April 21. Phil Handler of the Cardinals and Walt Kiesling of the Steelers served as co-coaches. The merger automatically dissolved the last day of the season, December 3.

In the NFL Championship Game, Green Bay defeated the New York Giants 14-7, December 17.

1945
The inbounds lines or hashmarks were moved from 15 yards away from the sidelines to nearer the center of the field—20 yards from the sidelines.

Brooklyn and Boston merged into a team that played home games in both cities and was known simply as The Yanks. The team was coached by former Boston head coach Herb Kopf. In December, the Brooklyn franchise withdrew from the NFL to join the new All-America Football Conference; all the players on its active and reserve lists were assigned to The Yanks, who once again became the Boston Yanks.

Halas rejoined the Bears late in the season after service with the U.S. Navy. Although Halas took over much of the coaching duties, Anderson and Johnsos remained the coaches of record throughout the season.

Steve Van Buren of Philadelphia led the NFL in rushing, kickoff returns, and scoring.

After the Japanese surrendered ending World War II, a count showed that the NFL service roster, limited to men who had played in league games, totaled 638, 21 of whom had died in action.

Rookie quarterback Bob Waterfield led Cleveland to a 15-14 victory over Washington in the NFL Championship Game, December 16.

1946
The contract of Commissioner Layden was not renewed, and Bert Bell, the co-owner of the Steelers, replaced him, January 11. Bell moved the league headquarters from Chicago to the Philadelphia suburb of Bala-Cynwyd.

Free substitution was withdrawn and substitutions were limited to no more than three men at a time. Forward passes were made automatically incomplete upon striking the goal posts, January 11.

The NFL took on a truly national appearance for the first time when Reeves was granted permission by the league to move his NFL champion Rams to Los Angeles.

Halfback Kenny Washington (March 21) and end Woody Strode (May 7) signed with the Los Angeles Rams to become the first African-Americans to play in the NFL in the modern era. Guard Bill Willis (August 6) and running back Marion Motley (August 9) joined the AAFC with the Cleveland Browns.

The rival All-America Football Conference began play with eight teams. The Cleveland Browns, coached by Paul Brown, won the AAFC's first championship, defeating the New York Yankees 14-9.

Bill Dudley of the Steelers led the NFL in rushing, interceptions, and punt returns, and won the league's most valuable player award.

Backs Frank Filchock and Merle Hapes of the Giants were questioned about an attempt by a New York man to fix the championship game with the Bears. Bell suspended Hapes but allowed Filchock to play; he played well, but Chicago won 24-14, December 15.

1947
The NFL added a fifth official, the back judge.

A bonus choice was made for the first time in the NFL draft. One team each year would select the special choice before the first round began. The Chicago Bears won a lottery and the rights to the first choice and drafted back Bob Fenimore of Oklahoma A&M.

The Cleveland Browns again won the AAFC title, defeating the New York Yankees 14-3.

Charles Bidwill, Sr., owner of the Cardinals, died April 19, but his wife and sons retained ownership of the team. On December 28, the Cardinals won the NFL Championship Game 28-21 over the Philadelphia Eagles, who had beaten Pittsburgh 21-0 in a playoff.

1948
Plastic helmets were prohibited. A flexible artificial tee was permitted at the kickoff. Officials other than the referee were equipped with whistles, not horns, January 14.

Fred Mandel sold the Detroit Lions to a syndicate headed by D. Lyle Fife, January 15.

Halfback Fred Gehrke of the Los Angeles Rams painted horns on the Rams' helmets, the first modern helmet emblems in pro football.

The Cleveland Browns won their third straight championship in the AAFC, going 14-0 and then defeating the Buffalo Bills 49-7.

In a blizzard, the Eagles defeated the Cardinals 7-0 in the NFL Championship Game, December 19.

1949
Alexis Thompson sold the champion Eagles to a syndicate headed by James P. Clark, January 15. The Boston Yanks became the New York Bulldogs, sharing the Polo Grounds with the Giants.

Free substitution was adopted for one year, January 20.

The NFL had two 1,000-yard rushers in the same season for the first time—Steve Van Buren of Philadelphia and Tony Canadeo of Green Bay.

The AAFC played its season with a one-division, seven-team format. On December 9, Bell announced a merger agreement in which three AAFC franchises—Cleveland, San Francisco, and Baltimore—would join the NFL in 1950. The Browns won their fourth consecutive AAFC title, defeating the 49ers 21-7, December 11.

In a heavy rain, the Eagles defeated the Rams 14-0 in the NFL Championship Game, December 18.

1950
Unlimited free substitution was restored, opening the way for the era of two platoons and specialization in pro football, January 20.

Curly Lambeau, founder of the franchise and Green Bay's head coach since 1921, resigned under fire, February 1.

The name National Football League was restored after about three months as the National-American Football League. The American and National conferences were created to replace the Eastern and Western divisions, March 3.

The New York Bulldogs became the Yanks and divided the players of the former AAFC Yankees with the Giants. A special allocation draft was held in which the 13 teams drafted the remaining AAFC players, with special consideration for Baltimore, which received 15 choices compared to 10 for other teams.

The Los Angeles Rams became the first NFL team to have all of its games—both home and away—televised. The Washington Redskins followed the Rams in arranging to televise their games; other teams made deals to put selected games on television.

In the first game of the season, former AAFC champion Cleveland defeated NFL champion Philadelphia 35-10. For the first time, deadlocks occurred in both conferences and playoffs were necessary. The Browns defeated the Giants in the American and the Rams defeated the Bears in the National. Cleveland defeated Los Angeles 30-28 in the NFL Championship Game, December 24.

1951
The Pro Bowl game, dormant since 1942, was revived under a new format matching the all-stars of each conference at the Los Angeles Memorial Coliseum. The American Conference defeated the National Conference 28-27, January 14.

Abraham Watner returned the Baltimore franchise and its player contracts back to the NFL for $50,000. Baltimore's former players were made available for drafting at the same time as college players, January 18.

A rule was passed that no tackle, guard, or center would be eligible to catch a forward pass, January 18.

The Rams reversed their television policy and televised only road games.

The NFL Championship Game was televised coast-to-coast for the first time, December 23. The DuMont Network paid $75,000 for the rights to the game, in which the Rams defeated the Browns 24-17.

1952
Ted Collins sold the New York Yanks' franchise back to the NFL, January 19. A new fran-

chise was awarded to a group in Dallas after it purchased the assets of the Yanks, January 24. The new Texans went 1-11, with the owners turning the franchise back to the league in midseason. For the last five games of the season, the commissioner's office operated the Texans as a road team, using Hershey, Pennsylvania, as a home base. At the end of the season the franchise was canceled, the last time an NFL team failed.

The Pittsburgh Steelers abandoned the Single-Wing for the T-formation, the last pro team to do so.

The Detroit Lions won their first NFL championship in 17 years, defeating the Browns 17-7 in the title game, December 28.

1953
A Baltimore group headed by Carroll Rosenbloom was granted a franchise and was awarded the holdings of the defunct Dallas organization, January 23. The team, named the Colts, put together the largest trade in league history, acquiring 10 players from Cleveland in exchange for five.

The names of the American and National conferences were changed to the Eastern and Western conferences, January 24.

Jim Thorpe died, March 28.

Mickey McBride, founder of the Cleveland Browns, sold the franchise to a syndicate headed by Dave R. Jones, June 10.

The NFL policy of blacking out home games was upheld by Judge Allan K. Grim of the U.S. District Court in Philadelphia, November 12.

The Lions again defeated the Browns in the NFL Championship Game, winning 17-16, December 27.

1954
The Canadian Football League began a series of raids on NFL teams, signing quarterback Eddie LeBaron and defensive end Gene Brito of Washington and defensive tackle Arnie Weinmeister of the Giants, among others.

Fullback Joe Perry of the 49ers became the first player in league history to gain 1,000 yards rushing in consecutive seasons.

Cleveland defeated Detroit 56-10 in the NFL Championship Game, December 26.

1955
The sudden-death overtime rule was used for the first time in a preseason game between the Rams and Giants at Portland, Oregon, August 28. The Rams won 23-17 three minutes into overtime.

A rule change declared the ball dead immediately if the ball carrier touched the ground with any part of his body except his hands or feet while in the grasp of an opponent.

The Baltimore Colts made an 80-cent phone call to Johnny Unitas and signed him as a free agent. Another quarterback, Otto Graham, played his last game as the Browns defeated the Rams 38-14 in the NFL Championship Game, December 26. Graham had quarterbacked the Browns to 10 championship-game appearances in 10 years.

NBC replaced DuMont as the network for the title game, paying a rights fee of $100,000.

1956
The NFL Players Association was founded.

Grabbing an opponent's facemask (other than the ball carrier) was made illegal. Using radio receivers to communicate with players on the field was prohibited. A natural leather ball with white end stripes replaced the white ball with black stripes for night games.

The Giants moved from the Polo Grounds to Yankee Stadium.

Halas retired as coach of the Bears, and was replaced by Paddy Driscoll.

CBS became the first network to broadcast some NFL regular-season games to selected television markets across the nation.

The Giants routed the Bears 47-7 in the NFL Championship Game, December 30.

1957
Pete Rozelle was named general manager of the Rams. Anthony J. Morabito, founder and co-owner of the 49ers, died of a heart attack during a game against the Bears at Kezar Stadium, October 28. An NFL-record crowd of 102,368 saw the 49ers-Rams game at the Los Angeles Memorial Coliseum, November 10.

The Lions came from 20 points down to post a 31-27 playoff victory over the 49ers, December 22. Detroit defeated Cleveland 59-14 in the NFL Championship Game, December 29.

1958
The bonus selection in the draft was eliminated, January 29. The last selection was quarterback King Hill of Rice by the Chicago Cardinals.

Halas reinstated himself as coach of the Bears.

Jim Brown of Cleveland gained an NFL-record 1,527 yards rushing. In a divisional playoff game, the Giants held Brown to eight yards and defeated Cleveland 10-0.

Baltimore, coached by Weeb Ewbank, defeated the Giants 23-17 in the first sudden-death overtime in an NFL Championship Game, December 28. The game ended when Colts fullback Alan Ameche scored on a one-yard touchdown run after 8:15 of overtime.

1959
Vince Lombardi was named head coach of the Green Bay Packers, January 28. Tim Mara, the co-founder of the Giants, died, February 17.

Lamar Hunt of Dallas announced his intentions to form a second pro football league. The first meeting was held in Chicago, August 14, and consisted of Hunt representing Dallas; Bob Howsam, Denver; K.S. (Bud) Adams, Houston; Barron Hilton, Los Angeles; Max Winter and Bill Boyer, Minneapolis; and Harry Wismer, New York City. They made plans to begin play in 1960.

The new league was named the American Football League, August 22. Buffalo, owned by Ralph Wilson, became the seventh franchise, October 28. Boston, owned by William H. Sullivan, became the eighth team, November 22. The first AFL draft, lasting 33 rounds, was held, November 22. Joe Foss was named AFL Commissioner, November 30. An additional draft of 20 rounds was held by the AFL, December 2.

NFL Commissioner Bert Bell died of a heart attack suffered at Franklin Field, Philadelphia, during the last two minutes of a game between the Eagles and the Steelers, October 11. Treasurer Austin Gunsel was named president in the office of the commissioner, October 14.

The Colts again defeated the Giants in the NFL Championship Game, 31-16, December 27.

1960
Pete Rozelle was elected NFL Commissioner as a compromise choice on the twenty-third ballot, January 26. Rozelle moved the league offices to New York City.

Hunt was elected AFL president for 1960, January 26. Minneapolis withdrew from the AFL, January 27, and the same ownership was given an NFL franchise for Minnesota (to start in 1961), January 28. Dallas received an NFL franchise for 1960, January 28. Oakland received an AFL franchise, January 30.

The AFL adopted the two-point option on points after touchdown, January 28. A no-tampering verbal pact, relative to players' contracts, was agreed to between the NFL and AFL, February 9.

The NFL owners voted to allow the transfer of the Chicago Cardinals to St. Louis, March 13.

The AFL signed a five-year television contract with ABC, June 9.

The Boston Patriots defeated the Buffalo Bills 28-7 before 16,000 at Buffalo in the first AFL preseason game, July 30. The Denver Broncos defeated the Patriots 13-10 before 21,597 at Boston in the first AFL regular-season game, September 9.

Philadelphia defeated Green Bay 17-13 in the NFL Championship Game, December 26.

1961
The Houston Oilers defeated the Los Angeles Chargers 24-16 before 32,183 in the first AFL Championship Game, January 1.

Detroit defeated Cleveland 17-16 in the first Playoff Bowl, or Bert Bell Benefit Bowl, between second-place teams in each conference in Miami, January 7.

End Willard Dewveall of the Bears played out his option and joined the Oilers, becoming the first player to play out his contract and jump from the NFL to the AFL, January 14.

Ed McGah, Wayne Valley, and Robert Osborne bought out their partners in the ownership of the Raiders, January 17. The Chargers were transferred to San Diego, February 10. Dave R. Jones sold the Browns to a group headed by Arthur B. Modell, March 22. The Howsam brothers sold the Broncos to a group headed by Calvin Kunz and Gerry Phipps, May 26.

NBC was awarded a two-year contract for radio and television rights to the NFL Championship Game for $615,000 annually, $300,000 of which was to go directly into the NFL Player Benefit Plan, April 5.

Canton, Ohio, where the league that became the NFL was formed in 1920, was chosen as the site of the Pro Football Hall of Fame, April 27. Dick McCann, a former Redskins executive, was named executive director.

A bill legalizing single-network television contracts by professional sports leagues was introduced in Congress by Representative Emanuel Celler. It passed the House and Senate and was signed into law by President John F. Kennedy, September 30.

Houston defeated San Diego 10-3 for the AFL championship, December 24. Green Bay won its first NFL championship since 1944, defeating the New York Giants 37-0, December 31.

1962
The Western Division defeated the Eastern Division 47-27 in the first AFL All-Star Game, played before 20,973 in San Diego, January 7.

Both leagues prohibited grabbing any player's facemask. The AFL voted to make the scoreboard clock the official timer of the game.

The NFL entered into a single-network agreement with CBS for telecasting all regular-season games for $4.65 million annually, January 10.

Judge Roszel Thompson of the U.S. District Court in Baltimore ruled against the AFL in its antitrust suit against the NFL, May 21. The AFL had charged the NFL with monopoly and conspiracy in areas of expansion, television, and player signings. The case lasted two and a half years, the trial two months.

McGah and Valley acquired controlling interest in the Raiders, May 24. The AFL assumed financial responsibility for the New York Titans, November 8. With Commissioner Rozelle as referee, Daniel F. Reeves regained the ownership of the Rams, outbidding his partners in sealed-envelope bidding for the team, November 27.

The Dallas Texans defeated the Oilers 20-17 for the AFL championship at Houston after 17 minutes, 54 seconds of overtime on a 25-yard field goal by Tommy Brooker, December 23. The game lasted a record 77 minutes, 54 seconds.

Judge Edward Weinfeld of the U.S. District Court in New York City upheld the legality of the NFL's television blackout within a 75-mile radius of home games and denied an injunction that would have forced the championship game between the Giants and the Packers to be televised in the New York City area, December 28. The Packers beat the Giants 16-7 for the NFL title, December 30.

1963
The Dallas Texans transferred to Kansas City, becoming the Chiefs, February 8. The New York Titans were sold to a five-man syndicate headed by David (Sonny) Werblin, March 28. Weeb Ewbank became the Titans' new head coach and the team's name was changed to the Jets, April 15. They began play in the Polo Grounds.

NFL Properties, Inc., was founded to serve as the licensing arm of the NFL.

Rozelle indefinitely suspended Green Bay halfback Paul Hornung and Detroit defensive tackle Alex Karras for placing bets on their own teams and on other NFL games; he also fined five other Detroit players $2,000 each for betting on one game in which they did not participate, and the Detroit Lions Football Company $2,000 on each of two counts for failure to report information promptly and for lack of sideline supervision.

Paul Brown, head coach of the Browns since their inception, was fired and replaced by Blanton Collier. Don Shula replaced Weeb Ewbank as head coach of the Colts.

The AFL allowed the Jets and Raiders to select players from other franchises in hopes of giving the league more competitive balance, May 11.

NBC was awarded exclusive network broadcasting rights for the 1963 NFL Championship Game for $926,000, May 23.

The Pro Football Hall of Fame was dedicated at Canton, Ohio, September 7.

The U.S. Fourth Circuit Court of Appeals reaffirmed the lower court's finding for the NFL in the $10-million suit brought by the AFL, ending three and a half years of litigation, November 21.

Jim Brown of Cleveland rushed for an NFL single-season record 1,863 yards.

Boston defeated Buffalo 26-8 in the first divisional playoff game in AFL history, December 28.

The Bears defeated the Giants 14-10 in the NFL Championship Game, a record sixth and last title for Halas in his thirty-sixth season as the Bears' coach, December 29.

1964
The Chargers defeated the Patriots 51-10 in the AFL Championship Game, January 5.

William Clay Ford, the Lions' president since 1961, purchased the team, January 10. A group representing the late James P. Clark sold the Eagles to a group headed by Jerry Wolman, January 21. Carroll Rosenbloom, the majority owner of the Colts since 1953, acquired complete ownership of the team, January 23.

The AFL signed a five-year, $36-million television contract with NBC to begin with the 1965 season, January 29.

Hornung and Karras were reinstated by Rozelle, March 16.

CBS submitted the winning bid of $14.1 million per year for the NFL regular-season television rights for 1964 and 1965, January 24. CBS acquired the rights to the championship games for 1964 and 1965 for $1.8 million per game, April 17.

Pete Gogolak of Cornell signed a contract with Buffalo, becoming the first soccer-style kicker in pro football.

Buffalo defeated San Diego 20-7 in the AFL Championship Game, December 26. Cleveland defeated Baltimore 27-0 in the NFL Championship Game, December 27.

1965
The NFL teams pledged not to sign college seniors until completion of all their games, including bowl games, and empowered the Commissioner to discipline the clubs up to as much as the loss of an entire draft list for a violation of the pledge, February 15.

The NFL added a sixth official, the line judge, February 19. The color of the officials' penalty flags was changed from white to bright gold, April 5.

Commissioner Rozelle negotiated an agreement on behalf of the NFL clubs to purchase Ed Sabol's Blair Motion Pictures, which was renamed NFL Films, April.

Atlanta was awarded an NFL franchise for 1966, with Rankin Smith, Sr., as owner, June 30. Miami was awarded an AFL franchise for 1966, with Joe Robbie and Danny Thomas as owners, August 16.

Field Judge Burl Toler became the first black official in NFL history, September 19.

According to a Harris survey, sports fans chose professional football (41 percent) as their favorite sport, overtaking baseball (38 percent) for the first time, October.

Green Bay defeated Baltimore 13-10 in sudden-death overtime in a Western Conference playoff game. Don Chandler kicked a 25-yard field goal for the Packers after 13 minutes, 39 seconds of overtime, December 26. The Packers then defeated the Browns 23-12 in the NFL Championship Game, January 2.

In the AFL Championship Game, the Bills defeated the Chargers, 23-0, December 26.

CBS acquired the rights to

the NFL regular-season games in 1966 and 1967, with an option for 1968, for $18.8 million per year, December 29.

1966
The AFL-NFL war reached its peak, as the leagues spent a combined $7 million to sign their 1966 draft choices. The NFL signed 75 percent of its 232 draftees, the AFL 46 percent of its 181. Of the 111 common draft choices, 79 signed with the NFL, 28 with the AFL, and 4 went unsigned.

Buddy Young became the first African-American to work in the league office when Commissioner Rozelle named him director of player relations, February 1.

The rights to the 1966 and 1967 NFL Championship Games were sold to CBS for $2 million per game, February 14.

Foss resigned as AFL Commissioner, April 7. Al Davis, the head coach and general manager of the Raiders, was named to replace him, April 8.

Goal posts offset from the goal line, painted bright yellow, and with uprights 20 feet above the cross-bar were made standard in the NFL, May 16.

A series of secret meetings regarding a possible AFL-NFL merger were held in the spring between Hunt of Kansas City and Tex Schramm of Dallas. Rozelle announced the merger, June 8. Under the agreement, the two leagues would combine to form an expanded league with 24 teams, to be increased to 26 in 1968 and to 28 by 1970 or soon thereafter. All existing franchises would be retained, and no franchises would be transferred outside their metropolitan areas. While maintaining separate schedules through 1969, the leagues agreed to play an annual AFL-NFL World Championship Game beginning in January, 1967, and to hold a combined draft, also beginning in 1967. Preseason games would be held between teams of each league starting in 1967. Official regular-season play would start in 1970 when the two leagues would officially merge to form one league with two conferences. Rozelle was named Commissioner of the expanded league setup.

Davis rejoined the Raiders, and Milt Woodard was named president of the AFL, July 25.

The St. Louis Cardinals moved into newly constructed Busch Memorial Stadium.

Barron Hilton sold the Chargers to a group headed by Eugene Klein and Sam Schulman, August 25.

Congress approved the AFL-NFL merger, passing legislation exempting the agreement itself from antitrust action, October 21.

New Orleans was awarded an NFL franchise to begin play in 1967, November 1. John Mecom, Jr., of Houston was designated majority stockholder and president of the franchise, December 15.

The NFL was realigned for the 1967-69 seasons into the Capitol and Century Divisions in the Eastern Conference and the Central and Coastal Divisions in the Western Conference, December 2. New Orleans and the New York Giants agreed to switch divisions in 1968 and return to the 1967 alignment in 1969.

The rights to the Super Bowl for four years were sold to CBS and NBC for $9.5 million, December 13.

1967
Green Bay earned the right to represent the NFL in the first AFL-NFL World Championship Game by defeating Dallas 34-27, January 1. The same day, Kansas City defeated Buffalo 31-7 to represent the AFL. The Packers defeated the Chiefs 35-10 before 61,946 fans at the Los Angeles Memorial Coliseum in the first game between AFL and NFL teams, January 15. The winning players' share for the Packers was $15,000 each, and the losing players' share for the Chiefs was $7,500 each. The game was televised by both CBS and NBC.

The "sling-shot" goal post and a six-foot-wide border around the field were made standard in the NFL, February 22.

Baltimore made Bubba Smith, a Michigan State defensive lineman, the first choice in the first combined AFL-NFL draft, March 14.

The AFL awarded a franchise to begin play in 1968 to Cincinnati, May 23. A group with Paul Brown as part owner, general manager, and head coach, was awarded the Cincinnati franchise, September 27.

Arthur B. Modell, the president of the Cleveland Browns, was elected president of the NFL, May 28.

Defensive back Emlen Tunnell of the New York Giants became the first black player to enter the Pro Football Hall of Fame, August 5.

An AFL team defeated an NFL team for the first time, when Denver beat Detroit 13-7 in a preseason game, August 5.

Green Bay defeated Dallas 21-17 for the NFL championship on a last-minute 1-yard quarterback sneak by Bart Starr in 13-below-zero temperature at Green Bay, December 31. The same day, Oakland defeated Houston 40-7 for the AFL championship.

1968
Green Bay defeated Oakland 33-14 in Super Bowl II at Miami, January 14. The game had the first $3-million gate in pro football history.

Vince Lombardi resigned as head coach of the Packers, but remained as general manager, January 28.

Werblin sold his shares in the Jets to his partners Don Lillis, Leon Hess, Townsend Martin, and Phil Iselin, May 21. Lillis assumed the presidency of the club, but then died July 23. Iselin was appointed president, August 6.

Halas retired for the fourth and last time as head coach of the Bears, May 27.

The Oilers left Rice Stadium for the Astrodome and became the first NFL team to play its home games in a domed stadium.

The movie *Heidi* became a footnote in sports history when NBC didn't show the last 50 seconds of the Jets-Raiders game in order to permit the children's special to begin on time. The Raiders scored two touchdowns in the last 42 seconds to win 43-32, November 17.

Ewbank became the first coach to win titles in both the NFL and AFL when his Jets defeated the Raiders 27-23 for the AFL championship, December 29. The same day, Baltimore defeated Cleveland 34-0.

1969
The AFL established a playoff format for the 1969 season, with the winner in one division playing the runner-up in the other, January 11.

An AFL team won the Super Bowl for the first time, as the Jets defeated the Colts 16-7 at Miami, January 12 in Super Bowl III. The title Super Bowl was recognized by the NFL for the first time.

Vince Lombardi became part owner, executive vice-president, and head coach of the Washington Redskins, February 7.

Wolman sold the Eagles to Leonard Tose, May 1.

Baltimore, Cleveland, and Pittsburgh agreed to join the AFL teams to form the 13-team American Football Conference of the NFL in 1970, May 17. The NFL also agreed on a playoff format that would include one "wild-card" team per conference—the second-place team with the best record.

The NFL announced a three-year agreement with ABC to televise *Monday Night Football*. The new series makes the NFL the first league with a regular series of national telecasts in prime time, May 26.

George Preston Marshall, president emeritus of the Redskins, died at 72, August 9.

The NFL marked its fiftieth year by the wearing of a special patch by each of the 16 teams.

1970
Kansas City defeated Minnesota 23-7 in Super Bowl IV at New Orleans, January 11. The gross receipts of approximately $3.8 million were the largest ever for a one-day sports event.

Four-year television contracts, under which CBS would televise all NFC games and NBC all AFC games (except Monday night games) and the two would divide televising the Super Bowl and AFC-NFC Pro Bowl games, were announced, January 26.

Art Modell resigned as president of the NFL, March 12. Milt Woodard resigned as president of the AFL, March

13. Lamar Hunt was elected president of the AFC and George Halas was elected president of the NFC, March 19.

The merged 26-team league adopted rules changes putting names on the backs of players' jerseys, making a point after touchdown worth only one point, and making the scoreboard clock the official timing device of the game, March 18.

The Players Negotiating Committee and the NFL Players Association announced a four-year agreement guaranteeing approximately $4,535,000 annually to player pension and insurance benefits, August 3. The owners also agreed to contribute $250,000 annually to improve or implement items such as disability payments, widows' benefits, maternity benefits, and dental benefits. The agreement also provided for increased preseason game and per diem payments, averaging approximately $2.6 million annually.

The Pittsburgh Steelers moved into Three Rivers Stadium. The Cincinnati Bengals moved to Riverfront Stadium.

Vince Lombardi died of cancer at 57, September 3.

The Super Bowl trophy was renamed the Vince Lombardi trophy, September 10.

Tom Dempsey of New Orleans kicked a game-winning NFL-record 63-yard field goal against Detroit, November 8.

1971

Baltimore defeated Dallas 16-13 on Jim O'Brien's 32-yard field goal with five seconds to go in Super Bowl V at Miami, January 17.

The NFC defeated the AFC 27-6 in the first AFC-NFC Pro Bowl at Los Angeles, January 24.

The Boston Patriots changed their name to the New England Patriots, March 25. Their new stadium, Schaefer Stadium, was dedicated in a 20-14 preseason victory over the Giants.

The Philadelphia Eagles left Franklin Field and played their games at the new Veterans Stadium.

The San Francisco 49ers left Kezar Stadium and moved their games to Candlestick Park.

Daniel F. Reeves, the president and general manager of the Rams, died at 58, April 15.

The Dallas Cowboys moved from the Cotton Bowl into their new home, Texas Stadium, October 24.

Miami defeated Kansas City 27-24 in sudden-death overtime in an AFC Divisional Playoff Game, December 25. Garo Yepremian kicked a 37-yard field goal for the Dolphins after 22 minutes, 40 seconds of overtime, as the game lasted 82 minutes, 40 seconds overall, making it the longest game in history.

1972

Dallas defeated Miami 24-3 in Super Bowl VI at New Orleans, January 16.

The inbounds lines or hashmarks were moved nearer the center of the field, 23 yards, 1 foot, 9 inches from the sidelines, March 23. The method of determining won-lost percentage in standings changed. Tie games, previously not counted in the standings, were made equal to a half-game won and a half-game lost, May 24.

Robert Irsay purchased the Los Angeles Rams and transferred ownership of the club to Carroll Rosenbloom in exchange for the Baltimore Colts, July 13.

William V. Bidwill purchased the stock of his brother Charles (Stormy) Bidwill to become the sole owner of the St. Louis Cardinals, September 2.

The National District Attorneys Association endorsed the position of professional leagues in opposing proposed legalization of gambling on professional team sports, September 28.

Franco Harris' "Immaculate Reception" gave the Steelers their first postseason win ever, 13-7 over the Raiders, December 23.

1973

Rozelle announced that all Super Bowl VII tickets were sold and that the game would be telecast in Los Angeles, the site of the game, on an experimental basis, January 3.

Miami defeated Washington 14-7 in Super Bowl VII at Los Angeles, completing a 17-0 season, the first perfect-record regular-season and postseason mark in NFL history, January 14.

The AFC defeated the NFC 33-28 in the Pro Bowl in Dallas, the first time since 1942 that the game was played outside Los Angeles, January 21.

A jersey numbering system was adopted, April 5: 1-19 for quarterbacks and specialists, 20-49 for running backs and defensive backs, 50-59 for centers and linebackers, 60-79 for defensive linemen and interior offensive linemen other than centers, and 80-89 for wide receivers and tight ends. Players who had been in the NFL in 1972 could continue to use old numbers.

NFL Charities, a nonprofit organization, was created to derive an income from monies generated from NFL Properties' licensing of NFL trademarks and team names, June 26. NFL Charities was set up to support education and charitable activities and to supply economic support to persons formerly associated with professional football who were no longer able to support themselves.

Congress adopted experimental legislation (for three years) requiring any NFL game that had been declared a sellout 72 hours prior to kickoff to be made available for local televising, September 14. The legislation provided for an annual review to be made by the Federal Communications Commission.

The Buffalo Bills moved their home games from War Memorial Stadium to Rich Stadium in nearby Orchard Park. The Giants tied the Eagles 23-23 in the final game in Yankee Stadium, September 23. The Giants played the rest of their home games at the Yale Bowl in New Haven, Connecticut.

A rival league, the World Football League, was formed and was reported in operation, October 2. It had plans to start play in 1974.

O.J. Simpson of Buffalo became the first player to rush for more than 2,000 yards in a season, gaining 2,003.

1974

Miami defeated Minnesota 24-7 in Super Bowl VIII at Houston, the second consecutive Super Bowl championship for the Dolphins, January 13.

Rozelle was given a 10-year contract effective January 1, 1973, February 27.

Tampa Bay was awarded the twenty-seventh franchise to begin operation in 1976, April 24.

Sweeping rules changes were adopted to add action and tempo to games: one sudden-death overtime period was added for preseason and regular-season games; the goal posts were moved from the goal line to the end lines; kickoffs were moved from the 40- to the 35-yard line; after missed field goals from beyond the 20, the ball was to be returned to the line of scrimmage; restrictions were placed on members of the punting team to open up return possibilities; roll-blocking and cutting of wide receivers was eliminated; the extent of downfield contact a defender could have with an eligible receiver was restricted; the penalties for offensive holding, illegal use of the hands, and tripping were reduced from 15 to 10 yards; wide receivers blocking back toward the ball within three yards of the line of scrimmage were prevented from blocking below the waist, April 25.

Seattle was awarded the twenty-eighth NFL franchise to begin play in 1976, June 4. Lloyd W. Nordstrom, president of the Seattle Seahawks, and Hugh Culverhouse, president of the Tampa Bay Buccaneers, signed franchise agreements, December 5.

The Birmingham Americans defeated the Florida Blazers 22-21 in the WFL World Bowl, winning the league championship, December 5.

1975

Pittsburgh defeated Minnesota 16-6 in Super Bowl IX at New Orleans, the Steelers' first championship since entering the NFL in 1933, January 12.

The Memphis Southmen of the WFL signed Larry Csonka, Jim Kiick, and Paul Warfield of Miami, March 31.

The divisional winners with the highest won-loss percentage were made the home team for the divisional playoffs, and the surviving winners with the highest percentage made home teams for the championship games. Previously, the home sites were pre-determined by division on a rotating basis, June 26.

Referees were equipped with wireless microphones for all preseason, regular-season, and playoff games.

The Lions moved to the new Pontiac Silverdome. The Giants played their home games in Shea Stadium. The Saints moved into the Louisiana Superdome.

The World Football League folded, October 22.

1976
Pittsburgh defeated Dallas 21-17 in Super Bowl X in Miami. The Steelers joined Green Bay and Miami as the only teams to win two Super Bowls; the Cowboys became the first wild-card team to play in the Super Bowl, January 18.

Lloyd Nordstrom, the president of the Seahawks, died at 66, January 20. His brother Elmer succeeded him as majority representative of the team.

The owners adopted the use of two 30-second clocks for all games, visible to both players and fans to note the official time between the ready-for-play signal and snap of the ball, March 16.

A veteran player allocation was held to stock the Seattle and Tampa Bay franchises with 39 players each, March 30-31. In the college draft, Seattle and Tampa Bay each received eight extra choices, April 8-9.

The Giants moved into new Giants Stadium in East Rutherford, New Jersey.

The Steelers defeated the College All-Stars in a storm-shortened Chicago College All-Star Game, the last of the series, July 23. St. Louis defeated San Diego 20-10 in a preseason game before 38,000 in Korakuen Stadium, Tokyo, in the first NFL game outside of North America, August 16.

1977
Oakland defeated Minnesota 32-14 in Super Bowl XI at Pasadena, January 9. The paid attendance was a pro record 103,438.

The NFL Players Association and the NFL Management Council ratified a collective bargaining agreement extending until 1982, covering five football seasons while continuing the pension plan—including years 1974, 1975, and 1976—with contributions totaling more than $55 million. The total cost of the agreement was estimated at $107 million. The agreement called for a college draft at least through 1986; contained a no-strike, no-suit clause; established a 43-man active player limit; reduced pension vesting to four years; provided for increases in minimum salaries and preseason and postseason pay; improved insurance, medical, and dental benefits; modified previous practices in player movement and control; and reaffirmed the NFL Commissioner's disciplinary authority. Additionally, the agreement called for the NFL member clubs to make payments totaling $16 million the next 10 years to settle various legal disputes, February 25.

The San Francisco 49ers were sold to Edward J. DeBartolo, Jr., March 28.

A 16-game regular season, 4-game preseason was adopted to begin in 1978, March 29. A second wild-card team was adopted for the playoffs beginning in 1978, with the wild-card teams to play each other and the winners advancing to a round of eight postseason series.

The Seahawks were permanently aligned in the AFC Western Division and the Buccaneers in the NFC Central Division, March 31.

Rules changes were adopted to open up the passing game and to cut down on injuries. Defenders were permitted to make contact with eligible receivers only once; the head slap was outlawed; offensive linemen were prohibited from thrusting their hands to an opponent's neck, face, or head; and wide receivers were prohibited from clipping, even in the legal clipping zone.

Rozelle negotiated contracts with the three television networks to televise all NFL regular-season and postseason games, plus selected preseason games, for four years beginning with the 1978 season. ABC was awarded yearly rights to 16 Monday night games, four primetime games, the AFC-NFC Pro Bowl, and the Hall of Fame games. CBS received the rights to all NFC regular-season and postseason games (except those in the ABC package) and to Super Bowls XIV and XVI. NBC received the rights to all AFC regular-season and postseason games (except those in the ABC package) and to Super Bowls XIII and XV. Industry sources considered it the largest single television package ever negotiated, October 12.

1978
Dallas defeated Denver 27-10 in Super Bowl XII, held indoors for the first time, at the Louisiana Superdome in New Orleans, January 15. Dallas' victory was the first for the NFC in six years.

According to a Louis Harris Sports Survey, 70 percent of the nation's sports fans said they followed football, compared to 54 percent who followed baseball. Football increased its lead as the country's favorite, 26 percent to 16 percent for baseball, January 19.

A seventh official, the side judge, was added to the officiating crew, March 14.

The NFL continued a trend toward opening up the game. Rules changes permitted a defender to maintain contact with a receiver within five yards of the line of scrimmage, but restricted contact beyond that point. The pass-blocking rule was interpreted to permit the extending of arms and open hands, March 17.

A study on the use of instant replay as an officiating aid was made during seven nationally televised preseason games.

The NFL played for the first time in Mexico City, with the Saints defeating the Eagles 14-7 in a preseason game, August 5.

Bolstered by the expansion of the regular-season schedule from 14 to 16 weeks, NFL paid attendance exceeded 12 million (12,771,800) for the first time. The per-game average of 57,017 was the third-highest in league history and the most since 1973.

1979
Pittsburgh defeated Dallas 35-31 in Super Bowl XIII at Miami to become the first team ever to win three Super Bowls, January 21.

NFL rules changes emphasized additional player safety. The changes prohibited players on the receiving team from blocking below the waist during kickoffs, punts, and field-goal attempts; prohibited the wearing of torn or altered equipment and exposed pads that could be hazardous; extended the zone in which there could be no crackback blocks; and instructed officials to quickly whistle a play dead when a quarterback was clearly in the grasp of a tackler, March 16.

Carroll Rosenbloom, the president of the Rams, drowned at 72, April 2. His widow, Georgia, assumed control of the club.

1980
Pittsburgh defeated the Los Angeles Rams 31-19 in Super Bowl XIV at Pasadena to become the first team to win four Super Bowls, January 20.

The AFC-NFC Pro Bowl, won 37-27 by the NFC, was played before 48,060 fans at Aloha Stadium in Honolulu, Hawaii. It was the first time in the 30-year history of the Pro Bowl that the game was played in a non-NFL city.

Rules changes placed greater restrictions on contact in the area of the head, neck, and face. Under the heading of "personal foul," players were prohibited from directly striking, swinging, or clubbing on the head, neck, or face. Starting in 1980, a penalty could be called for such contact whether or not the initial contact was made below the neck area.

CBS, with a record bid of $12 million, won the national radio rights to 26 NFL regular-season games, including Monday Night Football, and all 10 postseason games for the 1980-83 seasons.

The Los Angeles Rams moved their home games to Anaheim Stadium in nearby Orange County, California.

The Oakland Raiders joined

the Los Angeles Coliseum Commission's antitrust suit against the NFL. The suit contended the league violated antitrust laws in declining to approve a proposed move by the Raiders from Oakland to Los Angeles.

The NFL Draft is televised for the first time by ESPN, April 29.

Television ratings in 1980 were the second-best in NFL history, trailing only the combined ratings of the 1976 season. All three networks posted gains, and NBC's 15.0 rating was its best ever. CBS and ABC had their best ratings since 1977, with 15.3 and 20.8 ratings, respectively. CBS Radio reported a record audience of 7 million for Monday night and special games.

1981

Oakland defeated Philadelphia 27-10 in Super Bowl XV at the Louisiana Superdome in New Orleans, to become the first wild-card team to win a Super Bowl, January 25.

Edgar F. Kaiser, Jr., purchased the Denver Broncos from Gerald and Allan Phipps, February 26.

The owners adopted a disaster plan for re-stocking a team should the club be involved in a fatal accident, March 20.

A CBS-New York Times poll showed that 48 percent of sports fans preferred football to 31 percent for baseball.

The NFL teams hosted 167 representatives from 44 predominantly black colleges during training camps for a total of 289 days. The program was adopted for renewal during each training camp period.

ABC and CBS set all-time rating highs. ABC finished with a 21.7 rating and CBS with a 17.5 rating. NBC was down slightly to 13.9.

1982

San Francisco defeated Cincinnati 26-21 in Super Bowl XVI at the Pontiac Silverdome, in the first Super Bowl held in the North, January 24. The CBS telecast achieved the highest rating of any televised sports event ever, 49.1 with a 73.0 share.

The NFL signed a five-year contract with the three television networks (ABC, CBS, and NBC) to televise all NFL regular-season and postseason games starting with the 1982 season.

A jury ruled against the NFL in the antitrust trial brought by the Los Angeles Coliseum Commission and the Oakland Raiders, May 7. The verdict cleared the way for the Raiders to move to Los Angeles, where they defeated Green Bay 24-3 in their first preseason game, August 29.

The 1982 season was reduced from a 16-game schedule to nine as the result of a 57-day players' strike. The strike was called by the NFLPA at midnight on Monday, September 20, following the Green Bay at New York Giants game. Play resumed November 21-22 following ratification of the Collective Bargaining Agreement by NFL owners, November 17 in New York.

Under the Collective Bargaining Agreement, which was to run through the 1986 season, the NFL draft was extended through 1992 and the veteran free-agent system was left basically unchanged. A minimum salary schedule for years of experience was established; training camp and postseason pay were increased; players' medical, insurance, and retirement benefits were increased; and a severance-pay system was introduced to aid in career transition, a first in professional sports.

Despite the players' strike, the average paid attendance in 1982 was 58,472, the fifth-highest in league history.

1983

Because of the shortened season, the NFL adopted a format of 16 teams competing in a Super Bowl Tournament for the 1982 playoffs. The NFC's number-one seed, Washington, defeated the AFC's number-two seed, Miami, 27-17 in Super Bowl XVII at the Rose Bowl in Pasadena, January 30.

Super Bowl XVII was the second-highest rated live television program of all time, giving the NFL a sweep of the top 10 live programs in television history.

George Halas, the owner of the Bears and the last surviving member of the NFL's second organizational meeting, died at 88, October 31.

1984

The Los Angeles Raiders defeated Washington 38-9 in Super Bowl XVIII at Tampa Stadium, January 22.

An 11-man group headed by H.R. (Bum) Bright purchased the Dallas Cowboys from Clint Murchison, Jr., March 20. Club president Tex Schramm was designated as managing general partner.

Wellington Mara was named president of the NFC, March 20.

Patrick Bowlen purchased a majority interest in the Denver Broncos from Edgar Kaiser, Jr., March 21.

The Colts relocated to Indianapolis, March 28. Their new home became the Hoosier Dome.

The New York Jets moved their home games to Giants Stadium in East Rutherford, New Jersey.

Alex G. Spanos purchased a majority interest in the San Diego Chargers from Eugene V. Klein, August 28.

Houston defeated Pittsburgh 23-20 to mark the one-hundredth overtime game in regular-season play since overtime was adopted in 1974, December 2.

On the field, many all-time records were set: Dan Marino of Miami passed for 5,084 yards and 48 touchdowns; Eric Dickerson of the Los Angeles Rams rushed for 2,105 yards; Art Monk of Washington caught 106 passes; and Walter Payton of Chicago broke Jim Brown's career rushing mark, finishing the season with 13,309 yards.

According to a CBS Sports/*New York Times* survey, 53 percent of the nation's sports fans said they most enjoyed watching football, compared to 18 percent for baseball, December 2-4.

1985

San Francisco defeated Miami 38-16 in Super Bowl XIX at Stanford Stadium in Stanford, California, January 20. President Ronald Reagan, who took his second oath of office before tossing the coin for the game, was one of 115,936,000 viewers. Super Bowl XIX had a direct economic impact of $113.5 million on the San Francisco Bay area.

NBC Radio and the NFL entered into a two-year agreement granting NBC the radio rights to a 37-game package in each of the 1985-86 seasons, March 6. The package included 27 regular-season games and 10 postseason games.

Norman Braman, in partnership with Edward Leibowitz, bought the Philadelphia Eagles from Leonard Tose, April 29.

A group headed by Tom Benson, Jr., was approved to purchase the New Orleans Saints from John W. Mecom, Jr., June 3.

The NFL owners adopted a resolution calling for a series of overseas preseason games, beginning in 1986, with one game to be played in England/Europe and/or one game in Japan each year. The game would be a fifth preseason game for the clubs involved and all arrangements and selection of the clubs would be under the control of the Commissioner, May 23.

The league-wide conversion to videotape from movie film for coaching study was approved.

A Louis Harris poll in December revealed that pro football remained the sport most followed by Americans. Fifty-nine percent of those surveyed followed pro football, compared with 54 percent who followed baseball.

The Chicago-Miami Monday game had the highest rating, 29.6, and share, 46.0, of any primetime game in NFL history, December 2. The game was viewed in more than 25 million homes.

The NFL showed a ratings increase on all three networks for the season, gaining 4 percent on NBC, 10 on CBS, and 16 on ABC.

1986

Chicago defeated New England 46-10 in Super Bowl XX at the Louisiana Superdome, January 26. The Patriots had earned the right to play the Bears by becoming the first wild-card team to win three consecutive games on the road. The NBC telecast replaced the final episode of

*M*A*S*H* as the most-viewed television program in history, with an audience of 127 million viewers, according to A.C. Nielsen figures. In addition to drawing a 48.3 rating and a 70 percent share in the United States, Super Bowl XX was televised to 59 foreign countries and beamed via satellite to the QE II.

The owners adopted limited use of instant replay as an officiating aid, prohibited players from wearing or otherwise displaying equipment, apparel, or other items that carry commercial names, names of organizations, or personal messages of any type, March 11.

After an 11-week trial, a jury in U.S. District Court in New York awarded the United States Football League one dollar in its $1.7 billion antitrust suit against the NFL. The jury rejected all of the USFL's television-related claims, which were the self-proclaimed heart of the USFL's case. The jury deliberated five days, July 29.

Chicago defeated Dallas 17-6 at Wembley Stadium in London in the first American Bowl. The game drew a sellout crowd of 82,699 and the NBC national telecast in this country produced a 12.4 rating and 36 percent share, making it the highest daytime preseason television audience ever with 10.65-million viewers, August 3.

ABC's *NFL Monday Night Football,* in its seventeenth season, became the longest-running primetime series in the history of the network.

1987
The New York Giants defeated Denver 39-20 in Super Bowl XXI and captured their first NFL title since 1956. The game, played in Pasadena's Rose Bowl, drew a sellout crowd of 101,063, January 25.

New three-year TV contracts with ABC, CBS, and NBC were announced for 1987-89 at the NFL annual meeting in Maui, Hawaii, March 15. Commissioner Rozelle and Broadcast Committee Chairman Art Modell also announced a three-year contract with ESPN to televise 13 primetime games each season. The ESPN contract was the first with a cable network. However, NFL games on ESPN also were scheduled for regular television in the city of the visiting team and in the home city if the game was sold out 72 hours in advance.

A special payment program was adopted to benefit nearly 1,000 former NFL players who participated in the League before the current Bert Bell NFL Pension Plan was created and made retroactive to the 1959 season. Players covered by the new program spent at least five years in the League and played all or part of their career prior to 1959. Each vested player would receive $60 per month for each year of service in the League for life.

NFL and CBS Radio jointly announced agreement granting CBS the radio rights to a 40-game package in each of the next three NFL seasons, 1987-89, April 7.

Over 400 former NFL players from the pre-1959 era received first payments from NFL owners, July 1.

The NFL's debut on ESPN produced the two highest-rated and most-watched sports programs in basic cable history. The Chicago at Miami game on August 16 drew an 8.9 rating in 3.81 million homes. Those records fell two weeks later when the Los Angeles Raiders at Dallas game achieved a 10.2 cable rating in 4.36 million homes.

The 1987 season was reduced from a 16-game season to 15 as the result of a 24-day players' strike. The strike was called by the NFLPA on Tuesday, September 22, following the New England at New York Jets game. Games scheduled for the third weekend were canceled but the games of weeks four, five, and six were played with replacement teams. Striking players returned for the seventh week of the season, October 25.

In a three-team deal involving 10 players and/or draft choices, the Los Angeles Rams traded running back Eric Dickerson to the Indianapolis Colts for six draft choices and two players. Buffalo obtained the rights to linebacker Cornelius Bennett from Indianapolis, sending Greg Bell and three draft choices to the Rams. The Colts added Owen Gill and three draft choices of their own to complete the deal with the Rams, October 31.

The Chicago at Minnesota game became the highest-rated and most-watched sports program in basic cable history when it drew a 14.4 cable rating in 6.5 million homes, December 6.

1988
Washington defeated Denver 42-10 in Super Bowl XXII to earn its second victory this decade in the NFL Championship Game. The game, played for the first time in San Diego Jack Murphy Stadium, drew a sellout crowd of 73,302. Doug Williams, the game's MVP, became the first African-American quarterback to play in a Super Bowl, January 31.

In a unanimous 3-0 decision, the 2nd Circuit Court of Appeals in New York upheld the verdict of the jury that in July, 1986, had awarded the United States Football League one dollar in its $1.7 billion antitrust suit against the NFL. In a 91-page opinion, Judge Ralph K. Winter said the USFL sought through court decree the success it failed to gain among football fans, March 10.

By a 23-5 margin, owners voted to continue the instant replay system for the third consecutive season with the Instant Replay Official to be assigned to a regular seven-man, on-the-field crew. At the NFL annual meeting in Phoenix, Arizona, a 45-second clock was also approved to replace the 30-second clock. For a normal sequence of plays, the interval between plays was changed to 45 seconds from the time the ball is signaled dead until it is snapped on the succeeding play.

NFL owners approved the transfer of the Cardinals' franchise from St. Louis to Phoenix; approved two supplemental drafts each year—one prior to training camp and one prior to the regular season; and voted to initiate an annual series of games in Japan/Asia as early as the 1989 preseason, March 14-18.

The NFL Annual Selection Meeting returned to a separate two-day format and for the first time originated on a Sunday. ESPN drew a 3.6 rating during their seven-hour coverage of the draft, which was viewed in 1.6 million homes, April 24-25.

Art Rooney, founder and owner of the Steelers, died at 87, August 25.

Johnny Grier became the first African-American referee in NFL history, September 4.

Commissioner Rozelle announced that two teams would play a preseason game as part of the American Bowl series on August 6, 1989, in the Korakuen Tokyo Dome in Japan, December 16.

1989
San Francisco defeated Cincinnati 20-16 in Super Bowl XXIII. The game, played for the first time at Joe Robbie Stadium in Miami, was attended by a sellout crowd of 75,129, January 22.

Commissioner Rozelle announced his retirement, pending the naming of a successor, March 22 at the NFL annual meeting in Palm Desert, California.

Following the announcement, AFC president Lamar Hunt and NFC president Wellington Mara announced the formation of a six-man search committee composed of Art Modell, Robert Parins, Dan Rooney, and Ralph Wilson. Hunt and Mara served as co-chairmen.

By a 24-4 margin, owners voted to continue the instant replay system for the fourth straight season. A strengthened policy regarding anabolic steroids and masking agents was announced by Commissioner Rozelle. NFL clubs called for strong disciplinary measures in cases of feigned injuries and adopted a joint proposal by the Long-Range Planning and Finance committees regarding player personnel rules, March 19-23.

Two hundred twenty-nine unconditional free agents signed with new teams under management's Plan B system, April 1.

Jerry Jones purchased a majority interest in the Dallas Cowboys from H.R. (Bum)

Bright, April 18.

Tex Schramm was named president of the new World League of American Football to work with a six-man committee of Dan Rooney, chairman; Norman Braman, Lamar Hunt, Victor Kiam, Mike Lynn, and Bill Walsh, April 18.

NFL and CBS Radio jointly announced agreement extending CBS's radio rights to an annual 40-game package through the 1994 season, April 18.

As of opening day, September 10, of the 229 Plan B free agents, 111 were active and 23 others were on teams' reserve lists. Ninety-two others were waived and three retired.

Art Shell was named head coach of the Los Angeles Raiders making him the NFL's first black head coach since Fritz Pollard coached the Akron Pros in 1921, October 3.

The site of the New England Patriots at San Francisco 49ers game scheduled for Candlestick Park on October 22 was switched to Stanford Stadium in the aftermath of the Bay Area Earthquake of October 17. The change was announced on October 19.

Paul Tagliabue became the seventh chief executive of the NFL on October 26 when he was chosen to succeed Commissioner Pete Rozelle on the sixth ballot of a three-day meeting in Cleveland, Ohio.

In all, 12 ballots were required to select Tagliabue. Two were conducted at a meeting in Chicago on July 6, and four at a meeting in Dallas on October 10-11. On the twelfth ballot, with Seattle absent, Tagliabue received more than the 19 affirmative votes required for election from among the 27 clubs present.

The transfer from Commissioner Rozelle to Commissioner Tagliabue took place at 12:01 A.M. on Sunday, November 5.

NFL Charities donated $1 million through United Way to benefit Bay Area earthquake victims, November 6.

1990

San Francisco defeated Denver 55-10 in Super Bowl XXIV at the Louisiana Superdome, January 28. San Francisco joined Pittsburgh as the NFL's only teams to win four Super Bowls.

The NFL announced revisions in its 1990 draft eligibility rules. College juniors became eligible but must renounce their collegiate football eligibility before applying for the NFL Draft, February 16.

Commissioner Tagliabue announced NFL teams will play their 16-game schedule over 17 weeks in 1990-92 and 16 games over 18 weeks in 1993, February 27.

The NFL revised its playoff format to include two additional wild-card teams (one per conference), which raised the total to six wild-card teams.

Commissioner Tagliabue and Broadcast Committee Chairman Art Modell announced a four-year contract with Turner Broadcasting to televise nine Sunday-night games.

New four-year TV agreements were ratified for 1990-93 for ABC, CBS, NBC, ESPN, and TNT at the NFL annual meeting in Orlando, Florida, March 12. The contracts totaled $3.6 billion, the largest in TV history.

The NFL announced plans to expand its American Bowl series of preseason games. In addition to games in London and Tokyo, American Bowl games were scheduled for Berlin, Germany, and Montreal, Canada, in 1990.

For the fifth straight year, NFL owners voted to continue a limited system of Instant Replay. Beginning in 1990, the replay official will have a two-minute time limit to make a decision. The vote was 21-7, March 12.

Commissioner Tagliabue announced the formation of a Committee on Expansion and Realignment, March 13. He also named a Player Advisory Council, comprised of 12 former NFL players, March 14.

One-hundred eighty-four Plan B unconditional free agents signed with new teams, April 2.

Commissioner Tagliabue appointed Dr. John Lombardo as the League's Drug Advisor for Anabolic Steroids, April 25 and named Dr. Lawrence Brown as the League's Advisor for Drugs of Abuse, May 17.

NFL International Week was celebrated with four preseason games in seven days in Tokyo, London, Berlin, and Montreal. More than 200,000 fans on three continents attended the four games, August 4-11.

Commissioner Tagliabue announced the NFL Teacher of the Month program in which the League furnishes grants and scholarships in recognition of teachers who provided a positive influence upon NFL players in elementary and secondary schools, September 20.

For the first time since 1957, every NFL club won at least one of its first four games, October 1.

The Super Bowl Most Valuable Player trophy was renamed the Pete Rozelle trophy, October 8.

1991

The New York Giants defeated Buffalo 20-19 in Super Bowl XXV to capture their second title in five years. The game was played before a sellout crowd of 73,813 at Tampa Stadium and became the first Super Bowl decided by one point, January 26.

New York businessman Robert Tisch purchased a 50 percent interest in the New York Giants from Mrs. Helen Mara Nugent and her children, Tim Mara and Maura Mara Concannon, February 2.

NFL clubs voted to continue a limited system of Instant Replay for the sixth consecutive year. The vote was 21-7, March 19.

The NFL launched the World League of American Football, the first sports league to operate on a weekly basis on two separate continents, March 23.

NFL Charities presented a $250,000 donation to the United Service Organization. The donation was the second largest single grant ever by NFL Charities, April 5.

Commissioner Tagliabue named Harold Henderson as Executive Vice President for Labor Relations and Chairman of the NFL Management Council Executive Committee, April 8.

NFL clubs approved a recommendation by the Expansion and Realignment Committee to add two teams for the 1994 season, resulting in six divisions of five teams each, May 22.

"NFL International Week" featured six 1990 playoff teams playing nationally televised games in London, Berlin, and Tokyo on July 28 and August 3-4. The games drew more than 150,000 fans.

Paul Brown, founder of the Cleveland Browns and Cincinnati Bengals, died at age 82, August 5.

NFL clubs approved a resolution establishing an international division. A three-year financial plan for the World League was approved by NFL clubs at a meeting in Dallas, October 23.

1992

The NFL agreed to provide a minimum of $2.5 million in financial support to the NFL Alumni Association and assistance to NFL Alumni-related programs. The agreement included contributions from NFL Charities to the Pre-59ers and Dire Need Programs for former players, January 25.

The Washington Redskins defeated the Buffalo Bills 37-24 in Super Bowl XXVI to capture their third world championship in 10 years, January 26. The game was played before a sellout crowd of 63,130 at the Hubert H. Humphrey Metrodome in Minneapolis.

The use in officiating of a limited system of Instant Replay was not approved. The vote was 17-11 in favor of approval (21 votes were required). Instant Replay had been used for six consecutive years (1986-1991), March 18.

St. Louis businessman James Orthwein purchased controlling interest in the New England Patriots from Victor Kiam, May 11.

In a Harris Poll taken during the NFL offseason, professional football again was declared the nation's most popular sport. Professional football finished atop similar surveys conducted by Harris in 1985 and 1989, May 23.

NFL clubs accepted the report of the Expansion Committee at a league meeting in Pasadena. The report names five cities as finalists for the two expansion teams—Baltimore, Charlotte, Jacksonville, Memphis, and St. Louis, May 19.

At a league meeting in Dallas, NFL clubs approved a proposal by the World League Board of Directors to restructure the World League and place future emphasis on its international success, September 17.

The Professional and Amateur Sports Protection Act made it unlawful for a government entity to operate a lottery or other betting scheme based on pro or collegiate games. Four states that already had such betting were grandfathered, October 6.

NFL teams played their 16-game regular-season schedule over 18 weeks for the only time in league history.

1993
The NFL and lawyers for the players announced a settlement of various lawsuits and an agreement on the terms of a seven-year deal that included a new player system to be in place through the 1999 season, January 6.

Commissioner Tagliabue announced the establishment of the "NFL World Partnership Program" to develop amateur football internationally through a series of clinics conducted by former NFL players and coaches, January 14.

As part of Super Bowl XXVII, the NFL announced the creation of the first NFL Youth Education Town, a facility located in south central Los Angeles for inner city youth. January 25.

The Dallas Cowboys defeated the Buffalo Bills 52-17 in Super Bowl XXVII to capture their first NFL title since 1978. The game was played before a crowd of 98,374 at the Rose Bowl in Pasadena, California, January 31.

The NFL and the NFL Players Association officially signed a 7-year Collective Bargaining Agreement in Washington, D.C., which guarantees more than $1 billion in pension, health, and post-career benefits for current and retired players—the most extensive benefits plan in pro sports. It was the NFL's first CBA since the 1982 agreement expired in 1987, June 29.

NFL Enterprises, a newly formed division of the NFL responsible for NFL Films, home video, and special domestic and international television programming was announced, August 19.

NFL announced plans to allow fans, for the first time ever, to join players and coaches in selecting the annual AFC and NFC Pro Bowl teams, October 12.

NFL clubs unanimously awarded the league's twenty-ninth franchise to the Carolina Panthers and owner Jerry Richardson at a meeting in Chicago, October 26.

At the same meeting in Chicago, NFL clubs approved a plan to form a European league with joint venture partners, October 27.

Don Shula became the winningest coach in NFL history when Miami beat Philadelphia to give Shula his 325th victory, one more than George Halas, November 14.

NFL clubs awarded the league's thirtieth franchise to the Jacksonville Jaguars and owner Wayne Weaver at a meeting in Chicago, November 30.

The NFL announced new 4-year television agreements with NBC, ABC, ESPN, TNT, and NFL newcomer FOX, which took over the NFC package from CBS, December 18.

The NFL completed its new TV agreements by announcing that NBC would retain the rights to the AFC package, December 20.

1994
The Dallas Cowboys defeated the Buffalo Bills 30-13 in Super Bowl XXVIII to become the fifth team to win back-to-back Super Bowl titles, January 30.

NFL clubs unanimously approved the transfer of the New England Patriots from James Orthwein to Robert Kraft at a meeting in Orlando, February 22.

In a move to increase offensive production, NFL clubs at the league's annual meeting in Orlando adopted a package of changes, including modifications in line play, chucking rules, and the roughing-the-passer rule, plus the adoption of the two-point conversion and moving the spot of the kickoff back to the 30-yard line, March 22.

NFL clubs approved the transfer of the majority interest in the Miami Dolphins from the Robbie family to H. Wayne Huizenga, March 23.

The NFL and FOX announced the formation of a joint venture to create a six-team World League to begin play in Europe in April, 1995, March 23.

The Carolina Panthers earned the right to select first in the 1995 NFL draft by winning a coin toss with the Jacksonville Jaguars. The Jaguars received the second selection in the 1995 draft, April 24.

NFL clubs approved the transfer of the Philadelphia Eagles from Norman Braman to Jeffrey Lurie, May 6.

The NFL launched "NFL Sunday Ticket," a new season subscription service for satellite television dish owners, June 1.

An all-time NFL record crowd of 112,376 attended the American Bowl game between Dallas and Houston in Mexico City. It concluded the biggest American Bowl series in NFL history with four games attracting a record 256,666 fans, August 15.

The NFL reached agreement on a new seven-year contract with its game officials, September 22.

The NFL Management Council and the NFL Players Association announced an agreement on the formulation and implementation of the most comprehensive drug and alcohol policy in sports, October 28.

At an NFL meeting in Chicago, Commissioner Tagliabue slotted the two new expansion teams into the AFC Central (Jacksonville Jaguars) and NFC West (Carolina Panthers) for the 1995 season only. He also appointed a special committee on realignment to make recommendations on the 1996 season and beyond, November 2.

1995
The San Francisco 49ers became the first team to win five Super Bowls when they defeated the San Diego Chargers 49-26 in Super Bowl XXIX at Joe Robbie Stadium in Miami, January 29.

Carolina and Jacksonville stocked their expansion rosters with a total of 66 players from other NFL teams in a veteran player allocation draft in New York, February 16.

CBS Radio and the NFL agreed to a new four-year contract for an annual 53-game package of games, continuing a relationship that spanned 15 of the past 17 years, February 22.

NFL clubs approved the transfer of the Tampa Bay Buccaneers from the estate of the late Hugh Culverhouse to South Florida businessman Malcolm Glazer, March 13.

After a two-year hiatus, the World League of American Football returned to action with six teams in Europe, April 8.

The NFL became the first major sports league to establish a site on the Internet system of on-line computer communication, April 10.

The transfer of the Rams from Los Angeles to St. Louis was approved by a vote of the NFL clubs at a meeting in Dallas, April 12.

ABC's *NFL Monday Night Football* finished the 1994-95 television season as the fifth highest-rated show out of 146 with a 17.8 average rating, the highest finish in the 25-year history of the series, April 18.

The Frankfurt Galaxy defeated the Amsterdam Admirals 26-22 to win the 1995 World Bowl before a crowd of 23,847 in Amsterdam's Olympic Stadium, June 23.

The transfer of the Raiders from Los Angeles to Oakland was approved by a vote of the NFL clubs at a meeting in Chicago, July 22.

Jacksonville Municipal Stadium opened in Jacksonville, Florida before a sold-out crowd of more than 70,000 as the St. Louis Rams defeated the Jacksonville Jaguars 27-10 in their first preseason game, August 18.

NFL Charities and 50 NFL players donated $1 million to the United Negro College Fund in honor of the fiftieth anniversary of the UNCF and the integration of the modern NFL, September 15.

The Trans World Dome opened in St. Louis with a sold-out crowd of 65,598 as the Rams defeated the Carolina Panthers 28-17, November 12.

On the field, many significant records and milestones were achieved: Miami's Dan Marino surpassed Pro Football Hall of Famer Fran Tarkenton in four major passing categories—attempts, completions, yards, and touchdowns—to become the NFL's all-time career leader. San Francisco's Jerry Rice became the all-time reception and receiving-yardage leader.

1996
The Dallas Cowboys won their third Super Bowl title in four years when they defeated the Pittsburgh Steelers 27-17 in Super Bowl XXX at Sun Devil Stadium in Tempe, Arizona, January 28.

An agreement between the NFL and the city of Cleveland regarding the Cleveland Browns' relocation was approved by a vote of the NFL clubs, February 9. According to the agreement, the city of Cleveland retained the Browns' heritage and records, including the name, logo, colors, history, playing records, trophies, and memorabilia, and committed to building a new 72,000-seat stadium for a reactivated Browns' franchise to begin play there no later than 1999. Art Modell received approval to move his franchise to Baltimore and rename it.

The transfer of the Oilers from Houston to Nashville for the 1998 season was approved by a vote of the NFL clubs at a meeting in Atlanta, April 30.

The Scottish Claymores defeated the Frankfurt Galaxy 32-27 to win the 1996 World Bowl in front of 38,982 at Murrayfield Stadium in Edinburgh, Scotland, June 23.

The NFL returned to Baltimore when the new Baltimore Ravens defeated the Philadelphia Eagles 17-9 in a preseason game before a crowd of 63,804 at Memorial Stadium, August 3.

Ericsson Stadium opened in Charlotte, North Carolina with a crowd of 65,350 as the Carolina Panthers defeated the Chicago Bears 30-12 in a preseason game, August 3.

Former NFL Commissioner Pete Rozelle died at his home in Rancho Santa Fe, California. Rozelle, regarded as the premiere commissioner in sports history, led the NFL for 29 years, from 1960-1989, December 6.

1997
Indianapolis Colts owner Robert Irsay died from complications related to a stroke he suffered in 1995. Irsay acquired the club in 1972 when he traded his Los Angeles Rams to Carrol Rosenbloom for the Colts. He later moved the Colts from Baltimore to Indianapolis in 1984, January 14.

The Green Bay Packers won their first NFL title in 29 years by defeating the New England Patriots 35-21 in Super Bowl XXXI at the Louisiana Superdome in New Orleans, January 26.

The rules governing cross-ownership were modified, permitting NFL club owners to also own teams in other sports in their home market or markets without NFL teams. The vote was 24-5 (one abstention) in favor of approval, March 11.

Washington Redskins owner Jack Kent Cooke died at his home in Washington, D.C. Cooke became majority owner in 1974 and the Redskins won three Super Bowls under his leadership, April 6.

The Barcelona Dragons defeated the Rhein Fire 38-24 to win the 1997 World Bowl in front of 31,100 fans at Estadi Olimpic de Montjuic in Barcelona, Spain, June 22.

NFL clubs approved the transfer of the Seattle Seahawks from Ken Behring to Paul Allen, August 19.

Jack Kent Cooke Stadium opened in Raljon, Maryland with a crowd of 78,270 as the Washington Redskins defeated the Arizona Cardinals 19-13 in overtime, September 14.

The 10,000th regular-season game in NFL history was played when the Seattle Seahawks defeated the Tennessee Oilers 16-13 at the Kingdome in Seattle, October 5.

Atlanta Falcons owner Rankin Smith died of heart failure three days prior to his seventy-third birthday. Smith was the founder of the Falcons and was instrumental in bringing Super Bowls XXVIII and XXXIV to Atlanta, October 26.

1998
The NFL reached agreement on record eight-year television contracts with four networks. ABC (*NFL Monday Night Football*) and FOX (NFC) retained their previous rights, CBS took over the AFC package from NBC, and ESPN won the right to broadcast the entire Sunday night cable package, January 13.

The World League was renamed the NFL Europe League, January 22.

The Denver Broncos won their first Super Bowl by defeating the defending champion Green Bay Packers 31-24 in Super Bowl XXXII at Qualcomm Stadium in San Diego, January 25.

The NFL clubs approved an extension of the Collective Bargaining Agreement through 2003. The extended CBA also created a $100 million fund for youth football, March 22.

The NFL clubs unanimously approved an expansion team for Cleveland to fulfill the commitment to return the Browns to the field in 1999, March 23.

The Rhein Fire defeated the Frankfurt Galaxy 34-10 to win the 1998 World Bowl in front of 47,846 fans in Frankfurt's Waldstadion—the biggest crowd to witness a World Bowl since 1991, June 14.

NFL clubs approved the transfer of the Minnesota Vikings from a 10-man ownership group to Red McCombs, July 28.

The NFL Stadium at Camden Yards opened in Baltimore, Maryland before a crowd of 65,938 as the Baltimore Ravens defeated the Chicago Bears 19-14 in a preseason game, August 8.

Raymond James Stadium opened in Tampa, Florida before a crowd of 62,410 as the Tampa Bay Buccaneers defeated the Chicago Bears 27-15, September 20.

Tennessee Oilers owner Bud Adams announced the team will change its name to the Tennessee Titans following the 1998 season. The NFL announced that the name Oilers will be retired—a first in league history, November 14.

1999
The Denver Broncos won their second consecutive Super Bowl title by defeating the NFC champion Atlanta Falcons 34-19 in Super Bowl XXXIII at Pro Player Stadium in Miami, January 31.

Jim Pyne, a center allocated by the Detroit Lions, was the first selection of the Cleveland Browns in the 1999 NFL Expansion Draft. The Browns eventually selected 37 players, February 9.

CBS Radio/Westwood One agreed to a 3-year extension of their exclusive national radio rights to NFL games, March 11.

By a vote of 28-3, the owners adopted an instant replay system as an officiating aid for the 1999 season, March 17.

New York Jets owner Leon Hess died from complications of a blood disease. Hess had been involved in the ownership of the Jets since 1963 and was sole owner of the club since 1984, May 9.

A group led by Washington area businessman Daniel Snyder is approved by NFL clubs as the new owner of the Washington Redskins at a league meeting in Atlanta, May 25.

The Frankfurt Galaxy became the first team in NFL Europe League history to win a second World Bowl by defeating the Barcelona Dragons 38-24 at Rheinstadion, in Düsseldorf, Germany, June 27.

The Cleveland Browns returned to the field for the first time since 1995 and defeated the Dallas Cowboys 20-17 in overtime in the annual Hall of Fame Game at Canton, Ohio, August 9.

Cleveland Browns Stadium opened in Cleveland, Ohio before a crowd of 71,398 as the Minnesota Vikings defeated the Browns in a preseason game, 24-17, August 21.

Adelphia Coliseum opened in Nashville, Tennessee before a crowd of 65,729 with the Tennessee Titans defeating the Atlanta Falcons 17-3 in a preseason game, August 26.

Houston, Texas and owner Robert McNair were awarded the NFL's thirty-second franchise in a vote of the NFL clubs at a league meeting in Atlanta. The team will begin play in 2002. The NFL clubs also voted to realign into eight divisions of four teams each for the 2002 season, October 6.

Walter Payton, the NFL's all-time leading rusher, died of liver cancer at the age of 45. Payton played for the Chicago Bears from 1975-1987 and rushed for an NFL-record 16,726 yards, November 1.

Former NFL Commissioner Pete Rozelle, who guided a still-developing league to its position today as America's most popular sport, was named by *The Sporting News* as the most powerful person in sports in the 20th Century, December 15.

2000

New York businessman Robert Wood Johnson IV was approved by NFL clubs as the new owner of the New York Jets at a league meeting, January 18.

The St. Louis Rams won their first Super Bowl by defeating the AFC champion Tennessee Titans 23-16 in Super Bowl XXXIV at the Georgia Dome in Atlanta, January 30.

For the first time in league history, paid attendance topped 16 million for the regular season and more than 65,000 per game, an increase of 1,300 per game over 1998. Paid attendance for all NFL games increased in 1999 for the third year in a row and was the highest ever in the 80-year history of the league. It marked the first time in league history that the 20-million paid attendance mark was reached for all games in a season, March 27.

The Rhein Fire won their second World Bowl in three years, defeating the Scottish Claymores 13-10 to win World Bowl 2000 in front of 35,680 at Frankfurt's Waldstadion, June 25.

More than 100 of the 136 living members of the Pro Football Hall of Fame gathered to celebrate Pro Football's Greatest Reunion in Canton, Ohio, July 28-31.

Paul Brown Stadium opened in Cincinnati, Ohio with a crowd of 56,180 as the Cincinnati Bengals defeated the Chicago Bears 24-20 in a preseason game, August 19.

Minnesota's Gary Anderson converted a 21-yard field goal against Buffalo to pass George Blanda as the NFL's all-time scoring leader with 2,004 points, October 22.

San Francisco's Terrell Owens set a single-game receiving record with 20 receptions (283 yards) against Chicago, surpassing the previous mark of 18 by Tom Fears of the Los Angeles Rams in 1950, December 17.

2001

NFL clubs approved additional league-wide revenue sharing at a special league meeting in Dallas. The teams agreed to pool the visiting team share of gate receipts for all preseason and regular-season games and divide the pool equally starting in 2002, January 17.

The Baltimore Ravens won their first Super Bowl by defeating the NFC champion New York Giants 34-7 in Super Bowl XXXV at Raymond James Stadium in Tampa Bay, January 28.

The *Sports Business Daily* named NFL Commissioner Paul Tagliabue the 2000 Sports Industrialist of the Year, February 28.

NFL owners unanimously approved a realignment plan for the league starting in 2002. With the addition of the Houston Texans, the league's 32 teams will be divided into eight four-team divisions. Seven clubs change divisions, and the Seattle Seahawks change conferences, moving from the AFC to the NFC. A new scheduling format ensures that every team meets every other team in the league at least once every four years, May 22.

The Berlin Thunder won their first World Bowl, defeating the Barcelona Dragons 24-17 to win World Bowl IX in front of 32,116 at Amsterdam ArenA, June 30.

Heinz Field opened in Pittsburgh, Pennsylvania before a crowd of 57,829 with the Pittsburgh Steelers defeating the Detroit Lions 20-7 in a preseason game; and INVESCO Field at Mile High opened in Denver, Colorado before a crowd of 74,063 with the Denver Broncos defeating the New Orleans Saints 31-24 in a preseason game, August 25.

President George W. Bush became the first United States President to be involved in an NFL regular-season pregame coin toss as he helped kick off the 2001 season from the White House. Via satellite, President Bush tossed the coin for the 10 regular-season games that started at 1:00 P.M. ET, September 9.

In the wake of the September 11 terrorist attacks, Commissioner Paul Tagliabue postponed the games scheduled for September 16-17, September 13.

The league's 16-game regular season was retained when the postponed Week 2 games were rescheduled for the weekend of January 6-7, September 18.

The NFL and its game officials agreed to a new six-year Collective Bargaining Agreement, ending a two-week lockout of the regular officials, who returned to work on September 23, September 19.

The NFL announced that the league's prohibition of anabolic steroids and related substances had been strengthened to include supplements containing ephedrine and other high-risk supplements, September 27.

The NFL announced that the Super Bowl would be rescheduled from January 27 to February 3 in order to retain the full playoff format for the 2002 season. It will be the first Super Bowl played in February, October 3.

President Bush designated Super Bowl XXXVI as a "National Special Security Event," allowing all security for the game to be coordinated by the Secret Service, November 26.

2002

The NFL and the NFL Players Association agreed to a fourth extension of the 1993 Collective Bargaining Agreement through 2007, January 7.

In an AFC Wild Card matchup, the Oakland Raiders defeated the New York Jets 38-24 in the NFL's first-ever primetime playoff game, January 12.

In a special meeting in New Orleans, NFL owners voted unanimously to approve the purchase of the Atlanta Falcons to Home Depot co-founder Arthur Blank, February 2.

The New England Patriots won their first Super Bowl by defeating the NFC champion St. Louis Rams 20-17 in Super Bowl XXXVI at the Louisiana Superdome in New Orleans. The game marked the first time in Super Bowl history that the winning points came on the final play, a 48-yard field goal by Patriots kicker Adam Vinatieri, February 3.

Tony Boselli, a five-time Pro Bowl tackle allocated by the Jacksonville Jaguars, was the first selection of the Houston Texans in the 2002 NFL Expansion Draft. The Texans selected 19 players, February 18.

The NFL and Westwood One/CBS Radio Sports announced the renewal of a multiyear agreement for Westwood One/CBS Radio Sports to continue as the exclusive network radio home of the NFL, April 9.

NFL Europe kicked off its tenth season with a record 254 players allocated by NFL clubs, April 13-14.

The Berlin Thunder became the first team to win consecutive World Bowls, defeating the Rhein Fire 26-20 to win World Bowl X in front of 53,109 fans at Rheinstadion, June 22.

Seahawks Stadium opened in Seattle, Washington with an attendance of 52,902 fans as the Indianapolis Colts defeated the Seattle Seahawks 28-10 in a preseason game, August 10.

Gillette Stadium opened in Foxboro, Massachusetts with a crowd of 68,436 fans as the New England Patriots defeated the Philadelphia Eagles 16-15 in a preseason game, August 17.

Reliant Stadium opened in Houston, Texas with 69,432 fans in attendance, the largest non-Super Bowl crowd to ever watch an NFL game in Houston as the Miami Dolphins defeated the Houston Texans 24-3 in a preseason game, August 24.

For the first time, the NFL season kicked off on a Thursday night in prime time as the San Francisco 49ers defeated the New York Giants 16-13 at Giants Stadium. The game was preceded by "NFL Kickoff Live From Times Square," presented by New York City and the NFL, a football and music festival honoring the resilient spirit of New York and America, September 5.

Week 1 of the 2002 season produced the highest-scoring and most competitive Kickoff Weekend in NFL history. The 16 games averaged 49.3 points per game. A total of 788 points and 89 touchdowns were scored, the most in league history for an opening weekend. Eleven of the 16 games were decided by one score (eight points or less), a Kickoff Weekend record, September 5-9.

Johnny Unitas, the legendary quarterback for the Baltimore Colts and a Pro Football Hall of Fame member, died of a heart attack at the age of 69, September 11.

Oakland Raiders wide receiver Jerry Rice became the all-time leader in yards from scrimmage, surpassing Pro Football Hall of Fame running back Walter Payton (21,281 yards), September 29.

Cleveland Browns owner Al Lerner, the NFL Finance Committee Chairman and Chairman and CEO of MBNA Corporation, died at the age of 69, October 23.

Dallas Cowboys running back Emmitt Smith became the NFL's all-time rushing leader, surpassing Pro Football Hall of Fame running back Walter Payton (16,726 yards), October 27.

The NFL and NFLPA announced the creation of USA Football, the first national advocacy organization representing all levels of amateur football, December 5.

The 2002 season concluded with 25 overtime games, the most in NFL history, December 30.

2003

The Tampa Bay Buccaneers won their first Super Bowl by defeating the AFC champion Oakland Raiders 48-21 in Super Bowl XXXVII at Qualcomm Stadium in San Diego, January 26.

Chicago Bears chairman emeritus Edward W. McCaskey died at the age of 83, April 8.

The Frankfurt Galaxy became the first team to win three World Bowls, defeating the Rhein Fire 35-16 to win World Bowl XI in front of 28,138 fans at Hampden Park, June 14.

Tex Schramm, the legendary team president and general manager of the Dallas Cowboys and a member of the Pro Football Hall of Fame, died at the age of 83, July 15.

Lincoln Financial Field opened in Philadelphia, Pennsylvania with an attendance of 66,279 fans as the New England Patriots defeated the Philadelphia Eagles 24-12 in a preseason game, August 22.

A renovated Lambeau Field opened in Green Bay, Wisconsin with a crowd of 69,831 fans as the Carolina Panthers defeated the Green Bay Packers 20-7 in a preseason game, August 23.

A renovated Soldier Field opened in Chicago, Illinois with an attendance of 61,500 fans as the Green Bay Packers defeated the Chicago Bears 38-23 in a regular season game on ABC's *NFL Monday Night Football*, September 29.

NFL Network, the first 24-hour, year-round television channel dedicated to the NFL and the sport of football, launched on DirecTV, November 4.

2004

The New England Patriots won their second Super Bowl in three years by defeating the NFC champion Carolina Panthers 32-29 in Super Bowl XXXVIII at Reliant Stadium in Houston, February 1.

By a vote of 29-3, NFL owners extended the instant replay system for another five seasons through 2008, March 30.

Steve Bisciotti took over as the controlling owner of the Baltimore Ravens, succeeding Art Modell, who operated the franchise for 43 years, April 8.

Former Arizona Cardinals safety Pat Tillman was killed in a firefight while on combat patrol with the U.S. Army Rangers in Afghanistan, April 22.

A federal appeals court formally ruled in favor of the NFL's draft eligibility rule in Maurice Clarett's lawsuit, citing federal labor policy in permitting the NFL and the Players Association to set rules for when players can enter the league, May 24.

The Berlin Thunder defeated the Frankfurt Galaxy 30-24 to win World Bowl XII in front of 35,413 fans at Arena AufSchalke, June 12.

The New England Patriots defeated the New York Jets 13-7 for their NFL-record 18th consecutive regular-season victory, October 24.

The NFL reached an agreement on six-year contract extensions with two of its network television partners—CBS and FOX—to run through the 2011 season, November 8.

The NFL and DirecTV announced a five-year extension on the NFL Sunday Ticket subscription television package to run through the 2010 season, November 8.

NFL Europe named the Hamburg Sea Devils as the league's newest team, November 24.

2005

Indianapolis Colts quarterback Peyton Manning set the NFL single-season record with 49 touchdown passes, January 2.

The New England Patriots became the second team in NFL history to win three Super Bowls in four seasons by defeating the Philadelphia Eagles 24-21 in Super Bowl XXXIX at ALLTEL Stadium in Jacksonville, February 6.

The Pat Tillman USO Center opened in Afghanistan. The NFL donated $250,000 to the USO to honor the memory of the former Arizona Cardinals player who died in Afghanistan while serving in the U.S. Army, April 1.

The NFL reached long-term agreements for its Sunday and Monday primetime TV packages. NBC returned to the NFL by acquiring the Sunday night package for six years (2006-2011). ESPN agreed on an eight-year deal to televise *Monday Night Football* from 2006-2013, April 18.

The NFL strengthened its steroids program by adopting the Olympic testosterone testing standard, tripling the number of times a player can be randomly tested during the offseason from two to six, adding substances to the list of banned substances, and putting new language in the policy to allow for testing of designer drugs and other substances that may have evaded detection, April 27.

NFL owners voted unanimously to approve the sale of the Minnesota Vikings to real-estate developer Zygi Wilf, May 25.

The Amsterdam Admirals defeated the Berlin Thunder 27-21 to win World Bowl XIII in front of 35,134 fans at LTU Arena in Dússeldorf, Germany, June 11.

The NFL designated September 18-19 as "Hurricane Relief Weekend," which concluded with a telethon in conjunction with a Monday Night Football doubleheader on ABC and ESPN. The New York Giants-New Orleans Saints game, originally scheduled for the Louisiana Superdome, was moved to Giants Stadium following Hurricane Katrina. In total, the NFL, its owners, teams, players, and fans contributed $21 million to aid the Hurricane Katrina rebuilding effort, September 19.

An NFL record 103,467 fans attended the Arizona Cardinals' 31-14 victory over the San Francisco 49ers at Mexico City's Azteca Stadium, the first-ever regular-season NFL game played outside the United States, October 2.

Wellington Mara, the New York Giants' president and co-chief executive officer, died at the age of 89, October 25.

Preston Robert Tisch, the Giants' chairman and co-chief executive officer, died at the age of 79, November 15.

2006

The NFL announced that NFL Network would begin airing a "Road To The Playoffs" package of eight primetime regular season NFL games starting in 2006, January 28.

The Pittsburgh Steelers won their fifth Super Bowl, defeating the Seattle Seahawks 21-10 in Super Bowl XL at Ford Field in Detroit, Michigan, February 5.

The NFL clubs approved an extension of the Collective Bargaining Agreement through 2012, March 8.

Commissioner Tagliabue announced his decision to retire by the end of July. The NFL enjoyed an era of unrivaled prosperity in the Tagliabue Era, including labor peace throughout his 17-year tenure, March 20.

NFL clubs unanimously decided to return the name of the official game ball to "The Duke" in honor of the late New York Giants owner Wellington Mara, March 27.

The Amsterdam Admirals defeated the Berlin Thunder 22-7 to win World Bowl XIV in front of 36,286 fans at LTU Arena in Düsseldorf, Germany, May 27.

Roger Goodell became the eighth chief executive of the NFL on August 8 when he was chosen to succeed Paul Tagliabue as commissioner by a unanimous vote of the clubs at a three-day meeting in Chicago, Illinois. The transfer from Commissioner Tagliabue to Commissioner Goodell took place at 6:00 A.M. on Friday, September 1.

Cardinals Stadium opened in Glendale, Arizona with a crowd of 63,400 fans on August 12 as the Arizona Cardinals defeated the Pittsburgh Steelers 21-13 in a preseason game. The facility was later renamed University of Phoenix Stadium on September 26.

President George W. Bush signed into law HR 4954, which included the Internet Gambling Prohibition and Enforcement Act. The bill prohibits online gamblers from using credit cards, checks and electronic fund transfers to place and settle bets, strengthening enforcement of federal and state gambling laws that had been evaded by overseas gambling operations using the Internet, October 13.

NFL owners approved a resolution to stage a limited number of international regular-season games—up to two per season—beginning in 2007 and continuing through 2011, October 24.

The NFL Network broadcast its first-ever regular-season game as the Kansas City Chiefs defeated the Denver Broncos 19-10 at Arrowhead Stadium on Thanksgiving night, November 23.

San Diego Chargers running back LaDainian Tomlinson set the NFL single-season record for touchdowns with 29 on December 10. He finished the season with 31 touchdowns and also set a single-season record for points with 186.

Lamar Hunt, founder of the Kansas City Chiefs and the American Football League, died at the age of 74, December 13.

2007

The Indianapolis Colts won their second Super Bowl, defeating the Chicago Bears 29-17 in Super Bowl XLI at Dolphin Stadium in South Florida, February 4. Both teams were coached by African-Americans: Tony Dungy of the Colts and Lovie Smith of the Bears.

NFL clubs approved additional league-wide revenue sharing at a league meeting in Phoenix, Arizona. The teams agreed to redistribute up to $430 million over a four-year span, retroactive to 2006, March 26.

The NFL announced changes to its long-standing personal conduct policy and programs for players, coaches, and other team and league employees. The modifications focus on expanded educational and support programs in addition to increased levels of discipline for violations of the policy, April 10.

The NFL, NFL Players Association, NFL Retired Players Association, NFL Alumni Association, NFL Charities and Pro Football Hall of Fame formed the first-ever Alliance to coordinate medical support services for former players, May 22.

The Hamburg Sea Devils defeated the Frankfurt Galaxy 37-28 to win World Bowl XV in front of 48,125 fans at Commerzbank-Arena in Frankfurt, Germany, June 23.

The NFL announced it will focus its international business strategy on reaching the widest possible global audience, including the staging of international regular-season games, and discontinued NFL Europa after 15 seasons of operation, June 29.

NFL owners unanimously approved $10 million in additional Alliance funding for retired players to help pay for joint replacement surgeries and other medical assistance, supplementing the initial $7 million committed in July by Alliance members, October 24.

The New York Giants defeated the Miami Dolphins 13-10 at London's in front of 81,176 fans at Wembley Stadium in the first regular-season game played outside of North America, October 28.

On the field in the 2007 season, many significant records and milestones were achieved: Green Bay quarterback Brett Favre surpassed Pro Football Hall of Famer Dan Marino in both passing categories—touchdowns and yards—to become the NFL's all-time career leader. Patriots quarterback Tom Brady set the single-season record with 50 touchdown passes, including 23 to wide receiver Randy Moss—also a record. New England, which became the first team ever to finish 16-0 in the regular season, scored a record 589 points.

2008

The NFL, United States Olympic Committee, United States Anti-Doping Agency and MLB announced a partnership to form a clean competition anti-doping research collaborative, January 10.

Georgia Frontiere, majority owner of the St. Louis Rams, died at the age of 80, January 18.

The NFL announced it will stage a regular-season game in the United Kingdom during each of the next three seasons, beginning with the New Orleans Saints hosting the San Diego Chargers on October 26, 2008 at London's Wembley Stadium, February 1.

The New York Giants scored with 35 seconds remaining to win their third Super Bowl, defeating the New England Patriots 17-14 in Super Bowl XLII at University of Phoenix Stadium in Glendale, Arizona, February 3.

The NFL set an all-time paid attendance record in 2007 for the sixth consecutive season. Attendance for all 2007 games was 22,256,502, an increase of 56,790 over the previous mark. The Washington Redskins set an all-time NFL regular-season home paid attendance record of 711,471 for eight games, breaking their own record of 708,852 in 2006.

NFL clubs voted unanimously to exercise their option to shorten by two years the current Collective Bargaining Agreement, which now will run through the 2010 season and 2011 NFL Draft, May 20.

Lucas Oil Stadium opened in Indianapolis, Indiana with a crowd of 65,333 as the Buffalo Bills defeated the Indianapolis Colts by a score of 20-7 in a preseason game, August 24.

The NFL established a new fan code of conduct to help support a positive fan environment at all NFL stadiums, August 5.

NFLPA Executive Director and Pro Football Hall of Famer Gene Upshaw died at the age of 63, August 20.

For the first time, an NFL game was broadcast on NBC and also streamed live in its entirety to fans on the Internet via NFL.com and NBCSports.com as the Giants beat the Redskins 16-7 in the 2009 NFL Kickoff game, September 4.

Owners approved a restructured ownership plan for the Pittsburgh Steelers that will keep the team under the control of chairman Dan Rooney and team president Art Rooney II, December 17.

The NFL announced that the 2010 Pro Bowl will be played a week prior to Super Bowl XLIV on Sunday, January 31, 2010. Both games will be played in South Florida, December 30.

In the 256 regular-season games of 2008, 44.1 points per game were scored—the highest average since 1970.

2009

Stephen M. Ross purchased an additional 45 percent of the Miami Dolphins from Wayne Huizenga and became the team's managing partner. Coupled with his April 1, 2008 purchase of 50 percent of the franchise, the stadium, and the excess developable land, Ross now owns 95 percent of the Dolphins and the stadium while Huizenga retains a five percent share of both and remains a 50 percent partner in that land, January 20.

The NFL re-named its minority coaching internship program the Bill Walsh NFL Minority Coaching Fellowship, honoring the Pro Football Hall of Fame coach who conceived of the program, January 29.

The Pittsburgh Steelers

scored a touchdown with 42 seconds remaining to claim their NFL-record sixth Super Bowl title, defeating the Arizona Cardinals 27-23 in Super Bowl XLIII at Raymond James Stadium in Tampa Bay, February 1.

The NFL and Westwood One announced a new two-year agreement for Westwood One to continue as the exclusive network radio partner of the NFL, March 12.

The NFLPA selected Washington-based attorney DeMaurice Smith as its new executive director, March 16.

The NFL and DIRECTV announced an agreement to extend DIRECTV's rights to carry NFL Sunday Ticket through the 2014 season, March 23.

The NFL reached an agreement on two-year contract extensions with two of its network television partners – CBS and FOX – to run through the 2013 season, May 19.

The NFL extended by two years its broadcast partnership with NBC to televise the Sunday night package through the 2013 season, August 19.

Cowboys Stadium opened in Arlington, Texas with a crowd of 75,720 as the Dallas Cowboys defeated the Tennessee Titans by a score of 30-10 in a preseason game, August 21.

The NFL announced games that were blacked out in home team markets during the 2009 season would be shown on NFL.com in their entirety on a delayed basis, September 10.

The NFL launched a new "Red Zone Channel," offering fans crucial live action cut-ins of all Sunday afternoon games, September 13.

Pro Football Hall of Fame head coach and broadcaster John Madden was appointed special advisor to Commissioner Goodell, September 10.

NFL appointed former head coach Tony Dungy to lead a new NFL Player Advisory Forum and serve as a special advisor to Commissioner Goodell, November 19.

Commissioner Goodell notified NFL teams of new and expanded guidelines on return-to-play for any player who sustains a concussion, December 2.

2010

For the first time, the Pro Bowl was played in the Super Bowl city the week before the Super Bowl, as the AFC All-Stars beat the NFC All-Stars 41-34 in the 2010 Pro Bowl at Sun Life Stadium in South Florida. The game drew 70,697 fans – the highest attendance for a Pro Bowl since 1959, January 31.

The New Orleans Saints won their first Super Bowl title, defeating the Indianapolis Colts 31-17 in Super Bowl XLIV at Sun Life Stadium in South Florida. The game was viewed by 153.4 million people, making it the most-watched program in U.S. television history, February 7.

Dr. Hunt Batjer of Northwestern University Feinberg School of Medicine and Dr. Richard G. Ellenbogen of the University of Washington School of Medicine were named the new co-chairs of the NFL Head, Neck and Spine Medical Committee, March 16.

NFL owners voted to amend postseason overtime rules to a modified sudden death format, guaranteeing at least one possession for each club if the receiving team fails to score a touchdown on its first overtime possession, March 23.

The NFL and NFL Alumni Association announced a new neurological care program for retired players, one of a series of NFL initiatives addressing the quality of life of retired players, March 24.

NFL rules changes emphasized additional player safety. Protection for defenseless players was standardized and expanded, protecting a player who has just completed a catch from blows to the head or neck by an opponent who launches. Additional protection was also given to longsnappers. Play will now stop if a ball carrier's helmet is removed, March 24.

The NFL Draft debuted a new three-day format, with the first two days broadcast in primetime. A record combined total of 45.4 million viewers tuned in to watch the 75th NFL Draft on NFL Network, ESPN and ESPN2, April 22-24.

NFL COMMISSIONERS AND PRESIDENTS*

1920 ....Jim Thorpe, President
1921-39....Joe Carr, President
1939-41 .Carl Storck, President
1941-46 ....Elmer Layden, Commissioner
1946-1959 ....Bert Bell, Commissioner
1960-1989.........Pete Rozelle, Commissioner
1989-2006 .....Paul Tagliabue, Commissioner
2006-present ..Roger Goodell, Commissioner

**NFL treasurer Austin Gunsel served as president in the office of the commissioner following the death of Bert Bell (Oct. 11, 1959) until the election of Pete Rozelle (Jan. 26, 1960).*

2009

AMERICAN CONFERENCE

East Division

	W	L	T	Pct.	Pts.	OP
New England	10	6	0	.625	427	285
New York Jets*	9	7	0	.563	348	236
Miami	7	9	0	.438	360	390
Buffalo	6	10	0	.375	258	326

North Division

	W	L	T	Pct.	Pts.	OP
Cincinnati	10	6	0	.625	305	291
Baltimore*	9	7	0	.563	391	261
Pittsburgh	9	7	0	.563	368	324
Cleveland	5	11	0	.313	245	375

South Division

	W	L	T	Pct.	Pts.	OP
Indianapolis#	14	2	0	.875	416	307
Houston	9	7	0	.563	388	333
Tennessee	8	8	0	.500	354	402
Jacksonville	7	9	0	.438	290	380

West Division

	W	L	T	Pct.	Pts.	OP
San Diego	13	3	0	.813	454	320
Denver	8	8	0	.500	326	324
Oakland	5	11	0	.313	197	379
Kansas City	4	12	0	.250	294	424

NATIONAL CONFERENCE

East Division

	W	L	T	Pct.	Pts.	OP
Dallas	11	5	0	.688	361	250
Philadelphia*	11	5	0	.688	429	337
New York Giants	8	8	0	.500	402	427
Washington	4	12	0	.250	266	336

North Division

	W	L	T	Pct.	Pts.	OP
Minnesota	12	4	0	.750	470	312
Green Bay*	11	5	0	.688	461	297
Chicago	7	9	0	.438	327	375
Detroit	2	14	0	.125	262	494

South Division

	W	L	T	Pct.	Pts.	OP
New Orleans#	13	3	0	.813	510	341
Atlanta	9	7	0	.563	363	325
Carolina	8	8	0	.500	315	308
Tampa Bay	3	13	0	.188	244	400

West Division

	W	L	T	Pct.	Pts.	OP
Arizona	10	6	0	.625	375	325
San Francisco	8	8	0	.500	330	281
Seattle	5	11	0	.313	280	390
St. Louis	1	15	0	.063	175	436

**Wild Card qualifier for playoffs; #Top playoff seed in conference*

New England finished ahead of Cincinnati based on better strength of victory (.450 to Bengals' .438). Baltimore finished ahead of Pittsburgh based on better division record (3-3 to Steelers' 2-4). N.Y. Jets finished ahead of Baltimore for first Wild Card based on better record vs. common opponents (4-1 to Ravens' 1-4) and ahead of Houston based on better conference record (7-5 to Texans' 6-6). Baltimore was second Wild Card based on better conference record than Houston (7-5 to Texans' 6-6). Dallas finished ahead of Philadelphia based on head-to-head sweep (2-0). Green Bay was first Wild Card ahead of Philadelphia based on better record vs. common opponents (4-1 to Eagles' 3-2).

Wild Card Playoff: New York Jets 24, CINCINNATI 14
Baltimore 33, NEW ENGLAND 14

Divisional Playoff: INDIANAPOLIS 20, Baltimore 3
New York Jets 17, SAN DIEGO 14

AFC Championship: INDIANAPOLIS 30, New York Jets 17

Wild Card Playoff: DALLAS 34, Philadelphia 14
ARIZONA 51, Green Bay 45 (OT)

Divisional Playoff Games: NEW ORLEANS 45, Arizona 14
MINNESOTA 34, Dallas 3

NFC Championship Game: NEW ORLEANS 31, Minnesota 28 (OT)

Super Bowl XLIV: New Orleans (NFC) 31, Indianapolis (AFC) 17
at Sun Life Stadium, Miami, Florida

In Past Standings section, home teams in playoff games are indicated by capital letters.

Playoff Seeds

AFC

1. Indianapolis
2. San Diego
3. New England
4. Cincinnati
5. New York Jets
6. Baltimore

NFC

1. New Orleans
2. Minnesota
3. Dallas
4. Arizona
5. Green Bay
6. Philadelphia

2008

AMERICAN CONFERENCE

East Division

	W	L	T	Pct.	Pts.	OP
Miami	11	5	0	.688	345	317
New England	11	5	0	.688	410	309
New York Jets	9	7	0	.563	405	356
Buffalo	7	9	0	.438	336	342

North Division

	W	L	T	Pct.	Pts.	OP
Pittsburgh	12	4	0	.750	347	223
Baltimore*	11	5	0	.688	385	244
Cincinnati	4	11	1	.281	204	364
Cleveland	4	12	0	.250	232	350

South Division

	W	L	T	Pct.	Pts.	OP
Tennessee#	13	3	0	.813	375	234
Indianapolis*	12	4	0	.750	377	298
Houston	8	8	0	.500	366	394
Jacksonville	5	11	0	.313	302	367

West Division

	W	L	T	Pct.	Pts.	OP
San Diego	8	8	0	.500	439	347
Denver	8	8	0	.500	370	448
Oakland	5	11	0	.313	263	388
Kansas City	2	14	0	.125	291	440

NATIONAL CONFERENCE

East Division

	W	L	T	Pct.	Pts.	OP
New York Giants#	12	4	0	.750	427	294
Philadelphia*	9	6	1	.594	416	289
Dallas	9	7	0	.563	362	365
Washington	8	8	0	.500	265	296

North Division

	W	L	T	Pct.	Pts.	OP
Minnesota	10	6	0	.625	379	333
Chicago	9	7	0	.563	375	350
Green Bay	6	10	0	.375	419	380
Detroit	0	16	0	.000	268	517

South Division

	W	L	T	Pct.	Pts.	OP
Carolina	12	4	0	.750	414	329
Atlanta*	11	5	0	.688	391	325
Tampa Bay	9	7	0	.563	361	323
New Orleans	8	8	0	.500	463	393

West Division

	W	L	T	Pct.	Pts.	OP
Arizona	9	7	0	.563	427	426
San Francisco	7	9	0	.438	339	381
Seattle	4	12	0	.250	294	392
St. Louis	2	14	0	.125	232	465

**Wild Card qualifier for playoffs; #Top playoff seed in conference*

Miami finished ahead of New England based on better conference record (8-4 to Patriots' 7-5). Baltimore was second Wild Card ahead of New England based on better conference record (8-4 to Patriots' 7-5). San Diego finished ahead of Denver based on better division record (5-1 to Broncos' 3-3). N.Y. Giants finished ahead of Carolina based on head-to-head victory.

Wild Card Playoff: SAN DIEGO 23, Indianapolis 17 (OT);
Baltimore 27, MIAMI 9

Divisional Playoff: Baltimore 13, TENNESSEE 10
PITTSBURGH 35, San Diego 24

AFC Championship: PITTSBURGH 23, Baltimore 14

Wild Card Playoff: ARIZONA 30, Atlanta 24;
Philadelphia 26, MINNESOTA 14

Divisional Playoff: Arizona 33, CAROLINA 13;
Philadelphia 23, N.Y. GIANTS 11

NFC Championship: ARIZONA 32, Philadelphia 25

Super Bowl XLIII: Pittsburgh (AFC) 27, Arizona (NFC) 23
at Raymond James Stadium, Tampa, Florida

Playoff Seeds

AFC

1. Tennessee
2. Pittsburgh
3. Miami
4. San Diego
5. Indianapolis
6. Baltimore

NFC

1. N.Y. Giants
2. Carolina
3. Minnesota
4. Arizona
5. Atlanta
6. Philadelphia

2007

AMERICAN CONFERENCE

East Division

	W	L	T	Pct.	Pts.	OP
New England#	16	0	0	1.000	589	274
Buffalo	7	9	0	.438	252	354
New York Jets	4	12	0	.250	268	355
Miami	1	15	0	.063	267	437

North Division

	W	L	T	Pct.	Pts.	OP
Pittsburgh	10	6	0	.625	393	269
Cleveland	10	6	0	.625	402	382
Cincinnati	7	9	0	.438	380	385
Baltimore	5	11	0	.313	275	384

South Division

	W	L	T	Pct.	Pts.	OP
Indianapolis	13	3	0	.813	450	262
Jacksonville*	11	5	0	.688	411	304
Tennessee*	10	6	0	.625	301	297
Houston	8	8	0	.500	379	384

West Division

	W	L	T	Pct.	Pts.	OP
San Diego	11	5	0	.688	412	284
Denver	7	9	0	.438	320	409
Kansas City	4	12	0	.250	226	335
Oakland	4	12	0	.250	283	398

NATIONAL CONFERENCE

East Division

	W	L	T	Pct.	Pts.	OP
Dallas#	13	3	0	.813	455	325
New York Giants*	10	6	0	.625	373	351
Washington*	9	7	0	.563	334	310
Philadelphia	8	8	0	.500	336	300

North Division

	W	L	T	Pct.	Pts.	OP
Green Bay	13	3	0	.813	435	291
Minnesota	8	8	0	.500	365	311
Detroit	7	9	0	.438	346	444
Chicago	7	9	0	.438	334	348

South Division

	W	L	T	Pct.	Pts.	OP
Tampa Bay	9	7	0	.563	334	270
Carolina	7	9	0	.438	267	347
New Orleans	7	9	0	.438	379	388
Atlanta	4	12	0	.250	259	414

West Division

	W	L	T	Pct.	Pts.	OP
Seattle	10	6	0	.625	393	291
Arizona	8	8	0	.500	404	399
San Francisco	5	11	0	.313	219	364
St. Louis	3	13	0	.188	263	438

**Wild Card qualifier for playoffs; #Top playoff seed in conference*

Pittsburgh finished ahead of Cleveland based on head-to-head sweep (2-0). Tennessee finished ahead of Cleveland based on better record vs. common opponents (4-1 to Browns' 3-2). Kansas City finished ahead of Oakland based on better record vs. common opponents (2-10 to Raiders' 1-11). Dallas finished ahead of Green Bay based on head-to-head victory. Detroit finished ahead of Chicago based on head-to-head sweep (2-0). Carolina finished ahead of New Orleans based on better conference record (7-5 to Saints' 6-6).

Wild Card Playoff: Jacksonville 31, PITTSBURGH 29
SAN DIEGO 17, Tennessee 6
Divisional Playoff: NEW ENGLAND 31, Jacksonville 20
San Diego 28, INDIANAPOLIS 24
AFC Championship: NEW ENGLAND 21, San Diego 12
Wild Card Playoff: SEATTLE 35, Washington 14
N.Y. Giants 24, TAMPA BAY 14
Divisional Playoff: GREEN BAY 42, Seattle 20
N.Y. Giants 21, DALLAS 17
NFC Championship: N.Y. Giants 23, GREEN BAY 20 (OT)
Super Bowl XLII: N.Y. Giants (NFC) 17, New England (AFC) 14 at University of Phoenix Stadium, Glendale, Arizona

Playoff Seeds

AFC
1. New England
2. Indianapolis
3. San Diego
4. Pittsburgh
5. Jacksonville
6. Tennessee

NFC
1. Dallas
2. Green Bay
3. Seattle
4. Tampa Bay
5. N.Y. Giants
6. Washington

2006

AMERICAN CONFERENCE

East Division

	W	L	T	Pct.	Pts.	OP
New England	12	4	0	.750	385	237
New York Jets*	10	6	0	.625	316	295
Buffalo	7	9	0	.438	300	311
Miami	6	10	0	.375	260	283

North Division

	W	L	T	Pct.	Pts.	OP
Baltimore	13	3	0	.813	353	201
Cincinnati	8	8	0	.500	373	331
Pittsburgh	8	8	0	.500	353	315
Cleveland	4	12	0	.250	238	356

South Division

	W	L	T	Pct.	Pts.	OP
Indianapolis	12	4	0	.750	427	360
Tennessee	8	8	0	.500	324	400
Jacksonville	8	8	0	.500	371	274
Houston	6	10	0	.375	267	366

West Division

	W	L	T	Pct.	Pts.	OP
San Diego#	14	2	0	.875	492	303
Kansas City*	9	7	0	.563	331	315
Denver	9	7	0	.563	319	305
Oakland	2	14	0	.125	168	332

NATIONAL CONFERENCE

East Division

	W	L	T	Pct.	Pts.	OP
Philadelphia	10	6	0	.625	398	328
Dallas*	9	7	0	.563	425	350
New York Giants*	8	8	0	.500	355	362
Washington	5	11	0	.313	307	376

North Division

	W	L	T	Pct.	Pts.	OP
Chicago#	13	3	0	.813	427	255
Green Bay	8	8	0	.500	301	366
Minnesota	6	10	0	.375	282	327
Detroit	3	13	0	.188	305	398

South Division

	W	L	T	Pct.	Pts.	OP
New Orleans	10	6	0	.625	413	322
Carolina	8	8	0	.500	270	305
Atlanta	7	9	0	.438	292	328
Tampa Bay	4	12	0	.250	211	353

West Division

	W	L	T	Pct.	Pts.	OP
Seattle	9	7	0	.563	335	341
St. Louis	8	8	0	.500	367	381
San Francisco	7	9	0	.438	298	412
Arizona	5	11	0	.313	314	389

**Wild Card qualifier for playoffs; #Top playoff seed in conference*

Indianapolis finished ahead of New England based on head-to-head victory. Cincinnati finished ahead of Pittsburgh based on better division record (4-2 to Steelers' 3-3). Tennessee finished ahead of Jacksonville based on better division record (4-2 to Jaguars' 2-4). Kansas City finished ahead of Denver based on better division record (4-2 to Broncos' 3-3). New Orleans finished ahead of Philadelphia based on head-to-head victory. N.Y. Giants finished ahead of Carolina and St. Louis based on better conference record (Giants' 7-5 to Panthers' 6-6 and Rams' 6-6) and ahead of Green Bay based on strength of victory (.422 to Packers' .383).

Wild Card Playoff: INDIANAPOLIS 23, Kansas City 8
NEW ENGLAND 37, N.Y. Jets 16
Divisional Playoff: Indianapolis 15, BALTIMORE 6
New England 24, SAN DIEGO 21
AFC Championship: INDIANAPOLIS 38, New England 34
Wild Card Playoff: SEATTLE 21, Dallas 20
PHILADELPHIA 23, N.Y. Giants 20
Divisional Playoff: NEW ORLEANS 27, Philadelphia 24
CHICAGO 27, Seattle 24 (OT)
NFC Championship: CHICAGO 39, New Orleans 14
Super Bowl XLI: Indianapolis (AFC) 29, Chicago (NFC) 17 at Dolphin Stadium, Miami, Florida

Playoff Seeds

AFC
1. San Diego
2. Baltimore
3. Indianapolis
4. New England
5. N.Y. Jets
6. Kansas City

NFC
1. Chicago
2. New Orleans
3. Philadelphia
4. Seattle
5. Dallas
6. N.Y. Giants

2005

AMERICAN CONFERENCE

East Division

	W	L	T	Pct.	Pts.	OP
New England	10	6	0	.625	379	338
Miami	9	7	0	.563	318	317
Buffalo	5	11	0	.313	271	367
N.Y. Jets	4	12	0	.250	240	355

North Division

	W	L	T	Pct.	Pts.	OP
Cincinnati	11	5	0	.688	421	350
Pittsburgh*	11	5	0	.688	389	258
Baltimore	6	10	0	.375	265	299
Cleveland	6	10	0	.375	232	301

South Division

	W	L	T	Pct.	Pts.	OP
Indianapolis#	14	2	0	.875	439	247
Jacksonville*	12	4	0	.750	361	269
Tennessee	4	12	0	.250	299	421
Houston	2	14	0	.125	260	431

West Division

	W	L	T	Pct.	Pts.	OP
Denver	13	3	0	.813	395	258
Kansas City	10	6	0	.625	403	325
San Diego	9	7	0	.563	418	312
Oakland	4	12	0	.250	290	383

NATIONAL CONFERENCE

East Division

	W	L	T	Pct.	Pts.	OP
N.Y. Giants	11	5	0	.688	422	314
Washington*	10	6	0	.625	359	293
Dallas	9	7	0	.563	325	308
Philadelphia	6	10	0	.375	310	388

North Division

	W	L	T	Pct.	Pts.	OP
Chicago	11	5	0	.688	260	202
Minnesota	9	7	0	.563	306	344
Detroit	5	11	0	.313	254	345
Green Bay	4	12	0	.250	298	344

South Division

	W	L	T	Pct.	Pts.	OP
Tampa Bay	11	5	0	.688	300	274
Carolina*	11	5	0	.688	391	259
Atlanta	8	8	0	.500	351	341
New Orleans	3	13	0	.188	235	398

West Division

	W	L	T	Pct.	Pts.	OP
Seattle#	13	3	0	.813	452	271
St. Louis	6	10	0	.375	363	429
Arizona	5	11	0	.313	311	387
San Francisco	4	12	0	.250	239	428

**Wild Card qualifier for playoffs; #Top playoff seed in conference*

Cincinnati finished ahead of Pittsburgh based on better division record (5-1 to Steelers' 4-2). Baltimore finished ahead of Cleveland based on better division record (2-4 to Browns' 1-5). Tampa Bay finished ahead of Carolina based on better division record (5-1 to Panthers' 4-2). Chicago finished ahead of Tampa Bay, and Tampa Bay finished ahead of the N.Y. Giants, based on better conference record (Bears' 10-2 to Buccaneers' 9-3 to Giants' 8-4).

Wild Card playoff: NEW ENGLAND 28, Jacksonville 3
Pittsburgh 31, CINCINNATI 17
Divisional playoff: DENVER 27, New England 13
Pittsburgh 21, INDIANAPOLIS 18
AFC Championship: Pittsburgh 34, DENVER 17
Wild Card playoffs: Washington 17, TAMPA BAY 10
Carolina 23, NEW YORK GIANTS 0
Divisional playoff: SEATTLE 20, Washington 10
Carolina 29, CHICAGO 21
NFC Championship: SEATTLE 34, Carolina 14
Super Bowl XL: Pittsburgh (AFC) 21, Seattle (NFC) 10
at Ford Field, Detroit, Michigan

Playoff Seeds

AFC
1. Indianapolis
2. Denver
3. Cincinnati
4. New England
5. Jacksonville
6. **Pittsburgh**

NFC
1. **Seattle**
2. Chicago
3. Tampa Bay
4. New York Giants
5. Carolina
6. Washington

2004

AMERICAN CONFERENCE

East Division

	W	L	T	Pct.	Pts.	OP
New England	14	2	0	.875	437	260
N.Y. Jets*	10	6	0	.625	333	261
Buffalo	9	7	0	.563	395	284
Miami	4	12	0	.250	275	354

North Division

	W	L	T	Pct.	Pts.	OP
Pittsburgh#	15	1	0	.938	372	251
Baltimore	9	7	0	.563	317	268
Cincinnati	8	8	0	.500	374	372
Cleveland	4	12	0	.250	276	390

South Division

	W	L	T	Pct.	Pts.	OP
Indianapolis	12	4	0	.750	522	351
Jacksonville	9	7	0	.563	261	280
Houston	7	9	0	.438	309	339
Tennessee	5	11	0	.313	344	439

West Division

	W	L	T	Pct.	Pts.	OP
San Diego	12	4	0	.750	446	313
Denver*	10	6	0	.625	381	304
Kansas City	7	9	0	.438	483	435
Oakland	5	11	0	.313	320	442

NATIONAL CONFERENCE

East Division

	W	L	T	Pct.	Pts.	OP
Philadelphia#	13	3	0	.813	386	260
N.Y. Giants	6	10	0	.375	303	347
Dallas	6	10	0	.375	293	405
Washington	6	10	0	.375	240	265

North Division

	W	L	T	Pct.	Pts.	OP
Green Bay	10	6	0	.625	424	380
Minnesota*	8	8	0	.500	405	395
Detroit	6	10	0	.375	296	350
Chicago	5	11	0	.313	231	331

South Division

	W	L	T	Pct.	Pts.	OP
Atlanta	11	5	0	.688	340	337
New Orleans	8	8	0	.500	348	405
Carolina	7	9	0	.438	355	339
Tampa Bay	5	11	0	.313	301	304

West Division

	W	L	T	Pct.	Pts.	OP
Seattle	9	7	0	.563	371	373
St. Louis*	8	8	0	.500	319	392
Arizona	6	10	0	.375	284	322
San Francisco	2	14	0	.125	259	452

**Wild Card qualifier for playoffs; #Top playoff seed in conference*

Indianapolis finished ahead of San Diego based on head-to-head victory. N.Y. Jets finished ahead of Denver based on better record vs. common opponents (5-0 to Broncos' 3-2). St. Louis finished ahead of New Orleans and Minnesota based on best conference record (7-5 to Saints' 6-6 to Vikings' 5-7), and Minnesota finished ahead of New Orleans based on head-to-head victory. N.Y. Giants finished ahead of Dallas and Washington based on better head-to-head record (3-1 to Cowboys' 2-2 to Redskins' 1-3), and Dallas finished ahead of Washington based on head-to-head sweep (2-0).

Wild Card playoffs: N.Y. Jets 20, SAN DIEGO 17 (OT)
INDIANAPOLIS 49, Denver 24
Divisional playoffs: PITTSBURGH 20, N.Y. Jets 17 (OT)
NEW ENGLAND 20, Indianapolis 3
AFC Championship: New England 41, PITTSBURGH 27
Wild Card playoffs: St. Louis 27, SEATTLE 20
Minnesota 31, GREEN BAY 17
Divisional playoffs: ATLANTA 47, St. Louis 17
PHILADELPHIA 27, Minnesota 14
NFC Championship: PHILADELPHIA 27, Atlanta 10
Super Bowl XXXIX: New England (AFC) 24, Philadelphia (NFC) 21
at Alltel Stadium, Jacksonville, Florida

Playoff Seeds

AFC
1. Pittsburgh
2. **New England**
3. Indianapolis
4. San Diego
5. N.Y. Jets
6. Denver

NFC
1. **Philadelphia**
2. Atlanta
3. Green Bay
4. Seattle
5. St. Louis
6. Minnesota

2003

AMERICAN CONFERENCE

East Division

	W	L	T	Pct.	Pts.	OP
New England#	14	2	0	.875	348	238
Miami	10	6	0	.625	311	261
Buffalo	6	10	0	.375	243	279
N.Y. Jets	6	10	0	.375	283	299

North Division

	W	L	T	Pct.	Pts.	OP
Baltimore	10	6	0	.625	391	281
Cincinnati	8	8	0	.500	346	384
Pittsburgh	6	10	0	.375	300	327
Cleveland	5	11	0	.313	254	322

South Division

	W	L	T	Pct.	Pts.	OP
Indianapolis	12	4	0	.750	447	336
Tennessee*	12	4	0	.750	435	324
Jacksonville	5	11	0	.313	276	331
Houston	5	11	0	.313	255	380

West Division

	W	L	T	Pct.	Pts.	OP
Kansas City	13	3	0	.813	484	332
Denver*	10	6	0	.625	381	301
Oakland	4	12	0	.250	270	379
San Diego	4	12	0	.250	313	441

NATIONAL CONFERENCE

East Division

	W	L	T	Pct.	Pts.	OP
Philadelphia#	12	4	0	.750	374	287
Dallas*	10	6	0	.625	289	260
Washington	5	11	0	.313	287	372
N.Y. Giants	4	12	0	.250	243	387

North Division

	W	L	T	Pct.	Pts.	OP
Green Bay	10	6	0	.625	442	307
Minnesota	9	7	0	.563	416	353
Chicago	7	9	0	.438	283	346
Detroit	5	11	0	.313	270	379

South Division

	W	L	T	Pct.	Pts.	OP
Carolina	11	5	0	.688	325	304
New Orleans	8	8	0	.500	340	326
Tampa Bay	7	9	0	.438	301	264
Atlanta	5	11	0	.313	299	422

West Division

	W	L	T	Pct.	Pts.	OP
St. Louis	12	4	0	.750	447	328
Seattle*	10	6	0	.625	404	327
San Francisco	7	9	0	.438	384	337
Arizona	4	12	0	.250	225	452

**Wild Card qualifier for playoffs; #Top playoff seed in conference*

Buffalo finished ahead of N.Y. Jets based on better division record (2-4 to Jets' 1-5). Indianapolis finished ahead of Tennessee based on head-to-head sweep (2-0). Jacksonville finished ahead of Houston based on better division record (2-4 to Texans' 1-5). Denver finished ahead of Miami based on better conference record (9-3 to Dolphins' 7-5). Oakland finished ahead of San Diego based on better conference record (3-9 to Chargers' 2-10). Philadelphia finished ahead of St. Louis based on better conference record (9-3 to Rams' 8-4). Seattle finished ahead of Dallas based on better strength of victory (65-95 to Cowboys' 62-98).

Wild Card playoffs: Tennessee 20, BALTIMORE 17; INDIANAPOLIS 41, Denver 10

Divisional playoffs: NEW ENGLAND 17, Tennessee 14; Indianapolis 38, KANSAS CITY 31

AFC Championship: NEW ENGLAND 24, Indianapolis 14

Wild Card playoffs: CAROLINA 29, Dallas 10; GREEN BAY 33, Seattle 27 (OT)

Divisional playoffs: Carolina 29, ST. LOUIS 23 (2OT); PHILADELPHIA 20, Green Bay 17 (OT)

NFC Championship: Carolina 14, PHILADELPHIA 3

Super Bowl XXXVIII: New England (AFC) 32, Carolina (NFC) 29 at Reliant Stadium, Houston, Texas

Playoff Seeds

AFC	NFC
1. New England	1. Philadelphia
2. Kansas City	2. St. Louis
3. Indianapolis	**3. Carolina**
4. Baltimore	4. Green Bay
5. Tennessee	5. Seattle
6. Denver	6. Dallas

2002

AMERICAN CONFERENCE

East Division

	W	L	T	Pct.	Pts.	OP
N.Y. Jets	9	7	0	.563	359	336
New England	9	7	0	.563	381	346
Miami	9	7	0	.563	378	301
Buffalo	8	8	0	.500	379	397

North Division

	W	L	T	Pct.	Pts.	OP
Pittsburgh	10	5	1	.656	390	345
Cleveland*	9	7	0	.563	344	320
Baltimore	7	9	0	.438	316	354
Cincinnati	2	14	0	.125	279	456

South Division

	W	L	T	Pct.	Pts.	OP
Tennessee	11	5	0	.688	367	324
Indianapolis*	10	6	0	.625	349	313
Jacksonville	6	10	0	.375	328	315
Houston	4	12	0	.250	213	356

West Division

	W	L	T	Pct.	Pts.	OP
Oakland#	11	5	0	.688	450	304
Denver	9	7	0	.563	392	344
San Diego	8	8	0	.500	333	367
Kansas City	8	8	0	.500	467	399

NATIONAL CONFERENCE

East Division

	W	L	T	Pct.	Pts.	OP
Philadelphia#	12	4	0	.750	415	241
N.Y. Giants*	10	6	0	.625	320	279
Washington	7	9	0	.438	307	365
Dallas	5	11	0	.313	217	329

North Division

	W	L	T	Pct.	Pts.	OP
Green Bay	12	4	0	.750	398	328
Minnesota	6	10	0	.375	390	442
Chicago	4	12	0	.250	281	379
Detroit	3	13	0	.188	306	451

South Division

	W	L	T	Pct.	Pts.	OP
Tampa Bay	12	4	0	.750	346	196
Atlanta*	9	6	1	.594	402	314
New Orleans	9	7	0	.563	432	388
Carolina	7	9	0	.438	258	302

West Division

	W	L	T	Pct.	Pts.	OP
San Francisco	10	6	0	.625	367	351
St. Louis	7	9	0	.438	316	369
Seattle	7	9	0	.438	355	369
Arizona	5	11	0	.313	262	417

**Wild Card qualifier for playoffs; #Top playoff seed in conference*

New York Jets finished ahead of New England based on better record in common games (8-4 to Patriots' 7-5) and Miami based on better division record (4-2 to Dolphins' 2-4). New England finished ahead of Miami based on better division record (4-2 to Dolphins' 2-4). Cleveland finished ahead of Denver and New England based on better conference record (7-5 to Broncos' 5-7 and Patriots' 6-6). Oakland finished ahead of Tennessee based on better head-to-head record (1-0). San Diego finished ahead of Kansas City based on better division record (3-3 to Chiefs' 2-4). Philadelphia finished ahead of Green Bay and Tampa Bay based on better conference record (11-1 to Packers' 9-3 and Buccaneers' 9-3). Tampa Bay finished ahead of Green Bay based on better head-to-head record (1-0). St. Louis finished ahead of Seattle based on better division record (4-2 to Seahawks' 2-4).

Wild Card playoffs: N.Y. JETS 41, Indianapolis 0; PITTSBURGH 36, Cleveland 33

Divisional playoffs: TENNESSEE 34, Pittsburgh 31 (OT); OAKLAND 30, N.Y. Jets 10

AFC Championship: OAKLAND 41, Tennessee 24

Wild Card playoffs: Atlanta 27, GREEN BAY 7; SAN FRANCISCO 39, N.Y. Giants 38

Divisional playoffs: PHILADELPHIA 20, Atlanta 6; TAMPA BAY 31, San Francisco 6

NFC Championship: Tampa Bay 27, PHILADELPHIA 10

Super Bowl XXXVII: Tampa Bay (NFC) 48, Oakland (AFC) 21 at Qualcomm Stadium, San Diego, California

Playoff Seeds

AFC	NFC
1. Oakland	1. Philadelphia
2. Tennessee	**2. Tampa Bay**
3. Pittsburgh	3. Green Bay
4. N.Y. Jets	4. San Francisco
5. Indianapolis	5. N.Y. Giants
6. Cleveland	6. Atlanta

2001

AMERICAN CONFERENCE

Eastern Division

	W	L	T	Pct.	Pts.	OP
New England	11	5	0	.688	371	272
Miami*	11	5	0	.688	344	290
N.Y. Jets*	10	6	0	.625	308	295
Indianapolis	6	10	0	.375	413	486
Buffalo	3	13	0	.188	265	420

Central Division

	W	L	T	Pct.	Pts.	OP
Pittsburgh#	13	3	0	.813	352	212
Baltimore*	10	6	0	.625	303	265
Cleveland	7	9	0	.438	285	319
Tennessee	7	9	0	.438	336	388
Jacksonville	6	10	0	.375	294	286
Cincinnati	6	10	0	.375	226	309

Western Division

	W	L	T	Pct.	Pts.	OP
Oakland	10	6	0	.625	399	327
Seattle	9	7	0	.563	301	324
Denver	8	8	0	.500	340	339
Kansas City	6	10	0	.375	320	344
San Diego	5	11	0	.313	332	321

NATIONAL CONFERENCE

Eastern Division

	W	L	T	Pct.	Pts.	OP
Philadelphia	11	5	0	.688	343	208
Washington	8	8	0	.500	256	303
N.Y. Giants	7	9	0	.438	294	321
Arizona	7	9	0	.438	295	343
Dallas	5	11	0	.313	246	338

Central Division

	W	L	T	Pct.	Pts.	OP
Chicago	13	3	0	.813	338	203
Green Bay*	12	4	0	.750	390	266
Tampa Bay*	9	7	0	.563	324	280
Minnesota	5	11	0	.313	290	390
Detroit	2	14	0	.125	270	424

Western Division

	W	L	T	Pct.	Pts.	OP
St. Louis#	14	2	0	.875	503	273
San Francisco*	12	4	0	.750	409	282
New Orleans	7	9	0	.438	333	409
Atlanta	7	9	0	.438	291	377
Carolina	1	15	0	.063	253	410

**Wild Card qualifier for playoffs; #Top playoff seed in conference*

New England finished ahead of Miami based on better division record (6-2 to Dolphins' 5-3). Baltimore was second Wild Card ahead of N.Y. Jets based on better record against common opponents (3-2 to Jets' 2-2). Cleveland finished ahead of Tennessee based on better division record (5-5 to Titans' 3-7). Jacksonville finished ahead of Cincinnati based on head-to-head record (2-0). N.Y. Giants finished ahead of Arizona based on head-to-head record (2-0). Green Bay was first Wild Card ahead of San Francisco based on better conference record (9-3 to 49ers' 8-4). New Orleans finished ahead of Atlanta based on better division record (4-4 to Falcons' 3-5).

Wild Card playoffs: OAKLAND 38, N.Y. Jets 24; Baltimore 20, MIAMI 3

Divisional playoffs: NEW ENGLAND 16, Oakland 13 (OT); PITTSBURGH 27, Baltimore 10

AFC Championship: New England 24, PITTSBURGH 17

Wild Card playoffs: PHILADELPHIA 31, Tampa Bay 9; GREEN BAY 25, San Francisco 15

Divisional playoffs: Philadelphia 33, CHICAGO 19; ST. LOUIS 45, Green Bay 17

NFC Championship: ST. LOUIS 29, Philadelphia 24

Super Bowl XXXVI: New England (AFC) 20, St. Louis (NFC) 17 at Louisiana Superdome, New Orleans, Louisiana

Playoff Seeds

AFC
1. Pittsburgh
2. **New England**
3. Oakland
4. Miami
5. Baltimore
6. N.Y. Jets

NFC
1. **St. Louis**
2. Chicago
3. Philadelphia
4. Green Bay
5. San Francisco
6. Tampa Bay

2000

AMERICAN CONFERENCE

Eastern Division

	W	L	T	Pct.	Pts.	OP
Miami	11	5	0	.688	323	226
Indianapolis*	10	6	0	.625	429	326
N.Y. Jets	9	7	0	.563	321	321
Buffalo	8	8	0	.500	315	350
New England	5	11	0	.313	276	338

Central Division

	W	L	T	Pct.	Pts.	OP
Tennessee#	13	3	0	.813	346	191
Baltimore*	12	4	0	.750	333	165
Pittsburgh	9	7	0	.563	321	255
Jacksonville	7	9	0	.438	367	327
Cincinnati	4	12	0	.250	185	359
Cleveland	3	13	0	.188	161	419

Western Division

	W	L	T	Pct.	Pts.	OP
Oakland	12	4	0	.750	479	299
Denver*	11	5	0	.688	485	369
Kansas City	7	9	0	.438	355	354
Seattle	6	10	0	.375	320	405
San Diego	1	15	0	.063	269	440

NATIONAL CONFERENCE

Eastern Division

	W	L	T	Pct.	Pts.	OP
N.Y. Giants#	12	4	0	.750	328	246
Philadelphia*	11	5	0	.688	351	245
Washington	8	8	0	.500	281	269
Dallas	5	11	0	.313	294	361
Arizona	3	13	0	.188	210	443

Central Division

	W	L	T	Pct.	Pts.	OP
Minnesota	11	5	0	.688	397	371
Tampa Bay*	10	6	0	.625	388	269
Green Bay	9	7	0	.563	353	323
Detroit	9	7	0	.563	307	307
Chicago	5	11	0	.313	216	355

Western Division

	W	L	T	Pct.	Pts.	OP
New Orleans	10	6	0	.625	354	305
St. Louis*	10	6	0	.625	540	471
Carolina	7	9	0	.438	310	310
San Francisco	6	10	0	.375	388	422
Atlanta	4	12	0	.250	252	413

**Wild Card qualifier for playoffs; #Top playoff seed in conference*

Green Bay finished ahead of Detroit based on better division record (5-3 to Lions' 3-5). New Orleans finished ahead of St. Louis based on better division record (7-1 to Rams' 5-3). Tampa Bay was second Wild Card based on head-to-head victory over St. Louis (1-0).

Wild Card playoffs: MIAMI 23, Indianapolis 17 (OT); BALTIMORE 21, Denver 3

Divisional playoffs: OAKLAND 27, Miami 0; Baltimore 24, TENNESSEE 10

AFC Championship: Baltimore 16, OAKLAND 3

Wild Card playoffs: NEW ORLEANS 31, St. Louis 28; PHILADELPHIA 21, Tampa Bay 3

Divisional playoffs: MINNESOTA 34, New Orleans 16; N.Y. GIANTS 20, Philadelphia 10

NFC Championship: N.Y. GIANTS 41, Minnesota 0

Super Bowl XXXV: Baltimore (AFC) 34, N.Y. Giants (NFC) 7 at Raymond James Stadium, Tampa, Florida

Playoff Seeds

AFC
1. Tennessee
2. Oakland
3. Miami
4. **Baltimore**
5. Denver
6. Indianapolis

NFC
1. **N.Y. Giants**
2. Minnesota
3. New Orleans
4. Philadelphia
5. Tampa Bay
6. St. Louis

1999

AMERICAN CONFERENCE

Eastern Division

	W	L	T	Pct.	Pts.	OP
Indianapolis	13	3	0	.813	423	333
Buffalo*	11	5	0	.688	320	229
Miami*	9	7	0	.563	326	336
N.Y. Jets	8	8	0	.500	308	309
New England	8	8	0	.500	299	284

Central Division

	W	L	T	Pct.	Pts.	OP
Jacksonville#	14	2	0	.875	396	217
Tennessee*	13	3	0	.813	392	324
Baltimore	8	8	0	.500	324	277
Pittsburgh	6	10	0	.375	317	320
Cincinnati	4	12	0	.250	283	460
Cleveland	2	14	0	.125	217	437

Western Division

	W	L	T	Pct.	Pts.	OP
Seattle	9	7	0	.563	338	298
Kansas City	9	7	0	.563	390	322
San Diego	8	8	0	.500	269	316
Oakland	8	8	0	.500	390	329
Denver	6	10	0	.375	314	318

NATIONAL CONFERENCE

Eastern Division

	W	L	T	Pct.	Pts.	OP
Washington	10	6	0	.625	443	377
Dallas*	8	8	0	.500	352	276
N.Y. Giants	7	9	0	.438	299	358
Arizona	6	10	0	.375	245	382
Philadelphia	5	11	0	.313	272	357

Central Division

	W	L	T	Pct.	Pts.	OP
Tampa Bay	11	5	0	.688	270	235
Minnesota*	10	6	0	.625	399	335
Detroit*	8	8	0	.500	322	323
Green Bay	8	8	0	.500	357	341
Chicago	6	10	0	.375	272	341

Western Division

	W	L	T	Pct.	Pts.	OP
St. Louis#	13	3	0	.813	526	242
Carolina	8	8	0	.500	421	381
Atlanta	5	11	0	.313	285	380
San Francisco	4	12	0	.250	295	453
New Orleans	3	13	0	.188	260	434

**Wild Card qualifier for playoffs; #Top playoff seed in conference*
Miami was third Wild Card ahead of Kansas City based on better record against common opponents (6-1 to Chiefs' 5-3). N.Y. Jets finished ahead of New England based on better division record (4-4 to Patriots' 2-6). Seattle finished ahead of Kansas City based on head-to-head sweep (2-0). San Diego finished ahead of Oakland based on better division record (5-3 to Raiders' 3-5). Dallas was second Wild Card based on better record against common opponents (4-2 to Lions' 3-3) and better conference record than Carolina (7-5 to Panthers' 6-6). Detroit was third Wild Card based on better conference record than Green Bay (7-5 to Packers' 6-6) and head-to-head victory over Carolina.

Wild Card playoffs: TENNESSEE 22, Buffalo 16; Miami 20, SEATTLE 17
Divisional playoffs: JACKSONVILLE 62, Miami 7; Tennessee 19, INDIANAPOLIS 16
AFC Championship: Tennessee 33, JACKSONVILLE 14
Wild Card playoffs: WASHINGTON 27, Detroit 13; MINNESOTA 27, Dallas 10
Divisional playoffs: TAMPA BAY 14, Washington 13; ST. LOUIS 49, Minnesota 37
NFC Championship: ST. LOUIS 11, Tampa Bay 6
Super Bowl XXXIV: St. Louis (NFC) 23, Tennessee (AFC) 16 at Georgia Dome, Atlanta, Georgia

Playoff Seeds

AFC	NFC
1. Jacksonville	**1. St. Louis**
2. Indianapolis	2. Tampa Bay
3. Seattle	3. Washington
4. Tennessee	4. Minnesota
5. Buffalo	5. Dallas
6. Miami	6. Detroit

1998

AMERICAN CONFERENCE

Eastern Division

	W	L	T	Pct.	Pts.	OP
N.Y. Jets	12	4	0	.750	416	266
Miami*	10	6	0	.625	321	265
Buffalo*	10	6	0	.625	400	333
New England*	9	7	0	.563	337	329
Indianapolis	3	13	0	.188	310	444

Central Division

	W	L	T	Pct.	Pts.	OP
Jacksonville	11	5	0	.688	392	338
Tennessee	8	8	0	.500	330	320
Pittsburgh	7	9	0	.438	263	303
Baltimore	6	10	0	.375	269	335
Cincinnati	3	13	0	.188	268	452

Western Division

	W	L	T	Pct.	Pts.	OP
Denver#	14	2	0	.875	501	309
Oakland	8	8	0	.500	288	356
Seattle	8	8	0	.500	372	310
Kansas City	7	9	0	.438	327	363
San Diego	5	11	0	.313	241	342

NATIONAL CONFERENCE

Eastern Division

	W	L	T	Pct.	Pts.	OP
Dallas	10	6	0	.625	381	275
Arizona*	9	7	0	.563	325	378
N.Y. Giants	8	8	0	.500	287	309
Washington	6	10	0	.375	319	421
Philadelphia	3	13	0	.188	161	344

Central Division

	W	L	T	Pct.	Pts.	OP
Minnesota#	15	1	0	.938	556	296
Green Bay*	11	5	0	.688	408	319
Tampa Bay	8	8	0	.500	314	295
Detroit	5	11	0	.313	306	378
Chicago	4	12	0	.250	276	368

Western Division

	W	L	T	Pct.	Pts.	OP
Atlanta	14	2	0	.875	442	289
San Francisco*	12	4	0	.750	479	328
New Orleans	6	10	0	.375	305	359
Carolina	4	12	0	.250	336	413
St. Louis	4	12	0	.250	285	378

**Wild Card qualifier for playoffs; #Top playoff seed in conference*
Miami finished ahead of Buffalo based on better net division points (6 to Bills' 0). Oakland finished ahead of Seattle based on head-to-head sweep (2-0). Carolina finished ahead of St. Louis based on head-to-head sweep (2-0).

Wild Card playoffs: MIAMI 24, Buffalo 17; JACKSONVILLE 25, New England 10
Divisional playoffs: DENVER 38, Miami 3; N.Y. JETS 34, Jacksonville 24
AFC Championship: DENVER 23, N.Y. Jets 10
Wild Card playoffs: Arizona 20, DALLAS 7; SAN FRANCISCO 30, Green Bay 27
Divisional playoffs: ATLANTA 20, San Francisco 18; MINNESOTA 41, Arizona 21
NFC Championship: Atlanta 30, MINNESOTA 27 (OT)
Super Bowl XXXIII: Denver (AFC) 34, Atlanta (NFC) 19, at Pro Player Stadium, Miami, Florida

Playoff Seeds

AFC	NFC
1. Denver	1. Minnesota
2. N.Y. Jets	**2. Atlanta**
3. Jacksonville	3. Dallas
4. Miami	4. San Francisco
5. Buffalo	5. Green Bay
6. New England	6. Arizona

1997

AMERICAN CONFERENCE

Eastern Division

	W	L	T	Pct.	Pts.	OP
New England	10	6	0	.625	369	289
Miami*	9	7	0	.563	339	327
N.Y. Jets	9	7	0	.563	348	287
Buffalo	6	10	0	.375	255	367
Indianapolis	3	13	0	.188	313	401

Central Division

	W	L	T	Pct.	Pts.	OP
Pittsburgh	11	5	0	.688	372	307
Jacksonville*	11	5	0	.688	394	318
Tennessee	8	8	0	.500	333	310
Cincinnati	7	9	0	.438	355	405
Baltimore	6	9	1	.406	326	345

Western Division

	W	L	T	Pct.	Pts.	OP
Kansas City#	13	3	0	.813	375	232
Denver*	12	4	0	.750	472	287
Seattle	8	8	0	.500	365	362
Oakland	4	12	0	.250	324	419
San Diego	4	12	0	.250	266	425

NATIONAL CONFERENCE

Eastern Division

	W	L	T	Pct.	Pts.	OP
N.Y. Giants	10	5	1	.656	307	265
Washington	8	7	1	.531	327	289
Philadelphia	6	9	1	.406	317	372
Dallas	6	10	0	.375	304	314
Arizona	4	12	0	.250	283	379

Central Division

	W	L	T	Pct.	Pts.	OP
Green Bay	13	3	0	.813	422	282
Tampa Bay*	10	6	0	.625	299	263
Detroit*	9	7	0	.563	379	306
Minnesota*	9	7	0	.563	354	359
Chicago	4	12	0	.250	263	421

Western Division

	W	L	T	Pct.	Pts.	OP
San Francisco#	13	3	0	.813	375	265
Carolina	7	9	0	.438	265	314
Atlanta	7	9	0	.438	320	361
New Orleans	6	10	0	.375	237	327
St. Louis	5	11	0	.313	299	359

**Wild Card qualifier for playoffs; #Top playoff seed in conference*
Miami finished ahead of N.Y. Jets based on head-to-head sweep (2-0). Pittsburgh finished ahead of Jacksonville based on better net division points (78 to Jaguars' 23). Oakland finished ahead of San Diego based on better division record (2-6 to Chargers' 1-7). San Francisco was top playoff seed based on better conference record than Green Bay (11-1 to Packers' 10-2). Detroit finished ahead of Minnesota based on head-to-head sweep (2-0). Carolina finished ahead of Atlanta based on head-to-head sweep (2-0).

Wild Card playoffs: DENVER 42, Jacksonville 17; NEW ENGLAND 17, Miami 3
Divisional playoffs: PITTSBURGH 7, New England 6; Denver 14, KANSAS CITY 10
AFC Championship: Denver 24, PITTSBURGH 21
Wild Card playoffs: Minnesota 23, N.Y. GIANTS 22; TAMPA BAY 20, Detroit 10
Divisional playoffs: SAN FRANCISCO 38, Minnesota 22; GREEN BAY 21, Tampa Bay 7
NFC Championship: Green Bay 23, SAN FRANCISCO 10
Super Bowl XXXII: Denver (AFC) 31, Green Bay (NFC) 24, at Qualcomm Stadium, San Diego, California

Playoff Seeds

AFC
1. Kansas City
2. Pittsburgh
3. New England
4. **Denver**
5. Jacksonville
6. Miami

NFC
1. San Francisco
2. **Green Bay**
3. N.Y. Giants
4. Tampa Bay
5. Detroit
6. Minnesota

1996

AMERICAN CONFERENCE

Eastern Division

	W	L	T	Pct.	Pts.	OP
New England	11	5	0	.688	418	313
Buffalo*	10	6	0	.625	319	266
Indianapolis*	9	7	0	.563	317	334
Miami	8	8	0	.500	339	325
N.Y. Jets	1	15	0	.063	279	454

Central Division

	W	L	T	Pct.	Pts.	OP
Pittsburgh	10	6	0	.625	344	257
Jacksonville*	9	7	0	.563	325	335
Cincinnati	8	8	0	.500	372	369
Houston	8	8	0	.500	345	319
Baltimore	4	12	0	.250	371	441

Western Division

	W	L	T	Pct.	Pts.	OP
Denver#	13	3	0	.813	391	275
Kansas City	9	7	0	.563	297	300
San Diego	8	8	0	.500	310	376
Oakland	7	9	0	.438	340	293
Seattle	7	9	0	.438	317	376

NATIONAL CONFERENCE

Eastern Division

	W	L	T	Pct.	Pts.	OP
Dallas	10	6	0	.625	286	250
Philadelphia*	10	6	0	.625	363	341
Washington	9	7	0	.563	364	312
Arizona	7	9	0	.438	300	397
N.Y. Giants	6	10	0	.375	242	297

Central Division

	W	L	T	Pct.	Pts.	OP
Green Bay#	13	3	0	.813	456	210
Minnesota*	9	7	0	.563	298	315
Chicago	7	9	0	.438	283	305
Tampa Bay	6	10	0	.375	221	293
Detroit	5	11	0	.313	302	368

Western Division

	W	L	T	Pct.	Pts.	OP
Carolina	12	4	0	.750	367	218
San Francisco*	12	4	0	.750	398	257
St. Louis	6	10	0	.375	303	409
Atlanta	3	13	0	.188	309	461
New Orleans	3	13	0	.188	229	339

**Wild Card qualifier for playoffs; #Top playoff seed in conference*
Jacksonville was second Wild Card ahead of Indianapolis and Kansas City based on better conference record (7-5 to Colts' 6-6 and Chiefs' 5-7). Indianapolis was third Wild Card based on head-to-head victory over Kansas City (1-0). Cincinnati finished ahead of Houston based on better net division points (19 to Oilers' 11). Oakland finished ahead of Seattle based on better division record (3-5 to Seahawks' 2-6). Dallas finished ahead of Philadelphia based on better record against common opponents (7-4 to Eagles' 6-5). Minnesota was third Wild Card based on better conference record than Washington (8-4 to Redskins' 6-6). Carolina finished ahead of San Francisco based on head-to-head sweep (2-0). Atlanta finished ahead of New Orleans based on head-to-head sweep (2-0).

Wild Card playoffs: Jacksonville 30, BUFFALO 27; PITTSBURGH 42, Indianapolis 14
Divisional playoffs: Jacksonville 30, DENVER 27; NEW ENGLAND 28, Pittsburgh 3
AFC Championship: NEW ENGLAND 20, Jacksonville 6
Wild Card playoffs: DALLAS 40, Minnesota 15; SAN FRANCISCO 14, Philadelphia 0
Divisional playoffs: GREEN BAY 35, San Francisco 14; CAROLINA 26, Dallas 17
NFC Championship: GREEN BAY 30, Carolina 13
Super Bowl XXXI: Green Bay (NFC) 35, New England (AFC) 21, at Louisiana Superdome, New Orleans, Louisiana

Playoff Seeds

AFC
1. Denver
2. **New England**
3. Pittsburgh
4. Buffalo
5. Jacksonville
6. Indianapolis

NFC
1. **Green Bay**
2. Carolina
3. Dallas
4. San Francisco
5. Philadelphia
6. Minnesota

PAST STANDINGS

1995

AMERICAN CONFERENCE

Eastern Division

	W	L	T	Pct.	Pts.	OP
Buffalo	10	6	0	.625	350	335
Indianapolis*	9	7	0	.563	331	316
Miami*	9	7	0	.563	398	332
New England	6	10	0	.375	294	377
N.Y. Jets	3	13	0	.188	233	384

Central Division

	W	L	T	Pct.	Pts.	OP
Pittsburgh	11	5	0	.688	407	327
Cincinnati	7	9	0	.438	349	374
Houston	7	9	0	.438	348	324
Cleveland	5	11	0	.313	289	356
Jacksonville	4	12	0	.250	275	404

Western Division

	W	L	T	Pct.	Pts.	OP
Kansas City#	13	3	0	.813	358	241
San Diego*	9	7	0	.563	321	323
Seattle	8	8	0	.500	363	366
Denver	8	8	0	.500	388	345
Oakland	8	8	0	.500	348	332

NATIONAL CONFERENCE

Eastern Division

	W	L	T	Pct.	Pts.	OP
Dallas#	12	4	0	.750	435	291
Philadelphia*	10	6	0	.625	318	338
Washington	6	10	0	.375	326	359
N.Y. Giants	5	11	0	.313	290	340
Arizona	4	12	0	.250	275	422

Central Division

	W	L	T	Pct.	Pts.	OP
Green Bay	11	5	0	.688	404	314
Detroit*	10	6	0	.625	436	336
Chicago	9	7	0	.563	392	360
Minnesota	8	8	0	.500	412	385
Tampa Bay	7	9	0	.438	238	335

Western Division

	W	L	T	Pct.	Pts.	OP
San Francisco	11	5	0	.688	457	258
Atlanta*	9	7	0	.563	362	349
St. Louis	7	9	0	.438	309	418
Carolina	7	9	0	.438	289	325
New Orleans	7	9	0	.438	319	348

**Wild Card qualifier for playoffs; #Top playoff seed in conference*

Indianapolis finished ahead of Miami based on head-to-head sweep (2-0). San Diego was first Wild Card based on head-to-head victory over Indianapolis (1-0). Cincinnati finished ahead of Houston based on better division record (4-4 to Oilers' 3-5). Seattle finished ahead of Denver and Oakland based on best head-to-head record (3-1 to Broncos' 2-2 and Raiders' 1-3). Denver finished ahead of Oakland based on head-to-head sweep (2-0). Philadelphia was first Wild Card ahead of Detroit based on better conference record (9-3 to Lions' 7-5). San Francisco was second playoff seed ahead of Green Bay based on better conference record (8-4 to Packers' 7-5). Atlanta was third Wild Card ahead of Chicago based on better record against common opponents (4-2 to Bears' 3-3). St. Louis finished ahead of Carolina and New Orleans based on best head-to-head record (3-1 to Panthers' 1-3 and Saints' 2-2). Carolina finished ahead of New Orleans based on better conference record (4-8 to 3-9).

Wild Card playoffs: BUFFALO 37, Miami 22; Indianapolis 35, SAN DIEGO 20

Divisional playoffs: PITTSBURGH 40, Buffalo 21; Indianapolis 10, KANSAS CITY 7

AFC Championship: PITTSBURGH 20, Indianapolis 16

Wild Card playoffs: PHILADELPHIA 58, Detroit 37; GREEN BAY 37, Atlanta 20

Divisional playoffs: Green Bay 27, SAN FRANCISCO 17; DALLAS 30, Philadelphia 11

NFC Championship: DALLAS 38, Green Bay 27

Super Bowl XXX: Dallas (NFC) 27, Pittsburgh (AFC) 17, at Sun Devil Stadium, Tempe, Arizona

Playoff Seeds

AFC
1. Kansas City
2. **Pittsburgh**
3. Buffalo
4. San Diego
5. Indianapolis
6. Miami

NFC
1. **Dallas**
2. San Francisco
3. Green Bay
4. Philadelphia
5. Detroit
6. Atlanta

1994

AMERICAN CONFERENCE

Eastern Division

	W	L	T	Pct.	Pts.	OP
Miami	10	6	0	.625	389	327
New England*	10	6	0	.625	351	312
Indianapolis	8	8	0	.500	307	320
Buffalo	7	9	0	.438	340	356
N.Y. Jets	6	10	0	.375	264	320

Central Division

	W	L	T	Pct.	Pts.	OP
Pittsburgh#	12	4	0	.750	316	234
Cleveland*	11	5	0	.688	340	204
Cincinnati	3	13	0	.188	276	406
Houston	2	14	0	.125	226	352

Western Division

	W	L	T	Pct.	Pts.	OP
San Diego	11	5	0	.688	381	306
Kansas City*	9	7	0	.563	319	298
L.A. Raiders	9	7	0	.563	303	327
Denver	7	9	0	.438	347	396
Seattle	6	10	0	.375	287	323

NATIONAL CONFERENCE

Eastern Division

	W	L	T	Pct.	Pts.	OP
Dallas	12	4	0	.750	414	248
N.Y. Giants	9	7	0	.563	279	305
Arizona	8	8	0	.500	235	267
Philadelphia	7	9	0	.438	308	308
Washington	3	13	0	.188	320	412

Central Division

	W	L	T	Pct.	Pts.	OP
Minnesota	10	6	0	.625	356	314
Green Bay*	9	7	0	.563	382	287
Detroit*	9	7	0	.563	357	342
Chicago*	9	7	0	.563	271	307
Tampa Bay	6	10	0	.375	251	351

Western Division

	W	L	T	Pct.	Pts.	OP
San Francisco#	13	3	0	.813	505	296
New Orleans	7	9	0	.438	348	407
Atlanta	7	9	0	.438	317	385
L.A. Rams	4	12	0	.250	286	365

**Wild Card qualifier for playoffs; #Top playoff seed in conference*

Miami finished ahead of New England based on head-to-head sweep (2-0). Kansas City finished ahead of L.A. Raiders based on head-to-head sweep (2-0). Green Bay was first Wild Card based on best head-to-head record (3-1) vs. Detroit (2-2) and Chicago (1-3) and better conference record (8-4) than N.Y. Giants (6-6). Detroit was second Wild Card based on better division record (4-4) than Chicago (3-5) and head-to-head victory over N.Y. Giants (1-0). Chicago was third Wild Card based on better record against common opponents (4-4) than N.Y. Giants (3-5). New Orleans finished ahead of Atlanta based on head-to-head sweep (2-0).

Wild Card playoffs: MIAMI 27, Kansas City 17; CLEVELAND 20, New England 13

Divisional playoffs: PITTSBURGH 29, Cleveland 9; SAN DIEGO 22, Miami 21

AFC Championship: San Diego 17, PITTSBURGH 13

Wild Card playoffs: GREEN BAY 16, Detroit 12; Chicago 35, MINNESOTA 18

Divisional playoffs: SAN FRANCISCO 44, Chicago 15; DALLAS 35, Green Bay 9

NFC Championship: SAN FRANCISCO 38, Dallas 28

Super Bowl XXIX: San Francisco (NFC) 49, San Diego (AFC) 26, at Joe Robbie Stadium, Miami, Florida

Playoff Seeds

AFC
1. Pittsburgh
2. **San Diego**
3. Miami
4. Cleveland
5. New England
6. Kansas City

NFC
1. **San Francisco**
2. Dallas
3. Minnesota
4. Green Bay
5. Detroit
6. Chicago

1993

AMERICAN CONFERENCE

Eastern Division

	W	L	T	Pct.	Pts.	OP
Buffalo#	12	4	0	.750	329	242
Miami	9	7	0	.563	349	351
N.Y. Jets	8	8	0	.500	270	247
New England	5	11	0	.313	238	286
Indianapolis	4	12	0	.250	189	378

Central Division

	W	L	T	Pct.	Pts.	OP
Houston	12	4	0	.750	368	238
Pittsburgh*	9	7	0	.563	308	281
Cleveland	7	9	0	.438	304	307
Cincinnati	3	13	0	.188	187	319

Western Division

	W	L	T	Pct.	Pts.	OP
Kansas City	11	5	0	.688	328	291
L.A. Raiders*	10	6	0	.625	306	326
Denver*	9	7	0	.563	373	284
San Diego	8	8	0	.500	322	290
Seattle	6	10	0	.375	280	314

NATIONAL CONFERENCE

Eastern Division

	W	L	T	Pct.	Pts.	OP
Dallas#	12	4	0	.750	376	229
N.Y. Giants*	11	5	0	.688	288	205
Philadelphia	8	8	0	.500	293	315
Phoenix	7	9	0	.438	326	269
Washington	4	12	0	.250	230	345

Central Division

	W	L	T	Pct.	Pts.	OP
Detroit	10	6	0	.625	298	292
Minnesota*	9	7	0	.563	277	290
Green Bay*	9	7	0	.563	340	282
Chicago	7	9	0	.438	234	230
Tampa Bay	5	11	0	.313	237	376

Western Division

	W	L	T	Pct.	Pts.	OP
San Francisco	10	6	0	.625	473	295
New Orleans	8	8	0	.500	317	343
Atlanta	6	10	0	.375	316	385
L.A. Rams	5	11	0	.313	221	367

**Wild Card qualifier for playoffs; #Top playoff seed in conference*

Buffalo was top playoff seed based on head-to-head victory over Houston (1-0). Denver was second Wild Card ahead of Pittsburgh and Miami based on better conference record (8-4 to Steelers' 7-5 to Dolphins' 6-6). Pittsburgh was third Wild Card ahead of Miami based on head-to-head victory. San Francisco was second playoff seed based on head-to-head victory over Detroit (1-0). Minnesota finished ahead of Green Bay based on head-to-head sweep (2-0).

Wild Card playoffs: KANSAS CITY 27, Pittsburgh 24 (OT); L.A. RAIDERS 42, Denver 24

Divisional playoffs: BUFFALO 29, L.A. Raiders 23; Kansas City 28, HOUSTON 20

AFC Championship: BUFFALO 30, Kansas City 13

Wild Card playoffs: Green Bay 28, DETROIT 24; N.Y. GIANTS 17, Minnesota 10

Divisional playoffs: SAN FRANCISCO 44, N.Y. Giants 3; DALLAS 27, Green Bay 17

NFC Championship: DALLAS 38, San Francisco 21

Super Bowl XXVIII: Dallas (NFC) 30, Buffalo (AFC) 13, at Georgia Dome, Atlanta, Georgia

Playoff Seeds

AFC

1. Buffalo
2. Houston
3. Kansas City
4. L.A. Raiders
5. Denver
6. Pittsburgh

NFC

1. Dallas
2. San Francisco
3. Detroit
4. N.Y. Giants
5. Minnesota
6. Green Bay

1992

AMERICAN CONFERENCE

Eastern Division

	W	L	T	Pct.	Pts.	OP
Miami	11	5	0	.688	340	281
Buffalo*	11	5	0	.688	381	283
Indianapolis	9	7	0	.563	216	302
N.Y. Jets	4	12	0	.250	220	315
New England	2	14	0	.125	205	363

Central Division

	W	L	T	Pct.	Pts.	OP
Pittsburgh#	11	5	0	.688	299	225
Houston*	10	6	0	.625	352	258
Cleveland	7	9	0	.438	272	275
Cincinnati	5	11	0	.313	274	364

Western Division

	W	L	T	Pct.	Pts.	OP
San Diego	11	5	0	.688	335	241
Kansas City*	10	6	0	.625	348	282
Denver	8	8	0	.500	262	329
L.A. Raiders	7	9	0	.438	249	281
Seattle	2	14	0	.125	140	312

NATIONAL CONFERENCE

Eastern Division

	W	L	T	Pct.	Pts.	OP
Dallas	13	3	0	.813	409	243
Philadelphia*	11	5	0	.688	354	245
Washington*	9	7	0	.563	300	255
N.Y. Giants	6	10	0	.375	306	367
Phoenix	4	12	0	.250	243	332

Central Division

	W	L	T	Pct.	Pts.	OP
Minnesota	11	5	0	.688	374	249
Green Bay	9	7	0	.563	276	296
Tampa Bay	5	11	0	.313	267	365
Chicago	5	11	0	.313	295	361
Detroit	5	11	0	.313	273	332

Western Division

	W	L	T	Pct.	Pts.	OP
San Francisco#	14	2	0	.875	431	236
New Orleans*	12	4	0	.750	330	202
Atlanta	6	10	0	.375	327	414
L.A. Rams	6	10	0	.375	313	383

**Wild Card qualifier for playoffs; #Top playoff seed in conference*

Pittsburgh was top playoff seed, and Miami was second playoff seed ahead of San Diego, based on conference record (10-2 to Dolphins' 9-3 to Chargers' 9-5). Miami finished ahead of Buffalo based on better conference record (9-3 to Bills' 7-5). Houston was second Wild Card based on head-to-head victory over Kansas City (1-0). Washington was third Wild Card based on better conference record than Green Bay (7-5 to Packers' 6-6). Tampa Bay finished ahead of Chicago and Chicago finished ahead of Detroit based on better conference record (5-9 to Bears' 4-8 and Lions' 3-9). Atlanta finished ahead of L.A. Rams based on better record against common opponents (5-7 to Rams' 4-8).

Wild Card playoffs: SAN DIEGO 17, Kansas City 0; BUFFALO 41, Houston 38 (OT)

Divisional playoffs: Buffalo 24, PITTSBURGH 3; MIAMI 31, San Diego 0

AFC Championship: Buffalo 29, MIAMI 10

Wild Card playoffs: Washington 24, MINNESOTA 7; Philadelphia 36, NEW ORLEANS 20

Divisional playoffs: SAN FRANCISCO 20, Washington 13; DALLAS 34, Philadelphia 10

NFC Championship: Dallas 30, SAN FRANCISCO 20

Super Bowl XXVII: Dallas (NFC) 52, Buffalo (AFC) 17, at Rose Bowl, Pasadena, California

Playoff Seeds

AFC

1. Pittsburgh
2. Miami
3. San Diego
4. Buffalo
5. Houston
6. Kansas City

NFC

1. San Francisco
2. Dallas
3. Minnesota
4. New Orleans
5. Philadelphia
6. Washington

1991

AMERICAN CONFERENCE

Eastern Division

	W	L	T	Pct.	Pts.	OP
Buffalo#	13	3	0	.813	458	318
N.Y. Jets*	8	8	0	.500	314	293
Miami	8	8	0	.500	343	349
New England	6	10	0	.375	211	305
Indianapolis	1	15	0	.063	143	381

Central Division

	W	L	T	Pct.	Pts.	OP
Houston	11	5	0	.688	386	251
Pittsburgh	7	9	0	.438	292	344
Cleveland	6	10	0	.375	293	298
Cincinnati	3	13	0	.188	263	435

Western Division

	W	L	T	Pct.	Pts.	OP
Denver	12	4	0	.750	304	235
Kansas City*	10	6	0	.625	322	252
L.A. Raiders*	9	7	0	.563	298	297
Seattle	7	9	0	.438	276	261
San Diego	4	12	0	.250	274	342

NATIONAL CONFERENCE

Eastern Division

	W	L	T	Pct.	Pts.	OP
Washington#	14	2	0	.875	485	224
Dallas*	11	5	0	.688	342	310
Philadelphia	10	6	0	.625	285	244
N.Y. Giants	8	8	0	.500	281	297
Phoenix	4	12	0	.250	196	344

Central Division

	W	L	T	Pct.	Pts.	OP
Detroit	12	4	0	.750	339	295
Chicago*	11	5	0	.688	299	269
Minnesota	8	8	0	.500	301	306
Green Bay	4	12	0	.250	273	313
Tampa Bay	3	13	0	.188	199	365

Western Division

	W	L	T	Pct.	Pts.	OP
New Orleans	11	5	0	.688	341	211
Atlanta*	10	6	0	.625	361	338
San Francisco	10	6	0	.625	393	239
L.A. Rams	3	13	0	.188	234	390

**Wild Card qualifier for playoffs; #Top playoff seed in conference*

N.Y. Jets finished ahead of Miami based on head-to-head sweep (2-0). Chicago was first Wild Card based on better conference record than Dallas (9-3 to Cowboys' 8-4). Atlanta finished ahead of San Francisco based on head-to-head sweep (2-0), and was third Wild Card ahead of Philadelphia based on better conference record (7-5 to Eagles' 6-6).

Wild Card playoffs: KANSAS CITY 10, L.A. Raiders 6; HOUSTON 17, N.Y. Jets 10

Divisional playoffs: DENVER 26, Houston 24; BUFFALO 37, Kansas City 14

AFC Championship: BUFFALO 10, Denver 7

Wild Card playoffs: Atlanta 27, NEW ORLEANS 20; Dallas 17, CHICAGO 13

Divisional playoffs: WASHINGTON 24, Atlanta 7; DETROIT 38, Dallas 6

NFC Championship: WASHINGTON 41, Detroit 10

Super Bowl XXVI: Washington (NFC) 37, Buffalo (AFC) 24, at Hubert H. Humphrey Metrodome, Minneapolis, Minnesota

Playoff Seeds

AFC

1. Buffalo
2. Denver
3. Houston
4. Kansas City
5. L.A. Raiders
6. N.Y. Jets

NFC

1. Washington
2. Detroit
3. New Orleans
4. Chicago
5. Dallas
6. Atlanta

1990

AMERICAN CONFERENCE

Eastern Division

	W	L	T	Pct.	Pts.	OP
Buffalo#	13	3	0	.813	428	263
Miami*	12	4	0	.750	336	242
Indianapolis	7	9	0	.438	281	353
N.Y. Jets	6	10	0	.375	295	345
New England	1	15	0	.063	181	446

Central Division

	W	L	T	Pct.	Pts.	OP
Cincinnati	9	7	0	.563	360	352
Houston*	9	7	0	.563	405	307
Pittsburgh	9	7	0	.563	292	240
Cleveland	3	13	0	.188	228	462

Western Division

	W	L	T	Pct.	Pts.	OP
L.A. Raiders	12	4	0	.750	337	268
Kansas City*	11	5	0	.688	369	257
Seattle	9	7	0	.563	306	286
San Diego	6	10	0	.375	315	281
Denver	5	11	0	.313	331	374

NATIONAL CONFERENCE

Eastern Division

	W	L	T	Pct.	Pts.	OP
N.Y. Giants	13	3	0	.813	335	211
Philadelphia*	10	6	0	.625	396	299
Washington*	10	6	0	.625	381	301
Dallas	7	9	0	.438	244	308
Phoenix	5	11	0	.313	268	396

Central Division

	W	L	T	Pct.	Pts.	OP
Chicago	11	5	0	.688	348	280
Tampa Bay	6	10	0	.375	264	367
Detroit	6	10	0	.375	373	413
Green Bay	6	10	0	.375	271	347
Minnesota	6	10	0	.375	351	326

Western Division

	W	L	T	Pct.	Pts.	OP
San Francisco#	14	2	0	.875	353	239
New Orleans*	8	8	0	.500	274	275
L.A. Rams	5	11	0	.313	345	412
Atlanta	5	11	0	.313	348	365

**Wild Card qualifier for playoffs; #Top playoff seed in conference*

Cincinnati finished ahead of Houston and Pittsburgh based on best head-to-head record (3-1 to Oilers' 2-2 to Steelers' 1-3). Houston was Wild Card based on better conference record (8-4) than Seattle (7-5) and Pittsburgh (6-6). Philadelphia finished ahead of Washington based on better division record (5-3 to Redskins' 4-4). Tampa Bay was second in NFC Central based on best head-to-head record (5-1) against Detroit (2-4), Green Bay (3-3), and Minnesota (2-4). Detroit finished third based on best net division points (minus 8) against Green Bay (minus 40). Green Bay finished ahead of Minnesota based on better conference record (5-7 to Vikings' 4-8). The L.A. Rams finished ahead of Atlanta based on net points in division (plus 1 to Falcons' minus 31).

Wild Card playoffs: MIAMI 17, Kansas City 16; CINCINNATI 41, Houston 14

Divisional playoffs: BUFFALO 44, Miami 34; L.A. RAIDERS 20, Cincinnati 10

AFC Championship: BUFFALO 51, L.A. Raiders 3

Wild Card playoffs: Washington 20, PHILADELPHIA 6; CHICAGO 16, New Orleans 6

Divisional playoffs: SAN FRANCISCO 28, Washington 10; N.Y. GIANTS 31, Chicago 3

NFC Championship: N.Y. Giants 15, SAN FRANCISCO 13

Super Bowl XXV: N.Y. Giants (NFC) 20, Buffalo (AFC) 19, at Tampa Stadium, Tampa, Florida

Playoff Seeds

AFC

1. Buffalo
2. L.A. Raiders
3. Cincinnati
4. Miami
5. Kansas City
6. Houston

NFC

1. San Francisco
2. N.Y. Giants
3. Chicago
4. Philadelphia
5. Washington
6. New Orleans

1989

AMERICAN CONFERENCE

Eastern Division

	W	L	T	Pct.	Pts.	OP
Buffalo	9	7	0	.563	409	317
Indianapolis	8	8	0	.500	298	301
Miami	8	8	0	.500	331	379
New England	5	11	0	.313	297	391
N.Y. Jets	4	12	0	.250	253	411

Central Division

	W	L	T	Pct.	Pts.	OP
Cleveland	9	6	1	.594	334	254
Houston*	9	7	0	.563	365	412
Pittsburgh*	9	7	0	.563	265	326
Cincinnati	8	8	0	.500	404	285

Western Division

	W	L	T	Pct.	Pts.	OP
Denver#	11	5	0	.688	362	226
Kansas City	8	7	1	.531	318	286
L.A. Raiders	8	8	0	.500	315	297
Seattle	7	9	0	.438	241	327
San Diego	6	10	0	.375	266	290

NATIONAL CONFERENCE

Eastern Division

	W	L	T	Pct.	Pts.	OP
N.Y. Giants	12	4	0	.750	348	252
Philadelphia*	11	5	0	.688	342	274
Washington	10	6	0	.625	386	308
Phoenix	5	11	0	.313	258	377
Dallas	1	15	0	.063	204	393

Central Division

	W	L	T	Pct.	Pts.	OP
Minnesota	10	6	0	.625	351	275
Green Bay	10	6	0	.625	362	356
Detroit	7	9	0	.438	312	364
Chicago	6	10	0	.375	358	377
Tampa Bay	5	11	0	.313	320	419

Western Division

	W	L	T	Pct.	Pts.	OP
San Francisco#	14	2	0	.875	442	253
L.A. Rams*	11	5	0	.688	426	344
New Orleans	9	7	0	.563	386	301
Atlanta	3	13	0	.188	279	437

**Wild Card qualifier for playoffs; #Top playoff seed in conference*

Indianapolis finished ahead of Miami based on better conference record (7-5 vs. Dolphins' 6-8). Houston finished ahead of Pittsburgh based on head-to-head sweep (2-0). The L.A. Rams did not play San Francisco in the divisional playoffs because, from 1970-1989, two teams from the same division could not meet prior to the conference championship game. Philadelphia was first Wild Card ahead of L.A. Rams based on better record against common opponents (7-3 to Rams' 5-4). Minnesota finished ahead of Green Bay based on better division record (6-2 vs. Packers' 5-3).

Wild Card playoff: Pittsburgh 26, HOUSTON 23 (OT)
Divisional playoffs: CLEVELAND 34, Buffalo 30;
DENVER 24, Pittsburgh 23
AFC Championship: DENVER 37, Cleveland 21
Wild Card playoff: L.A. Rams 21, PHILADELPHIA 7
Divisional playoffs: L.A. Rams 19, N.Y. GIANTS 13 (OT);
SAN FRANCISCO 41, Minnesota 13
NFC Championship: SAN FRANCISCO 30, L.A. Rams 3
Super Bowl XXIV: San Francisco (NFC) 55, Denver (AFC) 10, at Louisiana Superdome, New Orleans, Louisiana

1988

AMERICAN CONFERENCE

Eastern Division

	W	L	T	Pct.	Pts.	OP
Buffalo	12	4	0	.750	329	237
Indianapolis	9	7	0	.563	354	315
New England	9	7	0	.563	250	284
N.Y. Jets	8	7	1	.531	372	354
Miami	6	10	0	.375	319	380

Central Division

	W	L	T	Pct.	Pts.	OP
Cincinnati#	12	4	0	.750	448	329
Cleveland*	10	6	0	.625	304	288
Houston*	10	6	0	.625	424	365
Pittsburgh	5	11	0	.313	336	421

Western Division

	W	L	T	Pct.	Pts.	OP
Seattle	9	7	0	.563	339	329
Denver	8	8	0	.500	327	352
L.A. Raiders	7	9	0	.438	325	369
San Diego	6	10	0	.375	231	332
Kansas City	4	11	1	.281	254	320

NATIONAL CONFERENCE

Eastern Division

	W	L	T	Pct.	Pts.	OP
Philadelphia	10	6	0	.625	379	319
N.Y. Giants	10	6	0	.625	359	304
Washington	7	9	0	.438	345	387
Phoenix	7	9	0	.438	344	398
Dallas	3	13	0	.188	265	381

Central Division

	W	L	T	Pct.	Pts.	OP
Chicago#	12	4	0	.750	312	215
Minnesota*	11	5	0	.688	406	233
Tampa Bay	5	11	0	.313	261	350
Detroit	4	12	0	.250	220	313
Green Bay	4	12	0	.250	240	315

Western Division

	W	L	T	Pct.	Pts.	OP
San Francisco	10	6	0	.625	369	294
L.A. Rams*	10	6	0	.625	407	293
New Orleans	10	6	0	.625	312	283
Atlanta	5	11	0	.313	244	315

**Wild Card qualifier for playoffs; #Top playoff seed in conference*

Cincinnati was top playoff seed ahead of Buffalo based on head-to-head victory (1-0). Indianapolis finished ahead of New England based on better record against common opponents (7-5 to Patriots' 6-6). Cleveland finished ahead of Houston based on better division record (4-2 to Oilers' 3-3). Houston did not play Cincinnati, and Minnesota did not play Chicago in the divisional playoffs because, from 1970-1989, two teams from the same division could not meet prior to the conference championship game. Philadelphia finished first in NFC East based on head-to-head sweep of N.Y. Giants (2-0). Washington finished third in NFC East based on better division record (4-4) than Phoenix (3-5). Detroit finished fourth in NFC Central based on head-to-head sweep of Green Bay (2-0). San Francisco finished first in NFC West based on better head-to-head record (3-1) against L.A. Rams (2-2) and New Orleans (1-3). San Francisco finished with second playoff seed ahead of Philadelphia based on better record against common opponents (5-3 to Eagles' 5-4). L.A. Rams finished second in NFC West based on better division record (4-2) than New Orleans (3-3) and earned Wild-Card position based on better conference record (8-4) than N.Y. Giants (9-5) and New Orleans (6-6).

Wild Card playoff: Houston 24, CLEVELAND 23
Divisional playoffs: CINCINNATI 21, Seattle 13;
BUFFALO 17, Houston 10
AFC Championship: CINCINNATI 21, Buffalo 10
Wild Card playoff: MINNESOTA 28, L.A. Rams 17
Divisional playoffs: CHICAGO 20, Philadelphia 12;
SAN FRANCISCO 34, Minnesota 9
NFC Championship: San Francisco 28, CHICAGO 3
Super Bowl XXIII: San Francisco (NFC) 20, Cincinnati (AFC) 16, at Joe Robbie Stadium, Miami, Florida

1987

AMERICAN CONFERENCE

Eastern Division

	W	L	T	Pct.	Pts.	OP
Indianapolis	9	6	0	.600	300	238
New England	8	7	0	.533	320	293
Miami	8	7	0	.533	362	335
Buffalo	7	8	0	.467	270	305
N.Y. Jets	6	9	0	.400	334	360

Central Division

	W	L	T	Pct.	Pts.	OP
Cleveland	10	5	0	.667	390	239
Houston*	9	6	0	.600	345	349
Pittsburgh	8	7	0	.533	285	299
Cincinnati	4	11	0	.267	285	370

Western Division

	W	L	T	Pct.	Pts.	OP
Denver#	10	4	1	.700	379	288
Seattle*	9	6	0	.600	371	314
San Diego	8	7	0	.533	253	317
L.A. Raiders	5	10	0	.333	301	289
Kansas City	4	11	0	.267	273	388

NATIONAL CONFERENCE

Eastern Division

	W	L	T	Pct.	Pts.	OP
Washington	11	4	0	.733	379	285
Dallas	7	8	0	.467	340	348
St. Louis	7	8	0	.467	362	368
Philadelphia	7	8	0	.467	337	380
N.Y. Giants	6	9	0	.400	280	312

Central Division

	W	L	T	Pct.	Pts.	OP
Chicago	11	4	0	.733	356	282
Minnesota*	8	7	0	.533	336	335
Green Bay	5	9	1	.367	255	300
Tampa Bay	4	11	0	.267	286	360
Detroit	4	11	0	.267	269	384

Western Division

	W	L	T	Pct.	Pts.	OP
San Francisco#	13	2	0	.867	459	253
New Orleans*	12	3	0	.800	422	283
L.A. Rams	6	9	0	.400	317	361
Atlanta	3	12	0	.200	205	436

**Wild Card qualifier for playoffs; #Top playoff seed in conference*

New England finished ahead of Miami based on head-to-head sweep (2-0). Houston was first Wild Card ahead of Seattle based on better conference record (7-4 to Seahawks' 5-6). Chicago was second playoff seed ahead of Washington based on better conference record (9-2 to Redskins' 9-3). Dallas finished ahead of St. Louis and Philadelphia based on better division record (4-4 to Cardinals' 3-5 and Eagles' 3-5). St. Louis finished ahead of Philadelphia based on better conference record (7-7 to Eagles' 4-7). Tampa Bay finished ahead of Detroit based on better division record (3-4 to Lions' 2-5).

Wild Card playoff: HOUSTON 23, Seattle 20 (OT)

Divisional playoffs: CLEVELAND 38, Indianapolis 21; DENVER 34, Houston 10

AFC Championship: DENVER 38, Cleveland 33

Wild Card playoff: Minnesota 44, NEW ORLEANS 10

Divisional playoffs: Minnesota 36, SAN FRANCISCO 24; Washington 21, CHICAGO 17

NFC Championship: WASHINGTON 17, Minnesota 10

Super Bowl XXII: Washington (NFC) 42, Denver (AFC) 10, at San Diego Jack Murphy Stadium, San Diego, California

Note: 1987 regular season was reduced from 16 to 15 games for each team due to players' strike.

1986

AMERICAN CONFERENCE

Eastern Division

	W	L	T	Pct.	Pts.	OP
New England	11	5	0	.688	412	307
N.Y. Jets*	10	6	0	.625	364	386
Miami	8	8	0	.500	430	405
Buffalo	4	12	0	.250	287	348
Indianapolis	3	13	0	.188	229	400

Central Division

	W	L	T	Pct.	Pts.	OP
Cleveland#	12	4	0	.750	391	310
Cincinnati	10	6	0	.625	409	394
Pittsburgh	6	10	0	.375	307	336
Houston	5	11	0	.313	274	329

Western Division

	W	L	T	Pct.	Pts.	OP
Denver	11	5	0	.688	378	327
Kansas City*	10	6	0	.625	358	326
Seattle	10	6	0	.625	366	293
L.A. Raiders	8	8	0	.500	323	346
San Diego	4	12	0	.250	335	396

NATIONAL CONFERENCE

Eastern Division

	W	L	T	Pct.	Pts.	OP
N.Y. Giants#	14	2	0	.875	371	236
Washington*	12	4	0	.750	368	296
Dallas	7	9	0	.438	346	337
Philadelphia	5	10	1	.344	256	312
St. Louis	4	11	1	.281	218	351

Central Division

	W	L	T	Pct.	Pts.	OP
Chicago	14	2	0	.875	352	187
Minnesota	9	7	0	.563	398	273
Detroit	5	11	0	.313	277	326
Green Bay	4	12	0	.250	254	418
Tampa Bay	2	14	0	.125	239	473

Western Division

	W	L	T	Pct.	Pts.	OP
San Francisco	10	5	1	.656	374	247
L.A. Rams*	10	6	0	.625	309	267
Atlanta	7	8	1	.469	280	280
New Orleans	7	9	0	.438	288	287

**Wild Card qualifier for playoffs; #Top playoff seed in conference*

Denver was second playoff seed ahead of New England based on head-to-head victory (1-0). N.Y. Jets were first Wild Card based on better conference record (8-4) than Kansas City (9-5), Seattle (7-5), and Cincinnati (7-5). Kansas City was second Wild Card based on better conference record (9-5) than Seattle (7-5) and Cincinnati (7-5). N.Y. Giants were top playoff seed based on better conference record than Chicago (11-1 to Bears' 10-2). Washington did not play the N.Y. Giants in the divisional playoffs because, from 1970-1989, two teams from the same division could not meet prior to the conference championship game.

Wild Card playoff: N.Y. JETS 35, Kansas City 15

Divisional playoffs: CLEVELAND 23, N.Y. Jets 20 (OT); DENVER 22, New England 17

AFC Championship: Denver 23, CLEVELAND 20 (OT)

Wild Card playoff: WASHINGTON 19, L.A. Rams 7

Divisional playoffs: Washington 27, CHICAGO 13; N.Y. GIANTS 49, San Francisco 3

NFC Championship: N.Y. GIANTS 17, Washington 0

Super Bowl XXI: N.Y. Giants (NFC) 39, Denver (AFC) 20, at Rose Bowl, Pasadena, California

1985

AMERICAN CONFERENCE

Eastern Division

	W	L	T	Pct.	Pts.	OP
Miami	12	4	0	.750	428	320
N.Y. Jets*	11	5	0	.688	393	264
New England*	11	5	0	.688	362	290
Indianapolis	5	11	0	.313	320	386
Buffalo	2	14	0	.125	200	381

Central Division

	W	L	T	Pct.	Pts.	OP
Cleveland	8	8	0	.500	287	294
Cincinnati	7	9	0	.438	441	437
Pittsburgh	7	9	0	.438	379	355
Houston	5	11	0	.313	284	412

Western Division

	W	L	T	Pct.	Pts.	OP
L.A. Raiders#	12	4	0	.750	354	308
Denver	11	5	0	.688	380	329
Seattle	8	8	0	.500	349	303
San Diego	8	8	0	.500	467	435
Kansas City	6	10	0	.375	317	360

NATIONAL CONFERENCE

Eastern Division

	W	L	T	Pct.	Pts.	OP
Dallas	10	6	0	.625	357	333
N.Y. Giants*	10	6	0	.625	399	283
Washington	10	6	0	.625	297	312
Philadelphia	7	9	0	.438	286	310
St. Louis	5	11	0	.313	278	414

Central Division

	W	L	T	Pct.	Pts.	OP
Chicago#	15	1	0	.938	456	198
Green Bay	8	8	0	.500	337	355
Minnesota	7	9	0	.438	346	359
Detroit	7	9	0	.438	307	366
Tampa Bay	2	14	0	.125	294	448

Western Division

	W	L	T	Pct.	Pts.	OP
L.A. Rams	11	5	0	.688	340	277
San Francisco*	10	6	0	.625	411	263
New Orleans	5	11	0	.313	294	401
Atlanta	4	12	0	.250	282	452

**Wild Card qualifier for playoffs; #Top playoff seed in conference*

L.A. Raiders were top playoff seed ahead of Miami based on better record against common opponents (5-1 to 4-2). N.Y. Jets were first Wild Card based on better conference record (9-3) than New England (8-4) and Denver (8-4). New England was second Wild Card ahead of Denver based on better record against common opponents (4-2 to Broncos' 3-3). Cincinnati finished ahead of Pittsburgh based on head-to-head sweep (2-0). Seattle finished ahead of San Diego based on head-to-head sweep (2-0). Dallas finished ahead of N.Y. Giants and Washington based on better head-to-head record (4-0 to Giants' 1-3 and Redskins' 1-3). N.Y. Giants were first Wild Card based on better conference record (8-4) than San Francisco (7-5) and Washington (6-6). San Francisco was second Wild Card based on head-to-head victory over Washington (1-0). Minnesota finished ahead of Detroit based on better division record (3-5 to Lions' 2-6).

Wild Card playoff: New England 26, N.Y. JETS 14

Divisional playoffs: MIAMI 24, Cleveland 21;
New England 27, L.A. RAIDERS 20

AFC Championship: New England 31, MIAMI 14

Wild Card playoff: N.Y. GIANTS 17, San Francisco 3

Divisional playoffs: L.A. RAMS 20, Dallas 0;
CHICAGO 21, N.Y. Giants 0

NFC Championship: CHICAGO 24, L.A. Rams 0

Super Bowl XX: Chicago (NFC) 46, New England (AFC) 10, at Louisiana Superdome, New Orleans, Louisiana

1984

AMERICAN CONFERENCE

Eastern Division

	W	L	T	Pct.	Pts.	OP
Miami#	14	2	0	.875	513	298
New England	9	7	0	.563	362	352
N.Y. Jets	7	9	0	.438	332	364
Indianapolis	4	12	0	.250	239	414
Buffalo	2	14	0	.125	250	454

Central Division

	W	L	T	Pct.	Pts.	OP
Pittsburgh	9	7	0	.563	387	310
Cincinnati	8	8	0	.500	339	339
Cleveland	5	11	0	.313	250	297
Houston	3	13	0	.188	240	437

Western Division

	W	L	T	Pct.	Pts.	OP
Denver	13	3	0	.813	353	241
Seattle*	12	4	0	.750	418	282
L.A. Raiders*	11	5	0	.688	368	278
Kansas City	8	8	0	.500	314	324
San Diego	7	9	0	.438	394	413

NATIONAL CONFERENCE

Eastern Division

	W	L	T	Pct.	Pts.	OP
Washington	11	5	0	.688	426	310
N.Y. Giants*	9	7	0	.563	299	301
St. Louis	9	7	0	.563	423	345
Dallas	9	7	0	.563	308	308
Philadelphia	6	9	1	.406	278	320

Central Division

	W	L	T	Pct.	Pts.	OP
Chicago	10	6	0	.625	325	248
Green Bay	8	8	0	.500	390	309
Tampa Bay	6	10	0	.375	335	380
Detroit	4	11	1	.281	283	408
Minnesota	3	13	0	.188	276	484

Western Division

	W	L	T	Pct.	Pts.	OP
San Francisco#	15	1	0	.938	475	227
L.A. Rams*	10	6	0	.625	346	316
New Orleans	7	9	0	.438	298	361
Atlanta	4	12	0	.250	281	382

**Wild Card qualifier for playoffs; #Top playoff seed in conference*

N.Y. Giants finished ahead of St. Louis and Dallas based on best head-to-head record (3-1 to Cardinals' 2-2 and Cowboys' 1-3). St. Louis finished ahead of Dallas based on better division record (5-3 to Cowboys' 3-5).

Wild Card playoff: SEATTLE 13, L.A. Raiders 7

Divisional playoffs: MIAMI 31, Seattle 10;
Pittsburgh 24, DENVER 17

AFC Championship: MIAMI 45, Pittsburgh 28

Wild Card playoff: N.Y. Giants 16, L.A. RAMS 13

Divisional playoffs: SAN FRANCISCO 21, N.Y. Giants 10;
Chicago 23, WASHINGTON 19

NFC Championship: SAN FRANCISCO 23, Chicago 0

Super Bowl XIX: San Francisco (NFC) 38, Miami (AFC) 16, at Stanford Stadium, Stanford, California

1983

AMERICAN CONFERENCE

Eastern Division

	W	L	T	Pct.	Pts.	OP
Miami	12	4	0	.750	389	250
New England	8	8	0	.500	274	289
Buffalo	8	8	0	.500	283	351
Baltimore	7	9	0	.438	264	354
N.Y. Jets	7	9	0	.438	313	331

Central Division

	W	L	T	Pct.	Pts.	OP
Pittsburgh	10	6	0	.625	355	303
Cleveland	9	7	0	.563	356	342
Cincinnati	7	9	0	.438	346	302
Houston	2	14	0	.125	288	460

Western Division

	W	L	T	Pct.	Pts.	OP
L.A. Raiders#	12	4	0	.750	442	338
Seattle*	9	7	0	.563	403	397
Denver*	9	7	0	.563	302	327
San Diego	6	10	0	.375	358	462
Kansas City	6	10	0	.375	386	367

NATIONAL CONFERENCE

Eastern Division

	W	L	T	Pct.	Pts.	OP
Washington#	14	2	0	.875	541	332
Dallas*	12	4	0	.750	479	360
St. Louis	8	7	1	.531	374	428
Philadelphia	5	11	0	.313	233	322
N.Y. Giants	3	12	1	.219	267	347

Central Division

	W	L	T	Pct.	Pts.	OP
Detroit	9	7	0	.563	347	286
Green Bay	8	8	0	.500	429	439
Chicago	8	8	0	.500	311	301
Minnesota	8	8	0	.500	316	348
Tampa Bay	2	14	0	.125	241	380

Western Division

	W	L	T	Pct.	Pts.	OP
San Francisco	10	6	0	.625	432	293
L.A. Rams*	9	7	0	.563	361	344
New Orleans	8	8	0	.500	319	337
Atlanta	7	9	0	.438	370	389

**Wild Card qualifier for playoffs; #Top playoff seed in conference*

L.A. Raiders were top playoff seed ahead of Miami based on head-to-head victory (1-0). Seattle was first Wild Card ahead of Denver based on better division record (5-3 to Broncos' 3-5) after Cleveland was eliminated from three-way tie based on losing head-to-head to both Seattle and Denver. Seattle did not play the L.A. Raiders in the divisional playoffs because, from 1970-1989, two teams from the same division could not meet prior to the conference championship game. New England finished ahead of Buffalo based on head-to-head sweep (2-0). Baltimore finished ahead of N.Y. Jets based on better conference record (5-9 to Jets' 4-8). San Diego finished ahead of Kansas City based on head-to-head sweep (2-0). Green Bay finished ahead of Chicago based on better record against common opponents (4-4 to Bears' 3-5) after Minnesota was eliminated from three-way tie based on conference record (Chicago 7-7 and Green Bay 6-6 to Vikings' 4-8).

Wild Card playoff: SEATTLE 31, Denver 7
Divisional playoffs: Seattle 27, MIAMI 20;
L.A. RAIDERS 38, Pittsburgh 10
AFC Championship: L.A. RAIDERS 30, Seattle 14
Wild Card playoff: L.A. Rams 24, DALLAS 17
Divisional playoffs: SAN FRANCISCO 24, Detroit 23;
WASHINGTON 51, L.A. Rams 7
NFC Championship: WASHINGTON 24, San Francisco 21
Super Bowl XVIII: L.A. Raiders (AFC) 38, Washington (NFC) 9, at Tampa Stadium, Tampa, Florida

1982

AMERICAN CONFERENCE

	W	L	T	Pct.	Pts.	OP
L.A. Raiders#	8	1	0	.889	260	200
Miami	7	2	0	.778	198	131
Cincinnati	7	2	0	.778	232	177
Pittsburgh	6	3	0	.667	204	146
San Diego	6	3	0	.667	288	221
N.Y. Jets	6	3	0	.667	245	166
New England	5	4	0	.556	143	157
Cleveland	4	5	0	.444	140	182
Buffalo	4	5	0	.444	150	154
Seattle	4	5	0	.444	127	147
Kansas City	3	6	0	.333	176	184
Denver	2	7	0	.222	148	226
Houston	1	8	0	.111	136	245
Baltimore	0	8	1	.056	113	236

NATIONAL CONFERENCE

	W	L	T	Pct.	Pts.	OP
Washington#	8	1	0	.889	190	128
Dallas	6	3	0	.667	226	145
Green Bay	5	3	1	.611	226	169
Minnesota	5	4	0	.556	187	198
Atlanta	5	4	0	.556	183	199
St. Louis	5	4	0	.556	135	170
Tampa Bay	5	4	0	.556	158	178
Detroit	4	5	0	.444	181	176
New Orleans	4	5	0	.444	129	160
N.Y. Giants	4	5	0	.444	164	160
San Francisco	3	6	0	.333	209	206
Chicago	3	6	0	.333	141	174
Philadelphia	3	6	0	.333	191	195
L.A. Rams	2	7	0	.222	200	250

As the result of a 57-day players' strike, the 1982 NFL regular season schedule was reduced from 16 weeks to 9. At the conclusion of the regular season, the NFL conducted a 16-team postseason Super Bowl Tournament. Eight teams from each conference were seeded 1-8 based on their records during the season.

#Top playoff seed in conference

Miami finished ahead of Cincinnati based on better conference record (6-1 to Bengals' 6-2). Pittsburgh finished ahead of San Diego based on better record against common opponents (3-1 to Chargers' 2-1) after N.Y. Jets were eliminated from three-way tie based on conference record (Pittsburgh and San Diego 5-3 to Jets' 2-3). Cleveland finished ahead of Buffalo and Seattle based on better conference record (4-3 to Bills' 3-3 to Seahawks' 3-5). Buffalo finished ahead of Seattle based on better conference record (3-3 to Seahawks' 3-5). Minnesota (4-1), Atlanta (4-3), St. Louis (5-4), Tampa Bay (3-3) seeds were determined by best won-lost record in conference games. Detroit finished ahead of New Orleans and the N.Y. Giants based on best conference record (4-4 to Saints' 3-5 to Giants' 3-5). New Orleans finished ahead of N.Y. Giants based on better record against common opponents (1-3 to Giants' 0-4). San Francisco finished ahead of Chicago, and Chicago finished ahead of Philadelphia, based on conference record (49ers' 2-3 to Bears' 2-5 to Eagles' 1-5).

First round playoff: MIAMI 28, New England 13;
L.A. RAIDERS 27, Cleveland 10;
N.Y. Jets 44, CINCINNATI 17;
San Diego 31, PITTSBURGH 28
Second round playoff: N.Y. Jets 17, L.A. RAIDERS 14;
MIAMI 34, San Diego 13
AFC Championship: MIAMI 14, N.Y. Jets 0
First round playoff: WASHINGTON 31, Detroit 7;
GREEN BAY 41, St. Louis 16;
MINNESOTA 30, Atlanta 24;
DALLAS 30, Tampa Bay 17
Second round playoff: WASHINGTON 21, Minnesota 7;
DALLAS 37, Green Bay 26
NFC Championship: WASHINGTON 31, Dallas 17
Super Bowl XVII: Washington (NFC) 27, Miami (AFC) 17, at Rose Bowl, Pasadena, California

1981

AMERICAN CONFERENCE

Eastern Division

	W	L	T	Pct.	Pts.	OP
Miami	11	4	1	.719	345	275
N.Y. Jets*	10	5	1	.656	355	287
Buffalo*	10	6	0	.625	311	276
Baltimore	2	14	0	.125	259	533
New England	2	14	0	.125	322	370

Central Division

	W	L	T	Pct.	Pts.	OP
Cincinnati#	12	4	0	.750	421	304
Pittsburgh	8	8	0	.500	356	297
Houston	7	9	0	.438	281	355
Cleveland	5	11	0	.313	276	375

Western Division

	W	L	T	Pct.	Pts.	OP
San Diego	10	6	0	.625	478	390
Denver	10	6	0	.625	321	289
Kansas City	9	7	0	.563	343	290
Oakland	7	9	0	.438	273	343
Seattle	6	10	0	.375	322	388

NATIONAL CONFERENCE

Eastern Division

	W	L	T	Pct.	Pts.	OP
Dallas	12	4	0	.750	367	277
Philadelphia*	10	6	0	.625	368	221
N.Y. Giants*	9	7	0	.563	295	257
Washington	8	8	0	.500	347	349
St. Louis	7	9	0	.438	315	408

Central Division

	W	L	T	Pct.	Pts.	OP
Tampa Bay	9	7	0	.563	315	268
Detroit	8	8	0	.500	397	322
Green Bay	8	8	0	.500	324	361
Minnesota	7	9	0	.438	325	369
Chicago	6	10	0	.375	253	324

Western Division

	W	L	T	Pct.	Pts.	OP
San Francisco#	13	3	0	.813	357	250
Atlanta	7	9	0	.438	426	355
Los Angeles	6	10	0	.375	303	351
New Orleans	4	12	0	.250	207	378

**Wild Card qualifier for playoffs; #Top playoff seed in conference*

Baltimore finished ahead of New England based on head-to-head sweep (2-0). San Diego finished ahead of Denver based on better division record (6-2 to Broncos' 5-3). Buffalo was second Wild Card based on head-to-head victory over Denver (1-0). Detroit finished ahead of Green Bay based on better record against common opponents (4-4 to Packers' 3-5).

Wild Card playoff: Buffalo 31, N.Y. JETS 27

Divisional playoffs: San Diego 41, MIAMI 38 (OT); CINCINNATI 28, Buffalo 21

AFC Championship: CINCINNATI 27, San Diego 7

Wild Card playoff: N.Y. Giants 27, PHILADELPHIA 21

Divisional playoffs: DALLAS 38, Tampa Bay 0; SAN FRANCISCO 38, N.Y. Giants 24

NFC Championship: SAN FRANCISCO 28, Dallas 27

Super Bowl XVI: San Francisco (NFC) 26, Cincinnati (AFC) 21, at Silverdome, Pontiac, Michigan

1980

AMERICAN CONFERENCE

Eastern Division

	W	L	T	Pct.	Pts.	OP
Buffalo	11	5	0	.688	320	260
New England	10	6	0	.625	441	325
Miami	8	8	0	.500	266	305
Baltimore	7	9	0	.438	355	387
N.Y. Jets	4	12	0	.250	302	395

Central Division

	W	L	T	Pct.	Pts.	OP
Cleveland	11	5	0	.688	357	310
Houston*	11	5	0	.688	295	251
Pittsburgh	9	7	0	.563	352	313
Cincinnati	6	10	0	.375	244	312

Western Division

	W	L	T	Pct.	Pts.	OP
San Diego#	11	5	0	.688	418	327
Oakland*	11	5	0	.688	364	306
Kansas City	8	8	0	.500	319	336
Denver	8	8	0	.500	310	323
Seattle	4	12	0	.250	291	408

NATIONAL CONFERENCE

Eastern Division

	W	L	T	Pct.	Pts.	OP
Philadelphia	12	4	0	.750	384	222
Dallas*	12	4	0	.750	454	311
Washington	6	10	0	.375	261	293
St. Louis	5	11	0	.313	299	350
N.Y. Giants	4	12	0	.250	249	425

Central Division

	W	L	T	Pct.	Pts.	OP
Minnesota	9	7	0	.563	317	308
Detroit	9	7	0	.563	334	272
Chicago	7	9	0	.438	304	264
Tampa Bay	5	10	1	.344	271	341
Green Bay	5	10	1	.344	231	371

Western Division

	W	L	T	Pct.	Pts.	OP
Atlanta#	12	4	0	.750	405	272
Los Angeles*	11	5	0	.688	424	289
San Francisco	6	10	0	.375	320	415
New Orleans	1	15	0	.063	291	487

**Wild Card qualifier for playoffs; #Top playoff seed in conference*

San Diego was top playoff seed based on better conference record than Cleveland and Buffalo (9-3 to Browns' 8-4 and Bills' 8-4). Cleveland was second playoff seed based on better record against common opponents (5-2 to Bills' 5-3). Cleveland finished ahead of Houston based on better conference record (8-4 to Oilers' 7-5). Oakland was first Wild Card based on better conference record than Houston (9-3 to Oilers' 7-5). San Diego finished ahead of Oakland based on better net points in division games (plus 60 net points to Raiders' plus 37). Oakland did not play San Diego in the divisional playoffs because, from 1970-1989, two teams from the same division could not meet prior to the conference championship game. Kansas City finished ahead of Denver based on head-to-head sweep (2-0). Atlanta was top playoff seed based on head-to-head victory over Philadelphia (1-0). Philadelphia finished ahead of Dallas based on better net points in division games (plus 84 net points to Cowboys' plus 50). Minnesota finished ahead of Detroit based on better conference record (8-4 to Lions' 9-5). Tampa Bay finished ahead of Green Bay based on better head-to-head record (1-0-1 to Packers' 0-1-1).

Wild Card playoff: OAKLAND 27, Houston 7

Divisional playoffs: SAN DIEGO 20, Buffalo 14; Oakland 14, CLEVELAND 12

AFC Championship: Oakland 34, SAN DIEGO 27

Wild Card playoff: DALLAS 34, Los Angeles 13

Divisional playoffs: PHILADELPHIA 31, Minnesota 16; Dallas 30, ATLANTA 27

NFC Championship: PHILADELPHIA 20, Dallas 7

Super Bowl XV: Oakland (AFC) 27, Philadelphia (NFC) 10, at Louisiana Superdome, New Orleans, Louisiana

1979

AMERICAN CONFERENCE

Eastern Division

	W	L	T	Pct.	Pts.	OP
Miami	10	6	0	.625	341	257
New England	9	7	0	.563	411	326
N.Y. Jets	8	8	0	.500	337	383
Buffalo	7	9	0	.438	268	279
Baltimore	5	11	0	.313	271	351

Central Division

	W	L	T	Pct.	Pts.	OP
Pittsburgh	12	4	0	.750	416	262
Houston*	11	5	0	.688	362	331
Cleveland	9	7	0	.563	359	352
Cincinnati	4	12	0	.250	337	421

Western Division

	W	L	T	Pct.	Pts.	OP
San Diego#	12	4	0	.750	411	246
Denver*	10	6	0	.625	289	262
Seattle	9	7	0	.563	378	372
Oakland	9	7	0	.563	365	337
Kansas City	7	9	0	.438	238	262

NATIONAL CONFERENCE

Eastern Division

	W	L	T	Pct.	Pts.	OP
Dallas#	11	5	0	.688	371	313
Philadelphia*	11	5	0	.688	339	282
Washington	10	6	0	.625	348	295
N.Y. Giants	6	10	0	.375	237	323
St. Louis	5	11	0	.313	307	358

Central Division

	W	L	T	Pct.	Pts.	OP
Tampa Bay	10	6	0	.625	273	237
Chicago*	10	6	0	.625	306	249
Minnesota	7	9	0	.438	259	337
Green Bay	5	11	0	.313	246	316
Detroit	2	14	0	.125	219	365

Western Division

	W	L	T	Pct.	Pts.	OP
Los Angeles	9	7	0	.563	323	309
New Orleans	8	8	0	.500	370	360
Atlanta	6	10	0	.375	300	388
San Francisco	2	14	0	.125	308	416

**Wild Card qualifier for playoffs; #Top playoff seed in conference*

San Diego was top playoff seed based on head-to-head victory over Pittsburgh (1-0). Seattle finished ahead of Oakland based on head-to-head sweep (2-0). Dallas finished ahead of Philadelphia based on better conference record (10-2 to Eagles' 9-3). Philadelphia did not play Dallas in the divisional playoffs because, from 1970-1989, two teams from the same division could not meet prior to the conference championship game. Tampa Bay finished ahead of Chicago based on a better division record (6-2 to Bears' 5-3). Chicago was second Wild Card ahead of Washington based on better net points in all games (57 to Redskins' 53).

Wild Card playoff: HOUSTON 13, Denver 7

Divisional playoffs: Houston 17, SAN DIEGO 14; PITTSBURGH 34, Miami 14

AFC Championship: PITTSBURGH 27, Houston 13

Wild Card playoff: PHILADELPHIA 27, Chicago 17

Divisional playoffs: TAMPA BAY 24, Philadelphia 17; Los Angeles 21, DALLAS 19

NFC Championship: Los Angeles 9, TAMPA BAY 0

Super Bowl XIV: Pittsburgh (AFC) 31, Los Angeles (NFC) 19, at Rose Bowl, Pasadena, California

1978

AMERICAN CONFERENCE

Eastern Division

	W	L	T	Pct.	Pts.	OP
New England	11	5	0	.688	358	286
Miami*	11	5	0	.688	372	254
N.Y. Jets	8	8	0	.500	359	364
Buffalo	5	11	0	.313	302	354
Baltimore	5	11	0	.313	239	421

Central Division

	W	L	T	Pct.	Pts.	OP
Pittsburgh#	14	2	0	.875	356	195
Houston*	10	6	0	.625	283	298
Cleveland	8	8	0	.500	334	356
Cincinnati	4	12	0	.250	252	284

Western Division

	W	L	T	Pct.	Pts.	OP
Denver	10	6	0	.625	282	198
Oakland	9	7	0	.563	311	283
Seattle	9	7	0	.563	345	358
San Diego	9	7	0	.563	355	309
Kansas City	4	12	0	.250	243	327

NATIONAL CONFERENCE

Eastern Division

	W	L	T	Pct.	Pts.	OP
Dallas	12	4	0	.750	384	208
Philadelphia*	9	7	0	.563	270	250
Washington	8	8	0	.500	273	283
St. Louis	6	10	0	.375	248	296
N.Y. Giants	6	10	0	.375	264	298

Central Division

	W	L	T	Pct.	Pts.	OP
Minnesota	8	7	1	.531	294	306
Green Bay	8	7	1	.531	249	269
Detroit	7	9	0	.438	290	300
Chicago	7	9	0	.438	253	274
Tampa Bay	5	11	0	.313	241	259

Western Division

	W	L	T	Pct.	Pts.	OP
Los Angeles#	12	4	0	.750	316	245
Atlanta*	9	7	0	.563	240	290
New Orleans	7	9	0	.438	281	298
San Francisco	2	14	0	.125	219	350

**Wild Card qualifier for playoffs; #Top playoff seed in conference*

New England finished ahead of Miami based on better division record (6-2 to Dolphins' 5-3). Buffalo finished ahead of Baltimore based on head-to-head sweep (2-0). Oakland finished ahead of Seattle and San Diego based on better record against common opponents (6-2 to Seahawks' 5-3 and Chargers' 4-4). Atlanta was first Wild Card ahead of Philadelphia based on better record against common opponents (5-2 to Eagles' 5-3). Houston did not play Pittsburgh, and Atlanta did not play Los Angeles in the divisional playoffs because, from 1970-1989, two teams from the same division could not meet prior to the conference championship game. Los Angeles was top playoff seed based on head-to-head victory over Dallas (1-0). St. Louis finished ahead of N.Y. Giants based on better division record (3-5 to Giants' 2-6). Minnesota finished ahead of Green Bay based on better head-to-head record (1-0-1). Detroit finished ahead of Chicago based on better division record (4-4 to Bears' 3-5).

Wild Card playoff: Houston 17, MIAMI 9

Divisional playoffs: Houston 31, NEW ENGLAND 14; PITTSBURGH 33, Denver 10

AFC Championship: PITTSBURGH 34, Houston 5

Wild Card playoff: ATLANTA 14, Philadelphia 13

Divisional playoffs: DALLAS 27, Atlanta 20; LOS ANGELES 34, Minnesota 10

NFC Championship: Dallas 28, LOS ANGELES 0

Super Bowl XIII: Pittsburgh (AFC) 35, Dallas (NFC) 31, at Orange Bowl, Miami, Florida

1977

AMERICAN CONFERENCE

Eastern Division

	W	L	T	Pct.	Pts.	OP
Baltimore	10	4	0	.714	295	221
Miami	10	4	0	.714	313	197
New England	9	5	0	.643	278	217
N.Y. Jets	3	11	0	.214	191	300
Buffalo	3	11	0	.214	160	313

Central Division

	W	L	T	Pct.	Pts.	OP
Pittsburgh	9	5	0	.643	283	243
Houston	8	6	0	.571	299	230
Cincinnati	8	6	0	.571	238	235
Cleveland	6	8	0	.429	269	267

Western Division

	W	L	T	Pct.	Pts.	OP
Denver#	12	2	0	.857	274	148
Oakland*	11	3	0	.786	351	230
San Diego	7	7	0	.500	222	205
Seattle	5	9	0	.357	282	373
Kansas City	2	12	0	.143	225	349

NATIONAL CONFERENCE

Eastern Division

	W	L	T	Pct.	Pts.	OP
Dallas#	12	2	0	.857	345	212
Washington	9	5	0	.643	196	189
St. Louis	7	7	0	.500	272	287
Philadelphia	5	9	0	.357	220	207
N.Y. Giants	5	9	0	.357	181	265

Central Division

	W	L	T	Pct.	Pts.	OP
Minnesota	9	5	0	.643	231	227
Chicago*	9	5	0	.643	255	253
Detroit	6	8	0	.429	183	252
Green Bay	4	10	0	.286	134	219
Tampa Bay	2	12	0	.143	103	223

Western Division

	W	L	T	Pct.	Pts.	OP
Los Angeles	10	4	0	.714	302	146
Atlanta	7	7	0	.500	179	129
San Francisco	5	9	0	.357	220	260
New Orleans	3	11	0	.214	232	336

**Wild Card qualifier for playoffs; #Top playoff seed in conference*

Baltimore finished ahead of Miami based on better conference record (9-3 to Dolphins' 8-4). N.Y. Jets finished ahead of Buffalo based on better point-differential in head-to-head competition (1 point). Houston finished ahead of Cincinnati based on better point-differential in head-to-head competition (2 points). Oakland did not play Denver in the divisional playoffs because, from 1970-1989, two teams from the same division could not meet prior to the conference championship game. Minnesota finished ahead of Chicago based on better point-differential in head-to-head competition (3 points). Chicago won Wild Card ahead of Washington based on better net points in conference games (48 to Redskins' 4). Philadelphia finished ahead of N.Y. Giants based on head-to-head sweep (2-0).

Divisional playoffs: DENVER 34, Pittsburgh 21; Oakland 37, BALTIMORE 31 (OT)

AFC Championship: DENVER 20, Oakland 17

Divisional playoffs: DALLAS 37, Chicago 7; Minnesota 14, LOS ANGELES 7

NFC Championship: DALLAS 23, Minnesota 6

Super Bowl XII: Dallas (NFC) 27, Denver (AFC) 10, at Louisiana Superdome, New Orleans, Louisiana

1976

AMERICAN CONFERENCE

Eastern Division

	W	L	T	Pct.	Pts.	OP
Baltimore	11	3	0	.786	417	246
New England*	11	3	0	.786	376	236
Miami	6	8	0	.429	263	264
N.Y. Jets	3	11	0	.214	169	383
Buffalo	2	12	0	.143	245	363

Central Division

	W	L	T	Pct.	Pts.	OP
Pittsburgh	10	4	0	.714	342	138
Cincinnati	10	4	0	.714	335	210
Cleveland	9	5	0	.643	267	287
Houston	5	9	0	.357	222	273

Western Division

	W	L	T	Pct.	Pts.	OP
Oakland#	13	1	0	.929	350	237
Denver	9	5	0	.643	315	206
San Diego	6	8	0	.429	248	285
Kansas City	5	9	0	.357	290	376
Tampa Bay	0	14	0	.000	125	412

NATIONAL CONFERENCE

Eastern Division

	W	L	T	Pct.	Pts.	OP
Dallas	11	3	0	.786	296	194
Washington*	10	4	0	.714	291	217
St. Louis	10	4	0	.714	309	267
Philadelphia	4	10	0	.286	165	286
N.Y. Giants	3	11	0	.214	170	250

Central Division

	W	L	T	Pct.	Pts.	OP
Minnesota#	11	2	1	.821	305	176
Chicago	7	7	0	.500	253	216
Detroit	6	8	0	.429	262	220
Green Bay	5	9	0	.357	218	299

Western Division

	W	L	T	Pct.	Pts.	OP
Los Angeles	10	3	1	.750	351	190
San Francisco	8	6	0	.571	270	190
New Orleans	4	10	0	.286	253	346
Atlanta	4	10	0	.286	172	312
Seattle	2	12	0	.143	229	429

**Wild Card qualifier for playoffs; #Top playoff seed in conference*

Baltimore finished ahead of New England based on better division record (7-1 to Patriots' 6-2). Pittsburgh finished ahead of Cincinnati based on head-to-head sweep (2-0). Washington finished ahead of St. Louis based on head-to-head sweep (2-0). New Orleans finished ahead of Atlanta based on better point-differential in head-to-head competition (27 points).

Divisional playoffs: OAKLAND 24, New England 21; Pittsburgh 40, BALTIMORE 14

AFC Championship: OAKLAND 24, Pittsburgh 7

Divisional playoffs: MINNESOTA 35, Washington 20; Los Angeles 14, DALLAS 12

NFC Championship: MINNESOTA 24, Los Angeles 13

Super Bowl XI: Oakland (AFC) 32, Minnesota (NFC) 14, at Rose Bowl, Pasadena, California

1975

AMERICAN CONFERENCE

Eastern Division

	W	L	T	Pct.	Pts.	OP
Baltimore	10	4	0	.714	395	269
Miami	10	4	0	.714	357	222
Buffalo	8	6	0	.571	420	355
N.Y. Jets	3	11	0	.214	258	433
New England	3	11	0	.214	258	358

Central Division

	W	L	T	Pct.	Pts.	OP
Pittsburgh#	12	2	0	.857	373	162
Cincinnati*	11	3	0	.786	340	246
Houston	10	4	0	.714	293	226
Cleveland	3	11	0	.214	218	372

Western Division

	W	L	T	Pct.	Pts.	OP
Oakland	11	3	0	.786	375	255
Denver	6	8	0	.429	254	307
Kansas City	5	9	0	.357	282	341
San Diego	2	12	0	.143	189	345

NATIONAL CONFERENCE

Eastern Division

	W	L	T	Pct.	Pts.	OP
St. Louis	11	3	0	.786	356	276
Dallas*	10	4	0	.714	350	268
Washington	8	6	0	.571	325	276
N.Y. Giants	5	9	0	.357	216	306
Philadelphia	4	10	0	.286	225	302

Central Division

	W	L	T	Pct.	Pts.	OP
Minnesota#	12	2	0	.857	377	180
Detroit	7	7	0	.500	245	262
Chicago	4	10	0	.286	191	379
Green Bay	4	10	0	.286	226	285

Western Division

	W	L	T	Pct.	Pts.	OP
Los Angeles	12	2	0	.857	312	135
San Francisco	5	9	0	.357	255	286
Atlanta	4	10	0	.286	240	289
New Orleans	2	12	0	.143	165	360

**Wild Card qualifier for playoffs; #Top playoff seed in conference*

Baltimore finished ahead of Miami based on head-to-head sweep (2-0). Cincinnati did not play Pittsburgh in the divisional playoffs because, from 1970-1989, two teams from the same division could not meet prior to the conference championship game. N.Y. Jets finished ahead of New England based on head-to-head sweep (2-0). Minnesota was top playoff seed based on better Point Rating system than Los Angeles (3 to 6). Chicago finished ahead of Green Bay based on better division record (2-4 to Bears' 1-5).

Divisional playoffs: PITTSBURGH 28, Baltimore 10; OAKLAND 31, Cincinnati 28

AFC Championship: PITTSBURGH 16, Oakland 10

Divisional playoffs: LOS ANGELES 35, St. Louis 23; Dallas 17, MINNESOTA 14

NFC Championship: Dallas 37, LOS ANGELES 7

Super Bowl X: Pittsburgh (AFC) 21, Dallas (NFC) 17, at Orange Bowl, Miami, Florida

1974

AMERICAN CONFERENCE

Eastern Division

	W	L	T	Pct.	Pts.	OP
Miami	11	3	0	.786	327	216
Buffalo*	9	5	0	.643	264	244
N.Y. Jets	7	7	0	.500	279	300
New England	7	7	0	.500	348	289
Baltimore	2	12	0	.143	190	329

Central Division

	W	L	T	Pct.	Pts.	OP
Pittsburgh	10	3	1	.750	305	189
Houston	7	7	0	.500	236	282
Cincinnati	7	7	0	.500	283	259
Cleveland	4	10	0	.286	251	344

Western Division

	W	L	T	Pct.	Pts.	OP
Oakland	12	2	0	.857	355	228
Denver	7	6	1	.536	302	294
Kansas City	5	9	0	.357	233	293
San Diego	5	9	0	.357	212	285

NATIONAL CONFERENCE

Eastern Division

	W	L	T	Pct.	Pts.	OP
St. Louis	10	4	0	.714	285	218
Washington*	10	4	0	.714	320	196
Dallas	8	6	0	.571	297	235
Philadelphia	7	7	0	.500	242	217
N.Y. Giants	2	12	0	.143	195	299

Central Division

	W	L	T	Pct.	Pts.	OP
Minnesota	10	4	0	.714	310	195
Detroit	7	7	0	.500	256	270
Green Bay	6	8	0	.429	210	206
Chicago	4	10	0	.286	152	279

Western Division

	W	L	T	Pct.	Pts.	OP
Los Angeles	10	4	0	.714	263	181
San Francisco	6	8	0	.429	226	236
New Orleans	5	9	0	.357	166	263
Atlanta	3	11	0	.214	111	271

**Wild Card qualifier for playoffs*

N.Y. Jets finished ahead of New England based on better conference record (5-6 to Patriots' 4-7). Houston finished ahead of Cincinnati based on head-to-head sweep (2-0). Kansas City finished ahead of San Diego based on better point-differential in head-to-head competition (3 points). St. Louis finished ahead of Washington based on head-to-head sweep (2-0).

Divisional playoffs: OAKLAND 28, Miami 26; PITTSBURGH 32, Buffalo 14

AFC Championship: Pittsburgh 24, OAKLAND 13

Divisional playoffs: MINNESOTA 30, St. Louis 14; LOS ANGELES 19, Washington 10

NFC Championship: MINNESOTA 14, Los Angeles 10

Super Bowl IX: Pittsburgh (AFC) 16, Minnesota (NFC) 6, at Tulane Stadium, New Orleans, Louisiana

From 1933-1974, sites for league/conference championship games alternated by division.

1973

AMERICAN CONFERENCE

Eastern Division

	W	L	T	Pct.	Pts.	OP
Miami	12	2	0	.857	343	150
Buffalo	9	5	0	.643	259	230
New England	5	9	0	.357	258	300
N.Y. Jets	4	10	0	.286	240	306
Baltimore	4	10	0	.286	226	341

Central Division

	W	L	T	Pct.	Pts.	OP
Cincinnati	10	4	0	.714	286	231
Pittsburgh*	10	4	0	.714	347	210
Cleveland	7	5	2	.571	234	255
Houston	1	13	0	.071	199	447

Western Division

	W	L	T	Pct.	Pts.	OP
Oakland	9	4	1	.679	292	175
Kansas City	7	5	2	.571	231	192
Denver	7	5	2	.571	354	296
San Diego	2	11	1	.179	188	386

NATIONAL CONFERENCE

Eastern Division

	W	L	T	Pct.	Pts.	OP
Dallas	10	4	0	.714	382	203
Washington*	10	4	0	.714	325	198
Philadelphia	5	8	1	.393	310	393
St. Louis	4	9	1	.321	286	365
N.Y. Giants	2	11	1	.179	226	362

Central Division

	W	L	T	Pct.	Pts.	OP
Minnesota	12	2	0	.857	296	168
Detroit	6	7	1	.464	271	247
Green Bay	5	7	2	.429	202	259
Chicago	3	11	0	.214	195	334

Western Division

	W	L	T	Pct.	Pts.	OP
Los Angeles	12	2	0	.857	388	178
Atlanta	9	5	0	.643	318	224
San Francisco	5	9	0	.357	262	319
New Orleans	5	9	0	.357	163	312

**Wild Card qualifier for playoffs*

Cincinnati finished ahead of Pittsburgh based on better conference record (8-3 to Steelers' 7-4). N.Y. Jets finished ahead of Baltimore based on head-to-head sweep (2-0). Kansas City finished ahead of Denver based on better division record (4-2 to Broncos' 3-2-1). Dallas finished ahead of Washington based on better point differential in head-to-head games (13 points). San Francisco finished ahead of New Orleans based on better division record (2-4 to Saints' 1-5).

Divisional playoffs: OAKLAND 33, Pittsburgh 14; MIAMI 34, Cincinnati 16

AFC Championship: MIAMI 27, Oakland 10

Divisional playoffs: MINNESOTA 27, Washington 20; DALLAS 27, Los Angeles 16

NFC Championship: Minnesota 27, DALLAS 10

Super Bowl VIII: Miami (AFC) 24, Minnesota (NFC) 7, at Rice Stadium, Houston, Texas

1972

AMERICAN CONFERENCE

Eastern Division

	W	L	T	Pct.	Pts.	OP
Miami	14	0	0	1.000	385	171
N.Y. Jets	7	7	0	.500	367	324
Baltimore	5	9	0	.357	235	252
Buffalo	4	9	1	.321	257	377
New England	3	11	0	.214	192	446

Central Division

	W	L	T	Pct.	Pts.	OP
Pittsburgh	11	3	0	.786	343	175
Cleveland*	10	4	0	.714	268	249
Cincinnati	8	6	0	.571	299	229
Houston	1	13	0	.071	164	380

Western Division

	W	L	T	Pct.	Pts.	OP
Oakland	10	3	1	.750	365	248
Kansas City	8	6	0	.571	287	254
Denver	5	9	0	.357	325	350
San Diego	4	9	1	.321	264	344

NATIONAL CONFERENCE

Eastern Division

	W	L	T	Pct.	Pts.	OP
Washington	11	3	0	.786	336	218
Dallas*	10	4	0	.714	319	240
N.Y. Giants	8	6	0	.571	331	247
St. Louis	4	9	1	.321	193	303
Philadelphia	2	11	1	.179	145	352

Central Division

	W	L	T	Pct.	Pts.	OP
Green Bay	10	4	0	.714	304	226
Detroit	8	5	1	.607	339	290
Minnesota	7	7	0	.500	301	252
Chicago	4	9	1	.321	225	275

Western Division

	W	L	T	Pct.	Pts.	OP
San Francisco	8	5	1	.607	353	249
Atlanta	7	7	0	.500	269	274
Los Angeles	6	7	1	.464	291	286
New Orleans	2	11	1	.179	215	361

**Wild Card qualifier for playoffs*

Dallas did not play Washington in the divisional playoffs because, from 1970-1989, two teams from the same division could not meet prior to the conference championship game.

Divisional playoffs: PITTSBURGH 13, Oakland 7; MIAMI 20, Cleveland 14

AFC Championship: Miami 21, PITTSBURGH 17

Divisional playoffs: Dallas 30, SAN FRANCISCO 28; WASHINGTON 16, Green Bay 3

NFC Championship: WASHINGTON 26, Dallas 3

Super Bowl VII: Miami (AFC) 14, Washington (NFC) 7, at Memorial Coliseum, Los Angeles, California

1971

AMERICAN CONFERENCE

Eastern Division

	W	L	T	Pct.	Pts.	OP
Miami	10	3	1	.769	315	174
Baltimore*	10	4	0	.714	313	140
New England	6	8	0	.429	238	325
N.Y. Jets	6	8	0	.429	212	299
Buffalo	1	13	0	.071	184	394

Central Division

	W	L	T	Pct.	Pts.	OP
Cleveland	9	5	0	.643	285	273
Pittsburgh	6	8	0	.429	246	292
Houston	4	9	1	.308	251	330
Cincinnati	4	10	0	.286	284	265

Western Division

	W	L	T	Pct.	Pts.	OP
Kansas City	10	3	1	.769	302	208
Oakland	8	4	2	.667	344	278
San Diego	6	8	0	.429	311	341
Denver	4	9	1	.308	203	275

NATIONAL CONFERENCE

Eastern Division

	W	L	T	Pct.	Pts.	OP
Dallas	11	3	0	.786	406	222
Washington*	9	4	1	.692	276	190
Philadelphia	6	7	1	.462	221	302
St. Louis	4	9	1	.308	231	279
N.Y. Giants	4	10	0	.286	228	362

Central Division

	W	L	T	Pct.	Pts.	OP
Minnesota	11	3	0	.786	245	139
Detroit	7	6	1	.538	341	286
Chicago	6	8	0	.429	185	276
Green Bay	4	8	2	.333	274	298

Western Division

	W	L	T	Pct.	Pts.	OP
San Francisco	9	5	0	.643	300	216
Los Angeles	8	5	1	.615	313	260
Atlanta	7	6	1	.538	274	277
New Orleans	4	8	2	.333	266	347

**Wild Card qualifier for playoffs*

New England finished ahead of N.Y. Jets based on better point-differential in head-to-head competition (13 points).

Divisional playoffs: Miami 27, KANSAS CITY 24 (OT); Baltimore 20, CLEVELAND 3

AFC Championship: MIAMI 21, Baltimore 0

Divisional playoffs: Dallas 20, MINNESOTA 12; SAN FRANCISCO 24, Washington 20

NFC Championship: DALLAS 14, San Francisco 3

Super Bowl VI: Dallas (NFC) 24, Miami (AFC) 3, at Tulane Stadium, New Orleans, Louisiana

From 1920-1971, tie games were not included in winning percentage.

1970

AMERICAN CONFERENCE

Eastern Division

	W	L	T	Pct.	Pts.	OP
Baltimore	11	2	1	.846	321	234
Miami*	10	4	0	.714	297	228
N.Y. Jets	4	10	0	.286	255	286
Buffalo	3	10	1	.231	204	337
Boston Patriots	2	12	0	.143	149	361

Central Division

	W	L	T	Pct.	Pts.	OP
Cincinnati	8	6	0	.571	312	255
Cleveland	7	7	0	.500	286	265
Pittsburgh	5	9	0	.357	210	272
Houston	3	10	1	.231	217	352

Western Division

	W	L	T	Pct.	Pts.	OP
Oakland	8	4	2	.667	300	293
Kansas City	7	5	2	.583	272	244
San Diego	5	6	3	.455	282	278
Denver	5	8	1	.385	253	264

NATIONAL CONFERENCE

Eastern Division

	W	L	T	Pct.	Pts.	OP
Dallas	10	4	0	.714	299	221
N.Y. Giants	9	5	0	.643	301	270
St. Louis	8	5	1	.615	325	228
Washington	6	8	0	.429	297	314
Philadelphia	3	10	1	.231	241	332

Central Division

	W	L	T	Pct.	Pts.	OP
Minnesota	12	2	0	.857	335	143
Detroit*	10	4	0	.714	347	202
Green Bay	6	8	0	.429	196	293
Chicago	6	8	0	.429	256	261

Western Division

	W	L	T	Pct.	Pts.	OP
San Francisco	10	3	1	.769	352	267
Los Angeles	9	4	1	.692	325	202
Atlanta	4	8	2	.333	206	261
New Orleans	2	11	1	.154	172	347

**Wild Card qualifier for playoffs*

Miami did not play Baltimore, and Detroit did not play Minnesota, in the divisional playoffs because, from 1970-1989, two teams from the same division could not meet prior to the conference championship game. Green Bay finished ahead of Chicago based on better division record (2-4 to Bears' 1-5).

Divisional playoffs: BALTIMORE 17, Cincinnati 0; OAKLAND 21, Miami 14

AFC Championship: BALTIMORE 27, Oakland 17

Divisional playoffs: DALLAS 5, Detroit 0; San Francisco 17, MINNESOTA 14

NFC Championship: Dallas 17, SAN FRANCISCO 10

Super Bowl V: Baltimore (AFC) 16, Dallas (NFC) 13, at Orange Bowl, Miami, Florida

1969 NFL

EASTERN CONFERENCE

Capitol Division

	W	L	T	Pct.	Pts.	OP
Dallas	11	2	1	.846	369	223
Washington	7	5	2	.583	307	319
New Orleans	5	9	0	.357	311	393
Philadelphia	4	9	1	.308	279	377

Century Division

	W	L	T	Pct.	Pts.	OP
Cleveland	10	3	1	.769	351	300
N.Y. Giants	6	8	0	.429	264	298
St. Louis	4	9	1	.308	314	389
Pittsburgh	1	13	0	.071	218	404

WESTERN CONFERENCE

Coastal Division

	W	L	T	Pct.	Pts.	OP
Los Angeles	11	3	0	.786	320	243
Baltimore	8	5	1	.615	279	268
Atlanta	6	8	0	.429	276	268
San Francisco	4	8	2	.333	277	319

Central Division

	W	L	T	Pct.	Pts.	OP
Minnesota	12	2	0	.857	379	133
Detroit	9	4	1	.692	259	188
Green Bay	8	6	0	.571	269	221
Chicago	1	13	0	.071	210	339

Conference championships: Cleveland 38, DALLAS 14; MINNESOTA 23, Los Angeles 20
NFL championship: MINNESOTA 27, Cleveland 7
Super Bowl IV: Kansas City (AFL) 23, Minnesota (NFL) 7, at Tulane Stadium, New Orleans, Louisiana

1969 AFL

EASTERN DIVISION

	W	L	T	Pct.	Pts.	OP
N.Y. Jets	10	4	0	.714	353	269
Houston	6	6	2	.500	278	279
Boston Patriots	4	10	0	.286	266	316
Buffalo	4	10	0	.286	230	359
Miami	3	10	1	.231	233	332

WESTERN DIVISION

	W	L	T	Pct.	Pts.	OP
Oakland	12	1	1	.923	377	242
Kansas City	11	3	0	.786	359	177
San Diego	8	6	0	.571	288	276
Denver	5	8	1	.385	297	344
Cincinnati	4	9	1	.308	280	367

Divisional playoffs: Kansas City 13, N.Y. JETS 6; OAKLAND 56, Houston 7
AFL championship: Kansas City 17, OAKLAND 7

1968 NFL

EASTERN CONFERENCE

Capitol Division

	W	L	T	Pct.	Pts.	OP
Dallas	12	2	0	.857	431	186
N.Y. Giants	7	7	0	.500	294	325
Washington	5	9	0	.357	249	358
Philadelphia	2	12	0	.143	202	351

Century Division

	W	L	T	Pct.	Pts.	OP
Cleveland	10	4	0	.714	394	273
St. Louis	9	4	1	.692	325	289
New Orleans	4	9	1	.308	246	327
Pittsburgh	2	11	1	.154	244	397

WESTERN CONFERENCE

Coastal Division

	W	L	T	Pct.	Pts.	OP
Baltimore	13	1	0	.929	402	144
Los Angeles	10	3	1	.769	312	200
San Francisco	7	6	1	.538	303	310
Atlanta	2	12	0	.143	170	389

Central Division

	W	L	T	Pct.	Pts.	OP
Minnesota	8	6	0	.571	282	242
Chicago	7	7	0	.500	250	333
Green Bay	6	7	1	.462	281	227
Detroit	4	8	2	.333	207	241

Conference championships: CLEVELAND 31, Dallas 20; BALTIMORE 24, Minnesota 14
NFL championship: Baltimore 34, CLEVELAND 0
Super Bowl III: N.Y. Jets (AFL) 16, Baltimore (NFL) 7, at Orange Bowl, Miami, Florida

1968 AFL

EASTERN DIVISION

	W	L	T	Pct.	Pts.	OP
N.Y. Jets	11	3	0	.786	419	280
Houston	7	7	0	.500	303	248
Miami	5	8	1	.385	276	355
Boston Patriots	4	10	0	.286	229	406
Buffalo	1	12	1	.077	199	367

WESTERN DIVISION

	W	L	T	Pct.	Pts.	OP
Oakland	12	2	0	.857	453	233
Kansas City	12	2	0	.857	371	170
San Diego	9	5	0	.643	382	310
Denver	5	9	0	.357	255	404
Cincinnati	3	11	0	.214	215	329

Western Division playoff: OAKLAND 41, Kansas City 6
AFL championship: N.Y. JETS 27, Oakland 23

1967 NFL

EASTERN CONFERENCE

Capitol Division

	W	L	T	Pct.	Pts.	OP
Dallas	9	5	0	.643	342	268
Philadelphia	6	7	1	.462	351	409
Washington	5	6	3	.455	347	353
New Orleans	3	11	0	.214	233	379

Century Division

	W	L	T	Pct.	Pts.	OP
Cleveland	9	5	0	.643	334	297
N.Y. Giants	7	7	0	.500	369	379
St. Louis	6	7	1	.462	333	356
Pittsburgh	4	9	1	.308	281	320

WESTERN CONFERENCE

Coastal Division

	W	L	T	Pct.	Pts.	OP
Los Angeles	11	1	2	.917	398	196
Baltimore	11	1	2	.917	394	198
San Francisco	7	7	0	.500	273	337
Atlanta	1	12	1	.077	175	422

Central Division

	W	L	T	Pct.	Pts.	OP
Green Bay	9	4	1	.692	332	209
Chicago	7	6	1	.538	239	218
Detroit	5	7	2	.417	260	259
Minnesota	3	8	3	.273	233	294

Los Angeles finished ahead of Baltimore based on better point differential in head-to-head games (net 24 points).
Conference championships: DALLAS 52, Cleveland 14; GREEN BAY 28, Los Angeles 7
NFL championship: GREEN BAY 21, Dallas 17
Super Bowl II: Green Bay (NFL) 33, Oakland (AFL) 14, at Orange Bowl, Miami, Florida

1967 AFL

EASTERN DIVISION

	W	L	T	Pct.	Pts.	OP
Houston	9	4	1	.692	258	199
N.Y. Jets	8	5	1	.615	371	329
Buffalo	4	10	0	.286	237	285
Miami	4	10	0	.286	219	407
Boston Patriots	3	10	1	.231	280	389

WESTERN DIVISION

	W	L	T	Pct.	Pts.	OP
Oakland	13	1	0	.929	468	233
Kansas City	9	5	0	.643	408	254
San Diego	8	5	1	.615	360	352
Denver	3	11	0	.214	256	409

AFL championship: OAKLAND 40, Houston 7

1966 NFL

EASTERN CONFERENCE

	W	L	T	Pct.	Pts.	OP
Dallas	10	3	1	.769	445	239
Cleveland	9	5	0	.643	403	259
Philadelphia	9	5	0	.643	326	340
St. Louis	8	5	1	.615	264	265
Washington	7	7	0	.500	351	355
Pittsburgh	5	8	1	.385	316	347
Atlanta	3	11	0	.214	204	437
N.Y. Giants	1	12	1	.077	263	501

WESTERN CONFERENCE

	W	L	T	Pct.	Pts.	OP
Green Bay	12	2	0	.857	335	163
Baltimore	9	5	0	.643	314	226
Los Angeles	8	6	0	.571	289	212
San Francisco	6	6	2	.500	320	325
Chicago	5	7	2	.417	234	272
Detroit	4	9	1	.308	206	317
Minnesota	4	9	1	.308	292	304

NFL championship: Green Bay 34, DALLAS 27
Super Bowl I: Green Bay (NFL) 35, Kansas City (AFL) 10, at Memorial Coliseum, Los Angeles, California

1966 AFL

EASTERN DIVISION

	W	L	T	Pct.	Pts.	OP
Buffalo	9	4	1	.692	358	255
Boston Patriots	8	4	2	.677	315	283
N.Y. Jets	6	6	2	.500	322	312
Houston	3	11	0	.214	335	396
Miami	3	11	0	.214	213	362

WESTERN DIVISION

	W	L	T	Pct.	Pts.	OP
Kansas City	11	2	1	.846	448	276
Oakland	8	5	1	.615	315	288
San Diego	7	6	1	.538	335	284
Denver	4	10	0	.286	196	381

AFL championship: Kansas City 31, BUFFALO 7

1965 NFL

EASTERN CONFERENCE

	W	L	T	Pct.	Pts.	OP
Cleveland	11	3	0	.786	363	325
Dallas	7	7	0	.500	325	280
N.Y. Giants	7	7	0	.500	270	338
Washington	6	8	0	.429	257	301
Philadelphia	5	9	0	.357	363	359
St. Louis	5	9	0	.357	296	309
Pittsburgh	2	12	0	.143	202	397

WESTERN CONFERENCE

	W	L	T	Pct.	Pts.	OP
Green Bay	10	3	1	.769	316	224
Baltimore	10	3	1	.769	389	284
Chicago	9	5	0	.643	409	275
San Francisco	7	6	1	.538	421	402
Minnesota	7	7	0	.500	383	403
Detroit	6	7	1	.462	257	295
Los Angeles	4	10	0	.286	269	328

Western Conference playoff: GREEN BAY 13, Baltimore 10 (OT)
NFL championship: GREEN BAY 23, Cleveland 12

1965 AFL

EASTERN DIVISION

	W	L	T	Pct.	Pts.	OP
Buffalo	10	3	1	.769	313	226
N.Y. Jets	5	8	1	.385	285	303
Boston Patriots	4	8	2	.333	244	302
Houston	4	10	0	.286	298	429

WESTERN DIVISION

	W	L	T	Pct.	Pts.	OP
San Diego	9	2	3	.818	340	227
Oakland	8	5	1	.615	298	239
Kansas City	7	5	2	.583	322	285
Denver	4	10	0	.286	303	392

AFL championship: Buffalo 23, SAN DIEGO 0

1964 NFL

EASTERN CONFERENCE

	W	L	T	Pct.	Pts.	OP
Cleveland	10	3	1	.769	415	293
St. Louis	9	3	2	.750	357	331
Philadelphia	6	8	0	.429	312	313
Washington	6	8	0	.429	307	305
Dallas	5	8	1	.385	250	289
Pittsburgh	5	9	0	.357	253	315
N.Y. Giants	2	10	2	.167	241	399

WESTERN CONFERENCE

	W	L	T	Pct.	Pts.	OP
Baltimore	12	2	0	.857	428	225
Green Bay	8	5	1	.615	342	245
Minnesota	8	5	1	.615	355	296
Detroit	7	5	2	.583	280	260
Los Angeles	5	7	2	.417	283	339
Chicago	5	9	0	.357	260	379
San Francisco	4	10	0	.286	236	330

NFL championship: CLEVELAND 27, Baltimore 0

1964 AFL

EASTERN DIVISION

	W	L	T	Pct.	Pts.	OP
Buffalo	12	2	0	.857	400	242
Boston Patriots	10	3	1	.769	365	297
N.Y. Jets	5	8	1	.385	278	315
Houston	4	10	0	.286	310	355

WESTERN DIVISION

	W	L	T	Pct.	Pts.	OP
San Diego	8	5	1	.615	341	300
Kansas City	7	7	0	.500	366	306
Oakland	5	7	2	.417	303	350
Denver	2	11	1	.154	240	438

AFL championship: BUFFALO 20, San Diego 7

1963 NFL

EASTERN CONFERENCE

	W	L	T	Pct.	Pts.	OP
N.Y. Giants	11	3	0	.786	448	280
Cleveland	10	4	0	.714	343	262
St. Louis	9	5	0	.643	341	283
Pittsburgh	7	4	3	.636	321	295
Dallas	4	10	0	.286	305	378
Washington	3	11	0	.214	279	398
Philadelphia	2	10	2	.167	242	381

WESTERN CONFERENCE

	W	L	T	Pct.	Pts.	OP
Chicago	11	1	2	.917	301	144
Green Bay	11	2	1	.846	369	206
Baltimore	8	6	0	.571	316	285
Detroit	5	8	1	.385	326	265
Minnesota	5	8	1	.385	309	390
Los Angeles	5	9	0	.357	210	350
San Francisco	2	12	0	.143	198	391

NFL championship: CHICAGO 14, N.Y. Giants 10

1963 AFL

EASTERN DIVISION

	W	L	T	Pct.	Pts.	OP
Boston Patriots	7	6	1	.538	327	257
Buffalo	7	6	1	.538	304	291
Houston	6	8	0	.429	302	372
N.Y. Jets	5	8	1	.385	249	399

WESTERN DIVISION

	W	L	T	Pct.	Pts.	OP
San Diego	11	3	0	.786	399	255
Oakland	10	4	0	.714	363	282
Kansas City	5	7	2	.417	347	263
Denver	2	11	1	.154	301	473

Eastern Division playoff: Boston 26, BUFFALO 8
AFL championship: SAN DIEGO 51, Boston 10

1962 NFL

EASTERN CONFERENCE

	W	L	T	Pct.	Pts.	OP
N.Y. Giants	12	2	0	.857	398	283
Pittsburgh	9	5	0	.643	312	363
Cleveland	7	6	1	.538	291	257
Washington	5	7	2	.417	305	376
Dallas Cowboys	5	8	1	.385	398	402
St. Louis	4	9	1	.308	287	361
Philadelphia	3	10	1	.231	282	356

WESTERN CONFERENCE

	W	L	T	Pct.	Pts.	OP
Green Bay	13	1	0	.929	415	148
Detroit	11	3	0	.786	315	177
Chicago	9	5	0	.643	321	287
Baltimore	7	7	0	.500	293	288
San Francisco	6	8	0	.429	282	331
Minnesota	2	11	1	.154	254	410
Los Angeles	1	12	1	.077	220	334

NFL championship: Green Bay 16, N.Y. GIANTS 7

1962 AFL

EASTERN DIVISION

	W	L	T	Pct.	Pts.	OP
Houston	11	3	0	.786	387	270
Boston Patriots	9	4	1	.692	346	295
Buffalo	7	6	1	.538	309	272
N.Y. Titans	5	9	0	.357	278	423

WESTERN DIVISION

	W	L	T	Pct.	Pts.	OP
Dallas Texans	11	3	0	.786	389	233
Denver	7	7	0	.500	353	334
San Diego	4	10	0	.286	314	392
Oakland	1	13	0	.071	213	370

AFL championship: Dallas Texans 20, HOUSTON 17 (OT)

1961 NFL

EASTERN CONFERENCE

	W	L	T	Pct.	Pts.	OP
N.Y. Giants	10	3	1	.769	368	220
Philadelphia	10	4	0	.714	361	297
Cleveland	8	5	1	.615	319	270
St. Louis	7	7	0	.500	279	267
Pittsburgh	6	8	0	.429	295	287
Dallas Cowboys	4	9	1	.308	236	380
Washington	1	12	1	.077	174	392

WESTERN CONFERENCE

	W	L	T	Pct.	Pts.	OP
Green Bay	11	3	0	.786	391	223
Detroit	8	5	1	.615	270	258
Baltimore	8	6	0	.571	302	307
Chicago	8	6	0	.571	326	302
San Francisco	7	6	1	.538	346	272
Los Angeles	4	10	0	.286	263	333
Minnesota	3	11	0	.214	285	407

NFL championship: GREEN BAY 37, N.Y. Giants 0

1961 AFL

EASTERN DIVISION

	W	L	T	Pct.	Pts.	OP
Houston	10	3	1	.769	513	242
Boston Patriots	9	4	1	.692	413	313
N.Y. Titans	7	7	0	.500	301	390
Buffalo	6	8	0	.429	294	342

WESTERN DIVISION

	W	L	T	Pct.	Pts.	OP
San Diego	12	2	0	.857	396	219
Dallas Texans	6	8	0	.429	334	343
Denver	3	11	0	.214	251	432
Oakland	2	12	0	.143	237	458

AFL championship: Houston 10, SAN DIEGO 3

1960 NFL

EASTERN CONFERENCE

	W	L	T	Pct.	Pts.	OP
Philadelphia	10	2	0	.833	321	246
Cleveland	8	3	1	.727	362	217
N.Y. Giants	6	4	2	.600	271	261
St. Louis	6	5	1	.545	288	230
Pittsburgh	5	6	1	.455	240	275
Washington	1	9	2	.100	178	309

WESTERN CONFERENCE

	W	L	T	Pct.	Pts.	OP
Green Bay	8	4	0	.667	332	209
Detroit	7	5	0	.583	239	212
San Francisco	7	5	0	.583	208	205
Baltimore	6	6	0	.500	288	234
Chicago	5	6	1	.455	194	299
L.A. Rams	4	7	1	.364	265	297
Dallas Cowboys	0	11	1	.000	177	369

NFL championship: PHILADELPHIA 17, Green Bay 13

1960 AFL

EASTERN CONFERENCE

	W	L	T	Pct.	Pts.	OP
Houston	10	4	0	.714	379	285
N.Y. Titans	7	7	0	.500	382	399
Buffalo	5	8	1	.385	296	303
Boston Patriots	5	9	0	.357	286	349

WESTERN CONFERENCE

	W	L	T	Pct.	Pts.	OP
L.A. Chargers	10	4	0	.714	373	336
Dallas Texans	8	6	0	.571	362	253
Oakland	6	8	0	.429	319	388
Denver	4	9	1	.308	309	393

AFL championship: HOUSTON 24, L.A. Chargers 16

1959

EASTERN CONFERENCE	W	L	T	Pct.	Pts.	OP	WESTERN CONFERENCE	W	L	T	Pct.	Pts.	OP
N.Y. Giants	10	2	0	.833	284	170	Baltimore	9	3	0	.750	374	251
Cleveland	7	5	0	.583	270	214	Chi. Bears	8	4	0	.667	252	196
Philadelphia	7	5	0	.583	268	278	Green Bay	7	5	0	.583	248	246
Pittsburgh	6	5	1	.545	257	216	San Francisco	7	5	0	.583	255	237
Washington	3	9	0	.250	185	350	Detroit	3	8	1	.273	203	275
Chi. Cardinals	2	10	0	.167	234	324	Los Angeles	2	10	0	.167	242	315

NFL championship: BALTIMORE 31, N.Y. Giants 16

1958

EASTERN CONFERENCE	W	L	T	Pct.	Pts.	OP	WESTERN CONFERENCE	W	L	T	Pct.	Pts.	OP
N.Y. Giants	9	3	0	.750	246	183	Baltimore	9	3	0	.750	381	203
Cleveland	9	3	0	.750	302	217	Chi. Bears	8	4	0	.667	298	230
Pittsburgh	7	4	1	.636	261	230	Los Angeles	8	4	0	.667	344	278
Washington	4	7	1	.364	214	268	San Francisco	6	6	0	.500	257	324
Chi. Cardinals	2	9	1	.182	261	356	Detroit	4	7	1	.364	261	276
Philadelphia	2	9	1	.182	235	306	Green Bay	1	10	1	.091	193	382

Eastern Conference playoff: N.Y. GIANTS 10, Cleveland 0
NFL championship: Baltimore 23, N.Y. GIANTS 17 (OT)

1957

EASTERN CONFERENCE	W	L	T	Pct.	Pts.	OP	WESTERN CONFERENCE	W	L	T	Pct.	Pts.	OP
Cleveland	9	2	1	.818	269	172	Detroit	8	4	0	.667	251	231
N.Y. Giants	7	5	0	.583	254	211	San Francisco	8	4	0	.667	260	264
Pittsburgh	6	6	0	.500	161	178	Baltimore	7	5	0	.583	303	235
Washington	5	6	1	.455	251	230	Los Angeles	6	6	0	.500	307	278
Philadelphia	4	8	0	.333	173	230	Chi. Bears	5	7	0	.417	203	211
Chi. Cardinals	3	9	0	.250	200	299	Green Bay	3	9	0	.250	218	311

Western Conference playoff: Detroit 31, SAN FRANCISCO 27
NFL championship: DETROIT 59, Cleveland 14

1956

EASTERN CONFERENCE	W	L	T	Pct.	Pts.	OP	WESTERN CONFERENCE	W	L	T	Pct.	Pts.	OP
N.Y. Giants	8	3	1	.727	264	197	Chi. Bears	9	2	1	.818	363	246
Chi. Cardinals	7	5	0	.583	240	182	Detroit	9	3	0	.750	300	188
Washington	6	6	0	.500	183	225	San Francisco	5	6	1	.455	233	284
Cleveland	5	7	0	.417	167	177	Baltimore	5	7	0	.417	270	322
Pittsburgh	5	7	0	.417	217	250	Green Bay	4	8	0	.333	264	342
Philadelphia	3	8	1	.273	143	215	Los Angeles	4	8	0	.333	291	307

NFL championship: N.Y. GIANTS 47, Chi. Bears 7

1955

EASTERN CONFERENCE	W	L	T	Pct.	Pts.	OP	WESTERN CONFERENCE	W	L	T	Pct.	Pts.	OP
Cleveland	9	2	1	.818	349	218	Los Angeles	8	3	1	.727	260	231
Washington	8	4	0	.667	246	222	Chi. Bears	8	4	0	.667	294	251
N.Y. Giants	6	5	1	.545	267	223	Green Bay	6	6	0	.500	258	276
Chi. Cardinals	4	7	1	.364	224	252	Baltimore	5	6	1	.455	214	239
Philadelphia	4	7	1	.364	248	231	San Francisco	4	8	0	.333	216	298
Pittsburgh	4	8	0	.333	195	285	Detroit	3	9	0	.250	230	275

NFL championship: Cleveland 38, LOS ANGELES 14

1954

EASTERN CONFERENCE	W	L	T	Pct.	Pts.	OP	WESTERN CONFERENCE	W	L	T	Pct.	Pts.	OP
Cleveland	9	3	0	.750	336	162	Detroit	9	2	1	.818	337	189
Philadelphia	7	4	1	.636	284	230	Chi. Bears	8	4	0	.667	301	279
N.Y. Giants	7	5	0	.583	293	184	San Francisco	7	4	1	.636	313	251
Pittsburgh	5	7	0	.417	219	263	Los Angeles	6	5	1	.545	314	285
Washington	3	9	0	.250	207	432	Green Bay	4	8	0	.333	234	251
Chi. Cardinals	2	10	0	.167	183	347	Baltimore	3	9	0	.250	131	279

NFL championship: CLEVELAND 56, Detroit 10

1953

EASTERN CONFERENCE	W	L	T	Pct.	Pts.	OP	WESTERN CONFERENCE	W	L	T	Pct.	Pts.	OP
Cleveland	11	1	0	.917	348	162	Detroit	10	2	0	.833	271	205
Philadelphia	7	4	1	.636	352	215	San Francisco	9	3	0	.750	372	237
Washington	6	5	1	.545	208	215	Los Angeles	8	3	1	.727	366	236
Pittsburgh	6	6	0	.500	211	263	Chi. Bears	3	8	1	.273	218	262
N.Y. Giants	3	9	0	.250	179	277	Baltimore	3	9	0	.250	182	350
Chi. Cardinals	1	10	1	.091	190	337	Green Bay	2	9	1	.182	200	338

NFL championship: DETROIT 17, Cleveland 16

1952

AMERICAN CONFERENCE	W	L	T	Pct.	Pts.	OP	NATIONAL CONFERENCE	W	L	T	Pct.	Pts.	OP
Cleveland	8	4	0	.667	310	213	Detroit	9	3	0	.750	344	192
N.Y. Giants	7	5	0	.583	234	231	Los Angeles	9	3	0	.750	349	234
Philadelphia	7	5	0	.583	252	271	San Francisco	7	5	0	.583	285	221
Pittsburgh	5	7	0	.417	300	273	Green Bay	6	6	0	.500	295	312
Chi. Cardinals	4	8	0	.333	172	221	Chi. Bears	5	7	0	.417	245	326
Washington	4	8	0	.333	240	287	Dallas Texans	1	11	0	.083	182	427

National Conference playoff: DETROIT 31, Los Angeles 21
NFL championship: Detroit 17, CLEVELAND 7

1951

AMERICAN CONFERENCE	W	L	T	Pct.	Pts.	OP	NATIONAL CONFERENCE	W	L	T	Pct.	Pts.	OP
Cleveland	11	1	0	.917	331	152	Los Angeles	8	4	0	.667	392	261
N.Y. Giants	9	2	1	.818	254	161	Detroit	7	4	1	.636	336	259
Washington	5	7	0	.417	183	296	San Francisco	7	4	1	.636	255	205
Pittsburgh	4	7	1	.364	183	235	Chi. Bears	7	5	0	.583	286	282
Philadelphia	4	8	0	.333	234	264	Green Bay	3	9	0	.250	254	375
Chi. Cardinals	3	9	0	.250	210	287	N.Y. Yanks	1	9	2	.100	241	382

NFL championship: LOS ANGELES 24, Cleveland 17

1950

AMERICAN CONFERENCE	W	L	T	Pct.	Pts.	OP	NATIONAL CONFERENCE	W	L	T	Pct.	Pts.	OP
Cleveland	10	2	0	.833	310	144	Los Angeles	9	3	0	.750	466	309
N.Y. Giants	10	2	0	.833	268	150	Chi. Bears	9	3	0	.750	279	207
Philadelphia	6	6	0	.500	254	141	N.Y. Yanks	7	5	0	.583	366	367
Pittsburgh	6	6	0	.500	180	195	Detroit	6	6	0	.500	321	285
Chi. Cardinals	5	7	0	.417	233	287	Green Bay	3	9	0	.250	244	406
Washington	3	9	0	.250	232	326	San Francisco	3	9	0	.250	213	300
							Baltimore	1	11	0	.083	213	462

American Conference playoff: CLEVELAND 8, N.Y. Giants 3
National Conference playoff: LOS ANGELES 24, Chi. Bears 14
NFL championship: CLEVELAND 30, Los Angeles 28

1949

EASTERN DIVISION	W	L	T	Pct.	Pts.	OP	WESTERN DIVISION	W	L	T	Pct.	Pts.	OP
Philadelphia	11	1	0	.917	364	134	Los Angeles	8	2	2	.800	360	239
Pittsburgh	6	5	1	.545	224	214	Chi. Bears	9	3	0	.750	332	218
N.Y. Giants	6	6	0	.500	287	298	Chi. Cardinals	6	5	1	.545	360	301
Washington	4	7	1	.364	268	339	Detroit	4	8	0	.333	237	259
N.Y. Bulldogs	1	10	1	.091	153	368	Green Bay	2	10	0	.167	114	329

NFL championship: Philadelphia 14, LOS ANGELES 0

1948

EASTERN DIVISION	W	L	T	Pct.	Pts.	OP	WESTERN DIVISION	W	L	T	Pct.	Pts.	OP
Philadelphia	9	2	1	.818	376	156	Chi. Cardinals	11	1	0	.917	395	226
Washington	7	5	0	.583	291	287	Chi. Bears	10	2	0	.833	375	151
N.Y. Giants	4	8	0	.333	297	388	Los Angeles	6	5	1	.545	327	269
Pittsburgh	4	8	0	.333	200	243	Green Bay	3	9	0	.250	154	290
Boston	3	9	0	.250	174	372	Detroit	2	10	0	.167	200	407

NFL championship: PHILADELPHIA 7, Chi. Cardinals 0

1947

EASTERN DIVISION	W	L	T	Pct.	Pts.	OP	WESTERN DIVISION	W	L	T	Pct.	Pts.	OP
Philadelphia	8	4	0	.667	308	242	Chi. Cardinals	9	3	0	.750	306	231
Pittsburgh	8	4	0	.667	240	259	Chi. Bears	8	4	0	.667	363	241
Boston	4	7	1	.364	168	256	Green Bay	6	5	1	.545	274	210
Washington	4	8	0	.333	295	367	Los Angeles	6	6	0	.500	259	214
N.Y. Giants	2	8	2	.200	190	309	Detroit	3	9	0	.250	231	305

Eastern Division playoff: Philadelphia 21, PITTSBURGH 0
NFL championship: CHI. CARDINALS 28, Philadelphia 21

1946

EASTERN DIVISION	W	L	T	Pct.	Pts.	OP	WESTERN DIVISION	W	L	T	Pct.	Pts.	OP
N.Y. Giants	7	3	1	.700	236	162	Chi. Bears	8	2	1	.800	289	193
Philadelphia	6	5	0	.545	231	220	Los Angeles	6	4	1	.600	277	257
Washington	5	5	1	.500	171	191	Green Bay	6	5	0	.545	148	158
Pittsburgh	5	5	1	.500	136	117	Chi. Cardinals	6	5	0	.545	260	198
Boston	2	8	1	.200	189	273	Detroit	1	10	0	.091	142	310

NFL championship: Chi. Bears 24, N.Y. GIANTS 14

1945

EASTERN DIVISION	W	L	T	Pct.	Pts.	OP	WESTERN DIVISION	W	L	T	Pct.	Pts.	OP
Washington	8	2	0	.800	209	121	Cleveland	9	1	0	.900	244	136
Philadelphia	7	3	0	.700	272	133	Detroit	7	3	0	.700	195	194
N.Y. Giants	3	6	1	.333	179	198	Green Bay	6	4	0	.600	258	173
Boston	3	6	1	.333	123	211	Chi. Bears	3	7	0	.300	192	235
Pittsburgh	2	8	0	.200	79	220	Chi. Cardinals	1	9	0	.100	98	228

NFL championship: CLEVELAND 15, Washington 14

1944

EASTERN DIVISION	W	L	T	Pct.	Pts.	OP	WESTERN DIVISION	W	L	T	Pct.	Pts.	OP
N.Y. Giants	8	1	1	.889	206	75	Green Bay	8	2	0	.800	238	141
Philadelphia	7	1	2	.875	267	131	Chi. Bears	6	3	1	.667	258	172
Washington	6	3	1	.667	169	180	Detroit	6	3	1	.667	216	151
Boston	2	8	0	.200	82	233	Cleveland	4	6	0	.400	188	224
Brooklyn	0	10	0	.000	69	166	Card-Pitt	0	10	0	.000	108	328

NFL championship: Green Bay 14, N.Y. GIANTS 7

1943

EASTERN DIVISION	W	L	T	Pct.	Pts.	OP	WESTERN DIVISION	W	L	T	Pct.	Pts.	OP
Washington	6	3	1	.667	229	137	Chi. Bears	8	1	1	.889	303	157
N.Y. Giants	6	3	1	.667	197	170	Green Bay	7	2	1	.778	264	172
Phil-Pitt	5	4	1	.556	225	230	Detroit	3	6	1	.333	178	218
Brooklyn	2	8	0	.200	65	234	Chi. Cardinals	0	10	0	.000	95	238

Eastern Division playoff: Washington 28, N.Y. GIANTS 0
NFL championship: CHI. BEARS 41, Washington 21

1942

EASTERN DIVISION	W	L	T	Pct.	Pts.	OP	WESTERN DIVISION	W	L	T	Pct.	Pts.	OP
Washington	10	1	0	.909	227	102	Chi. Bears	11	0	0	1.000	376	84
Pittsburgh	7	4	0	.636	167	119	Green Bay	8	2	1	.800	300	215
N.Y. Giants	5	5	1	.500	155	139	Cleveland	5	6	0	.455	150	207
Brooklyn	3	8	0	.273	100	168	Chi. Cardinals	3	8	0	.273	98	209
Philadelphia	2	9	0	.182	134	239	Detroit	0	11	0	.000	38	263

NFL championship: WASHINGTON 14, Chi. Bears 6

1941

EASTERN DIVISION	W	L	T	Pct.	Pts.	OP	WESTERN DIVISION	W	L	T	Pct.	Pts.	OP
N.Y. Giants	8	3	0	.727	238	114	Chi. Bears	10	1	0	.909	396	147
Brooklyn	7	4	0	.636	158	127	Green Bay	10	1	0	.909	258	120
Washington	6	5	0	.545	176	174	Detroit	4	6	1	.400	121	195
Philadelphia	2	8	1	.200	119	218	Chi. Cardinals	3	7	1	.300	127	197
Pittsburgh	1	9	1	.100	103	276	Cleveland	2	9	0	.182	116	244

Western Division playoff: CHI. BEARS 33, Green Bay 14
NFL championship: CHI. BEARS 37, N.Y. Giants 9

1940

EASTERN DIVISION	W	L	T	Pct.	Pts.	OP	WESTERN DIVISION	W	L	T	Pct.	Pts.	OP
Washington	9	2	0	.818	245	142	Chi. Bears	8	3	0	.727	238	152
Brooklyn	8	3	0	.727	186	120	Green Bay	6	4	1	.600	238	155
N.Y. Giants	6	4	1	.600	131	133	Detroit	5	5	1	.500	138	153
Pittsburgh	2	7	2	.222	60	178	Cleveland	4	6	1	.400	171	191
Philadelphia	1	10	0	.091	111	211	Chi. Cardinals	2	7	2	.222	139	222

NFL championship: Chi. Bears 73, WASHINGTON 0

1939

EASTERN DIVISION	W	L	T	Pct.	Pts.	OP	WESTERN DIVISION	W	L	T	Pct.	Pts.	OP
N.Y. Giants	9	1	1	.900	168	85	Green Bay	9	2	0	.818	233	153
Washington	8	2	1	.800	242	94	Chi. Bears	8	3	0	.727	298	157
Brooklyn	4	6	1	.400	108	219	Detroit	6	5	0	.545	145	150
Philadelphia	1	9	1	.100	105	200	Cleveland	5	5	1	.500	195	164
Pittsburgh	1	9	1	.100	114	216	Chi. Cardinals	1	10	0	.091	84	254

NFL championship: GREEN BAY 27, N.Y. Giants 0

1938

EASTERN DIVISION	W	L	T	Pct.	Pts.	OP	WESTERN DIVISION	W	L	T	Pct.	Pts.	OP
N.Y. Giants	8	2	1	.800	194	79	Green Bay	8	3	0	.727	223	118
Washington	6	3	2	.667	148	154	Detroit	7	4	0	.636	119	108
Brooklyn	4	4	3	.500	131	161	Chi. Bears	6	5	0	.545	194	148
Philadelphia	5	6	0	.455	154	164	Cleveland	4	7	0	.364	131	215
Pittsburgh	2	9	0	.182	79	169	Chi. Cardinals	2	9	0	.182	111	168

NFL championship: N.Y. GIANTS 23, Green Bay 17

1937

EASTERN DIVISION

	W	L	T	Pct.	Pts.	OP
Washington	8	3	0	.727	195	120
N.Y. Giants	6	3	2	.667	128	109
Pittsburgh	4	7	0	.364	122	145
Brooklyn	3	7	1	.300	82	174
Philadelphia	2	8	1	.200	86	177

WESTERN DIVISION

	W	L	T	Pct.	Pts.	OP
Chi. Bears	9	1	1	.900	201	100
Green Bay	7	4	0	.636	220	122
Detroit	7	4	0	.636	180	105
Chi. Cardinals	5	5	1	.500	135	165
Cleveland	1	10	0	.091	75	207

NFL championship: Washington 28, CHI. BEARS 21

1936

EASTERN DIVISION

	W	L	T	Pct.	Pts.	OP
Boston	7	5	0	.583	149	110
Pittsburgh	6	6	0	.500	98	187
N.Y. Giants	5	6	1	.455	115	163
Brooklyn	3	8	1	.273	92	161
Philadelphia	1	11	0	.083	51	206

WESTERN DIVISION

	W	L	T	Pct.	Pts.	OP
Green Bay	10	1	1	.909	248	118
Chi. Bears	9	3	0	.750	222	94
Detroit	8	4	0	.667	235	102
Chi. Cardinals	3	8	1	.273	74	143

NFL championship: Green Bay 21, Boston 6, at Polo Grounds, N.Y.

1935

EASTERN DIVISION

	W	L	T	Pct.	Pts.	OP
N.Y. Giants	9	3	0	.750	180	96
Brooklyn	5	6	1	.455	90	141
Pittsburgh	4	8	0	.333	100	209
Boston	2	8	1	.200	65	123
Philadelphia	2	9	0	.182	60	179

WESTERN DIVISION

	W	L	T	Pct.	Pts.	OP
Detroit	7	3	2	.700	191	111
Green Bay	8	4	0	.667	181	96
Chi. Bears	6	4	2	.600	192	106
Chi. Cardinals	6	4	2	.600	99	97

NFL championship: DETROIT 26, N.Y. Giants 7
One game between Boston and Philadelphia was canceled.

1934

EASTERN DIVISION

	W	L	T	Pct.	Pts.	OP
N.Y. Giants	8	5	0	.615	147	107
Boston	6	6	0	.500	107	94
Brooklyn	4	7	0	.364	61	153
Philadelphia	4	7	0	.364	127	85
Pittsburgh	2	10	0	.167	51	206

WESTERN DIVISION

	W	L	T	Pct.	Pts.	OP
Chi. Bears	13	0	0	1.000	286	86
Detroit	10	3	0	.769	238	59
Green Bay	7	6	0	.538	156	112
Chi. Cardinals	5	6	0	.455	80	84
St. Louis	1	2	0	.333	27	61
Cincinnati	0	8	0	.000	10	243

NFL championship: N.Y. GIANTS 30, Chi. Bears 13

1933

EASTERN DIVISION

	W	L	T	Pct.	Pts.	OP
N.Y. Giants	11	3	0	.786	244	101
Brooklyn	5	4	1	.556	93	54
Boston	5	5	2	.500	103	97
Philadelphia	3	5	1	.375	77	158
Pittsburgh	3	6	2	.333	67	208

WESTERN DIVISION

	W	L	T	Pct.	Pts.	OP
Chi. Bears	10	2	1	.833	133	82
Portsmouth	6	5	0	.545	128	87
Green Bay	5	7	1	.417	170	107
Cincinnati	3	6	1	.333	38	110
Chi. Cardinals	1	9	1	.100	52	101

NFL championship: CHI. BEARS 23, N.Y. Giants 21

1932

	W	L	T	Pct.
Chicago Bears	7	1	6	.875
Green Bay Packers	10	3	1	.769
Portsmouth Spartans	6	2	4	.750
Boston Braves	4	4	2	.500
New York Giants	4	6	2	.400
Brooklyn Dodgers	3	9	0	.250
Chicago Cardinals	2	6	2	.250
Staten Island Stapletons	2	7	3	.222

Chicago Bears and Portsmouth finished regularly scheduled games tied for first place. Bears won playoff game, which counted in standings, 9-0.

1931

	W	L	T	Pct.
Green Bay Packers	12	2	0	.857
Portsmouth Spartans	11	3	0	.786
Chicago Bears	8	5	0	.615
Chicago Cardinals	5	4	0	.556
New York Giants	7	6	1	.538
Providence Steam Roller	4	4	3	.500
Staten Island Stapletons	4	6	1	.400
Cleveland Indians	2	8	0	.200
Brooklyn Dodgers	2	12	0	.143
Frankford Yellow Jackets	1	6	1	.143

1930

	W	L	T	Pct.
Green Bay Packers	10	3	1	.769
New York Giants	13	4	0	.765
Chicago Bears	9	4	1	.692
Brooklyn Dodgers	7	4	1	.636
Providence Steam Roller	6	4	1	.600
Staten Island Stapletons	5	5	2	.500
Chicago Cardinals	5	6	2	.455
Portsmouth Spartans	5	6	3	.455
Frankford Yellow Jackets	4	13	1	.222
Minneapolis Red Jackets	1	7	1	.125
Newark Tornadoes	1	10	1	.091

1929

	W	L	T	Pct.
Green Bay Packers	12	0	1	1.000
New York Giants	13	1	1	.929
Frankford Yellow Jackets	10	4	5	.714
Chicago Cardinals	6	6	1	.500
Boston Bulldogs	4	4	0	.500
Staten Island Stapletons	3	4	3	.429
Providence Steam Roller	4	6	2	.400
Orange Tornadoes	3	5	4	.375
Chicago Bears	4	9	2	.308
Buffalo Bisons	1	7	1	.125
Minneapolis Red Jackets	1	9	0	.100
Dayton Triangles	0	6	0	.000

1928

	W	L	T	Pct.
Providence Steam Roller	8	1	2	.889
Frankford Yellow Jackets	11	3	2	.786
Detroit Wolverines	7	2	1	.778
Green Bay Packers	6	4	3	.600
Chicago Bears	7	5	1	.583
New York Giants	4	7	2	.364
New York Yankees	4	8	1	.333
Pottsville Maroons	2	8	0	.200
Chicago Cardinals	1	5	0	.167
Dayton Triangles	0	7	0	.000

1927

	W	L	T	Pct.
New York Giants	11	1	1	.917
Green Bay Packers	7	2	1	.778
Chicago Bears	9	3	2	.750
Cleveland Bulldogs	8	4	1	.667
Providence Steam Roller	8	5	1	.615
New York Yankees	7	8	1	.467
Frankford Yellow Jackets	6	9	3	.400
Pottsville Maroons	5	8	0	.385
Chicago Cardinals	3	7	1	.300
Dayton Triangles	1	6	1	.143
Duluth Eskimos	1	8	0	.111
Buffalo Bisons	0	5	0	.000

1926

	W	L	T	Pct.
Frankford Yellow Jackets	14	1	2	.933
Chicago Bears	12	1	3	.923
Pottsville Maroons	10	2	2	.833
Kansas City Cowboys	8	3	0	.727
Green Bay Packers	7	3	3	.700
Los Angeles Buccaneers	6	3	1	.667
New York Giants	8	4	1	.667
Duluth Eskimos	6	5	3	.545
Buffalo Rangers	4	4	2	.500
Chicago Cardinals	5	6	1	.455
Providence Steam Roller	5	7	1	.417
Detroit Panthers	4	6	2	.400
Hartford Blues	3	7	0	.300
Brooklyn Lions	3	8	0	.273
Milwaukee Badgers	2	7	0	.222
Akron Indians	1	4	3	.200
Dayton Triangles	1	4	1	.200
Racine Tornadoes	1	4	0	.200
Columbus Tigers	1	6	0	.143
Canton Bulldogs	1	9	3	.100
Hammond Pros	0	4	0	.000
Louisville Colonels	0	4	0	.000

1925

	W	L	T	Pct.
Chicago Cardinals	11	2	1	.846
Pottsville Maroons	10	2	0	.833
Detroit Panthers	8	2	2	.800
New York Giants	8	4	0	.667
Akron Indians	4	2	2	.667
Frankford Yellow Jackets	13	7	0	.650
Chicago Bears	9	5	3	.643
Rock Island Independents	5	3	3	.625
Green Bay Packers	8	5	0	.615
Providence Steam Roller	6	5	1	.545
Canton Bulldogs	4	4	0	.500
Cleveland Bulldogs	5	8	1	.385
Kansas City Cowboys	2	5	1	.286
Hammond Pros	1	4	0	.200
Buffalo Bisons	1	6	2	.143
Duluth Kelleys	0	3	0	.000
Rochester Jeffersons	0	6	1	.000
Milwaukee Badgers	0	6	0	.000
Dayton Triangles	0	7	1	.000
Columbus Tigers	0	9	0	.000

1924

	W	L	T	Pct.
Cleveland Bulldogs	7	1	1	.875
Chicago Bears	6	1	4	.857
Frankford Yellow Jackets	11	2	1	.846
Duluth Kelleys	5	1	0	.833
Rock Island Independents	5	2	2	.714
Green Bay Packers	7	4	0	.636
Racine Legion	4	3	3	.571
Chicago Cardinals	5	4	1	.556
Buffalo Bisons	6	5	0	.545
Columbus Tigers	4	4	0	.500
Hammond Pros	2	2	1	.500
Milwaukee Badgers	5	8	0	.385
Akron Indians	2	6	0	.250
Dayton Triangles	2	6	0	.250
Kansas City Blues	2	7	0	.222
Kenosha Maroons	0	4	1	.000
Minneapolis Marines	0	6	0	.000
Rochester Jeffersons	0	7	0	.000

1923

	W	L	T	Pct.
Canton Bulldogs	11	0	1	1.000
Chicago Bears	9	2	1	.818
Green Bay Packers	7	2	1	.778
Milwaukee Badgers	7	2	3	.778
Cleveland Indians	3	1	3	.750
Chicago Cardinals	8	4	0	.667
Duluth Kelleys	4	3	0	.571
Buffalo All-Americans	5	4	3	.556
Columbus Tigers	5	4	1	.556
Racine Legion	4	4	2	.500
Toledo Maroons	3	3	2	.500
Rock Island Independents	2	3	3	.400
Minneapolis Marines	2	5	2	.286
St. Louis All-Stars	1	4	2	.200
Hammond Pros	1	5	1	.167
Dayton Triangles	1	6	1	.143
Akron Indians	1	6	0	.143
Oorang Indians	1	10	0	.091
Louisville Brecks	0	3	0	.000
Rochester Jeffersons	0	4	0	.000

1922

	W	L	T	Pct.
Canton Bulldogs	10	0	2	1.000
Chicago Bears	9	3	0	.750
Chicago Cardinals	8	3	0	.727
Toledo Maroons	5	2	2	.714
Rock Island Independents	4	2	1	.667
Racine Legion	6	4	1	.600
Dayton Triangles	4	3	1	.571
Green Bay Packers	4	3	3	.571
Buffalo All-Americans	5	4	1	.556
Akron Pros	3	5	2	.375
Milwaukee Badgers	2	4	3	.333
Oorang Indians	3	6	0	.333
Minneapolis Marines	1	3	0	.250
Louisville Brecks	1	3	0	.250
Evansville Crimson Giants	0	3	0	.000
Rochester Jeffersons	0	4	1	.000
Hammond Pros	0	5	1	.000
Columbus Panhandles	0	8	0	.000

1921

	W	L	T	Pct.
Chicago Staleys	9	1	1	.900
Buffalo All-Americans	9	1	2	.900
Akron Pros	8	3	1	.727
Canton Bulldogs	5	2	3	.714
Rock Island Independents	4	2	1	.667
Evansville Crimson Giants	3	2	0	.600
Green Bay Packers	3	2	1	.600
Dayton Triangles	4	4	1	.500
Chicago Cardinals	3	3	2	.500
Rochester Jeffersons	2	3	0	.400
Cleveland Indians	3	5	0	.375
Washington Senators	1	2	0	.333
Cincinnati Celts	1	3	0	.250
Hammond Pros	1	3	1	.250
Minneapolis Marines	1	3	0	.250
Detroit Tigers	1	5	1	.167
Columbus Panhandles	1	8	0	.111
Tonawanda Kardex	0	1	0	.000
Muncie Flyers	0	2	0	.000
Louisville Brecks	0	2	0	.000
New York Giants	0	2	0	.000

1920*

	W	L	T	Pct.
Akron Pros	8	0	3	1.000
Decatur Staleys	10	1	2	.909
Buffalo All-Americans	9	1	1	.900
Chicago Cardinals	6	2	2	.750
Rock Island Independents	6	2	2	.750
Dayton Triangles	5	2	2	.714
Rochester Jeffersons	6	3	2	.667
Canton Bulldogs	7	4	2	.636
Detroit Heralds	2	3	3	.400
Cleveland Tigers	2	4	2	.333
Chicago Tigers	2	5	1	.286
Hammond Pros	2	5	0	.286
Columbus Panhandles	2	6	2	.250
Muncie Flyers	0	1	0	.000

**No official standings were maintained for the 1920 season, and the championship was awarded to the Akron Pros in a League meeting on April 30, 1921. Clubs played schedules that included games against nonleague opponents.*

RS=REGULAR SEASON
PS=POSTSEASON

***ARIZONA vs. ATLANTA**
RS: Cardinals lead series, 14-10
PS: Cardinals lead series, 1-0
1966—Falcons, 16-10 (A)
1968—Cardinals, 17-12 (StL)
1971—Cardinals, 26-9 (A)
1973—Cardinals, 32-10 (A)
1975—Cardinals, 23-20 (StL)
1978—Cardinals, 42-21 (StL)
1980—Falcons, 33-27 (StL) OT
1981—Falcons, 41-20 (A)
1982—Cardinals, 23-20 (A)
1986—Falcons, 33-13 (A)
1987—Cardinals, 34-21 (A)
1989—Cardinals, 34-20 (P)
1990—Cardinals, 24-13 (A)
1991—Cardinals, 16-10 (P)
1992—Falcons, 20-17 (A)
1993—Cardinals, 27-10 (A)
1994—Falcons, 10-6 (Atl)
1995—Cardinals, 40-37 (Ariz) OT
1997—Cardinals, 29-26 (Ariz)
1999—Falcons, 37-14 (Atl)
2001—Falcons, 34-14 (Ariz)
2004—Falcons, 6-3 (Atl)
2006—Falcons, 32-10 (Atl)
2007—Cardinals, 30-27 (Ariz) OT
2008—**Cardinals, 30-24 (Ariz)
(RS Pts.—Cardinals 531, Falcons 518)
(PS Pts.—Cardinals 30, Falcons 24)
**Franchise known as Phoenix prior to 1994 and in St. Louis prior to 1988*
***NFC First-Round Playoff*

***ARIZONA vs. BALTIMORE**
RS: Ravens lead series, 3-1
1997—Cardinals, 16-13 (B)
2000—Ravens, 13-7 (A)
2003—Ravens, 26-18 (A)
2007—Ravens, 26-23 (B)
(RS Pts.—Ravens 78, Cardinals 64)

***ARIZONA vs. BUFFALO**
RS: Bills lead series, 5-4
1971—Cardinals, 28-23 (B)
1975—Bills, 32-14 (StL)
1981—Cardinals, 24-0 (StL)
1984—Cardinals, 37-7 (StL)
1986—Bills, 17-10 (B)
1990—Bills, 45-14 (B)
1999—Bills, 31-21 (A)
2004—Bills, 38-14 (B)
2008—Cardinals, 41-17 (A)
(RS Pts.—Bills 210, Cardinals 203)
**Franchise known as Phoenix prior to 1994 and in St. Louis prior to 1988*

ARIZONA vs. CAROLINA
RS: Panthers lead series, 7-2
PS: Cardinals lead series, 1-0
1995—Panthers, 27-7 (C)
2001—Cardinals, 30-7 (C)
2002—Cardinals, 16-13 (C)
2003—Panthers, 20-17 (A)
2004—Panthers, 35-10 (C)
2005—Panthers, 24-20 (A)
2007—Panthers, 25-10 (A)
2008—Panthers, 27-23 (C)
*Cardinals, 33-13 (C)
2009—Panthers, 34-21 (A)
(RS Pts.—Panthers 212, Cardinals 154)
(PS Pts.—Cardinals 33, Panthers 13)
**NFC Divisional Playoff*

***ARIZONA vs. **CHICAGO**
RS: Bears lead series, 55-27-6
(NP denotes Normal Park;
Wr denotes Wrigley Field;
Co denotes Comiskey Park;
So denotes Soldier Field;
all Chicago)
1920—Cardinals, 7-6 (NP)
Staleys, 10-0 (Wr)
1921—Tie, 0-0 (Wr)
1922—Cardinals, 6-0 (Co)
Cardinals, 9-0 (Co)
1923—Bears, 3-0 (Wr)
1924—Bears, 6-0 (Wr)
Bears, 21-0 (Co)
1925—Cardinals, 9-0 (Co)
Tie, 0-0 (Wr)
1926—Bears, 16-0 (Wr)
Bears, 10-0 (So)
Tie, 0-0 (Wr)
1927—Bears, 9-0 (NP)
Cardinals, 3-0 (Wr)
1928—Bears, 15-0 (NP)
Bears, 34-0 (Wr)
1929—Tie, 0-0 (Wr)
Cardinals, 40-6 (Co)
1930—Bears, 32-6 (Co)
Bears, 6-0 (Wr)
1931—Bears, 26-13 (Wr)
Bears, 18-7 (Wr)
1932—Tie, 0-0 (Wr)
Bears, 34-0 (Wr)
1933—Bears, 12-9 (Wr)
Bears, 22-6 (Wr)
1934—Bears, 20-0 (Wr)
Bears, 17-6 (Wr)
1935—Tie, 7-7 (Wr)
Bears, 13-0 (Wr)
1936—Bears, 7-3 (Wr)
Cardinals, 14-7 (Wr)
1937—Bears, 16-7 (Wr)
Bears, 42-28 (Wr)
1938—Bears, 16-13 (So)
Bears, 34-28 (Wr)
1939—Bears, 44-7 (Wr)
Bears, 48-7 (Co)
1940—Cardinals, 21-7 (Co)
Bears, 31-23 (Wr)
1941—Bears, 53-7 (Wr)
Bears, 34-24 (Co)
1942—Bears, 41-14 (Wr)
Bears, 21-7 (Co)
1943—Bears, 20-0 (Wr)
Bears, 35-24 (Co)
1945—Cardinals, 16-7 (Wr)
Bears, 28-20 (Co)
1946—Bears, 34-17 (Co)
Cardinals, 35-28 (Wr)
1947—Cardinals, 31-7 (Co)
Cardinals, 30-21 (Wr)
1948—Bears, 28-17 (Co)
Cardinals, 24-21 (Wr)
1949—Bears, 17-7 (Co)
Bears, 52-21 (Wr)
1950—Bears, 27-6 (Wr)
Cardinals, 20-10 (Co)
1951—Cardinals, 28-14 (Co)
Cardinals, 24-14 (Wr)
1952—Cardinals, 21-10 (Co)
Bears, 10-7 (Wr)
1953—Cardinals, 24-17 (Wr)
1954—Bears, 29-7 (Co)
1955—Cardinals, 53-14 (Co)
1956—Bears, 10-3 (Wr)
1957—Bears, 14-6 (Co)
1958—Bears, 30-14 (Wr)
1959—Bears, 31-7 (So)
1965—Bears, 34-13 (Wr)
1966—Cardinals, 24-17 (StL)
1967—Bears, 30-3 (Wr)
1969—Cardinals, 20-17 (StL)
1972—Bears, 27-10 (StL)
1975—Cardinals, 34-20 (So)
1977—Cardinals, 16-13 (StL)
1978—Bears, 17-10 (So)
1979—Bears, 42-6 (So)
1982—Cardinals, 10-7 (So)
1984—Cardinals, 38-21 (StL)
1990—Bears, 31-21 (P)
1994—Bears, 19-16 (A) OT
1998—Cardinals, 20-7 (A)
2001—Bears, 20-13 (C)
2003—Bears, 28-3 (C)
2006—Bears, 24-23 (A)
2009—Cardinals, 41-21 (C)
(RS Pts.—Bears 1,667, Cardinals 1,114)
**Franchise known as Phoenix prior to 1994, in St. Louis prior to 1988, and in Chicago prior to 1960*
***Franchise in Decatur prior to 1921 and known as Staleys prior to 1922*

***ARIZONA vs. CINCINNATI**
RS: Bengals lead series, 5-4
1973—Bengals, 42-24 (C)
1979—Bengals, 34-28 (C)
1985—Cardinals, 41-27 (StL)
1988—Bengals, 21-14 (C)
1994—Cardinals, 28-7 (A)
1997—Bengals, 24-21 (C)
2000—Bengals, 24-13 (C)
2003—Cardinals, 17-14 (A)
2007—Cardinals, 35-27 (C)
(RS Pts.—Cardinals 221, Bengals 220)
**Franchise known as Phoenix prior to 1994 and in St. Louis prior to 1988*

***ARIZONA vs. CLEVELAND**
RS: Browns lead series, 33-12-3
1950—Browns, 34-24 (Cle)
Browns, 10-7 (Chi)
1951—Browns, 34-17 (Chi)
Browns, 49-28 (Cle)
1952—Browns, 28-13 (Cle)
Browns, 10-0 (Chi)
1953—Browns, 27-7 (Chi)
Browns, 27-16 (Cle)
1954—Browns, 31-7 (Cle)
Browns, 35-3 (Chi)
1955—Browns, 26-20 (Chi)
Browns, 35-24 (Cle)
1956—Cardinals, 9-7 (Chi)
Cardinals, 24-7 (Cle)
1957—Browns, 17-7 (Chi)
Browns, 31-0 (Cle)
1958—Browns, 35-28 (Cle)
Browns, 38-24 (Chi)
1959—Browns, 34-7 (Chi)
Browns, 17-7 (Cle)
1960—Browns, 28-27 (Cle)
Tie, 17-17 (StL)
1961—Browns, 20-17 (Cle)
Browns, 21-10 (StL)

1962—Browns, 34-7 (StL)
Browns, 38-14 (Cle)
1963—Cardinals, 20-14 (Cle)
Browns, 24-10 (StL)
1964—Tie, 33-33 (Cle)
Cardinals, 28-19 (StL)
1965—Cardinals, 49-13 (Cle)
Browns, 27-24 (StL)
1966—Cardinals, 34-28 (Cle)
Browns, 38-10 (StL)
1967—Browns, 20-16 (Cle)
Browns, 20-16 (StL)
1968—Cardinals, 27-21 (Cle)
Cardinals, 27-16 (StL)
1969—Tie, 21-21 (Cle)
Browns, 27-21 (StL)
1974—Cardinals, 29-7 (StL)
1979—Browns, 38-20 (StL)
1985—Cardinals, 27-24 (Cle) OT
1988—Browns, 29-21 (P)
1994—Browns, 32-0 (Cle)
2000—Cardinals, 29-21 (A)
2003—Browns, 44-6 (Cle)
2007—Cardinals, 27-21 (A)
(RS Pts.—Browns 1,227, Cardinals 859)
Franchise known as Phoenix prior to 1994, in St. Louis prior to 1988, and in Chicago prior to 1960

***ARIZONA vs. DALLAS**
RS: Cowboys lead series, 55-28-1
PS: Cardinals lead series, 1-0
1960—Cardinals, 12-10 (StL)
1961—Cardinals, 31-17 (D)
Cardinals, 31-13 (StL)
1962—Cardinals, 28-24 (D)
Cardinals, 52-20 (StL)
1963—Cardinals, 34-7 (D)
Cowboys, 28-24 (StL)
1964—Cardinals, 16-6 (D)
Cowboys, 31-13 (StL)
1965—Cardinals, 20-13 (StL)
Cowboys, 27-13 (D)
1966—Tie, 10-10 (StL)
Cowboys, 31-17 (D)
1967—Cowboys, 46-21 (D)
1968—Cowboys, 27-10 (StL)
1969—Cowboys, 24-3 (D)
1970—Cardinals, 20-7 (StL)
Cardinals, 38-0 (D)
1971—Cowboys, 16-13 (StL)
Cowboys, 31-12 (D)
1972—Cowboys, 33-24 (D)
Cowboys, 27-6 (StL)
1973—Cowboys, 45-10 (D)
Cowboys, 30-3 (StL)
1974—Cardinals, 31-28 (StL)
Cowboys, 17-14 (D)
1975—Cowboys, 37-31 (D) OT
Cardinals, 31-17 (StL)
1976—Cardinals, 21-17 (StL)
Cowboys, 19-14 (D)
1977—Cowboys, 30-24 (StL)
Cardinals, 24-17 (D)
1978—Cowboys, 21-12 (D)
Cowboys, 24-21 (StL) OT
1979—Cowboys, 22-21 (StL)
Cowboys, 22-13 (D)
1980—Cowboys, 27-24 (StL)
Cowboys, 31-21 (D)
1981—Cowboys, 30-17 (D)
Cardinals, 20-17 (StL)
1982—Cowboys, 24-7 (StL)
1983—Cowboys, 34-17 (StL)
Cowboys, 35-17 (D)
1984—Cardinals, 31-20 (D)
Cowboys, 24-17 (StL)
1985—Cardinals, 21-10 (StL)
Cowboys, 35-17 (D)
1986—Cowboys, 31-7 (StL)
Cowboys, 37-6 (D)
1987—Cardinals, 24-13 (StL)
Cowboys, 21-16 (D)
1988—Cowboys, 17-14 (P)
Cardinals, 16-10 (D)
1989—Cardinals, 19-10 (D)
Cardinals, 24-20 (P)
1990—Cardinals, 20-3 (P)
Cowboys, 41-10 (D)
1991—Cowboys, 17-9 (P)
Cowboys, 27-7 (D)
1992—Cowboys, 31-20 (D)
Cowboys, 16-10 (P)
1993—Cowboys, 17-10 (P)
Cowboys, 20-15 (D)
1994—Cowboys, 38-3 (D)
Cowboys, 28-21 (A)
1995—Cowboys, 34-20 (D)
Cowboys, 37-13 (A)
1996—Cowboys, 17-3 (D)
Cowboys, 10-6 (A)
1997—Cardinals, 25-22 (A) OT
Cowboys, 24-6 (D)
1998—Cowboys, 38-10 (D)
Cowboys, 35-28 (A)
**Cardinals, 20-7 (D)
1999—Cowboys, 35-7 (D)
Cardinals, 13-9 (A)
2000—Cardinals, 32-31 (A)
Cowboys, 48-7 (D)
2001—Cowboys, 17-3 (D)
Cardinals, 17-10 (A)
2002—Cardinals, 9-6 (A) OT
2003—Cowboys, 24-7 (D)
2005—Cowboys, 34-13 (D)
2006—Cowboys, 27-10 (A)
2008—Cardinals, 30-24 (A) OT
(RS Pts.—Cowboys 1,960, Cardinals 1,437)
(PS Pts.—Cardinals 20, Cowboys 7)
Franchise known as Phoenix prior to 1994 and in St. Louis prior to 1988
***NFC First-Round Playoff*

***ARIZONA vs. DENVER**
RS: Broncos lead series, 7-0-1
1973—Tie, 17-17 (StL)
1977—Broncos, 7-0 (D)
1989—Broncos, 37-0 (P)
1991—Broncos, 24-19 (D)
1995—Broncos, 38-6 (D)
2001—Broncos, 38-17 (A)
2002—Broncos, 37-7 (D)
2006—Broncos, 37-20 (A)
(RS Pts.—Broncos 235, Cardinals 86)
Franchise known as Phoenix prior to 1994 and in St. Louis prior to 1988

***ARIZONA vs. **DETROIT**
RS: Lions lead series, 31-24-5
1930—Tie, 0-0 (Port)
Cardinals, 23-0 (C)
1931—Spartans, 13-3 (Port)
Cardinals, 20-19 (C)
1932—Tie, 7-7 (Port)
1933—Spartans, 7-6 (Port)
1934—Lions, 6-0 (D)
Lions, 17-13 (C)
1935—Tie, 10-10 (D)
Lions, 7-6 (C)
1936—Lions, 39-0 (D)
Lions, 14-7 (C)
1937—Lions, 16-7 (C)
Lions, 16-7 (D)
1938—Lions, 10-0 (D)
Lions, 7-3 (C)
1939—Lions, 21-3 (D)
Lions, 17-3 (C)
1940—Tie, 0-0 (Buffalo)
Lions, 43-14 (C)
1941—Tie, 14-14 (C)
Lions, 21-3 (D)
1942—Cardinals, 13-0 (C)
Cardinals, 7-0 (D)
1943—Lions, 35-17 (D)
Lions, 7-0 (Buffalo)
1945—Lions, 10-0 (Milwaukee)
Lions, 26-0 (D)
1946—Cardinals, 34-14 (C)
Cardinals, 36-14 (D)
1947—Cardinals, 45-21 (C)
Cardinals, 17-7 (D)
1948—Cardinals, 56-20 (C)
Cardinals, 28-14 (D)
1949—Lions, 24-7 (C)
Cardinals, 42-19 (D)
1959—Lions, 45-21 (D)
1961—Lions, 45-14 (StL)
1967—Cardinals, 38-28 (StL)
1969—Lions, 20-0 (D)
1970—Lions, 16-3 (D)
1973—Lions, 20-16 (StL)
1975—Cardinals, 24-13 (D)
1978—Cardinals, 21-14 (StL)
1980—Lions, 20-7 (D)
Cardinals, 24-23 (StL)
1989—Cardinals, 16-13 (D)
1993—Lions, 26-20 (D)
Lions, 21-14 (Phx)
1995—Cardinals, 20-17 (D)
1998—Cardinals, 17-15 (D)
1999—Cardinals, 23-19 (A)
2001—Cardinals, 45-38 (A)
2002—Cardinals, 23-20 (A) OT
2003—Lions, 42-24 (D)
2004—Lions, 26-12 (D)
2005—Lions, 29-21 (D)
2006—Cardinals, 17-10 (A)
2007—Cardinals, 31-21 (A)
2009—Cardinals, 31-24 (D)
(RS Pts.—Lions 1,093, Cardinals 943)
Franchise known as Phoenix prior to 1994, in St. Louis prior to 1988, and in Chicago prior to 1960
***Franchise in Portsmouth prior to 1934 and known as the Spartans*

***ARIZONA vs. GREEN BAY**
RS: Packers lead series, 43-22-4
PS: Series tied, 1-1
1921—Tie, 3-3 (C)
1922—Cardinals, 16-3 (C)
1924—Cardinals, 3-0 (C)
1925—Cardinals, 9-6 (C)
1926—Cardinals, 13-7 (GB)
Packers, 3-0 (C)
1927—Packers, 13-0 (GB)
Tie, 6-6 (C)

1928—Packers, 20-0 (GB)
1929—Packers, 9-2 (GB)
Packers, 7-6 (C)
Packers, 12-0 (C)
1930—Packers, 14-0 (GB)
Cardinals, 13-6 (C)
1931—Packers, 26-7 (GB)
Cardinals, 21-13 (C)
1932—Packers, 15-7 (GB)
Packers, 19-9 (C)
1933—Packers, 14-6 (C)
1934—Packers, 15-0 (GB)
Cardinals, 9-0 (Mil)
Cardinals, 6-0 (C)
1935—Cardinals, 7-6 (GB)
Cardinals, 3-0 (Mil)
Cardinals, 9-7 (C)
1936—Packers, 10-7 (GB)
Packers, 24-0 (Mil)
Tie, 0-0 (C)
1937—Cardinals, 14-7 (GB)
Packers, 34-13 (Mil)
1938—Packers, 28-7 (Mil)
Packers, 24-22 (Buffalo)
1939—Packers, 14-10 (GB)
Packers, 27-20 (Mil)
1940—Packers, 31-6 (Mil)
Packers, 28-7 (C)
1941—Packers, 14-13 (Mil)
Packers, 17-9 (GB)
1942—Packers, 17-13 (C)
Packers, 55-24 (GB)
1943—Packers, 28-7 (C)
Packers, 35-14 (Mil)
1945—Packers, 33-14 (GB)
1946—Packers, 19-7 (C)
Cardinals, 24-6 (GB)
1947—Cardinals, 14-10 (GB)
Cardinals, 21-20 (C)
1948—Cardinals, 17-7 (Mil)
Cardinals, 42-7 (C)
1949—Cardinals, 39-17 (Mil)
Cardinals, 41-21 (C)
1955—Packers, 31-14 (GB)
1956—Packers, 24-21 (C)
1962—Packers, 17-0 (Mil)
1963—Packers, 30-7 (StL)
1967—Packers, 31-23 (StL)
1969—Packers, 45-28 (GB)
1971—Tie, 16-16 (StL)
1973—Packers, 25-21 (GB)
1976—Cardinals, 29-0 (StL)
1982—**Packers, 41-16 (GB)
1984—Packers, 24-23 (GB)
1985—Cardinals, 43-28 (StL)
1988—Packers, 26-17 (P)
1990—Packers, 24-21 (P)
1999—Packers, 49-24 (GB)
2000—Packers, 29-3 (A)
2003—Cardinals, 20-13 (A)
2006—Packers, 31-14 (GB)
2009—Packers, 33-7 (A)
**Cardinals, 51-45 (A) OT
(RS Pts.—Packers 1,233, Cardinals 891)
(PS Pts.—Packers 86, Cardinals 67)
Franchise known as Phoenix prior to 1994, in St. Louis prior to 1988, and in Chicago prior to 1960
***NFC First-Round Playoff*

ARIZONA vs. HOUSTON
RS: Series tied, 1-1
2005—Texans, 30-19 (H)
2009—Cardinals, 28-21 (A)
(RS Pts.—Texans 51, Cardinals 47)

***ARIZONA vs. **INDIANAPOLIS**
RS: Colts lead series, 8-6
1961—Colts, 16-0 (B)
1964—Colts, 47-27 (B)
1968—Colts, 27-0 (B)
1972—Cardinals, 10-3 (B)
1976—Cardinals, 24-17 (StL)
1978—Colts, 30-17 (StL)
1980—Cardinals, 17-10 (B)
1981—Cardinals, 35-24 (B)
1984—Cardinals, 34-33 (I)
1990—Cardinals, 20-17 (P)
1992—Colts, 16-13 (I)
1996—Colts, 20-13 (I)
2005—Colts, 17-13 (I)
2009—Colts, 31-10 (A)
(RS Pts.—Colts 308, Cardinals 233)
Franchise known as Phoenix prior to 1994 and in St. Louis prior to 1988
***Franchise in Baltimore prior to 1984*

ARIZONA vs. JACKSONVILLE
RS: Jaguars lead series, 2-1
2000—Jaguars, 44-10 (J)
2005—Jaguars, 24-17 (A)
2009—Cardinals, 31-17 (J)
(RS Pts.—Jaguars 85, Cardinals 58)

***ARIZONA vs. KANSAS CITY**
RS: Chiefs lead series, 7-2-1
1970—Tie, 6-6 (KC)
1974—Chiefs, 17-13 (StL)
1980—Chiefs, 21-13 (StL)
1983—Chiefs, 38-14 (KC)
1986—Cardinals, 23-14 (StL)
1995—Chiefs, 24-3 (A)
1998—Chiefs, 34-24 (KC)
2001—Cardinals, 24-16 (A)
2002—Chiefs, 49-0 (KC)
2006—Chiefs, 23-20 (A)
(RS Pts.—Chiefs 242, Cardinals 140)
Franchise known as Phoenix prior to 1994 and in St. Louis prior to 1988

***ARIZONA vs. MIAMI**
RS: Dolphins lead series, 8-2
1972—Dolphins, 31-10 (M)
1977—Dolphins, 55-14 (StL)
1978—Dolphins, 24-10 (M)
1981—Dolphins, 20-7 (StL)
1984—Dolphins, 36-28 (StL)
1990—Dolphins, 23-3 (M)
1996—Dolphins, 38-10 (A)
1999—Dolphins, 19-16 (M)
2004—Cardinals, 24-23 (M)
2008—Cardinals, 31-10 (A)
(RS Pts.—Dolphins 279, Cardinals 153)
Franchise known as Phoenix prior to 1994 and in St. Louis prior to 1988

***ARIZONA vs. MINNESOTA**
RS: Series tied, 10-10
PS: Vikings lead series, 2-0
1963—Cardinals, 56-14 (M)
1967—Cardinals, 34-24 (M)
1969—Vikings, 27-10 (StL)
1972—Cardinals, 19-17 (M)
1974—Vikings, 28-24 (StL)
**Vikings, 30-14 (M)
1977—Cardinals, 27-7 (M)
1979—Cardinals, 37-7 (StL)
1981—Cardinals, 30-17 (StL)
1983—Cardinals, 41-31 (StL)
1991—Vikings, 34-7 (M)
Vikings, 28-0 (P)
1994—Cardinals, 17-7 (A)
1995—Vikings, 30-24 (A) OT
1996—Vikings, 41-17 (M)
1997—Vikings, 20-19 (A)
1998—**Vikings, 41-21 (M)
2000—Vikings, 31-14 (M)
2003—Cardinals, 18-17 (A)
2006—Vikings, 31-26 (M)
2008—Vikings, 35-14 (A)
2009—Cardinals, 30-17 (A)
(RS Pts.—Cardinals 464, Vikings 463)
(PS Pts.—Vikings 71, Cardinals 35)
Franchise known as Phoenix prior to 1994 and in St. Louis prior to 1988
***NFC Divisional Playoff*

***ARIZONA vs. **NEW ENGLAND**
RS: Series tied, 6-6
1970—Cardinals, 31-0 (StL)
1975—Cardinals, 24-17 (StL)
1978—Patriots, 16-6 (StL)
1981—Cardinals, 27-20 (NE)
1984—Cardinals, 33-10 (NE)
1990—Cardinals, 34-14 (P)
1991—Cardinals, 24-10 (P)
1993—Patriots, 23-21 (P)
1996—Patriots, 31-0 (NE)
1999—Patriots, 27-3 (A)
2004—Patriots, 23-12 (A)
2008—Patriots, 47-7 (NE)
(RS Pts.—Patriots 238, Cardinals 222)
Franchise known as Phoenix prior to 1994 and in St. Louis prior to 1988
***Franchise in Boston prior to 1971*

***ARIZONA vs. NEW ORLEANS**
RS: Cardinals lead series, 13-12
PS: Saints lead series, 1-0
1967—Cardinals, 31-20 (StL)
1968—Cardinals, 21-20 (NO)
Cardinals, 31-17 (StL)
1969—Saints, 51-42 (StL)
1970—Cardinals, 24-17 (StL)
1974—Saints, 14-0 (NO)
1977—Cardinals, 49-31 (StL)
1980—Cardinals, 40-7 (NO)
1981—Cardinals, 30-3 (StL)
1982—Cardinals, 21-7 (NO)
1983—Saints, 28-17 (NO)
1984—Saints, 34-24 (NO)
1985—Cardinals, 28-16 (StL)
1986—Saints, 16-7 (StL)
1987—Cardinals, 24-19 (StL)
1990—Saints, 28-7 (NO)
1991—Saints, 27-3 (P)
1992—Saints, 30-21 (P)
1993—Saints, 20-17 (P)
1996—Cardinals, 28-14 (NO)
1997—Saints, 27-10 (NO)
1998—Cardinals, 19-17 (A)
2000—Saints, 21-10 (A)
2004—Cardinals, 34-10 (A)
2007—Saints, 31-24 (NO)
2009—**Saints, 45-14 (NO)
(RS Pts.—Cardinals 562, Saints 525)
(PS Pts.—Saints 45, Cardinals 14)
Franchise known as Phoenix prior to 1994 and in St. Louis prior to 1988
***NFC Divisional Playoff*

***ARIZONA vs. N.Y. GIANTS**
RS: Giants lead series, 79-42-2
1926—Giants, 20-0 (NY)
1927—Giants, 28-7 (NY)
1929—Giants, 24-21 (NY)
1930—Giants, 25-12 (NY)
Giants, 13-7 (C)
1935—Cardinals, 14-13 (NY)
1936—Giants, 14-6 (NY)
1938—Giants, 6-0 (NY)
1939—Giants, 17-7 (NY)
1941—Cardinals, 10-7 (NY)
1942—Giants, 21-7 (NY)
1943—Giants, 24-13 (NY)
1946—Giants, 28-24 (NY)
1947—Giants, 35-31 (NY)
1948—Cardinals, 63-35 (NY)
1949—Giants, 41-38 (C)
1950—Cardinals, 17-3 (C)
Giants, 51-21 (NY)
1951—Giants, 28-17 (NY)
Giants, 10-0 (C)
1952—Cardinals, 24-23 (NY)
Giants, 28-6 (C)
1953—Giants, 21-7 (NY)
Giants, 23-20 (C)
1954—Giants, 41-10 (C)
Giants, 31-17 (NY)
1955—Cardinals, 28-17 (C)
Giants, 10-0 (NY)
1956—Cardinals, 35-27 (C)
Giants, 23-10 (NY)
1957—Giants, 27-14 (NY)
Giants, 28-21 (C)
1958—Giants, 37-7 (Buffalo)
Cardinals, 23-6 (NY)
1959—Giants, 9-3 (NY)
Giants, 30-20 (Minn)
1960—Giants, 35-14 (StL)
Cardinals, 20-13 (NY)
1961—Cardinals, 21-10 (NY)
Giants, 24-9 (StL)
1962—Giants, 31-14 (StL)
Giants, 31-28 (NY)
1963—Giants, 38-21 (StL)
Cardinals, 24-17 (NY)
1964—Giants, 34-17 (NY)
Tie, 10-10 (StL)
1965—Giants, 14-10 (NY)
Giants, 28-15 (StL)
1966—Cardinals, 24-19 (StL)
Cardinals, 20-17 (NY)
1967—Giants, 37-20 (StL)
Giants, 37-14 (NY)
1968—Cardinals, 28-21 (NY)
1969—Cardinals, 42-17 (StL)
Giants, 49-6 (NY)
1970—Giants, 35-17 (NY)
Giants, 34-17 (StL)
1971—Giants, 21-20 (StL)
Cardinals, 24-7 (NY)
1972—Giants, 27-21 (NY)
Giants, 13-7 (StL)
1973—Cardinals, 35-27 (StL)
Giants, 24-13 (New Haven)
1974—Cardinals, 23-21 (New Haven)
Cardinals, 26-14 (StL)
1975—Cardinals, 26-14 (StL)
Cardinals, 20-13 (NY)
1976—Cardinals, 27-21 (StL)
Cardinals, 17-14 (NY)
1977—Cardinals, 28-0 (StL)
Giants, 27-7 (NY)
1978—Cardinals, 20-10 (StL)
Giants, 17-0 (NY)
1979—Cardinals, 27-14 (NY)
Cardinals, 29-20 (StL)
1980—Giants, 41-35 (StL)
Cardinals, 23-7 (NY)
1981—Giants, 34-14 (NY)
Giants, 20-10 (StL)
1982—Cardinals, 24-21 (StL)
1983—Tie, 20-20 (StL) OT
Cardinals, 10-6 (NY)
1984—Giants, 16-10 (NY)
Cardinals, 31-21 (StL)
1985—Giants, 27-17 (NY)
Giants, 34-3 (StL)
1986—Giants, 13-6 (StL)
Giants, 27-7 (NY)
1987—Giants, 30-7 (NY)
Cardinals, 27-24 (StL)
1988—Cardinals, 24-17 (P)
Giants, 44-7 (NY)
1989—Giants, 35-7 (NY)
Giants, 20-13 (P)
1990—Giants, 20-19 (NY)
Giants, 24-21 (P)
1991—Giants, 20-9 (NY)
Giants, 21-14 (P)
1992—Giants, 31-21 (NY)
Cardinals, 19-0 (P)
1993—Giants, 19-17 (NY)
Cardinals, 17-6 (P)
1994—Giants, 20-17 (A)
Cardinals, 10-9 (NY)
1995—Giants, 27-21 (NY) OT
Giants, 10-6 (A)
1996—Giants, 16-8 (NY)
Cardinals, 31-23 (A)
1997—Giants, 27-13 (A)
Giants, 19-10 (NY)
1998—Giants, 34-7 (NY)
Giants, 23-19 (A)
1999—Cardinals, 14-3 (A)
Cardinals, 34-24 (NY)
2000—Giants, 21-16 (NY)
Giants, 31-7 (A)
2001—Giants, 17-10 (A)
Giants, 17-13 (NY)
2002—Cardinals, 21-7 (A)
2004—Cardinals, 17-14 (A)
2005—Giants, 42-19 (NY)
2008—Giants, 37-29 (A)
2009—Cardinals, 24-17 (NY)
(RS Pts.—Giants 2,715, Cardinals 2,099)
**Franchise known as Phoenix prior to 1994, in St. Louis prior to 1988, and in Chicago prior to 1960*

***ARIZONA vs. N.Y. JETS**
RS: Jets lead series, 5-2
1971—Cardinals, 17-10 (StL)
1975—Cardinals, 37-6 (NY)
1978—Jets, 23-10 (NY)
1996—Jets, 31-21 (A)
1999—Jets, 12-7 (NY)
2004—Jets, 13-3 (A)
2008—Jets, 56-35 (NY)
(RS Pts.—Jets 151, Cardinals 130)
**Franchise known as Phoenix prior to 1994 and in St. Louis prior to 1988*

***ARIZONA vs. **OAKLAND**
RS: Raiders lead series, 5-2
1973—Raiders, 17-10 (StL)
1983—Cardinals, 34-24 (LA)
1989—Raiders, 16-14 (LA)
1998—Raiders, 23-20 (A)
2001—Cardinals, 34-31 (O) OT
2002—Raiders, 41-20 (A)
2006—Raiders, 22-9 (O)
(RS Pts.— Raiders 174, Cardinals 141)
**Franchise known as Phoenix prior to 1994 and in St. Louis prior to 1988*
***Franchise in Los Angeles from 1982-1994*

***ARIZONA vs. PHILADELPHIA**
RS: Series tied, 53-53-5
PS: Cardinals lead series, 2-1
1935—Cardinals, 12-3 (C)
1936—Cardinals, 13-0 (C)
1937—Tie, 6-6 (P)
1938—Eagles, 7-0 (Erie, Pa.)
1941—Eagles, 21-14 (P)
1945—Eagles, 21-6 (P)
1947—Cardinals, 45-21 (P)
**Cardinals, 28-21 (C)
1948—Cardinals, 21-14 (C)
**Eagles, 7-0 (P)
1949—Eagles, 28-3 (P)
1950—Eagles, 45-7 (C)
Cardinals, 14-10 (P)
1951—Eagles, 17-14 (C)
1952—Eagles, 10-7 (P)
Cardinals, 28-22 (C)
1953—Eagles, 56-17 (C)
Eagles, 38-0 (P)
1954—Eagles, 35-16 (C)
Eagles, 30-14 (P)
1955—Tie, 24-24 (C)
Eagles, 27-3 (P)
1956—Cardinals, 20-6 (P)
Cardinals, 28-17 (C)
1957—Eagles, 38-21 (C)
Cardinals, 31-27 (P)
1958—Tie, 21-21 (C)
Eagles, 49-21 (P)
1959—Eagles, 28-24 (Minn)
Eagles, 27-17 (P)
1960—Eagles, 31-27 (P)
Eagles, 20-6 (StL)
1961—Cardinals, 30-27 (P)
Eagles, 20-7 (StL)
1962—Cardinals, 27-21 (P)
Cardinals, 45-35 (StL)
1963—Cardinals, 28-24 (P)
Cardinals, 38-14 (StL)
1964—Cardinals, 38-13 (P)
Cardinals, 36-34 (StL)
1965—Eagles, 34-27 (P)
Eagles, 28-24 (StL)
1966—Cardinals, 16-13 (StL)
Cardinals, 41-10 (P)
1967—Cardinals, 48-14 (StL)
1968—Cardinals, 45-17 (P)
1969—Eagles, 34-30 (StL)
1970—Cardinals, 35-20 (P)
Cardinals, 23-14 (StL)
1971—Eagles, 37-20 (StL)
Eagles, 19-7 (P)
1972—Tie, 6-6 (P)
Cardinals, 24-23 (StL)
1973—Cardinals, 34-23 (P)

Eagles, 27-24 (StL)
1974—Cardinals, 7-3 (StL)
Cardinals, 13-3 (P)
1975—Cardinals, 31-20 (StL)
Cardinals, 24-23 (P)
1976—Cardinals, 33-14 (StL)
Cardinals, 17-14 (P)
1977—Cardinals, 21-17 (P)
Cardinals, 21-16 (StL)
1978—Cardinals, 16-10 (P)
Eagles, 14-10 (StL)
1979—Eagles, 24-20 (StL)
Eagles, 16-13 (P)
1980—Cardinals, 24-14 (StL)
Eagles, 17-3 (P)
1981—Eagles, 52-10 (StL)
Eagles, 38-0 (P)
1982—Cardinals, 23-20 (P)
1983—Cardinals, 14-11 (P)
Cardinals, 31-7 (StL)
1984—Cardinals, 34-14 (P)
Cardinals, 17-16 (StL)
1985—Eagles, 30-7 (P)
Eagles, 24-14 (StL)
1986—Cardinals, 13-10 (StL)
Tie, 10-10 (P) OT
1987—Eagles, 28-23 (StL)
Cardinals, 31-19 (P)
1988—Eagles, 31-21 (P)
Eagles, 23-17 (Phx)
1989—Eagles, 17-5 (Phx)
Eagles, 31-14 (P)
1990—Cardinals, 23-21 (P)
Eagles, 23-21 (Phx)
1991—Cardinals, 26-10 (P)
Eagles, 34-14 (Phx)
1992—Eagles, 31-14 (Phx)
Eagles, 7-3 (P)
1993—Eagles, 23-17 (P)
Cardinals, 16-3 (Phx)
1994—Eagles, 17-7 (P)
Cardinals, 12-6 (A)
1995—Eagles, 31-19 (A)
Eagles, 21-20 (P)
1996—Cardinals, 36-30 (A)
Eagles, 29-19 (P)
1997—Eagles, 13-10 (P) OT
Cardinals, 31-21 (A)
1998—Cardinals, 17-3 (A)
Cardinals, 20-17 (P) OT
1999—Cardinals, 25-24 (P)
Cardinals, 21-17 (A)
2000—Eagles, 33-14 (A)
Eagles, 34-9 (P)
2001—Cardinals, 21-20 (P)
Eagles, 21-7 (A)
2002—Eagles, 38-14 (P)
2005—Cardinals, 27-21 (A)
2008—Eagles, 48-20 (P)
***Cardinals, 32-25 (A)
(RS Pts.—Eagles 2,388, Cardinals 2,153)
(PS Pts.—Cardinals 60, Eagles 53)
Franchise known as Phoenix prior to 1994, in St. Louis prior to 1988, and in Chicago prior to 1960
***NFL Championship*
****NFC Championship*

***ARIZONA vs. **PITTSBURGH**
RS: Steelers lead series, 31-23-3
PS: Steelers lead series, 1-0
1933—Pirates, 14-13 (P)
1935—Pirates, 17-13 (P)
1936—Cardinals, 14-6 (C)
1937—Cardinals, 13-7 (P)
1939—Cardinals, 10-0 (P)
1940—Tie, 7-7 (P)
1942—Steelers, 19-3 (P)
1945—Steelers, 23-0 (P)
1946—Steelers, 14-7 (P)
1948—Cardinals, 24-7 (P)
1950—Steelers, 28-17 (C)
Steelers, 28-7 (P)
1951—Steelers, 28-14 (C)
1952—Steelers, 34-28 (C)
Steelers, 17-14 (P)
1953—Steelers, 31-28 (P)
Steelers, 21-17 (C)
1954—Cardinals, 17-14 (C)
Steelers, 20-17 (P)
1955—Steelers, 14-7 (P)
Cardinals, 27-13 (C)
1956—Steelers, 14-7 (P)
Cardinals, 38-27 (C)
1957—Steelers, 29-20 (P)
Steelers, 27-2 (C)
1958—Steelers, 27-20 (C)
Steelers, 38-21 (P)
1959—Cardinals, 45-24 (C)
Steelers, 35-20 (P)
1960—Steelers, 27-14 (P)
Cardinals, 38-7 (StL)
1961—Steelers, 30-27 (P)
Cardinals, 20-0 (StL)
1962—Steelers, 26-17 (StL)
Steelers, 19-7 (P)
1963—Steelers, 23-10 (P)
Cardinals, 24-23 (StL)
1964—Cardinals, 34-30 (StL)
Cardinals, 21-20 (P)
1965—Cardinals, 20-7 (P)
Cardinals, 21-17 (StL)
1966—Steelers, 30-9 (P)
Cardinals, 6-3 (StL)
1967—Cardinals, 28-14 (P)
Tie, 14-14 (StL)
1968—Tie, 28-28 (StL)
Cardinals, 20-10 (P)
1969—Cardinals, 27-14 (P)
Cardinals, 47-10 (StL)
1972—Steelers, 25-19 (StL)
1979—Steelers, 24-21 (StL)
1985—Steelers, 23-10 (P)
1988—Cardinals, 31-14 (Phx)
1994—Cardinals, 20-17 (A) OT
1997—Steelers, 26-20 (A) OT
2003—Steelers, 28-15 (P)
2007—Cardinals, 21-14 (A)
2008—***Steelers, 27-23 (Tampa Bay)
(RS Pts.—Steelers 1,106, Cardinals 1,059)
(PS Pts.—Steelers 27, Cardinals 23)
Franchise known as Phoenix prior to 1994, in St. Louis prior to 1988, and in Chicago prior to 1960
***Steelers known as Pirates prior to 1940*
****Super Bowl XLIII*

***ARIZONA vs. **ST. LOUIS**
RS: Series tied, 30-30-2
PS: Rams lead series, 1-0
1937—Cardinals, 6-0 (Cle)
Cardinals, 13-7 (Chi)
1938—Cardinals, 7-6 (Cle)
Cardinals, 31-17 (Chi)
1939—Rams, 24-0 (Chi)
Rams, 14-0 (Cle)
1940—Rams, 26-14 (Cle)
Cardinals, 17-7 (Chi)
1941—Rams, 10-6 (Cle)
Cardinals, 7-0 (Chi)
1942—Cardinals, 7-0 (Buffalo)
Rams, 7-3 (Cle)
1945—Rams, 21-0 (Cle)
Rams, 35-21 (Chi)
1946—Cardinals, 34-10 (Chi)
Rams, 17-14 (LA)
1947—Rams, 27-7 (LA)
Cardinals, 17-10 (Chi)
1948—Cardinals, 27-22 (LA)
Cardinals, 27-24 (Chi)
1949—Tie, 28-28 (Chi)
Cardinals, 31-27 (LA)
1951—Rams, 45-21 (LA)
1953—Tie, 24-24 (Chi)
1954—Rams, 28-17 (LA)
1958—Rams, 20-14 (Chi)
1960—Cardinals, 43-21 (LA)
1965—Rams, 27-3 (StL)
1968—Rams, 24-13 (StL)
1970—Rams, 34-13 (LA)
1972—Cardinals, 24-14 (StL)
1975—***Rams, 35-23 (LA)
1976—Cardinals, 30-28 (LA)
1979—Rams, 21-0 (LA)
1980—Rams, 21-13 (StL)
1984—Rams, 16-13 (StL)
1985—Rams, 46-14 (LA)
1986—Rams, 16-10 (StL)
1987—Rams, 27-24 (StL)
1988—Cardinals, 41-27 (LA)
1989—Rams, 37-14 (LA)
1991—Cardinals, 24-14 (LA)
1992—Cardinals, 20-14 (LA)
1993—Cardinals, 38-10 (P)
1994—Rams, 14-12 (LA)
1996—Cardinals, 31-28 (A) OT
1998—Cardinals, 20-17 (StL)
2002—Rams, 27-14 (A)
Rams, 30-28 (StL)
2003—Rams, 37-13 (StL)
Rams, 30-27 (A) OT
2004—Rams, 17-10 (StL)
Cardinals, 31-7 (A)
2005—Rams, 17-12 (A)
Cardinals, 38-28 (StL)
2006—Rams, 16-14 (A)
Cardinals, 34-20 (StL)
2007—Cardinals, 34-31 (StL)
Cardinals, 48-19 (A)
2008—Cardinals, 34-13 (StL)
Cardinals, 34-10 (A)
2009—Cardinals, 21-13 (StL)
Cardinals, 31-10 (A)
(RS Pts.—Rams 1,237, Cardinals 1,216)
(PS Pts.—Rams 35, Cardinals 23)
Franchise known as Phoenix prior to 1994, in St. Louis prior to 1988, and in Chicago prior to 1960
***Franchise in Los Angeles prior to 1995 and in Cleveland prior to 1946*
****NFC Divisional Playoff*

***ARIZONA vs. SAN DIEGO**
RS: Chargers lead series, 8-3
1971—Chargers, 20-17 (SD)
1976—Chargers, 43-24 (SD)

1983—Cardinals, 44-14 (StL)
1987—Chargers, 28-24 (SD)
1989—Chargers, 24-13 (P)
1992—Chargers, 27-21 (P)
1995—Chargers, 28-25 (SD)
1998—Cardinals, 16-13 (A)
2001—Cardinals, 20-17 (SD)
2002—Chargers, 23-15 (A)
2006—Chargers, 27-20 (SD)
(RS Pts.—Chargers 264, Cardinals 239)
Franchise known as Phoenix prior to 1994, in St. Louis prior to 1988,

***ARIZONA vs. SAN FRANCISCO**
RS: 49ers lead series, 21-16
1951—Cardinals, 27-21 (SF)
1957—Cardinals, 20-10 (SF)
1962—49ers, 24-17 (StL)
1964—Cardinals, 23-13 (SF)
1968—49ers, 35-17 (SF)
1971—49ers, 26-14 (StL)
1974—Cardinals, 34-9 (SF)
1976—Cardinals, 23-20 (StL) OT
1978—Cardinals, 16-10 (SF)
1979—Cardinals, 13-10 (StL)
1980—49ers, 24-21 (SF) OT
1982—49ers, 31-20 (StL)
1983—49ers, 42-27 (StL)
1986—49ers, 43-17 (SF)
1987—49ers, 34-28 (SF)
1988—Cardinals, 24-23 (P)
1991—49ers, 14-10 (SF)
1992—Cardinals, 24-14 (P)
1993—49ers, 28-14 (SF)
1999—49ers, 24-10 (A)
2000—49ers, 27-20 (SF)
2002—49ers, 38-28 (SF)
49ers, 17-14 (A)
2003—Cardinals, 16-13 (A) OT
49ers, 50-14 (SF)
2004—49ers, 31-28 (SF) OT
49ers, 31-28 (A) OT
2005—Cardinals, 31-14 (Mex. City)
Cardinals, 17-10 (SF)
2006—Cardinals, 34-27 (A)
Cardinals, 26-20 (SF)
2007—49ers, 20-17 (SF)
49ers, 37-31 (A) OT
2008—Cardinals, 23-13 (SF)
Cardinals, 29-24 (A)
2009—49ers, 20-16 (A)
49ers, 24-9 (SF)
(RS Pts.—49ers 871, Cardinals 780)
Franchise known as Phoenix prior to 1994, in St. Louis prior to 1988, and in Chicago prior to 1960

***ARIZONA vs. SEATTLE**
RS: Cardinals lead series, 13-9
1976—Cardinals, 30-24 (S)
1983—Cardinals, 33-28 (StL)
1989—Cardinals, 34-24 (S)
1993—Cardinals, 30-27 (S) OT
1995—Cardinals, 20-14 (A) OT
1998—Seahawks, 33-14 (S)
2002—Cardinals, 24-13 (S)
Seahawks, 27-6 (A)
2003—Seahawks, 38-0 (A)
Seahawks, 28-10 (S)
2004—Cardinals, 25-17 (A)
Seahawks, 24-21 (S)
2005—Seahawks, 37-12 (S)
Seahawks, 33-19 (A)
2006—Seahawks, 21-10 (S)
Cardinals, 27-21 (A)
2007—Cardinals, 23-20 (A)
Seahawks, 42-21 (S)
2008—Cardinals, 26-20 (S)
Cardinals, 34-21 (A)
2009—Cardinals, 27-3 (S)
Cardinals, 31-20 (A)
(RS Pts.—Seahawks 535, Cardinals 477)
Franchise known as Phoenix prior to 1994 and in St. Louis prior to 1988

***ARIZONA vs. TAMPA BAY**
RS: Series tied, 8-8
1977—Buccaneers, 17-7 (TB)
1981—Buccaneers, 20-10 (TB)
1983—Cardinals, 34-27 (TB)
1985—Buccaneers, 16-0 (TB)
1986—Cardinals, 30-19 (TB)
Cardinals, 21-17 (StL)
1987—Cardinals, 31-28 (StL)
Cardinals, 31-14 (TB)
1988—Cardinals, 30-24 (TB)
1989—Buccaneers, 14-13 (P)
1992—Buccaneers, 23-7 (TB)
Buccaneers, 7-3 (P)
1996—Cardinals, 13-9 (A)
1997—Buccaneers, 19-18 (TB)
2004—Cardinals, 12-7 (A)
2007—Buccaneers, 17-10 (TB)
(RS Pts.—Buccaneers 278, Cardinals 270)
Franchise known as Phoenix prior to 1994 and in St. Louis prior to 1988

***ARIZONA vs. **TENNESSEE**
RS: Cardinals lead series, 5-4
1970—Cardinals, 44-0 (StL)
1974—Cardinals, 31-27 (H)
1979—Cardinals, 24-17 (H)
1985—Oilers, 20-10 (StL)
1988—Oilers, 38-20 (H)
1994—Cardinals, 30-12 (H)
1997—Oilers, 41-14 (A)
2005—Cardinals, 20-10 (A)
2009—Titans, 20-17 (T)
(RS Pts.—Cardinals 210, Titans 185)
Franchise known as Phoenix prior to 1994 and in St. Louis prior to 1988
***Franchise in Houston prior to 1997; known as Oilers prior to 1999*

***ARIZONA vs. **WASHINGTON**
RS: Redskins lead series, 73-44-2
1932—Cardinals, 9-0 (B)
Braves, 8-6 (C)
1933—Redskins, 10-0 (C)
Tie, 0-0 (B)
1934—Redskins, 9-0 (B)
1935—Cardinals, 6-0 (B)
1936—Redskins, 13-10 (B)
1937—Cardinals, 21-14 (W)
1939—Redskins, 28-7 (W)
1940—Redskins, 28-21 (W)
1942—Redskins, 28-0 (W)
1943—Redskins, 13-7 (W)
1945—Redskins, 24-21 (W)
1947—Redskins, 45-21 (W)
1949—Cardinals, 38-7 (C)
1950—Cardinals, 38-28 (W)
1951—Redskins, 7-3 (C)
Redskins, 20-17 (W)
1952—Redskins, 23-7 (C)
Cardinals, 17-6 (W)
1953—Redskins, 24-13 (C)
Redskins, 28-17 (W)
1954—Cardinals, 38-16 (C)
Redskins, 37-20 (W)
1955—Cardinals, 24-10 (W)
Redskins, 31-0 (C)
1956—Cardinals, 31-3 (W)
Redskins, 17-14 (C)
1957—Redskins, 37-14 (C)
Cardinals, 44-14 (W)
1958—Cardinals, 37-10 (C)
Redskins, 45-31 (W)
1959—Cardinals, 49-21 (C)
Redskins, 23-14 (W)
1960—Cardinals, 44-7 (StL)
Cardinals, 26-14 (W)
1961—Cardinals, 24-0 (W)
Cardinals, 38-24 (StL)
1962—Redskins, 24-14 (W)
Tie, 17-17 (StL)
1963—Cardinals, 21-7 (W)
Cardinals, 24-20 (StL)
1964—Cardinals, 23-17 (W)
Cardinals, 38-24 (StL)
1965—Cardinals, 37-16 (W)
Redskins, 24-20 (StL)
1966—Cardinals, 23-7 (StL)
Redskins, 26-20 (W)
1967—Cardinals, 27-21 (W)
1968—Cardinals, 41-14 (StL)
1969—Redskins, 33-17 (W)
1970—Cardinals, 27-17 (StL)
Redskins, 28-27 (W)
1971—Redskins, 24-17 (StL)
Redskins, 20-0 (W)
1972—Redskins, 24-10 (W)
Redskins, 33-3 (StL)
1973—Cardinals, 34-27 (StL)
Redskins, 31-13 (W)
1974—Cardinals, 17-10 (W)
Cardinals, 23-20 (StL)
1975—Redskins, 27-17 (W)
Cardinals, 20-17 (StL) OT
1976—Redskins, 20-10 (W)
Redskins, 16-10 (StL)
1977—Redskins, 24-14 (W)
Redskins, 26-20 (StL)
1978—Redskins, 28-10 (StL)
Cardinals, 27-17 (W)
1979—Redskins, 17-7 (StL)
Redskins, 30-28 (W)
1980—Redskins, 23-0 (W)
Redskins, 31-7 (StL)
1981—Cardinals, 40-30 (StL)
Redskins, 42-21 (W)
1982—Redskins, 12-7 (StL)
Redskins, 28-0 (W)
1983—Redskins, 38-14 (StL)
Redskins, 45-7 (W)
1984—Cardinals, 26-24 (StL)
Redskins, 29-27 (W)
1985—Redskins, 27-10 (W)
Redskins, 27-16 (StL)
1986—Redskins, 28-21 (W)
Redskins, 20-17 (StL)
1987—Redskins, 28-21 (W)
Redskins, 34-17 (StL)
1988—Cardinals, 30-21 (P)
Redskins, 33-17 (W)
1989—Redskins, 30-28 (W)
Redskins, 29-10 (P)
1990—Redskins, 31-0 (W)

Redskins, 38-10 (P)
1991—Redskins, 34-0 (W)
Redskins, 20-14 (P)
1992—Cardinals, 27-24 (P)
Redskins, 41-3 (W)
1993—Cardinals, 17-10 (W)
Cardinals, 36-6 (P)
1994—Cardinals, 19-16 (W) OT
Cardinals, 17-15 (A)
1995—Redskins, 27-7 (W)
Cardinals, 24-20 (A)
1996—Cardinals, 37-34 (W) OT
Cardinals, 27-26 (A)
1997—Redskins, 19-13 (W) OT
Redskins, 38-28 (A)
1998—Cardinals, 29-27 (A)
Cardinals, 45-42 (W)
1999—Redskins, 24-10 (A)
Redskins, 28-3 (W)
2000—Cardinals, 16-15 (A)
Redskins, 20-3 (W)
2001—Redskins, 20-10 (A)
Redskins, 20-17 (W)
2002—Redskins, 31-23 (W)
2005—Redskins, 17-13 (A)
2007—Redskins, 21-19 (W)
2008—Redskins, 24-17 (W)
(RS Pts.—Redskins 2,645, Cardinals 2,203)
Franchise known as Phoenix prior to 1994, in St. Louis prior to 1988, and in Chicago prior to 1960
***Franchise in Boston prior to 1937 and known as Braves prior to 1933*

ATLANTA vs. ARIZONA
RS: Cardinals lead series, 14-10
PS: Cardinals lead series, 1-0;
See Arizona vs. Atlanta

ATLANTA vs. BALTIMORE
RS: Ravens lead series, 2-1
1999—Ravens, 19-13 (A) OT
2002—Falcons, 20-17 (A)
2006—Ravens, 24-10 (B)
(RS Pts.—Ravens 60, Falcons 43)

ATLANTA vs. BUFFALO
RS: Falcons lead series, 6-4
1973—Bills, 17-6 (A)
1977—Bills, 3-0 (B)
1980—Falcons, 30-14 (B)
1983—Falcons, 31-14 (A)
1989—Falcons, 30-28 (A)
1992—Bills, 41-14 (B)
1995—Bills, 23-17 (B)
2001—Falcons, 33-30 (A)
2005—Falcons, 24-16 (B)
2009—Falcons, 31-3 (A)
(RS Pts.—Falcons 216, Bills 189)

ATLANTA vs. CAROLINA
RS: Falcons lead series, 18-12
1995—Falcons, 23-20 (A) OT
Panthers, 21-17 (C)
1996—Panthers, 29-6 (C)
Falcons, 20-17 (A)
1997—Panthers, 9-6 (A)
Panthers, 21-12 (C)
1998—Falcons, 19-14 (C)
Falcons, 51-23 (A)
1999—Falcons, 27-20 (A)
Panthers, 34-28 (C)
2000—Falcons, 15-10 (C)
Falcons, 13-12 (A)
2001—Falcons, 24-16 (A)
Falcons, 10-7 (C)
2002—Falcons, 30-0 (A)
Falcons, 41-0 (C)
2003—Panthers, 23-3 (C)
Falcons, 20-14 (A) OT
2004—Falcons, 27-10 (C)
Falcons, 34-31 (A) OT
2005—Panthers, 24-6 (C)
Panthers, 44-11 (A)
2006—Falcons, 20-6 (C)
Panthers, 10-3 (A)
2007—Panthers, 27-20 (A)
Falcons, 20-13 (C)
2008—Panthers, 24-9 (C)
Falcons, 45-28 (A)
2009—Falcons, 28-20 (A)
Panthers, 28-19 (C)
(RS Pts.—Falcons 607, Panthers 555)

ATLANTA vs. CHICAGO
RS: Series tied, 12-12
1966—Bears, 23-6 (C)
1967—Bears, 23-14 (A)
1968—Falcons, 16-13 (C)
1969—Falcons, 48-31 (A)
1970—Bears, 23-14 (A)
1972—Falcons, 37-21 (C)
1973—Falcons, 46-6 (A)
1974—Falcons, 13-10 (A)
1976—Falcons, 10-0 (C)
1977—Falcons, 16-10 (C)
1978—Bears, 13-7 (C)
1980—Falcons, 28-17 (A)
1983—Falcons, 20-17 (C)
1985—Bears, 36-0 (C)
1986—Bears, 13-10 (A)
1990—Bears, 30-24 (C)
1992—Bears, 41-31 (C)
1993—Bears, 6-0 (C)
1998—Falcons, 20-13 (A)
2001—Bears, 31-3 (A)
2002—Bears, 14-13 (A)
2005—Bears, 16-3 (C)
2008—Falcons, 22-20 (A)
2009—Falcons, 21-14 (A)
(RS Pts.—Bears 441, Falcons 422)

ATLANTA vs. CINCINNATI
RS: Bengals lead series, 7-4
1971—Falcons, 9-6 (C)
1975—Bengals, 21-14 (A)
1978—Bengals, 37-7 (C)
1981—Bengals, 30-28 (A)
1984—Bengals, 35-14 (C)
1987—Bengals, 16-10 (A)
1990—Falcons, 38-17 (A)
1993—Bengals, 21-17 (C)
1996—Bengals, 41-31 (C)
2002—Falcons, 30-3 (A)
2006—Falcons, 29-27 (C)
(RS Pts.—Bengals 254, Falcons 227)

ATLANTA vs. CLEVELAND
RS: Browns lead series, 10-2
1966—Browns, 49-17 (A)
1968—Browns, 30-7 (C)
1971—Falcons, 31-14 (C)
1976—Browns, 20-17 (A)
1978—Browns, 24-16 (A)
1981—Browns, 28-17 (C)
1984—Browns, 23-7 (A)
1987—Browns, 38-3 (C)
1990—Browns, 13-10 (C)
1993—Falcons, 17-14 (A)
2002—Browns, 24-16 (C)
2006—Browns, 17-13 (A)
(RS Pts.—Browns 294, Falcons 171)

ATLANTA vs. DALLAS
RS: Cowboys lead series, 14-8
PS: Cowboys lead series, 2-0
1966—Cowboys, 47-14 (A)
1967—Cowboys, 37-7 (D)
1969—Cowboys, 24-17 (A)
1970—Cowboys, 13-0 (D)
1974—Cowboys, 24-0 (A)
1976—Falcons, 17-10 (A)
1978—*Cowboys, 27-20 (D)
1980—*Cowboys, 30-27 (A)
1985—Cowboys, 24-10 (D)
1986—Falcons, 37-35 (D)
1987—Falcons, 21-10 (D)
1988—Cowboys, 26-20 (D)
1989—Falcons 27-21 (A)
1990—Falcons, 26-7 (A)
1991—Cowboys, 31-27 (D)
1992—Cowboys, 41-17 (A)
1993—Falcons, 27-14 (A)
1995—Cowboys, 28-13 (A)
1996—Cowboys, 32-28 (D)
1999—Cowboys, 24-7 (D)
2001—Falcons, 20-13 (A)
2003—Falcons, 27-13 (D)
2006—Cowboys, 38-28 (A)
2009—Cowboys, 37-21 (D)
(RS Pts.—Cowboys 549, Falcons 411)
(PS Pts.—Cowboys 57, Falcons 47)
**NFC Divisional Playoff*

ATLANTA vs. DENVER
RS: Broncos lead series, 8-4
PS: Broncos lead series, 1-0
1970—Broncos, 24-10 (D)
1972—Falcons, 23-20 (A)
1975—Falcons, 35-21 (A)
1979—Broncos, 20-17 (A) OT
1982—Falcons, 34-27 (D)
1985—Broncos, 44-28 (A)
1988—Broncos, 30-14 (D)
1994—Broncos, 32-28 (D)
1997—Broncos, 29-21 (A)
1998—*Broncos, 34-19 (South Florida)
2000—Broncos, 42-14 (D)
2004—Falcons, 41-28 (D)
2008—Broncos, 24-20 (A)
(RS Pts.—Broncos 341, Falcons 285)
(PS Pts.—Broncos 34, Falcons 19)
**Super Bowl XXXIII*

ATLANTA vs. DETROIT
RS: Lions lead series, 23-10
1966—Lions, 28-10 (D)
1967—Lions, 24-3 (D)
1968—Lions, 24-7 (A)
1969—Lions, 27-21 (D)
1971—Lions, 41-38 (D)
1972—Lions, 26-23 (A)
1973—Lions, 31-6 (D)
1975—Lions, 17-14 (A)
1976—Lions, 24-10 (D)
1977—Falcons, 17-6 (A)
1978—Falcons, 14-0 (A)
1979—Lions, 24-23 (D)
1980—Falcons, 43-28 (A)
1983—Falcons, 30-14 (D)
1984—Lions, 27-24 (A) OT
1985—Lions, 28-27 (A)

1986—Falcons, 20-6 (D)
1987—Lions, 30-13 (A)
1988—Lions, 31-17 (D)
1989—Lions, 31-24 (A)
1990—Lions, 21-14 (D)
1993—Lions, 30-13 (D)
1994—Lions, 31-28 (D) OT
1995—Falcons, 34-22 (A)
1996—Lions, 28-24 (D)
1997—Lions, 28-17 (D)
1998—Falcons, 24-17 (D)
2000—Lions, 13-10 (D)
2002—Falcons, 36-15 (A)
2004—Lions, 17-10 (A)
2005—Falcons, 27-7 (D)
2006—Lions, 30-14 (D)
2008—Falcons, 34-21 (A)
(RS Pts.—Lions 747, Falcons 669)

ATLANTA vs. GREEN BAY
RS: Packers lead series, 12-11
PS: Series tied, 1-1
1966—Packers, 56-3 (Mil)
1967—Packers, 23-0 (Mil)
1968—Packers, 38-7 (A)
1969—Packers, 28-10 (GB)
1970—Packers, 27-24 (GB)
1971—Falcons, 28-21 (A)
1972—Falcons, 10-9 (Mil)
1974—Falcons, 10-3 (A)
1975—Packers, 22-13 (GB)
1976—Packers, 24-20 (A)
1979—Falcons, 25-7 (A)
1981—Falcons, 31-17 (GB)
1982—Packers, 38-7 (A)
1983—Falcons, 47-41 (A) OT
1988—Falcons, 20-0 (A)
1989—Packers, 23-21 (Mil)
1991—Falcons, 35-31 (A)
1992—Falcons, 24-10 (A)
1994—Packers, 21-17 (Mil)
1995—*Packers, 37-20 (GB)
2001—Falcons, 23-20 (GB)
2002—Packers, 37-34 (GB) OT
*Falcons, 27-7 (GB)
2005—Packers, 33-25 (A)
2008—Falcons, 27-24 (GB)
(RS Pts.—Packers 553, Falcons 461)
(PS Pts.—Falcons 47, Packers 44)
NFC First-Round Playoff

ATLANTA vs. HOUSTON
RS: Series tied, 1-1
2003—Texans, 17-13 (H)
2007—Falcons, 26-16 (A)
(RS Pts.—Falcons 39, Texans 33)

ATLANTA vs. *INDIANAPOLIS
RS: Colts lead series, 13-1
1966—Colts, 19-7 (A)
1967—Colts, 38-31 (B)
Colts, 49-7 (A)
1968—Colts, 28-20 (A)
Colts, 44-0 (B)
1969—Colts, 21-14 (A)
Colts, 13-6 (B)
1974—Colts, 17-7 (A)
1986—Colts, 28-23 (A)
1989—Colts, 13-9 (I)
1998—Falcons, 28-21 (A)
2001—Colts, 41-27 (I)
2003—Colts, 38-7 (I)
2007—Colts, 31-13 (A)
(RS Pts.—Colts 401, Falcons 199)
Franchise in Baltimore prior to 1984

ATLANTA vs. JACKSONVILLE
RS: Jaguars lead series, 3-1
1996—Jaguars, 19-17 (J)
1999—Jaguars, 30-7 (A)
2003—Falcons, 21-14 (A)
2007—Jaguars, 13-7 (J)
(RS Pts.—Jaguars 76, Falcons 52)

ATLANTA vs. KANSAS CITY
RS: Chiefs lead series, 5-2
1972—Chiefs, 17-14 (A)
1985—Chiefs, 38-10 (KC)
1991—Chiefs, 14-3 (KC)
1994—Chiefs, 30-10 (A)
2000—Falcons, 29-13 (A)
2004—Chiefs, 56-10 (KC)
2008—Falcons, 38-14 (A)
(RS Pts.—Chiefs 182, Falcons 114)

ATLANTA vs. MIAMI
RS: Dolphins lead series, 7-4
1970—Dolphins, 20-7 (A)
1974—Dolphins, 42-7 (M)
1980—Dolphins, 20-17 (A)
1983—Dolphins, 31-24 (M)
1986—Falcons, 20-14 (M)
1992—Dolphins, 21-17 (M)
1995—Dolphins, 21-20 (M)
1998—Falcons, 38-16 (A)
2001—Dolphins, 21-14 (M)
2005—Falcons, 17-10 (M)
2009—Falcons, 19-7 (A)
(RS Pts.—Dolphins 223, Falcons 200)

ATLANTA vs. MINNESOTA
RS: Vikings lead series, 15-9
PS: Series tied, 1-1
1966—Falcons, 20-13 (M)
1967—Falcons, 21-20 (A)
1968—Vikings, 47-7 (M)
1969—Falcons, 10-3 (A)
1970—Vikings, 37-7 (A)
1971—Vikings, 24-7 (M)
1973—Falcons, 20-14 (A)
1974—Vikings, 23-10 (M)
1975—Vikings, 38-0 (M)
1977—Vikings, 14-7 (A)
1980—Vikings, 24-23 (M)
1981—Falcons, 31-30 (A)
1982—*Vikings, 30-24 (M)
1984—Vikings, 27-20 (M)
1985—Falcons, 14-13 (A)
1987—Vikings, 24-13 (M)
1989—Vikings, 43-17 (M)
1991—Vikings, 20-19 (A)
1996—Vikings, 23-17 (A)
1998—**Falcons, 30-27 (M) OT
1999—Vikings, 17-14 (A)
2002—Falcons, 30-24 (M) OT
2003—Vikings, 39-26 (A)
2005—Falcons, 30-10 (A)
2007—Vikings, 24-3 (M)
2008—Falcons, 24-17 (M)
(RS Pts.—Vikings 568, Falcons 390)
(PS Pts.—Vikings 57, Falcons 54)
NFC First-Round Playoff
***NFC Championship*

ATLANTA vs. NEW ENGLAND
RS: Series tied, 6-6
1972—Patriots, 21-20 (NE)
1977—Patriots, 16-10 (A)
1980—Falcons, 37-21 (NE)
1983—Falcons, 24-13 (A)
1986—Patriots, 25-17 (NE)
1989—Falcons, 16-15 (A)
1992—Falcons, 34-0 (A)
1995—Falcons, 30-17 (A)
1998—Falcons, 41-10 (NE)
2001—Patriots, 24-10 (A)
2005—Patriots, 31-28 (A)
2009—Patriots, 26-10 (NE)
(RS Pts.—Falcons 277, Patriots 219)

ATLANTA vs. NEW ORLEANS
RS: Falcons lead series, 44-37
PS: Falcons lead series, 1-0
1967—Saints, 27-24 (NO)
1969—Falcons, 45-17 (A)
1970—Falcons, 14-3 (NO)
Falcons, 32-14 (A)
1971—Falcons, 28-6 (A)
Falcons, 24-20 (NO)
1972—Falcons, 21-14 (NO)
Falcons, 36-20 (A)
1973—Falcons, 62-7 (NO)
Falcons, 14-10 (A)
1974—Saints, 14-13 (NO)
Saints, 13-3 (A)
1975—Falcons, 14-7 (A)
Saints, 23-7 (NO)
1976—Saints, 30-0 (NO)
Falcons, 23-20 (A)
1977—Saints, 21-20 (NO)
Falcons, 35-7 (A)
1978—Falcons, 20-17 (NO)
Falcons, 20-17 (A)
1979—Falcons, 40-34 (NO) OT
Saints, 37-6 (A)
1980—Falcons, 41-14 (NO)
Falcons, 31-13 (A)
1981—Falcons, 27-0 (A)
Falcons, 41-10 (NO)
1982—Falcons, 35-0 (A)
Saints, 35-6 (NO)
1983—Saints, 19-17 (A)
Saints, 27-10 (NO)
1984—Falcons, 36-28 (NO)
Saints, 17-13 (A)
1985—Falcons, 31-24 (A)
Falcons, 16-10 (NO)
1986—Falcons, 31-10 (NO)
Saints, 14-9 (A)
1987—Saints, 38-0 (A)
1988—Saints, 29-21 (A)
Saints, 10-9 (NO)
1989—Saints, 20-13 (NO)
Saints, 26-17 (A)
1990—Falcons, 28-27 (A)
Saints, 10-7 (NO)
1991—Saints, 27-6 (A)
Falcons, 23-20 (NO) OT
*Falcons, 27-20 (NO)
1992—Saints, 10-7 (A)
Saints, 22-14 (NO)
1993—Saints, 34-31 (A)
Falcons, 26-15 (NO)
1994—Saints, 33-32 (NO)
Saints, 29-20 (A)
1995—Falcons, 27-24 (NO) OT
Falcons, 19-14 (A)
1996—Falcons, 17-15 (A)
Falcons, 31-15 (NO)
1997—Falcons, 23-17 (NO)
Falcons, 20-3 (A)
1998—Falcons, 31-23 (A)

Falcons, 27-17 (NO)
1999—Falcons, 20-17 (NO)
Falcons, 35-12 (A)
2000—Saints, 21-19 (A)
Saints, 23-7 (NO)
2001—Falcons, 20-13 (NO)
Saints, 28-10 (NO)
2002—Falcons, 37-35 (NO)
Falcons, 24-17 (A)
2003—Saints, 45-17 (A)
Saints, 23-20 (NO) OT
2004—Falcons, 24-21 (A)
Saints, 26-13 (NO)
2005—Falcons, 34-31 (San Antonio)
Falcons, 36-17 (A)
2006—Saints, 23-3 (NO)
Saints, 31-13 (A)
2007—Saints, 22-16 (NO)
Saints, 34-14 (A)
2008—Falcons, 34-20 (A)
Saints, 29-25 (NO)
2009—Saints, 35-27 (NO)
Saints, 26-23 (A)
(RS Pts.—Falcons 1,765, Saints 1,626)
(PS Pts.—Falcons 27, Saints 20)
NFC First-Round Playoff

ATLANTA vs. N.Y. GIANTS
RS: Series tied, 10-10
1966—Falcons, 27-16 (NY)
1968—Falcons, 24-21 (A)
1971—Giants, 21-17 (A)
1974—Falcons, 14-7 (New Haven)
1977—Falcons, 17-3 (A)
1978—Falcons, 23-20 (A)
1979—Giants, 24-3 (NY)
1981—Giants, 27-24 (A) OT
1982—Falcons, 16-14 (NY)
1983—Giants, 16-13 (A) OT
1984—Giants, 19-7 (A)
1988—Giants, 23-16 (A)
1998—Falcons, 34-20 (NY)
2000—Giants, 13-6 (A)
2002—Falcons, 17-10 (NY)
2003—Falcons, 27-7 (NY)
2004—Falcons, 14-10 (NY)
2006—Giants, 27-14 (A)
2007—Giants, 31-10 (A)
2009—Giants, 34-31 (NY) OT
(RS Pts.—Giants 363, Falcons 354)

ATLANTA vs. N.Y. JETS
RS: Falcons lead series, 6-4
1973—Falcons, 28-20 (NY)
1980—Jets, 14-7 (A)
1983—Falcons, 27-21 (NY)
1986—Jets, 28-14 (A)
1989—Jets, 27-7 (NY)
1992—Falcons, 20-17 (A)
1995—Falcons, 13-3 (A)
1998—Jets, 28-3 (NY)
2005—Falcons, 27-14 (A)
2009—Falcons, 10-7 (NY)
(RS Pts.—Jets 179, Falcons 156)

ATLANTA vs. *OAKLAND
RS: Raiders lead series, 7-5
1971—Falcons, 24-13 (A)
1975—Raiders, 37-34 (O) OT
1979—Raiders, 50-19 (O)
1982—Raiders, 38-14 (A)
1985—Raiders, 34-24 (A)
1988—Falcons, 12-6 (LA)
1991—Falcons, 21-17 (A)
1994—Raiders, 30-17 (LA)
1997—Raiders, 36-31 (A)
2000—Raiders, 41-14 (O)
2004—Falcons, 35-10 (A)
2008—Falcons, 24-0 (O)
(RS Pts.—Raiders 312, Falcons 269)
Franchise in Los Angeles from 1982-1994

ATLANTA vs. PHILADELPHIA
RS: Eagles lead series, 14-10-1
PS: Eagles lead series, 2-1
1966—Eagles, 23-10 (P)
1967—Eagles, 38-7 (A)
1969—Falcons, 27-3 (P)
1970—Tie, 13-13 (P)
1973—Falcons, 44-27 (P)
1976—Eagles, 14-13 (A)
1978—*Falcons, 14-13 (A)
1979—Falcons, 14-10 (P)
1980—Falcons, 20-17 (P)
1981—Eagles, 16-13 (P)
1983—Eagles, 28-24 (A)
1984—Falcons, 26-10 (A)
1985—Eagles, 23-17 (P) OT
1986—Eagles, 16-0 (A)
1988—Falcons, 27-24 (P)
1990—Eagles, 24-23 (A)
1994—Falcons, 28-21 (A)
1996—Eagles, 33-18 (A)
1997—Falcons, 20-17 (A)
1998—Falcons, 17-12 (A)
2000—Eagles, 38-10 (P)
2002—**Eagles, 20-6 (P)
2003—Eagles, 23-16 (A)
2004—***Eagles, 27-10 (P)
2005—Falcons, 14-10 (A)
2006—Eagles, 24-17 (P)
2008—Eagles, 27-14 (P)
2009—Eagles, 34-7 (P)
(RS Pts.—Eagles 525, Falcons 439)
(PS Pts.—Eagles 60, Falcons 30)
**NFC First-Round Playoff*
***NFC Divisional Playoff*
****NFC Championship*

ATLANTA vs. PITTSBURGH
RS: Steelers lead series, 11-2-1
1966—Steelers, 57-33 (A)
1968—Steelers, 41-21 (A)
1970—Falcons, 27-16 (A)
1974—Steelers, 24-17 (P)
1978—Steelers, 31-7 (P)
1981—Steelers, 34-20 (A)
1984—Steelers, 35-10 (P)
1987—Steelers, 28-12 (A)
1990—Steelers, 21-9 (P)
1993—Steelers, 45-17 (A)
1996—Steelers, 20-17 (A)
1999—Steelers, 13-9 (P)
2002—Tie, 34-34 (P) OT
2006—Falcons, 41-38 (A) OT
(RS Pts.—Steelers 437, Falcons 274)

ATLANTA vs. *ST. LOUIS
RS: Rams lead series, 47-25-2
PS: Falcons lead series, 1-0
1966—Rams, 19-14 (A)
1967—Rams, 31-3 (A)
Rams, 20-3 (LA)
1968—Rams, 27-14 (LA)
Rams, 17-10 (A)
1969—Rams, 17-7 (LA)
Rams, 38-6 (A)
1970—Tie, 10-10 (LA)
Rams, 17-7 (A)
1971—Tie, 20-20 (LA)
Rams, 24-16 (A)
1972—Falcons, 31-3 (A)
Rams, 20-7 (LA)
1973—Rams, 31-0 (LA)
Falcons, 15-13 (A)
1974—Rams, 21-0 (LA)
Rams, 30-7 (A)
1975—Rams, 22-7 (LA)
Rams, 16-7 (A)
1976—Rams, 30-14 (A)
Rams, 59-0 (LA)
1977—Falcons, 17-6 (A)
Rams, 23-7 (LA)
1978—Rams, 10-0 (LA)
Falcons, 15-7 (A)
1979—Rams, 20-14 (LA)
Rams, 34-13 (A)
1980—Falcons, 13-10 (A)
Rams, 20-17 (LA) OT
1981—Rams, 37-35 (A)
Rams, 21-16 (LA)
1982—Falcons, 34-17 (A)
1983—Rams, 27-21 (LA)
Rams, 36-13 (A)
1984—Falcons, 30-28 (LA)
Rams, 24-10 (A)
1985—Rams, 17-6 (LA)
Falcons, 30-14 (A)
1986—Falcons, 26-14 (A)
Rams, 14-7 (LA)
1987—Falcons, 24-20 (A)
Rams, 33-0 (LA)
1988—Rams, 33-0 (A)
Rams, 22-7 (LA)
1989—Rams, 31-21 (A)
Rams, 26-14 (LA)
1990—Rams, 44-24 (LA)
Falcons, 20-13 (A)
1991—Falcons, 31-14 (A)
Falcons, 31-14 (LA)
1992—Falcons, 30-28 (A)
Rams, 38-27 (LA)
1993—Falcons, 30-24 (A)
Falcons, 13-0 (LA)
1994—Falcons, 31-13 (A)
Falcons, 8-5 (LA)
1995—Rams, 21-19 (StL)
Falcons, 31-6 (A)
1996—Rams, 59-16 (StL)
Rams, 34-27 (A)
1997—Falcons, 34-31 (A)
Falcons, 27-21 (StL)
1998—Falcons, 37-15 (A)
Falcons, 21-10 (StL)
1999—Rams, 35-7 (StL)
Rams, 41-13 (A)
2000—Rams, 41-20 (A)
Rams, 45-29 (StL)
2001—Rams, 35-6 (A)
Rams, 31-13 (StL)
2003—Rams, 36-0 (StL)
2004—Falcons, 34-17 (A)
**Falcons, 47-17 (A)
2007—Rams, 28-16 (StL)
2008—Falcons, 31-27 (A)
(RS Pts.—Rams 1,755, Falcons 1,214)
(PS Pts.—Falcons 47, Rams 17)
**Franchise in Los Angeles prior to 1995*
***NFC Divisional Playoff*

ALL-TIME TEAM VS. TEAM RESULTS

ATLANTA vs. SAN DIEGO
RS: Falcons lead series, 7-1
1973—Falcons, 41-0 (SD)
1979—Falcons, 28-26 (SD)
1988—Chargers, 10-7 (A)
1991—Falcons, 13-10 (SD)
1994—Falcons, 10-9 (A)
1997—Falcons, 14-3 (SD)
2004—Falcons, 21-20 (A)
2008—Falcons, 22-16 (SD)
(RS Pts.—Falcons 156, Chargers 94)

ATLANTA vs. SAN FRANCISCO
RS: 49ers lead series, 44-28-1
PS: Falcons lead series, 1-0
1966—49ers, 44-7 (A)
1967—49ers, 38-7 (SF)
49ers, 34-28 (A)
1968—49ers, 28-13 (SF)
49ers, 14-12 (A)
1969—Falcons, 24-12 (A)
Falcons, 21-7 (SF)
1970—Falcons, 21-20 (A)
49ers, 24-20 (SF)
1971—Falcons, 20-17 (A)
49ers, 24-3 (SF)
1972—49ers, 49-14 (A)
49ers, 20-0 (SF)
1973—49ers, 13-9 (A)
Falcons, 17-3 (SF)
1974—49ers, 16-10 (A)
49ers, 27-0 (SF)
1975—Falcons, 17-3 (SF)
Falcons, 31-9 (A)
1976—49ers, 15-0 (SF)
Falcons, 21-16 (A)
1977—Falcons, 7-0 (SF)
49ers, 10-3 (A)
1978—Falcons, 20-17 (SF)
Falcons, 21-10 (A)
1979—49ers, 20-15 (SF)
Falcons, 31-21 (A)
1980—Falcons, 20-17 (SF)
Falcons, 35-10 (A)
1981—Falcons, 34-17 (A)
49ers, 17-14 (SF)
1982—Falcons, 17-7 (SF)
1983—49ers, 24-20 (SF)
Falcons, 28-24 (A)
1984—49ers, 14-5 (SF)
49ers, 35-17 (A)
1985—49ers, 35-16 (SF)
49ers, 38-17 (A)
1986—Tie, 10-10 (A) OT
49ers, 20-0 (SF)
1987—49ers, 25-17 (A)
49ers, 35-7 (SF)
1988—Falcons, 34-17 (SF)
49ers, 13-3 (A)
1989—49ers, 45-3 (SF)
49ers, 23-10 (A)
1990—49ers, 19-13 (SF)
49ers, 45-35 (A)
1991—Falcons, 39-34 (SF)
Falcons, 17-14 (A)
1992—49ers, 56-17 (SF)
49ers, 41-3 (A)
1993—49ers, 37-30 (SF)
Falcons, 27-24 (A)
1994—49ers, 42-3 (A)
49ers, 50-14 (SF)
1995—49ers, 41-10 (SF)
Falcons, 28-27 (A)
1996—49ers, 39-17 (SF)
49ers, 34-10 (A)
1997—49ers, 34-7 (SF)
49ers, 35-28 (A)
1998—49ers, 31-20 (SF)
Falcons, 31-19 (A)
*Falcons, 20-18 (A)
1999—49ers, 26-7 (SF)
Falcons, 34-29 (A)
2000—Falcons, 36-28 (A)
49ers, 16-6 (SF)
2001—49ers, 16-13 (SF) OT
49ers, 37-31 (A) OT
2004—Falcons, 21-19 (SF)
2007—Falcons, 20-16 (A)
2009—Falcons, 45-10 (SF)
(RS Pts.—49ers 1,756, Falcons 1,261)
(PS Pts.—Falcons 20, 49ers 18)
NFC Divisional Playoff

ATLANTA vs. SEATTLE
RS: Seahawks lead series, 8-3
1976—Seahawks, 30-13 (S)
1979—Seahawks, 31-28 (A)
1985—Seahawks, 30-26 (S)
1988—Seahawks, 31-20 (A)
1991—Falcons, 26-13 (A)
1997—Falcons, 24-17 (S)
2000—Seahawks, 30-10 (A)
2002—Seahawks, 30-24 (A) OT
2004—Seahawks, 28-26 (S)
2005—Seahawks, 21-18 (S)
2007—Falcons, 44-41 (A)
(RS Pts.—Seahawks 302, Falcons 259)

ATLANTA vs. TAMPA BAY
RS: Buccaneers lead series, 18-15
1977—Falcons, 17-0 (TB)
1978—Buccaneers, 14-9 (TB)
1979—Falcons, 17-14 (A)
1981—Buccaneers, 24-23 (TB)
1984—Buccaneers, 23-6 (TB)
1986—Falcons, 23-20 (TB) OT
1987—Buccaneers, 48-10 (TB)
1988—Falcons, 17-10 (A)
1990—Buccaneers, 23-17 (TB)
1991—Falcons, 43-7 (A)
1992—Falcons, 35-7 (TB)
1993—Buccaneers, 31-24 (A)
1994—Falcons, 34-13 (A)
1995—Falcons, 24-21 (TB)
1997—Buccaneers, 31-10 (A)
1999—Buccaneers, 19-10 (TB)
2000—Buccaneers, 27-14 (A)
2002—Buccaneers, 20-6 (A)
Buccaneers, 34-10 (TB)
2003—Buccaneers, 31-10 (A)
Falcons, 30-28 (TB)
2004—Falcons, 24-14 (A)
Buccaneers, 27-0 (TB)
2005—Buccaneers, 30-27 (A)
Buccaneers, 27-24 (TB) OT
2006—Falcons, 14-3 (A)
Falcons, 17-6 (TB)
2007—Buccaneers, 31-7 (A)
Buccaneers, 37-3 (TB)
2008—Buccaneers, 24-9 (TB)
Falcons, 13-10 (A) OT
2009—Falcons, 20-17 (A)
Falcons, 20-10 (TB)
(RS Pts.—Buccaneers 681, Falcons 567)

ATLANTA vs. *TENNESSEE
RS: Titans lead series, 7-5
1972—Falcons, 20-10 (A)
1976—Oilers, 20-14 (H)
1978—Falcons, 20-14 (A)
1981—Falcons, 31-27 (H)
1984—Falcons, 42-10 (A)
1987—Oilers, 37-33 (H)
1990—Falcons, 47-27 (A)
1993—Oilers, 33-17 (H)
1996—Oilers, 23-13 (A)
1999—Titans, 30-17 (T)
2003—Titans, 38-31 (A)
2007—Titans, 20-13 (T)
(RS Pts.—Falcons 298, Titans 289)
Franchise in Houston prior to 1997; known as Oilers prior to 1999

ATLANTA vs. WASHINGTON
RS: Redskins lead series, 14-6-1
PS: Redskins lead series, 1-0
1966—Redskins, 33-20 (W)
1967—Tie, 20-20 (A)
1969—Redskins, 27-20 (W)
1972—Redskins, 24-13 (W)
1975—Redskins, 30-27 (A)
1977—Redskins, 10-6 (W)
1978—Falcons, 20-17 (A)
1979—Redskins, 16-7 (A)
1980—Falcons, 10-6 (A)
1983—Redskins, 37-21 (W)
1984—Redskins, 27-14 (W)
1985—Redskins, 44-10 (A)
1987—Falcons, 21-20 (A)
1989—Redskins, 31-30 (A)
1991—Redskins, 56-17 (W)
*Redskins, 24-7 (W)
1992—Redskins, 24-17 (W)
1993—Redskins, 30-17 (W)
1994—Falcons, 27-20 (W)
2003—Redskins, 33-31 (A)
2006—Falcons, 24-14 (W)
2009—Falcons, 31-17 (W)
(RS Pts.—Redskins 536, Falcons 403)
(PS Pts.—Redskins 24, Falcons 7)
NFC Divisional Playoff

BALTIMORE vs. ARIZONA
RS: Ravens lead series, 3-1;
See Arizona vs. Baltimore

BALTIMORE vs. ATLANTA
RS: Ravens lead series, 2-1;
See Atlanta vs. Baltimore

BALTIMORE vs. BUFFALO
RS: Series tied, 2-2
1999—Bills, 13-10 (Balt)
2004—Ravens, 20-6 (Balt)
2006—Ravens, 19-7 (Balt)
2007—Bills, 19-14 (Buf)
(RS Pts.—Ravens 63, Bills 45)

BALTIMORE vs. CAROLINA
RS: Panthers lead series, 3-0
1996—Panthers, 27-16 (C)
2002—Panthers, 10-7 (C)
2006—Panthers, 23-21 (B)
(RS Pts.—Panthers 60, Ravens 44)

BALTIMORE vs. CHICAGO
RS: Series tied, 2-2
1998—Bears, 24-3 (C)
2001—Ravens, 17-6 (B)
2005—Bears, 10-6 (C)
2009—Ravens, 31-7 (C)

(RS Pts.—Ravens 57, Bears 47)

BALTIMORE vs. CINCINNATI

RS: Ravens lead series, 15-13

1996—Bengals, 24-21 (B)
Bengals, 21-14 (C)
1997—Ravens, 23-10 (B)
Bengals, 16-14 (C)
1998—Ravens, 31-24 (B)
Ravens, 20-13 (C)
1999—Ravens, 34-31 (C)
Ravens, 22-0 (B)
2000—Ravens, 37-0 (B)
Ravens, 27-7 (C)
2001—Bengals, 21-10 (C)
Ravens, 16-0 (B)
2002—Ravens, 38-27 (B)
Ravens, 27-23 (C)
2003—Bengals, 34-26 (C)
Ravens, 31-13 (B)
2004—Ravens, 23-9 (C)
Bengals, 27-26 (B)
2005—Bengals, 21-9 (B)
Bengals, 42-29 (C)
2006—Ravens, 26-20 (B)
Bengals, 13-7 (C)
2007—Bengals, 27-20 (C)
Bengals, 21-7 (B)
2008—Ravens, 17-10 (B)
Ravens, 34-3 (C)
2009—Bengals, 17-14 (B)
Bengals, 17-7 (C)

(RS Pts.—Ravens 610, Bengals 491)

BALTIMORE vs. CLEVELAND

RS: Ravens lead series, 15-7

1999—Ravens, 17-10 (B)
Ravens, 41-9 (C)
2000—Ravens, 12-0 (C)
Ravens, 44-7 (B)
2001—Browns, 24-14 (C)
Browns, 27-17 (B)
2002—Ravens, 26-21 (C)
Browns, 14-13 (B)
2003—Ravens, 33-13 (B)
Ravens, 35-0 (C)
2004—Browns, 20-3 (C)
Ravens, 27-13 (B)
2005—Ravens, 16-3 (B)
Browns, 20-16 (C)
2006—Ravens, 15-14 (C)
Ravens, 27-17 (B)
2007—Browns, 27-13 (C)
Browns, 33-30 (B) OT
2008—Ravens, 28-10 (B)
Ravens, 37-27 (C)
2009—Ravens, 34-3 (B)
Ravens, 16-0 (C)

(RS Pts.—Ravens 514, Browns 312)

BALTIMORE vs. DALLAS

RS: Ravens lead series, 3-0

2000—Ravens, 27-0 (B)
2004—Ravens, 30-10 (B)
2008—Ravens, 33-24 (D)

(RS Pts.—Ravens 90, Cowboys 34)

BALTIMORE vs. DENVER

RS: Ravens lead series, 4-3
PS: Ravens lead series, 1-0

1996—Broncos, 45-34 (D)
2000—*Ravens, 21-3 (B)
2001—Ravens, 20-13 (D)
2002—Ravens, 34-23 (B)
2003—Ravens, 26-6 (B)
2005—Broncos, 12-10 (D)
2006—Broncos, 13-3 (D)
2009—Ravens, 30-7 (B)

(RS Pts.—Ravens 157, Broncos 119)
(PS Pts.—Ravens 21, Broncos 3)
AFC First-Round Playoff

BALTIMORE vs. DETROIT

RS: Ravens lead series, 2-1

1998—Ravens, 19-10 (B)
2005—Lions, 35-17 (D)
2009—Ravens, 48-3 (B)

(RS Pts.—Ravens 84, Lions 48)

BALTIMORE vs. GREEN BAY

RS: Packers lead series, 3-1

1998—Packers, 28-10 (GB)
2001—Packers, 31-23 (GB)
2005—Ravens, 48-3 (B)
2009—Packers, 27-14 (GB)

(RS Pts.—Ravens 95, Packers 89)

BALTIMORE vs. HOUSTON

RS: Ravens lead series, 3-0

2002—Ravens, 23-19 (H)
2005—Ravens, 16-15 (B)
2008—Ravens, 41-13 (H)

(RS Pts.—Ravens 80, Texans 47)

BALTIMORE vs. INDIANAPOLIS

RS: Colts lead series, 7-2
PS: Colts lead series, 2-0

1996—Colts, 26-21 (I)
1998—Ravens, 38-31 (B)
2001—Ravens, 39-27 (B)
2002—Colts, 22-20 (I)
2004—Colts, 20-10 (I)
2005—Colts, 24-7 (B)
2006—*Colts, 15-6 (B)
2007—Colts, 44-20 (B)
2008—Colts, 31-3 (I)
2009—Colts, 17-15 (B)
*Colts, 20-3 (I)

(RS Pts.—Colts 242, Ravens 173)
(PS Pts.—Colts 35, Ravens 9)
AFC Divisional Playoff

BALTIMORE vs. JACKSONVILLE

RS: Jaguars lead series, 9-7

1996—Jaguars, 30-27 (J)
Jaguars, 28-25 (B) OT
1997—Jaguars, 28-27 (B)
Jaguars, 29-27 (J)
1998—Jaguars, 24-10 (J)
Jaguars, 45-19 (B)
1999—Jaguars, 6-3 (J)
Jaguars, 30-23 (B)
2000—Ravens, 39-36 (B)
Ravens, 15-10 (J)
2001—Ravens, 18-17 (B)
Ravens, 24-21 (J)
2002—Ravens, 17-10 (B)
2003—Ravens, 24-17 (B)
2005—Jaguars, 30-3 (J)
2008—Ravens, 27-7 (B)

(RS Pts.—Jaguars 368, Ravens 328)

BALTIMORE vs. KANSAS CITY

RS: Chiefs lead series, 3-2

1999—Chiefs, 35-8 (B)
2003—Chiefs, 17-10 (B)
2004—Chiefs, 27-24 (B)
2006—Ravens, 20-10 (KC)
2009—Ravens, 38-24 (B)

(RS Pts.—Chiefs 113, Ravens 100)

BALTIMORE vs. MIAMI

RS: Dolphins lead series, 5-2
PS: Ravens lead series, 2-0

1997—Dolphins, 24-13 (B)
2000—Dolphins, 19-6 (M)
2001—*Ravens, 20-3 (M)
2002—Dolphins, 26-7 (M)
2003—Dolphins, 9-6 (M) OT
2004—Ravens, 30-23 (B)
2007—Dolphins, 22-16 (M) OT
2008—Ravens, 27-13 (M)
*Ravens, 27-9 (M)

(RS Pts.—Dolphins 136, Ravens 105)
(PS Pts.—Ravens 47, Dolphins 12)
AFC First-Round Playoff

BALTIMORE vs. MINNESOTA

RS: Series tied, 2-2

1998—Vikings, 38-28 (B)
2001—Ravens, 19-3 (B)
2005—Ravens, 30-23 (B)
2009—Vikings, 33-31 (M)

(RS Pts.—Ravens 108, Vikings 97)

BALTIMORE vs. NEW ENGLAND

RS: Patriots lead series, 5-0
PS: Ravens lead series, 1-0

1996—Patriots, 46-38 (B)
1999—Patriots, 20-3 (NE)
2004—Patriots, 24-3 (NE)
2007—Patriots, 27-24 (B)
2009—Patriots, 27-21 (NE)
*Ravens, 33-14 (NE)

(RS Pts.—Patriots 144, Ravens 89)
(PS Pts.—Ravens 33, Patriots 14)
AFC First-Round Playoff

BALTIMORE vs. NEW ORLEANS

RS: Ravens lead series, 3-1

1996—Ravens, 17-10 (B)
1999—Ravens, 31-8 (B)
2002—Saints, 37-25 (B)
2006—Ravens, 35-22 (NO)

(RS Pts.—Ravens 108, Saints 77)

BALTIMORE vs. N.Y. GIANTS

RS: Ravens lead series, 2-1
PS: Ravens lead series, 1-0

1997—Ravens, 24-23 (NY)
2000—*Ravens, 34-7 (Tampa)
2004—Ravens, 37-14 (B)
2008—Giants, 30-10 (NY)

(RS Pts.—Ravens 71, Giants 67)
(PS Pts.—Ravens 34, Giants 7)
Super Bowl XXXV

BALTIMORE vs. N.Y. JETS

RS: Ravens lead series, 5-1

1997—Jets, 19-16 (NY) OT
1998—Ravens, 24-10 (NY)
2000—Ravens, 34-20 (B)
2004—Ravens, 20-17 (NY) OT
2005—Ravens, 13-3 (B)
2007—Ravens, 20-13 (B)

(RS Pts.—Ravens 127, Jets 82)

BALTIMORE vs. OAKLAND

RS: Ravens lead series, 5-1
PS: Ravens lead series, 1-0

1996—Ravens, 19-14 (B)
1998—Ravens, 13-10 (B)
2000—*Ravens, 16-3 (O)
2003—Raiders, 20-12 (O)
2006—Ravens, 28-6 (B)
2008—Ravens, 29-10 (B)
2009—Ravens, 21-13 (O)

(RS Pts.—Ravens 122, Raiders 73)
(PS Pts.—Ravens 16, Raiders 3)
AFC Championship

BALTIMORE vs. PHILADELPHIA
RS: Series tied, 1-1-1
1997—Tie, 10-10 (B) OT
2004—Eagles, 15-10 (P)
2008—Ravens, 36-7 (B)
(RS Pts.—Eagles 56, Ravens 32)

BALTIMORE vs. PITTSBURGH
RS: Steelers lead series, 17-11
PS: Steelers lead series, 2-0
1996—Steelers, 31-17 (P)
Ravens, 31-17 (B)
1997—Steelers, 42-34 (B)
Steelers, 37-0 (P)
1998—Steelers, 20-13 (B)
Steelers, 16-6 (P)
1999—Steelers, 23-20 (B)
Ravens, 31-24 (P)
2000—Ravens, 16-0 (P)
Steelers, 9-6 (B)
2001—Ravens, 13-10 (P)
Steelers, 26-21 (B)
*Steelers, 27-10 (P)
2002—Steelers, 31-18 (B)
Steelers, 34-31 (P)
2003—Steelers, 34-15 (P)
Ravens, 13-10 (B) OT
2004—Ravens, 30-13 (B)
Steelers, 20-7 (P)
2005—Steelers, 20-19 (P)
Ravens, 16-13 (B) OT
2006—Ravens, 27-0 (B)
Ravens, 31-7 (P)
2007—Steelers, 38-7 (P)
Ravens, 27-21 (B)
2008—Steelers, 23-20 (P) OT
Steelers, 13-9 (B)
**Steelers, 23-14 (P)
2009—Ravens, 20-17 (B) OT
Steelers, 23-20 (P)
(RS Pts.—Steelers 572, Ravens 518)
(PS Pts.—Steelers 50, Ravens 24)
**AFC Divisional Playoff*
***AFC Championship*

BALTIMORE vs. ST. LOUIS
RS: Series tied, 2-2
1996—Ravens, 37-31 (B) OT
1999—Rams, 27-10 (StL)
2003—Rams, 33-22 (StL)
2007—Ravens, 22-3 (B)
(RS Pts.—Rams 94, Ravens 91)

BALTIMORE vs. SAN DIEGO
RS: Ravens lead series, 4-3
1997—Chargers, 21-17 (SD)
1998—Chargers, 14-13 (SD)
2000—Ravens, 24-3 (B)
2003—Ravens, 24-10 (SD)
2006—Ravens, 16-13 (B)
2007—Chargers, 32-14 (SD)
2009—Ravens, 31-26 (SD)
(RS Pts.—Ravens 139, Chargers 119)

BALTIMORE vs. SAN FRANCISCO
RS: Ravens lead series, 2-1
1996—49ers, 38-20 (SF)
2003—Ravens, 44-6 (B)
2007—Ravens, 9-7 (SF)
(RS Pts.—Ravens 73, 49ers 51)

BALTIMORE vs. SEATTLE
RS: Ravens lead series, 2-1
1997—Ravens, 31-24 (B)
2003—Ravens, 44-41 (B) OT
2007—Seahawks, 27-6 (S)
(RS Pts.—Seahawks 92, Ravens 81)

BALTIMORE vs. TAMPA BAY
RS: Buccaneers lead series, 2-1
2001—Buccaneers, 22-10 (TB)
2002—Buccaneers, 25-0 (B)
2006—Ravens, 27-0 (TB)
(RS Pts.—Buccaneers 47, Ravens 37)

BALTIMORE vs. *TENNESSEE
RS: Series tied, 8-8
PS: Ravens lead series, 2-1
1996—Oilers, 29-13 (H)
Oilers, 24-21 (B)
1997—Ravens, 36-10 (T)
Ravens, 21-19 (B)
1998—Oilers, 12-8 (B)
Oilers, 16-14 (T)
1999—Titans, 14-11 (T)
Ravens, 41-14 (B)
2000—Titans, 14-6 (B)
Ravens, 24-23 (T)
**Ravens, 24-10 (T)
2001—Ravens, 26-7 (B)
Ravens, 16-10 (T)
2002—Ravens, 13-12 (B)
2003—***Titans, 20-17 (B)
2005—Titans, 25-10 (T)
2006—Ravens, 27-26 (T)
2008—Titans, 13-10 (B)
**Ravens, 13-10 (T)
(RS Pts.—Ravens 297, Titans 268)
(PS Pts.—Ravens 54, Titans 40)
**Franchise in Houston prior to 1997; known as Oilers prior to 1999*
***AFC Divisional Playoff*
****AFC First-Round Playoff*

BALTIMORE vs. WASHINGTON
RS: Ravens lead series, 3-1
1997—Ravens, 20-17 (W)
2000—Redskins, 10-3 (W)
2004—Ravens, 17-10 (W)
2008—Ravens, 24-10 (B)
(RS Pts.—Ravens 64, Redskins 47)

BUFFALO vs. ARIZONA
RS: Bills lead series, 5-4;
See Arizona vs. Buffalo

BUFFALO vs. ATLANTA
RS: Falcons lead series, 6-4;
See Atlanta vs. Buffalo

BUFFALO vs. BALTIMORE
RS: Series tied, 2-2;
See Baltimore vs. Buffalo

BUFFALO vs. CAROLINA
RS: Bills lead series, 4-1
1995—Bills, 31-9 (B)
1998—Bills, 30-14 (C)
2001—Bills, 25-24 (B)
2005—Panthers, 13-9 (B)
2009—Bills, 20-9 (C)
(RS Pts.—Bills 115, Panthers 69)

BUFFALO vs. CHICAGO
RS: Bears lead series, 6-4
1970—Bears, 31-13 (C)
1974—Bills, 16-6 (B)
1979—Bears, 7-0 (B)
1988—Bears, 24-3 (C)
1991—Bills, 35-20 (B)
1994—Bears, 20-13 (C)
1997—Bears, 20-3 (C)
2000—Bills, 20-3 (B)
2002—Bills, 33-27 (B) OT
2006—Bears, 40-7 (C)
(RS Pts.—Bears 198, Bills 143)

BUFFALO vs. CINCINNATI
RS: Bills lead series, 14-9
PS: Bengals lead series, 2-0
1968—Bengals, 34-23 (C)
1969—Bills, 16-13 (B)
1970—Bengals, 43-14 (B)
1973—Bengals, 16-13 (B)
1975—Bengals, 33-24 (C)
1978—Bills, 5-0 (B)
1979—Bills, 51-24 (B)
1980—Bills, 14-0 (C)
1981—Bengals, 27-24 (C) OT
*Bengals, 28-21 (C)
1983—Bills, 10-6 (C)
1984—Bengals, 52-21 (C)
1985—Bengals, 23-17 (B)
1986—Bengals, 36-33 (C) OT
1988—Bengals, 35-21 (C)
**Bengals, 21-10 (C)
1989—Bills, 24-7 (B)
1991—Bills, 35-16 (B)
1996—Bills, 31-17 (B)
1998—Bills, 33-20 (C)
2002—Bills, 27-9 (B)
2003—Bills, 22-16 (B) OT
2004—Bills, 33-17 (C)
2005—Bills, 37-27 (C)
2007—Bills, 33-21 (B)
(RS Pts.—Bills 561, Bengals 492)
(PS Pts.—Bengals 49, Bills 31)
**AFC Divisional Playoff*
***AFC Championship*

BUFFALO vs. CLEVELAND
RS: Browns lead series, 10-5
PS: Browns lead series, 1-0
1972—Browns, 27-10 (C)
1974—Bills, 15-10 (C)
1977—Browns, 27-16 (B)
1978—Browns, 41-20 (C)
1981—Bills, 22-13 (B)
1984—Browns, 13-10 (B)
1985—Browns, 17-7 (C)
1986—Browns, 21-17 (B)
1987—Browns, 27-21 (C)
1989—*Browns, 34-30 (C)
1990—Bills, 42-0 (C)
1995—Bills, 22-19 (C)
2004—Bills, 37-7 (B)
2007—Browns, 8-0 (C)
2008—Browns, 29-27 (B)
2009—Browns, 6-3 (B)
(RS Pts.—Bills 269, Browns 265)
(PS Pts.—Browns 34, Bills 30)
**AFC Divisional Playoff*

BUFFALO vs. DALLAS
RS: Cowboys lead series, 5-3
PS: Cowboys lead series, 2-0
1971—Cowboys, 49-37 (B)
1976—Cowboys, 17-10 (D)
1981—Cowboys, 27-14 (D)
1984—Bills, 14-3 (B)
1992—*Cowboys, 52-17 (Pasadena)
1993—Bills, 13-10 (D)
**Cowboys, 30-13 (Atlanta)
1996—Bills, 10-7 (B)
2003—Cowboys, 10-6 (D)
2007—Cowboys, 25-24 (B)
(RS Pts.—Cowboys 148, Bills 128)
(PS Pts.—Cowboys 82, Bills 30)

**Super Bowl XXVII*
***Super Bowl XXVIII*

BUFFALO vs. DENVER
RS: Bills lead series, 18-15-1
PS: Bills lead series, 1-0
1960—Broncos, 27-21 (B)
Tie, 38-38 (D)
1961—Broncos, 22-10 (B)
Bills, 23-10 (D)
1962—Broncos, 23-20 (B)
Bills, 45-38 (D)
1963—Bills, 30-28 (D)
Bills, 27-17 (B)
1964—Bills, 30-13 (B)
Bills, 30-19 (D)
1965—Bills, 30-15 (D)
Bills, 31-13 (B)
1966—Bills, 38-21 (B)
1967—Bills, 17-16 (D)
Broncos, 21-20 (B)
1968—Broncos, 34-32 (D)
1969—Bills, 41-28 (B)
1970—Broncos, 25-10 (B)
1975—Bills, 38-14 (B)
1977—Broncos, 26-6 (D)
1979—Broncos, 19-16 (B)
1981—Bills, 9-7 (B)
1984—Broncos, 37-7 (B)
1987—Bills, 21-14 (B)
1989—Broncos, 28-14 (B)
1990—Bills, 29-28 (B)
1991—*Bills, 10-7 (B)
1992—Bills, 27-17 (B)
1994—Bills, 27-20 (B)
1995—Broncos, 22-7 (D)
1997—Broncos, 23-20 (B) OT
2002—Broncos, 28-23 (D)
2005—Broncos, 28-17 (B)
2007—Broncos, 15-14 (B)
2008—Bills, 30-23 (D)
(RS Pts.—Bills 798, Broncos 757)
(PS Pts.—Bills 10, Broncos 7)
**AFC Championship*

BUFFALO vs. DETROIT
RS: Lions lead series, 4-3-1
1972—Tie, 21-21 (B)
1976—Lions, 27-14 (D)
1979—Bills, 20-17 (D)
1991—Lions, 17-14 (B) OT
1994—Lions, 35-21 (D)
1997—Bills, 22-13 (B)
2002—Bills, 24-17 (B)
2006—Lions, 20-17 (D)
(RS Pts.—Lions 167, Bills 153)

BUFFALO vs. GREEN BAY
RS: Bills lead series, 7-3
1974—Bills, 27-7 (GB)
1979—Bills, 19-12 (B)
1982—Packers, 33-21 (Mil)
1988—Bills, 28-0 (B)
1991—Bills, 34-24 (Mil)
1994—Bills 29-20 (B)
1997—Packers, 31-21 (GB)
2000—Bills 27-18 (B)
2002—Packers, 10-0 (GB)
2006—Bills, 24-10 (B)
(RS Pts.—Bills 230, Packers 165)

BUFFALO vs. HOUSTON
RS: Bills lead series, 3-2
2002—Bills, 31-24 (H)
2003—Texans, 12-10 (B)
2005—Bills, 22-7 (B)
2006—Bills, 24-21 (H)
2009—Texans, 31-10 (B)
(RS Pts.—Bills 97, Texans 95)

BUFFALO vs. *INDIANAPOLIS
RS: Bills lead series, 35-30-1
1970—Tie, 17-17 (Balt)
Colts, 20-14 (Buff)
1971—Colts, 43-0 (Buff)
Colts, 24-0 (Balt)
1972—Colts, 17-0 (Buff)
Colts, 35-7 (Balt)
1973—Bills, 31-13 (Buff)
Bills, 24-17 (Balt)
1974—Bills, 27-14 (Balt)
Bills, 6-0 (Buff)
1975—Bills, 38-31 (Balt)
Colts, 42-35 (Buff)
1976—Colts, 31-13 (Buff)
Colts, 58-20 (Balt)
1977—Colts, 17-14 (Balt)
Colts, 31-13 (Buff)
1978—Bills, 24-17 (Buff)
Bills, 21-14 (Balt)
1979—Bills, 31-13 (Balt)
Colts, 14-13 (Buff)
1980—Colts, 17-12 (Buff)
Colts, 28-24 (Balt)
1981—Bills, 35-3 (Balt)
Bills, 23-17 (Buff)
1982—Bills, 20-0 (Buff)
1983—Bills, 28-23 (Buff)
Bills, 30-7 (Balt)
1984—Colts, 31-17 (I)
Bills, 21-15 (Buff)
1985—Colts, 49-17 (I)
Bills, 21-9 (Buff)
1986—Bills, 24-13 (Buff)
Colts, 24-14 (I)
1987—Colts, 47-6 (Buff)
Bills, 27-3 (I)
1988—Bills, 34-23 (Buff)
Colts, 17-14 (I)
1989—Colts, 37-14 (I)
Bills, 30-7 (Buff)
1990—Bills, 26-10 (Buff)
Bills, 31-7 (I)
1991—Bills, 42-6 (Buff)
Bills, 35-7 (I)
1992—Bills, 38-0 (Buff)
Colts, 16-13 (I) OT
1993—Bills, 23-9 (Buff)
Bills, 30-10 (I)
1994—Colts, 27-17 (Buff)
Colts, 10-9 (I)
1995—Bills, 20-14 (Buff)
Bills, 16-10 (I)
1996—Bills, 16-13 (Buff) OT
Colts, 13-10 (I) OT
1997—Bills, 37-35 (B)
Bills, 9-6 (I)
1998—Bills, 31-24 (I)
Bills, 34-11 (B)
1999—Colts, 31-14 (I)
Bills, 31-6 (B)
2000—Colts, 18-16 (B)
Colts, 44-20 (I)
2001—Colts, 42-26 (I)
Colts, 30-14 (B)
2003—Colts, 17-14 (B)
2006—Colts, 17-16 (I)
2009—Bills, 30-7 (B)
(RS Pts.—Bills 1,377, Colts 1,278)
**Franchise in Baltimore prior to 1984*

BUFFALO vs. JACKSONVILLE
RS: Bills lead series, 5-4
PS: Jaguars lead series, 1-0
1996—*Jaguars, 30-27 (B)
1997—Jaguars, 20-14 (B)
1998—Bills, 17-16 (B)
2001—Bills, 13-10 (J)
2003—Bills, 38-17 (J)
2004—Jaguars, 13-10 (B)
2006—Bills, 27-24 (B)
2007—Jaguars, 36-14 (J)
2008—Bills, 20-16 (J)
2009—Jaguars, 18-15 (J)
(RS Pts.—Jaguars 170, Bills 168)
(PS Pts.—Jaguars 30, Bills 27)
**AFC First-Round Playoff*

BUFFALO vs. *KANSAS CITY
RS: Bills lead series, 21-16-1
PS: Bills lead series, 2-1
1960—Texans, 45-28 (B)
Texans, 24-7 (D)
1961—Bills, 27-24 (B)
Bills, 30-20 (D)
1962—Texans, 41-21 (D)
Bills, 23-14 (B)
1963—Tie, 27-27 (B)
Bills, 35-26 (KC)
1964—Bills, 34-17 (B)
Bills, 35-22 (KC)
1965—Bills, 23-7 (KC)
Bills, 34-25 (B)
1966—Chiefs, 42-20 (B)
Bills, 29-14 (KC)
**Chiefs, 31-7 (B)
1967—Chiefs, 23-13 (KC)
1968—Chiefs, 18-7 (B)
1969—Chiefs, 29-7 (B)
Chiefs, 22-19 (KC)
1971—Chiefs, 22-9 (KC)
1973—Bills, 23-14 (B)
1976—Bills, 50-17 (B)
1978—Bills, 28-13 (B)
Chiefs, 14-10 (KC)
1982—Bills, 14-9 (B)
1983—Bills, 14-9 (KC)
1986—Chiefs, 20-17 (B)
Bills, 17-14 (KC)
1991—Chiefs, 33-6 (KC)
***Bills, 37-14 (B)
1993—Chiefs, 23-7 (KC)
****Bills, 30-13 (B)
1994—Bills, 44-10 (B)
1996—Bills, 20-9 (B)
1997—Chiefs, 22-16 (KC)
2000—Bills, 21-17 (KC)
2002—Chiefs, 17-16 (KC)
2003—Chiefs, 38-5 (KC)
2005—Bills, 14-3 (B)
2008—Bills, 54-31 (KC)
2009—Bills, 16-10 (KC)
(RS Pts.—Bills 820, Chiefs 785)
(PS Pts.—Bills 74, Chiefs 58)
**Franchise in Dallas prior to 1963 and known as Texans*
***AFL Championship*
****AFC Divisional Playoff*
*****AFC Championship*

BUFFALO vs. MIAMI
RS: Dolphins lead series, 52-35-1
PS: Bills lead series, 3-1
1966—Bills, 58-24 (B)
Bills, 29-0 (M)
1967—Bills, 35-13 (B)
Dolphins, 17-14 (M)
1968—Tie, 14-14 (M)
Dolphins, 21-17 (B)
1969—Dolphins, 24-6 (M)
Bills, 28-3 (B)
1970—Dolphins, 33-14 (B)
Dolphins, 45-7 (M)
1971—Dolphins, 29-14 (B)
Dolphins, 34-0 (M)
1972—Dolphins, 24-23 (M)
Dolphins, 30-16 (B)
1973—Dolphins, 27-6 (M)
Dolphins, 17-0 (B)
1974—Dolphins, 24-16 (B)
Dolphins, 35-28 (M)
1975—Dolphins, 35-30 (B)
Dolphins, 31-21 (M)
1976—Dolphins, 30-21 (B)
Dolphins, 45-27 (M)
1977—Dolphins, 13-0 (B)
Dolphins, 31-14 (M)
1978—Dolphins, 31-24 (M)
Dolphins, 25-24 (B)
1979—Dolphins, 9-7 (B)
Dolphins, 17-7 (M)
1980—Bills, 17-7 (B)
Dolphins, 17-14 (M)
1981—Bills, 31-21 (B)
Dolphins, 16-6 (M)
1982—Dolphins, 9-7 (B)
Dolphins, 27-10 (M)
1983—Dolphins, 12-0 (B)
Bills, 38-35 (M) OT
1984—Dolphins, 21-17 (B)
Dolphins, 38-7 (M)
1985—Dolphins, 23-14 (B)
Dolphins, 28-0 (M)
1986—Dolphins, 27-14 (M)
Dolphins, 34-24 (B)
1987—Bills, 34-31 (M) OT
Bills, 27-0 (B)
1988—Bills, 9-6 (B)
Bills, 31-6 (M)
1989—Bills, 27-24 (M)
Bills, 31-17 (B)
1990—Dolphins, 30-7 (M)
Bills, 24-14 (B)
*Bills, 44-34 (B)
1991—Bills, 35-31 (B)
Bills, 41-27 (M)
1992—Dolphins, 37-10 (B)
Bills, 26-20 (M)
**Bills, 29-10 (M)
1993—Dolphins, 22-13 (B)
Bills, 47-34 (M)
1994—Bills, 21-11 (B)
Bills, 42-31 (M)
1995—Dolphins, 23-6 (M)
Bills, 23-20 (B)
***Bills, 37-22 (B)
1996—Dolphins, 21-7 (B)
Dolphins, 16-14 (M)
1997—Bills, 9-6 (B)
Dolphins, 30-13 (M)
1998—Dolphins, 13-7 (M)
Bills, 30-24 (B)
***Dolphins, 24-17 (M)
1999—Bills, 23-18 (M)
Bills, 23-3 (B)
2000—Dolphins, 22-13 (M)
Dolphins, 33-6 (B)
2001—Dolphins, 34-27 (B)
Dolphins, 34-7 (M)
2002—Bills, 23-10 (M)
Bills, 38-21 (B)
2003—Dolphins, 17-7 (M)
Dolphins, 20-3 (B)
2004—Bills, 20-13 (B)
Bills, 42-32 (M)
2005—Bills, 20-14 (B)
Dolphins, 24-23 (M)
2006—Bills, 16-6 (M)
Bills, 21-0 (B)
2007—Bills, 13-10 (M)
Bills, 38-17 (B)
2008—Dolphins, 25-16 (M)
Dolphins, 16-3 (Toronto)
2009—Dolphins, 38-10 (M)
Bills, 31-14 (B)
(RS Pts.—Dolphins 1,911, Bills 1,656)
(PS Pts.—Bills 127, Dolphins 90)
**AFC Divisional Playoff*
***AFC Championship*
****AFC First-Round Playoff*

BUFFALO vs. MINNESOTA
RS: Vikings lead series, 7-4
1971—Vikings, 19-0 (M)
1975—Vikings, 35-13 (B)
1979—Vikings, 10-3 (M)
1982—Bills, 23-22 (B)
1985—Vikings, 27-20 (B)
1988—Bills, 13-10 (B)
1994—Vikings, 21-17 (B)
1997—Vikings, 34-13 (B)
2000—Vikings, 31-27 (M)
2002—Bills, 45-39 (M) OT
2006—Bills, 17-12 (B)
(RS Pts.—Vikings 260, Bills 191)

BUFFALO vs. *NEW ENGLAND
RS: Patriots lead series, 58-40-1
PS: Patriots lead series, 1-0
1960—Bills, 13-0 (Bos)
Bills, 38-14 (Buff)
1961—Patriots, 23-21 (Buff)
Patriots, 52-21 (Bos)
1962—Tie, 28-28 (Buff)
Patriots, 21-10 (Bos)
1963—Bills, 28-21 (Buff)
Patriots, 17-7 (Bos)
**Patriots, 26-8 (Buff)
1964—Patriots, 36-28 (Buff)
Bills, 24-14 (Bos)
1965—Bills, 24-7 (Buff)
Bills, 23-7 (Bos)
1966—Patriots, 20-10 (Buff)
Patriots, 14-3 (Bos)
1967—Patriots, 23-0 (Buff)
Bills, 44-16 (Bos)
1968—Patriots, 16-7 (Buff)
Patriots, 23-6 (Bos)
1969—Bills, 23-16 (Buff)
Patriots, 35-21 (Bos)
1970—Bills, 45-10 (Bos)
Patriots, 14-10 (Buff)
1971—Patriots, 38-33 (NE)
Bills, 27-20 (Buff)
1972—Bills, 38-14 (Buff)
Bills, 27-24 (NE)
1973—Bills, 31-13 (NE)
Bills, 37-13 (Buff)
1974—Bills, 30-28 (Buff)
Bills, 29-28 (NE)
1975—Bills, 45-31 (Buff)
Bills, 34-14 (NE)
1976—Patriots, 26-22 (Buff)
Patriots, 20-10 (NE)
1977—Bills, 24-14 (NE)
Patriots, 20-7 (Buff)
1978—Patriots, 14-10 (Buff)
Patriots, 26-24 (NE)
1979—Patriots, 26-6 (Buff)
Bills, 16-13 (NE) OT
1980—Bills, 31-13 (Buff)
Patriots, 24-2 (NE)
1981—Bills, 20-17 (Buff)
Bills, 19-10 (NE)
1982—Patriots, 30-19 (NE)
1983—Patriots, 31-0 (Buff)
Patriots, 21-7 (NE)
1984—Patriots, 21-17 (Buff)
Patriots, 38-10 (NE)
1985—Patriots, 17-14 (Buff)
Patriots, 14-3 (NE)
1986—Patriots, 23-3 (Buff)
Patriots, 22-19 (NE)
1987—Patriots, 14-7 (NE)
Patriots, 13-7 (Buff)
1988—Bills, 16-14 (NE)
Bills, 23-20 (Buff)
1989—Bills, 31-10 (Buff)
Patriots, 33-24 (NE)
1990—Bills, 27-10 (NE)
Bills, 14-0 (Buff)
1991—Bills, 22-17 (Buff)
Patriots, 16-13 (NE)
1992—Bills, 41-7 (NE)
Bills, 16-7 (Buff)
1993—Bills, 38-14 (Buff)
Bills, 13-10 (NE) OT
1994—Bills, 38-35 (NE)
Patriots, 41-17 (Buff)
1995—Patriots, 27-14 (NE)
Patriots, 35-25 (Buff)
1996—Bills, 17-10 (Buff)
Patriots, 28-25 (NE)
1997—Patriots, 33-6 (NE)
Patriots, 31-10 (Buff)
1998—Bills, 13-10 (Buff)
Patriots, 25-21 (NE)
1999—Bills, 17-7 (Buff)
Bills, 13-10 (NE) OT
2000—Bills, 16-13 (NE) OT
Patriots, 13-10 (Buff) OT
2001—Patriots, 21-11 (NE)
Patriots, 12-9 (Buff) OT
2002—Patriots, 38-7 (Buff)
Patriots, 27-17 (NE)
2003—Bills, 31-0 (Buff)
Patriots, 31-0 (NE)
2004—Patriots, 31-17 (Buff)
Patriots, 29-6 (NE)
2005—Patriots, 21-16 (NE)
Patriots, 35-7 (Buff)
2006—Patriots, 19-17 (NE)
Patriots, 28-6 (B)
2007—Patriots, 38-7 (NE)
Patriots, 56-10 (Buff)

2008—Patriots, 20-10 (NE)
Patriots, 13-0 (B)
2009—Patriots, 25-24 (NE)
Patriots, 17-10 (Buff)
(RS Pts.—Patriots 2,054, Bills 1,787)
(PS Pts.—Patriots 26, Bills 8)
Franchise in Boston prior to 1971
***Division Playoff*

BUFFALO vs. NEW ORLEANS
RS: Saints lead series, 5-4
1973—Saints, 13-0 (NO)
1980—Bills, 35-26 (NO)
1983—Bills, 27-21 (B)
1989—Saints, 22-19 (B)
1992—Bills, 20-16 (NO)
1998—Bills, 45-33 (NO)
2001—Saints, 24-6 (B)
2005—Saints, 19-7 (San Antonio)
2009—Saints, 27-7 (B)
(RS Pts.—Saints 201, Bills 166)

BUFFALO vs. N.Y. GIANTS
RS: Bills lead series, 6-4
PS: Giants lead series, 1-0
1970—Giants, 20-6 (NY)
1975—Giants, 17-14 (B)
1978—Bills, 41-17 (B)
1987—Bills, 6-3 (B) OT
1990—Bills, 17-13 (NY)
*Giants, 20-19 (Tampa)
1993—Bills, 17-14 (B)
1996—Bills, 23-20 (NY) OT
1999—Giants, 19-17 (B)
2003—Bills, 24-7 (NY)
2007—Giants, 38-21 (B)
(RS Pts.—Bills 186, Giants 168)
(PS Pts.—Giants 20, Bills 19)
**Super Bowl XXV*

BUFFALO vs. *N.Y. JETS
RS: Bills lead series, 53-45
PS: Bills lead series, 1-0
1960—Titans, 27-3 (NY)
Titans, 17-13 (B)
1961—Bills, 41-31 (B)
Titans, 21-14 (NY)
1962—Titans, 17-6 (B)
Bills, 20-3 (NY)
1963—Bills, 45-14 (B)
Bills, 19-10 (NY)
1964—Bills, 34-24 (B)
Bills, 20-7 (NY)
1965—Bills, 33-21 (B)
Jets, 14-12 (NY)
1966—Bills, 33-23 (NY)
Bills, 14-3 (B)
1967—Bills, 20-17 (B)
Jets, 20-10 (NY)
1968—Bills, 37-35 (B)
Jets, 25-21 (NY)
1969—Jets, 33-19 (B)
Jets, 16-6 (NY)
1970—Bills, 34-31 (B)
Bills, 10-6 (NY)
1971—Jets, 28-17 (NY)
Jets, 20-7 (B)
1972—Jets, 41-24 (B)
Jets, 41-3 (NY)
1973—Bills, 9-7 (B)
Bills, 34-14 (NY)
1974—Bills, 16-12 (B)
Jets, 20-10 (NY)
1975—Bills, 42-14 (B)
Bills, 24-23 (NY)
1976—Jets, 17-14 (NY)
Jets, 19-14 (B)
1977—Jets, 24-19 (B)
Bills, 14-10 (NY)
1978—Jets, 21-20 (B)
Jets, 45-14 (NY)
1979—Bills, 46-31 (B)
Bills, 14-12 (NY)
1980—Bills, 20-10 (B)
Bills, 31-24 (NY)
1981—Bills, 31-0 (B)
Jets, 33-14 (NY)
**Bills, 31-27 (NY)
1983—Jets, 34-10 (B)
Bills, 24-17 (NY)
1984—Jets, 28-26 (B)
Jets, 21-17 (NY)
1985—Jets, 42-3 (NY)
Jets, 27-7 (B)
1986—Jets, 28-24 (B)
Jets, 14-13 (NY)
1987—Jets, 31-28 (B)
Bills, 17-14 (NY)
1988—Bills, 37-14 (NY)
Bills, 9-6 (B) OT
1989—Bills, 34-3 (B)
Bills, 37-0 (NY)
1990—Bills, 30-7 (NY)
Bills, 30-27 (B)
1991—Bills, 23-20 (NY)
Bills, 24-13 (B)
1992—Bills, 24-20 (NY)
Jets, 24-17 (B)
1993—Bills, 19-10 (NY)
Bills, 16-14 (B)
1994—Jets, 23-3 (B)
Jets, 22-17 (NY)
1995—Bills, 29-10 (B)
Bills, 28-26 (NY)
1996—Bills, 25-22 (NY)
Bills, 35-10 (B)
1997—Bills, 28-22 (NY)
Bills, 20-10 (B)
1998—Jets, 34-12 (NY)
Jets, 17-10 (B)
1999—Bills, 17-3 (B)
Jets, 17-7 (NY)
2000—Jets, 27-14 (NY)
Bills, 23-20 (B)
2001—Jets, 42-36 (B)
Bills, 14-9 (NY)
2002—Jets, 37-31 (B) OT
Jets, 31-13 (NY)
2003—Jets, 30-3 (NY)
Bills, 17-6 (B)
2004—Jets, 16-14 (NY)
Bills, 22-17 (B)
2005—Bills, 27-17 (B)
Jets, 30-26 (NY)
2006—Jets, 28-20 (B)
Bills, 31-13 (NY)
2007—Bills, 17-14 (B)
Bills, 13-3 (NY)
2008—Jets, 26-17 (B)
Jets, 31-27 (NY)
2009—Bills, 16-13 (NY) OT
Jets, 19-13 (Toronto)
(RS Pts.—Bills 1,995, Jets 1,940)
(PS Pts.—Bills 31, Jets 27)
**Jets known as Titans prior to 1963*
***AFC First-Round Playoff*

BUFFALO vs. *OAKLAND
RS: Raiders lead series, 19-16
PS: Bills lead series, 2-0
1960—Bills, 38-9 (B)
Raiders, 20-7 (O)
1961—Raiders, 31-22 (B)
Bills, 26-21 (O)
1962—Bills, 14-6 (B)
Bills, 10-6 (O)
1963—Raiders, 35-17 (O)
Bills, 12-0 (B)
1964—Bills, 23-20 (B)
Raiders, 16-13 (O)
1965—Bills, 17-12 (B)
Bills, 17-14 (O)
1966—Bills, 31-10 (O)
1967—Raiders, 24-20 (B)
Raiders, 28-21 (O)
1968—Raiders, 48-6 (B)
Raiders, 13-10 (O)
1969—Raiders, 50-21 (O)
1972—Raiders, 28-16 (O)
1974—Bills, 21-20 (B)
1977—Raiders, 34-13 (O)
1980—Bills, 24-7 (B)
1983—Raiders, 27-24 (B)
1987—Raiders, 34-21 (LA)
1988—Bills, 37-21 (B)
1990—Bills, 38-24 (B)
**Bills, 51-3 (B)
1991—Bills, 30-27 (LA) OT
1992—Raiders, 20-3 (LA)
1993—Raiders, 25-24 (B)
***Bills, 29-23 (B)
1998—Bills, 44-21 (B)
1999—Raiders, 20-14 (B)
2002—Raiders, 49-31 (B)
2004—Raiders, 13-10 (O)
2005—Raiders, 38-17 (O)
2008—Bills, 24-23 (B)
(RS Pts.—Raiders 794, Bills 716)
(PS Pts.—Bills 80, Raiders 26)
**Franchise in Los Angeles from 1982-1994*
***AFC Championship*
****AFC Divisional Playoff*

BUFFALO vs. PHILADELPHIA
RS: Eagles lead series, 6-5
1973—Bills, 27-26 (B)
1981—Eagles, 20-14 (B)
1984—Eagles, 27-17 (B)
1985—Eagles, 21-17 (P)
1987—Eagles, 17-7 (P)
1990—Bills, 30-23 (B)
1993—Bills, 10-7 (P)
1996—Bills, 24-17 (P)
1999—Bills, 26-0 (B)
2003—Eagles, 23-13 (B)
2007—Eagles, 17-9 (P)
(RS Pts.—Eagles 198, Bills 194)

BUFFALO vs. PITTSBURGH
RS: Steelers lead series, 11-8
PS: Steelers lead series, 2-1
1970—Steelers, 23-10 (P)
1972—Steelers, 38-21 (B)
1974—*Steelers, 32-14 (P)
1975—Bills, 30-21 (P)
1978—Steelers, 28-17 (B)
1979—Steelers, 28-0 (P)
1980—Bills, 28-13 (B)
1982—Bills, 13-0 (B)

1985—Steelers, 30-24 (P)
1986—Bills, 16-12 (B)
1988—Bills, 36-28 (B)
1991—Bills, 52-34 (B)
1992—Bills, 28-20 (B)
*Bills, 24-3 (P)
1993—Steelers, 23-0 (P)
1994—Steelers, 23-10 (P)
1995—*Steelers, 40-21 (P)
1996—Steelers, 24-6 (P)
1999—Bills, 24-21 (B)
2001—Steelers, 20-3 (B)
2004—Steelers, 29-24 (B)
2007—Steelers, 26-3 (P)
(RS Pts.—Steelers 441, Bills 345)
(PS Pts.—Steelers 75, Bills 59)
AFC Divisional Playoff

BUFFALO vs. *ST. LOUIS
RS: Bills lead series, 6-4
1970—Rams, 19-0 (B)
1974—Rams, 19-14 (LA)
1980—Bills, 10-7 (B) OT
1983—Rams, 41-17 (LA)
1989—Bills, 23-20 (B)
1992—Bills, 40-7 (B)
1995—Bills, 45-27 (StL)
1998—Rams, 34-33 (B)
2004—Bills, 37-17 (B)
2008—Bills, 31-14 (StL)
(RS Pts.—Bills 250, Rams 205)
Franchise in Los Angeles prior to 1995

BUFFALO vs. *SAN DIEGO
RS: Chargers lead series, 20-10-2
PS: Bills lead series, 2-1
1960—Chargers, 24-10 (B)
Bills, 32-3 (LA)
1961—Chargers, 19-11 (B)
Chargers, 28-10 (SD)
1962—Bills, 35-10 (B)
Bills, 40-20 (SD)
1963—Chargers, 14-10 (SD)
Chargers, 23-13 (B)
1964—Bills, 30-3 (B)
Bills, 27-24 (SD)
**Bills, 20-7 (B)
1965—Chargers, 34-3 (B)
Tie, 20-20 (SD)
**Bills, 23-0 (SD)
1966—Chargers, 27-7 (SD)
Tie, 17-17 (B)
1967—Chargers, 37-17 (B)
1968—Chargers, 21-6 (B)
1969—Chargers, 45-6 (SD)
1971—Chargers, 20-3 (SD)
1973—Chargers, 34-7 (SD)
1976—Chargers, 34-13 (B)
1979—Chargers, 27-19 (SD)
1980—Bills, 26-24 (SD)
***Chargers, 20-14 (SD)
1981—Bills, 28-27 (SD)
1985—Chargers, 14-9 (B)
Chargers, 40-7 (SD)
1998—Chargers, 16-14 (SD)
2000—Bills, 27-24 (B) OT
2001—Chargers, 27-24 (SD)
2002—Bills, 20-13 (B)
2005—Chargers, 48-10 (SD)
2006—Chargers, 24-21 (B)
2008—Bills, 23-14 (B)
(RS Pts.—Chargers 755, Bills 545)
(PS Pts.—Bills 57, Chargers 27)
Franchise in Los Angeles prior to 1961
***AFL Championship*
****AFC Divisional Playoff*

BUFFALO vs. SAN FRANCISCO
RS: Series tied, 5-5
1972—Bills, 27-20 (B)
1980—Bills, 18-13 (SF)
1983—49ers, 23-10 (B)
1989—49ers, 21-10 (SF)
1992—Bills, 34-31 (SF)
1995—49ers, 27-17 (SF)
1998—Bills, 26-21 (B)
2001—49ers, 35-0 (SF)
2004—Bills, 41-7 (SF)
2008—49ers, 10-3 (B)
(RS Pts.—49ers 208, Bills 186)

BUFFALO vs. SEATTLE
RS: Seahawks lead series, 6-5
1977—Seahawks, 56-17 (S)
1984—Seahawks, 31-28 (S)
1988—Bills, 13-3 (S)
1989—Seahawks, 17-16 (S)
1995—Bills, 27-21 (B)
1996—Seahawks, 26-18 (S)
1999—Seahawks, 26-16 (S)
2000—Bills, 42-23 (S)
2001—Seahawks, 23-20 (B)
2004—Bills, 38-9 (S)
2008—Bills, 34-10 (B)
(RS Pts.—Bills 269, Seahawks 245)

BUFFALO vs. TAMPA BAY
RS: Buccaneers lead series, 6-3
1976—Bills, 14-9 (TB)
1978—Buccaneers, 31-10 (TB)
1982—Buccaneers, 24-23 (TB)
1986—Buccaneers, 34-28 (TB)
1988—Buccaneers, 10-5 (TB)
1991—Bills, 17-10 (TB)
2000—Buccaneers, 31-17 (TB)
2005—Buccaneers, 19-3 (TB)
2009—Bills, 33-20 (B)
(RS Pts.—Buccaneers 188, Bills 150)

BUFFALO vs. *TENNESSEE
RS: Titans lead series, 25-14
PS: Bills lead series, 2-1
1960—Bills, 25-24 (B)
Oilers, 31-23 (H)
1961—Bills, 22-12 (H)
Oilers, 28-16 (B)
1962—Oilers, 28-23 (B)
Oilers, 17-14 (H)
1963—Oilers, 31-20 (B)
Oilers, 28-14 (H)
1964—Bills, 48-17 (H)
Bills, 24-10 (B)
1965—Oilers, 19-17 (B)
Bills, 29-18 (H)
1966—Bills, 27-20 (B)
Bills, 42-20 (H)
1967—Oilers, 20-3 (B)
Oilers, 10-3 (H)
1968—Oilers, 30-7 (B)
Oilers, 35-6 (H)
1969—Oilers, 17-3 (B)
Oilers, 28-14 (H)
1971—Oilers, 20-14 (B)
1974—Oilers, 21-9 (B)
1976—Oilers, 13-3 (B)
1978—Oilers, 17-10 (H)
1983—Bills, 30-13 (B)
1985—Bills, 20-0 (B)
1986—Oilers, 16-7 (H)
1987—Bills, 34-30 (B)
1988—**Bills, 17-10 (B)
1989—Bills, 47-41 (H) OT
1990—Oilers, 27-24 (H)
1992—Oilers, 27-3 (H)
***Bills, 41-38 (B) OT
1993—Bills, 35-7 (B)
1994—Bills, 15-7 (H)
1995—Oilers, 28-17 (B)
1997—Oilers, 31-14 (T)
1999—***Titans, 22-16 (T)
2000—Bills, 16-13 (B)
2003—Titans, 28-26 (T)
2006—Titans, 30-29 (B)
2009—Titans, 41-17 (T)
(RS Pts.—Titans 853, Bills 750)
(PS Pts.—Bills 74, Titans 70)
Franchise in Houston prior to 1997; known as Oilers prior to 1999
***AFC Divisional Playoff*
****AFC First-Round Playoff*

BUFFALO vs. WASHINGTON
RS: Bills lead series, 7-4
PS: Redskins lead series, 1-0
1972—Bills, 24-17 (W)
1977—Redskins, 10-0 (B)
1981—Bills, 21-14 (B)
1984—Redskins, 41-14 (W)
1987—Redskins, 27-7 (B)
1990—Redskins, 29-14 (W)
1991—*Redskins, 37-24 (Minneapolis)
1993—Bills, 24-10 (B)
1996—Bills, 38-13 (B)
1999—Bills, 34-17 (W)
2003—Bills, 24-7 (B)
2007—Bills, 17-16 (W)
(RS Pts.—Bills 217, Redskins 201)
(PS Pts.—Redskins 37, Bills 24)
Super Bowl XXVI

CAROLINA vs. ARIZONA
RS: Panthers lead series, 7-2
PS: Cardinals lead series, 1-0;
See Arizona vs. Carolina

CAROLINA vs. ATLANTA
RS: Falcons lead series, 18-12;
See Atlanta vs. Carolina

CAROLINA vs. BALTIMORE
RS: Panthers lead series, 3-0;
See Baltimore vs. Carolina

CAROLINA vs. BUFFALO
RS: Bills lead series, 4-1;
See Buffalo vs. Carolina

CAROLINA vs. CHICAGO
RS: Series tied, 2-2
PS: Panthers lead series, 1-0
1995—Bears, 31-27 (Chi)
2002—Panthers, 24-14 (Car)
2005—Bears, 13-3 (Chi)
*Panthers, 29-21 (Chi)
2008—Panthers, 20-17 (Car)
(RS Pts.—Bears 75, Panthers 74)
(PS Pts.—Panthers 29, Bears 21)
NFC Divisional Playoff

CAROLINA vs. CINCINNATI
RS: Panthers lead series, 2-1
1999—Panthers, 27-3 (Car)
2002—Panthers, 52-31 (Car)
2006—Bengals, 17-14 (Cin)
(RS Pts.—Panthers 93, Bengals 51)

CAROLINA vs. CLEVELAND
RS: Panthers lead series, 3-0
1999—Panthers, 31-17 (Cle)
2002—Panthers, 13-6 (Cle)
2006—Panthers, 20-12 (Car)
(RS Pts.—Panthers 64, Browns 35)

CAROLINA vs. DALLAS
RS: Cowboys lead series, 8-1
PS: Panthers lead series, 2-0
1996—*Panthers, 26-17 (C)
1997—Panthers, 23-13 (D)
1998—Cowboys, 27-20 (D)
2000—Cowboys, 16-13 (C) OT
2002—Cowboys, 14-13 (D)
2003—Cowboys, 24-20 (D)
**Panthers, 29-10 (C)
2005—Cowboys, 24-20 (C)
2006—Cowboys, 35-14 (C)
2007—Cowboys, 20-13 (C)
2009—Cowboys, 21-7 (D)
(RS Pts.—Cowboys 194, Panthers 143)
(PS Pts.—Panthers 55, Cowboys 27)
NFC Divisional Playoff
NFC First-Round Playoff

CAROLINA vs. DENVER
RS: Broncos lead series, 2-1
1997—Broncos, 34-0 (D)
2004—Broncos, 20-17 (D)
2008—Panthers, 30-10 (C)
(RS Pts.—Broncos 64, Panthers 47)

CAROLINA vs. DETROIT
RS: Panthers lead series, 4-1
1999—Lions, 24-9 (C)
2002—Panthers, 31-7 (C)
2003—Panthers, 20-14 (C)
2005—Panthers, 21-20 (D)
2008—Panthers, 31-22 (C)
(RS Pts.—Panthers 112, Lions 87)

CAROLINA vs. GREEN BAY
RS: Packers lead series, 6-4
PS: Packers lead series, 1-0
1996—*Packers, 30-13 (GB)
1997—Packers, 31-10 (C)
1998—Packers, 37-30 (C)
1999—Panthers, 33-31 (GB)
2000—Panthers, 31-14 (C)
2001—Packers, 28-7 (C)
2002—Packers, 17-14 (GB)
2004—Packers, 24-14 (C)
2005—Panthers, 32-29 (C)
2007—Packers, 31-17 (GB)
2008—Panthers, 35-31 (GB)
(RS Pts.—Packers 273, Panthers 223)
(PS Pts.—Packers 30, Panthers 13)
NFC Championship

CAROLINA vs. HOUSTON
RS: Texans lead series, 2-0
2003—Texans, 14-10 (H)
2007—Texans, 34-21 (C)
(RS Pts.—Texans 48, Panthers 31)

CAROLINA vs. INDIANAPOLIS
RS: Panthers lead series, 3-1
1995—Panthers, 13-10 (C)
1998—Panthers, 27-19 (I)
2003—Panthers, 23-20 (I) OT
2007—Colts, 31-7 (C)
(RS Pts.—Colts 80, Panthers 70)

CAROLINA vs. JACKSONVILLE
RS: Jaguars lead series, 3-1
1996—Jaguars, 24-14 (J)
1999—Jaguars, 22-20 (C)
2003—Panthers, 24-23 (C)
2007—Jaguars, 37-6 (J)
(RS Pts.—Jaguars 106, Panthers 64)

CAROLINA vs. KANSAS CITY
RS: Series tied, 2-2
1997—Chiefs, 35-14 (C)
2000—Chiefs, 15-14 (KC)
2004—Panthers, 28-17 (KC)
2008—Panthers, 34-0 (C)
(RS Pts.—Panthers 90, Chiefs 67)

CAROLINA vs. MIAMI
RS: Dolphins lead series, 4-0
1998—Dolphins, 13-9 (C)
2001—Dolphins, 23-6 (M)
2005—Dolphins, 27-24 (M)
2009—Dolphins, 24-17 (C)
(RS Pts.—Dolphins 87, Panthers 56)

CAROLINA vs. MINNESOTA
RS: Vikings lead series, 5-4
1996—Vikings, 14-12 (M)
1997—Vikings, 21-14 (M)
2000—Vikings, 31-17 (M)
2001—Panthers, 24-13 (M)
2002—Panthers, 21-14 (M)
2005—Panthers, 38-13 (C)
2006—Vikings, 16-13 (M) OT
2008—Vikings, 20-10 (M)
2009—Panthers, 26-7 (C)
(RS Pts.—Panthers 175, Vikings 149)

CAROLINA vs. NEW ENGLAND
RS: Series tied, 2-2
PS: Patriots lead series, 1-0
1995—Panthers, 20-17 (NE) OT
2001—Patriots, 38-6 (C)
2003—*Patriots, 32-29 (Houston)
2005—Panthers, 27-17 (C)
2009—Patriots, 20-10 (NE)
(RS Pts.—Patriots 92, Panthers 63)
(PS Pts.—Patriots 32, Panthers 29)
Super Bowl XXXVIII

CAROLINA vs. NEW ORLEANS
RS: Panthers lead series, 17-13
1995—Panthers, 20-3 (C)
Saints, 34-26 (NO)
1996—Panthers, 22-20 (NO)
Panthers, 19-7 (C)
1997—Panthers, 13-0 (NO)
Saints, 16-13 (C)
1998—Saints, 19-14 (NO)
Panthers, 31-17 (C)
1999—Saints, 19-10 (NO)
Panthers, 45-13 (C)
2000—Saints, 24-6 (NO)
Saints, 20-10 (C)
2001—Saints, 27-25 (C)
Saints, 27-23 (NO)
2002—Saints, 34-24 (C)
Panthers, 10-6 (NO)
2003—Panthers, 19-13 (C)
Panthers, 23-20 (NO) OT
2004—Panthers, 32-21 (NO)
Saints, 21-18 (C)
2005—Saints, 23-20 (C)
Panthers, 27-10 (Baton Rouge)
2006—Panthers, 21-18 (C)
Panthers, 31-21 (NO)
2007—Panthers, 16-13 (NO)
Saints, 31-6 (C)
2008—Panthers, 30-7 (C)
Panthers, 33-31 (NO)
2009—Saints, 30-20 (NO)
Panthers, 23-10 (C)
(RS Pts.—Panthers 630, Saints 555)

CAROLINA vs. N.Y. GIANTS
RS: Panthers lead series, 3-2
PS: Panthers lead series, 1-0
1996—Panthers, 27-17 (C)
2003—Panthers, 37-24 (NY)
2005—*Panthers, 23-0 (NY)
2006—Giants, 27-13 (C)
2008—Giants, 34-28 (NY) OT
2009—Panthers, 41-9 (NY)
(RS Pts.—Panthers 146, Giants 111)
(PS Pts.—Panthers 23, Giants 0)
NFC First-Round Playoff

CAROLINA vs. N.Y. JETS
RS: Jets lead series, 3-2
1995—Panthers, 26-15 (C)
1998—Jets, 48-21 (NY)
2001—Jets, 13-12 (C)
2005—Panthers, 30-3 (C)
2009—Jets, 17-6 (NY)
(RS Pts.—Jets 96, Panthers 95)

CAROLINA vs. OAKLAND
RS: Series tied, 2-2
1997—Panthers, 38-14 (C)
2000—Raiders, 52-9 (O)
2004—Raiders, 27-24 (C)
2008—Panthers, 17-6 (O)
(RS Pts.— Raiders 99, Panthers 88)

CAROLINA vs. PHILADELPHIA
RS: Eagles lead series, 5-1
PS: Panthers lead series, 1-0
1996—Eagles, 20-9 (P)
1999—Panthers, 33-7 (C)
2003—Eagles, 25-16 (C)
*Panthers, 14-3 (P)
2004—Eagles, 30-8 (P)
2006—Eagles, 27-24 (P)
2009—Eagles, 38-10 (C)
(RS Pts.—Eagles 147, Panthers 100)
(PS Pts.—Panthers 14, Eagles 3)
NFC Championship

CAROLINA vs. PITTSBURGH
RS: Steelers lead series, 3-1
1996—Panthers, 18-14 (C)
1999—Steelers, 30-20 (P)
2002—Steelers, 30-14 (P)
2006—Steelers, 37-3 (C)
(RS Pts.—Steelers 111, Panthers 55)

CAROLINA vs. ST. LOUIS
RS: Panthers lead series, 10-7
PS: Panthers lead series, 1-0
1995—Rams, 31-10 (C)
Rams, 28-17 (StL)
1996—Panthers, 45-13 (C)
Panthers, 20-10 (StL)
1997—Panthers, 16-10 (StL)
Rams, 30-18 (C)
1998—Panthers, 24-20 (StL)
Panthers, 20-13 (C)
1999—Rams, 35-10 (StL)
Rams, 34-21 (C)
2000—Panthers, 27-24 (StL)
Panthers, 16-3 (C)
2001—Rams, 48-14 (StL)
Rams, 38-32 (C)
2003—*Panthers, 29-23 (StL) 2OT
2004—Panthers, 20-7 (C)
2006—Panthers, 15-0 (C)
2007—Panthers, 27-13 (StL)
(RS Pts.—Rams 357, Panthers 352)

(PS Pts.—Panthers 29, Rams 23)
*NFC Divisional Playoff

CAROLINA vs. SAN DIEGO
RS: Panthers lead series, 3-1
1997—Panthers, 26-7 (SD)
2000—Panthers, 30-22 (C)
2004—Chargers, 17-6 (C)
2008—Panthers, 26-24 (SD)
(RS Pts.—Panthers 88, Chargers 70)

CAROLINA vs. SAN FRANCISCO
RS: Panthers lead series, 9-7
1995—Panthers, 13-7 (SF)
49ers, 31-10 (C)
1996—Panthers, 23-7 (C)
Panthers, 30-24 (SF)
1997—49ers, 34-21 (C)
49ers, 27-19 (SF)
1998—49ers, 25-23 (SF)
49ers, 31-28 (C) OT
1999—Panthers, 31-29 (SF)
Panthers, 41-24 (C)
2000—Panthers, 38-22 (SF)
Panthers, 34-16 (C)
2001—49ers, 24-14 (SF)
49ers, 25-22 (C) OT
2004—Panthers, 37-27 (SF)
2007—Panthers, 31-14 (C)
(RS Pts.—Panthers 415, 49ers 367)

CAROLINA vs. SEATTLE
RS: Panthers lead series, 2-1
PS: Seahawks lead series, 1-0
2000—Panthers, 26-3 (C)
2004—Seahawks, 23-17 (S)
2005—*Seahawks, 34-14 (S)
2007—Panthers, 13-10 (C)
(RS Pts.—Panthers 56, Seahawks 36)
(PS Pts.—Seahawks 34, Panthers 14)
*NFC Championship

CAROLINA vs. TAMPA BAY
RS: Panthers lead series, 12-7
1995—Buccaneers, 20-13 (C)
1996—Panthers, 24-0 (C)
1998—Buccaneers, 16-13 (TB)
2002—Buccaneers, 12-9 (C)
Buccaneers, 23-10 (TB)
2003—Panthers, 12-9 (TB) OT
Panthers, 27-24 (C)
2004—Panthers, 21-14 (C)
Panthers, 37-20 (TB)
2005—Panthers, 34-14 (TB)
Buccaneers, 20-10 (C)
2006—Panthers, 26-24 (TB)
Panthers, 24-10 (C)
2007—Buccaneers, 20-7 (C)
Panthers, 31-23 (TB)
2008—Buccaneers, 27-3 (TB)
Panthers, 38-23 (C)
2009—Panthers, 28-21 (TB)
Panthers, 16-6 (C)
(RS Pts.—Panthers 383, Buccaneers 326)

CAROLINA vs. *TENNESSEE
RS: Titans lead series, 2-1
1996—Panthers, 31-6 (H)
2003—Titans, 37-17 (C)
2006—Panthers, 26-24 (TB)
Panthers, 24-10 (C)
2007—Titans, 20-7 (T)
(RS Pts.—Titans 63, Panthers 55)
*Franchise in Houston prior to 1997; known as Oilers prior to 1999

CAROLINA vs. WASHINGTON
RS: Redskins lead series, 7-2
1995—Redskins, 20-17 (W)
1997—Redskins, 24-10 (C)
1998—Redskins, 28-25 (C)
1999—Redskins, 38-36 (W)
2000—Redskins, 20-17 (W)
2001—Redskins, 17-14 (W) OT
2003—Panthers, 20-17 (C)
2006—Redskins, 17-13 (W)
2009—Panthers, 20-17 (C)
(RS Pts.—Redskins 198, Panthers 172)

CHICAGO vs. ARIZONA
RS: Bears lead series, 55-27-6;
See Arizona vs. Chicago

CHICAGO vs. ATLANTA
RS: Series tied, 12-12;
See Atlanta vs. Chicago

CHICAGO vs. BALTIMORE
RS: Series tied, 2-2;
See Baltimore vs. Chicago

CHICAGO vs. BUFFALO
RS: Bears lead series, 6-4;
See Buffalo vs. Chicago

CHICAGO vs. CAROLINA
RS: Series tied, 2-2
PS: Panthers lead series, 1-0;
See Carolina vs. Chicago

CHICAGO vs. CINCINNATI
RS: Bengals lead series, 6-3
1972—Bengals, 13-3 (Chi)
1980—Bengals, 17-14 (Chi) OT
1986—Bears, 44-7 (Cin)
1989—Bears, 17-14 (Chi)
1992—Bengals, 31-28 (Chi) OT
1995—Bengals, 16-10 (Cin)
2001—Bears, 24-0 (Cin)
2005—Bengals, 24-7 (Chi)
2009—Bengals, 45-10 (Cin)
(RS Pts.—Bengals 167, Bears 157)

CHICAGO vs. CLEVELAND
RS: Browns lead series, 9-5
1951—Browns, 42-21 (Cle)
1954—Browns, 39-10 (Chi)
1960—Browns, 42-0 (Cle)
1961—Bears, 17-14 (Chi)
1967—Browns, 24-0 (Cle)
1969—Browns, 28-24 (Chi)
1972—Bears, 17-0 (Cle)
1980—Browns, 27-21 (Cle)
1986—Bears, 41-31 (Chi)
1989—Browns, 27-7 (Cle)
1992—Browns, 27-14 (Cle)
2001—Bears, 27-21 (Chi) OT
2005—Browns, 20-10 (Cle)
2009—Bears, 30-6 (Chi)
(RS Pts.—Browns 348, Bears 239)

CHICAGO vs. DALLAS
RS: Cowboys lead series, 11-8
PS: Cowboys lead series, 2-0
1960—Bears, 17-7 (C)
1962—Bears, 34-33 (D)
1964—Cowboys, 24-10 (C)
1968—Cowboys, 34-3 (C)
1971—Bears, 23-19 (C)
1973—Cowboys, 20-17 (C)
1976—Cowboys, 31-21 (D)
1977—*Cowboys, 37-7 (D)
1979—Cowboys, 24-20 (D)
1981—Cowboys, 10-9 (D)
1984—Cowboys, 23-14 (C)
1985—Bears, 44-0 (D)
1986—Bears, 24-10 (D)
1988—Bears, 17-7 (C)
1991—**Cowboys, 17-13 (C)
1992—Cowboys, 27-14 (D)
1996—Bears, 22-6 (C)
1997—Cowboys, 27-3 (D)
1998—Bears, 13-12 (C)
2004—Cowboys, 21-7 (D)
2007—Cowboys, 34-10 (C)
(RS Pts.—Cowboys 369, Bears 322)
(PS Pts.—Cowboys 54, Bears 20)
*NFC Divisional Playoff
**NFC First-Round Playoff

CHICAGO vs. DENVER
RS: Bears lead series, 7-6
1971—Broncos, 6-3 (D)
1973—Bears, 33-14 (D)
1976—Broncos, 28-14 (C)
1978—Broncos, 16-7 (D)
1981—Bears, 35-24 (C)
1983—Bears, 31-14 (C)
1984—Bears, 27-0 (C)
1987—Broncos, 31-29 (D)
1990—Bears, 16-13 (D) OT
1993—Broncos, 13-3 (C)
1996—Broncos, 17-12 (D)
2003—Bears, 19-10 (D)
2007—Bears, 37-34 (C) OT
(RS Pts.—Bears 266, Broncos 220)

CHICAGO vs. *DETROIT
RS: Bears lead series, 91-64-5
1930—Spartans, 7-6 (P)
Bears, 14-6 (C)
1931—Bears, 9-6 (C)
Spartans, 3-0 (P)
1932—Tie, 13-13 (C)
Tie, 7-7 (P)
Bears, 9-0 (C)
1933—Bears, 17-14 (C)
Bears, 17-7 (P)
1934—Bears, 19-16 (D)
Bears, 10-7 (C)
1935—Tie, 20-20 (C)
Lions, 14-2 (D)
1936—Bears, 12-10 (C)
Lions, 13-7 (D)
1937—Bears, 28-20 (C)
Bears, 13-0 (D)
1938—Lions, 13-7 (C)
Lions, 14-7 (D)
1939—Lions, 10-0 (C)
Bears, 23-13 (D)
1940—Bears, 7-0 (C)
Lions, 17-14 (D)
1941—Bears, 49-0 (C)
Bears, 24-7 (D)
1942—Bears, 16-0 (C)
Bears, 42-0 (D)
1943—Bears, 27-21 (D)
Bears, 35-14 (C)
1944—Tie, 21-21 (C)
Lions, 41-21 (D)
1945—Lions, 16-10 (D)
Lions, 35-28 (C)
1946—Bears, 42-6 (C)
Bears, 45-24 (D)
1947—Bears, 33-24 (C)
Bears, 34-14 (D)
1948—Bears, 28-0 (C)

Bears, 42-14 (D)
1949—Bears, 27-24 (C)
Bears, 28-7 (D)
1950—Bears, 35-21 (D)
Bears, 6-3 (C)
1951—Bears, 28-23 (D)
Lions, 41-28 (C)
1952—Bears, 24-23 (C)
Lions, 45-21 (D)
1953—Lions, 20-16 (C)
Lions, 13-7 (D)
1954—Lions, 48-23 (D)
Bears, 28-24 (C)
1955—Bears, 24-14 (D)
Bears, 21-20 (C)
1956—Lions, 42-10 (D)
Bears, 38-21 (C)
1957—Bears, 27-7 (D)
Lions, 21-13 (C)
1958—Bears, 20-7 (D)
Bears, 21-16 (C)
1959—Bears, 24-14 (D)
Bears, 25-14 (C)
1960—Bears, 28-7 (C)
Lions, 36-0 (D)
1961—Bears, 31-17 (D)
Lions, 16-15 (C)
1962—Lions, 11-3 (D)
Bears, 3-0 (C)
1963—Bears, 37-21 (D)
Bears, 24-14 (C)
1964—Lions, 10-0 (C)
Bears, 27-24 (D)
1965—Bears, 38-10 (C)
Bears, 17-10 (D)
1966—Lions, 14-3 (D)
Tie, 10-10 (C)
1967—Bears, 14-3 (C)
Bears, 27-13 (D)
1968—Lions, 42-0 (D)
Lions, 28-10 (C)
1969—Lions, 13-7 (D)
Lions, 20-3 (C)
1970—Lions, 28-14 (D)
Lions, 16-10 (C)
1971—Bears, 28-23 (D)
Lions, 28-3 (C)
1972—Lions, 38-24 (C)
Lions, 14-0 (D)
1973—Lions, 30-7 (C)
Lions, 40-7 (D)
1974—Bears, 17-9 (C)
Lions, 34-17 (D)
1975—Lions, 27-7 (D)
Bears, 25-21 (C)
1976—Bears, 10-3 (C)
Lions, 14-10 (D)
1977—Bears, 30-20 (C)
Bears, 31-14 (D)
1978—Bears, 19-0 (D)
Lions, 21-17 (C)
1979—Bears, 35-7 (C)
Lions, 20-0 (D)
1980—Bears, 24-7 (C)
Bears, 23-17 (D) OT
1981—Lions, 48-17 (D)
Lions, 23-7 (C)
1982—Lions, 17-10 (D)
Bears, 20-17 (C)
1983—Lions, 31-17 (D)
Lions, 38-17 (C)
1984—Bears, 16-14 (C)
Bears, 30-13 (D)
1985—Bears, 24-3 (C)
Bears, 37-17 (D)
1986—Bears, 13-7 (C)
Bears, 16-13 (D)
1987—Bears, 30-10 (C)
1988—Bears, 24-7 (D)
Bears, 13-12 (C)
1989—Bears, 47-27 (D)
Lions, 27-17 (C)
1990—Bears, 23-17 (C) OT
Lions, 38-21 (D)
1991—Bears, 20-10 (C)
Lions, 16-6 (D)
1992—Bears, 27-24 (C)
Lions, 16-3 (D)
1993—Bears, 10-6 (D)
Lions, 20-14 (C)
1994—Lions, 21-16 (D)
Bears, 20-10 (C)
1995—Lions, 24-17 (C)
Lions, 27-7 (D)
1996—Lions, 35-16 (D)
Bears, 31-14 (C)
1997—Lions, 32-7 (C)
Lions, 55-20 (D)
1998—Bears, 31-27 (C)
Lions, 26-3 (D)
1999—Lions, 21-17 (D)
Bears, 28-10 (C)
2000—Lions, 21-14 (C)
Bears, 23-20 (D)
2001—Bears, 13-10 (C)
Bears, 24-0 (D)
2002—Lions, 23-20 (D) OT
Bears, 20-17 (C) OT
2003—Bears, 24-16 (C)
Lions, 12-10 (D)
2004—Lions, 20-16 (C)
Lions, 19-13 (D)
2005—Bears, 38-6 (C)
Bears, 19-13 (D) OT
2006—Bears, 34-7 (C)
Bears, 26-21 (D)
2007—Lions, 37-27 (D)
Lions, 16-7 (C)
2008—Bears, 34-7 (D)
Bears, 27-23 (C)
2009—Bears, 48-24 (C)
Bears, 37-23 (D)
(RS Pts.—Bears 3,073, Lions 2,793)
Franchise in Portsmouth prior to 1934 and known as the Spartans

***CHICAGO vs. GREEN BAY**
RS: Bears lead series, 90-82-6
PS: Bears lead series, 1-0
1921—Staleys, 20-0 (C)
1923—Bears, 3-0 (GB)
1924—Bears, 3-0 (C)
1925—Packers, 14-10 (GB)
Bears, 21-0 (C)
1926—Tie, 6-6 (GB)
Bears, 19-13 (C)
Tie, 3-3 (C)
1927—Bears, 7-6 (GB)
Bears, 14-6 (C)
1928—Tie, 12-12 (GB)
Packers, 16-6 (C)
Packers, 6-0 (C)
1929—Packers, 23-0 (GB)
Packers, 14-0 (C)
Packers, 25-0 (C)
1930—Packers, 7-0 (GB)
Packers, 13-12 (C)
Bears, 21-0 (C)
1931—Packers, 7-0 (GB)
Packers, 6-2 (C)
Bears, 7-6 (C)
1932—Tie, 0-0 (GB)
Packers, 2-0 (C)
Bears, 9-0 (C)
1933—Bears, 14-7 (GB)
Bears, 10-7 (C)
Bears, 7-6 (C)
1934—Bears, 24-10 (GB)
Bears, 27-14 (C)
1935—Packers, 7-0 (GB)
Packers, 17-14 (C)
1936—Bears, 30-3 (GB)
Packers, 21-10 (C)
1937—Bears, 14-2 (GB)
Packers, 24-14 (C)
1938—Bears, 2-0 (GB)
Packers, 24-17 (C)
1939—Packers, 21-16 (GB)
Bears, 30-27 (C)
1940—Bears, 41-10 (GB)
Bears, 14-7 (C)
1941—Bears, 25-17 (GB)
Packers, 16-14 (C)
**Bears, 33-14 (C)
1942—Bears, 44-28 (GB)
Bears, 38-7 (C)
1943—Tie, 21-21 (GB)
Bears, 21-7 (C)
1944—Packers, 42-28 (GB)
Bears, 21-0 (C)
1945—Packers, 31-21 (GB)
Bears, 28-24 (C)
1946—Bears, 30-7 (GB)
Bears, 10-7 (C)
1947—Packers, 29-20 (GB)
Bears, 20-17 (C)
1948—Bears, 45-7 (GB)
Bears, 7-6 (C)
1949—Bears, 17-0 (GB)
Bears, 24-3 (C)
1950—Packers, 31-21 (GB)
Bears, 28-14 (C)
1951—Bears, 31-20 (GB)
Bears, 24-13 (C)
1952—Bears, 24-14 (GB)
Packers, 41-28 (C)
1953—Bears, 17-13 (GB)
Tie, 21-21 (C)
1954—Bears, 10-3 (GB)
Bears, 28-23 (C)
1955—Packers, 24-3 (GB)
Bears, 52-31 (C)
1956—Bears, 37-21 (GB)
Bears, 38-14 (C)
1957—Packers, 21-17 (GB)
Bears, 21-14 (C)
1958—Bears, 34-20 (GB)
Bears, 24-10 (C)
1959—Packers, 9-6 (GB)
Bears, 28-17 (C)
1960—Bears, 17-14 (GB)
Packers, 41-13 (C)
1961—Packers, 24-0 (GB)
Packers, 31-28 (C)

1962—Packers, 49-0 (GB)
Packers, 38-7 (C)
1963—Bears, 10-3 (GB)
Bears, 26-7 (C)
1964—Packers, 23-12 (GB)
Packers, 17-3 (C)
1965—Packers, 23-14 (GB)
Bears, 31-10 (C)
1966—Packers, 17-0 (C)
Packers, 13-6 (GB)
1967—Packers, 13-10 (GB)
Packers, 17-13 (C)
1968—Bears, 13-10 (GB)
Packers, 28-27 (C)
1969—Packers, 17-0 (GB)
Packers, 21-3 (C)
1970—Packers, 20-19 (GB)
Bears, 35-17 (C)
1971—Packers, 17-14 (C)
Packers, 31-10 (GB)
1972—Packers, 20-17 (GB)
Packers, 23-17 (C)
1973—Bears, 31-17 (GB)
Packers, 21-0 (C)
1974—Bears, 10-9 (C)
Packers, 20-3 (Mil)
1975—Bears, 27-14 (C)
Packers, 28-7 (GB)
1976—Bears, 24-13 (C)
Bears, 16-10 (GB)
1977—Bears, 26-0 (GB)
Bears, 21-10 (C)
1978—Packers, 24-14 (GB)
Bears, 14-0 (C)
1979—Bears, 6-3 (C)
Bears, 15-14 (GB)
1980—Packers, 12-6 (GB) OT
Bears, 61-7 (C)
1981—Packers, 16-9 (C)
Packers, 21-17 (GB)
1983—Packers, 31-28 (GB)
Bears, 23-21 (C)
1984—Bears, 9-7 (GB)
Packers, 20-14 (C)
1985—Bears, 23-7 (C)
Bears, 16-10 (GB)
1986—Bears, 25-12 (GB)
Bears, 12-10 (C)
1987—Bears, 26-24 (GB)
Bears, 23-10 (C)
1988—Bears, 24-6 (GB)
Bears, 16-0 (C)
1989—Packers, 14-13 (GB)
Packers, 40-28 (C)
1990—Bears, 31-13 (GB)
Bears, 27-13 (C)
1991—Bears, 10-0 (GB)
Bears, 27-13 (C)
1992—Bears, 30-10 (GB)
Packers, 17-3 (C)
1993—Packers, 17-3 (GB)
Bears, 30-17 (C)
1994—Packers, 33-6 (C)
Packers, 40-3 (GB)
1995—Packers, 27-24 (C)
Packers, 35-28 (GB)
1996—Packers, 37-6 (C)
Packers, 28-17 (GB)
1997—Packers, 38-24 (GB)
Packers, 24-23 (C)
1998—Packers, 26-20 (GB)
Packers, 16-13 (C)
1999—Bears, 14-13 (GB)
Packers, 35-19 (C)
2000—Bears, 27-24 (GB)
Packers, 28-6 (C)
2001—Packers, 20-12 (C)
Packers, 17-7 (GB)
2002—Packers, 34-21 (C)
Packers, 30-20 (GB)
2003—Packers, 38-23 (C)
Packers, 34-21 (GB)
2004—Bears, 21-10 (GB)
Packers, 31-14 (C)
2005—Bears, 19-7 (C)
Bears, 24-17 (GB)
2006—Bears, 26-0 (GB)
Packers, 26-7 (C)
2007—Bears, 27-20 (GB)
Bears, 35-7 (C)
2008—Packers, 37-3 (GB)
Bears, 20-17 (C) OT
2009—Packers, 21-15 (GB)
Packers, 21-14 (C)
(RS Pts.—Bears 3,037, Packers 2,921)
(PS Pts.—Bears 33, Packers 14)
Bears known as Staleys prior to 1922
**Division Playoff*

CHICAGO vs. HOUSTON
RS: Texans lead series, 2-0
2004—Texans, 24-5 (C)
2008—Texans, 31-24 (H)
(RS Pts.—Texans 55, Bears 29)

CHICAGO vs. *INDIANAPOLIS
RS: Colts lead series, 22-18
PS: Colts lead series, 1-0
1953—Colts, 13-9 (B)
Colts, 16-14 (C)
1954—Bears, 28-9 (C)
Bears, 28-13 (B)
1955—Colts, 23-17 (B)
Bears, 38-10 (C)
1956—Colts, 28-21 (B)
Bears, 58-27 (C)
1957—Colts, 21-10 (B)
Colts, 29-14 (C)
1958—Colts, 51-38 (B)
Colts, 17-0 (C)
1959—Bears, 26-21 (B)
Colts, 21-7 (C)
1960—Colts, 42-7 (B)
Colts, 24-20 (C)
1961—Bears, 24-10 (C)
Bears, 21-20 (B)
1962—Bears, 35-15 (C)
Bears, 57-0 (B)
1963—Bears, 10-3 (C)
Bears, 17-7 (B)
1964—Colts, 52-0 (B)
Colts, 40-24 (C)
1965—Colts, 26-21 (C)
Bears, 13-0 (B)
1966—Bears, 27-17 (C)
Colts, 21-16 (B)
1967—Colts, 24-3 (C)
1968—Colts, 28-7 (B)
1969—Colts, 24-21 (C)
1970—Colts, 21-20 (B)
1975—Colts, 35-7 (C)
1983—Colts, 22-19 (B) OT
1985—Bears, 17-10 (C)
1988—Bears, 17-13 (I)
1991—Bears, 31-17 (I)
2000—Bears, 27-24 (C)
2004—Colts, 41-10 (C)
2006—**Colts, 29-17 (South Florida)
2008—Bears, 29-13 (I)
(RS Pts.—Colts 848, Bears 808)
(PS: Pts.—Colts 29, Bears 17)
Franchise in Baltimore prior to 1984
***Super Bowl XLI*

CHICAGO vs. JACKSONVILLE
RS: Bears lead series, 3-2
1995—Bears, 30-27 (J)
1998—Jaguars, 24-23 (C)
2001—Bears, 33-13 (C)
2004—Jaguars, 22-3 (J)
2008—Bears, 23-10 (C)
(RS Pts.—Bears 112, Jaguars 96)

CHICAGO vs. KANSAS CITY
RS: Bears lead series, 6-4
1973—Chiefs, 19-7 (KC)
1977—Bears, 28-27 (C)
1981—Bears, 16-13 (KC) OT
1987—Bears, 31-28 (C)
1990—Chiefs, 21-10 (C)
1993—Bears, 19-17 (KC)
1996—Chiefs, 14-10 (KC)
1999—Bears, 20-17 (C)
2003—Chiefs, 31-3 (KC)
2007—Bears, 20-10 (C)
(RS Pts.—Chiefs 197, Bears 164)

CHICAGO vs. MIAMI
RS: Dolphins lead series, 7-3
1971—Dolphins, 34-3 (M)
1975—Dolphins, 46-13 (C)
1979—Dolphins, 31-16 (M)
1985—Dolphins, 38-24 (M)
1988—Bears, 34-7 (C)
1991—Dolphins, 16-13 (C) OT
1994—Bears, 17-14 (M)
1997—Bears, 36-33 (M) OT
2002—Dolphins, 27-9 (M)
2006—Dolphins, 31-13 (C)
(RS Pts.—Dolphins 277, Bears 178)

CHICAGO vs. MINNESOTA
RS: Vikings lead series, 52-43-2
PS: Bears lead series, 1-0
1961—Vikings, 37-13 (M)
Bears, 52-35 (C)
1962—Bears, 13-0 (M)
Bears, 31-30 (C)
1963—Bears, 28-7 (M)
Tie, 17-17 (C)
1964—Bears, 34-28 (M)
Vikings, 41-14 (C)
1965—Bears, 45-37 (M)
Vikings, 24-17 (C)
1966—Bears, 13-10 (M)
Bears, 41-28 (C)
1967—Bears, 17-7 (M)
Tie, 10-10 (C)
1968—Bears, 27-17 (M)
Bears, 26-24 (C)
1969—Vikings, 31-0 (C)
Vikings, 31-14 (M)
1970—Vikings, 24-0 (C)
Vikings, 16-13 (M)
1971—Bears, 20-17 (M)
Vikings, 27-10 (C)
1972—Bears, 13-10 (C)
Vikings, 23-10 (M)
1973—Vikings, 22-13 (C)

Vikings, 31-13 (M)
1974—Vikings, 11-7 (M)
Vikings, 17-0 (C)
1975—Vikings, 28-3 (M)
Vikings, 13-9 (C)
1976—Vikings, 20-19 (M)
Bears, 14-13 (C)
1977—Vikings, 22-16 (M) OT
Bears, 10-7 (C)
1978—Vikings, 24-20 (C)
Vikings, 17-14 (M)
1979—Bears, 26-7 (C)
Vikings, 30-27 (M)
1980—Vikings, 34-14 (C)
Vikings, 13-7 (M)
1981—Vikings, 24-21 (M)
Bears, 10-9 (C)
1982—Vikings, 35-7 (M)
1983—Vikings, 23-14 (C)
Bears, 19-13 (M)
1984—Bears, 16-7 (C)
Bears, 34-3 (M)
1985—Bears, 33-24 (M)
Bears, 27-9 (C)
1986—Bears, 23-0 (C)
Vikings, 23-7 (M)
1987—Bears, 27-7 (C)
Bears, 30-24 (M)
1988—Vikings, 31-7 (C)
Vikings, 28-27 (M)
1989—Bears, 38-7 (C)
Vikings, 27-16 (M)
1990—Bears, 19-16 (C)
Vikings, 41-13 (M)
1991—Bears, 10-6 (C)
Bears, 34-17 (M)
1992—Vikings, 21-20 (M)
Vikings, 38-10 (C)
1993—Vikings, 10-7 (M)
Vikings, 19-12 (C)
1994—Vikings, 42-14 (C)
Vikings, 33-27 (M) OT
*Bears, 35-18 (M)
1995—Bears, 31-14 (C)
Bears, 14-6 (M)
1996—Vikings, 20-14 (C)
Bears, 15-13 (M)
1997—Vikings, 27-24 (C)
Vikings, 29-22 (M)
1998—Vikings, 31-28 (C)
Vikings, 48-22 (M)
1999—Bears, 24-22 (M)
Vikings, 27-24 (C) OT
2000—Vikings, 30-27 (M)
Vikings, 28-16 (C)
2001—Bears, 17-10 (C)
Bears, 13-6 (M)
2002—Bears, 27-23 (C)
Vikings, 25-7 (M)
2003—Vikings, 24-13 (M)
Bears, 13-10 (C)
2004—Vikings, 27-22 (M)
Bears, 24-14 (C)
2005—Bears, 28-3 (C)
Vikings, 34-10 (M)
2006—Bears, 19-16 (M)
Bears, 23-13 (C)
2007—Vikings, 34-31 (C)
Vikings, 20-13 (M)
2008—Bears, 48-41 (C)
Vikings, 34-14 (M)
2009—Vikings, 36-10 (M)
Bears, 36-30 (C) OT
RS Pts.—Vikings 2,072, Bears 1,841)
(PS Pts.—Bears 35, Vikings 18)
NFC First-Round Playoff

CHICAGO vs. NEW ENGLAND
RS: Patriots lead series, 7-3
PS: Bears lead series, 1-0
1973—Patriots, 13-10 (C)
1979—Patriots, 27-7 (C)
1982—Bears, 26-13 (C)
1985—Bears, 20-7 (C)
*Bears, 46-10 (New Orleans)
1988—Patriots, 30-7 (NE)
1994—Patriots, 13-3 (C)
1997—Patriots, 31-3 (NE)
2000—Bears, 24-17 (C)
2002—Patriots, 33-30 (C)
2006—Patriots, 17-13 (NE)
(RS Pts.—Patriots 201, Bears 143)
(PS Pts.—Bears 46, Patriots 10)
Super Bowl XX

CHICAGO vs. NEW ORLEANS
RS: Bears lead series, 13-11
PS: Bears lead series, 2-0
1968—Bears, 23-17 (NO)
1970—Bears, 24-3 (NO)
1971—Bears, 35-14 (C)
1973—Saints, 21-16 (NO)
1974—Bears, 24-10 (C)
1975—Bears, 42-17 (NO)
1977—Saints, 42-24 (C)
1980—Bears, 22-3 (C)
1982—Saints, 10-0 (C)
1983—Saints, 34-31 (NO) OT
1984—Bears, 20-7 (C)
1987—Saints, 19-17 (C)
1990—*Bears, 16-6 (C)
1991—Bears, 20-17 (NO)
1992—Saints, 28-6 (NO)
1994—Bears, 17-7 (C)
1996—Saints, 27-24 (NO)
1997—Saints, 20-17 (C)
1999—Bears, 14-10 (C)
2000—Saints, 31-10 (C)
2002—Saints, 29-23 (C)
2003—Saints, 20-13 (NO)
2005—Bears, 20-17 (Baton Rouge)
2006—**Bears, 39-14 (C)
2007—Bears, 33-25 (C)
2008—Bears, 27-24 (C) OT
(RS Pts.—Bears 502, Saints 452)
(PS Pts.—Bears 55, Saints 20)
NFC First-Round Playoff
***NFC Championship*

CHICAGO vs. N.Y. GIANTS
RS: Bears lead series, 27-18-2
PS: Bears lead series, 5-3
1925—Bears, 19-7 (NY)
Giants, 9-0 (C)
1926—Bears, 7-0 (C)
1927—Giants, 13-7 (NY)
1928—Bears, 13-0 (C)
1929—Giants, 26-14 (C)
Giants, 34-0 (NY)
Giants, 14-9 (C)
1930—Giants, 12-0 (C)
Bears, 12-0 (NY)
1931—Bears, 6-0 (C)
Bears, 12-6 (NY)
Giants, 25-6 (C)
1932—Bears, 28-8 (NY)
Bears, 6-0 (C)
1933—Bears, 14-10 (C)
Giants, 3-0 (NY)
*Bears, 23-21 (C)
1934—Bears, 27-7 (C)
Bears, 10-9 (NY)
*Giants, 30-13 (NY)
1935—Bears, 20-3 (NY)
Giants, 3-0 (C)
1936—Bears, 25-7 (NY)
1937—Tie, 3-3 (NY)
1939—Giants, 16-13 (NY)
1940—Bears, 37-21 (NY)
1941—*Bears, 37-9 (C)
1942—Bears, 26-7 (NY)
1943—Bears, 56-7 (NY)
1946—Giants, 14-0 (NY)
*Bears, 24-14 (NY)
1948—Bears, 35-14 (C)
1949—Giants, 35-28 (NY)
1956—Tie, 17-17 (NY)
*Giants, 47-7 (NY)
1962—Giants, 26-24 (C)
1963—*Bears, 14-10 (C)
1965—Bears, 35-14 (NY)
1967—Bears, 34-7 (C)
1969—Giants, 28-24 (NY)
1970—Bears, 24-16 (NY)
1974—Bears, 16-13 (C)
1977—Bears, 12-9 (NY) OT
1985—**Bears, 21-0 (C)
1987—Bears, 34-19 (C)
1990—**Giants, 31-3 (NY)
1991—Bears, 20-17 (C)
1992—Giants, 27-14 (C)
1993—Giants, 26-20 (C)
1995—Bears, 27-24 (NY)
2000—Giants, 14-7 (C)
2004—Bears, 28-21 (NY)
2006—Bears, 38-20 (NY)
2007—Giants, 21-16 (C)
(RS Pts.—Bears 823, Giants 632)
(PS Pts.—Giants 162, Bears 142)
NFL Championship
***NFC Divisional Playoff*

CHICAGO vs. N.Y. JETS
RS: Bears lead series, 6-3
1974—Jets, 23-21 (C)
1979—Bears, 23-13 (C)
1985—Bears, 19-6 (NY)
1991—Bears, 19-13 (C) OT
1994—Bears, 19-7 (NY)
1997—Jets, 23-15 (C)
2000—Jets, 17-10 (NY)
2002—Bears, 20-13 (C)
2006—Bears, 10-0 (NY)
(RS Pts.—Bears 156, Jets 115)

CHICAGO vs. *OAKLAND
RS: Series tied, 6-6
1972—Raiders, 28-21 (O)
1976—Raiders, 28-27 (C)
1978—Raiders, 25-19 (C) OT
1981—Bears, 23-6 (O)
1984—Bears, 17-6 (C)
1987—Bears, 6-3 (LA)
1990—Raiders, 24-10 (LA)
1993—Raiders, 16-14 (C)
1996—Bears, 19-17 (C)
1999—Raiders, 24-17 (O)
2003—Bears, 24-21 (C)

2007—Bears, 17-6 (O)
(RS Pts.—Bears 214, Raiders 204)
Franchise in Los Angeles from 1982-1994

CHICAGO vs. PHILADELPHIA
RS: Bears lead series, 26-9-1
PS: Eagles lead series, 2-1
1933—Tie, 3-3 (P)
1935—Bears, 39-0 (P)
1936—Bears, 17-0 (P)
Bears, 28-7 (P)
1938—Bears, 28-6 (P)
1939—Bears, 27-14 (C)
1941—Bears, 49-14 (P)
1942—Bears, 45-14 (C)
1944—Bears, 28-7 (P)
1946—Bears, 21-14 (C)
1947—Bears, 40-7 (C)
1948—Eagles, 12-7 (P)
1949—Bears, 38-21 (C)
1955—Bears, 17-10 (C)
1961—Eagles, 16-14 (P)
1963—Bears, 16-7 (C)
1968—Bears, 29-16 (P)
1970—Bears, 20-16 (C)
1972—Bears, 21-12 (P)
1975—Bears, 15-13 (C)
1979—*Eagles, 27-17 (P)
1980—Eagles, 17-14 (P)
1983—Bears, 7-6 (P)
Bears, 17-14 (C)
1986—Bears, 13-10 (C) OT
1987—Bears, 35-3 (P)
1988—**Bears, 20-12 (C)
1989—Bears, 27-13 (C)
1993—Bears, 17-6 (P)
1994—Eagles, 30-22 (P)
1995—Bears, 20-14 (C)
1999—Eagles, 20-16 (C)
2000—Eagles, 13-9 (P)
2001—**Eagles, 33-19 (C)
2002—Eagles, 19-13 (C)
2004—Eagles, 19-9 (C)
2007—Bears, 19-16 (P)
2008—Bears, 24-20 (C)
2009—Eagles, 24-20 (C)
(RS Pts.—Bears 784, Eagles 453)
(PS Pts.—Eagles 72, Bears 56)
NFC First-Round Playoff
**NFC Divisional Playoff*

CHICAGO vs. *PITTSBURGH
RS: Bears lead series, 17-7-1
1934—Bears, 28-0 (P)
1935—Bears, 23-7 (P)
1936—Bears, 27-9 (P)
Bears, 26-7 (C)
1937—Bears, 7-0 (P)
1939—Bears, 32-0 (P)
1941—Bears, 34-7 (C)
1945—Bears, 28-7 (C)
1947—Bears, 49-7 (C)
1949—Bears, 30-21 (C)
1958—Steelers, 24-10 (P)
1959—Bears, 27-21 (C)
1963—Tie, 17-17 (P)
1967—Steelers, 41-13 (P)
1969—Bears, 38-7 (C)
1971—Bears, 17-15 (C)
1975—Steelers, 34-3 (P)
1980—Steelers, 38-3 (P)
1986—Bears, 13-10 (C) OT
1989—Bears, 20-0 (P)
1992—Bears, 30-6 (C)
1995—Steelers, 37-34 (C) OT
1998—Steelers, 17-12 (P)
2005—Steelers, 21-9 (P)
2009—Bears, 17-14 (C)
(RS Pts.—Bears 547, Steelers 367)
Steelers known as Pirates prior to 1940

CHICAGO vs. *ST. LOUIS
RS: Bears lead series, 50-34-3
PS: Series tied, 1-1
1937—Bears, 20-2 (Cle)
Bears, 15-7 (C)
1938—Rams, 14-7 (C)
Rams, 23-21 (Cle)
1939—Bears, 30-21 (Cle)
Bears, 35-21 (C)
1940—Bears, 21-14 (Cle)
Bears, 47-25 (C)
1941—Bears, 48-21 (Cle)
Bears, 31-13 (C)
1942—Bears, 21-7 (Cle)
Bears, 47-0 (C)
1944—Rams, 19-7 (Cle)
Bears, 28-21 (C)
1945—Rams, 17-0 (Cle)
Rams, 41-21 (C)
1946—Tie, 28-28 (C)
Bears, 27-21 (LA)
1947—Bears, 41-21 (LA)
Rams, 17-14 (C)
1948—Bears, 42-21 (C)
Bears, 21-6 (LA)
1949—Rams, 31-16 (C)
Rams, 27-24 (LA)
1950—Bears, 24-20 (LA)
Bears, 24-14 (C)
**Rams, 24-14 (LA)
1951—Rams, 42-17 (C)
1952—Rams, 31-7 (LA)
Rams, 40-24 (C)
1953—Rams, 38-24 (LA)
Bears, 24-21 (C)
1954—Rams, 42-38 (LA)
Bears, 24-13 (C)
1955—Bears, 31-20 (LA)
Bears, 24-3 (C)
1956—Bears, 35-24 (LA)
Bears, 30-21 (C)
1957—Bears, 34-26 (C)
Bears, 16-10 (LA)
1958—Bears, 31-10 (C)
Rams, 41-35 (LA)
1959—Rams, 28-21 (C)
Bears, 26-21 (LA)
1960—Bears, 34-27 (C)
Tie, 24-24 (LA)
1961—Bears, 21-17 (LA)
Bears, 28-24 (C)
1962—Bears, 27-23 (LA)
Bears, 30-14 (C)
1963—Bears, 52-14 (LA)
Bears, 6-0 (C)
1964—Bears, 38-17 (C)
Bears, 34-24 (LA)
1965—Rams, 30-28 (LA)
Bears, 31-6 (C)
1966—Rams, 31-17 (LA)
Bears, 17-10 (C)
1967—Rams, 28-17 (C)
1968—Bears, 17-16 (LA)
1969—Rams, 9-7 (C)
1971—Rams, 17-3 (LA)
1972—Tie, 13-13 (C)
1973—Rams, 26-0 (C)
1975—Rams, 38-10 (LA)
1976—Rams, 20-12 (LA)
1977—Bears, 24-23 (C)
1979—Bears, 27-23 (C)
1981—Rams, 24-7 (C)
1982—Bears, 34-26 (LA)
1983—Rams, 21-14 (LA)
1984—Rams, 29-13 (LA)
1985—***Bears, 24-0 (C)
1986—Rams, 20-17 (C)
1988—Rams, 23-3 (LA)
1989—Bears, 20-10 (C)
1990—Bears, 38-9 (C)
1993—Rams, 20-6 (LA)
1994—Bears, 27-13 (C)
1995—Rams, 34-28 (StL)
1996—Bears, 35-9 (C)
1997—Bears, 13-10 (StL)
1998—Rams, 20-12 (C)
1999—Rams, 34-12 (StL)
2002—Rams, 21-16 (StL)
2003—Rams, 23-21 (C)
2006—Bears, 42-27 (StL)
2008—Bears, 27-3 (StL)
2009—Bears, 17-9 (C)
(RS Pts.—Bears 2,020, Rams 1,762)
(PS Pts.—Bears 38, Rams 24)
Franchise in Los Angeles prior to 1995 and in Cleveland prior to 1946
**Conference Playoff*
***NFC Championship*

CHICAGO vs. SAN DIEGO
RS: Series tied, 5-5
1970—Chargers, 20-7 (C)
1974—Chargers, 28-21 (SD)
1978—Chargers, 40-7 (SD)
1981—Bears, 20-17 (C) OT
1984—Chargers, 20-7 (SD)
1993—Bears, 16-13 (SD)
1996—Bears, 27-14 (C)
1999—Bears, 23-20 (SD) OT
2003—Bears, 20-7 (C)
2007—Chargers, 14-3 (SD)
(RS Pts.—Chargers 193, Bears 151)

CHICAGO vs. SAN FRANCISCO
RS: Bears lead series, 29-28-1
PS: 49ers lead series, 3-0
1950—Bears, 32-20 (SF)
Bears, 17-0 (C)
1951—Bears, 13-7 (C)
1952—49ers, 40-16 (C)
Bears, 20-17 (SF)
1953—49ers, 35-28 (C)
49ers, 24-14 (SF)
1954—49ers, 31-24 (C)
Bears, 31-27 (SF)
1955—49ers, 20-19 (C)
Bears, 34-23 (SF)
1956—Bears, 31-7 (C)
Bears, 38-21 (SF)
1957—49ers, 21-17 (C)
49ers, 21-17 (SF)
1958—Bears, 28-6 (C)
Bears, 27-14 (SF)
1959—49ers, 20-17 (SF)
Bears, 14-3 (C)
1960—Bears, 27-10 (C)
49ers, 25-7 (SF)

1961—Bears, 31-0 (C)
49ers, 41-31 (SF)
1962—Bears, 30-14 (SF)
49ers, 34-27 (C)
1963—49ers, 20-14 (SF)
Bears, 27-7 (C)
1964—49ers, 31-21 (SF)
Bears, 23-21 (C)
1965—49ers, 52-24 (SF)
Bears, 61-20 (C)
1966—Tie, 30-30 (C)
49ers, 41-14 (SF)
1967—Bears, 28-14 (SF)
1968—Bears, 27-19 (C)
1969—49ers, 42-21 (SF)
1970—49ers, 37-16 (C)
1971—49ers, 13-0 (SF)
1972—49ers, 34-21 (C)
1974—49ers, 34-0 (C)
1975—49ers, 31-3 (SF)
1976—Bears, 19-12 (SF)
1978—Bears, 16-13 (SF)
1979—Bears, 28-27 (SF)
1981—49ers, 28-17 (SF)
1983—Bears, 13-3 (C)
1984—*49ers, 23-0 (SF)
1985—Bears, 26-10 (SF)
1987—49ers, 41-0 (SF)
1988—Bears, 10-9 (C)
*49ers, 28-3 (C)
1989—49ers, 26-0 (SF)
1991—49ers, 52-14 (SF)
1994—**49ers, 44-15 (SF)
2000—49ers, 17-0 (SF)
2001—Bears, 37-31 (C) OT
2003—49ers, 49-7 (SF)
2004—Bears, 23-13 (C)
2005—Bears, 17-9 (C)
2006—Bears, 41-10 (C)
2009—49ers, 10-6 (SF)
(RS Pts.—49ers 1,287, Bears 1,194)
(PS Pts.—49ers 95, Bears 18)
NFC Championship
***NFC Divisional Playoff*

CHICAGO vs. SEATTLE
RS: Seahawks lead series, 7-4
PS: Bears lead series, 1-0
1976—Bears, 34-7 (S)
1978—Seahawks, 31-29 (C)
1982—Seahawks, 20-14 (S)
1984—Seahawks, 38-9 (S)
1987—Seahawks, 34-21 (C)
1990—Bears, 17-0 (C)
1999—Seahawks, 14-13 (C)
2003—Seahawks, 24-17 (S)
2006—Bears, 37-6 (C)
*Bears, 27-24 (C) OT
2007—Seahawks, 30-23 (S)
2009—Bears, 25-19 (S)
(RS Pts.—Bears 239, Seahawks 223)
(PS Pts.—Bears 27, Seahawks 24)
NFC Divisional Playoff

CHICAGO vs. TAMPA BAY
RS: Bears lead series, 35-18
1977—Bears, 10-0 (TB)
1978—Buccaneers, 33-19 (TB)
Bears, 14-3 (C)
1979—Buccaneers, 17-13 (C)
Bears, 14-0 (TB)
1980—Bears, 23-0 (C)
Bears, 14-13 (TB)
1981—Bears, 28-17 (C)
Buccaneers, 20-10 (TB)
1982—Buccaneers, 26-23 (TB) OT
1983—Bears, 17-10 (C)
Bears, 27-0 (TB)
1984—Bears, 34-14 (C)
Bears, 44-9 (TB)
1985—Bears, 38-28 (C)
Bears, 27-19 (TB)
1986—Bears, 23-3 (TB)
Bears, 48-14 (C)
1987—Bears, 20-3 (C)
Bears, 27-26 (TB)
1988—Bears, 28-10 (C)
Bears, 27-15 (TB)
1989—Buccaneers, 42-35 (TB)
Buccaneers, 32-31 (C)
1990—Bears, 26-6 (TB)
Bears, 27-14 (C)
1991—Bears, 21-20 (TB)
Bears, 27-0 (C)
1992—Bears, 31-14 (C)
Buccaneers, 20-17 (TB)
1993—Bears, 47-17 (C)
Buccaneers, 13-10 (TB)
1994—Bears, 21-9 (C)
Bears, 20-6 (TB)
1995—Bears, 25-6 (TB)
Bears, 31-10 (C)
1996—Bears, 13-10 (C)
Buccaneers, 34-19 (TB)
1997—Bears, 13-7 (C)
Buccaneers, 31-15 (TB)
1998—Buccaneers, 27-15 (TB)
Buccaneers, 31-17 (C)
1999—Buccaneers, 6-3 (TB)
Buccaneers, 20-6 (C)
2000—Buccaneers, 41-0 (TB)
Bears, 13-10 (C)
2001—Bears, 27-24 (TB)
Bears, 27-3 (C)
2002—Buccaneers, 15-0 (C)
2004—Buccaneers, 19-7 (TB)
2005—Bears, 13-10 (TB)
2006—Bears, 34-31 (C) OT
2008—Buccaneers, 27-24 (C) OT
(RS Pts.—Bears 1,143, Buccaneers 835)

CHICAGO vs. *TENNESSEE
RS: Series tied, 5-5
1973—Bears, 35-14 (C)
1977—Oilers, 47-0 (H)
1980—Oilers, 10-6 (C)
1986—Bears, 20-7 (H)
1989—Oilers, 33-28 (C)
1992—Oilers, 24-7 (H)
1995—Bears, 35-32 (C)
1998—Bears, 23-20 (T)
2004—Bears, 19-17 (T) OT
2008—Titans, 21-14 (C)
(RS Pts.—Titans 225, Bears 187)
Franchise in Houston prior to 1997; known as Oilers prior to 1999

CHICAGO vs. *WASHINGTON
RS: Bears lead series, 20-18-1
PS: Redskins lead series, 4-3
1932—Tie, 7-7 (B)
1933—Bears, 7-0 (C)
Redskins, 10-0 (B)
1934—Bears, 21-0 (B)
1935—Bears, 30-14 (B)
1936—Bears, 26-0 (B)
1937—**Redskins, 28-21 (C)
1938—Bears, 31-7 (C)
1940—Redskins, 7-3 (W)
**Bears, 73-0 (W)
1941—Bears, 35-21 (C)
1942—**Redskins, 14-6 (W)
1943—Redskins, 21-7 (W)
**Bears, 41-21 (C)
1945—Redskins, 28-21 (W)
1946—Bears, 24-20 (C)
1947—Bears, 56-20 (W)
1948—Bears, 48-13 (C)
1949—Bears, 31-21 (W)
1951—Bears, 27-0 (W)
1953—Bears, 27-24 (W)
1957—Redskins, 14-3 (C)
1964—Redskins, 27-20 (W)
1968—Redskins, 38-28 (C)
1971—Bears, 16-15 (C)
1974—Redskins, 42-0 (W)
1976—Bears, 33-7 (C)
1978—Bears, 14-10 (W)
1980—Bears, 35-21 (C)
1981—Redskins, 24-7 (C)
1984—***Bears, 23-19 (W)
1985—Bears, 45-10 (C)
1986—***Redskins, 27-13 (C)
1987—***Redskins, 21-17 (C)
1988—Bears, 34-14 (W)
1989—Redskins, 38-14 (W)
1990—Redskins, 10-9 (W)
1991—Redskins, 20-7 (C)
1996—Redskins, 10-3 (W)
1997—Redskins, 31-8 (C)
1999—Redskins, 48-22 (W)
2001—Bears, 20-15 (W)
2003—Bears, 27-24 (C)
2004—Redskins, 13-10 (C)
2005—Redskins, 9-7 (W)
2007—Redskins, 24-16 (W)
(RS Pts.—Bears 779, Redskins 677)
(PS Pts.—Bears 194, Redskins 130)
Franchise in Boston prior to 1937 and known as Braves prior to 1933
***NFL Championship*
****NFC Divisional Playoff*

CINCINNATI vs. ARIZONA
RS: Bengals lead series, 5-4;
See Arizona vs. Cincinnati

CINCINNATI vs. ATLANTA
RS: Bengals lead series, 7-4;
See Atlanta vs. Cincinnati

CINCINNATI vs. BALTIMORE
RS: Ravens lead series, 15-13;
See Baltimore vs. Cincinnati

CINCINNATI vs. BUFFALO
RS: Bills lead series, 14-9
PS: Bengals lead series, 2-0;
See Buffalo vs. Cincinnati

CINCINNATI vs. CAROLINA
RS: Panthers lead series, 2-1;
See Carolina vs. Cincinnati

CINCINNATI vs. CHICAGO
RS: Bengals lead series, 6-3;
See Chicago vs. Cincinnati

CINCINNATI vs. CLEVELAND
RS: Bengals lead series, 38-35
1970—Browns, 30-27 (Cle)
Bengals, 14-10 (Cin)
1971—Browns, 27-24 (Cin)

Browns, 31-27 (Cle)
1972—Browns, 27-6 (Cle)
Browns, 27-24 (Cin)
1973—Browns, 17-10 (Cle)
Bengals, 34-17 (Cin)
1974—Bengals, 33-7 (Cin)
Bengals, 34-24 (Cle)
1975—Bengals, 24-17 (Cin)
Browns, 35-23 (Cle)
1976—Bengals, 45-24 (Cle)
Bengals, 21-6 (Cin)
1977—Browns, 13-3 (Cin)
Bengals, 10-7 (Cle)
1978—Browns, 13-10 (Cle) OT
Bengals, 48-16 (Cin)
1979—Browns, 28-27 (Cle)
Bengals, 16-12 (Cin)
1980—Browns, 31-7 (Cle)
Browns, 27-24 (Cin)
1981—Browns, 20-17 (Cin)
Bengals, 41-21 (Cle)
1982—Bengals, 23-10 (Cin)
1983—Browns, 17-7 (Cle)
Bengals, 28-21 (Cin)
1984—Bengals, 12-9 (Cin)
Bengals, 20-17 (Cle) OT
1985—Bengals, 27-10 (Cin)
Browns, 24-6 (Cle)
1986—Bengals, 30-13 (Cle)
Browns, 34-3 (Cin)
1987—Browns, 34-0 (Cin)
Browns, 38-24 (Cle)
1988—Bengals, 24-17 (Cin)
Browns, 23-16 (Cle)
1989—Bengals, 21-14 (Cin)
Bengals, 21-0 (Cle)
1990—Bengals, 34-13 (Cle)
Bengals, 21-14 (Cin)
1991—Browns, 14-13 (Cle)
Bengals, 23-21 (Cin)
1992—Bengals, 30-10 (Cin)
Browns, 37-21 (Cle)
1993—Browns, 27-14 (Cle)
Browns, 28-17 (Cin)
1994—Browns, 28-20 (Cin)
Browns, 37-13 (Cle)
1995—Browns, 29-26 (Cin) OT
Browns, 26-10 (Cle)
1999—Bengals, 18-17 (Cle)
Bengals, 44-28 (Cin)
2000—Browns, 24-7 (Cin)
Bengals, 12-3 (Cle)
2001—Bengals, 24-14 (Cin)
Browns, 18-0 (Cle)
2002—Browns, 20-7 (Cle)
Browns, 27-20 (Cin)
2003—Bengals, 21-14 (Cle)
Browns, 22-14 (Cin)
2004—Browns, 34-17 (Cle)
Bengals, 58-48 (Cin)
2005—Bengals, 27-13 (Cle)
Bengals, 23-20 (Cin)
2006—Bengals, 34-17 (Cin)
Bengals, 30-0 (Cle)
2007—Browns, 51-45 (Cle)
Bengals, 19-14 (Cin)
2008—Browns, 20-12 (Cin)
Bengals, 14-0 (Cle)
2009—Bengals, 23-20 (Cle) OT
Bengals, 16-7 (Cin)
(RS Pts.—Bengals 1,538, Browns 1,483)

CINCINNATI vs. DALLAS
RS: Cowboys lead series, 6-4
1973—Cowboys, 38-10 (D)
1979—Cowboys, 38-13 (D)
1985—Bengals, 50-24 (C)
1988—Bengals, 38-24 (D)
1991—Cowboys, 35-23 (D)
1994—Cowboys, 23-20 (C)
1997—Bengals, 31-24 (C)
2000—Cowboys, 23-6 (D)
2004—Bengals, 26-3 (C)
2008—Cowboys, 31-22 (D)
(RS Pts.—Cowboys 263, Bengals 239)

CINCINNATI vs. DENVER
RS: Broncos lead series, 17-8
1968—Bengals, 24-10 (C)
Broncos, 10-7 (D)
1969—Broncos, 30-23 (C)
Broncos, 27-16 (D)
1971—Bengals, 24-10 (D)
1972—Bengals, 21-10 (C)
1973—Broncos, 28-10 (D)
1975—Bengals, 17-16 (D)
1976—Bengals, 17-7 (C)
1977—Broncos, 24-13 (C)
1979—Broncos, 10-0 (D)
1981—Bengals, 38-21 (C)
1983—Broncos, 24-17 (D)
1984—Broncos, 20-17 (D)
1986—Broncos, 34-28 (D)
1991—Broncos, 45-14 (D)
1994—Broncos, 15-13 (D)
1996—Broncos, 14-10 (C)
1997—Broncos, 38-20 (D)
1998—Broncos, 33-26 (C)
2000—Bengals, 31-21 (C)
2003—Broncos, 30-10 (C)
2004—Bengals, 23-10 (C)
2006—Broncos, 24-23 (D)
2009—Broncos, 12-7 (C)
(RS Pts.—Broncos 523, Bengals 449)

CINCINNATI vs. DETROIT
RS: Bengals lead series, 7-3
1970—Lions, 38-3 (D)
1974—Lions, 23-19 (C)
1983—Bengals, 17-9 (C)
1986—Bengals, 24-17 (D)
1989—Bengals, 42-7 (C)
1992—Lions, 19-13 (C)
1998—Bengals, 34-28 (D) OT
2001—Bengals, 31-27 (D)
2005—Bengals, 41-17 (D)
2009—Bengals, 23-13 (C)
(RS Pts.—Bengals 247, Lions 198)

CINCINNATI vs. GREEN BAY
RS: Bengals lead series, 6-5
1971—Packers, 20-17 (GB)
1976—Bengals, 28-7 (C)
1977—Bengals, 17-7 (Mil)
1980—Packers, 14-9 (GB)
1983—Bengals, 34-14 (C)
1986—Bengals, 34-28 (Mil)
1992—Packers, 24-23 (GB)
1995—Packers, 24-10 (GB)
1998—Packers, 13-6 (C)
2005—Bengals, 21-14 (C)
2009—Bengals, 31-24 (GB)
(RS Pts.—Bengals 230, Packers 189)

CINCINNATI vs. HOUSTON
RS: Bengals lead series, 3-2
2002—Bengals, 38-3 (H)
2003—Bengals, 34-27 (C)
2005—Bengals, 16-10 (C)
2008—Texans, 35-6 (H)
2009—Texans, 28-17 (C)
(RS Pts.—Bengals 111, Texans 103)

CINCINNATI vs. *INDIANAPOLIS
RS: Colts lead series, 15-8
PS: Colts lead series, 1-0
1970—**Colts, 17-0 (B)
1972—Colts, 20-19 (C)
1974—Bengals, 24-14 (B)
1976—Colts, 28-27 (B)
1979—Colts, 38-28 (B)
1980—Bengals, 34-33 (C)
1981—Bengals, 41-19 (B)
1982—Bengals, 20-17 (B)
1983—Colts, 34-31 (C)
1987—Bengals, 23-21 (I)
1989—Colts, 23-12 (C)
1990—Colts, 34-20 (C)
1992—Colts, 21-17 (C)
1993—Colts, 9-6 (C)
1994—Colts, 17-13 (C)
1995—Bengals, 24-21 (I) OT
1996—Bengals, 31-24 (C)
1997—Bengals, 28-13 (I)
1998—Colts, 39-26 (I)
1999—Colts, 31-10 (I)
2002—Colts, 28-21 (I)
2005—Colts, 45-37 (C)
2006—Colts, 34-16 (I)
2008—Colts, 35-3 (I)
(RS Pts.—Colts 598, Bengals 511)
(PS Pts.—Colts 17, Bengals 0)
Franchise in Baltimore prior to 1984
***AFC Divisional Playoff*

CINCINNATI vs. JACKSONVILLE
RS: Jaguars lead series, 11-6
1995—Bengals, 24-17 (C)
Bengals, 17-13 (J)
1996—Bengals, 28-21 (C)
Jaguars, 30-27 (J)
1997—Jaguars, 21-13 (J)
Bengals, 31-26 (C)
1998—Jaguars, 24-11 (J)
Jaguars, 34-17 (C)
1999—Jaguars, 41-10 (C)
Jaguars, 24-7 (J)
2000—Jaguars, 13-0 (J)
Bengals, 17-14 (C)
2001—Jaguars, 30-13 (J)
Jaguars, 14-10 (C)
2002—Jaguars, 29-15 (C)
2005—Jaguars, 23-20 (J)
2008—Bengals, 21-19 (C)
(RS Pts.—Jaguars 393, Bengals 281)

CINCINNATI vs. KANSAS CITY
RS: Series tied, 13-13
1968—Chiefs, 13-3 (KC)
Chiefs, 16-9 (C)
1969—Bengals, 24-19 (C)
Chiefs, 42-22 (KC)
1970—Chiefs, 27-19 (C)
1972—Bengals, 23-16 (KC)
1973—Bengals, 14-6 (C)
1974—Bengals, 33-6 (C)
1976—Bengals, 27-24 (KC)
1977—Bengals, 27-7 (KC)
1978—Chiefs, 24-23 (C)
1979—Chiefs, 10-7 (C)
1980—Bengals, 20-6 (KC)

1983—Chiefs, 20-15 (KC)
1984—Chiefs, 27-22 (C)
1986—Chiefs, 24-14 (KC)
1987—Bengals, 30-27 (C) OT
1988—Chiefs, 31-28 (KC)
1989—Bengals, 21-17 (KC)
1993—Chiefs, 17-15 (KC)
2003—Bengals, 24-19 (C)
2005—Chiefs, 37-3 (KC)
2006—Bengals, 23-10 (KC)
2007—Chiefs, 27-20 (KC)
2008—Bengals, 16-6 (C)
2009—Bengals, 17-10 (C)
(RS Pts.—Bengals 499, Chiefs 488)

CINCINNATI vs. MIAMI
RS: Dolphins lead series, 12-5
PS: Dolphins lead series, 1-0
1968—Dolphins, 24-22 (C)
Bengals, 38-21 (M)
1969—Bengals, 27-21 (C)
1971—Dolphins, 23-13 (C)
1973—*Dolphins, 34-16 (M)
1974—Dolphins, 24-3 (M)
1977—Bengals, 23-17 (C)
1978—Dolphins, 21-0 (M)
1980—Dolphins, 17-16 (M)
1983—Dolphins, 38-14 (M)
1987—Dolphins, 20-14 (C)
1989—Dolphins, 20-13 (C)
1991—Dolphins, 37-13 (M)
1994—Dolphins, 23-7 (C)
1995—Dolphins, 26-23 (C)
2000—Dolphins, 31-16 (C)
2004—Bengals, 16-13 (C)
2007—Bengals, 38-25 (M)
(RS Pts.—Dolphins 401, Bengals 296)
(PS Pts.—Dolphins 34, Bengals 16)
AFC Divisional Playoff

CINCINNATI vs. MINNESOTA
RS: Vikings lead series, 6-5
1973—Bengals, 27-0 (C)
1977—Vikings, 42-10 (M)
1980—Bengals, 14-0 (C)
1983—Vikings, 20-14 (M)
1986—Bengals, 24-20 (C)
1989—Vikings, 29-21 (M)
1992—Vikings, 42-7 (C)
1995—Bengals, 27-24 (C)
1998—Vikings, 24-3 (M)
2005—Bengals, 37-8 (C)
2009—Vikings, 30-10 (M)
(RS Pts.—Vikings 239, Bengals 194)

CINCINNATI vs. *NEW ENGLAND
RS: Patriots lead series, 13-8
1968—Patriots, 33-14 (B)
1969—Patriots, 25-14 (C)
1970—Bengals, 45-7 (C)
1972—Bengals, 31-7 (NE)
1975—Bengals, 27-10 (C)
1978—Patriots, 10-3 (C)
1979—Patriots, 20-14 (C)
1984—Patriots, 20-14 (NE)
1985—Patriots, 34-23 (NE)
1986—Bengals, 31-7 (NE)
1988—Patriots, 27-21 (NE)
1990—Bengals, 41-7 (C)
1991—Bengals, 29-7 (C)
1992—Bengals, 20-10 (C)
1993—Patriots, 7-2 (NE)
1994—Patriots, 31-28 (C)
2000—Patriots, 16-13 (NE)
2001—Bengals, 23-17 (C)
2004—Patriots, 35-28 (NE)
2006—Patriots, 38-13 (C)
2007—Patriots, 34-13 (C)
(RS Pts.—Bengals 447, Patriots 402)
Franchise in Boston prior to 1971

CINCINNATI vs. NEW ORLEANS
RS: Bengals lead series, 6-5
1970—Bengals, 26-6 (C)
1975—Bengals, 21-0 (NO)
1978—Saints, 20-18 (C)
1981—Saints, 17-7 (NO)
1984—Bengals, 24-21 (NO)
1987—Saints, 41-24 (C)
1990—Saints, 21-7 (C)
1993—Saints, 20-13 (NO)
1996—Bengals, 30-15 (C)
2002—Bengals, 20-13 (C)
2006—Bengals, 31-16 (NO)
(RS Pts.—Bengals 221, Saints 190)

CINCINNATI vs. N.Y. GIANTS
RS: Bengals lead series, 5-3
1972—Bengals, 13-10 (C)
1977—Bengals, 30-13 (C)
1985—Bengals, 35-30 (C)
1991—Bengals, 27-24 (C)
1994—Giants, 27-20 (NY)
1997—Giants, 29-27 (NY)
2004—Bengals, 23-22 (C)
2008—Giants, 26-23 (NY) OT
(RS Pts.—Bengals 198, Giants 181)

CINCINNATI vs. N.Y. JETS
RS: Jets lead series, 14-7
PS: Jets lead series, 2-0
1968—Jets, 27-14 (NY)
1969—Jets, 21-7 (C)
Jets, 40-7 (NY)
1971—Jets, 35-21 (NY)
1973—Bengals, 20-14 (C)
1976—Bengals, 42-3 (NY)
1981—Bengals, 31-30 (NY)
1982—*Jets, 44-17 (C)
1984—Jets, 43-23 (NY)
1985—Jets, 29-20 (C)
1986—Bengals, 52-21 (C)
1987—Jets, 27-20 (NY)
1988—Bengals, 36-19 (C)
1990—Bengals, 25-20 (C)
1992—Jets, 17-14 (NY)
1993—Jets, 17-12 (NY)
1997—Jets, 31-14 (C)
2001—Jets, 15-14 (NY)
2004—Jets, 31-24 (NY)
2007—Bengals, 38-31 (C)
2008—Jets, 26-14 (NY)
2009—Jets, 37-0 (NY)
*Jets, 24-14 (C)
(RS Pts.—Jets 534, Bengals 448)
(PS Pts.—Jets 68, Bengals 31)
AFC First-Round Playoff

CINCINNATI vs. *OAKLAND
RS: Raiders lead series, 18-8
PS: Raiders lead series, 2-0
1968—Raiders, 31-10 (O)
Raiders, 34-0 (C)
1969—Bengals, 31-17 (C)
Raiders, 37-17 (O)
1970—Bengals, 31-21 (C)
1971—Raiders, 31-27 (O)
1972—Raiders, 20-14 (C)
1974—Raiders, 30-27 (O)
1975—Bengals, 14-10 (C)
**Raiders, 31-28 (O)
1976—Raiders, 35-20 (O)
1978—Raiders, 34-21 (C)
1980—Raiders, 28-17 (O)
1982—Bengals, 31-17 (C)
1983—Raiders, 20-10 (C)
1985—Raiders, 13-6 (LA)
1988—Bengals, 45-21 (LA)
1989—Raiders, 28-7 (LA)
1990—Raiders, 24-7 (LA)
**Raiders, 20-10 (LA)
1991—Raiders, 38-14 (C)
1992—Bengals, 24-21 (C) OT
1993—Bengals, 16-10 (C)
1995—Raiders, 20-17 (C)
1998—Raiders, 27-10 (O)
2003—Raiders, 23-20 (O)
2006—Bengals, 27-10 (C)
2009—Raiders, 20-17 (O)
(RS Pts.—Raiders 620, Bengals 480)
(PS Pts.—Raiders 51, Bengals 38)
Franchise in Los Angeles from 1982-1994
***AFC Divisional Playoff*

CINCINNATI vs. PHILADELPHIA
RS: Bengals lead series, 7-3-1
1971—Bengals, 37-14 (C)
1975—Bengals, 31-0 (P)
1979—Bengals, 37-13 (C)
1982—Bengals, 18-14 (P)
1988—Bengals, 28-24 (P)
1991—Eagles, 17-10 (P)
1994—Bengals, 33-30 (C)
1997—Eagles, 44-42 (P)
2000—Eagles, 16-7 (P)
2004—Bengals, 38-10 (P)
2008—Tie, 13-13 (C) OT
(RS Pts.—Bengals 294, Eagles 195)

CINCINNATI vs. PITTSBURGH
RS: Steelers lead series, 47-32
PS: Steelers lead series, 1-0
1970—Steelers, 21-10 (P)
Bengals, 34-7 (C)
1971—Steelers, 21-10 (P)
Steelers, 21-13 (C)
1972—Bengals, 15-10 (C)
Steelers, 40-17 (P)
1973—Bengals, 19-7 (C)
Steelers, 20-13 (P)
1974—Bengals, 17-10 (C)
Steelers, 27-3 (P)
1975—Steelers, 30-24 (C)
Steelers, 35-14 (P)
1976—Steelers, 23-6 (P)
Steelers, 7-3 (C)
1977—Steelers, 20-14 (P)
Bengals, 17-10 (C)
1978—Steelers, 28-3 (C)
Steelers, 7-6 (P)
1979—Bengals, 34-10 (C)
Steelers, 37-17 (P)
1980—Bengals, 30-28 (C)
Bengals, 17-16 (P)
1981—Bengals, 34-7 (C)
Bengals, 17-10 (P)
1982—Steelers, 26-20 (P) OT
1983—Steelers, 24-14 (C)
Bengals, 23-10 (P)
1984—Steelers, 38-17 (P)
Bengals, 22-20 (C)
1985—Bengals, 37-24 (P)

Bengals, 26-21 (C)
1986—Bengals, 24-22 (C)
Steelers, 30-9 (P)
1987—Steelers, 23-20 (P)
Steelers, 30-16 (C)
1988—Bengals, 17-12 (P)
Bengals, 42-7 (C)
1989—Bengals, 41-10 (C)
Bengals, 26-16 (P)
1990—Bengals, 27-3 (C)
Bengals, 16-12 (P)
1991—Steelers, 33-27 (C) OT
Steelers, 17-10 (P)
1992—Steelers, 20-0 (P)
Steelers, 21-9 (C)
1993—Steelers, 34-7 (P)
Steelers, 24-16 (C)
1994—Steelers, 14-10 (P)
Steelers, 38-15 (C)
1995—Bengals, 27-9 (P)
Steelers, 49-31 (C)
1996—Steelers, 20-10 (P)
Bengals, 34-24 (C)
1997—Steelers, 26-10 (C)
Steelers, 20-3 (P)
1998—Bengals, 25-20 (C)
Bengals, 25-24 (P)
1999—Steelers, 17-3 (C)
Bengals, 27-20 (P)
2000—Steelers, 15-0 (P)
Steelers, 48-28 (C)
2001—Steelers, 16-7 (P)
Bengals, 26-23 (C) OT
2002—Steelers, 34-7 (C)
Steelers, 29-21 (P)
2003—Steelers, 17-10 (C)
Bengals, 24-20 (P)
2004—Steelers, 28-17 (P)
Steelers, 19-14 (C)
2005—Steelers, 27-13 (C)
Bengals, 38-31 (P)
*Steelers, 31-17 (C)
2006—Bengals, 28-20 (P)
Steelers, 23-17 (C) OT
2007—Steelers, 24-13 (C)
Steelers, 24-10 (P)
2008—Steelers, 38-10 (C)
Steelers, 27-10 (P)
2009—Bengals, 23-20 (C)
Bengals, 18-12 (P)
(RS Pts.—Steelers 1,705, Bengals 1,407)
(PS Pts.—Steelers 31, Bengals 17)
AFC First-Round Playoff

CINCINNATI vs. *ST. LOUIS
RS: Bengals lead series, 6-5
1972—Rams, 15-12 (LA)
1976—Bengals, 20-12 (C)
1978—Bengals, 20-19 (LA)
1981—Bengals, 24-10 (C)
1984—Rams, 24-14 (C)
1990—Bengals, 34-31 (LA) OT
1993—Bengals, 15-3 (C)
1996—Rams, 26-16 (StL)
1999—Rams, 38-10 (C)
2003—Rams, 27-10 (StL)
2007—Bengals, 19-10 (C)
(RS Pts.—Rams 215, Bengals 194)
Franchise in Los Angeles prior to 1995

CINCINNATI vs. SAN DIEGO
RS: Chargers lead series, 19-10
PS: Bengals lead series, 1-0
1968—Chargers, 29-13 (SD)
Chargers, 31-10 (C)
1969—Bengals, 34-20 (C)
Chargers, 21-14 (SD)
1970—Bengals, 17-14 (SD)
1971—Bengals, 31-0 (C)
1973—Bengals, 20-13 (SD)
1974—Chargers, 20-17 (C)
1975—Bengals, 47-17 (C)
1977—Chargers, 24-3 (SD)
1978—Chargers, 22-13 (SD)
1979—Chargers, 26-24 (C)
1980—Chargers, 31-14 (C)
1981—Bengals, 40-17 (SD)
*Bengals, 27-7 (C)
1982—Chargers, 50-34 (SD)
1985—Chargers, 44-41 (C)
1987—Chargers, 10-9 (C)
1988—Bengals, 27-10 (C)
1990—Bengals, 21-16 (SD)
1992—Chargers, 27-10 (SD)
1994—Chargers, 27-10 (SD)
1996—Chargers, 27-14 (SD)
1997—Bengals, 38-31 (C)
1999—Chargers, 34-7 (C)
2001—Chargers, 28-14 (SD)
2002—Chargers, 34-6 (C)
2003—Bengals, 34-27 (SD)
2006—Chargers, 49-41 (C)
2009—Chargers, 27-24 (SD)
(RS Pts.—Chargers 726, Bengals 627)
(PS Pts.—Bengals 27, Chargers 7)
AFC Championship

CINCINNATI vs. SAN FRANCISCO
RS: 49ers lead series, 8-3
PS: 49ers lead series, 2-0
1974—Bengals, 21-3 (SF)
1978—49ers, 28-12 (SF)
1981—49ers, 21-3 (C)
*49ers, 26-21 (Detroit)
1984—49ers, 23-17 (SF)
1987—49ers, 27-26 (C)
1988—**49ers, 20-16 (South Florida)
1990—49ers, 20-17 (C) OT
1993—49ers, 21-8 (SF)
1996—49ers, 28-21 (SF)
1999—Bengals, 44-30 (C)
2003—Bengals, 41-38 (C)
2007—49ers, 20-13 (SF)
(RS Pts.—49ers 259, Bengals 223)
(PS Pts.—49ers 46, Bengals 37)
*Super Bowl XVI
**Super Bowl XXIII

CINCINNATI vs. SEATTLE
RS: Seahawks lead series, 9-8
PS: Bengals lead series, 1-0
1977—Bengals, 42-20 (C)
1981—Bengals, 27-21 (C)
1982—Bengals, 24-10 (C)
1984—Seahawks, 26-6 (C)
1985—Seahawks, 28-24 (C)
1986—Bengals, 34-7 (C)
1987—Bengals, 17-10 (S)
1988—*Bengals, 21-13 (C)
1989—Seahawks, 24-17 (C)
1990—Seahawks, 31-16 (S)
1991—Seahawks, 13-7 (C)
1992—Bengals, 21-3 (S)
1993—Seahawks, 19-10 (C)
1994—Bengals, 20-17 (S) OT
1995—Seahawks, 24-21 (S)
1999—Seahawks, 37-20 (S)
2003—Bengals, 27-24 (C)
2007—Seahawks, 24-21 (S)
(RS Pts.—Bengals 354, Seahawks 338)
(PS Pts.—Bengals 21, Seahawks 13)
AFC Divisional Playoff

CINCINNATI vs. TAMPA BAY
RS: Buccaneers lead series, 6-3
1976—Bengals, 21-0 (C)
1980—Buccaneers, 17-12 (C)
1983—Bengals, 23-17 (TB)
1989—Bengals, 56-23 (C)
1995—Buccaneers, 19-16 (TB)
1998—Buccaneers, 35-0 (C)
2001—Buccaneers, 16-13 (C) OT
2002—Buccaneers, 35-7 (C)
2006—Buccaneers, 14-13 (TB)
(RS Pts.— Buccaneers 176, Bengals 161)

CINCINNATI vs. *TENNESSEE
RS: Titans lead series, 39-31-1
PS: Bengals lead series, 1-0
1968—Oilers, 27-17 (C)
1969—Tie, 31-31 (H)
1970—Oilers, 20-13 (C)
Bengals, 30-20 (H)
1971—Oilers, 10-6 (H)
Bengals, 28-13 (C)
1972—Bengals, 30-7 (C)
Bengals, 61-17 (H)
1973—Bengals, 24-10 (C)
Bengals, 27-24 (H)
1974—Oilers, 34-21 (C)
Oilers, 20-3 (H)
1975—Bengals, 21-19 (H)
Bengals, 23-19 (C)
1976—Bengals, 27-7 (H)
Bengals, 31-27 (C)
1977—Bengals, 13-10 (C) OT
Oilers, 21-16 (H)
1978—Bengals, 28-13 (C)
Oilers, 17-10 (H)
1979—Oilers, 30-27 (C) OT
Oilers, 42-21 (H)
1980—Oilers, 13-10 (C)
Oilers, 23-3 (H)
1981—Oilers, 17-10 (H)
Bengals, 34-21 (C)
1982—Bengals, 27-6 (C)
Bengals, 35-27 (H)
1983—Bengals, 55-14 (H)
Bengals, 38-10 (C)
1984—Bengals, 13-3 (C)
Bengals, 31-13 (H)
1985—Oilers, 44-27 (H)
Bengals, 45-27 (C)
1986—Bengals, 31-28 (C)
Oilers, 32-28 (H)
1987—Oilers, 31-29 (C)
Oilers, 21-17 (H)
1988—Bengals, 44-21 (C)
Oilers, 41-6 (H)
1989—Oilers, 26-24 (H)
Bengals, 61-7 (C)
1990—Oilers, 48-17 (H)
Bengals, 40-20 (C)
**Bengals, 41-14 (C)
1991—Oilers, 30-7 (C)
Oilers, 35-3 (H)
1992—Oilers, 38-24 (C)
Oilers, 26-10 (H)
1993—Oilers, 28-12 (H)

Oilers, 38-3 (C)
1994—Oilers, 20-13 (H)
Bengals, 34-31 (C)
1995—Oilers, 38-28 (C)
Bengals, 32-25 (H)
1996—Oilers, 30-27 (C) OT
Bengals, 21-13 (H)
1997—Oilers, 30-7 (T)
Bengals, 41-14 (C)
1998—Oilers, 23-14 (C)
Oilers, 44-14 (T)
1999—Titans, 36-35 (T)
Titans, 24-14 (C)
2000—Titans, 23-14 (C)
Titans, 35-3 (T)
2001—Titans, 20-7 (C)
Bengals, 23-21 (T)
2002—Titans, 30-24 (C)
2004—Titans, 27-20 (T)
2005—Bengals, 31-23 (T)
2007—Bengals, 35-6 (C)
2008—Titans, 24-7 (C)
(RS Pts.—Titans 1,663, Bengals 1,636)
(PS Pts.—Bengals 41, Titans 14)
Franchise in Houston prior to 1997; known as Oilers prior to 1999
**AFC First-Round Playoff*

CINCINNATI vs. WASHINGTON
RS: Series tied, 4-4
1970—Redskins, 20-0 (W)
1974—Bengals, 28-17 (C)
1979—Redskins, 28-14 (W)
1985—Redskins, 27-24 (W)
1988—Bengals, 20-17 (C) OT
1991—Redskins, 34-27 (C)
2004—Bengals, 17-10 (W)
2008—Bengals, 20-13 (C)
(RS Pts.—Redskins 166, Bengals 150)

CLEVELAND vs. ARIZONA
RS: Browns lead series, 33-12-3;
See Arizona vs. Cleveland

CLEVELAND vs. ATLANTA
RS: Browns lead series, 10-2;
See Atlanta vs. Cleveland

CLEVELAND vs. BALTIMORE
RS: Ravens lead series, 15-7;
See Baltimore vs. Cleveland

CLEVELAND vs. BUFFALO
RS: Browns lead series, 10-5
PS: Browns lead series, 1-0;
See Buffalo vs. Cleveland

CLEVELAND vs. CAROLINA
RS: Panthers lead series, 3-0;
See Carolina vs. Cleveland

CLEVELAND vs. CHICAGO
RS: Browns lead series, 9-5;
See Chicago vs. Cleveland

CLEVELAND vs. CINCINNATI
RS: Bengals lead series, 38-35;
See Cincinnati vs. Cleveland

CLEVELAND vs. DALLAS
RS: Browns lead series, 15-11
PS: Browns lead series, 2-1
1960—Browns, 48-7 (D)
1961—Browns, 25-7 (C)
Browns, 38-17 (D)
1962—Browns, 19-10 (C)
Cowboys, 45-21 (D)
1963—Browns, 41-24 (D)
Browns, 27-17 (C)
1964—Browns, 27-6 (C)
Browns, 20-16 (D)
1965—Browns, 23-17 (C)
Browns, 24-17 (D)
1966—Browns, 30-21 (C)
Cowboys, 26-14 (D)
1967—Cowboys, 21-14 (C)
*Cowboys, 52-14 (D)
1968—Cowboys, 28-7 (D)
*Browns, 31-20 (C)
1969—Browns, 42-10 (C)
*Browns, 38-14 (D)
1970—Cowboys, 6-2 (C)
1974—Cowboys, 41-17 (D)
1979—Browns, 26-7 (C)
1982—Cowboys, 31-14 (D)
1985—Cowboys, 20-7 (D)
1988—Browns, 24-21 (C)
1991—Cowboys, 26-14 (C)
1994—Browns, 19-14 (D)
2004—Cowboys, 19-12 (D)
2008—Cowboys, 28-10 (C)
(RS Pts.—Browns 565, Cowboys 502)
(PS Pts.—Cowboys 86, Browns 83)
Conference Championship

CLEVELAND vs. DENVER
RS: Broncos lead series, 18-5
PS: Broncos lead series, 3-0
1970—Browns, 27-13 (D)
1971—Broncos, 27-0 (C)
1972—Browns, 27-20 (D)
1974—Browns, 23-21 (C)
1975—Broncos, 16-15 (D)
1976—Broncos, 44-13 (D)
1978—Broncos, 19-7 (C)
1980—Broncos, 19-16 (C)
1981—Broncos, 23-20 (D) OT
1983—Broncos, 27-6 (D)
1984—Broncos, 24-14 (C)
1986—*Broncos, 23-20 (C) OT
1987—*Broncos, 38-33 (D)
1988—Broncos, 30-7 (D)
1989—Browns, 16-13 (C)
*Broncos, 37-21 (D)
1990—Browns, 30-29 (D)
1991—Broncos, 17-7 (C)
1992—Broncos, 12-0 (C)
1993—Broncos, 29-14 (C)
1994—Broncos, 26-14 (D)
2000—Broncos, 44-10 (D)
2003—Broncos, 23-20 (D) OT
2006—Broncos, 17-7 (C)
2008—Broncos, 34-30 (C)
2009—Broncos, 27-6 (D)
(RS Pts.—Broncos 554, Browns 329)
(PS Pts.—Broncos 98, Browns 74)
AFC Championship

CLEVELAND vs. DETROIT
RS: Lions lead series, 14-4
PS: Lions lead series, 3-1
1952—Lions, 17-6 (D)
*Lions, 17-7 (C)
1953—*Lions, 17-16 (D)
1954—Lions, 14-10 (C)
*Browns, 56-10 (C)
1957—Lions, 20-7 (D)
*Lions, 59-14 (D)
1958—Lions, 30-10 (C)
1963—Lions, 38-10 (D)
1964—Browns, 37-21 (C)
1967—Lions, 31-14 (D)
1969—Lions, 28-21 (C)
1970—Lions, 41-24 (C)
1975—Lions, 21-10 (D)
1983—Browns, 31-26 (D)
1986—Browns, 24-21 (C)
1989—Lions, 13-10 (D)
1992—Lions, 24-14 (D)
1995—Lions, 38-20 (D)
2001—Browns, 24-14 (C)
2005—Lions, 13-10 (C)
2009—Lions, 38-37 (D)
(RS Pts.—Lions 448, Browns 319)
(PS Pts.—Lions 103, Browns 93)
NFL Championship

CLEVELAND vs. GREEN BAY
RS: Packers lead series, 10-7
PS: Packers lead series, 1-0
1953—Browns, 27-0 (Mil)
1955—Browns, 41-10 (C)
1956—Browns, 24-7 (Mil)
1961—Packers, 49-17 (C)
1964—Packers, 28-21 (Mil)
1965—*Packers, 23-12 (GB)
1966—Packers, 21-20 (C)
1967—Packers, 55-7 (Mil)
1969—Browns, 20-7 (C)
1972—Packers, 26-10 (C)
1980—Browns, 26-21 (C)
1983—Packers, 35-21 (Mil)
1986—Packers, 17-14 (C)
1992—Browns, 17-6 (C)
1995—Packers, 31-20 (C)
2001—Packers, 30-7 (GB)
2005—Browns, 26-24 (GB)
2009—Packers, 31-3 (C)
(RS Pts.—Packers 398, Browns 321)
(PS Pts.—Packers 23, Browns 12)
NFL Championship

CLEVELAND vs. HOUSTON
RS: Series tied, 3-3
2002—Browns, 34-17 (C)
2004—Browns, 22-14 (H)
2005—Texans, 19-16 (H)
2006—Texans, 14-6 (H)
2007—Browns, 27-17 (C)
2008—Texans, 16-6 (C)
(RS Pts.—Browns 111, Texans 97)

CLEVELAND vs. *INDIANAPOLIS
RS: Browns lead series, 13-12
PS: Series tied, 2-2
1956—Colts, 21-7 (C)
1959—Browns, 38-31 (B)
1962—Colts, 36-14 (C)
1964—**Browns, 27-0 (C)
1968—Browns, 30-20 (B)
**Colts, 34-0 (C)
1971—Browns, 14-13 (B)
***Colts, 20-3 (C)
1973—Browns, 24-14 (C)
1975—Colts, 21-7 (B)
1978—Browns, 45-24 (B)
1979—Browns, 13-10 (C)
1980—Browns, 28-27 (B)
1981—Browns, 42-28 (C)
1983—Browns, 41-23 (C)
1986—Browns, 24-9 (I)
1987—Colts, 9-7 (C)
***Browns, 38-21 (C)
1988—Browns, 23-17 (C)
1989—Colts, 23-17 (I) OT
1991—Browns, 31-0 (I)

1992—Colts, 14-3 (I)
1993—Colts, 23-10 (I)
1994—Browns, 21-14 (I)
1999—Colts, 29-28 (C)
2002—Colts, 28-23 (C)
2003—Colts, 9-6 (C)
2005—Colts, 13-6 (I)
2008—Colts, 10-6 (C)
(RS Pts.—Browns 508, Colts 466)
(PS Pts.—Colts 75, Browns 68)
Franchise in Baltimore prior to 1984
***NFL Championship*
****AFC Divisional Playoff*

CLEVELAND vs. JACKSONVILLE
RS: Jaguars lead series, 8-4
1995—Jaguars, 23-15 (C)
Jaguars, 24-21 (J)
1999—Jaguars, 24-7 (J)
Jaguars, 24-14 (C)
2000—Jaguars, 27-7 (C)
Jaguars, 48-0 (J)
2001—Browns, 23-14 (J)
Jaguars, 15-10 (C)
2002—Browns, 21-20 (J)
2005—Jaguars, 20-14 (C)
2008—Browns, 23-17 (J)
2009—Browns, 23-17 (C)
(RS Pts.—Jaguars 273, Browns 178)

CLEVELAND vs. KANSAS CITY
RS: Browns lead series, 10-9-2
1971—Chiefs, 13-7 (KC)
1972—Chiefs, 31-7 (C)
1973—Tie, 20-20 (KC)
1975—Browns, 40-14 (C)
1976—Chiefs, 39-14 (KC)
1977—Browns, 44-7 (C)
1978—Chiefs, 17-3 (KC)
1979—Browns, 27-24 (KC)
1980—Browns, 20-13 (C)
1984—Chiefs, 10-6 (KC)
1986—Browns, 20-7 (C)
1988—Browns, 6-3 (KC)
1989—Tie, 10-10 (C) OT
1990—Chiefs, 34-0 (KC)
1991—Browns, 20-15 (C)
1994—Chiefs, 20-13 (KC)
1995—Browns, 35-17 (C)
2002—Chiefs, 40-39 (C)
2003—Chiefs, 41-20 (KC)
2006—Browns, 31-28 (C) OT
2009—Browns, 41-34 (KC)
(RS Pts.—Chiefs 437, Browns 423)

CLEVELAND vs. MIAMI
RS: Dolphins lead series, 7-6
PS: Dolphins lead series, 2-0
1970—Browns, 28-0 (M)
1972—*Dolphins, 20-14 (M)
1973—Dolphins, 17-9 (C)
1976—Browns, 17-13 (C)
1979—Browns, 30-24 (C) OT
1985—*Dolphins, 24-21 (M)
1986—Browns, 26-16 (C)
1988—Dolphins, 38-31 (M)
1989—Dolphins, 13-10 (M) OT
1990—Dolphins, 30-13 (C)
1992—Dolphins, 27-23 (C)
1993—Dolphins, 24-14 (C)
2004—Dolphins, 10-7 (M)
2005—Browns, 22-0 (C)
2007—Browns, 41-31 (C)
(RS Pts.—Browns 271, Dolphins 243)
(PS Pts.—Dolphins 44, Browns 35)
**AFC Divisional Playoff*

CLEVELAND vs. MINNESOTA
RS: Vikings lead series, 10-3
PS: Vikings lead series, 1-0
1965—Vikings, 27-17 (C)
1967—Browns, 14-10 (C)
1969—Vikings, 51-3 (M)
*Vikings, 27-7 (M)
1973—Vikings, 26-3 (M)
1975—Vikings, 42-10 (C)
1980—Vikings, 28-23 (M)
1983—Vikings, 27-21 (C)
1986—Browns, 23-20 (M)
1989—Browns, 23-17 (C) OT
1992—Vikings, 17-13 (M)
1995—Vikings, 27-11 (M)
2005—Vikings, 24-12 (M)
2009—Vikings, 34-20 (C)
(RS Pts.—Vikings 350, Browns 193)
(PS Pts.—Vikings 27, Browns 7)
**NFL Championship*

CLEVELAND vs. NEW ENGLAND
RS: Browns lead series, 11-9
PS: Browns lead series, 1-0
1971—Browns, 27-7 (C)
1974—Browns, 21-14 (NE)
1977—Browns, 30-27 (C) OT
1980—Patriots, 34-17 (NE)
1982—Browns, 10-7 (C)
1983—Browns, 30-0 (NE)
1984—Patriots, 17-16 (C)
1985—Browns, 24-20 (C)
1987—Browns, 20-10 (NE)
1991—Browns, 20-0 (NE)
1992—Browns, 19-17 (NE)
1993—Patriots, 20-17 (C)
1994—Browns, 13-6 (C)
*Browns, 20-13 (C)
1995—Patriots, 17-14 (NE)
1999—Patriots, 19-7 (C)
2000—Browns, 19-11 (C)
2001—Patriots, 27-16 (NE)
2003—Patriots, 9-3 (NE)
2004—Patriots, 42-15 (C)
2007—Patriots, 34-17 (NE)
(RS Pts.—Browns 355, Patriots 338)
(PS Pts.—Browns 20, Patriots 13)
**AFC First-Round Playoff*

CLEVELAND vs. NEW ORLEANS
RS: Browns lead series, 11-4
1967—Browns, 42-7 (NO)
1968—Browns, 24-10 (NO)
Browns, 35-17 (C)
1969—Browns, 27-17 (NO)
1971—Browns, 21-17 (NO)
1975—Browns, 17-16 (C)
1978—Browns, 24-16 (NO)
1981—Browns, 20-17 (C)
1984—Saints, 16-14 (C)
1987—Saints, 28-21 (NO)
1990—Saints, 25-20 (NO)
1993—Browns, 17-13 (C)
1999—Browns, 21-16 (NO)
2002—Browns, 24-15 (NO)
2006—Saints, 19-14 (C)
(RS Pts.—Browns 341, Saints 249)

CLEVELAND vs. N.Y. GIANTS
RS: Browns lead series, 26-19-2
PS: Series tied, 1-1
1950—Giants, 6-0 (C)
Giants, 17-13 (NY)
*Browns, 8-3 (C)
1951—Browns, 14-13 (C)
Browns, 10-0 (NY)
1952—Giants, 17-9 (C)
Giants, 37-34 (NY)
1953—Browns, 7-0 (NY)
Browns, 62-14 (C)
1954—Browns, 24-14 (C)
Browns, 16-7 (NY)
1955—Browns, 24-14 (C)
Tie, 35-35 (NY)
1956—Giants, 21-9 (C)
Browns, 24-7 (NY)
1957—Browns, 6-3 (C)
Browns, 34-28 (NY)
1958—Giants, 21-17 (C)
Giants, 13-10 (NY)
*Giants, 10-0 (NY)
1959—Giants, 10-6 (C)
Giants, 48-7 (NY)
1960—Giants, 17-13 (C)
Browns, 48-34 (NY)
1961—Giants, 37-21 (C)
Tie, 7-7 (NY)
1962—Browns, 17-7 (C)
Giants, 17-13 (NY)
1963—Browns, 35-24 (NY)
Giants, 33-6 (C)
1964—Browns, 42-20 (C)
Browns, 52-20 (NY)
1965—Browns, 38-14 (NY)
Browns, 34-21 (C)
1966—Browns, 28-7 (NY)
Browns, 49-40 (C)
1967—Giants, 38-34 (NY)
Browns, 24-14 (C)
1968—Browns, 45-10 (C)
1969—Browns, 28-17 (C)
Giants, 27-14 (NY)
1973—Browns, 12-10 (C)
1977—Browns, 21-7 (NY)
1985—Browns, 35-33 (NY)
1991—Giants, 13-10 (NY)
1994—Giants, 16-13 (C)
2000—Giants, 24-3 (C)
2004—Giants, 27-10 (NY)
2008—Browns, 35-14 (C)
(RS Pts.—Browns 1,048, Giants 873)
(PS Pts.—Giants 13, Browns 8)
**Conference Playoff*

CLEVELAND vs. N.Y. JETS
RS: Browns lead series, 12-7
PS: Browns lead series, 1-0
1970—Browns, 31-21 (C)
1972—Browns, 26-10 (NY)
1976—Browns, 38-17 (C)
1978—Browns, 37-34 (C) OT
1979—Browns, 25-22 (NY) OT
1980—Browns, 17-14 (C)
1981—Jets, 14-13 (C)
1983—Browns, 10-7 (C)
1984—Jets, 24-20 (C)
1985—Jets, 37-10 (NY)
1986—*Browns, 23-20 (C) OT
1988—Jets, 23-3 (C)
1989—Browns, 38-24 (C)
1990—Jets, 24-21 (NY)
1991—Jets, 17-14 (C)
1994—Browns, 27-7 (C)
2002—Browns, 24-21 (NY)

2004—Jets, 10-7 (C)
2006—Browns, 20-13 (C)
2007—Browns, 24-18 (NY)
(RS Pts.—Browns 405, Jets 357)
(PS Pts.—Browns 23, Jets 20)
AFC Divisional Playoff

CLEVELAND vs. *OAKLAND
RS: Raiders lead series, 10-8
PS: Raiders lead series, 2-0
1970—Raiders, 23-20 (O)
1971—Raiders, 34-20 (C)
1973—Browns, 7-3 (O)
1974—Raiders, 40-24 (C)
1975—Raiders, 38-17 (O)
1977—Raiders, 26-10 (C)
1979—Raiders, 19-14 (O)
1980—**Raiders, 14-12 (C)
1982—***Raiders, 27-10 (LA)
1985—Raiders, 21-20 (C)
1986—Raiders, 27-14 (LA)
1987—Browns, 24-17 (LA)
1992—Browns, 28-16 (LA)
1993—Browns, 19-16 (LA)
2000—Raiders, 36-10 (O)
2003—Browns, 13-7 (C)
2005—Browns, 9-7 (O)
2006—Browns, 24-21 (O)
2007—Raiders, 26-24 (O)
2009—Browns, 23-9 (C)
(RS Pts.—Raiders 386, Browns 320)
(PS Pts.—Raiders 41, Browns 22)
Franchise in Los Angeles from 1982-1994
***AFC Divisional Playoff*
****AFC First-Round Playoff*

CLEVELAND vs. PHILADELPHIA
RS: Browns lead series, 31-15-1
1950—Browns, 35-10 (P)
Browns, 13-7 (C)
1951—Browns, 20-17 (C)
Browns, 24-9 (P)
1952—Browns, 49-7 (P)
Eagles, 28-20 (C)
1953—Browns, 37-13 (C)
Eagles, 42-27 (P)
1954—Eagles, 28-10 (P)
Browns, 6-0 (C)
1955—Browns, 21-17 (C)
Eagles, 33-17 (P)
1956—Browns, 16-0 (P)
Browns, 17-14 (C)
1957—Browns, 24-7 (C)
Eagles, 17-7 (P)
1958—Browns, 28-14 (C)
Browns, 21-14 (P)
1959—Browns, 28-7 (C)
Browns, 28-21 (P)
1960—Browns, 41-24 (P)
Eagles, 31-29 (C)
1961—Eagles, 27-20 (P)
Browns, 45-24 (C)
1962—Eagles, 35-7 (P)
Tie, 14-14 (C)
1963—Browns, 37-7 (C)
Browns, 23-17 (P)
1964—Browns, 28-20 (P)
Browns, 38-24 (C)
1965—Browns, 35-17 (P)
Browns, 38-34 (C)
1966—Browns, 27-7 (C)
Eagles, 33-21 (P)
1967—Eagles, 28-24 (P)
1968—Browns, 47-13 (C)
1969—Browns, 27-20 (P)
1972—Browns, 27-17 (P)
1976—Browns, 24-3 (C)
1979—Browns, 24-19 (P)
1982—Eagles, 24-21 (C)
1988—Browns, 19-3 (C)
1991—Eagles, 32-30 (C)
1994—Browns, 26-7 (P)
2000—Eagles, 35-24 (C)
2004—Eagles, 34-31 (C) OT
2008—Eagles, 30-10 (P)
(RS Pts.—Browns 1,185, Eagles 884)

CLEVELAND vs. PITTSBURGH
RS: Steelers lead series, 58-56
PS: Steelers lead series, 2-0
1950—Browns, 30-17 (P)
Browns, 45-7 (C)
1951—Browns, 17-0 (C)
Browns, 28-0 (P)
1952—Browns, 21-20 (P)
Browns, 29-28 (C)
1953—Browns, 34-16 (C)
Browns, 20-16 (P)
1954—Steelers, 55-27 (P)
Browns, 42-7 (C)
1955—Browns, 41-14 (C)
Browns, 30-7 (P)
1956—Browns, 14-10 (P)
Steelers, 24-16 (C)
1957—Browns, 23-12 (P)
Browns, 24-0 (C)
1958—Browns, 45-12 (P)
Browns, 27-10 (C)
1959—Steelers, 17-7 (P)
Steelers, 21-20 (C)
1960—Browns, 28-20 (C)
Steelers, 14-10 (P)
1961—Browns, 30-28 (P)
Steelers, 17-13 (C)
1962—Browns, 41-14 (P)
Browns, 35-14 (C)
1963—Browns, 35-23 (C)
Steelers, 9-7 (P)
1964—Steelers, 23-7 (C)
Browns, 30-17 (P)
1965—Browns, 24-19 (C)
Browns, 42-21 (P)
1966—Browns, 41-10 (C)
Steelers, 16-6 (P)
1967—Browns, 21-10 (C)
Browns, 34-14 (P)
1968—Browns, 31-24 (C)
Browns, 45-24 (P)
1969—Browns, 42-31 (C)
Browns, 24-3 (P)
1970—Browns, 15-7 (C)
Steelers, 28-9 (P)
1971—Browns, 27-17 (C)
Steelers, 26-9 (P)
1972—Browns, 26-24 (C)
Steelers, 30-0 (P)
1973—Steelers, 33-6 (P)
Browns, 21-16 (C)
1974—Steelers, 20-16 (P)
Steelers, 26-16 (C)
1975—Steelers, 42-6 (C)
Steelers, 31-17 (P)
1976—Steelers, 31-14 (P)
Browns, 18-16 (C)
1977—Steelers, 28-14 (C)
Steelers, 35-31 (P)
1978—Steelers, 15-9 (P) OT
Steelers, 34-14 (C)
1979—Steelers, 51-35 (C)
Steelers, 33-30 (P) OT
1980—Browns, 27-26 (C)
Steelers, 16-13 (P)
1981—Steelers, 13-7 (P)
Steelers, 32-10 (C)
1982—Browns, 10-9 (C)
Steelers, 37-21 (P)
1983—Steelers, 44-17 (P)
Browns, 30-17 (C)
1984—Browns, 20-10 (C)
Steelers, 23-20 (P)
1985—Browns, 17-7 (C)
Steelers, 10-9 (P)
1986—Browns, 27-24 (P)
Browns, 37-31 (C) OT
1987—Browns, 34-10 (C)
Browns, 19-13 (P)
1988—Browns, 23-9 (P)
Browns, 27-7 (C)
1989—Browns, 51-0 (P)
Steelers, 17-7 (C)
1990—Browns, 13-3 (C)
Steelers, 35-0 (P)
1991—Browns, 17-14 (C)
Steelers, 17-10 (P)
1992—Browns, 17-9 (C)
Steelers, 23-13 (P)
1993—Browns, 28-23 (C)
Steelers, 16-9 (P)
1994—Steelers, 17-10 (C)
Steelers, 17-7 (P)
*Steelers, 29-9 (P)
1995—Steelers, 20-3 (P)
Steelers, 20-17 (C)
1999—Steelers, 43-0 (C)
Browns, 16-15 (P)
2000—Browns, 23-20 (C)
Steelers, 22-0 (P)
2001—Steelers, 15-12 (C) OT
Steelers, 28-7 (P)
2002—Steelers, 16-13 (P) OT
Steelers, 23-20 (C)
**Steelers, 36-33 (P)
2003—Browns, 33-13 (P)
Steelers, 13-6 (C)
2004—Steelers, 34-23 (P)
Steelers, 24-10 (C)
2005—Steelers, 34-21 (P)
Steelers, 41-0 (C)
2006—Steelers, 24-20 (C)
Steelers, 27-7 (P)
2007—Steelers, 34-7 (C)
Steelers, 31-28 (P)
2008—Steelers, 10-6 (C)
Steelers, 31-0 (P)
2009—Steelers, 27-14 (P)
Browns, 13-6 (C)
(RS Pts.—Steelers 2,287, Browns 2,268)
(PS Pts.—Steelers 65, Browns 42)
**AFC Divisional Playoff*
***AFC First-Round Playoff*

CLEVELAND vs. *ST. LOUIS
RS: Series tied, 9-9
PS: Browns lead series, 2-1
1950—**Browns, 30-28 (C)
1951—Browns, 38-23 (LA)
**Rams, 24-17 (LA)

1952—Browns, 37-7 (C)
1955—**Browns, 38-14 (LA)
1957—Browns, 45-31 (C)
1958—Browns, 30-27 (LA)
1963—Browns, 20-6 (C)
1965—Rams, 42-7 (LA)
1968—Rams, 24-6 (C)
1973—Rams, 30-17 (LA)
1977—Rams, 9-0 (C)
1978—Browns, 30-19 (C)
1981—Rams, 27-16 (LA)
1984—Rams, 20-17 (LA)
1987—Browns, 30-17 (C)
1990—Rams, 38-23 (C)
1993—Browns, 42-14 (LA)
1999—Rams, 34-3 (StL)
2003—Rams, 26-20 (C)
2007—Browns, 27-20 (StL)
(RS Pts.—Rams 414, Browns 408)
(PS Pts.—Browns 85, Rams 66)
Franchise in Los Angeles prior to 1995
***NFL Championship*

CLEVELAND vs. SAN DIEGO
RS: Chargers lead series, 14-7-1
1970—Chargers, 27-10 (C)
1972—Browns, 21-17 (SD)
1973—Tie, 16-16 (C)
1974—Chargers, 36-35 (SD)
1976—Browns, 21-17 (C)
1977—Chargers, 37-14 (SD)
1981—Chargers, 44-14 (C)
1982—Chargers, 30-13 (C)
1983—Browns, 30-24 (SD) OT
1985—Browns, 21-7 (SD)
1986—Browns, 47-17 (C)
1987—Chargers, 27-24 (SD) OT
1990—Chargers, 24-14 (C)
1991—Browns, 30-24 (SD) OT
1992—Chargers, 14-13 (C)
1995—Chargers, 31-13 (SD)
1999—Chargers, 23-10 (SD)
2001—Browns, 20-16 (C)
2003—Chargers, 26-20 (C)
2004—Chargers, 21-0 (C)
2006—Chargers, 32-25 (SD)
2009—Chargers, 30-23 (C)
(RS Pts.—Chargers 540, Browns 434)

CLEVELAND vs. SAN FRANCISCO
RS: Browns lead series, 11-6
1950—Browns, 34-14 (C)
1951—49ers, 24-10 (SF)
1953—Browns, 23-21 (C)
1955—Browns, 38-3 (SF)
1959—49ers, 21-20 (C)
1962—Browns, 13-10 (SF)
1968—Browns, 33-21 (SF)
1970—49ers, 34-31 (SF)
1974—Browns, 7-0 (C)
1978—Browns, 24-7 (C)
1981—Browns, 15-12 (SF)
1984—49ers, 41-7 (C)
1987—49ers, 38-24 (SF)
1990—49ers, 20-17 (SF)
1993—Browns, 23-13 (C)
2003—Browns, 13-12 (SF)
2007—Browns, 20-7 (C)
(RS Pts.—Browns 352, 49ers 298)

CLEVELAND vs. SEATTLE
RS: Seahawks lead series, 11-5
1977—Seahawks, 20-19 (S)
1978—Seahawks, 47-24 (S)
1979—Seahawks, 29-24 (C)
1980—Browns, 27-3 (S)
1981—Seahawks, 42-21 (S)
1982—Browns, 21-7 (S)
1983—Seahawks, 24-9 (C)
1984—Seahawks, 33-0 (S)
1985—Seahawks, 31-13 (S)
1988—Seahawks, 16-10 (C)
1989—Browns, 17-7 (S)
1993—Seahawks, 22-5 (S)
1994—Browns, 35-9 (C)
2001—Seahawks, 9-6 (C)
2003—Seahawks, 34-7 (S)
2007—Browns, 33-30 (C) OT
(RS Pts.—Seahawks 363, Browns 271)

CLEVELAND vs. TAMPA BAY
RS: Browns lead series, 5-2
1976—Browns, 24-7 (TB)
1980—Browns, 34-27 (TB)
1983—Browns, 20-0 (C)
1989—Browns, 42-31 (TB)
1995—Browns, 22-6 (C)
2002—Buccaneers 17-3 (TB)
2006—Buccaneers, 22-7 (C)
(RS Pts.—Browns 152, Buccaneers 110)

CLEVELAND vs. *TENNESSEE
RS: Browns lead series, 33-27
PS: Titans lead series, 1-0
1970—Browns, 28-14 (C)
Browns, 21-10 (H)
1971—Browns, 31-0 (C)
Browns, 37-24 (H)
1972—Browns, 23-17 (H)
Browns, 20-0 (C)
1973—Browns, 42-13 (C)
Browns, 23-13 (H)
1974—Browns, 20-7 (C)
Oilers, 28-24 (H)
1975—Oilers, 40-10 (C)
Oilers, 21-10 (H)
1976—Browns, 21-7 (H)
Browns, 13-10 (C)
1977—Browns, 24-23 (H)
Oilers, 19-15 (C)
1978—Oilers, 16-13 (C)
Oilers, 14-10 (H)
1979—Oilers, 31-10 (H)
Browns, 14-7 (C)
1980—Oilers, 16-7 (C)
Browns, 17-14 (H)
1981—Oilers, 9-3 (C)
Oilers, 17-13 (H)
1982—Browns, 20-14 (H)
1983—Browns, 25-19 (C) OT
Oilers, 34-27 (H)
1984—Browns, 27-10 (C)
Browns, 27-20 (H)
1985—Browns, 21-6 (H)
Browns, 28-21 (C)
1986—Browns, 23-20 (H)
Browns, 13-10 (C) OT
1987—Oilers, 15-10 (C)
Browns, 40-7 (H)
1988—Oilers, 24-17 (H)
Browns, 28-23 (C)
**Oilers, 24-23 (C)
1989—Browns, 28-17 (C)
Browns, 24-20 (H)
1990—Oilers, 35-23 (C)
Oilers, 58-14 (H)
1991—Oilers, 28-24 (H)
Oilers, 17-14 (C)
1992—Browns, 24-14 (H)
Oilers, 17-14 (C)
1993—Oilers, 27-20 (C)
Oilers, 19-17 (H)
1994—Browns, 11-8 (H)
Browns, 34-10 (C)
1995—Browns, 14-7 (H)
Oilers, 37-10 (C)
1999—Titans, 26-9 (T)
Titans, 33-21 (C)
2000—Titans, 24-10 (T)
Titans, 24-0 (C)
2001—Titans, 31-15 (C)
Browns, 41-38 (T)
2002—Browns, 31-28 (T) OT
2005—Browns, 20-14 (C)
2008—Titans, 28-9 (T)
(RS Pts.—Browns 1,182, Titans 1,153)
(PS Pts.—Titans 24, Browns 23)
Franchise in Houston prior to 1997; known as Oilers prior to 1999
***AFC First-Round Playoff*

CLEVELAND vs. WASHINGTON
RS: Browns lead series, 33-10-1
1950—Browns, 20-14 (C)
Browns, 45-21 (W)
1951—Browns, 45-0 (C)
1952—Browns, 19-15 (C)
Browns, 48-24 (W)
1953—Browns, 30-14 (W)
Browns, 27-3 (C)
1954—Browns, 62-3 (C)
Browns, 34-14 (W)
1955—Redskins, 27-17 (C)
Browns, 24-14 (W)
1956—Redskins, 20-9 (W)
Redskins, 20-17 (C)
1957—Browns, 21-17 (C)
Tie, 30-30 (W)
1958—Browns, 20-10 (W)
Browns, 21-14 (C)
1959—Browns, 34-7 (C)
Browns, 31-17 (W)
1960—Browns, 31-10 (W)
Browns, 27-16 (C)
1961—Browns, 31-7 (C)
Browns, 17-6 (W)
1962—Redskins, 17-16 (C)
Redskins, 17-9 (W)
1963—Browns, 37-14 (C)
Browns, 27-20 (W)
1964—Browns, 27-13 (W)
Browns, 34-24 (C)
1965—Browns, 17-7 (W)
Browns, 24-16 (C)
1966—Browns, 38-14 (W)
Browns, 14-3 (C)
1967—Browns, 42-37 (C)
1968—Browns, 24-21 (W)
1969—Browns, 27-23 (C)
1971—Browns, 20-13 (W)
1975—Redskins, 23-7 (C)
1979—Redskins, 13-9 (C)
1985—Redskins, 14-7 (C)
1988—Browns, 17-13 (W)
1991—Redskins, 42-17 (W)
2004—Browns, 17-13 (C)
2008—Redskins, 14-11 (W)
(RS Pts.—Browns 1,101, Redskins 694)

DALLAS vs. ARIZONA
RS: Cowboys lead series, 55-28-1
PS: Cardinals lead series, 1-0;
See Arizona vs. Dallas
DALLAS vs. ATLANTA
RS: Cowboys lead series, 14-8
PS: Cowboys lead series, 2-0;
See Atlanta vs. Dallas
DALLAS vs. BALTIMORE
RS: Ravens lead series, 3-0;
See Baltimore vs. Dallas
DALLAS vs. BUFFALO
RS: Cowboys lead series, 5-3
PS: Cowboys lead series, 2-0;
See Buffalo vs. Dallas
DALLAS vs. CAROLINA
RS: Cowboys lead series, 8-1
PS: Panthers lead series, 2-0;
See Carolina vs. Dallas
DALLAS vs. CHICAGO
RS: Cowboys lead series, 11-8
PS: Cowboys lead series, 2-0;
See Chicago vs. Dallas
DALLAS vs. CINCINNATI
RS: Cowboys lead series, 6-4;
See Cincinnati vs. Dallas
DALLAS vs. CLEVELAND
RS: Browns lead series, 15-11
PS: Browns lead series, 2-1;
See Cleveland vs. Dallas
DALLAS vs. DENVER
RS: Broncos lead series, 6-4
PS: Cowboys lead series, 1-0
1973—Cowboys, 22-10 (Den)
1977—Cowboys, 14-6 (Dal)
*Cowboys, 27-10 (New Orleans)
1980—Broncos, 41-20 (Den)
1986—Broncos, 29-14 (Den)
1992—Cowboys, 31-27 (Den)
1995—Cowboys, 31-21 (Dal)
1998—Broncos, 42-23 (Den)
2001—Broncos, 26-24 (Dal)
2005—Broncos, 24-21 (Dal) OT
2009—Broncos, 17-10 (Den)
(RS Pts.—Broncos 243, Cowboys 210)
(PS Pts.—Cowboys 27, Broncos 10)
**Super Bowl XII*
DALLAS vs. DETROIT
RS: Cowboys lead series, 11-9
PS: Series tied, 1-1
1960—Lions, 23-14 (Det)
1963—Cowboys, 17-14 (Dal)
1968—Cowboys, 59-13 (Dal)
1970—*Cowboys, 5-0 (Dal)
1972—Cowboys, 28-24 (Dal)
1975—Cowboys, 36-10 (Det)
1977—Cowboys, 37-0 (Dal)
1981—Lions, 27-24 (Det)
1985—Lions, 26-21 (Det)
1986—Cowboys, 31-7 (Det)
1987—Lions, 27-17 (Det)
1991—Lions, 34-10 (Det)
*Lions, 38-6 (Det)
1992—Cowboys, 37-3 (Det)
1994—Lions, 20-17 (Dal) OT
2001—Lions, 15-10 (Det)
2002—Lions, 9-7 (Det)
2003—Cowboys, 38-7 (Det)
2004—Cowboys, 31-21 (Dal)
2005—Cowboys, 20-7 (Dal)
2006—Lions, 39-31 (Dal)
2007—Cowboys, 28-27 (Det)
(RS Pts.—Cowboys 513, Lions 353)
(PS Pts.—Lions 38, Cowboys 11)
**NFC Divisional Playoff*
DALLAS vs. GREEN BAY
RS: Cowboys lead series, 12-11
PS: Cowboys lead series, 4-2
1960—Packers, 41-7 (GB)
1964—Packers, 45-21 (D)
1965—Packers, 13-3 (Mil)
1966—*Packers, 34-27 (D)
1967—*Packers, 21-17 (GB)
1968—Packers, 28-17 (D)
1970—Cowboys, 16-3 (D)
1972—Packers, 16-13 (Mil)
1975—Packers, 19-17 (D)
1978—Cowboys, 42-14 (Mil)
1980—Cowboys, 28-7 (Mil)
1982—**Cowboys, 37-26 (D)
1984—Cowboys, 20-6 (D)
1989—Packers, 31-13 (GB)
Packers, 20-10 (D)
1991—Cowboys, 20-17 (Mil)
1993—Cowboys, 36-14 (D)
***Cowboys, 27-17 (D)
1994—Cowboys, 42-31 (D)
***Cowboys, 35-9 (D)
1995—Cowboys, 34-24 (D)
****Cowboys, 38-27 (D)
1996—Cowboys, 21-6 (D)
1997—Packers, 45-17 (GB)
1999—Cowboys, 27-13 (D)
2004—Packers, 41-20 (GB)
2007—Cowboys, 37-27 (D)
2008—Cowboys, 27-16 (GB)
2009—Packers, 17-7 (GB)
(RS Pts.—Cowboys 495, Packers 494)
(PS Pts.—Cowboys 181, Packers 134)
**NFL Championship*
***NFC Second-Round Playoff*
****NFC Divisional Playoff*
*****NFC Championship*
DALLAS vs. HOUSTON
RS: Series tied, 1-1
2002—Texans, 19-10 (H)
2006—Cowboys, 34-6 (D)
(RS Pts.—Cowboys 44, Texans 25)
DALLAS vs. *INDIANAPOLIS
RS: Cowboys lead series, 8-5
PS: Colts lead series, 1-0
1960—Colts, 45-7 (D)
1967—Colts, 23-17 (B)
1969—Cowboys, 27-10 (D)
1970—**Colts, 16-13 (Miami)
1972—Cowboys, 21-0 (B)
1976—Cowboys, 30-27 (D)
1978—Cowboys, 38-0 (D)
1981—Cowboys, 37-13 (B)
1984—Cowboys, 22-3 (D)
1993—Cowboys, 27-3 (I)
1996—Colts, 25-24 (D)
1999—Colts, 34-24 (I)
2002—Colts, 20-3 (I)
2006—Cowboys, 21-14 (D)
(RS Pts.—Cowboys 298, Colts 217)
(PS Pts.—Colts 16, Cowboys 13)
**Franchise in Baltimore prior to 1984*
***Super Bowl V*
DALLAS vs. JACKSONVILLE
RS: Series tied, 2-2
1997—Cowboys, 26-22 (D)
2000—Jaguars, 23-17 (D) OT
2002—Cowboys, 21-19 (D)
2006—Jaguars, 24-17 (J)
(RS Pts.—Jaguars 88, Cowboys 81)
DALLAS vs. KANSAS CITY
RS: Cowboys lead series, 6-3
1970—Cowboys, 27-16 (KC)
1975—Chiefs, 34-31 (D)
1983—Cowboys, 41-21 (D)
1989—Chiefs, 36-28 (KC)
1992—Cowboys, 17-10 (D)
1995—Cowboys, 24-12 (D)
1998—Chiefs, 20-17 (KC)
2005—Cowboys, 31-28 (D)
2009—Cowboys, 26-20 (KC) OT
(RS Pts.—Cowboys 242, Chiefs 197)
DALLAS vs. MIAMI
RS: Dolphins lead series, 7-4
PS: Cowboys lead series, 1-0
1971—*Cowboys, 24-3 (New Orleans)
1973—Dolphins, 14-7 (D)
1978—Dolphins, 23-16 (M)
1981—Cowboys, 28-27 (D)
1984—Dolphins, 28-21 (M)
1987—Dolphins, 20-14 (D)
1989—Dolphins, 17-14 (D)
1993—Dolphins, 16-14 (D)
1996—Cowboys, 29-10 (M)
1999—Cowboys, 20-0 (D)
2003—Dolphins, 40-21 (D)
2007—Cowboys, 37-20 (M)
(RS Pts.—Cowboys 221, Dolphins 215)
(PS Pts.—Cowboys 24, Dolphins 3)
**Super Bowl VI*
DALLAS vs. MINNESOTA
RS: Series tied, 10-10
PS: Cowboys lead series, 4-3
1961—Cowboys, 21-7 (D)
Cowboys, 28-0 (M)
1966—Cowboys, 28-17 (D)
1968—Cowboys, 20-7 (M)
1970—Vikings, 54-13 (M)
1971—*Cowboys, 20-12 (M)
1973—**Vikings, 27-10 (D)
1974—Vikings, 23-21 (D)
1975—*Cowboys, 17-14 (M)
1977—Cowboys, 16-10 (M) OT
**Cowboys, 23-6 (D)
1978—Vikings, 21-10 (D)
1979—Cowboys, 36-20 (M)
1982—Vikings, 31-27 (M)
1983—Cowboys, 37-24 (M)
1987—Vikings, 44-38 (D) OT
1988—Vikings, 43-3 (D)
1993—Cowboys, 37-20 (M)
1995—Cowboys, 23-17 (M) OT
1996—***Cowboys, 40-15 (D)
1998—Vikings, 46-36 (D)
1999—Vikings, 27-17 (M)
***Vikings, 27-10 (M)
2000—Vikings, 27-15 (D)
2004—Vikings, 35-17 (M)
2007—Cowboys, 24-14 (D)
2009—*Vikings, 34-3 (M)
(RS Pts.—Vikings 487, Cowboys 467)
(PS Pts.—Cowboys 135, Vikings 123)
**NFC Divisional Playoff*
***NFC Championship*
****NFC First-Round Playoff*

DALLAS vs. NEW ENGLAND
RS: Cowboys lead series, 7-3
1971—Cowboys, 44-21 (D)
1975—Cowboys, 34-31 (NE)
1978—Cowboys, 17-10 (D)
1981—Cowboys, 35-21 (NE)
1984—Cowboys, 20-17 (D)
1987—Cowboys, 23-17 (NE) OT
1996—Cowboys, 12-6 (D)
1999—Patriots, 13-6 (NE)
2003—Patriots, 12-0 (NE)
2007—Patriots, 48-27 (D)
(RS Pts.—Cowboys 218, Patriots 196)

DALLAS vs. NEW ORLEANS
RS: Cowboys lead series, 15-8
1967—Cowboys, 14-10 (D)
Cowboys, 27-10 (NO)
1968—Cowboys, 17-3 (NO)
1969—Cowboys, 21-17 (NO)
Cowboys, 33-17 (D)
1971—Saints, 24-14 (NO)
1973—Cowboys, 40-3 (D)
1976—Cowboys, 24-6 (NO)
1978—Cowboys, 27-7 (D)
1982—Cowboys, 21-7 (D)
1983—Cowboys, 21-20 (D)
1984—Cowboys, 30-27 (D) OT
1988—Saints, 20-17 (NO)
1989—Saints, 28-0 (NO)
1990—Cowboys, 17-13 (D)
1991—Cowboys, 23-14 (D)
1994—Cowboys, 24-16 (NO)
1998—Saints, 22-3 (NO)
1999—Saints, 31-24 (NO)
2003—Saints, 13-7 (NO)
2004—Saints, 27-13 (D)
2006—Saints, 42-17 (D)
2009—Cowboys, 24-17 (NO)
(RS Pts.—Cowboys 458, Saints 394)

DALLAS vs. N.Y. GIANTS
RS: Cowboys lead series, 55-38-2
PS: Giants lead series, 1-0
1960—Tie, 31-31 (NY)
1961—Giants, 31-10 (D)
Cowboys, 17-16 (NY)
1962—Giants, 41-10 (D)
Giants, 41-31 (NY)
1963—Giants, 37-21 (NY)
Giants, 34-27 (D)
1964—Tie, 13-13 (D)
Cowboys, 31-21 (NY)
1965—Cowboys, 31-2 (D)
Cowboys, 38-20 (NY)
1966—Cowboys, 52-7 (D)
Cowboys, 17-7 (NY)
1967—Cowboys, 38-24 (D)
1968—Giants, 27-21 (D)
Cowboys, 28-10 (NY)
1969—Cowboys, 25-3 (D)
1970—Cowboys, 28-10 (D)
Giants, 23-20 (NY)
1971—Cowboys, 20-13 (D)
Cowboys, 42-14 (NY)
1972—Cowboys, 23-14 (NY)
Giants, 23-3 (D)
1973—Cowboys, 45-28 (D)
Cowboys, 23-10 (New Haven)
1974—Giants, 14-6 (D)
Cowboys, 21-7 (New Haven)
1975—Cowboys, 13-7 (NY)
Cowboys, 14-3 (D)
1976—Cowboys, 24-14 (NY)
Cowboys, 9-3 (D)
1977—Cowboys, 41-21 (D)
Cowboys, 24-10 (NY)
1978—Cowboys, 34-24 (NY)
Cowboys, 24-3 (D)
1979—Cowboys, 16-14 (NY)
Cowboys, 28-7 (D)
1980—Cowboys, 24-3 (D)
Giants, 38-35 (NY)
1981—Cowboys, 18-10 (D)
Giants, 13-10 (NY) OT
1983—Cowboys, 28-13 (D)
Cowboys, 38-20 (NY)
1984—Giants, 28-7 (NY)
Giants, 19-7 (D)
1985—Cowboys, 30-29 (NY)
Cowboys, 28-21 (D)
1986—Cowboys, 31-28 (D)
Giants, 17-14 (NY)
1987—Cowboys, 16-14 (NY)
Cowboys, 33-24 (D)
1988—Giants, 12-10 (D)
Giants, 29-21 (NY)
1989—Giants, 30-13 (D)
Giants, 15-0 (NY)
1990—Giants, 28-7 (D)
Giants, 31-17 (NY)
1991—Cowboys, 21-16 (D)
Giants, 22-9 (NY)
1992—Cowboys, 34-28 (NY)
Cowboys, 30-3 (D)
1993—Cowboys, 31-9 (D)
Cowboys, 16-13 (NY) OT
1994—Cowboys, 38-10 (D)
Giants, 15-10 (NY)
1995—Cowboys, 35-0 (NY)
Cowboys, 21-20 (D)
1996—Cowboys, 27-0 (D)
Giants, 20-6 (NY)
1997—Giants, 20-17 (NY)
Giants, 20-7 (D)
1998—Cowboys, 31-7 (NY)
Cowboys, 16-6 (D)
1999—Giants, 13-10 (NY)
Cowboys, 26-18 (D)
2000—Giants, 19-14 (NY)
Giants, 17-13 (D)
2001—Giants, 27-24 (NY) OT
Cowboys, 20-13 (D)
2002—Giants, 21-17 (D)
Giants, 37-7 (NY)
2003—Cowboys, 35-32 (NY) OT
Cowboys, 19-3 (D)
2004—Giants, 26-10 (D)
Giants, 28-24 (NY)
2005—Cowboys, 16-13 (D) OT
Giants, 17-10 (NY)
2006—Giants, 36-22 (D)
Cowboys, 23-20 (NY)
2007—Cowboys, 45-35 (D)
Cowboys, 31-20 (NY)
*Giants, 21-17 (D)
2008—Giants, 35-14 (NY)
Cowboys, 20-8 (D)
2009—Giants, 33-31 (D)
Giants, 31-24 (NY)
(RS Pts.—Cowboys 2,090, Giants 1,760)
(PS Pts.—Giants 21, Cowboys 17)
**NFC Divisional Playoff*

DALLAS vs. N.Y. JETS
RS: Cowboys lead series, 7-2
1971—Cowboys, 52-10 (D)
1975—Cowboys, 31-21 (NY)
1978—Cowboys, 30-7 (NY)
1987—Cowboys, 38-24 (NY)
1990—Jets, 24-9 (NY)
1993—Cowboys, 28-7 (NY)
1999—Jets, 22-21 (D)
2003—Cowboys, 17-6 (NY)
2007—Cowboys, 34-3 (D)
(RS Pts.—Cowboys 260, Jets 124)

DALLAS vs. *OAKLAND
RS: Raiders lead series, 6-4
1974—Raiders, 27-23 (O)
1980—Cowboys, 19-13 (O)
1983—Raiders, 40-38 (D)
1986—Raiders, 17-13 (D)
1992—Cowboys, 28-13 (LA)
1995—Cowboys, 34-21 (O)
1998—Raiders, 13-12 (D)
2001—Raiders, 28-21 (O)
2005—Raiders, 19-13 (O)
2009—Cowboys, 24-7 (D)
(RS Pts.—Cowboys 225, Raiders 198)
**Franchise in Los Angeles from 1982-1994*

DALLAS vs. PHILADELPHIA
RS: Cowboys lead series, 55-43
PS: Cowboys lead series, 3-1
1960—Eagles, 27-25 (D)
1961—Eagles, 43-7 (D)
Eagles, 35-13 (P)
1962—Cowboys, 41-19 (D)
Eagles, 28-14 (P)
1963—Eagles, 24-21 (P)
Cowboys, 27-20 (D)
1964—Eagles, 17-14 (D)
Eagles, 24-14 (P)
1965—Eagles, 35-24 (D)
Cowboys, 21-19 (P)
1966—Cowboys, 56-7 (D)
Eagles, 24-23 (P)
1967—Eagles, 21-14 (P)
Cowboys, 38-17 (D)
1968—Cowboys, 45-13 (P)
Cowboys, 34-14 (D)
1969—Cowboys, 38-7 (P)
Cowboys, 49-14 (D)
1970—Cowboys, 17-7 (P)
Cowboys, 21-17 (D)
1971—Cowboys, 42-7 (P)
Cowboys, 20-7 (D)
1972—Cowboys, 28-6 (D)
Cowboys, 28-7 (P)
1973—Eagles, 30-16 (P)
Cowboys, 31-10 (D)
1974—Eagles, 13-10 (P)
Cowboys, 31-24 (D)
1975—Cowboys, 20-17 (P)
Cowboys, 27-17 (D)
1976—Cowboys, 27-7 (D)
Cowboys, 26-7 (P)
1977—Cowboys, 16-10 (P)
Cowboys, 24-14 (D)
1978—Cowboys, 14-7 (D)
Cowboys, 31-13 (P)
1979—Eagles, 31-21 (D)
Cowboys, 24-17 (P)
1980—Eagles, 17-10 (P)
Cowboys, 35-27 (D)
*Eagles, 20-7 (P)

1981—Cowboys, 17-14 (P)
Cowboys, 21-10 (D)
1982—Eagles, 24-20 (D)
1983—Cowboys, 37-7 (D)
Cowboys, 27-20 (P)
1984—Cowboys, 23-17 (D)
Cowboys, 26-10 (P)
1985—Eagles, 16-14 (P)
Cowboys, 34-17 (D)
1986—Cowboys, 17-14 (P)
Eagles, 23-21 (D)
1987—Cowboys, 41-22 (D)
Eagles, 37-20 (P)
1988—Eagles, 24-23 (P)
Eagles, 23-7 (D)
1989—Eagles, 27-0 (D)
Eagles, 20-10 (P)
1990—Eagles, 21-20 (D)
Eagles, 17-3 (P)
1991—Eagles, 24-0 (D)
Cowboys, 25-13 (P)
1992—Eagles, 31-7 (P)
Cowboys, 20-10 (D)
**Cowboys, 34-10 (D)
1993—Cowboys, 23-10 (P)
Cowboys, 23-17 (D)
1994—Cowboys, 24-13 (D)
Cowboys, 31-19 (P)
1995—Cowboys, 34-12 (D)
Eagles, 20-17 (P)
**Cowboys, 30-11 (D)
1996—Cowboys, 23-19 (P)
Eagles, 31-21 (D)
1997—Cowboys, 21-20 (D)
Eagles, 13-12 (P)
1998—Cowboys, 34-0 (P)
Cowboys, 13-9 (D)
1999—Eagles, 13-10 (P)
Cowboys, 20-10 (D)
2000—Eagles, 41-14 (D)
Eagles, 16-13 (P) OT
2001—Eagles, 40-18 (P)
Eagles, 36-3 (D)
2002—Eagles, 44-13 (P)
Eagles, 27-3 (D)
2003—Cowboys, 23-21 (D)
Eagles, 36-10 (P)
2004—Eagles, 49-21 (D)
Eagles, 12-7 (P)
2005—Cowboys, 33-10 (D)
Cowboys, 21-20 (P)
2006—Eagles, 38-24 (P)
Eagles, 23-7 (D)
2007—Cowboys, 38-17 (P)
Eagles, 10-6 (D)
2008—Cowboys, 41-37 (D)
Eagles, 44-6 (P)
2009—Cowboys, 20-16 (P)
Cowboys, 24-0 (D)
***Cowboys, 34-14 (D)
(RS Pts.—Cowboys 2,121, Eagles 1,904)
(PS Pts.—Cowboys 105, Eagles 55)
NFC Championship
***NFC Divisional Playoff*
****NFC First-Round Playoff*

DALLAS vs. PITTSBURGH
RS: Cowboys lead series, 14-13
PS: Steelers lead series, 2-1
1960—Steelers, 35-28 (D)
1961—Cowboys, 27-24 (D)
Steelers, 37-7 (P)
1962—Steelers, 30-28 (D)
Cowboys, 42-27 (P)
1963—Steelers, 27-21 (P)
Steelers, 24-19 (D)
1964—Steelers, 23-17 (P)
Cowboys, 17-14 (D)
1965—Steelers, 22-13 (P)
Cowboys, 24-17 (D)
1966—Cowboys, 52-21 (D)
Cowboys, 20-7 (P)
1967—Cowboys, 24-21 (P)
1968—Cowboys, 28-7 (D)
1969—Cowboys, 10-7 (P)
1972—Cowboys, 17-13 (D)
1975—*Steelers, 21-17 (Miami)
1977—Steelers, 28-13 (P)
1978—**Steelers, 35-31 (Miami)
1979—Steelers, 14-3 (P)
1982—Steelers, 36-28 (D)
1985—Cowboys, 27-13 (D)
1988—Steelers, 24-21 (P)
1991—Cowboys, 20-10 (D)
1994—Cowboys, 26-9 (P)
1995—***Cowboys, 27-17 (Tempe)
1997—Cowboys, 37-7 (P)
2004—Steelers, 24-20 (D)
2008—Steelers, 20-13 (P)
(RS Pts.—Cowboys 602, Steelers 541)
(PS Pts.—Cowboys 75, Steelers 73)
Super Bowl X
***Super Bowl XIII*
****Super Bowl XXX*

DALLAS vs. *ST. LOUIS
RS: Rams lead series, 11-10
PS: Series tied, 4-4
1960—Rams, 38-13 (D)
1962—Cowboys, 27-17 (LA)
1967—Rams, 35-13 (D)
1969—Rams, 24-23 (LA)
1971—Cowboys, 28-21 (D)
1973—Rams, 37-31 (LA)
**Cowboys, 27-16 (D)
1975—Cowboys, 18-7 (D)
***Cowboys, 37-7 (LA)
1976—**Rams, 14-12 (D)
1978—Rams, 27-14 (LA)
***Cowboys, 28-0 (LA)
1979—Cowboys, 30-6 (D)
**Rams, 21-19 (D)
1980—Rams, 38-14 (LA)
****Cowboys, 34-13 (D)
1981—Cowboys, 29-17 (D)
1983—****Rams, 24-17 (D)
1984—Cowboys, 20-13 (LA)
1985—**Rams, 20-0 (LA)
1986—Rams, 29-10 (LA)
1987—Cowboys, 29-21 (LA)
1989—Rams, 35-31 (D)
1990—Cowboys, 24-21 (LA)
1992—Rams, 27-23 (D)
2002—Cowboys, 13-10 (StL)
2005—Rams, 20-10 (D)
2007—Cowboys, 35-7 (D)
2008—Rams, 34-14 (StL)
(RS Pts.—Rams 484, Cowboys 449)
(PS Pts.—Cowboys 174, Rams 115)
**Franchise in Los Angeles prior to 1995*
***NFC Divisional Playoff*
****NFC Championship*
*****NFC First-Round Playoff*

DALLAS vs. SAN DIEGO
RS: Cowboys lead series, 6-3
1972—Cowboys, 34-28 (SD)
1980—Cowboys, 42-31 (D)
1983—Chargers, 24-23 (SD)
1986—Cowboys, 24-21 (SD)
1990—Cowboys, 17-14 (D)
1995—Cowboys, 23-9 (SD)
2001—Chargers, 32-21 (D)
2005—Cowboys, 28-24 (SD)
2009—Chargers, 20-17 (D)
(RS Pts.—Cowboys 229, Chargers 203)

DALLAS vs. SAN FRANCISCO
RS: 49ers lead series, 14-10-1
PS: Cowboys lead series, 5-2
1960—49ers, 26-14 (D)
1963—49ers, 31-24 (SF)
1965—Cowboys, 39-31 (D)
1967—49ers, 24-16 (SF)
1969—Tie, 24-24 (D)
1970—*Cowboys, 17-10 (SF)
1971—*Cowboys, 14-3 (D)
1972—49ers, 31-10 (D)
**Cowboys, 30-28 (SF)
1974—Cowboys, 20-14 (D)
1977—Cowboys, 42-35 (SF)
1979—Cowboys, 21-13 (SF)
1980—Cowboys, 59-14 (D)
1981—49ers, 45-14 (SF)
*49ers, 28-27 (SF)
1983—49ers, 42-17 (SF)
1985—49ers, 31-16 (SF)
1989—49ers, 31-14 (D)
1990—49ers, 24-6 (D)
1992—*Cowboys, 30-20 (SF)
1993—Cowboys, 26-17 (D)
*Cowboys, 38-21 (D)
1994—49ers, 21-14 (SF)
*49ers, 38-28 (SF)
1995—49ers, 38-20 (D)
1996—Cowboys, 20-17 (SF) OT
1997—49ers, 17-10 (SF)
2000—49ers, 41-24 (D)
2001—Cowboys, 27-21 (D)
2002—49ers, 31-27 (D)
2005—Cowboys, 34-31 (SF)
2008—Cowboys, 35-22 (D)
(RS Pts.—49ers 672, Cowboys 573)
(PS Pts.—Cowboys 184, 49ers 148)
**NFC Championship*
***NFC Divisional Playoff*

DALLAS vs. SEATTLE
RS: Cowboys lead series, 8-4
PS: Seahawks lead series, 1-0
1976—Cowboys, 28-13 (S)
1980—Cowboys, 51-7 (D)
1983—Cowboys, 35-10 (S)
1986—Seahawks, 31-14 (D)
1992—Cowboys, 27-0 (D)
1998—Cowboys, 30-22 (D)
2001—Seahawks, 29-3 (S)
2002—Seahawks, 17-14 (D)
2004—Cowboys, 43-39 (S)
2005—Seahawks, 13-10 (S)
2006—*Seahawks, 21-20 (S)
2008—Cowboys, 34-9 (D)
2009—Cowboys, 38-17 (D)
(RS Pts.—Cowboys 327, Seahawks 207)
(PS Pts.—Seahawks 21, Cowboys 20)
**NFC First-Round Playoff*

DALLAS vs. TAMPA BAY
RS: Cowboys lead series, 9-3
PS: Cowboys lead series, 2-0
1977—Cowboys, 23-7 (D)
1980—Cowboys, 28-17 (D)
1981—*Cowboys, 38-0 (D)
1982—Cowboys, 14-9 (D)
**Cowboys, 30-17 (D)
1983—Cowboys, 27-24 (D) OT
1990—Cowboys, 14-10 (D)
Cowboys, 17-13 (TB)
2000—Buccaneers, 27-7 (TB)
2001—Buccaneers, 10-6 (D)
2003—Buccaneers, 16-0 (TB)
2006—Cowboys, 38-10 (D)
2008—Cowboys, 13-9 (D)
2009—Cowboys, 34-21 (TB)
(RS Pts.—Cowboys 221, Buccaneers 173)
(PS Pts.—Cowboys 68, Buccaneers 17)
**NFC Divisional Playoff*
***NFC First-Round Playoff*

DALLAS vs. *TENNESSEE
RS: Cowboys lead series, 7-5
1970—Cowboys, 52-10 (D)
1974—Cowboys, 10-0 (H)
1979—Oilers, 30-24 (D)
1982—Cowboys, 37-7 (H)
1985—Cowboys, 17-10 (H)
1988—Oilers, 25-17 (D)
1991—Oilers, 26-23 (H) OT
1994—Cowboys, 20-17 (D)
1997—Oilers, 27-14 (D)
2000—Titans, 31-0 (T)
2002—Cowboys, 21-13 (D)
2006—Cowboys, 45-14 (T)
(RS Pts.—Cowboys 280, Titans 210)
**Franchise in Houston prior to 1997; known as Oilers prior to 1999*

DALLAS vs. WASHINGTON
RS: Cowboys lead series, 59-37-2
PS: Redskins lead series, 2-0
1960—Redskins, 26-14 (W)
1961—Tie, 28-28 (D)
Redskins, 34-24 (W)
1962—Tie, 35-35 (D)
Cowboys, 38-10 (W)
1963—Redskins, 21-17 (W)
Cowboys, 35-20 (D)
1964—Cowboys, 24-18 (D)
Redskins, 28-16 (W)
1965—Cowboys, 27-7 (D)
Redskins, 34-31 (W)
1966—Cowboys, 31-30 (W)
Redskins, 34-31 (D)
1967—Cowboys, 17-14 (W)
Redskins, 27-20 (D)
1968—Cowboys, 44-24 (W)
Cowboys, 29-20 (D)
1969—Cowboys, 41-28 (W)
Cowboys, 20-10 (D)
1970—Cowboys, 45-21 (W)
Cowboys, 34-0 (D)
1971—Redskins, 20-16 (D)
Cowboys, 13-0 (W)
1972—Redskins, 24-20 (W)
Cowboys, 34-24 (D)
*Redskins, 26-3 (W)
1973—Redskins, 14-7 (W)
Cowboys, 27-7 (D)
1974—Redskins, 28-21 (W)
Cowboys, 24-23 (D)
1975—Redskins, 30-24 (W) OT
Cowboys, 31-10 (D)
1976—Cowboys, 20-7 (W)
Redskins, 27-14 (D)
1977—Cowboys, 34-16 (D)
Cowboys, 14-7 (W)
1978—Redskins, 9-5 (W)
Cowboys, 37-10 (D)
1979—Redskins, 34-20 (W)
Cowboys, 35-34 (D)
1980—Cowboys, 17-3 (W)
Cowboys, 14-10 (D)
1981—Cowboys, 26-10 (W)
Cowboys, 24-10 (D)
1982—Cowboys, 24-10 (W)
*Redskins, 31-17 (W)
1983—Cowboys, 31-30 (W)
Redskins, 31-10 (D)
1984—Redskins, 34-14 (W)
Redskins, 30-28 (D)
1985—Cowboys, 44-14 (D)
Cowboys, 13-7 (W)
1986—Cowboys, 30-6 (D)
Redskins, 41-14 (W)
1987—Redskins, 13-7 (D)
Redskins, 24-20 (W)
1988—Redskins, 35-17 (D)
Cowboys, 24-17 (W)
1989—Redskins, 30-7 (D)
Cowboys, 13-3 (W)
1990—Redskins, 19-15 (W)
Cowboys, 27-17 (D)
1991—Redskins, 33-31 (D)
Cowboys, 24-21 (W)
1992—Cowboys, 23-10 (D)
Redskins, 20-17 (W)
1993—Redskins, 35-16 (W)
Cowboys, 38-3 (D)
1994—Cowboys, 34-7 (W)
Cowboys, 31-7 (D)
1995—Redskins, 27-23 (W)
Redskins, 24-17 (D)
1996—Cowboys, 21-10 (D)
Redskins, 37-10 (W)
1997—Redskins, 21-16 (W)
Cowboys, 17-14 (D)
1998—Cowboys, 31-10 (W)
Cowboys, 23-7 (D)
1999—Cowboys, 41-35 (W) OT
Cowboys, 38-20 (D)
2000—Cowboys, 27-21 (W)
Cowboys, 32-13 (D)
2001—Cowboys, 9-7 (D)
Cowboys, 20-14 (W)
2002—Cowboys, 27-20 (D)
Redskins, 20-14 (W)
2003—Cowboys, 21-14 (D)
Cowboys, 27-0 (W)
2004—Cowboys, 21-18 (W)
Cowboys, 13-10 (D)
2005—Redskins, 14-13 (D)
Redskins, 35-7 (W)
2006—Cowboys, 27-10 (D)
Redskins, 22-19 (W)
2007—Cowboys, 28-23 (D)
Redskins, 27-6 (W)
2008—Redskins, 26-24 (D)
Cowboys, 14-10 (W)
2009—Cowboys, 7-6 (D)
Cowboys, 17-0 (W)
(RS Pts.—Cowboys 2,240, Redskins 1,838)
(PS Pts.—Redskins 57, Cowboys 20)
**NFC Championship*

DENVER vs. ARIZONA
RS: Broncos lead series, 7-0-1;
See Arizona vs. Denver

DENVER vs. ATLANTA
RS: Broncos lead series, 8-4
PS: Broncos lead series, 1-0;
See Atlanta vs. Denver

DENVER vs. BALTIMORE
RS: Ravens lead series, 4-3
PS: Ravens lead series, 1-0;
See Baltimore vs. Denver

DENVER vs. BUFFALO
RS: Bills lead series, 18-15-1
PS: Bills lead series, 1-0;
See Buffalo vs. Denver

DENVER vs. CAROLINA
RS: Broncos lead series, 2-1;
See Carolina vs. Denver

DENVER vs. CHICAGO
RS: Bears lead series, 7-6;
See Chicago vs. Denver

DENVER vs. CINCINNATI
RS: Broncos lead series, 17-8;
See Cincinnati vs. Denver

DENVER vs. CLEVELAND
RS: Broncos lead series, 18-5
PS: Broncos lead series, 3-0;
See Cleveland vs. Denver

DENVER vs. DALLAS
RS: Broncos lead series, 6-4
PS: Cowboys lead series, 1-0;
See Dallas vs. Denver

DENVER vs. DETROIT
RS: Broncos lead series, 6-4
1971—Lions, 24-20 (Den)
1974—Broncos, 31-27 (Det)
1978—Lions, 17-14 (Det)
1981—Broncos, 27-21 (Den)
1984—Broncos, 28-7 (Det)
1987—Broncos, 34-0 (Den)
1990—Lions, 40-27 (Det)
1999—Broncos, 17-7 (Det)
2003—Broncos, 20-16 (Den)
2007—Lions, 44-7 (Det)
(RS Pts.—Broncos 225, Lions 203)

DENVER vs. GREEN BAY
RS: Series tied, 5-5-1
PS: Broncos lead series, 1-0
1971—Packers, 34-13 (Mil)
1975—Broncos, 23-13 (D)
1978—Broncos, 16-3 (D)
1984—Broncos, 17-14 (D)
1987—Tie, 17-17 (Mil) OT
1990—Broncos, 22-13 (D)
1993—Packers, 30-27 (GB)
1996—Packers, 41-6 (GB)
1997—*Broncos, 31-24 (San Diego)
1999—Broncos, 31-10 (D)
2003—Packers, 31-3 (GB)
2007—Packers, 19-13 (D) OT
(RS Pts.—Packers 225, Broncos 188)
(PS Pts.—Broncos 31, Packers 24)
**Super Bowl XXXII*

DENVER vs. HOUSTON
RS: Series tied, 1-1
2004—Broncos, 31-13 (D)
2007—Texans, 31-13 (H)
(RS Pts.—Broncos 44, Texans 44)

DENVER vs. *INDIANAPOLIS
RS: Broncos lead series, 11-7
PS: Colts lead series, 2-0
1974—Broncos, 17-6 (B)
1977—Broncos, 27-13 (D)
1978—Colts, 7-6 (B)
1981—Broncos, 28-10 (D)
1983—Broncos, 17-10 (B)
Broncos, 21-19 (D)
1985—Broncos, 15-10 (I)
1988—Colts, 55-23 (I)
1989—Broncos, 14-3 (D)
1990—Broncos, 27-17 (I)
1993—Broncos, 35-13 (D)
2001—Colts, 29-10 (I)
2002—Colts, 23-20 (D) OT
2003—Broncos, 31-17 (I)
**Colts, 41-10 (I)
2004—Broncos, 33-14 (D)
**Colts, 49-24 (I)
2006—Colts, 34-31 (D)
2007—Colts, 38-20 (I)
2009—Colts, 28-16 (I)
(RS Pts.—Broncos 391, Colts 346)
(PS Pts.—Colts 90, Broncos 34)
Franchise in Baltimore prior to 1984
***AFC First-Round Playoff*

DENVER vs. JACKSONVILLE
RS: Jaguars lead series, 4-3
PS: Series tied, 1-1
1995—Broncos, 31-23 (D)
1996—*Jaguars, 30-27 (D)
1997—**Broncos, 42-17 (D)
1998—Broncos, 37-24 (D)
1999—Jaguars, 27-24 (J)
2004—Jaguars, 7-6 (J)
2005—Broncos, 20-7 (J)
2007—Jaguars, 23-14 (D)
2008—Jaguars, 24-17 (D)
(RS Pts.—Broncos 149, Jaguars 135)
(PS Pts.—Broncos 69, Jaguars 47)
**AFC Divisional Playoff*
***AFC First-Round Playoff*

DENVER vs. *KANSAS CITY
RS: Chiefs lead series, 54-45
PS: Broncos lead series, 1-0
1960—Texans, 17-14 (D)
Texans, 34-7 (Dal)
1961—Texans, 19-12 (D)
Texans, 49-21 (Dal)
1962—Texans, 24-3 (D)
Texans, 17-10 (Dal)
1963—Chiefs, 59-7 (D)
Chiefs, 52-21 (KC)
1964—Broncos, 33-27 (D)
Chiefs, 49-39 (KC)
1965—Chiefs, 31-23 (D)
Chiefs, 45-35 (KC)
1966—Chiefs, 37-10 (KC)
Chiefs, 56-10 (D)
1967—Chiefs, 52-9 (KC)
Chiefs, 38-24 (D)
1968—Chiefs, 34-2 (KC)
Chiefs, 30-7 (D)
1969—Chiefs, 26-13 (D)
Chiefs, 31-17 (KC)
1970—Broncos, 26-13 (D)
Chiefs, 16-0 (KC)
1971—Chiefs, 16-3 (D)
Chiefs, 28-10 (KC)
1972—Chiefs, 45-24 (D)
Chiefs, 24-21 (KC)
1973—Chiefs, 16-14 (KC)
Broncos, 14-10 (D)
1974—Broncos, 17-14 (KC)
Chiefs, 42-34 (D)
1975—Broncos, 37-33 (D)
Chiefs, 26-13 (KC)
1976—Broncos, 35-26 (KC)
Broncos, 17-16 (D)
1977—Broncos, 23-7 (D)
Broncos, 14-7 (KC)
1978—Broncos, 23-17 (KC) OT
Broncos, 24-3 (D)
1979—Broncos, 24-10 (KC)
Broncos, 20-3 (D)
1980—Chiefs, 23-17 (D)
Chiefs, 31-14 (KC)
1981—Chiefs, 28-14 (KC)
Broncos, 16-13 (D)
1982—Chiefs, 37-16 (D)
1983—Broncos, 27-24 (D)
Chiefs, 48-17 (KC)
1984—Broncos, 21-0 (D)
Chiefs, 16-13 (KC)
1985—Broncos, 30-10 (KC)
Broncos, 14-13 (D)
1986—Broncos, 38-17 (D)
Chiefs, 37-10 (KC)
1987—Broncos, 26-17 (KC)
Broncos, 20-17 (D)
1988—Chiefs, 20-13 (KC)
Broncos, 17-11 (D)
1989—Broncos, 34-20 (D)
Broncos, 16-13 (KC)
1990—Broncos, 24-23 (D)
Chiefs, 31-20 (KC)
1991—Broncos, 19-16 (D)
Broncos, 24-20 (KC)
1992—Broncos, 20-19 (D)
Chiefs, 42-20 (KC)
1993—Chiefs, 15-7 (KC)
Broncos, 27-21 (D)
1994—Chiefs, 31-28 (D)
Broncos, 20-17 (KC) OT
1995—Chiefs, 21-7 (D)
Chiefs, 20-17 (KC)
1996—Chiefs, 17-14 (KC)
Broncos, 34-7 (D)
1997—Broncos, 19-3 (D)
Chiefs, 24-22 (KC)
**Broncos, 14-10 (KC)
1998—Broncos, 30-7 (KC)
Broncos, 35-31 (D)
1999—Chiefs, 26-10 (KC)
Chiefs, 16-10 (D)
2000—Chiefs, 23-22 (D)
Chiefs, 20-7 (KC)
2001—Broncos, 20-6 (D)
Chiefs, 26-23 (KC) OT
2002—Broncos, 37-34 (KC) OT
Broncos, 31-24 (D)
2003—Chiefs, 24-23 (KC)
Broncos, 45-27 (D)
2004—Broncos, 34-24 (D)
Chiefs, 45-17 (KC)
2005—Broncos, 30-10 (D)
Chiefs, 31-27 (KC)
2006—Broncos, 9-6 (D) OT
Chiefs, 19-10 (KC)
2007—Broncos, 27-11 (KC)
Broncos, 41-7 (D)
2008—Chiefs, 33-19 (KC)
Broncos, 24-17 (D)
2009—Broncos, 44-13 (KC)
Chiefs, 44-24 (D)
(RS Pts.—Chiefs 2,345, Broncos 2,004)
(PS Pts.—Broncos 14, Chiefs 10)
**Franchise in Dallas prior to 1963 and known as Texans*
***AFC Divisional Playoff*

DENVER vs. MIAMI
RS: Dolphins lead series, 11-3-1
PS: Broncos lead series, 1-0
1966—Dolphins, 24-7 (M)
Broncos, 17-7 (D)
1967—Dolphins, 35-21 (M)
1968—Broncos, 21-14 (D)
1969—Dolphins, 27-24 (M)
1971—Tie, 10-10 (D)
1975—Dolphins, 14-13 (M)
1985—Dolphins, 30-26 (D)
1998—Dolphins, 31-21 (M)
*Broncos, 38-3 (D)
1999—Dolphins, 38-21 (D)
2001—Dolphins, 21-10 (M)
2002—Dolphins, 24-22 (D)
2004—Broncos, 20-17 (D)
2005—Dolphins, 34-10 (M)
2008—Dolphins, 26-17 (D)
(RS Pts.—Dolphins 352, Broncos 260)
(PS Pts.—Broncos 38, Dolphins 3)
**AFC Divisional Playoff*

DENVER vs. MINNESOTA
RS: Vikings lead series, 7-5
1972—Vikings, 23-20 (D)
1978—Vikings, 12-9 (M) OT
1981—Broncos, 19-17 (D)
1984—Broncos, 42-21 (D)
1987—Vikings, 34-27 (M)
1990—Vikings, 27-22 (M)
1991—Broncos, 13-6 (M)
1993—Vikings, 26-23 (D)
1996—Broncos, 21-17 (M)
1999—Vikings, 23-20 (D)
2003—Vikings, 28-20 (M)
2007—Broncos, 22-19 (D) OT
(RS Pts.—Broncos 258, Vikings 253)

DENVER vs. *NEW ENGLAND
RS: Broncos lead series, 25-16
PS: Broncos lead series, 2-0
1960—Broncos, 13-10 (B)
Broncos, 31-24 (D)
1961—Patriots, 45-17 (B)
Patriots, 28-24 (D)
1962—Patriots, 41-16 (B)
Patriots, 33-29 (D)
1963—Broncos, 14-10 (D)
Patriots, 40-21 (B)
1964—Patriots, 39-10 (D)
Patriots, 12-7 (B)
1965—Broncos, 27-10 (B)
Patriots, 28-20 (D)
1966—Patriots, 24-10 (D)
Broncos, 17-10 (B)
1967—Broncos, 26-21 (D)
1968—Patriots, 20-17 (D)
Broncos, 35-14 (B)
1969—Broncos, 35-7 (D)
1972—Broncos, 45-21 (D)
1976—Patriots, 38-14 (NE)
1979—Broncos, 45-10 (D)
1980—Patriots, 23-14 (NE)

1984—Broncos, 26-19 (D)
1986—Broncos, 27-20 (D)
**Broncos, 22-17 (D)
1987—Broncos, 31-20 (D)
1988—Broncos, 21-10 (D)
1991—Broncos, 9-6 (NE)
Broncos, 20-3 (D)
1995—Broncos, 37-3 (NE)
1996—Broncos, 34-8 (NE)
1997—Broncos, 34-13 (D)
1998—Broncos, 27-21 (D)
1999—Patriots, 24-23 (NE)
2000—Patriots, 28-19 (D)
2001—Broncos, 31-20 (D)
2002—Broncos, 24-16 (NE)
2003—Patriots, 30-26 (D)
2005—Broncos, 28-20 (D)
**Broncos, 27-13 (D)
2006—Broncos, 17-7 (NE)
2008—Patriots, 41-7 (NE)
2009—Broncos, 20-17 (D) OT
(RS Pts.—Broncos 948, Patriots 834)
(PS Pts.—Broncos 49, Patriots 30)
Franchise in Boston prior to 1971
***AFC Divisional Playoff*

DENVER vs. NEW ORLEANS
RS: Broncos lead series, 7-2
1970—Broncos, 31-6 (NO)
1974—Broncos, 33-17 (D)
1979—Broncos, 10-3 (D)
1985—Broncos, 34-23 (D)
1988—Saints, 42-0 (NO)
1994—Saints, 30-28 (D)
2000—Broncos, 38-23 (NO)
2004—Broncos, 34-13 (NO)
2008—Broncos, 34-32 (D)
(RS Pts.—Broncos 242, Saints 189)

DENVER vs. N.Y. GIANTS
RS: Series tied, 5-5
PS: Giants lead series, 1-0
1972—Giants, 29-17 (NY)
1976—Broncos, 14-13 (D)
1980—Broncos, 14-9 (NY)
1986—Giants, 19-16 (NY)
*Giants, 39-20 (Pasadena)
1989—Giants, 14-7 (D)
1992—Broncos, 27-13 (D)
1998—Giants, 20-16 (NY)
2001—Broncos, 31-20 (D)
2005—Giants, 24-23 (NY)
2009—Broncos, 26-6 (D)
(RS Pts.—Broncos 191, Giants 167)
(PS Pts.—Giants 39, Broncos 20)
**Super Bowl XXI*

DENVER vs. *N.Y. JETS
RS: Broncos lead series, 16-14-1
PS: Broncos lead series, 1-0
1960—Titans, 28-24 (NY)
Titans, 30-27 (D)
1961—Titans, 35-28 (NY)
Broncos, 27-10 (D)
1962—Broncos, 32-10 (NY)
Titans, 46-45 (D)
1963—Tie, 35-35 (NY)
Jets, 14-9 (D)
1964—Jets, 30-6 (NY)
Broncos, 20-16 (D)
1965—Broncos, 16-13 (D)
Jets, 45-10 (NY)
1966—Jets, 16-7 (D)
1967—Jets, 38-24 (D)
Broncos, 33-24 (NY)
1968—Broncos, 21-13 (NY)
1969—Broncos, 21-19 (D)
1973—Broncos, 40-28 (NY)
1976—Broncos, 46-3 (D)
1978—Jets, 31-28 (D)
1980—Broncos, 31-24 (D)
1986—Jets, 22-10 (NY)
1992—Broncos, 27-16 (D)
1993—Broncos, 26-20 (NY)
1994—Jets, 25-22 (NY) OT
1996—Broncos, 31-6 (D)
1998—**Broncos, 23-10 (D)
1999—Jets, 21-13 (D)
2000—Broncos, 30-23 (NY)
2002—Jets, 19-13 (NY)
2005—Broncos, 27-0 (D)
2008—Broncos, 34-17 (NY)
(RS Pts.—Broncos 763, Jets 677)
(PS Pts.—Broncos 23, Jets 10)
**Jets known as Titans prior to 1963*
***AFC Championship*

DENVER vs. *OAKLAND
RS: Raiders lead series, 56-41-2
PS: Series tied, 1-1
1960—Broncos, 31-14 (D)
Raiders, 48-10 (O)
1961—Raiders, 33-19 (O)
Broncos, 27-24 (D)
1962—Broncos, 44-7 (D)
Broncos, 23-6 (O)
1963—Raiders, 26-10 (D)
Raiders, 35-31 (O)
1964—Raiders, 40-7 (O)
Tie, 20-20 (D)
1965—Raiders, 28-20 (D)
Raiders, 24-13 (O)
1966—Raiders, 17-3 (D)
Raiders, 28-10 (O)
1967—Raiders, 51-0 (O)
Raiders, 21-17 (D)
1968—Raiders, 43-7 (D)
Raiders, 33-27 (O)
1969—Raiders, 24-14 (D)
Raiders, 41-10 (O)
1970—Raiders, 35-23 (O)
Raiders, 24-19 (D)
1971—Raiders, 27-16 (D)
Raiders, 21-13 (O)
1972—Broncos, 30-23 (O)
Raiders, 37-20 (D)
1973—Tie, 23-23 (D)
Raiders, 21-17 (O)
1974—Raiders, 28-17 (D)
Broncos, 20-17 (O)
1975—Raiders, 42-17 (D)
Raiders, 17-10 (O)
1976—Raiders, 17-10 (D)
Raiders, 19-6 (O)
1977—Broncos, 30-7 (O)
Raiders, 24-14 (D)
**Broncos, 20-17 (D)
1978—Broncos, 14-6 (D)
Broncos, 21-6 (O)
1979—Raiders, 27-3 (O)
Raiders, 14-10 (D)
1980—Raiders, 9-3 (O)
Raiders, 24-21 (D)
1981—Broncos, 9-7 (D)
Broncos, 17-0 (O)
1982—Raiders, 27-10 (LA)
1983—Raiders, 22-7 (D)
Raiders, 22-20 (LA)
1984—Broncos, 16-13 (D)
Broncos, 22-19 (LA) OT
1985—Raiders, 31-28 (LA) OT
Raiders, 17-14 (D) OT
1986—Broncos, 38-36 (D)
Broncos, 21-10 (LA)
1987—Broncos, 30-14 (D)
Broncos, 23-17 (LA)
1988—Raiders, 30-27 (D) OT
Raiders, 21-20 (LA)
1989—Broncos, 31-21 (D)
Raiders, 16-13 (LA) OT
1990—Raiders, 14-9 (LA)
Raiders, 23-20 (D)
1991—Raiders, 16-13 (LA)
Raiders, 17-16 (D)
1992—Broncos, 17-13 (D)
Raiders, 24-0 (LA)
1993—Raiders, 23-20 (D)
Raiders, 33-30 (LA) OT
***Raiders, 42-24 (LA)
1994—Raiders, 48-16 (D)
Raiders, 23-13 (LA)
1995—Broncos, 27-0 (D)
Broncos, 31-28 (O)
1996—Broncos, 22-21 (O)
Broncos, 24-19 (D)
1997—Raiders, 28-25 (O)
Broncos, 31-3 (D)
1998—Broncos, 34-17 (O)
Broncos, 40-14 (D)
1999—Broncos, 16-13 (O)
Broncos, 27-21 (D) OT
2000—Broncos, 33-24 (O)
Broncos, 27-24 (D)
2001—Raiders, 38-28 (O)
Broncos, 23-17 (D)
2002—Raiders, 34-10 (D)
Raiders, 28-16 (O)
2003—Broncos, 31-10 (D)
Broncos, 22-8 (O)
2004—Broncos, 31-3 (O)
Raiders, 25-24 (D)
2005—Broncos, 31-17 (O)
Broncos, 22-3 (D)
2006—Broncos, 13-3 (D)
Broncos, 17-13 (O)
2007—Broncos, 23-20 (D) OT
Raiders, 34-20 (O)
2008—Broncos, 41-14 (O)
Raiders, 31-10 (D)
2009—Broncos, 23-3 (O)
Raiders, 20-19 (D)
(RS Pts.—Raiders 2,121, Broncos 1,941)
(PS Pts.—Raiders 59, Broncos 44)
**Franchise in Los Angeles from 1982-1994*
***AFC Championship*
****AFC First-Round Playoff*

DENVER vs. PHILADELPHIA
RS: Eagles lead series, 7-4
1971—Eagles, 17-16 (P)
1975—Broncos, 25-10 (D)
1980—Eagles, 27-6 (P)
1983—Eagles, 13-10 (D)
1986—Broncos, 33-7 (P)
1989—Eagles, 28-24 (D)
1992—Eagles, 30-0 (P)
1995—Eagles, 31-13 (P)
1998—Broncos, 41-16 (D)

2005—Broncos, 49-21 (D)
2009—Eagles, 30-27 (P)
(RS Pts.—Broncos 244, Eagles 230)

DENVER vs. PITTSBURGH
RS: Broncos lead series, 13-7-1
PS: Series tied, 3-3
1970—Broncos, 16-13 (D)
1971—Broncos, 22-10 (P)
1973—Broncos, 23-13 (P)
1974—Tie, 35-35 (D) OT
1975—Steelers, 20-9 (P)
1977—Broncos, 21-7 (D)
*Broncos, 34-21 (D)
1978—Steelers, 21-17 (D)
*Steelers, 33-10 (P)
1979—Steelers, 42-7 (P)
1983—Broncos, 14-10 (P)
1984—*Steelers, 24-17 (D)
1985—Broncos, 31-23 (P)
1986—Broncos, 21-10 (P)
1988—Steelers, 39-21 (P)
1989—Broncos, 34-7 (D)
*Broncos, 24-23 (D)
1990—Steelers, 34-17 (D)
1991—Broncos, 20-13 (D)
1993—Broncos, 37-13 (D)
1997—Steelers, 35-24 (P)
**Broncos, 24-21 (P)
2003—Broncos, 17-14 (D)
2005—**Steelers, 34-17 (D)
2006—Broncos, 31-20 (P)
2007—Broncos, 31-28 (D)
2009—Steelers, 28-10 (D)
(RS Pts.—Broncos 458, Steelers 435)
(PS Pts.—Steelers 156, Broncos 126)
AFC Divisional Playoff
***AFC Championship*

DENVER vs. *ST. LOUIS
RS: Rams lead series, 6-5
1972—Broncos, 16-10 (LA)
1974—Rams, 17-10 (D)
1979—Rams, 13-9 (D)
1982—Broncos, 27-24 (LA)
1985—Rams, 20-16 (LA)
1988—Broncos, 35-24 (D)
1994—Rams, 27-21 (LA)
1997—Broncos, 35-14 (D)
2000—Rams, 41-36 (StL)
2002—Broncos, 23-16 (D)
2006—Rams, 18-10 (StL)
(RS Pts.—Broncos 238, Rams 224)
Franchise in Los Angeles prior to 1995

DENVER vs. *SAN DIEGO
RS: Broncos lead series, 54-45-1
1960—Chargers, 23-19 (D)
Chargers, 41-33 (LA)
1961—Chargers, 37-0 (SD)
Chargers, 19-16 (D)
1962—Broncos, 30-21 (D)
Broncos, 23-20 (SD)
1963—Broncos, 50-34 (D)
Chargers, 58-20 (SD)
1964—Chargers, 42-14 (SD)
Chargers, 31-20 (D)
1965—Chargers, 34-31 (SD)
Chargers, 33-21 (D)
1966—Chargers, 24-17 (SD)
Broncos, 20-17 (D)
1967—Chargers, 38-21 (D)
Chargers, 24-20 (SD)
1968—Chargers, 55-24 (SD)
Chargers, 47-23 (D)
1969—Broncos, 13-0 (D)
Chargers, 45-24 (SD)
1970—Chargers, 24-21 (SD)
Tie, 17-17 (D)
1971—Broncos, 20-16 (D)
Chargers, 45-17 (SD)
1972—Chargers, 37-14 (SD)
Broncos, 38-13 (D)
1973—Broncos, 30-19 (D)
Broncos, 42-28 (SD)
1974—Broncos, 27-7 (D)
Chargers, 17-0 (SD)
1975—Broncos, 27-17 (SD)
Broncos, 13-10 (D) OT
1976—Broncos, 26-0 (D)
Broncos, 17-0 (SD)
1977—Broncos, 17-14 (SD)
Broncos, 17-9 (D)
1978—Broncos, 27-14 (D)
Chargers, 23-0 (SD)
1979—Broncos, 7-0 (D)
Chargers, 17-7 (SD)
1980—Chargers, 30-13 (D)
Broncos, 20-13 (SD)
1981—Broncos, 42-24 (D)
Chargers, 34-17 (SD)
1982—Chargers, 23-3 (D)
Chargers, 30-20 (SD)
1983—Broncos, 14-6 (D)
Chargers, 31-7 (SD)
1984—Broncos, 16-13 (SD)
Broncos, 16-13 (D)
1985—Chargers, 30-10 (SD)
Broncos, 30-24 (D) OT
1986—Broncos, 31-14 (SD)
Chargers, 9-3 (D)
1987—Broncos, 31-17 (SD)
Broncos, 24-0 (D)
1988—Broncos, 34-3 (D)
Broncos, 12-0 (SD)
1989—Broncos, 16-10 (D)
Chargers, 19-16 (SD)
1990—Chargers, 19-7 (SD)
Broncos, 20-10 (D)
1991—Broncos, 27-19 (D)
Broncos, 17-14 (SD)
1992—Broncos, 21-13 (D)
Chargers, 24-21 (SD)
1993—Broncos, 34-17 (D)
Chargers, 13-10 (SD)
1994—Chargers, 37-34 (D)
Broncos, 20-15 (SD)
1995—Chargers, 17-6 (SD)
Broncos, 30-27 (D)
1996—Broncos, 28-17 (D)
Chargers, 16-10 (SD)
1997—Broncos, 38-28 (SD)
Broncos, 38-3 (D)
1998—Broncos, 27-10 (D)
Broncos, 31-16 (SD)
1999—Broncos, 33-17 (SD)
Chargers, 12-6 (D)
2000—Broncos, 21-7 (SD)
Broncos, 38-37 (D)
2001—Chargers, 27-10 (SD)
Broncos, 26-16 (D)
2002—Broncos, 26-9 (D)
Chargers, 30-27 (SD) OT
2003—Broncos, 37-13 (SD)
Broncos, 37-8 (D)
2004—Broncos, 23-13 (D)
Chargers, 20-17 (SD)
2005—Broncos, 20-17 (D)
Broncos, 23-7 (SD)
2006—Chargers, 35-27 (D)
Chargers, 48-20 (SD)
2007—Chargers, 41-3 (D)
Chargers, 23-3 (SD)
2008—Broncos, 39-38 (D)
Chargers, 52-21 (SD)
2009—Broncos, 34-23 (SD)
Chargers, 32-3 (D)
(RS Pts.—Chargers 2,155, Broncos 2,111)
Franchise in Los Angeles prior to 1961

DENVER vs. SAN FRANCISCO
RS: Broncos lead series, 6-5
PS: 49ers lead series, 1-0
1970—49ers, 19-14 (SF)
1973—49ers, 36-34 (D)
1979—Broncos, 38-28 (SF)
1982—Broncos, 24-21 (D)
1985—Broncos, 17-16 (D)
1988—Broncos, 16-13 (SF) OT
1989—*49ers, 55-10 (New Orleans)
1994—49ers, 42-19 (SF)
1997—49ers, 34-17 (SF)
2000—Broncos, 38-9 (D)
2002—Broncos, 24-14 (SF)
2006—49ers, 26-23 (D) OT
(RS Pts.—Broncos 264, 49ers 258)
(PS Pts.—49ers 55, Broncos 10)
Super Bowl XXIV

DENVER vs. SEATTLE
RS: Broncos lead series, 33-18
PS: Seahawks lead series, 1-0
1977—Broncos, 24-13 (S)
1978—Broncos, 28-7 (D)
Broncos, 20-17 (S) OT
1979—Broncos, 37-34 (D)
Seahawks, 28-23 (S)
1980—Broncos, 36-20 (D)
Broncos, 25-17 (S)
1981—Seahawks, 13-10 (S)
Broncos, 23-13 (D)
1982—Seahawks, 17-10 (D)
Seahawks, 13-11 (S)
1983—Seahawks, 27-19 (S)
Broncos, 38-27 (D)
*Seahawks, 31-7 (S)
1984—Seahawks, 27-24 (D)
Broncos, 31-14 (S)
1985—Broncos, 13-10 (D) OT
Broncos, 27-24 (S)
1986—Broncos, 20-13 (D)
Seahawks, 41-16 (S)
1987—Broncos, 40-17 (D)
Seahawks, 28-21 (S)
1988—Seahawks, 21-14 (D)
Seahawks, 42-14 (S)
1989—Broncos, 24-21 (S) OT
Broncos, 41-14 (D)
1990—Broncos, 34-31 (D) OT
Seahawks, 17-12 (S)
1991—Broncos, 16-10 (D)
Seahawks, 13-10 (S)
1992—Seahawks, 16-13 (S) OT
Broncos, 10-6 (D)
1993—Broncos, 28-17 (D)
Broncos, 17-9 (S)
1994—Broncos, 16-9 (S)
Broncos, 17-10 (D)

1995—Seahawks, 27-10 (S)
Seahawks, 31-27 (D)
1996—Broncos, 30-20 (S)
Broncos, 34-7 (D)
1997—Broncos, 35-14 (S)
Broncos, 30-27 (D)
1998—Broncos, 21-16 (S)
Broncos, 28-21 (D)
1999—Seahawks, 20-17 (S)
Broncos, 36-30 (D) OT
2000—Broncos, 38-31 (S)
Broncos, 31-24 (D)
2001—Seahawks, 34-21 (S)
Broncos, 20-7 (D)
2002—Broncos, 31-9 (S)
2006—Seahawks, 23-20 (D)
(RS Pts.—Broncos 1,191, Seahawks 997)
(PS Pts.—Seahawks 31, Broncos 7)
AFC First-Round Playoff

DENVER vs. TAMPA BAY
RS: Broncos lead series, 5-2
1976—Broncos, 48-13 (D)
1981—Broncos, 24-7 (TB)
1993—Buccaneers, 17-10 (D)
1996—Broncos, 27-23 (D)
1999—Buccaneers, 13-10 (TB)
2004—Broncos, 16-13 (TB)
2008—Broncos, 16-13 (D)
(RS Pts.—Broncos 151, Buccaneers 99)

DENVER vs. *TENNESSEE
RS: Titans lead series, 20-13-1
PS: Broncos lead series, 2-1
1960—Oilers, 45-25 (D)
Oilers, 20-10 (H)
1961—Oilers, 55-14 (D)
Oilers, 45-14 (H)
1962—Broncos, 20-10 (D)
Oilers, 34-17 (H)
1963—Oilers, 20-14 (H)
Oilers, 33-24 (D)
1964—Oilers, 38-17 (D)
Oilers, 34-15 (H)
1965—Broncos, 28-17 (D)
Broncos, 31-21 (H)
1966—Oilers, 45-7 (H)
Broncos, 40-38 (D)
1967—Oilers, 10-6 (H)
Oilers, 20-18 (D)
1968—Oilers, 38-17 (H)
1969—Oilers, 24-21 (H)
Tie, 20-20 (D)
1970—Oilers, 31-21 (H)
1972—Broncos, 30-17 (D)
1973—Broncos, 48-20 (H)
1974—Broncos, 37-14 (D)
1976—Oilers, 17-3 (H)
1977—Broncos, 24-14 (H)
1979—**Oilers, 13-7 (H)
1980—Oilers, 20-16 (D)
1983—Broncos, 26-14 (H)
1985—Broncos, 31-20 (D)
1987—Oilers, 40-10 (D)
***Broncos, 34-10 (D)
1991—Oilers, 42-14 (H)
***Broncos, 26-24 (D)
1992—Broncos, 27-21 (D)
1995—Oilers, 42-33 (H)
2004—Broncos, 37-16 (T)
2007—Broncos, 34-20 (D)
(RS Pts.—Titans 915, Broncos 749)
(PS Pts.—Broncos 67, Titans 47)
**Franchise in Houston prior to 1997; known as the Oilers prior to 1999*
***AFC First-Round Playoff*
****AFC Divisional Playoff*

DENVER vs. WASHINGTON
RS: Broncos lead series, 6-5
PS: Redskins lead series, 1-0
1970—Redskins, 19-3 (D)
1974—Redskins, 30-3 (W)
1980—Broncos, 20-17 (D)
1986—Broncos, 31-30 (D)
1987—*Redskins, 42-10 (San Diego)
1989—Broncos, 14-10 (W)
1992—Redskins, 34-3 (W)
1995—Broncos, 38-31 (D)
1998—Broncos, 38-16 (W)
2001—Redskins, 17-10 (D)
2005—Broncos, 21-19 (D)
2009—Redskins, 27-17 (W)
(RS Pts.—Redskins 250, Broncos 198)
(PS Pts.—Redskins 42, Broncos 10)
**Super Bowl XXII*

DETROIT vs. ARIZONA
RS: Lions lead series, 31-24-5;
See Arizona vs. Detroit

DETROIT vs. ATLANTA
RS: Lions lead series, 23-10;
See Atlanta vs. Detroit

DETROIT vs. BALTIMORE
RS: Ravens lead series, 2-1;
See Baltimore vs. Detroit

DETROIT vs. BUFFALO
RS: Lions lead series, 4-3-1;
See Buffalo vs. Detroit

DETROIT vs. CAROLINA
RS: Panthers lead series, 4-1;
See Carolina vs. Detroit

DETROIT vs. CHICAGO
RS: Bears lead series, 91-64-5;
See Chicago vs. Detroit

DETROIT vs. CINCINNATI
RS: Bengals lead series, 7-3;
See Cincinnati vs. Detroit

DETROIT vs. CLEVELAND
RS: Lions lead series, 14-4
PS: Lions lead series, 3-1;
See Cleveland vs. Detroit

DETROIT vs. DALLAS
RS: Cowboys lead series, 11-9
PS: Series tied, 1-1;
See Dallas vs. Detroit

DETROIT vs. DENVER
RS: Broncos lead series, 6-4;
See Denver vs. Detroit

***DETROIT vs. GREEN BAY**
RS: Packers lead series, 88-64-7
PS: Packers lead series, 2-0
1930—Packers, 47-13 (GB)
Tie, 6-6 (P)
1932—Packers, 15-10 (GB)
Spartans, 19-0 (P)
1933—Packers, 17-0 (GB)
Spartans, 7-0 (P)
1934—Lions, 3-0 (GB)
Packers, 3-0 (D)
1935—Packers, 13-9 (Mil)
Packers, 31-7 (GB)
Lions, 20-10 (D)
1936—Packers, 20-18 (GB)
Packers, 26-17 (D)
1937—Packers, 26-6 (GB)
Packers, 14-13 (D)
1938—Lions, 17-7 (GB)
Packers, 28-7 (D)
1939—Packers, 26-7 (GB)
Packers, 12-7 (D)
1940—Lions, 23-14 (GB)
Packers, 50-7 (D)
1941—Packers, 23-0 (GB)
Packers, 24-7 (D)
1942—Packers, 38-7 (Mil)
Packers, 28-7 (D)
1943—Packers, 35-14 (GB)
Packers, 27-6 (D)
1944—Packers, 27-6 (Mil)
Packers, 14-0 (D)
1945—Packers, 57-21 (Mil)
Lions, 14-3 (D)
1946—Packers, 10-7 (Mil)
Packers, 9-0 (D)
1947—Packers, 34-17 (GB)
Packers, 35-14 (D)
1948—Packers, 33-21 (GB)
Lions, 24-20 (D)
1949—Packers, 16-14 (Mil)
Lions, 21-7 (D)
1950—Lions, 45-7 (GB)
Lions, 24-21 (D)
1951—Lions, 24-17 (GB)
Lions, 52-35 (D)
1952—Lions, 52-17 (GB)
Lions, 48-24 (D)
1953—Lions, 14-7 (GB)
Lions, 34-15 (D)
1954—Lions, 21-17 (GB)
Lions, 28-24 (D)
1955—Packers, 20-17 (GB)
Lions, 24-10 (D)
1956—Lions, 20-16 (GB)
Packers, 24-20 (D)
1957—Lions, 24-14 (GB)
Lions, 18-6 (D)
1958—Tie, 13-13 (GB)
Lions, 24-14 (D)
1959—Packers, 28-10 (GB)
Packers, 24-17 (D)
1960—Packers, 28-9 (GB)
Lions, 23-10 (D)
1961—Lions, 17-13 (Mil)
Packers, 17-9 (D)
1962—Packers, 9-7 (GB)
Lions, 26-14 (D)
1963—Packers, 31-10 (Mil)
Tie, 13-13 (D)
1964—Packers, 14-10 (D)
Packers, 30-7 (GB)
1965—Packers, 31-21 (D)
Lions, 12-7 (GB)
1966—Packers, 23-14 (GB)
Packers, 31-7 (D)
1967—Tie, 17-17 (GB)
Packers, 27-17 (D)
1968—Lions, 23-17 (GB)
Tie, 14-14 (D)
1969—Packers, 28-17 (D)
Lions, 16-10 (GB)
1970—Lions, 40-0 (GB)
Lions, 20-0 (D)
1971—Lions, 31-28 (D)
Tie, 14-14 (Mil)
1972—Packers, 24-23 (D)

Packers, 33-7 (GB)
1973—Tie, 13-13 (GB)
Lions, 34-0 (D)
1974—Packers, 21-19 (Mil)
Lions, 19-17 (D)
1975—Lions, 30-16 (Mil)
Lions, 13-10 (D)
1976—Packers, 24-14 (GB)
Lions, 27-6 (D)
1977—Lions, 10-6 (D)
Packers, 10-9 (GB)
1978—Packers, 13-7 (D)
Packers, 35-14 (Mil)
1979—Packers, 24-16 (Mil)
Packers, 18-13 (D)
1980—Lions, 29-7 (Mil)
Lions, 24-3 (D)
1981—Lions, 31-27 (D)
Packers, 31-17 (GB)
1982—Lions, 30-10 (GB)
Lions, 27-24 (D)
1983—Lions, 38-14 (D)
Lions, 23-20 (Mil) OT
1984—Packers, 41-9 (GB)
Lions, 31-28 (D)
1985—Packers, 43-10 (GB)
Packers, 26-23 (D)
1986—Lions, 21-14 (GB)
Packers, 44-40 (D)
1987—Lions, 19-16 (GB) OT
Packers, 34-33 (D)
1988—Lions, 19-9 (Mil)
Lions, 30-14 (D)
1989—Packers, 23-20 (Mil) OT
Lions, 31-22 (D)
1990—Packers, 24-21 (D)
Lions, 24-17 (GB)
1991—Lions, 23-14 (D)
Lions, 21-17 (GB)
1992—Packers, 27-13 (D)
Packers, 38-10 (Mil)
1993—Packers, 26-17 (Mil)
Lions, 30-20 (D)
**Packers, 28-24 (D)
1994—Packers, 38-30 (Mil)
Lions, 34-31 (D)
**Packers, 16-12 (GB)
1995—Packers, 30-21 (GB)
Lions, 24-16 (D)
1996—Packers, 28-18 (GB)
Packers, 31-3 (D)
1997—Lions, 26-15 (D)
Packers, 20-10 (GB)
1998—Packers, 38-19 (GB)
Lions, 27-20 (D)
1999—Lions, 23-15 (D)
Packers, 26-17 (GB)
2000—Lions, 31-24 (D)
Packers, 26-13 (GB)
2001—Packers, 28-6 (GB)
Packers, 29-27 (D)
2002—Packers, 37-31 (D)
Packers, 40-14 (GB)
2003—Packers, 31-6 (GB)
Lions, 22-14 (D)
2004—Packers, 38-10 (D)
Packers, 16-13 (GB)
2005—Lions, 17-3 (D)
Packers, 16-13 (GB) OT
2006—Packers, 31-24 (D)
Packers, 17-9 (GB)
2007—Packers, 37-26 (D)
Packers, 34-13 (GB)
2008—Packers, 48-25 (D)
Packers, 31-21 (GB)
2009—Packers, 26-0 (GB)
Packers, 34-12 (D)
(RS Pts.—Packers 3,355, Lions 2,856)
(PS Pts.—Packers 44, Lions 36)
**Franchise in Portsmouth prior to 1934 and known as the Spartans*
***NFC First-Round Playoff*

DETROIT vs. HOUSTON
RS: Series tied, 1-1
2004—Lions, 28-16 (D)
2008—Texans, 28-21 (H)
(RS Pts.—Lions 49, Texans 44)

DETROIT vs. *INDIANAPOLIS
RS: Colts lead series, 20-18-2
1953—Lions, 27-17 (B)
Lions, 17-7 (D)
1954—Lions, 35-0 (D)
Lions, 27-3 (B)
1955—Colts, 28-13 (B)
Lions, 24-14 (D)
1956—Lions, 31-14 (B)
Lions, 27-3 (D)
1957—Colts, 34-14 (B)
Lions, 31-27 (D)
1958—Colts, 28-15 (B)
Colts, 40-14 (D)
1959—Colts, 21-9 (B)
Colts, 31-24 (D)
1960—Lions, 30-17 (D)
Lions, 20-15 (B)
1961—Lions, 16-15 (B)
Colts, 17-14 (D)
1962—Lions, 29-20 (B)
Lions, 21-14 (D)
1963—Colts, 25-21 (D)
Colts, 24-21 (B)
1964—Colts, 34-0 (D)
Lions, 31-14 (B)
1965—Colts, 31-7 (B)
Tie, 24-24 (D)
1966—Colts, 45-14 (B)
Lions, 20-14 (D)
1967—Colts, 41-7 (B)
1968—Colts, 27-10 (D)
1969—Tie, 17-17 (B)
1973—Colts, 29-27 (D)
1977—Lions, 13-10 (B)
1980—Colts, 10-9 (D)
1985—Colts, 14-6 (I)
1991—Lions, 33-24 (I)
1997—Lions, 32-10 (D)
2000—Colts, 30-18 (I)
2004—Colts, 41-9 (D)
2008—Colts, 31-21 (I)
(RS Pts.—Colts 860, Lions 778)
**Franchise in Baltimore prior to 1984*

DETROIT vs. JACKSONVILLE
RS: Jaguars lead series, 3-1
1995—Lions, 44-0 (D)
1998—Jaguars, 37-22 (J)
2004—Jaguars, 23-17 (J) OT
2008—Jaguars, 38-14 (D)
(RS Pts.—Jaguars 98, Lions 97)

DETROIT vs. KANSAS CITY
RS: Chiefs lead series, 7-4
1971—Lions, 32-21 (D)
1975—Chiefs, 24-21 (KC) OT
1980—Chiefs, 20-17 (KC)
1981—Lions, 27-10 (D)
1987—Chiefs, 27-20 (D)
1988—Lions, 7-6 (KC)
1990—Chiefs, 43-24 (KC)
1996—Chiefs, 28-24 (D)
1999—Chiefs, 31-21 (KC)
2003—Chiefs, 45-17 (KC)
2007—Lions, 25-20 (D)
(RS Pts.—Chiefs 275, Lions 235)

DETROIT vs. MIAMI
RS: Dolphins lead series, 7-2
1973—Dolphins, 34-7 (M)
1979—Dolphins, 28-10 (D)
1985—Lions, 31-21 (D)
1991—Lions, 17-13 (D)
1994—Dolphins, 27-20 (M)
1997—Dolphins, 33-30 (M)
2000—Dolphins, 23-8 (D)
2002—Dolphins, 49-21 (M)
2006—Dolphins, 27-10 (D)
(RS Pts.—Dolphins 255, Lions 154)

DETROIT vs. MINNESOTA
RS: Vikings lead series, 65-30-2
1961—Lions, 37-10 (M)
Lions, 13-7 (D)
1962—Lions, 17-6 (M)
Lions, 37-23 (D)
1963—Lions, 28-10 (D)
Vikings, 34-31 (M)
1964—Lions, 24-20 (M)
Tie, 23-23 (D)
1965—Lions, 31-29 (M)
Vikings, 29-7 (D)
1966—Lions, 32-31 (M)
Vikings, 28-16 (D)
1967—Tie, 10-10 (M)
Lions, 14-3 (D)
1968—Vikings, 24-10 (M)
Vikings, 13-6 (D)
1969—Vikings, 24-10 (M)
Vikings, 27-0 (D)
1970—Vikings, 30-17 (D)
Vikings, 24-20 (M)
1971—Vikings, 16-13 (D)
Vikings, 29-10 (M)
1972—Vikings, 34-10 (D)
Vikings, 16-14 (M)
1973—Vikings, 23-9 (D)
Vikings, 28-7 (M)
1974—Vikings, 7-6 (D)
Lions, 20-16 (M)
1975—Vikings, 25-19 (M)
Lions, 17-10 (D)
1976—Vikings, 10-9 (D)
Vikings, 31-23 (M)
1977—Vikings, 14-7 (M)
Vikings, 30-21 (D)
1978—Vikings, 17-7 (M)
Lions, 45-14 (D)
1979—Vikings, 13-10 (D)
Vikings, 14-7 (M)
1980—Lions, 27-7 (D)
Vikings, 34-0 (M)
1981—Vikings, 26-24 (M)
Lions, 45-7 (D)
1982—Vikings, 34-31 (D)
1983—Vikings, 20-17 (M)
Lions, 13-2 (D)
1984—Vikings, 29-28 (D)
Lions, 16-14 (M)

1985—Vikings, 16-13 (M)
Lions, 41-21 (D)
1986—Lions, 13-10 (M)
Vikings, 24-10 (D)
1987—Vikings, 34-19 (M)
Vikings, 17-14 (D)
1988—Vikings, 44-17 (M)
Vikings, 23-0 (D)
1989—Vikings, 24-17 (M)
Vikings, 20-7 (D)
1990—Lions, 34-27 (M)
Vikings, 17-7 (D)
1991—Lions, 24-20 (D)
Lions, 34-14 (M)
1992—Lions, 31-17 (D)
Vikings, 31-14 (M)
1993—Lions, 30-27 (M)
Vikings, 13-0 (D)
1994—Vikings, 10-3 (M)
Lions, 41-19 (D)
1995—Vikings, 20-10 (M)
Lions, 44-38 (D)
1996—Vikings, 17-13 (M)
Vikings, 24-22 (D)
1997—Lions, 38-15 (D)
Lions, 14-13 (M)
1998—Vikings, 29-6 (M)
Vikings, 34-13 (D)
1999—Lions, 25-23 (D)
Vikings, 24-17 (M)
2000—Vikings, 31-24 (D)
Vikings, 24-17 (M)
2001—Vikings, 31-26 (M)
Lions, 27-24 (D)
2002—Vikings, 31-24 (M)
Vikings, 38-36 (D)
2003—Vikings, 23-13 (D)
Vikings, 24-14 (M)
2004—Vikings, 22-19 (M)
Vikings, 28-27 (D)
2005—Vikings, 27-14 (M)
Vikings, 21-16 (D)
2006—Vikings, 26-17 (M)
Vikings, 30-20 (D)
2007—Lions, 20-17 (D) OT
Vikings, 42-10 (M)
2008—Vikings, 12-10 (M)
Vikings, 20-16 (D)
2009—Vikings, 27-13 (D)
Vikings, 27-10 (M)
(RS Pts.—Vikings 2,115, Lions 1,782)

DETROIT vs. NEW ENGLAND
RS: Patriots lead series, 5-4
1971—Lions, 34-7 (NE)
1976—Lions, 30-10 (D)
1979—Patriots, 24-17 (NE)
1985—Patriots, 23-6 (NE)
1993—Lions, 19-16 (NE) OT
1994—Patriots, 23-17 (D)
2000—Lions, 34-9 (D)
2002—Patriots, 20-12 (D)
2006—Patriots, 28-21 (NE)
(RS Pts.—Lions 190, Patriots 160)

DETROIT vs. NEW ORLEANS
RS: Saints lead series, 10-9-1
1968—Tie, 20-20 (D)
1970—Saints, 19-17 (NO)
1972—Lions, 27-14 (D)
1973—Saints, 20-13 (NO)
1974—Lions, 19-14 (D)
1976—Saints, 17-16 (NO)
1977—Lions, 23-19 (D)
1979—Saints, 17-7 (NO)
1980—Lions, 24-13 (D)
1988—Saints, 22-14 (D)
1989—Lions, 21-14 (D)
1990—Lions, 27-10 (NO)
1992—Saints, 13-7 (D)
1993—Saints, 14-3 (NO)
1997—Saints, 35-17 (NO)
2000—Lions, 14-10 (NO)
2002—Lions, 26-21 (D)
2005—Lions, 13-12 (San Antonio)
2008—Saints, 42-7 (D)
2009—Saints, 45-27 (NO)
(RS Pts.—Saints 391, Lions 342)

***DETROIT vs. N.Y. GIANTS**
RS: Lions lead series, 20-18-1
PS: Lions lead series, 1-0
1930—Giants, 19-6 (P)
1931—Spartans, 14-6 (P)
Giants, 14-0 (NY)
1932—Spartans, 7-0 (P)
Spartans, 6-0 (NY)
1933—Spartans, 17-7 (P)
Giants, 13-10 (NY)
1934—Lions, 9-0 (D)
1935—**Lions, 26-7 (D)
1936—Giants, 14-7 (NY)
Lions, 38-0 (D)
1937—Lions, 17-0 (NY)
1939—Lions, 18-14 (D)
1941—Giants, 20-13 (NY)
1943—Tie, 0-0 (D)
1945—Giants, 35-14 (NY)
1947—Lions, 35-7 (D)
1949—Lions, 45-21 (NY)
1953—Lions, 27-16 (NY)
1955—Giants, 24-19 (D)
1958—Giants, 19-17 (D)
1962—Giants, 17-14 (NY)
1964—Lions, 26-3 (D)
1967—Lions, 30-7 (NY)
1969—Lions, 24-0 (D)
1972—Lions, 30-16 (D)
1974—Lions, 20-19 (D)
1976—Giants, 24-10 (NY)
1982—Giants, 13-6 (D)
1983—Lions, 15-9 (D)
1988—Giants, 30-10 (NY)
Giants, 13-10 (D) OT
1989—Giants, 24-14 (NY)
1990—Giants, 20-0 (NY)
1994—Lions, 28-25 (NY) OT
1996—Giants, 35-7 (D)
1997—Giants, 26-20 (D) OT
2000—Lions, 31-21 (NY)
2004—Lions, 28-13 (NY)
2007—Giants, 16-10 (D)
(RS Pts.—Lions 652, Giants 560)
(PS Pts.—Lions 26, Giants 7)
Franchise in Portsmouth prior to 1934 and known as the Spartans
***NFL Championship*

DETROIT vs. N.Y. JETS
RS: Lions lead series, 6-5
1972—Lions, 37-20 (D)
1979—Jets, 31-10 (NY)
1982—Jets, 28-13 (D)
1985—Lions, 31-20 (D)
1988—Jets, 17-10 (D)
1991—Lions, 34-20 (D)
1994—Lions, 18-7 (NY)
1997—Lions, 13-10 (D)
2000—Lions, 10-7 (NY)
2002—Jets, 31-14 (D)
2006—Jets, 31-24 (NY)
(RS Pts.—Jets 222, Lions 214)

DETROIT vs. *OAKLAND
RS: Raiders lead series, 6-4
1970—Lions, 28-14 (D)
1974—Raiders, 35-13 (O)
1978—Raiders, 29-17 (O)
1981—Lions, 16-0 (D)
1984—Raiders, 24-3 (D)
1987—Raiders, 27-7 (LA)
1990—Raiders, 38-31 (D)
1996—Raiders, 37-21 (O)
2003—Lions, 23-13 (D)
2007—Lions, 36-21 (O)
(RS Pts.—Raiders 238, Lions 195)
Franchise in Los Angeles from 1982-1994

***DETROIT vs. PHILADELPHIA**
RS: Eagles lead series, 13-12-2
PS: Eagles lead series, 1-0
1933—Spartans, 25-0 (P)
1934—Lions, 10-0 (P)
1935—Lions, 35-0 (D)
1936—Lions, 23-0 (P)
1938—Eagles, 21-7 (D)
1940—Lions, 21-0 (P)
1941—Lions, 21-17 (D)
1945—Lions, 28-24 (D)
1948—Eagles, 45-21 (P)
1949—Eagles, 22-14 (D)
1951—Lions, 28-10 (P)
1954—Tie, 13-13 (D)
1957—Lions, 27-16 (P)
1960—Eagles, 28-10 (P)
1961—Eagles, 27-24 (D)
1965—Lions, 35-28 (P)
1968—Eagles, 12-0 (D)
1971—Eagles, 23-20 (D)
1974—Eagles, 28-17 (P)
1977—Lions, 17-13 (D)
1979—Eagles, 44-7 (P)
1984—Tie, 23-23 (D) OT
1986—Lions, 13-11 (P)
1995—**Eagles, 58-37 (P)
1996—Eagles, 24-17 (P)
1998—Eagles, 10-9 (P)
2004—Eagles, 30-13 (D)
2007—Eagles, 56-21 (P)
(RS Pts.—Eagles 525, Lions 499)
(PS Pts.—Eagles 58, Lions 37)
Franchise in Portsmouth prior to 1934 and known as the Spartans
***NFC First-Round Playoff*

DETROIT vs. *PITTSBURGH
RS: Steelers lead series, 15-14-1
1934—Lions, 40-7 (D)
1936—Lions, 28-3 (D)
1937—Lions, 7-3 (D)
1938—Lions, 16-7 (D)
1940—Steelers, 10-7 (D)
1942—Steelers, 35-7 (D)
1946—Lions, 17-7 (D)
1947—Steelers, 17-10 (P)
1948—Lions, 17-14 (D)
1949—Steelers, 14-7 (P)
1950—Lions, 10-7 (D)
1952—Lions, 31-6 (P)
1953—Lions, 38-21 (D)

1955—Lions, 31-28 (P)
1956—Lions, 45-7 (D)
1959—Tie, 10-10 (P)
1962—Lions, 45-7 (D)
1966—Steelers, 17-3 (P)
1967—Steelers, 24-14 (D)
1969—Steelers, 16-13 (P)
1973—Steelers, 24-10 (P)
1983—Lions, 45-3 (D)
1986—Steelers, 27-17 (P)
1989—Steelers, 23-3 (D)
1992—Steelers, 17-14 (P)
1995—Steelers, 23-20 (P)
1998—Lions, 19-16 (D) OT
2001—Steelers, 47-14 (P)
2005—Steelers, 35-21 (P)
2009—Steelers, 28-20 (D)
(RS Pts.—Lions 579, Steelers 503)
Steelers known as Pirates prior to 1940

DETROIT vs. *ST. LOUIS
RS: Rams lead series, 42-37-1
PS: Lions lead series, 1-0
1937—Lions, 28-0 (C)
Lions, 27-7 (D)
1938—Rams, 21-17 (C)
Lions, 6-0 (D)
1939—Lions, 15-7 (D)
Rams, 14-3 (C)
1940—Lions, 6-0 (D)
Rams, 24-0 (C)
1941—Lions, 17-7 (D)
Lions, 14-0 (C)
1942—Rams, 14-0 (D)
Rams, 27-7 (C)
1944—Rams, 20-17 (D)
Lions, 26-14 (C)
1945—Rams, 28-21 (D)
1946—Rams, 35-14 (LA)
Rams, 41-20 (D)
1947—Rams, 27-13 (D)
Rams, 28-17 (LA)
1948—Rams, 44-7 (LA)
Rams, 34-27 (D)
1949—Rams, 27-24 (LA)
Rams, 21-10 (D)
1950—Rams, 30-28 (D)
Rams, 65-24 (LA)
1951—Rams, 27-21 (D)
Lions, 24-22 (LA)
1952—Lions, 17-14 (LA)
Lions, 24-16 (D)
**Lions, 31-21 (D)
1953—Rams, 31-19 (D)
Rams, 37-24 (LA)
1954—Lions, 21-3 (D)
Lions, 27-24 (LA)
1955—Rams, 17-10 (D)
Rams, 24-13 (LA)
1956—Lions, 24-21 (D)
Lions, 16-7 (LA)
1957—Lions, 10-7 (D)
Rams, 35-17 (LA)
1958—Rams, 42-28 (D)
Lions, 41-24 (LA)
1959—Lions, 17-7 (LA)
Lions, 23-17 (D)
1960—Rams, 48-35 (LA)
Lions, 12-10 (D)
1961—Lions, 14-13 (D)
Lions, 28-10 (LA)
1962—Lions, 13-10 (D)
Lions, 12-3 (LA)
1963—Lions, 23-2 (LA)
Rams, 28-21 (D)
1964—Tie, 17-17 (LA)
Lions, 37-17 (D)
1965—Lions, 20-0 (D)
Lions, 31-7 (LA)
1966—Rams, 14-7 (D)
Rams, 23-3 (LA)
1967—Rams, 31-7 (D)
1968—Rams, 10-7 (LA)
1969—Lions, 28-0 (D)
1970—Lions, 28-23 (LA)
1971—Rams, 21-13 (D)
1972—Lions, 34-17 (LA)
1974—Rams, 16-13 (LA)
1975—Rams, 20-0 (D)
1976—Rams, 20-17 (D)
1980—Lions, 41-20 (LA)
1981—Rams, 20-13 (LA)
1982—Lions, 19-14 (LA)
1983—Rams, 21-10 (LA)
1986—Rams, 14-10 (LA)
1987—Rams, 37-16 (D)
1988—Rams, 17-10 (LA)
1991—Lions, 21-10 (D)
1993—Lions, 16-13 (LA)
1999—Lions, 31-27 (D)
2001—Rams, 35-0 (D)
2003—Lions, 30-20 (D)
2006—Rams, 41-34 (StL)
2009—Rams, 17-10 (D)
(RS Pts.—Rams 1,576, Lions 1,445)
(PS Pts.—Lions 31, Rams 21)
Franchise in Los Angeles prior to 1995 and in Cleveland prior to 1946
***Conference Playoff*

DETROIT vs. SAN DIEGO
RS: Chargers lead series, 6-3
1972—Lions, 34-20 (D)
1977—Lions, 20-0 (D)
1978—Lions, 31-14 (D)
1981—Chargers, 28-23 (SD)
1984—Chargers, 27-24 (SD)
1996—Chargers, 27-21 (SD)
1999—Chargers, 20-10 (D)
2003—Chargers, 14-7 (D)
2007—Chargers, 51-14 (SD)
(RS Pts.—Chargers 201, Lions 184)

DETROIT vs. SAN FRANCISCO
RS: 49ers lead series, 34-26-1
PS: Series tied, 1-1
1950—Lions, 24-7 (D)
49ers, 28-27 (SF)
1951—49ers, 20-10 (D)
49ers, 21-17 (SF)
1952—49ers, 17-3 (SF)
49ers, 28-0 (D)
1953—Lions, 24-21 (D)
Lions, 14-10 (SF)
1954—49ers, 37-31 (SF)
Lions, 48-7 (D)
1955—49ers, 27-24 (D)
49ers, 38-21 (SF)
1956—Lions, 20-17 (D)
Lions, 17-13 (SF)
1957—49ers, 35-31 (SF)
Lions, 31-10 (D)
*Lions, 31-27 (SF)
1958—49ers, 24-21 (SF)
Lions, 35-21 (D)
1959—49ers, 34-13 (D)
49ers, 33-7 (SF)
1960—49ers, 14-10 (D)
Lions, 24-0 (SF)
1961—49ers, 49-0 (D)
Tie, 20-20 (SF)
1962—Lions, 45-24 (D)
Lions, 38-24 (SF)
1963—Lions, 26-3 (D)
Lions, 45-7 (SF)
1964—Lions, 26-17 (SF)
Lions, 24-7 (D)
1965—49ers, 27-21 (D)
49ers, 17-14 (SF)
1966—49ers, 27-24 (SF)
49ers, 41-14 (D)
1967—Lions, 45-3 (SF)
1968—49ers, 14-7 (D)
1969—Lions, 26-14 (SF)
1970—Lions, 28-7 (D)
1971—49ers, 31-27 (SF)
1973—Lions, 30-20 (D)
1974—Lions, 17-13 (D)
1975—Lions, 28-17 (SF)
1977—49ers, 28-7 (SF)
1978—Lions, 33-14 (D)
1980—Lions, 17-13 (D)
1981—Lions, 24-17 (D)
1983—**49ers, 24-23 (SF)
1984—49ers, 30-27 (D)
1985—Lions, 23-21 (D)
1988—49ers, 20-13 (SF)
1991—49ers, 35-3 (SF)
1992—49ers, 24-6 (SF)
1993—49ers, 55-17 (D)
1994—49ers, 27-21 (D)
1995—Lions, 27-24 (D)
1996—49ers, 24-14 (SF)
1998—49ers, 35-13 (SF)
2001—49ers, 21-13 (SF)
2003—49ers, 24-17 (SF)
2006—49ers, 19-13 (D)
2008—49ers, 31-13 (SF)
2009—49ers, 20-6 (SF)
(RS Pts.—49ers 1,326, Lions 1,264)
(PS Pts.—Lions 54, 49ers 51)
Conference Playoff
***NFC Divisional Playoff*

DETROIT vs. SEATTLE
RS: Seahawks lead series, 7-4
1976—Lions, 41-14 (S)
1978—Seahawks, 28-16 (S)
1984—Seahawks, 38-17 (S)
1987—Seahawks, 37-14 (D)
1990—Seahawks, 30-10 (S)
1993—Lions, 30-10 (D)
1996—Lions, 17-16 (D)
1999—Lions, 28-20 (S)
2003—Seahawks, 35-14 (S)
2006—Seahawks, 9-6 (D)
2009—Seahawks, 32-20 (S)
(RS Pts.—Seahawks 269, Lions 213)

DETROIT vs. TAMPA BAY
RS: Lions lead series, 27-25
PS: Buccaneers lead series, 1-0
1977—Lions, 16-7 (D)
1978—Lions, 15-7 (TB)
Lions, 34-23 (D)
1979—Buccaneers, 31-16 (TB)
Buccaneers, 16-14 (D)
1980—Lions, 24-10 (TB)

Lions, 27-14 (D)
1981—Buccaneers, 28-10 (TB)
Buccaneers, 20-17 (D)
1982—Buccaneers, 23-21 (TB)
1983—Lions, 11-0 (TB)
Lions, 23-20 (D)
1984—Buccaneers, 21-17 (TB)
Lions, 13-7 (D) OT
1985—Lions, 30-9 (D)
Buccaneers, 19-16 (TB) OT
1986—Buccaneers, 24-20 (D)
Lions, 38-17 (TB)
1987—Buccaneers, 31-27 (D)
Lions, 20-10 (TB)
1988—Buccaneers, 23-20 (D)
Buccaneers, 21-10 (TB)
1989—Lions, 17-16 (TB)
Lions, 33-7 (D)
1990—Buccaneers, 38-21 (D)
Buccaneers, 23-20 (TB)
1991—Lions, 31-3 (D)
Buccaneers, 30-21 (TB)
1992—Buccaneers, 27-23 (D)
Lions, 38-7 (TB)
1993—Buccaneers, 27-10 (TB)
Lions, 23-0 (D)
1994—Buccaneers, 24-14 (TB)
Lions, 14-9 (D)
1995—Lions, 27-24 (D)
Lions, 37-10 (TB)
1996—Lions, 21-6 (D)
Lions, 27-0 (TB)
1997—Buccaneers, 24-17 (D)
Lions, 27-9 (TB)
*Buccaneers, 20-10 (TB)
1998—Lions, 27-6 (D)
Lions, 28-25 (TB)
1999—Lions, 20-3 (D)
Buccaneers, 23-16 (TB)
2000—Buccaneers, 31-10 (D)
Lions, 28-14 (TB)
2001—Buccaneers, 20-17 (D)
Buccaneers, 15-12 (TB)
2002—Buccaneers, 23-20 (D)
2005—Buccaneers, 17-13 (TB)
2007—Lions, 23-16 (D)
2008—Buccaneers, 38-20 (D)
(RS Pts—Lions 1,094, Buccaneers 896)
(PS Pts.—Buccaneers 20, Lions 10)
NFC First-Round Playoff

DETROIT vs. *TENNESSEE
RS: Titans lead series, 7-3
1971—Lions, 31-7 (H)
1975—Oilers, 24-8 (H)
1983—Oilers, 27-17 (H)
1986—Lions, 24-13 (D)
1989—Oilers, 35-31 (H)
1992—Oilers, 24-21 (D)
1995—Lions, 24-17 (H)
2001—Titans, 27-24 (D)
2004—Titans, 24-19 (T)
2008—Titans, 47-10 (D)
(RS Pts.—Titans 245, Lions 209)
**Franchise in Houston prior to 1997; known as Oilers prior to 1999*

***DETROIT vs. **WASHINGTON**
RS: Redskins lead series, 27-11
PS: Redskins lead series, 3-0
1932—Spartans, 10-0 (P)
1933—Spartans, 13-0 (B)
1934—Lions, 24-0 (D)
1935—Lions, 17-7 (B)
Lions, 14-0 (D)
1938—Redskins, 7-5 (D)
1939—Redskins, 31-7 (W)
1940—Redskins, 20-14 (D)
1942—Redskins, 15-3 (D)
1943—Redskins, 42-20 (W)
1946—Redskins, 17-16 (W)
1947—Lions, 38-21 (D)
1948—Redskins, 46-21 (W)
1951—Lions, 35-17 (D)
1956—Redskins, 18-17 (W)
1965—Lions, 14-10 (D)
1968—Redskins, 14-3 (W)
1970—Redskins, 31-10 (W)
1973—Redskins, 20-0 (D)
1976—Redskins, 20-7 (W)
1978—Redskins, 21-19 (D)
1979—Redskins, 27-24 (D)
1981—Redskins, 33-31 (W)
1982—***Redskins, 31-7 (W)
1983—Redskins, 38-17 (W)
1984—Redskins, 28-14 (W)
1985—Redskins, 24-3 (W)
1987—Redskins, 20-13 (W)
1990—Redskins, 41-38 (D) OT
1991—Redskins, 45-0 (W)
****Redskins, 41-10 (W)
1992—Redskins, 13-10 (W)
1995—Redskins, 36-30 (W) OT
1997—Redskins, 30-7 (W)
1999—Lions, 33-17 (D)
***Redskins, 27-13 (W)
2000—Lions, 15-10 (D)
2004—Redskins, 17-10 (D)
2007—Redskins, 34-3 (W)
2008—Redskins, 25-17 (D)
2009—Lions, 19-14 (D)
(RS Pts.—Redskins 809, Lions 591)
(PS Pts.—Redskins 99, Lions 30)
**Franchise in Portsmouth prior to 1934 and known as the Spartans.*
***Franchise in Boston prior to 1937*
****NFC First-Round Playoff*
*****NFC Championship*

GREEN BAY vs. ARIZONA
RS: Packers lead series, 43-22-4
PS: Series tied, 1-1;
See Arizona vs. Green Bay

GREEN BAY vs. ATLANTA
RS: Packers lead series, 12-11
PS: Series tied, 1-1;
See Atlanta vs. Green Bay

GREEN BAY vs. BALTIMORE
RS: Packers lead series, 3-1;
See Baltimore vs. Green Bay

GREEN BAY vs. BUFFALO
RS: Bills lead series, 7-3;
See Buffalo vs. Green Bay

GREEN BAY vs. CAROLINA
RS: Packers lead series, 6-4
PS: Packers lead series, 1-0;
See Carolina vs. Green Bay

GREEN BAY vs. CHICAGO
RS: Bears lead series, 90-82-6
PS: Bears lead series, 1-0;
See Chicago vs. Green Bay

GREEN BAY vs. CINCINNATI
RS: Bengals lead series, 6-5;
See Cincinnati vs. Green Bay

GREEN BAY vs. CLEVELAND
RS: Packers lead series, 10-7
PS: Packers lead series, 1-0;
See Cleveland vs. Green Bay

GREEN BAY vs. DALLAS
RS: Cowboys lead series, 12-11
PS: Cowboys lead series, 4-2;
See Dallas vs. Green Bay

GREEN BAY vs. DENVER
RS: Series tied, 5-5-1
PS: Broncos lead series, 1-0;
See Denver vs. Green Bay

GREEN BAY vs. DETROIT
RS: Packers lead series, 88-64-7
PS: Packers lead series, 2-0;
See Detroit vs. Green Bay

GREEN BAY vs. HOUSTON
RS: Series tied, 1-1
2004—Packers, 16-13 (H)
2008—Texans, 24-21 (GB)
(RS Pts.—Packers 37, Texans 37)

GREEN BAY vs. *INDIANAPOLIS
RS: Series tied, 20-20-1
PS: Packers lead series, 1-0
1953—Packers, 37-14 (GB)
Packers, 35-24 (B)
1954—Packers, 7-6 (B)
Packers, 24-13 (Mil)
1955—Colts, 24-20 (Mil)
Colts, 14-10 (B)
1956—Packers, 38-33 (Mil)
Colts, 28-21 (B)
1957—Colts, 45-17 (Mil)
Packers, 24-21 (B)
1958—Colts, 24-17 (Mil)
Colts, 56-0 (B)
1959—Colts, 38-21 (B)
Colts, 28-24 (Mil)
1960—Packers, 35-21 (GB)
Colts, 38-24 (B)
1961—Packers, 45-7 (GB)
Colts, 45-21 (B)
1962—Packers, 17-6 (B)
Packers, 17-13 (GB)
1963—Packers, 31-20 (GB)
Packers, 34-20 (B)
1964—Colts, 21-20 (GB)
Colts, 24-21 (B)
1965—Packers, 20-17 (Mil)
Packers, 42-27 (B)
**Packers, 13-10 (GB) OT
1966—Packers, 24-3 (Mil)
Packers, 14-10 (B)
1967—Colts, 13-10 (B)
1968—Colts, 16-3 (GB)
1969—Colts, 14-6 (B)
1970—Colts, 13-10 (Mil)
1974—Packers, 20-13 (B)
1982—Tie, 20-20 (B) OT
1985—Colts, 37-10 (I)
1988—Colts, 20-13 (GB)
1991—Packers, 14-10 (Mil)
1997—Colts, 41-38 (I)
2000—Packers, 26-24 (GB)
2004—Colts, 45-31 (I)
2008—Packers, 34-14 (GB)
(RS Pts.—Colts 920, Packers 895)
(PS Pts.—Packers 13, Colts 10)
**Franchise in Baltimore prior to 1984*
***Conference Playoff*

GREEN BAY vs. JACKSONVILLE
RS: Series tied, 2-2
1995—Packers, 24-14 (J)
2001—Packers, 28-21 (J)
2004—Jaguars, 28-25 (GB)
2008—Jaguars, 20-16 (J)
(RS Pts.—Packers 93, Jaguars 83)

GREEN BAY vs. KANSAS CITY
RS: Chiefs lead series, 6-2-1
PS: Packers lead series, 1-0
1966—*Packers, 35-10 (Los Angeles)
1973—Tie, 10-10 (Mil)
1977—Chiefs, 20-10 (KC)
1987—Packers, 23-3 (KC)
1989—Chiefs, 21-3 (GB)
1990—Chiefs, 17-3 (GB)
1993—Chiefs, 23-16 (KC)
1996—Chiefs, 27-20 (KC)
2003—Chiefs, 40-34 (GB) OT
2007—Packers, 33-22 (KC)
(RS Pts.—Chiefs 183, Packers 152)
(PS Pts.—Packers 35, Chiefs 10)
**Super Bowl I*

GREEN BAY vs. MIAMI
RS: Dolphins lead series, 9-3
1971—Dolphins, 27-6 (Mia)
1975—Dolphins, 31-7 (GB)
1979—Dolphins, 27-7 (Mia)
1985—Dolphins, 34-24 (GB)
1988—Dolphins, 24-17 (Mia)
1989—Dolphins, 23-20 (Mia)
1991—Dolphins, 16-13 (Mia)
1994—Dolphins, 24-14 (Mil)
1997—Packers, 23-18 (GB)
2000—Dolphins, 28-20 (Mia)
2002—Packers, 24-10 (GB)
2006—Packers, 34-24 (M)
(RS Pts.—Dolphins 286, Packers 209)

GREEN BAY vs. MINNESOTA
RS: Packers lead series, 49-47-1
PS: Vikings lead series, 1-0
1961—Packers, 33-7 (Minn)
Packers, 28-10 (Mil)
1962—Packers, 34-7 (GB)
Packers, 48-21 (Minn)
1963—Packers, 37-28 (Minn)
Packers, 28-7 (GB)
1964—Vikings, 24-23 (GB)
Packers, 42-13 (Minn)
1965—Packers, 38-13 (Minn)
Packers, 24-19 (GB)
1966—Vikings, 20-17 (GB)
Packers, 28-16 (Minn)
1967—Vikings, 10-7 (Mil)
Packers, 30-27 (Minn)
1968—Vikings, 26-13 (Mil)
Vikings, 14-10 (Minn)
1969—Vikings, 19-7 (Minn)
Vikings, 9-7 (Mil)
1970—Packers, 13-10 (Mil)
Vikings, 10-3 (Minn)
1971—Vikings, 24-13 (GB)
Vikings, 3-0 (Minn)
1972—Vikings, 27-13 (GB)
Packers, 23-7 (Minn)
1973—Vikings, 11-3 (Minn)
Vikings, 31-7 (GB)
1974—Vikings, 32-17 (GB)
Packers, 19-7 (Minn)
1975—Vikings, 28-17 (GB)
Vikings, 24-3 (Minn)
1976—Vikings, 17-10 (Mil)
Vikings, 20-9 (Minn)
1977—Vikings, 19-7 (Minn)
Vikings, 13-6 (GB)
1978—Vikings, 21-7 (Minn)
Tie, 10-10 (GB) OT
1979—Vikings, 27-21 (Minn) OT
Packers, 19-7 (Mil)
1980—Packers, 16-3 (GB)
Packers, 25-13 (Minn)
1981—Vikings, 30-13 (Mil)
Packers, 35-23 (Minn)
1982—Packers, 26-7 (Mil)
1983—Vikings, 20-17 (GB) OT
Packers, 29-21 (Minn)
1984—Packers, 45-17 (Mil)
Packers, 38-14 (Minn)
1985—Packers, 20-17 (Mil)
Packers, 27-17 (Minn)
1986—Vikings, 42-7 (Minn)
Vikings, 32-6 (GB)
1987—Packers, 23-16 (Minn)
Packers, 16-10 (Mil)
1988—Packers, 34-14 (Minn)
Packers, 18-6 (GB)
1989—Vikings, 26-14 (Minn)
Packers, 20-19 (Mil)
1990—Packers, 24-10 (Mil)
Vikings, 23-7 (Minn)
1991—Vikings, 35-21 (GB)
Packers, 27-7 (Minn)
1992—Vikings, 23-20 (GB) OT
Vikings, 27-7 (Minn)
1993—Vikings, 15-13 (Minn)
Vikings, 21-17 (Mil)
1994—Packers, 16-10 (GB)
Vikings, 13-10 (Minn) OT
1995—Packers, 38-21 (GB)
Vikings, 27-24 (Minn)
1996—Vikings, 30-21 (Minn)
Packers, 38-10 (GB)
1997—Packers, 38-32 (GB)
Packers, 27-11 (Minn)
1998—Vikings, 37-24 (GB)
Vikings, 28-14 (Minn)
1999—Packers, 23-20 (GB)
Vikings, 24-20 (Minn)
2000—Packers, 26-20 (GB) OT
Packers, 33-28 (Minn)
2001—Vikings, 35-13 (Minn)
Packers, 24-13 (GB)
2002—Vikings, 31-21 (Minn)
Packers, 26-22 (GB)
2003—Vikings, 30-25 (GB)
Packers, 30-27 (Minn)
2004—Packers, 34-31 (GB)
Packers, 34-31 (Minn)
*Vikings, 31-17 (GB)
2005—Vikings, 23-20 (Minn)
Vikings, 20-17 (GB)
2006—Packers, 23-17 (Minn)
Packers, 9-7 (GB)
2007—Packers, 23-16 (Minn)
Packers, 34-0 (GB)
2008—Packers, 24-19 (GB)
Vikings, 28-27 (Minn)
2009—Vikings, 30-23 (Minn)
Vikings, 38-26 (GB)
(RS Pts.—Packers 2,024, Vikings 1,875)
(PS Pts.—Vikings 31, Packers 17)
**NFC First-Round Playoff*

GREEN BAY vs. NEW ENGLAND
RS: Series tied, 4-4
PS: Packers lead series, 1-0
1973—Patriots, 33-24 (NE)
1979—Packers, 27-14 (GB)
1985—Patriots, 26-20 (NE)
1988—Packers, 45-3 (Mil)
1994—Patriots, 17-16 (NE)
1996—*Packers, 35-21 (New Orleans)
1997—Packers, 28-10 (NE)
2002—Packers, 28-10 (NE)
2006—Patriots, 35-0 (GB)
(RS Pts.—Packers 188, Patriots 148)
(PS Pts.—Packers 35, Patriots 21)
**Super Bowl XXXI*

GREEN BAY vs. NEW ORLEANS
RS: Packers lead series, 14-7
1968—Packers, 29-7 (Mil)
1971—Saints, 29-21 (Mil)
1972—Packers, 30-20 (NO)
1973—Packers, 30-10 (Mil)
1975—Saints, 20-19 (NO)
1976—Packers, 32-27 (Mil)
1977—Packers, 24-20 (NO)
1978—Packers, 28-17 (Mil)
1979—Packers, 28-19 (Mil)
1981—Packers, 35-7 (NO)
1984—Packers, 23-13 (NO)
1985—Packers, 38-14 (Mil)
1986—Saints, 24-10 (NO)
1987—Saints, 33-24 (NO)
1989—Packers, 35-34 (GB)
1993—Packers, 19-17 (NO)
1995—Packers, 34-23 (NO)
2002—Saints, 35-20 (NO)
2005—Packers, 52-3 (GB)
2006—Saints, 34-27 (GB)
2008—Saints, 51-29 (NO)
(RS Pts.—Packers 587, Saints 457)

GREEN BAY vs. N.Y. GIANTS
RS: Packers lead series, 25-21-2
PS: Packers lead series, 4-2
1928—Giants, 6-0 (GB)
Packers, 7-0 (NY)
1929—Packers, 20-6 (NY)
1930—Packers, 14-7 (GB)
Giants, 13-6 (NY)
1931—Packers, 27-7 (GB)
Packers, 14-10 (NY)
1932—Packers, 13-0 (GB)
Giants, 6-0 (NY)
1933—Giants, 10-7 (Mil)
Giants, 17-6 (NY)
1934—Packers, 20-6 (Mil)
Giants, 17-3 (NY)
1935—Packers, 16-7 (GB)
1936—Packers, 26-14 (NY)
1937—Giants, 10-0 (NY)
1938—Giants, 15-3 (NY)
*Giants, 23-17 (NY)
1939—*Packers, 27-0 (Mil)
1940—Giants, 7-3 (NY)
1942—Tie, 21-21 (NY)
1943—Packers, 35-21 (NY)
1944—Giants, 24-0 (NY)
*Packers, 14-7 (NY)
1945—Packers, 23-14 (NY)
1947—Tie, 24-24 (NY)
1948—Giants, 49-3 (Mil)
1949—Giants, 30-10 (GB)
1952—Packers, 17-3 (NY)

1957—Giants, 31-17 (GB)
1959—Giants, 20-3 (NY)
1961—Packers, 20-17 (Mil)
*Packers, 37-0 (GB)
1962—*Packers, 16-7 (NY)
1967—Packers, 48-21 (NY)
1969—Packers, 20-10 (Mil)
1971—Giants, 42-40 (GB)
1973—Packers, 16-14 (New Haven)
1975—Packers, 40-14 (Mil)
1980—Giants, 27-21 (NY)
1981—Packers, 27-14 (NY)
Packers, 26-24 (Mil)
1982—Packers, 27-19 (NY)
1983—Giants, 27-3 (NY)
1985—Packers, 23-20 (GB)
1986—Giants, 55-24 (NY)
1987—Giants, 20-10 (NY)
1992—Giants, 27-7 (NY)
1995—Packers, 14-6 (GB)
1998—Packers, 37-3 (NY)
2001—Packers, 34-25 (NY)
2004—Giants, 14-7 (GB)
2007—Packers, 35-13 (NY)
**Giants, 23-20 (GB) OT
(RS Pts.—Packers 817, Giants 807)
(PS Pts.—Packers 131, Giants 60)
NFL Championship
***NFC Championship Game*

GREEN BAY vs. N.Y. JETS
RS: Jets lead series, 8-2
1973—Packers, 23-7 (Mil)
1979—Jets, 27-22 (GB)
1981—Jets, 28-3 (NY)
1982—Jets, 15-13 (NY)
1985—Jets, 24-3 (Mil)
1991—Jets, 19-16 (NY) OT
1994—Packers, 17-10 (GB)
2000—Jets, 20-16 (GB)
2002—Jets, 42-17 (NY)
2006—Jets, 38-10 (GB)
(RS Pts.—Jets 230, Packers 140)

GREEN BAY vs. *OAKLAND
RS: Series tied, 5-5
PS: Packers lead series, 1-0
1967—**Packers, 33-14 (Miami)
1972—Raiders, 20-14 (GB)
1976—Raiders, 18-14 (O)
1978—Raiders, 28-3 (GB)
1984—Raiders, 28-7 (LA)
1987—Raiders, 20-0 (GB)
1990—Packers, 29-16 (LA)
1993—Packers, 28-0 (GB)
1999—Packers, 28-24 (GB)
2003—Packers, 41-7 (O)
2007—Packers, 38-7 (GB)
(RS Pts.—Packers 202, Raiders 168)
(PS Pts.—Packers 33, Raiders 14)
**Franchise in Los Angeles from 1982-1994*
***Super Bowl II*

GREEN BAY vs. PHILADELPHIA
RS: Packers lead series, 23-13
PS: Eagles lead series, 2-0
1933—Packers, 35-9 (GB)
Packers, 10-0 (P)
1934—Packers, 19-6 (GB)
1935—Packers, 13-6 (P)
1937—Packers, 37-7 (Mil)
1939—Packers, 23-16 (P)
1940—Packers, 27-20 (GB)
1942—Packers, 7-0 (P)
1946—Packers, 19-7 (P)
1947—Eagles, 28-14 (P)
1951—Packers, 37-24 (GB)
1952—Packers, 12-10 (Mil)
1954—Packers, 37-14 (P)
1958—Packers, 38-35 (GB)
1960—*Eagles, 17-13 (P)
1962—Packers, 49-0 (P)
1968—Packers, 30-13 (GB)
1970—Packers, 30-17 (Mil)
1974—Eagles, 36-14 (P)
1976—Packers, 28-13 (GB)
1978—Eagles, 10-3 (P)
1979—Eagles, 21-10 (GB)
1987—Packers, 16-10 (GB) OT
1990—Eagles, 31-0 (P)
1991—Eagles, 20-3 (GB)
1992—Packers, 27-24 (Mil)
1993—Eagles, 20-17 (GB)
1994—Eagles, 13-7 (P)
1996—Packers, 39-13 (GB)
1997—Eagles, 10-9 (P)
1998—Packers, 24-16 (GB)
2000—Packers, 6-3 (GB)
2003—Eagles, 17-14 (GB)
**Eagles, 20-17 (P) OT
2004—Eagles, 47-17 (P)
2005—Eagles, 19-14 (P)
2006—Eagles, 31-9 (P)
2007—Packers, 16-13 (GB)
(RS Pts.—Packers 710, Eagles 579)
(PS Pts.—Eagles 37, Packers 30)
NFL Championship
***NFC Divisional Playoff*

GREEN BAY vs. *PITTSBURGH
RS: Packers lead series, 18-14
1933—Packers, 47-0 (GB)
1935—Packers, 27-0 (GB)
Packers, 34-14 (P)
1936—Packers, 42-10 (Mil)
1938—Packers, 20-0 (GB)
1940—Packers, 24-3 (Mil)
1941—Packers, 54-7 (P)
1942—Packers, 24-21 (Mil)
1946—Packers, 17-7 (GB)
1947—Steelers, 18-17 (Mil)
1948—Steelers, 38-7 (P)
1949—Steelers, 30-7 (Mil)
1951—Packers, 35-33 (Mil)
Steelers, 28-7 (P)
1953—Steelers, 31-14 (P)
1954—Steelers, 21-20 (GB)
1957—Packers, 27-10 (P)
1960—Packers, 19-13 (P)
1963—Packers, 33-14 (Mil)
1965—Packers, 41-9 (P)
1967—Steelers, 24-17 (GB)
1969—Packers, 38-34 (P)
1970—Packers, 20-12 (P)
1975—Steelers, 16-13 (Mil)
1980—Steelers, 22-20 (P)
1983—Steelers, 25-21 (GB)
1986—Steelers, 27-3 (P)
1992—Packers, 17-3 (GB)
1995—Packers, 24-19 (GB)
1998—Steelers, 27-20 (P)
2005—Steelers, 20-10 (GB)
2009—Steelers, 37-36 (P)
(RS Pts.—Packers 755, Steelers 573)
**Steelers known as Pirates prior to 1940*

GREEN BAY vs. *ST. LOUIS
RS: Rams lead series, 45-42-2
PS: Series tied, 1-1
1937—Packers, 35-10 (C)
Packers, 35-7 (GB)
1938—Packers, 26-17 (GB)
Packers, 28-7 (C)
1939—Rams, 27-24 (GB)
Packers, 7-6 (C)
1940—Packers, 31-14 (GB)
Tie, 13-13 (C)
1941—Packers, 24-7 (Mil)
Packers, 17-14 (C)
1942—Packers, 45-28 (GB)
Packers, 30-12 (C)
1944—Packers, 30-21 (GB)
Packers, 42-7 (C)
1945—Rams, 27-14 (GB)
Rams, 20-7 (C)
1946—Rams, 21-17 (Mil)
Rams, 38-17 (LA)
1947—Packers, 17-14 (Mil)
Packers, 30-10 (LA)
1948—Packers, 16-0 (GB)
Rams, 24-10 (LA)
1949—Rams, 48-7 (GB)
Rams, 35-7 (LA)
1950—Rams, 45-14 (Mil)
Rams, 51-14 (LA)
1951—Rams, 28-0 (Mil)
Rams, 42-14 (LA)
1952—Rams, 30-28 (Mil)
Rams, 45-27 (LA)
1953—Rams, 38-20 (Mil)
Rams, 33-17 (LA)
1954—Packers, 35-17 (Mil)
Rams, 35-27 (LA)
1955—Packers, 30-28 (Mil)
Rams, 31-17 (LA)
1956—Packers, 42-17 (Mil)
Rams, 49-21 (LA)
1957—Rams, 31-27 (Mil)
Rams, 42-17 (LA)
1958—Rams, 20-7 (GB)
Rams, 34-20 (LA)
1959—Rams, 45-6 (Mil)
Packers, 38-20 (LA)
1960—Rams, 33-31 (Mil)
Packers, 35-21 (LA)
1961—Packers, 35-17 (GB)
Packers, 24-17 (LA)
1962—Packers, 41-10 (Mil)
Packers, 20-17 (LA)
1963—Packers, 42-10 (GB)
Packers, 31-14 (LA)
1964—Rams, 27-17 (Mil)
Tie, 24-24 (LA)
1965—Packers, 6-3 (Mil)
Rams, 21-10 (LA)
1966—Packers, 24-13 (GB)
Packers, 27-23 (LA)
1967—Rams, 27-24 (LA)
**Packers, 28-7 (Mil)
1968—Rams, 16-14 (Mil)
1969—Rams, 34-21 (LA)
1970—Rams, 31-21 (GB)
1971—Rams, 30-13 (LA)
1973—Rams, 24-7 (LA)
1974—Packers, 17-6 (Mil)
1975—Rams, 22-5 (LA)
1977—Rams, 24-6 (Mil)

1978—Rams, 31-14 (LA)
1980—Rams, 51-21 (LA)
1981—Rams, 35-23 (LA)
1982—Packers, 35-23 (Mil)
1983—Packers, 27-24 (Mil)
1984—Packers, 31-6 (Mil)
1985—Rams, 34-17 (LA)
1988—Rams, 34-7 (GB)
1989—Rams, 41-38 (LA)
1990—Packers, 36-24 (GB)
1991—Rams, 23-21 (LA)
1992—Packers, 28-13 (GB)
1993—Packers, 36-6 (Mil)
1994—Packers, 24-17 (GB)
1995—Rams, 17-14 (GB)
1996—Packers, 24-9 (StL)
1997—Packers, 17-7 (GB)
2001—***Rams, 45-17 (StL)
2003—Rams, 34-24 (StL)
2004—Packers, 45-17 (GB)
2006—Rams, 23-20 (GB)
2007—Packers, 33-14 (StL)
2009—Packers, 36-17 (StL)
(RS Pts.—Rams 2,072, Packers 2,016)
(PS Pts.—Rams 52, Packers 45)
Franchise in Los Angeles prior to 1995 and in Cleveland prior to 1946
***Conference Championship*
****NFC Divisional Playoff*

GREEN BAY vs. SAN DIEGO
RS: Packers lead series, 8-1
1970—Packers, 22-20 (SD)
1974—Packers, 34-0 (GB)
1978—Packers, 24-3 (SD)
1984—Chargers, 34-28 (GB)
1993—Packers, 20-13 (SD)
1996—Packers, 42-10 (GB)
1999—Packers, 31-3 (SD)
2003—Packers, 38-21 (SD)
2007—Packers, 31-24 (GB)
(RS Pts.—Packers 270, Chargers 128)

GREEN BAY vs. SAN FRANCISCO
RS: Packers lead series, 29-25-1
PS: Packers lead series, 4-1
1950—Packers, 25-21 (GB)
49ers, 30-14 (SF)
1951—49ers, 31-19 (SF)
1952—49ers, 24-14 (SF)
1953—49ers, 37-7 (Mil)
49ers, 48-14 (SF)
1954—49ers, 23-17 (Mil)
49ers, 35-0 (SF)
1955—Packers, 27-21 (Mil)
Packers, 28-7 (SF)
1956—49ers, 17-16 (GB)
49ers, 38-20 (SF)
1957—49ers, 24-14 (Mil)
49ers, 27-20 (SF)
1958—49ers, 33-12 (Mil)
49ers, 48-21 (SF)
1959—Packers, 21-20 (GB)
Packers, 36-14 (SF)
1960—Packers, 41-14 (Mil)
Packers, 13-0 (SF)
1961—Packers, 30-10 (GB)
49ers, 22-21 (SF)
1962—Packers, 31-13 (Mil)
Packers, 31-21 (SF)
1963—Packers, 28-10 (Mil)
Packers, 21-17 (SF)
1964—Packers, 24-14 (Mil)
49ers, 24-14 (SF)
1965—Packers, 27-10 (GB)
Tie, 24-24 (SF)
1966—49ers, 21-20 (SF)
Packers, 20-7 (Mil)
1967—Packers, 13-0 (GB)
1968—49ers, 27-20 (SF)
1969—Packers, 14-7 (Mil)
1970—49ers, 26-10 (SF)
1972—Packers, 34-24 (Mil)
1973—49ers, 20-6 (SF)
1974—49ers, 7-6 (SF)
1976—49ers, 26-14 (GB)
1977—Packers, 16-14 (Mil)
1980—Packers, 23-16 (Mil)
1981—49ers, 13-3 (Mil)
1986—49ers, 31-17 (Mil)
1987—49ers, 23-12 (GB)
1989—Packers, 21-17 (SF)
1990—49ers, 24-20 (GB)
1995—*Packers, 27-17 (SF)
1996—Packers, 23-20 (GB) OT
*Packers, 35-14 (GB)
1997—**Packers, 23-10 (SF)
1998—Packers, 36-22 (GB)
***49ers, 30-27 (SF)
1999—Packers, 20-3 (SF)
2000—Packers, 31-28 (GB)
2001—***Packers, 25-15 (GB)
2002—Packers, 20-14 (SF)
2003—Packers, 20-10 (GB)
2006—Packers, 30-19 (SF)
2009—Packers, 30-24 (GB)
(RS Pts.—49ers 1,120, Packers 1,109)
(PS Pts.—Packers 137, 49ers 86)
**NFC Divisional Playoff*
***NFC Championship*
****NFC First-Round Playoff*

GREEN BAY vs. SEATTLE
RS: Packers lead series, 8-5
PS: Packers lead series, 2-0
1976—Packers, 27-20 (Mil)
1978—Packers, 45-28 (Mil)
1981—Packers, 34-24 (GB)
1984—Seahawks, 30-24 (Mil)
1987—Seahawks, 24-13 (S)
1990—Seahawks, 20-14 (Mil)
1996—Packers, 31-10 (S)
1999—Seahawks, 27-7 (GB)
2003—Packers, 35-13 (GB)
*Packers, 33-27 (GB) OT
2005—Packers, 23-17 (GB)
2006—Seahawks, 34-24 (S)
2007—**Packers, 42-20 (GB)
2008—Packers, 27-17 (S)
2009—Packers, 48-10 (GB)
(RS Pts.—Packers 352, Seahawks 274)
(PS Pts.—Packers 75, Seahawks 47)
**NFC First-Round Playoff*
***NFC Divisional Playoff*

GREEN BAY vs. TAMPA BAY
RS: Packers lead series, 29-21-1
PS: Packers lead series, 1-0
1977—Packers, 13-0 (TB)
1978—Packers, 9-7 (GB)
Packers, 17-7 (TB)
1979—Buccaneers, 21-10 (GB)
Buccaneers, 21-3 (TB)
1980—Tie, 14-14 (TB) OT
Buccaneers, 20-17 (Mil)
1981—Buccaneers, 21-10 (GB)
Buccaneers, 37-3 (TB)
1983—Packers, 55-14 (GB)
Packers, 12-9 (TB) OT
1984—Buccaneers, 30-27 (TB) OT
Packers, 27-14 (GB)
1985—Packers, 21-0 (GB)
Packers, 20-17 (TB)
1986—Packers, 31-7 (Mil)
Packers, 21-7 (TB)
1987—Buccaneers, 23-17 (Mil)
1988—Buccaneers, 13-10 (GB)
Buccaneers, 27-24 (TB)
1989—Buccaneers, 23-21 (GB)
Packers, 17-16 (TB)
1990—Buccaneers, 26-14 (TB)
Packers, 20-10 (Mil)
1991—Packers, 15-13 (GB)
Packers, 27-0 (TB)
1992—Buccaneers, 31-3 (TB)
Packers, 19-14 (Mil)
1993—Packers, 37-14 (TB)
Packers, 13-10 (GB)
1994—Packers, 30-3 (GB)
Packers, 34-19 (TB)
1995—Packers, 35-13 (GB)
Buccaneers, 13-10 (TB) OT
1996—Packers, 34-3 (TB)
Packers, 13-7 (GB)
1997—Packers, 21-16 (GB)
Packers, 17-6 (TB)
*Packers, 21-7 (GB)
1998—Packers, 23-15 (GB)
Buccaneers, 24-22 (TB)
1999—Packers, 26-23 (GB)
Buccaneers, 29-10 (TB)
2000—Buccaneers, 20-15 (TB)
Packers, 17-14 (GB) OT
2001—Buccaneers, 14-10 (TB)
Packers, 21-20 (GB)
2002—Buccaneers, 21-7 (TB)
2003—Packers, 20-13 (TB)
2005—Buccaneers, 17-16 (GB)
2008—Buccaneers, 30-21 (TB)
2009—Buccaneers, 38-28 (TB)
(RS Pts.—Packers 977, Buccaneers 824)
(PS Pts.—Packers 21, Buccaneers 7)
**NFC Divisional Playoff*

GREEN BAY vs. *TENNESSEE
RS: Titans lead series, 6-4
1972—Packers, 23-10 (H)
1977—Oilers, 16-10 (GB)
1980—Oilers, 22-3 (GB)
1983—Packers, 41-38 (H) OT
1986—Oilers, 31-3 (GB)
1992—Packers, 16-14 (H)
1998—Packers, 30-22 (GB)
2001—Titans, 26-20 (T)
2004—Titans, 48-27 (GB)
2008—Titans, 19-16 (T) OT
(RS Pts.—Titans 246, Packers 189)
**Franchise in Houston prior to 1997; known as Oilers prior to 1999*

GREEN BAY vs. *WASHINGTON
RS: Packers lead series, 17-12-1
PS: Series tied, 1-1
1932—Packers, 21-0 (B)
1933—Tie, 7-7 (GB)
Redskins, 20-7 (B)
1934—Packers, 10-0 (B)
1936—Packers, 31-2 (GB)
Packers, 7-3 (B)

**Packers, 21-6 (New York)
1937—Redskins, 14-6 (W)
1939—Packers, 24-14 (Mil)
1941—Packers, 22-17 (W)
1943—Redskins, 33-7 (Mil)
1946—Packers, 20-7 (W)
1947—Packers, 27-10 (Mil)
1948—Redskins, 23-7 (Mil)
1949—Redskins, 30-0 (W)
1950—Packers, 35-21 (Mil)
1952—Packers, 35-20 (Mil)
1958—Redskins, 37-21 (W)
1959—Packers, 21-0 (GB)
1968—Packers, 27-7 (W)
1972—Redskins, 21-16 (W)
***Redskins, 16-3 (W)
1974—Redskins, 17-6 (GB)
1977—Redskins, 10-9 (W)
1979—Redskins, 38-21 (W)
1983—Packers, 48-47 (GB)
1986—Redskins, 16-7 (GB)
1988—Redskins, 20-17 (Mil)
2001—Packers, 37-0 (GB)
2002—Packers, 30-9 (GB)
2004—Packers, 28-14 (W)
2007—Packers, 17-14 (GB)
(RS Pts.—Packers 571, Redskins 471)
(PS Pts.—Packers 24, Redskins 22)
Franchise in Boston prior to 1937 and known as Braves prior to 1933
***NFL Championship*
****NFC Divisional Playoff*

HOUSTON vs. ARIZONA
RS: Series tied, 1-1;
See Arizona vs. Houston
HOUSTON vs. ATLANTA
RS: Series tied, 1-1;
See Atlanta vs. Houston
HOUSTON vs. BALTIMORE
RS: Ravens lead series, 3-0;
See Baltimore vs. Houston
HOUSTON vs. BUFFALO
RS: Bills lead series, 3-2;
See Buffalo vs. Houston
HOUSTON vs. CAROLINA
RS: Texans lead series, 2-0;
See Carolina vs. Houston
HOUSTON vs. CHICAGO
RS: Texans lead series, 2-0;
See Chicago vs. Houston
HOUSTON vs. CINCINNATI
RS: Bengals lead series, 3-2;
See Cincinnati vs. Houston
HOUSTON vs. CLEVELAND
RS: Series tied, 3-3;
See Cleveland vs. Houston
HOUSTON vs. DALLAS
RS: Series tied, 1-1;
See Dallas vs. Houston
HOUSTON vs. DENVER
RS: Series tied, 1-1;
See Denver vs. Houston
HOUSTON vs. DETROIT
RS: Series tied, 1-1;
See Detroit vs. Houston
HOUSTON vs. GREEN BAY
RS: Series tied, 1-1;
See Green Bay vs. Houston
HOUSTON vs. INDIANAPOLIS
RS: Colts lead series, 15-1
2002—Colts, 23-3 (H)
Colts, 19-3 (I)
2003—Colts, 30-21 (I)
Colts, 20-17 (H)
2004—Colts, 49-14 (I)
Colts, 23-14 (H)
2005—Colts, 38-20 (H)
Colts, 31-17 (I)
2006—Colts, 43-24 (I)
Texans, 27-24 (H)
2007—Colts, 30-24 (H)
Colts, 38-15 (I)
2008—Colts, 31-27 (H)
Colts, 33-27 (I)
2009—Colts, 20-17 (I)
Colts, 35-27 (H)
(RS Pts.—Colts 487, Texans 297)
HOUSTON vs. JACKSONVILLE
RS: Series tied, 8-8
2002—Texans, 21-19 (J)
Jaguars, 24-21 (H)
2003—Texans, 24-20 (H)
Jaguars, 27-0 (J)
2004—Texans, 20-6 (H)
Texans, 21-0 (J)
2005—Jaguars, 21-14 (J)
Jaguars, 38-20 (H)
2006—Texans, 27-7 (H)
Texans, 13-10 (J)
2007—Jaguars, 37-17 (J)
Texans, 42-28 (H)
2008—Jaguars, 30-27 (J) OT
Texans, 30-17 (H)
2009—Jaguars, 31-24 (H)
Jaguars, 23-18 (J)
(RS Pts.—Texans 339, Jaguars 338)
HOUSTON vs. KANSAS CITY
RS: Series tied, 2-2
2003—Chiefs, 42-14 (H)
2004—Texans, 24-21 (KC)
2005—Chiefs, 45-17 (H)
2007—Texans, 20-3 (H)
(RS Pts.—Chiefs 111, Texans 75)
HOUSTON vs. MIAMI
RS: Texans lead series, 5-0
2003—Texans, 21-20 (M)
2006—Texans, 17-15 (H)
2007—Texans, 22-19 (H)
2008—Texans, 29-28 (H)
2009—Texans, 27-20 (M)
(RS Pts.—Texans 116, Dolphins 102)
HOUSTON vs. MINNESOTA
RS: Vikings lead series, 2-0
2004—Vikings, 34-28 (H) OT
2008—Vikings, 28-21 (M)
(RS Pts.—Vikings 62, Texans 49)
HOUSTON vs. NEW ENGLAND
RS: Patriots lead series, 2-1
2003—Patriots, 23-20 (H) OT
2006—Patriots, 40-7 (NE)
2009—Texans, 34-27 (H)
(RS Pts.—Patriots 90, Texans 61)
HOUSTON vs. NEW ORLEANS
RS: Series tied, 1-1
2003—Saints, 31-10 (NO)
2007—Texans, 23-10 (H)
(RS Pts.—Saints 41, Texans 33)
HOUSTON vs. N.Y. GIANTS
RS: Series tied, 1-1
2002—Texans, 16-14 (H)
2006—Giants, 14-10 (NY)
(RS Pts.—Giants 28, Texans 26)
HOUSTON vs. N.Y. JETS
RS: Jets lead series, 4-0
2003—Jets, 19-14 (H)
2004—Jets, 29-7 (NY)
2006—Jets, 26-11 (NY)
2009—Jets, 24-7 (H)
(RS Pts.—Jets 98, Texans 39)
HOUSTON vs. OAKLAND
RS: Texans lead series, 4-1
2004—Texans, 30-17 (H)
2006—Texans, 23-14 (O)
2007—Texans, 24-17 (O)
2008—Raiders, 27-16 (O)
2009—Texans, 29-6 (H)
(RS Pts.—Texans 122, Raiders 81)
HOUSTON vs. PHILADELPHIA
RS: Eagles lead series, 2-0
2002—Eagles, 35-17 (P)
2006—Eagles, 24-10 (H)
(RS Pts.—Eagles 59, Texans 27)
HOUSTON vs. PITTSBURGH
RS: Steelers lead series, 2-1
2002—Texans, 24-6 (P)
2005—Steelers, 27-7 (H)
2008—Steelers, 38-17 (P)
(RS Pts.—Steelers 71, Texans 48)
HOUSTON vs. ST. LOUIS
RS: Series tied, 1-1
2005—Rams, 33-27 (H) OT
2009—Texans, 16-13 (StL)
(RS Pts.—Rams 46, Texans 43)
HOUSTON vs. SAN DIEGO
RS: Chargers lead series, 3-0
2002—Chargers, 24-3 (SD)
2004—Chargers, 27-20 (H)
2007—Chargers, 35-10 (SD)
(RS Pts.—Chargers 86, Texans 33)
HOUSTON vs. SAN FRANCISCO
RS: Series tied, 1-1
2005—49ers, 20-17 (SF) OT
2009—Texans, 24-21 (H)
(RS Pts.—Texans 41, 49ers 41)
HOUSTON vs. SEATTLE
RS: Series tied, 1-1
2005—Seahawks, 42-10 (S)
2009—Texans, 34-7 (H)
(RS Pts.—Seahawks 49, Texans 44)
HOUSTON vs. TAMPA BAY
RS: Series tied, 1-1
2003—Buccaneers, 16-3 (TB)
2007—Texans, 28-14 (H)
(RS Pts.—Texans 31, Buccaneers 30)
HOUSTON vs. TENNESSEE
RS: Titans lead series, 12-4
2002—Titans, 17-10 (T)
Titans, 13-3 (H)
2003—Titans, 38-17 (T)
Titans, 27-24 (H)
2004—Texans, 20-10 (T)
Texans, 31-21 (H)
2005—Titans, 34-20 (H)
Titans, 13-10 (T)
2006—Titans, 28-22 (T)
Titans, 26-20 (H) OT
2007—Titans, 38-36 (H)
Titans, 28-20 (T)
2008—Titans, 31-12 (T)
Texans, 13-12 (H)
2009—Texans, 34-31 (T)
Titans, 20-17 (H)

(RS Pts.—Titans 387, Texans 309)

HOUSTON vs. WASHINGTON
RS: Redskins lead series, 2-0
2002—Redskins, 26-10 (W)
2006—Redskins, 31-15 (H)
(RS Pts.—Redskins 57, Texans 25)

INDIANAPOLIS vs. ARIZONA
RS: Colts lead series, 8-6;
See Arizona vs. Indianapolis

INDIANAPOLIS vs. ATLANTA
RS: Colts lead series, 13-1;
See Atlanta vs. Indianapolis

INDIANAPOLIS vs. BALTIMORE
RS: Colts lead series, 7-2
PS: Colts lead series, 2-0;
See Baltimore vs. Indianapolis

INDIANAPOLIS vs. BUFFALO
RS: Bills lead series, 35-30-1;
See Buffalo vs. Indianapolis

INDIANAPOLIS vs. CAROLINA
RS: Panthers lead series, 3-1;
See Carolina vs. Indianapolis

INDIANAPOLIS vs. CHICAGO
RS: Colts lead series, 22-18
PS: Colts lead series, 1-0;
See Chicago vs. Indianapolis

INDIANAPOLIS vs. CINCINNATI
RS: Colts lead series, 15-8
PS: Colts lead series, 1-0;
See Cincinnati vs. Indianapolis

INDIANAPOLIS vs. CLEVELAND
RS: Browns lead series, 13-12
PS: Series tied, 2-2;
See Cleveland vs. Indianapolis

INDIANAPOLIS vs. DALLAS
RS: Cowboys lead series, 8-5
PS: Colts lead series, 1-0;
See Dallas vs. Indianapolis

INDIANAPOLIS vs. DENVER
RS: Broncos lead series, 11-7
PS: Colts lead series, 2-0;
See Denver vs. Indianapolis

INDIANAPOLIS vs. DETROIT
RS: Colts lead series, 20-18-2;
See Detroit vs. Indianapolis

INDIANAPOLIS vs. GREEN BAY
RS: Series tied, 20-20-1
PS: Packers lead series, 1-0;
See Green Bay vs. Indianapolis

INDIANAPOLIS vs. HOUSTON
RS: Colts lead series, 15-1;
See Houston vs. Indianapolis

INDIANAPOLIS vs. JACKSONVILLE
RS: Colts lead series, 14-4
1995—Colts, 41-31 (J)
2000—Colts, 43-14 (I)
2002—Colts, 28-25 (J)
Colts, 20-13 (I)
2003—Colts, 23-13 (I)
Jaguars, 28-23 (J)
2004—Colts, 24-17 (J)
Jaguars, 27-24 (I)
2005—Colts, 10-3 (I)
Colts, 26-18 (J)
2006—Colts, 21-14 (I)
Jaguars, 44-17 (J)
2007—Colts, 29-7 (J)
Colts, 28-25 (I)
2008—Jaguars, 23-21 (I)
Colts, 31-24 (J)
2009—Colts, 14-12 (I)
Colts, 35-31 (J)
(RS Pts.—Colts 458, Jaguars 369)

***INDIANAPOLIS vs. KANSAS CITY**
RS: Colts lead series, 9-7
PS: Colts lead series, 3-0
1970—Chiefs, 44-24 (B)
1972—Chiefs, 24-10 (KC)
1975—Colts, 28-14 (B)
1977—Colts, 17-6 (KC)
1979—Chiefs, 14-0 (KC)
Chiefs, 10-7 (B)
1980—Colts, 31-24 (KC)
Chiefs, 38-28 (B)
1985—Chiefs, 20-7 (KC)
1990—Colts, 23-19 (I)
1995—**Colts, 10-7 (KC)
1996—Colts, 24-19 (KC)
1999—Colts, 25-17 (I)
2000—Colts, 27-14 (KC)
2001—Colts, 35-28 (KC)
2003—**Colts, 38-31 (KC)
2004—Chiefs, 45-35 (KC)
2006—***Colts, 23-8 (I)
2007—Colts, 13-10 (I)
(RS Pts.—Chiefs 346, Colts 334)
(PS Pts.—Colts 71, Chiefs 46)
**Franchise in Baltimore prior to 1984*
***AFC Divisional Playoff*
****AFC First-Round Playoff*

***INDIANAPOLIS vs. MIAMI**
RS: Dolphins lead series, 44-24
PS: Dolphins lead series, 2-0
1970—Colts, 35-0 (B)
Dolphins, 34-17 (M)
1971—Dolphins, 17-14 (M)
Colts, 14-3 (B)
**Dolphins, 21-0 (M)
1972—Dolphins, 23-0 (B)
Dolphins, 16-0 (M)
1973—Dolphins, 44-0 (M)
Colts, 16-3 (B)
1974—Dolphins, 17-7 (M)
Dolphins, 17-16 (B)
1975—Colts, 33-17 (M)
Colts, 10-7 (B) OT
1976—Colts, 28-14 (B)
Colts, 17-16 (M)
1977—Colts, 45-28 (B)
Dolphins, 17-6 (M)
1978—Dolphins, 42-0 (B)
Dolphins, 26-8 (M)
1979—Dolphins, 19-0 (M)
Dolphins, 28-24 (B)
1980—Colts, 30-17 (M)
Dolphins, 24-14 (B)
1981—Dolphins, 31-28 (B)
Dolphins, 27-10 (M)
1982—Dolphins, 24-20 (M)
Dolphins, 34-7 (B)
1983—Dolphins, 21-7 (B)
Dolphins, 37-0 (M)
1984—Dolphins, 44-7 (M)
Dolphins, 35-17 (I)
1985—Dolphins, 30-13 (M)
Dolphins, 34-20 (I)
1986—Dolphins, 30-10 (M)
Dolphins, 17-13 (I)
1987—Dolphins, 23-10 (I)
Colts, 40-21 (M)
1988—Colts, 15-13 (I)
Colts, 31-28 (M)
1989—Dolphins, 19-13 (M)
Colts, 42-13 (I)
1990—Dolphins, 27-7 (I)
Dolphins, 23-17 (M)
1991—Dolphins, 17-6 (M)
Dolphins, 10-6 (I)
1992—Colts, 31-20 (M)
Dolphins, 28-0 (I)
1993—Dolphins, 24-20 (I)
Dolphins, 41-27 (M)
1994—Dolphins, 22-21 (M)
Colts, 10-6 (I)
1995—Colts, 27-24 (M) OT
Colts, 36-28 (I)
1996—Colts, 10-6 (I)
Dolphins, 37-13 (M)
1997—Dolphins, 16-10 (M)
Colts, 41-0 (I)
1998—Dolphins, 24-15 (I)
Dolphins, 27-14 (M)
1999—Dolphins, 34-31 (I)
Colts, 37-34 (M)
2000—Dolphins, 17-14 (I)
Colts, 20-13 (M)
***Dolphins 23-17 (M) OT
2001—Dolphins, 27-24 (I)
Dolphins, 41-6 (M)
2002—Dolphins, 21-13 (I)
2003—Colts, 23-17 (M)
2006—Colts, 27-22 (I)
2009—Colts, 27-23 (M)
(RS Pts.—Dolphins 1,539, Colts 1,170)
(PS Pts.—Dolphins 44, Colts 17)
**Franchise in Baltimore prior to 1984*
***AFC Championship*
****AFC First-Round Playoff*

***INDIANAPOLIS vs. MINNESOTA**
RS: Colts lead series, 14-7-1
PS: Colts lead series, 1-0
1961—Colts, 34-33 (B)
Vikings, 28-20 (M)
1962—Colts, 34-7 (M)
Colts, 42-17 (B)
1963—Colts, 37-34 (M)
Colts, 41-10 (B)
1964—Vikings, 34-24 (M)
Colts, 17-14 (B)
1965—Colts, 35-16 (B)
Colts, 41-21 (M)
1966—Colts, 38-23 (M)
Colts, 20-17 (B)
1967—Tie, 20-20 (M)
1968—Colts, 21-9 (B)
**Colts, 24-14 (B)
1969—Vikings, 52-14 (M)
1971—Vikings, 10-3 (M)
1982—Vikings, 13-10 (M)
1988—Vikings, 12-3 (M)
1997—Vikings, 39-28 (M)
2000—Colts, 31-10 (I)
2004—Colts, 31-28 (I)
2008—Colts, 18-15 (M)
(RS Pts.—Colts 562, Vikings 462)
(PS Pts.—Colts 24, Vikings 14)
**Franchise in Baltimore prior to 1984*
***Conference Championship*

***INDIANAPOLIS vs. **NEW ENGLAND**
RS: Patriots lead series, 42-28
PS: Patriots lead series, 2-1
1970—Colts, 14-6 (Bos)

Colts, 27-3 (Balt)
1971—Colts, 23-3 (NE)
Patriots, 21-17 (Balt)
1972—Colts, 24-17 (NE)
Colts, 31-0 (Balt)
1973—Patriots, 24-16 (NE)
Colts, 18-13 (Balt)
1974—Patriots, 42-3 (NE)
Patriots, 27-17 (Balt)
1975—Patriots, 21-10 (NE)
Colts, 34-21 (Balt)
1976—Colts, 27-13 (NE)
Patriots, 21-14 (Balt)
1977—Patriots, 17-3 (NE)
Colts, 30-24 (Balt)
1978—Colts, 34-27 (NE)
Patriots, 35-14 (Balt)
1979—Colts, 31-26 (Balt)
Patriots, 50-21 (NE)
1980—Patriots, 37-21 (Balt)
Patriots, 47-21 (NE)
1981—Colts, 29-28 (NE)
Colts, 23-21 (Balt)
1982—Patriots, 24-13 (Balt)
1983—Colts, 29-23 (NE) OT
Colts, 12-7 (Balt)
1984—Patriots, 50-17 (I)
Patriots, 16-10 (NE)
1985—Patriots, 34-15 (NE)
Patriots, 38-31 (I)
1986—Patriots, 33-3 (NE)
Patriots, 30-21 (I)
1987—Colts, 30-16 (I)
Patriots, 24-0 (NE)
1988—Patriots, 21-17 (NE)
Colts, 24-21 (I)
1989—Patriots, 23-20 (I) OT
Patriots, 22-16 (NE)
1990—Patriots, 16-14 (I)
Colts, 13-10 (NE)
1991—Patriots, 16-7 (I)
Patriots, 23-17 (NE) OT
1992—Patriots, 37-34 (I) OT
Colts, 6-0 (NE)
1993—Colts, 9-6 (I)
Patriots, 38-0 (NE)
1994—Patriots, 12-10 (I)
Patriots, 28-13 (NE)
1995—Colts, 24-10 (NE)
Colts, 10-7 (I)
1996—Patriots, 27-9 (I)
Patriots, 27-13 (NE)
1997—Patriots, 31-6 (I)
Patriots, 20-17 (NE)
1998—Patriots, 29-6 (NE)
Patriots, 21-16 (I)
1999—Patriots, 31-28 (NE)
Colts, 20-15 (I)
2000—Patriots, 24-16 (NE)
Colts, 30-23 (I)
2001—Patriots, 44-13 (NE)
Patriots, 38-17 (I)
2003—Patriots, 38-34 (I)
***Patriots, 24-14 (NE)
2004—Patriots, 27-24 (NE)
****Patriots, 20-3 (NE)
2005—Colts, 40-21 (NE)
2006—Colts, 27-20 (NE)
***Colts, 38-34 (I)
2007—Patriots, 24-20 (I)
2008—Colts, 18-15 (I)
2009—Colts, 35-34 (I)
(RS Pts.—Patriots 1,638, Colts 1,306)
(PS Pts.—Patriots 78, Colts 55)
Franchise in Baltimore prior to 1984
***Franchise in Boston prior to 1971*
****AFC Championship*
*****AFC Divisional Playoff*

***INDIANAPOLIS vs. NEW ORLEANS**
RS: Series tied, 5-5
PS: Saints lead series, 1-0
1967—Colts, 30-10 (B)
1969—Colts, 30-10 (NO)
1973—Colts, 14-10 (B)
1986—Saints, 17-14 (I)
1989—Saints, 41-6 (NO)
1995—Saints, 17-14 (NO)
1998—Saints, 19-13 (I) OT
2001—Saints, 34-20 (NO)
2003—Colts, 55-21 (NO)
2007—Colts, 41-10 (I)
2009—**Saints 31-17 (South Florida)
(RS Pts.—Colts 237, Saints 189)
(PS Pts.—Saints 31, Colts 17)
Franchise in Baltimore prior to 1984
***Super Bowl XLIV*

***INDIANAPOLIS vs. N.Y. GIANTS**
RS: Colts lead series, 7-6
PS: Colts lead series, 2-0
1954—Colts, 20-14 (B)
1955—Giants, 17-7 (NY)
1958—Giants, 24-21 (NY)
**Colts, 23-17 (NY) OT
1959—**Colts, 31-16 (B)
1963—Giants, 37-28 (B)
1968—Colts, 26-0 (NY)
1971—Colts, 31-7 (NY)
1975—Colts, 21-0 (NY)
1979—Colts, 31-7 (NY)
1990—Giants, 24-7 (I)
1993—Giants, 20-6 (NY)
1999—Colts, 27-19 (NY)
2002—Giants, 44-27 (I)
2006—Colts, 26-21 (NY)
(RS Pts.—Colts 278, Giants 234)
(PS Pts.—Colts 54, Giants 33)
Franchise in Baltimore prior to 1984
***NFL Championship*

***INDIANAPOLIS vs. N.Y. JETS**
RS: Colts lead series, 40-26
PS: Jets lead series, 2-1
1968—**Jets 16-7 (Miami)
1970—Colts, 29-22 (NY)
Colts, 35-20 (B)
1971—Colts, 22-0 (B)
Colts, 14-13 (NY)
1972—Jets, 44-34 (B)
Jets, 24-20 (NY)
1973—Jets, 34-10 (B)
Jets, 20-17 (NY)
1974—Colts, 35-20 (NY)
Jets, 45-38 (B)
1975—Colts, 45-28 (NY)
Colts, 52-19 (B)
1976—Colts, 20-0 (NY)
Colts, 33-16 (B)
1977—Colts, 20-12 (NY)
Colts, 33-12 (B)
1978—Jets, 33-10 (B)
Jets, 24-16 (NY)
1979—Colts, 10-8 (B)
Jets, 30-17 (NY)
1980—Colts, 17-14 (NY)
Colts, 35-21 (B)
1981—Jets, 41-14 (B)
Jets, 25-0 (NY)
1982—Jets, 37-0 (NY)
1983—Colts, 17-14 (NY)
Jets, 10-6 (B)
1984—Jets, 23-14 (I)
Colts, 9-5 (NY)
1985—Jets, 25-20 (NY)
Jets, 35-17 (I)
1986—Jets, 26-7 (I)
Jets, 31-16 (NY)
1987—Colts, 6-0 (I)
Colts, 19-14 (NY)
1988—Colts, 38-14 (I)
Jets, 34-16 (NY)
1989—Colts, 17-10 (NY)
Colts, 27-10 (I)
1990—Colts, 17-14 (I)
Colts, 29-21 (NY)
1991—Jets, 17-6 (I)
Colts, 28-27 (NY)
1992—Colts, 6-3 (I) OT
Colts, 10-6 (NY)
1993—Jets, 31-17 (I)
Colts, 9-6 (NY)
1994—Jets, 16-6 (NY)
Colts, 28-25 (I)
1995—Colts, 27-24 (NY) OT
Colts, 17-10 (I)
1996—Colts, 21-7 (NY)
Colts, 34-29 (I)
1997—Jets, 16-12 (I)
Colts, 22-14 (NY)
1998—Jets, 44-6 (NY)
Colts, 24-23 (I)
1999—Colts, 16-13 (NY)
Colts, 13-6 (I)
2000—Colts, 23-15 (I)
Jets, 27-17 (NY)
2001—Colts, 45-24 (NY)
Jets, 29-28 (I)
2002—***Jets, 41-0 (NY)
2003—Colts, 38-31 (I)
2006—Colts, 31-28 (NY)
2009—Jets, 29-15 (I)
****Colts, 30-17 (I)
(RS Pts.—Colts 1,350, Jets 1,348)
(PS Pts.—Jets 74, Colts 37)
Franchise in Baltimore prior to 1984
***Super Bowl III*
****AFC First-Round Playoff*
*****AFC Championship*

***INDIANAPOLIS vs. **OAKLAND**
RS: Raiders lead series, 7-4
PS: Series tied, 1-1
1970—***Colts, 27-17 (B)
1971—Colts, 37-14 (O)
1973—Raiders, 34-21 (B)
1975—Raiders, 31-20 (B)
1977—****Raiders, 37-31 (B) OT
1984—Raiders, 21-7 (LA)
1986—Colts, 30-24 (LA)
1991—Raiders, 16-0 (LA)
1995—Raiders, 30-17 (O)
2000—Raiders, 38-31 (I)
2001—Raiders, 23-18 (I)
2004—Colts, 35-14 (I)
2007—Colts, 21-14 (O)
(RS Pts.—Raiders 259, Colts 237)

(PS Pts.—Colts 58, Raiders 54)
Franchise in Baltimore prior to 1984
***Franchise in Los Angeles from 1982-1994*
****AFC Championship*
*****AFC Divisional Playoff*

***INDIANAPOLIS vs. PHILADELPHIA**
RS: Colts lead series, 10-6
1953—Eagles, 45-14 (P)
1965—Colts, 34-24 (B)
1967—Colts, 38-6 (P)
1969—Colts, 24-20 (B)
1970—Colts, 29-10 (B)
1974—Eagles, 30-10 (P)
1978—Eagles, 17-14 (B)
1981—Eagles, 38-13 (P)
1983—Colts, 22-21 (P)
1984—Eagles, 16-7 (P)
1990—Colts, 24-23 (P)
1993—Eagles, 20-10 (I)
1996—Colts, 37-10 (I)
1999—Colts, 44-17 (P)
2002—Colts, 35-13 (P)
2006—Colts, 45-21 (I)
(RS Pts.—Colts 400, Eagles 331)
**Franchise in Baltimore prior to 1984*

***INDIANAPOLIS vs. PITTSBURGH**
RS: Steelers lead series, 13-6
PS: Steelers lead series, 5-0
1957—Steelers, 19-13 (B)
1968—Colts, 41-7 (P)
1971—Colts, 34-21 (B)
1974—Steelers, 30-0 (P)
1975—**Steelers, 28-10 (P)
1976—**Steelers, 40-14 (B)
1977—Colts, 31-21 (B)
1978—Steelers, 35-13 (P)
1979—Steelers, 17-13 (P)
1980—Steelers, 20-17 (B)
1983—Steelers, 24-13 (B)
1984—Colts, 17-16 (I)
1985—Steelers, 45-3 (P)
1987—Steelers, 21-7 (P)
1991—Steelers, 21-3 (I)
1992—Steelers, 30-14 (P)
1994—Steelers, 31-21 (P)
1995—***Steelers, 20-16 (P)
1996—****Steelers, 42-14 (P)
1997—Steelers, 24-22 (P)
2002—Steelers, 28-10 (P)
2005—Colts, 26-7 (I)
**Steelers, 21-18 (I)
2008—Colts, 24-20 (P)
(RS Pts.—Steelers 437, Colts 322)
(PS Pts.—Steelers 151, Colts 72)
**Franchise in Baltimore prior to 1984*
***AFC Divisional Playoff*
****AFC Championship*
*****AFC First-Round Playoff*

***INDIANAPOLIS vs. **ST. LOUIS**
RS: Colts lead series, 23-17-2
1953—Rams, 21-13 (B)
Rams, 45-2 (LA)
1954—Rams, 48-0 (B)
Colts, 22-21 (LA)
1955—Tie, 17-17 (B)
Rams, 20-14 (LA)
1956—Colts, 56-21 (B)
Rams, 31-7 (LA)
1957—Colts, 31-14 (B)
Rams, 37-21 (LA)
1958—Colts, 34-7 (B)
Rams, 30-28 (LA)
1959—Colts, 35-21 (B)
Colts, 45-26 (LA)
1960—Colts, 31-17 (B)
Rams, 10-3 (LA)
1961—Colts, 27-24 (B)
Rams, 34-17 (LA)
1962—Colts, 30-27 (B)
Colts, 14-2 (LA)
1963—Rams, 17-16 (LA)
Colts, 19-16 (B)
1964—Colts, 35-20 (B)
Colts, 24-7 (LA)
1965—Colts, 35-20 (B)
Colts, 20-17 (LA)
1966—Colts, 17-3 (LA)
Rams, 23-7 (B)
1967—Tie, 24-24 (B)
Rams, 34-10 (LA)
1968—Colts, 27-10 (B)
Colts, 28-24 (LA)
1969—Rams, 27-20 (B)
Colts, 13-7 (LA)
1971—Colts, 24-17 (B)
1975—Rams, 24-13 (LA)
1986—Rams, 24-7 (I)
1989—Rams, 31-17 (LA)
1995—Colts, 21-18 (I)
2001—Rams, 42-17 (StL)
2005—Colts, 45-28 (I)
2009—Colts, 42-6 (StL)
(RS Pts.—Colts 928, Rams 912)
**Franchise in Baltimore prior to 1984*
***Franchise in Los Angeles prior to 1995*

***INDIANAPOLIS vs. SAN DIEGO**
RS: Chargers lead series, 14-9
PS: Chargers lead series, 2-1
1970—Colts, 16-14 (SD)
1972—Chargers, 23-20 (B)
1976—Colts, 37-21 (SD)
1981—Chargers, 43-14 (B)
1982—Chargers, 44-26 (SD)
1984—Chargers, 38-10 (I)
1986—Chargers, 17-3 (I)
1987—Chargers, 16-13 (I)
Colts, 20-7 (SD)
1988—Colts, 16-0 (SD)
1989—Colts, 10-6 (I)
1992—Chargers, 34-14 (I)
Chargers, 26-0 (SD)
1993—Chargers, 31-0 (I)
1995—Chargers, 27-24 (I)
**Colts, 35-20 (SD)
1996—Chargers, 26-19 (I)
1997—Chargers, 35-19 (SD)
1998—Colts, 17-12 (I)
1999—Colts, 27-19 (SD)
2004—Colts, 34-31 (I) OT
2005—Chargers, 26-17 (I)
2007—Chargers, 23-21 (SD)
***Chargers, 28-24 (I)
2008—Colts, 23-20 (SD)
**Chargers, 23-17 (SD) OT
(RS Pts.—Chargers 539, Colts 400)
(PS Pts.—Colts 76, Chargers 71)
**Franchise in Baltimore prior to 1984*
***AFC First-Round Playoff*
****AFC Divisional Playoff*

***INDIANAPOLIS vs. SAN FRANCISCO**
RS: Colts lead series, 24-18
1953—49ers, 38-21 (B)
49ers, 45-14 (SF)
1954—Colts, 17-13 (B)
49ers, 10-7 (SF)
1955—Colts, 26-14 (B)
49ers, 35-24 (SF)
1956—49ers, 20-17 (B)
49ers, 30-17 (SF)
1957—Colts, 27-21 (B)
49ers, 17-13 (SF)
1958—Colts, 35-27 (B)
49ers, 21-12 (SF)
1959—Colts, 45-14 (B)
Colts, 34-14 (SF)
1960—49ers, 30-22 (B)
49ers, 34-10 (SF)
1961—Colts, 20-17 (B)
Colts, 27-24 (SF)
1962—49ers, 21-13 (B)
Colts, 22-3 (SF)
1963—Colts, 20-14 (SF)
Colts, 20-3 (B)
1964—Colts, 37-7 (B)
Colts, 14-3 (SF)
1965—Colts, 27-24 (B)
Colts, 34-28 (SF)
1966—Colts, 36-14 (B)
Colts, 30-14 (SF)
1967—Colts, 41-7 (B)
Colts, 26-9 (SF)
1968—Colts, 27-10 (B)
Colts, 42-14 (SF)
1969—49ers, 24-21 (B)
49ers, 20-17 (SF)
1972—49ers, 24-21 (SF)
1986—49ers, 35-14 (SF)
1989—49ers, 30-24 (I)
1995—Colts, 18-17 (I)
1998—49ers, 34-31 (SF)
2001—49ers, 40-21 (I)
2005—Colts, 28-3 (SF)
2009—Colts, 18-14 (I)
(RS Pts.—Colts 990, 49ers 836)
**Franchise in Baltimore prior to 1984*

***INDIANAPOLIS vs. SEATTLE**
RS: Colts lead series, 6-4
1977—Colts, 29-14 (S)
1978—Colts, 17-14 (S)
1991—Seahawks, 31-3 (S)
1994—Colts, 17-15 (I)
Colts, 31-19 (S)
1997—Seahawks, 31-3 (I)
1998—Seahawks, 27-23 (S)
2000—Colts, 37-24 (S)
2005—Seahawks, 28-13 (S)
2009—Colts, 34-17 (I)
(RS Pts.—Seahawks 220, Colts 207)
**Franchise in Baltimore prior to 1984*

***INDIANAPOLIS vs. TAMPA BAY**
RS: Colts lead series, 7-4
1976—Colts, 42-17 (B)
1979—Buccaneers, 29-26 (B) OT
1985—Colts, 31-23 (TB)
1987—Colts, 24-6 (I)
1988—Colts, 35-31 (I)
1991—Buccaneers, 17-3 (TB)
1992—Colts, 24-14 (TB)
1994—Buccaneers, 24-10 (TB)
1997—Buccaneers, 31-28 (I)
2003—Colts, 38-35 (TB) OT
2007—Colts, 33-14 (I)

(RS Pts.—Colts 294, Buccaneers 241)
Franchise in Baltimore prior to 1984

***INDIANAPOLIS vs. **TENNESSEE**
RS: Colts lead series, 18-12
PS: Titans lead series, 1-0
1970—Colts, 24-20 (H)
1973—Oilers, 31-27 (B)
1976—Colts, 38-14 (B)
1979—Oilers, 28-16 (B)
1980—Oilers, 21-16 (H)
1983—Colts, 20-10 (B)
1984—Colts, 35-21 (H)
1985—Colts, 34-16 (I)
1986—Oilers, 31-17 (H)
1987—Colts, 51-27 (I)
1988—Oilers, 17-14 (I) OT
1990—Oilers, 24-10 (H)
1992—Oilers, 20-10 (I)
1994—Colts, 45-21 (I)
1999—***Titans, 19-16 (I)
2002—Titans, 23-15 (I)
Titans, 27-17 (T)
2003—Colts, 33-7 (I)
Colts, 29-27 (T)
2004—Colts, 31-17 (T)
Colts, 51-24 (I)
2005—Colts, 31-10 (T)
Colts, 35-3 (I)
2006—Colts, 14-13 (I)
Titans, 20-17 (T)
2007—Colts, 22-20 (T)
Titans, 16-10 (I)
2008—Titans, 31-21 (T)
Colts, 23-0 (I)
2009—Colts, 31-9 (T)
Colts, 27-17 (I)
(RS Pts.—Colts 764, Titans 565)
(PS Pts.—Titans 19, Colts 16)
**Franchise in Baltimore prior to 1984*
***Franchise in Houston prior to 1997; known as Oilers prior to 1999*
****AFC Divisional Playoff*

***INDIANAPOLIS vs. WASHINGTON**
RS: Colts lead series, 18-10
1953—Colts, 27-17 (B)
1954—Redskins, 24-21 (W)
1955—Redskins, 14-13 (B)
1956—Colts, 19-17 (B)
1957—Colts, 21-17 (W)
1958—Colts, 35-10 (B)
1959—Redskins, 27-24 (W)
1960—Colts, 20-0 (B)
1961—Colts, 27-6 (W)
1962—Colts, 34-21 (B)
1963—Colts, 36-20 (W)
1964—Colts, 45-17 (B)
1965—Colts, 38-7 (W)
1966—Colts, 37-10 (B)
1967—Colts, 17-13 (W)
1969—Colts, 41-17 (B)
1973—Redskins, 22-14 (W)
1977—Colts, 10-3 (B)
1978—Colts, 21-17 (B)
1981—Redskins, 38-14 (W)
1984—Redskins, 35-7 (I)
1990—Colts, 35-28 (I)
1993—Redskins, 30-24 (W)
1994—Redskins, 41-27 (I)
1996—Redskins, 31-16 (W)
1999—Colts, 24-21 (I)
2002—Redskins, 26-21 (W)
2006—Colts, 36-22 (I)
(RS Pts.—Colts 704, Redskins 551)
**Franchise in Baltimore prior to 1984*

JACKSONVILLE vs. ARIZONA
RS: Jaguars lead series, 2-1;
See Arizona vs. Jacksonville

JACKSONVILLE vs. ATLANTA
RS: Jaguars lead series, 3-1;
See Atlanta vs. Jacksonville

JACKSONVILLE vs. BALTIMORE
RS: Jaguars lead series, 9-7;
See Baltimore vs. Jacksonville

JACKSONVILLE vs. BUFFALO
RS: Bills lead series, 5-4
PS: Jaguars lead series, 1-0;
See Buffalo vs. Jacksonville

JACKSONVILLE vs. CAROLINA
RS: Jaguars lead series, 3-1;
See Carolina vs. Jacksonville

JACKSONVILLE vs. CHICAGO
RS: Bears lead series, 3-2;
See Chicago vs. Jacksonville

JACKSONVILLE vs. CINCINNATI
RS: Jaguars lead series, 11-6;
See Cincinnati vs. Jacksonville

JACKSONVILLE vs. CLEVELAND
RS: Jaguars lead series, 8-4;
See Cleveland vs. Jacksonville

JACKSONVILLE vs. DALLAS
RS: Series tied, 2-2;
See Dallas vs. Jacksonville

JACKSONVILLE vs. DENVER
RS: Jaguars lead series, 4-3
PS: Series tied, 1-1;
See Denver vs. Jacksonville

JACKSONVILLE vs. DETROIT
RS: Jaguars lead series, 3-1;
See Detroit vs. Jacksonville

JACKSONVILLE vs. GREEN BAY
RS: Series tied, 2-2;
See Green Bay vs. Jacksonville

JACKSONVILLE vs. HOUSTON
RS: Series tied, 8-8;
See Houston vs. Jacksonville

JACKSONVILLE vs. INDIANAPOLIS
RS: Colts lead series, 14-4;
See Indianapolis vs. Jacksonville

JACKSONVILLE vs. KANSAS CITY
RS: Jaguars lead series, 6-2
1997—Jaguars, 24-10 (J)
1998—Jaguars, 21-16 (J)
2001—Chiefs, 30-26 (J)
2002—Jaguars, 23-16 (KC)
2004—Jaguars, 22-16 (J)
2006—Chiefs, 35-30 (KC)
2007—Jaguars, 17-7 (KC)
2009—Jaguars, 24-21 (KC)
(RS Pts.—Jaguars 187, Chiefs 151)

JACKSONVILLE vs. MIAMI
RS: Series tied, 2-2
PS: Jaguars lead series, 1-0
1998—Jaguars, 28-21 (J)
1999—*Jaguars, 62-7 (J)
2003—Dolphins, 24-10 (J)
2006—Jaguars, 24-10 (M)
2009—Dolphins, 14-10 (J)
(RS Pts.—Jaguars 72, Dolphins 69)
(PS Pts.—Jaguars 62, Dolphins 7)
**AFC Divisional Playoff*

JACKSONVILLE vs. MINNESOTA
RS: Vikings lead series, 3-1
1998—Vikings, 50-10 (M)
2001—Jaguars, 33-3 (M)
2004—Vikings, 27-16 (M)
2008—Vikings, 30-12 (J)
(RS Pts.—Vikings 110, Jaguars 71)

JACKSONVILLE vs. NEW ENGLAND
RS: Patriots lead series, 5-0
PS: Patriots lead series, 3-1
1996—Patriots, 28-25 (NE) OT
*Patriots, 20-6 (NE)
1997—Patriots, 26-20 (J)
1998—**Jaguars, 25-10 (J)
2003—Patriots, 27-13 (NE)
2005—**Patriots, 28-3 (NE)
2006—Patriots, 24-21 (J)
2007—***Patriots, 31-20 (NE)
2009—Patriots, 35-7 (NE)
(RS Pts.—Patriots 140, Jaguars 86)
(PS Pts.—Patriots 89, Jaguars 54)
**AFC Championship*
***AFC First-Round Playoff*
****AFC Divisional Playoff*

JACKSONVILLE vs. NEW ORLEANS
RS: Series tied, 2-2
1996—Saints, 17-13 (NO)
1999—Jaguars, 41-23 (J)
2003—Jaguars, 20-19 (J)
2007—Saints, 41-24 (NO)
(RS Pts.—Saints 100, Jaguars 98)

JACKSONVILLE vs. N.Y. GIANTS
RS: Series tied, 2-2
1997—Jaguars, 40-13 (J)
2000—Giants, 28-25 (NY)
2002—Giants, 24-17 (NY)
2006—Jaguars, 26-10 (J)
(RS Pts.—Jaguars 108, Giants 75)

JACKSONVILLE vs. N.Y. JETS
RS: Jaguars lead series, 6-2
PS: Jets lead series, 1-0
1995—Jets, 27-10 (NY)
1996—Jaguars, 21-17 (J)
1998—*Jets, 34-24 (NY)
1999—Jaguars, 16-6 (NY)
2002—Jaguars, 28-3 (J)
2003—Jets, 13-10 (NY)
2005—Jaguars, 26-20 (NY) OT
2006—Jaguars, 41-0 (J)
2009—Jaguars, 24-22 (NY)
(RS Pts.—Jaguars 176, Jets 108)
(PS Pts.—Jets 34, Jaguars 24)
**AFC Divisional Playoff*

JACKSONVILLE vs. OAKLAND
RS: Jaguars lead series, 3-1
1996—Raiders, 17-3 (O)
1997—Jaguars, 20-9 (O)
2004—Jaguars, 13-6 (O)
2007—Jaguars, 49-11 (J)
(RS Pts.—Jaguars 85, Raiders 43)

JACKSONVILLE vs. PHILADELPHIA
RS: Jaguars lead series, 3-0
1997—Jaguars, 38-21 (J)
2002—Jaguars, 28-25 (J)
2006—Jaguars, 13-6 (P)
(RS Pts.—Jaguars 79, Eagles 52)

JACKSONVILLE vs. PITTSBURGH
RS: Jaguars lead series, 11-9
PS: Jaguars lead series, 1-0
1995—Jaguars, 20-16 (J)
Steelers, 24-7 (P)

1996—Jaguars, 24-9 (J)
Steelers, 28-3 (P)
1997—Jaguars, 30-21 (J)
Steelers, 23-17 (P) OT
1998—Steelers, 30-15 (P)
Jaguars, 21-3 (J)
1999—Jaguars, 17-3 (P)
Jaguars, 20-6 (J)
2000—Steelers, 24-13 (J)
Jaguars, 34-24 (P)
2001—Jaguars, 21-3 (J)
Steelers, 20-7 (P)
2002—Steelers, 25-23 (J)
2004—Steelers, 17-16 (J)
2005—Jaguars, 23-17 (P) OT
2006—Jaguars, 9-0 (J)
2007—Jaguars, 29-22 (P)
*Jaguars, 31-29 (P)
2008—Steelers, 26-21 (J)
(RS Pts.—Jaguars 370, Steelers 341)
(PS Pts.—Jaguars 31, Steelers 29)
AFC First-Round Playoff

JACKSONVILLE vs. ST. LOUIS
RS: Rams lead series, 2-1
1996—Rams, 17-14 (StL)
2005—Rams, 24-21 (StL)
2009—Jaguars, 23-20 (J) OT
(RS Pts.—Rams 61, Jaguars 58)

JACKSONVILLE vs. SAN DIEGO
RS: Jaguars lead series, 2-1
2003—Jaguars, 27-21 (J)
2004—Chargers, 34-21 (SD)
2007—Jaguars, 24-17 (J)
(RS Pts.—Chargers 72, Jaguars 72)

JACKSONVILLE vs. SAN FRANCISCO
RS: Jaguars lead series, 2-1
1999—Jaguars, 41-3 (J)
2005—Jaguars, 10-9 (J)
2009—49ers, 20-3 (SF)
(RS Pts.—Jaguars 54, 49ers 32)

JACKSONVILLE vs. SEATTLE
RS: Seahawks lead series, 4-2
1995—Seahawks, 47-30 (J)
1996—Jaguars, 20-13 (J)
2000—Seahawks, 28-21 (J)
2001—Seahawks, 24-15 (S)
2005—Jaguars, 26-14 (J)
2009—Seahawks, 41-0 (S)
(RS Pts.—Seahawks 167, Jaguars 112)

JACKSONVILLE vs. TAMPA BAY
RS: Jaguars lead series, 3-1
1995—Buccaneers, 17-16 (TB)
1998—Jaguars, 29-24 (J)
2003—Jaguars, 17-10 (J)
2007—Jaguars, 24-23 (TB)
(RS Pts.—Jaguars 86, Buccaneers 74)

JACKSONVILLE vs. *TENNESSEE
RS: Titans lead series, 17-13
PS: Titans lead, 1-0
1995—Oilers, 10-3 (J)
Jaguars, 17-16 (H)
1996—Oilers, 34-27 (J)
Jaguars, 23-17 (H)
1997—Jaguars, 30-24 (T)
Jaguars, 17-9 (J)
1998—Jaguars, 27-22 (T)
Oilers, 16-13 (J)
1999—Titans, 20-19 (J)
Titans, 41-14 (T)
**Titans, 33-14 (J)
2000—Titans, 27-13 (T)
Jaguars, 16-13 (J)
2001—Jaguars, 13-6 (J)
Titans, 28-24 (T)
2002—Titans, 23-14 (T)
Titans, 28-10 (J)
2003—Titans, 30-17 (J)
Titans, 10-3 (T)
2004—Jaguars, 15-12 (T)
Titans, 18-15 (J)
2005—Jaguars, 31-28 (T)
Jaguars, 40-13 (J)
2006—Jaguars, 37-7 (J)
Titans, 24-17 (T)
2007—Titans, 13-10 (J)
Jaguars, 28-13 (T)
2008—Titans, 17-10 (T)
Titans, 24-14 (J)
2009—Jaguars, 37-17 (J)
Titans, 30-13 (T)
(RS Pts.—Titans 590, Jaguars 567)
(PS Pts.—Titans 33, Jaguars 14)
Franchise in Houston prior to 1997; known as Oilers prior to 1999
***AFC Championship*

JACKSONVILLE vs. WASHINGTON
RS: Redskins lead series, 3-1
1997—Redskins, 24-12 (W)
2000—Redskins, 35-16 (J)
2002—Jaguars, 26-7 (J)
2006—Redskins, 36-30 (W) OT
(RS Pts.—Redskins 102, Jaguars 84)

KANSAS CITY vs. ARIZONA
RS: Chiefs lead series, 7-2-1;
See Arizona vs. Kansas City

KANSAS CITY vs. ATLANTA
RS: Chiefs lead series, 5-2;
See Atlanta vs. Kansas City

KANSAS CITY vs. BALTIMORE
RS: Chiefs lead series, 3-2;
See Baltimore vs. Kansas City

KANSAS CITY vs. BUFFALO
RS: Bills lead series, 21-16-1
PS: Bills lead series, 2-1;
See Buffalo vs. Kansas City

KANSAS CITY vs. CAROLINA
RS: Series tied, 2-2;
See Carolina vs. Kansas City

KANSAS CITY vs. CHICAGO
RS: Bears lead series, 6-4;
See Chicago vs. Kansas City

KANSAS CITY vs. CINCINNATI
RS: Series tied, 13-13;
See Cincinnati vs. Kansas City

KANSAS CITY vs. CLEVELAND
RS: Browns lead series, 10-9-2;
See Cleveland vs. Kansas City

KANSAS CITY vs. DALLAS
RS: Cowboys lead series, 6-3;
See Dallas vs. Kansas City

KANSAS CITY vs. DENVER
RS: Chiefs lead series, 54-45
PS: Broncos lead series, 1-0;
See Denver vs. Kansas City

KANSAS CITY vs. DETROIT
RS: Chiefs lead series, 7-4;
See Detroit vs. Kansas City

KANSAS CITY vs. GREEN BAY
RS: Chiefs lead series, 6-2-1
PS: Packers lead series, 1-0;
See Green Bay vs. Kansas City

KANSAS CITY vs. HOUSTON
RS: Series tied, 2-2;
See Houston vs. Kansas City

KANSAS CITY vs. INDIANAPOLIS
RS: Colts lead series, 9-7
PS: Colts lead series, 3-0;
See Indianapolis vs. Kansas City

KANSAS CITY vs. JACKSONVILLE
RS: Jaguars lead series, 6-2;
See Jacksonville vs. Kansas City

KANSAS CITY vs. MIAMI
RS: Series tied, 12-12
PS: Dolphins lead series, 3-0
1966—Chiefs, 34-16 (KC)
Chiefs, 19-18 (M)
1967—Chiefs, 24-0 (M)
Chiefs, 41-0 (KC)
1968—Chiefs, 48-3 (M)
1969—Chiefs, 17-10 (KC)
1971—*Dolphins, 27-24 (KC) OT
1972—Dolphins, 20-10 (KC)
1974—Dolphins, 9-3 (M)
1976—Chiefs, 20-17 (M) OT
1981—Dolphins, 17-7 (KC)
1983—Dolphins, 14-6 (M)
1985—Dolphins, 31-0 (M)
1987—Dolphins, 42-0 (M)
1989—Chiefs, 26-21 (KC)
Chiefs, 27-24 (M)
1990—**Dolphins, 17-16 (M)
1991—Chiefs, 42-7 (KC)
1993—Dolphins, 30-10 (M)
1994—Dolphins, 45-28 (M)
**Dolphins, 27-17 (M)
1995—Dolphins, 13-6 (M)
1997—Dolphins, 17-14 (M)
2002—Chiefs, 48-30 (KC)
2005—Chiefs, 30-20 (M)
2006—Dolphins, 13-10 (M)
2008—Dolphins, 38-31 (KC)
(RS Pts.—Chiefs 501, Dolphins 455)
(PS Pts.—Dolphins 71, Chiefs 57)
AFC Divisional Playoff
***AFC First-Round Playoff*

KANSAS CITY vs. MINNESOTA
RS: Chiefs lead series, 5-4
PS: Chiefs lead series, 1-0
1969—*Chiefs, 23-7 (New Orleans)
1970—Vikings, 27-10 (M)
1974—Vikings, 35-15 (KC)
1981—Chiefs, 10-6 (M)
1990—Chiefs, 24-21 (KC)
1993—Vikings, 30-10 (M)
1996—Chiefs, 21-6 (M)
1999—Chiefs, 31-28 (KC)
2003—Vikings, 45-20 (M)
2007—Chiefs, 13-10 (KC)
(RS Pts.—Vikings 208, Chiefs 154)
(PS Pts.—Chiefs 23, Vikings 7)
Super Bowl IV

***KANSAS CITY vs. **NEW ENGLAND**
RS: Chiefs lead series, 16-12-3
1960—Patriots, 42-14 (B)
Texans, 34-0 (D)
1961—Patriots, 18-17 (D)
Patriots, 28-21 (B)
1962—Texans, 42-28 (D)
Texans, 27-7 (B)
1963—Tie, 24-24 (B)
Chiefs, 35-3 (KC)
1964—Patriots, 24-7 (B)

Patriots, 31-24 (KC)
1965—Chiefs, 27-17 (KC)
Tie, 10-10 (B)
1966—Chiefs, 43-24 (B)
Tie, 27-27 (KC)
1967—Chiefs, 33-10 (B)
1968—Chiefs, 31-17 (KC)
1969—Chiefs, 31-0 (B)
1970—Chiefs, 23-10 (KC)
1973—Chiefs, 10-7 (NE)
1977—Patriots, 21-17 (NE)
1981—Patriots, 33-17 (NE)
1990—Chiefs, 37-7 (NE)
1992—Chiefs, 27-20 (KC)
1995—Chiefs, 31-26 (KC)
1998—Patriots, 40-10 (NE)
1999—Chiefs, 16-14 (KC)
2000—Patriots, 30-24 (NE)
2002—Patriots, 41-38 (NE) OT
2004—Patriots, 27-19 (KC)
2005—Chiefs, 26-16 (KC)
2008—Patriots, 17-10 (NE)
(RS Pts.—Chiefs 752, Patriots 619)
Franchise located in Dallas prior to 1963 and known as Texans
**Franchise in Boston prior to 1971*

KANSAS CITY vs. NEW ORLEANS
RS: Saints lead series, 5-4
1972—Chiefs, 20-17 (NO)
1976—Saints, 27-17 (KC)
1982—Saints, 27-17 (NO)
1985—Chiefs, 47-27 (NO)
1991—Saints, 17-10 (KC)
1994—Chiefs, 30-17 (NO)
1997—Chiefs, 25-13 (KC)
2004—Saints, 27-20 (NO)
2008—Saints, 30-20 (KC)
(RS Pts.—Chiefs 206, Saints 202)

KANSAS CITY vs. N.Y. GIANTS
RS: Giants lead series, 10-2
1974—Giants, 33-27 (KC)
1978—Giants, 26-10 (NY)
1979—Giants, 21-17 (KC)
1983—Chiefs, 38-17 (KC)
1984—Giants, 28-27 (NY)
1988—Giants, 28-12 (NY)
1992—Giants, 35-21 (NY)
1995—Chiefs, 20-17 (KC) OT
1998—Giants, 28-7 (NY)
2001—Giants, 13-3 (KC)
2005—Giants, 27-17 (NY)
2009—Giants, 27-16 (KC)
(RS Pts.—Giants 300, Chiefs 215)

***KANSAS CITY vs. **N.Y. JETS**
RS: Series tied, 16-16-1
PS: Series tied, 1-1
1960—Titans, 37-35 (D)
Titans, 41-35 (NY)
1961—Titans, 28-7 (NY)
Texans, 35-24 (D)
1962—Texans, 20-17 (D)
Texans, 52-31 (NY)
1963—Jets, 17-0 (NY)
Chiefs, 48-0 (KC)
1964—Jets, 27-14 (NY)
Chiefs, 24-7 (KC)
1965—Chiefs, 14-10 (NY)
Jets, 13-10 (KC)
1966—Chiefs, 32-24 (NY)
1967—Chiefs, 42-18 (KC)
Chiefs, 21-7 (NY)
1968—Jets, 20-19 (KC)
1969—Chiefs, 34-16 (NY)
***Chiefs, 13-6 (NY)
1971—Jets, 13-10 (NY)
1974—Chiefs, 24-16 (KC)
1975—Jets, 30-24 (KC)
1982—Chiefs, 37-13 (KC)
1984—Jets, 17-16 (KC)
Jets, 28-7 (NY)
1986—****Jets, 35-15 (NY)
1987—Jets, 16-9 (KC)
1988—Tie, 17-17 (NY)
Chiefs, 38-34 (KC)
1992—Chiefs, 23-7 (NY)
1998—Jets, 20-17 (KC)
2001—Jets, 27-7 (NY)
2002—Chiefs, 29-25 (NY)
2005—Chiefs, 27-7 (KC)
2007—Jets, 13-10 (NY) OT
2008—Jets, 28-24 (NY)
(RS Pts.—Chiefs 761, Jets 648)
(PS Pts.—Jets 41, Chiefs 28)
Franchise in Dallas prior to 1963 and known as Texans
**Jets known as Titans prior to 1963*
***Inter-Divisional Playoff*
****AFC First-Round Playoff*

***KANSAS CITY vs. **OAKLAND**
RS: Chiefs lead series, 52-45-2
PS: Chiefs lead series, 2-1
1960—Texans, 34-16 (O)
Raiders, 20-19 (D)
1961—Texans, 42-35 (O)
Texans, 43-11 (D)
1962—Texans, 26-16 (O)
Texans, 35-7 (D)
1963—Raiders, 10-7 (O)
Raiders, 22-7 (KC)
1964—Chiefs, 21-9 (O)
Chiefs, 42-7 (KC)
1965—Raiders, 37-10 (O)
Chiefs, 14-7 (KC)
1966—Chiefs, 32-10 (O)
Raiders, 34-13 (KC)
1967—Raiders, 23-21 (O)
Raiders, 44-22 (KC)
1968—Chiefs, 24-10 (KC)
Raiders, 38-21 (O)
***Raiders, 41-6 (O)
1969—Raiders, 27-24 (KC)
Raiders, 10-6 (O)
****Chiefs, 17-7 (O)
1970—Tie, 17-17 (KC)
Raiders, 20-6 (O)
1971—Tie, 20-20 (O)
Chiefs, 16-14 (KC)
1972—Chiefs, 27-14 (KC)
Raiders, 26-3 (O)
1973—Chiefs, 16-3 (KC)
Raiders, 37-7 (O)
1974—Raiders, 27-7 (O)
Raiders, 7-6 (KC)
1975—Chiefs, 42-10 (KC)
Raiders, 28-20 (O)
1976—Raiders, 24-21 (KC)
Raiders, 21-10 (O)
1977—Raiders, 37-28 (KC)
Raiders, 21-20 (O)
1978—Raiders, 28-6 (O)
Raiders, 20-10 (KC)
1979—Chiefs, 35-7 (KC)
Chiefs, 24-21 (O)
1980—Raiders, 27-14 (KC)
Chiefs, 31-17 (O)
1981—Chiefs, 27-0 (KC)
Chiefs, 28-17 (O)
1982—Raiders, 21-16 (KC)
1983—Raiders, 21-20 (LA)
Raiders, 28-20 (KC)
1984—Raiders, 22-20 (KC)
Raiders, 17-7 (LA)
1985—Chiefs, 36-20 (KC)
Raiders, 19-10 (LA)
1986—Raiders, 24-17 (KC)
Chiefs, 20-17 (LA)
1987—Raiders, 35-17 (LA)
Chiefs, 16-10 (KC)
1988—Raiders, 27-17 (KC)
Raiders, 17-10 (LA)
1989—Chiefs, 24-19 (KC)
Raiders, 20-14 (LA)
1990—Chiefs, 9-7 (KC)
Chiefs, 27-24 (LA)
1991—Chiefs, 24-21 (KC)
Chiefs, 27-21 (LA)
*****Chiefs, 10-6 (KC)
1992—Chiefs, 27-7 (KC)
Raiders, 28-7 (LA)
1993—Chiefs, 24-9 (KC)
Chiefs, 31-20 (LA)
1994—Chiefs, 13-3 (KC)
Chiefs, 19-9 (LA)
1995—Chiefs, 23-17 (KC) OT
Chiefs, 29-23 (O)
1996—Chiefs, 19-3 (KC)
Raiders, 26-7 (O)
1997—Chiefs, 28-27 (O)
Chiefs, 30-0 (KC)
1998—Chiefs, 28-8 (KC)
Chiefs, 31-24 (O)
1999—Chiefs, 37-34 (O)
Raiders, 41-38 (KC) OT
2000—Raiders, 20-17 (KC)
Raiders, 49-31 (O)
2001—Raiders, 27-24 (KC)
Raiders, 28-26 (O)
2002—Chiefs, 20-10 (KC)
Raiders, 24-0 (O)
2003—Chiefs, 17-10 (O)
Chiefs, 27-24 (KC)
2004—Chiefs, 34-27 (O)
Chiefs, 31-30 (KC)
2005—Chiefs, 23-17 (O)
Chiefs, 27-23 (KC)
2006—Chiefs, 17-13 (KC)
Chiefs, 20-9 (O)
2007—Chiefs, 12-10 (O)
Raiders, 20-17 (KC)
2008—Raiders, 23-8 (KC)
Chiefs, 20-13 (O)
2009—Raiders, 13-10 (KC)
Chiefs, 16-10 (O)
(RS Pts.—Chiefs 2,043, Raiders 1,925)
(PS Pts.—Raiders 54, Chiefs 33)
Franchise in Dallas prior to 1963 and known as Texans
**Franchise in Los Angeles from 1982-1994*
***Division Playoff*
****AFL Championship*
*****AFC First-Round Playoff*

KANSAS CITY vs. PHILADELPHIA
RS: Eagles lead series, 4-2
1972—Eagles, 21-20 (KC)
1992—Chiefs, 24-17 (KC)
1998—Chiefs, 24-21 (P)
2001—Eagles, 23-10 (KC)
2005—Eagles, 37-31 (KC)
2009—Eagles, 34-14 (P)
(RS Pts.—Eagles 153, Chiefs 123)

KANSAS CITY vs. PITTSBURGH
RS: Steelers lead series, 17-9
PS: Chiefs lead series, 1-0
1970—Chiefs, 31-14 (P)
1971—Chiefs, 38-16 (KC)
1972—Steelers, 16-7 (P)
1974—Steelers, 34-24 (KC)
1975—Steelers, 28-3 (P)
1976—Steelers, 45-0 (KC)
1978—Steelers, 27-24 (P)
1979—Steelers, 30-3 (KC)
1980—Steelers, 21-16 (P)
1981—Chiefs, 37-33 (P)
1982—Steelers, 35-14 (P)
1984—Chiefs, 37-27 (P)
1985—Steelers, 36-28 (KC)
1986—Chiefs, 24-19 (P)
1987—Steelers, 17-16 (KC)
1988—Steelers, 16-10 (P)
1989—Steelers, 23-17 (P)
1992—Steelers, 27-3 (KC)
1993—*Chiefs, 27-24 (KC) OT
1996—Steelers, 17-7 (KC)
1997—Chiefs, 13-10 (KC)
1998—Steelers, 20-13 (KC)
1999—Chiefs, 35-19 (KC)
2001—Steelers, 20-17 (KC)
2003—Chiefs, 41-20 (KC)
2006—Steelers, 45-7 (P)
2009—Chiefs, 27-24 (KC) OT
(RS Pts.—Steelers 639, Chiefs 492)
(PS Pts.—Chiefs 27, Steelers 24)
**AFC First-Round Playoff*

KANSAS CITY vs. *ST. LOUIS
RS: Chiefs lead series, 5-4
1973—Rams, 23-13 (KC)
1982—Rams, 20-14 (LA)
1985—Rams, 16-0 (KC)
1991—Chiefs, 27-20 (LA)
1994—Rams, 16-0 (KC)
1997—Chiefs, 28-20 (StL)
2000—Chiefs, 54-34 (KC)
2002—Chiefs, 49-10 (KC)
2006—Chiefs, 31-17 (StL)
(RS Pts.—Chiefs 216, Rams 176)
**Franchise in Los Angeles prior to 1995*

***KANSAS CITY vs. **SAN DIEGO**
RS: Chiefs lead series, 50-48-1
PS: Chargers lead series, 1-0
1960—Chargers, 21-20 (LA)
Texans, 17-0 (D)
1961—Chargers, 26-10 (D)
Chargers, 24-14 (SD)
1962—Chargers, 32-28 (SD)
Texans, 26-17 (D)
1963—Chargers, 24-10 (SD)
Chargers, 38-17 (KC)
1964—Chargers, 28-14 (KC)
Chiefs, 49-6 (SD)
1965—Tie, 10-10 (SD)
Chiefs, 31-7 (KC)
1966—Chiefs, 24-14 (KC)
Chiefs, 27-17 (SD)
1967—Chargers, 45-31 (SD)
Chargers, 17-16 (KC)
1968—Chiefs, 27-20 (KC)
Chiefs, 40-3 (SD)
1969—Chiefs, 27-9 (SD)
Chiefs, 27-3 (KC)
1970—Chiefs, 26-14 (KC)
Chargers, 31-13 (SD)
1971—Chargers, 21-14 (SD)
Chiefs, 31-10 (KC)
1972—Chiefs, 26-14 (SD)
Chargers, 27-17 (KC)
1973—Chiefs, 19-0 (SD)
Chiefs, 33-6 (KC)
1974—Chiefs, 24-14 (SD)
Chargers, 14-7 (KC)
1975—Chiefs, 12-10 (SD)
Chargers, 28-20 (KC)
1976—Chargers, 30-16 (KC)
Chiefs, 23-20 (SD)
1977—Chargers, 23-7 (KC)
Chiefs, 21-16 (SD)
1978—Chargers, 29-23 (SD) OT
Chiefs, 23-0 (KC)
1979—Chargers, 20-14 (KC)
Chargers, 28-7 (SD)
1980—Chargers, 24-7 (KC)
Chargers, 20-7 (SD)
1981—Chargers, 42-31 (KC)
Chargers, 22-20 (SD)
1982—Chiefs, 19-12 (KC)
1983—Chargers, 17-14 (KC)
Chargers, 41-38 (SD)
1984—Chiefs, 31-13 (KC)
Chiefs, 42-21 (SD)
1985—Chargers, 31-20 (SD)
Chiefs, 38-34 (KC)
1986—Chiefs, 42-41 (KC)
Chiefs, 24-23 (SD)
1987—Chiefs, 20-13 (KC)
Chargers, 42-21 (SD)
1988—Chargers, 24-23 (KC)
Chargers, 24-13 (SD)
1989—Chargers, 21-6 (SD)
Chargers, 20-13 (KC)
1990—Chiefs, 27-10 (KC)
Chiefs, 24-21 (SD)
1991—Chiefs, 14-13 (SD)
Chiefs, 20-17 (KC) OT
1992—Chiefs, 24-10 (SD)
Chiefs, 16-14 (KC)
***Chargers, 17-0 (SD)
1993—Chiefs, 17-14 (SD)
Chiefs, 28-24 (KC)
1994—Chargers, 20-6 (SD)
Chargers, 14-13 (KC)
1995—Chiefs, 29-23 (KC) OT
Chiefs, 22-7 (SD)
1996—Chargers, 22-19 (SD)
Chargers, 28-14 (KC)
1997—Chiefs, 31-3 (KC)
Chiefs, 29-7 (SD)
1998—Chiefs, 23-7 (KC)
Chargers, 38-37 (SD)
1999—Chargers, 21-14 (SD)
Chiefs, 34-0 (KC)
2000—Chiefs, 42-10 (KC)
Chargers, 17-16 (SD)
2001—Chiefs, 25-20 (SD)
Chiefs, 20-17 (KC)
2002—Chargers, 35-34 (SD)
Chiefs, 24-22 (KC)
2003—Chiefs, 27-14 (KC)
Chiefs, 28-24 (SD)
2004—Chargers, 34-31 (KC)
Chargers, 24-17 (SD)
2005—Chargers, 28-20 (SD)
Chiefs, 20-7 (KC)
2006—Chiefs, 30-27 (KC)
Chargers, 20-9 (SD)
2007—Chiefs, 30-16 (SD)
Chargers, 24-10 (KC)
2008—Chargers, 20-19 (SD)
Chargers, 22-21 (KC)
2009—Chargers, 37-7 (KC)
Chargers, 43-14 (SD)
(RS Pts.—Chiefs 2,155, Chargers 1,975)
(PS Pts.—Chargers 17, Chiefs 0)
**Franchise in Dallas prior to 1963 and known as Texans*
***Franchise in Los Angeles prior to 1961*
****AFC First-Round Playoff*

KANSAS CITY vs. SAN FRANCISCO
RS: 49ers lead series, 6-4
1971—Chiefs, 26-17 (SF)
1975—49ers, 20-3 (KC)
1982—49ers, 26-13 (KC)
1985—49ers, 31-3 (SF)
1991—49ers, 28-14 (SF)
1994—Chiefs, 24-17 (KC)
1997—Chiefs, 44-9 (KC)
2000—49ers, 21-7 (SF)
2002—49ers, 17-13 (SF)
2006—Chiefs, 41-10 (KC)
(PS Pts.—Chiefs 188, 49ers 186)

KANSAS CITY vs. SEATTLE
RS: Chiefs lead series, 31-18
1977—Seahawks, 34-31 (KC)
1978—Seahawks, 13-10 (KC)
Seahawks, 23-19 (S)
1979—Chiefs, 24-6 (S)
Chiefs, 37-21 (KC)
1980—Seahawks, 17-16 (KC)
Chiefs, 31-30 (S)
1981—Chiefs, 20-14 (S)
Chiefs, 40-13 (KC)
1983—Chiefs, 17-13 (KC)
Seahawks, 51-48 (S) OT
1984—Seahawks, 45-0 (S)
Chiefs, 34-7 (KC)
1985—Chiefs, 28-7 (KC)
Seahawks, 24-6 (S)
1986—Seahawks, 23-17 (S)
Chiefs, 27-7 (KC)
1987—Seahawks, 43-14 (S)
Chiefs, 41-20 (KC)
1988—Seahawks, 31-10 (S)
Chiefs, 27-24 (KC)
1989—Chiefs, 20-16 (S)
Chiefs, 20-10 (KC)
1990—Seahawks, 19-7 (S)
Seahawks, 17-16 (KC)
1991—Chiefs, 20-13 (KC)
Chiefs, 19-6 (S)
1992—Chiefs, 26-7 (KC)
Chiefs, 24-14 (S)
1993—Chiefs, 31-16 (S)
Chiefs, 34-24 (KC)
1994—Chiefs, 38-23 (KC)
Seahawks, 10-9 (S)
1995—Chiefs, 34-10 (S)

Chiefs, 26-3 (KC)
1996—Chiefs, 35-17 (S)
Chiefs, 34-16 (KC)
1997—Chiefs, 20-17 (KC) OT
Chiefs, 19-14 (S)
1998—Chiefs, 17-6 (KC)
Seahawks, 24-12 (S)
1999—Seahawks, 31-19 (KC)
Seahawks, 23-14 (S)
2000—Chiefs, 24-17 (KC)
Chiefs, 24-19 (S)
2001—Chiefs, 19-7 (KC)
Seahawks, 21-18 (S)
2002—Seahawks, 39-32 (S)
2006—Chiefs, 35-28 (KC)
(RS Pts.—Chiefs 1,143, Seahawks 933)

KANSAS CITY vs. TAMPA BAY
RS: Series tied, 5-5
1976—Chiefs, 28-19 (TB)
1978—Buccaneers, 30-13 (KC)
1979—Buccaneers, 3-0 (TB)
1981—Chiefs, 19-10 (KC)
1984—Chiefs, 24-20 (KC)
1986—Chiefs, 27-20 (KC)
1993—Chiefs, 27-3 (TB)
1999—Buccaneers, 17-10 (TB)
2004—Buccaneers, 34-31 (TB)
2008—Buccaneers, 30-27 (KC) OT
(RS Pts.—Chiefs 206, Buccaneers 186)

***KANSAS CITY vs. **TENNESSEE**
RS: Chiefs lead series, 25-20
PS: Chiefs lead series, 2-0
1960—Oilers, 20-10 (H)
Texans, 24-0 (D)
1961—Texans, 26-21 (D)
Oilers, 38-7 (H)
1962—Texans, 31-7 (H)
Oilers, 14-6 (D)
***Texans, 20-17 (H) OT
1963—Chiefs, 28-7 (KC)
Oilers, 28-7 (H)
1964—Chiefs, 28-7 (KC)
Chiefs, 28-19 (H)
1965—Chiefs, 52-21 (KC)
Oilers, 38-36 (H)
1966—Chiefs, 48-23 (KC)
1967—Chiefs, 25-20 (H)
Oilers, 24-19 (KC)
1968—Chiefs, 26-21 (H)
Chiefs, 24-10 (KC)
1969—Chiefs, 24-0 (KC)
1970—Chiefs, 24-9 (KC)
1971—Chiefs, 20-16 (H)
1973—Chiefs, 38-14 (KC)
1974—Chiefs, 17-7 (H)
1975—Oilers, 17-13 (KC)
1977—Oilers, 34-20 (H)
1978—Oilers, 20-17 (KC)
1979—Oilers, 20-6 (H)
1980—Chiefs, 21-20 (KC)
1981—Chiefs, 23-10 (KC)
1983—Chiefs, 13-10 (H) OT
1984—Oilers, 17-16 (KC)
1985—Oilers, 23-20 (H)
1986—Chiefs, 27-13 (KC)
1988—Oilers, 7-6 (H)
1989—Chiefs, 34-0 (KC)
1990—Oilers, 27-10 (KC)
1991—Oilers, 17-7 (H)
1992—Oilers, 23-20 (H) OT
1993—Oilers, 30-0 (H)
****Chiefs, 28-20 (H)
1994—Chiefs, 31-9 (KC)
1995—Chiefs, 20-13 (KC)
1996—Chiefs, 20-19 (H)
2000—Titans, 17-14 (T) OT
2004—Chiefs, 49-38 (T)
2007—Titans, 26-17 (KC)
2008—Titans, 34-10 (KC)
(RS Pts.—Chiefs 962, Titans 808)
(PS Pts.—Chiefs 48, Titans 37)
**Franchise in Dallas prior to 1963 and known as Texans*
***Franchise in Houston prior to 1997; known as Oilers prior to 1999*
****AFL Championship*
*****AFC Divisional Playoff*

KANSAS CITY vs. WASHINGTON
RS: Chiefs lead series, 7-1
1971—Chiefs, 27-20 (KC)
1976—Chiefs, 33-30 (W)
1983—Redskins, 27-12 (W)
1992—Chiefs, 35-16 (KC)
1995—Chiefs, 24-3 (KC)
2001—Chiefs, 45-13 (W)
2005—Chiefs, 28-21, (KC)
2009—Chiefs, 14-6 (W)
(RS Pts.—Chiefs 218, Redskins 136)

MIAMI vs. ARIZONA
RS: Dolphins lead series, 8-2;
See Arizona vs. Miami

MIAMI vs. ATLANTA
RS: Dolphins lead series, 7-4;
See Atlanta vs. Miami

MIAMI vs. BALTIMORE
RS: Dolphins lead series, 5-2
PS: Ravens lead series, 2-0;
See Baltimore vs. Miami

MIAMI vs. BUFFALO
RS: Dolphins lead series, 52-35-1
PS: Bills lead series, 3-1;
See Buffalo vs. Miami

MIAMI vs. CAROLINA
RS: Dolphins lead series, 4-0;
See Carolina vs. Miami

MIAMI vs. CHICAGO
RS: Dolphins lead series, 7-3;
See Chicago vs. Miami

MIAMI vs. CINCINNATI
RS: Dolphins lead series, 12-5
PS: Dolphins lead series, 1-0;
See Cincinnati vs. Miami

MIAMI vs. CLEVELAND
RS: Dolphins lead series, 7-6
PS: Dolphins lead series, 2-0;
See Cleveland vs. Miami

MIAMI vs. DALLAS
RS: Dolphins lead series, 7-4
PS: Cowboys lead series, 1-0;
See Dallas vs. Miami

MIAMI vs. DENVER
RS: Dolphins lead series, 11-3-1
PS: Broncos lead series, 1-0;
See Denver vs. Miami

MIAMI vs. DETROIT
RS: Dolphins lead series, 7-2;
See Detroit vs. Miami

MIAMI vs. GREEN BAY
RS: Dolphins lead series, 9-3;
See Green Bay vs. Miami

MIAMI vs. HOUSTON
RS: Texans lead series, 5-0;
See Houston vs. Miami

MIAMI vs. INDIANAPOLIS
RS: Dolphins lead series, 44-24
PS: Dolphins lead series, 2-0;
See Indianapolis vs. Miami

MIAMI vs. JACKSONVILLE
RS: Series tied, 2-2
PS: Jaguars lead series, 1-0;
See Jacksonville vs. Miami

MIAMI vs. KANSAS CITY
RS: Series tied, 12-12
PS: Dolphins lead series, 3-0;
See Kansas City vs. Miami

MIAMI vs. MINNESOTA
RS: Dolphins lead series, 5-4
PS: Dolphins lead series, 1-0
1972—Dolphins, 16-14 (Minn)
1973—*Dolphins, 24-7 (Houston)
1976—Vikings, 29-7 (Mia)
1979—Dolphins, 27-12 (Minn)
1982—Dolphins, 22-14 (Mia)
1988—Dolphins, 24-7 (Mia)
1994—Vikings, 38-35 (Minn)
2000—Vikings, 13-7 (Minn)
2002—Vikings, 20-17 (Minn)
2006—Dolphins, 24-20 (Mia)
(RS Pts.—Dolphins 179, Vikings 167)
(PS Pts.—Dolphins 24, Vikings 7)
**Super Bowl VIII*

MIAMI vs. *NEW ENGLAND
RS: Dolphins lead series, 49-37
PS: Patriots lead series, 2-1
1966—Patriots, 20-14 (M)
1967—Patriots, 41-10 (B)
Dolphins, 41-32 (M)
1968—Dolphins, 34-10 (B)
Dolphins, 38-7 (M)
1969—Dolphins, 17-16 (B)
Patriots, 38-23 (Tampa)
1970—Patriots, 27-14 (B)
Dolphins, 37-20 (M)
1971—Dolphins, 41-3 (M)
Patriots, 34-13 (NE)
1972—Dolphins, 52-0 (M)
Dolphins, 37-21 (NE)
1973—Dolphins, 44-23 (M)
Dolphins, 30-14 (NE)
1974—Patriots, 34-24 (NE)
Dolphins, 34-27 (M)
1975—Dolphins, 22-14 (NE)
Dolphins, 20-7 (M)
1976—Patriots, 30-14 (NE)
Dolphins, 10-3 (M)
1977—Dolphins, 17-5 (M)
Patriots, 14-10 (NE)
1978—Patriots, 33-24 (NE)
Dolphins, 23-3 (M)
1979—Patriots, 28-13 (NE)
Dolphins, 39-24 (M)
1980—Patriots, 34-0 (NE)
Dolphins, 16-13 (M) OT
1981—Dolphins, 30-27 (NE) OT
Dolphins, 24-14 (M)
1982—Patriots, 3-0 (NE)
**Dolphins, 28-13 (M)
1983—Dolphins, 34-24 (M)
Patriots, 17-6 (NE)
1984—Dolphins, 28-7 (M)
Dolphins, 44-24 (NE)

1985—Patriots, 17-13 (NE)
Dolphins, 30-27 (M)
***Patriots, 31-14 (M)
1986—Patriots, 34-7 (NE)
Patriots, 34-27 (M)
1987—Patriots, 28-21 (NE)
Patriots, 24-10 (M)
1988—Patriots, 21-10 (NE)
Patriots, 6-3 (M)
1989—Dolphins, 24-10 (NE)
Dolphins, 31-10 (M)
1990—Dolphins, 27-24 (NE)
Dolphins, 17-10 (M)
1991—Dolphins, 20-10 (NE)
Dolphins, 30-20 (M)
1992—Dolphins, 38-17 (M)
Dolphins, 16-13 (NE) OT
1993—Dolphins, 17-13 (M)
Patriots, 33-27 (NE) OT
1994—Dolphins, 39-35 (M)
Dolphins, 23-3 (NE)
1995—Dolphins, 20-3 (NE)
Patriots, 34-17 (M)
1996—Dolphins, 24-10 (M)
Patriots, 42-23 (NE)
1997—Patriots, 27-24 (NE)
Patriots, 14-12 (M)
**Patriots, 17-3 (NE)
1998—Dolphins, 12-9 (M) OT
Patriots, 26-23 (NE)
1999—Dolphins, 31-30 (NE)
Dolphins, 27-17 (M)
2000—Dolphins, 10-3 (M)
Dolphins, 27-24 (NE)
2001—Dolphins, 30-10 (M)
Patriots, 20-13 (NE)
2002—Dolphins, 26-13 (M)
Patriots, 27-24 (NE) OT
2003—Patriots, 19-13 (M) OT
Patriots, 12-0 (NE)
2004—Patriots, 24-10 (NE)
Dolphins, 29-28 (M)
2005—Patriots, 23-16 (M)
Dolphins, 28-26 (NE)
2006—Patriots, 20-10 (NE)
Dolphins, 21-0 (M)
2007—Patriots, 49-28 (M)
Patriots, 28-7 (NE)
2008—Dolphins, 38-13 (NE)
Patriots, 48-28 (M)
2009—Patriots, 27-17 (NE)
Dolphins, 22-21 (M)
(RS Pts.—Dolphins 1,917, Patriots 1,727)
(PS Pts.—Patriots 61, Dolphins 45)
Franchise in Boston prior to 1971
***AFC First-Round Playoff*
****AFC Championship*

MIAMI vs. NEW ORLEANS
RS: Dolphins lead series, 6-4
1970—Dolphins, 21-10 (M)
1974—Dolphins, 21-0 (NO)
1980—Dolphins, 21-16 (M)
1983—Saints, 17-7 (NO)
1986—Dolphins, 31-27 (NO)
1992—Saints, 24-13 (NO)
1995—Saints, 33-30 (NO)
1998—Dolphins, 30-10 (M)
2005—Dolphins, 21-6 (Baton Rouge)
2009—Saints, 46-34 (M)
(RS Pts.—Dolphins 229, Saints 189)

MIAMI vs. N.Y. GIANTS
RS: Giants lead series, 4-2
1972—Dolphins, 23-13 (NY)
1990—Giants, 20-3 (NY)
1993—Giants, 19-14 (M)
1996—Giants, 17-7 (M)
2003—Dolphins, 23-10 (NY)
2007—Giants, 13-10 (London)
(RS Pts.—Giants 92, Dolphins 80)

MIAMI vs. N.Y. JETS
RS: Jets lead series, 46-41-1
PS: Dolphins lead series, 1-0
1966—Jets, 19-14 (M)
Jets, 30-13 (NY)
1967—Jets, 29-7 (NY)
Jets, 33-14 (M)
1968—Jets, 35-17 (NY)
Jets, 31-7 (M)
1969—Jets, 34-31 (NY)
Jets, 27-9 (M)
1970—Dolphins, 20-6 (NY)
Dolphins, 16-10 (M)
1971—Jets, 14-10 (M)
Dolphins, 30-14 (NY)
1972—Dolphins, 27-17 (NY)
Dolphins, 28-24 (M)
1973—Dolphins, 31-3 (M)
Dolphins, 24-14 (NY)
1974—Dolphins, 21-17 (M)
Jets, 17-14 (NY)
1975—Dolphins, 43-0 (NY)
Dolphins, 27-7 (M)
1976—Dolphins, 16-0 (M)
Dolphins, 27-7 (NY)
1977—Dolphins, 21-17 (M)
Dolphins, 14-10 (NY)
1978—Jets, 33-20 (NY)
Jets, 24-13 (M)
1979—Jets, 33-27 (NY)
Jets, 27-24 (M)
1980—Jets, 17-14 (NY)
Jets, 24-17 (M)
1981—Tie, 28-28 (M) OT
Jets, 16-15 (NY)
1982—Dolphins, 45-28 (NY)
Dolphins, 20-19 (M)
*Dolphins, 14-0 (M)
1983—Dolphins, 32-14 (NY)
Dolphins, 34-14 (M)
1984—Dolphins, 31-17 (NY)
Dolphins, 28-17 (M)
1985—Jets, 23-7 (NY)
Dolphins, 21-17 (M)
1986—Jets, 51-45 (NY) OT
Dolphins, 45-3 (M)
1987—Jets, 37-31 (NY) OT
Dolphins, 37-28 (M)
1988—Jets, 44-30 (M)
Jets, 38-34 (NY)
1989—Jets, 40-33 (M)
Dolphins, 31-23 (NY)
1990—Dolphins, 20-16 (M)
Dolphins, 17-3 (NY)
1991—Jets, 41-23 (NY)
Jets, 23-20 (M) OT
1992—Jets, 26-14 (NY)
Dolphins, 19-17 (M)
1993—Jets, 24-14 (M)
Jets, 27-10 (NY)
1994—Dolphins, 28-14 (M)
Dolphins, 28-24 (NY)
1995—Dolphins, 52-14 (M)
Jets, 17-16 (NY)
1996—Dolphins, 36-27 (M)
Dolphins, 31-28 (NY)
1997—Dolphins, 31-20 (NY)
Dolphins, 24-17 (M)
1998—Jets, 20-9 (NY)
Jets, 21-16 (M)
1999—Jets, 28-20 (NY)
Jets, 38-31 (M)
2000—Jets, 40-37 (NY) OT
Jets, 20-3 (M)
2001—Jets, 21-17 (NY)
Jets, 24-0 (M)
2002—Dolphins, 30-3 (M)
Jets, 13-10 (NY)
2003—Dolphins, 21-10 (NY)
Dolphins, 23-21 (M)
2004—Jets, 17-9 (M)
Jets, 41-14 (NY)
2005—Jets, 17-7 (NY)
Dolphins, 24-20 (M)
2006—Jets, 20-17 (NY)
Jets, 13-10 (M)
2007—Jets, 31-28 (NY)
Jets, 40-13 (M)
2008—Jets, 20-14 (M)
Dolphins, 24-17 (NY)
2009—Dolphins, 31-27 (M)
Dolphins, 30-25 (NY)
(RS Pts.—Dolphins 1,964, Jets 1,915)
(PS Pts.—Dolphins 14, Jets 0)
**AFC Championship*

MIAMI vs. *OAKLAND
RS: Raiders lead series, 16-12-1
PS: Raiders lead series, 3-1
1966—Raiders, 23-14 (M)
Raiders, 21-10 (O)
1967—Raiders, 31-17 (O)
1968—Raiders, 47-21 (M)
1969—Raiders, 20-17 (O)
Tie, 20-20 (M)
1970—Dolphins, 20-13 (M)
**Raiders, 21-14 (O)
1973—Raiders, 12-7 (O)
***Dolphins, 27-10 (M)
1974—**Raiders, 28-26 (O)
1975—Raiders, 31-21 (M)
1978—Dolphins, 23-6 (M)
1979—Raiders, 13-3 (O)
1980—Raiders, 16-10 (O)
1981—Raiders, 33-17 (M)
1983—Raiders, 27-14 (LA)
1984—Raiders, 45-34 (M)
1986—Raiders, 30-28 (M)
1988—Dolphins, 24-14 (LA)
1990—Raiders, 13-10 (M)
1992—Dolphins, 20-7 (M)
1994—Dolphins, 20-17 (M) OT
1996—Raiders, 17-7 (O)
1997—Dolphins, 34-16 (O)
1998—Dolphins, 27-17 (O)
1999—Dolphins, 16-9 (O)
2000—**Raiders, 27-0 (O)
2001—Dolphins, 18-15 (M)
2002—Dolphins, 23-17 (M)
2005—Dolphins, 33-21 (O)
2007—Raiders, 35-17 (M)
2008—Dolphins, 17-15 (M)
(RS Pts.—Raiders 601, Dolphins 542)
(PS Pts.—Raiders 86, Dolphins 67)

**Franchise in Los Angeles from 1982-1994*
***AFC Divisional Playoff*
****AFC Championship*

MIAMI vs. PHILADELPHIA
RS: Dolphins lead series, 7-5
1970—Eagles, 24-17 (P)
1975—Dolphins, 24-16 (M)
1978—Eagles, 17-3 (P)
1981—Dolphins, 13-10 (M)
1984—Dolphins, 24-23 (M)
1987—Dolphins, 28-10 (P)
1990—Dolphins, 23-20 (M) OT
1993—Dolphins, 19-14 (P)
1996—Eagles, 35-28 (P)
1999—Dolphins, 16-13 (M)
2003—Eagles, 34-27 (M)
2007—Eagles, 17-7 (P)
(RS Pts.—Eagles 233, Dolphins 229)

MIAMI vs. PITTSBURGH
RS: Steelers lead series, 11-9
PS: Dolphins lead series, 2-1
1971—Dolphins, 24-21 (M)
1972—*Dolphins, 21-17 (P)
1973—Dolphins, 30-26 (M)
1976—Steelers, 14-3 (P)
1979—**Steelers, 34-14 (P)
1980—Steelers, 23-10 (P)
1981—Dolphins, 30-10 (M)
1984—Dolphins, 31-7 (P)
*Dolphins, 45-28 (M)
1985—Dolphins, 24-20 (M)
1987—Dolphins, 35-24 (M)
1988—Steelers, 40-24 (P)
1989—Steelers, 34-14 (M)
1990—Dolphins, 28-6 (P)
1993—Steelers, 21-20 (M)
1994—Steelers, 16-13 (P) OT
1995—Dolphins, 23-10 (M)
1996—Steelers, 24-17 (M)
1998—Dolphins, 21-0 (M)
2004—Steelers, 13-3 (M)
2006—Steelers, 28-17 (P)
2007—Steelers, 3-0 (P)
2009—Steelers, 30-24 (M)
(RS Pts.—Dolphins 391, Steelers 370)
(PS Pts.—Dolphins 80, Steelers 79)
**AFC Championship*
***AFC Divisional Playoff*

MIAMI vs. *ST. LOUIS
RS: Dolphins lead series, 9-2
1971—Dolphins, 20-14 (LA)
1976—Rams, 31-28 (M)
1980—Dolphins, 35-14 (LA)
1983—Dolphins, 30-14 (M)
1986—Dolphins, 37-31 (LA) OT
1992—Dolphins, 26-10 (M)
1995—Dolphins, 41-22 (StL)
1998—Dolphins, 14-0 (M)
2001—Rams, 42-10 (StL)
2004—Dolphins, 31-14 (M)
2008—Dolphins, 16-12 (StL)
(RS Pts.—Dolphins 288, Rams 204)
**Franchise in Los Angeles prior to 1995*

MIAMI vs. SAN DIEGO
RS: Dolphins lead series, 12-11
PS: Series tied, 2-2
1966—Chargers, 44-10 (SD)
1967—Chargers, 24-0 (SD)
Dolphins, 41-24 (M)
1968—Chargers, 34-28 (SD)
1969—Chargers, 21-14 (M)
1972—Dolphins, 24-10 (M)
1974—Dolphins, 28-21 (SD)
1977—Chargers, 14-13 (M)
1978—Dolphins, 28-21 (SD)
1980—Chargers, 27-24 (M) OT
1981—*Chargers, 41-38 (M) OT
1982—**Dolphins, 34-13 (M)
1984—Chargers, 34-28 (SD) OT
1986—Chargers, 50-28 (SD)
1988—Dolphins, 31-28 (M)
1991—Chargers, 38-30 (SD)
1992—*Dolphins, 31-0 (M)
1993—Chargers, 45-20 (SD)
1994—*Chargers, 22-21 (SD)
1995—Dolphins, 24-14 (SD)
1999—Dolphins, 12-9 (M)
2000—Dolphins, 17-7 (SD)
2002—Dolphins, 30-3 (M)
2003—Dolphins, 26-10 (Ariz)
2005—Dolphins, 23-21 (SD)
2008—Dolphins, 17-10 (M)
2009—Chargers, 23-13 (SD)
(RS Pts.—Chargers 532, Dolphins 509)
(PS Pts.—Dolphins 124, Chargers 76)
**AFC Divisional Playoff*
***AFC Second-Round Playoff*

MIAMI vs. SAN FRANCISCO
RS: Dolphins lead series, 6-4
PS: 49ers lead series, 1-0
1973—Dolphins, 21-13 (M)
1977—Dolphins, 19-15 (SF)
1980—Dolphins, 17-13 (M)
1983—Dolphins, 20-17 (SF)
1984—*49ers, 38-16 (Stanford)
1986—49ers, 31-16 (M)
1992—49ers, 27-3 (SF)
1995—49ers, 44-20 (M)
2001—49ers, 21-0 (SF)
2004—Dolphins, 24-17 (SF)
2008—Dolphins, 14-9 (M)
(RS Pts.—49ers 207, Dolphins 154)
(PS Pts.—49ers 38, Dolphins 16)
**Super Bowl XIX*

MIAMI vs. SEATTLE
RS: Dolphins lead series, 7-3
PS: Dolphins lead series, 2-1
1977—Dolphins, 31-13 (M)
1979—Dolphins, 19-10 (M)
1983—*Seahawks, 27-20 (M)
1984—*Dolphins, 31-10 (M)
1987—Seahawks, 24-20 (S)
1990—Dolphins, 24-17 (M)
1992—Dolphins, 19-17 (S)
1996—Seahawks, 22-15 (M)
1999—**Dolphins, 20-17 (S)
2000—Dolphins, 23-0 (M)
2001—Dolphins, 24-20 (S)
2004—Seahawks, 24-17 (S)
2008—Dolphins, 21-19 (M)
(RS Pts.—Dolphins 213, Seahawks 166)
(PS Pts.—Dolphins 71, Seahawks 54)
**AFC Divisional Playoff*
***AFC First-Round Playoff*

MIAMI vs. TAMPA BAY
RS: Dolphins lead series, 5-4
1976—Dolphins, 23-20 (TB)
1982—Buccaneers, 23-17 (TB)
1985—Dolphins, 41-38 (M)
1988—Dolphins, 17-14 (TB)
1991—Dolphins, 33-14 (M)
1997—Buccaneers, 31-21 (TB)
2000—Buccaneers, 16-13 (M)
2005—Buccaneers, 27-13 (TB)
2009—Dolphins, 25-23 (M)
(RS Pts.—Buccaneers 206, Dolphins 203)

MIAMI vs. *TENNESSEE
RS: Dolphins lead series, 17-14
PS: Titans lead series, 1-0
1966—Dolphins, 20-13 (H)
Dolphins, 29-28 (M)
1967—Oilers, 17-14 (H)
Oilers, 41-10 (M)
1968—Oilers, 24-10 (M)
Dolphins, 24-7 (H)
1969—Oilers, 22-10 (H)
Oilers, 32-7 (M)
1970—Dolphins, 20-10 (H)
1972—Dolphins, 34-13 (M)
1975—Oilers, 20-19 (H)
1977—Dolphins, 27-7 (M)
1978—Oilers, 35-30 (H)
**Oilers, 17-9 (M)
1979—Oilers, 9-6 (M)
1981—Dolphins, 16-10 (H)
1983—Dolphins, 24-17 (H)
1984—Dolphins, 28-10 (M)
1985—Oilers, 26-23 (H)
1986—Dolphins, 28-7 (M)
1989—Oilers, 39-7 (H)
1991—Oilers, 17-13 (M)
1992—Dolphins, 19-16 (M)
1996—Dolphins, 23-20 (H)
1997—Dolphins, 16-13 (M) OT
1999—Dolphins, 17-0 (M)
2001—Dolphins, 31-23 (T)
2003—Titans, 31-7 (T)
2004—Titans, 17-7 (M)
2005—Dolphins, 24-10 (M)
2006—Dolphins, 13-10 (M)
2009—Titans, 27-24 (T) OT
(RS Pts.—Dolphins 580, Titans 571)
(PS Pts.—Titans 17, Dolphins 9)
**Franchise in Houston prior to 1997; known as Oilers prior to 1999*
***AFC First-Round Playoff*

MIAMI vs. WASHINGTON
RS: Dolphins lead series, 6-4
PS: Series tied, 1-1
1972—*Dolphins, 14-7 (Los Angeles)
1974—Redskins, 20-17 (W)
1978—Dolphins, 16-0 (W)
1981—Dolphins, 13-10 (M)
1982—**Redskins, 27-17 (Pasadena)
1984—Dolphins, 35-17 (W)
1987—Dolphins, 23-21 (M)
1990—Redskins, 42-20 (W)
1993—Dolphins, 17-10 (M)
1999—Redskins, 21-10 (W)
2003—Dolphins, 24-23 (M)
2007—Redskins, 16-13 (W) OT
(RS Pts.—Dolphins 188, Redskins 180)
(PS Pts.—Redskins 34, Dolphins 31)
**Super Bowl VII*
***Super Bowl XVII*

MINNESOTA vs. ARIZONA
RS: Series tied, 10-10
PS: Vikings lead series, 2-0;
See Arizona vs. Minnesota

MINNESOTA vs. ATLANTA
RS: Vikings lead series, 15-9
PS: Series tied, 1-1;

See Atlanta vs. Minnesota

MINNESOTA vs. BALTIMORE
RS: Series tied, 2-2;
See Baltimore vs. Minnesota

MINNESOTA vs. BUFFALO
RS: Vikings lead series, 7-4;
See Buffalo vs. Minnesota

MINNESOTA vs. CAROLINA
RS: Vikings lead series, 5-4;
See Carolina vs. Minnesota

MINNESOTA vs. CHICAGO
RS: Vikings lead series, 52-43-2
PS: Bears lead series, 1-0;
See Chicago vs. Minnesota

MINNESOTA vs. CINCINNATI
RS: Vikings lead series, 6-5;
See Cincinnati vs. Minnesota

MINNESOTA vs. CLEVELAND
RS: Vikings lead series, 10-3
PS: Vikings lead series, 1-0;
See Cleveland vs. Minnesota

MINNESOTA vs. DALLAS
RS: Series tied, 10-10
PS: Cowboys lead series, 4-3;
See Dallas vs. Minnesota

MINNESOTA vs. DENVER
RS: Vikings lead series, 7-5;
See Denver vs. Minnesota

MINNESOTA vs. DETROIT
RS: Vikings lead series, 65-30-2;
See Detroit vs. Minnesota

MINNESOTA vs. GREEN BAY
RS: Packers lead series, 49-47-1
PS: Vikings lead series, 1-0;
See Green Bay vs. Minnesota

MINNESOTA vs. HOUSTON
RS: Vikings lead series, 2-0;
See Houston vs. Minnesota

MINNESOTA vs. INDIANAPOLIS
RS: Colts lead series, 14-7-1
PS: Colts lead series, 1-0;
See Indianapolis vs. Minnesota

MINNESOTA vs. JACKSONVILLE
RS: Vikings lead series, 3-1;
See Jacksonville vs. Minnesota

MINNESOTA vs. KANSAS CITY
RS: Chiefs lead series, 5-4
PS: Chiefs lead series, 1-0;
See Kansas City vs. Minnesota

MINNESOTA vs. MIAMI
RS: Dolphins lead series, 5-4
PS: Dolphins lead series, 1-0;
See Miami vs. Minnesota

MINNESOTA vs. *NEW ENGLAND
RS: Patriots lead series, 6-4
1970—Vikings, 35-14 (B)
1974—Patriots, 17-14 (M)
1979—Patriots, 27-23 (NE)
1988—Vikings, 36-6 (M)
1991—Patriots, 26-23 (NE) OT
1994—Patriots, 26-20 (NE) OT
1997—Vikings, 23-18 (M)
2000—Vikings, 21-13 (NE)
2002—Patriots, 24-17 (NE)
2006—Patriots, 31-7 (M)
(RS Pts.—Vikings 219, Patriots 202)
**Franchise in Boston prior to 1971*

MINNESOTA vs. NEW ORLEANS
RS: Vikings lead series, 18-7
PS: Vikings lead series, 2-1
1968—Saints, 20-17 (NO)
1970—Vikings, 26-0 (M)
1971—Vikings, 23-10 (NO)
1972—Vikings, 37-6 (M)
1974—Vikings, 29-9 (M)
1975—Vikings, 20-7 (NO)
1976—Vikings, 40-9 (NO)
1978—Saints, 31-24 (NO)
1980—Vikings, 23-20 (NO)
1981—Vikings, 20-10 (M)
1983—Saints, 17-16 (NO)
1985—Saints, 30-23 (M)
1986—Vikings, 33-17 (M)
1987—*Vikings, 44-10 (NO)
1988—Vikings, 45-3 (M)
1990—Vikings, 32-3 (M)
1991—Saints, 26-0 (NO)
1993—Saints, 17-14 (M)
1994—Vikings, 21-20 (M)
1995—Vikings, 43-24 (M)
1998—Vikings, 31-24 (M)
2000—**Vikings, 34-16 (M)
2001—Saints, 28-15 (NO)
2002—Vikings, 32-31 (NO)
2004—Vikings, 38-31 (NO)
2005—Vikings, 33-16 (M)
2008—Vikings, 30-27 (NO)
2009—***Saints, 31-28 (NO) OT
(RS Pts.—Vikings 665, Saints 436)
(PS Pts.—Vikings 106, Saints 57)
**NFC First-Round Playoff*
***NFC Divisional Playoff*
****NFC Championship*

MINNESOTA vs. N.Y. GIANTS
RS: Vikings lead series, 13-8
PS: Giants lead series, 2-1
1964—Vikings, 30-21 (NY)
1965—Vikings, 40-14 (M)
1967—Vikings, 27-24 (M)
1969—Giants, 24-23 (NY)
1971—Vikings, 17-10 (NY)
1973—Vikings, 31-7 (New Haven)
1976—Vikings, 24-7 (M)
1986—Giants, 22-20 (M)
1989—Giants, 24-14 (NY)
1990—Giants, 23-15 (NY)
1993—*Giants, 17-10 (NY)
1994—Vikings, 27-10 (NY)
1996—Giants, 15-10 (NY)
1997—*Vikings, 23-22 (NY)
1999—Vikings, 34-17 (NY)
2000—**Giants, 41-0 (NY)
2001—Vikings, 28-16 (M)
2002—Giants, 27-20 (M)
2003—Giants, 29-17 (M)
2004—Giants, 34-13 (M)
2005—Vikings, 24-21 (NY)
2007—Vikings, 41-17 (NY)
2008—Vikings, 20-19 (M)
2009—Vikings, 44-7 (M)
(RS Pts.—Vikings 519, Giants 388)
(PS Pts.—Giants 80, Vikings 33)
**NFC First-Round Playoff*
***NFC Championship*

MINNESOTA vs. N.Y. JETS
RS: Jets lead series, 7-1
1970—Jets, 20-10 (NY)
1975—Vikings, 29-21 (M)
1979—Jets, 14-7 (NY)
1982—Jets, 42-14 (M)
1994—Jets, 31-21 (M)
1997—Jets, 23-21 (NY)
2002—Jets, 20-7 (NY)
2006—Jets, 26-13 (M)
(RS Pts.—Jets 197, Vikings 122)

MINNESOTA vs. *OAKLAND
RS: Raiders lead series, 8-4
PS: Raiders lead series, 1-0
1973—Vikings, 24-16 (M)
1976—**Raiders, 32-14 (Pasadena)
1977—Raiders, 35-13 (O)
1978—Raiders, 27-20 (O)
1981—Raiders, 36-10 (M)
1984—Raiders, 23-20 (LA)
1987—Vikings, 31-20 (M)
1990—Raiders, 28-24 (M)
1993—Raiders, 24-7 (LA)
1996—Vikings, 16-13 (O) OT
1999—Raiders, 22-17 (M)
2003—Raiders, 28-18 (O)
2007—Vikings, 29-22 (M)
(RS Pts.—Raiders 294, Vikings 229)
(PS Pts.—Raiders 32, Vikings 14)
**Franchise in Los Angeles from 1982-1994*
***Super Bowl XI*

MINNESOTA vs. PHILADELPHIA
RS: Vikings lead series, 11-9
PS: Eagles lead series, 3-0
1962—Vikings, 31-21 (M)
1963—Vikings, 34-13 (P)
1968—Vikings, 24-17 (P)
1971—Vikings, 13-0 (P)
1973—Vikings, 28-21 (M)
1976—Vikings, 31-12 (P)
1978—Vikings, 28-27 (M)
1980—Eagles, 42-7 (M)
*Eagles, 31-16 (P)
1981—Vikings, 35-23 (M)
1984—Eagles, 19-17 (P)
1985—Vikings, 28-23 (P)
Eagles, 37-35 (M)
1988—Vikings, 23-21 (M)
1989—Eagles, 10-9 (P)
1990—Eagles, 32-24 (P)
1992—Eagles, 28-17 (P)
1997—Vikings, 28-19 (M)
2001—Eagles, 48-17 (P)
2004—Eagles, 27-16 (P)
*Eagles, 27-14 (P)
2007—Eagles, 23-16 (M)
2008—**Eagles, 26-14 (M)
(RS Pts.—Eagles 463, Vikings 461)
(PS Pts.—Eagles 84, Vikings 44)
**NFC Divisional Playoff*
***NFC First-Round Playoff*

MINNESOTA vs. PITTSBURGH
RS: Vikings lead series, 8-7
PS: Steelers lead series, 1-0
1962—Steelers, 39-31 (P)
1964—Vikings, 30-10 (M)
1967—Vikings, 41-27 (P)
1969—Vikings, 52-14 (M)
1972—Steelers, 23-10 (P)
1974—*Steelers, 16-6 (New Orleans)
1976—Vikings, 17-6 (M)
1980—Steelers, 23-17 (M)
1983—Vikings, 17-14 (P)
1986—Vikings, 31-7 (M)
1989—Steelers, 27-14 (P)
1992—Vikings, 6-3 (P)
1995—Vikings, 44-24 (P)
2001—Steelers, 21-16 (P)
2005—Steelers, 18-3 (M)

2009—Steelers, 27-17 (P)
(RS Pts.—Vikings 346, Steelers 283)
(PS Pts.—Steelers 16, Vikings 6)
*Super Bowl IX

MINNESOTA vs. *ST. LOUIS
RS: Vikings lead series, 18-14-2
PS: Vikings lead series, 5-2
1961—Rams, 31-17 (LA)
Vikings, 42-21 (M)
1962—Vikings, 38-14 (LA)
Tie, 24-24 (M)
1963—Rams, 27-24 (LA)
Vikings, 21-13 (M)
1964—Rams, 22-13 (LA)
Vikings, 34-13 (M)
1965—Vikings, 38-35 (LA)
Vikings, 24-13 (M)
1966—Vikings, 35-7 (M)
Rams, 21-6 (LA)
1967—Rams, 39-3 (LA)
1968—Rams, 31-3 (M)
1969—Vikings, 20-13 (LA)
**Vikings, 23-20 (M)
1970—Vikings, 13-3 (M)
1972—Vikings, 45-41 (LA)
1973—Vikings, 10-9 (M)
1974—Rams, 20-17 (LA)
***Vikings, 14-10 (M)
1976—Tie, 10-10 (M) OT
***Vikings, 24-13 (M)
1977—Rams, 35-3 (LA)
****Vikings, 14-7 (LA)
1978—Rams, 34-17 (M)
****Rams, 34-10 (LA)
1979—Rams, 27-21 (LA) OT
1985—Rams, 13-10 (LA)
1987—Vikings, 21-16 (LA)
1988—*****Vikings, 28-17 (M)
1989—Vikings, 23-21 (M) OT
1991—Vikings, 20-14 (M)
1992—Vikings, 31-17 (LA)
1998—Vikings, 38-31 (StL)
1999—****Rams, 49-37 (StL)
2000—Rams, 40-29 (StL)
2003—Rams, 48-17 (StL)
2005—Vikings, 27-13 (M)
2006—Rams, 41-21 (M)
2009—Vikings, 38-10 (StL)
(RS Pts.—Rams 767, Vikings 753)
(PS Pts.—Rams 150, Vikings 150)
*Franchise in Los Angeles prior to 1995
**Conference Championship
***NFC Championship
****NFC Divisional Playoff
*****NFC First-Round Playoff

MINNESOTA vs. SAN DIEGO
RS: Series tied, 5-5
1971—Chargers, 30-14 (SD)
1975—Vikings, 28-13 (M)
1978—Chargers, 13-7 (M)
1981—Vikings, 33-31 (SD)
1984—Chargers, 42-13 (M)
1985—Vikings, 21-17 (M)
1993—Chargers, 30-17 (M)
1999—Vikings, 35-27 (M)
2003—Chargers, 42-28 (SD)
2007—Vikings, 35-17 (M)
(RS Pts.—Chargers 262, Vikings 231)

MINNESOTA vs. SAN FRANCISCO
RS: Vikings lead series, 20-18-1
PS: 49ers lead series, 4-1
1961—49ers, 38-24 (M)
49ers, 38-28 (SF)
1962—49ers, 21-7 (SF)
49ers, 35-12 (M)
1963—Vikings, 24-20 (SF)
Vikings, 45-14 (M)
1964—Vikings, 27-22 (SF)
Vikings, 24-7 (M)
1965—Vikings, 42-41 (SF)
49ers, 45-24 (M)
1966—Tie, 20-20 (SF)
Vikings, 28-3 (M)
1967—49ers, 27-21 (M)
1968—Vikings, 30-20 (SF)
1969—Vikings, 10-7 (M)
1970—*49ers, 17-14 (M)
1971—49ers, 13-9 (M)
1972—49ers, 20-17 (SF)
1973—Vikings, 17-13 (SF)
1975—Vikings, 27-17 (M)
1976—49ers, 20-16 (SF)
1977—Vikings, 28-27 (M)
1979—Vikings, 28-22 (M)
1983—49ers, 48-17 (M)
1984—49ers, 51-7 (SF)
1985—Vikings, 28-21 (M)
1986—Vikings, 27-24 (SF) OT
1987—*Vikings, 36-24 (SF)
1988—49ers, 24-21 (SF)
*49ers, 34-9 (SF)
1989—*49ers, 41-13 (SF)
1990—49ers, 20-17 (M)
1991—Vikings, 17-14 (M)
1992—49ers, 20-17 (M)
1993—49ers, 38-19 (SF)
1994—Vikings, 21-14 (M)
1995—49ers, 37-30 (SF)
1997—49ers, 28-17 (SF)
*49ers, 38-22 (SF)
1999—Vikings, 40-16 (M)
2003—Vikings, 35-7 (M)
2006—49ers, 9-3 (SF)
2007—Vikings, 27-7 (SF)
2009—Vikings, 27-24 (M)
(RS Pts.—49ers 892, Vikings 878)
(PS Pts.—49ers 154, Vikings 94)
*NFC Divisional Playoff

MINNESOTA vs. SEATTLE
RS: Seahawks lead series, 6-5
1976—Vikings, 27-21 (M)
1978—Seahawks, 29-28 (S)
1984—Seahawks, 20-12 (M)
1987—Seahawks, 28-17 (S)
1990—Vikings, 24-21 (S)
1996—Seahawks, 42-23 (S)
2002—Seahawks, 48-23 (S)
2003—Vikings, 34-7 (M)
2004—Seahawks, 27-23 (M)
2006—Vikings, 31-13 (S)
2009—Vikings, 35-9 (M)
(RS Pts.—Vikings 277, Seahawks 265)

MINNESOTA vs. TAMPA BAY
RS: Vikings lead series, 31-20
1977—Vikings, 9-3 (TB)
1978—Buccaneers, 16-10 (M)
Vikings, 24-7 (TB)
1979—Buccaneers, 12-10 (M)
Vikings, 23-22 (TB)
1980—Vikings, 38-30 (M)
Vikings, 21-10 (TB)
1981—Buccaneers, 21-13 (TB)
Vikings, 25-10 (M)
1982—Vikings, 17-10 (M)
1983—Vikings, 19-16 (TB) OT
Buccaneers, 17-12 (M)
1984—Buccaneers, 35-31 (TB)
Vikings, 27-24 (M)
1985—Vikings, 31-16 (TB)
Vikings, 26-7 (M)
1986—Vikings, 23-10 (TB)
Vikings, 45-13 (M)
1987—Buccaneers, 20-10 (TB)
Vikings, 23-17 (M)
1988—Vikings, 14-13 (M)
Vikings, 49-20 (TB)
1989—Vikings, 17-3 (M)
Vikings, 24-10 (TB)
1990—Buccaneers, 23-20 (M) OT
Buccaneers, 26-13 (TB)
1991—Vikings, 28-13 (M)
Vikings, 26-24 (TB)
1992—Vikings, 26-20 (M)
Vikings, 35-7 (TB)
1993—Vikings, 15-0 (M)
Buccaneers, 23-10 (TB)
1994—Vikings, 36-13 (TB)
Buccaneers, 20-17 (M) OT
1995—Buccaneers, 20-17 (TB) OT
Vikings, 31-17 (M)
1996—Buccaneers, 24-13 (TB)
Vikings, 21-10 (M)
1997—Buccaneers, 28-14 (M)
Vikings, 10-6 (TB)
1998—Vikings, 31-7 (M)
Buccaneers, 27-24 (TB)
1999—Vikings, 21-14 (M)
Buccaneers, 24-17 (TB)
2000—Vikings, 30-23 (M)
Buccaneers, 41-13 (TB)
2001—Vikings, 20-16 (M)
Buccaneers, 41-14 (TB)
2002—Buccaneers, 38-24 (TB)
2005—Buccaneers, 24-13 (M)
2008—Buccaneers, 19-13 (TB)
(RS Pts.—Vikings 1,093, Buccaneers 910)

MINNESOTA vs. *TENNESSEE
RS: Vikings lead series, 7-4
1974—Vikings, 51-10 (M)
1980—Oilers, 20-16 (H)
1983—Vikings, 34-14 (M)
1986—Oilers, 23-10 (H)
1989—Vikings, 38-7 (M)
1992—Oilers, 17-13 (M)
1995—Vikings, 23-17 (M) OT
1998—Vikings, 26-16 (T)
2001—Vikings, 42-24 (M)
2004—Vikings, 20-3 (M)
2008—Titans, 30-17 (T)
(RS Pts.—Vikings 290, Titans 181)
*Franchise in Houston prior to 1997; known as Oilers prior to 1999

MINNESOTA vs. WASHINGTON
RS: Redskins lead series, 8-6
PS: Redskins lead series, 3-2
1968—Vikings, 27-14 (M)
1970—Vikings, 19-10 (W)
1972—Redskins, 24-21 (M)
1973—*Vikings, 27-20 (M)
1975—Redskins, 31-30 (W)
1976—*Vikings, 35-20 (M)
1980—Vikings, 39-14 (W)
1982—**Redskins, 21-7 (W)

1984—Redskins, 31-17 (M)
1986—Redskins, 44-38 (W) OT
1987—Redskins, 27-24 (M) OT
***Redskins, 17-10 (W)
1992—Redskins, 15-13 (M)
****Redskins, 24-7 (M)
1993—Vikings, 14-9 (W)
1998—Vikings, 41-7 (M)
2004—Redskins, 21-18 (W)
2006—Vikings, 19-16 (W)
2007—Redskins, 32-21 (M)
(RS Pts.—Vikings 341, Redskins 295)
(PS Pts.—Redskins 102, Vikings 86)
NFC Divisional Playoff
***NFC Second-Round Playoff*
****NFC Championship*
*****NFC First-Round Playoff*

NEW ENGLAND vs. ARIZONA
RS: Series tied, 6-6;
See Arizona vs. New England
NEW ENGLAND vs. ATLANTA
RS: Series tied, 6-6;
See Atlanta vs. New England
NEW ENGLAND vs. BALTIMORE
RS: Patriots lead series, 5-0
PS: Ravens lead series, 1-0;
See Baltimore vs. New England
NEW ENGLAND vs. BUFFALO
RS: Patriots lead series, 58-40-1
PS: Patriots lead series, 1-0;
See Buffalo vs. New England
NEW ENGLAND vs. CAROLINA
RS: Series tied, 2-2
PS: Patriots lead series, 1-0;
See Carolina vs. New England
NEW ENGLAND vs. CHICAGO
RS: Patriots lead series, 7-3
PS: Bears lead series, 1-0;
See Chicago vs. New England
NEW ENGLAND vs. CINCINNATI
RS: Patriots lead series, 13-8;
See Cincinnati vs. New England
NEW ENGLAND vs. CLEVELAND
RS: Browns lead series, 11-9
PS: Browns lead series, 1-0;
See Cleveland vs. New England
NEW ENGLAND vs. DALLAS
RS: Cowboys lead series, 7-3;
See Dallas vs. New England
NEW ENGLAND vs. DENVER
RS: Broncos lead series, 25-16
PS: Broncos lead series, 2-0;
See Denver vs. New England
NEW ENGLAND vs. DETROIT
RS: Patriots lead series, 5-4;
See Detroit vs. New England
NEW ENGLAND vs. GREEN BAY
RS: Series tied, 4-4
PS: Packers lead series, 1-0;
See Green Bay vs. New England
NEW ENGLAND vs. HOUSTON
RS: Patriots lead series, 2-1;
See Houston vs. New England
NEW ENGLAND vs. INDIANAPOLIS
RS: Patriots lead series, 42-28
PS: Patriots lead series, 2-1;
See Indianapolis vs. New England
NEW ENGLAND vs. JACKSONVILLE
RS: Patriots lead series, 5-0
PS: Patriots lead series, 3-1;
See Jacksonville vs. New England
NEW ENGLAND vs. KANSAS CITY
RS: Chiefs lead series, 16-12-3;
See Kansas City vs. New England
NEW ENGLAND vs. MIAMI
RS: Dolphins lead series, 49-37
PS: Patriots lead series, 2-1;
See Miami vs. New England
NEW ENGLAND vs. MINNESOTA
RS: Patriots lead series, 6-4;
See Minnesota vs. New England
NEW ENGLAND vs. NEW ORLEANS
RS: Patriots lead series, 8-4
1972—Patriots, 17-10 (NO)
1976—Patriots, 27-6 (NE)
1980—Patriots, 38-27 (NO)
1983—Patriots, 7-0 (NE)
1986—Patriots, 21-20 (NO)
1989—Saints, 28-24 (NE)
1992—Saints, 31-14 (NE)
1995—Saints, 31-17 (NE)
1998—Patriots, 30-27 (NO)
2001—Patriots, 34-17 (NE)
2005—Patriots, 24-17 (NE)
2009—Saints, 38-17 (NO)
(RS Pts.—Patriots 270, Saints 252)
***NEW ENGLAND vs. N.Y. GIANTS**
RS: Patriots lead series, 5-3
PS: Giants lead series, 1-0;
1970—Giants, 16-0 (B)
1974—Patriots, 28-20 (New Haven)
1987—Giants, 17-10 (NY)
1990—Giants, 13-10 (NE)
1996—Patriots, 23-22 (NY)
1999—Patriots, 16-14 (NE)
2003—Patriots, 17-6 (NE)
2007—Patriots, 38-35 (NY)
**Giants, 17-14 (Arizona)
(RS Pts.—Giants 143, Patriots 142)
(PS Pts.—Giants 17, Patriots 14)
**Franchise in Boston prior to 1971*
***Super Bowl XLII*
***NEW ENGLAND vs. **N.Y. JETS**
RS: Jets lead series, 50-48-1
PS: Patriots lead series, 2-0
1960—Patriots, 28-24 (NY)
Patriots, 38-21 (B)
1961—Titans, 21-20 (B)
Titans, 37-30 (NY)
1962—Patriots, 43-14 (NY)
Patriots, 24-17 (B)
1963—Patriots, 38-14 (B)
Jets, 31-24 (NY)
1964—Patriots, 26-10 (B)
Jets, 35-14 (NY)
1965—Jets, 30-20 (B)
Patriots, 27-23 (NY)
1966—Tie, 24-24 (B)
Jets, 38-28 (NY)
1967—Jets, 30-23 (NY)
Jets, 29-24 (B)
1968—Jets, 47-31 (Birmingham)
Jets, 48-14 (NY)
1969—Jets, 23-14 (B)
Jets, 23-17 (NY)
1970—Jets, 31-21 (B)
Jets, 17-3 (NY)
1971—Patriots, 20-0 (NE)
Jets, 13-6 (NY)
1972—Jets, 41-13 (NE)
Jets, 34-10 (NY)
1973—Jets, 9-7 (NE)
Jets, 33-13 (NY)
1974—Patriots, 24-0 (NY)
Jets, 21-16 (NE)
1975—Jets, 36-7 (NY)
Jets, 30-28 (NE)
1976—Patriots, 41-7 (NE)
Patriots, 38-24 (NY)
1977—Jets, 30-27 (NY)
Patriots, 24-13 (NE)
1978—Patriots, 55-21 (NE)
Patriots, 19-17 (NY)
1979—Patriots, 56-3 (NE)
Jets, 27-26 (NY)
1980—Patriots, 21-11 (NY)
Patriots, 34-21 (NE)
1981—Jets, 28-24 (NY)
Jets, 17-6 (NE)
1982—Jets, 31-7 (NE)
1983—Patriots, 23-13 (NE)
Jets, 26-3 (NY)
1984—Patriots, 28-21 (NY)
Patriots, 30-20 (NE)
1985—Patriots, 20-13 (NE)
Jets, 16-13 (NY) OT
***Patriots, 26-14 (NY)
1986—Patriots, 20-6 (NY)
Jets, 31-24 (NE)
1987—Jets, 43-24 (NY)
Patriots, 42-20 (NE)
1988—Patriots, 28-3 (NE)
Patriots, 14-13 (NY)
1989—Patriots, 27-24 (NY)
Jets, 27-26 (NE)
1990—Jets, 37-13 (NE)
Jets, 42-7 (NY)
1991—Jets, 28-21 (NE)
Patriots, 6-3 (NY)
1992—Jets, 30-21 (NY)
Patriots, 24-3 (NE)
1993—Jets, 45-7 (NY)
Jets, 6-0 (NE)
1994—Jets, 24-17 (NY)
Patriots, 24-13 (NE)
1995—Patriots, 20-7 (NY)
Patriots, 31-28 (NE)
1996—Patriots, 31-27 (NY)
Patriots, 34-10 (NE)
1997—Patriots, 27-24 (NE) OT
Jets, 24-19 (NY)
1998—Jets, 24-14 (NE)
Jets, 31-10 (NY)
1999—Patriots, 30-28 (NY)
Jets, 24-17 (NE)
2000—Jets, 20-19 (NY)
Jets, 34-17 (NE)
2001—Jets, 10-3 (NE)
Patriots, 17-16 (NY)
2002—Patriots, 44-7 (NY)
Jets, 30-17 (NE)
2003—Patriots, 23-16 (NE)
Patriots, 21-16 (NY)
2004—Patriots, 13-7 (NE)
Patriots, 23-7 (NY)
2005—Patriots, 16-3 (NE)
Patriots, 31-21 (NY)
2006—Patriots, 24-17 (NY)
Jets, 17-14 (NE)
***Patriots, 37-16 (NE)
2007—Patriots, 38-14 (NY)
Patriots, 20-10 (NE)

2008—Patriots, 19-10 (NY)
Jets, 34-31 (NE) OT
2009—Jets, 16-9 (NY)
Patriots, 31-14 (NE)
(RS Pts.—Patriots 2,178, Jets 2,107)
(PS Pts.—Patriots 63, Jets 30)
Franchise in Boston prior to 1971
**Jets known as Titans prior to 1963*
***AFC First-Round Playoff*

***NEW ENGLAND vs. **OAKLAND**
RS: Series tied, 14-14-1
PS: Patriots lead series, 2-1
1960—Raiders, 27-14 (O)
Patriots, 34-28 (B)
1961—Patriots, 20-17 (B)
Patriots, 35-21 (O)
1962—Patriots, 26-16 (B)
Raiders, 20-0 (O)
1963—Patriots, 20-14 (O)
Patriots, 20-14 (B)
1964—Patriots, 17-14 (O)
Tie, 43-43 (B)
1965—Raiders, 24-10 (B)
Raiders, 30-21 (O)
1966—Patriots, 24-21 (B)
1967—Raiders, 35-7 (O)
Raiders, 48-14 (B)
1968—Raiders, 41-10 (O)
1969—Raiders, 38-23 (B)
1971—Patriots, 20-6 (NE)
1974—Raiders, 41-26 (O)
1976—Patriots, 48-17 (NE)
***Raiders, 24-21 (O)
1978—Patriots, 21-14 (O)
1981—Raiders, 27-17 (O)
1985—Raiders, 35-20 (NE)
***Patriots, 27-20 (LA)
1987—Patriots, 26-23 (NE)
1989—Raiders, 24-21 (LA)
1994—Raiders, 21-17 (NE)
2001—***Patriots, 16-13 (NE) OT
2002—Raiders, 27-20 (O)
2005—Patriots, 30-20 (NE)
2008—Patriots, 49-26 (O)
(RS Pts.—Raiders 732, Patriots 653)
(PS Pts.—Patriots 64, Raiders 57)
Franchise in Boston prior to 1971
**Franchise in Los Angeles from 1982-1994*
***AFC Divisional Playoff*

NEW ENGLAND vs. PHILADELPHIA
RS: Eagles lead series, 6-4
PS: Patriots lead series, 1-0
1973—Eagles, 24-23 (P)
1977—Patriots, 14-6 (NE)
1978—Patriots, 24-14 (NE)
1981—Eagles, 13-3 (P)
1984—Eagles, 27-17 (P)
1987—Eagles, 34-31 (NE) OT
1990—Eagles, 48-20 (P)
1999—Eagles, 24-9 (P)
2003—Patriots, 31-10 (P)
2004—*Patriots, 24-21 (Jacksonville)
2007—Patriots, 31-28 (NE)
(RS Pts.—Eagles 228, Patriots 203)
(PS Pts.—Patriots 24, Eagles 21)
Super Bowl XXXIX

NEW ENGLAND vs. PITTSBURGH
RS: Steelers lead series, 13-7
PS: Patriots lead series, 3-1
1972—Steelers, 33-3 (P)
1974—Steelers, 21-17 (NE)
1976—Patriots, 30-27 (P)
1979—Steelers, 16-13 (NE) OT
1981—Steelers, 27-21 (P) OT
1982—Steelers, 37-14 (P)
1983—Patriots, 28-23 (P)
1986—Patriots, 34-0 (P)
1989—Steelers, 28-10 (P)
1990—Steelers, 24-3 (P)
1991—Steelers, 20-6 (P)
1993—Steelers, 17-14 (P)
1995—Steelers, 41-27 (P)
1996—*Patriots, 28-3 (NE)
1997—Steelers, 24-21 (NE) OT
*Steelers, 7-6 (P)
1998—Patriots, 23-9 (P)
2001—**Patriots, 24-17 (P)
2002—Patriots, 30-14 (NE)
2004—Steelers, 34-20 (P)
**Patriots, 41-27 (P)
2005—Patriots, 23-20 (P)
2007—Patriots, 34-13 (NE)
2008—Steelers, 33-10 (NE)
(RS Pts.—Steelers 461, Patriots 381)
(PS Pts.—Patriots 99, Steelers 54)
AFC Divisional Playoff
**AFC Championship*

NEW ENGLAND vs. *ST. LOUIS
RS: Series tied, 5-5
PS: Patriots lead series, 1-0
1974—Patriots, 20-14 (NE)
1980—Rams, 17-14 (NE)
1983—Patriots, 21-7 (LA)
1986—Patriots, 30-28 (LA)
1989—Rams, 24-20 (NE)
1992—Rams, 14-0 (LA)
1998—Rams, 32-18 (StL)
2001—Rams, 24-17 (NE)
**Patriots, 20-17 (New Orleans)
2004—Patriots, 40-22 (StL)
2008—Patriots, 23-16 (NE)
(RS Pts.—Patriots 203, Rams 198)
(PS Pts.—Patriots 20, Rams 17)
Franchise in Los Angeles prior to 1995
**Super Bowl XXXVI*

***NEW ENGLAND vs. **SAN DIEGO**
RS: Patriots lead series, 18-14-2
PS: Patriots lead series, 2-1
1960—Patriots, 35-0 (LA)
Chargers, 45-16 (B)
1961—Chargers, 38-27 (B)
Patriots, 41-0 (SD)
1962—Patriots, 24-20 (B)
Patriots, 20-14 (SD)
1963—Chargers, 17-13 (SD)
Chargers, 7-6 (B)
***Chargers, 51-10 (SD)
1964—Patriots, 33-28 (SD)
Chargers, 26-17 (B)
1965—Tie, 10-10 (B)
Patriots, 22-6 (SD)
1966—Chargers, 24-0 (SD)
Patriots, 35-17 (B)
1967—Chargers, 28-14 (SD)
Tie, 31-31 (SD)
1968—Chargers, 27-17 (B)
1969—Chargers, 13-10 (B)
Chargers, 28-18 (SD)
1970—Chargers, 16-14 (B)
1973—Patriots, 30-14 (NE)
1975—Patriots, 33-19 (SD)
1977—Patriots, 24-20 (SD)
1978—Patriots, 28-23 (NE)
1979—Patriots, 27-21 (NE)
1983—Patriots, 37-21 (NE)
1994—Patriots, 23-17 (NE)
1996—Patriots, 45-7 (SD)
1997—Patriots, 41-7 (NE)
2001—Patriots, 29-26 (NE) OT
2002—Chargers, 21-14 (SD)
2005—Chargers, 41-17 (NE)
2006—****Patriots, 24-21 (SD)
2007—Patriots, 38-14 (NE)
*****Patriots, 21-12 (NE)
2008—Chargers, 30-10 (SD)
(RS Pts.—Patriots 802, Chargers 679)
(PS Pts.—Chargers 84, Patriots 55)
Franchise in Boston prior to 1971
**Franchise in Los Angeles prior to 1961*
***AFL Championship*
****AFC Divisional Playoff*
*****AFC Championship*

NEW ENGLAND vs. SAN FRANCISCO
RS: 49ers lead series, 7-4
1971—49ers, 27-10 (SF)
1975—Patriots, 24-16 (NE)
1980—49ers, 21-17 (SF)
1983—49ers, 33-13 (NE)
1986—49ers, 29-24 (NE)
1989—49ers, 37-20 (SF)
1992—49ers, 24-12 (NE)
1995—49ers, 28-3 (SF)
1998—Patriots, 24-21 (NE)
2004—Patriots, 21-7 (NE)
2008—Patriots, 30-21 (SF)
(RS Pts.—49ers 264, Patriots 198)

NEW ENGLAND vs. SEATTLE
RS: Patriots lead series, 8-7
1977—Patriots, 31-0 (NE)
1980—Patriots, 37-31 (S)
1982—Patriots, 16-0 (S)
1983—Seahawks, 24-6 (S)
1984—Patriots, 38-23 (NE)
1985—Patriots, 20-13 (S)
1986—Seahawks, 38-31 (NE)
1988—Patriots, 13-7 (NE)
1989—Seahawks, 24-3 (NE)
1990—Seahawks, 33-20 (NE)
1992—Seahawks, 10-6 (NE)
1993—Seahawks, 17-14 (NE)
Seahawks, 10-9 (S)
2004—Patriots, 30-20 (NE)
2008—Patriots, 24-21 (S)
(RS Pts.—Patriots 298, Seahawks 271)

NEW ENGLAND vs. TAMPA BAY
RS: Patriots lead series, 5-2
1976—Patriots, 31-14 (TB)
1985—Patriots, 32-14 (TB)
1988—Patriots, 10-7 (NE) OT
1997—Buccaneers, 27-7 (TB)
2000—Buccaneers, 21-16 (NE)
2005—Patriots, 28-0 (NE)
2009—Patriots, 35-7 (London)
(RS Pts.—Patriots 159, Buccaneers 90)

***NEW ENGLAND vs. **TENNESSEE**
RS: Patriots lead series, 21-15-1
PS: Series tied, 1-1
1960—Oilers, 24-10 (B)
Oilers, 37-21 (H)
1961—Tie, 31-31 (B)
Oilers, 27-15 (H)
1962—Patriots, 34-21 (B)

Oilers, 21-17 (H)
1963—Patriots, 45-3 (B)
Patriots, 46-28 (H)
1964—Patriots, 25-24 (B)
Patriots, 34-17 (H)
1965—Oilers, 31-10 (H)
Patriots, 42-14 (B)
1966—Patriots, 27-21 (B)
Patriots, 38-14 (H)
1967—Patriots, 18-7 (B)
Oilers, 27-6 (H)
1968—Oilers, 16-0 (B)
Oilers, 45-17 (H)
1969—Patriots, 24-0 (B)
Oilers, 27-23 (H)
1971—Patriots, 28-20 (NE)
1973—Patriots, 32-0 (H)
1975—Oilers, 7-0 (NE)
1978—Oilers, 26-23 (NE)
***Oilers, 31-14 (NE)
1980—Oilers, 38-34 (H)
1981—Patriots, 38-10 (NE)
1982—Patriots, 29-21 (NE)
1987—Patriots, 21-7 (H)
1988—Oilers, 31-6 (H)
1989—Patriots, 23-13 (NE)
1991—Patriots, 24-20 (NE)
1993—Oilers, 28-14 (NE)
1998—Patriots, 27-16 (NE)
2002—Titans, 24-7 (T)
2003—Patriots, 38-30 (NE)
***Patriots, 17-14 (NE)
2006—Patriots, 40-23 (T)
2009—Patriots, 59-0 (NE)
(RS Pts.—Patriots 926, Titans 749)
(PS Pts.—Titans 45, Patriots 31)
Franchise in Boston prior to 1971
***Franchise in Houston prior to 1997; known as Oilers prior to 1999*
****AFC Divisional Playoff*

NEW ENGLAND vs. WASHINGTON
RS: Redskins lead series, 6-2
1972—Patriots, 24-23 (NE)
1978—Redskins, 16-14 (NE)
1981—Redskins, 24-22 (W)
1984—Redskins, 26-10 (NE)
1990—Redskins, 25-10 (NE)
1996—Redskins, 27-22 (NE)
2003—Redskins, 20-17 (W)
2007—Patriots, 52-7 (NE)
(RS Pts.—Patriots 171, Redskins 168)

NEW ORLEANS vs. ARIZONA
RS: Cardinals lead series, 13-12
PS: Saints lead series, 1-0;
See Arizona vs. New Orleans

NEW ORLEANS vs. ATLANTA
RS: Falcons lead series, 44-37
PS: Falcons lead series, 1-0;
See Atlanta vs. New Orleans

NEW ORLEANS vs. BALTIMORE
RS: Ravens lead series, 3-1;
See Baltimore vs. New Orleans

NEW ORLEANS vs. BUFFALO
RS: Saints lead series, 5-4;
See Buffalo vs. New Orleans

NEW ORLEANS vs. CAROLINA
RS: Panthers lead series, 17-13;
See Carolina vs. New Orleans

NEW ORLEANS vs. CHICAGO
RS: Bears lead series, 13-11
PS: Bears lead series, 2-0;
See Chicago vs. New Orleans

NEW ORLEANS vs. CINCINNATI
RS: Bengals lead series, 6-5;
See Cincinnati vs. New Orleans

NEW ORLEANS vs. CLEVELAND
RS: Browns lead series, 11-4;
See Cleveland vs. New Orleans

NEW ORLEANS vs. DALLAS
RS: Cowboys lead series, 15-8;
See Dallas vs. New Orleans

NEW ORLEANS vs. DENVER
RS: Broncos lead series, 7-2;
See Denver vs. New Orleans

NEW ORLEANS vs. DETROIT
RS: Saints lead series, 10-9-1;
See Detroit vs. New Orleans

NEW ORLEANS vs. GREEN BAY
RS: Packers lead series, 14-7;
See Green Bay vs. New Orleans

NEW ORLEANS vs. HOUSTON
RS: Series tied, 1-1;
See Houston vs. New Orleans

NEW ORLEANS vs. INDIANAPOLIS
RS: Series tied, 5-5
PS: Saints lead series, 1-0;
See Indianapolis vs. New Orleans

NEW ORLEANS vs. JACKSONVILLE
RS: Series tied, 2-2;
See Jacksonville vs. New Orleans

NEW ORLEANS vs. KANSAS CITY
RS: Saints lead series, 5-4;
See Kansas City vs. New Orleans

NEW ORLEANS vs. MIAMI
RS: Dolphins lead series, 6-4;
See Miami vs. New Orleans

NEW ORLEANS vs. MINNESOTA
RS: Vikings lead series, 18-7
PS: Vikings lead series, 2-1;
See Minnesota vs. New Orleans

NEW ORLEANS vs. NEW ENGLAND
RS: Patriots lead series, 8-4;
See New England vs. New Orleans

NEW ORLEANS vs. N.Y. GIANTS
RS: Giants lead series, 14-11
1967—Giants, 27-21 (NY)
1968—Giants, 38-21 (NY)
1969—Saints, 25-24 (NY)
1970—Saints, 14-10 (NO)
1972—Giants, 45-21 (NY)
1975—Giants, 28-14 (NY)
1978—Saints, 28-17 (NO)
1979—Saints, 24-14 (NO)
1981—Giants, 20-7 (NY)
1984—Saints, 10-3 (NY)
1985—Giants, 21-13 (NO)
1986—Giants, 20-17 (NY)
1987—Saints, 23-14 (NO)
1988—Giants, 13-12 (NO)
1993—Giants, 24-14 (NO)
1994—Saints, 27-22 (NO)
1995—Giants, 45-29 (NY)
1996—Saints 17-3 (NY)
1997—Giants, 14-9 (NY)
1999—Giants, 31-3 (NY)
2001—Giants, 21-13 (NY)
2003—Saints, 45-7 (NO)
2005—Giants, 27-10 (NY*)
2006—Saints, 30-7 (NY)
2009—Saints, 48-27 (NO)
(RS Pts.—Giants 522, Saints 495)
**Saints home game*

NEW ORLEANS vs. N.Y. JETS
RS: Saints lead series, 6-5
1972—Jets, 18-17 (NY)
1977—Jets, 16-13 (NO)
1980—Saints, 21-20 (NY)
1983—Jets, 31-28 (NO)
1986—Jets, 28-23 (NY)
1989—Saints, 29-14 (NO)
1992—Saints, 20-0 (NY)
1995—Saints, 12-0 (NY)
2001—Jets, 16-9 (NO)
2005—Saints, 21-19 (NY)
2009—Saints, 24-10 (NO)
(RS Pts.—Saints 217, Jets 172)

NEW ORLEANS vs. *OAKLAND
RS: Series tied, 5-5-1
1971—Tie, 21-21 (NO)
1975—Raiders, 48-10 (O)
1979—Raiders, 42-35 (NO)
1985—Raiders, 23-13 (LA)
1988—Saints, 20-6 (NO)
1991—Saints, 27-0 (NO)
1994—Raiders, 24-19 (LA)
1997—Saints, 13-10 (O)
2000—Raiders, 31-22 (NO)
2004—Saints, 31-26 (O)
2008—Saints, 34-3 (NO)
(RS Pts.—Saints 245, Raiders 234)
**Franchise in Los Angeles from 1982-1994*

NEW ORLEANS vs. PHILADELPHIA
RS: Eagles lead series, 15-10
PS: Series tied, 1-1
1967—Saints, 31-24 (NO)
Eagles, 48-21 (P)
1968—Eagles, 29-17 (P)
1969—Eagles, 13-10 (P)
Saints, 26-17 (NO)
1972—Saints, 21-3 (NO)
1974—Saints, 14-10 (NO)
1977—Eagles, 28-7 (P)
1978—Eagles, 24-17 (NO)
1979—Eagles, 26-14 (NO)
1980—Eagles, 34-21 (NO)
1981—Eagles, 31-14 (NO)
1983—Saints, 20-17 (P) OT
1985—Saints, 23-21 (NO)
1987—Eagles, 27-17 (P)
1989—Saints, 30-20 (NO)
1991—Saints, 13-6 (P)
1992—Eagles, 15-13 (P)
*Eagles, 36-20 (NO)
1993—Eagles, 37-26 (P)
1995—Eagles, 15-10 (NO)
2000—Eagles, 21-7 (NO)
2003—Eagles, 33-20 (P)
2006—Saints, 27-24 (NO)
**Saints, 27-24 (NO)
2007—Eagles, 38-23 (NO)
2009—Saints, 48-22 (P)
(RS Pts.—Eagles 583, Saints 490)
(PS Pts.—Eagles 60, Saints 47)
**NFC First-Round Playoff*
***NFC Divisional Playoff*

NEW ORLEANS vs. PITTSBURGH
RS: Steelers lead series, 7-6
1967—Steelers, 14-10 (NO)
1968—Saints, 16-12 (P)
Saints, 24-14 (NO)
1969—Saints, 27-24 (NO)
1974—Steelers, 28-7 (NO)

1978—Steelers, 20-14 (P)
1981—Steelers, 20-6 (NO)
1984—Saints, 27-24 (NO)
1987—Saints, 20-16 (P)
1990—Steelers, 9-6 (NO)
1993—Steelers, 37-14 (P)
2002—Saints, 32-29 (NO)
2006—Steelers, 38-31 (P)
(RS Pts.—Steelers 285, Saints 234)

NEW ORLEANS vs. *ST. LOUIS
RS: Rams lead series, 38-30
PS: Saints lead series, 1-0
1967—Rams, 27-13 (NO)
1969—Rams, 36-17 (LA)
1970—Rams, 30-17 (NO)
Rams, 34-16 (LA)
1971—Saints, 24-20 (NO)
Rams, 45-28 (LA)
1972—Rams, 34-14 (LA)
Saints, 19-16 (NO)
1973—Rams, 29-7 (LA)
Rams, 24-13 (NO)
1974—Rams, 24-0 (LA)
Saints, 20-7 (NO)
1975—Rams, 38-14 (LA)
Rams, 14-7 (NO)
1976—Rams, 16-10 (NO)
Rams, 33-14 (LA)
1977—Rams, 14-7 (LA)
Saints, 27-26 (NO)
1978—Rams, 26-20 (NO)
Saints, 10-3 (LA)
1979—Rams, 35-17 (NO)
Saints, 29-14 (LA)
1980—Rams, 45-31 (LA)
Rams, 27-7 (NO)
1981—Saints, 23-17 (NO)
Saints, 21-13 (LA)
1983—Rams, 30-27 (LA)
Rams, 26-24 (NO)
1984—Rams, 28-10 (NO)
Rams, 34-21 (LA)
1985—Rams, 28-10 (LA)
Saints, 29-3 (NO)
1986—Saints, 6-0 (NO)
Rams, 26-13 (LA)
1987—Saints, 37-10 (NO)
Saints, 31-14 (LA)
1988—Rams, 12-10 (NO)
Saints, 14-10 (LA)
1989—Saints, 40-21 (LA)
Rams, 20-17 (NO) OT
1990—Saints, 24-20 (LA)
Saints, 20-17 (NO)
1991—Saints, 24-7 (NO)
Saints, 24-17 (LA)
1992—Saints, 13-10 (NO)
Saints, 37-14 (LA)
1993—Saints, 37-6 (LA)
Rams, 23-20 (NO)
1994—Saints, 37-34 (NO)
Saints, 31-15 (LA)
1995—Rams, 17-13 (StL)
Saints, 19-10 (NO)
1996—Rams, 26-10 (NO)
Rams, 14-13 (StL)
1997—Rams, 38-24 (StL)
Rams, 34-27 (NO)
1998—Saints, 24-17 (StL)
Saints, 24-3 (NO)
1999—Rams, 43-12 (StL)
Rams, 30-14 (NO)
2000—Saints, 31-24 (StL)
Rams, 26-21 (NO)
**Saints, 31-28 (NO)
2001—Saints, 34-31 (StL)
Rams, 34-21 (NO)
2004—Saints, 28-25 (StL) OT
2005—Rams, 28-17 (StL)
2007—Rams, 37-29 (NO)
2009—Saints, 28-23 (StL)
(RS Pts.—Rams 1,532, Saints 1,370)
(PS Pts.—Saints 31, Rams 28)
Franchise in Los Angeles prior to 1995
***NFC First-Round Playoff*

NEW ORLEANS vs. SAN DIEGO
RS: Chargers lead series, 7-3
1973—Chargers, 17-14 (SD)
1977—Chargers, 14-0 (NO)
1979—Chargers, 35-0 (NO)
1988—Saints, 23-17 (SD)
1991—Chargers, 24-21 (SD)
1994—Chargers, 36-22 (NO)
1997—Chargers, 20-6 (NO)
2000—Saints, 28-27 (SD)
2004—Chargers, 43-17 (SD)
2008—Saints, 37-32 (London)
(RS Pts.—Chargers 265, Saints 168)

NEW ORLEANS vs. SAN FRANCISCO
RS: 49ers lead series, 45-23-2
1967—49ers, 27-13 (SF)
1969—Saints, 43-38 (NO)
1970—Tie, 20-20 (SF)
49ers, 38-27 (NO)
1971—49ers, 38-20 (NO)
Saints, 26-20 (SF)
1972—49ers, 37-2 (NO)
Tie, 20-20 (SF)
1973—49ers, 40-0 (SF)
Saints, 16-10 (NO)
1974—49ers, 17-13 (NO)
49ers, 35-21 (SF)
1975—49ers, 35-21 (SF)
49ers, 16-6 (NO)
1976—49ers, 33-3 (SF)
49ers, 27-7 (NO)
1977—49ers, 10-7 (NO) OT
49ers, 20-17 (SF)
1978—Saints, 14-7 (SF)
Saints, 24-13 (NO)
1979—Saints, 30-21 (SF)
Saints, 31-20 (NO)
1980—49ers, 26-23 (NO)
49ers, 38-35 (SF) OT
1981—49ers, 21-14 (SF)
49ers, 21-17 (NO)
1982—Saints, 23-20 (SF)
1983—49ers, 32-13 (NO)
49ers, 27-0 (SF)
1984—49ers, 30-20 (SF)
49ers, 35-3 (NO)
1985—Saints, 20-17 (SF)
49ers, 31-19 (NO)
1986—49ers, 26-17 (SF)
Saints, 23-10 (NO)
1987—49ers, 24-22 (NO)
Saints, 26-24 (SF)
1988—49ers, 34-33 (NO)
49ers, 30-17 (SF)
1989—49ers, 24-20 (NO)
49ers, 31-13 (SF)
1990—49ers, 13-12 (NO)
Saints, 13-10 (SF)
1991—Saints, 10-3 (NO)
49ers, 38-24 (SF)
1992—49ers, 16-10 (NO)
49ers, 21-20 (SF)
1993—Saints, 16-13 (NO)
49ers, 42-7 (SF)
1994—49ers, 24-13 (SF)
49ers, 35-14 (NO)
1995—49ers, 24-22 (NO)
Saints, 11-7 (SF)
1996—49ers, 27-11 (SF)
49ers, 24-17 (NO)
1997—49ers, 33-7 (SF)
49ers, 23-0 (NO)
1998—49ers, 31-0 (NO)
49ers, 31-20 (SF)
1999—49ers, 28-21 (SF)
Saints, 24-6 (NO)
2000—Saints, 31-15 (NO)
Saints, 31-27 (SF)
2001—49ers, 28-27 (SF)
49ers, 38-0 (NO)
2002—Saints, 35-27 (NO)
2004—Saints, 30-27 (NO)
2006—Saints, 34-10 (NO)
2007—Saints, 31-10 (SF)
2008—Saints, 31-17 (NO)
(RS Pts.—49ers 1,691, Saints 1,261)

NEW ORLEANS vs. SEATTLE
RS: Series tied, 5-5
1976—Saints, 51-27 (S)
1979—Seahawks, 38-24 (S)
1985—Seahawks, 27-3 (NO)
1988—Saints, 20-19 (S)
1991—Saints, 27-24 (NO)
1997—Saints, 20-17 (NO) OT
2000—Seahawks, 20-10 (S)
2003—Seahawks, 27-10 (S)
2004—Seahawks, 21-7 (NO)
2007—Saints, 28-17 (S)
(RS Pts.—Seahawks 237, Saints 200)

NEW ORLEANS vs. TAMPA BAY
RS: Saints lead series, 21-15
1977—Buccaneers, 33-14 (NO)
1978—Saints, 17-10 (TB)
1979—Saints, 42-14 (TB)
1981—Buccaneers, 31-14 (NO)
1982—Buccaneers, 13-10 (NO)
1983—Saints, 24-21 (TB)
1984—Saints, 17-13 (NO)
1985—Saints, 20-13 (NO)
1986—Saints, 38-7 (NO)
1987—Saints, 44-34 (NO)
1988—Saints, 13-9 (NO)
1989—Buccaneers, 20-10 (TB)
1990—Saints, 35-7 (NO)
1991—Saints, 23-7 (NO)
1992—Saints, 23-21 (NO)
1994—Saints, 9-7 (TB)
1996—Buccaneers, 13-7 (TB)
1998—Saints, 9-3 (NO)
1999—Buccaneers, 31-16 (NO)
2001—Buccaneers, 48-21 (TB)
2002—Saints, 26-20 (TB) OT
Saints, 23-20 (NO)
2003—Saints, 17-14 (TB)
Buccaneers, 14-7 (NO)
2004—Buccaneers, 20-17 (NO)
Saints, 21-17 (TB)
2005—Buccaneers, 10-3 (Baton Rouge)

Buccaneers, 27-13 (TB)
2006—Saints, 24-21 (NO)
Saints, 31-14 (TB)
2007—Buccaneers, 31-14 (TB)
Buccaneers, 27-23 (NO)
2008—Saints, 24-20 (NO)
Buccaneers, 23-20 (TB)
2009—Saints, 38-7 (TB)
Buccaneers, 20-17 (NO) OT
(RS Pts.—Saints 724, Buccaneers 660)

NEW ORLEANS vs. *TENNESSEE
RS: Titans lead series, 7-4-1
1971—Tie, 13-13 (H)
1976—Oilers, 31-26 (NO)
1978—Oilers, 17-12 (NO)
1981—Saints, 27-24 (H)
1984—Saints, 27-10 (H)
1987—Saints, 24-10 (NO)
1990—Oilers, 23-10 (H)
1993—Saints, 33-21 (NO)
1996—Oilers, 31-14 (NO)
1999—Titans, 24-21 (NO)
2003—Titans, 27-12 (T)
2007—Titans, 31-14 (NO)
(RS Pts.—Titans 262, Saints 233)
**Franchise in Houston prior to 1997; known as Oilers prior to 1999*

NEW ORLEANS vs. WASHINGTON
RS: Redskins lead series, 15-8
1967—Redskins, 30-10 (NO)
Saints, 30-14 (W)
1968—Saints, 37-17 (NO)
1969—Redskins, 26-20 (NO)
Redskins, 17-14 (W)
1971—Redskins, 24-14 (W)
1973—Saints, 19-3 (NO)
1975—Redskins, 41-3 (W)
1979—Saints, 14-10 (W)
1980—Redskins, 22-14 (W)
1982—Redskins, 27-10 (NO)
1986—Redskins, 14-6 (NO)
1988—Redskins, 27-24 (W)
1989—Redskins, 16-14 (NO)
1990—Redskins, 31-17 (W)
1992—Saints, 20-3 (NO)
1994—Redskins, 38-24 (NO)
2001—Redskins, 40-10 (NO)
2002—Saints, 43-27 (W)
2003—Saints, 24-20 (W)
2006—Redskins, 16-10 (NO)
2008—Redskins, 29-24 (W)
2009—Saints, 33-30 (W) OT
(RS Pts.—Redskins 522, Saints 434)

N.Y. GIANTS vs. ARIZONA
RS: Giants lead series, 79-42-2;
See Arizona vs. N.Y. Giants

N.Y. GIANTS vs. ATLANTA
RS: Series tied, 10-10;
See Atlanta vs. N.Y. Giants

N.Y. GIANTS vs. BALTIMORE
RS: Ravens lead series, 2-1
PS: Ravens lead series, 1-0;
See Baltimore vs. N.Y. Giants

N.Y. GIANTS vs. BUFFALO
RS: Bills lead series, 6-4
PS: Giants lead series, 1-0;
See Buffalo vs. N.Y. Giants

N.Y. GIANTS vs. CAROLINA
RS: Panthers lead series, 3-2
PS: Panthers lead series, 1-0;
See Carolina vs. N.Y. Giants

N.Y. GIANTS vs. CHICAGO
RS: Bears lead series, 27-18-2
PS: Bears lead series, 5-3;
See Chicago vs. N.Y. Giants

N.Y. GIANTS vs. CINCINNATI
RS: Bengals lead series, 5-3;
See Cincinnati vs. N.Y. Giants

N.Y. GIANTS vs. CLEVELAND
RS: Browns lead series, 26-19-2
PS: Series tied, 1-1;
See Cleveland vs. N.Y. Giants

N.Y. GIANTS vs. DALLAS
RS: Cowboys lead series, 55-38-2
PS: Giants lead series, 1-0;
See Dallas vs. N.Y. Giants

N.Y. GIANTS vs. DENVER
RS: Series tied, 5-5
PS: Giants lead series, 1-0;
See Denver vs. N.Y. Giants

N.Y. GIANTS vs. DETROIT
RS: Lions lead series, 20-18-1
PS: Lions lead series, 1-0;
See Detroit vs. N.Y. Giants

N.Y. GIANTS vs. GREEN BAY
RS: Packers lead series, 25-21-2
PS: Packers lead series, 4-2;
See Green Bay vs. N.Y. Giants

N.Y. GIANTS vs. HOUSTON
RS: Series tied, 1-1;
See Houston vs. N.Y. Giants

N.Y. GIANTS vs. INDIANAPOLIS
RS: Colts lead series, 7-6
PS: Colts lead series, 2-0;
See Indianapolis vs. N.Y. Giants

N.Y. GIANTS vs. JACKSONVILLE
RS: Series tied, 2-2;
See Jacksonville vs. N.Y. Giants

N.Y. GIANTS vs. KANSAS CITY
RS: Giants lead series, 10-2;
See Kansas City vs. N.Y. Giants

N.Y. GIANTS vs. MIAMI
RS: Giants lead series, 4-2;
See Miami vs. N.Y. Giants

N.Y. GIANTS vs. MINNESOTA
RS: Vikings lead series, 13-8
PS: Giants lead series, 2-1;
See Minnesota vs. N.Y. Giants

N.Y. GIANTS vs. NEW ENGLAND
RS: Patriots lead series, 5-3
PS: Giants lead series, 1-0;
See New England vs. N.Y. Giants

N.Y. GIANTS vs. NEW ORLEANS
RS: Giants lead series, 14-11;
See New Orleans vs. N.Y. Giants

N.Y. GIANTS vs. N.Y. JETS
RS: Giants lead series, 7-4
1970—Giants, 22-10 (NYJ)
1974—Jets, 26-20 (New Haven) OT
1981—Jets, 26-7 (NYG)
1984—Giants, 20-10 (NYJ)
1987—Giants, 20-7 (NYG)
1988—Jets, 27-21 (NYJ)
1993—Jets, 10-6 (NYG)
1996—Giants, 13-6 (NYJ)
1999—Giants, 41-28 (NYG)
2003—Giants, 31-28 (NYJ) OT
2007—Giants, 35-24 (NYG)
(RS Pts.—Giants 236, Jets 202)

N.Y. GIANTS vs. *OAKLAND
RS: Raiders lead series, 7-4
1973—Raiders, 42-0 (O)
1980—Raiders, 33-17 (NY)
1983—Raiders, 27-12 (LA)
1986—Giants, 14-9 (LA)
1989—Giants, 34-17 (NY)
1992—Raiders, 13-10 (LA)
1995—Raiders, 17-13 (NY)
1998—Raiders, 20-17 (O)
2001—Raiders, 28-10 (NY)
2005—Giants, 30-21 (O)
2009—Giants, 44-7 (NY)
(RS Pts.—Raiders 234, Giants 201)
**Franchise in Los Angeles from 1982-1994*

N.Y. GIANTS vs. PHILADELPHIA
RS: Giants lead series, 79-69-2
PS: Series tied, 2-2
1933—Giants, 56-0 (NY)
Giants, 20-14 (P)
1934—Giants, 17-0 (NY)
Eagles, 6-0 (P)
1935—Giants, 10-0 (NY)
Giants, 21-14 (P)
1936—Eagles, 10-7 (P)
Giants, 21-17 (NY)
1937—Giants, 16-7 (P)
Giants, 21-0 (NY)
1938—Eagles, 14-10 (P)
Giants, 17-7 (NY)
1939—Giants, 13-3 (P)
Giants, 27-10 (NY)
1940—Giants, 20-14 (P)
Giants, 17-7 (NY)
1941—Giants, 24-0 (P)
Giants, 16-0 (NY)
1942—Giants, 35-17 (NY)
Giants, 14-0 (P)
1944—Eagles, 24-17 (NY)
Tie, 21-21 (P)
1945—Eagles, 38-17 (P)
Giants, 28-21 (NY)
1946—Eagles, 24-14 (P)
Giants, 45-17 (NY)
1947—Eagles, 23-0 (P)
Eagles, 41-24 (NY)
1948—Eagles, 45-0 (P)
Eagles, 35-14 (NY)
1949—Eagles, 24-3 (NY)
Eagles, 17-3 (P)
1950—Giants, 7-3 (NY)
Giants, 9-7 (P)
1951—Giants, 26-24 (NY)
Giants, 23-7 (P)
1952—Giants, 31-7 (P)
Eagles, 14-10 (NY)
1953—Eagles, 30-7 (P)
Giants, 37-28 (NY)
1954—Giants, 27-14 (NY)
Eagles, 29-14 (P)
1955—Eagles, 27-17 (P)
Giants, 31-7 (NY)
1956—Giants, 20-3 (NY)
Giants, 21-7 (P)
1957—Giants, 24-20 (P)
Giants, 13-0 (NY)
1958—Eagles, 27-24 (P)
Giants, 24-10 (NY)
1959—Eagles, 49-21 (P)
Giants, 24-7 (NY)
1960—Eagles, 17-10 (NY)
Eagles, 31-23 (P)
1961—Giants, 38-21 (NY)

Giants, 28-24 (P)
1962—Giants, 29-13 (P)
Giants, 19-14 (NY)
1963—Giants, 37-14 (P)
Giants, 42-14 (NY)
1964—Eagles, 38-7 (P)
Eagles, 23-17 (NY)
1965—Giants, 16-14 (P)
Giants, 35-27 (NY)
1966—Eagles, 35-17 (P)
Eagles, 31-3 (NY)
1967—Giants, 44-7 (NY)
1968—Giants, 34-25 (P)
Giants, 7-6 (NY)
1969—Eagles, 23-20 (NY)
1970—Giants, 30-23 (NY)
Eagles, 23-20 (P)
1971—Eagles, 23-7 (P)
Eagles, 41-28 (NY)
1972—Giants, 27-12 (P)
Giants, 62-10 (NY)
1973—Tie, 23-23 (NY)
Eagles, 20-16 (P)
1974—Eagles, 35-7 (P)
Eagles, 20-7 (New Haven)
1975—Giants, 23-14 (P)
Eagles, 13-10 (NY)
1976—Eagles, 20-7 (P)
Eagles, 10-0 (NY)
1977—Eagles, 28-10 (NY)
Eagles, 17-14 (P)
1978—Eagles, 19-17 (NY)
Eagles, 20-3 (P)
1979—Eagles, 23-17 (P)
Eagles, 17-13 (NY)
1980—Eagles, 35-3 (P)
Eagles, 31-16 (NY)
1981—Eagles, 24-10 (NY)
Giants, 20-10 (P)
*Giants, 27-21 (P)
1982—Giants, 23-7 (NY)
Giants, 26-24 (P)
1983—Eagles, 17-13 (NY)
Giants, 23-0 (P)
1984—Giants, 28-27 (NY)
Eagles, 24-10 (P)
1985—Giants, 21-0 (NY)
Giants, 16-10 (P) OT
1986—Giants, 35-3 (NY)
Giants, 17-14 (P)
1987—Giants, 20-17 (P)
Giants, 23-20 (NY) OT
1988—Eagles, 24-13 (P)
Eagles, 23-17 (NY) OT
1989—Eagles, 21-19 (P)
Eagles, 24-17 (NY)
1990—Giants, 27-20 (NY)
Eagles, 31-13 (P)
1991—Eagles, 30-7 (P)
Eagles, 19-14 (NY)
1992—Eagles, 47-34 (NY)
Eagles, 20-10 (P)
1993—Giants, 21-10 (NY)
Giants, 7-3 (P)
1994—Giants, 28-23 (NY)
Giants, 16-13 (P)
1995—Eagles, 17-14 (NY)
Eagles, 28-19 (P)
1996—Eagles, 19-10 (NY)
Eagles, 24-0 (P)
1997—Giants, 31-17 (NY)
Giants, 31-21 (P)
1998—Giants, 20-0 (NY)
Giants, 20-10 (P)
1999—Giants, 16-15 (NY)
Giants, 23-17 (P) OT
2000—Giants, 33-18 (P)
Giants, 24-7 (NY)
**Giants, 20-10 (NY)
2001—Eagles, 10-9 (NY)
Eagles, 24-21 (P)
2002—Eagles, 17-3 (P)
Giants, 10-7 (NY) OT
2003—Eagles, 14-10 (NY)
Eagles, 28-10 (P)
2004—Eagles, 31-17 (P)
Eagles, 27-6 (NY)
2005—Giants, 27-17 (NY)
Giants, 26-23 (P) OT
2006—Giants, 30-24 (P) OT
Eagles, 36-22 (NY)
*Eagles, 23-20 (P)
2007—Giants, 16-3 (NY)
Giants, 16-13 (P)
2008—Giants, 36-31 (P)
Eagles, 20-14 (NY)
**Eagles, 23-11 (NY)
2009—Eagles, 40-17 (P)
Eagles, 45-38 (NY)
(RS Pts.—Giants 2,861, Eagles 2,752)
(PS Pts.—Giants 78, Eagles 77)
NFC First-Round Playoff
***NFC Divisional Playoff*

N.Y. GIANTS vs. *PITTSBURGH
RS: Giants lead series, 44-28-3
1933—Giants, 23-2 (P)
Giants, 27-3 (NY)
1934—Giants, 14-12 (P)
Giants, 17-7 (NY)
1935—Giants, 42-7 (P)
Giants, 13-0 (NY)
1936—Pirates, 10-7 (P)
1937—Giants, 10-7 (P)
Giants, 17-0 (NY)
1938—Giants, 27-14 (P)
Pirates, 13-10 (NY)
1939—Giants, 14-7 (P)
Giants, 23-7 (NY)
1940—Tie, 10-10 (P)
Giants, 12-0 (NY)
1941—Giants, 37-10 (P)
Giants, 28-7 (NY)
1942—Steelers, 13-10 (P)
Steelers, 17-9 (NY)
1945—Giants, 34-6 (P)
Steelers, 21-7 (NY)
1946—Giants, 17-14 (P)
Giants, 7-0 (NY)
1947—Steelers, 38-21 (NY)
Steelers, 24-7 (P)
1948—Giants, 34-27 (NY)
Steelers, 38-28 (P)
1949—Steelers, 28-7 (P)
Steelers, 21-17 (NY)
1950—Giants, 18-7 (P)
Steelers, 17-6 (NY)
1951—Tie, 13-13 (P)
Giants, 14-0 (NY)
1952—Steelers, 63-7 (P)
1953—Steelers, 24-14 (P)
Steelers, 14-10 (NY)
1954—Giants, 30-6 (P)
Giants, 24-3 (NY)
1955—Steelers, 30-23 (P)
Steelers, 19-17 (NY)
1956—Giants, 38-10 (NY)
Giants, 17-14 (P)
1957—Giants, 35-0 (NY)
Steelers, 21-10 (P)
1958—Giants, 17-6 (NY)
Steelers, 31-10 (P)
1959—Giants, 21-16 (P)
Steelers, 14-9 (NY)
1960—Giants, 19-17 (P)
Giants, 27-24 (NY)
1961—Giants, 17-14 (P)
Giants, 42-21 (NY)
1962—Giants, 31-27 (P)
Steelers, 20-17 (NY)
1963—Steelers, 31-0 (P)
Giants, 33-17 (NY)
1964—Steelers, 27-24 (P)
Steelers, 44-17 (NY)
1965—Giants, 23-13 (P)
Giants, 35-10 (NY)
1966—Tie, 34-34 (P)
Steelers, 47-28 (NY)
1967—Giants, 27-24 (P)
Giants, 28-20 (NY)
1968—Giants, 34-20 (P)
1969—Giants, 10-7 (NY)
Giants, 21-17 (P)
1971—Steelers, 17-13 (P)
1976—Steelers, 27-0 (NY)
1985—Giants, 28-10 (NY)
1991—Giants, 23-20 (P)
1994—Steelers, 10-6 (NY)
2000—Giants, 30-10 (NY)
2004—Steelers, 33-30 (NY)
2008—Giants, 21-14 (P)
(RS Pts.—Giants 1,480, Steelers 1,246)
**Steelers known as Pirates prior to 1940*

N.Y. GIANTS vs. *ST. LOUIS
RS: Rams lead series, 25-13
PS: Series tied, 1-1
1938—Giants, 28-0 (NY)
1940—Rams, 13-0 (NY)
1941—Giants, 49-14 (NY)
1945—Rams, 21-17 (NY)
1946—Rams, 31-21 (NY)
1947—Rams, 34-10 (LA)
1948—Rams, 52-37 (NY)
1953—Rams, 21-7 (LA)
1954—Rams, 17-16 (NY)
1959—Giants, 23-21 (LA)
1961—Giants, 24-14 (NY)
1966—Rams, 55-14 (LA)
1968—Rams, 24-21 (LA)
1970—Rams, 31-3 (NY)
1973—Rams, 40-6 (LA)
1976—Rams, 24-10 (LA)
1978—Rams, 20-17 (NY)
1979—Giants, 20-14 (LA)
1980—Rams, 28-7 (NY)
1981—Giants, 10-7 (NY)
1983—Rams, 16-6 (NY)
1984—Rams, 33-12 (LA)
**Giants, 16-13 (LA)
1985—Giants, 24-19 (NY)
1988—Rams, 45-31 (NY)
1989—Rams, 31-10 (LA)
***Rams, 19-13 (NY) OT
1990—Giants, 31-7 (LA)

1991—Rams, 19-13 (NY)
1992—Rams, 38-17 (LA)
1993—Giants, 20-10 (NY)
1994—Rams, 17-10 (LA)
1997—Rams, 13-3 (StL)
1999—Rams, 31-10 (StL)
2000—Rams, 38-24 (NY)
2001—Rams, 15-14 (StL)
2002—Giants, 26-21 (StL)
2003—Giants, 23-13 (NY)
2005—Giants, 44-24 (NY)
2008—Giants, 41-13 (StL)
(RS Pts.—Rams 884, Giants 699)
(PS Pts.—Rams 32, Giants 29)
Franchise in Los Angeles prior to 1995 and in Cleveland prior to 1946
***NFC First-Round Playoff*
****NFC Divisional Playoff*

N.Y. GIANTS vs. SAN DIEGO
RS: Series tied, 5-5
1971—Giants, 35-17 (NY)
1975—Giants, 35-24 (NY)
1980—Chargers, 44-7 (SD)
1983—Chargers, 41-34 (NY)
1986—Giants, 20-7 (NY)
1989—Giants, 20-13 (SD)
1995—Chargers, 27-17 (NY)
1998—Giants, 34-16 (SD)
2005—Chargers, 45-23 (SD)
2009—Chargers, 21-20 (NY)
(RS Pts.—Chargers 255, Giants 245)

N.Y. GIANTS vs. SAN FRANCISCO
RS: Giants lead series, 14-13
PS: 49ers lead series, 4-3
1952—Giants, 23-14 (NY)
1956—Giants, 38-21 (SF)
1957—49ers, 27-17 (NY)
1960—Giants, 21-19 (SF)
1963—Giants, 48-14 (NY)
1968—49ers, 26-10 (NY)
1972—Giants, 23-17 (SF)
1975—Giants, 26-23 (SF)
1977—Giants, 20-17 (NY)
1978—Giants, 27-10 (NY)
1979—Giants, 32-16 (NY)
1980—49ers, 12-0 (SF)
1981—49ers, 17-10 (SF)
*49ers, 38-24 (SF)
1984—49ers, 31-10 (NY)
*49ers, 21-10 (SF)
1985—**Giants, 17-3 (NY)
1986—Giants, 21-17 (SF)
*Giants, 49-3 (NY)
1987—49ers, 41-21 (NY)
1988—49ers, 20-17 (NY)
1989—49ers, 34-24 (SF)
1990—49ers, 7-3 (SF)
***Giants, 15-13 (SF)
1991—Giants, 16-14 (NY)
1992—49ers, 31-14 (NY)
1993—*49ers, 44-3 (SF)
1995—49ers, 20-6 (SF)
1998—49ers, 31-7 (SF)
2002—49ers, 16-13 (NY)
**49ers, 39-38 (SF)
2005—Giants, 24-6 (SF)
2007—Giants, 33-15 (NY)
2008—Giants, 29-17 (NY)
(RS Pts.—49ers 533, Giants 533)
(PS Pts.—49ers 161, Giants 156)
**NFC Divisional Playoff*
***NFC First-Round Playoff*
****NFC Championship*

N.Y. GIANTS vs. SEATTLE
RS: Giants lead series, 8-5
1976—Giants, 28-16 (NY)
1980—Giants, 27-21 (S)
1981—Giants, 32-0 (S)
1983—Seahawks, 17-12 (NY)
1986—Seahawks, 17-12 (S)
1989—Giants, 15-3 (NY)
1992—Giants, 23-10 (NY)
1995—Seahawks, 30-28 (S)
2001—Giants, 27-24 (NY)
2002—Giants, 9-6 (NY)
2005—Seahawks, 24-21 (S) OT
2006—Seahawks, 42-30 (S)
2008—Giants, 44-6 (NY)
(RS Pts.—Giants 308, Seahawks 216)

N.Y. GIANTS vs. TAMPA BAY
RS: Giants lead series, 11-6
PS: Giants lead series, 1-0
1977—Giants, 10-0 (TB)
1978—Giants, 19-13 (TB)
Giants, 17-14 (NY)
1979—Giants, 17-14 (NY)
Buccaneers, 31-3 (TB)
1980—Buccaneers, 30-13 (TB)
1984—Giants, 17-14 (NY)
Buccaneers, 20-17 (TB)
1985—Giants, 22-20 (NY)
1991—Giants, 21-14 (TB)
1993—Giants, 23-7 (NY)
1997—Buccaneers, 20-8 (NY)
1998—Buccaneers, 20-3 (TB)
1999—Giants, 17-13 (TB)
2003—Buccaneers, 19-13 (TB)
2006—Giants, 17-3 (NY)
2007—*Giants, 24-14 (TB)
2009—Giants, 24-0 (TB)
(RS Pts.—Giants 261, Buccaneers 252)
(PS Pts.—Giants 24, Buccaneers 14)
**NFC First-Round Playoff*

N.Y. GIANTS vs. *TENNESSEE
RS: Giants lead series, 5-4
1973—Giants, 34-14 (NY)
1982—Giants, 17-14 (NY)
1985—Giants, 35-14 (H)
1991—Giants, 24-20 (NY)
1994—Giants, 13-10 (H)
1997—Oilers, 10-6 (T)
2000—Titans, 28-14 (T)
2002—Titans, 32-29 (NY) OT
2006—Titans, 24-21 (T)
(RS Pts.—Giants 193, Titans 166)
Franchise in Houston prior to 1997; known as Oilers prior to 1999

N.Y. GIANTS vs. *WASHINGTON
RS: Giants lead series, 89-61-4
PS: Series tied, 1-1
1932—Braves, 14-6 (B)
Tie, 0-0 (NY)
1933—Redskins, 21-20 (B)
Giants, 7-0 (NY)
1934—Giants, 16-13 (B)
Giants, 3-0 (NY)
1935—Giants, 20-12 (B)
Giants, 17-6 (NY)
1936—Giants, 7-0 (B)
Redskins, 14-0 (NY)
1937—Redskins, 13-3 (W)
Redskins, 49-14 (NY)
1938—Giants, 10-7 (W)
Giants, 36-0 (NY)
1939—Tie, 0-0 (W)
Giants, 9-7 (NY)
1940—Redskins, 21-7 (W)
Giants, 21-7 (NY)
1941—Giants, 17-10 (W)
Giants, 20-13 (NY)
1942—Giants, 14-7 (W)
Redskins, 14-7 (NY)
1943—Giants, 14-10 (NY)
Giants, 31-7 (W)
**Redskins, 28-0 (NY)
1944—Giants, 16-13 (NY)
Giants, 31-0 (W)
1945—Redskins, 24-14 (NY)
Redskins, 17-0 (W)
1946—Redskins, 24-14 (W)
Giants, 31-0 (NY)
1947—Redskins, 28-20 (W)
Giants, 35-10 (NY)
1948—Redskins, 41-10 (W)
Redskins, 28-21 (NY)
1949—Giants, 45-35 (W)
Giants, 23-7 (NY)
1950—Giants, 21-17 (W)
Giants, 24-21 (NY)
1951—Giants, 35-14 (W)
Giants, 28-14 (NY)
1952—Giants, 14-10 (W)
Redskins, 27-17 (NY)
1953—Redskins, 13-9 (W)
Redskins, 24-21 (NY)
1954—Giants, 51-21 (W)
Giants, 24-7 (NY)
1955—Giants, 35-7 (NY)
Giants, 27-20 (W)
1956—Redskins, 33-7 (W)
Giants, 28-14 (NY)
1957—Giants, 24-20 (W)
Redskins, 31-14 (NY)
1958—Giants, 21-14 (W)
Giants, 30-0 (NY)
1959—Giants, 45-14 (NY)
Giants, 24-10 (W)
1960—Tie, 24-24 (NY)
Giants, 17-3 (W)
1961—Giants, 24-21 (W)
Giants, 53-0 (NY)
1962—Giants, 49-34 (NY)
Giants, 42-24 (W)
1963—Giants, 24-14 (W)
Giants, 44-14 (NY)
1964—Giants, 13-10 (NY)
Redskins, 36-21 (W)
1965—Redskins, 23-7 (NY)
Giants, 27-10 (W)
1966—Giants, 13-10 (NY)
Redskins, 72-41 (W)
1967—Redskins, 38-34 (W)
1968—Giants, 48-21 (NY)
Giants, 13-10 (W)
1969—Redskins, 20-14 (W)
1970—Giants, 35-33 (NY)
Giants, 27-24 (W)
1971—Redskins, 30-3 (NY)
Redskins, 23-7 (W)
1972—Redskins, 23-16 (NY)
Redskins, 27-13 (W)
1973—Redskins, 21-3 (New Haven)
Redskins, 27-24 (W)

1974—Redskins, 13-10 (New Haven)
Redskins, 24-3 (W)
1975—Redskins, 49-13 (W)
Redskins, 21-13 (NY)
1976—Redskins, 19-17 (W)
Giants, 12-9 (NY)
1977—Giants, 20-17 (NY)
Giants, 17-6 (W)
1978—Giants, 17-6 (NY)
Redskins, 16-13 (W) OT
1979—Redskins, 27-0 (W)
Giants, 14-6 (NY)
1980—Redskins, 23-21 (NY)
Redskins, 16-13 (W)
1981—Giants, 17-7 (W)
Redskins, 30-27 (NY) OT
1982—Redskins, 27-17 (NY)
Redskins, 15-14 (W)
1983—Redskins, 33-17 (NY)
Redskins, 31-22 (W)
1984—Redskins, 30-14 (W)
Giants, 37-13 (NY)
1985—Giants, 17-3 (NY)
Redskins, 23-21 (W)
1986—Giants, 27-20 (NY)
Giants, 24-14 (W)
***Giants, 17-0 (NY)
1987—Redskins, 38-12 (NY)
Redskins, 23-19 (W)
1988—Giants, 27-20 (NY)
Giants, 24-23 (W)
1989—Giants, 27-24 (W)
Giants, 20-17 (NY)
1990—Giants, 24-20 (W)
Giants, 21-10 (NY)
1991—Redskins, 17-13 (NY)
Redskins, 34-17 (W)
1992—Giants, 24-7 (W)
Redskins, 28-10 (NY)
1993—Giants, 41-7 (W)
Giants, 20-6 (NY)
1994—Giants, 31-23 (NY)
Giants, 21-19 (W)
1995—Giants, 24-15 (W)
Giants, 20-13 (NY)
1996—Redskins, 31-10 (NY)
Redskins, 31-21 (W)
1997—Tie, 7-7 (W) OT
Giants, 30-10 (NY)
1998—Giants, 31-24 (NY)
Redskins, 21-14 (W)
1999—Redskins, 50-21 (NY)
Redskins, 23-13 (W)
2000—Redskins, 16-6 (NY)
Giants, 9-7 (W)
2001—Giants, 23-9 (NY)
Redskins, 35-21 (W)
2002—Giants, 19-17 (NY)
Giants, 27-21 (W)
2003—Giants, 24-21 (W) OT
Redskins, 20-7 (NY)
2004—Giants, 20-14 (NY)
Redskins, 31-7 (W)
2005—Giants, 36-0 (NY)
Redskins, 35-20 (W)
2006—Giants, 19-3 (NY)
Giants, 34-28 (W)
2007—Giants, 24-17 (W)
Redskins, 22-10 (NY)
2008—Giants, 16-7 (NY)
Giants, 23-7 (W)
2009—Giants, 23-17 (NY)
Giants, 45-12 (W)
(RS Pts.—Giants 3,086, Redskins 2,773)
(PS Pts.—Redskins 28, Giants 17)
Franchise in Boston prior to 1937 and known as Braves prior to 1933
***Division Playoff*
****NFC Championship*

N.Y. JETS vs. ARIZONA
RS: Jets lead series, 5-2;
See Arizona vs. N.Y. Jets

N.Y. JETS vs. ATLANTA
RS: Falcons lead series, 6-4;
See Atlanta vs. N.Y. Jets

N.Y. JETS vs. BALTIMORE
RS: Ravens lead series, 5-1;
See Baltimore vs. N.Y. Jets

N.Y. JETS vs. BUFFALO
RS: Bills lead series, 53-45
PS: Bills lead series, 1-0;
See Buffalo vs. N.Y. Jets

N.Y. JETS vs. CAROLINA
RS: Jets lead series, 3-2;
See Carolina vs. N.Y. Jets

N.Y. JETS vs. CHICAGO
RS: Bears lead series, 6-3;
See Chicago vs. N.Y. Jets

N.Y. JETS vs. CINCINNATI
RS: Jets lead series, 14-7
PS: Jets lead series, 2-0;
See Cincinnati vs. N.Y. Jets

N.Y. JETS vs. CLEVELAND
RS: Browns lead series, 12-7
PS: Browns lead series, 1-0;
See Cleveland vs. N.Y. Jets

N.Y. JETS vs. DALLAS
RS: Cowboys lead series, 7-2;
See Dallas vs. N.Y. Jets

N.Y. JETS vs. DENVER
RS: Broncos lead series, 16-14-1
PS: Broncos lead series, 1-0;
See Denver vs. N.Y. Jets

N.Y. JETS vs. DETROIT
RS: Lions lead series, 6-5;
See Detroit vs. N.Y. Jets

N.Y. JETS vs. GREEN BAY
RS: Jets lead series, 8-2;
See Green Bay vs. N.Y. Jets

N.Y. JETS vs. HOUSTON
RS: Jets lead series, 4-0;
See Houston vs. N.Y. Jets

N.Y. JETS vs. INDIANAPOLIS
RS: Colts lead series, 40-26
PS: Jets lead series, 2-1;
See Indianapolis vs. N.Y. Jets

N.Y. JETS vs. JACKSONVILLE
RS: Jaguars lead series, 6-2
PS: Jets lead series, 1-0;
See Jacksonville vs. N.Y. Jets

N.Y. JETS vs. KANSAS CITY
RS: Series tied, 16-16-1
PS: Series tied, 1-1;
See Kansas City vs. N.Y. Jets

N.Y. JETS vs. MIAMI
RS: Jets lead series, 46-41-1
PS: Dolphins lead series, 1-0;
See Miami vs. N.Y. Jets

N.Y. JETS vs. MINNESOTA
RS: Jets lead series, 7-1;
See Minnesota vs. N.Y. Jets

N.Y. JETS vs. NEW ENGLAND
RS: Jets lead series, 50-48-1
PS: Patriots lead series, 2-0;
See New England vs. N.Y. Jets

N.Y. JETS vs. NEW ORLEANS
RS: Saints lead series, 6-5;
See New Orleans vs. N.Y. Jets

N.Y. JETS vs. N.Y. GIANTS
RS: Giants lead series, 7-4;
See N.Y. Giants vs. N.Y. Jets

***N.Y. JETS vs. **OAKLAND**
RS: Raiders lead series, 20-15-2
PS: Series tied, 2-2
1960—Raiders, 28-27 (NY)
Titans, 31-28 (O)
1961—Titans, 14-6 (O)
Titans, 23-12 (NY)
1962—Titans, 28-17 (O)
Titans, 31-21 (NY)
1963—Jets, 10-7 (NY)
Raiders, 49-26 (O)
1964—Jets, 35-13 (NY)
Raiders, 35-26 (O)
1965—Tie, 24-24 (NY)
Raiders, 24-14 (O)
1966—Raiders, 24-21 (NY)
Tie, 28-28 (O)
1967—Jets, 27-14 (NY)
Raiders, 38-29 (O)
1968—Raiders, 43-32 (O)
***Jets, 27-23 (NY)
1969—Raiders, 27-14 (NY)
1970—Raiders, 14-13 (NY)
1972—Raiders, 24-16 (O)
1977—Raiders, 28-27 (NY)
1979—Jets, 28-19 (NY)
1982—****Jets, 17-14 (LA)
1985—Raiders, 31-0 (LA)
1989—Raiders, 14-7 (NY)
1993—Raiders, 24-20 (LA)
1995—Raiders, 47-10 (NY)
1996—Raiders, 34-13 (NY)
1997—Jets 23-22 (NY)
1999—Raiders, 24-23 (O)
2000—Raiders, 31-7 (O)
2001—Jets, 24-22 (O)
*****Raiders, 38-24 (O)
2002—Raiders, 26-20 (O)
****Raiders, 30-10 (O)
2003—Jets, 27-24 (O) OT
2005—Jets, 26-10 (NY)
2006—Jets, 23-3 (NY)
2008—Raiders, 16-13 (O) OT
2009—Jets, 38-0 (O)
(RS Pts.—Raiders 851, Jets 798)
(PS Pts.—Raiders 105, Jets 78)
Jets known as Titans prior to 1963
***Franchise in Los Angeles from 1982-1994*
****AFL Championship*
*****AFC Second-Round Playoff*
******AFC First-Round Playoff*

N.Y. JETS vs. PHILADELPHIA
RS: Eagles lead series, 8-0
1973—Eagles, 24-23 (P)
1977—Eagles, 27-0 (P)
1978—Eagles, 17-9 (P)
1987—Eagles, 38-27 (NY)
1993—Eagles, 35-30 (NY)
1996—Eagles, 21-20 (NY)
2003—Eagles, 24-17 (P)

2007—Eagles, 16-9 (NY)
(RS Pts.—Eagles 202, Jets 135)

N.Y. JETS vs. PITTSBURGH
RS: Steelers lead series, 15-3
PS: Steelers lead series, 1-0
1970—Steelers, 21-17 (P)
1973—Steelers, 26-14 (P)
1975—Steelers, 20-7 (NY)
1977—Steelers, 23-20 (NY)
1978—Steelers, 28-17 (NY)
1981—Steelers, 38-10 (P)
1983—Steelers, 34-7 (NY)
1984—Steelers, 23-17 (NY)
1986—Steelers, 45-24 (NY)
1988—Jets, 24-20 (NY)
1989—Steelers, 13-0 (NY)
1990—Steelers, 24-7 (NY)
1992—Steelers, 27-10 (P)
2000—Steelers, 20-3 (NY)
2001—Steelers, 18-7 (P)
2003—Jets, 6-0 (NY)
2004—Steelers, 17-6 (P)
*Steelers, 20-17 (P) OT
2007—Jets, 19-16 (NY) OT
(RS Pts.—Steelers 413, Jets 215)
(PS Pts.—Steelers 20, Jets 17)
AFC Divisional Playoff

N.Y. JETS vs. *ST. LOUIS
RS: Rams lead series, 9-3
1970—Jets, 31-20 (LA)
1974—Rams, 20-13 (NY)
1980—Rams, 38-13 (LA)
1983—Jets, 27-24 (NY) OT
1986—Rams, 17-3 (NY)
1989—Rams, 38-14 (LA)
1992—Rams, 18-10 (LA)
1995—Rams, 23-20 (NY)
1998—Rams, 30-10 (StL)
2001—Rams, 34-14 (NY)
2004—Rams, 32-29 (StL) OT
2008—Jets, 47-3 (NY)
(RS Pts.—Rams 297, Jets 231)
Franchise in Los Angeles prior to 1995

***N.Y. JETS vs. **SAN DIEGO**
RS: Chargers lead series, 19-11-1
PS: Jets lead series, 2-0
1960—Chargers, 21-7 (NY)
Chargers, 50-43 (LA)
1961—Chargers, 25-10 (NY)
Chargers, 48-13 (SD)
1962—Chargers, 40-14 (SD)
Titans, 23-3 (NY)
1963—Chargers, 24-20 (SD)
Chargers, 53-7 (NY)
1964—Tie, 17-17 (NY)
Chargers, 38-3 (SD)
1965—Chargers, 34-9 (NY)
Chargers, 38-7 (SD)
1966—Jets, 17-16 (NY)
Chargers, 42-27 (SD)
1967—Jets, 42-31 (SD)
1968—Jets, 23-20 (NY)
Jets, 37-15 (SD)
1969—Chargers, 34-27 (SD)
1971—Chargers, 49-21 (SD)
1974—Jets, 27-14 (NY)
1975—Chargers, 24-16 (SD)
1983—Jets, 41-29 (SD)
1989—Jets, 20-17 (SD)
1990—Chargers, 39-3 (NY)
Chargers, 38-17 (SD)
1991—Jets, 24-3 (NY)
1994—Chargers, 21-6 (NY)
2002—Jets, 44-13 (SD)
2004—Jets, 34-28 (SD)
***Jets, 20-17 (SD) OT
2005—Chargers, 31-26 (NY)
2008—Chargers, 48-29 (SD)
2009—****Jets, 17-14 (SD)
(RS Pts.—Chargers 903, Jets 654)
(PS Pts.—Jets 37, Chargers 31)
Jets known as Titans prior to 1963
***Franchise in Los Angeles prior to 1961*
****AFC First-Round Playoff*
*****AFC Divisional Playoff*

N.Y. JETS vs. SAN FRANCISCO
RS: 49ers lead series, 9-2
1971—49ers, 24-21 (NY)
1976—49ers, 17-6 (SF)
1980—49ers, 37-27 (NY)
1983—Jets, 27-13 (SF)
1986—49ers, 24-10 (SF)
1989—49ers, 23-10 (NY)
1992—49ers, 31-14 (NY)
1998—49ers, 36-30 (SF) OT
2001—49ers, 19-17 (NY)
2004—Jets, 22-14 (NY)
2008—49ers, 24-14 (SF)
(RS Pts.—49ers 262, Jets 198)

N.Y. JETS vs. SEATTLE
RS: Seahawks lead series, 9-8
1977—Seahawks, 17-0 (NY)
1978—Seahawks, 24-17 (NY)
1979—Seahawks, 30-7 (S)
1980—Seahawks, 27-17 (NY)
1981—Seahawks, 19-3 (NY)
Seahawks, 27-23 (S)
1983—Seahawks, 17-10 (NY)
1985—Jets, 17-14 (NY)
1986—Jets, 38-7 (S)
1987—Jets, 30-14 (NY)
1991—Seahawks, 20-13 (S)
1995—Jets, 16-10 (S)
1997—Jets, 41-3 (S)
1998—Jets, 32-31 (NY)
1999—Jets, 19-9 (NY)
2004—Jets, 37-14 (NY)
2008—Seahawks, 13-3 (S)
(RS Pts.—Jets 323, Seahawks 296)

N.Y. JETS vs. TAMPA BAY
RS: Jets lead series, 9-1
1976—Jets, 34-0 (NY)
1982—Jets, 32-17 (NY)
1984—Buccaneers, 41-21 (TB)
1985—Jets, 62-28 (NY)
1990—Jets, 16-14 (TB)
1991—Jets, 16-13 (NY)
1997—Jets, 31-0 (NY)
2000—Jets, 21-17 (TB)
2005—Jets, 14-12 (NY)
2009—Jets, 26-3 (TB)
(RS Pts.—Jets 273, Buccaneers 145)

***N.Y. JETS vs. **TENNESSEE**
RS: Titans lead series, 21-17-1
PS: Titans lead series, 1-0
1960—Oilers, 27-21 (H)
Oilers, 42-28 (NY)
1961—Oilers, 49-13 (H)
Oilers, 48-21 (NY)
1962—Oilers, 56-17 (H)
Oilers, 44-10 (NY)
1963—Jets, 24-17 (NY)
Oilers, 31-27 (H)
1964—Jets, 24-21 (NY)
Oilers, 33-17 (H)
1965—Oilers, 27-21 (H)
Jets, 41-14 (NY)
1966—Jets, 52-13 (NY)
Oilers, 24-0 (H)
1967—Tie, 28-28 (NY)
1968—Jets, 20-14 (H)
Jets, 26-7 (NY)
1969—Jets, 26-17 (NY)
Jets, 34-26 (H)
1972—Oilers, 26-20 (H)
1974—Oilers, 27-22 (NY)
1977—Oilers, 20-0 (H)
1979—Oilers, 27-24 (H) OT
1980—Jets, 31-28 (NY) OT
1981—Jets, 33-17 (NY)
1984—Oilers, 31-20 (H)
1988—Jets, 45-3 (NY)
1990—Jets, 17-12 (H)
1991—Oilers, 23-20 (NY)
***Oilers, 17-10 (H)
1993—Oilers, 24-0 (H)
1994—Oilers, 24-10 (H)
1995—Oilers, 23-6 (H)
1996—Oilers, 35-10 (NY)
1998—Jets, 24-3 (T)
2003—Jets, 24-17 (NY)
2006—Jets, 23-16 (T)
2007—Titans, 10-6 (T)
2008—Jets, 34-13 (T)
2009—Jets, 24-17 (NY)
(RS Pts.—Titans 934, Jets 843)
(PS Pts.—Titans 17, Jets 10)
Jets known as Titans prior to 1963
***Franchise in Houston prior to 1997; known as Oilers prior to 1999*
****AFC First-Round Playoff*

N.Y. JETS vs. WASHINGTON
RS: Redskins lead series, 8-1
1972—Redskins, 35-17 (NY)
1976—Redskins, 37-16 (NY)
1978—Redskins, 23-3 (W)
1987—Redskins, 17-16 (W)
1993—Jets, 3-0 (W)
1996—Redskins, 31-16 (W)
1999—Redskins, 27-20 (NY)
2003—Redskins, 16-13 (W)
2007—Redskins 23-20 (NY) OT
(RS Pts.—Redskins 209, Jets 124)

OAKLAND vs. ARIZONA
RS: Raiders lead series, 5-2;
See Arizona vs. Oakland

OAKLAND vs. ATLANTA
RS: Raiders lead series, 7-5;
See Atlanta vs. Oakland

OAKLAND vs. BALTIMORE
RS: Ravens lead series, 5-1
PS: Ravens lead series, 1-0;
See Baltimore vs. Oakland

OAKLAND vs. BUFFALO
RS: Raiders lead series, 19-16
PS: Bills lead series, 2-0;
See Buffalo vs. Oakland

OAKLAND vs. CAROLINA
RS: Series tied, 2-2;
See Carolina vs. Oakland

OAKLAND vs. CHICAGO
RS: Series tied, 6-6;

See Chicago vs. Oakland
OAKLAND vs. CINCINNATI
RS: Raiders lead series, 18-8
PS: Raiders lead series, 2-0;
See Cincinnati vs. Oakland
OAKLAND vs. CLEVELAND
RS: Raiders lead series, 10-8
PS: Raiders lead series, 2-0;
See Cleveland vs. Oakland
OAKLAND vs. DALLAS
RS: Raiders lead series, 6-4;
See Dallas vs. Oakland
OAKLAND vs. DENVER
RS: Raiders lead series, 56-41-2
PS: Series tied, 1-1;
See Denver vs. Oakland
OAKLAND vs. DETROIT
RS: Raiders lead series, 6-4;
See Detroit vs. Oakland
OAKLAND vs. GREEN BAY
RS: Series tied, 5-5
PS: Packers lead series, 1-0;
See Green Bay vs. Oakland
OAKLAND vs. HOUSTON
RS: Texans lead series, 4-1;
See Houston vs. Oakland
OAKLAND vs. INDIANAPOLIS
RS: Raiders lead series, 7-4
PS: Series tied, 1-1;
See Indianapolis vs. Oakland
OAKLAND vs. JACKSONVILLE
RS: Jaguars lead series, 3-1;
See Jacksonville vs. Oakland
OAKLAND vs. KANSAS CITY
RS: Chiefs lead series, 52-45-2
PS: Chiefs lead series, 2-1;
See Kansas City vs. Oakland
OAKLAND vs. MIAMI
RS: Raiders lead series, 16-12-1
PS: Raiders lead series, 3-1;
See Miami vs. Oakland
OAKLAND vs. MINNESOTA
RS: Raiders lead series, 8-4
PS: Raiders lead series, 1-0;
See Minnesota vs. Oakland
OAKLAND vs. NEW ENGLAND
RS: Series tied, 14-14-1
PS: Patriots lead series, 2-1;
See New England vs. Oakland
OAKLAND vs. NEW ORLEANS
RS: Series tied, 5-5-1;
See New Orleans vs. Oakland
OAKLAND vs. N.Y. GIANTS
RS: Raiders lead series, 7-4;
See N.Y. Giants vs. Oakland
OAKLAND vs. N.Y. JETS
RS: Raiders lead series, 20-15-2
PS: Series tied, 2-2;
See N.Y. Jets vs. Oakland
***OAKLAND vs. PHILADELPHIA**
RS: Series tied, 5-5
PS: Raiders lead series, 1-0
1971—Raiders, 34-10 (O)
1976—Raiders, 26-7 (P)
1980—Eagles, 10-7 (P)
**Raiders, 27-10 (New Orleans)
1986—Eagles, 33-27 (LA) OT
1989—Eagles, 10-7 (P)
1992—Eagles, 31-10 (P)
1995—Raiders, 48-17 (O)
2001—Raiders, 20-10 (P)
2005—Eagles, 23-20 (P)
2009—Raiders, 13-9 (O)
(RS Pts.—Raiders 212, Eagles 160)
(PS Pts.—Raiders 27, Eagles 10)
**Franchise in Los Angeles from 1982-1994*
***Super Bowl XV*
***OAKLAND vs. PITTSBURGH**
RS: Raiders lead series, 10-8
PS: Series tied, 3-3
1970—Raiders, 31-14 (O)
1972—Steelers, 34-28 (P)
**Steelers, 13-7 (P)
1973—Steelers, 17-9 (O)
**Raiders, 33-14 (O)
1974—Raiders, 17-0 (P)
***Steelers, 24-13 (O)
1975—***Steelers, 16-10 (P)
1976—Raiders, 31-28 (O)
***Raiders, 24-7 (O)
1977—Raiders, 16-7 (P)
1980—Raiders, 45-34 (P)
1981—Raiders, 30-27 (O)
1983—**Raiders, 38-10 (LA)
1984—Steelers, 13-7 (LA)
1990—Raiders, 20-3 (LA)
1994—Steelers, 21-3 (LA)
1995—Steelers, 29-10 (O)
2000—Steelers, 21-20 (P)
2002—Raiders, 30-17 (P)
2003—Steelers, 27-7 (P)
2004—Steelers, 24-21 (P)
2006—Raiders, 20-13 (O)
2009—Raiders, 27-24 (P)
(RS Pts.—Raiders 372, Steelers 353)
(PS Pts.—Raiders 125, Steelers 84)
**Franchise in Los Angeles from 1982-1994*
***AFC Divisional Playoff*
****AFC Championship*
***OAKLAND vs. **ST. LOUIS**
RS: Raiders lead series, 7-4
1972—Raiders, 45-17 (O)
1977—Rams, 20-14 (LA)
1979—Raiders, 24-17 (LA)
1982—Raiders, 37-31 (LA Raiders)
1985—Raiders, 16-6 (LA Rams)
1988—Rams, 22-17 (LA Raiders)
1991—Raiders, 20-17 (LA Raiders)
1994—Raiders, 20-17 (LA Rams)
1997—Raiders, 35-17 (O)
2002—Rams, 28-13 (StL)
2006—Rams, 20-0 (O)
(RS Pts.—Raiders 241, Rams 212)
**Franchise in Los Angeles from 1982-1994*
***Franchise in Los Angeles prior to 1995*
***OAKLAND vs. **SAN DIEGO**
RS: Raiders lead series, 54-44-2
PS: Raiders lead series, 1-0
1960—Chargers, 52-28 (LA)
Chargers, 41-17 (O)
1961—Chargers, 44-0 (SD)
Chargers, 41-10 (O)
1962—Chargers, 42-33 (O)
Chargers, 31-21 (SD)
1963—Raiders, 34-33 (SD)
Raiders, 41-27 (O)
1964—Chargers, 31-17 (SD)
Raiders, 21-20 (O)
1965—Chargers, 17-6 (O)
Chargers, 24-14 (SD)
1966—Chargers, 29-20 (O)
Raiders, 41-19 (SD)
1967—Raiders, 51-10 (O)
Raiders, 41-21 (SD)
1968—Chargers, 23-14 (O)
Raiders, 34-27 (SD)
1969—Raiders, 24-12 (SD)
Raiders, 21-16 (O)
1970—Tie, 27-27 (SD)
Raiders, 20-17 (O)
1971—Raiders, 34-0 (SD)
Raiders, 34-33 (O)
1972—Tie, 17-17 (O)
Raiders, 21-19 (SD)
1973—Raiders, 27-17 (SD)
Raiders, 31-3 (O)
1974—Raiders, 14-10 (SD)
Raiders, 17-10 (O)
1975—Raiders, 6-0 (SD)
Raiders, 25-0 (O)
1976—Raiders, 27-17 (SD)
Raiders, 24-0 (O)
1977—Raiders, 24-0 (O)
Chargers, 12-7 (SD)
1978—Raiders, 21-20 (SD)
Chargers, 27-23 (O)
1979—Chargers, 30-10 (SD)
Raiders, 45-22 (O)
1980—Chargers, 30-24 (SD) OT
Raiders, 38-24 (O)
***Raiders, 34-27 (SD)
1981—Chargers, 55-21 (O)
Chargers, 23-10 (SD)
1982—Raiders, 28-24 (LA)
Raiders, 41-34 (SD)
1983—Raiders, 42-10 (SD)
Raiders, 30-14 (LA)
1984—Raiders, 33-30 (LA)
Raiders, 44-37 (SD)
1985—Raiders, 34-21 (LA)
Chargers, 40-34 (SD) OT
1986—Raiders, 17-13 (LA)
Raiders, 37-31 (SD) OT
1987—Chargers, 23-17 (LA)
Chargers, 16-14 (SD)
1988—Raiders, 24-13 (LA)
Raiders, 13-3 (SD)
1989—Raiders, 40-14 (LA)
Chargers, 14-12 (SD)
1990—Raiders, 24-9 (SD)
Raiders, 17-12 (LA)
1991—Chargers, 21-13 (LA)
Raiders, 9-7 (SD)
1992—Chargers, 27-3 (SD)
Chargers, 36-14 (LA)
1993—Chargers, 30-23 (LA)
Raiders, 12-7 (SD)
1994—Chargers, 26-24 (LA)
Raiders, 24-17 (SD)
1995—Raiders, 17-7 (O)
Chargers, 12-6 (SD)
1996—Chargers, 40-34 (O)
Raiders, 23-14 (SD)
1997—Chargers, 25-10 (O)
Raiders, 38-13 (SD)
1998—Raiders, 7-6 (O)
Raiders, 17-10 (SD)
1999—Raiders, 28-9 (O)
Chargers, 23-20 (SD)
2000—Raiders, 9-6 (O)
Raiders, 15-13 (SD)
2001—Raiders, 34-24 (O)
Raiders, 13-6 (SD)

2002—Chargers, 27-21 (O) OT
Raiders, 27-7 (SD)
2003—Raiders, 34-31 (O) OT
Chargers, 21-14 (SD)
2004—Chargers, 42-14 (SD)
Chargers, 23-17 (O)
2005—Chargers, 27-14 (O)
Chargers, 34-10 (SD)
2006—Chargers, 27-0 (O)
Chargers, 21-14 (SD)
2007—Chargers, 28-14 ((SD)
Chargers, 30-17 (O)
2008—Chargers, 28-18 (O)
Chargers, 34-7 (SD)
2009—Chargers, 24-20 (O)
Chargers, 24-16 (SD)
(RS Pts.—Raiders 2,186, Chargers 2,138)
(PS Pts.—Raiders 34, Chargers 27)
Franchise in Los Angeles from 1982-1994
***Franchise in Los Angeles prior to 1961*
****AFC Championship*

***OAKLAND vs. SAN FRANCISCO**
RS: Raiders lead series, 6-5
1970—49ers, 38-7 (O)
1974—Raiders, 35-24 (SF)
1979—Raiders, 23-10 (O)
1982—Raiders, 23-17 (SF)
1985—49ers, 34-10 (LA)
1988—Raiders, 9-3 (SF)
1991—Raiders, 12-6 (LA)
1994—49ers, 44-14 (SF)
2000—Raiders, 34-28 (SF) OT
2002—49ers, 23-20 (O) OT
2006—49ers, 34-20 (SF)
(RS Pts.—49ers 261, Raiders 207)
Franchise in Los Angeles from 1982-1994

***OAKLAND vs. SEATTLE**
RS: Raiders lead series, 27-23
PS: Series tied, 1-1
1977—Raiders, 44-7 (O)
1978—Seahawks, 27-7 (S)
Seahawks, 17-16 (O)
1979—Seahawks, 27-10 (S)
Seahawks, 29-24 (O)
1980—Raiders, 33-14 (O)
Raiders, 19-17 (S)
1981—Raiders, 20-10 (O)
Raiders, 32-31 (S)
1982—Raiders, 28-23 (LA)
1983—Seahawks, 38-36 (S)
Seahawks, 34-21 (LA)
**Raiders, 30-14 (LA)
1984—Raiders, 28-14 (LA)
Seahawks, 17-14 (S)
***Seahawks, 13-7 (S)
1985—Seahawks, 33-3 (S)
Raiders, 13-3 (LA)
1986—Raiders, 14-10 (LA)
Seahawks, 37-0 (S)
1987—Seahawks, 35-13 (LA)
Raiders, 37-14 (S)
1988—Seahawks, 35-27 (S)
Seahawks, 43-37 (LA)
1989—Seahawks, 24-20 (LA)
Seahawks, 23-17 (S)
1990—Raiders, 17-13 (S)
Raiders, 24-17 (LA)
1991—Raiders, 23-20 (S) OT
Raiders, 31-7 (LA)
1992—Raiders, 19-0 (S)
Raiders, 20-3 (LA)
1993—Raiders, 17-13 (S)
Raiders, 27-23 (LA)
1994—Seahawks, 38-9 (LA)
Raiders, 17-16 (S)
1995—Raiders, 34-14 (O)
Seahawks, 44-10 (S)
1996—Raiders, 27-21 (S)
Seahawks, 28-21 (O)
1997—Seahawks, 45-34 (S)
Seahawks, 22-21 (O)
1998—Raiders, 31-18 (S)
Raiders, 20-17 (O)
1999—Seahawks, 22-21 (S)
Raiders, 30-21 (O)
2000—Raiders, 31-3 (O)
Seahawks, 27-24 (S)
2001—Raiders, 38-14 (O)
Seahawks, 34-27 (S)
2002—Raiders, 31-17 (O)
2006—Seahawks, 16-0 (S)
(RS Pts.—Raiders 1,117, Seahawks 1,075)
(PS Pts.—Raiders 37, Seahawks 27)
Franchise in Los Angeles from 1982-1994
***AFC Championship*
****AFC First-Round Playoff*

***OAKLAND vs. TAMPA BAY**
RS: Raiders lead series, 6-1
PS: Buccaneers lead series, 1-0
1976—Raiders, 49-16 (O)
1981—Raiders, 18-16 (O)
1993—Raiders, 27-20 (LA)
1996—Buccaneers, 20-17 (TB) OT
1999—Raiders, 45-0 (O)
2002—**Buccaneers, 48-21 (San Diego)
2004—Raiders, 30-20 (O)
2008—Raiders, 31-24 (TB)
(RS Pts.—Raiders 217, Buccaneers 116)
(PS Pts.—Buccaneers 48, Raiders 21)
Franchise in Los Angeles from 1982-1994
***Super Bowl XXXVII*

***OAKLAND vs. **TENNESSEE**
RS: Raiders lead series, 23-18
PS: Raiders lead series, 4-0
1960—Oilers, 37-22 (O)
Raiders, 14-13 (H)
1961—Oilers, 55-0 (H)
Oilers, 47-16 (O)
1962—Oilers, 28-20 (O)
Oilers, 32-17 (H)
1963—Raiders, 24-13 (H)
Raiders, 52-49 (O)
1964—Oilers, 42-28 (H)
Raiders, 20-10 (O)
1965—Raiders, 21-17 (O)
Raiders, 33-21 (H)
1966—Oilers, 31-0 (H)
Raiders, 38-23 (O)
1967—Raiders, 19-7 (H)
***Raiders, 40-7 (O)
1968—Raiders, 24-15 (H)
1969—Raiders, 21-17 (O)
****Raiders, 56-7 (O)
1971—Raiders, 41-21 (O)
1972—Raiders, 34-0 (H)
1973—Raiders, 17-6 (H)
1975—Oilers, 27-26 (O)
1976—Raiders, 14-13 (H)
1977—Raiders, 34-29 (O)
1978—Raiders, 21-17 (O)
1979—Oilers, 31-17 (H)
1980—*****Raiders, 27-7 (O)
1981—Oilers, 17-16 (H)
1983—Raiders, 20-6 (LA)
1984—Raiders, 24-14 (H)
1986—Raiders, 28-17 (H)
1988—Oilers, 38-35 (H)
1989—Oilers, 23-7 (H)
1991—Oilers, 47-17 (H)
1994—Raiders, 17-14 (LA)
1997—Oilers, 24-21 (T) OT
1999—Titans, 21-14 (T)
2001—Titans, 13-10 (O)
2002—Raiders, 52-25 (O)
******Raiders, 41-24 (O)
2003—Titans, 25-20 (T)
2004—Raiders, 40-35 (O)
2005—Raiders, 34-25 (T)
2007—Titans, 13-9 (T)
(RS Pts.—Titans 958, Raiders 937)
(PS Pts.—Raiders 164, Titans 45)
Franchise in Los Angeles from 1982-1994
***Franchise in Houston prior to 1997; known as Oilers prior to 1999*
****AFL Championship*
*****Inter-Divisional Playoff*
******AFC First-Round Playoff*
*******AFC Championship*

***OAKLAND vs. WASHINGTON**
RS: Raiders lead series, 7-4
PS: Raiders lead series, 1-0
1970—Raiders, 34-20 (O)
1975—Raiders, 26-23 (W) OT
1980—Raiders, 24-21 (O)
1983—Redskins, 37-35 (W)
**Raiders, 38-9 (Tampa)
1986—Redskins, 10-6 (W)
1989—Raiders, 37-24 (LA)
1992—Raiders, 21-20 (W)
1995—Raiders, 20-8 (W)
1998—Redskins, 29-19 (O)
2005—Raiders, 16-13 (W)
2009—Redskins, 34-13 (O)
(RS Pts.—Raiders 251, Redskins 239)
(PS Pts.—Raiders 38, Redskins 9)
Franchise in Los Angeles from 1982-1994
***Super Bowl XVIII*

PHILADELPHIA vs. ARIZONA
RS: Series tied, 53-53-5
PS: Cardinals lead series, 2-1;
See Arizona vs. Philadelphia

PHILADELPHIA vs. ATLANTA
RS: Eagles lead series, 14-10-1
PS: Eagles lead series, 2-1;
See Atlanta vs. Philadelphia

PHILADELPHIA vs. BALTIMORE
RS: Series tied, 1-1-1;
See Baltimore vs. Philadelphia

PHILADELPHIA vs. BUFFALO
RS: Eagles lead series, 6-5;
See Buffalo vs. Philadelphia

PHILADELPHIA vs. CAROLINA
RS: Eagles lead series, 5-1
PS: Panthers lead series, 1-0;
See Carolina vs. Philadelphia

PHILADELPHIA vs. CHICAGO
RS: Bears lead series, 26-9-1
PS: Eagles lead series, 2-1;
See Chicago vs. Philadelphia

PHILADELPHIA vs. CINCINNATI
RS: Bengals lead series, 7-3-1;

See Cincinnati vs. Philadelphia

PHILADELPHIA vs. CLEVELAND
RS: Browns lead series, 31-15-1;
See Cleveland vs. Philadelphia

PHILADELPHIA vs. DALLAS
RS: Cowboys lead series, 55-43
PS: Cowboys lead series, 3-1;
See Dallas vs. Philadelphia

PHILADELPHIA vs. DENVER
RS: Eagles lead series, 7-4;
See Denver vs. Philadelphia

PHILADELPHIA vs. DETROIT
RS: Eagles lead series, 13-12-2
PS: Eagles lead series, 1-0;
See Detroit vs. Philadelphia

PHILADELPHIA vs. GREEN BAY
RS: Packers lead series, 23-13
PS: Eagles lead series, 2-0;
See Green Bay vs. Philadelphia

PHILADELPHIA vs. HOUSTON
RS: Eagles lead series, 2-0;
See Houston vs. Philadelphia

PHILADELPHIA vs. INDIANAPOLIS
RS: Colts lead series, 10-6;
See Indianapolis vs. Philadelphia

PHILADELPHIA vs. JACKSONVILLE
RS: Jaguars lead series, 3-0;
See Jacksonville vs. Philadelphia

PHILADELPHIA vs. KANSAS CITY
RS: Eagles lead series, 4-2;
See Kansas City vs. Philadelphia

PHILADELPHIA vs. MIAMI
RS: Dolphins lead series, 7-5;
See Miami vs. Philadelphia

PHILADELPHIA vs. MINNESOTA
RS: Vikings lead series, 11-9
PS: Eagles lead series, 3-0;
See Minnesota vs. Philadelphia

PHILADELPHIA vs. NEW ENGLAND
RS: Eagles lead series, 6-4
PS: Patriots lead series, 1-0;
See New England vs. Philadelphia

PHILADELPHIA vs. NEW ORLEANS
RS: Eagles lead series, 15-10
PS; Series tied, 1-1;
See New Orleans vs. Philadelphia

PHILADELPHIA vs. N.Y. GIANTS
RS: Giants lead series, 79-69-2
PS: Series tied, 2-2;
See N.Y. Giants vs. Philadelphia

PHILADELPHIA vs. N.Y. JETS
RS: Eagles lead series, 8-0;
See N.Y. Jets vs. Philadelphia

PHILADELPHIA vs. OAKLAND
RS: Series tied, 5-5
PS: Raiders lead series, 1-0;
See Oakland vs. Philadelphia

PHILADELPHIA vs. *PITTSBURGH
RS: Eagles lead series, 46-27-3
PS: Eagles lead series, 1-0
1933—Eagles, 25-6 (Phila)
1934—Eagles, 17-0 (Pitt)
Pirates, 9-7 (Phila)
1935—Pirates, 17-7 (Phila)
Eagles, 17-6 (Pitt)
1936—Pirates, 17-0 (Pitt)
Pirates, 6-0 (Johnstown, Pa.)
1937—Pirates, 27-14 (Pitt)
Pirates, 16-7 (Pitt)
1938—Eagles, 27-7 (Buffalo)
Eagles, 14-7 (Charleston, W. Va.)
1939—Eagles, 17-14 (Phila)
Pirates, 24-12 (Pitt)
1940—Steelers, 7-3 (Pitt)
Eagles, 7-0 (Phila)
1941—Eagles, 10-7 (Pitt)
Tie, 7-7 (Phila)
1942—Eagles, 24-14 (Pitt)
Steelers, 14-0 (Phila)
1945—Eagles, 45-3 (Pitt)
Eagles, 30-6 (Phila)
1946—Steelers, 10-7 (Pitt)
Eagles, 10-7 (Phila)
1947—Steelers, 35-24 (Pitt)
Eagles, 21-0 (Phila)
**Eagles, 21-0 (Pitt)
1948—Eagles, 34-7 (Pitt)
Eagles, 17-0 (Phila)
1949—Eagles, 38-7 (Pitt)
Eagles, 34-17 (Phila)
1950—Eagles, 17-10 (Pitt)
Steelers, 9-7 (Phila)
1951—Eagles, 34-13 (Pitt)
Steelers, 17-13 (Phila)
1952—Eagles, 31-25 (Pitt)
Eagles, 26-21 (Phila)
1953—Eagles, 23-17 (Phila)
Eagles, 35-7 (Pitt)
1954—Eagles, 24-22 (Phila)
Steelers, 17-7 (Pitt)
1955—Steelers, 13-7 (Pitt)
Eagles, 24-0 (Phila)
1956—Eagles, 35-21 (Pitt)
Eagles, 14-7 (Phila)
1957—Steelers, 6-0 (Pitt)
Eagles, 7-6 (Phila)
1958—Steelers, 24-3 (Pitt)
Steelers, 31-24 (Phila)
1959—Eagles, 28-24 (Phila)
Steelers, 31-0 (Pitt)
1960—Eagles, 34-7 (Phila)
Steelers, 27-21 (Pitt)
1961—Eagles, 21-16 (Phila)
Eagles, 35-24 (Pitt)
1962—Steelers, 13-7 (Pitt)
Steelers, 26-17 (Phila)
1963—Tie, 21-21 (Phila)
Tie, 20-20 (Pitt)
1964—Eagles, 21-7 (Phila)
Eagles, 34-10 (Pitt)
1965—Steelers, 20-14 (Phila)
Eagles, 47-13 (Pitt)
1966—Eagles, 31-14 (Pitt)
Eagles, 27-23 (Phila)
1967—Eagles, 34-24 (Phila)
1968—Steelers, 6-3 (Pitt)
1969—Eagles, 41-27 (Phila)
1970—Eagles, 30-20 (Phila)
1974—Steelers, 27-0 (Pitt)
1979—Eagles, 17-14 (Phila)
1988—Eagles, 27-26 (Pitt)
1991—Eagles, 23-14 (Phila)
1994—Steelers, 14-3 (Pitt)
1997—Eagles, 23-20 (Phila)
2000—Eagles, 26-23 (Pitt) OT
2004—Steelers, 27-3 (Pitt)
2008—Eagles, 15-6 (Phila)
(RS Pts.—Eagles 1,429, Steelers 1,097)
(PS Pts.—Eagles 21, Steelers 0)
**Steelers known as Pirates prior to 1940*
***Division Playoff*

PHILADELPHIA vs. *ST. LOUIS
RS: Series tied, 17-17-1
PS: Rams lead series, 2-1
1937—Rams, 21-3 (P)
1939—Rams, 35-13 (Colorado Springs)
1940—Rams, 21-13 (C)
1942—Rams, 24-14 (Akron)
1944—Eagles, 26-13 (P)
1945—Eagles, 28-14 (P)
1946—Eagles, 25-14 (LA)
1947—Eagles, 14-7 (P)
1948—Tie, 28-28 (LA)
1949—Eagles, 38-14 (P)
**Eagles, 14-0 (LA)
1950—Eagles, 56-20 (P)
1955—Rams, 23-21 (P)
1956—Rams, 27-7 (LA)
1957—Rams, 17-13 (LA)
1959—Eagles, 23-20 (P)
1964—Rams, 20-10 (LA)
1967—Rams, 33-17 (LA)
1969—Rams, 23-17 (P)
1972—Rams, 34-3 (P)
1975—Rams, 42-3 (P)
1977—Rams, 20-0 (LA)
1978—Rams, 16-14 (P)
1983—Eagles, 13-9 (P)
1985—Rams, 17-6 (P)
1986—Eagles, 34-20 (P)
1988—Eagles, 30-24 (P)
1989—***Rams, 21-7 (P)
1990—Eagles, 27-21 (LA)
1995—Eagles, 20-9 (P)
1998—Eagles, 17-14 (P)
1999—Eagles, 38-31 (P)
2001—Rams, 20-17 (P) OT
****Rams, 29-24 (StL)
2002—Eagles, 10-3 (P)
2004—Rams, 20-7 (StL)
2005—Eagles, 17-16 (StL)
2008—Eagles, 38-3 (P)
(RS Pts.—Rams 693, Eagles 660)
(PS Pts.—Rams 50, Eagles 45)
**Franchise in Los Angeles prior to 1995 and in Cleveland prior to 1946*
***NFL Championship*
****NFC First-Round Playoff*
*****NFC Championship*

PHILADELPHIA vs. SAN DIEGO
RS: Chargers lead series, 6-4
1974—Eagles, 13-7 (SD)
1980—Chargers, 22-21 (SD)
1985—Chargers, 20-14 (SD)
1986—Eagles, 23-7 (P)
1989—Chargers, 20-17 (SD)
1995—Chargers, 27-21 (P)
1998—Chargers, 13-10 (SD)
2001—Eagles, 24-14 (P)
2005—Eagles, 20-17 (P)
2009—Chargers, 31-23 (SD)
(RS Pts.—Eagles 186, Chargers 178)

PHILADELPHIA vs. SAN FRANCISCO
RS: 49ers lead series, 16-11-1
PS: 49ers lead series, 1-0
1951—Eagles, 21-14 (P)
1953—49ers, 31-21 (SF)
1956—Tie, 10-10 (P)
1958—49ers, 30-24 (P)
1959—49ers, 24-14 (SF)
1964—49ers, 28-24 (P)
1966—Eagles, 35-34 (SF)

1967—49ers, 28-27 (P)
1969—49ers, 14-13 (SF)
1971—49ers, 31-3 (P)
1973—49ers, 38-28 (SF)
1975—Eagles, 27-17 (P)
1983—Eagles, 22-17 (SF)
1984—49ers, 21-9 (P)
1985—49ers, 24-13 (SF)
1989—49ers, 38-28 (P)
1991—49ers, 23-7 (P)
1992—49ers, 20-14 (SF)
1993—Eagles, 37-34 (SF) OT
1994—Eagles, 40-8 (SF)
1996—*49ers, 14-0 (SF)
1997—49ers, 24-12 (P)
2001—49ers, 13-3 (SF)
2002—Eagles, 38-17 (SF)
2003—49ers, 31-28 (P) OT
2005—Eagles, 42-3 (P)
2006—Eagles, 38-24 (SF)
2008—Eagles, 40-26 (SF)
2009—Eagles, 27-13 (P)
(RS Pts.—Eagles 645, 49ers 635)
(PS Pts.—49ers 14, Eagles 0)
NFC First-Round Playoff

PHILADELPHIA vs. SEATTLE
RS: Eagles lead series, 7-5
1976—Eagles, 27-10 (P)
1980—Eagles, 27-20 (S)
1986—Seahawks, 24-20 (S)
1989—Eagles, 31-7 (P)
1992—Eagles, 20-17 (S) OT
1995—Seahawks, 26-14 (S)
1998—Seahawks, 38-0 (P)
2001—Eagles, 27-3 (S)
2002—Eagles, 27-20 (S)
2005—Seahawks, 42-0 (P)
2007—Seahawks, 28-24 (P)
2008—Eagles, 26-7 (S)
(RS Pts.—Eagles 243, Seahawks 242)

PHILADELPHIA vs. TAMPA BAY
RS: Eagles lead series, 6-5
PS: Series tied, 2-2
1977—Eagles, 13-3 (P)
1979—*Buccaneers, 24-17 (TB)
1981—Eagles, 20-10 (P)
1988—Eagles, 41-14 (TB)
1991—Buccaneers, 14-13 (TB)
1995—Buccaneers, 21-6 (P)
1999—Buccaneers, 19-5 (P)
2000—**Eagles, 21-3 (P)
2001—Eagles, 17-13 (TB)
**Eagles, 31-9 (P)
2002—Eagles, 20-10 (P)
***Buccaneers, 27-10 (P)
2003—Buccaneers, 17-0 (P)
2006—Buccaneers, 23-21 (TB)
2009—Eagles, 33-14 (P)
(RS Pts.—Eagles 189, Buccaneers 158)
(PS Pts.—Eagles 79, Buccaneers 63)
NFC Divisional Playoff
***NFC First-Round Playoff*
****NFC Championship*

PHILADELPHIA vs. *TENNESSEE
RS: Eagles lead series, 6-3
1972—Eagles, 18-17 (H)
1979—Eagles, 26-20 (H)
1982—Eagles, 35-14 (P)
1988—Eagles, 32-23 (P)
1991—Eagles, 13-6 (H)
1994—Eagles, 21-6 (P)
2000—Titans, 15-13 (P)
2002—Titans, 27-24 (T)
2006—Titans, 31-13 (P)
(RS Pts.—Eagles 195, Titans 159)
**Franchise in Houston prior to 1997; known as Oilers prior to 1999*

PHILADELPHIA vs. *WASHINGTON
RS: Redskins lead series, 77-67-5
PS: Redskins lead series, 1-0
1934—Redskins, 6-0 (B)
Redskins, 14-7 (P)
1935—Eagles, 7-6 (B)
1936—Redskins, 26-3 (P)
Redskins, 17-7 (B)
1937—Eagles, 14-0 (W)
Redskins, 10-7 (P)
1938—Redskins, 26-23 (P)
Redskins, 20-14 (W)
1939—Redskins, 7-0 (P)
Redskins, 7-6 (W)
1940—Redskins, 34-17 (P)
Redskins, 13-6 (W)
1941—Redskins, 21-17 (P)
Redskins, 20-14 (W)
1942—Redskins, 14-10 (P)
Redskins, 30-27 (W)
1944—Tie, 31-31 (P)
Eagles, 37-7 (W)
1945—Redskins, 24-14 (W)
Eagles, 16-0 (P)
1946—Eagles, 28-24 (W)
Redskins, 27-10 (P)
1947—Eagles, 45-42 (P)
Eagles, 38-14 (W)
1948—Eagles, 45-0 (W)
Eagles, 42-21 (P)
1949—Eagles, 49-14 (P)
Eagles, 44-21 (W)
1950—Eagles, 35-3 (P)
Eagles, 33-0 (W)
1951—Redskins, 27-23 (P)
Eagles, 35-21 (W)
1952—Eagles, 38-20 (P)
Redskins, 27-21 (W)
1953—Tie, 21-21 (P)
Redskins, 10-0 (W)
1954—Eagles, 49-21 (W)
Eagles, 41-33 (P)
1955—Redskins, 31-30 (P)
Redskins, 34-21 (W)
1956—Eagles, 13-9 (P)
Redskins, 19-17 (W)
1957—Eagles, 21-12 (P)
Redskins, 42-7 (W)
1958—Redskins, 24-14 (P)
Redskins, 20-0 (W)
1959—Eagles, 30-23 (P)
Eagles, 34-14 (W)
1960—Eagles, 19-13 (P)
Eagles, 38-28 (W)
1961—Eagles, 14-7 (P)
Eagles, 27-24 (W)
1962—Redskins, 27-21 (P)
Eagles, 37-14 (W)
1963—Eagles, 37-24 (W)
Redskins, 13-10 (P)
1964—Redskins, 35-20 (W)
Redskins, 21-10 (P)
1965—Redskins, 23-21 (W)
Eagles, 21-14 (P)
1966—Redskins, 27-13 (P)
Eagles, 37-28 (W)
1967—Eagles, 35-24 (P)
Tie, 35-35 (W)
1968—Redskins, 17-14 (W)
Redskins, 16-10 (P)
1969—Tie, 28-28 (W)
Redskins, 34-29 (P)
1970—Redskins, 33-21 (P)
Redskins, 24-6 (W)
1971—Tie, 7-7 (W)
Redskins, 20-13 (P)
1972—Redskins, 14-0 (W)
Redskins, 23-7 (P)
1973—Redskins, 28-7 (P)
Redskins, 38-20 (W)
1974—Redskins, 27-20 (P)
Redskins, 26-7 (W)
1975—Eagles, 26-10 (P)
Eagles, 26-3 (W)
1976—Redskins, 20-17 (P) OT
Redskins, 24-0 (W)
1977—Redskins, 23-17 (W)
Redskins, 17-14 (P)
1978—Redskins, 35-30 (W)
Eagles, 17-10 (P)
1979—Eagles, 28-17 (P)
Redskins, 17-7 (W)
1980—Eagles, 24-14 (P)
Eagles, 24-0 (W)
1981—Eagles, 36-13 (P)
Redskins, 15-13 (W)
1982—Redskins, 37-34 (P) OT
Redskins, 13-9 (W)
1983—Redskins, 23-13 (P)
Redskins, 28-24 (W)
1984—Redskins, 20-0 (W)
Eagles, 16-10 (P)
1985—Eagles, 19-6 (W)
Redskins, 17-12 (P)
1986—Redskins, 41-14 (W)
Redskins, 21-14 (P)
1987—Redskins, 34-24 (W)
Eagles, 31-27 (P)
1988—Redskins, 17-10 (W)
Redskins, 20-19 (P)
1989—Eagles, 42-37 (W)
Redskins, 10-3 (P)
1990—Redskins, 13-7 (W)
Eagles, 28-14 (P)
**Redskins, 20-6 (P)
1991—Redskins, 23-0 (W)
Eagles, 24-22 (P)
1992—Redskins, 16-12 (W)
Eagles, 17-13 (P)
1993—Eagles, 34-31 (P)
Eagles, 17-14 (W)
1994—Eagles, 21-17 (P)
Eagles, 31-29 (W)
1995—Eagles, 37-34 (P) OT
Eagles, 14-7 (W)
1996—Eagles, 17-14 (W)
Redskins, 26-21 (P)
1997—Eagles, 24-10 (P)
Redskins, 35-32 (W)
1998—Eagles, 17-12 (P)
Redskins, 28-3 (W)
1999—Eagles, 35-28 (P)
Redskins, 20-17 (W) OT
2000—Redskins, 17-14 (P)
Eagles, 23-20 (W)

2001—Redskins, 13-3 (P)
Eagles, 20-6 (W)
2002—Eagles, 37-7 (W)
Eagles, 34-21 (P)
2003—Eagles, 27-25 (P)
Eagles, 31-7 (W)
2004—Eagles, 28-6 (P)
Eagles, 17-14 (W)
2005—Redskins, 17-10 (W)
Redskins, 31-20 (P)
2006—Eagles, 27-3 (P)
Eagles, 21-19 (W)
2007—Redskins, 20-12 (P)
Eagles, 33-25 (W)
2008—Redskins, 23-17 (P)
Redskins, 10-3 (W)
2009—Eagles, 27-17 (W)
Eagles, 27-24 (P)
(RS Pts.—Eagles 3,047, Redskins 2,909)
(PS Pts.—Redskins 20, Eagles 6)
**Franchise in Boston prior to 1937*
***NFC First-Round Playoff*

PITTSBURGH vs. ARIZONA
RS: Steelers lead series, 31-23-3
PS: Steelers lead series, 1-0;
See Arizona vs. Pittsburgh
PITTSBURGH vs. ATLANTA
RS: Steelers lead series, 11-2-1;
See Atlanta vs. Pittsburgh
PITTSBURGH vs. BALTIMORE
RS: Steelers lead series, 17-11
PS: Steelers lead series, 2-0;
See Baltimore vs. Pittsburgh
PITTSBURGH vs. BUFFALO
RS: Steelers lead series, 11-8
PS: Steelers lead series, 2-1;
See Buffalo vs. Pittsburgh
PITTSBURGH vs. CAROLINA
RS: Steelers lead series, 3-1;
See Carolina vs. Pittsburgh
PITTSBURGH vs. CHICAGO
RS: Bears lead series, 17-7-1;
See Chicago vs. Pittsburgh
PITTSBURGH vs. CINCINNATI
RS: Steelers lead series, 47-32
PS: Steelers lead series, 1-0;
See Cincinnati vs. Pittsburgh
PITTSBURGH vs. CLEVELAND
RS: Steelers lead series, 58-56
PS: Steelers lead series, 2-0;
See Cleveland vs. Pittsburgh
PITTSBURGH vs. DALLAS
RS: Cowboys lead series, 14-13
PS: Steelers lead series, 2-1;
See Dallas vs. Pittsburgh
PITTSBURGH vs. DENVER
RS: Broncos lead series, 13-7-1
PS: Series tied, 3-3;
See Denver vs. Pittsburgh
PITTSBURGH vs. DETROIT
RS: Steelers lead series, 15-14-1;
See Detroit vs. Pittsburgh
PITTSBURGH vs. GREEN BAY
RS: Packers lead series, 18-14;
See Green Bay vs. Pittsburgh
PITTSBURGH vs. HOUSTON
RS: Steelers lead series 2-1;
See Houston vs. Pittsburgh
PITTSBURGH vs. INDIANAPOLIS
RS: Steelers lead series, 13-6
PS: Steelers lead series, 5-0;
See Indianapolis vs. Pittsburgh
PITTSBURGH vs. JACKSONVILLE
RS: Jaguars lead series, 11-9
PS: Jaguars lead series, 1-0;
See Jacksonville vs. Pittsburgh
PITTSBURGH vs. KANSAS CITY
RS: Steelers lead series, 17-9
PS: Chiefs lead series, 1-0;
See Kansas City vs. Pittsburgh
PITTSBURGH vs. MIAMI
RS: Steelers lead series, 11-9
PS: Dolphins lead series, 2-1;
See Miami vs. Pittsburgh
PITTSBURGH vs. MINNESOTA
RS: Vikings lead series, 8-7
PS: Steelers lead series, 1-0;
See Minnesota vs. Pittsburgh
PITTSBURGH vs. NEW ENGLAND
RS: Steelers lead series, 13-7
PS: Patriots lead series, 3-1;
See New England vs. Pittsburgh
PITTSBURGH vs. NEW ORLEANS
RS: Steelers lead series, 7-6;
See New Orleans vs. Pittsburgh
PITTSBURGH vs. N.Y. GIANTS
RS: Giants lead series, 44-28-3;
See N.Y. Giants vs. Pittsburgh
PITTSBURGH vs. N.Y. JETS
RS: Steelers lead series, 15-3
PS: Steelers lead series, 1-0;
See N.Y. Jets vs. Pittsburgh
PITTSBURGH vs. OAKLAND
RS: Raiders lead series, 10-8
PS: Series tied, 3-3;
See Oakland vs. Pittsburgh
PITTSBURGH vs. PHILADELPHIA
RS: Eagles lead series, 46-27-3
PS: Eagles lead series, 1-0;
See Philadelphia vs. Pittsburgh
***PITTSBURGH vs. **ST. LOUIS**
RS: Rams lead series, 15-6-2
PS: Steelers lead series, 1-0
1938—Rams, 13-7 (New Orleans)
1939—Tie, 14-14 (C)
1941—Rams, 17-14 (Akron)
1947—Rams, 48-7 (P)
1948—Rams, 31-14 (LA)
1949—Tie, 7-7 (P)
1952—Rams, 28-14 (LA)
1955—Rams, 27-26 (LA)
1956—Steelers, 30-13 (P)
1961—Rams, 24-14 (LA)
1964—Rams, 26-14 (P)
1968—Rams, 45-10 (LA)
1971—Rams, 23-14 (P)
1975—Rams, 10-3 (LA)
1978—Rams, 10-7 (LA)
1979—***Steelers, 31-19 (Pasadena)
1981—Steelers, 24-0 (P)
1984—Steelers, 24-14 (P)
1987—Rams, 31-21 (LA)
1990—Steelers, 41-10 (P)
1993—Rams, 27-0 (LA)
1996—Steelers, 42-6 (P)
2003—Rams, 33-21 (P)
2007—Steelers, 41-24 (StL)
(RS Pts.—Rams 481, Steelers 409)
(PS Pts.—Steelers 31, Rams 19)
**Steelers known as Pirates prior to 1940*
***Franchise in Los Angeles prior to 1995 and in Cleveland prior to 1946*
****Super Bowl XIV*
PITTSBURGH vs. SAN DIEGO
RS: Steelers lead series, 21-6
PS: Chargers lead series, 2-1
1971—Steelers, 21-17 (P)
1972—Steelers, 24-2 (SD)
1973—Steelers, 38-21 (P)
1975—Steelers, 37-0 (SD)
1976—Steelers, 23-0 (P)
1977—Steelers, 10-9 (SD)
1979—Chargers, 35-7 (SD)
1980—Chargers, 26-17 (SD)
1982—*Chargers, 31-28 (P)
1983—Steelers, 26-3 (P)
1984—Steelers, 52-24 (P)
1985—Chargers, 54-44 (SD)
1987—Steelers, 20-16 (SD)
1988—Chargers, 20-14 (SD)
1989—Steelers, 20-17 (P)
1990—Steelers, 36-14 (P)
1991—Steelers, 26-20 (P)
1992—Steelers, 23-6 (SD)
1993—Steelers,.16-3 (P)
1994—Chargers, 37-34 (SD)
**Chargers, 17-13 (P)
1995—Steelers, 31-16 (P)
1996—Steelers, 16-3 (P)
2000—Steelers, 34-21 (SD)
2003—Steelers, 40-24 (P)
2005—Steelers, 24-22 (SD)
2006—Chargers, 23-13 (SD)
2008—Steelers, 11-10 (P)
***Steelers, 35-24 (P)
2009—Steelers, 38-28 (P)
(RS Pts.—Steelers 695, Chargers 471)
(PS Pts.—Steelers 76, Chargers 72)
**AFC First-Round Playoff*
***AFC Championship*
****AFC Divisional Playoff*
PITTSBURGH vs. SAN FRANCISCO
RS: 49ers lead series, 10-9
1951—49ers, 28-24 (P)
1952—Steelers, 24-7 (SF)
1954—49ers, 31-3 (SF)
1958—49ers, 23-20 (SF)
1961—Steelers, 20-10 (P)
1965—49ers, 27-17 (SF)
1968—49ers, 45-28 (P)
1973—Steelers, 37-14 (SF)
1977—Steelers, 27-0 (P)
1978—Steelers, 24-7 (SF)
1981—49ers, 17-14 (P)
1984—Steelers, 20-17 (SF)
1987—Steelers, 30-17 (P)
1990—49ers, 27-7 (SF)
1993—49ers, 24-13 (P)
1996—49ers, 25-15 (P)
1999—Steelers, 27-6 (SF)
2003—49ers, 30-14 (SF)
2007—Steelers, 37-16 (P)
(RS Pts.—Steelers 401, 49ers 371)
PITTSBURGH vs. SEATTLE
RS: Seahawks lead series, 8-7
PS: Steelers lead series, 1-0
1977—Steelers, 30-20 (P)
1978—Steelers, 21-10 (P)
1981—Seahawks, 24-21 (S)
1982—Seahawks, 16-0 (S)
1983—Steelers, 27-21 (S)

1986—Seahawks, 30-0 (S)
1987—Steelers, 13-9 (P)
1991—Seahawks, 27-7 (P)
1992—Steelers, 20-14 (P)
1993—Seahawks, 16-6 (S)
1994—Seahawks, 30-13 (S)
1998—Steelers, 13-10 (P)
1999—Seahawks, 29-10 (P)
2003—Seahawks, 23-16 (S)
2005—*Steelers, 21-10 (Detroit)
2007—Steelers, 21-0 (P)
(RS Pts.—Seahawks 279, Steelers 218)
(PS Pts.—Steelers 21, Seahawks 10)
Super Bowl XL

PITTSBURGH vs. TAMPA BAY
RS: Steelers lead series, 7-1
1976—Steelers, 42-0 (P)
1980—Steelers, 24-21 (TB)
1983—Steelers, 17-12 (P)
1989—Steelers, 31-22 (TB)
1998—Buccaneers, 16-3 (TB)
2001—Steelers, 17-10 (TB)
2002—Steelers, 17-7 (TB)
2006—Steelers, 20-3 (P)
(RS Pts.—Steelers 171, Buccaneers 91)

PITTSBURGH vs. *TENNESSEE
RS: Steelers lead series, 39-29
PS: Steelers lead series, 3-1
1970—Oilers, 19-7 (P)
Steelers, 7-3 (H)
1971—Steelers, 23-16 (P)
Oilers, 29-3 (H)
1972—Steelers, 24-7 (P)
Steelers, 9-3 (H)
1973—Steelers, 36-7 (H)
Steelers, 33-7 (P)
1974—Steelers, 13-7 (H)
Oilers, 13-10 (P)
1975—Steelers, 24-17 (P)
Steelers, 32-9 (H)
1976—Steelers, 32-16 (P)
Steelers, 21-0 (H)
1977—Oilers, 27-10 (H)
Steelers, 27-10 (P)
1978—Oilers, 24-17 (P)
Steelers, 13-3 (H)
**Steelers, 34-5 (P)
1979—Steelers, 38-7 (P)
Oilers, 20-17 (H)
**Steelers, 27-13 (P)
1980—Steelers, 31-17 (P)
Oilers, 6-0 (H)
1981—Steelers, 26-13 (P)
Oilers, 21-20 (H)
1982—Steelers, 24-10 (H)
1983—Steelers, 40-28 (H)
Steelers, 17-10 (P)
1984—Steelers, 35-7 (P)
Oilers, 23-20 (H) OT
1985—Steelers, 20-0 (P)
Steelers, 30-7 (H)
1986—Steelers, 22-16 (H) OT
Steelers, 21-10 (P)
1987—Oilers, 23-3 (P)
Oilers, 24-16 (H)
1988—Oilers, 34-14 (P)
Steelers, 37-34 (H)
1989—Oilers, 27-0 (H)
Oilers, 23-16 (P)
***Steelers, 26-23 (H) OT
1990—Steelers, 20-9 (P)
Oilers, 34-14 (H)
1991—Steelers, 26-14 (P)
Oilers, 31-6 (H)
1992—Steelers, 29-24 (H)
Steelers, 21-20 (P)
1993—Oilers, 23-3 (H)
Oilers, 26-17 (P)
1994—Steelers, 30-14 (P)
Steelers, 12-9 (H) OT
1995—Steelers, 34-17 (H)
Steelers, 21-7 (P)
1996—Steelers, 30-16 (P)
Oilers, 23-13 (H)
1997—Steelers, 37-24 (P)
Oilers, 16-6 (T)
1998—Oilers, 41-31 (P)
Oilers, 23-14 (T)
1999—Titans, 16-10 (T)
Titans, 47-36 (P)
2000—Titans, 23-20 (P)
Titans, 9-7 (T)
2001—Steelers, 34-7 (P)
Steelers, 34-24 (T)
2002—Titans, 31-23 (T)
****Titans, 34-31 (T) OT
2003—Titans, 30-13 (P)
2005—Steelers, 34-7 (P)
2008—Titans, 31-14 (T)
2009—Steelers, 13-10 (P) OT
(RS Pts.—Steelers 1,390, Titans 1,183)
(PS Pts.—Steelers 118, Titans 75)
Franchise in Houston prior to 1997; known as Oilers prior to 1999
***AFC Championship*
****AFC First-Round Playoff*
*****AFC Divisional Playoff*

***PITTSBURGH vs. **WASHINGTON**
RS: Redskins lead series, 42-31-3
1933—Redskins, 21-6 (P)
Pirates, 16-14 (B)
1934—Redskins, 7-0 (P)
Redskins, 39-0 (B)
1935—Pirates, 6-0 (P)
Redskins, 13-3 (B)
1936—Pirates, 10-0 (P)
Redskins, 30-0 (B)
1937—Redskins, 34-20 (W)
Pirates, 21-13 (P)
1938—Redskins, 7-0 (P)
Redskins, 15-0 (W)
1939—Redskins, 44-14 (W)
Redskins, 21-14 (P)
1940—Redskins, 40-10 (P)
Redskins, 37-10 (W)
1941—Redskins, 24-20 (P)
Redskins, 23-3 (W)
1942—Redskins, 28-14 (W)
Redskins, 14-0 (P)
1945—Redskins, 14-0 (P)
Redskins, 24-0 (W)
1946—Tie, 14-14 (W)
Steelers, 14-7 (P)
1947—Redskins, 27-26 (W)
Steelers, 21-14 (P)
1948—Redskins, 17-14 (W)
Steelers, 10-7 (P)
1949—Redskins, 27-14 (P)
Redskins, 27-14 (W)
1950—Steelers, 26-7 (W)
Redskins, 24-7 (P)
1951—Redskins, 22-7 (P)
Steelers, 20-10 (W)
1952—Redskins, 28-24 (P)
Steelers, 24-23 (W)
1953—Redskins, 17-9 (P)
Steelers, 14-13 (W)
1954—Steelers, 37-7 (P)
Redskins, 17-14 (W)
1955—Redskins, 23-14 (P)
Redskins, 28-17 (W)
1956—Steelers, 30-13 (P)
Steelers, 23-0 (W)
1957—Steelers, 28-7 (P)
Redskins, 10-3 (W)
1958—Steelers, 24-16 (P)
Tie, 14-14 (W)
1959—Redskins, 23-17 (P)
Steelers, 27-6 (W)
1960—Tie, 27-27 (W)
Steelers, 22-10 (P)
1961—Steelers, 20-0 (P)
Steelers, 30-14 (W)
1962—Steelers, 23-21 (P)
Steelers, 27-24 (W)
1963—Steelers, 38-27 (P)
Steelers, 34-28 (W)
1964—Redskins, 30-0 (P)
Steelers, 14-7 (W)
1965—Redskins, 31-3 (P)
Redskins, 35-14 (W)
1966—Redskins, 33-27 (P)
Redskins, 24-10 (W)
1967—Redskins, 15-10 (P)
1968—Redskins, 16-13 (W)
1969—Redskins, 14-7 (P)
1973—Steelers, 21-16 (P)
1979—Steelers, 38-7 (P)
1985—Redskins, 30-23 (P)
1988—Redskins, 30-29 (W)
1991—Redskins, 41-14 (P)
1997—Steelers, 14-13 (P)
2000—Steelers, 24-3 (P)
2004—Steelers, 16-7 (P)
2008—Steelers, 23-6 (W)
(RS Pts.—Redskins 1,419, Steelers 1,194)
**Steelers known as Pirates prior to 1940*
***Franchise in Boston prior to 1937*

ST. LOUIS vs. ARIZONA
RS: Series tied, 30-30-2
PS: Rams lead series, 1-0;
See Arizona vs. St. Louis

ST. LOUIS vs. ATLANTA
RS: Rams lead series, 47-25-2
PS: Falcons lead series, 1-0;
See Atlanta vs. St. Louis

ST. LOUIS vs. BALTIMORE
RS: Series tied, 2-2;
See Baltimore vs. St. Louis

ST. LOUIS vs. BUFFALO
RS: Bills lead series, 6-4;
See Buffalo vs. St. Louis

ST. LOUIS vs. CAROLINA
RS: Panthers lead series, 10-7
PS: Panthers lead series, 1-0;
See Carolina vs. St. Louis

ST. LOUIS vs. CHICAGO
RS: Bears lead series, 50-34-3
PS: Series tied, 1-1;
See Chicago vs. St. Louis

ST. LOUIS vs. CINCINNATI
RS: Bengals lead series, 6-5;

See Cincinnati vs. St. Louis

ST. LOUIS vs. CLEVELAND
RS: Series tied, 9-9
PS: Browns lead series, 2-1;
See Cleveland vs. St. Louis

ST. LOUIS vs. DALLAS
RS: Rams lead series, 11-10
PS: Series tied, 4-4;
See Dallas vs. St. Louis

ST. LOUIS vs. DENVER
RS: Rams lead series, 6-5;
See Denver vs. St. Louis

ST. LOUIS vs. DETROIT
RS: Rams lead series, 42-37-1
PS: Lions lead series, 1-0;
See Detroit vs. St. Louis

ST. LOUIS vs. GREEN BAY
RS: Rams lead series, 45-42-2
PS: Series tied, 1-1;
See Green Bay vs. St. Louis

ST. LOUIS vs. HOUSTON
RS: Series tied, 1-1;
See Houston vs. St. Louis

ST. LOUIS vs. INDIANAPOLIS
RS: Colts lead series, 23-17-2;
See Indianapolis vs. St. Louis

ST. LOUIS vs. JACKSONVILLE
RS: Rams lead series, 2-1;
See Jacksonville vs. St. Louis

ST. LOUIS vs. KANSAS CITY
RS: Chiefs lead series; 5-4;
See Kansas City vs. St. Louis

ST. LOUIS vs. MIAMI
RS: Dolphins lead series, 9-2;
See Miami vs. St. Louis

ST. LOUIS vs. MINNESOTA
RS: Vikings lead series, 18-14-2
PS: Vikings lead series, 5-2;
See Minnesota vs. St. Louis

ST. LOUIS vs. NEW ENGLAND
RS: Series tied, 5-5
PS: Patriots lead series, 1-0;
See New England vs. St. Louis

ST. LOUIS vs. NEW ORLEANS
RS: Rams lead series, 38-30
PS: Saints lead series, 1-0;
See New Orleans vs. St. Louis

ST. LOUIS vs. N.Y. GIANTS
RS: Rams lead series, 25-13
PS: Series tied, 1-1;
See N.Y. Giants vs. St. Louis

ST. LOUIS vs. N.Y. JETS
RS: Rams lead series, 9-3;
See N.Y. Jets vs. St. Louis

ST. LOUIS vs. OAKLAND
RS: Raiders lead series, 7-4;
See Oakland vs. St. Louis

ST. LOUIS vs. PHILADELPHIA
RS: Series tied, 17-17-1
PS: Rams lead series, 2-1;
See Philadelphia vs. St. Louis

ST. LOUIS vs. PITTSBURGH
RS: Rams lead series, 15-6-2
PS: Steelers lead series, 1-0;
See Pittsburgh vs. St. Louis

***ST. LOUIS vs. SAN DIEGO**
RS: Rams lead series, 5-4
1970—Rams, 37-10 (LA)
1975—Rams, 13-10 (SD) OT
1979—Chargers, 40-16 (LA)
1988—Chargers, 38-24 (LA)
1991—Rams, 30-24 (LA)
1994—Chargers, 31-17 (SD)
2000—Rams, 57-31 (StL)
2002—Rams, 28-24 (StL)
2006—Chargers, 38-24 (SD)
(RS Pts.—Rams 246, Chargers 246)
**Franchise in Los Angeles prior to 1995*

***ST. LOUIS vs. SAN FRANCISCO**
RS: Rams lead series, 60-58-2
PS: 49ers lead series, 1-0
1950—Rams, 35-14 (SF)
Rams, 28-21 (LA)
1951—49ers, 44-17 (SF)
Rams, 23-16 (LA)
1952—Rams, 35-9 (LA)
Rams, 34-21 (SF)
1953—49ers, 31-30 (SF)
49ers, 31-27 (LA)
1954—Tie, 24-24 (LA)
Rams, 42-34 (SF)
1955—Rams, 23-14 (SF)
Rams, 27-14 (LA)
1956—49ers, 33-30 (SF)
Rams, 30-6 (LA)
1957—49ers, 23-20 (SF)
Rams, 37-24 (LA)
1958—Rams, 33-3 (SF)
Rams, 56-7 (LA)
1959—49ers, 34-0 (SF)
49ers, 24-16 (LA)
1960—49ers, 13-9 (SF)
49ers, 23-7 (LA)
1961—49ers, 35-0 (SF)
Rams, 17-7 (LA)
1962—Rams, 28-14 (SF)
49ers, 24-17 (LA)
1963—Rams, 28-21 (LA)
Rams, 21-17 (SF)
1964—Rams, 42-14 (LA)
49ers, 28-7 (SF)
1965—49ers, 45-21 (LA)
49ers, 30-27 (SF)
1966—Rams, 34-3 (LA)
49ers, 21-13 (SF)
1967—49ers, 27-24 (LA)
Rams, 17-7 (SF)
1968—Rams, 24-10 (LA)
Tie, 20-20 (SF)
1969—Rams, 27-21 (SF)
Rams, 41-30 (LA)
1970—49ers, 20-6 (LA)
Rams, 30-13 (SF)
1971—Rams, 20-13 (SF)
Rams, 17-6 (LA)
1972—Rams, 31-7 (LA)
Rams, 26-16 (SF)
1973—Rams, 40-20 (SF)
Rams, 31-13 (LA)
1974—Rams, 37-14 (LA)
Rams, 15-13 (SF)
1975—Rams, 23-14 (SF)
49ers, 24-23 (LA)
1976—49ers, 16-0 (LA)
Rams, 23-3 (SF)
1977—Rams, 34-14 (LA)
Rams, 23-10 (SF)
1978—Rams, 27-10 (LA)
Rams, 31-28 (SF)
1979—Rams, 27-24 (LA)
Rams, 26-20 (SF)
1980—Rams, 48-26 (LA)
Rams, 31-17 (SF)
1981—49ers, 20-17 (SF)
49ers, 33-31 (LA)
1982—49ers, 30-24 (LA)
Rams, 21-20 (SF)
1983—Rams, 10-7 (SF)
49ers, 45-35 (LA)
1984—49ers, 33-0 (LA)
49ers, 19-16 (SF)
1985—49ers, 28-14 (LA)
Rams, 27-20 (SF)
1986—Rams, 16-13 (LA)
49ers, 24-14 (SF)
1987—49ers, 31-10 (LA)
49ers, 48-0 (SF)
1988—49ers, 24-21 (LA)
Rams, 38-16 (SF)
1989—Rams, 13-12 (SF)
49ers, 30-27 (LA)
**49ers, 30-3 (SF)
1990—Rams, 28-17 (SF)
49ers, 26-10 (LA)
1991—49ers, 27-10 (SF)
49ers, 33-10 (LA)
1992—49ers, 27-24 (SF)
49ers, 27-10 (LA)
1993—49ers, 40-17 (SF)
49ers, 35-10 (LA)
1994—49ers, 34-19 (LA)
49ers, 31-27 (SF)
1995—49ers, 44-10 (StL)
49ers, 41-13 (SF)
1996—49ers, 34-0 (SF)
49ers, 28-11 (StL)
1997—49ers, 15-12 (StL)
49ers, 30-10 (SF)
1998—49ers, 28-10 (StL)
49ers, 38-19 (SF)
1999—Rams, 42-20 (StL)
Rams, 23-7 (SF)
2000—Rams, 41-24 (StL)
Rams, 34-24 (SF)
2001—Rams, 30-26 (SF)
Rams, 27-14 (StL)
2002—49ers, 37-13 (SF)
Rams, 31-20 (StL)
2003—Rams, 27-24 (StL) OT
49ers, 30-10 (SF)
2004—Rams, 24-14 (SF)
Rams, 16-6 (StL)
2005—49ers, 28-25 (SF)
49ers, 24-20 (StL)
2006—49ers, 20-13 (SF)
Rams, 20-17 (StL)
2007—49ers, 17-16 (StL)
Rams, 13-9 (SF)
2008—49ers, 35-16 (SF)
49ers, 17-16 (StL)
2009—49ers, 35-0 (SF)
49ers, 28-6 (StL)
(RS Pts.—49ers 2,662, Rams 2,607)
(PS Pts.—49ers 30, Rams 3)
**Franchise in Los Angeles prior to 1995*
***NFC Championship*

***ST. LOUIS vs. SEATTLE**
RS: Seahawks lead series, 14-9
PS: Rams lead series, 1-0
1976—Rams, 45-6 (LA)
1979—Rams, 24-0 (S)
1985—Rams, 35-24 (S)
1988—Rams, 31-10 (LA)

1991—Seahawks, 23-9 (S)
1997—Seahawks, 17-9 (StL)
2000—Rams, 37-34 (Sea)
2002—Rams, 37-20 (StL)
Seahawks, 30-10 (Sea)
2003—Seahawks, 24-23 (Sea)
Rams, 27-22 (StL)
2004—Rams, 33-27 (Sea) OT
Rams, 23-12 (StL)
**Rams, 27-20 (Sea)
2005—Seahawks, 37-31 (StL)
Seahawks, 31-16 (Sea)
2006—Seahawks, 30-28 (StL)
Seahawks, 24-22 (Sea)
2007—Seahawks, 33-6 (Sea)
Seahawks, 24-19 (StL)
2008—Seahawks, 37-13 (Sea)
Seahawks, 23-20 (StL)
2009—Seahawks, 28-0 (Sea)
Seahawks, 27-17 (StL)
(RS Pts.—Rams 543, Seahawks 515)
(PS Pts.—Rams 27, Seahawks 20)
Franchise in Los Angeles prior to 1995
***NFC First-Round Playoff*

***ST. LOUIS vs. TAMPA BAY**
RS: Rams lead series, 9-7
PS: Rams lead series, 2-0
1977—Rams, 31-0 (LA)
1978—Rams, 26-23 (LA)
1979—Buccaneers, 21-6 (TB)
**Rams, 9-0 (TB)
1980—Buccaneers, 10-9 (TB)
1984—Rams, 34-33 (TB)
1985—Rams, 31-27 (TB)
1986—Rams, 26-20 (LA) OT
1987—Rams, 35-3 (LA)
1990—Rams, 35-14 (TB)
1992—Rams, 31-27 (TB)
1994—Buccaneers, 24-14 (TB)
1999—**Rams, 11-6 (StL)
2000—Buccaneers, 38-35 (TB)
2001—Buccaneers, 24-17 (StL)
2002—Buccaneers, 26-14 (TB)
2004—Rams, 28-21 (StL)
2007—Buccaneers, 24-3 (TB)
(RS Pts.—Rams 375, Buccaneers 335)
(PS Pts.—Rams 20, Buccaneers 6)
Franchise in Los Angeles prior to 1995
***NFC Championship*

***ST. LOUIS vs. **TENNESSEE**
RS: Rams lead series, 6-4
PS: Rams lead series, 1-0
1973—Rams, 31-26 (H)
1978—Rams, 10-6 (H)
1981—Oilers, 27-20 (LA)
1984—Rams, 27-16 (LA)
1987—Oilers, 20-16 (H)
1990—Rams, 17-13 (LA)
1993—Rams, 28-13 (H)
1999—Titans, 24-21 (T)
***Rams, 23-16 (Atlanta)
2005—Rams, 31-27 (StL)
2009—Titans, 47-7 (T)
(RS Pts.—Titans, 219, Rams 208)
(PS Pts.—Rams 23, Titans 16)
Franchise in Los Angeles prior to 1995
***Franchise in Houston prior to 1997; known as Oilers prior to 1999*
****Super Bowl XXXIV*

***ST. LOUIS vs. WASHINGTON**
RS: Redskins lead series, 21-8-1
PS: Series tied, 2-2
1937—Redskins, 16-7 (C)
1938—Redskins, 37-13 (W)
1941—Redskins, 17-13 (W)
1942—Redskins, 33-14 (W)
1944—Redskins, 14-10 (W)
1945—**Rams, 15-14 (C)
1948—Rams, 41-13 (W)
1949—Rams, 53-27 (LA)
1951—Redskins, 31-21 (W)
1962—Redskins, 20-14 (W)
1963—Redskins, 37-14 (LA)
1967—Tie, 28-28 (LA)
1969—Rams, 24-13 (W)
1971—Redskins, 38-24 (LA)
1974—Redskins, 23-17 (LA)
***Rams, 19-10 (LA)
1977—Redskins, 17-14 (W)
1981—Redskins, 30-7 (LA)
1983—Redskins, 42-20 (LA)
***Redskins, 51-7 (W)
1986—****Redskins, 19-7 (W)
1987—Rams, 30-26 (W)
1991—Redskins, 27-6 (LA)
1993—Rams, 10-6 (LA)
1994—Redskins, 24-21 (LA)
1995—Redskins, 35-23 (StL)
1996—Redskins, 17-10 (StL)
1997—Rams, 23-20 (W)
2000—Redskins, 33-20 (StL)
2002—Redskins, 20-17 (W)
2005—Redskins, 24-9 (StL)
2006—Rams, 37-31 (StL) OT
2008—Rams, 19-17 (W)
2009—Redskins, 9-7 (W)
(RS Pts.—Redskins 725, Rams 566)
(PS Pts.—Redskins 94, Rams 48)
Franchise in Los Angeles prior to 1995 and in Cleveland prior to 1946
***NFL Championship*
****NFC Divisional Playoff*
*****NFC First-Round Playoff*

SAN DIEGO vs. ARIZONA
RS: Chargers lead series, 8-3;
See Arizona vs. San Diego

SAN DIEGO vs. ATLANTA
RS: Falcons lead series, 7-1;
See Atlanta vs. San Diego

SAN DIEGO vs. BALTIMORE
RS: Ravens lead series, 4-3;
See Baltimore vs. San Diego

SAN DIEGO vs. BUFFALO
RS: Chargers lead series, 20-10-2
PS: Bills lead series, 2-1;
See Buffalo vs. San Diego

SAN DIEGO vs. CAROLINA
RS: Panthers lead series, 3-1;
See Carolina vs. San Diego

SAN DIEGO vs. CHICAGO
RS: Series tied, 5-5;
See Chicago vs. San Diego

SAN DIEGO vs. CINCINNATI
RS: Chargers lead series, 19-10
PS: Bengals lead series, 1-0;
See Cincinnati vs. San Diego

SAN DIEGO vs. CLEVELAND
RS: Chargers lead series, 14-7-1;
See Cleveland vs. San Diego

SAN DIEGO vs. DALLAS
RS: Cowboys lead series, 6-3;
See Dallas vs. San Diego

SAN DIEGO vs. DENVER
RS: Broncos lead series, 54-45-1;
See Denver vs. San Diego

SAN DIEGO vs. DETROIT
RS: Chargers lead series, 6-3;
See Detroit vs. San Diego

SAN DIEGO vs. GREEN BAY
RS: Packers lead series, 8-1;
See Green Bay vs. San Diego

SAN DIEGO vs. HOUSTON
RS: Chargers lead series, 3-0;
See Houston vs. San Diego

SAN DIEGO vs. INDIANAPOLIS
RS: Chargers lead series, 14-9
PS: Chargers lead series, 2-1;
See Indianapolis vs. San Diego

SAN DIEGO vs. JACKSONVILLE
RS: Jaguars lead series, 2-1;
See Jacksonville vs. San Diego

SAN DIEGO vs. KANSAS CITY
RS: Chiefs lead series, 50-48-1
PS: Chargers lead series, 1-0;
See Kansas City vs. San Diego

SAN DIEGO vs. MIAMI
RS: Dolphins lead series, 12-11
PS: Series tied, 2-2;
See Miami vs. San Diego

SAN DIEGO vs. MINNESOTA
RS: Series tied, 5-5;
See Minnesota vs. San Diego

SAN DIEGO vs. NEW ENGLAND
RS: Patriots lead series, 18-14-2
PS: Patriots lead series, 2-1;
See New England vs. San Diego

SAN DIEGO vs. NEW ORLEANS
RS: Chargers lead series, 7-3;
See New Orleans vs. San Diego

SAN DIEGO vs. N.Y. GIANTS
RS: Series tied, 5-5;
See N.Y. Giants vs. San Diego

SAN DIEGO vs. N.Y. JETS
RS: Chargers lead series, 19-11-1
PS: Jets lead series, 2-0;
See N.Y. Jets vs. San Diego

SAN DIEGO vs. OAKLAND
RS: Raiders lead series, 54-44-2
PS: Raiders lead series, 1-0;
See Oakland vs. San Diego

SAN DIEGO vs. PHILADELPHIA
RS: Chargers lead series, 6-4;
See Philadelphia vs. San Diego

SAN DIEGO vs. PITTSBURGH
RS: Steelers lead series, 21-6
PS: Chargers lead series, 2-1;
See Pittsburgh vs. San Diego

SAN DIEGO vs. ST. LOUIS
RS: Rams lead series, 5-4;
See St. Louis vs. San Diego

SAN DIEGO vs. SAN FRANCISCO
RS: 49ers lead series, 6-5
PS: 49ers lead series, 1-0
1972—49ers, 34-3 (SF)
1976—Chargers, 13-7 (SD) OT
1979—Chargers, 31-9 (SD)
1982—Chargers, 41-37 (SF)
1988—49ers, 48-10 (SD)
1991—49ers, 34-14 (SF)
1994—49ers, 38-15 (SD)
*49ers, 49-26 (South Florida)
1997—49ers, 17-10 (SF)

2000—49ers, 45-17 (SD)
2002—Chargers, 20-17 (SD) OT
2006—Chargers, 48-19 (SF)
(RS Pts.—49ers 305, Chargers 222)
(PS Pts.—49ers 49, Chargers 26)
Super Bowl XXIX

SAN DIEGO vs. SEATTLE
RS: Seahawks lead series, 25-23
1977—Chargers, 30-28 (S)
1978—Chargers, 24-20 (S)
Chargers, 37-10 (SD)
1979—Chargers, 33-16 (S)
Chargers, 20-10 (SD)
1980—Chargers, 34-13 (S)
Chargers, 21-14 (SD)
1981—Chargers, 24-10 (SD)
Seahawks, 44-23 (S)
1983—Seahawks, 34-31 (S)
Chargers, 28-21 (SD)
1984—Seahawks, 31-17 (S)
Seahawks, 24-0 (SD)
1985—Seahawks, 49-35 (SD)
Seahawks, 26-21 (S)
1986—Seahawks, 33-7 (S)
Seahawks, 34-24 (SD)
1987—Seahawks, 34-3 (S)
1988—Chargers, 17-6 (SD)
Seahawks, 17-14 (S)
1989—Seahawks, 17-16 (SD)
Seahawks, 10-7 (S)
1990—Chargers, 31-14 (S)
Seahawks, 13-10 (SD) OT
1991—Seahawks, 20-9 (S)
Chargers, 17-14 (SD)
1992—Chargers, 17-6 (SD)
Chargers, 31-14 (S)
1993—Chargers, 18-12 (SD)
Seahawks, 31-14 (S)
1994—Chargers, 24-10 (S)
Chargers, 35-15 (SD)
1995—Chargers, 14-10 (SD)
Chargers, 35-25 (S)
1996—Chargers, 29-7 (SD)
Seahawks, 32-13 (S)
1997—Seahawks, 26-22 (S)
Seahawks, 37-31 (SD)
1998—Seahawks, 27-20 (SD)
Seahawks, 38-17 (S)
1999—Chargers, 13-10 (SD)
Chargers, 19-16 (S)
2000—Seahawks, 20-12 (SD)
Seahawks, 17-15 (S)
2001—Seahawks, 13-10 (S) OT
Seahawks, 25-22 (SD)
2002—Seahawks, 31-28 (SD) OT
2006—Chargers, 20-17 (Sea)
(RS Pts.—Seahawks 1,001, Chargers 992)

SAN DIEGO vs. TAMPA BAY
RS: Chargers lead series, 8-1
1976—Chargers, 23-0 (TB)
1981—Chargers, 24-23 (TB)
1987—Chargers, 17-13 (TB)
1990—Chargers, 41-10 (SD)
1992—Chargers, 29-14 (SD)
1993—Chargers, 32-17 (TB)
1996—Buccaneers, 25-17 (SD)
2004—Chargers, 31-24 (SD)
2008—Chargers, 41-24 (TB)
(RS Pts.—Chargers 255, Buccaneers 150)

***SAN DIEGO vs. **TENNESSEE**
RS: Chargers lead series, 23-13-1
PS: Titans lead series, 3-1
1960—Oilers, 38-28 (H)
Chargers, 24-21 (LA)
***Oilers, 24-16 (H)
1961—Chargers, 34-24 (SD)
Oilers, 33-13 (H)
***Oilers, 10-3 (SD)
1962—Oilers, 42-17 (SD)
Oilers, 33-27 (H)
1963—Chargers, 27-0 (SD)
Chargers 20-14 (H)
1964—Chargers, 27-21 (SD)
Chargers, 20-17 (H)
1965—Chargers, 31-14 (SD)
Chargers, 37-26 (H)
1966—Chargers, 28-22 (H)
1967—Chargers, 13-3 (SD)
Oilers, 24-17 (H)
1968—Chargers, 30-14 (SD)
1969—Chargers, 21-17 (H)
1970—Tie, 31-31 (SD)
1971—Oilers, 49-33 (H)
1972—Chargers, 34-20 (SD)
1974—Oilers, 21-14 (H)
1975—Oilers, 33-17 (H)
1976—Chargers, 30-27 (SD)
1978—Chargers, 45-24 (H)
1979—****Oilers, 17-14 (SD)
1984—Chargers, 31-14 (SD)
1985—Oilers, 37-35 (H)
1986—Chargers, 27-0 (SD)
1987—Oilers, 33-18 (H)
1989—Oilers, 34-27 (SD)
1990—Oilers, 17-7 (SD)
1992—Oilers, 27-0 (H)
1993—Chargers, 18-17 (SD)
1998—Chargers, 13-7 (T)
2004—Chargers, 38-17 (SD)
2006—Chargers, 40-7 (SD)
2007—Chargers, 23-17 (T) OT
*****Chargers, 17-6 (SD)
2009—Chargers, 42-17 (T)
(RS Pts.—Chargers 937, Titans 812)
(PS Pts.—Titans 57, Chargers 50)
**Franchise in Los Angeles prior to 1961*
***Franchise in Houston prior to 1997; known as Oilers prior to 1999*
****AFL Championship*
*****AFC Divisional Playoff*
******AFC First-Round Playoff*

SAN DIEGO vs. WASHINGTON
RS: Redskins lead series, 6-3
1973—Redskins, 38-0 (W)
1980—Redskins, 40-17 (W)
1983—Redskins, 27-24 (SD)
1986—Redskins, 30-27 (SD)
1989—Redskins, 26-21 (W)
1998—Redskins, 24-20 (W)
2001—Chargers, 30-3 (SD)
2005—Chargers, 23-17 (W) OT
2009—Chargers, 23-20 (SD)
(RS Pts.—Redskins 225, Chargers 185)

SAN FRANCISCO vs. ARIZONA
RS: 49ers lead series, 21-16;
See Arizona vs. San Francisco

SAN FRANCISCO vs. ATLANTA
RS: 49ers lead series, 44-28-1
PS: Falcons lead series, 1-0;
See Atlanta vs. San Francisco

SAN FRANCISCO vs. BALTIMORE
RS: Ravens lead series, 2-1;
See Baltimore vs. San Francisco

SAN FRANCISCO vs. BUFFALO
RS: Series tied, 5-5;
See Buffalo vs. San Francisco

SAN FRANCISCO vs. CAROLINA
RS: Panthers lead series, 9-7;
See Carolina vs. San Francisco

SAN FRANCISCO vs. CHICAGO
RS: Bears lead series, 29-28-1
PS: 49ers lead series, 3-0;
See Chicago vs. San Francisco

SAN FRANCISCO vs. CINCINNATI
RS: 49ers lead series, 8-3
PS: 49ers lead series, 2-0;
See Cincinnati vs. San Francisco

SAN FRANCISCO vs. CLEVELAND
RS: Browns lead series, 11-6;
See Cleveland vs. San Francisco

SAN FRANCISCO vs. DALLAS
RS: 49ers lead series, 14-10-1
PS: Cowboys lead series, 5-2;
See Dallas vs. San Francisco

SAN FRANCISCO vs. DENVER
RS: Broncos lead series, 6-5
PS: 49ers lead series, 1-0;
See Denver vs. San Francisco

SAN FRANCISCO vs. DETROIT
RS: 49ers lead series, 34-26-1
PS: Series tied, 1-1;
See Detroit vs. San Francisco

SAN FRANCISCO vs. GREEN BAY
RS: Packers lead series, 29-25-1
PS: Packers lead series, 4-1;
See Green Bay vs. San Francisco

SAN FRANCISCO vs. HOUSTON
RS: Series tied, 1-1;
See Houston vs. San Francisco

SAN FRANCISCO vs. INDIANAPOLIS
RS: Colts lead series, 24-18;
See Indianapolis vs. San Francisco

SAN FRANCISCO vs. JACKSONVILLE
RS: Jaguars lead series, 2-1;
See Jacksonville vs. San Francisco

SAN FRANCISCO vs. KANSAS CITY
RS: 49ers lead series, 6-4;
See Kansas City vs. San Francisco

SAN FRANCISCO vs. MIAMI
RS: Dolphins lead series, 6-4
PS: 49ers lead series, 1-0;
See Miami vs. San Francisco

SAN FRANCISCO vs. MINNESOTA
RS: Vikings lead series, 20-18-1
PS: 49ers lead series, 4-1;
See Minnesota vs. San Francisco

SAN FRANCISCO vs. NEW ENGLAND
RS: 49ers lead series, 7-4;
See New England vs. San Francisco

SAN FRANCISCO vs. NEW ORLEANS
RS: 49ers lead series, 45-23-2;
See New Orleans vs. San Francisco

SAN FRANCISCO vs. N.Y. GIANTS
RS: Giants lead series, 14-13
PS: 49ers lead series, 4-3;
See N.Y. Giants vs. San Francisco

SAN FRANCISCO vs. N.Y. JETS
RS: 49ers lead series, 9-2;
See N.Y. Jets vs. San Francisco

SAN FRANCISCO vs. OAKLAND
RS: Raiders lead series, 6-5;

See Oakland vs. San Francisco

SAN FRANCISCO vs. PHILADELPHIA
RS: 49ers lead series, 16-11-1
PS: 49ers lead series, 1-0;
See Philadelphia vs. San Francisco

SAN FRANCISCO vs. PITTSBURGH
RS: 49ers lead series, 10-9;
See Pittsburgh vs. San Francisco

SAN FRANCISCO vs. ST. LOUIS
RS: Rams lead series, 60-58-2
PS: 49ers lead series, 1-0;
See St. Louis vs. San Francisco

SAN FRANCISCO vs. SAN DIEGO
RS: 49ers lead series, 6-5
PS: 49ers lead series, 1-0;
See San Diego vs. San Francisco

SAN FRANCISCO vs. SEATTLE
RS: Seahawks lead series, 12-10
1976—49ers, 37-21 (Sea)
1979—Seahawks, 35-24 (SF)
1985—49ers, 19-6 (SF)
1988—49ers, 38-7 (Sea)
1991—49ers, 24-22 (Sea)
1997—Seahawks, 38-9 (Sea)
2002—49ers, 28-21 (Sea)
49ers, 31-24 (SF)
2003—Seahawks, 20-19 (Sea)
Seahawks, 24-17 (SF)
2004—Seahawks, 34-0 (Sea)
Seahawks, 42-27 (SF)
2005—Seahawks, 27-25 (SF)
Seahawks, 41-3 (Sea)
2006—49ers, 20-14 (SF)
49ers, 24-14 (Sea)
2007—Seahawks, 23-3 (SF)
Seahawks, 24-0 (Sea)
2008—49ers, 33-30 (Sea) OT
Seahawks, 34-13 (SF)
2009—49ers, 23-10 (SF)
Seahawks, 20-17 (Sea)
(RS Pts.—Seahawks 531, 49ers 434)

SAN FRANCISCO vs. TAMPA BAY
RS: 49ers lead series, 15-3
PS: Buccaneers lead series, 1-0
1977—49ers, 20-10 (SF)
1978—49ers, 6-3 (SF)
1979—49ers, 23-7 (SF)
1980—Buccaneers, 24-23 (SF)
1983—49ers, 35-21 (SF)
1984—49ers, 24-17 (SF)
1986—49ers, 31-7 (TB)
1987—49ers, 24-10 (TB)
1989—49ers, 20-16 (TB)
1990—49ers, 31-7 (SF)
1992—49ers, 21-14 (SF)
1993—49ers, 45-21 (TB)
1994—49ers, 41-16 (SF)
1997—Buccaneers, 13-6 (TB)
2002—*Buccaneers, 31-6 (TB)
2003—49ers, 24-7 (SF)
2004—Buccaneers, 35-3 (TB)
2005—49ers, 15-10 (SF)
2007—49ers, 21-19 (SF)
(RS Pts.—49ers 413, Buccaneers 257)
(PS Pts.—Buccaneers 31, 49ers 6)
NFC Divisional Playoff

SAN FRANCISCO vs. *TENNESSEE
RS: 49ers lead series, 7-5
1970—49ers, 30-20 (H)
1975—Oilers, 27-13 (SF)
1978—Oilers, 20-19 (H)
1981—49ers, 28-6 (SF)
1984—49ers, 34-21 (H)
1987—49ers, 27-20 (SF)
1990—49ers, 24-21 (H)
1993—Oilers, 10-7 (SF)
1996—49ers, 10-9 (H)
1999—49ers, 24-22 (SF)
2005—Titans, 33-22 (T)
2009—Titans, 34-27 (SF)
(RS Pts.—49ers 265, Titans 243)
**Franchise in Houston prior to 1997; known as Oilers prior to 1999*

SAN FRANCISCO vs. WASHINGTON
RS: 49ers lead series, 14-9-1
PS: 49ers lead series, 3-1
1952—49ers, 23-17 (W)
1954—49ers, 41-7 (SF)
1955—Redskins, 7-0 (W)
1961—49ers, 35-3 (SF)
1967—Redskins, 31-28 (W)
1969—Tie, 17-17 (SF)
1970—49ers, 26-17 (SF)
1971—*49ers, 24-20 (SF)
1973—Redskins, 33-9 (W)
1976—Redskins, 24-21 (SF)
1978—Redskins, 38-20 (W)
1981—49ers, 30-17 (W)
1983—**Redskins, 24-21 (W)
1984—49ers, 37-31 (SF)
1985—49ers, 35-8 (W)
1986—Redskins, 14-6 (W)
1988—49ers, 37-21 (SF)
1990—49ers, 26-13 (SF)
*49ers, 28-10 (SF)
1992—*49ers, 20-13 (SF)
1994—49ers, 37-22 (W)
1996—49ers, 19-16 (W) OT
1998—49ers, 45-10 (W)
1999—Redskins, 26-20 (SF) OT
2002—49ers, 20-10 (SF)
2004—Redskins, 26-16 (SF)
2005—Redskins, 52-17 (W)
2008—49ers, 27-24 (SF)
(RS Pts.—49ers 592, Redskins 484)
(PS Pts.—49ers 93, Redskins 67)
**NFC Divisional Playoff*
***NFC Championship*

SEATTLE vs. ARIZONA
RS: Cardinals lead series, 13-9;
See Arizona vs. Seattle

SEATTLE vs. ATLANTA
RS: Seahawks lead series, 8-3;
See Atlanta vs. Seattle

SEATTLE vs. BALTIMORE
RS: Ravens lead series, 2-1;
See Baltimore vs. Seattle

SEATTLE vs. BUFFALO
RS: Seahawks lead series, 6-5;
See Buffalo vs. Seattle

SEATTLE vs. CAROLINA
RS: Panthers lead series, 2-1
PS: Seahawks lead series, 1-0;
See Carolina vs. Seattle

SEATTLE vs. CHICAGO
RS: Seahawks lead series, 7-4
PS: Bears lead series, 1-0;
See Chicago vs. Seattle

SEATTLE vs. CINCINNATI
RS: Seahawks lead series, 9-8
PS: Bengals lead series, 1-0;
See Cincinnati vs. Seattle

SEATTLE vs. CLEVELAND
RS: Seahawks lead series, 11-5;
See Cleveland vs. Seattle

SEATTLE vs. DALLAS
RS: Cowboys lead series, 8-4
PS: Seahawks lead series, 1-0;
See Dallas vs. Seattle

SEATTLE vs. DENVER
RS: Broncos lead series, 33-18
PS: Seahawks lead series, 1-0;
See Denver vs. Seattle

SEATTLE vs. DETROIT
RS: Seahawks lead series, 7-4;
See Detroit vs. Seattle

SEATTLE vs. GREEN BAY
RS: Packers lead series, 8-5
PS: Packers lead series, 2-0;
See Green Bay vs. Seattle

SEATTLE vs. HOUSTON
RS: Series tied, 1-1;
See Houston vs. Seattle

SEATTLE vs. INDIANAPOLIS
RS: Colts lead series, 6-4;
See Indianapolis vs. Seattle

SEATTLE vs. JACKSONVILLE
RS: Seahawks lead series, 4-2;
See Jacksonville vs. Seattle

SEATTLE vs. KANSAS CITY
RS: Chiefs lead series, 31-18;
See Kansas City vs. Seattle

SEATTLE vs. MIAMI
RS: Dolphins lead series, 7-3
PS: Dolphins lead series, 2-1;
See Miami vs. Seattle

SEATTLE vs. MINNESOTA
RS: Seahawks lead series, 6-5;
See Minnesota vs. Seattle

SEATTLE vs. NEW ENGLAND
RS: Patriots lead series, 8-7;
See New England vs. Seattle

SEATTLE vs. NEW ORLEANS
RS: Series tied, 5-5;
See New Orleans vs. Seattle

SEATTLE vs. N.Y. GIANTS
RS: Giants lead series, 8-5;
See N.Y. Giants vs. Seattle

SEATTLE vs. N.Y. JETS
RS: Seahawks lead series, 9-8;
See N.Y. Jets vs. Seattle

SEATTLE vs. OAKLAND
RS: Raiders lead series, 27-23
PS: Series tied, 1-1;
See Oakland vs. Seattle

SEATTLE vs. PHILADELPHIA
RS: Eagles lead series, 7-5;
See Philadelphia vs. Seattle

SEATTLE vs. PITTSBURGH
RS: Seahawks lead series, 8-7
PS: Steelers lead series, 1-0;
See Pittsburgh vs. Seattle

SEATTLE vs. ST. LOUIS
RS: Seahawks lead series, 14-9
PS: Rams lead series, 1-0;
See St. Louis vs. Seattle

SEATTLE vs. SAN DIEGO
RS: Seahawks lead series, 25-23;
See San Diego vs. Seattle

SEATTLE vs. SAN FRANCISCO
RS: Seahawks lead series, 12-10;
See San Francisco vs. Seattle

ALL-TIME TEAM VS. TEAM RESULTS

SEATTLE vs. TAMPA BAY
RS: Seahawks lead series, 7-3
1976—Seahawks, 13-10 (TB)
1977—Seahawks, 30-23 (S)
1994—Seahawks, 22-21 (S)
1996—Seahawks, 17-13 (TB)
1999—Buccaneers, 16-3 (S)
2004—Seahawks, 10-6 (TB)
2006—Seahawks, 23-7 (TB)
2007—Seahawks, 20-6 (S)
2008—Buccaneers, 20-10 (TB)
2009—Buccaneers, 24-7 (S)
(RS Pts.—Seahawks 155, Buccaneers 146)

SEATTLE vs. *TENNESSEE
RS: Seahawks lead series, 9-5
PS: Titans lead series, 1-0
1977—Oilers, 22-10 (S)
1979—Seahawks, 34-14 (S)
1980—Seahawks, 26-7 (H)
1981—Oilers, 35-17 (H)
1982—Oilers, 23-21 (H)
1987—**Oilers, 23-20 (H) OT
1988—Seahawks, 27-24 (S)
1990—Seahawks, 13-10 (S) OT
1993—Oilers, 24-14 (H)
1994—Seahawks, 16-14 (H)
1996—Seahawks, 23-16 (S)
1997—Seahawks, 16-13 (S)
1998—Seahawks, 20-18 (S)
2005—Seahawks, 28-24 (T)
2009—Titans, 17-13 (S)
(RS Pts.—Seahawks 278, Titans 261)
(PS Pts.—Titans 23, Seahawks 20)
**Franchise in Houston prior to 1997; known as Oilers prior to 1999*
***AFC First-Round Playoff*

SEATTLE vs. WASHINGTON
RS: Redskins lead series, 10-4
PS: Seahawks lead series, 2-0
1976—Redskins, 31-7 (W)
1980—Seahawks, 14-0 (W)
1983—Redskins, 27-17 (S)
1986—Redskins, 19-14 (W)
1989—Redskins, 29-0 (S)
1992—Redskins, 16-3 (S)
1994—Seahawks, 28-7 (W)
1995—Seahawks, 27-20 (W)
1998—Seahawks, 24-14 (S)
2001—Redskins, 27-14 (W)
2002—Redskins, 14-3 (S)
2003—Redskins, 27-20 (W)
2005—Redskins, 20-17 (W) OT
*Seahawks, 20-10 (S)
2007—**Seahawks, 35-14 (S)
2008—Redskins, 20-17 (S)
(RS Pts.—Redskins 271, Seahawks 205)
(PS Pts.—Seahawks 55, Redskins 24)
**NFC Divisional Playoff*
***NFC First-Round Playoff*

TAMPA BAY vs. ARIZONA
RS: Series tied, 8-8;
See Arizona vs. Tampa Bay

TAMPA BAY vs. ATLANTA
RS: Buccaneers lead series, 18-15;
See Atlanta vs. Tampa Bay

TAMPA BAY vs. BALTIMORE
RS: Buccaneers lead series, 2-1;
See Baltimore vs. Tampa Bay

TAMPA BAY vs. BUFFALO
RS: Buccaneers lead series, 6-3;
See Buffalo vs. Tampa Bay

TAMPA BAY vs. CAROLINA
RS: Panthers lead series, 12-7;
See Carolina vs. Tampa Bay

TAMPA BAY vs. CHICAGO
RS: Bears lead series, 35-18;
See Chicago vs. Tampa Bay

TAMPA BAY vs. CINCINNATI
RS: Buccaneers lead series, 6-3;
See Cincinnati vs. Tampa Bay

TAMPA BAY vs. CLEVELAND
RS: Browns lead series, 5-2;
See Cleveland vs. Tampa Bay

TAMPA BAY vs. DALLAS
RS: Cowboys lead series, 9-3
PS: Cowboys lead series, 2-0;
See Dallas vs. Tampa Bay

TAMPA BAY vs. DENVER
RS: Broncos lead series, 5-2;
See Denver vs. Tampa Bay

TAMPA BAY vs. DETROIT
RS: Lions lead series, 27-25
PS: Buccaneers lead series, 1-0;
See Detroit vs. Tampa Bay

TAMPA BAY vs. GREEN BAY
RS: Packers lead series, 29-21-1
PS: Packers lead series, 1-0;
See Green Bay vs. Tampa Bay

TAMPA BAY vs. HOUSTON
RS: Series tied, 1-1;
See Houston vs. Tampa Bay

TAMPA BAY vs. INDIANAPOLIS
RS: Colts lead series, 7-4;
See Indianapolis vs. Tampa Bay

TAMPA BAY vs. JACKSONVILLE
RS: Jaguars lead series, 3-1;
See Jacksonville vs. Tampa Bay

TAMPA BAY vs. KANSAS CITY
RS: Series tied, 5-5;
See Kansas City vs. Tampa Bay

TAMPA BAY vs. MIAMI
RS: Dolphins lead series, 5-4;
See Miami vs. Tampa Bay

TAMPA BAY vs. MINNESOTA
RS: Vikings lead series, 31-20;
See Minnesota vs. Tampa Bay

TAMPA BAY vs. NEW ENGLAND
RS: Patriots lead series, 5-2;
See New England vs. Tampa Bay

TAMPA BAY vs. NEW ORLEANS
RS: Saints lead series, 21-15;
See New Orleans vs. Tampa Bay

TAMPA BAY vs. N.Y. GIANTS
RS: Giants lead series, 11-6
PS: Giants lead series, 1-0;
See N.Y. Giants vs. Tampa Bay

TAMPA BAY vs. N.Y. JETS
RS: Jets lead series, 9-1;
See N.Y. Jets vs. Tampa Bay

TAMPA BAY vs. OAKLAND
RS: Raiders lead series, 6-1
PS: Buccaneers lead series, 1-0;
See Oakland vs. Tampa Bay

TAMPA BAY vs. PHILADELPHIA
RS: Eagles lead series, 6-5
PS: Series tied, 2-2;
See Philadelphia vs. Tampa Bay

TAMPA BAY vs. PITTSBURGH
RS: Steelers lead series, 7-1;
See Pittsburgh vs. Tampa Bay

TAMPA BAY vs. ST. LOUIS
RS: Rams lead series, 9-7
PS: Rams lead series, 2-0;
See St. Louis vs. Tampa Bay

TAMPA BAY vs. SAN DIEGO
RS: Chargers lead series, 8-1;
See San Diego vs. Tampa Bay

TAMPA BAY vs. SAN FRANCISCO
RS: 49ers lead series, 15-3
PS: Buccaneers lead series, 1-0;
See San Francisco vs. Tampa Bay

TAMPA BAY vs. SEATTLE
RS: Seahawks lead series, 7-3;
See Seattle vs. Tampa Bay

TAMPA BAY vs. *TENNESSEE
RS: Titans lead series, 7-2
1976—Oilers, 20-0 (H)
1980—Oilers, 20-14 (H)
1983—Buccaneers, 33-24 (TB)
1989—Oilers, 20-17 (H)
1995—Oilers, 19-7 (H)
1998—Oilers, 31-22 (TB)
2001—Titans, 31-28 (Tenn) OT
2003—Titans, 33-13 (Tenn)
2007—Buccaneers, 13-10 (TB)
(RS Pts.—Titans 208, Buccaneers 147)
**Franchise in Houston prior to 1997; known as Oilers prior to 1999*

TAMPA BAY vs. WASHINGTON
RS: Series tied, 8-8
PS: Series tied, 1-1
1977—Redskins, 10-0 (TB)
1982—Redskins, 21-13 (TB)
1989—Redskins, 32-28 (W)
1993—Redskins, 23-17 (TB)
1994—Buccaneers, 26-21 (TB)
Buccaneers, 17-14 (W)
1995—Buccaneers, 14-6 (TB)
1996—Buccaneers, 24-10 (TB)
1998—Redskins, 20-16 (W)
1999—*Buccaneers, 14-13 (TB)
2000—Redskins, 20-17 (W) OT
2003—Buccaneers, 35-13 (W)
2004—Redskins, 16-10 (W)
2005—Buccaneers, 36-35 (TB)
**Redskins, 17-10 (TB)
2006—Buccaneers, 20-17 (TB)
2007—Buccaneers, 19-13 (TB)
2009—Redskins, 16-13 (W)
(RS Pts.—Buccaneers 305, Redskins 287)
(PS Pts.—Redskins 30, Buccaneers 24)
**NFC Divisional Playoff*
***NFC First-Round Playoff*

TENNESSEE VS. ARIZONA
RS: Cardinals lead series, 5-4;
See Arizona vs. Tennessee

TENNESSEE vs. ATLANTA
RS: Titans lead series, 7-5;
See Atlanta vs. Tennessee

TENNESSEE vs. BALTIMORE
RS: Series tied, 8-8
PS: Ravens lead series, 2-1;
See Baltimore vs. Tennessee

TENNESSEE vs. BUFFALO
RS: Titans lead series, 25-14
PS: Bills lead series, 2-1;
See Buffalo vs. Tennessee

TENNESSEE vs. CAROLINA
RS: Titans lead series, 2-1;
See Carolina vs. Tennessee

TENNESSEE vs. CHICAGO
RS: Series tied, 5-5;
See Chicago vs. Tennessee
TENNESSEE vs. CINCINNATI
RS: Titans lead series, 39-31-1
PS: Bengals lead series, 1-0;
See Cincinnati vs. Tennessee
TENNESSEE vs. CLEVELAND
RS: Browns lead series, 33-27
PS: Titans lead series, 1-0;
See Cleveland vs. Tennessee
TENNESSEE vs. DALLAS
RS: Cowboys lead series, 7-5;
See Dallas vs. Tennessee
TENNESSEE vs. DENVER
RS: Titans lead series, 20-13-1
PS: Broncos lead series, 2-1;
See Denver vs. Tennessee
TENNESSEE vs. DETROIT
RS: Titans lead series, 7-3;
See Detroit vs. Tennessee
TENNESSEE vs. GREEN BAY
RS: Titans lead series, 6-4;
See Green Bay vs. Tennessee
TENNESSEE vs. HOUSTON
RS: Titans lead series, 12-4;
See Houston vs. Tennessee
TENNESSEE vs. INDIANAPOLIS
RS: Colts lead series, 18-12
PS: Titans lead series, 1-0;
See Indianapolis vs. Tennessee
TENNESSEE vs. JACKSONVILLE
RS: Titans lead series, 17-13
PS: Titans lead series, 1-0;
See Jacksonville vs. Tennessee
TENNESSEE vs. KANSAS CITY
RS: Chiefs lead series, 25-20
PS: Chiefs lead series, 2-0;
See Kansas City vs. Tennessee
TENNESSEE vs. MIAMI
RS: Dolphins lead series, 17-14
PS: Titans lead series, 1-0;
See Miami vs. Tennessee
TENNESSEE vs. MINNESOTA
RS: Vikings lead series, 7-4;
See Minnesota vs. Tennessee
TENNESSEE vs. NEW ENGLAND
RS: Patriots lead series, 21-15-1
PS: Series tied, 1-1;
See New England vs. Tennessee
TENNESSEE vs. NEW ORLEANS
RS: Titans lead series, 7-4-1;
See New Orleans vs. Tennessee
TENNESSEE vs. N.Y. GIANTS
RS: Giants lead series, 5-4;
See N.Y. Giants vs. Tennessee
TENNESSEE vs. N.Y. JETS
RS: Titans lead series, 21-17-1
PS: Titans lead series, 1-0;
See N.Y. Jets vs. Tennessee
TENNESSEE vs. OAKLAND
RS: Raiders lead series, 23-18
PS: Raiders lead series, 4-0;
See Oakland vs. Tennessee
TENNESSEE vs. PHILADELPHIA
RS: Eagles lead series, 6-3;
See Philadelphia vs. Tennessee
TENNESSEE vs. PITTSBURGH
RS: Steelers lead series, 39-29
PS: Steelers lead series, 3-1;
See Pittsburgh vs. Tennessee
TENNESSEE vs. ST. LOUIS
RS: Rams lead series, 6-4
PS: Rams lead series, 1-0;
See St. Louis vs. Tennessee
TENNESSEE vs. SAN DIEGO
RS: Chargers lead series, 23-13-1
PS: Titans lead series, 3-1;
See San Diego vs. Tennessee
TENNESSEE vs. SAN FRANCISCO
RS: 49ers lead series, 7-5;
See San Francisco vs. Tennessee
TENNESSEE vs. SEATTLE
RS: Seahawks lead series, 9-5
PS: Titans lead series, 1-0;
See Seattle vs. Tennessee
TENNESSEE vs. TAMPA BAY
RS: Titans lead series, 7-2;
See Tampa Bay vs. Tennessee
***TENNESSEE vs. WASHINGTON**
RS: Titans lead series, 6-4
1971—Redskins, 22-13 (W)
1975—Oilers, 13-10 (H)
1979—Oilers, 29-27 (W)
1985—Redskins, 16-13 (W)
1988—Oilers, 41-17 (H)
1991—Redskins, 16-13 (W) OT
1997—Oilers, 28-14 (T)
2000—Titans, 27-21 (W)
2002—Redskins, 31-14 (T)
2006—Titans, 25-22 (W)
(RS—Titans 216, Redskins 196)
**Franchise in Houston prior to 1997; known as Oilers prior to 1999*

WASHINGTON vs. ARIZONA
RS: Redskins lead series, 73-44-2;
See Arizona vs. Washington
WASHINGTON vs. ATLANTA
RS: Redskins lead series, 14-6-1
PS: Redskins lead series, 1-0;
See Atlanta vs. Washington
WASHINGTON vs. BALTIMORE
RS: Ravens lead series, 3-1;
See Baltimore vs. Washington
WASHINGTON vs. BUFFALO
RS: Bills lead series, 7-4
PS: Redskins lead series, 1-0;
See Buffalo vs. Washington
WASHINGTON vs. CAROLINA
RS: Redskins lead series, 7-2;
See Carolina vs. Washington
WASHINGTON vs. CHICAGO
RS: Bears lead series, 20-18-1
PS: Redskins lead series, 4-3;
See Chicago vs. Washington
WASHINGTON vs. CINCINNATI
RS: Series tied, 4-4;
See Cincinnati vs. Washington
WASHINGTON vs. CLEVELAND
RS: Browns lead series, 33-10-1;
See Cleveland vs. Washington
WASHINGTON vs. DALLAS
RS: Cowboys lead series, 59-37-2
PS: Redskins lead series, 2-0;
See Dallas vs. Washington
WASHINGTON vs. DENVER
RS: Broncos lead series, 6-5
PS: Redskins lead series, 1-0;
See Denver vs. Washington
WASHINGTON vs. DETROIT
RS: Redskins lead series, 27-11
PS: Redskins lead series, 3-0;
See Detroit vs. Washington
WASHINGTON vs. GREEN BAY
RS: Packers lead series, 17-12-1
PS: Series tied, 1-1;
See Green Bay vs. Washington
WASHINGTON vs. HOUSTON
RS: Redskins lead series, 2-0;
See Houston vs. Washington
WASHINGTON vs. INDIANAPOLIS
RS: Colts lead series, 18-10;
See Indianapolis vs. Washington
WASHINGTON vs. JACKSONVILLE
RS: Redskins lead series, 3-1;
See Jacksonville vs. Washington
WASHINGTON vs. KANSAS CITY
RS: Chiefs lead series, 7-1;
See Kansas City vs. Washington
WASHINGTON vs. MIAMI
RS: Dolphins lead series, 6-4
PS: Series tied, 1-1;
See Miami vs. Washington
WASHINGTON vs. MINNESOTA
RS: Redskins lead series, 8-6
PS: Redskins lead series, 3-2;
See Minnesota vs. Washington
WASHINGTON vs. NEW ENGLAND
RS: Redskins lead series, 6-2;
See New England vs. Washington
WASHINGTON vs. NEW ORLEANS
RS: Redskins lead series, 15-8;
See New Orleans vs. Washington
WASHINGTON vs. N.Y. GIANTS
RS: Giants lead series, 89-61-4
PS: Series tied, 1-1;
See N.Y. Giants vs. Washington
WASHINGTON vs. N.Y. JETS
RS: Redskins lead series, 8-1;
See N.Y. Jets vs. Washington
WASHINGTON vs. OAKLAND
RS: Raiders lead series, 7-4
PS: Raiders lead series, 1-0;
See Oakland vs. Washington
WASHINGTON vs. PHILADELPHIA
RS: Redskins lead series, 77-67-5
PS: Redskins lead series, 1-0;
See Philadelphia vs. Washington
WASHINGTON vs. PITTSBURGH
RS: Redskins lead series, 42-31-3;
See Pittsburgh vs. Washington
WASHINGTON vs. ST. LOUIS
RS: Redskins lead series, 21-8-1
PS: Series tied, 2-2;
See St. Louis vs. Washington
WASHINGTON vs. SAN DIEGO
RS: Redskins lead series, 6-3;
See San Diego vs. Washington
WASHINGTON vs. SAN FRANCISCO
RS: 49ers lead series, 14-9-1
PS: 49ers lead series, 3-1;
See San Francisco vs. Washington
WASHINGTON vs. SEATTLE
RS: Redskins lead series, 10-4
PS: Seahawks lead series, 2-0;
See Seattle vs. Washington
WASHINGTON vs. TAMPA BAY
RS: Series tied, 8-8
PS: Series tied, 1-1;
See Tampa Bay vs. Washington
WASHINGTON vs. TENNESSEE
RS: Titans lead series, 6-4;
See Tennessee vs. Washington

NFL OPENING KICKOFF WEEKEND

NFL OPENING KICKOFF GAMES (8)
(Home Team in capitals)

Date	Sites*	Teams
Sept. 5, 2002	Giants Stadium (East Rutherford, New Jersey) Times Square (New York, New York)	San Francisco 16, N.Y. GIANTS 13
Sept. 4, 2003	FedExField (Landover, Maryland) National Mall (Washington, D.C.)	WASHINGTON 16, N.Y. Jets 13
Sept. 9, 2004	Gillette Stadium (Foxboro, Massachusetts) Metropolitan Park (Jacksonville, Florida)	NEW ENGLAND 27, Indianapolis 24
Sept. 8, 2005	Gillette Stadium (Foxboro, Massachusetts) Detroit, Michigan Los Angeles Coliseum (Los Angeles, California)	NEW ENGLAND 30, Oakland 20
Sept. 7, 2006	Heinz Field (Pittsburgh, Pennsylvania) Miami, Florida	PITTSBURGH 28, Miami 17
Sept. 6, 2007	RCA Dome (Indianapolis, Indianapolis)	INDIANAPOLIS 41, New Orleans 10
Sept. 4, 2008	Giants Stadium (East Rutherford, New Jersey) Columbus Circle (New York, New York)	N.Y. GIANTS 16, Washington 7
Sept. 10, 2009	Heinz Field (Pittsburgh, Pennsylvania) Point State Park (Pittsburgh, Pennsylvania)	PITTSBURGH 13, Tennessee 10 (OT)

**The first site listed each year designates location of Thursday Night NFL Kickoff Weekend game; subsequent locations indicate site(s) of NFL Kickoff Weekend concert.*

SUPER BOWL COMPOSITE STANDINGS

	W	L	Pct.	Pts.	OP
San Francisco 49ers	5	0	1.000	188	89
Baltimore Ravens	1	0	1.000	34	7
New Orleans Saints	1	0	1.000	31	17
New York Jets	1	0	1.000	16	7
Tampa Bay Buccaneers	1	0	1.000	48	21
Pittsburgh Steelers	6	1	.857	168	133
Green Bay Packers	3	1	.750	127	76
New York Giants	3	1	.750	83	87
Dallas Cowboys	5	3	.625	221	132
Oakland/L.A. Raiders	3	2	.600	132	114
Washington Redskins	3	2	.600	122	103
New England Patriots	3	3	.500	121	165
Indianapolis/Baltimore Colts	2	2	.500	69	77
Chicago Bears	1	1	.500	63	39
Kansas City Chiefs	1	1	.500	33	42
Miami Dolphins	2	3	.400	74	103
Denver Broncos	2	4	.333	115	206
St. Louis/L.A. Rams	1	2	.333	59	67
Arizona Cardinals	0	1	.000	23	27
Atlanta Falcons	0	1	.000	19	34
Carolina Panthers	0	1	.000	29	32
San Diego Chargers	0	1	.000	26	49
Seattle Seahawks	0	1	.000	10	21
Tennessee Titans	0	1	.000	16	23
Cincinnati Bengals	0	2	.000	37	46
Philadelphia Eagles	0	2	.000	31	51
Buffalo Bills	0	4	.000	73	139
Minnesota Vikings	0	4	.000	34	95

SUPER BOWL HOST CITIES

South Florida	10	
New Orleans	9	
Los Angeles	7	(LA Coliseum 2, Rose Bowl 5)
Tampa Bay	4	
San Diego	3	
Arizona	2	
Atlanta	2	
Detroit	2	
Houston	2	
Jacksonville	1	
Minneapolis	1	
Stanford	1	

FUTURE SUPER BOWL SITES

Super Bowl XLV	Feb. 6, 2011	Cowboys Stadium, North Texas
Super Bowl XLVI	Feb. 5, 2012 *	Lucas Oil Stadium, Indianapolis, Indiana
Super Bowl XLVII	Feb. 3, 2013 *	Louisiana Superdome New Orleans, Louisiana
Super Bowl XLVIII	Feb. 2, 2014 *	New Meadowlands Stadium New York - New Jersey

**Tentative date*

PETE ROZELLE TROPHY/SUPER BOWL MVPs*

Super Bowl I	— QB Bart Starr, Green Bay
Super Bowl II	— QB Bart Starr, Green Bay
Super Bowl III	— QB Joe Namath, N.Y. Jets
Super Bowl IV	— QB Len Dawson, Kansas City
Super Bowl V	— LB Chuck Howley, Dallas
Super Bowl VI	— QB Roger Staubach, Dallas
Super Bowl VII	— S Jake Scott, Miami
Super Bowl VIII	— RB Larry Csonka, Miami
Super Bowl IX	— RB Franco Harris, Pittsburgh
Super Bowl X	— WR Lynn Swann, Pittsburgh
Super Bowl XI	— WR Fred Biletnikoff, Oakland
Super Bowl XII	— DT Randy White and DE Harvey Martin, Dallas
Super Bowl XIII	— QB Terry Bradshaw, Pittsburgh
Super Bowl XIV	— QB Terry Bradshaw, Pittsburgh
Super Bowl XV	— QB Jim Plunkett, Oakland
Super Bowl XVI	— QB Joe Montana, San Francisco
Super Bowl XVII	— RB John Riggins, Washington
Super Bowl XVIII	— RB Marcus Allen, L.A. Raiders
Super Bowl XIX	— QB Joe Montana, San Francisco
Super Bowl XX	— DE Richard Dent, Chicago
Super Bowl XXI	— QB Phil Simms, N.Y. Giants
Super Bowl XXII	— QB Doug Williams, Washington
Super Bowl XXIII	— WR Jerry Rice, San Francisco
Super Bowl XXIV	— QB Joe Montana, San Francisco
Super Bowl XXV	— RB Ottis Anderson, N.Y. Giants
Super Bowl XXVI	— QB Mark Rypien, Washington
Super Bowl XXVII	— QB Troy Aikman, Dallas
Super Bowl XXVIII	— RB Emmitt Smith, Dallas
Super Bowl XXIX	— QB Steve Young, San Francisco
Super Bowl XXX	— CB Larry Brown, Dallas
Super Bowl XXXI	— KR-PR Desmond Howard, Green Bay
Super Bowl XXXII	— RB Terrell Davis, Denver
Super Bowl XXXIII	— QB John Elway, Denver
Super Bowl XXXIV	— QB Kurt Warner, St. Louis
Super Bowl XXXV	— LB Ray Lewis, Baltimore
Super Bowl XXXVI	— QB Tom Brady, New England
Super Bowl XXXVII	— S Dexter Jackson, Tampa Bay
Super Bowl XXXVIII	— QB Tom Brady, New England
Super Bowl XXXIX	— WR Deion Branch, New England
Super Bowl XL	— WR Hines Ward, Pittsburgh
Super Bowl XLI	— QB Peyton Manning, Indianapolis
Super Bowl XLII	— QB Eli Manning, N.Y. Giants
Super Bowl XLIII	— WR Santonio Holmes, Pittsburgh
Super Bowl XLIV	— QB Drew Brees, New Orleans

** Award named Pete Rozelle Trophy since Super Bowl XXV.*

SUPER BOWL MVP BY POSITION

Quarterback	23
Running Back	7
Wide Receiver	6
Defensive End	2
Linebacker	2
Safety	2
Cornerback	1
Defensive Tackle	1
Kick Returner-Punt Returner	1

A defensive end and defensive tackle shared the Super Bowl XII MVP award.

RESULTS

NFC leads AFC, 23-21

Super Bowl	Date	Winner (Share)	Loser (Share)	Score	Site	Attendance
XLIV	2-7-10	New Orleans ($83,000)	Indianapolis ($42,000)	31-17	South Florida	74,059
XLIII	2-1-09	Pittsburgh ($78,000)	Arizona ($40,000)	27-23	Tampa Bay	70,774
XLII	2-3-08	N.Y. Giants ($78,000)	New England ($40,000)	17-14	Arizona	71,101
XLI	2-4-07	Indianapolis ($73,000)	Chicago ($38,000)	29-17	South Florida	74,512
XL	2-5-06	Pittsburgh ($73,000)	Seattle ($38,000)	21-10	Detroit	68,206
XXXIX	2-6-05	New England ($68,000)	Philadelphia ($36,500)	24-21	Jacksonville	78,125
XXXVIII	2-1-04	New England ($68,000)	Carolina ($36,500)	32-29	Houston	71,525
* XXXVII	1-26-03	Tampa Bay ($63,000)	Oakland ($35,000)	48-21	San Diego	67,603
* XXXVI	2-3-02	New England ($63,000)	St. Louis ($34,500)	20-17	New Orleans	72,922
XXXV	1-28-01	Baltimore ($58,000)	N.Y. Giants ($34,500)	34-7	Tampa Bay	71,921
* XXXIV	1-30-00	St. Louis ($58,000)	Tennessee ($33,000)	23-16	Atlanta	72,625
XXXIII	1-31-99	Denver ($53,000)	Atlanta ($32,500)	34-19	South Florida	74,803
XXXII	1-25-98	Denver ($48,000)	Green Bay ($29,000)	31-24	San Diego	68,912
XXXI	1-26-97	Green Bay ($48,000)	New England ($29,000)	35-21	New Orleans	72,301
XXX	1-28-96	Dallas ($42,000)	Pittsburgh ($27,000)	27-17	Arizona	76,347
XXIX	1-29-95	San Francisco ($42,000)	San Diego ($26,000)	49-26	South Florida	74,107
* XXVIII	1-30-94	Dallas ($38,000)	Buffalo ($23,500)	30-13	Atlanta	72,817
XXVII	1-31-93	Dallas ($36,000)	Buffalo ($18,000)	52-17	Pasadena	98,374
XXVI	1-26-92	Washington ($36,000)	Buffalo ($18,000)	37-24	Minneapolis	63,130
* XXV	1-27-91	N.Y. Giants ($36,000)	Buffalo ($18,000)	20-19	Tampa Bay	73,813
XXIV	1-28-90	San Francisco ($36,000)	Denver ($18,000)	55-10	New Orleans	72,919
XXIII	1-22-89	San Francisco ($36,000)	Cincinnati ($18,000)	20-16	South Florida	75,129
XXII	1-31-88	Washington ($36,000)	Denver ($18,000)	42-10	San Diego	73,302
XXI	1-25-87	N.Y. Giants ($36,000)	Denver ($18,000)	39-20	Pasadena	101,063
XX	1-26-86	Chicago ($36,000)	New England ($18,000)	46-10	New Orleans	73,818
XIX	1-20-85	San Francisco ($36,000)	Miami ($18,000)	38-16	Stanford	84,059
XVIII	1-22-84	L.A. Raiders ($36,000)	Washington ($18,000)	38-9	Tampa Bay	72,920
* XVII	1-30-83	Washington ($36,000)	Miami ($18,000)	27-17	Pasadena	103,667
XVI	1-24-82	San Francisco ($18,000)	Cincinnati ($9,000)	26-21	Pontiac	81,270
XV	1-25-81	Oakland ($18,000)	Philadelphia ($9,000)	27-10	New Orleans	76,135
XIV	1-20-80	Pittsburgh ($18,000)	Los Angeles ($9,000)	31-19	Pasadena	103,985
XIII	1-21-79	Pittsburgh ($18,000)	Dallas ($9,000)	35-31	South Florida	79,484
XII	1-15-78	Dallas ($18,000)	Denver ($9,000)	27-10	New Orleans	75,583
XI	1-9-77	Oakland ($15,000)	Minnesota ($7,500)	32-14	Pasadena	103,438
X	1-18-76	Pittsburgh ($15,000)	Dallas ($7,500)	21-17	South Florida	80,187
IX	1-12-75	Pittsburgh ($15,000)	Minnesota ($7,500)	16-6	New Orleans	80,997
VIII	1-13-74	Miami ($15,000)	Minnesota ($7,500)	24-7	Houston	71,882
VII	1-14-73	Miami ($15,000)	Washington ($7,500)	14-7	Los Angeles	90,182
VI	1-16-72	Dallas ($15,000)	Miami ($7,500)	24-3	New Orleans	81,023
V	1-17-71	Baltimore ($15,000)	Dallas ($7,500)	16-13	South Florida	79,204
* IV	1-11-70	Kansas City ($15,000)	Minnesota ($7,500)	23-7	New Orleans	80,562
III	1-12-69	N.Y. Jets ($15,000)	Baltimore ($7,500)	16-7	South Florida	75,389
II	1-14-68	Green Bay ($15,000)	Oakland ($7,500)	33-14	South Florida	75,546
I	1-15-67	Green Bay ($15,000)	Kansas City ($7,500)	35-10	Los Angeles	61,946

** One week between conference championship games and Super Bowl; all others had two weeks between conference championship games and Super Bowl.*

For historical Super Bowl game recaps, box scores, and video highlights, please visit www.SuperBowl.com.

SUPER BOWL XLIV

Sun Life Stadium, South Florida

February 7, 2010, Attendance: 74,059

NEW ORLEANS 31, INDIANAPOLIS 17—Tracy Porter's 74-yard interception return with 3:12 remaining capped a fourth-quarter comeback and lifted the Saints to their first Super Bowl title. The Colts, who won their first 14 regular-season games, forced a three-and-out on the Saints' opening possession. Peyton Manning completed two third-down passes to set up Matt Stover's 38-yard field goal. Following a second Saints' punt, the Colts drove 96 yards in 11 plays, keyed by runs of 16, 11, and 26 yards by Joseph Addai, and capped by Manning's 19-yard touchdown pass to Pierre Garcon on third-and-6 to stake the Colts to a 10-0 lead. The Saints, who had won their first 13 games of the season, answered with a a drive of 6:02, using Garrett Hartley's 46-yard field goal to get on the scoreboard. After a three-and-out, the Saints held the ball for 6:25. However, the drive resulted in zero points as Gary Brackett and Clint Session stopped Pierre Thomas for no gain on fourth-and-goal from the Colts' 1 with 1:49 left in the half. The Colts ran three times, failed to gain a first down, and were forced to punt. From their own 48-yard line with 35 seconds left in the half, Drew Brees connected on passes of 19 and 6 yards to Devery Henderson that led to Hartley's 44-yard field goal as the half expired, trimming the deficit to 10-6. The Saints then surprised everyone with an onside kick to begin the second half. Rookie punter Thomas Morstead's first-ever onside kick was perfect, and Chris Reis of the Saints eventually emerged from the intense scramble with the ball. Brees completed all five of his pass attempts on the drive, capped by Thomas' 16-yard touchdown catch on a screen pass to give the Saints their first lead. The Colts drove 76 yards on the ensuing possession, keyed by Manning's 27-yard pass to Dallas Clark on third-and-4, which resulted in Addai's 4-yard run for a 17-13 Indianapolis lead with 6:15 left in the third quarter. Courtney Roby returned the kickoff 34 yards and Brees completed four of five passes on the next drive set up Hartley's third long-range field goal, this one from 47 yards, to pull the Saints to within one point. On the Colts' next drive, Manning completed a 14-yard pass to Reggie Wayne on fourth-down near midfield. However, four plays later, faced with fourth-and-11, Stover missed a 51-yard field-goal attempt with 10:39 to play. Brees completed all seven pass attempts on the ensuing drive, capped by Jeremy Shockey's 2-yard scoring catch with 5:42 remaining. The Saints went for the 2-point conversion, and Lance Moore made a spectacular catch and reached across the goal-line with the reception to give New Orleans a 24-17 lead. The Colts quickly drove to the Saints' 31, but on third-and-5 Manning's short pass to the left side intended for Wayne was intercepted by Porter, who sprinted untouched 74 yards for a touchdown and 31-17 lead with 3:12 to play. Manning connected with Austin Collie on a 40-yard pass play to help the Colts get downfield. Indianapolis reached the Saints' 3 with 1:33 to play, but a 10-yard pass interference penalty on Garcon moved them back. On fourth-and-goal from the 5-yard line with 50 seconds to play, Manning's pass for Wayne was incomplete, and the Saints clinched their first-ever NFL championship. Brees, who was named Super Bowl MVP, was 32 of 39 for 288 yards and 2 touchdowns. Manning was 31 of 45 for 333 yards and 1 touchdown, with 1 interception.

New Orleans (31)		Indianapolis (17)
	Offense	
Marques Colston	WR	Reggie Wayne
Jermon Bushrod	LT	Charlie Johnson
Carl Nicks	LG	Ryan Lilja
Jonathan Goodwin	C	Jeff Saturday
Jahri Evans	RG	Kyle DeVan
Jon Stinchcomb	RT	Ryan Diem
Jeremy Shockey	TE	Dallas Clark
Devery Henderson	WR	Pierre Garcon
Drew Brees	QB	Peyton Manning
Pierre Thomas	RB	Joseph Addai
Reggie Bush	RB/H-B	Gijon Robinson
	Defense	
Bobby McCray	DE/LDE	Robert Mathis
Marvin Mitchell	LB/LDT	Daniel Muir
Sedrick Ellis	DT/RDT	Antonio Johnson
Will Smith	RDE	Dwight Freeney
Scott Fujita	SLB	Philip Wheeler
Jonathan Vilma	MLB	Gary Brackett
Scott Shanle	WLB	Clint Session
Jabari Greer	LCB	Kelvin Hayden
Tracy Porter	RCB	Jacob Lacey
Roman Harper	SS	Melvin Bullitt
Darren Sharper	FS	Antoine Bethea

SUBSTITUTIONS

NEW ORLEANS—Specialists: K—Garrett Hartley. P—Thomas Morstead. LS—Jason Kyle. Offense: QB—Mark Brunell. RB—Mike Bell. FB—Kyle Eckel. WR—Robert Meachem, Lance Moore, Courtney Roby. TE—David Thomas. T—Zach Strief. C—Nick Leckey. Defense: DT—Remi Ayodele. DE—Jeff Charleston, Anthony Hargrove. LB—Jonathan Casillas, Troy Evans. CB—Randall Gay, Malcolm Jenkins, Usama Young. S—Pierson Prioleau, Chris Reis. DNP: DT—DeMario Pressley. Not Active: QB—Chase Daniel. RB—Lynell Hamilton. WR—Adrian Arrington. TE—Darnell Dinkins, Tory Humphrey. G—Jamar Nesbit. DE—Paul Spicer. LB—Anthony Waters.

INDIANAPOLIS—Specialists: K—Matt Stover. P—Pat McAfee. LS/TE—Justin Snow. Offense: RB—Donald Brown, Mike Hart, Chad Simpson. WR—Hank Baskett, Austin Collie. TE—Jacob Tamme. G—Jamey Richard. T—Tony Ugoh. Defense: DT—Eric Foster. DE—Raheem Brock, Keyunta Dawson. LB—Cody Glenn, Ramon Humber, Freddy Keiaho. DB—Aaron Francisco, Tim Jennings, Jerraud Powers, T.J. Rushing, Jamie Silva. DNP: QB—Curtis Painter. Not Active: K—Adam Vinatieri. WR—Sam Giguere. TE—Colin Cloherty. G—Mike Pollak. T—Michael Toudouze. DT—John Gill, Fili Moala. DE—Ervin Baldwin.

OFFICIALS

Referee—Scott Green. Umpire—Undrey Wash. Head Linesman—John McGrath. Line Judge—Jeff Seeman. Side Judge—Greg Meyer. Field Judge—Rob Vernatchi. Back Judge—Gregory Steed. Replay Official—Jim Lapetina.

SCORING

New Orleans (NFC)	0	6	10	15	—31
Indianapolis (AFC)	10	0	7	0	—17

Ind — FG Stover 38 (7:29)
Ind — Garcon 19 pass from Manning (Stover kick) (0:36)
NO — FG Hartley 46 (9:34)
NO — FG Hartley 44 (0:00)
NO — P. Thomas 16 pass from Brees (Hartley kick) (11:41)
Ind — Addai 4 run (Stover kick) (6:15)
NO — FG Hartley 47 (2:01)
NO — Shockey 2 pass from Brees (Moore pass from Brees) (5:42)
NO — Porter 74 interception return (Hartley kick) (3:12)

TEAM STATISTICS	NO	IND
Total First Downs	20	23
Rushing	3	6
Passing	16	16
Penalty	1	1
Total Net Yardage	332	432
Total Offensive Plays	58	64
Avg. Gain Per Offensive Play	5.7	6.8
Rushes	18	19
Yards Gained Rushing (Net)	51	99
Avg. Yards per Rush	2.8	5.2
Passes Attempted	39	45
Passes Completed	32	31
Had Intercepted	0	1
Tackled Attempting to Pass	1	0
Yards Lost Attempting to Pass	7	0
Yards Gained Passing (Net)	281	333
Punts	2	2
Avg. Distance	44.0	45.0
Punt Returns	1	1
Punt Return Yardage	4	0
Kickoff Returns	4	5
Kickoff Return Yardage	102	111
Interception Return Yardage	74	0
Total Return Yardage (excl. Kickoff)	78	0
Fumbles	0	0
Fumbles Lost	0	0
Own Fumbles Recovered	0	0
Opponent Fumbles Recovered	0	0
Penalties	3	5
Yards Penalized	19	45
Field Goals	3	1
Field Goals Attempted	3	2
Third-Down Efficiency	3/9	6-13
Fourth-Down Efficiency	0/1	1/2
Time of Possession	30:11	29:49

INDIVIDUAL STATISTICS

RUSHING: NO: P. Thomas 9-30-0, Bush 5-25-0, Bell 2-4-0, Brees 1-(-1)-0, Henderson 1-(-7)-0. IND: Addai 13-77-1, Brown 4-18-0, Hart 2-4-0.
PASSING: NO: Brees 39-32-288-2-0. IND: Manning 45-31-333-1-1.
RECEIVING: NO: Colston 7-83-0, Henderson 7-63-0, P. Thomas 6-55-1, Bush 4-38-0, Shockey 3-13-1, Moore 2-21-0, Meachem 2-6-0, D. Thomas 1-9-0. IND: Clark 7-86-0, Addai 7-58-0, Collie 6-66-0, Garcon 5-66-1, Wayne 5-46-0, Brown 1-11-0.
KICKOFF RETURNS: NO: Roby 4-102-0. IND: Simpson 5-111-0.
PUNT RETURNS: NO: Bush 1-4-0. IND: Rushing 1-0-0.
PUNTING: NO: Morstead 2-88-44.0. IND: McAfee 2-90-45.0.
INTERCEPTIONS: NO: Porter 1-74-1. IND: None.
SACKS: NO: None. IND: Freeney 1.

AFC CHAMPIONSHIP GAME RESULTS

Includes AFL Championship Games (1960-69)

Season	Date	Winner (Share)	Loser (Share)	Score	Site	Attendance
2009	Jan. 24	Indianapolis ($38,000)	N.Y. Jets ($38,000)	30-17	Indianapolis	67,650
2008	Jan. 18	Pittsburgh ($37,500)	Baltimore ($37,500)	23-14	Pittsburgh	65,350
2007	Jan. 20	New England ($37,500)	San Diego ($37,500)	21-12	Foxborough	68,756
2006	Jan. 21	Indianapolis ($37,000)	New England ($37,000)	38-34	Indianapolis	57,433
2005	Jan. 22	Pittsburgh ($37,000)	Denver ($37,000)	34-17	Denver	76,775
2004	Jan. 23	New England ($36,500)	Pittsburgh ($36,500)	41-27	Pittsburgh	65,242
2003	Jan. 18	New England ($36,500)	Indianapolis ($36,500)	24-14	Foxborough	68,436
2002	Jan. 19	Oakland ($35,000)	Tennessee ($35,000)	41-24	Oakland	62,544
2001	Jan. 27	New England ($34,500)	Pittsburgh ($34,500)	24-17	Pittsburgh	64,704
2000	Jan. 14	Baltimore ($34,500)	Oakland ($34,500)	16-3	Oakland	62,784
1999	Jan. 23	Tennessee ($33,000)	Jacksonville ($33,000)	33-14	Jacksonville	75,206
1998	Jan. 17	Denver ($32,500)	N.Y. Jets ($32,500)	23-10	Denver	75,482
1997	Jan. 11	Denver ($30,000)	Pittsburgh ($30,000)	24-21	Pittsburgh	61,382
1996	Jan. 12	New England ($29,000)	Jacksonville ($29,000)	20-6	Foxborough	60,190
1995	Jan. 14	Pittsburgh ($27,000)	Indianapolis ($27,000)	20-16	Pittsburgh	61,062
1994	Jan. 15	San Diego ($26,000)	Pittsburgh ($26,000)	17-13	Pittsburgh	61,545
1993	Jan. 23	Buffalo ($23,500)	Kansas City ($23,500)	30-13	Buffalo	76,642
1992	Jan. 17	Buffalo ($18,000)	Miami ($18,000)	29-10	Miami	72,703
1991	Jan. 12	Buffalo ($18,000)	Denver ($18,000)	10-7	Buffalo	80,272
1990	Jan. 20	Buffalo ($18,000)	L.A. Raiders ($18,000)	51-3	Buffalo	80,325
1989	Jan. 14	Denver ($18,000)	Cleveland ($18,000)	37-21	Denver	76,046
1988	Jan. 8	Cincinnati ($18,000)	Buffalo ($18,000)	21-10	Cincinnati	59,747
1987	Jan. 17	Denver ($18,000)	Cleveland ($18,000)	38-33	Denver	76,197
1986	Jan. 11	Denver ($18,000)	Cleveland ($18,000)	23-20*	Cleveland	79,973
1985	Jan. 12	New England ($18,000)	Miami ($18,000)	31-14	Miami	75,662
1984	Jan. 6	Miami ($18,000)	Pittsburgh ($18,000)	45-28	Miami	76,029
1983	Jan. 8	L.A. Raiders ($18,000)	Seattle ($18,000)	30-14	Los Angeles	91,445
1982	Jan. 23	Miami ($18,000)	N.Y. Jets ($18,000)	14-0	Miami	67,396
1981	Jan. 10	Cincinnati ($9,000)	San Diego ($9,000)	27-7	Cincinnati	46,302
1980	Jan. 11	Oakland ($9,000)	San Diego ($9,000)	34-27	San Diego	52,675
1979	Jan. 6	Pittsburgh ($9,000)	Houston ($9,000)	27-13	Pittsburgh	50,475
1978	Jan. 7	Pittsburgh ($9,000)	Houston ($9,000)	34-5	Pittsburgh	50,725
1977	Jan. 1	Denver ($9,000)	Oakland ($9,000)	20-17	Denver	75,044
1976	Dec. 26	Oakland ($8,500)	Pittsburgh ($5,500)	24-7	Oakland	53,821
1975	Jan. 4	Pittsburgh ($8,500)	Oakland ($5,500)	16-10	Pittsburgh	50,609
1974	Dec. 29	Pittsburgh ($8,500)	Oakland ($5,500)	24-13	Oakland	53,800
1973	Dec. 30	Miami ($8,500)	Oakland ($5,500)	27-10	Miami	79,325
1972	Dec. 31	Miami ($8,500)	Pittsburgh ($5,500)	21-17	Pittsburgh	50,845
1971	Jan. 2	Miami ($8,500)	Baltimore ($5,500)	21-0	Miami	76,622
1970	Jan. 3	Baltimore ($8,500)	Oakland ($5,500)	27-17	Baltimore	54,799
1969	Jan. 4	Kansas City ($7,755)	Oakland ($6,252)	17-7	Oakland	53,564
1968	Dec. 29	N.Y. Jets ($7,007)	Oakland ($5,349)	27-23	New York	62,627
1967	Dec. 31	Oakland ($6,321)	Houston ($4,996)	40-7	Oakland	53,330
1966	Jan. 1	Kansas City ($5,309)	Buffalo ($3,799)	31-7	Buffalo	42,080
1965	Dec. 26	Buffalo ($5,189)	San Diego ($3,447)	23-0	San Diego	30,361
1964	Dec. 26	Buffalo ($2,668)	San Diego ($1,738)	20-7	Buffalo	40,242
1963	Jan. 5	San Diego ($2,498)	Boston ($1,596)	51-10	San Diego	30,127
1962	Dec. 23	Dallas ($2,206)	Houston ($1,471)	20-17*	Houston	37,981
1961	Dec. 24	Houston ($1,792)	San Diego ($1,111)	10-3	San Diego	29,556
1960	Jan. 1	Houston ($1,025)	L.A. Chargers ($718)	24-16	Houston	32,183

Sudden death overtime

AFC CHAMPIONSHIP GAME COMPOSITE STANDINGS

	W	L	Pct.	Pts.	OP
Cincinnati Bengals	2	0	1.000	48	17
Buffalo Bills	6	2	.750	180	92
Denver Broncos	6	2	.750	189	166
New England Patriots**	6	2	.750	205	179
Kansas City Chiefs*	3	1	.750	81	61
Miami Dolphins	5	2	.714	152	115
Pittsburgh Steelers	7	7	.500	308	284
Indianapolis Colts#	3	3	.500	125	133
Baltimore Ravens	1	1	.500	30	26
Tennessee Titans##	3	5	.375	133	195
Oakland Raiders###	5	9	.357	272	304
New York Jets	1	3	.250	54	90
San Diego Chargers***	2	7	.222	140	182
Seattle Seahawks	0	1	.000	14	30
Jacksonville Jaguars	0	2	.000	20	53
Cleveland Browns	0	3	.000	74	98

* *One game played when franchise was in Dallas (Texans) (Won 20-17)*

** *One game played when franchise was in Boston (Lost 51-10)*

*** *One game played when franchise was in Los Angeles (Lost 24-16)*

\# *Two games played when franchise was in Baltimore (Won 27-17, lost 21-0)*

\## *Six games played when franchise was in Houston and known as Oilers (Won 2, lost 4)*

\### *Two games played when franchise was in Los Angeles (Won 30-14, lost 51-3)*

2009 AFC CHAMPIONSHIP GAME

Lucas Oil Stadium, Indianapolis, Indiana
January 24, 2010, Attendance: 67,650

INDIANAPOLIS 30, NEW YORK JETS 17—Peyton Manning passed for 377 yards and 3 touchdowns as the Colts advanced to the Super Bowl for the second time in four years. Jay Feely missed a 44-yard field goal in the first quarter. Later in the quarter, the Colts drove 82 yards, capped by Matt Stover's 25-yard field goal on the first play of the second quarter. On the next play from scrimmage, Mark Sanchez connected with Braylon Edwards deep down the left sideline for an 80-yard touchdown. The Colts answered with a field goal, but the Jets drove 77 yards on their next possession, keyed by Brad Smith's 45-yard pass to Jerricho Cotchery out of the Wildcat formation, and culminated with Dustin Keller's 9-yard touchdown catch on third-and-7, to give the Jets a 14-6 lead. Three plays later, Calvin Pace forced Joseph Addai to fumble. Jim Leonhard recovered, and Feely made a 48-yard field goal. The Jets led 17-6 with 2:11 left in the half. After an incompletion, Manning completed consecutive passes of 18, 46, and 16 yards, the latter two to Austin Collie, to cut the deficit to 17-13 at the half. Feely missed a 52-yard field goal to begin the third quarter. Manning completed 6 of 8 passes on the next drive, and Pierre Garcon's 4-yard touchdown catch gave the Colts a 20-17 lead. Early in the fourth quarter, Manning completed 5 of 6 passes, capped by Dallas Clark's 15-yard scoring grab, for a 27-17 lead with 8:52 to play. The Colts' defense forced a three-and-out, and Indianapolis' offense drove 71 yards and took five minutes, 33 seconds off the clock. Stover's 21-yard field goal increased the lead to 30-17 with 2:29 to play. Kelvin Hayden intercepted Sanchez's pass three plays later to secure the victory. Manning was 26 of 39 for 377 yards and 3 touchdowns. Garcon had 11 catches for 151 yards, and Collie added 7 receptions for 123 yards. Sanchez was 17 of 30 for 257 yards and 2 touchdowns, with 1 interception. Cotchery had 5 catches for 102 yards and Edwards caught 2 passes for 100 yards.

New York Jets (17)	Offense	Indianapolis (30)
Jerricho Cotchery	WR	Reggie Wayne
D'Brickashaw Ferguson	LT	Charlie Johnson
Alan Faneca	LG	Ryan Lilja
Nick Mangold	C	Jeff Saturday
Brandon Moore	RG	Kyle DeVan
Damien Woody	RT	Ryan Diem
Ben Hartsock	TE	Dallas Clark
Braylon Edwards	WR	Pierre Garcon
Mark Sanchez	QB	Peyton Manning
Tony Richardson	FB/H-B	Gijon Robinson
Thomas Jones	RB	Joseph Addai
	Defense	
Shaun Ellis	DE/LE	Robert Mathis
Sione Pouha	NT/LT	Daniel Muir
Bryan Thomas	OLB/RT	Antonio Johnson
Bart Scott	WILL/RE	Dwight Freeney
David Harris	MIKE/SLB	Philip Wheeler
Calvin Pace	OLB/MLB	Gary Brackett
Darrelle Revis	CB/WLB	Clint Session
Dwight Lowery	CB/LCB	Kelvin Hayden
Donald Strickland	CB/RCB	Jacob Lacey
Jim Leonhard	S/SS	Melvin Bullitt
Kerry Rhodes	S/FS	Antoine Bethea

SUBSTITUTIONS

NEW YORK JETS—Specialists: K—Jay Feely. P—Steve Weatherford. LS—James Dearth. Offense: QB—Kellen Clemens. RB—Shonn Greene. WR—David Clowney, Brad Smith, Wallace Wright. TE—Dustin Keller, Matthew Mulligan. T—Wayne Hunter. OL—Robert Turner. Defense: DE—Mike DeVito, Marques Douglas. LB—Ryan Fowler, Vernon Gholston, Marques Murrell, Jamaal Westerman. CB—Marquice Cole, Drew Coleman, Lito Sheppard. S—James Ihedigbo, Eric Smith. Not Active: QB—Erik Ainge, Kevin O'Connell. RB—Chauncey Washington. WR—Danny Woodhead. G—Matt Slauson. DE—Ropati Pitoitua. DT—Howard Green. LB—Kenwin Cummings.

INDIANAPOLIS—Specialists: K—Matt Stover. P—Pat McAfee. LS—Justin Snow. Offense: RB—Donald Brown, Mike Hart, Chad Simpson. WR—Hank Baskett, Austin Collie. TE—Jacob Tamme. G—Jamey Richard. T—Tony Ugoh. Defense: DE—Raheem Brock, Keyunta Dawson. DT—Eric Foster. LB—Cody Glenn, Ramon Humber, Freddy Keiaho. CB—Aaron Francisco, Tim Jennings, T.J. Rushing, Jamie Silva. DNP: QB—Curtis Painter. DT—John Gill. Not Active: K—Adam Vinatieri. WR—Sam Giguere. TE—Colin Cloherty. G—Mike Pollak. T—Michael Toudouze. DE—Ervin Baldwin. DT—Fili Moala. DB—Jerraud Powers.

OFFICIALS

Referee—Tony Corrente. Umpire—Ruben Fowler.
Line Judge—Gary Arthur. Side Judge—Jeff Lamberth.
Head Linesman—Jim Mello. Back Judge—Scott Helverson.
Field Judge—Gary Cavaletto.

SCORING

New York Jets	0	17	0	0	—	17
Indianapolis	0	13	7	10	—	30

Ind — FG Stover 25
NYJ — Edwards 80 pass from Sanchez (Feely kick)
Ind — FG Stover 19
NYJ — Keller 9 pass from Sanchez (Feely kick)
NYJ — FG Feely 48
Ind — Collie 16 pass from Manning (Stover kick)
Ind — Garcon 4 pass from Manning (Stover kick)
Ind — Clark 15 pass from Manning (Stover kick)
Ind — FG Stover 21

TEAM STATISTICS	NYJ	IND
Total First Downs	17	27
Rushing	4	5
Passing	13	19
Penalty	0	3
Total Net Yardage	388	461
Total Offensive Plays	60	65
Average Gain Per Offensive Play	6.5	7.1
Rushes	29	24
Yards Gained Rushing (Net)	86	101
Average Yards per Rush	3.0	4.2
Passes Attempted	31	39
Passes Completed	18	26
Had Intercepted	1	0
Tackled Attempting to Pass	0	2
Yards Lost Attempting to Pass	0	17
Yards Gained Passing (Net)	302	360
Punts	4	4
Average Distance	51.0	46.3
Punt Returns	1	1
Punt Return Yardage	12	4
Kickoff Returns	5	3
Kickoff Return Yardage	139	83
Interception Return Yardage	0	3
Total Return Yardage (not incl. kickoffs)	12	7
Fumbles	0	2
Fumbles Lost	0	1
Own Fumbles Recovered	0	1
Opponent Fumbles Recovered	1	0
Penalties	6	1
Yards Penalized	46	5
Field Goals	1	3
Field Goals Attempted	3	3
Third-Down Efficiency	6/14	4/11
Fourth-Down Efficiency	0/0	0/0
Time of Possession	28:35	31:25

INDIVIDUAL STATISTICS

RUSHING: NYJ: Jones 16-42-0, Greene 10-41-0, Richardson 1-2-0, Sanchez 2-1-0. IND: Addai 16-80-0, Brown 6-18-0, Hart 1-3-0, Manning 1-0-0.

PASSING: NYJ: Sanchez 30-17-257-2-1, Smith 1-1-45-0-0.

IND: Manning 39-26-377-3-0.
RECEIVING: NYJ: Keller 6-63-1, Cotchery 5-102-0, Edwards 2-100-1, Jones 2-28-0, Smith 2-7-0, Richardson 1-2-0. IND: Garcon 11-151-1, Collie 7-123-1, Clark 4-35-1, Wayne 3-55-0, Addai 1-13-0.
KICKOFF RETURNS: NYJ: Smith 5-139-0. IND: Simpson 3-83-0.
PUNT RETURNS: NYJ: Cotchery 1-12-0. IND: Rushing 1-4-0.
PUNTING: NYJ: Weatherford 4-204-45.0. IND: McAfee 4-185-43.3.
INTERCEPTIONS: NYJ: None. IND: Hayden 1-3-0.
SACKS: NYJ: Harris 2. IND: None.

NFC CHAMPIONSHIP GAME RESULTS

Includes NFL Championship Games (1933-1969)

Season	Date	Winner (Share)	Loser (Share)	Score	Site	Attendance
2009	Jan. 24	New Orleans ($38,000)	Minnesota ($38,000)	31-28*	New Orleans	71,276
2008	Jan. 18	Arizona ($37,500)	Philadelphia ($37,500)	32-25	Glendale	70,650
2007	Jan. 20	N.Y. Giants ($37,500)	Green Bay ($37,500)	23-20*	Green Bay	72,740
2006	Jan. 21	Chicago ($37,000)	New Orleans ($37,000)	39-14	Chicago	61,817
2005	Jan. 22	Seattle ($37,000)	Carolina ($37,000)	34-14	Seattle	67,837
2004	Jan. 23	Philadelphia ($36,500)	Atlanta ($36,500)	27-10	Philadelphia	67,717
2003	Jan. 18	Carolina ($36,500)	Philadelphia ($36,500)	14-3	Philadelphia	67,862
2002	Jan. 19	Tampa Bay ($35,000)	Philadelphia ($35,000)	27-10	Philadelphia	66,713
2001	Jan. 27	St. Louis ($34,500)	Philadelphia ($34,500)	29-24	St. Louis	66,502
2000	Jan. 14	N.Y. Giants ($34,500)	Minnesota ($34,500)	41-0	East Rutherford	79,310
1999	Jan. 23	St. Louis ($33,000)	Tampa Bay ($33,000)	11-6	St. Louis	66,396
1998	Jan. 17	Atlanta ($32,500)	Minnesota ($32,500)	30-27*	Minneapolis	64,060
1997	Jan. 11	Green Bay ($30,000)	San Francisco ($30,000)	23-10	San Francisco	68,987
1996	Jan. 12	Green Bay ($29,000)	Carolina ($29,000)	30-13	Green Bay	60,216
1995	Jan. 14	Dallas ($27,000)	Green Bay ($27,000)	38-27	Dallas	65,135
1994	Jan. 15	San Francisco ($26,000)	Dallas ($26,000)	38-28	San Francisco	69,125
1993	Jan. 23	Dallas ($23,500)	San Francisco ($23,500)	38-21	Dallas	64,902
1992	Jan. 17	Dallas ($18,000)	San Francisco ($18,000)	30-20	San Francisco	64,920
1991	Jan. 12	Washington ($18,000)	Detroit ($18,000)	41-10	Washington	55,585
1990	Jan. 20	N.Y. Giants ($18,000)	San Francisco ($18,000)	15-13	San Francisco	65,750
1989	Jan. 14	San Francisco ($18,000)	L.A. Rams ($18,000)	30-3	San Francisco	65,634
1988	Jan. 8	San Francisco ($18,000)	Chicago ($18,000)	28-3	Chicago	66,946
1987	Jan. 17	Washington ($18,000)	Minnesota ($18,000)	17-10	Washington	55,212
1986	Jan. 11	New York Giants ($18,000)	Washington ($18,000)	17-0	East Rutherford	76,891
1985	Jan. 12	Chicago ($18,000)	L.A. Rams ($18,000)	24-0	Chicago	66,030
1984	Jan. 6	San Francisco ($18,000)	Chicago ($18,000)	23-0	San Francisco	61,336
1983	Jan. 8	Washington ($18,000)	San Francisco ($18,000)	24-21	Washington	55,363
1982	Jan. 22	Washington ($18,000)	Dallas ($18,000)	31-17	Washington	55,045
1981	Jan. 10	San Francisco ($9,000)	Dallas ($9,000)	28-27	San Francisco	60,525
1980	Jan. 11	Philadelphia ($9,000)	Dallas ($9,000)	20-7	Philadelphia	71,522
1979	Jan. 6	Los Angeles ($9,000)	Tampa Bay ($9,000)	9-0	Tampa	72,033
1978	Jan. 7	Dallas ($9,000)	Los Angeles ($9,000)	28-0	Los Angeles	71,086
1977	Jan. 1	Dallas ($9,000)	Minnesota ($9,000)	23-6	Dallas	64,293
1976	Dec. 26	Minnesota ($8,500)	Los Angeles ($5,500)	24-13	Minneapolis	48,379
1975	Jan. 4	Dallas ($8,500)	Los Angeles ($5,500)	37-7	Los Angeles	88,919
1974	Dec. 29	Minnesota ($8,500)	Los Angeles ($5,500)	14-10	Minneapolis	48,444
1973	Dec. 30	Minnesota ($8,500)	Dallas ($5,500)	27-10	Dallas	64,422
1972	Dec. 31	Washington ($8,500)	Dallas ($5,500)	26-3	Washington	53,129
1971	Jan. 2	Dallas ($8,500)	San Francisco ($5,500)	14-3	Dallas	63,409
1970	Jan. 3	Dallas ($8,500)	San Francisco ($5,500)	17-10	San Francisco	59,364
1969	Jan. 4	Minnesota ($7,930)	Cleveland ($5,118)	27-7	Minneapolis	46,503
1968	Dec. 29	Baltimore ($9,306)	Cleveland ($5,963)	34-0	Cleveland	78,410
1967	Dec. 31	Green Bay ($7,950)	Dallas ($5,299)	21-17	Green Bay	50,861
1966	Jan. 1	Green Bay ($9,813)	Dallas ($6,527)	34-27	Dallas	74,152
1965	Jan. 2	Green Bay ($7,819)	Cleveland ($5,288)	23-12	Green Bay	50,777
1964	Dec. 27	Cleveland ($8,052)	Baltimore ($5,571)	27-0	Cleveland	79,544
1963	Dec. 29	Chicago ($5,899)	New York ($4,218)	14-10	Chicago	45,801
1962	Dec. 30	Green Bay ($5,888)	New York ($4,166)	16-7	New York	64,892
1961	Dec. 31	Green Bay ($5,195)	New York ($3,339)	37-0	Green Bay	39,029
1960	Dec. 26	Philadelphia ($5,116)	Green Bay ($3,105)	17-13	Philadelphia	67,325
1959	Dec. 27	Baltimore ($4,674)	New York ($3,083)	31-16	Baltimore	57,545
1958	Dec. 28	Baltimore ($4,718)	New York ($3,111)	23-17*	New York	64,185
1957	Dec. 29	Detroit ($4,295)	Cleveland ($2,750)	59-14	Detroit	55,263
1956	Dec. 30	New York ($3,779)	Chi. Bears ($2,485)	47-7	New York	56,836
1955	Dec. 26	Cleveland ($3,508)	Los Angeles ($2,316)	38-14	Los Angeles	85,693
1954	Dec. 26	Cleveland ($2,478)	Detroit ($1,585)	56-10	Cleveland	43,827
1953	Dec. 27	Detroit ($2,424)	Cleveland ($1,654)	17-16	Detroit	54,577
1952	Dec. 28	Detroit ($2,274)	Cleveland ($1,712)	17-7	Cleveland	50,934
1951	Dec. 23	Los Angeles ($2,108)	Cleveland ($1,483)	24-17	Los Angeles	57,522
1950	Dec. 24	Cleveland ($1,113)	Los Angeles ($686)	30-28	Cleveland	29,751
1949	Dec. 18	Philadelphia ($1,094)	Los Angeles ($739)	14-0	Los Angeles	27,980
1948	Dec. 19	Philadelphia ($1,540)	Chi. Cardinals ($874)	7-0	Philadelphia	36,309
1947	Dec. 28	Chi. Cardinals ($1,132)	Philadelphia ($754)	28-21	Chicago	30,759

Season	Date	Winner (Share)	Loser (Share)	Score	Site	Attendance
1946	Dec. 15	Chi. Bears ($1,975)	New York ($1,295)	24-14	New York	58,346
1945	Dec. 16	Cleveland ($1,469)	Washington ($902)	15-14	Cleveland	32,178
1944	Dec. 17	Green Bay ($1,449)	New York ($814)	14-7	New York	46,016
1943	Dec. 26	Chi. Bears ($1,146)	Washington ($765)	41-21	Chicago	34,320
1942	Dec. 13	Washington ($965)	Chi. Bears ($637)	14-6	Washington	36,006
1941	Dec. 21	Chi. Bears ($430)	New York ($288)	37-9	Chicago	13,341
1940	Dec. 8	Chi. Bears ($873)	Washington ($606)	73-0	Washington	36,034
1939	Dec. 10	Green Bay ($703.97)	New York ($455.57)	27-0	Milwaukee	32,279
1938	Dec. 11	New York ($504.45)	Green Bay ($368.81)	23-17	New York	48,120
1937	Dec. 12	Washington ($225.90)	Chi. Bears ($127.78)	28-21	Chicago	15,870
1936	Dec. 13	Green Bay ($250)	Boston ($180)	21-6	New York	29,545
1935	Dec. 15	Detroit ($313.35)	New York ($200.20)	26-7	Detroit	15,000
1934	Dec. 9	New York ($621)	Chi. Bears ($414.02)	30-13	New York	35,059
1933	Dec. 17	Chi. Bears ($210.34)	New York ($140.22)	23-21	Chicago	26,000

**Sudden death overtime*

NFC CHAMPIONSHIP GAME COMPOSITE STANDINGS

	W	L	Pct.	Pts.	OP
Seattle Seahawks	1	0	1.000	34	14
Baltimore Colts	3	1	.750	88	60
Green Bay Packers	10	4	.714	323	200
Detroit Lions	4	2	.667	139	141
Arizona Cardinals**	2	1	.667	60	53
Washington Redskins*	7	5	.583	222	255
Chicago Bears	8	6	.571	325	259
Dallas Cowboys	8	8	.500	361	319
Philadelphia Eagles	5	5	.500	168	160
Atlanta Falcons	1	1	.500	40	54
New Orleans Saints	1	1	.500	45	67
Minnesota Vikings	4	5	.444	163	182
San Francisco 49ers	5	7	.417	245	222
New York Giants	7	11	.389	304	342
Cleveland Browns	4	7	.364	224	253
St. Louis Rams***	5	9	.357	163	300
Carolina Panthers	1	2	.333	41	67
Tampa Bay Buccaneers	1	2	.333	33	30

**One game played when franchise was in Boston (Lost 21-6)*

***Both games played when franchise was in Chicago(Won 28-21, lost 7-0)*

****One game played when franchise was in Cleveland (Won 15-14), and 11 games when franchise was in Los Angeles (Won 2, lost 9, scored 108 points, allowed 256 points).*

2009 NFC CHAMPIONSHIP GAME

Louisiana Superdome, New Orleans, Louisiana
January 24, 2010, Attendance: 71,276

NEW ORLEANS 31, MINNESOTA 28 (OT)—Garrett Hartley made a 40-yard field goal on the first possession of overtime and the Saints' defense forced 5 turnovers en route to earning the franchise's first-ever Super Bowl appearance. The Vikings scored on their first two possessions, driving 80 and 76 yards, to take a 14-7 lead. In the second quarter, Drew Brees completed a 28-yard pass to Reggie Bush on third-and-10 to set up Devery Henderson's game-tying 9-yard touchdown grab. Just before halftime, Bush muffed a punt and Kenny Onatolu recovered at the Saints' 10. However, two plays later, Brett Favre and Adrian Peterson had trouble with a handoff, and Scott Fujita recovered to keep the score 14-14 at halftime. Courtney Roby returned the second half's opening kickoff 61 yards to set up Pierre Thomas' 9-yard touchdown run for the Saints' first lead. The Vikings responded with an 80-yard touchdown drive to tie the game. Late in the third quarter, Jonathan Vilma intercepted Favre's short pass at the Saints' 28 to quell a drive. The Vikings' defense forced a punt, but two plays later, Will Smith forced Percy Harvin to fumble, and Remi Ayodele recovered and returned the ball five yards to the Vikings' 7. Brees completed a 5-yard touchdown pass to Bush for a 28-21 lead with 12:39 to play. The Vikings drove to the Saints' 18, but Tracy Porter forced Bernard Berrian to fumble at the Saints' 10. Vilma recovered to end another scoring threat. Peterson scored on a 2-yard run with 4:58 remaining, capping a drive that was highlighted by Visanthe Shiancoe's 16-yard yard catch on third-and-6, to tie the game 28-28. The Vikings' defense forced its fourth three-and-out of the second half. Favre completed a 10-yard pass to Berrian and 20-yard toss to Sidney Rice, and Chester Taylor gained 14 yards to the Saints' 33 with 1:06 left. Back-to-back running plays gained no yards. On third-and-10, a 12-men-in-the-huddle penalty pushed the Vikings back to the Saints' 38. With 19 seconds left, Favre rolled right and threw across the middle. Porter intercepted the pass to force overtime. The Saints won the coin toss, and Thomas returned the kickoff 40 yards. Facing fourth-and-1 from the Vikings' 43, Thomas gained 2 yards. Brees completed a key 12-yard pass to Robert Meachem to set up Hartley's winning kick. Brees was 17 of 31 for 197 yards and 3 touchdowns. Favre was 28 of 46 for 310 yards and 1 touchdown, with 2 interceptions. Peterson rushed 25 times for 122 yards. Berrian had 9 receptions for 102 yards.

Minnesota (28)	Offense	New Orleans (31)
Bernard Berrian	WR	Marques Colston
Bryant McKinnie	LT	Jermon Bushrod
Steve Hutchinson	LG	Carl Nicks
John Sullivan	C	Jonathan Goodwin
Anthony Herrera	RG	Jahri Evans
Phil Loadholt	RT	Jon Stinchcomb
Visanthe Shiancoe	TE	Dave Thomas
Sidney Rice	WR	Devery Henderson
Brett Favre	QB	Drew Brees
Adrian Peterson	RB/WR	Lance Moore
Percy Harvin	FB	Reggie Bush
	Defense	
Ray Edwards	LDE	Bobby McCray
Pat Williams	NT	Remi Ayodele
Kevin Williams	UT/DT	Sedrick Ellis
Jared Allen	RDE	Will Smith
Chad Greenway	SLB	Scott Fujita
Ben Leber	WLB/MLB	Jonathan Vilma
Benny Sapp	NB/WLB	Scott Shanle
Antoine Winfield	LCB	Jabari Greer
Cedric Griffin	RCB	Tracy Porter
Tyrell Johnson	SS	Randall Gay
Madieu Williams	FS	Darren Sharper

SUBSTITUTIONS

MINNESOTA—Specialists: K—Ryan Longwell. P—Chris Kluwe. LS—Cullen Loeffler. Offense: RB—Chester Taylor. FB—Naufahu Tahi. WR—Greg Lewis, Darius Reynaud. TE—Jeff Dugan, Jim Kleinsasser. G—Artis Hicks. T—Ryan Cook. Defense: DE—Jayme Mitchell, Brian Robison. DT—Fred Evans, Jimmy Kennedy. LB—Jasper Brinkley, Heath Farwell, Kenny Onatolu. CB—Asher Allen. S—Husain Abdullah, Eric Frampton, Jamarca Sanford. DNP: QB—

Tarvaris Jackson. Not Active: QB—Sage Rosenfels. RB—Albert Young. WR—Jaymar Johnson. TE—Garrett Mills. C—Jon Cooper. DT—Letroy Guion. LB—Jeremy Leman. CB—Karl Paymah.

NEW ORLEANS—Specialists: K—Garrett Hartley. P—Thomas Morstead. LS—Jason Kyle. Offense: QB—Mark Brunell. RB—Mike Bell, Lynell Hamilton, Pierre Thomas. FB—Kyle Eckel. WR—Robert Meachem, Courtney Roby. TE—Jeremy Shockey. T—Zach Strief. C—Nick Leckey. Defense: DE—Jeff Charleston, Anthony Hargrove. DT—DeMario Pressley. LB—Jonathan Casillas, Troy Evans, Marvin Mitchell. CB—Usama Young. S—Roman Harper, Pierson Prioleau, Chris Reis. Not Active: QB—Chase Daniel. FB—Adrian Arrington. TE—Darnell Dinkins, Tory Humphrey. G—Jamar Nesbit. DE—Paul Spicer. LB—Anthony Waters. CB—Malcolm Jenkins.

OFFICIALS

Referee—Peter Morelli. Umpire—Roy Ellison. Line Judge—Byron Boston. Side Judge—Tom Hill. Head Linesman—Mark Hittner. Back Judge—Bill Schmitz. Field Judge—Dyrol Prioleau.

SCORING

Minnesota	14	0	7	7	0	—	28
New Orleans	7	7	7	7	3	—	31

Minn — Peterson 19 run (Longwell kick)
NO — P. Thomas 38 pass from Brees (Hartley kick)
Minn — Rice 5 pass from Favre (Longwell kick)
NO — Henderson 9 pass from Brees (Hartley kick)
NO — P. Thomas 9 run (Hartley kick)
Minn — Peterson 1 run (Longwell kick)
NO — Bush 5 pass from Brees (Hartley kick)
Minn — Peterson 2 run (Longwell kick)
NO — FG Hartley 40

TEAM STATISTICS	MINN	NO
Total First Downs	31	15
Rushing	10	4
Passing	17	8
Penalty	4	3
Total Net Yardage	475	257
Total Offensive Plays	82	55
Average Gain Per Offensive Play	5.8	4.7
Rushes	36	23
Yards Gained Rushing (Net)	165	68
Average Yards per Rush	4.6	3.0
Passes Attempted	46	31
Passes Completed	28	17
Had Intercepted	2	0
Tackled Attempting to Pass	0	1
Yards Lost Attempting to Pass	0	8
Yards Gained Passing (Net)	310	189
Punts	4	7
Average Distance	39.0	51.3
Punt Returns	3	1
Punt Return Yardage	15	0
Kickoff Returns	2	6
Kickoff Return Yardage	33	183
Interception Return Yardage	0	29
Total Return Yardage (excluding Kickoffs)	15	29
Fumbles	6	3
Fumbles Lost	3	1
Own Fumbles Recovered	3	2
Opponent Fumbles Recovered	1	3
Penalties	5	9
Yards Penalized	32	88
Field Goals	0	1
Field Goals Attempted	0	1
Third-Down Efficiency	7/12	3/12
Fourth-Down Efficiency	0/0	1/1
Time of Possession	36:49	27:56

INDIVIDUAL STATISTICS

RUSHING: MINN: Peterson 25-122-3, Taylor 6-28-0, Harvin 4-15-0, Favre 1-0-0. NO: P. Thomas 14-61-1, Bush 7-8-0, Brees 1-0-0, Hamilton 1-(-1)-0.

PASSING: MINN: Favre 46-28-310-1-2. NO: Brees 31-17-197-3-0.

RECEIVING: MINN: Berrian 9-102-0, Harvin 5-38-0, Shiancoe 4-83-0, Rice 4-43-1, Taylor 3-18-0, Peterson 2-14-0, Kleinsasser 1-12-0. NO: Henderson 4-39-1, D. Thomas 3-32-0, P. Thomas 2-38-1, Bush 2-33-1, Colston 2-22-0, Meachem 2-19-0, Shockey 1-9-0, Moore 1-5-0

KICKOFF RETURNS: MINN: Harvin 2-33-0. NO: Roby 5-143-0, P. Thomas 1-40-0.

PUNT RETURNS: MINN: Reynaud 3-15-0. NO: Bush 1-0-0.

PUNTING: MINN: Kluwe 4-156-39.0. NO: Morstead 7-359-51.3.

INTERCEPTIONS: MINN: None. NO: Porter 1-26-0,Vilma 1-3-0.

SACKS: MINN: Edwards. NO: None.

AFC DIVISIONAL PLAYOFFS RESULTS

Includes Second-Round Playoff Games (1982), AFC Inter-Divisional Games (1969), and special playoff games to break ties for AFL Division Championships (1963, 1968)

Season	Date	Winner (Share)	Loser (Share)	Score	Site	Attendance
2009	Jan. 17	N.Y. Jets ($21,000)	San Diego ($21,000)	17-14	San Diego	69,498
	Jan. 16	Indianapolis ($21,000)	Baltimore ($21,000)	20-3	Indianapolis	67,535
2008	Jan. 11	Pittsburgh ($20,000)	San Diego ($20,000)	35-24	Pittsburgh	63,899
	Jan. 10	Baltimore ($20,000)	Tennessee ($20,000)	13-10	Nashville	69,143
2007	Jan. 13	San Diego ($20,000)	Indianapolis ($20,000)	28-24	Indianapolis	56,950
	Jan. 12	New England ($20,000)	Jacksonville ($20,000)	31-20	Foxborough	68,756
2006	Jan. 14	New England ($19,000)	San Diego ($19,000)	24-21	San Diego	68,810
	Jan. 13	Indianapolis ($19,000)	Baltimore ($19,000)	15-6	Baltimore	71,162
2005	Jan. 15	Pittsburgh ($19,000)	Indianapolis ($19,000)	21-18	Indianapolis	57,449
	Jan. 14	Denver ($19,000)	New England ($19,000)	27-13	Denver	76,238
2004	Jan. 16	New England ($18,000)	Indianapolis ($18,000)	20-3	Foxborough	68,756
	Jan. 15	Pittsburgh ($18,000)	N.Y. Jets ($18,000)	20-17*	Pittsburgh	64,915
2003	Jan. 11	Indianapolis ($18,000)	Kansas City ($18,000)	38-31	Kansas City	79,159
	Jan. 10	New England ($18,000)	Tennessee ($18,000)	17-14	Foxborough	68,436
2002	Jan. 12	Oakland ($17,000)	N.Y. Jets ($17,000)	30-10	Oakland	62,207
	Jan. 11	Tennessee ($17,000)	Pittsburgh ($17,000)	34-31*	Nashville	68,809
2001	Jan. 20	Pittsburgh ($17,000)	Baltimore ($17,000)	27-10	Pittsburgh	63,976
	Jan. 19	New England ($17,000)	Oakland ($17,000)	16-13*	Foxborough	60,292
2000	Jan. 7	Baltimore ($16,000)	Tennessee ($16,000)	24-10	Nashville	68,527
	Jan. 6	Oakland ($16,000)	Miami ($16,000)	27-0	Oakland	61,998
1999	Jan. 16	Tennessee ($16,000)	Indianapolis ($16,000)	19-16	Indianapolis	57,097
	Jan. 15	Jacksonville ($16,000)	Miami ($16,000)	62-7	Jacksonville	75,173

Season	Date	Winner (Share)	Loser (Share)	Score	Site	Attendance
1998	Jan. 10	N.Y. Jets ($15,000)	Jacksonville ($15,000)	34-24	East Rutherford	78,817
	Jan. 9	Denver ($15,000)	Miami ($15,000)	38-3	Denver	75,729
1997	Jan. 4	Denver ($15,000)	Kansas City ($15,000)	14-10	Kansas City	76,965
	Jan. 3	Pittsburgh ($15,000)	New England ($15,000)	7-6	Pittsburgh	61,228
1996	Jan. 5	New England ($14,000)	Pittsburgh ($14,000)	28-3	Foxborough	60,188
	Jan. 4	Jacksonville ($14,000)	Denver ($14,000)	30-27	Denver	75,678
1995	Jan. 7	Indianapolis ($13,000)	Kansas City ($13,000)	10-7	Kansas City	77,594
	Jan. 6	Pittsburgh ($13,000)	Buffalo ($13,000)	40-21	Pittsburgh	59,072
1994	Jan. 8	San Diego ($12,000)	Miami ($12,000)	22-21	San Diego	63,381
	Jan. 7	Pittsburgh ($12,000)	Cleveland ($12,000)	29-9	Pittsburgh	58,185
1993	Jan. 16	Kansas City ($12,000)	Houston ($12,000)	28-20	Houston	64,011
	Jan. 15	Buffalo ($12,000)	L.A. Raiders ($12,000)	29-23	Buffalo	61,923
1992	Jan. 10	Miami ($10,000)	San Diego ($10,000)	31-0	Miami	71,224
	Jan. 9	Buffalo ($10,000)	Pittsburgh ($10,000)	24-3	Pittsburgh	60,407
1991	Jan. 5	Buffalo ($10,000)	Kansas City ($10,000)	37-14	Buffalo	80,182
	Jan. 4	Denver ($10,000)	Houston ($10,000)	26-24	Denver	75,301
1990	Jan. 13	L.A. Raiders ($10,000)	Cincinnati ($10,000)	20-10	Los Angeles	92,045
	Jan. 12	Buffalo ($10,000)	Miami ($10,000)	44-34	Buffalo	77,087
1989	Jan. 7	Denver ($10,000)	Pittsburgh ($10,000)	24-23	Denver	75,477
	Jan. 6	Cleveland ($10,000)	Buffalo ($10,000)	34-30	Cleveland	78,921
1988	Jan. 1	Buffalo ($10,000)	Houston ($10,000)	17-10	Buffalo	79,532
	Dec. 31	Cincinnati ($10,000)	Seattle ($10,000)	21-13	Cincinnati	58,560
1987	Jan. 10	Denver ($10,000)	Houston ($10,000)	34-10	Denver	75,440
	Jan. 9	Cleveland ($10,000)	Indianapolis ($10,000)	38-21	Cleveland	79,372
1986	Jan. 4	Denver ($10,000)	New England ($10,000)	22-17	Denver	75,262
	Jan. 3	Cleveland ($10,000)	N.Y. Jets ($10,000)	23-20*	Cleveland	79,720
1985	Jan. 5	New England ($10,000)	L.A. Raiders ($10,000)	27-20	Los Angeles	87,163
	Jan. 4	Miami ($10,000)	Cleveland ($10,000)	24-21	Miami	74,667
1984	Dec. 30	Pittsburgh ($10,000)	Denver ($10,000)	24-17	Denver	74,981
	Dec. 29	Miami ($10,000)	Seattle ($10,000)	31-10	Miami	73,469
1983	Jan. 1	L.A. Raiders ($10,000)	Pittsburgh ($10,000)	38-10	Los Angeles	90,380
	Dec. 31	Seattle ($10,000)	Miami ($10,000)	27-20	Miami	74,136
1982	Jan. 16	Miami ($10,000)	San Diego ($10,000)	34-13	Miami	71,383
	Jan. 15	N.Y. Jets ($10,000)	L.A. Raiders ($10,000)	17-14	Los Angeles	90,038
1981	Jan. 3	Cincinnati ($5,000)	Buffalo ($5,000)	28-21	Cincinnati	55,420
	Jan. 2	San Diego ($5,000)	Miami ($5,000)	41-38*	Miami	73,735
1980	Jan. 4	Oakland ($5,000)	Cleveland ($5,000)	14-12	Cleveland	78,245
	Jan. 3	San Diego ($5,000)	Buffalo ($5,000)	20-14	San Diego	52,253
1979	Dec. 30	Pittsburgh ($5,000)	Miami ($5,000)	34-14	Pittsburgh	50,214
	Dec. 29	Houston ($5,000)	San Diego ($5,000)	17-14	San Diego	51,192
1978	Dec. 31	Houston ($5,000)	New England ($5,000)	31-14	Foxborough	60,735
	Dec. 30	Pittsburgh ($5,000)	Denver ($5,000)	33-10	Pittsburgh	50,230
1977	Dec. 24	Oakland ($5,000)	Baltimore ($5,000)	37-31*	Baltimore	59,925
	Dec. 24	Denver ($5,000)	Pittsburgh ($5,000)	34-21	Denver	75,059
1976	Dec. 19	Pittsburgh [$]	Baltimore [$]	40-14	Baltimore	59,296
	Dec. 18	Oakland [$]	New England [$]	24-21	Oakland	53,050
1975	Dec. 28	Oakland [$]	Cincinnati [$]	31-28	Oakland	53,030
	Dec. 27	Pittsburgh [$]	Baltimore [$]	28-10	Pittsburgh	49,557
1974	Dec. 22	Pittsburgh [$]	Buffalo [$]	32-14	Pittsburgh	49,841
	Dec. 21	Oakland [$]	Miami [$]	28-26	Oakland	53,023
1973	Dec. 23	Miami [$]	Cincinnati [$]	34-16	Miami	78,928
	Dec. 22	Oakland [$]	Pittsburgh [$]	33-14	Oakland	52,646
1972	Dec. 24	Miami [$]	Cleveland [$]	20-14	Miami	78,916
	Dec. 23	Pittsburgh [$]	Oakland [$]	13-7	Pittsburgh	50,327
1971	Dec. 26	Baltimore [$]	Cleveland [$]	20-3	Cleveland	70,734
	Dec. 25	Miami [$]	Kansas City [$]	27-24*	Kansas City	50,374
1970	Dec. 27	Oakland [$]	Miami [$]	21-14	Oakland	52,594
	Dec. 26	Baltimore [$]	Cincinnati [$]	17-0	Baltimore	49,694
1969	Dec. 21	Oakland [$]	Houston [$]	56-7	Oakland	53,539
	Dec. 20	Kansas City [$]	N.Y. Jets [$]	13-6	New York	62,977
1968	Dec. 22	Oakland [$]	Kansas City [$]	41-6	Oakland	53,605
1963	Dec. 28	Boston [$]	Buffalo [$]	26-8	Buffalo	33,044

**Sudden death overtime*

$ Players received 1/14 of annual salary for playoff appearances.

PLAYOFF GAME SUMMARIES

2009 AFC DIVISIONAL PLAYOFF GAME
Qualcomm Stadium, San Diego, California
January 17, 2010, Attendance: 69,498
NEW YORK JETS 17, SAN DIEGO 14—Shonn Green rushed for 128 yards and scored the decisive touchdown on a 53-yard run as the Jets beat the Chargers. San Diego entered the game having won its last 11 regular-season games. The Chargers' defense forced the Jets to punt on all six of their first-half possessions, but San Diego led just 7-0 at halftime. Brad Smith returned the opening kickoff of the second half 36 yards to set up Jay Feely's 46-yard field goal. Late in the third quarter, Steve Weatherford's 51-yard punt was downed at the 4-yard line. Two plays later, Jim Leonhard intercepted Philip Rivers' pass at the Chargers' 27 and returned it 11 yards to the 16-yard line. On third-and-goal from the Chargers' 2, Mark Sanchez rolled right and found Dustin Keller in the end zone for a 2-yard touchdown to give the Jets a 10-7 lead 1:25 into the fourth quarter. The Jets' defense forced a punt, and Jerricho Cotchery returned it 25 yards. Sanchez completed a key third-down pass to Cotchery before Greene raced up the middle 53 yards for a touchdown and 17-7 lead with 7:17 to play. Nate Kaeding, who had entered the game with 20 consecutive field goals made but missed two in the first half, missed a 40-yard attempt with 4:38 to play. The Chargers' defense forced a punt, and Rivers scored on a 1-yard run with 2:14 remaining to pull within 17-14. Kerry Rhodes recovered the onside kick. On fourth-and-1 from the Chargers' 29 with 1:09 to play, Thomas Jones gained 2 yards to seal the victory. Sanchez was 12 of 23 for 100 yards and 1 touchdown, with 1 interception. Greene rushed 23 times for 128 yards. Rivers was 27 of 40 for 298 yards and 1 touchdown, with 2 interceptions. Vincent Jackson had 7 receptions for 111 yards.

New York Jets	0	0	3	14	—	17
San Diego	0	7	0	7	—	14

SD — Wilson 13 pass from Rivers (Kaeding kick)
NYJ — FG Feely 46
NYJ — Keller 2 pass from Sanchez (Feely kick)
NYJ — Greene 53 run (Feely kick)
SD — Rivers 1 run (Kaeding kick)

Lucas Oil Stadium, Indianapolis, Indiana
January 16, 2010, Attendance: 67,535
INDIANAPOLIS 20, BALTIMORE 3—Peyton Manning passed for 2 touchdowns and the Colts' defense forced four turnovers as Indianapolis advanced to the AFC Championship Game. The Colts took a quick 3-0 lead, and Baltimore responded with a 15-play, 87-yard drive, capped by Billy Cundiff's 25-yard field goal, to tie the game. Following that score, the Colts' defense did not allow another drive of more than 43 yards the rest of the game. In the second quarter, faced with fourth-and-4 from the Colts' 35-yard line, Manning completed a 4-yard pass to Joseph Addai to keep alive a 14-play, 75-yard drive that ended with Austin Collie's 10-yard touchdown catch with 2:00 left in the half for a 10-3 lead. The Colts' defense forced a three-and-out, and Manning completed 6 of 7 passes on the ensuing 8-play, 64-yard drive that culminated with Reggie Wayne's 3-yard touchdown catch with three seconds left in the half for a 17-3 lead. In the third quarter, Ed Reed intercepted a pass and returned it 38 yards to the Colts' 27, but Pierre Garcon forced Reed to fumble and Dallas Clark recovered. Indianapolis drove 56 yards to set up Matt Stover's second field goal, and Antoine Bethea intercepted Joe Flacco's long pass at the Colts' 2 with 4:53 to play. Jerraud Powers intercepted Flacco at the Colts' 14 with 1:07 remaining to seal the victory. Manning was 30 of 44 for 246 yards and 2 touchdowns, with 1 interception. Flacco was 20 of 35 for 189 yards, with 2 interceptions.

Baltimore	3	0	0	0	—	3
Indianapolis	3	14	0	3	—	20

Ind — FG Stover 44
Balt — FG Cundiff 25
Ind — Collie 10 pass from Manning (Stover kick)
Ind — Wayne 3 pass from Manning (Stover kick)
Ind — FG Stover 33

NFC DIVISIONAL PLAYOFFS RESULTS
Includes Second-Round Playoff Games (1982), NFL Conference Championship Games (1967-69), and special playoff games to break ties for NFL Division or Conference Championships (1941, 1943, 1947, 1950, 1952, 1957, 1958, 1965)

Season	Date	Winner (Share)	Loser (Share)	Score	Site	Attendance
2009	Jan. 17	Minnesota ($21,000)	Dallas ($21,000)	34-3	Minneapolis	63,547
	Jan. 16	New Orleans ($21,000)	Arizona ($21,000)	45-14	New Orleans	70,149
2008	Jan. 11	Philadelphia ($20,000)	N.Y. Giants ($20,000)	23-11	East Rutherford	79,193
	Jan. 10	Arizona ($20,000)	Carolina ($20,000)	33-13	Charlotte	73,695
2007	Jan. 13	N.Y. Giants ($20,000)	Dallas ($20,000)	21-17	Dallas	63,660
	Jan. 12	Green Bay ($20,000)	Seattle ($20,000)	42-20	Green Bay	72,168
2006	Jan. 14	Chicago ($19,000)	Seattle ($19,000)	27-24*	Chicago	62,184
	Jan. 13	New Orleans ($19,000)	Philadelphia ($19,000)	27-24	New Orleans	70,001
2005	Jan. 15	Carolina ($19,000)	Chicago ($19,000)	29-21	Chicago	62,209
	Jan. 14	Seattle ($19,000)	Washington ($19,000)	20-10	Seattle	67,551
2004	Jan. 16	Philadelphia ($18,000)	Minnesota ($18,000)	27-14	Philadelphia	67,722
	Jan. 15	Atlanta ($18,000)	St. Louis ($18,000)	47-17	Atlanta	70,709
2003	Jan. 11	Philadelphia ($18,000)	Green Bay ($18,000)	20-17*	Philadelphia	67,707
	Jan. 10	Carolina ($18,000)	St. Louis ($18,000)	29-23*	St. Louis	66,165
2002	Jan. 12	Tampa Bay ($17,000)	San Francisco ($17,000)	31-6	Tampa	65,599
	Jan. 11	Philadelphia ($17,000)	Atlanta ($17,000)	20-6	Philadelphia	66,452
2001	Jan. 20	St. Louis ($17,000)	Green Bay ($17,000)	45-17	St. Louis	66,338
	Jan. 19	Philadelphia ($17,000)	Chicago ($17,000)	33-19	Chicago	66,944
2000	Jan. 7	N.Y. Giants ($16,000)	Philadelphia ($16,000)	20-10	East Rutherford	78,765
	Jan. 6	Minnesota ($16,000)	New Orleans ($16,000)	34-16	Minneapolis	63,881
1999	Jan. 16	St. Louis ($16,000)	Minnesota ($16,000)	49-37	St. Louis	66,194
	Jan. 15	Tampa Bay ($16,000)	Washington ($16,000)	14-13	Tampa	65,835
1998	Jan. 10	Minnesota ($15,000)	Arizona ($15,000)	41-21	Minneapolis	63,760
	Jan. 9	Atlanta ($15,000)	San Francisco ($15,000)	20-18	Atlanta	70,262
1997	Jan. 4	Green Bay ($15,000)	Tampa Bay ($15,000)	21-7	Green Bay	60,327
	Jan. 3	San Francisco ($15,000)	Minnesota ($15,000)	38-22	San Francisco	65,018

Season	Date	Winner (Share)	Loser (Share)	Score	Site	Attendance
1996	Jan. 5	Carolina ($14,000)	Dallas ($14,000)	26-17	Charlotte	72,808
	Jan. 4	Green Bay ($14,000)	San Francisco ($14,000)	35-14	Green Bay	60,787
1995	Jan. 7	Dallas ($13,000)	Philadelphia ($13,000)	30-11	Dallas	64,371
	Jan. 6	Green Bay ($13,000)	San Francisco ($13,000)	27-17	San Francisco	69,311
1994	Jan. 8	Dallas ($12,000)	Green Bay ($12,000)	35-9	Dallas	64,745
	Jan. 7	San Francisco ($12,000)	Chicago ($12,000)	44-15	San Francisco	64,644
1993	Jan. 16	Dallas ($12,000)	Green Bay ($12,000)	27-17	Dallas	64,790
	Jan. 15	San Francisco ($12,000)	N.Y. Giants ($12,000)	44-3	San Francisco	67,143
1992	Jan. 10	Dallas ($10,000)	Philadelphia ($10,000)	34-10	Dallas	63,721
	Jan. 9	San Francisco ($10,000)	Washington ($10,000)	20-13	San Francisco	64,991
1991	Jan. 5	Detroit ($10,000)	Dallas ($10,000)	38-6	Detroit	78,290
	Jan. 4	Washington ($10,000)	Atlanta ($10,000)	24-7	Washington	55,181
1990	Jan. 13	N.Y. Giants ($10,000)	Chicago ($10,000)	31-3	East Rutherford	77,025
	Jan. 12	San Francisco ($10,000)	Washington ($10,000)	28-10	San Francisco	65,292
1989	Jan. 7	L.A. Rams ($10,000)	N.Y. Giants ($10,000)	19-13*	East Rutherford	76,526
	Jan. 6	San Francisco ($10,000)	Minnesota ($10,000)	41-13	San Francisco	64,918
1988	Jan. 1	San Francisco ($10,000)	Minnesota ($10,000)	34-9	San Francisco	61,848
	Dec. 31	Chicago ($10,000)	Philadelphia ($10,000)	20-12	Chicago	65,534
1987	Jan. 10	Washington ($10,000)	Chicago ($10,000)	21-17	Chicago	65,268
	Jan. 9	Minnesota ($10,000)	San Francisco ($10,000)	36-24	San Francisco	63,008
1986	Jan. 4	N.Y. Giants ($10,000)	San Francisco ($10,000)	49-3	East Rutherford	75,691
	Jan. 3	Washington ($10,000)	Chicago ($10,000)	27-13	Chicago	65,524
1985	Jan. 5	Chicago ($10,000)	N.Y. Giants ($10,000)	21-0	Chicago	65,670
	Jan. 4	L.A. Rams ($10,000)	Dallas ($10,000)	20-0	Anaheim	66,581
1984	Dec. 30	Chicago ($10,000)	Washington ($10,000)	23-19	Washington	55,431
	Dec. 29	San Francisco ($10,000)	N.Y. Giants ($10,000)	21-10	San Francisco	60,303
1983	Jan. 1	Washington ($10,000)	L.A. Rams ($10,000)	51-7	Washington	54,440
	Dec. 31	San Francisco ($10,000)	Detroit ($10,000)	24-23	San Francisco	59,979
1982	Jan. 16	Dallas ($10,000)	Green Bay ($10,000)	37-26	Dallas	63,972
	Jan. 15	Washington ($10,000)	Minnesota ($10,000)	21-7	Washington	54,593
1981	Jan. 3	San Francisco ($5,000)	N.Y. Giants ($5,000)	38-24	San Francisco	58,360
	Jan. 2	Dallas ($5,000)	Tampa Bay ($5,000)	38-0	Dallas	64,848
1980	Jan. 4	Dallas ($5,000)	Atlanta ($5,000)	30-27	Atlanta	59,793
	Jan. 3	Philadelphia ($5,000)	Minnesota ($5,000)	31-16	Philadelphia	70,178
1979	Dec. 30	Los Angeles ($5,000)	Dallas ($5,000)	21-19	Dallas	64,792
	Dec. 29	Tampa Bay ($5,000)	Philadelphia ($5,000)	24-17	Tampa	71,402
1978	Dec. 31	Los Angeles ($5,000)	Minnesota ($5,000)	34-10	Los Angeles	70,436
	Dec. 30	Dallas ($5,000)	Atlanta ($5,000)	27-20	Dallas	63,406
1977	Dec. 26	Dallas ($5,000)	Chicago ($5,000)	37-7	Dallas	63,260
	Dec. 26	Minnesota ($5,000)	Los Angeles ($5,000)	14-7	Los Angeles	70,203
1976	Dec. 19	Los Angeles [$]	Dallas [$]	14-12	Dallas	63,283
	Dec. 18	Minnesota [$]	Washington [$]	35-20	Minneapolis	47,466
1975	Dec. 28	Dallas [$]	Minnesota [$]	17-14	Minneapolis	48,050
	Dec. 27	Los Angeles [$]	St. Louis [$]	35-23	Los Angeles	73,459
1974	Dec. 22	Los Angeles [$]	Washington [$]	19-10	Los Angeles	77,925
	Dec. 21	Minnesota [$]	St. Louis [$]	30-14	Minneapolis	48,150
1973	Dec. 23	Dallas [$]	Los Angeles [$]	27-16	Dallas	63,272
	Dec. 22	Minnesota [$]	Washington [$]	27-20	Minneapolis	48,040
1972	Dec. 24	Washington [$]	Green Bay [$]	16-3	Washington	52,321
	Dec. 23	Dallas [$]	San Francisco [$]	30-28	San Francisco	59,746
1971	Dec. 26	San Francisco [$]	Washington [$]	24-20	San Francisco	45,327
	Dec. 25	Dallas [$]	Minnesota [$]	20-12	Minneapolis	47,307
1970	Dec. 27	San Francisco [$]	Minnesota [$]	17-14	Minneapolis	45,103
	Dec. 26	Dallas [$]	Detroit [$]	5-0	Dallas	69,613
1969	Dec. 28	Cleveland [$]	Dallas [$]	38-14	Dallas	69,321
	Dec. 27	Minnesota [$]	Los Angeles [$]	23-20	Minneapolis	47,900
1968	Dec. 22	Baltimore [$]	Minnesota [$]	24-14	Baltimore	60,238
	Dec. 21	Cleveland [$]	Dallas [$]	31-20	Cleveland	81,497
1967	Dec. 24	Dallas [$]	Cleveland [$]	52-14	Dallas	70,786
	Dec. 23	Green Bay [$]	Los Angeles [$]	28-7	Milwaukee	49,861
1965	Dec. 26	Green Bay [$]	Baltimore [$]	13-10*	Green Bay	50,484
1958	Dec. 21	N.Y. Giants (#)	Cleveland (#)	10-0	New York	61,274
1957	Dec. 22	Detroit (#)	San Francisco (#)	31-27	San Francisco	60,118
1952	Dec. 21	Detroit (#)	Los Angeles (#)	31-21	Detroit	47,645
1950	Dec. 17	Los Angeles (#)	Chicago Bears (#)	24-14	Los Angeles	83,501
	Dec. 17	Cleveland (#)	N.Y. Giants (#)	8-3	Cleveland	33,054
1947	Dec. 21	Philadelphia (#)	Pittsburgh (#)	21-0	Pittsburgh	35,729
1943	Dec. 19	Washington (¢)	N.Y. Giants (¢)	28-0	New York	42,800
1941	Dec. 14	Chicago Bears (¢)	Green Bay (¢)	33-14	Chicago	43,425

**Sudden death overtime*

$ Players received 1/14 of annual salary for playoff appearances.

 # Players received 1/12 of annual salary for playoff appearances.

¢ Players received 1/10 of annual salary for playoff appearances.

2009 NFC DIVISIONAL PLAYOFF GAMES
Mall of America Field at HHH Metrodome,
Minneapolis, Minnesota
January 17, 2010, Attendance: 63,547

MINNESOTA 34, DALLAS 3—Brett Favre threw a playoff-career-high 4 touchdowns, 3 to Sidney Rice, and the Vikings' defense registered 6 sacks, 3 by Ray Edwards, as Minnesota advanced. Edwards sacked Tony Romo and forced him to fumble to thwart Dallas' game-opening drive. Shaun Suisham missed a 48-yard field-goal attempt on the Cowboys' next possession, and Favre connected with Rice for a 47-yard touchdown deep down the right side three plays later for a 7-0 lead. Suisham made a 33-yard field goal on Dallas' next drive, but the Vikings converted two third-down situations on their ensuing possession, capped by Rice's 16-yard touchdown grab, for a 14-3 lead. Two plays later, Jared Allen sacked Romo, forced him to fumble, and recovered the ball to set up Ryan Longwell's 23-yard field goal. Ben Leber's interception late in the third quarter led to Longwell's second field goal, and Rice's 45-yard scoring catch deep down the left sideline midway through the fourth quarter extended the lead to 27-3. Favre's fourth touchdown pass came on fourth-and-3 with 1:55 to play, an 11-yard pass to Visanthe Shiancoe. Favre was 15 of 24 for 234 yards and 4 touchdowns. Rice had 6 catches for 141 yards. Romo was 22 of 35 for 198 yards, with 1 interception. Jason Witten had 10 receptions for 98 yards.

Dallas	0	3	0	0	—	3
Minnesota	7	10	0	17	—	34

Minn — Rice 47 pass from Favre (Longwell kick)
Dall — FG Suisham 33
Minn — Rice 16 pass from Favre (Longwell kick)
Minn — FG Longwell 23
Minn — FG Longwell 28
Minn — Rice 45 pass from Favre (Longwell kick)
Minn — Shiancoe 11 pass from Favre (Longwell kick)

Louisiana Superdome, New Orleans, Louisiana
January 16, 2010, Attendance: 70,149

NEW ORLEANS 45, ARIZONA 14—The Saints' offense scored touchdowns on five of its six first-half possessions en route to victory. On the first play from scrimmage, however, it was Arizona's Tim Hightower who scored on a 70-yard touchdown run. New Orleans answered with a 72-yard touchdown drive. On the next play from scrimmage, Randall Gay forced Jerheme Urban to fumble. Darren Sharper recovered, and Drew Brees completed a 17-yard touchdown pass to Jeremy Shockey four plays later for a 14-7 lead with 7:02 left in the quarter. The Saints' defense forced a three-and-out, and Reggie Bush capped the ensuing 77-yard drive with a spectacular 46-yard touchdown run. After an exchange of punts, Kurt Warner engineered an 80-yard drive capped by Beanie Wells' 4-yard touchdown run to pull within 21-14. Six plays later, Brees and Pierre Thomas utilized the flea-flicker, with Brees completing a long 44-yard touchdown pass to Devery Henderson for a 28-14 advantage. Will Smith intercepted Warner two plays later to set up Marques Colston's 2-yard touchdown catch with 1:10 left in the half for a 35-14 lead. Bush ended the Saints' scoring with the third-longest punt return, 83 yards, in postseason history. Brees was 23 of 32 for 247 yards and 3 touchdowns. Warner, playing in his final NFL game, was 17 of 26 for 205 yards, with 1 interception. Matt Leinart was 7 of 10 for 61 yards.

Arizona	7	7	0	0	—	14
New Orleans	21	14	10	0	—	45

Ariz — Hightower 70 run (Rackers kick)
NO — Hamilton 1 run (Hartley kick)
NO — Shockey 17 pass from Brees (Hartley kick)
NO — Bush 46 run (Hartley kick)
Ariz — Wells 4 run (Rackers kick)
NO — Henderson 44 pass from Brees (Hartley kick)
NO — Colston 2 pass from Brees (Hartley kick)
NO — FG Hartley 43
NO — Bush 83 punt return (Hartley kick)

AFC WILD CARD PLAYOFF GAMES RESULTS

Season	Date	Winner (Share)	Loser (Share)	Score	Site	Attendance
2009	Jan. 10	Baltimore ($19,000)	New England ($21,000)	33-14	Foxborough	68,756
	Jan. 9	N.Y. Jets ($19,000)	Cincinnati ($21,000)	24-14	Cincinnati	63,686
2008	Jan. 4	Baltimore ($18,000)	Miami ($20,000)	27-9	Miami	74,240
	Jan. 3	San Diego ($20,000)	Indianapolis ($18,000)	23-17*	San Diego	68,082
2007	Jan. 6	San Diego ($20,000)	Tennessee ($18,000)	17-6	San Diego	65,640
	Jan. 5	Jacksonville ($18,000)	Pittsburgh ($20,000)	31-29	Pittsburgh	63,629
2006	Jan. 7	New England ($19,000)	N.Y. Jets ($17,000)	37-16	Foxborough	68,756
	Jan. 6	Indianapolis ($19,000)	Kansas City ($17,000)	23-8	Indianapolis	57,215
2005	Jan. 8	Pittsburgh ($17,000)	Cincinnati ($19,000)	31-17	Cincinnati	65,870
	Jan. 7	New England ($19,000)	Jacksonville ($17,000)	28-3	Foxborough	68,756
2004	Jan. 9	Indianapolis ($18,000)	Denver ($15,000)	49-24	Indianapolis	56,609
	Jan. 8	N.Y. Jets ($15,000)	San Diego ($18,000)	20-17*	San Diego	67,536
2003	Jan. 4	Indianapolis ($18,000)	Denver ($15,000)	41-10	Indianapolis	56,586
	Jan. 3	Tennessee ($15,000)	Baltimore ($18,000)	20-17	Baltimore	69,452
2002	Jan. 5	Pittsburgh ($17,000)	Cleveland ($12,500)	36-33	Pittsburgh	62,595
	Jan. 4	N.Y. Jets ($17,000)	Indianapolis ($12,500)	41-0	East Rutherford	78,524
2001	Jan. 13	Baltimore ($12,500)	Miami ($12,500)	20-3	Miami	72,251
	Jan. 12	Oakland ($17,000)	N.Y. Jets ($12,500)	38-24	Oakland	61,503
2000	Dec. 31	Baltimore (12,500)	Denver ($12,500)	21-3	Baltimore	69,638
	Dec. 30	Miami ($16,000)	Indianapolis ($12,500)	23-17*	Miami	73,193
1999	Jan. 9	Miami ($10,000)	Seattle ($16,000)	20-17	Seattle	66,170
	Jan. 8	Tennessee ($10,000)	Buffalo ($10,000)	22-16	Nashville	66,672
1998	Jan. 3	Jacksonville ($15,000)	New England ($10,000)	25-10	Jacksonville	71,139
	Jan. 2	Miami ($10,000)	Buffalo ($10,000)	24-17	Miami	72,698
1997	Dec. 28	New England ($15,000)	Miami ($10,000)	17-3	Foxborough	60,041
	Dec. 27	Denver ($10,000)	Jacksonville ($10,000)	42-17	Denver	74,481
1996	Dec. 29	Pittsburgh ($14,000)	Indianapolis ($10,000)	42-14	Pittsburgh	58,078
	Dec. 28	Jacksonville ($10,000)	Buffalo ($10,000)	30-27	Buffalo	70,213
1995	Dec. 31	Indianapolis ($7,500)	San Diego ($7,500)	35-20	San Diego	61,182
	Dec. 30	Buffalo ($13,000)	Miami ($7,500)	37-22	Buffalo	73,103

Season	Date	Winner (Share)	Loser (Share)	Score	Site	Attendance
1994	Jan. 1	Cleveland ($7,500)	New England ($7,500)	20-13	Cleveland	77,452
	Dec. 31	Miami ($12,000)	Kansas City ($7,500)	27-17	Miami	67,487
1993	Jan. 9	L.A. Raiders ($7,500)	Denver ($7,500)	42-24	Los Angeles	65,314
	Jan. 8	Kansas City ($12,000)	Pittsburgh ($7,500)	27-24*	Kansas City	74,515
1992	Jan. 3	Buffalo ($6,000)	Houston ($6,000)	41-38*	Buffalo	75,141
	Jan. 2	San Diego ($10,000)	Kansas City ($6,000)	17-0	San Diego	58,278
1991	Dec. 29	Houston ($10,000)	N.Y. Jets ($6,000)	17-10	Houston	61,485
	Dec. 28	Kansas City ($6,000)	L.A. Raiders ($6,000)	10-6	Kansas City	75,827
1990	Jan. 6	Cincinnati ($10,000)	Houston ($6,000)	41-14	Cincinnati	60,012
	Jan. 5	Miami ($6,000)	Kansas City ($6,000)	17-16	Miami	67,276
1989	Dec. 31	Pittsburgh ($6,000)	Houston ($6,000)	26-23*	Houston	59,406
1988	Dec. 26	Houston ($6,000)	Cleveland ($6,000)	24-23	Cleveland	75,896
1987	Jan. 3	Houston ($6,000)	Seattle ($6,000)	23-20*	Houston	50,519
1986	Dec. 28	N.Y. Jets ($6,000)	Kansas City ($6,000)	35-15	East Rutherford	75,210
1985	Dec. 28	New England ($6,000)	N.Y. Jets ($6,000)	26-14	East Rutherford	75,945
1984	Dec. 22	Seattle ($6,000)	L.A. Raiders ($6,000)	13-7	Seattle	62,049
1983	Dec. 24	Seattle ($6,000)	Denver ($6,000)	31-7	Seattle	64,275
1982	Jan. 9	N.Y. Jets ($6,000)	Cincinnati ($6,000)	44-17	Cincinnati	57,560
	Jan. 9	San Diego ($6,000)	Pittsburgh ($6,000)	31-28	Pittsburgh	53,546
	Jan. 8	L.A. Raiders ($6,000)	Cleveland ($6,000)	27-10	Los Angeles	56,555
	Jan. 8	Miami ($6,000)	New England ($6,000)	28-13	Miami	68,842
1981	Dec. 27	Buffalo ($3,000)	N.Y. Jets ($3,000)	31-27	New York	57,050
1980	Dec. 28	Oakland ($3,000)	Houston ($3,000)	27-7	Oakland	53,333
1979	Dec. 23	Houston ($3,000)	Denver ($3,000)	13-7	Houston	48,776
1978	Dec. 24	Houston ($3,000)	Miami ($3,000)	17-9	Miami	72,445

**Sudden death overtime*

2009 AFC WILD CARD PLAYOFF GAMES

Gillette Stadium, Foxborough, Massachusetts
January 10, 2010, Attendance: 68,756

BALTIMORE 33, NEW ENGLAND 14—Ray Rice ran 83 yards for a touchdown on the Ravens' first play from scrimmage and the Ravens scored 24 first-quarter points, equaling the second-most in NFL postseason history for the opening quarter, to defeat the Patriots. The Ravens' defense held New England to 196 yards, registered 3 sacks and forced 4 turnovers. Rice's 83-yard run 17 seconds into the game was the second-longest run in postseason history. Three plays later, Terrell Suggs sacked Tom Brady, forced him to fumble, and recovered the ball. Le'Ron McClain scored five plays later for a 14-0 lead just 4:31 into the game. Chris Carr intercepted Brady at the Patriots' 25 midway through the quarter, and Rice scored six plays later for a 21-0 lead. Ed Reed then intercepted a pass to set up Billy Cundiff's 27-yard field goal for a 24-0 lead with 1:19 left in the first quarter. The Patriots took advantage of a muffed punt to score their first touchdown and cut the deficit to 27-14 late in the third quarter with a 53-yard touchdown drive. The Ravens were faced with three third-down situations on their ensuing possession, and Joe Flacco converted all three, completing two passes and scrambling for seven yards, to set up Willis McGahee's 3-yard touchdown run with 10:32 to play. Flacco was 4 of 10 for 34 yards, with 1 interception. Rice carried 22 times for 159 yards. Brady was 23 of 42 for 154 yards and 2 touchdowns, with 3 interceptions.

Baltimore	24	0	3	6	—	33
Miami	0	7	7	0	—	14

Balt — Rice 83 run (Cundiff kick)
Balt — McClain 1 run (Cundiff kick)
Balt — Rice 1 run (Cundiff kick)
Balt — FG Cundiff 27
NE — Edelman 6 pass from Brady (Gostkowski kick)
Balt — FG Cundiff 23
NE — Edelman 1 pass from Brady (Gostkowski kick)
Balt — McGahee 3 run (run failed)

Paul Brown Stadium, Cincinnati, Ohio
January 9, 2010, Attendance: 63,686

NEW YORK JETS 24, CINCINNATI 14—Shonn Greene rushed for 135 yards as the Jets defeated the Bengals for the second consecutive week. New York had defeated Cincinnati the previous week to advance to the playoffs. For Cincinnati, the Bengals were playing in just their second postseason game since 1990. Greene's 39-yard touchdown run early in the second quarter tied the game 7-7. Darrelle Revis intercepted a pass on the Bengals' next possession, and four plays later Mark Sanchez connected deep down the right side with Dustin Keller on a 45-yard touchdown for a 14-7 lead. The Jets made a field goal to begin the third quarter, which was nullified by a holding penalty. The Jets punted, and the Bengals drove down field, but Shayne Graham's 35-yard field-goal attempt sailed wide left. On the ensuing drive, Sanchez completed a 16-yard pass to Braylon Edwards on third-and-6 to set up Thomas Jones' 9-yard touchdown run for a 21-7 lead. Cedric Benson broke free for a 47-yard touchdown early in the fourth quarter. The Jets answered with a field goal, and the Bengals then drove to the Jets' 11 with 3:58 to play. However, Graham pushed a 28-yard field-goal attempt wide right. The Bengals did force a punt, but the Jets' 2009 number-one ranked defense sacked Carson Palmer on each of the final two plays to secure the victory. Sanchez was 12 of 15 for 182 yards and 1 touchdown. Greene had 21 carries for 135 yards. Palmer was 18 of 36 for 146 yards and 1 touchdown, with 1 interception. Benson carried 21 times for 169 yards.

New York Jets	0	14	7	3	—	24
Cincinnati	7	0	0	7	—	14

Cin — Coles 11 pass from Palmer (Graham kick)
NYJ — Greene 39 run (Feely kick)
NYJ — Keller 45 pass from Sanchez (Feely kick)
NYJ — Jones 9 run (Feely kick)
Cin — Benson 47 run (Graham kick)
NYJ — FG Feely 20

NFC WILD CARD PLAYOFF GAMES RESULTS

Season	Date	Winner (Share)	Loser (Share)	Score	Site	Attendance
2009	Jan. 10	Arizona ($21,000)	Green Bay ($19,000)	51-45*	Glendale	61,926
	Jan. 9	Dallas ($21,000)	Philadelphia ($19,000)	34-14	Dallas	92,951
2008	Jan. 4	Philadelphia ($18,000)	Minnesota ($20,000)	26-14	Minneapolis	61,746
	Jan. 3	Arizona ($20,000)	Atlanta ($18,000)	30-24	Glendale	62,848
2007	Jan. 6	N.Y. Giants ($18,000)	Tampa Bay ($20,000)	24-14	Tampa	65,621
	Jan. 5	Seattle ($20,000)	Washington ($18,000)	35-14	Seattle	68,297
2006	Jan. 7	Philadelphia ($19,000)	N.Y. Giants ($17,000)	23-20	Philadelphia	69,094
	Jan. 6	Seattle ($19,000)	Dallas ($17,000)	21-20	Seattle	68,058
2005	Jan. 8	Carolina ($17,000)	N.Y. Giants ($19,000)	23-0	East Rutherford	79,378
	Jan. 7	Washington ($17,000)	Tampa Bay ($19,000)	17-10	Tampa	65,514
2004	Jan. 9	Minnesota ($15,000)	Green Bay ($18,000)	31-17	Green Bay	71,075
	Jan. 8	St. Louis ($15,000)	Seattle ($18,000)	27-20	Seattle	65,397
2003	Jan. 4	Green Bay ($18,000)	Seattle ($15,000)	33-27*	Green Bay	71,457
	Jan. 3	Carolina ($18,000)	Dallas ($15,000)	29-10	Charlotte	73,014
2002	Jan. 5	San Francisco ($17,000)	N.Y. Giants ($12,500)	39-38	San Francisco	66,318
	Jan. 4	Atlanta ($12,500)	Green Bay ($17,000)	27-7	Green Bay	65,358
2001	Jan. 13	Green Bay ($12,500)	San Francisco ($12,500)	25-15	Green Bay	59,825
	Jan. 12	Philadelphia ($17,000)	Tampa Bay ($12,500)	31-9	Philadelphia	65,847
2000	Dec. 31	Philadelphia ($12,500)	Tampa Bay ($12,500)	21-3	Philadelphia	65,813
	Dec. 30	New Orleans ($16,000)	St. Louis ($12,500)	31-28	New Orleans	64,900
1999	Jan. 9	Minnesota ($10,000)	Dallas ($10,000)	27-10	Minneapolis	64,056
	Jan. 8	Washington ($16,000)	Detroit ($10,000)	27-13	Washington	79,411
1998	Jan. 3	San Francisco ($10,000)	Green Bay ($10,000)	30-27	San Francisco	66,506
	Jan. 2	Arizona ($10,000)	Dallas ($15,000)	20-7	Dallas	62,969
1997	Dec. 28	Tampa Bay ($10,000)	Detroit ($10,000)	20-10	Tampa	73,361
	Dec. 27	Minnesota ($10,000)	N.Y. Giants ($15,000)	23-22	East Rutherford	77,497
1996	Dec. 29	San Francisco ($10,000)	Philadelphia ($10,000)	14-0	San Francisco	56,460
	Dec. 28	Dallas ($14,000)	Minnesota ($10,000)	40-15	Dallas	64,682
1995	Dec. 31	Green Bay ($13,000)	Atlanta ($7,500)	37-20	Green Bay	60,453
	Dec. 30	Philadelphia ($7,500)	Detroit ($7,500)	58-37	Philadelphia	66,099
1994	Jan. 1	Chicago ($7,500)	Minnesota ($12,000)	35-18	Minnesota	60,347
	Dec. 31	Green Bay ($7,500)	Detroit ($7,500)	16-12	Green Bay	58,125
1993	Jan. 9	N.Y. Giants ($7,500)	Minnesota ($7,500)	17-10	East Rutherford	75,089
	Jan. 8	Green Bay ($7,500)	Detroit ($12,000)	28-24	Detroit	68,479
1992	Jan. 3	Philadelphia ($6,000)	New Orleans ($6,000)	36-20	New Orleans	68,893
	Jan. 2	Washington ($6,000)	Minnesota ($10,000)	24-7	Minnesota	57,353
1991	Dec. 29	Dallas ($6,000)	Chicago ($6,000)	17-13	Chicago	62,594
	Dec. 28	Atlanta ($6,000)	New Orleans ($10,000)	27-20	New Orleans	68,794
1990	Jan. 6	Chicago ($10,000)	New Orleans ($6,000)	16-6	Chicago	60,767
	Jan. 5	Washington ($6,000)	Philadelphia ($6,000)	20-6	Philadelphia	65,287
1989	Dec. 31	L.A. Rams ($6,000)	Philadelphia ($6,000)	21-7	Philadelphia	65,479
1988	Dec. 26	Minnesota ($6,000)	L.A. Rams ($6,000)	28-17	Minnesota	61,204
1987	Jan. 3	Minnesota ($6,000)	New Orleans ($6,000)	44-10	New Orleans	68,546
1986	Dec. 28	Washington ($6,000)	L.A. Rams ($6,000)	19-7	Washington	54,567
1985	Dec. 29	N.Y. Giants ($6,000)	San Francisco ($6,000)	17-3	East Rutherford	75,131
1984	Dec. 23	N.Y. Giants ($6,000)	L.A. Rams ($6,000)	16-13	Anaheim	67,037
1983	Dec. 26	L.A. Rams ($6,000)	Dallas ($6,000)	24-17	Dallas	62,118
1982	Jan. 9	Dallas ($6,000)	Tampa Bay ($6,000)	30-17	Dallas	65,042
	Jan. 9	Minnesota ($6,000)	Atlanta ($6,000)	30-24	Minnesota	60,560
	Jan. 8	Green Bay ($6,000)	St. Louis ($6,000)	41-16	Green Bay	54,282
	Jan. 8	Washington ($6,000)	Detroit ($6,000)	31-7	Washington	55,045
1981	Dec. 27	N.Y. Giants ($3,000)	Philadelphia ($3,000)	27-21	Philadelphia	71,611
1980	Dec. 28	Dallas ($3,000)	Los Angeles ($3,000)	34-13	Dallas	63,052
1979	Dec. 23	Philadelphia ($3,000)	Chicago ($3,000)	27-17	Philadelphia	69,397
1978	Dec. 24	Atlanta ($3,000)	Philadelphia ($3,000)	14-13	Atlanta	59,403

**Sudden death overtime*

2009 NFC WILD CARD PLAYOFF GAMES

University of Phoenix Stadium, Glendale, Arizona
January 10, 2010, Attendance: 61,926

ARIZONA 51, GREEN BAY 45 (OT)—Michael Adams stripped Aaron Rodgers of the ball, and Karlos Dansby recovered the fumble in midair and ran 17 yards for the game-winning touchdown in overtime as Arizona won the highest-scoring postseason game in NFL history. Kurt Warner, who threw more touchdowns (5) than incompletions (4), was nearly flawless. Warner's 87.9 completion percentage (29 of 33) was the third-best in NFL postseason history. Not to be outdone, Aaron Rodgers, who was making his first playoff start, passed for 423 yards and 4 touchdowns. The two teams combined for a NFL-postseason-record 62 first downs. Turnovers on two of the Packers' first three plays from scrimmage led directly to Arizona touchdowns and a 14-0 lead. Arizona led 24-10 at halftime, and needed just six plays to drive 80 yards, capped by Larry Fitzgerald's 33-yard touchdown catch, for a 31-10 third-quarter lead. Rodgers responded with a 6-yard touchdown pass to Greg Jennings on third-and-goal to cut the deficit to 31-17 with 7:20 left in the third quarter. Mason Crosby then attempted an onside kick and Brandon Underwood recovered for the Packers. Ahman Green gained four yards on fourth-

and-1, and Jordy Nelson's 11-yard touchdown catch moments later pulled the Packers to within 31-24. Beanie Wells' 42-yard run set up Fitzgerald's second touchdown grab of the quarter for a 38-24 lead. Green Bay drove to the Arizona 30-yard line. Facing fourth-and-5 early in the fourth quarter and trailing by 14, Rodgers completed a short pass to James Jones that resulted in a 30-yard touchdown. The Packers' defense forced a punt, and Rodgers completed consecutive passes of 38 yards (to Jermichael Finley) and 28 yards (to Donald Driver) that led to John Kuhn's 1-yard game-tying scoring run with 10:57 to play. Green Bay had scored 28 points in 11 minutes, 23 seconds. Warner completed 6 of 7 passes on the next drive and took more than six minutes off the clock, capped by Steve Breaston's 17-yard touchdown catch, for a 45-38 lead with 4:55 left. Finley had a key 9-yard catch on the following drive to set up Spencer Havner's game-tying grab with 1:52 to play. Arizona drove to the Packers' 16, but Neil Rackers' 34-yard field-goal attempt sailed wide left. In overtime, Green Bay won the toss, but on third-and-6, a blitzing Adams stripped Rodgers of the ball. Dansby had the ball fall into his hands, and he ran untouched for the game-winning touchdown just 1:18 into overtime. Warner was 29 of 33 for 379 yards and 5 touchdowns. Breaston had 7 catches for 125 yards. Rodgers was 28 of 42 for 423 yards, 4 touchdowns, and 1 interception. Finley had 6 receptions for 159 yards and Jennings added 8 catches for 130 yards.

Green Bay	0	10	14	21	0	—	45
Arizona	17	7	14	7	6	—	51

Ariz — Hightower 1 run (Rackers kick)
Ariz — Doucet 15 pass from Warner (Rackers kick)
Ariz — FG Rackers 23
GB — Rodgers 1 run (Crosby kick)
Ariz — Doucet 15 pass from Warner (Rackers kick)
GB — FG Crosby 20
Ariz — Fitzgerald 33 pass from Warner (Rackers kick)
GB — Jennings 6 pass from Rodgers (Crosby kick)
GB — Nelson 11 pass from Rodgers (Crosby kick)
Ariz — Fitzgerald 11 pass from Warner (Rackers kick)
GB — Jones 30 pass from Rodgers (Crosby kick)
GB — Kuhn 1 run (Crosby kick)
Ariz — Breaston 17 pass from Warner (Rackers kick)
GB — Havner 11 pass from Rodgers (Crosby kick)
Ariz — Dansby 17 fumble return

Cowboys Stadium, Arlington, Texas
January 9, 2010, Attendance: 92,951

DALLAS 34, PHILADELPHIA 14—Tony Romo passed for 2 touchdowns and the Cowboys scored on all five of their second-quarter possessions to post the franchise's first playoff victory since 1996. The Cowboys converted 9 of 16 third-down situations, while permitting Philadelphia to convert just 2 of 11 third downs, allowing Dallas to maintain possession for 39 minutes, 34 seconds. A 40-yard pass interference penalty gave Dallas the ball at the Eagles' 1-yard line two plays into the second quarter. Rookie John Phillips caught Romo's 1-yard touchdown pass on the next play for a 7-0 lead. Two plays later, out of the Wildcat formation, Michael Vick completed a 76-yard touchdown pass deep down the left sideline to Jeremy Maclin to tie the game. Romo completed passes on third-and-9 and third-and-7 on the next possession, and Tashard Choice capped the 10-play, 85-yard drive with a 1-yard run for a 14-7 lead. The Cowboys' defense then forced a punt, and Patrick Crayton returned it 31 yards, which led to Shaun Suisham's field goal with 3:39 left in the half. Two plays later, Vick came in but fumbled the Shotgun snap. Bobby Carpenter recovered at the Eagles' 18, and Romo's 6-yard touchdown pass to Miles Austin three plays later made it 24-7 with 1:55 remaining in the second quarter. Five plays later, Bradie James forced Leonard Weaver to fumble. James also recovered the ball, and Suisham's 48-yard field goal just before halftime gave Dallas a 27-7 lead. Felix Jones' 73-yard touchdown run in the third quarter helped secure the victory. Romo was 23 of 35 for 244 yards and 2 touchdowns. Jones rushed 16 times for 148 yards. Donovan McNabb was 17 of 39 for 230 yards and 1 touchdown, with 1 interception. Maclin had 7 catches for 146 yards.

Philadelphia	0	7	0	7	—	14
Dallas	0	27	7	0	—	34

Dall — Phillips 1 pass from Romo (Suisham kick)
Phil — Maclin 76 pass from Vick (Akers kick)
Dall — Choice 1 run (Suisham kick)
Dall — FG Suisham 25
Dall — Austin 6 pass from Romo (Suisham kick)
Dall — FG Suisham 48
Dall — Jones 73 run (Suisham kick)
Phil — D. Jackson 4 pass from McNabb (Akers kick)

AFC-NFC PRO BOWL RESULTS (1971-2010)

Series tied, 20-20

Year	Date	Winner (Share)	Loser (Share)	Score	Site	Attendance
2010	Jan. 31	AFC ($45,000)	NFC ($22,500)	41-34	Miami	70,697
2009	Feb. 8	NFC ($45,000)	AFC ($22,500)	30-21	Honolulu	49,958
2008	Feb. 10	NFC ($40,000)	AFC ($20,000)	42-30	Honolulu	50,044
2007	Feb. 10	AFC ($40,000)	NFC ($20,000)	31-28	Honolulu	50,410
2006	Feb. 12	NFC ($40,000)	AFC ($20,000)	23-17	Honolulu	50,190
2005	Feb. 13	AFC ($35,000)	NFC ($17,500)	38-27	Honolulu	50,225
2004	Feb. 8	NFC ($35,000)	AFC ($17,500)	55-52	Honolulu	50,127
2003	Feb. 2	AFC ($30,000)	NFC ($15,000)	45-20	Honolulu	50,125
2002	Feb. 9	AFC ($30,000)	NFC ($15,000)	38-30	Honolulu	50,301
2001	Feb. 4	AFC ($30,000)	NFC ($15,000)	38-17	Honolulu	50,128
2000	Feb. 6	NFC ($25,000)	AFC ($12,500)	51-31	Honolulu	50,112
1999	Feb. 7	AFC ($25,000)	NFC ($12,500)	23-10	Honolulu	50,075
1998	Feb. 1	AFC ($25,000)	NFC ($12,500)	29-24	Honolulu	49,995
1997	Feb. 2	AFC ($20,000)	NFC ($10,000)	26-23 (OT)	Honolulu	50,031
1996	Feb. 4	NFC ($20,000)	AFC ($10,000)	20-13	Honolulu	50,034
1995	Feb. 5	AFC ($20,000)	NFC ($10,000)	41-13	Honolulu	50,529
1994	Feb. 6	NFC ($20,000)	AFC ($10,000)	17-3	Honolulu	50,026
1993	Feb. 7	AFC ($10,000)	NFC ($5,000)	23-20 (OT)	Honolulu	50,007
1992	Feb. 2	NFC ($10,000)	AFC ($5,000)	21-15	Honolulu	50,209
1991	Feb. 3	AFC ($10,000)	NFC ($5,000)	23-21	Honolulu	50,345
1990	Feb. 4	NFC ($10,000)	AFC ($5,000)	27-21	Honolulu	50,445
1989	Jan. 29	NFC ($10,000)	AFC ($5,000)	34-3	Honolulu	50,113
1988	Feb. 7	AFC ($10,000)	NFC ($5,000)	15-6	Honolulu	50,113
1987	Feb. 1	AFC ($10,000)	NFC ($5,000)	10-6	Honolulu	50,101
1986	Feb. 2	NFC ($10,000)	AFC ($5,000)	28-24	Honolulu	50,101
1985	Jan. 27	AFC ($10,000)	NFC ($5,000)	22-14	Honolulu	50,385
1984	Jan. 29	NFC ($10,000)	AFC ($5,000)	45-3	Honolulu	50,445
1983	Feb. 6	NFC ($10,000)	AFC ($5,000)	20-19	Honolulu	49,883
1982	Jan. 31	AFC ($5,000)	NFC ($2,500)	16-13	Honolulu	50,402
1981	Feb. 1	NFC ($5,000)	AFC ($2,500)	21-7	Honolulu	50,360
1980	Jan. 27	NFC ($5,000)	AFC ($2,500)	37-27	Honolulu	49,800
1979	Jan. 29	NFC ($5,000)	AFC ($2,500)	13-7	Los Angeles	46,281
1978	Jan. 23	NFC ($5,000)	AFC ($2,500)	14-13	Tampa	51,337
1977	Jan. 17	AFC ($2,000)	NFC ($1,500)	24-14	Seattle	64,752
1976	Jan. 26	NFC ($2,000)	AFC ($1,500)	23-20	New Orleans	30,546
1975	Jan. 20	NFC ($2,000)	AFC ($1,500)	17-10	Miami	26,484
1974	Jan. 20	AFC ($2,000)	NFC ($1,500)	15-13	Kansas City	66,918
1973	Jan. 21	AFC ($2,000)	NFC ($1,500)	33-28	Dallas	37,091
1972	Jan. 23	AFC ($2,000)	NFC ($1,500)	26-13	Los Angeles	53,647
1971	Jan. 24	NFC ($2,000)	AFC ($1,500)	27-6	Los Angeles	48,222

2010 AFC-NFC PRO BOWL

Sun Life Stadium, Miami, Florida
January 31, 2010, Attendance: 70,697

AFC 41, NFC 34—Matt Schaub passed for 2 scores and Chris Johnson scored the tie-breaking touchdown with 5:59 to play as the AFC defeated the NFC. This marked the first time the Pro Bowl was played prior to the Super Bowl. The AFC began the game with identical 5-play, 65-yard scoring drives that ended with Schaub touchdown passes to take a 14-3 lead just eight minutes, one second into the game. Aaron Rodgers answered with back-to-back scoring drives of 80 and 78 yards, the latter of which featured a 12-yard pass from Rodgers to DeSean Jackson on fourth-and-7, and was capped by the duo's 7-yard touchdown, for a 17-14 NFC lead. With the score 17-17, Josh Cribbs returned a punt 65 yards just before halftime, but Dan Carpenter's 36-yard field-goal attempt sailed wide right as the half expired. The NFC scored on the second play of the third quarter, as Jackson took a short pass from Donovan McNabb and sprinted for a 58-yard touchdown. Undeterred, David Garrard needed just two plays to tie the game on his deep 48-yard touchdown toss to Vincent Jackson. The AFC defense made a key play on the next play from scrimmage, as Brian Dawkins intercepted McNabb's pass to set up Maurice Jones-Drew's 4-yard touchdown run. The AFC defense then forced a punt, and Dan Carpenter made a 26-yard field goal to give the AFC a 34-24 lead with 5:09 left in the third quarter. Tony Romo entered the game and completed six consecutive passes to set up DeAngelo Williams' touchdown to pull within three points. Asante Samuel then intercepted Vince Young's pass and returned it 35 yards. David Akers made a 39-yard field goal moments later to tie the score 34-34 with 11:43 to play. Schaub re-entered the game and led the AFC on an 11-play, 76-yard march, highlighted by Andre Johnson's 7-yard catch on fourth-and-2, and capped by Chris Johnson's 2-yard run with 5:59 to play. Romo drove the NFC to the AFC 31-yard line, but on third down James Harrison intercepted Romo's pass and returned it 34 yards. Le'Ron McClain clinched the victory with his 3-yard run on fourth-and-1 with 1:40 remaining, allowing the AFC to run out the clock. Schaub, who was named the MVP, was 13 of 17 for 189 yards and 2 touchdowns and Garrard was 8 of 14 for 183 yards and a score. Vincent Jackson had 7 receptions for 122 yards. For the NFC, Rodgers was 15 of 19 for 197 yards and 2 touchdowns. DeSean Jackson had 6 catches for 101 yards.

NFC (34)	Offense	AFC (41)
DeSean Jackson (Philadelphia)	WR	Andre Johnson (Houston)
Jason Peters (Philadelphia)	LT	Ryan Clady (Denver)
Steve Hutchinson (Minnesota)	LG	Logan Mankins (New England)
Shaun O'Hara (N.Y. Giants)	C	Nick Mangold (N.Y. Jets)
Leonard Davis (Dallas)	RG	Alan Faneca (N.Y. Jets)
David Diehl (N.Y. Giants)	RT	Joe Thomas (Cleveland)
Vernon Davis (San Francisco)	TE	Antonio Gates (San Diego)
Miles Austin (Dallas)	WR	Brandon Marshall (Denver)
Aaron Rodgers (Green Bay)	QB	Matt Schaub (Houston)
Jason Witten (Dallas)	TE/FB	Le'Ron McClain (Baltimore)
Adrian Peterson (Minnesota)	RB	Chris Johnson (Tennessee)
	Defense	
Jared Allen (Minnesota)	DE	Mario Williams (Houston)
Jay Ratliff (Dallas)	UT	Haloti Ngata (Baltimore)
Darnell Dockett (Arizona)	NT	Vince Wilfork (New England)
Julius Peppers (Carolina)	DE	Kyle Vanden Bosch (Tennessee)
DeMarcus Ware (Dallas)	SLB	Elvis Dumervil (Denver)
London Fletcher (Washington)	MLB	Ray Lewis (Baltimore)
Brian Orakpo (Washington)	WLB	James Harrison (Pittsburgh)
Asante Samuel (Philadelphia)	CB	Nnamdi Asomugha (Oakland)
Terence Newman (Dallas)	CB	Darrelle Revis (N.Y. Jets)
Nick Collins (Green Bay)	FS	Brandon Meriweather (New England)
Quintin Mikell (Philadelphia)	SS	Brian Dawkins (Denver)

SUBSTITUTIONS

NFC—Specialists: K—David Akers (Philadelphia). P—Andy Lee (San Francisco). KR—Johnny Knox (Chicago). LS—Jon Dorenbos (Philadelphia). ST—Heath Farwell (Minnesota). Offense: QB—Donovan McNabb (Philadelphia), Tony Romo (Dallas). RB—Frank Gore (San Francisco), DeAngelo Williams (Carolina). FB—Leonard Weaver (Philadelphia). WR—Steve Smith (N.Y. Giants), Roddy White (Atlanta). G—Chris Snee (N.Y. Giants). C—Jonathan Goodwin (New Orleans), Ryan Kalil (Carolina). Defense: DE—Trent Cole (Philadelphia), Justin Smith (San Francisco). LB—Jon Beason (Carolina), Clay Matthews (Green Bay). CB—Mike Jenkins (Dallas). S—Antrel Rolle (Arizona). Not Active: QB—Drew Brees (New Orleans), Brett Favre (Minnesota). RB—Steven Jackson (St. Louis). WR—Larry Fitzgerald (Arizona), Sidney Rice (Minnesota). G—Jahri Evans (New Orleans). T—Bryant McKinnie (Minnesota), Jon Stinchcomb (New Orleans). C—Andre Gurode (Dallas). DT—Kevin Williams (Minnesota). LB—Jonathan Vilma (New Orleans), Lance Briggs (Chicago). CB—Dominique Rodgers-Cromartie (Arizona), Charles Woodson (Green Bay). S—Roman Harper (New Orleans), Darren Sharper (New Orleans), Adrian Wilson (Arizona).

AFC—Specialists: K—Dan Carpenter (Miami). P—Shane Lechler (Oakland). KR—Josh Cribbs (Cleveland). LS—Jon Condo (Oakland). ST—Kassim Osgood (San Diego). Offense: QB—David Garrard (Jacksonville), Vince Young (Tennessee). RB—Maurice Jones-Drew (Jacksonville), Ray Rice (Baltimore). WR—Vincent Jackson (San Diego), Chad Ochocinco (Cincinnati). TE—Heath Miller (Pittsburgh). G—Kris Dielman (San Diego). T—D'Brickashaw Ferguson (N.Y. Jets). C—Kevin Mawae (Tennessee). Defense: DT—Casey Hampton (Pittsburgh). DE—Shaun Ellis (N.Y. Jets). LB—DeMeco Ryans (Houston), LaMarr Woodley (Pittsburgh). CB—Champ Bailey (Denver). S—Yeremiah Bell (Miami). Not Active: K—Nate Kaeding (San Diego). QB—Tom Brady (New England), Peyton Manning (Indianapolis), Philip Rivers (San Diego). WR—Reggie Wayne (Indianapolis), Wes Welker (New England). TE—Dallas Clark (Indianapolis). T—Jake Long (Miami). C—Jeff Saturday (Indianapolis). DE—Dwight Freeney (Indianapolis), Robert Mathis (Indianapolis). LB—Brian Cushing (Houston). S—Antoine Bethea (Indianapolis), Jairus Byrd (Buffalo), Ed Reed (Baltimore).

HEAD COACHES

NFC—Wade Phillips (Dallas)
AFC—Norv Turner (San Diego)

OFFICIALS

Referee—Jeff Triplette. Umpire—Carl Paganelli. Side Judge—David Wyant. Field Judge—Scott Steenson. Head Linesman—Tony Veteri. Back Judge—Perry Paganelli. Line Judge—Ron Phares.

NFC	10	7	14	3	—	34
AFC	14	3	17	7	—	41

AFC — A. Johnson 33 pass from Schaub (Carpenter kick)
NFC — FG Akers 47
AFC — Marshall 23 pass from Schaub (Carpenter kick)
NFC — Smith 48 pass from Rodgers (Akers kick)
NFC — D. Jackson 7 pass from Rodgers (Akers kick)
AFC — FG Carpenter 30
NFC — D. Jackson 58 pass from McNabb (Akers kick)
AFC — V. Jackson 48 pass from Garrard (Carpenter kick)
AFC — Jones-Drew 4 run (Carpenter kick)
AFC — FG Carpenter 26
NFC — D. Williams 7 run (Akers kick)
NFC — FG Akers 39
AFC — C. Johnson 2 run (Carpenter kick)

TEAM STATISTICS	NFC	AFC
Total First Downs	22	26
Rushing	3	6
Passing	18	19
Penalty	1	1
Total Net Yardage	470	517
Total Offensive Plays	62	67
Avg. Gain Per Offensive Play	7.6	7.7
Rushes	11	22
Yards Gained Rushing (Net)	53	99
Avg. Yards per Rush	4.8	4.5
Passes Attempted	48	43
Passes Completed	31	27
Had Intercepted	2	1
Tackled Attempting to Pass	3	2
Yards Lost Attempting to Pass	12	1
Yards Gained Passing (Net)	429	419
Punts	2	1
Avg. Distance	45.0	54.0
Punt Returns	1	1
Punt Return Yardage	8	65
Kickoff Returns	6	7
Kickoff Return Yardage	133	214
Interception Return Yardage	35	40
Total Return Yardage (KO excluded)	43	105
Fumbles	0	2
Fumbles Lost	0	0
Own Fumbles Recovered	0	2
Opponent Fumbles Recovered	0	0
Penalties	1	1
Yards Penalized	12	13
Field Goals	2	2
Field Goals Attempted	2	3
Third-Down Efficiency	5/12	4/11
Fourth-Down Efficiency	1/2	3/4
Time of Possession	29:02	30:58

INDIVIDUAL STATISTICS

RUSHING: NFC: McNabb 4-26-0, Peterson 3-17-0, Williams 2-6-1, Gore 2-4-0. AFC: Rice 7-42-0, Jones-Drew 5-30-1, C. Johnson 4-19-1, McClain 2-6-0, Young 1-2-0, Garrard 1-2-0, Schaub 2-(-2)-0.

PASSING: NFC: Rodgers 19-15-197-2-0, Romo 18-13-154-0-1, McNabb 10-3-78-1-1, D. Jackson 1-0-0-0-0. AFC: Schaub 17-13-189-2-0, Garrard 14-8-183-1-0, Young 12-6-47-0-1.

RECEIVING: NFC: White 8-84-0, D. Jackson 6-101-2, Austin 6-49-0, Davis 3-67-0, Witten 3-49-0, Gore 2-11-0, Smith 1-48-1, Williams 1-15-0, Peterson 2-5-0. AFC: V. Jackson 7-122-1, Ochocinco 4-80-0, C. Johnson 4-48-0, A. Johnson 3-71-1, Gates 3-29-0, Rice 3-15-0, Marshall 1-23-1, Osgood 1-18-0, Miller 1-13-0.

KICKOFF RETURNS: NFC: Knox 4-103-0, Newman 1-15-0, Austin 1-15-0. AFC: Cribbs 7-214-0.

PUNT RETURNS: NFC: D. Jackson 1-8-0. AFC: Cribbs 1-65-0.

PUNTING: NFC: Lee 2-90-45.0. AFC: Lechler 1-54-54.0.

INTERCEPTIONS: NFC: Samuel 1-35. AFC: Harrison 1-34, Dawkins 1-3, Bailey 0-3.

SACKS: NFC: J. Smith 1, Ware 1. AFC: M. Williams 2, Dumervil 1.

PRO BOWL ALL-TIME RESULTS

Includes AFL All-Star Game played after the 1961-69 seasons.

Date	Result/Honored players	Site (attendance)
Jan. 15, 1939	New York Giants 13, Pro All-Stars 10	Wrigley Field, Los Angeles (20,000)
Jan. 14, 1940	Green Bay 16, NFL All-Stars 7	Gilmore Stadium, Los Angeles (18,000)
Dec. 29, 1940	Chicago Bears 28, NFL All-Stars 14	Gilmore Stadium, Los Angeles (21,624)
Jan. 4, 1942	Chicago Bears 35, NFL All-Stars 24	Polo Grounds, New York (17,725)
Dec. 27, 1942	NFL All-Stars 17, Washington 14	Shibe Park, Philadelphia (18,671)
Jan. 14, 1951	American Conf. 28, National Conf. 27 Otto Graham, Cleveland, player of the game	Los Angeles Memorial Coliseum (53,676)
Jan. 12, 1952	National Conf. 30, American Conf. 13 Dan Towler, Los Angeles, player of the game	Los Angeles Memorial Coliseum (19,400)
Jan. 10, 1953	National Conf. 27, American Conf. 7 Don Doll, Detroit, player of the game	Los Angeles Memorial Coliseum (34,208)
Jan. 17, 1954	East 20, West 9 Chuck Bednarik, Philadelphia, player of the game	Los Angeles Memorial Coliseum (44,214)
Jan. 16, 1955	West 26, East 19 Billy Wilson, San Francisco, player of the game	Los Angeles Memorial Coliseum (43,972)
Jan. 15, 1956	East 31, West 30 Ollie Matson, Chi. Cardinals, player of the game	Los Angeles Memorial Coliseum (37,867)
Jan. 13, 1957	West 19, East 10 Bert Rechichar, Baltimore, outstanding back Ernie Stautner, Pittsburgh, outstanding lineman	Los Angeles Memorial Coliseum (44,177)
Jan. 12, 1958	West 26, East 7 Hugh McElhenny, San Francisco, outstanding back Gene Brito, Washington, outstanding lineman	Los Angeles Memorial Coliseum (66,634)
Jan. 11, 1959	East 28, West 21 Frank Gifford, N.Y. Giants, outstanding back Doug Atkins, Chi. Bears, outstanding lineman	Los Angeles Memorial Coliseum (72,250)
Jan. 17, 1960	West 38, East 21 Johnny Unitas, Baltimore, outstanding back Gene (Big Daddy) Lipscomb, Baltimore, outstanding lineman	Los Angeles Memorial Coliseum (56,876)
Jan. 15, 1961	West 35, East 31 Johnny Unitas, Baltimore, outstanding back Sam Huff, N.Y. Giants, outstanding lineman	Los Angeles Memorial Coliseum (62,971)
Jan. 7, 1962	AFL West 47, East 27 Cotton Davidson, Dallas Texans, player of the game	Balboa Stadium, San Diego (20,973)
Jan. 14, 1962	NFL West 31, East 30 Jim Brown, Cleveland, outstanding back Henry Jordan, Green Bay, outstanding lineman	Los Angeles Memorial Coliseum (57,409)
Jan. 13, 1963	AFL West 21, East 14 Curtis McClinton, Dallas Texans, outstanding offensive player Earl Faison, San Diego, outstanding defensive player	Balboa Stadium, San Diego (27,641)
Jan. 13, 1963	NFL East 30, West 20 Jim Brown, Cleveland, outstanding back Gene (Big Daddy) Lipscomb, Pittsburgh, outstanding lineman	Los Angeles Memorial Coliseum (61,374)
Jan. 12, 1964	NFL West 31, East 17 Johnny Unitas, Baltimore, player of the game Gino Marchetti, Baltimore, outstanding lineman	Los Angeles Memorial Coliseum (67,242)
Jan. 19, 1964	AFL West 27, East 24 Keith Lincoln, San Diego, outstanding offensive player Archie Matsos, Oakland, outstanding defensive player	Balboa Stadium, San Diego (20,016)
Jan. 10, 1965	NFL West 34, East 14 Fran Tarkenton, Minnesota, outstanding back Terry Barr, Detroit, outstanding lineman	Los Angeles Memorial Coliseum (60,598)
Jan. 16, 1965	AFL West 38, East 14 Keith Lincoln, San Diego, outstanding offensive player Willie Brown, Denver, outstanding defensive player	Jeppesen Stadium, Houston (15,446)
Jan. 15, 1966	AFL All-Stars 30, Buffalo 19 Joe Namath, N.Y. Jets, most valuable player, offense Frank Buncom, San Diego, most valuable player, defense	Rice Stadium, Houston (35,572)
Jan. 15, 1966	NFL East 36, West 7 Jim Brown, Cleveland, outstanding back Dale Meinert, St. Louis, outstanding lineman	Los Angeles Memorial Coliseum (60,124)
Jan. 21, 1967	AFL East 30, West 23 Babe Parilli, Boston, outstanding offensive player Verlon Biggs, N.Y. Jets, outstanding defensive player	Oakland-Alameda County Coliseum (18,876)
Jan. 22, 1967	NFL East 20, West 10 Gale Sayers, Chicago, outstanding back Floyd Peters, Philadelphia, outstanding lineman	Los Angeles Memorial Coliseum (15,062)

Jan. 21, 1968 AFL East 25, West 24 ....Gator Bowl, Jacksonville, Fla. (40,103)
Joe Namath and Don Maynard, N.Y. Jets, out. off. players
Leslie (Speedy) Duncan, San Diego, out. def. player

Jan. 21, 1968 NFL West 38, East 20 ....Los Angeles Memorial Coliseum (53,289)
Gale Sayers, Chicago, outstanding back
Dave Robinson, Green Bay, outstanding lineman

Jan. 19, 1969 AFL West 38, East 25 ....Gator Bowl, Jacksonville, Fla. (41,058)
Len Dawson, Kansas City, outstanding offensive player
George Webster, Houston, outstanding defensive player

Jan. 19, 1969 NFL West 10, East 7 ....Los Angeles Memorial Coliseum (32,050)
Roman Gabriel, Los Angeles, outstanding back
Merlin Olsen, Los Angeles, outstanding lineman

Jan. 17, 1970 AFL West 26, East 3 ....Astrodome, Houston (30,170)
John Hadl, San Diego, player of the game

Jan. 18, 1970 NFL West 16, East 13 ....Los Angeles Memorial Coliseum (57,786)
Gale Sayers, Chicago, outstanding back
George Andrie, Dallas, outstanding lineman

Jan. 24, 1971 NFC 27, AFC 6 ....Los Angeles Memorial Coliseum (48,222)
Mel Renfro, Dallas, outstanding back
Fred Carr, Green Bay, outstanding lineman

Jan. 23, 1972 AFC 26, NFC 13 ....Los Angeles Memorial Coliseum (53,647)
Jan Stenerud, Kansas City, outstanding offensive player
Willie Lanier, Kansas City, outstanding defensive player

Jan. 21, 1973 AFC 33, NFC 28 ....Texas Stadium, Irving (37,091)
O.J. Simpson, Buffalo, player of the game

Jan. 20, 1974 AFC 15, NFC 13 ....Arrowhead Stadium, Kansas City (66,918)
Garo Yepremian, Miami, player of the game

Jan. 20, 1975 NFC 17, AFC 10 ....Orange Bowl, Miami (26,484)
James Harris, Los Angeles, player of the game

Jan. 26, 1976 NFC 23, AFC 20 ....Louisiana Superdome, New Orleans (30,546)
Billy Johnson, Houston, player of the game

Jan. 17, 1977 AFC 24, NFC 14 ....Kingdome, Seattle (64,752)
Mel Blount, Pittsburgh, player of the game

Jan. 23, 1978 NFC 14, AFC 13 ....Tampa Stadium (51,337)
Walter Payton, Chicago, player of the game

Jan. 29, 1979 NFC 13, AFC 7 ....Los Angeles Memorial Coliseum (46,281)
Ahmad Rashad, Minnesota, player of the game

Jan. 27, 1980 NFC 37, AFC 27 ....Aloha Stadium, Honolulu (49,800)
Chuck Muncie, New Orleans, player of the game

Feb. 1, 1981 NFC 21, AFC 7 ....Aloha Stadium, Honolulu (50,360)
Eddie Murray, Detroit, player of the game

Jan. 31, 1982 AFC 16, NFC 13 ....Aloha Stadium, Honolulu (50,402)
Kellen Winslow, San Diego, and Lee Roy Selmon, Tampa Bay, players of the game

Feb. 6, 1983 NFC 20, AFC 19 ....Aloha Stadium, Honolulu (49,883)
Dan Fouts, San Diego, and John Jefferson, Green Bay, players of the game

Jan. 29, 1984 NFC 45, AFC 3 ....Aloha Stadium, Honolulu (50,445)
Joe Theismann, Washington, player of the game

Jan. 27, 1985 AFC 22, NFC 14 ....Aloha Stadium, Honolulu (50,385)
Mark Gastineau, N.Y. Jets, player of the game

Feb. 2, 1986 NFC 28, AFC 24 ....Aloha Stadium, Honolulu (50,101)
Phil Simms, N.Y. Giants, player of the game

Feb. 1, 1987 AFC 10, NFC 6 ....Aloha Stadium, Honolulu (50,101)
Reggie White, Philadelphia, player of the game

Feb. 7, 1988 AFC 15, NFC 6 ....Aloha Stadium, Honolulu (50,113)
Bruce Smith, Buffalo, player of the game

Jan. 29, 1989 NFC 34, AFC 3 ....Aloha Stadium, Honolulu (50,113)
Randall Cunningham, Philadelphia, player of the game

Feb. 4, 1990 NFC 27, AFC 21 ....Aloha Stadium, Honolulu (50,445)
Jerry Gray, L.A. Rams, player of the game

Feb. 3, 1991 AFC 23, NFC 21 ....Aloha Stadium, Honolulu (50,345)
Jim Kelly, Buffalo, player of the game

Feb. 2, 1992 NFC 21, AFC 15 ....Aloha Stadium, Honolulu (50,209)
Michael Irvin, Dallas, player of the game

Feb. 7, 1993 AFC 23, NFC 20 (OT) ....Aloha Stadium, Honolulu (50,007)
Steve Tasker, Buffalo, player of the game

Feb. 6, 1994 NFC 17, AFC 3 ....Aloha Stadium, Honolulu (50,026)
Andre Rison, Atlanta, player of the game

Feb. 5, 1995 AFC 41, NFC 13 ....Aloha Stadium, Honolulu (50,529)
Marshall Faulk, Indianapolis, player of the game

PRO BOWL ALL-TIME RESULTS

Feb. 4, 1996	NFC 20, AFC 13 Jerry Rice, San Francisco, player of the game	Aloha Stadium, Honolulu (50,034)
Feb. 2, 1997	AFC 26, NFC 23 (OT) Mark Brunell, Jacksonville, player of the game	Aloha Stadium, Honolulu (50,031)
Feb. 1, 1998	AFC 29, NFC 24 Warren Moon, Seattle, player of the game	Aloha Stadium, Honolulu (49,995)
Feb. 7, 1999	AFC 23, NFC 10 Keyshawn Johnson, N.Y. Jets and Ty Law, New England, co-players of the game	Aloha Stadium, Honolulu (50,075)
Feb. 6, 2000	NFC 51, AFC 31 Randy Moss, Minnesota, player of the game	Aloha Stadium, Honolulu (50,112)
Feb. 4, 2001	AFC 38, NFC 17 Rich Gannon, Oakland, player of the game	Aloha Stadium, Honolulu (50,128)
Feb. 9, 2002	AFC 38, NFC 30 Rich Gannon, Oakland, player of the game	Aloha Stadium, Honolulu (50,301)
Feb. 2, 2003	AFC 45, NFC 20 Ricky Williams, Miami, player of the game	Aloha Stadium, Honolulu (50,125)
Feb. 8, 2004	NFC 55, AFC 52 Marc Bulger, St. Louis, player of the game	Aloha Stadium, Honolulu (50,127)
Feb. 13, 2005	AFC 38, NFC 27 Peyton Manning, Indianapolis, player of the game	Aloha Stadium, Honolulu (50,225)
Feb. 12, 2006	NFC 23, AFC 17 Derrick Brooks, Tampa Bay, player of the game	Aloha Stadium, Honolulu (50,190)
Feb. 10, 2007	AFC 31, NFC 28 Carson Palmer, Cincinnati, player of the game	Aloha Stadium, Honolulu (50,410)
Feb. 10, 2008	NFC 42, AFC 30 Adrian Peterson, Minnesota, most valuable player	Aloha Stadium, Honolulu (50,044)
Feb. 8, 2009	NFC 30, AFC 21 Larry Fitzgerald, Arizona, most valuable player	Aloha Stadium, Honolulu (49,958)
Jan. 31, 2010	AFC 41, NFC 34 Matt Schaub, Houston, most valuable player	Sun Life Stadium, South Florida (70,697)

2009 PRIMETIME GAMES
(Home Team in capitals, games listed in chronological order.)

SUNDAY NIGHT FOOTBALL
GREEN BAY 21, Chicago 15
New York Giants 33, DALLAS 31
Indianapolis 31, ARIZONA 10
PITTSBURGH 38, San Diego 28
Indianapolis 31, TENNESSEE 9
ATLANTA 21, Chicago 14
Arizona 24, NEW YORK GIANTS 17
Dallas 20, PHILADELPHIA 16
INDIANAPOLIS 35, New England 34
Philadelphia 24, CHICAGO 20
BALTIMORE 20, Pittsburgh 17 (OT)
ARIZONA 30, Minnesota 17
Philadelphia 45, NEW YORK GIANTS 38
CAROLINA 26, Minnesota 7
Dallas 17, WASHINGTON 0
NEW YORK JETS 37, Cincinnati 0

MONDAY NIGHT FOOTBALL
NEW ENGLAND 25, Buffalo 24
San Diego 24, OAKLAND 20
Indianapolis 27, MIAMI 23
DALLAS 21, Carolina 7
MINNESOTA 30, Green Bay 23
MIAMI 31, New York Jets 27
Denver 34, SAN DIEGO 23
Philadelphia 27, WASHINGTON 17
NEW ORLEANS 35, Atlanta 27
Pittsburgh 28, DENVER 10
Baltimore 16, CLEVELAND 0
Tennessee 20, HOUSTON 17
NEW ORLEANS 38, New England 17
GREEN BAY 27, Baltimore 14
SAN FRANCISCO 24, Arizona 9
New York Giants 45, WASHINGTON 12
CHICAGO 36, Minnesota 30 (OT)

THURSDAY-SATURDAY NIGHT FOOTBALL
PITTSBURGH 13, Tennessee 10 (OT) (Thurs.)
SAN FRANCISCO 10, Chicago 6 (Thurs.)
Miami 24, CAROLINA 17 (Thurs.)
DENVER 26, New York Giants 6 (Thurs.)
New York Jets 19, BUFFALO 13 in Toronto (Thurs.)
CLEVELAND 13, Pittsburgh 6 (Thurs.)
Indianapolis 35, JACKSONVILLE 31 (Thurs.)
Dallas 24, NEW ORLEANS 17 (Sat.)
San Diego 42, TENNESSEE 17 (Fri.)

SUNDAY NIGHT FOOTBALL

SUNDAY NIGHT WON-LOST RECORDS, 1978-2009

AMERICAN FOOTBALL CONFERENCE

	Balt.	Buff.	Cin.	Clev.	Den.	Hou.	Ind.	Jax.	K.C.	Mia.	N.E.	N.Y.J.	Oak.	Pitt.	S.D.	Tenn.
Total	9-8	10-10	3-10	1-9	18-15	1-3	16-16	5-6	10-4	19-7	15-14	8-11	16-18	15-14	14-15	11-9
2009	1-0		0-1				3-0				0-1	1-0		1-1	0-1	0-1
2008	1-0			0-1	0-1		2-1	0-1			0-2			2-0	2-1	
2007	0-1	0-1	0-1		1-0		1-2				3-0			1-1	1-1	1-0
2006					2-2		3-0		0-1		0-2		0-1	0-1	3-0	
2005	1-1	0-1	0-1	0-1		0-2	1-0	1-0	2-0		1-0	0-1	0-2	1-0	2-0	
2004	2-1	0-1	1-0	0-2	1-1	0-1	1-0	0-1	0-1	1-2	1-0		2-0	2-0		
2003	1-1	0-2		1-0	1-0		1-1	1-0	1-0	2-0	1-0		0-1	0-2		1-0
2002	1-0		0-1	0-1	0-2	1-0	1-1	0-1		1-1	0-2	2-0	2-0	0-1		
2001	0-1	0-1			2-0		0-2			1-0	0-1	2-0	1-1	1-0		0-1
2000	1-1	1-0					1-0	1-1		1-0		0-2	2-0	0-1	0-1	0-1
1999		2-0		0-1	0-1			1-0	1-0	1-0	2-0	0-1	0-1	1-0		0-1
1998	1-0	1-0	0-1		1-0		0-1	0-1	2-0	0-1	1-0	1-0	1-1		0-1	1-0
1997	0-1				1-0		0-1			1-1	1-0	0-1	1-0	2-0	0-2	
1996	0-1	1-1	0-1		1-1		1-0	1-0		1-0	2-0	0-1	0-1		1-1	1-0
1995		0-2			2-1			0-1	1-0	1-0	0-1	0-1	1-1		0-1	0-1
1994		1-0	0-1		0-1		0-1		2-0	2-1	1-0	0-1	1-1	0-1	1-0	
1993		1-0	0-1		0-1		0-3		0-1	1-0	0-1	1-1	1-0	0-1	0-2	2-1
1992		1-1	1-0		2-0		0-1		1-1	1-0	0-1	1-1	0-2	1-0	1-0	1-1
1991		1-0	0-1	0-1	2-0		0-2			1-0	0-1		2-0	1-1	0-1	2-0
1990		1-0	1-1		0-2					1-0			0-1	1-2	0-1	1-1
1989							1-0			1-0	0-1	0-1	0-2		1-0	
1988					0-1					0-1	1-0		1-0	1-0	0-1	1-1
1987				0-1	0-1					2-0	0-1		0-1		1-0	
1986																
1985														0-1	1-0	
1984				0-1	1-0											
1983													1-0			
1982																
1981																
1980															0-1	
1979																
1978					1-0						1-0		0-2	0-1		

SUNDAY NIGHT FOOTBALL ALL-TIME STANDINGS

AMERICAN FOOTBALL CONFERENCE

East	W	L	T	Pct.
Miami	19	7	0	.731
New England	15	14	0	.517
Buffalo	10	10	0	.500
New York Jets	8	11	0	.421

North	W	L	T	Pct.
Baltimore	9	8	0	.529
Pittsburgh	15	14	0	.517
Cincinnati	3	10	0	.231
Cleveland	1	9	0	.100

South	W	L	T	Pct.
Tennessee	11	9	0	.550
Indianapolis	16	16	0	.500
Jacksonville	5	6	0	.455
Houston	1	3	0	.250

West	W	L	T	Pct.
Kansas City	10	4	0	.714
Denver	18	15	0	.545
San Diego	14	15	0	.483
Oakland	16	18	0	.471

SUNDAY NIGHT WON-LOST RECORDS, 1978-2009

NATIONAL FOOTBALL CONFERENCE

	Ariz.	Atl.	Car.	Chi.	Dall.	Det.	G.B.	Minn.	N.O.	N.Y.G.	Phil.	St. L.	S.F.	Sea.	T.B.	Wash.
Total	7-13	7-7	5-7	13-16	20-16	5-7	14-4	15-14	11-12	14-18-1	12-12	10-11	11-8	15-11	6-11	14-14-1
2009	2-1	1-0	1-0	0-3	2-1		1-0	0-2		1-2	2-1					0-1
2008			0-1	2-1	3-0		0-1	1-0		2-1	0-2			0-1	1-0	0-2
2007				1-1	3-0		0-1	0-1	1-0	1-2	0-3			0-1		2-0
2006			0-1	2-1	2-1		1-0		1-0	0-2	0-1			1-1		0-1
2005	1-0	0-1		1-0	0-1	0-1	1-0	0-1	1-0	0-1	0-1	1-0	0-1	1-0		1-0
2004				1-0	0-1		1-0	1-0	0-1	1-0	1-0	1-0	0-2		0-1	0-2
2003		1-0	0-1	0-1	0-1		1-0	1-1	1-1	0-1		1-0	0-1	1-0	0-1	0-1
2002	0-1	1-0		0-1	0-1		1-0	0-2	1-0	1-0		1-0		1-0	1-1	1-0
2001	0-1		0-1	1-0	0-1			0-1	0-2		2-0	1-0	2-0	1-1	0-1	1-0
2000	1-1	0-1	1-0	0-2	0-2		1-0	1-0		2-1	1-0	0-1				1-0
1999	0-2	0-1	1-0		0-1	1-0	1-0	0-1	0-1	0-1			0-1	2-0	0-2	2-0
1998	1-0	1-0	0-1	0-2	1-0	1-0		2-0	0-1	0-1	0-1		1-0	0-2	0-1	0-1
1997	1-0	0-1	1-1	1-1	0-1	0-2	1-0	1-0	1-0	0-0-1	0-1	0-1	0-1	1-0	1-0	1-0-1
1996	0-1	0-1	1-0			0-1	1-0	2-0	0-1	0-2	1-0	0-1	1-0	0-1	0-1	1-0
1995	0-1	0-2	0-1		1-0		1-1	0-1	1-0	1-0	2-0		1-0	1-0	1-0	0-1
1994	1-1			1-0		1-1			1-0	1-0	1-0	0-1	1-0	0-1	0-1	0-1
1993	0-1			1-0	1-0	1-0	2-0	1-2	1-0	0-1	1-0		1-0	0-1	1-0	1-0
1992	0-1			0-1			1-0		1-1	1-1	1-0	1-1	1-0	0-1	0-1	0-1
1991	0-1	1-0			1-0	0-1		1-1	1-1	0-1		0-2		1-1	0-1	2-0
1990	0-1	1-0		1-1	0-1	1-1	0-1	2-0		1-0	0-2	0-1	1-0	2-0	1-0	1-0
1989				0-1	1-0			1-0	0-1			1-0		1-0		0-1
1988					0-1			1-0	0-1	1-0		1-0	0-1	1-0		0-1
1987				1-0	0-1			0-1		1-0		0-1	2-0	1-0		0-1
1986					0-1							1-0				
1985					1-0					0-1						
1984					1-0				0-1							
1983					0-1											
1982		1-0											0-1			
1981					1-0							0-1				
1980					1-0											
1979					1-0							0-1				
1978												1-0				

SUNDAY NIGHT FOOTBALL ALL-TIME STANDINGS

NATIONAL FOOTBALL CONFERENCE

East	W	L	T	Pct.
Dallas	20	16	0	.556
Philadelphia	12	12	0	.500
Washington	14	14	1	.500
New York Giants	14	18	1	.439

North	W	L	T	Pct.
Green Bay	14	4	0	.778
Minnesota	15	14	0	.517
Chicago	13	16	0	.448
Detroit	5	7	0	.417

South	W	L	T	Pct.
Atlanta	7	7	0	.500
New Orleans	11	12	0	.478
Carolina	5	7	0	.417
Tampa Bay	6	11	0	.353

West	W	L	T	Pct.
San Francisco	11	8	0	.579
Seattle	15	11	0	.577
St. Louis	10	11	0	.476
Arizona	7	13	0	.350

MONDAY NIGHT FOOTBALL

MONDAY NIGHT WON-LOST RECORDS, 1970-2009

AMERICAN FOOTBALL CONFERENCE

	Balt.	Buff.	Cin.	Cle.	Den.	Hou.	Ind.	Jax.	K.C.	Mia.	N.E.	N.Y.J.	Oak.	Pitt.	S.D.	Tenn.
Total	5-8	17-23	9-18	15-14	27-33-1	1-1	20-11	7-5	20-15	40-35	17-22	17-23	36-25-1	38-22	18-15	19-16
2009	1-1	0-1		0-1	1-1	0-1	1-0			1-1	1-1	0-1	0-1	1-0	1-1	1-0
2008	0-1	0-1		2-1	1-1	1-0	0-1	0-1			1-0	0-1	0-1	2-0	1-0	1-0
2007	0-3	0-1	1-1		1-2		1-0	0-1		0-1	2-0			2-0	1-0	1-1
2006	0-1		0-1		1-0		1-0	2-0	0-1	0-1	1-0	1-0	0-2	0-1	1-0	
2005	1-1				1-0		3-0		0-1		1-1	0-2		2-1	0-1	
2004	0-1		1-0		0-1		1-0		2-1	1-1	1-1	1-0				1-1
2003				0-1	1-1		1-0		1-0	1-1	1-0	1-0	0-3	0-1	0-1	0-1
2002	1-0				0-2		0-1			1-1	1-1	0-1	2-0	2-1		1-0
2001	2-0				1-1		0-1	0-1		1-0		0-1	1-0	1-0		0-2
2000		0-1			1-1		2-0	0-2	1-1	0-1	1-1	2-0	0-1			3-0
1999		1-0			1-2			2-0		1-2	0-1	2-1	0-1	1-0		
1998					2-1			2-0	0-2	1-2	1-2	1-0		2-1		
1997		1-1			2-1		0-1	1-0	2-0	1-2	1-2		0-2	0-2		
1996		0-2			1-0		1-0		0-2	1-2			2-1	3-0	1-1	
1995		1-1		0-2	1-0				1-1	2-1	1-0		0-2	1-1	1-1	
1994		1-1			0-2				1-1	1-0			1-1	2-0	0-1	0-3
1993		2-1		1-0	0-2		0-1		2-0	1-2			1-0	3-0	2-0	0-1
1992		2-0	0-1	0-1	0-2				1-0	2-1		0-1	0-2	1-0		1-0
1991		2-1	0-2						2-1	1-1		0-1	0-2	0-1		1-1
1990		1-1	1-1	1-1	1-1		0-1		0-1	0-1		0-1	2-0	1-0		1-0
1989		1-2	1-2	1-1	2-0							0-1	1-0			1-0
1988		2-0		1-2	0-2		1-1			1-1		0-1	1-1			1-0
1987				1-0	2-1					1-1	1-1	2-1	1-1			
1986			1-0	1-0	1-1					1-2	1-0	1-1	0-1	0-2	0-1	
1985			1-0	1-0	1-0					2-1	0-1	1-0	2-0	0-2	0-1	
1984		0-1	0-1		1-0					3-0		0-1	2-1	1-1	1-2	
1983		0-1	0-2						0-1	1-1		2-0	1-0	1-0	1-1	
1982		0-1	0-1							1-1		1-0	1-0	1-0	1-1	0-1
1981		1-1		0-1	1-0					1-1	0-1		2-1	1-1	2-1	0-1
1980				1-1	1-2					1-1	1-2	1-0	3-0	0-2	1-0	2-0
1979				1-0	0-2					0-2	0-2	1-1	2-0	2-1	1-0	2-0
1978			1-2		1-1		2-1			2-1	0-2		1-0	1-1	1-0	2-0
1977		0-1	0-1	1-0			1-1		0-1	1-0	0-1		2-0	2-0		
1976		0-2	1-1				2-0		0-1	1-1	1-0	0-1	2-0	0-1		0-1
1975		0-2	1-0		1-1				1-0	1-1	0-1	0-1	2-0	1-0	1-0	0-1
1974		1-0	0-1		0-2				1-0	2-0		0-1	0-1	2-0		
1973		1-0		0-1	0-0-1				1-1	2-0		0-1	0-0-1	1-1		
1972				1-0			1-0		1-0	1-0	0-1	0-1	2-0		0-1	0-1
1971				0-1			1-1		2-0	1-0		0-1	1-0	0-1	1-0	
1970			0-1	2-0			1-1		1-0	1-0		0-1	1-0	1-0	0-1	0-1

MONDAY NIGHT FOOTBALL ALL-TIME STANDINGS

AMERICAN FOOTBALL CONFERENCE

East	W	L	T	Pct.
Miami	40	35	0	.533
New England	17	22	0	.436
Buffalo	17	23	0	.425
New York Jets	17	23	0	.425

North	W	L	T	Pct.
Pittsburgh	38	22	0	.633
Cleveland	15	14	0	.517
Baltimore	5	8	0	.385
Cincinnati	9	18	0	.333

South	W	L	T	Pct.
Indianapolis	20	11	0	.645
Jacksonville	7	5	0	.583
Tennessee	19	16	0	.543
Houston	1	1	0	.500

West	W	L	T	Pct.
Oakland	36	25	1	.589
Kansas City	20	15	0	.571
San Diego	18	15	0	.545
Denver	27	33	1	.451

From 1970-71, tie games were not included in winning percentage.

MONDAY NIGHT WON-LOST RECORDS, 1970-2009

NATIONAL FOOTBALL CONFERENCE

	Ariz.	Atl.	Car.	Chi.	Dall.	Det.	G.B.	Minn.	N.O.	N.Y.G.	Phil.	St.L.	S.F.	Sea.	T.B.	Wash.
Total	6-13-1	9-22	5-4	20-33	42-29	11-13-1	27-28-1	26-25	12-16	19-31-1	26-22	26-27	39-24	16-8	8-9	26-32
2009	0-1	0-1	0-1	1-0	1-0		1-1	1-1	2-0	1-0	1-0		1-0			0-2
2008	1-0		1-0	1-0	1-0		1-2	1-1	1-1	0-1	1-1		0-1		0-1	0-1
2007	0-1	0-2		0-1	1-0		1-0	1-0	2-0	1-0	0-1		1-1	1-0		1-0
2006	0-1	0-1	1-1	2-0	0-1		0-2	1-1	1-0	1-1	2-0	0-1		2-0	0-1	0-1
2005		3-0	1-0		1-1		0-3	1-0	0-2	1-0	0-3	0-1		1-0		1-0
2004			0-1		2-1		2-1	0-2			2-1	2-1		0-1	0-1	0-1
2003		0-1		0-1	1-0		2-1			0-2	2-1	2-0	1-0		2-1	
2002				0-3			2-0			0-1	3-0	2-1	1-2	0-1	1-1	0-1
2001					1-0	0-1	2-0	1-1	0-1	0-3	1-0	2-1	1-0		1-0	0-2
2000			1-0		1-1		1-1	1-1				1-2		0-1	1-1	1-2
1999	0-1	1-2			1-2		1-2	2-1		1-0			1-2	1-0	1-0	
1998					2-0	1-1	0-3	1-0		0-2	0-1		3-0		1-1	0-1
1997			1-1	1-1	1-2		3-0	0-1			0-2		3-0			1-0
1996		0-1		2-0	2-1	0-2	2-1	0-1			0-2		2-1			
1995	0-1			1-2	3-0	2-0	1-0	0-2		0-1	0-1		2-1			
1994				0-2	2-1	1-0	1-0	2-0	0-2	1-2	2-0		2-1			
1993		0-1		0-1	1-1		0-1	1-0	0-2	1-0	1-1		1-2			1-2
1992		0-2		0-3	2-1	0-1		1-0	1-0	1-0	1-0		2-0	1-0		1-2
1991				2-1	0-1			0-1	1-0	2-1	2-1	0-1	2-1			2-0
1990						0-1		0-1	1-1	1-1	2-0	0-3	3-0	1-0		0-1
1989				1-1				1-1	1-1	2-1	0-2	0-2	3-0	1-0		0-2
1988	0-1			1-2	1-1			1-0	1-0	1-1	1-0	1-0	1-1	1-0		0-2
1987				1-2	2-1			1-0		0-3		1-2	2-0	0-2		1-1
1986	0-1			2-1	2-0	0-1	0-1			2-1		1-0	0-2	2-0		1-1
1985	1-1			1-1	1-1		0-1			0-1		2-1	1-2	0-2		2-1
1984		0-2		0-1	1-1	0-1	0-1		1-0	0-1		1-1	2-0	2-0		1-1
1983	0-0-1	0-1			1-1	2-0	2-1	0-1	0-1	1-1-1		1-0	1-0		0-1	1-2
1982					1-2	0-1	1-0	1-0		0-1					1-0	
1981		1-2		0-2	2-0	1-0		0-3			1-1	2-0		1-0		
1980				1-1	1-1				0-1	0-1	1-0	2-0		0-1	0-1	0-2
1979		1-2			0-2		1-0	0-1	0-1	0-1	1-1	1-0		2-0		1-0
1978		1-0		0-3	1-1			2-0				0-2	0-1			1-1
1977	2-0			1-0	1-1		0-1	0-1		0-1		1-1	0-2			1-1
1976	0-1				1-0			1-1			0-1	0-2	2-0			2-0
1975	0-1			0-1	1-1	0-1	0-1	1-0		1-0	0-1	1-0				1-0
1974	0-1	0-1		1-0	0-1	1-0	0-1	1-0	0-1		1-0	1-1	0-2			2-0
1973		1-1		0-1	1-1	1-0	1-1	0-1	0-1	0-1		1-0	1-0			1-1
1972	0-1	0-1		1-0	1-0	0-2	1-0	0-2	0-1	1-0	0-1	1-0	0-1			2-0
1971	1-1	1-0		0-1	1-0	0-1-1	0-1-1	2-0		0-1		0-2	0-1			1-0
1970	1-0	0-1		0-1	0-1	2-0	1-1	1-0		0-1	1-0	0-2				0-1

MONDAY NIGHT FOOTBALL ALL-TIME STANDINGS

NATIONAL FOOTBALL CONFERENCE

East	W	L	T	Pct.
Dallas	42	29	0	.592
Philadelphia	26	22	0	.542
Washington	26	32	0	.448
New York Giants	19	31	1	.382

North	W	L	T	Pct.
Minnesota	26	25	0	.510
Green Bay	27	28	1	.491
Detroit	11	13	1	.458
Chicago	20	33	0	.377

South	W	L	T	Pct.
Carolina	5	4	0	.556
Tampa Bay	8	9	0	.471
New Orleans	12	16	0	.429
Atlanta	9	22	0	.290

West	W	L	T	Pct.
Seattle	16	8	0	.667
San Francisco	39	24	0	.619
St. Louis	26	27	0	.491
Arizona	6	13	1	.325

From 1970-71, tie games were not included in winning percentage.

MONDAY NIGHT RECORDS

Compiled by Elias Sports Bureau
*NFL record.

MONDAY NIGHT RECORDS

SCORING
TOUCHDOWNS

Most Touchdowns, Career

36 Jerry Rice, San Francisco, 1985-2000; Oakland, 2001-04; Seattle 2004
24 Emmitt Smith, Dallas, 1990-2002; Arizona 2003-04
19 Marcus Allen, L.A. Raiders, 1982-1992; Kansas City, 1993-97

Most Touchdowns, Game

4 Ron Johnson, N.Y. Giants at Philadelphia, Oct. 2, 1972
Earl Campbell, Houston vs. Miami, Nov. 20, 1978
Marcus Allen, L.A. Raiders vs. San Diego, Sept. 24, 1984
Eric Dickerson, Indianapolis vs. Denver, Oct. 31, 1988
Emmitt Smith, Dallas at N.Y. Giants, Sept. 4, 1995
Marshall Faulk, St. Louis at Tampa Bay, Dec. 18, 2000

FIELD GOALS

Most Field Goals, Career

51 Gary Anderson, Pittsburgh, 1982-1994; Philadelphia, 1995-96; San Francisco, 1997; Minnesota, 1998-2002; Tennessee, 2003-04
50 Jason Elam, Denver, 1993-2007; Atlanta, 2008-09
42 Ryan Longwell, Green Bay, 1997-2005; Minnesota, 2006-09

Most Field Goals, Game

7 Chris Boniol, Dallas vs. Green Bay, Nov. 18, 1996*
Billy Cundiff, Dallas at N.Y. Giants, Sept. 15, 2003 (OT)*
5 Tim Mazzetti, Atlanta vs. Los Angeles, Oct. 30, 1978
Roger Ruzek, Dallas at L.A. Rams, Dec. 21, 1987
Rich Karlis, Minnesota vs. Cincinnati, Dec. 25, 1989
Nick Lowery, Kansas City vs. Denver, Sept. 20, 1993
Chris Jacke, Green Bay vs. San Francisco, Oct. 14, 1996 (OT)
Richie Cunningham, Dallas vs. Philadelphia, Sept. 15, 1997
Phil Dawson, Cleveland vs. Buffalo, Nov. 17, 2008

RUSHING
YARDS GAINED

Most Yards Gained, Career

2,434 Emmitt Smith, Dallas, 1990-2002; Arizona, 2003-04
1,897 Tony Dorsett, Dallas, 1977-1987; Denver, 1988
1,769 Thurman Thomas, Buffalo, 1988-1999; Miami, 2000

Most Yards Gained, Game

221 Bo Jackson, L.A. Raiders at Seattle, Nov. 30, 1987
216 Ricky Williams, Miami vs. Chicago, Dec. 9, 2002
214 Thurman Thomas, Buffalo at N.Y. Jets, Sept. 24, 1990

Longest Run From Scrimmage, Game

99 Tony Dorsett, Dallas at Minnesota, Jan. 3, 1983 (TD)*
91 Bo Jackson, L.A. Raiders at Seattle, Nov. 30, 1987 (TD)
83 James Lofton, Green Bay at N.Y. Giants, Sept. 20, 1982 (TD)

TOUCHDOWNS

Most Rushing Touchdowns, Career

23 Emmitt Smith, Dallas, 1990-2002; Arizona, 2003-04
17 Marcus Allen, L.A. Raiders, 1982-1992; Kansas City, 1993-97
14 Eric Dickerson, L.A. Rams, 1983-87; Indianapolis, 1987-1991; L.A. Raiders, 1992; Atlanta, 1993

Most Rushing Touchdowns, Game

4 Earl Campbell, Houston vs. Miami, Nov. 20, 1978
Eric Dickerson, Indianapolis vs. Denver, Oct. 31, 1988
Emmitt Smith, Dallas at N.Y. Giants, Sept. 4, 1995

PASSING
YARDS GAINED

Most Yards Gained, Career

9,654 Dan Marino, Miami, 1983-1999
8,741 Brett Favre, Atlanta, 1991; Green Bay, 1992-2007; N.Y. Jets, 2008; Minnesota, 2009
5,148 Joe Montana, San Francisco, 1979-1992; Kansas City, 1993-94

Most Yards Gained, Game

458 Joe Montana, San Francisco at L.A. Rams, Dec. 11, 1989
448 Marc Bulger, St. Louis at Green Bay, Nov. 29, 2004
447 Ken Anderson, Cincinnati vs. Buffalo, Nov. 17, 1975

Longest Pass Play

99 Brett Favre to Robert Brooks, Green Bay at Chicago, Sept. 11, 1995 (TD)*
97 Bernie Kosar to Webster Slaughter, Cleveland vs. Chicago, Oct. 23, 1989 (TD)
95 Joe Montana to John Taylor, San Francisco at L.A. Rams, Dec. 11, 1989 (TD)

TOUCHDOWNS

Most Touchdown Passes, Career

74 Dan Marino, Miami, 1983-1999
65 Brett Favre, Atlanta, 1991; Green Bay, 1992-2007; N.Y. Jets, 2008; Minnesota, 2009
42 Steve Young, Tampa Bay, 1985-86; San Francisco, 1987-1999

Most Touchdown Passes, Game

5 Dave Krieg, Seattle vs. L.A. Raiders, Nov. 28, 1988
Jim Kelly, Buffalo vs. Cincinnati, Oct. 21, 1991
Vinny Testaverde, N.Y. Jets vs. Miami, Oct. 23, 2000 (OT)
Ben Roethlisberger, Pittsburgh vs. Baltimore, Nov. 5, 2007
Drew Brees, New Orleans vs. New England, Nov. 30, 2009

RECEIVING
PASS RECEPTIONS

Most Pass Receptions, Career

254 Jerry Rice, San Francisco, 1985-2000; Oakland, 2001-04; Seattle, 2004
124 Andre Reed, Buffalo, 1985-1999; Washington, 2000
123 Cris Carter, Philadelphia, 1987-89; Minnesota, 1990-2001; Miami, 2002

Most Pass Receptions, Game

14 Herman Moore, Detroit vs. Chicago, Dec. 4, 1995
Jerry Rice, San Francisco vs. Minnesota, Dec. 18, 1995
13 Andre Reed, Buffalo vs. Denver, Sept. 18, 1989
Terrell Owens, San Francisco vs. Philadelphia, Nov. 25, 2002

YARDS GAINED

Most Yards Gained, Career

4,029 Jerry Rice, San Francisco, 1985-2000; Oakland, 2001-04; Seattle, 2004
1,783 Andre Reed, Buffalo, 1985-1999; Washington, 2000
1,556 Terrell Owens, San Francisco, 1996-2003; Philadelphia, 2004-05; Dallas, 2006-08; Buffalo, 2009

Most Yards Gained, Game

289 Jerry Rice, San Francisco vs. Minnesota, Dec. 18, 1995

286 John Taylor, San Francisco at L.A. Rams, Dec. 11, 1989
260 Wes Chandler, San Diego vs. Cincinnati, Dec. 20, 1982

TOUCHDOWN

Most Receiving Touchdowns, Career

34 Jerry Rice, San Francisco, 1985-2000; Oakland, 2001-04; Seattle, 2004
18 Terrell Owens, San Francisco, 1996-2003; Philadelphia, 2004-05; Dallas, 2006-08; Buffalo, 2009
16 Randy Moss, Minnesota, 1998-2004; Oakland, 2005-06; New England, 2007-09

Most Receiving Touchdowns, Game

3 Ron Johnson, N.Y. Giants at Philadelphia, Oct. 2, 1972
Wesley Walker, N.Y. Jets at Detroit, Dec. 6, 1982
Steve Largent, Seattle at San Diego, Oct. 29, 1984
Mark Clayton, Miami vs. Dallas, Dec. 17, 1984
Jerry Rice, San Francisco vs. Chicago, Dec. 14, 1987
Jerry Rice, San Francisco vs. Minnesota, Dec. 18, 1995
Lamar Thomas, Miami vs. Denver, Dec. 21, 1998
Ed McCaffrey, Denver vs. Miami, Sept. 13, 1999
Randy Moss, Minnesota vs. N.Y. Giants, Nov. 19, 2001
Isaac Bruce, St. Louis at New Orleans, Dec. 17, 2001
Terrell Owens, Philadelphia at Dallas, Nov. 15, 2004
Drew Bennett, Tennessee vs. Kansas City, Dec. 13, 2004
Marvin Harrison, Indianapolis vs. Cincinnati, Dec. 18, 2006

YARDS FROM SCRIMMAGE

Most Scrimmage Yards, Career

4,116 Jerry Rice, San Francisco, 1985-2000; Oakland, 2001-04; Seattle, 2004
2,836 Emmitt Smith, Dallas, 1990-2002; Arizona, 2003-04
2,567 Tony Dorsett, Dallas, 1977-1987; Denver, 1988

INTERCEPTIONS BY

Most Interceptions, Career

11 Everson Walls, Dallas, 1981-89; N.Y. Giants, 1990-92; Cleveland, 1992-93
9 Merton Hanks, San Francisco, 1991-98; Seattle, 1999
8 Emmitt Thomas, Kansas City, 1966-1978
Darren Sharper, Green Bay, 1997-2004; Minnesota, 2005-08; New Orleans, 2009

Most Interceptions, Game

4 Dick Anderson, Miami vs. Pittsburgh, Dec. 3, 1973*
3 Johnny Robinson, Kansas City at Baltimore, Sept. 28, 1970
Charlie Babb, Miami vs. Oakland, Sept. 22, 1975
Charles Phillips, Oakland vs. Denver, Dec. 8, 1975
Mark Murphy, Washington at San Diego, Oct. 31, 1983
Ken Easley, Seattle at San Diego, Oct. 29, 1984
Dwayne Harper, San Diego vs. Oakland, Nov. 27, 1995
Marcus Coleman, N.Y. Jets vs. Miami, Oct. 23, 2000 (OT)
Keith Bulluck, Tennessee vs. New Orleans, Sept. 24, 2007

Longest Interception Return

102 Eddie Anderson, L.A. Raiders at Miami, Dec. 14, 1992 (TD)
101 Lito Sheppard, Philadelphia at Dallas, Nov. 15, 2004 (TD)
98 Marcus Coleman, N.Y. Jets vs. Miami, Dec. 27, 1999 (TD)
Rod Woodson, Oakland at Denver, Nov. 11, 2002 (TD)
Brandon McDonald, Cleveland vs. Philadelphia, Dec. 15, 2008

SACKS

Most Sacks, Career

24.5 Bruce Smith, Buffalo, 1985-1999; Washington, 2000-03
20.0 Richard Dent, Chicago, 1983-1993, 1995; San Francisco, 1994; Indianapolis, 1996; Philadelphia, 1997
18.0 Kevin Greene, L.A. Rams, 1985-1992; Pittsburgh, 1993-95; Carolina, 1996, 1998-99; San Francisco, 1997

PUNTING

Highest Punt Average, Career (Minimum: 25 Punts)

47.2 Shane Lechler, Oakland, 2000-09
45.8 Dave Zastudil, Baltimore, 2002-05; Cleveland, 2006-09
44.5 Tom Tupa, Phoenix, 1988-1991; Indianapolis, 1992; Cleveland, 1994-95; New England, 1996-98; N.Y. Jets, 1999-2001; Tampa Bay, 2002-03; Washington, 2004

Longest Punt

90 Rodney Williams, N.Y. Giants at Denver, Sept. 10, 2001
83 Bryan Barker, Jacksonville vs. N.Y. Jets, Oct. 11, 1999
75 Craig Hentrich, Indianapolis vs. Tennessee, Oct. 27, 2008

PUNT RETURNS

Longest Punt Return

95 John Taylor, San Francisco vs. Washington, Nov. 21, 1988 (TD)
94 Dennis McKinnon, Chicago vs. N.Y. Giants, Sept. 14, 1987 (TD)
91 JoJo Townsell, N.Y. Jets vs. Seattle, Nov. 9, 1987 (TD)
Nate Burleson, Minnesota at Indianapolis, Nov. 8, 2004 (TD)

KICKOFF RETURNS

Longest Kickoff Return

105 Terry Fair, Detroit vs. Tampa Bay, Sept. 28, 1998 (TD)
104 Allen Rossum, San Francisco vs. Arizona, Nov. 10, 2008 (TD)
103 Terrence McGee, Buffalo vs. Dallas, Oct. 8, 2007 (TD)

FUMBLES

Longest Fumble Return

99 Don Griffin, San Francisco vs. Chicago, Dec. 23, 1991 (TD)
96 Joe Lavender, Philadelphia vs. Dallas, Sept. 23, 1974 (TD)
93 Adam Archuleta, St. Louis vs. Tampa Bay, Oct. 18, 2004 (TD)

THANKSGIVING DAY FOOTBALL

THANKSGIVING DAY FOOTBALL, 1920-2009

(Home Team in capitals, games listed in chronological order.)
(AFL)-American Football League, 1960-69.

Nov. 25, 1920	AKRON PROS 7, Canton Bulldogs 0 Decatur Staleys 6, CHICAGO TIGERS 0 ELYRIA (OH) ATHLETICS* 0, Columbus Panhandles 0 DAYTON TRIANGLES 28, Detroit Heralds 0 CHICAGO BOOSTERS* 27, Hammond Pros 0 All-Tonawanda (NY) 14, ROCHESTER JEFFERSONS 3 * Non league team. Games between league teams and non league teams counted in standings in 1920.
Nov. 24, 1921	Canton Bulldogs 14, AKRON PROS 0 Buffalo All-Americans 7, CHICAGO STALEYS 6
Nov. 30, 1922	Buffalo All-Americans 21, ROCHESTER JEFFERSONS 0 CHICAGO CARDINALS 6, Chicago Bears 0 RACINE LEGION 3, Milwaukee Badgers 0 Oorang Indians 18, COLUMBUS PANHANDLES 6 CANTON BULLDOGS 14, Akron Pros 0
Nov. 29, 1923	CANTON BULLDOGS 28, Toledo Maroons 0 CHICAGO BEARS 3, Chicago Cardinals 0 GREEN BAY PACKERS 19, Hammond Pros 0 Milwaukee Badgers 16, RACINE LEGION 0 AKRON PROS 2, Buffalo All-Americans 0
Nov. 27, 1924	AKRON PROS 22, Buffalo Bisons 0 Chicago Bears 21, CHICAGO CARDINALS 0 FRANKFORD YELLOWJACKETS 32, Dayton Triangles 7 CLEVELAND BULLDOGS 53, Milwaukee Badgers 10 (at Canton, Ohio) Green Bay Packers 17, KANSAS CITY BLUES 6
Nov. 26, 1925	CHICAGO BEARS 0, Chicago Cardinals 0 Kansas City Cowboys 17, CLEVELAND BULLDOGS 0 (at Hartford, Connecticut) Rock Island Independents 6, DETROIT PANTHERS 3 POTTSVILLE MAROONS 31, Green Bay Packers 0
Nov. 25, 1926	New York Giants 17, BROOKLYN LIONS 0 Los Angeles Buccaneers 9, DETROIT PANTHERS 6 CHICAGO BEARS 0, Chicago Cardinals 0 FRANKFORD YELLOWJACKETS 20, Green Bay Packers 14 POTTSVILLE MAROONS 8, Providence Steam Roller 0 CANTON BULLDOGS 0, Akron Pros 0
Nov. 24, 1927	Chicago Cardinals 3, CHICAGO BEARS 0 POTTSVILLE MAROONS 6, Providence Steam Roller 0 Green Bay Packers 17, FRANKFORD YELLOWJACKETS 9 Cleveland Bulldogs 30, NEW YORK YANKEES 19
Nov. 29, 1928	Providence Steam Roller 7, POTTSVILLE MAROONS 0 DETROIT WOLVERINES 33, Dayton Triangles 0 FRANKFORD YELLOWJACKETS 2, Green Bay Packers 0 CHICAGO BEARS 34, Chicago Cardinals 0
Nov. 28, 1929	New York Giants 21, STATEN ISLAND STAPLETONS 7 FRANKFORD YELLOWJACKETS 0, Green Bay Packers 0 Chicago Cardinals 40, CHICAGO BEARS 6
Nov. 27, 1930	STATEN ISLAND STAPLETONS 7, New York Giants 6 BROOKLYN DODGERS 33, Providence Steam Roller 12 Green Bay Packers 25, FRANKFORD YELLOWJACKETS 7 CHICAGO BEARS 6, Chicago Cardinals 0
Nov. 26, 1931	Green Bay Packers 38, PROVIDENCE STEAM ROLLER 7 STATEN ISLAND STAPLETONS 9, New York Giants 6 CHICAGO BEARS 18, Chicago Cardinals 7
Nov. 24, 1932	CHICAGO BEARS 34, Chicago Cardinals 0 Green Bay Packers 7, BROOKLYN DODGERS 0 STATEN ISLAND STAPLETONS 13, New York Giants 13
Nov. 30, 1933	Chicago Bears 22, CHICAGO CARDINALS 6 New York Giants 10, BROOKLYN DODGERS 0

Nov. 29, 1934	CHICAGO CARDINALS 6, Green Bay Packers 0 Chicago Bears 19, DETROIT LIONS 16 New York Giants 27, BROOKLYN DODGERS 0
Nov. 28, 1935	New York Giants 21, BROOKLYN DODGERS 0 CHICAGO CARDINALS 9, Green Bay Packers 7 DETROIT LIONS 14, Chicago Bears 2
Nov. 26, 1936	DETROIT LIONS 13, Chicago Bears 7 New York Giants 14, BROOKLYN DODGERS 0
Nov. 25, 1937	Chicago Bears 13, DETROIT LIONS 0 BROOKLYN DODGERS 13, New York Giants 13
Nov. 24, 1938	DETROIT LIONS 14, Chicago Bears 7 BROOKLYN DODGERS 7, New York Giants 7
Nov. 23, 1939#	PHILADELPHIA EAGLES 17, Pittsburgh Steelers 14
Nov. 28, 1940#	PHILADELPHIA EAGLES 7, Pittsburgh Steelers 0

In 1939 and 1940, President Roosevelt moved Thanksgiving one week earlier. Various states celebrated on the date declared by the President, while other states recognized the traditional fourth Thursday of the month. In 1941, Thanksgiving was sanctioned by Congress to be celebrated on the fourth Thursday of November, which it has been ever since.

Nov. 22, 1945	Cleveland Rams 28, DETROIT LIONS 21
Nov. 28, 1946	Boston Yanks 34, DETROIT LIONS 10
Nov. 27, 1947	Chicago Bears 34, DETROIT LIONS 14
Nov. 25, 1948	Chicago Cardinals 28, DETROIT LIONS 14
Nov. 24, 1949	Chicago Bears 28, DETROIT LIONS 7
Nov. 23, 1950	DETROIT LIONS 49, New York Yanks 14 Pittsburgh Steelers 28, CHICAGO CARDINALS 17
Nov. 22, 1951	DETROIT LIONS 52, Green Bay Packers 35
Nov. 27, 1952	DETROIT LIONS 48, Green Bay Packers 24 DALLAS TEXANS 27, Chicago Bears 23 (at Akron, Ohio)
Nov. 26, 1953	DETROIT LIONS 34, Green Bay Packers 15
Nov. 25, 1954	DETROIT LIONS 28, Green Bay Packers 24
Nov. 24, 1955	DETROIT LIONS 24, Green Bay Packers 10
Nov. 22, 1956	Green Bay Packers 24, DETROIT LIONS 20
Nov. 28, 1957	DETROIT LIONS 18, Green Bay Packers 6
Nov. 27, 1958	DETROIT LIONS 24, Green Bay Packers 14
Nov. 26, 1959	Green Bay Packers 24, DETROIT LIONS 17
Nov. 24, 1960	DETROIT LIONS 23, Green Bay Packers 10 (AFL) - NEW YORK TITANS 41, Dallas Texans 35
Nov. 23, 1961	Green Bay Packers 17, DETROIT LIONS 9 (AFL) - NEW YORK TITANS 21, Buffalo Bills 14
Nov. 22, 1962	DETROIT LIONS 26, Green Bay Packers 14 (AFL) - New York Titans 46, DENVER BRONCOS 45
Nov. 28, 1963	DETROIT LIONS 13, Green Bay Packers 13 (AFL) - Oakland Raiders 26, DENVER BRONCOS 10
Nov. 26, 1964	Chicago Bears 27, DETROIT LIONS 24 (AFL) - Buffalo Bills 27, SAN DIEGO CHARGERS 24
Nov. 25, 1965	DETROIT LIONS 24, Baltimore Colts 24 (AFL) - SAN DIEGO CHARGERS 20, Buffalo Bills 20
Nov. 24, 1966	San Francisco 49ers 41, DETROIT LIONS 14 DALLAS COWBOYS 26, Cleveland Browns 14 (AFL) - Buffalo Bills 31, OAKLAND RAIDERS 10

THANKSGIVING DAY FOOTBALL

Nov. 23, 1967	Los Angeles Rams 31, DETROIT LIONS 7 DALLAS COWBOYS 46, St. Louis Cardinals 21 (AFL) - Oakland Raiders 44, KANSAS CITY CHIEFS 22 (AFL) - SAN DIEGO CHARGERS 24, Denver Broncos 20
Nov. 28, 1968	Philadelphia Eagles 12, DETROIT LIONS 0 DALLAS COWBOYS 29, Washington Redskins 20 (AFL) - OAKLAND RAIDERS 13, Buffalo Bills 10 (AFL) - KANSAS CITY CHIEFS 24, Houston Oilers 10
Nov. 27, 1969	Minnesota Vikings 27, DETROIT LIONS 0 DALLAS COWBOYS 24, San Francisco 49ers 24 (AFL) - KANSAS CITY CHIEFS 31, Denver Broncos 17 (AFL) - San Diego Chargers 21, HOUSTON OILERS 17
Nov. 26, 1970	DETROIT LIONS 28, Oakland Raiders 14 DALLAS COWBOYS 16, Green Bay Packers 3
Nov. 25, 1971	DETROIT LIONS 32, Kansas City Chiefs 21 DALLAS COWBOYS 28, Los Angeles Rams 21
Nov. 23, 1972	DETROIT LIONS 37, New York Jets 20 San Francisco 49ers 31, DALLAS COWBOYS 10
Nov. 22, 1973	Washington Redskins 20, DETROIT LIONS 0 Miami Dolphins 14, DALLAS COWBOYS 7
Nov. 28, 1974	Denver Broncos 31, DETROIT LIONS 27 DALLAS COWBOYS 24, Washington Redskins 23
Nov. 27, 1975	Los Angeles Rams 20, DETROIT LIONS 0 Buffalo Bills 32, ST. LOUIS CARDINALS 14
Nov. 25, 1976	DETROIT LIONS 27, Buffalo Bills 14 DALLAS COWBOYS 19, St. Louis Cardinals 14
Nov. 24, 1977	Chicago Bears 31, DETROIT LIONS 14 Miami Dolphins 55, ST. LOUIS CARDINALS 14
Nov. 23, 1978	DETROIT LIONS 17, Denver Broncos 14 DALLAS COWBOYS 37, Washington Redskins 10
Nov. 22, 1979	DETROIT LIONS 20, Chicago Bears 0 Houston Oilers 30, DALLAS COWBOYS 24
Nov. 27, 1980	Chicago Bears 23, DETROIT LIONS 17 (OT) DALLAS COWBOYS 51, Seattle Seahawks 7
Nov. 26, 1981	DETROIT LIONS 27, Kansas City Chiefs 10 DALLAS COWBOYS 10, Chicago Bears 9
Nov. 25, 1982	New York Giants 13, DETROIT LIONS 6 DALLAS COWBOYS 31, Cleveland Browns 14
Nov. 24, 1983	DETROIT LIONS 45, Pittsburgh Steelers 3 DALLAS COWBOYS 35, St. Louis Cardinals 17
Nov. 22, 1984	DETROIT LIONS 31, Green Bay Packers 28 DALLAS COWBOYS 20, New England Patriots 17
Nov. 28, 1985	DETROIT LIONS 31, New York Jets 20 DALLAS COWBOYS 35, St. Louis Cardinals 17
Nov. 27, 1986	Green Bay Packers 44, DETROIT LIONS 40 Seattle Seahawks 31, DALLAS COWBOYS 14
Nov. 26, 1987	Kansas City Chiefs 27, DETROIT LIONS 20 Minnesota Vikings 44, DALLAS COWBOYS 38 (OT)
Nov. 24, 1988	Minnesota Vikings 23, DETROIT LIONS 0 Houston Oilers 25, DALLAS COWBOYS 17
Nov. 23, 1989	DETROIT LIONS 13, Cleveland Browns 10 Philadelphia Eagles 27, DALLAS COWBOYS 0
Nov. 22, 1990	DETROIT LIONS 40, Denver Broncos 27 DALLAS COWBOYS 27, Washington Redskins 17

Nov. 28, 1991	DETROIT LIONS 16, Chicago Bears 6 DALLAS COWBOYS 20, Pittsburgh Steelers 10
Nov. 26, 1992	Houston Oilers 24, DETROIT LIONS 21 DALLAS COWBOYS 30, New York Giants 3
Nov. 25, 1993	Chicago Bears 10, DETROIT LIONS 6 Miami Dolphins 16, DALLAS COWBOYS 14
Nov. 24, 1994	DETROIT LIONS 35, Buffalo Bills 21 DALLAS COWBOYS 42, Green Bay Packers 31
Nov. 23, 1995	DETROIT LIONS 44, Minnesota Vikings 38 DALLAS COWBOYS 24, Kansas City Chiefs 12
Nov. 28, 1996	Kansas City Chiefs 28, DETROIT LIONS 24 DALLAS COWBOYS 21, Washington Redskins 10
Nov. 27, 1997	DETROIT LIONS 55, Chicago Bears 20 Tennessee Titans 27, DALLAS COWBOYS 14
Nov. 26, 1998	DETROIT LIONS 19, Pittsburgh Steelers 16 (OT) Minnesota Vikings 46, DALLAS COWBOYS 36
Nov. 25, 1999	DETROIT LIONS 21, Chicago Bears 17 DALLAS COWBOYS 20, Miami Dolphins 0
Nov. 23, 2000	DETROIT LIONS 34, New England Patriots 9 Minnesota Vikings 27, DALLAS COWBOYS 15
Nov. 22, 2001	Green Bay Packers 29, DETROIT LIONS 27 Denver Broncos 26, DALLAS COWBOYS 24
Nov. 28, 2002	New England Patriots 20, DETROIT LIONS 12 DALLAS COWBOYS 27, Washington Redskins 20
Nov. 27, 2003	DETROIT LIONS 22, Green Bay Packers 14 Miami Dolphins 40, DALLAS COWBOYS 21
Nov. 25, 2004	Indianapolis Colts 41, DETROIT LIONS 9 DALLAS COWBOYS 21, Chicago Bears 7
Nov. 24, 2005	Atlanta Falcons 27, DETROIT LIONS 7 Denver Broncos 24, DALLAS COWBOYS 21 (OT)
Nov. 23, 2006	Miami Dolphins 27, DETROIT LIONS 10 DALLAS COWBOYS 38, Tampa Bay Buccaneers 10 KANSAS CITY CHIEFS 19, Denver Broncos 10
Nov. 22, 2007	Green Bay Packers 37, DETROIT LIONS 26 DALLAS COWBOYS 34, New York Jets 3 Indianapolis Colts 31, ATLANTA FALCONS 13
Nov. 27, 2008	Tennessee Titans 41, DETROIT LIONS 10 DALLAS COWBOYS 34, Seattle Seahawks 9 PHILADELPHIA EAGLES 48, Arizona Cardinals 20
Nov. 26, 2009	Green Bay Packers 34, DETROIT LIONS 12 DALLAS COWBOYS 24, Oakland Raiders 7 DENVER BRONCOS 26, New York Giants 6

THANKSGIVING DAY RECORDS

*NFL record; stats compiled by Elias Sports Bureau.

SCORING / Most Touchdowns, Game

6 Ernie Nevers, Chi. Cardinals vs. Chi. Bears, Nov. 28, 1929*
4 Sterling Sharpe, Green Bay at Dallas, Nov. 24, 1994
3 By many players

RUSHING / Most Yards Rushing, Game

273 O.J. Simpson, Buffalo at Detroit, Nov. 25, 1976
198 Bob Hoernschemeyer, Detroit vs. N.Y. Yankees, Nov. 23, 1950
195 Earl Campbell, Houston at Dallas, Nov. 22, 1979

PASSING / Most Yards Passing, Game

455 Troy Aikman, Dallas vs. Minnesota, Nov. 26, 1998
410 Scott Mitchell, Detroit vs. Minnesota, Nov. 23, 1995
384 Warren Moon, Minnesota at Detroit, Nov. 23, 1995

PASS RECEIVING

RECEPTIONS / Most Pass Receptions, Game

12 Brett Perriman, Detroit vs. Minnesota, Nov. 23, 1995
Marvin Harrison, Indianapolis at Detroit, Nov. 25, 2004
11 Daryl Johnston, Dallas vs. Miami, Nov. 25, 1993
Michael Irvin, Dallas vs. Kansas City, Nov. 23, 1995

YARDS GAINED / Most Yards on Pass Receptions, Game

303 Jim Benton, Cleveland at Detroit, Nov. 22, 1945
185 Lance Alworth, San Diego vs. Buffalo, Nov. 26, 1964
184 Anthony Carter, Minnesota at Dallas, Nov. 26, 1987 (OT)

INTERNATIONAL GAMES

NFL INTERNATIONAL GAMES (62)

REGULAR SEASON GAMES (6)

(Home Team in capitals)

Date	Site	Teams
October 2, 2005	Mexico City, Mexico	ARIZONA 31, San Francisco 14
October 28, 2007	London, England	N.Y. Giants 13, MIAMI 10
October 26, 2008	London, England	NEW ORLEANS 37, San Diego 32
December 7, 2008	Toronto, Canada	Miami 16, BUFFALO 3
October 25, 2009	London, England	New England 35, TAMPA BAY 7
December 3, 2009	Toronto, Canada	N.Y. Jets 19, BUFFALO 13

PRESEASON GAMES (56)

Date	Site	Teams
August 12, 1950	Ottawa, Canada	N.Y. Giants 27, Ottawa Rough Riders 6
August 11, 1951	Ottawa, Canada	N.Y. Giants 41, Ottawa Rough Riders 18
August 5, 1959	Toronto, Canada	Chi. Cardinals 55, Tor. Argonauts 26
August 3, 1960	Toronto, Canada	Pittsburgh 43, Toronto Argonauts 16
August 15, 1960	Toronto, Canada	Chicago 16, N.Y. Giants 7
August 2, 1961	Toronto, Canada	St. Louis 36, Toronto Argonauts 7
August 5, 1961	Montreal, Canada	Chicago 34, Montreal Alouettes 16
August 8, 1961	Hamilton, Canada	Hamilton Tiger-Cats 38, Buffalo 21
August 25, 1969	Montreal, Canada	Detroit 22, Boston 9
September 11, 1969	Montreal, Canada	Pittsburgh 17, N.Y. Giants 13
August 16, 1976	Tokyo, Japan	St. Louis 20, San Diego 10
August 5, 1978	Mexico City, Mexico	New Orleans 14, Philadelphia 7
August 6, 1983	London, England	Minnesota 28, St. Louis 10
* August 3, 1986	London, England	Chicago 17, Dallas 6
* August 9, 1987	London, England	L.A. Rams 28, Denver 27
* July 31, 1988	London, England	Miami 27, San Francisco 21
August 14, 1988	Goteborg, Sweden	Minnesota 28, Chicago 21
August 18, 1988	Montreal, Canada	N.Y. Jets 11, Cleveland 7
* August 5, 1989	Tokyo, Japan	L.A. Rams 16, San Francisco 13 (OT)
* August 6, 1989	London, England	Philadelphia 17, Cleveland 13
* August 4, 1990	Tokyo, Japan	Denver 10, Seattle 7
* August 5, 1990	London, England	New Orleans 17, L.A. Raiders 10
* August 9, 1990	Montreal, Canada	Pittsburgh 30, New England 14
* August 11, 1990	Berlin, Germany	L.A. Rams 19, Kansas City 3
* July 28, 1991	London, England	Buffalo 17, Philadelphia 13
* August 3, 1991	Berlin, Germany	San Francisco 21, Chicago 7
* August 3, 1991	Tokyo, Japan	Miami 19, L.A. Raiders 17
* August 1, 1992	Tokyo, Japan	Houston 34, Dallas 23
* August 15, 1992	Berlin, Germany	Miami 31, Denver 27
* August 16, 1992	London, England	San Francisco 17, Washington 15
* July 31, 1993	Tokyo, Japan	New Orleans 28, Philadelphia 16
* August 1, 1993	Barcelona, Spain	San Francisco 21, Pittsburgh 14
* August 7, 1993	Berlin, Germany	Minnesota 20, Buffalo 6
* August 8, 1993	London, England	Dallas 13, Detroit 13 (OT)
August 14, 1993	Toronto, Canada	Cleveland 12, New England 9
* July 31, 1994	Barcelona, Spain	L.A. Raiders 25, Denver 22
* August 6, 1994	Tokyo, Japan	Minnesota 17, Kansas City 9
* August 13, 1994	Berlin, Germany	N.Y. Giants 28, San Diego 20
* August 15, 1994	Mexico City, Mexico	Houston 6, Dallas 0
* August 5, 1995	Tokyo, Japan	Denver 24, San Francisco 10
* August 12, 1995	Toronto, Canada	Buffalo 9, Dallas 7
* July 27, 1996	Tokyo, Japan	San Diego 20, Pittsburgh 10
* August 5, 1996	Monterrey, Mexico	Kansas City 32, Dallas 6
* July 27, 1997	Dublin, Ireland	Pittsburgh 30, Chicago 17
* August 4, 1997	Mexico City, Mexico	Miami 38, Denver 19
* August 16, 1997	Toronto, Canada	Green Bay 35, Buffalo 3
* August 1, 1998	Tokyo, Japan	Green Bay 27, Kansas City 24 (OT)
* August 15, 1998	Vancouver, Canada	San Francisco 24, Seattle 21
* August 17, 1998	Mexico City, Mexico	New England 21, Dallas 3
* August 7, 1999	Sydney, Australia	Denver 20, San Diego 17
* August 5, 2000	Tokyo, Japan	Atlanta 20, Dallas 9
* August 19, 2000	Mexico City, Mexico	Indianapolis 24, Pittsburgh 23
* August 27, 2001	Mexico City, Mexico	Dallas 21, Oakland 6
* August 3, 2002	Osaka, Japan	Washington 38, San Francisco 7
* August 2, 2003	Tokyo, Japan	Tampa Bay 30, N.Y. Jets 14
* August 6, 2005	Tokyo, Japan	Atlanta 27, Indianapolis 21
August 14, 2008	Toronto, Canada	Buffalo 34, Pittsburgh 21

* *American Bowl Game*

WALTER PAYTON NFL MAN OF THE YEAR

The Walter Payton NFL Man of the Year Award is the only NFL award that recognizes a player for his community service activities as well as his excellence on the field. Renamed in 1999 for the legendary Chicago Bears Pro Football Hall of Fame running back, the Walter Payton NFL Man of the Year Award has been given annually since 1970.

YEAR	PLAYER	POS.	TEAM
1970	Johnny Unitas	QB	Baltimore Colts
1971	John Hadl	QB	San Diego Chargers
1972	Willie Lanier	LB	Kansas City Chiefs
1973	Len Dawson	QB	Kansas City Chiefs
1974	George Blanda	QB	Oakland Raiders
1975	Ken Anderson	QB	Cincinnati Bengals
1976	Franco Harris	RB	Pittsburgh Steelers
1977	Walter Payton	RB	Chicago Bears
1978	Roger Staubach	QB	Dallas Cowboys
1979	Joe Greene	DT	Pittsburgh Steelers
1980	Harold Carmichael	WR	Philadelphia Eagles
1981	Lynn Swann	WR	Pittsburgh Steelers
1982	Joe Theismann	QB	Washington Redskins
1983	Rolf Benirschke	K	San Diego Chargers
1984	Marty Lyons	T	New York Jets
1985	Dwight Stephenson	C	Miami Dolphins
1986	Reggie Williams	LB	Cincinnati Bengals
1987	Dave Duerson	S	Chicago Bears
1988	Steve Largent	WR	Seattle Seahawks
1989	Warren Moon	QB	Houston Oilers
1990	Mike Singletary	LB	Chicago Bears
1991	Anthony Muñoz	T	Cincinnati Bengals
1992	John Elway	QB	Denver Broncos
1993	Derrick Thomas	LB	Kansas City Chiefs
1994	Junior Seau	LB	San Diego Chargers
1995	Boomer Esiason	QB	New York Jets
1996	Darrell Green	CB	Washington Redskins
1997	Troy Aikman	QB	Dallas Cowboys
1998	Dan Marino	QB	Miami Dolphins
1999	Cris Carter	WR	Minnesota Vikings
2000*	Derrick Brooks	LB	Tampa Bay Buccaneers
	Jim Flanigan	DT	Chicago Bears
2001	Jerome Bettis	RB	Pittsburgh Steelers
2002	Troy Vincent	CB	Philadelphia Eagles
2003	Will Shields	G	Kansas City Chiefs
2004	Warrick Dunn	RB	Atlanta Falcons
2005	Peyton Manning	QB	Indianapolis Colts
2006*	Drew Brees	QB	New Orleans Saints
	LaDainian Tomlinson	RB	San Diego Chargers
2007	Jason Taylor	DE	Miami Dolphins
2008	Kurt Warner	QB	Arizona Cardinals
2009	Brian Waters	G	Kansas City Chiefs

* The award was shared in 2000 and 2006.

INTERCONFERENCE GAMES

AFC VS. NFC (REGULAR SEASON), 1970-2009

	Balt	Buff	Cin	Cle	Den	Hou	Ind	Jax	KC	Mia
1970		0-3	1-2	0-3	2-2		3-0		0-2-1	2-1
1971		0-3	1-2	2-1	1-3		2-1		2-1	3-0
1972		2-0-1	2-1	1-2	1-3		0-3		2-1	3-0
1973		2-1	2-1	1-2	0-3-1		2-1		1-1-1	3-0
1974		2-1	2-1	1-2	2-2		1-2		1-2	2-1
1975		1-2	3-0	1-3	2-1		2-1		2-1	3-0
1976		0-2	2-0	2-0	2-0		0-2		1-1	0-2
1977		1-1	2-1	1-1	1-1		1-1		1-1	2-0
1978		1-1	2-2	4-0	2-2		2-2		0-2	3-1
1979		2-2	2-2	3-1	3-1		1-1		0-2	4-0
1980		3-1	2-2	3-1	3-1		1-1		2-0	4-0
1981		1-3	2-2	3-1	3-1		0-4		2-2	3-1
1982		1-2	1-0	0-2	2-1		0-1-1		0-3	1-1
1983		1-3	3-1	2-2	0-2		2-0		2-2	3-1
1984		1-3	2-2	1-3	3-1		0-4		1-1	4-0
1985		0-2	2-2	1-3	3-1		3-1		2-2	3-1
1986		1-1	3-1	2-2	3-1		1-3		1-1	2-2
1987		1-2	1-2	2-2	2-1-1		1-0		1-2	3-0
1988		2-2	4-0	4-0	3-1		2-2		0-2	3-1
1989		1-3	2-2	3-1	2-2		1-3		2-0	2-0
1990		3-1	1-3	1-3	1-3		2-2		4-0	2-2
1991		3-1	1-3	0-4	2-0		0-4		2-2	3-1
1992		4-0	1-3	2-2	1-3		2-0		2-2	2-2
1993		4-0	2-2	3-1	1-3		0-4		2-2	3-1
1994		1-3	1-3	3-1	1-3		0-2		3-1	2-2
1995		3-1	2-2	1-3	2-2		2-2	0-4	3-1	2-2
1996	2-2	4-0	2-2		3-1		3-1	2-2	4-0	1-3
1997	2-1-1	1-3	2-2		3-1		1-3	2-2	4-0	1-3
1998	1-3	3-1	1-3		3-1		0-4	3-1	3-1	3-1
1999	2-1	3-1	1-2	1-2	2-2		4-0	4-0	2-2	2-2
2000	2-1	2-2	1-2	0-3	3-1		2-2	2-2	2-2	2-2
2001	2-2	1-3	1-2	1-2	3-1		1-3	1-2	1-3	2-2
2002	0-4	3-1	1-3	2-2	4-0	2-2	2-2	2-2	2-2	2-2
2003	3-1	2-2	2-2	2-2	1-3	2-2	3-1	2-2	3-1	3-1
2004	3-1	4-0	4-0	1-3	3-1	1-3	4-0	3-1	1-3	2-2
2005	2-2	0-4	4-0	2-2	3-1	1-3	3-1	3-1	1-3	2-2
2006	3-1	2-2	2-2	1-3	1-3	0-4	3-1	3-1	4-0	3-1
2007	3-1	1-3	1-3	3-1	1-3	3-1	4-0	3-1	1-3	0-4
2008	3-1	2-2	1-2-1	1-3	3-1	3-1	2-2	2-2	0-4	3-1
2009	2-2	2-2	3-1	0-4	2-2	3-1	4-0	1-3	1-3	2-2
Total	**30-23-1**	**71-70-1**	**75-68-1**	**61-73**	**83-65-2**	**15-17**	**67-67-1**	**33-26**	**68-64-2**	**95-50**

	NE	NYJ	Oak	Pitt	SD	Sea	TB	Tenn	TOTALS
1970	0-3	2-1	1-2	0-3	1-2			0-3	12-27-1
1971	0-3	0-3	1-1-1	1-2	2-1			0-2-1	15-23-2
1972	3-0	1-2	3-0	2-1	0-3			0-3	20-19-1
1973	2-1	0-3	2-1	3-0	1-2			0-3	19-19-2
1974	3-0	2-1	3-0	3-0	1-2			0-3	23-17
1975	1-2	0-3	3-0	2-1	0-3			3-0	23-17
1976	1-1	0-2	3-0	1-1	2-0		0-1	2-0	16-12
1977	2-0	1-1	1-1	2-0	1-1	1-0		2-0	19-9
1978	2-2	1-3	4-0	3-1	2-2	3-1		2-2	31-21
1979	3-1	3-1	4-0	3-1	3-1	3-1		2-2	36-16
1980	1-3	1-3	2-2	4-0	2-2	1-3		4-0	33-19
1981	0-4	2-0	2-2	3-1	2-2	0-2		1-3	24-28
1982	0-1	4-0	3-0	1-0	1-0	1-0		0-3	15-14-1
1983	2-2	3-1	2-2	2-2	2-2	1-3		1-3	26-26
1984	0-4	0-2	3-1	3-1	4-0	4-0		0-4	26-26
1985	3-1	2-2	3-1	1-3	1-1	2-2		1-3	27-25
1986	3-1	2-2	1-3	2-2	0-4	3-1		2-2	26-26
1987	0-3	0-4	2-2	2-2	2-0	4-0		2-2	23-22-1
1988	2-2	2-0	1-3	1-3	2-2	1-3		3-1	30-22
1989	0-4	1-3	2-2	3-1	2-2	0-4		3-1	24-28
1990	0-4	2-0	3-1	3-1	1-1	2-2		1-3	26-26
1991	1-1	2-2	2-2	0-4	1-3	1-3		1-3	19-33
1992	0-4	0-4	2-2	1-3	2-0	0-4		3-1	22-30
1993	1-1	2-2	3-1	2-2	2-2	0-2		2-2	27-25
1994	4-0	1-3	3-1	2-2	2-2	2-0		0-4	25-27
1995	0-4	0-4	3-1	2-2	3-1	3-1		1-3	27-33
1996	2-2	1-3	1-3	2-2	1-3	2-2		2-2	32-28
1997	1-3	3-1	2-2	2-2	1-3	2-2		4-0	31-28-1
1998	2-2	2-2	3-1	2-2	1-3	3-1		1-3	31-29
1999	3-1	2-2	3-1	3-0	1-3	2-2		3-1	38-22
2000	0-4	3-1	4-0	1-2	0-4	2-2		4-0	30-30
2001	3-1	2-2	3-1	3-0	2-2	1-3		3-1	30-30
2002	3-1	3-1	2-2	2-1-1	2-2			2-2	34-29-1
2003	3-1	0-4	1-3	1-3	2-2			4-0	34-30
2004	4-0	3-1	2-2	4-0	3-1			2-2	44-20
2005	3-1	1-3	2-2	4-0	2-2			1-3	34-30
2006	4-0	3-1	1-3	3-1	4-0			3-1	40-24
2007	4-0	0-4	0-4	3-1	2-2			3-1	32-32
2008	4-0	2-2	1-3	2-2	1-3			4-0	34-29-1
2009	3-1	2-2	1-3	3-1	4-0			4-0	37-27
Total	**73-69**	**61-81**	**88-61-1**	**87-56-1**	**68-71**	**44-44**	**0-1**	**76-72-1**	**1095-978-11**

NFC VS. AFC (REGULAR SEASON), 1970-2009

	Ariz	Atl	Car	Chi	Dall	Det	GB	Minn	NO
1970	2-0-1	1-2		1-2	3-0	3-0	2-1	2-1	0-3
1971	2-1	3-0		1-2	3-0	4-0	2-1	2-1	0-1-2
1972	1-2	2-2		1-2	3-0	2-0-1	2-1	1-2	0-3
1973	0-2-1	2-1		2-2	2-1	0-3	1-1-1	2-1	1-2
1974	2-1	0-3		0-3	2-1	1-2	2-1	2-1	0-3
1975	2-1	1-2		0-3	2-1	1-2	0-3	4-0	0-3
1976	1-1	0-2		0-2	2-0	2-0	0-2	2-0	1-2
1977	0-2	0-2		1-1	1-1	2-0	0-3	1-1	0-2
1978	0-4	1-3		0-4	3-1	2-2	2-2	1-3	1-3
1979	1-3	1-3		2-2	1-3	0-4	1-3	1-3	0-4
1980	1-1	2-2		0-4	3-1	0-2	1-3	1-3	1-3
1981	3-1	1-3		4-0	4-0	2-2	1-1	1-3	2-2
1982		1-1		1-1	2-1	0-1	1-1-1	1-3	1-0
1983	3-1	3-1		1-1	2-2	1-3	2-2	4-0	1-3
1984	3-1	1-3		2-2	2-2	0-4	0-4	0-4	3-1
1985	2-2	0-4		3-1	3-1	2-2	0-4	2-0	0-4
1986	1-1	1-3		4-0	1-3	1-3	1-3	1-3	1-3
1987	0-1	0-4		2-2	2-1	0-4	1-2-1	2-1	4-0
1988	1-3	1-3		3-1	0-4	1-1	1-3	2-2	4-0
1989	1-3	2-2		2-2	0-2	1-3	0-2	2-2	4-0
1990	2-2	2-2		2-2	1-1	1-3	1-3	2-2	2-2
1991	1-1	3-1		2-2	3-1	4-0	1-3	0-2	3-1
1992	0-2	2-2		1-3	4-0	2-2	3-1	3-1	3-1
1993	1-1	1-3		2-2	2-2	2-0	3-1	2-2	2-2
1994	3-1	1-3		3-1	3-1	2-2	1-3	2-2	1-3
1995	1-3	2-2	3-1	2-2	4-0	3-1	4-0	3-1	4-0
1996	0-4	0-4	3-1	2-2	2-2	1-3	3-1	1-3	1-3
1997	1-3	2-2	2-2	2-2	2-2	2-2	3-1	3-1	2-2
1998	1-3	3-1	1-3	2-2	1-3	1-3	3-1	4-0	1-3
1999	0-4	0-4	2-2	2-2	1-3	1-3	2-2	2-2	0-4
2000	1-3	1-3	2-2	2-2	1-3	2-2	1-3	3-1	1-3
2001	3-1	1-3	0-4	3-1	0-4	0-4	3-1	1-3	2-2
2002	0-4	2-1-1	3-1	1-3	2-2	0-4	3-1	1-3	2-2
2003	1-3	1-3	2-2	3-1	2-2	1-3	3-1	2-2	1-3
2004	1-3	3-1	1-3	1-3	1-3	1-3	1-3	3-1	2-2
2005	1-3	3-1	3-1	1-3	2-2	2-2	0-4	1-3	2-2
2006	0-4	2-2	2-2	2-2	3-1	1-3	1-3	0-4	1-3
2007	3-1	1-3	0-4	3-1	3-1	3-1	4-0	2-2	1-3
2008	2-2	3-1	4-0	2-2	2-2	0-4	1-3	2-2	3-1
2009	2-2	3-1	0-4	2-2	2-2	1-3	2-2	3-1	4-0
Total	**50-81-2**	**59-89-1**	**28-32**	**70-77**	**82-62**	**55-86-1**	**63-80-3**	**74-72**	**62-84-2**

	NYG	Phil	StL	SF	Sea	TB	Wash	TOTALS
1970	3-0	2-1	2-1	4-0			2-1	27-12-1
1971	1-2	1-2	1-2	2-1			1-2	23-15-2
1972	1-2	2-1	1-2	2-1			1-2	19-20-1
1973	1-2	2-1	3-0	1-2			2-1	19-19-2
1974	1-2	2-1	3-1	0-3			2-1	17-23
1975	2-1	0-3	3-0	1-2			1-2	17-23
1976	0-2	0-2	1-1	1-1	1-0		1-1	12-16
1977	0-2	1-1	2-0	0-2		0-1	1-1	9-19
1978	1-1	3-1	2-2	1-3		2-0	2-2	21-31
1979	1-1	2-2	2-2	0-4		2-0	2-2	16-36
1980	1-3	3-1	2-2	2-2		1-3	1-3	19-33
1981	1-1	3-1	1-3	3-1		0-4	2-2	28-24
1982	1-0	2-1	1-2	1-3		2-1		14-15-1
1983	0-4	1-1	1-3	2-2		1-3	4-0	26-26
1984	2-0	3-1	3-1	3-1		1-1	3-1	26-26
1985	2-2	1-1	3-1	3-1		0-4	4-0	25-27
1986	3-1	2-2	2-2	4-0		1-1	3-1	26-26
1987	2-1	3-1	1-2	3-1		0-2	2-1	22-23-1
1988	1-1	2-2	2-2	2-2		1-3	1-3	22-30
1989	4-0	3-1	3-1	4-0		0-4	2-2	28-24
1990	3-1	1-3	2-2	4-0		0-2	3-1	26-26
1991	3-1	4-0	1-3	3-1		1-3	4-0	33-19
1992	2-2	3-1	2-2	3-1		0-2	2-2	30-22
1993	2-2	2-2	2-2	2-2		1-3	1-3	25-27
1994	3-1	1-3	2-2	3-1		1-1	1-1	27-25
1995	0-4	1-3	1-3	3-1		2-2	0-4	33-27
1996	2-2	2-2	2-2	4-0		2-2	3-1	28-32
1997	1-3	2-1-1	0-4	2-2		3-1	1-3	28-31-1
1998	3-1	0-4	3-1	2-2		2-2	2-2	29-31
1999	2-2	1-3	3-1	1-3		3-1	2-2	22-38
2000	3-1	3-1	3-1	2-2		3-1	2-2	30-30
2001	2-2	3-1	4-0	4-0		2-2	2-2	30-30
2002	2-2	1-3	2-2	2-2	2-2	3-1	3-1	29-34-1
2003	1-3	3-1	4-0	1-3	2-2	1-3	2-2	30-34
2004	1-3	2-2	1-3	0-4	1-3	1-3	0-4	20-44
2005	3-1	3-1	3-1	1-3	3-1	2-2	0-4	30-34
2006	1-3	1-3	2-2	2-2	2-2	2-2	2-2	24-40
2007	3-1	3-1	0-4	1-3	2-2	1-3	2-2	32-32
2008	3-1	2-1-1	0-4	2-2	1-3	1-3	1-3	29-34-1
2009	2-2	2-2	0-4	1-3	1-3	0-4	2-2	27-37
Total	**70-66**	**78-65-2**	**76-73**	**82-69**	**15-18**	**42-70**	**72-71**	**978-1095-11**

INTERCONFERENCE GAMES

2009 INTERCONFERENCE GAMES

(Home Team in capital letters)

AFC 37, NFC 27

AFC Victories

Cincinnati 31, GREEN BAY 24
BUFFALO 33, Tampa Bay 20
NEW ENGLAND 26, Atlanta 10
Indianapolis 31, ARIZONA 10
INDIANAPOLIS 34, Seattle 17
DENVER 17, Dallas 10
Pittsburgh 28, DETROIT 20
JACKSONVILLE 23, St. Louis 20 (OT)
Kansas City 14, WASHINGTON 6
OAKLAND 13, Philadelphia 9
HOUSTON 24, San Francisco 21
PITTSBURGH 27, Minnesota 17
Indianapolis 42, ST. LOUIS 6
New England 35, TAMPA BAY 7
Buffalo 20, CAROLINA 9
CINCINNATI 45, Chicago 10
INDIANAPOLIS 18, San Francisco 14
San Diego 21, N.Y. GIANTS 20
Tennessee 34, SAN FRANCISCO 27
MIAMI 25, Tampa Bay 23
SAN DIEGO 31, Philadelphia 23
Miami 24, CAROLINA 17
DENVER 26, N.Y. Giants 6
N.Y. JETS 17, Carolina 6
TENNESSEE 20, Arizona 17
CINCINNATI 23, Detroit 13
BALTIMORE 48, Detroit 3
HOUSTON 34, Seattle 7
NEW ENGLAND 20, Carolina 10
N.Y. Jets 26, TAMPA BAY 3
TENNESSEE 47, St. Louis 7
San Diego 20, DALLAS 17
Houston 16, ST. LOUIS 13
BALTIMORE 31, Chicago 7
PITTSBURGH 37, Green Bay 36
SAN DIEGO 23, Washington 20
Tennessee 17, SEATTLE 13

NFC Victories

ATLANTA 19, Miami 7
Minnesota 34, CLEVELAND 20
Arizona 31, JACKSONVILLE 17
CHICAGO 17, Pittsburgh 14
PHILADELPHIA 34, Kansas City 14
New Orleans 27, BUFFALO 7
N.Y. Giants 27, KANSAS CITY 16
NEW ORLEANS 24, N.Y. Jets 10
Dallas 26, KANSAS CITY 20 (OT)
N.Y. GIANTS 44, Oakland 7
ARIZONA 28, Houston 21
SEATTLE 41, Jacksonville 0
MINNESOTA 33, Baltimore 31
Green Bay 31, CLEVELAND 3
New Orleans 46, MIAMI 34
CHICAGO 30, Cleveland 6
WASHINGTON 27, Denver 17
DETROIT 38, Cleveland 37
DALLAS 24, Oakland 7
SAN FRANCISCO 20, Jacksonville 3
NEW ORLEANS 38, New England 17
GREEN BAY 27, Baltimore 14
MINNESOTA 30, Cincinnati 10
Washington 34, OAKLAND 13
Atlanta 10, N.Y. JETS 7
ATLANTA 31, Buffalo 3
PHILADELPHIA 30, Denver 27

REGULAR SEASON INTERCONFERENCE RECORDS, 1970-2009

AMERICAN FOOTBALL CONFERENCE

East	**W**	**L**	**T**	**Pct.**
Miami	95	50	0	.655
New England	73	69	0	.514
Buffalo	71	70	1	.504
New York Jets	61	81	0	.430
North	**W**	**L**	**T**	**Pct.**
Pittsburgh	87	56	1	.608
Baltimore	30	23	1	.565
Cincinnati	75	68	1	.524
Cleveland	61	73	0	.455
South	**W**	**L**	**T**	**Pct.**
Jacksonville	33	26	0	.559
Tennessee	76	72	1	.514
Indianapolis	67	67	1	.500
Houston	15	17	0	.469
West	**W**	**L**	**T**	**Pct.**
Oakland	88	61	1	.591
Denver	83	65	2	.560
Kansas City	68	64	2	.515
San Diego	68	71	0	.489

NATIONAL FOOTBALL CONFERENCE

East	**W**	**L**	**T**	**Pct.**
Dallas	82	62	0	.569
Philadelphia	78	65	2	.545
New York Giants	70	66	0	.515
Washington	72	71	0	.503
North	**W**	**L**	**T**	**Pct.**
Minnesota	74	72	0	.507
Chicago	70	77	0	.476
Green Bay	63	80	3	.442
Detroit	55	86	1	.391
South	**W**	**L**	**T**	**Pct.**
Carolina	28	32	0	.467
New Orleans	62	84	2	.425
Atlanta	59	89	1	.399
Tampa Bay*	42	71	0	.372
West	**W**	**L**	**T**	**Pct.**
San Francisco	82	69	0	.543
St. Louis	76	73	0	.510
Seattle* #	59	62	0	.488
Arizona	50	81	2	.383

* Records include one game played between Seattle and Tampa Bay, won by the Seahawks 13-10, in their inaugural season (1976) when Seattle competed in the NFC and Tampa Bay in the AFC.

\# Seattle was a member of the AFC from 1977-2001.

From 1970-71, tie games were not included in winning percentage.

INTERCONFERENCE VICTORIES, 1970-2009

REGULAR SEASON

	AFC	NFC	Tie
1970	12	27	1
1971	15	23	2
1972	20	19	1
1973	19	19	2
1974	23	17	0
1975	23	17	0
1976	16	12	0
1977	19	9	0
1978	31	21	0
1979	36	16	0
1980	33	19	0
1981	24	28	0
1982	15	14	1
1983	26	26	0
1984	26	26	0
1985	27	25	0
1986	26	26	0
1987	23	22	1
1988	30	22	0
1989	24	28	0
1990	26	26	0
1991	19	33	0
1992	22	30	0
1993	27	25	0
1994	25	27	0
1995	27	33	0
1996	32	28	0
1997	31	28	1
1998	31	29	0
1999	38	22	0
2000	30	30	0
2001	30	30	0
2002	34	29	1
2003	34	30	0
2004	44	20	0
2005	34	30	0
2006	40	24	0
2007	32	32	0
2008	34	29	1
2009	37	27	0
Total	1,095	978	11

PRESEASON

	AFC	NFC	Tie
1970	21	28	1
1971	28	28	3
1972	27	25	4
1973	23	35	2
1974	35	25	0
1975	30	26	1
1976	30	31	0
1977	38	25	0
1978	20	19	0
1979	25	18	0
1980	22	20	1
1981	18	19	0
1982	25	16	0
1983	15	24	0
1984	16	19	0
1985	10	22	1
1986	22	17	0
1987	22	22	0
1988	23	16	1
1989	16	27	0
1990	15	29	0
1991	19	27	0
1992	30	22	0
1993	17	22	0
1994	22	16	0
1995	19	26	0
1996	27	19	0
1997	26	17	0
1998	34	16	0
1999	22	25	0
2000	34	17	0
2001	28	23	0
2002	25	24	0
2003	25	21	0
2004	21	18	0
2005	21	29	0
2006	27	24	0
2007	27	24	0
2008	21	27	0
2009	24	26	0
Total	950	914	14

NFL ALL-DECADE TEAM – 2000s

Offense

Quarterback	Tom Brady
Quarterback	Peyton Manning
Running Back	Shaun Alexander
Running Back	Jamal Lewis
Running Back	Edgerrin James
Running Back	LaDainian Tomlinson
Fullback	Lorenzo Neal
Wide Receiver	Marvin Harrison
Wide Receiver	Torry Holt
Wide Receiver	Randy Moss
Wide Receiver	Terrell Owens
Tight End	Antonio Gates
Tight End	Tony Gonzalez
Tackle	Walter Jones
Tackle	Jonathan Ogden
Tackle	Orlando Pace
Tackle	William Roaf
Guard	Larry Allen
Guard	Alan Faneca
Guard	Steve Hutchinson
Guard	Will Shields
Center	Olin Kreutz
Center	Kevin Mawae

Head Coach	Bill Belichick
Head Coach	Tony Dungy

Specialists

Punter	Shane Lechler
Punter	Brian Moorman
Kicker	David Akers
Kicker	Adam Vinatieri
Punt Returner	Dante Hall
Punt Returner	Devin Hester
Kick Returner	Joshua Cribbs
Kick Returner	Dante Hall

Defense

Defensive End	Dwight Freeney
Defensive End	Julius Peppers
Defensive End	Michael Strahan
Defensive End	Jason Taylor
Defensive Tackle	La'Roi Glover
Defensive Tackle	Warren Sapp
Defensive Tackle	Richard Seymour
Defensive Tackle	Kevin Williams
Linebacker	Derrick Brooks
Linebacker	Ray Lewis
Linebacker	Joey Porter
Linebacker	Zach Thomas
Linebacker	Brian Urlacher
Linebacker	DeMarcus Ware
Cornerback	Ronde Barber
Cornerback	Champ Bailey
Cornerback	Ty Law
Cornerback	Charles Woodson
Safety	Brian Dawkins
Safety	Troy Polamalu
Safety	Ed Reed
Safety	Darren Sharper

The NFL All-Decade teams are chosen every 10 years by the Pro Football Hall of Fame Selection Committee members. For a complete listing and expanded summary of each of the nine NFL All-Decade teams dating back to the 1920s, please visit http://www.profootballhof.com/story/2010/1/27/nfls-all-decade-teams/.

NUMBER-ONE DRAFT CHOICES

NUMBER-ONE DRAFT CHOICES

Season	Date	Team	Player	Position	College
2010	April 22-24	St. Louis	Sam Bradford	QB	Oklahoma
2009	April 25-26	Detroit	Matthew Stafford	QB	Georgia
2008	April 26-27	Miami	Jake Long	T	Michigan
2007	April 28-29	Oakland	JaMarcus Russell	QB	Louisiana State
2006	April 29-30	Houston	Mario Williams	DE	North Carolina State
2005	April 23-24	San Francisco	Alex Smith	QB	Utah
2004	April 24-25	San Diego	Eli Manning	QB	Mississippi
2003	April 26-27	Cincinnati	Carson Palmer	QB	Southern California
2002	April 20-21	Houston	David Carr	QB	Fresno State
2001	April 21-22	Atlanta	Michael Vick	QB	Virginia Tech
2000	April 15-16	Cleveland	Courtney Brown	DE	Penn State
1999	April 17-18	Cleveland	Tim Couch	QB	Kentucky
1998	April 18-19	Indianapolis	Peyton Manning	QB	Tennessee
1997	April 19-20	St. Louis	Orlando Pace	T	Ohio State
1996	April 20-21	New York Jets	Keyshawn Johnson	WR	Southern California
1995	April 22-23	Cincinnati	Ki-Jana Carter	RB	Penn State
1994	April 24-25	Cincinnati	Dan Wilkinson	DT	Ohio State
1993	April 25-26	New England	Drew Bledsoe	QB	Washington State
1992	April 26-27	Indianapolis	Steve Emtman	DT	Washington
1991	April 21-22	Dallas	Russell Maryland	DT	Miami
1990	April 22-23	Indianapolis	Jeff George	QB	Illinois
1989	April 23-24	Dallas	Troy Aikman	QB	UCLA
1988	April 24-25	Atlanta	Aundray Bruce	LB	Auburn
1987	April 28-29	Tampa Bay	Vinny Testaverde	QB	Miami
1986	April 29-30	Tampa Bay	Bo Jackson	RB	Auburn
1985	April 30-May 1	Buffalo	Bruce Smith	DE	Virginia Tech
1984	May 1-2	New England	Irving Fryar	WR	Nebraska
1983	April 26-27	Baltimore	John Elway	QB	Stanford
1982	April 27-28	New England	Kenneth Sims	DT	Texas
1981	April 28-29	New Orleans	George Rogers	RB	South Carolina
1980	April 29-30	Detroit	Billy Sims	RB	Oklahoma
1979	May 3-4	Buffalo	Tom Cousineau	LB	Ohio State
1978	May 2-3	Houston	Earl Campbell	RB	Texas
1977	May 3-4	Tampa Bay	Ricky Bell	RB	Southern California
1976	April 8-9	Tampa Bay	Lee Roy Selmon	DE	Oklahoma
1975	January 28-29	Atlanta	Steve Bartkowski	QB	California
1974	January 29-30	Dallas	Ed Jones	DE	Tennessee State
1973	January 30-31	Houston	John Matuszak	DE	Tampa
1972	February 1-2	Buffalo	Walt Patulski	DE	Notre Dame
1971	January 28-29	New England	Jim Plunkett	QB	Stanford
1970	January 27-28	Pittsburgh	Terry Bradshaw	QB	Louisiana Tech
1969	January 28-29	Buffalo (AFL)	O.J. Simpson	RB	Southern California
1968	January 30-31	Minnesota	Ron Yary	T	Southern California
1967	March 14	Baltimore	Bubba Smith	DT	Michigan State
1966	November 27, 1965	Atlanta	Tommy Nobis	LB	Texas
	November 28, 1965	Miami (AFL)	Jim Grabowski	RB	Illinois
1965	November 28, 1964	New York Giants	Tucker Frederickson	RB	Auburn
	November 28, 1964	Houston (AFL)	Lawrence Elkins	E	Baylor
1964	December 2, 1963	San Francisco	Dave Parks	E	Texas Tech
	November 30, 1963	Boston (AFL)	Jack Concannon	QB	Boston College
1963	December 3, 1962	Los Angeles	Terry Baker	QB	Oregon State
	December 1, 1962	Kansas City (AFL)	Buck Buchanan	DT	Grambling
1962	December 4, 1961	Washington	Ernie Davis	RB	Syracuse
	December 2, 1961	Oakland (AFL)	Roman Gabriel	QB	North Carolina State
1961	December 27-28, 1960	Minnesota	Tommy Mason	RB	Tulane
	November 23, 1960	Buffalo (AFL)	Ken Rice	G	Auburn
1960	Secret Draft	Los Angeles	Billy Cannon	RB	Louisiana State
	November 22, December 2, 1959	(AFL had no formal first pick)			
1959	December 2, 1958	Green Bay	Randy Duncan	QB	Iowa
1958	December 2, 1957	Chicago Cardinals	King Hill	QB	Rice
1957	November 27, 1956	Green Bay	Paul Hornung	HB	Notre Dame

NUMBER-ONE DRAFT CHOICES

Season	Date	Team	Player	Position	College
1956	November 29, 1955	Pittsburgh	Gary Glick	DB	Colorado A&M
1955	January 27-28	Baltimore	George Shaw	QB	Oregon
1954	January 28	Cleveland	Bobby Garrett	QB	Stanford
1953	January 22	San Francisco	Harry Babcock	E	Georgia
1952	January 17	Los Angeles	Bill Wade	QB	Vanderbilt
1951	January 18-19	New York Giants	Kyle Rote	HB	Southern Methodist
1950	January 21-22	Detroit	Leon Hart	E	Notre Dame
1949	December 21, 1948	Philadelphia	Chuck Bednarik	C	Pennsylvania
1948	December 19, 1947	Washington	Harry Gilmer	QB	Alabama
1947	December 16, 1946	Chicago Bears	Bob Fenimore	HB	Oklahoma A&M
1946	January 14	Boston	Frank Dancewicz	QB	Notre Dame
1945	April 6	Chicago Cardinals	Charley Trippi	HB	Georgia
1944	April 19	Boston	Angelo Bertelli	QB	Notre Dame
1943	April 8	Detroit	Frank Sinkwich	HB	Georgia
1942	December 22, 1941	Pittsburgh	Bill Dudley	HB	Virginia
1941	December 10, 1940	Chicago Bears	Tom Harmon	HB	Michigan
1940	December 9, 1939	Chicago Cardinals	George Cafego	HB	Tennessee
1939	December 8, 1938	Chicago Cardinals	Ki Aldrich	C	Texas Christian
1938	December 12, 1937	Cleveland	Corbett Davis	FB	Indiana
1937	December 12, 1936	Philadelphia	Sam Francis	FB	Nebraska
1936	February 8	Philadelphia	Jay Berwanger	HB	Chicago

Note: From 1947 through 1958, the first selection in the draft was a Bonus pick, awarded to the winner of a random draw. That club, in turn, forfeited its last-round draft choice. The winner of the Bonus choice was eliminated from future draws. The system was abolished after 1958, by which time all clubs had received a Bonus choice.

NUMBER-ONE DRAFT CHOICES BY POSITION

Quarterbacks:	29
Running Backs:	23
Defensive Linemen:	13
Offensive Linemen:	6
Wide Receivers:	6
Linebackers:	3
Defensive Backs:	1

FIRST-ROUND SELECTIONS

If club had no first-round selection, first player drafted is listed with round in parentheses.

ARIZONA CARDINALS

Year Player, College, Position

1936 Jim Lawrence, Texas Christian, B
1937 Ray Buivid, Marquette, B
1938 Jack Robbins, Arkansas, B
1939 Charles (Ki) Aldrich, TCU, C
1940 George Cafego, Tennessee, B
1941 John Kimbrough, Texas A&M, B
1942 Steve Lach, Duke, B
1943 Glenn Dobbs, Tulsa, B
1944 Pat Harder, Wisconsin, B
1945 Charley Trippi, Georgia, B
1946 Dub Jones, Louisiana State, B
1947 DeWitt (Tex) Coulter, Army, T
1948 Jim Spavital, Oklahoma A&M, B
1949 Bill Fischer, Notre Dame, G
1950 Jack Jennings, Ohio State, T (2)
1951 Jerry Groom, Notre Dame, C
1952 Ollie Matson, San Francisco, B
1953 Johnny Olszewski, California, B
1954 Lamar McHan, Arkansas, B
1955 Max Boydston, Oklahoma, E
1956 Joe Childress, Auburn, B
1957 Jerry Tubbs, Oklahoma, C
1958 King Hill, Rice, B
John David Crow, Texas A&M, B
1959 Bill Stacy, Mississippi State, B
1960 George Izo, Notre Dame, QB
1961 Ken Rice, Auburn, T
1962 Fate Echols, Northwestern, DT
Irv Goode, Kentucky, C
1963 Jerry Stovall, Louisiana State, S
Don Brumm, Purdue, DE
1964 Ken Kortas, Louisville, DT
1965 Joe Namath, Alabama, QB
1966 Carl McAdams, Oklahoma, LB
1967 Dave Williams, Washington, WR
1968 MacArthur Lane, Utah State, RB
1969 Roger Wehrli, Missouri, DB
1970 Larry Stegent, Texas A&M, RB
1971 Norm Thompson, Utah, CB
1972 Bobby Moore, Oregon, RB-WR
1973 Dave Butz, Purdue, DT
1974 J.V. Cain, Colorado, TE
1975 Tim Gray, Texas A&M, DB
1976 Mike Dawson, Arizona, DT
1977 Steve Pisarkiewicz, Missouri, QB
1978 Steve Little, Arkansas, K
Ken Greene, Washington State, DB
1979 Ottis Anderson, Miami, RB
1980 Curtis Greer, Michigan, DE
1981 E.J. Junior, Alabama, LB
1982 Luis Sharpe, UCLA, T
1983 Leonard Smith, McNeese St., DB
1984 Clyde Duncan, Tennessee, WR
1985 Freddie Joe Nunn, Mississippi, LB
1986 Anthony Bell, Michigan State, LB
1987 Kelly Stouffer, Colorado State, QB
1988 Ken Harvey, California, LB
1989 Eric Hill, Louisiana State, LB
Joe Wolf, Boston College, G
1990 Anthony Thompson, Indiana, RB (2)
1991 Eric Swann, No College, DE
1992 Tony Sacca, Penn State, QB (2)
1993 Garrison Hearst, Georgia, RB
Ernest Dye, South Carolina, T
1994 Jamir Miller, UCLA, LB
1995 Frank Sanders, Auburn, WR (2)
1996 Simeon Rice, Illinois, DE
1997 Tom Knight, Iowa, DB
1998 Andre Wadsworth, Florida St., DE
1999 David Boston, Ohio State, WR
L.J. Shelton, Eastern Michigan, T
2000 Thomas Jones, Virginia, RB
2001 Leonard Davis, Texas, T
2002 Wendell Bryant, Wisconsin, DT
2003 Bryant Johnson, Penn State, WR
Calvin Pace, Wake Forest, DE
2004 Larry Fitzgerald, Pittsburgh, WR
2005 Antrel Rolle, Miami, DB
2006 Matt Leinart, So. California, QB
2007 Levi Brown, Penn State, T
2008 Dominique Rodgers-Cromartie, Tenn. St., DB
2009 Beanie Wells, Ohio State, RB
2010 Dan Williams, Tennessee, DT

ATLANTA FALCONS

Year Player, College, Position

1966 Tommy Nobis, Texas, LB
Randy Johnson, Texas A&I, QB
1967 Leo Carroll, San Diego St., DE (2)
1968 Claude Humphrey, Tennessee St., DE
1969 George Kunz, Notre Dame, T
1970 John Small, Citadel, LB
1971 Joe Profit, Northeast Louisiana, RB
1972 Clarence Ellis, Notre Dame, DB
1973 Greg Marx, Notre Dame, DT (2)
1974 Gerald Tinker, Kent State, WR (2)
1975 Steve Bartkowski, California, QB
1976 Bubba Bean, Texas A&M, RB
1977 Warren Bryant, Kentucky, T
Wilson Faumuina, San Jose St., DT
1978 Mike Kenn, Michigan, T
1979 Don Smith, Miami, DE
1980 Junior Miller, Nebraska, TE
1981 Bobby Butler, Florida State, DB
1982 Gerald Riggs, Arizona State, RB
1983 Mike Pitts, Alabama, DE
1984 Rick Bryan, Oklahoma, DT
1985 Bill Fralic, Pittsburgh, T
1986 Tony Casillas, Oklahoma, NT
Tim Green, Syracuse, LB
1987 Chris Miller, Oregon, QB
1988 Aundray Bruce, Auburn, LB
1989 Deion Sanders, Florida State, DB
Shawn Collins, No. Arizona, WR
1990 Steve Broussard, Washington St., RB
1991 Bruce Pickens, Nebraska, DB
Mike Pritchard, Colorado, WR
1992 Bob Whitfield, Stanford, T
Tony Smith, So. Mississippi, RB
1993 Lincoln Kennedy, Washington, T
1994 Bert Emanuel, Rice, WR (2)
1995 Devin Bush, Florida State, DB
1996 Shannon Brown, Alabama, DT (3)
1997 Michael Booker, Nebraska, DB
1998 Keith Brooking, Georgia Tech, LB
1999 Patrick Kerney, Virginia, DE
2000 Travis Claridge, So. California, T (2)
2001 Michael Vick, Virginia Tech, QB
2002 T.J. Duckett, Michigan State, RB
2003 Bryan Scott, Penn State, DB (2)
2004 DeAngelo Hall, Virginia Tech, DB
Michael Jenkins, Ohio State, WR
2005 Roddy White, Ala.-Birmingham, WR
2006 Jimmy Williams, Virginia Tech, DB (2)
2007 Jamaal Anderson, Arkansas, DE
2008 Matt Ryan, Boston College, QB
Sam Baker, So. California, T
2009 Peria Jerry, Mississippi, DT
2010 Sean Weatherspoon, Missouri, LB

BALTIMORE RAVENS

Year Player, College, Position

1996 Jonathan Ogden, UCLA, T
Ray Lewis, Miami, LB
1997 Peter Boulware, Florida State, DE
1998 Duane Starks, Miami, DB
1999 Chris McAlister, Arizona, DB
2000 Jamal Lewis, Tennessee, RB
Travis Taylor, Florida, WR
2001 Todd Heap, Arizona State, TE
2002 Ed Reed, Miami, DB
2003 Terrell Suggs, Arizona State, DE
Kyle Boller, California, QB
2004 Dwan Edwards, Oregon St., DT (2)
2005 Mark Clayton, Oklahoma, WR
2006 Haloti Ngata, Oregon, DT
2007 Ben Grubbs, Auburn, G
2008 Joe Flacco, Delaware, QB
2009 Michael Oher, Mississippi, T
2010 Sergio Kindle, Texas, LB (2)

BUFFALO BILLS

Year Player, College, Position

1960 Richie Lucas, Penn State, QB
1961 Ken Rice, Auburn, T
1962 Ernie Davis, Syracuse, RB
1963 Dave Behrman, Michigan State, C
1964 Carl Eller, Minnesota, DE
1965 Jim Davidson, Ohio State, T
1966 Mike Dennis, Mississippi, RB
1967 John Pitts, Arizona State, S
1968 Haven Moses, San Diego St., WR
1969 O.J. Simpson, So. California, RB
1970 Al Cowlings, So. California, DE
1971 J.D. Hill, Arizona State, WR
1972 Walt Patulski, Notre Dame, DE
1973 Paul Seymour, Michigan, TE
Joe DeLamielleure, Michigan St., G
1974 Reuben Gant, Oklahoma State, TE
1975 Tom Ruud, Nebraska, LB
1976 Mario Clark, Oregon, DB
1977 Phil Dokes, Oklahoma State, DT
1978 Terry Miller, Oklahoma State, RB
1979 Tom Cousineau, Ohio State, LB
Jerry Butler, Clemson, WR
1980 Jim Ritcher, North Carolina St., C
1981 Booker Moore, Penn State, RB
1982 Perry Tuttle, Clemson, WR
1983 Tony Hunter, Notre Dame, TE
Jim Kelly, Miami, QB
1984 Greg Bell, Notre Dame, RB
1985 Bruce Smith, Virginia Tech, DE
Derrick Burroughs, Memphis St., DB
1986 Ronnie Harmon, Iowa, RB
Will Wolford, Vanderbilt, T
1987 Shane Conlan, Penn State, LB
1988 Thurman Thomas, Oklahoma St., RB (2)
1989 Don Beebe, Chadron, Neb., WR (3)
1990 James Williams, Fresno State, DB
1991 Henry Jones, Illinois, DB
1992 John Fina, Arizona, T
1993 Thomas Smith, North Carolina, DB

1994 Jeff Burris, Notre Dame, DB
1995 Ruben Brown, Pittsburgh, G
1996 Eric Moulds, Mississippi St., WR
1997 Antowain Smith, Houston, RB
1998 Sam Cowart, Florida State, LB (2)
1999 Antoine Winfield, Ohio State, DB
2000 Erik Flowers, Arizona State, DE
2001 Nate Clements, Ohio State, DB
2002 Mike Williams, Texas, T
2003 Willis McGahee, Miami, RB
2004 Lee Evans, Wisconsin, WR
J.P. Losman, Tulane, QB
2005 Roscoe Parrish, Miami, WR (2)
2006 Donte' Whitner, Ohio State, DB
John McCargo, North Carolina St., DT
2007 Marshawn Lynch, California, RB
2008 Leodis McKelvin, Troy, DB
2009 Aaron Maybin, Penn State, DE
Eric Wood, Louisville, C
2010 C.J. Spiller, Clemson, RB

CAROLINA PANTHERS

Year Player, College, Position
1995 Kerry Collins, Penn State, QB
Tyrone Poole, Ft. Valley State, DB
Blake Brockermeyer, Texas, T
1996 Tim Biakabutuka, Michigan, RB
1997 Rae Carruth, Colorado, WR
1998 Jason Peter, Nebraska, DT
1999 Chris Terry, Georgia, T (2)
2000 Rashard Anderson, Jackson St., DB
2001 Dan Morgan, Miami, LB
2002 Julius Peppers, North Carolina, DE
2003 Jordan Gross, Utah, T
2004 Chris Gamble, Ohio State, DB
2005 Thomas Davis, Georgia, DB
2006 DeAngelo Williams, Memphis, RB
2007 Jon Beason, Miami, LB
2008 Jonathan Stewart, Oregon, RB
Jeff Otah, Pittsburgh, T
2009 Everette Brown, Florida St., DE (2)
2010 Jimmy Clausen, Notre Dame, QB (2)

CHICAGO BEARS

Year Player, College, Position
1936 Joe Stydahar, West Virginia, T
1937 Les McDonald, Nebraska, E
1938 Joe Gray, Oregon State, B
1939 Sid Luckman, Columbia, QB
Bill Osmanski, Holy Cross, B
1940 Clyde (Bulldog) Turner, Hardin-Simmons, C
1941 Tom Harmon, Michigan, B
Norm Standlee, Stanford, B
Don Scott, Ohio State, B
1942 Frankie Albert, Stanford, B
1943 Bob Steber, Missouri, B
1944 Ray Evans, Kansas, B
1945 Don Lund, Michigan, B
1946 Johnny Lujack, Notre Dame, QB
1947 Bob Fenimore, Oklahoma State, B
Don Kindt, Wisconsin, B
1948 Bobby Layne, Texas, QB
Max Bumgardner, Texas, E
1949 Dick Harris, Texas, C
1950 Chuck Hunsinger, Florida, B
Fred Morrison, Ohio State, B
1951 Bob Williams, Notre Dame, B
Billy Stone, Bradley, B
Gene Schroeder, Virginia, E
1952 Jim Dooley, Miami, B
1953 Billy Anderson, Compton (Calif.) J.C., B
1954 Stan Wallace, Illinois, B
1955 Ron Drzewiecki, Marquette, B
1956 Menan (Tex) Schriewer, Texas, E
1957 Earl Leggett, Louisiana State, T
1958 Chuck Howley, West Virginia, G
1959 Don Clark, Ohio State, B
1960 Roger Davis, Syracuse, G
1961 Mike Ditka, Pittsburgh, E
1962 Ronnie Bull, Baylor, RB
1963 Dave Behrman, Michigan State, C
1964 Dick Evey, Tennessee, DT
1965 Dick Butkus, Illinois, LB
Gale Sayers, Kansas, RB
Steve DeLong, Tennessee, T
1966 George Rice, Louisiana State, DT
1967 Loyd Phillips, Arkansas, DE
1968 Mike Hull, Southern California, RB
1969 Rufus Mayes, Ohio State, T
1970 George Farmer, UCLA, WR (3)
1971 Joe Moore, Missouri, RB
1972 Lionel Antoine, Southern Illinois, T
Craig Clemons, Iowa, DB
1973 Wally Chambers, Eastern Kentucky, DE
1974 Waymond Bryant, Tennessee St., LB
Dave Gallagher, Michigan, DT
1975 Walter Payton, Jackson State, RB
1976 Dennis Lick, Wisconsin, T
1977 Ted Albrecht, California, T
1978 Brad Shearer, Texas, DT (3)
1979 Dan Hampton, Arkansas, DT
Al Harris, Arizona State, DE
1980 Otis Wilson, Louisville, LB
1981 Keith Van Horne, So. California, T
1982 Jim McMahon, Brigham Young, QB
1983 Jim Covert, Pittsburgh, T
Willie Gault, Tennessee, WR
1984 Wilber Marshall, Florida, LB
1985 William Perry, Clemson, DT
1986 Neal Anderson, Florida, RB
1987 Jim Harbaugh, Michigan, QB
1988 Brad Muster, Stanford, RB
Wendell Davis, Louisiana St., WR
1989 Donnell Woolford, Clemson, DB
Trace Armstrong, Florida, DE
1990 Mark Carrier, So. California, DB
1991 Stan Thomas, Texas, T
1992 Alonzo Spellman, Ohio State, DE
1993 Curtis Conway, So. California, WR
1994 John Thierry, Alcorn State, DE
1995 Rashaan Salaam, Colorado, RB
1996 Walt Harris, Mississippi State, DB
1997 John Allred, So. California, TE (2)
1998 Curtis Enis, Penn State, RB
1999 Cade McNown, UCLA, QB
2000 Brian Urlacher, New Mexico, LB
2001 David Terrell, Michigan, WR
2002 Marc Colombo, Boston College, T
2003 Michael Haynes, Penn State, DE
Rex Grossman, Florida, QB
2004 Tommie Harris, Oklahoma, DT
2005 Cedric Benson, Texas, RB
2006 Danieal Manning, Abilene Christian, DB (2)
2007 Greg Olsen, Miami, TE
2008 Chris Williams, Vanderbilt, T
2009 Jarron Gilbert, San Jose State, DT (3)
2010 Major Wright, Florida, DB (3)

CINCINNATI BENGALS

Year Player, College, Position
1968 Bob Johnson, Tennessee, C
1969 Greg Cook, Cincinnati, QB
1970 Mike Reid, Penn State, DT
1971 Vernon Holland, Tennessee St., T
1972 Sherman White, California, DE
1973 Isaac Curtis, San Diego State, WR
1974 Bill Kollar, Montana State, DT
1975 Glenn Cameron, Florida, LB
1976 Billy Brooks, Oklahoma, WR
Archie Griffin, Ohio State, RB
1977 Eddie Edwards, Miami, DT
Wilson Whitley, Houston, DT
Mike Cobb, Michigan State, TE
1978 Ross Browner, Notre Dame, DT
Blair Bush, Washington, C
1979 Jack Thompson, Washington St., QB
Charles Alexander, Louisiana St., RB
1980 Anthony Muñoz, So. California, T
1981 David Verser, Kansas, WR
1982 Glen Collins, Mississippi State, DE
1983 Dave Rimington, Nebraska, C
1984 Ricky Hunley, Arizona, LB
Pete Koch, Maryland, DE
Brian Blados, North Carolina, T
1985 Eddie Brown, Miami, WR
Emanuel King, Alabama, LB
1986 Joe Kelly, Washington, LB
Tim McGee, Tennessee, WR
1987 Jason Buck, Brigham Young, DE
1988 Rickey Dixon, Oklahoma, DB
1989 Eric Ball, UCLA, RB (2)
1990 James Francis, Baylor, LB
1991 Alfred Williams, Colorado, LB
1992 David Klingler, Houston, QB
Darryl Williams, Miami, DB
1993 John Copeland, Alabama, DE
1994 Dan Wilkinson, Ohio State, DT
1995 Ki-Jana Carter, Penn State, RB
1996 Willie Anderson, Auburn, T
1997 Reinard Wilson, Florida State, LB
1998 Takeo Spikes, Auburn, LB
Brian Simmons, North Carolina, LB
1999 Akili Smith, Oregon, QB
2000 Peter Warrick, Florida State, WR
2001 Justin Smith, Missouri, DE
2002 Levi Jones, Arizona State, T
2003 Carson Palmer, Southern California, QB
2004 Chris Perry, Michigan, RB
2005 David Pollack, Georgia, LB
2006 Johnathan Joseph, South Carolina, DB
2007 Leon Hall, Michigan, DB
2008 Keith Rivers, So. California, LB
2009 Andre Smith, Alabama, T
2010 Jermaine Gresham, Oklahoma, TE

CLEVELAND BROWNS

Year Player, College, Position
1950 Ken Carpenter, Oregon State, B
1951 Ken Konz, Louisiana State, B
1952 Bert Rechichar, Tennessee, DB
Harry Agganis, Boston U., QB
1953 Doug Atkins, Tennessee, DE
1954 Bobby Garrett, Stanford, QB
John Bauer, Illinois, G
1955 Kurt Burris, Oklahoma, C
1956 Preston Carpenter, Arkansas, B
1957 Jim Brown, Syracuse, RB
1958 Jim Shofner, Texas Christian, DB

1959 Rich Kreitling, Illinois, DE
1960 Jim Houston, Ohio State, DE
1961 Bobby Crespino, Mississippi, TE
1962 Gary Collins, Maryland, WR
Leroy Jackson, Western Illinois, RB
1963 Tom Hutchinson, Kentucky, WR
1964 Paul Warfield, Ohio State, WR
1965 James Garcia, Purdue, T (2)
1966 Milt Morin, Massachusetts, TE
1967 Bob Matheson, Duke, LB
1968 Marvin Upshaw, Trinity, Tex., DT-DE
1969 Ron Johnson, Michigan, RB
1970 Mike Phipps, Purdue, QB
Bob McKay, Texas, T
1971 Clarence Scott, Kansas State, CB
1972 Thom Darden, Michigan, DB
1973 Steve Holden, Arizona State, WR
Pete Adams, Southern California, T
1974 Billy Corbett, Johnson C. Smith, T (2)
1975 Mack Mitchell, Houston, DE
1976 Mike Pruitt, Purdue, RB
1977 Robert Jackson, Texas A&M, LB
1978 Clay Matthews, So. California, LB
Ozzie Newsome, Alabama, TE
1979 Willis Adams, Houston, WR
1980 Charles White, So. California, RB
1981 Hanford Dixon, So. Mississippi, DB
1982 Chip Banks, So. California, LB
1983 Ron Brown, Arizona State, WR (2)
1984 Don Rogers, UCLA, DB
1985 Greg Allen, Florida State, RB (2)
1986 Webster Slaughter, San Diego St., WR (2)
1987 Mike Junkin, Duke, LB
1988 Clifford Charlton, Florida, LB
1989 Eric Metcalf, Texas, RB
1990 Leroy Hoard, Michigan, RB (2)
1991 Eric Turner, UCLA, DB
1992 Tommy Vardell, Stanford, RB
1993 Steve Everitt, Michigan, C
1994 Antonio Langham, Alabama, DB
Derrick Alexander, Michigan, WR
1995 Craig Powell, Ohio State, LB
1999 Tim Couch, Kentucky, QB
2000 Courtney Brown, Penn State, DE
2001 Gerard Warren, Florida, DT
2002 William Green, Boston College, RB
2003 Jeff Faine, Norte Dame, C
2004 Kellen Winslow, Miami, TE
2005 Braylon Edwards, Michigan, WR
2006 Kamerion Wimbley, Florida St., DE
2007 Joe Thomas, Wisconsin, T
Brady Quinn, Notre Dame, QB
2008 Beau Bell, Nevada-Las Vegas, LB (4)
2009 Alex Mack, California, C
2010 Joe Haden, Florida, DB

DALLAS COWBOYS

Year Player, College, Position

1960 None
1961 Bob Lilly, Texas Christian, DT
1962 Sonny Gibbs, TCU, QB (2)
1963 Lee Roy Jordan, Alabama, LB
1964 Scott Appleton, Texas, DT
1965 Craig Morton, California, QB
1966 John Niland, Iowa, G
1967 Phil Clark, Northwestern, DB (3)
1968 Dennis Homan, Alabama, WR
1969 Calvin Hill, Yale, RB
1970 Duane Thomas, West Texas St., RB
1971 Tody Smith, So. California, DE
1972 Bill Thomas, Boston College, RB
1973 Billy Joe DuPree, Michigan St., TE
1974 Ed (Too Tall) Jones, Tennessee St., DE
Charley Young, North Carolina St., RB
1975 Randy White, Maryland, LB
Thomas Henderson, Langston, LB
1976 Aaron Kyle, Wyoming, DB
1977 Tony Dorsett, Pittsburgh, RB
1978 Larry Bethea, Michigan State, DE
1979 Robert Shaw, Tennessee, C
1980 Bill Roe, Colorado, LB (3)
1981 Howard Richards, Missouri, T
1982 Rod Hill, Kentucky State, DB
1983 Jim Jeffcoat, Arizona State, DE
1984 Billy Cannon, Jr., Texas A&M, LB
1985 Kevin Brooks, Michigan, DE
1986 Mike Sherrard, UCLA, WR
1987 Danny Noonan, Nebraska, DT
1988 Michael Irvin, Miami, WR
1989 Troy Aikman, UCLA, QB
1990 Emmitt Smith, Florida, RB
1991 Russell Maryland, Miami, DT
Alvin Harper, Tennessee, WR
Kelvin Pritchett, Mississippi, DT
1992 Kevin Smith, Texas A&M, DB
Robert Jones, East Carolina, LB
1993 Kevin Williams, Miami, WR (2)
1994 Shante Carver, Arizona State, DE
1995 Sherman Williams, Alabama, RB (2)
1996 Kavika Pittman, McNeese St., DE (2)
1997 David LaFleur, Louisiana State, TE
1998 Greg Ellis, North Carolina, DE
1999 Ebenezer Ekuban, North Carolina, DE
2000 Dwayne Goodrich, Tennessee, DB (2)
2001 Quincy Carter, Georgia, QB (2)
2002 Roy Williams, Oklahoma, DB
2003 Terence Newman, Kansas State, DB
2004 Julius Jones, Notre Dame, RB (2)
2005 DeMarcus Ware, Troy, DE
Marcus Spears, Louisiana St., DE
2006 Bobby Carpenter, Ohio State, LB
2007 Anthony Spencer, Purdue, LB
2008 Felix Jones, Arkansas, RB
Mike Jenkins, South Florida, DB
2009 Jason Williams, Western Illinois, LB (3)
2010 Dez Bryant, Oklahoma State, WR

DENVER BRONCOS

Year Player, College, Position

1960 Roger LeClerc, Trinity, Conn., C
1961 Bob Gaiters, New Mexico St., RB
1962 Merlin Olsen, Utah State, DT
1963 Kermit Alexander, UCLA, CB
1964 Bob Brown, Nebraska, T
1965 Dick Butkus, Illinois, LB (2)
1966 Jerry Shay, Purdue, DT
1967 Floyd Little, Syracuse, RB
1968 Curley Culp, Arizona State, DE (2)
1969 Grady Cavness, Texas-El Paso, DB (2)
1970 Bob Anderson, Colorado, RB
1971 Marv Montgomery, So. California, T
1972 Riley Odoms, Houston, TE
1973 Otis Armstrong, Purdue, RB
1974 Randy Gradishar, Ohio State, LB
1975 Louis Wright, San Jose State, DB
1976 Tom Glassic, Virginia, G
1977 Steve Schindler, Boston College, G
1978 Don Latimer, Miami, DT
1979 Kelvin Clark, Nebraska, T
1980 Rulon Jones, Utah State, DE (2)
1981 Dennis Smith, So. California, DB
1982 Gerald Willhite, San Jose St., RB
1983 Chris Hinton, Northwestern, G
1984 Andre Townsend, Mississippi, DE (2)
1985 Steve Sewell, Oklahoma, RB
1986 Jim Juriga, Illinois, T (4)
1987 Ricky Nattiel, Florida, WR
1988 Ted Gregory, Syracuse, NT
1989 Steve Atwater, Arkansas, DB
1990 Alton Montgomery, Houston, DB (2)
1991 Mike Croel, Nebraska, LB
1992 Tommy Maddox, UCLA, QB
1993 Dan Williams, Toledo, DE
1994 Allen Aldridge, Houston, LB (2)
1995 Jamie Brown, Florida A&M, T (4)
1996 John Mobley, Kutztown, LB
1997 Trevor Pryce, Clemson, DT
1998 Marcus Nash, Tennessee, WR
1999 Al Wilson, Tennessee, LB
2000 Deltha O'Neal, California, DB
2001 Willie Middlebrooks, Minnesota, DB
2002 Ashley Lelie, Hawaii, WR
2003 George Foster, Georgia, T
2004 D.J. Williams, Miami, LB
2005 Darrent Williams, Oklahoma St., DB (2)
2006 Jay Cutler, Vanderbilt, QB
2007 Jarvis Moss, Florida, DE
2008 Ryan Clady, Boise State, T
2009 Knowshon Moreno, Georgia, RB
Robert Ayers, Tennessee, DE
2010 Demaryius Thomas, Georgia Tech, WR
Tim Tebow, Florida, QB

DETROIT LIONS

Year Player, College, Position

1936 Sid Wagner, Michigan State, G
1937 Lloyd Cardwell, Nebraska, B
1938 Alex Wojciechowicz, Fordham, C
1939 John Pingel, Michigan State, B
1940 Doyle Nave, Southern California, B
1941 Jim Thomason, Texas A&M, B
1942 Bob Westfall, Michigan, B
1943 Frank Sinkwich, Georgia, B
1944 Otto Graham, Northwestern, B
1945 Frank Szymanski, Notre Dame, C
1946 Bill Dellastatious, Missouri, B
1947 Glenn Davis, Army, B
1948 Y.A. Tittle, Louisiana State, B
1949 John Rauch, Georgia, B
1950 Leon Hart, Notre Dame, E
Joe Watson, Rice, C
1951 Dick Stanfel, San Francisco, G (2)
1952 Yale Lary, Texas A&M, B (3)
1953 Harley Sewell, Texas, G
1954 Dick Chapman, Rice, T
1955 Dave Middleton, Auburn, B
1956 Hopalong Cassady, Ohio State, B
1957 Bill Glass, Baylor, G
1958 Alex Karras, Iowa, T
1959 Nick Pietrosante, Notre Dame, B
1960 John Robinson, Louisiana State, S
1961 Danny LaRose, Missouri, T (2)
1962 John Hadl, Kansas, QB
1963 Daryl Sanders, Ohio State, T
1964 Pete Beathard, So. California, QB
1965 Tom Nowatzke, Indiana, RB
1966 Nick Eddy, Notre Dame, RB (2)
1967 Mel Farr, UCLA, RB
1968 Greg Landry, Massachusetts, QB
Earl McCullouch, So. California, WR

1969 Altie Taylor, Utah State, RB (2)
1970 Steve Owens, Oklahoma, RB
1971 Bob Bell, Cincinnati, DT
1972 Herb Orvis, Colorado, DE
1973 Ernie Price, Texas A&I, DE
1974 Ed O'Neil, Penn State, LB
1975 Lynn Boden, South Dakota St., G
1976 James Hunter, Grambling, DB
Lawrence Gaines, Wyoming, RB
1977 Walt Williams, New Mexico St., DB (2)
1978 Luther Bradley, Notre Dame, DB
1979 Keith Dorney, Penn State, T
1980 Billy Sims, Oklahoma, RB
1981 Mark Nichols, San Jose State, WR
1982 Jimmy Williams, Nebraska, LB
1983 James Jones, Florida, RB
1984 David Lewis, California, TE
1985 Lomas Brown, Florida, T
1986 Chuck Long, Iowa, QB
1987 Reggie Rogers, Washington, DE
1988 Bennie Blades, Miami, DB
1989 Barry Sanders, Oklahoma St., RB
1990 Andre Ware, Houston, QB
1991 Herman Moore, Virginia, WR
1992 Robert Porcher, South Carolina St., DE
1993 Ryan McNeil, Miami, DB (2)
1994 Johnnie Morton, So. California, WR
1995 Luther Elliss, Utah, DT
1996 Reggie Brown, Texas A&M, LB
Jeff Hartings, Penn State, G
1997 Bryant Westbrook, Texas, DB
1998 Terry Fair, Tennessee, DB
1999 Chris Claiborne, So. California, LB
Aaron Gibson, Wisconsin, T
2000 Stockar McDougle, Oklahoma, T
2001 Jeff Backus, Michigan, T
2002 Joey Harrington, Oregon, QB
2003 Charles Rogers, Michigan State, WR
2004 Roy Williams, Texas, WR
Kevin Jones, Virginia Tech, RB
2005 Mike Williams, So. California, WR
2006 Ernie Sims, Florida State, LB
2007 Calvin Johnson, Georgia Tech, WR
2008 Gosder Cherilus, Boson College, T
2009 Matthew Stafford, Georgia, QB
Brandon Pettigrew, Oklahoma St., TE
2010 Ndamukong Suh, Nebraska, DT
Jahvid Best, California, RB

GREEN BAY PACKERS

Year Player, College, Position

1936 Russ Letlow, San Francisco, G
1937 Eddie Jankowski, Wisconsin, B
1938 Cecil Isbell, Purdue, B
1939 Larry Buhler, Minnesota, B
1940 Harold Van Every, Minnesota, B
1941 George Paskvan, Wisconsin, B
1942 Urban Odson, Minnesota, T
1943 Dick Wildung, Minnesota, T
1944 Merv Pregulman, Michigan, G
1945 Walt Schlinkman, Texas Tech, B
1946 Johnny Strzykalski, Marquette, B
1947 Ernie Case, UCLA, B
1948 Earl (Jug) Girard, Wisconsin, B
1949 Stan Heath, Nevada, B
1950 Clayton Tonnemaker, Minnesota, C
1951 Bob Gain, Kentucky, T
1952 Babe Parilli, Kentucky, QB
1953 Al Carmichael, So. California, B
1954 Art Hunter, Notre Dame, T
Veryl Switzer, Kansas State, B
1955 Tom Bettis, Purdue, G
1956 Jack Losch, Miami, B
1957 Paul Hornung, Notre Dame, B
Ron Kramer, Michigan, E
1958 Dan Currie, Michigan State, C
1959 Randy Duncan, Iowa, B
1960 Tom Moore, Vanderbilt, RB
1961 Herb Adderley, Michigan State, CB
1962 Earl Gros, Louisiana State, RB
1963 Dave Robinson, Penn State, LB
1964 Lloyd Voss, Nebraska, DT
1965 Donny Anderson, Texas Tech, RB
Lawrence Elkins, Baylor, E
1966 Jim Grabowski, Illinois, RB
Gale Gillingham, Minnesota, T
1967 Bob Hyland, Boston College, C
Don Horn, San Diego State, QB
1968 Fred Carr, Texas-El Paso, LB
Bill Lueck, Arizona, G
1969 Rich Moore, Villanova, DT
1970 Mike McCoy, Notre Dame, DT
Rich McGeorge, Elon, TE
1971 John Brockington, Ohio State, RB
1972 Willie Buchanon, San Diego St., DB
Jerry Tagge, Nebraska, QB
1973 Barry Smith, Florida State, WR
1974 Barty Smith, Richmond, RB
1975 Bill Bain, So. California, G (2)
1976 Mark Koncar, Colorado, T
1977 Mike Butler, Kansas, DE
Ezra Johnson, Morris Brown, DE
1978 James Lofton, Stanford, WR
John Anderson, Michigan, LB
1979 Eddie Lee Ivery, Georgia Tech, RB
1980 Bruce Clark, Penn State, DE
George Cumby, Oklahoma, LB
1981 Rich Campbell, California, QB
1982 Ron Hallstrom, Iowa, G
1983 Tim Lewis, Pittsburgh, DB
1984 Alphonso Carreker, Florida St., DE
1985 Ken Ruettgers, So. California, T
1986 Kenneth Davis, TCU, RB (2)
1987 Brent Fullwood, Auburn, RB
1988 Sterling Sharpe, South Carolina, WR
1989 Tony Mandarich, Michigan State, T
1990 Tony Bennett, Mississippi, LB
Darrell Thompson, Minnesota, RB
1991 Vinnie Clark, Ohio State, DB
1992 Terrell Buckley, Florida State, DB
1993 Wayne Simmons, Clemson, LB
George Teague, Alabama, DB
1994 Aaron Taylor, Notre Dame, T
1995 Craig Newsome, Arizona State, DB
1996 John Michels, Southern California, T
1997 Ross Verba, Iowa, T
1998 Vonnie Holliday, North Carolina, DT
1999 Antuan Edwards, Clemson, DB
2000 Bubba Franks, Miami, TE
2001 Jamal Reynolds, Florida State, DE
2002 Javon Walker, Florida State, WR
2003 Nick Barnett, Oregon State, LB
2004 Ahmad Carroll, Arkansas, DB
2005 Aaron Rodgers, California, QB
2006 A.J. Hawk, Ohio State, LB
2007 Justin Harrell, Tennessee, DT
2008 Jordy Nelson, Kansas State, WR (2)
2009 B.J. Raji, Boston College, DT
Clay Matthews, So. California, LB
2010 Bryan Bulaga, Iowa, T

HOUSTON TEXANS

Year Player, College, Position

2002 David Carr, Fresno State, QB
2003 Andre Johnson, Miami, WR
2004 Dunta Robinson, South Carolina, DB
Jason Babin, Western Michigan, LB
2005 Travis Johnson, Florida State, DE
2006 Mario Williams, North Carolina St., DE
2007 Amobi Okoye, Louisville, DT
2008 Duane Brown, Virginia Tech, T
2009 Brian Cushing, So. California, LB
2010 Kareem Jackson, Alabama, DB

INDIANAPOLIS COLTS

Year Player, College, Position

1953 Billy Vessels, Oklahoma, B
1954 Cotton Davidson, Baylor, B
1955 George Shaw, Oregon, B
Alan Ameche, Wisconsin, FB
1956 Lenny Moore, Penn State, B
1957 Jim Parker, Ohio State, G
1958 Lenny Lyles, Louisville, B
1959 Jackie Burkett, Auburn, C
1960 Ron Mix, Southern California, T
1961 Tom Matte, Ohio State, RB
1962 Wendell Harris, Louisiana State, S
1963 Bob Vogel, Ohio State, T
1964 Marv Woodson, Indiana, CB
1965 Mike Curtis, Duke, LB
1966 Sam Ball, Kentucky, T
1967 Bubba Smith, Michigan State, DT
Jim Detwiler, Michigan, RB
1968 John Williams, Minnesota, G
1969 Eddie Hinton, Oklahoma, WR
1970 Norman Bulaich, Texas Christian, RB
1971 Don McCauley, North Carolina, RB
Leonard Dunlap, North Texas St., DB
1972 Tom Drougas, Oregon, T
1973 Bert Jones, Louisiana State, QB
Joe Ehrmann, Syracuse, DT
1974 John Dutton, Nebraska, DE
Roger Carr, Louisiana Tech, WR
1975 Ken Huff, North Carolina, G
1976 Ken Novak, Purdue, DT
1977 Randy Burke, Kentucky, WR
1978 Reese McCall, Auburn, TE
1979 Barry Krauss, Alabama, LB
1980 Curtis Dickey, Texas A&M, RB
Derrick Hatchett, Texas, DB
1981 Randy McMillan, Pittsburgh, RB
Donnell Thompson, North Carolina, DT
1982 Johnie Cooks, Mississippi St., LB
Art Schlichter, Ohio State, QB
1983 John Elway, Stanford, QB
1984 Leonard Coleman, Vanderbilt, DB
Ron Solt, Maryland, G
1985 Duane Bickett, So. California, LB
1986 Jon Hand, Alabama, DE
1987 Cornelius Bennett, Alabama, LB
1988 Chris Chandler, Washington, QB (3)
1989 Andre Rison, Michigan State, WR
1990 Jeff George, Illinois, QB
1991 Shane Curry, Miami, DE (2)
1992 Steve Emtman, Washington, DT
Quentin Coryatt, Texas A&M, LB
1993 Sean Dawkins, California, WR
1994 Marshall Faulk, San Diego St., RB
Trev Alberts, Nebraska, LB

1995 Ellis Johnson, Florida, DT
1996 Marvin Harrison, Syracuse, WR
1997 Tarik Glenn, California, T
1998 Peyton Manning, Tennessee, QB
1999 Edgerrin James, Miami, RB
2000 Rob Morris, Brigham Young, LB
2001 Reggie Wayne, Miami, WR
2002 Dwight Freeney, Syracuse, DE
2003 Dallas Clark, Iowa, TE
2004 Bob Sanders, Iowa, DB (2)
2005 Marlin Jackson, Michigan, DB
2006 Joseph Addai, Louisiana State, RB
2007 Anthony Gonzalez, Ohio State, WR
2008 Mike Pollak, Arizona State, G (2)
2009 Donald Brown, Connecticut, RB
2010 Jerry Hughes, Texas Christian, DE

JACKSONVILLE JAGUARS

Year Player, College, Position
1995 Tony Boselli, Southern California, T
James Stewart, Tennessee, RB
1996 Kevin Hardy, Illinois, LB
1997 Renaldo Wynn, Notre Dame, DT
1998 Fred Taylor, Florida, RB
Donovin Darius, Syracuse, DB
1999 Fernando Bryant, Alabama, DB
2000 R. Jay Soward, So. California, WR
2001 Marcus Stroud, Georgia, DT
2002 John Henderson, Tennessee, DT
2003 Byron Leftwich, Marshall, QB
2004 Reggie Williams, Washington, WR
2005 Matt Jones, Arkansas, WR
2006 Marcedes Lewis, UCLA, TE
2007 Reggie Nelson, Florida, DB
2008 Derrick Harvey, Florida, DE
2009 Eugene Monroe, Virginia, T
2010 Tyson Alualu, Jacksonville, DT

KANSAS CITY CHIEFS

Year Player, College, Position
1960 Don Meredith, So. Methodist, QB
1961 E.J. Holub, Texas Tech, C
1962 Ronnie Bull, Baylor, RB
1963 Buck Buchanan, Grambling, DT
Ed Budde, Michigan State, G
1964 Pete Beathard, So. California, QB
1965 Gale Sayers, Kansas, RB
1966 Aaron Brown, Minnesota, DE
1967 Gene Trosch, Miami, DE-DT
1968 Mo Moorman, Texas A&M, G
George Daney, Texas-El Paso, G
1969 Jim Marsalis, Tennessee State, CB
1970 Sid Smith, Southern California, T
1971 Elmo Wright, Houston, WR
1972 Jeff Kinney, Nebraska, RB
1973 Gary Butler, Rice, TE (2)
1974 Woody Green, Arizona State, RB
1975 Elmore Stephens, Kentucky, TE (2)
1976 Rod Walters, Iowa, G
1977 Gary Green, Baylor, DB
1978 Art Still, Kentucky, DE
1979 Mike Bell, Colorado State, DE
Steve Fuller, Clemson, QB
1980 Brad Budde, Southern California, G
1981 Willie Scott, South Carolina, TE
1982 Anthony Hancock, Tennessee, WR
1983 Todd Blackledge, Penn State, QB
1984 Bill Maas, Pittsburgh, DT
John Alt, Iowa, T
1985 Ethan Horton, North Carolina, RB
1986 Brian Jozwiak, West Virginia, T
1987 Paul Palmer, Temple, RB
1988 Neil Smith, Nebraska, DE
1989 Derrick Thomas, Alabama, LB
1990 Percy Snow, Michigan State, LB
1991 Harvey Williams, Louisiana St., RB
1992 Dale Carter, Tennessee, DB
1993 Will Shields, Nebraska, G (3)
1994 Greg Hill, Texas A&M, RB
1995 Trezelle Jenkins, Michigan, T
1996 Jerome Woods, Memphis, DB
1997 Tony Gonzalez, California, TE
1998 Victor Riley, Auburn, T
1999 John Tait, Brigham Young, T
2000 Sylvester Morris, Jackson St., WR
2001 Eric Downing, Syracuse, DT (3)
2002 Ryan Sims, North Carolina, DT
2003 Larry Johnson, Penn State, RB
2004 Junior Siavii, Oregon, DT (2)
2005 Derrick Johnson, Texas, LB
2006 Tamba Hali, Penn State, DE
2007 Dwayne Bowe, Louisiana State, WR
2008 Glenn Dorsey, Louisiana State, DT
Branden Albert, Virginia, T
2009 Tyson Jackson, Louisiana State, DE
2010 Eric Berry, Tennessee, DB

MIAMI DOLPHINS

Year Player, College, Position
1966 Jim Grabowski, Illinois, RB
Rick Norton, Kentucky, QB
1967 Bob Griese, Purdue, QB
1968 Larry Csonka, Syracuse, RB
Doug Crusan, Indiana, T
1969 Bill Stanfill, Georgia, DE
1970 Jim Mandich, Michigan, TE (2)
1971 Otto Stowe, Iowa State, WR (2)
1972 Mike Kadish, Notre Dame, DT
1973 Chuck Bradley, Oregon, C (2)
1974 Donald Reese, Jackson State, DE
1975 Darryl Carlton, Tampa, T
1976 Larry Gordon, Arizona State, LB
Kim Bokamper, San Jose State, LB
1977 A.J. Duhe, Louisiana State, DT
1978 Guy Benjamin, Stanford, QB (2)
1979 Jon Giesler, Michigan, T
1980 Don McNeal, Alabama, DB
1981 David Overstreet, Oklahoma, RB
1982 Roy Foster, Southern California, G
1983 Dan Marino, Pittsburgh, QB
1984 Jackie Shipp, Oklahoma, LB
1985 Lorenzo Hampton, Florida, RB
1986 John Offerdahl, Western Michigan, LB (2)
1987 John Bosa, Boston College, DE
1988 Eric Kumerow, Ohio State, DE
1989 Sammie Smith, Florida State, RB
Louis Oliver, Florida, DB
1990 Richmond Webb, Texas A&M, T
1991 Randal Hill, Miami, WR
1992 Troy Vincent, Wisconsin, DB
Marco Coleman, Georgia Tech, LB
1993 O.J. McDuffie, Penn State, WR
1994 Tim Bowens, Mississippi, DT
1995 Billy Milner, Houston, T
1996 Daryl Gardener, Baylor, DT
1997 Yatil Green, Miami, WR
1998 John Avery, Mississippi, RB
1999 J.J. Johnson, Mississippi St., RB (2)
2000 Todd Wade, Mississippi, T (2)
2001 Jamar Fletcher, Wisconsin, DB
2002 Seth McKinney, Texas A&M, C (3)
2003 Eddie Moore, Tennessee, LB (2)
2004 Vernon Carey, Miami, T
2005 Ronnie Brown, Auburn, RB
2006 Jason Allen, Tennessee, DB
2007 Ted Ginn, Ohio State, WR
2008 Jake Long, Michigan, T
2009 Vontae Davis, Illinois, DB
2010 Jared Odrick, Penn State, DT

MINNESOTA VIKINGS

Year Player, College, Position
1961 Tommy Mason, Tulane, RB
1962 Bill Miller, Miami, WR (3)
1963 Jim Dunaway, Mississippi, T
1964 Carl Eller, Minnesota, DE
1965 Jack Snow, Notre Dame, WR
1966 Jerry Shay, Purdue, DT
1967 Clint Jones, Michigan State, RB
Gene Washington, Michigan St., WR
Alan Page, Notre Dame, DT
1968 Ron Yary, Southern California, T
1969 Ed White, California, G (2)
1970 John Ward, Oklahoma State, DT
1971 Leo Hayden, Ohio State, RB
1972 Jeff Siemon, Stanford, LB
1973 Chuck Foreman, Miami, RB
1974 Fred McNeill, UCLA, LB
Steve Riley, Southern California, T
1975 Mark Mullaney, Colorado State, DE
1976 James White, Oklahoma State, DT
1977 Tommy Kramer, Rice, QB
1978 Randy Holloway, Pittsburgh, DE
1979 Ted Brown, North Carolina St., RB
1980 Doug Martin, Washington, DT
1981 Mardye McDole, Mississippi St., WR (2)
1982 Darrin Nelson, Stanford, RB
1983 Joey Browner, So. California, DB
1984 Keith Millard, Washington St., DE
1985 Chris Doleman, Pittsburgh, LB
1986 Gerald Robinson, Auburn, DE
1987 D.J. Dozier, Penn State, RB
1988 Randall McDaniel, Arizona State, G
1989 David Braxton, Wake Forest, LB (2)
1990 Mike Jones, Texas A&M, TE (3)
1991 Carlos Jenkins, Michigan St., LB (3)
1992 Robert Harris, Southern Univ., DE (2)
1993 Robert Smith, Ohio State, RB
1994 DeWayne Washington, N. Carolina St., DB
Todd Steussie, California, T
1995 Derrick Alexander, Florida St., DE
Korey Stringer, Ohio State, T
1996 Duane Clemons, California, DE
1997 Dwayne Rudd, Alabama, LB
1998 Randy Moss, Marshall, WR
1999 Daunte Culpepper, Central Florida, QB
Dimitrius Underwood, Michigan St., DE
2000 Chris Hovan, Boston College, DT
2001 Michael Bennett, Wisconsin, RB
2002 Bryant McKinnie, Miami, T
2003 Kevin Williams, Oklahoma State, DT
2004 Kenechi Udeze, Southern California, DE
2005 Troy Williamson, South Carolina, WR
Erasmus James, Wisconsin, DE
2006 Chad Greenway, Iowa, LB
2007 Adrian Peterson, Oklahoma, RB
2008 Tyrell Johnson, Arkansas State, DB (2)
2009 Percy Harvin, Florida, WR
2010 Chris Cook, Virginia, DB (2)

NEW ENGLAND PATRIOTS

Year Player, College, Position
1960 Ron Burton, Northwestern, RB
1961 Tommy Mason, Tulane, RB
1962 Gary Collins, Maryland, WR
1963 Art Graham, Boston College, WR
1964 Jack Concannon, Boston College, QB
1965 Jerry Rush, Michigan State, DE
1966 Karl Singer, Purdue, T
1967 John Charles, Purdue, S
1968 Dennis Byrd, North Carolina St., DE
1969 Ron Sellers, Florida State, WR
1970 Phil Olsen, Utah State, DE
1971 Jim Plunkett, Stanford, QB
1972 Tom Reynolds, San Diego St., WR (2)
1973 John Hannah, Alabama, G
Sam Cunningham, So. California, RB
Darryl Stingley, Purdue, WR
1974 Steve Corbett, Boston College, G (2)
1975 Russ Francis, Oregon, TE
1976 Mike Haynes, Arizona State, DB
Pete Brock, Colorado, C
Tim Fox, Ohio State, DB
1977 Raymond Clayborn, Texas, DB
Stanley Morgan, Tennessee, WR
1978 Bob Cryder, Alabama, G
1979 Rick Sanford, South Carolina, DB
1980 Roland James, Tennessee, DB
Vagas Ferguson, Notre Dame, RB
1981 Brian Holloway, Stanford, T
1982 Kenneth Sims, Texas, DT
Lester Williams, Miami, DT
1983 Tony Eason, Illinois, QB
1984 Irving Fryar, Nebraska, WR
1985 Trevor Matich, Brigham Young, C
1986 Reggie Dupard, So. Methodist, RB
1987 Bruce Armstrong, Louisville, T
1988 John Stephens, Northwestern St., La., RB
1989 Hart Lee Dykes, Oklahoma St., WR
1990 Chris Singleton, Arizona, LB
Ray Agnew, North Carolina St., DE
1991 Pat Harlow, Southern California, T
Leonard Russell, Arizona St., RB
1992 Eugene Chung, Virginia Tech, T
1993 Drew Bledsoe, Washington St., QB
1994 Willie McGinest, So. California, DE
1995 Ty Law, Michigan, DB
1996 Terry Glenn, Ohio State, WR
1997 Chris Canty, Kansas State, DB
1998 Robert Edwards, Georgia, RB
Tebucky Jones, Syracuse, DB
1999 Damien Woody, Boston College, C
Andy Katzenmoyer, Ohio State, LB
2000 Adrian Klemm, Hawaii, T (2)
2001 Richard Seymour, Georgia, DT
2002 Daniel Graham, Colorado, TE
2003 Ty Warren, Texas A&M, DT
2004 Vince Wilfork, Miami, DT
Ben Watson, Georgia, TE
2005 Logan Mankins, Fresno State, G
2006 Laurence Maroney, Minnesota, RB
2007 Brandon Meriweather, Miami, DB
2008 Jerod Mayo, Tennessee, LB
2009 Patrick Chung, Oregon, DB (2)
2010 Devin McCourty, Rutgers, DB

NEW ORLEANS SAINTS

Year Player, College, Position
1967 Les Kelley, Alabama, RB
1968 Kevin Hardy, Notre Dame, DE
1969 John Shinners, Xavier, G
1970 Ken Burrough, Texas Southern, WR
1971 Archie Manning, Mississippi, QB
1972 Royce Smith, Georgia, G
1973 Derland Moore, Oklahoma, DE (2)
1974 Rick Middleton, Ohio State, LB
1975 Larry Burton, Purdue, WR
Kurt Schumacher, Ohio State, T
1976 Chuck Muncie, California, RB
1977 Joe Campbell, Maryland, DE
1978 Wes Chandler, Florida, WR
1979 Russell Erxleben, Texas, P-K
1980 Stan Brock, Colorado, T
1981 George Rogers, South Carolina, RB
1982 Lindsay Scott, Georgia, WR
1983 Steve Korte, Arkansas, G (2)
1984 James Geathers, Wichita State, DE
1985 Alvin Toles, Tennessee, LB
1986 Jim Dombrowski, Virginia, T
1987 Shawn Knight, Brigham Young, DT
1988 Craig Heyward, Pittsburgh, RB
1989 Wayne Martin, Arkansas, DE
1990 Renaldo Turnbull, West Virginia, DE
1991 Wesley Carroll, Miami, WR (2)
1992 Vaughn Dunbar, Indiana, RB
1993 Willie Roaf, Louisiana Tech, T
Irv Smith, Notre Dame, TE
1994 Joe Johnson, Louisville, DE
1995 Mark Fields, Washington State, LB
1996 Alex Molden, Oregon, DB
1997 Chris Naeole, Colorado, G
1998 Kyle Turley, San Diego State, T
1999 Ricky Williams, Texas, RB
2000 Darren Howard, Kansas St., DE (2)
2001 Deuce McAllister, Mississippi, RB
2002 Donte' Stallworth, Tennessee, WR
Charles Grant, Georgia, DE
2003 Johnathan Sullivan, Georgia, DT
2004 Will Smith, Ohio State, DE
2005 Jammal Brown, Oklahoma, T
2006 Reggie Bush, So. California, RB
2007 Robert Meachem, Tennessee, WR
2008 Sedrick Ellis, So. California, DT
2009 Malcolm Jenkins, Ohio State, DB
2010 Patrick Robinson, Florida State, DB

NEW YORK GIANTS

Year Player, College, Position
1936 Art Lewis, Ohio U., T
1937 Ed Widseth, Minnesota, T
1938 George Karamatic, Gonzaga, B
1939 Walt Neilson, Arizona, B
1940 Grenville Lansdell, So. California, B
1941 George Franck, Minnesota, B
1942 Merle Hapes, Mississippi, B
1943 Steve Filipowicz, Fordham, B
1944 Billy Hillenbrand, Indiana, B
1945 Elmer Barbour, Wake Forest, B
1946 George Connor, Notre Dame, T
1947 Vic Schwall, Northwestern, B
1948 Tony Minisi, Pennsylvania, B
1949 Paul Page, Southern Methodist, B
1950 Travis Tidwell, Auburn, B
1951 Kyle Rote, Southern Methodist, B
Jim Spavital, Oklahoma A&M, B
1952 Frank Gifford, Southern California, B
1953 Bobby Marlow, Alabama, B
1954 Ken Buck, Pacific, C (2)
1955 Joe Heap, Notre Dame, B
1956 Henry Moore, Arkansas, B (2)
1957 Sam DeLuca, South Carolina, T (2)
1958 Phil King, Vanderbilt, B
1959 Lee Grosscup, Utah, B
1960 Lou Cordileone, Clemson, G
1961 Bruce Tarbox, Syracuse, G (2)
1962 Jerry Hillebrand, Colorado, LB
1963 Frank Lasky, Florida, T (2)
1964 Joe Don Looney, Oklahoma, RB
1965 Tucker Frederickson, Auburn, RB
1966 Francis Peay, Missouri, T
1967 Louis Thompson, Alabama, DT (4)
1968 Dick Buzin, Penn State, T (2)
1969 Fred Dryer, San Diego State, DE
1970 Jim Files, Oklahoma, LB
1971 Rocky Thompson, West Texas St., WR
1972 Eldridge Small, Texas A&I, DB
Larry Jacobson, Nebraska, DE
1973 Brad Van Pelt, Michigan St., LB (2)
1974 John Hicks, Ohio State, G
1975 Al Simpson, Colorado State, T (2)
1976 Troy Archer, Colorado, DE
1977 Gary Jeter, Southern California, DT
1978 Gordon King, Stanford, T
1979 Phil Simms, Morehead State, QB
1980 Mark Haynes, Colorado, DB
1981 Lawrence Taylor, North Carolina, LB
1982 Butch Woolfolk, Michigan, RB
1983 Terry Kinard, Clemson, DB
1984 Carl Banks, Michigan State, LB
William Roberts, Ohio State, T
1985 George Adams, Kentucky, RB
1986 Eric Dorsey, Notre Dame, DE
1987 Mark Ingram, Michigan State, WR
1988 Eric Moore, Indiana, T
1989 Brian Williams, Minnesota, C-G
1990 Rodney Hampton, Georgia, RB
1991 Jarrod Bunch, Michigan, RB
1992 Derek Brown, Notre Dame, TE
1993 Michael Strahan, Texas Southern, DE (2)
1994 Thomas Lewis, Indiana, WR
1995 Tyrone Wheatley, Michigan, RB
1996 Cedric Jones, Oklahoma, DE
1997 Ike Hilliard, Florida, WR
1998 Shaun Williams, UCLA, DB
1999 Luke Petitgout, Notre Dame, T
2000 Ron Dayne, Wisconsin, RB
2001 Will Allen, Syracuse, DB
2002 Jeremy Shockey, Miami, TE
2003 William Joseph, Miami, DT
2004 Philip Rivers, North Carolina St., QB
2005 Corey Webster, Louisiana St., DB (2)
2006 Mathias Kiwanuka, Boston College, DE
2007 Aaron Ross, Texas, DB
2008 Kenny Phillips, Miami, DB
2009 Hakeem Nicks, North Carolina, WR
2010 Jason Pierre-Paul, South Florida, DE

NEW YORK JETS

Year Player, College, Position
1960 George Izo, Notre Dame, QB
1961 Tom Brown, Minnesota, G
1962 Sandy Stephens, Minnesota, QB
1963 Jerry Stovall, Louisiana State, S
1964 Matt Snell, Ohio State, RB
1965 Joe Namath, Alabama, QB
Tom Nowatzke, Indiana, RB
1966 Bill Yearby, Michigan, DT
1967 Paul Seiler, Notre Dame, T
1968 Lee White, Weber State, RB
1969 Dave Foley, Ohio State, T

FIRST-ROUND SELECTIONS

1970 Steve Tannen, Florida, CB
1971 John Riggins, Kansas, RB
1972 Jerome Barkum, Jackson St., WR
Mike Taylor, Michigan, LB
1973 Burgess Owens, Miami, DB
1974 Carl Barzilauskas, Indiana, DT
1975 Anthony Davis, So. California, RB (2)
1976 Richard Todd, Alabama, QB
1977 Marvin Powell, So. California, T
1978 Chris Ward, Ohio State, T
1979 Marty Lyons, Alabama, DE
1980 Johnny (Lam) Jones, Texas, WR
1981 Freeman McNeil, UCLA, RB
1982 Bob Crable, Notre Dame, LB
1983 Ken O'Brien, Cal-Davis, QB
1984 Russell Carter, So. Methodist, DB
Ron Faurot, Arkansas, DE
1985 Al Toon, Wisconsin, WR
1986 Mike Haight, Iowa, T
1987 Roger Vick, Texas A&M, RB
1988 Dave Cadigan, So. California, T
1989 Jeff Lageman, Virginia, LB
1990 Blair Thomas, Penn State, RB
1991 Browning Nagle, Louisville, QB (2)
1992 Johnny Mitchell, Nebraska, TE
1993 Marvin Jones, Florida State, LB
1994 Aaron Glenn, Texas A&M, DB
1995 Kyle Brady, Penn State, TE
Hugh Douglas, Central St., Ohio, DE
1996 Keyshawn Johnson, So. California, WR
1997 James Farrior, Virginia, LB
1998 Dorian Boose, Washington St., DE (2)
1999 Randy Thomas, Mississippi St., G (2)
2000 Shaun Ellis, Tennessee, DE
John Abraham, South Carolina, LB
Chad Pennington, Marshall, QB
Anthony Becht, West Virginia, TE
2001 Santana Moss, Miami, WR
2002 Bryan Thomas, Ala.-Birmingham, DE
2003 Dewayne Robertson, Kentucky, DT
2004 Jonathan Vilma, Miami, LB
2005 Mike Nugent, Ohio State, K (2)
2006 D'Brickashaw Ferguson, Virginia, T
Nick Mangold, Ohio State, C
2007 Darrelle Revis, Pittsburgh, DB
2008 Vernon Gholston, Ohio State, LB
Dustin Keller, Purdue, TE
2009 Mark Sanchez, So. California, QB
2010 Kyle Wilson, Boise State, DB

OAKLAND RAIDERS

Year Player, College, Position
1960 Dale Hackbart, Wisconsin, CB
1961 Joe Rutgens, Illinois, DT
1962 Roman Gabriel, North Carolina St., QB
1963 George Wilson, Alabama, RB (6)
1964 Tony Lorick, Arizona State, RB
1965 Harry Schuh, Memphis State, T
1966 Rodger Bird, Kentucky, S
1967 Gene Upshaw, Texas A&I, G
1968 Eldridge Dickey, Tennessee St., QB
1969 Art Thoms, Syracuse, DT
1970 Raymond Chester, Morgan St., TE
1971 Jack Tatum, Ohio State, S
1972 Mike Siani, Villanova, WR
1973 Ray Guy, Southern Mississippi, P
1974 Henry Lawrence, Florida A&M, T
1975 Neal Colzie, Ohio State, DB
1976 Charles Philyaw, Texas Southern, DT (2)
1977 Mike Davis, Colorado, DB (2)
1978 Dave Browning, Washington, DE (2)
1979 Willie Jones, Florida State, DE (2)
1980 Marc Wilson, Brigham Young, QB
1981 Ted Watts, Texas Tech, DB
Curt Marsh, Washington, T
1982 Marcus Allen, So. California, RB
1983 Don Mosebar, So. California, T
1984 Sean Jones, Northeastern, DE (2)
1985 Jessie Hester, Florida State, WR
1986 Bob Buczkowski, Pittsburgh, DE
1987 John Clay, Missouri, T
1988 Tim Brown, Notre Dame, WR
Terry McDaniel, Tennessee, DB
Scott Davis, Illinois, DE
1989 Jeff Francis, Tennessee, QB (6)
1990 Anthony Smith, Arizona, DE
1991 Todd Marinovich, So. California, QB
1992 Chester McGlockton, Clemson, DE
1993 Patrick Bates, Texas A&M, DB
1994 Rob Fredrickson, Michigan St., LB
1995 Napoleon Kaufman, Washington, RB
1996 Rickey Dudley, Ohio State, TE
1997 Darrell Russell, Southern California, DT
1998 Charles Woodson, Michigan, DB
Mo Collins, Florida, T
1999 Matt Stinchcomb, Georgia, T
2000 Sebastian Janikowski, Florida St., K
2001 Derrick Gibson, Florida State, DB
2002 Phillip Buchanon, Miami, DB
Napoleon Harris, Northwestern, LB
2003 Nnamdi Asomugha, California, DB
Tyler Brayton, Colorado, DE
2004 Robert Gallery, Iowa, T
2005 Fabian Washington, Nebraska, DB
2006 Michael Huff, Texas, DB
2007 JaMarcus Russell, Louisiana State, QB
2008 Darren McFadden, Arkansas, RB
2009 Darrius Heyward-Bey, Maryland, WR
2010 Rolando McClain, Alabama, LB

PHILADELPHIA EAGLES

Year Player, College, Position
1936 Jay Berwanger, Chicago, B
1937 Sam Francis, Nebraska, B
1938 Jim McDonald, Ohio State, B
1939 Davey O'Brien, Texas Christian, B
1940 George McAfee, Duke, B
1941 Art Jones, Richmond, B (2)
1942 Pete Kmetovic, Stanford, B
1943 Joe Muha, Virginia Military, B
1944 Steve Van Buren, Louisiana St., B
1945 John Yonaker, Notre Dame, E
1946 Leo Riggs, Southern California, B
1947 Neill Armstrong, Oklahoma A&M, E
1948 Clyde (Smackover) Scott, Arkansas, B
1949 Chuck Bednarik, Pennsylvania, C
Frank Tripucka, Notre Dame, B
1950 Harry (Bud) Grant, Minnesota, E
1951 Ebert Van Buren, Louisiana St., B
Chet Mutryn, Xavier, B
1952 Johnny Bright, Drake, B
1953 Al Conway, Army, B (2)
1954 Neil Worden, Notre Dame, B
1955 Dick Bielski, Maryland, B
1956 Bob Pellegrini, Maryland, C
1957 Clarence Peaks, Michigan State, B
1958 Walt Kowalczyk, Michigan State, B
1959 J.D. Smith, Rice, T (2)
1960 Ron Burton, Northwestern, RB
1961 Art Baker, Syracuse, RB
1962 Pete Case, Georgia, G (2)
1963 Ed Budde, Michigan State, G
1964 Bob Brown, Nebraska, T
1965 Ray Rissmiller, Georgia, T (2)
1966 Randy Beisler, Indiana, DE
1967 Harry Jones, Arkansas, RB
1968 Tim Rossovich, So. California, DE
1969 Leroy Keyes, Purdue, RB
1970 Steve Zabel, Oklahoma, TE
1971 Richard Harris, Grambling, DE
1972 John Reaves, Florida, QB
1973 Jerry Sisemore, Texas, T
Charle Young, So. California, TE
1974 Mitch Sutton, Kansas, DT (3)
1975 Bill Capraun, Miami, T (7)
1976 Mike Smith, Florida, DE (4)
1977 Skip Sharp, Kansas, DB (5)
1978 Reggie Wilkes, Georgia Tech, LB (3)
1979 Jerry Robinson, UCLA, LB
1980 Roynell Young, Alcorn State, DB
1981 Leonard Mitchell, Houston, DE
1982 Mike Quick, North Carolina St., WR
1983 Michael Haddix, Mississippi St., RB
1984 Kenny Jackson, Penn State, WR
1985 Kevin Allen, Indiana, T
1986 Keith Byars, Ohio State, RB
1987 Jerome Brown, Miami, DT
1988 Keith Jackson, Oklahoma, TE
1989 Jessie Small, Eastern Kentucky, LB (2)
1990 Ben Smith, Georgia, DB
1991 Antone Davis, Tennessee, T
1992 Siran Stacy, Alabama, RB (2)
1993 Lester Holmes, Jackson State, T
Leonard Renfro, Colorado, DT
1994 Bernard Williams, Georgia, T
1995 Mike Mamula, Boston College, DE
1996 Jermane Mayberry, Texas A&M-Kingsville, T
1997 Jon Harris, Virginia, DE
1998 Tra Thomas, Florida State, T
1999 Donovan McNabb, Syracuse, QB
2000 Corey Simon, Florida State, DT
2001 Freddie Mitchell, UCLA, WR
2002 Lito Sheppard, Florida, DB
2003 Jerome McDougle, Miami, DE
2004 Shawn Andrews, Arkansas, T
2005 Mike Patterson, So. California, DT
2006 Brodrick Bunkley, Florida State, DT
2007 Kevin Kolb, Houston, QB (2)
2008 Trevor Laws, Notre Dame, DT (2)
2009 Jeremy Maclin, Missouri, WR
2010 Brandon Graham, Michigan, DE

PITTSBURGH STEELERS

Year Player, College, Position
1936 Bill Shakespeare, Notre Dame, B
1937 Mike Basrak, Duquesne, C
1938 Byron (Whizzer) White, Colorado, B
1939 Bill Patterson, Baylor, B (3)
1940 Kay Eakin, Arkansas, B
1941 Chet Gladchuk, Boston College, C (2)
1942 Bill Dudley, Virginia, B
1943 Bill Daley, Minnesota, B
1944 Johnny Podesto, St. Mary's, Calif., B
1945 Paul Duhart, Florida, B
1946 Felix (Doc) Blanchard, Army, B
1947 Hub Bechtol, Texas, E
1948 Dan Edwards, Georgia, E
1949 Bobby Gage, Clemson, B
1950 Lynn Chandnois, Michigan St., B
1951 Butch Avinger, Alabama, B

1952 Ed Modzelewski, Maryland, B
1953 Ted Marchibroda, St. Bonaventure, B
1954 Johnny Lattner, Notre Dame, B
1955 Frank Varrichione, Notre Dame, T
1956 Gary Glick, Colorado A&M, B
Art Davis, Mississippi State, B
1957 Len Dawson, Purdue, B
1958 Larry Krutko, West Virginia, B (2)
1959 Tom Barnett, Purdue, B (8)
1960 Jack Spikes, Texas Christian, RB
1961 Myron Pottios, Notre Dame, LB (2)
1962 Bob Ferguson, Ohio State, RB
1963 Frank Atkinson, Stanford, T (8)
1964 Paul Martha, Pittsburgh, S
1965 Roy Jefferson, Utah, WR (2)
1966 Dick Leftridge, West Virginia, RB
1967 Don Shy, San Diego State, RB (2)
1968 Mike Taylor, Southern California, T
1969 Joe Greene, North Texas State, DT
1970 Terry Bradshaw, Louisiana Tech, QB
1971 Frank Lewis, Grambling, WR
1972 Franco Harris, Penn State, RB
1973 J.T. Thomas, Florida State, DB
1974 Lynn Swann, So. California, WR
1975 Dave Brown, Michigan, DB
1976 Bennie Cunningham, Clemson, TE
1977 Robin Cole, New Mexico, LB
1978 Ron Johnson, Eastern Michigan, DB
1979 Greg Hawthorne, Baylor, RB
1980 Mark Malone, Arizona State, QB
1981 Keith Gary, Oklahoma, DE
1982 Walter Abercrombie, Baylor, RB
1983 Gabriel Rivera, Texas Tech, DT
1984 Louis Lipps, So. Mississippi, WR
1985 Darryl Sims, Wisconsin, DE
1986 John Rienstra, Temple, G
1987 Rod Woodson, Purdue, DB
1988 Aaron Jones, Eastern Kentucky, DE
1989 Tim Worley, Georgia, RB
Tom Ricketts, Pittsburgh, T
1990 Eric Green, Liberty, TE
1991 Huey Richardson, Florida, DE
1992 Leon Searcy, Miami, T
1993 Deon Figures, Colorado, DB
1994 Charles Johnson, Colorado, WR
1995 Mark Bruener, Washington, TE
1996 Jamain Stephens, North Carolina A&T, T
1997 Chad Scott, Maryland, DB
1998 Alan Faneca, Louisiana State, G
1999 Troy Edwards, Louisiana Tech, WR
2000 Plaxico Burress, Michigan St., WR
2001 Casey Hampton, Texas, DT
2002 Kendall Simmons, Auburn, G
2003 Troy Polamalu, Southern California, DB
2004 Ben Roethlisberger, Miami (OH), QB
2005 Heath Miller, Virginia, TE
2006 Santonio Holmes, Ohio State, WR
2007 Lawrence Timmons, Florida State, LB
2008 Rashard Mendenhall, Illinois, RB
2009 Evander Hood, Missouri, DE
2010 Maurkice Pouncey, Florida, C

ST. LOUIS RAMS

Year Player, College, Position

1937 Johnny Drake, Purdue, B
1938 Corbett Davis, Indiana, B
1939 Parker Hall, Mississippi, B
1940 Ollie Cordill, Rice, B
1941 Rudy Mucha, Washington, C
1942 Jack Wilson, Baylor, B
1943 Mike Holovak, Boston College, B
1944 Tony Butkovich, Illinois, B
1945 Elroy (Crazylegs) Hirsch, Wisconsin, B
1946 Emil Sitko, Notre Dame, B
1947 Herman Wedemeyer, St. Mary's, Calif., B
1948 Tom Keane, West Virginia, B (2)
1949 Bobby Thomason, Virginia Military, B
1950 Ralph Pasquariello, Villanova, B
Stan West, Oklahoma, G
1951 Bud McFadin, Texas, G
1952 Bill Wade, Vanderbilt, QB
Bob Carey, Michigan State, E
1953 Donn Moomaw, UCLA, C
Ed Barker, Washington State, E
1954 Ed Beatty, Cincinnati, C
1955 Larry Morris, Georgia Tech, C
1956 Joe Marconi, West Virginia, B
Charles Horton, Vanderbilt, B
1957 Jon Arnett, Southern California, B
Del Shofner, Baylor, E
1958 Lou Michaels, Kentucky, T
Jim Phillips, Auburn, E
1959 Dick Bass, Pacific, B
Paul Dickson, Baylor, T
1960 Billy Cannon, Louisiana State, RB
1961 Marlin McKeever, So. California, E-LB
1962 Roman Gabriel, North Carolina St., QB
Merlin Olsen, Utah State, DT
1963 Terry Baker, Oregon State, QB
Rufus Guthrie, Georgia Tech, G
1964 Bill Munson, Utah State, QB
1965 Clancy Williams, Washington St., CB
1966 Tom Mack, Michigan, G
1967 Willie Ellison, Texas Southern, RB (2)
1968 Gary Beban, UCLA, QB (2)
1969 Larry Smith, Florida, RB
Jim Seymour, Notre Dame, WR
Bob Klein, Southern California, TE
1970 Jack Reynolds, Tennessee, LB
1971 Isiah Robertson, Southern, LB
Jack Youngblood, Florida, DE
1972 Jim Bertelsen, Texas, RB (2)
1973 Cullen Bryant, Colorado, DB (2)
1974 John Cappelletti, Penn State, RB
1975 Mike Fanning, Notre Dame, DT
Dennis Harrah, Miami, T
Doug France, Ohio State, T
1976 Kevin McLain, Colorado State, LB
1977 Bob Brudzinski, Ohio State, LB
1978 Elvis Peacock, Oklahoma, RB
1979 George Andrews, Nebraska, LB
Kent Hill, Georgia Tech, T
1980 Johnnie Johnson, Texas, DB
1981 Mel Owens, Michigan, LB
1982 Barry Redden, Richmond, RB
1983 Eric Dickerson, So. Methodist, RB
1984 Hal Stephens, East Carolina, DE (5)
1985 Jerry Gray, Texas, DB
1986 Mike Schad, Queen's Univ., Canada, T
1987 Donald Evans, Winston-Salem, DE (2)
1988 Gaston Green, UCLA, RB
Aaron Cox, Arizona State, WR
1989 Bill Hawkins, Miami, DE
Cleveland Gary, Miami, RB
1990 Bern Brostek, Washington, C
1991 Todd Lyght, Notre Dame, DB
1992 Sean Gilbert, Pittsburgh, DE
1993 Jerome Bettis, Notre Dame, RB
1994 Wayne Gandy, Auburn, T
1995 Kevin Carter, Florida, DE
1996 Lawrence Phillips, Nebraska, RB
Eddie Kennison, Louisiana St., WR
1997 Orlando Pace, Ohio State, T
1998 Grant Wistrom, Nebraska, DE
1999 Torry Holt, North Carolina St., WR
2000 Trung Canidate, Arizona, RB
2001 Damione Lewis, Miami, DT
Adam Archuleta, Arizona State, DB
Ryan Pickett, Ohio State, DT
2002 Robert Thomas, UCLA, LB
2003 Jimmy Kennedy, Penn State, DT
2004 Steven Jackson, Oregon State, RB
2005 Alex Barron, Florida State, T
2006 Tye Hill, Clemson, DB
2007 Adam Carriker, Nebraska, DE
2008 Chris Long, Virginia, DE
2009 Jason Smith, Baylor, T
2010 Sam Bradford, Oklahoma, QB

SAN DIEGO CHARGERS

Year Player, College, Position

1960 Monty Stickles, Notre Dame, E
1961 Earl Faison, Indiana, DE
1962 Bob Ferguson, Ohio State, RB
1963 Walt Sweeney, Syracuse, G
1964 Ted Davis, Georgia Tech, LB
1965 Steve DeLong, Tennessee, DE
1966 Don Davis, Cal St.-Los Angeles, DT
1967 Ron Billingsley, Wyoming, DE
1968 Russ Washington, Missouri, DT
Jimmy Hill, Texas A&I, DB
1969 Marty Domres, Columbia, QB
Bob Babich, Miami, Ohio, LB
1970 Walker Gillette, Richmond, WR
1971 Leon Burns, Long Beach State, RB
1972 Pete Lazetich, Stanford, DE (2)
1973 Johnny Rodgers, Nebraska, WR
1974 Bo Matthews, Colorado, RB
Don Goode, Kansas, LB
1975 Gary Johnson, Grambling, DT
Mike Williams, Louisiana State, DB
1976 Joe Washington, Oklahoma, RB
1977 Bob Rush, Memphis State, C
1978 John Jefferson, Arizona State, WR
1979 Kellen Winslow, Missouri, TE
1980 Ed Luther, San Jose State, QB (4)
1981 James Brooks, Auburn, RB
1982 Hollis Hall, Clemson, DB (7)
1983 Billy Ray Smith, Arkansas, LB
Gary Anderson, Arkansas, WR
Gill Byrd, San Jose State, DB
1984 Mossy Cade, Texas, DB
1985 Jim Lachey, Ohio State, G
1986 Leslie O'Neal, Oklahoma State, DE
James FitzPatrick, So. California, T
1987 Rod Bernstine, Texas A&M, TE
1988 Anthony Miller, Tennessee, WR
1989 Burt Grossman, Pittsburgh, DE
1990 Junior Seau, So. California, LB
1991 Stanley Richard, Texas, DB
1992 Chris Mims, Tennessee, DE
1993 Darrien Gordon, Stanford, DB
1994 Isaac Davis, Arkansas, G (2)
1995 Terrance Shaw, Stephen F. Austin, DB (2)
1996 Bryan Still, Virginia Tech, WR (2)
1997 Freddie Jones, North Carolina, TE (2)
1998 Ryan Leaf, Washington State, QB
1999 Jermaine Fazande, Oklahoma, RB (2)
2000 Rogers Beckett, Marshall, DB (2)
2001 LaDainian Tomlinson, TCU, RB

2002 Quentin Jammer, Texas, DB
2003 Sammy Davis, Texas A&M, DB
2004 Eli Manning, Mississippi, QB
2005 Shawne Merriman, Maryland, LB
Luis Castillo, Northwestern, DT
2006 Antonio Cromartie, Florida State, DB
2007 Craig Davis, Louisiana State, WR
2008 Antoine Cason, Arizona, DB
2009 Larry English, Northern Illinois, LB
2010 Ryan Mathews, Fresno State, RB

SAN FRANCISCO 49ERS

Year Player, College, Position
1950 Leo Nomellini, Minnesota, T
1951 Y.A. Tittle, Louisiana State, B
1952 Hugh McElhenny, Washington, B
1953 Harry Babcock, Georgia, E
Tom Stolhandske, Texas, E
1954 Bernie Faloney, Maryland, B
1955 Dickie Moegle, Rice, B
1956 Earl Morrall, Michigan State, B
1957 John Brodie, Stanford, B
1958 Jim Pace, Michigan, B
Charlie Krueger, Texas A&M, T
1959 Dave Baker, Oklahoma, B
Dan James, Ohio State, C
1960 Monty Stickles, Notre Dame, E
1961 Jimmy Johnson, UCLA, CB
Bernie Casey, Bowling Green, WR
Bill Kilmer, UCLA, QB
1962 Lance Alworth, Arkansas, WR
1963 Kermit Alexander, UCLA, CB
1964 Dave Parks, Texas Tech, WR
1965 Ken Willard, North Carolina, RB
George Donnelly, Illinois, DB
1966 Stan Hindman, Mississippi, DE
1967 Steve Spurrier, Florida, QB
Cas Banaszek, Northwestern, T
1968 Forrest Blue, Auburn, C
1969 Ted Kwalick, Penn State, TE
Gene Washington, Stanford, WR
1970 Cedrick Hardman, North Texas St., DE
Bruce Taylor, Boston U., DB
1971 Tim Anderson, Ohio State, DB
1972 Terry Beasley, Auburn, WR
1973 Mike Holmes, Texas Southern, DB
1974 Wilbur Jackson, Alabama, RB
Bill Sandifer, UCLA, DT
1975 Jimmy Webb, Mississippi St., DT
1976 Randy Cross, UCLA, C (2)
1977 Elmo Boyd, Eastern Kentucky, WR (3)
1978 Ken MacAfee, Notre Dame, TE
Dan Bunz, Cal St.-Long Beach, LB
1979 James Owens, UCLA, WR (2)
1980 Earl Cooper, Rice, RB
Jim Stuckey, Clemson, DT
1981 Ronnie Lott, So. California, DB
1982 Bubba Paris, Michigan, T (2)
1983 Roger Craig, Nebraska, RB (2)
1984 Todd Shell, Brigham Young, LB
1985 Jerry Rice, Mississippi Valley St., WR
1986 Larry Roberts, Alabama, DE (2)
1987 Harris Barton, North Carolina, T
Terrence Flagler, Clemson, RB
1988 Danny Stubbs, Miami, DE (2)
1989 Keith DeLong, Tennessee, LB
1990 Dexter Carter, Florida State, RB
1991 Ted Washington, Louisville, DT
1992 Dana Hall, Washington, DB
1993 Dana Stubblefield, Kansas, DT
Todd Kelly, Tennessee, DE
1994 Bryant Young, Notre Dame, DT
William Floyd, Florida State, RB
1995 J.J. Stokes, UCLA, WR
1996 Israel Ifeanyi, So.California, DE (2)
1997 Jim Druckenmiller, Virginia Tech, QB
1998 R.W. McQuarters, Oklahoma St., DB
1999 Reggie McGrew, Florida, DT
2000 Julian Peterson, Michigan St., LB
Ahmed Plummer, Ohio State, DB
2001 Andre Carter, California, DE
2002 Mike Rumph, Miami, DB
2003 Kwame Harris, Stanford, T
2004 Rashaun Woods, Oklahoma St., WR
2005 Alex Smith, Utah, QB
2006 Vernon Davis, Maryland, TE
Manny Lawson, North Carolina St., DE
2007 Patrick Willis, Mississippi, LB
Joe Staley, Central Michigan, T
2008 Kentwan Balmer, North Carolina, DT
2009 Michael Crabtree, Texas Tech, WR
2010 Anthony Davis, Rutgers, T
Mike Iupati, Idaho, G

SEATTLE SEAHAWKS

Year Player, College, Position
1976 Steve Niehaus, Notre Dame, DT
1977 Steve August, Tulsa, G
1978 Keith Simpson, Memphis St., DB
1979 Manu Tuiasosopo, UCLA, DT
1980 Jacob Green, Texas A&M, DE
1981 Ken Easley, UCLA, DB
1982 Jeff Bryant, Clemson, DE
1983 Curt Warner, Penn State, RB
1984 Terry Taylor, Southern Illinois, DB
1985 Owen Gill, Iowa, RB (2)
1986 John L. Williams, Florida, RB
1987 Tony Woods, Pittsburgh, LB
1988 Brian Blades, Miami, WR (2)
1989 Andy Heck, Notre Dame, T
1990 Cortez Kennedy, Miami, DT
1991 Dan McGwire, San Diego St., QB
1992 Ray Roberts, Virginia, T
1993 Rick Mirer, Notre Dame, QB
1994 Sam Adams, Texas A&M, DT
1995 Joey Galloway, Ohio State, WR
1996 Pete Kendall, Boston College, T
1997 Shawn Springs, Ohio State, DB
Walter Jones, Florida State, T
1998 Anthony Simmons, Clemson, LB
1999 Lamar King, Saginaw Valley St., DE
2000 Shaun Alexander, Alabama, RB
Chris McIntosh, Wisconsin, T
2001 Koren Robinson, North Carolina St., WR
Steve Hutchinson, Michigan, G
2002 Jerramy Stevens, Washington, TE
2003 Marcus Trufant, Washington State, DB
2004 Marcus Tubbs, Texas, DT
2005 Chris Spencer, Mississippi, C
2006 Kelly Jennings, Miami, DB
2007 Josh Wilson, Maryland, DB (2)
2008 Lawrence Jackson, So. California, DE
2009 Aaron Curry, Wake Forest, LB
2010 Russell Okung, Oklahoma State, T
Earl Thomas, Texas, DB

TAMPA BAY BUCCANEERS

Year Player, College, Position
1976 Lee Roy Selmon, Oklahoma, DT
1977 Ricky Bell, Southern California, RB
1978 Doug Williams, Grambling, QB
1979 Greg Roberts, Oklahoma, G (2)
1980 Ray Snell, Wisconsin, G
1981 Hugh Green, Pittsburgh, LB
1982 Sean Farrell, Penn State, G
1983 Randy Grimes, Baylor, C (2)
1984 Keith Browner, So. California, LB (2)
1985 Ron Holmes, Washington, DE
1986 Bo Jackson, Auburn, RB
Roderick Jones, So. Methodist, DB
1987 Vinny Testaverde, Miami, QB
1988 Paul Gruber, Wisconsin, T
1989 Broderick Thomas, Nebraska, LB
1990 Keith McCants, Alabama, LB
1991 Charles McRae, Tennessee, T
1992 Courtney Hawkins, Michigan St., WR (2)
1993 Eric Curry, Alabama, DE
1994 Trent Dilfer, Fresno State, QB
1995 Warren Sapp, Miami, DT
Derrick Brooks, Florida State, LB
1996 Regan Upshaw, California, DE
Marcus Jones, North Carolina, DT
1997 Warrick Dunn, Florida State, RB
Reidel Anthony, Florida, WR
1998 Jacquez Green, Florida, WR (2)
1999 Anthony McFarland, Louisiana St., DT
2000 Cosey Coleman, Tennessee, G (2)
2001 Kenyatta Walker, Florida, T
2002 Marquise Walker, Michigan, WR (3)
2003 Dewayne White, Louisville, DE (2)
2004 Michael Clayton, Louisiana St., WR
2005 Carnell Williams, Auburn, RB
2006 Davin Joseph, Oklahoma, G
2007 Gaines Adams, Clemson, DE
2008 Aqib Talib, Kansas, DB
2009 Josh Freeman, Kansas State, QB
2010 Gerald McCoy, Oklahoma, DT

TENNESSEE TITANS

Year Player, College, Position
1960 Billy Cannon, Louisiana State, RB
1961 Mike Ditka, Pittsburgh, E
1962 Ray Jacobs, Howard Payne, DT
1963 Danny Brabham, Arkansas, LB
1964 Scott Appleton, Texas, DT
1965 Lawrence Elkins, Baylor, WR
1966 Tommy Nobis, Texas, LB
1967 George Webster, Michigan St., LB
Tom Regner, Notre Dame, G
1968 Mac Haik, Mississippi, WR (2)
1969 Ron Pritchard, Arizona State, LB
1970 Doug Wilkerson, N. Carolina Central, G
1971 Dan Pastorini, Santa Clara, QB
1972 Greg Sampson, Stanford, DE
1973 John Matuszak, Tampa, DE
George Amundson, Iowa State, RB
1974 Steve Manstedt, Nebraska, LB (4)
1975 Robert Brazile, Jackson State, LB
Don Hardeman, Texas A&I, RB
1976 Mike Barber, Louisiana Tech, TE (2)
1977 Morris Towns, Missouri, T
1978 Earl Campbell, Texas, RB
1979 Mike Stensrud, Iowa State, DE (2)
1980 Angelo Fields, Michigan St., T (2)
1981 Michael Holston, Morgan St., WR (3)
1982 Mike Munchak, Penn State, G

1983 Bruce Matthews, So. California, T
1984 Dean Steinkuhler, Nebraska, T
1985 Ray Childress, Texas A&M, DE
Richard Johnson, Wisconsin, DB
1986 Jim Everett, Purdue, QB
1987 Alonzo Highsmith, Miami, RB
Haywood Jeffires, North Carolina St., WR
1988 Lorenzo White, Michigan State, RB
1989 David Williams, Florida, T
1990 Lamar Lathon, Houston, LB
1991 Mike Dumas, Indiana, DB (2)
1992 Eddie Robinson, Alabama St., LB (2)
1993 Brad Hopkins, Illinois, T
1994 Henry Ford, Arkansas, DE
1995 Steve McNair, Alcorn State, QB
1996 Eddie George, Ohio State, RB
1997 Kenny Holmes, Miami, DE
1998 Kevin Dyson, Utah, WR
1999 Jevon Kearse, Florida, DE
2000 Keith Bulluck, Syracuse, LB
2001 Andre Dyson, Utah, DB (2)
2002 Albert Haynesworth, Tennessee, DT
2003 Andre Woolfolk, Oklahoma, DB
2004 Ben Troupe, Florida, TE (2)
2005 Adam Jones, West Virginia, DB
2006 Vince Young, Texas, QB
2007 Michael Griffin, Texas, DB
2008 Chris Johnson, East Carolina, RB
2009 Kenny Britt, Rutgers, WR
2010 Derrick Morgan, Georgia Tech, DE

WASHINGTON REDSKINS

Year Player, College, Position
1936 Riley Smith, Alabama, B
1937 Sammy Baugh, Texas Christian, B
1938 Andy Farkas, Detroit, B
1939 I.B. Hale, Texas Christian, T
1940 Ed Boell, New York U., B
1941 Forest Evashevski, Michigan, B
1942 Orban (Spec) Sanders, Texas, B
1943 Jack Jenkins, Missouri, B
1944 Mike Micka, Colgate, B
1945 Jim Hardy, Southern California, B
1946 Cal Rossi, UCLA, B*
1947 Cal Rossi, UCLA, B
1948 Harry Gilmer, Alabama, B
Lowell Tew, Alabama, B
1949 Rob Goode, Texas A&M, B
1950 George Thomas, Oklahoma, B
1951 Leon Heath, Oklahoma, B
1952 Larry Isbell, Baylor, B
1953 Jack Scarbath, Maryland, B
1954 Steve Meilinger, Kentucky, E
1955 Ralph Guglielmi, Notre Dame, B
1956 Ed Vereb, Maryland, B
1957 Don Bosseler, Miami, B
1958 Mike Sommer, George Washington, B (2)
1959 Don Allard, Boston College, B
1960 Richie Lucas, Penn State, QB
1961 Norman Snead, Wake Forest, QB
Joe Rutgens, Illinois, DT
1962 Ernie Davis, Syracuse, RB
1963 Pat Richter, Wisconsin, TE
1964 Charley Taylor, Arizona St., RB-WR
1965 Bob Breitenstein, Tulsa, T (2)
1966 Charlie Gogolak, Princeton, K
1967 Ray McDonald, Idaho, RB
1968 Jim Smith, Oregon, DB
1969 Eugene Epps, Texas-El Paso, DB (2)
1970 Bill Bundige, Colorado, DT (2)
1971 Cotton Speyrer, Texas, WR (2)
1972 Moses Denson, Maryland St., RB (8)
1973 Charles Cantrell, Lamar, G (5)
1974 Jon Keyworth, Colorado, TE (6)
1975 Mike Thomas, Nevada-Las Vegas, RB (6)
1976 Mike Hughes, Baylor, G (5)
1977 Duncan McColl, Stanford, DE (4)
1978 Tony Green, Florida, RB (6)
1979 Don Warren, San Diego St., TE (4)
1980 Art Monk, Syracuse, WR
1981 Mark May, Pittsburgh, T
1982 Vernon Dean, San Diego St., DB (2)
1983 Darrell Green, Texas A&I, DB
1984 Bob Slater, Oklahoma, DT (2)
1985 Tory Nixon, San Diego St., DB (2)
1986 Markus Koch, Boise State, DE (2)
1987 Brian Davis, Nebraska, DB (2)
1988 Chip Lohmiller, Minnesota, K (2)
1989 Tracy Rocker, Auburn, DT (3)
1990 Andre Collins, Penn State, LB (2)
1991 Bobby Wilson, Michigan State, DT
1992 Desmond Howard, Michigan, WR
1993 Tom Carter, Notre Dame, DB
1994 Heath Shuler, Tennessee, QB
1995 Michael Westbrook, Colorado, WR
1996 Andre Johnson, Penn State, T
1997 Kenard Lang, Miami, DE
1998 Stephen Alexander, Oklahoma, TE (2)
1999 Champ Bailey, Georgia, DB
2000 LaVar Arrington, Penn State, LB
Chris Samuels, Alabama, T
2001 Rod Gardner, Clemson, WR
2002 Patrick Ramsey, Tulane, QB
2003 Taylor Jacobs, Florida, WR (2)
2004 Sean Taylor, Miami, DB
2005 Carlos Rogers, Auburn, DB
Jason Campbell, Auburn, QB
2006 Rocky McIntosh, Miami, LB (2)
2007 LaRon Landry, Louisiana State, DB
2008 Devin Thomas, Michigan State, WR (2)
2009 Brian Orakpo, Texas, DE
2010 Trent Williams, Oklahoma, T

**Choice lost because of ineligibility*

NFL'S 10 HIGHEST SCORING WEEKENDS

Point Total	Date	Weekend
837	November 20-24, 2008	12th
788	December 29-30, 2007	17th
788	December 5-6, 2004	13th
788	September 5, 8-9, 2002	1st
762	November 10-11, 1996	11th
761	October 16-17, 1983	7th
753	December 8-9, 2002	14th
752	November 29, December 2-3, 2007	13th
751	September 23-24, 2007	3rd
748	December 18-20, 2004	15th

TOP 10 TELEVISED SPORTS EVENTS OF ALL-TIME

(Based on A.C. Nielsen Figures)

Program	Date	Network	Share	Rating
Super Bowl XVI	1/24/82	CBS	73%	49.1
Super Bowl XVII	1/30/83	NBC	69%	48.6
Winter Olympics	2/23/94	CBS	64%	48.5
Super Bowl XX	1/26/86	NBC	70%	48.3
Super Bowl XII	1/15/78	CBS	67%	47.2
Super Bowl XIII	1/21/79	NBC	74%	47.1
Super Bowl XVIII	1/22/84	CBS	71%	46.4
Super Bowl XIX	1/20/85	ABC	63%	46.4
Super Bowl XIV	1/20/80	CBS	67%	46.3
Super Bowl XXX	1/28/96	NBC	68%	46.0

TEN MOST WATCHED TV PROGRAMS & ESTIMATED TOTAL NUMBER OF VIEWERS

(Based on A.C. Nielsen Figures)

Program	Date	Network	*Total Viewers
Super Bowl XLIV	Feb. 7, 2010	CBS	153,400,000
Super Bowl XLIII	Feb. 1, 2009	NBC	151,600,000
Super Bowl XLII	Feb. 3, 2008	FOX	148,300,000
Super Bowl XXXVIII	Feb. 1, 2004	CBS	144,400,000
Super Bowl XL	Feb. 5, 2006	ABC	141,400,000
Super Bowl XLI	Feb. 4, 2007	CBS	139,800,000
Super Bowl XXXVII	Jan. 26, 2003	ABC	138,900,000
Super Bowl XXX	Jan. 28, 1996	NBC	138,488,000
Super Bowl XXVIII	Jan. 30, 1994	NBC	134,800,000
Super Bowl XXXIX	Feb. 6, 2005	FOX	133,700,000

**Watched some portion of the broadcast*

NFL'S TOP FIVE PAID ATTENDANCE TOTALS FOR ALL GAMES

Year	Preseason	Regular Season	Postseason	All Games
2007	4,119,278	17,345,205	792,019	22,256,502
2006	4,083,282	17,340,879	775,551	22,199,712
2008	3,995,942	17,055,982	806,840	21,858,764
2005	3,977,388	17,012,453	802,255	21,792,096
2004	3,918,848	17,000,811	788,965	21,708,624

TEN HIGHEST-RATED *NFL MONDAY NIGHT FOOTBALL* GAMES OF ALL-TIME

(Based on A.C. Nielsen Figures)

Game	Date	Share	Rating
Chicago at Miami	12/2/85	46%	29.6
N.Y. Giants at San Francisco	12/3/90	42%	26.9
Dallas at Washington	10/2/78	43%	26.8
Pittsburgh at San Diego	12/22/80	40%	25.3
Philadelphia at Miami	11/30/81	40%	25.3
Pittsburgh at Houston	12/10/79	40%	25.1
Dallas at Miami	12/17/84	40%	25.1
Pittsburgh at Dallas	9/13/82	42%	24.9
Cincinnati at Oakland	12/6/76	40%	24.7
Dallas at Washington	10/8/73	40%	24.6
Minnesota at Atlanta	11/19/73	40%	24.6

NFL'S 10 BIGGEST SINGLE-GAME ATTENDANCE TOTALS

Date	Site	Game	Teams	Attendance
August 15, 1994	Azteca Stadium	American Bowl (Mexico City)	Cowboys vs. Oilers	112,376
August 17, 1998	Azteca Stadium	American Bowl (Mexico City)	Cowboys vs. Patriots	106,424
August 22, 1947	Soldier Field	College All-Star	Bears vs. All-Stars	105,840
September 20, 2009	Cowboys Stadium	Regular Season	Cowboys vs. Giants	105,121
August 4, 1997	Estadio Guillermo Canedo	American Bowl (Mexico City)	Broncos vs. Dolphins	104,629
January 20, 1980	Rose Bowl	Super Bowl XIV	Steelers vs. Rams	103,985
January 30, 1983	Rose Bowl	Super Bowl XVII	Redskins vs. Dolphins	103,667
October 2, 2005	Azteca Stadium	Regular Season	49ers at Cardinals	103,467
January 9, 1977	Rose Bowl	Super Bowl XI	Raiders vs. Vikings	103,438
November 10, 1957	L.A. Coliseum	Regular Season	49ers at Rams	102,368

NFL'S TOP 10 PAID ATTENDANCE WEEKENDS

Weekend	Games	Attendance
September 8, 11-12, 2005	16	1,115,018
December 6, 9-10, 2007	16	1,113,376
November 20-21, 2005	16	1,112,555
December 27-28, 2003	16	1,106,818
November 19-20, 2006	16	1,106,739
September 23-24, 2007	16	1,103,570
December 24-26, 2005	16	1,102,701
September 7, 10-11, 2006	16	1,102,102
September 9, 12-13, 2004	16	1,101,332
December 7, 10-11, 2006	16	1,099,794

NFL'S TOP 10 TEAM SINGLE-SEASON HOME PAID ATTENDANCE TOTALS

Year	Club	Games	Attendance
2007	Washington Redskins	8	711,471
2008	Washington Redskins	8	710,049
2006	Washington Redskins	8	708,952
2004	Washington Redskins	8	707,920
2005	Washington Redskins	8	707,614
2009	Washington Redskins	8	681,703
2003	Washington Redskins	8	667,033
2002	Washington Redskins	8	663,536
2001	Washington Redskins	8	661,970
2000	Washington Redskins	8	656,599

NFL PAID ATTENDANCE

For detailed 2009 attendance, see page 244.

Year	Regular Season			Average	Postseason	Total
2009	16,651,126	(256 games)		65,043	823,882 (12)	17,475,008
2008	17,055,982	(256 games)		66,625	806,840 (12)	17,862,822
2007	17,345,205	(256 games)		#67,755	792,019 (12)	#18,137,224
2006	17,340,879	(256 games)		67,738	775,551 (12)	18,116,430
2005	17,012,453	(256 games)		66,455	802,255 (12)	17,814,708
2004	17,000,811	(256 games)		66,409	788,965 (12)	17,789,776
2003	16,913,584	(255 games***)		66,328	805,546 (12)	17,719,130
2002	16,833,310	(256 games)		65,755	781,944 (12)	17,615,254
2001	16,166,258	(248 games)		65,187	766,905 (12)	16,933,163
2000	16,387,289	(248 games)		66,078	809,132 (12)	17,196,421
1999	16,206,640	(248 games)		65,349	793,759 (12)	17,000,399
1998	15,364,873	(240 games)		64,020	822,885 (12)	16,187,758
1997	14,967,314	(240 games)		62,364	801,879 (12)	15,769,193
1996	14,612,417	(240 games)		60,885	769,310 (12)	15,381,727
1995	15,043,562	(240 games)		62,682	790,906 (12)	15,834,468
1994	14,030,435	(224 games)		62,636	779,738 (12)	14,810,173
1993	13,966,843	(224 games)		62,352	814,607 (12)	14,781,450
1992	13,828,887	(224 games)		61,736	815,910 (12)	14,644,797
1991	13,841,459	(224 games)		61,792	813,247 (12)	14,654,706
1990	13,959,896	(224 games)		62,321	847,543 (12)	14,807,439
1989	13,625,662	(224 games)		60,829	685,771 (10)	14,311,433
1988	13,539,848	(224 games)		60,446	658,317 (10)	14,198,165
1987	11,406,166	(210 games**)		54,315	656,977 (10)	12,063,143
1986	13,588,551	(224 games)		60,663	734,002 (10)	14,322,553
1985	13,345,047	(224 games)		59,567	710,768 (10)	14,055,815
1984	13,398,112	(224 games)		59,813	665,194 (10)	14,063,306
1983	13,277,222	(224 games)		59,273	675,513 (10)	13,952,735
1982	7,367,438	(126 games*)		58,472	#1,033,153 (16)	8,400,591
1981	13,606,990	(224 games)		60,745	637,763 (10)	14,244,753
1980	13,392,230	(224 games)		59,787	624,430 (10)	14,016,660
1979	13,182,039	(224 games)		58,848	630,326 (10)	13,812,365
1978	12,771,800	(224 games)		57,017	624,388 (10)	13,396,188
1977	11,018,632	(196 games)		56,218	534,925 (8)	11,553,557
1976	11,070,543	(196 games)		56,482	492,884 (8)	11,563,427
1975	10,213,193	(182 games)		56,116	475,919 (8)	10,689,112
1974	10,236,322	(182 games)		56,244	438,664 (8)	10,674,986
1973	10,730,933	(182 games)		58,961	525,433 (8)	11,256,366
1972	10,445,827	(182 games)		57,395	483,345 (8)	10,929,172
1971	10,076,035	(182 games)		55,363	483,891 (8)	10,559,926
1970	9,533,333	(182 games)		52,381	458,493 (8)	9,991,826
1969	6,096,127	(112 games)	NFL	54,430	162,279 (3)	6,258,406
	2,843,373	(70 games)	AFL	40,620	167,088 (3)	3,010,461
1968	5,882,313	(112 games)	NFL	52,521	215,902 (3)	6,098,215
	2,635,004	(70 games)	AFL	37,643	114,438 (2)	2,749,442
1967	5,938,924	(112 games)	NFL	53,026	166,208 (3)	6,105,132
	2,295,697	(63 games)	AFL	36,439	53,330 (1)	2,349,027
1966	5,337,044	(105 games)	NFL	50,829	74,152 (1)	5,411,196
	2,160,369	(63 games)	AFL	34,291	42,080 (1)	2,202,449
1965	4,634,021	(98 games)	NFL	47,286	100,304 (2)	4,734,325
	1,782,384	(56 games)	AFL	31,828	30,361 (1)	1,812,745
1964	4,563,049	(98 games)	NFL	46,562	79,544 (1)	4,642,593
	1,447,875	(56 games)	AFL	25,855	40,242 (1)	1,488,117

PAID ATTENDANCE

Year	Regular Season			Average	Postseason	Total
1963	4,163,643	(98 games)	NFL	42,486	45,801 (1)	4,209,444
	1,208,697	(56 games)	AFL	21,584	63,171 (2)	1,271,868
1962	4,003,421	(98 games)	NFL	40,851	64,892 (1)	4,068,313
	1,147,302	(56 games)	AFL	20,487	37,981 (1)	1,185,283
1961	3,986,159	(98 games)	NFL	40,675	39,029 (1)	4,025,188
	1,002,657	(56 games)	AFL	17,904	29,556 (1)	1,032,213
1960	3,128,296	(78 games)	NFL	40,106	67,325 (1)	3,195,621
	926,156	(56 games)	AFL	16,538	32,183 (1)	958,339
1959	3,140,000	(72 games)		43,617	57,545 (1)	3,197,545
1958	3,006,124	(72 games)		41,752	123,659 (2)	3,129,783
1957	2,836,318	(72 games)		39,393	119,579 (2)	2,955,897
1956	2,551,263	(72 games)		35,434	56,836 (1)	2,608,099
1955	2,521,836	(72 games)		35,026	85,693 (1)	2,607,529
1954	2,190,571	(72 games)		30,425	43,827 (1)	2,234,398
1953	2,164,585	(72 games)		30,064	54,577 (1)	2,219,162
1952	2,052,126	(72 games)		28,502	97,507 (2)	2,149,633
1951	1,913,019	(72 games)		26,570	57,522 (1)	1,970,541
1950	1,977,753	(78 games)		25,356	136,647 (3)	2,114,400
1949	1,391,735	(60 games)		23,196	27,980 (1)	1,419,715
1948	1,525,243	(60 games)		25,421	36,309 (1)	1,561,552
1947	1,837,437	(60 games)		30,624	66,268 (2)	1,903,705
1946	1,732,135	(55 games)		31,493	58,346 (1)	1,790,481
1945	1,270,401	(50 games)		25,408	32,178 (1)	1,302,579
1944	1,019,649	(50 games)		20,393	46,016 (1)	1,065,665
1943	969,128	(40 games)		24,228	71,315 (2)	1,040,443
1942	887,920	(55 games)		16,144	36,006 (1)	923,926
1941	1,108,615	(55 games)		20,157	55,870 (2)	1,164,485
1940	1,063,025	(55 games)		19,328	36,034 (1)	1,099,059
1939	1,071,200	(55 games)		19,476	32,279 (1)	1,103,479
1938	937,197	(55 games)		17,040	48,120 (1)	985,317
1937	963,039	(55 games)		17,510	15,878 (1)	978,917
1936	816,007	(54 games)		15,111	29,545 (1)	845,552
1935	638,178	(53 games)		12,041	15,000 (1)	653,178
1934	492,684	(60 games)		8,211	35,059 (1)	527,743

 # Record

**Players' 57-day strike reduced 224-game schedule to 126 games.*

***Players' 24-day strike reduced 224-game schedule to 210 games.*

****The Week 8 Miami at San Diego game is not included. The game was moved to Arizona due to the San Diego wildfires and tickets were distributed at no charge.*

PRESEASON AND REGULAR SEASON – SUDDEN DEATH

The sudden death system of determining the winner shall prevail when the score is tied at the end of the regulation playing time of preseason and regular-season NFL games. The team scoring first during overtime play shall be the winner and the game automatically ends upon any score (by safety, field goal, or touchdown) or when a score is awarded by Referee for a palpably unfair act.

- At the end of regulation time the Referee will immediately toss coin at center of field in accordance with rules pertaining to the usual pregame toss. The captain of the visiting team will call the toss prior to the coin being flipped.
- Following a three-minute intermission after the end of the regulation game, play will continue for one 15-minute period or until there is a score. Each team has two time outs. General timing provisions that apply for the fourth quarter will prevail. Try is not attempted if touchdown scored. Disqualified players are not allowed to return.
- **Instant Replay:** No challenges. Reviews to be initiated by the replay assistant.

POSTSEASON – MODIFIED SUDDEN DEATH

NFL owners voted in 2010 to install a modified sudden death system to determine the winner when the score is tied at the end of regulation playing time of postseason NFL games. The system guarantees each team a possession or the opportunity to possess, unless the team that receives the opening kickoff scores a touchdown on its initial possession.

- At the end of regulation time the Referee will immediately toss coin at center of field in accordance with rules pertaining to the usual pregame toss. The captain of the visiting team will call the toss prior to the coin being flipped.
- Following a three-minute intermission after the end of the regulation game, play will be continued in 15-minute periods until a winner is declared. Each team must possess or have the opportunity to possess the ball unless the team that has the ball first scores a touchdown on its initial possession. Play continues in sudden death until a winner is determined, and the game automatically ends upon any score (by safety, field goal, or touchdown) or when a score is awarded by Referee for a palpably unfair act. Each team has three time outs per half and all general timing provisions apply as during a regular game. Try is not attempted if touchdown scored. Disqualified players are not allowed to return.
- **Instant Replay:** No challenges. Reviews to be initiated by the replay assistant.

Key Definitions:

Possession: Actual possession of the ball with complete control. The defense gains possession when it catches, intercepts, or recovers a loose ball.

Opportunity to possess: The opportunity to possess occurs only during kicking plays. A kickoff is an opportunity to possess for the receiving team. If the kicking team legally recovers the kick, the receiving team is considered to have had its opportunity. A punt or a field goal that crosses the line of scrimmage and is muffed by the receiving team is considered to be an opportunity to possess for the receivers. Normal touching rules by the kicking team apply.

2009/POSTSEASON OVERTIME GAMES

* *indicates Monday-night game*
\# *indicates Thursday/Saturday/Sunday-night game*
\+ *indicates Thanksgiving Day game*

REGULAR SEASON

\# **Sept. 10, 2009—Pittsburgh 13, Tennessee 10,** at Pittsburgh; Steelers win toss. Logan returns kickoff 20 yards. Drive begins at Steelers 22. Reed kicks 33-yard field goal at 4:32.

Oct. 4, 2009—Cincinnati 23, Cleveland 20, at Cleveland; Bengals win toss. Scott returns kickoff 28 yards. Drive begins on Bengals 30. Drive ends on Bengals 42. Huber punts 41 yards out of bounds. Drive begins on Browns 17. Drive ends on Browns 21. Zastudil punts 55 yards. Drive begins at Bengals 24. Drive ends at Bengals 41. Huber punts 43 yards. Drive begins on Browns 16. Drive ends on Browns 27. Zastudil punts 58 yards. Cosby returns 10 yards. Drive begins at Bengals 25. Drive ends at Bengals 31. Huber punts 49 yards. Cribbs returns 11 yards. Drive begins on Browns 31. Drive ends on Browns 49. Zastudil punts 51 yards to end zone. Drive begins on Bengals 20. Graham kicks 31-yard field goal at 14:53.

Oct. 11, 2009—Dallas 26, Kansas City 20, at Kansas City; Chiefs win toss. Charles returns kickoff 19 yards. Drive begins on Chiefs 27. Drive ends on Chiefs 46. Colquitt punts 38 yards. Fair catch. Drive begins on Cowboys 16. Drive ends on Cowboys 17. McBriar punts 41 yards. Wade returns 7 yards. Drive begins on Chiefs 49. Drive ends at midfield. Colquitt punts 29 yards. Fair catch. Drive begins on Cowboys 21. Tony Romo completes 60-yard touchdown pass to Miles Austin at 6:27.

Oct. 11, 2009—Denver 20, New England 17, at Denver; Broncos win toss. Touchback. Drive begins on Broncos 20. Prater kicks 41-yard field goal at 4:45.

Oct. 18, 2009—Jacksonville 23, St. Louis 20, at Jacksonville; Jaguars win the toss. Touchback. Drive begins on Jaguars 20. Scobee kicks 36-yard field goal at 6:56.

Oct. 18, 2009—Buffalo 16, N.Y. Jets 13, at N.Y. Jets; Jets win toss. Washington returns kickoff 27 yards. Drive begins on Jets 29. Drive ends on Bills 32 as botched snap on attempted field goal results in interception by Wendling. Drive starts on Bills 35. Drive ends on Bills 38. Moorman punts 45 yards. Leonhard returns -2 yards (holding penalty on Jets). Drive starts at Jets 8. Drive ends at Jets 12. Weatherford punts 43 yards. Fair catch. Drive starts at Bills 45. Lowery intercepts Fitzpatrick's pass at Bills 47 (no return). Drive starts at Bills 47. Posluszny intercepts Sanchez's pass at Bills 39 and returns 3 yards. Drive starts at Bills 42. Lindell kicks 47-yard field goal at 12:11.

Nov. 22, 2009—N.Y. Giants 34, Atlanta Falcons 31, at N.Y. Giants; Giants win toss. Hixon returns kickoff 33 yards. Drive begins on Giants 34. Tynes kicks 36-yard field goal at 3:49.

Nov. 22, 2009—Kansas City Chiefs 27, Pittsburgh Steelers 24, at Kansas City; Steelers win toss. Touchback. Drive begins on Steelers 20. Drive ends on Kansas City 38. Sepulveda punts 38 yards to end zone. Touchback. Drive begins on Chiefs 20. Succop kicks 22-yard field goal at 7:32.

\# **Nov. 29, 2009—Baltimore Ravens 20, Pittsburgh Steelers 17,** at Baltimore; Steelers win toss. Logan returns 17 yards. Drive begins on Steelers 23. Drive ends on Steelers 37. Sepulveda punts 46 yards. Out of bounds. Drive begins on Ravens 17. Drive ends on Ravens 17. Koch punts 38 yards. Fair catch. Drive begins on Steelers 45. Kruger intercepts Dixon's pass at Ravens 46 and returns 28 yards. Drive begins on Steelers 28. Cundiff kicks 29-yard field goal at 7:35.

Dec. 6, 2009—New Orleans Saints 33, Washington Redskins 30, at Washington; Redskins win toss. Thomas returns kickoff 23 yards. Drive begins on Redskins 20. McAlister recovers fumble by Sellers (no return). Drive begins on Redskins 37. Hartley kicks 18-yard field goal at 6:20.

Dec. 20, 2009—Tennessee Titans 27, Miami Dolphins 24, at Tennessee; Dolphins win toss. Ginn returns kickoff 23 yards. Drive begins on Dolphins 23. M. Griffin intercepts Henne's pass at Dolphins 45 and returns 3 yards. Dolphins' Camarillo penalized 15 yards for unnecessary roughness. Drive begins on Dolphins 27. Bironas kicks 46-yard field goal at 3:36.

Dec. 27, 2009—Tampa Bay Buccaneers 20, New Orleans Saints 17, at New Orleans; Buccaneers win toss. Spurlock returns kick 19 yards. Drive begins at Buccaneers 23. Barth kicks 47-yard field goal at 6:54.

* **Dec. 28, 2009—Chicago Bears 36, Minnesota Vikings 30,** at Chicago; Bears win toss. E. Bennett returns kick 22 yards. Drive begins at Bears 32. Drive ends on Vikings 35 as Gould missed 45-yard field goal attempt. Drive begins on Vikings 35. Drive ends at Vikings 21. Kluwe punts 43 yards to Bears 36. No return. Drive begins on Bears 36. Drive ends on Bears 39. Maynard punts 47 yards to Vikings 14. Reynaud returns 3 yards. Drive begins on Vikings 17. Peterson fumbles, Bears recover. Drive begins on Vikings 39. Cutler passes deep right to Aromashodu for 39-yard touchdown at 5:39.

POSTSEASON

Dec. 28, 1958—Baltimore 23, New York Giants 17, at New York in NFL Championship Game; Giants win toss. Maynard returns kickoff to Giants' 20. Chandler punts and Taseff returns one yard to Colts' 20. Ameche scores on 1-yard run at 8:15.

Dec. 23, 1962—Dallas Texans 20, Houston Oilers 17, at Houston in AFL Championship Game; Texans win toss and kick off. Jancik returns kickoff to Oilers' 33. Norton punts and Jackson makes fair catch on Texans' 22. Wilson punts and Jancik makes fair catch on Oilers' 45. Robinson intercepts Blanda's pass and returns 13 yards to Oilers' 47. Wilson's punt rolls dead at Oilers' 12. Hull intercepts Blanda's pass and returns 23 yards to midfield. Brooker kicks 25-yard field goal at 17:54.

Dec. 26, 1965—Green Bay 13, Baltimore 10, at Green Bay in NFL Divisional Playoff Game; Packers win toss. Moore returns kickoff to Packers' 22. Chandler punts and Haymond returns nine yards to Colts' 41. Gilburg punts and Wood makes fair catch at Packers' 21. Chandler punts and Haymond returns one yard to Colts' 41. Michaels misses 47-yard field goal. Chandler kicks 25-yard field goal at 13:39.

Dec. 25, 1971—Miami 27, Kansas City 24, at Kansas City in AFC Divisional Playoff Game; Chiefs win toss. Podolak, after a lateral from Buchanan, returns kickoff to Chiefs' 46. Stenerud's 42-yard field goal is blocked. Seiple punts and Podolak makes fair catch at Chiefs' 17. Wilson punts and Scott returns 18 yards to Dolphins' 39. Yepremian misses 62-yard field goal. Scott intercepts Dawson's pass and returns 13 yards to Dolphins' 46. Seiple punts and Podolak loses one yard to Chiefs' 15. Wilson punts and Scott makes fair catch on Dolphins' 30. Yepremian kicks 37-yard field goal at 22:40.

Dec. 24, 1977—Oakland 37, Baltimore 31, at Baltimore in AFC Divisional Playoff Game; Colts win toss. Raiders start on own 42 following a punt late in the first overtime. Oakland works way into field-goal range on Stabler's 19-yard pass to Branch at Colts' 26. Four plays later, on the second play of the second overtime, Stabler hits Casper with a 10-yard touchdown pass at 15:43.

Jan. 2, 1982—San Diego 41, Miami 38, at Miami in AFC Divisional Playoff Game; Chargers win toss. San Diego drives from its 13 to Miami 8. On second-and-goal, Benirschke misses 27-yard field goal attempt wide left at 9:15. Miami has the ball twice and San Diego twice more before the Dolphins get their third possession. Miami drives from the San Diego 46 to Chargers' 17 and on fourth-and-two, von Schamann's 34-yard field goal attempt is blocked by San Diego's Winslow after 11:27. Fouts then completes four of five passes, including a 39-yarder to Joiner that puts the ball on Dolphins' 10. On first down, Benirschke kicks a 29-yard field goal at 13:52.

Jan. 3, 1987—Cleveland 23, New York Jets 20, at Cleveland in AFC Divisional Playoff Game; Jets win toss. Jets' punt downed at Browns' 26. Moseley's 23-yard field goal attempt is wide right. Teams trade punts. Jets' second punt downed at Browns' 31. First overtime period expires eight plays later with Browns in possession at Jets' 42. Moseley kicks 27-yard field goal four plays into second overtime at 17:02.

Jan. 11, 1987—Denver 23, Cleveland 20, at Cleveland in AFC Championship Game; Browns win toss. Broncos hold Browns on four downs. Browns' punt returned four yards to Denver's 25. Elway completes 22- and 28-yard passes to set up Karlis's 33-yard field goal nine plays into drive at 5:38.

Jan. 3, 1988—Houston 23, Seattle 20, at Houston in AFC Wild Card Game; Seahawks win toss. Rodriguez punts to K. Johnson who returns one yard to Houston 15. Zendejas kicks 32-yard field goal 12 plays later at 8:05.

Dec. 31, 1989—Pittsburgh 26, Houston 23, at Houston in AFC Wild Card Playoff Game; Steelers win toss. Steelers punt to Oilers. Oilers' fumble recovered by Woodson and returned three yards. Four plays and 13 yards later, Anderson kicks a 50-yard field goal at 3:26.

Jan. 7, 1990—Los Angeles Rams 19, New York Giants 13, at New York in NFC Divisional Game; Rams win toss. Everett completes two passes to move ball to Giants' 48. White called for pass interference; ball spotted on Giants' 25. Everett hits Anderson with a 30-yard touchdown pass at 1:06.
Jan. 3, 1993—Buffalo 41, Houston 38, at Buffalo in AFC Wild Card Game; Oilers win toss. Oilers begin at 20. After 2 plays, Moon's pass is intercepted by Odomes who returns ball 2 yards to Houston 35. After 2 plays, Christie kicks 32-yard field goal at 3:06.
Jan. 8, 1994—Kansas City 27, Pittsburgh 24, at Kansas City in AFC Wild Card Game; Chiefs win toss. Hughes returns kick-off 20 yards to Kansas City 25. After 3 plays, Barker punts 48 yards to Pittsburgh 18 where Woodson returns 8 yards to the 26. After 6 plays, Royals punts 30 yards to Kansas City 20. Kansas City drives to Pittsburgh 14 where Lowery kicks 32-yard field goal at 11:03.
Jan. 17, 1999—Atlanta 30, Minnesota 27, at Minnesota in NFC Championship Game; Vikings win toss. Palmer returns kickoff 30 yards to Minnesota 29. After four plays, Berger punts 51 yards to Atlanta 7 where Dwight returns 8 yards to Atlanta 15. Falcons drive to Atlanta 36. Stryzinski punts 37 yards to Vikings' 27. Palmer calls fair catch. Vikings drive to Minnesota 39. Berger punts 52 yards to Atlanta 9. Downed by Vikings. Atlanta drives to Minnesota 21 where Andersen kicks 38-yard field goal at 11:52.
Dec. 30, 2000—Miami 23, Indianapolis 17, at Miami in AFC Wild Card Game; Dolphins win toss. Williams returns kickoff 18 yards to Miami 20. Offensive holding penalty on Freeman, 10 yards, ball spotted on Miami 10. Dolphins drive to Miami 29 where Turk punts 53 yards to Indianapolis 18. Colts drive to Miami 31 where Vanderjagt misses 49-yard field-goal attempt wide right. Dolphins drive to Indianapolis 17 where Smith rushes for a 17-yard touchdown at 11:16.
Jan. 19, 2002—New England 16, Oakland 13, at New England in AFC Divisional Playoff Game; Patriots win toss. Pass returns kickoff 24 yards to New England 34. Patriots drive to Oakland 5. Vinatieri kicks 23-yard field goal at 8:29.
Jan. 11, 2003—Tennessee 34, Pittsburgh 31, at Tennessee in AFC Divisional Playoff Game; Tennessee wins toss. Reed kicks 60 yards. Returned by Simon 21 yards to Tennessee 31. Titans drive to Pittsburgh 8. Nedney's 26-yard field goal is good at 2:15.
Jan. 4, 2004—Green Bay 33, Seattle 27, at Green Bay in NFC Wild Card Game; Seahawks win toss. Morris returns kick to Seattle 33. Seahawks drive to Seattle 42. Rouen's 44-yard punt returned by Chatman to Green Bay 26. Packers drive to Green Bay 31. Bidwell punts 35 yards to Seattle 34. Seahawks drive to Seattle 45. Hasselbeck's pass to Bannister intercepted by Packers' Harris and returned 52 yards for touchdown at 4:25.
Jan. 10, 2004—Carolina 29, St. Louis 23, at St. Louis in NFC Divisional Game; Panthers win toss. Smart returns kick to Carolina 32. Panthers drive to St. Louis 27. Kasay's 45-yard field-goal attempt no good. Rams take over at own 35 and drive to Carolina 35. Wilkins' 53-yard field-goal attempt no good. Panthers take over at Carolina 43, drive to Carolina 47. Sauerbrun punts 40 yards to St. Louis 13. Rams drive to Carolina 38. Bulger's pass intercepted by Manning at Carolina 35. Panthers drive to Carolina 31. First overtime ends. On first play of second overtime, Delhomme passes to Smith for 69-yard touchdown at 15:10.
Jan. 11, 2004—Philadelphia 20, Green Bay 17, at Philadelphia in NFC Divisional Game; Eagles win toss. Thrash returns kick to Philadelphia 28. Eagles drive to Philadelphia 24. Johnson punts 49 yards and Packers start at own 32 after holding penalty. Favre's pass intercepted by Dawkins at Philadelphia 31 and returned to Green Bay 34. Eagles drive to Green Bay 13. Akers kicks 31-yard field goal at 4:48.
Jan. 8, 2005—New York Jets 20, San Diego 17, at San Diego in AFC Wild Card Game; Chargers win toss. Dwight returns kick to San Diego 26. Chargers drive to San Diego 35. Scifres punts 39 yards and ball is downed at the New York 26. Jets gain no yards. Gowin punts 41 yards. Parker loses 3 yards on return. San Diego starts on own 30. Chargers drive to New York 22. Kaeding's 40-yard field-goal attempt no good. Jets drive to San Diego 10. Brien kicks 28-yard field goal at 14:55.
Jan. 15, 2005—Pittsburgh 20, New York Jets 17, at Pittsburgh in AFC Divisional Game; Jets win toss. Cotchery returns kick to New York 31. Jets drive to New York 41. Gowin punts 54 yards. Randle El returns 8 yards to Pittsburgh 13. Steelers drive to New York 15. Reed kicks 33-yard field goal at 11:04.
Jan. 14, 2007—Chicago 27, Seattle 24, at Chicago in NFC Divisional Playoff Game; Seahawks win the toss. Burleson returns kickoff 25 yards to Seahawks 30. Plackemeier punts 18 yards. Drive begins at Bears 34. Gould kicks 49-yard field goal at 4:53.
Jan. 20, 2008—New York Giants 23, Green Bay 20, at Green Bay in NFC Championship Game; Packers win toss. K. Robinson returns kick 19 yards to Green Bay 26. Favre pass intercepted by Webster and returned 9 yards to Green Bay 34. Tynes kicks 47-yard field goal at 12:34.
Jan. 3, 2009—San Diego Chargers 23, Indianapolis 17, at San Diego in AFC Wild Card Playoffs; Chargers win toss. Sproles returns kick 31 yards to San Diego 25. Sproles scores on 22-yard touchdown run at 6:12.
Jan. 10, 2010—Arizona Cardinals 51, Green Bay Packers 45, at Arizona in Wild Card Playoffs; Packers win toss. Touchback. Rodgers is sacked and fumbles, recovered by Dansby for 17-yard touchdown at 1:18.
Jan. 24, 2010—New Orleans Saints 31, Minnesota Vikings 28, at New Orleans in NFC Championship; Saints win toss. Thomas returns kick 40 yards. Drive begins at Saints 39. Hartley kicks 40-yard field goal at 4:45.

NFL POSTSEASON OVERTIME GAMES (BY LENGTH OF GAME)

Date	Game	Length
Dec. 25, 1971	Miami 27, KANSAS CITY 24	82:40
Dec. 23, 1962	Dallas Texans 20, HOUSTON 17	77:54
Jan. 3 1987	CLEVELAND 23, N.Y. Jets 20	77:02
Dec. 24, 1977	Oakland 37, BALTIMORE 31	75:43
Jan. 10, 2004	Carolina 29, ST. LOUIS 23	75:10
Jan. 8, 2005	N.Y. Jets 20, SAN DIEGO 17	74:55
Jan 2, 1982	San Diego 41, MIAMI 38	73:52
Dec. 26, 1965	GREEN BAY 13, Baltimore 10	73:39
Jan 17, 1999	Atlanta 30, MINNESOTA 27	71:52
Dec. 30, 2000	MIAMI 23, Indianapolis 17	71:16
Jan. 15, 2005	PITTSBURGH 20, N.Y. Jets 17	71:04
Jan 8, 1994	KANSAS CITY 27, Pittsburgh 24	71:03
Jan. 19, 2002	NEW ENGLAND 16, Oakland 13	68:29
Dec. 28, 1958	Baltimore 23, N.Y. GIANTS 17	68:15
Jan. 3, 1988	HOUSTON 23, Seattle 20	68:05
Jan. 3, 2009	SAN DIEGO 23, Indianapolis 17	66:12
Jan. 11, 1987	Denver 23, CLEVELAND 20	65:38
Jan. 14, 2007	CHICAGO 27, Seattle 24	64:53
Jan. 11, 2004	PHILADELPHIA 20, Green Bay 17	64:48
Jan. 24, 2010	NEW ORLEANS 31, Minnesota 28	64:45
Jan. 4, 2004	GREEN BAY 33, Seattle 27	64:25
Dec. 31, 1989	Pittsburgh 26, HOUSTON 23	63:26
Jan. 3, 1993	BUFFALO 41, Houston 38	63:06
Jan. 20, 2008	N.Y. Giants 23, GREEN BAY 20	62:26
Jan. 11, 2003	TENNESSEE 34, Pittsburgh 31	62:15
Jan. 10, 2010	ARIZONA 51, Green Bay 45	61:18
Jan. 7, 1990	L.A. Rams 19, N.Y. GIANTS 13	61:06

Home team in CAPS

There have been 27 overtime postseason games dating back to 1958. In 22 cases, both teams had at least one possession. Last time: 1/10/10, ARIZONA 51, Green Bay 45.

OVERTIME GAMES

OVERTIME WON-LOST RECORDS, 1974-2009 (REGULAR SEASON)

Team	Win	Loss	Tie	Pct.
AFC				
Baltimore	7	6	1	.536
Buffalo	18	9	0	.667
Cincinnati	15	11	1	.574
Cleveland	16	14	1	.532
Denver	22	15	2	.590
Houston	0	6	0	.000
Indianapolis	12	9	1	.568
Jacksonville	7	3	0	.700
Kansas City	11	16	2	.414
Miami	12	19	1	.391
New England	16	20	0	.444
N.Y. Jets	16	16	2	.500
Oakland	14	17	0	.452
Pittsburgh	18	14	2	.559
San Diego	12	17	0	.414
Tennessee	14	17	0	.452
NFC				
Arizona	18	14	2	.559
Atlanta	12	18	2	.406
Carolina	4	9	0	.308
Chicago	22	15	0	.595
Dallas	14	12	0	.538
Detroit	12	15	1	.446
Green Bay	11	13	4	.464
Minnesota	17	17	2	.500
New Orleans	8	10	0	.444
N.Y. Giants	18	14	2	.559
Philadelphia	11	16	4	.419
St. Louis	12	9	1	.568
San Francisco	18	13	1	.578
Seattle	8	17	0	.320
Tampa Bay	14	15	1	.483
Washington	19	12	1	.609

OVERTIME GAMES BY YEAR (REGULAR SEASON)

2009-13	2000-13	1991-15	1982- 4
2008-15	1999-11	1990-10	1981-10
2007-15	1998-7	1989-11	1980-13
2006-11	1997-17	1988- 9	1979-12
2005-14	1996-14	1987-13	1978-11
2004-12	1995-21	1986-16	1977-6
2003-23	1994-16	1985-10	1976-5
2002-25*	1993-7	1984- 9	1975-9
2001-17	1992-10	1983-19	1974-2

**Record*

OVERTIME GAME SUMMARY—1974-2009

There have been 445 overtime games in regular season play since the rule was adopted in 1974 (13 in 2009 season). Breakdown follows:

RESULTS

240 (7) times the team which won the toss won the game (53.9%)

188 (6) times the team which lost the toss won the game (42.2%)

17 (0) games ended tied (3.8%). Last time: Nov. 16, 2008, Philadelphia 13 at Cincinnati 13.

POSSESSIONS

310 (8) times both teams had at least one possession (69.7%)

135 (5) times the team which won the toss drove for winning score (100 FG, 35 TD) (30.3%)

Of the 445 overtime games, there were 13 miscellaneous situations in which non-standard possessions took place:

9 (0) times the defense or special teams won without registering an official possession (5 INT, 2 blocked punts, 1 FR, 1 blocked FG) (2.0%)

1 (0) times the special teams forced a fumble on the opening kickoff and drove for winning score (0.23%)

1 (0) times the punting team recovered a muffed punt and drove for winning score with team muffing punt having no official possessions (0.23%)

2 (0) times the team that won the toss elected to kick and the team receiving the ball drove for winning score (0.45%)

SCORING

312(11) games were decided by a field goal (70.1%)

114 (2) games were decided by a touchdown (25.6%)

2 (0) games were decided by a safety (0.45%)

17 (0) games ended tied (3.8%). Last time: Nov. 16, 2008, Philadelphia 13 at Cincinnati 13.

COIN TOSS

436(13) times the team which won the toss elected to receive (98.0%)

9 (0) times the team which won the toss elected to kick off (4 wins) (2.0%)

Note: The number in parentheses is the 2009 Season Total.

MOST OVERTIME GAMES, SEASON

5 Green Bay Packers, 1983

4 Denver Broncos, 1985, 2007
Cleveland Browns, 1989
Minnesota Vikings, 1994
Arizona Cardinals, 1995
Minnesota Vikings, 1995
Arizona Cardinals, 1997
San Francisco 49ers, 2001
Atlanta Falcons, 2002
San Diego Chargers, 2002
Carolina Panthers, 2003

LONGEST CONSECUTIVE GAME STREAKS WITHOUT OVERTIME (Current)

81 Indianapolis Colts (Last OT Game, 12/26/04 vs. San Diego Chargers)

(Record: 110, St. Louis/Phoenix Cardinals, 12/7/86-12/19/93)

There have been 27 overtime postseason games dating back to 1958. In 22 cases, both teams had at least one possession. Last time: 1/10/10, ARIZONA 51, Green Bay 45.

SHORTEST OVERTIME GAMES

0:14 New York Jets 37, BUFFALO 31; 9/8/02
0:16 CHICAGO 37, San Francisco 31; 10/28/01
0:16 Green Bay 19, DENVER 13; 10/29/07
0:17 NEW ORLEANS 20, Seattle 17; 11/16/97
0:21 Chicago 23, DETROIT 17; 11/27/80
0:30 Baltimore 29, NEW ENGLAND 23; 9/4/83
0:34 San Diego 23, WASHINGTON 17; 11/27/05
0:55 New York Giants 16, PHILADELPHIA 10; 9/29/85

LONGEST OVERTIME GAMES (ALL POSTSEASON GAMES)

22:40 Miami 27, KANSAS CITY 24; 12/25/71
17:54 Dallas Texans 20, HOUSTON 17; 12/23/62
17:02 CLEVELAND 23, New York Jets 20; 1/3/87
15:43 Oakland 37, BALTIMORE 31; 12/24/77
15:10 Carolina 29, ST. LOUIS 23; 1/10/04

OVERTIME SCORING SUMMARY

312 were decided by a field goal
53 were decided by a touchdown pass
31 were decided by a touchdown run
17 were decided by an interception (Atlanta 40, New Orleans 34, 9/2/79; Atlanta 47, Green Bay 41, 11/27/83; New York Giants 16, Philadelphia 10, 9/29/85; Indianapolis 23, Cleveland 17, 12/10/89; Cleveland 30, San Diego 24, 10/20/91; Kansas City 23, Oakland 17, 9/17/95; New York Giants 27, Arizona 21, 10/8/95; Washington 36, Detroit 30, 10/22/95; Arizona 20, Seattle 14, 10/29/95; Cincinnati 34, Detroit 28, 9/13/98; New York Giants 23, Philadelphia 17, 10/31/99; Chicago 37, San Francisco 31, 10/28/01; Chicago 27, Cleveland 21, 11/4/01; New Orleans 26, Tampa Bay 20, 9/8/02; Atlanta 20, Carolina 14, 12/7/03; Jacksonville 23, Pittsburgh 17, 10/16/05; Chicago 19, Detroit 13, 10/30/05)
3 were decided by a fumble recovery (Baltimore 29, New England 23, 9/4/83; Denver 36, Seattle 30, 12/19/99; San Francisco 37, Arizona 31, 11/24/07)
2 were decided on a fake field goal/touchdown pass (Minnesota 22, Chicago 16, 10/16/77; Cleveland 23, Minnesota 17, 12/17/89)
2 were decided by a kickoff return (Chicago 23, Detroit 17, 11/27/80; New York Jets 37, Buffalo 31, 9/8/02)
2 were decided by a safety (Minnesota 23, Los Angeles Rams 21, 11/5/89; Chicago 19, Tennessee 17, 11/14/04)
1 was decided by a punt return (Kansas City 29, San Diego 23, 10/9/95)
1 was decided on a fake field goal/touchdown run (Los Angeles Rams 27, Minnesota 21, 12/2/79)
1 was decided on a blocked field goal (Denver 30, San Diego 24, 11/17/85)
1 was decided on a blocked field goal/recovery by kicker (Green Bay 12, Chicago 6, 9/7/80)
1 was decided on a blocked field goal/recovery by kicking team (Philadelphia 23, New York Giants 17, 11/20/88)
1 was decided by a blocked punt (Arizona 30, Dallas 24, 10/12/08)
17 ended tied

OVERTIME RECORDS

Longest Touchdown Pass

99 Yards — Ron Jaworski to Mike Quick, Philadelphia 23, Atlanta 17 (11/10/85)
82 Yards — Tom Brady to Troy Brown, New England 19, Miami 13 (10/19/03); Brett Favre to Greg Jennings, Green Bay 19, Denver 13 (10/29/07)
76 Yards — Troy Aikman to Raghib Ismail, Dallas 41, Washington 35 (9/12/99)

Longest Touchdown Run

96 Yards — Garrison Hearst, San Francisco 36, New York Jets 30 (9/6/98)
60 Yards — Herschel Walker, Dallas 23, New England 17 (11/15/87)
46 Yards — Michael Vick, Atlanta 30, Minnesota 24 (12/1/02)

Longest Field Goal

57 Yards — Sebastian Janikowski, Oakland 16, New York Jets 13 (10/19/08)
53 Yards — Chris Jacke, Green Bay 23, San Francisco 20 (10/4/96)
52 Yards — Mike Cofer, Indianapolis 27, New York Jets 24 (9/10/95)

Longest Touchdown Plays

99 Yards — (Pass) Ron Jaworski to Mike Quick, Philadelphia 23, Atlanta 17 (11/10/85)
96 Yards — (Run) Garrison Hearst, San Francisco 36, New York Jets 30 (9/6/98)
96 Yards — (Kickoff return) Chad Morton, New York Jets 37, Buffalo 31 (9/8/02)
95 Yards — (Kickoff return) Dave Williams, Chicago 23, Detroit 17 (11/27/80)
86 Yards — (Punt return) Tamarick Vanover, Kansas City 29, San Diego 23 (10/9/95)

ASSOCIATED PRESS NFL MOST OUTSTANDING/VALUABLE PLAYERS

THE FOLLOWING AWARDS WERE NAMED BY ASSOCIATED PRESS IN BALLOTING BY A NATIONWIDE PANEL OF MEDIA.

NFL MOST OUTSTANDING PLAYER AWARD

YEAR	PLAYER	POS.	TEAM	ACCOMPLISHMENTS
1957	Jim Brown	RB	Cleveland Browns	Rushed for league-leading 942 yards and added 9 touchdowns as a rookie.
1958	Jim Brown	RB	Cleveland Browns	Rushed for NFL-record 1,527 yards and added 17 touchdowns. Led Browns to 9-3 record.
1959	Charley Conerly	QB	New York Giants	Passed for 14 touchdowns and only 4 interceptions. Led offense to division-leading 284 points.
1960	Norm Van Brocklin	QB	Philadelphia Eagles	Guided Eagles to first division title since 1949. Passed for 2,471 yards and 24 touchdowns.

NFL MOST VALUABLE PLAYER AWARD

YEAR	PLAYER	POS.	TEAM	ACCOMPLISHMENTS
1961	Paul Hornung	RB	Green Bay Packers	Led league in scoring for second straight season with 146 points (10 TD, 15 FG, 41 PAT).
1962	Jim Taylor	RB	Green Bay Packers	League rushing champion with 1,474 yards. Scored all-time record 19 touchdowns.
1963	Y.A. Tittle	QB	New York Giants	Set all-time season record with 36 touchdown passes. Guided league's top offense (5,024 yards).
1964	Johnny Unitas	QB	Baltimore Colts	Guided Colts to NFL's best record (12-2) and league's top offensive attack (4,779 yards).
1965	Jim Brown	RB	Cleveland Browns	Leader of NFL's top rushing attack. Led league with 1,544 yards, added 21 total touchdowns.
1966	Bart Starr	QB	Green Bay Packers	Passed for 14 touchdowns and only 3 interceptions. Led Packers to league-best 12-2 record.
1967	Johnny Unitas	QB	Baltimore Colts	Passed for 3,428 yards and 20 touchdowns. Led Colts to 11-1-2 record.
1968	Earl Morrall	QB	Baltimore Colts	Guided Colts to NFL-best 13-1 record. Led league with 26 touchdown passes.
1969	Roman Gabriel	QB	Los Angeles Rams	Led NFL with 24 touchdown passes. Guided Rams to 11-3 record.
1970	John Brodie	QB	San Francisco 49ers	Took 49ers to first division title. Threw NFL-best 24 touchdown passes.
1971	Alan Page	DT	Minnesota Vikings	Led defense that allowed NFL-low 139 points. Vikings won fourth straight NFC Central title.
1972	Larry Brown	RB	Washington Redskins	Led conference with 1,216 rushing yards. Redskins had NFC-best 11-3 record.
1973	O.J. Simpson	RB	Buffalo Bills	Rushed for all-time record 2,003 yards, including three 200-yard performances.
1974	Ken Stabler	QB	Oakland Raiders	Led league with 26 touchdown passes and only 12 interceptions. Raiders had NFL-best 12-2 record.
1975	Fran Tarkenton	QB	Minnesota Vikings	Tied for league-best 12-2 record. Led NFC with 91.7 passer rating.
1976	Bert Jones	QB	Baltimore Colts	Threw 24 touchdowns and only 9 interceptions for 102.5 passer rating.
1977	Walter Payton	RB	Chicago Bears	Rushed for league-leading 1,852 yards and 16 total touchdowns.
1978	Terry Bradshaw	QB	Pittsburgh Steelers	Led Steelers to league-leading 14-2 mark. Set club record with 28 touchdown passes.
1979	Earl Campbell	RB	Houston Oilers	Led league with 1,697 rushing yards and 19 touchdowns.
1980	Brian Sipe	QB	Cleveland Browns	NFL-best 91.4 passer rating. Set Browns' records with 30 touchdown passes and 4,132 yards.
1981	Ken Anderson	QB	Cincinnati Bengals	Led Bengals to first division title since 1973. NFL-high 98.5 passer rating.
1982	Mark Moseley	K	Washington Redskins	Converted 20 of 21 FGs. Set consecutive field-goal record at 23 (including last three in '81).
1983	Joe Theismann	QB	Washington Redskins	Leader of offense that scored NFL record 541 points. Redskins had NFL-best 14-2 record.
1984	Dan Marino	QB	Miami Dolphins	Set NFL records with 5,084 yards and 48 touchdown passes. Led Dolphins to AFC-best 14-2 mark.
1985	Marcus Allen	RB	Los Angeles Raiders	Rushed for league-leading 1,759 yards. Tied for AFC lead with 11 rushing touchdowns.
1986	Lawrence Taylor	LB	New York Giants	Recorded league-high 20.5 sacks, and led Giants' second-ranked defense (297.3).
1987	John Elway	QB	Denver Broncos	In 12 games, passed for 19 touchdowns and 3,198 yards, including four 300-yard games.
1988	Boomer Esiason	QB	Cincinnati Bengals	Led NFL with 97.4 passer rating. Tied for AFC lead with 28 TD passes.
1989	Joe Montana	QB	San Francisco 49ers	Set NFL record with 112.4 passer rating, including 70.2 completion percentage.
1990	Joe Montana	QB	San Francisco 49ers	Led 49ers to league-best 14-2 record. Completed NFC-high 61.7 percent of passes.
1991	Thurman Thomas	RB	Buffalo Bills	Recorded league-high 2,038 yards from scrimmage (1,407 rushing, 631 receiving).
1992	Steve Young	QB	San Francisco 49ers	NFL's top passer with 107.0 rating. Led 49ers to NFL-best 14-2 record.

ASSOCIATED PRESS NFL MOST OUTSTANDING/VALUABLE PLAYERS

1993	Emmitt Smith	RB	Dallas Cowboys	Led league in rushing (1,486 yards) for third straight year despite missing first two games.
1994	Steve Young	QB	San Francisco 49ers	Compiled NFL all-time best 112.8 passer rating. Completed more than 70 percent of his passes.
1995	Brett Favre	QB	Green Bay Packers	Led league with 38 touchdown passes and NFC with 99.5 passer rating.
1996	Brett Favre	QB	Green Bay Packers	Led Packers to top conference record (13-3). Threw NFL-best 39 touchdown passes.
1997*	Brett Favre	QB	Green Bay Packers	Led league with 35 touchdown passes. Led NFC with 3,867 passing yards.
	Barry Sanders	RB	Detroit Lions	Rushed for all-time second-best 2,053 yards, including record 14 straight 100-yard games.
1998	Terrell Davis	RB	Denver Broncos	Rushed for 2,008 yards and scored league-best 23 total touchdowns.
1999	Kurt Warner	QB	St. Louis Rams	Became the second QB in history to have 40 touchdown passes in a season (41).
2000	Marshall Faulk	RB	St. Louis Rams	Set NFL record with 26 touchdowns and led NFC with 2,189 yards from scrimmage.
2001	Kurt Warner	QB	St. Louis Rams	Led NFL with 4,830 passing yards, 36 touchdowns, 68.7 completion percentage, and 101.4 passer rating.
2002	Rich Gannon	QB	Oakland Raiders	Set single-season records with 10 300-yard passing games and 418 completions, and led NFL with 4,689 passing yards.
2003*	Peyton Manning	QB	Indianapolis Colts	Led NFL with 4,267 passing yards, had AFC-best 29 touchdown passes, and posted 99.0 passer rating.
	Steve McNair	QB	Tennessee Titans	Posted NFL-best 100.4 passer rating, passing for 3,215 yards with 24 touchdowns against 7 interceptions.
2004	Peyton Manning	QB	Indianapolis Colts	Set NFL records with 49 touchdown passes and 121.1 passer rating while passing for 4,557 yards.
2005	Shaun Alexander	RB	Seattle Seahawks	Set NFL record with 28 touchdowns and led league with 1,880 rushing yards.
2006	LaDainian Tomlinson	RB	San Diego Chargers	Set NFL record for touchdowns (31) and points scored (186). Rushed for team-record 1,815 yards.
2007	Tom Brady	QB	New England Patriots	Set NFL record with 50 passing touchdowns. Led New England to first 16-0 regular-season record in league history.
2008	Peyton Manning	QB	Indianapolis Colts	Threw for 4,002 yards and 27 touchdowns and 95.0 passer rating. Led Indianapolis to 12-4 record.
2009	Peyton Manning	QB	Indianapolis Colts	Threw for 4,500 yards with 33 touchdowns for 99.9 passer rating while leading Colts to NFL-best 14-2 record.

Total Associated Press NFL MVPs: 51
Four-time Winner: Peyton Manning
Three-time Winner: Brett Favre
Two-time Winners: Joe Montana, Johnny Unitas, Kurt Warner, Steve Young
* The award was shared in 1997 and 2003.

ASSOCIATED PRESS MVPs WHO WON SUPER BOWL/ NFL CHAMPIONSHIP IN SAME SEASON: 14

1960	Norm Van Brocklin	Philadelphia Eagles
1961	Paul Hornung	Green Bay Packers
1962	Jim Taylor	Green Bay Packers
1966	Bart Starr	Green Bay Packers
1968	Earl Morrall	Baltimore Colts
1978	Terry Bradshaw	Pittsburgh Steelers
1982	Mark Moseley	Washington Redskins
1986	Lawrence Taylor	New York Giants
1989	Joe Montana	San Francisco 49ers
1993	Emmitt Smith	Dallas Cowboys
1994	Steve Young	San Francisco 49ers
1996	Brett Favre	Green Bay Packers
1998	Terrell Davis	Denver Broncos
1999	Kurt Warner	St. Louis Rams

ASSOCIATED PRESS NFL MVP BY POSITION

Quarterback:	33	**Kicker:**	1
Running Back:	15	**Linebacker:**	1
Defensive Tackle:	1		

ASSOCIATED PRESS MVPs BY TEAM

8 Indianapolis/Baltimore Colts

6 Green Bay Packers

5 San Francisco 49ers

4 St. Louis/Los Angeles Rams

3 Oakland/Los Angeles Raiders
Washington Redskins

2 Buffalo Bills
Cincinnati Bengals
Cleveland Browns
Denver Broncos
Houston Oilers/Tennessee Titans
Minnesota Vikings
New York Giants

1 Chicago Bears
Dallas Cowboys
Detroit Lions
Miami Dolphins
New England Patriots
Pittsburgh Steelers
San Diego Chargers
Seattle Seahawks

ASSOCIATED PRESS NFL AWARDS

AP OFFENSIVE PLAYER OF THE YEAR

1973	O.J. Simpson	RB	Buffalo Bills
1974	Ken Stabler	QB	Oakland Raiders
1975	Fran Tarkenton	QB	Minnesota Vikings
1976	Bert Jones	QB	Baltimore Colts
1977	Walter Payton	RB	Chicago Bears
1978	Earl Campbell	RB	Houston Oilers
1979	Earl Campbell	RB	Houston Oilers
1980	Earl Campbell	RB	Houston Oilers
1981	Ken Anderson	QB	Cincinnati Bengals
1982	Dan Fouts	QB	San Diego Chargers
1983	Joe Theismann	QB	Washington Redskins
1984	Dan Marino	QB	Miami Dolphins
1985	Marcus Allen	RB	Los Angeles Raiders
1986	Eric Dickerson	RB	Los Angeles Rams
1987	Jerry Rice	WR	San Francisco 49ers
1988	Roger Craig	RB	San Francisco 49ers
1989	Joe Montana	QB	San Francisco 49ers
1990	Warren Moon	QB	Houston Oilers
1991	Thurman Thomas	RB	Buffalo Bills
1992	Steve Young	QB	San Francisco 49ers
1993	Jerry Rice	WR	San Francisco 49ers
1994	Barry Sanders	RB	Detroit Lions
1995	Brett Favre	QB	Green Bay Packers
1996	Terrell Davis	RB	Denver Broncos
1997	Barry Sanders	RB	Detroit Lions
1998	Terrell Davis	RB	Denver Broncos
1999	Marshall Faulk	RB	St. Louis Rams
2000	Marshall Faulk	RB	St. Louis Rams
2001	Marshall Faulk	RB	St. Louis Rams
2002	Priest Holmes	RB	Kansas City Chiefs
2003	Jamal Lewis	RB	Baltimore Ravens
2004	Peyton Manning	QB	Indianapolis Colts
2005	Shaun Alexander	RB	Seattle Seahawks
2006	LaDainian Tomlinson	RB	San Diego Chargers
2007	Tom Brady	QB	New England Patriots
2008	Drew Brees	QB	New Orleans Saints
2009	Chris Johnson	RB	Tennessee Titans

AP OFFENSIVE ROOKIE OF THE YEAR

1957	Jim Brown	RB	Cleveland Browns
1958	Jimmy Orr	WR	Pittsburgh Steelers
1959	Nick Pietrosante	RB	Detroit Lions
1960	Gail Cogdill	WR	Detroit Lions
1961	Mike Ditka	TE	Chicago Bears
1962	Ron Bull	RB	Chicago Bears
1963	Paul Flatley	WR	Minnesota Vikings
1964	Charley Taylor	WR	Washington Redskins
1965	Gale Sayers	RB	Chicago Bears
1966	Johnny Roland	RB	St. Louis Cardinals
1967	Mel Farr	RB	Detroit Lions
1968	Earl McCullouch	WR	Detroit Lions
1969	Calvin Hill	RB	Dallas Cowboys
1970	Duane Thomas	RB	Dallas Cowboys
1971	John Brockington	RB	Green Bay Packers
1972	Franco Harris	RB	Pittsburgh Steelers
1973	Chuck Foreman	RB	Minnesota Vikings
1974	Don Woods	RB	San Diego Chargers
1975	Mike Thomas	RB	Washington Redskins
1976	Sammy White	WR	Minnesota Vikings
1977	Tony Dorsett	RB	Dallas Cowboys
1978	Earl Campbell	RB	Houston Oilers
1979	Ottis Anderson	RB	St. Louis Cardinals
1980	Billy Sims	RB	Detroit Lions
1981	George Rogers	RB	New Orleans Saints
1982	Marcus Allen	RB	Los Angeles Raiders
1983	Eric Dickerson	RB	Los Angeles Rams
1984	Louis Lipps	WR	Pittsburgh Steelers
1985	Eddie Brown	WR	Cincinnati Bengals
1986	Rueben Mayes	RB	New Orleans Saints
1987	Troy Stradford	RB	Miami Dolphins
1988	John Stephens	RB	New England Patriots
1989	Barry Sanders	RB	Detroit Lions
1990	Emmitt Smith	RB	Dallas Cowboys
1991	Leonard Russell	RB	New England Patriots
1992	Carl Pickens	WR	Cincinnati Bengals
1993	Jerome Bettis	RB	Los Angeles Rams
1994	Marshall Faulk	RB	Indianapolis Colts
1995	Curtis Martin	RB	New England Patriots
1996	Eddie George	RB	Houston Oilers
1997	Warrick Dunn	RB	Tampa Bay Buccaneers
1998	Randy Moss	WR	Minnesota Vikings
1999	Edgerrin James	RB	Indianapolis Colts
2000	Mike Anderson	RB	Denver Broncos
2001	Anthony Thomas	RB	Chicago Bears
2002	Clinton Portis	RB	Denver Broncos
2003	Anquan Boldin	WR	Arizona Cardinals
2004	Ben Roethlisberger	QB	Pittsburgh Steelers
2005	Carnell Williams	RB	Tampa Bay Buccaneers
2006	Vince Young	QB	Tennessee Titans
2007	Adrian Peterson	RB	Minnesota Vikings
2008	Matt Ryan	QB	Atlanta Falcons
2009	Percy Harvin	WR	Minnesota Vikings

AP DEFENSIVE PLAYER OF THE YEAR

1971	Alan Page	DT	Minnesota Vikings
1972	Joe Greene	DT	Pittsburgh Steelers
1973	Dick Anderson	S	Miami Dolphins
1974	Joe Greene	DT	Pittsburgh Steelers
1975	Mel Blount	CB	Pittsburgh Steelers
1976	Jack Lambert	LB	Pittsburgh Steelers
1977	Harvey Martin	DE	Dallas Cowboys
1978	Randy Gradishar	LB	Denver Broncos
1979	Lee Roy Selmon	DE	Tampa Bay Buccaneers
1980	Lester Hayes	CB	Oakland Raiders
1981	Lawrence Taylor	LB	New York Giants
1982	Lawrence Taylor	LB	New York Giants
1983	Doug Betters	DE	Miami Dolphins
1984	Kenny Easley	S	Seattle Seahawks
1985	Mike Singletary	LB	Chicago Bears
1986	Lawrence Taylor	LB	New York Giants
1987	Reggie White	DT	Philadelphia Eagles
1988	Mike Singletary	LB	Chicago Bears
1989	Keith Millard	DT	Minnesota Vikings
1990	Bruce Smith	DE	Buffalo Bills
1991	Pat Swilling	LB	New Orleans Saints
1992	Cortez Kennedy	DT	Seattle Seahawks
1993	Rod Woodson	CB	Pittsburgh Steelers
1994	Deion Sanders	CB	San Francisco 49ers
1995	Bryce Paup	LB	Buffalo Bills
1996	Bruce Smith	DE	Buffalo Bills
1997	Dana Stubblefield	DT	San Francisco 49ers
1998	Reggie White	DE	Green Bay Packers
1999	Warren Sapp	DT	Tampa Bay Buccaneers
2000	Ray Lewis	LB	Baltimore Ravens
2001	Michael Strahan	DE	New York Giants
2002	Derrick Brooks	LB	Tampa Bay Buccaneers
2003	Ray Lewis	LB	Baltimore Ravens
2004	Ed Reed	S	Baltimore Ravens
2005	Brian Urlacher	LB	Chicago Bears
2006	Jason Taylor	DE	Miami Dolphins
2007	Bob Sanders	S	Indianapolis Colts
2008	James Harrison	LB	Pittsburgh Steelers
2009	Charles Woodson	CB	Green Bay Packers

AP DEFENSIVE ROOKIE OF THE YEAR

1967	Lem Barney	CB	Detroit Lions
1968	Claude Humphrey	DE	Atlanta Falcons
1969	Joe Greene	DT	Pittsburgh Steelers
1970	Bruce Taylor	CB	San Francisco 49ers
1971	Isiah Robertson	LB	Los Angeles Rams
1972	Willie Buchanon	CB	Green Bay Packers
1973	Wally Chambers	DT	Chicago Bears
1974	Jack Lambert	LB	Pittsburgh Steelers
1975	Robert Brazile	LB	Houston Oilers
1976	Mike Haynes	S	New England Patriots
1977	A.J. Duhe	DT	Miami Dolphins
1978	Al Baker	DE	Detroit Lions
1979	Jim Haslett	LB	Buffalo Bills
1980*	Buddy Curry	LB	Atlanta Falcons
	Al Richardson	LB	Atlanta Falcons
1981	Lawrence Taylor	LB	New York Giants
1982	Chip Banks	LB	Cleveland Browns
1983	Vernon Maxwell	LB	Baltimore Colts
1984	Bill Maas	NT	Kansas City Chiefs
1985	Duane Bickett	LB	Indianapolis Colts
1986	John Offerdahl	LB	Miami Dolphins
1987	Shane Conlan	LB	Buffalo Bills
1988	Erik McMillan	S	New York Jets
1989	Derrick Thomas	LB	Kansas City Chiefs
1990	Mark Carrier	S	Chicago Bears
1991	Mike Croel	LB	Denver Broncos
1992	Dale Carter	CB	Kansas City Chiefs
1993	Dana Stubblefield	DT	San Francisco 49ers
1994	Tim Bowens	DT	Miami Dolphins
1995	Hugh Douglas	DE	New York Jets
1996	Simeon Rice	DE	Arizona Cardinals
1997	Peter Boulware	LB	Baltimore Ravens
1998	Charles Woodson	CB	Oakland Raiders
1999	Jevon Kearse	DE	Tennessee Titans
2000	Brian Urlacher	LB	Chicago Bears
2001	Kendrell Bell	LB	Pittsburgh Steelers
2002	Julius Peppers	DE	Carolina Panthers
2003	Terrell Suggs	LB	Baltimore Ravens
2004	Jonathan Vilma	LB	New York Jets
2005	Shawne Merriman	LB	San Diego Chargers
2006	DeMeco Ryans	LB	Houston Texans
2007	Patrick Willis	LB	San Francisco 49ers
2008	Jerod Mayo	LB	New England Patriots
2009	Brian Cushing	LB	Houston Texans

*The award was shared in 1980.

AP COMEBACK PLAYER OF THE YEAR

1998	Doug Flutie	QB	Buffalo Bills
1999	Bryant Young	DT	San Francisco 49ers
2000	Joe Johnson	DE	New Orleans Saints
2001	Garrison Hearst	RB	San Francisco 49ers
2002	Tommy Maddox	QB	Pittsburgh Steelers
2003	Jon Kitna	QB	Cincinnati Bengals
2004	Drew Brees	QB	San Diego Chargers
2005*	Steve Smith	WR	Carolina Panthers
	Tedy Bruschi	LB	New England Patriots
2006	Chad Pennington	QB	New York Jets
2007	Greg Ellis	DE	Dallas Cowboys
2008	Chad Pennington	QB	Miami Dolphins
2009	Tom Brady	QB	New England Patriots

*The award was shared in 2005.

AP COACH OF THE YEAR

1957	George Wilson	Detroit Lions
1958	Weeb Ewbank	Baltimore Colts
1959	Vince Lombardi	Green Bay Packers
1960	Buck Shaw	Philadelphia Eagles
1961	Allie Sherman	New York Giants
1962	Allie Sherman	New York Giants
1963	George Halas	Chicago Bears
1964	Don Shula	Baltimore Colts
1965	George Halas	Chicago Bears
1966	Tom Landry	Dallas Cowboys
1967*	George Allen	Los Angeles Rams
	Don Shula	Baltimore Colts
1968	Don Shula	Baltimore Colts
1969	Bud Grant	Minnesota Vikings
1970	Paul Brown	Cincinnati Bengals
1971	George Allen	Washington Redskins
1972	Don Shula	Miami Dolphins
1973	Chuck Knox	Los Angeles Rams
1974	Don Coryell	St. Louis Cardinals
1975	Ted Marchibroda	Baltimore Colts
1976	Forrest Gregg	Cleveland Browns
1977	Red Miller	Denver Broncos
1978	Jack Patera	Seattle Seahawks
1979	Jack Pardee	Washington Redskins
1980	Chuck Knox	Buffalo Bills
1981	Bill Walsh	San Francisco 49ers
1982	Joe Gibbs	Washington Redskins
1983	Joe Gibbs	Washington Redskins
1984	Chuck Knox	Seattle Seahawks
1985	Mike Ditka	Chicago Bears
1986	Bill Parcells	New York Giants
1987	Jim Mora	New Orleans Saints
1988	Mike Ditka	Chicago Bears
1989	Lindy Infante	Green Bay Packers
1990	Jimmy Johnson	Dallas Cowboys
1991	Wayne Fontes	Detroit Lions
1992	Bill Cowher	Pittsburgh Steelers
1993	Dan Reeves	New York Giants
1994	Bill Parcells	New England Patriots
1995	Ray Rhodes	Philadelphia Eagles
1996	Dom Capers	Carolina Panthers
1997	Jim Fassel	New York Giants
1998	Dan Reeves	Atlanta Falcons
1999	Dick Vermeil	St. Louis Rams
2000	Jim Haslett	New Orleans Saints
2001	Dick Jauron	Chicago Bears
2002	Andy Reid	Philadelphia Eagles
2003	Bill Belichick	New England Patriots
2004	Marty Schottenheimer	San Diego Chargers
2005	Lovie Smith	Chicago Bears
2006	Sean Payton	New Orleans Saints
2007	Bill Belichick	New England Patriots
2008	Mike Smith	Atlanta Falcons
2009	Marvin Lewis	Cincinnati Bengals

*The award was shared in 1967.

Records

Compiled by Elias Sports Bureau.

The following records reflect all available official information on the National Football League from its formation in 1920 to date. Also included are all applicable records from the American Football League, 1960-69.

Individuals eligible for Rookie records are players who were in their first season of professional football and had not been on the roster of another professional football team, including teams in other leagues, for any regular-season or postseason games in a previous season. Eligible players, therefore, include those who were under contract to a National Football League club for a previous season but were terminated prior to their club's first regular-season game and not re-signed, or who were placed on Reserve/Injured (or another category of the Reserve List) prior to their club's first regular-season game and were not activated during the rest of the regular season or postseason.

INDIVIDUAL RECORDS

SERVICE

Most Seasons

26 George Blanda, Chi. Bears, 1949, 1950-58; Baltimore, 1950; Houston, 1960-66; Oakland, 1967-1975
25 Morten Andersen, New Orleans, 1982-1994; Atlanta, 1995-2000; N.Y. Giants, 2001; Kansas City, 2002-03; Minnesota, 2004; Atlanta, 2006-07
23 Gary Anderson, Pittsburgh, 1982-1994; Philadelphia, 1995-96; San Francisco, 1997; Minnesota, 1998-2002; Tennessee, 2003-04

Most Seasons, One Club

20 Jackie Slater, L.A. Rams, 1976-1994; St. Louis, 1995
Darrell Green, Washington, 1983-2002
19 Jim Marshall, Minnesota, 1961-1979
Bruce Matthews, Houston, 1983-1996; Tennessee, 1997-2001
18 Jim Hart, St. Louis, 1966-1983
Jeff Van Note, Atlanta, 1969-1986
Pat Leahy, N.Y. Jets, 1974-1991
Jason Hanson, Detroit, 1992-2009

Most Games Played, Career

382 Morten Andersen, New Orleans, 1982-1994; Atlanta, 1995-2000; N.Y. Giants, 2001; Kansas City, 2002-03; Minnesota, 2004; Atlanta, 2006-07
353 Gary Anderson, Pittsburgh, 1982-1994; Philadelphia, 1995-96; San Francisco, 1997; Minnesota, 1998-2002; Tennessee, 2003-04
352 Jeff Feagles, New England, 1988-89; Philadelphia, 1990-93; Arizona, 1994-97; Seattle, 1998-2002; N.Y. Giants, 2003-09

Most Consecutive Games Played, Career

336 Jeff Feagles, New England, 1988-89; Philadelphia, 1990-93; Arizona, 1994-97; Seattle, 1998-2002; N.Y. Giants, 2003-09 (current)
287 Brett Favre, Green Bay, 1992-2007; N.Y. Jets, 2008; Minnesota, 2009 (current)
282 Jim Marshall, Cleveland, 1960; Minnesota, 1961-1979

SCORING

Most Seasons Leading League

5 Don Hutson, Green Bay, 1940-44
Gino Cappelletti, Boston, 1961, 1963-66
3 Earl (Dutch) Clark, Portsmouth, 1932; Detroit, 1935-36
Pat Harder, Chi. Cardinals, 1947-49
Paul Hornung, Green Bay, 1959-1961
2 Jack Manders, Chi. Bears, 1934, 1937
Gordy Soltau, San Francisco, 1952-53
Doak Walker, Detroit, 1950, 1955
Gene Mingo, Denver, 1960, 1962
Jim Turner, N.Y. Jets, 1968-69
Fred Cox, Minnesota, 1969-1970
Chester Marcol, Green Bay, 1972, 1974
John Smith, New England, 1979-1980
Marshall Faulk, St. Louis, 2000-01

Most Consecutive Seasons Leading League

5 Don Hutson, Green Bay, 1940-44
4 Gino Cappelletti, Boston, 1963-66
3 Pat Harder, Chi. Cardinals, 1947-49
Paul Hornung, Green Bay, 1959-1961

POINTS

Most Points, Career

2,544 Morten Andersen, New Orleans, 1982-1994; Atlanta, 1995-2000; N.Y. Giants, 2001; Kansas City, 2002-03; Minnesota, 2004; Atlanta, 2006-07 (849-pat, 565-fg)
2,434 Gary Anderson, Pittsburgh, 1982-1994; Philadelphia 1995-96; San Francisco, 1997; Minnesota, 1998-2002; Tennessee, 2003-04 (820-pat, 538-fg)
2,044 John Carney, Tampa Bay, 1988-89; L.A. Rams, 1990; San Diego, 1990-2000; New Orleans, 2001-06; Jacksonville, 2007; Kansas City, 2007; N.Y. Giants, 2008; New Orleans, 2009 (625-pat, 473-fg)

Most Points, Season

186 LaDainian Tomlinson, San Diego, 2006 (31-td)
176 Paul Hornung, Green Bay, 1960 (15-td, 41-pat, 15-fg)
168 Shaun Alexander, Seattle, 2005 (28-td)

Most Point, No Touchdowns, Season

164 Gary Anderson, Minnesota, 1998 (59-pat, 35-fg)
163 Jeff Wilkins, St. Louis, 2003 (46-pat, 39-fg)
161 Mark Moseley, Washington, 1983 (62-pat, 33-fg)

Most Seasons, 100 or More Points

16 Jason Elam, Denver, 1993-2007; Atlanta, 2008
14 Gary Anderson, Pittsburgh, 1983-85, 1988, 1991-94; Philadelphia 1996; San Francisco, 1997; Minnesota, 1998-2000; Tennessee, 2003
Morten Andersen, New Orleans, 1985-89, 1991-94; Atlanta, 1995, 1997-98; Kansas City, 2002-03
13 Adam Vinatieri, New England, 1996-2005; Indianapolis, 2006-08

Most Points, Rookie Season

144 Kevin Butler, Chicago, 1985 (51-pat, 31-fg)
141 Mason Crosby, Green Bay, 2007 (48-pat, 31-fg)
132 Gale Sayers, Chicago, 1965 (22-td)

Most Points, Game

40 Ernie Nevers, Chi. Cardinals vs. Chi. Bears, Nov. 28, 1929 (6-td, 4-pat)
36 Dub Jones, Cleveland vs. Chi. Bears, Nov. 25, 1951 (6-td)
Gale Sayers, Chicago vs. San Francisco, Dec. 12, 1965 (6-td)
33 Paul Hornung, Green Bay vs. Baltimore, Oct. 8, 1961 (4-td, 6-pat, 1-fg)

Most Consecutive Games Scoring

360 Morten Andersen, New Orleans, 1983-1994; Atlanta, 1995-2000; N.Y. Giants, 2001; Kansas City, 2002-03; Minnesota, 2004; Atlanta, 2006-07
263 Jason Elam, Denver, 1993-2007; Atlanta, 2008-09 (current)
186 Jim Breech, Oakland, 1979; Cincinnati, 1980-1992

TOUCHDOWNS

Most Seasons Leading League

8 Don Hutson, Green Bay, 1935-38, 1941-44
3 Jim Brown, Cleveland, 1958-59, 1963
Lance Alworth, San Diego, 1964-66

Emmitt Smith, Dallas, 1992, 1994-95
2 By many players

Most Consecutive Seasons Leading League
4 Don Hutson, Green Bay, 1935-38, 1941-44
3 Lance Alworth, San Diego, 1964-66
2 By many players

Most Touchdowns, Career
208 Jerry Rice, San Francisco, 1985-2000; Oakland, 2001-04; Seattle, 2004 (10-r, 197-p, 1-ret)
175 Emmitt Smith, Dallas, 1990-2002; Arizona, 2003-04 (164-r, 11-p)
153 LaDainian Tomlinson, San Diego, 2001-09 (138-r, 15-p)

Most Touchdowns, Season
31 LaDainian Tomlinson, San Diego, 2006 (28-r, 3-p)
28 Shaun Alexander, Seattle, 2005 (27-r, 1-p)
27 Priest Holmes, Kansas City, 2003 (27-r)

Most Touchdowns, Rookie, Season
22 Gale Sayers. Chicago, 1965 (14-r, 6-p)
20 Eric Dickerson, Rams, 1983 (18-r, 2-p)
17 Fred Taylor, Jacksonville, 1998 (14-r, 3-p)
Randy Moss, Minnesota, 1998 (17-p)
Edgerrin James, Indianapolis, 1999 (13-r, 4-p)
Clinton Portis, Denver, 2002 (15-r, 2-p)

Most Touchdowns, Game
6 Ernie Nevers, Chi. Cardinals vs. Chi. Bears, Nov. 28, 1929 (6-r)
Dub Jones, Cleveland vs. Chi. Bears, Nov. 25, 1951 (4-r, 2-p)
Gale Sayers, Chicago vs. San Francisco, Dec. 12, 1965 (4-r, 1-p, 1-ret)
5 Jimmy Conzelman, Rhode Island vs. Evansville, Oct. 15, 1922 (5-r)
Bob Shaw, Chi. Cardinals vs. Baltimore, Oct. 2, 1950 (5-p)
Jim Brown, Cleveland vs. Baltimore, Nov. 1, 1959 (5-r)
Abner Haynes, Dall. Texans vs. Oakland, Nov. 26, 1961 (4-r, 1-p)
Billy Cannon, Houston vs. N.Y. Titans, Dec. 10, 1961 (3-r, 2-p)
Cookie Gilchrist, Buffalo vs. N.Y. Jets, Dec. 8, 1963 (5-r)
Paul Hornung, Green Bay vs. Baltimore, Dec. 12, 1965 (3-r, 2-p)
Kellen Winslow, San Diego vs. Oakland, Nov. 22, 1981 (5-p)
Jerry Rice, San Francisco vs. Atlanta, Oct. 14, 1990 (5-p)
James Stewart, Jacksonville vs. Philadelphia, Oct. 12, 1997 (5-r)
Shaun Alexander, Seattle vs. Minnesota, Sept. 29, 2002 (4-r, 1-p)
Clinton Portis, Denver vs. Kansas City, Dec. 7, 2003 (5-r)
4 By many players. Last time: DeAngelo Williams, Carolina vs. N.Y. Giants, Dec. 21, 2008 (ot) (4-r)

Most Consecutive Games Scoring Touchdowns
18 Lenny Moore, Baltimore, 1963-65
LaDainian Tomlinson, San Diego, 2004-05
14 O.J. Simpson, Buffalo, 1975
13 John Riggins, Washington, 1982-83
George Rogers, Washington, 1985-86
Jerry Rice, San Francisco, 1986-87

POINTS AFTER TOUCHDOWN

Most Seasons Leading League
8 George Blanda, Chi. Bears, 1956; Houston, 1961-62; Oakland, 1967-69, 1972, 1974
4 Bob Waterfield, Cleveland, 1945; Los Angeles, 1946, 1950, 1952
3 Earl (Dutch) Clark, Portsmouth, 1932; Detroit, 1935-36 Jack Manders, Chi. Bears, 1933-35
Don Hutson, Green Bay, 1941-42, 1945

Most (Kicking) Points After Touchdown Attempted, Career
959 George Blanda, Chi. Bears, 1949, 1950-58; Baltimore, 1950; Houston, 1960-66; Oakland, 1967-1975
859 Morten Andersen, New Orleans, 1982-1994; Atlanta, 1995-2000; N.Y. Giants, 2001; Kansas City, 2002-03; Minnesota, 2004; Atlanta, 2006-07
827 Gary Anderson, Pittsburgh, 1982-1994; Philadelphia 1995-96; San Francisco, 1997; Minnesota, 1998-2002; Tennessee, 2003-04

Most (Kicking) Points After Touchdown Attempted, Season
74 Stephen Gostkowski, New England, 2007
70 Uwe von Schamann, Miami, 1984
65 George Blanda, Houston, 1961

Most (Kicking) Points After Touchdown Attempted, Game
10 Charlie Gogolak, Washington vs. N.Y. Giants, Nov. 27, 1966
9 Pat Harder, Chi. Cardinals vs. N.Y. Giants, Oct. 17, 1948; vs. N.Y. Bulldogs, Nov. 13, 1949
Bob Waterfield, Los Angeles vs. Baltimore, Oct. 22, 1950
Bob Thomas, Chicago vs. Green Bay, Dec. 7, 1980
8 By many players

Most (One-Point) Points After Touchdown, Career
943 George Blanda, Chi. Bears, 1949, 1950-58; Baltimore, 1950; Houston, 1960-66; Oakland, 1967-1975
849 Morten Andersen, New Orleans, 1982-1994; Atlanta, 1995-2000; N.Y. Giants, 2001; Kansas City, 2002-03; Minnesota, 2004, Atlanta, 2006-07
820 Gary Anderson, Pittsburgh, 1982-1994; Philadelphia 1995-96; San Francisco, 1997; Minnesota, 1998-2002; Tennessee, 2003-04

Most (One-Point) Points After Touchdown, Season
74 Stephen Gostkowski, New England, 2007
66 Uwe von Schamann, Miami, 1984
64 George Blanda, Houston, 1961
Jeff Wilkins, St. Louis, 1999

Most (One-Point) Points After Touchdown, Game
9 Pat Harder, Chi. Cardinals vs. N.Y. Giants, Oct. 17, 1948
Bob Waterfield, Los Angeles vs. Baltimore, Oct. 22, 1950
Charlie Gogolak, Washington vs. N.Y. Giants, Nov. 27, 1966
8 By many players

Most Consecutive (Kicking) Points After Touchdown
422 Matt Stover, Baltimore, 1996-2008; Indianapolis, 2009 (current)
371 Jason Elam, Denver, 1993-2002
Jeff Wilkins, St. Louis, 1999-2007
306 Rian Lindell, Seattle, 2000-02; Buffalo, 2003-09 (current)

Highest (Kicking) Points After Touchdown Percentage, Career (200 points after touchdown)
100.00 Rian Lindell, Seattle, 2000-02; Buffalo, 2003-09 (306-306)
99.61 Josh Brown, Seattle, 2003-07; St. Louis, 2008-09 (258-259)
99.51 Stephen Gostkowski, New England, 2006-09 (204-205)

Most (Kicking) Points After Touchdown, No Misses, Season
74 Stephen Gostkowski, New England, 2007
64 Jeff Wilkins, St. Louis, 1999
59 Gary Anderson, Minnesota, 1998

Most (Kicking) Points After Touchdown, No Misses, Game

9 Pat Harder, Chi. Cardinals vs. N.Y. Giants, Oct. 17, 1948
Bob Waterfield, Los Angeles vs. Baltimore, Oct. 22, 1950
8 By many players

Most Two-Point Conversions, Career

Two-point conversions include AFL (1960-69) and NFL (since 1994).

7 Marshall Faulk, Indianapolis, 1994-98; St. Louis, 1999-2005
6 Terance Mathis, Atlanta, 1994-2001; Pittsburgh, 2002
5 Cris Carter, Minnesota, 1994-2001; Miami, 2002
Rob Moore, N.Y. Jets, 1994; Arizona, 1995-99
Willie Jackson, Jacksonville, 1995-97; Cincinnati, 1998-99; New Orleans, 2000-01; Washington, 2002
Keenan McCardell, Cleveland, 1994-95; Jacksonville, 1996-2001; Tampa Bay, 2002-03; San Diego, 2004-06, Washington, 2007
Marvin Harrison, Indianapolis, 1996-2008
Marcus Pollard, Indianapolis, 1995-2004; Detroit, 2005-06; Seattle, 2007; Atlanta, 2008
Todd Heap, Baltimore, 2001-09
Hines Ward, Pittsburgh, 1998-2009
Edgerrin James, Indianapolis, 1999-2005; Arizona, 2006-08; Seattle, 2009

Most Two-Point Conversions, Season

4 Todd Heap, Baltimore, 2003
3 Gino Cappelletti, Boston, 1960
Richie Lucas, Buffalo, 1961
Ronnie Harmon, San Diego, 1994
Haywood Jeffires, Houston, 1994
Tom Tupa, Cleveland, 1994
Terance Mathis, Atlanta, 1995
Lamar Smith, Seattle, 1996
Cris Carter, Minnesota, 1997
Terrell Davis, Denver, 1997
James Stewart, Detroit, 2000
Hines Ward, Pittsburgh, 2002
Brian Finneran, Atlanta, 2005
Reggie Bush, New Orleans, 2007
2 By many players

Most Two-Point Conversions, Game

2 Brett Perriman, Detroit vs. Green Bay, Nov. 6, 1994
Michael Jackson, Baltimore vs. New England, Oct. 6, 1996
Terrell Davis, Denver vs. Atlanta, Sept. 28, 1997
Charles Johnson, Pittsburgh vs. Tennessee, Nov. 1, 1998
Marshall Faulk, St. Louis vs. Atlanta, Oct. 15, 2000
Todd Heap, Baltimore vs. Cincinnati, Oct. 19, 2003
Reggie Bush, New Orleans vs. St. Louis, Nov. 11, 2007
Tarvaris Jackson, Minnesota vs. Denver, Dec. 30, 2007 (ot)

FIELD GOALS

Most Seasons Leading League

5 Lou Groza, Cleveland, 1950, 1952-54, 1957
4 Jack Manders, Chi. Bears, 1933-34, 1936-37
Ward Cuff, N.Y. Giants, 1938-39, 1943; Green Bay, 1947
Mark Moseley, Washington, 1976-77, 1979, 1982
3 Bob Waterfield, Los Angeles, 1947, 1949, 1951
Gino Cappelletti, Boston, 1961, 1963-64
Fred Cox, Minnesota, 1965, 1969-1970
Jan Stenerud, Kansas City, 1967, 1970, 1975

Most Consecutive Seasons Leading League

3 Lou Groza, Cleveland, 1952-54
2 Jack Manders, Chi. Bears, 1933-34
Armand Niccolai, Pittsburgh, 1935-36
Jack Manders, Chi. Bears, 1936-37
Ward Cuff, N.Y. Giants, 1938-39
Clark Hinkle, Green Bay, 1940-41
Cliff Patton, Philadelphia, 1948-49
Gino Cappelletti, Boston, 1963-64
Jim Turner, N.Y. Jets, 1968-69
Fred Cox, Minnesota, 1969-1970
Mark Moseley, Washington, 1976-77
Chip Lohmiller, Washington, 1991-92
Pete Stoyanovich, Miami, 1991-92

Most Field Goals Attempted, Career

709 Morten Andersen, New Orleans, 1982-1994; Atlanta, 1995-2000; N.Y. Giants, 2001; Kansas City, 2002-03; Minnesota, 2004; Atlanta, 2006-07
672 Gary Anderson, Pittsburgh, 1982-1994; Philadelphia, 1995-96; San Francisco, 1997; Minnesota, 1998-2002; Tennessee, 2003-04
641 George Blanda, Chi. Bears, 1949, 1950-58; Baltimore, 1950; Houston, 1960-66; Oakland, 1967-1975

Most Field Goals Attempted, Season

49 Bruce Gossett, Los Angeles, 1966
Curt Knight, Washington, 1971
48 Chester Marcol, Green Bay, 1972
47 Jim Turner, N.Y. Jets, 1969
David Ray, Los Angeles, 1973
Mark Moseley, Washington, 1983

Most Field Goals Attempted, Game

9 Jim Bakken, St. Louis vs. Pittsburgh, Sept. 24, 1967
8 Lou Michaels, Pittsburgh vs. St. Louis, Dec. 2, 1962
Garo Yepremian, Detroit vs. Minnesota, Nov. 13, 1966
Jim Turner, N.Y. Jets vs. Buffalo, Nov. 3, 1968
Billy Cundiff, Dallas vs. N.Y. Giants, Sept. 15, 2003 (ot)
Rob Bironas, Tennessee vs. Houston, Oct. 21, 2007
7 By many players

Most Field Goals, Career

565 Morten Andersen, New Orleans, 1982-1994; Atlanta, 1995-2000; N.Y. Giants, 2001; Kansas City, 2002-03; Minnesota, 2004; Atlanta, 2006-07
538 Gary Anderson, Pittsburgh, 1982-1994; Philadelphia, 1995-96; San Francisco, 1997; Minnesota, 1998-2002; Tennessee, 2003-04
473 John Carney, Tampa Bay, 1988-89; L.A. Rams, 1990; San Diego, 1990-2000; New Orleans, 2001-06; Jacksonville, 2007; Kansas City, 2007; N.Y. Giants, 2008; New Orleans, 2009

Most Field Goals, Season

40 Neil Rackers, Arizona, 2005
39 Olindo Mare, Miami, 1999
Jeff Wilkins, St. Louis, 2003
37 John Kasay, Carolina, 1996
Mike Vanderjagt, Indianapolis, 2003

Most Field Goals, Rookie, Season

35 Ali Haji-Sheikh, N.Y. Giants, 1983
34 Richie Cunningham, Dallas, 1997
33 Chester Marcol, Green Bay, 1972

Most Field Goals, Game

8 Rob Bironas, Tennessee vs. Houston, Oct. 21, 2007
7 Jim Bakken, St. Louis vs. Pittsburgh, Sept. 24, 1967
Rich Karlis, Minnesota vs. L.A. Rams, Nov. 5, 1989 (ot)
Chris Boniol, Dallas vs. Green Bay, Nov. 18, 1996
Billy Cundiff, Dallas vs. N.Y. Giants, Sept. 15, 2003 (ot)
Shayne Graham, Cincinnati vs. Baltimore, Nov. 11, 2007
6 By many players

Most Field Goals, One Quarter

4 Garo Yepremian, Detroit vs. Minnesota, Nov. 13, 1966 (second quarter)

Curt Knight, Washington vs. N.Y. Giants, Nov. 15, 1970 (second quarter)
Roger Ruzek, Dallas vs. N.Y. Giants, Nov. 2, 1987 (fourth quarter)
Cary Blanchard, Indianapolis vs. Buffalo, Sept. 21 1997 (second quarter)
Sebastian Janikowski, Oakland vs. Chicago, Oct. 5, 2003 (second quarter)
Jeff Wilkins, St. Louis vs. Baltimore, Nov. 9, 2003 (fourth quarter)
Lawrence Tynes, Kansas City vs. New England, Nov. 27, 2005 (second quarter)
Shayne Graham, Cincinnati vs. Baltimore, Nov. 11, 2007 (fourth quarter)
3 By many players

Most Consecutive Games Scoring Field Goals
38 Matt Stover, Baltimore, 1999-2001
31 Fred Cox, Minnesota, 1968-1970
28 Jim Turner, N.Y. Jets, 1970; Denver, 1971-72
Chip Lohmiller, Washington, 1988-1990

Most Consecutive Field Goals
42 Mike Vanderjagt, Indianapolis, 2002-04
40 Gary Anderson, San Francisco, 1997; Minnesota, 1998
36 Matt Stover, Baltimore, 2005-06

Longest Field Goal
63 Tom Dempsey, New Orleans vs. Detroit, Nov. 8, 1970
Jason Elam, Denver vs. Jacksonville, Oct. 25, 1998
62 Matt Bryant, Tampa Bay vs. Philadelphia, Oct. 22, 2006
61 Sebastian Janikowski, Oakland vs. Cleveland, Dec. 27, 2009

Highest Field Goal Pct., Career (100 field goals)
87.21 Nate Kaeding, San Diego, 2004-09 (150-172)
86.47 Mike Vanderjagt, Indianapolis, 1998-2005; Dallas, 2006 (230-266)
85.90 Robbie Gould, Chicago, 2005-09 (134-156)

Highest Field Goal Pct., Season (Qualifiers)
100.00 Tony Zendejas, L.A. Rams, 1991 (17-17)
Gary Anderson, Minnesota, 1998 (35-35)
Jeff Wilkins, St. Louis, 2000 (17-17)
Mike Vanderjagt, Indianapolis, 2003 (37-37)
96.43 Chris Boniol, Dallas, 1995 (28-27)
96.30 Norm Johnson, Atlanta, 1993 (27-26)
Pete Stoyanovich, Kansas City, 1997 (27-26)

Most Field Goals, No Misses, Game
8 Rob Bironas, Tennessee vs. Houston, Oct. 21, 2007
7 Rich Karlis, Minnesota vs. L.A. Rams, Nov. 5, 1989 (ot)
Chris Boniol, Dallas vs. Green Bay, Nov. 18, 1996
Shayne Graham, Cincinnati vs. Baltimore, Nov. 11, 2007
6 By many players

Most Field Goals, 50 or More Yards, Career
42 Jason Hanson, Detroit, 1992-2009
40 Morten Andersen, New Orleans, 1982-1994; Atlanta, 1995-2000; N.Y. Giants, 2001; Kansas City, 2002-03; Minnesota, 2004; Atlanta, 2006-07
39 Jason Elam, Denver, 1993-2007; Atlanta, 2008-09

Most Field Goals, 50 or More Yards, Season
8 Morten Andersen, Atlanta, 1995
Jason Hanson, Detroit, 2008
6 Dean Biasucci, Indianapolis, 1988
Chris Jacke, Green Bay, 1993
Tony Zendejas, L.A. Rams, 1993
Mike Vanderjagt, Indianapolis, 1998
Neil Rackers, Arizona, 2005
Sebastian Janikowski, Oakland, 2007
Josh Brown, St. Louis, 2008
Ryan Longwell, Minnesota, 2008
Josh Brown, St. Louis, 2009
Sebastian Janikowski, Oakland, 2009
5 Fred Steinfort, Denver, 1980
Norm Johnson, Seattle, 1986
Kevin Butler, Chicago, 1993
Jason Elam, Denver, 1995, 1999
Cary Blanchard, Indianapolis, 1996
Martín Gramatica, Tampa Bay, 2000, 2002
Paul Edinger, Chicago, 2002
Neil Rackers, Arizona, 2004
Josh Brown, Seattle, 2005
Kris Brown, Houston, 2007
Matt Prater, Denver, 2008
Rob Bironas, Tennessee, 2009

Most Field Goals, 50 or More Yards, Game
3 Morten Andersen, Atlanta vs. New Orleans, Dec. 10, 1995
Neil Rackers, Arizona vs. Seattle, Oct. 24, 2004
Kris Brown, Houston vs. Miami, Oct. 7, 2007
Conner Barth, Tampa Bay vs. Miami, Nov. 15, 2009
2 By many players. Last time: Rob Bironas, Tennessee vs. Houston, Nov. 23, 2009

SAFETIES

Most Safeties, Career
4 Ted Hendricks, Baltimore, 1969-1973; Green Bay, 1974; Oakland, 1975-1981; L.A. Raiders, 1982-83
Doug English, Detroit, 1975-79, 1981-85
3 Bill McPeak, Pittsburgh, 1949-1957
Charlie Krueger, San Francisco, 1959-1973
Ernie Stautner, Pittsburgh, 1950-1963
Jim Katcavage, N.Y. Giants, 1956-1968
Roger Brown, Detroit, 1960-66; Los Angeles, 1967-69
Bruce Maher, Detroit, 1960-67; N.Y. Giants, 1968-69
Ron McDole, St. Louis, 1961; Houston, 1962; Buffalo, 1963-1970; Washington, 1971-78
Alan Page, Minnesota, 1967-1978; Chicago, 1979-1981
Lyle Alzado, Denver, 1971-78; Cleveland, 1979-1981; L.A. Raiders, 1982-85
Rulon Jones, Denver, 1980-88
Steve McMichael, New England, 1980; Chicago, 1981-1993; Green Bay, 1994
Kevin Greene, L.A. Rams, 1985-1992; Pittsburgh, 1993-95; Carolina, 1996, 1998-99; San Francisco, 1997
Burt Grossman, San Diego, 1989-1993; Philadelphia, 1994
Eric Swann, Phoenix, 1991-93; Arizona, 1994-99; Carolina, 2000
Dan Saleaumua, Detroit, 1987-88; Kansas City, 1989-1996; Seattle, 1997-98
Derrick Thomas, Kansas City, 1989-1999
Bryant Young, San Francisco, 1994-2007
Jared Allen, Kansas City, 2004-07; Minnesota, 2008-09
2 By many players

Most Safeties, Season
2 Tom Nash, Green Bay, 1932
Roger Brown, Detroit, 1962
Ron McDole, Buffalo, 1964
Alan Page, Minnesota, 1971
Fred Dryer, Los Angeles, 1973
Benny Barnes, Dallas, 1973
James Young, Houston, 1977
Doug English, Detroit, 1983
Don Blackmon, New England, 1985
Tim Harris, Green Bay, 1988

Brian Jordan, Atlanta, 1991
Burt Grossman, San Diego, 1992
Rod Stephens, Seattle, 1993
Bryant Young, San Francisco, 1996
Jared Allen, Minnesota, 2008
Jameel McClain, Baltimore, 2008

Most Safeties, Game
2 Fred Dryer, Los Angeles vs. Green Bay, Oct. 21, 1973

RUSHING

Most Seasons Leading League
8 Jim Brown, Cleveland, 1957-1961, 1963-65
4 Steve Van Buren, Philadelphia, 1945, 1947-49
O.J. Simpson, Buffalo, 1972-73, 1975-76
Eric Dickerson, L.A. Rams, 1983-84, 1986; Indianapolis, 1988
Emmitt Smith, Dallas, 1991-93, 1995
Barry Sanders, Detroit, 1990, 1994, 1996-97
3 Earl Campbell, Houston, 1978-1980

Most Consecutive Seasons Leading League
5 Jim Brown, Cleveland, 1957-1961
3 Steve Van Buren, Philadelphia, 1947-49
Jim Brown, Cleveland, 1963-65
Earl Campbell, Houston, 1978-1980
Emmitt Smith, Dallas, 1991-93
2 By many players

ATTEMPTS

Most Seasons Leading League
6 Jim Brown, Cleveland, 1958-59, 1961, 1963-65
4 Steve Van Buren, Philadelphia, 1947-1950
Walter Payton, Chicago, 1976-79
3 Cookie Gilchrist, Buffalo, 1963-64; Denver, 1965
Jim Nance, Boston, 1966-67, 1969
O.J. Simpson, Buffalo, 1973-75
Eric Dickerson, L.A. Rams, 1983, 1986; Indianapolis, 1988
Emmitt Smith, Dallas, 1991, 1994-95

Most Consecutive Seasons Leading League
4 Steve Van Buren, Philadelphia, 1947-1950
Walter Payton, Chicago, 1976-79
3 Jim Brown, Cleveland, 1963-65
Cookie Gilchrist, Buffalo, 1963-64; Denver, 1965
O.J. Simpson, Buffalo, 1973-75
2 By many players

Most Attempts, Career
4,409 Emmitt Smith, Dallas, 1990-2002; Arizona, 2003-04
3,838 Walter Payton, Chicago, 1975-1987
3,518 Curtis Martin, New England, 1995-97; N.Y. Jets, 1998-2005

Most Attempts, Season
416 Larry Johnson, Kansas City, 2006
410 Jamal Anderson, Atlanta, 1998
407 James Wilder, Tampa Bay, 1984

Most Attempts, Rookie, Season
390 Eric Dickerson, L.A. Rams, 1983
378 George Rogers, New Orleans, 1981
369 Edgerrin James, Indianapolis, 1999

Most Attempts, Game
45 Jamie Morris, Washington vs. Cincinnati, Dec. 17, 1988 (ot)
43 Butch Woolfolk, N.Y. Giants vs. Philadelphia, Nov. 20, 1983
James Wilder, Tampa Bay vs. Green Bay, Sept. 30, 1984 (ot)
Rudi Johnson, Cincinnati vs. Houston, Nov. 9, 2003
42 James Wilder, Tampa Bay vs. Pittsburgh, Oct. 30, 1983
Terrell Davis, Denver vs. Buffalo, Oct. 26, 1997 (ot)
Ricky Williams, Miami vs. Buffalo, Sept. 21, 2003

YARDS GAINED

Most Yards Gained, Career
18,355 Emmitt Smith, Dallas, 1990-2002; Arizona, 2003-04
16,726 Walter Payton, Chicago, 1975-1987
15,269 Barry Sanders, Detroit, 1989-1998

Most Seasons, 1,000 or More Yards Rushing
11 Emmitt Smith, Dallas, 1991-2001
10 Walter Payton, Chicago, 1976-1981, 1983-86
Barry Sanders, Detroit, 1989-1998
Curtis Martin, New England, 1995-97; N.Y. Jets, 1998-2004
8 Franco Harris, Pittsburgh, 1972, 1974-79, 1983
Tony Dorsett, Dallas, 1977-1981, 1983-85
Thurman Thomas, Buffalo, 1989-1996
Jerome Bettis, L.A. Rams, 1993-94; Pittsburgh, 1996-2001
LaDainian Tomlinson, San Diego, 2001-08

Most Consecutive Seasons, 1,000 or More Yards Rushing
11 Emmitt Smith, Dallas, 1991-2001
10 Barry Sanders, Detroit, 1989-1998
Curtis Martin, New England, 1995-97; N.Y. Jets, 1998-2004
8 Thurman Thomas, Buffalo, 1989-1996
LaDainian Tomlinson, San Diego, 2001-08

Most Yards Gained, Season
2,105 Eric Dickerson, L.A. Rams, 1984
2,066 Jamal Lewis, Baltimore, 2003
2,053 Barry Sanders, Detroit, 1997

Most Yards Gained, Rookie, Season
1,808 Eric Dickerson, L.A. Rams, 1983
1,674 George Rogers, New Orleans, 1981
1,605 Ottis Anderson, St. Louis, 1979

Most Yards Gained, Game
296 Adrian Peterson, Minnesota vs. San Diego, Nov. 4, 2007
295 Jamal Lewis, Baltimore vs. Cleveland, Sept. 14, 2003
286 Jerome Harrison, Cleveland vs. Kansas City, Dec. 20, 2009

Most Games, 200 or More Yards Rushing, Career
6 O.J. Simpson, Buffalo, 1969-1977; San Francisco, 1978-79
5 Tiki Barber, N.Y. Giants, 1997-2006
4 Jim Brown, Cleveland, 1957-1965
Earl Campbell, Houston, 1978-1984; New Orleans, 1984-85
Barry Sanders, Detroit, 1989-1998
LaDainian Tomlinson, San Diego, 2001-09

Most Games, 200 or More Yards Rushing, Season
4 Earl Campbell, Houston, 1980
3 O.J. Simpson, Buffalo, 1973
Tiki Barber, N.Y. Giants, 2005
2 Jim Brown, Cleveland, 1963
O.J. Simpson, Buffalo, 1976
Walter Payton, Chicago, 1977
Eric Dickerson, L.A. Rams, 1984
Greg Bell, L.A. Rams, 1989
Terrell Davis, Denver, 1997
Barry Sanders, Detroit, 1997
Corey Dillon, Cincinnati, 2000
Marshall Faulk, St. Louis, 2000
LaDainian Tomlinson, San Diego, 2002
Ricky Williams, Miami, 2002
Jamal Lewis, Baltimore, 2003
LaDainian Tomlinson, San Diego, 2003
Larry Johnson, Kansas City, 2005
Willie Parker, Pittsburgh, 2006
Adrian Peterson, Minnesota, 2007

Michael Turner, Atlanta, 2008

Most Consecutive Games, 200 or More Yards Rushing

2 O.J. Simpson, Buffalo, 1973, 1976
Earl Campbell, Houston, 1980
Ricky Williams, Miami, 2002

Most Games, 100 or more Yards Rushing, Career

78 Emmitt Smith, Dallas, 1990-2002; Arizona, 2003-04
77 Walter Payton, Chicago, 1975-1987
76 Barry Sanders, Detroit, 1989-1998

Most Games, 100 or More Yards Rushing, Season

14 Barry Sanders, Detroit, 1997
12 Eric Dickerson, L.A. Rams, 1984
Barry Foster, Pittsburgh, 1992
Jamal Anderson, Atlanta, 1998
Jamal Lewis, Baltimore, 2003
Chris Johnson, Tennessee, 2009
11 O.J. Simpson, Buffalo, 1973
Earl Campbell, Houston, 1979
Marcus Allen, L.A. Raiders, 1985
Eric Dickerson, L.A. Rams, 1986
Emmitt Smith, Dallas, 1995
Terrell Davis, Denver, 1998
Shaun Alexander, Seattle, 2005
Larry Johnson, Kansas City, 2006

Most Consecutive Games, 100 or More Yards Rushing

14 Barry Sanders, Detroit, 1997
11 Marcus Allen, L.A. Raiders, 1985-86
Chris Johnson, Tennessee, 2009 (current)
9 Walter Payton, Chicago, 1985
Fred Taylor, Jacksonville, 2000
Deuce McAllister, New Orleans, 2003
Larry Johnson, Kansas City, 2005
LaDainian Tomlinson, San Diego, 2006

Longest Run from Scrimmage

99 Tony Dorsett, Dallas vs. Minnesota, Jan. 3, 1983 (TD)
98 Ahman Green, Green Bay vs. Denver, Dec. 28, 2003 (TD)
97 Andy Uram, Green Bay vs. Chi. Cardinals, Oct. 8, 1939 (TD)
Bob Gage, Pittsburgh vs. Chi. Bears, Dec. 4, 1949 (TD)

AVERAGE GAIN

Highest Average Gain, Career (750 attempts)

6.36 Randall Cunningham, Philadelphia, 1985-1995; Minnesota, 1997-99; Dallas, 2000; Baltimore, 2001 (775-4,928)
5.22 Jim Brown, Cleveland, 1957-1965 (2,359-12,312)
5.14 Mercury Morris, Miami, 1969-1975; San Diego, 1976 (804-1,433)

Highest Average Gain, Season (Qualifiers)

8.45 Michael Vick, Atlanta, 2006 (123-1,039)
8.44 Beattie Feathers, Chi. Bears, 1934 (119-1,004)
7.98 Randall Cunningham, Philadelphia, 1990 (118-942)

Highest Average Gain, Game (10 attempts)

17.30 Michael Vick, Atlanta vs. Minnesota, Dec. 1, 2002 (10-173)
17.09 Marion Motley, Cleveland vs. Pittsburgh, Oct. 29, 1950 (11-188)
16.70 Billy Grimes, Green Bay vs. N.Y. Yanks, Oct. 8, 1950 (10-167)

TOUCHDOWNS

Most Seasons Leading League

5 Jim Brown, Cleveland, 1957-59, 1963, 1965
4 Steve Van Buren, Philadelphia, 1945, 1947-49
3 Abner Haynes, Dall. Texans, 1960-62
Cookie Gilchrist, Buffalo, 1962-64
Paul Lowe, L.A. Chargers, 1960; San Diego, 1961, 1965
Leroy Kelly, Cleveland, 1966-68
Emmitt Smith, Dallas, 1992, 1994-95
LaDainian Tomlinson, San Diego, 2004, 2006-07

Most Consecutive Seasons Leading League

3 Steve Van Buren, Philadelphia, 1947-49
Jim Brown, Cleveland, 1957-59
Abner Haynes, Dall. Texans, 1960-62
Cookie Gilchrist, Buffalo, 1962-64
Leroy Kelly, Cleveland, 1966-68

Most Touchdowns, Career

164 Emmitt Smith, Dallas, 1990-2002; Arizona, 2003-04
138 LaDainian Tomlinson, San Diego, 2001-09
123 Marcus Allen, L.A. Raiders, 1982-1992; Kansas City, 1993-97

Most Rushing Touchdowns, Season

28 LaDainian Tomlinson, San Diego, 2006
27 Priest Holmes, Kansas City, 2003
Shaun Alexander, Seattle, 2005
25 Emmitt Smith, Dallas, 1995

Most Touchdowns, Rookie, Season

18 Eric Dickerson, L.A. Rams, 1983
15 Ickey Woods, Cincinnati, 1988
Mike Anderson, Denver, 2000
Clinton Portis, Denver, 2002
14 Gale Sayers, Chicago, 1965
Barry Sanders, Detroit, 1989
Curtis Martin, New England, 1995
Fred Taylor, Jacksonville, 1998

Most Touchdowns, Game

6 Ernie Nevers, Chi. Cardinals vs. Chi. Bears, Nov. 28, 1929
5 Jimmy Conzelman, Rhode Island vs. Evansville, Oct. 15, 1922
Jim Brown, Cleveland vs. Baltimore, Nov. 1, 1959
Cookie Gilchrist, Buffalo vs. N.Y. Jets, Dec. 8, 1963
James Stewart, Jacksonville vs. Philadelphia, Oct. 12, 1997
Clinton Portis, Denver vs. Kansas City, Dec. 7, 2003
4 By many players

Most Consecutive Games Rushing for Touchdowns

18 LaDainian Tomlinson, San Diego, 2004-05
13 John Riggins, Washington, 1982-83
George Rogers, Washington, 1985-86
11 Lenny Moore, Baltimore, 1963-64
Emmitt Smith, Dallas, 1994-95
Emmitt Smith, Dallas, 1995
Priest Holmes, Kansas City, 2002

PASSING

Most Seasons Leading League

6 Sammy Baugh, Washington, 1937, 1940, 1943, 1945, 1947, 1949
Steve Young San Francisco, 1991-94, 1996-97
4 Len Dawson, Dall. Texans; 1962; Kansas City, 1964, 1966, 1968
Roger Staubach, Dallas, 1971, 1973, 1978-79
Ken Anderson, Cincinnati, 1974-75, 1981-82
3 Arnie Herber, Green Bay, 1932, 1934, 1936
Norm Van Brocklin, Los Angeles, 1950, 1952, 1954
Bart Starr, Green Bay, 1962, 1964, 1966
Peyton Manning, Indianapolis, 2004-06

Most Consecutive Seasons Leading League

4 Steve Young, San Francisco, 1991-94
3 Peyton Manning, Indianapolis, 2004-06
2 Cecil Isbell, Green Bay, 1941-42
Milt Plum, Cleveland, 1960-61
Ken Anderson, Cincinnati, 1974-75, 1981-82
Roger Staubach, Dallas, 1978-79

Steve Young, San Francisco, 1996-97

PASSER RATING

Highest Passer Rating, Career (1,500 attempts)

96.8 Steve Young, Tampa Bay, 1985-86; San Francisco, 1987-1999
95.8 Philip Rivers, San Diego, 2004-09
95.6 Tony Romo, Dallas, 2004-09

Highest Passer Rating, Season (Qualifiers)

121.1 Peyton Manning, Indianapolis, 2004
117.2 Tom Brady, New England, 2007
112.8 Steve Young, San Francisco, 1994

Highest Passer Rating, Rookie, Season (Qualifiers)

98.1 Ben Roethlisberger, Pittsburgh, 2004
96.0 Dan Marino, Miami, 1983
88.3 Greg Cook, Cincinnati, 1969

ATTEMPTS

Most Seasons Leading League

5 Dan Marino, Miami, 1984, 1986, 1988, 1992, 1997
4 Sammy Baugh, Washington, 1937, 1943, 1947-48
Johnny Unitas, Baltimore, 1957, 1959-1961
George Blanda, Chi. Bears, 1953; Houston, 1963-65
3 Arnie Herber, Green Bay, 1932, 1934, 1936
Sonny Jurgensen, Washington, 1966-67, 1969
Drew Bledsoe, New England, 1994-96
Brett Favre, Green Bay, 1999, 2005-06

Most Consecutive Seasons Leading League

3 Johnny Unitas, Baltimore, 1959-1961
George Blanda, Houston, 1963-65
Drew Bledsoe, New England, 1994-96
2 By many players

Most Passes Attempted, Career

9,811 Brett Favre, Atlanta, 1991; Green Bay, 1992-2007; N.Y. Jets, 2008; Minnesota, 2009
8,358 Dan Marino, Miami, 1983-1999
7,250 John Elway, Denver, 1983-1998

Most Passes Attempted, Season

691 Drew Bledsoe, New England, 1994
655 Warren Moon, Houston, 1991
652 Drew Brees, New Orleans, 2007

Most Passes Attempted, Rookie, Season

575 Peyton Manning, Indianapolis, 1998
540 Chris Weinke, Carolina, 2001
486 Rick Mirer, Seattle, 1993

Most Passes Attempted, Game

70 Drew Bledsoe, New England vs. Minnesota, Nov. 13, 1994
69 Vinny Testaverde, N.Y. Jets vs. Baltimore, Dec. 24, 2000
68 George Blanda, Houston vs. Buffalo, Nov. 1, 1964
Jon Kitna, Cincinnati vs. Pittsburgh, Dec. 30, 2001

COMPLETIONS

Most Seasons Leading League

6 Dan Marino, Miami, 1984-86, 1988, 1992, 1997
5 Sammy Baugh, Washington, 1937, 1943, 1945, 1947-48
4 George Blanda, Chi. Bears, 1953; Houston, 1963-65
Sonny Jurgensen, Philadelphia, 1961; Washington, 1966-67, 1969

Most Consecutive Seasons Leading League

3 George Blanda, Houston, 1963-65
Dan Marino, Miami, 1984-86
2 By many players

Most Passes Completed, Career

6,083 Brett Favre, Atlanta, 1991; Green Bay, 1992-2007; N.Y. Jets, 2008, Minnesota, 2009
4,967 Dan Marino, Miami, 1983-1999
4,232 Peyton Manning, Indianapolis, 1998-2009

Most Passes Completed, Season

440 Drew Brees, New Orleans, 2007
418 Rich Gannon, Oakland, 2002
413 Drew Brees, New Orleans, 2008

Most Passes Completed, Rookie, Season

326 Peyton Manning, Indianapolis, 1998
293 Chris Weinke, Carolina, 2001
274 Rick Mirer, Seattle, 1993

Most Passes Completed, Game

45 Drew Bledsoe, New England vs. Minnesota, Nov. 13, 1994 (ot)
43 Rich Gannon, Oakland vs. Pittsburgh, Sept. 15, 2002
42 Richard Todd, N.Y. Jets vs. San Francisco, Sept. 21, 1980
Vinny Testaverde, N.Y. Jets vs. Seattle, Dec. 6, 1998

Most Consecutive Passes Completed

24 Donovan McNabb, Philadelphia vs. N.Y. Giants (10), Nov. 28, 2004; vs. Green Bay (14), Dec. 5, 2004
23 Peyton Manning, Indianapolis vs. Detroit (6), Dec. 14, 2008; vs. Jacksonville (17), Dec. 18, 2008
22 Joe Montana, San Francisco vs. Cleveland (5), Nov. 29, 1987; vs. Green Bay (17), Dec. 6, 1987
Mark Brunell, Washington vs. Houston, Sept. 24, 2006
David Carr, Houston vs. Buffalo, Nov. 19, 2006

COMPLETION PERCENTAGE

Most Seasons Leading League

8 Len Dawson, Dall. Texans, 1962; Kansas City, 1964-69, 1975
7 Sammy Baugh, Washington, 1940, 1942-43, 1945, 1947-49
5 Joe Montana, San Francisco, 1980-81, 1985, 1987, 1989
Steve Young, San Francisco, 1992, 1994-97

Most Consecutive Seasons Leading League

6 Len Dawson, Kansas City, 1964-69
4 Steve Young, San Francisco, 1994-97
3 Sammy Baugh, Washington, 1947-49
Otto Graham, Cleveland, 1953-55
Milt Plum, Cleveland, 1959-1961
Kurt Warner, St. Louis, 1999-2001

Highest Completion Percentage, Career (1,500 attempts)

66.06 Chad Pennington, N.Y. Jets, 2000-07; Miami, 2008-09 (2,469-1,631)
65.50 Kurt Warner, St. Louis, 1998-2003; N.Y. Giants, 2004; Arizona, 2005-09 (4,070-2,666)
64.80 Peyton Manning, Indianapolis, 1998-2009 (6,531-4,232)

Highest Completion Percentage, Season (Qualifiers)

70.62 Drew Brees, New Orleans, 2009 (514-363)
70.55 Ken Anderson, Cincinnati, 1982 (309-218)
70.33 Sammy Baugh, Washington, 1945 (182-128)

Highest Completion Percentage, Rookie, Season (Qualifiers)

66.44 Ben Roethlisberger, Pittsburgh, 2004 (295-196)
61.06 Matt Ryan, Atlanta, 2008 (434-265)
60.05 Joe Flacco, Baltimore, 2008 (428-257)

Highest Completion Percentage, Game (20 attempts)

92.31 Kurt Warner, Arizona vs. Jacksonville, Sept. 20, 2009 (26-24)
91.30 Vinny Testaverde, Cleveland vs. L.A. Rams, Dec. 26, 1993 (23-21)
90.91 Ken Anderson, Cincinnati vs. Pittsburgh, Nov. 10, 1974 (22-20)

YARDS GAINED

Most Seasons Leading League

5 Sonny Jurgensen, Philadelphia, 1961-62; Washington, 1966-67, 1969
Dan Marino, Miami, 1984-86, 1988, 1992
4 Sammy Baugh, Washington, 1937, 1940, 1947-48
Johnny Unitas, Baltimore, 1957, 1959-1960, 1963
Dan Fouts, San Diego, 1979-1982
3 Arnie Herber, Green Bay, 1932, 1934, 1936
Sid Luckman, Chi. Bears, 1943, 1945-46
John Brodie, San Francisco, 1965, 1968, 1970
John Hadl, San Diego, 1965, 1968, 1971
Joe Namath, N.Y. Jets, 1966-67, 1972

Most Consecutive Seasons Leading League

4 Dan Fouts, San Diego, 1979-1982
3 Dan Marino, Miami, 1984-86
2 By many players

Most Yards Gained, Career

69,329 Brett Favre, Atlanta, 1991; Green Bay, 1992-2007; N.Y. Jets, 2008, Minnesota, 2009
61,361 Dan Marino, Miami, 1983-1999
51,475 John Elway, Denver, 1983-1998

Most Seasons, 3,000 or More Yards Passing

18 Brett Favre, Green Bay, 1992-2007; N.Y. Jets, 2008; Minnesota, 2009
13 Dan Marino, Miami, 1984-1992, 1994-95, 1997-98
12 John Elway, Denver, 1985-1991, 1993-97
Peyton Manning, Indianapolis, 1998-2009

Most Yards Gained, Season

5,084 Dan Marino, Miami, 1984
5,069 Drew Brees, New Orleans, 2008
4,830 Kurt Warner, St. Louis, 2001

Most Yards Gained, Rookie, Season

3,739 Peyton Manning, Indianapolis, 1998
3,440 Matt Ryan, Atlanta, 2008
2,971 Joe Flacco, Baltimore, 2008

Most Yards Gained, Game

554 Norm Van Brocklin, Los Angeles vs. N.Y. Yanks, Sept. 28, 1951
527 Warren Moon, Houston vs. Kansas City, Dec. 16, 1990
522 Boomer Esiason, Arizona vs. Washington, Nov. 10, 1996 (ot)

Most Games, 400 or More Yards Passing, Career

13 Dan Marino, Miami, 1983-1999
7 Joe Montana, San Francisco, 1979-1990, 1992; Kansas City, 1993-94
Warren Moon, Houston, 1984-1993; Minnesota, 1994-96; Seattle, 1997-98; Kansas City, 1999-2000
Peyton Manning, Indianapolis, 1998-2009
6 Dan Fouts, San Diego, 1973-1987
Drew Bledsoe, New England, 1993-2001; Buffalo, 2002-04; Dallas, 2005-06

Most Games, 400 or More Yards Passing, Season

4 Dan Marino, Miami, 1984
3 Dan Marino, Miami, 1986
2 By many players

Most Consecutive Games, 400 or More Yards Passing

2 Dan Fouts, San Diego, 1982
Dan Marino, Miami, 1984
Phil Simms, N.Y. Giants, 1985
Billy Volek, Tennessee, 2004
Matt Cassel, New England, 2008

Most Games, 300 or More Yards Passing, Career

63 Dan Marino, Miami, 1983-1999
61 Brett Favre, Atlanta, 1991; Green Bay, 1992-2007; N.Y. Jets, 2008; Minnesota, 2009
56 Peyton Manning, Indianapolis, 1998-2009

Most Games, 300 or More Yards Passing, Season

10 Rich Gannon, Oakland, 2002
Drew Brees, New Orleans, 2008
9 Dan Marino, Miami, 1984
Warren Moon, Houston, 1990
Kurt Warner, St. Louis, 1999
Kurt Warner, St. Louis, 2001
Peyton Manning, Indianapolis, 2009
Matt Schaub, Houston, 2009
8 Dan Fouts, San Diego, 1980
Kurt Warner, St. Louis, 2000
Trent Green, Kansas City, 2004
Marc Bulger, St. Louis, 2006
Drew Brees, New Orleans, 2006
Tom Brady, New England, 2007
Jay Cutler, Denver, 2008
Tony Romo, Dallas, 2009

Most Consecutive Games, 300 or More Yards Passing

6 Steve Young, San Francisco, 1998
Kurt Warner, St. Louis, 2000
Rich Gannon, Oakland, 2002
5 Joe Montana, San Francisco, 1982
Kerry Collins, N.Y. Giants, 2001-02
Drew Brees, New Orleans, 2006
Kurt Warner, Arizona, 2008
Tom Brady, New England, 2009
Peyton Manning, Indianapolis, 2009
4 Dan Fouts, San Diego, 1979
Dan Fouts, San Diego, 1980-81
Bill Kenney, Kansas City, 1983
Joe Montana, San Francisco, 1985-86
Joe Montana, San Francisco, 1990
Warren Moon, Houston, 1990
Drew Bledsoe, New England, 1993-94
Kurt Warner, St. Louis, 1999
Brian Griese, Denver, 2002
Daunte Culpepper, Minnesota, 2004
Trent Green, Kansas City, 2004
Drew Brees, New Orleans, 2008-09

Longest Pass Completion (All TDs except as noted)

99 Frank Filchock (to Farkas), Washington vs. Pittsburgh, Oct. 15, 1939
George Izo (to Mitchell), Washington vs. Cleveland, Sept. 15, 1963
Karl Sweetan (to Studstill), Detroit vs. Baltimore, Oct. 16, 1966
Sonny Jurgensen (to Allen), Washington vs. Chicago, Sept. 15, 1968
Jim Plunkett (to Branch), L.A. Raiders vs. Washington, Oct. 2, 1983
Ron Jaworski (to Quick), Philadelphia vs. Atlanta, Nov. 10, 1985
Stan Humphries (to Martin), San Diego vs. Seattle, Sept. 18, 1994
Brett Favre (to Brooks), Green Bay vs. Chicago, Sept. 11, 1995
Trent Green (to Boerigter), Kansas City vs. San Diego, Dec. 22, 2002
Jeff Garcia (to Davis), Cleveland vs. Cincinnati, Oct. 17, 2004
Gus Frerotte (to Berrian), Minnesota vs. Chicago, Nov. 30, 2008
98 Doug Russell (to Tinsley), Chi. Cardinals vs. Cleveland, Nov. 27, 1938
Ogden Compton (to Lane), Chi. Cardinals vs. Green Bay, Nov. 13, 1955
Bill Wade (to Farrington), Chicago Bears vs. Detroit, Oct. 8, 1961
Jacky Lee (to Dewveall), Houston vs. San Diego, Nov. 25, 1962

Earl Morrall (to Jones), N.Y. Giants vs. Pittsburgh, Sept. 11, 1966
Jim Hart (to Moore), St. Louis vs. Los Angeles, Dec. 10, 1972 (no TD)
Bobby Hebert (to Haynes), Atlanta vs. New Orleans, Sept. 12, 1993
Charlie Batch (to Morton), Detroit vs. Chicago, Oct. 4, 1998
Ryan Fitzpatrick (to Owens), Buffalo vs. Jacksonville, Nov. 22, 2009
97 Pat Coffee (to Tinsley), Chi. Cardinals vs. Chi. Bears, Dec. 5, 1937
Bobby Layne (to Box), Detroit vs. Green Bay, Nov. 26, 1953
George Shaw (to Tarr), Denver vs. Boston, Sept. 21, 1962
Bernie Kosar (to Slaughter), Cleveland vs. Chicago, Oct. 23, 1989
Steve Young (to Taylor), San Francisco vs. Atlanta, Nov. 3, 1991

AVERAGE GAIN

Most Seasons Leading League
7 Sid Luckman, Chi. Bears, 1939-1943, 1946-47
5 Steve Young, San Francisco, 1991-94, 1997
3 Arnie Herber, Green Bay, 1932, 1934, 1936
Norm Van Brocklin, Los Angeles, 1950, 1952, 1954
Len Dawson, Dall. Texans, 1962; Kansas City, 1966, 1968
Bart Starr, Green Bay, 1966-68
Kurt Warner, St. Louis, 1999-2001

Most Consecutive Seasons Leading League
5 Sid Luckman, Chi. Bears, 1939-1943
4 Steve Young, San Francisco, 1991-94
3 Bart Starr, Green Bay, 1966-68
Kurt Warner, St. Louis, 1999-2001

Highest Average Gain, Career (1,500 Attempts)
8.63 Otto Graham, Cleveland, 1950-55 (1,565-13,499)
8.42 Sid Luckman, Chi. Bears, 1939-1950 (1,744-14,686)
8.16 Norm Van Brocklin, Los Angeles, 1949-1957; Philadelphia, 1958-1960 (2,895-23,611)

Highest Average Gain, Season (Qualifiers)
11.17 Tommy O'Connell, Cleveland, 1957 (110-1,229)
10.86 Sid Luckman, Chi. Bears, 1943 (202-2,194)
10.55 Otto Graham, Cleveland, 1953 (258-2,722)

Highest Average Gain, Rookie, Season (Qualifiers)
9.411 Greg Cook, Cincinnati, 1969 (197-1,854)
9.409 Bob Waterfield, Cleveland, 1945 (171-1,609)
8.88 Ben Roethlisberger, Pittsburgh, 2004 (295-2,621)

Highest Average Gain, Game (20 attempts)
18.58 Sammy Baugh, Washington vs. Boston, Oct. 31, 1948 (24-446)
18.50 Johnny Unitas, Baltimore vs. Atlanta, Nov. 12, 1967 (20-370)
17.71 Joe Namath, N.Y. Jets vs. Baltimore, Sept. 24, 1972 (28-496)

TOUCHDOWNS

Most Seasons Leading League
4 Johnny Unitas, Baltimore, 1957-1960
Len Dawson, Dall. Texans, 1962; Kansas City, 1963, 1965-66
Steve Young, San Francisco, 1992-94, 1998
Brett Favre, Green Bay, 1995-97, 2003
3 Arnie Herber, Green Bay, 1932, 1934, 1936
Sid Luckman, Chi. Bears, 1943, 1945-46
Y.A. Tittle, San Francisco, 1955; N.Y. Giants, 1962-63
Dan Marino, Miami, 1984-86
Peyton Manning, Indianapolis, 2000, 2004, 2006
2 By many players

Most Consecutive Seasons Leading League
4 Johnny Unitas, Baltimore, 1957-1960
3 Dan Marino, Miami, 1984-86
Steve Young, San Francisco, 1992-94
Brett Favre, Green Bay, 1995-97
2 By many players

Most Touchdown Passes, Career
497 Brett Favre, Atlanta, 1991; Green Bay, 1992-2007; N.Y. Jets, 2008, Minnesota, 2009
420 Dan Marino, Miami, 1983-1999
366 Peyton Manning, Indianapolis, 1998-2009

Most Touchdown Passes, Season
50 Tom Brady, New England, 2007
49 Peyton Manning, Indianapolis, 2004
48 Dan Marino, Miami, 1984

Most Touchdown Passes, Rookie, Season
26 Peyton Manning, Indianapolis, 1998
22 Charlie Conerly, N.Y. Giants, 1948
20 Dan Marino, Miami, 1983

Most Touchdown Passes, Game
7 Sid Luckman, Chi. Bears vs. N.Y. Giants, Nov. 14, 1943
Adrian Burk, Philadelphia vs. Washington, Oct. 17, 1954
George Blanda, Houston vs. N.Y. Titans, Nov. 19, 1961
Y.A. Tittle, N.Y. Giants vs. Washington, Oct. 28, 1962
Joe Kapp, Minnesota vs. Baltimore, Sept. 28, 1969
6 By many players. Last time:
Tom Brady, New England vs. Tennessee, Oct. 18, 2009

Most Games, Four or More Touchdown Passes, Career
23 Brett Favre, Atlanta, 1991; Green Bay, 1992-2007; N.Y. Jets, 2008; Minnesota, 2009
21 Dan Marino, Miami, 1983-1999
Peyton Manning, Indianapolis, 1998-2009
17 Johnny Unitas, Baltimore, 1956-1972; San Diego, 1973

Most Games, Four or More Touchdown Passes, Season
6 Dan Marino, Miami, 1984
Peyton Manning, Indianapolis, 2004
5 Dan Marino, Miami, 1986
Brett Favre, Green Bay, 1996
Donovan McNabb, Philadelphia, 2004
Tom Brady, New England, 2007
4 George Blanda, Houston, 1961
Vince Ferragamo, Los Angeles, 1980
Steve Young, San Francisco, 1994
Randall Cunningham, Minnesota, 1998
Daunte Culpepper, Minnesota, 2004
Tony Romo, Dallas, 2007
Peyton Manning, Indianapolis, 2009

Most Consecutive Games, Four or More Touchdown Passes
5 Peyton Manning, Indianapolis, 2004
4 Dan Marino, Miami, 1984
2 By many players

Most Consecutive Games, Touchdown Passes
47 Johnny Unitas, Baltimore, 1956-1960
36 Brett Favre, Green Bay, 2002-2004
30 Dan Marino, Miami, 1985-87

HAD INTERCEPTED

Most Consecutive Passes Attempted, None Intercepted
308 Bernie Kosar, Cleveland, 1990-91
294 Bart Starr, Green Bay, 1964-65
279 Jeff George, Indianapolis-Atlanta, 1993-94

Most Passes Had Intercepted, Career
317 Brett Favre, Atlanta, 1991; Green Bay, 1992-2007; N.Y. Jets, 2008; Minnesota, 2009

277 George Blanda, Chi. Bears, 1949, 1950-58; Baltimore, 1950; Houston, 1960-66; Oakland, 1967-1975
268 John Hadl, San Diego, 1962-1972; Los Angeles, 1973-74; Green Bay, 1974-75; Houston, 1976-77

Most Passes Had Intercepted, Season
42 George Blanda, Houston, 1962
35 Vinny Testaverde, Tampa Bay, 1988
34 Frank Tripucka, Denver, 1960

Most Passes Had Intercepted, Game
8 Jim Hardy, Chi. Cardinals vs. Philadelphia, Sept. 24, 1950
7 Parker Hall, Cleveland vs. Green Bay, Nov. 8, 1942
Frank Sinkwich, Detroit vs. Green Bay, Oct. 24, 1943
Bob Waterfield, Los Angeles vs. Green Bay, Oct. 17, 1948
Zeke Bratkowski, Chicago vs. Baltimore, Oct. 2, 1960
Tommy Wade, Pittsburgh vs. Philadelphia, Dec. 12, 1965
Ken Stabler, Oakland vs. Denver, Oct. 16, 1977
Steve DeBerg, Tampa Bay vs. San Francisco, Sept. 7, 1986
Ty Detmer, Detroit vs. Cleveland, Sept. 23, 2001
6 By many players

Most Attempts, No Interceptions, Game
70 Drew Bledsoe, New England vs. Minnesota, Nov. 13, 1994 (ot)
63 Rich Gannon, Minnesota vs. New England, Oct. 20, 1991 (ot)
60 Davey O'Brien, Philadelphia vs. Washington, Dec. 1, 1940

LOWEST PERCENTAGE, PASSES HAD INTERCEPTED

Most Seasons Leading League, Lowest Percentage, Passes Had Intercepted
5 Sammy Baugh, Washington, 1940, 1942, 1944-45, 1947
3 Charlie Conerly, N.Y. Giants, 1950, 1956, 1959
Bart Starr, Green Bay, 1962, 1964, 1966
Roger Staubach, Dallas, 1971, 1977, 1979
Ken Anderson, Cincinnati, 1972, 1981-82
Ken O'Brien, N.Y. Jets, 1985, 1987-88
2 By many players

Lowest Pct., Passes Had Intercepted, Career (1,500 attempts)
2.04 David Garrard, Jacksonville, 2002-09 (1,915-39)
2.106 Neil O'Donnell, Pittsburgh, 1991-95; N.Y. Jets, 1996-97; Cincinnati, 1998; Tennessee, 1999-2003 (3,229-68)
2.107 Donovan McNabb, Philadelphia, 1999-2009 (4,746-100)

Lowest Pct., Passes Had Intercepted, Season (Qualifiers)
0.41 Damon Huard, Kansas City, 2006 (244-1)
0.66 Joe Ferguson, Buffalo, 1976 (151-1)
0.90 Steve DeBerg, Kansas City, 1990 (444-4)

Lowest Pct., Passes Had Intercepted, Rookie, Season (Qualifiers)
1.98 Charlie Batch, Detroit, 1998 (303-6)
2.03 Dan Marino, Miami, 1983 (296-6)
2.10 Gary Wood, N.Y. Giants, 1964 (143-3)

TIMES SACKED

Times Sacked has been compiled since 1963.

Most Times Sacked, Career
516 John Elway, Denver, 1983-1998
503 Brett Favre, Atlanta, 1991; Green Bay, 1992-2007; N.Y. Jets, 2008; Minnesota, 2009
494 Dave Krieg, Seattle, 1980-1991; Kansas City, 1992-93; Detroit, 1994; Arizona, 1995; Chicago, 1996; Tennessee, 1997-98

Most Times Sacked, Season
76 David Carr, Houston, 2002
72 Randall Cunningham, Philadelphia, 1986
68 David Carr, Houston, 2005

Most Times Sacked, Game
12 Bert Jones, Baltimore vs. St. Louis, Oct. 26, 1980
Warren Moon, Houston vs. Dallas, Sept. 29, 1985
Donovan McNabb, Philadelphia vs. N.Y. Giants, Sept. 30, 2007
11 Charley Johnson, St. Louis vs. N.Y. Giants, Nov. 1, 1964
Bart Starr, Green Bay vs. Detroit, Nov. 7, 1965
Jack Kemp, Buffalo vs. Oakland, Oct. 15, 1967
Bob Berry, Atlanta vs. St. Louis, Nov. 24, 1968
Greg Landry, Detroit vs. Dallas, Oct. 6, 1975
Ron Jaworski, Philadelphia vs. St. Louis, Dec. 18, 1983
Paul McDonald, Cleveland vs. Kansas City, Sept. 30, 1984
Archie Manning, Minnesota vs. Chicago, Oct. 28, 1984
Steve Pelluer, Dallas vs. San Diego, Nov. 16, 1986
Randall Cunningham, Philadelphia vs. L.A. Raiders, Nov. 30, 1986 (ot)
David Norrie, N.Y. Jets vs. Dallas, Oct. 4, 1987
Troy Aikman, Dallas vs. Philadelphia, Sept. 15, 1991
Bernie Kosar, Cleveland vs. Indianapolis, Sept. 6, 1992
10 By many players

RECEIVING

Most Seasons Leading League
8 Don Hutson, Green Bay, 1936-37, 1939, 1941-45
5 Lionel Taylor, Denver, 1960-63, 1965
3 Tom Fears, Los Angeles, 1948-1950
Pete Pihos, Philadelphia, 1953-55
Billy Wilson, San Francisco, 1954, 1956-57
Raymond Berry, Baltimore, 1958-1960
Lance Alworth, San Diego, 1966, 1968-69
Sterling Sharpe, Green Bay, 1989, 1992-93

Most Consecutive Seasons Leading League
5 Don Hutson, Green Bay, 1941-45
4 Lionel Taylor, Denver, 1960-63
3 Tom Fears, Los Angeles, 1948-1950
Pete Pihos, Philadelphia, 1953-55
Raymond Berry, Baltimore, 1958-1960

Most Pass Receptions, Career
1,549 Jerry Rice, San Francisco, 1985-2000; Oakland, 2001-04; Seattle, 2004
1,102 Marvin Harrison, Indianapolis, 1996-2008
1,101 Cris Carter, Philadelphia, 1987-89; Minnesota, 1990-2001; Miami, 2002

Most Seasons, 50 or More Pass Receptions
17 Jerry Rice, San Francisco, 1986-1996, 1998-2000; Oakland, 2001-03
13 Andre Reed, Buffalo, 1986-1994, 1996-99
12 Isaac Bruce, St. Louis, 1995-97, 1999-2004, 2006-07; San Francisco, 2008
Marvin Harrison, Indianapolis, 1996-2006, 2008
Tony Gonzalez, Kansas City, 1998-2008; Atlanta, 2009
Terrell Owens, San Francisco, 1997-2003; Philadelphia, 2004; Dallas, 2006-08; Buffalo, 2009

Most Pass Receptions, Season
143 Marvin Harrison, Indianapolis, 2002
123 Herman Moore, Detroit, 1995
Wes Welker, New England, 2009
122 Cris Carter, Minnesota, 1994
Jerry Rice, San Francisco, 1995

Cris Carter, Minnesota, 1995

Most Pass Receptions, Rookie, Season

101 Anquan Boldin, Arizona, 2003
91 Eddie Royal, Denver, 2008
90 Terry Glenn, New England, 1996

Most Pass Receptions, Game

21 Brandon Marshall, Denver vs. Indianapolis, Dec. 13, 2009
20 Terrell Owens, San Francisco vs. Chicago, Dec. 17, 2000
18 Tom Fears, Los Angeles vs. Green Bay, Dec. 3, 1950
Brandon Marshall, Denver vs. San Diego, Sept. 14, 2008

Most Consecutive Games, Pass Receptions

274 Jerry Rice, San Francisco, 1985-2000; Oakland, 2001-04
190 Marvin Harrison, Indianapolis, 1996-2008
185 Terrell Owens, San Francisco, 1996-2003; Philadelphia, 2004-05; Dallas, 2006-08; Buffalo, 2009

YARDS GAINED

Most Seasons Leading League

7 Don Hutson, Green Bay, 1936, 1938-39, 1941-44
6 Jerry Rice, San Francisco, 1986, 1989-1990, 1993-95
3 Raymond Berry, Baltimore, 1957, 1959-1960
Lance Alworth, San Diego, 1965-66, 1968

Most Consecutive Seasons Leading League

4 Don Hutson, Green Bay, 1941-44
3 Jerry Rice, San Francisco, 1993-95
2 By many players

Most Yards Gained, Career

22,895 Jerry Rice, San Francisco, 1985-2000; Oakland, 2001-04; Seattle, 2004
15,208 Isaac Bruce, L.A. Rams, 1994; St. Louis, 1995-2007; San Francisco, 2008-09
14,951 Terrell Owens, San Francisco, 1996-2003; Philadelphia, 2004-05; Dallas, 2006-08; Buffalo, 2009

Most Seasons, 1,000 or More Yards, Pass Receiving

14 Jerry Rice, San Francisco, 1986-1996, 1998; Oakland, 2001-02
10 Randy Moss, Minnesota, 1998-2003; Oakland, 2005; New England, 2007-09
9 Tim Brown, L.A. Raiders, 1993-94; Oakland, 1995-2001
Jimmy Smith, Jacksonville, 1996-2002, 2004-05
Terrell Owens, San Francisco, 1998, 2000-03; Philadelphia, 2004; Dallas, 2006-08

Most Yards Gained, Season

1,848 Jerry Rice, San Francisco, 1995
1,781 Isaac Bruce, St. Louis, 1995
1,746 Charley Hennigan, Houston, 1961

Most Yards Gained, Rookie, Season

1,473 Bill Groman, Houston, 1960
1,377 Anquan Boldin, Arizona, 2003
1,313 Randy Moss, Minnesota, 1998

Most Yards Gained, Game

336 Flipper Anderson, L.A. Rams vs. New Orleans, Nov. 26, 1989
309 Stephone Paige, Kansas City vs. San Diego, Dec. 22, 1985
303 Jim Benton, Cleveland vs. Detroit, Nov. 22, 1945

Most Games, 200 or More Yards Pass Receiving, Career

5 Lance Alworth, San Diego, 1962-1970; Dallas, 1971-72
4 Don Hutson, Green Bay, 1935-45
Charley Hennigan, Houston, 1960-66
Jerry Rice, San Francisco, 1985-2000; Oakland, 2001-04; Seattle, 2004
3 Don Maynard, N.Y. Giants, 1958; N.Y. Jets, 1960-1972; St. Louis, 1973
Wes Chandler, New Orleans, 1978-1981; San Diego, 1981-87; San Francisco, 1988
Isaac Bruce, L.A. Rams, 1994; St. Louis, 1995-2007; San Francisco, 2008

Most Games, 200 or More Yards Pass Receiving, Season

3 Charley Hennigan, Houston, 1961
2 Don Hutson, Green Bay, 1942
Gene Roberts, N.Y. Giants, 1949
Lance Alworth, San Diego, 1963
Don Maynard, N.Y. Jets, 1968

Most Games, 100 or More Yards Pass Receiving, Career

76 Jerry Rice, San Francisco, 1985-2000; Oakland, 2001-04; Seattle, 2004
64 Randy Moss, Minnesota, 1998-2004; Oakland, 2005-06; New England, 2007-09
59 Marvin Harrison, Indianapolis, 1996-2008

Most Games, 100 or More Yards Pass Receiving, Season

11 Michael Irvin, Dallas, 1995
10 Charley Hennigan, Houston, 1961
Herman Moore, Detroit, 1995
Marvin Harrison, Indianapolis, 2002
Torry Holt, St. Louis, 2003
9 Elroy (Crazylegs) Hirsch, Los Angeles, 1951
Bill Groman, Houston, 1960
Lance Alworth, San Diego, 1965
Don Maynard, N.Y. Jets, 1967
Stanley Morgan, New England, 1986
Mark Carrier, Tampa Bay, 1989
Robert Brooks, Green Bay, 1995
Isaac Bruce, St. Louis, 1995
Jerry Rice, San Francisco, 1995
Marvin Harrison, Indianapolis, 1999
Jimmy Smith, Jacksonville, 1999
David Boston, Arizona, 2001
Steve Smith, Carolina, 2005
Randy Moss, New England, 2007

Most Consecutive Games, 100 or More Yards Pass Receiving

7 Charley Hennigan, Houston, 1961
Michael Irvin, Dallas, 1995
6 Raymond Berry, Baltimore, 1960
Bill Groman, Houston, 1961
Pat Studstill, Detroit, 1966
Isaac Bruce, St. Louis, 1995
5 Elroy (Crazylegs) Hirsch, Los Angeles, 1951
Bob Boyd, Los Angeles, 1954
Terry Barr, Detroit, 1963
Lance Alworth, San Diego, 1966
Don Maynard, N.Y. Jets, 1968-69
Harold Jackson, Philadelphia, 1971-72
Patrick Jeffers, Carolina, 1999
Terrell Owens, Philadelphia, 2004
Anquan Boldin, Arizona, 2005

Longest Pass Reception (All TDs except as noted)

99 Andy Farkas (from Filchock), Washington vs. Pittsburgh, Oct. 15, 1939
Bobby Mitchell (from Izo), Washington vs. Cleveland, Sept. 15, 1963
Pat Studstill (from Sweetan), Detroit vs. Baltimore, Oct. 16, 1966
Gerry Allen (from Jurgensen), Washington vs. Chicago, Sept. 15, 1968
Cliff Branch (from Plunkett), L.A. Raiders vs. Washington, Oct. 2, 1983
Mike Quick (from Jaworski), Philadelphia vs. Atlanta, Nov. 10, 1985
Tony Martin (from Humphries), San Diego vs. Seattle, Sept. 18, 1994

Robert Brooks (from Favre), Green Bay vs. Chicago, Sept. 11, 1995
Marc Boerigter (from Green), Kansas City vs. San Diego, Dec. 22, 2002
Andre Davis (from Garcia), Cleveland vs. Cincinnati, Oct. 17, 2004
Bernard Berrian (from Frerotte), Minnesota vs. Chicago, Nov. 30, 2008
98 Gaynell Tinsley (from Russell), Chi. Cardinals vs. Cleveland, Nov. 17, 1938
Dick (Night Train) Lane (from Compton), Chi. Cardinals vs. Green Bay, Nov. 13, 1955
John Farrington (from Wade), Chicago vs. Detroit, Oct. 8, 1961
Willard Dewveall (from Lee), Houston vs. San Diego, Nov. 25, 1962
Homer Jones (from Morrall), N.Y. Giants vs. Pittsburgh, Sept. 11, 1966
Bobby Moore (from Hart), St. Louis vs. Los Angeles, Dec. 10, 1972 (no TD)
Michael Haynes (from Hebert), Atlanta vs. New Orleans, Sept. 12, 1993
Johnnie Morton (from Batch), Detroit vs. Chicago, Oct. 4, 1998
Terrell Owens (from Fitzpatrick), Buffalo vs. Jacksonville, Nov. 22, 2009
97 Gaynell Tinsley (from Coffee), Chi. Cardinals vs. Chi. Bears, Dec. 5, 1937
Cloyce Box (from Layne), Detroit vs. Green Bay, Nov. 26, 1953
Jerry Tarr (from Shaw), Denver vs. Boston, Sept. 21, 1962
Webster Slaughter (from Kosar), Cleveland vs. Chicago, Oct. 23, 1989
John Taylor (from Young), San Francisco vs. Atlanta, Nov. 3, 1991

AVERAGE GAIN

Highest Avg. Gain, Career (200 receptions)
22.26 Homer Jones, N.Y. Giants, 1964-69; Cleveland, 1970 (224-4,986)
20.83 Buddy Dial, Pittsburgh, 1959-1963; Dallas, 1964-66 (261-5,436)
20.24 Harlon Hill, Chi. Bears, 1954-1961; Pittsburgh, 1962; Detroit, 1962 (233-4,717)

Highest Avg. Gain, Season (24 receptions)
32.58 Don Currivan, Boston, 1947 (24-782)
31.44 Bucky Pope, Los Angeles, 1964 (25-786)
28.60 Bobby Duckworth, San Diego, 1984 (25-715)

Highest Average Gain, Game (3 receptions)
63.00 Torry Holt, St. Louis vs. Atlanta, Sept. 24, 2000 (3-189)
60.67 Bill Groman, Houston vs. Denver, Nov. 20, 1960 (3-182)
Homer Jones, N.Y. Giants vs. Washington, Dec. 12, 1965 (3-182)
60.33 Don Currivan, Boston vs. Washington, Nov. 30, 1947 (3-181)

TOUCHDOWNS

Most Seasons Leading League
9 Don Hutson, Green Bay, 1935-38, 1940-44
6 Jerry Rice, San Francisco, 1986-87, 1989-1991, 1993
5 Randy Moss, Minnesota, 1998, 2000, 2003; New England, 2007, 2009

Most Consecutive Seasons Leading League
5 Don Hutson, Green Bay, 1940-44
4 Don Hutson, Green Bay, 1935-38
3 Lance Alworth, San Diego, 1964-66
Jerry Rice, San Francisco, 1989-1991

Most Touchdowns, Career
197 Jerry Rice, San Francisco, 1985-2000; Oakland, 2001-04; Seattle, 2004
148 Randy Moss, Minnesota, 1998-2004; Oakland, 2005-06; New England, 2007-09
144 Terrell Owens, San Francisco, 1996-2003; Philadelphia, 2004-05; Dallas, 2006-08; Buffalo, 2009

Most Touchdowns, Season
23 Randy Moss, New England, 2007
22 Jerry Rice, San Francisco, 1987
18 Mark Clayton, Miami, 1984
Sterling Sharpe, Green Bay, 1994

Most Touchdowns, Rookie, Season
17 Randy Moss, Minnesota, 1998
13 Bill Howton, Green Bay, 1952
John Jefferson, San Diego, 1978
12 Harlon Hill, Chi. Bears, 1954
Bill Groman, Houston, 1960
Mike Ditka, Chicago, 1961
Bob Hayes, Dallas, 1965

Most Touchdowns, Game
5 Bob Shaw, Chi. Cardinals vs. Baltimore, Oct. 2, 1950
Kellen Winslow, San Diego vs. Oakland, Nov. 22, 1981
Jerry Rice, San Francisco vs. Atlanta, Oct. 14, 1990
4 By many players. Last time:
Randy Moss, New England vs. Buffalo, Nov. 18, 2007
Terrell Owens, Dallas vs. Washington, Nov. 18, 2007

Most Consecutive Games, Touchdowns
13 Jerry Rice, San Francisco, 1986-87
11 Elroy (Crazylegs) Hirsch, Los Angeles, 1950-51
Buddy Dial, Pittsburgh, 1959-1960
10 Carl Pickens, Cincinnati, 1994-95
Randy Moss, Minnesota, 2003-04

YARDS FROM SCRIMMAGE

Most Scrimmage Yards, Career
23,540 Jerry Rice, San Francisco 1985-2000; Oakland, 2001-04; Seattle, 2004
21,579 Emmitt Smith, Dallas, 1990-2002; Arizona, 2003-04
21,264 Walter Payton, Chicago, 1975-1987

Most Scrimmage Yards, Season
2,509 Chris Johnson, Tennessee, 2009
2,429 Marshall Faulk, St. Louis, 1999
2,390 Tiki Barber, N.Y. Giants, 2005

Most Scrimmage Yards, Rookie, Season
2,212 Eric Dickerson, L.A. Rams, 1983
2,139 Edgerrin James, Indianapolis, 1999
1,924 Billy Sims, Detroit, 1980

Most Scrimmage Yards, Game
336 Flipper Anderson, L.A. Rams vs. New Orleans, Nov. 26, 1989 (ot)
330 Billy Cannon, Houston vs. N.Y. Titans, Dec. 10, 1961
315 Adrian Peterson, Minnesota vs. San Diego, Nov. 4, 2007

INTERCEPTIONS BY

Most Seasons Leading League
3 Everson Walls, Dallas, 1981-82, 1985
2 Dick (Night Train) Lane, Los Angeles, 1952; Chi. Cardinals, 1954
Jack Christiansen, Detroit, 1953, 1957
Milt Davis, Baltimore, 1957, 1959
Dick Lynch, N.Y. Giants, 1961, 1963
Johnny Robinson, Kansas City, 1966, 1970
Bill Bradley, Philadelphia, 1971-72
Emmitt Thomas, Kansas City, 1969, 1974
Ronnie Lott, San Francisco, 1986; L.A. Raiders, 1991
Rod Woodson, Baltimore, 1999; Oakland, 2002

Ty Law, New England, 1998; N.Y. Jets, 2005
Ed Reed, Baltimore, 2004, 2008
Darren Sharper, Green Bay, 2000; New Orleans, 2009
Asante Samuel, New England, 2006; Philadelphia, 2009

Most Interceptions By, Career
81 Paul Krause, Washington, 1964-67; Minnesota, 1968-1979
79 Emlen Tunnell, N.Y. Giants, 1948-1958; Green Bay, 1959-1961
71 Rod Woodson, Pittsburgh, 1987-1996; San Francisco, 1997; Baltimore, 1998-2001; Oakland, 2002-03

Most Interceptions By, Season
14 Dick (Night Train) Lane, Los Angeles, 1952
13 Dan Sandifer, Washington, 1948
Orban (Spec) Sanders, N.Y. Yanks, 1950
Lester Hayes, Oakland, 1980
12 By nine players

Most Interceptions By, Rookie, Season
14 Dick (Night Train) Lane, Los Angeles, 1952
13 Dan Sandifer, Washington, 1948
12 Woodley Lewis, Los Angeles, 1950
Paul Krause, Washington, 1964

Most Interceptions By, Game
4 Sammy Baugh, Washington vs. Detroit, Nov. 14, 1943
Dan Sandifer, Washington vs. Boston, Oct. 31, 1948
Don Doll, Detroit vs. Chi. Cardinals, Oct. 23, 1949
Bob Nussbaumer, Chi. Cardinals vs. N.Y. Bulldogs, Nov. 13, 1949
Russ Craft, Philadelphia vs. Chi. Cardinals, Sept. 24, 1950
Bobby Dillon, Green Bay vs. Detroit, Nov. 26, 1953
Jack Butler, Pittsburgh vs. Washington, Dec. 13, 1953
Austin (Goose) Gonsoulin, Denver vs. Buffalo, Sept. 18, 1960
Jerry Norton, St. Louis vs. Washington, Nov. 20, 1960; vs. Pittsburgh, Nov. 26, 1961
Dave Baker, San Francisco vs. L.A. Rams, Dec. 4, 1960
Bobby Ply, Dall. Texans vs. San Diego, Dec. 16, 1962
Bobby Hunt, Kansas City vs. Houston, Oct. 4, 1964
Willie Brown, Denver vs. N.Y. Jets, Nov. 15, 1964
Dick Anderson, Miami vs. Pittsburgh, Dec. 3, 1973
Willie Buchanon, Green Bay vs. San Diego, Sept. 24, 1978
Deron Cherry, Kansas City vs. Seattle, Sept. 29, 1985
Kwamie Lassiter, Arizona vs. San Diego, Dec. 27, 1998
Deltha O'Neal, Denver vs. Kansas City, Oct. 7, 2001

Most Consecutive Games, Passes Intercepted By
8 Tom Morrow, Oakland, 1962-63
7 Tom Landry, N.Y. Giants, 1950-51
Paul Krause, Washington, 1964
Larry Wilson, St. Louis, 1966
Ben Davis, Cleveland, 1968
6 By many players.
Last time: Brian Russell, Minnesota, 2003

YARDS GAINED

Most Seasons Leading League
3 Darren Sharper, Green Bay, 2002; Minnesota, 2005; New Orleans, 2009
2 Dick (Night Train) Lane, Los Angeles, 1952; Chi. Cardinals, 1954
Herb Adderley, Green Bay, 1965, 1969
Dick Anderson, Miami, 1968, 1970

Most Yards Gained, Career
1,483 Rod Woodson, Pittsburgh, 1987-1996; San Francisco, 1997; Baltimore, 1998-2001; Oakland, 2002-03
1,412 Darren Sharper, Green Bay, 1997-2004; Minnesota, 2005-08; New Orleans, 2009
1,331 Deion Sanders, Atlanta, 1989-1993; San Francisco, 1994; Dallas, 1995-99; Washington, 2000; Baltimore, 2004-05

Most Yards Gained, Season
376 Darren Sharper, New Orleans, 2009
358 Ed Reed, Baltimore, 2004
349 Charlie McNeil, San Diego, 1961

Most Yards Gained, Rookie, Season
301 Don Doll, Detroit, 1949
298 Dick (Night Train) Lane, Los Angeles, 1952
275 Woodley Lewis, Los Angeles, 1950

Most Yards Gained, Game
177 Charlie McNeil, San Diego vs. Houston, Sept. 24, 1961
170 Louis Oliver, Miami vs. Buffalo, Oct. 4, 1992
167 Dick Jauron, Detroit vs. Chicago, Nov. 18, 1973

Longest Return (All TDs)
107 Ed Reed, Baltimore vs. Philadelphia, Nov. 23, 2008
106 Ed Reed, Baltimore vs. Cleveland, Nov. 7, 2004
103 Vencie Glenn, San Diego vs. Denver, Nov. 29, 1987
Louis Oliver, Miami vs. Buffalo, Oct. 4, 1992

TOUCHDOWNS

Most Touchdowns, Career
12 Rod Woodson, Pittsburgh, 1987-1996; San Francisco, 1997; Baltimore, 1998-2001; Oakland, 2002-03
11 Darren Sharper, Green Bay, 1997-2004; Minnesota, 2005-08; New Orleans, 2009
9 Ken Houston, Houston, 1967-1972; Washington, 1973-1980
Aeneas Williams, Phoenix, 1991-93; Arizona, 1994-2000; St. Louis, 2001-04
Deion Sanders, Atlanta, 1989-1993; San Francisco, 1994; Dallas, 1995-99; Washington, 2000; Baltimore, 2004-05
Charles Woodson, Oakland, 1998-2005; Green Bay, 2006-09

Most Touchdowns, Season
4 Ken Houston, Houston, 1971
Jim Kearney, Kansas City, 1972
Eric Allen, Philadelphia, 1993
3 Dick Harris, San Diego, 1961
Dick Lynch, N.Y. Giants, 1963
Herb Adderley, Green Bay, 1965
Lem Barney, Detroit, 1967
Miller Farr, Houston, 1967
Monte Jackson, Los Angeles, 1976
Rod Perry, Los Angeles, 1978
Ronnie Lott, San Francisco, 1981
Lloyd Burruss, Kansas City, 1986
Wayne Haddix, Tampa Bay, 1990
Robert Massey, Phoenix, 1992
Ray Buchanan, Indianapolis, 1994
Deion Sanders, San Francisco, 1994
Mark McMillian, Kansas City, 1997
Otis Smith, N.Y. Jets, 1997
Jimmy Hitchcock, Minnesota, 1998
Eric Allen, Oakland, 2000
Derrick Brooks, Tampa Bay, 2002
Antrel Rolle, Arizona, 2007
Nick Collins, Green Bay, 2008
Darren Sharper, New Orleans, 2009
Charles Woodson, Green Bay, 2009
2 By many players

Most Touchdowns, Rookie, Season
3 Lem Barney, Detroit, 1967
Ronnie Lott, San Francisco, 1981
2 By many players

Most Touchdowns, Game

2 Bill Blackburn, Chi. Cardinals vs. Boston, Oct. 24, 1948
Dan Sandifer, Washington vs. Boston, Oct. 31, 1948
Bob Franklin, Cleveland vs. Chicago, Dec. 11, 1960
Bill Stacy, St. Louis vs. Dall. Cowboys, Nov. 5, 1961
Jerry Norton, St. Louis vs. Pittsburgh, Nov. 26, 1961
Miller Farr, Houston vs. Buffalo, Dec. 7, 1968
Ken Houston, Houston vs. San Diego, Dec. 19, 1971
Jim Kearney, Kansas City vs. Denver, Oct. 1, 1972
Lemar Parrish, Cincinnati vs. Houston, Dec. 17, 1972
Dick Anderson, Miami vs. Pittsburgh, Dec. 3, 1973
Prentice McCray, New England vs. N.Y. Jets, Nov. 21, 1976
Kenny Johnson, Atlanta vs. Green Bay, Nov. 27, 1983 (ot)
Mike Kozlowski, Miami vs. N.Y. Jets, Dec. 16, 1983
Dave Brown, Seattle vs. Kansas City, Nov. 4, 1984
Lloyd Burruss, Kansas City vs. San Diego, Oct. 19, 1986
Henry Jones, Buffalo vs. Indianapolis, Sept. 20, 1992
Robert Massey, Phoenix vs. Washington, Oct. 4, 1992
Eric Allen, Philadelphia vs. New Orleans, Dec. 26, 1993
Ken Norton, San Francisco vs. St. Louis, Oct. 22, 1995
Otis Smith, N.Y. Jets vs. Tampa Bay, Dec. 14, 1997
Dewayne Washington, Pittsburgh vs. Jacksonville, Nov. 22, 1998
Aaron Glenn, Houston vs. Pittsburgh, Dec. 8, 2002
Ronde Barber, Tampa Bay vs. Philadelphia, Oct. 22, 2006
Antrel Rolle, Arizona vs. Cincinnati, Nov. 18, 2007
Derrick Johnson, Kansas City vs. Denver, Jan. 3, 2010

PUNTING

Most Punts, Career

1,713 Jeff Feagles, New England, 1988-89; Philadelphia, 1990-93; Arizona, 1994-97; Seattle, 1998-2002; N.Y. Giants, 2003-09
1,401 Sean Landeta, N.Y. Giants, 1985-1993; L.A. Rams, 1993-94; St. Louis, 1995-96; Tampa Bay, 1997; Green Bay, 1998; Philadelphia, 1999-2002; St. Louis, 2003-04; Philadelphia, 2005
1,226 Lee Johnson, Houston, 1985-87; Cleveland, 1987-88; Cincinnati, 1988-1998; New England, 1999-2001; Minnesota, 2001; Philadelphia, 2002

Most Punts, Season

114 Bob Parsons, Chicago, 1981
Chad Stanley, Houston, 2002
111 Brad Maynard, N.Y. Giants, 1997
109 John James, Atlanta, 1978

Most Punts, Rookie, Season

111 Brad Maynard, N.Y. Giants, 1997
108 John Teltschik, Philadelphia, 1986
101 Daniel Pope, Kansas City, 1999

Most Punts, Game

16 Leo Araguz, Oakland vs. San Diego, Oct. 11, 1998
15 John Teltschik, Philadelphia vs. N.Y. Giants, Dec. 6, 1987 (ot)
14 Dick Nesbitt, Chi. Cardinals vs. Chi. Bears, Nov. 30, 1933
Keith Molesworth, Chi. Bears vs. Green Bay, Dec. 10, 1933
Sammy Baugh, Washington vs. Philadelphia, Nov. 5, 1939
Carl Kinscherf, N.Y. Giants vs. Detroit, Nov. 7, 1943
George Taliaferro, N.Y. Yanks vs. Los Angeles, Sept. 28, 1951

Longest Punt

98 Steve O'Neal, N.Y. Jets vs. Denver, Sept. 21, 1969
94 Joe Lintzenich, Chi. Bears vs. N.Y. Giants, Nov. 16, 1931
93 Shawn McCarthy, New England vs. Buffalo, Nov. 3, 1991

AVERAGE YARDAGE

Highest Average, Punting, Career (250 punts)

47.31 Shane Lechler, Oakland, 2000-09 (778-36,811)
45.55 Donnie Jones, Seattle, 2004; Miami, 2005-06; St. Louis, 2007-09 (449-20,451)
45.25 Jon Ryan, Green Bay, 2006-07; Seattle, 2008-09 (310-14,028)

Highest Avg. Punting, Season (Qualifiers)

51.40 Sammy Baugh, Washington, 1940 (35-1,799)
51.14 Shane Lechler, Oakland, 2009 (96-4,909)
50.00 Donnie Jones, St. Louis, 2008 (82-4,100)

Highest Avg. Punting, Rookie, Season

46.74 Brett Kern, Denver, 2008 (46-2,150)
45.92 Frank Sinkwich, Detroit, 1943 (12-551)
45.91 Shane Lechler, Oakland, 2000 (65-2,984)

Highest Avg. Punting, Game (4 punts)

61.75 Bob Cifers, Detroit vs. Chi. Bears, Nov. 24, 1946 (4-247)
61.60 Roy McKay, Green Bay vs. Chi. Cardinals, Oct. 28, 1945 (5-308)
59.50 Darren Bennett, San Diego vs. Pittsburgh, Oct. 1, 1995 (4-238)

NET AVERAGE

Net average has been compiled since 1976.

Highest Net Average, Punting, Career (250 punts)

39.00 Donnie Jones, Seattle, 2004; Miami, 2005-06; St. Louis, 2007-09 (451-17,591)
38.97 Mike Scifres, San Diego, 2003-09 (394-15,354)
38.92 Dustin Colquitt, Kansas City, 2005-09 (399-15,528)

Highest Net Average, Punting, Season (Qualifiers)

43.85 Shane Lechler, Oakland, 2009 (96-4,210)
41.69 Donnie Jones, St. Louis, 2009 (90-3,752)
41.18 Shane Lechler, Oakland, 2008 (90-3,706)

Highest Net Average, Punting, Rookie, Season (Qualifiers)

38.00 Dale Hatcher, L.A. Rams, 1985 (88-3,344)
37.955 Shane Lechler, Oakland, 2000 (66-2,505)
37.946 Ben Graham, N.Y. Jets, 2005 (74-2,808)

Highest Net Average, Punting, Game (4 punts)

59.50 Rohn Stark, Indianapolis vs. Houston, Sept. 13, 1992 (4-238)
53.00 Brian Moorman, Buffalo vs. Kansas City, Dec. 13, 2009 (4-212)
52.80 Mike Horan, Denver vs. L.A. Raiders, Sept. 26, 1988 (ot) (5-264)
David Zastudil, Cleveland vs. Pittsburgh, Sept. 14, 2008 (5-264)

PUNTS HAD BLOCKED

Most Consecutive Punts, None Blocked

1,177 Chris Gardocki, Chicago, 1992-94; Indianapolis, 1995-98; Cleveland, 1999-2003; Pittsburgh, 2004-06
878 Bryan Barker, Kansas City, 1993; Philadelphia, 1994; Jacksonville, 1995-2000; Washington, 2001-03; Green Bay, 2004; St. Louis, 2005
638 Tom Tupa, New England, 1997-98; N.Y. Jets, 1999-2001; Tampa Bay, 2002-03; Washington, 2004

Most Punts Had Blocked, Career

14 Herman Weaver, Detroit, 1970-76; Seattle, 1977-1980
Harry Newsome, Pittsburgh, 1985-89; Minnesota, 1990-93
12 Jerrel Wilson, Kansas City, 1963-1977; New England, 1978

Tom Blanchard, N.Y. Giants, 1971-73; New Orleans, 1974-78; Tampa Bay, 1979-1981
Jeff Feagles, New England, 1988-89; Philadelphia, 1990-93; Arizona, 1994-97; Seattle, 1998-2002; N.Y. Giants, 2003-09
11 David Lee, Baltimore, 1966-1978

Most Punts Had Blocked, Season
6 Harry Newsome, Pittsburgh, 1988
4 Bryan Wagner, Cleveland, 1990
3 By many players

PUNTS INSIDE THE 20

Punts Inside the 20 have been compiled since 1976.

Most Punts Inside the 20, Career
554 Jeff Feagles, New England, 1988-89; Philadelphia, 1990-93; Arizona, 1994-97; Seattle, 1998-2002; N.Y. Giants, 2003-09
399 Craig Hentrich, Green Bay, 1994-97; Tennessee, 1998-2009
383 Brad Maynard, N.Y. Giants, 1997-2000; Chicago, 2001-09

Most Punts Inside the 20, Season
42 Andy Lee, San Francisco, 2007
Ben Graham, Arizona, 2009
41 Dustin Colquitt, Kansas City, 2009
40 Brad Maynard, Chicago, 2008

Most Punts Inside the 20, Game
8 Mark Royals, Pittsburgh vs. Houston, Nov. 6, 1994 (ot)
Bryan Barker, Jacksonville vs. Baltimore, Nov. 14, 1999
7 Josh Miller, Pittsburgh vs. Cincinnati, Dec. 20, 1998
David Zastudil. Cleveland vs. Buffalo, Oct. 11, 2009
Thomas Morstead, New Orleans vs. Carolina, Jan. 3, 2010
6 By many players

PUNT RETURNS

Most Seasons Leading League
3 Les (Speedy) Duncan, San Diego, 1965-66; Washington, 1971
Rick Upchurch, Denver, 1976, 1978, 1982
2 Dick Christy, N.Y. Titans, 1961-62
Claude Gibson, Oakland, 1963-64
Billy (White Shoes) Johnson, Houston, 1975, 1977
Mel Gray, New Orleans, 1987; Detroit, 1991
Jermaine Lewis, Baltimore, 1997, 2000
Roscoe Parrish, Buffalo, 2007-08

PUNT RETURNS

Most Punt Returns, Career
463 Brian Mitchell, Washington, 1990-99; Philadelphia, 2000-02; N.Y. Giants, 2003
351 Eric Metcalf, Cleveland, 1989-1994; Atlanta, 1995-96; San Diego, 1997; Arizona, 1998; Carolina, 1999; Washington, 2001; Green Bay, 2002
349 David Meggett, N.Y. Giants, 1989-1994; New England, 1995-97; N.Y. Jets, 1998

Most Punt Returns, Season
70 Danny Reece, Tampa Bay, 1979
62 Fulton Walker, Miami-L.A. Raiders, 1985
58 J.T. Smith, Kansas City, 1979
Greg Pruitt, L.A. Raiders, 1983
Leo Lewis, Minnesota, 1988
Desmond Howard, Green Bay, 1996
Nate Burleson, Seattle, 2007

Most Punt Returns, Rookie, Season
57 Lew Barnes, Chicago, 1986
55 B.J. Sams, Baltimore, 2004
54 James Jones, Dallas, 1980

Most Punt Returns, Game
11 Eddie Brown, Washington vs. Tampa Bay, Oct. 9, 1977
10 Theo Bell, Pittsburgh vs. Buffalo, Dec. 16, 1979
Mike Nelms, Washington vs. New Orleans, Dec. 26, 1982
Ronnie Harris, New England vs. Pittsburgh, Dec. 5, 1993
9 Rodger Bird, Oakland vs. Denver, Sept. 10, 1967
Ralph McGill, San Francisco vs. Atlanta, Oct. 29, 1972
Ed Podolak, Kansas City vs. San Diego, Nov. 10, 1974
Anthony Leonard, San Francisco vs. New Orleans, Oct. 17, 1976
Butch Johnson, Dallas vs. Buffalo, Nov. 15, 1976
Larry Marshall, Philadelphia vs. Tampa Bay, Sept. 18, 1977
Nesby Glasgow, Baltimore vs. Kansas City, Sept. 2, 1979
Mike Nelms, Washington vs. St. Louis, Dec. 21, 1980
Leon Bright, N.Y. Giants vs. Philadelphia, Dec. 11, 1982
Pete Shaw, N.Y. Giants vs. Philadelphia, Nov. 20, 1983
Cleotha Montgomery, L.A. Raiders vs. Detroit, Dec. 10, 1984
Phil McConkey, N.Y. Giants vs. Philadelphia, Dec. 6, 1987 (ot)
Andre Hastings, Pittsburgh vs. Cleveland, Nov. 13, 1995
Steve Smith, Carolina vs. Detroit, Sept. 15, 2002
Reggie Swinton, Arizona vs. Philadelphia, Dec. 24, 2005

FAIR CATCHES

Most Fair Catches, Career
231 Brian Mitchell, Washington, 1990-99; Philadelphia, 2000-02; N.Y. Giants, 2003
162 Tim Brown, L.A. Raiders, 1988-1994; Oakland, 1995-2003; Tampa Bay, 2004
144 Glyn Milburn, Denver, 1993-95; Detroit, 1996-97; Chicago, 1998-2001; San Diego, 2001

Most Fair Catches, Season
33 Brian Mitchell, Philadelphia, 2000
29 Wes Welker, Miami, 2006
27 Leo Lewis, Minnesota, 1989
Antonio Chatman, Green Bay, 2004

Most Fair Catches, Game
7 Bake Turner, N.Y. Jets vs. Miami, Nov. 20, 1966
Lem Barney, Detroit vs. Chicago, Nov. 21, 1976
Bobby Morse, Philadelphia vs. Buffalo, Dec. 27, 1987
Chris Carr, Tennessee vs. Jacksonville, Nov. 16, 2008
6 Jake Scott, Miami vs. Buffalo, Dec. 20, 1970
Greg Pruitt, L.A. Raiders vs. Seattle, Oct. 7, 1984
Phil McConkey, San Diego vs. Kansas City, Dec. 17, 1989
Gerald McNeil, Houston vs. Pittsburgh, Sept. 16, 1990
Bobby Engram, Chicago vs. Minnesota, Sept. 15, 1996
Eddie Kennison, New Orleans vs. Baltimore, Dec. 19, 1999
R.W. McQuarters, N.Y. Giants vs. Atlanta, Oct. 15, 2007
5 By many players

YARDS GAINED

Most Seasons Leading League

3 Alvin Haymond, Baltimore, 1965-66; Los Angeles, 1969
2 Bill Dudley, Pittsburgh, 1942, 1946
Emlen Tunnell, N.Y. Giants, 1951-52
Dick Christy, N.Y. Titans, 1961-62
Claude Gibson, Oakland, 1963-64
Rodger Bird, Oakland, 1966-67
J.T. Smith, Kansas City, 1979-1980
Vai Sikahema, St. Louis, 1986-87
David Meggett, N.Y. Giants, 1989-1990
Tamarick Vanover, Kansas City, 1995, 1999

Most Yards Gained, Career

4,999 Brian Mitchell, Washington, 1990-99; Philadelphia, 2000-02; N.Y. Giants, 2003
3,708 Dave Meggett, N.Y. Giants, 1989-1994; New England, 1995-97; N.Y. Jets, 1998
3,601 Darrien Gordon, San Diego, 1993-94, 1996; Denver, 1997-98; Oakland, 1999-2000; Atlanta, 2001; Green Bay, 2002

Most Yards Gained, Season

875 Desmond Howard, Green Bay, 1996
692 Fulton Walker, Miami-L.A. Raiders, 1985
666 Greg Pruitt, L.A. Raiders, 1983

Most Yards Gained, Rookie, Season

656 Louis Lipps, Pittsburgh, 1984
655 Neal Colzie, Oakland, 1975
619 Leon Johnson, N.Y. Jets, 1997

Most Yards Gained, Game

207 LeRoy Irvin, Los Angeles vs. Atlanta, Oct. 11, 1981
205 George Atkinson, Oakland vs. Buffalo, Sept. 15, 1968
199 Eddie Drummond, Detroit vs. Jacksonville, Nov. 14, 2004 (ot)

Longest Punt Return (All TDs)

103 Robert Bailey, L.A. Rams vs. New Orleans, Oct. 23, 1994
98 Gil LeFebvre, Cincinnati vs. Brooklyn, Dec. 3, 1933
Charlie West, Minnesota vs. Washington, Nov. 3, 1968
Dennis Morgan, Dallas vs. St. Louis, Oct. 13, 1974
Terance Mathis, N.Y. Jets vs. Dallas, Nov. 4, 1990
97 Greg Pruitt, L.A. Raiders vs. Washington, Oct. 2, 1983

AVERAGE YARDAGE

Highest Average, Career (75 returns)

12.78 George McAfee, Chi. Bears, 1940-41, 1945-1950 (112-1,431)
12.75 Jack Christiansen, Detroit, 1951-58 (85-1,084)
12.55 Claude Gibson, San Diego, 1961-62; Oakland, 1963-65 (110-1,381)

Highest Average, Season (Qualifiers)

23.00 Herb Rich, Baltimore, 1950 (12-276)
21.47 Jack Christiansen, Detroit, 1952 (15-322)
21.28 Dick Christy, N.Y. Titans, 1961 (18-383)

Highest Average, Rookie, Season (Qualifiers)

23.00 Herb Rich, Baltimore, 1950 (12-276)
20.88 Jerry Davis, Chi. Cardinals, 1948 (16-334)
20.73 Frankie Sinkwich, Detroit, 1943 (11-228)

Highest Average, Game

51.00 Steve Smith, Carolina vs. Cincinnati, Dec. 8, 2002 (3-153)
47.67 Chuck Latourette, St. Louis vs. New Orleans, Sept. 29, 1968 (3-143)
47.33 Johnny Roland, St. Louis vs. Philadelphia, Oct. 2, 1966 (3-142)

TOUCHDOWNS

Most Touchdowns, Career

10 Eric Metcalf, Cleveland, 1989-1994; Atlanta, 1995-96; San Diego, 1997; Arizona, 1998; Carolina, 1999; Washington, 2001; Green Bay, 2002
9 Brian Mitchell, Washington, 1990-99; Philadelphia 2000-02; N.Y. Giants, 2003
8 Jack Christiansen, Detroit, 1951-58
Rick Upchurch, Denver, 1975-1983
Desmond Howard, Washington, 1992-94; Jacksonville, 1995; Green Bay, 1996, 1999; Oakland, 1997-98; Detroit, 1999-2002

Most Touchdowns, Season

4 Jack Christiansen, Detroit, 1951
Rick Upchurch, Denver, 1976
Devin Hester, Chicago, 2007
3 Emlen Tunnell, N.Y. Giants, 1951
Billy (White Shoes) Johnson, Houston, 1975
LeRoy Irvin, Los Angeles, 1981
Desmond Howard, Green Bay, 1996
Darrien Gordon, Denver, 1997
Eric Metcalf, San Diego, 1997
Devin Hester, Chicago, 2006
Adam Jones, Tennessee, 2006
Reggie Bush, New Orleans, 2008
Johnnie Lee Higgins, Oakland, 2008
2 By many players

Most Touchdowns, Rookie, Season

4 Jack Christiansen, Detroit, 1951
3 Devin Hester, Chicago, 2006
2 By many players

Most Touchdowns, Game

2 Jack Christiansen, Detroit vs. Los Angeles, Oct. 14, 1951; vs. Green Bay, Nov. 22, 1951
Dick Christy, N.Y. Titans vs. Denver, Sept. 24, 1961
Rick Upchurch, Denver vs. Cleveland, Sept. 26, 1976
LeRoy Irvin, Los Angeles vs. Atlanta, Oct. 11, 1981
Vai Sikahema, St. Louis vs. Tampa Bay, Dec. 21, 1986
Todd Kinchen, L.A. Rams vs. Atlanta, Dec. 27, 1992
Eric Metcalf, Cleveland vs. Pittsburgh, Oct. 24, 1993; San Diego vs. Cincinnati, Nov. 2, 1997
Darrien Gordon, Denver vs. Carolina, Nov. 9, 1997
Jermaine Lewis, Baltimore vs. Seattle, Dec. 7, 1997; Baltimore vs. N.Y. Jets, Dec. 24, 2000
Steve Smith, Carolina vs. Cincinnati, Dec. 8, 2002
Eddie Drummond, Detroit vs. Jacksonville, Nov. 14, 2004 (ot)
Reggie Bush, New Orleans vs. Minnesota, Oct. 6, 2008

KICKOFF RETURNS

Most Seasons Leading League

3 Abe Woodson, San Francisco, 1959, 1962-63
2 Lynn Chandnois, Pittsburgh, 1951-52
Bobby Jancik, Houston, 1962-63
Travis Williams, Green Bay, 1967; Los Angeles, 1971
Mel Gray, Detroit, 1991, 1994
Michael Bates, Carolina, 1996-97

KICKOFF RETURNS

Most Kickoff Returns, Career

607 Brian Mitchell, Washington, 1990-99; Philadelphia, 2000-02; N.Y. Giants, 2003
514 Allen Rossum, Philadelphia, 1998-99; Green Bay, 2000-01; Atlanta, 2002-06; Pittsburgh, 2007; San Francisco, 2008-09; Dallas, 2009
426 Dante Hall, Kansas City, 2000-06; St. Louis, 2007-08

Most Kickoff Returns, Season
82 MarTay Jenkins, Arizona, 2000
73 Josh Scobey, Arizona, 2003
Chris Carr, Oakland, 2005
70 Tyrone Hughes, New Orleans, 1996
Michael Lewis, New Orleans, 2002

Most Kickoff Returns, Rookie, Season
73 Josh Scobey, Arizona, 2003
Chris Carr, Oakland, 2005
67 Ronney Jenkins, San Diego, 2000
64 Tab Perry, Cincinnati, 2005

Most Kickoff Returns, Game
10 Desmond Howard, Oakland vs. Seattle, Oct. 26, 1997
Richard Alston, Cleveland vs. Cincinnati, Nov. 28, 2004
9 Noland Smith, Kansas City vs. Oakland, Nov. 23, 1967
Dino Hall, Cleveland vs. Pittsburgh, Oct. 7, 1979
Paul Palmer, Kansas City vs. Seattle, Sept. 20, 1987
Eric Metcalf, Atlanta vs. San Francisco, Sept. 29, 1996; vs. St. Louis, Nov. 10, 1996
Michael Bates, Carolina vs. Atlanta, Oct. 4, 1998
Nate Jacquet, Minnesota vs. Philadelphia, Nov. 11, 2001
Ahmad Merritt, Chicago vs. San Francisco, Sept. 7, 2003
Josh Scobey, Arizona vs. Cleveland, Nov. 16, 2003
Maurice Hicks, San Francisco vs. San Diego, Oct. 15, 2006
Aveion Cason, Detroit vs. San Diego, Dec. 16, 2007
Allen Rossum, San Francisco vs. Philadelphia, Oct. 12, 2008
Steve Breaston, Arizona vs. New England, Dec. 21, 2008
Danny Amendola, St. Louis vs. Tennessee, Dec. 13, 2009
8 By many players

YARDS GAINED

Most Seasons Leading League
3 Bruce Harper, N.Y. Jets, 1977-79
Tyrone Hughes, New Orleans, 1994-96
2 Marshall Goldberg, Chi. Cardinals, 1941-42
Woodley Lewis, Los Angeles, 1953-54
Al Carmichael, Green Bay, 1956-57
Timmy Brown, Philadelphia, 1961, 1963
Bobby Jancik, Houston, 1963, 1966
Ron Smith, Atlanta, 1966-67
Chris Carr, Oakland, 2005-06

Most Yards Gained, Career
14,014 Brian Mitchell, Washington, 1990-99; Philadelphia, 2000-02; N.Y. Giants, 2003
11,947 Allen Rossum, Philadelphia, 1998-99; Green Bay, 2000-01; Atlanta, 2002-06; Pittsburgh, 2007; San Francisco, 2008-09; Dallas, 2009
10,250 Mel Gray, New Orleans, 1986-88; Detroit, 1989-1994; Houston, 1995-96; Tennessee, 1997; Philadelphia, 1997

Most Yards Gained, Season
2,186 MarTay Jenkins, Arizona, 2000
1,809 Josh Cribbs, Cleveland, 2007
1,807 Michael Lewis, New Orleans, 2002

Most Yards Gained, Rookie, Season
1,752 Chris Carr, Oakland, 2005
1,684 Josh Scobey, Arizona, 2003
1,577 Justin Miller, N.Y. Jets, 2005

Most Yards Gained, Game
304 Tyrone Hughes, New Orleans vs. L.A. Rams, Oct. 23, 1994
299 Ted Ginn, Jr., Miami vs. N.Y. Jets, Nov. 1, 2009
294 Wally Triplett, Detroit vs. Los Angeles, Oct. 29, 1950

Longest Kickoff Return (All TDs)
108 Ellis Hobbs, New England, vs. N.Y. Jets, Sept. 9, 2007
106 Al Carmichael, Green Bay vs. Chi. Bears, Oct. 7, 1956
Noland Smith, Kansas City vs. Denver, Dec. 17, 1967
Roy Green, St. Louis vs. Dallas, Oct. 21, 1979
Brad Smith, N.Y. Jets vs. Indianapolis, Dec. 27, 2009
105 Frank Seno, Chi. Cardinals vs. N.Y. Giants, Oct. 20, 1946
Ollie Matson, Chi. Cardinals vs. Washington, Oct. 14, 1956
Abe Woodson, San Francisco vs. Los Angeles, Nov. 8, 1959
Timmy Brown, Philadelphia vs. Cleveland, Sept. 17, 1961
Jon Arnett, Los Angeles vs. Detroit, Oct. 29, 1961
Eugene (Mercury) Morris, Miami vs. Cincinnati, Sept. 14, 1969
Travis Williams, Los Angeles vs. New Orleans, Dec. 5, 1971
Terry Fair, Detroit vs. Tampa Bay, Sept. 28, 1998

AVERAGE YARDAGE

Highest Average, Career (75 returns)
30.56 Gale Sayers, Chicago, 1965-1971 (91-2,781)
29.57 Lynn Chandnois, Pittsburgh, 1950-56 (92-2,720)
28.69 Abe Woodson, San Francisco, 1958-1964; St. Louis, 1965-66 (193-5,538)

Highest Average, Season (Qualifiers)
41.06 Travis Williams, Green Bay, 1967 (18-739)
37.69 Gale Sayers, Chicago, 1967 (16-603)
35.50 Ollie Matson, Chi. Cardinals, 1958 (14-497)

Highest Average, Rookie, Season (Qualifiers)
41.06 Travis Williams, Green Bay, 1967 (18-739)
33.08 Tom Moore, Green Bay, 1960 (12-397)
32.88 Duriel Harris, Miami, 1976 (17-559)

Highest Average, Game (3 returns)
73.50 Wally Triplett, Detroit vs. Los Angeles, Oct. 29, 1950 (4-294)
67.33 Lenny Lyles, San Francisco vs. Baltimore, Dec. 18, 1960 (3-202)
65.33 Ken Hall, Houston vs. N.Y. Titans, Oct. 23, 1960 (3-196)

TOUCHDOWNS

Most Touchdowns, Career
8 Josh Cribbs, Cleveland, 2005-09
6 Ollie Matson, Chi. Cardinals, 1952, 1954-58; L.A. Rams, 1959-1962; Detroit, 1963; Philadelphia, 1964
Gale Sayers, Chicago, 1965-1971
Travis Williams, Green Bay, 1967-1970; Los Angeles, 1971
Mel Gray, New Orleans, 1986-88; Detroit, 1989-1994; Houston, 1995-96; Tennessee, 1997; Philadelphia, 1997
Dante Hall, Kansas City, 2000-06; St. Louis, 2007-08
5 Bobby Mitchell, Cleveland, 1958-1961; Washington, 1962-68
Abe Woodson, San Francisco, 1958-1964; St. Louis, 1965-66
Timmy Brown, Green Bay, 1959; Philadelphia, 1960-67; Baltimore, 1968
Terrence McGee, Buffalo, 2003-09
Allen Rossum, Philadelphia, 1998-99; Green Bay, 2000-01; Atlanta, 2002-06; Pittsburgh, 2007; San Francisco, 2008-09; Dallas, 2009
Michael Bates, Seattle, 1993-94; Cleveland, 1995; Carolina, 1996-2000, 2002; Washington, 2001; N.Y. Jets, 2003; Dallas, 2003

Justin Miller, N.Y. Jets, 2005-08; Oakland, 2008-09; N.Y. Jets, 2009

Most Touchdowns, Season

4 Travis Williams, Green Bay, 1967
Cecil Turner, Chicago, 1970
3 Verda (Vitamin T) Smith, Los Angeles, 1950
Abe Woodson, San Francisco, 1963
Gale Sayers, Chicago, 1967
Raymond Clayborn, New England, 1977
Ron Brown, L.A. Rams, 1985
Mel Gray, Detroit, 1994
Darrick Vaughn, Atlanta, 2000
Terrence McGee, Buffalo, 2004
André Davis, Houston, 2007
Leon Washington, N.Y. Jets, 2007
Josh Cribbs, Cleveland, 2009
2 By many players

Most Touchdowns, Rookie, Season

4 Travis Williams, Green Bay, 1967
3 Raymond Clayborn, New England, 1977
Darrick Vaughn, Atlanta, 2000
2 By many players

Most Touchdowns, Game

2 Timmy Brown, Philadelphia vs. Dallas, Nov. 6, 1966
Travis Williams, Green Bay vs. Cleveland, Nov. 12, 1967
Ron Brown, L.A. Rams vs. Green Bay, Nov. 24, 1985
Tyrone Hughes, New Orleans vs. L.A. Rams, Oct. 23, 1994
Chad Morton, N.Y. Jets vs. Buffalo, Sept. 8, 2002 (ot)
Devin Hester, Chicago vs. St. Louis, Dec. 11, 2006
André Davis, Houston vs. Jacksonville, Dec. 30, 2007
Ted Ginn, Jr., Miami vs. N.Y. Jets, Nov. 1, 2009
Josh Cribbs, Cleveland vs. Kansas City, Dec. 20, 2009

COMBINED KICK RETURNS

Most Combined Kick Returns, Career

1,070 Brian Mitchell, Washington, 1990-99; Philadelphia, 2000-02; N.Y. Giants, 2003 (p-463, k-607)
821 Allen Rossum, Philadelphia, 1998-99; Green Bay, 2000-01; Atlanta, 2002-06; Pittsburgh, 2007; San Francisco, 2008-09; Dallas, 2009 (p-307, k-514)
711 Glyn Milburn, Denver, 1993-95; Detroit, 1996-97; Chicago, 1998-2001; San Diego, 2001 (p-304, k-407)

Most Combined Kick Returns, Season

114 Michael Lewis, New Orleans, 2002 (p-44, k-70)
B.J. Sams, Baltimore, 2004 (p-55, k-59)
107 Chris Carr, Oakland, 2005 (p-34, k-73)
Dante Hall, Kansas City, 2005 (p-42, k-65)
105 Reggie Swinton, Arizona, 2005 (p-42, k-63)

Most Combined Kick Returns, Game

13 Stump Mitchell, St. Louis vs. Atlanta, Oct. 18, 1981 (p-6, k-7)
Ronnie Harris, New England vs. Pittsburgh, Dec. 5, 1993 (p-10, k-3)
12 Mel Renfro, Dallas vs. Green Bay, Nov. 29, 1964 (p-4, k-8)
Larry Jones, Washington vs. Dallas, Dec. 13, 1975 (p-6, k-6)
Eddie Brown, Washington vs. Tampa Bay, Oct. 9, 1977 (p-11, k-1)
Nesby Glasgow, Baltimore vs. Denver, Sept. 2, 1979 (p-9, k-3)
Tim Dwight, Atlanta vs. Detroit, Nov. 12, 2000 (p-8, k-4)
Wes Welker, Miami vs. Buffalo, Dec. 5, 2004 (p-6, k-6)
Reggie Swinton, Arizona vs. Philadelphia, Dec. 24, 2005 (p-9, k-3)
Devin Hester, Chicago vs. Detroit, Sept. 30, 2007 (p-5, k-7)
11 By many players

YARDS GAINED

Most Yards Returned, Career

19,013 Brian Mitchell, Washington, 1990-99; Philadelphia, 2000-02; N.Y. Giants, 2003 (p-4,999; k-14,014)
15,003 Allen Rossum, Philadelphia, 1998-99; Green Bay, 2000-01; Atlanta, 2002-06; Pittsburgh, 2007; San Francisco, 2008-09; Dallas, 2009 (p-3,056; k-11,947)
13,003 Mel Gray, New Orleans, 1986-88; Detroit, 1989-1994; Houston, 1995-96; Tennessee, 1997; Philadelphia, 1997 (p-2,753; k-10,250)

Most Yards Returned, Season

2,432 Michael Lewis, New Orleans, 2002 (p-625; k-1,807)
2,214 Josh Cribbs, Cleveland, 2007 (p-405; k-1,809)
2,187 MarTay Jenkins, Arizona, 2000 (pr-1; k-2,186)

Most Yards Returned, Game

347 Tyrone Hughes, New Orleans vs. L.A. Rams, Oct. 23, 1994 (p-43; k-304)
314 Devin Hester, Chicago vs. Detroit, Sept. 30, 2007 (p-95; k-219)
306 Josh Cribbs, Cleveland vs. Baltimore, Nov. 18, 2007 (p-61; k-245) (ot)

TOUCHDOWNS

Most Touchdowns, Career

13 Brian Mitchell, Washington, 1990-99; Philadelphia, 2000-02; N.Y. Giants, 2003 (p-9, k-4)
12 Eric Metcalf, Cleveland, 1989-1994; Atlanta, 1995-96; San Diego, 1997; Arizona, 1998; Carolina, 1999; Washington, 2001; Green Bay, 2002 (p-10, k-2)
Dante Hall, Kansas City, 2000-06; St. Louis, 2007-08 (p-6, k-6)
11 Devin Hester, Chicago, 2006-09 (p-7, k-4)

Most Touchdowns, Season

6 Devin Hester, Chicago, 2007 (p-4, k-2)
5 Devin Hester, Chicago, 2006 (p-3, k-2)
4 Jack Christiansen, Detroit, 1951 (p-4)
Emlen Tunnell, N.Y. Giants, 1951 (p-3, k-1)
Gale Sayers, Chicago, 1967 (p-1, k-3)
Travis Williams, Green Bay, 1967 (k-4)
Cecil Turner, Chicago, 1970 (k-4)
Billy Johnson, Houston, 1975 (p-3, k-1)
Rick Upchurch, Denver, 1976 (p-4)
Dante Hall, Kansas City, 2003 (p-2, r-2)
Eddie Drummond, Detroit, 2004 (p-2, k-2)
Josh Cribbs, Cleveland, 2009 (p-1, k-3)

Most Touchdowns, Game

2 Jack Christiansen, Detroit vs. Los Angeles, Oct. 14, 1951 (p-2); vs. Green Bay, Nov. 22, 1951 (p-2)
Jim Patton, N.Y. Giants vs. Washington, Oct. 30, 1955 (p-1, k-1)
Bobby Mitchell, Cleveland vs. Philadelphia, Nov. 23, 1958 (p-1, k-1)
Dick Christy, N.Y. Titans vs. Denver, Sept. 24, 1961 (p-2)
Al Frazier, Denver vs. Boston, Dec. 3, 1961 (p-1, k-1)
Timmy Brown, Philadelphia vs. Dallas, Nov. 6, 1966 (k-2)
Travis Williams, Green Bay vs. Cleveland, Nov. 12, 1967 (k-2); vs. Pittsburgh, Nov. 2, 1969 (p-1, k-1)

Gale Sayers, Chicago vs. San Francisco, Dec. 3, 1967 (p-1, k-1)
Rick Upchurch, Denver vs. Cleveland, Sept. 26, 1976 (p-2)
Eddie Payton, Detroit vs. Minnesota, Dec. 17, 1977 (p-1, k-1)
LeRoy Irvin, Los Angeles vs. Atlanta, Oct. 11, 1981 (p-2)
Ron Brown, L.A. Rams vs. Green Bay, Nov. 24, 1985 (k-2)
Vai Sikahema, St. Louis vs. Tampa Bay, Dec. 21, 1986 (p-2)
Todd Kinchen, L.A. Rams vs. Atlanta, Dec. 27, 1992 (p-2)
Eric Metcalf, Cleveland vs. Pittsburgh, Oct. 24, 1993 (p-2); San Diego vs. Cincinnati, Nov. 2, 1997 (p-2)
Tyrone Hughes, New Orleans vs. L.A. Rams, Oct. 23, 1994 (k-2)
Darrien Gordon, Denver vs. Carolina, Nov. 9, 1997 (p-2)
Jermaine Lewis, Baltimore vs. Seattle, Dec. 7, 1997 (p-2); Baltimore vs. N.Y. Jets, Dec. 24, 2000 (p-2)
Chad Morton, N.Y. Jets vs. Buffalo, Sept. 8, 2002 (ot) (k-2)
Michael Lewis, New Orleans vs. Washington, Oct. 13, 2002 (p-1, k-1)
Dante Hall, Kansas City vs. St. Louis, Dec. 8, 2002 (p-1, k-1)
Steve Smith, Carolina vs. Cincinnati, Dec. 8, 2002 (p-2)
Eddie Drummond, Detroit vs. Jacksonville, Nov. 14, 2004 (ot) (p-2)
Devin Hester, Chicago vs. St. Louis, Dec. 11, 2006 (k-2)
Darren Sproles, San Diego vs. Indianapolis, Nov. 11, 2007 (p-1, k-1)
Devin Hester, Chicago vs. Denver, Nov. 25, 2007 (p-1, k-1)
André Davis, Houston vs. Jacksonville, Dec. 30, 2007 (k-2)
Reggie Bush, New Orleans vs. Minnesota, Oct. 6, 2008
Eddie Royal, Denver vs. San Diego, Oct. 19, 2009 (p-1, k-1)
Ted Ginn, Jr., Miami vs. N.Y. Jets, Nov. 1, 2009 (k-2)
Josh Cribbs, Cleveland vs. Kansas City, Dec. 20, 2009 (k-2)

FUMBLES

Most Fumbles, Career

161 Warren Moon, Houston, 1984-1993; Minnesota, 1994-96; Seattle, 1997-98; Kansas City, 1999-2000
159 Brett Favre, Atlanta, 1991; Green Bay, 1992-2007; N.Y. Jets, 2008; Minnesota, 2009
153 Dave Krieg, Seattle, 1980-1991; Kansas City, 1992-93; Detroit, 1994; Arizona, 1995; Chicago, 1996; Tennessee, 1997-98

Most Fumbles, Season

23 Kerry Collins, N.Y. Giants, 2001
Daunte Culpepper, Minnesota, 2002
21 Tony Banks, St. Louis, 1996
David Carr, Houston, 2002
18 Dave Krieg, Seattle, 1989
Warren Moon, Houston, 1990

Most Fumbles, Game

7 Len Dawson, Kansas City vs. San Diego, Nov. 15, 1964
6 Sam Etcheverry, St. Louis vs. N.Y. Giants, Sept, 17, 1961
Dave Krieg, Seattle vs. Kansas City, Nov. 5, 1989
Brett Favre, Green Bay vs. Tampa Bay, Dec. 7, 1998
Kurt Warner, St. Louis vs. N.Y. Giants, Sept. 7, 2003
Chad Pennington, N.Y. Jets vs. Kansas City, Sept. 11, 2005
5 Paul Christman, Chi. Cardinals vs. Green Bay, Nov. 10, 1946
Joe Perry, San Francisco vs. Cleveland, Nov. 12, 1950
Charlie Conerly, N.Y. Giants vs. San Francisco, Dec. 1, 1957
Tom Yewcic, Boston vs. Oakland, Dec. 16, 1962
Jack Kemp, Buffalo vs. Houston, Oct. 29, 1967
Roman Gabriel, Philadelphia vs. Oakland, Nov. 21, 1976
Randall Cunningham, Philadelphia vs. L.A. Raiders, Nov. 30, 1986 (ot)
Willie Totten, Buffalo vs. Indianapolis, Oct. 4, 1987
Dave Walter, Cincinnati vs. Seattle, Oct. 11, 1987
Dave Krieg, Seattle vs. San Diego, Nov. 25, 1990 (ot)
Andre Ware, Detroit vs. Green Bay, Dec. 6, 1992
Steve Beuerlein, Carolina vs. San Francisco, Nov. 8, 1998
Patrick Ramsey, Washington vs. Green Bay, Oct. 20, 2002
Eli Manning, N.Y. Giants vs. Buffalo, Dec. 23, 2007
Josh Johnson, Tampa Bay vs. Carolina, Oct. 18, 2009

FUMBLES RECOVERED

Most Fumbles Recovered, Career, Own and Opponents'

56 Warren Moon, Houston, 1984-1993; Minnesota, 1994-96; Seattle, 1997-98; Kansas City, 1999-2000 (56 own)
47 Dave Krieg, Seattle, 1980-1991; Kansas City, 1992-93; Detroit, 1994; Arizona, 1995; Chicago, 1996; Tennessee, 1997-98 (47 own)
45 Boomer Esiason, Cincinnati, 1984-1992, 1997; N.Y. Jets, 1993-95; Arizona, 1996 (45 own)

Most Fumbles Recovered, Season, Own and Opponents'

12 David Carr, Houston, 2002 (12 own)
9 Don Hultz, Minnesota, 1963 (9 opp)
Dave Krieg, Seattle, 1989 (9 own)
Brian Griese, Denver, 1999 (9 own)
Jon Kitna, Seattle, 2000 (9 own)
8 Paul Christman, Chi. Cardinals, 1945 (8 own)
Joe Schmidt, Detroit, 1955 (8 opp)
Bill Butler, Minnesota, 1963 (8 own)
Kermit Alexander, San Francisco, 1965 (4 own, 4 opp)
Jack Lambert, Pittsburgh, 1976 (1 own, 7 opp)
Danny White, Dallas, 1981 (8 own)
Dan Marino, Miami, 1988 (7 own, 1 opp)
Tony Banks, St. Louis, 1998 (8 own)
Ryan Fitzpatrick, Cincinnati, 2008 (8 own)

Most Fumbles Recovered, Game, Own and Opponents'

4 Otto Graham, Cleveland vs. N.Y. Giants, Oct. 25, 1953 (4 own)
Sam Etcheverry, St. Louis vs. N.Y. Giants, Sept. 17, 1961 (4 own)
Roman Gabriel, Los Angeles vs. San Francisco, Oct. 12, 1969 (4 own)
Randall Cunningham, Philadelphia vs. L.A. Raiders, Nov. 30, 1986 (ot) (4 own)

Joe Ferguson, Buffalo vs. Miami, Sept. 18, 1977 (4 own)
3 By many players

OWN FUMBLES RECOVERED

Most Own Fumbles Recovered, Career

56 Warren Moon, Houston, 1984-1993; Minnesota, 1994-96; Seattle, 1997-98; Kansas City, 1999-2000
47 Dave Krieg, Seattle, 1980-1991; Kansas City, 1992-93; Detroit, 1994; Arizona, 1995; Chicago, 1996; Tennessee, 1997-98
45 Boomer Esiason, Cincinnati, 1984-1992, 1997; N.Y. Jets, 1993-95; Arizona, 1996

Most Own Fumbles Recovered, Season

12 David Carr, Houston, 2002
9 Dave Krieg, Seattle, 1989
Brian Griese, Denver, 1999
Jon Kitna, Seattle, 2000
8 Paul Christman, Chi. Cardinals, 1945
Bill Butler, Minnesota, 1963
Danny White, Dallas, 1981
Tony Banks, St. Louis, 1998
Ryan Fitzpatrick, Cincinnati, 2008

Most Own Fumbles Recovered, Game

4 Otto Graham, Cleveland vs. N.Y. Giants, Oct. 25, 1953
Sam Etcheverry, St. Louis vs. N.Y. Giants, Sept. 17, 1961
Roman Gabriel, Los Angeles vs. San Francisco, Oct. 12, 1969
Joe Ferguson, Buffalo vs. Miami, Sept. 18, 1977
Randall Cunningham, Philadelphia vs. L.A. Raiders, Nov. 30, 1986 (ot)
3 By many players

OPPONENTS' FUMBLES RECOVERED

Most Opponents' Fumbles Recovered, Career

29 Jim Marshall, Cleveland, 1960; Minnesota, 1961-1979
28 Rickey Jackson, New Orleans, 1981-1993; San Francisco, 1994-95
27 Jason Taylor, Miami, 1997-2007; Washington, 2008; Miami, 2009

Most Opponents' Fumbles Recovered, Season

9 Don Hultz, Minnesota, 1963
8 Joe Schmidt, Detroit, 1955
7 Alan Page, Minnesota, 1970
Jack Lambert, Pittsburgh, 1976
Ray Childress, Houston, 1988
Rickey Jackson, New Orleans, 1990

Most Opponents' Fumbles Recovered, Game

3 Corwin Clatt, Chi. Cardinals vs. Detroit, Nov. 6, 1949
Vic Sears, Philadelphia vs. Green Bay, Nov. 2, 1952
Ed Beatty, San Francisco vs. Los Angeles, Oct. 7, 1956
Ron Carroll, Houston vs. Cincinnati, Oct. 27, 1974
Maurice Spencer, New Orleans vs. Atlanta, Oct. 10, 1976
Steve Nelson, New England vs. Philadelphia, Oct. 8, 1978
Charles Jackson, Kansas City vs. Pittsburgh, Sept. 6, 1981
Willie Buchanon, San Diego vs. Denver, Sept. 27, 1981
Joey Browner, Minnesota vs. San Francisco, Sept. 8, 1985
Ray Childress, Houston vs. Washington, Oct. 30, 1988
John Thierry, Chicago vs. Houston, Oct. 22, 1995
Stephen Boyd, Detroit vs. Chicago, Oct. 4, 1998
Darryl Williams, Seattle vs. Kansas City, Oct. 4, 1998
Rod Woodson, Oakland vs. Pittsburgh, Sept. 15, 2002
Brian Young, St. Louis vs. Baltimore, Nov. 9, 2003
2 By many players

YARDS RETURNING FUMBLES

Longest Fumble Run (All TDs)

104 Jack Tatum, Oakland vs. Green Bay, Sept. 24, 1972
Aeneas Williams, Arizona vs. Washington, Nov. 5, 2000
102 Travis Davis, Pittsburgh vs. Carolina, Dec. 26, 1999
100 Chris Martin, Kansas City vs. Miami, Oct. 13, 1991

TOUCHDOWNS

Most Touchdowns, Career (Total)

6 Jason Taylor, Miami, 1997-2007; Washington, 2008; Miami, 2009
5 Jessie Tuggle, Atlanta, 1987-2000
4 Bill Thompson, Denver, 1969-1981
Derrick Thomas, Kansas City, 1989-1999
Keith Bulluck, Tennessee, 2000-09
Ronde Barber, Tampa Bay, 1997-2009

Most Touchdowns, Season (Total)

2 Harold McPhail, Boston, 1934
Harry Ebding, Detroit, 1937
John Morelli, Boston, 1944
Frank Maznicki, Boston, 1947
Fred (Dippy) Evans, Chi. Bears, 1948
Ralph Heywood, Boston, 1948
Art Tait, N.Y. Yanks, 1951
John Dwyer, Los Angeles, 1952
Leo Sugar, Chi. Cardinals, 1957
Doug Cline, Houston, 1961
Jim Bradshaw, Pittsburgh, 1964
Royce Berry, Cincinnati, 1970
Ahmad Rashad, Buffalo, 1974
Tim Gray, Kansas City, 1977
Charles Phillips, Oakland, 1978
Kenny Johnson, Atlanta, 1981
George Martin, N.Y. Giants, 1981
Del Rodgers, Green Bay, 1982
Mike Douglass, Green Bay, 1983
Shelton Robinson, Seattle, 1983
Erik McMillan, N.Y. Jets, 1989
Les Miller, San Diego, 1990
Seth Joyner, Philadelphia, 1991
Robert Goff, New Orleans, 1992
Willie Clay, Detroit, 1993
Tyrone Hughes, New Orleans, 1994
Chad Brown, Seattle, 1997
Marcus Robertson, Tennessee, 1997
Dwayne Rudd, Minnesota, 1998
Keith McKenzie, Green Bay, 1999
Ronde Barber, Tampa Bay, 2004
Leonard Little, St. Louis, 2004
Antwan Odom, Tennessee, 2005
Adalius Thomas, Baltimore, 2005
Kevin Curtis, Philadelphia, 2007

Most Touchdowns, Career (Own recovered)

2 Ken Kavanaugh, Chi. Bears, 1940-41, 1945-1950
Mike Ditka, Chicago, 1961-66; Philadelphia, 1967-68; Dallas, 1969-1972
Gail Cogdill, Detroit, 1960-68; Baltimore, 1968; Atlanta, 1969-1970
Ahmad Rashad, St. Louis, 1972-73; Buffalo, 1974; Minnesota, 1976-1982
Jim Mitchell, Atlanta, 1969-1979
Drew Pearson, Dallas, 1973-1983

Del Rodgers, Green Bay, 1982, 1984; San Francisco, 1987-88
Alan Ricard, Baltimore, 2001-05
Kevin Curtis, St. Louis, 2003-06; Philadelphia, 2007-09

Most Touchdowns, Season (Own recovered)
2 Ahmad Rashad, Buffalo, 1974
Del Rodgers, Green Bay, 1982
Kevin Curtis, Philadelphia, 2007
1 By many players

Most Touchdowns, Career (Opponents' recovered)
6 Jason Taylor, Miami, 1997-2007; Washington, 2008; Miami, 2009
5 Jessie Tuggle, Atlanta, 1987-2000
4 Derrick Thomas, Kansas City, 1989-1999
Keith Bulluck, Tennessee, 2000-09
Ronde Barber, Tampa Bay, 1997-2009

Most Touchdowns, Season (Opponents' recovered)
2 Harold McPhail, Boston, 1934
Harry Ebding, Detroit, 1937
John Morelli, Boston, 1944
Frank Maznicki, Boston, 1947
Fred (Dippy) Evans, Chi. Bears, 1948
Ralph Heywood, Boston, 1948
Art Tait, N.Y. Yanks, 1951
John Dwyer, Los Angeles, 1952
Leo Sugar, Chi. Cardinals, 1957
Doug Cline, Houston, 1961
Jim Bradshaw, Pittsburgh, 1964
Royce Berry, Cincinnati, 1970
Tim Gray, Kansas City, 1977
Charles Phillips, Oakland, 1978
Kenny Johnson, Atlanta, 1981
George Martin, N.Y. Giants, 1981
Mike Douglass, Green Bay, 1983
Shelton Robinson, Seattle, 1983
Erik McMillan, N.Y. Jets, 1989
Les Miller, San Diego, 1990
Seth Joyner, Philadelphia, 1991
Robert Goff, New Orleans, 1992
Willie Clay, Detroit, 1993
Tyrone Hughes, New Orleans, 1994
Chad Brown, Seattle, 1997
Marcus Robertson, Tennessee, 1997
Dwayne Rudd, Minnesota, 1998
Keith McKenzie, Green Bay, 1999
Ronde Barber, Tampa Bay, 2004
Leonard Little, St. Louis, 2004
Antwan Odom, Tennessee, 2005
Adalius Thomas, Baltimore, 2005

Most Touchdowns, Game (Opponents' recovered)
2 Fred (Dippy) Evans, Chi. Bears vs. Washington, Nov. 28, 1948

COMBINED NET YARDS GAINED

Rushing, receiving, interception returns, punt returns, kickoff returns, and fumble returns

Most Seasons Leading League
5 Jim Brown, Cleveland, 1958-1961, 1964
4 Brian Mitchell, Washington, 1994-96, 1998
3 Cliff Battles, Boston, 1932-33; Washington, 1937
Gale Sayers, Chicago, 1965-67
Eric Dickerson, L.A. Rams, 1983-84, 1986
Thurman Thomas, Buffalo, 1989, 1991-92

Most Consecutive Seasons Leading League
4 Jim Brown, Cleveland, 1958-1961
3 Gale Sayers, Chicago, 1965-67
Brian Mitchell, Washington, 1994-96
2 Cliff Battles, Boston, 1932-33
Charley Trippi, Chi. Cardinals, 1948-49
Timmy Brown, Philadelphia, 1962-63
Floyd Little, Denver, 1967-68
James Brooks, San Diego, 1981-82
Eric Dickerson, L.A. Rams, 1983-84
Thurman Thomas, Buffalo, 1991-92
Dante Hall, Kansas City, 2003-04

ATTEMPTS

Most Attempts, Career
4,939 Emmitt Smith. Dallas, 1990-2002; Arizona, 2003-04
4,368 Walter Payton, Chicago, 1975-1987
4,016 Curtis Martin, New England, 1995-97; N.Y. Jets, 1998-2005

Most Attempts, Season
496 James Wilder, Tamp Bay, 1984
458 Larry Johnson, Kansas City, 2006
455 Eddie George, Tennessee, 2000

Most Attempts, Rookie, Season
442 Eric Dickerson, L.A. Rams, 1983
433 Edgerrin James, Indianapolis, 1999
401 Curtis Martin, New England, 1995

Most Attempts, Game
48 James Wilder, Tampa Bay vs. Pittsburgh, Oct. 30, 1983
LaDainian Tomlinson, San Diego vs. Denver, Dec. 1, 2002 (ot)
47 James Wilder, Tampa Bay vs. Green Bay, Sept. 30, 1984 (ot)
Terrell Davis, Denver vs. Buffalo, Oct. 26, 1997 (ot)
46 Gerald Riggs, Atlanta vs. L.A. Rams, Nov. 17, 1985

YARDS GAINED

Most Yards Gained, Career
23,546 Jerry Rice, San Francisco, 1985-2000; Oakland, 2001-04; Seattle, 2004
23,330 Brian Mitchell, Washington, 1990-99; Philadelphia, 2000-02; N.Y. Giants, 2003
21,803 Walter Payton, Chicago, 1975-1987

Most Yards Gained, Season
2,690 Derrick Mason, Tennessee, 2000
2,647 Michael Lewis, New Orleans, 2002
2,535 Lionel James, San Diego, 1985

Most Yards Gained, Rookie, Season
2,317 Tim Brown, L.A. Raiders, 1988
2,272 Gale Sayers, Chicago, 1965
2,250 Maurice Jones-Drew, Jacksonville, 2006

Most Yards Gained, Game
404 Glyn Milburn, Denver vs. Seattle, Dec. 10, 1995
373 Billy Cannon, Houston vs. N.Y. Titans, Dec. 10. 1961
361 Adrian Peterson, Minnesota vs. Chicago, Oct. 14, 2007

SACKS

Sacks have been compiled since 1982.

Most Seasons Leading League
2 Mark Gastineau, N.Y. Jets, 1983-84
Reggie White, Philadelphia, 1987-88
Kevin Greene, Pittsburgh, 1994; Carolina, 1996
Michael Strahan, N.Y. Giants, 2001, 2003

Most Sacks, Career
200.0 Bruce Smith, Buffalo, 1985-1999; Washington, 2000-03
198.0 Reggie White, Philadelphia, 1985-1992; Green Bay, 1993-98; Carolina, 2000
160.0 Kevin Greene, L.A. Rams, 1985-1992; Pittsburgh, 1993-95; Carolina, 1996, 1998-99; San Francisco, 1997

Most Sacks, Season
22.5 Michael Strahan, N.Y. Giants, 2001
22.0 Mark Gastineau, N.Y. Jets, 1984
21.0 Reggie White, Philadelphia, 1987

Chris Doleman, Minnesota, 1989

Most Sacks, Rookie, Season
14.5 Jevon Kearse, Tennessee, 1999
13.0 Dwight Freeney, Indianapolis, 2002
12.5 Leslie O'Neal, San Diego, 1986
Simeon Rice, Arizona, 1996

Most Sacks, Game
7.0 Derrick Thomas, Kansas City vs. Seattle, Nov. 11, 1990
6.0 Fred Dean, San Francisco vs. New Orleans, Nov. 13, 1983
Derrick Thomas, Kansas City vs. Oakland, Sept. 6, 1998
Osi Umenyiora, N.Y. Giants vs. Philadelphia, Sept. 30, 2007
5.5 William Gay, Detroit vs. Tampa Bay, Sept. 4, 1983

Most Seasons, 10 or More Sacks
13 Bruce Smith, Buffalo, 1986-1990, 1992-98; Washington, 2000
12 Reggie White, Philadelphia, 1985-1992; Green Bay, 1993, 1995, 1997-98
10 Kevin Greene, L.A. Rams, 1988-1990, 1992; Pittsburgh, 1993-94; Carolina, 1996, 1998-99; San Francisco, 1997

Most Consecutive Seasons, 10 or More Sacks
9 Reggie White, Philadelphia, 1985-1992; Green Bay, 1993
8 John Randle, Minnesota, 1992-99
7 Lawrence Taylor, N.Y. Giants, 1984-1990
Bruce Smith, Buffalo, 1992-98

Most Consecutive Games, Sack
10 Simon Fletcher, Denver, Nov. 15, 1992-Sept. 20, 1993
DeMarcus Ware, Dallas, Dec. 16, 2007-Oct. 19, 2008
9 Bruce Smith, Buffalo, Nov. 16, 1986-Oct. 25, 1987
Kevin Greene, San Francisco-Carolina, Dec. 7, 1997-Oct. 18, 1998
Dwight Freeney, Indianapolis, Dec. 18, 2008-Nov. 8, 2009
8 By many players

MISCELLANEOUS

Longest Return of Missed Field Goal (All TDs)
109 Antonio Cromartie, San Diego vs. Minnesota, Nov. 4, 2007
108 Nathan Vasher, Chicago vs. San Francisco, Nov. 13, 2005
Devin Hester, Chicago vs. N.Y. Giants, Nov. 12, 2006
107 Chris McAlister, Baltimore vs. Denver, Sept. 30, 2002

TEAM RECORDS

CHAMPIONSHIPS

Most Seasons League Champion
12 Green Bay, 1929-1931, 1936, 1939, 1944, 1961-62, 1965-67, 1996
9 Chi. Bears, 1921, 1932-33, 1940-41, 1943, 1946, 1963, 1985
7 N.Y. Giants, 1927, 1934, 1938, 1956, 1986, 1990, 2007

Most Consecutive Seasons League Champion
3 Green Bay, 1929-1931
Green Bay, 1965-67
2 Canton, 1922-23
Chi. Bears, 1932-33
Chi. Bears, 1940-41
Philadelphia, 1948-49
Detroit, 1952-53
Cleveland, 1954-55
Baltimore, 1958-59
Houston, 1960-61
Green Bay, 1961-62
Buffalo, 1964-65
Miami, 1972-73
Pittsburgh, 1974-75
Pittsburgh, 1978-79
San Francisco, 1988-89
Dallas, 1992-93
Denver, 1997-98
New England, 2003-04

Most Times Finishing First, Regular Season
22 N.Y. Giants, 1927, 1933-35, 1938-39, 1941, 1944, 1946, 1956, 1958-59, 1961-63, 1986, 1989-1990, 1997, 2000, 2005, 2008
21 Chi. Bears, 1921, 1932-34, 1937, 1940-43, 1946, 1956, 1963, 1984-88, 1990, 2001, 2005-06
Green Bay, 1929-1931, 1936, 1938-39, 1944, 1960-62, 1965-67, 1972, 1995-97, 2002-04, 2007
Dallas, 1966-1971, 1973, 1976-79, 1981, 1985, 1992-96, 1998, 2007, 2009
19 Pittsburgh, 1972, 1974-79, 1983-84, 1992, 1994-97, 2001-02, 2004, 2007-08

Most Consecutive Times Finishing First, Regular Season
7 Los Angeles, 1973-79
6 Cleveland, 1950-55
Dallas, 1966-1971
Minnesota, 1973-78
Pittsburgh, 1974-79
5 Oakland, 1972-76
Chicago, 1984-88
San Francisco, 1986-1990
Dallas, 1992-96
Indianapolis, 2003-07
New England, 2003-07

GAMES WON

Most Consecutive Games Won
23 Indianapolis, 2008-09
21 New England, 2006-08
18 New England, 2003-04

Most Consecutive Games Without Defeat
25 Canton, 1921-23 (won 22, tied 3)
24 Chi. Bears, 1941-43 (won 23, tied 1)
23 Green Bay, 1928-1930 (won 21, tied 2)
Indianapolis, 2009 (won 23)

Most Games Won, Season
16 New England, 2007
15 San Francisco, 1984
Chicago, 1985
Minnesota, 1998
Pittsburgh, 2004
14 By many teams

Most Consecutive Games Won, Season
16 New England, 2007, entire season
14 Miami, 1972, entire season
Pittsburgh, 2004
Indianapolis, 2009
13 Chi. Bears, 1934, entire season
Denver, 1998
Indianapolis, 2005
New Orleans, 2009

Most Consecutive Games Won, Start of Season
16 New England, 2007, entire season
14 Miami, 1972, entire season
Indianapolis, 2009
13 Chi. Bears, 1934, entire season
Denver, 1998
Indianapolis, 2005
New Orleans, 2009

Most Consecutive Games Won, End of Season
16 New England, 2007, entire season
14 Miami, 1972, entire season
Pittsburgh, 2004
13 Chi. Bears, 1934, entire season

Most Consecutive Games Without Defeat, Season
16 New England, 2007 (won 16), entire season
14 Miami, 1972 (won 14), entire season
Pittsburgh, 2004 (won 14)
Indianapolis, 2009 (won 14)
13 Chi. Bears, 1926 (won 11, tied 2)
Green Bay, 1929 (won 12, tied 1)
Chi. Bears, 1934 (won 13), entire season
Baltimore, 1967 (won 11, tied 2)
Denver, 1998 (won 13)
Indianapolis, 2005 (won 13)
New Orleans, 2009 (won 13)

Most Consecutive Games Without Defeat, Start of Season
16 New England, 2007 (won 16), entire season
14 Miami, 1972 (won 14), entire season
Indianapolis, 2009 (won 14)
13 Chi. Bears, 1926 (won 11, tied 2)
Green Bay, 1929 (won 12, tied 1), entire season
Chi. Bears, 1934 (won 13), entire season
Baltimore, 1967 (won 11, tied 2)
Denver, 1998 (won 13)
Indianapolis, 2005 (won 13)
New Orleans, 2009 (won 13)

Most Consecutive Games Without Defeat, End of Season
16 New England, 2007 (won 16), entire season
14 Miami, 1972 (won 14), entire season
Pittsburgh, 2004 (won 14)
13 Green Bay, 1929 (won 12, tied 1), entire season
Chi. Bears, 1934 (won 13), entire season

Most Consecutive Home Games Won
27 Miami, 1971-74
25 Green Bay, 1995-98
24 Denver, 1996-98

Most Consecutive Home Games Without Defeat
29 Green Bay, 1928-1933 (won 26, tied 3)
27 Miami, 1971-74 (won 27)
25 Green Bay, 1995-98 (won 25)

Most Consecutive Road Games Won
18 San Francisco, 1988-1990
12 New England, 2006-08
11 L.A. Chargers/San Diego, 1960-61
San Francisco, 1987-88
Pittsburgh, 2004-05
Indianapolis, 2008-09

Most Consecutive Road Games Without Defeat
18 San Francisco, 1988-1990 (won 18)
13 Chi. Bears, 1941-43 (won 12, tied 1)
12 Green Bay, 1928-1930 (won 10, tied 2)
New England, 2006-08 (won 12)

Most Shutout Games Won or Tied, Season
10 Pottsville, 1926 (won 9, tied 1)
N.Y. Giants, 1927 (won 9, tied 1)
9 Akron, 1921 (won 8, tied 1)
Canton, 1922 (won 7, tied 2)
Frankford, 1926 (won 9)
Frankford, 1929 (won 6, tied 3)

Most Consecutive Shutout Games Won or Tied
13 Akron, 1920-21 (won 10, tied 3)
7 Pottsville, 1926 (won 6, tied 1)
Detroit, 1934 (won 7)
6 Buffalo, 1920-21 (won 5, tied 1)
Frankford, 1926 (won 6)
Detroit, 1926 (won 4, tied 2)
N.Y. Giants, 1926-27 (won 5, tied 1)

GAMES LOST

Most Consecutive Games Lost
26 Tampa Bay, 1976-1977
19 Chi. Cardinals, 1942-43, 1945
Oakland, 1961-62
Detroit, 2007-09
18 Houston, 1972-73

Most Consecutive Games Without Victory
26 Tampa Bay, 1976-77 (lost 26)
23 Rochester, 1922-25 (lost 21, tied 2)
Washington, 1960-61 (lost 20, tied 3)
19 Dayton, 1927-29 (lost 18, tied 1)
Chi. Cardinals, 1942-43, 1945 (lost 19)
Oakland, 1961-62 (lost 19)
Detroit, 2007-09 (lost 19)

Most Games Lost, Season
16 Detroit, 2008
15 New Orleans, 1980
Dallas, 1989
New England, 1990
Indianapolis, 1991
N.Y. Jets, 1996
San Diego, 2000
Carolina, 2001
Miami, 2007
St. Louis, 2009
14 By many teams

Most Consecutive Games Lost, Season
16 Detroit, 2008, entire season
15 Carolina, 2001
14 Tampa Bay, 1976
New Orleans, 1980
Baltimore, 1981
New England, 1990

Most Consecutive Games Lost, Start of Season
16 Detroit, 2008, entire season
14 Tampa Bay, 1976, entire season
New Orleans, 1980
13 Oakland, 1962
Indianapolis, 1986
Miami, 2007

Most Consecutive Games Lost, End of Season
16 Detroit, 2008, entire season
15 Carolina, 2001
14 Tampa Bay, 1976, entire season
New England, 1990

Most Consecutive Games Without Victory, Season
16 Detroit, 2008 (lost 16), entire season
15 Carolina, 2001 (lost 15)
14 Tampa Bay, 1976 (lost 14), entire season
New Orleans, 1980 (lost 14)
Baltimore, 1981 (lost 14)
New England, 1990 (lost 14)

Most Consecutive Games Without Victory, Start of Season
16 Detroit, 2008 (lost 16), entire season
14 Tampa Bay, 1976 (lost 14), entire season
New Orleans, 1980 (lost 14)
13 Washington, 1961 (lost 12, tied 1)
Oakland, 1962 (lost 13)
Indianapolis, 1986 (lost 13)
Miami, 2007 (lost 13)

Most Consecutive Games Without Victory, End of Season
16 Detroit, 2008 (lost 16), entire season
15 Carolina, 2001
14 Tampa Bay, 1976, (lost 14), entire season
New England, 1990 (lost 14)

Most Consecutive Home Games Lost
14 Dallas, 1988-89
13 Houston, 1972-73

Tampa Bay, 1976-77
N.Y. Jets, 1995-97
St. Louis, 2008-09 (current)
11 Oakland, 1961-62
Los Angeles, 1961-63
Cincinnati, 1998-99

Most Consecutive Home Games Without Victory
14 Dallas, 1988-89 (lost 14)
13 Houston, 1972-73 (lost 13)
Tampa Bay, 1976-77 (lost 13)
N.Y. Jets, 1995-97 (lost 13)
Philadelphia, 1936-38 (lost 12, tied 1)
St. Louis, 2008-09 (lost 13) (current)

Most Consecutive Road Games Lost
24 Detroit, 2001-03
23 Houston, 1981-84
22 Buffalo, 1983-86

Most Consecutive Road Games Without Victory
24 Detroit, 2001-03 (lost 24)
23 Houston, 1981-84 (lost 23)
22 Buffalo, 1983-86 (lost 22)

Most Shutout Games Lost or Tied, Season
8 Frankford, 1927 (lost 6, tied 2)
Brooklyn, 1931 (lost 8)
7 Dayton, 1925 (lost 6, tied 1)
Orange, 1929 (lost 4, tied 3)
Frankford, 1931 (lost 6, tied 1)
6 By many teams

Most Consecutive Shutout Games Lost or Tied
8 Rochester, 1922-24 (lost 8)
7 Hammond, 1922-23 (lost 6, tied 1)
6 Providence, 1926-27 (lost 5, tied 1)
Brooklyn, 1942-43 (lost 6)

TIE GAMES

Most Tie Games, Season
6 Chi. Bears, 1932
5 Frankford, 1929
4 Chi. Bears, 1924
Orange, 1929
Portsmouth, 1932

Most Consecutive Tie Games
3 Chi. Bears, 1932
2 By many teams

SCORING

Most Seasons Leading League
10 Chi. Bears, 1932, 1934-35, 1939, 1941-43, 1946-47, 1956
9 San Francisco, 1953, 1965, 1970, 1987, 1989, 1992-95
L.A./St. Louis Rams, 1950-52, 1957, 1967, 1973, 1999-2001
7 Green Bay, 1931, 1936-38, 1961-62, 1996

Most Consecutive Seasons Leading League
4 San Francisco, 1992-1995
3 Green Bay, 1936-38
Chi. Bears, 1941-43
Los Angeles, 1950-52
Oakland, 1967-69
St. Louis, 1999-2001
2 By many teams

POINTS

Most Points, Season
589 New England, 2007
556 Minnesota, 1998
541 Washington, 1983

Fewest Points, Season (Since 1932)
37 Cincinnati/St. Louis, 1934
38 Cincinnati, 1933
Detroit, 1942
51 Pittsburgh, 1934
Philadelphia, 1936

Most Points, Game
72 Washington vs. N.Y. Giants, Nov. 27, 1966
70 Los Angeles vs. Baltimore, Oct. 22, 1950
66 Rochester vs. *Fort Porter, Oct. 10, 1920
**Not a member of the American Professional Football Association*

Most Points, Both Teams, Game
113 Washington (72) vs. N.Y. Giants (41), Nov. 27, 1966
106 Cincinnati (58) vs. Cleveland (48), Nov. 28, 2004
101 Oakland (52) vs. Houston (49), Dec. 22, 1963

Fewest Points, Both Teams, Game
0 In many games. Last time: N.Y. Giants vs. Detroit, Nov. 7, 1943

Most Points, Shutout Victory Game
66 Rochester vs. *Fort Porter, Oct. 10, 1920
**Not a member of the American Professional Football Association*
64 Philadelphia vs. Cincinnati, Nov. 6, 1934
62 Akron vs. Oorang, Oct. 29, 1922

Most Consecutive Games Scoring
420 San Francisco, 1977-2004
277 Denver, 1992-2009 (current)
274 Cleveland, 1950-1971

Fewest Points, Shutout Victory, Game
2 Akron vs. Buffalo, Nov. 29, 1923
Kansas City vs. Buffalo, Nov. 21, 1926
Frankford vs. Green Bay, Nov. 29, 1928
Green Bay vs. Chi. Bears, Oct. 16, 1932
Chi. Bears vs. Green Bay, Sept. 18, 1938

Most Points Overcome to Win Game
28 San Francisco vs. New Orleans, Dec. 7, 1980 (ot) (trailed 7-35, won 38-35)
26 Buffalo vs. Indianapolis, Sept., 21, 1997 (trailed 0-26, won 37-35)
25 St. Louis vs. Tampa Bay, Nov. 8, 1987 (trailed 3-28, won 31-28)

Most Points Overcome to Tie Game
31 Denver vs. Buffalo, Nov. 27, 1960 (trailed 7-38, tied 38-38)
28 Los Angeles vs. Philadelphia, Oct. 3, 1948 (trailed 0-28, tied 28-28)

Most Points, Each Half
1st: 49 Green Bay vs. Tampa Bay, Oct. 2, 1983
48 Buffalo vs. Miami, Sept. 18, 1966
45 Green Bay vs. Cleveland, Nov. 12, 1967
Indianapolis vs. Denver, Oct. 31, 1988
Houston vs. Cleveland, Dec. 9, 1990
Seattle vs. Minnesota, Sept. 29, 2002
New England vs. Tennessee, Oct. 18, 2009
2nd: 49 Chi. Bears vs. Philadelphia, Nov. 30, 1941
48 Chi. Cardinals vs. Baltimore, Oct. 2, 1950
N.Y. Giants vs. Baltimore, Nov. 19, 1950
45 Cincinnati vs. Houston, Dec. 17, 1972

Most Points, Both Teams, Each Half
1st: 70 Houston (35) vs. Oakland (35), Dec. 22, 1963
63 Philadelphia (42) vs. Detroit (21), Sept. 23, 2007
62 N.Y. Jets (41) vs. Tampa Bay (21), Nov. 17, 1985
Indianapolis (35) vs. Cincinnati (27), Nov. 20, 2005
2nd: 66 Cleveland (35) vs. Cincinnati (31), Nov. 28, 2004
65 Washington (38) vs. N.Y. Giants (27), Nov. 27, 1966
62 L.A. Raiders (31) vs. San Diego (31), Jan. 2, 1983
Baltimore (38) vs. Seattle (24), Nov. 23, 2003

Most Points, One Quarter
41 Green Bay vs. Detroit, Oct. 7, 1945 (second quarter)
Los Angeles vs. Detroit, Oct. 29, 1950 (third quarter)

37 Los Angeles vs. Green Bay, Sept. 21, 1980 (second quarter)
35 Chi. Cardinals vs. Boston, Oct. 24, 1948 (third quarter)
Green Bay vs. Cleveland, Nov. 12, 1967 (first quarter)
Green Bay vs. Tampa Bay, Oct. 2, 1983 (second quarter)
New England vs. Tennessee, Oct. 18, 2009 (second quarter)

Most Points, Both Teams, One Quarter
49 Oakland (28) vs. Houston (21), Dec. 22, 1963 (second quarter)
48 Green Bay (41) vs. Detroit (7), Oct. 7, 1945 (second quarter)
Los Angeles (41) vs. Detroit (7), Oct. 29, 1950 (third quarter)
Detroit (34) vs. Chicago (14), Sept. 30, 2007 (fourth quarter)
47 St. Louis (27) vs. Philadelphia (20), Dec. 13, 1964 (second quarter)

Most Points, Each Quarter
1st: 35 Green Bay vs. Cleveland, Nov. 12, 1967
31 Buffalo vs. Kansas City, Sept. 13, 1964
28 By eight teams
2nd: 41 Green Bay vs. Detroit, Oct. 7, 1945
37 Los Angeles vs. Green Bay, Sept. 21, 1980
35 Green Bay vs. Tampa Bay, Oct. 2, 1983
New England vs. Tennessee, Oct. 18, 2009
3rd: 41 Los Angeles vs. Detroit, Oct. 29, 1950
35 Chi. Cardinals vs. Boston, Oct. 24, 1948
28 By 10 teams
4th: 34 Detroit vs. Chicago, Sept. 30, 2007
31 Oakland vs. Denver, Dec. 17, 1960
Oakland vs. San Diego, Dec. 8, 1963
Atlanta vs. Green Bay, Sept. 13, 1981
30 N.Y. Jets vs. Miami, Oct. 23, 2000

Most Points, Both Teams, Each Quarter
1st: 42 Green Bay (35) vs. Cleveland (7), Nov. 12, 1967
41 Tennessee (24) vs. Indianapolis (17), Dec. 5, 2004
35 Dall. Texans (21) vs. N.Y. Titans (14), Nov. 11, 1962
Dallas (28) vs. Philadelphia (7), Oct. 19, 1969
Kansas City (21) vs. Seattle (14), Dec. 11, 1977
Detroit (21) vs. L.A. Raiders (14), Dec. 10, 1990
Dallas (21) vs. Atlanta (14), Dec. 22, 1991
Indianapolis (21) vs. Green Bay (14), Sept 26, 2004
Miami (21) vs. Buffalo (14), Dec. 5, 2004
Philadelphia (21) vs. New Orleans (14), Dec. 23, 2007
2nd: 49 Oakland (28) vs. Houston (21), Dec. 22, 1963
48 Green Bay (41) vs. Detroit (7), Oct. 7, 1945
47 St. Louis (27) vs. Philadelphia (20), Dec. 13, 1964
3rd: 48 Los Angeles (41) vs. Detroit (7), Oct. 29, 1950
42 Washington (28) vs. Philadelphia (14), Oct. 1, 1955
41 Green Bay (21) vs. N.Y. Yanks (20), Oct. 8, 1950
4th: 48 Detroit (34) vs. Chicago (14), Sept. 30, 2007
43 Atlanta (28) vs. Carolina (15), Nov. 23, 2008
42 Chi. Cardinals (28) vs. Philadelphia (14), Dec. 7, 1947
Green Bay (28) vs. Chi. Bears (14), Nov. 6, 1955
N.Y. Jets (28) vs. Boston (14), Oct. 27, 1968
Pittsburgh (21) vs. Cleveland (21), Oct. 18, 1969
New England (21) vs. Kansas City (21), Sept. 22, 2002

TOUCHDOWNS

Most Seasons Leading League, Touchdowns
13 Chi. Bears, 1932, 1934-35, 1939, 1941-44, 1946-48, 1956, 1965
7 Dallas, 1966, 1968, 1971, 1973, 1977-78, 1980
San Francisco, 1953, 1970, 1987, 1992-95
L.A./St. Louis Rams, 1949-1952, 1999-2001
San Diego, 1963, 1965, 1979, 1981-82, 1985, 2006
6 Oakland, 1967-69, 1972, 1974, 1977
Green Bay, 1932, 1937-38, 1961-62, 1996
Baltimore/Indianapolis Colts, 1957-59, 1964, 1976, 2004

Most Consecutive Seasons Leading League, Touchdowns
4 Chi. Bears, 1941-44
Los Angeles, 1949-1952
San Francisco, 1992-95
3 Chi. Bears, 1946-48
Baltimore, 1957-59
Oakland, 1967-69
St. Louis, 1999-2001
2 By many teams

Most Touchdowns, Season
75 New England, 2007
70 Miami, 1984
67 St. Louis, 2000

Fewest Touchdowns, Season (Since 1932)
3 Cincinnati, 1933
4 Cincinnati/St. Louis, 1934
5 Detroit, 1942

Most Touchdowns, Game
10 Rochester vs. *Fort Porter, Oct. 10, 1920
**Not a member of the American Professional Football Association*
Philadelphia vs. Cincinnati, Nov. 6, 1934
Los Angeles vs. Baltimore, Oct. 22, 1950
Washington vs. N.Y. Giants, Nov. 27, 1966
9 Rock Island vs. Evansville, Oct. 15, 1922
Akron vs. Oorang, Oct. 29, 1922
Racine vs. Louisville, Nov. 5, 1922
Chi. Cardinals vs. Rochester, Oct. 7, 1923
Chi. Cardinals vs. Milwaukee, Dec. 10, 1925
Chi. Cardinals vs. N.Y. Giants, Oct. 17, 1948
Chi. Cardinals vs. N.Y. Bulldogs, Nov. 13, 1949
Los Angeles vs. Detroit, Oct. 29, 1950
Pittsburgh vs. N.Y. Giants, Nov. 30, 1952
Chicago vs. San Francisco, Dec. 12, 1965
Chicago vs. Green Bay, Dec. 7, 1980
8 By many teams

Most Touchdowns, Both Teams, Game
16 Washington (10) vs. N.Y. Giants (6), Nov. 27, 1966
14 Chi. Cardinals (9) vs. N.Y. Giants (5), Oct. 17, 1948
Los Angeles (10) vs. Baltimore (4), Oct. 22, 1950
Houston (7) vs. Oakland (7), Dec. 22, 1963
13 New Orleans (7) vs. St. Louis (6), Nov. 2, 1969
Kansas City (7) vs. Seattle (6), Nov. 27, 1983 (ot)
San Diego (8) vs. Pittsburgh (5), Dec. 8, 1985
N.Y. Jets (7) vs. Miami (6), Sept. 21, 1986 (ot)
Cincinnati (7) vs. Cleveland (6), Nov. 28, 2004

Most Consecutive Games Scoring Touchdowns
166 Cleveland, 1957-1969
117 San Diego, 2002-09 (current)
111 Indianapolis, 2003-09 (current)

POINTS AFTER TOUCHDOWN

Most (One-Point) Points After Touchdown, Season
74 New England, 2007
66 Miami, 1984
65 Houston, 1961

Fewest (One-Point) Points After Touchdown, Season
2 Chi. Cardinals, 1933
3 Cincinnati, 1933
Pittsburgh, 1934
4 Cincinnati/St. Louis, 1934

Most (One-Point) Points After Touchdown, Game
10 Los Angeles vs. Baltimore, Oct. 22, 1950
9 Chi. Cardinals vs. N.Y. Giants, Oct. 17, 1948

Pittsburgh vs. N.Y. Giants, Nov. 30, 1952
Washington vs. N.Y. Giants, Nov. 27, 1966
8 By many teams

Most (One-Point) Points After Touchdown, Both Teams, Game
14 Chi. Cardinals (9) vs. N.Y. Giants (5), Oct. 17, 1948
Houston (7) vs. Oakland (7), Dec. 22, 1963
Washington (9) vs. N.Y. Giants (5), Nov. 27, 1966
13 Los Angeles (10) vs. Baltimore (3), Oct. 22, 1950
Cincinnati (7) vs. Cleveland (6), Nov. 28, 2004
12 In many games

Most Two-Point Conversions, Season
6 Miami, 1994
Minnesota, 1997
5 Arizona, 1995
Baltimore, 1996
Jacksonville, 1996
Chicago, 1997
San Francisco, 1998
Pittsburgh, 2002
4 By many teams

Most Two-Point Conversions, Game
4 St. Louis vs. Atlanta, Oct. 15, 2000
3 Baltimore vs. New England, Oct. 6, 1996
Pittsburgh vs. Tennessee, Nov. 1, 1998
2 By many teams

Most Two-Point Conversions, Both Teams, Game
5 Baltimore (3) vs. New England (2), Oct. 6, 1996
St. Louis (4) vs. Atlanta (1), Oct. 15, 2000
3 Seattle (2) vs. Kansas City (1), Oct. 23, 1994
Minnesota (2) vs. Seattle (1), Nov. 10, 1996
Pittsburgh (3) vs. Tennessee (0), Nov. 1, 1998
2 In many games

FIELD GOALS

Most Seasons Leading League, Field Goals
11 Green Bay, 1935-36, 1940-43, 1946-47, 1955, 1972, 1974
8 Washington, 1945, 1956, 1971, 1976-77, 1979, 1982, 1992
L.A./St. Louis Rams, 1949, 1951, 1958, 1966, 1973, 1978, 2003, 2006
N.Y. Giants, 1933, 1937, 1939, 1941, 1944, 1959, 1983, 2008
6 Boston/New England Patriots, 1961, 1963, 1964, 1986, 2004, 2008

Most Consecutive Seasons Leading League, Field Goals
4 Green Bay, 1940-43
3 Cleveland, 1952-54
2 By many teams

Most Field Goals Attempted, Season
49 Los Angeles, 1966
Washington, 1971
48 Green Bay, 1972
47 N.Y. Jets, 1969
Los Angeles, 1973
Washington, 1983

Fewest Field Goals Attempted, Season (Since 1938)
0 Chi. Bears, 1944
2 Cleveland, 1939
Card-Pitt, 1944
Boston, 1946
Chi. Bears, 1947
3 Chi. Bears, 1945
Cleveland, 1945

Most Field Goals Attempted, Game
9 St. Louis vs. Pittsburgh, Sept. 24, 1967
8 Pittsburgh vs. St. Louis, Dec. 2, 1962
Detroit vs. Minnesota, Nov. 13, 1966
N.Y. Jets vs. Buffalo, Nov. 3, 1968
Dallas vs. N.Y. Giants, Sept. 15, 2003 (ot)
Tennessee vs. Houston, Oct. 21, 2007
7 By many teams

Most Field Goals Attempted, Both Teams, Game
11 St. Louis (6) vs. Pittsburgh (5), Nov. 13, 1966
Washington (6) vs. Chicago (5), Nov. 14, 1971
Green Bay (6) vs. Detroit (5), Sept. 29, 1974
Washington (6) vs. N.Y. Giants (5), Nov. 14, 1976
10 In many games

Most Field Goals, Season
43 Arizona, 2005
39 Miami, 1999
St. Louis, 2003
37 Carolina, 1996
Indianapolis, 2003

Fewest Field Goals, Season (Since 1932)
0 Boston, 1932, 1935
Chi. Cardinals, 1932, 1945
Green Bay, 1932, 1944
N.Y. Giants, 1932
Brooklyn, 1944
Card-Pitt, 1944
Chi. Bears, 1944, 1947
Boston, 1946
Baltimore, 1950
Dallas, 1952

Most Field Goals, Game
8 Tennessee vs. Houston, Oct. 21, 2007
7 St. Louis vs. Pittsburgh, Sept. 24, 1967
Minnesota vs. L.A. Rams, Nov. 5, 1989 (ot)
Dallas vs. Green Bay, Nov. 18, 1996
Dallas vs. N.Y. Giants, Sept. 15, 2003 (ot)
Cincinnati vs. Baltimore, Nov. 11, 2007
6 By many teams

Most Field Goals, Both Teams, Game
9 San Diego (5) vs. Kansas City (4), Sept. 29, 1996
Miami (6) vs. New England (3), Oct. 17, 1999
Houston (5) vs. Miami (4), Oct. 7, 2007
8 Cleveland (4) vs. St. Louis (4), Sept. 20, 1964
Chicago (5) vs. Philadelphia (3), Oct. 20, 1968
Washington (5) vs. Chicago (3), Nov. 14, 1971
Kansas City (5) vs. Buffalo (3), Dec. 19, 1971
Detroit (4) vs. Green Bay (4), Sept. 29, 1974
Cleveland (5) vs. Denver (3), Oct. 19, 1975
New England (4) vs. San Diego (4), Nov. 9, 1975
San Francisco (6) vs. New Orleans (2), Oct. 16, 1983
Seattle (5) vs. L.A. Raiders (3), Dec. 18, 1988
Atlanta (6) vs. New Orleans (2), Nov. 13, 1994
Indianapolis (4) vs. San Diego (4), Nov. 3, 1996
Dallas (7) vs. N.Y. Giants (1), Sept. 15, 2003 (ot)
Oakland (5) vs. Chicago (3), Oct. 5, 2003
Buffalo (5) vs. Tennessee (3), Dec. 24, 2006
Tennessee (8) vs. Houston (0), Oct. 21, 2007
Buffalo (5) vs. Washington (3), Dec. 2, 2007
Kansas City (4) vs. Denver (4), Sept. 28, 2008
San Francisco (4) vs. Philadelphia (4), Oct. 12, 2008
Pittsburgh (4) vs. Cincinnati (4), Nov. 15, 2009
7 In many games

Most Consecutive Games Scoring Field Goals
38 Baltimore, 1999-2001
31 Minnesota, 1968-1970
28 Washington, 1988-1990

SAFETIES

Most Safeties, Season
4 Cleveland, 1927
Detroit, 1962
Seattle, 1993
San Francisco, 1996
Tennessee, 1999
3 By many teams

Most Safeties, Game

3 L.A. Rams vs. N.Y. Giants, Sept. 30, 1984
2 N.Y. Giants vs. Pottsville, Oct. 30, 1927
Chi. Bears vs. Pottsville, Nov. 13, 1927
Detroit vs. Brooklyn, Dec. 1, 1935
N.Y. Giants vs. Pittsburgh, Sept. 17, 1950
N.Y. Giants vs. Washington, Nov. 5, 1961
Chicago vs. Pittsburgh, Nov. 9, 1969
Dallas vs. Philadelphia, Nov. 19, 1972
Los Angeles vs. Green Bay, Oct. 21, 1973
Oakland vs. San Diego, Oct. 26, 1975
Denver vs. Seattle, Jan. 2, 1983
New Orleans vs. Cleveland, Sept. 13, 1987
Buffalo vs. Denver, Nov. 8, 1987
San Francisco vs. St. Louis, Sept. 8, 1996
Jacksonville vs. Pittsburgh, Oct. 3, 1999
Minnesota vs. Atlanta, Oct. 5, 2003
Dallas vs. Arizona, Oct. 5, 2003
Buffalo vs. Houston, Nov. 16, 2003
Minnesota vs. Green Bay, Nov. 9, 2008

Most Safeties, Both Teams, Game

3 L.A. Rams (3) vs. N.Y. Giants (0), Sept. 30, 1984
2 Chi. Cardinals (1) vs. Frankford (1), Nov. 19, 1927
Chi. Cardinals (1) vs. Cincinnati (1), Nov. 12, 1933
Chi. Bears (1) vs. San Francisco (1), Oct. 19, 1952
Cincinnati (1) vs. Los Angeles (1), Oct. 22, 1972
Chi. Bears (1) vs. San Francisco (1), Sept. 19, 1976
Baltimore (1) vs. Miami (1), Oct. 29, 1978
Atlanta (1) vs. Detroit (1), Oct. 5, 1980
Houston (1) vs. Philadelphia (1), Oct. 2, 1988
Cleveland (1) vs. Seattle (1), Nov. 14, 1993
Arizona (1) vs. Houston (1), Dec. 4, 1994
(Also see previous record)

FIRST DOWNS

Most Seasons Leading League

9 Chi. Bears, 1935, 1939, 1941, 1943, 1945, 1947-49, 1955
7 San Diego, 1965, 1969, 1980-83, 1985
L.A./St. Louis Rams, 1946, 1950-51, 1954, 1957, 1973, 2001
6 San Francisco, 1965, 1987, 1989, 1993-94, 1998
Baltimore/Indianapolis Colts, 1958-59, 1967, 2003, 2005-06

Most Consecutive Seasons Leading League

4 San Diego, 1980-83
3 Chi. Bears, 1947-49
New England, 2007-09
2 By many teams

Most First Downs, Season

398 Kansas City, 2004
393 New England, 2007
387 Miami, 1984

Fewest First Downs, Season

51 Cincinnati, 1933
64 Pittsburgh, 1935
67 Philadelphia, 1937

Most First Downs, Game

39 N.Y. Jets vs. Miami, Nov. 27, 1988
Washington vs. Detroit, Nov. 4, 1990 (ot)
38 Los Angeles vs. N.Y. Giants, Nov. 13, 1966
37 Green Bay vs. Philadelphia, Nov. 11, 1962

Fewest First Downs, Game

0 N.Y. Giants vs. Green Bay, Oct. 1, 1933
Pittsburgh vs. Boston, Oct. 29, 1933
Philadelphia vs. Detroit, Sept. 20, 1935
N.Y. Giants vs. Washington, Sept. 27, 1942
Denver vs. Houston, Sept. 3, 1966

Most First Downs, Both Teams, Game

64 Seattle (32) vs. Kansas City (32), Nov. 24, 2002
62 San Diego (32) vs. Seattle (30), Sept. 15, 1985
Oakland (31) vs. Kansas City (31), Nov. 5, 2000
59 Miami (31) vs. Buffalo (28), Oct. 9, 1983 (ot)
Seattle (33) vs. Kansas City (26), Nov. 27, 1983 (ot)
N.Y. Jets (32) vs. Miami (27), Sept. 21, 1986 (ot)
N.Y. Jets (39) vs. Miami (20), Nov. 27, 1988
Oakland (31) vs. San Francisco (28), Oct. 8, 2000 (ot)

Fewest First Downs, Both Teams, Game

7 Chi. Cardinals (2) vs. Detroit (5), Sept. 15, 1940
9 Pittsburgh (1) vs. Boston (8), Oct. 27, 1935
Boston (4) vs. Brooklyn (5), Nov. 24, 1935
N.Y. Giants (3) vs. Detroit (6), Nov. 7, 1943
Pittsburgh (4) vs. Chi. Cardinals (5), Nov. 11, 1945
N.Y. Bulldogs (1) vs. Philadelphia (8), Sept. 22, 1949
10 Philadelphia (4) vs. Brooklyn (6), Nov. 5, 1944
N.Y. Giants (4) vs. Washington (6), Dec. 11, 1960

Most First Downs, Rushing, Season

181 New England, 1978
177 Los Angeles, 1973
176 Chicago, 1985

Fewest First Downs, Rushing, Season

36 Cleveland, 1942
Boston, 1944
39 Brooklyn, 1943
40 Philadelphia, 1940
Detroit, 1945

Most First Downs, Rushing, Game

25 Philadelphia vs. Washington, Dec. 2, 1951
23 St. Louis vs. New Orleans, Oct. 5, 1980
21 Cleveland vs. Philadelphia, Dec. 13, 1959
Green Bay vs. Philadelphia, Nov. 11, 1962
Los Angeles vs. New Orleans, Nov. 25, 1973
Pittsburgh vs. Kansas City, Nov. 7, 1976
New England vs. Denver, Nov. 28, 1976
Oakland vs. Green Bay, Sept. 17, 1978
Buffalo vs. Washington, Nov. 3, 1996
San Francisco vs. Detroit, Dec. 14, 1998
Kansas City vs. Atlanta, Oct. 24, 2004

Fewest First Downs, Rushing, Game

0 By many teams. Last time:
Chicago vs. Minnesota, Nov. 29, 2009

Most First Downs, Rushing, Both Teams, Game

36 Philadelphia (25) vs. Washington (11), Dec. 2, 1951
31 Detroit (18) vs. Washington (13), Sept. 30, 1951
30 Los Angeles (17) vs. Minnesota (13), Nov. 5, 1961
New Orleans (17) vs. Green Bay (13), Sept. 9, 1979
New Orleans (16) vs. San Francisco (14), Nov. 11, 1979
New England (16) vs. Kansas City (14), Oct. 4, 1981
Indianapolis (18) vs. Denver (12), Sept. 30, 2007

Fewest First Downs, Rushing, Both Teams, Game

1 Oakland (0) vs. Tennessee (1), Sept. 7, 2003
Carolina (0) vs. Detroit (1), Oct. 16, 2005
2 Houston (0) vs. Denver (2), Dec. 2, 1962
N.Y. Jets, (1) vs. St. Louis (1), Dec. 3, 1995
Miami (1) vs. San Diego (1), Dec. 19, 1999
New Orleans (0) vs. Baltimore (2), Dec. 19, 1999
Baltimore (0) vs. Tennessee (2), Sept. 18, 2005
Pittsburgh (1) vs. Baltimore (1), Nov. 5, 2007
Arizona (1) vs. San Francisco (1), Sept. 13, 2009
3 In many games

Most First Downs, Passing, Season

259 San Diego, 1985
251 Houston, 1990
250 Miami, 1986

Fewest First Downs, Passing, Season

18 Pittsburgh, 1941
23 Brooklyn, 1942
N.Y. Giants, 1944
24 N.Y. Giants, 1943

Most First Downs, Passing, Game
29 N.Y. Giants vs. Cincinnati, Oct. 13, 1985
28 Tennessee vs. Oakland, Dec. 19, 2004
27 San Diego vs. Seattle, Sept. 15, 1985

Fewest First Downs, Passing, Game
0 By many teams. Last time:
Oakland vs. Atlanta, Nov. 2, 2008

Most First Downs, Passing, Both Teams, Game
43 San Diego (23) vs. Cincinnati (20), Dec. 20, 1982
Miami (24) vs. N.Y. Jets (19), Sept. 21, 1986 (ot)
Tennessee (28) vs. Oakland (15), Dec. 19, 2004
42 San Francisco (22) vs. San Diego (20), Dec. 11, 1982
Seattle (22) vs. Cleveland (20), Nov. 4, 2007 (ot)
41 San Diego (27) vs. Seattle (14), Sept. 15, 1985
Miami (26) vs. Cleveland (15), Dec. 12, 1988
Kansas City (23) vs. Oakland (18), Nov. 5, 2000

Fewest First Downs, Passing, Both Teams, Game
0 Brooklyn vs. Pittsburgh, Nov. 29, 1942
1 Green Bay (0) vs. Cleveland (1), Sept. 21, 1941
Pittsburgh (0) vs. Brooklyn (1), Oct. 11, 1942
N.Y. Giants (0) vs. Detroit (1), Nov. 7, 1943
Pittsburgh (0) vs. Chi. Cardinals (1), Nov. 11, 1945
N.Y. Bulldogs (0) vs. Philadelphia (1), Sept. 22, 1949
Chicago (0) vs. Buffalo (1), Oct. 7, 1979
2 In many games

Most First Downs, Penalty, Season
47 Buffalo, 2002
Indianapolis, 2004
44 Dallas, 2005
43 Denver, 1994

Fewest First Downs, Penalty, Season
2 Brooklyn, 1940
4 Chi. Cardinals, 1940
N.Y. Giants, 1942, 1944
Washington, 1944
Cleveland, 1952
Kansas City, 1969
5 Brooklyn, 1939
Chi. Bears, 1939
Detroit, 1953
Los Angeles, 1953
Houston, 1982

Most First Downs, Penalty, Game
11 Denver vs. Houston, Oct. 6, 1985
9 Chi. Bears vs. Cleveland, Nov. 25, 1951
Baltimore vs. Pittsburgh, Oct. 30, 1977
N.Y. Jets vs. Houston, Sept. 18, 1988
Dallas vs. Detroit, Nov. 20, 2005
8 Philadelphia vs. Detroit, Dec. 2, 1979
Cincinnati vs. N.Y. Jets, Oct. 6, 1985
Buffalo vs. Houston, Sept. 20, 1987
Houston vs. Atlanta, Sept. 9, 1990
Kansas City vs. L.A. Raiders, Oct. 3, 1993
San Francisco vs. New Orleans, Oct. 11, 1998
Oakland vs. San Francisco, Oct. 8, 2000 (ot)
Philadelphia vs. Chicago, Nov. 3, 2002
Detroit vs. Baltimore, Oct. 9, 2005

Most First Downs, Penalty, Both Teams, Game
12 Buffalo (7) vs. San Francisco (5), Oct. 4, 1998
Detroit (8) vs. Baltimore (4), Oct. 9, 2005
11 Chi. Bears (9) vs. Cleveland (2), Nov. 25, 1951
Cincinnati (8) vs. N.Y. Jets (3), Oct. 6, 1985
Denver (11) vs. Houston (0), Oct. 6, 1985
Detroit (6) vs. Dallas (5), Nov. 8, 1987
N.Y. Jets (9) vs. Houston (2), Sept. 18, 1988
Kansas City (8) vs. L.A. Raiders (3), Oct. 3, 1993
Detroit (6) vs. San Diego (5), Nov. 11, 1996
Philadelphia (8) vs. Chicago (3), Nov. 3, 2002
Arizona (6) vs. St. Louis (5), Dec. 3, 2006
Indianapolis (6) vs. Green Bay (5), Oct. 19, 2008
10 In many games

NET YARDS GAINED RUSHING AND PASSING

Most Seasons Leading League
12 Chi. Bears, 1932, 1934-35, 1939, 1941-44, 1947, 1949, 1955-56
9 L.A./St. Louis Rams, 1946, 1950-51, 1954, 1957, 1973, 1999-2001
7 San Diego, 1963, 1965, 1980-83, 1985

Most Consecutive Seasons Leading League
4 Chi. Bears, 1941-44
San Diego, 1980-83
3 Baltimore, 1958-1960
Houston, 1960-62
Oakland, 1968-1970
St. Louis, 1999-2001
2 By many teams

Most Yards Gained, Season
7,075 St. Louis, 2000
6,936 Miami, 1984
6,800 San Francisco, 1998

Fewest Yards Gained, Season
1,150 Cincinnati, 1933
1,443 Chi. Cardinals, 1934
1,486 Chi. Cardinals, 1933

Most Yards Gained, Game
735 Los Angeles vs. N.Y. Yanks, Sept. 28, 1951
683 Pittsburgh vs. Chi. Cardinals, Dec. 13, 1958
682 Chi. Bears vs. N.Y. Giants, Nov. 14, 1943

Fewest Yards Gained, Game
–7 Seattle vs. Los Angeles, Nov. 4, 1979
–5 Denver vs. Oakland, Sept. 10, 1967
14 Chi. Cardinals vs. Detroit, Sept. 15, 1940

Most Yards Gained, Both Teams, Game
1,133 Los Angeles (636) vs. N.Y. Yanks (497), Nov. 19, 1950
1.102 San Diego (661) vs. Cincinnati (441), Dec. 20, 1982
1,095 Kansas City (590) vs. Indianapolis (505), Oct. 31, 2004

Fewest Yards Gained, Both Teams, Game
30 Chi. Cardinals (14) vs. Detroit (16), Sept. 15, 1940
136 Chi. Cardinals (50) vs. Green Bay (86), Nov. 18, 1934
154 N.Y. Giants (51) vs. Washington (103), Dec. 11, 1960

Most Consecutive Games, 400 or More Yards Gained
11 San Diego, 1982-83
9 New England, 2006-07
8 St. Louis, 1999-2000

Most Consecutive Games, 300 or More Yards Gained
36 Minnesota, 2002-04
30 Minnesota, 1999-2000
St. Louis, 2000-02
29 Los Angeles, 1949-1951
New Orleans, 2008-09

RUSHING

Most Seasons Leading League
16 Chi. Bears, 1932, 1934-35, 1939-1942, 1951, 1955-56, 1968, 1977, 1983-86
7 Buffalo, 1962, 1964, 1973, 1975, 1982, 1991-92
6 Cleveland, 1958-59, 1963, 1965-67
San Francisco, 1952-54, 1987, 1998-99

Most Consecutive Seasons Leading League
4 Chi. Bears, 1939-1942
Chi. Bears, 1983-86
3 Detroit, 1936-38
San Francisco, 1952-54
Cleveland, 1965-67
Atlanta, 2004-06
2 By many teams

ATTEMPTS

Most Rushing Attempts, Season
681 Oakland, 1977
674 Chicago, 1984
671 New England, 1978

Fewest Rushing Attempts, Season
211 Philadelphia, 1982
219 San Francisco, 1982
225 Houston, 1982

Most Rushing Attempts, Game
72 Chi. Bears vs. Brooklyn, Oct. 20, 1935
70 Chi. Cardinals vs. Green Bay, Dec. 5, 1948
69 Chi. Cardinals vs. Green Bay, Dec. 6, 1936
Kansas City vs. Cincinnati, Sept. 3, 1978

Fewest Rushing Attempts, Game
6 Chi. Cardinals vs. Boston, Oct. 29, 1933
New England vs. Pittsburgh, Oct. 31, 2004
Arizona vs. Minnesota, Nov. 26, 2006
7 Oakland vs. Buffalo, Oct. 5, 1963
Houston vs. N.Y. Giants, Dec. 8, 1985
Seattle vs. L.A. Raiders, Nov. 17, 1991
Green Bay vs. Miami, Sept. 11, 1994
Detroit vs. Minnesota, Dec. 2, 2007
Arizona vs. Minnesota, Dec. 14, 2008
8 Denver vs. Oakland, Dec. 17, 1960
Buffalo vs. St. Louis, Sept. 9, 1984
Detroit vs. San Francisco, Oct. 20, 1991
Atlanta vs. Detroit, Sept. 5, 1993
St. Louis vs. San Francisco, Nov. 2, 2003
N.Y. Jets vs. Denver, Nov. 20, 2005
St. Louis vs. Carolina, Nov. 19, 2006
Detroit vs. Arizona, Nov. 11, 2007
San Diego vs. Pittsburgh, Oct. 4, 2009

Most Rushing Attempts, Both Teams, Game
108 Chi. Bears (70) vs. Green Bay (38), Dec. 5, 1948
105 Oakland (62) vs. Atlanta (43), Nov. 30, 1975 (ot)
104 Chi. Bears (64) vs. Pittsburgh (40), Oct. 18, 1936

Fewest Rushing Attempts, Both Teams, Game
16 Chi. Cardinals (6) vs. Boston (10), Oct. 22, 1933
30 Minnesota (15) vs. New England (15), Oct. 30, 2006
31 Green Bay (12) vs. Pittsburgh (19), Dec. 20, 2009

YARDS GAINED

Most Yards Gained Rushing, Season
3,165 New England, 1978
3,088 Buffalo, 1973
2,986 Kansas City, 1978

Fewest Yards Gained Rushing, Season
298 Philadelphia, 1940
467 Detroit, 1946
471 Boston, 1944

Most Yards Gained Rushing, Game
426 Detroit vs. Pittsburgh, Nov. 4, 1934
423 N.Y. Giants vs. Baltimore, Nov. 19, 1950
420 Boston vs. N.Y. Giants, Oct. 8, 1933

Fewest Yards Gained Rushing, Game
–53 Detroit vs. Chi. Cardinals, Oct. 17, 1943
–36 Philadelphia vs. Chi. Bears, Nov. 19, 1939
–33 Brooklyn vs. Phil-Pitt, Oct. 2, 1943

Most Yards Gained Rushing, Both Teams, Game
595 Los Angeles (371) vs. N.Y. Yankees (224), Nov. 18, 1951
574 Chi. Bears (396) vs. Pittsburgh (178), Oct. 10, 1934
558 Boston (420) vs. N.Y. Giants (138), Oct. 8, 1933

Fewest Yards Gained Rushing, Both Teams, Game
–15 Detroit (–53) vs. Chi. Cardinals (38), Oct. 17, 1943
4 Detroit (–10) vs. Chi. Cardinals (14), Sept. 15, 1940
45 San Diego (21) vs. Philadelphia (24), Oct. 23, 2005

AVERAGE GAIN

Highest Average Gain, Rushing, Season
5.74 Cleveland, 1963
5.65 San Francisco, 1954
5.56 San Diego, 1963

Lowest Average Gain, Rushing, Season
0.94 Philadelphia, 1940
1.45 Boston, 1944
1.55 Pittsburgh, 1935

TOUCHDOWNS

Most Touchdowns, Rushing, Season
36 Green Bay, 1962
33 Pittsburgh, 1976
32 Kansas City, 2003

Fewest Touchdowns, Rushing, Season
1 Brooklyn, 1934
2 Chi. Cardinals, 1933
Cincinnati, 1933
Pittsburgh, 1934
Philadelphia, 1935
Philadelphia, 1936
Philadelphia, 1937
Philadelphia, 1938
Pittsburgh, 1940
Philadelphia, 1972
N.Y. Jets, 1995
Arizona, 2005
3 By many teams

Most Touchdowns, Rushing, Game
9 Rock Island vs. Evansville, Oct. 15, 1922
Racine vs. Louisville, Nov. 5, 1922
8 Chi. Cardinals vs. Rochester, Oct. 7, 1923
Kansas City vs. Atlanta, Oct. 24, 2004
7 By many teams

Most Touchdowns, Rushing, Both Teams, Game
9 Rock Island (9) vs. Evansville (0), Oct. 15, 1922
Racine (9) vs. Louisville (0), Nov. 5, 1922
8 Chi. Cardinals (8) vs. Rochester (0), Oct. 7, 1923
Canton (7) vs. Cleveland (1), Nov. 25, 1923
Los Angeles (6) vs. N.Y. Yanks (2), Nov. 18, 1951
Chi. Bears (5) vs. Green Bay (3), Nov. 6, 1955
Denver (5) vs. Kansas City (3), Dec. 7, 2003
Kansas City (8) vs. Atlanta (0), Oct. 24, 2004
7 In many games

PASSING

ATTEMPTS

Most Passes Attempted, Season
709 Minnesota, 1981
699 New England, 1994
686 New England, 1995

Fewest Passes Attempted, Season
102 Cincinnati, 1933
106 Boston, 1933
120 Detroit, 1937

Most Passes Attempted, Game
70 New England vs. Minnesota, Nov. 13, 1994 (ot)
69 N.Y. Jets vs. Baltimore, Dec. 24, 2000
68 Houston vs. Buffalo, Nov 1, 1964
Cincinnati vs. Pittsburgh, Dec. 30, 2001 (ot)

Fewest Passes Attempted, Game
0 Green Bay vs. Portsmouth, Oct. 8, 1933
Detroit vs. Cleveland, Sept. 10, 1937
Pittsburgh vs. Brooklyn, Nov. 16, 1941
Pittsburgh vs. Los Angeles, Nov. 13, 1949
Cleveland vs. Philadelphia, Dec. 3, 1950

Most Passes Attempted, Both Teams, Game
112 New England (70) vs. Minnesota (42), Nov. 13, 1994 (ot)
104 Miami (55) vs. N.Y. Jets (49), Oct. 18. 1987 (ot)
N.Y. Jets (58) vs. San Francisco (46), Sept. 6, 1998 (ot)
103 Cincinnati (68) vs. Pittsburgh (35), Dec. 30, 2001 (ot)
Seattle (53) vs. San Diego (50), Dec. 29, 2002 (ot)

Fewest Passes Attempted, Both Teams, Game
4 Chi. Cardinals (1) vs. Detroit (3), Nov. 3, 1935
Detroit (0) vs. Cleveland (4), Sept. 10, 1937
6 Chi. Cardinals (2) vs. Detroit (4), Sept. 15, 1940
8 Brooklyn (2) vs. Philadelphia (6), Oct. 1, 1939

COMPLETIONS

Most Passes Completed, Season
440 New Orleans, 2007
432 San Francisco, 1995
419 Arizona, 2005

Fewest Passes Completed, Season
25 Cincinnati, 1933
33 Boston, 1933
34 Chi. Cardinals, 1934

Most Passes Completed, Game
45 New England vs. Minnesota, Nov. 13, 1994 (ot)
43 Washington vs. Detroit, Nov. 4, 1990 (ot)
Oakland vs. Pittsburgh, Sept. 15, 2002
42 N.Y. Jets vs. San Francisco, Sept. 21, 1980
N.Y. Jets vs. Seattle, Dec. 6, 1998

Fewest Passes Completed, Game
0 By many teams. Last time: Buffalo vs. N.Y. Jets, Sept. 29, 1974

Most Passes Completed, Both Teams, Game
71 New England (45) vs. Minnesota (26), Nov. 13, 1994 (ot)
68 San Francisco (37) vs. Atlanta (31), Oct. 6, 1985
Denver (34) vs. Oakland (34), Nov. 11, 2002
66 Cincinnati (40) vs. San Diego (26), Dec. 20, 1982
Indianapolis (34) vs. Houston (32), Nov. 8, 2009

Fewest Passes Completed, Both Teams, Game
1 Chi. Cardinals (0) vs. Philadelphia (1), Nov. 8, 1936
Detroit (0) vs. Cleveland (1), Sept. 10, 1937
Chi. Cardinals (0) vs. Detroit (1), Sept. 15, 1940
Brooklyn (0) vs. Pittsburgh (1), Nov. 29, 1942
2 Chi. Cardinals (0) vs. Detroit (2), Nov. 3, 1935
Buffalo (0) vs. N.Y. Jets (2), Sept. 29, 1974
Chi. Cardinals (0) vs. Green Bay (2), Nov. 18, 1934
3 In seven games

YARDS GAINED

Most Seasons Leading League, Passing Yardage
10 San Diego, 1965, 1968, 1971, 1978-1983, 1985
8 Chi. Bears, 1932, 1939, 1941, 1943, 1945, 1949, 1954, 1964
Washington, 1938, 1940, 1944, 1947-48, 1967, 1974, 1989
7 Houston, 1960-61, 1963-64, 1990-92
L.A./St. Louis Rams, 1946, 1950-51, 1956, 1999-2001
Balt./Indianapolis, 1957, 1959, 1960, 1963, 1976, 2003-04

Most Consecutive Seasons Leading League, Passing Yardage
6 San Diego, 1978-1983
4 Green Bay, 1934-37
3 Miami, 1986-88
Houston, 1990-92
St. Louis, 1999-2001

Most Yards Gained, Passing, Season
5,232 St. Louis, 2000
5,018 Miami, 1984
4,977 New Orleans, 2008

Fewest Yards Gained, Passing, Season
302 Chi. Cardinals, 1934
357 Cincinnati, 1933
459 Boston, 1934

Most Yards Gained Passing, Game
541 Los Angeles vs. N.Y. Yankees, Sept. 28, 1951
530 Minnesota vs. Baltimore, Sept. 28, 1969
521 Miami vs. N.Y. Jets, Oct. 23, 1988

Fewest Yards Gained, Passing, Game
–53 Denver vs. Oakland, Sept. 10, 1967
–52 Cincinnati vs. Houston, Oct. 31, 1971
–39 Atlanta vs. San Francisco, Oct. 23, 1976

Most Yards Gained, Passing, Both Teams, Game
884 N.Y. Jets (449) vs. Miami (435), Sept. 21, 1986 (ot)
883 San Diego (486) vs. Cincinnati (397), Dec. 20, 1982
874 Miami (456) vs. New England (418), Sept. 4, 1994

Fewest Yards Gained, Passing, Both Teams, Game
–11 Green Bay (–10) vs. Dallas (–1), Oct. 24, 1965
1 Chi. Cardinals (0) vs. Philadelphia (1), Nov. 8, 1936
7 Brooklyn (0) vs. Pittsburgh (7), Nov. 29, 1942

TIMES SACKED

Most Seasons Leading League, Fewest Times Sacked
10 Miami, 1973, 1982-1990
6 Indianapolis, 1999-2000, 2004-06, 2009
5 N.Y. Jets, 1965-66, 1968, 1993, 2000

Most Consecutive Seasons Leading League, Fewest Times Sacked
9 Miami, 1982-1990
3 St. Louis, 1974-76
Indianapolis, 2004-06
2 By many teams

Most Times Sacked, Season
104 Philadelphia, 1986
78 Arizona, 1997
76 Houston, 2002

Fewest Times Sacked, Season
7 Miami, 1988
8 San Francisco, 1970
St. Louis, 1975
9 N.Y. Jets, 1966
Washington, 1991

Most Times Sacked, Game
12 Pittsburgh vs. Dallas, Nov. 20, 1966
Baltimore vs. St. Louis, Oct. 26, 1980
Detroit vs. Chicago, Dec. 16, 1984
Houston vs. Dallas, Sept. 29, 1985
Philadelphia vs. N.Y. Giants, Sept. 30, 2007
11 St. Louis vs. N.Y. Giants, Nov. 1, 1964
Los Angeles vs. Baltimore, Nov. 22, 1964
Denver vs. Buffalo, Dec. 13, 1964
Green Bay vs. Detroit, Nov. 7, 1965
Buffalo vs. Oakland, Oct. 15, 1967
Denver vs. Oakland, Nov. 5, 1967
Atlanta vs. St. Louis, Nov. 24, 1968
Detroit vs. Dallas, Oct. 6, 1975
Philadelphia vs. St. Louis, Dec. 18, 1983
Cleveland vs. Kansas City, Sept. 30, 1984
Minnesota vs. Chicago, Oct. 28, 1984
Atlanta vs. Cleveland, Nov. 18, 1984
Dallas vs. San Diego, Nov. 16, 1986
Philadelphia vs. Detroit, Nov. 16, 1986
Philadelphia vs. L.A. Raiders, Nov. 30, 1986 (ot)
L.A. Raiders vs. Seattle, Dec. 8, 1986
N.Y. Jets vs. Dallas, Oct. 4, 1987
Philadelphia vs. Chicago, Oct. 4, 1987
Dallas vs. Philadelphia, Sept. 15, 1991
Cleveland vs. Indianapolis, Sept. 6, 1992
10 By many teams

Most Times Sacked, Both Teams, Game
18 Green Bay (10) vs. San Diego (8), Sept. 24, 1978
17 Buffalo (10) vs. N.Y. Titans (7), Nov. 23, 1961
Pittsburgh (12) vs. Dallas (5), Nov. 20, 1966
Atlanta (9) vs. Philadelphia (8), Dec. 16, 1984
Philadelphia (11) vs. L.A. Raiders (6), Nov. 30, 1986 (ot)
16 Los Angeles (11) vs. Baltimore (5), Nov. 22, 1964
Buffalo (11) vs. Oakland (5), Oct. 15, 1967

COMPLETION PERCENTAGE

Most Seasons Leading League, Completion Percentage
14 San Francisco, 1952, 1957-58, 1965, 1981, 1983, 1987, 1989, 1992-97
11 Washington, 1937, 1939-1940, 1942-45, 1947-48, 1969-1970
8 Green Bay, 1936, 1941, 1961-62, 1964, 1966, 1968, 1998

Most Consecutive Seasons Leading League, Completion Percentage
6 San Francisco, 1992-97
4 Washington, 1942-45
Kansas City, 1966-69
3 Cleveland, 1953-55
St. Louis, 1999-2001

Highest Completion Percentage, Season
70.65 Cincinnati, 1982 (310-219)
70.25 San Francisco, 1994 (511-359)
70.19 San Francisco, 1989 (483-339)

Lowest Completion Percentage, Season
22.9 Philadelphia, 1936 (170-39)
24.5 Cincinnati, 1933 (102-25)
25.0 Pittsburgh, 1941 (168-42)

TOUCHDOWNS

Most Touchdowns, Passing, Season
51 Indianapolis, 2004
50 New England, 2007
49 Miami, 1984

Fewest Touchdowns, Passing, Season
0 Cincinnati, 1933
Pittsburgh, 1945
1 Boston, 1932
Boston, 1933
Chi. Cardinals, 1934
Cincinnati/St. Louis, 1934
Detroit, 1942
2 Chi. Cardinals, 1932
Stapleton, 1932
Chi. Cardinals, 1935
Brooklyn, 1936
Pittsburgh, 1942

Most Touchdowns, Passing, Game
7 Chi. Bears vs. N.Y. Giants, Nov. 14, 1943
Philadelphia vs. Washington, Oct. 17, 1954
Houston vs. N.Y. Titans, Nov. 19, 1961
Houston vs. N.Y. Titans, Oct. 14, 1962
N.Y. Giants vs. Washington, Oct. 28, 1962
Minnesota vs. Baltimore, Sept. 28, 1969
San Diego vs. Oakland, Nov. 22, 1981
6 By many teams

Most Touchdowns, Passing, Both Teams, Game
12 New Orleans (6) vs. St. Louis (6), Nov. 2, 1969
11 N.Y. Giants (7) vs. Washington (4), Oct. 28, 1962
Oakland (6) vs. Houston (5), Dec. 22, 1963
Cincinnati (6) vs. Cleveland, (5), Sept. 16, 2007
10 San Diego (5) vs. Seattle (5), Sept. 15, 1985
Miami (6) vs. N.Y. Jets (4), Sept. 21, 1986 (ot)
San Francisco (6) vs. Atlanta (4), Oct. 14, 1990

PASSES HAD INTERCEPTED

Most Passes Had Intercepted, Season
48 Houston, 1962
45 Denver, 1961
41 Card-Pitt, 1944

Fewest Passes Had Intercepted, Season
5 Cleveland, 1960
Green Bay, 1966
Kansas City, 1990
N.Y. Giants, 1990
6 Green Bay, 1964
St. Louis, 1982
Dallas, 1993
Jacksonville, 2005
Washington, 2008
7 Los Angeles, 1969
Denver, 2005
Miami, 2008
Minnesota, 2009

Most Passes Had Intercepted, Game
9 Detroit vs. Green Bay, Oct. 24, 1943
Pittsburgh vs. Philadelphia, Dec. 12, 1965
8 Green Bay vs. N.Y. Giants, Nov. 21, 1948
Chi. Cardinals vs. Philadelphia, Sept. 24, 1950
N.Y. Yanks vs. N.Y. Giants, Dec. 16, 1951
Denver vs. Houston, Dec. 2, 1962
Chi. Bears vs. Detroit, Sept. 22, 1968
Baltimore vs. N.Y. Jets, Sept. 23, 1973
7 By many teams. Last time: Detroit vs. Cleveland, Sept. 23, 2001

Most Passes Had Intercepted, Both Teams, Game
13 Denver (8) vs. Houston (5), Dec. 2, 1962
11 Philadelphia (7) vs. Boston (4), Nov. 3, 1935
Boston (6) vs. Pittsburgh (5), Dec. 1, 1935
Cleveland (7) vs. Green Bay (4), Oct. 30, 1938
Green Bay (7) vs. Detroit (4), Oct. 20, 1940
Detroit (7) vs. Chi. Bears (4), Nov. 22, 1942
Detroit (7) vs. Cleveland (4), Nov. 26, 1944
Chi. Cardinals (8) vs. Philadelphia (3), Sept. 24, 1950
Washington (7) vs. N.Y. Giants (4), Dec. 8, 1963
Pittsburgh (9) vs. Philadelphia (2), Dec 12, 1965
10 In many games

PUNTING

Most Seasons Leading League (Average Distance)
8 Oakland, 1974-75, 1977-78, 2003-04, 2007, 2009
7 Denver 1962-64, 1966-67, 1982, 1999
6 Washington, 1940-43, 1945, 1958
Kansas City, 1968, 1971-73, 1979, 1984
L.A. Rams, 1946, 1949, 1955-56, 1994, 2008

Most Consecutive Seasons Leading League (Average Distance)
4 Washington, 1940-43
3 Cleveland, 1950-52
Denver, 1962-64
Kansas City, 1971-73

Most Punts, Season
116 Houston, 2002
114 Chicago, 1981
113 Boston, 1934
Brooklyn, 1934
Dallas, 2002

Fewest Punts, Season
23 San Diego, 1982
31 Cincinnati, 1982
32 Chi. Bears, 1941

Most Punts, Game
17 Chi. Bears vs. Green Bay, Oct. 22, 1933
Cincinnati vs. Pittsburgh, Oct. 22, 1933
16 Cincinnati vs. Portsmouth, Sept. 17, 1933

Chi. Cardinals vs. Chi. Bears, Nov. 30, 1933
Chi. Cardinals vs. Detroit, Sept. 15, 1940
Oakland vs. San Diego, Oct. 11, 1998
15 Chi. Cardinals vs. Cincinnati, Nov. 12, 1933
N.Y. Giants vs. Chi. Bears, Nov. 17, 1935
Philadelphia vs. N.Y. Giants, Dec. 6, 1987 (ot)

Fewest Punts, Game
0 By many teams. Last time:
Denver vs. Buffalo, Dec. 21, 2008
New Orleans vs. Detroit, Dec. 21, 2008

Most Punts, Both Teams, Game
31 Chi. Bears (17) vs. Green Bay (14), Oct. 22, 1933
Cincinnati (17), vs. Pittsburgh (14), Oct. 22, 1933
29 Chi. Cardinals (15) vs. Cincinnati (14), Nov. 12, 1933
Chi. Cardinals (16) vs. Chi. Bears (13), Nov. 30, 1933
Chi. Cardinals (16) vs. Detroit (13), Sept. 15, 1940
28 Philadelphia (14) vs. Washington (14), Nov. 5, 1939

Fewest Punts, Both Teams, Game
0 Buffalo vs. San Francisco, Sept. 13, 1992
1 Baltimore (0) vs. Cleveland (1), Nov. 1, 1959
Dall. Cowboys (0) vs. Cleveland (1), Dec. 3, 1961
Chicago (0) vs. Detroit (1), Oct. 1, 1972
San Francisco (0) vs. N.Y. Giants (1), Oct. 15, 1972
Green Bay (0) vs. Buffalo (1), Dec. 5, 1982
Miami (0) vs. Buffalo (1), Oct. 12, 1986
Green Bay (0) vs. Chicago (1), Dec. 17, 1989
Oakland (0) vs. Seattle (1), Dec. 5, 1999
Tampa Bay (0) vs. Minnesota (1), Oct. 29, 2000
New Orleans (0) vs. San Francisco (1), Oct. 20, 2002
2 In many games

AVERAGE YARDAGE

Highest Avg. Distance, Punting, Season
51.1 Oakland, 2009
49.6 St. Louis, 2008
49.1 Oakland, 2007

Lowest Average Distance, Punting, Season
32.7 Card-Pitt, 1944 (60-1,964)
33.8 Cincinnati, 1986 (59-1,996)
33.9 Detroit, 1969 (74-2,510)

PUNT RETURNS

Most Seasons Leading League (Average Return)
9 Detroit, 1943-45, 1951-52, 1962, 1966, 1969, 1991
7 Chi. Cardinals/St. Louis, 1948-49, 1955-56, 1959, 1986-87
6 Green Bay, 1950, 1953-54, 1961, 1972, 1996
Dallas/Kansas City, 1960, 1968, 1970, 1979-1980, 2003

Most Consecutive Seasons Leading League (Average Return)
3 Detroit, 1943-45
2 By many teams

Most Punt Returns, Season
71 Pittsburgh, 1976
Tampa Bay, 1979
L.A. Raiders, 1985
67 Pittsburgh, 1974
Los Angeles, 1978
L.A. Raiders, 1984
65 San Francisco, 1976

Fewest Punt Returns, Season
12 Baltimore, 1981
San Diego, 1982
14 Los Angeles, 1961
Philadelphia, 1962
Baltimore, 1982
15 Houston, 1960
Washington, 1960
Oakland, 1961
N.Y. Giants, 1969
Philadelphia, 1973
Kansas City, 1982

Most Punt Returns, Game
12 Philadelphia vs. Cleveland, Dec. 3, 1950
11 Chi. Bears vs. Chi. Cardinals, Oct. 8, 1950
Washington vs. Tampa Bay, Oct. 9, 1977
10 Philadelphia vs. N.Y. Giants, Nov. 26, 1950
Philadelphia vs. Tampa Bay, Sept. 18, 1977
Pittsburgh vs. Buffalo, Dec. 16, 1979
Washington vs. New Orleans, Dec. 26, 1982
Philadelphia vs. Seattle, Dec. 13, 1992 (ot)
New England vs. Pittsburgh, Dec. 5, 1993

Most Punt Returns, Both Teams, Game
17 Philadelphia (12) vs. Cleveland (5), Dec. 3, 1950
16 N.Y. Giants (9) vs. Philadelphia (7), Dec. 12, 1954
Washington (11) vs. Tampa Bay (5), Oct. 9, 1977
Oakland (8) vs. San Diego (8), Oct. 11, 1998
15 Detroit (8) vs. Cleveland (7), Sept. 27, 1942
Los Angeles (8) vs. Baltimore (7), Nov. 27, 1966
Pittsburgh (8) vs. Houston (7), Dec. 1, 1974
Philadelphia (10) vs. Tampa Bay (5), Sept. 18, 1977
Baltimore (9) vs. Kansas City (6), Sept. 2, 1979
Washington (10) vs. New Orleans (5), Dec. 26, 1982
L.A. Raiders (8) vs. Cleveland (7), Nov. 16, 1986
Indianapolis (34) vs. Houston (32), Nov. 8, 2009

FAIR CATCHES

Most Fair Catches, Season
34 Baltimore, 1971
33 Philadelphia, 2000
32 San Diego, 1969
Oakland, 2001

Fewest Fair Catches, Season
0 San Diego, 1975
New England, 1976
Tampa Bay, 1976
Pittsburgh, 1977
Dallas, 1982
1 Cleveland, 1974
San Francisco, 1975
Kansas City, 1976
St. Louis, 1976
San Diego, 1976
L.A. Rams, 1982
St. Louis, 1982
Tampa Bay, 1982
Arizona, 2001
2 By many teams

Most Fair Catches, Game
7 Minnesota vs. Dallas, Sept. 25, 1966
N.Y. Jets vs. Miami, Nov. 20, 1966
Detroit vs. Chicago, Nov. 21, 1976
Philadelphia vs. Buffalo, Dec. 27, 1987
Tennessee vs. Jacksonville, Nov. 16, 2008
6 By many teams

YARDS GAINED

Most Yards, Punt Returns, Season
875 Green Bay, 1996
785 L.A. Raiders, 1985
781 Chi. Bears, 1948

Fewest Yards, Punt Returns, Season
27 St. Louis, 1965
35 N.Y. Giants, 1965
37 New England, 1972

Most Yards, Punt Returns, Game
231 Detroit vs. San Francisco, Oct. 6, 1963
225 Oakland vs. Buffalo, Sept. 15, 1968
219 L.A. Rams vs. Atlanta, Oct. 11, 1981

Fewest Yards, Punt Returns, Game
-28 Washington vs. Dallas, Dec. 11, 1966
-23 N.Y. Giants vs. Buffalo, Oct. 20, 1975
Pittsburgh vs. Houston, Sept. 20, 1970
-20 New Orleans vs. Pittsburgh, Oct. 20, 1968

Most Yards, Punt Returns, Both Teams, Game
282 L.A. Rams (219) vs. Atlanta (63), Oct. 11, 1981
245 Detroit (231) vs. San Francisco (14), Oct. 6, 1963
244 Oakland (225) vs. Buffalo (19), Sept. 15, 1968

Fewest Yards, Punt Returns, Both Teams, Game
-18 Buffalo (-18) vs. Pittsburgh (0), Oct. 29, 1972
-14 Miami (-14) vs. Boston (0), Nov. 30, 1969
Tennessee (-14) vs. New Orleans (0), Sept. 21, 2003
-13 N.Y. Giants (-13) vs. Cleveland (0), Nov. 14, 1965

AVERAGE YARDS RETURNING PUNTS

Highest Average, Punt Returns, Season
20.2 Chi. Bears, 1941
19.1 Chi. Cardinals, 1948
18.2 Chi. Cardinals, 1949

Lowest Average, Punt Returns, Season
1.2 St. Louis, 1965 (23-27)
1.5 N.Y. Giants, 1965 (24-35)
1.7 Washington, 1970 (27-45)

TOUCHDOWNS RETURNING PUNTS

Most Touchdowns, Punt Returns, Season
5 Chi. Cardinals, 1959
4 Chi. Cardinals, 1948
Detroit, 1951
N.Y. Giants, 1951
Denver, 1976
Chicago, 2007
3 Washington, 1941
Detroit, 1952
Pittsburgh, 1952
Houston, 1975
Los Angeles, 1981
Cleveland, 1993
Green Bay, 1996
Denver, 1997
San Diego, 1997
Chicago, 2006
Tennessee, 2006
New Orleans, 2008
Oakland, 2008

Most Touchdowns, Punt Returns, Game
2 Detroit vs. Los Angeles, Oct. 14, 1951
Detroit vs. Green Bay, Nov. 22, 1951
Chi. Cardinals vs. Pittsburgh, Nov. 1, 1959
Chi. Cardinals vs. N.Y. Giants, Nov. 22, 1959
N.Y. Titans vs. Denver, Sept. 24, 1961
Denver vs. Cleveland, Sept. 26, 1976
Los Angeles vs. Atlanta, Oct. 11, 1981
St. Louis vs. Tampa Bay, Dec. 21, 1986
L.A. Rams vs. Atlanta, Dec. 27, 1992
Cleveland vs. Pittsburgh, Oct. 24, 1993
San Diego vs. Cincinnati, Nov. 2, 1997
Denver vs. Carolina, Nov. 9, 1997
Baltimore vs. Seattle, Dec. 7, 1997
Baltimore vs. N.Y. Jets, Dec. 24, 2000
Oakland vs. Tennessee, Sept. 29, 2002
Carolina vs. Cincinnati, Dec. 8, 2002
Detroit at Jacksonville, Nov. 14, 2004 (ot)
New Orleans vs. Minnesota, Oct. 6, 2008

Most Touchdowns, Punt Returns, Both Teams, Game
2 Philadelphia (1) vs. Washington (1), Nov. 9, 1952
Kansas City (1) vs. Buffalo (1), Sept. 11, 1966
Baltimore (1) vs. New England (1), Nov. 18, 1979
L.A. Raiders (1) vs. Philadelphia (1), Nov. 30, 1986 (ot)
Cincinnati (1) vs. Green Bay (1), Sept. 20, 1992
Oakland (1) vs. Seattle (1), Nov. 15, 1998
Atlanta (1) vs. Tennessee (1), Nov. 23, 2003
San Diego (1) vs. Denver (1), Oct. 19, 2009
(Also see previous record)

KICKOFF RETURNS

Most Seasons Leading League (Average Return)
8 Washington, 1942, 1947, 1962-63, 1973-74, 1981, 1995
6 Chicago Bears, 1943, 1948, 1958, 1966, 1972, 1985
N.Y. Giants, 1944, 1946, 1949, 1951, 1953, 2004
5 Green Bay, 1954, 1964, 1967, 1993, 1998
New England, 1977, 1980, 1982, 1997, 2006
Hou. Oilers/ Tenn. Titans, 1960, 1962-63, 1968, 2008

Most Consecutive Seasons Leading League (Average Return)
3 Denver, 1965-67
2 By many teams

Most Kickoff Returns, Season
96 Detroit, 2009
89 Cleveland, 1999
88 New Orleans, 1980

Fewest Kickoff Returns, Season
17 N.Y. Giants, 1944
20 N.Y. Giants, 1941, 1943
Chi. Bears, 1942
23 Washington, 1942

Most Kickoff Returns, Game
12 N.Y. Giants vs. Washington, Nov. 27, 1966
11 Kansas City vs. Buffalo, Nov. 23, 2008
10 By many teams

Most Kickoff Returns, Both Teams, Game
19 N.Y. Giants (12) vs. Washington (7), Nov. 27, 1966
Cleveland (10) vs. Cincinnati (9), Nov. 28, 2004
18 Houston (10) vs. Oakland (8), Dec. 22, 1963
17 Washington (9) vs. Green Bay (8), Oct. 17, 1983
San Diego (9) vs. Pittsburgh (8), Dec. 8, 1985
Detroit (9) vs. Green Bay (8), Nov. 27, 1986
L.A. Raiders (9) vs. Seattle (8), Dec. 18, 1988
Oakland (10) vs. Seattle (7), Oct. 26, 1997
Buffalo (9) vs. Minnesota (8), Sept. 15, 2002 (ot)
Cincinnati (10) vs. Cleveland (7), Sept. 16, 2007
Kansas City (11) vs. Buffalo (6), Nov. 23, 2008

YARDS GAINED

Most Yards, Kickoff Returns, Season
2,296 Arizona, 2000
2,173 Houston, 2005
2,050 Detroit, 2009

Fewest Yards, Kickoff Returns, Season
282 N.Y. Giants, 1940
381 Green Bay, 1940
424 Chicago, 1963

Most Yards, Kickoff Returns, Game
367 Baltimore vs. Minnesota, Dec. 13, 1998
362 Detroit vs. Los Angeles, Oct. 29, 1950
304 Chi. Bears vs. Green Bay, Nov. 9, 1952
New Orleans vs. L.A. Rams, Oct. 23, 1994

Most Yards, Kickoff Returns, Both Teams, Game
560 Detroit (362) vs. L.A. Rams (198), Oct. 29, 1950
511 Baltimore (367) vs. Minnesota (144), Dec. 13, 1998
501 New Orleans (304) vs. L.A. Rams (197), Oct. 23, 1994

AVERAGE YARDAGE

Highest Average, Kickoff Returns, Season
29.4 Chicago, 1972
28.9 Pittsburgh, 1952

28.2 Washington, 1962

Lowest Average, Kickoff Returns, Season
14.7 N.Y. Jets, 1993 (46-675)
15.8 N.Y. Giants, 1993 (32-507)
15.9 Tampa Bay, 1993 (58-922)

TOUCHDOWNS

Most Touchdowns, Kickoff Returns, Season
4 Green Bay, 1967
Chicago, 1970
Detroit, 1994
Houston, 2007
3 Los Angeles, 1950
Chi. Cardinals, 1954
San Francisco, 1963
Denver, 1966
Chicago, 1967
New England, 1977
L.A. Rams, 1985
Atlanta, 2000
Buffalo, 2004
N.Y. Jets, 2007
Cleveland, 2009
2 By many teams

Most Touchdowns, Kickoff Returns, Game
2 Chi. Bears vs. Green Bay, Sept. 22, 1940
Chi. Bears vs. Green Bay, Nov. 9, 1952
Philadelphia vs. Dallas, Nov. 6, 1966
Green Bay vs. Cleveland, Nov. 12, 1967
L.A. Rams vs. Green Bay, Nov. 24, 1985
New Orleans vs. L.A. Rams, Oct. 23, 1994
Baltimore vs. Minnesota, Dec. 13, 1998
N.Y. Jets vs. Buffalo, Sept. 8, 2002 (ot)
Chicago vs. St. Louis, Dec. 11, 2006
Houston vs. Jacksonville, Dec. 30, 2007
Miami vs. N.Y. Jets, Nov. 1, 2009
Cleveland vs. Kansas City, Dec. 20, 2009

Most Touchdowns, Kickoff Returns, Both Teams, Game
3 Baltimore (2) vs. Minnesota (1), Dec. 13, 1998
2 In many games

FUMBLES

Most Fumbles, Season
56 Chi. Bears, 1938
San Francisco, 1978
54 Philadelphia, 1946
51 New England, 1973

Fewest Fumbles, Season
7 Kansas City, 2002
8 Cleveland, 1959
10 Indianapolis, 1998
Minnesota, 1998

Most Fumbles, Game
10 Phil-Pitt vs. N.Y. Giants, Oct. 9, 1943
Detroit vs. Minnesota, Nov. 12, 1967
Kansas City vs. Houston, Oct. 12, 1969
San Francisco vs. Detroit, Dec. 17, 1978
9 Philadelphia vs. Green Bay, Oct. 13, 1946
Boston at Oakland, Dec. 16, 1962
Kansas City vs. San Diego, Nov. 15, 1964
N.Y. Giants vs. Buffalo, Oct. 20, 1975
St. Louis vs. Washington, Oct. 25, 1976
San Diego vs. Green Bay, Sept. 24, 1978
Pittsburgh vs. Cincinnati, Oct. 14, 1979
Cleveland vs. Seattle, Dec. 20, 1981
Cleveland vs. Pittsburgh, Dec. 23, 1990
Oakland vs. Seattle, Dec. 22, 1996
8 By many teams

Most Fumbles, Both Teams, Game
14 Chi. Bears (7) vs. Cleveland (7), Nov. 24, 1940
St. Louis (8) vs. N.Y. Giants (6), Sept. 17, 1961
Kansas City (10) vs. Houston (4), Oct. 12, 1969
13 Washington (8) vs. Pittsburgh (5), Nov. 14, 1937
Philadelphia (7) vs. Boston (6), Dec. 8, 1946
N.Y. Giants (7) vs. Washington (6), Nov. 5, 1950
Kansas City (9) vs. San Diego (4), Nov. 15, 1964
Buffalo (7) vs. Denver (6), Dec. 13, 1964
N.Y. Jets (7) vs. Houston (6), Sept. 12, 1965
Cleveland (7) vs. New Orleans (6), Dec. 12, 1971
Houston (8) vs. Pittsburgh (5), Dec. 9, 1973
St. Louis (9) vs. Washington (4), Oct. 25, 1976
Cleveland (9) vs. Seattle (4), Dec. 20, 1981
Green Bay (7) vs. Detroit (6), Oct. 6, 1985
12 In many games

FUMBLES LOST

Most Fumbles Lost, Season
36 Chi. Cardinals, 1959
31 Green Bay, 1952
29 Chi. Cardinals, 1946
Pittsburgh, 1950
Cleveland, 1978

Fewest Fumbles Lost, Season
2 Kansas City, 2002
3 Philadelphia, 1938
Minnesota, 1980
N.Y. Giants, 2008
4 San Francisco, 1960
Kansas City, 1982
Minnesota, 1998
Detroit, 2003

Most Fumbles Lost, Game
8 St. Louis vs. Washington, Oct. 25, 1976
Cleveland vs. Pittsburgh, Dec. 23, 1990
7 Cincinnati vs. Buffalo, Nov. 30, 1969
Pittsburgh vs. Cincinnati, Oct. 14, 1979
Cleveland vs. Seattle, Dec. 20, 1981
6 By many teams

FUMBLES RECOVERED

Most Fumbles Recovered, Season, Own and Opponents'
58 Minnesota, 1963 (27 own, 31 opp)
51 Chi. Bears, 1938 (37 own, 14 opp)
San Francisco, 1978 (24 own, 27 opp)
50 Philadelphia, 1987 (23 own, 27 opp)

Fewest Fumbles Recovered, Season, Own and Opponents'
9 San Francisco, 1982 (5 own, 4 opp)
10 Jacksonville, 2006 (6 own, 4 opp)
11 Cincinnati, 1982 (5 own, 6 opp)
Denver, 2008 (4 own, 7 opp)
Washington, 2008 (6 own, 5 opp)

Most Fumbles Recovered, Game, Own and Opponents'
10 Denver vs. Buffalo, Dec. 13, 1964 (5 own, 5 opp)
Pittsburgh vs. Houston, Dec. 9, 1973 (5 own, 5 opp)
Washington vs. St. Louis, Oct. 25, 1976 (2 own, 8 opp)
9 St. Louis vs. N.Y. Giants, Sept. 17, 1961 (6 own, 3 opp)
Houston vs. Cincinnati, Oct. 27, 1974 (4 own, 5 opp)
Kansas City vs. Dallas, Nov. 10, 1975 (4 own, 5 opp)
Green Bay vs. Detroit, Oct. 6, 1985 (5 own, 4 opp)
Pittsburgh vs. Cleveland, Dec. 23, 1990 (1 own, 8 opp)
8 By many teams

Most Own Fumbles Recovered, Season
37 Chi. Bears, 1938
28 Pittsburgh, 1987
27 Philadelphia, 1946
Minnesota, 1963

Fewest Own Fumbles Recovered, Season
1 Indianapolis, 2006
Philadelphia, 2008
2 Washington, 1958
Miami, 2000
3 Detroit, 1956
Cleveland, 1959
Houston, 1982
New Orleans, 2005

Most Opponents' Fumbles Recovered, Season
31 Minnesota, 1963
29 Cleveland, 1951
28 Green Bay, 1946
Houston, 1977
Seattle, 1983

Fewest Opponents' Fumbles Recovered, Season
3 Los Angeles, 1974
Green Bay, 1995
4 Philadelphia, 1944
San Francisco, 1982
Jacksonville, 2006
Jacksonville, 2008
5 Baltimore, 1982
Arizona, 1997
Baltimore, 1998
Chicago, 2003
Oakland, 2006
N.Y. Giants, 2008
Washington, 2008
Buffalo, 2009

Most Opponents' Fumbles Recovered, Game
8 Washington vs. St. Louis, Oct. 25, 1976
Pittsburgh vs. Cleveland, Dec. 23, 1990
7 Buffalo vs. Cincinnati, Nov. 30, 1969
Cincinnati vs. Pittsburgh, Oct. 14, 1979
Seattle vs. Cleveland, Dec. 20, 1981
6 By many teams

TOUCHDOWNS

Most Touchdowns, Fumbles Recovered, Season, Own and Opponents'
5 Chi. Bears, 1942 (1 own, 4 opp)
Los Angeles, 1952 (1 own, 4 opp)
San Francisco, 1965 (1 own, 4 opp)
Oakland, 1978 (2 own, 3 opp)
4 Chi. Bears, 1948 (1 own, 3 opp)
Boston, 1948 (4 opp)
Denver, 1979 (1 own, 3 opp)
Atlanta, 1981 (1 own, 3 opp)
Denver, 1984 (4 opp)
St. Louis, 1987 (4 opp)
Minnesota, 1989 (4 opp)
Atlanta, 1991 (4 opp)
Philadelphia, 1995 (4 opp)
Atlanta, 1998 (4 opp)
New Orleans, 1998 (4 opp)
Kansas City, 1999 (4 opp)
3 By many teams

Most Touchdowns, Own Fumbles Recovered, Season
2 Chi. Bears, 1953
New England, 1973
Buffalo, 1974
Denver, 1975
Oakland, 1978
Green Bay, 1982
New Orleans, 1983
Cleveland, 1986
Green Bay, 1989
Miami, 1996
Buffalo, 2000
Philadelphia, 2007

Most Touchdowns, Opponents' Fumbles Recovered, Season
4 Detroit, 1937
Chi. Bears, 1942
Boston, 1948
Los Angeles, 1952
San Francisco, 1965
Denver, 1984
St. Louis, 1987
Minnesota, 1989
Atlanta, 1991
Philadelphia, 1995
Atlanta, 1998
New Orleans, 1998
Kansas City, 1999
3 By many teams

Most Touchdowns, Fumbles Recovered, Game, Own and Opponents'
2 By many teams

Most Touchdowns, Fumbles Recovered, Game, Both Teams, Own and Opponents'
3 Detroit (2) vs. Minnesota (1), Dec. 9, 1962 (2 own, 1 opp)
Green Bay (2) vs. Dallas (1), Nov. 29, 1964 (3 opp)
Oakland (2) vs. Buffalo (1), Dec. 24, 1967 (3 opp)
Oakland (2) vs. Philadelphia (1), Sept. 24, 1995 (3 opp)
Tennessee (2) vs. Pittsburgh (1), Jan. 2, 2000 (3 opp)

Most Touchdowns, Own Fumbles Recovered, Game
2 Miami vs. New England, Sept.1, 1996

Most Touchdowns, Opponents' Fumbles Recovered, Game
2 Many times. Last time:
San Francisco vs. St. Louis, Oct. 4, 2009

Most Touchdowns, Opponents' Fumbles Recovered, Game, Both Teams
3 Green Bay (2) vs. Dallas (1), Nov. 29, 1964
Oakland (2) vs. Buffalo (1), Dec. 24, 1967
Oakland (2) vs. Philadelphia (1), Sept. 24, 1995
Tennessee (2) vs. Pittsburgh (1), Jan. 2, 2000

TURNOVERS

(Number of times losing the ball on interceptions and fumbles.)

Most Turnovers, Season
65 Denver, 1961
63 San Francisco, 1978
58 Chi. Bears, 1947
Pittsburgh, 1950
N.Y. Giants, 1983

Fewest Turnovers, Season
12 Kansas City, 1982
13 Miami, 2008
N.Y. Giants, 2008
14 N.Y. Giants, 1943
Cleveland, 1959
N.Y. Giants, 1990

Most Turnovers, Game
12 Detroit vs. Chi. Bears, Nov. 22, 1942
Chi. Cardinals vs. Philadelphia, Sept. 24, 1950
Pittsburgh vs. Philadelphia, Dec. 12, 1965
11 San Diego vs. Green Bay, Sept. 24, 1978
10 Washington vs. N.Y. Giants, Dec. 4, 1938
Pittsburgh vs. Green Bay, Nov. 23, 1941
Detroit vs. Green Bay, Oct. 24, 1943
Chi. Cardinals vs. Green Bay, Nov. 10, 1946
Chi. Cardinals vs. N.Y. Giants, Nov. 2, 1952
Minnesota vs. Detroit, Dec. 9, 1962
Houston vs. Oakland, Sept. 7, 1963
Washington vs. N.Y. Giants, Dec. 8, 1963
Chicago vs. Detroit, Sept. 22, 1968

St. Louis vs. Washington, Oct. 25, 1976
N.Y. Jets vs. New England, Nov. 21, 1976
San Francisco vs. Dallas, Oct. 12, 1980
Cleveland vs. Seattle, Dec. 20, 1981
Detroit vs. Denver, Oct. 7, 1984

Most Turnovers, Both Teams, Game
17 Detroit (12) vs. Chi. Bears (5), Nov. 22, 1942
Boston (9) vs. Philadelphia (8), Dec. 8, 1946
16 Chi. Cardinals (12) vs. Philadelphia (4), Sept. 24, 1950
Chi. Cardinals (8) vs. Chi. Bears (8), Dec. 7, 1958
Minnesota (10) vs. Detroit (6), Dec. 9, 1962
Houston (9) vs. Kansas City (7), Oct. 12, 1969
15 Philadelphia (8) vs. Chi. Cardinals (7), Oct. 3, 1954
Denver (9) vs. Houston (6), Dec. 2, 1962
Washington (10) vs. N.Y. Giants (5), Dec. 8, 1963
St. Louis (9) vs. Kansas City (6), Oct. 2, 1983

PENALTIES

Most Seasons Leading League, Fewest Penalties
13 Miami, 1968, 1976-1984, 1986, 1990-91
9 Pittsburgh, 1946-47, 1950-52, 1954, 1963, 1965, 1968
8 Boston/New England, 1962, 1964-65, 1973, 1987, 1989, 1993, 2008

Most Consecutive Seasons Leading League, Fewest Penalties
9 Miami, 1976-1984
3 Pittsburgh, 1950-52
2 By many teams

Most Seasons Leading League, Most Penalties
16 Chi. Bears, 1941-44, 1946-49, 1951, 1959-1961, 1963, 1965, 1968, 1976
15 Oakland/L.A. Raiders, 1963, 1966, 1968-69, 1975, 1982, 1984, 1991, 1993-96, 2003-05
7 L.A./St. Louis Rams, 1950, 1952, 1962, 1969, 1978, 1980, 1997

Most Consecutive Seasons Leading League, Most Penalties
4 Chi. Bears, 1941-44, 1946-49
Oakland/L.A. Raiders, 1993-96
3 Chi. Cardinals, 1954-56
Chi. Bears, 1959-1961
Oakland, 2003-05

Fewest Penalties, Season
19 Detroit, 1937
21 Boston, 1935
24 Philadelphia, 1936

Most Penalties, Season
158 Kansas City, 1998
156 L.A. Raiders, 1994
Oakland, 1996
149 Houston, 1989

Fewest Penalties, Game
0 By many teams. Last time:
New England vs. New Orleans, Nov. 30, 2009

Most Penalties, Game
22 Brooklyn vs. Green Bay, Sept. 17, 1944
Chi. Bears vs. Philadelphia, Nov. 26, 1944
San Francisco vs. Buffalo, Oct. 4, 1998
21 Cleveland vs. Chi. Bears, Nov. 25, 1951
Baltimore vs. Detroit, Oct. 9, 2005
20 Tampa Bay vs. Seattle, Oct. 17, 1976
Oakland vs. Denver, Dec. 15, 1996

Fewest Penalties, Both Teams, Game
0 Brooklyn vs. Pittsburgh, Oct. 28, 1934
Brooklyn vs. Boston, Sept. 28, 1936
Cleveland vs. Chi. Bears, Oct. 9, 1938
Pittsburgh vs. Philadelphia, Nov. 10, 1940

Most Penalties, Both Teams, Game
37 Cleveland (21) vs. Chi. Bears (16), Nov. 25, 1951
35 Tampa Bay (20) vs. Seattle (15), Oct. 17, 1976
34 San Francisco (22) vs. Buffalo (12), Oct. 4, 1998

YARDS PENALIZED

Most Seasons Leading League, Fewest Yards Penalized
13 Miami, 1967-68, 1973, 1977-1984, 1990-91
10 Boston/Washington, 1935, 1953-54, 1956-58, 1970, 1985, 1995, 1997
8 Boston/New England, 1962, 1964-66, 1987, 1989, 1993, 2008

Most Consecutive Seasons Leading League, Fewest Yards Penalized
8 Miami, 1977-1984
3 Washington, 1956-58
Boston, 1964-66
2 By many teams

Most Seasons Leading League, Most Yards Penalized
15 Chi. Bears, 1935, 1937, 1939-1944, 1946-47, 1949, 1951, 1961-62, 1968
12 Oakland/L.A. Raiders, 1963-64, 1968-69, 1975, 1982, 1984, 1991, 1993-94, 1996, 2003
6 Buffalo, 1962, 1967, 1970, 1972, 1981, 1983
Houston, 1961, 1985-86, 1988-1990

Most Consecutive Seasons Leading League, Most Yards Penalized
6 Chi. Bears, 1939-1944
3 Houston, 1988-1990
2 By many teams

Fewest Yards Penalized, Season
139 Detroit, 1937
146 Philadelphia, 1937
159 Philadelphia, 1936

Most Yards Penalized, Season
1,304 Kansas City, 1998
1,274 Oakland, 1969
1,266 Oakland, 1996

Fewest Yards Penalized, Game
0 By many teams. Last time:
New England vs. New Orleans, Nov. 30, 2009

Most Yards Penalized, Game
212 Tennessee vs. Baltimore, Oct. 10, 1999
209 Cleveland vs. Chi. Bears, Nov. 25, 1951
191 Philadelphia vs. Seattle, Dec. 13, 1992 (ot)

Fewest Yards Penalized, Both Teams, Game
0 Brooklyn vs. Pittsburgh, Oct. 28, 1934
Brooklyn vs. Boston, Sept. 28, 1936
Cleveland vs. Chi. Bears, Oct. 9, 1938
Pittsburgh vs. Philadelphia, Nov. 10, 1940

Most Yards Penalized, Both Teams, Game
374 Cleveland (209) vs. Chi. Bears (165), Nov. 25, 1951
310 Tampa Bay (190) vs. Seattle (120), Oct. 17, 1976
Green Bay (175) vs. Baltimore (135), Dec. 7, 2009
309 Green Bay (184) vs. Boston (125), Oct. 21, 1945

DEFENSE

SCORING

Most Seasons Leading League, Fewest Points Allowed
11 N.Y. Giants, 1927, 1935, 1938-39, 1941, 1944, 1958-59, 1961, 1990, 1993
Chi. Bears, 1932, 1936-37, 1942, 1948, 1963, 1985-86, 1988, 2001, 2005
7 Cleveland, 1951, 1953-57, 1994
Green Bay, 1929, 1935, 1947, 1962, 1965-66, 1996
6 Dallas/Kansas City, 1960, 1962, 1968-69, 1995, 1997

Most Consecutive Seasons Leading League, Fewest Points Allowed
5 Cleveland, 1953-57
3 Buffalo, 1964-66
Minnesota, 1969-1971

2 By many teams

Fewest Points Allowed, Season (Since 1932)

44 Chi. Bears, 1932
54 Brooklyn, 1933
59 Detroit, 1934

Most Points Allowed, Season

533 Baltimore, 1981
517 Detroit, 2008
501 N.Y. Giants, 1966

Fewest TDs Allowed, Season (Since 1932)

6 Chi. Bears, 1932
Brooklyn, 1933
7 Detroit, 1934
8 Green Bay, 1932
9 St. Louis, 1934
N.Y. Giants, 1939
N.Y. Giants, 1944

Most Touchdowns Allowed, Season

68 Baltimore, 1981
66 N.Y. Giants, 1966
63 Baltimore, 1950
Detroit, 2008

FIRST DOWNS

Fewest First Downs Allowed, Season

77 Detroit, 1935
79 Boston, 1935
82 Washington, 1937

Most First Downs Allowed, Season

406 Baltimore, 1981
371 Seattle, 1981
368 Cleveland, 1999

Fewest First Downs Allowed, Rushing, Season

35 Chi. Bears, 1942
40 Green Bay, 1939
41 Brooklyn, 1944

Most First Downs Allowed, Rushing, Season

179 Detroit, 1985
178 New Orleans, 1980
175 Seattle, 1981

Fewest First Downs Allowed, Passing, Season

33 Chi. Bears, 1943
34 Pittsburgh, 1941
Washington, 1943
35 Detroit, 1940
Philadelphia, 1940
Philadelphia, 1944

Most First Downs Allowed, Passing, Season

230 Atlanta, 1995
227 Kansas City, 2002
222 Minnesota, 2007

Fewest First Downs Allowed, Penalty, Season

1 Boston, 1944
3 Philadelphia, 1940
Pittsburgh, 1945
Washington, 1957
4 Cleveland, 1940
Green Bay, 1943
N.Y. Giants, 1943

Most First Downs Allowed, Penalty, Season

56 Kansas City, 1998
48 Houston, 1985
46 Houston, 1986

NET YARDS ALLOWED RUSHING AND PASSING

Most Seasons Leading League, Fewest Yards Allowed

8 Chi. Bears, 1942-43, 1948, 1958, 1963, 1984-86
Pittsburgh, 1957, 1974, 1976, 1990, 2001, 2004, 2007-08
6 N.Y. Giants, 1938, 1940-41, 1951, 1956, 1959
Philadelphia, 1944-45, 1949, 1953, 1981, 1991
Minnesota, 1969-1970, 1975, 1988-89, 1993

Most Consecutive Seasons Leading League, Fewest Yards Allowed

3 Boston/Washington, 1935-37
Chicago, 1984-86
2 By many teams

Fewest Yards Allowed, Season

1,539 Chi. Cardinals, 1934
1,703 Chi. Bears, 1942
1,789 Brooklyn, 1933

Most Yards Allowed, Season

6,793 Baltimore, 1981
6,470 Detroit, 2008
6,403 Green Bay, 1983

RUSHING

Most Seasons Leading League, Fewest Yards Allowed

10 Chi. Bears, 1937, 1939, 1942, 1946, 1949, 1963, 1984-85, 1987-88
7 Detroit, 1938, 1950, 1952, 1962, 1970, 1980-81
Philadelphia, 1944-45, 1947-48, 1953, 1990-91
Dallas, 1966-69, 1972, 1978, 1992
Pittsburgh, 1961, 1976, 1982, 1997, 2001-02, 2004
5 N.Y. Giants, 1940, 1951, 1956, 1959, 1986
L.A./St. Louis Rams, 1964-65, 1973-74, 1999
Minnesota, 1975, 1994, 2006-08

Most Consecutive Seasons Leading League, Fewest Yards Allowed

4 Dallas, 1966-69
3 Minnesota, 2006-08
2 By many teams

Fewest Yards Allowed, Rushing, Season

519 Chi. Bears, 1942
558 Philadelphia, 1944
762 Pittsburgh, 1982

Most Yards Allowed, Rushing, Season

3,228 Buffalo, 1978
3,106 New Orleans, 1980
3,010 Baltimore, 1978

Fewest Touchdowns Allowed, Rushing, Season

2 Detroit, 1934
N.Y. Giants, 1944
Dallas, 1968
Minnesota, 1971
3 By many teams

Most Touchdowns Allowed, Rushing, Season

36 Oakland, 1961
31 N.Y. Giants, 1980
Tampa Bay, 1986
Detroit, 2008
30 Baltimore, 1981

PASSING

Most Seasons Leading League, Fewest Yards Allowed

10 Green Bay, 1947-48, 1962, 1964-68, 1996, 2005
7 Washington, 1939, 1942, 1945, 1952-53, 1980, 1985
Philadelphia 1934, 1936, 1940, 1949, 1981, 1991, 1998
Pittsburgh, 1941, 1946, 1951, 1955, 1974, 1990, 2008
6 Chi. Bears, 1938, 1943-44, 1958, 1960, 1963
Minnesota, 1969-1970, 1972, 1975-76, 1989

Most Consecutive Seasons Leading League, Fewest Yards Allowed

5 Green Bay, 1964-68
2 By many teams

Fewest Yards Allowed Passing, Season

545 Philadelphia, 1934

558 Portsmouth, 1933
585 Chi. Cardinals, 1934

Most Yards Allowed, Passing, Season
4,541 Atlanta, 1995
4.427 San Francisco, 2005
4,389 N.Y. Jets, 1986

Fewest Touchdowns Allowed, Passing, Season
1 Portsmouth, 1932
Philadelphia, 1934
2 Brooklyn, 1933
Chi. Bears, 1934
3 Chi. Bears, 1932
Green Bay, 1932
Green Bay, 1934
Chi. Bears, 1936
New York, 1939
New York, 1944

Most Touchdowns Allowed, Passing, Season
40 Denver, 1963
38 St. Louis, 1969
37 Washington, 1961
Baltimore, 1981

SACKS

Most Seasons Leading League
5 Oakland/L.A. Raiders, 1966-68, 1982, 1986
Dallas, 1966, 1968-69, 1978, 2008
4 New England/Boston, 1961, 1963, 1977, 1979
Dallas/Kansas City, 1960, 1965, 1969, 1990
L.A./St. Louis Rams, 1968, 1970, 1988, 1999
N.Y. Giants, 1963, 1985, 1998, 2007
3 San Francisco, 1967, 1972, 1976
N.Y. Giants, 1963, 1985, 1998
New Orleans, 1992, 1997, 2000
Pittsburgh, 1974, 1994, 2001
San Diego, 1962, 1980, 2006

Most Consecutive Seasons Leading League
3 Oakland, 1966-68
2 Dallas, 1968-69

Most Sacks, Season
72 Chicago, 1984
71 Minnesota, 1989
70 Chicago, 1987

Fewest Sacks, Season
10 Kansas City, 2008
11 Baltimore, 1982
12 Buffalo, 1982

Most Sacks, Game
12 Dallas vs. Pittsburgh, Nov. 20, 1966
St. Louis vs. Baltimore, Oct. 26, 1980
Chicago vs. Detroit, Dec. 16, 1984
Dallas vs. Houston, Sept. 29, 1985
N.Y. Giants vs. Philadelphia, Sept. 30, 2007
11 N.Y. Giants vs. St. Louis, Nov. 1, 1964
Baltimore vs. Los Angeles, Nov. 22, 1964
Buffalo vs. Denver, Dec. 13, 1964
Detroit vs. Green Bay, Nov. 7, 1965
Oakland vs. Buffalo, Oct. 15, 1967
Oakland vs. Denver, Nov. 5, 1967
St. Louis vs. Atlanta, Nov. 24, 1968
Dallas vs. Detroit, Oct. 6, 1975
St. Louis vs. Philadelphia, Dec. 18, 1983
Kansas City vs. Cleveland, Sept. 30, 1984
Chicago vs. Minnesota, Oct. 28, 1984
Cleveland vs. Atlanta, Nov. 18, 1984
Detroit vs. Philadelphia, Nov. 16, 1986
San Diego vs. Dallas, Nov. 16, 1986
L.A. Raiders vs. Philadelphia, Nov. 30, 1986 (ot)
Seattle vs. L.A. Raiders, Dec. 8, 1986
Chicago vs. Philadelphia, Oct. 4, 1987
Dallas vs. N.Y. Jets, Oct. 4, 1987
Philadelphia vs. Dallas, Sept. 15, 1991
Indianapolis vs. Cleveland, Sept. 6, 1992
10 By many teams

Most Opponents Yards Lost Attempting to Pass, Season
666 Oakland, 1967
583 Chicago, 1984
573 San Francisco, 1976

Fewest Opponents Yards Lost Attempting to Pass, Season
62 Kansas City, 2008
72 Jacksonville, 1995
75 Green Bay, 1956

INTERCEPTIONS BY

Most Seasons Leading League
10 N.Y. Giants, 1933, 1937-39, 1944, 1948, 1951, 1954, 1961, 1997
9 Green Bay, 1940, 1942-43, 1947, 1955, 1957, 1962, 1965, 2009
8 Chi. Bears, 1935-36, 1941-42, 1946, 1963, 1985, 1990

Most Consecutive Seasons Leading League
5 Kansas City, 1966-1970
3 N.Y. Giants, 1937-39
2 By many teams

Most Passes Intercepted, Season
49 San Diego, 1961
42 Green Bay, 1943
41 N.Y. Giants, 1951

Fewest Passes Intercepted By, Season
3 Houston, 1982
4 Detroit, 2008
5 Baltimore, 1982
Oakland, 2005

Most Passes Intercepted By, Game
9 Green Bay vs. Detroit, Oct. 24, 1943
Philadelphia vs. Pittsburgh, Dec. 12, 1965
8 N.Y. Giants vs. Green Bay, Nov. 21, 1948
Philadelphia vs. Chi. Cardinals, Sept. 24, 1950
N.Y. Giants vs. N.Y. Yanks, Dec. 16, 1951
Houston vs. Denver, Dec. 2, 1962
Detroit vs. Chicago, Sept. 22, 1968
N.Y. Jets vs. Baltimore, Sept. 23, 1973
7 By many teams. Last time:
Cleveland vs. Detroit, Sept. 23, 2001

Most Consecutive Games, One or More Interceptions By
46 L.A. Chargers/San Diego, 1960-63
37 Detroit, 1960-63
36 Boston, 1944-47

Most Yards Returning Interceptions, Season
929 San Diego, 1961
712 Los Angeles, 1952
700 Baltimore, 2004

Fewest Yards Returning Interceptions, Season
5 Los Angeles, 1959
16 Detroit, 2008
25 Washington, 2006

Most Yards Returning Interceptions, Game
325 Seattle vs. Kansas City, Nov. 4, 1984
314 Los Angeles vs. San Francisco, Oct. 18, 1964
245 Houston vs. N.Y. Jets, Oct. 15, 1967

Most Yards Returning Interceptions, Both Teams, Game
356 Seattle (325) vs. Kansas City (31), Nov. 4, 1984
338 Los Angeles (314) vs. San Francisco (24), Oct. 18, 1964
308 Dallas (182) vs. Los Angeles (126), Nov. 2, 1952

Most Touchdowns, Returning Interceptions, Season
9 San Diego, 1961
8 Seattle, 1998

7 Seattle, 1984
St. Louis, 1999

Most Touchdowns Returning Interceptions, Game

4 Seattle vs. Kansas City, Nov. 4, 1984
3 Baltimore vs. Green Bay, Nov. 5, 1950
Cleveland vs. Chicago, Dec. 11, 1960
Philadelphia vs. Pittsburgh, Dec. 12, 1965
Baltimore vs. Pittsburgh, Sept. 29, 1968
Buffalo vs. N.Y. Jets, Sept. 29, 1968
Houston vs. San Diego, Dec. 19, 1971
Cincinnati vs. Houston, Dec. 17, 1972
Tampa Bay vs. New Orleans, Dec. 11, 1977
Minnesota vs. N.Y. Giants, Nov. 25, 2007
2 By many teams

Most Touchdown Returning Interceptions, Both Teams, Game

4 Philadelphia (3) vs. Pittsburgh (1), Dec. 12, 1965
Seattle (4) vs. Kansas City (0), Nov. 4, 1984
3 Los Angeles (2) vs. Detroit (1), Nov. 1, 1953
Cleveland (2) vs. N.Y. Giants (1), Dec. 18, 1960
Pittsburgh (2) vs. Cincinnati (1), Oct. 10, 1983
Kansas City (2) vs. San Diego (1), Oct. 19, 1986
Arizona (2) vs. St. Louis (1), Dec. 30, 2007
(Also see previous record)

PUNT RETURNS

Fewest Opponents Punt Returns, Season

7 Washington, 1962
San Diego, 1982
10 Buffalo, 1982
11 Boston, 1962
New England, 2008

Most Opponents Punt Returns, Season

71 Tampa Bay, 1976, 1977
69 N.Y. Giants, 1953
Cleveland, 2000
68 Cleveland, 1974
Cleveland, 1999

Fewest Yards Allowed, Punt Returns, Season

22 Green Bay, 1967
30 Buffalo, 1982
34 Washington, 1962

Most Yards Allowed, Punt Returns, Season

932 Green Bay, 1949
913 Boston, 1947
906 New Orleans, 1974

Lowest Avg. Allowed, Punt Returns, Season

1.20 Chi. Cardinals, 1954
1.22 Cleveland, 1959
1.55 Chi. Cardinals, 1953

Highest Average Allowed, Punt Returns, Season

18.6 Green Bay, 1949 (50-932)
18.0 Cleveland, 1977 (31-558)
17.9 Boston, 1960 (20-357)

Most Touchdowns Allowed, Punt Returns, Season

4 Los Angeles, 1951
N.Y. Giants, 1959
Atlanta, 1992
Minnesota, 2008
3 Green Bay, 1949
Chi. Cardinals, 1951
L.A. Rams, 1951, 1994
Washington, 1952
Dallas, 1952
Pittsburgh, 1959, 1993
N.Y. Jets, 1968
Cleveland, 1977
Atlanta, 1986
Tampa Bay, 1986
Arizona, 2002
Cincinnati, 2002
Tennessee, 2002
2 By many teams

KICKOFF RETURNS

Fewest Opponents Kickoff Returns, Season

10 Brooklyn, 1943
13 Denver, 1992
15 Detroit, 1942
Brooklyn, 1944

Most Opponents Kickoff Returns, Season

93 Indianapolis, 2003
92 Indianapolis, 2004
New England, 2007
91 Washington, 1983
Minnesota, 2009

Fewest Yards Allowed, Kickoff Returns, Season

225 Brooklyn, 1943
254 Denver, 1992
293 Brooklyn, 1944

Most Yards Allowed, Kickoff Returns, Season

2,194 St. Louis, 2001
2,115 St. Louis, 1999
2,060 Minnesota, 2009

Lowest Average Allowed, Kickoff Returns, Season

14.3 Cleveland, 1980
14.9 Indianapolis, 1993
15.0 Seattle, 1982

Highest Average Allowed, Kickoff Returns, Season

29.5 N.Y. Jets, 1972 (47-1,386)
29.4 Los Angeles, 1950 (48-1,411)
29.1 New England, 1971 (49-1,427)

Most Touchdowns Allowed, Kickoff Returns, Season

4 Minnesota, 1998
Pittsburgh, 2009
3 Minnesota, 1963, 1970
Dallas, 1966
Detroit, 1980
Pittsburgh, 1986
Buffalo, 1997
Atlanta, 2000
Arizona, 2005
Indianapolis, 2007
2 By many teams

FUMBLES

Fewest Opponents Fumbles, Season

11 Cleveland, 1956
Baltimore, 1982
Tennessee, 1998
12 Green Bay, 1995
Cincinnati, 1998
Jacksonville, 2006
Baltimore, 2007
13 Los Angeles, 1956
Chicago, 1960
Cleveland, 1963
Cleveland, 1965
Detroit, 1967
San Diego, 1969
New England, 2005
Cleveland, 2006

Most Opponents Fumbles, Season

50 Minnesota, 1963
San Francisco, 1978
48 N.Y. Giants, 1980
N.Y. Jets, 1986
47 N.Y. Giants, 1977
Seattle, 1984

TURNOVERS

(Number of times losing the ball on interceptions and fumbles.)

Fewest Opponents Turnovers, Season

11 Baltimore, 1982
12 Washington, 2006
13 San Francisco, 1982
Denver, 2008

Most Opponent Turnovers, Season

66 San Diego, 1961
63 Seattle, 1984
61 Washington, 1983
57 Detroit, 1952
Buffalo, 1965

Most Opponent Turnovers, Game

12 Chi. Bears vs. Detroit, Nov. 22, 1942
Philadelphia vs. Chi. Cardinals, Sept. 24, 1950
Philadelphia vs. Pittsburgh, Dec. 12, 1965
11 Green Bay vs. San Diego, Sept. 24, 1978
10 By 14 teams

OUTSTANDING PERFORMERS

1,000 YARDS RUSHING IN A SEASON

Year	Player, Team	Att.	Yards	Avg.	Long	TD
2009	Chris Johnson, Tennessee[2]	358	2,006	5.6	91	14
	Steven Jackson, St. Louis[5]	324	1,416	4.8	58	4
	Thomas Jones, N.Y. Jets[5]	331	1,402	4.2	71	14
	Maurice Jones-Drew, Jacksonville	312	1,391	4.5	80	15
	Adrian Peterson, Minnesota[3]	314	1,383	4.4	64	18
	Ray Rice, Baltimore	254	1,339	5.3	59	7
	Ryan Grant, Green Bay[2]	282	1,253	4.4	62	11
	Cedric Benson, Cincinnati	301	1,251	4.2	42	6
	Jonathan Stewart, Carolina	221	1,133	5.1	67	10
	Ricky Williams, Miami[5]	241	1,121	4.6	68	11
	Jamaal Charles, Kansas City	190	1,120	5.9	76	7
	Frank Gore, San Francisco[4]	229	1,120	4.9	80	10
	DeAngelo Williams, Carolina[2]	216	1,117	5.2	77	7
	Rashard Mendenhall, Pittsburgh	242	1,108	4.6	60	7
	Fred Jackson, Buffalo	237	1,062	4.5	43	2
2008	Adrian Peterson, Minnesota[2]	363	1,760	4.9	67	10
	Michael Turner, Atlanta	376	1,699	4.5	70	17
	DeAngelo Williams, Carolina	273	1,515	5.6	69	18
	Clinton Portis, Washington[6]	342	1,487	4.4	31	9
	Thomas Jones, N.Y. Jets[4]	290	1,312	4.5	59	13
	*Steve Slaton, Houston	268	1,282	4.8	71	9
	*Matt Forté, Chicago	316	1,238	3.9	50	8
	*Chris Johnson, Tennessee	251	1,228	4.9	66	9
	Ryan Grant, Green Bay	312	1,203	3.9	57	4
	LaDainian Tomlinson, San Diego[8]	292	1,110	3.8	45	11
	Brandon Jacobs, N.Y. Giants[2]	219	1,089	5.0	44	15
	Steven Jackson, St. Louis[4]	253	1,042	4.1	56	7
	Frank Gore, San Francisco[3]	240	1,036	4.3	41	6
	Marshawn Lynch, Buffalo[2]	250	1,036	4.1	50	8
	Derrick Ward, N.Y. Giants	182	1,025	5.6	51	2
	Jamal Lewis, Cleveland[7]	279	1,002	3.6	29	4
2007	LaDainian Tomlinson, San Diego[7]	315	1,474	4.7	49	15
	*Adrian Peterson, Minnesota	238	1,341	5.6	73	12
	Brian Westbrook, Philadelphia[2]	278	1,333	4.8	36	7
	Willie Parker, Pittsburgh[3]	321	1,316	4.1	32	2
	Jamal Lewis, Cleveland[6]	298	1,304	4.4	66	9
	Clinton Portis, Washington[5]	325	1,262	3.9	32	11
	Edgerrin James, Arizona[7]	324	1,222	3.8	27	7
	Willis McGahee, Baltimore[3]	294	1,207	4.1	46	7
	Fred Taylor, Jacksonville[7]	223	1,202	5.4	80	5
	Thomas Jones, N.Y. Jets[3]	310	1,119	3.6	36	1
	*Marshawn Lynch, Buffalo	280	1,115	4.0	56	7
	LenDale White, Tennessee	303	1,110	3.7	28	7
	Frank Gore, San Francisco[2]	260	1,102	4.2	43	5
	Joseph Addai, Indianapolis[2]	261	1,072	4.1	23	12
	Justin Fargas, Oakland	222	1,009	4.6	48	4
	Brandon Jacobs, N.Y. Giants	202	1,009	5.0	43	4
	Steven Jackson, St. Louis[3]	237	1,002	4.2	54	5
2006	LaDainian Tomlinson, San Diego[6]	348	1,815	5.2	85	28
	Larry Johnson, Kansas City[2]	416	1,789	4.3	47	17
	Frank Gore, San Francisco	312	1,695	5.4	72	8
	Tiki Barber, N.Y. Giants[6]	327	1,662	5.1	55	5
	Steven Jackson, St. Louis[2]	346	1,528	4.4	59	13
	Willie Parker, Pittsburgh[2]	337	1,494	4.4	76	13
	Rudi Johnson, Cincinnati[3]	341	1,309	3.8	22	12
	Brian Westbrook, Philadelphia	240	1,217	5.1	71	7
	Chester Taylor, Minnesota	303	1,216	4.0	95	6
	Travis Henry, Tennessee[3]	270	1,211	4.5	70	7
	Thomas Jones, Chicago[2]	296	1,210	4.1	30	6
	Edgerrin James, Arizona[6]	337	1,159	3.4	18	6
	Ladell Betts, Washington	245	1,154	4.7	26	4
	Fred Taylor, Jacksonville[6]	231	1,146	5.0	76	5
	Warrick Dunn, Atlanta[5]	286	1,140	4.0	90	4
	Jamal Lewis, Baltimore[5]	314	1,132	3.6	52	9
	Julius Jones, Dallas	267	1,084	4.1	77	4
	*Joseph Addai, Indianapolis	226	1,081	4.8	41	7
	Ahman Green, Green Bay[6]	266	1,059	4.0	70	5
	Deuce McAllister, New Orleans[4]	244	1,057	4.3	57	10

Year	Player, Team	Att.	Yards	Avg.	Long	TD
	Michael Vick, Atlanta	123	1,039	8.5	51	2
	Tatum Bell, Denver	233	1,025	4.4	51	2
	Ronnie Brown, Miami	241	1,008	4.2	47	5
2005	Shaun Alexander, Seattle[5]	370	1,880	5.1	88	27
	Tiki Barber, N.Y. Giants[5]	357	1,860	5.2	95	9
	Larry Johnson, Kansas City	336	1,750	5.2	49	20
	Clinton Portis, Washington[4]	352	1,516	4.3	47	11
	Edgerrin James, Indianapolis[5]	360	1,506	4.2	33	13
	LaDainian Tomlinson, San Diego[5]	339	1,462	4.3	62	18
	Rudi Johnson, Cincinnati[2]	337	1,458	4.3	33	12
	Warrick Dunn, Atlanta[4]	280	1,416	5.1	65	3
	Thomas Jones, Chicago	314	1,335	4.3	42	9
	Willis McGahee, Buffalo[2]	325	1,247	3.8	27	5
	Reuben Droughns, Cleveland[2]	309	1,232	4.0	75	2
	Willie Parker, Pittsburgh	255	1,202	4.7	80	4
	*Carnell Williams, Tampa Bay	290	1,178	4.1	71	6
	Steven Jackson, St. Louis	254	1,046	4.1	51	8
	LaMont Jordan, Oakland	272	1,025	3.8	26	9
	Mike Anderson, Denver[2]	239	1,014	4.2	44	12
2004	Curtis Martin, N.Y. Jets[10]	371	1,697	4.6	25	12
	Shaun Alexander, Seattle[4]	353	1,696	4.8	44	16
	Corey Dillon, New England[7]	345	1,635	4.7	44	12
	Edgerrin James, Indianapolis[4]	334	1,548	4.6	40	9
	Tiki Barber, N.Y. Giants[4]	322	1,518	4.7	72	13
	Rudi Johnson, Cincinnati	361	1,454	4.0	52	12
	LaDainian Tomlinson, San Diego[4]	339	1,335	3.9	42	17
	Clinton Portis, Washington[3]	343	1,315	3.8	64	5
	Reuben Droughns, Denver	275	1,240	4.5	51	6
	Fred Taylor, Jacksonville[5]	260	1,224	4.7	46	2
	Domanick Davis, Houston[2]	302	1,188	3.9	44	13
	Ahman Green, Green Bay[5]	259	1,163	4.5	90	7
	*Kevin Jones, Detroit	241	1,133	4.7	74	5
	Willis McGahee, Buffalo	284	1,128	4.0	41	13
	Warrick Dunn, Atlanta[3]	265	1,106	4.2	60	9
	Deuce McAllister, New Orleans[3]	269	1,074	4.0	71	9
	Chris Brown, Tennessee	220	1,067	4.9	52	6
	Jamal Lewis, Baltimore[4]	235	1,006	4.3	75	7
2003	Jamal Lewis, Baltimore[3]	387	2,066	5.3	82	14
	Ahman Green, Green Bay[4]	355	1,883	5.3	98	15
	LaDainian Tomlinson, San Diego[3]	313	1,645	5.3	73	13
	Deuce McAllister, New Orleans[2]	351	1,641	4.7	76	8
	Clinton Portis, Denver[2]	290	1,591	5.5	65	14
	Fred Taylor, Jacksonville[4]	345	1,572	4.6	62	6
	Stephen Davis, Carolina[4]	318	1,444	4.5	40	8
	Shaun Alexander, Seattle[3]	326	1,435	4.4	55	14
	Priest Holmes, Kansas City[4]	320	1,420	4.4	31	27
	Ricky Williams, Miami[4]	392	1,372	3.5	45	9
	Travis Henry, Buffalo[2]	331	1,356	4.1	64	10
	Curtis Martin, N.Y. Jets[9]	323	1,308	4.1	56	2
	Edgerrin James, Indianapolis[3]	310	1,259	4.1	43	11
	Tiki Barber, N.Y. Giants[3]	278	1,216	4.4	27	2
	*Domanick Davis, Houston	238	1,031	4.3	51	8
	Eddie George, Tennessee[7]	312	1,031	3.3	27	5
	Kevan Barlow, San Francisco	201	1,024	5.1	78	6
	Anthony Thomas, Chicago[2]	244	1,024	4.2	67	6
2002	Ricky Williams, Miami[3]	383	1,853	4.8	63	16
	LaDainian Tomlinson, San Diego[2]	372	1,683	4.5	76	14
	Priest Holmes, Kansas City[3]	313	1,615	5.2	56	21
	*Clinton Portis, Denver	273	1,508	5.5	59	15
	Travis Henry, Buffalo	325	1,438	4.4	34	13
	Deuce McAllister, New Orleans	325	1,388	4.3	62	13
	Tiki Barber, N.Y. Giants[2]	304	1,387	4.6	70	11
	Jamal Lewis, Baltimore[2]	308	1,327	4.3	75	6
	Fred Taylor, Jacksonville[3]	287	1,314	4.6	63	8
	Corey Dillon, Cincinnati[6]	314	1,311	4.2	67	7
	Michael Bennett, Minnesota	255	1,296	5.1	85	5
	Ahman Green, Green Bay[3]	286	1,240	4.3	43	7
	Shaun Alexander, Seattle[2]	295	1,175	4.0	58	16
	Eddie George, Tennessee[6]	343	1,165	3.4	35	12

OUTSTANDING PERFORMERS

Year	Player, Team	Att.	Yards	Avg.	Long	TD
	Curtis Martin, N.Y. Jets[8]	261	1,094	4.2	35	7
	Duce Staley, Philadelphia[3]	269	1,029	3.8	57	5
	James Stewart, Detroit[2]	231	1,021	4.4	56	4
2001	Priest Holmes, Kansas City[2]	327	1,555	4.8	41	8
	Curtis Martin, N.Y. Jets[7]	333	1,513	4.5	47	10
	Stephen Davis, Washington[3]	356	1,432	4.0	32	5
	Ahman Green, Green Bay[2]	304	1,387	4.6	83	9
	Marshall Faulk, St. Louis[7]	260	1,382	5.3	71	12
	Shaun Alexander, Seattle	309	1,318	4.3	88	14
	Corey Dillon, Cincinnati[5]	340	1,315	3.9	96	10
	Ricky Williams, New Orleans[2]	313	1,245	4.0	46	6
	*LaDainian Tomlinson, San Diego	339	1,236	3.6	54	10
	Garrison Hearst, San Francisco[4]	252	1,206	4.8	43	4
	*Anthony Thomas, Chicago	278	1,183	4.3	46	7
	Antowain Smith, New England[2]	287	1,157	4.0	44	12
	*Dominic Rhodes, Indianapolis	233	1,104	4.7	77	9
	Jerome Bettis, Pittsburgh[8]	225	1,072	4.8	48	4
	Emmitt Smith, Dallas[11]	261	1,021	3.9	44	3
2000	Edgerrin James, Indianapolis[2]	387	1,709	4.4	30	13
	Robert Smith, Minnesota[4]	295	1,521	5.2	72	7
	Eddie George, Tennessee[5]	403	1,509	3.7	35	14
	*Mike Anderson, Denver	297	1,487	5.0	80	15
	Corey Dillon, Cincinnati[4]	315	1,435	4.6	80	7
	Fred Taylor, Jacksonville[2]	292	1,399	4.8	71	12
	*Jamal Lewis, Baltimore	309	1,364	4.4	45	6
	Marshall Faulk, St. Louis[6]	253	1,359	5.4	36	18
	Jerome Bettis, Pittsburgh[7]	355	1,341	3.8	30	8
	Stephen Davis, Washington[2]	332	1,318	4.0	50	11
	Ricky Watters, Seattle[7]	278	1,242	4.5	55	7
	Curtis Martin, N.Y. Jets[6]	316	1,204	3.8	55	9
	Emmitt Smith, Dallas[10]	294	1,203	4.1	52	9
	James Stewart, Detroit	339	1,184	3.5	34	10
	Ahman Green, Green Bay	263	1,175	4.5	39	10
	Charlie Garner, San Francisco[2]	258	1,142	4.4	42	7
	Lamar Smith, Miami	309	1,139	3.7	68	14
	Warrick Dunn, Tampa Bay[2]	248	1,133	4.6	70	8
	James Allen, Chicago	290	1,120	3.9	29	2
	Tyrone Wheatley, Oakland	232	1,046	4.5	80	9
	Jamal Anderson, Atlanta[4]	282	1,024	3.6	42	6
	Tiki Barber, N.Y. Giants	213	1,006	4.7	78	8
	Ricky Williams, New Orleans	248	1,000	4.0	26	8
1999	*Edgerrin James, Indianapolis	369	1,553	4.2	72	13
	Curtis Martin, N.Y. Jets[5]	367	1,464	4.0	50	5
	Stephen Davis, Washington	290	1,405	4.8	76	17
	Emmitt Smith, Dallas[9]	329	1,397	4.3	63	11
	Marshall Faulk, St. Louis[5]	253	1,381	5.5	58	7
	Eddie George, Tennessee[4]	320	1,304	4.1	40	9
	Duce Staley, Philadelphia[2]	325	1,273	3.9	29	4
	Charlie Garner, San Francisco	241	1,229	5.1	53	4
	Ricky Watters, Seattle[6]	325	1,210	3.7	45	5
	Corey Dillon, Cincinnati[3]	263	1,200	4.6	50	5
	*Olandis Gary, Denver	276	1,159	4.2	71	7
	Jerome Bettis, Pittsburgh[6]	299	1,091	3.7	35	7
	Dorsey Levens, Green Bay[2]	279	1,034	3.7	36	9
	Robert Smith, Minnesota[3]	221	1,015	4.6	70	2
1998	Terrell Davis, Denver[4]	392	2,008	5.1	70	21
	Jamal Anderson, Atlanta[3]	410	1,846	4.5	48	14
	Garrison Hearst, San Francisco[3]	310	1,570	5.1	96	7
	Barry Sanders, Detroit[10]	343	1,491	4.3	73	4
	Emmitt Smith, Dallas[8]	319	1,332	4.2	32	13
	Marshall Faulk, Indianapolis[4]	324	1,319	4.1	68	6
	Eddie George, Tennessee[3]	348	1,294	3.7	37	5
	Curtis Martin, N.Y. Jets[4]	369	1,287	3.5	60	8
	Ricky Watters, Seattle[5]	319	1,239	3.9	39	9
	*Fred Taylor, Jacksonville	264	1,223	4.6	77	14
	Robert Smith, Minnesota[2]	249	1,187	4.8	74	6
	Jerome Bettis, Pittsburgh[5]	316	1,185	3.8	42	3
	Corey Dillon, Cincinnati[2]	262	1,130	4.3	66	4
	Antowain Smith, Buffalo	300	1,124	3.7	30	8

Year	Player, Team	Att.	Yards	Avg.	Long	TD
	*Robert Edwards, New England	291	1,115	3.8	53	9
	Duce Staley, Philadelphia	258	1,065	4.1	64	5
	Gary Brown, N.Y. Giants[2]	247	1,063	4.3	45	5
	Adrian Murrell, Arizona[3]	274	1,042	3.8	32	8
	Warrick Dunn, Tampa Bay	245	1,026	4.2	50	2
	Priest Holmes, Baltimore	233	1,008	4.3	56	7
1997	Barry Sanders, Detroit[9]	335	2,053	6.1	82	11
	Terrell Davis, Denver[3]	369	1,750	4.7	50	15
	Jerome Bettis, Pittsburgh[4]	375	1,665	4.4	34	7
	Dorsey Levens, Green Bay	329	1,435	4.4	52	7
	Eddie George, Tennessee[2]	357	1,399	3.9	30	6
	Napoleon Kaufman, Oakland	272	1,294	4.8	83	6
	Robert Smith, Minnesota	232	1,266	5.5	78	6
	Curtis Martin, New England[3]	274	1,160	4.2	70	4
	*Corey Dillon, Cincinnati	233	1,129	4.8	71	10
	Ricky Watters, Philadelphia[4]	285	1,110	3.9	28	7
	Adrian Murrell, N.Y. Jets[2]	300	1,086	3.6	43	7
	Emmitt Smith, Dallas[7]	261	1,074	4.1	44	4
	Marshall Faulk, Indianapolis[3]	264	1,054	4.0	45	7
	Raymont Harris, Chicago	275	1,033	3.8	68	10
	Garrison Hearst, San Francisco[2]	234	1,019	4.4	51	4
	Jamal Anderson, Atlanta[2]	290	1,002	3.5	39	7
1996	Barry Sanders, Detroit[8]	307	1,553	5.1	54	11
	Terrell Davis, Denver[2]	345	1,538	4.5	71	13
	Jerome Bettis, Pittsburgh[3]	320	1,431	4.5	50	11
	Ricky Watters, Philadelphia[3]	353	1,411	4.0	56	13
	*Eddie George, Houston	335	1,368	4.1	76	8
	Terry Allen, Washington[4]	347	1,353	3.9	49	21
	Adrian Murrell, N.Y. Jets	301	1,249	4.1	78	6
	Emmitt Smith, Dallas[6]	327	1,204	3.7	42	12
	Curtis Martin, New England[2]	316	1,152	3.6	57	14
	Anthony Johnson, Carolina	300	1,120	3.7	29	6
	*Karim Abdul-Jabbar, Miami	307	1,116	3.6	29	11
	Jamal Anderson, Atlanta	232	1,055	4.5	32	5
	Thurman Thomas, Buffalo[8]	281	1,033	3.7	36	8
1995	Emmitt Smith, Dallas[5]	377	1,773	4.7	60	25
	Barry Sanders, Detroit[7]	314	1,500	4.8	75	11
	*Curtis Martin, New England	368	1,487	4.0	49	14
	Chris Warren, Seattle[4]	310	1,346	4.3	52	15
	Terry Allen, Washington[3]	338	1,309	3.9	28	10
	Ricky Watters, Philadelphia[2]	337	1,273	3.8	57	11
	Errict Rhett, Tampa Bay[2]	332	1,207	3.6	21	11
	Rodney Hampton, N.Y. Giants[5]	306	1,182	3.9	32	10
	*Terrell Davis, Denver	237	1,117	4.7	60	7
	Harvey Williams, Oakland	255	1,114	4.4	60	9
	Craig Heyward, Atlanta	236	1,083	4.6	31	6
	Marshall Faulk, Indianapolis[2]	289	1,078	3.7	40	11
	*Rashaan Salaam, Chicago	296	1,074	3.6	42	10
	Garrison Hearst, Arizona	284	1,070	3.8	38	1
	Edgar Bennett, Green Bay	316	1,067	3.4	23	3
	Thurman Thomas, Buffalo[7]	267	1,005	3.8	49	6
1994	Barry Sanders, Detroit[6]	331	1,883	5.7	85	7
	Chris Warren, Seattle[3]	333	1,545	4.6	41	9
	Emmitt Smith, Dallas[4]	368	1,484	4.0	46	21
	Natrone Means, San Diego	343	1,350	3.9	25	12
	*Marshall Faulk, Indianapolis	314	1,282	4.1	52	11
	Thurman Thomas, Buffalo[6]	287	1,093	3.8	29	7
	Rodney Hampton, N.Y. Giants[4]	327	1,075	3.3	27	6
	Terry Allen, Minnesota[2]	255	1,031	4.0	45	8
	Jerome Bettis, L.A. Rams[2]	319	1,025	3.2	19	3
	*Errict Rhett, Tampa Bay	284	1,011	3.6	27	7
1993	Emmitt Smith, Dallas[3]	283	1,486	5.3	62	9
	*Jerome Bettis, L.A. Rams	294	1,429	4.9	71	7
	Thurman Thomas, Buffalo[5]	355	1,315	3.7	27	6
	Erric Pegram, Atlanta	292	1,185	4.1	29	3
	Barry Sanders, Detroit[5]	243	1,115	4.6	42	3
	Leonard Russell, New England	300	1,088	3.6	21	7
	Rodney Hampton, N.Y. Giants[3]	292	1,077	3.7	20	5
	Chris Warren, Seattle[2]	273	1,072	3.9	45	7

Year	Player, Team	Att.	Yards	Avg.	Long	TD
	*Reggie Brooks, Washington	223	1,063	4.8	85	3
	*Ron Moore, Phoenix	263	1,018	3.9	20	9
	Gary Brown, Houston	195	1,002	5.1	26	6
1992	Emmitt Smith, Dallas[2]	373	1,713	4.6	68	18
	Barry Foster, Pittsburgh	390	1,690	4.3	69	11
	Thurman Thomas, Buffalo[4]	312	1,487	4.8	44	9
	Barry Sanders, Detroit[4]	312	1,352	4.3	55	9
	Lorenzo White, Houston	265	1,226	4.6	44	7
	Terry Allen, Minnesota	266	1,201	4.5	51	13
	Reggie Cobb, Tampa Bay	310	1,171	3.8	25	9
	Harold Green, Cincinnati	265	1,170	4.4	53	2
	Rodney Hampton, N.Y. Giants[2]	257	1,141	4.4	63	14
	Cleveland Gary, L.A. Rams	279	1,125	4.0	63	7
	Herschel Walker, Philadelphia[2]	267	1,070	4.0	38	8
	Chris Warren, Seattle	223	1,017	4.6	52	3
	Ricky Watters, San Francisco	206	1,013	4.9	43	9
1991	Emmitt Smith, Dallas	365	1,563	4.3	75	12
	Barry Sanders, Detroit[3]	342	1,548	4.5	69	16
	Thurman Thomas, Buffalo[3]	288	1,407	4.9	33	7
	Rodney Hampton, N.Y. Giants	256	1,059	4.1	44	10
	Earnest Byner, Washington[3]	274	1,048	3.8	32	5
	Gaston Green, Denver	261	1,037	4.0	63	4
	Christian Okoye, Kansas City[2]	225	1,031	4.6	48	9
1990	Barry Sanders, Detroit[2]	255	1,304	5.1	45	13
	Thurman Thomas, Buffalo[2]	271	1,297	4.8	80	11
	Marion Butts, San Diego	265	1,225	4.6	52	8
	Earnest Byner, Washington[2]	297	1,219	4.1	22	6
	Bobby Humphrey, Denver[2]	288	1,202	4.2	37	7
	Neal Anderson, Chicago[3]	260	1,078	4.1	52	10
	Barry Word, Kansas City	204	1,015	5.0	53	4
	James Brooks, Cincinnati[3]	195	1,004	5.1	56	5
1989	Christian Okoye, Kansas City	370	1,480	4.0	59	12
	*Barry Sanders, Detroit	280	1,470	5.3	34	14
	Eric Dickerson, Indianapolis[7]	314	1,311	4.2	21	7
	Neal Anderson, Chicago[2]	274	1,275	4.7	73	11
	Dalton Hilliard, New Orleans	344	1,262	3.7	40	13
	Thurman Thomas, Buffalo	298	1,244	4.2	38	6
	James Brooks, Cincinnati[2]	221	1,239	5.6	65	7
	*Bobby Humphrey, Denver	294	1,151	3.9	40	7
	Greg Bell, L.A. Rams[3]	272	1,137	4.2	47	15
	Roger Craig, San Francisco[3]	271	1,054	3.9	27	6
	Ottis Anderson, N.Y. Giants[6]	325	1,023	3.1	36	14
1988	Eric Dickerson, Indianapolis[6]	388	1,659	4.3	41	14
	Herschel Walker, Dallas	361	1,514	4.2	38	5
	Roger Craig, San Francisco[2]	310	1,502	4.8	46	9
	Greg Bell, L.A. Rams[2]	288	1,212	4.2	44	16
	*John Stephens, New England	297	1,168	3.9	52	4
	Gary Anderson, San Diego	225	1,119	5.0	36	3
	Neal Anderson, Chicago	249	1,106	4.4	80	12
	Joe Morris, N.Y. Giants[3]	307	1,083	3.5	27	5
	*Ickey Woods, Cincinnati	203	1,066	5.3	56	15
	Curt Warner, Seattle[4]	266	1,025	3.9	29	10
	John Settle, Atlanta	232	1,024	4.4	62	7
	Mike Rozier, Houston	251	1,002	4.0	28	10
1987	Charles White, L.A. Rams	324	1,374	4.2	58	11
	Eric Dickerson, L.A. Rams-Indianapolis[5]	283	1,288	4.6	57	6
1986	Eric Dickerson, L.A. Rams[4]	404	1,821	4.5	42	11
	Joe Morris, N.Y. Giants[2]	341	1,516	4.4	54	14
	Curt Warner, Seattle[3]	319	1,481	4.6	60	13
	*Rueben Mayes, New Orleans	286	1,353	4.7	50	8
	Walter Payton, Chicago[10]	321	1,333	4.2	41	8
	Gerald Riggs, Atlanta[3]	343	1,327	3.9	31	9
	George Rogers, Washington[4]	303	1,203	4.0	42	18
	James Brooks, Cincinnati	205	1,087	5.3	56	5
1985	Marcus Allen, L.A. Raiders[3]	390	1,759	4.6	61	11
	Gerald Riggs, Atlanta[2]	397	1,719	4.3	50	10
	Walter Payton, Chicago[9]	324	1,551	4.8	40	9
	Joe Morris, N.Y. Giants	294	1,336	4.5	65	21
	Freeman McNeil, N.Y. Jets[2]	294	1,331	4.5	69	3

Year	Player, Team	Att.	Yards	Avg.	Long	TD
	Tony Dorsett, Dallas[8]	305	1,307	4.3	60	7
	James Wilder, Tampa Bay[2]	365	1,300	3.6	28	10
	Eric Dickerson, L.A. Rams[3]	292	1,234	4.2	43	12
	Craig James, New England	263	1,227	4.7	65	5
	Kevin Mack, Cleveland	222	1,104	5.0	61	7
	Curt Warner, Seattle[2]	291	1,094	3.8	38	8
	George Rogers, Washington[3]	231	1,093	4.7	35	7
	Roger Craig, San Francisco	214	1,050	4.9	62	9
	Earnest Jackson, Philadelphia[2]	282	1,028	3.6	59	5
	Stump Mitchell, St. Louis	183	1,006	5.5	64	7
	Earnest Byner, Cleveland	244	1,002	4.1	36	8
1984	Eric Dickerson, L.A. Rams[2]	379	2,105	5.6	66	14
	Walter Payton, Chicago[8]	381	1,684	4.4	72	11
	James Wilder, Tampa Bay	407	1,544	3.8	37	13
	Gerald Riggs, Atlanta	353	1,486	4.2	57	13
	Wendell Tyler, San Francisco[3]	246	1,262	5.1	40	7
	John Riggins, Washington[5]	327	1,239	3.8	24	14
	Tony Dorsett, Dallas[7]	302	1,189	3.9	31	6
	Earnest Jackson, San Diego	296	1,179	4.0	32	8
	Ottis Anderson, St. Louis[5]	289	1,174	4.1	24	6
	Marcus Allen, L.A. Raiders[2]	275	1,168	4.2	52	13
	Sammy Winder, Denver	296	1,153	3.9	24	4
	*Greg Bell, Buffalo	262	1,100	4.2	85	7
	Freeman McNeil, N.Y. Jets	229	1,070	4.7	53	5
1983	*Eric Dickerson, L.A. Rams	390	1,808	4.6	85	18
	William Andrews, Atlanta[4]	331	1,567	4.7	27	7
	*Curt Warner, Seattle	335	1,449	4.3	60	13
	Walter Payton, Chicago[7]	314	1,421	4.5	49	6
	John Riggins, Washington[4]	375	1,347	3.6	44	24
	Tony Dorsett, Dallas[6]	289	1,321	4.6	77	8
	Earl Campbell, Houston[5]	322	1,301	4.0	42	12
	Ottis Anderson, St. Louis[4]	296	1,270	4.3	43	5
	Mike Pruitt, Cleveland[4]	293	1,184	4.0	27	10
	George Rogers, New Orleans[2]	256	1,144	4.5	76	5
	Joe Cribbs, Buffalo[3]	263	1,131	4.3	45	3
	Curtis Dickey, Baltimore	254	1,122	4.4	56	4
	Tony Collins, New England	219	1,049	4.8	50	10
	Billy Sims, Detroit[3]	220	1,040	4.7	41	7
	Marcus Allen, L.A. Raiders	266	1,014	3.8	19	9
	Franco Harris, Pittsburgh[8]	279	1,007	3.6	19	5
1981	*George Rogers, New Orleans	378	1,674	4.4	79	13
	Tony Dorsett, Dallas[5]	342	1,646	4.8	75	4
	Billy Sims, Detroit[2]	296	1,437	4.9	51	13
	Wilbert Montgomery, Philadelphia[3]	286	1,402	4.9	41	8
	Ottis Anderson, St. Louis[3]	328	1,376	4.2	28	9
	Earl Campbell, Houston[4]	361	1,376	3.8	43	10
	William Andrews, Atlanta[3]	289	1,301	4.5	29	10
	Walter Payton, Chicago[6]	339	1,222	3.6	39	6
	Chuck Muncie, San Diego[2]	251	1,144	4.6	73	19
	*Joe Delaney, Kansas City	234	1,121	4.8	82	3
	Mike Pruitt, Cleveland[3]	247	1,103	4.5	21	7
	Joe Cribbs, Buffalo[2]	257	1,097	4.3	35	3
	Pete Johnson, Cincinnati	274	1,077	3.9	39	12
	Wendell Tyler, Los Angeles[2]	260	1,074	4.1	69	12
	Ted Brown, Minnesota	274	1,063	3.9	34	6
1980	Earl Campbell, Houston[3]	373	1,934	5.2	55	13
	Walter Payton, Chicago[5]	317	1,460	4.6	69	6
	Ottis Anderson, St. Louis[2]	301	1,352	4.5	52	9
	William Andrews, Atlanta[2]	265	1,308	4.9	33	4
	*Billy Sims, Detroit	313	1,303	4.2	52	13
	Tony Dorsett, Dallas[4]	278	1,185	4.3	56	11
	*Joe Cribbs, Buffalo	306	1,185	3.9	48	11
	Mike Pruitt, Cleveland[2]	249	1,034	4.2	56	6
1979	Earl Campbell, Houston[2]	368	1,697	4.6	61	19
	Walter Payton, Chicago[4]	369	1,610	4.4	43	14
	*Ottis Anderson, St. Louis	331	1,605	4.8	76	8
	Wilbert Montgomery, Philadelphia[2]	338	1,512	4.5	62	9
	Mike Pruitt, Cleveland	264	1,294	4.9	77	9
	Ricky Bell, Tampa Bay	283	1,263	4.5	49	7

OUTSTANDING PERFORMERS

Year	Player, Team	Att.	Yards	Avg.	Long	TD
	Chuck Muncie, New Orleans	238	1,198	5.0	69	11
	Franco Harris, Pittsburgh[7]	267	1,186	4.4	71	11
	John Riggins, Washington[3]	260	1,153	4.4	66	9
	Wendell Tyler, Los Angeles	218	1,109	5.1	63	9
	Tony Dorsett, Dallas[3]	250	1,107	4.4	41	6
	*William Andrews, Atlanta	239	1,023	4.3	23	3
1978	*Earl Campbell, Houston	302	1,450	4.8	81	13
	Walter Payton, Chicago[3]	333	1,395	4.2	76	11
	Tony Dorsett, Dallas[2]	290	1,325	4.6	63	7
	Delvin Williams, Miami[2]	272	1,258	4.6	58	8
	Wilbert Montgomery, Philadelphia	259	1,220	4.7	47	9
	Terdell Middleton, Green Bay	284	1,116	3.9	76	11
	Franco Harris, Pittsburgh[6]	310	1,082	3.5	37	8
	Mark van Eeghen, Oakland[3]	270	1,080	4.0	34	9
	*Terry Miller, Buffalo	238	1,060	4.5	60	7
	Tony Reed, Kansas City	206	1,053	5.1	62	5
	John Riggins, Washington[2]	248	1,014	4.1	31	5
1977	Walter Payton, Chicago[2]	339	1,852	5.5	73	14
	Mark van Eeghen, Oakland[2]	324	1,273	3.9	27	7
	Lawrence McCutcheon, Los Angeles[4]	294	1,238	4.2	48	7
	Franco Harris, Pittsburgh[5]	300	1,162	3.9	61	11
	Lydell Mitchell, Baltimore[3]	301	1,159	3.9	64	3
	Chuck Foreman, Minnesota[3]	270	1,112	4.1	51	6
	Greg Pruitt, Cleveland[3]	236	1,086	4.6	78	3
	Sam Cunningham, New England	270	1,015	3.8	31	4
	*Tony Dorsett, Dallas	208	1,007	4.8	84	12
1976	O.J. Simpson, Buffalo[5]	290	1,503	5.2	75	8
	Walter Payton, Chicago	311	1,390	4.5	60	13
	Delvin Williams, San Francisco	248	1,203	4.9	80	7
	Lydell Mitchell, Baltimore[2]	289	1,200	4.2	43	5
	Lawrence McCutcheon, Los Angeles[3]	291	1,168	4.0	40	9
	Chuck Foreman, Minnesota[2]	278	1,155	4.2	46	13
	Franco Harris, Pittsburgh[4]	289	1,128	3.9	30	14
	Mike Thomas, Washington	254	1,101	4.3	28	5
	Rocky Bleier, Pittsburgh	220	1,036	4.7	28	5
	Mark van Eeghen, Oakland	233	1,012	4.3	21	3
	Otis Armstrong, Denver[2]	247	1,008	4.1	31	5
	Greg Pruitt, Cleveland[2]	209	1,000	4.8	64	4
1975	O.J. Simpson, Buffalo[4]	329	1,817	5.5	88	16
	Franco Harris, Pittsburgh[3]	262	1,246	4.8	36	10
	Lydell Mitchell, Baltimore	289	1,193	4.1	70	11
	Jim Otis, St. Louis	269	1,076	4.0	30	5
	Chuck Foreman, Minnesota	280	1,070	3.8	31	13
	Greg Pruitt, Cleveland	217	1,067	4.9	50	8
	John Riggins, N.Y. Jets	238	1,005	4.2	42	8
	Dave Hampton, Atlanta	250	1,002	4.0	22	5
1974	Otis Armstrong, Denver	263	1,407	5.3	43	9
	*Don Woods, San Diego	227	1,162	5.1	56	7
	O.J. Simpson, Buffalo[3]	270	1,125	4.2	41	3
	Lawrence McCutcheon, Los Angeles[2]	236	1,109	4.7	23	3
	Franco Harris, Pittsburgh[2]	208	1,006	4.8	54	5
1973	O.J. Simpson, Buffalo[2]	332	2,003	6.0	80	12
	John Brockington, Green Bay[3]	265	1,144	4.3	53	3
	Calvin Hill, Dallas[2]	273	1,142	4.2	21	6
	Lawrence McCutcheon, Los Angeles	210	1,097	5.2	37	2
	Larry Csonka, Miami[3]	219	1,003	4.6	25	5
1972	O.J. Simpson, Buffalo	292	1,251	4.3	94	6
	Larry Brown, Washington[2]	285	1,216	4.3	38	8
	Ron Johnson, N.Y. Giants[2]	298	1,182	4.0	35	9
	Larry Csonka, Miami[2]	213	1,117	5.2	45	6
	Marv Hubbard, Oakland	219	1,100	5.0	39	4
	*Franco Harris, Pittsburgh	188	1,055	5.6	75	10
	Calvin Hill, Dallas	245	1,036	4.2	26	6
	Mike Garrett, San Diego[2]	272	1,031	3.8	41	6
	John Brockington, Green Bay[2]	274	1,027	3.7	30	8
	Eugene (Mercury) Morris, Miami	190	1,000	5.3	33	12
1971	Floyd Little, Denver	284	1,133	4.0	40	6
	*John Brockington, Green Bay	216	1,105	5.1	52	4
	Larry Csonka, Miami	195	1,051	5.4	28	7

Year	Player, Team	Att.	Yards	Avg.	Long	TD
	Steve Owens, Detroit	246	1,035	4.2	23	8
	Willie Ellison, Los Angeles	211	1,000	4.7	80	4
1970	Larry Brown, Washington	237	1,125	4.7	75	5
	Ron Johnson, N.Y. Giants	263	1,027	3.9	68	8
1969	Gale Sayers, Chicago[2]	236	1,032	4.4	28	8
1968	Leroy Kelly, Cleveland[3]	248	1,239	5.0	65	16
	*Paul Robinson, Cincinnati	238	1,023	4.3	87	8
1967	Jim Nance, Boston[2]	269	1,216	4.5	53	7
	Leroy Kelly, Cleveland[2]	235	1,205	5.1	42	11
	Hoyle Granger, Houston	236	1,194	5.1	67	6
	Mike Garrett, Kansas City	236	1,087	4.6	58	9
1966	Jim Nance, Boston	299	1,458	4.9	65	11
	Gale Sayers, Chicago	229	1,231	5.4	58	8
	Leroy Kelly, Cleveland	209	1,141	5.5	70	15
	Dick Bass, Los Angeles[2]	248	1,090	4.4	50	8
1965	Jim Brown, Cleveland[7]	289	1,544	5.3	67	17
	Paul Lowe, San Diego[2]	222	1,121	5.0	59	7
1964	Jim Brown, Cleveland[6]	280	1,446	5.2	71	7
	Jim Taylor, Green Bay[5]	235	1,169	5.0	84	12
	John Henry Johnson, Pittsburgh[2]	235	1,048	4.5	45	7
1963	Jim Brown, Cleveland[5]	291	1,863	6.4	80	12
	Clem Daniels, Oakland	215	1,099	5.1	74	3
	Jim Taylor, Green Bay[4]	248	1,018	4.1	40	9
	Paul Lowe, San Diego	177	1,010	5.7	66	8
1962	Jim Taylor, Green Bay[3]	272	1,474	5.4	51	19
	John Henry Johnson, Pittsburgh	251	1,141	4.5	40	7
	Cookie Gilchrist, Buffalo	214	1,096	5.1	44	13
	Abner Haynes, Dall. Texans	221	1,049	4.7	71	13
	Dick Bass, Los Angeles	196	1,033	5.3	57	6
	Charlie Tolar, Houston	244	1,012	4.1	25	7
1961	Jim Brown, Cleveland[4]	305	1,408	4.6	38	8
	Jim Taylor, Green Bay[2]	243	1,307	5.4	53	15
1960	Jim Brown, Cleveland[3]	215	1,257	5.8	71	9
	Jim Taylor, Green Bay	230	1,101	4.8	32	11
	John David Crow, St. Louis	183	1,071	5.9	57	6
1959	Jim Brown, Cleveland[2]	290	1,329	4.6	70	14
	J.D. Smith, San Francisco	207	1,036	5.0	73	10
1958	Jim Brown, Cleveland	257	1,527	5.9	65	17
1956	Rick Casares, Chi. Bears	234	1,126	4.8	68	12
1954	Joe Perry, San Francisco[2]	173	1,049	6.1	58	8
1953	Joe Perry, San Francisco	192	1,018	5.3	51	10
1949	Steve Van Buren, Philadelphia[2]	263	1,146	4.4	41	11
	Tony Canadeo, Green Bay	208	1,052	5.1	54	4
1947	Steve Van Buren, Philadelphia	217	1,008	4.6	45	13
1934	*Beattie Feathers, Chi. Bears	119	1,004	8.4	82	8

**First season of professional football.*

200 YARDS RUSHING IN A GAME

Date	Player, Team, Opponent	Att.	Yards	TD
Jan. 3, 2010	Jamaal Charles, Kansas City vs. Denver	25	259	2
Jan. 3, 2010	Fred Jackson, Buffalo vs. Indianapolis	33	212	0
Dec. 27, 2009	Jonathan Stewart, Carolina vs. N.Y. Giants	28	206	1
Dec. 20, 2009	Jerome Harrison, Cleveland vs. Kansas City	34	286	3
Nov. 1, 2009	Chris Johnson, Tennessee vs. Jacksonville	24	228	2
Oct. 18, 2009	Thomas Jones, N.Y. Jets vs. Buffalo (OT)	22	210	1
Sept. 20, 2009	Frank Gore, San Francisco vs. Seattle	16	207	2
Dec. 28, 2008	Michael Turner, Atlanta vs. St. Louis	25	208	1
Dec. 21, 2008	Derrick Ward, N.Y. Giants vs. Carolina (OT)	15	215	0
Sept. 7, 2008	Michael Turner, Atlanta vs. Detroit	22	220	2
Nov. 4, 2007	*Adrian Peterson, Minnesota vs. San Diego	30	296	3
Oct. 14, 2007	*Adrian Peterson, Minnesota vs. Chicago	20	224	3
Sept. 16, 2007	Jamal Lewis, Cleveland vs. Cincinnati	27	216	1
Dec. 30, 2006	Tiki Barber, N.Y. Giants vs. Washington	23	234	3
Dec. 7, 2006	Willie Parker, Pittsburgh vs. Cleveland	32	223	1
Nov. 27, 2006	Shaun Alexander, Seattle vs. Green Bay	40	201	0
Nov. 19, 2006	Frank Gore, San Francisco vs. Seattle	24	212	0
Nov. 12, 2006	Willie Parker, Pittsburgh vs. New Orleans	22	213	2
Jan. 1, 2006	Larry Johnson, Kansas City vs. Cincinnati	26	201	3
Dec. 31, 2005	Tiki Barber, N.Y. Giants vs. Oakland	28	203	1

OUTSTANDING PERFORMERS

Date	Player, Team, Opponent	Att.	Yards	TD
Dec. 17, 2005	Tiki Barber, N.Y. Giants vs. Kansas City	29	220	2
Nov. 20, 2005	Larry Johnson, Kansas City vs. Houston	36	211	2
Oct. 30, 2005	Tiki Barber, N.Y. Giants vs. Washington	24	206	1
Nov. 28, 2004	Rudi Johnson, Cincinnati vs. Cleveland	26	202	2
Nov. 21, 2004	Edgerrin James, Indianapolis vs. Chicago	23	204	1
Dec. 28, 2003	Ahman Green, Green Bay vs. Denver	20	218	2
Dec. 28, 2003	LaDainian Tomlinson, San Diego vs. Oakland	31	243	2
Dec. 21, 2003	Jamal Lewis, Baltimore vs. Cleveland	22	205	2
Dec. 7, 2003	Clinton Portis, Denver vs. Kansas City	22	218	5
Oct. 19, 2003	LaDainian Tomlinson, San Diego vs. Cleveland	26	200	1
Sept. 14, 2003	Jamal Lewis, Baltimore vs. Cleveland	30	295	2
Dec. 29, 2002	*Clinton Portis, Denver vs. Arizona	24	228	2
Dec. 28, 2002	Tiki Barber, N.Y. Giants vs. Philadelphia	32	203	0
Dec. 9, 2002	Ricky Williams, Miami vs. Chicago	31	216	2
Dec. 1, 2002	LaDainian Tomlinson, San Diego vs. Denver	37	220	3
Dec. 1, 2002	Ricky Williams, Miami vs. Buffalo	27	228	2
Sept. 29, 2002	LaDainian Tomlinson, San Diego vs. New England	27	217	2
Dec. 23, 2001	Marshall Faulk, St. Louis vs. Carolina	30	202	2
Nov. 11, 2001	Shaun Alexander, Seattle vs. Oakland	35	266	3
Dec. 24, 2000	Marshall Faulk, St. Louis vs. New Orleans	32	220	2
Dec. 3, 2000	Corey Dillon, Cincinnati vs. Arizona	35	216	1
Dec. 3, 2000	Warrick Dunn, Tampa Bay vs. Dallas	22	210	2
Dec. 3, 2000	*Mike Anderson, Denver vs. New Orleans	37	251	4
Dec. 3, 2000	Curtis Martin, N.Y. Jets vs. Indianapolis	30	203	1
Nov. 19, 2000	Fred Taylor, Jacksonville vs. Pittsburgh	30	234	3
Oct. 22, 2000	Corey Dillon, Cincinnati vs. Denver	22	278	2
Oct. 15, 2000	Marshall Faulk, St. Louis vs. Atlanta	25	208	1
Oct. 15, 2000	Edgerrin James, Indianapolis vs. Seattle	38	219	3
Sept. 24, 2000	Charlie Garner, San Francisco vs. Dallas	36	201	1
Sept. 3, 2000	Duce Staley, Philadelphia vs. Dallas	26	201	1
Nov. 22, 1998	Priest Holmes, Baltimore vs. Cincinnati	36	227	1
Oct. 11, 1998	Terrell Davis, Denver vs. Seattle	30	208	1
Dec. 4, 1997	*Corey Dillon, Cincinnati vs. Tennessee	39	246	4
Nov. 23, 1997	Barry Sanders, Detroit vs. Indianapolis	24	216	2
Oct. 26, 1997	Terrell Davis, Denver vs. Buffalo (OT)	42	207	1
Oct. 19, 1997	Napoleon Kaufman, Oakland vs. Denver	28	227	1
Oct. 12, 1997	Barry Sanders, Detroit vs. Tampa Bay	24	215	2
Sept. 21, 1997	Terrell Davis, Denver vs. Cincinnati	27	215	1
Aug. 31, 1997	Eddie George, Tennessee vs. Oakland (OT)	35	216	1
Sept. 22, 1996	LeShon Johnson, Arizona vs. New Orleans	21	214	2
Nov. 13, 1994	Barry Sanders, Detroit vs. Tampa Bay	26	237	0
Dec. 12, 1993	*Jerome Bettis, L.A. Rams vs. New Orleans	28	212	1
Oct. 31, 1993	Emmitt Smith, Dallas vs. Philadelphia	30	237	1
Nov. 24, 1991	Barry Sanders, Detroit vs. Minnesota	23	220	4
Dec. 23, 1990	James Brooks, Cincinnati vs. Houston	20	201	1
Oct. 14, 1990	Barry Word, Kansas City vs. Detroit	18	200	2
Sept. 24, 1990	Thurman Thomas, Buffalo vs. N.Y. Jets	18	214	0
Dec. 24, 1989	Greg Bell, L.A. Rams vs. New England	26	210	1
Sept. 24, 1989	Greg Bell, L.A. Rams vs. Green Bay	28	221	2
Sept. 17, 1989	Gerald Riggs, Washington vs. Philadelphia	29	221	1
Dec. 18, 1988	Gary Anderson, San Diego vs. Kansas City	34	217	1
Nov. 30, 1987	*Bo Jackson, L.A. Raiders vs. Seattle	18	221	2
Nov. 15, 1987	Charles White, L.A. Rams vs. St. Louis	34	213	1
Dec. 7, 1986	Rueben Mayes, New Orleans vs. Miami	28	203	2
Oct. 5, 1986	Eric Dickerson, L.A. Rams vs. Tampa Bay (OT)	30	207	2
Dec. 21, 1985	George Rogers, Washington vs. St. Louis	34	206	1
Dec. 21, 1985	Joe Morris, N.Y. Giants vs. Pittsburgh	36	202	3
Dec. 9, 1984	Eric Dickerson, L.A. Rams vs. Houston	27	215	2
Nov. 18, 1984	*Greg Bell, Buffalo vs. Dallas	27	206	1
Nov. 4, 1984	Eric Dickerson, L.A. Rams vs. St. Louis	21	208	0
Sept. 2, 1984	Gerald Riggs, Atlanta vs. New Orleans	35	202	2
Nov. 27, 1983	*Curt Warner, Seattle vs. Kansas City (OT)	32	207	3
Nov. 6, 1983	James Wilder, Tampa Bay vs. Minnesota	31	219	1
Sept. 18, 1983	Tony Collins, New England vs. N.Y. Jets	23	212	3
Sept. 4, 1983	George Rogers, New Orleans vs. St. Louis	24	206	2
Dec. 21, 1980	Earl Campbell, Houston vs. Minnesota	29	203	1
Nov. 16, 1980	Earl Campbell, Houston vs. Chicago	31	206	0
Oct. 26, 1980	Earl Campbell, Houston vs. Cincinnati	27	202	2
Oct. 19, 1980	Earl Campbell, Houston vs. Tampa Bay	33	203	0
Nov. 26, 1978	*Terry Miller, Buffalo vs. N.Y. Giants	21	208	2
Dec. 4, 1977	*Tony Dorsett, Dallas vs. Philadelphia	23	206	2

Date	Player, Team, Opponent	Att.	Yards	TD
Nov. 20, 1977	Walter Payton, Chicago vs. Minnesota	40	275	1
Oct. 30, 1977	Walter Payton, Chicago vs. Green Bay	23	205	2
Dec. 5, 1976	O.J. Simpson, Buffalo vs. Miami	24	203	1
Nov. 25, 1976	O.J. Simpson, Buffalo vs. Detroit	29	273	2
Oct. 24, 1976	Chuck Foreman, Minnesota vs. Philadelphia	28	200	2
Dec. 14, 1975	Greg Pruitt, Cleveland vs. Kansas City	26	214	3
Sept. 28, 1975	O.J. Simpson, Buffalo vs. Pittsburgh	28	227	1
Dec. 16, 1973	O.J. Simpson, Buffalo vs. N.Y. Jets	34	200	1
Dec. 9, 1973	O.J. Simpson, Buffalo vs. New England	22	219	1
Sept. 16, 1973	O.J. Simpson, Buffalo vs. New England	29	250	2
Dec. 5, 1971	Willie Ellison, Los Angeles vs. New Orleans	26	247	1
Dec. 20, 1970	John (Frenchy) Fuqua, Pittsburgh vs. Philadelphia	20	218	2
Nov. 3, 1968	Gale Sayers, Chicago vs. Green Bay	24	205	0
Oct. 30, 1966	Jim Nance, Boston vs. Oakland	38	208	2
Oct. 10, 1964	John Henry Johnson, Pittsburgh vs. Cleveland	30	200	3
Dec. 8, 1963	Cookie Gilchrist, Buffalo vs. N.Y. Jets	36	243	5
Nov. 3, 1963	Jim Brown, Cleveland vs. Philadelphia	28	223	1
Oct. 20, 1963	Clem Daniels, Oakland vs. N.Y. Jets	27	200	2
Sept. 22, 1963	Jim Brown, Cleveland vs. Dallas	20	232	2
Dec. 10, 1961	Billy Cannon, Houston vs. N.Y. Titans	25	216	3
Nov. 19, 1961	Jim Brown, Cleveland vs. Philadelphia	34	237	4
Dec. 18, 1960	John David Crow, St. Louis vs. Pittsburgh	24	203	0
Nov. 15, 1959	Bobby Mitchell, Cleveland vs. Washington	14	232	3
Nov. 24, 1957	*Jim Brown, Cleveland vs. Los Angeles	31	237	4
Dec. 16, 1956	*Tom Wilson, Los Angeles vs. Green Bay	23	223	0
Nov. 22, 1953	Dan Towler, Los Angeles vs. Baltimore	14	205	1
Nov. 12, 1950	Gene Roberts, N.Y. Giants vs. Chi. Cardinals	26	218	2
Nov. 27, 1949	Steve Van Buren, Philadelphia vs. Pittsburgh	27	205	0
Oct. 8, 1933	Cliff Battles, Boston vs. N.Y. Giants	16	215	1

First season of professional football.

TIMES 200 OR MORE

120 times by 75 players…Simpson 6; Barber 5; Brown, Campbell, Sanders, Tomlinson 4; Bell, Davis, Dickerson, Dillon, Faulk, Lewis 3; Alexander, Gore, James, L. Johnson, Parker, Payton, Peterson, Portis, Riggs, Rogers, Turner, Williams 2.

4,000 YARDS PASSING IN A SEASON

Year	Player, Team	Att.	Comp.	Pct.	Yards	TD	Int.
2009	Matt Schaub, Houston	583	396	67.9	4,770	29	15
	Peyton Manning, Indianapolis[10]	571	393	68.8	4,500	33	16
	Tony Romo, Dallas[2]	550	347	63.1	4,483	26	9
	Aaron Rodgers, Green Bay[2]	541	350	64.7	4,434	30	7
	Tom Brady, New England[3]	565	371	65.7	4,398	28	13
	Drew Brees, New Orleans[4]	514	363	70.6	4,388	34	11
	Ben Roethlisberger, Pittsburgh	506	337	66.6	4,328	26	12
	Philip Rivers, San Diego[2]	486	317	65.2	4,254	28	9
	Brett Favre, Minnesota[6]	531	363	68.4	4,202	33	7
	Eli Manning, N.Y. Giants	509	317	62.3	4,021	27	14
2008	Drew Brees, New Orleans[3]	635	413	65.0	5,069	34	17
	Kurt Warner, Arizona[3]	598	401	67.1	4,583	30	14
	Jay Cutler, Denver	616	384	62.3	4,526	25	18
	Aaron Rodgers, Green Bay	536	341	63.6	4,038	28	13
	Philip Rivers, San Diego	478	312	65.3	4,009	34	11
	Peyton Manning, Indianapolis[9]	555	371	66.8	4,002	27	12
2007	Tom Brady, New England[2]	578	398	68.9	4,806	50	8
	Drew Brees, New Orleans[2]	652	440	67.5	4,423	28	18
	Tony Romo, Dallas	520	335	64.4	4,211	36	19
	Brett Favre, Green Bay[5]	535	356	66.5	4,155	28	15
	Carson Palmer, Cincinnati[2]	575	373	64.9	4,131	26	20
	Jon Kitna, Detroit[2]	561	355	63.3	4,068	18	20
	Peyton Manning, Indianapolis[8]	515	337	65.4	4,040	31	14
2006	Drew Brees, New Orleans	554	356	64.3	4,418	26	11
	Peyton Manning, Indianapolis[7]	557	362	65.0	4,397	31	9
	Marc Bulger, St. Louis	588	370	62.9	4,301	24	8
	Jon Kitna, Detroit	596	372	62.4	4,208	21	22
	Carson Palmer, Cincinnati	520	324	62.3	4,035	28	13
2005	Tom Brady, New England	530	334	63.0	4,110	26	14
	Trent Green, Kansas City[3]	507	317	62.5	4,014	17	10

OUTSTANDING PERFORMERS

Year	Player, Team	Att.	Comp.	Pct.	Yards	TD	Int.
2004	Daunte Culpepper, Minnesota	548	379	69.2	4,717	39	11
	Trent Green, Kansas City[2]	556	369	66.4	4,591	27	17
	Peyton Manning, Indianapolis[6]	497	336	67.6	4,557	49	10
	Jake Plummer, Denver	521	303	58.2	4,089	27	20
	Brett Favre, Green Bay[4]	540	346	64.1	4,088	30	17
2003	Peyton Manning, Indianapolis[5]	566	379	67.0	4,267	29	10
	Trent Green, Kansas City	523	330	63.1	4,039	24	12
2002	Rich Gannon, Oakland	618	418	67.6	4,689	26	10
	Drew Bledsoe, Buffalo[3]	610	375	61.5	4,359	24	15
	Peyton Manning, Indianapolis[4]	591	392	66.3	4,200	27	19
	Kerry Collins, N.Y. Giants	545	335	61.5	4,073	19	14
2001	Kurt Warner, St. Louis[2]	546	375	68.7	4,830	36	22
	Peyton Manning, Indianapolis[3]	547	343	62.7	4,131	26	23
2000	Peyton Manning, Indianapolis[2]	571	357	62.5	4,413	33	15
	Jeff Garcia, San Francisco	561	355	63.3	4,278	31	10
	Elvis Grbac, Kansas City	547	326	59.6	4,169	28	14
1999	Steve Beuerlein, Carolina	571	343	60.1	4,436	36	15
	Kurt Warner, St. Louis	499	325	65.1	4,353	41	13
	Peyton Manning, Indianapolis	533	331	62.1	4,135	26	15
	Brett Favre, Green Bay[3]	595	341	57.3	4,091	22	23
	Brad Johnson, Washington	519	316	60.9	4,005	24	13
1998	Brett Favre, Green Bay[2]	551	347	63.0	4,212	31	23
	Steve Young, San Francisco[2]	517	322	62.3	4,170	36	12
1996	Mark Brunell, Jacksonville	557	353	63.4	4,367	19	20
	Vinny Testaverde, Baltimore	549	325	59.2	4,177	33	19
	Drew Bledsoe, New England[2]	623	373	59.9	4,086	27	15
1995	Brett Favre, Green Bay	570	359	63.0	4,413	38	13
	Scott Mitchell, Detroit	583	346	59.3	4,338	32	12
	Warren Moon, Minnesota[4]	606	377	62.2	4,228	33	14
	Jeff George, Atlanta	557	336	60.3	4,143	24	11
1994	Drew Bledsoe, New England	691	400	57.9	4,555	25	27
	Dan Marino, Miami[6]	615	385	62.6	4,453	30	17
	Warren Moon, Minnesota[3]	601	371	61.7	4,264	18	19
1993	John Elway, Denver	551	348	63.2	4,030	25	10
	Steve Young, San Francisco	462	314	68.0	4,023	29	16
1992	Dan Marino, Miami[5]	554	330	59.6	4,116	24	16
1991	Warren Moon, Houston[2]	655	404	61.7	4,690	23	21
1990	Warren Moon, Houston	584	362	62.0	4,689	33	13
1989	Don Majkowski, Green Bay	599	353	58.9	4,318	27	20
	Jim Everett, L.A. Rams	518	304	58.7	4,310	29	17
1988	Dan Marino, Miami[4]	606	354	58.4	4,434	28	23
1986	Dan Marino, Miami[3]	623	378	60.7	4,746	44	23
	Jay Schroeder, Washington	541	276	51.0	4,109	22	22
1985	Dan Marino, Miami[2]	567	336	59.3	4,137	30	21
1984	Dan Marino, Miami	564	362	64.2	5,084	48	17
	Neil Lomax, St. Louis	560	345	61.6	4,614	28	16
	Phil Simms, N.Y. Giants	533	286	53.7	4,044	22	18
1983	Lynn Dickey, Green Bay	484	289	59.7	4,458	32	29
	Bill Kenney, Kansas City	603	346	57.4	4,348	24	18
1981	Dan Fouts, San Diego[3]	609	360	59.1	4,802	33	17
1980	Dan Fouts, San Diego[2]	589	348	59.1	4,715	30	24
	Brian Sipe, Cleveland	554	337	60.8	4,132	30	14
1979	Dan Fouts, San Diego	530	332	62.6	4,082	24	24
1967	Joe Namath, N.Y. Jets	491	258	52.5	4,007	26	28

400 YARDS PASSING IN A GAME

Date	Player, Team, Opponent	Att.	Comp.	Yards	TD
Jan. 3, 2010	Kyle Orton, Denver vs. Kansas City	56	32	431	1
Dec. 20, 2009	Ben Roethlisberger, Pittsburgh vs. Green Bay	46	29	503	3
Dec. 6, 2009	Drew Brees, New Orleans vs. Washington (OT)	49	35	419	2
Nov. 22, 2009	Matthew Stafford, Detroit vs. Cleveland	43	26	422	5
Nov. 15, 2009	Donovan McNabb, Philadelphia vs. San Diego	55	35	450	2
Oct. 18, 2009	Ben Roethlisberger, Pittsburgh vs. Cleveland	35	23	417	2
Sept. 20, 2009	Philip Rivers, San Diego vs. Baltimore	45	25	436	2
Dec. 7, 2008	Matt Schaub, Houston vs. Green Bay	42	28	414	2
Nov. 23, 2008	Matt Cassel, New England vs. Miami	43	30	415	3
Nov. 13, 2008	Matt Cassel, New England vs. N.Y. Jets (OT)	51	30	400	3
Nov. 9, 2008	Drew Brees, New Orleans vs. Atlanta	58	31	422	2
Nov. 6, 2008	Jay Cutler, Denver vs. Cleveland	42	24	447	3

Date	Player, Team, Opponent	Att.	Comp.	Yards	TD
Sept. 28, 2008	Kurt Warner, Arizona vs. N.Y. Jets	57	40	472	2
Sept. 21, 2008	Drew Brees, New Orleans vs. Denver	48	39	421	1
Sept. 21, 2008	Brian Griese, Tampa Bay vs. Chicago (OT)	67	38	407	2
Nov. 25, 2007	Kurt Warner, Arizona vs. San Francisco (OT)	48	34	484	2
Nov. 4, 2007	Drew Brees, New Orleans vs. Jacksonville	49	35	445	3
Sept. 23, 2007	Jon Kitna, Detroit vs. Philadelphia	46	29	446	2
Sept. 16, 2007	Carson Palmer, Cincinnati vs. Cleveland	50	33	401	6
Dec. 10, 2006	Chris Weinke, Carolina vs. N.Y. Giants	61	34	423	1
Nov. 26, 2006	Matt Leinart, Arizona vs. Minnesota	51	31	405	1
Nov. 19, 2006	Drew Brees, New Orleans vs. Cincinnati	52	37	510	2
Nov. 12, 2006	Carson Palmer, Cincinnati vs. San Diego	42	31	440	3
Nov. 5, 2006	Ben Roethlisberger, Pittsburgh vs. Denver	54	38	433	1
Oct. 22, 2006	Joey Harrington, Miami vs. Green Bay	62	33	414	2
Sept. 17, 2006	Peyton Manning, Indianapolis vs. Houston	38	26	400	3
Oct. 2, 2005	Marc Bulger, St. Louis vs. N.Y. Giants	62	40	442	2
Jan. 2, 2005	Marc Bulger, St. Louis vs. N.Y. Jets (OT)	39	29	450	3
Dec. 19, 2004	Daunte Culpepper, Minnesota vs. Detroit	35	25	404	3
Dec. 19, 2004	Billy Volek, Tennessee vs. Oakland	60	40	492	4
Dec. 13, 2004	Billy Volek, Tennessee vs. Kansas City	43	29	426	4
Dec. 6, 2004	Matt Hasselbeck, Seattle vs. Dallas	40	28	414	3
Dec. 5, 2004	Peyton Manning, Indianapolis vs. Tennessee	33	25	425	3
Dec. 5, 2004	Donovan McNabb, Philadelphia vs. Green Bay	43	32	464	5
Nov. 29, 2004	Marc Bulger, St. Louis vs. Green Bay	53	35	448	2
Nov. 28, 2004	Kelly Holcomb, Cleveland vs. Cincinnati	39	30	413	5
Oct. 31, 2004	Peyton Manning, Indianapolis vs. Kansas City	44	25	472	5
Oct. 31, 2004	Jake Plummer, Denver vs. Atlanta	55	31	499	4
Oct. 17, 2004	Daunte Culpepper, Minnesota vs. New Orleans	37	26	425	5
Oct. 10. 2004	Tim Rattay, San Francisco vs. Arizona (OT)	57	38	417	2
Nov. 16, 2003	Peyton Manning, Indianapolis vs. N.Y. Jets	36	27	401	1
Oct. 12, 2003	Trent Green, Kansas City vs. Green Bay (OT)	45	27	400	3
Oct. 12, 2003	Steve McNair, Tennessee vs. Houston	27	18	421	3
Dec. 29, 2002	Matt Hasselbeck, Seattle vs. San Diego (OT)	53	36	449	2
Dec. 1, 2002	Matt Hasselbeck, Seattle vs. San Francisco	55	30	427	3
Nov. 10, 2002	Marc Bulger, St. Louis vs. San Diego	48	36	453	4
Nov. 10, 2002	Tommy Maddox, Pittsburgh vs. Atlanta (OT)	41	28	473	4
Oct. 6, 2002	Drew Bledsoe, Buffalo vs. Oakland	53	32	417	2
Sept. 22, 2002	Tom Brady, New England vs. Kansas City (OT)	54	39	410	4
Sept. 15, 2002	Drew Bledsoe, Buffalo vs. Minnesota (OT)	49	35	463	3
Sept. 15, 2002	Rich Gannon, Oakland vs. Pittsburgh	64	43	403	1
Dec. 30, 2001	Jon Kitna, Cincinnati vs. Pittsburgh	68	35	411	2
Dec. 23, 2001	Chris Chandler, Atlanta vs. Buffalo	40	28	431	2
Nov. 18, 2001	Charlie Batch, Detroit vs. Arizona	62	36	436	3
Nov. 18, 2001	Kurt Warner, St. Louis vs. New England	42	30	401	3
Sept. 23, 2001	Peyton Manning, Indianapolis vs. Buffalo	29	23	421	4
Dec. 24, 2000	Vinny Testaverde, N.Y. Jets vs. Baltimore	69	36	481	2
Dec. 17, 2000	Jeff Garcia, San Francisco vs. Chicago	44	36	402	2
Dec. 3, 2000	Aaron Brooks, New Orleans vs. Denver	48	30	441	2
Nov. 19, 2000	Gus Frerotte, Denver vs. San Diego	58	36	462	5
Nov. 5, 2000	Elvis Grbac, Kansas City vs. Oakland	53	39	504	2
Nov. 5, 2000	Trent Green, St. Louis vs. Carolina	42	29	431	2
Sept. 25, 2000	Peyton Manning, Indianapolis vs. Jacksonville	36	23	440	4
Sept. 4, 2000	Kurt Warner, St. Louis vs. Denver	35	25	441	3
Dec. 26, 1999	Brad Johnson, Washington vs. San Francisco (OT)	47	32	471	2
Dec. 5, 1999	Jeff Garcia, San Francisco vs. Cincinnati	49	33	437	3
Nov. 28, 1999	Jim Harbaugh, San Diego vs. Minnesota	39	25	404	1
Nov. 14, 1999	Jim Miller, Chicago vs. Minnesota (OT)	48	34	422	3
Sept. 26, 1999	Peyton Manning, Indianapolis vs. San Diego	54	29	404	2
Dec. 6, 1998	Vinny Testaverde, N.Y. Jets vs. Seattle	63	42	418	2
Dec. 6, 1998	John Elway, Denver vs. Kansas City	32	22	400	2
Nov. 26, 1998	Troy Aikman, Dallas vs. Minnesota	57	34	455	1
Nov. 23, 1998	Drew Bledsoe, New England vs. Miami	54	28	423	2
Nov. 15, 1998	Jake Plummer, Arizona vs. Dallas	56	31	465	3
Oct. 5, 1998	Randall Cunningham, Minnesota vs. Green Bay	32	20	442	4
Sept. 6, 1998	Glenn Foley, N.Y. Jets vs. San Francisco (OT)	58	30	415	3
Nov. 2, 1997	Tony Banks, St. Louis vs. Atlanta	34	23	401	2
Oct. 26, 1997	Warren Moon, Seattle vs. Oakland	44	28	409	5
Nov. 10, 1996	Boomer Esiason, Arizona vs. Washington (OT)	59	35	522	3
Nov. 3, 1996	Drew Bledsoe, New England vs. Miami	41	30	419	3

OUTSTANDING PERFORMERS

Date	Player, Team, Opponent	Att.	Comp.	Yards	TD
Oct. 27, 1996	Vinny Testaverde, Baltimore vs. St. Louis (OT)	51	31	429	3
Oct. 20, 1996	Mark Brunell, Jacksonville vs. St. Louis	52	37	421	0
Sept. 22, 1996	Mark Brunell, Jacksonville vs. New England (OT)	39	23	432	3
Dec. 18, 1995	Steve Young, San Francisco vs. Minnesota	49	30	425	3
Nov. 26, 1995	Dave Krieg, Arizona vs. Atlanta (OT)	43	27	413	4
Nov. 23, 1995	Scott Mitchell, Detroit vs. Minnesota	45	30	410	4
Oct. 1, 1995	Dan Marino, Miami vs. Cincinnati	48	33	450	2
Nov. 20, 1994	Warren Moon, Minnesota vs. N.Y. Jets	50	33	400	2
Nov. 13, 1994	Drew Bledsoe, New England vs. Minnesota (OT)	70	45	426	3
Nov. 6, 1994	Warren Moon, Minnesota vs. New Orleans	57	33	420	3
Sept. 25, 1994	Dan Marino, Miami vs. Minnesota	54	29	431	3
Sept. 4, 1994	Dan Marino, Miami vs. New England (OT)	42	23	473	5
Sept. 4, 1994	Drew Bledsoe, New England vs. Miami (OT)	51	32	421	4
Dec. 19, 1993	Steve Beuerlein, Phoenix vs. Seattle	53	34	431	3
Dec. 5, 1993	Brett Favre, Green Bay vs. Chicago	54	36	402	2
Nov. 28, 1993	Steve Young, San Francisco vs. L.A. Rams	32	26	462	4
Oct. 31, 1993	Jeff Hostetler, L.A. Raiders vs. San Diego	32	20	424	2
Sept. 13, 1992	Steve Young, San Francisco vs. Buffalo	37	26	449	3
Sept. 13, 1992	Jim Kelly, Buffalo vs. San Francisco	33	22	403	3
Nov. 10, 1991	Warren Moon, Houston vs. Dallas (OT)	56	41	432	0
Nov. 10, 1991	Mark Rypien, Washington vs. Atlanta	31	16	442	6
Oct. 13, 1991	Warren Moon, Houston vs. N.Y. Jets	50	35	423	2
Dec. 16, 1990	Warren Moon, Houston vs. Kansas City	45	27	527	3
Nov. 4, 1990	Joe Montana, San Francisco vs. Green Bay	40	25	411	3
Oct. 14, 1990	Joe Montana, San Francisco vs. Atlanta	49	32	476	6
Oct. 7, 1990	Boomer Esiason, Cincinnati vs. L.A. Rams (OT)	45	31	490	3
Dec. 23, 1989	Warren Moon, Houston vs. Cleveland	51	32	414	2
Dec. 11, 1989	Joe Montana, San Francisco vs. L.A. Rams	42	30	458	3
Nov. 26, 1989	Jim Everett, L.A. Rams vs. New Orleans (OT)	51	29	454	1
Nov. 26, 1989	Mark Rypien, Washington vs. Chicago	47	30	401	4
Oct. 2, 1989	Randall Cunningham, Philadelphia vs. Chicago	62	32	401	1
Sept. 24, 1989	Joe Montana, San Francisco vs. Philadelphia	34	25	428	5
Sept. 24, 1989	Dan Marino, Miami vs. N.Y. Jets	55	33	427	3
Sept. 17, 1989	Randall Cunningham, Philadelphia vs. Washington	46	34	447	5
Dec. 18, 1988	Dave Krieg, Seattle vs. L.A. Raiders	32	19	410	4
Dec. 12, 1988	Dan Marino, Miami vs. Cleveland	50	30	404	4
Oct. 23, 1988	Dan Marino, Miami vs. N.Y. Jets	60	35	521	3
Oct. 16, 1988	Vinny Testaverde, Tampa Bay vs. Indianapolis	42	25	469	2
Sept. 11, 1988	Doug Williams, Washington vs. Pittsburgh	52	30	430	2
Nov. 29, 1987	Tom Ramsey, New England vs. Philadelphia	53	34	402	3
Nov. 22, 1987	Boomer Esiason, Cincinnati vs. Pittsburgh	53	30	409	0
Sept. 20, 1987	Neil Lomax, St. Louis vs. San Diego	61	32	457	3
Dec. 21, 1986	Boomer Esiason, Cincinnati vs. N.Y. Jets	30	23	425	5
Dec. 14, 1986	Dan Marino, Miami vs. L.A. Rams (OT)	46	29	403	5
Nov. 23, 1986	Bernie Kosar, Cleveland vs. Pittsburgh (OT)	46	28	414	2
Nov. 17, 1986	Joe Montana, San Francisco vs. Washington	60	33	441	0
Nov. 16, 1986	Dan Marino, Miami vs. Buffalo	54	39	404	4
Nov. 10, 1986	Bernie Kosar, Cleveland vs. Miami	50	32	401	0
Nov. 2, 1986	Tommy Kramer, Minnesota vs. Washington (OT)	35	20	490	4
Nov. 2, 1986	Ken O'Brien, N.Y. Jets vs. Seattle	32	26	431	4
Oct. 27, 1986	Jay Schroeder, Washington vs. N.Y. Giants	40	22	420	1
Oct. 12, 1986	Steve Grogan, New England vs. N.Y. Jets	42	23	401	3
Sept. 21, 1986	Ken O'Brien, N.Y. Jets vs. Miami (OT)	43	29	479	4
Sept. 21, 1986	Dan Marino, Miami vs. N.Y. Jets (OT)	50	30	448	6
Sept. 21, 1986	Tony Eason, New England vs. Seattle	45	26	414	3
Dec. 20, 1985	John Elway, Denver vs. Seattle	42	24	432	1
Nov. 10, 1985	Dan Fouts, San Diego vs. L.A. Raiders (OT)	41	26	436	4
Oct. 13, 1985	Phil Simms, N.Y. Giants vs. Cincinnati	62	40	513	1
Oct. 13, 1985	Dave Krieg, Seattle vs. Atlanta	51	33	405	4
Oct. 6, 1985	Phil Simms, N.Y. Giants vs. Dallas	36	18	432	3
Oct. 6, 1985	Joe Montana, San Francisco vs. Atlanta	57	37	429	5
Sept. 19, 1985	Tommy Kramer, Minnesota vs. Chicago	55	28	436	3
Sept. 15, 1985	Dan Fouts, San Diego vs. Seattle	43	29	440	4
Dec. 16, 1984	Neil Lomax, St. Louis vs. Washington	46	37	468	2
Dec. 9, 1984	Dan Marino, Miami vs. Indianapolis	41	29	404	4
Dec. 2, 1984	Dan Marino, Miami vs. L.A. Raiders	57	35	470	4
Nov. 25, 1984	Dave Krieg, Seattle vs. Denver	44	30	406	3
Nov. 4, 1984	Dan Marino, Miami vs. N.Y. Jets	42	23	422	2

Date	Player, Team, Opponent	Att.	Comp.	Yards	TD
Oct. 21, 1984	Dan Fouts, San Diego vs. L.A. Raiders	45	24	410	3
Sept. 30, 1984	Dan Marino, Miami vs. St. Louis	36	24	429	3
Sept. 2, 1984	Phil Simms, N.Y. Giants vs. Philadelphia	30	23	409	4
Dec. 11, 1983	Bill Kenney, Kansas City vs. San Diego	41	31	411	4
Nov. 20, 1983	Dave Krieg, Seattle vs. Denver	42	31	418	3
Oct. 9, 1983	Joe Ferguson, Buffalo vs. Miami (OT)	55	38	419	5
Oct. 2, 1983	Joe Theismann, Washington vs. L.A. Raiders	39	23	417	3
Sept. 25, 1983	Richard Todd, N.Y. Jets vs. L.A. Rams (OT)	50	37	446	2
Dec. 26, 1982	Vince Ferragamo, L.A. Rams vs. Chicago	46	30	509	3
Dec. 20, 1982	Dan Fouts, San Diego vs. Cincinnati	40	25	435	1
Dec. 20, 1982	Ken Anderson, Cincinnati vs. San Diego	56	40	416	2
Dec. 11, 1982	Dan Fouts, San Diego vs. San Francisco	48	33	444	5
Nov. 21, 1982	Joe Montana, San Francisco vs. St. Louis	39	26	408	3
Nov. 15, 1981	Steve Bartkowski, Atlanta vs. Pittsburgh	50	33	416	2
Oct. 25, 1981	Brian Sipe, Cleveland vs. Baltimore	41	30	444	4
Oct. 25, 1981	David Woodley, Miami vs. Dallas	37	21	408	3
Oct. 11, 1981	Tommy Kramer, Minnesota vs. San Diego	43	27	444	4
Dec. 14, 1980	Tommy Kramer, Minnesota vs. Cleveland	49	38	456	4
Nov. 16, 1980	Doug Williams, Tampa Bay vs. Minnesota	55	30	486	4
Oct. 19, 1980	Dan Fouts, San Diego vs. N.Y. Giants	41	26	444	3
Oct. 12, 1980	Lynn Dickey, Green Bay vs. Tampa Bay (OT)	51	35	418	1
Sept. 21, 1980	Richard Todd, N.Y. Jets vs. San Francisco	60	42	447	3
Oct. 3, 1976	James Harris, Los Angeles vs. Miami	29	17	436	2
Nov. 17, 1975	Ken Anderson, Cincinnati vs. Buffalo	46	30	447	2
Nov. 18, 1974	Charley Johnson, Denver vs. Kansas City	42	28	445	2
Dec. 11, 1972	Joe Namath, N.Y. Jets vs. Oakland	46	25	403	1
Sept. 24, 1972	Joe Namath, N.Y. Jets vs. Baltimore	28	15	496	6
Dec. 21, 1969	Don Horn, Green Bay vs. St. Louis	31	22	410	5
Sept. 28, 1969	Joe Kapp, Minnesota vs. Baltimore	43	28	449	7
Sept. 9, 1968	Pete Beathard, Houston vs. Kansas City	48	23	413	2
Nov. 26, 1967	Sonny Jurgensen, Washington vs. Cleveland	50	32	418	3
Oct. 1, 1967	Joe Namath, N.Y. Jets vs. Miami	39	23	415	3
Sept. 17, 1967	Johnny Unitas, Baltimore vs. Atlanta	32	22	401	2
Nov. 13, 1966	Don Meredith, Dallas vs. Washington	29	21	406	2
Nov. 28, 1965	Sonny Jurgensen, Washington vs. Dallas	43	26	411	3
Oct. 24, 1965	Fran Tarkenton, Minnesota vs. San Francisco	35	21	407	3
Nov. 1, 1964	Len Dawson, Kansas City vs. Denver	38	23	435	6
Oct. 25, 1964	Cotton Davidson, Oakland vs. Denver	36	23	427	5
Oct. 16, 1964	Babe Parilli, Boston vs. Oakland	47	25	422	4
Dec. 22, 1963	Tom Flores, Oakland vs. Houston	29	17	407	6
Nov. 17, 1963	Norm Snead, Washington vs. Pittsburgh	40	23	424	2
Nov. 10, 1963	Don Meredith, Dallas vs. San Francisco	48	30	460	3
Oct. 13, 1963	Charley Johnson, St. Louis vs. Pittsburgh	41	20	428	2
Dec. 16, 1962	Sonny Jurgensen, Philadelphia vs. St. Louis	34	15	419	5
Nov. 18, 1962	Bill Wade, Chicago vs. Dall. Cowboys	46	28	466	2
Oct. 28, 1962	Y.A. Tittle, N.Y. Giants vs. Washington	39	27	505	7
Sept. 15, 1962	Frank Tripucka, Denver vs. Buffalo	56	29	447	2
Dec. 17, 1961	Sonny Jurgensen, Philadelphia vs. Detroit	42	27	403	3
Nov. 19, 1961	George Blanda, Houston vs. N.Y. Titans	32	20	418	7
Oct. 29, 1961	George Blanda, Houston vs. Buffalo	32	18	464	4
Oct. 29, 1961	Sonny Jurgensen, Philadelphia vs. Washington	41	27	436	3
Oct. 13, 1961	Jacky Lee, Houston vs. Boston	41	27	457	2
Dec. 13, 1958	Bobby Layne, Pittsburgh vs. Chi. Cardinals	49	23	409	2
Nov. 8, 1953	Bobby Thomason, Philadelphia vs. N.Y. Giants	44	22	437	4
Oct. 4, 1952	Otto Graham, Cleveland vs. Pittsburgh	49	21	401	3
Sept. 28, 1951	Norm Van Brocklin, Los Angeles vs. N.Y. Yanks	41	27	554	5
Dec. 11, 1949	Johnny Lujack, Chi. Bears vs. Chi. Cardinals	39	24	468	6
Oct. 31, 1948	Sammy Baugh, Washington vs. Boston	24	17	446	4
Oct. 31, 1948	Jim Hardy, Los Angeles vs. Chi. Cardinals	53	28	406	3
Nov. 14, 1943	Sid Luckman, Chi. Bears vs. N.Y. Giants	32	21	433	7

TIMES 400 OR MORE

208 times by 108 players…Marino 13; P. Manning, Montana, Moon 7; Bledsoe, Fouts 6; Brees, Jurgensen, Krieg 5; Bulger, Esiason, Kramer, Testaverde, Warner 4; Cunningham, Hasselbeck, Namath, Roethlisberger, Simms, Young 3; Anderson, Blanda, Brunell, Cassel, Culpepper, Elway, Garcia, Green, C. Johnson, Kitna, Kosar, Lomax, McNabb, Meredith, O'Brien, Palmer, Plummer, Rypien, Todd, Volek, Williams 2.

OUTSTANDING PERFORMERS

100 PASS RECEPTIONS IN A SEASON

Year	Player, Team	No.	Yards	Avg.	Long	TD
2009	Wes Welker, New England[3]	123	1,348	11.0	58	4
	Steve Smith, N.Y. Giants	107	1,220	11.4	51	7
	Andre Johnson, Houston[3]	101	1,569	15.5	72	9
	Brandon Marshall, Denver[3]	101	1,120	11.1	75	10
	Dallas Clark, Indianapolis	100	1,106	11.1	80	10
	Reggie Wayne, Indianapolis[2]	100	1,264	12.6	65	10
2008	Andre Johnson, Houston[2]	115	1,575	13.7	65	8
	Wes Welker, New England[2]	111	1,165	10.5	64	3
	Brandon Marshall, Denver[2]	104	1,265	12.2	47	6
2007	T.J. Houshmandzadeh, Cincinnati	112	1,143	10.2	42	12
	Wes Welker, New England	112	1,175	10.5	42	8
	Reggie Wayne, Indianapolis	104	1,510	14.5	64	10
	Derrick Mason, Baltimore	103	1,087	10.6	79	5
	Brandon Marshall, Denver	102	1,325	13.0	68	7
	Larry Fitzgerald, Arizona[2]	100	1,409	14.1	48	10
2006	Andre Johnson, Houston	103	1,147	11.1	53	5
2005	Larry Fitzgerald, Arizona	103	1,409	13.7	47	10
	Steve Smith, Carolina	103	1,563	15.2	80	12
	Anquan Boldin, Arizona[2]	102	1,402	13.7	54	7
	Torry Holt, St. Louis[2]	102	1,331	13.0	44	9
2004	Tony Gonzalez, Kansas City	102	1,258	12.3	32	7
2003	Torry Holt, St. Louis	117	1,696	14.5	48	12
	Randy Moss, Minnesota[2]	111	1,632	14.7	72	17
	*Anquan Boldin, Arizona	101	1,377	13.6	71	8
	LaDainian Tomlinson, San Diego	100	725	7.3	73	4
2002	Marvin Harrison, Indianapolis[4]	143	1,722	12.0	69	11
	Hines Ward, Pittsburgh	112	1,329	11.9	72	12
	Randy Moss, Minnesota	106	1,347	12.7	60	7
	Eric Moulds, Buffalo	100	1,292	12.9	70	10
	Terrell Owens, San Francisco	100	1,300	13.0	76	13
2001	Rod Smith, Denver[2]	113	1,343	11.9	65	11
	Jimmy Smith, Jacksonville[2]	112	1,373	12.3	35	8
	Marvin Harrison, Indianapolis[3]	109	1,524	14.0	68	15
	Keyshawn Johnson, Tampa Bay	106	1,266	11.9	47	1
	Troy Brown, New England	101	1,199	11.9	60	5
	Marty Booker, Chicago	100	1,071	10.7	66	8
2000	Marvin Harrison, Indianapolis[2]	102	1,413	13.9	78	14
	Muhsin Muhammad, Carolina	102	1,183	11.6	36	6
	Ed McCaffrey, Denver	101	1,317	13.0	61	9
	Rod Smith, Denver	100	1,602	16.0	49	8
1999	Jimmy Smith, Jacksonville	116	1,636	14.1	62	6
	Marvin Harrison, Indianapolis	115	1,663	14.5	57	12
1997	Tim Brown, Oakland	104	1,408	13.5	59	5
	Herman Moore, Detroit[3]	104	1,293	12.4	79	8
1996	Jerry Rice, San Francisco[4]	108	1,254	11.6	39	8
	Herman Moore, Detroit[2]	106	1,296	12.2	50	9
	Carl Pickens, Cincinnati	100	1,180	11.8	61	12
1995	Herman Moore, Detroit	123	1,686	13.7	69	14
	Jerry Rice, San Francisco[3]	122	1,848	15.1	81	15
	Cris Carter, Minnesota[2]	122	1,371	11.2	60	17
	Isaac Bruce, St. Louis	119	1,781	15.0	72	13
	Michael Irvin, Dallas	111	1,603	14.4	50	10
	Brett Perriman, Detroit	108	1,488	13.8	91	9
	Eric Metcalf, Atlanta	104	1,189	11.4	62	8
	Robert Brooks, Green Bay	102	1,497	14.7	99	13
	Larry Centers, Arizona	101	962	9.5	32	2
1994	Cris Carter, Minnesota	122	1,256	10.3	65	7
	Jerry Rice, San Francisco[2]	112	1,499	13.4	69	13
	Terance Mathis, Atlanta	111	1,342	12.1	81	11
1993	Sterling Sharpe, Green Bay[2]	112	1,274	11.4	54	11
1992	Sterling Sharpe, Green Bay	108	1,461	13.5	76	13
1991	Haywood Jeffires, Houston	100	1,181	11.8	44	7
1990	Jerry Rice, San Francisco	100	1,502	15.0	64	13
1984	Art Monk, Washington	106	1,372	12.9	72	7
1964	Charley Hennigan, Houston	101	1,546	15.3	53	8
1961	Lionel Taylor, Denver	100	1,176	11.8	52	4

**First season of professional football.*

1,000 YARDS PASS RECEIVING IN A SEASON

Year	Player, Team	No.	Yards	Avg.	Long	TD
2009	Andre Johnson, Houston[4]	101	1,569	15.5	72	9
	Wes Welker, New England[3]	123	1,348	11.0	58	4
	Miles Austin, Dallas	81	1,320	16.3	60	11
	Sidney Rice, Minnesota	83	1,321	15.8	63	8
	Randy Moss, New England[10]	83	1,264	15.2	71	13
	Reggie Wayne, Indianapolis[6]	100	1,264	12.6	65	10
	Santonio Holmes, Pittsburgh	79	1,248	15.8	57	5
	Steve Smith, N.Y. Giants	107	1,220	11.4	51	7
	Vincent Jackson, San Diego[2]	68	1,167	17.2	55	9
	Hines Ward, Pittsburgh[6]	95	1,167	12.3	54	6
	Antonio Gates, San Diego[2]	79	1,157	14.6	56	8
	DeSean Jackson, Philadelphia	62	1,156	18.6	71	9
	Roddy White, Atlanta[3]	85	1,153	13.6	90	11
	Brandon Marshall, Denver[3]	101	1,120	11.1	75	10
	Greg Jennings, Green Bay[2]	68	1,113	16.4	83	4
	Dallas Clark, Indianapolis	100	1,106	11.1	80	10
	Larry Fitzgerald, Arizona[4]	97	1,092	11.3	34	13
	Marques Colston, New Orleans[3]	70	1,074	15.3	68	9
	Donald Driver, Green Bay[7]	70	1,061	15.2	71	6
	Chad Ochocinco, Cincinnati[7]	72	1,047	14.5	50	9
	Jason Witten, Dallas[2]	94	1,030	11.0	69	2
	Derrick Mason, Baltimore[8]	73	1,028	14.1	72	7
	Anquan Boldin, Arizona[5]	84	1,024	12.2	44	4
2008	Andre Johnson, Houston[3]	115	1,575	13.7	65	8
	Larry Fitzgerald, Arizona[3]	96	1,431	14.9	78	12
	Steve Smith, Carolina[5]	78	1,421	18.2	65	6
	Roddy White, Atlanta[2]	88	1,382	15.7	70	7
	Calvin Johnson, Detroit	78	1,331	17.1	96	12
	Greg Jennings, Green Bay	80	1,292	16.1	63	9
	Brandon Marshall, Denver[2]	104	1,265	12.2	47	6
	Antonio Bryant, Tampa Bay[2]	83	1,248	15.0	71	7
	Wes Welker, New England[2]	111	1,165	10.5	64	3
	Reggie Wayne, Indianapolis[5]	82	1,145	14.0	65	6
	Vincent Jackson, San Diego	59	1,098	18.6	60	7
	Tony Gonzalez, Kansas City[4]	96	1,058	11.0	35	10
	Terrell Owens, Dallas[9]	69	1,052	15.2	75	10
	Santana Moss, Washington[3]	79	1,044	13.2	67	6
	Hines Ward, Pittsburgh[5]	81	1,043	12.9	49	7
	Anquan Boldin, Arizona[4]	89	1,038	11.7	79	11
	Derrick Mason, Baltimore[7]	80	1,037	13.0	54	5
	Dwayne Bowe, Kansas City	86	1,022	11.9	36	7
	Lee Evans, Buffalo[2]	63	1,017	16.1	87	3
	Donald Driver, Green Bay[6]	74	1,012	13.7	71	5
	Randy Moss, New England[9]	69	1,008	14.6	76	11
	Steve Breaston, Arizona	77	1,006	13.1	58	3
2007	Reggie Wayne, Indianapolis[4]	104	1,510	14.5	64	10
	Randy Moss, New England[8]	98	1,493	15.2	65	23
	Chad Ochocinco, Cincinnati[6]	93	1,440	15.5	70	8
	Larry Fitzgerald, Arizona[2]	100	1,409	14.1	48	10
	Terrell Owens, Dallas[8]	81	1,355	16.7	52	15
	Brandon Marshall, Denver	102	1,325	13.0	68	7
	Braylon Edwards, Cleveland	80	1,289	16.1	78	16
	Marques Colston, New Orleans[2]	98	1,202	12.3	45	11
	Roddy White, Atlanta	83	1,202	14.5	69	6
	Torry Holt, St. Louis[8]	93	1,189	12.8	40	7
	Wes Welker, New England	112	1,175	10.5	42	8
	Tony Gonzalez, Kansas City[3]	99	1,172	11.8	31	5
	Bobby Engram, Seattle	94	1,147	12.2	49	6
	Jason Witten, Dallas	96	1,145	11.9	53	7
	T.J. Houshmandzadeh, Cincinnati[2]	112	1,143	10.2	42	12
	Jerricho Cotchery, N.Y. Jets	82	1,130	13.8	50	2
	Kevin Curtis, Philadelphia	77	1,110	14.4	75	6
	Kellen Winslow, Cleveland	82	1,106	13.5	49	5
	Derrick Mason, Baltimore[6]	103	1,087	10.6	79	5
	Donald Driver, Green Bay[5]	82	1,048	12.8	47	2
	Plaxico Burress, N.Y. Giants[4]	70	1,025	14.6	60	12
	Joey Galloway, Tampa Bay[6]	57	1,014	17.8	69	6
	Steve Smith, Carolina[4]	87	1,002	11.5	74	7

OUTSTANDING PERFORMERS

Year	Player, Team	No.	Yards	Avg.	Long	TD
2006	Chad Ochocinco, Cincinnati[5]	87	1,369	15.7	74	7
	Marvin Harrison, Indianapolis[8]	95	1,366	14.4	68	12
	Reggie Wayne, Indianapolis[3]	86	1,310	15.2	51	9
	Roy Williams, Detroit	82	1,310	16.0	60	7
	Donald Driver, Green Bay[4]	92	1,295	14.1	82	8
	Lee Evans, Buffalo	82	1,292	15.8	83	8
	Anquan Boldin, Arizona[3]	83	1,203	14.5	64	4
	Torry Holt, St. Louis[7]	93	1,188	12.8	67	10
	Terrell Owens, Dallas[7]	85	1,180	13.9	56	13
	Steve Smith, Carolina[3]	83	1,166	14.1	72	8
	Andre Johnson, Houston[2]	103	1,147	11.1	53	5
	Isaac Bruce, St. Louis[8]	74	1,098	14.8	45	3
	Laveranues Coles, N.Y. Jets[2]	91	1,098	12.1	58	6
	Mike Furrey, Detroit	98	1,086	11.1	31	6
	Javon Walker, Denver[2]	69	1,084	15.7	83	8
	T.J. Houshmandzadeh, Cincinnati	90	1,081	12.0	40	9
	Joey Galloway, Tampa Bay[5]	62	1,057	17.1	64	7
	Terry Glenn, Dallas[4]	70	1,047	15.0	54	6
	*Marques Colston, New Orleans	70	1,038	14.8	86	8
2005	Steve Smith, Carolina[2]	103	1,563	15.2	80	12
	Santana Moss, Washington[2]	84	1,483	17.7	78	9
	Chad Ochocinco, Cincinnati[4]	97	1,432	14.8	70	9
	Larry Fitzgerald, Arizona	103	1,409	13.7	47	10
	Anquan Boldin, Arizona[2]	102	1,402	13.7	54	7
	Torry Holt, St. Louis[6]	102	1,331	13.0	44	9
	Joey Galloway, Tampa Bay[4]	83	1,287	15.5	80	10
	Donald Driver, Green Bay[3]	86	1,221	14.2	59	5
	Plaxico Burress, N.Y. Giants[3]	76	1,214	16.0	78	7
	Marvin Harrison, Indianapolis[7]	82	1,146	14.0	80	12
	Terry Glenn, Dallas[3]	62	1,136	18.3	71	7
	Chris Chambers, Miami	82	1,118	13.6	77	11
	Rod Smith, Denver[8]	85	1,105	13.0	72	6
	Eddie Kennison, Kansas City[2]	68	1,102	16.2	55	5
	Antonio Gates, San Diego	89	1,101	12.4	38	10
	Derrick Mason, Baltimore[5]	86	1,073	12.5	39	3
	Reggie Wayne, Indianapolis[2]	83	1,055	12.7	66	5
	Jimmy Smith, Jacksonville[9]	70	1,023	14.6	45	6
	Antonio Bryant, Cleveland	69	1,009	14.6	54	4
	Randy Moss, Oakland[7]	60	1,005	16.8	79	8
2004	Muhsin Muhammad, Carolina[3]	93	1,405	15.1	51	16
	Joe Horn, New Orleans[4]	94	1,399	14.9	57	11
	Javon Walker, Green Bay	89	1,382	15.5	79	12
	Torry Holt, St. Louis[5]	94	1,372	14.6	75	10
	Isaac Bruce, St. Louis[7]	89	1,292	14.5	56	6
	Chad Ochocinco, Cincinnati[3]	95	1,274	13.4	53	9
	Tony Gonzalez, Kansas City[2]	102	1,258	12.3	32	7
	Drew Bennett, Tennessee	80	1,247	15.6	48	11
	Reggie Wayne, Indianapolis	77	1,210	15.7	71	12
	Donald Driver, Green Bay[2]	84	1,208	14.4	50	9
	Terrell Owens, Philadelphia[6]	77	1,200	15.6	59	14
	Darrell Jackson, Seattle[3]	87	1,199	13.8	56	7
	*Michael Clayton, Tampa Bay	80	1,193	14.9	75	7
	Jimmy Smith, Jacksonville[8]	74	1,172	15.8	65	6
	Derrick Mason, Tennessee[4]	96	1,168	12.2	37	7
	Rod Smith, Denver[7]	79	1,144	14.5	85	7
	Andre Johnson, Houston	79	1,142	14.5	54	6
	Marvin Harrison, Indianapolis[6]	86	1,113	12.9	59	15
	Eddie Kennison, Kansas City	62	1,086	17.5	70	8
	Ashley Lelie, Denver	54	1,084	20.1	58	7
	Brandon Stokley, Indianapolis	68	1,077	15.8	69	10
	Eric Moulds, Buffalo[4]	88	1,043	11.9	49	5
	Nate Burleson, Minnesota	68	1,006	14.8	68	9
	Hines Ward, Pittsburgh[4]	80	1,004	12.6	58	4
2003	Torry Holt, St. Louis[4]	117	1,696	14.5	48	12
	Randy Moss, Minnesota[6]	111	1,632	14.7	72	17
	*Anquan Boldin, Arizona	101	1,377	13.6	71	8
	Chad Ochocinco, Cincinnati[2]	90	1,355	15.1	82	10
	Derrick Mason, Tennessee[3]	95	1,303	13.7	50	8
	Marvin Harrison, Indianapolis[5]	94	1,272	13.5	79	10

Year	Player, Team	No.	Yards	Avg.	Long	TD
	Laveranues Coles, Washington[2]	82	1,204	14.7	64	6
	Keenan McCardell, Tampa Bay[5]	84	1,174	14.0	76	8
	Hines Ward, Pittsburgh[3]	95	1,163	12.2	50	10
	Darrell Jackson, Seattle[2]	68	1,137	16.7	80	9
	Steve Smith, Carolina	88	1,110	12.6	67	7
	Santana Moss, N.Y. Jets	74	1,105	14.9	65	10
	Terrell Owens, San Francisco[5]	80	1,102	13.8	75	9
	Amani Toomer, N.Y. Giants[5]	63	1,057	16.8	77	5
2002	Marvin Harrison, Indianapolis[4]	143	1,722	12.0	69	11
	Randy Moss, Minnesota[5]	106	1,347	12.7	60	7
	Amani Toomer, N.Y. Giants[4]	82	1,343	16.4	82	8
	Hines Ward, Pittsburgh[2]	112	1,329	11.9	72	12
	Plaxico Burress, Pittsburgh[2]	78	1,325	17.0	62	7
	Joe Horn, New Orleans[3]	88	1,312	14.9	63	7
	Torry Holt, St. Louis[3]	91	1,302	14.3	58	4
	Terrell Owens, San Francisco[4]	100	1,300	13.0	76	13
	Eric Moulds, Buffalo[3]	100	1,292	12.9	70	10
	Laveranues Coles, N.Y. Jets	89	1,264	14.2	43	5
	Peerless Price, Buffalo	94	1,252	13.3	73	9
	Koren Robinson, Seattle	78	1,240	15.9	83	5
	Jerry Rice, Oakland[14]	92	1,211	13.2	75	7
	Marty Booker, Chicago[2]	97	1,189	12.3	54	6
	Chad Ochocinco, Cincinnati	69	1,166	16.9	72	5
	Keyshawn Johnson, Tampa Bay[4]	76	1,088	14.3	76	5
	Isaac Bruce, St. Louis[6]	79	1,075	13.6	34	7
	Donald Driver, Green Bay	70	1,064	15.2	85	9
	Jimmy Smith, Jacksonville[7]	80	1,027	12.8	47	7
	Rod Smith, Denver[6]	89	1,027	11.5	46	5
	Derrick Mason, Tennessee[2]	79	1,012	12.8	40	5
	Rod Gardner, Washington	71	1,006	14.2	43	8
2001	David Boston, Arizona[2]	98	1,598	16.3	61	8
	Marvin Harrison, Indianapolis[3]	109	1,524	14.0	68	15
	Terrell Owens, San Francisco[3]	93	1,412	15.2	60	16
	Jimmy Smith, Jacksonville[6]	112	1,373	12.3	35	8
	Torry Holt, St. Louis[2]	81	1,363	16.8	51	7
	Rod Smith, Denver[5]	113	1,343	11.9	65	11
	Keyshawn Johnson, Tampa Bay[3]	106	1,266	11.9	47	1
	Joe Horn, New Orleans[2]	83	1,265	15.2	56	9
	Randy Moss, Minnesota[4]	82	1,233	15.0	73	10
	Troy Brown, New England	101	1,199	11.9	60	5
	Tim Brown, Oakland[9]	91	1,165	12.8	46	9
	Johnnie Morton, Detroit[4]	77	1,154	15.0	76	4
	Jerry Rice, Oakland[13]	83	1,139	13.7	40	9
	Derrick Mason, Tennessee	73	1,128	15.5	71	9
	Curtis Conway, San Diego[3]	71	1,125	15.8	72	6
	Keenan McCardell, Jacksonville[4]	93	1,110	11.9	45	6
	Isaac Bruce, St. Louis[5]	64	1,106	17.3	51	6
	Kevin Johnson, Cleveland	84	1,097	13.1	55	9
	Darrell Jackson, Seattle	70	1,081	15.4	64	8
	Marty Booker, Chicago	100	1,071	10.7	66	8
	Qadry Ismail, Baltimore[2]	74	1,059	14.3	77	7
	Amani Toomer, N.Y. Giants[3]	72	1,054	14.6	60	5
	Willie Jackson, New Orleans	81	1,046	12.9	63	5
	Plaxico Burress, Pittsburgh	66	1,008	15.3	43	6
	Hines Ward, Pittsburgh	94	1,003	10.7	34	4
2000	Torry Holt, St. Louis	82	1,635	19.9	85	6
	Rod Smith, Denver[4]	100	1,602	16.0	49	8
	Isaac Bruce, St. Louis[4]	87	1,471	16.9	78	9
	Terrell Owens, San Francisco[2]	97	1,451	15.0	69	13
	Randy Moss, Minnesota[3]	77	1,437	18.7	78	15
	Marvin Harrison, Indianapolis[2]	102	1,413	13.9	78	14
	Derrick Alexander, Kansas City[3]	78	1,391	17.8	81	10
	Joe Horn, New Orleans	94	1,340	14.3	52	8
	Eric Moulds, Buffalo[2]	94	1,326	14.1	52	5
	Ed McCaffrey, Denver[3]	101	1,317	13.0	61	9
	Cris Carter, Minnesota[8]	96	1,274	13.3	53	9
	Jimmy Smith, Jacksonville[5]	91	1,213	13.3	65	8
	Keenan McCardell, Jacksonville[3]	94	1,207	12.8	67	5
	Tony Gonzalez, Kansas City	93	1,203	12.9	39	9

Year	Player, Team	No.	Yards	Avg.	Long	TD
	Muhsin Muhammad, Carolina[2]	102	1,183	11.6	36	6
	David Boston, Arizona	71	1,156	16.3	70	7
	Tim Brown, Oakland[8]	76	1,128	14.8	45	11
	Amani Toomer, N.Y. Giants[2]	78	1,094	14.0	54	7
1999	Marvin Harrison, Indianapolis	115	1,663	14.5	57	12
	Jimmy Smith, Jacksonville[4]	116	1,636	14.1	62	6
	Randy Moss, Minnesota[2]	80	1,413	17.7	67	11
	Marcus Robinson, Chicago	84	1,400	16.7	80	9
	Tim Brown, Oakland[7]	90	1,344	14.9	47	6
	Germane Crowell, Detroit	81	1,338	16.5	77	7
	Muhsin Muhammad, Carolina	96	1,253	13.1	60	8
	Cris Carter, Minnesota[7]	90	1,241	13.8	68	13
	Michael Westbrook, Washington	65	1,191	18.3	65	9
	Amani Toomer, N.Y. Giants	79	1,183	15.0	80	6
	Keyshawn Johnson, N.Y. Jets[2]	89	1,170	13.2	65	8
	Isaac Bruce, St. Louis[3]	77	1,165	15.1	60	12
	Terry Glenn, New England[2]	69	1,147	16.6	67	4
	Albert Connell, Washington	62	1,132	18.3	62	7
	Johnnie Morton, Detroit[3]	80	1,129	14.1	48	5
	Qadry Ismail, Baltimore	68	1,105	16.3	76	6
	Raghib Ismail, Dallas[2]	80	1,097	13.7	76	6
	Patrick Jeffers, Carolina	63	1,082	17.2	88	12
	Antonio Freeman, Green Bay[3]	74	1,074	14.5	51	6
	Bill Schroeder, Green Bay	74	1,051	14.2	51	5
	Marshall Faulk, St. Louis	87	1,048	12.1	57	5
	Tony Martin, Miami[4]	67	1,037	15.5	69	5
	Darnay Scott, Cincinnati	68	1,022	15.0	76	7
	Rod Smith, Denver[3]	79	1,020	12.9	71	4
	Ed McCaffrey, Denver[2]	71	1,018	14.3	78	7
	Terance Mathis, Atlanta[4]	81	1,016	12.5	52	6
1998	Antonio Freeman, Green Bay[2]	84	1,424	17.0	84	14
	Eric Moulds, Buffalo	67	1,368	20.4	84	9
	*Randy Moss, Minnesota	69	1,313	19.0	61	17
	Rod Smith, Denver[2]	86	1,222	14.2	58	6
	Jimmy Smith, Jacksonville[3]	78	1,182	15.2	72	8
	Tony Martin, Atlanta[3]	66	1,181	17.9	62	6
	Jerry Rice, San Francisco[12]	82	1,157	14.1	75	9
	Frank Sanders, Arizona[2]	89	1,145	12.9	42	3
	Terance Mathis, Atlanta[3]	64	1,136	17.8	78	11
	Keyshawn Johnson, N.Y. Jets	83	1,131	13.6	41	10
	Terrell Owens, San Francisco	67	1,097	16.4	79	14
	Wayne Chrebet, N.Y. Jets	75	1,083	14.4	63	8
	Michael Irvin, Dallas[7]	74	1,057	14.3	51	1
	Ed McCaffrey, Denver	64	1,053	16.5	48	10
	O.J. McDuffie, Miami	90	1,050	11.7	61	7
	Joey Galloway, Seattle[3]	65	1,047	16.1	81	10
	Johnnie Morton, Detroit[2]	69	1,028	14.9	98	2
	Raghib Ismail, Carolina	69	1,024	14.8	62	8
	Carl Pickens, Cincinnati[4]	82	1,023	12.5	67	5
	Tim Brown, Oakland[6]	81	1,012	12.5	49	9
	Cris Carter, Minnesota[6]	78	1,011	13.0	54	12
1997	Rob Moore, Arizona[3]	97	1,584	16.3	47	8
	Tim Brown, Oakland[5]	104	1,408	13.5	59	5
	Yancey Thigpen, Pittsburgh[2]	79	1,398	17.7	69	7
	Jimmy Smith, Jacksonville[2]	82	1,324	16.1	75	4
	Irving Fryar, Philadelphia[5]	86	1,316	15.3	72	6
	Herman Moore, Detroit[4]	104	1,293	12.4	79	8
	Antonio Freeman, Green Bay	81	1,243	15.3	58	12
	Michael Irvin, Dallas[6]	75	1,180	15.7	55	9
	Rod Smith, Denver	70	1,180	16.9	78	12
	Keenan McCardell, Jacksonville[2]	85	1,164	13.7	60	5
	Jake Reed, Minnesota[4]	68	1,138	16.7	56	6
	Shannon Sharpe, Denver[3]	72	1,107	15.4	68	3
	Andre Rison, Kansas City[5]	72	1,092	15.2	45	7
	Cris Carter, Minnesota[5]	89	1,069	12.0	43	13
	Johnnie Morton, Detroit	80	1,057	13.2	73	6
	Joey Galloway, Seattle[2]	72	1,049	14.6	53	12
	Frank Sanders, Arizona	75	1,017	13.6	70	4
	Robert Brooks, Green Bay[2]	60	1,010	16.8	48	7

Year	Player, Team	No.	Yards	Avg.	Long	TD
	Derrick Alexander, Baltimore[2]	65	1,009	15.5	92	9
1996	Isaac Bruce, St. Louis[2]	84	1,338	15.9	70	7
	Jake Reed, Minnesota[3]	72	1,320	18.3	82	7
	Herman Moore, Detroit[3]	106	1,296	12.2	50	9
	Jerry Rice, San Francisco[11]	108	1,254	11.6	39	8
	Jimmy Smith, Jacksonville	83	1,244	15.0	62	7
	Michael Jackson, Baltimore	76	1,201	15.8	86	14
	Irving Fryar, Philadelphia[4]	88	1,195	13.6	42	11
	Carl Pickens, Cincinnati[3]	100	1,180	11.8	61	12
	Tony Martin, San Diego[2]	85	1,171	13.8	55	14
	Cris Carter, Minnesota[4]	96	1,163	12.1	43	10
	*Terry Glenn, New England	90	1,132	12.6	37	6
	Keenan McCardell, Jacksonville	85	1,129	13.3	52	3
	Tim Brown, Oakland[4]	90	1,104	12.3	42	9
	Derrick Alexander, Baltimore	62	1,099	17.7	64	9
	Shannon Sharpe, Denver[2]	80	1,062	13.3	51	10
	Curtis Conway, Chicago[2]	81	1,049	13.0	58	7
	Andre Reed, Buffalo[4]	66	1,036	15.7	67	6
	Brett Perriman, Detroit[2]	94	1,021	10.9	44	5
	Rob Moore, Arizona[2]	58	1,016	17.5	69	4
	Henry Ellard, Washington[7]	52	1,014	19.5	51	2
	Charles Johnson, Pittsburgh	60	1,008	16.8	70	3
1995	Jerry Rice, San Francisco[10]	122	1,848	15.1	81	15
	Isaac Bruce, St. Louis	119	1,781	15.0	72	13
	Herman Moore, Detroit[2]	123	1,686	13.7	69	14
	Michael Irvin, Dallas[5]	111	1,603	14.4	50	10
	Robert Brooks, Green Bay	102	1,497	14.7	99	13
	Brett Perriman, Detroit	108	1,488	13.8	91	9
	Cris Carter, Minnesota[3]	122	1,371	11.2	60	17
	Tim Brown, Oakland[3]	89	1,342	15.1	80	10
	Yancey Thigpen, Pittsburgh	85	1,307	15.4	43	5
	Jeff Graham, Chicago	82	1,301	15.9	51	4
	Carl Pickens, Cincinnati[2]	99	1,234	12.5	68	17
	Tony Martin, San Diego	90	1,224	13.6	51	6
	Eric Metcalf, Atlanta	104	1,189	11.4	62	8
	Jake Reed, Minnesota[2]	72	1,167	16.2	55	9
	Quinn Early, New Orleans	81	1,087	13.4	70	8
	Anthony Miller, Denver[5]	59	1,079	18.3	62	14
	Bert Emanuel, Atlanta	74	1,039	14.0	52	5
	*Joey Galloway, Seattle	67	1,039	15.5	59	7
	Terance Mathis, Atlanta[2]	78	1,039	13.3	54	9
	Curtis Conway, Chicago	62	1,037	16.7	76	12
	Henry Ellard, Washington[6]	56	1,005	17.9	59	5
	Mark Carrier, Carolina[2]	66	1,002	15.2	66	3
	Brian Blades, Seattle[4]	77	1,001	13.0	49	4
1994	Jerry Rice, San Francisco[9]	112	1,499	13.4	69	13
	Henry Ellard, Washington[5]	74	1,397	18.9	73	6
	Terance Mathis, Atlanta	111	1,342	12.1	81	11
	Tim Brown, L.A. Raiders[2]	89	1,309	14.7	77	9
	Andre Reed, Buffalo[2]	90	1,303	14.5	83	8
	Irving Fryar, Miami[3]	73	1,270	17.4	54	7
	Cris Carter, Minnesota[2]	122	1,256	10.3	65	7
	Michael Irvin, Dallas[4]	79	1,241	15.7	65	6
	Jake Reed, Minnesota	85	1,175	13.8	59	4
	Ben Coates, New England	96	1,174	12.2	62	7
	Herman Moore, Detroit	72	1,173	16.3	51	11
	Fred Barnett, Philadelphia[2]	78	1,127	14.4	54	5
	Carl Pickens, Cincinnati	71	1,127	15.9	70	11
	Sterling Sharpe, Green Bay[4]	94	1,119	11.9	49	18
	Anthony Miller, Denver[4]	60	1,107	18.5	76	5
	Andre Rison, Atlanta[3]	81	1,088	13.4	69	8
	Brian Blades, Seattle[3]	81	1,088	13.4	45	4
	Rob Moore, N.Y. Jets	78	1,010	12.9	41	6
	Shannon Sharpe, Denver	87	1,010	11.6	44	4
1993	Jerry Rice, San Francisco[8]	98	1,503	15.3	80	15
	Michael Irvin, Dallas[3]	88	1,330	15.1	61	7
	Sterling Sharpe, Green Bay[4]	112	1,274	11.4	54	11
	Andre Rison, Atlanta[3]	86	1,242	14.4	53	15
	Tim Brown, L.A. Raiders	80	1,180	14.8	71	7

Year	Player, Team	No.	Yards	Avg.	Long	TD
	Anthony Miller, San Diego[3]	84	1,162	13.8	66	7
	Cris Carter, Minnesota	86	1,071	12.5	58	9
	Reggie Langhorne, Indianapolis	85	1,038	12.2	72	3
	Irving Fryar, Miami[2]	64	1,010	15.8	65	5
1992	Sterling Sharpe, Green Bay[3]	108	1,461	13.5	76	13
	Michael Irvin, Dallas[2]	78	1,396	17.9	87	7
	Jerry Rice, San Francisco[7]	84	1,201	14.3	80	10
	Andre Rison, Atlanta[2]	93	1,119	12.0	71	11
	Fred Barnett, Philadelphia	67	1,083	16.2	71	6
	Anthony Miller, San Diego[2]	72	1,060	14.7	67	7
	Eric Martin, New Orleans[3]	68	1,041	15.3	52	5
1991	Michael Irvin, Dallas	93	1,523	16.4	66	8
	Gary Clark, Washington[5]	70	1,340	19.1	82	10
	Jerry Rice, San Francisco[6]	80	1,206	15.1	73	14
	Haywood Jeffires, Houston[2]	100	1,181	11.8	44	7
	Michael Haynes, Atlanta	50	1,122	22.4	80	11
	Andre Reed, Buffalo[2]	81	1,113	13.7	55	10
	Drew Hill, Houston[5]	90	1,109	12.3	61	4
	Mark Duper, Miami[4]	70	1,085	15.5	43	5
	James Lofton, Buffalo[6]	57	1,072	18.8	77	8
	Mark Clayton, Miami[5]	70	1,053	15.0	43	12
	Henry Ellard, L.A. Rams[4]	64	1,052	16.4	38	3
	Art Monk, Washington[5]	71	1,049	14.8	64	8
	Irving Fryar, New England	68	1,014	14.9	56	3
	John Taylor, San Francisco[2]	64	1,011	15.8	97	9
	Brian Blades, Seattle[2]	70	1,003	14.3	52	2
1990	Jerry Rice, San Francisco[5]	100	1,502	15.0	64	13
	Henry Ellard, L.A. Rams[3]	76	1,294	17.0	50	4
	Andre Rison, Atlanta	82	1,208	14.7	75	10
	Gary Clark, Washington[4]	75	1,112	14.8	53	8
	Sterling Sharpe, Green Bay[2]	67	1,105	16.5	76	6
	Willie Anderson, L.A. Rams[2]	51	1,097	21.5	55	4
	Haywood Jeffires, Houston	74	1,048	14.2	87	8
	Stephone Paige, Kansas City	65	1,021	15.7	86	5
	Drew Hill, Houston[4]	74	1,019	13.8	57	5
	Anthony Carter, Minnesota[3]	70	1,008	14.4	56	8
1989	Jerry Rice, San Francisco[4]	82	1,483	18.1	68	17
	Sterling Sharpe, Green Bay	90	1,423	15.8	79	12
	Mark Carrier, Tampa Bay	86	1,422	16.5	78	9
	Henry Ellard, L.A. Rams[2]	70	1,382	19.7	53	8
	Andre Reed, Buffalo	88	1,312	14.9	78	9
	Anthony Miller, San Diego	75	1,252	16.7	69	10
	Webster Slaughter, Cleveland	65	1,236	19.0	97	6
	Gary Clark, Washington[3]	79	1,229	15.6	80	9
	Tim McGee, Cincinnati	65	1,211	18.6	74	8
	Art Monk, Washington[4]	86	1,186	13.8	60	8
	Willie Anderson, L.A. Rams	44	1,146	26.0	78	5
	Ricky Sanders, Washington[2]	80	1,138	14.2	68	4
	Vance Johnson, Denver	76	1,095	14.4	69	7
	Richard Johnson, Detroit	70	1,091	15.6	75	8
	Eric Martin, New Orleans[2]	68	1,090	16.0	53	8
	John Taylor, San Francisco	60	1,077	18.0	95	10
	Mervyn Fernandez, L.A. Raiders	57	1,069	18.8	75	9
	Anthony Carter, Minnesota[2]	65	1,066	16.4	50	4
	Brian Blades, Seattle	77	1,063	13.8	60	5
	Mark Clayton, Miami[4]	64	1,011	15.8	78	9
1988	Henry Ellard, L.A. Rams	86	1,414	16.4	68	10
	Jerry Rice, San Francisco[3]	64	1,306	20.4	96	9
	Eddie Brown, Cincinnati	53	1,273	24.0	86	9
	Anthony Carter, Minnesota	72	1,225	17.0	67	6
	Ricky Sanders, Washington	73	1,148	15.7	55	12
	Drew Hill, Houston[3]	72	1,141	15.8	57	10
	Mark Clayton, Miami[3]	86	1,129	13.1	45	14
	Roy Green, Phoenix[3]	68	1,097	16.1	52	7
	Eric Martin, New Orleans	85	1,083	12.7	40	7
	Al Toon, N.Y. Jets[2]	93	1,067	11.5	42	5
	Bruce Hill, Tampa Bay	58	1,040	17.9	42	9
	Lionel Manuel, N.Y. Giants	65	1,029	15.8	46	4
1987	J.T. Smith, St. Louis[2]	91	1,117	12.3	38	8

Year	Player, Team	No.	Yards	Avg.	Long	TD
	Jerry Rice, San Francisco[2]	65	1,078	16.6	57	22
	Gary Clark, Washington[2]	56	1,066	19.0	84	7
	Carlos Carson, Kansas City[3]	55	1,044	19.0	81	7
1986	Jerry Rice, San Francisco	86	1,570	18.3	66	15
	Stanley Morgan, New England[3]	84	1,491	17.8	44	10
	Mark Duper, Miami[3]	67	1,313	19.6	85	11
	Gary Clark, Washington	74	1,265	17.1	55	7
	Al Toon, N.Y. Jets	85	1,176	13.8	62	8
	Todd Christensen, L.A. Raiders[3]	95	1,153	12.1	35	8
	Mark Clayton, Miami[2]	60	1,150	19.2	68	10
	*Bill Brooks, Indianapolis	65	1,131	17.4	84	8
	Drew Hill, Houston[2]	65	1,112	17.1	81	5
	Steve Largent, Seattle[8]	70	1,070	15.3	38	9
	Art Monk, Washington[3]	73	1,068	14.6	69	4
	*Ernest Givins, Houston	61	1,062	17.4	60	3
	Cris Collinsworth, Cincinnati[4]	62	1,024	16.5	46	10
	Wesley Walker, N.Y. Jets[2]	49	1,016	20.7	83	12
	J.T. Smith, St. Louis	80	1,014	12.7	45	6
	Mark Bavaro, N.Y. Giants	66	1,001	15.2	41	4
1985	Steve Largent, Seattle[7]	79	1,287	16.3	43	6
	Mike Quick, Philadelphia[3]	73	1,247	17.1	99	11
	Art Monk, Washington[2]	91	1,226	13.5	53	2
	Wes Chandler, San Diego[4]	67	1,199	17.9	75	10
	Drew Hill, Houston	64	1,169	18.3	57	9
	James Lofton, Green Bay[5]	69	1,153	16.7	56	4
	Louis Lipps, Pittsburgh	59	1,134	19.2	51	12
	Cris Collinsworth, Cincinnati[3]	65	1,125	17.3	71	5
	Tony Hill, Dallas[3]	74	1,113	15.0	53	7
	Lionel James, San Diego	86	1,027	11.9	67	6
	Roger Craig, San Francisco	92	1,016	11.0	73	6
1984	Roy Green, St. Louis[2]	78	1,555	19.9	83	12
	John Stallworth, Pittsburgh[3]	80	1,395	17.4	51	11
	Mark Clayton, Miami	73	1,389	19.0	65	18
	Art Monk, Washington	106	1,372	12.9	72	7
	James Lofton, Green Bay[4]	62	1,361	22.0	79	7
	Mark Duper, Miami[2]	71	1,306	18.4	80	8
	Steve Watson, Denver[3]	69	1,170	17.0	73	7
	Steve Largent, Seattle[6]	74	1,164	15.7	65	12
	Tim Smith, Houston[2]	69	1,141	16.5	75	4
	Stacey Bailey, Atlanta	67	1,138	17.0	61	6
	Carlos Carson, Kansas City[2]	57	1,078	18.9	57	4
	Mike Quick, Philadelphia[2]	61	1,052	17.2	90	9
	Todd Christensen, L.A. Raiders[2]	80	1,007	12.6	38	7
	Kevin House, Tampa Bay[2]	76	1,005	13.2	55	5
	Ozzie Newsome, Cleveland[2]	89	1,001	11.2	52	5
1983	Mike Quick, Philadelphia	69	1,409	20.4	83	13
	Carlos Carson, Kansas City	80	1,351	16.9	50	7
	James Lofton, Green Bay[3]	58	1,300	22.4	74	8
	Todd Christensen, L.A. Raiders	92	1,247	13.6	45	12
	Roy Green, St. Louis	78	1,227	15.7	71	14
	Charlie Brown, Washington	78	1,225	15.7	75	8
	Tim Smith, Houston	83	1,176	14.2	47	6
	Kellen Winslow, San Diego[3]	88	1,172	13.3	46	8
	Earnest Gray, N.Y. Giants	78	1,139	14.6	62	5
	Steve Watson, Denver[2]	59	1,133	19.2	78	5
	Cris Collinsworth, Cincinnati[2]	66	1,130	17.1	63	5
	Steve Largent, Seattle[5]	72	1,074	14.9	46	11
	Mark Duper, Miami	51	1,003	19.7	85	10
1982	Wes Chandler, San Diego[3]	49	1,032	21.1	66	9
1981	Alfred Jenkins, Atlanta[2]	70	1,358	19.4	67	13
	James Lofton, Green Bay[2]	71	1,294	18.2	75	8
	Steve Watson, Denver	60	1,244	20.7	95	13
	Frank Lewis, Buffalo[2]	70	1,244	17.8	33	4
	Steve Largent, Seattle[4]	75	1,224	16.3	57	9
	Charlie Joiner, San Diego[4]	70	1,188	17.0	57	7
	Kevin House, Tampa Bay	56	1,176	21.0	84	9
	Wes Chandler, New Orleans/San Diego[2]	69	1,142	16.6	51	6
	Dwight Clark, San Francisco	85	1,105	13.0	78	4
	John Stallworth, Pittsburgh[2]	63	1,098	17.4	55	5

OUTSTANDING PERFORMERS

Year	Player, Team	No.	Yards	Avg.	Long	TD
	Kellen Winslow, San Diego[2]	88	1,075	12.2	67	10
	Pat Tilley, St. Louis	66	1,040	15.8	75	3
	Stanley Morgan, New England[2]	44	1,029	23.4	76	6
	Harold Carmichael, Philadelphia[3]	61	1,028	16.9	85	6
	Freddie Scott, Detroit	53	1,022	19.3	48	5
	*Cris Collinsworth, Cincinnati	67	1,009	15.1	74	8
	Joe Senser, Minnesota	79	1,004	12.7	53	8
	Ozzie Newsome, Cleveland	69	1,002	14.5	62	6
	Sammy White, Minnesota	66	1,001	15.2	53	3
1980	John Jefferson, San Diego[3]	82	1,340	16.3	58	13
	Kellen Winslow, San Diego	89	1,290	14.5	65	9
	James Lofton, Green Bay	71	1,226	17.3	47	4
	Charlie Joiner, San Diego[3]	71	1,132	15.9	51	4
	Ahmad Rashad, Minnesota[2]	69	1,095	15.9	76	5
	Steve Largent, Seattle[3]	66	1,064	16.1	67	6
	Tony Hill, Dallas[2]	60	1,055	17.6	58	8
	Alfred Jenkins, Atlanta	57	1,026	18.0	57	6
1979	Steve Largent, Seattle[2]	66	1,237	18.7	55	9
	John Stallworth, Pittsburgh	70	1,183	16.9	65	8
	Ahmad Rashad, Minnesota	80	1,156	14.5	52	9
	John Jefferson, San Diego[2]	61	1,090	17.9	65	10
	Frank Lewis, Buffalo	54	1,082	20.0	55	2
	Wes Chandler, New Orleans	65	1,069	16.4	85	6
	Tony Hill, Dallas	60	1,062	17.7	75	10
	Drew Pearson, Dallas[2]	55	1,026	18.7	56	8
	Wallace Francis, Atlanta	74	1,013	13.7	42	8
	Harold Jackson, New England[3]	45	1,013	22.5	59	7
	Charlie Joiner, San Diego[2]	72	1,008	14.0	39	4
	Stanley Morgan, New England	44	1,002	22.8	63	12
1978	Wesley Walker, N.Y. Jets	48	1,169	24.4	77	8
	Steve Largent, Seattle	71	1,168	16.5	57	8
	Harold Carmichael, Philadelphia[2]	55	1,072	19.5	56	8
	*John Jefferson, San Diego	56	1,001	17.9	46	13
1976	Roger Carr, Baltimore	43	1,112	25.9	79	11
	Cliff Branch, Oakland[2]	46	1,111	24.2	88	12
	Charlie Joiner, San Diego	50	1,056	21.1	81	7
1975	Ken Burrough, Houston	53	1,063	20.1	77	8
1974	Cliff Branch, Oakland	60	1,092	18.2	67	13
	Drew Pearson, Dallas	62	1,087	17.5	50	2
1973	Harold Carmichael, Philadelphia	67	1,116	16.7	73	9
1972	Harold Jackson, Philadelphia[2]	62	1,048	16.9	77	4
	John Gilliam, Minnesota	47	1,035	22.0	66	7
1971	Otis Taylor, Kansas City[2]	57	1,110	19.5	82	7
1970	Gene Washington, San Francisco	53	1,100	20.8	79	12
	Marlin Briscoe, Buffalo	57	1,036	18.2	48	8
	Dick Gordon, Chicago	71	1,026	14.5	69	13
	Gary Garrison, San Diego[2]	44	1,006	22.9	67	12
1969	Warren Wells, Oakland[2]	47	1,260	26.8	80	14
	Harold Jackson, Philadelphia	65	1,116	17.2	65	9
	Roy Jefferson, Pittsburgh[2]	67	1,079	16.1	63	9
	Dan Abramowicz, New Orleans	73	1,015	13.9	49	7
	Lance Alworth, San Diego[7]	64	1,003	15.7	76	4
1968	Lance Alworth, San Diego[6]	68	1,312	19.3	80	10
	Don Maynard, N.Y. Jets[5]	57	1,297	22.8	87	10
	George Sauer, N.Y. Jets[3]	66	1,141	17.3	43	3
	Warren Wells, Oakland	53	1,137	21.5	94	11
	Gary Garrison, San Diego	52	1,103	21.2	84	10
	Roy Jefferson, Pittsburgh	58	1,074	18.5	62	11
	Paul Warfield, Cleveland	50	1,067	21.3	65	12
	Homer Jones, N.Y. Giants[3]	45	1,057	23.5	84	7
	Fred Biletnikoff, Oakland	61	1,037	17.0	82	6
	Lance Rentzel, Dallas	54	1,009	18.7	65	6
1967	Don Maynard, N.Y. Jets[4]	71	1,434	20.2	75	10
	Ben Hawkins, Philadelphia	59	1,265	21.4	87	10
	Homer Jones, N.Y. Giants[2]	49	1,209	24.7	70	13
	Jackie Smith, St. Louis	56	1,205	21.5	76	9
	George Sauer, N.Y. Jets[2]	75	1,189	15.9	61	6
	Lance Alworth, San Diego[5]	52	1,010	19.4	71	9
1966	Lance Alworth, San Diego[4]	73	1,383	18.9	78	13

Year	Player, Team	No.	Yards	Avg.	Long	TD
	Otis Taylor, Kansas City	58	1,297	22.4	89	8
	Pat Studstill, Detroit	67	1,266	18.9	99	5
	Bob Hayes, Dallas[2]	64	1,232	19.3	95	13
	Charlie Frazier, Houston	57	1,129	19.8	79	12
	Charley Taylor, Washington	72	1,119	15.5	86	12
	George Sauer, N.Y. Jets	63	1,081	17.2	77	5
	Homer Jones, N.Y. Giants	48	1,044	21.8	98	8
	Art Powell, Oakland[5]	53	1,026	19.4	46	11
1965	Lance Alworth, San Diego[3]	69	1,602	23.2	85	14
	Dave Parks, San Francisco	80	1,344	16.8	53	12
	Don Maynard, N.Y. Jets[3]	68	1,218	17.9	56	14
	Pete Retzlaff, Philadelphia	66	1,190	18.0	78	10
	Lionel Taylor, Denver[4]	85	1,131	13.3	63	6
	Tommy McDonald, Los Angeles[3]	67	1,036	15.5	51	9
	*Bob Hayes, Dallas	46	1,003	21.8	82	12
1964	Charley Hennigan, Houston[3]	101	1,546	15.3	53	8
	Art Powell, Oakland[4]	76	1,361	17.9	77	11
	Lance Alworth, San Diego[2]	61	1,235	20.2	82	13
	Johnny Morris, Chicago	93	1,200	12.9	63	10
	Elbert Dubenion, Buffalo	42	1,139	27.1	72	10
	Terry Barr, Detroit[2]	57	1,030	18.1	58	9
1963	Bobby Mitchell, Washington[2]	69	1,436	20.8	99	7
	Art Powell, Oakland[3]	73	1,304	17.9	85	16
	Buddy Dial, Pittsburgh[2]	60	1,295	21.6	83	9
	Lance Alworth, San Diego	61	1,205	19.8	85	11
	Del Shofner, N.Y. Giants[4]	64	1,181	18.5	70	9
	Lionel Taylor, Denver[3]	78	1,101	14.1	72	10
	Terry Barr, Detroit	66	1,086	16.5	75	13
	Charley Hennigan, Houston[2]	61	1,051	17.2	83	10
	Sonny Randle, St. Louis[2]	51	1,014	19.9	68	12
	Bake Turner, N.Y. Jets	71	1,009	14.2	53	6
1962	Bobby Mitchell, Washington	72	1,384	19.2	81	11
	Sonny Randle, St. Louis	63	1,158	18.4	86	7
	Tommy McDonald, Philadelphia[2]	58	1,146	19.8	60	10
	Del Shofner, N.Y. Giants[3]	53	1,133	21.4	69	12
	Art Powell, N.Y. Titans[2]	64	1,130	17.7	80	8
	Frank Clarke, Dall. Cowboys	47	1,043	22.2	66	14
	Don Maynard, N.Y. Titans[2]	56	1,041	18.6	86	8
1961	Charley Hennigan, Houston	82	1,746	21.3	80	12
	Lionel Taylor, Denver[2]	100	1,176	11.8	52	4
	Bill Groman, Houston[2]	50	1,175	23.5	80	17
	Tommy McDonald, Philadelphia	64	1,144	17.9	66	13
	Del Shofner, N.Y. Giants[2]	68	1,125	16.5	46	11
	Jim Phillips, Los Angeles	78	1,092	14.0	69	5
	*Mike Ditka, Chicago	56	1,076	19.2	76	12
	Dave Kocourek, San Diego	55	1,055	19.2	76	4
	Buddy Dial, Pittsburgh	53	1,047	19.8	88	12
	R.C. Owens, San Francisco	55	1,032	18.8	54	5
1960	*Bill Groman, Houston	72	1,473	20.5	92	12
	Raymond Berry, Baltimore	74	1,298	17.5	70	10
	Don Maynard, N.Y. Titans	72	1,265	17.6	65	6
	Lionel Taylor, Denver	92	1,235	13.4	80	12
	Art Powell, N.Y. Titans	69	1,167	16.9	76	14
1958	Del Shofner, Los Angeles	51	1,097	21.5	92	8
1956	Bill Howton, Green Bay[2]	55	1,188	21.6	66	12
	Harlon Hill, Chi. Bears[2]	47	1,128	24.0	79	11
1954	Bob Boyd, Los Angeles	53	1,212	22.9	80	6
	*Harlon Hill, Chi. Bears	45	1,124	25.0	76	12
1953	Pete Pihos, Philadelphia	63	1,049	16.7	59	10
1952	*Bill Howton, Green Bay	53	1,231	23.2	90	13
1951	Elroy (Crazylegs) Hirsch, Los Angeles	66	1,495	22.7	91	17
1950	Tom Fears, Los Angeles[2]	84	1,116	13.3	53	7
	Cloyce Box, Detroit	50	1,009	20.2	82	11
1949	Bob Mann, Detroit	66	1,014	15.4	64	4
	Tom Fears, Los Angeles	77	1,013	13.2	51	9
1945	Jim Benton, Cleveland	45	1,067	23.7	84	8
1942	Don Hutson, Green Bay	74	1,211	16.4	73	17

**First season of professional football.*

OUTSTANDING PERFORMERS

250 YARDS PASS RECEIVING IN A GAME

Date	Player, Team, Opponent	No.	Yards	TD
Oct. 11, 2009	Miles Austin, Dallas vs. Kansas City (OT)	10	250	2
Nov. 19, 2006	Lee Evans, Buffalo vs. Houston	11	265	2
Nov. 12, 2006	Chad Ochocinco, Cincinnati vs. San Diego	11	260	2
Nov. 10, 2002	Plaxico Burress, Pittsburgh vs. Atlanta (OT)	9	253	2
Dec. 17, 2000	Terrell Owens, San Francisco vs. Chicago	20	283	1
Sept. 10, 2000	Jimmy Smith, Jacksonville vs. Baltimore	15	291	3
Dec. 12, 1999	Qadry Ismail, Baltimore vs. Pittsburgh	6	258	3
Dec. 18, 1995	Jerry Rice, San Francisco vs. Minnesota	14	289	3
Dec. 11, 1989	John Taylor, San Francisco vs. L.A. Rams	11	286	2
Nov. 26, 1989	Willie Anderson, L.A. Rams vs. New Orleans (OT)	15	336	1
Oct. 18, 1987	Steve Largent, Seattle vs. Detroit	15	261	3
Oct. 4, 1987	Anthony Allen, Washington vs. St. Louis	7	255	3
Dec. 22, 1985	Stephone Paige, Kansas City vs. San Diego	8	309	2
Dec. 20, 1982	Wes Chandler, San Diego vs. Cincinnati	10	260	2
Sept. 23, 1979	*Jerry Butler, Buffalo vs. N.Y. Jets	10	255	4
Nov. 4, 1962	Sonny Randle, St. Louis vs. N.Y. Giants	16	256	1
Oct. 28, 1962	Del Shofner, N.Y. Giants vs. Washington	11	269	1
Oct. 13, 1961	Charley Hennigan, Houston vs. Boston	13	272	1
Oct. 21, 1956	Billy Howton, Green Bay vs. Los Angeles	7	257	2
Dec. 3, 1950	Cloyce Box, Detroit vs. Baltimore	12	302	4
Nov. 22, 1945	Jim Benton, Cleveland vs. Detroit	10	303	1

First season of professional football.

2,000 COMBINED NET YARDS GAINED IN A SEASON

Year	Player, Team	Rushing Att.-Yds.	Pass Rec.	Punt Ret.	Kickoff Ret.	Fum. Ret.	Total Yds.
2009	Fred Jackson, Buffalo	237-1,062	46-371	6-69	41-1,014	0-0	330-2,516
	Josh Cribbs, Cleveland[2]	55-381	20-135	38-452	56-1,542	2-0	171-2,510
	Chris Johnson, Tennessee	358-2,006	50-503	0-0	0-0	1-0	409-2,509
	Jamaal Charles, Kansas City	190-1,120	40-297	0-0	36-925	3-0	269-2,342
	Darren Sproles, San Diego[2]	93-343	45-497	26-183	54-1,300	1-0	219-2,323
	Danny Amendola, St. Louis	3-2	43-326	31-360	66-1,618	1-0	144-2,302
	*Percy Harvin, Minnesota	15-135	60-790	0-0	42-1,156	0-0	117-2,081
	Ray Rice, Baltimore	254-1,339	78-702	0-0	0-0	1-2	333-2,043
2008	Leon Washington, N.Y. Jets[2]	76-448	47-355	29-303	48-1,231	4-(-5)	204-2,332
	Darren Sproles, San Diego	61-330	29-342	22-249	53-1,376	1-(-2)	166-2,295
	Jerious Norwood, Atlanta[2]	95-489	36-338	0-0	51-1,311	0-0	182-2,138
2007	Josh Cribbs, Cleveland	9-61	3-37	30-405	59-1,809	2-0	103-2,312
	Jerious Norwood, Atlanta	103-613	28-277	0-0	52-1,317	0-0	183-2,207
	Brian Westbrook, Philadelphia	278-1,333	90-771	4-79	0-0	0-0	372-2,183
	*Ted Ginn Jr., Miami	4-3	34-420	24-230	63-1,433	2-(-9)	127-2,077
	Leon Washington, N.Y. Jets	71-353	36-213	20-183	47-1,291	1-0	175-2,040
	*Adrian Peterson, Minnesota	238-1,341	19-268	0-0	16-412	3-0	276-2,014
	Maurice Jones-Drew, Jacksonville[2]	167-768	40-407	3-28	31-811	0-0	241-2,014
2006	Steven Jackson, St. Louis	346-1,528	90,806	0-0	0-0	2-0	438-2,334
	LaDainian Tomlinson, San Diego[3]	348-1,815	56-508	0-0	0-0	1-0	405-2,323
	*Maurice Jones-Drew, Jacksonville	166-941	46-436	1-13	31-860	0-0	244-2,250
	Larry Johnson, Kansas City[2]	416-1,789	41-410	0-0	0-0	1-0	458-2,199
	Frank Gore, San Francisco	312-1,695	61-485	0-0	0-0	0-0	373-2,180
	Wes Welker, Miami[2]	0-0	67-687	41-378	48-1,064	1-0	157-2,129
	Tiki Barber, N.Y. Giants[4]	327-1,662	58-465	0-0	0-0	1-0	386-2,127
	Chris Carr, Oakland	0-0	0-0	35-216	69-1,762	1-0	106-2,078
2005	Tiki Barber, N.Y. Giants[3]	357-1,860	54-530	0-0	0-0	1-0	412-2,390
	Dante Hall, Kansas City[4]	7-11	34-436	42-276	65-1,560	2-0	150-2,283
	Wes Welker, Miami	1-5	29-434	43-390	61-1,379	4-0	138-2,208
	Larry Johnson, Kansas City	336-1,750	33-343	0-0	0-0	3-0	372-2,093
2004	Dante Hall, Kansas City[3]	8-56	25-230	23-232	68-1,718	0-0	124-2,236
	Tiki Barber, N.Y. Giants[2]	322-1,518	52-578	0-0	0-0	2-0	376-2,096
	Edgerrin James, Indianapolis[3]	334-1,548	51-483	0-0	0-0	1-0	386-2,031
2003	Dante Hall, Kansas City[2]	16-73	40-423	29-472	57-1,478	0-0	142-2,446
	LaDainian Tomlinson, San Diego[2]	313-1,645	100-725	0-0	0-0	2-0	415-2,370
	Jamal Lewis, Baltimore	387-2,066	26-205	0-0	0-0	1-0	414-2,271
	Ahman Green, Green Bay	355-1,883	50-367	0-0	0-0	2-0	407-2,250
	Deuce McAllister, New Orleans	351-1,641	69-516	0-0	0-0	3-(-3)	423-2,154
	Priest Holmes, Kansas City[3]	320-1,420	74-690	0-0	0-0	0-0	394-2,110
2002	Michael Lewis, New Orleans	1-15	8-200	44-625	70-1,807	2-0	125-2,647
	Priest Holmes, Kansas City[2]	313-1,615	70-672	0-0	0-0	0-0	383-2,287
	Ricky Williams, Miami	383-1,853	47-363	0-0	0-0	1-0	431-2,216

Year	Player, Team	Rushing Att.-Yds.	Pass Rec.	Punt Ret.	Kickoff Ret.	Fum. Ret.	Total Yds.
	LaDainian Tomlinson, San Diego	372-1,683	79-489	0-0	0-0	0-0	451-2,172
	Dante Hall, Kansas City	11-54	20-322	29-390	57-1,354	1-0	118-2,120
2001	Priest Holmes, Kansas City	327-1,555	62-614	0-0	0-0	0-0	389-2,169
	Marshall Faulk, St. Louis[4]	260-1,382	83-765	0-0	0-0	2-0	345-2,147
	Derrick Mason, Tennessee[2]	0-0	73-1,128	20-128	34-748	1-0	128-2,004
2000	Derrick Mason, Tennessee	1-1	63-895	51-662	42-1,132	1-0	158-2,690
	MarTay Jenkins, Arizona	1-(-4)	17-219	1-1	82-2,186	0-0	101-2,402
	Edgerrin James, Indianapolis[2]	387-1,709	63-594	0-0	0-0	0-0	450-2,303
	Marshall Faulk, St. Louis[3]	253-1,359	81-830	0-0	1-18	2-0	337-2,207
	Tiki Barber, N.Y. Giants	213-1,006	70-719	39-332	1-28	5-0	328-2,085
1999	Marshall Faulk, St. Louis[2]	253-1,381	87-1,048	0-0	0-0	0-0	340-2,429
	*Edgerrin James, Indianapolis	369-1,553	62-586	0-0	0-0	2-0	433-2,139
	*Terrence Wilkins, Indianapolis	1-2	42-565	41-388	51-1,134	1-0	136-2,089
	Glyn Milburn, Chicago[2]	16-102	20-151	30-346	61-1,426	2-0	129-2,025
1998	Brian Mitchell, Washington[4]	39-208	44-306	44-506	59-1,337	0-0	186-2,357
	Marshall Faulk, Indianapolis	324-1,319	86-908	0-0	0-0	2-13	412-2,240
	Terrell Davis, Denver[2]	392-2,008	25-217	0-0	0-0	1-0	418-2,225
	Jamal Anderson, Atlanta	410-1,846	27-319	0-0	0-0	1-0	438-2,165
	Garrison Hearst, San Francisco	310-1,570	39-535	0-0	0-0	1-0	350-2,105
1997	Barry Sanders, Detroit[2]	335-2,053	33-305	0-0	0-0	1-0	369-2,358
	Kevin Williams, Arizona	1-(-2)	20-273	40-462	59-1,458	1-0	121-2,191
	Brian Mitchell, Washington[3]	23-107	36-438	38-442	47-1,094	0-0	144-2,081
	Terrell Davis, Denver	369-1,750	42-287	0-0	0-0	2-(-7)	413-2,030
	Jermaine Lewis, Baltimore	3-35	42-648	28-437	41-905	2-0	116-2,025
1995	Brian Mitchell, Washington[2]	46-301	38-324	25-315	55-1,408	0-0	164-2,348
	Emmitt Smith, Dallas[2]	377-1,773	62-375	0-0	0-0	0-0	439-2,148
	Glyn Milburn, Denver	49-266	22-191	31-354	47-1,269	0-0	149-2,080
	Ernie Mills, Pittsburgh	5-39	39-679	0-0	54-1,306	0-0	98-2,024
1994	Brian Mitchell, Washington	78-311	26-236	32-452	58-1,478	0-0	194-2,477
	Barry Sanders, Detroit	331-1,883	44-283	0-0	0-0	0-0	375-2,166
1992	Thurman Thomas, Buffalo[2]	312-1,487	58-626	0-0	0-0	1-0	371-2,113
	Emmitt Smith, Dallas	373-1,713	59-335	0-0	0-0	1-0	433-2,048
	Barry Foster, Pittsburgh	390-1,690	36-344	0-0	0-0	2-(–20)	428-2,014
1991	Thurman Thomas, Buffalo	288-1,407	62-631	0-0	0-0	0-0	350-2,038
1990	Herschel Walker, Minnesota[2]	184-770	35-315	0-0	44-966	4-0	267-2,051
1988	*Tim Brown, L.A. Raiders	14-50	43-725	49-444	41-1,098	7-0	154-2,317
	Roger Craig, San Francisco[2]	310-1,502	76-534	0-0	2-32	2-0	390-2,068
	Eric Dickerson, Indianapolis[4]	388-1,659	36-377	0-0	0-0	1-0	425-2,036
	Herschel Walker, Dallas	361-1,514	53-505	0-0	0-0	3-0	417-2,019
1986	Eric Dickerson, L.A. Rams[3]	404-1,821	26-205	0-0	0-0	2-0	432-2,026
	Gary Anderson, San Diego	127-442	80-871	25-227	24-482	2-0	258-2,022
1985	Lionel James, San Diego	105-516	86-1,027	25-213	36-779	1-0	253-2,535
	Marcus Allen, L.A. Raiders	380-1,759	67-555	0-0	0-0	2-(–6)	449-2,308
	Roger Craig, San Francisco	214-1,050	92-1,016	0-0	0-0	0-0	306-2,066
	Walter Payton, Chicago[4]	324-1,551	49-483	0-0	0-0	1-0	374-2,034
1984	Eric Dickerson, L.A. Rams[2]	379-2,105	21-139	0-0	0-0	4-15	404-2,259
	James Wilder, Tampa Bay	407-1,544	85-685	0-0	0-0	4-0	496-2,229
	Walter Payton, Chicago[3]	381-1,684	45-368	0-0	0-0	1-0	427-2,052
1983	*Eric Dickerson, L.A. Rams	390-1,808	51-404	0-0	0-0	1-0	442-2,212
	William Andrews, Atlanta[2]	331-1,567	59-609	0-0	0-0	2-0	392-2,176
	Walter Payton, Chicago[2]	314-1,421	53-607	0-0	0-0	2-0	369-2,028
1981	*James Brooks, San Diego	109-525	46-329	22-290	40-949	2-0	219-2,093
	William Andrews, Atlanta	289-1,301	81-735	0-0	0-0	0-0	370-2,036
1980	Bruce Harper, N.Y. Jets[2]	45-126	50-634	28-242	49-1,070	3-0	175-2,072
1979	Wilbert Montgomery, Philadelphia	338-1,512	41-494	0-0	1-6	2-0	382-2,012
1978	Bruce Harper, N.Y. Jets	58-303	13-196	30-378	55-1,280	1-0	157-2,157
1977	Walter Payton, Chicago	339-1,852	27-269	0-0	2-95	5-0	373-2,216
	Terry Metcalf, St. Louis[3]	149-739	34-403	14-108	32-772	1-0	230-2,022
1975	Terry Metcalf, St. Louis[2]	165-816	43-378	23-285	35-960	2-23	268-2,462
	O.J. Simpson, Buffalo[2]	329-1,817	28-426	0-0	0-0	1-0	358-2,243
1974	Mack Herron, New England	231-824	38-474	35-517	28-629	3-0	335-2,444
	Otis Armstrong, Denver	263-1,407	38-405	0-0	16-386	1-0	318-2,198
	Terry Metcalf, St. Louis	152-718	50-377	26-340	20-623	7-0	255-2,058
1973	O.J. Simpson, Buffalo	332-2,003	6-70	0-0	0-0	0-0	338-2,073
1966	Gale Sayers, Chicago[2]	229-1,231	34-447	6-44	23-718	3-0	295-2,440
	Leroy Kelly, Cleveland	209-1,141	32-366	13-104	19-403	0-0	273-2,014
1965	*Gale Sayers, Chicago	166-867	29-507	16-238	21-660	4-0	236-2,272
1963	Timmy Brown, Philadelphia[2]	192-841	36-487	16-152	33-945	2-3	279-2,428

OUTSTANDING PERFORMERS

Year	Player, Team	Rushing Att.-Yds.	Pass Rec.	Punt Ret.	Kickoff Ret.	Fum. Ret.	Total Yds.
	Jim Brown, Cleveland	291-1,863	24-268	0-0	0-0	0-0	315-2,131
1962	Timmy Brown, Philadelphia	137-545	52-849	6-81	30-831	4-0	229-2,306
	Dick Christy, N.Y. Titans	114-535	62-538	15-250	38-824	2-0	231-2,147
1961	Billy Cannon, Houston	200-948	43-586	9-70	18-439	2-0	272-2,043
1960	*Abner Haynes, Dallas Texans	156-875	55-576	14-215	19-434	4-0	248-2,100

First season of professional football.

300 COMBINED NET YARDS GAINED IN A GAME

Date	Player, Team, Opponent	No.	Yards	TD
Dec. 20, 2009	Josh Cribbs, Cleveland vs. Kansas City	14	316	2
Oct. 18, 2009	Domenik Hixon, N.Y. Giants vs. New Orleans	12	303	0
Sept. 28, 2008	Steve Breaston, Arizona vs. N.Y. Jets	19	324	0
Sept. 14, 2008	Darren Sproles, San Diego vs. Denver	14	317	2
Nov. 18, 2007	Josh Cribbs, Cleveland vs. Baltimore (OT)	12	309	0
Nov. 4, 2007	*Adrian Peterson, Minnesota vs. San Diego	31	315	3
Oct. 14, 2007	*Adrian Peterson, Minnesota vs. Chicago	25	361	3
Sept. 30, 2007	Devin Hester, Chicago vs. Detroit	13	317	1
Dec. 10, 2006	*Maurice Jones-Drew, Jacksonville vs. Indianapolis	19	303	3
Dec. 14, 2003	Derrick Mason, Tennessee vs. Buffalo	21	302	0
Nov. 16, 2003	Jonathan Carter, N.Y. Jets vs. Indianapolis	7	304	2
Dec. 8, 2002	Steve Smith, Carolina vs. Cincinnati	9	313	3
Nov. 24, 2002	Priest Holmes, Kansas City vs. Seattle	30	307	3
Oct. 13, 2002	Michael Lewis, New Orleans vs. Washington	8	356	2
Dec. 24, 1999	Jason Tucker, Dallas vs. New Orleans	13	331	1
Dec. 7, 1997	Jermaine Lewis, Baltimore vs. Seattle	10	308	3
Dec. 25, 1995	Kevin Williams, Dallas vs. Arizona	16	307	2
Dec. 10, 1995	Glyn Milburn, Denver vs. Seattle	33	404	0
Oct. 23, 1994	Tyrone Hughes, New Orleans vs. L.A. Rams	11	347	2
Dec. 11, 1989	John Taylor, San Francisco vs. L.A. Rams	14	321	2
Nov. 26, 1989	Willie Anderson, L.A. Rams vs. New Orleans (OT)	15	336	1
Nov. 28, 1988	*Tim Brown, L.A. Raiders vs. Seattle	12	308	1
Dec. 22, 1985	Stephone Paige, Kansas City vs. San Diego	8	309	2
Nov. 10, 1985	Lionel James, San Diego vs. L.A. Raiders (OT)	23	345	0
Sept. 22, 1985	Lionel James, San Diego vs. Cincinnati	20	316	2
Dec. 21, 1975	*Walter Payton, Chicago vs. New Orleans	32	300	1
Nov. 23, 1975	Greg Pruitt, Cleveland vs. Cincinnati	28	304	2
Nov. 1, 1970	Eugene (Mercury) Morris, Miami vs. Baltimore	17	302	0
Oct. 4, 1970	O.J. Simpson, Buffalo vs. N.Y. Jets	26	303	2
Dec. 6, 1969	Jerry LeVias, Houston vs. N.Y. Jets	18	329	1
Nov. 2, 1969	Travis Williams, Green Bay vs. Pittsburgh	11	314	3
Dec. 18, 1966	Gale Sayers, Chicago vs. Minnesota	20	339	2
Dec. 12, 1965	*Gale Sayers, Chicago vs. San Francisco	17	336	6
Nov. 17, 1963	Gary Ballman, Pittsburgh vs. Washington	12	320	2
Dec. 16, 1962	Timmy Brown, Philadelphia vs. St. Louis	19	341	2
Dec. 10, 1961	Billy Cannon, Houston vs. N.Y. Titans	32	373	5
Nov. 19, 1961	Jim Brown, Cleveland vs. Philadelphia	38	313	4
Dec. 3, 1950	Cloyce Box, Detroit vs. Baltimore	13	302	4
Oct. 29, 1950	Wally Triplett, Detroit vs. Los Angeles	11	331	1
Nov. 22, 1945	Jim Benton, Cleveland vs. Detroit	10	303	1

First season of professional football.

2,000 SCRIMMAGE YARDS GAINED IN A SEASON

Year	Player, Team	Att.	Rushing Yards	Receptions	Receiving Yards	Scrimm. Yards
2009	Chris Johnson, Tennessee	358	2,006	50	503	2,509
	Ray Rice, Baltimore	254	1,339	78	702	2,041
2007	Brian Westbrook, Philadelphia	278	1,333	90	771	2,104
2006	Steven Jackson, St. Louis	346	1,528	90	806	2,334
	LaDainian Tomlinson, San Diego[3]	348	1,815	56	508	2,323
	Larry Johnson, Kansas City[2]	416	1,789	41	410	2,199
	Frank Gore, San Francisco	312	1,695	61	485	2,180
	Tiki Barber, N.Y. Giants[3]	327	1,662	58	465	2,127
2005	Tiki Barber, N.Y. Giants[2]	357	1,860	54	530	2,390
	Larry Johnson, Kansas City	336	1,750	33	343	2,093
2004	Tiki Barber, N.Y. Giants	322	1.518	52	578	2,096
	Edgerrin James, Indianapolis[3]	334	1,548	51	483	2,031
2003	LaDainian Tomlinson, San Diego[2]	313	1,645	100	725	2,370
	Jamal Lewis, Baltimore	387	2,066	26	205	2,271
	Ahman Green, Green Bay	355	1,883	50	367	2,250

Year	Player, Team	Att.	Rushing Yards	Receptions	Receiving Yards	Scrimm. Yards
	Deuce McAllister, New Orleans	351	1,641	69	516	2,157
	Priest Holmes, Kansas City[3]	320	1,420	74	690	2,110
2002	Priest Holmes, Kansas City[2]	313	1,615	70	672	2,287
	Ricky Williams, Miami	383	1,853	47	363	2,216
	LaDainian Tomlinson, San Diego	372	1,683	79	489	2,172
2001	Priest Holmes, Kansas City	327	1,555	62	614	2,169
	Marshall Faulk, St. Louis[4]	260	1,382	83	765	2,147
2000	Edgerrin James, Indianapolis[2]	387	1,709	63	594	2,303
	Marshall Faulk, St. Louis[3]	253	1,359	81	830	2,189
1999	Marshall Faulk, St. Louis[2]	253	1,381	87	1,048	2,429
	*Edgerrin James, Indianapolis	369	1,553	62	586	2,139
1998	Marshall Faulk, Indianapolis	324	1,319	86	908	2,227
	Terrell Davis, Denver[2]	392	2,008	25	217	2,225
	Jamal Anderson, Atlanta	410	1,846	27	319	2,165
	Garrison Hearst, San Francisco	310	1,570	39	535	2,105
1997	Barry Sanders, Detroit[2]	335	2,053	33	305	2,358
	Terrell Davis, Denver	369	1,750	42	287	2,037
1995	Emmitt Smith, Dallas[2]	377	1,773	62	375	2,148
1994	Barry Sanders, Detroit	331	1,883	44	283	2,166
1992	Thurman Thomas, Buffalo[2]	312	1,487	58	626	2,113
	Emmitt Smith, Dallas	373	1,713	59	335	2,048
	Barry Foster, Pittsburgh	390	1,690	36	344	2,034
1991	Thurman Thomas, Buffalo	288	1,407	62	631	2,038
1988	Roger Craig, San Francisco[2]	310	1,502	76	534	2,036
	Eric Dickerson, Indianapolis[4]	388	1,659	36	377	2,036
	Herschel Walker, Dallas	361	1,514	53	505	2,019
1986	Eric Dickerson, L.A. Rams[3]	404	1,821	26	205	2,026
1985	Marcus Allen, L.A. Raiders	380	1,759	67	555	2,314
	Roger Craig, San Francisco	214	1,050	92	1,016	2,066
	Walter Payton, Chicago[4]	324	1,551	49	483	2,034
1984	Eric Dickerson, L. A. Rams[2]	379	2,105	21	139	2,244
	James Wilder, Tampa Bay	407	1,544	85	685	2,229
	Walter Payton, Chicago[3]	381	1,684	45	368	2,052
1983	*Eric Dickerson, L.A. Rams	390	1,808	51	404	2,212
	William Andrews, Atlanta[2]	331	1,567	59	609	2,176
	Walter Payton, Chicago[2]	314	1,421	53	607	2,028
1981	William Andrews, Atlanta	289	1,301	81	735	2,036
1979	Wilbert Montgomery, Philadelphia	338	1,512	41	494	2,006
1977	Walter Payton, Chicago	339	1,852	27	269	2,121
1975	O.J. Simpson, Buffalo[2]	329	1,817	28	426	2,243
1973	O.J. Simpson, Buffalo	332	2,003	6	70	2,073
1963	Jim Brown, Cleveland	291	1,863	24	268	2,131

First season of professional football.

300 SCRIMMAGE YARDS GAINED IN A GAME

Date	Player, Team, Opponent	Att.	Yards	TD
Nov. 4, 2007	*Adrian Peterson, Minnesota vs. San Diego	31	315	3
Nov. 24, 2002	Priest Holmes, Kansas City vs. Seattle	30	307	3
Nov. 26, 1989	Flipper Anderson, L.A. Rams vs. New Orleans (OT)	15	336	1
Dec. 22, 1985	Stephone Paige, Kansas City vs. San Diego	8	309	2
Dec. 10, 1961	Billy Cannon, Houston vs. N.Y. Titans	30	330	5
Dec. 3, 1950	Cloyce Box, Detroit vs. Baltimore	12	302	4
Nov. 22, 1945	Jim Benton, Cleveland vs. Detroit	10	303	1

First season of professional football.

OUTSTANDING PERFORMERS

TOP 20 SCORERS

Player	Years	TD	FG	PAT	TP
1. Morten Andersen	25	0	565	849	2,544
2. Gary Anderson	23	0	538	820	2,434
3. John Carney	22	0	473	625	2,044
4. Matt Stover	19	0	471	591	2,004
5. George Blanda	26	9	335	943	2,002
6. Jason Elam	17	0	436	675	1,983
7. Jason Hanson	18	0	427	554	1,835
8. Norm Johnson	18	0	366	638	1,736
9. John Kasay	18	0	408	507	1,731
10. Nick Lowery	18	0	383	562	1,711
11. Jan Stenerud	19	0	373	580	1,699
12. Eddie Murray	19	0	352	538	1,594
13. Al Del Greco	17	0	347	543	1,584
14. Adam Vinatieri	14	0	338	514	1,530
15. Ryan Longwell	13	0	322	536	1,502
16. Steve Christie	15	0	336	468	1,476
17. Pat Leahy	18	0	304	558	1,470
18. Jim Turner	16	1	304	521	1,439
19. Matt Bahr	17	0	300	522	1,422
20. Jeff Wilkins	14	0	307	495	1,416

TOP 20 TOUCHDOWN SCORERS

Player	Years	Rush	Rec.	Total Returns	TD
1. Jerry Rice	20	10	197	1	208
2. Emmitt Smith	15	164	11	0	175
3. LaDainian Tomlinson	9	138	15	0	153
4. Randy Moss	12	0	148	1	149
5. Terrell Owens	14	3	144	0	147
6. Marcus Allen	16	123	21	1	145
7. Marshall Faulk	12	100	36	0	136
8. Cris Carter	16	0	130	1	131
9. Marvin Harrison	13	0	128	0	128
10. Jim Brown	9	106	20	0	126
11. Walter Payton	13	110	15	0	125
12. John Riggins	14	104	12	0	116
13. Lenny Moore	12	63	48	2	113
14. Shaun Alexander	9	100	12	0	112
15. Barry Sanders	10	99	10	0	109
16. Tim Brown	17	1	100	4	105
Don Hutson	11	3	99	3	105
18. Steve Largent	14	1	100	0	101
19. Franco Harris	13	91	9	0	100
Curtis Martin	11	90	10	0	100

TOP 20 RUSHERS

Player	Years	Att.	Yards	Avg.	Long	TD
1. Emmitt Smith	15	4,409	18,355	4.2	75	164
2. Walter Payton	13	3,838	16,726	4.4	76	110
3. Barry Sanders	10	3,062	15,269	5.0	85	99
4. Curtis Martin	11	3,518	14,101	4.0	70	90
5. Jerome Bettis	13	3,479	13,662	3.9	71	91
6. Eric Dickerson	11	2,996	13,259	4.4	85	90
7. Tony Dorsett	12	2,936	12,739	4.3	99	77
8. LaDainian Tomlinson	9	2,880	12,490	4.3	85	138
9. Jim Brown	9	2,359	12,312	5.2	80	106
10. Marshall Faulk	12	2,836	12,279	4.3	71	100
11. Edgerrin James	11	3,028	12,246	4.0	72	80
12. Marcus Allen	16	3,022	12,243	4.1	61	123
13. Franco Harris	13	2,949	12,120	4.1	75	91
14. Thurman Thomas	13	2,877	12,074	4.2	80	65
15. Fred Taylor	12	2,491	11,540	4.6	80	66
16. John Riggins	14	2,916	11,352	3.9	66	104
17. Corey Dillon	10	2,618	11,241	4.3	96	82
18. O.J. Simpson	11	2,404	11,236	4.7	94	61
19. Warrick Dunn	12	2,669	10,967	4.1	90	49
20. Ricky Watters	10	2,622	10,643	4.1	57	78

TOP 20 LEADERS IN PASSES COMPLETED

1.	Brett Favre	6,083
2.	Dan Marino	4,967
3.	Peyton Manning	4,232
4.	John Elway	4,123
5.	Warren Moon	3,988
6.	Drew Bledsoe	3,839
7.	Vinny Testaverde	3,787
8.	Fran Tarkenton	3,686
9.	Joe Montana	3,409
10.	Dan Fouts	3,297
11.	Kerry Collins	3,279
12.	Dave Krieg	3,105
13.	Boomer Esiason	2,969
14.	Troy Aikman	2,898
15.	Steve DeBerg	2,874
	Jim Kelly	2,874
17.	Jim Everett	2,841
18.	Johnny Unitas	2,830
19.	Donovan McNabb	2,801
20.	Mark Brunell	2,753

TOP 20 LEADERS IN PASSING YARDS

1.	Brett Favre	69,329
2.	Dan Marino	61,361
3.	John Elway	51,475
4.	Peyton Manning	50,128
5.	Warren Moon	49,325
6.	Fran Tarkenton	47,003
7.	Vinny Testaverde	46,233
8.	Drew Bledsoe	44,611
9.	Dan Fouts	43,040
10.	Joe Montana	40,551
11.	Johnny Unitas	40,239
12.	Kerry Collins	38,618
13.	Dave Krieg	38,147
14.	Boomer Esiason	37,920
15.	Jim Kelly	35,467
16.	Jim Everett	34,837
17.	Jim Hart	34,665
18.	Steve DeBerg	34,241
19.	John Hadl	33,503
20.	Phil Simms	33,462

TOP 20 LEADERS IN TOUCHDOWN PASSES

Rank	Player	TD Passes
1.	Brett Favre	497
2.	Dan Marino	420
3.	Peyton Manning	366
4.	Fran Tarkenton	342
5.	John Elway	300
6.	Warren Moon	291
7.	Johnny Unitas	290
8.	Vinny Testaverde	275
9.	Joe Montana	273
10.	Dave Krieg	261
11.	Sonny Jurgensen	255
12.	Dan Fouts	254
13.	Drew Bledsoe	251
14.	Boomer Esiason	247
15.	John Hadl	244
16.	Len Dawson	239
17.	Jim Kelly	237
18.	George Blanda	236
19.	Steve Young	232
20.	Tom Brady	225

TOP 20 LEADERS IN RECEPTION YARDS

1.	Jerry Rice	22,895
2.	Isaac Bruce	15,208
3.	Terrell Owens	14,951
4.	Tim Brown	14,934
5.	Marvin Harrison	14,580
6.	Randy Moss	14,465
7.	James Lofton	14,004
8.	Cris Carter	13,899
9.	Henry Ellard	13,777
10.	Torry Holt	13,382
11.	Andre Reed	13,198
12.	Steve Largent	13,089
13.	Irving Fryar	12,785
14.	Art Monk	12,721
15.	Jimmy Smith	12,287
16.	Charlie Joiner	12,146
17.	Michael Irvin	11,904
18.	Don Maynard	11,834
19.	Tony Gonzalez	11,807
20.	Muhsin Muhammad	11,438

OUTSTANDING PERFORMERS

TOP 20 COMBINED YARDS GAINED

Player	Years	Tot.	Rush.	Rec.	Int. Ret.	Punt Ret.	Kickoff Ret.	Fumble Ret.
1. Jerry Rice	20	23,546	645	22,895	0	0	6	0
2. Brian Mitchell	14	23,330	1,967	2,336	0	4,999	14,014	14
3. Walter Payton	13	21,803	16,726	4,538	0	0	539	0
4. Emmitt Smith	15	21,564	18,355	3,224	0	0	0	-15
5. Tim Brown	17	19,682	190	14,934	0	3,320	1,235	3
6. Marshall Faulk	12	19,190	12,279	6,875	0	0	18	18
7. Barry Sanders	10	18,308	15,269	2,921	0	0	118	0
8. Herschel Walker	12	18,168	8,225	4,859	0	0	5,084	0
9. Marcus Allen	16	17,648	12,243	5,411	0	0	0	-6
10. Curtis Martin	11	17,421	14,101	3,329	0	0	0	-9
11. Tiki Barber	10	17,359	10,449	5,183	0	1,181	544	2
12. Eric Metcalf	13	17,230	2,392	5,572	0	3,453	5,813	0
13. Thurman Thomas	13	16,532	12,074	4,458	0	0	0	0
14. LaDainian Tomlinson	9	16,445	12,490	3,955	0	0	0	0
15. Tony Dorsett	12	16,326	12,739	3,554	0	0	0	54
16. Derrick Mason	13	16,178	3	11,089	0	1,590	3,496	0
17. Henry Ellard	16	15,718	50	13,777	0	1,527	364	0
18. Warrick Dunn	12	15,665	10,967	4,339	0	48	310	1
19. Edgerrin James	11	15,610	12,246	3,364	0	0	0	0
20. Irving Fryar	17	15,594	242	12,785	0	2,055	505	7

TOP 20 YARDS FROM SCRIMMAGE

Player	Years	Scrimmage Yards	Rushing Yards	Receiving Yards
1. Jerry Rice	20	23,540	645	22,895
2. Emmitt Smith	15	21,579	18,355	3,224
3. Walter Payton	13	21,264	16,726	4,538
4. Marshall Faulk	12	19,154	12,279	6,875
5. Barry Sanders	10	18,190	15,269	2,921
6. Marcus Allen	16	17,654	12,243	5,411
7. Curtis Martin	11	17,430	14,101	3,329
8. Thurman Thomas	13	16,532	12,074	4,458
9. LaDainian Tomlinson	9	16,445	12,490	3,955
10. Tony Dorsett	12	16,293	12,739	3,554
11. Tiki Barber	10	15,632	10,449	5,183
12. Edgerrin James	11	15,610	12,246	3,364
13. Eric Dickerson	11	15,347	13,259	2,137
14. Isaac Bruce	16	15,347	139	15,208
15. Warrick Dunn	12	15,306	10,967	4,339
16. Terrell Owens	14	15,202	251	14,951
17. Tim Brown	17	15,124	190	14,934
18. Jerome Bettis	13	15,111	13,662	1,449
19. Ricky Watters	10	14,891	10,643	4,248
20. Jim Brown	9	14,811	12,312	2,499

TOP 20 PASSERS

Player	Years	Att.	Comp.	Pct. Comp.	Yards	Avg. Gain	TD	Pct. TD	Int.	Pct. Int.	Rating
1. Steve Young	15	4,149	2,667	64.3	33,124	7.98	232	5.6	107	2.6	96.8
2. Philip Rivers	6	1,914	1,207	63.1	14,951	7.81	106	5.5	45	2.4	95.8
3. Tony Romo	6	1,857	1,178	63.4	15,045	8.10	107	5.8	55	3.0	95.6
4. Peyton Manning	12	6,531	4,232	64.8	50,128	7.68	366	5.6	181	2.8	95.2
5. Kurt Warner	12	4,070	2,666	65.5	32,344	7.95	208	5.1	128	3.1	93.7
6. Tom Brady	10	4,218	2,672	63.3	30,844	7.31	225	5.3	99	2.3	93.3
7. Joe Montana	15	5,391	3,409	63.2	40,551	7.52	273	5.1	139	2.6	92.3
8. Drew Brees	9	4,164	2,697	64.8	30,646	7.36	202	4.9	110	2.6	91.9
9. Ben Roethlisberger	6	2,411	1,526	63.3	19,302	8.01	127	5.3	81	3.4	91.7
10. Chad Pennington	10	2,469	1,631	66.1	17,804	7.21	102	4.1	64	2.6	90.1
11. Carson Palmer	6	2,631	1,662	63.2	18,724	7.12	128	4.9	80	3.0	87.9
12. Daunte Culpepper	11	3,199	2,016	63.0	24,153	7.55	149	4.7	106	3.3	87.8
13. Jeff Garcia	11	3,676	2,264	61.6	25,537	6.95	161	4.4	83	2.3	87.5
14. Brett Favre	19	9,811	6,083	62.0	69,329	7.07	497	5.1	317	3.2	86.6
15. Donovan McNabb	11	4,746	2,801	59.0	32,873	6.93	216	4.6	100	2.1	86.5
16. Dan Marino	17	8,358	4,967	59.4	61,361	7.34	420	5.0	252	3.0	86.4
17. Trent Green	11	3,740	2,266	60.6	28,475	7.61	162	4.3	114	3.0	86.0
18. David Garrard	8	1,915	1,170	61.1	13,269	6.93	66	3.4	39	2.0	84.9
19. Rich Gannon	16	4,206	2,533	60.2	28,743	6.83	180	4.3	104	2.5	84.7
20. Marc Bulger	8	3,171	1,969	62.1	22,814	7.19	122	3.8	93	2.9	84.4

1,500 or more attempts. The passing ratings are based on performance standards established for completion percentage, interception percentage, touchdown percentage, and average gain. Please consult page 312 for more information.

TOP 20 PASS RECEIVERS

	Player	Years	No.	Yards	Avg.	Long	TD
1.	Jerry Rice	20	1,549	22,895	14.8	96	197
2.	Marvin Harrison	13	1,102	14,580	13.2	80	128
3.	Cris Carter	16	1,101	13,899	12.6	80	130
4.	Tim Brown	17	1,094	14,934	13.7	80	100
5.	Isaac Bruce	16	1,024	15,208	14.9	80	91
6.	Terrell Owens	14	1,006	14,951	14.9	98	144
7.	Tony Gonzalez	13	999	11,807	11.8	73	82
8.	Andre Reed	16	951	13,198	13.9	83	87
9.	Art Monk	16	940	12,721	13.5	79	68
10.	Randy Moss	12	926	14,465	15.6	82	148
11.	Torry Holt	11	920	13,382	14.5	85	74
12.	Hines Ward	12	895	10,947	12.2	85	78
13.	Keenan McCardell	16	883	11,373	12.9	76	63
14.	Derrick Mason	13	863	11,089	12.8	79	59
15.	Jimmy Smith	12	862	12,287	14.3	75	67
16.	Muhsin Muhammad	14	860	11,438	13.3	72	62
17.	Irving Fryar	17	851	12,785	15.0	80	84
18.	Rod Smith	12	849	11,389	13.4	85	68
19.	Larry Centers	14	827	6,797	8.2	54	28
20.	Steve Largent	14	819	13,089	16.0	74	100

TOP 20 INTERCEPTORS

	Player	Years	No.	Yards	Avg.	Long	TD
1.	Paul Krause	16	81	1,185	14.6	81	3
2.	Emlen Tunnell	14	79	1,282	16.2	55	4
3.	Rod Woodson	17	71	1,483	20.9	98	12
4.	Dick (Night Train) Lane	14	68	1,207	17.8	80	5
5.	Ken Riley	15	65	596	9.2	66	5
6.	Ronnie Lott	14	63	730	11.6	83	5
	Darren Sharper	13	63	1,412	22.4	99	11
7.	Dave Brown	15	62	698	11.3	90	5
	Dick LeBeau	14	62	762	12.3	70	3
9.	Emmitt Thomas	13	58	937	16.2	73	5
10.	Mel Blount	14	57	736	12.9	52	2
	Bobby Boyd	9	57	994	17.4	74	4
	Eugene Robinson	16	57	762	13.4	49	1
	Johnny Robinson	12	57	741	13.0	57	1
	Everson Walls	13	57	504	8.8	40	1
15.	Lem Barney	11	56	1,077	19.2	71	7
	Pat Fischer	17	56	941	16.8	69	4
17.	Aeneas Williams	14	55	807	14.7	65	9
18.	Eric Allen	14	54	826	15.3	94	8
	Willie Brown	16	54	472	8.7	45	2
	Darrell Green	20	54	621	11.5	83	6

TOP 20 PUNTERS (MINIMUM 250 PUNTS)

	Player	Years	No.	Yards	Avg.	Long	Blk.
1.	Shane Lechler	10	778	36,811	47.3	73	3
2.	Donnie Jones	6	449	20,451	45.5	80	2
3.	Jon Ryan	4	310	14,028	45.3	72	3
4.	Sammy Baugh	16	338	15,245	45.1	85	9
5.	Mat McBriar	6	371	16,712	45.0	75	1
6.	Andy Lee	6	554	24,896	44.9	82	2
7.	Tommy Davis	11	511	22,833	44.7	82	2
8.	Ben Graham	5	335	14,886	44.4	69	2
9.	Chris Kluwe	5	391	17,360	44.4	70	1
10.	Yale Lary	11	503	22,279	44.3	74	4
11.	Mike Scifres	7	393	17,380	44.2	71	1
12.	Todd Sauerbrun	13	889	39,208	44.1	73	9
13.	Dustin Colquitt	5	397	17,502	44.1	81	2
14.	Bob Scarpitto	8	283	12,408	43.8	87	4
15.	Horace Gillom	7	385	16,872	43.8	80	5
16.	Sam Koch	4	321	14,057	43.8	74	2
17.	Jerry Norton	11	358	15,671	43.8	78	2
18.	Dave Lewis	4	285	12,447	43.7	63	0
19.	Brian Moorman	9	700	30,524	43.6	84	1
20.	Greg Montgomery	9	524	22,831	43.6	77	8

OUTSTANDING PERFORMERS

TOP 20 KICKOFF RETURNERS (MINIMUM 75 RETURNS)

Player	Years	No.	Yards	Avg.	Long	TD
1. Gale Sayers	7	91	2,781	30.6	103	6
2. Lynn Chandnois	7	92	2,720	29.6	93	3
3. Abe Woodson	9	193	5,538	28.7	105	5
4. Buddy Young	6	90	2,514	27.9	104	2
5. Travis Williams	5	102	2,801	27.5	105	6
6. Joe Arenas	7	139	3,798	27.3	96	1
7. Ellis Hobbs	5	125	3,394	27.2	108	3
8. Clarence Davis	8	79	2,140	27.1	76	0
9. Steve Van Buren	8	76	2,030	26.7	98	3
10. Lenny Lyles	12	81	2,161	26.7	103	3
11. Josh Cribbs	5	265	7,049	26.6	103	8
12. Mercury Morris	8	111	2,947	26.5	105	3
13. Bobby Jancik	6	158	4,185	26.5	61	0
14. Mel Renfro	14	85	2,246	26.4	100	2
15. Bobby Mitchell	14	102	2,690	26.4	98	5
16. Terrence McGee	7	207	5,450	26.3	104	5
17. Ollie Matson	14	143	3,746	26.2	105	6
18. Alvin Haymond	10	170	4,438	26.1	98	2
19. Justin Miller	5	152	3,966	26.1	103	5
20. Noland Smith	3	82	2,137	26.1	106	1

TOP 20 PUNT RETURNERS (MINIMUM 75 RETURNS)

Player	Years	No.	Yards	Avg.	Long	TD
1. George McAfee	8	112	1,431	12.8	74	2
2. Jack Christiansen	8	85	1,084	12.8	89	8
3. Claude Gibson	5	110	1,381	12.6	85	3
4. Roscoe Parrish	5	118	1,445	12.2	82	3
5. Bill Dudley	9	124	1,515	12.2	96	3
6. Rick Upchurch	9	248	3,008	12.1	92	8
7. Desmond Howard	11	244	2,895	11.9	95	8
8. Billy Johnson	14	282	3,317	11.8	87	6
9. Mack Herron	3	84	982	11.7	66	0
10. Billy Thompson	13	157	1,814	11.6	60	0
11. Darrien Gordon	9	314	3,601	11.5	94	6
12. Santana Moss	9	112	1,268	11.3	80	3
13. Henry Ellard	16	135	1,527	11.3	83	4
14. Rodger Bird	3	94	1,063	11.3	78	0
15. Bosh Pritchard	6	95	1,072	11.3	81	2
16. Devin Hester	4	145	1,636	11.3	89	7
17. DeSean Jackson	2	79	881	11.2	85	3
18. Terry Metcalf	6	84	936	11.1	69	1
19. Bob Hayes	11	104	1,158	11.1	90	3
20. Jermaine Lewis	9	295	3,282	11.1	89	6

TOP 20 LEADERS IN SACKS

Player	*Years	No.
1. Bruce Smith	19	200.0
2. Reggie White	15	198.0
3. Kevin Greene	15	160.0
4. Chris Doleman	15	150.5
5. Michael Strahan	15	141.5
6. Richard Dent	15	137.5
John Randle	14	137.5
8. Leslie O'Neal	13	132.5
Lawrence Taylor	12	132.5
10. Rickey Jackson	14	128.0
11. Jason Taylor	13	127.5
12. Derrick Thomas	11	126.5
13. Simeon Rice	12	122.0
14. Clyde Simmons	15	121.5
15. Sean Jones	13	113.0
16. Greg Townsend	13	109.5
17. Pat Swilling	12	107.5
18. Trace Armstrong	15	106.0
19. Kevin Carter	14	104.5
Neil Smith	13	104.5

**Years played since 1982 when sacks became an official statistic.*

POSTSEASON LEADERS

TOP 10 POSTSEASON RUSHERS

Player	Att.	Yards	Avg.	Long	TD
1. Emmitt Smith	349	1,586	4.5	65	19
2. Franco Harris	400	1,556	3.9	50	16
3. Thurman Thomas	339	1,442	4.3	40	16
4. Tony Dorsett	302	1,383	4.6	53	9
5. Marcus Allen	267	1,347	5.0	74	11
6. Terrell Davis	204	1,140	5.6	62	12
7. John Riggins	251	996	4.0	43	12
8. Larry Csonka	225	891	4.0	49	9
9. Chuck Foreman	229	860	3.8	62	7
10. Edgerrin James	218	852	3.9	34	6

TOP 10 POSTSEASON PASSERS

Player	Att.	Comp.	Pct. Comp.	Yards	Avg. Gain	TD	Pct. TD	Int.	Pct. Int.	Rating
1. Bart Starr	213	130	61.0	1,753	8.23	15	7.0	3	1.4	104.8
2. Drew Brees	225	150	66.7	1,648	7.32	13	5.8	2	0.9	103.7
3. Kurt Warner	462	307	66.5	3,952	8.55	31	6.7	14	3.0	102.8
4. Joe Montana	734	460	62.7	5,772	7.86	45	6.1	21	2.9	95.6
5. Ken Anderson	166	110	66.3	1,321	7.96	9	5.4	6	3.6	93.5
6. Joe Theismann	211	128	60.7	1,782	8.45	11	5.2	7	3.3	91.4
7. Troy Aikman	502	320	63.7	3,849	7.67	23	4.6	17	3.4	88.3
8. Peyton Manning	692	435	62.9	5,164	7.46	28	4.0	19	2.7	87.6
9. Ben Roethlisberger	278	172	61.9	2,239	8.05	15	5.4	12	4.3	87.2
10. Brett Favre	791	481	60.8	5,855	7.40	44	5.6	30	3.8	86.3

TOP 10 POSTSEASON PASS RECEIVERS

Player	No.	Yards	Avg.	Long	TD
1. Jerry Rice	151	2,245	14.9	72	22
2. Michael Irvin	87	1,315	15.1	53	8
3. Andre Reed	85	1,229	14.5	72	9
4. Reggie Wayne	82	1,127	13.7	72	9
5. Thurman Thomas	76	672	8.8	27	5
Hines Ward	76	1,064	14.0	45	8
7. Cliff Branch	73	1,289	17.7	72	5
8. Fred Biletnikoff	70	1,167	16.7	57	10
9. Art Monk	69	1,062	15.4	48	7
10. Drew Pearson	67	1,105	16.5	83	8

TOP 10 POSTSEASON INTERCEPTION LEADERS

Player	Interceptions
1. Ronnie Lott	9
Bill Simpson	9
Charlie Waters	9
4. Lester Hayes	8
5. Willie Brown	7
Rodney Harrison	7
Ed Reed	7
Asante Samuel	7
Dennis Thurman	7
9. Bobby Bryant	6
Eric Davis	6
Glen Edwards	6
Darrell Green	6
Cliff Harris	6
Ty Law	6
Vernon Perry	6
Aeneas Williams	6

TOP 10 POSTSEASON SACK LEADERS

Player	Sacks
1. Willie McGinest	16.0
2. Bruce Smith	14.5
3. Reggie White	12.0
4. Charles Haley	11.0
5. Richard Dent	10.5
6. Trace Armstrong	10.0
Charles Mann	10.0
Tony Tolbert	10.0
9. Neil Smith	9.5
Michael Strahan	9.5

**Sacks became an official statistic in 1982.*

YEARLY STATISTICAL LEADERS

ANNUAL SCORING LEADERS

Year	Player, Team	TD	FG	PAT	TP
2009	Nate Kaeding, San Diego, AFC	0	32	50	146
	David Akers, Philadelphia, NFC	0	32	43	139
2008	Stephen Gostkowski, New England, AFC	0	36	40	148
	David Akers, Philadelphia, NFC	0	33	45	144
2007	*Mason Crosby, Green Bay, NFC	0	31	48	141
	Randy Moss, New England, AFC	23	0	0	138
2006	LaDainian Tomlinson, AFC	31	0	0	186
	Robbie Gould, Chicago, NFC	0	32	47	143
2005	Shaun Alexander, Seattle, NFC	28	0	0	168
	Shayne Graham, Cincinnati, AFC	0	28	47	131
2004	Adam Vinatieri, New England, AFC	0	31	48	141
	David Akers, Philadelphia, NFC	0	27	41	122
2003	Jeff Wilkins, St. Louis, NFC	0	39	46	163
	Priest Holmes, Kansas City, AFC	27	0	0	162
2002	Priest Holmes, Kansas City, AFC	24	0	0	144
	Jay Feely, Atlanta, NFC	0	32	42	138
2001	Marshall Faulk, St. Louis, NFC	21	0	0	#128
	Mike Vanderjagt, Indianapolis, AFC	0	28	41	125
2000	Marshall Faulk, St. Louis, NFC	26	0	0	##160
	Matt Stover, Baltimore, AFC	0	35	30	135
1999	Mike Vanderjagt, Indianapolis, AFC	0	34	43	145
	Jeff Wilkins, St. Louis, NFC	0	20	64	124
1998	Gary Anderson, Minnesota, NFC	0	35	59	164
	Steve Christie, Buffalo, AFC	0	33	41	140
1997	Mike Hollis, Jacksonville, AFC	0	31	41	134
	Richie Cunningham, Dallas, NFC	0	34	24	126
1996	John Kasay, Carolina, NFC	0	37	34	145
	Cary Blanchard, Indianapolis, AFC	0	36	27	135
1995	Emmitt Smith, Dallas, NFC	25	0	0	150
	Norm Johnson, Pittsburgh, AFC	0	34	39	141
1994	John Carney, San Diego, AFC	0	34	33	135
	Fuad Reveiz, Minnesota, NFC	0	34	30	132
1993	Jeff Jaeger, L.A. Raiders, AFC	0	35	27	132
	Jason Hanson, Detroit, NFC	0	34	28	130
1992	Pete Stoyanovich, Miami, AFC	0	30	34	124
	Morten Andersen, New Orleans, NFC	0	29	33	120
	Chip Lohmiller, Washington, NFC	0	30	30	120
1991	Chip Lohmiller, Washington, NFC	0	31	56	149
	Pete Stoyanovich, Miami, AFC	0	31	28	121
1990	Nick Lowery, Kansas City, AFC	0	34	37	139
	Chip Lohmiller, Washington, NFC	0	30	41	131
1989	Mike Cofer, San Francisco, NFC	0	29	49	136
	*David Treadwell, Denver, AFC	0	27	39	120
1988	Scott Norwood, Buffalo, AFC	0	32	33	129
	Mike Cofer, San Francisco, NFC	0	27	40	121
1987	Jerry Rice, San Francisco, NFC	23	0	0	138
	Jim Breech, Cincinnati, AFC	0	24	25	97
1986	Tony Franklin, New England, AFC	0	32	44	140
	Kevin Butler, Chicago, NFC	0	28	36	120
1985	*Kevin Butler, Chicago, NFC	0	31	51	144
	Gary Anderson, Pittsburgh, AFC	0	33	40	139
1984	Ray Wersching, San Francisco, NFC	0	25	56	131
	Gary Anderson, Pittsburgh, AFC	0	24	45	117
1983	Mark Moseley, Washington, NFC	0	33	62	161
	Gary Anderson, Pittsburgh, AFC	0	27	38	119
1982	*Marcus Allen, L.A. Raiders, AFC	14	0	0	84
	Wendell Tyler, L.A. Rams, NFC	13	0	0	78
1981	Ed Murray, Detroit, NFC	0	25	46	121
	Rafael Septien, Dallas, NFC	0	27	40	121
	Jim Breech, Cincinnati, AFC	0	22	49	115
	Nick Lowery, Kansas City, AFC	0	26	37	115
1980	John Smith, New England, AFC	0	26	51	129
	*Ed Murray, Detroit, NFC	0	27	35	116
1979	John Smith, New England, AFC	0	23	46	115
	Mark Moseley, Washington, NFC	0	25	39	114
1978	*Frank Corral, Los Angeles, NFC	0	29	31	118
	Pat Leahy, N.Y. Jets, AFC	0	22	41	107

Year	Player, Team	TD	FG	PAT	TP
1977	Errol Mann, Oakland, AFC	0	20	39	99
	Walter Payton, Chicago, NFC	16	0	0	96
1976	Toni Linhart, Baltimore, AFC	0	20	49	109
	Mark Moseley, Washington, NFC	0	22	31	97
1975	O.J. Simpson, Buffalo, AFC	23	0	0	138
	Chuck Foreman, Minnesota, NFC	22	0	0	132
1974	Chester Marcol, Green Bay, NFC	0	25	19	94
	Roy Gerela, Pittsburgh, AFC	0	20	33	93
1973	David Ray, Los Angeles, NFC	0	30	40	130
	Roy Gerela, Pittsburgh, AFC	0	29	36	123
1972	*Chester Marcol, Green Bay, NFC	0	33	29	128
	Bobby Howfield, N.Y. Jets, AFC	0	27	40	121
1971	Garo Yepremian, Miami, AFC	0	28	33	117
	Curt Knight, Washington, NFC	0	29	27	114
1970	Fred Cox, Minnesota, NFC	0	30	35	125
	Jan Stenerud, Kansas City, AFC	0	30	26	116
1969	Jim Turner, N.Y. Jets, AFL	0	32	33	129
	Fred Cox, Minnesota, NFL	0	26	43	121
1968	Jim Turner, N.Y. Jets, AFL	0	34	43	145
	Leroy Kelly, Cleveland, NFL	20	0	0	120
1967	Jim Bakken, St. Louis, NFL	0	27	36	117
	George Blanda, Oakland, AFL	0	20	56	116
1966	Gino Cappelletti, Boston, AFL	6	16	35	119
	Bruce Gossett, Los Angeles, NFL	0	28	29	113
1965	*Gale Sayers, Chicago, NFL	22	0	0	132
	Gino Cappelletti, Boston, AFL	9	17	27	132
1964	Gino Cappelletti, Boston, AFL	7	25	36	#155
	Lenny Moore, Baltimore, NFL	20	0	0	120
1963	Gino Cappelletti, Boston, AFL	2	22	35	113
	Don Chandler, N.Y. Giants, NFL	0	18	52	106
1962	Gene Mingo, Denver, AFL	4	27	32	137
	Jim Taylor, Green Bay, NFL	19	0	0	114
1961	Gino Cappelletti, Boston, AFL	8	17	48	147
	Paul Hornung, Green Bay, NFL	10	15	41	146
1960	Paul Hornung, Green Bay, NFL	15	15	41	176
	*Gene Mingo, Denver, AFL	6	18	33	123
1959	Paul Hornung, Green Bay	7	7	31	94
1958	Jim Brown, Cleveland	18	0	0	108
1957	Sam Baker, Washington	1	14	29	77
	Lou Groza, Cleveland	0	15	32	77
1956	Bobby Layne, Detroit	5	12	33	99
1955	Doak Walker, Detroit	7	9	27	96
1954	Bobby Walston, Philadelphia	11	4	36	114
1953	Gordy Soltau, San Francisco	6	10	48	114
1952	Gordy Soltau, San Francisco	7	6	34	94
1951	Elroy (Crazylegs) Hirsch, Los Angeles	17	0	0	102
1950	*Doak Walker, Detroit	11	8	38	128
1949	Pat Harder, Chi. Cardinals	8	3	45	102
	Gene Roberts, N.Y. Giants	17	0	0	102
1948	Pat Harder, Chi. Cardinals	6	7	53	110
1947	Pat Harder, Chi. Cardinals	7	7	39	102
1946	Ted Fritsch, Green Bay	10	9	13	100
1945	Steve Van Buren, Philadelphia	18	0	2	110
1944	Don Hutson, Green Bay	9	0	31	85
1943	Don Hutson, Green Bay	12	3	36	117
1942	Don Hutson, Green Bay	17	1	33	138
1941	Don Hutson, Green Bay	12	1	20	95
1940	Don Hutson, Green Bay	7	0	15	57
1939	Andy Farkas, Washington	11	0	2	68
1938	Clarke Hinkle, Green Bay	7	3	7	58
1937	Jack Manders, Chi. Bears	5	8	15	69
1936	Earl (Dutch) Clark, Detroit	7	4	19	73
1935	Earl (Dutch) Clark, Detroit	6	1	16	55
1934	Jack Manders, Chi. Bears	3	10	31	79
1933	Ken Strong, N.Y. Giants	6	5	13	64
	Glenn Presnell, Portsmouth	6	6	10	64
1932	Earl (Dutch) Clark, Portsmouth	6	3	10	55

**First season of professional football.*
#Cappelletti's total and Faulk's total in 2001 include a two-point conversion.
##Faulk's total in 2000 includes 2 two-point conversions.

YEARLY STATISTICAL LEADERS

ANNUAL TOUCHDOWN LEADERS

Year	Player, Team	TD	Rush	Pass	Ret.
2009	Adrian Peterson, Minnesota, NFC	18	18	0	0
	Chris Johnson, Tennessee, AFC	16	14	2	0
	Maurice Jones-Drew, Jacksonville, AFC	16	15	1	0
2008	DeAngelo Williams, Carolina, NFC	20	18	2	0
	Thomas Jones, N.Y. Jets, AFC	15	13	2	0
	LenDale White, Tennessee, AFC	15	15	0	0
2007	Randy Moss, New England, AFC	23	0	23	0
	Terrell Owens, Dallas, NFC	15	0	15	0
2006	LaDainian Tomlinson, San Diego, AFC	31	28	3	0
	Marion Barber, Dallas, NFC	16	14	2	0
	Steven Jackson, St. Louis, NFC	16	13	3	0
2005	Shaun Alexander, Seattle, NFC	28	27	1	0
	Larry Johnson, Kansas City, AFC	21	20	1	0
2004	Shaun Alexander, Seattle, NFC	20	16	4	0
	LaDainian Tomlinson, San Diego, AFC	18	17	1	0
2003	Priest Holmes, Kansas City, AFC	27	27	0	0
	Ahman Green, Green Bay, NFC	20	15	5	0
2002	Priest Holmes, Kansas City, AFC	24	21	3	0
	Shaun Alexander, Seattle, NFC	18	16	2	0
2001	Marshall Faulk, St. Louis, NFC	21	12	9	0
	Shaun Alexander, Seattle, AFC	16	14	2	0
2000	Marshall Faulk, St. Louis, NFC	26	18	8	0
	Edgerrin James, Indianapolis, AFC	18	13	5	0
1999	Stephen Davis, Washington, NFC	17	17	0	0
	*Edgerrin James, Indianapolis, AFC	17	13	4	0
1998	Terrell Davis, Denver, AFC	23	21	2	0
	*Randy Moss, Minnesota, NFC	17	0	17	0
1997	Karim Abdul-Jabbar, Miami, AFC	16	15	1	0
	Barry Sanders, Detroit, NFC	14	11	3	0
1996	Terry Allen, Washington, NFC	21	21	0	0
	Curtis Martin, New England, AFC	17	14	3	0
1995	Emmitt Smith, Dallas, NFC	25	25	0	0
	Carl Pickens, Cincinnati, AFC	17	0	17	0
1994	Emmitt Smith, Dallas, NFC	22	21	1	0
	*Marshall Faulk, Indianapolis, AFC	12	11	1	0
	Natrone Means, San Diego, AFC	12	12	0	0
1993	Jerry Rice, San Francisco, NFC	16	1	15	0
	Marcus Allen, Kansas City, AFC	15	12	3	0
1992	Emmitt Smith, Dallas, NFC	19	18	1	0
	Thurman Thomas, Buffalo, AFC	12	9	3	0
1991	Barry Sanders, Detroit, NFC	17	16	1	0
	Mark Clayton, Miami, AFC	12	0	12	0
	Thurman Thomas, Buffalo, AFC	12	7	5	0
1990	Barry Sanders, Detroit, NFC	16	13	3	0
	Derrick Fenner, Seattle, AFC	15	14	1	0
1989	Dalton Hilliard, New Orleans, NFC	18	13	5	0
	Christian Okoye, Kansas City, AFC	12	12	0	0
	Thurman Thomas, Buffalo, AFC	12	6	6	0
1988	Greg Bell, L.A. Rams, NFC	18	16	2	0
	Eric Dickerson, Indianapolis, AFC	15	14	1	0
	*Ickey Woods, Cincinnati, AFC	15	15	0	0
1987	Jerry Rice, San Francisco, NFC	23	1	22	0
	Johnny Hector, N.Y. Jets, AFC	11	11	0	0
1986	George Rogers, Washington, NFC	18	18	0	0
	Sammy Winder, Denver, AFC	14	9	5	0
1985	Joe Morris, N.Y. Giants, NFC	21	21	0	0
	Louis Lipps, Pittsburgh, AFC	15	1	12	2
1984	Marcus Allen, L.A. Raiders, AFC	18	13	5	0
	Mark Clayton, Miami, AFC	18	0	18	0
	Eric Dickerson, L.A. Rams, NFC	14	14	0	0
	John Riggins, Washington, NFC	14	14	0	0
1983	John Riggins, Washington, NFC	24	24	0	0
	Pete Johnson, Cincinnati, AFC	14	14	0	0
	*Curt Warner, Seattle, AFC	14	13	1	0
1982	*Marcus Allen, L.A. Raiders, AFC	14	11	3	0
	Wendell Tyler, L.A. Rams, NFC	13	9	4	0
1981	Chuck Muncie, San Diego, AFC	19	19	0	0
	Wendell Tyler, Los Angeles, NFC	17	12	5	0

Year	Player, Team	TD	Rush	Pass	Ret.
1980	*Billy Sims, Detroit, NFC	16	13	3	0
	Earl Campbell, Houston, AFC	13	13	0	0
	*Curtis Dickey, Baltimore, AFC	13	11	2	0
	John Jefferson, San Diego, AFC	13	0	13	0
1979	Earl Campbell, Houston, AFC	19	19	0	0
	Walter Payton, Chicago, NFC	16	14	2	0
1978	David Sims, Seattle, AFC	15	14	1	0
	Terdell Middleton, Green Bay, NFC	12	11	1	0
1977	Walter Payton, Chicago, NFC	16	14	2	0
	Nat Moore, Miami, AFC	13	1	12	0
1976	Chuck Foreman, Minnesota, NFC	14	13	1	0
	Franco Harris, Pittsburgh, AFC	14	14	0	0
1975	O.J. Simpson, Buffalo, AFC	23	16	7	0
	Chuck Foreman, Minnesota, NFC	22	13	9	0
1974	Chuck Foreman, Minnesota, NFC	15	9	6	0
	Cliff Branch, Oakland, AFC	13	0	13	0
1973	Larry Brown, Washington, NFC	14	8	6	0
	Floyd Little, Denver, AFC	13	12	1	0
1972	Emerson Boozer, N.Y. Jets, AFC	14	11	3	0
	Ron Johnson, N.Y. Giants, NFC	14	9	5	0
1971	Duane Thomas, Dallas, NFC	13	11	2	0
	Leroy Kelly, Cleveland, AFC	12	10	2	0
1970	Dick Gordon, Chicago, NFC	13	0	13	0
	MacArthur Lane, St. Louis, NFC	13	11	2	0
	Gary Garrison, San Diego, AFC	12	0	12	0
1969	Warren Wells, Oakland, AFL	14	0	14	0
	Tom Matte, Baltimore, NFL	13	11	2	0
	Lance Rentzel, Dallas, NFL	13	0	12	1
1968	Leroy Kelly, Cleveland, NFL	20	16	4	0
	Warren Wells, Oakland, AFL	12	1	11	0
1967	Homer Jones, N.Y. Giants, NFL	14	1	13	0
	Emerson Boozer, N.Y. Jets, AFL	13	10	3	0
1966	Leroy Kelly, Cleveland, NFL	16	15	1	0
	Dan Reeves, Dallas, NFL	16	8	8	0
	Lance Alworth, San Diego, AFL	13	0	13	0
1965	*Gale Sayers, Chicago, NFL	22	14	6	2
	Lance Alworth, San Diego, AFL	14	0	14	0
	Don Maynard, N.Y. Jets, AFL	14	0	14	0
1964	Lenny Moore, Baltimore, NFL	20	16	3	1
	Lance Alworth, San Diego, AFL	15	2	13	0
1963	Art Powell, Oakland, AFL	16	0	16	0
	Jim Brown, Cleveland, NFL	15	12	3	0
1962	Abner Haynes, Dallas, AFL	19	13	6	0
	Jim Taylor, Green Bay, NFL	19	19	0	0
1961	Bill Groman, Houston, AFL	18	1	17	0
	Jim Taylor, Green Bay, NFL	16	15	1	0
1960	Paul Hornung, Green Bay, NFL	15	13	2	0
	Sonny Randle, St. Louis, NFL	15	0	15	0
	Art Powell, N.Y. Titans, AFL	14	0	14	0
1959	Raymond Berry, Baltimore	14	0	14	0
	Jim Brown, Cleveland	14	14	0	0
1958	Jim Brown, Cleveland	18	17	1	0
1957	Lenny Moore, Baltimore	11	3	7	1
1956	Rick Casares, Chi. Bears	14	12	2	0
1955	*Alan Ameche, Baltimore	9	9	0	0
	Harlon Hill, Chi. Bears	9	0	9	0
1954	*Harlon Hill, Chi. Bears	12	0	12	0
1953	Joseph Perry, San Francisco	13	10	3	0
1952	Cloyce Box, Detroit	15	0	15	0
1951	Elroy (Crazylegs) Hirsch, Los Angeles	17	0	17	0
1950	Bob Shaw, Chi. Cardinals	12	0	12	0
1949	Gene Roberts, N.Y. Giants	17	9	8	0
1948	Mal Kutner, Chi. Cardinals	15	1	14	0
1947	Steve Van Buren, Philadelphia	14	13	0	1
1946	Ted Fritsch, Green Bay	10	9	1	0
1945	Steve Van Buren, Philadelphia	18	15	2	1
1944	Don Hutson, Green Bay	9	0	9	0
	Bill Paschal, N.Y. Giants	9	9	0	0

Year	Player, Team	TD	Rush	Pass	Ret.
1943	Don Hutson, Green Bay	12	0	11	1
	*Bill Paschal, N.Y. Giants	12	10	2	0
1942	Don Hutson, Green Bay	17	0	17	0
1941	Don Hutson, Green Bay	12	2	10	0
	George McAfee, Chi. Bears	12	6	3	3
1940	John Drake, Cleveland	9	9	0	0
	Richard Todd, Washington	9	4	4	1
1939	Andrew Farkas, Washington	11	5	5	1
1938	Don Hutson, Green Bay	9	0	9	0
1937	Cliff Battles, Washington	7	5	1	1
	Clarke Hinkle, Green Bay	7	5	2	0
	Don Hutson, Green Bay	7	0	7	0
1936	Don Hutson, Green Bay	9	0	8	1
1935	*Don Hutson, Green Bay	7	0	6	1
1934	*Beattie Feathers, Chi. Bears	9	8	1	0
1933	*Charlie (Buckets) Goldenberg, Green Bay	7	4	1	2
	John (Shipwreck) Kelly, Brooklyn	7	2	3	2
	*Elvin (Kink) Richards, N.Y. Giants	7	4	3	0
1932	Earl (Dutch) Clark, Portsmouth	6	3	3	0
	Red Grange, Chi. Bears	6	3	3	0

**First season of professional football.*

ANNUAL LEADERS—MOST FIELD GOALS MADE

Year	Player, Team	Att.	Made	Pct.
2009	Nate Kaeding, San Diego, AFC	35	32	91.4
	David Akers, Philadelphia, NFC	37	32	86.5
2008	Stephen Gostkowski, New England, AFC	40	36	90.0
	John Carney, N.Y. Giants, NFC	38	35	92.1
2007	Rob Bironas, Tennessee, AFC	39	35	89.7
	*Mason Crosby, Green Bay, NFC	39	31	79.5
	Robbie Gould, Chicago, NFC	36	31	86.1
2006	Robbie Gould, Chicago, NFC	36	32	88.9
	Jeff Wilkins, St. Louis, NFC	37	32	86.5
	Matt Stover, Baltimore, AFC	30	28	93.3
2005	Neil Rackers, Arizona, NFC	42	40	95.2
	Matt Stover, Baltimore, AFC	34	30	88.2
2004	Adam Vinatieri, New England, AFC	33	31	93.9
	David Akers, Philadelphia, NFC	32	27	84.4
2003	Jeff Wilkins, St. Louis, NFC	42	39	92.9
	Mike Vanderjagt, Indianapolis, AFC	37	37	100.0
2002	Jay Feely, Atlanta, NFC	40	32	80.0
	Martín Gramatica, Tampa Bay, NFC	39	32	82.1
	Adam Vinatieri, New England, AFC	30	27	90.0
2001	Jason Elam, Denver, AFC	36	31	86.1
	*Jay Feely, Atlanta, NFC	37	29	78.4
2000	Matt Stover, Baltimore, AFC	39	35	89.7
	Ryan Longwell, Green Bay, NFC	38	33	86.8
1999	Olindo Mare, Miami, AFC	46	39	84.8
	*Martin Gramatica, Tampa Bay, NFC	32	27	84.4
1998	Al Del Greco, Tennessee, AFC	39	36	92.3
	Gary Anderson, Minnesota, NFC	35	35	100.0
1997	Richie Cunningham, Dallas, NFC	37	34	91.9
	Cary Blanchard, Indianapolis, AFC	41	32	78.1
1996	John Kasay, Carolina, NFC	45	37	82.2
	Cary Blanchard, Indianapolis, AFC	40	36	90.0
1995	Norm Johnson, Pittsburgh, AFC	41	34	82.9
	Morten Andersen, Atlanta, NFC	37	31	83.8
1994	John Carney, San Diego, AFC	38	34	89.5
	Fuad Reveiz, Minnesota, NFC	39	34	87.2
1993	Jeff Jaeger, L.A. Raiders, AFC	44	35	79.5
	Jason Hanson, Detroit, NFC	43	34	79.1
1992	Pete Stoyanovich, Miami, AFC	37	30	81.1
	Chip Lohmiller, Washington, NFC	40	30	75.0
1991	Pete Stoyanovich, Miami, AFC	37	31	83.8
	Chip Lohmiller, Washington, NFC	43	31	72.1
1990	Nick Lowery, Kansas City, AFC	37	34	91.9
	Chip Lohmiller, Washington, NFC	40	30	75.0
1989	Rich Karlis, Minnesota, NFC	39	31	79.5
	*David Treadwell, Denver, AFC	33	27	81.8

Year	Player, Team	Att.	Made	Pct.
1988	Scott Norwood, Buffalo, AFC	37	32	86.5
	Mike Cofer, San Francisco, NFC	38	27	71.1
1987	Morten Andersen, New Orleans, NFC	36	28	77.8
	Dean Biasucci, Indianapolis, AFC	27	24	88.9
	Jim Breech, Cincinnati, AFC	30	24	80.0
1986	Tony Franklin, New England, AFC	41	32	78.0
	Kevin Butler, Chicago, NFC	41	28	68.3
1985	Gary Anderson, Pittsburgh, AFC	42	33	78.6
	Morten Andersen, New Orleans, NFC	35	31	88.6
	*Kevin Butler, Chicago, NFC	37	31	83.8
1984	*Paul McFadden, Philadelphia, NFC	37	30	81.1
	Gary Anderson, Pittsburgh, AFC	32	24	75.0
	Matt Bahr, Cleveland, AFC	32	24	75.0
1983	*Ali-Haji-Sheikh, N.Y. Giants, NFC	42	35	83.3
	*Raul Allegre, Baltimore, AFC	35	30	85.7
1982	Mark Moseley, Washington, NFC	21	20	95.2
	Nick Lowery, Kansas City, AFC	24	19	79.2
1981	Rafael Septien, Dallas, NFC	35	27	77.1
	Nick Lowery, Kansas City, AFC	36	26	72.2
1980	*Ed Murray, Detroit, NFC	42	27	64.3
	John Smith, New England, AFC	34	26	76.5
	Fred Steinfort, Denver, AFC	34	26	76.5
1979	Mark Moseley, Washington, NFC	33	25	75.8
	John Smith, New England, AFC	33	23	69.7
1978	*Frank Corral, Los Angeles, NFC	43	29	67.4
	Pat Leahy, N.Y. Jets, AFC	30	22	73.3
1977	Mark Moseley, Washington, NFC	37	21	56.8
	Errol Mann, Oakland, AFC	28	20	71.4
1976	Mark Moseley, Washington, NFC	34	22	64.7
	Jan Stenerud, Kansas City, AFC	38	21	55.3
1975	Jan Stenerud, Kansas City, AFC	32	22	68.8
	Toni Fritsch, Dallas, NFC	35	22	62.9
1974	Chester Marcol, Green Bay, NFC	39	25	64.1
	Roy Gerela, Pittsburgh, AFC	29	20	69.0
1973	David Ray, Los Angeles, NFC	47	30	63.8
	Roy Gerela, Pittsburgh, AFC	43	29	67.4
1972	*Chester Marcol, Green Bay, NFC	48	33	68.8
	Roy Gerela, Pittsburgh, AFC	41	28	68.3
1971	Curt Knight, Washington, NFC	49	29	59.2
	Garo Yepremian, Miami, AFC	40	28	70.0
1970	Jan Stenerud, Kansas City, AFC	42	30	71.4
	Fred Cox, Minnesota, NFC	46	30	65.2
1969	Jim Turner, N.Y. Jets, AFL	47	32	68.1
	Fred Cox, Minnesota, NFL	37	26	70.3
1968	Jim Turner, N.Y. Jets, AFL	46	34	73.9
	Mac Percival, Chicago, NFL	36	25	69.4
1967	Jim Bakken, St. Louis, NFL	39	27	69.2
	Jan Stenerud, Kansas City, AFL	36	21	58.3
1966	Bruce Gossett, Los Angeles, NFL	49	28	57.1
	Mike Mercer, Oakland-Kansas City, AFL	30	21	70.0
1965	Pete Gogolak, Buffalo, AFL	46	28	60.9
	Fred Cox, Minnesota, NFL	35	23	65.7
1964	Jim Bakken, St. Louis, NFL	38	25	65.8
	Gino Cappelletti, Boston, AFL	39	25	64.1
1963	Jim Martin, Baltimore, NFL	39	24	61.5
	Gino Cappelletti, Boston, AFL	38	22	57.9
1962	Gene Mingo, Denver, AFL	39	27	69.2
	Lou Michaels, Pittsburgh, NFL	42	26	61.9
1961	Steve Myhra, Baltimore, NFL	39	21	53.8
	Gino Cappelletti, Boston, AFL	32	17	53.1
1960	Tommy Davis, San Francisco, NFL	32	19	59.4
	*Gene Mingo, Denver, AFL	28	18	64.3
1959	Pat Summerall, N.Y. Giants	29	20	69.0
1958	Paige Cothren, Los Angeles	25	14	56.0
	*Tom Miner, Pittsburgh	28	14	50.0
1957	Lou Groza, Cleveland	22	15	68.2
1956	Sam Baker, Washington	25	17	68.0
1955	Fred Cone, Green Bay	24	16	66.7
1954	Lou Groza, Cleveland	24	16	66.7

Year	Player, Team	Att.	Made	Pct.
1953	Lou Groza, Cleveland	26	23	88.5
1952	Lou Groza, Cleveland	33	19	57.6
1951	Bob Waterfield, Los Angeles	23	13	56.5
1950	Lou Groza, Cleveland	19	13	68.4
1949	Cliff Patton, Philadelphia	18	9	50.0
	Bob Waterfield, Los Angeles	16	9	56.3
1948	Cliff Patton, Philadelphia	12	8	66.7
1947	Ward Cuff, Green Bay	16	7	43.8
	Pat Harder, Chi. Cardinals	10	7	70.0
	Bob Waterfield, Los Angeles	16	7	43.8
1946	Ted Fritsch, Green Bay	17	9	52.9
1945	Joe Aguirre, Washington	13	7	53.8
1944	Ken Strong, N.Y. Giants	12	6	50.0
1943	Ward Cuff, N.Y. Giants	9	3	33.3
	Don Hutson, Green Bay	5	3	60.0
1942	Bill Daddio, Chi. Cardinals	10	5	50.0
1941	Clarke Hinkle, Green Bay	14	6	42.9
1940	Clarke Hinkle, Green Bay	14	9	64.3
1939	Ward Cuff, N.Y. Giants	16	7	43.8
1938	Ward Cuff, N.Y. Giants	9	5	55.6
	Ralph Kercheval, Brooklyn	13	5	38.5
1937	Jack Manders, Chi. Bears		8	
1936	Jack Manders, Chi. Bears		7	
	Armand Niccolai, Pittsburgh		7	
1935	Armand Niccolai, Pittsburgh		6	
	Bill Smith, Chi. Cardinals		6	
1934	Jack Manders, Chi. Bears		10	
1933	*Jack Manders, Chi. Bears		6	
	Glenn Presnell, Portsmouth		6	
1932	Earl (Dutch) Clark, Portsmouth		3	

**First season of professional football.*

ANNUAL RUSHING LEADERS

Year	Player, Team	Att.	Yards	Avg.	TD
2009	Chris Johnson, Tennessee, AFC	358	2,006	5.6	14
	Steven Jackson, St. Louis, NFC	324	1,416	4.4	4
2008	Adrian Peterson, Minnesota, NFC	363	1,760	4.9	10
	Thomas Jones, N.Y. Jets, AFC	290	1,312	4.5	13
2007	LaDainian Tomlinson, San Diego, AFC	315	1,474	4.7	15
	*Adrian Peterson, Minnesota, NFC	238	1,341	5.6	12
2006	LaDainian Tomlinson, San Diego, AFC	348	1,815	5.2	28
	Frank Gore, San Francisco, NFC	312	1,695	5.4	8
2005	Shaun Alexander, Seattle, NFC	370	1,880	5.1	27
	Larry Johnson, Kansas City, AFC	336	1,750	5.2	20
2004	Curtis Martin, N.Y. Jets, AFC	371	1,697	4.6	12
	Shaun Alexander, Seattle, NFC	353	1,696	4.8	16
2003	Jamal Lewis, Baltimore, AFC	387	2,066	5.3	14
	Ahman Green, Green Bay, NFC	355	1,883	5.3	15
2002	Ricky Williams, Miami, AFC	383	1,853	4.8	16
	Deuce McAllister, New Orleans, NFC	325	1,388	4.3	13
2001	Priest Holmes, Kansas City, AFC	327	1,555	4.8	8
	Stephen Davis, Washington, NFC	356	1,432	4.0	5
2000	Edgerrin James, Indianapolis, AFC	387	1,709	4.4	13
	Robert Smith, Minnesota, NFC	295	1,521	5.2	7
1999	*Edgerrin James, Indianapolis, AFC	369	1,553	4.2	13
	Stephen Davis, Washington, NFC	290	1,405	4.8	17
1998	Terrell Davis, Denver, AFC	392	2,008	5.1	21
	Jamal Anderson, Atlanta, NFC	410	1,846	4.5	14
1997	Barry Sanders, Detroit, NFC	335	2,053	6.1	11
	Terrell Davis, Denver, AFC	369	1,750	4.7	15
1996	Barry Sanders, Detroit, NFC	307	1,553	5.1	11
	Terrell Davis, Denver, AFC	345	1,538	4.5	13
1995	Emmitt Smith, Dallas, NFC	377	1,773	4.7	25
	*Curtis Martin, New England, AFC	368	1,487	4.0	14
1994	Barry Sanders, Detroit, NFC	331	1,883	5.7	7
	Chris Warren, Seattle, AFC	333	1,545	4.6	9
1993	Emmitt Smith, Dallas, NFC	283	1,486	5.3	9
	Thurman Thomas, Buffalo, AFC	355	1,315	3.7	6

Year	Player, Team	Att.	Yards	Avg.	TD
1992	Emmitt Smith, Dallas, NFC	373	1,713	4.6	18
	Barry Foster, Pittsburgh, AFC	390	1,690	4.3	11
1991	Emmitt Smith, Dallas, NFC	365	1,563	4.3	12
	Thurman Thomas, Buffalo, AFC	288	1,407	4.9	7
1990	Barry Sanders, Detroit, NFC	255	1,304	5.1	13
	Thurman Thomas, Buffalo, AFC	271	1,297	4.8	11
1989	Christian Okoye, Kansas City, AFC	370	1,480	4.0	12
	*Barry Sanders, Detroit, NFC	280	1,470	5.3	14
1988	Eric Dickerson, Indianapolis, AFC	388	1,659	4.3	14
	Herschel Walker, Dallas, NFC	361	1,514	4.2	5
1987	Charles White, L.A. Rams, NFC	324	1,374	4.2	11
	Eric Dickerson, Indianapolis, AFC	223	1,011	4.5	5
1986	Eric Dickerson, L.A. Rams, NFC	404	1,821	4.5	11
	Curt Warner, Seattle, AFC	319	1,481	4.6	13
1985	Marcus Allen, L.A. Raiders, AFC	380	1,759	4.6	11
	Gerald Riggs, Atlanta, NFC	397	1,719	4.3	10
1984	Eric Dickerson, L.A. Rams, NFC	379	2,105	5.6	14
	Earnest Jackson, San Diego, AFC	296	1,179	4.0	8
1983	*Eric Dickerson, L.A. Rams, NFC	390	1,808	4.6	18
	*Curt Warner, Seattle, AFC	335	1,449	4.3	13
1982	Freeman McNeil, N.Y. Jets, AFC	151	786	5.2	6
	Tony Dorsett, Dallas, NFC	177	745	4.2	5
1981	*George Rogers, New Orleans, NFC	378	1,674	4.4	13
	Earl Campbell, Houston, AFC	361	1,376	3.8	10
1980	Earl Campbell, Houston, AFC	373	1,934	5.2	13
	Walter Payton, Chicago, NFC	317	1,460	4.6	6
1979	Earl Campbell, Houston, AFC	368	1,697	4.6	19
	Walter Payton, Chicago, NFC	369	1,610	4.4	14
1978	*Earl Campbell, Houston, AFC	302	1,450	4.8	13
	Walter Payton, Chicago, NFC	333	1,395	4.2	11
1977	Walter Payton, Chicago, NFC	339	1,852	5.5	14
	Mark van Eeghen, Oakland, AFC	324	1,273	3.9	7
1976	O.J. Simpson, Buffalo, AFC	290	1,503	5.2	8
	Walter Payton, Chicago, NFC	311	1,390	4.5	13
1975	O.J. Simpson, Buffalo, AFC	329	1,817	5.5	16
	Jim Otis, St. Louis, NFC	269	1,076	4.0	5
1974	Otis Armstrong, Denver, AFC	263	1,407	5.3	9
	Lawrence McCutcheon, Los Angeles, NFC	236	1,109	4.7	3
1973	O.J. Simpson, Buffalo, AFC	332	2,003	6.0	12
	John Brockington, Green Bay, NFC	265	1,144	4.3	3
1972	O.J. Simpson, Buffalo, AFC	292	1,251	4.3	6
	Larry Brown, Washington, NFC	285	1,216	4.3	8
1971	Floyd Little, Denver, AFC	284	1,133	4.0	6
	*John Brockington, Green Bay, NFC	216	1,105	5.1	4
1970	Larry Brown, Washington, NFC	237	1,125	4.7	5
	Floyd Little, Denver, AFC	209	901	4.3	3
1969	Gale Sayers, Chicago, NFL	236	1,032	4.4	8
	Dickie Post, San Diego, AFL	182	873	4.8	6
1968	Leroy Kelly, Cleveland, NFL	248	1,239	5.0	16
	*Paul Robinson, Cincinnati, AFL	238	1,023	4.3	8
1967	Jim Nance, Boston, AFL	269	1,216	4.5	7
	Leroy Kelly, Cleveland, NFL	235	1,205	5.1	11
1966	Jim Nance, Boston, AFL	299	1,458	4.9	11
	Gale Sayers, Chicago, NFL	229	1,231	5.4	8
1965	Jim Brown, Cleveland, NFL	289	1,544	5.3	17
	Paul Lowe, San Diego, AFL	222	1,121	5.0	7
1964	Jim Brown, Cleveland, NFL	280	1,446	5.2	7
	Cookie Gilchrist, Buffalo, AFL	230	981	4.3	6
1963	Jim Brown, Cleveland, NFL	291	1,863	6.4	12
	Clem Daniels, Oakland, AFL	215	1,099	5.1	3
1962	Jim Taylor, Green Bay, NFL	272	1,474	5.4	19
	Cookie Gilchrist, Buffalo, AFL	214	1,096	5.1	13
1961	Jim Brown, Cleveland, NFL	305	1,408	4.6	8
	Billy Cannon, Houston, AFL	200	948	4.7	6
1960	Jim Brown, Cleveland, NFL	215	1,257	5.8	9
	*Abner Haynes, Dall. Texans, AFL	156	875	5.6	9
1959	Jim Brown, Cleveland	290	1,329	4.6	14
1958	Jim Brown, Cleveland	257	1,527	5.9	17
1957	*Jim Brown, Cleveland	202	942	4.7	9

Year	Player, Team	Att.	Yards	Avg.	TD
1956	Rick Casares, Chi. Bears	234	1,126	4.8	12
1955	*Alan Ameche, Baltimore	213	961	4.5	9
1954	Joe Perry, San Francisco	173	1,049	6.1	8
1953	Joe Perry, San Francisco	192	1,018	5.3	10
1952	Dan Towler, Los Angeles	156	894	5.7	10
1951	Eddie Price, N.Y. Giants	271	971	3.6	7
1950	Marion Motley, Cleveland	140	810	5.8	3
1949	Steve Van Buren, Philadelphia	263	1,146	4.4	11
1948	Steve Van Buren, Philadelphia	201	945	4.7	10
1947	Steve Van Buren, Philadelphia	217	1,008	4.6	13
1946	Bill Dudley, Pittsburgh	146	604	4.1	3
1945	Steve Van Buren, Philadelphia	143	832	5.8	15
1944	Bill Paschal, N.Y. Giants	196	737	3.8	9
1943	*Bill Paschal, N.Y. Giants	147	572	3.9	10
1942	*Bill Dudley, Pittsburgh	162	696	4.3	5
1941	Clarence (Pug) Manders, Brooklyn	111	486	4.4	5
1940	Byron (Whizzer) White, Detroit	146	514	3.5	5
1939	*Bill Osmanski, Chicago	121	699	5.8	7
1938	*Byron (Whizzer) White, Pittsburgh	152	567	3.7	4
1937	Cliff Battles, Washington	216	874	4.0	5
1936	*Alphonse (Tuffy) Leemans, N.Y. Giants	206	830	4.0	2
1935	Doug Russell, Chi. Cardinals	140	499	3.6	0
1934	*Beattie Feathers, Chi. Bears	119	1,004	8.4	8
1933	Jim Musick, Boston	173	809	4.7	5
1932	*Cliff Battles, Boston	148	576	3.9	3

**First season of professional football.*

ANNUAL PASSING LEADERS

(Current rating system implemented in 1973)

Year	Player, Team	Att.	Comp.	Yards	TD	Int.	Rating
2009	Drew Brees, New Orleans, NFC	514	363	4,388	34	11	109.6
	Philip Rivers, San Diego, AFC	486	317	4,254	28	9	104.4
2008	Philip Rivers, San Diego, AFC	478	312	4,009	34	11	105.5
	Kurt Warner, Arizona, NFC	598	401	4,583	30	14	96.9
2007	Tom Brady, New England, AFC	578	398	4,806	50	8	117.2
	Tony Romo, Dallas, NFC	520	335	4,211	36	19	97.4
2006	Peyton Manning, Indianapolis, AFC	557	362	4,397	31	9	101.0
	Drew Brees, New Orleans, NFC	554	356	4,418	26	11	96.2
2005	Peyton Manning, Indianapolis, AFC	453	305	3,747	28	10	104.1
	Matt Hasselbeck, Seattle, NFC	449	294	3,459	24	9	98.2
2004	Peyton Manning, Indianapolis, AFC	497	336	4,557	49	10	121.1
	Daunte Culpepper, Minnesota, NFC	548	379	4,717	39	11	110.9
2003	Steve McNair, Tennessee, AFC	400	250	3,215	24	7	100.4
	Daunte Culpepper, Minnesota, NFC	454	295	3,479	25	11	96.4
2002	Chad Pennington, N.Y. Jets, AFC	399	275	3,120	22	6	104.2
	Brad Johnson, Tampa Bay, NFC	451	281	3,049	22	6	92.9
2001	Kurt Warner, St. Louis, NFC	546	375	4,830	36	22	101.4
	Rich Gannon, Oakland, AFC	549	361	3,828	27	9	95.5
2000	Brian Griese, Denver, AFC	336	216	2,688	19	4	102.9
	Trent Green, St. Louis, NFC	240	145	2,063	16	5	101.8
1999	Kurt Warner, St. Louis, NFC	499	325	4,353	41	13	109.2
	Peyton Manning, Indianapolis, AFC	533	331	4,135	26	15	90.7
1998	Randall Cunningham, Minnesota, NFC	425	259	3,704	34	10	106.0
	Vinny Testaverde, N.Y. Jets, AFC	421	259	3,256	29	7	101.6
1997	Steve Young, San Francisco, NFC	356	241	3,029	19	6	104.7
	Mark Brunell, Jacksonville, AFC	435	264	3,281	18	7	91.2
1996	Steve Young, San Francisco NFC	316	214	2,410	14	6	97.2
	John Elway, Denver, AFC	466	287	3,328	26	14	89.2
1995	Jim Harbaugh, Indianapolis, AFC	314	200	2,575	17	5	100.7
	Brett Favre, Green Bay, NFC	570	359	4,413	38	13	99.5
1994	Steve Young, San Francisco, NFC	461	324	3,969	35	10	112.8
	Dan Marino, Miami, AFC	615	385	4,453	30	17	89.2
1993	Steve Young, San Francisco, NFC	462	314	4,023	29	16	101.5
	John Elway, Denver, AFC	551	348	4,030	25	10	92.8
1992	Steve Young, San Francisco, NFC	402	268	3,465	25	7	107.0
	Warren Moon, Houston, AFC	346	224	2,521	18	12	89.3
1991	Steve Young, San Francisco, NFC	279	180	2,517	17	8	101.8
	Jim Kelly, Buffalo, AFC	474	304	3,844	33	17	97.6

Year	Player, Team	Att.	Comp.	Yards	TD	Int.	Rating
1990	Jim Kelly, Buffalo, AFC	346	219	2,829	24	9	101.2
	Phil Simms, N.Y. Giants, NFC	311	184	2,284	15	4	92.7
1989	Joe Montana, San Francisco, NFC	386	271	3,521	26	8	112.4
	Boomer Esiason, Cincinnati, AFC	455	258	3,525	28	11	92.1
1988	Boomer Esiason, Cincinnati, AFC	388	223	3,572	28	14	97.4
	Wade Wilson, Minnesota, NFC	332	204	2,746	15	9	91.5
1987	Joe Montana, San Francisco, NFC	398	266	3,054	31	13	102.1
	Bernie Kosar, Cleveland, AFC	389	241	3,033	22	9	95.4
1986	Tommy Kramer, Minnesota, NFC	372	208	3,000	24	10	92.6
	Dan Marino, Miami, AFC	623	378	4,746	44	23	92.5
1985	Ken O'Brien, N.Y. Jets, AFC	488	297	3,888	25	8	96.2
	Joe Montana, San Francisco, NFC	494	303	3,653	27	13	91.3
1984	Dan Marino, Miami, AFC	564	362	5,084	48	17	108.9
	Joe Montana, San Francisco, NFC	432	279	3,630	28	10	102.9
1983	Steve Bartkowski, Atlanta, NFC	432	274	3,167	22	5	97.6
	*Dan Marino, Miami, AFC	296	173	2,210	20	6	96.0
1982	Ken Anderson, Cincinnati, AFC	309	218	2,495	12	9	95.3
	Joe Theismann, Washington, NFC	252	161	2,033	13	9	91.3
1981	Ken Anderson, Cincinnati, AFC	479	300	3,754	29	10	98.4
	Joe Montana, San Francisco, NFC	488	311	3,565	19	12	88.4
1980	Brian Sipe, Cleveland, AFC	554	337	4,132	30	14	91.4
	Ron Jaworski, Philadelphia, NFC	451	257	3,529	27	12	91.0
1979	Roger Staubach, Dallas, NFC	461	267	3,586	27	11	92.3
	Dan Fouts, San Diego, AFC	530	332	4,082	24	24	82.6
1978	Roger Staubach, Dallas, NFC	413	231	3,190	25	16	84.9
	Terry Bradshaw, Pittsburgh, AFC	368	207	2,915	28	20	84.7
1977	Bob Griese, Miami, AFC	307	180	2,252	22	13	87.8
	Roger Staubach, Dallas, NFC	361	210	2,620	18	9	87.0
1976	Ken Stabler, Oakland, AFC	291	194	2,737	27	17	103.4
	James Harris, Los Angeles, NFC	158	91	1,460	8	6	89.6
1975	Ken Anderson, Cincinnati, AFC	377	228	3,169	21	11	93.9
	Fran Tarkenton, Minnesota, NFC	425	273	2,994	25	13	91.8
1974	Ken Anderson, Cincinnati, AFC	328	213	2,667	18	10	95.7
	Sonny Jurgensen, Washington, NFC	167	107	1,185	11	5	94.5
1973	Roger Staubach, Dallas, NFC	286	179	2,428	23	15	94.6
	Ken Stabler, Oakland, AFC	260	163	1,997	14	10	88.3
1972	Norm Snead, N.Y. Giants, NFC	325	196	2,307	17	12	
	Earl Morrall, Miami, AFC	150	83	1,360	11	7	
1971	Roger Staubach, Dallas, NFC	211	126	1,882	15	4	
	Bob Griese, Miami, AFC	263	145	2,089	19	9	
1970	John Brodie, San Francisco, NFC	378	223	2,941	24	10	
	Daryle Lamonica, Oakland, AFC	356	179	2,516	22	15	
1969	Sonny Jurgensen, Washington, NFL	442	274	3,102	22	15	
	*Greg Cook, Cincinnati, AFL	197	106	1,854	15	11	
1968	Len Dawson, Kansas City, AFL	224	131	2,109	17	9	
	Earl Morrall, Baltimore, NFL	317	182	2,909	26	17	
1967	Sonny Jurgensen, Washington, NFL	508	288	3,747	31	16	
	Daryle Lamonica, Oakland, AFL	425	220	3,228	30	20	
1966	Bart Starr, Green Bay, NFL	251	156	2,257	14	3	
	Len Dawson, Kansas City, AFL	284	159	2,527	26	10	
1965	Rudy Bukich, Chicago, NFL	312	176	2,641	20	9	
	John Hadl, San Diego, AFL	348	174	2,798	20	21	
1964	Len Dawson, Kansas City, AFL	354	199	2,879	30	18	
	Bart Starr, Green Bay, NFL	272	163	2,144	15	4	
1963	Y.A. Tittle, N.Y. Giants, NFL	367	221	3,145	36	14	
	Tobin Rote, San Diego, AFL	286	170	2,510	20	17	
1962	Len Dawson, Dallas Texans, AFL	310	189	2,759	29	17	
	Bart Starr, Green Bay, NFL	285	178	2,438	12	9	
1961	George Blanda, Houston, AFL	362	187	3,330	36	22	
	Milt Plum, Cleveland, NFL	302	177	2,416	18	10	
1960	Milt Plum, Cleveland, NFL	250	151	2,297	21	5	
	Jack Kemp, L.A. Chargers, AFL	406	211	3,018	20	25	
1959	Charlie Conerly, N.Y. Giants	194	113	1,706	14	4	
1958	Eddie LeBaron, Washington	145	79	1,365	11	10	
1957	Tommy O'Connell, Cleveland	110	63	1,229	9	8	
1956	Ed Brown, Chicago Bears	168	96	1,667	11	12	
1955	Otto Graham, Cleveland	185	98	1,721	15	8	
1954	Norm Van Brocklin, Los Angeles	260	139	2,637	13	21	
1953	Otto Graham, Cleveland	258	167	2,722	11	9	

YEARLY STATISTICAL LEADERS

Year	Player, Team	Att.	Comp.	Yards	TD	Int.	Rating
1952	Norm Van Brocklin, Los Angeles	205	113	1,736	14	17	
1951	Bob Waterfield, Los Angeles	176	88	1,566	13	10	
1950	Norm Van Brocklin, Los Angeles	233	127	2,061	18	14	
1949	Sammy Baugh, Washington	255	145	1,903	18	14	
1948	Tommy Thompson, Philadelphia	246	141	1,965	25	11	
1947	Sammy Baugh, Washington	354	210	2,938	25	15	
1946	Bob Waterfield, Los Angeles	251	127	1,747	18	17	
1945	Sammy Baugh, Washington	182	128	1,669	11	4	
	Sid Luckman, Chicago Bears	217	117	1,725	14	10	
1944	Frank Filchock, Washington	147	84	1,139	13	9	
1943	Sammy Baugh, Washington	239	133	1,754	23	19	
1942	Cecil Isbell, Green Bay	268	146	2,021	24	14	
1941	Cecil Isbell, Green Bay	206	117	1,479	15	11	
1940	Sammy Baugh, Washington	177	111	1,367	12	10	
1939	*Parker Hall, Cleveland	208	106	1,227	9	13	
1938	Ed Danowski, N.Y. Giants	129	70	848	7	8	
1937	*Sammy Baugh, Washington	171	81	1,127	8	14	
1936	Arnie Herber, Green Bay	173	77	1,239	11	13	
1935	Ed Danowski, N.Y. Giants	113	57	794	10	9	
1934	Arnie Herber, Green Bay	115	42	799	8	12	
1933	*Harry Newman, N.Y. Giants	136	53	973	11	17	
1932	Arnie Herber, Green Bay	101	37	639	9	9	

**First season of professional football.*

ANNUAL PASSING TOUCHDOWN LEADERS

Year	Player, Team	TD
2009	Drew Brees, New Orleans, NFC	34
	Peyton Manning, Indianapolis, AFC	33
2008	Drew Brees, New Orleans, NFC	34
	Philip Rivers, San Diego, AFC	34
2007	Tom Brady, New England, AFC	50
	Tony Romo, Dallas, NFC	36
2006	Peyton Manning, Indianapolis, AFC	31
	Drew Brees, New Orleans, NFC	26
2005	Carson Palmer, Cincinnati, AFC	32
	Jake Delhomme, Carolina, NFC	24
	Matt Hasselbeck, Seattle, NFC	24
	Eli Manning, N.Y. Giants, NFC	24
2004	Peyton Manning, Indianapolis, AFC	49
	Daunte Culpepper, Minnesota, NFC	39
2003	Brett Favre, Green Bay, NFC	32
	Peyton Manning, Indianapolis, AFC	29
2002	Tom Brady, New England, AFC	28
	Aaron Brooks, New Orleans, NFC	27
	Brett Favre, Green Bay, NFC	27
2001	Kurt Warner, St. Louis, NFC	36
	Rich Gannon, Oakland, AFC	27
2000	Daunte Culpepper, Minnesota, NFC	33
	Peyton Manning, Indianapolis, AFC	33
1999	Kurt Warner, St. Louis, NFC	41
	Peyton Manning, Indianapolis, AFC	26
1998	Steve Young, San Francisco, NFC	36
	Vinny Testaverde, N.Y. Jets, AFC	29
1997	Brett Favre, Green Bay, NFC	35
	Jeff George, Oakland, AFC	29
1996	Brett Favre, Green Bay, NFC	39
	Vinny Testaverde, Baltimore, AFC	33
1995	Brett Favre, Green Bay, NFC	38
	Jeff Blake, Cincinnati, AFC	28
1994	Steve Young, San Francisco, NFC	35
	Dan Marino, Miami, AFC	30
1993	Steve Young, San Francisco, NFC	29
	John Elway, Denver, AFC	25
1992	Steve Young, San Francisco, NFC	25
	Dan Marino, Miami, AFC	24
1991	Jim Kelly, Buffalo, AFC	33
	Mark Rypien, Washington, NFC	28
1990	Warren Moon, Houston, AFC	33
	Randall Cunningham, Philadelphia, NFC	30
1989	Jim Everett, L.A. Rams, NFC	29
	Boomer Esiason, Cincinnati, AFC	28
1988	Jim Everett, L.A. Rams, NFC	31
	Boomer Esiason, Cincinnati, AFC	28
	Dan Marino, Miami, AFC	28
1987	Joe Montana, San Francisco, NFC	31
	Dan Marino, Miami, AFC	26
1986	Dan Marino, Miami, AFC	44
	Tommy Kramer, Minnesota, NFC	24
1985	Dan Marino, Miami, AFC	30
	Joe Montana, San Francisco, NFC	27
1984	Dan Marino, Miami, AFC	48
	Neil Lomax, St. Louis, NFC	28
	Joe Montana, San Francisco, NFC	28
1983	Lynn Dickey, Green Bay, NFC	32
	Joe Ferguson, Buffalo, AFC	26
	Brian Sipe, Cleveland, AFC	26
1982	Terry Bradshaw, Pittsburgh, AFC	17
	Dan Fouts, San Diego, AFC	17
	Joe Montana, San Francisco, NFC	17
1981	Dan Fouts, San Diego, AFC	33
	Steve Bartkowski, Atlanta, NFC	30
1980	Steve Bartkowski, Atlanta, NFC	31
	Dan Fouts, San Diego, AFC	30
	Brian Sipe, Cleveland, AFC	30
1979	Steve Grogan, New England, AFC	28
	Brian Sipe, Cleveland, AFC	28
	Roger Staubach, Dallas, NFC	27
1978	Terry Bradshaw, Pittsburgh, AFC	28
	Roger Staubach, Dallas, NFC	25
	Fran Tarkenton, Minnesota, NFC	25
1977	Bob Griese, Miami, AFC	22
	Ron Jaworski, Philadelphia, NFC	18
	Roger Staubach, Dallas, NFC	18
1976	Ken Stabler, Oakland, AFC	27
	Jim Hart, St. Louis, NFC	18
1975	Joe Ferguson, Buffalo, AFC	25
	Fran Tarkenton, Minnesota, NFC	25
1974	Ken Stabler, Oakland, AFC	26
	Jim Hart, St. Louis, NFC	20
1973	Roman Gabriel, Philadelphia, NFC	23
	Roger Staubach, Dallas, NFC	23
	Charley Johnson, Denver, AFC	20
1972	Billy Kilmer, Washington, NFC	19
	Joe Namath, N.Y. Jets, AFC	19
1971	John Hadl, San Diego, AFC	21
	John Brodie, San Francisco, NFC	18

Year	Player, Team	TD
1970	John Brodie, San Francisco, NFC	24
	John Hadl, San Diego, AFC	22
	Daryle Lamonica, Oakland, AFC	22
1969	Daryle Lamonica, Oakland, AFL	34
	Roman Gabriel, Los Angeles, NFL	24
1968	John Hadl, San Diego, AFL	27
	Earl Morrall, Baltimore, NFL	26
1967	Sonny Jurgensen, Washington, NFL	31
	Daryle Lamonica, Oakland, AFL	30
1966	Frank Ryan, Cleveland, NFL	29
	Len Dawson, Kansas City, AFL	26
1965	John Brodie, San Francisco, NFL	30
	Len Dawson, Kansas City, AFL	21
1964	Babe Parilli, Boston, AFL	31
	Frank Ryan, Cleveland, NFL	25
1963	Y.A. Tittle, N.Y. Giants, NFL	36
	Len Dawson, Kansas City, AFL	26
1962	Y.A. Tittle, N.Y. Giants, NFL	33
	Len Dawson, Dallas, AFL	29
1961	George Blanda, Houston, AFL	36
	Sonny Jurgensen, Philadelphia, NFL	32
1960	Al Dorow, N.Y. Titans, AFL	26
	Johnny Unitas, Baltimore, NFL	25
1959	Johnny Unitas, Baltimore	32
1958	Johnny Unitas, Baltimore	19
1957	Johnny Unitas, Baltimore	24
1956	Tobin Rote, Green Bay	18
1955	Tobin Rote, Green Bay	17
	Y.A. Tittle, San Francisco	17

Year	Player, Team	TD
1954	Adrian Burk, Philadelphia	23
1953	Robert Thomason, Philadelphia	21
1952	Jim Finks, Pittsburgh	20
	Otto Graham, Cleveland	20
1951	Bobby Layne, Detroit	26
1950	George Ratterman, N.Y. Yanks	22
1949	Johnny Lujack, Chi. Bears	23
1948	Tommy Thompson, Philadelphia	25
1947	Sammy Baugh, Washington	25
1946	Sid Luckman, Chi. Bears	17
	Bob Waterfield, Los Angeles	17
1945	Sid Luckman, Chi. Bears	14
	*Bob Waterfield, Cleveland	14
1944	Frank Filchock, Washington	13
1943	Sid Luckman, Chi. Bears	28
1942	Cecil Isbell, Green Bay	24
1941	Cecil Isbell, Green Bay	15
1940	Sammy Baugh, Washington	12
1939	Frank Filchock, Washington	11
1938	Bob Monnett, Green Bay	9
1937	Bernie Masterson, Chi. Bears	9
1936	Arnie Herber, Green Bay	11
1935	Ed Danowski, N.Y. Giants	10
1934	Arnie Herber, Green Bay	8
1933	*Harry Newman, N.Y. Giants	11
1932	Arnie Herber, Green Bay	9

First season of professional football.

ANNUAL PASS RECEIVING LEADERS

Year	Player, Team	No.	Yards	Avg.	TD
2009	Wes Welker, New England, AFC	123	1,348	11.0	4
	Steve Smith, N.Y. Giants, NFC	107	1,220	11.4	7
2008	Andre Johnson, Houston, AFC	115	1,575	13.7	8
	Larry Fitzgerald, Arizona, NFC	96	1,431	14.9	12
2007	T.J. Houshmandzadeh, Cincinnati, AFC	112	1,143	10.2	12
	Wes Welker, New England, AFC	112	1,175	10.5	8
	Larry Fitzgerald, Arizona, NFC	100	1,409	14.1	10
2006	Andre Johnson, Houston, AFC	103	1,147	11.1	5
	Mike Furrey, Detroit, NFC	98	1,086	11.1	6
2005	Steve Smith, Carolina, NFC	103	1,563	15.2	12
	Larry Fitzgerald, Arizona, NFC	103	1,409	13.7	10
	Chad Ochocinco, Cincinnati, AFC	97	1,432	14.8	9
2004	Tony Gonzalez, Kansas City, AFC	102	1,258	12.3	7
	Joe Horn, New Orleans, NFC	94	1,399	14.9	11
	Torry Holt, St. Louis, NFC	94	1,372	14.6	10
2003	Torry Holt, St. Louis, NFC	117	1,696	14.5	12
	LaDainian Tomlinson, San Diego, AFC	100	725	7.3	4
2002	Marvin Harrison, Indianapolis, AFC	143	1,722	12.0	11
	Randy Moss, Minnesota, NFC	106	1,347	12.7	7
2001	Rod Smith, Denver, AFC	113	1,343	11.9	11
	Keyshawn Johnson, Tampa Bay, NFC	106	1,266	11.9	1
2000	Marvin Harrison, Indianapolis, AFC	102	1,413	13.9	14
	Muhsin Muhammad, Carolina, NFC	102	1,183	11.6	6
1999	Jimmy Smith, Jacksonville, AFC	116	1,636	14.1	6
	Muhsin Muhammad, Carolina, NFC	96	1,253	13.1	8
1998	O.J. McDuffie, Miami, AFC	90	1,050	11.7	7
	Frank Sanders, Arizona, NFC	89	1,145	12.9	3
1997	Tim Brown, Oakland, AFC	104	1,408	13.5	5
	Herman Moore, Detroit, NFC	104	1,293	12.4	8
1996	Jerry Rice, San Francisco, NFC	108	1,254	11.6	8
	Carl Pickens, Cincinnati, AFC	100	1,180	11.8	12
1995	Herman Moore, Detroit, NFC	123	1,686	13.7	14
	Carl Pickens, Cincinnati, AFC	99	1,234	12.5	17
1994	Cris Carter, Minnesota, NFC	122	1,256	10.3	7
	Ben Coates, New England, AFC	96	1,174	12.2	7
1993	Sterling Sharpe, Green Bay, NFC	112	1,274	11.4	11
	Reggie Langhorne, Indianapolis, AFC	85	1,038	12.2	3
1992	Sterling Sharpe, Green Bay, NFC	108	1,461	13.5	13

YEARLY STATISTICAL LEADERS

Year	Player, Team	No.	Yards	Avg.	TD
	Haywood Jeffires, Houston, AFC	90	913	10.1	9
1991	Haywood Jeffires, Houston, AFC	100	1,181	11.8	7
	Michael Irvin, Dallas, NFC	93	1,523	16.4	8
1990	Jerry Rice, San Francisco, NFC	100	1,502	15.0	13
	Haywood Jeffires, Houston, AFC	74	1,048	14.2	8
	Drew Hill, Houston, AFC	74	1,019	13.8	5
1989	Sterling Sharpe, Green Bay, NFC	90	1,423	15.8	12
	Andre Reed, Buffalo, AFC	88	1,312	14.9	9
1988	Al Toon, N.Y. Jets, AFC	93	1,067	11.5	5
	Henry Ellard, L.A. Rams, NFC	86	1,414	16.4	10
1987	J.T. Smith, St. Louis, NFC	91	1,117	12.3	8
	Al Toon, N.Y. Jets, AFC	68	976	14.4	5
1986	Todd Christensen, L.A. Raiders, AFC	95	1,153	12.1	8
	Jerry Rice, San Francisco, NFC	86	1,570	18.3	15
1985	Roger Craig, San Francisco, NFC	92	1,016	11.0	6
	Lionel James, San Diego, AFC	86	1,027	11.9	6
1984	Art Monk, Washington, NFC	106	1,372	12.9	7
	Ozzie Newsome, Cleveland, AFC	89	1,001	11.2	5
1983	Todd Christensen, L.A. Raiders, AFC	92	1,247	13.6	12
	Roy Green, St. Louis, NFC	78	1,227	15.7	14
	Charlie Brown, Washington, NFC	78	1,225	15.7	8
	Earnest Gray, N.Y. Giants, NFC	78	1,139	14.6	5
1982	Dwight Clark, San Francisco, NFC	60	913	15.2	5
	Kellen Winslow, San Diego, AFC	54	721	13.4	6
1981	Kellen Winslow, San Diego, AFC	88	1,075	12.2	10
	Dwight Clark, San Francisco, NFC	85	1,105	13.0	4
1980	Kellen Winslow, San Diego, AFC	89	1,290	14.5	9
	*Earl Cooper, San Francisco, NFC	83	567	6.8	4
1979	Joe Washington, Baltimore, AFC	82	750	9.1	3
	Ahmad Rashad, Minnesota, NFC	80	1,156	14.5	9
1978	Rickey Young, Minnesota, NFC	88	704	8.0	5
	Steve Largent, Seattle, AFC	71	1,168	16.5	8
1977	Lydell Mitchell, Baltimore, AFC	71	620	8.7	4
	Ahmad Rashad, Minnesota, NFC	51	681	13.4	2
1976	MacArthur Lane, Kansas City, AFC	66	686	10.4	1
	Drew Pearson, Dallas, NFC	58	806	13.9	6
1975	Chuck Foreman, Minnesota, NFC	73	691	9.5	9
	Reggie Rucker, Cleveland, AFC	60	770	12.8	3
	Lydell Mitchell, Baltimore, AFC	60	544	9.1	4
1974	Lydell Mitchell, Baltimore, AFC	72	544	7.6	2
	Charles Young, Philadelphia, NFC	63	696	11.0	3
1973	Harold Carmichael, Philadelphia, NFC	67	1,116	16.7	9
	Fred Willis, Houston, AFC	57	371	6.5	1
1972	Harold Jackson, Philadelphia, NFC	62	1,048	16.9	4
	Fred Biletnikoff, Oakland, AFC	58	802	13.8	7
1971	Fred Biletnikoff, Oakland, AFC	61	929	15.2	9
	Bob Tucker, N.Y. Giants, NFC	59	791	13.4	4
1970	Dick Gordon, Chicago, NFC	71	1,026	14.5	13
	Marlin Briscoe, Buffalo, AFC	57	1,036	18.2	8
1969	Dan Abramowicz, New Orleans, NFL	73	1,015	13.9	7
	Lance Alworth, San Diego, AFL	64	1,003	15.7	4
1968	Clifton McNeil, San Francisco, NFL	71	994	14.0	7
	Lance Alworth, San Diego, AFL	68	1,312	19.3	10
1967	George Sauer, N.Y. Jets, AFL	75	1,189	15.9	6
	Charley Taylor, Washington, NFL	70	990	14.1	9
1966	Lance Alworth, San Diego, AFL	73	1,383	18.9	13
	Charley Taylor, Washington, NFL	72	1,119	15.5	12
1965	Lionel Taylor, Denver, AFL	85	1,131	13.3	6
	Dave Parks, San Francisco, NFL	80	1,344	16.8	12
1964	Charley Hennigan, Houston, AFL	101	1,546	15.3	8
	Johnny Morris, Chicago, NFL	93	1,200	12.9	10
1963	Lionel Taylor, Denver, AFL	78	1,101	14.1	10
	Bobby Joe Conrad, St. Louis, NFL	73	967	13.2	10
1962	Lionel Taylor, Denver, AFL	77	908	11.8	4
	Bobby Mitchell, Washington, NFL	72	1,384	19.2	11
1961	Lionel Taylor, Denver, AFL	100	1,176	11.8	4
	Jim (Red) Phillips, Los Angeles, NFL	78	1,092	14.0	5
1960	Lionel Taylor, Denver, AFL	92	1,235	13.4	12
	Raymond Berry, Baltimore, NFL	74	1,298	17.5	10

Year	Player, Team	No.	Yards	Avg.	TD
1959	Raymond Berry, Baltimore	66	959	14.5	14
1958	Raymond Berry, Baltimore	56	794	14.2	9
	Pete Retzlaff, Philadelphia	56	766	13.7	2
1957	Billy Wilson, San Francisco	52	757	14.6	6
1956	Billy Wilson, San Francisco	60	889	14.8	5
1955	Pete Pihos, Philadelphia	62	864	13.9	7
1954	Pete Pihos, Philadelphia	60	872	14.5	10
	Billy Wilson, San Francisco	60	830	13.8	5
1953	Pete Pihos, Philadelphia	63	1,049	16.7	10
1952	Mac Speedie, Cleveland	62	911	14.7	5
1951	Elroy (Crazylegs) Hirsch, Los Angeles	66	1,495	22.7	17
1950	Tom Fears, Los Angeles	84	1,116	13.3	7
1949	Tom Fears, Los Angeles	77	1,013	13.2	9
1948	*Tom Fears, Los Angeles	51	698	13.7	4
1947	Jim Keane, Chi. Bears	64	910	14.2	10
1946	Jim Benton, Los Angeles	63	981	15.6	6
1945	Don Hutson, Green Bay	47	834	17.7	9
1944	Don Hutson, Green Bay	58	866	14.9	9
1943	Don Hutson, Green Bay	47	776	16.5	11
1942	Don Hutson, Green Bay	74	1,211	16.4	17
1941	Don Hutson, Green Bay	58	738	12.7	10
1940	*Don Looney, Philadelphia	58	707	12.2	4
1939	Don Hutson, Green Bay	34	846	24.9	6
1938	Gaynell Tinsley, Chi. Cardinals	41	516	12.6	1
1937	Don Hutson, Green Bay	41	552	13.5	7
1936	Don Hutson, Green Bay	34	536	15.8	8
1935	*Tod Goodwin, N.Y. Giants	26	432	16.6	4
1934	Joe Carter, Philadelphia	16	238	14.9	4
	Morris (Red) Badgro, N.Y. Giants	16	206	12.9	1
1933	John (Shipwreck) Kelly, Brooklyn	22	246	11.2	3
1932	Ray Flaherty, N.Y. Giants	21	350	16.7	3

**First season of professional football.*

ANNUAL PASS RECEIVING LEADERS (YARDS)

Year	Player, Team	No.	Yards	Avg.	TD
2009	Andre Johnson, Houston, AFC	101	1,569	15.5	9
	Miles Austin, Dallas, NFC	81	1,320	16.3	11
2008	Andre Johnson, Houston, AFC	115	1,575	13.7	8
	Larry Fitzgerald, Arizona, NFC	96	1,431	14.9	12
2007	Reggie Wayne, Indianapolis, AFC	104	1,510	14.5	10
	Larry Fitzgerald, Arizona, NFC	100	1,409	14.1	10
2006	Chad Ochocinco, Cincinnati, AFC	87	1,369	15.7	7
	Roy Williams, Detroit, NFC	82	1,310	16.0	7
2005	Steve Smith, Carolina, NFC	103	1,563	15.2	12
	Chad Ochocinco, Cincinnati, AFC	97	1,432	14.8	9
2004	Muhsin Muhammad, Carolina, NFC	93	1,405	15.1	16
	Chad Ochocinco, Cincinnati, AFC	95	1,274	13.4	9
2003	Torry Holt, St. Louis, NFC	117	1,696	14.5	12
	Chad Ochocinco, Cincinnati, AFC	90	1,355	15.1	10
2002	Marvin Harrison, Indianapolis, AFC	143	1,722	12.0	11
	Randy Moss, Minnesota, NFC	106	1,347	12.7	7
2001	David Boston, Arizona, NFC	98	1,598	16.3	8
	Marvin Harrison, Indianapolis, AFC	109	1,524	14.0	15
2000	Torry Holt, St. Louis, NFC	82	1,635	19.9	6
	Rod Smith, Denver, AFC	100	1,602	16.0	8
1999	Marvin Harrison, Indianapolis, AFC	115	1,663	14.5	12
	Randy Moss, Minnesota, NFC	80	1,413	17.7	11
1998	Antonio Freeman, Green Bay, NFC	84	1,424	17.0	14
	Eric Moulds, Buffalo, AFC	67	1,368	20.4	9
1997	Rob Moore, Arizona, NFC	97	1,584	16.3	8
	Tim Brown, Oakland, AFC	104	1,408	13.5	5
1996	Isaac Bruce, St. Louis, NFC	84	1,338	15.9	7
	Jimmy Smith, Jacksonville, AFC	83	1,244	15.0	7
1995	Jerry Rice, San Francisco, NFC	122	1,848	15.1	15
	Tim Brown, Oakland, AFC	89	1,342	15.1	10
1994	Jerry Rice, San Francisco, NFC	112	1,499	13.4	13
	Tim Brown, L.A. Raiders, AFC	89	1,309	14.7	9
1993	Jerry Rice, San Francisco, NFC	98	1,503	15.3	15
	Tim Brown, L.A. Raiders, AFC	80	1,180	14.8	7

YEARLY STATISTICAL LEADERS

Year	Player, Team	No.	Yards	Avg.	TD
1992	Sterling Sharpe, Green Bay, NFC	108	1,461	13.5	13
	Anthony Miller, San Diego, AFC	72	1,060	14.7	7
1991	Michael Irvin, Dallas, NFC	93	1,523	16.4	8
	Haywood Jeffires, Houston, AFC	100	1,181	11.8	7
1990	Jerry Rice, San Francisco, NFC	100	1,502	15.0	13
	Haywood Jeffires, Houston, AFC	74	1,048	14.2	8
1989	Jerry Rice, San Francisco, NFC	82	1,483	18.1	17
	Andre Reed, Buffalo, AFC	88	1,312	14.9	9
1988	Henry Ellard, L.A. Rams, NFC	86	1,414	16.4	10
	Eddie Brown, Cincinnati, AFC	53	1,273	24.0	9
1987	J.T. Smith, St. Louis, NFC	91	1,117	12.3	8
	Carlos Carson, Kansas City, AFC	55	1,044	19.0	7
1986	Jerry Rice, San Francisco, NFC	86	1,570	18.3	15
	Stanley Morgan, New England, AFC	84	1,491	17.8	10
1985	Steve Largent, Seattle, AFC	79	1,287	16.3	6
	Mike Quick, Philadelphia, NFC	73	1,247	17.1	11
1984	Roy Green, St. Louis, NFC	78	1,555	19.9	12
	John Stallworth, Pittsburgh, AFC	80	1,395	17.4	11
1983	Mike Quick, Philadelphia, NFC	69	1,409	20.4	13
	Carlos Carson, Kansas City, AFC	80	1,351	16.9	7
1982	Wes Chandler, San Diego, AFC	49	1,032	21.1	9
	Dwight Clark, San Francisco, NFC	60	913	15.2	5
1981	Alfred Jenkins, Atlanta, NFC	70	1,358	19.4	13
	Frank Lewis, Buffalo, AFC	70	1,244	17.8	4
	Steve Watson, Denver, AFC	60	1,244	20.7	13
1980	John Jefferson, San Diego, AFC	82	1,340	16.3	13
	James Lofton, Green Bay, NFC	71	1,226	17.3	4
1979	Steve Largent, Seattle, AFC	66	1,237	18.7	9
	Ahmad Rashad, Minnesota, NFC	80	1,156	14.5	9
1978	Wesley Walker, N.Y. Jets, AFC	48	1,169	24.4	8
	Harold Carmichael, Philadelphia, NFC	55	1,072	19.5	8
1977	Drew Pearson, Dallas, NFC	48	870	18.1	2
	Ken Burrough, Houston, AFC	43	816	19.0	8
1976	Roger Carr, Baltimore, AFC	43	1,112	25.9	11
	*Sammy White, Minnesota, NFC	51	906	17.8	10
1975	Ken Burrough, Houston, AFC	53	1,063	20.1	8
	Mel Gray, St. Louis, NFC	48	926	19.3	11
1974	Cliff Branch, Oakland, AFC	60	1,092	18.2	13
	Drew Pearson, Dallas, NFC	62	1,087	17.5	2
1973	Harold Carmichael, Philadelphia, NFC	67	1,116	16.7	9
	*Isaac Curtis, Cincinnati, AFC	45	843	18.7	9
1972	Harold Jackson, Philadelphia, NFC	62	1,048	16.9	4
	Rich Caster, N.Y. Jets, AFC	39	833	21.4	10
1971	Otis Taylor, Kansas City, AFC	57	1,110	19.5	7
	Gene Washington, San Francisco, NFC	46	884	19.2	4
1970	Gene Washington, San Francisco, NFC	53	1,100	20.8	12
	Marlin Briscoe, Buffalo, AFC	57	1,036	18.2	8
1969	Warren Wells, Oakland, AFL	47	1,260	26.8	14
	Harold Jackson, Philadelphia, NFL	65	1,116	17.2	9
1968	Lance Alworth, San Diego, AFL	68	1,312	19.3	10
	Roy Jefferson, Pittsburgh, NFL	58	1,074	18.5	11
1967	Don Maynard, N.Y. Jets, AFL	71	1,434	20.3	10
	Ben Hawkins, Philadelphia, NFL	59	1,265	21.4	10
1966	Lance Alworth, San Diego, AFL	73	1,383	18.9	13
	Pat Studstill, Detroit, NFL	67	1,266	18.9	5
1965	Lance Alworth, San Diego, AFL	69	1,602	23.2	14
	Dave Parks, San Francisco, NFL	80	1,344	16.8	12
1964	Charley Hennigan, Houston, AFL	101	1,546	15.3	8
	Johnny Morris, Chicago, NFL	93	1,200	12.9	10
1963	Bobby Mitchell, Washington, NFL	69	1,436	20.8	7
	Art Powell, Oakland, AFL	73	1,304	17.8	16
1962	Bobby Mitchell, Washington, NFL	72	1,384	19.2	11
	Art Powell, N.Y. Titans, AFL	64	1,130	17.6	8
1961	Charley Hennigan, Houston, AFL	82	1,746	21.3	12
	Tommy McDonald, Philadelphia, NFL	64	1,144	17.9	13
1960	*Bill Groman, Houston, AFL	72	1,473	20.5	12
	Raymond Berry, Baltimore, NFL	74	1,298	17.5	10
1959	Raymond Berry, Baltimore	66	959	14.5	14
1958	Del Shofner, Los Angeles	51	1,097	21.5	8

Year	Player, Team	No.	Yards	Avg.	TD
1957	Raymond Berry, Baltimore	47	800	17.0	6
1956	Billy Howton, Green Bay	55	1,188	21.6	12
1955	Pete Pihos, Philadelphia	62	864	13.9	7
1954	Bob Boyd, Los Angeles	53	1,212	22.9	6
1953	Pete Pihos, Philadelphia	63	1,049	16.7	10
1952	*Billy Howton, Green Bay	53	1,231	23.2	13
1951	Elroy (Crazylegs) Hirsch, Los Angeles	66	1,495	22.7	17
1950	Tom Fears, Los Angeles	84	1,116	13.3	7
1949	Bob Mann, Detroit	66	1,014	15.4	4
1948	Mal Kutner, Chi. Cardinals	41	943	23.0	14
1947	Mal Kutner, Chi. Cardinals	43	944	21.9	7
1946	Jim Benton, Los Angeles	63	981	15.5	6
1945	Jim Benton, Cleveland	45	1,067	23.7	8
1944	Don Hutson, Green Bay	58	866	14.6	9
1943	Don Hutson, Green Bay	47	776	16.5	11
1942	Don Hutson, Green Bay	74	1,211	16.4	17
1941	Don Hutson, Green Bay	58	738	12.7	10
1940	*Don Looney, Philadelphia	58	707	12.2	4
1939	Don Hutson, Green Bay	34	846	24.9	6
1938	Don Hutson, Green Bay	32	548	17.1	9
1937	*Gaynell Tinsley, Chi. Cardinals	36	675	18.8	5
1936	Don Hutson, Green Bay	34	526	15.5	8
1935	Charley Malone, Boston	22	433	19.7	2
1934	Harry Ebding, Detroit	9	257	28.6	2
1933	*Paul Moss, Pittsburgh	18	383	21.3	2
1932	Johnny (Blood) McNally, Green Bay	19	326	17.2	3

**First season of professional football.*

ANNUAL PUNT RETURN LEADERS

Year	Player, Team	No.	Yards	Avg.	Long	TD
2009	DeSean Jackson, Philadelphia, NFC	29	441	15.2	85	2
	Wes Welker, New England, AFC	27	338	12.5	69	0
2008	Roscoe Parrish, Buffalo, AFC	21	322	15.3	63	1
	*Clifton Smith, Tampa Bay, NFC	23	324	14.1	70	1
2007	Roscoe Parrish, Buffalo, AFC	27	440	16.3	74	1
	Devin Hester, Chicago, NFC	42	651	15.5	89	4
2006	Adam Jones, Tennessee, AFC	34	440	12.9	90	3
	*Devin Hester, Chicago, NFC	47	600	12.8	84	3
2005	Reno Mahe, Philadelphia, NFC	21	269	12.8	44	0
	B.J. Sams, Baltimore, AFC	33	401	12.2	51	0
2004	Eddie Drummond, Detroit, NFC	24	316	13.2	83	2
	Dennis Northcutt, Cleveland, AFC	36	432	12.0	44	0
2003	Dante Hall, Kansas City, AFC	29	472	16.3	93	2
	Brian Westbrook, Philadelphia, NFC	20	306	15.3	84	2
2002	Jimmy Williams, San Francisco, NFC	20	336	16.8	89	1
	Santana Moss, N.Y. Jets, AFC	25	413	16.5	63	2
2001	Troy Brown, New England, AFC	29	413	14.2	85	2
	Darrien Gordon, Atlanta, NFC	31	437	14.1	74	0
2000	Jermaine Lewis, Baltimore, AFC	36	578	16.1	89	2
	Az-Zahir Hakim, St. Louis, NFC	32	489	15.3	86	1
1999	*Charlie Rogers, Seattle, AFC	22	318	14.5	94	1
	*Mac Cody, Arizona, NFC	32	373	11.7	31	0
1998	Deion Sanders, Dallas, NFC	24	375	15.6	69	2
	Reggie Barlow, Jacksonville, AFC	43	555	12.9	85	1
1997	Jermaine Lewis, Baltimore, AFC	28	437	15.6	89	2
	David Palmer, Minnesota, NFC	34	444	13.1	57	0
1996	Desmond Howard, Green Bay, NFC	58	875	15.1	92	3
	Darrien Gordon, San Diego, AFC	36	537	14.9	81	1
1995	David Palmer, Minnesota, NFC	26	342	13.2	74	1
	Andre Coleman, San Diego, AFC	28	326	11.6	88	1
1994	Brian Mitchell, Washington, NFC	32	452	14.1	78	2
	Darrien Gordon, San Diego, AFC	36	475	13.2	90	2
1993	*Tyrone Hughes, New Orleans, NFC	37	503	13.6	83	2
	Eric Metcalf, Cleveland, AFC	36	464	12.9	91	2
1992	Johnny Bailey, Phoenix, NFC	20	263	13.2	65	0
	Rod Woodson, Pittsburgh, AFC	32	364	11.4	80	1
1991	Mel Gray, Detroit, NFC	25	385	15.4	78	1
	Rod Woodson, Pittsburgh, AFC	28	320	11.4	40	0

YEARLY STATISTICAL LEADERS

Year	Player, Team	No.	Yards	Avg.	Long	TD
1990	Clarence Verdin, Indianapolis, AFC	31	396	12.8	36	0
	*Johnny Bailey, Chicago, NFC	36	399	11.1	95	1
1989	Walter Stanley, Detroit, NFC	36	496	13.8	74	0
	Clarence Verdin, Indianapolis, AFC	23	296	12.9	49	1
1988	John Taylor, San Francisco, NFC	44	556	12.6	95	2
	JoJo Townsell, N.Y. Jets, AFC	35	409	11.7	59	1
1987	Mel Gray, New Orleans, NFC	24	352	14.7	80	0
	Bobby Joe Edmonds, Seattle, AFC	20	251	12.6	40	0
1986	*Bobby Joe Edmonds, Seattle, AFC	34	419	12.3	75	1
	*Vai Sikahema, St. Louis, NFC	43	522	12.1	71	2
1985	Irving Fryar, New England, AFC	37	520	14.1	85	2
	Henry Ellard, L.A. Rams, NFC	37	501	13.5	80	1
1984	Mike Martin, Cincinnati, AFC	24	376	15.7	55	0
	Henry Ellard, L.A. Rams, NFC	30	403	13.4	83	2
1983	*Henry Ellard, L.A. Rams, NFC	16	217	13.6	72	1
	Kirk Springs, N.Y. Jets, AFC	23	287	12.5	76	1
1982	Rick Upchurch, Denver, AFC	15	242	16.1	78	2
	Billy Johnson, Atlanta, NFC	24	273	11.4	71	0
1981	LeRoy Irvin, Los Angeles, NFC	46	615	13.4	84	3
	*James Brooks, San Diego, AFC	22	290	13.2	42	0
1980	J.T. Smith, Kansas City, AFC	40	581	14.5	75	2
	*Kenny Johnson, Atlanta, NFC	23	281	12.2	56	0
1979	John Sciarra, Philadelphia, NFC	16	182	11.4	38	0
	*Tony Nathan, Miami, AFC	28	306	10.9	86	1
1978	Rick Upchurch, Denver, AFC	36	493	13.7	75	1
	Jackie Wallace, Los Angeles, NFC	52	618	11.9	58	0
1977	Billy Johnson, Houston, AFC	35	539	15.4	87	2
	Larry Marshall, Philadelphia, NFC	46	489	10.6	48	0
1976	Rick Upchurch, Denver, AFC	39	536	13.7	92	4
	Eddie Brown, Washington, NFC	48	646	13.5	71	1
1975	Billy Johnson, Houston, AFC	40	612	15.3	83	3
	Terry Metcalf, St. Louis, NFC	23	285	12.4	69	1
1974	Lemar Parrish, Cincinnati, AFC	18	338	18.8	90	2
	Dick Jauron, Detroit, NFC	17	286	16.8	58	0
1973	Bruce Taylor, San Francisco, NFC	15	207	13.8	61	0
	Ron Smith, San Diego, AFC	27	352	13.0	84	2
1972	Ken Ellis, Green Bay, NFC	14	215	15.4	80	1
	Chris Farasopoulos, N.Y. Jets, AFC	17	179	10.5	65	1
1971	Les (Speedy) Duncan, Washington, NFC	22	233	10.6	33	0
	Leroy Kelly, Cleveland, AFC	30	292	9.7	74	0
1970	Ed Podolak, Kansas City, AFC	23	311	13.5	60	0
	*Bruce Taylor, San Francisco, NFC	43	516	12.0	76	0
1969	Alvin Haymond, Los Angeles, NFL	33	435	13.2	52	0
	*Bill Thompson, Denver, AFL	25	288	11.5	40	0
1968	Bob Hayes, Dallas, NFL	15	312	20.8	90	2
	Noland Smith, Kansas City, AFL	18	270	15.0	80	1
1967	Floyd Little, Denver, AFL	16	270	16.9	72	1
	Ben Davis, Cleveland, NFL	18	229	12.7	52	1
1966	Les (Speedy) Duncan, San Diego, AFL	18	238	13.2	81	1
	Johnny Roland, St. Louis, NFL	20	221	11.1	86	1
1965	Leroy Kelly, Cleveland, NFL	17	265	15.6	67	2
	Les (Speedy) Duncan, San Diego, AFL	30	464	15.5	66	2
1964	Bobby Jancik, Houston, AFL	12	220	18.3	82	1
	Tommy Watkins, Detroit, NFL	16	238	14.9	68	2
1963	Dick James, Washington, NFL	16	214	13.4	39	0
	Claude (Hoot) Gibson, Oakland, AFL	26	307	11.8	85	2
1962	Dick Christy, N.Y. Titans, AFL	15	250	16.7	73	2
	Pat Studstill, Detroit, NFL	29	457	15.8	44	0
1961	Dick Christy, N.Y. Titans, AFL	18	383	21.3	70	2
	Willie Wood, Green Bay, NFL	14	225	16.1	72	2
1960	*Abner Haynes, Dall. Texans, AFL	14	215	15.4	46	0
	Abe Woodson, San Francisco, NFL	13	174	13.4	48	0
1959	Johnny Morris, Chi. Bears	14	171	12.2	78	1
1958	Jon Arnett, Los Angeles	18	223	12.4	58	0
1957	Bert Zagers, Washington	14	217	15.5	76	2
1956	Ken Konz, Cleveland	13	187	14.4	65	1
1955	Ollie Matson, Chi. Cardinals	13	245	18.8	78	2
1954	*Veryl Switzer, Green Bay	24	306	12.8	93	1
1953	Charley Trippi, Chi. Cardinals	21	239	11.4	38	0

Year	Player, Team	No.	Yards	Avg.	Long	TD
1952	Jack Christiansen, Detroit	15	322	21.5	79	2
1951	Claude (Buddy) Young, N.Y. Yanks	12	231	19.3	79	1
1950	*Herb Rich, Baltimore	12	276	23.0	86	1
1949	Verda (Vitamin T) Smith, Los Angeles	27	427	15.8	85	1
1948	George McAfee, Chi. Bears	30	417	13.9	60	1
1947	*Walt Slater, Pittsburgh	28	435	15.5	33	0
1946	Bill Dudley, Pittsburgh	27	385	14.3	52	0
1945	*Dave Ryan, Detroit	15	220	14.7	56	0
1944	*Steve Van Buren, Philadelphia	15	230	15.3	55	1
1943	Andy Farkas, Washington	15	168	11.2	33	0
1942	Merlyn Condit, Brooklyn	21	210	10.0	23	0
1941	Byron (Whizzer) White, Detroit	19	262	13.8	64	0

**First season of professional football.*

ANNUAL KICKOFF RETURN LEADERS

Year	Player, Team	No.	Yards	Avg.	Long	TD
2009	Clifton Smith, Tampa Bay, NFC	31	902	29.1	83	0
	Josh Cribbs, Cleveland, AFC	56	1,542	27.5	103	3
2008	Danieal Manning, Chicago, NFC	36	1,070	29.7	83	1
	Ellis Hobbs, New England, AFC	45	1,281	28.5	95	1
2007	Josh Cribbs, Cleveland, AFC	59	1,809	30.7	100	2
	*Aundrae Allison, Minnesota, NFC	20	574	28.7	104	1
2006	Justin Miller, N.Y. Jets, AFC	46	1,304	28.3	103	2
	*Devin Hester, Chicago, NFC	20	528	26.4	96	2
2005	Terrence McGee, Buffalo, AFC	46	1,391	30.2	99	1
	Koren Robinson, Minnesota, NFC	47	1,221	26.0	86	1
2004	Willie Ponder, N.Y. Giants, NFC	36	967	26.9	91	1
	Terrence McGee, Buffalo, AFC	52	1,370	26.3	104	3
2003	Jerry Azumah, Chicago, NFC	41	1,191	29.0	89	2
	*Bethel Johnson, New England, AFC	30	847	28.2	92	1
2002	MarTay Jenkins, Arizona, NFC	20	559	28.0	95	1
	Kevin Faulk, New England, AFC	26	725	27.9	87	2
2001	Ronney Jenkins, San Diego, AFC	58	1,541	26.6	93	2
	*Steve Smith, Carolina, NFC	56	1,431	25.6	99	2
2000	*Darrick Vaughn, Atlanta, NFC	39	1,082	27.7	100	3
	Derrick Mason, Tennessee, AFC	42	1,132	27.0	66	0
1999	Tony Horne, St. Louis, NFC	30	892	29.7	101	2
	Tremain Mack, Cincinnati, AFC	51	1,382	27.1	99	1
1998	*Terry Fair, Detroit, NFC	51	1,428	28.0	105	2
	Corey Harris, Baltimore, AFC	35	965	27.6	95	1
1997	Michael Bates, Carolina, NFC	47	1,281	27.3	56	0
	Aaron Glenn, N.Y. Jets, AFC	28	741	26.5	96	1
1996	Michael Bates, Carolina, NFC	33	998	30.2	93	1
	Tamarick Vanover, Kansas City, AFC	33	854	25.9	97	1
1995	Ron Carpenter, N.Y. Jets, AFC	20	553	27.7	58	0
	Brian Mitchell, Washington, NFC	55	1,408	25.6	59	0
1994	Mel Gray, Detroit, NFC	45	1,276	28.4	102	3
	Randy Baldwin, Cleveland, AFC	28	753	26.9	85	1
1993	Robert Brooks, Green Bay, NFC	23	611	26.6	95	1
	*Raghib Ismail, L.A. Raiders, AFC	25	605	24.2	66	0
1992	Jon Vaughn, New England, AFC	20	564	28.2	100	1
	Deion Sanders, Atlanta, NFC	40	1,067	26.7	99	2
1991	Mel Gray, Detroit, NFC	36	929	25.8	71	0
	Nate Lewis, San Diego, AFC	23	578	25.1	95	1
1990	Kevin Clark, Denver, AFC	20	505	25.3	75	0
	David Meggett, N.Y. Giants, NFC	21	492	23.4	58	0
1989	Rod Woodson, Pittsburgh, AFC	36	982	27.3	84	1
	Mel Gray, Detroit, NFC	24	640	26.7	57	0
1988	*Tim Brown, L.A. Raiders, AFC	41	1,098	26.8	97	1
	Donnie Elder, Tampa Bay, NFC	34	772	22.7	51	0
1987	Sylvester Stamps, Atlanta, NFC	24	660	27.5	97	1
	Paul Palmer, Kansas City, AFC	38	923	24.3	95	2
1986	Dennis Gentry, Chicago, NFC	20	576	28.8	91	1
	Lupe Sanchez, Pittsburgh, AFC	25	591	23.6	64	0
1985	Ron Brown, L.A. Rams, NFC	28	918	32.8	98	3
	Glen Young, Cleveland, AFC	35	898	25.7	63	0
1984	*Bobby Humphery, N.Y. Jets, AFC	22	675	30.7	97	1
	Barry Redden, L.A. Rams, NFC	23	530	23.0	40	0

YEARLY STATISTICAL LEADERS

Year	Player, Team	No.	Yards	Avg.	Long	TD
1983	Fulton Walker, Miami, AFC	36	962	26.7	78	0
	Darrin Nelson, Minnesota, NFC	18	445	24.7	50	0
1982	*Mike Mosley, Buffalo, AFC	18	487	27.1	66	0
	Alvin Hall, Detroit, NFC	16	426	26.6	96	1
1981	Mike Nelms, Washington, NFC	37	1,099	29.7	84	0
	Carl Roaches, Houston, AFC	28	769	27.5	96	1
1980	Horace Ivory, New England, AFC	36	992	27.6	98	1
	Rich Mauti, New Orleans, NFC	31	798	25.7	52	0
1979	Larry Brunson, Oakland, AFC	17	441	25.9	89	0
	Jimmy Edwards, Minnesota, NFC	44	1,103	25.1	83	0
1978	Steve Odom, Green Bay, NFC	25	677	27.1	95	1
	*Keith Wright, Cleveland, AFC	30	789	26.3	86	0
1977	*Raymond Clayborn, New England, AFC	28	869	31.0	101	3
	*Wilbert Montgomery, Philadelphia, NFC	23	619	26.9	99	1
1976	*Duriel Harris, Miami, AFC	17	559	32.9	69	0
	Cullen Bryant, Los Angeles, NFC	16	459	28.7	90	1
1975	*Walter Payton, Chicago, NFC	14	444	31.7	70	0
	Harold Hart, Oakland, AFC	17	518	30.5	102	1
1974	Terry Metcalf, St. Louis, NFC	20	623	31.2	94	1
	Greg Pruitt, Cleveland, AFC	22	606	27.5	88	1
1973	Carl Garrett, Chicago, NFC	16	486	30.4	67	0
	*Wallace Francis, Buffalo, AFC	23	687	29.9	101	2
1972	Ron Smith, Chicago, NFC	30	924	30.8	94	1
	*Bruce Laird, Baltimore, AFC	29	843	29.1	73	0
1971	Travis Williams, Los Angeles, NFC	25	743	29.7	105	1
	Eugene (Mercury) Morris, Miami, AFC	15	423	28.2	94	1
1970	Jim Duncan, Baltimore, AFC	20	707	35.4	99	1
	Cecil Turner, Chicago, NFC	23	752	32.7	96	4
1969	Bobby Williams, Detroit, NFL	17	563	33.1	96	1
	*Bill Thompson, Denver, AFL	18	513	28.5	63	0
1968	Preston Pearson, Baltimore, NFL	15	527	35.1	102	2
	*George Atkinson, Oakland, AFL	32	802	25.1	60	0
1967	*Travis Williams, Green Bay, NFL	18	739	41.1	104	4
	*Zeke Moore, Houston, AFL	14	405	28.9	92	1
1966	Gale Sayers, Chicago, NFL	23	718	31.2	93	2
	*Goldie Sellers, Denver, AFL	19	541	28.5	100	2
1965	Tommy Watkins, Detroit, NFL	17	584	34.4	94	0
	Abner Haynes, Denver, AFL	34	901	26.5	60	0
1964	*Clarence Childs, N.Y. Giants, NFL	34	987	29.0	100	1
	Bo Roberson, Oakland, AFL	36	975	27.1	59	0
1963	Abe Woodson, San Francisco, NFL	29	935	32.2	103	3
	Bobby Jancik, Houston, AFL	45	1,317	29.3	53	0
1962	Abe Woodson, San Francisco, NFL	37	1,157	31.3	79	0
	*Bobby Jancik, Houston, AFL	24	826	30.3	61	0
1961	Dick Bass, Los Angeles, NFL	23	698	30.3	64	0
	*Dave Grayson, Dall. Texans, AFL	16	453	28.3	73	0
1960	*Tom Moore, Green Bay, NFL	12	397	33.1	84	0
	Ken Hall, Houston, AFL	19	594	31.3	104	1
1959	Abe Woodson, San Francisco	13	382	29.4	105	1
1958	Ollie Matson, Chi. Cardinals	14	497	35.5	101	2
1957	*Jon Arnett, Los Angeles	18	504	28.0	98	1
1956	*Tom Wilson, Los Angeles	15	477	31.8	103	1
1955	Al Carmichael, Green Bay	14	418	29.9	100	1
1954	Billy Reynolds, Cleveland	14	413	29.5	51	0
1953	Joe Arenas, San Francisco	16	551	34.4	82	0
1952	Lynn Chandnois, Pittsburgh	17	599	35.2	93	2
1951	Lynn Chandnois, Pittsburgh	12	390	32.5	55	0
1950	Verda (Vitamin T) Smith, Los Angeles	22	742	33.7	97	3
1949	*Don Doll, Detroit	21	536	25.5	56	0
1948	*Joe Scott, N.Y. Giants	20	569	28.5	99	1
1947	Eddie Saenz, Washington	29	797	27.5	94	2
1946	Abe Karnofsky, Boston	21	599	28.5	97	1
1945	Steve Van Buren, Philadelphia	13	373	28.7	98	1
1944	Bob Thurbon, Card.-Pitt.	12	291	24.3	55	0
1943	Ken Heineman, Brooklyn	16	444	27.8	69	0
1942	Marshall Goldberg, Chi. Cardinals	15	393	26.2	95	1
1941	Marshall Goldberg, Chi. Cardinals	12	290	24.2	41	0

**First season of professional football.*

ANNUAL INTERCEPTION LEADERS

Year	Player, Team	No.	Yards	TD
2009	*Jairus Byrd, Buffalo, AFC	9	118	0
	Asante Samuel, Philadelphia, NFC	9	117	0
	Darren Sharper, New Orleans, NFC	9	376	3
	Charles Woodson, Green Bay, NFC	9	179	3
2008	Ed Reed, Baltimore, AFC	9	264	2
	Nick Collins, Green Bay, NFC	7	295	3
	Charles Woodson, Green Bay, NFC	7	169	2
2007	Antonio Cromartie, San Diego, AFC	10	144	1
	O.J. Atogwe, St. Louis, NFC	8	125	1
2006	Champ Bailey, Denver, AFC	10	162	1
	Asante Samuel, New England, AFC	10	120	0
	Walt Harris, San Francisco, NFC	8	84	1
	Charles Woodson, Green Bay, NFC	8	61	1
2005	Ty Law, N.Y. Jets, AFC	10	195	1
	Deltha O'Neal, Cincinnati, AFC	10	103	0
	Darren Sharper, Minnesota, NFC	9	276	2
2004	Ed Reed, Baltimore, AFC	9	358	1
	Ken Lucas, Seattle, NFC	6	46	1
	*Chris Gamble, Carolina, NFC	6	15	0
2003	Tony Parrish, San Francisco, NFC	9	202	0
	Brian Russell, Minnesota, NFC	9	185	0
	Ed Reed, Baltimore, AFC	7	132	1
	Marcus Coleman, Houston, AFC	7	95	0
	Patrick Surtain, Miami, AFC	7	59	0
2002	Rod Woodson, Oakland, AFC	8	225	2
	Brian Kelly, Tampa Bay, NFC	8	68	0
2001	*Anthony Henry, Cleveland, AFC	10	177	1
	Ronde Barber, Tampa Bay, NFC	10	86	1
2000	Darren Sharper, Green Bay, NFC	9	109	0
	Samari Rolle, Tennessee, AFC	7	140	1
	Brian Walker, Miami, AFC	7	80	0
1999	Rod Woodson, Baltimore, AFC	7	195	2
	Sam Madison, Miami, AFC	7	164	1
	James Hasty, Kansas City, AFC	7	98	2
	Donnie Abraham, Tampa Bay, NFC	7	115	2
	Troy Vincent, Philadelphia, NFC	7	91	0
1998	Ty Law, New England, AFC	9	133	1
	Kwamie Lassiter, Arizona, NFC	8	80	0
1997	Ryan McNeil, St. Louis, NFC	9	127	1
	Mark McMillian, Kansas City, AFC	8	274	3
	Darryl Williams, Seattle, AFC	8	172	1
1996	Tyrone Braxton, Denver, AFC	9	128	1
	Keith Lyle, St. Louis, NFC	9	152	0
1995	*Orlando Thomas, Minnesota, NFC	9	108	1
	Willie Williams, Pittsburgh, AFC	7	122	1
1994	Eric Turner, Cleveland, AFC	9	199	1
	Aeneas Williams, Arizona, NFC	9	89	0
1993	Eugene Robinson, Seattle, AFC	9	80	0
	Nate Odomes, Buffalo, AFC	9	65	0
	Deion Sanders, Atlanta, NFC	7	91	0
1992	Henry Jones, Buffalo, AFC	8	263	2
	Audray McMillian, Minnesota, NFC	8	157	2
1991	Ronnie Lott, L.A. Raiders, AFC	8	52	0
	Ray Crockett, Detroit, NFC	6	141	1
	Deion Sanders, Atlanta, NFC	6	119	1
	*Aeneas Williams, Phoenix, NFC	6	60	0
	Tim McKyer, Atlanta, NFC	6	24	0
1990	*Mark Carrier, Chicago, NFC	10	39	0
	Richard Johnson, Houston, AFC	8	100	1
1989	Felix Wright, Cleveland, AFC	9	91	1
	Eric Allen, Philadelphia, NFC	8	38	0
1988	Scott Case, Atlanta, NFC	10	47	0
	Erik McMillan, N.Y. Jets, AFC	8	168	2
1987	Barry Wilburn, Washington, NFC	9	135	1
	Mike Prior, Indianapolis, AFC	6	57	0
	Mark Kelso, Buffalo, AFC	6	25	0
	Keith Bostic, Houston, AFC	6	-14	0
1986	Ronnie Lott, San Francisco, NFC	10	134	1
	Deron Cherry, Kansas City, AFC	9	150	0
1985	Everson Walls, Dallas, NFC	9	31	0
	Albert Lewis, Kansas City, AFC	8	59	0
	Eugene Daniel, Indianapolis, AFC	8	53	0
1984	Ken Easley, Seattle, AFC	10	126	2
	*Tom Flynn, Green Bay, NFC	9	106	0
1983	Mark Murphy, Washington, NFC	9	127	0
	Ken Riley, Cincinnati, AFC	8	89	2
	Vann McElroy, L.A. Raiders, AFC	8	68	0
1982	Everson Walls, Dallas, NFC	7	61	0
	Ken Riley, Cincinnati, AFC	5	88	1
	Bobby Jackson, N.Y. Jets, AFC	5	84	1
	Dwayne Woodruff, Pittsburgh, AFC	5	53	0
	Donnie Shell, Pittsburgh, AFC	5	27	0
1981	*Everson Walls, Dallas, NFC	11	133	0
	John Harris, Seattle, AFC	10	155	2
1980	Lester Hayes, Oakland, AFC	13	273	1
	Nolan Cromwell, Los Angeles, NFC	8	140	1
1979	Mike Reinfeldt, Houston, AFC	12	205	0
	Lemar Parrish, Washington, NFC	9	65	0
1978	Thom Darden, Cleveland, AFC	10	200	0
	Ken Stone, St. Louis, NFC	9	139	0
	Willie Buchanon, Green Bay, NFC	9	93	1
1977	Lyle Blackwood, Baltimore, AFC	10	163	0
	Rolland Lawrence, Atlanta, NFC	7	138	0
1976	Monte Jackson, Los Angeles, NFC	10	173	3
	Ken Riley, Cincinnati, AFC	9	141	1
1975	Mel Blount, Pittsburgh, AFC	11	121	0
	Paul Krause, Minnesota, NFC	10	201	0
1974	Emmitt Thomas, Kansas City, AFC	12	214	2
	Ray Brown, Atlanta, NFC	8	164	1
1973	Dick Anderson, Miami, AFC	8	163	2
	Mike Wagner, Pittsburgh, AFC	8	134	0
	Bobby Bryant, Minnesota, NFC	7	105	1
1972	Bill Bradley, Philadelphia, NFC	9	73	0
	Mike Sensibaugh, Kansas City, AFC	8	65	0
1971	Bill Bradley, Philadelphia, NFC	11	248	0
	Ken Houston, Houston, AFC	9	220	4
1970	Johnny Robinson, Kansas City, AFC	10	155	0
	Dick LeBeau, Detroit, NFC	9	96	0
1969	Mel Renfro, Dallas, NFL	10	118	0
	Emmitt Thomas, Kansas City, AFL	9	146	1
1968	Dave Grayson, Oakland, AFL	10	195	1
	Willie Williams, N.Y. Giants, NFL	10	103	0
1967	Miller Farr, Houston, AFL	10	264	3
	*Lem Barney, Detroit, NFL	10	232	3
	Tom Janik, Buffalo, AFL	10	222	2
	Dave Whitsell, New Orleans, NFL	10	178	2
	Dick Westmoreland, Miami, AFL	10	127	1
1966	Larry Wilson, St. Louis, NFL	10	180	2
	Johnny Robinson, Kansas City, AFL	10	136	1
	Bobby Hunt, Kansas City, AFL	10	113	0
1965	W.K. Hicks, Houston, AFL	9	156	0
	Bobby Boyd, Baltimore, NFL	9	78	1
1964	Dainard Paulson, N.Y. Jets, AFL	12	157	1
	*Paul Krause, Washington, NFL	12	140	1
1963	Fred Glick, Houston, AFL	12	180	1
	Dick Lynch, N.Y. Giants, NFL	9	251	3
	Roosevelt Taylor, Chicago, NFL	9	172	1
1962	Lee Riley, N.Y. Titans, AFL	11	122	0
	Willie Wood, Green Bay, NFL	9	132	0
1961	Billy Atkins, Buffalo, AFL	10	158	0
	Dick Lynch, N.Y. Giants, NFL	9	60	0
1960	*Austin (Goose) Gonsoulin, Denver, AFL	11	98	0
	Dave Baker, San Francisco, NFL	10	96	0
	Jerry Norton, St. Louis, NFL	10	96	0

Year	Player, Team	No.	Yards	TD
1959	Dean Derby, Pittsburgh	7	127	0
	Milt Davis, Baltimore	7	119	1
	Don Shinnick, Baltimore	7	70	0
1958	Jim Patton, N.Y. Giants	11	183	0
1957	Milt Davis, Baltimore	10	219	2
	Jack Christiansen, Detroit	10	137	1
	Jack Butler, Pittsburgh	10	85	0
1956	Linden Crow, Chi. Cardinals	11	170	0
1955	Will Sherman, Los Angeles	11	101	0
1954	Dick (Night Train) Lane, Chi. Cardinals	10	181	0
1953	Jack Christiansen, Detroit	12	238	1
1952	*Dick (Night Train) Lane, Los Angeles	14	298	2
1951	Otto Schnellbacher, N.Y. Giants	11	194	2
1950	Orban (Spec) Sanders, N.Y. Yanks	13	199	0
1949	Bob Nussbaumer, Chi. Cardinals	12	157	0
1948	*Dan Sandifer, Washington	13	258	2
1947	Frank Reagan, N.Y. Giants	10	203	0
	Frank Seno, Boston	10	100	0
1946	Bill Dudley, Pittsburgh	10	242	1
1945	Roy Zimmerman, Philadelphia	7	90	0
1944	*Howard Livingston, N.Y. Giants	9	172	1
1943	Sammy Baugh, Washington	11	112	0
1942	Clyde (Bulldog) Turner, Chi. Bears	8	96	1
1941	Marshall Goldberg, Chi. Cardinals	7	54	0
	*Art Jones, Pittsburgh	7	35	0
1940	Clarence (Ace) Parker, Brooklyn	6	146	1
	Kent Ryan, Detroit	6	65	0
	Don Hutson, Green Bay	6	24	0

**First season of professional football.*

ANNUAL PUNTING LEADERS

Year	Player, Team	No.	Avg.	Long
2009	Shane Lechler, Oakland, AFC	96	51.1	70
	Andy Lee, San Francisco, NFC	99	47.6	64
2008	Donnie Jones, St. Louis, NFC	82	50.0	68
	Shane Lechler, Oakland, AFC	90	48.8	70
2007	Shane Lechler, Oakland, AFC	73	49.1	70
	Andy Lee, San Francisco, NFC	105	47.3	74
2006	Mat McBriar, Dallas, NFC	56	48.2	75
	Shane Lechler, Oakland, AFC	77	47.5	67
2005	Brian Moorman, Buffalo, AFC	71	45.7	68
	Josh Bidwell, Tampa Bay, NFC	90	45.6	61
2004	Shane Lechler, Oakland, AFC	73	46.7	67
	Tom Tupa, Washington, NFC	103	44.1	61
2003	Shane Lechler, Oakland, AFC	96	46.9	73
	Todd Sauerbrun, Carolina, NFC	77	44.6	64
2002	Todd Sauerbrun, Carolina, NFC	104	45.5	67
	Chris Hanson, Jacksonville, AFC	81	44.2	64
2001	Todd Sauerbrun, Carolina, NFC	93	47.5	73
	Shane Lechler, Oakland, AFC	73	46.2	65
2000	Darren Bennett, San Diego, AFC	92	46.2	66
	Mitch Berger, Minnesota, NFC	62	44.7	60
1999	Tom Rouen, Denver, AFC	84	46.5	65
	Mitch Berger, Minnesota, NFC	61	45.4	75
1998	Craig Hentrich, Tennessee, AFC	69	47.2	71
	Mark Royals, New Orleans, NFC	88	45.6	64
1997	Mark Royals, New Orleans, NFC	88	45.9	66
	Tom Tupa, New England, AFC	78	45.8	73
1996	John Kidd, Miami, AFC	78	46.3	63
	Matt Turk, Washington, NFC	75	45.1	63
1995	Rick Tuten, Seattle, AFC	83	45.0	73
	Sean Landeta, St. Louis, NFC	83	44.3	63
1994	Sean Landeta, L.A. Rams, NFC	78	44.8	62
	Jeff Gossett, L.A. Raiders, AFC	77	43.9	65
1993	Greg Montgomery, Houston, AFC	54	45.6	77
	Jim Arnold, Detroit, NFC	72	44.5	68
1992	Greg Montgomery, Houston, AFC	53	46.9	66
	Harry Newsome, Minnesota, NFC	72	45.0	84
1991	Reggie Roby, Miami, AFC	54	45.7	64
	Harry Newsome, Minnesota, AFC	68	45.5	65
1990	Mike Horan, Denver, AFC	58	44.4	67
	Sean Landeta, N.Y. Giants, NFC	75	44.1	67
1989	Rich Camarillo, Phoenix, NFC	76	43.4	58
	Greg Montgomery, Houston, AFC	56	43.3	63
1988	Harry Newsome, Pittsburgh, AFC	65	45.4	62
	Jim Arnold, Detroit, NFC	97	42.4	69
1987	Rick Donnelly, Atlanta, NFC	61	44.0	62
	Ralf Mojsiejenko, San Diego, AFC	67	42.9	57
1986	Rohn Stark, Indianapolis, AFC	76	45.2	63
	Sean Landeta, N.Y. Giants, NFC	79	44.8	61
1985	Rohn Stark, Indianapolis, AFC	78	45.9	68
	*Rick Donnelly, Atlanta, NFC	59	43.6	68
1984	Jim Arnold, Kansas City, AFC	98	44.9	63
	*Brian Hansen, New Orleans, NFC	69	43.8	66
1983	Rohn Stark, Baltimore, AFC	91	45.3	68
	Frank Garcia, Tampa Bay, NFC	95	42.2	64
1982	Luke Prestridge, Denver, AFC	45	45.0	65
	Carl Birdsong, St. Louis, NFC	54	43.8	65
1981	Pat McInally, Cincinnati, AFC	72	45.4	62
	Tom Skladany, Detroit, NFC	64	43.5	74
1980	Dave Jennings, N.Y. Giants, NFC	94	44.8	63
	Luke Prestridge, Denver, AFC	70	43.9	57
1979	*Bob Grupp, Kansas City, AFC	89	43.6	74
	Dave Jennings, N.Y. Giants, NFC	104	42.7	72
1978	Pat McInally, Cincinnati, AFC	91	43.1	65
	*Tom Skladany, Detroit, NFC	86	42.5	63
1977	Ray Guy, Oakland, AFC	59	43.3	74
	Tom Blanchard, New Orleans, NFC	82	42.4	66
1976	Marv Bateman, Buffalo, AFC	86	42.8	78
	John James, Atlanta, NFC	101	42.1	67
1975	Ray Guy, Oakland, AFC	68	43.8	64
	Herman Weaver, Detroit, NFC	80	42.0	61
1974	Ray Guy, Oakland, AFC	74	42.2	66
	Tom Blanchard, New Orleans, NFC	88	42.1	71
1973	Jerrel Wilson, Kansas City, AFC	80	45.5	68
	*Tom Wittum, San Francisco, NFC	79	43.7	62
1972	Jerrel Wilson, Kansas City, AFC	66	44.8	69
	Dave Chapple, Los Angeles, NFC	53	44.2	70
1971	Dave Lewis, Cincinnati, AFC	72	44.8	56
	Tom McNeill, Philadelphia, NFC	73	42.0	64
1970	Dave Lewis, Cincinnati, AFC	79	46.2	63
	*Julian Fagan, New Orleans, NFC	77	42.5	64
1969	David Lee, Baltimore, NFL	57	45.3	66
	Dennis Partee, San Diego, AFL	71	44.6	62
1968	Jerrel Wilson, Kansas City, AFL	63	45.1	70
	Billy Lothridge, Atlanta, NFL	75	44.3	70
1967	Bob Scarpitto, Denver, AFL	105	44.9	73
	Billy Lothridge, Atlanta, NFL	87	43.7	62
1966	Bob Scarpitto, Denver, AFL	76	45.8	70
	*David Lee, Baltimore, NFL	49	45.6	64
1965	Gary Collins, Cleveland, NFL	65	46.7	71
	Jerrel Wilson, Kansas City, AFL	69	45.4	64
1964	Bobby Walden, Minnesota, NFL	72	46.4	73
	Jim Fraser, Denver, AFL	73	44.2	67
1963	Yale Lary, Detroit, NFL	35	48.9	73
	Jim Fraser, Denver, AFL	81	44.4	66
1962	Tommy Davis, San Francisco, NFL	48	45.6	82
	Jim Fraser, Denver, AFL	55	43.6	75
1961	Yale Lary, Detroit, NFL	52	48.4	71
	Billy Atkins, Buffalo, AFL	85	44.5	70
1960	Jerry Norton, St. Louis, NFL	39	45.6	62
	*Paul Maguire, L.A. Chargers, AFL	43	40.5	61
1959	Yale Lary, Detroit	45	47.1	67
1958	Sam Baker, Washington	48	45.4	64
1957	Don Chandler, N.Y. Giants	60	44.6	61
1956	Norm Van Brocklin, Los Angeles	48	43.1	72
1955	Norm Van Brocklin, Los Angeles	60	44.6	61

Year	Player, Team	No.	Avg.	Long
1954	Pat Brady, Pittsburgh	66	43.2	72
1953	Pat Brady, Pittsburgh	80	46.9	64
1952	Horace Gillom, Cleveland	61	45.7	73
1951	Horace Gillom, Cleveland	73	45.5	66
1950	*Fred (Curly) Morrison, Chi. Bears	57	43.3	65
1949	*Mike Boyda, N.Y. Bulldogs	56	44.2	61
1948	Joe Muha, Philadelphia	57	47.3	82
1947	Jack Jacobs, Green Bay	57	43.5	74
1946	Roy McKay, Green Bay	64	42.7	64
1945	Roy McKay, Green Bay	44	41.2	73
1944	Frank Sinkwich, Detroit	45	41.0	73
1943	Sammy Baugh, Washington	50	45.9	81
1942	Sammy Baugh, Washington	37	48.2	74
1941	Sammy Baugh, Washington	30	48.7	75
1940	Sammy Baugh, Washington	35	51.4	85
1939	*Parker Hall, Cleveland	58	40.8	80

First season of professional football.

ANNUAL LEADERS IN SACKS (SINCE 1982)

Year	Player, Team	Sacks
2009	Elvis Dumervil, Denver, AFC	17.0
	Jared Allen, Minnesota, NFC	14.5
2008	DeMarcus Ware, Dallas, NFC	20.0
	Joey Porter, Miami, AFC	17.5
2007	Jared Allen, Kansas City, AFC	15.5
	Patrick Kerney, Seattle, NFC	14.5
2006	Shawne Merriman, San Diego, AFC	17.0
	Aaron Kampman, Green Bay, NFC	15.5
2005	Derrick Burgess, Oakland, AFC	16.0
	Osi Umenyiora, N.Y. Giants, NFC	14.5
2004	Dwight Freeney, Indianapolis, AFC	16.0
	Bertrand Berry, Arizona, NFC	14.5
2003	Michael Strahan, N.Y. Giants, NFC	18.5
	Adewale Ogunleye, Miami, AFC	15.0
2002	Jason Taylor, Miami, AFC	18.5
	Simeon Rice, Tampa Bay, NFC	15.5
2001	Michael Strahan, N.Y. Giants, NFC	22.5
	Peter Boulware, Baltimore, AFC	15.0
2000	La'Roi Glover, New Orleans, NFC	17.0
	Trace Armstrong, Miami, AFC	16.5
1999	Kevin Carter, St. Louis, NFC	17.0
	*Jevon Kearse, Tennessee, AFC	14.5
1998	Michael Sinclair, Seattle, AFC	16.5
	Reggie White, Green Bay, NFC	16.0
1997	John Randle, Minnesota, NFC	15.5
	Bruce Smith, Buffalo, AFC	14.0
1996	Kevin Greene, Carolina, NFC	14.5
	Michael McCrary, Seattle, AFC	13.5
	Bruce Smith, Buffalo, AFC	13.5
1995	Bryce Paup, Buffalo, AFC	17.5
	William Fuller, Philadelphia, NFC	13.0
	Wayne Martin, New Orleans, NFC	13.0
1994	Kevin Greene, Pittsburgh, AFC	14.0
	Ken Harvey, Washington, NFC	13.5
	John Randle, Minnesota, NFC	13.5
1993	Neil Smith, Kansas City, AFC	15.0
	Renaldo Turnbull, New Orleans, NFC	13.0
	Reggie White, Green Bay, NFC	13.0
1992	Clyde Simmons, Philadelphia, NFC	19.0
	Leslie O'Neal, San Diego, AFC	17.0
1991	Pat Swilling, New Orleans, NFC	17.0
	William Fuller, Houston, AFC	15.0
1990	Derrick Thomas, Kansas City, AFC	20.0
	Charles Haley, San Francisco, NFC	16.0
1989	Chris Doleman, Minnesota, NFC	21.0
	Lee Williams, San Diego, AFC	14.0
1988	Reggie White, Philadelphia, NFC	18.0
	Greg Townsend, L.A. Raiders, AFC	11.5
1987	Reggie White, Philadelphia, NFC	21.0
	Andre Tippett, New England, AFC	12.5
1986	Lawrence Taylor, N.Y. Giants, NFC	20.5
	Sean Jones, L.A. Raiders, AFC	15.5
1985	Richard Dent, Chicago, NFC	17.0
	Andre Tippett, New England, AFC	16.5
1984	Mark Gastineau, N.Y. Jets, AFC	22.0
	Richard Dent, Chicago, NFC	17.5
1983	Mark Gastineau, N.Y. Jets, AFC	19.0
	Fred Dean, San Francisco, NFC	17.5
1982	Doug Martin, Minnesota, NFC	11.5
	Jesse Baker, Houston, AFC	7.5

First season of professional football.

POINTS SCORED

Year	Team	Points
2009	New Orleans, NFC	510
	San Diego, AFC	454
2008	New Orleans, NFC	463
	San Diego, AFC	439
2007	New England, AFC	589
	Dallas, NFC	455
2006	San Diego, AFC	492
	Chicago, NFC	427
2005	Seattle, NFC	452
	Indianapolis, AFC	439
2004	Indianapolis, AFC	522
	Green Bay, NFC	424
2003	Kansas City, AFC	484
	St. Louis, NFC	447
2002	Kansas City, AFC	467
	New Orleans, NFC	432
2001	St. Louis, NFC	503
	Indianapolis, AFC	413
2000	St. Louis, NFC	540
	Denver, AFC	485
1999	St. Louis, NFC	526
	Indianapolis, AFC	423
1998	Minnesota, NFC	556
	Denver, AFC	501
1997	Denver, AFC	472
	Green Bay, NFC	422
1996	Green Bay, NFC	456
	New England, AFC	418
1995	San Francisco, NFC	457
	Pittsburgh, AFC	407
1994	San Francisco, NFC	505
	Miami, AFC	389
1993	San Francisco, NFC	473
	Denver, AFC	373
1992	San Francisco, NFC	431
	Buffalo, AFC	381
1991	Washington, NFC	485
	Buffalo, AFC	458
1990	Buffalo, AFC	428
	Philadelphia, NFC	396
1989	San Francisco, NFC	442
	Buffalo, AFC	409
1988	Cincinnati, AFC	448
	L.A. Rams, NFC	407
1987	San Francisco, NFC	459
	Cleveland, AFC	390
1986	Miami, AFC	430
	Minnesota, NFC	398
1985	San Diego, AFC	467
	Chicago, NFC	456
1984	Miami, AFC	513
	San Francisco, NFC	475
1983	Washington, NFC	541
	L.A. Raiders, AFC	442
1982	San Diego, AFC	288
	Dallas, NFC	226

Year	Team	Points
	Green Bay, NFC	226
1981	San Diego, AFC	478
	Atlanta, NFC	426
1980	Dallas, NFC	454
	New England, AFC	441
1979	Pittsburgh, AFC	416
	Dallas, NFC	371
1978	Dallas, NFC	384
	Miami, AFC	372
1977	Oakland, AFC	351
	Dallas, NFC	345
1976	Baltimore, AFC	417
	Los Angeles, NFC	351
1975	Buffalo, AFC	420
	Minnesota, NFC	377
1974	Oakland, AFC	355
	Washington, NFC	320
1973	Los Angeles, NFC	388
	Denver, AFC	354
1972	Miami, AFC	385
	San Francisco, NFC	353
1971	Dallas, NFC	406
	Oakland, AFC	344
1970	San Francisco, NFC	352
	Baltimore, AFC	321
1969	Minnesota, NFL	379
	Oakland, AFL	377
1968	Oakland, AFL	453
	Dallas, NFL	431
1967	Oakland, AFL	468
	Los Angeles, NFL	398
1966	Kansas City, AFL	448
	Dallas, NFL	445
1965	San Francisco, NFL	421
	San Diego, AFL	340
1964	Baltimore, NFL	428
	Buffalo, AFL	400
1963	N.Y. Giants, NFL	448
	San Diego, AFL	399
1962	Green Bay, NFL	415
	Dall. Texans, AFL	389
1961	Houston, AFL	513
	Green Bay, NFL	391
1960	N.Y. Titans, AFL	382
	Cleveland, NFL	362
1959	Baltimore	374
1958	Baltimore	381
1957	Los Angeles	307
1956	Chi. Bears	363
1955	Cleveland	349
1954	Detroit	337
1953	San Francisco	372
1952	Los Angeles	349
1951	Los Angeles	392
1950	Los Angeles	466
1949	Philadelphia	364
1948	Chi. Cardinals	395
1947	Chi. Bears	363
1946	Chi. Bears	289
1945	Philadelphia	272
1944	Philadelphia	267
1943	Chi. Bears	303
1942	Chi. Bears	376
1941	Chi. Bears	396
1940	Washington	245
1939	Chi. Bears	298
1938	Green Bay	223
1937	Green Bay	220
1936	Green Bay	248
1935	Chi. Bears	192
1934	Chi. Bears	286
1933	N.Y. Giants	244
1932	Chi. Bears	160

TOTAL YARDS GAINED

Year	Team	Yards
2009	New Orleans, NFC	6,461
	New England, AFC	6,357
2008	New Orleans, NFC	6,571
	Denver, AFC	6,333
2007	New England, AFC	6,580
	Green Bay, NFC	5,931
2006	New Orleans, NFC	6,264
	Indianapolis, AFC	6,070
2005	Kansas City, AFC	6,192
	Seattle, NFC	5,915
2004	Kansas City, AFC	6,695
	Green Bay, NFC	6,357
2003	Minnesota, NFC	6,294
	Kansas City, AFC	5,910
2002	Oakland, AFC	6,237
	Minnesota, NFC	6,192
2001	St. Louis, NFC	6,690
	Indianapolis, AFC	5,955
2000	St. Louis, NFC	7,075
	Denver, AFC	6,554
1999	St. Louis, NFC	6,412
	Indianapolis, AFC	5,726
1998	San Francisco, NFC	6,800
	Denver, AFC	6,092
1997	Denver, AFC	5,872
	Detroit, NFC	5,798
1996	Denver, AFC	5,791
	Philadelphia, NFC	5,627
1995	Detroit, NFC	6,113
	Denver, AFC	6,040
1994	Miami, AFC	6,078
	San Francisco, NFC	6,060
1993	San Francisco, NFC	6,435
	Miami, AFC	5,812
1992	San Francisco, NFC	6,195
	Buffalo, AFC	5,893
1991	Buffalo, AFC	6,252
	San Francisco, NFC	5,858
1990	Houston, AFC	6,222
	San Francisco, NFC	5,895
1989	San Francisco, NFC	6,268
	Cincinnati, AFC	6,101
1988	Cincinnati, AFC	6,057
	San Francisco, NFC	5,900
1987	San Francisco, NFC	5,987
	Denver, AFC	5,624
1986	Cincinnati, AFC	6,490
	San Francisco, NFC	6,082
1985	San Diego, AFC	6,535
	San Francisco, NFC	5,920
1984	Miami, AFC	6,936
	San Francisco, NFC	6,366
1983	San Diego, AFC	6,197
	Green Bay, NFC	6,172
1982	San Diego, AFC	4,048
	San Francisco, NFC	3,242
1981	San Diego, AFC	6,744
	Detroit, NFC	5,933
1980	San Diego, AFC	6,410
	Los Angeles, NFC	6,006
1979	Pittsburgh, AFC	6,258
	Dallas, NFC	5,968
1978	New England, AFC	5,965
	Dallas, NFC	5,959
1977	Dallas, NFC	4,812
	Oakland, AFC	4,736

Year	Team	Yards
1976	Baltimore, AFC	5,236
	St. Louis, NFC	5,136
1975	Buffalo, AFC	5,467
	Dallas, NFC	5,025
1974	Dallas, NFC	4,983
	Oakland, AFC	4,718
1973	Los Angeles, NFC	4,906
	Oakland, AFC	4,773
1972	Miami, AFC	5,036
	N.Y. Giants, NFC	4,483
1971	Dallas, NFC	5,035
	San Diego, AFC	4,738
1970	Oakland, AFC	4,829
	San Francisco, NFC	4,503
1969	Dallas, NFL	5,122
	Oakland, AFL	5,036
1968	Oakland, AFL	5,696
	Dallas, NFL	5,117
1967	N.Y. Jets, AFL	5,152
	Baltimore, NFL	5,008
1966	Dallas, NFL	5,145
	Kansas City, AFL	5,114
1965	San Francisco, NFL	5,270
	San Diego, AFL	5,188
1964	Buffalo, AFL	5,206
	Baltimore, NFL	4,779
1963	San Diego, AFL	5,153
	N.Y. Giants, NFL	5,024
1962	N.Y. Giants, NFL	5,005
	Houston, AFL	4,971
1961	Houston, AFL	6,288
	Philadelphia, NFL	5,112
1960	Houston, AFL	4,936
	Baltimore, NFL	4,245
1959	Baltimore	4,458
1958	Baltimore	4,539
1957	Los Angeles	4,143
1956	Chi. Bears	4,537
1955	Chi. Bears	4,316
1954	Los Angeles	5,187
1953	Philadelphia	4,811
1952	Cleveland	4,352
1951	Los Angeles	5,506
1950	Los Angeles	5,420
1949	Chi. Bears	4,873
1948	Chi. Cardinals	4,705
1947	Chi. Bears	5,053
1946	Los Angeles	3,793
1945	Washington	3,549
1944	Chi. Bears	3,239
1943	Chi. Bears	4,045
1942	Chi. Bears	3,900
1941	Chi. Bears	4,265
1940	Green Bay	3,400
1939	Chi. Bears	3,988
1938	Green Bay	3,037
1937	Green Bay	3,201
1936	Detroit	3,703
1935	Chi. Bears	3,454
1934	Chi. Bears	3,900
1933	N.Y. Giants	2,973
1932	Chi. Bears	2,755

YARDS RUSHING

Year	Team	Yards
2009	N.Y. Jets, AFC	2,756
	Carolina, NFC	2,498
2008	N.Y. Giants, NFC	2,518
	Baltimore, AFC	2,376
2007	Minnesota, NFC	2,634
	Jacksonville, AFC	2,391
2006	Atlanta, NFC	2,939
	San Diego, AFC	2,578
2005	Atlanta, NFC	2,546
	Denver, AFC	2,539
2004	Atlanta, NFC	2,672
	Pittsburgh, AFC	2,464
2003	Baltimore, AFC	2,674
	Green Bay, NFC	2,558
2002	Minnesota, NFC	2,507
	Miami, AFC	2,502
2001	Pittsburgh, AFC	2,774
	San Francisco, NFC	2,244
2000	Oakland, AFC	2,470
	Minnesota, NFC	2,129
1999	San Francisco, NFC	2,095
	Jacksonville, AFC	2,091
1998	San Francisco, NFC	2,544
	Denver, AFC	2,468
1997	Pittsburgh, AFC	2,479
	Detroit, NFC	2,464
1996	Denver, AFC	2,362
	Washington, NFC	1,910
1995	Kansas City, AFC	2,222
	Dallas, NFC	2,201
1994	Pittsburgh, AFC	2,180
	Detroit, NFC	2,080
1993	N.Y. Giants, NFC	2,210
	Seattle, AFC	2,015
1992	Buffalo, AFC	2,436
	Philadelphia, NFC	2,388
1991	Buffalo, AFC	2,381
	Minnesota, NFC	2,201
1990	Philadelphia, NFC	2,556
	San Diego, AFC	2,257
1989	Cincinnati, AFC	2,483
	Chicago, NFC	2,287
1988	Cincinnati, AFC	2,710
	San Francisco, NFC	2,523
1987	San Francisco, NFC	2,237
	L.A. Raiders, AFC	2,197
1986	Chicago, NFC	2,700
	Cincinnati, AFC	2,533
1985	Chicago, NFC	2,761
	Indianapolis, AFC	2,439
1984	Chicago, NFC	2,974
	N.Y. Jets, AFC	2,189
1983	Chicago, NFC	2,727
	Baltimore, AFC	2,695
1982	Buffalo, AFC	1,371
	Dallas, NFC	1,313
1981	Detroit, NFC	2,795
	Kansas City, AFC	2,633
1980	Los Angeles, NFC	2,799
	Houston, AFC	2,635
1979	N.Y. Jets, AFC	2,646
	St. Louis, NFC	2,582
1978	New England, AFC	3,165
	Dallas, NFC	2,783
1977	Chicago, NFC	2,811
	Oakland, AFC	2,627
1976	Pittsburgh, AFC	2,971
	Los Angeles, NFC	2,528
1975	Buffalo, AFC	2,974
	Dallas, NFC	2,432
1974	Dallas, NFC	2,454
	Pittsburgh, AFC	2,417
1973	Buffalo, AFC	3,088
	Los Angeles, NFC	2,925
1972	Miami, AFC	2,960
	Chicago, NFC	2,360
1971	Miami, AFC	2,429

Year	Team	Yards
	Detroit, NFC	2,376
1970	Dallas, NFC	2,300
	Miami, AFC	2,082
1969	Dallas, NFL	2,276
	Kansas City, AFL	2,220
1968	Chicago, NFL	2,377
	Kansas City, AFL	2,227
1967	Cleveland, NFL	2,139
	Houston, AFL	2,122
1966	Kansas City, AFL	2,274
	Cleveland, NFL	2,166
1965	Cleveland, NFL	2,331
	San Diego, AFL	2,085
1964	Green Bay, NFL	2,276
	Buffalo, AFL	2,040
1963	Cleveland, NFL	2,639
	San Diego, AFL	2,203
1962	Buffalo, AFL	2,480
	Green Bay, NFL	2,460
1961	Green Bay, NFL	2,350
	Dall. Texans, AFL	2,189
1960	St. Louis, NFL	2,356
	Oakland, AFL	2,056
1959	Cleveland	2,149
1958	Cleveland	2,526
1957	Los Angeles	2,142
1956	Chi. Bears	2,468
1955	Chi. Bears	2,388
1954	San Francisco	2,498
1953	San Francisco	2,230
1952	San Francisco	1,905
1951	Chi. Bears	2,408
1950	N.Y. Giants	2,336
1949	Philadelphia	2,607
1948	Chi. Cardinals	2,560
1947	Los Angeles	2,171
1946	Green Bay	1,765
1945	Cleveland	1,714
1944	Philadelphia	1,661
1943	Phil-Pitt	1,730
1942	Chi. Bears	1,881
1941	Chi. Bears	2,263
1940	Chi. Bears	1,818
1939	Chi. Bears	2,043
1938	Detroit	1,893
1937	Detroit	2,074
1936	Detroit	2,885
1935	Chi. Bears	2,096
1934	Chi. Bears	2,847
1933	Boston	2,260
1932	Chi. Bears	1,770

YARDS PASSING

Leadership in this category has been based on net yards since 1952.

Year	Team	Yards
2009	Houston, AFC	4,654
	New Orleans, NFC	4,355
2008	New Orleans, NFC	4,977
	Denver, AFC	4,471
2007	New England, AFC	4,731
	Green Bay, NFC	4,334
2006	New Orleans, NFC	4,503
	Indianapolis, AFC	4,308
2005	Arizona, NFC	4,437
	New England, AFC	4,120
2004	Indianapolis, AFC	4,623
	Minnesota, NFC	4,516
2003	Indianapolis, AFC	4,179
	St. Louis, NFC	3,961
2002	Oakland, AFC	4,475
	St. Louis, NFC	4,154
2001	St. Louis, NFC	4,663
	Indianapolis, AFC	3,989
2000	St. Louis, NFC	5,232
	Indianapolis, AFC	4,282
1999	St. Louis, NFC	4,353
	Indianapolis, AFC	4,066
1998	Minnesota, NFC	4,328
	N.Y. Jets, AFC	3,836
1997	Seattle, AFC	3,959
	Green Bay, NFC	3,705
1996	Jacksonville, AFC	4,110
	Philadelphia, NFC	3,745
1995	San Francisco, NFC	4,608
	Miami, AFC	4,210
1994	New England, AFC	4,444
	Minnesota, NFC	4,324
1993	Miami, AFC	4,353
	San Francisco, NFC	4,302
1992	Houston, AFC	4,029
	San Francisco, NFC	3,880
1991	Houston, AFC	4,621
	San Francisco, NFC	3,997
1990	Houston, AFC	4,805
	San Francisco, NFC	4,177
1989	Washington, NFC	4,349
	Miami, AFC	4,216
1988	Miami, AFC	4,516
	Washington, NFC	4,136
1987	Miami, AFC	3,876
	San Francisco, NFC	3,750
1986	Miami, AFC	4,779
	San Francisco, NFC	4,096
1985	San Diego, AFC	4,870
	Dallas, NFC	3,861
1984	Miami, AFC	5,018
	St. Louis, NFC	4,257
1983	San Diego, AFC	4,661
	Green Bay, NFC	4,365
1982	San Diego, AFC	2,927
	San Francisco, NFC	2,502
1981	San Diego, AFC	4,739
	Minnesota, NFC	4,333
1980	San Diego, AFC	4,531
	Minnesota, NFC	3,688
1979	San Diego, AFC	3,915
	San Francisco, NFC	3,641
1978	San Diego, AFC	3,375
	Minnesota, NFC	3,243
1977	Buffalo, AFC	2,530
	St. Louis, NFC	2,499
1976	Baltimore, AFC	2,933
	Minnesota, NFC	2,855
1975	Cincinnati, AFC	3,241
	Washington, NFC	2,917
1974	Washington, NFC	2,978
	Cincinnati, AFC	2,804
1973	Philadelphia, NFC	2,998
	Denver, AFC	2,519
1972	N.Y. Jets, AFC	2,777
	San Francisco, NFC	2,735
1971	San Diego, AFC	3,134
	Dallas, NFC	2,786
1970	San Francisco, NFC	2,923
	Oakland, AFC	2,865
1969	Oakland, AFL	3,271
	San Francisco, NFL	3,158
1968	San Diego, AFL	3,623
	Dallas, NFL	3,026
1967	N.Y. Jets, AFL	3,845
	Washington, NFL	3,730

Year	Team	Yards
1966	N.Y. Jets, AFL	3,464
	Dallas, NFL	3,023
1965	San Francisco, NFL	3,487
	San Diego, AFL	3,103
1964	Houston, AFL	3,527
	Chicago, NFL	2,841
1963	Baltimore, NFL	3,296
	Houston, AFL	3,222
1962	Denver, AFL	3,404
	Philadelphia, NFL	3,385
1961	Houston, AFL	4,392
	Philadelphia, NFL	3,605
1960	Houston, AFL	3,203
	Baltimore, NFL	2,956
1959	Baltimore	2,753
1958	Pittsburgh	2,752
1957	Baltimore	2,388
1956	Los Angeles	2,419
1955	Philadelphia	2,472
1954	Chi. Bears	3,104
1953	Philadelphia	3,089
1952	Cleveland	2,566
1951	Los Angeles	3,296
1950	Los Angeles	3,709
1949	Chi. Bears	3,055
1948	Washington	2,861
1947	Washington	3,336
1946	Los Angeles	2,080
1945	Chi. Bears	1,857
1944	Washington	2,021
1943	Chi. Bears	2,310
1942	Green Bay	2,407
1941	Chi. Bears	2,002
1940	Washington	1,887
1939	Chi. Bears	1,965
1938	Washington	1,536
1937	Green Bay	1,398
1936	Green Bay	1,629
1935	Green Bay	1,449
1934	Green Bay	1,165
1933	N.Y. Giants	1,348
1932	Chi. Bears	1,013

FEWEST POINTS ALLOWED

Year	Team	Points
2009	N.Y. Jets, AFC	236
	Dallas, NFC	250
2008	Pittsburgh, AFC	223
	Philadelphia, NFC	289
2007	Indianapolis, AFC	262
	Tampa Bay, NFC	270
2006	Baltimore, AFC	201
	Chicago, NFC	255
2005	Chicago, NFC	202
	Indianapolis, AFC	247
2004	Pittsburgh, AFC	251
	Philadelphia, NFC	260
2003	New England, AFC	238
	Dallas, NFC	260
2002	Tampa Bay, NFC	196
	Miami, AFC	301
2001	Chicago, NFC	203
	Pittsburgh, AFC	212
2000	Baltimore, AFC	165
	Philadelphia, NFC	245
1999	Jacksonville, AFC	217
	Tampa Bay, NFC	235
1998	Miami, AFC	265
	Dallas, NFC	275
1997	Kansas City, AFC	232
	Tampa Bay, NFC	263

Year	Team	Points
1996	Green Bay, NFC	210
	Pittsburgh, AFC	257
1995	Kansas City, AFC	241
	San Francisco, NFC	258
1994	Cleveland, AFC	204
	Dallas, NFC	248
1993	N.Y. Giants, NFC	205
	Houston, AFC	238
1992	New Orleans, NFC	202
	Pittsburgh, AFC	225
1991	New Orleans, NFC	211
	Denver, AFC	235
1990	N.Y. Giants, NFC	211
	Pittsburgh, AFC	240
1989	Denver, AFC	226
	N.Y. Giants, NFC	252
1988	Chicago, NFC	215
	Buffalo, AFC	237
1987	Indianapolis, AFC	238
	San Francisco, NFC	253
1986	Chicago, NFC	187
	Seattle, AFC	293
1985	Chicago, NFC	198
	N.Y. Jets, AFC	264
1984	San Francisco, NFC	227
	Denver, AFC	241
1983	Miami, AFC	250
	Detroit, NFC	286
1982	Washington, NFC	128
	Miami, AFC	131
1981	Philadelphia, NFC	221
	Miami, AFC	275
1980	Philadelphia, NFC	222
	Houston, AFC	251
1979	Tampa Bay, NFC	237
	San Diego, AFC	246
1978	Pittsburgh, AFC	195
	Dallas, NFC	208
1977	Atlanta, NFC	129
	Denver, AFC	148
1976	Pittsburgh, AFC	138
	Minnesota, NFC	176
1975	Los Angeles, NFC	135
	Pittsburgh, AFC	162
1974	Los Angeles, NFC	181
	Pittsburgh, AFC	189
1973	Miami, AFC	150
	Minnesota, NFC	168
1972	Miami, AFC	171
	Washington, NFC	218
1971	Minnesota, NFC	139
	Baltimore, AFC	140
1970	Minnesota, NFC	143
	Miami, AFC	228
1969	Minnesota, NFL	133
	Kansas City, AFL	177
1968	Baltimore, NFL	144
	Kansas City, AFL	170
1967	Los Angeles, NFL	196
	Houston, AFL	199
1966	Green Bay, NFL	163
	Buffalo, AFL	255
1965	Green Bay, NFL	224
	Buffalo, AFL	226
1964	Baltimore, NFL	225
	Buffalo, AFL	242
1963	Chicago, NFL	144
	San Diego, AFL	255
1962	Green Bay, NFL	148
	Dall. Texans, AFL	233
1961	San Diego, AFL	219

Year	Team	Points
	N.Y. Giants, NFL	220
1960	San Francisco, NFL	205
	Dall. Texans, AFL	253
1959	N.Y. Giants	170
1958	N.Y. Giants	183
1957	Cleveland	172
1956	Cleveland	177
1955	Cleveland	218
1954	Cleveland	162
1953	Cleveland	162
1952	Detroit	192
1951	Cleveland	152
1950	Philadelphia	141
1949	Philadelphia	134
1948	Chi. Bears	151
1947	Green Bay	210
1946	Pittsburgh	117
1945	Washington	121
1944	N.Y. Giants	75
1943	Washington	137
1942	Chi. Bears	84
1941	N.Y. Giants	114
1940	Brooklyn	120
1939	N.Y. Giants	85
1938	N.Y. Giants	79
1937	Chi. Bears	100
1936	Chi. Bears	94
1935	Green Bay	96
	N.Y. Giants	96
1934	Detroit	59
1933	Brooklyn	54
1932	Chi. Bears	44

FEWEST TOTAL YARDS ALLOWED

Year	Team	Yards
2009	N.Y. Jets, AFC	4,037
	Green Bay, NFC	4,551
2008	Pittsburgh, AFC	3,795
	Philadelphia, NFC	4,389
2007	Pittsburgh, AFC	4,262
	Tampa Bay, NFC	4,454
2006	Baltimore, AFC	4,225
	Chicago, NFC	4,706
2005	Tampa Bay, NFC	4,444
	Pittsburgh, AFC	4,544
2004	Pittsburgh, AFC	4,134
	Washington, NFC	4,281
2003	Dallas, NFC	4,056
	Buffalo, AFC	4,313
2002	Tampa Bay, NFC	4,044
	Miami, AFC	4,656
2001	Pittsburgh, AFC	4,137
	St. Louis, NFC	4,471
2000	Tennessee, AFC	3,813
	Washington, NFC	4,474
1999	Buffalo, AFC	4,045
	Tampa Bay, NFC	4,280
1998	San Diego, AFC	4,208
	Tampa Bay, NFC	4,345
1997	San Francisco, NFC	4,013
	Denver, AFC	4,671
1996	Green Bay, NFC	4,156
	Pittsburgh, AFC	4,362
1995	San Francisco, NFC	4,398
	Kansas City, AFC	4,549
1994	Dallas, NFC	4,313
	Pittsburgh, AFC	4,326
1993	Minnesota, NFC	4,406
	Pittsburgh, AFC	4,531
1992	Dallas, NFC	3,931
	Houston, AFC	4,211
1991	Philadelphia, NFC	3,549
	Denver, AFC	4,549
1990	Pittsburgh, AFC	4,115
	N.Y. Giants, NFC	4,206
1989	Minnesota, NFC	4,184
	Kansas City, AFC	4,293
1988	Minnesota, NFC	4,091
	Buffalo, AFC	4,578
1987	San Francisco, NFC	4,095
	Cleveland, AFC	4,264
1986	Chicago, NFC	4,130
	L.A. Raiders, AFC	4,804
1985	Chicago, NFC	4,135
	L.A. Raiders, AFC	4,603
1984	Chicago, NFC	3,863
	Cleveland, AFC	4,641
1983	Cincinnati, AFC	4,327
	New Orleans, NFC	4,691
1982	Miami, AFC	2,312
	Tampa Bay, NFC	2,442
1981	Philadelphia, NFC	4,447
	N.Y. Jets, AFC	4,871
1980	Buffalo, AFC	4,101
	Philadelphia, NFC	4,443
1979	Tampa Bay, NFC	3,949
	Pittsburgh, AFC	4,270
1978	Los Angeles, NFC	3,893
	Pittsburgh, AFC	4,168
1977	Dallas, NFC	3,213
	New England, AFC	3,638
1976	Pittsburgh, AFC	3,323
	San Francisco, NFC	3,562
1975	Minnesota, NFC	3,153
	Oakland, AFC	3,629
1974	Pittsburgh, AFC	3,074
	Washington, NFC	3,285
1973	Los Angeles, NFC	2,951
	Oakland, AFC	3,160
1972	Miami, AFC	3,297
	Green Bay, NFC	3,474
1971	Baltimore, AFC	2,852
	Minnesota, NFC	3,406
1970	Minnesota, NFC	2,803
	N.Y. Jets, AFC	3,655
1969	Minnesota, NFL	2,720
	Kansas City, AFL	3,163
1968	Los Angeles, NFL	3,118
	N.Y. Jets, AFL	3,363
1967	Oakland, AFL	3,294
	Green Bay, NFL	3,300
1966	St. Louis, NFL	3,492
	Oakland, AFL	3,910
1965	San Diego, AFL	3,262
	Detroit, NFL	3,557
1964	Green Bay, NFL	3,179
	Buffalo, AFL	3,878
1963	Chicago, NFL	3,176
	Boston, AFL	3,834
1962	Detroit, NFL	3,217
	Dall. Texans, AFL	3,951
1961	San Diego, AFL	3,726
	Baltimore, NFL	3,782
1960	St. Louis, NFL	3,029
	Buffalo, AFL	3,866
1959	N.Y. Giants	2,843
1958	Chi. Bears	3,066
1957	Pittsburgh	2,791
1956	N.Y. Giants	3,081
1955	Cleveland	2,841
1954	Cleveland	2,658
1953	Philadelphia	2,998

Year	Team	Yards
1952	Cleveland	3,075
1951	N.Y. Giants	3,250
1950	Cleveland	3,154
1949	Philadelphia	2,831
1948	Chi. Bears	2,931
1947	Green Bay	3,396
1946	Washington	2,451
1945	Philadelphia	2,073
1944	Philadelphia	1,943
1943	Chi. Bears	2,262
1942	Chi. Bears	1,703
1941	N.Y. Giants	2,368
1940	N.Y. Giants	2,219
1939	Washington	2,116
1938	N.Y. Giants	2,029
1937	Washington	2,123
1936	Boston	2,181
1935	Boston	1,996
1934	Chi. Cardinals	1,539
1933	Brooklyn	1,789

FEWEST RUSHING YARDS ALLOWED

Year	Team	Yards
2009	Green Bay, NFC	1,333
	Pittsburgh, AFC	1,438
2008	Minnesota, NFC	1,230
	Pittsburgh, AFC	1,284
2007	Minnesota, NFC	1,185
	Baltimore, AFC	1,268
2006	Minnesota, NFC	985
	Baltimore, AFC	1,214
2005	San Diego, AFC	1,349
	Carolina, NFC	1,465
2004	Pittsburgh, AFC	1,299
	Washington, NFC	1,304
2003	Tennessee, AFC	1,295
	Dallas, NFC	1,425
2002	Pittsburgh, AFC	1,375
	Tampa Bay, NFC	1,554
2001	Pittsburgh, AFC	1,195
	Chicago, NFC	1,313
2000	Baltimore, AFC	970
	N.Y. Giants, NFC	1,156
1999	St. Louis, NFC	1,189
	Baltimore, AFC	1,231
1998	San Diego, AFC	1,140
	Atlanta, NFC	1,203
1997	Pittsburgh, AFC	1,318
	San Francisco, NFC	1,366
1996	Denver, AFC	1,331
	Green Bay, NFC	1,416
1995	San Francisco, NFC	1,061
	Pittsburgh, AFC	1,321
1994	Minnesota, NFC	1,090
	San Diego, AFC	1,404
1993	Houston, AFC	1,273
	Minnesota, NFC	1,536
1992	Dallas, NFC	1,244
	Buffalo, AFC	1,395
	San Diego, AFC	1,395
1991	Philadelphia, NFC	1,136
	N.Y. Jets, AFC	1,442
1990	Philadelphia, NFC	1,169
	San Diego, AFC	1,515
1989	New Orleans, NFC	1,326
	Denver, AFC	1,580
1988	Chicago, NFC	1,326
	Houston, AFC	1,592
1987	Chicago, NFC	1,413
	Cleveland, AFC	1,433
1986	N.Y. Giants, NFC	1,284
	Denver, AFC	1,651
1985	Chicago, NFC	1,319
	N.Y. Jets, AFC	1,516
1984	Chicago, NFC	1,377
	Pittsburgh, AFC	1,617
1983	Washington, NFC	1,289
	Cincinnati, AFC	1,499
1982	Pittsburgh, AFC	762
	Detroit, NFC	854
1981	Detroit, NFC	1,623
	Kansas City, AFC	1,747
1980	Detroit, NFC	1,599
	Cincinnati, AFC	1,680
1979	Denver, AFC	1,693
	Tampa Bay, NFC	1,873
1978	Dallas, NFC	1,721
	Pittsburgh, AFC	1,774
1977	Denver, AFC	1,531
	Dallas, NFC	1,651
1976	Pittsburgh, AFC	1,457
	Los Angeles, NFC	1,564
1975	Minnesota, NFC	1,532
	Houston, AFC	1,680
1974	Los Angeles, NFC	1,302
	New England, AFC	1,587
1973	Los Angeles, NFC	1,270
	Oakland, AFC	1,470
1972	Dallas, NFC	1,515
	Miami, AFC	1,548
1971	Baltimore, AFC	1,113
	Dallas, NFC	1,144
1970	Detroit, NFC	1,152
	N.Y. Jets, AFC	1,283
1969	Dallas, NFL	1,050
	Kansas City, AFL	1,091
1968	Dallas, NFL	1,195
	N.Y. Jets, AFL	1,195
1967	Dallas, NFL	1,081
	Oakland, AFL	1,129
1966	Buffalo, AFL	1,051
	Dallas, NFL	1,176
1965	San Diego, AFL	1,094
	Los Angeles, NFL	1,409
1964	Buffalo, AFL	913
	Los Angeles, NFL	1,501
1963	Boston, AFL	1,107
	Chicago, NFL	1,442
1962	Detroit, NFL	1,231
	Dall. Texans, AFL	1,250
1961	Boston, AFL	1,041
	Pittsburgh, NFL	1,463
1960	St. Louis, NFL	1,212
	Dall. Texans, AFL	1,338
1959	N.Y. Giants	1,261
1958	Baltimore	1,291
1957	Baltimore	1,174
1956	N.Y. Giants	1,443
1955	Cleveland	1,189
1954	Cleveland	1,050
1953	Philadelphia	1,117
1952	Detroit	1,145
1951	N.Y. Giants	913
1950	Detroit	1,367
1949	Chi. Bears	1,196
1948	Philadelphia	1,209
1947	Philadelphia	1,329
1946	Chi. Bears	1,060
1945	Philadelphia	817
1944	Philadelphia	558
1943	Phil-Pitt	793
1942	Chi. Bears	519

Year	Team	Yards
1941	Washington	1,042
1940	N.Y. Giants	977
1939	Chi. Bears	812
1938	Detroit	1,081
1937	Chi. Bears	933
1936	Boston	1,148
1935	Boston	998
1934	Chi. Cardinals	954
1933	Brooklyn	964

FEWEST PASSING YARDS ALLOWED

Leadership in this category has been based on net yards since 1952.

Year	Team	Yards
2009	N.Y. Jets, AFC	2,459
	Carolina, NFC	3,056
2008	Pittsburgh, AFC	2,511
	Philadelphia, NFC	2,913
2007	Tampa Bay, NFC	2,728
	Indianapolis, AFC	2,764
2006	Oakland, AFC	2,413
	New Orleans, NFC	2,854
2005	Green Bay, NFC	2,680
	N.Y. Jets, AFC	2,755
2004	Tampa Bay, NFC	2,579
	Miami, AFC	2,592
2003	Dallas, NFC	2,631
	Buffalo, AFC	2,707
2002	Tampa Bay, NFC	2,490
	Indianapolis, AFC	2,917
2001	Miami, AFC	2,829
	Philadelphia, NFC	2,864
2000	Tennessee, AFC	2,423
	Washington, NFC	2,621
1999	Buffalo, AFC	2,675
	Tampa Bay, NFC	2,873
1998	Philadelphia, NFC	2,720
	Oakland, AFC	2,876
1997	Dallas, NFC	2,522
	Indianapolis, AFC	2,820
1996	Green Bay, NFC	2,740
	Pittsburgh, AFC	2,947
1995	N.Y. Jets, AFC	2,740
	Philadelphia, NFC	2,816
1994	Dallas, NFC	2,752
	Houston, AFC	2,795
1993	New Orleans, NFC	2,606
	Cincinnati, AFC	2,798
1992	New Orleans, NFC	2,470
	Kansas City, AFC	2,537
1991	Philadelphia, NFC	2,413
	Denver, AFC	2,755
1990	Pittsburgh, AFC	2,500
	Dallas, NFC	2,639
1989	Minnesota, NFC	2,501
	Kansas City, AFC	2,527
1988	Kansas City, AFC	2,434
	Minnesota, NFC	2,489
1987	San Francisco, NFC	2,484
	L.A. Raiders, AFC	2,727
1986	St. Louis, NFC	2,637
	New England, AFC	2,978
1985	Washington, NFC	2,746
	Pittsburgh, AFC	2,783
1984	New Orleans, NFC	2,453
	Cleveland, AFC	2,696
1983	New Orleans, NFC	2,691
	Cincinnati, AFC	2,828
1982	Miami, AFC	1,027
	Tampa Bay, NFC	1,384
1981	Philadelphia, NFC	2,696
	Buffalo, AFC	2,870
1980	Washington, NFC	2,171
	Buffalo, AFC	2,282
1979	Tampa Bay, NFC	2,076
	Buffalo, AFC	2,530
1978	Buffalo, AFC	1,960
	Los Angeles, NFC	2,048
1977	Atlanta, NFC	1,384
	San Diego, AFC	1,725
1976	Minnesota, NFC	1,575
	Cincinnati, AFC	1,758
1975	Minnesota, NFC	1,621
	Cincinnati, AFC	1,729
1974	Pittsburgh, AFC	1,466
	Atlanta, NFC	1,572
1973	Miami, AFC	1,290
	Atlanta, NFC	1,430
1972	Minnesota, NFC	1,699
	Cleveland, AFC	1,736
1971	Atlanta, NFC	1,638
	Baltimore, AFC	1,739
1970	Minnesota, NFC	1,438
	Kansas City, AFC	2,010
1969	Minnesota, NFL	1,631
	Kansas City, AFL	2,072
1968	Houston, AFL	1,671
	Green Bay, NFL	1,796
1967	Green Bay, NFL	1,377
	Buffalo, AFL	1,825
1966	Green Bay, NFL	1,959
	Oakland, AFL	2,118
1965	Green Bay, NFL	1,981
	San Diego, AFL	2,168
1964	Green Bay, NFL	1,647
	San Diego, AFL	2,518
1963	Chicago, NFL	1,734
	Oakland, AFL	2,589
1962	Green Bay, NFL	1,746
	Oakland, AFL	2,306
1961	Baltimore, NFL	1,913
	San Diego, AFL	2,363
1960	Chicago, NFL	1,388
	Buffalo, AFL	2,124
1959	N.Y. Giants	1,582
1958	Chi. Bears	1,769
1957	Cleveland	1,300
1956	Cleveland	1,103
1955	Pittsburgh	1,295
1954	Cleveland	1,608
1953	Washington	1,751
1952	Washington	1,580
1951	Pittsburgh	1,687
1950	Cleveland	1,581
1949	Philadelphia	1,607
1948	Green Bay	1,626
1947	Green Bay	1,790
1946	Pittsburgh	939
1945	Washington	1,121
1944	Chi. Bears	1,052
1943	Chi. Bears	980
1942	Washington	1,093
1941	Pittsburgh	1,168
1940	Philadelphia	1,012
1939	Washington	1,116
1938	Chi. Bears	897
1937	Detroit	804
1936	Philadelphia	853
1935	Chi. Cardinals	793
1934	Philadelphia	545
1933	Portsmouth	558

Compiled by Elias Sports Bureau

Super Bowl I, 1/15/67
Super Bowl II, 1/14/68
Super Bowl III, 1/12/69
Super Bowl IV, 1/11/70
Super Bowl V, 1/17/71
Super Bowl VI, 1/16/72
Super Bowl VII, 1/14/73
Super Bowl VIII, 1/13/74
Super Bowl IX, 1/12/75
Super Bowl X, 1/18/76
Super Bowl XI, 1/9/77
Super Bowl XII, 1/15/78
Super Bowl XIII, 1/21/79
Super Bowl XIV, 1/20/80
Super Bowl XV, 1/25/81
Super Bowl XVI, 1/24/82
Super Bowl XVII, 1/30/83
Super Bowl XVIII, 1/22/84
Super Bowl XIX, 1/20/85
Super Bowl XX, 1/26/86
Super Bowl XXI, 1/25/87
Super Bowl XXII, 1/31/88
Super Bowl XXIII, 1/22/89
Super Bowl XXIV, 1/28/90
Super Bowl XXV, 1/27/91
Super Bowl XXVI, 1/26/92
Super Bowl XXVII, 1/31/93
Super Bowl XXVIII, 1/30/94
Super Bowl XXIX, 1/29/95
Super Bowl XXX, 1/28/96
Super Bowl XXXI, 1/26/97
Super Bowl XXXII, 1/25/98
Super Bowl XXXIII, 1/31/99
Super Bowl XXXIV, 1/30/00
Super Bowl XXXV, 1/28/01
Super Bowl XXXVI, 2/3/02
Super Bowl XXXVII, 1/26/03
Super Bowl XXXVIII, 2/1/04
Super Bowl XXXIX, 2/6/05
Super Bowl XL, 2/5/06
Super Bowl XLI, 2/4/07
Super Bowl XLII, 2/3/08
Super Bowl XLIII, 2/1/09
Super Bowl XLIV, 2/7/10

INDIVIDUAL RECORDS

SERVICE

Most Games

6 Mike Lodish, Buffalo, XXV-XXVIII; Denver, XXXII-XXXIII
5 Marv Fleming, Green Bay, I-II; Miami, VI-VIII
Larry Cole, Dallas, V-VI, X, XII-XIII
Cliff Harris, Dallas, V-VI, X, XII-XIII
Charles Haley, San Francisco, XXIII-XXIV; Dallas, XXVII-XXVIII, XXX
D.D. Lewis, Dallas, V-VI, X, XII-XIII
Preston Pearson, Baltimore, III; Pittsburgh, IX; Dallas, X, XII-XIII
Charlie Waters, Dallas, V-VI, X, XII-XIII
Rayfield Wright, Dallas, V-VI, X, XII-XIII
Cornelius Bennett, Buffalo, XXV-XXVIII; Atlanta, XXXIII
John Elway, Denver, XXI-XXII, XXIV, XXXII-XXXIII
Glenn Parker, Buffalo, XXV-XXVIII; N.Y. Giants, XXXV
Bill Romanowski, San Francisco, XXIII-XXIV; Denver, XXXII-XXXIII; Oakland, XXXVII
Adam Vinatieri, New England, XXXI, XXXVI, XXXVIII, XXXIX; Indianapolis, XLI
Tedy Bruschi, New England, XXXI, XXXVI, XXXVIII-XXXIX, XLII
4 By many players

Most Games, Winning Team

5 Charles Haley, San Francisco, XXIII-XXIV; Dallas, XXVII-XXVIII, XXX
4 By many players

Most Games, Coach

6 Don Shula, Baltimore, III; Miami, VI-VIII, XVII, XIX
5 Tom Landry, Dallas, V-VI, X, XII-XIII
4 Bud Grant, Minnesota, IV, VIII-IX, XI
Chuck Noll, Pittsburgh, IX-X, XIII-XIV
Joe Gibbs, Washington, XVII-XVIII, XXII, XXVI
Marv Levy, Buffalo, XXV-XXVIII
Dan Reeves, Denver, XXI-XXII, XXIV; Atlanta, XXXIII
Bill Belichick, New England, XXXVI, XXXVIII-XXXIX, XLII

Most Games, Winning Team, Coach

4 Chuck Noll, Pittsburgh, IX-X, XIII-XIV
3 Bill Walsh, San Francisco, XVI, XIX, XXIII
Joe Gibbs, Washington, XVII, XXII, XXVI
Bill Belichick, New England, XXXVI, XXXVIII-XXXIX
2 Vince Lombardi, Green Bay, I-II
Tom Landry, Dallas, VI, XII
Don Shula, Miami, VII-VIII
Tom Flores, Oakland, XV; L.A. Raiders, XVIII
Bill Parcells, N.Y. Giants, XXI, XXV
Jimmy Johnson, Dallas, XXVII-XXVIII
George Seifert, San Francisco, XXIV, XXIX
Mike Shanahan, Denver, XXXII-XXXIII

Most Games, Losing Team, Coach

4 Bud Grant, Minnesota, IV, VIII-IX, XI
Don Shula, Baltimore, III; Miami, VI, XVII, XIX
Marv Levy, Buffalo, XXV-XXVIII
Dan Reeves, Denver, XXI-XXII, XXIV; Atlanta, XXXIII
3 Tom Landry, Dallas, V, X, XIII

SCORING

POINTS

Most Points, Career

48 Jerry Rice, San Francisco-Oakland, 4 games (8-td)
34 Adam Vinatieri, New England-Indianapolis, 5 games (7-fg, 13-xp)
30 Emmitt Smith, Dallas, 3 games (5-td)

Most Points, Game

18 Roger Craig, San Francisco vs. Miami, XIX (3-td)
Jerry Rice, San Francisco vs. Denver, XXIV (3-td); vs. San Diego, XXIX (3-td)
Ricky Watters, San Francisco vs. San Diego, XXIX (3-td)
Terrell Davis, Denver vs. Green Bay, XXXII (3-td)
15 Don Chandler, Green Bay vs. Oakland, II (3-pat, 4-fg)
14 Ray Wersching, San Francisco vs. Cincinnati, XVI (2-pat, 4-fg)
Kevin Butler, Chicago vs. New England, XX (5-pat, 3-fg)

TOUCHDOWNS

Most Touchdowns, Career

8 Jerry Rice, San Francisco-Oakland, 4 games (8-p)
5 Emmitt Smith, Dallas, 3 games (5-r)
4 Franco Harris, Pittsburgh, 4 games (4-r)
Roger Craig, San Francisco, 3 games (2-r, 2-p)
Thurman Thomas, Buffalo, 4 games (4-r)
John Elway, Denver, 5 games (4-r)

Most Touchdowns, Game

3 Roger Craig, San Francisco vs. Miami, XIX (1-r, 2-p)
Jerry Rice, San Francisco. vs. Denver, XXIV (3-p); vs. San Diego, XXIX (3-p)
Ricky Watters, San Francisco vs. San Diego, XXIX (1-r, 2-p)
Terrell Davis, Denver vs. Green Bay, XXXII (3-r)
2 Max McGee, Green Bay vs. Kansas City, I (2-p)
Elijah Pitts, Green Bay vs. Kansas City, I (2-r)
Bill Miller, Oakland vs. Green Bay, II (2-p)
Larry Csonka, Miami vs. Minnesota, VIII (2-r)
Pete Banaszak, Oakland vs. Minnesota, XI (2-r)
John Stallworth, Pittsburgh vs. Dallas, XIII (2-p)
Franco Harris, Pittsburgh vs. Los Angeles, XIV (2-r)
Cliff Branch, Oakland vs. Philadelphia, XV (2-p)
Dan Ross, Cincinnati vs. San Francisco, XVI (2-p)
Marcus Allen, L.A. Raiders vs. Washington, XVIII (2-r)
Jim McMahon, Chicago vs. New England, XX (2-r)
Ricky Sanders, Washington vs. Denver, XXII (2-p)
Timmy Smith, Washington vs. Denver, XXII (2-r)
Tom Rathman, San Francisco vs. Denver, XXIV (2-r)
Gerald Riggs, Washington vs. Buffalo, XXVI (2-r)
Michael Irvin, Dallas vs. Buffalo, XXVII (2-p)
Emmitt Smith, Dallas vs. Buffalo, XXVIII (2-r)
Emmitt Smith, Dallas vs. Pittsburgh, XXX (2-r)
Antonio Freeman, Green Bay vs. Denver, XXXII (2-p)
Howard Griffith, Denver vs. Atlanta, XXXIII (2-r)
Eddie George, Tennessee vs. St. Louis, XXXIV (2-r)
Keenan McCardell, Tampa Bay vs. Oakland, XXXVII (2-r)

Dwight Smith, Tampa Bay vs. Oakland, XXXVII (2-ret)
Larry Fitzgerald, Arizona vs. Pittsburgh, XLIII (2-p)

POINTS AFTER TOUCHDOWN

Most (One-Point) Points After Touchdown, Career

13 Adam Vinatieri, New England-Indianapolis, 5 games (13 att)
9 Mike Cofer, San Francisco, 2 games (10 att)
8 Don Chandler, Green Bay, 2 games (8 att)
Roy Gerela, Pittsburgh, 3 games (9 att)
Chris Bahr, Oakland-L.A. Raiders, 2 games (8 att)
Jason Elam, Denver, 2 games (8 att)

Most (One-Point) Points After Touchdown, Game

7 Mike Cofer, San Francisco vs. Denver, XXIV (8 att)
Lin Elliott, Dallas vs. Buffalo, XXVII (7 att)
Doug Brien, San Francisco vs. San Diego, XXIX (7 att)
6 Ali Haji-Sheikh, Washington vs. Denver, XXII (6 att)
Martín Gramatica, Tampa Bay vs. Oakland, XXXVII (6 att)
5 Don Chandler, Green Bay vs. Kansas City, I (5 att)
Roy Gerela, Pittsburgh vs. Dallas, XIII (5 att)
Chris Bahr, L.A. Raiders vs. Washington, XVIII (5 att)
Ray Wersching, San Francisco vs. Miami, XIX (5 att)
Kevin Butler, Chicago vs. New England, XX (5 att)

Most Two-Point Conversions, Game

1 Mark Seay, San Diego vs. San Francisco, XXIX
Alfred Pupunu, San Diego vs. San Francisco, XXIX
Mark Chmura, Green Bay vs. New England, XXXI
Kevin Faulk, New England vs. Carolina, XXXVIII
Lance Moore, New Orleans vs. Indianapolis, XLIV

FIELD GOALS

Field Goals Attempted, Career

10 Adam Vinatieri, New England-Indianapolis, 5 games
6 Jim Turner, N.Y. Jets-Denver, 2 games
Roy Gerela, Pittsburgh, 3 games
Rich Karlis, Denver, 2 games
Jeff Wilkins, St. Louis, 2 games
5 Efren Herrera, Dallas, 1 game
Ray Wersching, San Francisco, 2 games
Jason Elam, Denver, 2 games
Matt Stover, Baltimore-Indianapolis, 2 games

Most Field Goals Attempted, Game

5 Jim Turner, N.Y. Jets vs. Baltimore, III
Efren Herrera, Dallas vs. Denver, XII
4 Don Chandler, Green Bay vs. Oakland, II
Roy Gerela, Pittsburgh vs. Dallas, X
Ray Wersching, San Francisco vs. Cincinnati, XVI
Rich Karlis, Denver vs. N.Y. Giants, XXI
Mike Cofer, San Francisco vs. Cincinnati, XXIII
Jason Elam, Denver vs. Atlanta, XXXIII
Jeff Wilkins, St. Louis vs. Tennessee, XXXIV
Adam Vinatieri, Indianapolis vs. Chicago, XLI

Most Field Goals, Career

7 Adam Vinatieri, New England-Indianapolis, 5 games (10 att)
5 Ray Wersching, San Francisco, 2 games (5 att)
4 Don Chandler, Green Bay, 2 games (4 att)
Jim Turner, N.Y. Jets-Denver, 2 games (6 att)
Uwe von Schamann, Miami, 2 games (4 att)
Jeff Wilkins, St. Louis, 2 games (6 att)

Most Field Goals, Game

4 Don Chandler, Green Bay vs. Oakland, II
Ray Wersching, San Francisco vs. Cincinnati, XVI
3 Jim Turner, N.Y. Jets vs. Baltimore, III
Jan Stenerud, Kansas City vs. Minnesota, IV
Uwe von Schamann, Miami vs. San Francisco, XIX
Kevin Butler, Chicago vs. New England, XX
Jim Breech, Cincinnati vs. San Francisco, XXIII
Chip Lohmiller, Washington vs. Buffalo, XXVI
Eddie Murray, Dallas vs. Buffalo, XXVIII
Jeff Wilkins, St. Louis vs. Tennessee, XXXIV
Adam Vinatieri, Indianapolis vs. Chicago, XLI
Garrett Hartley, New Orleans vs. Indianapolis, XLIV

Longest Field Goal

54 Steve Christie, Buffalo vs. Dallas, XXVIII
51 Jason Elam, Denver vs. Green Bay, XXXII
50 Jeff Wilkins, St. Louis vs. New England, XXXVI
John Kasay, Carolina vs. New England, XXXVIII

SAFETIES

Most Safeties, Game

1 Dwight White, Pittsburgh vs. Minnesota, IX
Reggie Harrison, Pittsburgh vs. Dallas, X
Henry Waechter, Chicago vs. New England, XX
George Martin, N.Y. Giants vs. Denver, XXI
Bruce Smith, Buffalo vs. N.Y. Giants, XXV

RUSHING

ATTEMPTS

Most Attempts, Career

101 Franco Harris, Pittsburgh, 4 games
70 Emmitt Smith, Dallas, 3 games
64 John Riggins, Washington, 2 games

Most Attempts, Game

38 John Riggins, Washington vs. Miami, XVII
34 Franco Harris, Pittsburgh vs. Minnesota, IX
33 Larry Csonka, Miami vs. Minnesota, VIII

YARDS GAINED

Most Yards Gained, Career

354 Franco Harris, Pittsburgh, 4 games
297 Larry Csonka, Miami, 3 games
289 Emmitt Smith, Dallas, 3 games

Most Yards Gained, Game

204 Timmy Smith, Washington vs. Denver, XXII
191 Marcus Allen, L.A. Raiders vs. Washington, XVIII
166 John Riggins, Washington vs. Miami, XVII

Longest Run From Scrimmage

75 Willie Parker, Pittsburgh vs. Seattle, XL (TD)
74 Marcus Allen, L.A. Raiders vs. Washington, XVIII (TD)
58 Tom Matte, Baltimore vs. N.Y. Jets, III
Timmy Smith, Washington vs. Denver, XXII (TD)

AVERAGE GAIN

Highest Average Gain, Career (20 attempts)

9.6 Marcus Allen, L.A. Raiders, 1 game (20-191)
9.3 Timmy Smith, Washington, 1 game (22-204)
5.4 Dominic Rhodes, Indianapolis, 1 game (21-113)

Highest Average Gain, Game (10 attempts)

10.5 Tom Matte, Baltimore vs. N.Y. Jets, III (11-116)
9.6 Marcus Allen, L.A. Raiders vs. Washington, XVIII (20-191)
9.3 Willie Parker, Pittsburgh vs. Seattle, XL (10-93)

TOUCHDOWNS

Most Touchdowns, Career

5 Emmitt Smith, Dallas, 3 games
4 Franco Harris, Pittsburgh, 4 games
Thurman Thomas, Buffalo, 4 games
John Elway, Denver, 5 games
3 Terrell Davis, Denver, 2 games

Most Touchdowns, Game

3 Terrell Davis, Denver vs. Green Bay, XXXII
2 Elijah Pitts, Green Bay vs. Kansas City, I
Larry Csonka, Miami vs. Minnesota, VIII
Pete Banaszak, Oakland vs. Minnesota, XI
Franco Harris, Pittsburgh vs. Los Angeles, XIV
Marcus Allen, L.A. Raiders vs. Washington, XVIII
Jim McMahon, Chicago vs. New England, XX

Timmy Smith, Washington vs. Denver, XXII
Tom Rathman, San Francisco vs. Denver, XXIV
Gerald Riggs, Washington vs. Buffalo, XXVI
Emmitt Smith, Dallas vs. Buffalo, XXVIII
Emmitt Smith, Dallas vs. Pittsburgh, XXX
Howard Griffith, Denver vs. Atlanta, XXXIII
Eddie George, Tennessee vs. St. Louis, XXXIV

PASSING

PASSER RATING

Highest Passer Rating, Career (40 attempts)
127.8 Joe Montana, San Francisco, 4 games
122.8 Jim Plunkett, Oakland-L.A. Raiders, 2 games
112.8 Terry Bradshaw, Pittsburgh, 4 games

ATTEMPTS

Most Passes Attempted, Career
156 Tom Brady, New England, 4 games
152 John Elway, Denver, 5 games
145 Jim Kelly, Buffalo, 4 games

Most Passes Attempted, Game
58 Jim Kelly, Buffalo vs. Washington, XXVI
51 Donovan McNabb, Philadelphia vs. New England, XXXIX
50 Dan Marino, Miami vs. San Francisco, XIX
Jim Kelly, Buffalo vs. Dallas, XXVIII

COMPLETIONS

Most Passes Completed, Career
100 Tom Brady, New England, 4 games
83 Joe Montana, San Francisco, 4 games
Kurt Warner, St. Louis-Arizona, 3 games
81 Jim Kelly, Buffalo, 4 games

Most Passes Completed, Game
32 Tom Brady, New England vs. Carolina, XXXVIII
Drew Brees, New Orleans vs. Indianapolis, XLIV
31 Jim Kelly, Buffalo vs. Dallas, XXVIII
Kurt Warner, Arizona vs. Pittsburgh, XLIII
Peyton Manning, Indianapolis vs. New Orleans, XLIV
30 Donovan McNabb, Philadelphia vs. New England, XXXIX

Most Consecutive Completions, Game
13 Joe Montana, San Francisco vs. Denver, XXIV
10 Phil Simms, N.Y. Giants vs. Denver, XXI
Troy Aikman, Dallas vs. Pittsburgh, XXX
Kurt Warner, Arizona vs. Pittsburgh, XLIII
Drew Brees, New Orleans vs. Indianapolis, XLIV
9 Jim Kelly, Buffalo vs. Dallas, XXVIII
Neil O'Donnell, Pittsburgh vs. Dallas, XXX
Steve McNair, Tennessee vs. St. Louis, XXXIV
Peyton Manning, Indianapolis vs. Chicago, XLI

COMPLETION PERCENTAGE

Highest Completion Percentage, Career (40 attempts)
70.0 Troy Aikman, Dallas, 3 games, (80-56)
68.0 Joe Montana, San Francisco, 4 games (122-83)
67.5 Peyton Manning, Indianapolis, 2 games (83-56)

Highest Completion Percentage, Game (20 attempts)
88.0 Phil Simms, N.Y. Giants vs. Denver, XXI (25-22)
82.1 Drew Brees, New Orleans vs. Indianapolis, XLIV (39-32)
75.9 Joe Montana, San Francisco vs. Denver, XXIV (29-22)

YARDS GAINED

Most Yards Gained, Career
1,156 Kurt Warner, St. Louis-Arizona, 3 games
1,142 Joe Montana, San Francisco, 4 games
1,128 John Elway, Denver, 5 games

Most Yards Gained, Game
414 Kurt Warner, St. Louis vs. Tennessee, XXXIV
377 Kurt Warner, Arizona vs. Pittsburgh, XLIII
365 Kurt Warner, St. Louis vs. New England, XXXVI

Longest Pass Completion
85 Jake Delhomme (to Muhammad), Carolina vs. New England, XXXVIII (TD)
81 Brett Favre (to Freeman), Green Bay vs. New England, XXXI (TD)
80 Jim Plunkett (to King), Oakland vs. Philadelphia, XV (TD)
Doug Williams (to Sanders), Washington vs. Denver, XXII (TD)
John Elway (to R. Smith), Denver vs. Atlanta, XXXIII (TD)

AVERAGE GAIN

Highest Average Gain, Career (40 attempts)
11.10 Terry Bradshaw, Pittsburgh, 4 games (84-932)
9.62 Bart Starr, Green Bay, 2 games (47-452)
9.41 Jim Plunkett, Oakland-L.A. Raiders, 2 games (46-433)

Highest Average Gain, Game (20 attempts)
14.71 Terry Bradshaw, Pittsburgh vs. Los Angeles, XIV (21-309)
12.80 Jim McMahon, Chicago vs. New England, XX (20-256)
12.43 Jim Plunkett, Oakland vs. Philadelphia, XV (21-261)

TOUCHDOWNS

Most Touchdown Passes, Career
11 Joe Montana, San Francisco, 4 games
9 Terry Bradshaw, Pittsburgh, 4 games
8 Roger Staubach, Dallas, 4 games

Most Touchdown Passes, Game
6 Steve Young, San Francisco vs. San Diego, XXIX
5 Joe Montana, San Francisco vs. Denver, XXIV
4 Terry Bradshaw, Pittsburgh vs. Dallas, XIII
Doug Williams, Washington vs. Denver, XXII
Troy Aikman, Dallas vs. Buffalo, XXVII

HAD INTERCEPTED

Lowest Percentage, Passes Had Intercepted, Career (40 attempts)
0.00 Jim Plunkett, Oakland-L.A. Raiders, 2 games (46-0)
Joe Montana, San Francisco, 4 games (122-0)
0.64 Tom Brady, New England, 4 games (156-1)
1.25 Troy Aikman, Dallas, 3 games (80-1)

Most Attempts, Without Interception, Game
48 Tom Brady, New England vs. N.Y. Giants, XLII
45 Kurt Warner, St. Louis vs. Tennessee, XXXIV
39 Drew Brees, New Orleans vs. Indianapolis, XLIV

Most Passes Had Intercepted, Career
8 John Elway, Denver, 5 games
7 Craig Morton, Dallas-Denver, 2 games
Jim Kelly, Buffalo, 4 games
6 Fran Tarkenton, Minnesota, 3 games

Most Passes Had Intercepted, Game
5 Rich Gannon, Oakland vs. Tampa Bay, XXXVII
4 Craig Morton, Denver vs. Dallas, XII
Jim Kelly, Buffalo vs. Washington, XXVI
Drew Bledsoe, New England vs. Green Bay, XXXI
Kerry Collins, N.Y. Giants vs. Baltimore, XXXV
3 By 11 players

PASS RECEIVING

RECEPTIONS

Most Receptions, Career
33 Jerry Rice, San Francisco-Oakland, 4 games
27 Andre Reed, Buffalo, 4 games
21 Deion Branch, New England, 2 games

Most Receptions, Game
11 Dan Ross, Cincinnati vs. San Francisco, XVI
Jerry Rice, San Francisco vs. Cincinnati, XXIII
Deion Branch, New England vs. Philadelphia, XXXIX

Wes Welker, New England vs. N.Y. Giants, XLII
10 Tony Nathan, Miami vs. San Francisco, XIX
Jerry Rice, San Francisco vs. San Diego, XXIX
Andre Hastings, Pittsburgh vs. Dallas, XXX
Deion Branch, New England vs. Carolina, XXXVIII
Joseph Addai, Indianapolis vs. Chicago, XLI
9 Ricky Sanders, Washington vs. Denver, XXII
Antonio Freeman, Green Bay vs. Denver, XXXII
Terrell Owens, Philadelphia vs. New England, XXXIX
Santonio Holmes, Pittsburgh vs. Arizona, XLIII

YARDS GAINED

Most Yards Gained, Career

589 Jerry Rice, San Francisco-Oakland, 4 games
364 Lynn Swann, Pittsburgh, 4 games
323 Andre Reed, Buffalo, 4 games

Most Yards Gained, Game

215 Jerry Rice, San Francisco vs. Cincinnati, XXIII
193 Ricky Sanders, Washington vs. Denver, XXII
162 Isaac Bruce, St. Louis vs. Tennessee, XXXIV

Longest Reception

85 Muhsin Muhammad (from Delhomme), Carolina vs. New England, XXXVIII
81 Antonio Freeman (from Favre), Green Bay vs. New England, XXXI (TD)
80 Kenny King (from Plunkett), Oakland vs. Philadelphia, XV (TD)
Ricky Sanders (from Williams), Washington vs. Denver, XXII (TD)
Rod Smith (from Elway), Denver vs. Atlanta, XXXIII

AVERAGE GAIN

Highest Average Gain, Career (8 receptions)

24.4 John Stallworth, Pittsburgh, 4 games (11-268)
23.4 Ricky Sanders, Washington, 2 games (10-234)
22.8 Lynn Swann, Pittsburgh, 4 games (16-364)

Highest Average Gain, Game (3 receptions)

40.33 John Stallworth, Pittsburgh vs. Los Angeles, XIV (3-121)
40.25 Lynn Swann, Pittsburgh vs. Dallas, X (4-161)
38.33 John Stallworth, Pittsburgh vs. Dallas, XIII (3-115)

TOUCHDOWNS

Most Touchdowns, Career

8 Jerry Rice, San Francisco-Oakland, 4 games
3 John Stallworth, Pittsburgh, 4 games
Lynn Swann, Pittsburgh, 4 games
Cliff Branch, Oakland-L.A. Raiders, 3 games
Antonio Freeman, Green Bay, 2 games
2 Max McGee, Green Bay, 2 games
Bill Miller, Oakland, 1 game
Butch Johnson, Dallas, 2 games
Dan Ross, Cincinnati, 1 game
Roger Craig, San Francisco, 3 games
Ricky Sanders, Washington, 2 games
John Taylor, San Francisco, 3 games
Gary Clark, Washington, 2 games
Don Beebe, Buffalo-Green Bay, 4 games
Michael Irvin, Dallas, 3 games
Ricky Watters, San Francisco, 1 game
Jay Novacek, Dallas, 3 games
Keenan McCardell, Tampa Bay, 1 game
Ricky Proehl, St. Louis-Carolina, 3 games
David Givens, New England, 2 games
Mike Vrabel, New England, 4 games
Muhsin Muhammad, Carolina-Chicago, 2 games
Larry Fitzgerald, Arizona, 1 game

Most Touchdowns, Game

3 Jerry Rice, San Francisco vs. Denver, XXIV; vs. San Diego, XXIX
2 Max McGee, Green Bay vs. Kansas City, I
Bill Miller, Oakland vs. Green Bay, II
John Stallworth, Pittsburgh vs. Dallas, XIII
Cliff Branch, Oakland vs. Philadelphia, XV
Dan Ross, Cincinnati vs. San Francisco, XVI
Roger Craig, San Francisco vs. Miami, XIX
Ricky Sanders, Washington vs. Denver, XXII
Michael Irvin, Dallas vs. Buffalo, XXVII
Ricky Watters, San Francisco vs. San Diego, XXIX
Antonio Freeman, Green Bay vs. Denver, XXXII
Keenan McCardell, Tampa Bay vs. Oakland, XXXVII
Larry Fitzgerald, Arizona vs. Pittsburgh, XLIII

INTERCEPTIONS BY

Most Interceptions By, Career

3 Chuck Howley, Dallas, 2 games
Rod Martin, Oakland-L.A. Raiders, 2 games
Larry Brown, Dallas, 3 games
2 Randy Beverly, N.Y. Jets, 1 game
Jake Scott, Miami, 3 games
Mike Wagner, Pittsburgh, 3 games
Mel Blount, Pittsburgh, 4 games
Eric Wright, San Francisco, 4 games
Barry Wilburn, Washington, 1 game
Brad Edwards, Washington, 1 game
Thomas Everett, Dallas, 2 games
James Washington, Dallas, 2 games
Darrien Gordon, San Diego-Denver-Oakland, 4 games
Dexter Jackson, Tampa Bay, 1 game
Dwight Smith, Tampa Bay, 1 game
Rodney Harrison, San Diego-New England, 4 games

Most Interceptions By, Game

3 Rod Martin, Oakland vs. Philadelphia, XV
2 Randy Beverly, N.Y. Jets vs. Baltimore, III
Chuck Howley, Dallas vs. Baltimore, V
Jake Scott, Miami vs. Washington, VII
Barry Wilburn, Washington vs. Denver, XXII
Brad Edwards, Washington vs. Buffalo, XXVI
Thomas Everett, Dallas vs. Buffalo, XXVII
Larry Brown, Dallas vs. Pittsburgh, XXX
Darrien Gordon, Denver vs. Atlanta, XXXIII
Dexter Jackson, Tampa Bay vs. Oakland, XXXVII
Dwight Smith, Tampa Bay vs. Oakland, XXXVII
Rodney Harrison, New England vs. Philadelphia, XXXIX

YARDS GAINED

Most Yards Gained, Career

108 Darrien Gordon, San Diego-Denver-Oakland, 4 games
100 James Harrison, Pittsburgh, 2 games
94 Dwight Smith, Tampa Bay, 1 game

Most Yards Gained, Game

108 Darrien Gordon, Denver vs. Atlanta, XXXIII
100 James Harrison, Pittsburgh vs. Arizona, XLIII
94 Dwight Smith, Tampa Bay vs. Oakland, XXXVII

Longest Return

100 James Harrison, Pittsburgh vs. Arizona, XLIII (TD)
76 Kelly Herndon, Seattle vs. Pittsburgh, XL
75 Willie Brown, Oakland vs. Minnesota, XI (TD)

TOUCHDOWNS

Most Touchdowns, Game

2 Dwight Smith, Tampa Bay vs. Oakland, XXXVII
1 Herb Adderley, Green Bay vs. Oakland, II
Willie Brown, Oakland vs. Minnesota, XI
Jack Squirek, L.A. Raiders vs. Washington, XVIII
Reggie Phillips, Chicago vs. New England, XX
Duane Starks, Baltimore vs. N.Y. Giants, XXXV

Ty Law, New England vs. St. Louis, XXXVI
Derrick Brooks, Tampa Bay vs. Oakland, XXXVII
Kelvin Hayden, Indianapolis vs. Chicago, XLI
James Harrison, Pittsburgh vs. Arizona, XLIII
Tracy Porter, New Orleans vs. Indianapolis, XLIV

PUNTING

Most Punts, Career
17 Mike Eischeid, Oakland-Minnesota, 3 games
Mike Horan, Denver-St. Louis, 4 games
16 Brad Maynard, N.Y. Giants-Chicago, 2 games
15 Larry Seiple, Miami, 3 games

Most Punts, Game
11 Brad Maynard, N.Y. Giants vs. Baltimore, XXXV
10 Kyle Richardson, Baltimore vs. N.Y. Giants, XXXV
9 Ron Widby, Dallas vs. Baltimore, V

Longest Punt
63 Lee Johnson, Cincinnati vs. San Francisco, XXIII
62 Rich Camarillo, New England vs. Chicago, XX
61 Jerrel Wilson, Kansas City vs. Green Bay, I

AVERAGE YARDAGE

Highest Average, Punting, Career (10 punts)
46.5 Jerrel Wilson, Kansas City, 2 games (11-511)
43.8 Tom Rouen, Denver-Seattle, 3 games (11-482)
43.0 Kyle Richardson, Baltimore, 1 game (10-430)
Tom Tupa, New England-Tampa Bay, 2 games (12-516)

Highest Average, Punting, Game (4 punts)
50.2 Tom Rouen, Seattle vs. Pittsburgh, XL (6-301)
48.8 Bryan Wagner, San Diego vs. San Francisco, XXIX (4-195)
48.7 Chris Gardocki, Pittsburgh vs. Seattle, XL (6-292)

PUNT RETURNS

Most Punt Returns, Career
8 Troy Brown, New England, 3 games
6 Willie Wood, Green Bay, 2 games
Jake Scott, Miami, 3 games
Theo Bell, Pittsburgh, 2 games
Mike Nelms, Washington, 1 game
John Taylor, San Francisco, 3 games
Desmond Howard, Green Bay, 1 game
David Meggett, N.Y. Giants-New England, 2 games
Darrien Gordon, San Diego-Denver-Oakland, 4 games
5 Dana McLemore, San Francisco, 1 game

Most Punt Returns, Game
6 Mike Nelms, Washington vs. Miami, XVII
Desmond Howard, Green Bay vs. New England, XXXI
5 Willie Wood, Green Bay vs. Oakland, II
Dana McLemore, San Francisco vs. Miami, XIX
4 By nine players

Most Fair Catches, Game
4 Jermaine Lewis, Baltimore vs. N.Y. Giants, XXXV
Karl Williams, Tampa Bay vs. Oakland, XXXVII
3 Ron Gardin, Baltimore vs. Dallas, V
Golden Richards, Dallas vs. Pittsburgh, X
Greg Pruitt, L.A. Raiders vs. Washington, XVIII
Al Edwards, Buffalo vs. N.Y. Giants, XXV
David Meggett, N.Y. Giants vs. Buffalo, XXV

YARDS GAINED

Most Yards Gained, Career
94 John Taylor, San Francisco, 3 games
90 Desmond Howard, Green Bay, 1 game
67 David Meggett, N.Y. Giants-New England, 2 games

Most Yards Gained, Game
90 Desmond Howard, Green Bay vs. New England, XXXI
56 John Taylor, San Francisco vs. Cincinnati, XXIII
52 Mike Nelms, Washington vs. Miami, XXII

Longest Return
45 John Taylor, San Francisco vs. Cincinnati, XXIII
34 Darrell Green, Washington vs. L.A. Raiders, XVIII
Desmond Howard, Green Bay vs. New England, XXXI
Jermaine Lewis, Baltimore vs. N.Y. Giants, XXXV
Steve Breaston, Arizona vs. Pittsburgh, XLIII
32 Desmond Howard, Green Bay vs. New England, XXXI

AVERAGE YARDAGE

Highest Average, Career (4 returns)
15.7 John Taylor, San Francisco, 3 games (6-94)
15.0 Desmond Howard, Green Bay, 1 game (6-90)
11.2 David Meggett, N.Y. Giants-New England, 2 games (6-67)

Highest Average, Game (3 returns)
18.7 John Taylor, San Francisco vs. Cincinnati, XXIII (3-56)
15.0 Desmond Howard, Green Bay vs. New England, XXXI (6-90)
14.0 Terrence Wilkins, Indianapolis vs. Chicago, XLI (3-42)

TOUCHDOWNS

Most Touchdowns, Game
None

KICKOFF RETURNS

Most Kickoff Returns, Career
10 Ken Bell, Denver, 3 games
8 Larry Anderson, Pittsburgh, 2 games
Fulton Walker, Miami, 2 games
Andre Coleman, San Diego, 1 game
Marcus Knight, Oakland, 1 game
7 Preston Pearson, Baltimore-Pittsburgh-Dallas, 5 games
Stephen Starring, New England, 1 game
David Meggett, N.Y. Giants-New England, 2 games

Most Kickoff Returns, Game
8 Andre Coleman, San Diego vs. San Francisco, XXIX
Marcus Knight, Oakland vs. Tampa Bay, XXXVII
7 Stephen Starring, New England vs. Chicago, XX
6 Darren Carrington, Denver vs. San Francisco, XXIV
Antonio Freeman, Green Bay vs. Denver, XXXII
Ron Dixon, N.Y. Giants vs. Baltimore, XXXV

YARDS GAINED

Most Yards Gained, Career
283 Fulton Walker, Miami, 2 games
244 Andre Coleman, San Diego, 1 game
210 Tim Dwight, Atlanta, 1 game

Most Yards Gained, Game
244 Andre Coleman, San Diego vs. San Francisco, XXIX
210 Tim Dwight, Atlanta vs. Denver, XXXIII
190 Fulton Walker, Miami vs. Washington, XVII

Longest Return
99 Desmond Howard, Green Bay vs. New England, XXXI (TD)
98 Fulton Walker, Miami vs. Washington, XVII (TD)
Andre Coleman, San Diego vs. San Francisco, XXIX (TD)
97 Ron Dixon, N.Y. Giants vs. Baltimore, XXXV (TD)

AVERAGE YARDAGE

Highest Average, Career (4 returns)
42.0 Tim Dwight, Atlanta, 1 game (5-210)
38.5 Desmond Howard, Green Bay, 1 game (4-154)
35.4 Fulton Walker, Miami, 2 games (8-283)

Highest Average, Game (3 returns)
47.5 Fulton Walker, Miami vs. Washington, XVII (4-190)
42.0 Tim Dwight, Atlanta vs. Denver, XXXIII (5-210)
38.5 Desmond Howard, Green Bay vs. New England, XXXI (4-154)

SUPER BOWL RECORDS

TOUCHDOWNS
Most Touchdowns, Game

1 Fulton Walker, Miami vs. Washington, XVII
Stanford Jennings, Cincinnati vs. San Francisco, XXIII
Andre Coleman, San Diego vs. San Francisco, XXIX
Desmond Howard, Green Bay vs. New England, XXXI
Tim Dwight, Atlanta vs. Denver, XXXIII
Ron Dixon, N.Y. Giants vs. Baltimore, XXXV
Jermaine Lewis, Baltimore vs. N.Y. Giants, XXXV
Devin Hester, Chicago vs. Indianapolis, XLI

FUMBLES
Most Fumbles, Career

5 Roger Staubach, Dallas, 4 games
4 Jim Kelly, Buffalo, 4 games
Kurt Warner, St. Louis-Arizona, 3 games
3 Franco Harris, Pittsburgh, 4 games
Terry Bradshaw, Pittsburgh, 4 games
John Elway, Denver, 5 games
Frank Reich, Buffalo, 4 games
Thurman Thomas, Buffalo, 4 games

Most Fumbles, Game

3 Roger Staubach, Dallas vs. Pittsburgh, X
Jim Kelly, Buffalo vs. Washington, XXVI
Frank Reich, Buffalo vs. Dallas, XXVII
2 Franco Harris, Pittsburgh vs. Minnesota, IX
Butch Johnson, Dallas vs. Denver, XII
Terry Bradshaw, Pittsburgh vs. Dallas, XIII
Joe Montana, San Francisco vs. Cincinnati, XXIII
John Elway, Denver vs. San Francisco, XXIV
Thurman Thomas, Buffalo vs. Dallas, XXVIII
Rex Grossman, Chicago vs. Indianapolis, XLI
Eli Manning, N.Y. Giants vs. New England, XLII
Kurt Warner, Arizona vs. Pittsburgh, XLIII

RECOVERIES
Most Fumbles Recovered, Career

2 Jake Scott, Miami, 3 games (1 own, 1 opp)
Fran Tarkenton, Minnesota, 3 games (2 own)
Franco Harris, Pittsburgh, 4 games (2 own)
Roger Staubach, Dallas, 4 games (2 own)
Bobby Walden, Pittsburgh, 2 games (2 own)
John Fitzgerald, Dallas, 4 games (2 own)
Randy Hughes, Dallas, 3 games (2 opp)
Butch Johnson, Dallas, 2 games (2 own)
Mike Singletary, Chicago, 1 game (2 opp)
John Elway, Denver, 5 games (2 own)
Jimmie Jones, Dallas, 2 games (2 opp)
Kenneth Davis, Buffalo, 4 games (2 own)
Kurt Warner, St. Louis-Arizona, 3 games (2 own)

Most Fumbles Recovered, Game

2 Jake Scott, Miami vs. Minnesota, VIII (1 own, 1 opp)
Roger Staubach, Dallas vs. Pittsburgh, X (2 own)
Randy Hughes, Dallas vs. Denver, XII (2 opp)
Butch Johnson, Dallas vs. Denver, XII (2 own)
Mike Singletary, Chicago vs. New England, XX (2 opp)
Jimmie Jones, Dallas vs. Buffalo, XXVII (2 opp)

YARDS GAINED
Most Yards Gained, Game

64 Leon Lett, Dallas vs. Buffalo, XXVII (opp)
49 Mike Bass, Washington vs. Miami, VII (opp)
46 James Washington, Dallas vs. Buffalo, XXVIII (opp)

Longest Return

64 Leon Lett, Dallas vs. Buffalo, XXVII
49 Mike Bass, Washington vs. Miami, VII (TD)
46 James Washington, Dallas vs. Buffalo, XXVIII (TD)

TOUCHDOWNS
Most Touchdowns, Game

1 Mike Bass, Washington vs. Miami, VII (opp 49 yds)
Mike Hegman, Dallas vs. Pittsburgh, XIII (opp 37 yds)
Jimmie Jones, Dallas vs. Buffalo, XXVII (opp 2 yds)
Ken Norton, Dallas vs. Buffalo, XXVII (opp 9 yds)
James Washington, Dallas vs. Buffalo, XXVIII (opp 46 yds)

COMBINED NET YARDS GAINED
(Rushing, receiving, interception returns, punt returns, kickoff returns, and fumble returns)

ATTEMPTS
Most Attempts, Career

108 Franco Harris, Pittsburgh, 4 games
81 Emmitt Smith, Dallas, 3 games
72 Roger Craig, San Francisco, 3 games
Thurman Thomas, Buffalo, 4 games

Most Attempts, Game

39 John Riggins, Washington vs. Miami, XVII
35 Franco Harris, Pittsburgh vs. Minnesota, IX
34 Matt Snell, N.Y. Jets vs. Baltimore, III
Emmitt Smith, Dallas vs. Buffalo, XXVIII

YARDS GAINED
Most Yards Gained, Career

604 Jerry Rice, San Francisco-Oakland, 4 games
468 Franco Harris, Pittsburgh, 4 games
410 Roger Craig, San Francisco, 3 games

Most Yards Gained, Game

244 Andre Coleman, San Diego vs. San Francisco, XXIX
Desmond Howard, Green Bay vs. New England, XXXI
235 Ricky Sanders, Washington vs. Denver, XXII
230 Antonio Freeman, Green Bay vs. Denver, XXXII

SACKS
Sacks have been compiled since XVII.

Most Sacks, Career

4.5 Charles Haley, San Francisco-Dallas, 5 games
3.0 Danny Stubbs, San Francisco, 2 games
Leonard Marshall, N.Y. Giants, 2 games
Jeff Wright, Buffalo, 4 games
Reggie White, Green Bay, 2 games
Willie McGinest, New England, 4 games
Tedy Bruschi, New England, 5 games
Mike Vrabel, New England, 4 games
Darnell Dockett, Arizona, 1 game
2.5 Dexter Manley, Washington, 3 games
Michael Strahan, N.Y. Giants, 2 games

Most Sacks, Game

3.0 Reggie White, Green Bay vs. New England, XXXI
Darnell Dockett, Arizona vs. Pittsburgh, XLIII
2.0 Dwaine Board, San Francisco vs. Miami, XIX
Dennis Owens, New England vs. Chicago, XX
Otis Wilson, Chicago vs. New England, XX
Leonard Marshall, N.Y. Giants vs. Denver, XXI
Alvin Walton, Washington vs. Denver, XXII
Charles Haley, San Francisco vs. Cincinnati, XXIII
Danny Stubbs, San Francisco vs. Denver, XXIV
Jeff Wright, Buffalo vs. Dallas, XXVIII
Raylee Johnson, San Diego vs. San Francisco, XXIX
Chad Hennings, Dallas vs. Pittsburgh, XXX
Tedy Bruschi, New England vs. Green Bay, XXXI
Michael McCrary, Baltimore vs. N.Y. Giants, XXXV
Simeon Rice, Tampa Bay vs. Oakland, XXXVII
Mike Vrabel, New England vs. Carolina, XXXVIII
Adalius Thomas, New England vs. N.Y. Giants, XLII
Justin Tuck, N.Y. Giants vs. New England, XLII
LaMarr Woodley, Pittsburgh vs. Arizona, XLIII

TEAM RECORDS

GAMES, VICTORIES, DEFEATS

Most Games
8 Dallas, V-VI, X, XII-XIII, XXVII-XXVIII, XXX
7 Pittsburgh, IX-X, XIII-XIV, XXX, XL, XLIII
6 Denver, XII, XXI-XXII, XXIV, XXXII-XXXIII
New England, XX, XXXI, XXXVI, XXXVIII-XXXIX, XLII

Most Consecutive Games
4 Buffalo, XXV-XXVIII
3 Miami, VI-VIII
2 Green Bay, I-II; XXXI-XXXII
Dallas, V-VI; XII-XIII; XXVII-XXVIII
Minnesota, VIII-IX
Pittsburgh, IX-X; XIII-XIV
Washington, XVII-XVIII
Denver, XXI-XXII; XXXII-XXXIII
San Francisco, XXIII-XXIV
New England, XXXVIII-XXXIX

Most Games Won
6 Pittsburgh, IX-X, XIII-XIV, XL, XLIII
5 San Francisco, XVI, XIX, XXIII-XXIV, XXIX
Dallas, VI, XII, XXVII-XXVIII, XXX
3 Oakland/L.A. Raiders, XI, XV, XVIII
Washington, XVII, XXII, XXVI
Green Bay, I-II, XXXI
New England, XXXVI, XXXVIII-XXXIX
N.Y. Giants, XXI, XXV, XLII

Most Consecutive Games Won
2 Green Bay, I-II
Miami, VII-VIII
Pittsburgh, IX-X, XIII-XIV
San Francisco, XXIII-XXIV
Dallas, XXVII-XXVIII
Denver, XXXII-XXXIII
New England, XXXVIII-XXXIX

Most Games Lost
4 Minnesota, IV, VIII-IX, XI
Denver, XII, XXI-XXII, XXIV
Buffalo, XXV-XXVIII
3 Dallas, V, X, XIII
Miami, VI, XVII, XIX
New England, XX, XXXI, XLII
2 Washington, VII, XVIII
Cincinnati, XVI, XXII
L.A./St. Louis Rams, XIV, XXXVI
Oakland/L.A. Raiders, II, XXXVII
Philadelphia, XV, XXXIX
Baltimore/Indianapolis, III, XLIV

Most Consecutive Games Lost
4 Buffalo, XXV-XXVIII
2 Minnesota, VIII-IX
Denver, XXI-XXII

SCORING

Most Points, Game
55 San Francisco vs. Denver, XXIV
52 Dallas vs. Buffalo, XXVII
49 San Francisco vs. San Diego, XXIX

Fewest Points, Game
3 Miami vs. Dallas, VI
6 Minnesota vs. Pittsburgh, IX
7 By five teams

Most Points, Both Teams, Game
75 San Francisco (49) vs. San Diego (26), XXIX
69 Dallas (52) vs. Buffalo (17), XXVII
Tampa Bay (48) vs. Oakland (21), XXXVII
66 Pittsburgh (35) vs. Dallas (31), XIII

Fewest Points, Both Teams, Game
21 Washington (7) vs. Miami (14), VII
22 Minnesota (6) vs. Pittsburgh (16), IX
23 Baltimore (7) vs. N.Y. Jets (16), III

Largest Margin of Victory, Game
45 San Francisco vs. Denver, XXIV (55-10)
36 Chicago vs. New England, XX (46-10)
35 Dallas vs. Buffalo, XXVII (52-17)

Most Points, Each Half
1st: 35 Washington vs. Denver, XXII
2nd: 30 N.Y. Giants vs. Denver, XXI

Most Points, Each Quarter
1st: 14 Miami vs. Minnesota, VIII
Oakland vs. Philadelphia, XV
Dallas vs. Buffalo, XXVII
San Francisco vs. San Diego, XXIX
New England vs. Green Bay, XXXI
Chicago vs. Indianapolis, XLI
2nd: 35 Washington vs. Denver, XXII
3rd: 21 Chicago vs. New England, XX
4th: 21 Dallas vs. Buffalo, XXVII

Most Points, Both Teams, Each Half
1st: 45 Washington (35) vs. Denver (10), XXII
2nd: 46 Tampa Bay (28) vs. Oakland (18), XXXVII

Fewest Points, Both Teams, Each Half
1st: 2 Minnesota (0) vs. Pittsburgh (2), IX
2nd: 7 Miami (0) vs. Washington (7), VII
Denver (0) vs. Washington (7), XXII

Most Points, Both Teams, Each Quarter
1st: 24 New England (14) vs. Green Bay (10), XXXI
2nd: 35 Washington (35) vs. Denver (0), XXII
3rd: 24 Washington (14) vs. Buffalo (10), XXVI
4th: 37 Carolina (19) vs. New England (18), XXXVIII

TOUCHDOWNS

Most Touchdowns, Game
8 San Francisco vs. Denver, XXIV
7 Dallas vs. Buffalo, XXVII
San Francisco vs. San Diego, XXIX
6 Washington vs. Denver, XXII
Tampa Bay vs. Oakland, XXXVII

Fewest Touchdowns, Game
0 Miami vs. Dallas, VI
1 By 19 teams

Most Touchdowns, Both Teams, Game
10 San Francisco (7) vs. San Diego (3), XXIX
9 Pittsburgh (5) vs. Dallas (4), XIII
San Francisco (8) vs. Denver (1), XXIV
Dallas (7) vs. Buffalo (2), XXVII
Tampa Bay (6) vs. Oakland (3), XXXVII
8 Carolina (4) vs. New England (4), XXXVIII

Fewest Touchdowns, Both Teams, Game
2 Baltimore (1) vs. N.Y. Jets (1), III
3 In six games

POINTS AFTER TOUCHDOWN

Most (One-Point) Points After Touchdown, Game
7 San Francisco vs. Denver, XXIV
Dallas vs. Buffalo, XXVII
San Francisco vs. San Diego, XXIX
6 Washington vs. Denver, XXII
Tampa Bay vs. Oakland, XXXVII
5 Green Bay vs. Kansas City, I
Pittsburgh vs. Dallas, XIII
L.A. Raiders vs. Washington, XVIII
San Francisco vs. Miami, XIX
Chicago vs. New England, XX

Most (One-Point) Points After Touchdown, Both Teams, Game
9 Pittsburgh (5) vs. Dallas (4), XIII
Dallas (7) vs. Buffalo (2), XXVII
8 San Francisco (7) vs. Denver (1), XXIV
San Francisco (7) vs. San Diego (1), XXIX

7 Washington (6) vs. Denver (1), XXII
Washington (4) vs. Buffalo (3), XXVI
Denver (4) vs. Green Bay (3), XXXII

Fewest (One-Point) Points After Touchdown, Both Teams, Game
2 Baltimore (1) vs. N.Y. Jets (1), III
Baltimore (1) vs. Dallas (1), V
Minnesota (0) vs. Pittsburgh (2), IX

Most Two-Point Conversions, Game
2 San Diego vs. San Francisco, XXIX

Most Two-Point Conversions, Both Teams, Game
2 San Diego (2) vs. San Francisco (0), XXIX

FIELD GOALS

Most Field Goals Attempted, Game
5 N.Y. Jets vs. Baltimore, III
Dallas vs. Denver, XII
4 Green Bay vs. Oakland, II
Pittsburgh vs. Dallas, XX
San Francisco vs. Cincinnati, XVI; XXIII
Denver vs. N.Y. Giants, XXI
Denver vs. Atlanta, XXXIII
St. Louis vs. Tennessee, XXXIV
Indianapolis vs. Chicago, XLI

Most Field Goals Attempted, Both Teams, Game
7 N.Y. Jets (5) vs. Baltimore (2), III
San Francisco (4) vs. Cincinnati (3), XXIII
St. Louis (4) vs. Tennessee (3), XXXIV
Denver (4) vs. Atlanta (3), XXXIII
6 Dallas (5) vs. Denver (1), XII
5 Green Bay (4) vs. Oakland (1), II
Pittsburgh (4) vs. Dallas (1), X
Oakland (3) vs. Philadelphia (2), XV
Denver (4) vs. N.Y. Giants (1), XXI
Dallas (3) vs. Buffalo (2), XXVIII
Indianapolis (4) vs. Chicago (1), XLI
New Orleans (3) vs. Indianapolis (2), XLIV

Fewest Field Goals Attempted, Both Teams, Game
1 Minnesota (0) vs. Miami (1), VIII
San Francisco (0) vs. Denver (1), XXIV
Philadelphia (0) vs. New England (1), XXXIX
New England (0) vs. N.Y. Giants (1), XLII
2 Green Bay (0) vs. Kansas City (2), I
Miami (1) vs. Washington (1), VII
Minnesota (1) vs. Pittsburgh (1), IX
Dallas (1) vs. Pittsburgh (1), XIII
Dallas (1) vs. Buffalo (1), XXVII
San Diego (1) vs. San Francisco (1), XXIX
Denver (1) vs. Green Bay (1), XXXII
Arizona (0) vs. Pittsburgh (2), XLIII

Most Field Goals, Game
4 Green Bay vs. Oakland, II
San Francisco vs. Cincinnati, XVI
3 N.Y. Jets vs. Baltimore, III
Kansas City vs. Minnesota, IV
Miami vs. San Francisco, XIX
Chicago vs. New England, XX
Cincinnati vs. San Francisco, XXIII
Washington vs. Buffalo, XXVI
Dallas vs. Buffalo, XXVIII
St. Louis vs. Tennessee, XXXIV
Indianapolis vs. Chicago, XLI
New Orleans vs. Indianapolis, XLIV

Most Field Goals, Both Teams, Game
5 Cincinnati (3) vs. San Francisco (2), XXIII
Dallas (3) vs. Buffalo (2), XXVIII
4 Green Bay (4) vs. Oakland (0), II
San Francisco (4) vs. Cincinnati (0), XVI
Miami (3) vs. San Francisco (1), XIX
Chicago (3) vs. New England (1), XX
Washington (3) vs. Buffalo (1), XXVI
Atlanta (2) vs. Denver (2), XXXIII
St. Louis (3) vs. Tennessee (1), XXXIV
Indianapolis (3) vs. Chicago (1), XLI
New Orleans (3) vs. Indianapolis (1), XLIV
3 In 13 games

Fewest Field Goals, Both Teams, Game
0 Miami vs. Washington, VII
Pittsburgh vs. Minnesota, IX
1 Green Bay (0) vs. Kansas City (1), I
Minnesota (0) vs. Miami (1), VIII
Pittsburgh (0) vs. Dallas (1), XIII
Washington (0) vs. Denver (1), XXII
San Francisco (0) vs. Denver (1), XXIV
San Francisco (0) vs. San Diego (1), XXIX
Philadelphia (0) vs. New England (1), XXXIX
Pittsburgh (0) vs. Seattle (1), XLI
New England (0) vs. N.Y. Giants (1), XLII

SAFETIES

Most Safeties, Game
1 Pittsburgh vs. Minnesota, IX; vs. Dallas, X
Chicago vs. New England, XX
N.Y. Giants vs. Denver, XXI
Buffalo vs. N.Y. Giants, XXV
Arizona vs. Pittsburgh, XLIII

FIRST DOWNS

Most First Downs, Game
31 San Francisco vs. Miami, XIX
29 New England vs. Carolina, XXXVIII
28 San Francisco vs. Denver, XXIV
San Francisco vs. San Diego, XXIX

Fewest First Downs, Game
9 Minnesota vs. Pittsburgh, IX
Miami vs. Washington, XVII
10 Dallas vs. Baltimore, V
Miami vs. Dallas, VI
11 Denver vs. Dallas, XII
N.Y. Giants vs. Baltimore, XXXV
Oakland vs. Tampa Bay, XXXVII
Chicago vs. Indianapolis, XLI

Most First Downs, Both Teams, Game
50 San Francisco (31) vs. Miami (19), XIX
Tennessee (27) vs. St. Louis (23), XXXIV
49 Buffalo (25) vs. Washington (24), XXVI
48 San Francisco (28) vs. San Diego (20), XXIX

Fewest First Downs, Both Teams, Game
24 Dallas (10) vs. Baltimore (14), V
N.Y. Giants (11) vs. Baltimore (13), XXXV
26 Minnesota (9) vs. Pittsburgh (17), IX
27 Pittsburgh (13) vs. Dallas (14), X

RUSHING

Most First Downs, Rushing, Game
16 San Francisco vs. Miami, XIX
15 Dallas vs. Miami, VI
14 Washington vs. Miami, XVII
San Francisco vs. Denver, XXIV
Denver vs. Green Bay, XXXII

Fewest First Downs, Rushing, Game
1 New England vs. Chicago, XX
St. Louis vs. Tennessee, XXXIV
Oakland vs. Tampa Bay, XXXVII
2 Minnesota vs. Kansas City, IV; vs. Pittsburgh, IX; vs. Oakland, XI
Pittsburgh vs. Dallas, XIII
Miami vs. San Francisco, XIX
N.Y. Giants vs. Baltimore, XXXV
Arizona vs. Pittsburgh, XLIII
3 Miami vs. Dallas, VI

Philadelphia vs. Oakland, XV
New England vs. Green Bay, XXXI
Carolina vs. New England, XXXVIII
Chicago vs. Indianapolis, XLII
New England vs. N.Y. Giants, XLII
New Orleans vs. Indianapolis, XLIV

Most First Downs, Rushing, Both Teams, Game

21 Washington (14) vs. Miami (7), XVII
19 Washington (13) vs. Denver (6), XXII
San Francisco (14) vs. Denver (5), XXIV
18 Dallas (15) vs. Miami (3), VI
Miami (13) vs. Minnesota (5), VIII
San Francisco (16) vs. Miami (2), XIX
N.Y. Giants (10) vs. Buffalo (8), XXV
Denver (14) vs. Green Bay (4), XXXII

Fewest First Downs, Rushing, Both Teams, Game

6 Arizona (2) vs. Pittsburgh (4), XLIII
7 Oakland (1) vs. Tampa Bay (6), XXXVIII
New England (3) vs. N.Y. Giants (4), XLII
8 Baltimore (4) vs. Dallas (4), V
Pittsburgh (2) vs. Dallas (6), XIII
N.Y. Giants (2) vs. Baltimore (6), XXXV

PASSING

Most First Downs, Passing, Game

20 Arizona vs. Pittsburgh, XLIII
19 New England vs. Carolina, XXXVIII
18 Buffalo vs. Washington, XXVI
St. Louis vs. Tennessee, XXXIV
Philadelphia vs. New England, XXXIX

Fewest First Downs, Passing, Game

1 Denver vs. Dallas, XII
2 Miami vs. Washington, XVII
4 Miami vs. Minnesota, VIII

Most First Downs, Passing, Both Teams, Game

32 Miami (17) vs. San Francisco (15), XIX
Philadelphia (18) vs. New England (14), XXXIX
Arizona (20) vs. Pittsburgh (12), XLIII
Indianapolis (16) vs. New Orleans (16), XLIV
31 San Francisco (17) vs. San Diego (14), XXIX
St. Louis (18) vs. Tennessee (13), XXXIV
New England (19) vs. Carolina (12), XXXVIII
30 Buffalo (18) vs. Washington (12), XXVII
New England (17) vs. N.Y. Giants (13), XLII

Fewest First Downs, Passing, Both Teams, Game

9 Denver (1) vs. Dallas (8), XII
10 Minnesota (5) vs. Pittsburgh (5), IX
11 Dallas (5) vs. Baltimore (6), V
Miami (2) vs. Washington (9), XVII

PENALTY

Most First Downs, Penalty, Game

4 Baltimore vs. Dallas, V
Miami vs. Minnesota, VIII
Cincinnati vs. San Francisco, XVI
Buffalo vs. Dallas, XXVII
St. Louis vs. Tennessee, XXXIV
Pittsburgh vs. Arizona, XLIII
3 Kansas City vs. Minnesota, IV
Minnesota vs. Oakland, XI
Buffalo vs. Washington, XXVI
Green Bay vs. Denver, XXXII
N.Y. Giants vs. Baltimore, XXXV
St. Louis vs. New England, XXXVI
Tampa Bay vs. Oakland, XXXVII
New England vs. Carolina, XXXVIII

Most First Downs, Penalty, Both Teams, Game

6 Cincinnati (4) vs. San Francisco (2), XVI
St. Louis (4) vs. Tennessee (2), XXXIV
5 Baltimore (4) vs. Dallas (1), V
Miami (4) vs. Minnesota (1), VIII
Buffalo (3) vs. Washington (2), XXVI
Green Bay (3) vs. Denver (2), XXXII
New England (3) vs. Carolina (2), XXXVIII
Pittsburgh (4) vs. Arizona (1), XLIII
4 Kansas City (3) vs. Minnesota (1), IV
Buffalo (4) vs. Dallas (0), XXVII
N.Y. Giants (3) vs. Baltimore (1), XXXV
St. Louis (3) vs. New England (1), XXXVI
Tampa Bay (3) vs. Oakland (1), XXXVII

Fewest First Downs, Penalty, Both Teams, Game

0 Dallas vs. Miami, VI
Miami vs. Washington, VII
Dallas vs. Pittsburgh, X
Miami vs. San Francisco, XIX
Pittsburgh vs. Seattle, XL
1 Green Bay (0) vs. Kansas City (1), I
Miami (0) vs. Washington (1), XVII
Cincinnati (0) vs. San Francisco (1), XXIII
San Francisco (0) vs. Denver (1), XXIV
Dallas (0) vs. Buffalo (1), XXVIII
Dallas (0) vs. Pittsburgh (1), XXX
Denver (0) vs. Atlanta (1), XXXIII
Chicago (0) vs. Indianapolis (1), XLI

NET YARDS GAINED RUSHING AND PASSING

Most Yards Gained, Game

602 Washington vs. Denver, XXII
537 San Francisco vs. Miami, XIX
481 New England vs. Carolina, XXXVIII

Fewest Yards Gained, Game

119 Minnesota vs. Pittsburgh, IX
123 New England vs. Chicago, XX
152 N.Y. Giants vs. Baltimore, XXXV

Most Yards Gained, Both Teams, Game

929 Washington (602) vs. Denver (327), XXII
868 New England (481) vs. Carolina (387), XXXVIII
851 San Francisco (537) vs. Miami (314), XIX

Fewest Yards Gained, Both Teams, Game

396 N.Y. Giants (152) vs. Baltimore (244), XXXV
452 Minnesota (119) vs. Pittsburgh (333), IX
481 Washington (228) vs. Miami (253), VII
Denver (156) vs. Dallas (325), XII

RUSHING

ATTEMPTS

Most Attempts, Game

57 Pittsburgh vs. Minnesota, IX
53 Miami vs. Minnesota, VIII
52 Oakland vs. Minnesota, XI
Washington vs. Miami, XVII

Fewest Attempts, Game

9 Miami vs. San Francisco, XIX
11 New England vs. Chicago, XX
Oakland vs. Tampa Bay, XXXVII
12 Arizona vs. Pittsburgh, XLIII

Most Attempts, Both Teams, Game

81 Washington (52) vs. Miami (29), XVII
78 Pittsburgh (57) vs. Minnesota (21), IX
Oakland (52) vs. Minnesota (26), XI
77 Miami (53) vs. Minnesota (24), VIII
Pittsburgh (46) vs. Dallas (31), X

Fewest Attempts, Both Teams, Game

37 Arizona (12) vs. Pittsburgh (25), XLIII
New Orleans (18) vs. Indianapolis (19), XLIV
42 New England (16) vs. N.Y. Giants (26), XLII
45 Philadelphia (17) vs. New England (28), XXXIX

SUPER BOWL RECORDS

YARDS GAINED

Most Yards Gained, Game
280 Washington vs. Denver, XXII
276 Washington vs. Miami, XVII
266 Oakland vs. Minnesota, XI

Fewest Yards Gained, Game
7 New England vs. Chicago, XX
17 Minnesota vs. Pittsburgh, IX
19 Oakland vs. Tampa Bay, XXXVII

Most Yards Gained, Both Teams, Game
377 Washington (280) vs. Denver (97), XXII
372 Washington (276) vs. Miami (96), XVII
338 N.Y. Giants (172) vs. Buffalo (166), XXV

Fewest Yards Gained, Both Teams, Game
91 Arizona (33) vs. Pittsburgh (58), XLIII
136 New England (45) vs. N.Y. Giants (91), XLII
150 New Orleans (51) vs. Indianapolis (99), XLIV

AVERAGE GAIN

Highest Average Gain, Game
7.00 L.A. Raiders vs. Washington, XVIII (33-231)
Washington vs. Denver, XXII (40-280)
6.64 Buffalo vs. N.Y. Giants, XXV (25-166)
6.22 Baltimore vs. N.Y. Jets, III (23-143)

Lowest Average Gain, Game
0.64 New England vs. Chicago, XX (11-7)
0.81 Minnesota vs. Pittsburgh, IX (21-17)
1.73 Oakland vs. Tampa Bay, XXXVII (11-19)

TOUCHDOWNS

Most Touchdowns, Game
4 Chicago vs. New England, XX
Denver vs. Green Bay, XXXII
3 Green Bay vs. Kansas City, I
Miami vs. Minnesota, VIII
San Francisco vs. Denver, XXIV
Denver vs. Atlanta, XXXIII
2 Oakland vs. Minnesota, XI
Pittsburgh vs. Los Angeles, XIV
L.A. Raiders vs. Washington, XVIII
San Francisco vs. Miami, XIX
N.Y. Giants vs. Denver, XXI
Washington vs. Denver, XXII; vs. Buffalo, XXVI
Buffalo vs. N.Y. Giants, XXV
Dallas vs. Buffalo, XXVIII; vs. Pittsburgh, XXX
Tennessee vs. St. Louis, XXXIV
Pittsburgh vs. Seattle, XL

Fewest Touchdowns, Game
0 By 30 teams

Most Touchdowns, Both Teams, Game
4 Miami (3) vs. Minnesota (1), VIII
Chicago (4) vs. New England (0), XX
San Francisco (3) vs. Denver (1), XXIV
Denver (4) vs. Green Bay (0), XXXII
3 In nine games

Fewest Touchdowns, Both Teams, Game
0 Pittsburgh vs. Dallas, X
Oakland vs. Philadelphia, XV
Cincinnati vs. San Francisco, XXIII
1 In 15 games

PASSING

ATTEMPTS

Most Passes Attempted, Game
59 Buffalo vs. Washington, XXVI
55 San Diego vs. San Francisco, XXIX
51 Philadelphia vs. New England, XXXIX

Fewest Passes Attempted, Game
7 Miami vs. Minnesota, VIII
11 Miami vs. Washington, VII
14 Pittsburgh vs. Minnesota, IX

Most Passes Attempted, Both Teams, Game
93 San Diego (55) vs. San Francisco (38), XXIX
92 Buffalo (59) vs. Washington (33), XXVI
85 Miami (50) vs. San Francisco (35), XIX

Fewest Passes Attempted, Both Teams, Game
35 Miami (7) vs. Minnesota (28), VIII
39 Miami (11) vs. Washington (28), VII
40 Pittsburgh (14) vs. Minnesota (26), IX
Miami (17) vs. Washington (23), XVII

COMPLETIONS

Most Passes Completed, Game
32 New England vs. Carolina, XXXVIII
New Orleans vs. Indianapolis, XLIV
31 Buffalo vs. Dallas, XXVIII
Arizona vs. Pittsburgh, XLIII
Indianapolis vs. New Orleans, XLIV
30 Philadelphia vs. New England, XXXIX

Fewest Passes Completed, Game
4 Miami vs. Washington, XVII
6 Miami vs. Minnesota, VIII
8 Miami vs. Washington, VII
Denver vs. Dallas, XII

Most Passes Completed, Both Teams, Game
63 New Orleans (32) vs. Indianapolis (31), XLIV
53 Miami (29) vs. San Francisco (24), XIX
Philadelphia (30) vs. New England (23), XXXIX
52 San Diego (27) vs. San Francisco (25), XXIX
Arizona (31) vs. Pittsburgh (21), XLIII

Fewest Passes Completed, Both Teams, Game
19 Miami (4) vs. Washington (15), XVII
20 Pittsburgh (9) vs. Minnesota (11), IX
22 Miami (8) vs. Washington (14), VII

COMPLETION PERCENTAGE

Highest Completion Percentage, Game (20 attempts)
88.0 N.Y. Giants vs. Denver, XXI (25-22)
82.1 New Orleans vs. Indianapolis, XLIV (39-32)
75.0 San Francisco vs. Denver, XXIV (32-24)

Lowest Completion Percentage, Game (20 attempts)
32.0 Denver vs. Dallas, XII (25-8)
37.9 Denver vs. San Francisco, XXIV (29-11)
38.5 Denver vs. Washington, XXII (39-15)
N.Y. Giants vs. Baltimore, XXXV (39-15)

YARDS GAINED

Most Yards Gained, Game
407 St. Louis vs. Tennessee, XXXIV
374 Arizona vs. Pittsburgh, XLIII
354 New England vs. Carolina, XXXVIII

Fewest Yards Gained, Game
35 Denver vs. Dallas, XII
63 Miami vs. Minnesota, VIII
69 Miami vs. Washington, VII

Most Yards Gained, Both Teams, Game
649 New England (354) vs. Carolina (295), XXXVIII
615 San Francisco (326) vs. Miami (289), XIX
St. Louis (407) vs. Tennessee (208), XXXIV
614 Indianapolis (333) vs. New Orleans (281), XLIV

Fewest Yards Gained, Both Teams, Game
156 Miami (69) vs. Washington (87), VII
186 Pittsburgh (84) vs. Minnesota (102), IX
204 Miami (80) vs. Washington (124), XVII

TIMES SACKED

Most Times Sacked, Game
7 Dallas vs. Pittsburgh, X
New England vs. Chicago, XX
6 Kansas City vs. Green Bay, I

Washington vs. L.A. Raiders, XVIII
Denver vs. San Francisco, XXIV
5 Dallas vs. Denver, XII; vs. Pittsburgh, XIII
Cincinnati vs. San Francisco, XVI; XXIII
Denver vs. Washington, XXII
Buffalo vs. Washington, XXVI
Green Bay vs. New England, XXXI
New England vs. Green Bay, XXXI
Oakland vs. Tampa Bay, XXXVIII
New England vs. N.Y. Giants, XLII

Fewest Times Sacked, Game

0 Baltimore vs. N.Y. Jets, III; vs. Dallas, V
Minnesota vs. Pittsburgh, IX
Pittsburgh vs. Los Angeles, XIV
Philadelphia vs. Oakland, XV
Washington vs. Buffalo, XXVI
Denver vs. Green Bay, XXXII; vs. Atlanta, XXXIII
Tampa Bay vs. Oakland, XXXVII
New England vs. Carolina, XXXVIII
Indianapolis vs. New Orleans, XLIV
1 By 17 teams

Most Times Sacked, Both Teams, Game

10 New England (7) vs. Chicago (3), XX
Green Bay (5) vs. New England (5), XXXI
9 Kansas City (6) vs. Green Bay (3), I
Dallas (7) vs. Pittsburgh (2), X
Dallas (5) vs. Denver (4), XII
Dallas (5) vs. Pittsburgh (4), XIII
Cincinnati (5) vs. San Francisco (4), XXIII
8 Washington (6) vs. L.A. Raiders (2), XVIII
New England (5) vs. N.Y. Giants (3), XLII

Fewest Times Sacked, Both Teams, Game

1 Philadelphia (0) vs. Oakland (1), XV
Denver (0) vs. Green Bay (1), XXXII
Indianapolis (0) vs. New Orleans (1), XLIV
2 Baltimore (0) vs. N.Y. Jets (2), III
Baltimore (0) vs. Dallas (2), V
Minnesota (0) vs. Pittsburgh (2), IX
Denver (0) vs. Atlanta (2), XXXIII
Chicago (1) vs. Indianapolis (1), XLI
3 In five games

TOUCHDOWNS

Most Touchdowns, Game

6 San Francisco vs. San Diego, XXIX
5 San Francisco vs. Denver, XXIV
4 Pittsburgh vs. Dallas, XIII
Washington vs. Denver, XXII
Dallas vs. Buffalo, XXVII

Fewest Touchdowns, Game

0 By 19 teams

Most Touchdowns, Both Teams, Game

7 Pittsburgh (4) vs. Dallas (3), XIII
San Francisco (6) vs. San Diego (1), XXIX
6 Carolina (3) vs. New England (3), XXXVIII
5 Washington (4) vs. Denver (1), XXII
San Francisco (5) vs. Denver (0), XXIV
Dallas (4) vs. Buffalo (1), XXVII
Philadelphia (3) vs. New England (2), XXXIX

Fewest Touchdowns, Both Teams, Game

0 N.Y. Jets vs. Baltimore, III
Miami vs. Minnesota, VIII
Buffalo vs. Dallas, XXVIII
1 In seven games

INTERCEPTIONS BY

Most Interceptions By, Game

5 Tampa Bay vs. Oakland, XXXVII
4 N.Y. Jets vs. Baltimore, III
Dallas vs. Denver, XII
Washington vs. Buffalo, XXVI
Dallas vs. Buffalo, XXVII
Green Bay vs. New England, XXXI
Baltimore vs. N.Y. Giants, XXXV
3 By 13 teams

Most Interceptions By, Both Teams, Game

6 Baltimore (3) vs. Dallas (3), V
Tampa Bay (5) vs. Oakland (1), XXXVII
5 Washington (4) vs. Buffalo (1), XXVI
4 In 10 games

Fewest Interceptions By, Both Teams, Game

0 Buffalo vs. N.Y. Giants, XXV
St. Louis vs. Tennessee, XXXIV
1 Oakland (0) vs. Green Bay (1), II
Miami (0) vs. Dallas (1), VI
Minnesota (0) vs. Miami (1), VIII
N.Y. Giants (0) vs. Denver (1), XXI
Cincinnati (0) vs. San Francisco (1), XXIII
New England (0) vs. Carolina (1), XXXVIII
N.Y. Giants (0) vs. New England (1), XLII
Indianapolis (0) vs. New Orleans (1), XLIV

YARDS GAINED

Most Yards Gained, Game

172 Tampa Bay vs. Oakland, XXXVII
136 Denver vs. Atlanta, XXXIII
100 Pittsburgh vs. Arizona, XLIII

Most Yards Gained, Both Teams, Game

184 Tampa Bay (172) vs. Oakland (12), XXXVII
137 Denver (136) vs. Atlanta (1), XXXIII
100 Seattle (76) vs. Pittsburgh (24), XL
Indianapolis (94) vs. Chicago (6), XLI

TOUCHDOWNS

Most Touchdowns, Game

3 Tampa Bay vs. Oakland, XXXVII
1 Green Bay vs. Oakland, II
Oakland vs. Minnesota, XI
L.A. Raiders vs. Washington, XVIII
Chicago vs. New England, XX
Baltimore vs. N.Y. Giants, XXXV
New England vs. St. Louis, XXXVI
Indianapolis vs. Chicago, XLI
Pittsburgh vs. Arizona, XLIII
New Orleans vs. Indianapolis, XLIV

PUNTING

Most Punts, Game

11 N.Y. Giants vs. Baltimore, XXXV
10 Baltimore vs. N.Y. Giants, XXXV
9 Dallas vs. Baltimore, V

Fewest Punts, Game

1 Atlanta vs. Denver, XXXIII
Denver vs. Atlanta, XXXIII
2 Pittsburgh vs. Los Angeles, XIV
Denver vs. N.Y. Giants, XXI
St. Louis vs. Tennessee, XXXIV
Indianapolis vs. New Orleans, XLIV
New Orleans vs. Indianapolis, XLIV
3 By 12 teams

Most Punts, Both Teams, Game

21 N.Y. Giants (11) vs. Baltimore (10), XXXV
15 Washington (8) vs. L.A. Raiders (7), XVIII
New England (8) vs. Green Bay (7), XXXI
13 Dallas (9) vs. Baltimore (4), V
Pittsburgh (7) vs. Minnesota (6), IX

Fewest Punts, Both Teams, Game

2 Atlanta (1) vs. Denver (1), XXXIII
4 Indianapolis (2) vs. New Orleans (2), XLIV
5 Denver (2) vs. N.Y. Giants (3), XXI
St. Louis (2) vs. Tennessee (3), XXXIV

AVERAGE YARDAGE
Highest Average, Game (4 punts)
50.17 Seattle vs. Pittsburgh, XL (6-301)
48.75 San Diego vs. San Francisco, XXIX (4-195)
48.67 Pittsburgh vs. Seattle, XL (6-292)
Lowest Average, Game (4 punts)
31.00 Tampa Bay vs. Oakland, XXXVII (5-155)
31.20 Washington vs. Miami, VII (5-156)
32.38 Washington vs. L.A. Raiders, XVIII (8-259)

PUNT RETURNS
Most Punt Returns, Game
6 Washington vs. Miami, XVII
Green Bay vs. New England, XXXI
5 By seven teams
Fewest Punt Returns, Game
0 Minnesota vs. Miami, VIII
Buffalo vs. N.Y. Giants, XXV
Washington vs. Buffalo, XXVI
Denver vs. Green Bay, XXXII
Green Bay vs. Denver, XXXII
Atlanta vs. Denver, XXXIII
Denver vs. Atlanta, XXXIII
1 By 23 teams
Most Punt Returns, Both Teams, Game
10 Green Bay (6) vs. New England (4), XXXI
9 Pittsburgh (5) vs. Minnesota (4), IX
8 Green Bay (5) vs. Oakland (3), II
Baltimore (5) vs. Dallas (3), V
Washington (6) vs. Miami (2), XVII
N.Y. Giants (5) vs. Baltimore (3), XXXV
Fewest Punt Returns, Both Teams, Game
0 Denver vs. Green Bay, XXXII
Atlanta vs. Denver, XXXIII
2 Dallas (1) vs. Miami (1), VI
Denver (1) vs. N.Y. Giants (1), XXI
Buffalo (0) vs. N.Y. Giants (2), XXV
Buffalo (1) vs. Dallas (1), XXVIII
Indianapolis (1) vs. New Orleans (1), XLIV
3 Kansas City (1) vs. Minnesota (2), IV
Minnesota (0) vs. Miami (3), VIII
Washington (1) vs. Denver (2), XXII
Washington (0) vs. Buffalo (3), XXVI
Dallas (1) vs. Pittsburgh (2), XXX
Tennessee (1) vs. St. Louis (2), XXXIV

YARDS GAINED
Most Yards Gained, Game
90 Green Bay vs. New England, XXXI
56 San Francisco vs. Cincinnati, XXIII
52 Washington vs. Miami, XVII
Fewest Yards Gained, Game
–1 Dallas vs. Miami, VI
Tennessee vs. St. Louis, XXXIV
0 By 13 teams
Most Yards Gained, Both Teams, Game
120 Green Bay (90) vs. New England (30), XXXI
80 N.Y. Giants (46) vs. Baltimore (34), XXXV
74 Washington (52) vs. Miami (22), XVII
Fewest Yards Gained, Both Teams, Game
0 Denver vs. Green Bay, XXXII
Atlanta vs. Denver, XXXIII
4 Indianapolis (0) vs. New Orleans (4), XLIV
7 Tennessee (-1) vs. St. Louis (8), XXXIV

AVERAGE RETURN
Highest Average, Game (3 returns)
18.7 San Francisco vs. Cincinnati, XXIII (3-56)
15.0 Green Bay vs. New England, XXXI (6-90)
14.0 Indianapolis vs. Chicago, XLI (3-42)

TOUCHDOWNS
Most Touchdowns, Game
None

KICKOFF RETURNS
Most Kickoff Returns, Game
9 Denver vs. San Francisco, XXIV
Oakland vs. Tampa Bay, XXXVII
8 San Diego vs. San Francisco, XXIX
7 By eight teams
Fewest Kickoff Returns, Game
1 N.Y. Jets vs. Baltimore, III
L.A. Raiders vs. Washington, XVIII
Washington vs. Buffalo, XXVI
2 By 10 teams
Most Kickoff Returns, Both Teams, Game
13 Oakland (9) vs. Tampa Bay (4), XXXVII
12 Denver (9) vs. San Francisco (3), XXIV
San Diego (8) vs. San Francisco (4), XXIX
11 Los Angeles (6) vs. Pittsburgh (5), XIV
Miami (7) vs. San Francisco (4), XIX
New England (7) vs. Chicago (4), XX
Green Bay (6) vs. Denver (5), XXXII
Fewest Kickoff Returns, Both Teams, Game
5 N.Y. Jets (1) vs. Baltimore (4), III
Miami (2) vs. Washington (3), VII
Washington (1) vs. Buffalo (4), XXVI
6 In five games

YARDS GAINED
Most Yards Gained, Game
244 San Diego vs. San Francisco, XXIX
227 Atlanta vs. Denver, XXXIII
222 Miami vs. Washington, XVII
Fewest Yards Gained, Game
16 Washington vs. Buffalo, XXVI
17 L.A. Raiders vs. Washington, XVIII
25 N.Y. Jets vs. Baltimore, III
Most Yards Gained, Both Teams, Game
292 San Diego (244) vs. San Francisco (48), XXIX
289 Green Bay (154) vs. New England (135), XXXI
281 N.Y. Giants (170) vs. Baltimore (111), XXXV
Fewest Yards Gained, Both Teams, Game
78 Miami (33) vs. Washington (45), VII
82 Pittsburgh (32) vs. Minnesota (50), IX
92 San Francisco (40) vs. Cincinnati (52), XVI

AVERAGE GAIN
Highest Average, Game (3 returns)
44.0 Cincinnati vs. San Francisco, XXIII (3-132)
38.5 Green Bay vs. New England, XXXI (4-154)
37.0 Miami vs. Washington, XVII (6-222)

TOUCHDOWNS
Most Touchdowns, Game
1 Miami vs. Washington, XVII
Cincinnati vs. San Francisco, XXIII
San Diego vs. San Francisco, XXIX
Green Bay vs. New England, XXXI
Atlanta vs. Denver, XXXIII
Baltimore vs. N.Y. Giants, XXXV
N.Y. Giants vs. Baltimore, XXXV
Chicago vs. Indianapolis, XLI
Most Touchdowns, Both Teams, Game
2 Baltimore (1) vs. N.Y. Giants (1), XXXV

PENALTIES
Most Penalties, Game
12 Dallas vs. Denver, XII
Carolina vs. New England, XXXVIII

11 Arizona vs. Pittsburgh, XLIII
10 Dallas vs. Baltimore, V

Fewest Penalties, Game
0 Miami vs. Dallas, VI
Pittsburgh vs. Dallas, X
Denver vs. San Francisco, XXIV
Atlanta vs. Denver, XXXIII
1 Green Bay vs. Oakland, II
Miami vs. Minnesota, VIII; vs. San Francisco, XIX
Buffalo vs. Dallas, XXVIII
2 By six teams

Most Penalties, Both Teams, Game
20 Dallas (12) vs. Denver (8), XII
Carolina (12) vs. New England (8), XXXVIII
18 Arizona (11) vs. Pittsburgh (7), XLIII
16 Cincinnati (8) vs. San Francisco (8), XVI
Green Bay (9) vs. Denver (7), XXXII

Fewest Penalties, Both Teams, Game
2 Pittsburgh (0) vs. Dallas (2), X
3 Miami (0) vs. Dallas (3), VI
Miami (1) vs. San Francisco (2), XIX
4 Denver (0) vs. San Francisco (4), XXIV
Atlanta (0) vs. Denver (4), XXXIII

YARDS PENALIZED

Most Yards Penalized, Game
133 Dallas vs. Baltimore, X
122 Pittsburgh vs. Minnesota, IX
106 Arizona vs. Pittsburgh, XLIII

Fewest Yards Penalized, Game
0 Miami vs. Dallas, VI
Pittsburgh vs. Dallas, X
Denver vs. San Francisco, XXIV
Atlanta vs. Denver, XXXIII
4 Miami vs. Minnesota, VIII
10 Miami vs. San Francisco, XIX
San Francisco vs. Miami, XIX
Buffalo vs. Dallas, XXVIII

Most Yards Penalized, Both Teams, Game
164 Dallas (133) vs. Baltimore (31), V
162 Arizona (106) vs. Pittsburgh (56), XLIII
154 Dallas (94) vs. Denver (60), XII

Fewest Yards Penalized, Both Teams, Game
15 Miami (0) vs. Dallas (15), VI
20 Pittsburgh (0) vs. Dallas (20), X
Miami (10) vs. San Francisco (10), XIX
38 Denver (0) vs. San Francisco (38), XXIV

FUMBLES

Most Fumbles, Game
8 Buffalo vs. Dallas, XXVII
6 Dallas vs. Denver, XII
Buffalo vs. Washington, XXVI
5 Baltimore vs. Dallas, V

Fewest Fumbles, Game
0 By 22 teams

Most Fumbles, Both Teams, Game
12 Buffalo (8) vs. Dallas (4), XXVII
10 Dallas (6) vs. Denver (4), XII
8 Dallas (4) vs. Pittsburgh (4), X

Fewest Fumbles, Both Teams, Game
0 Los Angeles vs. Pittsburgh, XIV
Green Bay vs. New England, XXXI
Pittsburgh vs. Seattle, XL
Indianapolis vs. New Orleans, XLIV
1 Oakland (0) vs. Minnesota (1), XI
Oakland (0) vs. Philadelphia (1), XV
Denver (0) vs. Washington (1), XXII
N.Y. Giants (0) vs. Buffalo (1), XXV
Denver (0) vs. Atlanta (1), XXXIII
2 In nine games

Most Fumbles Lost, Game
5 Buffalo vs. Dallas, XXVII
4 Baltimore vs. Dallas, V
Denver vs. Dallas, XII
New England vs. Chicago, XX
3 Chicago vs. Indianapolis, XLI

Most Fumbles Lost, Both Teams, Game
7 Buffalo (5) vs. Dallas (2), XXVII
6 Denver (4) vs. Dallas (2), XII
New England (4) vs. Chicago (2), XX
5 Baltimore (4) vs. Dallas (1), V
Chicago (3) vs. Indianapolis (2), XLI

Fewest Fumbles Lost, Both Teams, Game
0 Green Bay vs. Kansas City, I
Dallas vs. Pittsburgh, X
Los Angeles vs. Pittsburgh, XIV
Denver vs. N.Y. Giants, XXI; vs. Washington, XXII
Buffalo vs. N.Y. Giants, XXV
San Diego vs. San Francisco, XXIX
Dallas vs. Pittsburgh, XXX
Green Bay vs. New England, XXXI
St. Louis vs. Tennessee, XXXIV
Oakland vs. Tampa Bay, XXXVII
Pittsburgh vs. Seattle, XL
Indianapolis vs. New Orleans, XLIV

Most Fumbles Recovered, Game
8 Dallas vs. Denver, XII (4 own, 4 opp.)
6 Dallas vs. Buffalo, XXVII (1 own, 5 opp.)
5 Chicago vs. New England, XX (1 own, 4 opp.)

TURNOVERS

(Number of times losing the ball on interceptions and fumbles.)

Most Turnovers, Game
9 Buffalo vs. Dallas, XXVII
8 Denver vs. Dallas, XII
7 Baltimore vs. Dallas, V

Fewest Turnovers, Game
0 Green Bay vs. Oakland, II
Miami vs. Minnesota, VIII
Pittsburgh vs. Dallas, X
Oakland vs. Minnesota, XI; vs. Philadelphia, XV
N.Y. Giants vs. Denver, XXI; vs. Buffalo, XXV
San Francisco vs. Denver, XXIV; vs. San Diego, XXIX
Buffalo vs. N.Y. Giants, XXV
Dallas vs. Pittsburgh, XXX
Green Bay vs. New England, XXXI
St. Louis vs. Tennessee, XXXIV
Tennessee vs. St. Louis, XXXIV
Baltimore vs. N.Y. Giants, XXXV
New England vs. St. Louis, XXXVI
New Orleans vs. Indianapolis, XLIV
1 By many teams

Most Turnovers, Both Teams, Game
11 Baltimore (7) vs. Dallas (4), V
Buffalo (9) vs. Dallas (2), XXVII
10 Denver (8) vs. Dallas (2), XII
8 New England (6) vs. Chicago (2), XX
Chicago (5) vs. Indianapolis (3), XLI

Fewest Turnovers, Both Teams, Game
0 Buffalo vs. N.Y. Giants, XXV
St. Louis vs. Tennessee, XXXIV
1 N.Y. Giants (0) vs. Denver (1), XXI
New Orleans (0) vs. Indianapolis (1), XLIV
2 Green Bay (1) vs. Kansas City (1), I
Miami (0) vs. Minnesota (2), VIII
Cincinnati (1) vs. San Francisco (1), XXIII
Carolina (1) vs. New England (1), XXXVIII
New England (1) vs. N.Y. Giants (1), XLII

POSTSEASON RECORDS

Compiled by Elias Sports Bureau

Throughout this all-time postseason record section, the following abbreviations are used to indicate various levels of postseason games:

SB Super Bowl (1966 to date)

AFC AFC Championship Game (1970 to date) or AFL Championship Game (1960-69)

NFC NFC Championship Game (1970 to date) or NFL Championship Game (1933-69)

AFC-D AFC Divisional Playoff Game (1970 to date), AFC Second-Round Playoff Game (1982), AFL Inter-Divisional Playoff Game (1969), or special playoff game to break tie for AFL Division Championship (1963, 1968)

NFC-D NFC Divisional Playoff Game (1970 to date), NFC Second-Round Playoff Game (1982), NFL Conference Championship Game (1967-69), or special playoff game to break tie for NFL Division or Conference Championship (1941, 1943, 1947, 1950, 1952, 1957, 1958, 1965)

AFC-FR AFC First-Round Playoff Game (1978 to date)

NFC-FR NFC First-Round Playoff Game (1978 to date)

Year indicates season in which game took place and does not necessarily reflect calendar year.

POSTSEASON GAME COMPOSITE STANDINGS

	W	L	PCT.	PTS.	OP
Pittsburgh Steelers	31	19	.620	1,180	1,020
Baltimore Ravens	8	5	.615	238	164
Green Bay Packers	25	16	.610	995	817
Carolina Panthers	6	4	.600	219	203
New England Patriots#	21	14	.600	744	699
San Francisco 49ers	25	17	.595	1,044	853
Oakland Raiders**	25	18	.581	1,028	797
Washington Redskins*	23	17	.575	819	707
Dallas Cowboys	33	25	.569	1,355	1,098
Denver Broncos	17	15	.531	694	794
Indianapolis Colts***	19	19	.500	769	769
Miami Dolphins	20	20	.500	789	875
Philadelphia Eagles	19	19	.500	741	699
Chicago Bears	16	17	.485	702	681
Buffalo Bills	14	15	.483	681	658
Arizona Cardinals††††	6	7	.462	305	361
Jacksonville Jaguars	5	6	.455	262	288
New Orleans Saints	5	6	.455	251	307
New York Giants	20	24	.455	763	833
New York Jets	10	12	.455	446	447
St. Louis Rams††	19	24	.442	770	944
Tennessee Titans†	14	19	.424	579	762
Minnesota Vikings	19	26	.422	900	1,017
Detroit Lions	7	10	.412	365	404
Seattle Seahawks	7	10	.412	356	367
Atlanta Falcons	6	9	.400	322	361
Tampa Bay Buccaneers	6	9	.400	230	279
San Diego Chargers†††	10	16	.385	488	592
Kansas City Chiefs****	8	13	.381	340	445
Cincinnati Bengals	5	9	.357	277	312
Cleveland Browns	11	20	.355	629	728

* *One game played when franchise was in Boston (lost 21-6).*

** *12 games played when franchise was in Los Angeles (won 6, lost 6, 268 points scored, 224 points allowed).*

*** *15 games played when franchise was in Baltimore (won 8, lost 7, 264 points scored, 262 points allowed).*

**** *One game played when franchise was Dallas Texans (won 20-17).*

\# *Two games played when franchise was in Boston (won 26-8, lost 51-10).*

† *22 games played when franchise was in Houston and known as the Oilers (won 9, lost 13, 371 points scored, 533 points allowed).*

†† *One game played when franchise was in Cleveland (won 15-14), 32 games played when franchise was in Los Angeles (won 12, lost 20, 486 points scored, 683 points allowed).*

††† *One game played when franchise was in Los Angeles (lost 24-16).*

†††† *Two games played when franchise was in Chicago (won 28-21, lost 7-0), three games played when franchise was in St. Louis (lost 30-14, lost 35-23, lost 41-16).*

INDIVIDUAL RECORDS

SERVICE

Most Games, Career

29 Jerry Rice, San Francisco-Oakland-Seattle (SB 4, NFC 6, AFC 1, NFC-D 11, AFC-D 2, NFC-FR 4, AFC-FR 1)

27 D.D. Lewis, Dallas (SB 5, NFC 9, NFC-D 12, NFC-FR 1)

26 Larry Cole, Dallas (SB 5, NFC 8, NFC-D 12, NFC-FR 1)

Bill Romanowski, San Francisco-Philadelphia-Denver-Oakland (SB 5, NFC 5, AFC 3, NFC-D 6, AFC-D 4, NFC-FR 1, AFC-FR 2)

Most Games, Head Coach

36 Tom Landry, Dallas

Don Shula, Baltimore-Miami

24 Chuck Noll, Pittsburgh

Mike Holmgren, Green Bay-Seattle

Joe Gibbs, Washington

22 Bud Grant, Minnesota

Most Championships Won, Head Coach

6 George Halas, Chicago

Curly Lambeau, Green Bay

5 Vince Lombardi, Green Bay

4 Guy Chamberlin, Canton Bulldogs-Cleveland Bulldogs-Frankford Yellow Jackets

Chuck Noll, Pittsburgh

Most Games Won, Head Coach

20 Tom Landry, Dallas

19 Don Shula, Baltimore-Miami

17 Joe Gibbs, Washington

Most Games Lost, Head Coach

17 Don Shula, Baltimore-Miami

16 Tom Landry, Dallas

13 Marty Schottenheimer, Cleveland-Kansas City-San Diego

SCORING

POINTS

Most Points, Career

177 Adam Vinatieri, New England-Indianapolis, 23 games (51-pat, 42-fg)

153 Gary Anderson, Pittsburgh-Philadelphia-San Francisco-Minnesota-Tennessee, 22 games (57-pat, 32-fg)

132 Jerry Rice, San Francisco-Oakland-Seattle, 29 games (22-td)

Most Points, Game

30 Ricky Watters, NFC-D: San Francisco vs. N.Y. Giants, 1993 (5-td)

19 Pat Harder, NFC-D: Detroit vs. Los Angeles, 1952 (2-td, 4-pat, 1-fg)

Paul Hornung, NFC: Green Bay vs. N.Y. Giants, 1961 (1-td, 4-pat, 3-fg)

18 By many players

Most Consecutive Games Scoring

23 Adam Vinatieri, New England-Indianapolis, 1996-2008 (current)

19 George Blanda, Chi. Bears-Houston-Oakland, 1956-1975

18 David Akers, Philadelphia, 2000-06, 2008-09 (current)

TOUCHDOWNS

Most Touchdowns, Career

22 Jerry Rice, San Francisco-Oakland-Seattle, 29 games (22-p)

21 Thurman Thomas, Buffalo, 21 games (16-r, 5-p)

Emmitt Smith, Dallas, 17 games (19-r, 2-p)

17 Franco Harris, Pittsburgh, 19 games (16-r, 1-p)

Most Touchdowns, Game

5 Ricky Watters, NFC-D: San Francisco vs. N.Y. Giants, 1993 (5-r)

3 Andy Farkas, NFC-D: Washington vs. N.Y. Giants, 1943 (3-r)
Tom Fears, NFC-D: Los Angeles vs. Chi. Bears, 1950 (3-p)
Otto Graham, NFC: Cleveland vs. Detroit, 1954 (3-r)
Gary Collins, NFC: Cleveland vs. Baltimore, 1964 (3-p)
Craig Baynham, NFC-D: Dallas vs. Cleveland, 1967 (2-r, 1-p)
Fred Biletnikoff, AFC-D: Oakland vs. Kansas City, 1968 (3-p)
Tom Matte, NFC: Baltimore vs. Cleveland, 1968 (3-r)
Larry Schreiber, NFC-D: San Francisco vs. Dallas, 1972 (3-r)
Larry Csonka, AFC: Miami vs. Oakland, 1973 (3-r)
Franco Harris, AFC-D: Pittsburgh vs. Buffalo, 1974 (3-r)
Preston Pearson, NFC: Dallas vs. Los Angeles, 1975 (3-p)
Dave Casper, AFC-D: Oakland vs. Baltimore, 1977 (ot) (3-p)
Alvin Garrett, NFC-FR: Washington vs. Detroit, 1982 (3-p)
John Riggins, NFC-D: Washington vs. L.A. Rams, 1983 (3-r)
Roger Craig, SB: San Francisco vs. Miami, 1984 (1-r, 2-p)
Jerry Rice, NFC-D: San Francisco vs. Minnesota, 1988 (3-p)
Jerry Rice, SB: San Francisco vs. Denver, 1989 (3-p)
Kenneth Davis, AFC: Buffalo vs. L.A. Raiders, 1990 (3-r)
Andre Reed, AFC-FR: Buffalo vs. Houston, 1992 (ot) (3-p)
Sterling Sharpe, NFC-FR: Green Bay vs. Detroit, 1993 (3-p)
Napoleon McCallum, AFC-FR: L.A. Raiders vs. Denver, 1993 (3-r)
Thurman Thomas, AFC: Buffalo vs. Kansas City, 1993 (3-r)
William Floyd, NFC-D: San Francisco vs. Chicago, 1994 (3-r)
Ricky Watters, SB: San Francisco vs. San Diego, 1994 (1-r, 2-p)
Jerry Rice, SB: San Francisco vs. San Diego, 1994 (3-p)
Emmitt Smith, NFC: Dallas vs. Green Bay, 1995 (3-r)
Curtis Martin, AFC-D: New England vs. Pittsburgh, 1996 (3-r)
Terrell Davis, SB: Denver vs. Green Bay, 1997 (3-r)
Mario Bates, NFC-D: Arizona vs. Minnesota, 1998 (3-r)
Leroy Hoard, NFC-D: Minnesota vs. Arizona, 1998 (2-r, 1-p)
Willie Jackson, NFC-FR: New Orleans vs. St. Louis, 2000 (3-p)
Amani Toomer, NFC-FR: N.Y. Giants vs. San Francisco, 2002 (3-p)
Shaun Alexander, NFC-FR: Seattle vs. Green Bay, 2003 (ot) (3-r)
Ryan Grant, NFC-D: Green Bay vs. Seattle, 2007 (3-r)
Larry Fitzgerald, NFC: Arizona vs. Philadelphia, 2008 (3-p)
Sidney Rice, NFC-D: Minnesota vs. Dallas, 2009 (3-p)
Adrian Peterson, NFC: Minnesota vs. New Orleans, 2009 (3-r)

Most Consecutive Games Scoring Touchdowns

9 Thurman Thomas, Buffalo, 1992-98

8 John Stallworth, Pittsburgh, 1978-1983
Emmitt Smith, Dallas, 1993-96

7 John Riggins, Washington, 1982-84
Marcus Allen, L.A. Raiders, 1982-85
Terrell Davis, Denver, 1996-98
David Givens, New England, 2003-05

POINTS AFTER TOUCHDOWN

Most (One-Point) Points After Touchdown, Career

57 Gary Anderson, Pittsburgh-Philadelphia-San Francisco-Minnesota-Tennessee, 22 games (57 att)

51 Adam Vinatieri, New England-Indianapolis, 23 games (51 att)

49 George Blanda, Chi. Bears-Houston-Oakland, 19 games (49 att)

Most (One-Point) Points After Touchdown, Game

8 Lou Groza, NFC: Cleveland vs. Detroit, 1954 (8 att)
Jim Martin, NFC: Detroit vs. Cleveland, 1957 (8 att)
George Blanda, AFC-D: Oakland vs. Houston, 1969 (8 att)
Mike Hollis, AFC-D: Jacksonville vs. Miami, 1999 (8 att)

7 Danny Villanueva, NFC-D: Dallas vs. Cleveland, 1967 (7 att)
Raul Allegre, NFC-D: N.Y. Giants vs. San Francisco, 1986 (7 att)
Mike Cofer, SB: San Francisco vs. Denver, 1989 (8 att)
Lin Elliott, SB: Dallas vs. Buffalo, 1992 (7 att)
Doug Brien, SB: San Francisco vs. San Diego, 1994 (7 att)
Gary Anderson, NFC-FR: Philadelphia vs. Detroit, 1995 (7 att)
Jeff Wilkins, NFC-D: St. Louis vs. Minnesota, 1999 (7 att)
Mike Vanderjagt, AFC-FR: Indianapolis vs. Denver, 2004 (7 att)

6 George Blair, AFC: San Diego vs. Boston, 1963 (6 att)
Mark Moseley, NFC-D: Washington vs. L.A. Rams, 1983 (6 att)
Uwe von Schamann, AFC: Miami vs. Pittsburgh, 1984 (6 att)
Ali Haji-Sheikh, SB: Washington vs. Denver, 1987 (6 att)
Scott Norwood, AFC: Buffalo vs. L.A. Raiders, 1990 (7 att)
Jeff Jaeger, AFC-FR: L.A. Raiders vs. Denver, 1993 (6 att)
Jason Elam, AFC-FR: Denver vs. Jacksonville, 1997 (6 att)
Jeff Wilkins, NFC-D: St. Louis vs. Green Bay, 2001 (6 att)
Martín Gramatica, SB: Tampa Bay vs. Oakland, 2002 (6 att)
Jay Feely, NFC-D: Atlanta vs. St. Louis, 2004 (6 att)
Mason Crosby, NFC-D: Green Bay vs. Seattle, 2007 (6 att)
Neil Rackers, NFC-FR: Arizona vs. Green Bay, 2009 (ot) (6 att)
Mason Crosby, NFC-FR: Green Bay vs. Arizona, 2009 (ot) (6 att)
Garrett Hartley, NFC-D: New Orleans vs. Arizona, 2009 (6 att)

Most (Kicking) Points After Touchdown, No Misses, Career

57 Gary Anderson, Pittsburgh-Philadelphia-San Francisco-Minnesota-Tennessee, 22 games

51 Adam Vinatieri, New England-Indianapolis, 23 games

49 George Blanda, Chi. Bears-Houston-Oakland, 19 games

Most Two-Point Conversions, Career

2 Terrell Owens, San Francisco-Philadelphia-Dallas, 12 games
Kevin Faulk, New England, 18 games

Most Two-Point Conversions, Game

2 Terrell Owens, NFC-FR: San Francisco vs. N.Y. Giants, 2002

FIELD GOALS

Most Field Goals Attempted, Career

51 Adam Vinatieri, New England-Indianapolis, 23 games

40 Gary Anderson, Pittsburgh-Philadelphia-San Francisco-Minnesota-Tennessee, 22 games

39 George Blanda, Chi. Bears-Houston-Oakland, 19 games

Most Field Goals Attempted, Game

6 George Blanda, AFC: Oakland vs. Houston, 1967
David Ray, NFC-D: Los Angeles vs. Dallas, 1973
Mark Moseley, AFC-D: Cleveland vs. N.Y. Jets, 1986 (ot)
Matt Bahr, NFC: N.Y. Giants vs. San Francisco, 1990
Steve Christie, AFC: Buffalo vs. Miami, 1992
Jeff Wilkins, NFC-D: St. Louis vs. Carolina, 2003 (2 ot)

5 By many players

Most Field Goals, Career

42 Adam Vinatieri, New England-Indianapolis, 23 games

32 Gary Anderson, Pittsburgh-Philadelphia-San Francisco-Minnesota-Tennessee, 22 games

30 David Akers, Philadelphia, 18 games

Most Field Goals, Game

5 Chuck Nelson, NFC-D: Minnesota vs. San Francisco, 1987
Matt Bahr, NFC: N.Y. Giants vs. San Francisco, 1990
Steve Christie, AFC: Buffalo vs. Miami, 1992
Brad Daluiso, NFC-FR: N.Y. Giants vs. Minnesota, 1997
John Kasay, NFC-FR: Carolina vs. Dallas, 2003
Jeff Wilkins, NFC-D: St. Louis vs. Carolina, 2003 (2 ot)
Adam Vinatieri, AFC: New England vs. Indianapolis, 2003
Adam Vinatieri, AFC-D: Indianapolis vs. Baltimore, 2006

4 Gino Cappelletti, AFC-D: Boston vs. Buffalo, 1963
George Blanda, AFC: Oakland vs. Houston, 1967
Don Chandler, SB: Green Bay vs. Oakland, 1967
Curt Knight, NFC: Washington vs. Dallas, 1972

George Blanda, AFC-D: Oakland vs. Pittsburgh, 1973
Ray Wersching, SB: San Francisco vs. Cincinnati, 1981
Tony Franklin, AFC-FR: New England vs. N.Y. Jets, 1985
Jess Atkinson, NFC-FR: Washington vs. L.A. Rams, 1986
Luis Zendejas, NFC-D: Philadelphia vs. Chicago, 1988
Gary Anderson, AFC-FR: Pittsburgh vs. Houston, 1989 (ot)
Norm Johnson, AFC-D: Pittsburgh vs. Buffalo, 1995
Chris Boniol, NFC-FR: Dallas vs. Minnesota, 1996
John Kasay, NFC-D: Carolina vs. Dallas, 1996
Mike Hollis, AFC-D: Jacksonville vs. New England, 1998
Al Del Greco, AFC-D: Tennessee vs. Indianapolis, 1999
David Akers, NFC-D: Philadelphia vs. Chicago, 2001
Nate Kaeding, AFC-D: San Diego vs. New England, 2007
David Akers, NFC-FR: Philadelphia vs. Minnesota, 2008
Neil Rackers, NFC-D: Arizona vs. Carolina, 2008
3 By many players

Most Consecutive Games Scoring Field Goals
13 Toni Fritsch, Dallas-Houston, 1972-79
12 Adam Vinatieri, New England, 1997-2004
11 Jason Elam, Denver-Atlanta, 1997-2000, 2003-05, 2008 (current)

Most Consecutive Field Goals
19 David Akers, Philadelphia, 2000-04, 2006, 2008
16 Gary Anderson, Pittsburgh-Philadelphia, 1989-1995
Matt Stover, Baltimore, 2001, 2003, 2006, 2008; Indianapolis, 2009
15 Rafael Septien, Dallas, 1978-1982

Longest Field Goal
58 Pete Stoyanovich, AFC-FR: Miami vs. Kansas City, 1990
55 Jeff Wilkins, NFC-D: St. Louis vs. Atlanta, 2004
54 Ed Murray, NFC-D: Detroit vs. San Francisco, 1983
Steve Christie, SB: Buffalo vs. Dallas, 1993
John Carney, AFC-FR: San Diego vs. Indianapolis, 1995

Highest Field Goal Percentage, Career (10 field goals)
92.9 Martín Gramatica, Tampa Bay-Indianapolis-Dallas, 9 games (14-13)
91.3 John Kasay, Carolina, 10 games (23-21)
90.9 Chuck Nelson, L.A. Rams-Minnesota, 6 games (11-10)

SAFETIES

Most Safeties, Game
1 Bill Willis, NFC-D: Cleveland vs. N.Y. Giants, 1950
Carl Eller, NFC-D: Minnesota vs. Los Angeles, 1969
George Andrie, NFC-D: Dallas vs. Detroit, 1970
Alan Page, NFC-D: Minnesota vs. Dallas, 1971
Dwight White, SB: Pittsburgh vs. Minnesota, 1974
Reggie Harrison, SB: Pittsburgh vs. Dallas, 1975
Jim Jensen, NFC-D: Dallas vs. Los Angeles, 1976
Ted Washington, AFC: Houston vs. Pittsburgh, 1978
Randy White, NFC-D: Dallas vs. Los Angeles, 1979
Henry Waechter, SB: Chicago vs. New England, 1985
Rulon Jones, AFC-FR: Denver vs. New England, 1986
George Martin, SB: N.Y. Giants vs. Denver, 1986
D.D. Hoggard, AFC: Cleveland vs. Denver, 1987
Bruce Smith, SB: Buffalo vs. N.Y. Giants, 1990
Reggie White, NFC-FR: Philadelphia vs. New Orleans, 1992
Willie Clay, NFC-FR: Detroit vs. Green Bay, 1994
Carnell Lake, AFC-D: Pittsburgh vs. Cleveland, 1994
Reuben Davis, AFC-D: San Diego vs. Miami, 1994
Jevon Kearse, AFC-FR: Tennessee vs. Buffalo, 1999
Brady Smith, NFC-D: Atlanta vs. St. Louis, 2004
Antonio Smith, NFC-FR: Arizona vs. Atlanta, 2008

RUSHING

ATTEMPTS

Most Attempts, Career
400 Franco Harris, Pittsburgh, 19 games
349 Emmitt Smith, Dallas, 17 games
339 Thurman Thomas, Buffalo, 21 games

Most Attempts, Game
40 Lamar Smith, AFC-FR: Miami vs. Indianapolis, 2000 (ot)
38 Ricky Bell, NFC-D: Tampa Bay vs. Philadelphia, 1979
John Riggins, SB: Washington vs. Miami, 1982
37 Lawrence McCutcheon, NFC-D: Los Angeles vs. St. Louis, 1975
John Riggins, NFC-D: Washington vs. Minnesota, 1982

YARDS GAINED

Most Yards Gained, Career
1,586 Emmitt Smith, Dallas, 17 games
1,556 Franco Harris, Pittsburgh, 19 games
1,442 Thurman Thomas, Buffalo, 21 games

Most Yards Gained, Game
248 Eric Dickerson, NFC-D: L.A. Rams vs. Dallas, 1985
209 Lamar Smith, AFC-FR: Miami vs. Indianapolis, 2000 (ot)
206 Keith Lincoln, AFC: San Diego vs. Boston, 1963

Most Games, 100 or More Yards Rushing, Career
7 Emmitt Smith, Dallas, 17 games
Terrell Davis, Denver, 8 games
6 John Riggins, Washington, 9 games
Thurman Thomas, Buffalo, 21 games
5 Franco Harris, Pittsburgh, 19 games
Marcus Allen, L.A. Raiders-Kansas City, 16 games

Most Consecutive Games, 100 or More Yards Rushing
7 Terrell Davis, Denver, 1997-98
6 John Riggins, Washington, 1982-83
4 Thurman Thomas, Buffalo, 1990-91

Longest Run From Scrimmage
90 Fred Taylor, AFC-D: Jacksonville vs. Miami, 1999 (TD)
83 Ray Rice, AFC-FR: Baltimore vs. New England, 2009 (TD)
80 Roger Craig, NFC-D: San Francisco vs. Minnesota, 1988 (TD)
Charlie Garner, AFC-FR: Oakland vs. N.Y. Jets, 2001 (TD)

AVERAGE GAIN

Highest Average Gain, Career (100 attempts)
5.59 Terrell Davis, Denver, 8 games (204-1,140)
5.04 Marcus Allen, L.A. Raiders-Kansas City, 16 games (267-1,347)
4.89 Eric Dickerson, L.A. Rams-Indianapolis, 7 games (148-724)

Highest Average Gain, Game (10 attempts)
15.90 Elmer Angsman, NFC: Chi. Cardinals vs. Philadelphia, 1947 (10-159)
15.85 Keith Lincoln, AFC: San Diego vs. Boston, 1963 (13-206)
11.31 Zack Crockett, AFC-FR: Indianapolis vs. San Diego, 1995 (13-147)

TOUCHDOWNS

Most Touchdowns, Career
19 Emmitt Smith, Dallas, 17 games
16 Franco Harris, Pittsburgh, 19 games
Thurman Thomas, Buffalo, 21 games
12 John Riggins, Washington, 9 games
Terrell Davis, Denver, 8 games

Most Touchdowns, Game
5 Ricky Watters, NFC-D: San Francisco vs. N.Y. Giants, 1993
3 Andy Farkas, NFC-D: Washington vs. N.Y. Giants, 1943
Otto Graham, NFC: Cleveland vs. Detroit, 1954
Tom Matte, NFC: Baltimore vs. Cleveland, 1968
Larry Schreiber, NFC-D: San Francisco vs. Dallas, 1972
Larry Csonka, AFC: Miami vs. Oakland, 1973
Franco Harris, AFC-D: Pittsburgh vs. Buffalo, 1974
John Riggins, NFC-D: Washington vs. L.A. Rams, 1983
Kenneth Davis, AFC: Buffalo vs. L.A. Raiders, 1990
Napoleon McCallum, AFC-FR: L.A. Raiders vs. Denver, 1993
Thurman Thomas, AFC: Buffalo vs. Kansas City, 1993
William Floyd, NFC-D: San Francisco vs. Chicago, 1994
Emmitt Smith, NFC: Dallas vs. Green Bay, 1995
Curtis Martin, AFC-D: New England vs. Pittsburgh, 1996
Terrell Davis, SB: Denver vs. Green Bay, 1997
Mario Bates, NFC-D: Arizona vs. Minnesota, 1998
Shaun Alexander, NFC-FR: Seattle vs. Green Bay, 2003 (ot)
Ryan Grant, NFC-D: Green Bay vs. Seattle, 2007
Adrian Peterson, NFC: Minnesota vs. New Orleans, 2009 (ot)

Most Consecutive Games Rushing for Touchdowns
8 Emmitt Smith, Dallas, 1993-96
Thurman Thomas, Buffalo, 1992-98
7 John Riggins, Washington, 1982-84
Terrell Davis, Denver, 1996-98
5 Franco Harris, Pittsburgh, 1974-75
Franco Harris, Pittsburgh, 1977-79
Curtis Martin, New England-N.Y. Jets, 1996-98
Jerome Bettis, Pittsburgh, 2004-05

PASSING

PASSER RATING

Highest Passer Rating, Career (150 attempts)
104.8 Bart Starr, Green Bay, 10 games
103.7 Drew Brees, San Diego-New Orleans, 6 games
102.8 Kurt Warner, St. Louis-Arizona, 11 games

ATTEMPTS

Most Passes Attempted, Career
791 Brett Favre, Green Bay-Minnesota, 24 games
734 Joe Montana, San Francisco-Kansas City, 23 games
692 Peyton Manning, Indianapolis, 18 games

Most Passes Attempted, Game
65 Steve Young, NFC-D: San Francisco vs. Green Bay, 1995
64 Bernie Kosar, AFC-D: Cleveland vs. N.Y. Jets, 1986 (ot)
Dan Marino, AFC-FR: Miami vs. Buffalo, 1995
58 Jim Kelly, SB: Buffalo vs. Washington, 1991

COMPLETIONS

Most Passes Completed, Career
481 Brett Favre, Green Bay-Minnesota, 24 games
460 Joe Montana, San Francisco-Kansas City, 23 games
435 Peyton Manning, Indianapolis, 18 games

Most Passes Completed, Game
36 Warren Moon, AFC-FR: Houston vs. Buffalo, 1992 (ot)
33 Dan Fouts, AFC-D: San Diego vs. Miami, 1981 (ot)
Bernie Kosar, AFC-D: Cleveland vs. N.Y. Jets, 1986 (ot)
Dan Marino, AFC-FR: Miami vs. Buffalo, 1995
Peyton Manning, AFC-D: Indianapolis vs. San Diego, 2007
32 Neil Lomax, NFC-FR: St. Louis vs. Green Bay, 1982
Danny White, NFC-FR: Dallas vs. L.A. Rams, 1983
Warren Moon, AFC-D: Houston vs. Kansas City, 1993
Neil O'Donnell, AFC: Pittsburgh vs. San Diego, 1994
Steve Young, NFC-D: San Francisco vs. Green Bay, 1995
Tom Brady, AFC-D: New England vs. Oakland, 2001 (ot)
Tom Brady, SB: New England vs. Carolina, 2003
Drew Brees, SB: New Orleans vs. Indianapolis, 2009

COMPLETION PERCENTAGE

Highest Completion Percentage, Career (150 attempts)
66.7 Drew Brees, San Diego-New Orleans, 6 games (225-150)
66.5 Kurt Warner, St. Louis-Arizona, 13 games (462-307)
66.3 Ken Anderson, Cincinnati, 6 games (166-110)

Highest Completion Percentage, Game (15 completions)
92.9 Tom Brady, AFC-D: New England vs. Jacksonville, 2007 (28-26)
88.0 Phil Simms, SB: N.Y. Giants vs. Denver, 1986 (25-22)
87.9 Kurt Warner, NFC-FR: Arizona vs. Green Bay, 2009 (ot) (33-29)

YARDS GAINED

Most Yards Gained, Career
5,855 Brett Favre, Green Bay-Minnesota, 24 games
5,772 Joe Montana, San Francisco-Kansas City, 23 games
5,164 Peyton Manning, Indianapolis, 18 games

Most Yards Gained, Game
489 Bernie Kosar, AFC-D: Cleveland vs. N.Y. Jets, 1986 (ot)
458 Peyton Manning, AFC-FR: Indianapolis vs. Denver, 2004
433 Dan Fouts, AFC-D: San Diego vs. Miami, 1981 (ot)

Most Games, 300 or More Yards Passing, Career
8 Peyton Manning, Indianapolis, 18 games
6 Joe Montana, San Francisco-Kansas City, 23 games
Kurt Warner, St. Louis-Arizona, 13 games
5 Dan Fouts, San Diego, 7 games

Most Consecutive Games, 300 or More Yards Passing
4 Dan Fouts, San Diego, 1979-1981
3 Jim Kelly, Buffalo, 1989-1990
Warren Moon, Houston, 1991-93
2 Daryle Lamonica, Oakland, 1968
Ken Anderson, Cincinnati, 1981-82
Terry Bradshaw, Pittsburgh, 1979-1982
Joe Montana, San Francisco, 1983-84
Dan Marino, Miami, 1984
Troy Aikman, Dallas, 1994
Steve Young, San Francisco, 1994-95
Kurt Warner, St. Louis, 1999-2000
Peyton Manning, Indianapolis, 2003
Marc Bulger, St. Louis, 2003-04
Matt Hasselbeck, Seattle, 2003-04
Peyton Manning, Indianapolis, 2007-08
Donovan McNabb, Philadelphia, 2004, 2008
Kurt Warner, Arizona, 2008-09
Peyton Manning, Indianapolis, 2009 (current)

Longest Pass Completion
96 Trent Dilfer (to Sharpe), AFC: Baltimore vs. Oakland, 2000 (TD)
94 Troy Aikman (to Harper), NFC-D: Dallas vs. Green Bay, 1994 (TD)
93 Daryle Lamonica (to Dubenion), AFC-D: Buffalo vs. Boston, 1963 (TD)

AVERAGE GAIN

Highest Average Gain, Career (150 attempts)
8.55 Kurt Warner, St. Louis-Arizona, 13 games (462-3,952)
8.45 Joe Theismann, Washington, 10 games (211-1,782)
8.43 Jim Plunkett, Oakland/L.A. Raiders, 10 games (272-2,293)

Highest Average Gain, Game (20 attempts)
14.71 Terry Bradshaw, SB: Pittsburgh vs. Los Angeles, 1979 (21-309)
14.50 Peyton Manning, AFC-FR: Indianapolis vs. Denver, 2003 (26-377)
13.88 Peyton Manning, AFC-FR: Indianapolis vs. Denver, 2004 (33-458)

TOUCHDOWNS

Most Touchdown Passes, Career
45 Joe Montana, San Francisco-Kansas City, 23 games
44 Brett Favre, Green Bay-Minnesota, 24 games
32 Dan Marino, Miami, 18 games

Most Touchdown Passes, Game
6 Daryle Lamonica, AFC-D: Oakland vs. Houston, 1969
Steve Young, SB: San Francisco vs. San Diego, 1994
5 Sid Luckman, NFC: Chi. Bears vs. Washington, 1943
Daryle Lamonica, AFC-D: Oakland vs. Kansas City, 1968
Joe Montana, SB: San Francisco vs. Denver, 1989
Kurt Warner, NFC-D: St. Louis vs. Minnesota, 1999
Kerry Collins, NFC: N.Y. Giants vs. Minnesota, 2000
Peyton Manning, AFC-FR: Indianapolis vs. Denver, 2003
Kurt Warner, NFC-FR: Arizona vs. Green Bay, 2009 (ot)
4 Otto Graham, NFC: Cleveland vs. Los Angeles, 1950
Tobin Rote, NFC: Detroit vs. Cleveland, 1957
Bart Starr, NFC: Green Bay vs. Dallas, 1966
Ken Stabler, AFC-D: Oakland vs. Miami, 1974
Roger Staubach, NFC: Dallas vs. Los Angeles, 1975
Terry Bradshaw, SB: Pittsburgh vs. Dallas, 1978
Don Strock, AFC-D: Miami vs. San Diego, 1981 (ot)
Lynn Dickey, NFC-FR: Green Bay vs. St. Louis, 1982
Dan Marino, AFC: Miami vs. Pittsburgh, 1984
Phil Simms, NFC-D: N.Y. Giants vs. San Francisco, 1986
Doug Williams, SB: Washington vs. Denver, 1987
Jim Kelly, AFC-D: Buffalo vs. Cleveland, 1989
Joe Montana, NFC-D: San Francisco vs. Minnesota, 1989
Warren Moon, AFC-FR: Houston vs. Buffalo, 1992 (ot)
Frank Reich, AFC-FR: Buffalo vs. Houston, 1992 (ot)
Troy Aikman, SB: Dallas vs. Buffalo, 1992
Jeff George, NFC-D: Minnesota vs. St. Louis, 1999

Aaron Brooks, NFC-FR: New Orleans vs. St. Louis, 2000
Kerry Collins, NFC-FR: N.Y. Giants vs. San Francisco, 2002
Peyton Manning, AFC-FR: Indianapolis vs. Denver, 2004
Daunte Culpepper, NFC-FR: Minnesota vs. Green Bay, 2004
Kurt Warner, NFC: Arizona vs. Philadelphia, 2008
Aaron Rodgers, NFC-FR: Green Bay vs. Arizona, 2009 (ot)
Brett Favre, NFC-D: Minnesota vs. Dallas, 2009

Most Consecutive Games, Touchdown Passes
20 Brett Favre, Green Bay-Minnesota, 1995-2009 (current)
16 Tom Brady, New England, 2001-09 (current)
13 Dan Marino, Miami, 1983-1995

HAD INTERCEPTED

Lowest Percentage, Passes Had Intercepted, Career (150 attempts)
0.89 Drew Brees, San Diego-New Orleans, 6 games (225-2)
1.41 Bart Starr, Green Bay, 10 games (213-3)
2.15 Phil Simms, N.Y. Giants, 10 games (279-6)

Most Attempts Without Interception, Game
54 Neil O'Donnell, AFC: Pittsburgh vs. San Diego, 1994
48 Warren Moon, AFC-FR: Houston vs. Pittsburgh, 1989 (ot)
Randall Cunningham, NFC: Minnesota vs. Atlanta, 1998 (ot)
Tom Brady, SB: New England vs. N.Y. Giants, 2007
47 Daryle Lamonica, AFC: Oakland vs. N.Y. Jets, 1968

Most Passes Had Intercepted, Career
30 Brett Favre, Green Bay-Minnesota, 24 games
28 Jim Kelly, Buffalo, 17 games
26 Terry Bradshaw, Pittsburgh, 19 games

Most Passes Had Intercepted, Game
6 Frank Filchock, NFC: N.Y. Giants vs. Chi. Bears, 1946
Bobby Layne, NFC: Detroit vs. Cleveland, 1954
Norm Van Brocklin, NFC: Los Angeles vs. Cleveland, 1955
Brett Favre, NFC-D: Green Bay vs. St. Louis, 2001
5 Frank Filchock, NFC: Washington vs. Chi. Bears, 1940
George Blanda, AFC: Houston vs. San Diego, 1961
George Blanda, AFC: Houston vs. Dall. Texans, 1962 (ot)
Y.A. Tittle, NFC: N.Y. Giants vs. Chicago, 1963
Mike Phipps, AFC-D: Cleveland vs. Miami, 1972
Dan Pastorini, AFC: Houston vs. Pittsburgh, 1978
Dan Fouts, AFC-D: San Diego vs. Houston, 1979
Tommy Kramer, NFC-D: Minnesota vs. Philadelphia, 1980
Dan Fouts, AFC-D: San Diego vs. Miami, 1982
Richard Todd, AFC: N.Y. Jets vs. Miami, 1982
Gary Danielson, NFC-D: Detroit vs. San Francisco, 1983
Jay Schroeder, AFC: L.A. Raiders vs. Buffalo, 1990
Rich Gannon, SB: Oakland vs. Tampa Bay, 2002
Jake Delhomme, NFC-D: Carolina vs. Arizona, 2008
4 By many players

PASS RECEIVING

RECEPTIONS

Most Receptions, Career
151 Jerry Rice, San Francisco-Oakland-Seattle, 29 games
87 Michael Irvin, Dallas, 16 games
85 Andre Reed, Buffalo, 21 games

Most Receptions, Game
13 Kellen Winslow, AFC-D: San Diego vs. Miami, 1981 (ot)
Thurman Thomas, AFC-D: Buffalo vs. Cleveland, 1989
Shannon Sharpe, AFC-FR: Denver vs. L.A. Raiders, 1993
Chad Morton, NFC-D: New Orleans vs. Minnesota, 2000
12 Raymond Berry, NFC: Baltimore vs. N.Y. Giants, 1958
Michael Irvin, NFC: Dallas vs. San Francisco, 1994
Darrell Jackson, NFC-FR: Seattle vs. St. Louis, 2004
Steve Smith, NFC-D: Carolina vs. Chicago, 2005
11 Dante Lavelli, NFC: Cleveland vs. Los Angeles, 1950
Dan Ross, SB: Cincinnati vs. San Francisco, 1981
Franco Harris, AFC-FR: Pittsburgh vs. San Diego, 1982
Steve Watson, AFC-D: Denver vs. Pittsburgh, 1984
John L. Williams, AFC-D: Seattle vs. Cincinnati, 1988
Jerry Rice, SB: San Francisco vs. Cincinnati, 1988
Ernest Givins, AFC-FR: Houston vs. Pittsburgh, 1989 (ot)
Amp Lee, NFC-D: Minnesota vs. Chicago, 1994
Jay Novacek, NFC-D: Dallas vs. Green Bay, 1994
O.J. McDuffie, AFC-FR: Miami vs. Buffalo, 1995
Jerry Rice, NFC-D: San Francisco vs. Green Bay, 1995
Hines Ward, AFC-FR: Pittsburgh vs. Cleveland, 2002
Deion Branch, SB: New England vs. Philadelphia, 2004
Plaxico Burress, NFC: N.Y. Giants vs. Green Bay, 2007 (ot)
Wes Welker, SB: New England vs. N.Y. Giants, 2007
Roddy White, NFC-FR: Atlanta vs. Arizona, 2008
Pierre Garcon, AFC: Indianapolis vs. N.Y. Jets, 2009

Most Consecutive Games, Pass Receptions
28 Jerry Rice, San Francisco-Oakland, 1985-2002
22 Drew Pearson, Dallas, 1973-1983
18 Paul Warfield, Cleveland-Miami, 1964-1974
Cliff Branch, Oakland/L.A. Raiders, 1974-1983
Thurman Thomas, Buffalo, 1989-1998
Shannon Sharpe, Denver-Baltimore-Denver, 1991-2003

YARDS GAINED

Most Yards Gained, Career
2,245 Jerry Rice, San Francisco-Oakland-Seattle, 29 games
1,315 Michael Irvin, Dallas, 16 games
1,289 Cliff Branch, Oakland/L.A. Raiders, 22 games

Most Yards Gained, Game
240 Eric Moulds, AFC-FR: Buffalo vs. Miami, 1998
227 Anthony Carter, NFC-D: Minnesota vs. San Francisco, 1987
221 Reggie Wayne, AFC-FR: Indianapolis vs. Denver, 2004

Most Games, 100 or More Yards Receiving, Career
8 Jerry Rice, San Francisco-Oakland-Seattle, 29 games
6 Michael Irvin, Dallas, 16 games
5 John Stallworth, Pittsburgh, 18 games
Andre Reed, Buffalo, 21 games
Hines Ward, Pittsburgh, 14 games

Most Consecutive Games, 100 or More Yards Receiving, Career
4 Larry Fitzgerald, Arizona, 2008
3 Tom Fears, Los Angeles, 1950-51
Jerry Rice, San Francisco, 1988-89
Randy Moss, Minnesota, 1999-2000
2 By many players

Longest Reception
96 Shannon Sharpe (from Dilfer), AFC: Baltimore vs. Oakland, 2000 (TD)
94 Alvin Harper (from Aikman), NFC-D: Dallas vs. Green Bay, 1994 (TD)
93 Elbert Dubenion (from Lamonica), AFC-D: Buffalo vs. Boston, 1963 (TD)

AVERAGE GAIN

Highest Average Gain, Career (20 receptions)
27.3 Alvin Harper, Dallas, 10 games (24-655)
23.7 Willie Gault, Chicago-L.A. Raiders, 12 games (21-497)
22.8 Harold Jackson, L.A. Rams-New England-Minnesota-Seattle, 14 games (24-548)

Highest Average Gain, Game (3 receptions)
46.3 Harold Jackson, NFC: Los Angeles vs. Minnesota, 1974 (3-139)
42.7 Billy Cannon, AFC: Houston vs. L.A. Chargers, 1960 (3-128)
42.0 Lenny Moore, NFC: Baltimore vs. N.Y. Giants, 1959 (3-126)

TOUCHDOWNS

Most Touchdowns, Career
22 Jerry Rice, San Francisco-Oakland-Seattle, 29 games
12 John Stallworth, Pittsburgh, 18 games
10 Fred Biletnikoff, Oakland, 19 games
Antonio Freeman, Green Bay-Philadelphia-Green Bay, 16 games
Randy Moss, Minnesota-New England, 12 games

Most Touchdowns, Game
3 Tom Fears, NFC-D: Los Angeles vs. Chi. Bears, 1950
Gary Collins, NFC: Cleveland vs. Baltimore, 1964
Fred Biletnikoff, AFC-D: Oakland vs. Kansas City, 1968
Preston Pearson, NFC: Dallas vs. Los Angeles, 1975
Dave Casper, AFC-D: Oakland vs. Baltimore, 1977 (ot)
Alvin Garrett, NFC-FR: Washington vs. Detroit, 1982
Jerry Rice, NFC-D: San Francisco vs. Minnesota, 1988

Jerry Rice, SB: San Francisco vs. Denver, 1989
Andre Reed, AFC-FR: Buffalo vs. Houston, 1992 (ot)
Sterling Sharpe, NFC-FR: Green Bay vs. Detroit, 1993
Jerry Rice, SB: San Francisco vs. San Diego, 1994
Willie Jackson, NFC-FR: New Orleans vs. St. Louis, 2000
Amani Toomer, NFC-FR: N.Y. Giants vs. San Francisco, 2002
Larry Fitzgerald, NFC: Arizona vs. Philadelphia, 2008
Sidney Rice, NFC-D: Minnesota vs. Dallas, 2009

Most Consecutive Games, Touchdown Passes Caught
8 John Stallworth, Pittsburgh, 1978-1983
7 David Givens, New England, 2003-05)
5 James Lofton, Green Bay-Buffalo, 1982-1990
Randy Moss, Minnesota, 1998-2000
Antonio Freeman, Green Bay, 1997-2001
Hines Ward, Pittsburgh, 2002-05
Larry Fitzgerald, Arizona, 2008-09

INTERCEPTIONS BY

Most Interceptions, Career
9 Charlie Waters, Dallas, 25 games
Bill Simpson, Los Angeles-Buffalo, 11 games
Ronnie Lott, San Francisco-L.A. Raiders, 20 games
8 Lester Hayes, Oakland/L.A. Raiders, 13 games
7 Willie Brown, Oakland, 17 games
Dennis Thurman, Dallas, 14 games
Rodney Harrison, San Diego-New England, 13 games
Asante Samuel, New England-Philadelphia, 18 games
Ed Reed, Baltimore, 7 games

Most Interceptions, Game
4 Vernon Perry, AFC-D: Houston vs. San Diego, 1979
3 Joe Laws, NFC: Green Bay vs. N.Y. Giants, 1944
Charlie Waters, NFC-D: Dallas vs. Chicago, 1977
Rod Martin, SB: Oakland vs. Philadelphia, 1980
Dennis Thurman, NFC-D: Dallas vs. Green Bay, 1982
A.J. Duhe, AFC: Miami vs. N.Y. Jets, 1982
Ty Law, AFC: New England vs. Indianapolis, 2003
Ricky Manning Jr., NFC: Carolina vs. Philadelphia, 2003
2 By many players

Most Consecutive Games, Interceptions
4 Aeneas Williams, Arizona-St. Louis, 1998-2001
Rodney Harrison, New England, 2004, 2007
3 By many players. Last time:
Ed Reed, Baltimore, 2006, 2008

YARDS GAINED

Most Yards Gained, Career
227 Asante Samuel, New England-Philadelphia, 18 games
196 Willie Brown, Oakland, 17 games
187 Ronnie Lott, San Francisco-L.A.-Raiders, 20 games

Most Yards Gained, Game
108 Darrien Gordon, SB: Denver vs. Atlanta, 1998
101 George Teague, NFC-FR: Green Bay vs. Detroit, 1993
100 Champ Bailey, AFC-D: Denver vs. New England, 2005
James Harrison, SB: Pittsburgh vs. Arizona, 2008

Longest Return
101 George Teague, NFC-FR: Green Bay vs. Detroit, 1993 (TD)
100 Champ Bailey, AFC-D: Denver vs. New England, 2005
James Harrison, SB: Pittsburgh vs. Arizona, 2008 (TD)
98 Darrol Ray, AFC-FR: N.Y. Jets vs. Cincinnati, 1982 (TD)

TOUCHDOWNS

Most Touchdowns, Career
4 Asante Samuel, New England-Philadelphia, 18 games
3 Willie Brown, Oakland, 17 games
2 Lester Hayes, Oakland/L.A. Raiders, 13 games
Ronnie Lott, San Francisco-L.A. Raiders, 20 games
Darrell Green, Washington, 18 games
Melvin Jenkins, Seattle-Detroit, 5 games
George Teague, Green Bay-Dallas-Miami-Dallas, 12 games
Aeneas Williams, Arizona-St. Louis, 6 games
Dwight Smith, Tampa Bay, 4 games

Most Touchdowns, Game
2 Aeneas Williams, NFC-D: St. Louis vs. Green Bay, 2001
Dwight Smith, SB: Tampa Bay vs. Oakland, 2002
1 By many players

PUNTING

Most Punts, Career
111 Ray Guy, Oakland/L.A. Raiders, 22 games
101 Craig Hentrich, Green Bay-Tennessee, 22 games
84 Danny White, Dallas, 18 games
Sean Landeta, N.Y. Giants-Tampa Bay-Green Bay-Philadelphia-St. Louis, 18 games

Most Punts, Game
14 Dave Jennings, AFC-D: N.Y. Jets vs. Cleveland, 1986 (ot)
12 David Lee, AFC-D: Baltimore vs. Oakland, 1977 (ot)
11 Ken Strong, NFC: N.Y. Giants vs. Chi. Bears, 1933
Jim Norton, AFC: Houston vs. Oakland, 1967
Ode Burrell, AFC-D: Houston vs. Oakland, 1969
Dale Hatcher, NFC: L.A. Rams vs. Chicago, 1985
Brad Maynard, SB: N.Y. Giants vs. Baltimore, 2000

Longest Punt
76 Ed Danowski, NFC: N.Y. Giants vs. Detroit, 1935
Mike Horan, AFC: Denver vs. Buffalo, 1991
72 Charlie Conerly, NFC-D: N.Y. Giants vs. Cleveland, 1950
Yale Lary, NFC: Detroit vs. Cleveland, 1953
71 Ray Guy, AFC: Oakland vs. San Diego, 1980

AVERAGE YARDAGE

Highest Average, Career (25 punts)
44.5 Rich Camarillo, New England, 6 games (35-1,559)
44.44 Todd Sauerbrun, Carolina-Denver-New England, 9 games (43-1,911)
44.38 Mike Scifres, San Diego, 8 games (42-1,864)

Highest Average, Game (4 punts)
56.0 Ray Guy, AFC: Oakland vs. San Diego, 1980 (4-224)
53.3 Craig Hentrich, AFC-D: Tennessee vs. Baltimore, 2008 (4-213)
52.8 Hunter Smith, AFC: Indianapolis vs. New England, 2006 (4-211)

PUNT RETURNS

Most Punt Returns, Career
34 David Meggett, N.Y. Giants-New England-N.Y. Jets, 13 games
Brian Mitchell, Washington-Philadelphia, 16 games
33 Troy Brown, New England, 20 games
25 Theo Bell, Pittsburgh-Tampa Bay, 10 games

Most Punt Returns, Game
7 Ron Gardin, AFC-D: Baltimore vs. Cincinnati, 1970
Carl Roaches, AFC-FR: Houston vs. Oakland, 1980
Gerald McNeil, AFC-D: Cleveland vs. N.Y. Jets, 1986 (ot)
Phil McConkey, NFC-D: N.Y. Giants vs. San Francisco, 1986
David Meggett, AFC-D: New England vs. Pittsburgh, 1996
Reggie Barlow, AFC-FR: Jacksonville vs. New England, 1998
6 George McAfee, NFC-D: Chi. Bears vs. Los Angeles, 1950
Eddie Brown, NFC-D: Washington vs. Minnesota, 1976
Theo Bell, AFC: Pittsburgh vs. Houston, 1978
Eddie Brown, NFC: Los Angeles vs. Tampa Bay, 1979
John Sciarra, NFC: Philadelphia vs. Dallas, 1980
Kurt Sohn, AFC: N.Y. Jets vs. Miami, 1982
Mike Nelms, SB: Washington vs. Miami, 1982
Anthony Carter, NFC-FR: Minnesota vs. New Orleans, 1987
Desmond Howard, SB: Green Bay vs. New England, 1996
Nate Jacquet, AFC-FR: Miami vs. Seattle, 1999
Derrick Mason, AFC-FR: Tennessee vs. Baltimore, 2003
Antonio Chatman, AFC-D: Green Bay vs. Philadelphia, 2003
Nate Burleson, NFC-FR: Seattle vs. Washington, 2007
Jim Leonhard, AFC: Baltimore vs. Pittsburgh, 2008

5 By many players

YARDS GAINED

Most Yards Gained, Career

339 Brian Mitchell, Washington-Philadelphia, 16 games
315 Troy Brown, New England, 20 games
312 David Meggett, N.Y. Giants-New England-N.Y. Jets, 13 games

Most Yards Gained, Game

152 Allen Rossum, NFC-D: Atlanta vs. St. Louis, 2004
143 Anthony Carter, NFC-FR: Minnesota vs. New Orleans, 1987
141 Bob Hayes, NFC-D: Dallas vs. Cleveland, 1967

Longest Return

88 Jermaine Lewis, AFC-D: Baltimore vs. Pittsburgh, 2001 (TD)
84 Anthony Carter, NFC-FR: Minnesota vs. New Orleans, 1987 (TD)
83 Reggie Bush, NFC-D: New Orleans vs. Arizona, 2009 (TD)

AVERAGE YARDAGE

Highest Average, Career (10 returns)

23.9 Allen Rossum, Green Bay-Atlanta, 6 games (10-239)
15.3 Robert Brooks, Green Bay, 11 games (14-214)
15.2 Anthony Carter, Minnesota-Detroit, 9 games (17-259)

Highest Average Gain, Game (3 returns)

50.7 Allen Rossum, NFC-D: Atlanta vs. St. Louis, 2004 (3-152)
47.0 Bob Hayes, NFC-D: Dallas vs. Cleveland, 1967 (3-141)
36.3 Reggie Bush, NFC-D: New Orleans vs. Arizona, 2009 (3-109)

TOUCHDOWNS

Most Touchdowns

1 Hugh Gallarneau, NFC-D: Chicago Bears vs. Green Bay, 1941
Bosh Pritchard, NFC-D: Philadelphia vs. Pittsburgh, 1947
Charley Trippi, NFC: Chicago Cardinals vs. Philadelphia, 1947
Verda (Vitamin T) Smith, NFC-D: Los Angeles vs. Detroit, 1952
George (Butch) Byrd, AFC: Buffalo vs. San Diego, 1965
Golden Richards, NFC: Dallas vs. Minnesota, 1973
Wes Chandler, AFC-D: San Diego vs. Miami, 1981 (ot)
Shaun Gayle, NFC-D: Chicago vs. N.Y. Giants, 1985
Anthony Carter, NFC-FR: Minnesota vs. New Orleans, 1987
Darrell Green, NFC-D: Washington vs. Chicago, 1987
Antonio Freeman, NFC-FR: Green Bay vs. Atlanta, 1995
Desmond Howard, NFC-D: Green Bay vs. San Francisco, 1996
Jermaine Lewis, AFC-D: Baltimore vs. Pittsburgh, 2001
Troy Brown, AFC: New England vs. Pittsburgh, 2001
Antwaan Randle El, AFC-FR: Pittsburgh vs. Cleveland, 2002
Santana Moss, AFC-D: N.Y. Jets vs. Pittsburgh, 2004 (ot)
Allen Rossum, NFC-D: Atlanta vs. St. Louis, 2004
Steve Smith, NFC: Carolina vs. Seattle, 2005
Santonio Holmes, AFC: Pittsburgh vs. San Diego, 2008
Reggie Bush, NFC-D: New Orleans vs. Arizona, 2009

KICKOFF RETURNS

Most Kickoff Returns, Career

36 Brian Mitchell, Washington-Philadelphia, 16 games
31 Kevin Williams, Dallas-Buffalo, 12 games
29 Fulton Walker, Miami-L.A. Raiders, 10 games

Most Kickoff Returns, Game

8 Marc Logan, AFC-D: Miami vs. Buffalo, 1990
Andre Coleman, SB: San Diego vs. San Francisco, 1994
Marcus Knight, SB: Oakland vs. Tampa Bay, 2002
7 Don Bingham, NFC: Chi. Bears vs. N.Y. Giants, 1956
Reggie Brown, NFC-FR: Atlanta vs. Minnesota, 1982
David Verser, AFC-FR: Cincinnati vs. N.Y. Jets, 1982
Del Rodgers, NFC-D: Green Bay vs. Dallas, 1982
Henry Ellard, NFC-D: L.A. Rams vs. Washington, 1983
Stephen Starring, SB: New England vs. Chicago, 1985
Darick Holmes, AFC-D: Buffalo vs. Pittsburgh, 1995
Antonio Freeman, NFC: Green Bay vs. Dallas, 1995
Roell Preston, NFC-FR: Green Bay vs. San Francisco, 1998
Robert Tate, NFC-D: Minnesota vs. St. Louis, 1999
Fred McAfee, NFC-D: New Orleans vs. Minnesota, 2000
Michael Bates, NFC-FR: Dallas vs. Carolina, 2003
Dante Hall, AFC-D: Kansas City vs. Indianapolis, 2003
Michael Lewis, NFC: New Orleans vs. Chicago, 2006
6 By many players

YARDS GAINED

Most Yards Gained, Career

875 Brian Mitchell, Washington-Philadelphia, 16 games
677 Fulton Walker, Miami-L.A. Raiders, 10 games
632 Kevin Williams, Dallas-Buffalo, 12 games

Most Yards Gained, Game

244 Andre Coleman, SB: San Diego vs. San Francisco, 1994
220 Ellis Hobbs, AFC: New England vs. Indianapolis, 2006
210 Tim Dwight, SB: Atlanta vs. Denver, 1998

Longest Return

100 Brian Mitchell, NFC-D: Washington vs. Tampa Bay, 1999 (TD)
99 Desmond Howard, SB: Green Bay vs. New England, 1996 (TD)
98 Fulton Walker, SB: Miami vs. Washington, 1982 (TD)
Andre Coleman, SB: San Diego vs. San Francisco, 1994 (TD)

AVERAGE YARDAGE

Highest Average, Career (10 returns)

30.1 Carl Garrett, Oakland, 5 games (16-481)
30.0 Reggie Barlow, Jacksonville, 8 games (12-360)
29.2 Chad Morton, New Orleans-N.Y. Jets-N.Y. Giants, 6 games (14-409)

Highest Average, Game (3 returns)

56.7 Les (Speedy) Duncan, NFC-D: Washington vs. San Francisco, 1971 (3-170)
51.3 Ed Podolak, AFC-D: Kansas City vs. Miami, 1971 (ot) (3-154)
49.0 Les (Speedy) Duncan, AFC: San Diego vs. Buffalo, 1964 (3-147)

TOUCHDOWNS

Most Touchdowns, Career

2 Ron Dixon, N.Y. Giants, 4 games
1 By many players

Most Touchdowns, Game

1 Vic Washington, NFC-D: San Francisco vs. Dallas, 1972
Nat Moore, AFC-D: Miami vs. Oakland, 1974
Marshall Johnson, AFC-D: Baltimore vs. Oakland, 1977 (ot)
Fulton Walker, SB: Miami vs. Washington, 1982
Stanford Jennings, SB: Cincinnati vs. San Francisco, 1988
Eric Metcalf, AFC-D: Cleveland vs. Buffalo, 1989
Andre Coleman, SB: San Diego vs. San Francisco, 1994
Desmond Howard, SB: Green Bay vs. New England, 1996
Chuck Levy, NFC: San Francisco vs. Green Bay, 1997
Tim Dwight, SB: Atlanta vs. Denver, 1998
Kevin Dyson, AFC-FR: Tennessee vs. Buffalo, 1999
Charlie Rogers, AFC-FR: Seattle vs. Miami, 1999
Brian Mitchell, NFC-D: Washington vs. Tampa Bay, 1999
Tony Horne, NFC-D: St. Louis vs. Minnesota, 1999
Derrick Mason, AFC: Tennessee vs. Jacksonville, 1999
Ron Dixon, NFC-D: N.Y. Giants vs. Philadelphia, 2000; SB: N.Y. Giants vs. Baltimore, 2000
Jermaine Lewis, SB: Baltimore vs. N.Y. Giants, 2000
Dante Hall, AFC-D: Kansas City vs. Indianapolis, 2003
Miles Austin, NFC-FR: Dallas vs. Seattle, 2006
Devin Hester, SB: Chicago vs. Indianapolis, 2006

FUMBLES

Most Fumbles, Career

16 Warren Moon, Houston-Minnesota, 10 games
14 John Elway, Denver, 22 games
Donovan McNabb, Philadelphia, 16 games
13 Tony Dorsett, Dallas, 17 games

Most Fumbles, Game

5 Warren Moon, AFC-D: Houston vs. Kansas City, 1993
4 Brian Sipe, AFC-D: Cleveland vs. Oakland, 1980
Randall Cunningham, NFC-FR: Minnesota vs. N.Y. Giants, 1997
3 By many players

RECOVERIES

Most Own Fumbles Recovered, Career

8 Warren Moon, Houston-Minnesota, 10 games
7 John Elway, Denver, 22 games
6 Jim Kelly, Buffalo, 17 games

Most Opponents' Fumbles Recovered, Career

4 Cliff Harris, Dallas, 21 games
Harvey Martin, Dallas, 22 games
Ted Hendricks, Baltimore-Oakland/L.A. Raiders, 21 games
Alvin Walton, Washington, 9 games
Monte Coleman, Washington, 21 games
Dave Thomas, Dallas-Jacksonville-N.Y. Giants, 13 games
3 Paul Krause, Minnesota, 19 games
Jack Lambert, Pittsburgh, 18 games
Fred Dryer, Los Angeles, 14 games
Charlie Waters, Dallas, 25 games
Jack Ham, Pittsburgh, 16 games
Mike Hegman, Dallas, 16 games
Tom Jackson, Denver, 10 games
Rich Milot, Washington, 13 games
Mike Singletary, Chicago, 12 games
Darryl Grant, Washington, 16 games
Wes Hopkins, Philadelphia, 3 games
Wilber Marshall, Chicago-Washington, 15 games
Tyrone Braxton, Denver-Miami-Denver, 19 games
Neil Smith, Kansas City-Denver, 16 games
Tony Brackens, Jacksonville, 7 games
Phil Hansen, Buffalo, 14 games
Carnell Lake, Pittsburgh-Jacksonville-Baltimore, 17 games
Jason Gildon, Pittsburgh, 13 games
Tedy Bruschi, New England, 22 games
Jim Leonhard, Baltimore-N.Y. Jets, 6 games
2 By many players

Most Fumbles Recovered, Game, Own and Opponents'

3 Jack Lambert, AFC: Pittsburgh vs. Oakland, 1975 (3 opp)
Ron Jaworski, NFC-FR: Philadelphia vs. N.Y. Giants, 1981 (3 own)
Devin Hester, NFC-D: Chicago vs. Seattle, 2006 (3-own)
2 By many players

YARDS GAINED

Longest Return

93 Andy Russell, AFC-D: Pittsburgh vs. Baltimore, 1975 (opp, TD)
79 Neil Smith, AFC-D: Denver vs. Miami, 1998 (opp, TD)
64 Leon Lett, SB: Dallas vs. Buffalo, 1992 (opp)

TOUCHDOWNS

Most Touchdowns

1 By many players

COMBINED NET YARDS GAINED

Rushing, receiving, interception returns, punt returns, kickoff returns, and fumble returns.

ATTEMPTS

Most Attempts, Career

454 Franco Harris, Pittsburgh, 19 games
417 Thurman Thomas, Buffalo, 21 games
397 Emmitt Smith, Dallas, 17 games

Most Attempts, Game

43 Lamar Smith, AFC-FR: Miami vs. Indianapolis, 2000 (ot)
42 Curtis Martin, AFC-D: N.Y. Jets vs. Jacksonville, 1998
40 Lawrence McCutcheon, NFC-D: Los Angeles vs. St. Louis, 1975

YARDS GAINED

Most Yards Gained, Career

2,289 Jerry Rice, San Francisco-Oakland-Seattle, 29 games
2,124 Thurman Thomas, Buffalo, 21 games
2,060 Franco Harris, Pittsburgh, 19 games

Most Yards Gained, Game

350 Ed Podolak, AFC-D: Kansas City vs. Miami, 1971 (ot)
329 Keith Lincoln, AFC: San Diego vs. Boston, 1963
328 Darren Sproles, AFC-FR: San Diego vs. Indianapolis, 2008 (ot)

SACKS

Sacks have been compiled since 1982.

Most Sacks, Career

16.0 Willie McGinest, New England, 18 games
14.5 Bruce Smith, Buffalo, 20 games
12.0 Reggie White, Philadelphia-Green Bay, 19 games

Most Sacks, Game

4.5 Willie McGinest, AFC-FR: New England vs. Jacksonville, 2005
3.5 Rich Milot, NFC-D: Washington vs. Chicago, 1984
Richard Dent, NFC-D: Chicago vs. N.Y. Giants, 1985
3.0 Richard Dent, NFC-D: Chicago vs. Washington, 1984
Garin Veris, AFC-FR: New England vs. N.Y. Jets, 1985
Gary Jeter, NFC-D: L.A. Rams vs. Dallas, 1985
Carl Hairston, AFC-D: Cleveland vs. N.Y. Jets, 1986 (ot)
Charles Mann, NFC-D: Washington vs. Chicago, 1987
Kevin Greene, NFC-FR: L.A. Rams vs. Minnesota, 1988
Greg Townsend, AFC-D: L.A. Raiders vs. Cincinnati, 1990
Wilber Marshall, NFC: Washington vs. Detroit, 1991
Fred Stokes, NFC-FR: Washington vs. Minnesota, 1992
Pierce Holt, NFC-D: San Francisco vs. Washington, 1992
Tony Casillas, NFC: Dallas vs. San Francisco, 1992
Gerald Williams, AFC-FR: Pittsburgh vs. Kansas City, 1993
Chad Brown, AFC-FR: Pittsburgh vs. Indianapolis, 1996
Reggie White, SB: Green Bay vs. New England, 1996
Warren Sapp, NFC-D: Tampa Bay vs. Green Bay, 1997
Trace Armstrong, AFC-FR: Miami vs. Seattle, 1999
Michael McCrary, AFC-FR: Baltimore vs. Denver, 2000
Willie McGinest, AFC-D: New England vs. Tennessee, 2003
Darnell Dockett, SB: Arizona vs. Pittsburgh, 2008
Ray Edwards, NFC-D: Minnesota vs. Dallas, 2009

TEAM RECORDS

CHAMPIONSHIPS

Most Seasons League Champion

12 Green Bay, 1929-1931, 1936, 1939, 1944, 1961-62, 1965-67, 1996
9 Chi. Bears, 1921, 1932-33, 1940-41, 1943, 1946, 1963, 1985
7 N.Y. Giants, 1927, 1934, 1938, 1956, 1986, 1990, 2007

Most Consecutive Seasons League Champion

3 Green Bay, 1929-1931
Green Bay, 1965-67
2 Canton, 1922-23

Chi. Bears, 1932-33
Chi. Bears, 1940-41
Philadelphia, 1948-49
Detroit, 1952-53
Cleveland, 1954-55
Baltimore, 1958-59
Houston, 1960-61
Green Bay, 1961-62
Buffalo, 1964-65
Miami, 1972-73
Pittsburgh, 1974-75
Pittsburgh, 1978-79
San Francisco, 1988-89
Dallas, 1992-93
Denver, 1997-98
New England, 2003-04

GAMES, VICTORIES, DEFEATS

Most Seasons Participating in Postseason Games
30 N.Y. Giants, 1933-35, 1938-39, 1941, 1943-44, 1946, 1950, 1956, 1958-59, 1961-63, 1981, 1984-86, 1989-1990, 1993, 1997, 2000, 2002, 2005-08
Dallas, 1966-1973, 1975-1983, 1985, 1991-96, 1998-99, 2003, 2006-07, 2009
27 Cleveland/L.A./St. Louis Rams, 1945, 1949-1952, 1955, 1967, 1969, 1973-1980, 1983-86, 1988-89, 1999-2001, 2003-04
26 Minnesota, 1968-1971, 1973-78, 1980, 1982, 1987-89, 1992-94, 1996-2000, 2004, 2008-09

Most Consecutive Seasons Participating in Postseason Games
9 Dallas, 1975-1983
8 Dallas, 1966-1973
Pittsburgh, 1972-79
Los Angeles, 1973-1980
San Francisco, 1983-1990
Indianapolis, 2002-09 (current)
7 Houston, 1987-1993
San Francisco, 1992-98

Most Games
58 Dallas, 1966-1973, 1975-1983, 1985, 1991-96, 1998-99, 2003, 2006-07, 2009
50 Pittsburgh, 1947, 1972-79, 1982-84, 1989, 1992-97, 2001-02, 2004-05, 2007-08
45 Minnesota, 1968-1971, 1973-78, 1980, 1982, 1987-89, 1992-94, 1996-2000, 2004, 2008-09

Most Games Won
33 Dallas, 1967, 1970-73, 1975, 1977-78, 1980-82, 1991-96, 2009
31 Pittsburgh, 1972, 1974-76, 1978-79, 1984, 1989, 1994-97, 2001-02, 2004-05, 2008
25 Oakland/L.A. Raiders, 1967-1970, 1973-77, 1980, 1982-83, 1990, 1993, 2000-02
San Francisco, 1970-71, 1981, 1983-84, 1988-1990, 1992-94, 1996-98, 2002
Green Bay, 1936, 1939, 1944, 1961-62, 1965-67, 1982, 1993-97, 2001, 2003, 2007

Most Consecutive Games Won
10 New England, 2001, 2003-05
9 Green Bay, 1961-62, 1965-67
7 Pittsburgh, 1974-76
San Francisco, 1988-1990
Dallas, 1992-94
Denver, 1997-98

Most Games Lost
26 Minnesota, 1968-1971, 1973-78, 1980, 1982, 1987-89, 1992-94, 1996-2000, 2004, 2008-09
25 Dallas, 1966-1970, 1972-73, 1975-76, 1978-1983, 1985, 1991, 1994, 1996, 1998-99, 2003, 2006-07, 2009
24 L.A./St. Louis Rams, 1949-1950, 1952, 1955, 1967, 1969, 1973-1980, 1983-86, 1988-89, 2000-01, 2003-04
N.Y. Giants, 1933, 1935, 1939, 1941, 1943-44, 1946, 1950, 1958-59, 1961-63, 1981, 1984-85, 1989, 1993, 1997, 2000, 2002, 2005-06, 2008

Most Consecutive Games Lost
6 N.Y. Giants, 1939, 1941, 1943-44, 1946, 1950
Cleveland, 1969, 1971-72, 1980, 1982, 1985
Minnesota, 1988-89, 1992-94, 1996
Detroit, 1991, 1993-95, 1997, 1999 (current)
Seattle, 1984, 1987-88, 1999, 2003-04
Kansas City, 1993-95, 1997, 2003, 2006 (current))
Dallas, 1996, 1998-99, 2003, 2006-07 (current)
5 N.Y. Giants, 1958-59, 1961-63
Los Angeles, 1952, 1955, 1967, 1969, 1973
Denver, 1977-79, 1983-84
Baltimore/Indianapolis, 1971, 1975-77, 1987
Philadelphia, 1980-81, 1988-1990
Indianapolis, 1995-96, 1999-2000, 2002
4 Washington, 1972-74, 1976
Miami, 1974, 1978-79, 1981
Chi. Cardinals/St. Louis, 1948, 1974-75, 1982
Boston/New England, 1963, 1976, 1978, 1982
New Orleans, 1987, 1990-92
Buffalo, 1995-96, 1998-99 (current)
N.Y. Giants, 2000, 2002, 2005-06
San Diego, 1994-95, 2004, 2006

SCORING

Most Points, Game
73 NFC: Chi. Bears vs. Washington, 1940
62 AFC-D: Jacksonville vs. Miami, 1999
59 NFC: Detroit vs. Cleveland, 1957

Most Points, Both Teams, Game
96 NFC-FR: Arizona (51) vs. Green Bay (45), 2009
95 NFC-FR: Philadelphia (58) vs. Detroit (37), 1995
86 NFC-D: St. Louis (49) vs. Minnesota (37), 1999

Fewest Points, Both Teams, Game
5 NFC-D: Detroit (0) vs. Dallas (5), 1970
7 NFC: Chi. Cardinals (0) vs. Philadelphia (7), 1948
9 NFC: Tampa Bay (0) vs. Los Angeles (9), 1979

Largest Margin of Victory, Game
73 NFC: Chi. Bears vs. Washington, 1940 (73-0)
55 AFC-D: Jacksonville vs. Miami, 1999 (62-7)
49 AFC-D: Oakland vs. Houston, 1969 (56-7)

Most Points, Shutout Victory, Game
73 NFC: Chi. Bears vs. Washington, 1940
41 NFC: N.Y. Giants vs. Minnesota, 2000
AFC-FR: N.Y. Jets vs. Indianapolis, 2002
38 NFC-D: Dallas vs. Tampa Bay, 1981

Most Points Overcome to Win Game
32 AFC-FR: Buffalo vs. Houston, 1992 (trailed 3-35, won 41-38) (ot)
24 NFC-FR: San Francisco vs. N.Y. Giants, 2002 (trailed 14-38, won 39-38)
20 NFC-D: Detroit vs. San Francisco, 1957 (trailed 7-27, won 31-27)

Most Points, Each Half
1st: 41 AFC: Buffalo vs. L.A. Raiders, 1990
AFC-D: Jacksonville vs. Miami, 1999
38 NFC-D: Washington vs. L.A. Rams, 1983
NFC-FR: Philadelphia vs. Detroit, 1995
35 NFC: Cleveland vs. Detroit, 1954
AFC-D: Oakland vs. Houston, 1969
SB: Washington vs. Denver, 1987
AFC-FR: Indianapolis vs. Denver, 2004
NFC-D: New Orleans vs. Arizona, 2009
2nd: 45 NFC: Chi. Bears vs. Washington, 1940
35 AFC-FR: Buffalo vs. Houston, 1992
NFC-D: St. Louis vs. Minnesota, 1999
NFC-FR: Green Bay vs. Arizona, 2009
32 AFC: Indianapolis vs. New England, 2006

Most Points, Each Quarter
1st: 28 AFC-D: Oakland vs. Houston, 1969

24 AFC-D: San Diego vs. Miami, 1981
AFC-D: Jacksonville vs. Miami, 1999
AFC-D: Baltimore vs. New England, 2009
21 NFC: Chi. Bears vs. Washington, 1940
AFC: San Diego vs. Boston, 1963
AFC-D: Oakland vs. Kansas City, 1968
AFC: Oakland vs. San Diego, 1980
AFC: Buffalo vs. L.A. Raiders, 1990
NFC: San Francisco vs. Dallas, 1994
NFC-D: New Orleans vs. Arizona, 2009
2nd: 35 SB: Washington vs. Denver, 1987
31 NFC-FR: Philadelphia vs. Detroit, 1995
27 NFC-FR: Dallas vs. Philadelphia, 2009
3rd: 28 AFC-FR: Buffalo vs. Houston, 1992
26 NFC: Chi. Bears vs. Washington, 1940
21 NFC-D: Dallas vs. Cleveland, 1967
NFC-D: Dallas vs. Tampa Bay, 1981
AFC-D: L.A. Raiders vs. Pittsburgh, 1983
SB: Chicago vs. New England, 1985
NFC-D: N.Y. Giants vs. San Francisco, 1986
AFC: Cleveland vs. Denver, 1987
AFC: Cleveland vs. Denver, 1989
NFC-D: St. Louis vs. Minnesota, 1999
4th: 27 NFC: N.Y. Giants vs. Chi. Bears, 1934
26 NFC-FR: Philadelphia vs. New Orleans, 1992
24 NFC: Baltimore vs. N.Y. Giants, 1959
OT: 6 NFC: Baltimore vs. N.Y. Giants, 1958
AFC-D: Oakland vs. Baltimore, 1977
NFC-D: L.A. Rams vs. N.Y. Giants, 1989
AFC-FR: Miami vs. Indianapolis, 2000
NFC-FR: Green Bay vs. Seattle, 2003
NFC-D: Carolina vs. St. Louis, 2003
AFC-FR: San Diego vs. Indianapolis, 2008
NFC-FR: Arizona vs. Green Bay, 2009

TOUCHDOWNS

Most Touchdowns, Game

11 NFC: Chi. Bears vs. Washington, 1940
8 NFC: Cleveland vs. Detroit, 1954
NFC: Detroit vs. Cleveland, 1957
AFC-D: Oakland vs. Houston, 1969
SB: San Francisco vs. Denver, 1989
AFC-D: Jacksonville vs. Miami, 1999
7 AFC: San Diego vs. Boston, 1963
NFC-D: Dallas vs. Cleveland, 1967
NFC-D: N.Y. Giants vs. San Francisco, 1986
AFC: Buffalo vs. L.A. Raiders, 1990
SB: Dallas vs. Buffalo, 1992
SB: San Francisco vs. San Diego, 1994
NFC-FR: Philadelphia vs. Detroit, 1995
NFC-D: St. Louis vs. Minnesota, 1999
AFC-FR: Indianapolis vs. Denver, 2004
NFC-FR: Arizona vs. Green Bay, 2009 (ot)

Most Touchdowns, Both Teams, Game

13 NFC-FR: Arizona (7) vs. Green Bay (6), 2009 (ot)
12 NFC-FR: Philadelphia (7) vs. Detroit (5), 1995
NFC-D: St. Louis (7) vs. Minnesota (5), 1999
11 NFC: Chi. Bears (11) vs. Washington (0), 1940

Fewest Touchdowns, Both Teams, Game

0 NFC-D: N.Y. Giants vs. Cleveland, 1950
NFC-D: Dallas vs. Detroit, 1970
NFC: Los Angeles vs. Tampa Bay, 1979
AFC-D: Baltimore vs. Indianapolis, 2006
1 NFC: Chi. Cardinals (0) vs. Philadelphia (1), 1948
NFC-D: Cleveland (0) vs. N.Y. Giants (1), 1958
AFC: San Diego (0) vs. Houston (1), 1961
AFC-D: N.Y. Jets (0) vs. Kansas City (1), 1969
NFC-D: Green Bay (0) vs. Washington (1), 1972
NFC-FR: New Orleans (0) vs. Chicago (1), 1990
NFC: N.Y. Giants (0) vs. San Francisco (1), 1990
AFC-FR: L.A. Raiders (0) vs. Kansas City (1), 1991
AFC-D: New England (0) vs. Pittsburgh (1), 1997
NFC: Tampa Bay (0) vs. St. Louis (1), 1999
AFC: Oakland (0) vs. Baltimore (1), 2000
2 In many games

POINTS AFTER TOUCHDOWN

Most (One-Point) Points After Touchdown, Game

8 NFC: Cleveland vs. Detroit, 1954
NFC: Detroit vs. Cleveland, 1957
AFC-D: Oakland vs. Houston, 1969
AFC-D: Jacksonville vs. Miami, 1999
7 NFC: Chi. Bears vs. Washington, 1940
NFC-D: Dallas vs. Cleveland, 1967
NFC-D: N.Y. Giants vs. San Francisco, 1986
SB: San Francisco vs. Denver, 1989
SB: Dallas vs. Buffalo, 1992
SB: San Francisco vs. San Diego, 1994
NFC-FR: Philadelphia vs. Detroit, 1995
NFC-D: St. Louis vs. Minnesota, 1999
AFC-FR: Indianapolis vs. Denver, 2004
6 AFC: San Diego vs. Boston, 1963
NFC-D: Washington vs. L.A. Rams, 1983
AFC: Miami vs. Pittsburgh, 1984
SB: Washington vs. Denver, 1987
AFC: Buffalo vs. L.A. Raiders, 1990
AFC-FR: L.A. Raiders vs. Denver, 1993
AFC-FR: Denver vs. Jacksonville, 1997
NFC-D: St. Louis vs. Green Bay, 2001
SB: Tampa Bay vs. Oakland, 2002
NFC-D: Atlanta vs. St. Louis, 2004)
NFC-FR: Green Bay vs. Seattle, 2007
NFC-FR: Arizona vs. Green Bay, 2009 (ot)
NFC-FR: Green Bay vs. Arizona, 2009 (ot)
NFC-D: New Orleans vs. Arizona, 2009

Most (One-Point) Points After Touchdown, Both Teams, Game

12 NFC-FR: Arizona (6) vs. Green Bay (6), 2009
10 NFC: Detroit (8) vs. Cleveland (2), 1957
AFC-D: Miami (5) vs. San Diego (5), 1981 (ot)
AFC: Miami (6) vs. Pittsburgh (4), 1984
AFC-FR: Buffalo (5) vs. Houston (5), 1992 (ot)
NFC-FR: Philadelphia (7) vs. Detroit (3), 1995
AFC-FR: Indianapolis (7) vs. Denver (3), 2004
9 In many games

Fewest (One-Point) Points After Touchdown, Both Teams, Game

0 NFC-D: N.Y. Giants vs. Cleveland, 1950
NFC-D: Dallas vs. Detroit, 1970
NFC: Los Angeles vs. Tampa Bay, 1979
NFC: St. Louis vs. Tampa Bay, 1999
AFC-D: Baltimore vs. Indianapolis, 2006

Most Two-Point Conversions, Game

2 SB: San Diego vs. San Francisco, 1994
NFC-FR: Detroit vs. Philadelphia, 1995
NFC-FR: San Francisco vs.. N.Y. Giants, 2002
1 By many teams

FIELD GOALS

Most Field Goals, Game

5 NFC-D: Minnesota vs. San Francisco, 1987
NFC: N.Y. Giants vs. San Francisco, 1990
AFC: Buffalo vs. Miami, 1992
NFC-FR: N.Y. Giants vs. Minnesota, 1997
NFC-FR: Carolina vs. Dallas, 2003
NFC-D: St. Louis vs. Carolina, 2003 (2 ot)
AFC: New England vs. Indianapolis, 2003
AFC-D: Indianapolis vs. Baltimore, 2006
4 AFC-D: Boston vs. Buffalo, 1963
AFC: Oakland vs. Houston, 1967
SB: Green Bay vs. Oakland, 1967
NFC: Washington vs. Dallas, 1972
AFC-D: Oakland vs. Pittsburgh, 1973
SB: San Francisco vs. Cincinnati, 1981
AFC-FR: New England vs. N.Y. Jets, 1985
NFC-FR: Washington vs. L.A. Rams, 1986

NFC-D: Philadelphia vs. Chicago, 1988
AFC-FR: Pittsburgh vs. Houston, 1989 (ot)
AFC-D: Pittsburgh vs. Buffalo, 1995
NFC-FR: Dallas vs. Minnesota, 1996
NFC-D: Carolina vs. Dallas, 1996
AFC-FR: Jacksonville vs. New England, 1998
AFC-D: Tennessee vs. Indianapolis, 1999
NFC-D: Philadelphia vs. Chicago, 2001
AFC: San Diego vs. New England, 2007
NFC-FR: Philadelphia vs. Minnesota, 2008
NFC-D: Arizona vs. Carolina, 2008
3 By many teams

Most Field Goals, Both Teams, Game
8 NFC-FR: N.Y. Giants (5) vs. Minnesota (3), 1997
NFC-D: St. Louis (5) vs. Carolina (3), 2003 (2 ot)
7 AFC-FR: Pittsburgh (4) vs. Houston (3), 1989 (ot)
NFC: N.Y. Giants (5) vs. San Francisco (2), 1990
NFC-D: Carolina (4) vs. Dallas (3), 1996
AFC-D: Tennessee (4) vs. Indianapolis (3), 1999
AFC-D: Indianapolis (5) vs. Baltimore (2), 2006
6 NFC-D: Minnesota (5) vs. San Francisco (1), 1987
NFC-D: Philadelphia (4) vs. Chicago (2), 1988
AFC: Buffalo (5) vs. Miami (1), 1992
NFC-FR: Carolina (5) vs. Dallas (1), 2003
AFC-FR: New England (3) vs. N.Y. Jets (3), 2006
NFC-D: N.Y. Giants (3) vs. Philadelphia (3), 2008

Most Field Goals Attempted, Game
6 AFC: Oakland vs. Houston, 1967
NFC-D: Los Angeles vs. Dallas, 1973
AFC-D: Cleveland vs. N.Y. Jets, 1986 (ot)
NFC: N.Y. Giants vs. San Francisco, 1990
AFC: Buffalo vs. Miami, 1992
NFC-D: St. Louis vs. Carolina, 2003 (2 ot)
5 By many teams

Most Field Goals Attempted, Both Teams, Game
11 NFC-D: St. Louis (6) vs. Carolina (5), 2003 (2 ot)
9 NFC-D: Philadelphia (5) vs. Chicago (4), 1988
NFC-FR: N.Y. Giants (5) vs. Minnesota (4), 1997
8 NFC-D: Los Angeles (6) vs. Dallas (2), 1973
NFC-D: Detroit (5) vs. San Francisco (3), 1983
AFC-D: Cleveland (6) vs. N.Y. Jets (2), 1986 (ot)
NFC-D: Minnesota (5) vs. San Francisco (3), 1987
AFC-FR: Houston (4) vs. Pittsburgh (4), 1989 (ot)
NFC-FR: Chicago (4) vs. New Orleans (4), 1990
NFC: N.Y. Giants (6) vs. San Francisco (2), 1990
NFC-D: N.Y. Giants (5) vs. Philadelphia (3), 2008

SAFETIES

Most Safeties, Game
1 By many teams

Most Safeties, Both Teams, Game
1 In many games

FIRST DOWNS

Most First Downs, Game
34 AFC-D: San Diego vs. Miami, 1981 (ot)
33 AFC-D: Cleveland vs. N.Y. Jets, 1986 (ot)
32 AFC: Indianapolis vs. New England, 2006
NFC-FR: Green Bay vs. Arizona, 2009 (ot)

Fewest First Downs, Game
6 NFC: N.Y. Giants vs. Green Bay, 1961
AFC-D: Baltimore vs. Tennessee, 2000
7 NFC: Green Bay vs. Boston, 1936
NFC-D: Pittsburgh vs. Philadelphia, 1947
NFC: Chi. Cardinals vs. Philadelphia, 1948
NFC: Los Angeles vs. Philadelphia, 1949
NFC-D: Cleveland vs. N.Y. Giants, 1958
AFC-D: Cincinnati vs. Baltimore, 1970
NFC-D: Detroit vs. Dallas, 1970
NFC: Tampa Bay vs. Los Angeles, 1979
AFC-D: Baltimore vs. Pittsburgh, 2001
AFC-FR: Kansas City vs. Indianapolis, 2006
8 By many teams

Most First Downs, Both Teams, Game
62 NFC-FR: Green Bay (32) vs. Arizona (30), 2009 (ot)
59 AFC-D: San Diego (34) vs. Miami (25), 1981 (ot)
55 AFC-FR: San Diego (29) vs. Pittsburgh (26), 1982

Fewest First Downs, Both Teams, Game
15 NFC: Green Bay (7) vs. Boston (8), 1936
19 NFC: N.Y. Giants (9) vs. Green Bay (10), 1939
NFC: Washington (9) vs. Chi. Bears (10), 1942
20 NFC-D: Cleveland (9) vs. N.Y. Giants (11), 1950

RUSHING

Most First Downs, Rushing, Game
19 NFC-FR: Dallas vs. Los Angeles, 1980
18 AFC-D: Miami vs. Cincinnati, 1973
AFC: Miami vs. Oakland, 1973
AFC-D: Pittsburgh vs. Buffalo, 1974
AFC-FR: Buffalo vs. Miami, 1995
AFC-FR: Denver vs. Jacksonville, 1997
17 AFC-D: Cincinnati vs. Seattle, 1988
AFC: Buffalo vs. Kansas City, 1993

Fewest First Downs, Rushing, Game
0 NFC: Los Angeles vs. Philadelphia, 1949
AFC-D: Buffalo vs. Boston, 1963
AFC: Oakland vs. Pittsburgh, 1974
NFC-FR: New Orleans vs. Minnesota, 1987
NFC: L.A. Rams vs. San Francisco, 1989
NFC-D: Chicago vs. N.Y. Giants, 1990
AFC-FR: Indianapolis vs. Pittsburgh, 1996
AFC-FR: Seattle vs. Miami, 1999
AFC-D: Miami vs. Jacksonville, 1999
AFC-D: Miami vs. Oakland, 2000
AFC-D: Baltimore vs. Pittsburgh, 2001
AFC-D: Indianapolis vs. New England, 2004
NFC-FR: Philadelphia vs. Dallas, 2009
1 By many teams

Most First Downs, Rushing, Both Teams, Game
26 AFC: Buffalo (14) vs. L.A. Raiders (12), 1990
25 NFC-FR: Dallas (19) vs. Los Angeles (6), 1980
23 NFC: Cleveland (15) vs. Detroit (8), 1952
AFC-D: Miami (18) vs. Cincinnati (5), 1973
AFC-D: Pittsburgh (18) vs. Buffalo (5), 1974
AFC-FR: Buffalo (18) vs. Miami (5), 1995

Fewest First Downs, Rushing, Both Teams, Game
2 NFC-FR: New Orleans (1) vs. St. Louis (1), 2000
5 AFC-D: Buffalo (0) vs. Boston (5), 1963
NFC-D: Washington (1) vs. Tampa Bay (4), 1999
AFC-FR: Cleveland (2) vs. Pittsburgh (3), 2002
AFC-D: Baltimore (2) vs. Indianapolis (3), 2009
6 NFC: Green Bay (2) vs. Boston (4), 1936
NFC-D: Baltimore (2) vs. Minnesota (4), 1968
AFC-D: Houston (1) vs. Oakland (5), 1969
AFC-FR: N.Y. Jets (1) vs. Houston (5), 1991
AFC-FR: Denver (1) vs. Baltimore (5), 2000
AFC: Pittsburgh (1) vs. Baltimore (5), 2008
SB: Arizona (2) vs. Pittsburgh (4), 2008

PASSING

Most First Downs, Passing, Game
24 AFC-FR: Pittsburgh vs. Cleveland, 2002
21 AFC-D: Miami vs. San Diego, 1981 (ot)
AFC-D: San Diego vs. Miami, 1981 (ot)
AFC-D: Cleveland vs. N.Y. Jets, 1986 (ot)
NFC-D: Philadelphia vs. Chicago, 1988
AFC-D; Indianapolis vs. San Diego, 2007
NFC-FR: Arizona vs. Green Bay, 2009 (ot)
20 NFC-FR: Dallas vs. L.A. Rams, 1983
AFC-D: Buffalo vs. Cleveland, 1989
AFC-FR: Miami vs. Buffalo, 1995
NFC-FR: Detroit vs. Philadelphia, 1995
AFC-FR: San Diego vs. Indianapolis, 1995
NFC-D: Minnesota vs. St. Louis, 1999

AFC: Indianapolis vs. New England, 2006
SB: Arizona vs. Pittsburgh, 2008

Fewest First Downs, Passing, Game
0 NFC: Philadelphia vs. Chi. Cardinals, 1948
1 NFC-D: N.Y. Giants vs. Washington, 1943
NFC: Cleveland vs. Detroit, 1953
SB: Denver vs. Dallas, 1977
2 By many teams

Most First Downs, Passing, Both Teams, Game
42 AFC-D: Miami (21) vs. San Diego (21), 1981 (ot)
AFC-FR: Pittsburgh (24) vs. Cleveland (18), 2002
38 AFC-FR: Pittsburgh (19) vs. San Diego (19), 1982
NFC-D: Minnesota (20) vs. St. Louis (18), 1999
NFC-FR: Arizona (21) vs. Green Bay (17), 2009 (ot)
36 NFC: Minnesota (19) vs. Atlanta (17), 1998 (ot)

Fewest First Downs, Passing, Both Teams, Game
2 NFC: Philadelphia (0) vs. Chi. Cardinals (2), 1948
4 NFC-D: Cleveland (2) vs. N.Y. Giants (2), 1950
5 NFC: Detroit (2) vs. N.Y. Giants (3), 1935
NFC: Green Bay (2) vs. N.Y. Giants (3), 1939

PENALTY

Most First Downs, Penalty, Game
7 AFC-D: New England vs. Oakland, 1976
AFC: Tennessee vs. Oakland, 2002
6 AFC-D: Cleveland vs. N.Y. Jets, 1986 (ot)
NFC-D: Chicago vs. Carolina, 2005
NFC-FR: Green Bay vs. Arizona, 2009 (ot)
5 AFC-FR: Cleveland vs. L. A. Raiders, 1982
NFC-D: San Francisco vs. Minnesota, 1997
AFC-FR: Miami vs. Buffalo, 1998
NFC-D: Arizona vs. Minnesota, 1998
AFC: Pittsburgh vs. New England, 2001
AFC-D: Pittsburgh vs. Tennessee, 2002 (ot)
AFC-FR: Cincinnati vs. N.Y. Jets, 2009

Most First Downs, Penalty, Both Teams, Game
10 AFC: Tennessee (7) vs. Oakland (3), 2002
9 AFC-D: New England (7) vs. Oakland (2), 1976
8 NFC-FR: Atlanta (4) vs. Minnesota (4), 1982
AFC-FR: Miami (5) vs. Buffalo (3), 1998
NFC-FR: Dallas (4) vs. Philadelphia (4), 2009
NFC-FR: Green Bay (6) vs. Arizona (2), 2009 (ot)

NET YARDS GAINED RUSHING AND PASSING

Most Yards Gained, Game
610 AFC: San Diego vs. Boston, 1963
602 SB: Washington vs. Denver, 1987
569 AFC: Miami vs. Pittsburgh, 1984

Fewest Yards Gained, Game
86 NFC-D: Cleveland vs. N.Y. Giants, 1958
99 NFC: Chi. Cardinals vs. Philadelphia, 1948
112 NFC-D: N.Y. Giants vs. Washington, 1943

Most Yards Gained, Both Teams, Game
1,038 AFC-FR: Buffalo (536) vs. Miami (502), 1995
1,036 AFC-D: San Diego (564) vs. Miami (472), 1981 (ot)
1,024 AFC: Miami (569) vs. Pittsburgh (455), 1984
NFC-FR: Arizona (531) vs. Green Bay (493), 2009 (ot)

Fewest Yards Gained, Both Teams, Game
331 NFC: Chi. Cardinals (99) vs. Philadelphia (232), 1948
332 NFC-D: N.Y. Giants (150) vs. Cleveland (182), 1950
336 NFC: Boston (116) vs. Green Bay (220), 1936

RUSHING

ATTEMPTS

Most Attempts, Game
65 NFC: Detroit vs. N.Y. Giants, 1935
61 NFC: Philadelphia vs. Los Angeles, 1949
59 AFC: New England vs. Miami, 1985

Fewest Attempts, Game
8 AFC-D: Miami vs. San Diego, 1994
9 SB: Miami vs. San Francisco, 1984
NFC: Minnesota vs. N.Y. Giants, 2000
10 NFC: L.A. Rams vs. San Francisco, 1989
NFC-FR: Atlanta vs. Green Bay, 1995
NFC-FR: Detroit vs. Washington, 1999

Most Attempts, Both Teams, Game
109 NFC: Detroit (65) vs. N.Y. Giants (44), 1935
97 AFC-D: Baltimore (50) vs. Oakland (47), 1977 (ot)
91 NFC: Philadelphia (57) vs. Chi. Cardinals (34), 1948

Fewest Attempts, Both Teams, Game
32 AFC-D: Houston (14) vs. Kansas City (18), 1993
37 SB: Arizona (12) vs. Pittsburgh (25), 2008
SB: New Orleans (18) vs. Indianapolis (19), 2009
38 NFC-D: Detroit (16) vs. Dallas (22), 1991

YARDS GAINED

Most Yards Gained, Game
382 NFC: Chi. Bears vs. Washington, 1940
341 AFC-FR: Buffalo vs. Miami, 1995
338 NFC-FR: Dallas vs. Los Angeles, 1980

Fewest Yards Gained, Game
– 4 NFC-FR: Detroit vs. Green Bay, 1994
7 AFC-D: Buffalo vs. Boston, 1963
SB: New England vs. Chicago, 1985
14 AFC-D: Miami vs. Denver, 1998
AFC: N.Y. Jets vs. Denver, 1998

Most Yards Gained, Both Teams, Game
430 NFC-FR: Dallas (338) vs. Los Angeles (92), 1980
426 NFC: Cleveland (227) vs. Detroit (199), 1952
411 AFC-FR: Buffalo (341) vs. Miami (70), 1995

Fewest Yards Gained, Both Teams, Game
77 NFC-FR: Detroit (–4) vs. Green Bay (81), 1994
84 NFC-FR: St. Louis (34) vs. New Orleans (50), 2000
90 AFC-D: Buffalo (7) vs. Boston (83), 1963
NFC-D: Tampa Bay (44) vs. Washington (46), 1999

AVERAGE GAIN

Highest Average Gain, Game
9.94 AFC: San Diego vs. Boston, 1963 (32-318)
9.29 NFC-D: Green Bay vs. Dallas, 1982 (17-158)
8.18 NFC-D: Atlanta vs. St. Louis, 2004 (40-327)

Lowest Average Gain, Game
– 0.27 NFC-FR: Detroit vs. Green Bay, 1994 (15-(– 4))
0.58 AFC-D: Buffalo vs. Boston, 1963 (12-7)
0.64 SB: New England vs. Chicago, 1985 (11-7)

TOUCHDOWNS

Most Touchdowns, Game
7 NFC: Chi. Bears vs. Washington, 1940
6 NFC-D: San Francisco vs. N.Y. Giants, 1993
5 NFC: Cleveland vs. Detroit, 1954
NFC-D: San Francisco vs. Chicago, 1994
AFC-FR: Pittsburgh vs. Indianapolis, 1996
AFC-FR: Denver vs. Jacksonville, 1997

Most Touchdowns, Both Teams, Game
7 NFC: Chi. Bears (7) vs. Washington (0), 1940
6 NFC: Cleveland (5) vs. Detroit (1), 1954
NFC-D: San Francisco (6) vs. N.Y. Giants (0), 1993
NFC-D: San Francisco (5) vs. Chicago (1), 1994
AFC-FR: Denver (5) vs. Jacksonville (1), 1997
5 NFC: Chi. Cardinals (3) vs. Philadelphia (2), 1947
AFC: San Diego (4) vs. Boston (1), 1963
AFC-D: Cincinnati (3) vs. Buffalo (2), 1981
AFC-FR: Pittsburgh (5) vs. Indianapolis (0), 1996
NFC-D: Arizona (3) vs. Minnesota (2), 1998
NFC-FR: Seattle (3) vs. Green Bay (2), 2003 (ot)

PASSING

ATTEMPTS

Most Attempts, Game
66 AFC-FR: Miami vs. Buffalo, 1995
65 AFC-D: Cleveland vs. N.Y. Jets, 1986 (ot)
NFC-D: San Francisco vs. Green Bay, 1995
61 NFC-FR: Minnesota vs. Chicago, 1994

Fewest Attempts, Game

5 NFC: Detroit vs. N.Y. Giants, 1935
6 AFC: Miami vs. Oakland, 1973
7 SB: Miami vs. Minnesota, 1973

Most Attempts, Both Teams, Game

102 AFC-D: San Diego (54) vs. Miami (48), 1981 (ot)
96 AFC: N.Y. Jets (49) vs. Oakland (47), 1968
95 AFC-D: Cleveland (65) vs. N.Y. Jets (30), 1986 (ot)

Fewest Attempts, Both Teams, Game

18 NFC: Detroit (5) vs. N.Y. Giants (13), 1935
23 NFC: Chi. Cardinals (11) vs. Philadelphia (12), 1948
24 NFC-D: Cleveland (9) vs. N.Y. Giants (15), 1950

COMPLETIONS

Most Completions, Game

36 AFC-FR: Houston vs. Buffalo, 1992 (ot)
34 AFC-D: Cleveland vs. N.Y. Jets, 1986 (ot)
AFC-FR: Miami vs. Buffalo, 1995
33 AFC-D: San Diego vs. Miami, 1981 (ot)
NFC-FR: Minnesota vs. Chicago, 1994)
AFC-D: Indianapolis vs. San Diego, 2007

Fewest Completions, Game

2 NFC: Detroit vs. N.Y. Giants, 1935
NFC: Philadelphia vs. Chi. Cardinals, 1948
3 NFC: N.Y. Giants vs. Chi. Bears, 1941
NFC: Green Bay vs. N.Y. Giants, 1944
NFC: Chi. Cardinals vs. Philadelphia, 1947
NFC: Chi. Cardinals vs. Philadelphia, 1948
NFC-D: Cleveland vs. N.Y. Giants, 1950
NFC-D: N.Y. Giants vs. Cleveland, 1950
NFC: Cleveland vs. Detroit, 1953
AFC: Miami vs. Oakland, 1973
4 NFC: N.Y. Giants vs. Detroit, 1935
NFC-D: N.Y. Giants vs. Washington, 1943
NFC-D: Pittsburgh vs. Philadelphia, 1947
NFC-D: Dallas vs. Detroit, 1970
AFC: Miami vs. Baltimore, 1971
SB: Miami vs. Washington, 1982
AFC-FR: Seattle vs. L.A. Raiders, 1984
AFC-FR: Baltimore vs. New England, 2009

Most Completions, Both Teams, Game

64 AFC-D: San Diego (33) vs. Miami (31), 1981 (ot)
63 SB: New Orleans (32) vs. Indianapolis (31), 2009
57 AFC-FR: Houston (36) vs. Buffalo (21), 1992 (ot)
NFC-FR: N.Y. Giants (29) vs. San Francisco (28), 2002
NFC-FR: Arizona (29) vs. Green Bay (28), 2009 (ot)

Fewest Completions, Both Teams, Game

5 NFC: Philadelphia (2) vs. Chi. Cardinals (3), 1948
6 NFC: Detroit (2) vs. N.Y. Giants (4), 1935
NFC-D: Cleveland (3) vs. N.Y. Giants (3), 1950
11 NFC: Green Bay (3) vs. N.Y. Giants (8), 1944
NFC-D: Dallas (4) vs. Detroit (7), 1970

COMPLETION PERCENTAGE

Highest Completion Percentage, Game (20 attempts)

92.9 AFC-D: New England vs. Jacksonville, 2007 (28-26)
88.0 SB: N.Y. Giants vs. Denver, 1986 (25-22)
87.9 NFC-FR: Arizona vs. Green Bay, 2009 (33-29) (ot)

Lowest Completion Percentage, Game (20 attempts)

18.5 NFC: Tampa Bay vs. Los Angeles, 1979 (27-5)
20.0 NFC-D: N.Y. Giants vs. Washington, 1943 (20-4)
25.8 NFC: Chi. Bears vs. Washington, 1937 (31-8)

YARDS GAINED

Most Yards Gained, Game

483 AFC-D: Cleveland vs. N.Y. Jets, 1986 (ot)
454 AFC-FR: Indianapolis vs. Denver, 2004
435 AFC: Miami vs. Pittsburgh, 1984

Fewest Yards Gained, Game

3 NFC: Chi. Cardinals vs. Philadelphia, 1948
7 NFC: Philadelphia vs. Chi. Cardinals, 1948
9 NFC-D: N.Y. Giants vs. Cleveland, 1950
NFC: Cleveland vs. Detroit, 1953

Most Yards Gained, Both Teams, Game

809 AFC-D: San Diego (415) vs. Miami (394), 1981 (ot)
779 NFC-FR: Green Bay (404) vs. Arizona (375), 2009 (ot)
762 NFC-D: Minnesota (388) vs. St. Louis (374), 1999

Fewest Yards Gained, Both Teams, Game

10 NFC: Chi. Cardinals (3) vs. Philadelphia (7), 1948
38 NFC-D: N.Y. Giants (9) vs. Cleveland (29), 1950
102 NFC-D: Dallas (22) vs. Detroit (80), 1970

TIMES SACKED

Most Times Sacked, Game

9 AFC: Kansas City vs. Buffalo, 1966
NFC: Chicago vs. San Francisco, 1984
AFC-D: N.Y. Jets vs. Cleveland, 1986 (ot)
AFC-D: Houston vs. Kansas City, 1993
8 NFC: Green Bay vs. Dallas, 1967
NFC: Minnesota vs. Washington, 1987
NFC-D: Philadelphia vs. Green Bay, 2003 (ot)
7 NFC-D: Dallas vs. Los Angeles, 1973
SB: Dallas vs. Pittsburgh, 1975
AFC-FR: Houston vs. Oakland, 1980
NFC-D: Washington vs. Chicago, 1984
SB: New England vs. Chicago, 1985
AFC-FR: Kansas City vs. San Diego, 1992
AFC-D: Pittsburgh vs. Buffalo, 1992

Most Times Sacked, Both Teams, Game

13 AFC: Kansas City (9) vs. Buffalo (4), 1966
AFC-D: N.Y. Jets (9) vs. Cleveland (4), 1986 (ot)
12 NFC-D: Dallas (7) vs. Los Angeles (5), 1973
NFC-D: Washington (7) vs. Chicago (5), 1984
NFC: Chicago (9) vs. San Francisco (3), 1984
AFC-FR: Kansas City (7) vs. San Diego (5), 1992
11 AFC-D: Houston (9) vs. Kansas City (2), 1993

Fewest Times Sacked, Both Teams, Game

0 AFC-D: Buffalo vs. Pittsburgh, 1974
AFC-FR: Pittsburgh vs. San Diego, 1982
AFC: Miami vs. Pittsburgh, 1984
AFC-D: Buffalo vs. Miami, 1990
AFC-D: Denver vs. Houston, 1991
AFC-FR: Buffalo vs. Miami, 1995
AFC-D: Indianapolis vs. Tennessee, 1999
AFC-D: Indianapolis vs. San Diego, 2007
NFC-D: N.Y. Giants vs. Philadelphia, 2008
1 In many games

TOUCHDOWNS

Most Touchdowns, Game

6 AFC-D: Oakland vs. Houston, 1969
SB: San Francisco vs. San Diego, 1994
5 NFC: Chi. Bears vs. Washington, 1943
NFC: Detroit vs. Cleveland, 1957
AFC-D: Oakland vs. Kansas City, 1968
SB: San Francisco vs. Denver, 1989
NFC-D: St. Louis vs. Minnesota, 1999
NFC: N.Y. Giants vs. Minnesota, 2000
AFC-FR: Indianapolis vs. Denver, 2003
NFC-FR: Arizona vs. Green Bay, 2009 (ot)
4 By many teams

Most Touchdowns, Both Teams, Game

9 NFC-D: St. Louis (5) vs. Minnesota (4), 1999
NFC-FR: Arizona (5) vs. Green Bay (4), 2009 (ot)
8 AFC-FR: Buffalo (4) vs. Houston (4), 1992 (ot)
7 NFC: Chi. Bears (5) vs. Washington (2), 1943
AFC-D: Oakland (6) vs. Houston (1), 1969
SB: Pittsburgh (4) vs. Dallas (3), 1978
AFC-D: Miami (4) vs. San Diego (3), 1981 (ot)
AFC: Miami (4) vs. Pittsburgh (3), 1984
AFC-D: Buffalo (4) vs. Cleveland (3), 1989
SB: San Francisco (6) vs. San Diego (1), 1994
NFC-FR: Detroit (4) vs. Philadelphia (3), 1995
NFC-FR: New Orleans (4) vs. St. Louis (3), 2000

NFC-FR: N.Y. Giants (4) vs. San Francisco (3), 2002
NFC: Arizona (4) vs. Philadelphia (3), 2008

INTERCEPTIONS BY

Most Interceptions By, Game

8 NFC: Chi. Bears vs. Washington, 1940
7 NFC: Cleveland vs. Los Angeles, 1955
6 NFC: Green Bay vs. N.Y. Giants, 1939
NFC: Chi. Bears vs. N.Y. Giants, 1946
NFC: Cleveland vs. Detroit, 1954
AFC: San Diego vs. Houston, 1961
AFC: Buffalo vs. L.A. Raiders, 1990
NFC-FR: Philadelphia vs. Detroit, 1995
NFC-D: St. Louis vs. Green Bay, 2001

Most Interceptions By, Both Teams, Game

10 NFC: Cleveland (7) vs. Los Angeles (3), 1955
AFC: San Diego (6) vs. Houston (4), 1961
9 NFC: Green Bay (6) vs. N.Y. Giants (3), 1939
8 NFC: Chi. Bears (8) vs. Washington (0), 1940
NFC: Chi. Bears (6) vs. N.Y. Giants (2), 1946
NFC: Cleveland (6) vs. Detroit (2), 1954
AFC-FR: Buffalo (4) vs. N.Y. Jets (4), 1981
AFC: Miami (5) vs. N.Y. Jets (3), 1982

YARDS GAINED

Most Yards Gained, Game

172 SB: Tampa Bay vs. Oakland, 2002
161 NFC-D: St. Louis vs. Green Bay, 2001
138 AFC-FR: N.Y. Jets vs. Cincinnati, 1982

Most Yards Gained, Both Teams, Game

184 SB: Tampa Bay (172) vs. Oakland (12), 2002
161 NFC-D: St. Louis (161) vs. Green Bay (0), 2001
156 NFC: Green Bay (123) vs. N.Y. Giants (33), 1939

TOUCHDOWNS

Most Touchdowns, Game

3 NFC: Chi. Bears vs. Washington, 1940
NFC-D: St. Louis vs. Green Bay, 2001
SB: Tampa Bay vs. Oakland, 2002
2 NFC-D: Los Angeles vs. St. Louis, 1975
NFC-FR: Philadelphia vs. Detroit, 1995)
NFC-FR: Seattle vs. Washington, 2007
1 In many games

Most Touchdowns, Both Teams, Game

3 NFC: Chi. Bears (3) vs. Washington (0), 1940
NFC-D: St. Louis (3) vs. Green Bay (0), 2001
SB: Tampa Bay (3) vs. Oakland (0), 2002
2 NFC-D: Los Angeles (2) vs. St. Louis (0), 1975
NFC-D: Dallas (1) vs. Green Bay (1), 1982
NFC-D: Minnesota (1) vs. San Francisco (1), 1987
NFC-FR: Detroit (1) vs. Green Bay (1), 1993
NFC-FR: Philadelphia (2) vs. Detroit (0), 1995
AFC-FR: Buffalo (1) vs. Jacksonville (1), 1996)
NFC-FR: Seattle (2) vs. Washington (0), 2007
1 In many games

PUNTING

Most Punts, Game

14 AFC-D: N.Y. Jets vs. Cleveland, 1986 (ot)
13 NFC: N.Y. Giants vs. Chi. Bears, 1933
AFC-D: Baltimore vs. Oakland, 1977 (ot)
11 AFC: Houston vs. Oakland, 1967
AFC-D: Houston vs. Oakland, 1969
NFC: L.A. Rams vs. Chicago, 1985
SB: N.Y. Giants vs. Baltimore, 2000

Fewest Punts, Game

0 NFC-FR: St. Louis vs. Green Bay, 1982
AFC-FR: N.Y. Jets vs. Cincinnati, 1982
AFC-FR: Indianapolis vs. Denver, 2003
AFC-D: Kansas City vs. Indianapolis, 2003
AFC-D: Indianapolis vs. Kansas City, 2003
1 By many teams

Most Punts, Both Teams, Game

23 NFC: N.Y. Giants (13) vs. Chi. Bears (10), 1933
22 AFC-D: N.Y. Jets (14) vs. Cleveland (8), 1986 (ot)
21 AFC-D: Baltimore (13) vs. Oakland (8), 1977 (ot)
NFC: L.A. Rams (11) vs. Chicago (10), 1985
SB: N.Y. Giants (11) vs. Baltimore (10), 2000

Fewest Punts, Both Teams, Game

0 AFC-D: Kansas City vs. Indianapolis, 2003
1 NFC-FR: St. Louis (0) vs. Green Bay (1), 1982
2 AFC-FR: N.Y. Jets (0) vs. Cincinnati (2), 1982
SB: Atlanta (1) vs. Denver (1), 1998
AFC-FR: Indianapolis (0) vs. Denver (2), 2003)
AFC-D: New England (1) vs. Jacksonville (1), 2007
NFC-FR: Arizona (1) vs. Green Bay (1), 2009 (ot)

AVERAGE YARDAGE

Highest Average, Punting, Game (4 punts)

56.0 AFC: Oakland vs. San Diego, 1980
53.3 AFC-D: Tennessee vs. Baltimore, 2008
52.8 AFC: Indianapolis vs. New England, 2006

Lowest Average, Punting, Game (4 punts)

24.9 NFC: Washington vs. Chi. Bears, 1937
25.3 AFC-FR: Pittsburgh vs. Houston, 1989
25.5 NFC: Green Bay vs. N.Y. Giants, 1962

PUNT RETURNS

Most Punt Returns, Game

8 NFC: Green Bay vs. N.Y. Giants, 1944
7 By many teams

Most Punt Returns, Both Teams, Game

13 AFC-FR: Houston (7) vs. Oakland (6), 1980
12 AFC-D: New England (7) vs. Pittsburgh (5), 1996
11 NFC: Green Bay (8) vs. N.Y. Giants (3), 1944
NFC-D: Green Bay (6) vs. Baltimore (5), 1965
AFC-FR: Jacksonville (7) vs. New England (4), 1998
AFC: Baltimore (6) vs. Pittsburgh (5), 2008

Fewest Punt Returns, Both Teams, Game

0 NFC: Chi. Bears vs. N.Y. Giants, 1941
AFC: Boston vs. San Diego, 1963
NFC-FR: Green Bay vs. St. Louis, 1982
AFC-FR: Houston vs. N.Y. Jets, 1991
AFC-D: Denver vs. Houston, 1991
NFC-D: San Francisco vs. Washington, 1992
SB: Denver vs. Green Bay, 1997
SB: Atlanta vs. Denver, 1998
AFC-FR: Oakland vs. N.Y. Jets, 2001
AFC-D: N.Y. Jets vs. Oakland, 2002
AFC-FR: Denver vs. Indianapolis, 2003
NFC-D: Carolina vs. St. Louis, 2003
AFC-D: Indianapolis vs. Kansas City, 2003
1 In many games

YARDS GAINED

Most Yards Gained, Game

155 NFC-D: Dallas vs. Cleveland, 1967
152 NFC-D: Atlanta vs. St. Louis, 2004
150 NFC: Chi. Cardinals vs. Philadelphia, 1947

Fewest Yards Gained, Game

–10 NFC: Green Bay vs. Cleveland, 1965
–9 NFC: Dallas vs. Green Bay, 1966
AFC-D: Kansas City vs. Oakland, 1968
–7 NFC-D: San Francisco vs. Atlanta, 1998

Most Yards Gained, Both Teams, Game

166 NFC-D: Dallas (155) vs. Cleveland (11), 1967
AFC-D: Baltimore (99) vs. Pittsburgh (67), 2001
160 NFC: Chi. Cardinals (150) vs. Philadelphia (10), 1947
152 NFC-D: Atlanta (152) vs. St. Louis (0), 2004

Fewest Yards Gained, Both Teams, Game

–9 NFC: Dallas (–9) vs. Green Bay (0), 1966
–6 AFC-D: Miami (–5) vs. Oakland (–1), 1970
–3 NFC-D: San Francisco (–5) vs. Dallas (2), 1972

POSTSEASON RECORDS

TOUCHDOWNS
Most Touchdowns, Game
1 By 20 teams

KICKOFF RETURNS
Most Kickoff Returns, Game
10 NFC-D: L.A. Rams vs. Washington, 1983
NFC-FR: Detroit vs. Philadelphia, 1995
9 NFC: Chi. Bears vs. N.Y. Giants, 1956
AFC: Boston vs. San Diego, 1963
AFC: Houston vs. Oakland, 1967
SB: Denver vs. San Francisco, 1989
AFC-D: Miami vs. Buffalo, 1990
AFC: L.A. Raiders vs. Buffalo, 1990
AFC-D: Miami vs. Jacksonville, 1999
SB: Oakland vs. Tampa Bay, 2002
8 By many teams
Most Kickoff Returns, Both Teams, Game
15 AFC-D: Miami (9) vs. Buffalo (6), 1990
14 NFC-FR: Detroit (10) vs. Philadelphia (4), 1995
13 NFC-D: Green Bay (7) vs. Dallas (6), 1982
NFC-FR: Green Bay (7) vs. San Francisco (6), 1998
AFC-FR: N.Y. Jets (8) vs. Oakland (5), 2001
NFC-FR: San Francisco (7) vs. N.Y. Giants (6), 2002
AFC-D: Tennessee (7) vs. Pittsburgh (6), 2002
SB: Oakland (9) vs. Tampa Bay (4), 2002
NFC-FR: Seattle (7) vs. Green Bay (6), 2003 (ot)
AFC-D: Kansas City (7) vs. Indianapolis (6), 2003
AFC: Pittsburgh (8) vs. New England (5), 2004
AFC: New England (8) vs. Indianapolis (5), 2006
Fewest Kickoff Returns, Both Teams, Game
1 NFC: Green Bay (0) vs. Boston (1), 1936
AFC-FR: San Diego (0) vs. Kansas City (1), 1992
2 NFC-D: Los Angeles (0) vs. Chi. Bears (2), 1950
AFC: Houston (0) vs. San Diego (2), 1961
AFC-D: Oakland (1) vs. Pittsburgh (1), 1972
AFC-D: N.Y. Jets (0) vs. L.A. Raiders (2), 1982
AFC: Miami (1) vs. N.Y. Jets (1), 1982
NFC: N.Y. Giants (0) vs. Washington (2), 1986
3 In many games

YARDS GAINED
Most Yards Gained, Game
244 SB: San Diego vs. San Francisco, 1994
231 AFC: New England vs. Indianapolis, 2006
227 SB: Atlanta vs. Denver, 1998
Most Yards Gained, Both Teams, Game
379 AFC-D: Baltimore (193) vs. Oakland (186), 1977 (ot)
348 NFC-D: Minnesota (174) vs. St. Louis (174), 1999
323 AFC-D: New England (231) vs. Indianapolis (92), 2006
Fewest Yards Gained, Both Teams, Game
5 AFC-FR: San Diego (0) vs. Kansas City (5), 1992
15 NFC: N.Y. Giants (0) vs. Washington (15), 1986
31 NFC-D: Los Angeles (0) vs. Chi. Bears (31), 1950

TOUCHDOWNS
Most Touchdowns, Game
1 NFC-D: San Francisco vs. Dallas, 1972
AFC-D: Miami vs. Oakland, 1974
AFC-D: Baltimore vs. Oakland, 1977 (ot)
SB: Miami vs. Washington, 1982
SB: Cincinnati vs. San Francisco, 1988
AFC-D: Cleveland vs. Buffalo, 1989
SB: San Diego vs. San Francisco, 1994
SB: Green Bay vs. New England, 1996
NFC: San Francisco vs. Green Bay, 1997
SB: Atlanta vs. Denver, 1998
AFC-FR: Tennessee vs. Buffalo, 1999
AFC-FR: Seattle vs. Miami, 1999
NFC-D: Washington vs. Tampa Bay, 1999
NFC-D: St. Louis vs. Minnesota, 1999
AFC: Tennessee vs. Jacksonville, 1999
NFC-D: N.Y. Giants vs. Philadelphia, 2000
SB: Baltimore vs. N.Y. Giants, 2000
SB: N.Y. Giants vs. Baltimore, 2000
AFC-D: Kansas City vs. Indianapolis, 2003
NFC-FR: Dallas vs. Seattle, 2006
SB: Chicago vs. Indianapolis, 2006
Most Touchdowns, Both Teams, Game
2 SB: Baltimore (1) vs. N.Y. Giants (1), 2000

PENALTIES
Most Penalties, Game
17 AFC-FR: L.A. Raiders vs. Denver, 1993
14 AFC-FR: Oakland vs. Houston, 1980
NFC-D: San Francisco vs. N.Y. Giants, 1981
AFC: Oakland vs. Tennessee, 2002
NFC-FR: Dallas vs. Philadelphia, 2009
13 AFC-FR: Houston vs. Cleveland, 1988
AFC-D: Houston vs. Denver, 1991
NFC-D: Arizona vs. Minnesota, 1998
NFC-D: Carolina vs. St. Louis, 2003 (2 ot)
Fewest Penalties, Game
0 NFC: Philadelphia vs. Green Bay, 1960
NFC-D: Detroit vs. Dallas, 1970
AFC-D: Miami vs. Oakland, 1970
SB: Miami vs. Dallas, 1971
NFC-D: Washington vs. Minnesota, 1973
SB: Pittsburgh vs. Dallas, 1975
NFC: San Francisco vs. Chicago, 1988
SB: Denver vs. San Francisco, 1989
AFC-D: L.A. Raiders vs. Cincinnati, 1990
AFC-D: Miami vs. San Diego, 1992
SB: Atlanta vs. Denver, 1998
AFC-FR: N.Y. Jets vs. Oakland, 2001
NFC-FR: Carolina vs. Dallas, 2003
1 By many teams
Most Penalties, Both Teams, Game
27 AFC-FR: L.A. Raiders (17) vs. Denver (10), 1993
23 NFC-FR: Dallas (14) vs. Philadelphia (9), 2009
22 AFC-FR: Oakland (14) vs. Houston (8), 1980
NFC-D: San Francisco (14) vs. N.Y. Giants (8), 1981
AFC-FR: Houston (13) vs. Cleveland (9), 1988
NFC-D: Arizona (13) vs. Minnesota (9), 1998
Fewest Penalties, Both Teams, Game
1 AFC-D: L.A. Raiders (0) vs. Cincinnati (1), 1990
2 NFC: Washington (1) vs. Chi. Bears (1), 1937
NFC-D: Washington (0) vs. Minnesota (2), 1973
SB: Pittsburgh (0) vs. Dallas (2), 1975
NFC-FR: Carolina (0) vs. Dallas (2), 2003
3 AFC: Miami (1) vs. Baltimore (2), 1971
NFC: San Francisco (1) vs. Dallas (2), 1971
SB: Miami (0) vs. Dallas (3), 1971
AFC-D: Pittsburgh (1) vs. Oakland (2), 1972
AFC-D: Miami (1) vs. Cincinnati (2), 1973
SB: Miami (1) vs. San Francisco (2), 1984
NFC: San Francisco (0) vs. Chicago (3), 1988
AFC: New England (1) vs. Pittsburgh (2), 2004
AFC: San Diego (1) vs. New England (2), 2007

YARDS PENALIZED
Most Yards Penalized, Game
145 NFC-D: San Francisco vs. N.Y. Giants, 1981
133 SB: Dallas vs. Baltimore, 1970
130 AFC-FR: L.A. Raiders vs. Denver, 1993
Fewest Yards Penalized, Game
0 By many teams
Most Yards Penalized, Both Teams, Game
228 NFC-FR: Philadelphia (116) vs. Dallas (112), 2009
227 AFC-FR: L.A. Raiders (130) vs. Denver (97), 1993
206 NFC-D: San Francisco (145) vs. N.Y. Giants (61), 1981
Fewest Yards Penalized, Both Teams, Game
5 AFC-D: L.A. Raiders (0) vs. Cincinnati (5), 1990
9 NFC-D: Washington (0) vs. Minnesota (9), 1973

11 NFC-FR: Carolina (0) vs. Dallas (11), 2003

FUMBLES

Most Fumbles, Game

8 SB: Buffalo vs. Dallas, 1992
7 AFC-D: Houston vs. Kansas City, 1993
6 By 13 teams

Most Fumbles, Both Teams, Game

12 AFC: Houston (6) vs. Pittsburgh (6), 1978
SB: Buffalo (8) vs. Dallas (4), 1992
10 NFC: Chi. Bears (5) vs. N.Y. Giants (5), 1934
SB: Dallas (6) vs. Denver (4), 1977
AFC: Jacksonville (5) vs. Tennessee (5), 1999
9 NFC-D: San Francisco (6) vs. Detroit (3), 1957
NFC-D: San Francisco (5) vs. Dallas (4), 1972
NFC: Dallas (5) vs. Philadelphia (4), 1980
NFC: Minnesota (6) vs. Dallas (3), 2009

Most Fumbles Lost, Game

5 SB: Buffalo vs. Dallas, 1992
AFC-D: Miami vs. Jacksonville, 1999
4 NFC: N.Y. Giants vs. Baltimore, 1958 (ot)
AFC: Kansas City vs. Oakland, 1969
SB: Baltimore vs. Dallas, 1970
AFC: Pittsburgh vs. Oakland, 1975
SB: Denver vs. Dallas, 1977
AFC: Houston vs. Pittsburgh, 1978
AFC: Miami vs. New England, 1985
SB: New England vs. Chicago, 1985
NFC-FR: L.A. Rams vs. Washington, 1986
NFC-FR: Minnesota vs. Dallas, 1996
AFC-FR: Buffalo vs. Miami, 1998
AFC: N.Y. Jets vs. Denver, 1998
AFC: Jacksonville vs. Tennessee, 1999
3 By many teams

Fewest Fumbles, Both Teams, Game

0 NFC: Green Bay vs. Cleveland, 1965
AFC-D: Houston vs. San Diego, 1979
NFC-D: Dallas vs. Los Angeles, 1979
SB: Los Angeles vs. Pittsburgh, 1979
AFC-D: Buffalo vs. Cincinnati, 1981
NFC: Minnesota vs. Washington, 1987
NFC-D: San Francisco vs. Washington, 1990
NFC: Dallas vs. Green Bay, 1995
AFC-D: New England vs. Pittsburgh, 1996
SB: Green Bay vs. New England, 1996
AFC-FR: Miami vs. Seattle, 1999
AFC-FR: Miami vs. Indianapolis, 2000 (ot)
AFC-D: Baltimore vs. Tennessee, 2000
SB: Pittsburgh vs. Seattle, 2005
SB: Indianapolis vs. New Orleans, 2009
1 In many games

RECOVERIES

Most Total Fumbles Recovered, Game

8 SB: Dallas vs. Denver, 1977 (4 own, 4 opp)
7 NFC: Chi. Bears vs. N.Y. Giants, 1934 (5 own, 2 opp)
NFC-D: San Francisco vs. Detroit, 1957 (4 own, 3 opp)
NFC-D: San Francisco vs. Dallas, 1972 (4 own, 3 opp)
AFC: Pittsburgh vs. Houston, 1978 (3 own, 4 opp)
6 AFC: Houston vs. San Diego, 1961 (4 own, 2 opp)
AFC-D: Cleveland vs. Baltimore, 1971 (4 own, 2 opp)
AFC-D: Cleveland vs. Oakland, 1980 (5 own, 1 opp)
NFC: Philadelphia vs. Dallas, 1980 (3 own, 3 opp)
SB: Dallas vs. Buffalo, 1992 (1 own, 5 opp)
NFC-D: Green Bay vs. San Francisco, 1996 (4 own, 2 opp)
AFC: Denver vs. N.Y. Jets, 1998 (2 own, 4 opp)
AFC: Tennessee vs. Jacksonville, 1999 (2 own, 4 opp)

Most Own Fumbles Recovered, Game

5 NFC: Chi. Bears vs. N.Y. Giants, 1934
AFC-D: Cleveland vs. Oakland, 1980
4 By many teams

TOUCHDOWNS

Most Touchdowns, Game

2 SB: Dallas vs. Buffalo, 1992

TURNOVERS

Numbers of times losing the ball on interceptions and fumbles.

Most Turnovers, Game

9 NFC: Washington vs. Chi. Bears, 1940
NFC: Detroit vs. Cleveland, 1954
AFC: Houston vs. Pittsburgh, 1978
SB: Buffalo vs. Dallas, 1992
8 NFC: N.Y. Giants vs. Chi. Bears, 1946
NFC: Los Angeles vs. Cleveland, 1955
NFC: Cleveland vs. Detroit, 1957
SB: Denver vs. Dallas, 1977
NFC-D: Minnesota vs. Philadelphia, 1980
NFC-D: Green Bay vs. St. Louis, 2001
7 In many games

Fewest Turnovers, Game

0 By many teams

Most Turnovers, Both Teams, Game

14 AFC: Houston (9) vs. Pittsburgh (5), 1978
13 NFC: Detroit (9) vs. Cleveland (4), 1954
AFC: Houston (7) vs. San Diego (6), 1961
12 AFC: Pittsburgh (7) vs. Oakland (5), 1975

Fewest Turnovers, Both Teams, Game

0 SB: Buffalo vs. N.Y. Giants, 1990
AFC-FR: Kansas City vs. Pittsburgh, 1993 (ot)
NFC-FR: Detroit vs. Green Bay, 1994
AFC-FR: Denver vs. Jacksonville, 1996
SB: St. Louis vs. Tennessee, 1999
1 AFC-D: Baltimore (0) vs. Cincinnati (1), 1970
AFC-D: Pittsburgh (0) vs. Buffalo (1), 1974
AFC: Oakland (0) vs. Pittsburgh (1), 1976
NFC-D: Minnesota (0) vs. Washington (1), 1982
NFC-D: Chicago (0) vs. N.Y. Giants (1), 1985
SB: N.Y. Giants (0) vs. Denver (1), 1986
NFC: Washington (0) vs. Minnesota (1), 1987
AFC-D: Cincinnati (0) vs. L.A. Raiders (1), 1990
NFC: N.Y. Giants (0) vs. San Francisco (1), 1990
NFC-FR: N.Y. Giants (0) vs. Minnesota (1), 1993
AFC-FR: L.A. Raiders (0) vs. Denver (1), 1993
NFC: Dallas (0) vs. San Francisco (1), 1993
AFC: Indianapolis (0) vs. Pittsburgh (1), 1995
NFC-D: San Francisco (0) vs. Minnesota (1), 1997
AFC-D: Indianapolis (0) vs. Tennessee (1), 1999
AFC-FR: Baltimore (0) vs. Denver (1), 2000
AFC-D: Baltimore (0) vs. Tennessee (1), 2000
AFC-D: Oakland (0) vs. New England (1), 2001
NFC-FR: Green Bay (0) vs. Seattle (1), 2003 (ot)
AFC-D: Indianapolis (0) vs. Kansas City (1), 2003
AFC-FR: N.Y. Jets (0) vs. San Diego (1), 2004 (ot)
NFC: Philadelphia (0) vs. Atlanta (1), 2003
NFC-FR: Philadelphia (0) vs. N.Y. Giants (1), 2006
NFC-D: Philadelphia (0) vs. New Orleans (1), 2006
NFC-D: N.Y. Giants (0) vs. Dallas (1), 2007
SB: New Orleans (0) vs. Indianapolis (1), 2009
2 In many games

AFC-NFC PRO BOWL RECORDS

Includes records of AFC-NFC Pro Bowls, 1971-2010
Compiled by Elias Sports Bureau

INDIVIDUAL RECORDS

SERVICE

Most Games

12 Randall McDaniel, Minnesota 1990-2000; Tampa Bay 2001
Will Shields, Kansas City, 1996-2007

11 *Reggie White, Philadelphia, 1987-1993; Green Bay, 1994, 1996-97, 1999
Junior Seau, San Diego, 1992-2002
Rod Woodson, Pittsburgh, 1990-95, 1997; Baltimore, 2000-02; Oakland, 2003

10 Lawrence Taylor, N.Y. Giants, 1982-1991
Ronnie Lott, San Francisco, 1982-85, 1987-1991; L.A. Raiders 1992
Mike Singletary, Chicago, 1984-1993
**Bruce Matthews, Houston, 1989-1995, 1997; Tennessee, 2000, 2002
***Jerry Rice, San Francisco, 1987-88, 1990-94, 1996, 1999; Oakland, 2003

**Also selected, but did not play, in two additional games*
***Also selected, but did not play, in four additional games*
****Also selected but did not play, in three additional games*

SCORING

POINTS

Most Points, Career

45 Morten Andersen, New Orleans, 1986-89, 1991, 1993; Atlanta, 1996 (15-pat, 10-fg)

39 David Akers, Philadelphia, 2002-03, 2005, 2010 (12-pat, 9-fg)

30 Jan Stenerud, Kansas City, 1971-72, 1976; Minnesota, 1985 (6-pat, 8-fg)
Jimmy Smith, Jacksonville, 1998-2001 (5-td)
Marvin Harrison, Indianapolis, 2000-06 (5-td)
Tony Gonzalez, Kansas City, 2000-01, 2003-09 (5-td)

Most Points, Game

18 John Brockington, Green Bay, 1973 (3-td)
Mike Alstott, Tampa Bay, 2000 (3-td)
Jimmy Smith, Jacksonville, 2000 (3-td)
Shaun Alexander, Seattle, 2004 (3-td)

15 Garo Yepremian, Miami, 1974 (5-fg)
Jason Hanson, Detroit, 2000 (6-pat, 3-fg)

14 Jan Stenerud, Kansas City, 1972 (2-pat, 4-fg)

TOUCHDOWNS

Most Touchdowns, Career

5 Jimmy Smith, Jacksonville, 1998-2001 (5-p)
Marvin Harrison, Indianapolis, 2000-06 (5-p)
Tony Gonzalez, Kansas City, 2000-01, 2003-09 (5-p)

4 Mike Alstott, Tampa Bay, 1998-2003 (3-r, 1-p)
Hines Ward, Pittsburgh, 2002-05 (3-p, 1-ret)
Terrell Owens, San Francisco, 2001-04; Dallas, 2008 (4-p)

3 John Brockington, Green Bay, 1972-74 (2-r, 1-p)
Earl Campbell, Houston, 1979-1982, 1984 (3-r)
Chuck Muncie, New Orleans, 1980; San Diego, 1982-83 (3-r)
William Andrews, Atlanta, 1981-84 (1-r, 2-p)
Marcus Allen, L.A. Raiders, 1983, 1985-86, 1988; Kansas City, 1994 (2-r, 1-p)
Cris Carter, Minnesota, 1994-2001 (3-p)
Curtis Martin, New England, 1996-97; N.Y. Jets, 1999, 2002 (2-r, 1-p)
Shaun Alexander, Seattle, 2004 (2-r, 1-p)
Torry Holt, St. Louis, 2001-02, 2004-06, 2008 (3-p)
Larry Fitzgerald, Arizona, 2006, 2008-09 (3-p)
Adrian Peterson, Minnesota, 2008-2010 (3-r)

Most Touchdowns, Game

3 John Brockington, Green Bay, 1973 (2-r, 1-p)
Mike Alstott, Tampa Bay, 2000 (3-r)
Jimmy Smith, Jacksonville, 2000 (3-p)
Shaun Alexander, Seattle, 2004 (2-r, 1-p)

2 Mel Renfro, Dallas, 1971 (2-ret)
Earl Campbell, Houston, 1980 (2-r)
Chuck Muncie, New Orleans, 1980 (2-r)
William Andrews, Atlanta, 1984 (2-p)
Herschel Walker, Dallas, 1989 (2-r)
Johnny Johnson, Phoenix, 1991 (2-r)
Eric Green, Pittsburgh, 1995 (2-p)
Marvin Harrison, Indianapolis, 2001 (2-p)
Ricky Williams, Miami, 2003 (2-r)
Hines Ward, Pittsburgh, 2005 (1-p, 1-ret)
T.J. Houshmandzadeh, Cincinnati, 2008 (2-p)
Terrell Owens, Dallas, 2008 (2-p)
Adrian Peterson, Minnesota, 2008 (2-r)
Larry Fitzgerald, Arizona, 2009 (2-p)
DeSean Jackson, Philadelphia, 2010 (2-p)

POINTS AFTER TOUCHDOWN

Most Points After Touchdown, Career

15 Morten Andersen, New Orleans, 1986-89, 1991, 1993; Atlanta, 1996 (15 att)

12 David Akers, Philadelphia, 2002-03, 2005, 2010 (12 att)

11 Adam Vinatieri, New England, 2003, 2005 (11 att)

Most Points After Touchdown, Game

7 Mike Vanderjagt, Indianapolis, 2004 (7 att)

6 Ali Haji-Sheikh, N.Y. Giants, 1984 (6 att)
Jason Hanson, Detroit, 2000 (6 att)
Adam Vinatieri, New England, 2003 (6 att)
Nick Folk, Dallas, 2008 (6 att)

5 John Carney, San Diego, 1995 (5 att)
Matt Stover, Baltimore, 2001 (5 att)
Jason Elam, Denver, 2002 (5 att)
Jeff Wilkins, St. Louis, 2004 (5 att)
Adam Vinatieri, New England, 2005 (5 att)
Dan Carpenter, Miami, 2010 (5 att)

FIELD GOALS

Most Field Goals Attempted, Career

18 Morten Andersen, New Orleans, 1986-89, 1991, 1993; Atlanta, 1996

15 Jan Stenerud, Kansas City, 1971-72, 1976; Minnesota, 1985

11 David Akers, Philadelphia, 2002-03, 2005, 2010

Most Field Goals Attempted, Game

6 Jan Stenerud, Kansas City, 1972
Eddie Murray, Detroit, 1981
Mark Moseley, Washington, 1983

5 Garo Yepremian, Miami, 1974

4 Jan Stenerud, Kansas City, 1976
Nick Lowery, Kansas City, 1991, 1993
Morten Andersen, New Orleans, 1993
Cary Blanchard, Indianapolis, 1997
John Kasay, Carolina, 1997
David Akers, Philadelphia, 2002
Jeff Wilkins, St. Louis, 2004

Most Field Goals, Career

10 Morten Andersen, New Orleans, 1986-89, 1991, 1993; Atlanta, 1996

9 David Akers, Philadelphia, 2002-03, 2005, 2010

8 Jan Stenerud, Kansas City, 1971-72, 1976; Minnesota, 1985

Most Field Goals, Game

5 Garo Yepremian, Miami, 1974 (5 att)
4 Jan Stenerud, Kansas City, 1972 (6 att)
Eddie Murray, Detroit, 1981 (6 att)
3 Nick Lowery, Kansas City, 1991 (4 att)
Nick Lowery, Kansas City, 1993 (4 att)
Jason Elam, Denver, 1999 (3 att)
Jason Hanson, Detroit, 2000 (3 att)
David Akers, Philadelphia, 2002 (4 att)
Neil Rackers, Arizona, 2006 (3 att)
Rob Bironas, Tennessee, 2008 (3 att)
John Carney, N.Y. Giants, 2009 (3 att)

Longest Field Goal

53 David Akers, Philadelphia, 2003
51 Morten Andersen, New Orleans, 1989
Jason Hanson, Detroit, 2000
49 Fuad Reveiz, Minnesota, 1995
David Akers, Philadelphia, 2002

SAFETIES

Most Safeties, Game

1 Art Still, Kansas City, 1983
Mark Gastineau, N.Y. Jets, 1985
Greg Townsend, L.A. Raiders, 1992

RUSHING

ATTEMPTS

Most Attempts, Career

81 Walter Payton, Chicago, 1977-1981, 1984-87
68 O.J. Simpson, Buffalo, 1973-77
66 Barry Sanders, Detroit, 1990-93, 1995-98

Most Attempts, Game

19 O.J. Simpson, Buffalo, 1974
17 Marv Hubbard, Oakland, 1974
16 O.J. Simpson, Buffalo, 1973
Marcus Allen, L.A. Raiders, 1986
Adrian Peterson, Minnesota, 2008

YARDS GAINED

Most Yards Gained, Career

368 Walter Payton, Chicago, 1977-1981, 1984-87
356 O.J. Simpson, Buffalo, 1973-77
271 Marshall Faulk, Indianapolis, 1995-96, 1999; St. Louis, 2000, 2002-03

Most Yards Gained, Game

180 Marshall Faulk, Indianapolis, 1995
129 Adrian Peterson, Minnesota, 2008
127 Chris Warren, Seattle, 1995

Longest Run From Scrimmage

49 Marshall Faulk, Indianapolis, 1995 (TD)
41 Lawrence McCutcheon, Los Angeles, 1976
Natrone Means, San Diego, 1995
Marshall Faulk, Indianapolis, 1995
39 Chris Warren, Seattle, 1994
Priest Holmes, Kansas City, 2002
Adrian Peterson, Minnesota, 2008

AVERAGE GAIN

Highest Average Gain, Career (20 attempts)

9.36 Chris Warren, Seattle, 1994-96, (25-234)
7.19 Adrian Peterson, Minnesota, 2008-2010 (27-194)
6.45 Marshall Faulk, Indianapolis, 1995-96, 1999; St. Louis, 2000, 2002-03 (42-271)

Highest Average Gain, Game (10 attempts)

13.85 Marshall Faulk, Indianapolis, 1995 (13-180)
9.07 Chris Warren, Seattle, 1995 (14-127)
8.06 Adrian Peterson, Minnesota 2008 (16-129)

TOUCHDOWNS

Most Touchdowns, Career

3 Earl Campbell, Houston, 1979-1982, 1984
Chuck Muncie, New Orleans, 1980; San Diego, 1982-83
Mike Alstott, Tampa Bay, 1998-2003
Adrian Peterson, Minnesota, 2008-2010
2 John Brockington, Green Bay, 1972-74
O.J. Simpson, Buffalo, 1973-77
Walter Payton, Chicago, 1977-1981, 1984-87
Marcus Allen, L.A. Raiders, 1983, 1985-86, 1988; Kansas City, 1994
Herschel Walker, Dallas, 1988-89
Johnny Johnson, Phoenix, 1991
Barry Sanders, Detroit, 1990-93, 1995-98
Curtis Martin, New England, 1996-97; N.Y. Jets, 1999, 2002
Ricky Williams, Miami, 2003
Shaun Alexander, Seattle, 2004-06
LaDainian Tomlinson, San Diego, 2003, 2005-07

Most Touchdowns, Game

3 Mike Alstott, Tampa Bay, 2000
2 John Brockington, Green Bay, 1973
Earl Campbell, Houston, 1980
Chuck Muncie, New Orleans, 1980
Herschel Walker, Dallas, 1989
Johnny Johnson, Phoenix, 1991
Ricky Williams, Miami, 2003
Shaun Alexander, Seattle, 2004
Adrian Peterson, Minnesota, 2008

PASSING

ATTEMPTS

Most Attempts, Career

179 Peyton Manning, Indianapolis, 2000-01, 2003-09
120 Dan Fouts, San Diego, 1980-84, 1986
101 Steve Young, San Francisco, 1993-96, 1998-99

Most Attempts, Game

41 Peyton Manning, Indianapolis, 2004
32 Bill Kenney, Kansas City, 1984
Steve Young, San Francisco, 1993
30 Dan Fouts, San Diego, 1983

COMPLETIONS

Most Completions, Career

107 Peyton Manning, Indianapolis, 2000-01, 2003-09
63 Dan Fouts, San Diego, 1980-84, 1986
48 Steve Young, San Francisco, 1993-96, 1998-99

Most Completions, Game

22 Peyton Manning, Indianapolis, 2004
21 Joe Theismann, Washington, 1984
18 Steve Young, San Francisco, 1993

COMPLETION PERCENTAGE

Highest Completion Percentage, Career (40 attempts)

68.9 Joe Theismann, Washington, 1983-84 (45-31)
67.9 Rich Gannon, Oakland, 2000-03 (53-36)
64.4 Jim Kelly, Buffalo, 1988, 1991-92 (45-29)

Highest Completion Percentage, Game (10 attempts)

90.0 Archie Manning, New Orleans, 1980 (10-9)
85.7 Rich Gannon, Oakland, 2001 (14-12)
80.0 Rich Gannon, Oakland, 2002 (10-8)
Jeff Garcia, Tampa Bay, 2008 (10-8)

YARDS GAINED

Most Yards Gained, Career

1,496 Peyton Manning, Indianapolis, 2000-01, 2003-09
890 Dan Fouts, San Diego, 1980-84, 1986
614 Steve Young, San Francisco, 1993-96, 1998-99

AFC-NFC PRO BOWL RECORDS

Most Yards Gained, Game
342 Peyton Manning, Indianapolis, 2004
274 Dan Fouts, San Diego, 1983
270 Peyton Manning, Indianapolis, 2000

Longest Completion
93 Jeff Blake, Cincinnati (to Thigpen, Pittsburgh), 1996 (TD)
90 Steve McNair, Tennessee (to Johnson, Cincinnati), 2004 (TD)
80 Mark Brunell, Jacksonville (to Brown, Oakland), 1997 (TD)

AVERAGE GAIN

Highest Average Gain, Career (40 attempts)
8.36 Peyton Manning, Indianapolis, 2000-01, 2003-09 (179-1,496)
8.19 Rich Gannon, Oakland, 2000-03 (53-434)
8.12 Brett Favre, Green Bay, 1993-94, 1996-97 (57-463)

Highest Average Gain, Game (10 attempts)
15.27 Randall Cunningham, Philadelphia, 1991 (11-168)
13.70 Rich Gannon, Oakland, 2002 (10-137)
13.07 David Garrard, Jacksonville, 2010 (14-183)

TOUCHDOWNS

Most Touchdowns, Career
14 Peyton Manning, Indianapolis, 2000-01, 2003-09
7 Rich Gannon, Oakland, 2000-03
4 Steve Young, San Francisco, 1993-96, 1998-99
Marc Bulger, St. Louis, 2004, 2007
Donovan McNabb, Philadelphia, 2001-03, 2005, 2010

Most Touchdowns, Game
4 Marc Bulger, St. Louis, 2004
3 Joe Theismann, Washington, 1984
Phil Simms, N.Y. Giants, 1986
Peyton Manning, Indianapolis, 2004
Peyton Manning, Indianapolis, 2005
2 James Harris, Los Angeles, 1975
Mike Boryla, Philadelphia, 1976
Ken Anderson, Cincinnati, 1977
Jim Kelly, Buffalo, 1991
Mark Rypien, Washington, 1992
Steve Young, San Francisco, 1998
Peyton Manning, Indianapolis, 2000
Rich Gannon, Oakland, 2001
Peyton Manning, Indianapolis, 2001
Rich Gannon, Oakland, 2002
Donovan McNabb, Philadelphia, 2002
Rich Gannon, Oakland, 2003
Brad Johnson, Tampa Bay, 2003
Carson Palmer, Cincinnati, 2007
Tony Romo, Dallas, 2008
Aaron Rodgers, Green Bay, 2010
Matt Schaub, Houston, 2010

HAD INTERCEPTED

Most Passes Had Intercepted, Career
8 Dan Fouts, San Diego, 1980-84, 1986
Peyton Manning, Indianapolis, 2000-01, 2003-09
6 Jim Hart, St. Louis, 1975-78
Donovan McNabb, Philadelphia, 2001-03, 2005, 2010
5 Ken Stabler, Oakland, 1974-75, 1978
Jeff Garcia, San Francisco, 2001-03; Tampa Bay, 2008

Most Passes Had Intercepted, Game
5 Jim Hart, St. Louis, 1977
4 Ken Stabler, Oakland, 1974
3 Dan Fouts, San Diego, 1986
Mark Rypien, Washington, 1990
Steve Young, San Francisco, 1993
Jim Harbaugh, Indianapolis, 1996
Vinny Testaverde, N.Y. Jets, 1999
Jeff Garcia, San Francisco, 2003
Peyton Manning, Indianapolis, 2006

Most Attempts, Without Interception, Game
27 Joe Theismann, Washington, 1984
Phil Simms, N.Y. Giants, 1986
26 John Brodie, San Francisco, 1971
Danny White, Dallas, 1983
23 Dave Krieg, Seattle, 1990

PERCENTAGE, PASSES HAD INTERCEPTED

Lowest Percentage, Passes Had Intercepted, Career (40 attempts)
0.00 Joe Theismann, Washington, 1983-84 (45-0)
1.89 Rich Gannon, Oakland, 2000-03 (53-1)
2.13 Dave Krieg, Seattle, 1985, 1989-1990 (47-1)

PASS RECEIVING

RECEPTIONS

Most Receptions, Career
39 Tony Gonzalez, Kansas City, 2000-01, 2003-09
37 Jerry Rice, San Francisco, 1987-88, 1990-94, 1996, 1999; Oakland, 2003
30 Marvin Harrison, Indianapolis, 2000-06

Most Receptions, Game
9 Randy Moss, Minnesota, 2000
8 Steve Largent, Seattle, 1986
Michael Irvin, Dallas, 1992
Andre Rison, Atlanta, 1993
Jimmy Smith, Jacksonville, 2000
Marvin Harrison, Indianapolis, 2001
Terrell Owens, San Francisco, 2002
Steve Smith, Carolina, 2006
Terrell Owens, Dallas, 2008
Roddy White, Atlanta, 2010
7 John Stallworth, Pittsburgh, 1983
Jerry Rice, San Francisco, 1992
Isaac Bruce, St. Louis, 1997
Keyshawn Johnson, N.Y. Jets, 1999
Randy Moss, Minnesota, 1999
Warrick Dunn, Tampa Bay, 2001
Torry Holt, St. Louis, 2001
Torry Holt, St. Louis, 2004
Vincent Jackson, San Diego, 2010

YARDS GAINED

Most Yards Gained, Career
590 Tony Gonzalez, Kansas City, 2000-01, 2003-09
495 Jerry Rice, San Francisco, 1987-88, 1990-94, 1996, 1999; Oakland, 2003
462 Marvin Harrison, Indianapolis, 2000-06

Most Yards Gained, Game
212 Randy Moss, Minnesota, 2000
156 Chad Ochocinco, Cincinnati, 2004
137 Tim Brown, Oakland, 1997
Reggie Wayne, Indianapolis, 2007

Longest Reception
93 Yancey Thigpen, Pittsburgh (from Blake, Cincinnati), 1996 (TD)
90 Chad Ochocinco, Cincinnati (from McNair, Tennessee), 2004 (TD)
80 Tim Brown, Oakland (from Brunell, Jacksonville), 1997 (TD)

TOUCHDOWNS

Most Touchdowns, Career
5 Jimmy Smith, Jacksonville, 1998-2001
Marvin Harrison, Indianapolis, 2000-06

Tony Gonzalez, Kansas City, 2000-01, 2003-09
4 Terrell Owens, San Francisco, 2001-04; Dallas, 2008
3 Cris Carter, Minnesota, 1994-2001
Torry Holt, St. Louis, 2001-02, 2004-06, 2008
Hines Ward, Pittsburgh, 2002-05
Larry Fitzgerald, Arizona, 2006, 2008-09

Most Touchdowns, Game
3 Jimmy Smith, Jacksonville, 2000
2 William Andrews, Atlanta, 1984
Eric Green, Pittsburgh, 1995
Marvin Harrison, Indianapolis, 2001
T.J. Houshmandzadeh, Cincinnati, 2008
Terrell Owens, Dallas, 2008
Larry Fitzgerald, Arizona, 2009
DeSean Jackson, Philadelphia, 2010

INTERCEPTIONS BY

Most Interceptions By, Career
4 Everson Walls, Dallas, 1982-84, 1986
Deion Sanders, Atlanta, 1992-94; San Francisco, 1995; Dallas, 1999
Champ Bailey, Washington, 2001-04; Denver, 2005-08
3 Ken Houston, Houston, 1971-73; Washington, 1974-79
Jack Lambert, Pittsburgh, 1976-1984
Ted Hendricks, Baltimore, 1972-74; Green Bay, 1975; Oakland, 1981-82; L.A. Raiders, 1983-84
Mike Haynes, New England, 1978-1981, 1983; L.A. Raiders, 1985-87
Ty Law, New England, 1999, 2002-04; N.Y. Jets, 2006
Brian Dawkins, Philadelphia, 2000, 2002-03, 2005-06, 2009; Denver, 2010
2 By 20 players

Most Interceptions By, Game
2 Mel Blount, Pittsburgh, 1977
Everson Walls, Dallas, 1982, 1983
LeRoy Irvin, L.A. Rams, 1986
David Fulcher, Cincinnati, 1990
Brian Dawkins, Philadelphia, 2000
Rod Woodson, Oakland, 2003
Ed Reed, Baltimore, 2007
Antonio Cromartie, San Diego, 2008

YARDS GAINED

Most Yards Gained, Career
147 Ty Law, New England, 1999, 2002-04; N.Y. Jets, 2006
103 Deion Sanders, Atlanta, 1992-94; San Francisco, 1995; Dallas, 1999
88 Rod Woodson, Pittsburgh, 1990-95, 1997; Baltimore, 2000-02; Oakland, 2003

Most Yards Gained, Game
87 Deion Sanders, Dallas, 1999
77 Antonio Cromartie, San Diego, 2008
73 Rod Woodson, Pittsburgh, 1994

Longest Gain
87 Deion Sanders, Dallas, 1999
73 Rod Woodson, Pittsburgh, 1994 (lateral)
67 Ty Law, New England, 1999 (TD)

TOUCHDOWNS

Most Touchdowns, Career
2 Ty Law, New England, 1999, 2002-04; N.Y. Jets, 2006
Derrick Brooks, Tampa Bay, 1998-2001, 2003, 2006-07
1 By many

Most Touchdowns, Game
1 Bobby Bell, Kansas City, 1973
Nolan Cromwell, L.A. Rams, 1984
Joey Browner, Minnesota, 1986
Jerry Gray, L.A. Rams, 1990
Mike Johnson, Cleveland, 1990
Junior Seau, San Diego, 1993
Ken Harvey, Washington, 1996
Ashley Ambrose, Cincinnati, 1997
Ty Law, New England, 1999
Derrick Brooks, Tampa Bay, 2000
Aeneas Williams, Arizona, 2000
Ray Lewis, Baltimore, 2002
Ty Law, New England, 2003
Dre' Bly, Detroit, 2004
Derrick Brooks, Tampa Bay, 2006

PUNTING

Most Punts, Career
33 Ray Guy, Oakland, 1974-79, 1981
23 Rohn Stark, Indianapolis, 1986-87, 1991, 1993
22 Reggie Roby, Miami, 1985, 1990; Washington, 1995

Most Punts, Game
10 Reggie Roby, Miami, 1985
9 Tom Wittum, San Francisco, 1974
Rohn Stark, Indianapolis, 1987
8 Jerrel Wilson, Kansas City, 1971
Tom Skladany, Detroit, 1982
Reggie Roby, Washington, 1995

Longest Punt
73 Shane Lechler, Oakland, 2002
70 Shane Lechler, Oakland, 2002
65 Shane Lechler, Oakland, 2009

AVERAGE YARDAGE

Highest Average, Career (10 punts)
53.00 Shane Lechler, Oakland, 2002, 2005, 2008-2010 (11-583)
47.30 Jeff Feagles, Arizona, 1996; N.Y. Giants, 2009 (10-473)
46.73 Reggie Roby, Miami, 1985, 1990; Washington, 1995 (22-1,028)

Highest Average, Game (4 punts)
60.75 Shane Lechler, Oakland, 2002 (4-243)
55.50 Darren Bennett, San Diego, 1996 (4-222)
52.00 Matt Turk, Washington, 1999 (4-208)

PUNT RETURNS

Most Punt Returns, Career
13 Rick Upchurch, Denver, 1977, 1979-1980, 1983
11 Vai Sikahema, St. Louis, 1987-88
Eric Metcalf, Cleveland 1994-95; San Diego 1998
10 Mike Nelms, Washington, 1981-83

Most Punt Returns, Game
7 Vai Sikahema, St. Louis, 1987
6 Henry Ellard, L.A. Rams, 1985
Gerald McNeil, Cleveland, 1988
Eric Metcalf, Cleveland, 1995
5 Rick Upchurch, Denver, 1980
Mike Nelms, Washington, 1981
Carl Roaches, Houston, 1982
Johnny Bailey, Phoenix, 1993

Most Fair Catches, Game
2 Jerry Logan, Baltimore, 1971
Dick Anderson, Miami, 1974
Henry Ellard, L.A. Rams, 1985
Isaac Bruce, St. Louis, 1997
Desmond Howard, Detroit, 2001

YARDS GAINED

Most Yards Gained, Career
183 Billy Johnson, Houston, 1976, 1978; Atlanta, 1984

138 Mel Renfro, Dallas, 1971-72, 1974
Rick Upchurch, Denver, 1977, 1979-1980, 1983
135 Eric Metcalf, Cleveland, 1994-95; San Diego 1998

Most Yards Gained, Game
159 Billy Johnson, Houston, 1976
138 Mel Renfro, Dallas, 1971
117 Wally Henry, Philadelphia, 1980

Longest Punt Return
90 Billy Johnson, Houston, 1976 (TD)
86 Wally Henry, Philadelphia, 1980 (TD)
82 Mel Renfro, Dallas, 1971 (TD)

AVERAGE YARDAGE
Highest Average, Career (4 returns)
22.88 Billy Johnson, Houston, 1976, 1978; Atlanta, 1984 (8-183)
21.50 Tony Green, Washington, 1979 (4-86)
15.67 David Meggett, N.Y. Giants, 1990; New England, 1997

Highest Average, Game (3 returns)
39.75 Billy Johnson, Houston, 1976 (4-159)
39.00 Wally Henry, Philadelphia, 1980 (3-117)
21.50 Tony Green, Washington, 1979 (4-86)

TOUCHDOWNS
Most Touchdowns, Game
2 Mel Renfro, Dallas, 1971
1 Billy Johnson, Houston, 1976
Wally Henry, Philadelphia, 1980

KICKOFF RETURNS
Most Kickoff Returns, Career
17 Michael Bates, Carolina, 1997-2001
14 Mel Gray, Detroit, 1991-92, 1995
13 Josh Cribbs, Cleveland, 2008, 2010

Most Kickoff Returns, Game
8 Derrick Mason, Tennessee, 2004
7 Mel Gray, Detroit, 1995
Jerry Azumah, Chicago, 2004
Josh Cribbs, Cleveland, 2010
6 Greg Pruitt, L.A. Raiders, 1984
David Meggett, New England, 1997
Michael Bates, Carolina, 1998
Steve Smith, Carolina, 2002
Josh Cribbs, Cleveland, 2008

YARDS GAINED
Most Yards Gained, Career
488 Michael Bates, Carolina, 1997-2001
373 Josh Cribbs, Cleveland, 2008, 2010
309 Greg Pruitt, Cleveland, 1974-75, 1977-78; L.A. Raiders, 1984

Most Yards Gained, Game
228 Jerry Azumah, Chicago, 2004
217 Michael Lewis, New Orleans, 2003
214 Josh Cribbs, Cleveland, 2010

Longest Kickoff Return
66 Michael Bates, Carolina, 2000
62 Greg Pruitt, L.A. Raiders, 1984
61 Eugene (Mercury) Morris, Miami, 1972

AVERAGE YARDAGE
Highest Average, Career (4 returns)
43.40 Michael Lewis, New Orleans, 2003 (5-217)
35.00 Les (Speedy) Duncan, Washington, 1972 (5-175)
32.57 Jerry Azumah, Chicago, 2004 (7-228)

Highest Average, Game (3 returns)
43.40 Michael Lewis, New Orleans, 2003 (5-217)
42.67 Clifton Smith, Tampa Bay, 2009 (3-128)
42.00 Michael Bates, Carolina, 2000 (4-168)

TOUCHDOWNS
Most Touchdowns, Game
1 Hines Ward, Pittsburgh, 2005

FUMBLES
Most Fumbles, Career
6 Dan Fouts, San Diego, 1980-84, 1986
4 Lawrence McCutcheon, Los Angeles, 1974-78
Franco Harris, Pittsburgh, 1973-76, 1978-1981
Jay Schroeder, Washington, 1987
Vai Sikahema, St. Louis, 1987-88
Trent Green, Kansas City, 2004, 2006
3 By 9 players

Most Fumbles, Game
4 Jay Schroeder, Washington, 1987
Trent Green, Kansas City, 2004
3 Dan Fouts, San Diego, 1982
Vai Sikahema, St. Louis, 1987
2 By 19 players

RECOVERIES
Most Fumbles Recovered, Career
3 Harold Jackson, Philadelphia, 1973; Los Angeles, 1974, 1976, 1978 (3-own)
Dan Fouts, San Diego, 1980-84, 1986 (3-own)
Randy White, Dallas, 1978, 1980-86 (3-opp)
Trent Green, Kansas City, 2004, 2006 (3-own)
Peyton Manning, Indianapolis, 2000-01, 2003-09 (3-own)
2 By many players

Most Fumbles Recovered, Game
3 Trent Green, Kansas City, 2004 (3-own)
2 Dick Anderson, Miami, 1974 (1-own, 1-opp)
Harold Jackson, Los Angeles, 1974 (2-own)
Dan Fouts, San Diego, 1982 (2-own)
Joey Browner, Minnesota, 1990 (2-opp)
Jessie Armstead, N.Y. Giants, 1999 (1-own, 1-opp)
Steve Beuerlein, Carolina, 2000 (2-own)

YARDAGE
Longest Fumble Return
83 Art Still, Kansas City, 1985 (TD, opp)
70 Adalius Thomas, Baltimore, 2007 (TD, opp)
51 Phil Villapiano, Oakland, 1974 (opp)

TOUCHDOWNS
Most Touchdowns, Game
1 Art Still, Kansas City, 1985
Keith Millard, Minnesota, 1990
Adalius Thomas, Baltimore, 2007

SACKS
Sacks have been compiled since 1983.

Most Sacks, Career
9.5 Reggie White, Philadelphia, 1987-1993; Green Bay, 1994, 1996-97, 1999
9.0 Howie Long, L.A. Raiders, 1984-88, 1990, 1993-1994
7.5 Bruce Smith, Buffalo, 1988-1991, 1995-96, 1998-99

Most Sacks, Game
4 Mark Gastineau, N.Y. Jets, 1985
Reggie White, Philadelphia, 1987
3 Richard Dent, Chicago, 1985
Bruce Smith, Buffalo, 1991
2.5 Bruce Smith, Buffalo, 1998

Rules

2010 NFL ROSTER OF OFFICIALS

Carl Johnson, Vice President of Officiating
Ed Coukart, Supervisor of Officials
Neely Dunn, Supervisor of Officials
Johnny Grier, Supervisor of Officials
Gary Slaughter, Supervisor of Officials
Bill Vinovich, Supervisor of Officials

No.	Name	Position	College
20	Anderson, Barry	Side Judge	North Carolina State
66	Anderson, Walt	Referee	Texas
108	Arthur, Gary	Line Judge	Wright State
26	Baltz, Mark	Head Linesman	Ohio
72	Banks, Michael	Side Judge	Illinois State
55	Barnes, Tom	Line Judge	Minnesota
56	Baynes, Allen	Side Judge	Auburn
59	Baynes, Rusty	Line Judge	Auburn-Montgomery
32	Bergman, Jeff	Line Judge	Robert Morris
91	Bergman, Jerry	Head Linesman	Robert Morris
34	Blakeman, Clete	Referee	Nebraska
23	Boger, Jerome	Referee	Morehouse College
18	Boston, Byron	Line Judge	Austin
74	Bowers, Derick	Head Linesman	East Central
98	Bradley, Greg	Head Linesman	Tennessee
31	Brown, Chad	Umpire	East Texas State
43	Brown, Terry	Field Judge	Tennessee-Knoxville
11	Bryan, Fred	Umpire	Northern Iowa
86	Buchanan, Jimmy	Field Judge	South Carolina State
134	Camp, Ed	Head Linesman	William Paterson
126	Carey, Don	Back Judge	California-Riverside
94	Carey, Mike	Referee	Santa Clara
39	Carlsen, Don	Side Judge	Cal State-Chico
60	Cavaletto, Gary	Field Judge	Hancock
41	Cheek, Boris	Field Judge	Morgan State
51	Cheffers, Carl	Referee	California-Irvine
95	Coleman, James	Side Judge	Arkansas
65	Coleman, Walt	Referee	Arkansas
99	Corrente, Tony	Referee	Cal State-Fullerton
70	Dawson, Scott	Umpire	Virginia Tech
58	DeBell, Jimmy	Side Judge	SUNY-Brockport
53	DeFelice, Garth	Umpire	San Diego State
6	Dornan, Kirk	Back Judge	Central Washington
27	Dyer, Lee	Back Judge	Tennessee-Chattanooga
3	Edwards, Scott	Field Judge	Alabama
81	Ellison, Roy	Umpire	Savannah State
61	Ferguson, Keith	Back Judge	San Jose State
64	Ferrell, Dan	Umpire	Cal State-Fullerton
71	Fowler, Ruben	Umpire	Huston-Tillotson
133	Freeman, Steve	Back Judge	Mississippi State
80	Gautreaux, Greg	Field Judge	S.W. Louisiana
19	Green, Scott	Referee	Delaware
49	Hall, Rich	Umpire	Arizona
40	Hannah, Butch	Umpire	Middle Tennessee State
125	Hayes, Laird	Side Judge	Princeton
54	Hayward, George	Head Linesman	Missouri Western
93	Helverson, Scott	Back Judge	Iowa
29	Hill, Adrian	Line Judge	Buffalo
97	Hill, Tom	Side Judge	Carson Newman
28	Hittner, Mark	Head Linesman	Pittsburg State
85	Hochuli, Ed	Referee	Texas-El Paso
82	Horton, Buddy	Field Judge	Oregon State
37	Howey, Jim	Field Judge	Erskine College
35	Hussey, John	Line Judge	Idaho State
76	Jenkins, Darrell	Umpire	San Jose State
121	King, Paul	Umpire	Nicholls State
103	Lamberth, Jeff	Side Judge	Texas A&M
73	Larrew, Joe	Side Judge	St. Louis
127	Leavy, Bill	Referee	San Jose State
130	Lewis, Darryll	Line Judge	Dartmouth
89	Lucivansky, Jon	Field Judge	Minnesota
106	Mackie, Wayne	Head Linesman	Colgate
52	Mapp, Julian	Head Linesman	Grambling State
107	Marinucci, Ron	Line Judge	Glassboro State
77	McAulay, Terry	Referee	Louisiana State
5	McGrath, John	Head Linesman	Kentucky
8	McKenzie, Dana	Head Linesman	Toledo
110	McKinnely, Phil	Head Linesman	UCLA
48	Mello, Jim	Head Linesman	Northeastern
78	Meyer, Greg	Side Judge	Texas Christian
115	Michalek, Tony	Umpire	Indiana
111	Miles, Terrence	Back Judge	Arizona State
135	Morelli, Pete	Referee	St. Mary's
124	Paganelli, Carl	Umpire	Michigan State
105	Paganelli, Dino	Back Judge	Aquinas College
46	Paganelli, Perry	Back Judge	Hope College
132	Parry, John	Referee	Purdue
15	Patterson, Rick	Side Judge	Wofford
79	Payne, Kent	Head Linesman	Nebraska Wesleyan
9	Perlman, Mark	Line Judge	Salem
10	Phares, Ron	Line Judge	Virginia Tech
47	Podraza, Tim	Line Judge	Nebraska
109	Prioleau, Dyrol	Field Judge	Johnson C. Smith
30	Prukop, Todd	Back Judge	Cal State-Fullerton
63	Quirk, Jim	Field Judge	Middlebury
83	Reels, Richard	Back Judge	Chicago State
44	Rice, Jeff	Umpire	Northwestern
57	Riveron, Alberto	Referee	Miami
128	Rose, Larry	Side Judge	Florida
67	Rosenbaum, Doug	Field Judge	Illinois Wesleyan
129	Schuster, Bill	Umpire	Alfred
45	Seeman, Jeff	Line Judge	Minnesota
2	Smith, Billy	Back Judge	East Carolina
90	Spanier, Mike	Line Judge	St. Cloud State
24	Stabile, Tom	Head Linesman	Slippery Rock
12	Steed, Greg	Back Judge	Howard
88	Steenson, Scott	Field Judge	North Texas
84	Steinkerchner, Mark	Line Judge	Akron
22	Stelljes, Steve	Head Linesman	Friends
68	Stephan, Tom	Line Judge	Pittsburg State
114	Steratore, Gene	Referee	Kent State
112	Steratore, Tony	Back Judge	California
102	Stritesky, Bruce	Umpire	Embry Riddle
100	Symonette, Tom	Line Judge	Florida
62	Torbert, Ronald	Side Judge	Michigan State
42	Triplette, Jeff	Referee	Wake Forest
75	Vernatchi, Rob	Back Judge	California-Riverside
36	Veteri, Tony	Head Linesman	Manhattan College
25	Waggoner, Bob	Field Judge	Juniata College
96	Wash, Undrey	Umpire	Texas-Arlington
7	Washington, Keith	Side Judge	Virginia Military Institute
116	Weatherford, Mike	Side Judge	Oklahoma State
50	Weir, Mike	Field Judge	Missouri
119	Wilson, Greg	Back Judge	USC
14	Winter, Ron	Referee	Michigan State
4	Wrolstad, Craig	Field Judge	Washington
16	Wyant, David	Side Judge	Virginia
38	Yette, Greg	Back Judge	Howard
33	Zimmer, Steve	Field Judge	Hofstra

Roster as of May 2010

NUMERICAL ROSTER

No.	Name	Position
2	Billy Smith	BJ
3	Scott Edwards	FJ
4	Craig Wrolstad	FJ
5	John McGrath	HL
6	Kirk Dornan	BJ
7	Keith Washington	SJ
8	Dana McKenzie	HL
9	Mark Perlman	LJ
10	Ron Phares	LJ
11	Fred Bryan	U
12	Greg Steed	BJ
14	Ron Winter	R
15	Rick Patterson	SJ
16	David Wyant	SJ
18	Byron Boston	LJ
19	Scott Green	R
20	Barry Anderson	SJ
22	Steve Stelljes	HL
23	Jerome Boger	R
24	Tom Stabile	HL
25	Bob Waggoner	FJ
26	Mark Baltz	HL
27	Lee Dyer	BJ
28	Mark Hittner	HL
29	Adrian Hill	LJ
30	Todd Prukop	BJ
31	Chad Brown	U
32	Jeff Bergman	LJ
33	Steve Zimmer	FJ
34	Clete Blakeman	R
35	John Hussey	LJ
36	Tony Veteri	HL
37	Jim Howey	FJ
38	Greg Yette	BJ
39	Don Carlsen	SJ
40	Butch Hannah	U
41	Boris Cheek	FJ
42	Jeff Triplette	R
43	Terry Brown	FJ
44	Jeff Rice	U
45	Jeff Seeman	LJ
46	Perry Paganelli	BJ
47	Tim Podraza	LJ
48	Jim Mello	HL
49	Rich Hall	U
50	Mike Weir	FJ
51	Carl Cheffers	R
52	Julian Mapp	HL
53	Garth DeFelice	U
54	George Hayward	HL
55	Tom Barnes	LJ
56	Allen Baynes	SJ
57	Alberto Riveron	R
58	Jimmy DeBell	SJ
59	Rusty Baynes	LJ
60	Gary Cavaletto	FJ
61	Keith Ferguson	BJ
62	Ronald Torbert	SJ
63	Jim Quirk	FJ
64	Dan Ferrell	U
65	Walt Coleman	R
66	Walt Anderson	R
67	Doug Rosenbaum	FJ
68	Tom Stephan	LJ
70	Scott Dawson	U
71	Ruben Fowler	U
72	Michael Banks	SJ
73	Joe Larrew	SJ
74	Derick Bowers	HL
75	Rob Vernatchi	BJ
76	Darrell Jenkins	U
77	Terry McAulay	R
78	Greg Meyer	SJ
79	Kent Payne	HL
80	Greg Gautreaux	FJ
81	Roy Ellison	U
82	Buddy Horton	FJ
83	Richard Reels	BJ
84	Mark Steinkerchner	LJ
85	Ed Hochuli	R
86	Jimmy Buchanan	FJ
88	Scott Steenson	FJ
89	Jon Lucivansky	FJ
90	Mike Spanier	LJ
91	Jerry Bergman	HL
93	Scott Helverson	BJ
94	Mike Carey	R
95	James Coleman	SJ
96	Undrey Wash	U
97	Tom Hill	SJ
98	Greg Bradley	HL
99	Tony Corrente	R
100	Tom Symonette	LJ
102	Bruce Stritesky	U
103	Jeff Lamberth	SJ
105	Dino Paganelli	BJ
106	Wayne Mackie	HL
107	Ron Marinucci	LJ
108	Gary Arthur	LJ
109	Dyrol Prioleau	FJ
110	Phil McKinnely	HL
111	Terrence Miles	BJ
112	Tony Steratore	BJ
114	Gene Steratore	R
115	Tony Michalek	U
116	Mike Weatherford	SJ
119	Greg Wilson	BJ
121	Paul King	U
124	Carl Paganelli	U
125	Laird Hayes	SJ
126	Don Carey	BJ
127	Bill Leavy	R
128	Larry Rose	SJ
129	Bill Schuster	U
130	Darryll Lewis	LJ
132	John Parry	R
133	Steve Freeman	BJ
134	Ed Camp	HL
135	Pete Morelli	R

Roster as of May 2010

OFFICIALS

2010 OFFICIALS AT A GLANCE

REFEREES

Walt Anderson, No. **66,** Texas, college officiating coordinator, retired dentist, 15th year.
Clete Blakeman, No. **34,** Nebraska, attorney, 3rd year.
Jerome Boger, No. **23,** Morehouse College, commercial insurance underwriter, 7th year.
Mike Carey, No. **94,** Santa Clara, owner, skiing accessories, 21st year.
Carl Cheffers, No. **51,** California-Irvine, sales manager, 11th year.
Walt Coleman, No. **65,** Arkansas, manager dairy processor, 22nd year.
Tony Corrente, No. **99,** Cal State-Fullerton, educator, 16th year.
Scott Green, No. **19,** Delaware, president, government support services, 20th year.
Ed Hochuli, No. **85,** Texas-El Paso, attorney, 21st year.
Bill Leavy, No. **127,** San Jose State, retired firefighter, 16th year.
Terry McAulay, No. **77,** Louisiana State, college officiating coordinator, 13th year.
Pete Morelli, No. **135,** St. Mary's, high school principal, 14th year.
John Parry, No. **132,** Purdue, financial advisor, 11th year.
Alberto Riveron, No. **57,** Miami, sales, commercial restaurant equipment, 7th year.
Gene Steratore, No. **114,** Kent State, co-owner, supply company, 8th year.
Jeff Triplette, No. **42,** Wake Forest, restructuring consultant, 15th year.
Ron Winter, No. **14,** Michigan State, university professor, 16th year.

UMPIRES

Chad Brown, No. **31,** East Texas State, executive manager of facilities/student affairs administration, 19th year.
Fred Bryan, No. **11,** Northern Iowa, superintendent, juvenile correctional facility, 2nd year.
Scott Dawson, No. **70,** Virginia Tech, president/owner, commercial construction company, 16th year.
Garth DeFelice, No. **53,** San Diego State, distribution center manager, beverage company, 13th year.
Roy Ellison, No. **81,** Savannah State, technical staff member, 8th year.
Dan Ferrell, No. **64,** Cal State-Fullerton, director, parts logistics, 8th year.
Ruben Fowler, No. **71,** Huston-Tillotson, retired firefighter, 5th year.
Rich Hall, No. **49,** Arizona, custom cabinetry, 7th year.
Butch Hannah, No. **40,** Middle Tennessee State, retired federal probation officer, 12th year.
Darrell Jenkins, No. **76,** San Jose State, retired, 9th year.
Paul King, No. **121,** Nicholls State, teacher, 2nd year.
Tony Michalek, No. **115,** Indiana, USA Football officiating director, 9th year.
Carl Paganelli, No. **124,** Michigan State, federal probation officer, 12th year.
Jeff Rice, No. **44,** Northwestern, attorney, 16th year.
Bill Schuster, No. **129,** Alfred, insurance broker, 11th year.
Bruce Stritesky, No. **102,** Embry Riddle, airline pilot, 5th year.
Undrey Wash, No. **96,** Texas-Arlington, claims controller, 11th year.

HEAD LINESMEN

Mark Baltz, No. **26,** Ohio, sales consultant, 22nd year.
Jerry Bergman, No. **91,** Robert Morris, sales executive, 9th year.
Derick Bowers, No. **74,** East Central, sales representative, 8th year.
Greg Bradley, No. **98,** Tennessee, chemical engineer, 2nd year.
Ed Camp, No. **134,** William Paterson, physical education teacher, 11th year.
George Hayward, No. **54,** Missouri Western, vice-president and manager, warehouse company, 20th year.
Mark Hittner, No. **28,** Pittsburg State, investment broker, 14th year.
Wayne Mackie, No. **106,** Colgate, director of housing, 4th year.
Julian Mapp, No. **52,** Grambling State, project leader, 2nd year.
John McGrath, No. **5,** Kentucky, vice president of sales, 9th year.
Dana McKenzie, No. **8,** Toledo, claims adjuster, 3rd year.
Phil McKinnely, No. **110,** UCLA, inventory control, 8th year.
Jim Mello, No. **48,** Northeastern, facilities manager, 7th year.
Kent Payne, No. **79,** Nebraska Wesleyan, teacher, 7th year.
Tom Stabile, No. **24,** Slippery Rock, secondary educational administrator, 16th year.
Steve Stelljes, No. **22,** Friends, business planning manager, 9th year.
Tony Veteri, No. **36,** Manhattan College, physical education teacher, 19th year.

LINE JUDGES

Gary Arthur, No. **108,** Wright State, president, commercial printing company, 14th year.
Tom Barnes, No. **55,** Minnesota, manufacturing representative, 25th year.
Rusty Baynes, No. **59,** Auburn-Montgomery, general manager, safety services, 1st year.
Jeff Bergman, No. **32,** Robert Morris, president and chief executive officer, medical services, 19th year.
Byron Boston, No. **18,** Austin, tax consultant, 16th year.
Adrian Hill, No. **29,** Buffalo, software engineer, 1st year.
John Hussey, No. **35,** Idaho State, sales representative, retail logistics group, 9th year.
Darryll Lewis, No. **130,** Dartmouth, associate professor, 12th year.
Ron Marinucci, No. **107,** Glassboro State, vice president, novelty cone company, 14th year.
Mark Perlman, No. **9,** Salem, teacher, 10th year.
Ron Phares, No. **10,** Virginia Tech, president, construction company, 26th year.
Tim Podraza, No. **47,** Nebraska, banker, 3rd year.
Jeff Seeman, No. **45,** Minnesota, brokerage sales, 9th year.
Mike Spanier, No. **90,** St. Cloud State, middle school principal, 12th year.
Mark Steinkerchner, No. **84,** Akron, vice-president, 17th year.
Tom Stephan, No. **68,** Pittsburg State, president and CEO, 12th year.
Tom Symonette, No. **100,** Florida, certified public accountant, 7th year.

Roster as of May 2010

FIELD JUDGES

Terry Brown, No. **43,** Tennessee, probation supervisor, 5th year.
Jimmy Buchanan, No. **86,** South Carolina State, insurance agent, 2nd year.
Gary Cavaletto, No. **60,** Hancock, general manager, agricultural operations, 8th year.
Boris Cheek, No. **41,** Morgan State, director of operations and management, 15th year.
Scott Edwards, No. **3,** Alabama, environmental engineer, 12th year.
Greg Gautreaux, No. **80,** S.W. Louisiana, athletic programs manager, 9th year.
Buddy Horton, No. **82,** Oregon State, water service worker, 12th year.
Jim Howey, No. **37,** Erskine College, director of adult education, 12th year.
Jon Lucivansky, No. **89,** Minnesota, high school associate principal, 2nd year.
Dyrol Prioleau, No. **109,** Johnson C. Smith, manager, law firm, 4th year.
Jim Quirk, No. **63,** Middlebury, financial advisor, 1st year.
Doug Rosenbaum, No. **67,** Illinois Wesleyan, financial consultant, 10th year.
Scott Steenson, No. **88,** North Texas, commercial real estate broker, 20th year.
Bob Waggoner, No. **25,** Juniata College, probation officer, 14th year.
Mike Weir, No. **50,** Missouri, owner, sporting goods store, 9th year.
Craig Wrolstad, No. **4,** Washington, athletic director, 8th year.
Steve Zimmer, No. **33,** Hofstra, attorney, 14th year.

SIDE JUDGES

Barry Anderson, No. **20,** North Carolina State, builder/developer, 4th year.
Michael Banks, No. **72,** Illinois State, carpenter foreman, 9th year.
Allen Baynes, No. **56,** Auburn, realtor, 3rd year.
Don Carlsen, No. **39,** Cal State-Chico, retired county school superintendent, 22nd year.
James Coleman, No. **95,** Arkansas, electrical engineer, 6th year.
Jimmy DeBell, No. **58,** SUNY-Brockport, high school teacher, 2nd year.
Laird Hayes, No. **125,** Princeton, professor, physical education & athletics, 16th year.
Tom Hill, No. **97,** Carson Newman, teacher, 12th year.
Jeff Lamberth, No. **103,** Texas A&M, attorney, 9th year.
Joe Larrew, No. **73,** St. Louis, attorney, 9th year.
Greg Meyer, No. **78,** Texas Christian, banker, 9th year.
Rick Patterson, No. **15,** Wofford, banker, 15th year.
Larry Rose, No. **128,** Florida, financial planner, 14th year.
Ronald Torbert, No. **62,** Michigan State, attorney, 1st year.
Keith Washington, No. **7,** Virginia Military Institute, program financial analyst, 3rd year.
Mike Weatherford, No. **116,** Oklahoma State, energy trader, 9th year.
David Wyant, No. **16,** Virginia, consulting engineer, 20th year.

BACK JUDGES

Don Carey, No. **126,** California-Riverside, contract manager, 16th year.
Kirk Dornan, No. **6,** Central Washington, purchasing manager, 17th year.
Lee Dyer, No. **27,** Tennessee-Chattanooga, sales manager, 8th year.
Keith Ferguson, No. **61,** San Jose State, sales, 11th year.
Steve Freeman, No. **133,** Mississippi State, custom home builder, 10th year.
Scott Helverson, No. **93,** Iowa, sales, printing and promotions, 8th year.
Terrence Miles, No. **111,** Arizona State, quality control manager, 3rd year.
Dino Paganelli, No. **105,** Aquinas College, educator, 5th year.
Perry Paganelli, No. **46,** Hope College, retired high school administrator, 13th year.
Todd Prukop, No. **30,** Cal State-Fullerton, medical sales representative, 2nd year.
Richard Reels, No. **83,** Chicago State, director of security, court services, 18th year.
Billy Smith, No. **2,** East Carolina, retired federal government, 17th year.
Greg Steed, No. **12,** Howard, computer systems analyst, 8th year.
Tony Steratore, No. **112,** California, PA., co-owner, supply company, 11th year.
Rob Vernatchi, No. **75,** California-Riverside, enforcement investigator, 7th year.
Greg Wilson, No. **119,** USC, law enforcement, 3rd year.

Roster as of May 2010

OFFICIAL SIGNALS

1

TOUCHDOWN, FIELD GOAL, or SUCCESSFUL TRY
Both arms extended above head.

2

SAFETY
Palms together above head.

3

FIRST DOWN
Arm pointed toward defensive team's goal.

4

DEAD BALL or NEUTRAL ZONE ESTABLISHED
One arm above head with an open hand.
With fist closed: **Fourth Down.**

5

BALL ILLEGALLY TOUCHED, KICKED, or BATTED
Fingertips tap both shoulders.

6

TIME OUT
Hands crisscrossed above head.
Same signal followed by placing one hand on top of cap: **Referee's Time Out.**
Same signal followed by arm swung at side: **Touchback.**

7

NO TIME OUT or TIME IN WITH WHISTLE
Full arm circled to simulate moving clock.

8

DELAY OF GAME or EXCESS TIME OUT
Folded arms.

9

FALSE START, ILLEGAL FORMATION, or KICKOFF or SAFETY KICK OUT OF BOUNDS or KICKING TEAM PLAYER VOLUNTARILY OUT OF BOUNDS DURING A PUNT
Forearms rotated over and over in front of body.

10

PERSONAL FOUL
One wrist striking the other above head.
Same signal followed by swinging leg:
Roughing the Kicker.
Same signal followed by raised arm swinging forward:
Roughing the Passer.
Same signal followed by grasping facemask: **Major Facemask.**

11

HOLDING
Grasping one wrist, the fist clenched, in front of chest.

12

ILLEGAL USE OF HANDS, ARMS, or BODY
Grasping one wrist, the hand open and facing forward, in front of chest.

13

PENALTY REFUSED, INCOMPLETE PASS, PLAY OVER, or MISSED FIELD GOAL or EXTRA POINT
Hands shifted in horizontal plane.

14

PASS JUGGLED INBOUNDS AND CAUGHT OUT OF BOUNDS
Hands up and down in front of chest (following incomplete pass signal).

15

ILLEGAL FORWARD PASS
One hand waved behind back followed by loss of down signal (23), when appropriate.

16

INTENTIONAL GROUNDING OF PASS
Parallel arms waved in a diagonal plane across body. Followed by loss of down signal (23).

17

INTERFERENCE WITH FORWARD PASS or FAIR CATCH
Hands open and extended forward from shoulders with hands vertical.

18

INVALID FAIR-CATCH SIGNAL
One hand waved above head.

19

INELIGIBLE RECEIVER or INELIGIBLE MEMBER OF KICKING TEAM DOWNFIELD
Right hand touching top of cap.

20

ILLEGAL CONTACT
One open hand extended forward.

21

OFFSIDE, ENCROACHMENT, or NEUTRAL ZONE INFRACTION
Hands on hips.

22

ILLEGAL MOTION AT SNAP
Horizontal arc with one hand.

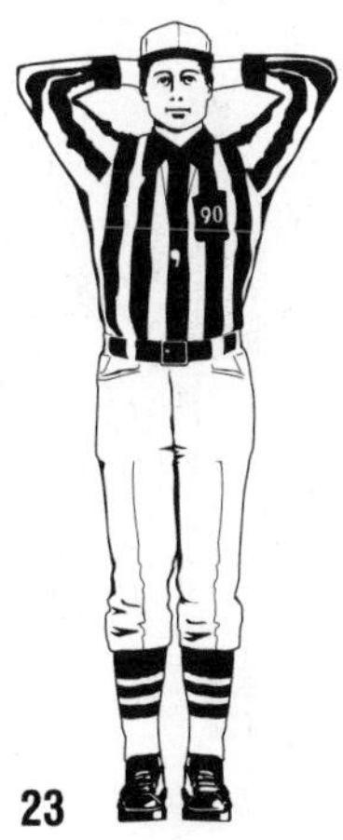

23

LOSS OF DOWN
Both hands held behind head.

24

INTERLOCKING INTERFERENCE, PUSHING, or HELPING RUNNER
Pushing movement of hands to front with arms downward.

25

TOUCHING A FORWARD PASS or SCRIMMAGE KICK
Diagonal motion of one hand across another.

26

UNSPORTSMANLIKE CONDUCT
Arms outstretched, palms down.

27

ILLEGAL CUT
Hand striking front of thigh.
ILLEGAL BLOCK BELOW THE WAIST
One hand striking front of thigh preceded by personal-foul signal (10).
CHOP BLOCK
Both hands striking side of thighs preceded by personal-foul signal (10).
CLIPPING
One hand striking back of calf preceded by personal-foul signal (10).

28

ILLEGAL CRACKBACK
Strike of an open right hand against the right mid-thigh preceded by personal foul signal (10).

29

PLAYER DISQUALIFIED
Ejection signal.

30

TRIPPING
Repeated action of right foot in back of left heel.

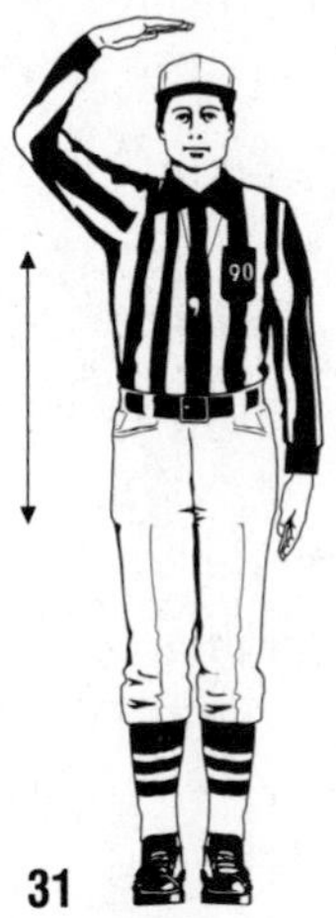

31

UNCATCHABLE FORWARD PASS
Palm of right hand held parallel to ground above head and moved back and forth.

32

TWELVE MEN IN OFFENSIVE HUDDLE or TOO MANY MEN ON THE FIELD
Both hands on top of head.

33

FACEMASK
Grasping facemask with one hand.

34

ILLEGAL SHIFT
Horizontal arcs with two hands.

35

RESET PLAY CLOCK– 25 SECONDS
Pump one arm vertically.

36

RESET PLAY CLOCK– 40 SECONDS
Pump two arms vertically.

NATIONAL FOOTBALL LEAGUE, 2010

280 Park Avenue, New York, New York 10017 (212) 450-2000

NFL Internet Network: www.NFL.com

Commissioner: Roger Goodell

Executive Vice President/Football Operations: Ray Anderson

Executive Vice President of Media/
President and Chief Executive Officer of NFL Network: Steve Bornstein

Executive Vice President of Communications and Public Affairs: Joe Browne

Executive Vice President of NFL Ventures and Business Operations: Eric Grubman

Executive Vice President of Finance/Chief Financial Officer: Anthony Noto

Executive Vice President of Labor/League Counsel: Jeff Pash